an
ian

written and researched by

Ros Belford, Martin Dunford
and Celia Woolfrey

with additional contributions from

iii

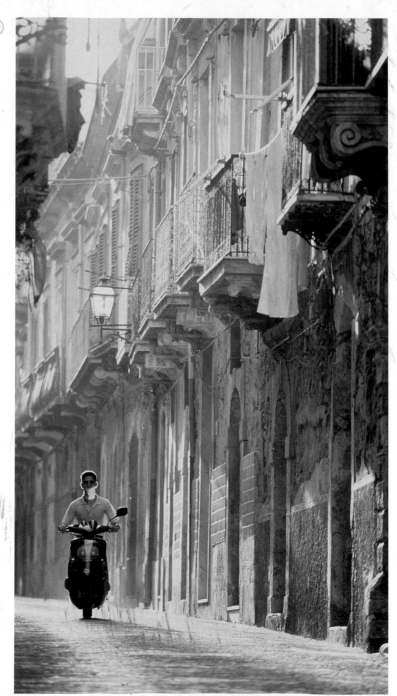

Introduction to

Italy

Italy is perhaps Europe's most complex and alluring destination. It is a modern, industrialized nation, but it is also, to an equal degree, a Mediterranean country, with a southern European sensibility. Agricultural land covers much of the country, a lot of which, especially in the south, is still owned under almost feudal conditions. In towns and villages all over the country, life grinds to a halt in the middle of the day for a siesta, and is strongly family-oriented, with an emphasis on the traditions and rituals of the Catholic Church, which, notwithstanding a growing scepticism among the country's youth, still dominates people's lives.

Above all, Italy provokes reaction. Its people are volatile, rarely indifferent, and on one and the same day you might encounter the kind of disdain dished out to tourist masses everywhere and an hour later be treated to embarrassingly generous hospitality. If there is a single national characteristic, it's to embrace life to the full: in the hundreds of local festivals taking place across the country on any given day, to celebrate a saint or the local harvest; in the importance placed on good food; in the obsession with clothes and image; and above all in the daily domestic ritual of the collective evening stroll or *passeggiata* – a sociable affair celebrated by young and old alike in every town and village across the country.

Italy only became a unified state in 1861, and, as a result, Italians often feel more loyalty to their region than to the nation as a whole – something manifest in different cuisines, dialects, landscape and often varying

v

Fact file

- Italy is a peninsula, shaped rather like a boot, jutting out into the Mediterranean Sea. It covers a surface area of 301,230 square km and includes the islands of Sardinia and Sicily. The distance from the tip of the country's "toe" to its northern border is about 1380km. Much of the land is mountainous, the highest point being Mont Blanc (4748m) in the north.

- Italy's population is nearly 58 million, with around 2.5 million living in the capital, Rome. The dominant ethnic group is Italian, with small clusters of German-, French- and Slovene-Italians in the north and Albanian- and Greek-Italians in the south. There is also a growing Muslim immigrant community.

- Italy has been a democratic republic since 1946, when the monarchy was abolished by popular referendum. The parliament consists of two houses, the Senate and the Chamber of Deputies, elected for five-year terms of office. The president is elected for a seven-year term by a joint session of parliament and regional representatives. Real power, however, is in the hands of the prime minister, who is generally the leader of the party with the biggest majority in the Chamber of Deputies.

standards of living. There is also, of course, the country's enormous cultural legacy: Tuscany alone has more classified historical monuments than any country in the world; there are considerable remnants of the Roman Empire all over the country, notably of course in Rome itself; and every region retains its own relics of an artistic tradition generally acknowledged to be among the world's richest.

Yet there's no reason to be intimidated by the art and architecture. If you want to lie on a beach, there are any number of places to do so: beaches are for the most part sandy; coastal development has been kept relatively under control, and many resorts are still largely the preserve of Italian tourists, while other parts of the coast, especially in the south of the country, are almost entirely undiscovered. Mountains, too, run the country's length – from the Alps and Dolomites in the north right along the Apennines, which form the spine of the peninsula – and are an important reference-point for most Italians. Skiing and other winter sports are practised avidly, and in the five national parks, protected from the national passion for hunting, wildlife of all sorts thrives.

Where to go

The north is "discovered" Italy. The regions of **Piemonte** and **Lombardy**, in the northwest, make up the richest and most cosmopolitan part of the country, and the two main centres, Turin and Milan, are its wealthiest cities. In their southern reaches, these regions are

Food and wine

Italy is a fantastic culinary experience even if you are already extremely familiar with Italian food. Not only does Italian food taste better in Italy, but there's a regional variety that makes travelling from place to place a source of pure, indulgent culinary pleasure. Everywhere in Liguria will serve pasta with pesto sauce, but you won't find it anywhere but tourist joints in the rest of the country; Piemonte is famous for its wine, meat dishes in rich, creamy sauces, its truffles, and some excellent wines; in Lombardy and some other parts of the north the staple is polenta rather than pasta; while down south you'll find pasta everywhere, best with baby clams and garlic or a simple tomato and basil sauce – and Naples is of course the home of the wood-fired pizza. Rome is known for its offal and Italian-Jewish cuisine, Emilia-Romagna for its pork dishes, rich pasta sauces, and some Italian food classics – salami, parma ham and parmesan cheese; Tuscany's trademark is its relatively simple food – great chargrilled steaks, for example, washed down with some of the country's best wines. Buon Appetito!

flat and scenically dull, especially Lombardy, but in the north the presence of the Alps shapes the character of each: skiing and hiking are prime activities, and the lakes and mountains of Lombardy are time-honoured tourist territory. **Liguria**, the small coastal province to the south, has long been known as the "Italian Riviera" and is accordingly crowded with sun-seeking holiday-makers for much of the summer season. Nonetheless, it's a beautiful stretch of coast, and its capital, Genoa, is a bustling port with a long seafaring tradition.

Much of the most dramatic mountain scenery lies within the smaller northern regions. In the far northwest, the tiny bilingual region of **Valle d'Aosta** is home to some of the country's most frequented ski resorts, and is bordered by the tallest of the Alps – the Matterhorn and Mont Blanc. In the northeast, **Trentino-Alto Adige**, another bilingual region, and one in which the national boundary is especially blurred, marks the beginning of the Dolomites mountain range, where Italy's largest national park, the Stelvio, lies amid some of the country's most memorable landscapes.

The Dolomites stretch into the northeastern regions of the **Veneto** and **Friuli-Venezia Giulia**. However, here the main focus of interest is, of course, Venice; a unique city, and every bit as beautiful as its reputation would suggest (although this means you won't be alone in appreciating it). If the crowds are too much, there's also the arc of historic towns outside the city – Verona, Padua and Vicenza, all centres of interest in their own right, although rather overshadowed by their illustrious neighbour. To the south, the region of **Emilia-Romagna** has been at the heart of Italy's postwar industrial boom and has a standard of living on a par with Piemonte and Lombardy, although it's also a traditional stronghold of the Italian Left. Its coast is popular among Italians, and Rimini is about Italy's brashest (and trendiest) seaside resort, with a high reputation on the clubbing scene. You may do better to ignore the beaches altogether, however, and concentrate on the ancient centres of Ravenna, Ferrara, Parma and the

Italy has an enormous cultural legacy: Tuscany alone has more classified historical monuments than any country in the world.

regional capital of Bologna, one of Italy's liveliest, most historic but least appreciated cities.

Central Italy represents perhaps the most commonly perceived image of the country, and **Tuscany**, with its classic rolling countryside and the art-packed towns of Florence, Pisa and Siena, to name only the three best-known centres, is one of its most visited regions. Neighbouring **Umbria** is similar in all but its tourist numbers, though it gets busier every year, as visitors flock into towns such as Perugia, Spoleto and Assisi. Further east still, **Marche** may in time go the same way, but for the moment is comparatively untouched, its highlights being the ancient towns of Urbino and Áscoli Piceno. South of Marche, the hills begin to pucker into mountains in the twin regions of **Abruzzo** and **Molise**, one of Italy's remotest areas, centring on one of the country's highest peaks – the Gran Sasso d'Italia. Molise, particularly, is a taster of the south, as is **Lazio** to the west, in part

Art

It's a safe bet that you're visiting the country with the world's greatest concentration of art treasures for just that – its art. And you won't be disappointed. Northern Italy on the whole has the country's richest concentration, but wherever you're travelling, even the smallest country church can boast a masterpiece or two; remote monasteries and small country towns can hold enticing museums; and the big city galleries – the Uffizi in Florence, Milan's Brera, too many to mention in Rome – are stacked full of beautiful paintings and sculptures. Like food, you can find different styles – and the work of different artists – in distinct regions. There's ancient art, most obviously the Roman mosaics and murals of Pompeii and Herculaneum, and the earlier funereal sculpture and applied arts of the Etruscans of northern Lazio. Siena was home to some of the earliest Gothic stylists of the fourteenth century; Florence bloomed most brightly during the Renaissance of the fifteenth century, while Rome's most characteristic style is the later Baroque look of the counter-reformation; Venice is not surprisingly the place to see the works of the great Venetian painters, Titian, Tintoretto, et al. Your only problem will be having the time to take it all in.

a poor and sometimes desolate region whose often rugged landscapes contrast with the more manicured beauty of the other central regions. Lazio's real focal point, though, is **Rome**, Italy's capital and the one city in the country which owes allegiance neither to the north or south, its people proudly aloof from the rest of the country's squabbles. Rome is a tremendous city quite unlike any other, and in terms of historical sights outstrips everywhere else in the country by some way.

The south proper begins below Rome, with the region of **Campania**, which is as far as many tourists get. Naples is a petulant, unforgettable city, the spiritual heart of the Italian south, and on hand nearby are some of Italy's finest ancient sites in Pompeii and Herculaneum, not to mention the country's most spectacular stretch of coast around Amalfi. **Basilicata** and **Calabria**, which make up the instep and toe of Italy's boot, are harder territory but still rewarding, the emphasis less on art, more on the landscape and quiet, unspoilt coastlines. **Puglia**, the "heel" of Italy, has underrated pleasures, notably the landscape of its Gargano peninsula, the souk-like quality of its capital Bari, and the Baroque glories of Lecce in the far south. As for **Sicily**, the island is really a law unto itself, with a wide mixture of attractions ranging from some of the finest preserved Hellenistic treasures in Europe, to a couple of Italy's fanciest beach resorts in Taormina and Cefalù, not to mention some gorgeous upland scenery. Come this far south and you're closer to Africa than Milan, and it shows – in the climate, the architecture and the cooking, with couscous featuring on many menus in the west of the island. **Sardinia**, too, feels far removed from the Italian mainland, especially in its relatively undiscovered interior, although you may be content to explore its fine beaches, which are among Italy's best.

Football

Calcio – or football, or soccer – is Italy's national sport, and enjoys a fanatical following across the country. It's usually possible to get tickets to see even one of the big sides – as long as they're not playing each other – and although not cheap, it's one of the best introductions to modern Italian culture you'll find. And the shirts and banners that you can buy outside the grounds make great souvenirs.

When to go

taly's **climate** is one of the most hospitable in the world, with a general pattern of warm, dry summers and mild winters. There are, however, marked regional variations, ranging from the more temperate northern part of the country to the firmly Mediterranean south. Summers are hot and dry along the coastal areas, especially as you move south, cool in the major mountain areas – the Alps and Apennines. Winters are mild in the south of the country, Rome and below, but in the north they can be at least as cold as anywhere in the northern hemisphere, sometimes worse, especially across the plains of Lombardy and Emilia-Romagna, which can be very inhospitable indeed in January.

As for **when to go**, if you're planning to visit fairly popular areas, especially beach resorts, avoid July and August, when the weather can be too hot and the crowds at their most congested. August is when the Italians go on holiday, so expect the crush to be especially bad in the resorts and the

Average temperatures
°C = (°F - 32) multiplied by 5/9

	Jan	Feb	Mar	Apr	May	Jun	Jul	Aug	Sep	Oct	Nov	Dec
Ancona												
	5.7	5.8	9.4	13.6	17.6	22.3	24.9	24.3	21.1	16.6	12.6	7.4
Bari												
	8.4	8.5	10.8	13.9	17.5	21.9	24.5	24.3	21.7	18.2	14.8	10.2
Bologna												
	2.5	3.4	8.6	13.8	18.1	23.3	26.0	25.4	21.3	15.2	9.7	3.9
Cágliari												
	10.5	11.0	13.0	15.0	18.5	22.5	25.5	25.5	23.0	19.0	15.0	12.5
Florence												
	5.6	5.8	9.9	13.3	17.4	22.1	25.0	24.5	21.2	15.8	11.2	6.0
Genoa												
	8.4	8.7	11.5	14.5	17.8	21.9	24.6	25.0	21.8	18.1	18.1	13.3
Milan												
	1.9	3.8	8.6	13.2	17.3	22.2	24.8	23.9	20.3	13.7	8.5	3.0
Naples												
	8.7	8.7	11.4	14.3	18.1	22.3	24.8	24.8	22.3	18.1	14.5	10.3
Palermo												
	10.3	10.4	13.0	16.2	18.7	23.0	25.3	25.1	23.2	19.9	16.8	12.6
Rome												
	7.4	8.0	11.5	14.4	18.4	22.9	25.7	25.5	22.4	17.7	13.4	8.9
Trieste												
	5.3	4.8	8.6	12.9	17.1	21.2	24.0	23.3	20.4	15.1	11.0	6.3
Venice												
	3.8	4.1	8.2	12.6	17.1	21.2	23.6	23.3	20.4	15.1	10.5	5.0

scene in the major historic cities – Rome, Florence, Venice – to be slightly artificial, as the only people around are fellow tourists. The nicest time to visit, in terms of the weather and lack of crowds, is April to late June, or September and October. If you're planning to swim, however, bear in mind that only the south of the country may be warm enough outside the May to September period.

things not to miss

It's not possible to see everything Italy has to offer in one trip – and we don't suggest you try. What follows is a selective taste of the country's highlights: outstanding buildings and ancient sites, natural wonders and colourful festivals. They're arranged in five colour-coded categories, which you can browse through to find the very best things to see and experience. All highlights have a page reference to take you straight into the guide, where you can find out more.

01 Mantua Page **191** • The Mantegna frescoes of Mantua's Palazzo Ducale, and the works of Guilio Romano in its Palazzo Te, make a visit to this ancient and alluring Lombard city hard to resist.

02 Basilica di San Francesco, Assisi Page 623
•The burial place of St Francis and one of Italy's greatest church buildings, with frescoes by Giotto, Simone Martini and others.

03 Città Alta, Bergamo Page 219
•Bergamo's medieval high town is an impossibly romantic spot to spend an evening.

04 Parco Nazionale d'Abruzzo Page 829
• Italy's third-largest national park, and probably its wildest, with marvellous walking and wildlife.

05 Food in Emilia-Romagna Page 412
• This region is known as Italy's gastronomic heart, home to Parma ham, Parmesan cheese, balsamic vinegar, great stuffed pasta dishes and underrated wines like Lambrusco, all on view at Bologna's marvellous indoor food market.

06 Sardinia's south coast Page 1123
•There are plenty of places to sun-worship in Italy, but this ranks among one of Italy's most memorable coastlines, with a handful of five-star beaches tucked between the rocky headlands.

07 Vatican Museums, Rome Page **767** • Put simply, this is the largest and richest collection of art and culture in the world. You'd be mad to miss it.

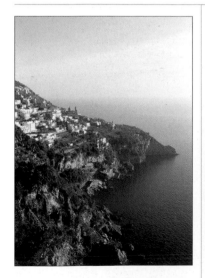

08 Amalfi Coast Page **896** • The views on the road that snakes along the Amalfi Coast, connecting the resorts of Positano, Amalfi and Ravello, can hardly be bettered anywhere in the world.

09 The Duomo, Florence Page **478** • Florence's cathedral dome is one of the most instantly recognizable images in the world – and one of its most significant engineering feats.

11 Paestum Page **904** •The majestic Greek temples of this Campanian site are the backdrop for a fine stretch of sandy beach.

10 Basilica di San Marco, Venice Page **299** • One of Europe's most exotic cathedrals, Venice's principal place of worship is a fabulous sight, with 4000 square metres of golden mosaics.

12 Matera Page **979** •A truly unique city, sliced by a ravine containing thousands of sassi – cave dwellings gouged out of the rock that were inhabited till the 1950s.

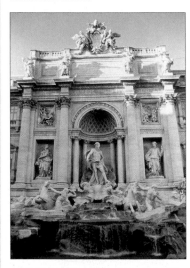

14 Centro Storico, Rome

Page **723** • There's so much to see in Rome that aimlessly wandering the city's fantastic old centre can turn up a surprise at every turn – whether it's an ancient statue, a marvellous Baroque fountain like the Trevi fountain shown here, or an art-packed Renaissance church.

13 Monreale Page **1014** • The extraordinary Greek and Byzantine mosaics in the Norman cathedral of the Sicilian hilltown of Monreale are one of the island's most unmissable attractions.

16 Sicily's Greek ruins Page **1044** • The ancient theatres at Siracusa and Taormina are magnificent summer stages for Greek drama, while the temple complex at nearby Agrigento is one of the finest such sites outside Greece itself.

15 Duomo, Orvieto Page **651** • One of the country's finest – and best-sited – cathedrals, with a marvellous fresco cycle by Luca Signorelli. -

17 Ravenna's mosaics Page
447 •Ravenna's Byzantine mosaics –
in the churches Sant'Apollinare Nuovo and
San Vitale – are a stunning testimony to the
city's ranking as the capital of Europe fifteen
hundred years ago.

**18 Shop till you drop in
Milan** Page **163** • If you're fond of
fashion, where better to flash the cash than
in its commercial home, Milan.

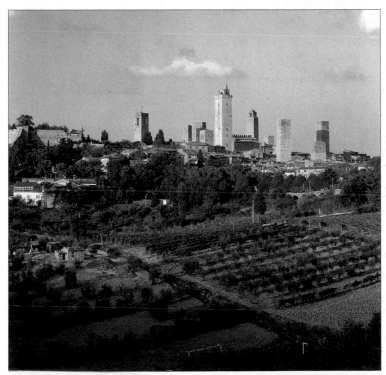

19 Tuscan hilltowns Page **461** •The campanile-spiked profile of a hilltown is
what many people think of when they think of Italy. And they're not wrong: in Montepulciano, Montalcino, and San Gimigniano, Tuscany in particular has some of the most beautiful,
if sometimes also most touristy, examples of ancient hilltowns in the world.

20 **Certosa di Pavia** Page **187** •This Carthusian monastery is a fantastic construction, rising out of the rice fields near Pavia.

21 **Cinque Terre** Page **144** •These five fishing villages are shoehorned picturesquely into one of the most rugged parts of Liguria's coastline, and linked by a highly scenic coastal walking path.

22 **Gran Paradiso National Park** Page **100** • The first Italian national park preserves an Alpine region of deep valleys and beautiful mountains that is home to ibex, chamois, and golden eagles.

23 **Urbino** Page **666** • This so-called 'ideal city' and art capital, created by Federico da Montefeltro, the ultimate Renaissance man, attracts people from miles around.

24 **Genoa** Page **109** • An old port par excellence, Genoa's rabbit-warren of medieval streets, revitalized harbour and first-rate museums and churches, make it one of Italy's most atmospheric cities.

25 Capitoline Museums, Rome Page 726

Separated by Michelangelo's elegant Campidoglio piazza, these make up the august and impressive home of some of Rome's finest ancient sculpture and paintings.

27 Cápri Page 883

Stay the night if you can, when the day-trippers have departed, to make the most of the island, with its stunning scenery and clifftop walks.

26 Palio, Siena Page 556

Perhaps the most fanatically followed and most violent horserace in the world – an amazing spectacle and a true slice of Sienese life.

28 Carnival Page 339

Venice's famous carnival is worth seeing for its costumes and crowds. But it is rather an exclusive affair, and events around the rest of the country – most notably in Verona, in the Veneto, and Viareggio, on the Tuscan coast – are more authentic and definitely more fun, with the entire town turning out for their raucous processions.

29 Cappella degli Scrovegni, Padua
Page **346** •The chapel frescoes here, by Giotto, constitute one of the great works of European art.

30 Mount Etna
Page **849** • It's an eerie climb up the blackened lunar landscape of this smoking volcano, which dominates the landscape of eastern Sicily.

32 Pizza
Page **849** •You can eat pizza all over Italy, but nowhere is it quite as good as in its home town of Naples, served sizzling hot straight from a wood-fired oven.

31 Duomo, Milan
Page **172** •The world's largest and perhaps most attention-grabbing Gothic cathedral.

33 Gubbio
Page **615** •The best-looking of Umbria's medieval hill towns, and without Assisi's crowds and commercialism.

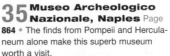

35 Museo Archeologico Nazionale, Naples Page
864 • The finds from Pompeii and Herculaneum alone make this superb museum worth a visit.

34 **Lecce** Page **945** •This exuberant city of Baroque architecture and opulent churches is one of the must-sees of the Italian South.

36 **Skiing** Page **51** •Whether you opt for the Alps or the Dolomites in the north, or the Abruzzo or Aspromonte mountains in the south, you're never far from somewhere decent to ski in Italy.

37 **The Uffizi, Florence** Page **486** • Italy's greatest collection of art, and – in a city not exactly short on things to see – perhaps the most essential attraction of them all.

38 **The Last Supper, Milan** Page **177** •Leonardo da Vinci's mural for the refectory wall of the Santa Maria delle Grazie is one of the world's most resonant images.

39 **Truffles** Page **67** • The speciality of the region around Alba in Piemonte is the astonishingly expensive white truffle, shaved onto pasta and washed down with the excellent local Barolo or Barbaresco wine.

40 **Pompeii and Hercula-neum** Page **874 & 877** • Probably the two best-preserved Roman sites in the country, destroyed and at the same time preserved by the eruption of Vesuvius in AD 79 and giving an amazing glimpse into the daily life and architecture of ancient Rome.

41 **Elba** Page **537** • This easily accessible, mountainous Tuscan island offers great beaches and some fantastic hiking opportunities.

Contents

Using this Rough Guide

We've tried to make this Rough Guide a good read and easy to use. The book is divided into five main sections, and you should be able to find whatever you want in one of them.

Colour section

The front colour section offers a quick tour of Italy. The **introduction** aims to give you a feel for the place, with suggestions on where to go. We also tell you what the weather is like and include a basic country fact file. Next, our authors round up their favourite aspects of Italy in the **things not to miss** section – whether it's great food, amazing sights or a special hotel. Right after this comes a full **contents** list.

Basics

The Basics section covers all the **pre-departure** nitty-gritty to help you plan your trip. This is where to find out which airlines fly to your destination, what paperwork you'll need, what to do about money and insurance, about Internet access, food, security, public transport, car rental – in fact just about every piece of **general practical information** you might need.

Guide

This is the heart of the Rough Guide, divided into user-friendly chapters, each of which covers a specific region. Every chapter starts with a list of **highlights** and an **introduction** that helps you to decide where to go, depending on your time and budget. Likewise, introductions to the various towns and smaller regions within each chapter should help you plan your itinerary. We start most town accounts with information on arrival and accommodation, followed by a tour of the sights, and finally reviews of places to eat and drink, and details of nightlife. Longer accounts also have a directory of practical listings. Each chapter concludes with **public transport** details for that region.

Contexts

Read Contexts to get a deeper understanding of what makes Italy tick. We include a brief history, articles about **art** and **architecture**, and a detailed further reading section that reviews dozens of **books** relating to the country.

Language

The **language** section gives useful guidance for speaking Italian and pulls together all the vocabulary you might need on your trip, including a comprehensive menu reader. Here you'll also find a glossary of words and terms peculiar to the country.

Index + small print

Apart from a **full index**, which includes maps as well as places, this section covers publishing information, credits and acknowledgements, and also has our contact details in case you want to send in updates and corrections to the book – or suggestions as to how we might improve it.

Chapter list and map

Contents

Colour section

Basics

The Guide

CONTENTS

5

Contexts   1105–1188

Language   1189–1200

Index and small print   1201–1215

Map symbols

maps are listed in the full index using coloured text

-----	International boundary	∴	Ruins
--- ...	Regional boundary	♛	Castle
----	Chapter boundary	⚱	Church (regional maps)
▬▬▬	Motorway	⚘	Monastery
═══	Major road	✡	Synagogue
───	Minor road	⚚	Fountain
⅏	Steps	⊞	Hospital
-----	Path	**P**	Parking
━▬━	Railway	Ⓜ	Metro station
··········	Funicular	★	Bus/taxi stop
━━●━━	Cable car	ⓘ	Information office
── ──	Ferry route	⊠	Post office
── ──	Hydrofoil route	Ⓒ	Telephone office
────	Waterway	@	Internet access
▪▪▪	Wall	◉	Accommodation
✈	Airport	▣	Restaurant
⋏⋏	Mountain range	■━	Gate
▲	Mountain peak	▬	Building
⌢⌣	Pass	✚	Cathedral/church (town maps)
◠	Cave	▦	Park
♦	Ancient site/ place of interest	⊡	Cemetery
⚠	Campsite		

Basics

Basics

Getting there

The easiest way to get to Italy from the UK and Ireland is to fly: and the lowest priced air tickets are generally cheaper than those for the long train or bus journey. Driving from the UK is also a viable, though expensive, option – you'd need to allow at least two days to reach central Italy.

The majority of flights go to Milan and Rome, with Bologna, Pisa, Naples, Turin and Venice in the second tier, frequent onward flights connect these gateway cities to smaller regional airports and to Sicily and Sardinia. **From the US and Canada** there are a number of direct flights to Milan and Rome, although you could consider flying via London and picking up a cheap onward flight from there. There are no direct flights to Italy **from Australia or New Zealand**, but plenty of airlines fly to Milan and Rome via an Asian or European city.

Airfares always depend on the **season**, with the highest being around June to August, when the weather is best; fares drop during the "shoulder" seasons – September to October and April to May – and you'll get the best prices during the low season, November to March (excluding Christmas and New Year when prices are hiked up and seats are at a premium). Note also that it is generally more expensive to fly at weekends; price ranges quoted below assume midweek travel.

You can often cut costs by going through a **specialist flight agent** – either a consolidator, who buys up blocks of tickets from the airlines and sells them at a discount, or a **discount agent**, who in addition to dealing with discounted flights may offer special student and youth fares and a range of other travel-related services such as travel insurance, rail passes, car rentals, tours and the like. Some agents specialize in **charter flights**, which may be cheaper than anything available on a scheduled flight, but again departure dates are fixed and withdrawal penalties are high. You may even find it cheaper to pick up a **package deal** which takes care of flights and accommodation for an all-in price.

If Italy is only one stop on a longer journey, you might want to consider buying a **Round-the-World** (RTW) ticket. Some travel agents can sell you an "off-the-shelf" RTW ticket that will have you touching down in about half a dozen cities; others will have to assemble one for you, which can be tailored to your needs but is apt to be more expensive. Figure on £950/US$1500 for a RTW ticket including Italy.

Booking flights online

Many airlines and discount travel websites offer you the opportunity to book your tickets online, cutting out the costs of agents and middlemen. Good deals can often be found through discount or auction sites, as well as through the airlines' own websites.

Online booking agents and general travel sites

Ⓦ **www.cheapflights.com** Bookings from the UK and Ireland only. Flight deals, travel agents, plus links to other travel sites.

Ⓦ **www.cheaptickets.com** Discount flight specialists.

Ⓦ **www.etn.nl/discount.htm** A hub of consolidator and discount agent Web links, maintained by the nonprofit European Travel Network.

Ⓦ **www.expedia.com** Discount airfares, all-airline search engine and daily deals.

Ⓦ **www.flyaow.com** Online air travel info and reservations site.

Ⓦ **www.geocities.com/Thavery2000/** Has an extensive list of airline toll-free numbers and websites.

Ⓦ **www.hotwire.com** Bookings from the US only. Last-minute savings of up to forty percent on regular published fares. Travellers must be at least 18 and there are no refunds, transfers or changes allowed. Log-in required.

ⓦ **www.lastminute.com** Bookings from the UK only. Offers good last-minute holiday package and flight-only deals.

ⓦ **www.priceline.com** Name-your-own-price website that has deals at around forty percent off standard fares. You cannot specify flight times (although you do specify dates) and the tickets are non-refundable, non-transferable and non-changeable.

ⓦ **www.skyauction.com** Bookings from the US only. Auctions tickets and travel packages using a "second bid" scheme. The best strategy is to bid the maximum you're willing to pay, since if you win you'll pay just enough to beat the runner-up regardless of your maximum bid.

ⓦ **www.smilinjack.com/airlines.htm** Lists an up-to-date compilation of airline website addresses.

ⓦ **http://travel.yahoo.com** Incorporates a lot of Rough Guide material in its coverage of destination countries and cities across the world, with information about places to eat, sleep etc.

ⓦ **www.travelocity.com** Destination guides, hot Web fares and best deals for car rental, accommodation and lodging as well as fares. Provides access to the travel agent system SABRE, the most comprehensive central reservations system in the US.

ⓦ **www.travelshop.com.au** Australian website offering discounted flights, packages, insurance, online bookings.

From the UK and Ireland

There are plenty of **flights** from the UK and Ireland to Italy. It's well worth checking out the offers of the **low cost**, no-frills airlines, easyJet and Ryanair, which fly regularly from Stansted to many Italian destinations – you can sometimes buy tickets for less than £60 return (including taxes) for a mid-week, off-peak flight. Other sources of cheap flights are travel agents, which can often give you a deal on a direct **charter flight**, although you'd be advised to make enquiries well in advance during peak season; you can also track down deals on charters direct through a number of specialist tour operators or by scouring the classified section of the Sunday papers and *Time Out* magazine.

Of the **scheduled airlines** flying the Italian routes, British Airways (BA) and Alitalia operate daily direct flights to the major Italian cities from London Heathrow and Gatwick. BA also has flights from Manchester to Rome and Milan and from Birmingham and Glasgow to Milan, although the Glasgow route is not direct.

The major **scheduled carriers** operate a system of first-come, first-served on the cheaper seats, and prices depend more on how far in advance you book and how popular the flight is than the season or even the distance. The cheapest scheduled tickets normally come with certain restrictions. Usually your trip has to include a Saturday night away and any changes to your ticket incur an additional fee; tickets are also rarely valid for longer than a month. Flights cost around £120–£160 (generally more for southern Italy) for a return fare in low season but be prepared to pay £250–300 in high season, when the cheaper seats get booked up months in advance.

Aer Lingus has daily direct flights **from Dublin** to Rome and Milan, and Alitalia covers the same route three to five times a week depending on the season. It is possible to find deals for around €270 if you book early, but prices are usually significantly higher (€345–500) and unless you're in a hurry it makes more sense to pick up an inexpensive flight to London or Birmingham and get a connecting flight from there. Ryanair, Aer Lingus, British Midland and British European operate regular daily flights from Dublin to London: the cheapest is Ryanair – starting at around €50 for a return to Stansted. Alternatively you could fly direct from Ireland to Brussels with Ryanair: they operate a cheap service from Brussels to Pisa, Venice and Rome.

Most airlines now offer direct phone or Internet booking, with many of the low-cost carriers operating a **ticketless system** – you are given a reference number to check in with at the airport.

There are a number of **flight specialists to Italy** offering a wide array of flights to a broad selection of Italian cities; or you could approach a **student/youth travel specialist** like STA Travel which offers all kinds of discounted fares, though these won't necessarily beat the deals you could find yourself. Using one of these outfits – and setting aside cut-price airlines – you can expect to pay £100–120 to one of the major gateways in low season and even during the height of summer you should be able to find something for significantly under £200.

Most agents, and some airlines, offer **"open-jaw"** deals, whereby you can fly into one Italian city and back from another – a good idea if you want to make your way across the country, and sometimes no more expensive than a **package deal** (see below), which takes care of flights and accommodation for an all-in price.

Airlines in the UK and Ireland

Aer Lingus UK ☎ 0845/9737 747, Republic of Ireland ☎ 0818/365 000, ⓦ www.aerlingus.ie.
Alitalia UK ☎ 0870/5448 259, Republic of Ireland ☎ 01/677 5171, ⓦ www.alitalia.it.
British Airways UK ☎ 0845/77 333 77, Republic of Ireland ☎ 1800/626 747,
ⓦ www.britishairways.com.
British Midland UK ☎ 0870/607 0555, Republic of Ireland ☎ 01/407 3036, ⓦ www.flybmi.com.
easyJet UK ☎ 0870/600 0000,
ⓦ www.easyjet.com.
Ryanair UK ☎ 0870/156 9569, Republic of Ireland ☎ 01/609 7800, ⓦ www.ryanair.com.

Flight and travel agents in the UK and Ireland

Co-op Travel Care Belfast ☎ 028/9047 1717,
ⓦ www.travelcareonline.com. Flights and package holidays to Italy.
Flightbookers UK ☎ 0870/010 7000,
ⓦ www.ebookers.com. Low fares on a selection of scheduled flights.
Go Holidays Dublin ☎ 01/874 4126,
ⓦ www.goholidays.ie. City break specialists to Florence, Rome and Venice.
Joe Walsh Tours Dublin ☎ 01/676 0991,
ⓦ www.joewalshtours.ie. General budget fares agent.
Lee Travel Cork ☎ 021/277 111,
ⓦ www.leetravel.ie. Flights and holidays in Italy.
Premier Travel Derry ☎ 028/7126 3333,
ⓦ www.premiertravel.uk.com. Discount flight specialists with hotel, insurance and car rental deals.
STA Travel UK ☎ 0870/1600 599,
ⓦ www.statravel.co.uk. Worldwide specialists in low-cost flights and tours for students and under-26s, though other customers welcome.
Trailfinders UK ☎ 020/7628 7628,
ⓦ www.trailfinders.com. One of the best-informed and most efficient agents for independent travellers.

usit NOW Dublin ☎ 01/602 1600,
ⓦ www.usitnow.ie. Student and youth specialists for flights and trains.

Packages and organized tours

Italy stands somewhat apart from other European package destinations: it's not especially cheap and has avoided the big hotel build-ups that have blighted parts of Spain and Greece. And it's as much a venue for specialist-interest and touring holidays as the standard sun-sand-sea packages. Having said that, there's no shortage of **travel-plus-accommodation** deals on the market, and if you're keen to stay in one (or two) places, they can work out to be very good value. Many companies offer travel at rates as competitive as you could find on your own, and any travel agent can fill you in on all the latest offers. Obviously it's cheapest to travel out of season, something we'd recommend anyway, as resorts and sights are much less crowded and the weather, in the south at least, is often still warm enough for swimming well into October. **Prices** for package deals start at about £450 per person per week for half-board in a hotel during May in Amalfi or Sorrento, and at least double that in high season although your travel agent might come up with some good last-minute deals. Restored **villas** and farmhouses are a popular option but are no bargain: you should reckon on about £600–800 per week to rent the average four-bedded Tuscan farmhouse in August, rather less out of season and in less popular areas. A cheaper alternative is agriturismo accommodation (see p.36).

An increasing number of operators organize **specialist holidays** to Italy – walking tours, art and archeology holidays, Italian food and wine jaunts, short breaks to coincide with opera festivals or even football matches. However they don't come cheap: accommodation, food, local transport and the services of a guide are nearly always included, and a week's half-board holiday can cost anything from £500 to £700 per person, rising to well over £1000 for full board. There's also a plethora of operators selling **short-break deals** to Italian cities: for these, reckon on spending upwards of £250 per person for three nights in Florence in a three-star hotel during low season and upwards of £350 between April and October, though special offers can sometimes cut prices drastically, especially for late bookings.

If you want to rent a car in Italy, it's well worth checking with tour operators (and flight agents) before you leave, as some **fly-drive** deals work out very cheaply. Crystal Holidays and Citalia have reasonable prices, starting at around £390 a week per person in summer for flight, car and accommodation. See p.32 for more on car rental.

Tour operators in the UK and Ireland

ACE Study Tours ☎01223/835 055, ⓦwww.study-tours.org. A variety of mainly art and architectural tours under the guidance of various experts.

Alternative Travel Group ☎01865/513 333, ⓦwww.atg-oxford.co.uk. All-inclusive walking holidays throughout Italy, including truffle- and flower-themed tours. Costly but well organized.

Arblaster & Clarke ☎01730/893 344, ⓦwww.arblasterandclarke.com. Upmarket wine and gourmet tours including wine cruise of Italian islands.

Citalia ☎020/8686 5533, ⓦwww.citalia.co.uk. Hotel and villa packages plus tailor-made itineraries, city breaks, self-catering holidays and car rental.

Cook Italy in Italy ☎0039/051-644 8612, ⓦwww.cookitaly.com. Cooking courses in Tuscany, Umbria, Sicily and Bologna.

Cottages to Castles ☎01622/775 217, ⓦwww.cottagestocastles.com. Specializes in exclusive property rental all over Italy.

Crystal Holidays ☎020/8939 5405, ⓦwww.crystalholidays.co.uk. Hotel packages, two-centre holidays, city breaks and fly-drives.

Eurobreak ☎020/8780 7700, ⓦwww.eurobreak.com. City breaks in nine major Italian cities.

Exclusive Italy ☎01892/619650, ⓦwww.exclusivedestinations.co.uk. Upmarket hotels and resorts.

Exodus UK ☎020/8675 5550, ⓦwww.thisamazingplanet.com. Walking and cycling in the Italian Lakes, the Dolomites and northern Tuscany.

Headwater ☎01606/720 033, ⓦwww.headwater.com. Walking tours in six regions of Italy and five Italian islands.

Italiatour ☎01883/625255, ⓦwww.italiatour.co.uk. Tours throughout Italy, special interest holidays and fly-drive.

Italian Connection ☎020/7520 0470, ⓦwww.italian-connection.co.uk. Specializing in tailor-made holidays throughout Italy.

Italian Life ☎0870/444 8811, ⓦwww.italianlife.co.uk. Large database of properties in central and southern Italy, with a comprehensive online search facility to find just the right one.

Magic of Italy ☎020/8939 5453, ⓦwww.magictravelgroup.co.uk. Hotel, villa packages and city breaks throughout Italy.

Martin Randall Travel ☎020/8742 3355, ⓦwww.martinrandall.com. Small-group cultural tours led by experts on art, archeology or music.

Saga Holidays ☎0130/377 1111, ⓦwww.sagaholidays.com. The country's biggest and most established specialist in tours and holidays aimed at older people

Simply Travel ☎020/8541 2200, ⓦwww.simply-travel.com. Upmarket tour company specializing in villas and hotels in the less touristy parts of Tuscany, Umbria and Sardinia.

Tasting Places ☎020/7460 0077, ⓦwww.tastingplaces.com. Week-long cooking holidays in Veneto, Sicily, Tuscany and Umbria.

Tabona & Walford ☎020/8870 6015, ⓦwww.tabonaandwalford.com. Bespoke walking tours in Tuscany, Sicily and Sardinia.

By rail from the UK and Ireland

Travelling **by train** to Italy won't save much money but it can be an enjoyable and leisurely way of getting to the country and you can stop off in other parts of Europe on the way. As you'd expect, the choice of routes and fares is hugely complex, but most trains pass through Paris and head down through France towards Milan. A return ticket to Milan, using Eurostar and the super-fast TGV through France, currently costs £172 and takes around twelve hours; the seventeen-hour journey to Florence costs £198 and for the same price you can extend the trip another two hours to Rome. Advance booking is essential and discounts (for under-26s) and special offers are legion. Using slower trains won't cut the cost very significantly and neither will the cross-Channel ferry route, which is now barely used and accordingly badly timetabled.

Bear in mind that if you travel via Paris on Eurostar you will have to change stations which means lugging your bags on the metro from the Gare du Nord to the Gare de

Lyon. Details on all international rail tickets and passes are best obtained by calling personally at major train stations or by contacting the agents listed below. Don't expect much help from travel agents on planning routes, however, or the Italian State Railways office to answer the phone.

If you are planning to include Italy as part of a longer European trip it might be worth investing in a **rail pass** – the **InterRail** and **Eurail** passes offer a month's unlimited rail travel throughout Europe, but note that they must be bought before leaving home. See "Getting Around" (p.28) for details of all rail passes available, including those for use solely on the Italian rail network.

Rail contacts in the UK

Eurostar ☎0870/160 6600,
ⓦwww.eurostar.com.
The Eurostar passenger train goes from Waterloo International in London to Paris (3hr) and Brussels (2hr 40min) via Ashford in Kent (1hr from London) and the Channel Tunnel. The cheapest return ticket to Paris is currently £79, though restrictions apply. You can get through-ticketing – including the tube journey to Waterloo International – from Eurostar, from most travel agents or from mainline train stations in Britain; typical add-on prices for a return ticket to Paris from Edinburgh or Glasgow are £30, from Manchester £20 and Birmingham £13.50. Note that InterRail passes give discounts on the Eurostar service.

See p.26 for information on **Italian State Railways** and other rail contacts in the UK.

By bus from the UK and Ireland

It's difficult to see why anyone would want to travel to Italy by **bus,** unless they had a phobia of flying – and of trains. National Express Eurolines do, however, have occasional bargain offers – at the time of writing a return ticket to Milan costs £69, if booked a week in advance; the normal price for under-26s is £98. The Milan service departs four times a week and takes twenty-three hours; the journey on to Rome will add a gruelling nine hours – and a light £10 – to the trip.

There are direct services **from London** to Turin, Milan, Bologna, Florence and Rome, with less frequent services to Parma, Siena, Venice, Verona, Genoa and Naples.

Eurolines also has a frequent service **from Dublin**, Cork, Limerick and Belfast to London. If you are really keen on buses the **Eurolines pass** gives you unlimited travel between forty-eight European cities for either fifteen, thirty or sixty days; high-season prices for under-26s or over-60s are £186 for thirty days, or £205 for sixty days; for adults £229 and £267 respectively. Alternatively you could consider the **Busabout** Flexipass option detailed below but note that their route does not cover southern Italy.

Bus contacts in the UK and Ireland

Busabout UK ☎020/7950 1661,
ⓦwww.busabout.com. Busabout runs every 2–3 days on 5 circuits in summer, fewer in winter, taking in 70 European cities, with add-on connections to 5 more, plus a link to London and through tickets from elsewhere in Britain and Ireland. Tickets are available in increments of 15 days, 21 days, 1 month, 2 months, or 3 months, with special deals on set itineraries. Busabout also sells Flexipasses, allowing 10 or 15 days' travel within 2 months, 21 days' travel within 3 months, or 30 days out of 4 months. The passes are available direct from the company or from any international branch of STA Travel.
Eurolines UK ☎0870/514 3219, Republic of Ireland ☎01/836 6111, ⓦwww.eurolines.co.uk. Tickets can also be purchased from any Eurolines or National Express agent (☎0870/580 8080, ⓦwww.nationalexpress.co.uk or ⓦwww.gobycoach.com).

By car and ferry from the UK and Ireland

There's no one fixed route to Italy if you're travelling with **your own vehicle**. The best cross-Channel options for most drivers will be the standard ferry/hovercraft links between Dover and Calais/Ostend, or between Newhaven and Dieppe. Crossing with Eurotunnel (24hr service departing every 15min at peak periods) will speed up the initial part of the journey, although overall there are no great savings on time to be made since there's still a long way to go once you reach France. The tunnel journey takes 35 minutes (45 minutes for some night departure times), though you must arrive at least 30min before departure. Rates depend on the time of year, time of day and length of stay and it's cheaper to travel between 10pm and 6am, while the highest fares are reserved for weekend departures and returns in July and August.

Any travel agent can provide up-to-date cross-Channel schedules and make advance bookings – which are essential in high season. As regards **routes** from northern France, the Alpine route via Germany and Switzerland is probably the shortest as the crow flies, but can be pretty arduous; most drivers hotfoot it to the south of France and then switch east into northern Italy. Both the AA and RAC provide comprehensive route-planning services, as well as offering insurance, general advice on all aspects of driving to Italy and details of useful contact organizations. The AA has special deals for Channel crossings, with an overnight stay and breakdown assistance policy included.

Cross-Channel routes

Brittany Ferries UK ☎0870/901 2400, Republic of Ireland ☎021/4277 801, ⊛www.brittanyferries.co.uk. Poole to Cherbourg; Portsmouth to Caen and St Malo; Plymouth to Roscoff (March–Nov/Dec); Cork to Roscoff (March–Oct only).
Eurotunnel UK ☎0870/535 3535, ⊛www.eurotunnel.com.
Hoverspeed UK ☎0870/240 8070, ⊛www.hoverspeed.co.uk. Twenty-four daily departures. Dover to Calais; Newhaven to Dieppe.
Irish Ferries UK ☎0870/517 1717, Republic of Ireland ☎01/661 0511, ⊛www.irishferries.com. Services from Rosslare to Cherbourg and Roscoff run from March to end Sept.
P&O Stena Line UK ☎0870/600 0600, ⊛www.posl.com. Dover to Calais.
Sea France ☎0870/571 1711, ⊛www.seafrance.com. Dover to Calais.

From the US and Canada

Alitalia and Delta Airlines fly the widest choice of direct routes between the **USA** and Italy with daily flights to Milan from New York, Miami, Chicago and Boston and to Rome from New York. American Airlines has a direct route from Chicago to Rome. In addition, many European carriers fly to Italy (via their capitals) from all major US and Canadian cities.

The **direct scheduled fares** charged by each airline don't vary as much as you might think, and you'll more often than not be basing your choice around things like flight timings, routes and gateway cities, ticket restrictions, and even the airline's reputation for comfort and service. It's a long flight, something like nine hours from New York, Boston and the eastern Canadian cities, twelve hours from Chicago, and fifteen hours from Los Angeles, so it's as well to be fairly comfortable and to arrive at a reasonably sociable hour.

The cheapest **round-trip fares** to Rome or Milan, travelling midweek in low season, start at around $650 from New York or Boston, rising to about $950 during the summer. Add another $100–200 for flights from LA, Miami and Chicago. Note that these prices do not include taxes.

Air Canada and Alitalia have **direct** flights from **Toronto** to Milan and Rome for a low-season fare of Can$950 midweek, increasing to around Can$1300 in high season without taxes.

Airlines in North America

Air Canada ☎1-888/247-2262, ⊛www.aircanada.ca.
Air France US ☎1-800/237-2747, Canada ☎1-800/667-2747, ⊛www.airfrance.com.
Alitalia US ☎1-800/223-5730, Canada ☎1-800/361-8336, ⊛www.alitalia.com.
American Airlines ☎1-800/433-7300, ⊛www.aa.com.
Austrian Airlines ☎1-800/843-0002, ⊛www.aua.com.
British Airways ☎1-800/247-9297, ⊛www.ba.com.
Continental Airlines ☎1-800/231-0856, ⊛www.continental.com.
Delta Air Lines ☎1-800/241-4141, ⊛www.delta.com.
Iberia ☎1-800/772-4642, ⊛www.iberia.com.
KLM/Northwest ☎1-800/447-4747, ⊛www.klm.com.
LOT Polish Airlines US ☎1-800/223-0593 or 718/264-6480, Canada ☎1-800/668-5928, ⊛www.lot.com.
Lufthansa US ☎1-800/645-3880, Canada ☎1-800/563-5954, ⊛www.lufthansa-usa.com.
Northwest/KLM Airlines ☎1-800/447-4747, ⊛www.nwa.com.
SAS (Scandinavian Airlines) ☎1-800/221-2350, ⊛www.scandinavian.net.

Swiss ☎1-800/221-4750, ⊛www.swiss.com.
TAP Air Portugal ☎1-800/221-7370,
⊛www.tap-airportugal.pt.

Discount travel companies in North America

Air Brokers International ☎1-800/883-3273,
⊛www.airbrokers.com. Consolidator and specialist
in round-the-world tickets.
Airtech ☎1-877-247-8324 or 212/219-7000,
⊛www.airtech.com. Standby seat broker; also
deals in consolidator fares and courier flights.
Council Travel ☎1-800/226-8624,
⊛www.counciltravel.com. Nationwide organization
that specializes mostly, but by no means
exclusively, in student/budget travel. Flights from
the US only.
Educational Travel Center ☎1-800/747-5551
or 608/256-5551, ⊛www.edtrav.com.
Student/youth discount agent.
High Adventure Travel ☎1-800/350-0612 or
415/912-5600, ⊛www.airtreks.com. Round-the-
world tickets. The website features an interactive
database that lets you build and price your own
round-the-world itinerary.
Skylink US ☎1-800/247-6659 or 212/573-8980,
Canada ☎1-800/759-5465,
⊛www.skylinkus.com. Consolidator.
STA Travel ☎1-800/777-0112 or 781-4040,
⊛www.sta-travel.com. Worldwide specialists in
independent travel; also student IDs, travel
insurance, car rental, rail passes, etc.
Student Flights ☎1-800/255-8000 or 480/951-
1177, ⊛www.isecard.com. Student/youth fares,
student IDs.
TFI Tours International ☎1-800/745-8000 or
212/736-1140, ⊛www.lowestairprice.com.
Consolidator.
Travac ☎1-800/872-8800,
⊛www.thetravelsite.com. Consolidator and
charter broker with offices in New York City and
Orlando.
Travelers Advantage ☎1-877/259-2691,
⊛www.travelersadvantage.com. Discount travel
club; annual membership fee required (currently $1
for 3 months' trial).
Travel Avenue ☎1-800/333-3335,
⊛www.travelavenue.com. Full-service travel agent
that offers discounts in the form of rebates.
Travel Cuts Canada ☎1-800/667-2887, US ☎1-
866/246-9762, ⊛www.travelcuts.com. Canadian
student-travel organization.
Worldtek Travel ☎1-800/243 1723,
⊛www.worldtek.com. Discount travel agency for
worldwide travelers.

Packages and organized tours

There are dozens of companies operating
group travel and tours in Italy, ranging from
full-blown luxury escorted tours to small
groups sticking to specialized itineraries.
Prices vary widely, so check what you are
getting for your money (many don't include
the cost of the airfare). Reckon on paying at
least US$1500/Can$2250 for a ten-day touring vacation, and as much as
US$5000/Can$7500 (not including flights) for
a fourteen-day escorted specialist package.

Tour operators in North America

Abercrombie & Kent ☎1-800/323-7308 or
630/954-2944, ⊛www.abercrombiekent.com.
Upmarket escorted or independent walking and
cultural tours of Italy.
Adventures Abroad ☎1-800/665-3998 or
604/303-1099, ⊛www.adventures-abroad.com.
Small-group tours throughout Italy.
Backroads ☎1-800/462-2848 or 510/527-1555,
⊛www.backroads.com. Cycling and hiking in
Veneto, Tuscany and Puglia.
BCT Scenic Walking ☎1-800/473-1210,
⊛www.bctwalk.com. Escorted walking tours.
Butterfield & Robinson ☎1-800/678-1147,
⊛www.butterfield.com. Escorted cycling and
walking tours.
Central Holidays ☎1-800-935/5000,
⊛www.CentralHolidays.com. Wide range of
independent or escorted tours and city breaks.
Classic Journeys ☎1-800/200-3887,
⊛www.classicjourneys.com. Cooking and hiking
throughout Italy.
Country Walkers ☎1-800/464-92255,
⊛www.countrywalkers.com. Small-group walking
tours throughout Italy.
Cross Culture ☎1-800/491-1148 or 413/256-
6303, ⊛www.crosscultureinc.com. Small-group
cultural tours.
Europe Through the Back Door ☎425/771-
8303, ⊛www.ricksteves.com.
20-day tour of Italy and 7-night tour of Rome,
Florence or Venice.
Geographic Expeditions ☎1-800/777-8183 or
415/922-0448, ⊛www.geoex.com. Cultural tours
of Sicily.
The International Kitchen ☎1-800/945-8606,
⊛www.intl-kitchen.com. Cooking school vacations
in Tuscany and Amalfi.
Italian Connection ☎1-800/462-7911, ⊛www
.italian-connection.com. Hiking and cooking in
Sicily, Tuscany, Piemonte and the Dolomites.

Journeys International ☎1-800/255-8735, ⓦwww.journeys-intl.com. Offers three tours of three very different regions of Italy.
Mountain Travel–Sobek ☎1-888/687-6235, ⓦwww.mtsobek.com. Hiking in Tuscany, Dolomites, Italian Lakes and the Mont Blanc circuit.
New Frontiers ☎1-800/366-6387, ⓦwww.newfrontiers.com. 5-night tour of Rome.

From Australia and New Zealand

Round-trip fares to Rome and Milan from the main cities in **Australia** cost A$1500–1850 in low season, and A$1700–2500 in high season. You are likely to get most **flexibility** by travelling with Alitalia, Thai, British Airways or Qantas, which offer a range of discounted Italian tour packages and air passes, although you can generally find cheaper offers with Garuda and Sri Lanka Airlines. There are no direct flights to Italy from Australia.

Round-trip fares to Rome from **New Zealand** cost from NZ$2000 low season to NZ$3200 high season. Alitalia flies in conjunction with other carriers (from Auckland via Sydney and Bangkok/Singapore to Rome or Milan); British Airways to Rome from Auckland via Singapore/Bangkok or LA; Qantas to Rome from Auckland, Christchurch or Wellington via Sydney or Melbourne; JAL to Rome from Auckland (with inclusive overnight stop in Tokyo/Osaka); Malaysia and Thai to Rome from Auckland via Kuala Lumpur and Bangkok respectively.

Airlines in Australia and New Zealand

Alitalia Australia ☎02/9262 3925, ⓦwww.alitalia.com
British Airways Australia ☎02/8904 8800, New Zealand ☎0800/274 847, ⓦwww.britishairways.com.
Cathay Pacific Australia ☎13 17 47, New Zealand ☎09/379 0861 or 0508/800 454, ⓦwww.cathaypacific.com.
Garuda Australia ☎02/9334 9970, New Zealand ☎09/366 1862, ⓦwww.garuda-indonesia.com.
Japan Airlines Australia ☎02/9272 1111, New Zealand ☎09/379 9906, ⓦwww.japanair.com.
KLM Australia ☎1300/303 747, New Zealand ☎09/309 1782, ⓦwww.klm.com.
Lufthansa Australia ☎1300/655 727, New Zealand ☎09/303 1529, ⓦwww.lufthansa.com.

Malaysia Airlines Australia ☎13 26 27, New Zealand ☎09/373 2741, ⓦwww.mas.com.my.
Qantas Australia ☎13 13 13, New Zealand ☎09/661 901, ⓦwww.qantas.com.au.
Singapore Airlines Australia ☎13 10 11, New Zealand ☎09/303 2129, ⓦwww.singaporeair.com.
Sri Lankan Airlines Australia ☎02/9244 2234, New Zealand ☎09/308 3353, ⓦwww.airlanka.com.
Thai Airways Australia ☎1300/651 960, New Zealand ☎09/377 3886, ⓦwww.thaiair.com.

General travel agents in Australia and New Zealand

Budget Travel New Zealand ☎09/366 0061 or 0800/808 040, ⓦwww.budgettravel.co.nz. Discount flight and holiday specialists.
Destinations Unlimited New Zealand ☎09/414 1680, ⓦwww.etravelnz.com. Web-based travel agency with flights, RTW tickets and European car rental.
Flight Centres Australia ☎13 31 33 or 02/9235 3522, New Zealand ☎09/358 4310, ⓦwww.flightcentre.com.au. Discount international airfares and holiday packages.
STA Travel Australia ☎1300/733 035, ⓦwww.statravel.com.au, New Zealand ☎0508/782 872, ⓦwww.statravel.co.nz. Worldwide specialists in low-cost flights and tours for students and under-26s.
Student Uni Travel Australia ☎02/9232 8444, ⓔaustralia@backpackers.net. Branches in Brisbane, Cairns, Darwin, Melbourne and Perth.
Trailfinders Australia ☎02/9247 7666, ⓦwww.trailfinders.com.au. One of the best-informed and most efficient agents for independent travellers.
Travel.com Australia ☎1300/130 482 or 02/9249 5444, ⓦwww.travel.com.au, New Zealand ☎09/359 3860, ⓦwww.travel.co.nz. Discount flights and holiday deals.

Specialist travel agents in Australia and New Zealand

Abercrombie and Kent Australia ☎03/9536 1800 or 1300/851 800, New Zealand ☎0800/441 638, ⓦwww.abercrombiekent.com.au. Upmarket escorted or independent walking and cultural tours of Italy.
Adventure Travel Company New Zealand ☎09/379 9755, ⓦwww.adventuretravel.co.nz. Car and villa rental, walking and cycling tours in Italy.

CIT Australia ☎02/9267 1255,
ⓦwww.cittravel.com.au. Italian specialists, with packages to Venice, Tuscany, Rome, Florence and the rest of the country.
Contiki Holidays Australia ☎02/9511 2200, New Zealand ☎09/309 8824, ⓦwww.contiki.com. Frenetic tours for 18–35 year-old party animals.

Explore Holidays Australia ☎02/9857 6200 or 1300/731 000, ⓦwww.exploreholidays.com.au. Accommodation and package tours to Italy.
Walkabout Gourmet Adventures Australia ☎03/5159 6556, ⓦwww.walkaboutgourmet.com. Classy food, wine and walking tours throughout Italy.

Red tape and visas

British, Irish and other EU citizens can enter Italy and stay as long as they like on production of a valid passport. Citizens of the United States, Canada, Australia and New Zealand need only a valid passport, too, but are limited to stays of three months. All other nationals should consult the relevant embassy about visa requirements.

Legally, you're required to register with the police within three days of entering Italy, though if you're staying at a hotel this will be done for you. Although the police in some towns have become more punctilious about this, most would still be amazed at any attempt to register yourself down at the local police station while on holiday. However, if you're going to be living here for a while, you'd be advised to do it. For more on living and working in Italy see p.54.

Italian embassies and consulates abroad

Australia Embassy: 12 Grey St, Deakin, Canberra, ACT 2600 ☎02/6273 3333, ⓦwww.ambitalia.org.au. Consulates in Melbourne

☎03/9867 5744 and Sydney ☎02/9392 7900.
Canada Embassy: 275 Slater St, Ottawa, ON, K1P 5H9 ☎613/232-2401, ⓦwww.italyincanada.com. Consulates in Montréal t514/849-8351 and Toronto ☎416/977-1566.
Ireland Embassy: 63–65 Northumberland Rd, 6365 Dublin 4 ☎01/660 1744.
New Zealand Embassy: 34–38 Grant Rd, PO Box 463, Thorndon, Wellington ☎04/473 5339, ⓦwww.italy-embassy.org.nz.
UK Embassy: 14 Three King's Yard, London W1Y 2EH ☎020/7312 2200, ⓦwww.embitaly.org.uk. Consulates in Edinburgh ☎0131/226 3695 and Manchester ☎0161/236 9024.
USA Embassy: 3000 Whitehaven St NW, Washington DC 20008 ☎202/612-4400, ⓦwww.italyemb.org. Consulates in Chicago ☎312/467-1550, New York ☎212/737-9100 and San Francisco ☎415/292-9210.

Information, websites and maps

Before you leave, it may be worth contacting the Italian State Tourist Office (ENIT, ⓦ www.enit.it) for a selection of maps and brochures, though you can usually pick up much the same information from tourist offices in Italy.

Tourist Offices

Most Italian towns, major train stations and airports have a **tourist office** or "APT" (Azienda Promozione Turistica), all of which vary in degree of usefulness (and helpfulness) but usually provide at least a town plan and local listings guide. In smaller villages there is sometimes a "Pro Loco" office which has much the same kind of information, but the staff are unlikely to speak English.

Opening hours vary: larger city and resort offices are likely to be open Monday to Saturday 9am to 1pm and 4 to 7pm, and sometimes for a short period on Sunday mornings; smaller offices may open weekdays only, while Pro Loco times are notoriously erratic – some open for only a couple of hours a day, even in summer. If the tourist office isn't open and all else fails, the local telephone office, most hotels, and bars with phones should all have a copy of the local *Tuttocittà* or similar (a supplement to the main telephone directories), which carries listings and phone numbers of essential services and adverts for restaurants and shops, together with indexed maps of the appropriate city.

Italian State Tourist Offices

Australia Level 26, 44 Market St, Sydney, NSW 2000 ☎ 02/9962 1666, ⓔ enitour@ihug.com.au.
Canada 175 Bloor St East, Suite 907, South Tower, Toronto, ON M4W 3R8 ☎ 416/925 4882, ⓦ www.italiantourism.com.
Ireland Italian Embassy, 63 Northumberland Rd, Dublin ☎ 01/660 1744.
New Zealand Italian Embassy, 34 Grant Rd, Thorndon, Wellington ☎ 04/473 5339.
UK 1 Princes St, London W1R 8AY ☎ 0207/339 3562, ⓔ italy@italiantouristboard.co.uk.
US 630 Fifth Avenue, Suite 1565, New York NY 10111 ☎ 212/245 4822; 500 North Michigan Avenue, Suite 2240, Chicago, Il 60611 ☎ 0996;12400 Wilshire Boulevard, Suite 550, Los Angeles, CA 90025 ☎ 310/820 1898, ⓦ www.italiantourism.com.

Useful websites

ⓦ **www.beniculturali.it** Italian Ministry for Arts and the Environment with details of museums, exhibitions and performances.
ⓦ **www.camping.it** Great site for campers covering virtually every campsite in Italy.
ⓦ **www.enit.it** Italian State Tourist Board with plenty of tourist information.
ⓦ **www.initaly.com** Travel tips and other information.
ⓦ **www.internettrain.it** Internet points in 60 Italian towns and cities.
ⓦ **www.italytour.com** Virtual tour of Italy.
ⓦ **www.meteo.it** Weather forecasts – in Italian but with self-explanatory symbols.
ⓦ **www.museionline.it** Links to museum and exhibition sites, dates, events.
ⓦ **www.paginegialle.it** Italian yellow pages online.
ⓦ **www.parks.it** National and regional parks, wildlife information.
wwww.room-service.co.uk Dedicated booking service for hotels in all categories across most of northern and central Italy.
ⓦ **www.traghetti.com** Links to main ferry operators to the Italian islands.
ⓦ **www.trenitalia.com** Italian State Railways with timetable information in English and Italian.
ⓦ **www.venere.it** Good site for accessing the Web pages of those hotels that have them – and booking rooms online.
ⓦ **www.zoomata.com** New ezine with lots of information about Italy today.

Maps

The **town plans** throughout the Guide should be fine for most purposes, and practically all tourist offices give out maps of their local area for free. The clearest and best-value large-scale commercial **road map** of Italy is the Michelin 1:1,000,000 which covers the whole country including Sicily and Sardinia. There are also the 1:800,000 and 1:400,000 maps produced by the Touring Club Italiano, covering north, south and central Italy, although these are a little more expensive; TCI also produce excellent 1:200,000 maps of the individual regions, which are indispensable if you are touring a specific area in depth. Alternatively, the Automobile Club d'Italia issues a good, free 1:275,000 road map, available from State Tourist Offices. Local tourist offices also often have road maps of varying quality to give away.

For **hiking** you'll need at least a scale of 1:50,000. Studio FMB and the TCI cover the major mountain areas of northern Italy to this scale, but for more detailed, down-to-scale 1:25,000 maps, both the Istituto Geografico Centrale and Kompass series cover central and northwest Italy and the Alps. The Apennines and Tuscany are covered by Multigraphic (Firenze), easiest bought in Italy, while Tabacco produce a good series detailing the Dolomites and the northeast of the country. In Italy, the Club Alpino Italiano (ⓦwww.cai.it) is a good source of hiking maps; we've supplied details of branches throughout the Guide.

Map outlets

In the UK and Ireland

Blackwell's Map and Travel Shop 50 Broad St, Oxford OX1 3BQ ☏01865/793 550, ⓦhttp://maps.blackwell.co.uk/index.html.
Easons Bookshop 40 O'Connell St, Dublin 1 ☏01/873 3811, ⓦwww.eason.ie.
Heffers Map and Travel 20 Trinity St, Cambridge CB2 1TJ ☏01865/333 536, ⓦwww.heffers.co.uk.
Hodges Figgis Bookshop 56–58 Dawson St, Dublin 2 ☏01/677 4754, ⓦwww.hodgesfiggis.com.
James Thin Booksellers 53–59 South Bridge Edinburgh EH1 1YS ☏0131/622 8222, ⓦwww.jthin.co.uk.
The Map Shop 30a Belvoir St, Leicester LE1 6QH ☏0116/247 1400, ⓦwww.mapshopleicester.co.uk.
National Map Centre 22–24 Caxton St, London SW1H 0QU ☏020/7222 2466, ⓦwww.mapsnmc.co.uk.
Newcastle Map Centre 55 Grey St, Newcastle upon Tyne, NE1 6EF ☏0191/261 5622.
Ordnance Survey Ireland Phoenix Park, Dublin 8 ☏01/8025 349, ⓦwww.irlgov.ie/osi.
Ordnance Survey of Northern Ireland Colby House, Stranmillis Ct, Belfast BT9 5BJ ☏028/9025 5755, ⓦwww.osni.gov.uk.
Stanfords 12–14 Long Acre, WC2E 9LP ☏020/7836 1321, ⓦwww.stanfords.co.uk. Maps available by mail, phone order, or email. Other

branches within British Airways offices at 156 Regent St, London W1R 5TA ☏020/7434 4744, and 29 Corn St, Bristol BS1 1HT ☏0117/929 9966.
The Travel Bookshop 13–15 Blenheim Crescent, W11 2EE ☏020/7229 5260, ⓦwww.thetravelbookshop.co.uk.

In the US and Canada

Adventurous Traveler Bookstore 102 Lake Street, Burlington, VT 05401 ☏1-800/282-3963, ⓦwww.adventuroustraveler.com.
Book Passage 51 Tamal Vista Blvd, Corte Madera, CA 94925 ☏1-800/999-7909, ⓦwww.bookpassage.com.
Distant Lands 56 S Raymond Ave, Pasadena, CA 91105 ☏1-800/310-3220, ⓦwww.distantlands.com.
Elliot Bay Book Company 101 S Main St, Seattle, WA 98104 ☏1-800/962-5311, ⓦwww.elliotbaybook.com.
Forsyth Travel Library 226 Westchester Ave, White Plains, NY 10604 ☏1-800/367-7984, ⓦwww.forsyth.com.
Globe Corner Bookstore 28 Church St, Cambridge, MA 02138 ☏1-800/358-6013, ⓦwww.globecorner.com.
GORP Travel ☏1-877/440-4677, ⓦwww.gorp.com/gorp/books/main.htm.
Map Link 30 S La Patera Lane, Unit 5, Santa Barbara, CA 93117 ☏805/692-6777, ⓦwww.maplink.com.
Rand McNally ☏1-800/333-0136, ⓦwww.randmcnally.com. Around thirty stores across the US; dial ext ☏2111 or check the website for the nearest location.
The Travel Bug Bookstore 2667 W Broadway, Vancouver V6K 2G2 ☏604/737-1122, ⓦwww.swifty.com/tbug.
World of Maps 1235 Wellington St, Ottawa, Ontario K1Y 3A3 ☏1-800/214-8524, ⓦwww.worldofmaps.com.

In Australia and New Zealand

The Map Shop 6–10 Peel St, Adelaide, SA 5000 ☏08/8231 2033, ⓦwww.mapshop.net.au.
Mapland 372 Little Bourke St, Melbourne, Victoria 3000, ☏03/9670 4383, ⓦwww.mapland.com.au.
MapWorld 173 Gloucester St, Christchurch, New Zealand ☏0800/627 967 or 03/374 5399, ⓦwww.mapworld.co.nz.
Perth Map Centre 1/884 Hay St, Perth, WA 6000, ☏08/9322 5733, ⓦwww.perthmap.com.au.
Specialty Maps 46 Albert St, Auckland 1001 ☏09/307 2217, ⓦwww.ubdonline.co.nz/maps.
Travel Bookshop Shop 3, 175 Liverpool St, Sydney ☏02/9261 8200.

Insurance

Even though EU health care privileges apply in Italy, you'd do well to take out an insurance policy before travelling to cover against theft, loss, illness or injury. Before paying for a new policy, however, it's worth checking whether you are already covered: some all-risks home insurance policies may cover your possessions when overseas, and many private medical schemes include cover when abroad. In Canada, for example, provincial health plans usually provide partial cover for medical mishaps overseas, while holders of official student/teacher/youth cards in both Canada and the US are entitled to meagre accident coverage and hospital in-patient benefits. Students will often find that their student health coverage extends during the vacations and for one term beyond the date of last enrolment.

If you're not already covered, you might want to contact a specialist travel insurance company, or consider the travel insurance deal we offer (see box below). A typical policy usually provides cover for the loss of baggage, tickets and – up to a certain limit – cash or cheques, as well as cancellation or curtailment of your journey. Most policies exclude so-called dangerous sports unless an extra premium is paid: in Italy this can mean scuba-diving, windsurfing and trekking. Many policies can be chopped and changed to exclude coverage you don't need – for example, sickness and accident benefits can often be excluded or included at will. If you do take medical coverage, ascertain whether benefits will be paid as treatment proceeds or only after your return home, and whether there is a 24-hour medical emergency number. When securing baggage cover, make sure that the per-article limit – typically under £500 – will cover your most valuable possession. If you need to make a claim, you should keep receipts for medicines and medical treatment, and in the event you have anything stolen, you must obtain an official statement from the police (*polizia* or *carabinieri*).

Rough Guides travel insurance

Rough Guides offers its own travel insurance, customized for our readers by a leading UK broker and backed by a Lloyd's underwriter. It's available for anyone, of any nationality and any age, travelling anywhere in the world.

There are two main Rough Guide insurance plans: **Essential**, for basic, no-frills cover; and **Premier** – with more generous and extensive benefits. Alternatively, you can take out **annual multi-trip insurance**, which covers you for any number of trips throughout the year (with a maximum of 60 days for any one trip). Unlike many policies, the Rough Guides schemes are calculated by the day, so if you're travelling for 27 days rather than a month, that's all you pay for. If you intend to be away for the whole year, the Adventurer policy will cover you for 365 days. Each plan can be supplemented with a "Hazardous Activities Premium" if you plan to indulge in sports considered dangerous, such as skiing, scuba-diving or trekking.

For a policy quote, call the Rough Guide Insurance Line on UK freefone ☏0800/015 0906; US toll-free ☏1-866/220 5588, or, if you're calling from elsewhere ☏+44 1243/621 046. Alternatively, get an online quote or buy online at ⓦwww.roughguidesinsurance.com.

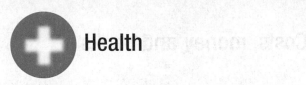

Health

EU citizens can take advantage of Italy's health services under the same terms as the residents of the country, but you'll need form E111, available from any main post office. The Australian Medicare system also has a reciprocal health-care arrangement with Italy.

Vaccinations are not required, and Italy doesn't present any more **health worries** than anywhere else in Europe; the worst that's likely to happen to you is suffering from the extreme heat in summer or from an upset stomach (shellfish is the usual culprit). The **water** is perfectly safe to drink and you'll find public fountains (usually button- or tap-operated) in squares and city streets everywhere, though look out for *acqua non potabile* signs, indicating that the water is unsafe to drink. It's worth taking insect repellent, as even inland towns, most notoriously Milan, suffer from a persistent **mosquito** problem, especially in summer.

Pharmacies

An Italian **pharmacist** (*farmacia*) is well qualified to give you advice on minor ailments and to dispense prescriptions and there's generally one open all night in the bigger towns and cities. A rota system operates, and you should find the address of the one currently open on any *farmacia* door or listed in the local paper.

Doctors and hospitals

If you need **treatment**, go to a doctor (*medico*); every town and village has one. Ask at a pharmacy, or consult the local Yellow Pages (under *Azienda Unità Sanitaria Locale* or *Unità Sanitaria Locale*). The Italian Yellow Pages (*Pagine Gialle*) also list some specialist practitioners in such fields as acupuncturo and homeopathy, the latter much more common in Italy than in some countries. If you're eligible, take your E111 with you to the doctor's: this should enable you to get free treatment and prescriptions for medicines at the local rate – about ten percent of the price of the medicine. For repeat medication, take any empty bottles or capsules with you to the doctor's – the brand names often differ.

If you are **seriously ill** or involved in an **accident**, go straight to the *Pronto Soccorso* (casualty) of the nearest hospital, or phone ☎113 and ask for *ospedale* or *ambulanza*. Throughout the Guide, you'll find listings for pharmacies, hospitals and emergency services in all the major cities. Major train stations and airports also often have first-aid stations with qualified doctors on hand.

Incidentally, try to avoid going to the **dentist** (*dentista*) while you're in Italy. These aren't covered by the *mutua* or health service, and for the smallest problem you'll pay through the teeth. Take local advice, or consult the local Yellow Pages.

If you don't have a spare pair of glasses, it's worth taking a copy of your prescription so that an **optician** (*ottico*) can make you up a new pair should you lose or damage them.

Costs, money and banks

In recent years the economic boom and the glut of visitors in the more touristy cities have conspired to increase prices in Italy; accommodation costs in particular have soared. Generally you'll find the south much less expensive than the north: as a broad guide, expect to pay most in Venice, Milan, Florence and Bologna, less in Rome, while in Naples and Sicily prices come down to fairly reasonable levels.

Average costs

Some **basics** are reasonably inexpensive: a pizza or plate of pasta with a beer (the staple cheap meal in a restaurant) will cost between £5/$8 and £10/$16 on average, though in some of the larger, more visited cities – Florence and Venice, for example – it can be difficult to find appealing venues in this price range; Rome and Naples, on the other hand, are no problem. Buses and trains are cheap too: for instance, a second-class return from Rome to Milan on an Intercity train – a five-and-a-half-hour, six-hundred-kilometre trip – costs just £46/$74. **Drinking**, by contrast, is pricey – unless you stick to wine. Soft drinks and coffee cost around the same as in Britain and more than in North America; a large glass of beer can cost up to £4/$6 if you decide to sit down. **Room rates** start at a bottom line of £20/$30 for the most basic double room in a one-star hotel, although again in Milan, Florence or Venice it's hard to find anything under £30/$44.

Overall, in central Italy, if you're watching your budget – camping, buying food from shops and markets – you could get by on around £25/$40 a day; a more realistic **average daily budget** – staying in one-star hotels, taking trains and eating one cheap meal out a day – would be approaching £40/$64, perhaps a little less in the south; while to live reasonably well you probably need to spend at least £50/$80 a day.

Bear in mind, too, that the **time of year** can make a big difference. During the height of summer, in July and August when the Italians take their holidays, hotel prices can escalate; outside the season, however, you can often negotiate much lower rates. There are a few **reductions** and discounts for ISIC members, under-18s and over-65s but only in the major cities and for entry into state museums and sites elsewhere (see below for details).

Youth and student discounts

Once obtained, various official and quasi-official **youth/student ID cards** soon pay for themselves in savings. Full-time students are eligible for the International Student ID Card (ISIC, ⓦwww.isiccard.com), which entitles the bearer to special discounts for transport, accommodation, entertainment, museums, sports clubs, some food outlets and courses in Rome, Milan, Bologna, Florence and other major Italian cities – check the ⓦwww.istc-net.org site for detailed information about which discounts you can get and where. For Americans there's also a health benefit, providing up to $3000 in emergency medical coverage and $100 a day for 60 days in the hospital, plus a 24-hour hotline to call in the event of a medical, legal or financial emergency. The card costs $22 for Americans; Can$16 for Canadians; AUS$16.50 for Australians; NZ$21 for New Zealanders; and £6 in the UK.

You only have to be 26 or under to qualify for the **International Youth Travel Card**, which costs US$22/£6 and carries the same benefits. Teachers qualify for the **International Teacher Card**, offering similar discounts and costing £6, US$22, Can$16, AUS$16.50 and NZ$21. All these cards are available in the US from Council Travel and STA and, in Canada, Travel Cuts (see p.17 for addresses); in Australia and New Zealand from STA or Campus Travel; and in the UK from CTS Travel (🌐 www.ctstravel.co.uk) or STA.

Several other travel organizations and accommodation groups also sell their own cards, good for various discounts. A university photo ID might open some doors, but is not as easily recognizable as the ISIC cards.

Currency

On January 1, 2002, Italy was one of twelve European Union countries to change over to a single currency, the **euro** (EU$). The euro is split into 100 cents. There are seven euro **notes** – in denominations of 500, 200, 100, 50, 20, 10, and 5 euros, each a different colour and size – and eight different **coin** denominations, including 2 and 1 euros, then 50, 20, 10, 5, 2, and 1 cents. Euro coins feature a common EU design on one face, but different country-specific designs on the other. At the time of writing the working **rate of exchange** is £1 = €1.56; US$1 = €1.06; Aus$1 = 0.55; NZ$ = 0.48.

Cash and travellers' cheques

Although it's a good idea to have some **cash** when you first arrive, it is safer to bring the bulk of your money in the form of **travellers' cheques,** available from any bank or post office in the UK. Most American and Canadian banks sell American Express cheques, and they're widely accepted; your local bank will probably also sell one or more of the other brands. Alternatively check the American Express 🌐 www.americanexpress.com, Thomas Cook 🌐 www.thomascook.com or Visa 🌐 www.visa.com websites direct.

The usual fee for travellers' cheque sales is one or two percent, though this may be waived if you buy the cheques through a bank where you have an account. It pays to get a selection of denominations. Make sure you keep the purchase agreement and a record of cheque serial numbers safe and separate from the cheques themselves. In the event that cheques are lost or stolen, the issuing company will expect you to report the loss forthwith to their office in Italy; most companies claim to replace lost or stolen cheques within 24 hours.

It's advisable to buy **euro traveller's cheques** rather than dollars or pound sterling, since you'll probably get a better rate of exchange this way, and you may not have to pay commission when you cash them, though this does depend on individual banks – if you do have to pay a fee it will usually be around one percent of the total. There is no commission on Thomas Cook euro travellers' cheques if you cash them at a Thomas Cook Exchange Bureau.

Credit and debit cards

Credit cards are a very handy backup source of funds, and can be used either over the counter or in ATMs (*bancomat*), providing you have a PIN number that's designed to work overseas. Mastercard, Visa and American Express are accepted just about everywhere in Italy. Remember that all cash advances are treated as loans, with interest accruing daily from the date of withdrawal; there is often a transaction fee on top of this. However, you may be able to make withdrawals from ATMs using your **debit card**, which is not liable to interest payments, and the flat transaction fee is usually quite small – your bank will be able to advise on this. Found even in small towns, the *bancomat* accepts all major cards, with a minimum withdrawal of €50 and a maximum of €250 per day.

A compromise between travellers' cheques and plastic is **Visa Travel Money**, a disposable pre-paid debit card with a PIN which works in all ATMs that take Visa cards. You load up your account with funds before leaving home, and when they run out, you simply throw the card away. You can buy up to nine cards to access the same funds – useful for couples or families travelling together – and it's a good idea to buy at least one extra as a back-up in case of loss or theft. There is also a 24-hour toll-free customer assistance number: ☎800-819-014 from Italy. The card is available in most countries from branches of Thomas Cook and Citicorp. For more information, check the Visa Travel Money website at 🌐 http://usa.visa.com/personal/cards/visa _travel_money.html.

Changing money

In Italy, you'll get the best rate of exchange (*cambio*) at a **bank**. There are a few nation-wide banking chains – the Banca Nazionale del Lavoro, Credito Italiano and Cassa di Risparmio, among others – as well as regional chains like the Banca di Roma, Banco di Napoli or Banco di Sicilia. **Banking hours** are normally Monday to Friday mornings from 8.30am until 1pm, and for an hour in the afternoon (usually 2.30–3.30pm). There are local variations on this and banks are usually open only in the morning on the day before a public holiday. Outside banking hours, the larger **hotels** will change money or travellers' cheques, although if you're staying in a reasonably large city the rate is invariably better at the train station **exchange bureaux** – normally open evenings and weekends. Check the "Listings" sections of the main city accounts in the Guide.

Wiring money

Having **money wired** from home using one of the companies listed below is never convenient or cheap, and should be considered a last resort. It's also possible to have money wired directly from a bank in your home country to a bank in Italy, although this is somewhat less reliable because it involves two separate institutions. If you choose this route, your home bank will need the address of the branch bank where you want to pick up the money and the address and telex number of the Rome or Milan head office, which will act as the clearing house; usually money takes two working days to arrive, and costs around £25/$40 per transaction.

Money-wiring companies

American Express Moneygram
US and Canada ☎1-800/926-9400, Australia ☎1800/230 100, New Zealand ☎09/379 8243 or 0800/262 263, UK and Republic of Ireland ☎0800/6663 9472, ⓦwww.moneygram.com.
Thomas Cook US ☎1-800/287-7362, Canada ☎1-888/823-4732, UK ☎01733/318 922, Belfast ☎028/9055 0030, Dublin ☎01/677 1721, ⓦwww.us.thomascook.com.
Western Union US and Canada ☎1-800/325-6000, Australia ☎1800/649 565, New Zealand ☎09/270 0050, UK ☎0800/833 833, Republic of Ireland ☎1800/395 395, ⓦwww.westernunion.com.

Getting around

The easiest way of travelling around Italy is by train. The Italian train system is one of the least expensive in Europe, reasonably comprehensive, and, in the north of the country at least, very efficient – and is far preferable over long distances to the fragmented, localized and sometimes grindingly slow bus service. Local buses, though, can be very efficient, and where it is actually a better idea to take a bus we've said as much in the text. Planes are expensive and best reserved for longer journeys where time is tight. Ferries go to all the Italian islands, and also ply routes to Greece, Albania, Croatia, Malta, Yugoslavia, Corsica and Tunisia (see pp.536, 681, 929, 941 & 1061). We've detailed train, bus and ferry frequencies in the "Travel Details" section at the end of each chapter of the Guide: note that these refer to regular working-day schedules (ie Monday to Saturday); services may be much reduced or even non-existent on Sundays.

By rail

Italian State Railways (Ferrovie dello Stato, or FS) operate eight types of train. At the top of the range are the **Pendolino** (CiS), a trans-Alpine service, the **Eurostar Italia** (ES), which runs between major cities, slightly faster and more efficient than the **Intercity** (IC), and the **Eurocity** trains which connect the major Italian cities with centres such as Paris, Vienna, Hamburg and Barcelona. Reservations are usually required for all of these services and a supplement in the region of thirty percent of the ordinary fare is payable. Make sure you pay your supplement before getting on board; otherwise you'll have to cough up a far bigger surcharge to the conductor.

Diretto, **Espresso** and **Interregionale** trains are the common-or-garden long-distance expresses, calling only at larger stations. Although reservations are not required for these trains, it's worth **reserving** seats if

you're making a long journey, especially in summer, when they can get very crowded. Reservations can be made at any major train station or travel agent in Italy or via Italian State Railways agents in the UK, US or Australia (see p.30).

Lastly, there are the **Regionale** services, which stop at every place with a population higher than zero (and on which smoking is not allowed).

For **information** on all the above trains call ☏ 8488.88088, or visit the useful FS website at Ⓦ www.trenitalia.com.

In addition to the routes operated by FS,

there are a number of **privately run** lines, using separate stations though charging similar fares. Where they're worth using, these are detailed in the text.

Timetables

Timings and route information for the FS network are posted up at train stations, and we give a rough idea of frequencies and journey times in the "Travel Details" sections at the end of each chapter. If you're travelling extensively it would be worth investing in a copy of the twice-yearly *In Treno In Tutt'Italia* timetable (€3.90), which covers the main routes and is normally on sale at train-station newspaper stands. Pay attention to the **timetable notes**, which may specify the dates between which some services run (*Si effetua dal . . . al . . .*), or whether a service is seasonal (*periodico*, denoted by a vertical squiggle); *laborativo* or *feriale* is the word for the Monday to Saturday service, represented by two crossed hammers; and *festivo* means that a train runs only on Sundays and holidays, symbolized by a cross.

Fares

Fares are inexpensive, calculated by the kilometre and easy to work out for each journey. The timetables give the prices per kilometre but as a rough guide, a second-class one-way fare from Rome to Milan currently costs about €38 by Intercity. **Sleepers** (*cuccetta*) are available on many long-distance services, and prices vary according to the length of journey and whether or not you're sharing. See above for how to make reservations.

All stations have yellow validating machines in which passengers must stamp their ticket before embarking on their journey. Look out for them as you come on to the platform: if you fail to **validate your ticket** you'll be given an on-the-spot-fine. Return tickets are valid within two months of the outward journey, but as two one-way tickets cost the same it's hardly worth bothering.

Rail passes

A rail pass is worth considering if you plan to travel extensively around Italy or are visiting the country as part of a wider tour of Europe. The Europe-wide **InterRail** and **Eurail** passes (see below) give unlimited travel on the FS network, though you'll be liable for supplements on the faster trains. Supplements tend to be quite cheap however, eg €3 on a Eurostar Italia from Venice to Verona, and can be worth paying for the time saved and comfort gained.

If you're travelling exclusively in Italy by train you might consider buying one of the following rail passes available on the FS system, though you'd have to cover a lot of ground to make the price worth it.

The **Italy Flexi Railcard** is available to all non-EU citizens and entitles you to a choice of 4, 8 or 12 days unlimited travel within a month. Second-class adult tickets start at US$191 for 4 days, US$334 for 8 days and US$343 for 12 days travel. The **Italy Flexi Railcard Youth** is the equivalent pass for under-26s and prices for the 4, 8 or 12 days start at US$159, US$223 and US$286 respectively. Note that these passes must be bought outside Italy, and US citizens will usually be charged an additional $15 issuing fee. (see p.30 for details of US and Australian rail contacts).

The **Italy Railcard** is only available to EU citizens and gives unlimited travel on all FS trains (expect to pay a supplement for some services), but unless you're constantly on the move it isn't likely to be worth the money. Prices are currently €210 for 8 days, €264 for 15 days, €306 for 21 days and €369 for 30 days travel.

The **Kilometric/Chilometrico** ticket gives 3000km worth of travel on a maximum of twenty separate journeys. It costs €116.72, but you have to pay supplements on faster trains and unless you're travelling in a group (the ticket is valid for five people) it probably isn't worth getting. You're unlikely to cover this sort of distance on an Italian holiday anyway.

Two discount cards – the **Cartaverde** for under-26s, and the **Carta d'argento** for over-65s – come into their own if you're going to be spending a long time in the country. Valid for one year, they give a twenty percent discount on any fare, cost €20, and are available from main train stations in Italy. Bear in mind, too, that **children aged 4–12 qualify for a fifty percent discount** on all journeys, and children under 4 (not occupying a seat) travel free.

InterRail pass

InterRail passes are only available to European residents, and you will be asked to provide proof of residency before being allowed to purchase one. They come in over-26 and (cheaper) under-26 versions, and cover 28 European countries (including Turkey and Morocco) grouped together in zones:

A Republic of Ireland/Britain
B Norway, Sweden, Finland
C Germany, Austria, Switzerland, Denmark
D Czech & Slovak Republics, Poland, Hungary, Croatia
E France, Belgium, Netherlands, Luxembourg
F Spain, Portugal, Morocco
G Italy, Greece, Turkey, Slovenia plus some ferry services between Italy and Greece
H Bulgaria, Romania, Yugoslavia, Macedonia

The passes are available for 22 days (one zone only), or one month and you can purchase up to three zones or a global pass covering all zones. You can save £5 by booking via the InterRail website (ⓦ www.inter-rail.co.uk). InterRail passes do not include travel between Britain and the continent, although InterRail Pass holders are eligible for discounts on rail travel In Britain and Northern Ireland and cross-Channel ferries and free travel on the Brindisi–Patras ferry between Italy and Greece. The InterRail Pass also gives a discount on the London–Paris Eurostar service.

Eurail passes

A **Eurail Pass** is not likely to pay for itself if you're planning to stick to Italy. The pass, which must be purchased before arrival in Europe, allows unlimited free first-class train travel in Italy and 16 other countries and is available in increments of 15 days, 21 days, 1 month, 2 months and 3 months. If you're under 26, you can save money with a **Eurail Youthpass**, which is valid for second-class travel, or, if you're travelling with 1–4 other companions, a joint **Eurail Saverpass**, both of which are available in the same increments as the Eurail Pass. You stand a better chance of getting your money's worth out of a **Eurail Flexipass**, which is good for 10 or 15 days' travel within a two-month period. This, too, comes in first-class, under-26/second-class (**Eurorail Youth Flexipass**) and group (**Eurail Saver Flexipass**) versions.

In addition, a scaled-down version of the Flexipass, the **Europass**, is available which allows first-class and youth (second-class) travel in France, Germany, Italy, Spain and Switzerland for any 5 days, 6 days, 8 days, 10 days or 15 days within 2 months. Up to four "associate" countries (Austria/Hungary, Benelux, Greece, Portugal) can be included for an additional fee. The **Europass Saverpass** is a version of the Europass for people travelling in groups of two or more that offers a saving of 15 percent per person on the regular fare.

Details of prices for all these passes can be found on ⓦ www.raileurope.com, and the passes can be purchased from one of the agents listed below.

Euro-Domino pass

Euro-Domino passes are valid on the Italian network but are only available to EU residents or to anyone living in Europe for at least six months prior to the date of travel. These passes are available for between three and eight days' travel in a specific country within a one-month period. Current prices work out at €139 adult/€104 under-26 for a three-day pass, €169/€128 for five days and €199/€152 for eight days. There is also a half-price child (age 4–11) fare. Passes are available from rail agents in the UK and Ireland (see overleaf).

Useful timetable publications

The red-covered **Thomas Cook European Timetables** (available from branches of Thomas Cook) details schedules of over 50,000 trains in Europe, as well as timings of over 200 ferry routes and rail-connecting bus services. It's updated and issued every month; main changes occur in the June edition (published end of May) with details of the summer European schedules, and October (published end of Sept) for the winter schedules; some have advance summer/winter timings also.

Rail contacts

In the UK and Ireland

Italian State Railways ☎020/7724 0011, ⓦwww.trenitalia.com. Tickets, timetables and passes for travel within Italy.

Northern Ireland Railways UK ☎028/9089 9411, ⓦwww.nirailways.co.uk. Sells InterRail passes.

Rail Europe UK ☎0870/584 8848, ⓦwww.raileurope.co.uk. Sells rail journeys for Italy, sleepers and couchettes. Discounted rail fares for under-26s on a variety of European routes; also agents for InterRail, Eurostar and Euro-Domino.

Trainseurope UK ☎020/8699 3654, ⓦwww.trainseurope.co.uk.
Sells rail passes, motorail tickets and makes reservations for any European train journey.

In North America

CIT Rail US ☎1-800/223-7987 or 212/730-2400, Canada ☎1-800/361-7799, ⓦwww.fs-on-line.com. Eurail, Europass and Italian passes.

DER Travel US ☎1-888/337-7350, ⓦwww.dertravel.com/rail. Eurail, Europass and many individual country passes.

European Rail Services Canada ☎1-800/205-5800 or 416/695-1211, ⓦwww.europeanrailservices.com. Eurail, Europass, and many individual country passes.

Europrail International Canada ☎1-888/667-9734, ⓦwww.europrail.net. Eurail, Europass and many individual country passes.

Online Travel US ☎1-800/660-5300, ⓦwww.eurorail.com. Eurail Pass, Europass and Italian network passes.

Rail Europe US ☎1-800/438-7245, Canada ☎1-800/361-7245, ⓦwww.raileurope.com/us. Official North American Eurail Pass agent; also sells Europass, multinational passes and most single-country passes.

ScanTours US ☎1-800/223-7226 or 310/636-4656, ⓦwww.scantours.com. Eurail, and many other European country passes.

In Australia and New Zealand

CIT World Travel Australia ☎02/9267 1255 or 03/9650 5510, ⓦwww.cittravel.com.au. Eurail, Europass and Italian rail passes.

Rail Plus Australia ☎1300/555 003 or 03/9642 8644, ⓔinfo@railplus.com.au. Sells Eurail and Europass passes.

Trailfinders Australia ☎02/9247 7666, ⓦwww.trailfinder.com.au. All Europe passes.

By bus

Trains don't go everywhere and sooner or later you'll have to use **regional buses** (*autobus*). Nearly all places are connected by some kind of bus service, but in out-of-the-way towns and villages schedules can be sketchy and are drastically reduced – sometimes non-existent – at weekends, especially on Sundays, something you need to watch out for on the timetable. Bear in mind also that in rural areas schedules are often designed with the working and/or school day in mind – meaning a frighteningly early start if you want to catch that day's one bus out of town, and occasionally a complete absence of services during school holidays.

There isn't a national **bus company**, although a few companies do operate services beyond their own immediate area. **Bus terminals** can be anywhere in larger towns, though often they're sensibly placed next door to the train station; wherever possible we've detailed their whereabouts in the text, but if you're not sure ask for directions to the *autostazione*. In smaller towns and villages, most buses pull in at the central piazza. **Timetables** are worth picking up from the local company's office, bus stations or on the bus. Buy **tickets** immediately before you travel from the bus station ticket office, or on the bus itself; on longer hauls you can try to buy them in advance direct from the bus company, but seat reservations are not normally possible. If you want to get off, ask *posso scendere?*; "the next stop" is *la prossima fermata*.

City buses are always cheap, usually costing a flat fare of €1; it's normally a bit cheaper in the south. **Tickets** are available from a variety of sources, commonly newsagents and tobacconists, but also from any shop displaying the *biglietti* symbol, including many campsite shops and hotel front desks. Once on board, you must cancel your ticket in the machine at the back of the bus. The whole system is based on trust, though in most cities checks for fare-dodging are regularly made, and hefty spot-fines are levied against offenders.

By plane

ATI, the domestic arm of Alitalia, operates **flights** all over Italy. However, it's only worth taking a plane within Italy if you want to cover a large distance quickly: ordinary prices are quite high, pricier than even the most expensive express train.

As an example of ordinary one-way fares, Venice–Rome will cost from around €150, Milan–Naples €190 without airport taxes. If you book a flight from London to Italy with Alitalia you qualify for their **Visit Italy Pass**, which gives you three internal flights for £135 or five for £198 – a bargain if you're making long hops from north to south.

By ferry and hydrofoil

Italy has a well-developed network of **ferries** and **hydrofoils** operated by a number of different private companies. Large car ferries connect the major islands of Sardinia and Sicily with the mainland ports of Genoa, Livorno, La Spezia, Civitavecchia, Fiumicino and Naples, while the smaller island groupings – the Tremiti islands, the Bay of Naples islands, the Pontine islands – are usually linked to a number of nearby mainland towns. Fares are reasonable, although on some of the more popular services – to Sardinia, certainly – you should book well in advance in summer, especially if you're taking a vehicle across. Remember, too, that frequencies are drastically reduced outside the summer months, and some services stop altogether. You'll find a broad guide to journey times and frequencies in the "Travel Details" section at the end of relevant chapters; for full up-to-date schedules and prices, check the Italian website Ⓦwww.traghetti.com which has links to all the main ferry companies, or contact one of the ferry agents in the UK below.

UK agents for Italian ferries

SMS Travel ☎0171/244 8422. Agents for Siremar and Tirrenia ferries Ⓦwww.siremar.it.
Viamare Travel Limited ☎020/7431 4560, Ⓦwww.viamare.com.

By car

Travelling **by car** in Italy is relatively painless, though cities can be hard work. The roads are good, the motorway, or *autostrada* network very comprehensive, and the notorious Italian drivers rather less erratic than their

reputation suggests – though their regard for the rules of the road is sometimes lax to say the least. The best plan is to avoid driving in cities as much as possible; the congestion, proliferation of complex one-way systems and occasional incidents of naked aggression can make it a nightmare.

Parking is very often a headache too. If you get fed up of driving around and settle for a space in a *zona di rimozione* (tow-away zone), don't expect your car to be there when you get back. A handy gadget to have is a small clock-like dial which you set and stick in the windscreen, to indicate when you parked and that you're still within the allowed limit: rental cars generally come equipped with these, and some tourist offices have them too. Parking at night is easier than during the day, but make sure you are not parked in a street that turns into a market in the morning. Increasing numbers of cities operate a colour-coded parking scheme: **blue zone** parking spaces (delineated by a blue line) usually have a maximum stay of one or two hours; they cost around €0.70–1.50 per hour (pay at meters or to attendants) but are sometimes free after 8pm and on Sundays. **White-zone** spaces (white lines) are free and unlimited zone spaces are almost always reserved for residents. Note that walled towns which exclude cars often allow tourists to drive into the city to drop off baggage at a hotel. Car parks, often small enclosed garages, are universally expensive, costing up to €20 a day in big cities; be aware that it's not unknown for hotels to state that they have parking and then direct you to the nearest paying garage.

Most **motorways** are **toll-roads**. Take a ticket as you come on and pay on exit; in automatic booths the amount due is flashed up on a screen in front of you. Major credit cards are accepted; follow the "Viacard" sign. Rates aren't especially high but they can mount up on a long journey: as a general rule, you'll pay around €18 driving a small car from Rome to Florence. Since other roads can be frustratingly slow, tolls are well worth it over long distances. At the time of writing unleaded **petrol** costs €1.05 per litre.

As regards **documentation**, if you're

bringing your own car you need a valid driving licence, an international green card of insurance, and an **international driving permit** if you're a non-EU licence holder. The local branch of your national motoring organization (see below) will usually issue this for you. It's compulsory to carry your car documents and passport while you're driving, and you may be required to present them if stopped by the police – not an uncommon occurrence.

Rules of the road are straightforward: drive on the right; at junctions, where there's any ambiguity, give precedence to vehicles coming from the right; observe the speed limits – 50kph in built-up areas, 110kph on dual carriage-ways and 130kph on motorways (for camper vans, these limits are reduced to 50kph, 80kph and 100kph respectively); and don't drink and drive.

If you **break down**, dial ☏116 and tell the operator where you are, the type of car and your registration number: the nearest office of the Automobile Club d'Italia (ACI) will send someone out to fix your car – although it's not a free service and can work out very expensive if you need a tow. For this reason you might consider arranging cover with a motoring organization in your home country before you leave. Any ACI office in Italy can tell you where to get **spare parts** for your particular car.

Car rental in Italy is pricey, especially in high season, at around £200/US$320 per week for a small hatchback, with unlimited mileage. The major chains have offices in all the larger cities and at airports, train stations, etc: addresses are detailed in the "Listings" sections at the end of city accounts throughout the Guide. Local firms can be less expensive and often have an office at the airport, but generally the best deals are to be had by arranging things in advance, through one of the agents listed below or with Italian specialist tour operators like Crystal or Citalia when you book your flight or holiday. You will need a credit card to act as a deposit when picking up your car.

Never leave anything visible in the car when you're not using it, including the radio. Certain economically depressed cities have appalling reputations for theft – in Naples,

some rental agencies won't insure a car left anywhere except in a locked garage. If you're taking your own vehicle, consider installing a detachable car-radio, and depress your aerial and tuck in your wing mirrors when you park. Most cities and ports have **garages** where you can leave your car; these are a safe enough option.

However you get around on the roads, bear in mind that the **traffic** can be heavy on main roads (particularly over bank holiday weekends and the first and last weekends of August) and appalling in city centres. Some measures to combat the problem have been initiated by the **Città Slow** movement (in association with Slow Food; see p.38) as part of its wider aim to preserve the unique character of member towns and to prevent their increasing standardization. There are currently thirty-two "Slow Towns" in Italy, all committed to improving the quality of life of their inhabitants by introducing, for example, alternate car-free Sundays and a ban on car alarms to reduce noise pollution.

Although Italians are by no means the world's worst drivers they don't win any **safety** prizes either. The secret is to make it very clear what you're going to do – and then do it. A particular danger for foreign drivers is the large number of scooters that can appear suddenly from the blind spot or dash across junctions and red lights with alarming recklessness. Contrary to popular belief, Italians don't go round sounding their horns all the time – in fact, it's taken as a sign of letting things get to you if you resort to such crude tactics. There are exceptions to this rule, though – notably in Naples, which has anarchic tendencies all of its own.

Finally, don't assume that as a **pedestrian** you're safe; even on crossings with traffic lights you can be subject to some close calls.

Car rental agencies

Avis UK ☏0870/606 0100, ⊛www.avis.co.uk, US ☏1-800/331-1084, Canada ☏1-800/272-5871, ⊛www.avis.com, Republic of Ireland ☏01/605 7500, ⊛www.avis.ie, Australia ☏13 63 33, ⊛www.avis.com.au, NZ ☏09/526 2847, ⊛www.avis.co.nz.

Budget UK ☏0800/181 181, ⊛www.budget.co.uk, Republic of Ireland

ⓣ0903/27711, ⓦwww.budget.ie, US ⓣ1-
800/527-0700, ⓦwww.budget.com, Australia
ⓣ1300/362 848, ⓦwww.budget.com.au, NZ
ⓣ09/976 2222, ⓦwww.budget.co.nz.
Europcar UK ⓣ0870/607 5000, Republic of
Ireland ⓣ01/614 2800, US & Canada ⓣ1-
877/940 6900, Australia ⓣ1300 13 13 90,
ⓦwww.europcar.com.
Hertz UK ⓣ0870/848 4848, ⓦwww.hertz.co.uk,
Republic of Ireland ⓣ01/676 7476,
ⓦwww.hertz.ie, US ⓣ1-800/654-3001, Canada
ⓣ1 800/263 0600, ⓦwww.hertz.com, Australia
ⓣ13 30 39, ⓦwww.hertz.com.au, NZ
ⓣ0800/654 321, ⓦwww.hertz.co.nz.
Holiday Autos UK ⓣ0870/400 0099, Republic of
Ireland ⓣ01/872 9366, US ⓣ1-800/422-7737,
Australia ⓣ1300/554 432, New Zealand
ⓣ0800/144 040, ⓦwww.holidayautos.com.
National UK ⓣ0870/536 5365,
ⓦwww.nationalcar.co.uk, US ⓣ1-800/227-7368,
ⓦwww.nationalcar.com, Australia ⓣ13 10 45,
ⓦwww.nationalcar.com.au, NZ ⓣ0800/800 115,
ⓦwww.nationalcar.co.nz.
Thrifty UK ⓣ01494/751 600,
ⓦwww.thrifty.co.uk, Republic of Ireland
ⓣ1800/515 800, ⓦwww.thrifty.ie, US ⓣ1-
800/367-2277, ⓦwww.thrifty.com, Australia
ⓣ1300/367 227, ⓦwww.thrifty.com.au, NZ
ⓣ09/309 0111, ⓦwww.thrifty.co.nz.

Motoring organizations

Australia AAA ⓣ02/6247 7311,
ⓦwww.aaa.asn.au.
Canada CAA ⓣ613/247-0117, ⓦwww.caa.ca.
Italy TCI ⓣ02.852.6304, ⓦwww.touringclub.it.
Ireland AA ⓣ01/617 9988, ⓦwww.aaireland.ie.
New Zealand AA ⓣ09/377 4660,
ⓦwww.nzaa.co.nz.
UK AA ⓣ0800/444 500, ⓦwww.theaa.co.uk; RAC
ⓣ0800/550 055, ⓦwww.rac.co.uk.
US AAA ⓣ1-800/222-4357, ⓦwww.aaa.com.

Hitchhiking

Hitchhiking (*autostop*) is moderately possible in Italy but, as elsewhere in Europe, is
generally inadvisable. If you're determined,
remember that hitching on motorways is illegal, eliciting an on-the-spot fine; stand on a

slip road or at one of the service areas. Bear
in mind also that you should **never hitch
alone** – this applies particularly to women in
the south. Always ask where the car is
headed (*Dov'è diretto?*) before you commit
yourself, and if you want to get out say *Mi fa
scendere.*

By bike

Cycling is seen as more of a sport than a
way of getting around in much of Italy, but as
well as racing clubs on the move you'll see
mountain bikes, touring cycles laden with
panniers, and people of all ages on shopping bikes, often with a toddler balanced on
the cross-bar. Italians in small towns and villages are welcoming to cyclists, and hotels
and hostels will take your bike in overnight
for safekeeping. On the islands, in the
mountains, in major resorts and larger cities
it's usually possible to **rent** a bike, but in
rural areas facilities for this are few and far
between.

The serious cyclist might consider staying
at one of a new chain of hotels that cater
specifically for cycling enthusiasts and their
bikes. Each hotel has a secure room for your
bike, a bike maintenance workshop,
overnight laundry facilities, suggested itineraries and group-tour possibilities, a doctor at
hand and even a special cyclists' diet.
Contact ⓣ0039/0541.660.410, ⓦwww.italy-
bikehotels.it for further information and a list
of hotels.

An alternative is to tour by **motorbike**,
though again there are relatively few places
to rent one. **Mopeds** and **scooters** on the
other hand are relatively easy to find: everyone in Italy, from kids to grannies, rides one
of these and although they're not really built
for any kind of long-distance travel, for shooting around towns and islands they're ideal.
We've detailed outlets in the text; roughly
speaking you should expect to pay up to
€35 a day for a machine. Crash helmets are
compulsory, though in the south at least it's a
law that seems to be largely ignored.

Accommodation

Accommodation in Italy is strictly regulated and, while never especially cheap, is at least fairly reliable: hotels are star-rated and are required to post their prices clearly in each room. Most tourist offices have details of hotel rates in their town or region, and you can usually expect them to be broadly accurate. Whatever happens, establish the *full* price of your room *before* you accept it. In popular resorts and the major cities booking ahead is advisable, particularly during July or August, while for Venice, Rome and Florence it's pretty well essential to book ahead from Easter until late September. You can do this relatively painlessly with hotel booking services online (see "useful websites" p.20) or with travel agents, but we've given phone numbers – and websites/email addresses where available – throughout the Guide if you want to book direct. Make sure you get confirmation of the booking by fax, email or letter; it is far from uncommon to arrive and find all knowledge of your booking is denied. The phrases on pp.1194–1196 should help you get over the language barrier, and in any case in many places you should be able to find someone who speaks at least some English.

Hotels

Hotels in Italy come tagged with a sometimes confusing variety of names, and, although the differences have become minimal of late, you will still find the various names used for what are always basically private hotel facilities. A **locanda** is historically perhaps the most basic option, although the word is, oddly enough, sometimes appropriated to denote somewhere quite fancy.

You will also find **pensione**, although there is nowadays very little difference between these and a regular **albergo** or **hotel**. **Prices** vary greatly between the south and north of Italy, as well as between well-touristed honeyspots and more rural areas. The official star system is based on facilities (TV in rooms, swimming pool, etc) rather than character or comfort – or even price.

In very busy places it's not unusual to have to stay for a minimum of three nights, and many proprietors will add the price of **breakfast** to your bill whether you want it or not; try to ask for accommodation only – you can always eat more cheaply in a bar. Be warned, too, that in major seaside resorts you will often be forced to take **half- or full-pension** in high season. You can cut costs slightly by cramming three into a double room, but most hotels will charge an extra thirty-five percent for this. Note also that people travelling alone may sometimes be clobbered for the price of a double room even when taking a single, though it can also work the other way round – if all their **single rooms** are taken, a hotelier may well put you in a double room but only charge the single rate.

Hostels

There are plenty of official **HI youth hostels** in Italy, charging around €12 per night for a dormitory bed. You can easily base a tour of the country around them, although for two people travelling together they don't always represent a massive saving on the cheapest double hotel room – especially if you take into account the bus fare you might have to fork out to reach some of them. If you're travelling on your own, on the other hand, hostels are usually more sociable and can work out a lot cheaper; many have facilities such as inexpensive restaurants and self-catering kitchens that enable you to cut costs further. In a few cases too – notably Castroreale in Sicily and Montagnana in the Veneto – the hostels are beautifully located and in many ways preferable to any hotel.

Virtually all of the Italian hostels are members of the official International Youth Hostel Federation, and strictly speaking you need to be a member of that organization in order to use them – you can join through your home country's youth hostelling organization (see below). You will need to reserve well ahead in the summer months, most efficiently by using Hostelling International's **International Booking Network** which, for a small fee, enables you to book (including online) at hostels in selected Italian cities from your home country up to six months in advance. For more out-of-the-way hostels, you need to contact the hostel direct at least fifteen days in advance, sending approximately a thirty-percent deposit with your booking. We've listed most of the hostels in the Guide, and you can find detailed information about each one on the Ostelli Online website, ⓦ www.ostellionline.org.

In some cities, including Rome, it's also possible to stay in **student accommodation** vacated by Italian students for the summer. This is usually confined to July and August, but accommodation is generally in individual rooms and can work out a lot cheaper than a straight hotel room. Again you'll need to book in advance: we've listed possible places in the text, and you should contact them as far ahead as possible to be sure of a room.

You will also come across accommodation operated by **religious organizations** – convents (normally for women only), welcome houses and the like, again with a mixture of dormitory and individual rooms, which can sometimes be a way of cutting costs as well as meeting like-minded people. Most

Accommodation price codes

Hotels in this guide have been categorized according to the price codes outlined below. They represent the cheapest rates for a double room in high season (July & August), although in places like Florence and Venice you can expect high season rates from March to November.

❶ Under €35 The cheapest kind of one-star hotels; most rooms will have shared facilities and may be quite bleak. You may find places in this category heavily booked owing to the fact that they're often used as cheap permanent accommodation. Credit cards are rarely accepted.

❷ €35–50 The standard one-star hotel, normally with a mixture of rooms with shared and private facilities, and in most cases comfortable enough for a shortish stay. This is probably the most commonly recommended category in this book, although in Venice, Florence and some other northern cities and resorts, you'll be extremely lucky to find one-star places at this price.

❸ €50–65 Mainly two-star hotels, which may have some rooms with shared facilities. You will sometimes have a TV and telephone at this price, too.

❹ €65–80 In Venice and Florence there are one-stars in this category. Elsewhere, this price will get you a room in an attractive two-star, or even a three-star hotel, generally with private bath, telephone and TV.

❺ €80–105 This should get you a room with private bath, TV and telephone pretty much everywhere in Italy, and in the south of the country and more remote places, you could be looking at something fairly swanky.

❻ €105–130 Usually a good three-star or moderate four-star; expect high standards and a range of facilities including a pool and formal restaurant.

❼ €130–160 These should be special hotels, either by virtue of their location or facilities. Again, in Venice and Florence, you'll be paying this sort of price for rooms that would fall into one of the lower categories elsewhere.

❽ €160–200 We have only recommended somewhere in this category if it is really special, if it enjoys a wonderful location, a superb site or building – perhaps an old convent or manor house – or if the service and food are just too good to miss.

❾ Over €200 The sky's-the-limit category, populated by a select few of the most celebrated hotels in Italy.

operate a curfew of some sort, and you should bear in mind that they don't always work out a great deal cheaper than a bottom-line one-star hotel. Information can be found in the local tourist offices or through the Associazione Cattólica Internazionale al Servizio della Giovane, ⓦ www.acisjf.it, which has offices in major towns.

Youth hostel associations

Australia ℡ 02/9261 1111, ⓦ www.yha.org.au.
Canada ℡ 1-800/663-5777, ⓦ www.hihostels.ca.
England & Wales ℡ 0870/770 8868,
ⓦ www.yha.org.uk.
Italy ℡ 06.487.1152, ⓦ www.ostellionline.org.
New Zealand ℡ 03/379 9970,
ⓦ www.yha.org.nz.
Northern Ireland ℡ 028/9032 4733,
ⓦ www.hini.org.uk.
Republic of Ireland ℡ 01/830 4555, ⓦ www.ire-landyha.org.
Scotland ℡ 0870/155 3255, ⓦ www.syha.org.uk.
USA ℡ 202/783-6161, ⓦ www.hiayh.org.

Camping

Camping is popular in Italy and there are plenty of sites, mostly on the coast and generally open April to September (though winter "camping" – in caravans and camper vans – is popular in ski areas). The majority are well equipped and often have bungalows, mainly with four to six beds. On the coast in high season you can expect to pay a daily rate of around €9 per person plus €10–12 per tent or caravan and €2.50 per vehicle. Local tourist offices have details of nearby sites, otherwise visit the Italian camping website, ⓦ www.camping.it, for information and booking facilities for campsites all over Italy.

Villas, agriturismo and rifugi

If you're not intending to travel around a lot it might be worth considering renting a villa or **farmhouse** for a week or two. Most tend to be located in the affluent northern areas of Italy – especially Tuscany and Umbria. They don't come cheap, but are of a very high standard and often enjoy marvellous locations; British-based tour operators which rent villas, either on their own or in conjunc-

tion with a flight or fly-drive package, are detailed on p.14.

Bed and breakfast schemes are a relatively new arrival, the best ones offering a good way to get a flavour of Italian home life; they're not necessarily cheaper than an inexpensive hotel, however, and they rarely accept credit cards. For a comprehensive list of Italy's B&Bs check the Caffelletto ⓦ www.caffelletto.it and BBItalia ⓦ www.bbitalia.it websites.

The **agriturismo** scheme, which has grown considerably in recent years, enables farmers to rent out converted barns and farm buildings to tourists through a centralized booking agency, and has found favour with city-bound Italians intent on rediscovering "country ways" and keen to feast on rustic delicacies. Some tourist apartments or other converted farm buildings cost about the same as a one-star hotel and are available for a minimum of a week, with rates starting from around €300 for places with two beds. Note that you're unlikely to be able to pay by credit card. There are often a wide range of activities on offer, such as horse riding, hunting and mountain biking, plus escorted walks and excursions. For a full list of properties, contact Agriturist, ℡ 06/852.1342, ⓦ www.agriturist.com, or consult one of the many publications about farmhouse holidays/agriturismo that are on sale at airports, newsstands and bookshops in Italy, or at any good travel bookshop before you leave home.

Finally, if you're planning on hiking and climbing there is the **rifugi** network, consisting of about five hundred mountain huts, owned by the Club Alpino Italiano (**CAI** ℡ 02.614.1378, ⓦ www.cai.it), that non-members can stay in for €16.50–20, a night, though you should book at least ten days in advance; there are also private *rifugi* that charge around double this. Most are fairly spartan, with bunks in unheated dorms, but their settings can be magnificent and usually leave you well placed to continue your hike the next day. Bear in mind that the word *rifugio* can be used for anything from a smart chalet-hotel to a snack bar at the top of a cable-car line. We've indicated in the text where this is the case.

Eating and drinking

Although it has long been popular primarily for its cheapness and convenience, Italian food occupies a revered place as one of the world's great cuisines. The southern Italian diet especially, with its emphasis on olive oil, fresh and plentiful fruit, vegetables and fish, is one of the healthiest in Europe, and there are few national cuisines that can boast so much variety in both ingredients and cooking methods. Italy's wines, too, are among the finest and most diverse in Europe and the international image of cheap fizz and rough reds is long out of date.

The basics of Italian cuisine

Some of the **regions** of Italy still preserve their own distinctive cuisines, with for example the French influence in Piemonte, Austrian flavours in Alto Adige, and even Greek in Calabria (regional cuisine and specialities to seek out are highlighted in "Regional Food and Wine" boxes at the beginning of Guide chapters). Italy has remained largely untouched by the latter-day boom in non-indigenous eating, partly owing to its lack of any substantial colonial legacy but also because of the innate chauvinism of Italian eating habits. The exceptions are the Chinese restaurants that crop up in every town, the ubiquitous burger bars, and the Spanish, Japanese and North African cuisine found in more cosmopolitan towns, especially, of course, Rome and Milan. More often than not the exotic option is to sample cooking from other parts of the country. Milan tends to be the favourite melting-pot, with restaurants specializing in food from all regions.

True to the stereotype that every Italian believes that Italian food is the best in the world and that mamma's is always the perfect example, many restaurants are simply an extension of the home dining table. Adventure is not usually on the menu. There has been some limited experimentation with new, "trendier" ingredients like wholewheat pasta and brown rice, but probably the best you'd get if you asked a waiter for any such thing would be a raised eyebrow; request a wholewheat pizza and you'd certainly be laughed out of sight. **Vegetarian restaurants**, too, have been slow to catch on, and you're only likely to find them in major cities, but there are always plenty of non-meat choices on every menu.

Perhaps the most striking thing about eating in Italy is how deeply embedded in the culture it really is. Food is celebrated with gusto: **traditional meals** tend to consist of many courses and can seem to last forever, starting with an antipasto, followed by a risotto or a pasta dish, leading on to a fish or meat course, cheese, and finished with fresh fruit and coffee. Even everyday meals are a scaled-down version of the full-blown affair.

Shopping for food is a serious matter. Supermarkets have yet to make any real impact on the dominance of the traditional store in town centres, and foodstores of every description abound. **Street** markets, too, can be exhilarating, selling bountiful, fresh and flavoursome produce. Happily, the Italians as yet haven't adopted the heavy cropping methods which result in completely tasteless produce – even a simple raw tomato can be a revelation.

Foods like bread and cheese are still made with an eye to quality. **Bread** is almost entirely made by small bakeries and tends to get heavier, crustier and saltier the further south you go (for eating with salty hams, salami and cheeses there is *pane senza sale*). **Cheese** is often factory produced, with large firms like the Milan-based Galbani marketing common varieties like Bel Paese, Gorgonzola and Taleggio. But cheese-making also remains in the hands of local farmers working to traditional recipes: local tastes are much in evidence.

> There's a detailed **menu reader** of Italian terms on pp.1194–1196.

It was precisely this appreciation of good-quality local products that led to the development of the **Slow Food** movement (ⓦwww.slowfood.com) in the 1980s. An organization with increasing recognition worldwide, it seeks to promote the genuine pleasures of food and drink by encouraging high-quality gastronomic production and the protection of traditional cuisine in the face of the "aggressive advance of food and cultural standardization". Two excellent Slow Food publications, *Osterie d'Italia* and *Vini d'Italia,* are on sale in most Italian bookshops.

Breakfast, snacks and ice cream

Most Italians start their day in a bar, their **breakfast** consisting of a coffee with hot milk (*cappuccino*) and a *brioche* or *cornetto* – a jam-, custard- or chocolate-filled croissant, which you usually help yourself to from the counter and eat standing at the bar. Breakfast in a hotel (*prima colazione*) is often a limp affair of bread and processed meats, often not worth the price.

At other times of the day, **sandwiches** (*panini*) can be pretty substantial, a bread stick or roll packed with any number of fillings (around €1.70–3 per sandwich). A sandwich bar (*paninoteca*) in larger towns and cities, and in smaller places a grocer's shop (*alimentari*) will normally make you up whatever you want. Bars may also offer *tramezzini*, ready-made sliced white bread with mixed fillings – less appetizing than the average panino but still tasty and slightly cheaper at around €1.50 a time. Toasted sandwiches (*toast*) are common, too: in a *paninoteca* you can get whatever you want toasted; in ordinary bars it's more likely to be a variation on cheese or ham with tomato.

When it comes to hot **takeaway food** there are a number of options. It's possible to find slices of pizza (*pizza rustica* or *pizza al taglio*) pretty much everywhere, and you can get most of the things already mentioned, plus pasta, chips, even full hot meals, in a **tavola calda**, a sort of stand-up snack bar that's at its best in the morning when everything is fresh. Some are self-service and have limited seating, too. The bigger towns have these, and there's often one inside larger train stations. Another alterna-

tive is a **rosticceria**, where the speciality is spit-roast chicken but other fast foods such as slices of pizza, chips and hamburgers, or stuffed roasted vegetables, are also often served.

Other sources of quick snacks are **markets**, some of which sell takeaway food from stalls, including *focacce* – oven-baked pastries topped with cheese or tomato or filled with spinach, fried offal or meat – and *arancini* or *suppli* – deep-fried balls of rice with meat (*rosso*) or butter and cheese (*bianco*) filling. **Supermarkets**, also, are an obvious stop for a picnic lunch: the major department store chains, Upim and Standa, often have food halls.

Italian **ice cream** (*gelato*) is justifiably famous: a cone (*un cono*) is an indispensable accessory to the evening *passeggiata*. Most bars have a fairly good selection, but for real choice go to a **gelateria**, where the range is a tribute to the Italian imagination and flair for display. You'll sometimes have to go by appearance rather than attempting to decipher their exotic names, many of which don't even mean much to Italians: often the basics – chocolate and strawberry – are best. There's no problem locating the finest *gelateria* in town – it's the one that draws the crowds – and we've noted the really special places throughout the Guide. If in doubt, go for the places that make their own ice cream, denoted by the sign "Produzione Propria" outside.

Pizza

Pizza is now a worldwide phenomenon, but Italy remains the best place to eat it. The creations served up here – especially in the city where pizza started, Naples – are wholly different from the soggy concoctions that have taken over the international fast-food market. Virtually everywhere in Italy pizza comes thin and flat, not deep-pan, and the choice of toppings is fairly limited, with none of the dubious pineapple and sweetcorn variations. It's easy to find pizzas cooked in the traditional way, in wood-fired ovens (*forno a legna*) rather than the squeaky-clean electric ones, so that the pizzas arrive blasted and bubbling on the surface and with a distinctive charcoal taste.

Pizzerias range from a stand-up counter

selling slices to a fully fledged sit-down restaurant, and on the whole they don't sell much else besides pizza, soft drinks and beer. Some straight restaurants often have pizza on the menu, too. A basic cheese and tomato pizza (*margherita*) costs around €4.60 (sometimes less in the south, often more in the north), a fancier variety €5–6, and it's quite acceptable to cut it into slices and eat it with your fingers. Consult our food glossary (see pp.1194–1196) for the different kinds of pizza.

Lunch and dinner

Full **meals** are often elaborate affairs, generally served in either a **trattoria** or a **ristorante**. Traditionally, a trattoria is a cheaper and more basic purveyor of homestyle cooking (*cucina casalinga*), while a *ristorante* is more upmarket, with aproned waiters and tablecloths, though these days the two are often interchangeable. The main differences you'll notice now are to do with opening times: often trattorias, at least in rural areas, will be open only at lunchtime – there won't be a menu and the waiter will simply reel off a list of what's on that day.

In large towns both will be open in the evening, but there'll be more choice in a *ristorante*, which will always have a menu and sometimes a help-yourself antipasto buffet. In either, pasta dishes go for around €5–8, and there's usually no problem just having this; the main fish or meat courses will normally be anything between €6.50 and €10.

At the end of the meal ask for the bill (*il conto*); bear in mind that almost everywhere you'll pay a cover charge (*coperto*) on top of your food of €1–3 a head. In many trattorias the bill amounts to little more than an illegible scrap of paper; if you want to check it, ask for a **receipt** (*ricevuta*), something all bars and restaurants are legally bound to provide anyway (indeed they – and you – can be fined if you don't take the receipt with you and the same applies to shops and bars). In more expensive places service (*servizio*) will often be added on top of the cover charge, generally about ten percent. If service isn't included you can choose to **tip** about the same amount, but unless you're particularly pleased with the service it's common just to leave a few coins.

Other types of eating places include those that bill themselves as everything – trattoria-ristorante-pizzeria – and perform no function very well, serving mediocre food that you could get at better prices elsewhere. Look out also for spaghetterias, bar-restaurants which serve basic pasta dishes and are often the hangout of the local youth. Osterie are common too, basically an old-fashioned restaurant or pub-like place specializing in home cooking, though some extremely upmarket places with pretensions to established antiquity borrow the name. In our listings, we've indicated the regular weekly **closing day**.

Traditionally a meal (lunch is *pranzo*, dinner is *cena*) starts with **antipasto** (literally "before the meal"), a course generally served only in ristoranti and consisting of various cold cuts of meat, seafood and various cold vegetable dishes. *Prosciutto* is a common antipasto dish, ham either cooked (*cotto*) or just cured and hung (*crudo*) and served alone or with mozzarella cheese. A plateful of various antipasti from a self-service buffet will set you back €5–6 a head, an item chosen from the menu a bit less. The next course, **il primo**, consists of a soup, risotto or pasta dish, and is followed by **il secondo** – the meat or fish course, usually served alone, except for perhaps a wedge of lemon or tomato. Watch out when ordering fish, which will either be served whole or by weight: 250g is usually plenty for one person, or ask to have a look at the fish before it's cooked. You may need quite an appetite to tackle all three courses; those on a budget will fill up best with just pasta, though portions can be quite small. Vegetables or salads – **contorni** – are ordered and served separately, and sometimes there won't be much choice: potatoes will usually come as chips (*patate fritte*), but you can also find boiled (*lesse*) or roast (*arrostite*), while salads are either green (*verde*) or mixed (*mista*). If there's no menu, the verbal list of what's available can be bewildering; if you don't understand, just ask for what you want. Everywhere will have pasta with tomato sauce (*pomodoro*) or meat sauce (*al ragù*). Afterwards you nearly always get a choice of fresh fruit (*frutta*) and a selection of **desserts** (*dolci*) – sometimes just ice cream or *mace-*

donia (fresh fruit salad), but often more elaborate items, like *cassata* (ice cream made with ricotta) or *zuppa inglese* (spongecake or trifle). Sadly, the indulgent dessert of *zabaglione* is rarely available at any but the most upmarket places.

Italy isn't a bad country to travel in if you're a **vegetarian**, but unless you're determined you can end up eating endless plates of pizza and pasta with tomato sauce. There are, however, other pasta sauces without meat, some superb vegetable antipasti and if you eat fish and seafood you should have no problem at all. Salads, too, are fresh and good. The only real difficulty is one of comprehension: Italians don't understand someone not eating meat, and stating the obvious doesn't always get the point across. Saying you're a vegetarian (*Sono vegetariano/a*) and asking if a dish has meat in it (*c'è carne dentro?*) might still turn up a poultry or prosciutto dish. Better is to ask what a dish is made with before you order (*com'è fatto?*) so that you can spot the non-meaty meat. **Vegans** will have a much harder time, though pizzas without cheese (*marinara* – nothing to do with fish – is a common option) are a good standby, vegetable soup is usually just that and the fruit is excellent.

Drinking

Although many Italian children are brought up on wine and a *mezzo* (half-litre carafe) is a standard accompaniment to any meal, there's not a great emphasis on dedicated **drinking** in Italy. You'll rarely see drunks in public, young people don't devote their nights to getting wasted, and women especially are frowned upon if they're seen to be overindulging. Nonetheless there's a wide choice of alcoholic drinks available, often at low prices; soft drinks come in multifarious hues, thanks to the abundance of fresh fruit; and there are also mineral water and crushed-ice drinks: you'll certainly never be stuck if you want to slake your thirst.

Where to drink

Traditional **bars** are less social centres than functional places and are all very similar to each other – brightly lit places, with a chrome counter, a Gaggia coffee machine

and a picture of the local football team on the wall. You'll come here for ordinary drinking: a coffee in the morning, a quick beer, a cup of tea, but people don't generally idle away the day or evening in bars. Indeed in some more rural areas it's difficult to find a bar open much after 9pm. Where these places do fit into the general Mediterranean pattern is with their lack of set licensing hours and the fact that children are always allowed in; there's often a telephone and you can buy snacks and ice creams as well as drinks.

An **osteria** can be a more congenial setting, often a traditional place where you can usually try local specialities with a glass of wine; real wine enthusiasts, however, should head for an **enoteca**, though many of these are more oriented towards selling wine by the case than by the glass. Cities offer a much greater variety of places to sit and drink in the evening, sometimes with live music or DJs. The more energetic or late-opening of these are have taken to calling themselves **pubs**, a spill-over from the outrageous success of Irish pubs, at least one of which you'll find in almost every city, packed to the rafters with the local talent. Beer, particularly in its draught form, *alla spina*, has become fashionable in recent years.

In **traditional bars**, the routine rarely varies. It's cheapest to drink standing at the counter (there's often nowhere to sit anyway), in which case you pay first at the cash desk (*la cassa*), present your receipt (*scontrino*) to the barperson and give your order. There's always a list of prices (*listino prezzi*) behind the bar. It's customary to leave a small coin on the counter for the barperson, although no one will object if you don't. If there's waiter service, just sit where you like, though bear in mind that to do this will cost perhaps twice as much, especially if you sit outside (*fuori*) – the difference is shown on the price list as *tavola* (table) or *terrazzo* (any outside seating area). Late-night bars and pubs rarely operate on the *scontrino* system; you may be asked to pay up front, in the English manner, or be presented with a bill. If not, head for the counter when you leave – the barperson will have kept a rough but surprisingly accurate tally.

Coffee, tea and soft drinks

One of the most distinctive smells in an Italian street is that of fresh **coffee**. It's always excellent: the basic choice is either small and black (*espresso*, or just *caffè*), which costs around €0.80 a cup, or white and frothy (*cappuccino*, for about €1.10), but there are scores of variations. If you want your espresso watered down, more like an American black coffee, ask for a *caffè lungo* or *Americano*; with a drop of milk is *caffè macchiato*; very milky coffee is *caffè latte*. Coffee with a shot of alcohol – and you can ask for just about anything in your coffee – is *caffè corretto*. Many places also now sell decaffeinated coffee (ask for Hag, even when it isn't); while in summer you might want to have your coffee cold (*caffè freddo*). For a real treat ask for *caffè granita* – cold coffee with crushed ice, usually topped with cream.

If you don't like coffee, there's always **tea**. In summer you can drink this cold too (*tè freddo*) – excellent for taking the heat off. Hot tea (*tè caldo*) comes with lemon (*con limone*) unless you ask for milk (*con latte*). Milk itself is drunk hot as often as cold, or you can get it with a dash of coffee (*latte macchiato*) and sometimes as milk shakes – *frappe* or *frullati*.

Alternatively, there are various **soft drinks** (*analcoliche*) to choose from. A **spremuta** is a fresh fruit juice, squeezed at the bar, usually orange, lemon or grapefruit. You might need to add sugar to the lemon juice (*di limone*), but the orange (*d'arancia*) is invariably sweet enough on its own, especially the crimson-red variety, made from blood oranges. There are also crushed-ice **granitas**, big in Sicily and offered in several flavours other than coffee, and available with or without whipped cream (*panna*) on top. Otherwise there's the usual range of fizzy drinks and concentrated juices: Coke is as prevalent as it is everywhere, though the diet or light versions less so; the home-grown Italian version, Chinotto, is less sweet – good with a slice of lemon. **Tap water** (*acqua normale*) is quite drinkable, and you won't pay for it in a bar. Italians drink more **mineral water** (*acqua minerale*) than any other country in Europe, certainly at least a bottle with every meal. Either still (*senza gas* or *naturale*) or sparkling (*con gas* or *frizzante*), it costs about €1.30 a bottle.

Beer and spirits

Beer (*birra*) is always a lager-type brew which usually comes in one-third or two-third litre bottles, or on tap (*alla spina*), measure for measure more expensive than the bottled variety. A small beer is a *piccola*, (20cl or 25cl), a larger one (usually 40cl) a *media*. The cheapest and most common brands are the Italian Morotti, Peroni and Dreher, all of which are very drinkable; if this is what you want, either state the brand name or ask for *birra nazionale* or *birra chiara* – otherwise you may be given the more expensive imported beer. You may also come across darker beers (*birra nera* or *birra rossa*), which have a sweeter, maltier taste and in appearance resemble stout or bitter.

All the usual **spirits** are on sale and known mostly by their generic names. There are also Italian brands of the main varieties: the best Italian brandies are Stock and Vecchia Romagna. A generous shot of these costs about €1.30–1.50, imported stuff much more.

The home-grown Italian firewater is **grappa**, originally from Bassano di Grappa in the Veneto but now available just about everywhere. It's made from the leftovers from the winemaking process (skins, stalks and the like) and is something of an acquired taste; should you acquire it, it's probably the cheapest way of getting plastered. The more expensive *distillato*, extravagantly made from the grape itself, will suit more refined tastes.

You'll also find **fortified wines** like Martini, Cinzano and Campari; ask for a Camparisoda and you'll get a ready-mixed version from a little bottle; a slice of lemon is a *spicchio di limone*, ice is *ghiaccio*. You might also try Cynar – believe it or not, an artichoke-based sherry often drunk as an aperitif. There's also a daunting selection of **liqueurs**. Amaro is a bitter after-dinner drink, Amaretto much sweeter with a strong taste of almond, Sambuca a sticky-sweet aniseed concoction, traditionally served with a coffee bean in it and set on fire (though, increasingly, this is something put on to impress tourists). Another sweet alternative, originally from Sorrento, is *Limoncello* or *limoncino*, a lemon-based liqueur best drunk in a frozen vase-shaped glass. Strega is another drink you'll see behind every bar, yellow, herb-and-saffron based stuff in tall, elongated bottles: about as sweet as it looks but not unpleasant.

Wine

Just as Italy's food has suffered from stereotyped images, so too has its **wine**. Lambrusco was one of the first Italian wines to sell well overseas, despite (or because of) its reputation as cheap party plonk, while inexpensive Soave, Valpolicella and Chianti continue to shift units. Some of the finer wines are now well established abroad, though often the very best wines are kept for the home market. A few pointers in the right direction are given in the "Regional Food and

Wine" box at the beginning of each chapter. Nudged along by the DOC laws (see box), standards have been steadily increasing in recent years. Many producers have been turning their hands to making higher **quality wines**, and besides the finer tuning of established names such as Barolo and Orvieto, there's a good deal of experimentation going on everywhere. Southern winemakers are no longer content to see nearly all of their produce going north to beef up table-wine blends, while in Tuscany, Trentino-Alto Adige and Friuli, French grape varieties such as Chardonnay, Sauvignon Blanc and the Pinots are joining old Italian favourites with startling success.

They don't waste drinking time in Italy with dialogue or veneration, however; neither is there much time for the snobbery often associated with "serious" wine drinking. Light **reds** such as those made from the dolcetto grape are hauled out of the fridge in hot weather, while some full-bodied **whites**

The Denominazione d'Origine system

The **Denominazione d'Origine** system is the key to understanding what to look for in Italian wine, but it shouldn't be seen as any sort of guarantee. The denomination is a certificate of origin, not of quality, and while it may mean a wine will be drinkable, stick to it too rigidly and you could be missing out on an awful lot. Denomination zones are set by governmental decree. They specify where a certain named wine may be made, what grape varieties may be used, the maximum yield of grapes per hectare and for how long the wine should be aged. **Denominazione d'Origine Controllata** (DOC) guarantees the origin of the wine and that it has been made to the specification of the rules for the zone in which it's produced. *Vino da tavola* is simply wine that does not conform to the DOC laws, though it's not necessarily wine you'd sooner pour down the sink than drink. **Denominazione d'Origine Controllata e Garantita** (DOCG) is the only designation at the moment that actually has any real meaning. Wines sold under this label not only have to conform to the ordinary DOC laws, but are also tested by government-appointed inspectors. There are currently twenty-one DOCG wines and three hundred DOC. Though it's undoubtedly true that the DOC system has helped lift standards, the laws have come under fire from both growers and critics for their rigidity, constraints and anomalies. Chianti, for instance, can be a quaffable lunchtime drink, a wine of pedigree to be treated with reverence, or – depending on the vintage – it can be appalling. All will have a DOC. Some claim too that the restrictions of the DOCG are losing their credibility. With big reds such as Barolo the ageing term can destroy all the fruitiness of the wine, while the entry of Albana di Romagna, a somewhat ordinary white, to DOCG status has caused consternation. Increasingly, producers eager to experiment have begun to disregard the regulations and make new wines that are sometimes expensive and among Italy's best wines, though they're still officially labelled *da távola* (the nickname *super vini da távola* has emerged). The Sicilian Corvo, red and white, is perhaps the best-known non-DOC label, a modern wine that goes for a little over twice the price of ordinary table plonk. Tuscany also produces some excellent table wines.

are drunk at near room temperature. Wine is still very cheap, though unless your aim is to get legless as cheaply as possible, it's wise to avoid the very cheapest plonk. In restaurants you'll invariably be offered red (*rosso*) or white (*bianco*) – rarely rosé (*rosato*). If you're unsure about what to order, don't be afraid to try the local stuff (ask for *vino sfuso*, or simply *un mezzo* – a half litre – or *un quar-*

to – a quarter), sometimes served straight from the barrel, particularly down south. It's often very good, and cheap at an average of around €4.10 a litre. Bottled wine is pricier but still very good value; expect to pay €8.20–10.30 a bottle in a restaurant, and less than half that from a shop or supermarket. In bars you can buy a glass of wine for about €0.60–2, depending on quality.

Communications

Mail

Post Office opening hours are usually Monday–Saturday 8.30am–7.30pm, though branches in smaller towns tend to close at 1pm. Note too that offices close an hour earlier on the last working day of the month. Stamps (*francobolli*), are sold in *tabacchi* too, as well as in some gift shops in the tourist resorts; they will often also weigh your letter. The Italian postal system is one of the slowest in Europe so if your letter is urgent make sure you send it "posta prioritaria" which has varying rates according to weight and destination. Letters can be sent poste restante to any Italian post office by addressing them "Fermo Posta" followed by the name of the town. When picking something up take your passport, and make sure they check under middle names and initials – and every other letter when all else fails – as filing is often diabolical.

Telephones

Public **telephones**, run by **Telecom Italia**, come in various forms, usually with clear instructions in English. Coin-operated machines are increasingly hard to find so you will probably have to buy a **telephone card** (*carta* or *scheda telefonica*), available from tabacchi and newsstands for €2.28 or €5.16. Note that the perforated corner of these cards must be torn off before they can be used. If you can't find a phone box, bars will often have a phone you can use – look for the yellow or red phone symbol.

Telephone numbers change with amazing frequency in Italy and codes are now an integral part of the number and always need to dialled, regardless of whether or not you are in the zone you are telephoning. All telephone numbers listed in the Guide include the relevant code. Numbers beginning ☎800 are free, ☎170 will get you through to an English-speaking operator, ☎176 to international directory enquiries.

Phone **tariffs** are among the most expensive in Europe, though there is a reduced rate for off-peak calls (weekdays 6.30pm–8am, weekends 1pm Saturday–8am Monday for national calls; 10pm–8am Monday–Saturday and all day Sunday for international calls).

Calling home from Italy

You can call abroad from most public phone boxes with an **international phone card**. These are on sale at main post offices and come in four denominations ranging from €6.45 to €51. The two most common phone cards are the *Columbus* card for calls to Western Europe and North America and the standard *Scheda Telefonica Internazionale* for the rest of the world. A slightly cheaper option at peak calling times is the *Europa Card* for calls to Europe, US and Canada only, costing €5; you don't insert it into the phone but dial a central number and then a pin code given on the reverse of the card.

Alternatively you could consider a **telephone charge card** from your phone company back home. Using a PIN number, you can make calls from most hotel, public and private phones that will be charged to your account. Most major charge cards are free to obtain but bear in mind that rates aren't necessarily cheaper than calling from a public phone.

In the **US and Canada**, AT&T, MCI, Sprint, Canada Direct and other North American long-distance companies all enable their customers to make credit-card calls while overseas, billed to your home number. Call your company's customer service line to find out if they provide a service from Italy and if so, what the toll-free access code is.

In **the UK and Ireland**, British Telecom (☎0800/345 144, ⊛www.chargecard.bt.com) will issue free to all BT customers the BT Charge Card, which can be used in 116 countries. AT&T (dial ☎0800/890 011, then 888/641-6123 when you hear the AT&T prompt to be transferred to the Florida Call Centre, free 24 hours) has the Global Calling Card; while NTL (☎0500/100 505) issues its own Global Calling Card, which can be used in more than sixty countries abroad, though the fees cannot be charged to a normal phone bill.

To call **Australia and New Zealand** from overseas, telephone charge cards such as Telstra Telecard or Optus Calling Card in Australia, and Telecom NZ's Calling Card, can be used to make calls abroad, which are charged back to a domestic account or credit card. Apply to Telstra (☎1800/038 000), Optus (☎1300/300 937), or Telecom NZ (☎04/801 9000).

You can make **international reversed charge** or **collect calls** (*chiamata con addebito destinatario*) by dialling ☎170 and following the recorded instructions.

International codes

UK and Northern Ireland international access code + 44 + city code.
Republic of Ireland international access code + 353 + city code.
USA and Canada international access code + 1 + area code.
Australia international access code + 61 + city code.
New Zealand international access code + 64 + city code.

Calling Italy from abroad

To call Italy **from abroad**, dial the access code ☎00 from the UK, Ireland and New Zealand, ☎011 from the US and Canada, ☎0011 from Australia, followed by 39, then the area code **including the first zero** (the major towns are listed below), and finally the subscriber number.

Mobile phones

Mobile phones in Italy work on the GSM European standard. You will hardly see an Italian without his or her *telefonino*, but if you are going to join them make sure you have made the necessary "roaming" arrangements before you leave home – which may involve paying a hefty (refundable) deposit. You are also likely to be charged extra for incoming calls when abroad, as the people calling you will be paying the usual rate. If you want to retrieve messages while you're away, you might have to ask your provider for a new access code. For further information about using your phone abroad, check out ⊛ www.telecomsadvice.org.uk/ features/using_your_mobile_abroad.htm.

Email

One of the best ways to keep in touch while travelling is to sign up for a free Internet **email address** that can be accessed from anywhere, for example YahooMail or Hotmail – accessible through ⊛www.yahoo.com and ⊛www.hotmail.com. Once you've set up an account, you can use these sites to pick up and send mail from any Internet café, or hotel with Internet access.

Most average-sized towns have at least one Internet point, though they are sometimes hidden inside a computer shop or newsagents. Internet cafés as such are found mainly in larger towns or cities. Expect to pay around €4 for thirty minutes; there are often discounts for students.

⊛www.kropla.com is a useful website giving details of how to plug your **lap-top** in when abroad, phone country codes around the world, and information about electrical systems in different countries.

The media

Newspapers

The **Italian press** is largely regionally based, but some newspapers are available all over the country. The centre-left *La Repubblica* and authoritative right-slanted *Corriere della Sera* are the two most widely read and available, published nationwide with local supplements. The traditionally radical *Il Manifesto* has in recent years lost ground to *L'Unità*, the party organ of the Democratic Left (formerly the Communist Party), which has won recognition as the best-designed and most readable newspaper. *Paese Sera* is another broadly left-wing daily read widely in the south. Other provincial newspapers include *La Stampa*, the daily of Turin, and *Il Messaggero* of Rome – both rather stuffy, establishment sheets. *Il Mattino* is the more readable organ of Naples and the Campania area, while other southern editions include the *Giornale di Sicilia and La Gazzetta del Sud*. Perhaps the most avidly read newspapers of all, however, are the specialist sports papers, most notably the *Corriere dello Sport* and the pink *Gazzetta dello Sport* – both essential reading if you want to get a handle on the Italian football scene.

English-language newspapers can be found for around three times their home cover price in all the larger cities and most of the more established resorts, usually a day late, though in Milan and Rome you can sometimes find papers on the day of publication. In remoter parts of the country it's not unusual for papers to be delayed by several days.

TV and radio

If you get the chance, try to watch some Italian **TV**, if only to size up the pros and cons of deregulation. Although the much-vaunted programmes with stripping housewives and the like do exist, the output is otherwise pretty bland, with the accent on ghastly quiz shows, shopping channels, cathartic chat shows in which the famous and not-so-famous air their dirty linen, and soaps, plus a heavy smattering of American imports. Nevertheless, the three national channels, RAI 1, 2 and 3, have the odd worthy programme; RAI 3 remains broadly left-wing, with its output leaning more towards the cultural and intellectual, and is the outlet for local news and features. Satellite television is fairly widely distributed, and three-star hotels and above almost always offer the usual mix of BBC World, CNN and French-, German- and Spanish-language news channels, as well as MTV and Eurosport.

The situation in **radio** is if anything even more anarchic, with the FM waves crowded to the extent that you continually pick up new stations whether you want to or not. This means there are generally some good stations if you search hard enough, but on the whole the RAI stations are again the more professional – though even with them daytime listening is virtually undiluted Euro-pop.

For **world service** stations check the following websites for details of their global frequencies:
BBC ⓦ www.bbc.co.uk/worldservice
Radio Canada ⓦ www.rcinet.ca
Voice of America ⓦ www.voa.gov

Opening hours, public holidays and festivals

Italian opening hours are becoming more flexible. Most shops and businesses in Italy open Monday to Saturday from around 8am until 1pm, and from about 4pm until 7pm, though many shops close on Saturday afternoons and Monday mornings, and in the south the day can begin and end an hour later. In the north some businesses work a 9-to-5 day to facilitate international dealings. Traditionally, everything except bars and restaurants closes on Sunday, though most towns have a *pasticceria* open in the mornings, while in large cities and tourist areas, Sunday opening is becoming more common.

The other factors that can disrupt your plans are **national holidays** and local **saints' days** and festivals. In **August**, particularly during the weeks either side of *Ferragosto*, when most of the country flees to the coast, many towns are left half-deserted, with shops, bars and restaurants closed and a reduced public transport service. Local religious holidays don't generally close down shops and businesses for the whole day, but they do mean that accommodation space may be tight. The country's official **national holidays**, on the other hand, close everything down except bars and restaurants.

Public holidays

January 1 (New Year's Day)
January 6 (Epiphany)
Pasquetta (Easter Monday)
April 25 (Liberation Day)
May 1 (Labour Day)
August 15 (*Ferragosto*; Assumption of the Blessed Virgin Mary)
November 1 (*Ognissanti*; All Souls Day)
December 8 (*Immaccolata*; Immaculate Conception of the Blessed Virgin Mary)
December 25 (*Natale*; Christmas)
December 26 (*Santo Stefano*; St Stephen's Day)

Churches, museums and archeological sites

The rules for visiting **churches** are much as they are all over the Mediterranean. **Dress modestly**, which usually means no shorts (not even Bermuda-length ones) for men or women and covered shoulders for women, and try to avoid wandering around during a service. Most churches open in the early morning, around 7 or 8am for Mass, and close around noon, opening up again at 4pm and closing at 7 or 8pm. In more remote places, some churches will only open for early morning and evening services, while others are closed at all times except Sundays and on religious holidays; if you're determined to take a look, you may have to ask around for the key.

Another problem you'll face – and this applies to the whole country – is that lots of churches, monasteries, convents and oratories are **closed for restoration** (*chiuso per restauro*). We've indicated in the text the more long-term closures, though you might be able to persuade a workman or priest/curator to show you around even if there's scaffolding everywhere.

Most museums and sites are closed on Mondays. **Opening hours** for state-run **museums** are generally from 9am until 7pm, Tuesday to Saturday, and from 9am until 1pm on Sunday. Most other museums roughly follow this pattern too, although they are more likely to close for a couple of hours in the afternoon, and have shorter opening hours in winter. Many large museums also run late-night openings in summer (till 10pm or later Tues–Sat, or 8pm Sun). The opening times of **archeological sites** are more flexible: most sites open every day, often Sunday included, from 9am until late evening – frequently specified as one hour before sunset, and thus changing according to the time of year. In winter, times are drastically cut, if only because of the darker evenings; 4pm is a common closing time.

Festivals

Whether for religious, traditional or cultural reasons, Italy has no shortage of **festivals** throughout the year, and at Christmas, Easter or during the summer months you are likely to come across at least one local festival celebrating an historic event, a patron saint's day, a town's local produce or some artistic talent.

Recently there's also been a revival of the carnival (*carnevale*), the last fling before Lent, although the anarchic fun that was enjoyed in the past has generally been replaced by elegant, self-conscious affairs, with ingenious costumes and handmade masks. The places to head for are Venice, Viareggio in Tuscany and Arcireale in Sicily, although smaller towns will often put on a parade.

Perhaps the most widespread local event in Italy is the **religious procession**, which can be a very dramatic affair. **Good Friday** is celebrated in many towns and villages – particularly in the south – by parading models of Christ through the streets accompanied by white-robed, hooded figures singing penitential hymns. Many processions have strong pagan roots, marking important dates on the calendar and only relatively recently sanctified by the Church. Superstition and a desire for good luck are very much part of these events.

Despite the dwindling number of practising Catholics in Italy there has been a revival of **pilgrimages** over the last decade or so. These are as much social occasions as spiritual journeys and as many as a million pilgrims travel through the night, mostly on foot, to the **Shrine of the Madonna di Polsi** in the inhospitable Aspromonte mountains in Calabria, while Sardinia's biggest festival, the **Festa di Sant'Efisio**, sees a four-day march from Cagliari to Pula and back, to commemorate the saint's martyrdom.

There are many festivals that evoke local pride in **tradition:** medieval contests like the **Palio** horse race in Siena perpetuating allegiances to certain competing clans. Other towns put on crossbow, jousting and flag-twirling contests, marching bands in full medieval costume accompanying the event with enthusiastic drumming; these are far from staged affairs, with fierce rivalry between participants.

Food-inspired *feste* are lower-key, but no less enjoyable, affairs, usually celebrating the local speciality of the region to the accompaniment of dancing, music from a local brass band and noisy fireworks at the end of the evening. There are literally hundreds of food festivals, sometimes advertised as *sagre*, and every region has them – look in the local papers or ask at the tourist office during summer and autumn and you're bound to find something going on. Most are modest affairs, meant for the locals and little publicized – but there are a few exceptions.

The home-town pride that sparks off many of the food festivals also expresses itself in some of the **arts festivals** spread across Italy, particularly in the central part of the country – based in ancient amphitheatres or between medieval walls and occasionally marking the work of a native composer. Major concerts and opera are usually well advertised but also extremely popular so you should book tickets well in advance.

Festivals diary

There are literally thousands of festivals in Italy and sometimes the best ones are those that you come across unexpectedly in the smaller towns. Here are just some of the highlights on the Italian festival calendar. Note that **dates change** from year to year, so it's best to contact the local tourist office for specific details.

January

Rome Toy and sweet fair in Piazza Navona, to celebrate the *Befana* (Jan 6).

February

Carnevale Carnival festivities in **Venice** ⓦ www.venice-carnival.com, **Viareggio** ⓦ www.ilcarnevale.com, **Foiano della Chiana** (Arezzo), **Cento** (Ferrara) plus many towns throughout Italy.
Ivrea Battle of the Oranges ⓦ www.carnevale.ivrea.it.
Agrigento Almond Blossom Festival (last 2 weeks of Feb).

March

Venice *Su e zo per i ponti* (2nd Sun) – a marathon "up and down the bridges".

April

Nocera Tirinese *Rito dei Battienti* (Easter Saturday) – a macabre parade of flagellants whipping themselves with shards of glass.
Florence *Lo Scoppio del Carro* (Easter Day) – a symbolic firework display outside the Duomo after Mass.

May

Cocullo (L'Aquila) Festival of snakes (1st week of May) – one of the most ancient Italian festivals celebrating the patron saint, San Domenico Abate, in which his statue is draped with live snakes and paraded through the streets.
Gubbio *Corsa dei Ceri* (1st Sun) – three 20ft-high wooden "ceri", repre-

senting three patron saints, are raced through the old town by "ceraioli" in medieval costume.
Camogli Fish festival of San Fortunato (2nd Sun) – the patron saint of fishermen; plenty of fried fish, fireworks and bonfires.
Florence Festa del Grillo (1st, 2nd & 3rd Sun) – celebration of the cricket; contestants bring along highly ornate boxes containing crickets which are judged according to beauty and singing voice.
International Wine Day (last Sun) – wine estates all over Italy open their cellars to the public.

June

Pisa *Luminaria di San Ranieri* (June 15) – the Arno glows in the reflected light of 70,000 "lumini" or small glass lamps displayed in windows and balconies of every palazzo bordering the river.
Florence *Calcio Storico Fiorentino* (June 24) – medieval-style football match and other festivities to celebrate San Giovanni, the patron saint.
Spoleto *Festival dei Due Mondi* – two months of theatre, concerts and street entertainment ⓦ www.spoletofestival.it.
Verona Verona Opera season starts ⓦ www.arena.it.
Positano Start of the Amalfi Coast Opera and Chamber Music Festival.

July

Siena Palio (July 2) – medieval bareback horse race in the Campo.
Matera *Festa della Madonna della*

Bruna (July 2) – statue of patron saint paraded around town on a float and then burned.

Palermo *Festino di Santa Rosalia* (2nd week) – a 5-day street party to celebrate the city's patron saint ⓦwww.santarosalia.it.

Perugia Umbria Jazz Festival ⓦwww.umbriajazz.com.

Bologna Porretta Soul Festival ⓦwww.porrettasoul.com.

Santarcangelo di Romagna Festival Internazionale del Teatro in Piazza ⓦwww.santarcangelofestival.com.

August
Ferragosto (Aug 15) – national holiday with local festivals, water fights and fireworks all over Italy.

Siena (Aug 16) – second Palio horse race.

Pesaro Rossini Opera Festival (mid-month) ⓦwww.rossinioperafestival.it.

Ferrara Ferrara Buskers Festival – gathering of some of the world's best street performers ⓦwww.ferrarabuskers.com.

Venice (end of month) – start of the oldest International Film Festival ⓦwww.labiennaledivenezia.net.

September
Venice *La Regatta di Venezia* (1st Sun) – gondola race in medieval costume along the Grand Canal.

Verona (Sept 12) – street entertainment and general partying to celebrate the birthday of the town's most famous lover, Juliet.

Naples *Festa di San Gennaro* (Sept 15) – patron saint – gathering in the cathedral to witness the liquefaction of the saint's blood.

San Giovanni Rotondo, Foggia (Sept 23) – thousands of followers commemorate the death of Padre Pio.

October
Marino, Rome *Sagra del Vino* (1st weekend) – one of the most famous among hundreds of wine festivals across the country with fountains flowing with wine.

Trieste *La Barcolana* (2nd Sun) – boat race ⓦwww.barcolana.it.

Perugia Eurochocolate (3rd & 4th weekend) – Italy's chocolate city celebrates ⓦwww.chocolate.perugia.it.

Acqualagna, Pesaro *Festa del Tartufo Bianco* (last Sun) – beginning of a month-long white truffle festival.

November
Olive oil Festivals all over Italy.

December
Stiffe, L'Aquila Bethlehem in the Grotto – life-size statues from the nativity scene are carried into a 650-metre-deep grotto and positioned for the month among stalagmites and a natural waterfall.

Suvereto, Livorno Festa del Cinghiale (Dec 1–10) – a 10-day festival in honour of the wild boar.

Orvieto Umbria Jazz Winter (end of month) ⓦwww.umbriajazz.com.

Sports and outdoor pursuits

Spectator sports are popular in Italy, especially the hallowed *calcio* (football), and there is undying national passion for frenetic motor and cycle races. When it comes to participation, though, you get the impression that there isn't the same compulsion to hit the hell out of a squash ball or sweat your way through an aerobics class after work as there is, say, in Britain or the States. All the same, the notion of staying fit has lately been absorbed into the general obsession with *bella figura* (looking good), especially when it offers the opportunity to wear the flashiest designer gear. Members-only sports clubs, gyms and public sports facilities have mushroomed over the last decade and it's usually possible to find places where you can work out or join in a competitive game. Otherwise, the country's natural advantages provide plenty of scope for keeping in trim in the most enjoyable ways possible.

For visitors to Italy, the most accessible activities are centred around the mountains – where you can climb, ski, paraglide, raft or simply explore on foot – and the coastal regions, with plenty of opportunities for swimming, sailing and windsurfing; Campania, Calabria and Sicily are particularly popular for scuba diving and snorkelling.

You can get a guide and map suggesting **sailing itineraries** round the coast of southern Italy from the Italian State Tourist Office (see p.20).

Sport

If you are at all interested in the game, it would be a shame to leave Italy without attending a *partita* or **football** match; *calcio* is the national sport and is followed fanatically by millions of Italians. The **season** starts around the end of August, takes a break during the latter part of December and early part of January, and finishes up, with the Italian Cup final, in June. The **Italian League** is split into four principal divisions, Serie A, Serie B, and Serie C1 and C2; matches are normally played on Sunday afternoons, occasionally Sunday evenings, and there is a good chance that on any weekend there will be a team from one of the above divisions playing not too far away. Serie A, is of course, the most prestigious division, comprising eighteen teams; the bottom-placed four are relegated each season, to be replaced by the top four from

Serie B. Inevitably **tickets** for Serie A matches are not cheap, starting at about €15 for "Curva" seats where the *tifosi* or hard-core fans go, rising to €40–50 for "Tribuna" seats along the side of the pitch, and anything up to €100 for the more comfortable "Poltroncina" cushioned-seats in the centre of the Tribuna. We've given details of where to buy tickets for the major clubs and how to get to their grounds in the "Listings" sections at the end of major city accounts. Once at the football match, get into the atmosphere of the occasion by knocking back *borghetti* – little vials of cold coffee with a drop of spirit added.

Italy's chosen sport after football is **basketball**, introduced from the United States after World War II. Most cities have a team, and Italy is now ranked among the foremost in the world. Other stateside imports are **baseball** and **American football**. In a country that has produced Ferrari, Maserati, Alfa Romeo and Fiat, it should come as no surprise that **motor racing** gives Italians such a buzz. There are grand prix tracks at Monza near Milan (home of the Italian Grand Prix) and at Ímola, where the San Marino Grand Prix is held.

The other sport popular with participants and crowds of spectators alike is **cycling.** At weekends especially, you'll often see a club pack out, dressed in bright team kit, whirring along on their slender machines. The annual Giro d'Italia in the second half of May is a prestige event that attracts scores of international participants each year, closing down roads and creating great excitement.

Outdoor pursuits

With the Alps right on the doorstep, it's easy to spend a weekend **skiing** or **snowboarding** from Milan, Turin, or Venice. Some of the most popular ski resorts are Sestriere and Bardonecchia in Piemonte, Cervinia and Courmayeur in Val d'Aosta and the Val Gardena and Val di Fassa in the stunning Dolomite mountains of Trentino Alto Adige and Veneto – home to one of Italy's best known and most exclusive resorts, Cortina d'Ampezzo. Further south you can ski at the small resorts of Abetone and Amiata in Tuscany, Monte Vettore in the Marche, Gran Sasso and Maiella in Abruzzo and on Mount Etna in Sicily. Contact the regional tourist offices for information about accommodation, ski schools and prices of lift passes. All of these mountain resorts are of course ideal bases for summer **hiking** and **climbing** and most areas have detailed maps with itineraries and marked paths. For less strenuous treks, the rolling hills of Tuscany and Umbria make perfect walking and **mountain bike** country and numerous tour operators offer independent or escorted tours throughout the region (see pp.14, 17 and 18). Many tourist offices also publish booklets suggesting itineraries.

If the heat of the summer lures you towards the extensive Italian coast you can expect to find all the usual seaside resort activity and plenty of opportunities for **sailing** and **windsurfing**. **Scuba diving** is popular in Sicily and off most of the smaller islands – you can either join a diving school or hire equipment from one if you're an experienced diver.

Watersports aren't just restricted to the coast so If you're not planning a beach holiday as such you could consider a detour to the Italian Lakes in the north or Trasimeno and Bolsena further south towards Rome. River **canoeing** and **rafting** are limited to the mountain areas of the North – contact the Monrosa rafting club near Turin, ⓦwww.monrosarafting.it, for details of their activities on the Sesia river.

Horse riding is becoming increasingly popular in rural areas of Italy and most tourist offices have lists of local stables (*maneggio*). Many agriturismi (see p.36) also have riding facilities and sometimes offer daily or weekly treks and night rides. Note that Italians rarely wear or provide riding hats.

Crime and personal safety

Despite what you hear about the Mafia, most of the crime you're likely to come across in Italy is of the small-time variety, prevalent in the major cities and the south of the country, where gangs of *scippatori* or "snatchers" operate. Crowded streets or markets and packed tourist sights are the places to be wary of; *scippatori* work on foot or on scooters, disappearing before you've had time to react. As well as handbags, they whip wallets, tear off visible jewellery and, if they're really adroit, unstrap watches.

You can minimize the risk of this happening by being discreet: don't flash anything of value, keep a firm hand on your camera, and carry shoulderbags, as Italian women do, slung across your body. It's a good idea, too, to entrust money and credit cards to hotel managers. Never leave anything valuable in your car, and try to park in car parks on well-lit, well-used streets. On the whole it's common sense to avoid badly lit areas completely at night and deserted inner-city areas by day. Confronted with a robber, your best bet is to submit meekly.

Emergencies

For help in an **emergency**, call one of the following national emergency telephone numbers:

℡112 for the police (Carabinieri).
℡113 for any emergency service, including ambulance (Soccorso Pubblico di Emergenza).
℡115 for the fire brigade (Vigili del Fuoco).℡116 for road assistance (Soccorso Stradale).
℡118 for an ambulance (Ambulanza).

The police

If the worst happens, you'll be forced to have some dealings with the **police**. In Italy these come in many forms, their power split ostensibly to prevent any seizure of power. You're not likely to have much contact with the **Guardia di Finanza**, responsible for investigating smuggling, tax evasion and other finance-related felonies; the **Vigili Urbani**, mainly concerned with directing traffic and issuing parking fines; or the **Polizia Stradale** who patrol the motorways. You may, however, have dealings with the **Carabinieri**, with their military-style uniforms and white shoulder belts, who deal with general crime, public order and drug control. These are the ones Italians are most rude about, but a lot of jokes concerning their supposed stupidity stem from the usual north-south prejudice. The Carabinieri tend to come from southern Italy – joining the police is one way to escape the poverty trap – and they are posted away from home so as to be well out of the sphere of influence of their families. The **Polizia Statale**, the other general crime-fighting force, enjoy a fierce rivalry with the **Carabinieri** and are the ones you'll perhaps have most chance of coming into contact with, since **thefts** should be reported to them. You'll find the address of the **Questura** or police station in the local telephone directory (in smaller places it may be just a local *commissariato*), and we've included details in the major city listings. The *Questura* is also where you're supposed to go to obtain a *permesso di soggiorno* **if you're staying** for any length of time, or a **visa extension** if you require one (see "Red Tape and Visas", p.19).

In any brush with the authorities, your experience will depend on the individuals you're dealing with. Apart from **topless bathing** (permitted, but don't try anything more daring) and **camping rough**, don't expect a soft touch if you're picked up for any offence, especially if it's drugs-related. **Drugs** are generally frowned upon by everyone above a certain age, and universal hysteria about *la droga*, fuelled by the serious problem of heroin addiction all over Italy, means that any distinction between the "hard" and "soft" variety has become blurred. Theoretically everything is illegal above the possession of a few grams of cannabis or marijuana "for personal use", though there's no agreed definition of what this means and you can expect at least a fine for this. In general the south of Italy is less tolerant than the north and, in any case, if found with suspicious substances you can be kept in jail for as long as it takes for them to analyse the stuff, draw up reports and wait for the bureaucratic wheels to grind – which could be several weeks and sometimes months. For the nearest **embassy or consulate** see "Listings" in the Rome, Milan and Naples accounts, though bear in mind that they're unlikely to be very sympathetic or do anything more than put you in touch with a lawyer.

Women and sexual harassment

The degree of freedom Italian women enjoy is comparable to that in Britain or the USA, despite the somewhat outdated reputation of Italian men as predatory Lotharios. It's true of course that some women do encounter whistling, hissing and catcalling, but actually this kind of behaviour is quite rare: you are just as likely to be treated with a great deal of respect and courtesy in day-to-day communications. It's all too easy to overreact to unwelcome overtures; don't take a little light-hearted flirting or an appreciative *ciao bella!* too seriously.

One thing that is dangerous is being drawn into making generalizations – the two female authors of this guide for example have had very different experiences researching the book – but Italy is an easy country to travel around for a woman, whether alone or with female friends. Certainly there is none of the alcohol-fuelled aggressive abuse from men that you might find in English cities; occasionally you might find yourself walking into a café and finding that you have invaded an all-male preserve, or be on the receiving end of a stupid comment from a group of adolescent boys. However, if you're on holiday without a male partner at any of the resorts popular with northern European tourists the assumption will be made that you are looking for a quick fling – fine if you are, but irritating if you're not. Basically, as long as you recognize that you are in a different culture, and as long as you only do what you feel comfortable doing, you don't need to be unduly concerned. Incidentally, greater respect seems to be accorded to older women – so, for once, age can work in your favour.

Contacts for women travellers

Few Italian women will actually admit to being feminist, a label that carries largely negative connotations in Italy. This social stigma has resulted in a low level of structured activity such as women's groups and helpline organizations; despite this, women have secured great advances in the fields of equality at work and good maternity rights. Another statistic that may confound your preconceptions is that Italy's birth rate is one of the lowest in Europe.

Periodicals such as **Noi Donne** are good sources of information on culture, news and politics relating to women. Rome, Bologna and Milan are the places with most action, although this is fairly limited: **il riflusso**, the general term to describe the fall-off in political activity since the Seventies, has affected the women's movement as it has others. Organizations with an academic or institutional slant on women's issues include the Centro Documentazione Donne ⓦ www.women.it, the Unione delle Donne Italiane ⓦ www .archividelledonne.it, and the Centro Studi Storiche sul Movimento di Liberazione delle Donne in Bologna ⓦ www.storiadelledonne.it. For contacts and Internet discussion groups try the **Spazio Donna** (women's space) in La Città Invisibile at ⓦ www.citinv.it.

Sexual harassment

If you do experience persistent **pestering** it isn't usually accompanied by any kind of violent intent, but it can be annoying and frustrating nevertheless. **Silent indifference** is often the most effective policy, as is looking as confident as possible – if you feel threatened it's always a good idea to look as though you know where you are going, even if you don't. Any attempt to hurl Italian insults in the direction of the transgressor is, at best, likely to cause ridicule – and at worst, could well inflame the situation further.

One thing that's worth mentioning is that the Italian **sex industry** is a thriving business, and a woman on her own wandering around a town may in some places be taken to be a prostitute looking for business. Even such an innocent occupation as waiting alone at a bus stop can bring unwelcome attention – this obviously doesn't mean every street or bus stop but there are certain places (one particular road in Rimini, for example) where car doors will mysteriously spring open as you pass by; you can pretty quickly work out what's going on and the

obvious thing to do is walk somewhere else.

Flashers in parks are another common occurrence, and, as parks are often a pick-up place, your motives for sitting quietly in the sun may be misconstrued. This doesn't mean it's impossible to go there, just that it's more relaxing if you pick a spot where there are other people around.

 # Work and study

All EU citizens are eligible to work in Italy. The two main bureaucratic requirements are a *libretto di lavoro* and *permesso di soggiorno*, respectively a work and residence permit, both available from the *Questura* (police station). For the first you must have a letter from your employers saying they are prepared to take you on; for the second you'll need a passport, passport photos, an E111 and a lot of patience. Work permits are pretty impossible for non-EU citizens to obtain: you must have the firm promise of a job that no Italian could do before you can even apply to the Italian embassy in your home country. A useful publication is *Live and Work in Italy* by Victoria Pybus – a comprehensive guide and full of practical information.

The obvious choice is to **teach English**, for which the demand has expanded enormously in recent years. You can do this in two ways: freelance private lessons, or through a language school. **Private lessons** generally pay best, and you can charge around €15–20 an hour, though there's scope for bargaining. Advertise in bars, shop windows and local newspapers, and, most importantly, get the news around by word-of-mouth that you're looking for work, emphasizing your excellent background, qualifications and experience. An advantage of private teaching is that you can start at any time of the year (summer especially is a good time for schoolchildren and students who have to retake exams in September); the main disadvantage is that it can take weeks to get off the ground, and you need enough money to support yourself until then. You'll find the best opportunities for this kind of work in the tourist resorts and the bigger towns and cities. **Teaching in schools**, you start earning immediately. It usually involves more hours per week, often in the evening, at a

lower rate per hour, though the amount you get depends on the school. Don't accept anything less than €8 an hour (approximately £5/US$8), while the bigger schools should pay much more than this. For the less reputable places, you can get away without any qualifications and a bit of bluff, but you'll need to show a TEFL (Teaching of English as a Foreign Language) certificate for the more professional establishments. For the main language schools, it's best to apply in writing before you leave (look for the ads in *The Guardian* and *Times Education Supplement*), preferably before the summer, though you can also find openings in September. If you're looking on the spot, sift through the phone books and do the rounds on foot, asking to speak to the *direttore* or his/her secretary; don't bother to try in August when everything is closed. The best teaching jobs of all are with a university as a *lettore*, a job requiring fewer hours than the language schools and generally providing a fuller pay-packet. Universities require English-language teachers in most faculties, and you can write to the individual faculties (addressed to Ufficio di Personale). Strictly speaking you could get by without any knowledge of Italian while teaching, though it obviously helps.

If teaching's not up your street, there's the possibility of **courier work** in the summer, especially around the seaside resorts. These are good places for finding **bar/restaurant work**, too – not the most lucrative of jobs, though you should make enough to keep you over the summer. You'll have to ask around for both types of work, and some knowledge of Italian is essential. **Au pairing** is another option: sift through the ads in *The Lady* to find openings.

Study and work programmes

One way of spending time in Italy is to combine a holiday with learning the language, enrolling in one of the many summer courses on Italian art and culture or joining an international work programme. There are many opportunities for studying Italian, either as part of an overseas study scheme or by applying directly to an Italian language school when you arrive. See below for useful contacts.

From the UK and Ireland

British Council 10 Spring Gardens, London SW1A 2BN ☎020/7930 8466. Produce a free leaflet which details study opportunities abroad. The Council's Central Management Direct Teaching (☎020/7389 4931) recruits TEFL teachers for posts worldwide (check ⓦ www.britishcouncil.org/work /jobs.htm for a current list of vacancies), and its Central Bureau for International Educational and Training (☎020/7389 4004; publications ☎020/7389 4880; ⓦ www.centralbureau.org.uk) enables those who already work as teachers to find out about teacher development programmes abroad.
Earthwatch Institute 57 Woodstock Rd, Oxford OX2 6HJ ☎01865/311 600, ⓦ www.earthwatch .org.
Erasmus EU-run student exchange programme enabling students at participating universities in Britain and Ireland to study in one of 26 European countries. Mobility grants available for three months to a full academic year. Anyone interested should contact their university's international relations office, or check the Erasmus website ⓦ http://europa.eu .int/comm/education/ erasmus.html.

Field Studies Council Overseas (FSCO) Montford Bridge, Shrewsbury SY4 1HW ☎01743/852 150, ⓦ www.fscoverseas.org.uk. Respected educational charity with over 20 years' experience of organizing specialized holidays with study tours worldwide. Studies include the flora of the Dolomites. Group size is generally limited to 10–15 people. *Overseas Experiences* brochure available.
International House 106 Piccadilly, London W1V 9NL ☎020/7518 6999, ⓦ www.ihlondon.com. Head office for reputable English-teaching organization which offers TEFL training leading to the award of a Certificate in English Language Teaching to Adults (CELTA), and recruits for teaching positions in Britain and abroad.
Italian Cultural Institute 39 Belgrave Square London SW1X 8NX ☎020/7235 1461, ⓦ www.italcultur.org.uk. The official Italian government agency for the promotion of cultural exchanges between Britain and Italy. A number of scholarships are available to British students wishing to study at Italian universities.

From the US

AFS Intercultural Programs 198 Madison Ave, 8th Floor, New York, NY 10016 ☎1-800/876-2377 or 212/299 9000, ⓦ www.afs.org/usa. Runs two-semester student exchange programs.
American Institute for Foreign Study River Plaza, 9 West Broad St, Stamford, CT 06902-3788 ☎1-800/727-2437, ⓦ www.aifs.com. Language study and cultural immersion for the summer or school year.
Earthwatch Institute 3 Clock Tower Place, Suite 100, Box 75, Maynard, MA 01754 ☎1-800/776-0188 or 978/461-0081, ⓦ www.earthwatch.org. International non-profit organization with offices in Boston, Oxford, England, Melbourne, Australia and Tokyo, Japan. Their fieldwork projects for volunteers include Italy's volcanic park survey and food and drink in ancient Pompeii.
Elderhostel 75 Federal St, Boston, MA 02110 ☎1/877-426-8056, ⓦ www.elderhostel.org. Runs educational and activity programs for over 60s. Programs generally last a week or more and costs are in line with those of commercial tours.

From Australia and New Zealand

Australians Studying Abroad 1/970 High St, Armadale, Melbourne ☎1800/645 755 or 03/9509 1955, ⓦ www.asatravinfo.com.au. Study tours focusing on art and culture.

Travellers with disabilities

Facilities in Italy aren't particularly geared towards disabled travellers, though people are helpful enough and progress is gradually being made in the areas of accessible accommodation, transport and public buildings. The historical and, in some cases, crumbling fabric of many of Italy's cities and villages presents particular problems.

The Italian State Tourist Office (see p.20 for addresses) can supply you with detailed information about facilities and accommodation in Rome and Florence and a booklet in English, *Servicing for Disabled People*, published by the Italian State Railways, listing their services. *Cooperativa Sociale* has a useful website ⓦ www.coinsociale.it, with some pages in English and a wealth of information, tips and links in Italian. If you do not use a wheelchair all the time but your walking capabilities are limited, remember that you are likely to need to cover greater distances while travelling (often over rougher terrain and in hotter temperatures) than you are used to. And if you use a wheelchair, have it serviced before you go and carry a repair kit.

Read your travel insurance small print carefully to check that pre-existing medical conditions are not excluded. And use your travel agent to make your journey simpler: airline or bus companies can cope better if they are expecting you, with a wheelchair provided at airports and staff primed to help. A medical certificate of your fitness to travel, provided by your doctor, is also extremely useful; some airlines or insurance companies may insist on it. Finally, don't forget any medication you may require and a prescription, including the generic name, in case of emergency.

Contacts for travellers with disabilities

In the UK and Ireland

Holiday Care 2nd floor, Imperial Building, Victoria Rd, Horley, Surrey RH6 7PZ ☏ 01293/774 535, Minicom ☏ 01293/776 943, ⓦ www.holidaycare .org.uk. Provides free lists of accessible accommodation abroad. Information on financial help for holidays available.

Irish Wheelchair Association Blackheath Drive, Clontarf, Dublin 3 ☏ 01/833 8241, ⓔ iwa@iol.ie. Useful information provided about travelling abroad with a wheelchair.
Tripscope Alexandra House, Albany Rd, Brentford, Middlesex TW8 0NE ☏ 0845/7585 641, ⓦ www.justmobility.co.uk/tripscope, ⓔ tripscope@cableinet.co.uk. This registered charity provides a national telephone information service offering free advice on international transport for those with a mobility problem.

In the US and Canada

Access-Able ⓦ www.access-able.com. Online resource for travellers with disabilities.
Directions Unlimited 123 Green Lane, Bedford Hills, NY 10507 ☏ 1-800/533-5343 or 914/241-1700. Tour operator specializing in custom tours for people with disabilities.
Mobility International USA 451 Broadway, Eugene, OR 97401, voice and TDD ☏ 541/343-1284, ⓦ www.miusa.org. Information and referral services, access guides, tours and exchange programmes. Annual membership $35 (includes quarterly newsletter).
Society for the Advancement of Travelers with Handicaps (SATH) 347 5th Ave, New York, NY 10016 ☏ 212/447-7284, ⓦ www.sath.org. Non-profit educational organization that has actively represented travellers with disabilities since 1976.
Travel Information Service ☏ 215/456-9600. Telephone-only information and referral service.
Wheels Up! ☏ 1-888/389-4335, ⓦ www.wheelsup.com. Provides discounted airfare, tour and cruise prices for disabled travellers, also publishes a free monthly newsletter and has a comprehensive website.

In Australia and New Zealand

ACROD (Australian Council for Rehabilitation of the Disabled) PO Box 60, Curtin ACT 2605 ☏ 02/6282 4333; Suite 103, 1st floor, 1–5 Commercial Rd, Kings Grove 2208 ☏ 02/9554

3666. Provides lists of travel agencies and tour operators for people with disabilities.
Disabled Persons Assembly 4/173–175 Victoria St, Wellington, New Zealand ☎04/801

9100. Resource centre with lists of travel agencies and tour operators for people with disabilities.

Travelling with children

Children are adored in Italy and will be made a fuss of in the street, and welcomed and catered for in bars and restaurants (though be warned that there's no such thing as a smoke-free environment, with chain-smoking the norm). Hotels normally charge around thirty percent extra to put a bed or cot in your room, though kids pay less on trains (see "Getting Around", p.26) and can generally expect discounts for museum entry: prices vary according to museum but 11–18 year olds are usually admitted at half-price on production of some form of ID (for places such as the Uffizi and the Colosseum this applies only to EU citizens). Under 11s – or sometimes only under 6s – have free entry.

The only hazards when travelling with children in summer are the heat and sun. Very high factor suncreams are quite difficult to find although chemists usually sell sunblock. Bonnets or straw hats are plentiful in local markets. Take advantage of the less intense periods – mornings and evenings – for travelling, and use the quiet of siesta-time to recover flagging energy. The rhythms of the southern climate soon modify established patterns, and you'll find it more natural carrying on later into the night, past normal bedtimes. In summer, it's not unusual to see Italian children out at midnight, and not looking any the worse for it.

Contacts for travellers with children

In the UK and Ireland

Club Med ☎0700/007 007 007, ⓦwww.clubmed.co.uk. Specializes in purpose-built

holiday resorts, with kids' club, entertainment and sports facilities on site.

Mark Warner Holidays ☎0870/770 4222, ⓦwww.markwarner.co.uk. Holiday villages with children's entertainment and childcare included.

Simply Travel ☎020/8541 2200, ⓦwww.simply-travel.com. Upmarket tour company offering villas and hotels in the less touristy parts of Italy. In some destinations they can provide qualified, English-speaking nannies to come to your villa and look after the children.

In the US

Families Welcome 92 N Main St, Ashland, OR 97520 ☎1-800/326-0724 or 541/482-6121. Vacations for parents and kids.

Travel With Your Children 40 Fifth Ave, New York, NY 10011 ☎212/477 5524 or 1-888/822-4388. Publish a regular newsletter, Family Travel Times (ⓦwww.familytraveltimes.com), as well as a series of books on travel with children including *Great Adventure Vacations With Your Children*.

Gay and lesbian travellers

Homosexuality is legal in Italy, and the age of consent is 16. The Gay World Pride march took place in Rome in July 2000, and although condemned, predictably enough, by the Pope, the size of the turnout (over a quarter of a million) and the largely sympathetic press coverage have been read as signs that homosexuality is becoming more widely accepted in Italy. Attitudes are most tolerant in the northern cities: Bologna is generally regarded as the gay capital, and Milan, Turin and Rome all have well-developed gay scenes; there are also a few *spiagge gay* (gay beaches) dotted along the coast: the more popular gay resorts include Taormina and Rimini. Away from the big cities and resorts, though, activity is more covert. You'll notice, in the South especially, that overt displays of affection between (all) men – linking arms during the *passeggiata*, kissing in greeting, etc – are common. The line determining what's acceptable, however, is finely drawn.

The national gay organization, ARCI-Gay ☎051/649 3055, ⓦwww.arcigay.it, is based in Bologna but has branches in most big towns; *Babilonia,* ⓦwww.babilonia.net, is the national gay magazine, published monthly, and the ⓦwww.gay.it website, in association with ⓦwww.gay.com, has a wealth of information for gays and lesbians in Italy.

Contacts for gay and lesbian travellers

In the UK

ⓦwww.gaytravel.co.uk Online gay and lesbian travel agent, offering good deals on all types of holiday. Also lists gay- and lesbian-friendly hotels around the world.

Madison Travel 118 Western Rd, Hove, East Sussex NN3 1DB ☎01273/202 532, ⓦwww.madisontravel.co.uk. Established travel agents specializing in packages to gay- and lesbian-friendly mainstream destinations, and also to gay/lesbian destinations.

In the US and Canada

Damron Company PO Box 422458, San Francisco CA 94142 ☎1-800/462-6654 or 415/255-0404, ⓦwww.damron.com. Publisher of the *Men's Travel Guide*, a pocket-sized yearbook full of listings of hotels, bars, clubs and resources for gay men; the *Women's Traveler*, which provides similar listings for lesbians; and *Damron Accommodations*, which provides detailed listings of over 1000 accommodations for gays and lesbians worldwide. All of these titles are offered at a discount on the website. No specific city guides – everything is incorporated in the yearbooks.

In Australia and New Zealand

Gay Travel ⓦwww.gaytravel.com. The site for trip planning, bookings, and general information about international travel.

Parkside Travel 70 Glen Osmond Rd, Parkside, SA 5063 ☎08/8274 1222, ⓔparkside@herveyworld.com.au. Gay travel agent associated with local branch of Hervey World Travel; all aspects of gay and lesbian travel worldwide.

Silke's Travel 263 Oxford St, Darlinghurst, NSW 2010 ☎02/8347 2000 or 1800/807 860, ⓦwww.silkes.com.au. Long-established gay and lesbian specialist, with the emphasis on women's travel.

Directory

Addresses These are usually written as the street name followed by the number – eg Via Roma 69. *Interno* refers to the flat number – eg *interno* 5 (often abbreviated as int.). Confusingly, some towns (notably Florence and Genoa) have two parallel systems for numbering properties, one for shops and restaurants and another for businesses and private residences; sometimes a shop or restaurant is suffixed by the letter "r", meaning that Via Garibaldi 15r might be in an entirely different place from Via Garibaldi 15. Watch out for addresses with "s/n" rather than a street number, which refers to the fact that they have no number, or are *senza numero*.

Bargaining Not really on in shops and restaurants, though you'll find you can get a "special price" for some rooms and cheap hotels if you're staying a few days or off season, and that things like boat or bike rental and guided tours (especially out of season) are negotiable. In markets, you can in theory haggle for everything except food.

Beaches Most beaches are clearly signposted *spiaggia* but you'll have to pay for access to the best parts of the better ones (referred to as lidos), plus a few euro to rent a sun bed and shade and use the showers all day. During winter most beaches look like rubbish dumps: it's not worth anyone's while to clean them until the season starts at Easter. Some beaches, particularly along the north coast of Sicily, are prone to invasions of jellyfish (*meduse*) from time to time. These are not dangerous, but can cause quite a sting, so take local advice and believe, if you will, the Italian train of thought that they are a sign of unpolluted water.

Camping gaz Easy enough to buy for the small, portable, camping stoves, either from a hardware store (*ferramenta*) or camping/sports shops; remember you can't carry canisters on aeroplanes.

Cigarettes The state monopoly brand – MS, jokingly referred to as *Morte Sicura* ("certain death") or *Merda Secca* ("dried shit") – are the most widely smoked cigarettes, strong and aromatic and selling for around €2.20 for a pack of twenty. Younger people tend to smoke imported brands these days – these are slightly more expensive, at around €2.94 per pack. You buy cigarettes from *tabacchi*, recognizable by a sign displaying a white "T" on a black or blue background, and some bars. After hours you'll have to use automatic, hole-in-the-wall vending machines; these are hardly more expensive than *tabacchi*, accept notes and are found on practically every street corner in major cities.

Contraception Condoms (*preservativi*, *profilittici*) are available over the counter from all pharmacies (some also have vending machines after hours) and some supermarkets; the pill (*la pillola*) is available from pharmacies by prescription only.

Department stores There are two main nationwide chains, Upim and Standa. Neither is particularly posh, and they're good places to stock up on toiletries and other basic supplies; branches of both stores sometimes have a food hall attached.

Electricity The supply is 220V, though anything requiring 240V will work. Most plugs are three round pins though you'll find the older 2-pin plug in some places: a travel plug adapter is useful.

Laundries Coin-operated laundromats, sometimes known as *tintorie,* are rare outside large cities, and even there numbers are sparse; see the "Listings" sections of the main city accounts for addresses. More common is a *lavanderia*, a service-wash laundry, but this will be more expensive. Although you can usually get away with it, washing clothes in your hotel room can cause an international incident – simply because the room's plumbing often can't cope with all the water. It's better to ask if there's somewhere you can wash your clothes.

Public toilets Almost unheard of outside train and bus stations, and usually the only alternative is to dive discreetly into a bar or restaurant. In stations and some smarter establishments, there might be an attendant who guards the facilities, dispenses paper (*carta*) and expects a tip of a few euro cents. Standards have improved over the last few years and you'll find most places to be very clean, though it's advisable not to be without your own toilet roll.

Time Italy is always one hour ahead of Britain, seven hours ahead of US Eastern Standard Time and ten hours ahead of Pacific Time.

War cemeteries Anzio and Cassino are just the best known of a number of fiercely contested battles on Italian soil during World War II. Information and a list of Allied cemeteries are available from the Commonwealth War Graves Commission, 2 Marlow Rd, Maidenhead, Berkshire SL6 7DX ☏01628/ 634 221.

Guide

Guide

Piemonte and Valle d'Aosta

CHAPTER 1 **Highlights**

* **Coffee and pastries in Turin** There are few better or more typically Italian ways to pass the time than sipping a coffee and nibbling a pastry in one of Turin's fin-de-siècle cafés. See p.80

* **Sacra di San Michele** The views of the surrounding valley from this fortified abbey are more than worth the long climb up via steps hewn into the rock. See p.83

* **Truffles** The speciality of the region around Alba in Piemonte is the expensive white truffle, shaved onto pasta and washed down with the excellent local Barolo or Barbaresco wine. See p.67

* **Parco Nazionale del Gran Paradiso** The first Italian national park preserves an Alpine region of deep valleys and beautiful mountains that is home to ibex, chamois and golden eagles. See p.100

* **Mont Blanc (Monte Bianco)** Excellent views of this awe-inspiring mountain are to be enjoyed from the Testa d'Arpy. See p.103

Piemonte and Valle d'Aosta

ringed by the French and Swiss Alps and grooved with mountain valleys, there are no less "Italian" regions than **Piemonte** and **Valle d'Aosta**, in the extreme northwest of the country. French was spoken in Piemonte until the end of the nineteenth century and still influences Piemontese dialects; Valle d'Aosta is bilingual and in some valleys the locals, whose ancestors emigrated from Switzerland, still speak a dialect based on German. Piemonte (literally "at the foot of the mountains") is one of Italy's wealthiest regions, known for its fine wines and food and for being home to key Italian corporations such as Fiat and Olivetti. The mighty River Po, Italy's longest, begins here, and the towns of its vast plain – which stretches right across northern Italy – have grown rich on both manufacturing and rice, cultivated in sweeping paddy fields.

Turin, on the main rail and road route from France to Milan, is the obvious first stop: despite being Italy's second industrial city, it retains a Baroque core and is well placed for days out. South of Turin, **Alba** and **Saluzzo** are perhaps the most enticing centres, the former a good base for visiting the wine cantinas, the latter convenient if you want to explore the western valleys; **Asti**, to the southeast, really comes to life during its famous medieval Palio. For the rest, winter sports and walking are the main activities, with **Sestriere** the main skiing centre and the ascent of Monviso in the far west appealing to the climbing fraternity.

Greater challenges – and more spectacular views – are to be found in the adjoining region of **Valle d'Aosta**. Fringed by Europe's highest mountains, Mont Blanc, Monte Rosa and the Matterhorn, veined with valleys and studded with castles, Valle d'Aosta is undeniably picturesque. The central Aosta valley cuts right across the region, following the River Dora to the foot of Mont Blanc on the French border. Along the river are most of the feudal castles for which Valle d'Aosta is famed – the majority built by the Challant family, who ruled the region for seven centuries. Although the castles are pretty from the outside, and easily accessible by bus or train, few are absorbing enough to warrant a special trip into the region. But as skiing and walking country, Valle d'Aosta is unsurpassed. The main valley, it has to be said, is for the most part rather bland, and it's in the more scenic tributary valleys that you'll want to spend most of your time. The eastern area is the most touristed, with ski resorts and narrow, winding roads that can get choked with holiday traffic. If you're walking, you're best off heading west for the protected zone of Italy's largest national park, the **Gran Paradiso**. The valleys here can also be busy – the mountain *rifugi* as well as the hotels get packed in summer – but development is restrained. **Aosta**, the regional capital, is the only town of any size and, with its attractive cobbled streets and good shopping, makes an excellent staging post on the way to the smaller mountain resorts.

Getting around Piemonte is fairly easy. The network of trains and buses is comprehensive, and your own transport is only necessary for the more out-of-the-way places. You can get to most places from Turin; Alba makes a good base

Regional food and wine

Piemonte and Valle d'Aosta are a paradise for gastronomes and connoisseurs of vintage wines. Rich Piemontese cuisine betrays close links with France through dishes like *fonduta* (fondue) and its preference for using **butter** and **cream** in cooking. As in most of the north, olive oil and tomatoes are relatively uncommon, although immigrants from the south have brought their cooking with them. Piemonte is perhaps most famous for its white **truffles**, the most exquisite of which come from around the town of Alba and are ferociously expensive. Their most usual use is a few shavings to subtly perfume a dish of pasta or a risotto. Watch out too for *porcini* mushrooms, chestnuts, and, more specifically, **bagna caöda** – a sociable local variation on the fondue in which everyone dips vegetables into a sauce of oil, anchovies, garlic, butter and cream. In Valle d'Aosta they prepare good rich **soups** like *soupe à la Valpellineuntze*, with cabbage, or *soupe à la cogneintze*, with rice.

The rolling vine-clad hills of Le Langhe and Monferrato produce classy, traditional **wines** like Barolo, Barbera and Nebbiolo. These fine reds need ageing, and Barolo in particular can be very expensive. More suitable for everyday drinking are wines made from the dolcetto grape, notably Dolcetto d'Alba, drunk young and lightly chilled. Probably the most famous is the sparkling Asti (wine makers dropped the "spumante" from the name in 1994 in a bid for a new image) – a sweet wine, though there has been a trend in recent years to make dry spumante. Martini and Cinzano vermouths are also produced in and around Turin, a fusion of the region's wines with at least thirteen of the wild herbs that grow on its mountains. The traditional version to drink, now a brand name, is Punt e Mes ("point and a half") – one part bitter to half-a-part sweet.

for exploring Le Langhe, Saluzzo for the western valleys. Exploring the Valle d'Aosta on public transport demands a bit more patience. Buses run from Piemonte along the main valley past most of the castles, but services connecting the many tributary valleys are rare. The road branches off at Aosta into Switzerland via the Grand-St-Bernard Pass and forks again some 30km further west at Pré-St-Didier: both branches run into France – the southern via the Petit-St-Bernard Pass to Chambéry, the northern to Chamonix through the Mont Blanc tunnel. Because of the border posts, the road is much used by long-distance lorries, which are something of an earache and eyesore. Trains are less regular and run only as far as Pré-St-Didier, so for serious exploration of the quieter valleys, your own vehicle is a definite advantage.

Although the western shore of **Lago Maggiore** is actually in Piemonte, we've treated all the lakes as a region and covered them in the "Lombardy and the lakes" chapter; the Maggiore account starts on p.200.

Turin (Torino)

"Do you know Turin?" asked Nietzsche. "It is a city after my own heart . . . a princely residence of the seventeenth century, which has only one taste giving commands to everything, the court and its nobility. Aristocratic calm is preserved in everything; there are no nasty suburbs." Although **TURIN**'s traffic-choked streets are no longer calm, and its suburbs are as dreary as any in Italy, the city centre's gracious Baroque thoroughfares, opulent palaces, sumptuous churches and splendid collections of Egyptian antiquities and northern European paintings are still there – a pleasant surprise to those who might have been expecting satanic factories and little else.

Turin's suburbs were built by a new dynasty, **Fiat** (Fabbrica Italiana di Automobili Torino), whose owner, Gianni Agnelli, is reckoned to be the most powerful man in Italy. Although the only sign of Agnelli's power appears to be the number of Fiats that cram Turin's streets (as they do those of every other Italian city), it's worth remembering that Fiat owns Alfa Romeo, Lancia, Autobianchi and Ferrari too, accounting for more than sixty percent of the Italian car market. But there are other, more hidden branches of the Agnelli empire. Stop for a Cinzano in one of the city's many *fin-de-siècle* cafés and you're drinking an Agnelli vermouth; buy the *La Stampa* or *Corriere della Sera* newspapers and you're reading newsprint produced by the Agnelli family. Support the Juventus football team and you're supporting the Agnellis who own it. Wielding such power, Agnelli and friends are seen as a political force in a country where governments are relatively transient. Foreign governments often take more notice of Agnelli than they do of Italy's elected leaders: as Henry Kissinger once said, Gianni Agnelli "is the permanent establishment". Terrorists, too, recognized where the roots of Italian power lay: the Red Brigade was founded on the factory floors of Fiat, and Fiat executives were as much targets as were politicians.

Some history

From 1574 Turin was the seat of the Savoy dukes, who persecuted Piemonte's Protestants and Jews, censored the press and placed education of the nobles in the extreme hands of the Jesuits. The Savoys gained a royal title in 1713, and a few years later acquired Sardinia, which whetted their appetite for more territory. After more than a century of military and diplomatic wrangling with foreign powers, the second monarch, Carlo Emanuele III (who promised to "eat Italy like an artichoke"), teamed up with the liberal politician of the Risorgimento, Cavour, who used the royal family to lend credibility to the Unification movement. In 1860 Garibaldi handed over Sicily and southern Italy to Vittorio Emanuele, and though it was to take a further ten years for him to seize the heart of the artichoke – Rome – he was declared king of Italy.

The capital was moved to Rome in 1870, leaving Turin in the hands of the Piemontese nobility. It became a provincial backwater where a tenth of the 200,000 population worked as domestic servants, with a centre decked out in elaborate finery, its cafés – decorated with chandeliers, carved wood, frescoes and gilt – only slightly less ostentatious than the rooms of the Savoy palaces. World War I brought plenty of work but also food shortages and, in 1917, street riots erupted, establishing Turin as a centre of labour activism. Gramsci led occupations of the Fiat factory here, going on to found the Communist Party.

By the Fifties Turin's population had soared to 700,000, the increase mainly made up of migrant workers from the poor south, who were housed in shanty towns outside the city and shunned as peasants by the Torinese. Blocks of flats were eventually built for the workers – the bleak Mirafiori housing estates – and by the Sixties Fiat was employing 130,000 workers, with a further half million dependent on the company in some way. Not surprisingly, Turin became known as Fiatville. Today there are fewer people involved in the industry, and Fiat's famous Lingotto factory has been turned into an arts centre, yet the gap left behind has been filled by some of the biggest names from other industries, especially those belonging to the worlds of textiles and fashion (Armani, Valentino, Cerruti and Ungaro), publishing (Einaudi and UTET), and banking.

Arrival, information and city transport

Turin's main **train station**, Porta Nuova, is on Corso Vittorio Emanuele II, at the foot of Via Roma – convenient for the city centre and hotels. Some trains also stop at Porta Susa on Corso Inghilterra, west of the centre. Close by, on the corner of Corso Inghilterra and Corso Vittorio Emanuele II, is the main **bus station**, the arrival and departure point for most intercity and all international coaches; buses to Saluzzo and Cúneo arrive at and leave from the top of Corso Marconi, near the junction with Via Nizza. The bus station is linked to Via Nizza (near Porta Nuova) and Porta Susa by bus #60. Turin's **airport**, Caselle (information ☎011.567.6361 or 011.567.6362), is 15km north of the city, connected by buses every 30 to 45 minutes with Porta Susa and Porta Nuova train stations (35-minute journey; tickets cost €4.13).

The main **tourist office** is on the corner of Piazza Castello and Via Garibaldi (daily 9am–7.30pm; ☎011.535.181, ⓦwww.turismotorino.org), with branches at the train station (daily 8.30am–7.30pm; ☎011.535.901) and the airport (daily 9am–7.30pm; ☎011.567.8124). All are well organized with detailed information and suggested itineraries, as well as a free hotel reservation service. They can also supply you with the **Torino card** (€14), which gives you entrance to 84 museums and access to all bus services for 48 hours. **What's on** listings and **ticket outlets** are detailed on p.81.

Most of Turin's sights are within walking distance of Porta Nuova station, although if you're pushed for time the **tram and bus** network provides a fast and efficient way of getting around. Tickets must be bought before you board – €0.77 from *tabacchi*, although it's worth asking at the tourist offices for details of current discount tickets. Of **routes** you might use a lot, tram #4 goes north through the city from Porta Nuova, along Via XX Settembre to Piazza della Repubblica. Other useful routes are tram #1 between Porta Susa and Porta Nuova, tram #15 from Porta Nuova to Via Pietro Micca, bus #61 from Porta Nuova across the river and bus #34 from Porta Nuova to the Museo dell'Automobile. A handy way to explore the city is the new **TurismoBus** which operates a hop-on-hop-off service. It runs a circular route around the city, taking in the major sights; tickets cost €5 and are valid all day. The main **taxi** ranks are at the bus and train stations and the airport, or dial ☎011.5730, 011.5737 or 011.3399.

Accommodation

The majority of the city's **hotels** – in all price ranges – are close by Porta Nuova station; while not the most salubrious part of town, it has been cleaned up in recent years. The streets opposite Porta Nuova, close to Piazza Carlo Felice, although slightly more expensive, are less eventful, and there are also other attractive options dotted around the city. Wherever you choose to stay, bear in mind that demand is usually high, especially during the skiing season and trade fairs (when prices also rise), and it's a good idea to phone in advance. As the majority of Turin's hotels cater to the business trade, however, at weekends and during August it's often possible to negotiate a discount. Bear in mind though that many hotels are closed in August, which is low season for Turin.

Hotels

Artua Via Brofferio 1 ☎011.517.5301, ⓕ011.517.5141. Comfortable hotel with air-conditioning, plus safe parking. Has a sister hotel, *Solferino* (☎011.561.3444, ⓕ011.562.2241), next door, with similar facilities. Both ❹

Astoria Via XX Settembre 4 ☎011 562.0653, ⓕ011.562.5866. Good-value hotel just off Piazza Carlo Felice, with very pleasant rooms, all with satellite TV, and extremely friendly management. ❹

Canelli Via San Dalmazzo 7 ☎011.537.166. A neat, simple but gloomy hotel close to the pedestrian area of Via Garibaldi. As the cheapest hotel in town, this place is often full – book well in advance. ❶

Conte Biancamano Corso Vittorio Emanuele II 73 ☎011.562.3281, ⓕ011.562.3789. If you feel like splashing out a bit, go for this hotel set in an old palace with panelled ceilings and large rooms. ❻

Hotel Liberty Via Pietro Micca 15 ☎011.562.8801, ⓕ011.562.8163. Comfortable belle époque-style rooms on the edge of the medieval quarter. ❺

Montevecchio Via Montevecchio 13 ☎011.562.0023, ⓕ011.562.3047. That rare thing – a quiet hotel near the train station. This one also has good facilities, with TV and telephone in all rooms. ❹

Roma & Rocca Cavour Piazza Carlo Felice 60 ☎011.561.2772, ⓕ011.562.8137. Old-style hotel close to the station, overlooking a noisy square with a small park and fountain. Generally good value, though avoid the poor breakfast, which is expensive (ask for the room "senza colazione"). ❹

San Carlo Piazza San Carlo 197 ☎011.562.7846. Well located in one of Turin's most representative central squares. Try to get a room with a view. ❸

Sila Piazza Carlo Felice 80 ☎011.544.086. Convenient location almost opposite the main train station. Good lodgings with decent facilities. ❹

Urbani Via Saluzzo 7 ☎011.669.9047, ⓕ011.669.3226. First choice for comfort and value in the station area. Very pleasant rooms, individually furnished, many with balconies overlooking the inner courtyard. Located on a quiet street a minute's walk from Porta Nuova. ❹

Villa Sassi Strada Traforo del Pino 47 ☎011.898.0556, ⓕ011.890.095, ⓦwww .villasassi.com. A luxurious eighteenth-century villa set in its own parkland in the hills above the city. Rooms are elegant, many with original features. Closed Aug. ❾

Hostel and campsite

Ostello Torino Via Alby 1 ☎011.660.2939. Bus #52 from Porta Nuova across the river. The official HI hostel, with beds in clean modern dormitories, and dinners for €8. Open mid-Feb to Christmas. €12, including breakfast.

Villa Rey Strada Val San Martino Superiore 27 ☎011.819.0117. The most convenient of the city's campsites, not far from the youth hostel. Take bus #61 from Porta Nuova, and then bus #54. End of March to end of Nov.

The City

The grid street-plan of Turin's Baroque centre makes it easy to find your way about. **Via Roma** is the central spine of the city, a grand affair lined with designer shops and ritzy cafés, although nowadays on the grubby side. It is punctuated by the city's most elegant piazzas, most notably **Piazza San Carlo**, close to which are some of the most prestigious museums. **Piazza Castello** forms a fittingly grandiose, if hectic, conclusion to Via Roma, with its royal palaces awash in a sea of traffic. From here you can walk in a number of directions. To the west, **Via Pietro Micca** leads to a cluster of pedestrianized shopping streets, more relaxed than Via Roma and a good area to head for during the evening passeggiata in summer. North lies **Piazza della Repubblica**, a vast square with calming fountains at its centre. To the southeast, the porticoes of **Via Po** forge down to the river, a short walk along which is the extensive **Parco del Valentino**, home to some of the city's best nightlife. Beyond lies the engaging **Museo dell'Automobile** and the **Pinacoteca Giovanni e Marella Agnelli**, a new art gallery displaying the superb private collection built up by the Fiat magnate, while the hills **across the river**, which are peppered with the Art Deco villas of the richest Torinese, shelter the **Basilica di Superga** and the **Stupinigi Palace**.

Porta Nuova and around

As you step out of **Porta Nuova** station, you'll notice immediately Turin's measured symmetry, although the area around the station is seedy, with prostitutes and street-hasslers cruising the once-elegant arcades of Via Nizza and Corso Vittorio Emanuele II.

To the west of here, the **Galleria Civica d'Arte Moderna e Contemporanea** at Via Magenta 31 (Tues–Sun 9am–7pm; €5.50) features a good selection of twentieth-century work by artists as varied as De Chirico, Chillida, Warhol, Fontana and Basilico. The overall quality of the permanent collection is tempered by an unexceptional floor-and-a-half of work from the last two hundred years of the Torinese school, but as the gallery is on the international circuit for touring exhibitions and loans there is often more than enough to compensate.

Back at Porta Nuova, crossing the road brings you to the neat gardens of **Piazza Carlo Felice**, beyond which lies **Via Roma**, the stamping ground of the well heeled. Halfway down Via Roma, **Piazza San Carlo** is known with some justification as the parlour of Turin, a grand oval space fronted by Baroque facades, the porticoes of which house elegant cafés. Holding court is an equestrian statue of the Savoy duke Emanuele Filiberto raising his sword in triumph after securing Turin's independence from the French and Spanish at the battle of San Quintino in 1574, while the entrance to the square is guarded by the twin Baroque churches of **San Carlo** and **Santa Cristina**. Behind the churches two nudes represent Turin's two rivers – the Po and the Dora.

Around the corner from Piazza San Carlo, the **Museo Egizio**, Via Accademia delle Scienze 6 (Tues–Sun 8.30am–7pm; €6.50), holds a superb collection of Egyptian antiquities, gathered together in the late eighteenth century under the aegis of Carlo Emanuele III. There are decorated mummy cases and an intriguing assortment of everyday objects, including castanets, sandals, a linen tunic dating from 2300 BC, and even food – eggs, pomegranates and grain, recognizable despite their shrivelled, darkened state. Also interesting is the small Nubian temple dedicated by Tutmosis III to Ellesija, although the undoubted highlights are a **statue of Ramses II**, very much praised by Champollion, and the **Tomb of Kha and Mirit**. The tomb, discovered in 1906 at Deir-el-Medina, home of the architects, masons and painters of the nearby royal necropoli, is that of a 1400 BC architect, Kha, and his wife Mirit. The burial chamber contains the tools of Kha's trade – cubits, a case for balances, pens and a writing tablet – and more ordinary daily items: a bed with a headrest, clothes, generous rations of food, even a board game to while away the posthumous hours. And to ensure that Mirit kept up appearances, she was provided with a cosmetic case, wig, comb and tweezers.

Above the museum, the **Galleria Sabauda** (Tues–Sun 8.30am–7pm; €4) was built around the Savoys' private collection and is still firmly stamped with their taste: a middling miscellany of Italian paintings – work from Piemontese, Florentine, Venetian and Bolognese schools – supplemented by a fine collection of Dutch and Flemish works. Of the Italian paintings, the most interesting is the fifteenth-century *Archangel Raphael and Tobias* by Antonio and Piero Pollaiuolo, an ultra-realistic work that amply demonstrates the Pollaiuolo brothers' studies in anatomy. Among the first artists to do this, the brothers were once considered ahead of their time, as a look at the rarefied, almost ethereal painting of the same subject by their contemporary, Filippino Lippi, shows. The northern European collection is more engaging. Alongside a number of French paintings, there are debauched peasant scenes by Flemish artists, notably works by Rembrandt, David Teniers Jnr, and a bucolic *Amarilli and Mirtillo* by van Dyck. Take a look too at the intriguing *Vanity of Human Life* by Jan Brueghel. On a more elevated level, Hans Memling's *Passion of Christ* tells the story of Christ's final days in a Renaissance city setting.

▲ Stadio delle Alpi & Stazione Dora

▼ Palazzina di Caccia di Stupinigi

Piazza Castello and around

Via Roma continues north through the heart of Turin, passing near some of
the key monuments of the Savoys and the Italian Unification. The **Museo
Nazionale del Risorgimento**, Via Accademia della Scienze 5 (Tues–Sun
9am–7pm; €4), housed in the star-flecked **Palazzo Carignano**, birthplace of
Vittorio Emanuele II, is worth a visit. The first meetings of the Italian parlia-

CORSO REGINA MARGHERITA

Parco Michelotti

LUNGO PO MACHIAVELLI

CORSO GABETTI

VIA ROSSINI

VIA MONTEBELLO

CORSO S. MAURIZIO

VIA JANZHOLIA

CORSO CASALE

Campsite ▶

Teatro Reggio   Auditorium RAI

Mole Antonelliana

VIA G. VERDI

▶ Via Strada San Martino Superiore

Palazzo Carignano
Museo Nazionale
del Risorgimento

LUNGO PO CADORNA

PIAZZA C.
CARLO ALBERTO

PIAZZA
VITTORIO VENETO

13

Gran Madre
di Dio

Villa della
Regina

14

VIA M. VITTORIA

PONTE REGINA
MARGHERITA

VIA VILLA DELLA REGINA

VIA GIOLITTI

River Po

PIAZZA
CAVOUR

19

VIA CAVOUR

Monte Dei
Cappuccini Museo
della Montagna

N

PIAZZA
BODONI

VIA DEI MILLE

VIA MAZZINI

24

PONTE VITTORIO
EMANUELE I

CORSO FIUME

0   200 m

VIA GALLIARI

VIA BERTHOLLET

RESTAURANTS AND CAFÉS

Arcadia	17
L'Arcimboldo	1
Baratti and Milano	9
Al Bicerin	2
Brek	21
Del Cambio	11
C'era una volta	24
Il Conte Verde	7
Cucco	13
Frullati Varturi	8
Mulassano	5
Papillon	12
Pepino	12
Platti	22
Porto di Savona	14
Quattri Soldi	23
Rosticeria	20
La Ruota	6
San Carlo	15
Stratta	16
La Taverna Rossa	25
Torino	18
Tre Galline	3
Vegetarian Club	19
Zucca	10

VIA S. PELLICO

Parco
del
Valentino

K

CORSO MARCONI

CORSO D'AZEGLIO

CORSO MONCALIERI

Castello
Valentino

ACCOMMODATION

Artua	D
Astoria	E
Canelli	A
Conte Bianamano	F
Liberty	B
Montevecchio	J
Roma & Rocca Cavour	G
San Carlo	C
Sila	H
Urbani	I
Youth Hostal	K

Borgo e
Castello
Medioevale

▼ Museo dell'Automobile & Lingotto Centre

ment were held in the palace's circular Chamber of the Subalpine Parliament, and the building was the powerbase of leaders like Cavour, who ousted the more radical Garibaldi to an early retirement on the island of Caprera near Sardinia. It's ironic, then, that the most interesting sections of the museum are those dedicated to Garibaldi: portraits showing him as a scruffy, long-haired revolutionary, some of his clothes – an embroidered fez, a long stripy scarf and one of the famous red shirts – adopted during his exile in South America, where he trained himself by fighting in various wars of independence. These shirts became the uniform of his army of a thousand volunteers who seized southern Italy and Sicily from the Bourbons.

What Vittorio Emanuele II made of the eccentrically dressed revolutionary who secured half the kingdom for him is undocumented, but you feel sure that his residence, the sixteenth-century **Palazzo Reale** (guided tours every 40min Tues–Sun 9am–7pm; €6.50), at the head of the sprawling, traffic-choked Piazza Castello, wouldn't have impressed Garibaldi. Designed by Castellamonte, to the specifications of Madama Reale Cristina of France, this nouveau-riche palace with an unexceptional facade hides glitzy rooms gilded virtually top-to-bottom and decorated with bombastic allegorical paintings. Around the rooms you'll find comical collections of chinoiserie, with lions, cockerels and fat laughing Chinamen, a thousand-piece dinner set and a particularly flashy vase of Meissen porcelain encrusted with golf balls and birds. If this isn't enough, look in also on the seventeenth-century church of **San Lorenzo**, tucked behind the left wing of the palace. Designed by Guarini, who was also responsible for the Palazzo Carignano, it's scalloped with chapels, crowned by a complex dome supported on overlapping semi-circles, and lined with multicoloured marble, frescoes and stucco festoons and statuettes.

On the right-hand side of the Palazzo Reale is the **Armeria Reale** (Tues–Sun 9am–7pm; €2), a collection of armour and weapons spanning seven centuries and several continents started by King Carlo Alberto in 1837. Pride of place is given to his stuffed horse, which stands among cases of guns and swords. There's also a gallery of suits of armour and a blood-curdling collection of oriental arms, including gorgeously jewelled Turkish sheaths and intimidating Japanese masks. The same building houses the **Biblioteca Reale** (open only to bona fide scholars, or for special exhibitions), which, along with countless volumes and manuscripts, has a collection of drawings by artists including Leonardo da Vinci, Bellini, Raphael, Tiepolo and Rembrandt, part of it sometimes on display.

Across the square from the Palazzo Reale, the **Palazzo Madama** is an altogether more appealing building, with an ornate Baroque facade by the early eighteenth-century architect Juvarra, who also redesigned the piazza and many of the streets leading off it. Inside, the originally fifteenth-century palace incorporates parts of a thirteenth-century castle and a Roman gate. It's worth looking in also for some of the building's original furniture and frescoes and the **Museo Civico dell'Arte Antica** (closed for restoration at the time of writing) – a collection that includes everything from early Christian gold jewellery and oriental ceramics to a famous *Portrait of an Unknown Man* by Antonello da Messina and an inlaid Gothic commode.

Behind the Palazzo Reale – and reached through a small passage – is the fifteenth-century **Duomo**, on Via XX Settembre. The only example of Renaissance architecture in Turin, it was severely damaged in a fire in 1997 but is open to visitors and worshippers despite being decked in purple satin to hide scaffolding and restoration work – the reconstruction of its fantastic Holy Shroud Chapel, designed by Guarini in 1668, will not be completed until at least 2010. Luckily a quick-thinking fireman rescued from the blazing chapel what has been called "the most remarkable forgery in history", the **Turin Shroud** – a piece of cloth imprinted with the image of a man's body that has been claimed as the shroud in which Christ was wrapped after his crucifixion. One of the most famous medieval relics, it made world headlines in 1989 after carbon-dating tests carried out by three universities all concluded it was a fake,

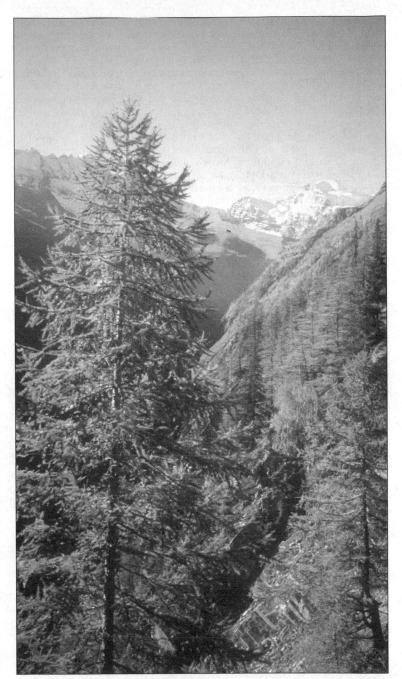

△ The Parco Nacionale del Gran Paradiso

made between 1260 and 1390 – although no one is any the wiser about how the medieval forgers actually managed to create the image. Most of the time you can't see the shroud itself; it is locked away and officially only on display once every twenty-five years, although in reality the possibility of a glimpse is more frequent, as it is sometimes brought out for special occasions (it's worth checking at the tourist office for details). If you don't get to see the real thing, head to the left of the nave, where there's a photographic reproduction, on which the face of a bearded man, crowned with thorns, is clearly visible, together with marks supposed to have been left by a double-thonged whip, spear wounds and bruises that could have been caused carrying a cross. For those whose interest is still not satiated, there is a museum that covers the history and science of the shroud, **Museo della Sindone** (daily 9am–noon & 3–7pm; €5.50), on Via S. Domenico 28.

The only relics of Turin's days as a small Roman colony are visible from outside the duomo: the scant remains of a **theatre** and the impressive **Porta Palatina** – two sixteen-sided towers flanking an arched passageway. Beyond, the massive and recently restored **Piazza della Repubblica** is another Juvarra design. Behind the Porta Palazzo is the Saturday-morning Balôn, or **flea market**, home to fortune-tellers (Turin is reputed to be the centre of the Italian occult) and black marketeers. On the second Sunday of each month there's a Gran Balôn with opportunities to buy collectable items including lace, toys, secondhand furniture and books.

Behind Piazza della Repubblica stands Turin's most elaborate church, the **Santuario della Consolata**, built to house an ancient statue of the Madonna, Maria Consolatrice, the protector of the city. Designed by Guarini, the church has an impressive decorative altar by Juvarra, and outside its pink-and-white Neoclassical facade there are shops crammed with votive objects, which the more devout Torinese buy to offer to the statue, housed in an ancient crypt below the church. Not to be missed is the series of paintings in the church, featuring people being "saved" from such disasters as being gored by a bull, cutting overhead electricity cables with garden shears, exploding chip pans, and numerous accidents involving prams and trams. After all this, you may well want to head across the road to the beautiful old café *Al Bicerin* (see p.80) for a pick-me-up.

Parco del Valentino, the Museo dell'Automobile and Pinacoteca Giovanni e Marella Agnelli

The scruffy porticoes of Via Po lead down to the river from Via Roma, ending just before the bridge in the vast arcaded Piazza Vittorio Veneto. Turn off halfway down, along Via Montebello, to the **Mole Antonelliana**, whose bishop's-hat dome, topped by a pagoda-like spire balancing on a mini-Greek temple, is a distinctive landmark and has been adopted as the city's emblem. Designed as a synagogue in the nineteenth century by the eccentric architect Antonelli, the building was ceded to the local council by Turin's Jewish community while still under construction because of escalating costs. The decision to house the new **Museo del Cinema** (Tues–Sun 9am–7pm; €5.20 or €6.80 with lift to top of Mole) in this rather preposterous white elephant seems a suitable way to celebrate the sheer spectacle of the building. Turin's involvement with cinema goes back to the early years of the twentieth century, when it was one of the first Italian cities to import and experiment with the new medium invented by the Lumière brothers. The interesting museum covers the early days of the magic lantern and experimental moving pictures, the development of the cinema as a global phenomenon, and twenty-first-century special effects.

Across the bridge from the **Piazza Vittorio Veneto** there is the Pantheon-like **Gran Madre di Dio** church. Behind the church, a path takes you up the hill to the **Museo Nazionale della Montagna Duca degli Abruzzi** at Via Giardino 39 (daily 9am–7pm; €5), a fascinating museum dedicated to the mountain environment and its people.

South along the river from Piazza Vittorio Veneto is the riverside **Parco del Valentino**, which you're most likely to visit at night, as it holds some of the best of Turin's clubs. But in the daytime it makes a pleasant place to wind down after the hum of the city centre, its curving lanes, formal flower beds and fake hills covering half a million square metres – making it one of Italy's largest parks. Within the grounds are two castles, one real, the other a fake. The ornate **Castello Valentino** was another Savoy residence, used mainly for wedding feasts and other extravagant parties, and nowadays seat of the university's faculty of architecture. The **Borgo e Castello Medioevale** (daily 9am–8pm; free) and, inside, the **Rocca Medioevale** (Tues–Sun 9am–7pm; €3) date from an industrial exhibition held in 1884 and are a synthesis of the best houses and castles of medieval Piemonte and Valle d'Aosta, built with the same materials as the originals and using the same construction techniques. You may balk at the bogusness of the thing, and it does feel a little like Disneyland, but it actually conjures up a picture of life in a fifteenth-century castle far better than many of the originals, kitted out as it is with painstaking replicas of intricately carved Gothic furniture. The castle is based on the one at Fénis (see p.97), and the frescoes are reproductions of those at Manta (see p.84).

A longish walk from here, along the river, takes you to the **Museo dell'Automobile** at Corso Unità d'Italia 40 (Tues–Sun 10am–6.30pm; €5; bus #34 from Via Nizza), Italy's only motor museum. Even if you know nothing about cars, this has some appeal – you'll spot models you haven't seen since your childhood and others familiar from films, as the museum traces the development from the early cars, handcrafted for a privileged minority, to the mass-produced family version. There's one of the first Fiats, a bulky 1899 model, close to a far sleeker version, built only two years later and, just three decades later, the first small Fiat family-targeted vehicle, a design which was still on the streets in the Sixties. Look also at the gleaming Isotta Fraschini driven by Gloria Swanson in *Sunset Boulevard*, still with the initials of Norma Desmond, the character she played, on the side. The pride of the collection is the 1907 Itala which won the Peking-to-Paris race in the same year; you can read of its adventures in Luigi Barzini's book *Peking to Paris*.

Walking a little further on and turning right down Via Garessio will take you to the newly opened **Pinacoteca Giovanni e Marella Agnelli** (Mon–Sat 10am–6pm; €4), a priceless collection of artworks donated by head of the Fiat dynasty, Gianni Agnelli. The paintings are housed in a glass-and-metal gallery, designed by Renzo Piano, which overlooks the test track on top of the **Lingotto Centre**, Via Nizza 250, the former Fiat car works, now Turin's main conference and exhibition space. The bulk of the collection consists of nineteenth- and twentieth-century masterpieces, including a number of Matisses and Picassos (*L'Hétaire* and *Homme Appuyé sur une Table*), as well as Modigliani's *Nu Couché* and Manet's *La Négresse*. The eighteenth century is represented by six Canalettos and Tiepolo's *Halberdier in a Landscape*.

Out from the centre: the Basilica di Superga and Stupinigi Palace

South of the river, Turin fades into decrepit suburbs, beyond which lie the wooded hills that conceal the fancy villas of the city's industrialists, including that of Gianni Agnelli. For a taste of the views enjoyed by Turin's mega-rich, take bus #70 up to the **Parco della Rimembranza**, with 10,000 trees planted in honour of the Torinese victims of World War I and crowned with an enormous light-flashing statue of Victory. Alternatively, head out to the grandiose Baroque **Basilica di Superga**, from which there are fine panoramas across the city to the Alps (tram #15 followed by a shuttle bus – #79.

The basilica, yet another design from Filippo Juvarra, stands high on a hill above the rest of the city, a position that is the key to its existence. In 1706 King Vittorio Amadeo climbed the hill in order to study the positions of the French and Spanish armies who had been besieging the city for four months, and vowed that he would erect a temple to the Madonna on this site if she were to aid him in the coming battle. Turin was spared, and the king immediately set Juvarra to work, flattening the top of the hill and producing over the next 25 years the circular basilica you see today. An elegant dome, pierced by windows and supported on pairs of white columns, is flanked by delicately scalloped onion-domed towers and rises above a Greek temple entrance, though the most striking thing about the building these days is the graffiti – names dating back to the beginning of the century scratched into the interior pillars. Many Torinese come here not to pay homage to the Virgin, nor even to the splendid tombs of the Savoys, but to visit the tomb of the 1949 Torino football team, all of whom were killed when their plane crashed into the side of the hill. If you happen to go to a match between Torino and Juventus, you may well hear the sinister chant from the Juventus supporters, "Superga, Superga".

A nearby attraction worth making a trip out of town for is the Savoy dynasty's luxurious hunting lodge, the **Palazzina di Caccia di Stupinigi** (Tues–Sun 10am–6pm; €6.20). Another Juvarra creation, built in the 1730s and perhaps his finest work, this symmetrical fantasy with a generous dash of Rococo was awarded UNESCO World Heritage status in 1997. The exterior of the palace has been restored, and the interior is as luxurious as it ever was: the most extravagant room, the oval Salone Centrale, is a dizzying triumph of optical illusion that merges fake features with real in a superb trompe l'oeil. Other rooms are decorated with hunting motifs: Diana, goddess of hunting, bathes on bedroom ceilings, hunting scenes process across walls, and even the chapel is dedicated to St Uberto, patron saint of the hunt. And everywhere there are opulent wall-coverings – gilded brocades, hand-painted silk, carefully inked rice paper – and delicate eighteenth-century furniture, including gilded four-posters, inlaid desks and cabinets, even a marvellous marble bath, decorated with a relief of an imperial eagle, installed by Pauline Bonaparte. To get there, take bus #41sb from Corso Vittorio Emanuele II; on the way you'll pass through the bleak Mirafiori suburbs on the west side of the city, built for workers at the nearby Fiat plant.

Another rewarding trip is west to **RIVOLI** and its **Museo dell'Arte Contemporaneo** housed in the baroque Castello di Rivoli (Tues–Fri 10am–5pm, Sat & Sun 10am–7pm; €6.20; Ⓦ www.castellodirivoli.org), one-time residence of the Savoy family. It's the most important collection of post-war art in Italy, ranging from works by Jeff Koons, Carl Andre and Claes Oldenburg to Arte Povera artists such as Mario Merz and Alighiero Boetti. On weekdays bus #36 (1hr) runs from Piazza Castello or Porta Susa station; at the weekend buses run infrequently from Piazza Castello and Porta Nuova.

Eating and drinking

Torinese **cuisine** shows strong French influences, especially evident in the winter dish of *bagna caöda* (see p.67). Fungi and game in autumn, and truffles used as flavouring, are also classics. *Agnolotti* and *cappelletti* are the best-known dishes, followed by meat *buji* (boiled) or braised in wine. Cheeses to look out for are *tomini*, *robiole* and *tume*. The humble *grissini* (bread sticks) found wrapped in greaseproof paper on every restaurant table across the land reach new heights in Turin (they were allegedly invented to tempt the appetite of the sickly boy-king Vittorio Amedeo II in the seventeenth century). The sweets, too, are marvellous, many of them invented in the Savoy kitchens to tempt the royal palates: among the decadent delights are *spumone piemontese*, a mousse of mascarpone cheese with rum; *panna cotta*, smooth, rich cooked cream; light pastries like *lingue di gatto* (cat's tongues) and *baci di dama* (lady's kisses). Turin is also credited as the home of *zabaglione*, used to fill *bignole*, or iced choux pastries; Spanish friar San Pasquale Bayon, a gifted cook and parish priest of the city's church of San Tommaso in the sixteenth century, is said to have invented the egg yolk, sugar and Marsala mixture. Make sure you leave some room to sample one of Turin's major products – **chocolate**. Best known is the hazelnut chocolate *Gianduiotto*, which dates back to the nineteenth century. Some even claim that it was the Torinese who introduced chocolate to France when chocolate making for export began in 1678. The best places to buy chocolate are listed on p.82.

There are plenty of **restaurants** in which to indulge in these dishes all over the city, as well as any number of cheaper eating places serving the kind of food you can find anywhere in the country. For food on the run, there are **snack bars** and **takeaways** on Via Nizza, some tempting **delicatessens** on Via Lagrange and a superb rosticceria on Corso Vittorio Emanuele II for DIY lunches. For a drink, a snack, a pastry or an ice cream, you should also look in on one of the city's *fin-de-siècle* **cafés**, which are a Turin institution. The prices are steep, but the atmosphere more than compensates.

Restaurants

Arcadia Galleria Subalpina 16. Try this place for an eclectic mix of Italian food and sushi. It's affordable at lunchtime, but pricier in the evening. Closed Sun & Aug.

L'Arcimboldo Via Santa Chiara 54. Specializes in *pasta fresca*, with a choice of a hundred sauces, all at low prices. Closed Sun.

Del Cambio Piazza Carignano 2 ☎011.546.690. Historic, formal shrine to Piemontese food much frequented by expense-account types. A great opportunity to feast on traditional dishes, such as beef in Barolo or Cavour's favourite of *fianziera* (veal, sweetbreads and *porcini*, cooked with butter and wine); prices are suitably extravagant and booking is advisable. Closed Mon, Sun & Aug.

C'era una volta Corso Vittorio Emanuele II 41. Simple, delicious Piemontese cuisine at moderate prices. Closed Sun.

Il Conte Verde Via Bellezia 15. Piemontese specialities – try the *tartrà*, a soufflé of cheese, herbs and cream. Closed Sun.

Cucco Corso Casale 89. A big Art Nouveau place near the river at Ponte Margherita serving typical Piemontese cooking at moderate prices with a choice of around 30 antipasti. Closed Mon.

Porto di Savona Piazza Vittorio Veneto 2. Cheap and cheerful restaurant very popular with students and businesspeople alike, attracted primarily by the bargain formula of *piatto unico* and dessert. Closed Tues lunchtime and all day Mon.

Quattro Soldi Corso Castelfidardo 7. Reliable, good-value neighbourhood pizzeria-ristorante in the southwest corner of town. Closed Wed.

La Taverna Rossa Via Valperga Caluso. Excellent pizza and simple dishes at low prices down by the Parco del Valentino. No closing day.

Tre Galline Via Bellezia 37 ☎011.436.6553. The oldest restaurant in Turin, with a lovely panelled interior. Don't miss the sweet-and-sour (*agrodolce*) rabbit. Reckon on €35 a head. Booking advisable. Closed Mon lunchtime, all day Sun & Aug.

Vegetarian Club Via San Massimo 17. Reasonably priced vegetarian restaurant with a good selection of dishes and a quiet outside terrace. Closed Mon.

Cafés

Baratti and Milano Piazza Castello 29. Established in 1873 and preserving its nineteenth-century interior of mirrors, chandeliers and carved wood, in which genteel Torinese ladies sip leisurely teas. Great hot chocolate.

Al Bicerin Piazza della Consolata 5. Walk into this tiny, beautiful place and you feel a bit like you're stepping into a museum. Try a *bicerin* – a Piemontese speciality of coffee fortified with brandy, cream and chocolate.

Mulassano Piazza Castello 15. A cosy café first opened in 1900, with marble fittings and a beautiful ceiling. Traditionally the favourite of actors and singers from the nearby Teatro Regio.

Pepin Piazza Carignano 8. Ritzy café with summer garden, famed for its ice creams. Try the violet-flavoured *pinguino* or the outrageously rich cream-and-chocolate concoction of *pezzo duro*.

Platti Corso Vittorio Emanuele II 72. Art Nouveau-furnished café dating from 1870 that hosts art exhibitions and occasional live music.

San Carlo Piazza San Carlo 156. Where the heroes of the Risorgimento met in the nineteenth century, this rather glitzily restored café with gilt pilasters and an immense chandelier combines a restaurant and ice cream parlour.

Stratta Piazza San Carlo 156. The oldest *confette-ria* in Turin, dating back to 1836. *Marron glacé* is a speciality.

Torino Piazza San Carlo 204. A good place for a leisurely aperitif or cocktail, of which the most popular is the *Torino's* very own "Elvira", made with Martini, vodka and various secret ingredients. Famous regulars were writer Cesare Pavese and Luigi Einaudi (a Torinese economist who became the second President of the Italian Republic).

Zucca Via Roma 294. Pastries and *tramezzini*, plus a famous *aperitivo della casa*.

Snacks, takeaways and self-service places

Brek Piazza Carlo Felice (closed Sun) and Piazza Solferino (closed Mon). Slick, high-quality self-service, with tables outside in summer.

Frullati Varturi Piazza Castello 15. Very central lunchtime option, with sandwiches and an array of fresh local and tropical fruits, ready for the liquidizer.

Papillon Via Corte d'Appello 3. Sandwiches, snacks and full meals.

Rosticceria Via Gramsci 12. Inexpensive place, very crowded at lunchtime, serving everything from *arancini* (fried rice balls) to whole roast chickens.

La Ruota Via Barbaroux 11. Good place for a quick lunch, eat in or takeaway.

Nightlife and entertainment

Turin's **nightlife** is more sedate than that of, say, Milan, but there is a reasonably varied mix of clubs and bars here, with the most lively spots down on the embankment bordered by the Parco del Valentino, known locally as the **Murazzi** – the best advice is just to wander down there and see what takes your fancy. Problems with drugs and theft have given the place a bit of a reputation and there's often quite a heavy police/carabinieri presence – so watch your wallet and take it easy. The area is especially popular on summer weekends when a big crowd spills out of the bars and onto the riverfront jetties. For a more tranquil alternative try the medieval area around Piazza Emanuele Filiberto and Via Santa Chiara.

Getting down to the business of **drinking**, you'll find that birrerias, extremely popular in the 1980s, have been supplemented by new vinerias – wine bars – where you can also order up a substantial snack (known locally as a *marenda sinoira*). Note that some **clubs** require membership cards, which cost between €5 and €10, but your first drink is usually included in this. After that, although drink prices can be inflated, the measures are relatively generous – bar staff usually keep pouring until they think it looks big enough.

The city has an impressive agenda of **live music** in July and September, with many well-publicized open-air performances, some of them free. The season kicks off with **jazz** in the second week of July courtesy of the JVC Jazz Festival (☎011.561.3926) at the Piazzetta and Giardini Reale, which attracts international names such as Tito Puente and João Gilberto. For **rock** fans, the Pellerossa Festival (☎011.434.3333) in the third and fourth weeks

of July offers an eclectic mix of Italian and foreign bands – previous head-
liners have included Bob Dylan and Sonic Youth – with affordable tickets.
However, the festival takes place outside town at the Certosa Reale and the
Parco dalla Chiesa, and you'll need a car to get there. For most of September
a major festival called, appropriately enough, Settembre Musica mixes **jazz**,
world music, **classical music** and **performance art** (T011.442.4777) at
various venues around town. Check the website W www.comune.torino.it
and links for listings.

Turin is also the home of the prestigious **RAI National Symphony
Orchestra**, which performs in, among other places, the Lingotto centre.
Turin's **opera** house, the Teatro Regio (T011.881.5241), is one of the best in
the country and is recognizable from its pod-like Seventies architecture.

The city's Il Teatro Stabile (T011.517.6246), one of Italy's principal publicly
funded **theatre** companies, is acclaimed for its productions of major works by
nineteenth- and twentieth-century European writers; they normally perform
at the Casignano Theatre on Piazza Carignano. For new writers and experimental work, look out for shows by the Gruppo della Rocca, the Teatro
dell'Angolo, the Teatro Juvarra and the Laboratorio Teatro Settimo. There are
also four international **film** festivals held in Turin each year, among them a
women's film festival in March and a "cinema of homosexual themes" in April;
contact the tourist office for details.

For **what's on listings**, opening hours and so on, check the pages of the Turin
daily, *La Stampa*, particularly its Tuesday and Friday supplements, or the weekly *News Spettacolo*. There's also a free monthly bilingual publication available in
hotels and bars, *Un Ospite a/A guest in Torino*, which has a list of events and
exhibitions as well as suggestions for itineraries. Failing that you can get information on events, exhibitions, festivals and the like from either the Informacittà
office, on Piazza Palazzo di Città (Mon–Fri 8.30am–4pm; T011.442.3602), or
the Vetrina per Torino office, Piazza San Carlo 159 (Mon 3–7pm, Tues–Sat
9am–1pm; T011.442.4740); the latter also sells tickets for most events.

Bars, birrerias, clubs and vinerias

AEIOU Via Spanzotti 3 T011.385.8580. Off Corso
Francia, this is a large, modern club in a former
warehouse, with a wide selection of cocktails –
and music. A good place to go if you just want to
dance.

Centralino Via delle Rosine 16 T011.837.500.
Jazz concerts and avant-garde productions; membership card required.

La Contea Corso Quintino Sella 132. Birreria situated across the river that features live jazz and
other styles under a trompe l'oeil fresco of a
square. Food, too, is served on the terrace under a
pergola in summer. Closed Sun.

Doctor Sax Murazzi di Lungo Po Cadorna 4.
African rhythms and contemporary art exhibitions.
Closed Mon.

Hiroshima Mon Amour Via Bossoli 83
T011.317.6636. Live music, avant-garde performances, alternative theatre and cabaret in a
converted school.

Jumping Jester Via Mazzini 2. Old-style wooden
interior with huge TV screen on which football

matches are shown live. Serves a top pint of cold
Caffreys or Tennants.

Lucky Nugget Saloon Corso Vittorio Emanuele
II 40. Open late and popular with an eclectic
bunch of customers – you can have just a drink
or choose from a full range of Mexican food.
There are three floors: chill out upstairs or downstairs, or if you're pining to dance on a few
tables, head straight for the central section.
Closed Mon.

Magazzino di Gilgamesh Piazza Moncenisio
13b. Birreria and coffee shop with music, plus a
international restaurant on the third floor, and
cabaret and country music. Closed Sun.

Nuev Caval Brons Piazza San Carlo 157. Bar (and
restaurant) with a help-yourself canapé selection
that Henry VIII would have been proud of. Closed
Sat lunch & all day Sun.

Roar Roads Via Carlo Alberta 3. Despite the dubious name, a very passable pub just off Via Po that
pulls in locals and foreigners. Closed Sun.

The Shamrock Inn Corso Vittorio Emanuele II 34.
The place for an authentic pint of Irish stout, frequented from about 10.30pm onwards by Torinese

and a smattering of Brits, Australians and Scandinavians. Good-value sandwiches. Closed Sun.

Tre Galli Via Sant'Agostino 25. Busy vineria with a long wine list of local and Italian wines by the bottle or glass (for the latter, ask for a *mescita a calice*) and plates of cheeses, ham, *salumi* and homemade *grissini*. Laid-back atmosphere and tables outside on the piazza in summer. Open until 2am. Closed Sun.

Listings

Books and newspapers Libreria Luxembourg, Via C. Battisti 7, has an excellent range of British and American paperbacks. English-language newspapers and magazines can be bought from the newsagents in Porta Nuova station and Libreria Internazionale de La Stampa, Via Roma 80.

Car parks The Porta Nuova car park (daily 7am–10pm) is the most central place to leave your vehicle.

Car rental Avis, Corso Turati 15 (☎011.501.107); Europcar, Via Madama Cristina 272 (☎011.650.3603); Hertz, Via Magellano 12 (☎011.502.080). All these companies also have desks at Porta Nuova station and the airport.

Chocolate The best shops are Peyrano at Corso Moncalieri 47 and Croci Bruno at Via Principessa Clotilde 61a; the latter is slightly less expensive.

Closing days Some shops are closed on Monday morning. Be prepared for the summer shutdown (first Mon–last Sat of Aug), when there's only a limited public transport service, and many restaurants, food shops and other businesses are closed.

Exchange Outside normal banking hours you can exchange money at Porta Nuova station (daily 7.10am–1.40pm & 2.10–8.30pm).

Football Turin's two teams, Juventus and Torino, play on Saturday and Sunday afternoons at the Stadio dell' Alpi, Strada Altessano 131, Continassa, Venaria Reale (☎011.738.0081), although it's rumoured that Torino may soon be moving to a new stadium. Stadio dell' Alpi is reachable by tram #9 only when there's a game on; at other times (to see the high-tech architecture of the stadium, for example) take bus #72. Although Juventus is the most popular team in Italy (a recent poll found that one-third of all Italians support them), most of the locals support the underdogs, Torino.

Hospital Ospedale Molinette, Corso Bramante 88–90 ☎011.633.1633; for 24hr emergency medical attention call ☎5747.

Internet access @h!, Via Montebello 13 (Mon–Fri 10am–1pm & 2–7pm).

Laundries Alba, Via San Secondo 1; Lava Aschiuga, Via Berthollet 18, with other branches at Via de Nanni 84 and Piazza della Repubblica 5.

Markets In addition to the Porta Palazzo on Piazza della Repubblica, and the weekly Balôn and monthly Gran Balôn markets behind Porta Palazzo (see p.76), there's often some heavily discounted designer fashion (the genuine thing, from end-of-line clearances) at the Crocetta market around Via Cassini and Via Marco Polo (Tues–Fri morning & all day Sat) – not exactly street market prices, but still much cheaper than in the shops.

Pharmacist Boniscontro, Corso Vittorio Emanuele II 66 (☎011.538.271), is an all-night chemist.

Police ☎113. City police station at Corso XI Febbraio 22 ☎011.460.6060. Dial ☎112 for Carabinieri.

Post office The central post office is at Via Alfieri 10 (Mon–Fri 8.30am–2.30pm, Sat 8.30am–1pm).

Shopping Via Roma is good for designer labels, and there is trendier, less expensive fare in the pedestrianized streets bordered by Via Pietro Micca, Via Monte Pietá, Via dei Mercanti and Via San Francesco d'Assisi. Sellers of secondhand clothes and costume jewellery, book binders and tailors cluster in the narrow streets around Via Barbaroux, Via San Tommaso and Via Monte di Pietá, off Via Garibaldi.

West of Turin: the Susa and Chisone valleys

The main route to France from Turin runs through the **Susa Valley**, passing the region's main ski resorts. The one real sight, the **Sacra di San Michele**, a forbidding fortified abbey anchored atop a rocky hill, is an easy day-trip from Turin. **Susa** itself, reached by a minor branch of the rail line, was once a modest Roman town and is now a modest provincial town – a pleasant stopover but with little else to lure you.

Sacra di San Michele

The closest town to the **Sacra di San Michele** is **AVIGLIANA**, half an hour by train from Turin and connected with the abbey by infrequent buses. It's a grotty sort of place, though, and if you don't mind walking it's much nicer to push on to the next stop on the train route, **SANT'AMBROGIO**, a small village at the foot of San Michele's hill, from where it's a very steep sixty- to ninety-minute hike to the abbey. The walk is worth it, both for the views and for the opportunity it affords to soak up the spooky atmosphere that surrounds the glowering abbey, reached by a long flight of stairs hewn into the rock – the *Scalone dei Morti* ("Stairs of the Dead"). Corpses used to be laid out here for local peasants to come and pay their respects, setting a morbid tone that's continued with the abbey buildings proper, from the Romanesque entrance arch carved with signs of the zodiac to the Gothic-Romanesque abbey church.

Susa

A further 25km down the valley from Sant'Ambrogio, **SUSA** is a possible stopover if it's late, a likeable, rather scruffy old town with a few **hotels**, such as the three-star *du Park*, Via Mazzini 15 (☎0122.622.273; ❹), and the three-star *Napoleon*, Via Mazzini 44 (☎0122.622.855; ❺).

While most of Italy was ruled by the Romans, Susa and western Piemonte remained in the hands of the Gauls. The best-known of its Gaulish leaders, Cottius, was much admired by the Romans, with whom he reached a peaceful arrangement, and there are a handful of Gaulish/Roman remains scattered around the town centre, notably in **Piazza San Giusto**, where there's a redoubtable defensive gate. The adjacent Romanesque **Cattedrale** has a fine campanile, but its most interesting features are the external frescoes – a *Crucifixion* and an *Entry into Jerusalem*. Just above the piazza, Cottius erected the **Arco di Augusto** in honour of the Roman emperor; its top is decorated with a processional frieze and gives views down into a small park laid out around the remains of some **Roman Baths**.

From Susa you can make an excursion to the **Abbey of Novalesa**, 10km away at the foot of Rocciamelone in the Cenischia Valley, close by the French border. The church here is a relatively recent, eighteenth-century structure, but parts of the cloister and walls date back to the eighth century, while the four chapels, one of which is decorated with frescoes, were built in the tenth century.

In the opposite direction, southeast, at the end of the Chisone Valley, **PINEROLO** is worth a short stop. It's a small town with a medieval centre that was for centuries the seat of the Acaia princedom, precursors of the House of Savoy. You can walk around the frescoed courtyard of their **palace**, halfway up the hill, where you'll also find the church of **San Maurizio**, burial place of the Acaia princes, decorated with fifteenth-century frescoes. In the town centre, there's a Gothic **Duomo** and the huge covered **Cavallerizza Caprilli** or parade ground for horses. The **Museo della Cavalleria** (Tues–Thurs 9–11am & 3–5pm, Fri–Sun 9–11.30am; free) gives a good sense of the town's glory days, with displays relating to the prestigious former cavalry school of Pinerolo. There are lots of objects – uniforms, arms and spurs, trophies and documents, even a stuffed horse – pertaining to the brilliance of the horsemen and their steeds, as well as displays of bridles, horseshoes, tools and the like, and a rather sad section devoted to the tanks and jeeps that have come to replace horses in the military.

The Piemontese ski resorts

Close to the French border are Piemonte's principal purpose-built ski resorts – well used by British tour operators and really far cheaper if you take a package. The snow is in any case notoriously unreliable, and resorts have been known to close down mid-season, though Sestriere has lately protected itself against the weather by installing Europe's largest artificial snow-machine.

Of the main three resorts, modern **BARDONECCHIA** is a weekenders' haunt, with small chalet-style hotels. **SAUZE D'OULX**, a little way south, is known as the Benidorm of the Alps and attracts hordes of youngsters who treat skiing as a hangover cure. Apart from a few winding streets of old houses, it's an ugly, sprawling place, and its lift-passes are expensive. Linked by lift to Sauze d'Oulx, **SESTRIERE** was the dream resort of Mussolini and the Fiat baron, Giovanni Agnelli, though it's now very overdeveloped. Agnelli conceived an aristocratic mountain retreat, favoured by the young and beautiful, though he was not unaware of the fast-growing tourist industry. The story goes that he insisted the height of the sinks be raised to prevent "common tourists" from pissing in them. Nowadays, the reality is a bland resort that dribbles over a bleak mountain, dominated by two cylindrical towers, both now owned by Club Med.

Saluzzo and the Valle Po

A flourishing medieval town, and later the seat of one of Piemonte's few Renaissance courts, **SALUZZO**, 57km south of Turin, retains much of its period appeal. Flaking ochre-washed terraces and Renaissance houses with painted trompe l'oeil landscapes line stepped cobbled streets climbing up to a castle, now a prison. A pleasant place to stay and wander, the town has the added attraction of regular bus services into the Po, Varaita and Maira valleys, which cut through the foothills of the Monviso mountain towards France.

There are a few things around town worth seeing. Just below the castle, the Gothic church of **San Giovanni** has a number of thirteenth- and fourteenth-century frescoes and the tomb of the leading light of Renaissance Saluzzo, Marchese Ludovico II, anachronistically depicted like a medieval knight beneath a fancily carved canopy. Close by, the Gothic **Casa Cavassa** is a fifteenth-century palace with an arcaded courtyard that doubled as home for one of Ludovico's ministers and now houses the town's **Museo Civico** (currently closed for restoration; check with the tourist office for latest information). Inside are period furniture and paintings, including the gorgeously gilded *Madonna della Misericordia*, with the Madonna sheltering Ludovico, his wife and the population of Saluzzo in the folds of her cloak.

That's about all there is to the town centre, but just to the south of Saluzzo, a five-minute bus ride from outside the train station, there's the **Castello della Manta** – a medieval fortress that was transformed into a refined residence by the Saluzzo marquises in the fifteenth century (Tues–Sun 10am–1pm & 2–5/6pm; €5). Though from the outside it's as plain and austere as Saluzzo's castle, it's worth visiting for the late-Gothic frescoes in the Baronial Hall. One of these illustrates the myth of the fountain of youth, elderly people processing towards the magical waters while others impatiently rip off their clothes to plunge in. The other, *Nine Heroes and Nine Heroines*, depicts idealized chivalrous courtiers and exquisite damsels, with china-pale faces and elaborate costumes, standing beneath stylized trees with coats of arms hanging from the branches.

Saluzzo's **tourist office** is at Via Griselda 6, in front of the town hall (Tues–Sun 9am–12.30pm & 3–5.30pm; ☎0175.46.710, ⓦwww.comune.saluzzo.cn.it), and can provide information on the whole of the western valleys region, including a lits of B&Bs. Among the **hotels**, the cheapest is the *Persico* in Vicolo Mercati (☎0175.41.213; ❸), which also has a very good **restaurant** serving traditional cuisine (closed Fri); or there are a couple of three-stars, the *Astor* at Piazza Garibaldi 39 (☎0175.45.506; ❺) and the *Griselda* at Corso XXVII Aprile 13 (☎0175.47.484; ❺).

Valle Po

West of Saluzzo, close to the French border, lies the source of the River Po, which flows right across industrial northern Italy, gathering the waste from its thousands of factories before finally discharging into the Adriatic. The Alpine style resort of **CRISSOLO** lies towards the end of the valley, and you can hike (or take a minibus in summer) to the **Pian del Re**, a grassy plain around the source of the Po, walking on to the entrance of the **Pertuis de la Traversette**, a 75-metre-long tunnel (open roughly July–September, closed by snow rest of year) built by Saluzzo's Marquis Ludovico to ease the trading route into France for his mule trains. According to one theory, the pre-tunnel pass was used by Hannibal and his elephants.

Crissolo is also a good base for climbing **Monviso**, Piemonte's highest mountain, reachable by way of a long rocky scramble in about six hours from the *Quintino Sella rifugio* (see below), two to three hours beyond the Pian del Re. Even if you don't want to scale the summit, the walk to the *rifugio* is lovely, passing a series of **mountain lakes**; or, if you prefer, it's possible to do a **circuit of the lakes**, turning off the main trail just before Lago Chiaretto, from where a path leads past Lago Superiore and back to Pian del Re. There are also **caves** near Crissolo, the **Grotta del Rio Martino** above the town, with stalactites and a subterranean lake and waterfall. The quick route here takes half an hour from Crissolo but is steep; the slower, easier route takes an hour. Unless you're an experienced caver, it's advisable to go with a guide, arranged through Crissolo's **tourist office** (June–Sept, Dec & Jan Mon–Sat 9.30am–12.30pm; ☎0175.940.131) at Via Umberto 139.

Crissolo's **hotels** are all on the main street, the Via Provinciale. The *Albergo Serenella* at no. 18 (☎0175.94.944; ❸) is cheap and open year-round, as is the *Club Alpino* at no. 32 (☎0175.94.925; ❸). Another small hotel at Pian del Re, the *Pian del Re* (☎0175.94.967; ❷), is open mid-June to mid-September, while the *Quintino Sella rifugio*, near the Lago Grande del Viso, is open at Easter and from June 26 to October 4, and sometimes in winter; at all times it's advisable to phone in advance (☎0175.94.943). The majority of **restaurants** are in the hotels, so you may find taking half board a better deal.

Cúneo and around

There's not much to bring you to **CÚNEO**, the main town of southern Piemonte. Its severely geometric modern centre has less appeal than its extensive bus and rail connections, and the old town – what there is left of it – is dark and gloomy. Even its one "sight", the museum (weekdays only) in the restored Gothic church of **San Francesco** behind the bus station, is only of limited interest: the collection ranges from medieval frescoes to a folk section with traditional costumes, kitchen utensils and an ancient bike.

The **tourist office** is at Via Roma 28 (Mon–Sun 9.30am–12.30pm & 2.30–5.30pm; ☎0171.693.358, ⊛www.cuneoholiday.com). If you want to stay, there are a couple of reasonable **hotels**: the *Cavallo Nero* at Piazza Seminario 8 (☎0171.692.168; ❷) and the similarly priced *Ligure* at Via Savigliano 11 (☎0171.681.942; ❷).

What does bring people to Cúneo are the **valleys** to the south of the town, which are popular for their sulphurous spas and summer and winter resorts. Of the main valleys, the **Valle Stura** is much visited by botanists for its many rare species of flowers; the **Valle Gesso**, whose name means gypsum or chalk, is characterized by its vast walls of limestone, unusual in Piemonte, and some of it has been set aside as the huge **Parco Naturale dell'Argentera-Valle Gesso**, in which you can stay in various refuges, take the waters at **TERME DI VALDIERI**, or visit the botanical gardens at **VALDIERI**. The **Valle del Pesio** shouldn't be missed in spring at least, when a waterfall, known for obvious reasons as the *Piss del Pesio*, is in full pelt; there's also a twelfth-century monastery, the **Certosa di Pesio**, which boasts a missionary museum. Trains to France run through the verdant **Valle Vermenagna**, part of which is given over to the **Parco Naturale di Palanfre**, visitable from **VERNANTE**. Again, the appeal is mainly botanical, with over 800 species of trees and flowers growing at some 3000m above sea level.

Val Maira, actually to the north of Cúneo but still considered one of its valleys, is a quiet and narrow valley, known as the "Emerald Valley" for its greenery. There's not much beyond this, though the villages, with their traditional rubble and wood houses perched high above the river, are very picturesque, particularly **ELVA**, in the hills above **STROPPO** (ask in the cafés for the unofficial taxi driver). If you're walking, it's best to get a **map** from Saluzzo before heading out. The best base is the *Gentil Locando* (☎0171.99.139; ❷), located at the Marmara Bridge, between Stroppo and the small village of Prazzo, with clean rooms and a good-value restaurant. There are no hotels at Stroppo, just a **campsite** near the turn-off for Elva.

Mondoví and around

Half an hour by train from Cúneo, **MONDOVÍ**, split into two parts – modern Breo and older Piazza – isn't especially exciting, though does give access to some interesting fifteenth-century frescoes, a sanctuary and some caves nearby. Time in Mondoví is best spent in the upper town, Piazza, built around a large square – Piazza Maggiore, on which stand a turretted medieval palace and an exotic Baroque church, the seventeenth-century **Chiesa della Missione**, whose interior is decorated with an incredible trompe l'oeil by Andrea Pozzo, a cloudy heaven with angels seemingly suspended in mid-air. If you've time, you can laze around in the **Belvedere**, to the north of Piazza, a garden occupying the site of a thirteenth-century church destroyed except for its campanile in the last century. The campanile was used by a physicist in the eighteenth century to establish topographical measurements; though you can't climb up, the views from garden-level stretch north to the hills of Le Langhe and south to the foothills of the Alps.

Bastia

One of the attractions of Mondoví is its proximity to the hamlet of **BASTIA**, 10km northeast, where the church of **San Fiorenzo** – from the outside a modest rustic structure – holds some brilliantly coloured late-Gothic frescoes. Completed around 1472, the panels were worked on by at least four artists;

they're absorbing pieces, with lively if predictable scenes from the lives of Christ and various saints, including a stunning hell, infested with vicious monsters. **Buses** run to Bastia from the train station at Mondoví but are badly timed for returning.

The Santuario di Vicoforte

A twenty-minute bus ride (from the train station) east of Mondoví, the **Santuario di Vicoforte** is another popular trip from the town, an imposing Baroque church crowned by what is claimed as the world's largest elliptical dome. It's liveliest on Sundays – like most Italian sanctuaries as much a place for a good day out as for devotions, purpose-built arcaded crescents housing restaurants, pastry, souvenir and clothes shops.

According to legend the sanctuary owes its existence to a hunter who, while out in the woods, discovered a pillar painted with a picture of the Madonna and Child – said to have been erected as a votive offering by a poor baker whose bread wouldn't rise. In fact, the sanctuary was begun in 1598 on the orders of King Carlo Emanuele I, and eventually finished in 1890. The frescoed pillar is nowhere to be seen, and the 36-metre dome is rather a disappointment. But the kitsch **museum** provides some compensation: a haphazard collection of ecclesiastical bric-a-brac laid out in a labyrinth of rooms around the dome and towers. The exhibits range from gaudy treasures to ceremonial costumes and photos of those cured of their ailments by a visit here.

Grotta di Bossea

Twenty-four kilometres south of Vicoforte, and difficult to reach unless you have your own transport, the **Grotta di Bossea** (Mon–Sat 10am–1.30pm & 3pm–4.30pm, Sun 10–11.30am & 2.30–5.30pm; guided visits €7.75) is the third of Mondoví's surrounding sights, a long-established subterranean tourist attraction filled with contorted stalactites and stalagmites, waterfalls and lakes and a subterranean scientific laboratory, set up to monitor the caves' wildlife – which includes seven unique species. On display is the skeleton of the *Ursius spelaeus*, an underground monster over 3m long and 2m high that lived here between 25,000 and 40,000 years ago.

Alba and Le Langhe

Northeast of Cúneo, the town of **Alba** and the surrounding **Le Langhe** hills mean two things to the Italians: white truffles and red wine. The region supplies some of the finest of both – the **truffles** are more delicate and aromatic than the black variety found further south, and the **wines** range from the "King of Italian reds", Barolo, to the light and fragrant Nebbiolo. There are a number of wine museums and cantinas in the hill-villages around Alba, the best being those at Barolo, Annunziata and Grinzane di Cavour – all accessible direct by bus from Alba.

Although these big cantinas all sell wine, you'll get a better deal at one of the smaller family-owned establishments scattered around the region. Most of the area's very different wines all come from the same grape, Nebbiolo, and the final taste is dependent on the soil: sandy soil produces the grapes for the light red **Nebbiolo**, calcium and mineral-rich soil those for the more robust **Barolo**.

Alba

Whether or not you want to taste wine, **ALBA** repays a visit, for its central core of red-brick medieval towers, Baroque and Renaissance palaces and cobbled streets lined with gastronomic shops is one of Piemonte's most alluring. And if you come in October, there's a chance to see the town's hilarious annual donkey race – a skit on nearby Asti's prestigious Palio.

The town's only sight as such is its late-Gothic **Duomo**, on the central Piazza Risorgimento, gaudily restored and holding some fine Renaissance stalls, inlaid with cityscapes, musical instruments, and fake cupboards whose contents seem to be on the verge of falling out. But Alba is primarily a place to stroll and eat. **Via Vittorio Emanuele**, the main drag, leads up to the centre from Piazza Savona, and is a fine, bustling street, with the most tempting of Alba's local produce on display – wines, truffles, cheeses, weird and wonderful varieties of mushroom, and the wickedly sticky *nocciola*, a nutty, chocolatey cake. **Via Cavour** is another pleasant medieval street with plenty of wine shops, behind which the **donkey race** and displays of medieval pageantry attract the crowds during the festival at the beginning of October. There's also an annual **truffle festival** later in the month, when you could blow your whole budget on a knobbly truffle or a meal in one of the many swanky restaurants. At the end of April/beginning of May, the Vinum festival gives you the chance to taste five hundred local wines.

Practicalities

The **tourist office** (Mon–Sat 9am–1pm & 2–6pm, Sun 10am–1pm & 2–5pm; ☎0173.36.2562, ⊛www.comune.alba.cn.it, ⊛www.turismodoc.it) is on Via Emanuele 19 and has maps of Alba and information on the surrounding area. If you want to **stay**, you could try the very basic *Leon d'Oro*, Piazza Marconi 2 (☎0173.441.901; ❷), or the *Hotel Savona*, a decent three-star handy for the train station, located at Piazza Savona 2 (☎0173.440.440; ❺), with especially good deals for triples. You'll need to plan ahead to be sure of a room, especially during the October festival. The best place to sample **Albese cooking** is the excellent *Osteria dell'Arco*, at Piazza Savona 5 (closed Mon lunchtime & all day Sun), which has a particularly fine selection of local cheeses. For wine by the glass try *Vincafe*, Via Vittorio Emanuele 12.

If you have your own transport, the village of **NEIVE**, about 13km north of Alba, makes a good alternative overnight stop. Here *Il Contea*, Piazza Cocito 8 (☎0173.67.126; ❸; in high season half-board compulsory), a **restaurant** with **rooms**, offers excellent food and some of the best Barbaresco, Dolcetto and Barolo wines from the vineyards around. Rooms are comfortable, with antique beds and whitewashed walls.

Around Alba: the hills of Le Langhe

Eight kilometres south of Alba, the castle of **Grinzane di Cavour** was rented by the Cavour family in the nineteenth century and served as a weekend retreat for Camillo Cavour. Nowadays it's the seat of Piemonte's regional *enoteca*, or winery, and has a pricey restaurant serving local specialities. The upstairs **folk museum** (☎0173.262.159; daily except Tues & Jan 9.30am–12.30pm & 2.30–6.30pm; €2.58) holds various bits of Cavour trivia and a surprisingly engaging display of agricultural equipment, ranging from a ferret trap and grappa distillery to winter boots made of hay and a contraption for cleaning the cocoons of silkworms. In the afternoons there are wine-tasting sessions, and although there are inevitably some extremely expensive wines, many are affordable.

A few kilometres southwest of Grinzane, in the heart of Le Langhe, **BARO-LO** is the best-known name among Italian wines, its peach- and ochre-washed houses set among extensive vineyards. It's a small village but very geared up to the steady stream of wealthy gastronomes and wine connoisseurs who come here. You can visit the *Enoteca Regionale del Barolo*, housed in a flaking turreted castle on Piazza Falletti (℡0173.562.277; daily except Thurs 10am–12.30pm & 3–6.30pm; free; tastings at weekends), or indulge yourself with a **night** and a **meal** at the *Hotel Barolo*, Via Lo Mondo 2 (℡0173.563.54, ⓦ www.hotelbarolo.it; ❹), whose restaurant – an imperious place with a stiff dress code – is renowned hereabouts.

Just north of Barolo, **LA MORRA** is an earthy old village, with good views over the undulating vineyards from outside the *Belvedere* **restaurant** (℡0173.50.190; closed Mon) on Piazza Castello, which offers classic Albese cooking including wonderful *agnolotti*. The village is home to the Cantina Comunale di La Morra (10am–noon & 2.30–6.30pm, closed Tues; free), in which you can taste and buy wine. There are also some good food shops, with a wide range of local cheeses, and if you're there on a Monday, you can pick up bargains at the market. As for staying over, there's the *Italia* **hotel** at Via Roma 30 (℡0173.50.609; ❸).

The Cantina Comunale has maps of **walks** through the vineyards, best of which is the one to **ANNUNZIATA**, about half an hour down the hill, where there's a private wine museum, the **Museo "Ratti" dei Vini d'Alba** at Frazione Annunziata 2 (Mon–Fri 8.30am–noon & 2–5pm, closed Aug; free), housed in a Renaissance abbey next to the firm's cantina. Laid out in a musty cellar, the museum has a number of intriguing exhibits – a massive barrel for treading grapes, a primitive wine tanker, consisting of an elongated barrel on a rickety cart, and a collection of Roman wine jugs found in the area. Best of all, there's a letter from an Arctic explorer, congratulating the Ratti on the fact that their Barolo had stood up to the rigours of travel and climate on an expedition to the North Pole. Wine at the Ratti cantina is expensive, and you can only buy it in lots of six. It's far cheaper and is sold in single bottles at the family cantina, Oberto Severino, 1km up the road back towards La Morra.

Asti and around

The wine connection continues in **Asti**, 30km north of Alba, and the capital of Italy's sparkling wine industry, being the most famous producer of *spumante*. For most of the year Asti itself is fairly sedate, a small town, not unattractive, but it becomes the focus of attention in September every year, as it gears up for its Palio. Though it's taken nothing like as seriously as Siena's more famous event (see p.556), and has to some extent been revived for tourists, you'd be mad to miss it if you're near here at the right time. The surrounding area hides a fine Romanesque abbey near **Albugnano**, the more profane attraction of steamy spa waters at **Acqui Terme**, and a rare glimpse of Italy's Jewish history in the grand synagogue of **Casale Monferrato**.

Asti

In the run-up to its annual Palio, **ASTI** throws off its sedate air and hosts street banquets and a medieval market. On the day of the race itself, the third Sunday in September, there's a thousand-strong procession of citizens dressed as their fourteenth-century ancestors, before the frenetic bare-backed horse race around the arena of the Campo del Palio – followed by the awarding of the *palio* (banner) to the winner and all-night feasting and boozing.

The rest of the year the Campo del Palio is a vast, bleak car park, and there's frankly not a lot to see. The arcaded **Piazza Alfieri** is officially the centre of town, behind which the **Collegiata di San Secondo** (Mon–Sun 8.30am–noon & 3.30–6.30pm) is dedicated to the city's patron saint, built on the site of the saint's martyrdom in the second century. There's nothing left of the second-century church but there is a fine sixth-century crypt, its columns so slender that they seem on the verge of toppling over. As for the rest of the church, it's a slick, early-Gothic construction, with neat red-brick columns topped with tidily carved capitals and in the left aisle a polyptych by one of Asti's Renaissance artists, Gandolfino d'Asti. The Palio banners are also kept here, housed in a heavily ornate Baroque chapel, along with the Carroccio – a sacred war chariot used in medieval times.

The main street, **Corso Alfieri**, slices through the town from the Piazza Alfieri, to the east of which the church of **San Pietro** at Corso Alfieri 2 (Tues–Sun 9am–1pm & 4–6/7pm) has a circular twelfth-century **Baptistry**, now used as an exhibition space, and a **museum** (€4) housed in what was a pilgrim's hospice, displaying an odd – and badly labelled – assortment of Roman and Egyptian artefacts. At the other end of the Corso is the **Torre Rossa**, a medieval tower with a chequered top, built on the foundations of the Roman tower in which San Secondo, a Roman soldier, was imprisoned before being killed.

Practicalities

Asti's **tourist office** is on Piazza Alfieri (Mon–Sat 9am–1pm & 2.30–6.30pm, plus occasional summer Sundays 10am–1pm; ☎0141.530.357, ⓦwww .terredasti.it), and has information on the Palio and maps of the town. If you're intending to go to Asti on the Palio weekend, book a **room** well in advance; at other times there should be little problem. The best of the affordable options are the conveniently sited *Cavour* at Piazza Marconi 18 (☎0141.530.222; ❸) and the slightly cheaper *Genova*, Corso Alessandria 26 (☎0141.593.197; ❸). As somewhere renowned for its food perhaps should, Asti has a wide choice of **restaurants**, ranging from basic and cheap pizzerias like *Monna Laura*, Via Cavour 30 (closed Mon), to places serving local cuisine like the excellent *Gener Neuv*, Lungotanaro dei Pescatori 4 (closed Sun eve & Mon). If you're into *spumante* or want to sample the other wines of the region, there is a **wine festival** from the second Friday to the third Sunday in September, the Festa della Douya d'Or, with wine tastings in the piazzas of the *centro storico* from early evening until midnight. The rest of the year, you can always try the *Tre Bicchieri*, Piazza Statuto 37, an atmospheric wine bar which has several hundred wines in stock.

Around Asti

North of Asti, **CASALE MONFERRATO** has the dubious distinction of being cement capital of Italy, but it's also home to the country's most sumptuous **synagogue**, tucked down an alley off Via Saloman Olmer, the first left off the main Via Roma (Sun 10am–noon & 3–5pm, on weekdays ring next door for entrance). A rich, gold-encrusted affair with a voluptuously curving pulpit and a "museum of treasures" laid out in the closed-off women's gallery, the synagogue is a leftover from the days when there was a sizeable Jewish population in Piemonte, most of whom had fled from Spain in the sixteenth century to escape persecution. Casale was home to nearly 200 Jewish families, who lived here in peace until Mussolini's racial laws (brought in mainly to appease Hitler) forced many to leave.

Between Asti and Casale Monferrato is the small town of **MONCALVO**, tucked into a fold in the hills and surrounded by fields of sunflowers, vineyards and acres of corn. If you have the cash and want to spoil yourself in restful sur-roundings, head for the *Locanda di Sant'Uffizio* (℡0141.916.292; ❾), 4km south of Moncalvo at Cioccaro di Penango, a luxury hotel in a seventeenth-century ecclesiastical palace, with antique-filled rooms, a gourmet restaurant and a swimming pool. If the *menu degustazione* seems a little excessive, there are plen-ty of agriturismo places to eat at nearby, or try the *Ametista* at Piazza Antico Castello 14 (closed Wed) in Moncalvo itself, which offers country dishes such as peperoni flan with *bagna caöda*.

Most easily reached with your own transport, the **Abbazia di Vezzolano** (daily 9am–1pm & 2–5pm), in the village of **ALBUGNANO**, deep in a val-ley to the northwest of Asti, displays some of the area's best late Romanesque architecture. According to legend the abbey was founded by Charlemagne, who had a religious vision on the site. Outside it has a fancily arcaded and sculpted facade and a Romanesque cloister. Inside, there's a stone rood screen carved with expressive scenes from the life of Mary, and a row of naive, rustic-looking saints.

Northern Piemonte: Biella, Varallo and Valsesia

The main attraction of northern Piemonte is really the mountains, especially the dramatic Alpine **Valsesia**, which winds up to the foot of Monte Rosa on the Swiss border. On the way, stop off at two of the region's most visited sanc-tuaries, the **Santuario d'Oropa** near **Biella** and the **Sacro Monte** at **Varallo**. From here you're well poised for either Piemonte's mountains or those of Valle d'Aosta, a few kilometres west. Worth a slight detour is the mag-ical train ride that starts at **Domodossola**, conveniently en route if you're heading for Switzerland or down to Milan.

Biella and Ivrea

A short train ride northwest from Novara, the provincial capital of **BIELLA** is known for its wool industry, its periphery choked with mills and the hilltop upper town with the mansions and villas of wool barons. It's not an especially rewarding place, apart perhaps from its small medieval quarter, reachable by funicular or by strolling up its many arcaded lanes. But it does give access to the **Santuario d'Oropa** (daily 7.30am–noon & 2–6pm; free), a forty-minute bus ride northwest of Biella at the foot of Monte Mucrone. Founded in the fourth century by St Eusebio to house a black statue of the Madonna and Child, this is an odd sort of attraction, and can't really compete with the sanc-tuary at Varallo (see p.93) for sheer sensationalism. But it's the most venerated of Piemonte's shrines, the main church an immense neo-Baroque concoction, and it's a good starting-point also for **walks** into the surrounding mountains. If you wish, you can **stay at the sanctuary** itself, which has around 700 rooms (book through the Biella tourist office; see overleaf). A cable car runs regularly up Monte Mucrone as far as the (closed) *Albergo Savoia*, where a network of marked trails begins. One of the nicest and easiest is to the **Lago Mucrone**, a small mountain lake; more energetic is the hike up to the summit of Monte Mucrone itself – a two-hour trek.

Biella's **tourist office** is at Piazza Vittorio Veneto 3 (Mon–Sat 9am–12.30pm & 2.30–5.30pm, Sun 9am–1pm; ☏015.351.128, ⓦwww.atl.biella.it). Though you should definitely move on if you can, you may need to stay overnight in Biella. Try the clean and modern *Bugella* (☏015.406.607; ❺), or ask about bed-and-breakfast options at the tourist office. If you do stay, swing by *La Baracca* at Via Costa di Riva 11b, a **nightclub** and art gallery in a converted nineteenth-century factory building that makes great use of light and glass.

IVREA, to the southwest of Biella, is well worth a visit in the week leading up to Shrove Tuesday, when there's a **carnival**, featuring piping, drumming, masked balls, historic processions and fireworks, culminating in a bizarre three-day "Battle of the Oranges" when the whole town and hundreds of spectators turn out to pelt each other with oranges; it's important to know that you have to wear a red hat if you don't want to be a target. At the end of each day, the town is covered in a thick carpet of orange pulp, and the following morning there's a traditional handing out of polenta and cod. For a **place to stay**, try the small *Luca* at Corso Garibaldi 58 (☏0125.48.697; ❸), or head 3km north-east out of town to the four-star *Castello San Giuseppe* at Chiaverano d'Ivrea (☏0125.424.370, ⓦwww.castellosangiuseppe.it; ❼), set in a converted Carmelite monastery.

Varallo and Sacro Monte

Some 50km by train north of Novara, **VARALLO** marks the beginning of northern Piemonte's more picturesque reaches, surrounded by steep wooded hills and filled with Art Deco villas and Baroque *palazzi*. It's a pretty place in itself, very pleasant for a short visit, but most people come to see the sanctuary of **Sacro Monte**, just outside the town and connected by bus five times daily from the train station.

If you've only come for Sacro Monte you could make straight there from the station; if you want to see the town first – and it is worth a wander – the centre is a five-minute walk to the right along Corso Roma. On the way you pass the church of **San Gaudenzio**, anchored to a creeper-covered cliff and surrounded by arcades. It's less impressive inside, though there's a polyptych by the sixteenth-century Varallo-born artist Gaudenzio Ferrari, responsible for much of the work at Sacro Monte. The main street, **Corso Umberto I**, lined with shuttered and balconied palaces, winds through the town from here towards the River Serio. There's more work by Gaudenzio Ferrari in the church of **Madonna delle Grazie**, off to the north of Corso Umberto I at the end of Via Don Maio, where an entire wall is covered with colourful and detailed scenes from the life of Christ.

The **tourist office** is at Corso Roma 38 (Tues–Sun except some winter Sundays 9am–1pm & 3–7pm; ☏0163.51.280 or 0163.53.091). If you want to **stay over** in Varallo, try the *Monte Rosa* at Via Regaldi 4 (☏0163.51.100; ❸), a wonderful, friendly, rambling old hotel a brisk five-minute walk away from the town centre. Or there is a **HI Hostel**, Varallo, at Via Scaranini (☏0163.510.36; €12.50). For **food**, the restaurant *Fra Dolcino*, opposite the station in Piazza Marconi 3, does falafel, couscous and kebabs, as well as good pizzas (closed Thurs).

Sacro Monte

Crowning the hill above Varallo, **Sacro Monte** (daily 7.30am–12.15pm & 2.15–6.30pm; free) is a complex of 45 chapels, each housing a 3-D tableau of painted statues against frescoed scenery representing a scene from the life of Christ. Founded in the fifteenth century by a friar anxious to popularize Catholicism in a region in which heresy was rife, Sacro Monte emphasizes sensationalism and spectacle, calculated to work upon the emotions of the uneducated. The sanctuary is at its best when busy: to get a measure of its continuing popularity, you need to visit on a Sunday, when it's full of families, pensioners and nuns, all of whom picnic in the shady grounds after finishing their pilgrimage.

Inevitably a bizarre spectacle, depicting the whole range of key biblical episodes from the Fall to Christ's birth, life and death, the tableaux don't pull any punches. The *Massacre of the Innocents* (#11) has a floor littered with dead babies, while Herod's army prepares to spear, hack and slash more. And the chapels (#30–41) that retell the events of Christ's passion are flagrant emotional manipulation, with crazed flagellators, spitting soldiers and a series of liberally blood-splattered Christs. By the time you reach the *Road to Calvary* (#36) you almost flinch at the sight of a flaked-out Christ being viciously kicked. Dominating the central piazza of the sanctuary, the Baroque **Basilica** offers some relief, the highlight being the cupola – a nice piece of optical trickery, encrusted with figures perched on bubblegum clouds.

Valsesia

From Varallo the main road follows the River Sesia to the foot of multipeaked Monte Rosa, whose massive bulk heads four Italian valleys and spreads north into Switzerland. **Valsesia**, the easternmost valley, is also the most dramatic – worth going for the ride even if you don't want to launch a hiking or skiing assault on the mountains.

Flanked by dark pine-wooded slopes crowned with a toothed ridge of rock, the road winds up the valley, the perspective changing at every turn. It's a well-touristed area (mainly by Italians and Germans), and traditional houses with slate roofs and wood-slatted balconies mingle with Alpine-style villas and apartments. The villages are crowded for much of the summer, and with weekend skiers in the winter. September is the quietest month, when many of the hotels close, but the weather up the mountains is unpredictable then, and hiking can be hazardous.

The Valsesia villages were founded in the thirteenth century by religious sects from the Swiss Valais, known as Walser, in search of land and the freedom to worship. There are reckoned to be around 3000 true Walsers in the valleys of Monte Rosa, and in most bars and shops you'll still hear people speaking a dialect based on ancient German. If you want to see how these isolated communities lived and worked, visit the **Walser Museum** (July daily 2–6pm; Aug 1–21 daily 10am–noon & 2–6pm; Aug 22–June Sat & Sun 2–6pm or by appointment, ☎0163.922.935; €2.07), a traditionally furnished seventeenth-century house in the hamlet of **PEDEMONTE**, ten minutes' walk from Alagna.

ALAGNA, at the head of the valley, right below Monte Rosa, is the most convenient place to stay, whether you want to ski or hike. Popular and predominantly modern, it has a cluster of wood-slatted Walser houses to the south, with a tiny network of overgrown tracks winding in between them. Some houses still function as farms, with hay hanging to dry on the slats and wood stacked behind, while others are holiday homes, with geraniums tumbling from window boxes. Alagna's cheapest **hotel** is the *Mirella*, in the suburb of Bonda (☎0163.922.965; ❸); there is also the more central but more expensive *Genzianella*, Via Centro 33 (☎0163.923.205; may insist on half-board; ❼). The **tourist office** (daily except Wed 9.30am–12.30pm & 3–6.30pm; ☎0163 .922.988) is on Piazza Grober.

There are lots of **walks** among the foothills, all of which are well marked from Alagna. If you're interested in seeing more than mountain scenery, follow a path 5km back down the valley to **RIVA VALDOBBIA**, whose church facade is covered with a colourful late sixteenth-century fresco of *The Last Judgement*. However, the toughest and most spectacular hikes are those on **Monte Rosa** itself. It's possible to save time and energy by taking the cable car up to Punta Indren (3260m), from where you can walk to one of the many *rifugi;* most of these are open from June to September, but check at the tourist office in Alagna before setting out. Failing that, you could walk down into the next valley, Val Gressoney in Valle d'Aosta (see opposite).

All these walks involve a good deal of scree-crossing and some sobering drops, and none is to be taken lightly – you'll need a good **map** (the FMB map of the four Monte Rosa valleys shows all paths, *rifugi* and pistes as does the Kompass *Monte Rosa* map), and you should monitor the weather carefully. There's also an ambitious long-distance circuit of Monte Rosa, starting at Alagna, taking in Val Gressoney, Val d'Ayas and Zermatt across the Swiss border: you'll need five days if you make use of ski-lifts and cable cars, and a good deal longer than that if you don't.

Skiing in the area is organized by Monterosa Ski, who have an office in Alagna, and equipment is available for rent in the village. However, the runs are narrow, and though experienced skiers can cross into Val Gressoney, it involves walking as well as off-piste skiing. The valleys are also popular for **canoeing and rafting**, and several centres organize classes and excursions. One such centre is Hidronica (☎0163.735.301, Ⓦwww.hidronica.com). Check Ⓦwww.alagna.it for more information.

Domodossola and over the border to Locarno

At the foot of the Simplon Pass, but handily situated on the main train line between Milan and Bern, in Switzerland, and with frequent trains (15 daily) from Novara, is the little town of **DOMODOSSOLA**. With its arcaded medieval centre and market square, it warrants a visit in its own right, but is more famous as the starting point of a scenic train ride. "La Vigezzina", a small, pale-blue train, connects Domodossola with Locarno, across the border in Switzerland, taking in the vineyards and chestnut forests of the Val Vigezzo and Centovalli along the way. The scenery is gorgeous, and, although the ride is pricier than the regular train, it is well worth it; InterRail passes are valid in any case, if you have one. The journey to Locarno takes an hour and a half, but you can get off and explore at any of the pretty flower-strewn stations en route; when you want the next train to stop, just remember to raise the red and white signal on the platform. An alternative way back is to take the hydrofoil from Locarno across Lago Maggiore to Arona, near the southern tip of the lake and on the railway line.

The road to Aosta and the eastern valleys

The tributary valleys in **eastern Valle d'Aosta** have suffered most from the skiing industry, although experienced mountain hikers may be lured by the challenge of climbing Monte Rosa and the Matterhorn from **Valtournenche**. Less ambitious walkers will find most to do in the **Val Gressoney**, which still has a number of traditional villages settled by the Swiss Walsers, while in the main Aosta valley you'll find one of the region's more interesting castles, **Fénis**.

Val Gressoney

The **Val Gressoney** is the first of the Valle d'Aosta valleys, but you could be forgiven for thinking you'd stepped into an ad-maker's Switzerland. The grass is velvety green, the River Lys crystal clear, the traditional houses wood-slatted and the modern ones gleaming Alpine chalets, while the craggy head of the valley is overlooked by one of Monte Rosa's shimmering glaciers. As you might expect from such natural advantages, the valley gets busy, especially at weekends and holidays: the walking is good, and the skiing isn't bad either, with pistes laid out on rocky south-facing slopes that are great for catching the sun but which get a little slushy by the afternoon in late season.

At the mouth of the valley, **PONT-ST-MARTIN**'s usefulness as a bus and train terminus outweighs its attractiveness, and there's little reason to hang around. The valley comes into its own at the popular but attractive resorts of **GRESSONEY-ST-JEAN** and especially **GRESSONEY-LA-TRINITÉ**, which is close to the head of the valley and is cheaper than St-Jean, with some good, homely hotels. It also makes a convenient starting-point for walks, though be warned that the true beginning of the summer walking season doesn't start until late June: between Easter and then, most hotels are closed. If you want to do more than wander along the river, a track leads up to the lovely mountain lake, **Gabiet** – a two- to three-hour walk (you can go part way by ski-lift or cable car) – from where you can continue over the mountain into the Valsesia, doing the last part of the descent by cable car if you're tired. Val Gressoney's Walser settlements can be reached by footpaths from La Trinité; one of the nicest is **BIEL**, with some eighteenth-century houses (maps available from La Trinité's tourist office; see below). The Walsers still speak their German dialect, and French and Italian too, and the trilingual signs you'll see are not only for the benefit of tourists.

La Trinité's **tourist office** (daily 9am–12.30pm & 2–6pm; ☎0125.366.143, ⓦwww.gressoneyonline.it) is on Piazza Tache, across the river from the bus stop. Most **hotels** in the area are quite expensive, but the *Gressoney*, for example, at Via Lys 3 in St-Jean (☎0125.355.986; ❺), has huge king-sized beds and is worth splashing out on if you feel like some four-star comfort (avoid eating there though and have a pizza in the village instead). At Gabiet is the one-star *Del Ponte* (☎0125.366.180; may insist on half-board; ❹), which you have to take the cable car to reach as it is up at 2000m, and there are a couple of places around St-Jean too: *La Stella* at località Steina (☎0125.355.068; may insist on half-board; ❺). There is a **campsite** just beyond St-Jean: *Camping Gressoney* (☎0125.355.264).

Val d'Ayas

Branching off the main valley and headed by the huge mass of Monte Rosa, **Val d'Ayas** is one of the region's most beautiful valleys – large, open and flanked by thickly wooded slopes. As a result, it tends to be overwhelmed by visitors, and the tourist-geared villages are chock-full of trippers and skiers at the weekend and during high season – and correspondingly dead at other times of the year.

The main ski resort, **CHAMPOLUC**, at the head of the valley, is connected by a series of chair lifts to Staffal in the Val Gressoney. It's also the base for the tough ascent (4hr minimum; route #62) of the **Testa Grigia** (3315m) – although you can cheat on this by taking the funicular and ski-lift part of the way. From the top there's a superb view across the peaks of the Matterhorn to Mont Blanc; however, the climb is strictly for the experienced unless you can afford a **guide** (contact the Alpine Guide Association of Champoluc on ☎0125.308.116, or the Champoluc tourist office, at Via Varasc 16, Mon–Sun 9am–12.30pm & 3–6pm; ☎0125.307.113, ⓕ0125.307.785).

BRUSSON, further down the valley, is a better base for less demanding walks. There's a trail (3hr 30min; route #6) up to seven mountain lakes, starting with a long climb through a dense wood up to a waterfall – the water drops 30m, and is most impressive in spring when the snow is melting.

The **hotel** *Beau Site* at Rue Trois Villages 2 (☎0125.300.144; may insist on half-board; ❺), on the edge of Brusson, is clean, simple and has a good **restaurant**. In Champoluc hotels are expensive, but the *Cré-Forné* hotel (☎0125.307.197; may insist on half-board; ❺) at **CREST** (connected with Champoluc by funicular) is a good alternative. There are also **campsites** between Brusson and Champoluc: try the *Camping Deans* (☎0125.300.297) in località Extrapieraz; facilities include a bar-restaurant.

Valtournenche and the Matterhorn (Cervino)

VALTOURNENCHE, headed by the Matterhorn, or Cervino as the Italians call it, should be one of the most spectacular of Italy's mountain valleys, but unfortunately the main towns are overdeveloped and hydroelectric works ruin the views on the plains. The international ski resort Breuil-Cervinia is a purely functional, modern resort, and even the Matterhorn is a letdown, with tribes of skiers ensuring that its glacier is grubby for much of the year. That said these are the Alps, and if you can't manage to carry on to the other valleys further west, you will at least get a taste of chocolate-box chalets and flower-covered meadows straight out of Heidi.

Breuil-Cervinia

BREUIL-CERVINIA was one of Italy's first ski resorts, built in the prewar years as part of Mussolini's drive for a healthy nation. In its day the ski lifts, soaring to 3500m, broke all records, and its grand hotels ensured the patronage of Europe's wealthy. Today the wealthy are cossetted in modern buildings outside the resort, leaving the tacky streets of the town for packaged hordes attracted by a large skiing area with lots of easy runs.

If you want to climb the **Matterhorn** (4476m), you should seriously consider approaching from Zermatt in Switzerland; the Italian route is strictly for experts. If undeterred, you'll need the FMB map, which covers Valtournenche and the Monte Rosa valleys, and to be very well equipped. There are two *rifugi* on the way, *Duca degli Abruzzi* (☎0166.949.145; mid-July to mid-Sept, closed at time of writing, but due to reopen in July 2003), two hours fifteen minutes from Breuil in Orionde (2800m), and the *Rifugio Jean A Carrel* (☎0166.948.169; open all year, a bivouac not a real *rifugio*: you need to take your own food and drink) – where most people stay the night – four hours beyond (3850m). From the *Carrel rifugio* it's a tough climb to the summit, even with the ropes that have been fitted along the more dangerous stretches of the route.

Nus and the Castello di Fénis

Further up the main valley from Chatillon and overlooked by a ruined castle is the small, pretty village of **FUS**, a good base for the **Castello di Fénis** 2km away (Wed–Mon 9am–7.30pm; ☎0165.764.263; €5). Backed by wooded hills and encircled by two rows of turreted walls, the castle is a fairy-tale cluster of towers decorated with scalloped arcades. These defences were primarily aes-thetic, with the real job of protecting the valley being left to the less prettified fortresses of nearby Nus and Quart, while the Fénis branch of the Challant counts concentrated on refining their living quarters with fine Gothic frescoes. The best of these is in the courtyard, above the elaborate twin staircase that leads to the upper storeys. A courtly St George rescues a damsel in distress from the clutches of a tremendous dragon, overlooked by a tribe of protective saints brandishing moral statements on curling scrolls.

There's a **hotel** in Fénis – *La Chatelaine* (☎0165.764.264), in località Chez Sapin, open year-round. However, as Nus has a train station and is close to the main road for buses, you may find it more convenient to sleep there: the *Florian* at Via Risorgimento 3 (☎0165.767.968; ❷) has clean and comfortable doubles and is also open all year.

Aosta and around

The attractive mountain town of **AOSTA** was founded by the Romans in 25 BC after they disposed of the local tribe by auctioning them off in a slave mar-ket. It was primarily a military camp, but little survives from the era. More remains of medieval Aosta, its narrow cobbled streets and overhanging upper storeys giving the place a very alpine air. The town's key attraction though is its position: encircled by the **Alps**, and with access to the lovely valleys of the **Parco Nazionale del Gran Paradiso**, the ski resorts of **Mont Blanc**, and a sprinkling of castles in between, it's an ideal base for exploring the northwest of the region, before heading on to Switzerland or France.

The Town

The centre of town is marked by **Piazza E. Chanoux** and its pavement cafés, from where Via Porta Pretoria and Via Sant'Anselmo lead east, forming the main axis of the town centre and the principal street for window-shopping and people-watching. At the far end, the **Porta Pretoria** is one of the town's most impressive sights: two parallel triple-arched gateways which formed the main entrance into the Roman town. The space in between was for soldiers to keep a check on visitors to the town, and a family of medieval nobles later made their home above it, building a tower which now houses temporary exhibi-tions.

North of the gate there are further relics of the Roman occupation in the **Teatro Romano** (daily: March–Sept 9am–8pm; rest of year 9am–6.30pm; free), of which a section of the four-storeyed facade remains, 22m high and pierced with arched windows. Unfortunately since 2000 it has been hidden behind scaffolding, and no one will risk estimating a date for completion of the restoration. Close by, the medieval **Torre Fromage** at Via du Baillage is now a contemporary art exhibition-space (daily 9.30am–12.30pm & 2.30–6.30pm).

A short walk east of here, outside the main town walls off Via Sant'Anselmo, the church of **Sant'Orso** houses a number of tenth-century frescoes behind its dull facade, hidden up in the roof where you can examine them at close quarters from specially constructed walkways – though you'll need to find the sacristan to get up there. If you can't find him, content yourself with the fifteenth-century choir stalls, carved with a menagerie of holy men and animals, ranging from bats and monkeys to a tonsured monk. There are even better carvings on the eye-level capitals of the intimate Romanesque **cloisters** (daily: March–Sept 10am–12.30pm & 1.30–7pm; Oct–Feb 10am–12.30pm & 1.30–5pm) – mostly scenes from the story of Christ, with an undue emphasis on donkeys and sheep. The **priorate** has terracotta decorations on its outside walls and an octagonal tower which rises above the complex. Nearby are the recently discovered fifth-century remains of the **Basilica of San Lorenzo** (daily 9am–7pm; free), which are well-explained (in Italian) and worth a peek on your way past.

At the far end of Via Sant'Anselmo, the **Arco di Augusto** was erected in 25 BC to celebrate the seizure of the territory from the local Salassi tribe and to honour Emperor Augustus, after whom the town was named Augusta Praetoria (Aosta is a corruption of Augusta). Though the arch loses something islanded in a sea of traffic and topped by an ugly eighteenth-century roof, it's a sturdy-looking monument, the mountains behind only adding to its measure of dignity. Beyond is a well-preserved **Roman bridge**, its single arch spanning the dried-up bed of the River Buthier.

On the other side of the centre of town, the **Foro Romano** on Piazza Giovanni XXIII is the misleading name for another Roman relic, a vaulted passage under the actual forum area, the purpose of which is unclear. Nearby is the **Museo Archeologico Regionale** (daily 9am–7pm; free), with interesting exhibits on the settlements based around Aosta since Celtic times. The **Cattedrale** next door looks unpromising from the outside, but masks a Gothic interior with even more fantastically carved choir stalls than Sant'Orso's, with a mermaid, lion and snail among the saints. Remains of a fourth-century baptistry are visible through the floor; better are the mosaics on the presbytery pavement showing the two rivers of earthly paradise and Christ, holding the sun and moon, surrounded by the symbols of the months. Like Saint Orso it has some impressive tenth-century frescoes hidden in the roof, saved for posterity by the lowering of the ceiling in the fourteenth century; you can visit these on a guided tour which leaves several times a day (€5.20). There are more treasures in the cathedral **museum** (€2.10) – gold-, silver- and gem-encrusted reliquaries and equally ornate chalices, crucifixes and caskets for relics.

Practicalities

Aosta's **tourist office** (daily 9am–8pm; ☎0165.236.627, ⓦwww .regione.vda.it/turismo) is at Piazza E. Chanoux 8 and has maps and other information on the town and around. You can get to most places within the region by bus from the **bus station** on Viale G. Carrel, but some of the more remote valleys are served by only one bus a week out of season. Trains run from the **train station** at Piazza Manzetti, south of the centre, west along the main valley only as far as Pré-St-Didier. The best bet is to arm yourself with the combined bus and train timetable from the tourist office and use both.

The first choice for a **hotel room** would be *La Belle Epoque* at Via d'Avise 8, off Via Aubert (☎0165.262.276, ⓦwww.labelleepoque.it, ❸), which is modern, clean and compact. Alternatively, the *Mochettaz*, Corso Ivrea 107 (☎0165.43.706; ❷), charges slightly less, while the *Albergo Pila*, Via Paravera 12b (☎0165.43.398; ❷), is good value, though it's a ten-minute walk from the centre of town on the far side of the train line. All these hotels are open year-round. There are a number of **campsites** nearby: *Milleluci*, about 1km away in località Roppoz (☎0165.235.278; year-round), is just on the outskirts of town, and has a swimming pool, a bar and playground. Finding **somewhere to eat** is no problem: you could try the *Praetoria*, Via Sant'Anselmo 9 (closed Thurs), a family-style trattoria; the intimate *Trattoria degli Artisti* at via Maillet 5/7 for traditional Aostan fare; or the friendly *Ostaria del Calvino* on Via Croce di Città. Otherwise Via E. Aubert and Via Porta Pretoria are the best streets to trawl. In the evening, a good place to sit with a glass of wine is *La Cave*, via Challand 34.

West from Aosta: Castello di Sarre

Both road and rail run west from Aosta through the main valley, passing a number of **castles**, the best of which is the thirteenth-century **Castello di Sarre**, accessible by bus or train from Aosta (Tues–Sun 9am–8pm; €5). It's a ten-minute walk up a hill covered with apple orchards from the St Maurice train station; coming by bus, walk from the bus stop up the main road and take the unmarked turning just before the toll-booth. Sarre is the former hunting lodge of Vittorio Emanuele II, who actually bought the castle by mistake. He had set his sights on the castle of Aymaville opposite, but the agent sent to buy the castle was confused about the direction in which the river flowed, and ended up buying Sarre instead.

Vittorio Emanuele made the best of a bad job, permanently stamping the halls of the castle with his astounding taste in interior decor, pushing the hunting-lodge motif to its limits, with horns of wild ibex lining the main gallery, thousands of white chamois skulls studding the stuccoed festoons and horn-sprouting medallions that surround the stuffed heads of ibex. Pride of place is given to the first ibex slain by the king. The custodian claims that many died a natural death, but this was hardly the impression that Vittorio Emanuele, in his guise as macho huntsman, intended to convey. The rest of the castle is well patronized by diehard Italian monarchists who come to pay their respects to Savoy family trees, portraits and photographs and walls plastered with magazine features on the now-exiled Italian royals.

North from Aosta: the Col di San Bernardo

Immediately north of Aosta, the **Col di San Bernardo** (2473m) leads the way into Switzerland; it was named after the legendary **monastery** that for centuries provided shelter to travellers on the main pilgrim route from Northern Europe to Rome, and was the home of the eponymous big brown-and-white dogs who rescued Alpine travellers in distress. The history of the mountain pass is well documented in the **museum** (June–Sept daily 9am–6pm; 6 Swiss francs) housed in the monastery, although you'll need your passport to visit as it's situated just over the border in Switzerland. The spectacular pass is open only during summer, but the border is open year-round by way of a tunnel.

The Gran Paradiso National Park

For some of Valle d'Aosta's most beautiful mountains and valleys you need to make for the south of the region, down to the **Parco Nazionale di Gran Paradiso** – Italy's first national park, spread around the valleys at the foot of 4061-metre-high Gran Paradiso mountain.

Oddly enough the park owes its foundation to King Vittorio Emanuele II, who donated his extensive hunting park to the state in 1922, ensuring that the population of ibex that he and his hunters had managed to reduce to near-extinction survived. There are now around 3500 ibex here and about 6000 chamois, living most of the year above the tree line but descending to the valleys in winter and spring. The most dramatic sightings are during the mating season in November and December, when you may see pairs of males fighting it out for the possession of a female. You might also see golden eagles nesting, and there are a number of rare types of alpine flower – most of which can be seen in the botanical garden in the Cogne Valley.

The park's three valleys – **Cogne**, **Valsavarenche** and **Val de Rhêmes** – are popular, but tourist development has been cautious and well organized. The hotels are good (you get far more for your money than you would in one of the nearby towns) and the campsites not too vast – though once you are inside the park boundaries you can pitch a tent between the hours of 9pm and 6am only. There are a few mountain *rifugi* and *bivacci* (unoccupied shelters) between which run well-marked footpaths. Though it's primarily a summer resort for walkers, the cross-country skiing is also good, and every winter a 45-kilometre Gran Paradiso Trek is organized at Cogne (contact the tourist office in Cogne for details – see opposite). The starting-point for the ascent of Gran

Paradiso itself is **Pont** in the Valsavarenche, while **Cogne** gives access to the Alta Via 2, a long, high-level mountain trail.

There are regular buses throughout the year from Aosta to Cogne, but Valsavarenche and Val de Rhêmes are served by buses only in summer. At other times driving into either of these valleys is easiest from the village of **INTROD**, about 2km from **VILLENEUVE**, which is on the main bus route and a walkable distance from the castles of Saint-Pierre and Sarriod de la Tour.

Val di Cogne

The **Val di Cogne** is the principal, most popular and most dramatic section of the park. Its lower reaches are narrow, the road running above the fast-flowing Grand Eyvia River overlooked by sheer wavy-ridged mountains. Further on, the valley broadens out around the main village, **COGNE**, which is surrounded by gentle green meadows with glacier-covered mountains rising beyond.

The **tourist office** here, in the centre of the village (Mon–Sun 9am–12.30pm & 3–5.30/6pm; ☎0165.74.040, ⓦwww.cogne.org), has maps with descriptions in English of walks, one of which is an easy, scenic stroll that follows the river, with the glaciers in view for most of the way. **VALNONTEY** is a small village and starting-point for the steep, three-hour walk up to the *Rifugio V. Sella* (☎0165.74.310; Easter–Sept), a demanding hike that is incredibly popular on summer Sundays and in early August. The path passes a **botanical garden** (mid-June to mid-Sept daily 10am–6.30pm; €2.10), with rare Alpine flora, then zigzags up through a forest and onto exposed mountainside before reaching the *rifugio*, set on a grassy plateau. At the mountain tarn of Lago Loson, a fifteen-minute walk from the *rifugio*, you may well spot **ibex** or more timid **chamois**, especially at sunset and sunrise, when there are fewer people around. Hardened hikers who can cope with a stretch of climbing can press on over the **Colle de Lauson** to the Val de Rhêmes.

There's a **campsite**, *Vallee de Cogne*, close to Cogne village in località Fabrique (☎0165.74.079; year-round), and two at Valnontey: *Lo Stambecco* (☎0165.74.152; mid-May to mid-Sept) and *Gran Paradiso* (☎0165.749.204; mid-May to mid-Sept). As for **hotels**, Cogne's most reasonable are the *Stambecco*, Rue des Clementines 21 (☎0165.74.068; ❹), and the *Bouton d'Or* at Viale Cavagnet 15 (☎0165.74.268; ❺), which also has very reasonable singles. Both are open all year, although they can get booked up quickly in high season, and it's advisable to call ahead. Groups of two to six people may want to consider staying in one of the *Bellevue* hotel's self-contained **chalets** on Rue des Clementines (☎0165.74.825), which work out at about €100 per person per night for half-board – not the budget option, but the food is excellent.

Staying in Valnontey may be a better bet if you want to do some walking. There are a handful of affordable **alberghi** in the cluster of stone and wood chalets that make up the village centre but they may insist you stay half-board: try *Herbetet* (☎0165.74.180; mid-May to mid-Sept; ❸), the *Petit Dahu* (☎0165.74.146; ❼), or the *Paradisia* (☎0165.74.158; April–Oct; ❺). Stock up on picnic food and provisions before you leave Cogne because all Valnontey has to offer in the way of shops are lots of souvenir stalls and some "panoramic" restaurants.

Cogne's choice of **restaurants** is more limited, since most people stay on a half-pension basis, but you could try the rustic *Brasserie Bon Bec* on Rue Bourgeo, or the couple of **takeaways** and plenty of *salumerie* that will make up sandwiches for you.

Valsavarenche

Although not as spectacular as the Val di Cogne, **Valsavarenche**, the next valley west, has its own kind of beauty, attracting seasoned walkers rather than gentle amblers. The most popular route is the **ascent of Gran Paradiso**, from **PONT** at the end of the valley. Though reckoned to be the easiest of the higher Alps to climb, it is nevertheless a climb rather than a hike, with no path marked beyond the *Rifugio Vittorio Emanuele II* (☎0165.95.920; March 23–Sept 19), two and a half hours from Pont.

If you feel safer walking along footpaths, the best of the hikes are from the main village of **DEGIOZ**, otherwise known as Valsavarenche, up to the *Rifugio Orvielles* (2hr 30min) and then on to a series of high mountain lakes. This takes seven hours, but you can shorten it a bit by taking path #3a down to Pont. Less taxing is the two-hour walk from Pont towards the glacier **Grand Etret** at the head of the valley, although the first stretch is boring.

The only **hotel** in Degioz is the *Parco Nazionale* (☎0165.905.706; New Year & mid-May to Sept; ❹), while in Pont there is the *Genzianella* which may insist on half-board (☎0165.95.393; June–Sept; ❻). The area is well supplied with **campsites**, of which perhaps the nicest is *Pont Breuil* (☎0165.95.458; June–Sept), actually in Pont, with a well-stocked site shop (there's no other for miles); ibex come down to graze on the grassy meadow around the tents. There's also a leafy site at località Pia de la Presse, *Gran Paradiso* (☎0165.905.801; June–Sept). There are **places to eat** in Degioz, but at Pont you'll have to cook for yourself, or ask at one of the hotels.

Val di Rhêmes

The least touristed but most open of the valleys, **Val di Rhêmes**, is also headed by glaciers. The best place to stay is **BREUIL**, a small hamlet outside Rhêmes-Notre-Dame at the end of the valley, from which most of the walks start. There's a fairly easy path along the river to a waterfall, the Cascata di Goletta, at its most spectacular after the spring snow-melt, and from here you can continue to the mountain lake of Goletta and the *Rifugio Albergo Benevolo* (☎0165.936.143; March 6–Sept 20). In Breuil, the *Hotel Breuil* (☎0166.949.537; ❻) is conveniently central and is open all year, as is the *Edelweiss*, Via Guido Rey 13 (☎0166.949.078; ❻), which has its own sauna and fitness facilities should hiking up and down mountains not prove exhausting enough. Further out, in Avouil, the *Leonardo Carrel* (☎0166.949.077; ❷) is a fine **pensione** with good food and appealingly wood-panelled, Alpine-style rooms.

Arvier and Valgrisenche

Valgrisenche, a few kilometres west from Val di Rhêmes, is the wildest and least accessible of Valle d'Aosta's valleys. It's stunningly beautiful, narrow with rocky snow-dusted ridges rising above dark pine woods, although the upper reaches are defaced by the concrete dam of a reservoir. The only buses from Aosta into the valley are at 7am and 6pm in summer, and at 5.30am in winter, although buses and trains stop year-round at **ARVIER** at the mouth of the valley – one of the region's most appealing villages, with a small medieval core of twisting streets and stone houses alongside a gorge spanned by a Roman bridge. Arvier produces *L'Enfer d'Arvier*, reckoned to be the region's best wine.

In the village of **VALGRISENCHE** itself, the *Frassy* hotel (☎0165.97.100; ❶) makes a good base, although it's only open July to mid-September. Nearby the hamlet of **BONNE** above the reservoir is a good starting point for **walks**. These include the four- to five-hour ascent of the glaciated Testa del Rutor (3486m). There are many other walks, but none of them is easy – make sure you carry the Kompass *Gran Paradiso* map. The only **hotel** in Bonne is the *Perret* (☎0165.97.107; ❻), open all year and with a restaurant and bar.

The northwest: around Mont Blanc

Dominated by the snowy peaks of **Mont Blanc** (Monte Bianco to the Italians), the northern reaches of Valle d'Aosta are scenically stunning but also very popular. The most sensational views are from the cable cars that glide and swoop (at times alarmingly so) across the mountain to Chamonix in France. However, the trip is expensive, even if you take a bus back to Italy through the eleven-kilometre-long Mont Blanc tunnel, and the service is often suspended because of bad weather.

If the cable car seems too pricey, you can walk up to the **Testa d'Arpy** from the sprawling resort of **LA THUILE**, on the road to the Petit-St-Bernard Pass into France, for sweeping views of the peaks and glaciers of Mont Blanc. Buses run from Pré-St-Didier at the end of the Valle d'Aosta railway line to La Thuile, from where it's just over two hours' walk by path or road to the old *La Genzianella* hotel at the top of the Colle San Carlo. From here a path leads through woods to Testa d'Arpy in around ten minutes, a natural balcony with a bird's-eye view up the valley to Mont Blanc. It's well worth having a good map (FSB *Monte Bianco*), not so much to find your way as to identify the peaks and glaciers spread out before you.

As for La Thuile, it's rather an overdeveloped resort, and it makes sense to pass through quickly, after calling in at the **tourist office**, at Via Collomb 4 (daily 9am–12.30pm & 3–6pm; ☎0165.884.179, ⓦwww.lathuile.it), for maps – and to sleep instead up the mountain at *Du Glacier* (☎0165.884.137; ❹), in the little hamlet of Golette; it's open all year but phone in advance to check that there's room, and in high season they may only take bookings for several days. Of the other walks starting from the hotel the most interesting is the 45-minute hike to **Lago d'Arpy**, from where a path leads down into La Thuile.

Courmayeur and Mont Blanc

COURMAYEUR is the smartest and most popular of Valle d'Aosta's ski resorts, much used by package tour operators. The skiing is good, though there's little to challenge experts, and the scenery is magnificent, but, predictably, what remains of the old village is enmeshed in a web of ersatz Alpine chalets and après-ski hangouts.

If you simply want a week of skiing, you'll probably do better to take a package; if you've come to hike or take the big-dipping cable cars across to Chamonix, the most convenient place to stay is **LA PALUD**, 5km outside Courmayeur (three buses a day).

The **cable car** runs from La Palud to Punta Helbronner all year round, but continues to Chamonix only between April and September. There are between ten and twelve departures a day, depending on the time of year, roughly hourly starting at 8.30am – although ultimately the regularity depends on the weather. To be sure of good views, you'll need to set out early since it's usually cloudy by midday; be sure also to get there in plenty of time, especially on summer weekends, as it's much used by summer skiers. Even if it's blazing hot in the valley, the temperature plunges to freezing-point at the top, so take some warm clothes.

There are good walks along the two valleys at the foot of the Mont Blanc glaciers, both of which have seasonal **campsites** accessible by bus from Courmayeur. Val Ferret to the west is the more interesting option – you can walk back from Frebouze over Monte de la Saxe, with some stunning views of Mont Blanc en route.

If you do end up having to spend a night in Courmayeur, the cheapest **hotel** is the *Venezia* at Via delle Villette 2 (☎0165.842.461; ❷); or there's the *Crampon*, on the same street at no. 8 (☎0165.842.385; ❻; Christmas–April & July to mid-Sept), which also has a **restaurant**. Hotels in La Palud include the *Chalet Joli* (☎0165.869.722; ❼) and the extremely comfortable *Vallee Blanche* (☎0165.89.7002; ❺).

Travel details

Trains

Alba to: Asti (8 daily; 1hr).
Aosta to: Pré-St-Didier (14 daily; 50min).
Asti to: Casale Monferrato (6 daily; 50min).
Cúneo to: Limone Piemonte (14 daily; 30min).
Novara to: Biella (20 daily; 1hr 10min); Varallo (9 daily; 1hr 30min).
Turin to: Aosta (17 daily; 2hr); Asti (33 daily; 30min–1hr); Cúneo (9 daily; 1hr 30min); Milan Centrale (24 daily; 1hr 45min); Modane (8 daily; 1hr 25min–2hr 25min); Novara (27 daily; 1hr 15min).

Buses

Alba to: Barolo (6 daily; 30min); Grinzane (6 daily; 1hr).
Aosta to: Aymavilles (22 daily; 25min); Cogne (6 daily; 50min); Courmayeur (20 daily; 1hr); Pont Valsavarenche (3 daily; 1hr 10min); Rhêmes St Georges (3 on weekdays Sept–June; 45min; July & Aug 2 daily, going on to Rhêmes Notre Dame; 1hr); Valgrisenche (mid-June to mid-Sept 2 daily; mid-Sept to mid-June Mon, Tues & Sat only; 1hr 30min).

Biella to: Ivrea (6 daily; 2hr 25min); Santuario di Oropa (9 daily; 40min).
Chatillon to: Breuil Cervinia (6 daily; 1hr–1hr 30min).
Cogne to: Valnontey (July & early Sept 9 daily; Aug 22 daily; 15 min).
Cúneo to: Dronero (Val Maira; 22 daily; 35min); Valle Stura (7 daily; 1hr–1hr 20min).
Mondoví to: Bastia (2 daily, 15min), Santuario di Vicoforte (45 daily; 10min).
Pont-St-Martin to: Gressoney La Trinité (7 daily; 1hr 20min).
Pré-St-Didier to: Courmayeur (15 daily; 10–25min); La Thuile (7 daily; 25min).
Saluzzo to: Crissolo (3 daily; 2hr); Cúneo (17 daily; 1hr); Val Varaita (3 daily; 1hr 15min).
Turin (Corso Inghilterra) to: Alagna (1 daily; 3hr); Aosta (12 daily; 2–3hr); Cervinia (1 daily; 2hr 15min); Chamonix/Geneva (1 daily; 3hr 15min–4hr 30min); Champoluc (2 daily; 3hr 30min); Courmayeur (7 daily; 3–4hr); Gressoney La Trinité (4 daily; 2hr 10min–3hr 10min); Ivrea (12 daily; 1hr 15min); Locarno (1 daily; 4hr); Lugano via Novara (1 daily; 3hr).
Turin (Corso Marconi) to: Cúneo (8 daily; 2hr 45min); Saluzzo (10 daily; 1hr 20min).

Liguria

CHAPTER 2 # Highlights

* **Cinque Terre** These five fishing villages are shoe-horned into one of the most rugged parts of Liguria's coastline and linked by a highly scenic coastal walking path. See p.144

* **San Remo** With its famous Art Nouveau Casino, grand seafront and characterful old quarter, San Remo affords a glimpse of old-style Riviera glamour. See p.130

* **Portofino** Nestling on a wooded promontory, Portofino is a playground of the international jet set to rival St Tropez. See p.140

* **Genoa** With its rabbit warren of medieval streets, revitalized port area and a clutch of first-rate museums and churches, Genoa could easily justify a week of your time. See p.109

* **The train from Genoa to Casella** This is an excellent way to escape the crowds on the coast and explore some of Italy's most spectacular mountain scenery. See p.127

Liguria

Sheltering on the seaward side of the mountains that divide Piemonte from the coast, **Liguria** is the classic introduction to Italy for travellers journeying overland through France. There's an unexpected change as you cross the border from Nice and Monaco: the **Italian Riviera** (as Liguria's commercially developed strip of coast is known) has more variety of landscape and architecture than its French counterpart, and is generally less frenetic. The mountains which, in places, drop sheer to the sea are treated as an irrelevance by most visitors eager to press on to their chosen resort, but Liguria's lofty hinterland can offer respite from the standard format of beach, beach and more beach. Teetering on slopes carpeted with olives and vines are isolated mountain villages that retain their own rural culture and cuisine.

The chief city of the region is **Genoa**, an ancient, sprawling port often acclaimed as the most atmospheric of all Italian cities. It has a dense and fascinating old quarter that is complemented by a vibrant social and ethnic mix and a newly energized dockside district. The city stands midway between two distinct stretches of coastline. To the west is the **Riviera di Ponente**, one long ribbon of hotels packed out in summer with Italian families who book a year ahead to stay in their favourite spot. Picking your route carefully means you can avoid the worst of it. **San Remo**, the *grande-dame* of Riviera resorts, is flanked by hillsides covered with glasshouses, and is a major centre for the worldwide export of flowers; **Albenga** and **Noli** are attractive medieval centres that have also retained a good deal of character; and **Finale Ligure** is a thoroughly pleasant Mediterranean seaside town.

On Genoa's eastern side is the more rugged **Riviera di Levante**. Umbrella pines grow horizontally on the cliff-faces overlooking the water, and in the evening a glassy calm falls over the little bays and inlets. Walks on **Monte di Portofino** and in the coastal scenery of the famed **Cinque Terre** take you through scrubland and vineyards for memorable vistas over broad gulfs and jutting headlands. This mix of mountains and fishing villages accessible only by boat appealed to the early nineteenth-century Romantics, who "discovered" the Riviera in the eighteenth century, preparing the way for other artists and poets and the first package tourists. Now the whole area explodes into quite a ruck every July and August, with resorts like **Portofino** qualifying as amongst the most expensive in the country – although nearby **Santa Margherita Ligure** has its unpretentious moments, and **Lévanto** is a great place to make for if you just want to soak up the sun on a budget. Visiting out of season, of course, is a peaceful way to enjoy the beauty without the hubbub.

In the summer months, though, the only real way to avoid the crowds is to travel inland. Minor roads and mule tracks link villages built spiral-fashion around hilltops, originally as protection against Saracen invasion. A testing long-distance footpath, the **Alta Via dei Monti Liguri**, runs from pass to mountain pass along the length of Liguria, but aside from the odd section accessible on public transport from the coast it's mainly for hardened pros. Nonetheless, high-altitude resorts such as **Santo Stefano d'Aveto** and **Torriglia** offer plenty of summer walking (and, in places, winter skiing) that can lift you a world away from the resorts down below on the sea.

In a **car**, the shore road is for the most part a disappointment: the coast is extremely built up, and in fact you get a much better sense of the beauty of the region by taking the east–west autostrada which cuts through the mountains a few kilometres inland by means of a mixture of tunnels and viaducts. Fleeting bursts of daylight between tunnels give glimpses of the string of resorts along the coast, silvery olive groves and a brilliant sea. However, the easiest way to take in the region is by **train**: there are regular services stopping just about everywhere and, because the track is forced to squeeze along the narrow coastal strip, stations are almost invariably centrally located in towns and villages.

Liguria's regional **tourist office** is based at Piazza Matteotti 9, Genoa (℡010.530.8201, Ⓦwww.turismo.liguriainrete.it) – check out their encyclopedic website, which has information in English on every town and village in the region, plus the option to reserve at any hotel, campsite or agriturismo farmhouse. The excellent spiral-bound **Liguria Tourist Atlas**, published by the regional government in collaboration with cartographers DeAgostini, is invaluable if you're spending any time in the area and has useful detailed plans of town centres.

Genoa

GENOA (**Genova** in Italian) is "the most winding, incoherent of cities, the most entangled topographical ravel in the world." So said Henry James, and the city is still marvellously eclectic, full of pace and rough-edged style. Sprawled behind the huge port – Italy's largest and an increasingly popular stopoff for international cruise liners – is a dense and fascinating warren of medieval alleyways, a district which has more zest than all the coastal resorts put together.

Genoa made its money at sea, through trade, colonial exploitation and piracy. By the thirteenth century, on the heels of a major role in the **Crusades**, the Genoese were roaming the Mediterranean, bringing back ideas as well as goods: the city's architects were using Arab pointed arches a century before the

Regional food and wine

Liguria belongs geographically to the north, but its benign Mediterranean climate, and to some extent its cooking, belong further south. Traditionally, the recipes from this region make something out of nothing; this is a legacy of the hardships of life here in the past, and is mirrored by a reserve in the Ligurian character that has given the people an undeserved reputation among other Italians for meanness. The best-known of all Ligurian specialities is **pesto**. Invented by the Genoese to help their long-term sailors fight off scurvy, it's made with chopped basil, garlic, pine-nuts and grated sharp cheese (pecorino or parmesan) ground up together in olive oil – traditionally with a pestle and mortar, from where the name arises. It's used as a sauce for pasta (often flat *trenette* noodles, or knobbly little potato-flour shapes known as **trofie**), or stirred into soup to make *minestrone alla genovese*. Otherwise, **fish** dominates – not surprising in a region where more than two-thirds of the population live on the coast. Local **anchovies** are a common antipasto, while pasta with a variety of fish and seafood sauces appears everywhere (mussels, scampi, octopus and clams are all excellent); there's also a host of specific dishes such as *ciuppin* or fish soup, *burrida di seppie* (cuttlefish stew), or fish *in carpione* (marinated in vinegar and herbs). Salt **cod** (*bacalà*) and wind-dried cod (*stoccofisso*) are big local favourites, often served fried. Other dishes to look out for are *cima alla genovese* (cold stuffed veal) and the widely available *torta pasqualina*, a spinach-and-cheese pie with eggs. The latter is served as fast food, as are other kinds of *torta* and golden **focaccia** bread, often flavoured with olives, sage or rosemary. Chickpeas grow abundantly along the coast and crop up in **farinata**, a kind of chickpea pancake displayed in broad round baking trays that you'll see everywhere, and in *zuppa di ceci*, another dish rarely found outside Liguria. Pastries, too, are excellent: Genoa is famous for its **pandolce**, a sweet cake laced with dried fruit, nuts and candied peel.

Liguria's soil and aspect aren't suited to vine-growing, although plenty of local **wine** – mainly white – is quite drinkable. The steep, terraced slopes of the Cinque Terre are home to an eponymous white wine and the sweet, expensive dessert wine called Sciacchetrà, made from partially dried grapes. From the Riviera di Ponente, look out for the crisp whites of Pigato (from Albenga) and Vermentino (from Imperia), as well as the acclaimed Rossese di Dolceacqua, Liguria's best red.

---

rest of Italy. The San Giorgio banking syndicate effectively controlled the city for much of the fifteenth century, and cold-shouldered **Columbus** (who had grown up in Genoa) when he sought funding for his voyages of exploration. With Spanish backing, he opened up new Atlantic trade routes which ironically reduced *Genova La Superba* ("the proud") to a backwater. Following foreign invasion, in 1768 the Banco di San Giorgio was forced to sell the Genoese colony of Corsica to the French, and a century later, the city became a hotbed of radicalism: **Mazzini**, one of the main protagonists of the Risorgimento, was born here, and in 1860 **Garibaldi** set sail for Sicily with his "Thousand" from the city's harbour. Around the same time, Italy's industrial revolution began in Genoa, with steelworks and shipyards spreading along the coast. These suffered heavy **bombing** in World War II, and the subsequent economic decline hobbled Genoa for decades.

Things started to look up in the 1990s. State funding to celebrate the 500th anniversary of Columbus's 1492 voyage paid to renovate some of the city's late-Renaissance palaces and the old port area, with Genoa's most famous son of modern times, **Renzo Piano** (best known as the co-designer of Paris's Pompidou Centre), taking a leading role. The results of a 46-million euro programme to prepare the city for a well-earned role as **European Capital of Culture** in 2004 are evident all over the city, especially in the old town. The

GENOA

▲ Train to Casella

◀ Pegli

▲ Albaro & Boccadasse ▲ **8**

ACCOMMODATION

Agnello d'Oro	2
Bel Soggiorno	7
Bristol Palace	5
La Capannina	8
Carletto	3
HI Hostel	1
Ricci	4
Soana	6

Stazione Brignole

PIAZZA VERDI

PIAZZA MANIN

Museo Americanisto

PIAZZA BRIGNOLE

PIAZZA DELLA VITTORIA

Mercato Orientale **4**

3

6 7

S. Stefano

Zeffirino

Da Genio

PIAZZA CORVETTO

5

PIAZZA DANTE

Villetta di Negro

Palazzo Bianco

Palazzo Rosso

Palazzo Spinola

Palazzo San Giorgio

Teatro Carlo Felice

Palazzo Ducale

PIAZZA FERRARI

PIAZZA MATTEOTTI

Porta Soprana

Sant' Agostino

Cattedrale

PIAZZA CAVOUR

Casa di Mazzini

PIAZZA CARICAMENTO

Bigo

San Marco

PORTO ANTICO

Aquarium

Porta dei Vacca

Padiglione del Mare

Porta Siberia

See 'Genoa Old Town' map for detail

1

CORSO FIRENZE

Orto Botanico

Palazzo Reale

Stazione Principe

PIAZZA ACQUAVERDE

S. Giovanni di Prè

Commenda

2

Stazione Marittima

PONTE DEI MILLE

N

0   200 m

111

city authorities must be hoping that 2004 will prove a less controversial moment in the limelight than the ill-fated G8 summit, held in Genoa in July 2001, which descended into chaos as police fought running battles on the streets with rioting anti-globalization protesters, and in which 23-year old Carlo Giuliani was shot dead by carabinieri.

The tidying-up hasn't sanitized the **old town**, however; the core of the city, between the two stations and the waterfront, is still dark and slightly threatening. But despite the sleaze, the overriding impression is of a buzzing hive of activity – food shops nestled in the portals of former palaces, carpenters' workshops sandwiched between designer furniture outlets, everything surrounded by a crush of people and the squashed vowels of the impenetrable Genoese dialect that has, over the centuries, absorbed elements of Neapolitan, Calabrese and Portuguese. Aside from the cosmopolitan street life, you should seek out the **Cattedrale di San Lorenzo** with its fabulous treasury, small medieval churches such as **San Donato** and **Santa Maria di Castello**, and the Renaissance *palazzi* that contain Genoa's **art** collections and furniture and decor from the grandest days of the city's illustrious past.

Arrival, transport and information

There are two big **train stations** in Genoa. **Stazione Principe**, on Piazza Acquaverde, just above the port on the west side of the centre, is the main one, although a number of mainline trains also pass through **Stazione Brignole** on Piazza Verdi, to the east of the centre. Buses #33 and #37, among others, ply between the two. There's a staffed left-luggage office at Principe (daily 6am–10pm; €2.58 per piece for 12hr), and lockers at Brignole (daily 24h; €2.58 for 6hr; 30hr maximum). If you're arriving at Principe after dark, cling on to your valuables while moving through the station and avoid the notorious Via di Prè alley nearby, which is the core territory of Genoa's lowlife. **Buses** arrive on Piazza della Vittoria, a few minutes' walk south of Brignole.

The **Aeroporto Cristoforo Colombo** (Ⓦwww.airport.genova.it) is 6km west of the city centre. "Volabus" #100 runs to Stazione Principe, Piazza de Ferrari, on the edge of the Old Town, and Piazza Verdi outside Stazione Brignole (every 30min; takes 25min; information ☎010.558.2414). Buy your €2.07 ticket on the bus.

Getting around the centre is best done **on foot**, resorting to Genoa's AMT **buses** (information ☎010.558.2414) only for trips to outlying sights. Public transport tickets, available from *tabacchi* and newspaper stands, cost €0.77 for 90 minutes, or €2.58 all day, and are valid on buses, all the city's various **funiculars** and **lifts**, the expanding metro system which serves the suburban commuter belt, and local trains between Voltri and Nervi (although not on the narrow-gauge mountain line to Casella; see p.127). AMT also runs the worthwhile **Girocittà** tour (€13; ☎010.558.2414), comprising a two-hour bus tour around the major city sights with multilingual guides aboard, followed by an optional one-hour walking tour of the *centro storico*. The bus tour starts outside Brignole station on Piazza Verdi at 9.30 each morning. Another good way to get a flavour of the city is from **a boat**; see "Listings" on p.126 for details.

The main **tourist office** (toll-free ☎1674.69.838, Ⓦwww.apt.genova.it) is at Stazione Principe (Mon–Sat 9.30am–1pm & 2.30–6pm; ☎010.246.2633); other branches can be found at the Porto Antico, in a small booth next to the aquarium (daily 9am–1pm & 2–6pm; ☎010.248.711), at the airport (Mon–Sat 9.30am–12.30pm & 1.30–5.30pm; ☎010.601.5247) and at Stazione Marittima near the cruise terminal (May–Sept daily 9am–6.30pm; ⓣ010.246.3686). Note, though, that Genoa's tourist industry is undergoing a complete overhaul in the build-up to the 2004 celebrations, which may well encompass new locations and changes in opening times; for details, contact the city's tourism administration, at Via Roma 11/3 (ⓣ010.576.791).

Accommodation

There's no shortage of **accommodation**, but many of the budget hotels – especially those around the train stations – are grimy and depressing, and you need to look hard to find the exceptions. The area just west of Stazione Brignole (Piazza Colombo and Via XX Settembre) is much preferable to anything around Stazione Principe. There's a handful of quality hotels in the old quarter – though you should steer clear of the one-star places down by the port (on and around Via di Prè), some of which are the haunts of drug-dealers and prostitutes.

Hotels

Agnello d'Oro Vico Monachette 6
ⓣ010.246.2084, ⓕ246.2327. Comfortable, modernized rooms – some with balconies – in a seventeenth-century palace alongside the Palazzo Reale and within spitting distance of Stazione Principe. ❹

Bel Soggiorno Via XX Settembre 19/2 ⓣ & ⓕ581.418. Run by a gregarious German woman (who speaks English), this is a welcoming place, although the standard of the rooms – both en suite and not – doesn't quite measure up to the cosiness of the lobby and breakfast room. ❷–❸

Bristol Palace Via XX Settembre 35 ⓣ010.592.541, ⓕ561.756. Grand old pile full of antique furniture, old masters and an Edwardian sense of order and discretion. Rooms are large, attractive and air-conditioned. ❼

Cairoli Via Cairoli 14/4 ⓣ010.246.1454, ⓕ246.7512, ⓔcairoli@rdn.it. A friendly two-star, whose brightly furnished, modern, soundproofed rooms all have private bath, TV and telephone. One of the city's best deals. ❸

La Capannina Via Tito Speri 7 ⓣ010.317.131, ⓕ362.2692. Down a side street off the river walkway near the charming fishing cove of Boccadasse, well east of the centre (bus #17).

Characterful rooms and a tranquil location make it something of a bargain. ❸

Carletto Via Colombo 16/4 ⓣ010.588.412, ⓕ589.615. Less than ten minutes' walk from Stazione Brignole, just off busy Via San Vincenzo, this has clean, ordinary rooms – some en suite, some with shared bathroom. ❷

City Via San Sebastiano 6 ⓣ010.55451, ⓕ586.301. Four-star Best Western hotel in a great central location, round the corner from the theatre. ❻

Major Vico Spada 4 ⓣ010.247.4174, ⓕ246.9898. A great location in the old town, just off Via Luccoli, along with clean and well-furnished rooms with TV and telephone, make this a great bargain. ❷

Ricci Piazza Colombo 4/8 ⓣ010.592.746, ⓕ590.380. A slightly institutional one-star in a rather grim apartment building. But it's handy for Stazione Brignole, and the rooms are clean enough. ❷

Soana Via XX Settembre 23/8 ⓣ010.562.814, ⓕ561.486. A good location right by the Porta Monumentale, and very friendly, with a mixture of rooms – some are plain and basic, others are lovely and fully modernized. One of the best choices in the area. ❷–❸

Camping and hostels

The few **campsites** within the city boundaries include *Villa Doria* at Via al Campeggio Villa Doria 15 in Pegli (ⓣ010.696.9600), though you'd do far better to stay at one of the coastal resorts and commute into town.

Genoa's HI **hostel** is a clean and well-run place situated up in the hills of Righi, north of the centre, at Via Costanzi 120 (ⓣ & ⓕ010.242.2457, ⓦwww .geocities.com/hostelge; closed late Dec & Jan). From Stazione Brignole, take bus #40, from Stazione Principe you need bus #35, then switch at the fifth stop onto bus #40. Bed and breakfast costs €12.91, and there are cheap meals, as well as maps and information on offer. Check-in is 3.30–6pm.

Genoa addresses

Genoa is one of the handful of Italian cities that, for some reason, has an unnecessarily complicated double system of street-numbering: commercial establishments, such as bars and restaurants, have **red** numbers (*rosso*), while all other buildings have **black** numbers (*nero*) – and the two systems don't run in tandem. This means, for example, that Via Banchi 35r might be next-door to Via Banchi 89n, but several hundred metres from Via Banchi 33n.

The City

Genoa's atmospheric **Old Town** spreads outwards from the port in a confusion of tiny alleyways (*caruggi*), bordered by **Via Gramsci** along the waterfront and by **Via Balbi** and **Via Garibaldi** to the north. The *caruggi* are lined with high buildings, usually six or seven storeys, set very close together. Tiny grocers, textile workshops and bakeries jostle for position with boutiques, design outlets and goldsmiths amidst a flurry of shouts, smells and scrawny cats. Not for nothing is Genoa the only European city to be mentioned in the *Arabian Nights*.

The cramped layout of the area reflects its medieval politics. Around the thirteenth and fourteenth centuries, the city's principal families – Doria, Spinola, Grimaldi and Fieschi – marked out certain streets and squares as their territory, even extending their domains to include churches: to pray in someone else's chapel was to risk being stabbed in the back. New buildings on each family's patch had to be slotted in wherever they could, resulting in a maze of crooked alleyways that was the battleground of dynastic feuds which lasted well into the eighteenth century. Genoa has, however, remained relatively free of fire, not least because each building's kitchens were invariably placed on the topmost storey.

The Palazzo Ducale and around

From 1384 to 1515, except for brief periods of foreign domination, Genoa was ruled by a doge, resident at the **Palazzo Ducale** in Piazza Matteotti, right in the heart of the old town. The present building, with its huge vaulted atrium, was built in the sixteenth century – its wide steps up from the courtyard were designed with the doge's grand processions in mind. The building now makes a splendid exhibition hall (times and prices vary; ⓦ www.palazzoducale.genova.it) and houses archives and libraries, as well as hosting shows and concerts; it was here that the G8 summit took place in July 2001. The dour **Gesù** church across the square, where locals come to siesta on hot summer afternoons, was designed by Pellegrino Tibaldi at the end of the sixteenth century and contains a mass of marble and gilt stucco and some fine Baroque paintings, including Guido Reni's *Assumption* in the right aisle and two works by Rubens: the *Miracles of St Ignatius* on the left and the *Circumcision* on the high altar.

An alley between the two leads through to **Piazza de Ferrari**, overlooked by a statue of Garibaldi in front of the grand facade of the Carlo Felice opera house; from here, Via XX Settembre heads east towards Brignole, while Via Roma cuts north to skirt the old town.

Cattedrale di San Lorenzo

West of Piazza Matteotti, bulking out the north side of Via San Lorenzo which cuts down to the port, is the **Cattedrale di San Lorenzo**. There's an entrance from the street, but you should first go round to take in the main western

GENOA OLD TOWN

0   100 m

Port

N

ACCOMMODATION

Cairoli	1
City	3
Major	2

RESTAURANTS				**BARS & CAFÉS**			
Antica Cantina	**B**	Da Rina	**I**	Bar Berto	**g**	Louisiana Jazz Club	**f**
La Berlocca	**C**	Squarciafico	**D**	La Bottega del Conto	**k**	Café La Madeleine	**a**
Mario Rivaro	**A**	Trattoria dei Genoani	**G**	Britannia	**e**	Caffè Mangini	**c**
Östaja dö Castello	**H**	Le Tre Finestre	**J**	Caffetteria Orefici	**d**	Moretti	**i**
Pansön	**E**	Ugo	**F**	Fitzcarraldo	**l**	Qualude	**n**
				Klainguti	**b**	Café Roger	**m**
				Le Corbusier	**j**	Caffè degli Specchi	**h**

facade, an elaborate confection of twisting, fluted columns and black-and-white striped stone – high-quality Carrara marble alternating with local slate – that was added by Gothic craftsmen from France in the early thirteenth century, a hundred years or so after the main building had been constructed. The **stripes** here, like other examples throughout the city, were a sign of prestige: families could use them only if they had a permit, awarded for "some illustrious deed to the advantage of their native city". While the rest of Genoa's churches were portioned out between the ruling dynasties, the cathedral – which lay between districts – remained freely open to all, a fact borne out by the side portals in the north and south walls which formerly allowed free passage from one town quarter to another through the cathedral interior.

The **interior** houses the Renaissance chapel of St John the Baptist, whose ashes – legend has it – once rested in the thirteenth-century sarcophagus. After a particularly bad storm in medieval times, priests carried his casket through the city down to the port to placate the sea, and a commemorative procession still takes place each June 24 in honour of the saint. The Baptist's reliquary is in the **Museo del Tesoro** (Mon–Sat 9–11.30am & 3–5.30pm; €5.16, visit with guided tour only; ⓦwww.comune.genova.it/turismo/musei), housed in an atmospheric crypt. Also on display are a polished quartz plate on which, legend says, Salome received John the Baptist's severed head, and a glass vessel said to have been given to Solomon by the Queen of Sheba and used at the Last Supper. Artefacts from Byzantine and later times include delicate jewelled crosses and reliquaries – along with a British artillery shell that was fired from the sea during World War II and fell through the roof, but miraculously failed to explode.

North of San Lorenzo

The district around the cathedral has changed dramatically in the last few years, with an influx of art shops and trendy fashion outlets along the main Via San Lorenzo. One block north, just off Piazza San Lorenzo, a narrow winding alley, **Vico del Filo**, doglegs its way down to Piazza Caricamento on the portside; a local insult for one who is particularly dim is to describe them as being "as stupid as the Vico del Filo".

An unnamed lane leads north from San Lorenzo through tiny **Piazza Invrea** to the rather swanky little shopping square of **Campetto** and adjacent **Via degli Orefici**, "Street of the Goldsmiths". Unlike the generic, machine-produced gold jewellery found in Florence, much of what is on offer in Genoa is still made by hand at upper-floor workshops in the area of Campetto, sold in shops such as *L'Oro degli Sforza* on the square at relatively affordable prices. Linked to Campetto is genteel **Piazza Soziglia**, with a good mixture of bars and places to eat, among them *Klainguti*, one of Genoa's oldest coffee-houses (see p.124). From here **Via Luccoli** heads north, with glitzy boutiques and design outlets galore, while a few steps to the west is **Piazza Lavagna**, home to the thriving Mercato dei Pulci, the daily flea market. Via Garibaldi, with its sixteenth-century *palazzi* of Genoa's mercantile dynasties, is a short stroll north (see p.118).

A little east of Campetto and Piazza Soziglia is the city's prettiest small square, **Piazza San Matteo**. This lay in the territory of the Doria family, who went one step further than merely striping the twelfth-century church of **San Matteo** in black and white: they ordered elaborate testimonials to the family's worthiness to be carved on the facade of the church and their adjoining palaces. Andrea Doria, the most illustrious of the clan, lived in the palace on the left corner of the square (the other palaces on the square were home to the rest of the family) before he built his lavish palace down on the waterfront (see p.120). He is now buried in the crypt, which the sacristan will open for you. Peek in too at the pretty little cloister adjoining the church.

Piazza Banchi and Piazza Caricamento

Heading west from Campetto on Via degli Orefici brings you out into a thriving commercial zone centred on **Piazza Banchi**, a tiny enclosed market square of secondhand books, records, fruit and flowers which was once the heart of the medieval city. The little church of **San Pietro in Banchi** overlooking the square was built in the sixteenth century after a plague: with little money to spare, the city authorities sold plots of commercial space in arcades around the church terrace in order to fund construction of the main building, an economic model that is familiar today but was virtually unknown at the time.

It's a short stroll west from Piazza Banchi out into the open spaces of Genoa's port. The sea once came up to the vaulted arcades of Via Sottoripa, which runs alongside the main **Piazza Caricamento**; these days the waterfront is blocked off by containers and fences, but there's been a market here since the twelfth century, when small boats used to come ashore from galleys at anchor. Fruit and vegetable stalls still line the arcade, now interspersed with fly pitches selling sunglasses and pirated CDs.

On the southern edge of the square is the **Palazzo di San Giorgio**, a brightly painted fortified palace built in 1260 from the stones of a captured Venetian fortress. After the great sea-battle of Curzola in 1298, the Genoese used the building to keep their Venetian prisoners under lock and key; among them was one **Marco Polo**, who met a Pisan writer named Rustichello inside and spun tales of adventure to him of worlds beyond the seas. After their release, Rustichello published the stories in a single volume that became one of the most famous books of all time, translated into English as *The Travels of Marco Polo*. In 1408, the building was taken over by the Banco di San Giorgio,

---

The cross of St George

If you're a football fan wandering around Genoa, you may legitimately be wondering why the locals seem so taken with the England team as to hang English flags of **St George** from every window. The truth is, however, that the flag – a red cross on a white background – was first acquired by the Genoese, and only came to be the English national emblem courtesy of some crafty deal-making.

The legend of St George originated in the early Christian era in the Middle East with tales of the bravery of an Arab or Turkish warrior: the hero is still venerated today in ordinary churches across Syria, Turkey, Palestine and as far afield as Armenia. The familiar story of dragon-baiting and princess-saving was brought to Europe during the Crusades. Genoese sailors, the master navigators of the day, safely escorted the waves of European armies to and from the Holy Land, and in gratitude, the newly – and temporarily – victorious Crusader kings of Middle Eastern territories granted the Genoese the honour of flying the flag of their local saint protector, St George.

For centuries afterwards, Genoese ships flying the St George's cross remained immune from attack by pirates – although whether it was respect for the saint, fear of violent retribution, or the attraction of Genoese payoffs which kept the bandits away is open to question. However, some time in the sixteenth or seventeenth centuries, English sea-captains, who had long suffered at the hands of pirates, formally requested the right to fly the favoured emblem. And never slow to spot a nice little earner, the Genoese agreed a price.

a syndicate established to finance the war against Venice, which in the sixteenth century steered the city from trading to banking, thus turning Genoa into the leading financial centre of the day. These days, the palazzo is home to the harbour authorities, but you can ask the guardian on the door to let you in to see the medieval Sala dei Protettori and beautiful Sala Manica Lunga, whose decor was restored to its thirteenth-century grandeur following bomb damage in World War II.

The Galleria Nazionale di Palazzo Spinola

From Piazza Banchi, the animated medieval **Via San Luca** heads north, lined with shops selling counterfeit designer clothes and accessories. This street was in Spinola family territory, and when the last of the family died, in 1958, their grand residence became the excellent **Galleria Nazionale di Palazzo Spinola**, located beside Piazza Pelliceria (Tues–Sat 9am–8pm, Sun 1–8pm; €4.13; under-25s half-price; joint ticket with Palazzo Reale €6.20). Room 2 holds portraits by van Dyck of Matthew, Mark, Luke and John as men of books, while on the upper floor are an intensely mournful *Ecce Homo* by the Sicilian master Antonello da Messina and the splendid *Adoration of the Magi* by Joos van Cleve, sawn into planks when stolen from the church of San Donato in the 1970s. Don't miss the little **terrace**, way up on the spine of the roof and shaded with orange and lemon trees.

The way north passes through a hectic and rather seedy neighbourhood centred on the vibrant **Via della Maddalena** alley, crowded with shops and stalls that ring with shouts in French and Arabic from the predominantly West and North African street-traders, doing business alongside Genoa's burgeoning red-light trade. Steep lanes rise north of Via della Maddalena, lifting you out of the mêlée and into the ordered calm of Via Garibaldi.

Along Via Garibaldi

When newly-made fortunes encouraged Genoa's merchant bankers to move out of the cramped old town in the mid-sixteenth century, artisans' houses were pulled down to make way for the Strada Nuova, later named **Via Garibaldi**, on the northern fringe of the quarter. To walk along the surprisingly narrow street is to stroll through a Renaissance architect's drawing pad – sculpted facades, stucco work and medallions decorate the exterior of the three-storey *palazzi*, while the big courtyards are almost like private squares. Take a look, for instance, at no. 7, the heavily stuccoed **Palazzo Podestà**, with its grotto and fountain on the far side of its small courtyard, or the splendid **Palazzo Tursi**, a few doors along, the largest of Genoa's palaces and now the town hall, with a glassed-in main courtyard.

The first building at the western end of Via Garibaldi is the **Galleria di Palazzo Bianco**, Genoa's finest art gallery (Tues–Fri 9am–7pm, Wed & Sat 10am–7pm; €3.10; joint ticket with Palazzo Rosso €5.16; free on Sun; Ⓦ www.comune.genova.it/turismo/musei). In room 1 a small but potent image of San Fabiano hangs alongside a strikingly similar portrait of San Antonio; the former is by Francesco Brea, the latter by his father Antonio Brea, both Genoese. At the top of the stairs is a radiant *SS Sebastian, Francis and John the Baptist* by Fra' Filippo Lippi, but most rooms on the upper floor are filled with Flemish works. Room 4 holds a *Madonna and Child* by Joos van Cleve and a dark, brooding Christ by Hans Memling, while room 6 has a gloriously detailed celebration of a Netherlandish winter by Jan Wildens, showing a woman tumbling immodestly on the ice and some poor character about to be pelted with snowballs while in the privy. The piercing gaze of van Dyck's

Christ dominates room 7, despite Rubens's ageing *Venus and Mars* cavorting bawdily nearby, while room 8 has some festive tavern scenes by Jan Steen. Room 9 holds Veronese's giant *Crucifixion*, and next door is a dramatic *Ecce Homo* by Caravaggio. A surfeit of work by the Genoese painter Bernardo Strozzi completes the collection.

Across the road at Via Garibaldi 18 is the less prestigious **Galleria di Palazzo Rosso** (same times and prices). Room 2 has an effeminate *St John the Baptist* by Leonardo da Vinci and a striking *Portrait of a Young Man* by Dürer, but it's the topmost floor that is the main attraction, with every room restored to its original Baroque grandeur and bedecked with chandeliers, mirrors and an excess of gilding. Frescoes cover the ceilings, while rooms 13 and 14 display a series of splendid portraits by van Dyck of the Brignole-Sale family, who built the palace in 1671.

Along Via Balbi

A few minutes' walk west of Via Garibaldi is the house at Via Lomellini 11 where Giuseppe Mazzini, one of the most influential activists of Italian Unification, was born in 1805; it now displays documents and relics from his life as the **Museo del Risorgimento** (Tues–Fri 9am–1pm, Sat 10am–7pm; €3.10). Past traffic-heavy Piazza della Nunziata, overlooked by the giant sixteenth-century church of **Santissima Annunziata del Vastato**, which boasts one of the most exuberantly decorated interiors in the city, you'll come to the main road of **Via Balbi**, laid out a few decades after Via Garibaldi.

The Palazzo Reale

At Via Balbi 10 sits the vast and absorbing **Palazzo Reale** (Mon & Tues 8.15am–1.45pm, Wed–Sun 8.15am–7.15pm; €4.13; under-25s half-price; joint ticket with Palazzo Spinola €6.20; ⓦ www.palazzorealegenova.it), built by the Balbi family in the early seventeenth century and later occupied by the Durazzo dynasty and the Savoyard royals. You enter through the huge atrium, which looks onto the elegant courtyard garden behind, and climb grand staircases. The first big room is the **ballroom**, with gilt stucco ceilings and Chinese vases. To the left are four drawing-rooms, featuring a huge watercolour of the crossing of the Red Sea painted on silk by Romanelli, grand marble fireplaces and bronze candelabra. These rooms lead through to the stunning hall of mirrors, where Joseph II, Emperor of Austria, is said to have remarked in 1784 – with a flourish of disingenuous flattery – that the palace appeared more of a royal residence than his own simple pad back in Vienna. The room was designed in the 1730s by Gerolamo Durazzo and the best of its statues are four exquisite works in marble and gold by Filippo Parodi: the first pair, facing each other nearest the door, are Hyacinth and Venus, while at the far end of the room are Adonis and Clizia. Doors lead through to the private quarters of the Duke of Genoa, with the **duke's bedchamber** featuring a sumptuous Baroque ceiling fresco and the duke's bathchamber holding elegant furniture carved in England in the 1820s.

On the way back through to the east wing of the building, you pass along a **chapel gallery** behind the ballroom, covered in trompe l'oeil frescoes by Lorenzo de Ferrari (1733). The adjacent **throne room**, its walls covered in deep red velvets and an excess of gold, is dotted with dozens of "C.A." monograms in honour of Carlo Alberto, King of Savoy. Continuing east, you come to the lavish **audience room**, with its dazzling Turkish carpet, silk curtains, and a grand portrait of a tight-lipped Caterina Durazzo-Balbi painted by van Dyck in 1624 during his six-year stay in Genoa. Alongside, the **king's bed-**

chamber has parquet wooden flooring made by English carpenters in 1843, an exquisite Murano glass chandelier, and van Dyck's first canvas of the *Crucifixion*, also dating from 1624, while the King's Bathchamber features the Savoyard motto *Je atans mon astre* ("I await my destiny" in archaic French) set into the floor. You then move into the **queen's quarters**, a series of rooms featuring a ghostly pale *Crucifixion* by the Neapolitan master Luca Giordano and a *St Lawrence* (1616) by Bernardo Strozzi. After another series of drawing-rooms, one hung with Parisian tapestries of 1610, double-doors open onto the **grand terrace** which runs on three sides of a rectangle above the garden courtyard, giving airy views out over the port. Adjacent on the east side is the crumbling Teatro Falcone, where once the virtuoso Genoese violinist Paganini played.

Around Stazione Principe

Via Balbi continues west to the grandiose **Stazione Principe**, fronted by Piazza Acquaverde with a central statue of Columbus. Immediately below the train station, the drab run of portfront buildings is broken by the elegant loggia of the twelfth-century **Commendà**, a former convent, hospital and lodging-house for crusading knights, now gutted and converted to a temporary exhibition space. The oddly double-apsed church of **San Giovanni di Prè**, whose landmark campanile was added in the late twelfth century, was originally reserved solely for the use of the Knights of Malta, or Knights Hospitallers, who ran the Commendà next door and who have left behind them the legacy of a host of Maltese crosses used as decoration on buildings all over town. From here, the busy and notoriously seedy **Via di Prè** runs parallel with the waterfront Via Gramsci and is the first real street of the old town; partway along is the Bagnaschi hardware shop, occupying a perfectly preserved former hospital dating from 1353. Via di Prè skirts the port as far as the twelfth-century **Porta dei Vacca**, from where alleys take you into the heart of the old quarter.

From Piazza Acquaverde, Via Doria runs west down to the ferry terminal, past the lavish gardens of the huge **Palazzo del Principe Doria Pamphilj**, built in the early 1530s by Andrea Doria, who made his reputation and fortune attacking Turkish fleets and Barbary pirates and liberating the Genoese republic from the French and Spanish. The gardens back onto the *fin-de-siècle* **Stazione Marìttima**, which was once the departure point for steamers to New York and Buenos Aires, but nowadays handles ferries to Corsica, Sardinia and Sicily (see p.126). It was from the **Ponte dei Mille** (Jetty of the Thousand) in front of the ferry terminal that **Giuseppe Garibaldi**, ex-mercenary and spaghetti salesman, persuaded his thousand Red Shirts to set off for Sicily in two clapped-out paddle steamers, armed with just a few rifles and no ammunition. Their mission, to support a Sicilian uprising and unite the island with the mainland states, greatly annoyed some northern politicians, who didn't want anything to do with the undeveloped south – an attitude which echoes in Italian politics to this day. About 1km further round the port is Genoa's restored sixteenth-century lighthouse, the **Lanterna**, as well as the **Matitone**, a postmodern polygonal tower housing municipal offices which comes to a sharp point above the industrial area of the port – giving rise to its sardonic nickname of "The Big Pencil".

The Porto Antico

The *sopraelevata*, or elevated highway, shoots along the waterfront above Piazza Caricamento, dividing the city from the ancient port, or **Porto Antico**, long

Whale-watching

The waters off the Ligurian coast as far south as Corsica comprise a World Wildlife Fund-monitored **International Whale Sanctuary**, home to twelve species of whale as well as dolphins and plenty of other marine life. It's easy to join summer boat excursions from towns along the Riviera for whale-watching in open sea (June–Sept at least once a week). All must be **booked in advance** and comprise a full day on board, including a light lunch and commentary from local WWF experts.

Main operators are Alimar (℡010.256.775; ⒲www.alimar.ge.it) and Cooperativa Battellieri (℡010.265.712, ⒲www.battellierigenova.it) – their boats start from **Genoa** (€30.99) and pick up from **Savona** (€28.41); Alimar's also pick up from **Alassio** (€25.82 with lunch, or €20.66 without). Different boats depart Porto Maurizio harbour in **Imperia** ℡0183.280.110; €25.82), while from **San Remo** the operator is Riviera Line ℡0184.505.055, ⒲www.rivieraline.it; €36.15).

since finished as a commercial concern but revitalized during the 1990s with the aim of bringing people down to the harbour again. Old warehouses have been converted into exhibition spaces, open stages host waterside performances, and there's an ice-skating rink, a cinema, a children's play area and a swimming pool. It's now a pleasant place to stroll, with cafés and pricey waterside bistros fronting the marina.

The visual centrepiece of the development is the **Bigo** – a curious multi-armed contraption, brainchild of Renzo Piano, intended to recall the harbour-side cranes of old. One of the arms hauls a circular elevator up more than 60m to give visitors a superb all-round view over the city (opening times vary, usually daily 10am–6pm; €3.36). South of the Bigo is the old Porta Siberia, with the **Molo Vecchio** (Old Wharf) just beyond; this was formerly where condemned prisoners would be led, to take the Last Sacrament at the little church of **San Marco** halfway along, before arriving at the gallows overlooking Piazza Cavour. The main feature of the area is a gigantic former cotton warehouse, now a commercial shopping centre with bars, cinemas, music stores and the **Padiglione del Mare e della Navigazione**, a small museum tracing the history of Genoa's relationship with the sea (Tues–Fri 10.30am–5.30pm, Sat & Sun 10.30am–6pm; €5.40; joint ticket with Aquarium €14.90).

Just north of the Bigo is the pride and joy of the city, the **Acquario di Genova** (Tues, Wed & Fri 9.30am–7.30pm, Thurs 9.30am–10pm, Sat & Sun 9.30am–8.30pm; also Nov–Feb Mon 10am–6pm, March–Oct Mon 9.30am–7.30pm; last entry 2hr before closing; €11.60; joint ticket with Padiglione €14.90; ⒲www.acquario.ge.it). This is Europe's largest aquarium, and houses sea creatures from all the world's major habitats. They have the world's largest reconstruction of a Caribbean coral reef, complete with moray eels, turtles and angelfish, and a growing number of species from the coral reefs and forests of Madagascar. Although the whole affair boasts a fashionably ecology-conscious slant and excellent background information (delivered in Italian and English), the larger beasts – including grey sharks, dolphins, seals and an enclosure containing a group of Humboldt penguins – can't help but seem pathetically imprisoned. It's best to avoid visiting on the weekend, when it can be a struggle just to glimpse the creatures between the human bodies. Alongside the aquarium is the newest addition to the seafront area, the futuristic-looking **Bolla** (Bubble), a steel and glass Renzo Piano-designed sphere housing a collection of outsized tree ferns (free).

South of San Lorenzo

The section of the old town south of the Cattedrale di San Lorenzo is less visited than the attraction-packed districts to the north, and more residential. Many of Genoa's students and young professionals live in the upper floors of the old buildings lining Via dei Giustiniani and Via San Bernardo, generating a lively bar culture in the surrounding alleys.

From the cathedral and Piazza Matteotti, narrow **Salita Pollaiuoli** plunges you into the gloom between high buildings down to a crossroads with **Via San Bernardo**, built by the Romans and now one of Genoa's most characterful old-town streets, with grocers and bakers trading behind the portals of palaces decorated in the fifteenth and sixteenth centuries. On the south side of the crossroads is tiny **Piazza San Donato**, a quiet square overlooked by the church of San Donato, a crumbly, bare Romanesque church with a Roman architrave surviving over its door and an octagonal Byzantine-style campanile. The stark simplicity is refreshing after the self-importance of the nearby Gesù on Piazza Matteotti.

Piazza Sarzano and around

A shrine stuck on the side wall of San Donato faces up Stradone Sant'Agostino, laid out in the eighteenth century and now home to a quirky array of bars and workshops. Partway up, stairs lead you into the university's **architecture faculty**, designed by Ignazio Gardella; its tranquil internal garden courtyard gives expansive views over the city. At the top of the street is the long, narrow bulge of **Piazza Sarzano**, originally home to Genoa's many ropemaking workshops and, owing to its enormous length, still the scene for medieval-style jousting tournaments. The piazza is marked by the mosaic spire of the newly rebuilt church of **Sant'Agostino**; alongside it is the unique triangular cloister of the thirteenth-century monastery, which now houses the **Museo di Sant'Agostino** (Tues–Sun 9am–7pm; €3.10), displaying Roman and Romanesque masonry fragments. The highlight is a fragment of the tomb of Margherita of Brabant, sculpted in 1312 by Giovanni Pisano.

Sneak down behind a remnant of the city wall at the southeastern corner of Piazza Sarzano alongside the church of San Antonio, and an alley lined with pretty houses will lead you down into the tranquil little enclosed piazza of **Campopisano**. It was here, during the wars between Genoa and Pisa, that Pisan prisoners were brought in chains, executed and buried; today, the pavement sports pretty mosaics in local *rissëu* style, using smooth white stones collected from the beach and black stones – or *serpentinita* – quarried from dark veins of slate that snake their way across nearby hillsides.

North from Piazza Sarzano streets connect to the **Porta Soprana**, a twin-towered stone gateway featuring impressive Gothic arches (surprisingly dating from as early as 1155) that now stands as the focus for a rather upmarket collection of bars and terrace cafés.

Modern Genoa

In the nineteenth century, Genoa began to expand beyond its old-town constraints. The newer districts begin with the large central **Piazza de Ferrari**, from where **Via XX Settembre** runs a straight course east through the commercial centre of the city towards Stazione Brignole. This grand boulevard features big department stores, shops selling designer clothes, and pavement cafés beneath its neon-lit arcades. There are prized delicatessens in the side streets around Stazione Brignole and Piazza Colombo, and a bustling covered **Mercato Orientale** partway along, in the cloisters of an old Augustinian monastery. At the eastern end of Via XX Settembre, the small park outside the Brignole train station (hub for city buses) extends south into **Piazza della Vittoria**, a huge and dazzling white square built during the Fascist period that now serves as the long-distance bus station.

Walking north from Piazza de Ferrari takes you up to **Piazza Corvetto** – built by the Austrians in the nineteenth century and now a major confluence of traffic and people. Across the other side of the square, a thoughtful-looking statue of Giuseppe Mazzini marks the entrance to the **Villetta di Negro**, a lushly landscaped park whose artificial waterfalls and grottoes scale the hill. At the top, the **Museo d'Arte Orientale Edoardo Chiossone** (Tues, Fri, Sat & Sun 10am–7pm; €3.10) holds a collection of oriental art that includes eighteenth-century sculpture and paintings and samurai armour. Chiossone was a printer and engraver for the Italian mint, and, on the strength of his banknote engraving skills, he was invited by the Meiji dynasty to establish the Japanese Imperial Mint. He lived in Japan from 1875 until his death in Tokyo in 1898, building up a fascinating and extensive collection.

If you're not satisfied with the view from the Villetta di Negro, you can take the Art Nouveau-style public lift from **Piazza del Portello** up to the **Castelletto**, which offers a great panorama over the port and the roofs of the old town; a **funicular** also leaves from the same place up to the residential **Sant'Anna** district, although the views from here aren't as good (ordinary bus tickets are valid for both). When Genoa ran out of building space, plots for houses were hewn out of the hillside behind, like the steps of an amphitheatre, and the funicular enables you to see this at close quarters, as the carriages edge past people's front windows. Another funicular runs from Largo Zecca, further west, to the suburb of **Righi**, where you can admire vistas of the city below and wander off on any of a number of paths all around, although most locals' motives for coming up here are more prosaic – to sit in the various panoramic restaurants for extended sessions of family dining.

The outskirts: Albaro, Boccadasse and Staglieno

For a spot of relaxation, head out of town to the eastern waterfront suburb of **Albaro**, at the end of Corso Italia, a broad boulevard that runs along the seafront beyond the giant Fiera exhibition area (bus #31 from Stazione Brignole). This is the place to jog, stroll, pose at one of the private lidos, or watch the sun set from a café table. From Albaro, you can walk or take bus #42 to **Boccadasse**. Once an outlying fishing port, this village is now part of the city, with boats pulled up on the pebble beach, nets hanging out to dry, some arty shops, and costly restaurants in which to sample the catch of the day.

Another good outing is to the **Staglieno cemetery** (daily 7.30am–5pm; free), on a hill northeast of the centre above the Bisagno valley. Bus #34 runs from Stazione Principe through Piazza Nunziata and Piazza Corvetto to the cemetery. This is still Genoa's major burial ground, laid out between 1844 and 1851, and is a veritable city of the dead, crammed with Neoclassical porticoes, Gothic chapels and statuary galore. The entrance gates lead you into a vast quadrangle dominated by a Neoclassical **Pantheon** holding monuments to a clutch of famous nineteenth-century Genoese, including **Nino Bixio**, second-in-command on Garibaldi's expedition to Sicily. Behind and to the right of the Pantheon is the mausoleum of **Giuseppe Mazzini**, fronted by two squat Doric columns. One of the most sentimental monuments is the statue of **Teresa Campodonico**, a seller of nuts, whose life savings went to reproduce her slight, bent figure; carved below is a poem recounting how she sold her nuts in sunshine and in rain so as to gain her daily bread and propel her image into future ages. In the Protestant section of the cemetery you'll find the grave of **Constance Lloyd**, Oscar Wilde's wife, who died in 1898 at the age of forty, less than a year after Wilde had been released from prison, having long since changed her name and the names of their two sons to Holland.

Eating, drinking and nightlife

You could spend several days checking out the scores of places to **eat** in Genoa, from basic trattorias to elegant nineteenth-century *caffès*. The cheapest, around the port, are often open only at lunchtime.

On first impressions, life **after dark** looks sparse, but a bit of time rooting around in the old town will turn up a good choice of convivial bars and small clubs, some of them with live music.

Drinks, snacks and light meals

Piazza Caricamento is one of the best places for a quick lunch on the hoof, the arcades (*sottoripe*) along the edge of the piazza lined with cafés serving **focaccia**, panini and deep-fried seafood. There are also lots of places in the old town selling **farinata** (Genoa's home-grown snack, made from chickpea flour and olive oil) – two that stand out are *Antica Sciamadda* at Via Ravecca 19r (closed Mon), and *Tugnin* on Piazza Tommaseo. *Forno Patrone*, Via Ravecca 72r (closed Wed afternoon) is one of the city's top bakeries. Centuries of Turkish influence have produced Genoese variations on Middle Eastern confectionery, including candied fruit (best sampled at *Romanengo* in Via Soziglia) and slabs of *pandolce* as served up at *Profumo* in Via del Portello.

Bars and cafés

Bar Berto Piazza delle Erbe 6r. Relaxed café-bar founded in 1904 by Signor Berto who walked some 15km west to the ceramics centre of Albisola in order to collect colourful bits of broken tile to decorate the walls of his new bar. With seating inside and out beneath the terrace awning, this is a trendy spot for coffee, beer or a reasonably priced light meal. Open daily.

La Bottega del Conte Mura delle Grazie. This cocktail bar is a dimly-lit Bohemian hangout in a street behind the Porto Antico. Once a delicatessen, antique culinary implements still adorn the walls. Live jazz on Tuesdays.

Klainguti Piazza Soziglia 98r. An Austrian-built *salon* dating from 1828, selling cakes and ice cream under chandeliers. They still produce the hazelnut croissant known as a *Falstaff*, which was much esteemed by Giuseppe Verdi, who spent forty winters in Genoa – "Thanks for the Falstaff, much better than mine," he wrote to the bakers. No closing day.

Café La Madeleine Via della Maddalena 103r. A wonderful little café-theatre, haunt of writers, poets, musicians and story-tellers, with plenty of readings and small concerts. Closed Mon.

Caffè Mangini Via Roma at Piazza Corvetto. One of Genoa's most venerable *pasticcerie*, in business since the early 1800s and still top-notch today. No closing day.

Caffetteria Orefici Via degli Orefici 25r. Fragrant temple to the art of coffee-making, with a range of specialist coffees and perfect results every time. Closed Sun.

Café Roger Stradone di Sant'Agostino. A quirky spot designed in riotous style after the Frank Zappa song "The Dangerous Kitchen" – every shelf is wonky, fake meat-cleavers dangle overhead, plastic sharks rise out of the sink, phoney electric cables snake around the basins, and so on. The staff, music, and clientele make this a fun stop for a daytime coffee or evening beer. No closing day.

Caffè degli Specchi Salita Pollaiuoli 43r. Hidden in an alley opposite the Palazzo Ducale, this has been a prime spot since 1917 for Genovese artists, writers and intellectuals to take coffee while admiring themselves in the mirrors (*specchi*) which cover the magnificent tiled interior. The place still offers much the same ambience and old-time service, along with some tapas in the evening. Closed Sun.

Restaurants

Antica Cantina I Tre Merli Via dietro il coro della Maddalena 6, ☎010.24.74.095, ☯www .itremerli.it. With 300 wines on the menu, all stored in a converted fourteenth-century well, the atmospheric surroundings, slick service and innovative approach to Ligurian cuisine – try the carpaccio di branzino – make for a memorable meal. Around €25 per head excluding wine. Closed Wed.

La Berlocca Via del Macelli di Soziglia 45r ⓣ010.247.4162. Young bistro-style establishment in the old town, offering something more adventurous than traditional Ligurian dishes. Closed Mon.

Da Genio Salita San Leonardo 61r ⓣ010.588.443. This long-established restaurant, off Via Fieschi at the top of a steep hill above Piazza Dante, is highly regarded for great Ligurian food, served in a reasonably informal atmosphere, at moderate prices. Closed Sun & Aug.

Mario Rivaro Via del Portello 16r. Decent local dishes and seafood soups, from €10 a dish. Closed Sun.

Östaja dö Castello Salita Santa Maria di Castello 32r. Great old-town family-run trattoria serving Genoese specialities – mainly, but not exclusively, fish. Moderate to low prices. Closed Sun.

Pansön Piazza delle Erbe 5r ⓣ010.246.8903. Venerable Genoese institution, in the same family since 1790; diners select from a fishy menu priced high to keep the riff-raff away. Closed Sun eve.

Da Rina Mura delle Grazie 3r. High-quality, simple Genoese cooking in fairly unpretentious surroundings down near the waterfront. Lots of fish and classic Ligurian dishes such as *cima alla genovese*. Moderately priced. Closed Mon.

Squarciafico Piazza Invrea 3r ⓣ010.247.0823, ⓦwww.squarciafico.it. Atmospheric cantina in the wine-cellar of a fifteenth-century mansion just off

Piazza San Lorenzo. Calm, modern decor and innovative, carefully prepared food complement each other perfectly; be prepared for €25 per person. Closed Aug.

Trattoria dei Genoani Piazza delle Erbe 8r. Sociable little trattoria in a lively area founded by supporters of the Genoa football club patronized by supporters of the Genoa football club – don't go shouting for Sampdoria here – which offers down-the-line takes on Genoese and Ligurian dishes, for affordable prices. Closed Sun & Mon.

Le Tre Finestre Scalinata di San Antonio 2a. A tiny old-time trattoria off Piazza Sarzano. There's no menu (the waitress will just rattle off the dishes of the day), and the food is cheap, plain and hearty. Join in the good old-fashioned accordion singalong on Friday nights. Closed Mon–Thurs eve, and all day Sun.

Ugo Via Giustiniani 86r. Convivial trattoria in the heart of the student quarter near San Donato, with a boisterous, friendly group of regulars who pack in at shared tables to wolf the Genoese and Ligurian nosh – heavy on pesto and seafood. A hearty meal for two can come in at under €15. Well worth checking out. Closed Sun & Mon.

Zeffirino Via XX Settembre 20r ⓣ010.591.990. Expensive – expect to pay around €45 (excluding wine) for a three- to four-course meal of between-two-stools trad/mod cuisine – but this is where Frank Sinatra and Pavarotti have also dined and so has ineffable star quality. Closed Wed.

Entertainment and nightlife

The best source of information on **nightlife** is the local daily paper *Il Secolo XIX*; in summer you can supplement this with *Genova by Night,* the tourist office's free what's-on guide. There are plenty of **bars** along the seamy waterfront Via Gramsci, in between the strip joints and brothels, but more attractive places to drink can be found on the side roads off Via XX Settembre and around Piazza delle Erbe. Recommended are *Moretti* on Piazza San Bernardo, a beery student dive; consistently popular *Le Corbusier*, Via San Donato 36r; and *Eprie Rosse*, Via Ravecca 54r, a characterful wine-bar. The *Britannia* pub at Vico Casana 76r, off Piazza de Ferrari, has pints of Guinness and burgers and chips. The *Louisiana* **club** on Via San Sebastiano hosts live trad jazz most nights from around 10pm, but you'll find more happening joints tucked away in the southern part of the old town: the *Quaalude*, beneath the "Massari" signboard at Piazza Sarzano 14, is an underground club that features live bands and/or dance parties on Fridays and Saturdays – ask around in local bars for the latest news – while the *Fitzcarraldo* on Piazza Cavour is the mainstay of Genoa's live alternative rock scene.

The two main **theatres** in Genoa are the Teatro della Corte, Via E.F. Duca d'Aosta, and the Teatro Duse, Via Bacigalupo, who advertise their performances on the same hoardings around town and sell tickets to both venues (ⓣ010.534.2200, ⓦwww.teatro-di-genova.it.net). The Teatro Carlo Felice in Piazza de Ferrari (ⓣ010.589.329, ⓦwww.carlofelice.it), is Genoa's main **opera**

house; its performances are often oversubscribed, but it's still worth an enquiry. Chamber-music concerts take place in some of Genoa's *palazzi* in summertime.

Listings

Airlines Alitalia, via XXII Ottobre 12 ☎1478.65.642; BA ☎1478.12.266; Delta ☎1678.64.114; Meridiana ☎0789.69.300.

Banks Plenty next to Stazione Principe in Piazza Acquaverde, on Via Balbi, and on Via XX Settembre.

Boats Alimar (☎010.256.775, ⓦwww.alimar.ge.it) and Cooperativa Battellieri (☎010.265.712, ⓦwww.battellierigenova.it) offer 45min tours by boat around the port, departing from alongside the aquarium (every 30min, daily 9.30am–5pm; €6). Alimar also do romantic tours by night (July & Aug daily 9pm). Both companies run plenty of summer excursions west and east along the Riviera (generally €8–13 one-way), departing either from the Aquarium or from Calata Zingari next to the Stazione Marittima. Routings along the eastern coast are also operated by Golfo Paradiso, based in Camogli (☎0185.772.091, ⓦwww.golfoparadiso.it), whose boats depart from Calata Mandraccio, just south of the Bigo. For whale-watching see p.121.

Bookshops Feltrinelli (ⓦwww.feltrinelli.it), Via XX Settembre 233, has some English-language paperbacks, but Di Stefano (ⓦwww.distefano.it), Porto Antico and Via Ceccardi 40r, has a better selection.

Car rental Europcar (airport ☎010.650.4881); Hertz, Via Casaregis 78 (☎010.570.2625; airport ☎010.651.2422); Maggiore, Corso Sardegna 275 (☎010.839.2153; airport ☎010.651.2467); Sixt, Via Montevideo 111r (☎010.315.166; airport ☎010.362.0846).

Consulates UK, Via di Francia 28 ☎010.416.958; USA, Via Dante 2 ☎010.584.492.

Doctor Call ☎010.354.022 for a doctor on call; First Aid emergency is on ☎113.

Ferries Any of the shipping agencies under the arcades along Piazza Caricamento can give current details of the long-distance ferries departing regularly to Bastia (Corsica), Olbia or Porto Torres (both Sardinia), Palermo (Sicily) and further afield to Barcelona, Tunis and around the Med. Main operators are: Grimaldi, Via Fieschi 17 (☎010.55091, ⓦwww.grimaldi.it); Moby, Via Milano 51 (☎010.253.4211, ⓦwww.mobylines.it); and Tirrenia, Ponte Colombo (☎010.254.3851).

Flight information ☎010.601.5410.

Football Genoa's premier side, Sampdoria, play at the Luigi Ferraris stadium, behind Stazione Brignole. They share the stadium with the city's other major team, Genoa – founded in 1893 as the Genoa Cricket and Athletic Club, originally for British expatriates only. Bus #12 from Piazza Caricamento, and bus #37 from Stazione Principe, both pass near the stadium; or you can walk it in 15–20min from Brignole.

Hospitals Ospedale Galliera, Mura delle Cappuccine 14 (☎010.56.321), is the city's most central hospital, situated just south of Piazza Vittoria, while Ospedale Evangelico, Corso Solferino 1a (☎010.55.221) is English-speaking. For an emergency ambulance, call ☎010.5551.

Internet access *Il Navigator* at Via Ravecca 25r (daily 9am–12.30pm & 2.30–7.30pm plus Fri 9pm–midnight) has several computers with fast ADSL connections as well as printing facilities.

Parking There are a dozen or so central car parks, all of which cost €16–20 per day; the largest is beneath Piazza della Vittoria (open 24hr). The old quarter is barred to traffic.

Pharmacies Ponte Monumentale, Via XX Settembre 115r (☎010.564.430), and Farmacia Pescetto, Via Balbi 185r (☎010.246.2697), are both English-speaking and open 24hr.

Police Carabinieri ☎112; Polizia ☎113; coastguard police ☎010.267.451. Genoa's police HQ is on ☎010.557.111.

Post office Via Dante 4 (Mon–Sat 8am–6.30pm; staff at window 15 speak English). Sub-post offices are at both train stations, open same hours.

Taxis Radio Taxi Genova ☎010.5966.

Train information ☎1478.88.088.

Around Genoa

Genoa has spilled over its old city limits to sprawl some 30km along the coast, with good bus and train connections to most of its outlying parts, including the popular parks and promenades at **Nervi** to the east and **Pegli** to the west. If you can, though, head north inland: the terraced hills are at their most verdant in spring, when the blossom is out and the vines are flourishing. Several small villages make good bases for scenic walking, or you can sit back and let the train take the strain with an hour-long ride on a clanky old narrow-gauge line from Genoa up to the rustic hill-village of **Casella**. See the box on p.128 for details of how to access hikes on the Alta Via long-distance mountain trail.

Nervi

Genoa's mainly residential suburbs extend east to **NERVI** (accessible by local train or bus #15 from Piazza Cavour), a neat resort spread around a small harbour with a handful of bars along the seafront. Much of the centre of Nervi is given over to exotic flowers and plants: walking left out of the train station brings you into the **Parco di Villa Gropallo**, with, alongside, the **Parco di Villa Serra**, which hosts an open-air cinema during August (information from the Genoa tourist office). The park slopes down to a romantic seafront promenade with a few bars and fish restaurants, while joining it to the east are the lavish rose-gardens of the **Parco di Villa Grimaldi**. Following the lovely **promenade** east around the cliffs of the Sant'Ilario headland brings you to the **Museo Civile G. Luxoro**, holding a small collection of furniture, textiles and clocks (Tues–Fri 9am–1pm, Sat 10am–1pm; €3.10). Semi-suburban though Nervi is, it still feels a long way from city life among the orange trees and the dreamy villa gardens.

Pegli

West of Genoa lies **PEGLI**, and the romantic **Villa Durazzo-Pallavicini**, which is set in lavish grounds landscaped in nineteenth-century fantasy style (gardens Tues–Sun: April–Sept 9am–7pm; Oct–March 9am–5pm; €3.50). The villa now houses the **Museo Civico di Archeologia Ligure** (Tues–Fri 9am–7pm, Sat & Sun 10am–7pm; €3.10), where items unearthed from cave burials in the hills along the west coast include the skeleton of a "Young Prince" with seashell crown and ceremonial dagger. You can get here by local train or slow buses #1, #2 or #3 from Piazza Caricamento.

Genoa's northern hinterland

Many Genoese escape the city in summer by heading for the hills. The Genoa **tourist office** has the useful *Antola and its Valleys* booklet in English, complete with itinerary suggestions, a map and details of walks. AMT **buses** from Genoa's Piazza della Vittoria serve all the larger villages. Look out wherever you are for breads and pastas made with local chestnut flour, as well as *scarpignon*, ravioli stuffed with a meat and walnut paste.

Narrow-gauge **trains** – worth taking just for the sake of it – leave roughly hourly from a station in Genoa's Piazza Manin, connected to Brignole by bus #33 and Principe by bus #34. They start off climbing through the Val Bisagno and coil northwards up to **CASELLA**, in a wooded dell at the foot of Monte Maggio (55min from Genoa). One-way fares to Casella are €1.80; the FGC trains (☎010.837.321) aren't covered by Genoa's normal bus tickets. Casella is the trailhead for a number of hiking routes in the picturesque **Valle Scrivia** (ⓦwww.altavallescrivia.it). If you show a train ticket at the *Cicli Cerati* office in front of Casella station, you can **rent a mountain-bike** for €4 per hour, or €10 per day (bookings on ☎010.967.7520). The town has a couple of **hotels**, of which the *Magenta* at Piazza XXV Aprile 20 is the better bet if you're there in summer (☎010.967.7113; ❸; July & Aug only); there are half-a-dozen **restaurants**, including *Camugin* (closed Mon) in front of the church, known for its fresh fish, and *Chiara* (closed Mon) with a wood-fired pizza oven.

Northeast of Genoa, buses follow the SS225 road over the Passo di Scoffera to little **Torriglia**, which offers the photogenic ruins of a medieval castle and

Walking the Alta Via

The **Alta Via dei Monti Liguri** is a long-distance high-level trail covering the length of Liguria, from Ventimiglia in the west all across the ridge-tops to Ceparana on the Tuscan border above La Spezia in the east, a total distance of some 440km. The mountains, which form the connection between the Alps and the Apennines, aren't high – rarely more than 1500m – and the scenic route, which makes full use of the many passes between peaks, is correspondingly easygoing. The whole thing, which would take weeks to complete in full, has been divided up into 43 stages of between about two and four hours each, making it easy to dip in and out. Trail support and maintenance is generally good, with *rifugi* dotted along the path and distinctive way-marks (red-white-red "AV" signs).

A sample walk starts from point 26 – **Crocetta d'Orero**, on the Genoa–Casella train line: heading east from Crocetta, an easy route covers 7.8km to point 27, **Colle di Creto** (2hr 30min, and served by Genoa buses), with a diversion along the way to a lovely botanical path in and around the deserted hamlet of **Ciaé**. Another sample walk, the very first stage of all, from **Ventimiglia** to La Colla, sidelining to **Dolceacqua**, is outlined on p.130. Unfortunately, access from the main coastal towns to most other parts of the Alta Via can be tricky, and requires juggling with route itineraries and bus timetables.

For information on the Alta Via, your best bet is the **Associazione Alta Via dei Monti Liguri**, based at the Centro Studi Unioncamere Liguri, Via San Lorenzo 15/1 in Genoa (℡010.247.1876, ℻010.247.1522, ⓦwww.lig.camcom.it), which pro-duces a full-colour wall-map of the route, along with detailed English descriptions and timings of all 43 stages (plus hotels and restaurants along the way). Books and an eight-pamphlet guide to the trail are on sale in bookshops. The same infor-mation is at ⓦwww.parks.it – click on "Grand Itineraries". **Club Alpino Italiano** offices in the major towns have information on *rifugi*, and the **Federazione Italiano Escursionismo** (FIE) publishes detailed guides to all the inland paths of Liguria.

plenty of hiking trails into the mountains of the **Parco Naturale dell'Antola** (ⓦwww.parks.it). The **tourist office** is at Via N.S. della Provvidenza 3 (Tues–Sun 9.30am–12.30pm & 3–6pm; ℡010.944.931), and the basic *Della Posta* **hotel** is at Via Matteotti 39 (℡010.944.050; ➋). From Torriglia, the SS45 heads northeast along the Val Trebbia through **Montebruno**, famed for its richly decorated fifteenth-century Santuario dell'Assunta (containing a Byzantine carving of the Madonna) and its mushroom-shaped chocolates called *funghetti*. Minor roads from Montebruno serve the mountain communi-ty of **FONTANIGORDA**, set further east amongst beech and chestnut woods and famous for its thirteen fountains. A scenic walking trail from here heads up and over the Passo di Esola to Rezzoáglio, which lies within striking distance of **Santo Stefano d'Aveto**. Fontanigorda's **hotels** include the good-value *La Fontanella*, Piazza Roma 7 (℡010.952.000, ℻010.542.825; ➋), with en-suite and shared-bath rooms, and the adequate *Augustus*, Via Fontana Vecchia 1 (℡010.952.014; ➌), both with **restaurants**.

Off to the west of Bolzaneto, a few kilometres north of Genoa, a minor road off the SS35 heads to the hilltop sanctuary of **Madonna della Guardia**, for centuries the prime pilgrimage spot for the Genoese. The SS35 continues north up the valley, with buses passing through tiny **Ronco Scrivia**, which has an attractive medieval bridge over the river with three pointed arches, and **Isole del Cantone**, where a minor road climbs right up a wild side-valley towards Vobbia; a few kilometres into the valley, high up on the left (north) side, you'll spot the towers of the **Castello della Pietra**, a thirteenth-century castle, which sits in a dramatic spot wedged between rock pinnacles above the thick forest; if you have the puff, climb the steep path up to it for spectacular valley views.

The Riviera di Ponente

The autostrada gives the most positive impression of the **Riviera di Ponente** ("Western Riviera"), the umbrella title for the stretch of Ligurian coast between the French border and Genoa. From its elevated viaducts, the marinas and resorts way below are mere specks in a stunning panorama of glittering sea and acres of glasshouses. If you exit the autostrada and venture down to the coastal road to see things close-up, you'll find that the Riviera towns are generally fairly functional places, occasionally sporting an attractive medieval quarter but always overflowing with hotels and apartment blocks. Yet these resorts have their good points – chiefly the sandy beaches, comparatively low prices and lack of pretentiousness.

Just about every settlement along this stretch of coast is a resort of some kind, either well-developed, family-targeted places like **Finale Ligure**, small, better-preserved villages like **Noli**, or grand old resorts like **San Remo**; the attractive medieval town of **Albenga** manages happily to fall somewhere in between. Some of these places – San Remo, for example, or the border town of **Ventimiglia** – also make good bases for travelling into the mountain areas behind the coast, where stone villages and agricultural communes reveal the more private side of the region. Walkers can explore sections of the Alta Via dei Monti Liguri (see box opposite) or loop through attractive and little-visited hill-towns like **Taggia** or **Dolceacqua**. In the large resort of **Alassio**, an organization of local hoteliers – the Consorzio Riviera Palmhotels, at Via Leonardo da Vinci 139 (℡0182.648.270, ℻600.961, 🌐www.palmhotels.it) – offers a booking service along the whole coast.

Ventimiglia and around

The first stop inside Italy, barely 6km east of the border, **VENTIMIGLIA** is a scruffy frontier town that enjoyed several centuries of minor prosperity courtesy of the constant border traffic. However, it's been experiencing hard times since the 1995 **Schengen** agreement, permitting unhindered passage between France and Italy, rendered the town's time-honoured role as customs post and refreshment point redundant. The town does make a good base for country **walks** though (see below), especially as the town's **hotels** offer considerably better value than those in other nearby resorts. The pleasant *Sea Gull*, Passeggiata Marconi 24 (℡0184.351.726, ℻231.217, 🌐www.seagullhotel.it; ❸), has its own patch of beach below the crumbling medieval quarter, while the *XX Settembre*, Via Roma 16 (℡0184.351.222; ❷), is the pick of the low-end choices. For **food**, you could try the *Usteria d'a Porta Marina* (closed Tues eve & Wed), overlooking the river at Via Trossarelli 22: the celebrated *branzino* (sea-bass) in local Rossese wine is expensive, but they have set menus for €18.

Mórtola Inferiore

From Via Cavour in front of Ventimiglia's train station, bus #1a heads west for 5km to the village of **MÓRTOLA INFERIORE**, famed for the spectacular hillside **Giardini Botanici "Hanbury"** (June–Sept Mon, Tues & Thurs–Sun

9am–7pm; Oct–May 10am–4pm; €6.20). These gardens were laid out in 1867 by Sir Thomas Hanbury, a London spice merchant, and are powerfully atmospheric, with hidden corners and pergola-covered walks tumbling down to the sea. A half-hour walk further west along the coast road – or a few minutes on bus #1a – is the frontier post. A scramble down the hillside brings you to the caves of **Balzi Rossi** (Tues–Sun 9am–7pm; free), where remains of prehistoric civilizations dating back to the Paleolithic age were discovered ; a small **Museo Preistorico** (same hours; €2) houses a collection of artefacts and crude fertility sculptures.

A walk to Dolceacqua

The area's best walk comprises Stage One of the **Alta Via dei Monti Liguri** hiking trail (see box on p.128). The ten-kilometre route (an easy 3hr) begins from Ventimiglia tourist office; walk east for a few minutes along Via Cavour, which becomes Corso Genova, and then duck north beneath the train tracks via an underpass which is marked with the first of the red-and-white "AV" waymarkers. From here, you climb out of the town through vineyards onto a ridge running between the valleys of the Roia and the Nervia, past the votive chapel of **San Giacomo**, through the ancient hamlet of **Ciaixe** and up to **La Colla**.

From La Colla, the trail continues along a side-path that takes you east down to the medieval riverside village of **DOLCEACQUA**, best-known for its excellent Rossese red wine and its olive oil. Piles of black olives crowd the village at harvest time, spread out on cloths on the ground prior to processing. The Nervia, crossed by an elegant 33-metre single-span medieval bridge, runs from the new part of town, or **borgo**, alongside the valley road, to the steep, stone alleyways of the older quarter, the **terra**, which are arranged in concentric circles around slopes topped by the blank-eyed ruins of a castle that once belonged to the Doria family. A theatre festival and concerts are staged here every summer (contact the tourist office for details, see below), and Dolceacqua is also the scene of a more ancient festival, rooted in fertility rites: on the Sunday nearest to January 20, a laurel tree hung with coloured Communion wafers is carried through the village as part of the procession of St Sebastian. For ideas on **walks** in the beautiful Upper Nervia Valley, ask at the **tourist office**, Via Patrioti Martiri 58 (daily 10am–1pm & 4–7pm; ☎0184.206.666). **Buses** run between Dolceacqua and Ventimiglia.

San Remo and around

Set on a broad sweeping bay between twin headlands, **SAN REMO** had its heyday as a classy resort in the sixty years or so up to the outbreak of World War II, when the Empress Maria Alexandrovna headed a substantial Russian community in the town (Tchaikovsky completed *Eugene Onegin* and wrote his Fourth Symphony in San Remo in 1878) and wealthy Europeans paraded on the Corso Imperatrice. Some of the grand hotels overlooking the sea, especially those near the train station, are now grimy and crumbling, but others in the ritzier western parts of town are still in pristine condition, opening their doors to Europe's blue-rinse nobility season after season. San Remo is blessed with the Riviera's most famous **casino** after the one in Monte Carlo, and it remains a showy, old-fashioned town, with a good deal of life.

San Remo's premier annual event is the **Festival della Canzone**, held every February, where Italy's finest pop performers compete for the giddy honour of representing the motherland in the Eurovision Song Contest. No less melodramatic is the **Campionato Mondiale di Fuochi d'Artificio**, or World

Fireworks Championship (W www.sanremo.it/fuochi), an annual fixture in late June and early July which sees lavish pyrotechnic displays bursting nightly over the port.

Arrival, information and accommodation

San Remo's ultra-modern new **train station** is east of the town centre on Corso Cavallotti. The **tourist office**, meanwhile, is at Largo Nuvoloni 1 (Mon–Sat 8am–7pm, Sun 9am–1pm; T 0184.571.571, W www.sanremonet.com and W www.apt.rivieradeifiori.it). Five minutes' walk east along Corso Matteotti on Piazza Colombo is the main **bus station**. Local Riviera Trasporti buses from here shuttle around town and up to Taggia (see p.133); one-hour tickets cost €0.85. **Boat** trips along the coast are run by Riviera Line, Molo di Levante 35 (March–Oct daily 10am & 3pm; lasts 1hr 30min; €11; T 0184.505.055, W www.rivieraline.it); they also do whale-watching excursions (see p.121). For **Internet** access, head to Mailboxes Etc at Corso Cavalotti 86, beside *Hotel Méditerranée* (Mon–Fri 9am–6.30pm, Sat 9am–1pm; €4 for 30min). For advice on **hiking**, visit the Club Alpino Italiano office, Piazza Cassini 13 (Tues & Fri 9.30am–10.30pm, Wed & Sat 6–7pm).

Finding **accommodation** should be no problem; note, though, the usual insistence on half- or full-board in high season. The *Royal Hotel*, Corso Imperatrice 80 (T 0184.5391, F 0184.661.445, W www.royalhotelsanremo.com; ➒), is probably the finest in Liguria, complete with a vast heated saltwater swimming pool set into its tropical garden and a resident orchestra to accompany afternoon tea and formal dinner. Cream of the four-star crop is the *Astoria West End*, Corso Matuzia 8 (T 0184.6554, F 0184.663.318, W www.astoriasanremo.it; ➐), dripping with *fin-de-siècle* elegance. The *Paradiso*, Via Roccasterone 12 (T 0184.571.211, F 0184.578.176, W www.paradisohotel.it; ➎), is in a quiet location above the town's bustle, with its own secluded garden and sunny, modern rooms, while nearer the station the *Alexander* is a comfortable option at Corso Garibaldi 123 (T 0184.504.591, F 0184.572.131; ➌). The *Maristella*, right by the sea at Corso dell'Imperatrice 77 (T 0184.667.881, F 0184.667.655, E hmcps@tin.it; ➋), is a friendly place with attractive Liberty-style decor. At the western end of the centre, on and between Corso Matteotti and Via Roma, you'll find a number of budget hotels, including the family-run *Al Dom* at Corso Mombello 13, with large and airy but noisy rooms (T 0184.501.460; E alxey@libero.it; ➋), and the welcoming *Matuzia* at Corso Matteotti 121, top floor (T & F 0184.577.070; ➋). There's a **campsite** west of town, *Villaggio dei Fiori*, Via Tiro a Volo 3 (T 0184.660.635, F 0184.662.377; open all year).

The Town

The tourist office is housed in the **Palazzo di Riviera**, a prime example of the kind of floral Liberty-style architecture that is arrayed all along the palm-lined **Corso Imperatrice** boulevard which stretches along the seafront west of the centre. Directly opposite the tourist office is an onion-domed **Russian Orthodox church** (Tues–Sun 9.30am–12.30pm & 3–6.30pm), built in the 1920s and more impressive on the outside than within. About 100m further east you'll come to San Remo's landmark **Casino**, a white Liberty-style palace with grand staircases and distinctive turrets that still stands as the epitome of the town's old-fashioned sense of monied leisure, playing an active part in its nightlife to this day (see overleaf). **Corso degli Inglesi** winds around and above the casino, home to dozens of villas in varying states of repair, including one close to the junction of Via Fratelli Asquascati complete with stained-glass irises and majolica tiles.

From the casino, the main **Corso Matteotti**, lined with cocktail bars, *gelaterie*, cinemas and clothes stores, heads east into the commercial centre of town. Lurid neon signs on side streets point to private clubs and by-the-hour hotels, all rubbing shoulders with a handful of expensive restaurants. The cross-street **Corso Mombello** connects south to the Giardini Veneto on the seafront alongside the harbour, and north to the main central square **Piazza Eroi Sanremesi**. This huge, rambling space is partly taken up by market-stalls and terrace cafés, and partly backs onto the Gothic **Cattedrale di San Siro** (daily 7–11.15am & 3–6pm), which features unusual twelfth-century bas reliefs above its side doors and a processional black crucifix within. A short way east of the cathedral, at Corso Matteotti 143, is the impressive Renaissance Palazzo Borea d'Olmo, still owned by the family of the same name and now housing the **Museo Civico** (Tues–Sat 9am–noon & 3–6pm; €2), but its array of local finds and paintings is less memorable than the sumptuous frescoed interior. **Piazza Colombo** is just east of the museum, with Via Asquasciati heading down to the sea. If you follow the harbourside promenade east for 1km, you'll come to the marina and – on the north side of the tracks – the **Giardino Ormond** (daily 9am–7pm), which is filled with date-palms, yuccas, olive-trees, jacaranda, bougainvillea and even a grand cedar of Lebanon.

San Remo's most fascinating quarter – which stands in stark contrast to the glamour and bustle of the seafront districts – is its **old town**, accessible up steep lanes north of Piazza Eroi Sanremesi and Piazza Cassini. Known as **La Pigna** or the "Pine-Cone", its kasbah-like arched passageways and alleys leading nowhere come as quite a surprise after the busy, modern streets below. From the gardens at the highest peak you get excellent views across the whole of the town and surrounding countryside.

If you can drag yourself out of bed early enough, San Remo offers one of the liveliest and most engaging spectacles on the Riviera: the **wholesale flower market** in Armea, 4km east of town (Mon–Fri 4am–8am). You'll know when you're approaching by the sight of waiters running around with trays of espresso, and the woven boxes for flowers attached to the vans and Vespas outside. Some eighty tonnes of flowers a day are shipped out of here, around Italy and the world. The market itself is strictly for trade, but no one minds bystanders as long as they don't get in the way.

Eating, drinking and nightlife

San Remo is well served for **restaurants**, most of which offer the local speciality of *sardenàira*, a kind of cheese-less pizza topped with tomatoes, olives, capers, garlic and fresh oregano. Piazza Eroi Sanremesi is ringed by pizzeria-restaurants, most with decent tourist menus; best is *Graziella* (closed Mon). Two excellent-value choices in the centre are *Piccolo Mondo*, Via Piave 7 (☎0184.509.012; closed Sun & Mon), a cosy little trattoria serving choice Ligurian dishes on an alley off Corso Matteotti, and the bright, modern *Don Fernando* at Via Bixio 77 (closed Mon) where enormous pans of fresh pasta and the sauce of your choice are brought to your table. *Vittorio*, round the corner at Piazza Bresca 16 (☎0184.501.924; closed Wed), is an excellent place for mid-price fish and seafood. *Bagatto*, Corso Matteotti 145 (☎0184.531.925; closed Sun & July), is the easiest-going of San Remo's many formal restaurants, serving top-quality local cuisine for around €37, excluding wine.

For **nightlife**, San Remo's famous **Casino** comes out tops every time (daily 2.30pm–3am). Admission is free to the slot machines, but not to the evocative Belle Époque gaming rooms (Mon–Thurs €2.58, Fri–Sun €7.75). The dress-code is jacket and tie for both American and French gaming rooms, but you can get away with jeans and sneakers in the slot machine area. It's worth the effort to get in, even if you then eschew the James Bondery downstairs in favour of a quiet evening on the roof garden (where drinks aren't too expensive). Elsewhere around town, there's no shortage of **clubs** and **bars**, and in summer there are open-air jazz, blues and folk **concerts** around the harbour and in the various parks.

The Valle Argentina

The Valle Argentina ("Silver Valley") heads inland from the bustling seaside resort of **Arma di Taggia**, 6km east of San Remo. Sleepy, crumbling **TAGGIA**, 3km north, is known for its sixteen-arched **Romanesque bridge**, the *taggiasca* black olive that is famed for giving top-quality oil, and a collection of work by Ligurian artists in the black-and-white stone convent church of **San Domenico** just outside the old walls (daily 9am–noon & 3–5pm; donations). If you can, time a visit for the third Sunday in July, when the ancient *festa* of the Magdalene culminates in a "Dance of Death" performed by two men, traditionally from the same two families, accompanied by the local brass and woodwind band.

Some 25km further up the valley is the tiny village of **TRIORA**. The trip here from San Remo (4 services daily from the main bus station) is worth doing in its own right, the bus wending its way past small settlements with ancient bridges and farms linked to the main road across the valley by a rope and pulley system. Triora is within sight of Monte Pietradura, which stays snowcapped until April. In 1588, after an unexpected famine, two hundred women in this isolated community were denounced by the Inquisition as **witches**: thirty were tortured, fourteen were burned at the stake, and one woman committed suicide before she could be executed. Documents from the trial are preserved in the **Museo Etnografico** in the village (May–Dec Mon–Sat 3–6.30pm, Sun 10.30am–noon & 3–6pm; Jan–April Sun only; €1.03), and a commemorative plaque adorns the overgrown Cabotina just outside the village, supposed scene of the witches' gatherings. Also worth seeking out is the celebrated Sienese painter Taddeo di Bartolo's *Baptism of Christ* (1397), hung in the baptistry of the Romanesque-Gothic **Collegiata** church. Triora is known for its flat bread, *Pane di Triora*, and the village has a single **hotel**, the peaceful *Colombo d'Oro*, Corso Italia 66 (☎0184.94.051, ⓕ0184 .94.089; ➋), converted from an old monastery.

From San Remo to Genoa

There's not a great deal to divert you on the first stretch of coast east of San Remo as far as Albenga. This stretch is shoulder-to-shoulder beach resorts, which offer little diversity and stay unrelentingly busy all summer long (when it can be hard to find accommodation, despite the hundreds of hotels), although the crush does ease a bit out of season.

Some 30km east of San Remo is the provincial capital of **IMPERIA**, formed in 1923 when Mussolini linked twin townships on either side of the River Impero. Imposing **Porto Maurizio**, on the western bank, is the more attractive of the two, ascending the hillside in a series of zigzags from a marina and small beach. Its stepped old quarter is dominated by a massive late-eighteenth-century cathedral and a series of Baroque churches and elegant villas. Quieter **Oneglia**, 2km east, is still very much wedded to the sea, with an active population of fisherfolk; just behind its station at Via Garessio 13 is the **Museo dell'Olivo**, paid for by the town's leading olive-oil dynasty, the Fratelli Carli (Mon–Sat 9am–noon & 3–6.30pm; free; ⓦ www.museodellolivo.com), housing modern displays devoted to the history of Liguria's green nectar. The **tourist office** is at Viale Matteotti 37 in Porto Maurizio (Mon–Sat 8am–7pm; ℡0183.660.140), where you'll also find the comfortable **hotels** *Croce di Malta*, overlooking the old harbour at Via Scarincio 148 (℡0183.667.020, ℉0183.63.687, ⓦwww.hotelcrocedimalta.com; ❹), and *Ambra*, on Via Rambaldo 9 (℡0183.63.715; ❷).

East of Imperia, olive plantations take over from flowers along what has been dubbed the **Riviera dei Olivi**. Two big beach resorts – Diano Marina and **ALASSIO**, the latter with a spectacular four-kilometre fine-sand beach and motorboat trips out to the Isola Gallinara island nature reserve – bookend a couple of slightly less frenetic spots: **Cervo** is a picturesque spiral of cottages that primps and preens itself for the tourist trade, while **LAIGUEGLIA**, a quiet ex-fishing port with a couple of porticoed streets to wander, offers a more palatable slice of beach life than its big-time neighbours.

A walk up the steps from the junction of Via Mimosa and the main Via Roma in Laigueglia takes you away from the coast through a cluster of holiday homes to the old **Roman road** near the top of the hill. From here, follow the *strada privata* into the woods and take the signposted path for the ruins of the **Castello di Andora** and what is held to be the best Romanesque church on the Riviera (a 45min walk). Even if you never get to the church and castle, the walk along mule tracks between olive groves and woods is one of the most appealing parts of this bit of coast, with plenty of shaded places to dream away the afternoon. From the castle you can either backtrack or walk on through the outskirts of the village of **Andora** to its train station.

Albenga

Beyond Alassio the terrain grows more mountainous, and the rail line and road stick close to the sea for the 8km journey to the small market town of **ALBENGA**. With silting up of the river estuary, Albenga long ago lost its port and merits a visit these days for its pleasingly business-like old quarter, still within medieval walls. The **train station** is 800m east of the old town via the twin parallel boulevards of Viale dei Mille and Viale Martiri della Libertà; the latter leads to the **tourist office** at no. 1 (Mon–Sat 9am–12.30pm & 3–6.30pm, Sun 9am–noon; ℡0182.558.444, ⓦwww.inforiviera.it), and on to **Piazza San Michele** at the heart of the old town. This small square is dominated by the elegant **cathedral**, the main part of which was built in the eleventh century and enlarged in the early fourteenth. Diagonally opposite in the Torre Comunale is the **Museo Civico Ingauno** (Tues–Sun 10am–noon & 3–6pm; €1.55), displaying interesting ancient artefacts and providing access to Albenga's big draw, the **Baptistry**. This ingenious building went up alongside the cathedral in the fifth century, and combines an unusual ten-sided exterior with a more orthodox octagonal interior. Inside are fragmentary mosaics showing the Apostles represented by twelve doves.

Behind the Baptistry to the north, the archbishop's palace houses the diverting **Museo Diocesano** (Tues–Sun 10am–noon & 3–6pm; donations). Taking pride of place are the remains of the fifteenth-century frescoes that adorned what used to be a chapel and the bishop's own bedchamber (the latter decorated by Provencal artists with a mixture of sombre and bright flower patterns to represent night and day). A few metres west, where Via Medaglie d'Oro crosses Via Ricci, is the thirteenth-century **Loggia dei Quattro Canti**, marking the town centre of Roman Albingaunum. Some 500m north of here, beyond Piazza Garibaldi and along Viale Pontelungo, you'll find the odd sight of an elegant, arched 150m bridge spanning nothing much: the **Pontelungo** was built here in the twelfth century to cross the river, which shifted course soon afterwards.

One of the cheapest **hotels** in the town is the pleasant, 1930-style *Italia*, Viale Martiri della Libertà 8 (℡0182.50.405, ℻0182.570.273; faustocarrara@libero.it; ❷), with only shared-bath rooms. Alternatively, down on the seafront *Sole Mare*, Lungomare Colombo 15 (℡0182.51.817, ℻0182.52.752; ❹), has a range of rooms. The *Lungomare* **campsite** is at the mouth of the river off Strada Vicinale Avarenna (℡0182.51.449, ℻0182.52.525; open all year). Albenga's least expensive **restaurants** are off Via Medaglie d'Oro on the alley Via Torlaro. *Da Puppo*, a characterful little place with a wood-burning pizza oven and good *farinata* is at no. 20, while at no. 13 is *Il Vecchio Mulino* (closed Thurs) serving basic trattoria food from €5. Pricey *Antica Osteria dei Leoni*, behind the Baptistry at Via Lengueglia 49 (closed Mon), has a good range of local dishes, while the popular *Babette*, Viale Pontelungo 26 (closed Mon & Tues), hosts Greek-, French- and Italian-themed dinners.

The caves of Toirano

Nurseries of artichokes and petunias, interspersed with garden centres and caravan sites, line the coast between Albenga and the town of **Borghetto Santo Spirito**, transfer point for buses a few kilometres inland to the spectacular caves of **TOIRANO**, set halfway up a rocky hillside outside the well-preserved medieval village centre. There are three main cave complexes (daily: July & Aug 9am–12.30pm & 3–6pm; rest of year 9–11.30am & 2.30–5.30pm; €7.75; Ⓦwww.toirano.it). The stalactite-adorned **Grotta della Bàsura** – dialect for "The Witch's Cave" – was the home of Stone Age inhabitants some eighty thousand years ago. These early troglodytes apparently shared their cave-dwellings with local bears: there's a mass of bear bones in the underground Bear Cemetery, and dozens of prehistoric foot- and pawprints left in what was once mud. A path leads on to the **Grotta di Santa Lucia**, containing remarkable stalagmite and stalactite formations, with a natural spring which was dedicated in the Middle Ages to St Lucy, patron saint of eyesight, after several miraculous cures were effected here. Further on, guided tours around **Grotta del Colombo** lead you through the beautiful caverns formed in the limestone over millions of years by the action of water.

Finale Ligure

Busy **FINALE LIGURE** is overtly committed to tourism, yet manages to remain attractive. The majority of tourists are Italian families; only around 10pm on summer nights does the place come alive, as people pack the outdoor restaurants, seafront fairground and open-air cinema, while an extended *passeggiata* fills the promenade and the old alleys. There are three parts to the town. **Finalmarina** is the main bit, with the **train station** at its western end, a good pebbly beach, a promenade lined with palms, and narrow shopping streets set back from the seafront that hold the **tourist office** at Via San Pietro 14 (Mon–Sat 9am–12.30pm & 3.30–7pm, Sun 9am–noon; ℡019.681.019, Ⓦwww.inforiviera.it). The bars in the vicinity of Piazza Vittorio Emanuele II and the adjoining Piazza di Spagna, the main public space in the centre of this spread-out resort, are the points to which everyone eventually gravitates. **Finalpia** is a small district five minutes' walk to the east on the other side of the River Sciusa focused around the twelfth-century church of Santa Maria di Pia (rebuilt in florid early-eighteenth-century style) and its adjacent sixteenth-century cloistered abbey. **Finalborgo** is a medieval walled quarter set on a slight hill 2km inland from Finalmarina and overlooked by bare rock-faces that are a favourite with free climbers, who gather at *Bar Gelateria Centrale* in Finalborgo's Piazza Garibaldi at weekends. The area's wider fame comes from the **Grotte delle Arene Candide**, among Europe's most important caves for prehistoric remains; they're closed for excavation, but some finds are on display at the **Museo Civico** in Finalborgo's church of Santa Caterina (July & Aug Tues–Sun 10am–noon & 4–7pm; rest of year Tues–Sun 10am–noon & 2.30–5pm; €3). The same church hosts an interesting bric-à-brac and antiques **market** on the first weekend of each month during summer.

In high season virtually all the hotels insist on full pension, and you'd do better staying up the coast at Noli (see below), unless you opt for the excellent *Castello Vuillermin* HI **hostel** which occupies an old castle high above the train station at Via Caviglia 46 and has marvellous views out to sea (☎019.690.515, ⓦwww.hostelfinaleligure.com; €11; mid-March to mid-Oct). *Eurocamping* is a well-run riverside **campsite** at Via Calvisio 37 in Finalpia (☎019.601.240; April–Sept). The best places **to eat** need some hunting out. *Da Tonino*, Via Bolla 5, has outside seating and good pizzas. *Gabbri*, next to the church of San Giovanni Battisti at Via Pollupice 1 (closed Thurs), is a friendly trattoria whose atmosphere and reasonably priced menu feel a million miles away from the brash seafront pizza parlours. Up in Finalborgo *Ai Torchi*, Via dell'Annunziata 12 (☎019.690.531; closed Tues & Jan; Aug open daily), occupies an ancient olive-oil factory and serves expensive pasta and fish dishes with care and some style.

The tourist office has information on picturesque inland **walks**, the **Sentieri Parlanti**, which zigzag across the hills past the excellent mid-priced *Osteria La Briga* restaurant (☎019.698.579; closed Tues & Wed and in winter), where you can fill up on *ortica* (nettle) and *tartufo nero* (black truffle) lasagne. You can rent **mountain-bikes** on Via Brunenghi in Finalborgo – from Raceware at no. 124, and R.C. Bike at no. 65.

Noli

The Via Aurelia heads northeast from Finale Ligure past the small Capo di Noli, where the sea is inviting and the inlets are accessible from the road. **NOLI**'s beaches aren't great but otherwise this is the nicest resort along this part of the Riviera, topped by a castle whose battlements march down the hill to meet the walls of the small but pretty old town. Aside from half-a-dozen medieval towers, Noli's grid of old streets hides the majestic Romanesque church of **San Paragorio** near the train station, notable for its crypt, frescoes, a thirteenth-century bishop's throne of inlaid wood kept behind glass in an interior chapel, and a twelfth-century *Volto Santo* (True Likeness of Christ) similar to the one at Lucca in Tuscany (see p.530). The **tourist office** faces the sea at Corso Italia 8 (Mon–Sat 9am–noon & 3.30–6.30pm, Sun 9am–noon; ☎019.749.9003), and a number of the town's thirteenth-century palaces have been converted into **hotels**, most of which have popular **restaurants** attached. *Miramare*, Corso Italia 2 (☎019.748.926; ❹), is top choice, an old fortress updated with all mod cons. *Albergo Triestina*, down a medieval street off the seafront at Via da Noli 16 (☎019.748.024; ❹), offers a personal, welcoming ambience, while *Da Ines* at Via Vignolo 1 (☎019.748.5428, Ⓕ019.748.086; ❸) has pleasant, well-equipped rooms, and is an especially convivial place to eat. The **beaches** are broad and sandy some 3km further up the coast at **SPOTORNO**, but this once-tranquil little place has lost just about all of the character it could claim in 1926, when D.H. Lawrence holed up there to write *Lady Chatterley's Lover*.

Savona

First impressions of **SAVONA**, 17km northeast of Noli, aren't up to much: it's a functional city much rebuilt after a hammering in World War II. However, its port infrastructure and ugly outskirts hide a picturesque **medieval centre** worth exploring – especially when it's taken over on summer Saturdays by a huge antiques and bric-à-brac market. The town's main claim to fame is as the *Città dei Papi*, City of Popes: local boy Francesco Della Rovere became **Pope Sixtus IV** in 1471, and had a large private chapel built within the Vatican (named the Sistine Chapel after himself), and his nephew Giuliano, who became **Pope Julius II** in 1503, commissioned Michelangelo to decorate the chapel's ceiling.

Savona lies at the southern end of a time-honoured route over the mountains, and the town's links with Turin are maintained to this day via the autostrada and main train line. The **train station** is in the west of town, across the River Letimbro from the old quarter which nestles in the curve of the old port and bristles with medieval towers. Via Don Minzoni, to the left of the station as you walk out, heads east across the river to the parks of Piazza del Popolo, from where the main **Via Paleocapa**, lined with Art Nouveau arcades, continues east to the port. Savona's **tourist office** is at Corso Italia 157r (summer Mon–Sat 9.30am–1pm & 3–6.30pm, Sun 9.30am–1pm; winter Tues–Sat 9.30am–1pm & 3–6.30pm; ☎019.840.2321). The Dominican church of San Giovanni marks the point where Via Pia heads south into the atmospheric old quarter, which is dominated by the **Duomo** and its attached **Cappella Sistina**, a Baroque extravaganza commissioned by Sixtus IV in memory of his parents.

Above the old town stands the huge **Priamàr** fortress, built in 1528 by the Genoese as a sign of their superiority over the defeated Savonese. These days it houses three major museums. The interesting **Museo d'Arte Sandro Pertini** (Mon–Sat 8.30am–1pm), displaying modern Italian art collected by Pertini, one-time President of Italy, and the **Museo Renata Cuneo** (currently closed for renovation) housing contemporary sculpture by Cuneo, a Savona local, share a joint €2.07 admission ticket. Completing the array is the **Museo Civico** (Tues–Sat 10am–noon & 3–5pm, Sun 3–5pm; €2.07), which has Greek and Etruscan bits and bobs along with some Islamic and Byzantine ceramics. Until recently, the **Pinacoteca Civica** was also housed here, but its collection – mostly mediocre Baroque paintings overshadowed by a striking Renaissance *Crucifixion* by Donato de' Bardi – is currently being transferred to Palazzo Gavotti on Piazza Chabrol and is due to reopen in its new home in early 2003 – ask at the tourist office for details.

There are no **hotels** in the old town, but the decent *Riviera Suisse*, Via Paleocapa 24 (☎019.850.853, ℱ019.853.435; ❹), is very close by. The more convenient and enticing of Savona's two HI **hostels** is *Fortezza del Priamar* in the old fortress (☎ & ℱ019.812.653, ℮priamarhostel@iol.it; €11.36; bus #2). The best **campsite** is *Buggi*, at Via N.S. del Monte 15 (☎019.804.573; open all year).

The Riviera di Levante

The glorious stretch of coast **east from Genoa**, dubbed the **Riviera di Levante**, is not the place to come for a relaxing beach holiday. As ever, visiting out of season eases the claustrophobia, but in summer, catching some rays in the most popular resort towns involves fighting for a small piece of pebble beach or concrete jetty (the beaches aren't as good as those on the other side of Genoa), while sitting in the waterfront restaurants and cafés means running the gauntlet of some highly competitive posing. Ports that once eked a living from fishing and coral diving have been transformed by a solid thirty years of tourism; the coastline is still wild and extremely beautiful in parts, but predictably the sense of remoteness has gone. It's pointless protesting against the stranglehold that tourism has: once you accept that wandering around ex-fishing villages with hordes of others is inevitable, you can appreciate the attractions this area still holds.

Away from the resorts, the cliffs and bays are covered with pine and olive trees, best seen from the vantage points along the footpaths criss-crossing the headland of the **Monte di Portofino**. The harbour towns of **Camogli** on the **Golfo Paradiso** and **Santa Margherita Ligure** on the Golfo Tigullio are favourite subjects for arty picture postcards, while super-chic **Portofino** on the southern tip of the headland effortlessly pulls in the international jetset. More digestible nightlife is better served at big, feisty resorts such as **Rapallo**. Further east, the main road heads inland, bypassing the spectacular **Cinque Terre** and joining the train line at the port of **La Spezia**, which stands at the head of the idyllic Golfo dei Poeti and gives access to romantic waterside villages such as **Portovénere**. From La Spezia, there's easy access by road or rail to Pisa or Parma, and by sea to Corsica.

Recco

Allied bombing in 1944 to cut the coastal rail line virtually destroyed **RECCO** – at the head of the gulf 18km east of Genoa – and the town that has sprung up in its place is unremarkable but for its gastronomy. People come here specifically to eat at some of the best **restaurants** in Liguria. If your wallet is fat, book a table at either *Da-ö Vittorió*, Via Roma 160 (℡0185.74.029, ℱ0185.723.605; ❺; closed Thurs), a renovated century-old building 500m north of the town centre, or the modern villa-style *Manuelina*, Via Roma 300 (℡0185.74.128, ℱ0185.721.095, ✉manuelina@manuelina.it; ❻; closed Wed), some 300m further north set in its own garden; both establishments are also hotels. They are acclaimed for their *focaccia al formaggio* (Recco's speciality), *minestrone alla genovese* and local *troffiette recchelline* (pasta with green beans, potatoes and pesto).

Camogli

CAMOGLI – 2km southeast of Recco – was the "saltiest, roughest, most piratical little place", according to Dickens when he visited in 1884. It's had its rough edges knocked off since then, and is one of the most attractive small resorts along this stretch of the coast, well connected by road, rail and boat. The town's name, a contraction of *Casa Mogli* (House of Wives), comes from the days when voyages lasted for years and the women ran the port while the men were away. In its day, Camogli supported a huge fleet of 700 vessels, which once saw off Napoleon. The town declined in the age of steam, but the crumbling arcades by the harbour and the dark flight of steps into the town centre still have the "smell of fish, and seaweed, and old rope" that Dickens relished.

The **train station** is just south of the beach; turn right towards the centre for the small **tourist office**, 50m north at Via XX Settembre 33 (Mon–Sat 8.30am–noon & 3–7pm, Sun 9am–1pm; ℡0185.771.066, ⊕www.camogli.it). Summer **boats** shuttle over from Genoa's Porto Antico in an hour (€8), using

Open or wrapped?

If you're visiting Camogli on the second Sunday in May, you won't be able to miss the **Sagra del Pesce**, preceded on the Saturday night by fireworks and a huge bonfire. This generous – and smelly – event has its origins in celebrating the munificence of the sea and retains its ancient resonance for Camogli's fisherfolk even today. Thousands of fish are plucked fresh from the waves, flipped into a giant frying-pan set up on the harbourfront and distributed free of charge to all and sundry as a demonstration of the sea's abundance (and in the hope for its continuation). In recent years the event has been beset by quibbles: bureaucrats have suggested that the frying-pan – some five metres across – is a health hazard, and there have even been allegations that frozen fish is defrosted out at sea and then passed off as fresh. For all that, local enthusiasm for the festival hasn't waned one bit.

the old harbour on the north side of town, separated from the unimpressive pebble beach to the south by a promontory occupied by the medieval **Castello della Dragonara**. You can wander up through the alleyways to the castle, though the aquarium it houses is currently closed for renovation.

The best **hotel** is the lavish *Cenobio dei Dogi*, in its own waterfront park at Via Cuneo 34 (℡0185.7241, ℻0185.772.796; ❽); once the summer palace of Genoa's doges, it boasts its own beach, pool, tennis courts, restaurants and tasteful guest rooms. *La Camogliese*, Via Garibaldi 55 (℡0185.771.402, ℻0185.774.024; ❸), is a friendly spot excellently situated by the water (take the steps down opposite the station); it has pleasant rooms and they don't insist on full pension. Otherwise, try the spartan *Selene*, Via Cuneo 15 (℡0185.770.149, ℻0185.770.195; ❷). The *Camogliese* hotel has a quality mid-priced **restaurant** (closed Wed in winter). The much pricier *Vento Ariel* on the harbourfront (℡0185.771.080; closed Wed) serves only fish brought that day directly from the nets into the kitchen. Away from the sea, *Don Ricardo* on Salita Priaro (the flight of steps up from the fishing harbour) does affordable Mexican food, and *Revello* is a fine bakery at Via Garibaldi 183.

Fish aside, Camogli makes its living from **ferries** operated by Golfo Paradiso, Via Scalo 3 (℡0185.772.091, Ⓦwww.golfoparadiso.it). Departures to tranquil **Punta Chiappa**, ideal for a spot of swimming and basking in the sun, and **San Fruttuoso** (see below), are most frequent (May–Sept at least hourly; Oct–April 3 weekdays, hourly at weekends; around €8 return), with a special **night excursion** offering the most romantic views of the gulf plus three hours in San Fruttuoso for dinner or a stroll (July & Aug 3 weekly; €9 return). There are also boats east to the **Cinque Terre** (July–Sept 2–4 weekly; €19 return), which stop beforehand at **Portofino** and continue to **Portovénere**, as well as plenty more west to **Recco** and **Genoa** (€8 return).

San Fruttuoso

The enchanting thousand-year-old abbey of **SAN FRUTTUOSO** is one of the principal draws along this stretch of the Riviera, occupying a picturesque little bay at the southern foot of Monte di Portofino. The only way to get there is **on foot** (see p.141) or **by boat**: dozens shuttle backwards and forwards from practically every harbour along the coast. On summer weekends, the tiny harbour and church may be uncomfortably crowded. Out of season, however (or at twilight, courtesy of the occasional night cruises), San Fruttuoso is peaceful and an excellent place for doing very little; while wandering through the abbey, the only sound is the waves on the beach outside.

The **Abbazia di San Fruttuoso** (June–Sept Tues–Sun 10am–6pm; March–May & Oct Tues–Sun 10am–4pm; Dec–Feb Sat & Sun 10am–4pm, closed Nov; €3.10) was originally built to house the relics of the third-century martyr St Fructuosus, which were brought here from Spain after the Moorish invasion in 711. It was rebuilt in 984 with an unusual Byzantine-style cupola and distinctive waterside arches. In later centuries it became a Benedictine abbey which exerted a sizeable degree of control over the surrounding countryside. The Doria family took over in the sixteenth century and added the defensive **Torre dei Doria** nearby. Find a quiet moment, if you can, to explore the small, elegant church, with its compact little cloister and half-dozen Doria tombs. Off the headland, a 1954 bronze statue known as the **Cristo degli Abissi** (Christ of the Depths) rests eight fathoms down on the seabed, to honour the memory of divers who have lost their lives at sea and to protect those still working beneath the waves.

There's a handful of simple **restaurants** on San Fruttuoso's beach serving fish and steamed mussels, and one place **to stay** – the tiny *Da Giovanni* (☎0185.770.047; ❹).

Portofino and the Golfo del Tigullio

Matching the Golfo Paradiso on the western side of the Monte di Portofino headland is the **Golfo del Tigullio** on the eastern side, a broad arc of a bay named after the local Tigullian tribe of pre-Roman antiquity. The gulf stretches 28km from the rocks and inlets around the millionaire's playground of **Portofino** and its friendlier neighbour **Santa Margherita Ligure** to head east along a dramatically beautiful – and densely touristed – coastline. In summer the main focus is the large resort of **Rapallo**.

The Consorzio Portofino Coast runs an **information** and hotel-booking service for the area, based at Via Lamarmora 17/6, Rapallo (☎0185.270.222, ℗0185.230.054, ⓦwww.portofinocoast.it). The Italian tourist office's website for the area is ⓦwww.apttigullio.liguria.it.

Portofino

There's no escaping the beauty of **PORTOFINO**, tucked into a protected inlet surrounded by lush cypress- and olive-clad slopes, yet it manages to be both attractive and off-putting at the same time. The village has been effortlessly drawing in Europe's jetset royals, filmstars and other glitterati since the *dolce vita* days of Bogart and Bacall, Sophia Loren, Burton and Taylor, and Princess Grace, all of whom holidayed here – its snob rating remains impeccable. The village lies at the end of a narrow and treacherously winding road 5km south from Santa Margherita, but thanks to continuous traffic the bus journey can take longer than the boats that shuttle regularly to and from all nearby ports. Once you've arrived and surveyed the expensive restaurants and lace shops by the water, there's not much to do other than watch everyone else do the same; bear in mind, though, that a couple of peaceful harbourside beers will leave you little change from €20.

To get a sense of Portofino's idyllic setting follow the footpath which heads south from the harbour up onto the headland. Five minutes from the village is the church of **San Giorgio**, said to contain relics of St George. A further ten minutes up is the **Castello Brown** – currently closed for restoration – but you can look down on pint-sized Portofino from the terrace outside. The scenic path continues south for a quarter-hour down to the **Faro** (lighthouse) on the very tip of the promontory. The only way back is up the same path. Northwest

The Portofino headland – protected as the Parco Naturale Regionale di Portofino (ⓦwww.parks.it) and encircled by cliffs and small coves – is one of the most rewarding areas for **walking** on the Riviera coast. At 612m, **Monte di Portofino** is high enough to be interesting but not so high as to demand any specialist hiking prowess. The trails cross slopes of wild thyme, pine and holm oak, enveloped in summer in the constant whirring of cicadas. From the summit, the view over successive headlands is breathtaking. Not many people walk these marked paths, maybe because their early stages are fairly steep – but they aren't particularly strenuous, levelling off later and with plenty of places to stop.

One of the best trails skirts the whole headland, beginning in Camogli, on the western side of the promontory. The path rises gently for 1km south to **San Rocco** (221m), then follows the coast south to a viewpoint above Punta Chiappa, before swinging east to the scenic **Passo del Bacio** (200m), rising to a ridge-top and then descending gently through the olive-trees and palms to **San Fruttuoso** (3hr from Camogli). It continues east over a little headland and onto the wild and beautiful cliff-tops above **Punta Carega**, before passing through the hamlets of Prato, Olmi (279m) and Cappelletta and down steps to **Portofino** (4hr 30min from Camogli).

There are plenty of alternative routes. About 1km south of San Rocco, an easier path forks inland up to **Portofino Vetta** and **Pietre Strette** (452m), before loading down again through the foliage to San Fruttuoso (2hr 30min from Camogli). **Ruta** is a small village 250m up on the north side of Monte di Portofino, served by buses from Camogli, Santa Margherita and Rapallo; a peaceful, little-trod trail from Ruta heads up to the summit of the mountain (2hr), or diverts partway along to take you across country to Olmi and on to Portofino (2hr 30min from Ruta).

from the village, steeply stepped paths head through vineyards and orchards to Olmi and on to San Fruttuoso (see box above for more). The best sandy **beach** is the sparkling cove at **Paraggi**, 3km north of Portofino on the corniche road (buses will stop on request) – not exactly remote, but less formal than Portofino, with a couple of bars set back from the water.

The **tourist office** is at Via Roma 35 (summer daily 10.30am–1.30pm & 2.30–7.30pm; winter Tues–Sun 10.30am–1.30pm & 2–5.30pm; ☏0185.269.024). **Accommodation** is absurdly expensive year-round. The *Eden* stands within its own delightful gardens in the centre at Vico Dritto 8 (☏0185.269.091, ⓕ0185.269.047, ⓦwww.hoteledenportofino.com; ❼), but if money is no object, you'll want to shell out at the *Splendido*, Viale Baratta 16 (☏0185.269.551, ⓕ0185.267.806, ⓔsplendido.orient-express.com; ❾) – prices are astronomical, but this is held to be one of Italy's best hotels. **Eating out**, whether at the hotels or, for example, at the super-chic seafood restaurant *Il Pitosforo* on the harbour (☏0185.269.020; closed Mon & Tues), which in summer opens only in the evening, is best left to those who don't read their credit-card statements.

Santa Margherita Ligure

SANTA MARGHERITA LIGURE is a thoroughly attractive, palm-laden small resort tucked into an inlet, replete with grand hotels, garden villas and views of the glittering bay. In the daytime, trendy young Italians cruise the streets or whizz around the harbour on jetskis, while the rest of the family sunbathes or crams the *gelaterie*. Santa Margherita is cheaper to stay in than Portofino and less crowded than Rapallo, and makes a good base both for taking boats and trains up and down the coast and for exploring the countryside on foot. The **train station**

Boats on the Tigullio coast

Dozens of **boats** serve all points on the Tigullio coast, run by companies based in Genoa (see p.126), Camogli (see p.139) and La Spezia (see p.152), along with the main local operator – Servizio Marittimo del Tigullio, Via Palestro 8/1b, Santa Margherita (℡0185.284.670, Ⓦwww.traghettiportofino.it). You should **book ahead** to guarantee a place in high summer.

The most popular line shuttles to and fro between **Rapallo**, **Santa Margherita**, **Portofino** and **San Fruttuoso**, taking 15min between each (summer: hourly every day; winter: 2 on Sun). There are also lovely **night excursions** on the same route (July & Aug 2–8 weekly). The most you'll pay for a one-way fare is €6.71. Boats also connect to the **Cinque Terre** (€13.94). Some continue to **Portovénere** and **Lérici** (€17.04). The best-value round-trip cruise ticket is the **"Super Cinque Terre"**, which gives stops of 1hr in Riomaggiore, 3hr for lunch in Monterosso and 1hr in Vernazza (June–Sept 2 weekly; €25.82).

overlooks the harbour from the north; behind the waterfront Piazza Veneto 250m south is the **tourist office**, Via XXV Aprile 2b (Mon–Sat 9am–12.30pm & 3.30–6.30pm, Sun 9.30am–12.30pm; ℡0185.287.485).

The town is also famous for its **watersports** – the European Dive-In Center, Via Canevaro 2 (℡0185.293.017, Ⓦwww.europeandc.com), is one outfit offering waterskiing, sailing and diving; the tourist office has a list of others and there's a handful of places on the harbourfront offering **boats for rent**. **Walking** trails cross the Monte di Portofino headland: marked paths from Santa Margherita to Pietre Strette (1hr 30min) and Olmi (1hr 40min) link in with the trails outlined in the box overleaf. The best **beaches** are out of town, accessible by bus: south towards Portofino is Paraggi (see overleaf), while to the north the road drops down to a patch of beach in the bay of **San Michele di Pagana**. In addition to its beach bars and crystal-clear water, a *Crucifixion* by van Dyck in the church of San Michele may prove an added incentive for a visit.

As ever, check in case the **hotels** insist on half- or full-pension. Good mid-price options are *Annabella*, Via Costasecca 10 (℡0185.286.531; ❸), which has attractive bathless rooms; and welcoming *Nuova Riviera*, Via Belvedere 10, off Piazza Mazzini (℡0185.287.403, Ⓕ0185.290.083, Ⓦwww.nuovariviera.com; ❸), on a quiet residential street. Although there are several stuffy grand hotels vying for top-dog status, you may prefer the pleasant, modern suite-style rooms at the seafront *Lido Palace*, Via Doria 3 (℡0185.285.821, Ⓕ0185.284.708; ❻), which also has private parking.

Trattoria Baicin, just back from the waterfront park at Via Algeria 5 (closed Mon), is a fine **restaurant**, with a three-course set menu for €18 and excellent seafood. *Da Pezzi*, Via Cavour 21 (closes 9pm & closed Sat), is a long-established locals' hangout serving basic pasta and grills. On the same street at no. 29 is a good *focacceria*, with opposite it a bar-*gelateria* that can make up a big salad for €4.50. Of the many seafront restaurants, one to aim for is *Da Alfredo*, Piazza Martiri 37 (closed Tues), which does good pizzas. Head south behind the squat harbourfront *castello* to reach the old port, where you'll find a clutch of old-style fish restaurants, including *L'Ancora*, Via Maragliano 7 (closed Tues), an excellent-value, mid-priced place; and the swankier *Dei Pescatori*, Via Bottaro 43 (℡0185.286.747; closed Wed & Thurs).

Rapallo

RAPALLO is a highly developed resort town – three times bigger than Santa Margherita – with an expanse of glass-fronted restaurants and plush hotels crowding around a south-facing bay. In the early part of the twentieth century it was a backwater, and writers in particular came for the bay's extraordinary beauty, of which you now get an inkling only early in the morning or at dusk. Max Beerbohm lived in Rapallo for the second half of his life, and attracted a literary circle to the town; Ezra Pound wrote the first thirty of his *Cantos* here between 1925 and 1930, D.H. Lawrence stayed for a while and Hemingway also dropped by (but came away muttering that the sea was flat and boring). The resort's striking landmarks are the large **marina** and the **castle**, now converted into an exhibition space, stuck out at the end of a small causeway. Unlike most of the Tigullio resorts, Rapallo does have an existence independent of its tourist trade, particularly around the **old town**, a grid of cobbled streets behind the stone Saline Gate: this is the commercial centre and venue for the Tuesday fish and vegetable market, while the busy Thursday market at Piazza Cile to the northwest of the centre beneath the train tracks is a good place to buy cheap clothing.

The **tourist office** is at Via Armanda Diaz 9 (Mon–Sat 9am 12.30pm & 3.30–6.30pm, Sun 9.30am–12.30pm; ☎0185.230.346), and can provide details of diving outfits in the town and places to rent boats. The **hotels** are headed by the lavish *Excelsior Palace*, Via San Michele di Pagana 8 (☎0185.230.666, ℗0185.230.214, Ⓦwww.thi.it; ⑨). Cheaper are the welcoming *Stella*, Via Aurelia Ponente 6 (☎0185.50.367, ℗0185.272.837, Ⓦwww.hotelstella-riviera.com; ④), and *Riviera*, nearby at Piazza IV Novembre 2 (☎0185.50.248, ℗0185.65.668, Ⓦwww.tigullio.net/hotelriviera; ⑤); both are converted villas a block in from the sea, the former with parking and some discount shared-bath rooms. Best bargain is the *Bandoni*, in a fine old *palazzo* within sight and smell of the sea at Via Marsala 24 (☎0185.50.423, ℗0185.57.206; ③); its modest rooms are tastefully furnished and the management are flexible about full pension. The *Rapallo* **campsite** is at Via San Lazzaro 4 (☎0185.262.018; June–Sept).

Many **restaurants** in Rapallo and along the Tigullio coast serve the local speciality *bagnun*, a dish based on anchovies, tomato, garlic, onion and white wine. You'll find good trattorias in the alleys behind the mediocre seafront restaurants: *Da Mario*, Piazza Garibaldi 23 (closed Wed), is moderately priced, with tables outside under medieval porticoes. *O Bansin*, Via Venezia 105 (closes 9.30pm & closed Sun), is an affordable old town restaurant. *Zi Teresa*, opposite the train station at Corso Italia 33 (closed Wed), has a good mixed menu of pizzas, pasta and more expensive fish dishes. *Nin Hao*, a pleasant Chinese with its own garden at Piazza Molfino 4 (open daily), has good-value set menus, from as little as €8 for lunch. For just a drink or a snack, try the pubby *Taverna Paradiso* down a side alley off Via Mazzini 73 (evenings only), the delightful *Il Castello* winebar at Lungomare Castello 6, with its waterfront terrace, or the *Gallo Nero* at Via Magenta 10.

Santuario di Montallegro

The best excursion from Rapallo is on the **cable car** (*funivia*; €7.75 return), which rises every thirty minutes from Via Castegneto, ten minutes' walk inland from Rapallo's castle, up to the **Santuario di Montallegro** (612m). The church was founded in 1557 when a Byzantine icon of the Madonna appeared miraculously in the hands of one Giovanni Chichizola, and it's in a superb setting overlooking a steep green valley, with views across the whole of the sparkling bay. A *festa* commemorating the miracle is held during the first three days of July, when the coffer of the Madonna is carried through Rapallo, and a fireworks contest culminates in the mock burning of the castle.

Alternative ways up to Montallegro include following a relatively easy foot-path from Rapallo station (1hr). This continues to the summit of Monte Rosa above the church (another 30min), or diverts east across the hilltops and down to the quiet town of **Chiávari** (4hr 30min from Rapallo and also on the train line). Bus #92 runs from Rapallo station to Montallegro.

The Cinque Terre

The stupendous folded coastline of the **Cinque Terre** ("Five Lands") stretch-es between the pleasant beach resort of **Lévanto** and the major port of La Spezia. The area is named for five tiny villages – **Monterosso**, **Vernazza**, **Corniglia**, **Manarola** and **Riomaggiore** – wedged into a series of coves between sheer cliffs; their comparative remoteness, and the dramatic nature of their position on a stunning coastline, make them the principal scenic highlight of the whole Riviera. They do inevitably get very crowded in summer and all the villages have lost a good deal of their character to a tide of kitschy souvenir shops and overpriced, under-quality restaurants, but even in August you really shouldn't bypass the area – the scenery is breathtaking, there is some lovely walking between villages, and nearby **Lévanto** is a comfortable base away from the worst of the crowds.

Principally fishing ports for centuries, in recent decades the five villages have diversified into **wine**. The Cinque Terre label is one of Liguria's better whites,

CINQUE TERRE & GOLFO DEI POETI

but is less famous than the dessert wine Sciacchetrà, made from grapes which are left to dry on open-air racks until late autumn; they end up much sweeter than normal, like raisins, and in turn produce a full-bodied, heavily alcoholic and (because of the quantity of grapes that goes into it) expensive wine that you savour sip by sip, or dunk dry *biscotti* into after a meal.

Local businesses have set up the Consorzio Turistico Cinque Terre as a central **information and booking service**, based at Piazza Garibaldi 29, Monterosso al Mare (☎0187.817.838 or 0187.778.336); their website Ⓦwww.cinqueterre is especially useful.

Transport around the Cinque Terre

The three principal ways to get to and around the villages of the Cinque Terre are trains, boats and Shanks's pony. If you're on a fast **train**, you'll zip through without seeing much more than a few tantalizing glimpses of turquoise water as the train speeds from one tunnel to the next. Regular slow trains stop at every village, and local stations sell a Cinque Terre day ticket (*biglietto giornaliero*) for €2.83, covering travel between all five villages and Lévanto until midnight.

Boats from every company on the Riviera shuttle along this bit of coast all summer long. Make sure to confirm which of the four waterside villages you'll be stopping at (Corniglia has no harbour), and specify if you want a one-way ticket, rather than the more usual round-trip cruise tickets. Hopping between

Cinque Terre villages by boat is easy, with between five and eight a day (April–Oct) going in both directions – although watch out for a lull between about noon and 2.30pm.

The most satisfactory way to get around is **on foot**: there's a network of trails (see box 148) linking the villages along the coast or up on the ridge-tops that offer spectacular views. However, the coastal path in particular can get uncomfortably crowded throughout the summer months.

Trying to tour the area by **car or motorbike** truly isn't worth the effort. All five villages do now have road access, although the roads are narrow, exceptionally steep, not very scenic and punctuated by corkscrew bends. There's also virtually no public parking anywhere (one small toll area at Riomaggiore and another at Monterosso, both of which fill up by mid-morning). To get to Vernazza, for instance, you must park way back at a barrier placed across the access road and then walk a steep kilometre down into the village. You'd do better to leave your vehicle in Lévanto or La Spezia.

Lévanto

Heading east out of the big resort of Sestri Levante, the train line and coastal road disappear into a series of tunnels that last almost until La Spezia. The slow bus route loops through coastal resorts and past red marble quarries inland before arriving at the unpretentious small town of **Lévanto**, last settlement before the Cinque Terre. Its sandy **beach** – the best for miles around – inexpensive hotels and good transport links make it a perfect base for exploring, more congenial than staying in one of the five villages themselves. The only real sights in the town are architectural remnants from Lévanto's thirteenth-century heyday, including the **Loggia Comunale** on the central Piazza del Popolo, the black-and-white striped church of **Sant'Andrea** above the piazza, and the odd surviving stretch of medieval wall here and there.

The **tourist office** is at the end of the main Via Roma at Piazza Mazzini 1 (Mon–Sat 9am–1pm & 3–6pm, Sun 9am–1pm; ☎0187.808.125), while the **train station** is ten minutes' walk inland from the seafront. Of the **hotels**, some of which insist on a minimum of two nights' stay in high season, the finest is *Stella Maris*, Via Marconi 4 (☎0187.808.258, ℱ0187.807.351, ⓦ www.hotelstellamaris .it; ⑥), with a handful of characterful rooms in the nineteenth-century Palazzo Vannoni, plus some others (④) in a more modern annexe on Piazza Staglieno. The *Europa*, Via Dante Alighieri 41 (☎0187.808.126, ℱ0187.808.594; ③), is another charmingly old-fashioned place with parking. The *Gentile*, a block back from the sea at Via Jacopo 27 (☎0187.808.551; ②), is a popular cheaper option, with some private rooms. There's also a clean, modern and central **youth hostel** on Via San Nicolò (☎0187.802.562; ①), with **Internet** access. The best of a handful of **campsites** is *Acqua Dolce*, Via Semenza 5 (☎0187.807.365, ℱ0187.808.465; closed mid-Nov to mid-Dec & mid-Jan to end Feb).

The town's best **restaurant** is the expensive *Araldo*, Via Jacopo 24 (closed Tues except in July & Aug), featuring fresh local ingredients beneath a vaulted, painted ceiling. Don't miss the specialities *gattafin*, deep-fried vegetable ravioli; and *cotolette di acciughe*, fried, stuffed anchovies. For more casual fare, *Caffè Roma*, Piazza Staglieno 10 (closed Tues), as well as being a popular hangout, has a small restaurant at the back that serves moderately priced pasta, pizzas and fish.

Monterosso al Mare

Tucked into a bay on the east side of the jutting headland of Punta Mesco, **MONTEROSSO** is the chief village of the Cinque Terre. It's also the largest of the five – population 1800 – and most developed, with the modern beach resort of **Fegina** occupying the shore just west of the old village. Beaches, both free and toll, are broad and picturesque; they're separated from the narrow lanes of the old quarter by a hill, atop which is the seventeenth-century **Convento dei Cappuccini**. In the centre of the old village is the striped thirteenth-century church of **San Giovanni Battista**. Monterosso's most recent claim to fame is as the hometown of the Nobel Prize-winning poet Eugenio Montale; his *Ossi di Seppia* (Cuttlefish Bones) is a collection of early poems about his youth in Monterosso.

Monterosso has the Cinque Terre's sole official **tourist office**, in the station (daily 9am–7pm; ☎0187.817.059, ⓦwww.aptcinqueterre.sp.it), as well as a Pro Loco tourist association office at Via Fegina 38 (☎0187.817.506). Top **hotel** is the *Porto Roca*, Via Corone 1 (☎0187.817.502, ⓕ0187.817.692, ⓦwww.por-toroca.it; ❼; March–Nov), in a blissful location with sea-views from most rooms. *Villa Adriana*, Via IV Novembre 23 (☎0187.818.109, ⓕ0187.818.128; ❻), has its own beach and even some car-parking space. The *Degli Amici*, Via Buranco 36 (☎0187.817.544, ⓕ0187.817.424, ⓦwww.cinqueterre.it /hotel_amici, ❹), is nicely situated away from the hubbub, its unremarkable rooms are all en suite. *Punta Mesco*, near the rail bridge at Via Molinelli 35 (☎ & ⓕ0187.817.495; ❹), has the cheapest rooms in town. Pick of the **restaurants** is *Il Gigante* on Via IV Novembre (☎0187.817.401; closed Mon), with pricey but excellent Ligurian cuisine.

Vernazza

A few headlands east is **VERNAZZA**, loveliest of the five villages, throwing a protective arm around the only natural harbour on this rocky coast. The narrow lanes with their tall, colourful houses are typical of the area, and the little cramped village is overlooked by stout medieval bastions and a watchtower, built by the Genoese after they'd destroyed the previous castle in 1182 to punish the locals for piracy. Down beside the main piazza overlooking the sea is the Gothic church of **Santa Margherita di Antiochia**, with an elegant octagonal campanile.

There are two **hotels**: plain, bathless rooms in the *Barbara*, Piazza Marconi 30 (☎ & ⓕ0187.812.398; ❷), occupy the top floor of one of the oldest buildings in the village, overlooking the main square beside the harbour, while the friendly *Sorriso*, further up into the village at Via Gavino 4 (☎0187.812.224; ❸), has both en-suite and bathless options. A handful of places offer **rooms** – in summer, ask at the Monterosso tourist office in advance for details, since you're likely to find them all full if you turn up without a booking. Poor-value **restaurants** ring the main Piazza Marconi; the *Sorriso* hotel is better value, and *Osteria Il Baretto*, Via Roma 31 (☎0187.812.381), may lack a sea view but has excellent *antipasti di mare* in recompense. The *Blue Marlin* bar at Via Roma 43 has **internet** access. Also on Via Roma you'll spot a sales outlet of the **Cooperativa Agricola Cinque Terre**, where you can sample the local wines.

Corniglia

CORNIGLIA is the smallest of the five, and also the remotest: the village clings to a high cliff 90m above the sea, and its only access to the water (and the train station) is via a long flight of steps. Floral-decorated squares fill the village, and the little Gothic church of **San Pietro** boasts an exquisite, marble rose window. There are no hotels, but plenty of places offering **rooms**, and a handful of unremarkable eateries. Oddly for a hilltop village, Corniglia stands out for its **beaches**. On the southern side of the village's rocky promontory is

There's plenty of **walking** to be done in and around the Cinque Terre, but you should note a couple of precautions. Most of the paths are unshaded, and in summer temperatures can soar: you should wear a hat and carry a water-bottle for even a short stroll. Walking shoes are also advisable – paths are rocky and uneven at the best of times. Take note of weather forecasts in spring and autumn, as rainstorms can brew up rapidly and make paths treacherously slippery. Tourist offices in Monterosso, Lévanto and La Spezia have plenty of maps and information, and can advise on good itineraries.

The most popular and accessible route is the 11km Blue Trail (*Sentiero Azzurro*), signed either with blue waymarkers or as route no. 2; this hugs the shoreline between all five villages, offering spectacular scenery the whole way along. Owing to the gradients, covering it from east to west (5hr) is considerably easier than from west to east; if you start early, walking west also means you'll have the sun behind you most of the way. Follow the red and white stripes painted on walls, trees and gates from **Riomaggiore** station to the start of the Blue Trail, a stretch called the **Via dell'Amore** (Lovers' Path), which winds above the waves past lemon trees in every backyard. In spring, before the sun has turned everything except the vines to dust, you'll walk beneath cliffs covered with wildflowers. An easy twenty minutes covers the kilometre west to **Manarola**, from where a less crowded and more spectacular path climbs slightly and then heads on for 3km to the station at **Corniglia**, passing rock-cut steps leading down to the pebbly beach. Steep steps lead up into the centre of Corniglia itself (1hr from Manarola). It's a fairly leisurely ninety-minute walk for the 4km on to **Vernazza**, with just a couple of difficult spots and the attraction of access to the lovely beach at Guvano. Note that if you're attempting things in the other direction, the Vernazza–Corniglia walk is a tough-going 2hr-plus hike. The walk from Vernazza to **Monterosso** is the hardest westbound stretch, two hours to cover 3km, with first a steep climb up to 180m and then a sharp descent into Monterosso.

Other routes run perpendicular to the coastline, heading steeply up the slopes to give breathtaking coastal views, often passing old churches in the hills above each township. These routes link up with the long trail no. 1, or *Sentiero Rosso*, that runs from Portovénere (east of Riomaggiore) along the ridge-tops to Lévanto, a full-day (9–10hr) hike covering some 23km. Nonetheless, it's easy to split things up manageably. As an example, trail no. 3 climbs from Riomaggiore past the Santuario di Montenero church up to the **Colle del Telegrafo** viewpoint (516m; 1hr 30min), from where trail no. 1 heads west, giving expansive views along the coast as far as Monterosso; through the chestnut woods, some 3km west of Colle del Telegrafo, is **La Croce** (637m; 1hr), where trail no. 01 returns you steeply down to Riomaggiore (1hr). Another, yet more scenic, option would be to follow trail no. 7 up from Vernazza 3km through vineyards and past dry stone walls to the church at San Bernardino, then Casa Fornacchi and the ridge-top at **Cigoletta** (612m; 1hr 30min). Cigoletta is another junction point on the *Sentiero Rosso*, from where a trail heads further up to the peak of **Monte Marvede** (667m; 45min) high above Corniglia, with panoramic vistas over the whole coast; the lovely trail no. 6 heads down from Marvede through more vineyards and patches of forest to Manarola (3.5km; 1hr 45min).

Another highly rewarding walk is trail no. 10, which leads from Monterosso station up through pine woods and onto a flight of steps that emerge at the San Antonio church on the high point of the **Punta Mesco** headland (1hr), giving a spectacular panorama along the length of the Cinque Terre coastline. The walk north along the tops from there to **Monte Vè o Focone**, and the descent on trail no. 14 into Lévanto, are both easy (total 3hr from Monterosso).

the **Spiaggone di Corniglia**, a narrow stretch of pebbles that has relatively easy access from the footpath towards Manarola. Here you'll find the **campsite** *Villaggio Marino Europa* (☎0187.812.279; April–Sept), with a set of spartan bungalows sleeping up to six (❸).

The Cinque Terre's best beach is the wild and tranquil **Spiaggia di Guvano**, on the northern side of Corniglia's promontory. Follow the signs from the north side of the train station, which will lead you to a disused rail tunnel with an entryphone: ask for the *spiaggia*, and you'll be buzzed through the gate for a long walk through the tunnel (1km or more) to the beach itself, where you must pay €3 admission. Once there, the attractions of warm, clear water, lovely scenery and relative peace and quiet might persuade you to throw off your social bonds – this is one of the few beaches in Liguria to permit **nudity** (although bear in mind that you are overlooked by walkers on the footpath to Vernazza).

Manarola

MANAROLA is almost as enchanting as Vernazza, its pastel-shaded houses crowded impossibly up the sides of a prominent headland of dark rock. The fourteenth-century church of San Lorenzo in the village has another beautiful rose window. On the road from Manarola to Corniglia above the village is the hamlet of **Groppo**, home to the **Cooperativa Agricola Cinque Terre**, which offers tastings and direct sale of the local wines (Mon–Sat 10am–noon & 2–6pm; ☎0187.920.435).

Manarola's two **hotels** are outstanding. Family-run *Ca' d'Andrean*, Via Discovolo 101 (☎0187.920.040, ℱ0187.920.452, ⓦwww.cadaandrean.it; ❸), takes a real pride in its service and its few, airy rooms (some with balcony); *Marina Piccola*, Via Discovolo 192 (☎0187.920.103, ℱ0187.920.966; ❹; closed Nov & Jan to mid-Feb), has six pleasant rooms in the main building and four in a less inviting, cheaper annexe. The small non-HI **hostel** *Ostello 5 Terre* is a clean, friendly place 300m up the hill from the station at Via Riccobaldi 21 (☎0187.920.215, ℱ0187.920.218, ⓦwww.cinqueterre.net/ostello; €16); you may need to book several weeks ahead in summer for dorm beds or en-suite rooms.

Riomaggiore

Lively **RIOMAGGIORE** is the easternmost of the Cinque Terre, with a relatively easy road link to the outside world that makes it also the most crowded of the five. Nonetheless, its vividly multicoloured houses piling up the steep slopes above the romantic little harbour, with no two on the same level, give the place a bizarre charm that remains untempered by the café crowds. Aside from the requisite rose window, the church of **San Giovanni Battista** houses a striking wooden *Crucifixion* by Maragliano. Riomaggiore is also the starting-point for the twenty-minute walk on the **Via dell'Amore** (Lovers' Path) to Manarola (see box opposite).

The only **hotel** is the pleasantly modern *Villa Argentina*, in a lovely spot at Via De Gasperi 37 (☎ & ℱ0187.920.213; ❹). Otherwise, your best bet is **private rooms**; English-speaking Roberto and Luciano Fazioli (Scalinata della Tagliata 6h; ☎0187.920.587; ❷) manage various properties in Riomaggiore and Manarola, from clean, simple rooms to self-catering apartments with terraced balconies overlooking the harbour; another good bet for similar-style rooms is *Mar Mar* at Via Malborghetto 8 (☎0187.920.932; ❷). For **food**, *La Lanterna* (closed Tues) has a good, moderately priced pasta and seafood menu, and a great location in the pinched harbour (to get there, walk under the train line from the bottom of the main street); while *Controvelaccio* on Via Colombo also has various inexpensive menus and delicious fresh anchovies. *Ripa del Sole*, Via De Gasperi 4 (☎0187.920.143), serves acclaimed gourmet menus for €45.

The Golfo dei Poeti

After the beauty of the Golfo Paradiso and Golfo del Tigullio, and the drama of the Cinque Terre, Liguria still has a final flourish. Hard up against the Tuscan border is the majestic Golfo di La Spezia, an impressive sweeping panorama of islands and rough headlands renamed the **Golfo dei Poeti** in 1919 by Italian playwright Sam Benelli for the succession of romantic souls who fell in love with the place. Petrarch was the first; Shelley lived and died on these shores; Byron was another regular; and D.H. Lawrence passed the pre-World War I years here. The town at the head of the gulf is workaday **La Spezia**, a major naval and shipbuilding centre with a fine art gallery. Small resorts line the fringes of the bay, linked by buses which swing around on twisting roads or boats which shuttle across the glittering blue water – **Portovénere**, sitting astride a spit of land to the southwest, and **Lérici** on the southeastern shore, both of them pleasant and highly picturesque stopovers.

Dozens of **boats** embark on rapid, half-day and all-day excursions throughout the summer – and on certain days in winter too – between just about every port along this coast. Local tourist offices have precise details of sailings. The principal operator is Navigazione Golfo dei Poeti, Via Mazzini 21, in La Spezia (☎0187.732.987, ⓦwww.navigazionegolfodeipoeti.it); others include In-Tur, Viale Italia (☎0187.24.324), and Battellieri del Golfo, Banchina Revel (☎0187.21.010). Fares are low: from La Spezia to Isola Palmaria costs €3.50; from Lérici across the bay to Portovénere €4.50; and from Portovénere around the three islands of Palmaria, Tino and Tinetto €8.

La Spezia

Up until a few years ago, most travel guides dismissed **LA SPEZIA** with a few curt comments. This ordinary working town was known mainly for its huge mercantile port and the largest naval base in the country – until the **Museo Amedeo Lia**, probably the finest collection of medieval and Renaissance art in Liguria, put it on the tourist map. Art aside, realistically priced hotels and restaurants make it a good base from which to explore both the Golfo dei Poeti and the Cinque Terre.

La Spezia's position, sandwiched between the hills and the sea, proved an early attraction to conquerors, with its strategic importance reflected in the number of Genoese castles that stud the hills. These were the town's first fortifications, yet it took **Napoleon** to capitalize on what is one of Europe's finest natural harbours and construct a naval and military complex at La Spezia early in the nineteenth century. The naval presence made the town a prime target in World War II and most of the centre had to be rebuilt following Allied **bombing**; it's now characterized by rather drab buildings lining a regular grid of streets behind the palm-fringed harbourfront promenade of **Viale Mazzini**. At the eastern end, opposite the Porto Mercantile, sits the 1970s **Cattedrale Cristo Re**, overlooking Piazza Europa and distinguished by a boldly minimalist white tower curving against a hilly backdrop. At the western end are some lovely **public gardens**, a short distance from **Piazza Chiodo** and La Spezia's *raison d'être* – the vast naval **Arsenale**, which was rebuilt after destruction in World War II. There's no public admittance to the complex itself, but just to the left of the entrance is the engaging **Museo Tecnico Navale** (Mon–Sat

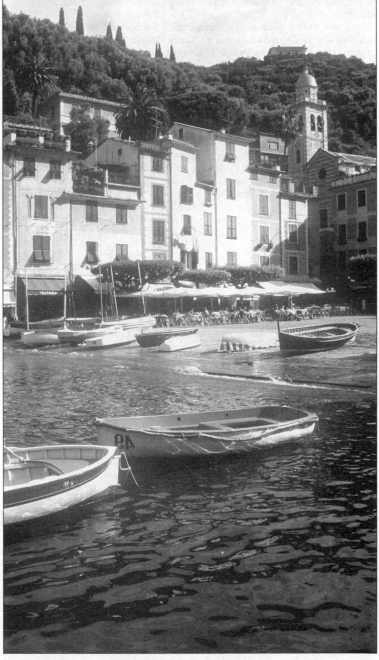

△ Portofino

8.30am–6pm, Sun 10.15am–3.45pm; €1.55), which contains battle relics and models.

From the public gardens it's a short stroll inland on Via Prione to Piazza Beverini and the striped Duomo of **Santa Maria Assunta** housing a polychrome terracotta by Andrea della Robbia. Behind the church is the lively marketplace of **Piazza Cavour**, some 100m east of which lies the **Museo Amedeo Lia**, Via Prione 234 (Tues–Sun 10am–6pm; €6; ⓦwww .castagna.it/mal). This impressive place occupies a seventeenth-century former Franciscan convent that has undergone careful and intelligent renovation. It was opened in December 1996 following the donation of more than a thousand artworks to the city by Lia, a private collector. The museum ticket allows you to go in and out as many times as you like during the day. A lovely *Madonna with Child* by Giampietrino launches the small but exceptionally high-quality sixteenth-century collection in Rooms VI and VII; other highlights are Pontormo's sharp-eyed *Self-Portrait*, a supremely self-assured *Portrait of a Gentleman* by Titian, and Bellini's *Portrait of an Attorney*. Upstairs in room XI are bronzes by Giambologna and Ammanati. Room XII houses the museum's most celebrated item, the famous *Addolorata*, a half-statue in polychrome terracotta of a sorrowful Madonna made by Benedetto da Maiano.

Practicalities

The **train station** is a steep ten-minute walk above the town centre – head left out of the station and then follow the curving Via XX Settembre all the way down until it hits the first of three long, parallel boulevards which run along the front of the port: these three are Via Chiodo, then palm-lined Viale Mazzini, and then the principal traffic street of Viale Italia. The **ferries** to Corsica, Sardinia, the Cinque Terre and around the Golfo dei Poeti leave from the Porto Mercantile, on the central waterfront.

The main **tourist office** is just back from the port at Viale Mazzini 47 (Mon–Sat 9am–1pm & 4–7pm & Sun 9am–1pm; ☎0187.770.900, ⓦwww.laspezianet.it), while the **bus station** is on Piazza Chiodo, at the western end of Via Chiodo in front of the naval arsenal, from where ATC buses leave for Tuscany and the countryside valleys. Buses to Portovénere and Lérici depart either from the train station forecourt or from Piazza Cavour.

There are several **hotels** near the train station: the *Terminus* is right outside at Via Paleocapa 21 (☎0187.703.436, ⓕ0187.714.935; ❶); the slightly more comfortable *Parma* is down the steps in front of the station at Via Fiume 143 (☎0187.743.010, ⓕ0187.743.240; ❷); while the *Venezia*, Via Paleocapa 10 (☎0187.733.465; ❸), is better in terms of decor and service. Near Piazza Cavour is the *Flavia*, Vicolo della Stagno 7 (☎0187.736.060; ❶), with bargain doubles. Closer to the water, on one of the old centre's few pretty streets, *Il Sole*, Via F. Cavalotti 31 (☎0187.735.164; ❷), has basic rooms furnished with a haphazard selection of ancient furniture. The *Jolly* overlooks the bay at Via XX Settembre 2 (☎0187.739.555, ⓕ0187.22.129; ❻), part of a chain and replete with all comforts.

For **food**, the daily covered market in Piazza Cavour is a good place to buy picnic supplies; it takes over the whole square on Saturday mornings. You can get *farinata* at *La Pia* on Via Magenta, and good pizzas at *Da Giulio*, Via San Agostino 29 (closed Wed). There's a cluster of restaurants between Via del Prione and the Arsenale, where prices are kept in check by the naval clientele (many are closed in August); *Da Luciano*, Via Colombo 27, is another low-priced possibility in this part of town. Down near the seafront lurks *Da Dino*, Via Da Passano 19 (closed Sun evening & Mon), a down-to-earth eatery offering good-

Ferrries to Corsica

Happy Lines is the main **ferry** operator between La Spezia and **Bastia** on the island of Corsica (France), running boats most days between mid-April and late September. The crossing takes five hours and costs €18 per person, rising to €27 on summer weekends, plus €40–73 for a car. Departures are all in the daytime, but you can book a bargain cabin onboard either for the night before you depart or for the night after you dock (checkout is at 6.30am, however); two-person cabins cost from €14, four-person ones from €25. You can get tickets from any travel agent in La Spezia, Happy Lines at Via Maralunga 45 (℡0187.564.530, ⊛www.happylines.it) or on the dockside.

There are also twelve-hour crossings to **Olbia** on Sardinia, but you'll find much lower prices, shorter crossing-times and more regular service from Piombino or Livorno in Tuscany.

value menus of fish and other local fare, and *La Posta*, Via Don Minzoni 24 (closed Sat & Sun), is in much the same mould. *La Grande Muraglia*, Via Prione 44 (no closing day), is an excellent, inexpensive Chinese with plenty of authentic dishes.

Portovénere

The ancient, narrow-laned village of **PORTOVÉNERE** sits astride a spit of land on the very tip of the southwestern arm of the bay, blessed with breathtaking views, a memorably tranquil atmosphere and a string of three islets just offshore, each smaller and rockier than the last. The **bus** ride from La Spezia is a frenetic affair, with some hair-raising bends, but it gives fine views of the bay and the islands; however, the views are just as good from the **boats** which depart as regularly as buses.

You enter through a twelfth-century towered **gate** built by the Genoese, who fortified this spot in opposition to Pisan forces that had taken Lérici across the bay. In the upper part of the village is the twelfth-century church of **San Lorenzo**, renowned for the remarkable treasures in its vestry, including four ivory caskets (three Syrian and one Byzantine) from about the year 1000. Higher up still is the sixteenth-century fortified **castello**, with panoramic views out over this most beautiful spot from its terraced gardens. Portovénere's characteristic rose- and yellow-painted tower-houses were aligned to form a defensive wall, now transformed into a trendy waterside strip known as the Palazzata, which spreads out at the end of the promontory to the church of **San Pietro** on the very tip of dry land, built with a banded facade and an elegant campanile in the thirteenth century over the ruins of a Roman **temple to Venus**; the village got its name from the Latin *Portus Veneris*, or Port of Venus. The views from the terrace in front of the church out to the three islands and across to the Cinque Terre coast are magnificent. One of the rocky coves around the base of the church is the **Grotto Arpaia**, a favoured spot of Lord Byron; he swam across the bay from here to visit Shelley at San Terenzo (see below). To this day, the gulf has the nickname of the "Baia di Byron", but swimming is discouraged in favour of the **boats** which shuttle regularly to and from Lérici.

Boats from Portovénere also tour the three **islands** that lie south of the peninsula, all but the nearest of which lie in a military zone and so can only be viewed from the water. (Note, though, that island excursions paid for in Portovénere cost quite a bit more than trips booked and begun in La Spezia – see opposite) **Isola Palmária** is the largest, 500m south of Portovénere, with the Grotta Azzurra cave as its star attraction. Next is the **Isola del Tino**, a rocky islet marked with a lighthouse and the remains of a Romanesque abbey. Finally comes the even tinier **Isola del Tinetto**, also home to a monastic community in centuries gone by.

Practicalities

Portovénere's **tourist office** is at Piazza Bastreri 7 (Mon–Sat 9am–noon & 3–6pm, Sun 9am–noon; ☎0187.790.691, ⒲www.aptcinqueterre.sp.it), alongside the least expensive **hotel**, two-star *Genio* (☎0187.790.611; ❹). Of the four upscale choices, the pick is the *Royal Sporting*, a short walk outside the village on the beach, Via dell'Olivo 345 (☎0187.790.326, Ⓕ0187.777.707, ⒲www .royalsporting.com; ❻), with pleasant, cool interior courtyards, spectacular views and a huge salt-water swimming pool. In a different vein, *Locanda Lorena* offers half-a-dozen simple rooms: nothing special but for its remote location on the Isola Palmaria, at Via Cavour 4 (☎0187.792.370; ❸; April–Sept).

There's a wealth of places to **eat**. The century-old *Antica Osteria del Carrugio* (closed Thurs) is at Via Capellini 66, in the shadow of the castle; its affordable specialities are anchovies, sheep's cheese and stuffed mussels (which are cultivated on poles in Portovénere's harbour). Down on the photogenic harbourfront Calata Doria are a handful of pricier places, including *La Taverna del Corsaro* (☎0187.900.622; closed Mon), famous for its version of Portovénere's *zuppa di datteri* (razor-clam soup), and the acclaimed *Iseo* (☎0187.790.610; closed Wed), the village's best restaurant.

Lérici and around

East of La Spezia, you'll pass several kilometres of dockyards, foundries and thriving heavy industry; the sprawl is eventually brought up short at the boundary of a protected nature reserve which covers the southern half of the gulf shore.

First of the string of small resorts here is **SAN TERENZO**, marked by its prominent castle. There's a good sandy beach and a choice of accommodation, but, predictably, most of the **hotels** will insist on full- or half-pension in high season. The best deals are right on the seafront, at the *Nettuno*, Via Mantegazza 1 (☎0187.971.093; ❷), and the *Trieste*, a few doors down at no. 13 (☎0187.970.610; ❷), alongside which is the **Villa Magni**, where Shelley spent some productive months in 1822, before setting off to meet Leigh Hunt at Livorno, "full of spirits and joy", according to Mary Shelley's account. On the way back, his boat, the *Ariel*, went down near Viareggio, and Shelley drowned, aged thirty. Plans to turn the house into a multimedia **Museo P.B. Shelley** are well under way.

About 2km south of San Terenzo lies **LÉRICI**, an upwardly mobile resort of garden villas, seafront bars, trattorias and gift shops. Piazza Garibaldi, behind the marina, acts as the bus station. The **tourist office** is on the seafront north of Piazza Garibaldi, at Via Biaggini 6 (Mon–Sat 9am–1pm & 4–7pm, Sun 9am–1pm; ☎0187.967.346, ⒲www.aptcinqueterre.sp.it), and has details of the regular **boats** across to Portovénere. The circuitous route up to the Pisan-built castle from Piazza Garibaldi passes through **Via del Ghetto**, the old Jewish quarter once populated by Livornese merchants, and up the steep **Salita Arpara**, derived from a medieval word meaning "the place where hawks nest". At the top, the **castle** (July & Aug Tues–Sun 10.30am–12.30pm & 6.30pm–midnight; rest of year Tues–Sun 10.30am–12.30pm & 2.30–5.30pm; €4.60) has fabulous views from the highest terrace right across to Portovénere and the three islands and back towards La Spezia. Inside, apart from a Gothic chapel, much of the interior is given over to a museum of geopaleontology, documenting prehistoric dinosaur life in the area.

Lérici's two pleasantest **hotels** are near the tourist office: the *Shelley & Delle Palme* is at Via Biaggini 5 (T0187.968.204, F0187.964.271; ❹) and the *Byron* at no. 19 (T0187.965.699, F0187.967.409, W www.cdh.it/hb; ❹); both have dreamy sea views from balconied rooms. The sole inexpensive option is the modern *Del Golfo*, inland at Via Gerini 37 (T0187.967.400, F0187.965.733; ❷). When it comes to **eating**, the outdoor pizzerias that line Lérici's harbour provide an attractive setting as the sun goes down. Amongst many are the popular *Il Giogo*, Via Petriccioli 44 (closed Mon), where you can indulge in pizzas, interesting seafood and home-made desserts; and the elegant *La Piccola Oasi*, Via Cavour 60 (closed Tues), which offers a simple set menu.

Travel details

Trains

Genoa to: Alassio (15 daily; 1hr 10min–1hr 25min); Albenga (16 daily; 1hr 10min–1hr 55min); Bologna (4 daily; 3-4hr); Camogli (every 20–30min; 30–50min); Finale Ligure (15 daily; 45min–1hr); Imperia (11 daily; 1hr 30min–2hr); La Spezia (hourly; 1hr 10min–2hr 10min); Milan (hourly; 2hr); Naples (every 2–3hr; 7–8hr); Pisa (14 daily; 2–3hr 30min); Rapallo (every 20min; 30min); Rome (every 1–2hr; 6hr); San Remo (hourly; 1hr 45–2hr 40min); Santa Margherita (every 20min; 20min–1hr); Ventimiglia (every 30min; 2hr 55min).

Buses

Camogli to: Ruta (every 30min–1hr; 25min).
Chiávari to: Rezzoaglio (6 daily; 1hr 25min); Bologna (2 daily; 4hr).
Finale Ligure to: Borghetto Santo Spirito (every 15min; 25min).

Genoa to: Rovegno (5 daily; 1hr 50min); Torriglia (hourly; 1hr 10min).
La Spezia to: Lérici (every 10min; 20min); Portovénere (every 30min; 20min).
Rapallo to: Chiávari (hourly; 30min); Montallegro (every 2hr; 40min); Santa Margherita (every 20min; 10min).
Santa Margherita to: Portofino (every 15–20min; 15min).
Ventimiglia to: Dolceacqua (14 daily; 18min); La Mortola (9 daily; 15min).

Ferries

Genoa to: Bastia (1 weekly; 4hr 30min); Cágliari (2 weekly in summer; 20hr); Olbia (at least 7 weekly in summer; 9hr 30min); Palermo (4 weekly; 20hr); Porto Torres (7 weekly; 12hr).
La Spezia to: Bastia (2–5 weekly; 5hr).

Lombardy
and the lakes

CHAPTER 3

Highlights

＊ **Roof of Milan's Duomo**
Wander around the roof
of the world's largest
Gothic cathedral with the
best views of the city
and the mountains
beyond. See p.172

＊ **The Last Supper**
Leonardo da Vinci's
mural for the refectory
wall of the Santa Maria
delle Grazie is one of the
world's most resonant
images. See p.177

＊ **Certosa di Pavia** This
Carthusian monastery is a
fantastic construction rising out of the rice fields
near Pavia. See p.187

＊ **Cycling round Mantua**
Rent a bike and explore

elegant Mantua and the
surrounding waterways.
See p.193

＊ **Ravioli alla zucca** Tuck
into a plate of delicious
pumpkin ravioli topped
with sage butter. See
p.162

＊ **Lake Como** Explore the
most romantic of the
lakes by ferry. See p.207

＊ **Città Alta, Bergamo**
Bergamo's medieval high
town is an impossibly
romantic spot to spend
an evening. See p.219

＊ **Villa Feltrinelli** A fabulous hotel in an enviable
position on the shores of
Lake Garda. See p.233

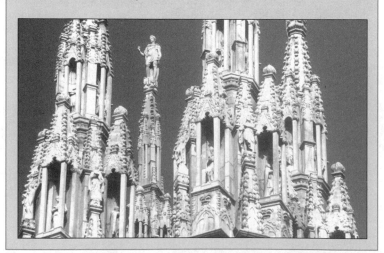

3

Lombardy
and the lakes

Lombardy, Italy's richest and most developed region, often seems to have more in common with its northern European neighbours than with the rest of Italy. Given its history, this is hardly surprising: it was ruled for almost two centuries by the French and Austrians and takes its name from the northern Lombards, who invaded the region and ousted the Romans. As a border region, accessible through numerous mountain passes, Lombardy has always been vulnerable to invasion, just as it has always profited by being a commercial crossroads. It was long viewed by northerners as the capital of Italy – emperors from Charlemagne to Napoleon came to Lombardy to be crowned king – and northern European business magnates continue to take Lombardy's capital, Milan, more seriously than Rome, the region's big businesses and banks wielding political as well as economic power across the nation.

The region's landscape has paid the price for economic success: industry chokes the peripheries of towns, sprawls across the Po plain in the south, and even spreads its polluting tentacles into the northern lakes and mountain valleys. Nonetheless Lombardy has its attractions: the upper reaches of its valleys are largely unspoilt; its towns and cities all retain wanderable medieval cores; and the stunning scenery and lush vegetation of the lakes make it easy to forget that the water is not sparkling clean.

As for Lombardy's people, from the cosseted residents of the provincial towns to Milan's workaholics, they hardly fit the popular image of Italians. In fact, they don't have much time for a substantial proportion of their compatriots: urban northerners are rather dismissive of the south and derisive of Rome. The last decade or so has even seen the rise of a political party – the Lega Nord – nominally demanding independence from Rome but successfully capitalizing on a wave of feeling that northern taxes sustain the inefficient, work-shy south.

Milan, a natural gateway to the region, and where you may well arrive, dominates the plain that forms the southern part of Lombardy. The towns across here – **Pavia**, **Cremona**, **Mantua** – flourished during the Middle Ages and Renaissance, and retain their historical character today, albeit encircled by burgeoning suburbs. To the north, Lombardy is quite different, the lakes and low mountains of the edge of the Alps sheltering fewer historic towns, though **Bergamo** and **Brescia** are notable exceptions. This has long been popular

SWITZERLAND

Chiavenna   Chiareggo

Locarno   Sórico
                    Gravedona   Cólico
Cannobio
              Luino Lugano   Bellano
Verbania   Lago di Lugano   Menaggio Varenna
        Laveno   Tremezzo Bellagio
Stresa   Lago di
            Ghirla
Lago   Cernobbio   Lecco   San
d'Orta   Varese   Como   Pellegrino
Orta San Giulio   Lago di Lago di Lago di
        Arona   Lago di   Lago di Alsério Pusiano Annone Garlate
                   Varese
                                                          Bergamo

        Malpensa

                A8
Turin
        Novara   Milan   Linate   Treviglio
                                                         Caravaggio
Vercelli   Crema

        Vigévano   River Ticino   A7   Lodi

                Certosa di Pavia

                        Pavia   River Adda

        River Po

Genoa   PIEMONTE   A21   Piacenza

        Alessandria   EMIL

160

Regional food and wine

Lombardy is distinctive in its variations in culinary habits – rice, for example, might form the bulk of the diet in some areas but would rarely be eaten in others, and food varies even from town to town. The short-grain rice used for risottos is grown in the paddy fields of the Ticino Valley, and other staples include green pasta and polenta. The latter is found all over northern Italy: made from maize meal boiled and patiently stirred for around forty minutes, watched with an eagle eye so it doesn't go lumpy. Polenta can be eaten straightaway, or else left to cool and then sliced and grilled and served as an accompaniment to meat.

The sophisticated recipes of Milanese urbanites contrast sharply with the more rustic dishes of the Alpine foothills and lakes. The latter are sometimes known as *piatti poveri* (poor food): devised over centuries, these employ imagination and often time-consuming techniques to make up for the lack of expensive ingredients. *Pizzoccheri*, buckwheat noodles found in the Valtellina Valley, are a good example of this. *Risotto alla Milanese*, on the other hand, golden yellow from saffron, is Milan's most renowned culinary invention, and, it is said, only truly Milanese if it has been cooked with the juices of roast veal flavoured with sage and rosemary. *Ossobuco* (shin of veal) is another Milanese favourite, as are *biscotti* – handmade biscuits flavoured with nuts, vanilla and lemon and sold by weight at specialist shops all over the city. *Panettone*, the soft, eggy cake with sultanas eaten at Christmas time, also originated here.

From Cremona comes *mostarda di frutta* (pickled fruit with mustard), the traditional condiment to serve with *bollito misto* (boiled meats). Another meaty dish is *La Casoêula*, a pork stew said to be of Spanish origin. Stuffed pastas – for example, around the Po valley, ravioli filled with pumpkin – and veal – either hot or cold in dishes like *vitello tonnato* (thin slices of cold veal covered with tuna mayonnaise) – are also popular, as are wild fungi.

Lombardy is also one of the largest cheese-making regions in the country. As well as Gorgonzola there are numerous other local cheeses, the parmesan-like Grana Padano and the smooth, rich Mascarpone (used in sweet dishes) and the strong soft cheese Taleggio being among the best known.

Although Lombardy is not well known internationally for its **wines**, Milan supermarket shelves bulge with decent wines from the Oltrepò Pavese, and the northern areas of Valtellina, while around Brescia, the Franciacorta area is beginning to earn more of an international profile for its good reds. For white wines, try the slightly sparkling Ca' Del Bosco.

tourist territory, particularly around the lakes of **Maggiore**, **Como** and **Garda**, and wealthy Italian holiday-makers and day-trippers are much in evidence. Although the western shore of Lago Maggiore and the eastern and northern shores of Lago di Garda are, strictly speaking, in Piemonte, Veneto and Trentino respectively, the **lakes region** and its resorts are all covered in this chapter.

Milan and southern Lombardy

Much of Lombardy's wealth is concentrated in the cities and towns of the broad Po plain, which forms the southern belt of the region. It's a wealth that is obvious throughout the area in the well-preserved medieval towns and the industrial estates that surround them, not to mention the pollution – the Po is Italy's most polluted river, and air pollution in Milan is still sometimes so dangerous that the traffic police don gas masks.

Despite all this, the area is well worth exploring. **Milan** may be polluted, but it's an upbeat city, with some great classical and contemporary art galleries and a splendid cathedral, as well as world-famous designer stores and a lively night scene. It certainly needn't be as daunting as its reputation suggests; given time, and taken on its own contemporary terms, it is a stimulating place to be. **Pavia**, to the south, is a pretty medieval town that makes an attractive introduction to this part of Lombardy, its cobbled streets and ancient churches taking a firm back seat in terms of sights to its fabulous **Certosa**, just outside. In the east, **Cremona** was the birthplace of the violin and home of Stradivari, and has a neat, well-preserved centre, though it's not the kind of place in which you'd want to stay long. **Mantua**, in the far eastern corner of the region, is by contrast Lombardy's most visually appealing city, at least from a distance, although what you really come for are the remains of the powerful Gonzaga family, who ruled here for three hundred years from their extravagant ducal palace and their later Palazzo Te, on the outskirts of the city, which contains some of the finest (and most steamily erotic) fresco-painting of the entire Renaissance.

Milan (Milano)

The dynamo behind the country's "economic miracle" in the Fifties, **MILAN** is a city like no other in Italy. It's foggy in winter, muggy in summer, and is closer in outlook, as well as distance, to London than to Palermo. This is no city of peeling *palazzi*, cobbled piazzas and *la dolce vita*, but one in which the pace is fast, and where consumerism and the work-ethic rule the lives of its well-dressed citizens.

Because of this most people pass straight through, and if it's summer and you're keen for sun and sea this might well be the best thing you can do; the weather, in August especially, can be off-puttingly humid. But at any other time of year it's well worth giving Milan more of a chance. It's a historic city, with enough churches and museums to keep you busy for a week – the Accademia Brera, duomo and the church of Santa Maria delle Grazie – but there are also parks and cafés to relax in, and the contemporary aspects of the place represent the leading edge of Italy's fashion and design industry.

Some history

Milan first stepped into the historical limelight in the fourth century when Emperor Constantine issued the **Edict of Milan** here, granting Christians

MILAN

BARS & CAFÉS

ATM	C
Le Biciclette	K
Corso Como 10	B
Lelephante	I
Luca's Bar	J

ACCOMMODATION

Antica Locanda Solferino	5
Arno	4
Casa Mia	6
La Cordata	9
Goloomina	3
Kennedy	7
San Francisco	2
Valley	1
Youth hostel	8

RESTAURANTS

L'Altro Luogo (Aimo e Nadia)	D
Joia	E
Milch	A
Oskar	F
Pizza OK	H
Al Pont de Ferr	L
Osteria delle Vigne	M
Warsa	G

0   200m

throughout the Roman Empire the freedom to worship for the first time. The city, under its charismatic bishop, Ambrogio (St Ambrose), swiftly became a major centre of Christianity – many of today's churches stand on the sites, or even retain parts, of fourth-century predecessors.

Medieval Milan rose to prominence under the ruthless regime of the Visconti dynasty, who founded what is still the city's most spectacular building, the florid late-Gothic **Duomo**, and built the first, heavily fortified nucleus of the **Castello** – which, under their successors, the Sforza, was extended to house what became one of the most luxurious courts of the Renaissance. This was a period of much building and rebuilding, notably under the last Sforza, Lodovico, who employed the architect **Bramante** to improve the city's churches and **Leonardo da Vinci** to paint *The Last Supper* and design war-machines to aid him in his struggles with foreign powers and other Italian states. Leonardo's inventions didn't prevent Milan falling to the French in 1499, marking the beginning of almost four centuries of foreign rule. Later, the Austrian Habsburgs took control, during their time commissioning the **Teatro della Scala** and founding the **Brera** art gallery, which, during Milan's short spell under Napoleon, was filled with paintings looted from churches and private collections.

Mussolini made his mark on the city too. Arrive by train and you emerge into the massive white megalith of the central **station** built on his orders; the town council offices are housed in the pompous twin **Arengario**, from which he would address crowds gathered in Piazza Duomo. And with stark irony it was on the now major road junction of **Piazzale Loreto** that the dead dictator was strung up for display to the baying mob.

Arrival

Most international and domestic **trains** pull in at the main **Stazione Centrale**, northeast of the city centre on Piazza Duca d'Aosta, at the hub of the metro network on lines MM2 and MM3. Quite a few trains, especially those from stations in the Milan region – Bergamo, Pavia, Como and the other western lakes – terminate at **Garibaldi**, **Lambrate**, **Porta Genova** and **Nord**, all on MM2 (the metro stop for Milan Nord is "Cadorna"), although these often also stop at Centrale. International and long-distance **buses** arrive at and depart from Piazza Castello, in front of the Castello Sforzesco. Information and tickets are available from the Autostradale bus office (☏02.801.161) on the piazza, or Zani Viaggi (☏02.867.131), on the corner of Piazza Castello and Foro Buonaparte. As for arrival by car, the city is encircled by a multi-laned toll road, the Tangenziale, from which there are links onto the autostradas for Venice and Turin (A4), Genoa (A7), and the "Autostrada del Sole" (A1) for Bologna, Florence, Rome and the south.

Milan has two **airports**, both used by domestic and international traffic. **Malpensa** (☏02.7485.2200), 50km northwest of the city, is the main one, connected by direct **bus** with the Stazione Centrale (every 20min 5.10am–11.30pm; 1hr; €5.50), and by the FNME **train**, the Malpensa Express (every 30min 6.30am–1.30am; 40min; information ☏02.27.723, ⓦwww.ferrovienord.it), with Milano Nord (the early morning and late evening services are replaced by a bus from Via Leopardi, just to the left of the station). Tickets cost €9 if bought beforehand, more if bought on the train, although Air Italia and Lufthansa passengers are entitled to discounts; check when you buy your ticket that your airline hasn't arranged a similar deal. A **taxi** costs around €80 depending on the traffic and where you're going in town. Milan's other airport, **Linate** (☎02.7485.2200), is just 7km east from the city centre: special airport buses connect it with the air terminal on Piazza Luigi di Savoia, on the east side of Stazione Centrale (every 20min 5.40am–9.30pm; 20min; €4.50). Ordinary ATM urban transport **buses** (#73) also run every ten minutes from 5.30am until around midnight between Linate and Piazza San Babila in the city centre, and they don't take much longer; tickets cost the usual €1 and should be bought before you get on the bus from the airport newsagent, or, if you have change, from the ticket machine at the bus stop. A **taxi** to the centre will cost around €30. Bear in mind, too, that there's a twice-daily connecting bus service between Linate and Malpensa, a 75-minute journey. A third airport **Bergamo Orio al Serio** is touted as Milan but is actually 45km northeast (see p.216).

Information

Milan has two main **tourist offices**, one tucked away between two jewellery shops down a corridor off the main upper level of the Stazione Centrale (Mon–Sat 9am–6pm; ☎02.7252.4360), and another, larger office in the city centre; there are also information desks at the airports (daily 9am–4pm). At the time of writing, the city centre office was at Via Marconi 1, on the corner of Piazza Duomo (Mon–Fri 8.45am–1pm & 2–6pm, Sat & Sun 9am–1pm & 2–5pm; ☎02.7252.4301, ⓕ02.7252.4350), but there are plans to move it whilst the building is renovated; the Galleria Vittorio Emanuele, across the square, was being mooted as the most likely new home. The tourist office publishes *Milano Mese* (ⓦwww.vivimilano.corriere.it), a monthly booklet, in Italian, which is worth picking up for its **listings** and general information. *Hello Milan* also gives good monthly rundowns of cultural events and the like, and *Milan Where, When, How*, has comprehensive listings concentrating on shopping, sport, bars, clubs and discos; both are available free in hotel lobbies, bars or the tourist office in Piazza Duomo. The pullouts in either *Corriere della Sera* on Wednesdays, or *La Repubblica* on Thursdays, are another valuable source of listings.

City transport

Milan's street-plan resembles a spider's web, with roads radiating out from the central Piazza Duomo. The bulk of the city is encircled by three concentric ring roads, although the suburbs and industrial estates are now spilling out towards a fourth ring, the Tangenziale, which links the main autostradas. The city centre is, however, fairly compact, and most of what you'll want to see is within the first or second rings, each of them marking ancient city boundaries.

In spite of this, the streets can be smoggy, and at some point you'll want to make use of the **public transport** system – an efficient network of trams, buses and metro. The **metro** is easiest to master (and the fastest and most useful). It's made up of four lines, the red MM1, green MM2, yellow MM3, and blue *passante ferroviario*, meeting at the four main hubs of Stazione Centrale, Duomo, Cadorna and Loreto (see map overleaf). The system is not comprehensive, but it's adequate for sightseeing. However, you may also want to use a **tram** or **bus**: the system is well organized and integrated with the metro. Buses, trams and the metro run from around 6am to midnight, after which **nightbuses** take over, following the metro routes until 1am.

For all **public transport enquiries** (ⓦwww.atm-mi.it) the information offices at the Duomo or Stazione Centrale metro stations are helpful, and have free route maps and English-speaking staff. **Tickets**, valid for 75 minutes, cost

€1 and can be used for one metro trip and as many bus and tram rides as you want. They are on sale at tobacconists, bars and at the metro station newsagents; most outlets close at 8pm so it's best to buy a few tickets in advance, or a carnet of ten for €8.50. Some stations have automatic ticket machines, although only the newer ones give change. You can also buy a one-day (€3) or two-day pass (€5.50) from the Stazione Centrale or Duomo metro stations.

Taxis don't cruise the streets, so don't bother trying to flag one down. Either head for a taxi rank – on Piazza Duomo, Largo Cairoli, Piazza San Babila, Stazione Centrale, etc – or phone one of the following numbers: ☎02.6767, 02.4040 or 02.8585. Apart from taxis, **driving** in the city is best avoided: the streets are congested and parking nigh on impossible. Parking in prohibited zones is not worth it; you'll be fined if caught and have your car impounded by the police (see "Listings", p.184, for details of city-centre car parks).

Accommodation

Milan is still more a business than a tourist city, and its **accommodation** is geared to the expense-account traveller: prices tend to be high and many hotels are booked up all year round. If you want to be sure of a room, phone ahead and get them to fax you back to confirm the reservation. The area around Stazione Centrale, and across to Corso Buenos Aires and Piazzale Loreto, is home to a good proportion of the city's cheaper hotels, and although many cater to the area's considerable red-light trade, you should be fine at any of the carefully chosen places below. As you go towards the centre, prices rise but there are still some good deals to be had in the side streets off the city's main thoroughfares.

Hotels

Antica Locanda dei Mercanti Via San Tomaso 6 ☎02.805.4080, ⊛www.locanda.it. A charming little spot where two of the individually decorated rooms even have their own roof terraces. Breakfast is served in the rooms. ❽

Antica Locanda Solferino Via Castelfidardo 2 ☎02.657.0129, ℮info@anticalocandasolferino.it.

Between the Giardini Pubblici and Parco Sempione, this select haven is favoured by models and left-leaning intellectuals alike, and only a stone's throw from shoppers' heaven. ❻

Ariston Largo Carobbio 2 ☎02.7200.0914, ⊛www.brerahotels.com. This modern hotel prides itself on an ecological construction but the best thing about it is its position – within walking distance of the Duomo and the Navigli – and the free bicycles. Rooms are a little cramped but all ensuite and there's a good breakfast included in the price. ⑥

Arno Via Lazzaretto 17 ⓣ & ⓕ 02.670.5509, ⓔ hotelarno@libero.it. Not far from Stazione Centrale, this very welcoming *pensione* has a washing machine, kitchen and Internet access for guests. The rooms are basic but clean and good value. ③

Casa Mia Viale Vittorio Veneto 30 t502.657.5249, ⓔ hotelcasamia@libero.it. A friendly, spotless hotel with bright, quiet en-suite rooms. One of the best options in the station area. Ten percent discount on presentation of this book. Breakfast included ⑥

Four Seasons Via Gesù 8 ⓣ 02.77.088, ⓦ www.fourseasons.com/milan. Housed in a fifteenth-century convent, Milan's top hotel offers luxurious rooms overlooking a cloistered courtyard. If your pockets are deep enough the elegantly elite atmosphere provides a perfect backdrop for a visit to Milan. ⑨

Gelsomina V. Piero della Francesca 4/7 ⓣ 02.3419.1742. A comfortable, friendly *pensione*; all rooms are en suite. Tram #33 or #29 from MM Garibaldi, or buses #57 or #94. ③

Kennedy Viale Tunisia 6 6th floor ⓣ 02.2940.0934, ⓦ www.kennedyhotel.it. A newly renovated one-star in the station area with simple rooms, some ensuite. Worth a try when all else is full. ④

London Via Rovello 3 ⓣ 02.720.166, ⓦ hote.london@traveleurope.it. A pleasant, family-run hotel in a good central position. There's a choice of singles and doubles with or without en-suite shower; the decor is standard but all rooms have air conditioning. Closed Aug. ⑤

Rovello Via Rovello 18a ⓣ 02.8646.4654, ⓕ 02.7202.3656. The newly refurbished rooms in this well-located hotel, close to Castello Sforzesco, are attractive and spacious with shiny new bathrooms. Prices may be negotiable in summer. Breakfast included. ⑥

San Francisco Viale Lombardia 55 ⓣ 02.236.1009, ⓕ 02.2668.0377. A family-run hotel with simple rooms and a small garden several blocks east of Piazzale Loreto, in the student area. Bus #56. ④

Santa Marta Via Santa Marta 4 ⓣ 02.804.567, ⓦ hotel-santamarta.it. A three-star in a great central location in the Roman part of town. The rooms are comfortable though plainly furnished. Breakfast included. ⑧

Valley Via Soperga 19 ⓣ 02.6698.7252. Two minutes' walk north of the Stazione Centrale, this simple little spot is a good choice if you're arriving late or leaving early. The airy no-frills rooms are mainly ensuite. ④

Hostels and campsites

Autodromo Parco di Monza, Monza ⓣ 039.387.771. A campsite in a park near the renowned Formula One circuit, north of Milan. Trains run from Stazione Centrale to Monza station, from where it's a short bus ride. Open from early May to the end of September only.

Città di Milano Via G. Airaghi 61 ⓣ 02.4820.0134, ⓦ www.parcoaquatica.com. The nearest campsite to the centre, but still a metro trip and a bus ride away. MM1 to De Angeli, then bus #72. Open all year.

La Cordata Via Burigozzo 11, off Corso Italia ⓣ 02.5831.4675, ⓦ www.lacordata.it. A clean, basic hostel run by a scout organization in a very good central location. Bunks are in 6-, 10- or 16-bed dorms, each dorm with its own shower room. There's a large kitchen and communal room for residents' use. 12.30am curfew. €15.50 with sheets.

Ostello Piero Rotta Viale Salmoiraghi 1, on the corner of Via Martino Bassi ⓣ 02.3926.7095. An institutional–feeling HI hostel housed in a large modern building with a garden, out in the northwest suburbs near the San Siro stadium. Open 7–9am and 3.30–11pm; 12.30am curfew. You can't book ahead, so it's best to arrive early, especially in summer. MM1 to QT8, then a couple of hundred metres straight ahead and the hostel is on your right. €16 including breakfast.

The City

Historic Milan lies at the centre of a web of streets, within the inner **Cerchia dei Navigli**, which follows the route of the medieval city walls. **Piazza del Duomo** is the city centre's main orientation point: most of the city's major sights lie within this area, as well as the swankiest designer shops and most elegant cafés. Visits to **art galleries and museums**, the **Duomo** and other churches can be punctuated with designer window-shopping in the so-called Quadrilatero d'Oro, or sipping overpriced drinks among the designer-dressed

CENTRAL MILAN

N

ACCOMMODATION
Antica Locanda
dei Mercanti   4
Ariston   6
Four Seasons   1
London   3
Rovello   2
Santa Marta   5

RESTAURANTS
Luini   E
Trattoria Milanese   H
Taverna Morigi   G
Premiata   I
Santa Lucia   C

CAFÉS & BARS
Arco della Pace   A
Bar Brera   B
Bar Magenta   D
Caffè Miani   F

Arena
Parco Sempione
Arco Pace A
Palazzo dell'Arte
Stazione Nord
Cadorna
Santa Maria delle Grazie
Museo Archeologico D
Monastero Maggiore G
Università Cattolica
S. Ambrogio
Sant'Ambrogio
Museo Nazionale della Scienza e della Tecnica
S. Vittorio al Corpo

Castello Sforzesco
Teatro Piccolo
Cairoli
Pinacoteca Brera
La Scala
Galleria Vittorio Emanuele II
Palazzo della Ragione
Pinacoteca Ambrosiana
San Satiro

Museo del Risorgimento
Museo Poldi Pezzoli
Duomo
Museo del Duomo
San Nazaro
Ospedale Maggiore

Giardini Pubblici
Museo del Cinema
Museo Civico di Storia Naturale
Sala Oberdan
Porta Venezia
Civica Galleria d'Arte Moderne
San Babila

VIALE PIAVE
VIALE MAJNO
VIALE PREMUDA
VIALE BIANCA MARIA
VIA DONIZETTI
PIAZZA DEL TRICOLORE
CORSO BUENOS AIRES
VIA PALESTRO
VIA SENATO
CORSO VENEZIA
VIA DELLA SPIGA
VIA S. ANDREA
VIA MANZONI
VIA MONTENAPOLEONE
CORSO MATTEOTTI
VIA VISCONTI MODRONE
CORSO MONFORTE
CORSO DI PORTA VITTORIA
CORSO PORTA ROMANA
VIA S. ANTONIO
VIA FRANCESCO SFORZA
VIA LARGA
VIA TORINO
CORSO MAGENTA
VIA CARDUCCI
VIALE PORTA VERCELLINA
VIA S. VITTORE
VIA G. CARDUCCI
VIA MERAVIGLI
VIA DANTE
FORO BUONAPARTE
CORSO GIUSEPPE GARIBALDI
VIA PONTACCIO
VIA BRERA
VIA SOLFERINO
VIA MOSCOVA
VIA MONTEBELLO
VIA FATEBENEFRATELLI
CORSO PORTA NUOVA
VIA STATUTO
VIA LEGNANO
VIALE MALTA
VIALE GADIO
SEMPIONE
VIALE EMILIO ALEMAGNA
VIALE SHAKESPEARE

0   200m

clientele of the pavement cafés of the **Galleria Vittorio Emanuele** or around the **Pinacoteca di Brera** art gallery. The second *cerchia*, the **Viali**, skirts behind the centre's two large parks – the **Parco Sempione** and **Giardini Pubblici** – to the canal sides of the **Navigli** in the south, following the tracks of defensive walls built during the Spanish occupation. Within lie the **Castello Sforzesco** and the church of **Santa Maria delle Grazie**, which houses Milan's most famous painting, Leonardo's *The Last Supper*. What follows is a wedge-by-wedge account of the city: Milan is not an easily wanderable city, so make a judicious selection, walking a little but where necessary hopping between places by way of the metro or other public transport.

Piazza del Duomo

The unquestioned hub of the city is **Piazza del Duomo**, a large, mostly pedestrianized square that's rarely quiet at any time of day. Milanese hurry out of the metro station deftly avoiding the pigeon-feed sellers and ice cream vendors; designer-dressed kids hang out on the steps of the cathedral; harassed tour guides gather together their flocks; and well-preserved women stiletto-click across the square to glitzy cafés.

The **Duomo** is the world's largest Gothic cathedral, begun in 1386 under the Viscontis and completed nearly five centuries later. The finishing touches to the facade were finally added in 1813, and from the outside at least it's an incredible building, notable as much for its decoration – a strange mixture of Baroque and Gothic – as its size. The marble, chosen specially by the Viscontis, comes from the quarries of Candoglia near Lago Maggiore and continues to be used in renovation today – the fabric not surprisingly under severe attack from Milan's polluted atmosphere. Restoration of the cathedral is ongoing and the magnificent facade is scheduled to be under scaffolding until at least late 2004.

Inside the Duomo, a green, almost subterranean half-light filters through the stained glass windows, lending the marble columns a bone-like hue that led the French writer Suarés to compare the interior to "the hollow of a colossal beast". By the entrance, the narrow brass strip embedded in the pavement with the signs of the zodiac alongside is Europe's largest sundial, laid out in 1786. A beam of light still falls on it through a hole in the ceiling, though changes in the Earth's axis mean that it's no longer accurate. To the left of the entrance you'll find the cathedral's fourth-century **Battistero Paleocristiano** (daily 9.30am–5.15pm; €1.50) where St Ambrose baptized St Augustine in 387 AD. Augustine had arrived in Milan three years earlier with his illegitimate son, and after sampling various religions, including paganism, was eventually converted to Christianity by Ambrose, then the city's bishop.

At the far end of the church, suspended high above the chancel, a large crucifix contains the most important of the Duomo's holy relics – a nail from Christ's cross, which was crafted to become the bit for the bridle of Emperor Constantine's horse. The cross is lowered once a year, on September 14, the Feast of the Cross, by a device invented by Leonardo da Vinci. Close by, beneath the presbytery, the **Scurolo di San Carlo** (daily 9am–noon & 2.30–6pm; €1) is an octagonal crypt housing the remains of St Charles Borromeo, the zealous sixteenth-century cardinal who was canonized for his unflinching work among the poor of the city and whose reforms antagonized the higher echelons of the corrupt Church. He lies here in a glass coffin, clothed, bejewelled, masked and gloved, wearing a gold crown attributed to Cellini. Borromeo was also responsible for the large altar in the north transept, erected in order to close off a door that allowed the locals to use the cathedral as a short cut to the market. Adjacent to Borromeo's resting-place, the **treasury** features extravagant evangelical covers, Byzantine ivory-work and heavily embroidered vestments. To the right of the chancel, by the door to the Palazzo Reale, the sixteenth-century statue of St Bartholomew, with his flayed skin thrown like a toga over his shoulder, is one of the church's more gruesome statues, with veins, muscles and bones sculpted with anatomical accuracy, the draped skin retaining the form of knee, foot, toes and toenails.

Outside again, from the northwest end of the cathedral you can get to the **cathedral roof** (daily: 17 Feb to 14 Nov 9am–5.45pm; 15 Nov to 16 Feb 9am–4.15pm; €3.50 to walk, €5 for the elevator), where you can stroll around the forest of tracery, pinnacles and statues while enjoying fine views of the city and on clear days even the Alps. The highlight is the central spire, its lacy marble crowned by a gilded statue of the Madonna looking out over the bodies of the roof sunbathers.

Across the way from the cathedral, the **Museo del Duomo** (daily 10am–1.15pm & 3–6pm; €6), housed in a wing of the Palazzo Reale on the southern side of the piazza, holds casts of a good many of the 3000 or so statues and gargoyles that spike the Duomo. You can also see how it might have ended up, in a display of entries for a late nineteenth-century competition of new designs for the facade. The scheme came to nothing – partly because the winner died, but mostly because the Milanese had grown attached to the duomo's distinctive hybrid frontage.

South of Piazza del Duomo

South of Piazza del Duomo there are several minor gems hidden among the shops and offices. The best of these is the charming church of **San Satiro** (daily 8–11am & 3.30–6.30pm), off the busy shopping street of Via Torino, a study in ingenuity, commissioned from Milan's foremost Renaissance architect, Bramante, in 1476. Originally the oratory of the adjacent ninth-century church of San Satiro, it was transformed by Bramante into a long-naved basilica by converting the long oblong oratory into the transept and adding a wonderful trompe l'oeil apse onto the back wall.

Five minutes west, just off Via Torino at Piazza Pio 2, the **Pinacoteca Ambrosiana** (Tues–Sun 10am–5.30pm; €7.50) was founded by another member of the Borromeo family, Cardinal Federico Borromeo, in the early seventeenth century. The cardinal collected ancient manuscripts, assembling one of the largest libraries in Europe, though what you come here for now is his art collection, stamped with his taste for Jan Brueghel, sixteenth-century Venetians and some of the more kitsch followers of Leonardo. Among many mediocre works, there is a rare painting by Leonardo da Vinci, *Portrait of a Musician*, a cartoon by Raphael for the School of Athens, and a Caravaggio considered to be Italy's first ever still life. The museum's quirkiest exhibit, however, is a lock of Lucrezia Borgia's hair – put for safe-keeping in a glass phial ever since Byron (having decided that her hair was the most beautiful he had ever seen) extracted one as a keepsake from the library downstairs where it used to be kept unprotected.

Cutting across Via Torino and Via Mazzini to Corso di Porta Romana, one of the city's busiest radial roads, takes you to the church of **San Nazaro**. Here the family chapel of one of the city's better-known traitors – the *condottiere* Giangiacomo Trivulzio, who led the French attack on Milan to spite his rival Lodovico Sforza and was rewarded by being made the city's French governor – was built arrogantly as a vestibule that everyone had to pass through on their way to church rather than as a more usual side chapel. His tomb and those of his family are contained in niches around the walls, the inscription above Giangiacomo's reading, "He who never rested now rests: silence."

Behind San Nazaro, the **Ospedale Maggiore** – once known locally as the "Ca' Granda" (Big House) – was an ambitious project undertaken by the Florentine architect Filarete to unite the city's numerous hospitals and charitable institutions on one site. His hopes of introducing Renaissance architecture to Milan were dampened by local architects who, as soon as Filarete returned to Florence, introduced the late-Gothic elements clearly visible on the facade. To get a clearer idea of Filarete's intentions, step inside to look at the courtyards – eight small ones formed by two crucifixes, separated by a ninth rectangular one. Today the building houses the city's university, and the courtyards make a perfect spot to rest your sightseeing-weary legs for half an hour or so.

North of Piazza del Duomo

Almost as famous a Milanese sight as the duomo is the gaudily opulent **Galleria Vittorio Emanuele II**, a cruciform glass-domed gallery designed in 1865 by Giuseppe Mengoni, who was killed when he fell from the roof a few days before the inaugural ceremony. Though the prices in its cafés are extortionate, you'll see what seems like the city's whole population shove or stroll through depending on the time of day. Be sure to also take a look at the circular mosaic beneath the glass cupola, composed of the symbols that made up the cities of the newly united Italy: Romulus and Remus for Rome, a fleur-de-lys for Florence, the white shield with a red cross for Milan and a bull for Turin – the indentation in the last is because it's considered good luck to spin round on the bull's testicles.

The left arm of the gallery leads towards **Piazza dei Mercanti**, surrounded by medieval palaces, which were once the seats of guilds and other city organizations. The square was the commercial centre of medieval Milan and the city's financial hub until the turn of the twentieth century, when the Borsa or Stock Exchange – then housed in the sixteenth-century **Palazzo dei Giureconsulti** on Via Mercanti – was moved north to Piazza degli Affari. Now the square is one of the city's more peaceful spots, dominated by the **Palazzo della Ragione**, built in the early thirteenth century to celebrate Milan winning autonomy from the emperor. The upper storey was added four centuries later, by another imperial figure, Empress Maria Theresa.

The main branch of Galleria Vittorio Emanuele leads through to Piazza della Scala and the world-famous **La Scala** opera house (℡02.860.775, ⓦwww.teatroallascala.org), designed by Piermarini and opened in 1778 with an opera by Antonio Salieri – a well-known name in his own right then, though more famous now (thanks to Peter Schaffer's play *Amadeus*) for his rivalry with Mozart than for his music. La Scala is still to a great extent the social and cultural centre of Milan's elite, and although Sixties protests have since led to a more open official policy on the arts in Milan, it remains as exclusive a venue as it ever was. Note however that the theatre is currently undergoing extensive renovation and will remain closed until 2005; its temporary home in the meantime is the new Arcimboldi Theatre; see p.183 for further details. The small **museum** (Tues–Sun 9am–6pm; €5), featuring costumes, sets, composers' death masks, plaster casts of conductors' hands, and a rugged statue of Puccini in a capacious overcoat, has been moved for the renovation period to Palazzo Busca, Corso Magenta 71, opposite Santa Maria delle Grazie (see p.177).

Heading north out of the piazza you come to the **Museo Poldi Pezzoli** at Via Manzoni 12 (Tues–Sun 10am–6pm; €6), comprising pieces assembled by the nineteenth-century collector Gian Giacomo Poldi Pezzoli. Much of this is made up of rather dull rooms of clocks, watches, cutlery and jewellery, but the Salone Dorato upstairs contains a number of intriguing paintings, including a portrait of a portly *San Nicola da Tolentino* by Piero della Francesca, part of an altarpiece on which he worked intermittently for fifteen years. St Nicholas looks across at two works by Botticelli, one a gentle *Madonna del Libro*, among the many variations of the Madonna and Child theme which he produced at the end of the fifteenth century, the other a mesmerizing *Deposition*, painted towards the end of his life in response to the monk Savonarola's crusade against his earlier, more humanistic canvases. Also in the room is the museum's best-known portrait, *Portrait of a Young Woman* by Pollaiuolo, whose anatomical studies are evidenced in the subtle suggestion of bone structure beneath the skin of this ideal Renaissance woman.

The Brera district and the Quadrilatero d'Oro

Due north of La Scala, **Via Brera** sets the tone for the city's arty quarter with its small galleries and art shops. There's nothing resembling an artist's garret, however: Via Brera and the streets around it are the terrain of the rich, reflected in the café prices and designer styles of those who can afford to sit outside them.

The Brera district gives its name to Milan's most prestigious art gallery, the **Pinacoteca di Brera** at Via Brera 28 (Tues–Sun 8.30am–7.30pm; €6.20), originally set up by Napoleon, who filled the building with works looted from the churches and aristocratic collections of French-occupied Italy, opening the museum to the public in 1809. It's a fine gallery, Milan's best by far, but it's also rather large, and so your visit will probably be more enjoyable if you're selective, dipping into the collection guided by your own personal tastes.

Not surprisingly, most of the museum's paintings are Italian and predate the twentieth century. The Brera does display modern work, including paintings by Modigliani, De Chirico and Carrà (Room 1), but it's the Renaissance which constitutes the museum's core. There's a good representation of Venetian painters – works by Bonifacio and, a century later, Paolo Veronese, the latter weighing in with a depiction of *Supper in the House of Simon* (Room IX) which got him into trouble with the Inquisition, who considered the introduction of frolicking animals and unruly kids unsuitable subject matter for a religious painting. Tintoretto's *Pietà* (Room IX) was more starkly in tune with requirements of the time, a scene of intense concentration and grief over Christ's body, painted in the 1560s. Gentile Bellini's *St Mark Preaching in St Euphemia Square* (Room VIII) introduces an exotic note, the square bustling with turbaned men, veiled women, camels and even a giraffe. There are also paintings by Gentile's follower, Carpaccio, namely *The Presentation of the Virgin* and *The Disputation of St Stephen* (Room VI), while the *Pietà* (Room VI) by Gentile's more talented brother, Giovanni, has been deemed "one of the most moving paintings in the history of art". Look out also for *The Dead Christ* (Room VI), a painting by Giovanni Bellini's brother-in-law, Mantegna: it's an ingenious composition – Christ, lying on a wooden slab, viewed from the wrinkled and pierced soles of his feet upwards. Although he was a contemporary of Mantegna, Crivelli's work, nearby, is quite different, his paintings creating a fairyland for his pale, perfect Madonnas, hermetically sealed from the realities of time and decay.

Later rooms hold yet more quality work, of which Piero della Francesca's haunting *Madonna with Angels, SS and Federigo da Montefeltro* (Room XXIV) is the most arresting. But take a look too at Raphael's *Marriage of the Virgin* (Room XXIV), whose lucid, languid Renaissance mood is in sharp contrast to the grim realism of Caravaggio's *Supper at Emmaus* (Room XXIX) set in a dark tavern. Less well known but equally realistic are the paintings of Lombardy's brilliant eighteenth-century realist, Ceruti – known as Il Pitochetto (The Little Beggar) for his unfashionable sympathy with the poor, who stare out with reproachful dignity from his canvases (Room XXXVI). As his main champion, Roberto Longhi, said, his figures are "dangerously larger than life", not easily transformed into "gay drawing room ornaments". The collection ends with the unfinished *Fuimaria* (Room XXXVII) by Giuseppe Pelizza da Volpedo, a composition showing the artist's socialist ideals and an emerging consciousness of people-power – a theme that he returned to for *The Fourth Estate* in the Civica Galleria d'Arte Moderna (see below), adopted as an emblem of the power of the populace.

Round the corner from the *pinacoteca*, the **Museo del Risorgimento** at Via Borgonuovo 23 (Tues–Sun 9am–1pm & 2–5.30pm; free) charts the course of Italian Unification through a well-presented combination of paintings, proclamations, cuttings and photographs – though it helps to have some knowledge of the Italian Unification to appreciate it.

A couple of blocks to the east across Via Manzoni lies the so-called **Quadrilatero d'Oro** – the few hundred square yards bordered by Via Monte Napoleone, Via Sant'Andrea, Via Spiga and Via Borgospesso – which is home to the shops of all the big designer names, along with design studios and contemporary art galleries. The area is well worth a stroll, if only to observe the better-heeled Milanese searching out the perfect *objet d'art* for their elegant pads. Indeed, to leave Milan without looking in the windows of its fashionable boutiques would be to miss out on a crucial aspect of the city.

The Giardini Pubblici and modern art galleries

Northeast from the Duomo, the heavily trafficked Piazza Cavour marks the corner of the city's oldest public park, the **Giardini Pubblici**, designed by Piermarini shortly after he completed La Scala. Relandscaped in the nineteenth century to give it a more rustic look, its shady avenues and small lake are ideal for recuperating from Milan's twin doses of culture and carbon monoxide fumes.

Across the road from the park in the Villa Reale, the **Civica Galleria d'Arte Moderna**, Via Palestro 16 (Tues–Sun 9am–5.30pm; free), is one of Milan's most palatable galleries, housed in Napoleon's former in-town residence, which now doubles as the civic registry office. The main building holds nineteenth-century Italian art and sculpture – including striking political works by the painter Giuseppe Pellizza da Volpedo, canvases by the self-styled romantic *scapigliati* (wild-haired) movement of the late nineteenth century, impressive sculptures by Marino Marini, and a less arcane selection of paintings by Corot, Millet and various French Impressionists. Also worth a look are the works of the Futurists – Boccioni, Balla and Morandi. In the grounds, the **Padiglione d'Arte Contemporanea** (Tues–Sun 9.30am–7pm; ⓦwww.pac-milano.org; €5.20) is a venue for temporary and often prestigious exhibitions of contemporary art. Overlooking the gardens, in a light airy annexe, the small **Collezione Vismara** has Picasso's *Battle of the Centaurs* – a spontaneously simple charcoal complete with finger smudges – and minor but appealing works by Matisse, Dufy and their Italian contemporaries.

Just to the northeast of the park is **Spazio Oberdan**, Viale Vittorio Veneto 2 (Tues & Thurs 10am–10pm, Wed & Fri–Sun 10am–7.30pm; ☎02.7740.6300,

The Castello Sforzesco

At the far end of Via Dante from Piazza del Duomo, **Castello Sforzesco** rises
imperiously from the mayhem of Foro Buonaparte, a congested and distinctly
un-forum-like road and bus terminus laid out by Napoleon in self-tribute. He
had a vision of a grand new centre for the Italian capital, laid out along Roman
lines, but he only got as far as constructing an arena, a triumphal arch and these
two semicircular roads before he lost Milan to the Austrians a few years later.
The arena and triumphal arch still stand behind the castle in the **Parco
Sempione**, a popular hangout for foreign tourists, junkies and prostitutes.

The red-brick castle, the result of numerous rebuildings, is, with its crenellated towers and fortified walls, one of Milan's most striking landmarks. Begun by
the Viscontis, it was destroyed by mobs rebelling against their regime in 1447,
and rebuilt by their successors, the Sforzas. Under Lodovico Sforza the court
became one of the most powerful, luxurious and cultured of the Renaissance,
renowned for its ostentatious wealth and court artists like Leonardo and
Bramante. Lodovico's days of glory came to an end when Milan was invaded by
the French in 1499, and from then until the end of the nineteenth century the
castle was used as a barracks by successive occupying armies. Just over a century ago it was converted into a series of museums. Note that in 2000 the council started a programme of technical work on the castle entailing temporary closures, so it's possible that parts of the complex will be closed during your visit.

The *castello*'s buildings are grouped around three courtyards, one of which,
the Corte Ducale, formed the centre of the residential quarters, which now
contain the **Museo d'Arte Antica** and the **Pinacoteca del Castello**
(Tues–Sun 9am–5.30pm; free). The Museo d'Arte Antica holds fragments of
sculpture from Milan's demolished churches and palaces, a run-of-the-mill collection saved by the inclusion of Michelangelo's *Rondanini Pietà*, which the
artist worked on for the last nine years of his life. It's an unfinished but oddly
powerful work, with much of the marble unpolished and a third arm (indicating a change of position for Christ's body) hanging limply from a block of
stone to his right.

The first room of the **Pinacoteca**, upstairs, contains a cycle of monochrome
frescoes illustrating the Griselda story from Boccaccio's *Decameron* – a catalogue
of indignities inflicted by a marquis on his wife in order to test her fidelity. It was
intended as a celebration of the patience and devotion of one Bianca Pellegrini,
and if you decide to push on into the first room of the main picture gallery, you'll
see what she looked like: Bianca was used as a model for the Madonna in a
polyptych by Benedetto Bembo. In the same room are works by Bellini, Crivelli
and Lippi, and one of Mantegna's last works, a dreamy evocation of the *Madonna
in Glory among Angels and SS*. There are also lots of paintings by Vincenzo Foppa,
the leading artist on the Milanese scene before Leonardo da Vinci, in the next
room; look out too for the polyptych by De' Tatti, in which the castle makes an
appearance as a fanciful setting for the Crucifixion, and for Arcimboldi's bizarre
Primavera – a portrait of a woman composed entirely of flowers, heralded as a sixteenth-century precursor of Surrealism.

The castle's other museums are housed in the Sforza fortress, the **Rocchetta**,
to the left of the Corte Ducale (same times). Of these, the **museum of
applied arts** is only really of specialist interest, containing wrought-iron work,
ceramics, ivory and musical instruments. The small, well-displayed **Egyptian
collection** is rather better, with impressive displays of mummies and sar-

③

cophagi and papyrus fragments from *The Book of the Dead*. There's also a small and deftly lit **prehistoric collection**, which has as its centrepiece an assortment of finds from the Iron Age burial grounds of the Golasecca civilization, south of Lago Maggiore.

Santa Maria delle Grazie and around

To the south of the castle, beyond the busy streets of the financial district, skirted by Corso Magenta, are some of Milan's richest cultural pickings. The **Museo Archeologico**, in the ex-Monastero Maggiore at Corso Magenta 15 (Tues–Sun 9.30am–5.30pm; free), is well worth a visit. The displays of glass phials, kitchen utensils and jewellery from Roman Milan are compelling, and though there's a scarcity of larger objects, there is a colossal head of Jove, found near the castle, a torso of Hercules and a smattering of mosaic pavements unearthed around the city.

But what really brings visitors into this part of town is the church of **Santa Maria delle Grazie** – famous for its mural of the *Last Supper* by Leonardo da Vinci. First built as a Gothic church by the fifteenth-century architect Solari, Santa Maria delle Grazie was partially rebuilt under a dissatisfied Lodovico Sforza by the more up-to-date Bramante, who tore down Solari's chancel and replaced it with a massive dome supported by an airy Renaissance cube. Lodovico also intended to replace the nave and facade, but was unable to do so before Milan fell to the French, leaving an odd combination of styles – Solari's Gothic vaults, decorated in powdery blues, reds and ochre, illuminated by the light that floods through the windows of Bramante's dome. A side door leads into Bramante's cool and tranquil cloisters, outside of which there's a good view of the sixteen-sided drum the architect placed around his dome.

Leonardo's *Last Supper* – signposted **Cenacolo Vinciano** – is one of the world's great paintings and most resonant images. However, art of this magnitude doesn't come easy: visits must be booked by telephone at least three or four days in advance (reservations on ℡02.8942.1146 Mon–Fri 9am–7pm; viewing Tues–Sun 8.15am–6.45pm; €6.50, plus €2 obligatory booking fee). Henry James likened the painting to an "illustrious invalid" that people visited with "leave-taking sighs and almost death-bed or tip-toe precautions"; certainly it's hard, when you visit the painting, decayed and faded on the refectory wall, not to feel that it's the last time you'll see it. Restoration is virtually perpetual owing to its fragile nature, but the main part of the fresco is free from scaffolding. That the work survived at all is something of a miracle. Leonardo's decision to use oil paint rather than the more usual faster-drying – and longer-lasting – fresco technique with watercolours led to the painting disintegrating within five years of its completion. A couple of centuries later Napoleonic troops billeted here used the wall for target practice. And in 1943 a bomb destroyed the building, amazingly leaving only the *Last Supper*'s wall standing. Well-meaning restoration over the centuries has also meant that little of Leonardo's original colouring has survived, but despite this the painting still retains its power. Leonardo spent two years on it, searching the streets of Milan for models. When the monks complained that the face of Judas was still unfinished, Leonardo replied that he had been searching for over a year among the city's criminals for a sufficiently evil face, and that if he didn't find one he would use the face of the prior. Whether or not Judas's face is modelled on the prior's is unrecorded, but Leonardo's Judas does seem, as Vasari wrote, "the very embodiment of treachery and inhumanity".

A couple of blocks south, at Via S. Vittore 21, the **Museo Nazionale della Scienza e della Tecnica** (Tues–Fri 9.30am–4.50pm, Sat & Sun 9.30am–

6.20pm; €6.20) is dedicated to Leonardo and is inspired by his inventions, with reconstructions of some of his wackier contraptions, including the famous flying machine. Less compelling are the general sections on physics, astronomy, telecommunications and musical instruments. There are also collections of steam trains, aeroplanes and even a full-scale reconstruction of the ballroom and bridge of an ocean liner.

The nearby church of **Sant'Ambrogio** (Mon–Sat 7am–noon & 3–7pm, Sun 7am–1pm & 3.30–8pm) was founded in the fourth century by Milan's patron saint. St Ambrose, as he's known in English, is even today an important name in the city: the Milanese refer to themselves as Ambrosiani, have named a chain of banks after him, and celebrate his feast day, December 7, with the opening of the Scala season and a big street market around the church. Ambrose's remains still lie in the church's crypt, but there's nothing left of the original church in which his most famous convert, St Augustine, first heard him preach.

The present church, the blueprint for many of Lombardy's Romanesque basilicas, is, however, one of the city's loveliest, reached through a colonnaded quadrangle with column capitals carved with rearing horses, contorted dragons and an assortment of bizarre predators. Inside, to the left of the nave, a freestanding Byzantine pillar is topped with a "magic" bronze serpent, flicked into a loop and symbolizing Aaron's rod – an ancient tradition held that on the Day of Judgement it would crawl back to the Valley of Jesophat. Look, too, at the pulpit, a superb piece of Romanesque carving decorated with reliefs of wild animals and the occasional human, most of whom are intent upon devouring one another. There are older relics further down the nave, notably the ciborium, reliefed with the figures of saints Gervasius and Protasius – martyred Roman soldiers whose clothed bodies flank that of St Ambrose in the crypt. A nineteenth-century autopsy revealed that they had been killed by having their throats cut. Similar investigations into St Ambrose's remains restored the reputation of the anonymous fifth-century artist responsible for the mosaic portrait of the saint in the Cappella di San Vittorio in Ciel d'Oro (to the right of the sacristy). Until then it was assumed that Ambrose owed his crooked face to a slip of the artist's hand, but the examination of his skull revealed an abnormally deep-set tooth, suggesting that his face would indeed have been slightly deformed.

Outside (entrance to the left of the choir) is Bramante's unfinished **Cortile della Canonica**. The side that Bramante did complete, a novel concoction incorporating knobbly "tree trunk" columns and a triumphal arch, was shattered by a bomb in the last war and reconstructed from the fragments. The second side was added only in 1955 and leads to a modest museum (Mon & Wed–Fri 10am–noon & 3–5pm, Sat & Sun 3–5pm; €2), whose only memorable exhibit is St Ambrose's bed.

South of the centre: Navigli and Ticinese

Flanking the city's two canals, just south of the Cerchia Viali, the streets of the **Navigli** quarter feel a long way from the city centre, their peeling houses and waterside views much sought after by the city's would-be Bohemians. A thriving inland port from the fifteenth century until the 1950s, the Naviglio Pavese – which links Milan with Pavia – and the Naviglio Grande – which runs to the west – are part of a network of rivers and canals covering the whole of Italy's northern plain, making ports or even naval bases of landlocked cities. They were also much used by travellers: the ruling families of the North used them to visit one another, Prospero and Miranda escaped along the Navigli in *The Tempest*, and they were still being used by Grand Tourists in the eighteenth century; Goethe, for example, describes the discomfort and hazards of jour-

△ Sant'Andrea and the Rotonda, Mantua

neying by canal. These days there's not much to do other than browse in its artists' studios and antique shops, but it's a peaceful area by day, good for idle strolling, and a lively one at night when its restaurants and bars fill up.

Back towards the centre, the **Ticinese** is another arty district, though as yet less a prey to regeneration than Navigli. On the southern edge of the quarter, at the bottom of Corso di Porta Ticinese, the nineteenth-century **Arco di Porta Ticinese** is an Ionic gateway on a noisy traffic island built to celebrate Napoleon's victory at Marengo – and, after his demise, dedicated to peace. In recent years the Corso has become a focus of alternative fashion and is lined with small boutique shops and bars and cafés that come alive at *aperitivo* time.

Ticinese also boasts two important churches. The first, **Sant'Eustorgio**, at the bottom end of the Corso, was built in the fourth century to house the bones of the Magi, said to have been brought here by St Ambrose. It was rebuilt in the eleventh century, but in the twelfth century was virtually destroyed by Barbarossa, who seized the Magi's bones and deposited them in Cologne Cathedral. Some of the bones were returned in 1903 and are kept in a Roman sarcophagus tucked away in the right transept. The main reason for visiting the church, however, is to see the **Portinari Chapel**, round to the left of the main entrance (Tues–Sun 4.30–6.30pm; €6), commissioned from the Florentine architect Michelozzi in the 1460s by one Portinari, an agent of the Medici bank, to house the remains of St Peter the Martyr. Peter, one of Catholicism's less attractive saints, was banned from the Church for allegedly entertaining women in his cell, then cleared of the charge and given a job as an Inquisitor. His death was particularly nasty – he was axed in the head by a member of the sect that he was persecuting – but the martyrdom led to almost immediate canonization and the dubious honour of being deemed Patron of Inquisitors. The chapel, with its simple geometric design, has been credited with being Milan's first real Renaissance building, although it was Bramante who really developed the style. Inside, you are treated to scenes from the life of St Peter in frescoes by Foppa and reliefs carved on the sides of his elaborate tomb.

Further up the Corso, the fourteenth-century **Porta Ticinese** and sixteen Corinthian columns – **the Colonne di San Lorenzo**, scavenged from a Roman ruin – stand outside the church of **San Lorenzo**. It's an evocative spot alive at all hours with an odd juxtaposition of rattling trams, bongo-banging youth and ancient monuments. San Lorenzo, apparently considered by Leonardo da Vinci to be the most beautiful church in Milan, was founded in the fourth century, when it was the largest centrally planned church in the western Roman Empire. The current structure is a sixteenth-century renovation of an eleventh-century rebuilding, a shaky edifice under threat from the vibrating tramlines outside. Inside, the most interesting feature is the **Cappella di San Aquilino** (daily 7.30am–6pm; €2), much of which has survived from the fourth century. There are fragments of fourth-century mosaics on the walls, including one in the left apse where the tiles have crumbled away, revealing the artist's original sketches. Behind the altar, steps lead down to what is left of the original foundations, a jigsaw of fragments of Roman architecture looted from an arena.

Eating

Milan may seem to live at a faster pace than much of Italy but it takes its food just as seriously. There are restaurants and cafés to suit every pocket and more choice of types of cuisine than you'll find anywhere else in the country apart from Rome. Whether you're looking for a neighbourhood trattoria, want to watch models pick at their salads or fancy well-priced ethnic food, Milan has it all – usually within easy reach of wherever you're staying. If you don't fancy a sit-down meal, make the most of the Milanese custom of **aperitivo** (see below) to curb your hunger.

Food markets and snacks

For real low-budget eating, there are **street markets** every day except Sunday scattered throughout the city, selling all the cheese, salami and fruit you need for a picnic lunch. A complete list is given daily in the *Corriere della Sera* under the heading "Mercati". The most central **supermarkets** are Standa at Via Torino 37 and in Piazza Castello, and the over-priced Centro Commerciale in the Stazione Centrale (daily 5.30am–midnight).

As well as all the usual fast-food joints around the Duomo, there is one special place to pop in for a **snack**. *Luini* at Via S. Radegonda 16, just east of the cathedral, has been serving delicious *panzerotti* (deep fried mini calzone) for over a hundred and fifty years. You almost have to fight your way through the crowds at lunchtime but it's worth it for a change from panini.

Restaurants

Predictably, the **centre** of Milan has numerous pricey, expense-account establishments, but usually, just round the corner, there is somewhere more atmospheric or better value. To the south of the centre, the area around the **Ticinese** and **Navigli** is full of restaurants and cafés but although very pleasant it's mainly a tourist preserve beyond Saturday and Sunday evenings. We've also included a couple of bargain places around the budget hotels near the **Stazione Centrale**, a relaxed immigrant area with a growing reputation for ethnic cuisine.

L'Altro Luogo (Aimo e Nadia) Piazza Repubblica 13 ☏02.2901.7038. A new restaurant from Milan's top culinary couple serving outstanding cuisine at top prices in elegant but relaxed surroundings. Closed Sat, Sun & Mon lunch.

Joia Via P. Castaldi 18 ☏02.2952.2124. A famous designer joint serving imaginative vegetarian food. Prices are steep, though the lunchtime menu is better value. Closed Sun & Aug.

Trattoria Milanese Via Santa Marta 11 ☏02.8645.1991. An authentic neighbourhood resturant in the labyrinth of ancient streets ten minutes' walk west of the Duomo. Understandably risotto and *osso buco* take pride of place among all that's best of Milanese cooking. Closed Tues.

Milch Via E Petrella 19. You don't get more Milanese than fusion food and this hip converted dairy certainly knows how to mix ingredients. Welcoming atmosphere just up from the main station. Closed Mon & Aug.

Taverna Morigi Via Morigi. Daily specials are chalked on the board in this famous 1920s *osteria* with a fine wine list. Good home cooking to a loyal clientele. Closed Mon.

Oskar Via Palazzi 4. A popular restaurant with plenty of local atmosphere, serving fantastic-value pasta dishes in huge portions. Don't be put off by the the voluble owners or the Mussolini memorabilia in one corner. Closed Sun.

Pizza OK Via Lambro 15. Basic and very popular pizzeria that serves some of the best – and biggest – pizzas in town. Huge choice of toppings and good prices. Closed Sun lunch.

Al Pont de Ferr Ripa di Porta Ticenese 55. An intimate restaurant right by the canal that offers an unusual take on local classics – try the delicious pumpkin risotto with pistachio. There's also an excellent cheese selection to complement the impressive wine list. Tram 3.

Premiata Alzaia Naviglio Grande 2. A loud, bustling pizzeria often with a queue running out of the door. There's a second branch a little further north at Via de Amicis 24, which is just as popular.

Santa Lucia Via S Pietro All'Orto ☏02.7602.3155. A classic Milanese institution frequented by post-opera goers. Traditional, quality food surrounded by black-and-white photos of the stars who've been here before you. Open until 1.30am. Closed Mon.

Osteria delle Vigne Ripa di Porta Ticenese 61. One of the best spots in the area for a tasty, relaxed meal. Good-value dishes and an impressive wine list. Closed Sun.

Warsa Via Melzo 16. An Eritrean restaurant in among the shops and bars of Milan's African community, serving very tasty bargain food; good variety of vegetarian dishes as well as various meat options. Closed Wed.

Nightlife: bars, clubs and live music

Milan has perhaps Italy's best **nightlife**. This centres on three main areas: the streets around the Brera gallery and north to Corso Como; the Porta Venezia area, with its alternative scene; and the canal-side Navigli and the adjacent Ticinese quarter, south of the city, where there are any number of lively bars, restaurants and nightclubs, some hosting regular live bands.

The city's **clubs** are at their hippest midweek, particularly on Thursdays – at weekends out-of-towners flood in and any self-respecting Milanese trendy either stays at home or hits a bar. Many places have obscure door policies, often dependent on the whim of the bouncer; assuming you get in, you can expect to pay €10–20 entry, which usually includes your first drink. As for **live music**, Milan scores high on jazz, and the pop scene is relatively good by Italian standards: there are regular gigs by local bands, and the city is a stop on the circuit for big-name touring bands.

If you need an antidote to the expensive designer side of Milan's nightlife, check out the very healthy alternative scene, which revolves around the city's many **Centri Sociali**. Born out of the student protests of the late Sixties, these centres are essentially squatted buildings, where committees organize cheap, sometimes free, entertainment, such as concerts and film showings. They also contain bars and – often good – vegetarian restaurants, and are an established part of the social scene, accepted by neighbours and even sometimes receiving local funding. Check out the historic *Leoncavallo*, at Via Watteau 7 (☎02.670.5185, ⓦwww.leoncavall.org), or look in the listings section of the newspaper *Il Manifesto* for other *centri*.

An Italian custom that has been honed to a fine art in Milan is the **aperitivo**. Between 6 and 9pm the city unwinds over a drink and a bite to eat. As well as another opportunity to preen and pose *aperitivo*-time is a boon for budget travellers: counters often groan under the weight of hot and cold food all of which is included in the price of your drink. Take a plate and help yourself, although if you're really planning to fill up, it'll go down better if you go back several times rather than piling your plate unseemingly high. If you choose your venue wisely you won't need to spend another penny on food all night. On Sundays, many places offer a **brunch** in a similar style – for a set price you can help yourself from the generous buffets.

Cafés and bars

Arco della Pace Piazza Sempione 2a. Located in the arch itself, this working men's club has become a hip spot for a drink. In the summer you can join the crowds on the pavement and listen to the concerts in the nearby park. Open Wed–Fri.

ATM Bastione di Porta Volta 15. A former tram station is the venue for this relaxed bar which has become a classic for a laid-back thirty-something crowd, especially popular at *aperitivo* time.

Bar Brera Via Brera 23. An unassuming staple for a drink or a snack right in the thick of things. Pick a table outside and people-watch or settle into the snug interior during the day with a drink and a paper.

Bar Magenta Via Carducci 13. An enduringly popular bar with Twenties decor that gets packed to the point of bursting on Friday nights and weekends. Closed Mon.

Caffè Miani Piazza Duomo 21. Probably Milan's oldest bar, also known as *Zucca in Galleria*. Once a favourite stop for those en route to the Scala, these days it's a little too touristy. Prices are high even by Milanese standards. Closed Wed.

10 Corso Como Corso Como 10. The bar is the best bit of this chi-chi set-up of exhibition space, boutiques, a restaurant and a courtyard café-bar. Prices are extortionate but the atmosphere is very chic.

Le Biciclette Conca del Naviglio 10. Smart young things prop up the bar in this swish modern joint in a leafy street near the Navigli. The definitive *aperitivo* bar.

Lelephante Via Melzo 22. Cocktails are the speciality at this good-time bar popular with a mixed crowd. Hardly a poseur in sight.

Luca's Bar Colonne di San Lorenzo. Unassuming by day, this Ticinese bar kicks into action in the evening, when an unpretentious crowd congregate on the pavement outside. Closed Sun.

Venues and clubs

Café L'Atlantique Viale Umbriale 42 ⓦ www.cafeatlantique.com. Achingly trendy spot where the slickest of Milan's slick meet. Top DJs regularly spin their stuff.

Hollywood Corso Como 15 ⓣ 02.659.8996. Long-established as the place to go if you want to be surrounded by beautiful people. Very Milanese but certainly no mould-breaker.

Magazzini Generali Via Pietrasanta 14 ⓣ 02.5521.1313. Ex-warehouse that's become a Milan institution with a mixture of popular club nights and live music.

Plastic Viale Umbria 120 ⓣ 02.733.996. Historical club that still draws in the crowds to dance to an eclectic mixture of sounds. Very strict door policy.

Scimmie Via Ascanio Sforza 49 ⓦ www.scimmie.it. Ticinese club that is one of Milan's most popular venues, with a different band every night and jazz-fusion predominating. Small and smoky, with a decent restaurant – and a barge on the canal in summer.

Tunnel Via Sammartini 30 ⓦ www.uscitanuovisuoni .com. A refreshingly alternative venue for national bands and occasional dance nights.

Opera, theatre and cinema

Many of Milan's tourists are in the city for just one reason – **La Scala**, Via dei Filodrammatici 2 (ⓣ 02.7200.3744, ⓦ www.lascala.milano.com), one of the world's most prestigious opera houses. The opera season runs from December through to July, and there's usually also a season of classical concerts between September and November. Note, however, that La Scala is currently closed for extensive **refurbishment**; see box for details.

Of Milan's **theatres**, the Teatro Piccolo, Via Rovello 2 (ⓣ 02.7233.3222, ⓦ www.piccoloteatro.org), is a classical theatre, with a traditional repertoire, and is reckoned to be one of Italy's best. Teatro dell'Elfo, Via Ciro Menotti 11 (ⓣ 02.716.791, ⓦ www.elfo.org), reachable on bus #60, puts on more original plays. Count on paying around €15 for a seat at either of these places. As for **cinema**, Sound and Motion Pictures (ⓦ www.anteospaziocinema.com; €6.70) show a selection of original language films at the following cinemas: the Arcobaleno, Viale Tunisia 11 (ⓣ 02.2940.6054; MM Porta Venezia), the Anteo, Via Milazzo 9 (ⓣ 02.659.7732), and the Mexico, Via Savona 57 (ⓣ 02.4895.1802). The Fondazione Cineteca Italiana is based at the Spazio Oberdan (see p.175; ⓦ www.cinetecamilano.it), and has an excellent programme of international art-house films. In the summer months outdoor cinema is organized at several venues around the city; see newspaper for listings.

La Scala refurbishment

La Scala closed in January 2002 for extensive refurbishment and is due to reopen in 2005. In the meantime, the opera company has taken up temporary residence at the **Arcimboldi Theatre** on the northern outskirts of the city. The programme continues as before, though inevitably the atmosphere in the brand-new auditorium is not the same.

Not surprisingly, seats for the opera sell out months in advance, but you can book tickets via the La Scala website (ⓦ www.lascala.milano.com) if you get in early enough. The average price of a ticket is about €40, but there is also often a reasonable chance of picking up a cheaper seat on the day; tickets are on sale from the Arcimboldi box office two hours before the start of the performance.

A bus shuttle service runs from Piazza Duomo to the Arcimboldi (6.45–7.15pm and after the show; valid public transport ticket). The information point in the Duomo metro has details of the service.

Listings

Airlines Aer Lingus, Galleria Passarella 2
☎02.7600.0080; Alitalia, Via Albricci 5
☎02.2499.2700; Air Canada, Viale Regina
Giovanna 8 ☎02.2940.9189; American Airlines,
Via Vittor Pisani 19 ☎02.6791.4400; British
Airways, Corso Italia 8 ☎147.812.266; Qantas,
Piazza Velasca 4 ☎02.864.287.

Airport enquiries ☎02.7485.2200 (daily
7am–11pm) for both Linate and Malpensa airports.

American Express Via Brera 3 ☎02.876.674
(Mon–Fri 9am–5pm).

Bicycle rental Despite the reputation of the city's
traffic, central Milan is an enjoyable place to negotiate by bicycle: it's mainly flat and motorists show
much more respect to cyclists than in London or
New York. AWS rents town and mountain bikes at
Via Ponte Seveso 33, down the west side of the
Stazione Centrale (Tues–Sun 9am–1pm & 3–7pm).

Books The English Bookshop, Via Mascheroni 12
(☎02.469.4468), is the best source of English-
language books in the city centre, but Libreria
Hoepli at Via Ulrico Hoepli 5, Libreria Feltrinelli at
Via Ugo Foscolo 1/3 and FNAC at Via Torino 5 all
have good, if more limited, selections.

Car parks Central car parks include Autosilo Diaz,
Piazza Diaz 6, just south of Piazza Duomo; Garage
Traversi, on Via Bagutta, close to Piazza San
Babila; and Garage Venezia, Corso Venezia 11,
near Piazza Oberdan. To park in the blue bays
around town get a "SostaMilano" card available
from the ATM Point in the Duomo metro station or
many bars and tobacconists.

Car rental Avis, Europcar, Hertz and Maggiore all
have desks at Stazione Centrale, and at both airports.

Consulates Australia, Via Borgogna 2
☎02.7770.4217; Canada, Via V. Pisani 19
☎02.67.581; UK, Via San Paolo 7 ☎02.723.001;
USA, Via Principe Amadeo 2/10 ☎02.290.351.

Doctors English-speaking doctors are available at
International Health Center, Via San Paolo 15
(☎02.7200.4080, ⓦwww.ihc.it), and The Milan
Clinic, Via Cerva 25 (☎02.7601.6047).

Exchange Banks usually offer the best rates, but
out of normal banking hours you can change
money and travellers' cheques at the Stazione
Centrale office (daily 7am–11pm), where there's
also a 24-hour automatic currency-exchange
machine. The airports all have exchange facilities.

Football Milan's two teams are Inter Milan and AC
Milan. They play on alternate Sundays at the G.
Meazza stadium (San Siro), Via Piccolomini 5
(☎02.4870.0457; MM Lotto, then a longish walk).
There are hourly guided tours around the stadium

(Mon–Sat 10am–5pm from Gate 4, Piazzale dello
Sport; Sun 9am–noon from Gate 21/22, Piazzale
Axum; €10). You can buy match tickets here and,
for AC Milan games, from Milan Point, on Via San
Gottardo 2 (☎02.8942.2711), or from branches of
Cariplo banks (☎02.88.661); and for Inter games,
from Ticket One, Viale Vittorio Veneto 2
(☎02.2953.6577), and branches of Banca
Popolare Milano (☎02.77.011).

Gay and Lesbian Milan The city is something of
a focus for Italian gays and lesbians, and the
Libreria Babele Galleria, Via San Nicolao 10
(☎02.8691.5597, ⓦwww.libreriababele.it), is a
good central source of information on the scene
here and in other northern Italian cities. Arcigay
has been at the centre of Italian gay life for
decades and their website ⓦwww.arigaymilano
.org is worth checking out before a visit to the
country. The sister organization ArciLesbica
(ⓦhttp://women.it/arciles) is also an active political force in the community. Although most of
Milan's bars and clubs welcome a mixed crowd,
for more select venues Via Sammartini, not far
from the Stazione Centrale, offers a choice of
locals, and the women-only disco at *Sottomarino
Giallo*, Via Donatello 2, has become an institution.

Hospital There is a 24-hour casualty service at
the Ospedale Maggiore Policlinico, Via Francesco
Sforza 35 (☎02.55.031), a short walk from Piazza
Duomo.

Internet access *Terzomillennio*, Via Lazzaretto
☎02.205.2121 (Mon–Fri 9am–9pm, Sat
9am–6pm); *Internet Enjoy*, Via Medici 6
☎02.7209.4544 (Mon–Sat 10am–midnight, Sun
3pm–midnight).

Laundries There's a coin-operated laundry in the
Brera district, Via Anfiteatro 9, and another, the
Lavanderia Automatica, on Via Lombardini 4. Near
the Stazione Centrale, try the Lavanderia, Via
Tadino 6.

Left luggage Stazione Centrale daily 4am–1am;
☎02.6371.2667.

Pharmacy The Stazione Centrale
(☎02.669.0935), which has English-speaking
assistants, and Carlo Erba, on Piazza Duomo
(☎02.8646.4832); both have 24-hour services.
Rotas are published in *Corriere della Sera*, and are
usually posted on farmacia doors.

Police Phone ☎113. Head office at Via
Fatebenefratelli 11 (☎02.62.261), near the Brera.

Post office Via Cordusio 4, off Piazza Cordusio –
not the building marked "Poste", but around the
corner (Mon–Fri 8am–2pm, Sat 8.30am–noon).

Shopping The "Quadrilatero d'Oro" – Via Monte

Napoleone and around – is the place for the big fashion designers (and their sky-high prices), while Corso di Porta Ticinese is the area to head for more alternative youth-oriented shops. If your budget is more restricted, Via Torino, Porta Vittoria and Corso Buenos Aires are home to more middle-range clothes stores and chains. If you're intent on finding designer labels at affordable prices, check out the *blochisti*, or warehouses, selling last season's lines at half-price: try Gastone, Via Vanzetti 20; Diffusione Tessile, Galleria San Carlo 6; or Il Salvagente, at Via Bronzetti 16.

Swimming pools Cozzi, Viale Tunisia 35 (☎02.659.9703), is perhaps the most convenient place, close to Stazione Centrale. There's also the Lido di Milano, Piazzale Lotto 15 (☎02.366.100), which has both indoor and open-air pools.

Telephones International calls can be made either from Telecom Italia offices in Galleria V. Emanuele II (8am–9.30pm) or at the Stazione Centrale (8am–8pm).

Train enquiries ⊛www.trenitalia.com; Ferrovie dello Stato ☎147.888.088 (daily 7am–9pm); Ferrovie Nord ☎02.20.222 (daily 9am–6pm).

Travel agents CTS, Via Sant'Antonio 2 (☎02.5830.4751), and CIT in the Galleria Vittorio Emanuele II (☎02.863.701, ⊛www.cititalia.net), are the best source of train tickets, cheap flights, etc.

South of Milan: Pavia and Vigévano

Furthest west of the string of historic towns that spread across the Lombardy plain, **Pavia** and **Vigévano** are close enough to Milan to be seen on a day-trip, but still retain clear identities of their own. Pavia should not be missed if you're in Milan for any length of time; Vigévano is more of a backwater, and as such hardly a place to stay, but its central Renaissance square and ramshackle castle could make a pleasant half-day out from either Pavia or Milan.

Pavia and around

Medieval **PAVIA** was known as the city of a hundred towers. And although only a handful remain – one of the best collapsed in 1989 – the medieval aspect is still strong, with numerous Romanesque and Gothic churches tucked away in a wanderable web of narrow streets and cobbled squares. The town is not, however, stranded in the past – its ancient university continues to thrive, ensuring an animated street life and reasonably lively night-time scene.

Pavia reached its zenith in the Dark Ages when it was capital of the Kingdom of the Lombards. After their downfall it remained a centre of power, and the succession of emperors who ruled northern Italy continued to come to the town to receive the Lombards' traditional iron crown. This all came to an end in the fourteenth century when Pavia was handed over to the Viscontis and became a satellite of Milan. The Viscontis, and later the Sforzas, did, however, found the university and provide the town with its prime tourist attraction – the nearby **Certosa di Pavia**.

Pavia

It's Pavia as a whole that appeals, rather than any specific sight. Just wandering around town is the nicest way to spend time here: pick any side street and you're almost bound to stumble on something of interest – a lofty medieval tower, a pretty Romanesque or Gothic church, or just a silent, sleepy piazza. Getting lost is difficult, as long as you bear in mind that the centre is quartered by the two main streets: Corso Cavour, which becomes Corso Mazzini, and Corso Strada Nuova.

One piazza that is neither sleepy nor silent is the central **Piazza della Vittoria**, a large cobbled rectangle surrounded by tatty buildings, housing bars, *gelaterie* and restaurants. At the eastern end steps lead down to an **underground market**, while at the square's southern end the **Broletto**, medieval Pavia's town hall, abuts the rear of the rambling and unwieldy **Duomo** – an early Renaissance sprawl of protruding curves and jutting angles that was only finally completed in the 1930s. The west front of the duomo, facing **Piazza del Duomo**, has been tidied up since the collapse of the adjacent Torre Civica in March 1989, which killed four people.

The best of the town's churches is the Romanesque **San Michele**, a five-minute walk away on Via Cavallotti. The friezes and capitals on its broad sandstone facade are carved into a menagerie of snake-tailed fish, griffins, dragons and other beasts, some locked in a struggle with humans, representing the fight between good and evil. It's also worth looking in on the church of **San Pietro in Ciel d'Oro**, on the other side of the centre at the top of Strada Nuova, dating from 1132 and containing a superb fourteenth-century altarpiece. Nearby, the **Castello Visconteo** (Tues–Sat 9am–1.30pm, Sun 9am–12.30pm; €2.50) was initiated by Galeazzo Il Visconti in 1360, and added to by the Sforzas. The austere exterior originally housed luxurious apartments, the majority of which were in the wing of the quadrangle destroyed by the French in 1527. But the castle was used as a barracks until 1921, and although it's been restored, the rooms that remain are hardly stunning. The **Museo Civico** inside includes an art gallery with a handful of Venetian paintings, an archeology collection with Roman jewellery, pottery and glassware, and a museum of sculpture displaying architectural fragments, mosaics and sculptures rescued from the town's demolished churches – most impressive of which are the reconstructed eleventh- and twelfth-century portals.

Practicalities

Regular **trains** make the thirty-minute journey between Pavia and Milan, but connections from Pavia to the other cities of the Lombardy plain are infrequent and slow. **Bus** services drop you at the bus station round the corner from the train station, on the western edge of the town centre. Buses #3 and #6 connect the train station with the centre, or it's about a ten-minute walk down Corso Cavour to Piazza della Vittoria. The **tourist office** is near Stazione Centrale – turn left as you leave the train station, then right after the bus station – at Via F. Filzi 2 (Mon–Sat 8.30am–12.30pm & 2–6pm; ☎0382.22.156, Ⓦwww.apt.pavia.it).

Pavia's few **hotels** tend to take the overspill from Milan's commercial fairs, and finding somewhere to stay can be more difficult than you might imagine, especially as there are very few cheap options. The most reasonable choices in town – both near the station – are the decent *Aurora*, Via Vittorio Emanuele 25 (☎0382.23.664, Ⓦwww.albergoaurora.com; ❹), and the 3-star *Excelsior*, Piazzale Stazione (☎0382 28 596; ❹), which is a bit pricier but clean and convenient. The best-value option is the *Hotel Ritz Pavia*, 3km north of Pavia (☎0382 580.280, Ⓦwww.hotelritzpavia.com; ❺), where the comfortable motel-like accommodation offers spacious, en-suite, modern rooms, including some with facilities for the disabled. There is a shuttle bus to and from the station and bicycles available for residents to cycle the 2km to the Certosa. There is also a **campsite**, the *Ticino*, Via Mascherpa 10 (☎0382.527.094; April–Nov) – take bus #4 from the train station.

For a quick **lunch**, the *Punto Bar*, Strada Nuova 9, is a good *paninoteca*, with at least thirty varieties of sandwich and plenty of space to sit down. Of regular **restaurants**, the *Osteria della Madonna del Peo* (☎0382.302.833) is one of the best central options with local specialities served in a cosy vaulted trattoria. If you're feeling flush, make for the *Bardelli*, Viale Lungoticino Visconti 2 (☎0382.274.441), where creative Italian cooking is served in a riverside villa. For more waterside options, head over the covered bridge to Via Milazzo where there are numerous popular eateries including the relaxed *Osteria della Malora*, Via Milazzo 79 (closed Mon & Sun eve), a favourite with locals.

The Certosa di Pavia

Ten kilometres from Pavia, the **Certosa di Pavia** (May–Sept Tues–Sun 9–11.30am & 2.30–6pm; April closes 5.30pm; Oct–March closes 4.30pm; free) is one of the most extravagant monasteries in Europe, commissioned by Gian Galeazzo Visconti in 1396 as the family mausoleum. Visconti intended the church here to resemble Milan's late-Gothic cathedral. It took a century to build, and by the time it was finished tastes had changed – and the Viscontis had been replaced by the Sforzas. But the architect appointed to finish the building, Amadeo, did so in style, festooning the facade with a fantasia of inlaid marble, twisted columns and friezes that say more about the wealth of the families that financed the complex than the contemplative Carthusian order it was built for. The Certosa is actually reachable from both Milan and Pavia, either by bus or by train. Buses are most frequent, hourly from Piazza Castello in Milan or from Pavia's bus station, dropping you a fifteen-minute walk from the Certosa. If you arrive by train, turn left out of the station and walk around the Certosa walls until you reach the entrance – also a fifteen-minute walk.

The monastery lies at the end of a tree-lined avenue, part of a former Visconti hunting range that stretched all the way from Pavia's *castello*. You can see the **church** unaccompanied, a Gothic building on the inside though no less splendid than the facade, its paintings, statues and vaults combining to create an almost ballroom glamour; look out for the tombs of Lodovico Il Moro and Gian Galeazzo Visconti, which are masterpieces of the early Renaissance. But to visit the rest of the monastery you need to join a **guided tour** of just under an hour, led by one of the monks released from the Carthusian strict vow of silence. It is in Italian, but well worth doing even if you don't understand a word. The tour begins in the church and then moves on to the **small cloister**, with fine terracotta decoration and a geometric garden around a fountain. Further on, the **great cloister** is stunning for its size and tranquillity, and also offers an insight into life in the complex. It is surrounded on three sides by the **monks' houses**, each consisting of two rooms, a chapel, a garden and a loggia, with a bedroom above. The hatches to the side of the entrances were to enable food to be passed through without any communication. There is also a **refectory** with a frescoed ceiling, which was used for occasional communal eating; the Bible was read throughout the silent meal from the pulpit (with a hidden entrance). The dining room is divided by a blind wall, which allowed the monastery to feed pilgrims staying in their guesthouse without compromising the rules of their closed order. The tour is free but voluntary contributions to upkeep are collected on your way out. The final call is the Certosa **shop**, stocked with honey, chocolate, souvenirs and the famous Chartreuse liqueur; give yourself time before leaving to sample the different varieties of the liqueur at the kiosk outside the entrance – yellow is strong, green stronger.

Vigévano

An hour by bus to the west of Pavia, **VIGÉVANO** is Lombardy at its most comfortably wealthy, a smug little town of boutiques, antiques dealers and – most significantly – shoe shops. The shoe industry is Vigévano's mainstay, and there are signs of the bedrock of the town's prosperity all over the centre. If you go on a Sunday, Italy's only **shoe museum** is open on Corso Cavour (Sun 10.30am–12.30pm & 3–6pm; closed Aug & Dec), with a collection of some of the weirdest and wackiest excesses of shoe design in the country.

As for the town itself, most of it is pretty unremarkable, and there'd be little reason to visit were it not for the **Piazza Ducale**, which is something special, surrounded on three sides by well-preserved and delicately frescoed arcades, the embodiment of Renaissance harmony. Designed by Bramante and heavily influenced by Leonardo, even the Baroque facade of the **Duomo** doesn't spoil the proportions, deftly curved to conceal the fact that the church is set at a slight angle to the square.

Otherwise the **Castello** (April–Sept Tues–Sun 8.30am–7pm; rest of year Sun & public holidays 8.30am–8pm; free) is about all Vigévano has to offer. A Visconti and later Sforza stronghold now in the final throes of a lengthy restoration, the castle's still semi-dilapidated state is part of its attraction: it's largely unsupervised, which means you can go just about wherever you want, scrambling up rickety flights of steps to the upper floors, or down dank passages to the dungeons. The oldest part of the castle is the Rocca Vecchia, a fort built by the Visconti to defend the road to Milan, to which it is connected by a covered walkway. The Sforzas retained the castle's military function, but added the elegant Palazzo Ducale, still mostly unrestored, the Loggia delle Dame, an open walkway for the noblewomen's evening passeggiata, and the Falconiera, another open gallery used for the training of falcons. On the right of the courtyard, the **stables** (summer Mon–Fri 2–8pm, Sat & Sun 2–10pm; winter daily 2–6pm; free), designed by Leonardo, offer some insight into how the Sforza troops lived and worked – cathedral-like quarters for the horses, and a loft above for soldiers and hay.

For a good overhead view of both the Castello and the Piazza Ducale, climb the **Torre del Bramante** (April, May, Aug & Sept Tues–Fri 10am–12.30pm & 3–5.30pm, Sat & Sun 10am–12.30pm & 2.30–6.30pm; rest of year Sat & Sun only 10am–6.30pm; €1), a tower that was begun in 1198, before the Castello, and completed by Bramante at the end of the fifteenth century. The entrance is next to that of the Castello.

Cremona

A cosy provincial town situated bang in the middle of the Po plain, **CREMONA** is known for its violins. Ever since Andrea Amati established the first violin workshop here in 1566, and his son Nicolo and pupils Stradivari and Guarneri continued and expanded the industry, Cremona has been a focus for the instrument, attracting both tourists and musicians worldwide. Today around a hundred violin makers maintain the tradition started by the Amati family: there's an internationally famous school of violin making here, and there are frequent classical concerts, as well as a string festival held every third October.

All this said, Cremona is a quiet, relatively unexciting town, and not an obvious place to spend a night, and most people treat it as a day-trip from Milan or as a stopover en route to the richer pickings of Mantua or Bergamo. However, its lack of overnight visitors can be appealing in itself – there are a few places to stay and a small crop of pleasant restaurants – and it can be a nice idea to give yourself time to wind down here, but not long enough to get bored.

Arrival, information and accommodation

Cremona's **train station** is on Via Dante, on the northern edge of the city centre, ten minutes' walk from the focal Piazza del Comune; bus #1 runs regular-

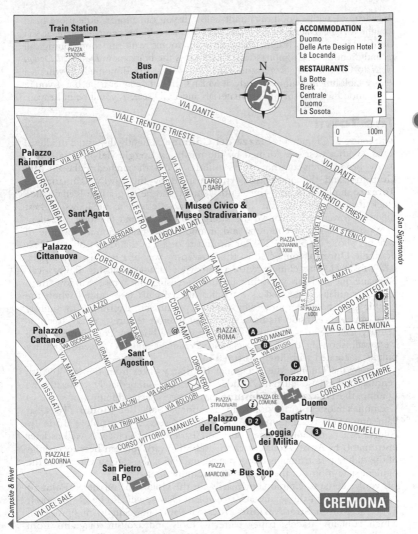

ACCOMMODATION
Duomo 2
Delle Arte Design Hotel 3
La Locanda 1

RESTAURANTS
La Botte C
Brek A
Centrale B
Duomo E
La Sosota D

Train Station

PIAZZA
STAZIONE

Bus
Station

N

VIA DANTE

VIALE TRENTO E TRIESTE

0   100m

Palazzo
Raimondi

VIA BERTESI

CORSO GARIBALDI

VIA BEMBO

VIA PALESTRO

VIA FAERIO

VIA GEROMINI

LARGO
P. SARPI

VIA DANTE

VIALE TRENTO E TRIESTE

▶ San Sigismondo

Sant'Agata

Museo Civico &
Museo Stradivariano

VIA OBERDAN

VIA UGOLANI DATI

PIAZZA
GIOVANNI
XXIII

VIA S. ANTONIO DEL FUOCO

VIA STENICO

Palazzo
Cittanuova

CORSO GARIBALDI

VIA MANZONI

VIA ASELLI

VIA AMATI

VIA BATTISTI

VIA S. TOMMASO

PIAZZA
LODI

CORSO MATTEOTTI

❶

PALLAVICINO

VIA MILAZZO

VIA INGEGNERI

CORSO CAMPI

VIA G. DA CREMONA

Palazzo
Cattaneo

VIA GUIDO GRANDI

VIA OSCASALI

VIA FLASIO

@

PIAZZA
ROMA

Ⓐ

CORSO MANZINI

Ⓑ

VIA PERTUSIO

Ⓒ

Sant'
Agostino

VIA MANNA

CORSO VERDI

VIA SOLFERINO

Torazzo

CORSO XX SETTEMBRE

VIA BISSOLATI

VIA JACINI

VIA CAVALOTTI

VIA BOLDORI

Ⓒ

PIAZZA
STRADIVARI

ⓘ

PIAZZA DEL
COMUNE

Duomo

VIA TRIBUNALI

CORSO VITTORIO EMANUELE

Ⓓ❷

Palazzo
del Comune

Baptistry

VIA BONOMELLI

❸

PIAZZALE
CADORNA

Loggia
dei Militia

Ⓔ

◀ Campsite & River

San Pietro
al Po

PIAZZA
MARCONI

★ Bus Stop

VIA DEL SALE

CREMONA

ly to the Piazza Cavour, also in the centre. Most intercity buses stop at the train station or at the **bus station** just one block east.

The **tourist office** is on the Piazza del Comune, opposite the Duomo (Mon–Sat 9.30am–12.30 & 3–6pm, Sun 9am–12.30pm; ☏0372 .23.233, ⓦ www.aptcremona.it), and has leaflets, details of classical concerts and a list of violin makers' workshops. The *Speed Café*, just off Corso Campi, at Via Sofonisba Anguissola 1, has **Internet** access (4.30pm–1am).

There's a variety of **accommodation** options if you want to stay over in Cremona, including a **campsite**, the *Parco al Po*, on Via Lungo Po Europa (☏0372.21.268, Ⓕ0372.27.137; May–Sept); take bus #1 (direction Viale Po) from the train station. If you prefer a roof over your head, five minutes' walk east of the main piazza is the family-run *La Locanda* (☏0372.457.834; ❸), at Via

Pallavicino 4, with a good restaurant below. If you can afford a little more head straight for the *Duomo* (℡0372.35.242; ❹), just off the central square at Via Gonfalonieri 13, for bright, clean en-suite rooms with air conditioning, all recently renovated. Cremona's top-class joint is the brand-new *Delle Arti Design Hotel* (℡0372 23131, ⓦwww.dellearti.com; ❼), at Via Bonomelli 8, where a sleek establishment is aimed mostly at Milan's chi-chi designer tribe, but if you're in the mood for state-of-the-art materials and LCD screens you'll be in heaven.

The Town

The centre of Cremona is **Piazza del Comune**, a slightly disjointed medieval square, with a west side formed by the red-brick **Loggia dei Militia** – formerly headquarters of the town's militia – and the arched **Palazzo del Comune**, and the northeast corner marked by the gawky Romanesque **Torazzo**, built in the mid-thirteenth century and bearing a fine Renaissance clock dating from 1583. At 112m, the Torazzo claims to be Italy's highest medieval tower, and if you've the energy you can ascend for some excellent views over the rest of Cremona and around (under restoration at the time of writing; phone ℡0372.23.233 for an update or ask at the tourist office). Next door, the **Duomo**, connected to the Torazzo by way of a Renaissance loggia, is a mixed-looking church, with a fine west facade made up of Classical, Romanesque and fancy Gothic features, focusing on a rose window from 1274. Originally conceived as a basilica, its transepts were added when the Gothic style became more fashionable – presumably explaining its slightly squat appearance inside. Its most significant interior features are its sixteenth-century nave frescoes, including a superb trompe l'oeil by Pordenone on the west wall, showing the *Crucifixion* and *Deposition*, and the fifteenth-century pulpits, decorated with finely tortured reliefs.

Next to the Duomo, the octagonal **Baptistry** dates from the late twelfth century, and is also currently under restoration. Immediately opposite the Duomo, the **Palazzo del Comune** has a very select exhibition of some of Cremona's most historic violins in its upstairs **Sala dei Violini** (Tues–Sat 9am–6pm, Sun 10am–6pm; €6), including a very early example made by Andrea Amati in 1566 for the court of Charles IX of France, as well as later instruments by Amati's son, Guarneri, and Stradivari. You can hear recordings of the different instruments being played and you'll also catch a glimpse of the opulent state rooms of the Palazzo del Comune itself.

If you've come to Cremona primarily for the violins, the pilastered **Palazzo Affaitati**, north of the square at Via Ugolani Dati 4, will also be of interest. It holds the **Museo Stradivariano** (Tues–Sat 9am–6pm, Sun 10am–6pm; €7), which contains models, paper patterns, tools and acoustic diagrams from Stradivari's workshop, along with more violins, violas, viols, cellos and guitars, many of which have elaborately carved scrolls, hanging impotently in glass cases; an enlightening video is also shown (alternately in English and Italian), which helps to unravel the mysteries of the violin maker's art. The instruments have to be played regularly to keep them in trim, and you could try asking the custodian when the next work-out is due. In the same building, the **Museo Civico** (same hours; joint ticket €10) is a decidedly provincial and rather pedestrian collection of mainly Cremonese art, redeemed only by being superbly displayed in striking galleries. Alongside the art are changing exhibitions drawn from the bizarre artefacts and natural history specimens accumulated by Ponzone, the museum's nineteenth-century founder.

Turning left off Via Palestro onto Via Bertesi, you approach the **Palazzo Raimondi**, a dignified building made distinctive by its frescoed cornice.

Conceived by the humanist Raimondi, it now houses the prestigious International School of Violin Making and its associated **Museo Organologico**, which is used mainly by the school, although visits can be arranged in advance (℗0372.386.89).

Southwest of Piazza del Comune, on Via Tibaldi, the church of **San Pietro al Po** has better (and more visible) frescoes than the Duomo; indeed its walls are coated with paintings and intricate stuccos, also dating from the sixteenth century. It's all pretty excessive, but there's sophisticated optical trickery in the trompe l'oeil work of Antonio Campi in the transept vaults. Look in also on the refectory next door for Bernadino Gatti's hearty fresco of the *Feeding of the Five Thousand*.

If you like the church of San Pietro al Po, you'll love that of **San Sigismondo** on the eastern edge of town (bus #3 from the train station, bus #2 from Piazza Cavour). Built by Francesco and Bianca Sforza in 1441 to commemorate their wedding – Cremona was Bianca's dowry – its Mannerist decor is among Italy's best, ranging from Camillo Boccaccino's soaring apse fresco to the *Pentecost* by Giulio Campi in the third bay of the nave, plagiarized from Mantegna's ceiling in the Camera degli Sposi at Mantua. Other highlights include Giulio's *Annunciation* on the entrance wall, in which Gabriel is seemingly suspended in mid-air, and the gory John the Baptist in the second left chapel, by Giulio's younger brother Antonio.

Eating and drinking

For **food**, the excellent *gastronomie* that cluster along Corso Garibaldi and the Corso Campi make good places to put together a picnic or, if you fancy a cheap salad, there's a branch of the good-value chain *Brek* at the beginning of Corso Manzini (Mon–Thurs 9am–3pm & 5.30–8pm, Fri & Sat open until 11.30pm, Sun 5.30–11.30pm). For more regional cuisine head for one of the cosy *osterie* dotted around the centre and, if it's on the menu, try a *bollito misto* – a mixture of boiled meats, served with Cremonese *mostarda di frutta*, consisting of fruit suspended in a sweet mustard syrup. An old staple that still serves well-priced traditional dishes is the *Ristorante Centrale*, off Via Solferino at Via Pertusio 4 (closed Thurs), while a couple of blocks east is one of the town's newer venues, *Taverna La Botte*, at Via Porta Marzia 5, where a hipper crowd tuck into local specialities. *La Sosota* on the other side of the main *piazza*, at Via Sicario 9, is an attractive *osteria* with a traditional atmosphere. For a crispy pizza, you can't get a much better spot than the tables outside the popular *Pizzeria Ristorante Duomo*, on Via Gonfalonieri 13, down the side of the Palazzo Comunale. Around Piazza del Comune and Piazza della Pace there are several very pleasant pavement cafés and *gelaterie* in which to while away the time.

Mantua (Mantova) and around

Aldous Huxley called it the most romantic city in the world; and with an Arabian nights skyline rising above its three encircling lakes, **MANTUA (MANTOVA)** is undeniably evocative. It was the scene of Verdi's *Rigoletto*, and its history is one of equally operatic plots, most of them perpetuated by the Gonzagas, one of Renaissance Italy's richest and most powerful families, who ruled the town for three centuries. Its centre of interlinking cobbled squares retains its medieval aspect, and there are two splendid palaces: the **Palazzo Ducale**, containing Mantegna's stunning fresco of the Gonzaga family and court, and **Palazzo Te**, whose frescoes by the flashy Mannerist Giulio Romano have entertained and outraged generations of visitors with their combination of steamy erotica and illusionistic fantasy. Around Mantua the flat, agricultural Mantuan plain offers a couple of half-day trips including a cycle ride to the quirky church at **Grazie** and the surrounding marsh lands, or for those interested in urban planning, **Sabbioneta**, to the southeast, will provide an interesting diversion.

Mantua's melodramatic history and the hazy sunsets reflected in tranquil lakes are only half the story. Outside the few traffic-free streets of the historic centre the roads are lined with Fascist-era buildings and jammed with cars, while the outskirts have been desecrated by chemical, plastics and paper works that are reputedly responsible for lining the bed of the largest lake, Superiore, with mercury. Nevertheless, the core of the city is still very appealing, especially on Thursdays when Piazza Mantegna, Piazza dell'Erbe and the streets around are filled with a large market.

The state of these same streets aroused the ire of a visiting pope in 1459, who complained that Mantua was muddy, marshy, riddled with fever and intensely hot. His host, Lodovico II Gonzaga, was spurred into action: he could do little about the heat (Mantua can still be unbearably hot and mosquito-ridden in summer) but he did give the city an elaborate facelift, ranging from paving the squares and repainting the shops, to engaging Mantegna as court artist and calling in the prestigious architectural theorist Alberti to design the monumental church of Sant'Andrea – one of the most influential buildings of the early Renaissance. Lodovico's successors continued the tradition of artistic patronage, and although most of the thousands of works of art once owned by the Gonzagas are now scattered around Europe, the town still has plenty of relics from the era.

Arrival, information and accommodation

Mantua's old centre is a ten-minute walk from the **train station** on Piazza Don E. Leoni and the **bus station**, just beyond on Piazza Mondadori, off Corso Vittorio Emanuele II. Bus #1 runs from the train station to the centre of town. The **tourist office**, in the centre of town at Piazza Mantegna 6 – the entrance is actually on Piazza dell'Erbe (Mon–Sat 8.30am–12.30pm & 3–6pm, Sun 9.30am–12.30pm; ☎0376.328.253) – has the usual maps and hotel lists as well as information on boat and cycle routes in the Po Valley and agriturismo in the region. Mantua is perfect for exploring on two wheels: **bicycles** can be rented by the hour or the day from La Rigola (☎0376.366.677) at the end of Via Accademia on the lake or, nearer the station, at Bike Hire Mantova, Viale Piave 22B (Mon–Sat 8am–12.30pm & 2.30–7.30pm; ☎0376.220.909).

As in most parts of northern Italy, **hotels** get booked up quickly, and it's advisable to phone ahead. Right opposite the station, the *ABC*, Piazza Don Leoni 25 (☎0376.322.329; ❸), has decent rooms mainly overlooking an internal courtyard, with breakfast included, while the very pleasant family-run *Bianchi Stazione*, next door at Piazza Don E. Leoni 24 (☎0376.326.465, ℱ0376.321.504; ❺), offers more comfort including some new suites and an attractive garden in the *cortile*. Another budget possibility, right in the centre of town, is the rather noisy rooms at the small, neat *Broletto* at Via Accademia 1 (☎0376.326.784; ❻). At the top end of the scale is the very attractive *San Lorenzo*, Piazza Concordia 14 (☎0376.220.500, ℱ0376.327.194; ❽), where the simply but elegantly furnished rooms have balconies overlooking the town. The tourist office also has information about various bed and breakfast options in the area and there's one small (ten plots only), expensive **campsite**, *Corte Chiara* (☎0376.390.804; May–Sept), north of Mantua, outside of Porto Mantovano on the road to Marmirolo.

The City

The centre of Mantua is made up of four interlinking squares, the first of which, **Piazza Mantegna**, is a small, wedge-shaped open space at the end of the arcaded shopping thoroughfare of **Corso Umberto**. It's dominated by the façade of Alberti's church of **Sant'Andrea**, an unfinished basilica that says a lot about the ego of Lodovico II Gonzaga, who commissioned it. He felt that the existing medieval church was neither impressive enough to represent the splendour of his state nor large enough to hold the droves of people who flocked to Sant'Andrea every Ascension Day to see the holy relic of Christ's blood which had been found on the site. The relic is still there, and after years of dispute about its authenticity (it was supposed to have been brought to Mantua by the soldier who pierced Christ's side), Pope Pius II settled the matter in the fifteenth century by declaring it had miraculously cured him of gout.

Work started on the church in 1472, with the court architect, Luca Fancelli, somewhat resentfully overseeing Alberti's plans. There was a bitchy rivalry between the two, and when, on one of his many visits, Alberti fell and hurt a testicle, Fancelli gleefully told him that "God lets men punish themselves in the place where they sin". Inside, the church is roofed with one immense barrel vault, echoing the triumphal arch of the facade, which gives it a rather cool and calculated feel. The octagonal balustrade at the crossing stands above the crypt where the holy relic is kept in two vases, copies of originals designed by Cellini and stolen by the Austrians in 1846; to see them, ask the sacristan. The painter Mantegna is buried in the first chapel on the left, his tomb topped with a bust of the artist that's said to be a self-portrait; the wall-paintings in the chapel were designed by the artist and executed by students, one of whom was Correggio.

Opposite Sant'Andrea, sunk below the present level of the adjoining **Piazza dell'Erbe**, is Mantua's oldest church, the eleventh-century **Rotonda** (daily 10am–noon & 2.30–4.30pm), which narrowly escaped destruction under Lodovico's city-improvement plans, only to be partially demolished in the sixteenth century and used as a courtyard by the surrounding houses. Rebuilt at the beginning of the last century and beautifully restored in the last few years, it still contains traces of twelfth- and thirteenth-century frescoes. Piazza dell'Erbe itself is one of the town's most characterful squares, with a small daily market and cafés and restaurants sheltering in the arcades below the thirteenth-century **Palazzo della Ragione**, whose impressive wooden-vaulted main hall is viewable during occasional temporary exhibitions. At the north end of the square, a passage leads under the red-brick **Broletto**, or medieval town hall, into the smaller **Piazza Broletto**, where you can view two reminders of how "criminals" were treated under the Gonzagas. The bridge to the right has metal rings embedded in its vault, to which victims were chained by the wrists, before being hauled up by a pulley and suspended in mid-air; while on your far left – actually on the corner of Piazza Sordello – the tall medieval **Torre della Gabbia** has a cage attached in which prisoners were displayed. The Broletto itself is more generous to deserving Mantuans, and is dedicated to the city's two most famous sons: Virgil, a statue of whom overlooks the square, and Tazio Nuvolari, Italy's most celebrated racing driver, whose career is mapped in a small **museum** (Tues, Wed & Fri–Sun 10am–1pm & 3.30–6.30pm; closed Jan & Feb; €3).

If you have the time, it's well worth making a short diversion off Via Broletto up Via Accademia to the eighteenth-century **Teatro Scientifico** or **Bibiena** (Tues–Sun 9.30am–12.30pm & 3–6pm; €2.50), the work of Antonio Bibiena, whose brother designed the Bayreuth Opera House. This is a much smaller theatre, at once intimate and splendid, its curved walls lined with boxes calculated to make their occupants more conspicuous than the performers. A thirteen-year-old Mozart gave the inaugural concert here: his impression is unrecorded, but his father was fulsome in his praise for the building, writing that he had never in his life seen anything more beautiful. Concerts are still given – details from the theatre or tourist office.

Beyond Piazza Broletto, **Piazza Sordello** is a large, sombre square, headed by the Baroque facade of the **Duomo** and flanked by grim crenellated palaces built by the Gonzagas' predecessors, the Bonalcosi. The Duomo conceals a rich interior, designed by Giulio Romano after the church had been gutted by fire. As for the palaces, the two on the left are now owned by the successors of Baldassare Castiglione, a relative of the Gonzagas, who made himself unpopular at the Mantuan court by setting his seminal handbook of Renaissance behaviour, *The Book of the Courtier*, in the rival court of Urbino. Opposite, the **Palazzo del Capitano** and **Magna Domus** were taken by Luigi Gonzaga when he seized Mantua from the Bonalcosi in 1328, the beginning of three hundred years of Gonzaga rule.

The Palazzo Ducale

The Palazzo del Capitano and Magna Domus form the core of the **Palazzo Ducale**, an enormous complex that was once the largest palace in Europe (Tues–Sun 8.45am–7.15pm; €6.50). At its height it covered 34,000 square metres, had a population of over a thousand, and when it was sacked by the Habsburgs in 1630 eighty carriages were needed to carry the two thousand works of art contained in its five hundred rooms. Only a proportion of these rooms are open to visitors, and numbers are restricted for some of them; to see them you have to take a **guided tour** (in Italian) that takes you through to the Sala dei Specchi and then allows you to wander freely through the grounds and the Castello di San Giorgio.

At the time of Luigi's coup of 1328, the Gonzagas were a family of wealthy local peasants, living outside the city on vast estates with an army of retainers. On seizing power Luigi immediately nominated himself Captain of the People ′ – an event pictured in one of the first paintings you'll see on your tour – and the role quickly became a hereditary one, eventually growing in grandeur to that of marquis. During this time the Gonzagas did their best to make Mantua into a city that was a suitable reflection of their increasing influence, commissioning sought-after Renaissance artists like Mantegna to depict them in their finery. Lodovico II's grandson, Francesco II, further swelled the Gonzagan coffers by hiring himself out as a mercenary for various other Italian city-states – money his wife, Isabella d'Este, spent amassing a prestigious collection of paintings, sculpture and *objets d'art*. Under Isabella's son, Federico II, Gonzaga fortunes reached their height; his marriage to the heiress of the duchy of Monferrato procured a ducal title for the family, while he continued the policy of self-glorification by commissioning an out-of-town villa for himself and his mistress. Federico's descendants were for the most part less colourful characters, one notable exception being Vincenzo I, whose debauchery and corruption provided the inspiration for Verdi's licentious duke in *Rigoletto*. After Vincenzo's death, the now bankrupt court was forced to sell many of the family treasures to England's King Charles I (many of the works are still in London's Victoria and Albert Museum) just three years before it was sacked by the Habsburgs.

The first rooms of the palace are the least impressive. There is a thirteenth-century sculpture of a seated Virgil, a painting from 1494 by Domenico Morone showing the *Expulsion of the Bonatosi* from the square outside, and, perhaps most interestingly, the fragments of a half-finished fresco by Pisanello, discovered in 1969 behind two layers of plaster and thought to depict either an episode from an Arthurian romance or the (idealized) military exploits of the first marquis, Gianfrancesco Gonzaga. Whatever its subject, it's a powerful piece of work, charged with energy, in which faces, costumes and landscape are minutely observed.

Further on, through the Sala dello Zodiaco, whose late sixteenth-century ceiling is spangled with stars and constellations, is the **Salone dei Fiume** ("Room of the Rivers"), in which Baroque trompe l'oeil goes over the top to create a mock garden complete with painted creepers and two ghastly fountains surrounded by stalactites and stalagmites. The **Sala dei Specchi** ("Hall of the Mirrors") has a notice outside signed by Monteverdi, who worked as court musician to Vincenzo I and gave frequent concerts of new works – notably the world's first modern opera, *L'Orfeo*, written in 1607. Vincenzo also employed Rubens, whose *Adoration of the Magi* in the **Salone degli Arcieri**, next door, shows the Gonzaga family of 1604, including Vincenzo with his handlebar moustache. The picture was originally part of a triptych, but Napoleonic troops carried off two-thirds of it after briefly occupying the town in 1797 and chopped the remaining third into saleable chunks of portraiture. Although most have been traced, and some returned to the palazzo, there are still a few gaps. Around the room is a curious frieze of horses, glimpsed behind curtains.

The Castello di San Giorgio contains the palace's principal treasure, however: Mantegna's frescoes of the Gonzaga family – among the painter's most famous works, splendidly restored in the so-called **Camera degli Sposi** and depicting the Marquis Lodovico and his wife Barbara with their family. They're naturalistic pieces of work, giving a vivid impression of real people, of the relationships between them and of the tensions surrounding something that is happening, or about to happen. In the main one Lodovico discusses a letter with a courtier while his wife looks on; their youngest daughter leans on her mother's lap, about to bite into an apple, while an older son and daughter (possibly Barbarina) look towards the door, where an ambassador from another court is being welcomed – lending some credence to the theory that negotiations are about to take place for Barbarina's marriage. The other fresco, *The Meeting*, takes place out of doors against a landscape of weird rock formations and an imaginary city with the Gonzagan arms above the gate. Divided into three sections by fake pilasters, it shows Gonzagan retainers with dogs and a horse in attendance on Lodovico, who is welcoming his son Francesco back from Rome, where he had just become the first Gonzaga to be made a cardinal. In the background are the Holy Roman Emperor Frederick III and the King of Denmark – a selection which apparently annoyed the Duke of Milan, who was incensed that the "two most wretched men in the world" had been included while he had been omitted. Lodovico's excuse was that he would have included the duke had he not objected so strongly to Mantegna's uncompromising portrait style. If you have time before the guide sweeps you out, have a look at the ceiling, another nice piece of trompe l'oeil, in which two women, peering down from a balustrade, have balanced a tub of plants on a pole and appear to be on the verge of letting it tumble into the room – an illusionism that was to be crucial in the development of the Gonzaga's next resident artist of any note, Giulio Romano, whose Palazzo Te – see opposite – should not be missed.

Finally, the private **apartments of Isabella d'Este**, on the ground floor, are sometimes on view. Though they once housed works by Michelangelo, Mantegna and Perugino, only the unmoveable decorations remain – inlaid cupboards and intricately carved ceilings and doors. A ruthless employer, Isabella would threaten her artists and craftsmen with the dungeon if she thought they were working too slowly, and had no compunction about bullying Mantegna on his death-bed to give her a piece of sculpture she particularly coveted. She was more deferential to Leonardo da Vinci, however, who did two drawings of her but ignored her suggestion that one be converted into a portrait of Christ. Isabella also collected dwarfs, whose job it was to cheer her up while her husband was away fighting. For centuries it was assumed that the suite of miniature rooms beyond Isabella's apartments was built for the dwarfs; in fact it's a scaled-down version of the St John Lateran basilica in Rome, built for Vincenzo.

South of the centre: to the Palazzo Te

A twenty-minute walk from the centre of Mantua, at the end of the long spine of Via Principe Amedeo and Via Acerbi, the Palazzo Te is the later of the city's two Gonzaga palaces, and equally compelling in its way; and you can take in a few of Mantua's more minor attractions on the way there.

The first thing to look at on the way is Giulio Romano's **Fish Market**, to the left off Piazza Martiri Belfiori, a short covered bridge over the river, which is still used as a market building. Following Via Principe Amedeo south, the **Casa di Giulio Romano**, off to the right at Via Poma 18, overshadowed by the monster-studded Palazzo di Giustizia, was also designed by Romano – like much of his Mantuan work, it was meant to impress the sophisticated, who would have found the licence taken with the Classical rules of architecture witty and amusing. A five-minute walk away on busy Via Giovanni Acerbi, the more austere brick **Casa del Mantegna** was also designed by the artist, both as a home and private museum, and is now used as a contemporary art-space and conference centre (during exhibitions daily 10am–12.30pm & 2.30–6.30pm). Across the road, the church of **San Sebastiano** (closed indefinitely; phone ℗0376.360.506 for details) was the work of Alberti, and is famous as the first Renaissance church to be built on a central Greek cross plan, described as "curiously pagan" by Nikolaus Pevsner. Lodovico II's son was less polite: "I could not understand whether it was meant to turn out as a church, a mosque or a synagogue." Its days as a consecrated building are over and it now contains commemorative plaques forming a monument to the fallen Mantuan soldiers of World War II.

At the end of Via Giovanni Acerbi, across Viale Te, the **Palazzo Te** (Mon 1–6pm, Tues–Sun 9am–6pm; €8) was designed for playboy Federico Gonzaga and his mistress, Isabella Boschetta, by Giulio Romano; it's the artist/architect's greatest work and a renowned Renaissance pleasure dome. When the palace was built, Te – or Tejeto, as it used to be known – was an island connected to the mainland by bridge, an ideal location for an amorous retreat away from Federico's wife and the restrictions of life in the Palazzo Ducale. Built around a square courtyard originally occupied by a labyrinth, these days it houses modest but appealing collections of Egyptian artefacts and modern art, although the main reason for visiting is to see Giulio's amazing decorative scheme.

A tour of the palace is like a voyage around Giulio's imagination, a sumptuous world where very little is what it seems. In the **Camera del Sole e delle Luna**, the sun and the moon are represented by a pair of horse-drawn chariots viewed from below, giving a fine array of bottoms on the ceiling; in the **Sala dei Cavalli**, dedicated to the prime specimens from the Gonzaga studfarm (which was also on the island), portraits of horses stand before an illusionistic background in which simulated marble, fake pilasters and mock reliefs surround views of painted landscapes through nonexistent windows. The function of the **Sala di Psiche**, further on, is undocumented, but the sultry frescoes, and the proximity to Federico's private quarters, might give a few clues, the ceiling paintings telling the story of Cupid and Psyche with some more dizzying "sotto in su" (from the bottom up) works by Giulio, among others clumsily executed by his pupils. On the walls, too, are racy pieces, covered with orgiastic wedding-feast scenes, at which drunk and languishing gods in various states of undress are attended by a menagerie of real and mythical beasts. Don't miss the severely incontinent river-god in the background, included either as a punning reference to Giulio's second name, Pippi (The Pisser), or as encouragement to Federico who, according to his doctors, suffered from the "obstinate retention of urine". Other scenes show Mars and Venus having a bath,

Olympia about to be raped by a half-serpentine Jupiter and Pasiphae disguising herself as a cow in order to seduce a bull – all watched over by the giant Polyphemus, perched above the fireplace, clutching the pan-pipes with which he sang of his love for Galatea before murdering her lover.

Polyphemus and his fellow giants are revenged in the extraordinary **Sala dei Giganti** beyond – "the most fantastic and frightening creation of the whole Renaissance", according to the critic Frederick Hartt – showing the destruction of the giants by the gods. As if at some kind of advanced disaster movie, the destruction appears to be all around: cracking pillars, toppling brickwork, and screaming giants, mangled and crushed by great chunks of architecture, appearing to crash down into the room. Stamp your feet and you'll discover another parallel to twentieth-century cinema – the sound-effects that Giulio created by making the room into an echo chamber.

Eating and drinking

Mantua is an easy place to **eat** well and cheaply, with plenty of reasonably priced restaurants throughout its centre, many serving Mantuan specialities like *spezzatino di Mantova* (donkey stew), *agnoli in brodo* (pasta stuffed with cheese and sausage in broth) or the delicious *tortelli di zucca* (pasta stuffed with pumpkin). If you want a **snack** when visiting Palazzo Te, head for one of the *kioskos* across the park, just off Viale Isonzo; they serve a wide choice of piadine and panini, with a view of the *palazzo*. In town the wine bar, *Buca della Gabbia,* at Via Cavour 98, is a good spot for an *aperitivo* in winter or something stonger after dinner.

Aquila Nigra Vicolo Bonaclosi 4 ☎0376.327.180. One of the top places in town, this formal restaurant, housed in an elegant palazzo just off Piazza Sordello, serves delicious fare complemented by an impressive wine list. Closed Sun, Mon & Aug.
Fragoletto Piazza Arche 5. Over towards the river, the *Fragoletto* is popular with locals for its well-priced regional cuisine. Closed Mon.
La Masseria Piazza Broletto 7. A popular, lively place with a wide selection of other dishes as well as good pizzas served at outside tables. Closed Thurs.

Al Quadrato Piazza Virgiliana 49. A tranquil spot away from the fray, overlooking the Piazza Virgiliana park; serves good pizzas and tasty fish dishes. Closed Mon.
Trattoria del Rio Via Pescheria 23. A relaxed trattoria right by the fish market serving traditional Mantuan dishes. Closed Fri.
Santa Barbara Piazza Santa Barbara 19. Inside the Palazzo Ducale complex itself, this is an atmospheric setting for local specialities. Closed Mon.

Grazie and Sabbioneta

There's not much to see within easy reach of Mantua, and the countryside – the Mantuan plain – is for the most part flat and dull. The closest real attraction is at **GRAZIE**, a ten-minute bus ride west, where the church of **Santa Maria delle Grazie** has an interior chock-full of weird votive offerings, wax and wooden mannequins in clothes petrified with age standing in niches, surrounded by wooden hearts, breasts, hands and feet nailed up by the recipients of miracle cures. There's even a stuffed crocodile hanging from the ceiling. Alongside the church, a path leads down to the marshes, rich in rare birds and wildlife. For **boat trips** along the Po contact Motonavi Andes at Piazza Sordello 8, Mantua (☎0376.322.875) or Motonave Sebastiano N. at Via Ostigliese est 272, Governolo (☎0376.668.134).

Further out, fifty minutes by bus from Mantua bus station (3–9 daily), **SABBIONETA** is a more interesting target, an odd little place with the air of an abandoned film set, where imperious Renaissance palaces gaze blankly over deserted and dusty piazzas. The town is the result of the obsessive dream of

Vespasiano Gonzaga, member of a minor branch of the Mantuan family, to create the ideal city, but it has now been abandoned by all but the oldest inhabitants, a handful of agricultural workers and the tourist board.

Sabbioneta was an anachronism even as it was being built. In the sixteenth century it was no more than an agricultural village, nominal capital of an insignificant state on the Mantuan border struggling to maintain its independence from the foreign powers who had colonized most of Lombardy. Unperturbed, its ruler, Duke Vespasiano, was keen to create an ideal state on the model of ancient Athens and Rome, and he uprooted his subjects from their farm cottages, forcing them to build and then inhabit the new city, which held a Greek and Latin Academy and a Palladian theatre as well as a couple of ducal residences. After Vespasiano's death, Sabbioneta returned to – and has remained in – its former state: a small agricultural village like hundreds of others throughout Italy.

The **tourist office** is at Piazza D'Armi 1 (Tues–Sat. April–Sept 9.30am–12.30pm & 2.30–6pm, Sun closes 7pm; Oct–March closes 5pm; ☎0375 .221.044; ⓦwww.sabbioneta.org) and they arrange guided tours (€7.20) around the most important buildings; entrance without a guide is €5.70 or €2.60 for each sight. The tours start with the **Palazzo del Giardino**, Vespasiano's private residence, decorated with frescoed models of civilized behaviour, ranging from Roman emperors to the Three Graces. Next stop is the **Teatro Olimpico**, copied from Palladio's theatre of the same name in Vicenza, in which the only spectators are pallid marble gods, fake-bronze emperors and ghostly painted courtiers. The **Palazzo Ducale**, around the corner, holds painted wooden statues of four of the Gonzagas, including Vespasiano (with the ruffle and beard), sitting imperiously on horseback. What remains of the palace's decor is likewise concerned with the show of strength – frescoed elephants and friezes of eagles and lions. Close by, the **Chiesa dell'Incoronata** (Sun & public holidays only 3–6pm) is remarkable mainly for its trompe l'oeil roof, which appears to be three times higher in than out – perhaps an apt comment on Vespasiano, a bronze statue of whom sits beneath, dressed as a Roman emperor and looking reluctant to leave his dream city.

Northern Lombardy: lakes and mountains

"One can't describe the beauty of the **Italian lakes**, nor would one try if one could." Henry James's sentiment hasn't stopped generations of writers trying to do just that in pages of purple prose. In fact, the lakes just about deserve it: their beauty is extravagant, and it's not surprising that the most melodramatic and romantic of Italy's opera composers – Verdi, Rossini and Bellini – rented lakeside villas in which to work. British and German Romantic poets also enthused about the area, and in doing so implanted them firmly in northern European imaginations. The result is a massive influx every summer of package tourists from cooler climes, come to savour the Italian dream and to take large gulps at what Keats called "the beaker of the warm south".

It would, however, be unwise literally to drink the lakes' waters, even though considerable efforts have been made in recent years to clean them up. Most *comunes* have installed purification plants, and although there is still some way to go before the lakes are totally clean, swimming is safe in most areas. Where it is not, the local *comune* is obliged to erect a warning notice. **Garda** is the cleanest lake, and one of the best centres in Europe for windsurfing and sailing, although you'll have to share the water with huge numbers of like-minded enthusiasts. If watersports don't appeal, **Como** is the most scenically stunning of the lakes: surrounded by tall peaks that rise more or less directly from the water's edge, the luxuriance of its vegetation is equalled by the opulence of the local villas and *palazzi*; and when such things begin to cloy, there are good hikes in its mountainous hinterland. The shores of **Maggiore** are much flatter, and many of its *fin-de-siècle* resorts are rather sedate. There are, however, some good walks, and you shouldn't miss the gardens on Isola Bella. Though the picture-postcard charms of Orta San Giulio, the main village on **Lago d'Orta**, ensure that it is thronged with people at Easter and in summer, it's a romantic base in spring or autumn, and while the other minor lakes – **Lago d'Iseo** and **Lago Ledro** – are tame by comparison, you might want to stay on Iseo's islet, where there are some pleasant hikes.

The hilly terrain between the lakes is sliced up by **mountain valleys**: their lower reaches are largely residential and harbour light industry, with their rivers frequently reduced to a trickle by hydroelectric works, but the upper reaches are mainly untouched, with plenty of possibilities for hikes. There are also numerous small ski resorts, but none worth going out of your way for. Of the two main cities, **Brescia** is really best avoided; **Bergamo** makes a much nicer place to stay, with an old walled hilltop centre that ranks as one of the loveliest in Italy. If you're lucky enough to find a room there, it's also a good base for trips to lakes Como and Iseo and the mountainous country in between.

Getting around the lakes

The three biggest lakes are all well served by **ferries**, which zigzag from shore to shore, docking at jetties that are usually conveniently positioned on the main lakeside piazzas or in the centre of the larger towns' promenades. Some of the regular boats are pretty slow, and if you're in a hurry, you might want to pay extra for a **hydrofoil**; timetables are available at all tourist offices and the ticket offices on the jetties themselves, and include a table of tariffs. Prices vary from lake to lake and various passes are available on all of them, although unless you're doing two or three long journeys with lots of stops, they're no bargain. Note that there is a discount for over-60 EU residents on Lake Como on presentation of proof of age. Check sailing times and prices for all the lakes online at ⓦ www.navigazionelaghi.it.

In addition, there are fairly regular **buses** up and down the shores, a cheaper but far less interesting way of travelling. Timetables are usually posted on bus stops, and again some of the better-organized tourist offices have copies. Be warned, though, that in Garda and Maggiore, which have one shoreline in Lombardy and another in, respectively, Veneto and Piemonte, it can be impossible to get hold of timetables for the "rival" region's buses.

Lago Maggiore and Lago d'Orta

For generations of overland travellers, **Lago Maggiore** has been the first taste of Italy. Road and railway from Switzerland run along its shores and, for travellers weary of the journey and the cool grandeur of the Alps, the first glimpse of Maggiore's limpid waters, gentle green hills and the hint of exotic vegetation can seem a promising taster of the country. Unmistakably Mediterranean in atmosphere, with citrus trees, palms and oleanders lining the lakeside proms and a peaceful, serene air, this is not somewhere for thrill-seekers, but is a beautiful place. Orange blossom, vines, clear air and the verbena that flourishes on its shores continue to draw the tourists, and you'll need to book in advance in peak season.

The western shore

The majority of the tourists who flock to Lago Maggiore head for the western shore, from where the jewel of the lake, the sumptuous gardens and villas of the **Isole Borromee**, is easily accessible. Miraculously, however, the area has not completely lost its charm and the *fin-de-siècle* resort of **Stresa** is still a good base for a visit to the area. It is the last lakeside stop on the trainline to Domodossola (see p.94), a taxi ride away from Lago d'Orta and, most importantly, has wonderful views and easy access to the lake's islands. Further north **Verbania** has ferry links to the eastern shore, plus the lake's only youth hostel, and **Cannobio**, the last stop before Switzerland, is a younger resort that's popular with families and a convenient pad for exploring Maggiore's hilly hinterland. The southern reaches of the shore are rather drab, but you'll have more chance of finding a room there in high season. All the resorts on the western shore of the lake are connected by regular bus and ferry services; the train line goes inland after Stresa.

Stresa

The Maggiore of the tourist brochures begins at **STRESA**, whose popularity as a resort began in 1906 with the construction of the Simplon Tunnel. Its elegant lakeside promenade is now trodden by elderly visitors for whose benefit the main square in its mellow old centre is filled with ranks of café tables dedicated to the mass consumption of outsize ice-cream sundaes. If you are here for any length of time, after strolling up and down the promenade past the *Grand Hotel des Iles Borromees*, which was used as a location by Hemingway in *A Farewell to Arms*, you might want to laze around at Stresa's **Lido** (open summer only) to the north, close to the Mottarone cable car station. From here, you can also catch a cable car up **Monte Mottarone** (daily every 20min 9.20am–noon & 1.40–5pm; €9 return). It's hardly the most sensational of hills, but undeserving of Ruskin's derision – he referred to it as "the stupidest of mountains" and thought the views of the Alps dull. Ruskin's mood or the weather must have been bad, for the views stretch from Monte Rosa on the Valle d'Aosta/Swiss border across to the Adamello. Its wooded western slopes are now a favourite destination for family outings, and on summer Sundays the roadside is lined with picnickers; the tourist office has leaflets detailing walks in the area. If you want to range a bit further, you can rent mountain bikes near the summit (€15 per day). Lago d'Orta lies on the other side of the mountain, and though it is possible to walk down to the lake, it's a tedious three-hour tramp.

Practicalities

Stresa's Pro Loco **tourist office** at Via Canonica 8 (Easter to 20 Oct daily 10am–12.20pm & 3–6.30pm, winter Mon–Fri 10am–12.30pm & 3–6.30pm, Sat 10am–12.30pm; ℡0323.31.308, ⟨W⟩www.lagomaggiore.it), as well as dispensing the usual local information, has programmes for the prestigious **international music festival** held annually in late July and early August.

If you want to **stay** in Stresa, you could choose to join the Brits and Americans at the lakefront grand hotels: the *Grand Hotel des Iles Borromees* (℡0323.938.938, ⓦwww.borromees.it; ❾) or the marginally more accessible *Regina Palace Hotel* (℡50323.936.936, ⓦwww.stresa.net/hotel/regina; ❾) where all conceivable comforts are catered for in opulent surroundings. At the other end of the scale is the friendly little *Albergo Ristorante Luina* (℡0323.30.285, ⓔluinastresa@yahoo.it; ❹), at Via Garibaldi 21 right in the centre of the village, which has diminutive en-suite rooms and a good-value restaurant downstairs with home cooking. For a little more money but still in the centre, make for the three-star *Hotel Primavera* (℡0323.31.286, ⓕ0323.33.458; ❺ with breakfast; closed mid-Nov to March), where spacious, modern, en-suite rooms have balconies – some with lake views. The most atmospheric of all the options in this part of the lake, however, is the *Albergo Ristorante Varenna* (℡0323.30.408, ⓦwww.hotelverbana.it; ❼) on the Isla Pescatori. The handsomely furnished rooms in this romantic little hotel have wonderful lake views and make a perfect bolthole at any time of year.

If you're looking for somewhere **to eat**, the best place to try regional Piemontese cooking is in the snug *La Botte* (closed Wed) on Via Mazzini 6/8, right in the village centre, where the friendly host serves up local game as well as a variety of tasty pasta dishes. A couple of doors away at number 25 the *Pietmontese* offers a more refined atmosphere in the elegant dining room or the pleasant garden, at correspondingly higher prices. The *Osteria degli Amici*, at Via Anna Maria Bolongaro 27 (closed Wed), on the other side of the main square, is a simple place with an attractive vine-covered terrace where a very tasty *risotto alle scampetti* is served, but service can be slow. For snacks and **drinks**, the *Red Baron*, five minutes' walk along from the train station at Via Roma 63, is an amiable place run by a friendly English woman who serves up great sandwiches, hearty *bruschette* and beer on tap.

The Isole Borromee

The three visitable **Isole Borromee** are all served by regular ferries from Stresa, either from Piazza Marconi or Piazzale Lido, further up the lakeside promenade. **Isola Bella** is home to a villa (24 March to 20 Oct daily 9am–noon & 1.30–5.30pm; gardens 9am–6.15pm; €8.50), reckoned by Robert Southey to be "one of the most costly efforts of bad taste in all Italy". It is best known, however, for the most gloriously excessive of all the lakes' gardens, though three centuries ago it was little more than a barren rock. In the seventeenth century Count Carlo III Borromeo decided to create an island paradise for his wife Isabella, and commissioned the architect, Angelo Crivelli, to transform it into a sumptuous Baroque oasis. Tons of soil were brought across from the mainland, a villa, fountains and statues were built, white peacocks imported, and ten terraces of orange and lemon trees, camellias, magnolias, box trees, laurels and cypresses carved out. The centrepiece, however, is a four-tiered confection of shell-, mirror- and marble-encrusted grottoes, topped with a suitably melodramatic unicorn, mini-obelisks, and various Greek gods and cute cherubs in attendance. Inside, ritzy rooms are opulently furnished, and there are more artificial grottoes and a collection of eighteenth-century marionettes in the cellar. Isola Bella really is worth seeing, though as Maggiore's main tourist attraction, every inch of the island not occupied by the palace and garden is taken up by restaurants with multilingual menus and stalls selling lace, pottery, the ubiquitous Pinochio puppet and assorted gimcrackery.

Hemingway's favourite island, **Isola dei Pescatori** (or Isola Superiore), once an island of fishermen, retains a certain charm, despite the regular invasions of sightseers. Along with the obligatory trinket stands and restaurants there are a few ordinary bars and shops, and it's a good spot to hang around for an hour or so or bring a picnic and settle down with splendid lake views to accompany your meal. Ferries move on to **Isola Madre**, larger and less visited than Isola Bella, with a small, tasteful *palazzo* (24 March to 20 Oct 9am–noon & 1.30–5pm; €8), stacked with portraits of the Borromeos in a luxuriant but less formal garden. Tiny **San Giovanni**, the fourth Borromean island, has a villa once owned by Toscanini, but is closed to the public.

Verbania

Half-way up the lake is **PALLANZA**, which along with the industrial quarters of Suna and Intra makes up the town of **VERBANIA**, whose name recalls *Verbanum* – the name used by the Romans for the whole, verbena-shored lake. Verbania's winter climate is the mildest on the lake, which enabled a retired Scottish soldier, Captain Neil McEachern, to create in the Thirties the most botanically prestigious garden of all the lakes, at the **Villa Táranto**. The grounds (April–Oct daily 8.30am–7.30pm; last admission 6.30pm; €7) contain 20,000 species of plant – including giant Amazonian lilies, lotus blossoms, Japanese maple, and *Melia azederach*, a sacred Indian tree – laid out with cool geometric accuracy around fountains and pools.

A half-hour walk south of Villa Táranto, Pallanza's lakefront is lined with manicured flower beds and dapper *gelaterie*, bars and hotels, but on the hill behind there's a more down-to-earth quarter in which the souvenir shops are almost outnumbered by *alimentari*, fruit shops and *pasticcerie*. The **tourist office** is on Corso Zanitello 8 (May–Sept Mon–Sat 9am–noon & 3–6pm, Sun 9am–noon; Oct–April Mon–Fri 9am–12.30pm &3–6pm, Sat 9am–12.30pm; ℡ & ℻0323.503249, ⓦwww.verbania.alpcom.it). From just opposite the entrance to the villa, the lake's only **car ferry** joins the east Piemonte coast with the western Lombardy shores at the town of Laveno (see p.205). Pallanza also boasts the only **youth hostel** (℡0323.501.648, ℻0323.507.877; March–Oct) on the lake, a signposted ten-minute uphill walk from Piazza Gramsci where the bus drops you. It's a friendly place and organizes activities in the area. It's set in an old villa that offers double rooms (€15.50), 4–8-bed dorms (€14) and larger 12-bed dorms (€12.50), breakfast included.

Cannobio

CANNOBIO is the most appealing place to stay on the western shore of the lake, its lakefront road of pastel-washed houses giving onto a series of stepped alleyways leading into a tightly tangled old village of stone houses. The only sight as such is the **Santuario della Pietà**, a Bramante-inspired church with a curious openwork cupola. It was built on the site of a 1522 miracle, when a picture of the *Pietà* suddenly began to bleed; shortly afterwards Cannobio remained unscathed while the plague ravished other villages nearby. How religious minds could do nothing but link the two events. Carlo Borromeo, anxious as ever to boost the morale of Catholics in the face of the snowballing power of the Protestant church, ordered a chapel to be built to house the painting. It's still there, though curiously there's no sign of blood stains.

At the head of Via Marconi is the SS34 coast road, on which you'll find the **tourist office** (Mon–Sat 9am–noon & 4–7pm, Sun 9am–noon; Oct–March closed Thurs; ℡0323.71.212) and a couple of supermarkets. At the northern end of the lakefront, past the car park, between the town and most of the campsites, lies the blue-flag winning public beach, backed by a pleasant grassy area with trees, picnic tables, showers and watersports. On Sundays, the local market takes over the waterfront area selling anything from fresh produce to leather and tacky imitation goods.

The cheapest **accommodation** in Cannobio is offered by the various lakeside campsites to the north of town, many of which have bungalows and caravans to rent; there are also plenty of rooms advertised along the main road. Tucked among the streets winding up from the lakeside is the charming *Hotel Pironi*, Via G. Marconi 35 (☎0323.706.24; ❼), where friendly staff welcome you to the wonderfully serene atmosphere and comfortable rooms of a converted fifteenth-century convent. The modern *Villa Belvedere* (☎0323.70.159, ✉info@villabelvederehotel.it; ❺), just out of town on the road to the Val Cannobina, is the sister hotel and has a swimming pool that residents at both hotels can use. A cheaper but still appealing option is the *Antica Stallera*, Via P. Zacchero (☎0323.715.95; ❺), which has a vine-covered garden restaurant overlooked by the simple, modern en-suite rooms. If the prices are getting too much for you, head out of town on the SS34: just past the River Cannobino is the very popular *La Residence* **campsite** (☎0323.71.190, ✉info@camping-campagna.it; March–Oct) where, in addition to tent pitches, there are **rooms** in a clean, modern villa (❸).

As for **eating**, *Lo Scalo* (closed Mon), on a corner site on the lakefront opposite the ferry port, is arguably the best place in town and is certainly one of the smarter. The food – which has been awarded three Michelin forks – is inventive and based on Piemontese specialities; you'll end up paying around €80 a head for a full meal with wine. If you're keeping to a tighter budget, *Osteria La Streccia*, up a narrow cobbled alley off the lakefront (closed Tues), offers good food in a rustic, low-ceilinged dining room, or head for the garden at the *Antica Stallera* (see above). In summer the *gelaterie* on the lakefront are a good spot for a **snack** or cappuccino, while the bar below the *Hotel Pironi* (see above) is a cosy spot for a **drink** in cooler weather.

Inland along the Val Cannobina

Cannobio is well served by both ferries and buses, and you could catch one of the latter from the jetty up the Val Cannobina, a rarely visited valley punctuated by a few ancient stone-built hamlets. From Falmonta at the end of the bus route you could walk or drive up to the winter resort of Malesco from where you can pick up the privately run FART train to Locarno in Switzerland (see p.94).

About 10km out of Cannobio along the Val Cannobina, the **Orrido di Santa Ana** is a spectacular narrow gorge surrounded by wooded slopes, which makes a good place for a picnic or a bathe if you have your own transport, or time the buses carefully. Beside the Roman bridge and the chapel is a small river beach and a wonderfully sited restaurant, the *Ristorante Grotto Sant'Anna* (☎0323.70.682; closed Mon), which offers tasty and reasonably priced food.

The eastern shore

In general there is little of great interest on the eastern side of Lago Maggiore, although any of the smaller centres make feasible bases for the rest of the lake, or for hiking into the hills behind. From **MACCAGNO**, an improbably steep track leads straight out from the village into the hills, from where there are paths to the Lago Delio and Valle Veddasca. Most interestingly, you can walk to the village of Curiglia, beyond which, from Ponte di Piero, an acute mule track climbs to the picturesque village of **MONTEVIASCO**, 500m above. There's no road to Monteviasco, and until recently the mule track was its only link with the world. Nowadays, however, there's a cable car.

Back in Maccagno, the *Albergo Torre Imperiale* on Piazza Roma (☎0332.51.000;

❹), at the foot of the village near the lake, has basic doubles above a simple restaurant and bar, and there's a **campsite** on the waterfront – *Camping Lido* (☎0332.560.250). Four kilometres further south is one of the most appealing places **to stay** in the area: the *Hotel Camin Colmegna* (03332.510.855; ❻) is a very friendly family hotel right on the waterfront. It's uncomfortably close to the main road but on a sunny day the extensive lakeside gardens and swimming areas are difficult to beat.

One and half kilometres south, **LUINO**, a sizeable town and tourist centre, is really only worth visiting on Wednesdays when it hosts Maggiore's biggest market, the usual mixture of local produce, plastic toys and cheap shoes. The *centro storico* (follow sign off the main road to the left of the *imbarcadero*) is no great shakes but is reasonably well stocked with food and especially wine shops. If you've spent any time in Lombardy's art galleries you may already be familiar with the work of Bernardino Luino, one of Leonardo's followers. It's assumed that he hailed from Luino, and if you like his work, you should take a look at the campanile he frescoed at the oratory of **SS Pietro e Paolo**. Luino's **tourist office** (Mon–Sat 9am–noon & 3–6.45pm; ☎0332.530.019) is across the road from the jetty and can help with a list of places to stay.

Twenty five kilometres south of Luino, **LAVENO** is also accessible by car ferry (€1.80 per person plus €4.80 for an average-sized car) from Intra in around 20min. From Laveno a cable car climbs up to the **Sasso del Ferro** for great views of the Alps. On its southern slopes, but visible only from the lake, is the **Santuario di Santa Caterina del Sasso** (daily 8.30am–noon & 2–6pm; free). In the early twelfth century a wealthy moneylender, Alberto Besozzi, was sailing on the lake when his boat sank. He prayed to St Catherine of Alexandria and was safely washed up on shore, afterwards giving up usury and becoming a hermit in a cave on the hillside. When his prayers averted a plague the locals built a church, which became popular with pilgrims, especially after a boulder fell on the roof but was miraculously wedged just above the altar instead of falling on the priest saying Mass. The boulder finally crashed through in 1910, and the church was closed until recently for fear of further rockfalls.

Lago d'Orta

The locals call **Lago d'Orta** "Cinderella", capturing perfectly the reticent beauty of this small lake with its deep blue waters and intriguing island. Orta is a popular target for the weekend-long passeggiata that occurs from Easter onwards, but nevertheless is one of the few places on the lakes which really has retained a faded nineteenth-century charm. Try, if you can, to go mid-week or out of season.

Orta San Giulio and the hinterland

Occupying the tip of a peninsula on the lake's eastern shore, **ORTA SAN GIULIO** is a romantic little village where narrow cobbled streets run between pastel-washed houses and palaces with elaborate wrought-iron balconies. It is, not surprisingly, Lago d'Orta's main attraction, and on summer Sundays the approach roads hum with traffic but, in the evening, the charm returns. Life centres on two piazzas: **Piazzetta Ernesto Ragazzoni**, and **Piazza Motta** – open to the lake and looking directly on to Isola San Giulio – where visitors congregate in three *gelaterie* (of which *Venus* is the best). Somewhat out of place among the pavement cafés is the **Palazzo della Comunità**, Orta's diminutive town hall, decorated with faded frescoes and supported on an arcaded loggia. From the piazza you can walk out of the village along Via Giovanetti to a lakeside promenade popular with smooching couples, or catch a boat to the island (see below).

Above the town is the **Sacro Monte**, 21 chapels dedicated to St Francis of Assisi and containing some awful tableaux of painted terracotta statues acting out scenes from the saint's life against frescoed B-movie backgrounds. They make up a devotional route still followed by pilgrims, though as many visitors come simply to picnic, admire the views of the lake and inhale the pine-scented air.

Orta-Misiano **station** is around 3km out of town, but it's downhill all the way. Turn left out of the station on to the main road and continue downhill for about twenty minutes, passing the eccentric *Villa Crespi* on your left. The **tourist office** is on your way, on Via Panoramica (Tues–Sat 9am–noon & 3–6pm, Sun 10am–noon & 3–5pm; ☎0322.905.614, ⓦwww.lagodorta.net), and is well organized, with bus timetables as well as information on places to stay.

There's a wide variety of **accommodation** on offer in or around Orta San Giulio, but you'd do best to book ahead in high season if you can. At the top end of the scale is the *San Rocco* where anonymous modern rooms are compensated for by a wonderful lakeside location; the position of the pool and café-bar are simply unbeatable. At the other end of the main drag, dominating the main piazza, *Hotel Orta* (☎0322.90.253; ⓦwww.hotelorta.it; ❸), a traditional family-run hotel, has seen better days. The en-suite rooms are pretty dated but many have lake-views and if you can manage to bag one of the three suites facing the island, with private terraces right over the water, you'll be in heaven. For a few more mod cons, try the *Hotel La Bussola* (☎0322.911.913 ⓦwww.emmeti.it/Hbussola) just above the village by the main car park, with a swimming pool and lovely views from the dining room and terrace. Just beside the *Olina* restaurant, at Via Olina 40 in the village centre, is a little office (☎0322.905.656, ⓕ0322.905.645) offering a collection of en-suite rooms, self-catering apartments and holiday lets, often unusually decorated with the owner's modern, quirky taste. There is also a **campsite**, *Camping Orta* (☎ & ⓕ0322.90.267), a little out of town sandwiched between the main road and the lake – it's about a fifteen-minute walk downhill from the station (turn right at the main crossroads opposite Hotel Crespi).

Finding good **snack** food in the village is a challenge, but the *Bar Edera*, signposted off Via Olina, does reasonably priced crepes, *piadine* and *pizzette*, while *Taverna Boeuc* on Via Bersani serves tasty morsels to accompany your wine. For more of a sit-down **meal**, you'll eat very well at the *Olina* (closed Wed), which serves excellent local specialities and thoughtful extras like aperitifs on the house; just beyond Piazzetta Ragazzoni in the *centro storico* is the smarter *Antico Agnello*, Via Olina 18 (booking advised at weekends, ☎0322.90.259; closed Tues), offering tasty Lombard and Piedmont dishes, great puddings and congenial service.

Isola San Giulio

Orta's highlight is the **Isola San Giulio**, a tiny island-village dominated by a severe white seminary and the tower of its twelfth-century basilica. Boats leave every fifteen minutes, and the return journey costs €2.50; the last boat back is at 7.30pm. The San Giulio of the town and island was a priest who in 390 AD decided to found a sanctuary on the island. The locals refused to row him over, as the island was supposedly seething with monsters and snakes, and Giulio is said to have crossed on foot using his staff as a rudder and his cloak as a sail. Once there, he banished the snakes, founded his sanctuary and earned himself a sainthood. The **Basilica** (May–Sept Mon–Sat 9.30am–noon & 2–6.45pm, Sun 9.30am–12.15pm & 2–6.45pm; Oct–April closes 5.30pm) has a redoubtable black marble pulpit, carved with venomous-looking griffins and serpents, recalling the myth. The massive vertebra in the sacristy is said to have belonged to one of the island's dragons; scientists reckon it's a whalebone.

The Varesotto

The **Varesotto** is the least attractive but richest of the lake provinces, a major industrial region that produces everything from shoes and silk to helicopters. Its three small lakes are badly polluted and, lying blandly on the plain, cannot compete with nearby Maggiore and Como for scenic splendour. The provincial capital, **Varese**, is worthy of a place on your itinerary only if you have to make train or bus connections on your way to hiking in the countryside around.

Varese

VARESE is a gracious purpose-built town of gardens, marble Fifties villas and rectangular Fascist-era buildings, fringed with shoe factories. Its inhabitants are every bit as obsessed with style as the Milanese and look almost as perfect as the window-display mannequins in the designer shops that line the main street, Corso Matteotti. The centre of town is Piazza Monte Grappa, not far from the city's main attraction, the formal gardens around the long, pink **Palazzo Estense**, built in the eighteenth century for the Este Dukes of Modena (daily 8am–sunset, until 11pm July & Aug; free). The *raison d'être* of modern Varese is to provide alternative accommodation for the thousands who visit Milan's trade fairs, especially the fashion shows in April and October. Consequently, the majority of the **hotels** are aimed at an expense-account clientele, though there are a half-dozen two-stars, and a cheaper option in the shape of the *Stadio*, Via Bolchini 24 (☎0332.224.069; ❷), which also has rooms for up to four people. For inexpensive meals and **snacks** such as roast beef and fresh salads, there's *Bistrot* on the corner of Via Manzoni and Via Mazzini. The **tourist office** at Via Carobbio 2 (June–Sept Mon–Fri 9am–noon & 3.15–7pm, Sat 9am–noon & 3–6pm; Oct–May Mon–Fri 9am–noon & 3–6.30pm, Sat 9am–noon; ❻varersottoturismo.com) can give the full picture.

North of Varese: hiking routes

More attractive than the three small lakes near Varese is **Lago di Ghirla**, a tarn deep in a valley, the Valganna, near the Swiss border. There's a **campsite** (☎0332.716.583; April–Sept) on the side away from the B37 road and plenty of opportunities for stiff hikes – it's best to avoid going on the weekends in summer though, when the area is very crowded.

There are a number of other country and forest **treks** to the north of Varese, the most interesting of which is the haul across to Maccagno on Lago Maggiore (see p.204). The walk starts at Porto Ceresio at the foot of Lago Lugano near the Swiss border and takes ten days; you could, though, pick it up at any point along the route. The booklet *Via Verde Varesina*, available only in Italian from local bookshops, is useful for information on how to get to starting-points on public transport and for places to eat and stay over; its maps, however, are poor, and unless you can read its route descriptions you'll need to buy a decent map as well.

Lago di Como

Of all the Italian lakes, it's the forked **Lago di Como** that comes most heavily praised. Wordsworth thought it "a treasure which the earth keeps to itself", though what he would think of the place now is anyone's guess: the lake is still surrounded by abundant vegetation but it can get very busy and the principal towns of **Como** or **Lecco**, in particular, are not especially appealing destinations these days. At times, though, as you're zigzagging up the lake on a steamer, it can seem almost ridiculously romantic, and if you want to do more than indulge in *belle époque* dreams, you could try one of several great walks through the lake's mountainous hinterland – and in most places the water is clean enough for swimming. Of the lake's other towns and villages, three are outstanding: **Varenna** and **Bellagio** for unrepentant romantics and **Menaggio** if you want a pleasant, affordable base for walking, swimming or cycling.

Como Town

COMO can be a dispiriting place to arrive, with little of the picture-postcard prettiness you may be expecting from a lakeside town. As the nearest resort to Milan and a popular stopoff on the main road into Switzerland, it's both heavily touristed – though the atmosphere doesn't feel as forced as in some of the other lake towns as many of the tourists are Italian – and, on the outskirts at least, fairly industrialized. Apart from tourism, the main industry is a rarefied one – Como is the main silk-supplier for Milan's fashion designers – but it doesn't make its factories any more endearing. If you have time to spare, the old town is pleasant to wander or eat in, and the funicular ride has great views across the lake, but really you'd do best using the town as a transport hub and moving on to one of the lake's more attractive resorts.

Lakeside **Piazza Cavour** is bounded by ugly metal-and-glass hotels and banks plus a couple of pricey pavement cafés. To the left is a little lakeside park set around a curious temple, now the **Museo Alessandro Volta** (April–Sept Tues–Sun 10am–noon & 3–6pm; Oct–March 10am–noon & 2–4pm; €2.50), dedicated to Como's most useful son, a pioneer in electricity who gave his name to the volt – some of the instruments he used to conduct his experiments are displayed inside. Beyond, compellingly illuminated at night, is the **Villa Olmo**, an eighteenth-century Neoclassical pile in magnificent grounds. The villa itself is a popular venue for congresses, but it's open to the public when it's delegate-free (Mon–Sat 9am–noon & 3–6pm), although it is the **gardens** that are the biggest draw (Mon–Sat: summer 8am–11pm; winter 7am–7pm).

From Piazza Cavour Via Plinio leads up to the **Broletto**, prettily striped in pink, white and grey, and with a fifteenth-century balcony designed for municipal orators. Next door, the splendid **Duomo** (daily 7.30am–noon & 3–7pm) was begun at the end of the fourteenth century but wasn't completed until the eighteenth, when the Baroque genius Juvarra added the cupola. The church is reckoned to be Italy's best example of Gothic-Renaissance fusion: the Gothic spirit clear in the fairy-tale pinnacles, rose windows and buffoonish gargoyles; that of the Renaissance in its portals (with rounded rather than ogival arches) and in the presence of the two pagans flanking the main west door – the Elder and Younger Plinys, both of whom were born in Como. There was nothing unusual in the sequestration of classical figures by Christians in the Renaissance, but the presence, especially of Pliny Junior, does seem somewhat inappropriate, since his only connection with Christianity was to order the assassination of two deaconesses. Inside, the Gothic aisles are hung with rich Renaissance tapestries (some woven with perspective scenes) and if you've a few spare coins you could illuminate a heavy-lidded Leonardesque *Madonna* and an *Adoration of the Magi* by Luini, and a languid *Flight to Egypt* by Gaudenzio Ferrari.

Behind the Duomo, on the other side of the railway tracks in Piazza del Popolo, is the definitive example of Rationalist architecture by Como-born

Giuseppe Terragni. Built as the headquarters for the local Fascist party in the Thirties it has been rechristened the **Palazzo Terragni** and is now home to the area Guardia di Finanza.

The second of Como's churches, the Romanesque **Sant'Abbondio**, left along Via Regina from the main train station, struggles to hold its own in a dreary suburb. Built in the eleventh century, it was stripped of later encrustations in the nineteenth century and returned to its original simplicity. Once inside you can forget the brutal surroundings as you wander down the serene aisles to the apse with its colourful fourteenth-century frescoes, the most appealing of which depicts the Magi dreaming of Christ under striped and patterned blankets.

If you have time, head down to the lake shore to the right of Piazza Cavour, by Como Lago station, and take a **funicular** (roughly every thirty minutes 6am–10.30pm; €3.70 return) up to **Brunate**, a small hilltop resort that has great views up the lake and is a good starting-point for hikes (the tourist office has free leaflets detailing routes).

Practicalities

Como has three **train stations**: Como San Giovanni, on the main line from Chiasso to Milan, and Como Borghi and Como Lago, from where trains run to Milan Nord, Saronno, Varese Nord and Novara Nord. Como Lago is, as its name suggests, on the lakeshore, opposite the **ferry jetty** and across the road from the **bus station**. Como San Giovanni, ten minutes' walk from the lake and old centre, is connected with the jetty (and the bus station across the road) by buses #4 and #7. Como Borghi is on the southern side of the town centre, a short walk down Via Sirtori from Viale Battisti. Como San Giovanni has a small **tourist office**, but the main office is situated on Piazza Cavour (Oct–May Mon–Sat 9am–1pm & 2.30–6pm, Sun 9.30am–12.30pm; June–Sept Mon–Sat same hours, Sun 2.30–6pm; ☎031.330.0111, ⓦwww.lakecomo.com).

Como's **youth hostel** is at the *Villa Olmo*, Via Bellinzona 6 (☎031.573.800, ⓔostellocomo@tin.it; €11.50; March–Nov); it also serves dinner (€10), has laundry facilities, rents out bikes, and can get you a discount on the funicular. To get there take bus #1 or #6 from Como San Giovanni or walk for twenty minutes along Via Borgo Vico (on the left as you walk down the steps from the main train station). Two more central places **to stay** are to be found in the pleasant Piazza Volta, just back from the water. Terragni's dingy-looking façade on the *Albergo Ristorante Posta* (☎031.26.6012, ⓦwww.hotelposta.net; ❺) belies a selection of clean, basic, en-suite rooms, including some triples and a quad. Across the square is the more upmarket *Albergo Firenze* (☎031.30.0333, ⓦwww.albergofirenze.it; ❻), where smart, comfortable rooms are set mainly around a quiet internal courtyard.

The liveliest of the cheaper **places to eat** is *La Scuderia*, Piazza Matteotti 4 (closed Tues), right next to the bus station; try the pasta dishes as the pizzas are pretty standard. Alternatively, down one side of the Duomo, the *Teatro Sociale*, at Via Maestri Comacini, serves a decent set meal for €15 (closed Tues). For something a little more upmarket, *Villa Olmo Parco*, at Via Cantoni 1, serves good food at an attractive spot by the lake (closed Tues). If you crave something sweet, try the pastries at *Belli* on Via Vittorio Emanuele, or the ice creams at *Bolla* on Via Pietro Boldoni. For an *aperitivo* or evening **drink**, the atmospheric wine-bar, *Osteria del Gallo*, at Via Vitani 16, serves a choice of tasty nibbles with a fine selection of wines or, if you'd prefer something livelier, head for the bars on the waterfront Lungo Lario Triest, round by the funicular station.

The western shore

The lower reaches of the western shore are the stuff of tourist brochures: wooded mountain slopes protect the lake from extremes of temperature and lush gardens abound. Many of the opulent villas that line the lakeside are still privately owned and on summer weekends the lakeside road is solid with day-trippers. The lake's only island, Isola Comacina, lies at the narrowest point of the lake, just before the waters open up to the warm climes of the nineteenth-century resorts of the **Tremezzino**. **Menaggio**, a little further north, makes a good base for trips into the mountains behind or across to Bellagio (see p.213) and Varenna (see p.212). As you continue up the lake the shore turns rockier and less accessible until the lake spreads out into the marshes and flatter territory that accommodates campsites and windsurfers around **Gravedona**.

Ferries and the C10 **bus** regularly ply their way from Como to Colico, and, from Cadenabbia and Menaggio, car and passenger **ferries** shuttle across to the central and eastern shores of the lake.

Cernobbio and Isola Comacina

The first port of call by steamer on the **western shore** of Lake Como is **Cernobbio** (also accessible by frequent bus from Como's Piazza Matteotti), whose main claim to fame is the swanky **Villa d'Este** hotel (☎031.34.81, ⓦ www.villadeste.it; ❾), a palatial sixteenth-century confection in an opulent garden. The hotel's extravagant gardens with statues, fountains and grottoes and its atmosphere of moneyed comfort make it very popular with Americans including stars from Greta Garbo to Woody Allen and Madonna. If your pockets aren't up to this, you'll have to content yourself with glimpses of its gardens from the steamer.

A little further north lies **Isola Comacina**, Como's only island and another retreat for the well-heeled. Anything further removed from the greenery of Maggiore's islands would be hard to imagine. Comacina, uninhabited save for a handful of artists, is a wild place where you can wander through the ruins of nine abandoned churches. One of the earliest settlements on the lake, it was conquered by the Romans, and, later, when the barbarians invaded, it became a refuge for the wealthy citizens of Como. It developed into a centre of resistance, and in the turmoil of the Middle Ages, attracted an eclectic mix of dethroned monarchs, future saints and the pirate Federico Barbarossa. Eventually it allied with Milan against Como, an unfortunate move, which led to the island being sacked by Como and razed to the ground. Abandoned for centuries, it was bought by a local, Auguste Caprini, who outraged Italy by selling it to the King of Belgium after World War I. Diplomatically, the king decided to return it, and the island is now administered by a joint Belgian/Italian commission. Since 1947 it has been home to an extremely exclusive restaurant, the *Locanda dell'Isola* (☎0344.55.083), whose former clients include Ursula Andress and the Duchess of Kent. If you don't wish to spend your entire budget on one meal, bring a picnic, as the snack bar by the jetty overcharges even for simple sandwiches.

The Tremezzina

Sheltered by a headland, the shore above Isola Comacina, known as the **Tremezzina**, is where Como's climate is at its gentlest, the lake at its most tranquil and the vegetation at its most lush. Lined with cypresses and palms, it's lovely at any time of year, but unbeatable in spring, when it's awash with colour and heady with the scent of flowering bushes.

Inland at **MEZZEGRA**, in 1944, two families of evacuees staying at the Villa Belmonte witnessed a less tranquil scene from their windows. A car drew up and a burly man in a black beret, nervously clutching the lapels of his coat, got out, followed by a woman and a tall pale man with a machine gun. The burly man was Mussolini, the woman his mistress, Claretta Petacci, and the tall man the partisan leader, Walter Audisio. Audisio pulled the trigger and Claretta flew at him, grasping the barrel of the gun; Audisio shot twice more, but the trigger jammed. He took his driver's machine gun and pointed it at Mussolini, who said "Shoot me in the chest"; Audisio shot first at Claretta, killing her outright, and then complied with Mussolini's last request.

TREMEZZO, like Como's other resorts, has its fair share of *belle époque* palaces, villas and hotels, but overall it's a sedate, rather middle-aged resort. The main reason to stop here is to visit the **Villa Carlotta** (daily: April–Sept 9am–6pm; March & Oct 9 11.30am & 2–4.30pm; €6.50), which has its own *imbarcadero* between Tremezzo and Cadenabbia. Pink, white and Neoclassical, it was built by a Prussian princess for her daughter, Carlotta, and now houses a collection of pompous eighteenth-century statues, including Canova's meltingly romantic *Cupid & Psyche* and a frieze of Alexander entering Babylon commissioned by Napoleon – though he was exiled before he could pay for it. The bill was picked up by a count, who in return got himself included as a member of Alexander's army (he's at the end, along with the artist). The villa's greatest attraction, however, is the fourteen-acre **garden**, a beautifully ordered collection of camellias, rhododendrons and azaleas.

Menaggio

MENAGGIO, 5km north, is a bustling village and lively resort that is a good base for hiking and cycling in the mountains as well as sunbathing and swimming. The **ferry jetty** is about five minutes' walk from the main square, Piazza Garibaldi, in and around which you'll find most of Menaggio's lakeside cafés and restaurants. The **tourist office** here (Mon–Sat 9am–noon & 3–6pm; ☎0344.32.924) is unusually well organized, with practical information on the town and maps on walks in the area and an **Internet** point. Swimming in the lake is safe here, and there's a beach and vast pool at the **Lido** (late-June to mid-Sept daily 9am–7pm), as well as **water-skiing** and other waterborne activities at the Centro Lago Service on Via Lago Castelli (☎0344.32.003). There's a good selection of **hikes** to be done around Menaggio, ranging from a two-and-a-half hour walk to the pretty village of Codogna, to the fifty-kilometre *Sentiero delle 4 Valli*, which leads through four valleys to Lago Lugano. The tourist office has descriptions of routes in English, including details of how to get to the various starting-points on public transport, but take a map as well.

Menaggio's **youth hostel**, the *Ostello La Primula*, Via IV Novembre 86 (☎0344.32.356, ⓦwww.menaggiohostel.com; €11.50 including breakfast; mid-March to mid-Nov), is just outside the village, overlooking the main road; reservations necessary. A couple of family rooms supplement the small, clean dorms. The hostel has its own small beach, rents out **bikes**, organizes hikes and can arrange discounts on boat rental, as well as serving excellent meals for €9.30. The nicer of the two **campsites** is the *Lido* (☎0344.31.150; May–Sept), on the road heading north out of town; the slightly cheaper *Europa* (☎0344.31.187; April–Sept) is just beforehand. If you'd prefer a **hotel**, try the *Hotel Garden* (☎0344.31616; ❹), right on the lake front, just a little out of town to the north, or, if you'd rather be in the centre of things, *Il Vapore* (☎0344.32.229; ❷), on Piazza T Grossi, has simple en-suite rooms.

The lakeside offers several options for set menus but if you want something a little less touristy, head for *Vecchia Menaggio* at Via al Lago 13 (closed Tues) for simple, good-value **meals**. Menaggio is a treasure trove for self-caterers, with a couple of big supermarkets and some excellent delicatessens, plus a *tavola calda* on the main road through town.

Gravedona and around

The next major steamer stop is **GRAVEDONA**, not a particularly pretty place but one of the few towns on the lake as old as Como. Wordsworth set off on a moonlight hike from here, got lost, and, stuck on a rock in the middle of nowhere, was unable to sleep because he was "tormented by the stings of insects". Medieval Gravedona, along with nearby Dongo and Sorico, formed part of an independent republic, victimized in the fifteenth century by the inquisitor Peter of Verona for daring to doubt that the pope was God's earthly representative. The people got rid of Peter by hacking him to death, but the pope rewarded him for his devotion to duty by swiftly canonizing him and deeming him Patron of Inquisitors. There's a prophetic twelfth-century carving in the lakeside church of **Santa Maria del Tiglio** (open July–Sept, at other times get the key from the green house on the road) – a centaur pursuing a deer, an early Christian symbol for the persecution of the Church.

If you want to stay over, the *Locanda Serenella* (℡0344.89.452; ❷) and the *Serenella* **campsite**, beyond the church and down towards the lake, are both open from April to October. Beyond Gravedona the lake sides flatten out and the building gets more haphazard, although as the winds are good for **sailing** and **windsurfing** there are a number of **campsites** and cheap, modern **hotels**; you'll find details on Ⓦ www.gravedona.it.

The eastern shore and Bellagio

The **eastern shore** of the lake, stretching from the flat marshes of the north to Como's right leg, **Lago Lecco**, overshadowed by the saw-like ridge of Monte Resegone, is often sunless and consequently less visited than the western shore. The triangle of land between the two branches – the **central zone** – is lusher and sunnier, busy on the coast but with plenty of quiet villages and three small lakes inland. There are fewer places to stay, however, and these are not easily accessible, except Colico, Bellano and **Varenna** on the main shore and **Bellagio** on the central triangle, which are all served by ferries. The **D20** bus runs between Lecco and Colico.

The north

At the top end of the lake's eastern shore – opposite Gravedona – **COLICO** is the final stop for Como steamers, a small industrial centre whose only attraction is a restored eleventh-century abbey, the **Abbazia di Piona**, on the tip of the promontory just above the steamer landing. From here, steamers and hydrofoils head back down the eastern shore, stopping off at **BELLANO**, a small workaday town of silk and cotton mills. From opposite the ferry jetty follow the signs for the three-mintue walk up behind Piazza San Giorgio to the **Orrido do Bellano** (June–Sept daily 10am–10.30pm; Oct–May Tues–Sat 10am–1pm & 3–6pm, Sun 10am–6pm), a steep gorge with a series of walkways suspended above a roaring river.

Varenna

Five kilometres further south, **VARENNA** is arguably the nicest place on the lake. Shaded by pines and planes, and almost completely free of souvenir shops the village falls down steep narrow alleyways to the lakefront. If you are feeling energetic, you could haul up the hill to the **Castello de Vezio**, allegedly founded by the Lombard Queen Theodolinda, for some great views. If you're not, it's a short walk south, past the **tourist office** on Piazza San Giorgio (summer Tues–Sat 10–noon & 3–6pm; winter Sun 10am–12.30pm; T0341.830.367, W www.varennaitaly.com), along the main road to the **Villa Cipressi**, a nineteenth-century villa now occupied by a hotel. For €2 (or €3 including Monastero, see below) you get access to its gardens (March–Oct daily 9am–7pm), which are voluptuously terraced and swooningly scented – enough to make even die-hard cynics gush. After this, the gardens of the **Villa Monastero** next door (April 15–Oct daily 10am–noon & 2–6.30pm; €2, or €3 for joint entry with the Cipressi) seem tame, so it's no great hardship if, as often happens, they are closed for conferences.

It's easy to be seduced into **staying** in Varenna but you'll need to make sure you book ahead in high season. The first place you'll see if you're arriving by ferry is the *Olivedo*, directly opposite the *imbarcadero* (T0341.830.115, W www.olivedo.it; ❹), a family-run *pensione* stuffed with old prints and knick-knacks. A cheaper option, that's more likely to have free rooms if you haven't booked, is the friendly *Albergo Beretta* on Via per Esino 1 (T & F0341.830.132, W www.varennaitaly.com; ❸), just up the road from the Lido. The rooms at the *Villa Cipressi* (see above; T0341.830.113; March to mid-Nov; ❺) are disappointingly modern and characterless but you do have the run of the gardens. A more attractive choice is the popular *Milano* (T0341.830.298, W www.varena.net; ❻), with great views from the rooms and breakfast terrace. The top spot in town is the *Hotel du Lac* (T0341.830238, W www.albergodu-lac.com; ❽), right on the waterfront on Via del Prestino 4.

The best place to **eat** is *Vecchia Varenna*, hidden in the arcades along the lakeside promenade (T & F0341.83.0793; closed Mon; book ahead in summer for a table on the terrace) – though it's not cheap, you may be tempted by such classic dishes as *gnocchi* with game sauce and trout with pine nuts. For snacks, *Il Mole*, a little further round the bay, is very pleasant, and has a good selection of salads.

Bellagio

Cradled by cypress-spiked hills on the tip of the triangle separating Como's two "legs", **BELLAGIO** has been called the most beautiful town in Italy. With a promenade planted with oleanders and limes, *fin-de-siècle* hotels painted shades of butterscotch, peach and cream, and a hilly old centre of steep cobbled streets and alleyways – to say nothing of its tremendous location – it's easy to see why Bellagio has become so popular. These days, however, the cobbled streets are lined with upmarket souvenir shops and village life very much plays second fiddle to the tourists.

The lake is clean enough to swim in here, which you can do from the **Lido** (Easter–Oct daily 8am–midnight) at the end of the promenade, or if you can't stand the piped music, do what the local kids do and have a dip at the tiny harbour less than 1km out of town in the other direction; follow the signs to the *Ristorante La Punta*. The gardens of the **Villa Melzi** behind (April–Oct daily 9am–6pm; €5.16) are no great shakes, but it's well worth making the effort to book onto a guided tour around the gorgeous gardens of the **Villa Serbelloni**, splendidly sited on a hill above the town. Built on the site of one of Pliny the Younger's villas, it is now owned by the Rockefeller Foundation, and is perhaps the best place to appreciate Bellagio's genteel English air. It was once a favourite haunt of European monarchs, and it's not hard to imagine them strolling among the grottoes and statues of the extravagant garden and gushing over the views of the two branches of the lake. The sumptuously frescoed interior is closed to visitors, but there are guided tours around the **gardens** (April–Oct Tues–Sun 11am & 4pm; book at the tourist office; €5.50). At the foot of the hill is a classy hotel, also called *Villa Serbelloni* (see below), whose guests numbered Churchill, recovering from the war in late 1945, and John F. Kennedy.

Practicalities

Bellagio's **tourist office**, in the *imbarcadero* on lakefront Piazza Mazzini (April–Oct Mon & Wed–Sat 9am–noon & 3–6pm; Nov–Easter Mon & Wed–Sat same hours; ☎031.950.204, ⓦ www.bellagiolakecomo.com), is a helpful source of information on activities in the area including hiking, horse riding, mountain biking and watersports. Car ferries pull into the jetty round past the main carpark, which is also the end of the line for the spectacular bus route from Como. As for somewhere to **stay**, *Villa Serbelloni* (☎031.950.216, ⓦ www.villaserbelloni.it; ❾) has been the top place in town for over a century. The deluxe rooms are individually furnished and there's a lakeside pool for use in the summer or an indoor one for cooler weather. At the top of the village, *Hotel Belvedere* (☎031.950.410, ⓦ www.belvederebellagio.com; ❼, with breakfast; April–Nov) is a modern hotel, again with a swimming pool and wonderful views over the Lecco arm of the lake. Just down the hill, and really requiring your own transport, *La Pergola* (☎031.950.263, ⓦ www.lapergolabellagio.it; ❺ with breakfast), in the stunning hamlet of Pescallo, offers stylish en-suite rooms with balconies overlooking the lake and the vine-covered restaurant below. The best of the economical rooms are at the friendly *Giardinetto*, Via Roncati 12 (☎031.950.168; ❷; mid-March to Oct; no credit cards), right at the top of Bellagio. Some rooms have lake views and there's a garden where you can picnic. There's a small, relaxed **campsite** (☎031.951.325, ⓦ www.ducati.karoo.net; June–Sept) run by an English woman and her Italian husband; the price includes entrance to the lido in Bellagio. If you don't have your own transport, you'll probably want to take a taxi up there to the Azenda Agricola, about ten minutes' drive out of town on Via Valassina.

Like everything in Bellagio, the **restaurants** can be pricey. For reasonable local dishes, *Bilacus*, at the top of Salita Serbelloni, is a good choice and has an attractive pergola for alfresco dining. One of the best bets in Bellagio, however, is five minutes' walk north of town at *La Punta* (☎031.951.888; you'll need to book at weekends and in high season), which serves excellent food at good prices and offers lovely views over the lake. The best places for ice cream are *Il Sorbetto* at the top of Salita Serbelloni and the *Gelateria del Borgo* at Via Garibaldi 46.

Lecco and around

Flanked by mountains of scored granite, Como's eastern fork is austere and fjord-like, at its most atmospheric in the morning mists. The villages wedged along the shoreline are far more workaday than those of the rest of the lake, and **LECCO**, at its foot, is a frantic commercial centre. You almost certainly won't want to stay in Lecco, but its public transport connections are good, and there are some challenging hikes in the nearby mountains. Trains run to Como, Milan and Bergamo, and back up the eastern shore by way of Varenna to Sondrio, and there are buses into the mountain villages. **Buses** leave from outside the **train station**, from where it's a brisk five-minute walk to the **ferry station** (go straight down the central street, Via Cavour, and across Piazza Garibaldi, to the shore and turn right). Lecco's business-like **tourist office** is on Via Nazario Sauro 6, off Piazza Garibaldi (Mon–Sat 9am–12.30pm & 2.30–6.30pm; June same hours plus Sun 9am–12.30pm; ☎0341.362.360,

ⓦwww.aptlecco.com). **Accommodation** is limited to one hotel – *Moderno* – on Piazza Diaz, outside the train station (ⓣ0341.286.519; ❸). There are a number of **snack bars** and pizzerias around the station, though none of them is particularly special.

If you've time to kill you could pop into Lecco's **Basilica**, which boasts a set of fourteenth-century Giottesque frescoes, and the birthplace of Alessandro Manzoni, author of the great nineteenth-century novel *I Promessi Sposi* ("The Betrothed"): the **Villa Manzoni**, on Via Amendola (head left out of the station along Via Sassi then Via Marconi), is open as a museum (Tues–Sun 9.30am–5pm; €4.13). You can see Manzoni's study and a chapel, decorated as they would have been when he sold the house in 1818.

Above Lecco at the end of the road to **MALNAGA** a **cable car** – and paths #1, #7 and #18 – climb up to the **Piani d'Erna**, from where trails lead further into the mountains. Alternatively, buses from outside the train station run up to **PIANI RESINELLI**, another starting-point for hikes. These are not Sunday afternoon strolls, however, and unless you are experienced, you really should get hold of a reliable walking book as well as a good map before you go. Many of the walks involve scaling a *via ferrata* (see box on p.246). Some stretches are vertical, and once you've started it's often impossible to turn back – the *vie ferrate* are popular and there will probably be a queue behind you.

The Valchiavenna and Valtellina

Trains run north of Colico into the **Valchiavenna**, a flat-bottomed valley into which Lake Como extended right up until Roman times. It left behind the **Lago di Mezzola** – not worth getting off the train for, but a pleasant enough distraction before you hit the rusty corrugated-iron buildings of Novate. Further on, you could stop at **CHIAVENNA**, at the end of the train line, to visit one of the many *crotti*, natural cellars in the rocks (across the rail line), which for centuries have been used for maturing wine, salami, cured meats and cheeses. Most are now inns and restaurants, the most authentic of which is the *Crotto al Prato*, on Via Picchi 13 (follow signs to the "*campo polisportivo*"), where you can sit at outdoor tables by the boules pitch with wonderful mountain views or in the cosy stone interior. The town is otherwise a quiet mountain resort and the very friendly **tourist office** (daily 10am–12.30pm & 3–7pm; ⓣ0343.37.485), on the main Via Consol Chiavennaschi, can give you information on things to see and do in town and the surrounding area.

For somewhere **to stay** try the pleasant little *Flora* at Via Don Guanella 10 (ⓣ0343.32.254; ❷), 150m right of the station. For a bit more, you can get the three-star treatment at the *Crimea*, Via Pratogiano 16 (ⓣ0343.34.343; ❸). Alternatively there's an attractive **campsite** (ⓣ0343.36.7555), 3km north of town, next to the impressive Acquafraggia waterfall.

Nearby there are interesting walks up to the **Marmitte dei Giganti**, potholes formed by glaciation. From Chiavenna you can catch a bus to St Moritz in **Switzerland**, from where the *trenino rosso* (see below) takes a scenic mountain route back across the border to Tirano.

Unless you're a keen skier, or are heading for eastern Switzerland or Trentino, there's little to draw you to the **Valtellina**, east of Lake Como, one of Italy's less appealing Alpine valleys. Cut through by road and rail, it's mined for minerals and iron ore and is prone to landslides. The train continues up from Lake Como to the region's main centre, **SONDRIO**, a modern and undistinguished town, but well known for its wine, which is on sale in many of its shops. The **tourist office** is at Via C. Battisti 12 (☎0342.512.500), though distractions are few – apart from the **Museo Valtellinese** at Via del Gesù 8 (Mon 2.30–4.30pm, Tues–Fri 9am–noon & 2.30–4.30pm, Sat 9am–noon; free), a museum of local traditions with small art and archeological sections. You'd do better to catch a train on to **TIRANO**, a similarly bland town, but one that gives access to the private **RhB trenino rosso del Bernina**, which follows a stunning route through the mountains to St Moritz in Switzerland (InterRail and Eurail passes are valid). If you wanted, you could pick up a bus in St Moritz and return to Italy via Chiavenna.

A prettier valley, the **Val Malenco**, runs off to one side of the Valtellina, and is easily accessible by bus from Sondrio. Head up as high as possible to the tiny village of **CHIAREGGIO**, where you can stay at *Locanda Pian del Lupo* (☎0342.451.601; ❷) before heading off on a network of footpaths past brilliantly clear tarns, well served by mountain *rifugi*. The tourist office in Sondrio (see above) has details, including maps, or you could buy the local Kompass map.

Further up Valtellina from Tirano, to which it's connected by bus, **BORMIO** is a very prestigious but snooty and unfriendly ski resort that was once an important stopover on the trade routes between Venice and Switzerland. It still retains a core of cobbled streets and frescoed palaces from the fifteenth and sixteenth centuries within a sprawl of hotels for its many skiers: it hosted the 1985 World Alpine Ski Championships and is now one of Europe's largest areas for summer skiing. Close by, the huge **Parco Nazionale dello Stelvio** (see p.269) is a good place for walks and challenging climbs, as well as skiing. Details can be gleaned from the **tourist office** in Bormio at Via Roma 131b (Mon–Sat 9am–12.30pm & 2.30–6pm, Sun 9.30am–12.30pm; ☎0342.903 .300, ⓦwww.bormio.info) – where you can also pick up maps, details of *rifugi*, and information on the town – or from the national park **visitors' centre**, Via Monte Braulio 56 (Mon–Fri 9am–1pm & 2.30–6.30pm, only until 5pm on Fri; plus Sat & Sun in summer 9am–12.30pm & 2–7pm; ☎0342.910.100, ⓦwww.passostevio.biz). If you're sleeping over in Bormio, the *Villa Rina*, at Via Milano 77 (☎0342.901.674; ❷), has reasonable doubles, but prices vary greatly with the time of year.

Bergamo

Just 50km northeast of Milan, yet much closer to the mountains in look and feel, **BERGAMO** is a city with a split identity, made up of two distinct parts – **Bergamo Bassa**, the lower, more modern centre, and **Bergamo Alta**, clinging to the hill 1200 feet above the Lombardian plain. Bergamo Bassa is an odd mixture of pompous Neoclassical town planning and medieval cobbled streets; but Bergamo Alta is one of northern Italy's loveliest city centres, a favourite retreat for the work-weary Milanese, who flock here at weekends seeking solace in its fresh mountain air, wanderable lanes and the lively, but easy-going pace of its life.

Bergamo owes much of its magic to the Venetians, who ruled the town for over 350 years, building houses and palaces with fancy Gothic windows and adorning many a facade and open space with the Venetian lion – symbol of the republic. The most striking feature, however, is the ring of gated walls. Now worn, mellow and overgrown with creepers, these kept alien armies out until

BERGAMO

BERGAMO ALTA

ACCOMMODATION
Agnello d'Oro	5
Cascina Grumello	6
Commercio	7
Gourmet	3
San Giorgio	8
San Vigilio	2
Sole	4
Youth hostel	1

RESTAURANTS & BARS
Baretto di San Vigilio	A
Bella Napoli	C
La Colombina	D
Cooperativa Citta Altà	F
Donizetti	D
Caffè Funicolare Sole	G
La Mariana	B
Vinoria Cozzi	E

BERGAMO ALTA

Funicular

GALLERIA
CONCA
D'ORO

Accademia
Carrara

Porta
Nuova

Bus
Stations

Train
Station

0   100m

BERGAMO ALTA

Castello & ②

Funicular

Cittadella
(Museums)

Palazzo
della
Ragione

Aula
della
Curia

Santa
Maria

Duomo

Museo Storico

Rocca

Sant' Agostino

San Michele al
Pozzo Bianco

Accademia
Carrara

Funicular

0   100m

1796, when French Revolutionary troops successfully stormed the city, throwing off centuries of Venetian rule.

Arrival and information

Bergamo's international **airport** Orio al Serio (☎035.326.111, ⓦwww
.milanoorio-airport.it) is 5km southeast of town; it's connected with regular
buses to the Autolinee station in Bergamo (every 30min Mon–Sat
5.30am–10.30pm, 8 buses on Sun 9.15am–7.15pm; €1.05) and the Stazione
Centrale in Milan (Mon–Sat 8 daily; €6.70; information ☎035.318.472).
Tickets can be bought on the bus if the office to the right of Arrivals is closed.
A taxi into central Milan from Orio will cost around €150.

The **train station** is right at the end of Bergamo Bassa's central avenue, Viale
Giovanni XXIII, which becomes Via Vittorio Emanuele II. To the right are the
two **bus stations**: the SAB, serving the northern mountains and valleys, and
the Stazione Autolinee, serving all other destinations. Bus #1 runs from right
outside the train station to the **funicular station** at the foot of the hill, from
where you can make the ascent by cable car to Piazza Mercato delle Scarpe for
no extra charge as long as you show your bus ticket – otherwise it costs €1.
Alternatively, you can stay on the bus until the end of the line at Colle Aperto
at the other end of the main drag in Bergamo Alta.

There are two branches of the **tourist office**, one at Viale Vittorio Emanuele
II 20 (Mon–Fri 9am–12.30pm & 2–5.30pm; ☎035.210.204, ⓦwww.apt.berg-
amo.it), a ten-minute walk up from the train station, and the main office up in
Bergamo Alta at Vicolo Aquila Nera 2, off Piazza Vecchia (April–Oct daily
9am–12.30pm & 2–5.30pm; ☎035.232.730). They both have maps and information on the town and province.

Accommodation

Bergamo is not somewhere to arrive on spec, even out of season: **accommodation** is pricey, and there is fairly limited choice beyond the business hotels
on the access roads to town. Help is at hand in the form of the very well run
youth hostel (☎035.361.724; ⓦwww.gigilander.iol.it/ostellobergamo;
€13.50 per person for dorm, €16 per person for a double, triple or quad
room; €18.50 for a single, all including breakfast). The hostel has won awards
for being the best in Europe and offers meals for €8, bathrooms and balconies
in every room, bicycles for rent (€8 per day), a garden to flop in, and facilities
for disabled – there's also a great view of the *città alta*. To get to the hostel, take
bus #14 from Porta Nuova, direction S. Colombana, and get off just after the
modern church at the stop signposted for the *ostello* – it's at the top of the
rather steep steps on the right.

Agnello d'Oro Via Gombito 22 ☎035.249.883,
ⓦagnellodoro.it. In the heart of the upper town,
this cosy hotel offers plain, comfortable en-suite
rooms. Some of the rooms have balconies on to
the tiny square below. Breakfast included. ❺
Cascina Grumello Frazione Nese, Alzano
Lombardo ☎0 35.510.060,
ⓦwww.agriegusta.com. On a hill 7km east of
Bergamo this sprawling fifteenth-century farmhouse offers a mixed bag of rooms and apartments especially suitable for families or small
groups. The rustic atmosphere and the tranquil

spot make an ideal base from which to explore the
area. €23.25 per person.
Commercio Via T. Tasso 88 ☎035.224.096,
ⓕ035.220.451. Well located on a quiet street in
Bergamo Bassa, this old convent with an attractive
courtyard garden was being renovated at the time
of writing but it is well worth finding out more
about the results of this. ❹
Gourmet Via San Vigilio 1 ☎035.437.3004. Just
above Città Alta, spacious, modern rooms with wonderful views; there are also two mini-apartments
and a restaurant with local staples down below. ❺

San Giorgio Via San Giorgio 10, the continuation of Via Paleocapa ☎035.212.043. A friendly, well-run lower town option, a five-minute walk from the station. Various sized rooms with or without bathrooms are available, all spotlessly clean and decently furnished. ❷

San Vigilio Via San Vigilio 15 ☎035.253.179, ⓕ035.402.081. Right at the top of town offering glorious views, this *fin-de-siècle* hotel was visited by Herman Hesse and still preserves some original features in its seven individually furnished en-suite rooms. Cooking in the restaurant and paintings are by the idiosyncratic proprietor. Turn left out of the second funicular and follow the road round or take bus #21 from Colle Aperto. ❺

Sole Via B Colleoni 1 ☎035.218.238, ⓕ035.240.011. Just off the main square, this traditional hotel offers simple en-suite rooms with little balconies facing an internal courtyard. ❹

The City

However you get to Bergamo, you'll arrive in **BERGAMO BASSA**, which spreads north from the railway station in a comfortable blend of Neoclassical ostentation, Fascist severity and tree-lined elegance. At the heart of things, the mock-Doric temples of the **Porta Nuova** mark the entrance to **Sentierone**, a spacious piazza with gardens, surrounded by nineteenth-century arcades and frowned down upon by the **Palazzo di Giustizia**, built in the bombastic rectangular style of the Mussolini era. This is one of the liveliest parts of the lower city, at its busiest during the evening passeggiata. Leading off to the west is Via XX Settembre, the city's main shopping street, full of high-street names and little boutiques. Bergamo's main appeal, however, lies in the upper town – **BERGAMO ALTA**, easily reached using the **funicular** at the top end of Viale Vittorio Emanuele II, or by taking bus #1 from the train station, which drops you just inside the northwestern gate of Porta Alessandro at Largo Colle Aperto. If your calf muscles are up to it though, the half hour uphill walk is well worthwhile. Head up Via Pignolo lined with sixteenth- and seventeeth-century *palazzi* to Porta Sant'Agostino in the Venetian walls. Follow Viale delle Mura round – with views over the orchards and private gardens of the villas – until you feel like diving into the heart of the upper town proper.

Bergamo Alta

From Piazza Mercato delle Scarpe, where the funicular arrives, Via Gombito leads up to **Piazza Vecchia**, enclosed by a harmonious miscellany of buildings, ranging from wrought-iron-balconied houses containing cafés and restaurants to the opulent Palladian-style civic library. Stendhal rather enthusiastically dubbed the square "the most beautiful place on earth", and certainly it's a striking open space, the most imposing building the medieval **Palazzo della Ragione**, a Venetian-Gothic-style structure that stretches right across the piazza, lending a stagey feel to things, especially at night when the wrought-iron lamps are switched on. Court cases used to be heard under the open arcades that form the ground floor, and, following a guilty verdict, condemned criminals were exhibited there. The piazza itself was the scene of more joyous celebrations in 1797, when the French formed the Republic of Bergamo. A "tree of liberty" was erected, and the square, carpeted with tapestries, was transformed into an open-air ballroom in which – as a symbol of the new democracy – dances were led by an aristocrat partnered by a butcher.

To the right of the Palazzo della Ragione is the entrance to the massive **Torre Civica**, or Torre del Campanone, which you can ascend by lift (May to mid-Sept daily 10am–8pm, Fri & Sat until 10pm; mid-Sept to Oct Mon–Fri 9.30am–12.30pm & 2–7pm, Sat & Sun 10am–7pm; Nov–Feb Sat & Sun 10.30am–12.30pm & 2–6pm; March & April Wed–Sun 10.30am–12.30pm & 2–8pm; €1). Its fifteenth-century bell, which narrowly escaped being melted down by the Germans to make arms during World War II, still tolls every half-hour. Afterwards, walk through the palazzo's arcades to the **Piazza del Duomo** and the **Duomo** on the left – though this is of less interest than the church of **Santa Maria Maggiore** in front, a rambling Romanesque church garnished with a scalloped Gothic porch crowned by two loggias sheltering statues of saints. Inside, Santa Maria is an extraordinarily elaborate church, its ceiling marzipanned with ornament in the worst tradition of Baroque excess, encrusted with gilded stucco, painted vignettes and languishing statues. There's a piece of nineteenth-century kitsch too – a monument to Donizetti, the Bergamo-based composer of highly popular romantic comedies with memorable melodies and predictable plots, who died from syphilis here in 1848. As the town's most famous son, his death was much grieved, and bas-relief *putti* stamp their feet and smash their lyres in misery over the event. More subtly, the intarsia biblical scenes on the choir stalls – designed by Lotto, and executed by a local craftsman – are remarkable not only for their intricacy but also for the incredible colour-range of the natural wood.

Even the glitziness of Santa Maria is overshadowed by the Renaissance decoration of the **Cappella Colleoni** next door (Tues–Sun: April–Oct 9am–12.30pm & 2–6.30pm; Nov–March 9am–12.30pm & 2–4.30pm). Built onto the church in the 1470s, the chapel is a gorgeously extravagant confection of pastel-coloured marble carved into an abundance of miniature arcades, balustrades and twisted columns, and capped with a mosque-like dome. Commissioned by Bartolomeo Colleoni, a Bergamo mercenary in the pay of Venice, it was designed by the Pavian sculptor Amadeo – responsible for the equally excessive Certosa di Pavia. The interior is almost as opulent, with a ceiling frescoed in the eighteenth century by Tiepolo sheltering Colleoni's sarcophagus, encrusted with reliefs and statuettes, and topped with a gleaming gilded equestrian statue. There's also the more modest tomb of his daughter, Medea, who died aged 15. Note Colleoni's coat-of-arms on the gate as you enter; the smoothness of the third "testicle" (supposedly biologically true) bears witness to the local tradition that rubbing it will bring you luck.

Take a look, too, at the nearby **Baptistry** (visits by appointment, ☎035.210.223), removed from the interior of Santa Maria Maggiore in the seventeenth century when christenings were transferred to the Duomo. After some time in storage it was eventually reconstructed outside the **Aula della Curia** ("Bishop's Court"; Mon–Fri 9am–12.30pm; free), alongside the Cappella Colleoni, which contains thirteenth- and fourteenth-century frescoes of the life of Christ, including an odd scene in which Christ judges the damned, holding a dagger, Damocles-like, in his teeth. Behind, at the back of Santa Maria Maggiore, is the bulging and recently restored, although still closed to the public, **Tempietto di Santa Croce**, dating from the tenth century.

Leading out of Piazza Vecchia, **Via Colleoni** also memorializes Bartolomeo Colleoni; it's a narrow street but one of the upper city's main pedestrian thoroughfares, leading to the brink of Bergamo Alta and lined with pastry shops selling chocolate and marzipan cakes topped with birds (*uccelli*). **Luogo Pio Colleoni**, Via Colleoni 9–11 (May–July Sun 10am–1pm & 2–7pm; €1), was Colleoni's Bergamo residence; it was also the headquarters of a charitable institution that he set up to provide dowries for poor women – the Venetians ruled that no woman could marry without one. Only two rooms of the original house still exist. The first displays the original Amadeo statues from the front of the Cappella Colleoni and some average frescoes depicting Colleoni; the second was once the meeting room for the charity's council members, who these days continue a modernized version of their good work from upstairs, giving financial aid and lodgings to widows. At the end of Via Colleoni, Piazza Mascheroni lies at the entrance to the **Cittadella**, a military stronghold built by Barnabo Visconti that originally occupied the entire western headland. The remaining buildings now house a small theatre and two well-organized, didactic (Italian only) **museums**: one of **archeology** (Tues–Sun 9am–noon & 2–6pm; free) and the other of **natural history** (Tues–Fri 9am–12.30pm & 2.30–6pm, Sat & Sun 9am–7.30pm; free).

There are good views from the Cittadella of **Colle Aperto** (Open Hill) outside the gate to Bergamo Bassa, though for really outstanding views you need to walk up to the **Castello**, perched on the summit of San Vigilio, which rises up from Porta Sant'Alessandro. A funicular operates in summer but the walk is pleasant, up a steep, narrow road overlooking the gardens of Bergamo's most desirable properties, and past very attractive but rather pricey bars and restaurants. In the grounds of the castle there's a maze of underground passages to explore that used to run right down to Bergamo Alta. If you're interested in the subterranean world, there are **guided tours** of the tunnels under the Venetian wall (the wall that encloses Bergamo Alta) organized by the Gruppo Speleologico Le Nottole (☎035.251.233; hours and price vary according to season and size of group).

Returning to the Colle Aperto, you can either walk back through the city or follow the old **walls** around its circumference – the whole circuit takes a couple of hours. The most picturesque stretch is between the Colle Aperto and Porta San Giacomo, from where a long flight of steps leads down into the lower city. Alternatively, returning through the upper city to Piazza Mercato delle Scarpe, you can turn down Via San Pancrazio and then into Piazza Mercato del Fieno, to see the **Museo Storico** (Tues–Sun 9.30am–1pm & 2.30–5.45pm; free). Housed in the ex-convent of San Francesco, it currently spans the history of the city during the Unification and is relatively small, but there are plans to display the rest of the collection, which covers the last hundred years, as and when funds allow. Heading east from here you'll climb to Via Rocca, which leads up to the grounds of the **Rocca**, where there is little to attract your attention, apart from a view over eastern Bergamo, before you delve into the twisting streets of the **medieval quarter** below.

The Accademia Carrara

Just below the upper town, close to the city walls, the **Accademia Carrara** (Tues–Sun: April–Sept 9.30am–1pm & 2.30–6.45pm; Oct–March 9.30am–1pm & 2–5.45pm; €2.58) is one of Bergamo's most important sights and among Lombardy's best collections of art. You can walk down here from the old city, along the steep Via Porta Dipinta and through the Porta Sant'Agostino, to see portraits by Pisanello and Botticelli, works by Giovanni Bellini and Crivelli, Carpaccio and Lotto – all carefully and imaginatively displayed with the layperson in mind. There are also paintings by the Lombard realists Foppa and Bergognone, Spanish-style portraits by Moroni, an elegant idealized *St Sebastian* by Raphael and canvases by Titian and Palma il Vecchio. Don't miss the room dedicated to works by the twentieth-century Bergamo-born sculptor Giacomo Manzù, best known for his stylized bronzes of cardinals. While you're in this area, take a stroll across the road to the **Galleria d'Arte Moderna e Contemporanea** (Ⓦ www.gamec.it; prices and times vary according to each exhibition), which hosts top-quality touring exhibitions of work by modern artists and designers.

Eating and drinking

One of the pleasures of Bergamo is its food, easily enjoyable whether you're on a tight budget and restricted to assembling picnics from the many *salumerie* and bakeries in the old town, or can afford to graze around the city's terrific **osterie**. For some, one of the town's attractions are the local game-bird specialities (hunting and devouring the wildlife around Bergamo is a major occupation).

For **picnic food**, stock up on rustic-style pies at the Salumeria Mangili at Via Gombito 8, or on *pane greco* (bread topped with aubergine and tomato) from Forno tre Soldi, Via Colleoni 13a, and decadent pastries at Nessi, Via Gombito 34, in Bergamo Bassa. You'll find the best **ice cream** in town under the luxuriant Lombardian balconies of *La Mariana*, in the corner of Colle Aperto in the *città alta*.

Antiva Trattoria la Colombina Via Borgo Canale 12 ☎035.261.402. A very appealing little trattoria with tasty, good-value food and wonderful views. Closed Mon & Aug.

Baretto di San Vigilio Via Castello 1 ☎035.253.191. An unbeatable choice on an attractive vine-covered terrace with wonderful views and excellent food. Prices reflect the location.

Bella Napoli Via Taramelli 5/7/9 ☎035.242.308. A wide choice of decent, wood-oven-cooked pizzas in a bright, modern pizzeria near the station. Eat in or take-away.

Caffè Funicolare in the funicular station on Piazza Mercato delle Scarpe. Good-value snacks served on a terrace with a great view over Città Bassa. Stays open until 2am. Closed Tues.

Cooperativa Città Alta Vicolo Sant'Agata, clearly signposted off Via Colleoni. A cheery amalgam of café, restaurant and bar open until 2am. This co-operative venture in Bergamo Alta boasts low prices, a happy hour on Thursdays, and a garden where you can idle away your time admiring the distant hills. Closed Wed.

Donizetti Via Gombito 17a. Excellent either for a slap-up meal or a *degustazione* platter of local meats and cheeses washed down with fine wine. Inside is warm and welcoming; in summer tables are laid out in the covered market space.

Sole Via B. Colleoni 1. A very popular restaurant serving traditional local specialities and fish served in an attractive garden in summer.

Vineria Cozzi Via Colleoni 22a. A classy wine bar in Bergamo Alta with around three hundred wines to choose from and an excellent cold buffet. Closed Wed.

Around Bergamo

Industrial development has done a pretty thorough job of ruining much of the countryside around Bergamo, although if you push on up the valleys things do improve. Northwest of Bergamo the **Val Brembana** follows a mountain-fringed route that was well-trodden in the Middle Ages by caravans of mules transporting minerals from the Valtellina to the cities of the plain. The road is now frequented mostly by weekend skiers heading up to Foppolo and by less energetic Italians en route to **SAN PELLEGRINO TERME** to take the waters. San Pellegrino has been Lombardy's most fashionable spa since the early 1900s, and it's from this period that its extravagant main buildings – the grand hotels and casino – date.

The **Val Cavallina** has also suffered from industrial development, with much of it ruined by small factories and tacky housing. The holiday area around Lago d'Endine isn't too bad, but you're more likely to pass through the valley only on your way up to Lago d'Iseo.

The **Valle Seriana**, northeast of the town, is probably the most developed, with factories and apartment blocks competing for space with forests and mountains, and rivers reduced to streams by hydroelectric power. The upper reaches of the valley are, however, still fairly unspoilt and can be a decent spot for a day or two's skiing and easily accessible by bus from Bergamo.

Clusone

CLUSONE is the main stop worth making in the Valle Seriana, a picturesque hilltop town where the **Chiesa dei Disciplini** (above the centre, a ten-minute walk from the bus station) draws people from all over. There's little of interest inside the church, but the two fifteenth-century frescoes on its outside wall more than compensate. The upper fresco, *The Triumph of Death*, concentrates on the attitude of the wealthy towards death, with three noblemen returning from the hunt, discovering an open tomb containing the worm-infested corpses of the pope and emperor. A huge skeleton, representing Death, balances on the edge of the tomb, while other skeletons take aim at people gathered around the tomb – incorruptible figures, uninterested in the bribes being offered them. The *Dance of Death* below continues the moral tale, contrasting the corrupt upper classes with a procession of contented commoners, each dancing his way towards death quite happily, above an inscription inviting those who have genuinely served God to approach without fear and join the dance.

Clusone itself is worth a wander, especially on Mondays when the steep curving streets are taken over by a market selling local sausage and cheeses. The **tourist office** (Mon, Tues, Thurs & Fri 10am–noon & 3–5pm, Sat 9am–noon & 3–6pm, Sun 9am–noon; ☎0346.21.113) is on Piazza dell'Orologio, named for the fiendishly complicated sixteenth century clock on the tower of the Palazzo Comunale. If you have the time and patience, you can work out the date, the sign of the zodiac, the duration of the night and the phase of the moon. The tourist office has information on local walks and hotels, and can provide details of the internationally renowned **jazz festival**, which is held in July. From Clusone you can take a bus to Lago d'Iseo (see below) or further up the Valle Seriana.

Lago d'Iseo and the Val Camonica

Lago d'Iseo raises your expectations: descending from Clusone, the road passes through steep gorges, thick forests and stark angular mountains, at the foot of which lies the lake. As it's the fifth largest of the northern lakes, and the least known outside Italy, you'd imagine it to be more undiscovered than the others but the apartment blocks, harbourside boutiques, ice cream parlours and heavy industry of **LOVERE** put paid to any notions that Iseo might have escaped either tourist exploitation or industrialization. This doesn't deter the Italians, who flock to Lago d'Iseo's resorts for its fish restaurants, watersports and low-key hikes, but unless any of these appeal, or you want to use it as a base for the ascent of Monte Gugliemo or for exploring the prehistoric rock carvings in the Val Camonica, there's little point in hanging around.

There is one retreat, however: the traffic-free **Monte Isola**, accessible by **ferry** (hourly) from Iseo town at the south of the lake. It's Italy's largest lake-island, over 3km long and rising to 600m. As there's a large campsite, and space in its hotels for two hundred people, you're unlikely to get much solitude in high season; but out of season it's well worth a visit, either to be utterly lazy or to take a walk right around the edge of the island, for great views across the lake. There are a couple of cheap **hotels**: the *Bellavista* (☎030.988.6106, ✉paolo.archini@libero.it; ❷) in the village of **SIVIANO** on the northwest corner of the island, and the *Sensole* (☎030.988.6203; ❹) in **SENSOLE**. The **campsite** (☎030.982.5221; April–Oct) is at **CARZANO** on the northeast tip of the island.

The attractions of **ISEO** town are purely practical: **trains** from Brescia stop here, as do buses. If you need to **stay** here, try the *Milano*, Lungolago Marconi 4 (℡030.980.449; ❸), a reasonably priced hotel in the centre, or the pricier but very pleasant option, the *Ambra*, Porta Gabriele Rosa 2 (℡030.980.130; ❹). Iseo's **tourist office** at Lungolago Marconi 23 (Mon–Sat 9am–12.30pm & 3–6pm, Sun 9am–noon; closed Sat pm and Sun in winter; ℡030.980.209, ⓦwww.lagoiseo.org) has maps and details of walks, the most worthwhile of which is the hike from Marone, halfway along the eastern side of the lake, up a steep and winding road to the village of **ZONE**. The reward is the extraordinary rock formations – soaring pinnacles formed by the erosion of the debris brought down by the glacier that gouged out the lake basin. If they look strangely familiar, it could be because Leonardo is said to have visited them, reproducing their peaks in his *Virgin of the Rocks* in the Louvre.

From Zone a track leads up to **Monte Guglielmo** (1949m), the ascent taking about three and a half hours. There's a *rifugio* near the summit: ask around in Zone before you leave to check it's open; if the warden's not there you'll be given the key.

Val Camonica

Like Lago d'Iseo, the **Val Camonica** would be outstandingly beautiful were it not for the indiscriminate scattering of light industry that mars its lower reaches. Road and railway run up from the lake, following the River Oglio through the spa town of Boario to **CAPO DI PONTE**, whose **national park** (Tues–Sun 9am–sunset; €4), a fifteen-minute walk uphill from the station (turn left out of the station and left again a couple of hundred metres further on when you see a sign), contains prehistoric rock carvings spanning an incredible 8000 years – remnants from the culture of the Camuni tribe who holed up here to escape northern invaders from 5000 BC until the Romans colonized the area several thousand years later, together with the even older works that inspired the Camuni's art. There are carvings throughout the valley, but the most concentrated group is in the park, beginning with the **Great Rock** in front of the site's shop, where a set of stick-and-blob figures gives a taste of Camuni life over a thousand-year period. There are hunters, agricultural workers, a religious ceremony presided over by priests, and a Bronze Age burial in which the corpse is surrounded by his weapons and tools. To see how the civilization developed into the Iron Age, head for Rock 35, carved with a blacksmith, and Rock 23, with a four-wheeled wagon transporting an urn. Carvings in other parts of the valley include some in the hamlet of **BEDOLINO** outside **CEMMO**, about 2km above Capo di Ponte on the other side of the Oglio, where, in someone's garden, there's a rock with a carving of a **Bronze Age map** showing huts, fields, walls, streams, canals and the Rosa Camuna, which has been adopted as the symbol of Lombardy.

Brescia and around

Located between two lakes and surrounded by vine-covered hills, the ancient settlement of **BRESCIA** is a wealthy town, famed for its arms industry. It has valuable Roman remains, Renaissance squares and a Medieval city centre juxtaposed with important twentieth-century architecture. Yet for all this, it's a scruffy and charmless town, lacking any of the elegance of other northern Italian cities. The gentle hills to the west are known as the **Franciacorta** and

BRESCIA

ACCOMMODATION
Antica Villa	**2**
Jolly Hotel Igea	**4**
Master	**1**
Solferino	**3**

RESTAURANTS
Trattoria Due Stelle	**A**
Osteria Al Bianchi	**B**

Castello

S. Pietro in Oliveto

PIAZZALE GARIBALDI

Torre dell' Orologio

Roman Theatre

Santa Giulia Civic Museum

Loggia

Capitolinn

Broletto

San Francesco

Duomo

Rotonda

S. M. dei Miracoli

Ss. Nazaro e Celso

Pinacoteca Tosio-Martinengo

PIAZZALE ARNALDO

PIAZZALE DELLA REPUBBLICA

Bus Station

Bus Station

Train Station

PIAZZALE CREMONA

0   200 m

▲ Autostrada ▼ Autostrada ▼ Cremona & Piacenza ▶ Verona, Venice & Trento

give their name to renowned wines made on the hillsides.

Brescia's centre is grouped around the four piazzas beyond the main Corso Palestro. **Piazza del Mercato** is a sprawling cobbled square of more interest to the stomach than the eye – there's a supermarket, and small shops selling local salamis and cheeses nestling under its dark porticoes. **Piazza della Vittoria** is quite different, a disquieting reminder of the Fascist regime embodied in the clinical austerity of Piacentrini's gleaming marble rectangles.

Alongside the monumental post office, Via 24 Maggio leads to Brescia's prettiest square, **Piazza della Loggia**, dating back to the fifteenth century, when the city invited Venice in to rule and protect it from Milan's power-hungry Viscontis. The Venetian influence is clearest in the fancily festooned **Loggia**, in which both Palladio and Titian had a hand, and in the **Torre dell'Orologio**, modelled on the campanile in Venice's Piazza San Marco. In the northeast corner is the **Porta Bruciata**, a defensive medieval tower-gate, which in 1974, as part of the Strategy of Tension, was the scene of a Fascist bomb attack during a trade union march, in which eight people were killed and over a hundred injured.

To the south of Porta Bruciata, a small side street leads to **Piazza Paolo VI**, one of the few squares in Italy to have two cathedrals – though, frankly, it would have been better off without the second, a heavy Mannerist monument that took over two hundred years to complete. The old twelfth-century cathedral, or **Rotonda** (April–Oct daily except Tues 9am–noon & 3–7pm; Nov–March Sat & Sun 10am–noon & 3–6pm), is quite a different matter, a simple circular building of local stone, whose fine proportions are sadly difficult to appreciate from the outside as it is sunk below the current level of the piazza. Inside, glass set into the transept pavement reveals the remains of Roman baths (a wall and geometrical mosaics) and the apse of an eighth-century basilica, which burned down in 1097. Most interesting is the fine red marble tomb of Berardo Maggi, a thirteenth-century Bishop of Brescia, opposite the entrance, decorated on one side with a full-length relief of the cleric, on the other by reliefs showing other ecclesiasts and dignitaries processing through a lively crowd of citizens to celebrate the peace Maggi had brought to the town's rival Guelph and Ghibelline factions.

Behind Piazza del Duomo, Via Mazzini leads to Via dei Musei – the *decumanus maximus* of the Roman town of Brixia, with Via Gallo the *cardus*. There's a **theatre**, but the most substantial monument is the **Capitolino**, a Roman temple built in 73 AD, now partly reconstructed with red brick. Behind the temple are three reconstructed *celle*, probably temples to the Capitoline trinity of Jupiter, Juno and Minerva.

Further along Via dei Musei is the civic museum in the monastery complex of **Santa Giulia** (Tues–Sun: April–Sept 10am–8pm; Fri until 10pm; Oct–March 9.30am–5.30pm; €6). Inside are three churches: the oldest being San Salvatore, whose present structure dates back to the twelfth century but includes the remains of an original crypt built in 762 to house the relics of St Julia; Santa Maria in Solario, built in the twelfth century as a private chapel for the Benedictine nuns who lived at the abbey, is covered in frescoes painted mainly by the Renaissance artist Floriano Ferramola; and the late-sixteenth-century church of **Santa Giulia** with further frescoes by Ferramola. The museum is a collection of artefacts chronicling the city's history from the Bronze Age to the end of the twentieth century. The highlights are undoubtedly the Roman rooms containing bronze objects found by the Capitolium including the life-sized winged *Victory* and the beautifully preserved mosaic floors of the Roman domus. Other prize exhibits include an eighth-century crucifix presented to the convent by Desiderius, King of the Lombards – made of wood overlaid with silver and encrusted with over two hundred gems and cameos and a collection of priceless glassware.

Behind the museum, Via Piamarta climbs up the **Cydnean Hill**, the core of early Roman Brixia, mentioned by Catullus, though again the remains are scanty. There are a few fragments of a gate just before you reach the sixteenth-century church of **San Pietro in Oliveto**, so called because of the olive grove surrounding it, and the hill itself is crowned by the **Castello** (daily 8am–8pm; free) – a monument to Brescia's various overlords, begun in the fifteenth century by Luchino Visconti and added to by the Venetians, French and Austrians over the years. The resultant confusion of towers, ramparts, halls and courtyards makes a good place for an atmospheric picnic, and holds a complex of museums including Italy's largest **museum of arms**, the **Museo del Risorgimento** (Sun: June–Sept 3–6pm; Oct–May 2.30–5.30pm; free) and a **model railway museum** (Tues–Sun: June–Sept 10am–5pm; Oct–May 9.30am–1pm & 2.30–5pm; €3).

More appealing perhaps is Brescia's main art gallery, the **Pinacoteca Tosio-Martinengo** (Tues–Sun: June–Sept 10am–5pm; Oct–May 9.30am–1pm & 2.30–5pm; €3), which consists of a well laid-out collection mainly made up of the works of minor local artists, including a beautiful black *Sant'Apollonia* by Vincenzo Foppa. The rooms devoted to the "Nativity" and "Town and Province" are worth a look, as are those of the seventeenth-century realist Ceruti, who, unusually for his time, specialized in painting the poor (see p.175).

Practicalities

Brescia's main advantage is the convenience of its transport connections: it is on the main Milan–Verona railway line, giving you access to the cities of the Veneto as well as those of Lombardy. The rest of the province, including the main resorts of Garda and several more distant destinations, is covered by direct buses, which leave from the two **bus terminals** outside the **train station**. This is south of the centre, a short bus ride or fifteen-minute walk from the city centre. The international **airport** at Montichiari (☎030.965.6511), 23km southeast, is connected by several buses daily (€7.50 return) or a taxi should cost around €30. Note that the airport is also connected by daily bus to Verona (see p.359).

Brescia has two **tourist offices**, one in the centre at Piazza Loggia 6 (April–Sept Mon–Sat 9.30am–6.30pm; Oct–March Mon–Fri 9.30am–12.30pm & 2–5pm, Sat 9.30am–12.30pm; ☎030.240.0357, ⓦwww.bresciaholiday.com, ⓦwww.comune.brescia.it), the other at Corso Zanardelli 34 (Mon–Fri 9am–12.30pm & 3–6pm, Sat 9am–12.30pm; ☎030.43.418). One particularly enlightened local initiative in Brescia is the blue bike scheme in which **bicycles** can be collected and dropped off at any of the designated points around town – ask at the tourist offices for details.

The bicycle scheme is particularly useful if you decide you want **to stay** in Brescia as all the decent options are outside the city centre. Brescia's hotels are aimed at business travellers and there is little choice when it comes to budget or characterful places. Across the road from the local bus station is the basic *Solferino*, Via Solferino 1 (☎030.46.300; ❷), with shared bathrooms; ask for an internal room. Practically next door, at Viale Stazione 15, the chain *Jolly Hotel Igea* (☎030.44.221, ⓦwww.jollyhotels.it; ❻) is clean and anonymous and often has deals at weekends. On the other side of the city centre, ten minutes' walk from the castle, is another business hotel, the *Master*, at Via Luigi Apollonio 72 (☎030.44.221, ⓦwww.hotelmaster.net; ❻), with ample parking and a garden. A more characterful option, a little further out of town in the same direction, at Via San Rocchino 90, is *Antica Villa* (☎030.31.86, ⓕ030.338.4312; ❺) with comfortable rooms.

Brescia has a good selection of reasonably priced **places to eat** in the centre of town specializing in local dishes like *casoncei* (large meat-filled ravioli) or game. One of the city's oldest institutions is *Trattoria Due Stelle*, at Via San Faustino 48 (closed Mon), serving traditional Brescian fare at outside tables in summer; there's a lively bar next door. Another tasty central option, which is very popular with locals, is *Osteria Al Bianchi* on Via Gasparo de Salò 42, just by Piazza della Loggia. Immediately east of Piazza della Loggia on Via Cesaria Beccharia there are plenty of less traditional places, popular with young Brescianos at the weekend.

Around Brescia

With Lago di Garda and the mountains of Val Trompia so easily accessible from Brescia, there seems little point in making do with the distinctly run-of-the-mill attractions of the countryside closest to the city. But if you're keen on wine you might want to make for the area between Brescia and Lago d'Iseo, known as the **Franciacorta** – a hilly wine-producing district, rising from the bland built-up lowlands around the city, which got its name from the religious communities that lived there from the eleventh century onwards. These communities and their land were exempt from tax and known as the Corti Franche, or free courts. The wine-producers soon moved in, attracted by the possibility of owning vineyards in a duty-free haven, and though the Franciacorta is no longer tax free, the extremely drinkable wine continues to flow – and is available from shops all over the region. For more information check out the website Ⓦ www.stradadelfranciacorta.it.

Val Trompia, Lago d'Idro and Lago di Ledro

You may be able to ignore the arms industry in Brescia, but its impact is unavoidable when you pass through the **Val Trompia**, directly north of the city. The industry dates back over four hundred years, started by the Venetians, keen to utilize the rich iron ore deposits of the area and to whom it became so indispensable that during the sixteenth century restrictions were actually placed on people's movements out of the region. The centre of today's (much diminished) arms industry is **GARDONE VAL TROMPIA**, where the Beretta company has its headquarters.

The valley beyond Gardone is crammed with industry as far as Lavone, and hiking becomes possible only at **BOVEGNO**. From this small village paths lead up to Monte Muffetto (4hr) and, even better, to Monte Crestoso and its tiny tarns (5hr 30min), though you'll need a tent, as there are no *rifugi*. If you're without a tent, there are two *rifugi* further on – *Croce Domini* (1992m) at the head of the valley, and *Bonardi* (1743m) above the lovely Passo del Maniva. From either base you can walk down to Lago d'Idro or climb Monte Colombino, again with a couple of tarns. The map to get is the Kompass Carta Turistica, *Le Tre Valli Bresciane*. There are also a few cheap hotels at the ski resorts of **COLLIO** and **SAN COLUMBANO**; try the tiny *Belvedere* (Ⓣ & Ⓕ 030 .927.259; ❷) in the latter.

From close to the *rifugio Croce Domini* a steep track climbs over into the broad Valle della Berga and up to **BAGOLINO** on the road to Lago d'Idro. Bagolino is quiet, preserving many of its medieval houses and a church, **San Rocco**, that has a startlingly realistic cycle of fifteenth-century frescoes. If you want to avoid Idro's unremarkable resorts, this is the place to stay: the *Cavallino* hotel at Via San Giorgio 164 (Ⓣ & Ⓕ 0365.99.103; ❷) is quite reasonable, and buses run fairly frequently to and from the lake.

Lago d'Idro is a reasonably pretty lake, except for its marshy upper reaches where the effect is spoiled by a sand-dredger. Tourism is family-oriented, but as there's no road running along the upper reaches of the east shore, you should be able to find a quiet beach there. Although bathing in the lake is said to induce a skin rash, few people are able to resist its cool, clear waters; there are also walks in the area if you want to do more than swim and laze around. Marked paths climb up into the hills from the east shore, and from **ANFO** on the west shore a track leads past the *rifugio Rosa di Baramone* to Bagolino. Again, you'll need the Kompass map mentioned above.

Idro's resorts are uniformly bland, but if you want to stay over, *Al Lago*, Via Lago 10 (Ⓣ & Ⓕ 0365.809.026; ❸), at Anfo, has cheap doubles, as does the *Geny*, Via Capovalle 7 (Ⓣ & Ⓕ 0365.823.380; ❷), at **CRONE**, on the bus route from Idray, 2km away. Of the **campsites**, the most convenient are the two at Anfo and a couple at Vantone on the east shore – both on the bus route from Brescia.

Northeast from Idro, via Ponte Caffaro, you reach the point where the Austrian border ran through until 1918. From here a road leads to tranquil

Lago di Ledro in the Val Sabbia, only 2km long and slightly less across, and a good bolt-hole if you want to get away from the frantic northwest of Lake Garda. Quieter than Idro, and far preferable, it has a couple of **campsites**, including the attractive *Al Sole* (☎0464.508.496, ⓦwww.campingalsole.it) right on the lakeside, and a good **hotel** – the 3-star *Mezzolago* (☎0464.508.181; ❷), with balconies on to the lake.

Lago di Garda

Lago di Garda is the largest and cleanest of the Italian lakes, and also the most popular. Tourism is relatively recent – beginning only in force last century when the road around its shores was completed, but the lake is now firmly on the tour operators' schedules, and much of the development has been feverish. Its resorts are each year invaded by a fair number of package-holiday clients, as well as huge numbers of Germans, Austrians and Italians attracted by some of Europe's best windsurfing and the gentle climate. Winters are mild, summers tempered by breezes – the northern *sover*, which blows down the lake from midnight and through the morning, and the *ova*, blowing from the south in the afternoon and evening. Along the so-called Riviera Bresciana, on the most sheltered stretch of the western shore, are lush groves of olives, vines and citrus trees – fruits used for Garda's main products: olive oil, citrus syrups and Bardolino, Soave and Valpolicella wines. Scenically the shores of the lake are varied: the rich vegetation of its middle reaches gives way to the rugged north, where the lake narrows and is tightly enclosed by craggy mountains; the southern shores, 16km at their widest, are backed by a gentle plain.

The waters of the lake lap onto the shores of three distinct administrative regions: the western shore north until Limone del Garda is in Lombardy (ⓦwww.bresciaholiday.com), the top of the lake is in Trentino (ⓦwww.gardatrentino.com), and the west side of the lake until Peschiera is in the Veneto (ⓦwww.aptgardaveneto.com). Regular **buses** ply their way between Desenzano and Riva on one shore and Riva and Peschiera on the other. The passenger **ferry** serves a similar service between Sirmione and Riva, with a car ferry crossing the middle of the lake between Toscolano-Maderno and Torri del Benaco.

The southern shore

Within easy striking distance of the Milan–Venice autostrada and railway and with regular buses from the main Lombardian towns, the **southern shore** of Lake Garda is predictably well-touristed. **DESENZANO DEL GARDA**, the lake's largest town, is a major rail junction and a good starting-point for visiting Garda. Buses tend to connect with trains, and there are several ferries daily up to Riva stopping off at other resorts on the way. The town itself holds little to detain you. The lakefront, lined with bars and restaurants, is quite attractive, though it's hard to ignore the busy main road running alongside. If you do end up with time to fill, head for the **castle**, from where there are spectacular views, or the **Roman villa** on Via Crocifisso: the villa is definitely worth visiting, a formerly large and luxurious home that preserves some good mosaics (Tues–Sat; March to mid-Oct 8.30am–7pm; mid-Oct to Feb 8.30am–5pm; €5).

SIRMIONE, 9km east, is spread along a narrow promontory protruding 4km into the lake. It is a popular spot, in a beautiful setting, though these days it's suffocated with luxury hotels, souvenir stands and tourists. You're unlikely to want to stay, and in any case most of the hotels are usually full with people on package tours, but it's worth a brief visit to take in the town's handful of sights and laze around on the surrounding lidos.

Inside the town's battlements stands the **Rocca Scaligera** (Tues–Sun: April–Sept 9am–7pm; Oct–March 8.30am–4.30pm; €4), a fairytale castle with boxy turreted towers almost entirely surrounded by water, built by the Veronese Scaligeri family in the thirteenth century when they ruled Garda. There's not much to see inside, although the views from its battlements are lovely.

You can escape the crowds by walking out beyond the town to the peninsula's triangular and traffic-free hilly head, covered in cypresses and olive groves. The church of **San Pietro** here has thirteenth-century frescoes, and its shady grounds make for a good picnic stop. A path leads along the edge of the peninsula, passing bubbling hot sulphur springs, to the **Spiaggia Lido delle Bionde** (May–Oct daily 8am–midnight) where you can eat, drink, swim in the lake or sunbathe on the pontoon or nearby rocks. If you continue, you'll reach a fenced-off area at the tip of the peninsula. The signs warn of landslides, but most people ignore these since the flat rocks are good for sun-soaking. Swimming or paddling is tricky, however, as underwater the rocks are slippery. There's a gate here up to the **Grotte di Catullo** (Tues–Sun: March to mid-Oct 8.30am–7pm; mid-Oct to Feb 8.30am–4.30pm; €4), touted as Catullus's villa, although the white ruins are actually of a Roman spa: there's a hot sulphur spring 300m under the lake, and people still come to Sirmione to take the waters. Catullus did, however, retire to the town, coming all the way from the Black Sea by boat, hauling it overland when necessary so that he could keep it on the lake. The ruins, scattered on the hillside among ancient olive trees, are lovely, and there are superb views across the lake to the mountains. There's a small antiquarium with fragments of mosaics and frescoes, and below the site, though not accessible from it, a beach.

If you want to stay in Sirmione, booking ahead is essential in July and August. If you haven't booked, the **tourist office** (April–Oct daily 10am–12.30pm & 3.30–9pm; Nov–March Mon–Fri 9am–12.30pm & 3–6pm, Sat 9am–12.30pm; ☎030.916.114), by the bus station and main car park, has a list of **rooms**, but don't count on these being free either. Of the **hotels**, the *Grifone*, Via Bocchio 4 (☎030.916.014; April–Oct; ❸), on the waterfront overlooking the castle, and *La Magnolia*, Via Vittorio Emanuele 43 (☎030.916.135; April–Oct; ❷), on the main thoroughfare beyond the castle, are both reasonably priced and pleasant. The nearest **campsite** is the *Sirmione*, Via Sirmioncino 9 (☎030.990.4665; March–Oct), at Colombare, 3km south of Sirmione, on the lakefront; head along Via Colombare out of town towards the mainland – though this too gets extremely crowded.

The western shore

The lower reaches of the **western shore** are a good place to stock up on some local produce, as much of the area is dedicated to vine and olive growing, although there are also plenty of campsites which make for cheap and reasonably convenient bases. A little further north from the old Venetian town of **Saló** stands the main sight of the lake, the exuberant **Il Vittoriale**, just outside the sedate resort of **Gardone Riviera**. After **Gargnano** – the most attractive and unspoilt of the lake villages – the shoreline has been dubbed the Riviera del Limone because of the citrus cultivation that lines the steep hillsides. The crop was reportedly introduced here by the Franciscans in the fourteenth century and was cultivated in the *lemonaias* that are still strewn across the landscape, although most are now abandoned. The tortuous winding road offers up tantalizing glimpses of the sparkling lake from between the *gallerie* and the lemon trees, but there is little reason to stop until you reach the nineteenth-century resort of **Riva del Garda** at the head of the lake.

Garda's only **car ferry** at Toscolano-Maderno, halfway up the shore, regularly plies across the lake to the eastern shore's most attractive village, Torri del Benaco (see p.234).

Saló, Gardone Riviera and Il Vittoriale

SALÓ, splendidly sited on a bay at the foot of the luxuriant Riviera Bresciana, is worth a brief stop. The town gave its name to Mussolini's short-lived last republic, instituted here after his rescue from the Abruzzi by the Nazis. Though it retains a handful of buildings from the fifteenth century – notably the Duomo and town hall – when it was the Venetian Empire's main garrison town, these are unlikely to detain you for long. Better to detour 6km inland to **PUEGNAGO DEL GARDA**, where you can sample the rosé wines – Grapello and Chiaretto – that the Comincioli vineyard has been producing since the sixteenth century.

A couple of kilometres further up the shore, **GARDONE RIVIERA** was once the most fashionable of Garda's resorts and still retains its symbols of sophistication, though the elegant promenade, lush gardens, opulent villas and ritzy hotels now have to compete with more recent – less tasteful – tourist tack. It is famous for the consistency of its climate, and has Garda's most exotic botanical garden, the **Giardino Botanico Hruska** (mid-March to mid-Oct daily 9am–6pm; €3), laid out among artificial cliffs and streams.

The highlight of Gardone, and indeed of the whole lake, is **Il Vittoriale** (April–Sept daily 9.30am–7pm; Oct–March Mon–Fri 9am–1pm & 2–5pm; ⓦwww.vittoriale.it; €16), the home of Italy's most notorious and extravagant twentieth-century writer, Gabriele D'Annunzio. Weight of numbers means that tickets for the house itself are restricted at peak times (Sundays, national holidays, some days in July & Aug), when you must arrive well before the opening times to be sure of a ticket for the house – even then, be prepared for a scrum. Once tickets for the house are sold out, you can only visit the grounds, the mausoleum, a small museum and the ship *Puglia*, beached incongruously among cypress trees in the park; the ticket for the grounds is €6.

Born in 1863, D'Annunzio was no ordinary writer. He did pen some exquisite poetry and a number of novels, but he became better known as a soldier and socialite, leading his own private army and indulging in much-publicized affairs with numerous women, including the actress Eleonora Duse. When berated by his friends for treating her cruelly, he simply replied, "I gave her everything, even suffering". He was a fervent supporter of Mussolini, providing the Fascist Party with their (meaningless) war cry, *eia! eia! alalá*, though Mussolini eventually found his excessive exhibitionism an embarrassment (his boasts of eating dead babies, certainly, were bad publicity), and in 1925 presented him with this villa – ostensibly as a reward for his patriotism, in reality to shut him up.

Once D'Annunzio had had the house "de-Germanized", as he put it (the house had been confiscated from the German art critic Henry Thode), it didn't take him long to transform Mussolini's Liberty-style gift into the Hollywood studio look-alike you see now. Outside, rammed into the cypress-covered hillside, is the prow of the battleship *Puglia* used in D'Annunzio's so-called "Fiume adventure". Fiume (now Rijeka), on the North Adriatic, had been promised to Italy before they entered World War I, but was eventually handed over to Yugoslavia instead. Incensed, D'Annunzio gathered together his army, occupied Fiume, and returned home a national hero. D'Annunzio's personality makes itself felt from the start in the two reception rooms – one a chilly and formal room for guests he didn't like, the other warm and inviting for those he did. Il Duce was apparently shown to the former, where the mirror has an inscription reputedly aimed at him – "Remember that you are made of glass and I of steel."

Nor was dining with D'Annunzio a reassuring experience: roast baby may not have featured on the menu, but in the glitzy dining room, as a warning to greedy guests, pride of place was given to a gilded and embalmed tortoise who had died of overeating. In fact D'Annunzio rarely ate with his guests, retreating instead to the Sala di Lebbroso, where he would lie on a bier surrounded by leopard skins and contemplate death. The rest of the house is no less bizarre: the bathroom has a bathtub hemmed in by hundreds of objects, ranging from Persian ceramic tiles, through Buddhas, to toy animals; and the Sala del Mappamondo, as well as the huge globe for which it is named, contains an Austrian machine-gun and books, including an immense version of *The Divine Comedy*. Suspended from the ceiling of the auditorium adjoining the house is the biplane that D'Annunzio used in a famous flight over Vienna in World War I.

Gardone's **tourist office** is at Via Repubblica 39, the cobbled street that runs parallel with the lakefront through the village (April–June Mon–Sat 9am–12.30pm & 4–7pm, closed Thurs afternoon; July–Sept same hours plus Thurs 4–7pm & Sun 9am–12.30pm; Oct–March Mon–Sat 9am–12.30pm & 3–6pm, closed Thurs afternoon; ⊤ & Ⓕ0365.20.347, ⓌWww.lagodigarda.it). If you want to **stay** over in Gardone, there are a couple of mid-range options: the lakefront *Diana*, Lungolago D'Annunzio 30 (⊤0365.21.815; ❸) offers rooms with balconies, or alternatively, walk up the hill on the other side of the main road towards Il Vittoriale until Via Roma meets Via dei Colli and you'll come to the pleasantly located *Hohl*, Via dei Colli 4 (⊤0365.20.160; ❸; March–Oct), which has a garden.

There are a couple of **places to eat** up in the old village around Il Vittoriale, including *La Stalla* on Via dei Colli, signposted off the road down from Il Vittoriale serving well priced staples in a tranquil garden setting. If you want to splash out, head for *Agli Angeli*, 2 Piazzetta Giuseppe Garibaldi, which has interesting pasta and fish courses. Down on the lakeside there are numerous cafés with attractive views across the lake where you can settle down for a cappuccino or a *gelato*.

San Michele

Up in the mountains behind Gardone is the little Alpine village of **SAN MICHELE**. There are six buses daily from Gardone and Saló, but as the views along the road are splendid, you might want to walk the hour or so uphill. The *Colomber Hotel* (⊤0365.21.108; ❷), 500m inland – follow the signs to the *Refugio G. Pirlo M. Spino* – has comfortable en-suite rooms – some with balconies overlooking the hills – and a good restaurant serving local specialities and well-chosen wine. It's a good base if you want to do some walking to the springs and waterfalls in the surrounding hills; the owners can give suggestions for **walks**, but for more ambitious hikes, there are maps marked with footpaths available from CAI, Via San Carlo 17, in Saló.

Gargnano and Limone

Twelve kilometres up the coast is **GARGNANO**, now famous for its annual sailing race – the Centomiglia – but once the headquarters of Mussolini's puppet Republic of Saló. The puppeteers were the Nazis, who placed him here in

Villa Feltrinelli largely to keep him out of harm's way. The dictator had by this time lost all credibility and he sank into depression; although he installed his mistress, Claretta Petacci, in nearby Il Vittoriale, the cold, damp rooms and heavy Nazi presence in the woods outside put paid to any passion.

Gargnano, tumbling down the hillside from the main road to the little fishing port, is still more a working village than a resort. It's the perfect spot to unwind for a day or two and wander around the abandoned olive factory or the lakefront villas with their boathouses, or just to relax with an ice cream or a drink in one of the waterfront cafés. It was here that DH Lawrence stayed while writing *Twilight in Italy*, a work which is beautifully evocative of the lake's attractions.

The main sight in the village is the thirteenth-century church of **San Francesco** – the columns in its cloisters are carved with citrus fruits, a reference to the Franciscans' introduction of the crop to Europe. A three-kilometre-stroll along the road which leads north from the port takes you through olive and lemon groves, past Il Duce's final home, the newly converted *Villa Feltrinelli* (see below), to the eleventh-century chapel of **San Giacoma Calina**. On the side facing the lake, under the portico where the fishermen keep their equipment, is a thirteenth-century fresco of St. Christopher, incredible for the fact that it is still visible despite the obvious lack of attention.

Gargnano's **tourist office** (Mon–Sat 10am–noon & 3.30–7pm; ☎0365 .71.222, ⓦwww.prolocogargnano.it) is housed in the ex-Palazzo Comunale, which has two cannonballs wedged in the lakeside of the building as a reminder of the naval bombings suffered in July 1866 during the war of independence from the Austrians. A new addition to the numerous **accommodation** options in Gargnano is the fabulous *Villa Feltrinelli* (☎0365.798.000, ⓦwww.villafeltrinelli.com; ⓽) – fast being recognized as one of the world's top hotels. Every detail has been considered in this elegant eleven-roomed villa with an enviable lakeside position; it's worth pawning all your worldly possessions for the view from the baths alone. Also on the lakefront, and probably in a slightly more realistic price range, is the very pleasant *Villa Giulia* on Viale Rimembranze 20 (☎0365.71.022, ⓦwww.villaguilia.it; ⓻). Otherwise try the friendly *Tiziana-Garnì* on Via Dosso 51 (☎0365.71.342, ⓦwww.albergo-tiziano.ocm; ⓷), a little too close to the main road, but offering comfortable modern rooms, most with lake views. There is also a campsite, *Rucc*, at Via Rimembranze 23 (☎0365.71.805), near the local beach.

Gargnano is also well served for good **places to eat**. For a snack or ice cream there are various places to try round the port, while the *Miralago*, next to the tourist office, offers excellent food at good prices. There's even the cosy little *La Tortuga*, just back from the lakefront on via XXIV Maggio, a Michelin-starred restaurant offering top food in a formal atmosphere.

Further north among citrus groves is **LIMONE SUL GARDA**, a pretty, stone-built village jammed on the slopes between the mountains and the lake, though unfortunately ruined by tourism. The steep cobbled streets are lined with stalls selling souvenirs, leather jackets and sequined T-shirts; the old stone facades are studded with plastic signs advertising restaurants and hotels; and as you elbow your way through the crowds you'll dig into more German and British than Italian ribs. Unless you're aching to eat chicken and chips, frankfurters and sauerkraut, you're better off staying away.

Riva del Garda

At the northwest tip of the lake, **RIVA DEL GARDA** is the best known of the lake's resorts. It started attracting visitors in the late nineteenth century and retains some stylish pastel-painted hotels. Its old town is pleasant enough and Riva is also cheaper than most of the other lake resorts; coupled with the fact that it boasts Garda's only youth hostel the town makes a good base for a budget holiday.

There's not a great deal to do or see, except for the severe moated **castle** (daily 9.30am–12.30pm & 2.30–5.30pm; €3) alongside the port, with its modest collection of local art. The entry ticket also allows you to climb the Torre Apponale in the main Piazza 3 Novembre, affording wonderful views of the lake (Tues–Sun: 16 June to 15 Sept 9.30am–6pm; 15 March to 15 June & 16 Sept to 3 Nov 9.30am–12.45 & 2.15–5.30pm).

If you're staying at Riva you'll need a map, available from the helpful **tourist office** in the Giardini di Porta Orientale, on the far side of the castle (May & June Mon–Sat 9am–noon & 3–6.30pm; July–Sept same hours plus Sun 10am–noon & 4–6.30pm; Oct–April Mon–Fri 8.30am–12.15pm & 2.30–5.15pm; ℡0464.554.444, ⓦwww.gardatrentino.com) – staff here can give you information on things to do in the area plus a list of **accommodation** options and should be able to find you somewhere to stay. Alternatively, the very central youth hostel at Piazza Cavour 10 (℡0464.554.911, ⓦwww.ostelloriva.com; €11; April–Oct), was being renovated at the time of writing to include more doubles and family rooms. If you fancy something more upmarket, head for the good-value, comfortable rooms at the *Albergo Ancora* (℡0464.522.131, ⓦwww.rivadelgarda.com/ancora; ❹), just west of Piazza Cavour.

The lakefront is lined with **gelaterie and pizzerias**, and there are numerous bars that open in the evening. If you want a more local experience, head for *Osteria del Gallo* under the portico in the corner of Piazza San Rocco. There's a short menu of simple local mountain staples and the owner will reel off many more. The good wine list of Trento wines and the relaxed atmosphere make this a good spot to settle down for the evening. For somewhere with a little more pretension make for *Café Italia* in Piazza Cavour – one of the few stylish places in town; they also offer rather pricey **Internet** access.

The eastern shore

Overlooked by the mountains of the Monte Baldo chain, the main resorts of Garda's **eastern shore** are heavily touristed and have none of the charming flaking palaces of the western side. Head for **Torbole** in the north if you're a keen windsurfer or attracted by any of the myriad of other activities on offer. Along the shore to the south, **Malcesine** has an appealing centre that is nowadays hidden under postcard stands and trilingual pizza menus. It is, however, still a good base for escapes by bike or on foot into the mountains. Further south still lies **Torri del Benaco**, a lovely old village, popular but not yet ruined by tourism, while **Garda** and **Bardolino** are bustling resorts, the former a favourite haunt of Italian holiday-makers.

Much of the inland side of the lake road on this shore is lined with campsites and, although there is plenty of **accommodation,** things get very busy. Between June and September it's advisable to book ahead or arrive early in the day.

Torbole
TORBOLE, at the top of the lake, 4km east of Riva, played an important role in the fifteenth-century war between the Viscontis and the Venetians, when a fleet of warships was dragged overland here and launched into the lake. Nowadays it's still the water that dominates, since Torbole's main diversions are sailing and windsurfing, and the place has a fresh feeling, something added to

by the suntanned faces you'll encounter in the many bars and fast-food joints. If you're a sports freak, this is a great place to stay, with numerous activities on offer both on the water and in the mountains behind. Windsurfing enthusiasts come here from all over Europe, attracted by the ideal wind conditions. It's also a good place for beginners, and in the mornings, when the wind is gentler, the water is full of wobbling novices attempting to circle their instructors.

The **tourist office** (April & May Mon–Sat 9am–noon & 3–6.15pm; June–Oct Mon–Sat 9am–noon & 3–6.30pm, Sun 10am–noon & 4–6.30pm; Nov–March 9am–noon & 2.30–5.15pm; ☎0464.505.177, Ⓦwww.torbole .com) is conveniently located on the lakefront between the jetty and the centre; it has a huge range of information on different courses, places to rent bikes and boards and routes for every imaginable sport. If it's closed, there is a freephone service outside to a substantial number of the **hotels** (phone numbers are listed on a board). The *Casa Nataly*, at Piazza Alpini 10 (☎0464.505.341, Ⓦwww.casanataly@tin.it; ❷), is just off the main road on the edge of town and also rents apartments by the week; the *Casa Romani* (☎0464.505.113; ❷) charges about the same and is in a handy location just off the main road directly opposite the ferry jetty; it has two swimming pools and some rooms with use of a kitchen. A more upmarket alternative is the modern *Villa Verde* (☎0464.505.74; ❸), on the other side of town from the tourist office, in a peaceful setting two minutes' walk from the centre. It has its own pool and garden, plus some of the rooms have balconies with lake views.

Malcesine

Backed by the slopes of Monte Baldo and blessed with the same windsurfer-friendly winds as Torbole, **MALCESINE**, 14km further south, has been inundated with British and German package tourists in the last few years and the crowds temper much of the appeal of what is left of the old town. The main sight is a thirteenth-century turreted **Castello** (April–Oct daily 9am–9pm; rest of year Sat & Sun only; €4), built, like Sirmione's, by the Scaligeri family. Goethe was imprisoned here briefly in 1786, having been arrested on suspicion of being a spy – he'd been caught making sketches of the lake castle's towers. In 1439, the warships of the Venetian fleet were transported over the 320-metre-high San Giovannia pass to Malcesine by means of filling in the small River Cameras with earth and hauling the ships uphill over tree-trunk rollers, *Fitzcarraldo*-style. They went on to rule the nearby towns of Lazise and Peschiera, and eventually Brescia (see p.224), but by May 1509 they lost their hard-won territory after battles with the army commanded by Louis XII of France.

For more active pursuits you need to head up Monte Baldo. Although there are well-marked trails up the mountain, you can save energy by taking the brand-new **funicular** (daily: April–Oct every 30min 8am–6pm; €13 return), but be prepared for long queues in summer. If you want to mountain bike, there are wheels for hire at G. Furioli in Piazza Matteotti, who even transport the bikes to the top, from where you can make a panoramic descent; you can also take your own bike up on one of the four trips – three in the morning and one at lunchtime – designed especially for cyclists.

The **tourist office** at Via Capitanato 6–8 (June–Oct Mon–Sat 10am–1pm & 4–7pm, Sun 9am–1pm; Nov–May closed Sun; ☎045.740.0044, Ⓕ045.740.1633), north along the lake from the port, has maps of signposted walks in the hills behind. Most **hotels** in Malcesine get swallowed up by package companies, so the choice is limited. In the centre of town, near the lake is the decent little *Hotel Modena* at Via Garibaldi 2 (☎ & Ⓕ045.740.0016; closed mid-Oct to Easter; ❶), which offers good-value en-suites. With your own transport or if you're prepared for a twenty-minute walk north of town, the modern *Hotel Florida* (☎0457.400.587, ⓦwww.villaflorida.it; closed Oct–Easter; min 3 days; ❷) is peacefully set among olive groves and has its own swimming pool and balconied rooms, some with lake views. There are also various places with **rooms** to let in this area: try *Casa Chincarni* (☎045.740.0375; ❷). Many of Malcesine's **restaurants** are aimed at the town's German visitors: the *Speck Stube*, Via Molina 1, is one of the better of the Teutonic-style eateries; or else try the *Agli Scaligeri*, at Via Caselunghe 12, for tasty, reasonably priced dishes.

Torri del Benaco and Punta San Vigilio

To the south of Malcesine, **TORRI DEL BENACO** is the prettiest and least spoilt of the villages on this side of the lake. Its old centre consists simply of one long cobbled street, Corso Dante, crisscrossed with tunnelling alleyways and lined with mellow stone *palazzi*. At one end of the street is the **castle**, illuminated at night and with a long glasshouse – or *lemonia* – built along one side to protect the lemon trees inside during cold weather. Inside the castle there is a small **anthropological museum** (April, May & Oct daily 9.30am–12.30pm & 2.30–6pm; June–Sept daily 9.30am–1pm & 4.30–7.30pm; Nov–March Sun 2.30–5.30pm; €2.50). Beyond the castle, the port area is a piazza planted with limes and chestnuts, at night the focus of the passeggiata.

Torri is a fine place to stay, and there are a number of reasonably priced **hotels**, the best of which is the *Onda*, located on Via per Albisano two minutes' walk from the village centre (☎045.722.5895, ⓦwww.ondagardi.com; ❷). Each spotlessly clean room has its own balcony or terrace and the friendly owners provide a first-rate breakfast. If there's no room, the newly renovated *Belvedere* opposite (☎045.722.5088; ❷) is also a good bet with lake-view balconies and a large garden. The top hotel in town is the elegant *Gardesana* (☎045.722.5411, ⓦwww.hotel-gardesana.com; ❻), right on the harbour at Piazza Calderini 20.

Just off the main road, by the castle is the **tourist office** (April–June & Sept Mon–Sat 9am–1pm & 3–6pm; July & Aug daily 9am–1pm & 3–7pm; ☎045.722.5120). One of the top **restaurants** in town is the *Gardesana* (closed Tues & Nov–Jan), where you can splash out on a romantic meal overlooking the lake. There are numerous other options among the warren of streets and along the waterfront, although bear in mind some of the lake-view spots are overpriced and poor quality. For a good pizza, the family-run restaurant on Viale Fosse (closed Tues), just off the main road, is a good choice, or, if you prefer, you can pick up a hearty sandwich at *La Regata* on the lakefront. For **drinks**, try *Don Diego* on Via Faese, an alleyway off Corso Dante, easily recognizable by the graffitied doors, where you can drink local Bardolino wine or the bar's notoriously heady and moderately priced *sangria*.

If you fancy a **swim**, there's a lido in Torri, but you'd probably be better off heading south for the white shingle beaches at **Punta San Vigilio**, a hilly headland a short bus ride away. There's an excellent pay beach, with sun loungers and picnic tables scattered on grassy slopes planted with pines and planes, or, if you want to save your money, you can take a footpath about 100m from the first gate to several smaller coves – one of which is unofficially nudist. There's also a charming restaurant and an extremely exclusive hotel here, which numbers Churchill and Prince Charles among its famous ex-guests.

Garda, Bardolino, Lazise and Gardaland

Like many of its neighbours, the attractive ex-fishing village of **GARDA**, 8km south, has seen its narrow, windy alleys and cottages encroached upon by snack bars, cheap leather and souvenir shops. Even the fifteenth-century **Loggia della Losa**, originally a dock for the palace behind, is now a *gelateria*. If you want to stay, the **tourist office**, on the waterfront at Lungolago 3 (April–Sept Mon–Sat 9am–7pm, Sun 9am–1pm; Oct–March Mon–Sat 9am–1pm & 3–6pm; ☎045.627.0384, ⓦwww.aptgardaveneto.com), has daily updated information on available accommodation and can also provide leaflets on walks in the hills behind.

Three kilometres away is the spruce little resort of **BARDOLINO**, popular with British and German visitors, and, as you might have guessed, the home of the light, red Bardolino wine – the town is at its most animated between mid-September and mid-October, when the *Festa di Uva* (Festival of the Grape) is held. At other times of year, apart from strolling along its lush palm- and pine-planted promenade, there's not a lot to do, although the church of **San Zeno**, tucked in the corner of a dusty yard just off the main coast road, is worth a brief look. It was built in the eighth century, and its Latin-cross form and high domed ceiling became a prototype for later Romanesque churches. Otherwise, concentrate on sampling Bardolino wine at the unlikely-looking bar on Via Cesare Battisti, which has no name outside but is commonly known as *Da Romaldì*, or try the ice cream at *Cristallo* on the lakefront near the ferry jetty, which sells the biggest and best ice creams on the lake, in a repertoire of flavours ranging from *mascarpone* to *panna cotta* with fresh forest fruits.

The walled village of **LAZISE**, further down the shore, was once a major Venetian port and retains a (privately owned) **castle** and, on the harbour, an arcaded medieval **customs house**. Originally used for building and repairing boats for the Venetian fleet, it later served as a shelter for sheep, whose urine was used to make nitrogen, a vital ingredient in gunpowder. Nowadays Lazise is crammed with cafés, pizzerias and *gelaterie* and plenty of summer visitors, but it's not a bad place to escape to out of season, when it reverts to being a sleepy lakeside village. If you want to **stay**, go for the *Tecla* at Via Cansignorio 12 (☎045.758.0032; ❷), above a wine shop just off Corso Cangrande. The **tourist office** (Mon–Sat: April–Oct 9am–1pm & 3–7pm; Nov–March closes one hour earlier; ☎045.758.0114) is on Via F. Fontana near the harbour, and has maps and leaflets about the village.

Finally, if you have kids to amuse, or just want a daft day out, you can catch a bus from any of the east-shore villages to **Gardaland**, Italy's most popular amusement park, at Castelnuovo del Garda (daily: April to June 21 10am–6pm; June 22 to Sept 10 9am–midnight; Sept 11–30 & Oct Sat & Sun 10am–6.30pm; ☎045.644.9777, ⓦwww.gardaland.it; €20.50, children under ten €17.25, under one-metre-tall free). It's pricey, and you pay extra for some of the attractions, but its various rides and themed entertainments attract around two million visitors a year; with restless children in tow, you might just want to join them.

Travel details

Trains

Bergamo to: Brescia (hourly; 50min); Cremona (3 daily; 1hr 30 min); Lecco (hourly; 35min); Verona (1 daily; 1hr 30 min).

Brescia to: Cremona (every 30min; 50min); Milan (every 30min; 1hr); Parma (9 daily; 1hr 30min–1hr 50min); Verona (every 20min; 40min).

Cremona to: Mantua (every 40min; 1hr 10min); Brescia (every 45min; 40min).

Lecco to: Bergamo (hourly; 45min); Sondrio (every 20min; 1hr 25min).

Mantua to: Bologna (2 daily; 1hr 35min); Milan (6 daily; 2hr); Modena (every 30min; 45min); Padua (2 daily; 1hr 55min); Rome (Mon–Sat 1 daily; 4hr 15min); Venezia (Mon–Sat 1 daily; 2hr 45min); Verona (every 50 min; 50 min).

Milan Centrale to: Bergamo (hourly; 50min); Brescia (every 30 min; 1hr 30min); Certosa di Pavia (6 daily; 25min); Como (hourly; 40min); Desenzano (hourly; 1hr 15min); Lecco (hourly; 1hr 20min); Pavia (every 15min; 25min); Peschiera (hourly; 1hr 25min); Stresa (hourly; 1hr 5min); Varenna (8 dailly; 1hr 20min).

Milan Lambrate to: Certosa di Pavia (9 daily; 20min); Cremona (3 daily; 1hr 35min); Pavia (every 15min; 25min).

Milan Porta Garibaldi to: Bergamo (every 40 min; 55min); Varese (17 daily; 1hr).

Milan Porta Genova to: Vigévano (hourly; 35min).

Pavia to: Certosa di Pavia (14 daily; 10min); Cremona (11 daily; 2hr 20min); Mantua (6 daily; 3hr).

Sondrio to: Tirano (every 50min; 35min).

Buses

Bergamo to: Clusone (every 20min; 1hr).

Brescia to: Gardone Riviera (every 25min; 1hr 5min); Iseo (2 daily; 45min).

Como to: Bellagio (every 30min; 1hr 10min); Cernobbio (every 30min; 20min); Colico (5 daily; 2hr 20min); Menaggio (every 20min; 1hr 10min);

Tremezzo (14 daily; 1hr); Varese (38 daily; 1hr 10min).

Cremona to: Bergamo (4 daily; 2hr 20min); Brescia (every 30min; 1hr 25min); Iseo (1 daily; 2hr).

Gardone Riviera to: Limone (3 daily; 1hr); Riva del Garda (5 daily; 1hr 15min).

Mantua to: Brescia (1hr; 1hr); Peschiera (9 daily; 1hr 10min); Sabbioneta (4 daily; 50min); Sirmione (1 daily; 1hr 15min); Verona (6 daily; 1hr 20min).

Menaggio to: Lugano (9 daily; 1hr).

Milan (Via Bligny) to: Certosa (Mon–Sat every 30min, Sun 7 daily; 30 min).

Pavia to: Certosa (Mon–Sat every 30min, Sun hourly; 20min); Milan (Mon–Sat every 30min, Sun 7 daily; 1hr); Vigévano (Mon–Fri hourly, Sat & Sun 8 daily; 1hr).

Peschiera to: Garda (every 30min; 30min).

Tirano to: Bormio (15 daily; 1hr).

Ferries

(The frequencies below are for summer sailings, for other times of year consult ⓦ www.nav-igazionelaghi.it.)

Cadenabbia to: Bellagio (every 25min; 10min); Varenna (every 25min; 25min).

Como to: Bellagio (8 daily; 2hr); Cernobbio (every 20min; 15min); Colico (10 daily; 4 hours); Menaggio (8 daily; 2hr 15min); Varenna (8 daily; 2hr 20min).

Desenzano to: Garda (8 daily; 1hr); Gardone Riviera (7 daily; 1hr 40min); Gargnano (5 daily; 2hr 30min); Malcesine (5 daily; 3hr 15min); Riva del Garda (7 daily; 3hr 30min); Saló (5 daily; 1hr 30min); Sirmione (every 45min; 20min).

Intra to Laveno (every 30min; 20min).

Maderno to Torri (every 40min; 30min).

Stresa to: Intra (12 daily; 50min); Isola Bella (every 30min; 10min); Isola dei Pescatori (every 30min; 15min); Isola Madre (every 30min; 30min); Pallanza (every 30min; 35min); Villa Taranto (hourly; 45min).

Trentino-Alto Adige

CHAPTER 4

Highlights

* **Castello Róncolo** A thirteenth-century castle decorated with beautiful frescoes of courtly life. See p.266

* **Ice Man** The chief exhibit in Bolzano's Museo Archeologico is the superbly preserved "Ice Man", an early Copper Age male, found in the Ötzaler Alps in 1991. See p.264

* **Trento's Piazza Duomo** Trento's pleasant central square, with its backdrop of mountains, is ringed by arcades, shops and cafés. See p.247

* **The Dolomites** The resort of Madonna di Campiglio makes a good base for some fine skiing and hiking in the Dolomites. See p.252

* **Strada di Vino** Follow the "wine road" through the Adige valley and sample some of the region's best food and wine. See p.249

Trentino-Alto Adige

T**rentino–Alto Adige** is something of an anomaly: a mixed **German-Italian** region, much of which has only been part of Italy since 1919. Before then Alto Adige was known as the South Tyrol and was part of Austria. At the end of World War I, Austria ceded South Tyrol to the Italians, and, in a bid to make the new territory instantly Italian, Mussolini turned the name on its head, naming it after the upper reaches of the Adige River, which bisects the region. Many Tyroleans opted for resettlement in Germany, but others stayed and have clung tenaciously to their language, culture and traditions.

Even now, one of the first things you'll notice about **Alto Adige** is its German character. Gothic onion-domed churches dot the landscape of vineyards and forests, street signs are in German, and there's sauerkraut and strudel on the menu. By contrast **Trentino**, just to the south, is 98 percent Italian-speaking, and the food and architecture belong more to the Mediterranean world than to the Alps. Both parts of the region enjoy semi-autonomy from central government, along with one of the highest standards of living in Italy, a consequence of special grants and aid they receive from Rome – intended to defuse the ethnic tension that has existed ever since enforced union took place.

If some German speakers are unwilling to remain part of Italy, there are right-wing Italian speakers who would be equally pleased to see them go. Friction between the two camps flared up in the Sixties, when Germanic activists staged disturbances. Talks between the Austrian and Italian governments brought about a package of concessions and promises from central government, known as the *pacchetto*, all the provisions of which have now been implemented. These days, the **political climate** has shifted slightly and many German speakers have moved away from the extreme nationalist Union Für Südtirol towards the Lega Nord.

Tourism (chiefly skiing and hiking), farming and wine production are the mainstays of the economy, and there are plenty of good, reasonably cheap guesthouses and agriturism places in the mountains and vineyards. Although the region's resorts can be lethargic, the landscape, dominated by the stark and jagged **Dolomites**, is among the most beautiful in the country. Circling the spiked towers of rock that characterize the range, a network of trails follows the ridges, varying in length from a day's walk to a two-week trek; the long-distance trails, called *alte vie*, can be picked up from the small resorts.

The chief towns of **Trento** and **Bolzano** are the transport hubs for the region. Trento gives access to most of the western Dolomites: the **Pale di San Martino**, a cluster of enormous peaks encircling the high, rocky plain above San Martino di Castrozza; the **Catinaccio** (or Rosengarten) range between

0   10 km

Passo di Brénnero 1357 m

▲ Gran Pilastro 3510 m

Campo Túres

AUSTRIA

Fúndres

Selva dei Molini

Val Pusteria

Brunico

San Lorenzo

Villabassa

Novacella

PARCO NATURALE FÁNES-SENNES-BRAIES

Dobbiaco

Bressanone

San Vigílio

PARCO NATURALE DOLOMITI DI SESTO

Fortezza

Croda Rossa 3139 m

PARCO NATURALE OLDE

Pederú

Val di Funes

Santa Maddalena

Pedráces

Cristallo 3221 m

Tre Cime di Lavaredo 2999 m

Ortisei

Passo di Gardena 2121 m

Lago di Misurina

Tofane 3243 m

Auronzo di Cadore

Siusi

Passo di Sella 2234 m

Corvara

Passo Tre Croci 1814 m

Sasso Lungo 3179 m

Selle 3151 m

Passo di Falzarago

Alpe di Siusi

Passo Pordio 2239 m

Arabba

Cortina d'Ampezzo

Rosengarten/ Catinaccio 2981 m

Canazei

Caprile

Antelao 3263 m

Vigo di Fassa

Marmolada 3343 m

Pieve di Cadore

Carezza al Lago

Passo di Costalunga 1745 m

Alleghe

Moena

Passo di San Pellegrino 1918 m

Civetta 3218 m

Val di Fassa

Panevéggio

Predazzo

Pale di San Martino 3192 m

Passo di Rolle 1970 m

FRIULI-VENEZIA GIULIA

Tésero

San Martino

PARCO NATURALE PANEVEGGIO

Passo di Cereda 1369 m

Cima d'Asta 2847 m

Fiera di Primiero

Mezzano

Imer

Belluno

Fonzaso

Feltre

Vittório Veneto

VENETO

▶ Lienz S Salzburg

▶ Udine

▶ Trieste

A27

▼ Venice

Regional food and wine

Trentino-Alto Adige, as its name suggests, is really two regions: Alto Adige with its unreservedly Germanic traditions, and Trentino, which mixes mountain influences with more Italian flavours from the south. Another influence is the weather: in this mountainous region, with only a couple of snow-free months a year, the diet tends to be dominated by carbohydrates. There's no such thing as a light supper in Trentino.

A **typical meal** starts with some kind of salami (*lucanicche* in local dialect), often paper-thin slices of salt beef, followed by Tyrolean *canederli* – bread dumplings flavoured with *speck* (smoked ham) and accompanied by a melted butter dressing – or *strangolapreti*, bread and spinach gnocchi. Game and rabbit with polenta are popular as *secondi*. Desserts are often based on apples, pears or plums, readily available from the local orchards. Other sweet treats include *Soffiato alla Trentina*, a meringue trifle, and *Zelten Trentino*, a rich fruitcake flavoured with grappa and usually eaten at Christmas.

As you travel north into Alto Adige the menu becomes more Germanic, with *knödel* (dumplings) and goulash, sausages with horseradish sauce (*salsa al cren*), sauerkraut, *apfel strudel*, *sachertorte* and all manner of sweet tarts and pastries. If you're really keen to sample some of Alto Adige's cuisine, try to co-ordinate your visit with the Törggelen season (see box on p.267).

Vines have been cultivated here since Roman times, and Trentino-Alto Adige produces more **DOC wines** than any other region in Italy. Most famous are the Pinot Grigios and Chardonnays, which are bright and aromatic from being grown at high altitudes and in cool conditions. These also provide wine makers with the raw material for some outstanding traditional-method sparkling wines, often marketed under the spumante Trentino Classico label. Despite the excellence of the whites, local wine makers actually make more reds, achieving considerable success with local varieties like Teróldego and Schiava (known as Vernatsch in German-speaking areas). Red wines made from Schiava are good when young: look out for the pale-red Kalterersee (Caldaro) and the fuller, more fruity St Magdalene (Santa Maddalena); those made from the Lagrein grape variety are more robust, such as the strong, dark Lagrein Dunkel, or the Kretzer rosé from Bolzano's vineyards at Gries. Also worth seeking out is the rare **vin santo** from Trentino's Valle dei Laghi – a luscious dessert wine made from local Nosiola grapes.

---

the Val di Fassa and Bolzano; the **Gruppo di Sella**, with its *vie ferrate* (see box on p.246); and the glacier-topped **Marmolada**. Still in the western Dolomites, but with easier access from Bolzano, are the **Alpe di Siusi**, a magical plateau of grass and wetland, high above the valley. The *alpe* are enclosed by the peaks of **Sasso Lungo** (or Langkofel) and **Sciliar** (or Schlern); to the north is the quieter Odle (or Geisler Gruppe). Even further to the west, on the other side of Trento, are the **Dolomiti di Brenta**, a collection of wild peaks above the meadows of Valle Rendena.

The eastern Dolomites start on the opposite side of the Adige Valley, past Passo di Campolongo and Corvara, with activity focusing on **Cortina d'Ampezzo**, self-styled "Queen of the Dolomite resorts" – though actually just across the regional border in the Veneto. In summer, avoid the overpopulated peaks like the **Tre Cime di Lavaredo** and head for **Sorapiss** or **Monte Pelmo** to the south, or **Le Tofane** and the mountains of the **Fánes–Sénnes–Bráies** group to the west. In winter, Cortina comes into its own as an upmarket ski resort with excellent, if expensive, facilities.

It's worth noting that provincial **bus** companies stick fairly rigidly to towns within their territory, so that some places which look like they should be easy to get to from Bolzano, say, often are not. For example, there are more frequent buses to Canazei from Trento, and this is the case for other towns in the northern part of Trentino. If you're **driving** outside the summer months, be aware that many passes can remain closed until well after Easter. Approach roads all have signs indicating whether the pass is open, or you can call Bolzano's information line on ☎0471.999.999. The Südtirol's official **website** ⓦwww.suedtirol.com has some useful links and reams of information about the province, with pages devoted to individual towns and resorts.

Hiking and skiing

The official **hiking** season lasts from June 20 to September 20; this is when most refuges and cable cars are open, though you'll find some also have a winter season. Cable cars sometimes close in mid-September. These dates may seem rigid, but they're based on long experience of climate in the area: snow can linger in the high country until late June, and winter closes in early. Some refuges open or close early or late according to local conditions. Nearby *rifugi* are the best place to phone for information on cable cars and weather conditions.

Routes are well-established, with a large number of well-marked day walks and a series of longer trails, known as **alte vie**. Four of these run north–south between the Val Pusteria (Pustertal) and the Veneto, and four from the Val d'Isarco (Eisacktal) south, each stage requiring five to eight hours' walking from one mountain refuge to the next. Some of the initial ascents are strenuous, but once you are up on the ridges the paths level out and give superb views across the valleys and glaciers. (As a rule of thumb, an averagely fit person takes around three hours to ascend 1000m.) Parts of the trails are exposed, or have snowfields across them, but alternative routes are always available. Alta Via 1, between the Lago di Bráies (Pragser Wildsee) and Belluno, is the most popular, so much so that you should think twice about going between mid-July and August because of the crowds, not to mention the summer heat.

There aren't many guides in English to the trails. Tourist offices usually have information on the day walks in the locality, often quite detailed and with good maps. The larger branches sometimes have guides to Alte Vie 1 and 2; Martin Collins's *Alta Via: High Level Walks in the Dolomites* (Cicerone) details walks along Alte Vie 1 and 2; and if you read Italian or German, Alpina Verlag's *Dolomite Alte Vie/Dolomiten Hohenwegel 1–10* is an extremely thorough option – available free from larger tourist offices. As for maps, the *alte vie* are marked on the Kompass 1:50,000 and Tabacco 1:25,000 maps, along with the multitude of other shorter trails which can be followed without guides. These maps are on sale everywhere in the Dolomites.

As for **skiing and winter sports**, Trento's excellent *Snow Info* brochure and Bolzano's skiing booklet (published by the provincial tourist offices) give details of chair lifts, altitude and length of runs in each resort, plus maps; try also ⓦwww.dolomitisuperski.com. From December, you can get the latest on snow conditions in Trentino on ☎0461.916.666 and in Bolzano on ☎0471.271.177; Bolzano's weather website, ⓦwww.provinz.bz.it/meteo, is very useful. *Settimane Bianche* ("White Weeks") are bargain package deals offering full- or half-board and a ski-pass: information is available from Italian tourist offices before you leave, and also from regional offices in Italy. For specific details of places to stay and prices, ask for the information leaflets published each October by local tourist offices. If you take a car and want to ski at more than one resort, the one-week Dolomiti Superski gives you access to 1200km of runs, 460 cable cars and chair lifts, and costs €35 per day, though the more days you buy the cheaper it gets – a week costs €186. Note that ski buses are free in some places.

Rifugi

The most convenient places to stay once you're high up are the **rifugi** (refuges). Solidly constructed, usually two- or three-storey buildings, they provide dormitory accommodation, meals and a bar. Some have hot showers, but just as many have only freezing cold water. Blankets are provided, and sheets can be rented for a nominal charge. All are open from June until around September or October, and some also operate in the skiing season; we've given opening periods as a guide, but these are still subject to prevailing weather conditions. If you're planning a long trek that relies on refuges for accommmodation, you should definitely call ahead; at the same time, you can check that the place isn't likely to be packed out by a large party – nobody is ever turned away, but overflow accommodation is either on a mattress in the bar or even in the hen house. If you are a member of the Club Alpino Italiano the overnight rate is around €8, if not, expect to pay around €16. **Emergency calls** can be made from the refuges; to call Soccorso Alpino (Alpine Rescue), dial ☎118. A full list of refuges, with phone numbers, is available from the provincial tourist offices in Bolzano and Trento. For more on *rifugi*, see "Accommodation" in Basics, p.36.

For those who shudder at the idea of walking boots and rucksacks, the region is also famous for its many varied and beautiful castles, some of which have fascinating Gothic fresco cycles. A handy publication is the *Guide to the Castles of Trentino* available from the tourist office in Trento.

Vie Ferrate

Vie ferrate (literally "iron ways") are a peculiarly Italian phenomenon. The easiest way to describe them is as aided rock-climbs. Consisting of permanently fixed metal ladders, pegs and cables, onto which climbers' karabiners can be clipped, they provide access to routes which would otherwise be too difficult. Many *vie ferrate* were begun as far back as the late nineteenth century as mountaineering really took off in Europe; others were put in place by the Alpini troops during World War I to assist the climbs that were a matter of survival for the soldiers fighting in the mountains. Many more have been created since by volunteers from local Club Alpino Italiano groups.

All are clearly marked on both Kompass and Tabacco maps as a line of little black dots or crosses, but *vie ferrate* are definitely not for beginners or vertigo-sufferers. You need to be confident belaying, have the proper equipment (including helmet, ropes, two self-locking karabiners and a chest- or seat-harness) – and you must know what you're doing. Incidentally, it's not advisable to climb a *via ferrata* in a thunderstorm either; it might just become one long lightning conductor.

Of course, once you've done a few straightforward paths up in the mountains you may be inspired to tackle some *ferrate*, and there are plenty of people around who will teach you. Individual guides charge by the hour, and so become more affordable if you can assemble a small group. Otherwise, enrol on a mountain skills course: both Trentino and Alto Adige provincial tourist offices keep lists of guides and mountaineering schools, but you'll need to book well in advance.

Guides and mountaineering schools

Alpinschule Südtirol Jungmannstrasse 8, Campo Tures ☎0474.690.012. Courses throughout the Dolomites, from ice-climbing to *vie ferrate*. The school is run by the famous mountaineer Hans Kammerlander.
Collegio Guide Alpine ☎0461.981.207. Central number for Alpine guides in the province of Trentino. For Alto Adige, call ☎0471.976.357.
Scuola Alpinismo Orizzonti Trentini, Via Petrarca 8 ☎0461.230.141. Trento-based guides.

TRENTINO-ALTO ADIGE

4

Trento

Straddling the Adige Valley, **TRENTO**, just three hours from Venice by train, is a quiet provincial centre that makes one of the best bases for exploring the region, not least because of its bus services to the mountains. Overshadowed by Monte Bondone, it's beautifully sited too, encircled by mountains and exuding a relaxed pace of life. It wasn't always so, however. From the tenth to the eighteenth centuries, Trento was a powerful bishopric ruled by a dynasty of princes; it was the venue of the Council of Trent in the sixteenth century, when the Catholic Church, threatened by the Reformation in northern Europe, met to plan its countermeasures – meetings that spanned a total of eighteen years. Later, throughout the nineteenth century, ownership of the city, which remained in Austrian hands, was hotly contested, and it only became properly part of Italy in 1918, after the conclusion of World War I.

Arrival, information and accommodation

Trento's main **bus and train stations** are almost next door to each other at Piazza Dante and Via Pozzo. A secondary, combined station – **Trento-Malé**, run by a private company – is on Via Dogana, just beyond the train station, with trains up to Cles in the Val di Non, Malé in the Vale di Sole and buses to Madonna di Campiglio and Molveno. Tickets and information on Trento-Malé connections can be had from the office at the station (℡0461.238.350, ⓦwww.fertm.it).

The **tourist office** at Via Alfieri 4, across the park from the main train station (daily 9am–7pm; ℡0461.983.880), has plenty of information on Trento, including copies of *Trentino Mese*, the town's monthly listings guide. The **regional information centre** (contactable by phone only: ℡0461.839.000) has details on mountain refuges, transport, hiking and skiing possibilities, and agriturismi in the province.

The cheapest **hotel** close to the centre is the *Venezia*, Piazza Duomo 45 (℡0461.234.559, Ⓕ0461.234.114; ④), plain but comfortable, with a few rooms overlooking the piazza and others in a thirteenth-century tower. Rather more luxurious is the *Aquila d'Oro*, next door, at Via Belenzani 76 (℡ & Ⓕ0461.986.282; ⓦwww.aquiladoro.it; ⑤). Close to the main station, the smart *Hotel America*, at Via Torre Verde 50 (℡0461.983.010, Ⓕ0461.230.603, ⓦwww.hotelamerica.it; ⑤), is the only other affordable hotel in town. If you don't mind staying further out, try the *Villa Madruzzo*, Via Ponto Alto 26 (℡0461.986.220, Ⓕ0461.986.361; ⑤), in Cagnola, in the hills overlooking Trento to the east, reached by bus #9 (20min); it's good value and serves regional cuisine. For visitors on a budget there's the clean, friendly **hostel** *Europa* at Via Torrevange no 9, 500m to your right out of the station (℡0461.263.484; from €12.50); as well as dormitory-style rooms they do singles and doubles. The nearest **campsite** is a stiff hike away at the end of a cable-car ride, on Monte Bondone, which overlooks town from across the river (see "Around Trento" on p.250).

The Town

Trento was known as Tridentum to the Romans, a name celebrated by the eighteenth-century Neptune fountain in the central **Piazza Duomo**, a pleasant square ringed by arcades, shops and cafés and giving onto streets lined with frescoed palaces, notably via Belanziani, many of them built in the sixteenth century when Trento was an important market town. Architecture buffs

ACCOMMODATION

Aquila d'Oro	3
America	1
Venezia	4
Youth Hostel	2

RESTAURANTS,
CAFÉS & BARS

Albergo Accademia	D E
Call Me	C
Chiesa	F
Due Giganti	
Due Spade	H I
Irish Pub	G
Murphy's	J
Pedavena	A
Pub Stube	
Primavera	B

might like to pick up an excellent guide to the palaces, *Renaissance Trento*, from the tourist information office. The three most significant meetings of the Council of Trent – convened to confront the growth of Protestantism and to establish the so-called Counter-Reformation – took place in the **Duomo** between 1545 and 1563. The building itself was begun in the thirteenth century, but wasn't completed until the sixteenth. Inside, the arched, colonnaded steps flanking the nave are a dramatic touch to an otherwise plain building. There are fresco fragments in the nave and an enormous carved marble baldachin over the altar – a replica of the one in St Peter's, Rome – although the most interesting part lies under the church, where a medieval crypt and foundations of an early Christian basilica (built over the tomb of St Vigilio, the third bishop of Trento) were discovered in 1977.

In the late 1970s, excavations uncovered the remains of an early Christian Basilica. The neighbouring **Museo Diocesano Tridentino e Basilica Paleocristiana** (Mon–Sat 9am–noon & 2–5.30pm; €3), housed in the Palazzo Pretorio, includes large annotated paintings of the sessions of the Council of Trent and some carved altarpieces from the church of San Zeno in the Val di Non. Hidden away in cell-like side rooms are some ornate reliquaries and an impressive cycle of fifteenth-century Flemish tapestries. The building is appealing in itself, too, with its fishtail battlements and heavy studded doors and a view from the upper floor of the frescoed palaces around the square.

The most powerful of the Trento princes was Bernardo Clesio, who in the late fifteenth and early sixteenth centuries built up much of the town's art collection, a good proportion of which is held in the **Castello del Buonconsiglio** (Tues–Sat 10am–6pm; €5), another venue of the Council of Trent, a short walk from Piazza Duomo on the eastern side of the town centre. It's two castles really: the thirteenth-century **Castelvecchio** and the extension built in 1530 called the **Magno Palazzo**, in which several rooms frescoed with classical subjects by the Dossi Family and Romanino lead off a quiet inner courtyard. Upstairs is the **Museo Provinciale d'Arte**, whose highlight is the *Ciclo dei Mesi* ("Cycle of the Months"), hidden at the end of a narrow passageway in the Torre d'Aquila (a tour of the *Ciclo* costs an extra €3). These frescoes, dating from 1400, show details from farming and courtly life and – reflecting the castle's role in the nineteenth century – soldiers confined to barracks; in a case of life imitating art, soldiers also added their own touches by scribbling on the borders and drawing in beards.

The ditch around the castle was the place of execution for two celebrated Trentese, Cesare Battisti and his comrade Fabio Filzi. Born in 1875, Battisti was a man of his times, a combination of romantic idealist and guerrilla fighter. He set up the socialist-irredentist newspaper *Il Popolo* as a forum for protest against Austrian rule, and used Italy's entry into World War I as an opportunity to step up his campaign to eject Austrian forces from the Tyrol. The stratagem was unsuccessful: in 1916 he led an attempt to take Monte Pasubio to the south of Trento, but he was arrested by the Austrians and shot as a traitor. You can visit his and Filzi's cells in the castle, as well as a small museum to the Risorgimento and Liberation of Trentino.

Eating, drinking and nightlife

You can **eat** well in Trento and the surrounding area, feasting on unfussy local specialities. Gourmands will appreciate the special four-course menus (around €30) at *Osteria a le due Spade* on Via Dom Archangelo Rizzi 11 (west of the duomo off Via G. Verdi), with sophisticated dishes to savour in a low-ceilinged, wood-panelled room. For about the same price, you can get marvellous local

---

Travelling the wine road

Wine enthusiasts are well catered for in Trentino, with a wine road (Strada di Vino or Südtiroler Weinstrasse) that enables you to indulge in a happy combination of sightseeing and **sampling local food and wine**. Head out of Trento on the trunk road to Bolzano, and take the right turning, signposted for Lavis, from where the wine road is clearly marked; Trento tourist office has a good guide to local grape types and wine producers.

The vines are often strung on wide pergolas, the traditional method of viticulture here since Roman times, which allows the breezes blowing up the Adige Valley from Lake Garda to circulate around the grapes, giving a beneficial cooling effect. Farmers and wine makers who are part of the agriturismo network advertise their establishments with a **yellow sign**: anything with a farm name and a knife and fork symbol is usually worth investigating. Often the owners will have converted a room in their farmhouse into a small informal restaurant, and will serve a set meal, accompanied by their own (or local) wine for around €10. Most of the goodies will be home-made: *nostra produzione* is the phrase to look out for, applied across the menu to anything from salami to sausages to goat's cheese. It helps to have a few words of Italian or German at your disposal so you can chat – you will probably be shown around the farm or cantina (winery) if you express an interest.

specialities in the restaurant attached to the *Albergo Accademia* at Vicolo Collico 6, off Piazza Santa Maria Maggiore (☎0461.981.580). Otherwise try the slightly less pricey *Chiesa*, on Via San Marco (closed Sun), with fish a speciality. At the budget end is *Due Giganti*, Via Simonino 14 (closed Sun), a good-value self-service chain, with all you can eat for €5.50. There are also a couple of good *rosticcerie* on Via Santa Croce, near the market, plus the lively *Pedavena* at Via Santa Croce 15 (closed Aug), which stays open until midnight and serves excellent, cheap Trentese dishes such as *canederli* and *strangolapreti* (spinach gnocchi). *Primavera*, at via Suffragio 92, is popular for inexpensive Italian standards and has outside seating under the arches.

Trento doesn't resound with **nightlife**, but there are a couple of good bars that stay open late. *Pub Stube*, at Via del Suffragio 51 (closed Sun), is the centre of the German-speaking scene, while inevitably, students head for one of the two Irish pubs, *Murphy's*, on Piazza Duomo, or the *Irish Pub* on Via G. Verdi. For **Internet access** try the good-value and friendly *Call Me*, Via Belezani 58.

Around Trento

Cable cars run from Ponte San Lorenzo, near Trento's bus station (every 15–30min; €0.80), to **SARDAGNA**, on the lower slopes of the towering Monte Bondone. There's some skiing in winter, and a scattering of holiday homes belonging mostly to Trentese; for committed **campers** there's *Camping Mezavia* (☎0461.948.178; June–Sept & Dec–April), two hours' trek from the top of the cable car. Also popular with locals are the resorts of **Lavarone** and **Folgaria** to the south, or **Pergine** to the west near **Lago di Caldonazzo**, where there is a free beach and lido (buses from Trento).

An enlightening half-day trip from the city (and reachable by local bus) is a visit to the **ethnographic museum** (Museo degli Usi e Costumi della Gente Trentina; Tues–Sat: summer 10am–12.30pm & 2.30–7pm; winter 9am–12.30pm & 2.30–6pm; €2.58) at **SAN MICHELE ALL'ADIGE**. One of the largest of its kind in Europe, with exhibits ranging from re-creations of village houses (complete with muddy boots drying by the stove) to displays on hunting, grazing and wine making, the museum gives a real flavour of what life in Trentino was like until the twentieth century.

The rail line south from Trento runs beneath the scree-covered slopes of the Adige Valley, where the only sight for miles might be a station platform in the middle of nowhere or the blank fortifications of a castle or World War I stronghold. Hanging on an outcrop above the village of **CALLIANO**, some way south of Trento, **Castel Beseno** is one of the few castles that have been restored and is open to the public (March–Oct Tues–Sun 9am–noon & 2–5.pm; Nov–Feb Tues–Sat 10am–6pm; ☎0464.846.000; €3.50). It's more of a fortified town than a castle in fact, spreading across the hilltop at the valley entrance and once providing a bulwark between the Venetians and the Tyrolese. A bloody but decisive battle was fought here in 1487, after which the Venetians gave up all hope of seizing Trentino at all. The castle is a twenty-minute walk from the village of **Besenello**, which is connected with Trento by bus. At weekends buses run all the way to the castle from Besenello's main piazza.

Monte Pasubio and Sentiero della Pace

Some of the bloodiest engagements of World War I took place around **Monte Pasubio**, to the southeast of Calliano. 460,000 lives were lost – many from the cold – and 947,000 were wounded on the Italian side alone. The recently created **Sentiero della Pace** ("Path of Peace") follows the front, from the Órtles mountains east across the ranges to Marmolada, the trail littered with old bullets and barbed wire. Tourist offices can provide free maps (Kompass, 1:50,000) of the entire route. The opposing armies dug fortresses in the rock and cut tunnels into the glaciers, but protection from enemy fire did not ensure safety – in the winter of 1916, one of the hardest in living memory, around 10,000 soldiers died in avalanches. The Campana dei Caduti, made out of melted-down cannon, tolls every evening in memory of the dead of both sides, from the Colle di Miravalle, a hill just outside the nearby town of Rovereto.

The Dolomiti di Brenta

The sawtoothed peaks and glaciers of the **Dolomiti di Brenta**, northwest of Trento, give these ranges a rougher character than the rest of the Dolomites, yet throughout you can choose your own level of walking. While steep, few peaks rise above 3000m, and the paths are easy to follow but strenuous, while less demanding trails circle the side valleys. The range is circled by a good slow road, the southern half of which passes through the quiet lake resort of **Malveno** before it is joined by the road from Trento. The circuit then turns north passing the frescoed churches and wooded valleys of the **Valle Rendena** before arriving at the main resort of **Madonna di Campiglio**, the best base for climbing, walking or skiing in the area. The northern half of the Brenta is bounded by **Val di Non** and **Val di Sole**, both served by the private Trento-Malé railway line and home to a smattering of castles and other sights.

Climbers come here for the towers of Cima Tosa and Cima Brenta, the original reason for *vie delle bochette* – iron ladders knocked into the rock to give access to these ascents; their position, clinging tenaciously to the rock walls, is sensational (see box on p.246 for more on these *vie ferrate*). There are enough regular, marked footpaths for two or three days' high-altitude walking; Kompass produce the best map for the area. Trento's tourist office has a free guide to the Dolomiti di Brenta in English.

Up the Valle Rendena

Buses from Trento to Madonna di Campiglio skirt Monte Bondone and wind their way past a series of patchy hills and villages, passing **Lago di Toblino**, just outside **VEZZANO**, where **Castel Toblino** – now a restaurant – sits on a spit of land jutting into the lake. The castle is steeped in the legend of a medieval love affair between one Claudia Particella and Carlo Emanuele Madruzzo, Prince-Bishop of Trento. The bishop apparently asked the pope, in vain, to allow him to leave the Church; undeterred, the two lovers returned to the castle, but one night, during a trip on the lake, they mysteriously drowned. Whether it was murder, accident or suicide is unknown. In the restaurant, a four-course meal is about €35, but there's also a lakeside bar selling beer, coffee and sandwiches for a fraction of the price.

From Lago di Toblino, the road continues west, turning into the **Valle Rendena** at Tione di Trento, where a more remote landscape of pasture and forest begins. This quiet valley is a good place to rest up, with a wonderfully eccentric roadside **hotel**, *Pub-Museum da Giorgio* (☎0465.321.541; ❷), at Iavré, 6km north of Tione, which the proprietor has packed with more than 5000 historical objects and curiosities including a collection of old keys and a watch that was recovered from the wreck of the Titanic. There are also a couple of small **campsites** reasonably close to villages; one of these is *Faè della Val*

Rendena (☎0465.507.178; June–Sept & Dec–April), north of Pinzolo, near **Sant'Antonio di Mavignola**.

Small churches like the lone Sant'Antonio, just before Borzago, are decorated with fresco cycles by Baschenis, one of the many Bergamasque artists who worked in the area. At **CARISOLO**, the church of **Santo Stefano** has frescoes of a *danse macabre* on an outside wall, and others inside depicting the legend of Charlemagne's passage through the Val di Campiglio on the way to his coronation in Rome. Before Madonna, several turnings off the main road lead high up west into the Adamello range, the most beautiful being the **Val di Genova**, which begins 2km from Carisolo. The road follows the cascading river up through a pine forest, along a deteriorating road past several waterfalls, spectacular in spring when the snow begins to melt. Most impressive is the **Cascata di Nárdis**, 4km from the turn-off, where several channels spill down the granite rock walls of the mountainside. Facing the waterfall is the *Albergo Cascate Nardis* (☎0465.501.454; ❷), with a restaurant; it's a good place to stop, though busy with day-trippers in summer. From here, it's another 13km to **BÉDOLE** (1614m), and a further two to three hours' hike from there along trail 212 to the *Rifugio Città di Trento* (☎0465.501.193; open April & June–Sept) at 2480m, within reach of the Adamello glaciers.

A short way before Carisolo, at **CADERZONE**, a turning off the Valle Rendena follows a much less trodden trail (221) which heads steeply up to the small lakes of **San Giuliano** and **Garzone** (two-and-a-half hours' walk). There's a small, very basic refuge between the two, and a second path (230) heads north then descends to the ski village of **PINZOLO** (two hours' descent). It's much smaller than its neighbour Madonna di Campiglio (ski-lift passes cover both resorts), but well worth a look for its church of San Vigilio, decorated with another sixteenth-century fresco of the *danse macabre* by Simone Baschenis.

Madonna di Campiglio

The major village in the Valle Rendena is **MADONNA DI CAMPIGLIO**, an upmarket ski resort with plenty of chair lifts and runs for all levels of skiing. About nine **buses** a day run from Trento to the main square, not far from the **tourist office** on Via Pradalago 4 (Mon–Sat 9am–noon & 3–6.30pm, Sun 9am–noon; ☎0465.442.000). Another service runs at about the same frequency to Malé, 23km north, from where you can pick up trains back to Trento. In summer, the climbing and walking in the Dolomiti di Brenta are superb, and you may want to stay at Madonna, if only to reach the trailheads. Luckily, out of the skiing season, the village tends to be deserted except for a sprinkling of walkers, and there are often good off-season deals to be had in three-star **hotels**. A decent, central place is *La Montanara* (☎0465.441.105; ⓦwww.lamontanara.it; ❺), though the least expensive places in town are a few minutes' walk down via Vallesina – follow the yellow signs for the *Rifugio Vallesinella*; try the *Garni Bucaneve* (☎0465.441.271; ❺), the *Garni dei Fiori* (☎0465.442.310; ❺) and the *Norma* (☎0465.441.110; ❻).

The best way to approach the trailheads is by cable car from **Carlo Magno**, 3km north of the village centre, to Grostè (mid-June to mid-Sept daily 8.30am–12.30pm & 2–5pm; €8 one way, €13 return) – see below. Another possibility is to head west, taking Funivia Cinque Laghi (July to mid-Sept, same times and prices as above) from the centre of town to *Rifugio Pancugolo* (☎0465.443.270; no accommodation) at 2064m, in the Presanella group. From the refuge, paths include a five-hour route via **Lago Ritorto** and **Lago Gelato** back down to the valley.

Trails from Grostè

Once you're at **GROSTÈ** (2437m) you can plan your own routes as long as you have a decent hiking map, such as the one produced by Kompass. By the cable-car terminus is the *Rifugio Graffer*, at 2262m (℡0465.441.358; June 20 to Sept 20 & Dec–April). It is close to the trails and has overnight accommodation and a restaurant. From the cable-car station, trail 316 sets out across boulder-strewn slopes towards refuges *Sella* and *Tuckett* (both ℡0465.507.287; June–Sept), about 5km (1hr 30min) away, where you can eat a large meal and bask on the veranda, thousands of feet above the valley.

Trail 328, which later becomes 318 (called the Sentiero Bogani), starts just past the refuges; there are difficult boulders to negotiate at first, but then there's an easy path which has been blasted out of the side of the rock walls. A shrine in a small overhang commemorates the lives lost in these peaks, but by this time, about four hours from Grostè, the *Rifugio Brentei* (℡0465.441.244; June–Sept), set at 2176m, is in sight, midway between Cima Brenta and Cima Tosa. There are some difficult ascents a short distance from the refuge, but it's more than likely that by this stage you won't be capable of anything other than staring across the vast ravine at the Adamello glaciers in the distance. Next day, if you can cope with snowfields, you could either trek up to the **Bocca di Brenta** and cross over the ridge to meet trail 319 down to Molveno (see below; 3hr 30min), or simply return to Madonna via trails 318 and 316 (3hr 30min).

Molveno

The lakeside village of **MOLVENO**, surrounded by the peaks of the Brenta Alta, is a marginally cheaper place to stay than Madonna. Although the cheapest places go quickly, particularly in high season, the **tourist office** here, above the lake in the small town centre, at Piazza Marconi 5 (Mon–Sat 9am–12.30pm & 3–6.30pm, Sun 9.30am–12.30pm; ℡0461.586.086, ⓦwww.dolomitimolveno.com) should be able to help you find a **room** for the night. *Albergo Italia* (℡0461.586.915; ❻) and the plainer *Garni Alpenrose*, just back from the campsite (℡0461.586.169; ❹), are both on Via Lungolago, with views of the lake. Failing these, there's a swish **campsite**, *Campeggio Spiaggia Lago di Molveno* (℡0461.586.978), on the water's edge, with a restaurant, bar and shop.

There are few **easy trails** from Molveno into the Brenta massif – paths often disappear into nothing but *vie ferrate* across the rocks; fortunately these are all marked on maps, so you just need to plan your route carefully. If you decide to approach the Brenta group from this side, a cable car runs from the village to **Pradel** (1500m), where there's an albergo, *Rifugio Pradel* (June–Sept; ℡0461.586.903), and from where trails lead through the beeches and pines of the **Val delle Seghe** in the shadow of Croz dell'Altissimo (2339m). An easy circular route winds back to Molveno (2hr 30min), or technically more demanding paths take you higher up, past *Rifugio Tosa* at 2439m, and *Rifugio Tommaso Pedrotti* at 2491m (both June–Sept; ℡0461.948.115).

The most prodigious of nineteenth-century climbers, Francis Fox Tuckett, opened up a difficult new route to Cima Brenta from Molveno, now known as the **Bochetta di Tuckett**. As ice axes hadn't been invented, he negotiated snowfields with a ladder and alpenstock, and carried joints of meat and bottles of wine for mountaintop breakfasts. The landscape where he "roamed amongst toppling rocks, and spires of white and brown and bronze coloured stone" is almost unchanged but for the *bochetta*, descending from the pass down to the *Tuckett* and *Sella* refuges (see above). More paths skirt Cima Tosa and lead to

Pinzolo via *Rifugio Dodici Apostoli* (June–Sept, ☎0465.501.309), a stone-built refuge for the hardy set at 2498m, with only cold water to wash in.

From Molveno, the road follows the lake south, then descends down to **Ponte Arche**, where you can pick up buses on the Madonna–Trento route. It's a beautiful trip through a valley which hasn't benefited from, or been blighted by, ski tourism, but there are only two buses daily.

East of Trento

To the **east of Trento**, the **Valsugana** and the **Val di Fiemme** are joined by road, making a wide loop. Halfway around, a group of stunning pinnacles and bare peaks called the **Pale di San Martino** appears: formed as a coral reef sixty million years ago, their rock is so pale it glares even at dawn. It is now incorporated in the **Parco Naturale Panevéggio**, a gentler, wooded area with many walks, trails and campsites. The nearest resort to the Pale is **San Martino di Castrozzo**, the terminus for buses travelling the loop in both directions.

Valsugana

Most people take the bus along the **Valsugana** to get to a market in one of its modern and busy towns, such as Caldonazzo. There's nothing to see between the towns except rows of fruit trees and vineyards, and later, as the Brenta Valley closes in to become a narrow gorge, a succession of hydroelectric plants. What makes the trip interesting is the terrain to the north, in particular the **Cima d'Asta**, a mountain dotted with bright-blue, icy tarns and crossed by the Sentiero della Pace ("Path of Peace", see p.250). You reach the westerly part of this from **Panarotta**, in the mountains above Lago di Caldonazzo, from where the trail – at this point an ancient ridgeway path and wartime patrol route – follows a course across the peaks towards Passo di Rolle (see "Parco Naturale Panevéggio", p.256).

If you're travelling by public transport from Trento to San Martino di Castrozza you have no choice but to go the long way round, via Fonzaso in the Veneto; most services head east by **train** from Trento to Primolano, where you have to change for the **bus** on to San Martino. By **car**, though, there's a short cut if you turn off at Borgo Valsugana and cut through the foothills, climbing through an increasingly Alpine landscape to rejoin the main road at Imer.

Imer, Mezzano and Fiera di Primiero

IMER and, a couple of kilometres east, **MEZZANO** are archetypal tourist villages, decked out with geraniums and credit-card stickers, attracting people by the busload, but away from the main roads you can easily escape the crowds. The valley itself is wide, with hay meadows spreading either side, and, outside from the main tourist centres, makes a good place to rest up, with easy paths running into the foothills. One possibility is the path east from Imer along the lush **Val Noana** to the reservoir under the slopes of Monte Pavione (a 3hr 30min round trip). As far as **accommodation** goes, self-sufficiency is an advantage, as you'll be competing with bus tours for the cheap hotels. An alternative to Alpine-style hotels in the villages is *Camping Calavise*, a (well-signposted) couple of kilometres off the main valley road which has a bar and playground (☎0439.67.468) or, further up the valley, *Rifugio Fonteghi*

(☎0439.67.043), a forty-five-minute walk along the path on the south side of the reservoir.

About 4km further on from Imer, **FIERA DI PRIMIERO** is a larger resort and market town with a tourist office (Mon–Sat 9am–noon & 3–7pm, Sun 9.30am–12.30pm and 4.15–7pm; ☎0439.62.407). It's a major crossroads in the area, from where buses run up to the beginning of the Val Canali and to Passo Cereda (1369m). The mountains around Fiera were worked for silver from the thirteenth century, and local miners paid for the town's fifteenth-century church. Now the ranges are crossed by hiking trails.

Trails to the north of Passo Cereda take you up into the high plateau of the **Pale di San Martino**. One path follows a long ridge of rock before passing down into **Val Canali**, described by Amelia Edwards in the nineteenth century as the most "lonely, desolate and tremendous scene . . . to be found this side of the Andes". Things have changed since the arrival of Alta Via 2 – followed by a bar, visitor centre, refuge and campsite – but the valley retains a feeling of isolation. The official campsite, the *Castelpietra* (☎0439.62.426, Ⓦwww.castelpietra.it; June–Sept), is opposite the National Park centre, and there are further places to camp at the head of the glen. *Rifugio Treviso* (☎0439.62.311; end of June–Sept) is a possible overnight stop, while the more luxurious *Cant del Gal* (☎0439.62.997; ❸), further down the valley, also has a good restaurant specializing in game and wild mushrooms, though it's fairly expensive.

A stiff ascent from *Rifugio Treviso* brings you onto the **Altopiano delle Pale** at Passo di Pradidali, where eagles can be seen circling above the barren plateau and the silence is broken every so often by a trickle of falling stones. Once you are at this altitude, there are many possibilities for linking up with other trails across the stark upland; local tourist offices publish a useful 1:35,000 map which shows the various paths, though you shouldn't rely on it for navigation. *Rifugio Pedrotti alla Rosetta* (☎0439.683.008; June–Sept), at 2581m, is the nearest place with accommodation (a 2hr 30min hike north); facilities include cold-water washbasins, a restaurant and bar. The rifugio is also the base of the Orizzonti Trentini alpine guides (see "Vie ferrate" box on p.246).

San Martino di Castrozza and around

The road into **SAN MARTINO DI CASTROZZA** twists and turns, and you feel like you're in the middle of nowhere until the resort's new hotels appear around the corner; the sensation is even more marked if you're heading up over the Passo di Rolle (see p.256). After Cortina d'Ampezzo, San Martino is one of the smarter Dolomite resorts, but it has a more relaxed atmosphere in its cafés and a less pretentious way of going about things. The **tourist office**, next to the bus stop, at Via Passo Rolle 165 (Mon–Sat 9am–noon & 3–7pm, Sun 9.30am–12.30pm & 4.15–7.30pm; ☎0439.768.867, Ⓦwww.sanmartino .com) may be able to help with finding a cheapish **room**. Otherwise, try the *Biancaneve* (☎0439.68.135; ❸) or the slightly more expensive *Suisse* (☎0439.68.087; ❸); both are on Via Dolomiti, which runs off the main square just up from the tourist office. The alternative is to pitch a tent at the village **campsite**, *Sass Maòr* (☎0439.68.347), about 1km from the centre. Heading out of San Martino, **buses** south to Fiera di Primiero and Imer run at least hourly. The service north over the Passo di Rolle runs less often, but you can count on at least six daily for much of the summer.

A number of **trails**, chair lifts and cable cars head off into the mountains, making San Martino one of the best bases in the area. The strongest attraction is again the **Pale di San Martino**; a cable-car ride from San Martino (daily 8am–5pm; journey up €9, down €8, return-trip €15) takes you up to *Rifugio Pedrotti alla Rosetta*, perched on the edge of the Altopiano – see p.255 for details. The Colverde cable car from the village runs to the foot of the Pale, from where the Rosetta cable car takes you up to the highland.

Up on the summits, even in the summer, you should be prepared for snow, wind and rain – as well as scorching sun and the most stupendous views. From the chair-lift terminus, you can make for *Rifugio Pradidali* at 2278m (☎0439.64.180), a walk and descent of three hours. A more ambitious walk would be to continue on from the refuge over the **Passo di Ball**, returning from there to San Martino or descending over into **Val Canali** at *Rifugio Cant del Gal* (see p.255). If you prefer the relative security of a guided trek, ask at the desk of the Gruppo Guide Alpine (daily 5.30–7.30pm; ☎0439.768.795), in the same building as the tourist office; they run graded excursions most days in July and August.

Parco Naturale Panevéggio

Out of San Martino, traffic files up to **Passo di Rolle**, a beautiful stretch of high moorland dotted with avalanche breaks and a few sheep. There are only two buses a day, so a car really helps here. At the pass, a chair lift takes you up to Baita Segantini, a log-cabin bar from where you can see **Cimon della Pala**'s summit. It takes thirty minutes or so to walk back down to the pass, where there are several more bars and restaurants.

The Passo di Rolle falls within the **Parco Naturale Panevéggio** (🌐www.parcopan.org), an area of firs, rowan and larch that once provided timber for the Venetian fleet and wood for Stradivarius violins. Skirted by nature trails, there are three **visitors' centres** (summer daily 9am–12.30pm & 3–7pm; winter Sat & Sun 9am–12.30pm & 2–6pm; ☎0439.648.54; €1.70), 7km on from the pass, outside **PANEVÉGGIO** village, with excellent displays on the wildlife of the area and offering guided walks into the forest (€2.50). In the remoter parts of the park you might catch a glimpse of white alpine hare or marmot – a creature resembling a large guinea pig, which stands up on its hind legs to act as sentinel for the burrow and emits a distinctive screech. After a few days trekking in the Pale, you may want to take it easy, and Panevéggio's fields are good for sunbathing and sleep. There's an unusually pleasant **camping area** next to Lago Panevéggio, though the atmosphere is spoiled when the lake is dry. The entrance is at the end of the track marked "Area della Sosta", just past the village; facilities are minimal and stays are limited to 24 hours. There's a proper campsite, *Bellamonte* (☎0462.576.119), 4km down the road to Predazzo (see below).

Val di Fiemme

Once you're out of the confines of the park, **PREDAZZO** is the first town you come to in the **Val di Fiemme**, at the turn-off for the Val di Fassa. The town itself has become something of a pilgrimage site for geologists, owing to the extensive collection of local rocks and fossils in the newly enlarged **Museo Civico** (closed at the time of writing but due to reopen in late 2003) on Piazza Santi Filippo e Giacomo. Surprisingly accessible to non-experts, the displays include samples of the Dolomitic calcite rock first identified by, and named after, the French mineralogist Dieudonné Sylvain Guy Tancrède de Gratet de Dolomieu.

Predazzo is a useful point to overnight, and **bus** connections to Trento and Bolzano are reasonable. A good **hotel** is the *Maria* (℡0462.501.203; may insist on half-board; ❺), five minutes' walk from the centre on the main Corso Dolomiti. *Camping Villa Verde* (℡0462.502.394) is a thirty-minute walk east, from the central bus station, but has spectacular views, and facilities include a restaurant and shop.

Throughout the valley, hotel hoardings are ubiquitous, and even the tiniest villages hereabouts have a plan of the mountain ranges with chair lifts marked, but behind the modern Dolomites tourist industry, this is an ancient region that from the twelfth to the seventeenth centuries was virtually autonomous. A local parliament met at the *Banco de la reson*, a circle of stone benches surrounded by trees in **CAVALESE**, the next town along, and the Magnifica Comunità of Cavalese is still relatively powerful, administering extensive communal land. A short way beyond the town centre, on the road to Tésero, is a small **tourist office** (Mon–Sat 9am–noon & 3.30–7pm; July & Aug also Sun 9am–noon) which can arrange visits to the medieval **Palazzo della Comunità**. This was the Bishop of Trento's summer palace, and now houses a small **museum and gallery** (guided tours only; July & Aug daily 4.30, 5.30 and 6.30pm; rest of year for hours contact the tourist office; free). Wood-panelled rooms redolent of sawdust and polish, with fine wooden ceilings and painted friezes, contain the original valley statutes, together with some unremarkable paintings by local seventeenth-century artists. The building's lack of fortifications indicates that Trento's bishop felt safe from the armed rebellions that had plagued him in the city, and its exterior is covered in frescoes depicting St Virgilio (Trento's patron saint) enthroned in the centre of a trompe l'oeil pediment.

Many people pause at Cavalese simply to stroll the cobbled streets, grazing at some of the cake and ice cream shops, or to take the cable car up to the **Catena dei Lagorai**. This mountain chain, concealing a string of lakes, is accessible on foot from any of the small villages along the main road. There was a tragic accident here in February 1998, in which a number of skiiers were killed when a low-flying US airforce aeroplane sliced through the wires of their cable-car; the lift has since re-opened (July, Aug & Dec–Easter; €12.50 return). Leisurely day-trips are feasible, but if you feel inspired once you're up on the ridges, either follow the paths towards Passo di Rolle, or go west. A day or two of walking west (via refuges) brings you to the Val dei Mócheni, which was colonized in medieval times by German farmers travelling south, and has kept its own language and Gothic script. The first farmers were joined later by speculators searching for the rich seams of copper and silver which lay in the mountains. For somewhere to **stay**, head for the recently refitted *Laurino* (℡0462.340.151; ❹) in Cavalese.

TÉSERO, 4km from Cavalese on the higher road, is, for most people, simply a staging post on their way to the mountains. The town's only attraction is the parish church, frescoed with *Cristo della Domenica* (Christ of the Sabbath) and symbols of everything banned on a Sunday.

The Catinaccio and Gruppo di Sella

North of Predazzo, the Val di Fassa penetrates deep into the western Dolomites, passing through one of the heartlands of **Ladino** culture (see box on p.260). Access to the famously roseate peaks of the **Catinaccio** (Rosengarten) range is simple enough from **Vigo di Fassa**, the valley's main resort. The area is popular with German walkers, drawn to the dramatic serrated peaks, but once you're above the whine of the cable cars there's plenty of wilderness to lose yourself in.

At the head of the Val di Fass, **Canazei** makes a good springboard for the high plateaus of the **Gruppo di Sella**, and the gentler trail of the **Viel del Pan**, which leads down to the tiny resort of **Arabba**. On the northern side of the Sella group, **Corvara** is a much larger resort with a sizeable Ladino population.

Catinaccio

The long belt of sheer rock walls and towers which makes up the **Catinaccio** (**Rosengarten**) range is an awesome sight, described by local judge and nineteenth-century writer Theodor Christomannos as a "gigantic fortification. . . the gate into the kingdom of immortal ghosts, of high-flying giants". Rosengarten gets its German name from the roses that legend says used to grow here. King Laurino, saddened when his daughter married and left him alone, put a spell on the roses so that no one would see them again by day or night, but forgot to include dawn and dusk in his curse, which is when the low sun gives the rock a roseate glow.

The trails across the range cater for all levels of hiking ability, but the going gets tough on the ridges, from where you can see as far as the Stubaier Alps, on the border with Austria. The most popular approach to Catinaccio is from **VIGO DI FASSA**, a bus stop on the Trento–Canazei route with a few three-star **hotels**; try the *Renato*, via Solar 15 (☎0462.764.006; ⓦwww.hotelrenato.it, ❻), with a pool and many rooms with balconies; the *Gambrinus* (☎0462.764.159; ❺) which has a sauna and runs guided walks; or the slightly more luxurious *Vael* (☎0462.764.110, ⓦwww.vael.it, ❼). Alternatively, there's the *Rifugio Roda de Vael* (☎0462.764.450; June–Sept), a ninety-minute walk away from the village along trails 547 and 545.

The trek to **Torri del Vájiolet** from Vigo di Fassa is the preferred route up onto the range; the cable car from the village to *Rifugio Ciampedie* (☎0462 .764.432; mid-June to mid-Oct) covers most of the ascent; a well-beaten trail leads from the terminus through the woods to the basic *Rifugio Gardeccia* (☎0462.763.152; mid-June to mid-Oct). From here it's a steep walk up to a refuge under the Torri, although the severity of the ascent doesn't discourage hordes of summer Sunday walkers. A stiff zigzagging climb from here brings you to *Rifugio Re Alberto* (☎0462.763.428; June–Sept), three hours from *Rifugio Ciampedie*; there's also alternative accommodation nearby at the *Rifugio Passo Santner* (☎0471.642.230; June–Sept) or the *Rifugio Vájiolet* (☎0462.763.292; mid-June to Sept).

Paths lead **south** across the range and eventually down to Passo di Costalunga and the Lago di Carezza, a beautiful little lake reflecting the peaks of the Latemar range, from where you can catch a bus to Bolzano. There are more choices to the **north**, where there are a number of trails onto Monte Sciliar (Schlern), with variations in height of no more than around 500m. *Rifugio Bolzano-Schlern* (☎0471.612.024; June–Sept), near the summit of Monte Sciliar, is a good two days' trek from *Rifugio Re Alberto*; you can stop overnight at *Rifugio Alpe di Tires* (*Tierser Alplhütte*; ☎0471.727.958), in between the two. From Sciliar, paths descend onto the wetland plateau of the Alpe di Siusi (see p.271).

For a change of pace, head to the **Museo Instituto Culturale Ladino** (Mon–Fri 3–7pm; €3) for an excellent introduction to Ladino culture (see box on p.260). Located in a renovated hayloft next to the parsonage of the parish

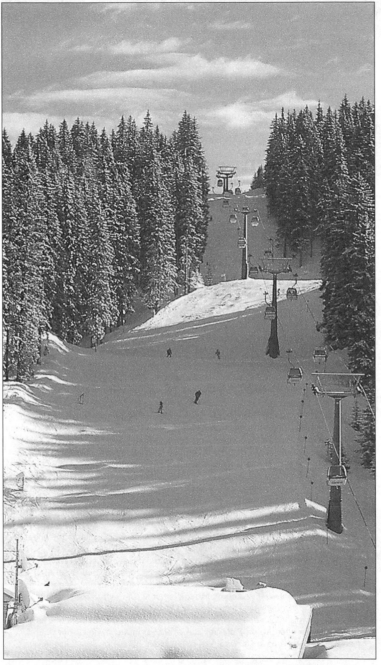

△Madonna di Campiglio

church of San Giovanni, the tiny village next to Vigo di Fassa (within walking distance), the museum has intriguing exhibits on the myths and rites of the Ladini.

Canazei

CANAZEI is a relatively modern town at the head of the Val di Fassa and, for the area, a buzzing summer and winter resort. It's from there that you head for the high passes – the **Gruppo di Sella** for hard trails, or the easier **Viel del Pan**, opposite Marmolada. The Sella Ronda Card entitles you to use of a selection of lifts and public transport (buses run by the SAD company) around the Gruppo di Sella and is available at ski lifts for €16. Canazei itself makes a good base to **stay**: *La Zondra* (☎0462.601.233; ❹), with balconied rooms, and the *Ciamorc* (☎0462.602.426; ❷) are both on Via Pareda, while the *Giardino delle Rose* (☎0462.602.221; ❷) and *Albergo Centrale* (☎0462.602.340; ❸) are pleasantly located on via Dolomiti, in the middle of the village; *Villa Ester* (☎0462.601.254; ❹) is also centrally located, next to the swimming pool. From Canazei a switchback road (of 27 bends) climbs relentlessly for 12km and is often busy with busloads of tourists heading for the scenic Great Dolomites Road (see p.276) and determined cyclists making the thousand-metre ascent.

Halfway up the switchback road out of Canazei, the cable car at Pradel leads to **Passo Sella** (2240m), one of the most impressive of the Dolomite passes.

Ladino country

The meeting-point of Trentino, Alto Adige and the Veneto is home to a distinct cultural group, the **Ladini**. Their language, Ladin, was once spoken over a wide area, from Austria down to the River Po (in what's now Emilia-Romagna), but now survives only in a few valleys in the Dolomites, and in Swiss Engadine, preserved by the relative remoteness of the mountainous territory. There are around 40,000 speakers, but Ladin is especially prevalent in the area around the Sella group – the Val di Fassa, the Val Badia, the Val Gardena and Livinallongo.

The history of the Ladini is recorded in their epics, which recount tales of battles, treachery and reversals of fortune. Around 4000 AD, the Ladini were constantly threatened with invasion by Germanic tribes from the north and others from the Po Valley. Christianity later emerged as a major threat, but the Ladini absorbed and transformed the new religion, investing the new saints with the powers of more ancient female divinities. The rudimentary Castello di Thurn at San Martino di Badia, a bleak outpost of the bishop-princes of Bressanone, is testimony to the Church's attempt to keep the Val di Badia under its control. In 1452, Bishop Nicolo Cusano railed against a woman from the Val di Fassa who said she had met the goddess Diana in the woods, and there was a strong pagan undercurrent to the cult of Santa Giuliana, whose sword-wielding image is painted on the plaster of houses in the Fassa and Badia valleys.

The Cësa di Ladins, in **Ortisei** (see p.271), and the Museo Instituto Culturale Ladino, near **Vigo di Fassa** (see previous page), are excellent places to find out more. Meanwhile, villages in the area around Vigo contain sections of the museum devoted to working life in Ladino country (mid-June to mid-Sept Mon–Sat 8.30am–noon & 3.30–7pm; outside season call tourist information in Vigo di Fassa ☎0462.764.093, ⓦwww.fassa.com). **Moena** is home to a restored nineteenth-century cooperage (*Botega da Pinter*) at Via Dolomiti 3; **Pera di Fassa** houses a restored watermill (*Molin de Pezol*) at Via Jumela 6; and a working, antique sawmill (*La Sia*) can be seen at Via Pian Trevisan at Penia, just outside **Canazei**. Tourist offices, notably the one in **Corvara** (see p.262), have details of occasional festivals, exhibitions and events.

Paths climb from here onto the jagged peaks of the **Sasso Lungo** (Langkofel) and follow the ridges down onto the Alpe di Siusi. Even up on the summits, saxifrage grows between cracks in the rock, and the silence is broken only by the occasional buzzing of a beetle. It takes two days to walk from the Sella pass, via *Rifugio Vicenza* (☎0471.792.323; June–Sept), into the Val Gardena (Grödnertal), where there are buses to Bolzano.

Just past Pradel the road forks. The right-hand turning takes you up to **Passo Pordoi** (2242m), an astonishing vantage point between the Gruppo di Sella and Marmolada – at 3246m the highest Dolomite, its rounded peak permanently shrouded by a glacier. From here, peaks radiate in every direction, giving you a chance to identify the distinctive shapes of each of the main Dolomite ranges. In the foreground, the Sasso Lungo mountains look like a jagged, gloved hand, flanked by two prominent peaks; the Gruppo di Sella is squat and chunky; and Scilar (Schlern), just visible in the distance, comprises a flat rocky tabletop, culminating in two peaks. A small road winds downwards to Passo Folzarego, and ultimately Cortina d'Ampezzo, but Passo Pordoi itself is where many of the trails start. It's also another occasion for joining Alta Via 2, which dips down to the main road here. Most of the tourist buses stop at this point, and a collection of cafés and stalls have taken advantage of their location around the trailheads to charge rather inflated prices; the **hotels** here may insist on half-board; try the *Pordoi* (☎0462.601.115; ❻).

The Gruppo di Sella

The **Gruppo di Sella** lies to the north of Passo Pordoi and resembles a lunar landscape, with an arid plateau surrounded by pink, dolomitic peaks and crisscrossed by many fairly difficult trails. For less confident walkers, there's a choice of two less demanding paths: either stick to the Alta Via 2, which crosses from one edge of the massif to the other, or break away at Sass de Mesdi, from where a trail circles down to the Sella pass. Both routes take a couple of days, with overnight stops at *Rifugio Cavazza* (*Pisciaduhütte*; ☎0471.836.292; July–Sept) or *Rifugio Boè* (*Boè Hütte*; ☎0471.847.303; June–Sept). The Gruppo di Sella is an excellent place to walk, with views across the ranges down to Passo Gardena (Sellajoch, 2137m), from where Corvara and the Val Badia are within striking distance, as are the Odle (Geisler) group across the valley. There are bus services to Sella Ronda, and you can also pick up buses to Bolzano from **Selva**, 11km away in the Val Gardena.

Viel del Pan

Some much less ambitious walking can be undertaken from Passo Pordoi, starting just past the *Albergo Savoia*, again following the route of Alta Via 2 but in the opposite direction. A narrow path cut into the turf traverses the mountainside opposite Marmolada, where Austrian battalions hid under the glacier in 8km of gallery during World War I. Even if you're not a great walker, a twenty-minute stroll along this easy trail is worthwhile for the views of the Dolomites, which are far better than those from the road.

From the seventeenth century this path was on the grain-smuggling route called the **Viel del Pan** ("trail of bread" in Venetian dialect), and it remained busy enough in the nineteenth century for the Guardia di Finanza to set up armed patrols along it. The contrast between the glacier on Marmolada and the peaks of the Sella group – 360 degrees of mountain – is superb. The path descends to **Lago Fedaia**, from where there are irregular buses in summer back to Canazei. The *Rifugio Marmolada Castiglioni* (☎0462.601.117) is on the edge of the reservoir. On the northern side of the ridge lies **ARABBA**, a small resort with family-run hotels in the centre and scattered in the peaceful pastures around, from where a cable-car system runs up to the Dolomites. For somewhere to **stay**, the *Albergo Posta* (℡0436.79.105; ❸) is basic but central and ageing gracefully, while the *Garni Emma* (℡0436.79.116; ❸) has a family atmosphere and sits beside a small stream. The larger, more professional *Pensione Marilena* (℡0436.79.128; ❸) is right at the foot of the cable car. The only bus service from here is the one that goes from Belluno to Corvara.

Corvara

The central town of the Ladini (see box on p.260), **CORVARA** is primarily a ski resort, and the most visible sign of the language is a page or two in Ladino in local newspapers. Corvara also makes a good base for the excellent trails of the nearby Fánes Park, a bus ride away, where most of the Ladini legends are based. The **tourist office** at Strada Col Alp 36 (Mon–Sat 8am–noon & 3–7pm, Sun 10am–noon & 4–6pm; ℡0471.836.176) has details of **hotels and rooms** in private houses. The *Monti Pallidi* (℡0471.836.081; ❸), Strada Col Alp 75, is good value, as is the *Laura* (℡0471.836.340; ❷), at no. 44, round the corner, opposite the church. There's also a **campsite**, *Camping Colfosco* (*Colfuschg*; ℡0471.836.515; June–Sept & Dec–Easter). A few buses leave for Brunico and Belluno from outside the tourist office.

Bolzano (Bozen)

Situated on the junction of the rivers Talvera (Talfer) and Isarco (Eisack) near the southern limit of the province, **BOLZANO** (BOZEN) is Alto Adige's chief town. For centuries a valley market town and way station, Bolzano's fortunes in the Middle Ages vacillated as the Counts of Tyrol and the Bishops of Trento competed for power. The town passed to the Habsburgs in the fourteenth century, then at the turn of the nineteenth century Bavaria took control, opposed by Tyrolese patriot and military leader Andreas Hofer. His battle in 1809 to keep the Tyrol under Austrian rule was only temporarily successful, as in the same year the Austrian Emperor ceded the Tyrol to the Napoleonic kingdom of Italy. More changes followed, as Bolzano was handed back to Austria until after World War I, whereupon it passed, like the rest of the province, to Italy. Nowadays, in both winter and summer, the town is a busy tourist resort, and its pavement cafés and generally relaxed pace of life make it a good, if uneventful, place to rest up or use as a base for trips into the mountains. An unmissable pleasure is the local wine: Bolzano is at the head of the wine road (Strada di Vino/Südtiroler Weinstrasse; see box on p.249), which runs south to the border with Trentino, and it's especially well known for its Chardonnay.

Arrival, information and accommodation

Bolzano's **bus station**, centrally placed at Via Perathoner 4, serves most of the small villages and resorts in the province; the **train station** is a few minutes' walk south of here through the park down via Stazione. There is a city **tourist office** at Piazza Walther 8 (Mon–Fri 9am–6.30pm, Sat 9am–12.30pm; ℡0471.307.001, ⓦwww.bolzano-bozen.it), and a **regional office** just off the square at Piazza Parrochia 11/12 (Mon–Thurs 8.30am–1pm & 3–6.30pm, Fri 8.30am–2.30pm; ℡0471.307.040). Their "Alpine Desk" (Mon–Fri 9am–noon

Cable car to Colle ▼

& 2–5pm; ☎0471.473.809) has information on weather conditions and advisability of routes. The Club Alpino Italiano at Piazza Erbe 46 (daily except Sat 11am–noon & 5–7pm; ☎0471.978.172), on the top end of the square, is also a good source of local hiking information. The best place for Internet access is *Vecchia Bolzano*, via Isarco 19, a pub popular with teenagers, opposite the Duomo.

The best budget **accommodation** is rooms to rent; you can get a list from the tourist office. Alternatively try *Kolpinghaus*, Via Ospedale 3, off Piazza Walther (☎0471.308.400, ☏0471.973.917, ⓦwww.kolping.it/bz; ❹), an imposing religious-run residence with single and double rooms, while the *Croce Bianca* on Piazza del Grano (*Weisses Kreuz*; ☎0471.977.552; ❷) is a more conventional cheap albergo. Convenient for transport, but characterless, are the inexpensive *Hotel Adria*, Via Perathoner 17 (☎0471.975.735, ⓦwww.sudtirol .com/adria; ❹), immediately opposite the bus station, and *Hotel Regina*, opposite the train station on Via Renon (☎0471.972.195, ☏0471.978.944, ⓦwww.hotelreginabz.it; ❺). For luxury, head for the *Parkhotel Laurin*, Via Laurin 4 (☎0471.311.000, ⓦwww.laurin.it; ❽), with a restaurant, garden and swimming pool. One way of escaping the summer humidity is to stay in the hills above town at Colle (Kohlern), reached by a ten-minute cable car (€2.70) from Via Campiglio, itself a twenty-minute walk from the train sttation. The *Klaushof*, Colle 14 (☎0471.329.999; ❷), is one of several hotels on the same road. The tourist office has details of rooms to let in farmhouses and in a few private houses in town. For **campers**, the *Moosbauer* site (☎0471.918.492) is on the main Bolzano–Merano road.

The Town

Central Bolzano definitely looks like a part of the German-speaking world. Restaurants serve *speck*, *gulasch* and *knödel*, and bakers sell black bread and *sachertorte*. The centre of town is **Piazza Walther**, whose pavement cafés, around its statue of the *minnesinger* (troubadour) Walther von der Vogelweide, are the town's favoured meeting places. Converted into a cathedral as recently as 1964, the **Duomo** (Dom), on the edge of the square, resembles a parish church: built in the fourteenth and fifteenth centuries, and restored after being bombed in World War II, it has a striking green-and-yellow mosaic roof and elaborately carved spire. The fourteenth-century **Franciscan church** on Via dei Francescani is also worth seeking out, embellished with a carved wooden altarpiece by Hans Klocher and with elegant, frescoed cloisters from the same period.

A couple of streets west of Piazza Walther, on Via Cappuccini, the **Chiesa dei Domenicani** (Dominican monastery) has frescoes of fifteenth-century courtly life painted on the walls of the decaying cloisters, framed by a growth of stone tracery. The Cappella di San Giovanni, built at the beginning of the fourteenth century, retains frescoes by painters of the Giotto school, including a *Triumph of Death* underneath a starry vault. Follow the street north to **Piazza Erbe**, site of a daily fruit and vegetable market, from where the oriel windows and eleventh-century arcades of **Via Portici** lead off to the right.

On the west side of the old town stands one of Alto Adige's more important museums, the recently opened **Museo Archeologico** (Tues–Sun 10am–5pm, Thurs until 7pm, ⓦ www.iceman.it; €8), a ten-minute walk west of the centre at Via Museo (Museumstrasse) 43. Once the seat of the Austro-Hungarian National Bank, and then the Banco d'Italia, the building's four floors trace the region's history and developing culture from the end of the last Ice Age to the early Middle Ages, through exhibits, reconstructions, models and multimedia presentations. At the heart of the museum is the Iceman, nicknamed "Ötzi", the superbly preserved mummy of an early Copper Age male discovered in the ice of the Ötzaler Alps in 1991. Visitors can only view the mummy through a small window in a high-tech refrigeration unit; its preservation depends on remaining in an identical climate to the one in which it was discovered. At around 5300 years old, "Ötzi", his clothing, and his attendant possessions provide an unprecedented insight into the everyday culture of his time. What the museum won't tell you is that "Ötzi" was found by Austrians on the Italo-Austrian border; Italy only won custody after an unseemly legal battle with Austria in the 1990s.

Continuing westwards down Via Museo takes you to a pleasant park alongside the River Talvera (Talfer). Bolzano's German and Gothic quarter ends on the other side of the Ponte Talvera, where **Piazza della Vittoria** signals the edge of the Italian town, much of it laid out by Mussolini's favourite architect, Marcello Piacentini. The epic triumphal arch on the square was commissioned by Mussolini in 1928 and is something of a controversial monument. Until a recent clean-up it was covered with graffiti and surrounded by low railings, and was even bombed by German-speaking separatists in the late-1980s. The piazza is now the site of relatively sedate activity, hosting a big general market on Saturdays.

Alto Adige (Südtirol) was Italy's prize for co-operation with the Allies in World War I. When the Fascists came to power in 1923, despite the fact that German speakers outnumbered Italian speakers by about ten to one, a process of Italianization was imposed on the area. Cartographers remade maps, substituting Italian place-names for German, people were stripped of their own names and forced to adopt Italian ones, the teaching of German in schools was banned and stonemasons were even brought in to chip away German inscriptions from tombstones. Most telling was the change of the region's name and orientation – what had been the *South* Tyrol became the *Upper* Adige. But colonization wasn't just linguistic, as Italian workers from other regions were encouraged to settle, particularly in the towns. A large number of German speakers took the hint and emigrated, but after World War II many remained – along with the rival claims of Austria and Italy for control over the area. Both parties came to an agreement ratified under the Paris Peace Treaty of 1946 that Austria would give up its claim to the region on condition that Italy took steps to redress some of the cultural damage perpetrated under Fascism.

In 1948 some fancy footwork by the Italian government led to the union of Italian-speaking Trentino with German-speaking Alto Adige. In the new Trentino-Alto Adige region, German speakers were a minority and, as such, were entitled to very few of the compensatory measures agreed under the Paris Peace Treaty. After violent protests in the Sixties, a package of concessions was hastily put together, including a statute drawn up in 1971 which deemed that two-thirds of all public jobs and houses should be reserved for German speakers (a fair reflection of the ethnic mix at the time) and that all public servants should be bilingual in German and Italian. This has since been upheld, partly owing to pressure from the SVP (Südtiroler Volkspartei). Funds have been channelled into the area by successive governments, with the result that unemployment is low compared with the national average, and per capita income high. However, the right-wing MSI (Movimento Sociale Italiano), which argues for repeal of the 1971 act, gained strength during the Eighties, commanding something like fifty percent of the local Italian vote in some places, and in 1987 secured the election of their first-ever local deputy, a lawyer who declared Mussolini "a great man", and actively encouraged neo-fascist sympathizers to move into the province to swell their numbers.

A petty apartheid still exists in the education system: for example, there are separate entrances to the German and Italian sections of the same school and many young German speakers commute across the Austrian border to Innsbruck University. But as Italy has moved closer into the European Union, the central and regional governments have become more tolerant of ethnic diversity, with German gaining ground as the official language of preference. But while political pressures may have declined, on social occasions the two groups remain surprisingly separate – some bars and restaurants, particularly in Bolzano, make their allegiances clear.

If you've time, follow Corso Libertà from the square to the leafy suburb of Gries, on the left bank, where the Gothic **Parrocchiale** in the main square, overshadowed by a Baroque church nearby, contains a richly carved and painted fifteenth-century altarpiece by Michael Pacher (see p.273 for more on this Tyrolean artist).

Eating and drinking

If you're just after a lunchtime snack, try *wurstel* and *apfel strudel,* the commonest **street foods**, available from stalls on Piazza Erbe, Piazza del Grano and via Stazione, and the cafés of Via dei Portici. Via Museo is a good source of decent local **restaurants**; the *Weisse Traube* (*Uva Bianca*) at no. 17a (closed Sun), for example, offers a good-value set lunch. Along Via dei Bottai there's the *Cavallino Bianco* (*Weisses Rössel*) at no. 6 (closed July), a *bierkeller* with a menu heavy on Tyrolean specialities. *Batzenhäusl*, Via A. Hofer 30 (closed Tues), is good too, an old wine bar with a lively atmosphere, as is *Lowengrube*, Piazza Dogana 3, a *bierlokal* with good food and *weissbier* on tap. *Hopfen*, a restaurant on the corner of the fruit market at Piazza Erbe, is highly recommended for its beer brewed on the premises and huge plates of meaty Tyrolean specialities. It's worth noting that despite being a tourist destination, Bolzano practically closes down on Sunday, supermarkets included, though on Sunday evenings, and late every night, it's possible to get **pizza** and ice cream from *Subito*, on Piazza Erbe.

If you're after **nightlife** Bolzano is surprisingly dull for a town of its size, but it's easy to meet young people, as there are only three venues. *Nadamas*, on Piazza Erbe 44, is a Latin-themed bar, while just off Via Museo, on Vicolo Erbe, are *Casanova* and the inevitable Irish pub next door, *Pogue Mahone's*.

Around Bolzano

Bolzano is hemmed in by mountains terraced high with vineyards, across which a couple of footpaths up from the valley basin give a brief taste of the countryside. The **Passeggiata del Guncinà** starts at the end of Via Knoller near Gries' Parrocchiale, while the other, the **Passeggiata Sant'Osvaldo**, begins at Via Rencio, behind the train station, traverses some hillside terraces, and brings you down to the path next to the River Talvera.

Just north of the town centre, the thirteenth-century **Castello Róncolo** (Schloss Runkelstein; Tues–Sun 10am–7pm; €8), reachable by bus #12 from the station, is covered with frescoes of courtly life showing people hunting and dancing as well as the legendary lovers Tristan and Isolde. Look out for a fresco showing a group of nobles fishing in the Sala del Torneo. In the background a noble is offering a fish to a lady – the medieval equivalent of an indecent proposal. The Castello also has an excellent trattoria in its courtyard.

There's a whole clutch of castles just southwest of Bolzano at **APPIANO** (EPPAN AN DER WEINSTRASSE). One of the few that hasn't fallen to rack and ruin or been turned into a hotel or restaurant is **Schloss Moos Schulthaus** (Tues–Sun, tours at 10am, 11am, 4pm and 5pm, ☎0471.660.139; €5), which was saved from crumbling away just in time and turned into a museum. Its original Tyrolean kitchen, complete with huge great hearth, has been kept intact, and there are some newly uncovered frescoes depicting "the war of cats and mice".

From the ruined battlements of nearby **Schloss Hocheppan** (now a restaurant, April–June & Sept–Nov daily except Tues 9am–5pm; July daily 9am–5pm) you can see thirty or so other fortresses and castles, testifying to the cut and thrust of medieval politics in these parts. Hocheppan was the stronghold of the Counts of Eppan, rulers of the area until the powerful Counts of Tyrol took over after a series of bloody battles. The Hocheppan chapel by the side of the ruins is worth a look for its very secular frescoes: women flirting at the altar, and one of the earliest representations of the ubiquitous *knödel*, or dumpling, which still features heavily on most South Tyrolean menus.

Monte Renòn (Rittner) gives a taste of the high peaks around Bolzano. A cable car (open all year dawn to dusk; every 20min) ascends from Via Renòn (Rittnerstrasse) to Soprabolzano (Oberbozen), from where a tram service or footpaths lead to some of the other small villages, past a forest of eroded earth pillars, thirty minutes' walk north of Collalbo. A good time to come up here is in summer, around St Bartholomew's Day (August 24), when hundreds of

Törggelen

To get a flavour of Alto Adige's edible specialities, it's well worth timing your visit for the Törggelen season. This roughly coincides with the grape harvest, from about the end of September to the beginning of December, and traditionally marked the passage of the year – celebrating a golden time of clear autumnal weather before winter really set in.

Farmers and innkeepers lay on a spread of *speck* (smoked ham), local cheese and roast chestnuts, accompanied by wines from the surrounding hills, to which you apply yourself after a walk (or just a cable-car ride) up the mountain. Good areas to embark on your Törggelen expedition are found just south of Bolzano, around the wine road (see p.249), and the villages of Termano (Tramin), Caldaro (Kaltern) and Appiano (Eppan), or the Valle d'Isarco around Bressanone (Brixen). Just a few suggestions to whet your appetite: *Törglkeller* at Località Bichl 2 at Caldaro (closed Sun); *Loosmannhof* (☏0471.365.551), Località Signato/Signat; and *Wieser* (☏0471.662.376; closed Wed) at Appiano (Eppan).

farmers from outlying villages congregate on Renòn for the annual horse fair.

You might also visit the area south of Bolzano to eat; some of the farmhouses serve typical South Tyrolean dishes in their wood-panelled dining rooms (see "Törggelen", above).

Merano and the Giogáia di Tessa

MERANO (MERAN) an hour north by train from Bolzano, lies close to two great mountain ranges. The closest, the **Giogáia di Tessa** (Texelgruppe), less than 10km away, is characterized by steep traverses across pastureland, with old snow still on the slopes in summer; watercourses irrigate the south-facing slopes, planted below with vines, peach and apple trees. Further west, the **Ortles** mountains – an unbelievable expanse of glaciers and rocky spurs – straddle the border with Valtellina and are included within the Parco Nazionale dello Stelvio, one of Italy's major national parks (see p.269). Both ranges offer isolated trails, away from tourist routes, with bus services to most villages.

Merano itself sits on a bend in the River Passirio, a sedate spa town surrounded by a ring of mountains, and, incongruously, by semitropical plants. Mild spring and autumn weather attracted Central Europeans at the turn of the last century, and a resort of *fin-de-siècle* hotels, neat gardens and promenades evolved. The town's old nucleus is **Via dei Portici**, running west from the Gothic **Duomo** and fifteenth-century castle; around it are plenty of shopping streets and the Thermal Centre, which still provides radioactive water cures. It's mainly a retirement resort, but you may decide to stay in Merano for bus connections to the Parco Naturale di Tessa to the north, or the Ortles mountains in the Parco Nazionale dello Stelvio to the southwest. If you're here on Easter Monday, head for the hippodrome to the south of the centre, where Tyrolean musicians astride huge Haflinger horses parade around the stadium, with much horn-blowing and flag-waving before the actual races start. In summer, twice-weekly classical concerts are held – some in atmospheric castles. Perhaps more tempting, though, is the **grape fest** in the third week of October, marked by a procession, concerts and stands groaning under the weight of gastronomic delights.

Buses arrive and leave directly outside the **train station** on Piazza Stazione, ten minutes' walk from the centre of town. The **tourist office** is at Corso Libertà 45 (March–Nov Mon–Fri 9am–6.30pm, Sat 9.30am–6pm, Sun

10am–12.30pm; Dec–Feb Mon–Fri 9am–12.30pm & 2.30–6.30pm; ☎0473 .272.000, ⓦwww.meraninfo.it).Three of the least expensive central **hotels** are the basic *Santer Klause* on Passeirerg, just off Pfarrplatz (☎0473.234.086; ❷); *Tyrol*, a quiet hotel with a garden, closer to the train station atVia XXX Aprile 8 (☎0473.449.719; ❷); and *Villa Betty*, just across the river from the station, on Via Petrarca (☎0473.233.949; ❹). The best places to **eat** in town are the *Weinstube Haisrainer*,Via dei Portici 100, serving Italian andTyrolean dishes, and the *Weinstube Batzenhäusl* a few doors along at no. 84. **Campers** should use *Camping Meran,*Via Piave 44 (☎0473.231.249; Easter–Nov) which has a swimming pool: turn right out of the station, cross the river by way ofVia Rezia and Via Petrarca, andVia Piave is the third turning on the right.

For **hiking** advice and information, consult the Club Alpino Italiano office, Via Carlo Wolff, or Merano's Alpine association, the Alpenverien Südtirol, at Via Galilei 45 (☎0473.237.134), an alley off Corso Libertà.

Parco Naturale di Tessa (Naturpark Texelgruppe)

The mountain chains around Merano belong to a separate geological period from the Dolomites, and are actually part of the Zillertaler and Ötztaler ranges of the eastern Alps.Their foothills, called the **Giogáia di Tessa** (Texelgruppe), begin immediately north of the town. Two high-level paths, the north and south sections of the **Meraner Höhenweg**, encircle this massif. The gentler **southern route** (marked as route 24 on signs) overlooks Merano, the built-up ValVenosta (Vinschgau), and the neighbouring peaks, and is crowded even out of season.The total walking time is 24 hours, and every few kilometres there's a dairy farm offering bed and breakfast or a *rifugio* for overnight stops. **Buses** go from Merano to the beginning of the route at Hof Unterpferl in Katherinaberg (#105), and to Ulfas, just west of Sankt Leonhard, where it ends – plus several points along the way, including **Castel Tirolo** (mid-March to mid-Nov Tues–Sun 10am–5pm, ☎0473.220.221; €2.60, guide an extra €1.60), where a cable car ascends to a couple of *rifugi* and souvenir shops at **Hochmuter**. The castle's tenth-century frescoed chapel is worth the visit, if you can fight your way through the crowds of other tourists who pack the lanes around. Below Tirolo Castle is **Brunnenburg**, a neo-Gothic pile that's all fishtail battlements and conical towers, where American poet Ezra Pound spent the last years of his life. His grandson now runs a rather surreal **art gallery** in the same building (April–Nov daily except Tues 9.30am–5pm; ☎0473.923.533; €2), all its works being linked by the theme of "bread".

The **northern** stretch of the Meraner Höhenweg is an entirely different trail, running at a higher altitude but still below the snowline, through isolated pastures and rocky terrain.The comparative scarcity of *rifugi* makes it necessary to plan overnight stops in advance. The first section of the trail, Katherinaberg–Montfert–Eishof, is a walk of four hours; you then pick up the path from Eishof to *Rifugio Stettiner* (no accommodation; 3hr 30min); Stettiner to Pfelders (3hr 30min) is the last part. For places to stay in **KATHERIN-ABERG**, try the *Hotel Am Fels* (☎0473.679.139; ❹), which has a swimming pool and sauna; in **PFELDERS**, there's *Edelweiss* (☎0473.646.713; ❸) and *Panorama* (☎0473.646.727; ❷) – all much of a muchness.

From *Rifugio Stettiner* there's another option, the **Pfelderer Höhenweg**, which runs east to the Zwickauer Shelter, crosses the path here, and traverses the pastures of Obere Schneid.There are some sheer drops down to the valley, and you need crampons above the snowline, but this is an excellent walk, which gives a hint of how isolated these small valleys were until recently. If you don't feel equipped for this, but want to extend the route, continue past Pfelders to Ulfas (4hr), and from there on to Vipiteno (2–3 days), where you either link up with the main Bolzano-to-Innsbruck railway or carry on eastwards along the **Pfunderer Höhenweg** (see p.275).

A bus travels north from Merano along the Val Passiria to **SANKT LEONHARD**, skirting the edge of the Texelgruppe, and, on the other side, Merano's ski resorts on the slopes of Punta Cervina (Hirzer Spitze). A network of paths cross the summer pastures around Sankt Leonhard: one of these leaves **Sankt Martino**, 4km south of Sankt Leonhard, and makes the steep ascent (2hr 30min) to **Pfandleralm**, the home village of Andreas Hofer. Originally an innkeeper, wine merchant and cattle dealer, he fought for the Tyrol's return to Austria after it had been ceded to Bavaria in 1805. After successful uprisings against occupying Bavarian and Napoleonic troops, he became self-styled commander-in-chief of the South Tyrol, attracting strong popular support. However, larger political forces overtook him. When the Tyrol was ceded to the French by Austria's Emperor Francis I, Hofer was arrested in 1810 and executed under Napoleon's orders in Mantua. At Pfandleralm a memorial to him stands on the edge of the meadow, and in the Sandwirt guesthouse at Sankt Leonhard, there's a small **museum** in his memory (Mon–Sat 8am–noon & 2–6pm; €1).

Parco Naturale dello Stelvio

The Parco Nazionale dello Stelvio (or the Stilfser National park) is one of Italy's major national parks; it covers the whole **Ortles** range, and is topped by one of Europe's largest glaciers (the Ghicciaio dei Forni) and crossed by the Passo dello Stelvio, which misses being the highest pass in the Alps by just twelve metres. Tourism has made its mark, and the park is as crisscrossed by ski lifts as anywhere in the Alps. But it's still a remarkable place. People come here for the high trails and glacier skiing in summer, or for the chance of seeing species such as the red and roe deer, elk, chamois, golden eagles and ibex. One of the best valleys for spotting wildlife is the sheer-sided Val Zebrù, off the Valfurva, the smallest of the valleys, accessible from Bormio (see p.216).

There are buses to the park's various points of access but perhaps the place to head for first is **SILANDRO (SCHLANDERS)**, in the long, relatively wide Val Venosta (Vinschgau), with its **visitors' centre** (Mon–Fri 8.30am–7pm, Sat 9am–noon, winter Mon–Fri 8.30am–noon, 2–6pm; ☎0473.730.155) and information on *rifugi* and trails. If you're all hiked out, there's a good castle, **Coira**, but more frequently known by its German name of **Churburg**, 20km away on the road to Malles (Mals; buses from Merano). It was owned by the Lords of Matsch at the turn of the thirteenth century, when it was just one castle in a whole chain stretching from Bavaria to just north of Milan and was battled over by various knights in armour – whose suits, some weighing nearly 25kg, can be seen in the **armoury** (March 20 to Oct 31 Tues–Sun 10am–noon & 2–4.30pm; €6).

The valleys

Three main valley roads thread their way from the Val Venosta (Vinschgau) into the foothills of the Ortles range: Val d'Ultimo, Val Martello (Martelltal) and Val di Solda (Suldental). A traditional place of hiding in an area renowned for mountain warfare, the isolated **Val d'Ultimo** was opened up in the last century, and buses now run from Merano to the village of **SANKT GERTRAUD**. Around the lower slopes are startling green pastures and some ancient larches, but the main attraction of coming here lies higher up, where trails lead over rock-strewn moorland to *Rifugio Canziani* (*Höchster Hütte*; 3hr; no accommodation), dramatically surrounded by the glaciers and peaks of **Zufrittspitze**. If you're feeling less energetic, the valley is still a good place for some shorter walks, using the village as base. *Utnerhof*, Hauptstrasse 114 (☏0473.798.117; ❸), is one of a handful of **hotels** in the village, and most rooms have balconies, while for **food** you should splash out at *Genziana*, Via Fontana Bianca 116 – amazing meals for around €20 a head.

Further west, **Val Martello** (Martelltal) is equally beautiful, its lower slopes covered with silver birches. A bus travels from Merano to Silandro, and another from Silandro into Val Martello, passing the ruins of Cartel Montani and an aviary for falcons at Morter. At the head of the valley, **PARADISO DEL CEVEDALE** (2088m) is one of the busiest bases for climbers and cross-country skiers, lying close to Monte Cevedale (Zufall Spitze; 3757m); other trails lead through high passes to Val d'Ultimo and Val di Solda.

One of the main roads through the park is the awe-inspiring route over the **Passo dello Stelvio** (2758m), one of the highest and last to open – it is known to stay closed until July. A single bus from Merano makes the journey to the pass (late June to mid-Sept), passing the turn-off to the Val di Solda on the way; an alternative route is to take the frequent service from Merano to **Spondigna** and wait for one of the two afternoon buses from Malles there. **TRAFOI**, up at 1543m, is a lonely hamlet perched by the side of the road towards the beginning of the main climb, but there are a few good pensions just short of the village and bus stop: try the *Tuckett* (☏0473.611.722; ❹) or the *Trafoi* (☏0473.611.728; ❷). A cable car leads up to *Rifugio Forcola* (no accommodation), at 2250m, from where a fine path continues up and round to the Passo dello Stelvio (4hr). The pass marked the frontier between Italy, Switzerland and Austria until 1918, and **Pizzo Garibaldi** (Dreisprachenspitze), a spur of rock fifteen minutes' walk from the pass, is the symbolic meeting place for the three main languages of the area. The road continues down through switchbacks and startling gradients to Bormio.

A better choice in this area is to turn off just short of Trafoi towards **SOLDA**, 8km west. Set in an isolated tributary valley hanging over the main road, it's been a major climbing and skiing centre since the nineteenth century – there's even a tiny, eccentric **museum** (daily 9am–7pm; free) celebrating Solda's existence as a mountain resort. There's now a helpful **tourist office** (Mon–Sat 9am–noon & 3–8pm, Aug also open Sun 9am–noon & 2–6pm; ☏0473 .613.015, ⓦwww.sulden.suedtirol.com) and a large range of **accommodation**. In the lower town, best for restaurants and services, are *Paulmichl* (☏0473.613.064; ❺), right next to the tourist office, and *Ortlerhof*, the first hotel on the way into town (summer only; ☏0473.613.052; ❷). Ten minutes' walk away, in the upper part of town, the *Garni des Alpes* (☏0473.613.062; ❸) is excellent value and has a resident climbing/skiing guide. Although Solda attracts fairly serious climbers and skiers, you don't have to be experienced to attempt some of the trails. There are easy paths (2hr) up to *Rifugio-Albergo Città di Milano* (*Schaubach Hütte*; ☏0473.613.002; June–Sept) at 2581m, or more difficult trails to *Rifugio Payer* (☏0473.613.010; July–Sept) at 3020m, a fantastic viewpoint and base for the ascent of **Ortles** (3905m).

Alpe di Siusi (Seiser Alm)

The grasslands of the **Alpe di Siusi** (Seiser Alm), to the north of Bolzano, are Europe's largest Alpine plateau, extending over sixty square kilometres high above the rest of the valley under the peaks of **Sciliar** (Schlern) national park. The valley roads give you little idea of what lies above.

The bus from Bolzano goes to Siusi, from where another service ascends to the Alpe. On the way, the road climbs through a series of loops past the Hauenstein forest, the ruins of a castle which was once the home of Osvald of Wolkenstein (1377–1445) – the last *minnesinger* (troubador) of the South Tyrol – and the onion-domed church of **San Valentino** (St Valentiskirchlein). Buses terminate at **SALTRIA** (SALTNER), at the heart of the wetlands in a relatively unspoilt area, where the only evidence of human activity is dairy farming and some logging in the woods. Horses graze on the tough grass which grows up here, picking their way between the bogs and streams; small huts and clumps of pine are dotted across the plateau. Paths lead off the Alpe di Siusi to *rifugi* in the peaks, or there are four **hotels** that are more or less the only buildings at Saltria: *Ritsch* is one of the simpler (☎0471.727.910; ❺).

Sciliar (Schlern) and Sasso Lungo (Langkofel)

The **Parco Nazionale dello Sciliar**, which spreads over this area, is named after **Sciliar** (Schlern), a flat-topped, sheer mountain which splits off at one end into two peaks, Cima Euringer and Santner. Trails lead onto Sciliar from Tires (Tiers), Fié Am Sciliar (Völs Am Schlern) or Siusi (Seis), all involving long, steep climbs up to the summit (2563m). In the heyday of the spa resort, **FIÉ AM SCILIAR** was famous for its curative hay baths – presumably only beneficial if you didn't suffer from hayfever. Schloss Prösels, the fairly simple **castle** (guided tours daily: April–Oct 3, 4 & 5pm; ☎0471.601.062; €3.50) here, was once the seat of the Lords of Völs, patrons of the arts and staunch campaigners against witchcraft and superstition.

Just before the peak of Sciliar is *Rifugio Bolzano al Monte Pez* (*Schlernhaus*; ☎0471.612.024; June–Oct), one of the original Alpine huts from the 1880s. The cable car from Hoferalp, above Umes di Fiè (Ums), cuts out 1000m of ascent. In summer, paths can be crowded, but the day-trippers tend to disappear back down into the valley by evening, when the teeth of **Sasso Lungo** (Langkofel) become blunted by cloud.

Trails onto Sasso Lungo spring from the path between Saltria and **Monte Pana**, above Santa Cristina in the Val Gardena (see below). Half a day's walking brings you to *Rifugio Vicenza* (*Langkofelhütte*; ☎0471.792.323; June 20–Sept); from here paths lead across the mountain down to Passo di Sella (Sellajoch).

Val Gardena (Grödnertal)

Trails and chair lifts connect the Alpe with the **Val Gardena** (Grödnertal), a valley of squeaky-clean guesthouses and a continuous stream of tourist buses. The main village in the valley, **ORTISEI** (SANKT ULRICH), has for centuries been a big producer of religious sculpture and, more recently, hand-carved wooden toys, several families each perpetuating a particular design. Three thousand woodcarvers in the valley still make furniture and religious statues, but Ortisei, like the neighbouring villages of **Santa Cristina** and

Selva (Wolkenstein), is now mainly a ski resort, within easy reach of the **Sella Ronda**, a route of ski-runs and lifts encircling the Gruppo di Sella that make up the heart of the Dolomite skiing area. The massive circuit takes at least a day to complete. The **Cësa di Ladins** at Reziastrasse 83 (summer Mon–Fri 10am–noon & 2–7pm; €3.50; for winter hours call ☎0471.797.554) celebrates local Ladino culture (see box on p.260), the natural history of the area and local-boy-made-good Luis Trenker, a documentary filmmaker in the 1930s. **Buses** make the journey back to Bolzano, or you can drive in the other direction towards the Passo di Sella or Passo di Gardena.

Valle d'Isarco and Val Pusteria

The attraction of the four-hour bus trip from Bolzano to Cortina d'Ampezzo isn't so much what you see of the **Valle d'Isarco** (Eisacktal) and **Val Pusteria** (Pusertal), but the access it gives to the beginning of the *alte vie* and quieter routes into the **Val di Funes** (Villnöss), the Odle group, and the isolated ridges to the north of Val Pusteria. Largely untouched by tourism, these are great places to walk. In the side valleys dippers dart in and out of the streams and the sawing of timber cuts through the air. Higher up, you're likely to see marmots, and chamoix betray their presence with a tumbling of stones.

The Valle d'Isarco (Eisacktal) and around

The main village of the southern Valle d'Isarco (Eisack), **CHIUSA** (KLAUSEN), is served by trains from Bolzano and Bressanone (Brixen), and buses that continue into the **Val di Funes**, a little to the north. **SANTA MADDALENA** (SANKT MAGDALENA), surrounded by tracts of pasture, lies 10km into the valley, at the base of Le Odle. This quiet village is a good place for an overnight stop with a few reasonable **hotels**, such as the two-star *Gasthof Hofmann* on Hofmann Johann (☎0474.948.014; ❺). Another bus climbs halfway up the mountain to Zanseralm, from where it's one hour's walk to *Rifugio Genova* (☎0472.840.132; July–Sept) at 2301m. The level paths take you above the larch forests that fill the valley, and give fantastic views of the peaks. A four-hour circular trail called the Sentiero delle Odle (Adolf Munkel Weg) traverses the grass slopes beneath the teeth of the range, from Zanseralm via Saint Renon or to Brogles-Alm, and back down to the valley. Alta Via 2 is a short walk from Saint Renon.

Bressanone (Brixen)

Alta Via 2 can also be picked up in the foothills above **BRESSANONE** (BRIXEN), whose bishops – in constant rivalry with the neighbouring Counts of Tyrol – ruled the area as an independent state for a thousand years. The complex of buildings which made up their base is still the focus of the town, centred on Piazza del Duomo (Dom Platz), and preserves a medieval character, though rather diluted by bourgeois tidiness.

The **Duomo**, modernized in the eighteenth century, is the most imposing building in the complex: the interesting part lies to the side, in the cloisters, which were frescoed in the fourteenth century. The cathedral **treasury** is now kept in the Museo Diocesano (see below), where vestments belonging to Bressanone's bishop-princes are hung. Their strong influence in the region is evident from the present given by Emperor Henry II to Bishop Albuino: a tenth-century Byzantine silk cloak, spread with the stylized eagle that was the bishop's personal emblem. The bishop's palace, next to the Duomo, houses the

Museo Diocesano (mid-March to Nov Tues–Sun 10am–5pm; €5), furnished in predictably grand style, with an overwhelming collection of crib scenes in the **crypt** (same ticket as Museo Diocesano). For more secular pleasures, head for the **Novacella Monastery** (Kloster Neustift), 3km away and reachable by bus (at least hourly), which produces well-regarded wine and sells direct to the public via its own cellar in the old smithy. If you can get a group together, take a guided tour around the beautifully frescoed medieval **cloisters** (Mon–Sat 9am–8pm; €4.40; ☎0472.836.189).

Bressanone's **tourist office** (Mon–Sat 8.30am–12.30pm & 2.30–6pm; ☎0472.836.401, ⓦwww.brixen.org), opposite the bus station, has information on trails around the town and further afield. There are some excellent, inexpensive **places to stay** in the old town, including *Golden Traube*, Via Portici Minori 9 (☎0472.833.689; ❹), *Tallero*, Via Mercato Vecchio 35 (☎0472.830.577; ❷), and the small, family-run *Mayrhofer*, Via Tratten 17 (☎0472.836.327; ⓦwww.mayrhofer.it; ❹). If you're feeling flush, the *Elephant*, Via Rio Bianco 4 (☎0472.832.750, ⓦwww.hotelelephant.com; ❽), is one of the longest-established grand hotels in the Dolomites, furnished in elegant Tyrolean style and with excellent food and service. There are two **campsites** 5km north in Varna (Vahrn): the *Löwenhof* (*Al Leone*) is at Via Lago di Varna 60 (☎0472.836.216; closed Nov), while the other, *Zum See* (*Al Lago*), is near Lake Varna, at Via Lago di Varna 129 (☎0472.832.169; April–Oct); several buses travel here on weekdays, fewer at weekends. The narrow streets around the edge of Piazza Duomo have some old-established Tyrolean **restaurants** – like *Fink*, Via Portici Minori 4 (closed Tues evening & all Wed), and *Oste Scuro* in front of the cathedral (closed Sun evening & all Mon), and there's a *mensa* on Via Fallmerayer. For picnics, try the shops in the old arcades or the Monday market on Brennerstrasse.

Val Pusteria (Pusertal)

The road through the **Val Pusteria** (Pusertal), a wide valley of maize fields and hay meadows, sweeps around the northern edge of the Dolomites. Most of the *alte vie* start from points along the main road through the valley, which is served by bus from Brunico. The train route branches off the main Bolzano–Innsbruck line at Fortezza, heading on to Bressanone and Brunico on its way to Innichen. For walkers, many of the *alte vie* start in the Val Pusteria: Alta Via 1 starts from Lago di Bráies (Pragser Wildsee), Alta Via 3 from Villabassa (Niederdorf), Alta Via 4 from San Candido (Innichen) and Alta Via 5 from Sesto (Sexten). There are also lesser-known trails to the north, for example the Alta Via Val di Fundres (Pfunderer Höhenweg) – see p.275 for details.

Brunico (Bruneck)

An influx of people from the surrounding villages arrives daily in the otherwise sleepy market town of **BRUNICO** (BRUNECK), which is also the transport centre of the region, with buses along the valley and to most of the small places higher up in the hills. Brunico was home of painter and sculptor Michael Pacher (c1435–98): if you have some time to kill, go and look at his *Vine Madonna* in the parish church of the village of San Lorenzo, 4km southwest of town. Pacher is probably the most famous Tyrolean painter and woodcarver, straddling German Gothic and the more spare Italian styles; there's something vaguely unsavoury about this particular Madonna and her pudgy child, gripping a bunch of black grapes, but it's refreshing to see work in its original setting rather than in a museum.

The Brunico **tourist office**, opposite the bus station in Via Europa (Mon–Fri

9am–12.30pm & 2–6pm, Sat 9am–noon; ☎0474.555.722), has details of **places to stay**. The central *Blitzburg*, Via Europa 10 (☎0474.555.837; ❹), and *Corona (Krone)* at Via Ragen di Sopra 8 (☎0474.411.108; ❹) are reasonable options. For **campers** there's the *Camping Scheisstand*, Via Dobbiaco 4 (☎0474.401.326; May–Sept). A stopping **train** makes the journey along the Val Pusteria from here to the end of the line at Dobbiaco.

Vipiteno (Sterzing)

Situated on the busy route north from Bolzano to Innsbruck, **VIPITENO** (STERZING) is easy enough to get to. This close to the Austrian border it's hardly surprising that much of Vipiteno is typically Tyrolean, with geranium-filled balconies and wood-panelled old inns. The porticoed main street, however, **Via Città Nuova** (Neustadtstrasse), is more reminiscent of places further south, lined with elegant, battlemented *palazzi* erected in Renaissance times by a locally based Florentine bank. At one end, the **Torre di Città** was rebuilt in 1867 after fire destroyed the fifteenth-century original. The late-Gothic **Palazzo Comunale** on the square behind is worth a visit for its attractive galleried courtyard and a collection of fifteenth- and sixteenth-century paintings and sculptures (Mon–Sat 8.30am–noon & 2.30–5.30pm; free). Also worth tracking down is the **Museo Civico**, on Via della Commenda (currently being restored, due to reopen July 2003; €2), five minutes' walk from the centre, near the hospital. The museum is essentially an exhibition of local carving, the highlight being an altarpiece by Hans Multscher, a fifteenth-century sculptor and painter from Ulm. His work shows a keen sense of realism, as exemplified in an altarpiece of 1459. Several of his carved wooden figures can be seen in the nearby parish church of **Santa Maria in Vibitin**.

The **tourist office** is at Piazza Città 3 (daily 8.30am–noon & 2.30–6pm; ☎0472.765.325). If you decide to **stay** in Vipiteno, the elegant, friendly *Wipptalerhof*, Via Città Nuova 4 (☎0472.765.428; ❸), is undoubtedly the first choice. If it's fully booked, the tranquil *Pension Schneider*, Eduard Ploner Strasse 1 (☎0472.765.288; ❸), is well situated on a quiet side street just above Via Città Vecchia, the extension of Via Città Nuova.

Parco Naturale Fánes-Sénnes-Bráies

If you have a limited amount of time to spend in the **Parco Naturale Fánes-Sénnes-Bráies**, east of Brunico, you should aim for the upper slopes of **Alpe di Fánes**, where you pick up some of the best ridgeway paths. You can get here by taking a bus from either Corvara (see p.262) or Brunico to **Longega** (Zwischenwasser), and then walking 4km to **San Vigilio Di Marebbe**, in a side valley, where the tourist office can advise on routes up into the mountains. A regular jeep taxi service runs from San Vigilio to *Rifugio Fánes* (☎0474.501.097; Dec 20 to April 30 & June 10 to Oct 15) and *Rifugio La Varella* (☎0474.501.079; March 19 to April 25 & June 19 to Oct 19), both around 2000m up on the Alpe di Fánes Piccola. Footpaths cross the grassy plateaus, passing small tarns and the rocks of **Castel de Fánes**, home of Dolasilla, the mythical princess of the Ladini. The lakes are fed by underground streams, which you can sometimes hear, burbling deep beneath your feet.

Perhaps the best way to see the park, however, is to walk the section of Alta Via 1 that runs through it, a hike which takes three to four days, with overnight stops at refuges. The trail starts at **Lago di Bráies** (Pragser Wildsee), a deep-green lake surrounded by pines, 8km off the main road through the Val Pusteria – an extraordinary place (according to legend, the lake is a gateway to underground caverns), although you should avoid it in July and August, when crowds descend on the trails. To get here, take a bus from **Corvara** to **Brunico** and then another bus towards **Dobbiaco**, asking the driver to drop you at the turn-off, which is between **Monguelfo** (Welsberg) and **Villabassa** (Niederdorf), around thirty minutes out of Brunico; buses also go all the way to the lake from Dobbiaco.

Also accessible from Brunico by cable car (€10 return) is the **Plan de Corones**, surrounded by jagged peaks. Here, legend has it, Dolasilla was crowned at the top of the mountain with the *raiëta* – a crystal that harnessed powerful forces.

Alta Via Val di Fundres (Pfunderer Höhenweg)

The high-level **Alta Via Val di Fundres** (Pfunderer Höhenweg) follows the ridges north of Brunico. Although it's in the lower part of the Zillertal Alps, the path gives a feeling of the high mountains, with views across to the glaciers of Gran Pilastro (Hochfeiler) on the Austrian border. It's an exhilarating area, often subject to snow, ice and scorching sun in the same day. Access to the path is at Kleines Tor (2374m) on Monte Sommo (Sambock), a steep climb along path 29 from **Selva Dei Molini** (Mühlwald), 24km from Brunico. The walk takes four to five days, with overnight stops in *rifugi* or *bivacci*. The nearest big village is **CAMPO TURES** (SAND IN TAUFERS), where the wonderfully evocative medieval castle, **Schloss Taufers** (daily 10am–5pm ℡0474.678.543; €4.50), has dozens of wood-panelled rooms, including one haunted by a woman whose husband was murdered on their wedding day. The dungeons boast a particularly gruesome array of torture instruments, but perhaps the most appealing aspect of the castle is its setting: stark grey walls, bristling with towers, stand in contrast to the glistening backdrop of the Zillertal glaciers.

From Kleines Tor the path drops down to the Winnebach Valley, then climbs to *Fritz Walde Hütte*. A steep path crosses the Hochsagescharte Col (2650m), drops to Passenjoch (2410m) and then, after a westerly descent to *Gampes Hütte* (2223m), makes a spectacular traverse across steep pasture that eventually descends to the Eisbrugger Valley. The end of the route at **Vipiteno** (see p.274) is reached via **Boden** and the Weitenber Valley. Early on the last day you can be descending across pasture just emerging from snow, and in the evening be eating pizza in town. It's possible to do half of the walk by joining the path above **Fundres**, or the top of the Val di Valles (Valser Tal), where there's accommodation at *Brixner Hütte* (℡0472.547.131; mid-June to October).

Cortina d'Ampezzo and around

The 1956 Winter Olympics were staged at **CORTINA D'AMPEZZO** (it still has the Pista Olimpica di Bob), an event which began the transformation of the town from a small resort to a city in the mountains. Its main reason for existing now is the skiing season – roughly Christmas to Easter – when the population rises from 7000 to around 40,000, packing out the designer-clothes and antiques shops, as well as the slopes around the city. Cortina is the Italian equivalent of Saint Moritz, attracting actors, artists – and the rich. The place encourages a kind of Hollywood existence: taking sleighs down the mountain after a meal at a glamorous restaurant, or renting helicopters to seek out off-piste skiing. Out of season the place is dead; although it has a summer hiking season of sorts, between July and September when the cable cars operate. The ranges are less crowded on the side that faces away from the city, and are better approached from the smaller resorts of Corvara, Alleghe and San Vigilio di Marebbe. The setting is stunning, however, surrounded by a great circle of mountains which includes Monte Pelmo and Antelao, the Gruppo delle Marmarole, and Monte Sorapiss, Cristallo and Tofane.

Cortina's **tourist office** is at Piazzetta San Francesco 8 (daily 9am–12.30pm & 3.30–6.30pm; ☎0436.3231, ⓦwww.infodolomiti.it). Their hiking map is good, with refuge phone numbers and an indication of how long trails take to walk. The bad news is that **staying** here is expensive: prices climb exponentially in August and during the peak ski season – but there are a lot of campsites. One of the cheaper places worth trying to book ahead is the central *Albergo Cavallino*, Corso Italia 142 (☎0436.2614; ❸), which was being refitted at the time of writing but is due to re-open soon. Otherwise try the large *Hotel Impero*, Via Cesare Battisti 66 (☎0436.4246; ❼), which sometimes has good deals, or the modern *Villa Nevada*, on Ronce 64 (☎0436.4778; ❼), across the other side of town. Women who write far enough in advance may be able to get a bed in the hostel run by the Rev. Suore Francescane, *Casa dello Studente San Francesco*, Via Cianderies 33. The tourist office has further details and lists of rooms available in private houses. In summer, there's the option of **camping** at one of a number of well-equipped sites, all with bar and shop: *Cortina* (☎0436.867.575), which also has a swimming pool, *Dolomiti* (☎0436.2485) and *Rochetta* (☎0436.5063) are all 2km to the south at **Campo**, while *Olympia* (☎0436.5057) is at **Fiames**, 5km north.

Away from the hotel dining rooms, cafés and ice cream parlours are about the only sources of sustenance, though the central *Croda Café*, Corso Italia 163, has good-value pizza and a wide, if more expensive, à la carte menu. Campers and self-caterers will appreciate the **food** section of the large Cooperativa department store in the centre of town.

Apart from the tortuous **bus** routes via Bolzano and Belluno, there are long-distance services to Cortina from Milan, Padua and Bologna; the **bus station** is on Via Marconi, above town. The nearest **train station** is Calalzo, 32km east; a connecting bus runs every hour.

Around Cortina

Cortina is better known for trips by road and cable car than for mountain trails, with many drivers heading for the **Great Dolomites Road** (a scenic route between Cortina and Bolzano) and its passes. In summer there are buses to the small lake at **Misurina** (3 or 4 daily) and to the **Tre Cime di Lavaredo**, three mountain peaks to the northeast of the city – both extremely busy areas in high season.

One of the alternatives is to head south by bus towards Belluno in the Veneto (see p.374), passing through Titian's home town of **PIEVE DI CADORE**, with many paintings attributed to him and his family in the Parrocchiale. The one most likely to be authentic is in the third chapel on the left, and the altarpiece of the *Last Supper*, by his cousin Cesare, is rather fine. **Titian's birthplace** is represented by a stone and wood house on Via Arsenale (late June to mid-Sept Tues–Sun 9.30am–12.30pm & 4–7pm; ☎0435.322.62; €1.50). Although it was been equipped with furniture and a fireplace from the fifteenth century, the present structure dates from the 1800s.

Sporting, Piazza Municipio 21 (☎0435.31.262; ❹), is the most comfortable of Pieve di Cadore's inexpensive **hotels**; the **tourist office** (Mon–Sat 9am–12.30pm & 3.30–6.30pm, closed Thurs; Sun 10am–12.30pm; ☎0435.31.644), just down the road in a village called **TAI DI CADORE**, has the full list of accommodation. Among the handful of cafés and **bars**, *Caffè Tiziano* (closed Mon), in the vaults of the old Palazzo della Magnifica Comunità Cadorina, offers snacks, great cocktails and pool on full-size tables.

Alleghe and Monte Civetta

Without your own vehicle, it can be difficult to reach the most interesting mountains in these parts. One place you can get to by bus is the small village of **ALLEGHE**. The lake here was created after a huge rock avalanche in the eighteenth century – a common occurrence in the area. Now a peaceful summer and winter resort, Alleghe borders the northeastern edge of the lake, its aquamarine waters reflecting the pine forests around. Towering above is Monte Civetta, essentially Alleghe's main attraction, and the village makes a good base in between walks or climbs. The best of several two-star **hotels** in Alleghe is the *Alpenrose*, a five-minute walk up from the village centre at Via Coldai 85 (℡0437.723.929; ❸); otherwise the *Garni La Nava*, Corso Italia 43 (℡0437.523.340; ❸), is in a good position right beside the lake, near the town centre. *Camping Alleghe*, 2km away at Masarè (June–Sept & Dec–April; ℡0437.723.737), is open for the summer and skiing seasons. **Places to eat** in town include the *enoteca* in Piazza Kennedy (closed Tues); don't miss the cakes in the pasticceria on the same square. Also on Piazza Kennedy is the **tourist office** (Mon–Sat 9am–12.30pm & 3.30–6.30pm; ℡0437.523.333), geared up to provide information on cable cars and difficulty of footpaths; it also sometimes has English-language guides to the *alta via* routes.

For trips around the lake, the *Hotel Alleghe*, at the bottom of town, rents mountain **bikes** at €20 per day. But the classic trip from Alleghe is the walk up to **Monte Civetta**: from Fontanive just above the village take footpath 564 all the way up through steep meadows and summer pastures until you join Alta Via 1 at the Pian dei Sech. From there it's a last haul (about an hour) to *Rifugio Sonino* at Coldai (also signposted as *Rifugio Coldai*; 2132m; ℡0437.789.160; late June to Sept). If avoiding the three- or four-hour slog up the mountain appeals, then take the **cable car** from the village to Piani di Pezze and the **chair lift** from there to Col dei Baldi (July–Aug daily 8.30am–5.30pm; €7 return). If you're lucky enough to be at the Col on a clear evening, head for Lago Coldai just beyond the refuge for views of the great rock wall of Civetta, rippling with rock chimneys and pipes, glowing red in the sunset.

Hardened hikers can continue on Alta Via 1, the next day of which takes you across small snowfields and past windows in the rock which offer dizzying glimpses of the valley and the Dolomite groups. A couple of hours from Coldai, *Rifugio Tissi* is perched improbably on an incline, on a vast slab of rock, and is cheerfully shambolic, with accommodation available (℡0437.721.644; late June to mid-Sept). From here you can continue on Alta Via 1, past *Rifugio Vazzoler* down to Listolade in the valley (5hr; hourly buses to Alleghe), or head straight down the steep trail 563 for three hours to Masare (20min walk from Alleghe), dipping your feet in a waterfall on the way.

Travel details

Trains

Bolzano to: Bressanone (25 daily; 30min); Merano (hourly; 40min); Trento (30 daily; 35–50min); Vipiteno (14 daily; 1hr).
Brunico to: Dobbiaco (15 daily; 30min).
Fortezza to: Brunico (15 daily; 40min); Dobbiaco (15 daily; 1hr).
Trento to: Bologna (10 daily; 3hrs); Bolzano (30 daily; 35–50min); Cles (Trento-Malé line; hourly; 1hr); Malé (Trento-Malé line; hourly; 1hr 35min); Rovereto (28 daily; 15min); Venice (3 daily; 2hr 45min); Verona (28 daily; 1hr 10min).

Buses

Note that buses are significantly less frequent on Saturdays, and rare on Sundays and public holidays.

Bolzano to: Canazei (3 daily; 1hr 45min); Corvara (7 daily; 1hr); Fiè (16 daily; 30min); Lago di Carezzo (5 daily; 55min); Merano (hourly; 1hr); Predazzo (7 daily; 2hr); Selva (8 daily; 1hr 20min); Siusi (every 30min; 45min); Vigo di Fassa (4 daily; 1hr 20min).

Bressanone to: Brunico (hourly; 1hr); San Pietro (3 daily; 45min); Santa Maddalena (2 daily; 55min); Siusi (6 daily; 40min).

Brunico to: Bressanone (hourly; 1hr); Campo Tures (every 30min; 20min); Corvara (hourly; 1hr 10min); Dobbiaco (10 daily; 45min); Plan de Corones cable-car terminal (8 daily; 15min); San Vigilio di Marebbe (6 daily; 35min); Siusi (3 daily; 1hr 30min; change at Prato Isarco).

Cortina d'Ampezzo to: Belluno (6 daily; 2hr); Calalzo (10 daily; 1hr); Dobbiaco (6 daily; 45min); Pieve di Cadore (10 daily; 50min).

Corvara to: Belluno (2 daily; 2hr 45min); Longega (8 daily; 45min).

Dobbiaco to: Brunico (10 daily; 45min); Cortina d'Ampezzo (6 daily; 45min); Lago Bráies (5 daily; 25min); Villabassa (10 daily; 10 min).

Fiera di Primiero to: Passo di Cereda (1–2 daily; 25min).

Merano to: Moso (at least hourly; 1hr 10min); Passo dello Stelvio (1 daily; 3hr); San Leonardo (every 30min; 50min); Katherinaberg (6 daily; 50min); Santa Geltrude (9 daily; 1hr 25min); Silandro (every 30min; 1hr); Solda (2 daily; 2hr 30min).

San Martino di Castrozza to: Feltre, Veneto (9 daily; 1hr 20min); Fiera di Primiero (9 daily; 30min); Imer (9 daily; 40min); Predazzo (2 daily; 1hr).

Siusi to: Ortisei (5 daily; 40min); Santa Cristina (4 daily; 1hr); Selva (4 daily; 1hr); Tires (4 daily; 45min).

Trento to: Belluno (1 daily; 2hr 40min); Canazei (6 daily; 2hr 40min); Fiera di Primiero (3 daily, bus and train connection; 2hr 30min); Madonna di Campiglio (9 daily; 2hr); Molveno (3 daily; 2hr); Predazzo (6 daily; 1hr 45min); Rovereto (hourly; 40min); San Martino di Castrozza (3 daily, bus and train connection; 3hr); Tione (11 daily; 1hr); Vigo di Fassa (6 daily; 2hr 15min).

Venice and
the Veneto

CHAPTER 5

Highlights

* **San Marco, Venice** San Marco is a fabulous sight with its 4000 square metres of golden mosaics – all you have to work out is how to beat the queues. See p.299

* **Itinerari Segreti del Palazzo Ducale** A fascinating tour that takes you behind the scenes of Venice's superb Gothic palace. See p.305

* **Venice by water** No Venice trip is complete without a ride down the Canal Grande. See p.290

* **Accademia** One of the finest specialist collections of European art anywhere. See p.309

* **Prosecco** Sit in any main square in the region and sip a glass of Prosecco, the local sparkling white wine. See p.282

* **Carnivals** Venice's carnival is famous for its costumes and crowds, but if you want a more local event, head for Verona, where the whole town turns out for a procession of more than 80 floats. See p.365

* **Giotto frescoes** Giotto's frescoes in Padua's Cappella degli Scrovegni constitute one of the great works of European art and exert a powerful presence. See p.346

Venice and the Veneto

T he first-time visitor to **Venice** arrives with a heavy freight of expectations, most of which turn out to be well founded. All the photographs
you've seen of the Palazzo Ducale, of the Basilica di San Marco, of the
palaces along the Canal Grande – they've simply been recording the
extraordinary truth. All the bad things you've heard about the city turn out to
be right as well. Economically and socially ossified, it is losing people by the year
and plays virtually no part in the life of modern Italy. It is deluged with tourists
– the annual influx exceeding Venice's population two-hundredfold.
Occasionally things get so bad that entry into the city is barred to those who
haven't already booked a room. And it is expensive – the price of a good meal
almost anywhere else in Italy will get you a lousy one in Venice, and its hoteliers make the most of a situation where demand will always far outstrip supply.

As soon as you begin to explore Venice, though, every day will bring its surprises, for this is an urban landscape so rich that you can't walk for a minute
without coming across something that's worth a stop. And although it's true
that Venice can be unbearably crowded, things aren't so bad beyond the magnetic field of San Marco and the kitsch-sellers of the vicinity, and in the off-
season (October to Christmas and January to Easter) it's even possible to have
parts of the centre virtually to yourself. As for keeping your costs down, Venice
has plenty of markets in addition to the celebrated Rialto, there are some
good-value eating places, and you can, with planning, find a bed without
spending a fortune.

Tourism is far from being the only strand to the economy of the **Veneto**,
however. The rich, flat land around the Po supports some of Italy's most productive farms and vineyards, and industrial development around the main
towns rivals even the better-known areas around Milan, making the region one
of the richest in Europe. At Marghera, just over the lagoon from Venice, the
Veneto has the largest industrial complex in the country, albeit one that is now
in decline. But tourism is important, and the region has more tourist accommodation than any other in Italy. After Venice, it's **Padua** and **Verona** that are
the main attractions, with their masterpieces by Giotto, Donatello and
Mantegna and a profusion of great buildings from Roman times to the
Renaissance. None of the other towns of the Veneto can match the cultural
wealth of these two former rivals to Venice, but there are nonetheless plenty of

The Veneto vies with Lombardy for the risotto-making crown, while Venice specializes in fish and **seafood**, together with exotic ingredients like pomegranates, pine nuts and raisins, harking back to its days as a port and merchant city. The **risottos** tend to be more liquid than those to the west, usually with a seafood base although peas (*bisi* in dialect) are also common, as are other seasonal vegetables – spinach, asparagus, pumpkin. The red salad leaf raddichio also has its home in the Veneto, as does the renowned Italian dessert, tiramisù. Polenta is eaten too, while **pork** in all forms features strongly, together with heavy **soups** of beans, rice and root vegetables. *Gnocchi* tend to be served in an unusual sweet-sour sauce.

Pastries and **sweets** are also an area of Venetian expertise. Look out for the thin oval biscuits called *baicoli*, the ring-shaped cinnamon-flavoured *bussolai* (a speciality of the Venetian island of Burano), and *mandolato* – a cross between nougat and toffee, made with almonds. The Austrian occupation has left its mark in the form of the ubiquitous strudel and the cream- or jam-filled *krapfen* (doughnuts).

The Veneto has been very successful at developing **wines** with French and German grape varieties, notably Merlot, Cabernet, Pinot Bianco, Pinot Grigio, Müller-Thurgau, Riesling, Chardonnay and Gewürztraminer. The quintessentially Italian Bardolino, Valpolicella and Soave are all from the Verona region and, like so many Italian wines, taste better near their region of origin. This is also true of the more rarely exported **Prosecco**, a light champagne-like wine from the area around Conegliano: don't miss the chance to sample Prosecco Rosé and the delicious Cartizze, the finest type of Prosecco. Grappa, the local firewater, is associated particularly with the upland town of Bassano di Grappa, where every *alimentari* is stocked with a dozen varieties. Made from grape husks, juniper berries or plums, grappa is very much an acquired taste, but beware – the acquisition can be a damaging process.

places between the plains of Polésine in the south and the mountains in the north that justify a detour – the Palladian city of **Vicenza**, for instance, the fortified settlements of **Castelfranco** and **Cittadella** or the idyllic upland town of **Ásolo**.

For outdoor types, much of the Veneto is dull, consisting of flatlands interrupted by gentle outcrops around Padua and Vicenza. The interesting terrain lies in its northern part, especially in the area above **Belluno** and **Vittorio Veneto**, where the wooded slopes of the foothills – excellent for walking – soon give way to the savage precipices of the eastern Dolomites. Because most of the high peaks of the Dolomites lie within Trentino-Alto Adige, and the mountains of the eastern Dolomites are most easily explored as part of a tour of the range as a whole, the area of the Veneto to the north of Belluno is covered in the "Trentino-Alto Adige" chapter, starting on p.239. Similarly, the eastern shore of Lago di Garda is covered as part of the lakes region in the "Lombardy and the Lakes" chapter, starting on p.157.

Venice (Venezia)

The monuments that draw the largest crowds are the **Basilica di San Marco** – the mausoleum of the city's patron saint – and the **Palazzo Ducale** – the home of the doge and all the governing councils. Certainly these are the most dramatic structures in the city: the first a mosaic-clad emblem of Venice's Byzantine origins, the second perhaps the finest of all secular Gothic buildings. Every parish rewards exploration, though – a roll-call of the churches worth visiting would feature over fifty names, and a list of the important paintings and sculptures they contain would be twice as long. Two of the distinctively Venetian institutions known as the **scuole** retain some of the outstanding examples of Italian Renaissance art – the **Scuola di San Rocco**, with its sequence of pictures by Tintoretto, and the **Scuola di San Giorgio degli Schiavoni**, decorated with a gorgeous sequence by Carpaccio.

Although many of the city's treasures remain in the buildings for which they were created, a sizeable number have been removed to one or other of Venice's **museums**. The one that should not be missed is the **Accademia**, an assembly of Venetian painting that consists of virtually nothing but masterpieces; other prominent collections include the museum of eighteenth century art in the **Ca'Rezzonico**, and the **Museo Correr**, the civic museum of Venice – but again, a comprehensive list would fill a page.

The cultural heritage preserved in the museums and churches is a source of endless fascination, but you should discard your worthy itineraries for a day and just wander – the anonymous parts of Venice reveal as much of the city's essence as the highlighted attractions. And equally indispensable for a full understanding of Venice's way of life and development are expeditions to the **northern and southern islands** of the lagoon, where the incursions of the tourist industry are on the whole less obtrusive.

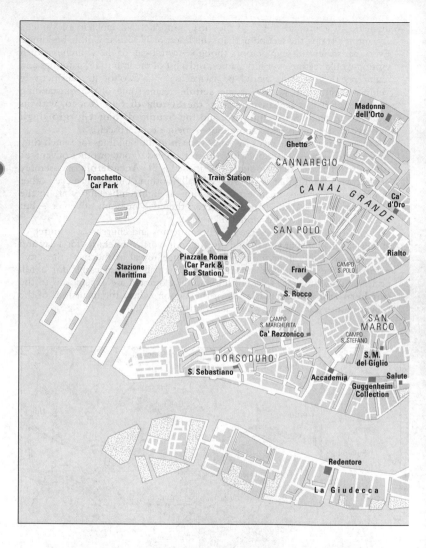

A brief history

Small groups of fishermen and hunters were living on the mudbanks of the Venetian lagoon at the start of the Christian era, but it was with the barbarian invasions of the fifth century that sizeable communities began to settle on the mudbanks. The first mass migration was provoked by the arrival in the Veneto of **Attila the Hun**'s hordes in 453, and the rate of settlement accelerated a century later, when, in 568, the **Lombards** swept into northern Italy.

The loose confederation of island communes that began to develop in the sixth century owed political allegiance to Byzantium, and until the end of the seventh century its senior officials were effectively controlled by the Byzantine hierarchy of Ravenna. But with the steep increase in the population of the islands which

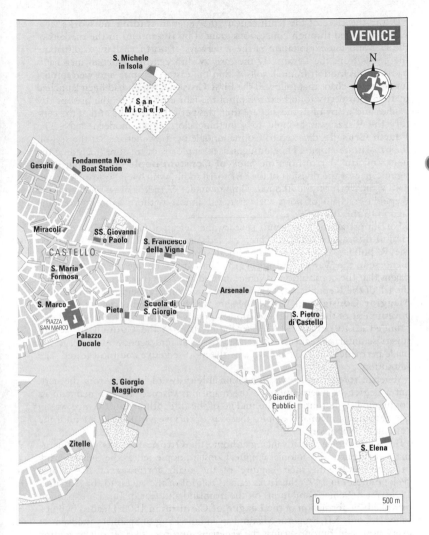

resulted from the strengthening of the Lombard grip on the Veneto in the later seventh century, the ties with the empire grew weaker, and in 726 the settlers chose their own leader of the provincial government – their first **doge**.

The control of Byzantium soon became no more than nominal, and the inhabitants of the lagoon signalled their independence through one great symbolic act – the theft of the body of **St Mark** from Alexandria in 828. St Mark displaced Byzantium's St Theodore as the city's patron, and a basilica was built alongside the doge's castle to accommodate the relics. These two buildings – the **Basilica di San Marco** and the **Palazzo Ducale** were to remain the emblems of the Venetian state and the repository of power within the city for almost one thousand years.

Before the close of the tenth century the Venetian **trading networks** were well established through concessions granted by Byzantium in the markets of the East and the exploitation of the waterways of northern Italy to distribute the goods from the Levant. By the early twelfth century Venetian merchants had won exemption from all tolls within the eastern empire and were profiting from the chaos that followed the **First Crusade**, which had been launched in 1095. Prosperity found expression in the fabric of the city: the present-day basilica and many of its mosaics are from this period; and at the end of the century the Piazza was brought to something close to its modern shape. The **Fourth Crusade**, diverted to Constantinople by the Venetians, set the seal on their maritime empire. They brought back shiploads of treasure (including the horses of San Marco) from the **Sack of Constantinople** in 1204, but more significant was the division of the territorial spoils, which left "one quarter and half a quarter" of the Roman Empire under Venice's sway and gave the Republic a chain of ports that stretched almost without a break from the lagoon to the Black Sea.

For almost all the fourteenth century, the defeat of Genoa – Venice's main rival in the eastern markets – preoccupied Venice's rulers, who finally secured the Republic's economic and political supremacy after the defeat of the Genoese in the **War of Chioggia** (1379–80). It was during the Genoese campaigns that the constitution of Venice arrived at a state that was to endure until the fall of the Republic, the largest step in this evolution being the **Serrata del Maggior Consiglio** of 1297, a measure which restricted participation in the government of the city to those families already involved in it. A revolt of disgruntled aristocrats in 1310 led to the creation of the **Council of Ten** to supervise internal security – intended to be an emergency measure, it was made permanent in 1334 and became the most secretive and most feared state institution.

Venetian foreign policy was predominantly eastward-looking from the start, but a degree of intervention on the mainland was necessary to maintain its continental trade routes. By the middle of the fifteenth century, Venice was in possession of a mainland empire that was to survive virtually intact until the coming of Napoleon.

But while Venice was advancing at home, the **Ottoman Turks** were emerging as a threat to the colonial empire. Constantinople fell to the Sultan's army in 1453, and with their capture of the main fortresses of the Morea (Peloponnese) in 1499, the Turks gained control of the access to the Adriatic.

Distrust of Venice's ambitions on the mainland and fear of Turkish expansion provoked the formation of the **League of Cambrai** in 1508. Headed by Pope Julius II, Louis XII, Emperor Maximilian and the King of Spain, it pitted almost every power in Europe against the Venetians, in a pact that set out to destroy Venice's empire as a prelude to conquering the Turks. When the fighting finished in 1516, Venice's subtle diplomacy had ensured that it still possessed nearly all the land it had held a decade before, but many of the cities of the Veneto had been sacked, great swaths of the countryside ruined, and the Venetian treasury bled almost dry. Worse was to come. After Vasco da Gama's voyage to India via the Cape of Good Hope, the slow and expensive land routes across Asia to the markets of Venice could now be bypassed by the merchants of northern Europe. The economic balance of Europe now began to tilt in favour of the Portuguese, the English and the Dutch.

After the **Sack of Rome** in 1527 the whole Italian peninsula, with the sole exception of Venice, came under the domination of Emperor Charles V. Hemmed in at home, Venice saw its overseas territory further whittled away by the Turks as the century progressed: by 1529 the Ottoman Empire extended right along the southern Mediterranean to Morocco, and even the great naval success at **Lepanto** in **1571** was quickly followed by the surrender of Cyprus.

At the start of the seventeenth century a row with Rome, concerning the extent of papal jurisdiction within the Republic, culminated in 1606 with the excommunication of the entire city. After a year of arguments the **Papal Interdict** was lifted, damaging the prestige of the papacy throughout Europe. Relations with the **Habsburgs** were no easier. The Austrian branch caused trouble by encouraging pirate raids on Venetian shipping, and in 1618 the more devious Spanish wing attempted to subvert the Venetian state by a wildly ambitious plot that has always been known as the **Spanish Conspiracy**. But the **Turks** caused the most lasting damage, taking the one remaining stronghold in the eastern Mediterranean, Crete, in 1669.

Venice in the eighteenth century became a political nonentity, reduced to pursuing a policy of unarmed neutrality. At home, the economy remained healthy, but the division between the upper stratum of the aristocracy and the ever-increasing poorer section was widening, and all attempts to dampen discontent within the city by democratizing its government were stifled by the conservative elite.

Politically moribund and constitutionally ossified, Venice was renowned not as one of the great powers of Europe, but rather as its playground, a city of casinos and perpetual festivals. **Napoleon** brought the show to an end. On May 12, 1797, the Maggior Consiglio met for the last time, voting to accede to Napoleon's demand that it dismantle the machinery of government. In October, Napoleon relinquished Venice to the Austrians, but returned in 1805 to join the city to his Kingdom of Italy, and it stayed under French rule until after Waterloo. It then passed back to the Austrians and remained a Habsburg province until united with the Kingdom of Italy in 1866.

During the French occupation a large number of buildings were demolished to facilitate urban improvement schemes, and modernization projects were continued under the Austrians. They created most of the *rio terrà* (infilled canals), constructed two new bridges across the Canal Grande, and built a rail link with the mainland.

Yet Venice in the nineteenth century was almost destitute. Eclipsed as an Adriatic port by Trieste (the Austrians' preference), Venice achieved large-scale expansion in the area of **tourism**, with the development of the **Lido** as Europe's most fashionable resort. It was the need for a more substantial economic base that led, in the wake of World War I, to the construction of the industrial complex on the marshland across the lagoon from Venice, at **Marghera**, a processing and refining centre to which raw materials would be brought by sea. In 1933 a road link was built to carry the workforce between Venice and the steadily expanding complex, but it was not until after World War II that Marghera's growth accelerated. The factories of Marghera are essential to the economy of the province, but they have caused terrible problems too: apart from polluting the environment of the lagoon, they have siphoned many people out of Venice and into the cheaper housing of Mestre, making Mestre-Marghera today more than three times larger than the historic centre of Venice, where the population has dropped since the last war from around 170,000 to about 80,000. No city has suffered more from the tourist industry than Venice – about ten million people visit the city each year, and around half of those don't even stay a night – though without them Venice would barely survive at all.

Arrival

If you are arriving **by air**, you'll touch down in one of two airports: **Treviso**, 30km inland from Venice, or at Venice's Marco Polo airport. The former is used chiefly by charter companies, many of whom provide a bus link from the airport into Venice – the ATVO bus that meets Ryanair flights, for example, costs €4.30 single and takes 1hr 10min. If such a service isn't provided, take the #6 bus from right outside the arrivals building into Treviso (20min), from where there are regular bus and train connections to Venice.

Nearly all scheduled flights and some charters arrive at **Marco Polo**, around 7km north of Venice, on the edge of the lagoon. If you're on a package holiday, the cost of transport to the city centre, either by land or by water, might already be covered. The cheapest alternatives are to take one of the hourly Alilaguna **water buses** to the landing stage near San Marco (€9.81; journey time 1hr; Ⓦ www.alilaguna.com), or one of the two road-going **bus services** to the terminal at Piazzale Roma: the ATVO (Azienda Trasporti Veneto Orientale; Ⓦ www.atvo.it) coach that departs every half hour (€2.70; 20min), or the cheaper ACTV (Azienda del Consorzio Trasporti Veneziano) bus #5 which is equally frequent and takes five minutes longer, but costs just €0.77 (plus a small supplement for large pieces of luggage). The ticket offices for the water buses and the land buses are in the arrivals hall; the latter will sell you a ticket for the ATVO rather than the ACTV bus unless you make clear your preference for *il cinque*. If you are staying for more than a couple of days it might be a wise investment to buy an ACTV pass (see p.291). You can also get ACTV bus tickets (but not passes) from the *tabacchi* in the departures area, which you reach by turning right outside the arrivals hall.

The most luxurious way to arrive is by **water-taxi**, which offers the best views of the city – and you can't beat the thrill of arriving at the water door of a hotel by taxi. The drivers tout for business in and around the arrivals hall and will charge around €80 for up to six people. Ordinary **car-taxis** are ranked outside the arrivals hall, and cost about €25 to Piazzale Roma, site of the Venice bus terminal.

Visitors arriving **by car** must leave their vehicle either on the mainland or in one of the city's car parks – at Piazzale Roma or the ever-expanding Tronchetto, Europe's largest car park. Prices at these two vary according to the time of year, the length of stay and the size of car, but it's never a cheap option (from about €18 per day), and in summer the tailbacks can be horrendous. It's better to use either the open-air San Giuliano car park at **Mestre** (open summer, Easter and during the Carnevale), linked by ACTV buses with central Venice, or the newly expanded terminal at **Fusina** open year-round and connected by ACTV water buses with Piazza San Marco, making this route one of the most pleasant ways to arrive in Venice (€4.13).

Arriving **by train or bus**, you simply get off at the end of the line. The Piazzale Roma bus station and Santa Lucia train station are just five minutes' walk from each other, at the top of the Canal Grande, and both are well served by *vaporetto* (water bus) services to the core of the city. The **left luggage** office at the train station charges €2.58 per item per twelve hours; it's found at the end of platform 14. The lockers alongside platform 1 are slightly more expensive at €1.55 per six hours.

Information, orientation and city transport

The main **tourist office**, known as the Venice Pavilion, is in the Palazzina del Santi, the waterfront building on the west side of the Giardinetti Reale, a minute's walk from the Piazza San Marco (Mon–Sat 10am–6pm; ☎041.529.8711, ⓦwww.turismovenezia.it). Smaller offices operate at the train station (daily 8am–7pm; ☎041.529.8727), on Calle dell'Ascension 71f in the corner of the Piazza San Marco (Mon–Sat 9.30am–5.30pm, in winter closes 3.15pm; ☎041.529.8740), in the airport arrivals area (Mon–Sat 9.30am–8pm) and on the Lido at Gran Viale S.M. Elisabetta 6 (May–Sept daily 9.30am–3.30pm; ☎041.526.5721). There are seasonal tourist information offices (green cabins) dotted around the city (Feb–Oct 10am–1pm & 1.30–5pm), on Campo San Felice (Cannaregio), Campo dei Frari (San Polo) and Riva dei Sette Martiri (Castello). The free **map** distributed by these offices is fine for general orientation, but not much else. The Touring Club Italiano (TCI) produces a good detailed map, as does Magnetic North, which usefully marks on a large number of the city's shops, restaurants and bars.

Worth looking out for is the English-Italian magazine *Un Ospite di Venezia*, produced weekly in summer and monthly in winter, which gives up-to-date **information** on exhibitions, special events and vaporetto timetables – it's free from the main tourist office, and from the receptions of the posher hotels. The tourist office also produces the *Leo Bussola*, a handy bi-monthly booklet with information on museums and events.

The transport system

Venice has two interlocking street systems – the canals and the pavements – and contrary to what you might expect, you'll be using the latter most of the time. Apart from services #1 and #82, which cut through the city along the Canal Grande, the water buses skirt the city centre, connecting points on the

---

Rolling Venice and Venice Cards

If you're aged between 14 and 29, you are eligible for a **Rolling Venice card**, which entitles you to discounts at some hostels, shops, restaurants, cinemas, museums and exhibitions, plus reductions on some transport services. The card costs €2.58, is valid for a year, and is worth buying if you're in town for a week or longer and aim to make the most of every minute. It's available from the following outlets: Agenzia Transalpino, at the train station; Assessorato alla Gioventù, Corte Contarina 1529 (just west of San Marco); Agenzia Arte e Storia, Santa Croce 659 (near Campo della Lana); Associazione Italiana Alberghi per la Gioventù, Calle del Castelforte 3101 (near the Scuola di San Rocco); and Agenzia Transalpino (in the train station).

Another discount scheme for all ages is the **Venice Card**, but you'll need to be an active sightseer to make it worthwhile. It comes in two sizes with a discount for under 30s: the blue one (1-day card €11 full price, €7 with discount; 3-day card €41/17 for three days) gives you free access to public transport and Amav public toilets, while the orange one (1-day card €26/16, 3-day card €58/30) also gives you free access to the museums covered by the Museum Pass (see p.299). Cards must be ordered up to 48 hours in advance on ⓦwww.venicecard.com, ☎899.909.090 in Italy or ☎00.39.041.271.4747 from abroad. You will be given a code number which you'll need to present when you pick up and pay for the ticket – either at the Alilaguna office at the airport, the VELA ticket office at the railway station or the San Giuliano car park.

periphery and the outer islands. In most cases the speediest way of **getting around** is on foot. Distances between major sights are extremely short (you can cross the whole city in an hour), and once you've got your general bearings you'll find that navigation is less daunting than it seems on arrival. The ACTV website for general information is ⓦ www.actv.it.

The water buses

There are two basic types of boat: the **vaporetti**, which are the lumbering workhorses used on the Canal Grande stopping service and other heavily used routes, and the **motoscafi**, smaller vessels employed on routes where the volume of traffic isn't as great. On both types there's a flat-rate fare of €3.10 for any one continuous journey, or €5.16 return unless it's a traghetto journey (see below), in which case the fare is €1.03. On return journeys (and some one-way routes – look at the top of your ticket to see if there is a date printed) you'll have to **stamp your ticket** in the yellow machine, usually placed right by the landing stage.

Water-bus routes

The **water-bus routes** operated by ACTV can seem bewilderingly complicated, and in the past the company has seemed bent on maximizing the confusion by altering routes and numbers for no readily apparent reason. Recent changes have rationalized the situation, but this is no guarantee for the future; in particular note that the water buses which currently make a circuit of the far eastern side of the city may return to their previous route through the Arsenale. As a rule, the routes displayed at each *vaporetto* stop are reliable, although in the outlying parishes they sometimes take a few months to get round to posting up the current map. The map handed out by the tourist offices never gives the complete picture.

What follows is a run-through of the most useful services. Times given are approximate, as it will depend on exactly where along the route you pick up the bus, so if you need to catch an early or late *vaporetto*, check at a ticket office; most of the vendors speak some English. Be warned that so many services call at San Marco, San Zaccaria, Rialto and the train station, that the bus stops at these points are spread out over a long stretch of waterfront, so you might have to walk past several stops before finding the one you need.

#1: The perversely named *accelerato* is the slowest of the water buses, the workhorse of the system, and the one you'll use most often; it's also one of the very few routes that seems exempt from alterations. It starts at the Piazzale Roma, calls at all stops bar San Samuele on the Canal Grande, works its way along the San Marco waterfront to Sant'Elena, and then goes over to the Lido. The #1 runs every 20min 5–6.30am, every 10min 6.30am–9.45pm, and every 20min 9.45–11.45pm. For the night service, see #N.

#82: This all-year service circles the southern island of San Polo/Dorsoduro, travelling in both directions along the route. What you'll most likely need to know is that it runs from the train and bus stations down the Canal Grande to San Marco, and it's faster than the #1, as there are fewer stops. It calls at San Zaccaria, San Giorgio Maggiore, Giudecca (Zitelle, Redentore and Palanca), Záttere, San Basilio, Sacca Fisola, Tronchetto, Piazzale Roma, train station, Canal Grande (usually Rialto, Sant' Angelo, San Tomà, San Samuele and Accademia) and San Marco at Vallaresso. The service runs every 10min from 6am–8.30pm, then every 20min until 11pm, though the section from San Tomà to San Marco runs only every 20min through the day. Earlier in the morning (from 5–8am) and later in the evening (after 8.30pm) there is a restricted service along this latter section – the #82 acting as a shuttle between San Zaccaria and Sant'Angelo. For the night service see #N.

Tickets are available from most landing stages, from *tabacchi*, from shops displaying the ACTV sign, and from the two ACTV public offices – at Piazzale Roma (daily summer 6am–midnight; winter 6am–8pm), and in Ramo dei Fuseri, close to the northwest corner of the Piazza (Mon–Fri 7.30am–6pm, Sat 7.30am–1pm). The latter is your best source of free up-to-date colour maps of the main routes – the tourist offices seem to run out of them very quickly. In the remoter parts of the city, you may not be able to find anywhere to buy a ticket, particularly after working hours, when the booths at the landing stages tend to close down. If necessary you can pay on board for the normal price, but make sure you ask the attendant immediately as there's a €23 spot-fine for not having a valid ticket and inspections are frequent.

ACTV produces three **travel passes**: a 24-hour ticket (€9.30); a three-day ticket (€18.08), and a seven-day ticket (€30.99), all of which are valid on all water- and land-buses within Venice. There are also three itinerary tickets covering particular routes: these cost €7.75 each and are valid for twelve hours

#41/42: The circular service, running right round the main island of Venice, with a short detour at the northern end to San Michele and Murano. The #41 travels anticlockwise, the #42 clockwise and both run every 20min from 7am to 8pm. Earlier and later in the day, a commuter service shuttles between Murano and Venice every 10–20min, following the #51/52 route on from the Fondamente Nove in the appropriate direction.

#51/52: Similar to the #41/42, this much-altered route also circles Venice, but heads out to the Lido (rather than Murano) at the easternmost end of the circle. The #51 runs anticlockwise, the #52 clockwise, and both run fast through the Guidecca canal, stopping only at Zattere and Santa Marta between San Marco and Piazzale Roma. Both run every 20min from 7am–9.30pm. Early in the morning and late in the evening a reduced service begins from and terminates at Murano instead of the Lido, cutting out the northeasternmost flank of Venice between Fondamente Nove and the Lido. This applies to the #51 in the mornings (4.30–7am) and evenings (8–11pm) and to the #52 after 8pm only. After 11pm the #52 becomes a shuttle between the Lido and the train station via the Guidecca canal; this route runs until 12.30pm and connects through to Rialto.

#12: for most of the day the #12 runs every half hour from Fondamente Nove (hourly early in the morning and evenings), calling first at Murano-Faro before heading on to Mazzorbo, Burano and Torcello (sometimes calling at Torcello before Burano).

#N: The night service (11.30pm–4.30am) is a selective fusion of the #1 and #82 routes, running from Piazzale Roma to the Lido, down the Canal Grande. Stops are as follows: Lido, Giardini, San Zaccaria, Vallaresso, Accademia, San Samuele, San Tomà, Rialto, Ca' d'Oro, San Stae, San Marcuola, train station, Piazzale Roma, Tronchetto, Sacca Fisola, San Basilio, Zattere, Palanca, Redentore, Zitelle, San Giorgio and San Zaccaria – then retracing its route. It runs along the whole of the route in both directions every 30–40min, and from Rialto to Tronchetto every 20min. Another night service connects Venice with the Murano stops, running to and from Fondamente Nove every 30min between midnight and 4am.

NB: In addition to the longer routes, some *vaporetti* and *motoscafi* operate as *traghetti* across the Canal Grande and over to the nearer islands: for example, if you want to go from San Zaccaria over to San Giorgio Maggiore, you need only pay the lower *traghetto* fare of €1.55. If your journey is a short single-stop trip across a body of water, a *traghetto* fare almost certainly applies – it'll be shown on the tariff list on the ticket booth.

unlimited use on either the Canal Grande or the islands of the Northern Lagoon (including Torcello, Burano and Murano). The Carta Venezia, which gives huge reductions on all ACTV buses, is not available to non-residents.

Traghetti

There are only three bridges on the Canal Grande – at the train station, Rialto and Accademia – so the **traghetti** (gondola ferries) that cross it can be useful time-savers. Costing just €0.40, they are also the only cheap way of getting a ride on a gondola – though it's *de rigueur* to stand in a *traghetto* rather than sit. They run between: San Marco–Salute; Santa Maria del Giglio–Salute; San Barnaba–San Samuele; San Tomà–Santo Stefano; Riva del Carbon–Riva del Vin (near Rialto); Santa Sofia–Pescerìa; San Marcuola–Fondaco dei Turchi; train station–San Simeone. All *traghetti* run Mon–Sat from early morning to noon, while those on the routes Santa Maria del Giglio–Salute, San Tomà–Santo Stefano and Santa Sofia–Pescerìa run till around 7–9pm daily, the last two on Sundays, as well; in the winter months some *traghetti* stop running earlier, while others are suspended altogether.

Gondolas

The **gondola** is no longer a form of transport but rather an adjunct of the tourist industry. That said, it can be a delightful way of relishing the sheer sense of being in Venice, and the cost isn't all that off-putting when split among a small group. To hire one costs €62 per fifty minutes for up to six passengers, rising to €77.45 between 8pm and 8am; you pay an extra €31 for every additional 25 minutes. Further hefty surcharges will be levied should you require the services of an on-board accordionist or tenor – and a surprising number of people do, despite the strangulated voices and hackneyed repertoire of most of the aquatic Carusos. Even though the tariff is set by the local authorities, it's been known for some gondoliers to try to extort even higher rates than these – if you do decide to go for a ride, establish the charge before setting off.

To minimize the chances of being ripped off by a private individual making a stash of euros on the side, only take a boat from one of the following **official gondola stands**: west of the Piazza at Calle Vallaresso, Campo San Moisè or Campo Santa Maria del Giglio; immediately north of the Piazza at Bacino Orseolo; on the Molo, in front of the Palazzo Ducale; outside the Danieli hotel on Riva degli Schiavoni; at the train station; at Piazzale Roma; at Campo Santa Sofia, near the Ca' d'Oro; at San Tomà; or by the Rialto Bridge on Riva Carbon.

Venice's **water-taxis** are sleek and speedy vehicles that can penetrate the shallowest of canals. Unfortunately they are perhaps the most expensive kind of taxi in western Europe, with high tariffs supplemented by extra charges – such as for luggage more that 50cm long and for rides between 10pm and 7am. The base rate is €14 for the first seven minutes, and then €0.25 for every fifteen seconds (that's €1 per minute). You can pick up a taxi at one of the taxi stands (such as in front of the Piazzetta or at the airport), grabbing one that is disgorging its passengers, or by phoning ☎041.522.2303 or 041.522.8538 (if ordered by phone it will have €4 on the clock when it arrives).

Accommodation

The virtually limitless demand for **accommodation** in Venice has pushed prices to such a level that it's possible to pay in excess of €120 for a double room in a one-star hotel in **high season**. What's more, high season here is

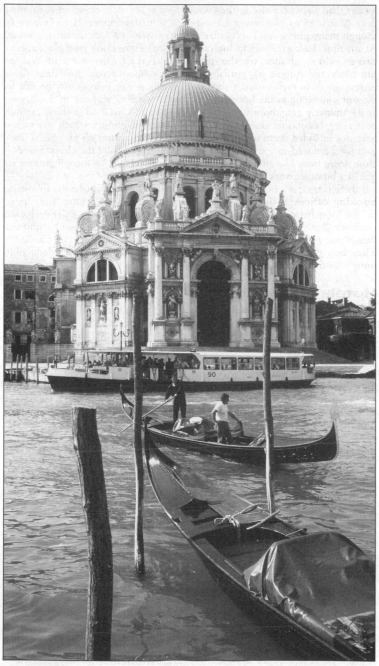

△ Santa Maria della Salute, Venice

longer than anywhere else in the country – it is officially classified as running from March 15 to November 15 and then from December 21 to January 6, though many places don't recognize the existence of a low season any more. At any time during the official high season it's wisest to book your place at least two months in advance, whether it's a hostel bed or a five-star suite, and for June, July and August it's virtually obligatory. Should you bowl into town unannounced in high summer, the booking offices (see below) may be able to dig out something in the hotels of mainland Mestre or way out in the lagoon at the unlovely neighbouring resorts of Jesolo and Cavallino (a thirty-minute boat ride), but rooms here would be nobody's free choice, which is why we have not included them in our listings. During the winter it's possible to bargain for a reduced-rate room, but many hotels – especially the cheaper ones – close down from November to February or even March, so you might have to put in a bit of legwork before finding somewhere.

If there is no space in any of the places listed below, try one of the following **booking offices**: at the train station (summer 8am–9pm; winter 8am–7pm); on the Tronchetto (9am–7pm) in the multistorey car park at Piazzale Roma (summer 9am–9pm; winter 9am–7pm); at Marco Polo airport (summer 9am–7pm; winter noon–7pm); or at the autostrada's Venice exit (11am–7pm). They only deal with hotels (not hostels) and take a deposit that's deductible from your first night's bill.

Hotels

Venice has around two hundred hotels, ranging from spartan one-star joints to five-star establishments charging €500 and more a night, and what follows is a rundown on the best choices in all categories. Though there are some typical anomalies, the star system is a broadly reliable indicator of quality, but always bear in mind that you pay through the nose for your proximity to the **Piazza San Marco**. So if you want maximum comfort for your money, decide how much you can afford and then look for a place outside the San Marco *sestiere* – after all, it's not far to walk, wherever you're staying.

Be warned that although **breakfast** should be optional, most hotels include it in their price and simply refuse to take guests who don't want to pay a ludicrous extra charge for a jug of coffee and a puny croissant – breakfast at the humblest one-star can add €10 per person onto your bill. By law, the price of a room must be displayed on the back of its door; if it's not, or if the price doesn't correspond to what you're being charged, complain first to the management and then to the Questura (see p.341).

San Marco

Ai Do Mori Calle Larga S. Marco 658 ☎041.520.4817, ℻041.520.5328, ⓦwww.hotelaidomori.com. Very friendly, and situated a few paces off the Piazza, this hotel is a top recommendation for budget travellers, with cheaper rooms having shared bathrooms. The top-floor room, with its private terrace looking over the roofs of the Basilica and the Torre dell'Orologio, is one of the most attractive one-star rooms in the city. ❺

Ala Campo S. Maria del Giglio 2494 ☎041.520.8333, ℻041.520.6390, ⓦwww.hotelala.com. If you want to stay in the city's aristocratic accommodation zone but can't stretch to the prices of the *Bauer Grünwald* and its coevals, the three-star *Ala* is a logical choice. There are more welcoming places in Venice, but the rooms are spacious and the *Ala* has a perfect location, on a square whose mouth opens onto the Canal Grande. ❾

Casa Petrarca Calle delle Colonne 4394 ☎041.520.0430. The cheapest hotel within a stone's throw of the Piazza. Phone first, as it only has seven rooms, two with shared bathrooms – including a minute single room – though they may be able to accommodate you nearby. Extremely hospitable, with English-speaking staff. ❺

La Fenice et des Artistes Campiello Fenice 1936 ☎041.523.2333, ⓕ041.520.3721, ⓦwww .fenicehotels.it. This large three-star was a favoured hangout of the opera crowd, performers and audience alike. Until La Fenice reopens, it might have more vacancies than it used to. Rooms have air-conditioning and safe, and the hotel has a small garden. Devoted guests come back regularly. ❾
Fiorita Campiello Nuovo 3457 ☎041.523.4754, ⓕ041.522.8043, ⓦwww.locandafiorita.com. Just nine rooms, some with shared bathrooms, in this one-star just off San Stefano but they have been refurbished in a beguiling Venetian style and have air-conditioning. Welcoming management, and there's a nearby *traghetto* across the Canal Grande. ❺
Al Gambero Calle dei Fabbri 4687 ☎041.522 .4384, ⓕ041.520.0431, ⓦwww.locandaalgambero .com. Large hotel in an excellent position a short distance off the north side of the Piazza; the rooms are well maintained, and many of them overlook a canal that's on the standard gondola route from the Bacino Orseolo. Has more single rooms than many

Venice hotels. There's a boisterous Franco-Italian bistro on the ground floor. ❺
Kette Piscina S. Moisè 2053 ☎041.520.7766, ⓕ041.522.8964 ⓦwww.hotelkette.com. Recently upped to a four-star hotel, it's a favourite with the upper-bracket tour companies, mainly on account of its quiet location in an alleyway parallel to Calle Larga XXII Marzo and close to La Fenice. In season there's nothing under €330, but out of season prices more than halve. ❾
Noemi Calle dei Fabbri 909 ☎041.523.8144, ⓦwww.hotelnoemi.com. The rooms are basic and the decor is a bit dowdy, but the *Noemi* is right in the thick of the action, just a minute's walk north of the Piazza, its staff are thoughtful and its prices are lower than rival one-stars. Half the rooms have safes and bathrooms, all have a/c. Also has an annexe. ❺
San Samuele Salizzada S. Samuele 3358 ☎ & ⓕ041.522.8045. A friendly one-star close to the Palazzo Grassi, with rooms distinctly less shabby than some at this end of the market, if not exactly plush. Some rooms have shared bathrooms. ❹

Dorsoduro

Accademia Villa Maravege Fondamenta Bollani 1058 ☎041.521.0188, ⓕ041.523.9152, ⓦwww.pensioneaccademia.it. Once the Russian embassy, this quiet seventeenth-century villa has a devoted following, not least on account of its courtyard, which occupies a promontory at the convergence of two canals, with a view of a small section of the Canal Grande, and its small garden. To be sure of a room, get your booking in at least three months ahead. ❻
Agli Alboretti Rio Terrà Foscarini 884 ☎041.523.0058, ⓕ041.521.0158, ⓦwww.agli-alboretti.com. Friendly two-star well situated right next to the Accademia. All rooms have air-conditioning and TV. Avoid murky room 19 and you can't go wrong. ❻
Antico Capon Campo S. Margherita 3004b ☎ & ⓕ041.528.5292 ⓦwww.anticocapon.com. Simply furnished small rooms above a pizzeria-restaurant on an atmospheric square in the heart of the student district. Pleasant staff. Rooms in the annexe on the other side of the square are noisier. ❺
La Calcina Zàttere ai Gesuati 780 ☎041.520.6466, ⓕ041.522.7045, ⓦwww.lacalcina.com. Unpretentious and charismatic three-star in the house where Ruskin wrote much of *The Stones of Venice*. A/c rooms have parquet flooring and safe. From the more expensive ones you can gaze across

to the Redentore. Also has cheaper singles with shared bathrooms. ❻
Ca-Pisani Rio Terà Foscarini, Dorsoduro 979a ☎041.240.1411 ⓦwww.capisanihotel.it. This very glamorous 29-room four-star created quite a stir when it opened next to the Accademia, partly because of its location – the opposite side of the Canal Grande from its top-ranking rivals – but mainly because of its retro style. Its 30s-40s looks with dark wood and chrome are a refreshing break from the Renaissance and Rococo competition. Highly recommended. ❾
Messner Rio Terà dei Catacumeni 216/237 ☎041.522.7443, ⓕ041.522.7266, ⓦwww.charmingvenice.com/messner. In an excellent, quiet location close to the Salute *vaporetto* stop, the *Messner* has modern, smart rooms with safes and is run by friendly staff. There are also cheaper rooms in the annexe round the corner: all have a private bathroom but for some rooms this is out on the corridor. ❻
Montin Fondamenta di Borgo 1147 ☎041.522.7151, ⓕ041.520.0255. On a quiet, small canal, the *Montin* is known principally for its upmarket and once-fashionable restaurant; few people realise that it offers some of Venice's most charismatic accommodation, though there are only eleven rooms, some sharing a bathroom. ❺

San Polo

Alex Rio Terrà Frari S. Polo 2606 ℗ &
🅕041.523.1341, ⓔ mariofiorentini@tiscalinet.it. A
longstanding budget-travellers' favourite, this one-
star hotel has recently been refurbished. The top
rooms have a small terrace, and some rooms
share bathrooms. The supermarket in front is useful for picnics and breakfast. ❹

Ca' Fóscari Calle della Frescada, Dorsoduro
3887b, ℗041.710.401, 🅕041.710.817, ⓔ valter-
sc@tin.it. Quiet, well decorated and relaxed one-
star, tucked away in a micro-alley near S. Tomà.
Just eleven rooms (some with shared bathrooms),
so it's quickly booked out. Closed last week July &
first week August. ❹

San Cassiano-Ca' Favretto Calle della Rosa, S.
Croce 2232, ℗041.524.1768, 🅕041.721.033,
ⓦ www.sancassiano.it. Beautiful three-star with

some rooms and the dining room looking across
the Canal Grande towards the Ca' d'Oro. Very helpful staff, courtyard garden and a grand entrance
hall. ❾

Sturion Calle del Sturion, S. Polo 679
℗041.523.6243, 🅕041.522.8378, ⓦ www.locan-
dasturion.com. Immaculate three-star on a wonderful site a few yards from the Canal Grande,
close to the Rialto. Run by an exceptionally welcoming management that offers free trips to
Murano, concert tickets and other goodies. ❽

Tivoli Crosera S. Pantalon, Dorsoduro 3638
℗041.524.2460, 🅕041.522.2656, ⓦ www.hotel-
tivoli.it. This two-star is the biggest moderately
priced hotel in the immediate vicinity of the Frari
and S. Rocco, so often has space when the rest
are full. Appealing, nicely furnished rooms. ❼

Cannaregio

Abbazia Calle Priuli 66 ℗041.717.333,
ⓦ www.abbaziahotel.com This fabulous three-star
hotel is in a former Carmelite monastery close to
the station, up an alley way by the Scalzi church.
Recent renovation has improved facilites.
Delightful garden. ❽

Adua Lista di Spagna 233a ℗041.716.184,
🅕041.244.0162. Clean third-floor one-star with
annexe. Friendly management and benign prices.
Rooms with own bathrooms cost €30 more. ❹

Bernardi Semenzato Calle dell'Oca 4363/66
℗041.522.7257, 🅕041.522.2424,
ⓔ mtfepoli@tin.it. The big advantages of this two-
star are its location (in a tiny alleyway close to
Campo S. Apostoli, with a cheaper annexe a couple of streets behind) and its owners, who speak
good English and are immensely helpful. Small
roof terrace. Cheapest rooms have shared bathrooms. ❸

Al Gobbo Campo S. Geremia 312,
℗041.715.001, 🅕041.714.765. Rather more
genteel than most of its fellow one-stars on the

adjacent Lista di Spagna; the better – and more
expensive – rooms overlook an attractive small
garden and include a bathroom. ❹

Hesperia Calle Riello 459 ℗041.715.251, 🅕041
.715.112, ⓦ www.venere.it/venezia/hesperia.
Sixteen-room two-star in a secluded alleyway just
beyond the Palazzo Savorgnan, close to the
Cannaregio canal. Rooms are small but very
homely, and come complete with Murano glass fittings (not the garish variety). Some rooms share
bathrooms. ❼

Villa Rosa Calle della Misericordia 389, ℗041.718
.976, 🅕041.716.569, ⓦ www.villarosahotel.com.
Clean, fairly large one-star secreted in a narrow
alley off the Lista di Spagna, well away from the
hubbub but still near the station. Air-conditioned
rooms – the best have a small terrace, and there is
a large terrace at the back for breakfast. If it's full,
you can try the modern, simply furnished and much
cheaper *Santa Lucia* next door (ⓦ www.hotelslucia
.com). ❻

Castello

Canada Campo S. Lio 5659 ℗041.522.9912,
🅕041.523.5852. Pristine two-star with more single rooms than most, some with air-conditioning.
Book well in advance for one of the two double
rooms with a roof terrace. ❼

Caneva Ramo Dietro la Fava 5515 ℗041.522.8118,
ⓦ www.hotelcaneva.com. Close to the Rialto, tucked
away behind the church of Santa Maria della Fava,
with a small courtyard. Well-appointed one-star, but
not the most genial of proprietors. Some rooms have
shared bathrooms. ❹

Casa Verardo Calle della Chiesa 4765 ℗041.528
.6127, 🅕041.523.2765, ⓦ www.casaverardo.it.
Just off Campo SS Filippo e Giacomo, a couple of
minutes from San Marco and from Campo Santa
Maria Formosa. Very fine, newly refurbished and
well-equipped three-star hotel with a breakfast
terrace downstairs, a sun lounge at the top and
another terrace attached to one of the rooms. ❻

Danieli Riva degli Schiavoni 4196
℗041.522.6480, 🅕041.520.0208, ⓦ www
.luxurycollection.com/danieli. No longer the most

expensive hotel in Venice, but no other place can compete with the glamour of the *Danieli*. Balzac stayed here, as did Wagner and Dickens. This magnificent Gothic palazzo affords just about the most sybaritic hotel experience on the Continent – provided you book a room in the old part of the building, not the modern extension. ❾

La Residenza Campo Bandiera e Moro 3608 ☎041.528.5315, ⓦwww.venicelaresidenza.com. This fourteenth-century *palazzo* – with a magnificent main hallway – is a mid-budget gem (in Venetian terms), occupying much of one side of a tranquil square just off the main waterfront. Rooms have period furniture, a/c, safe and minibar. ❼

Rio Campo SS Filippo e Giacomo 4356 ☎041.523.4810, ⓦwww.aciugheta-hotelrio.it. A couple of minutes' walk from the Piazza. Simply furnished, pleasant rooms, some sharing bathrooms. Rooms are air-conditioned and come with a safe, minibar and TV, though the ones overlooking the busy square can be noisy. ❺

Scandinavia Campo S. Maria Formosa 5240 ☎041.522.3507, ⓦwww.scandinaviahotel.com. Large, comfortable three-star on one of the liveliest squares in the city. Rooms, ranging from en-suites to private bathroom in the corridor, are decorated in eighteenth-century style with plenty of Murano glass. ❻–❾

Silva Fondamenta del Rimedio 4423 ☎041.523.7892, ⓕ041.528.6817. Fairly basic one-star overlooking a quiet canal very close to San Marco – just to the north – with singles and doubles with or without bathrooms. ❹

Wildner Riva degli Schiavoni 4161 ☎041.522.7463, ⓦwww.veneziahotele.com. Modestly attractive hotel that offers gorgeous views over to San Giorgio Maggiore. One of the cheapest hotels on the front, and one of the most expensive two-stars in town. Four of the rooms have a little cubby hole that almost makes them a suite. ❽

Hostels and institutions

Venice's hostels, most of which are run by religious foundations, are generally comfortable, well run and inexpensive by Venetian standards – moreover, even in the high season they might well have a place or two to spare. The tourist office regularly produces a simple typed list of all hostel accommodation in the city; if the places listed below are full up, ask for a copy of it at the San Marco branch.

Domus Civica Calle Campazzo, S. Polo 3082 ☎041.721.103. A student house in winter, but open to travellers July to October. A little awkward to find: it's off Calle della Lacca, to the west of San Giovanni Evangelista. Most rooms are double; showers free; no breakfast; 11.30pm curfew; single €28.50, double €52 with 20 percent discount for ISIC-card holders.

Ostello Santa Fosca S. Maria dei Servi, Cannaregio 2372 ☎041.715.775, ⓦwww.santafosca.com. Student-run hostel in an atmospheric former Servite convent in a quiet part of Cannaregio, with dorm beds, single and double rooms, but all with shared bathrooms and few locks on doors to rooms. Check-in 5–8pm, earlier in winter; 11.30pm curfew, later in summer. €18 dorm bed, €21 per head in smaller rooms. Worth booking ahead.

Foresteria Valdese S. Maria Formosa Castello 5170 ☎041.528.6797, ⓦwww.chiesavaldese .org/venezia. Installed in a *palazzo* at the end of Calle Lunga S. Maria Formosa, with flaking frescoes and a large salon. Run by Waldensians, it's principally a hostel for grown-ups, with occasional school groups. Two large dorms, and a couple of rooms for two to four people. It also has a couple of self-catering flats for three to six people. Registration 9am–1pm & 6–8pm. Prices range from €19 for a dorm bed to €70 for a double room with own bathroom. Reservations by phone only.

Ostello Venezia Fondamenta delle Zitelle, Giudecca 86 ☎041.523.8211, ⓕ041.523.5689. The city's large HI hostel occupies a superb location looking over to San Marco, but it's run with a certain briskness – notices demand "perfect sobriety and cleanliness". The waiting room opens at 1.30pm in summer and 4pm in winter for the 6pm registration. Curfew at 11.30pm, lock-out time 9.30am. Breakfast and sheets included in price, but bear in mind that you'll have to pay for a boat over to the main island. No kitchen, but full (and excellent) meals at €8. Luggage can be left here after you've checked out but you pay €2.50. Internet access (with phone card). €16 per bed, HI card necessary, but you can join on the spot for €15.50.

Suore Canossiane Fondamenta del Ponte Piccolo, Giudecca 428 ☎041.522.2157. Women-only hostel near the Palanca *vaporetto* stop. Open 8am–noon & 3–10pm – you must arrive in person, as there's no booking. €13 per bed.

Camping

If you're coming from the airport and want to pitch your tent promptly, you could settle for the large and friendly site nearby, the *Alba d'Oro*, Via Triestina 214b (☎041.541.5102, ⓦwww.evacanze.it; April–Sept), which at least has the benefit of frequent bus connections to Piazzale Roma. If you're coming from Venice itself, take bus #5 from Piazzale Roma to the airport, then walk or take bus #15 (every 20min) to Cá'Noghera, the fourth stop.

More attractive sites are to be found on the outer edge of the lagoon on the **Litorale del Cavallino**, which stretches from the Punta Sabbioni to Jésolo and has a total of around 60,000 pitches, many of them quite luxuriously appointed. The #14 vaporetto stops close to the relatively cheap *Miramare*, Lungomare Dante Alighieri 29 (☎041.966.150, ⓦwww.camping-miremare.it; April–Sept), and a bit further away the more luxurious and expensive *Marina di Venezia*, Via Montello 6 (☎041.966.146, ⓦwww.marinadivenezia.it; April–Sept). However, there's a minimum stay of three days here, and the price can be a problem; when you've added on the fare for the forty-minute boat trip into the city you're not left with a particularly economical proposition.

Alternatively, back on the mainland, the municipal site at **Fusina**, Via Moranzani 79 (☎041.547.0055, ⓦwww.camping-fusina.com; Feb–Nov), has 800 places and chalets too. *Vaporetti* connect Fusina to central Venice all year, or you can take the bus to Mestre and change there for bus #1.

The City

The 118 islands of central Venice are divided into six districts known as *sestieri*, and the houses within each *sestiere* are numbered in a sequence that makes sense solely to the functionaries of the post office – this explains how buildings facing each other across an alleyway can have numbers that are separated by hundreds.

Venice's main thoroughfare is the **Canal Grande**. Almost four kilometres long and between thirty and seventy metres wide (but at no point much deeper than five metres), it divides the city in half – three *sestieri* to the west and three to the east. The majority of the most important palaces in Venice stand on the Canal Grande, and the main facades of all of them are on the canalside, many properly visible only from the water.

On the east side of the Canal Grande is the *sestiere* of **San Marco**, the zone where the majority of the essential sights are clustered, and accordingly the most expensive and most crowded district of the city. On the east it's bordered by **Castello**, and on the north by **Cannaregio** – both of which become more residential, and poorer and quieter, the further you go from the centre. On the other side of the Canal Grande, the largest of the *sestieri* is Dorsoduro, stretching from the fashionable quarter at the southern tip of the canal to the docks in the west. **Santa Croce**, named after a now demolished church, roughly follows the curve of the Canal Grande from Piazzale Roma to a point just short of the Rialto, where it joins the smartest and commercially most active of the districts on this bank – **San Polo**.

To the uninitiated, the boundaries of the *sestieri* seem arbitrary. So, although in some instances we've used *sestieri* as broad indicators of location, the boundaries of our sections have been chosen for their practicality and do not, except in the case of San Marco, exactly follow the city's official divisions.

Museum and church passes

In an attempt to make sure that tourists go to see more than just the big central sights, entry to a number of sights is with a combined ticket only. The most popular is the **Museum Card**. Costing €9.50, the ticket allows one visit to each of the following attractions: the Palazzo Ducale, Museo Correr, Museo Archeologico and Biblioteca Nazionale Marciana. Two other museum cards are available: for the Museums of the Eighteenth Century (Ca'Rezzonico, Palazzo Mocenigo and the Casa Goldoni – €8) and the Island Museums (Museo del Merletto on Burano and Museo Vetrario on Murano – €6). If you are doing a lot of sightseeing, you might want to go for the **Museum Pass** (€15.50), which covers all three groups of museums and is valid for a year from purchase. The cards are available at all participating museums and are valid for up to three months.

In addition, fifteen churches that charge for entry (either to the whole structure or just part) are now part of the **Chorus Pass** scheme (ⓦ www.chorus-ve.org). For €8 you can buy a pass that allows one visit to each of the churches over a one-year period. Individual entrance fees at each of the participating churches are €2, and nearly all the churches observe the same opening hours: Monday to Saturday 10am to 5pm, and Sunday 1 to 5pm. The churches involved include Santa Maria del Giglio, Santo Stefano, Santa Maria Formosa, Santa Maria dei Miracoli, the Frari, San Polo, San Giacomo dell'Orio, San Stae, Sant'Alvise, Madonna dell'Orto, San Pietro di Castello, Redentore and San Sebastiano.

San Marco

The section of Venice enclosed by the lower loop of the Canal Grande – a rectangle smaller than 1000 metres by 500 – is, in essence, the Venice of the travel brochures. The plush hotels are concentrated here, in the sestiere of **SAN MARCO**, as are the swankier shops and the best-known cultural attractions of the city. But small though this area is, you can still lose the hordes within it.

"The finest drawing-room in Europe" was how Napoleon described its focal point, the **Piazza San Marco** – the only piazza in Venice, all other squares being *campi* or *campielli*. Less genteel phrases might seem appropriate on a suffocating summer afternoon, but you can take some slight consolation from the knowledge that the Piazza has always been congested. Neither is the influx of foreigners a modern phenomenon – its parades, festivities and markets have always drawn visitors from all over the Continent and beyond, the biggest attraction being a huge international trade fair known as the **Fiera della Sensa**, which kept the Piazza buzzing for the fortnight following the Ascension Day ceremony of the marriage of Venice to the sea. The coffee shops of the Piazza were a vital component of eighteenth-century high society, and the two survivors from that period – *Florian* and *Quadri* – are still the smartest and most expensive in town: an espresso in Florian will set you back at least €8, plus a supplement for the thrill of hearing the band's rendition of *My Way* or the best of Lloyd-Webber.

The Basilica di San Marco

The **Basilica di San Marco** is the most exotic of Europe's cathedrals, and no visitor can remain dispassionate when confronted by it. Herbert Spencer found it loathsome – "a fine sample of barbaric architecture", but to John Ruskin it was a "treasure-heap . . . a confusion of delight". Delightful or not, it's certainly confusing, increasingly so as you come nearer and the details emerge; some knowledge of the history of the building helps bring a little order out of chaos.

⑤

SAN MARCO

0   100 m

▲ **A**

Sant'Aponal

Rio di S. Polo

S. Silvestro

Rio di S. Stin

CAMPO
SAN POLO

Rio di S. Polo

R. della Madonnetta

R. di S. Apollinare

Frari

⑤

S. Polo

D

R. della Madonnetta

R. dei Meloni

CAMPO
DEI FRARI

E

S. Silvestro
1

R. di Fran

Palazzo
Grimani

R. di S. Toma

CANAL GRANDE

**Museo
Goldoni**

CAMPO
SAN TOMA

R. di S. Luca

⑥

San
Toma

S. Angelo 1

S. Benedetto

SALIZ. CHIESA S. LUCA

Rio di Ca' Michiel

Traghetto

⑩

S. Tomà
1, 82, N

Palazzo
Corner Spinelli

**Museo
Fortuny**

R. di S. Luca

H

R. TERRA ASSASSINI

R. della Verona

**Palazzo
Balbi**

R. di Ca' Garzoni

**Palazzi
Mocenigo**

R. di S. Angelo

CAMPO
S. ANGELO

C. DE LA MANDOLA

Ca'Foscari

P. S. SAMUELE

**Oratorio
Annunziata**

⑭

J

⑮

**Ca'
Rezzonico**

Palazzo Grassi

SAL. S. SAMUELE

C. NUOVO

⑯

C. BOTTEGHE

K

CALLE DE LA FENICE

**S.
Samuele
82, N**

CAMPO S.
SAMUELE

SAL. MALIPIERO

S. Samuele

C. TEATRO

S. Stefano

La Fenice

Traghetto

CAMPO
SANTO
STEFANO

CORTE
S. FORZA

**Ca'
Rezzonico
1**

**Ca'del
Duca**

C. CICOGNA

S. Maurizio

**S. Maria
del Giglio**

R. d. Fenice

R. del Duca

**Palazzo
Loredan**

CAMPO S.
MAURIZIO

R. di S. M. Zobenigo

⑲

⑳

R. S. Vidal

S. Vitale

CAMPO
PISANI

**Palazzo Corner
della Ca'Grande**

R. Corner Zaguri

CAMPO
DEL
TRAGHETTO

M

**Accademia
1, 82, N**

R. dell Orso

**Palazzo
Pisani**

R. di S. Stefano

CONTE D.
ACCADEMIA

S. M. del Giglio 1

Traghetto

Accademia

CANAL GRANDE

S. Trovaso

**Guggenheim
Collection**

▼ **22**   **21**

▼ **23**

San Giacomo

Rialto Market

Fondaco d. Tedeschi

R. d. Fontego d. Tedeschi

CALLE DE LA MADONA

CALLE DEL SCALOE

PONTE DI RIALTO

❶

S. Lio

SAL. DI S. LIO

CAMPO SANTA MARIA FORMOSA

❸

S. Maria Formosa

Rialto 1, 82, N

❷

S. Bartolomeo

C. D. STAGNERI

Rio delle rava

MERCERIA 2 APRILE

CAMPO S. BARTOLOMEO

CAMPO S. SALVADOR

S. Salvador

S. Maria della Fava

Traghetto

Palazzo Loredan (Municipio)

MERC. D. CAPITELLO

❹

Rio della Guerra

RIO ZULIAN

R. D. POLO GUERRA

Rio della Guerra

Palazzo Querini-Stampalia

❻

CALLE D. CAPITELLO

MER. D. S. SALVADOR

RIO D. Baratteri

Teatro Goldoni

Palazzo Farsetti

S. Giuliano

CAMPO S. LUCA

CALLE FIUBERA

RIO DI S. ZULIAN

CALLE SPADERIA

Rio dei Ferali

CALLE D. SPECHIERI

S. Luca

C. DEI FABBRI

CAMPO MANIN

F ❽

CALLE D. FABBRI

RIO DI S. ZULIAN

CALLE DE LA CASADA

LARGA SAN MARCO

❾ G ⑫

SALIZZ. S. PROVOLO

CALLE DELLA MANDOLA

Torre dell'Orologio

❶❶

Scala del Bovolo

R. dei Fuseri

CAMPO MANIN

RIO DEL CAPENTO

P. DEI LEONCINI

CALLE DEL CAVALLETTO

San Marco

Ateneo Veneto

CALLE D BARCAROLI

MERCERIA DELL'OROLOGIO

FREZZERIA

Bacino Orseolo

R. del Cavallero

Procuratie Vecchie

CAMPO S. FANTIN

CALLE VALLARESSO

S. Fantin

Campanile

PIAZZA SAN MARCO

Ponte dei Sospiri

Prigioni

R. d. Veste

E. del Barcaroli

❶❼

❶❸

PIAZZETTA

Libreria Sansoviniana

Rio di Palazzo

Palazzo Ducale

Ponte della Paglia

CALLE D. ASCENSION

Procuratie Nuove

i

C. D. VALLARESSO

SAL. S. MOISE

R. della Zecca

MOLO

S. Moise

Zecca

CAMPO S. MOISE

C. D. RIDOTTO

Giardinetti Reali

N

VISTE

C. LARGA XXII MARZO

❶❽

Rio dei S. Moise

i

Palazzo Giustinian

↪ **S. Marco 1, 82, N**

Traghetto

Salute 1

S. Maria della Salute

Dogana di Mare

Although San Marco is open from 6.30am on most days for prayer, tourists are asked not to enter before 9am and the main body of the church is often roped off before this time; the basilica usually closes at 5pm. Admission fees totalling €5 are charged for certain parts of the church. Sections of the basilica will almost certainly be under restoration or closed off for some other reason; though restoration of the Cappella Zen and Baptistry has at last been completed, there's no sign of either being reopened in the near future.

The story of the Basilica

According to the **legend of St Mark's annunciation**, the Evangelist was moored in the lagoon, on his way to Rome, when an angel appeared and told him that his body would rest there. (The angel's salute – *Pax tibi, Marce evangelista meus* – is the text cut into the book that the Lion of St Mark is always shown holding.) The founders of Venice, having persuaded themselves of the sacred ordination of their city, duly went about fulfilling the angelic prophecy, and in 828 the body of St Mark was stolen from Alexandria and brought here.

Modelled on Constantinople's Church of the Twelve Apostles, the shrine of St Mark was consecrated in 832, but in 976 both the church and the Palazzo Ducale were ruined by fire during an uprising against the doge. The present basilica was originally finished in 1094 and embellished over the succeeding centuries. The combination of ancient structure and later decorations is, to a great extent, what makes San Marco so bewildering, but the picture is made yet more complicated by the addition of ornaments looted from abroad that are sometimes older than the building itself and in some cases have nothing to do with the Church. Every trophy that the doge stuck onto his church (and bear in mind this church was not the cathedral of Venice but the doge's own chapel) was proof of Venice's secular might and so of the spiritual power of St Mark. Conversely, the Evangelist was invoked to sanctify political actions and rituals of state – the doge's investiture was consecrated in the church, and military commanders received their commissions at the altar.

The exterior, narthex and Loggia dei Cavalli

Of the exterior features that can be seen easily from the ground, the **Romanesque carvings** of the **central door** demand the closest attention – especially the middle arch's figures of The Months and Seasons and outer arch's series of *The Trades of Venice*. The carvings were begun around 1225 and finished in the early fourteenth century. Take a look also at the mosaic above the doorway on the far left – *The Arrival of the Body of St Mark* – which was made around 1260 (the only early mosaic left on the main facade) and includes the oldest known image of the basilica.

From the Piazza you pass into the vestibule known as the **narthex**, decorated with the first of the church's **mosaics**: Old Testament scenes on the domes and arches, together with *The Madonna with Apostles and Evangelists* in the niches of the bay in front of the main door – dating from the 1060s, the oldest mosaics in San Marco.

A steep staircase goes from the church's main door up to the **Museo Marciano** and the Loggia dei Cavalli (daily 9.45am–4.30pm; €1.50). Apart from giving you an all-round view, the loggia is also the best place from which to inspect the Gothic carvings along the apex of the facade. The **horses** outside are replicas, the genuine articles having been removed inside, allegedly to protect them from the risks of atmospheric pollution, although some cynics have insisted that the rescue mission had more to do with the marketing strategies of Olivetti, who sponsored the operation. You'll find the originals just behind the loggia, in the **Galleria**, along with oddments of mosaic and a fine polyptych by Paolo Veneziano. Thieved from the Hippodrome of Constantinople in 1204 during the Fourth Crusade, they are probably Roman works of the second century – the only such ancient group, or *quadriga*, to have survived – and are made of a bronze that is very rich in copper.

The interior

With its undulating floor of twelfth-century patterned marble, its plates of eastern stone on the lower walls, and its 4000 square metres of **mosaics** covering every other inch of wall and vaulting, the interior of San Marco is the most opulent of any cathedral. One visit is not enough – there's too much to take in at one go, and the shifting light reveals and hides parts of the decoration as the day progresses; try calling in for half an hour at the beginning and end of a couple of days.

The majority of the mosaics were in position by the middle of the thirteenth century; some date from the fourteenth and fifteenth centuries, and others were created in the sixteenth to replace damaged early sections. A thorough guide to them would take volumes, but an inventory of the very best might include the following. On the west wall, above the door – *Christ, the Virgin and St Mark* (thirteenth century); west dome – *Pentecost* (early twelfth century); arch between west and central domes – *Crucifixion, Resurrection* (the latter a fifteenth-century copy); central dome – *Ascension*; east dome – *Religion of Christ Foretold by the Prophets*; between windows of apse – *Four Patron SS of Venice*; north transept's dome – *Acts of St John the Evangelist*; arch to west of north transept's dome (and continued on upper part of adjacent wall) – *Life of the Virgin and Life of the Infant Christ*; wall of south aisle – *The Agony in the Garden*; west wall of south transept – *Rediscovery of the Body of St Mark*. This last scene refers to the story that St Mark's body was hidden during the rebuilding of the basilica in 1063 and was not found again until 1094, when it miraculously broke through the pillar in which it had been buried.

From the south transept you can enter the **Sanctuary** (Mon–Sat 9.45am–4.30pm, Sun 2–4.30pm; €1.50), where, behind the altar, you'll find the most precious of San Marco's treasures – the **Pala d'Oro** (Golden Altar Panel). Commissioned in 976 in Constantinople, the Pala was enlarged, enriched and rearranged by Byzantine goldsmiths in 1105, then by Venetians in 1209 (to incorporate some less cumbersome loot from the Fourth Crusade) and again (finally) in 1345. The completed screen holds 83 enamel plaques, 74 enamelled roundels, 38 chiselled figures, 300 sapphires, 300 emeralds, 400 garnets, 15 rubies, 1300 pearls and a couple of hundred other stones.

In a corner of the south transept is the door of the Treasury (same times as Sanctuary; €2), a small but dazzling line-up of chalices, reliquaries, candelabra and so on – a fair proportion of which owes its presence here to the great Constantinople robbery of 1204.

The **Baptistry** – off the south aisle – was altered to its present form by the fourteenth-century Doge Andrea Dandolo, whose tomb (facing the door) was thought by Ruskin to have the best monumental sculpture in the city. Dandolo also ordered the creation of the mosaics depicting *Scenes from the Lives of Christ* and *John the Baptist*, works in which the hieratic formality of Byzantine art is blended with the rich detail of the Gothic.

The adjoining **Cappella Zen** was created between 1504 and 1521 by enclosing the piazzetta entrance to the narthex, in order to house the tomb of Cardinal Giambattista Zen, whose estate was left to the city on condition that he was buried within San Marco. The late thirteenth-century **mosaics** on the vault show *Scenes from the Life of St Mark*. The chapel is sometimes known as the Chapel of the Madonna of the Shoe, taking its name from the *Virgin and Child* by Antonio Lombardo (1506) on the high altar.

Back in the main body of the church, there's still more to see on the lower levels of the building. Don't overlook the **rood screen**'s marble figures of *The Virgin, St Mark and the Apostles*, carved in 1394 by the dominant sculptors in Venice at that time, Jacobello and Pietro Paolo Dalle Masegne. The **pulpits** on each side of the screen were assembled in the early fourteenth century from miscellaneous panels (some from Constantinople); the new doge was presented to the people from the right-hand one. The tenth-century **Icon of the Madonna of Nicopeia** (in the chapel on east side of north transept) is the most revered religious image in Venice; it used to be one of the most revered in Constantinople. A beautiful mid-fifteenth-century mosaic cycle of *Scenes from the Life of the Virgin*, one of the earliest Renaissance works in Venice, is to be seen in the adjacent **Cappella della Madonna dei Mascoli**. And on the north side of the nave stands a marble kiosk fabricated to house a painting of the *Crucifix* on the altar; this arrived in Venice in 1205, and in 1290 achieved its current exalted status by spouting blood after an assault on it.

The Palazzo Ducale

The **Palazzo Ducale** (daily: April–Oct 9am–7pm; Nov–March 9am–4pm; entrance with Museum Card, see box on p.299) was far more than the residence of the doge – it was the home of all of Venice's governing councils, many of its courts, a sizeable number of its civil servants and even its prisons. The government of Venice was administered through an intricate system of elected committees and councils – a system designed to limit the power of any individual – but for the last 500 years of the republic's existence only those families listed in the register of noble births and marriages known as the *Libro d'Oro* (Golden Book) were entitled to play a part in the system.

At the head of the network sat the **doge**, the one politician to sit on all the major councils of state and the only one elected for life; he could be immensely influential in steering policy and in making appointments, and restrictions were accordingly imposed on his actions to reduce the possibility of his abusing that power – his letters were read by censors, for example, and he wasn't permitted to receive foreign delegations alone. The privileges of the job far outweighed the inconveniences, though, and men campaigned for years to increase their chances of election.

Like San Marco, the Palazzo Ducale has been rebuilt many times since its foundation in the first years of the ninth century. It was with the construction of a new hall for the Maggior Consiglio (Great Council) in 1340 that the *palazzo* began to take on its present shape. The hall was constructed parallel to the waterfront and was inaugurated in 1419; three years later, it was decided to extend the building along the piazzetta, copying the style of the fourteenth-century work – the slightly fatter column on the piazzetta side, under a tondo of Justice, is where the two wings meet.

The principal entrance to the *palazzo* – the **Porta della Carta** – is one of the most ornate Gothic works in the city. It was commissioned in 1438 by Doge Francesco Fóscari from Bartolomeo and Giovanni Bon, but the figures of Fóscari and his lion are replicas – the originals were pulverized in 1797 by the head of the stonemason's guild, as a favour to Napoleon. Fóscari's head survived the hammering, however, and is on display inside.

Tourists no longer enter the building by the Porta della Carta, but instead are herded through a doorway on the lagoon side. Once through the ticket hall you emerge in the courtyard, opposite the other end of the passageway into the *palazzo* – the **Arco Fóscari**. This also was commissioned from the Bons by Doge Fóscari but finished a few years after his death by Antonio Rizzo and Antonio Bregno. In 1483 a fire demolished most of the wing to your right, and led to more work for Rizzo – he designed the enormous staircase (Scala dei Giganti) and much of the new wing. Reconstruction continued under Pietro Lombardo, Spavento and Scarpagnino, and finally Bartolomeo Monopola, who completed the courtyard in about 1600 by extending the arcades along the other two sides.

Parts of the Palazzo Ducale can be marched through fairly briskly. Acres of canvas cover the walls, but many of the paintings are just wearisome exercises in self-aggrandizement. But other sections you will not want to rush, and, if you're there in the high season, it's a good idea to buy your ticket within half an hour of the opening time. A word of warning – restoration work is continually in progress in the Palazzo Ducale, and there's never any indication before you go in as to which bits are under wraps; it's a distinct possibility that some of the highlights will be hidden from view.

The itinerary begins on the left side of the courtyard, where the finest of the capitals from the *palazzo*'s exterior arcade are displayed in the **Museo dell'Opera**. Upstairs, the route takes you through the doge's private apartments then on to the **Anticollegio**, the room in which embassies had to wait before being admitted to the presence of the doge and his cabinet. As regards the quality of its paintings, this is one of the richest rooms in the Palazzo Ducale: four pictures by Tintoretto hang on the door walls, and facing the windows is Veronese's *Rape of Europa*.

The cycle of paintings on the ceiling of the adjoining **Sala del Collegio** is also by Veronese, and he features strongly again in the most stupendous room in the building – the **Sala del Maggior Consiglio**. Veronese's ceiling panel of *The Apotheosis of Venice* is suspended over the dais from which the doge oversaw the sessions of the city's general assembly; the backdrop is **Tintoretto**'s immense *Paradiso*, painted towards the end of his life, with the aid of his son, Domenico. At the opposite end there's a curiosity: the frieze of portraits of the first 76 doges (the series continues in the Sala dello Scrutinio – through the door at the far end) is interrupted by a painted black veil, marking the place where **Doge Marin Falier** would have been honoured had he not conspired against the state in 1355 and been beheaded for his crime.

From here you descend quickly to the underbelly of the Venetian state, crossing the **Ponte dei Sospiri** (Bridge of Sighs) to the prisons. Before the construction of these cells in the early seventeenth century all prisoners were kept in the Piombi (the Leads), under the roof of the Palazzo Ducale, or in the Pozzi (the Wells) in the bottom two storeys; the new block was occupied mainly by petty criminals. The route finishes with a detour through the Pozzi, but if you want to see the Piombi, and the rooms in which the day-to-day administration of Venice took place, you have to go on the **Itinerari Segreti del Palazzo Ducale**, an intriguing guided tour through the warren of offices and passageways that interlocks with the public rooms of the building. It's not cheap (€12.50), but well worth the price, and covers entry to the whole palace. Tickets must be booked in advance by asking at the Palazzo or phoning ☏041.522.4951; the tour is held every day except Wednesday at 9.45am, 10.45am and 11.35am in English.

The Campanile and Torre dell'Orologio

Most of the landscape of the Piazza dates from the great period of urban renewal that began at the end of the fifteenth century and went on for much of the following century. The one exception – excluding San Marco itself – is the **Campanile** (daily: July–Sept 9.30am–8pm; Oct–June 9.30am–5pm; €6), which began life as a lighthouse in the ninth century and was modified frequently up to the early sixteenth. The present structure is in fact a reconstruction: the original tower collapsed on July 14, 1902 – a catastrophe that injured nobody and is commemorated by faked postcard photos ostensibly taken at the very instant of the disaster. The collapse reduced to rubble the **Loggetta** at the base of the campanile, but somehow it was pieced together again; built between 1537 and 1549 by Sansovino, it has served as a meeting-room for the nobility, a guardhouse and the place at which the state lottery was drawn. At 99 metres, the campanile is the tallest structure in the city, and from the top (there is a lift) you can make out virtually every building, but not a single canal.

The other tower in the Piazza, the **Torre dell'Orologio**, was built between 1496 and 1506. A restoration lasting several years has prevented people from taking the staircase up past the innards of the clock and onto the terrace on which the so-called Moors stand.

The Procuratie and Museo Correr

Away to the left of the Torre dell'Orologio stretches the **Procuratie Vecchie**; begun around 1500 by Codussi, this block housed the offices of the **Procurators of St Mark**, a committee of nine men whose responsibilities included the upkeep of the basilica and other public buildings. A century or so after taking possession, the procurators were moved to the opposite side of the Piazza, into the **Procuratie Nuove**. Napoleon converted these apartments and offices into a royal palace and then, having realized that the building lacked a ballroom, remedied the deficiency by smashing down the church of San Geminiano in order to connect the two Procuratie with a new wing for dancing.

Generally known as the **Ala Napoleonica**, this short side of the Piazza is partly occupied by the **Museo Correr** (daily: April–Oct 9am–7pm; Nov–March 9am–5pm; entrance with Museum Card, see box on p.299), an immense triple-decker museum with a vast **historical collection** of coins, weapons, regalia, prints, paintings and miscellanea. Much of this is heavy going unless you have an intense interest in Venetian history, though there's an appealing exhibition of Venetian applied arts, and one show-stopping item in the form of the original blocks and a print of Jacopo de'Barbari's astonishing aerial view of Venice, engraved in 1500. The **Quadreria** on the second floor is no rival for the Accademia's collection (see p.309), but it does set out clearly the evolution of painting in Venice from the thirteenth century to around 1500 (though not all of its pictures are by Venetians), and it contains some gems. The Pietà by Cosmé Tura and the *Transfiguration* and *Dead Christ Supported by Angels* by Giovanni Bellini stand out, along with a **Carpaccio** picture usually known as *The Courtesans*, although its subjects are really a couple of terminally bored, bourgeois ladies dressed in the eccentric manner prevalent in the late fifteenth century.

Accessed from within the Correr is the **Museo Archeologico** (times and ticket as above). In many cities a collection of Greek and Roman sculpture as comprehensive as this one would merit a strong recommendation; in Venice you needn't feel guilty about leaving it for a rainy day. A further section is devoted to the **Museo del Risorgimento** (included in the Museo Correr ticket), which acts as a shrine to Daniele Manin, five of the fifteen rooms being devoted to his rebellion against the Austrians. The final part of the Correr, part of the Biblioteca Nazionale Marciana, is the **Libreria Sansoviniana** (times and ticket as above), which looks down onto the Piazzetta (see below). These historic rooms of the library were only recently opened to the public and it's worth perservering as far as this end of the museum if only to see the Staircase, stuccoed by Vittoria, and adjacent Antechamber. The latter, designed by Palladio's follower Scamaozzi, has a remarkable Titian *Wisdom* in the centre of the ceiling, surrounded by mesmerizing trompe l'oeil perspective. In the main hall are reproductions of some of the more precious of the library's million volumes, while staring down pensively from the walls are frescoes of philosophers and Virtues by Veronese, Tintoretto and others.

The Piazzetta

The **Piazzetta** – the open space between San Marco and the waterfront pavement known as the Molo – was the area where the politicians used to gather before meetings; known as the broglio, its wheeling and dealing probably gave rise to the English word "imbroglio". Facing the Palazzo Ducale is Sansovino's masterpiece and the most consistently admired Renaissance building in the city – the **Libreria Sansoviniana** (see above). Work was well advanced on the building when, in December 1545, a severe frost resulted in a major collapse, a setback that landed the architect in prison for a while. Completion came in 1591, two decades after Sansovino's death.

Attached to the library, with its main facade to the lagoon, Sansovino's first major building in Venice, the **Zecca** (Mint), was built between 1537 and 1545 on the site of the thirteenth-century mint. By the beginning of the fifteenth century the city's prosperity was such that the Venetian coinage was in use in every European exchange, and the doge could with some justification call Venice "the mistress of all the gold in Christendom".

The piazzetta's two **columns** were brought here from the Levant at the end of the twelfth century, in company with a third, which fell off the barge and still lies somewhere just off the Molo. The figures perched on top are St Theodore (it's a copy – the original is in the Palazzo Ducale), patron saint of Venice when it was dependent on Byzantium, and a Chimera, customized to look like the Lion of St Mark. Public executions were carried out between the columns, the techniques employed ranging from straightforward hanging to burial alive, head downwards. Superstitious Venetians avoid passing between them.

Sometimes the heads of freshly dispatched villains were mounted on the **Pietra del Bando**, the stump of porphyry at the other end of the piazzetta, against the corner of San Marco. Its routine use, however, was as one of the two stones from which the laws of the republic were proclaimed (the other is at the Rialto). The Pietra del Bando was brought back to Venice from Acre after the Venetian defeat of the Genoese there in 1256; the two square pillars near to it, with their fine fifth-century Syrian carving, were probably hauled away from Constantinople in 1204.

North of the Piazza

The Mercerie, a chain of glitzy streets that starts under the clock tower and finishes at the Campo San Bartolomeo, is the most direct route between the Rialto and San Marco and has therefore always been the main land thoroughfare of the city and a prime site for its shopkeepers. For those immune to the charms of window-shopping there's little reason to linger until you reach the church of **San Salvador** (Mon–Sat 10am–noon & 3 6pm, Sun 9am–12.30pm & 3–6pm; free), an early sixteenth-century church cleverly planned in the form of three Greek crosses placed end to end. It has a couple of Titian paintings – an altarpiece of the Transfiguration (1560) and an Annunciation (1566), whose awkwardly embarking angel is often blamed on the great man's assistants. The end of the south transept is filled by the tomb of Caterina Cornaro, who for a while was Queen of Cyprus before being manoeuvred into surrendering the island to Venice (see p.369).

The **Campo San Bartolomeo**, close to the foot of the Rialto bridge, is at its best in the evening, when it's as packed as any bar in town. For a crash-course in the Venetian character, hang around the statue of Goldoni for a while at about 7pm. If the crush gets a bit too much, you can retire to the nearby **Campo San Luca**, another focus of after-work gatherings but not as much of a pressure-cooker as San Bartolomeo.

Beyond Campo San Luca is **Campo Manin**, on the south side of which is a sign for the spiral staircase known as the **Scala del Bovolo** (*bovolo* means "snail shell" in Venetian dialect), a piece of flamboyant engineering dating from around 1500 (April–Oct daily 10am–5.30pm; Nov–March weekends only, but open during Carnival; €2.50). The **Museo Fortuny** (closed for repair, but sections sometimes open Tues–Sun 10am–6pm) is also close at hand, similarly tucked away in a spot you'd never accidentally pass, but signposted with the occasional yellow sign. In addition to making his famous silk dresses, which were said to be fine enough to be threaded through a wedding ring, Mariano Fortuny (1871–1949) was a painter, architect, engraver, photographer, theatre designer and sculptor; the museum reflects his versatility, but you'll probably come out wishing there were more of his frocks on display.

West of the Piazza

Although it too has its share of fashionable shops – much of the broad Calle Larga XXII Marzo, for example, is dedicated to the beautification of the well-heeled and their dwellings – the area to the **west of the Piazza** is less frenetic than the streets to the north. None of the first-division tourist sights are here, but the walk from the Piazza to the Accademia bridge, through a succession of campi each quite unlike its predecessor, isn't lacking in worthwhile diversions.

Heading west from the Piazza, you soon reach the hypnotically dreadful **San Moisè** (Mon–Sat 3.30–7pm, Sun 9am–noon; free), runaway winner of any poll for the ugliest church in Venice. The facade sculpture, featuring a species of camel unknown to zoology, was created in 1668 by Heinrich Meyring; and if you think this is in dubious taste, wait till you see his altarpiece of *Mount Sinai with Moses Receiving the Tablets*.

Halfway along the Calle Larga XXII Marzo, on the right, is the Calle del Sartor da Veste, which takes you over a canal and into the Campo San Fantin, where the Renaissance church of **San Fantin** has a graceful domed apse by Sansovino. Across the campo is the wreckage of Venice's largest and oldest theatre, **La Fenice**, opened in December 1792, rebuilt in 1836 after the place had been wrecked by fire, and now a burned-out husk once again, in the wake of the fire that ripped though the building on the night of January 29, 1996, just as a phase of restoration was coming to a close. Criminal investigations are proceeding (it seems almost certain that the fire was started deliberately), and La Fenice is officially supposed to be opening in 2003, but given the delays that have occurred so far, this seems somewhat unlikely. In the interim, opera and ballet performances are being held over on Tronchetto, in a vast tent called the Palafenice (see p.338), and in the Teatro Malibran (ask at tourist office for details).

Back on the main road to the Accademia, another very odd church awaits – **Santa Maria del Giglio**, otherwise known as Santa Maria del Zobenigo (see box on p.299 for times and ticket). You can stare at this all day and still not find a single Christian image. The statues are of the five Barbaro brothers who financed the rebuilding of the church in 1678; Virtue, Honour, Fame and Wisdom hover respectfully around them; and the maps in relief depict the towns the brothers graced in the course of their exemplary military and diplomatic careers.

The tilting campanile that soon looms into view over the vapid church of San Maurizio belongs to Santo Stefano, which stands at the end of the next campo – the **Campo Santo Stefano**. Large enough to hold several clusters of tourists and natives plus a kids' football match or two, the Campo Santo Stefano is always lively but never feels crowded, and has, in *Paolin*, one of the best ice cream places in Venice (see review on p.337). To those few non-Venetians to whom his name means anything, Francesco Morosini is known as the man who lobbed a missile through the roof of the Parthenon towards the end of the seventeenth century. He lived at the Canal Grande end of the campo (no. 2802) and is buried in **Santo Stefano** (see box on p.299 for times and ticket), a thirteenth-century church that was rebuilt in the fourteenth and altered again in the first half of the fifteenth; the Gothic doorway and the ship's keel roof both belong to this last phase. The best paintings are in the sacristy – *The Agony in the Garden*, *The Last Supper* and *The Washing of the Disciples' Feet*, all late works by Tintoretto.

Dorsoduro

Some of the finest architecture in Venice, both domestic and public, is to be found in the sestiere of **DORSODURO**, a situation partly attributable to the stability of its sandbanks – Dorsoduro means "hard back". Yet for all its attractions, not many visitors wander off the strip that runs between the main sights of the area – the Ca' Rezzonico, the Accademia and the Salute. The *sestiere* has a bafflingly complex border, so for clarity's sake we have taken the curve of the Canal Grande–Rio di Ca' Fóscari–Rio Nuovo as the boundary between Dorsoduro and the rest of central Venice.

The Galleria dell'Accademia

The **Galleria dell'Accademia** (Mon 8.15am–2pm, Tues–Sun 8.15am–7.15pm; €6.50) is one of the finest specialist collections of European art, following the history of Venetian painting from the fourteenth to the eighteenth centuries. When it was established in 1807, its exhibits came largely from churches and convents that were then being suppressed; indeed, the buildings that the Accademia has occupied since then include two former religious buildings – the church of Santa Maria della Carità, rebuilt by Bartolomeo Bon in the 1440s, and the incomplete Convento dei Canonici Lateranensi, partly built by Palladio in 1561.

The Accademia is the third component – with San Marco and the Palazzo Ducale – of the triad of obligatory tourist sights in Venice, but admissions are restricted to batches of 300 people at a time. So, if you're visiting in high summer and don't want to wait, get here about 1pm when most people are having lunch.

To the early Renaissance

The gallery is laid out in a roughly chronological succession of rooms going anticlockwise. The first room at the top of the stairs is the fifteenth century assembly room of the Scuola and houses works by the earliest known individual Venetian painters. **Paolo Veneziano** (from the first half of the fourteenth century) and his follower **Lorenzo Veneziano** are the most absorbing.

Room 2 moves on to works from the late fifteenth and early sixteenth centuries, with large altarpieces that are contemplative even when the scenes are far from calm. **Carpaccio**'s strange and gruesome *Crucifixion and Glorification of the Ten Thousand Martyrs of Mount Ararat* (painted around 1512) and his *Presentation of Jesus in the Temple* accompany works by **Giovanni Bellini** and **Cima da Conegliano**.

In the west room you can observe the emergence of the characteristically Venetian treatment of colour in works from the early Renaissance, but there's nothing here as exciting as the small paintings in rooms 4 and 5, a high point of the collection. Apart from an exquisite *St George* by **Mantegna** and a series of **Giovanni Bellini** Madonnas, this section contains **Giorgione**'s enigmatic *Tempest* – nobody has ever satisfactorily explained what, if anything, is going on here, and the picture may well have been equally opaque to the person for whom it was created in 1500.

High Renaissance

Room 6 introduces one of the heavyweights of Venetian painting, Jacopo Robusti, known as **Tintoretto**. The *Creation of the Animals* features a few species that must have followed the unicorn into extinction. Another big name represented here is **Titian** (Tiziano Vecellio), with a not particularly interesting *John the Baptist* (early 1540s). One of the most compelling paintings in the gallery is in room 7, the *Young Man in his Study* by **Lorenzo Lotto** (1528).

Room 10 is dominated by epic productions, and an entire wall is filled by **Paolo Veronese**'s *Christ in the House of Levi*. Originally called *The Last Supper*, this picture provoked a stern reaction from the Court of the Holy Office: it was too irreverent for such a holy subject, they insisted – why were there "Germans and buffoons and such-like things in this picture? Does it appear to you fitting that at our Lord's last supper you should paint buffoons, drunkards, Germans, dwarfs, and similar indecencies?" Veronese fielded all their questions and responded simply by changing the title, which made the work acceptable. The pieces by **Tintoretto** in here include three legends of St Mark: *St Mark Rescues a Slave* (1548), which was the painting that made his reputation, *The Theft of the Body of St Mark* and *St Mark Saves a Saracen* (both 1560s). All of these show Tintoretto's love of energy and drama – from the physical or psychological drama of the subject matter, emphasized by the twisting poses of the people depicted, to the technical energy of his brush strokes, perception of colour and use of light. Opposite is an emotional late **Titian**, a pietà (1570s) intended for his own tomb in the Frari (see p.315).

The eighteenth century

Room 11 contains a number of works by **Giambattista Tiepolo**, the most prominent painter of eighteenth-century Venice, including two shaped fragments rescued from the wreckage of the Scalzi (1743–45) and *The Translation of the Holy House of Loreto* (1743), a sketch for the same ceiling. There's also more from **Tintoretto**; the *Madonna dei Tesorieri* (1566), with its sumptuously painted velvets, shows facial types still found in Venice today.

The following stretch of seventeenth- and eighteenth-century paintings isn't too enthralling – the highlights are portraits by Rosalba Carriera and interiors by Pietro Longhi in room 17. Carriera's work popularized the use of pastel as a medium; look for her moving *Self-Portrait in Old Age* (1740s), executed just before she went blind. Longhi is not the most brilliant of painters in the Accademia, but his illustrative work is fascinating for the insights it gives into eighteenth-century Venice. (For more, including the famous *Rhinoceros*, go to the Ca' Rezzonico; see p.312).

The Vivarinis, the Bellinis and Carpaccio

Around the corner and to the right are more works from the fifteenth and early sixteenth centuries. Pieces by the Vivarini family feature strongly; **Alvise Vivarini**'s *Santa Chiara* is outstanding. **Giovanni Bellini** is represented by four triptychs painted, with workshop assistance, for this church in the 1460s. The extraordinary *Blessed Lorenzo Giustinian* is by his brother, **Gentile**; one of the oldest surviving Venetian canvases, and Gentile's earliest signed work, it was possibly used as a standard in processions, which would account for its state.

The magnificent cycle of pictures painted around 1500 for the Scuola di San Giovanni Evangelista, mainly illustrating the miracles of the Relic of the Cross, is displayed in room 20, off a corridor to the left. All of the paintings are replete with fascinating local details, but particularly rich are **Carpaccio**'s *Cure of a Lunatic* and **Gentile Bellini**'s *Recovery of the Relic from the Canale di San Lorenzo* and *Procession of the Relic in the Piazza*. The next room contains a complete cycle of pictures by **Carpaccio** illustrating the *Story of St Ursula*, painted for the Scuola di Sant'Orsola at San Zanipolo (1490–94). Restored in the mid-1980s, the paintings form one of Italy's most unforgettable groups. The legend is that Hereus, a British prince, proposed marriage to Ursula, a Breton princess. She accepted on two conditions: that Hereus convert to Christianity, and that he should wait for three years, while she went on a pilgrimage. The pilgrimage, undertaken with a company of 11,000 virgins, ended with a massacre near Cologne by the Huns – as Ursula had been forewarned in a dream.

Finally, in room 24 (the former hostel of the Scuola), there's **Titian**'s *Presentation of the Virgin* (dating from 1539). It was painted for the place where it hangs, as was the triptych by **Antonio Vivarini** and **Giovanni d'Alemagna** (1446), another of the oldest Venetian canvases.

The Guggenheim and the Salute

Within five minutes' walk of the Accademia, beyond the Campo San Vio, is the unfinished Palazzo Venier dei Leoni, home of Peggy Guggenheim for thirty years until her death in 1979, now the base for the **Guggenheim Collection** (daily except Tues 10am–6pm; April–Oct open Sat till 10pm; €8; ⓦwww.guggenheim.org). Her private collection is an eclectic, quirky choice of mainly excellent pieces from her favourite modernist movements and artists. Prime pieces include Brancusi's *Bird in Space* and *Maestra*, De Chirico's *Red Tower* and *Nostalgia of the Poet*, Max Ernst's *Robing of the Bride*, sculpture by Laurens and Lipchitz, paintings by Malevich and collages by Schwitters.

Continuing along the line of the Canal Grande, you come to Santa Maria della Salute, better known simply as the **Salute** (daily 9am–noon & 3–5pm, free), built to fulfil a Senate decree of October 22, 1630, that a new church would be dedicated to Mary if the city were delivered from the plague that was ravaging it – an outbreak that was to kill about a third of the population. Work began in 1631 on **Baldessare Longhena**'s design and was completed in 1681, though the church was not consecrated until November 9, 1687, five years before Longhena's death. Thereafter, every November 21, the Signoria headed a procession from San Marco to the Salute, over a specially constructed pontoon bridge, to give thanks for the city's good health (*salute* meaning "health" and "salvation") – and even today the festival of the Salute is a major event in the Venetian calendar.

In 1656, a hoard of **Titian** paintings from the suppressed church of Santo Spirito were moved here and are now housed in the sacristy (€1). The most prominent of these is the altarpiece of *St Mark Enthroned with SS Cosmas, Damian, Sebastian and Rocco* (the plague saints). The *Marriage at Cana*, with its dramatic lighting and perspective, is by **Tintoretto** (1561), and features likenesses of a number of the artist's friends.

The **Dogana di Mare** (Customs House), with its Doric facade (1676–82), occupies the spur formed by the meeting of the Canal Grande with the Giudecca canal; known as the Punta della Dogana, the very tip of the promontory is a great spot to have a picnic, particularly at sunset. The gold ball, noticeable from anywhere on this busy stretch of water, is a weathervane, topped by a figure representing either Justice or Fortune.

Along the Záttere to San Sebastiano

Stretching along the waterside from the Punta della Dogana to the Stazione Marittima, the **Záttere** (Rafts) was originally the place where most of the bulky goods coming into Venice were unloaded, and is now a popular place for a picnic lunch or a Sunday stroll. Its principal sight is the church of Santa Maria del Rosario, invariably known as the **Gesuati** (see box on p.299 for times and ticket) – worth a call for its paintings by **Giambattista Tiepolo**: three ceiling frescoes of *Scenes from the Life of St Dominic* and an altarpiece of *Madonna with three Dominican Saints*.

A diversion to the right straight after the Gesuati takes you past the **squero di San Trovaso**, the busiest gondola workshop left in Venice, and on to the church of **San Trovaso**. Venetian folklore has it that this church was the only neutral ground between the rival working-class factions of the Nicolotti and the Castellani, who would celebrate intermarriages and other services here, but came and went through separate doors. It is a large dark church, whose paintings are properly visible only in the morning; they include a pair of fine paintings by **Tintoretto** (*The Temptation of St Anthony* and *The Last Supper*), and the two large pictures begun by Tintoretto at the very end of his life, *The Adoration of the Magi* and *The Expulsion from the Temple*.

The church of **San Sebastiano** (see box on p.299 for times and ticket), right up by the Stazione Marittima (erratic opening hours), was built between 1505 and 1545 and was the parish church of **Paolo Veronese**, who provided most of its paintings and is buried here. He was first brought in to paint the ceiling of the sacristy with a *Coronation of the Virgin* and the *Four Evangelists*, followed by the *Scenes from the Life of St Esther* on the ceiling of the church. He then painted the dome of the chancel (since destroyed), and with the help of his brother, Benedetto, moved on to the walls of the church and the nuns' choir. The paintings around the high altar and the organ came last, painted in the 1560s.

Ca' Rezzonico and around

From San Sebastiano it's a straightforward walk back towards the Canal Grande along Calle Avogaria and Calle Lunga San Barnaba, a route that deposits you in Campo San Barnaba, just yards from the **Ca' Rezzonico**, now the **Museo del Settecento Veneziano** – the Museum of Eighteenth-Century Venice (daily except Tues: April–Oct 10am–5pm; Nov–March 10am–4pm; €6.50). Having acquired the Ca' Rezzonico in 1934, the *comune* of Venice set about furnishing and decorating it with eighteenth-century items and materials (or their closest modern equivalent), so giving the place the feel of a well-appointed house rather than of a formal museum. On the applied arts side of the collection, the plentiful and outlandish carvings by **Andrea Brustolon** are as likely to elicit revulsion as admiration. As for the paintings, the highlights are **Pietro Longhi**'s affectionate illustrations of Venice social life and the frescoes painted towards the end of his life by **Giandomenico Tiepolo**. Although painted at a time when this type of work was going out of fashion, these frescoes of clowns and carnival scenes (created originally for his own house) are among Giandomenico's best-known images. Fans of his father's slightly more flamboyant style won't come away disappointed either.

The nearby **Campo Santa Margherita** is a wide but friendly space, with a daily market and a clutch of shops that contribute to the quarter's distinctive atmosphere. The **Scuola Grande dei Carmini** (Mon–Sat 9am–6pm, Sun 9am–4pm; €5), on the west of the campo, is a showcase for Giambattista Tiepolo, whose ceiling paintings in the main upstairs hall, painted in the early 1740s, centre on a panel of *The Virgin in Glory*.

San Polo

For practical reasons, the district we have labelled **SAN POLO** covers an area over twice the size of the *sestiere* of the same name, including a huge chunk of the *sestiere* of Santa Croce and a bit of Dorsoduro, and is bounded by the Canal Grande and the Rio Nuovo–Rio di Ca' Fóscari. You cannot stray unwittingly over either of these canals, which is more than can be said for the boundaries of the *sestieri*, which zigzag wildly.

From the Rialto to the Gallery of Modern Art

Relatively stable building land and a good defensive position drew some of the earliest lagoon settlers to the high bank (*rivo alto*) above the Canal Grande that was to develop into the **Rialto** district. While the political centre of the new city grew up around San Marco, the Rialto became the commercial zone. In the twelfth century, Europe's first state bank was opened here, and the financiers of the district were the weightiest figures on the international exchanges for the next three centuries and more. The state offices that oversaw all maritime business were here as well, and in the early sixteenth century the offices of the exchequer were installed in the new **Palazzo dei Camerlenghi**, at the foot of the Rialto bridge.

The connection between wealth and moral turpitude was exemplified by the Rialto, where the fleshpots were as busy as the cash desks. A late sixteenth-century survey showed that there were about 3000 patrician women in the city, but well over 11,000 prostitutes, the majority of them based in the banking quarter. One Rialto brothel, the Casteletto, was especially esteemed for the literary, musical and sexual talents of its staff, and a perennial Venetian bestseller was a catalogue giving the addresses and prices of the city's most alluring courtesans.

It was through the markets of the Rialto that Venice earned its reputation as the bazaar of Europe. Virtually anything could be bought or sold here: Italian fabrics, precious stones, silver plate and gold jewellery, spices and dyes from the Orient. Trading had been going on here for over 400 years when, in 1514, a fire destroyed everything in the area except the church. The possibility of relocating the business centre was discussed but found little favour, so reconstruction began almost straight away, the **Fabbriche Vecchie** (the arcaded buildings along the Ruga degli Orefici and around the Campo San Giacomo) being finished five years after the fire, and Sansovino's **Fabbriche Nuove** (running along the Canal Grande from Campo Cesare Battisti) following about thirty years later.

Today's Rialto market is tamer than that of Venice at its peak, but it's still one of the liveliest spots in the city, and one of the few places where it's possible to stand in a crowd and hear nothing but Italian spoken. There's a shoal of memento-sellers by the church and along the Ruga degli Orefici; the market proper lies between them and the Canal Grande – mainly fruit stalls around the **Campo San Giacomo**, vegetable stalls and butchers' shops as you go through to the Campo Battisti, after which you come to the fish market. (The fish market and many of the other stalls close for the day at 1pm, but some reopen in the late afternoon.) There are excellent cheese shops around the junction of **Ruga degli Orefici** and **Ruga Vecchia San Giovanni**; the Ruga Vecchia has a number of good *alimentari* among the kitsch-merchants.

A popular Venetian legend asserts that the city was founded on Friday, March 25, 421 AD at exactly midday; from the same legend derives the claim that the church of **San Giacomo di Rialto** (daily 10am–noon; free) was founded in that year, and is thus the oldest church in Venice. It might actually be the oldest; what is not disputed is that the church was rebuilt in 1071 and that parts of the present structure date from then – for instance, the interior's six columns of ancient Greek marble have eleventh-century Veneto-Byzantine capitals. As you walk away from the Rialto, following roughly the curve of the Canal Grande, you enter a district which becomes labyrinthine even by Venetian standards. A directionless stroll between the Rio delle Beccerie and the Rio di San Zan Degolà will satisfy any addict of the picturesque: you cannot walk for more than a couple of minutes without coming across a workshop crammed into a ground-floor room or a garden spilling over a canalside wall.

The church of **San Cassiano** (Mon–Sat 9.45–11.30am & 4.30–7pm; free) is a building you're bound to pass as you wander out of the Rialto. Don't be put off by its barn-like appearance: it contains three paintings by **Tintoretto**, *The Resurrection*, *The Descent into Limbo* and *The Crucifixion*. The first two have been mauled by restorers, but the third is one of the greatest pictures in Venice, a startling composition dominated not by the cross but by the ladder on which the executioners stand.

Nearby, and signposted from San Cassiano, is the **Ca' Pésaro**, in which you'll find both the **Galleria d'Arte Moderna** (temporarily closed at time of writing) and **Museo Orientale** (Tues–Sun 9.15am–1.15pm; entry at quarter past the hour; €2.07, or €9.50 together with Accademia and Ca' d'Oro). Pieces bought from the Biennale make up much of the modern collection, and its backbone consists of work by a range of Italian artists, many of whom will be unfamiliar. As for the oriental galleries, the jumble of lacquer work, armour, screens, weaponry and so forth will appeal chiefly to the initiated.

Campo San Polo

The largest square in Venice after the Piazza, the **Campo San Polo** used to be the city's favourite bullfighting arena as well as the site of weekly markets and occasional fairs. Nowadays it's a combination of outdoor social centre and children's sports stadium.

The bleak interior of **San Polo** church (see box on p.299 for times and ticket) should be visited for a *Last Supper* by **Tintoretto** and **Giandomenico Tiepolo**'s paintings of the *Stations of the Cross*, a series painted when the artist was only twenty. The sober piety of these pictures will come as a surprise if you've been to the Ca' Rezzonico, though it often seems that his interest was less in the central drama than in the society portraits that occupy the edges of the stage.

Calle Madonetta, going off the campo in the direction of Rialto, is the beginning of a sequence of busy **shopping streets**, in which you'll find a couple of good *pasticcerie* and a host of shoe and clothes shops. Salizzada San Polo and Calle dei Saonéri, on the opposite side of the *campo*, are effectively a continuation of these streets, which together comprise this side of the Canal Grande's answer to the Mercerie.

The Frari

The Franciscans were granted a large plot of land near San Polo in about 1250, not long after the death of St Francis; replacement of their first church by the present Santa Maria Gloriosa dei Frari – more generally known simply as the **Frari** (Mon–Sat 9am–6pm, Sun 1–6pm; see box on p.299 for ticket details) – began in the mid-fourteenth century and took over a hundred years. This mountain of brick is not an immediately attractive building but, whatever your predilections, its collection of paintings, sculptures and monuments will gain the church a place on your list of Venetian highlights.

As every guide to the city points out, Venice is relatively impoverished as far as major paintings by **Titian** are concerned: apart from the Salute and the Accademia, the Frari is the only building in Venice with more than a single significant work by him. One of these – the *Assumption*, painted in 1518 – you will see almost immediately as you look towards the altar through the fifteenth-century monks' choir, a swirling, dazzling piece of compositional and colouristic bravura for which there was no precedent in Venetian art. The other Titian masterpiece here, the *Madonna di Ca' Pésaro*, is more static but was equally innovative in its displacement of the figure of the Virgin from the centre of the picture.

Wherever you stand in the Frari, you'll be facing something that deserves your attention, but three or four pieces apart from the Titians stand out from the rest. Two funerary monuments embodying the emergence in Venice of Renaissance sculptural technique flank the Titian *Assumption*: on the left the **tomb of Doge Niccolò Tron**, by **Antonio Rizzo** and assistants, dating from 1476; on the right, the more chaotic **tomb of Doge Francesco Fóscari**, carved by **Antonio and Paolo Bregno** shortly after Fóscari's death in 1457. The wooden statue of *St John the Baptist*, in the first chapel to the right, was commissioned from **Donatello** in 1438 by Florentine merchants in Padua; recent work has restored its luridly naturalistic appearance. Still moving to the right, the third chapel houses a typically vivid *Christ on the Sarcophagus* by **Bartolomeo Vivarini**. Head through the door on the right for the sacristy, where on the altar (the site for which it was created) is a picture that alone would justify a visit to the Frari – the *Madonna and Child with SS Nicholas of Bari, Peter, Mark and Benedict*, painted in 1488 by **Giovanni Bellini**. In the words of Henry James, "it is as solemn as it is gorgeous and as simple as it is deep".

Two massive tombs take up much of the nave. One is the bombastic monument to Titian, built in the mid-nineteenth century on the supposed site of his grave. He died in the 1576 plague epidemic, in around his ninetieth year, and was the only casualty of that outbreak to be given a church burial. Opposite is a tomb of similarly pompous dimensions but of redeeming peculiarity: the Mausoleum of Canova, erected in 1827 by pupils of the sculptor, following a design he had made for the tomb of Titian.

The Scuola Grande di San Rocco and San Rocco church

At the rear of the Frari is a place you should on no account miss: the **Scuola Grande di San Rocco** (daily: summer 9am–5.30pm; winter 10am–4pm; €5.16). St Rocco (St Roch) was attributed with the power to cure the plague and other serious illnesses, so when the saint's body was brought to Venice in 1485, this *scuola* began to profit from donations from people wishing to invoke his aid. In 1515 it commissioned this prestigious new building, and soon after its completion in 1560, work began on the decorative scheme that was to put the Scuola's rivals in the shade – a cycle of more than fifty major paintings by **Tintoretto**.

The Tintoretto paintings

To appreciate the evolution of Tintoretto's art you have to begin in the smaller room on the upper storey – the **Sala dell'Albergo**. In 1564 the Scuola held a competition for the contract to paint its first picture. The subject was to be *The Glorification of St Roch*, and Tintoretto won the contest by rigging up a finished painting in the very place for which the winning picture was destined – the centre of the ceiling. The protests of his rivals, who had simply submitted sketches, were to no avail. Virtually an entire wall of the Sala is occupied by the stupendous *Crucifixion*, a painting that reduced Ruskin to a state of dumbfounded wonder. His loquacious guide to the cycle concludes: "I must leave this picture to work its will on the spectator; for it is beyond all analysis, and above all praise." The pictures on the entrance wall – *Christ before Pilate*, *Christ Crowned with Thorns* and *The Way to Calvary* – inevitably suffer from such company, but they deserve close scrutiny.

Tintoretto finished the Sala in 1567 and eight years later he started on the main upper hall, a project he completed in 1581. The Old Testament subjects depicted in the three large panels of the **ceiling**, with their references to the

The Scuole

The institutions known as the **scuole** seem to have originated in the thirteenth century with the formation of the flagellant orders, whose public scourgings were intended to purge the sins of the world. The interaction between these societies of flagellants and the lay brotherhoods established by the city's branches of the mendicant orders (the Franciscans and the Dominicans) gave rise in 1260 to the formation of the confraternity called **Scuola di Santa Maria della Carità**, the first of the so-called **scuole grande**. By the middle of the sixteenth century there were five more of these major confraternities – **San Giovanni Evangelista**, **San Marco**, **Santa Maria della Misericordia**, **San Rocco** and **San Teodoro** – plus scores of smaller bodies known as the *scuole minore*, of which there were once as many as four hundred.

The *scuole grande*, drawing much of their membership from the wealthiest professional and mercantile groups, and with rosters of up to six hundred men, received subscriptions that allowed them to fund lavish architectural and artistic projects, of which the Scuola Grande di San Rocco is the most spectacular example. The *scuole minore*, united by membership of certain guilds (eg goldsmiths at the Scuola dei Battioro e Tiraori, shoemakers at the Scuola dei Calerghi), or by common nationality (as with San Giorgio degli Schiavoni, the Slavs' *scuola*), generally operated from far more modest bases. Yet all *scuole* had the same basic functions – to provide assistance for their members (eg dowries and medical aid), to offer a place of communal worship, and to distribute alms and services in emergencies (anything from plague relief to the provision of troops). To an extent, the *scuole* also acted as a kind of political safety valve. The councils of state were the unique preserve of the city's self-designated patrician class, but the *scuole* were open only to traders, doctors, lawyers, artisans and civil servants. They had no real power, but a wealthy private club like the Scuola Grande di San Rocco could, if it chose, act as an effective pressure group. Like all other Venetian institutions, the *scuole* came to an end with the coming of Napoleon, who disbanded them in 1806. Most of their possessions were scattered, and their headquarters were in time put to new uses – thus the Scuola Grande di San Marco became the city hospital, the Scuola Grande di Santa Maria della Carità became the galleries of the Accademia, the Scuola Grande di Maria della Misericordia has become a sports hall. Two of the *scuole*, however, were revived in the middle of the nineteenth century and continue to function as charitable bodies in the magnificently decorated buildings they commissioned centuries ago – they are the Scuola di San Giorgio degli Schiavoni and Scuola Grande di San Rocco.

alleviation of physical suffering, are coded declarations of the Scuola's charitable activities: *Moses Striking Water from the Rock*, *The Miracle of the Brazen Serpent* and *The Miraculous Fall of Manna*. The paintings around the walls, all based on the New Testament, are an amazing feat of sustained inventiveness, in which every convention of perspective, lighting, colour and even anatomy is defied. A caricature of the irascible Tintoretto (with a jarful of paint brushes) is incorporated into the trompe l'oeil carvings by the seventeenth-century sculptor Francesco Pianta.

Displayed on easels, either in the *sala* or main hall – they are often moved – are a handful of paintings that are understandably missed by many visitors, given the competition. *Christ Carrying the Cross* is now generally thought to be an early **Titian**, though some still maintain Giorgione's authorship; Titian's *Annunciation* is similarly influenced by the earlier master. Two early **Tiepolo** paintings, also on easels, relieve the eyes with a wash of airy colour.

The paintings on the ground floor were created between 1583 and 1587, when Tintoretto was in his late sixties. The turbulent *Annunciation* is one of the most arresting images of the event ever painted, and there are few Renaissance landscapes to match those of *The Flight into Egypt* and the small paintings of *St Mary Magdalen* and *St Mary of Egypt*.

The church

Yet more paintings by Tintoretto adorn the neighbouring church of **San Rocco** (8am–12.30pm & 3–5pm; free). On the south wall of the nave you'll find *St Roch Taken to Prison*, and below it *The Pool of Bethesda* – though only the latter is definitely by Tintoretto. In the chancel are four large works, all of them difficult to see properly: the best are *St Roch Curing the Plague Victims* (lower right) and *St Roch in Prison* (lower left); the two higher pictures are *St Roch in Solitude* and *St Roch Healing the Animals*, though the second is again a doubtful attribution.

San Pantaleone

To the south of San Rocco runs the teeming Crosera San Pantalon, the atmosphere in whose shops, cafés and bars has a lot to do with the proximity of the university. Between this street and the Rio di Ca' Fóscari stands the church of **San Pantaleone** (daily 4–6pm; free), which possesses a *Coronation of the Virgin* by Antonio Vivarini and Giovanni d'Alemagna (in the chapel to the left of the chancel) and Veronese's last painting, *San Pantaleone Healing a Boy* (second chapel on right). The church can also boast of having the most melodramatic ceiling in the city: *The Martyrdom and Apotheosis of San Pantaleone*. It kept Gian Antonio Fumiani busy from 1680 to 1704 but he never got the chance to bask in the glory of his labours – he died in a fall from the scaffolding on which he'd been working.

Southeast of San Pantaleone, the cluster of Gothic palaces fronting the Canal Grande constitutes one of the city's architectural glories. Built in 1435, the **Ca' Fóscari**, which Ruskin thought "the noblest example in Venice" of late Gothic, was the home of Doge Francesco Fóscari, whose extraordinarily long term of office came to an end with his forced resignation, an event partly attributable to the unrelenting feud conducted against him by the Loredan family and its allies. He died in 1457, only weeks after leaving the Palazzo Ducale. Adjoining the Ca' Fóscari are a pair of joined buildings of the same period – the **Palazzi Giustinian**. Wagner wrote the second act of *Tristan* while living here.

Cannaregio

In the northernmost section of Venice, **CANNAREGIO**, you can go from one extreme to another in a matter of minutes: it is a short distance from the bustle of the train station and the execrable Lista di Spagna to areas which, although no longer rural – Cannaregio comes from *canna*, meaning "reed" – are still among the quietest and prettiest parts of the whole city. The district also has the dubious distinction of containing the world's original ghetto.

The station area

The first building worth a look in the vicinity of the station is to the left as you come out of it – the **Scalzi** church, also called Santa Maria di Nazareth (daily 7–11.45am & 4–7pm; free). Built in the 1670s for the barefoot (*scalzi*) order of Carmelites, the interior, by Baldessare Longhena, is a joy for aficionados of the Baroque. There are frescoes by Giambattista Tiepolo in the first chapel on the left and the second on the right, but his major work in the church, the ceiling, was destroyed in 1915 by an Austrian bomb. A couple of fragments, now in the Accademia, were all that was salvaged.

Foreign embassies used to be concentrated in this area, so that the Venetian authorities could keep an eye on them all together, and the **Lista di Spagna** takes its name from the Spanish embassy, which used to be at no. 168. The street is now completely given over to the tourist trade, with shops and stalls, bars, restaurants and hotels all competing for the same desperate trade. If you are hunting for trinkets, food or a bed, you'll find things better and cheaper elsewhere.

The church of **San Geremia** (Mon–Sat 8am–noon & 3–7pm, Sun 9.15am–12.15pm & 3–7pm; free) is chiefly notable for being the present home of **St Lucy**, martyred in Syracuse in 304, stolen from Constantinople by Venetian crusaders in 1204, and ousted from her own Palladian church in 1863 when it was demolished to build the station. Lucy tore her own eyes out after an unwanted suitor kept complimenting her on their beauty, and hence became the patron saint of eyesight: the glass case on the high altar contains her desiccated body. Architecturally, the church's main point of interest is the twelfth-century campanile, one of the oldest in the city.

The ballroom of the **Palazzo Labia**, next door to the church, contains frescoes by Giambattista Tiepolo and his assistants (1745–50), illustrating the story of Antony and Cleopatra. The present owners, RAI (the state radio service), allow the public in to see them on Wednesdays, Thursdays and Fridays from 3 to 4pm (for an appointment call ☎041.781.277, but admission is often granted at the door).

The **Canale di Cannaregio** was the main entrance to Venice before the road and rail bridges were built; walk along it to get to the church of **San Giobbe** (Mon–Sat 10am–noon & 4–6pm). The physical afflictions with which God permitted Satan to test the faith of Job – he was smitten with "sore boils from the sole of his foot unto his crown" – made Job particularly popular with the Venetians, who suffered regularly from malaria, plague and a plethora of damp-related diseases. The church was built on the site of an oratory by the Venetian Gothic architect Antonio Gambello, later assisted by Pietro Lombardo, who introduced Tuscan Renaissance elements. Lombardo's contribution, his first work in Venice, consists of the doorway and, inside, the statues of SS Anthony, Bernardino and Louis and the chancel. Its choicest paintings – Giovanni Bellini's *Madonna Enthroned with Saints* and Carpaccio's *Presentation in the Temple* – have been removed to the drier atmosphere of the Accademia.

The Ghetto

The Venetian **Ghetto** was, in a sense, the first in the world: the word comes from the Venetian dialect getar (to found), or geto (foundry), which is what this area was until 1390. It was in 1516 that all the city's Jews were ordered to move to the island of the Ghetto Nuovo, an enclave that was sealed at night by Christian curfew guards – whose wages were paid for by the Jews. Distinctive badges or caps had to be worn by all Jews, and there were various economic and social restraints on the community, although oppression was lighter in Venice than in most other parts of Europe (it was one of the few states to tolerate the Jewish religion). When Jews were expelled en masse from Spain in 1492 and Portugal in 1497, many of them came here.

Each wave of Jewish immigrants established its own synagogues with their distinctive rites. The **Scola Levantina**, founded in 1538, and the **Scola Spagnola**, possibly founded about twenty years later, reflect the wealth of these particular groups, who were important traders within the Venetian state; the latter was redesigned around 1584 by Longhena (the profession of architect was barred to Jews), a project that influenced the alteration of the other synagogues. These two are still used today for services, the former in summer and the latter in winter, and, together with the beautiful Scola al Canton and the Scola Italiana, can be viewed in a fascinating hourly tour of the area (€8; tours in English start on the half hour) organized by the **Jewish Museum** in Campo Ghetto Nuovo (daily except Sat & Jewish hols: June–Sept 10am–7pm; Oct–May 10am–4.30pm; €3, or free with tour); the collection in the museum itself is mainly of silverware, embroidery and other liturgical objects. Try the excellent website, Ⓦ www.jewishvenice.org, for links and more information.

The Ghetto looks quite different from the rest of Venice. The Jewish population grew to about 4000 and, even though they were allowed to spread into the **Ghetto Vecchio** and the **Ghetto Nuovissima**, there was gross overcrowding. As the Ghetto buildings were not allowed to be more than one-third higher than the surrounding houses, the result was a stack of low-ceilinged storeys – seven is the usual number. Napoleon removed the gates of the Ghetto in 1797 but the Austrians replaced them in 1798, and Venice's Jews didn't achieve equal rights with other Venetians until Unification with Italy in 1866. After the depredations of the Holocaust, the Jewish population is now growing again, with many Hasidic Jews, often younger people from the US and Israel, once more living and working in and around the Ghetto.

Sant'Alvise, Madonna dell'Orto and around

The area northeast of the Ghetto is one of the most restful parts of Venice. The long *fondamente*, dotted with food shops, bars and trattorias; the red walls and green shutters of the houses; the blue and yellow hulls of the boats – together they create a scene reminiscent of Henry James's vision of the essence of Venice: "I simply see a narrow canal in the heart of the city – a patch of green water and a surface of pink wall."

A few minutes north of the Ghetto stands the church of **Sant'Alvise** (Mon–Sat 10am–5pm, Sun 3–5pm; see box on p.299 for ticket price). Commissioned by Antonia Venier, daughter of Doge Antonio Venier, after the saint appeared to her in a vision in 1388, the church has one outstanding picture, the *The Road to Calvary* by Giambattista Tiepolo, painted in 1743. His *Crown of Thorns* and *Flagellation*, slightly earlier works, are on the right-hand wall of the nave. Normally under the nuns' choir, to the right as you enter the church, but on view in the sacristy whilst restoration work is ongoing, are eight small tempera paintings, generally known as *The Baby Carpaccios* thanks to

Ruskin's speculative attribution; they do date from Carpaccio's infancy (around 1470), but they're not actually by him.

A circuitous stroll eastwards brings you to the Gothic church of **Madonna dell'Orto** (see box on p.299 for times and ticket). Dedicated to St Christopher in about 1350, the church was renamed after a large stone Madonna by Giovanni de'Santi, found discarded in a local vegetable garden (*orto*), began to work miracles; brought inside the church in 1377, the figure can still be seen (now heavily restored) in the Cappella di San Mauro through a door at the front end of the right aisle. The main sculpture on the facade is a fifteenth-century *St Christopher* by the Florentine Nicolò di Giovanni; Bartolomeo Bon designed the portal in 1460, shortly before his death. The **interior** was messed around in the 1860s, and although some of the overpainting was removed during restoration work of the 1930s, its appearance still owes much to nineteenth-century interference. Scraps of fresco on the arches and the painted beams give an idea of how it must have looked in the sixteenth century. This was the first church in Venice to be given a thorough restoration job after the floods of 1966; the floor was relaid, the lower walls rebuilt, chapels restored to their pre-1864 layout and all the paintings were cleaned. The *St Christopher* over the door was the first Istrian stonework to be restored in Venice.

This is Tintoretto's parish church: he is buried here, in the chapel to the right of the high altar. So too are his son and daughter, Domenico and Marietta. And there are a number of paintings by the artist here, notably the colossal *Making of the Golden Calf* and *The Last Judgement*, which flank the main altar. Others include Tintoretto's *The Presentation of the Virgin in the Temple*, at the end of the right aisle; *The Vision of the Cross to St Peter* and *The Beheading of St Paul*, on each side of the chancel's *Annunciation* by Palma il Giovane; and *St John the Baptist and Other SS* by Cima da Conegliano on the first altar on the right. In the first chapel on the left there should also be a *Madonna and Child* by Giovanni Bellini, but it was stolen in 1993.

From the Ca' d'Oro to the Gesuiti

Back towards the Canal Grande, the main thoroughfare of eastern Cannaregio, the **Strada Nova**, was carved through the houses in 1871–72, and is now a bustling and eclectic shopping street where you can buy anything from spaghetti to surgical trusses. Nearly halfway along is the inconspicuous *calle* named after, and leading to, the Ca' d'Oro – a Gothic palace much altered by restoration, and whose finest feature, the facade, is best seen from the water anyway. Inside the **Galleria Giorgio Franchetti** (Mon 8.15am–2pm, Tues–Sun 8.15am–7.15pm; €3 or €9.50 together with Accademia and Museo Orientale) is a museum put together from the bequest of the man who owned and repaired the house at the start of this century, and from a few state collections. One of the prize exhibits is in the courtyard – Bartolomeo Bon's sculpted well-head; others include a *St Sebastian* by Mantegna and a beautifully carved *Young Couple* by Tullio Lombardo. Big names such as Tintoretto and Titian are here, but not at their best; you'll get more out of pieces from less exalted artists – for instance, the views of *The Piazzetta facing San Giorgio* and *Quayside with the Salute* by Francesco Guardi.

At the eastern end of the Strada Nova you come to the Campo dei Santi Apostoli, a general meeting-point and crossroads, and the church of **Santi Apostoli** (daily 7.30–11.30am & 5–7pm; free). The exterior is unexceptional, other than the curious 24-hour clock on the campanile, but give the interior a look for the Cappella Corner: the design of the chapel is attributed to Mauro Codussi, the altar painting of the *Communion of St Lucy* is by Giambattista

5

Tiepolo, and the tomb of Marco Corner (father of Caterina Cornaro) is attributed to Tullio Lombardo.

Just inland from the Fondamente Nuove, the northern edge of this zone, is the **Gesuiti** church, as Santa Maria Assunta is familiarly known (daily: summer 10am–noon & 5–7pm; winter 10am–noon & 4–6pm; free). The Jesuits began work on their church in 1714, and it took fifteen years to inlay the marble walls of the interior and carve its marble "curtains" – with a result that is jaw-droppingly impressive even if you hate Baroque architecture. The *Martyrdom of St Lawrence* by Titian, on the first altar on the left, is a night scene made doubly obscure by the lighting arrangements.

Castello

Our designation of **CASTELLO** includes all the eastern section of the city, and is bounded in the northwest by the Rio dei Santi Apostoli and Rio dei Gesuiti, and in the southwest by the canal that winds from the side of the post office at the Rialto to the back of San Marco. In terms of its tourist appeal, centre stage is occupied by the huge **Santi Giovanni e Paolo**, a place saturated with the history and mythology of Venice. Within a few minutes' walk of here you will find a trio of fascinating churches, **Santa Maria dei Miracoli**, **Santa Maria Formosa** and **San Zaccaria**, as well as the beguiling Carpaccio paintings in the Scuola di San Giorgio degli Schiavoni, to name just the highlights of the western part of this district.

Once the industrial hub of the city and the largest manufacturing site in Europe, the **Arsenale** area (the eastern section of the Castello *sestiere*) is now predominantly a residential quarter and has little to offer of cultural significance. It would be a mistake, however, to leave it entirely unexplored. In the summer of odd-numbered years the Biennale art show sets up shop in its custom-built pavilions here, and at other times its open spaces – the **Giardini Garibaldi**, **Giardini Pubblici** and **Parco della Rimembranze** – are a good antidote to the claustrophobia that overtakes most visitors to Venice at some point.

The Miracoli and around

If you head into Castello by walking north from the Rialto bridge, you'll pass the cosy church of **San Giovanni Crisostomo** (Mon–Sat 8.15am–12.15pm & 3–7pm, Sun 3–7pm; free), built around 1500 to designs by Mauro Codussi. It has a magnificent late painting by Giovanni Bellini, *SS Jerome, Christopher and Augustine*, and a fine altarpiece by Sebastiano del Piombo – *St John Chrysostom with SS John the Baptist, Liberale, Mary Magdalene, Agnes and Catherine*. Round the back of the church is the Corte Seconda del Milion, a tiny courtyard hemmed in by ancient buildings, one of which – though nobody is sure which – was Marco Polo's family home.

Sitting on the lip of a canal just a minute to the north of Corte Seconda del Milion, the church of Santa Maria dei Miracoli – known simply as the **Miracoli** (see box on p.299 for times and ticket) – is one of the most attractive buildings in Europe. It was built in the 1480s to house a painting of the Madonna (still the altarpiece) which was believed to have performed a number of miracles, such as reviving a man who'd spent half an hour lying at the bottom of the Giudecca canal. The church is thought to have been designed by Pietro Lombardo; certainly he and his two sons Tullio and Antonio oversaw the building and executed much of the carving. Typically for Renaissance architecture in Venice, richness of effect takes precedence over classical correctness – the Corinthian pilasters are set below the Ionic, so that the viewer can better appreciate the carving on the Corinthian.

The marble-lined interior contains some of the most intricate decorative sculpture to be seen in Venice. The half-length figures of two saints and the *Annunciation* on the balustrade of the raised galleries at the east end are attributed to Tullio Lombardo; the rest of the attributions for the carvings at this end are arguable between the two brothers and their father. Ruskin was greatly distressed by the children's heads carved to the side of the top of the altar steps: "The man who could carve a child's head so perfectly must have been wanting in all human feeling, to cut it off, and tie it by the hair to a vine leaf."

Campo Santi Giovanni e Paolo

After the Piazza, the Campo Santi Giovanni e Paolo – or, in its Venetian dialect form, San Zanipolo – is the most impressive open space in Venice. Dominated by the huge brick church from which it gets its name, it also has the most beautiful facade of any of the *scuole grande* and one of the finest Renaissance equestrian monuments.

The Colleoni statue and the Scuola Grande di San Marco

The *condottiere* **Bartolomeo Colleoni** began his wayward career in Venice's army in 1429. In the succeeding years he defected to Milan, re-enlisted for Venice, fled again, and finally signed up for good in 1455 – whereupon Venice suffered an outbreak of peace, which meant that in the twenty years leading up to his death in 1475 (see p.220) Colleoni was called upon to fight only once. When he died, Colleoni left a handsome legacy to the republic on condition that a monument should be erected to him in the square before San Marco, an impossible proposition to Venice's rulers, with their cult of anonymity. They got around this dilemma with a splendid piece of disingenuousness, interpreting the will in a way that allowed them to raise the monument before the Scuola Grande di San Marco, rather than the basilica, and still claim the money.

The commission for the monument was won by **Andrea Verrocchio** in 1481, and difficulties dogged this stage of the proceedings too. Having virtually completed the horse, Verrocchio heard that another artist was being approached to sculpt the rider, and he retaliated by mutilating the work he'd done and galloping off to Florence. The matter was eventually smoothed over, and Verrocchio was working again on the piece when he died at the end of June 1488. **Alessandro Leopardi** was then called in to finish the work and produce the plinth for it, which he gladly did – even adding his signature on the horse's girth and appending *del Cavallo* to his name.

An unimprovable backdrop to Colleoni, the **Scuola Grande di San Marco** has provided a sumptuous facade and foyer for the Ospedale Civile since its suppression in the early nineteenth century. The facade was started by Pietro Lombardo and Giovanni Buora in 1487, and finished in 1495 by Mauro Codussi after a row between Pietro and Buora and the Scuola. It works better in sections rather than as a unity: the perspectival panels by Tullio and Antonio Lombardo don't quite bring off the intended illusion, but only the hardhearted will not be charmed by them individually.

The church of Santi Giovanni e Paolo

The church of **Santi Giovanni e Paolo** (Mon–Sat 7.30am–12.30pm & 3.30–6pm, Sun 3–6pm; free), the Dominican equivalent to the Frari, was founded in 1246, rebuilt and enlarged from 1333, and finally consecrated in 1430. The sarcophagus of Doge Giacomo Tiepolo, who originally gave the site to the Dominicans, is on the left of the door outside.

The **interior** is stunning for its sheer size: approximately 90 metres long, 38 metres wide at the transepts and 33 metres high in the centre. It seems more spacious now than it would have up to 1682, when the wooden choir, placed similarly to that of the Frari, was demolished. The simplicity of the design, a nave with two aisles and gracefully soaring arches, is offset by the huge number of tombs and monuments around the walls. Contrary to the impression created, not all of the doges are buried here, just 25 of them.

The **west wall** is devoted to the Mocenigo family: above the door is the tomb of Doge Alvise Mocenigo and his wife by Pietro Lombardo; to the right is the monument to Doge Giovanni Mocenigo by Tullio Lombardo; and on the left the superb monument to Doge Pietro Mocenigo by Pietro Lombardo, assisted by his sons.

In the **south aisle**, after the first altar, is the monument to the Venetian military commander Marcantonio Bragadin, to which is attached one of Venice's grisliest stories. In 1571 Bragadin was double-crossed by the Turks to whom he had been obliged to surrender Famagusta: tortured and humiliated for days by his captors, he was eventually skinned alive. Some years later the skin was brought back to Venice, and today it sits in that urn high up on the wall.

The next altar has a superb Giovanni Bellini polyptych, showing *St Vincent Ferrer, with SS Christopher and Sebastian*, and an *Annunciation* and pietà above, still in the original frame. At the far end of this aisle, before you turn into the transept, you'll see a small shrine with the **foot of St Catherine of Siena**: most of her body is in Rome, her head is in her house in Siena, one foot's here, and other little relics are scattered about Italy.

The **south transept** has a painting by Alvise Vivarini, *Christ Carrying the Cross* (1474), and Lorenzo Lotto's *St Antonine* (1542), painted in return for nothing more than his expenses and permission to be buried in the church. Sadly, Lotto was eventually driven from his home town by the jealousies and plots of other artists (including Titian), and died and was buried in the monastery at Loreto.

On the right of the chancel is the tomb of Doge Michele Morosini, selected by Ruskin as "the richest monument of the Gothic period in Venice". The tomb of Doge Andrea Vendramin, opposite, was singled out as its antithesis – only the half of the effigy's head that would be visible from below was completed by the artist, a short cut denounced by Ruskin as indicative of "an extreme of intellectual and moral degradation". Tullio Lombardo is thought to have been the culprit, with help from others – maybe his father and brother.

The **Cappella del Rosario**, at the end of the north transept, was virtually destroyed by fire in 1867; its paintings by Tintoretto, Palma il Giovane and others were lost. Of their replacements, the best are **Veronese**'s ceiling panels and *Adoration*.

Funerary sculpture is the main attraction of the north aisle. To the left of the sacristy door is the monument to Doge Pasquale Malipiero by Pietro Lombardo, one of the earliest in Renaissance style in Venice.

Santa Maria Formosa and around

South of San Zanipolo lies Campo di Santa Maria Formosa, an atmospheric square with a modest but mouthwatering morning market. The church of **Santa Maria Formosa** (see box on p.299 for times and ticket) was built by San Magno, Bishop of Oderzo, in the seventh century, who was inspired by a dream in which he saw a buxom (*formosa*) figure of the Madonna. The present building is another Codussi effort, dating from 1492. Palma il Vecchio's altarpiece of *St Barbara*, the church's outstanding picture, was admired by George Eliot as "an almost unique presentation of a hero-woman". Bartolomeo

Vivarini's *Madonna della Misericordia*, in a side chapel, is a fine example of one of the warmest Catholic symbols – here she's shown sheltering a group of parishioners under her cloak.

The Renaissance Palazzo Querini-Stampalia, just round the corner from Santa Maria Formosa, houses the **Pinacoteca Querini-Stampalia** (Tues–Thurs 10am–6pm, Fri & Sat 10am–10pm; €6). Unless you have a voracious appetite for seventeenth- and eighteenth-century Venetian painting, you'll get most pleasure from earlier pieces such as Palma il Vecchio's portraits of *Francesco Querini* and *Paola Priuli Querini* and Giovanni Bellini's *The Presentation in the Temple*. Apart from that, the main interest is in the eighteenth-century decor of the rooms, especially the library. It's worth taking advantage of the unusual late opening times at the weekend, when you can often savour the atmosphere of the palace in peace or take in a classical concert (included in the price; ☎041.271.1411). The basement and some of the entranceways were remodelled in 1963 by the Venetian architect **Carlo Scarpa**. Most impressive is his garden, a characteristically curious mixture of brutalism and whimsy.

San Zaccaria and the Riva

The Campo San Zaccaria, a few yards off the waterfront, has a more torrid past than most – the convent here was notorious for its libidinous goings-on (officials were once sent to close down the nuns' parlour, only to be met with a barrage of bricks), and in 864 Doge Pietro Tradonico was murdered here as he returned from vespers. The towering church of **San Zaccaria** (daily 10am–noon & 4–6pm; free), a pleasing mixture of Gothic and Renaissance, was started by Antonio Gambello and finished after his death in 1481 by Mauro Codussi, who was responsible for the facade from the first storey upwards. Inside is one of the city's most stunning altarpieces, a *Madonna and Four SS* by Giovanni Bellini. A small fee gets you into the rebuilt remnants of the old church, the Cappella di Sant'Atanasio and Cappella di San Tarasio; here you'll find an early Tintoretto, the *Birth of John the Baptist*, and three wonderful altarpieces by Antonio Vivarini and Giovanni d'Alemagna. Floor mosaics from the ninth and twelfth centuries can be seen through panels in the present floor level, and downstairs is a spooky, waterlogged, ninth-century crypt.

The principal waterfront of the area, the **Riva degli Schiavoni**, stretches right back to the Molo. It's a favourite walk, particularly as the sun goes down, and many notables have lived or stayed in houses and hotels here: Petrarch and his daughter lived at no. 4145 for a while, Henry James stayed nearby at no. 4161 when he was finishing *The Portrait of a Lady*, and the *Hotel Danieli*, at the far end, has accommodated George Sand, Charles Dickens, Proust, Wagner and the ever-present Ruskin.

Halfway along the Riva stands the **Pietà** church (or Santa Maria della Visitazione), famous as the place where Vivaldi was choirmaster – he was also violin teacher to the attached orphanage. Giorgio Massari won a competition to redesign the church in 1736, and it's possible that he consulted with Vivaldi on its acoustics; building didn't actually begin until 1745, and the facade was even more delayed – it was only finished in 1906. The church is still used for concerts (Ⓦwww.vivaldi.it; €25), and when the box office is open you can sometimes peer over the ropes at the interior, which, in its newly restored form, looks like a wedding-cake turned inside out – and it has one of Venice's most ostentatious ceiling paintings, Giambattista Tiepolo's *The Glory of Paradise*.

The Greek quarter and the Scuola di San Giorgio degli Schiavoni

Stroll north along the flank of the pietà and you'll enter the quarter of Venice's Greek community, identifiable from a distance by the alarmingly tilted campanile of **San Giorgio dei Greci**. The Greek presence was strong in Venice from the eleventh century, and grew stronger after Constantinople's capture by the Turks in 1453; by the close of the fifteenth century they had founded their own church, college and school here. The present *scuola*, designed (like the college) by Longhena in the seventeenth century, now houses the **Museo Dipinti Sacri Bizantini** (Mon–Sat 10am–12.30pm & 1.30–4.30pm, Sun 10am–5pm; €4). Although many of the most beautiful of the exhibited works (mainly fifteenth to eighteenth century) maintain the traditions of icon painting in terms of composition and use of symbolic figures rather than attempts at realism, it's fascinating to see how some of the artists absorbed Western influences. The **church** contains icons dating back to the twelfth century and a lot of work by Michael Danaskinàs, a sixteenth-century Cretan artist.

From here it's a hundred metres or so to the **Scuola di San Giorgio degli Schiavoni**, whose ground-floor hall (Tues–Sat 9.30am–12.30pm & 3.30–6.30pm, Sun 9.30am–12.30pm; €3) would get onto anyone's list of the ten most beautiful rooms in Europe. Venice's resident Slavs (*Schiavoni*), most of whom were traders, set up a *scuola* to look after their interests in 1451; the present building dates from the early sixteenth century, and the whole interior looks more or less as it would have then. Entering it, you step straight from the street into the superb lower hall, the walls of which are decorated with a cycle created by Vittore Carpaccio between 1502 and 1509. Originally painted for the upstairs room, but moved here when the building was rearranged in 1551, the sequence of pictures consists chiefly of scenes from the lives of SS George, Tryphone and Jerome, (the Dalmatian patron saints). Outstanding among them is *The Vision of St Augustine*, depicting the moment that Augustine, while writing to St Jerome, was told in a vision of Jerome's death.

San Francesco della Vigna

Somewhat stranded on the northern edge of Castello, the church of **San Francesco della Vigna** (daily 8am–noon & 3.30–7pm; free) takes its name from the vineyard that was here when the Franciscans were given the site in 1253. The present church building was begun in 1534, designed and supervised by Sansovino, but the design was modified during construction, and Palladio was later brought in to provide the facade. Although smaller than the two great mendicant churches of San Zanipolo and the Frari, it feels less welcoming – probably attributable to the cold colouring added to the more calculated Renaissance architecture. However, there are some fine works of art that make the trek worthwhile – but be sure to have a pocketful of coins for the (necessary) light boxes. The ones you shouldn't miss are: *SS Jerome, Bernard and Ludovic*, attributed to Antonio Vivarini (left of main door); the sculptures of Prophets and Evangelists by the Lombardo family (in the chapel left of the chancel); and a *Sacra Conversazione* by Veronese (fifth chapel on the north side).

The Arsenale and Museo Storico Navale

A corruption of the Arabic *darsin'a* (house of industry), the very name of the **Arsenale** is indicative of the strength of Venice's trading links with the eastern Mediterranean, and the workers of these dockyards and factories were the foundations upon which the city's mercantile and military supremacy rested. Construction of the Arsenale commenced in the early years of the twelfth century, and by the third decade of the fifteenth century it had become the base for some 300 shipping companies, operating around 3000 vessels in excess of 200 tons. The productivity of the Arsenale was legendary: for the visit of Henry III of France in 1574 the Arsenalotti built a complete ship while the state reception for the king was in progress – compare this to the six months it takes to build a gondola today.

Expansion of the Arsenale continued into the sixteenth century – Sanmicheli's covered dock for the state barge (the *Bucintoro*) was built in the 1540s, for example, and da Ponte's gigantic rope-factory (the Tana) in 1579. By then, though, the maritime strength of Venice was past its peak; militarily too, despite the conspicuous success at Lepanto in 1571, Venice was on the wane, and the recapture of the Morea at the end of the seventeenth century was little more than a glorious interlude in a longer story of decline. When Napoleon took over the city in 1797 he burned down the wharves, sank the last *Bucintoro* and confiscated the remnant of the Venetian navy.

Under Austrian occupation the docks were reconstructed, and they stayed in continuous service until the end of 1917, when, having built a number of ships for the Italian navy in World War I, they were dismantled to prevent them being of use to the enemy. Since then it has been used by the navy for storage and repairs, and as a venue for part of the Biennale, but plans exist to extend the Museo Storico Navale into the Arsenale buildings and to convert other parts into sports halls, accommodation for the University of Architecture and premises for ACTV.

There is no public access to the Arsenale complex. You can get a look at part of it, however, from the bridge connecting the Campo Arsenale and the Fondamenta dell'Arsenale. The main **gateway** to the Arsenale, built by Antonio Gambello in 1460, was the first structure in Venice to employ the classical vocabulary of Renaissance architecture. The four **lions** to the side of the gateway must be the most-photographed in the city: the two on the right were probably taken from Delos (at an unknown date), the left-hand one of the pair being positioned here to mark the recapture of Corfu in 1716; the larger pair were brought back from Piraeus in 1687 by Francesco Morosini after the reconquest of the Morea.

Nearby, on the other side of the Rio dell'Arsenale and facing the lagoon, is the **Museo Storico Navale** (Mon–Sat 8.45am–1pm; €1.55). Chiefly of interest for its models of Venetian craft from the gondola to the Bucintoro (these models were the equivalents of blueprints), the museum gives a comprehensive picture of the working life of the Arsenale and the smaller boatyards of Venice; but if you want to get a flavour of the city's history from a single museum visit, then you should give priority to the Correr (see p.306).

San Pietro di Castello

In 1808 the greater part of the canal connecting the Bacino di San Marco to the broad inlet of the Canale di San Pietro was filled in to form what is now **Via Garibaldi**, the widest street in the city and the busiest commercial area in the eastern district. If you follow your nose along the right-hand side of the street you'll soon be crossing the Ponte di Quintavalle onto the island of **San Pietro**, once the ecclesiastical centre of Venice, but nowadays a slightly down-at-heel place where the chief activity is the repairing of boats.

By 775 the settlement here had grown sufficiently to be granted the foundation of a bishopric under the authority of the Patriarch of Grado. From the beginning, the political and economic nucleus of the city was in the Rialto and San Marco areas, and the relationship between the Church and the geographically remote rulers of the city was never to be close. In 1451 the first **Patriarch of Venice** was invested, but still his seat remained at Castello, and things stayed that way until 1807 (ten years after the republic had ceased to exist), when the patriarch was at last permitted to install himself in San Marco.

As with the Arsenale, the hidden history of San Pietro is perhaps more interesting than what you can actually see. The church – which takes its name from the castle that used to stand here – is basically a grandiose derivative of a plan by Palladio and has little to recommend it. The most intriguing object inside is the so-called Throne of St Peter (in the south aisle), a marble seat made from an Arabic funeral stone inscribed with texts from the Koran. The lurching campanile, rebuilt by Codussi in the 1480s, was the first tower in Venice to be clad in stone.

Sant'Elena

Located at the eastern limit of the city, beyond the area in which the Biennale is held, the island of **Sant'Elena** was enlarged tenfold during the Austrian administration, partly to form exercise grounds for the troops. Much of the island used to be covered by the meadow of Sant'Elena, a favourite recreation area in the last century, but which has since been usurped by houses, leaving only a strip of park along the waterfront. Still, the walk out here is the nearest you'll get to country pleasures in Venice, and the **church of Sant'Elena** – next to the city's football stadium – is worth a visit.

A church was first erected here in the thirteenth century, following the acquisition of the body of St Helena (the mother of Constantine), and substantially rebuilt in 1435. The spartan Gothic interior has recently been restored, as have the cloister and campanile (the latter so zealously that it now looks like a power-station chimney), but the main attraction is the doorway to the church, an ensemble created in the 1470s by Antonio Rizzo. The sculptural group in the lunette – a monument to Comandante Vittore Cappello, showing him kneeling before St Helena – is the district's one major work of art.

The northern islands

The islands lying to the north of Venice – **San Michele**, **Murano**, **Burano** and **Torcello** – are the places to visit when the throng of tourists in the main part of the city becomes too oppressive, and are the source of much of the glass and lace work you will have seen in many shops in Venice.

To get to them, the main **vaporetto** stop is the Fondamente Nuove, though you can also get the #72 (every 20min) direct from the train station. From the Fondamente Nuove, the #41 (every 20min) will take you to San Michele and Murano. The #12 (every 30min) runs directly from the Fondamente Nuove to Murano's Faro stop, and straight on to Burano and then Torcello. It takes 45 minutes – but note that some boats go to Torcello first, then Burano.

San Michele

The high brick wall around the cemetery island of San Michele gives way by the landing stage to the elegant white facade of **San Michele in Isola**, designed by Mauro Codussi in 1469. With this building, Codussi not only helped introduce Renaissance architecture to Venice, but also promoted the use of Istrian stone. Easy to carve yet resistant to water, it had been used as damp-proofing at ground level, but never before for a complete facade; it was to be used on the facades of most major buildings in Venice from the Renaissance onwards.

The main part of the island, through the cloisters, is the city **cemetery** (daily: summer 7.30am–6pm; winter 7.30am–4pm), established by Napoleonic decree and nowadays maintained by the Franciscans, as is the church. The majority of Venetians lie here for just ten years or so, when their bones are dug up and removed to an ossuary and the land recycled. Only those who can afford it stay longer. The cemetery is laid out in sections – ask at the entrance for the little give-away map – the most dilapidated of which is for the Protestants (no. XV), where any admirers can find **Ezra Pound**'s grave. In section XIV are the Greek and Russian Orthodox graves, including the restrained memorial stones of **Igor and Vera Stravinsky** and the more elaborate tomb of **Serge Diaghilev** – always strewn with flowers.

Even with the grave-rotation system, the island is reaching full capacity, so in 1998 a competition was held for the **redevelopment** of San Michele. The winning entry, from English architect David Chipperfield, places a sequence of formal courtyards alongside a new funerary chapel and crematorium (the Church's line on space-saving cremation having become more flexible of late). On the eastern side of San Michele two footbridges will connect with a rectangular expanse of reclaimed land, site of a trio of tomb buildings overlooking two tiers of waterside gardens, which in turn will overlook central Venice. Making much use of Istrian stone and earthenware plasterwork, Chipperfield's creation promises to be an austerely beautiful addition to the cityscape – and there's a certain appropriateness to the fact that Venice's first great architectural project of the twenty-first century will be a cross between a necropolis and a philosopher's retreat.

Murano

Chiefly famed now as the home of Venice's **glass-blowing** industry, **Murano**'s main *fondamente* are crowded with shops selling the mostly revolting products of the furnaces. However, don't despair: Murano does have other things to offer.

The glass furnaces were moved to Murano from Venice as a safety measure in 1291, and so jealously did the Muranese guard their industrial secrets that for a long while they had the European monopoly on glass mirror-making. The glass-blowers of Murano were accorded various privileges not allowed to other artisans, such as being able to wear swords. From 1376 the offspring of a marriage between a Venetian nobleman and the daughter of a glass-worker were allowed to be entered into the Libro d'Oro, unlike the children of other cross-class matches.

Far more interesting than most of the finished products is the performance of their manufacture. There are numerous **furnaces** to visit, all free of charge on the assumption that you will then want to buy something, though you won't be pressed too hard to do so. Many of the workshops are to be found along Fondamenta dei Vetrai, traditionally a glassworking centre, as the name suggests.

When the Venetian Republic fell to Napoleon in 1797, there were seventeen churches on Murano; today only two are open. The first is San **Pietro Martire** (daily 9am–noon & 3–6pm; free), a Dominican Gothic church begun in 1363 and largely rebuilt after a fire in 1474. Its main attraction is a pair of paintings by Giovanni Bellini hanging on the right wall: on the left is the large and elegant *Madonna and Child with SS Mark and Augustine, and Doge Barbarigo*, and on the right an *Assumption*.

The Glass Museum

Close by, along Fondamenta Cavour, you'll find the **Museo Vetrario** in the Palazzo Giustinian (daily except Wed: summer 10am–5pm; winter 10am–4pm;

€4, or see Museum passes box on p.299). Perhaps the finest single item is the dark-blue Barovier marriage cup, dating from around 1470; it's on show in room 1 on the first floor, along with some splendid Renaissance enamelled and painted glass. But every room contains some amazing creations: glass beakers that look as if they are made from veined stone; sixteenth-century platters that look like discs of crackled ice; stupendously ugly nineteenth-century decorative pieces, with fat little birds enmeshed in trellises of glass. A separate room contains a fascinating exhibition on the history of Murano glass techniques, this time fully explained in English.

Santi Maria e Donato

Murano's main draw is the Veneto-Byzantine church of **Santi Maria e Donato**, which was founded in the seventh century and rebuilt in the twelfth (daily 8am–noon & 4–7pm; free). Its beautiful **mosaic floor**, dated 1141 in the nave, mingles abstract patterns with images of beasts and birds – an eagle carries off a deer; two roosters carry off a fox, slung from a pole. The church was originally dedicated to Mary, but in 1125 was rededicated when the relics of St Donato were brought here from Kefallonia. Four splendid bones from an unfortunate dragon that was slain by the holy spit of Donato are now hanging behind the altar. Above these, in the apse, is a twelfth-century **mosaic of the Madonna** and fifteenth-century frescoes of the Evangelists.

Burano

The main route into **Burano** is a narrow street full of lace shops which soon opens out to reveal the brightly painted houses of the village itself; the colours used to be symbolic, but the meanings have become muddled over time and people now paint their houses whatever colour takes their fancy.

This is still largely a fishing community, the lagoon's main yield being shellfish of various kinds, such as *vongole* (tiny clams) and small crabs. (The catch can be bought either here, on the Fondamenta Pescheria, or back in Venice, at the Rialto.) It's a solitary business; one or two people have even built themselves vulnerable-looking houses out on the slightly higher mud-flats, constructed largely from material scavenged from the lagoon tips.

As the men of Burano live mainly from the water, so the women are to a large extent dependent on **lace making**. Making Burano-point and Venetian-point lace is extremely exacting work – highly skilled, mind-bendingly repetitive, and taking an enormous toll on the eyesight. Each woman specializes in one particular stitch, and so each piece is passed along a sort of "production line" during its construction. The skills are taught at the **Scuola dei Merletti** (daily except Tues: April–Oct 10am–5pm; Nov–March 10am–4pm; €4, or see Museum passes box on p.299). It's in the spacious Piazza Baldessare Galuppi and combines a lace school with a museum, and is well worth a visit before you buy anything. (Much of the work in the shops is machine produced and imported.) The school was opened in 1872 after the indigenous crafting of lace nearly died out; the museum shows work dating back to the sixteenth century, but most was produced in the past hundred years. Across the square rises the leaning campanile – a useful landmark for those heading out to the island.

Torcello

Torcello has come full circle: settled as early as the fifth century, the seat of the Bishop of Altinum from 638, and the home of about 20,000 people by the fourteenth century, it was then eclipsed by Venice, and by 1600 was largely deserted. Today the total population is about 100, and there is little visible evidence of the island's prime – two churches and a couple of buildings round a dusty square, and pottery shards half-buried in the fields.

The main reason people come here today is to visit Venice's first cathedral, **Santa Maria dell'Assunta** (daily 10.30am–5.30pm, closes 5pm Nov–March; €3, including audio-guide, or €6 joint ticket with museum and campanile). An early church on the site became a cathedral after the Bishop of Altinum arrived with other emigrants from the mainland. The present Veneto-Byzantine building is on pretty much the same plan as the seventh-century one, but it was largely rebuilt in the 860s and altered again in 1008. Inside, the waterlogged crypt is the only survival of the body of the original church; the baptistry also dates from the seventh century, but circular foundations in front of the main doors are all that remain of it.

The dominant tone of the interior is created by its watery green-grey marble columns and panelling; the mosaic floor is eleventh-century, but two wooden panels lift to reveal the original floor underneath. A stunning twelfth-century **mosaic** of the Madonna and Child, on a pure gold background, covers the semi-dome of the apse, resting on an eleventh-century mosaic frieze of the Apostles. In the centre of the frieze, below the window, is an image of St Heliodorus, the first Bishop of Altinum, whose remains were brought here by the first settlers. It's interesting to compare this image with the gold-plated face mask given to his remains in a Roman sarcophagus in front of the original seventh-century altar. Ruskin described the view from the campanile (same times; €2, or €6 for joint ticket), completed in the twelfth century, as "one of the most notable scenes in this wide world", a verdict you can test yourself, as the campanile has now been reinforced, cleaned and reopened, after thirty years' service as a pigeon coop.

The church of **Santa Fosca** (same hours as Santa Maria; free) was built in the eleventh and twelfth centuries to house the body of the eponymous saint, brought to Torcello from Libya some time before 1011 and now resting under the altar. Much restored, the church retains the Greek cross form and a fine exterior apse, and inside, the elegant brick arches and cornerings leading up to its wooden dome. Despite the tourists, both these churches manage to maintain a meditative calm.

In the square outside sits the curious **chair of Attila**. Local legend has it that if you sit in it you will be wed within a year. Behind it, in two buildings round the square, is the **Museo dell'Estuario** (Tues–Sun: April–Oct 10.30am–5.30pm; Nov–March 10am–5pm; €2, or €6 for joint ticket), which includes thirteenth-century beaten gold figures, sections of mosaic heads, and jewellery. It's all nicely laid out, and worth a visit.

The southern islands

The section of the lagoon to the south of the city, enclosed by the long islands of the **Lido** and **Pellestrina**, has far fewer outcrops of solid land than the northern half: once you get past **Giudecca** and **San Giorgio Maggiore** – which are in effect detached pieces of central Venice – and clear of the smaller islands that dot the water off the middle section of the Lido, you could, on certain days, look in the direction of the mainland and think you were out in the open sea. The nearer islands are the more interesting: the farther-flung settlements of the southern lagoon have played as significant a role in the history of Venice as the better-known northern islands but nowadays they have little going for them other than the pleasure of the trip.

San Giorgio Maggiore

The prominence of Palladio's church of **San Giorgio Maggiore** (daily 9.30am–12.30pm & summer 2.30–6.30pm, winter 2.30–5pm; free) almost forces you to have an opinion as to its architectural merits. Ruskin didn't much care for it: "It is impossible to conceive a design more gross, more barbarous, more childish in conception, more servile in plagiarism, more insipid in result, more contemptible under every point of rational regard." Palladio's successors were more impressed, though, and it was to prove one of the most influential Renaissance church designs. For more on Palladio, see box on p.353.

The finely calculated proportions and Counter-Reformation austerity of the interior reminded Ruskin merely of an assembly room; in his opinion, its paintings were what justified opening the door. Two pictures by Tintoretto hang in the chancel: *The Fall of Manna* and *The Last Supper*, perhaps the most famous of all his images. They were painted as a pair in 1592–94, the last years of the artist's life; another Tintoretto of the same date – a *Deposition* – hangs in the Cappella dei Morti, approached through the door on the right of the choir.

On the left of the choir a corridor leads to the **campanile** (€3); rebuilt in 1791 after the collapse of its predecessor, it's the best vantage point in the city, with the whole of Venice spread out before you – and it also has a lift.

The ex-Benedictine monastery next door to the church, now the base of the combined arts research institute, craft school and naval college known as the **Fondazione Giorgio Cini**, is one of the architectural gems of Venice, and a regular venue for exhibitions (the only time when the Fondazione is open to the public; phone ☎041.528.9900 for details, ⦿www.cini.it). It incorporates a 128-metre-long dormitory, designed by Giovanni Buora around 1494, a double staircase and a library by Longhena, a magnificent refectory by Palladio and two adjoining cloisters, one planned by Giovanni Buora and built by his son, the other designed by Palladio.

Giudecca

In the earliest records of Venice, the island of **Giudecca** was known as Spina Longa, a name clearly derived from its shape; the modern name might refer to the Jews (*Giudei*) who were based here from the late thirteenth century, or to the disruptive noble families who, from the ninth century, were shoved onto this chain of islets to keep them quiet (*giudicati* meaning "judged"). Before the banks of the Brenta became the prestigious site for one's summer abode, Giudecca was where the wealthiest aristocrats of early Renaissance Venice built their villas, and in places you can still see traces of their gardens. The present-day suburb is a strange mixture of decrepitude and vitality: at the western edge is the neo-Gothic fortress of the Mulino Stucky, a long-derelict flour mill built in 1895 that is finally being restored, and at the other stands the *Cipriani*, the most expensive hotel in Venice.

The Franciscan church of the **Redentore** (see box on p.299 for times and ticket), designed by Palladio (see p.353) in 1577, is Giudecca's main monument. In 1575–76 Venice suffered an outbreak of bubonic plague that annihilated nearly 50,000 people – virtually a third of the city's population. The Redentore was built in thanks for Venice's deliverance, and every year until the downfall of the republic the doge and his senators attended a Mass in the church on the Feast of the Redentore to express their continuing gratitude. The procession walked to the church over a pontoon bridge from the Zattere, a ceremony perpetuated by the people of Venice on the third Sunday in July.

The long-overdue restoration of the interior has cleared the clutter, revealing the genius of Palladio's original conception. The bright, clean plasterwork, in particular, reflects the masterful use of different intensities of light in the various parts of the church to draw the eye – and the mind – inward and upward. As the architect wrote, "Among all colours, none can be more suitable for temples than white because the purity of the colour is more acceptable to God". The best paintings in the church, including a *Madonna with Child and Angels* by Alvise Vivarini, are in the sacristy, where you'll be greatly edified by a gallery of eighteenth-century wax heads of illustrious Franciscans, arranged in glass cases all round the room.

San Lazzaro degli Armeni

No foreign community has a longer pedigree in Venice than the Armenians: they were established by the end of the thirteenth century, and for around five hundred years have had a church within a few yards of the Piazza (in Calle degli Armeni). They are far less numerous now, and the most conspicuous sign of their presence is the Armenian island by the Lido, **San Lazzaro degli Armeni** (daily 3.25–5pm; €6; take *vaporetto* #20 just before 3pm), identifiable from the city by the onion-shaped top of its campanile. The Roman Catholic Armenian monastery here was founded in 1717 by Manug di Pietro (known as Mechitar – "The Consoler"), and derived its name from the island's past function as a leper colony – Lazarus being the patron saint of lepers.

The Armenian monks have always had a reputation as scholars and linguists, and the monastery's collection of precious manuscripts and books – the former going back to the fifth century – is a highlight, along with a Tiepolo ceiling panel and the room in which Byron stayed while lending a hand with the preparation of an Armenian–English dictionary.

The Lido and the southern lagoon

For about eight centuries, the **Lido** was the focus of the annual hullaballoo of Venice's "Marriage to the Sea", when the doge went out to the Porto di Lido to drop a gold ring into the brine and then disembarked for Mass at San Nicolò al Lido. It was then an unspoilt strip of land, and remained so into the last century. Within thirty years it had become the smartest bathing resort in Italy, and although it's no longer as chic as it was when Thomas Mann set *Death in Venice* here, there's less room on its beaches now than ever before. But unless you're staying at one of the flashy hotels that stand shoulder to shoulder along the seafront, or are prepared to pay a ludicrous fee to rent one of their beach hutches for the day, you won't be allowed to get the choicest Lido sand between your toes. The ungroomed public beaches are at the northern and southern ends of the island – though why people would want to jeopardize their health in these filthy waters is a mystery.

Eating and drinking

Unfortunately, there's more than an element of truth to Venice's reputation as a place where mass tourism has produced homogenized menus and slapdash standards. Venice has fewer good moderately priced **restaurants** than any other major Italian city, it has more really bad restaurants than any other, and in some of the very expensive establishments you're paying not for a fine culinary experience but for the event of dining in a posh Venetian restaurant. However, things have been getting better recently, an improvement due in part to the efforts of the Ristorante della Buona Accoglienza, an association of restaurateurs determined to present the best of genuine Venetian cuisine at sensible prices. In the Venetian context, "sensible" means in the region of €30 per person, but even in the lower price ranges there are plenty of acceptable little places hidden away in the city's quieter quarters – and some are rather more than merely acceptable.

More than anywhere else in Italy, the division between **bars** and restaurants is often difficult to draw – many of the places listed below under "Restaurants" have a bar area on the street side of the dining room, while some of the "Bars" have basic sit-down areas for eating. We've classified our bars and restaurants according to which aspect of the business draws most of the customers, but if you're looking for a simple meal in a particular area of the city, be sure to check both sets of listings.

Restaurants

Virtually every budget restaurant in Venice advertises a set-price **menù turistico** for as little as €12, which at its best will offer a choice of three or four dishes for each course. This can be a cheap way of sampling Venetian specialities (though you'd be better off with *cichetti*, tapas-like portions served in bars), but the quality and certainly the quantity won't be up to the mark of an **à la carte** meal. As a general rule, value for money tends to increase with the distance from San Marco; plenty of restaurants within a short radius of the Piazza offer menus that seem to be reasonable, but you'll probably find the food unappetizing, the portions tiny and the service abrupt. And quality of food aside, an evening expedition into the maze of **Dorsoduro** and San Polo or lively **Cannaregio**, the best *sestieri* for dining, is an excellent way to get yourself off the beaten track.

We've supplied the phone numbers for those places where **booking** is advisable; Sunday lunch is particularly busy. Wherever possible, we've also supplied the day of the week on which each restaurant is closed, but bear in mind that many restaurateurs take their annual holiday in August, and that quite a few places close down in the dead weeks of January and early February.

San Marco

Acqua Pazza Campo Sant'Angelo 3808 ☎041.277.0688. A classy, moderately expensive restaurant serving good seafood and Neapolitan pizzas in a spacious environment. Excellent homemade limoncello. Open till 11pm, closed Mon.

Al Bacareto Calle delle Botteghe 3447. Inexpensive to moderately priced dishes such as the excellent *risotto alla pescatore* (fisherman's risotto) can be eaten either in the dining room or standing at the bar area (the cheaper option). Handy for the Palazzo Grassi. Open till 11pm. Closed Sun.

Le Bistrot de Venise Calle dei Fabbri 4685 ⊛www.bistrotdevenise.com. In summer this is a rather tame restaurant, but from October to early May it becomes something of a community arts centre, with poetry readings, live music and exhibitions. It looks a bit like a French bistro, but the menu is based on old-style Venetian recipes. The reasonably priced food is fine, though the atmosphere has suffered by proximity to the tourist honeypot of the Piazza. The bar opens at 9am, the kitchen at noon, and food is served until 15min before closing. Open daily until 1am.

Da Fiore Calle delle Botteghe 3461. Established in the mid-1990s, this popular (and expensive) restaurant offers genuine Venetian cuisine in a classy trattoria-style setting. The ante-room is a nice small bar that's open to all, though most of the customers are waiting to go through. Not to be confused with the *Da Fiore* fish restaurant in San Polo. Open until midnight. Closed Tues.

Da Ivo Ramo dei Fuseri 1809 ☎041.528.5004. Has built up a big following with its Tuscan dishes. Recommended are the mussel soup and the bistecca. Expensive. Closed Sun.

Dorsoduro

Ai Carmini Calle delle Pazienze, Rio Terrà Scozzera 2893b. Located in the buzzy Campo S. Margherita, this restaurant is hard to beat if you're looking for a good, inexpensive tourist menu of Venetian specialties, and at €10.32 you certainly won't find a better price. Lies at one end of the buzzy Campo S. Margherita. Open until 2am. Closed Sun.

Ai Cugnai Piscina del Forner 857. A few yards to the east of the Accademia, but remarkably unspoilt considering how close it is to one of the city's biggest tourist draws, this is a moderately priced and very welcoming little trattoria, run by a family of gregarious Venetian senior citizens. Ordesrs are memorized rather than written down and can become scrambled, but that is part of the fun. Open till 9pm. Closed Mon.

Ai Quattro Ferri Calle Lunga S. Barnaba. One of several excellent places in this alley down from Campo S. Barnaba – *La Bitta* and *Da Sandro* are also recommended. Simple, easy-going and cheap osteria with delicious *cichetti* and a menu that changes daily. Attracts a lively young crowd, especially after 9pm. Open till midnight. Closed Sun.

San Trovaso Fondamenta Priuli 1016. An efficient two-storey restaurant-pizzeria which is packed most nights with a mix of tourists and locals. Straightforward food in robust portions. Open till 9.50pm. Closed Mon.

Alle Zattere Záttere ai Gesuati 795. An excellent pizzeria a short walk from the Accademia with large outdoor seating on the water with views over to Giudecca. Moderate prices.

San Polo

Arca Calle S. Pantalon 3760. A popular student hang-out serving superb pizzas and a good range of *cichetti*. Closed Sun.

Osteria da Fiore Calle dei Scaleter 2202a. An expensive.fish restaurant that some rank as the best in Venice. Closed Sun & Mon.

Jazz Club 900 Campiello del Sansoni, 900. Follow your nose towards one of the best pizza ovens you'll find in the city, or just follow the signpost off the Ruga Vecchia San Giovanni, by the Rialto bridge. The atmosphere is eccentric, with a dark, heavily panelled interior and non-stop jazz, usually live on Wed, but not in summer – check on Ⓦ www.jazz900.com. Inexpensive. Open until midnight. Closed Mon.

Al Nono Risorto Sottoportego de Siora Bettina 2338. Busy pizzeria-restaurant just off Campo S. Cassiano; has a pleasant garden and a predominantly twenty-something following. Live jazz and blues on Thursdays in winter. Moderate prices. Open until midnight. Closed Wed.

Osteria al Ponte "La Patatina" Calle dei Saoneri 2741a. Bustling osteria serving excellent *cichetti* and other Venetian specialities with set menus that change regularly. Open till 10.30pm. Closed Sun.

Da Sandro Campiello dei Meloni. Split-site pizzeria-trattoria, with rooms on both sides of the campiello and tables on the pavement. Often frenetic, though not aggressively so. The pizzas are the best thing they do. Inexpensive to moderate prices. Closed Fri.

Cannaregio

Anice Stellato Fondamenta Madonna dell'Orto ☎041.720.744. Hugely popular with Venetians for the superb, reasonably priced meals and unfussy atmosphere. Rather too far out for most tourists, though, situated as it is on the northernmost Cannaregio canal. If you can't get a table – it's frequently booked solid – drop by for the excellent *cichetti* at the bar. Open till midnight. Closed Mon.

Casa Mia Calle dell'Oca 4430. Always heaving with locals, who usually order from the pizza list rather than the menu, though the standard dishes are reliable enough. Inexpensive. Open till 11pm. Closed Tues.

Gam Gam Fondamenta di Cannaregio 122 Ⓦ www.jewishvenice.org. A rarity in Venice: a kosher restaurant, with an intriguing menu of Israeli, Eastern European and Venetian cuisine, and a mixed clientele of discerning New Yorkers and curious locals. The *cholent*, a chick pea stew, and *latkas*, potato balls, are particularly good. Excellent for vegetarians, too. Open till 10pm. Closed Fri eve and Sat.

Ai Promessi Sposi Calle dell'Orca 4367. A bar-trattoria specializing in *baccalà* and other traditional fish dishes. Excellent range of mouthwatering *cichetti* at the bar. Small garden at the back. Closed Wed,

Sahara Fondamenta della Misericorderia 2519 ☎041.721.077. Delicious Syrian dishes are served up at this lively restaurant, with belly dancing on Saturdays – for which booking is advisable. Outdoor seating on the canal in summer. Prices are relatively inexpensive. Open till 2am. Closed Mon.

Alla Vedova Ca' d'Oro Calle del Pistor 3912. Just off the Strada Nova, opposite the alley leading to the Ca' d'Oro, this trattoria is vaguely reminiscent of a Victorian parlour, albeit one that's heaving with Venetians, especially later on in the evening. A small blackboard acts as a menu, with a short list of Venetian standards. Open till 11pm. Closed Thurs and Sun lunch.

Castello

Aciugheta Campo S. Filippo e Giacomo 4357. A bar with a pizzeria-trattoria next door. The closest spot to San Marco to eat without paying through the nose. Closed Wed.

Corte Sconta Calle del Pestrin 3886 ☏041.522.7024. Secreted in a tiny lane to the east of San Giovanni in Brágora, this restaurant offers wonderful seafood dishes and far better than average house wine. The *menù degustazione*, costing €48 (without wine), is probably the best meal that sum will get you in the entire city. Booking absolutely essential. Open till 9.45pm. Closed Sun & Mon.

Fiaschetteria Toscana Salizzada S. Giovanni Crisostomo 5719. ☏041.528.5281. The name means "Tuscan wine shop" but the menu is true Venetian. Very highly rated for food, but also has good wine list, so it is worth booking. Closed Mon lunch, Tues and mid July–mid August.

Al Mascaron Calle Lunga S. Maria Formosa 5225 ☏041.522.5995. Has an arty feel and excellent food, but definitely two types of clientele – Italians and non-Italians – with service to match each. Has a good reputation among the locals though and gets very busy, so book if you can. Closed Sun.

Da Remigio Salizzada dei Greci 3416 ☏041.523.0089. Brilliant, good-value neighbourhood trattoria, serving gorgeous home-made gnocchi. Be sure to book – the locals pack this place every night. Closed Mon eve & Tues.

Dai Tosi Calle Secco Marina 738. Terrific and moderately priced pizzeria-trattoria – not to be confused with the friendly, run-down pizzeria of the same name a few doors along – with excellent home-made pasta as well as delicious pizzas. A really buzzing place when the Biennale is on, and devoid of tourists outside the festival. Open until 11.30pm. Closed Wed.

Giudecca

Altanella Calle delle Erbe 268 ☏041.522.7780. Highly recommended for its beautiful and reasonably priced fish dishes and the terrace overlooking the island's central canal. No credit cards. Worth booking. Closed Mon and Tues.

Harry's Dolci Fondamenta S. Biagio 773 ☏041.522.4844. Despite the name, sweets aren't the only things on offer here – the kitchen of this offshoot of *Harry's Bar* (see below) is rated by many as the equal of its ancestor. It's actually less expensive, but you're nonetheless talking about a place where the set menu costs €54 a head, drink excluded. Still, if you want to experience Venetian culinary refinement at its most exquisite, this is it. Closed Tues.

Bars and snacks

Stand at a traditional Venetian **bar**, known as a *bácaro*, any time of the day and you won't have to wait long before someone drops by for a reviving *ombra*, a tiny glass of wine customarily downed in one. The origins of the word are obscure, but may come from the tradition of wine-sellers in the Piazza keeping their bottles cool by standing in the *ombra*, or shade. Most bars also serve some kind of food, ranging from fat little sandwiches in soft white bread, Venice's famous **tramezzini**, through the traditional *cichetti*, tapas by another name, to proper cooked meals.

San Marco

Bácaro Jazz Salizzada Fondaco dei Tedeschi. Formerly a branch of *Wendy Burger* (who presumably found the going a bit tough when *McDonald's* moved into town), this place has been reborn as a jazz-themed bar with a menu of old-style *cichetti*, and is proving a big hit with cool Venetian kids. Open 11am–2am. Closed Wed.

Devil's Forest Calle Stagneri. The liveliest bar in the vicinity of Campo San Bartolomeo, and a convincing facsimile of a British pub, with a good range of beers and a dartboard – though the food is a lot better than you'd find in most real pubs. Open 8am–1am. Closed Sun.

Harry's Bar Calle Vallaresso 1323. The most glamorous bar in town since time immemorial; famed in equal measure for its cocktails, its sandwiches and its celebrity-league prices. Open 3pm–1am. Closed Mon.

Vino Vino Ponte delle Veste 2007. Very close to the Fenice opera house, this is a slightly posey wine bar, but it does stock more than 100 wines. It also serves relatively inexpensive meals as well.

Open 10am–midnight. Closed Tues.
Al Volto Calle Cavalli 4081. This dark little bar is an *enoteca* in the true sense of the word – 1300

Dorsoduro

Il Caffé Campo S. Margherita. Known as *Caffè Rosso*, this inviting café-bar with an elegant interior is a student favourite, with chairs outside and great music. Live jazz/blues/rock on Thurs. Open till 1am. Closed Sun.
Cantina del Vino già Schiavi Fondamenta Nani 992. Popular bar and wine shop opposite San Trovaso – do some sampling before you buy. Great place to graze on the bar snacks at lunchtime. Open till 8.30pm. Closed Sun.

San Polo

Bancogiro Sotoportego del Banco Giro 122. Popular bar by the Rialto market facing onto the square by San Giacomo, where the youthful clientele spill out onto the bank of the Canal Grande behind. Also serves good snacks. Open till midnight. Closed Sun eve and Monday.
Do Mori Calle Do Mori 429. Hidden just off Ruga Vecchia S. Giovanni, this is the best bar in the market area. Delicious snacks and terrific atmosphere. Open 9am–1pm & 5–8pm. Closed Wed afternoon and all day Sun.
Café Noir Crosera San Pantalon 3805. Along with

Cannaregio

Enoteca da Colonne 1814c. Delicious range of food in this busy bar just off Rio Terrà San Leonardo, and an impressive collection of corkscrews on the wall. Packed with regulars at lunchtime, small terrace out the front in summer.
Fiddler's Elbow Corte dei Pali. Self-styled "Irish pub"; usually has a few Venetian lads trying to act rowdily and a smattering of Brits showing them how it's really done, but most of the kids are content with sipping a small glass of Guinness for an hour. Open 5pm–midnight. Closed Wed.
Iguana Fondamenta della Misericordia 2517. Sits on the borderline between *bácaro* and Mexican cantina, serving reasonably-priced Tex-Mex fare to a young crowd. Live Latin and jazz Tues. Open until 1am. Closed Mon.
Paradiso Perduto Fondamenta della Misericordia 2540. Lashings of simple (but not inexpensive)

wines from Italy and elsewhere, some cheap, many not; good snacks, too. Open till 10pm. Closed Sun.

Corner Pub Calle della Chiesa 684. Very near the Guggenheim, this place usually has a few arty foreigners in attendance, but they are always outnumbered by locals. Open until 12.30am. Closed Mon.
Margaret Du Champ Campo S. Margherita 3019. Another very popular bar on the lively campo – but less studenty than others and slightly more showy. Open till 2am. Closed Wed.

the *Café Blue* a couple of doors away (which has live music in winter on Fridays), this is the absolute favourite student bar. Warm, cosmopolitan atmosphere, with a trendy crowd dropping in for a spritz or dabbling on the very cheap Internet in the small room at the back. Open 7am–2am, Sunday eves only.
Ruga Rialto Ruga Vecchia S. Giovanni. Lively bar – the area is full of them – with a young crowd, though lacking in atmosphere on quiet nights. Live blues/funk Fri. Good for *cichetti* and an *ombra*.

Venetian food are served at the refectory-like tables of *Paradiso Perduto*, but essentially this place is Venice's leading boho bar, attracting students, arty types and the gay community. The bar opens around 7.30pm, the kitchen gets going at 8pm, and the doors close at 2am. Bar prices are higher when live music is playing – usually Sun and sometimes Mon. Closed Tues and Wed.

Castello

Al Ponte Calle Larga G. Gallina 6378. Typical osteria off Santi Giovanni e Paolo, good for a glass of wine and a snack. Open till 8.30pm. Closed Sun.
Alla Rampa Salizzada S. Antonin 3607. Utterly traditional *bácaro* with a nautical flavour. Great for a cheap *ombra* (€0.60), if you don't mind being the only customer who isn't Venetian, male and over forty.

Cafés, pasticcerie and ice cream

As in every Italian city, the **cafés** are central to social life, and you'll never be more than a couple of minutes from a decent one. In addition to their marvellous local confections, many **pasticcerie** also serve coffee, but will have at most a few bar stools. Strict budgeting is further jeopardized by Venice's **gela-terie**, where ice cream comes in forms you're unlikely to have experienced before.

General areas in which to find good cafés and pasticcerie include **Campo Santa Margherita**, **Crosera San Pantalon**, running just south of San Rocco, and **Campiello Meloni** (between S. Polo and S. Aponal), which has a couple of excellent pasticcerie whose doors remain open on Sundays.

Florian Piazza S. Marco 56–59. Opened in 1720 by Florian Francesconi, and frescoed and mirrored in a passable pastiche of that period, this is the café to be seen in. A simple cappuccino will set you back a purseload if the band's performing, and you'll have to take out a mortgage for a cocktail. Closed Wed.

Nico Zàttere ai Gesuati; Dorsoduro. A high point of a wander in the area, celebrated for an artery-clogging creation called a *gianduiotto* – a paper cup containing a block of praline ice cream drowned in whipped cream. Open till 10pm. Closed Thurs.

Paolin Campo S. Stefano; San Marco. Thought by many to be the makers of the best ice cream in Venice; certainly their pistachio is amazing, and the outside tables have one of the finest settings in the city. Open till midnight daily.

Rizzardini Calle della Madonetta 1415. Founded in 1742, this is one of the best places for the less florid varieties of Venetian pastries. Closed Mon.

Rosa Salva Campo S. Luca, Calle Flubera and Merceria S. Salvador; all San Marco. Venice's premier chain of cafés: excellent coffee and very good pastries in unfussed surroundings.

Tonolo Crosera S. Pantalon; San Polo. The busiest café on one of the busiest streets of the student district; especially hectic on Sunday mornings, when the fancy Tonolo cakes are in high demand for the day's main meal. Closed Mon.

Markets and shops

The campi, parks and canalside steps make **picnicking** a pleasant alternative in Venice, and if you're venturing off to the outer islands it's often the only way of refuelling. Don't try to picnic in the *campi*, though – the bylaws against it are strictly enforced.

Open-air **markets** for fruit and vegetables are held in various squares every day except Sunday; check out Santa Maria Formosa, Santa Margherita, Campiello dell'Anconetta, Rio Terrà San Leonardo and the barge moored by Campo San Barnaba. The market of markets, however, is the one at the Rialto, where you can buy everything you need for an impromptu feast – it's open Monday to Saturday 8am to 1pm, with a few stalls opening again in the late afternoon.

Virtually every parish has its **alimentari** and most of them are good; one worth singling out is Aliani Gastronomia in Ruga Vecchia S. Giovanni (San Polo) – scores of cheeses, meats and salads that'll have you drooling. Alternatively, you could get everything from one of Venice's well-hidden **supermarkets**. Most central is Su.Ve., on the corner of Salizzada S. Lio and Calle Mondo Nuovo (Castello); others are on Campo S. Margherita (Dorsoduro), Rio Terrà Frari (San Polo), Zàttere Ponte Lungo (Dorsoduro) and close to the youth hostel on the main Giudecca waterfront.

Nightlife, shows and festivals

Except when the *Carnevale* is in full swing, Venice after dark is pretty moribund. Locals head to Mestre and the mainland for nightlife, as high rents and zealous noise policing close down as many late bars as manage to open. That said, the city's calendar of special events is often impressive, though the bias is definitely towards high culture. To find out what's on in the way of concerts and films, check *Un Ospite di Venezia* (Ⓦwww.unospitedivenezia.it), *Leo Bussola* or go to Ⓦwww.govenice.org; for news of events outside the mainstream, check the posters.

Concerts and cinema

Prior to the calamitous fire of 1996, **La Fenice** was the third-ranking Italian opera house after Milan's La Scala and Naples' San Carlo. While the building is being reconstructed, a process that is expected to last well into 2003 and possibly beyond, performances are being held in a vast marquee called the **Palafenice** (over on Tronchetto; a special water bus takes ticket-holders from Piazzale Roma to the tent) and in the **Teatro Malibran** by the church of S. Giovanni Crisostomo (special water buses operate from the Rialto bridge to the station, Piazzale Roma and the Tronchetto car park). Tickets for Palafenice can be bought at ticket offices in the Calle dei Fuseri, San Marco 1810, at Piazzale Roma, at the train station (all open Mon–Sat 8.30am–6.30pm; ☎041.786.580), or at Palafenice itself (☎041.786.511, ℱ041.786.505, Ⓦwww.teatrolafenice.it). Prices range from €18 to €93; the opera season runs from late November to the end of June, punctuated by ballet performances.

Music performances at the **Goldoni** (box office 9.30am–12.30pm & 4–6pm; ☎041.520.5422, Ⓔteatrogo@tin.it) are somewhat less frequent than at La Fenice; the repertoire here isn't as straitlaced, with a **jazz** series cropping up every now and then. For most of the year the Goldoni specializes in the works of the eponymous writer. **Classical** concerts, with a strong bias towards the eighteenth century, are also performed at three Scuole Grande (San Giovanni Evangelista, San Rocco and San Teodoro), at the Palazzo Querini-Stampalia (☎041.271.1411, Ⓦwww.querinistampalia.it), and at the churches of the Miracoli, the Frari, San Bartolomeo, San Rocco, Redentore, San Barnaba, the Ospedaletto and the Pietà (the most regularly used – it specializes in Vivaldi in particular). Ticket prices vary widely, from free performances to €25 in the Pietà – which is expensive for performances more often distinguished by enthusiasm than professionalism.

Venice's **cinemas** show a typically depressing selection of the worst Hollywood offering badly dubbed into Italian. During the Biennale, however, an open-air cinema in Campo S. Polo shows dubbed or Italian-language films to a high-spirited local audience. Films start each night at around 9pm, and it's worth the trip if only for the atmosphere.

Late bars

Upbeat and downmarket from the theatre and classical concerts, some bars play music late and approach a pub (current jargon for the ubiquitous "disco-bar") atmosphere. We've listed likely venues under bars (pp.335–6), but trends and nights change so fast that it can be best to head for one or two areas and just follow the noise. The best nightlife is found along the Fondamenta della Misericordia, in Cannaregio, where *Iguana* and *Paradiso Perduto* (see "Bars") stay open late and have occasional DJs or live music. Dorsoduro, on and around the studenty Campo S. Margherita, is another good bet, though many bars close earlier; try *Du Champ*, which stays open until 2am. There is more live music in *Ruga Rialto* and *Il Caffè* (see above), as well as at *Suzie Café* at Campo de S. Basilio 1527, Dorsoduro (near the San Basilio vaporetto stop) which has a reggae/ska session on Thursday or Friday. To really get down, however, there's only one option, *Casanova* (☎041.534.7479, Ⓦwww.casanova.it), on the Lista di Spagna. As a huge, old-fashioned **disco-club** it would be half empty anywhere

⑤

else. In Venice it's open Sunday to Wednesday till 2am, but the big days are Thursday to Saturday when it's open till past 4am and is packed. The current regime is student/indie-pop (Thurs), salsa till 2am and then revival (Fri), house (Sat).

Exhibitions – and the Biennale

In addition to those permanent museums that hold one-off exhibitions from time to time, Venice has numerous venues for temporary shows, of which the Fiat-owned **Palazzo Grassi** (℡199.139.139, ⓦwww.palazzograssi.it) maintains the highest standards. There's also the **Venice Biennale** (℡041.521.8711, ⓦwww.labiennale.org), set up in 1895 as a showpiece for international contemporary art and held from June to September of every odd-numbered year. Its permanent site in the Giardini Pubblici has pavilions for about forty countries (the largest for Italy's representatives), plus space for a thematic international exhibition. Supplementing this central part of the Biennale is the **Aperto** ("Open"), a mixed exhibition showing the work of younger, or less established artists – often more exciting than the main event. The Aperto takes over spaces all over the city: the salt warehouses on the Záttere, for instance, or the Corderie in the Arsenale. Exhibits from earlier years, plus a fabulous collection of magazines and catalogues from all over the world, are kept in the archive in the Palazzo Corner della Regina, close to Ca' Pésaro; entrance is free.

Festivals

The *Carnevale* and the Film Festival might be the best publicized of the city's festivals, but the calendar is strewn with other special events, most of them with religious or commemorative origins.

Carnevale

The Venice **Carnevale** occupies the ten days leading up to Lent, finishing on Shrove Tuesday with a masked ball for the glitterati and dancing in the Piazza for the plebs. Revived spontaneously in the 1970s, it is now supported by the city authorities, who organize various pageants and performances (details from the San Marco tourist office – see p.289). Apart from these events, Carnevale is an endless parade. During the day people don costumes and go to the Piazza to be photographed, while business types can be seen doing their shopping in the classic white mask, black cloak and tricorne hat. In the evening some congregate in the remoter squares, while those who have spent hundreds of pounds on their costumes install themselves in the windows of *Florian*'s and pose for a while. Many private palaces open their doors to themed feasts, some of which you'll be able to visit; ask at the tourist office for more details. Masks are on sale throughout the year in Venice, but special mask and costume shops magically appear during Carnevale, and Campo San Maurizio sprouts a marquee with mask-making demonstrations and a variety of designs for sale.

La Sensa

The feast of **La Sensa** happens in May on the Sunday after Ascension Day – the latter the day on which the doge performed the wedding of Venice to the sea. The ritual has recently been revived – a distinctly feeble procession that ends with the mayor and a gang of other dignitaries getting into a present-day approximation of the *Bucintoro* (the state barge) and sailing off to the Lido. Of more interest is the **Vogalonga** (long row), held on the same day. Open to any crew in any class of rowing boat, it covers a 32-kilometre course from the

Bacino di San Marco out to Burano and back; the competitors arrive at the mouth of the Canal Grande anywhere between about 11am and 3pm.

Santa Maria della Salute

Named after the church of the Salute, this centuries-old feast day is a reminder of the devastating plague of 1630–31. The church was built in thanks for deliverance from the outbreak, and every November 21 since then the Venetians have processed over a pontoon bridge across the Canal Grande to give thanks for their good health, or to pray for sick friends and relatives. It offers the only chance to see the church as it was designed to be seen – with its main doors open, and with hundreds of people milling up the steps and round the building.

La Festa del Redentore

Another plague-related festival, this time to mark the end of the 1576 epidemic. Celebrated on the third Sunday in July, the day is centred on Palladio's church of the Redentore, which was built by way of thanksgiving for the city's escape. A bridge of boats is strung across the Giudecca canal to allow the faithful to walk over to the church, and on the Saturday night hundreds of people row out for a picnic on the water. The night ends with a grand fireworks display, after which it's traditional to make for the Lido to watch the sun rise.

The Regata Storica

Held on the first Sunday in September, the **Regata Storica** is the annual trial of strength and skill for the city's gondoliers and other expert rowers. It starts with a procession of richly decorated historic craft along the Canal Grande course, their crews all decked out in period dress. Bystanders are expected to support contestants in the main event, and may even be issued with appropriate colours.

The Film Festival

The **Venice Film Festival** – the world's oldest – takes place on the Lido every year in late August and early September. The tourist office will have the festival programme a few weeks in advance, as will the two cinemas where the films are shown – the main Palazzo del Cinema (Lungomare G. Marconi) and the Astra (Via Corfu). Tickets are available for the general public, but you have to go along and queue for them on the day of performance. Outside the festival season, the Palazzo and Astra are run as ordinary commercial cinemas.

Listings

ACTV enquiries Piazzale Roma, daily 7.30am–8pm ☎041.528.7886, ⓦ www.actv.it.
Airlines Alitalia, Salizzada S. Moisè, San Marco 1463 ☎041.520.0355; British Airways, Riva degli Schiavoni, Castello 4191 ☎041.528.5026.
Airport enquiries ☎041.260.9260, ⓦ www.veniceairport.it.
American Express The American Express office is in Salizzada S. Moisè, a couple of minutes' walk west of the Piazza; Mon–Fri 9am–5.30pm, Sat 9am–12.30pm; emergency number

☎041.1678.72.000 (toll-free).
Banks Banca Commerciale Italiana, Calle Larga XXII Marzo, San Marco 2188; Banca d'Italia, Campo S. Bartolomeo, San Marco 4799; Banca Credito Italiano, Campo S. Salvador, San Marco; Banco Ambrosiano Veneto, Calle Goldoni, San Marco 4481; Banco di Roma, Mercerie dell'Orologio, San Marco 191; Banco San Marco, Calle Larga XXII Marzo, San Marco 383.
Car rental At Marco Polo airport: Eurodollar ☎041.541.5570; Hertz ☎041.541.6075; Italy by

Car ℡041.541.6049. At Piazzale Roma: Autorent ℡041.520.9907; Avis ℡041.522.5825; Eurodollar ℡041.528.9551; Europcar ℡041.523.8616; Hertz ℡041.528.3524; Mattiazzo ℡041.528.9494; Sixt ℡167.018.668.

Consulates and embassies The British consulate is by the Accademia in the Palazzo Querini, Dorsoduro 1051 ℡041.522.7207; this office is staffed by an honorary consul – the closest full consulate is in Milan. The nearest US consulate is also in Milan. Travellers from Ireland, Australia, New Zealand and Canada should contact their Rome embassies.

Exchange There are clusters of exchange bureaux (*cambios*) where most tourists gather – near San Marco, the Rialto and the train station. Open late every day of the week, they can be useful in emergencies, but their rates of commission and exchange tend to be steep. The best rates are at American Express and the main banks (see above).

Hospital Ospedale Civile, Campo SS. Giovanni e Paolo ℡041.523.0000.

Internet access A number of dedicated Internet points have opened in the last couple of years, most charging around €7–9 per 30min, though rates tend to drop the longer you stay online. Try *Venetian Navigator* on Casselleria between Piazza San Marco and Campo Santa Maria Formosa; *Net House* on Campo S. Stefano, near the Ponte dell'Accademia; *Play the Game*, Calle Lunga S. Maria Formosa, in Castello; *Omniservice*, on Fondamenta dei Tolentini; *Veniceconnection* (€5.70 per hour) at Calle Campaniel San Polo 2898a; and one of the cheapest at €2.50 an hour, the congenial *Café Noir* (see p.336) on Crosera S. Pantalon.

Laundries In Salizzada del Pistor, Cannaregio 4553, near SS Apostoli.

Left luggage The desk at the end of platform 14 in the train station charges €2.58 per item per 12 hours. The lockers alongside platform 1 are slightly more expensive at €1.55 per 6 hours. Both open 24hr, though the latter may be closed for security reasons.

Lost property If you lose anything on the train or at the station, call ℡041.785.238; at Piazzale Roma or on the bus, call ℡041.522.4576; at the airport, call ℡041.260.6436; on the *vaporetti*, call ℡041.780.310; and anywhere in the city itself, call the town hall on ℡041.520.8844.

Passports In the event of a lost passport, notify the Questura in Mestre, at Via Nicoldi 24 (℡041.271.5511) and then your consulate or embassy (see above).

Police To notify police of a theft, report to the carabinieri's Pronto Intervento Stranieri office on Fondamenta S. Lorenzo ℡041.528.4666; in emergencies, ring ℡113.

Post offices Venice's main post office is in the Fondaco dei Tedeschi, near the Rialto bridge. Any poste restante should be addressed to Fermo Posta, Fondaco dei Tedeschi, 80100 Venezia; it can be collected Mon–Sat 8.15am–6.45pm – take your passport with you. Stamps are on sale Mon–Sat 8.15am–7pm; the telegram service operates round the clock. The principal branch post offices are in Calle dell'Ascensione, immediately west of the Piazza (Mon–Fri 8.10am–1.25pm, Sat 8.10am–noon) and at Zàttere 1406 (same hours). Stamps can also be bought in *tabacchi*, as well as in some gift shops.

Public toilets On most campi you'll now see small, green, white and blue Amav signs directing you to the nearest toilet; you'll need a €0.50 piece to get through the turnstiles – an assistant should be at hand if you don't have the right change. The toilets by platform 1 at the train station cost €0.52. Toilets are to be found in most of the city's bars as well – it's diplomatic to buy a drink before availing yourself of the facility, but it's not a legal requirement. In practice it's best to ask in places off the main thoroughfares, if only for the sake of the long-suffering restaurateurs.

Telephones All Venice's public call-boxes accept phonecards (the vast majority accept nothing but cards), but for lengthy long-distance calls it might be best to go to one of the two main Telecom Italia offices, where you can dial direct and be charged afterwards. The offices are at Piazzale Roma (daily 8am–9.30pm) and adjoining the main post office (Mon–Fri 8.30am–12.30pm & 4–7pm).

The Veneto

Virtually every acre of the Veneto bears the imprint of Venetian rule. In **Belluno**, right under the crags of the Dolomites, the style of the buildings declares the town's former allegiance, while the Lion of St Mark looks over the market square of **Verona**, on the Veneto's western edge. On the flatlands of the Po basin (the southern border of the region) and on farming estates all over the Veneto, the elegant **villas** of the Venetian nobility are still standing.

Yet the Veneto is as diverse culturally as it is geographically. The aspects of Verona that make the city so attractive were created long before the expansion of Venice's terra firma empire, and in **Padua** – a university seat since the thirteenth century – the civilization of the Renaissance displays a character quite distinct from that which evolved in Venice. Even in **Vicenza**, which reached its present form mainly during its long period of subservience, the very appearance of the streets is proof of a fundamental independence.

Nowadays this is one of Italy's wealthiest regions. Verona, Padua, Vicenza and **Treviso**, 30km north of Venice, are all major industrial and commercial centres, while intensive dairies, fruit farms and vineyards (around Conegliano, for example) have made the Veneto a leading agricultural producer too.

The Veneto's densest concentration of industry is at **Mestre** and **Marghera**, the grim conurbation through which all road and rail lines from Venice pass before spreading out over the mainland. It's less a city than an economic life-support system for Venice, and the negative impression you get on your way through is entirely valid. Some people trim their holiday expenses by staying in Mestre's cheaper hotels (Venice's tourist offices will supply addresses), but venturing further inland is a more pleasurable cost-cutting exercise.

The Brenta

The southernmost of the three main rivers that empty into the Venetian lagoon, the **Brenta** caused no end of trouble to the earliest settlers on both the mainland and the islands, with its frequent flooding and its deposits of silt. By the sixteenth century, though, the canalization of the river had brought it under control, and it became a favoured building site for the Venetian aristocracy. Some of these Venetian villas were built as a combination of summer residence and farmhouse – many, however, were intended solely for the former function. The period from mid-June to mid-November was the season of the *villeggiatura*, when the patrician families of Venice would load their best furniture onto barges and set off for the relative coolness of the Brenta.

Around one hundred **villas** are left standing on the river between Padua and Venice: some are derelict, a large number are still inhabited and a handful are open to the public. Of this last category, two are outstanding – the **Villa Fóscari** and the **Villa Pisani** – both of which are easily accessible by bus from Venice: four ACTV buses go to the former (€0.80), and the hourly buses between Padua and Venice (ACTV bus, marked dolo Venezia in Padua bus station, not the SITA bus that goes on the motorway) go past both (€2). Don't be tempted by the widely advertised boat trips along the Brenta – they cost upwards of €62 and stop longer for lunch than at any of the villas.

Villa Fóscari

The **Villa Fóscari** at **MALCONTENTA** (May to mid-Nov Tues & Sat 9am–noon; €7) was designed in 1559 by Palladio (see box on p.353) and is the nearest of his villas to Venice. Most of Palladio's villas fall into two broad groups: those built on cohesive farming estates, with a central low block for living quarters and wings for storage and associated uses (the Villa Barbaro at Masèr and the Villa Emo near Castelfranco); and the large, single-block villas, built for landowners whose fields were dispersed or in some way unsuitable for the construction of a major building. The Villa Fóscari is the masterpiece of this second group, powerfully evoking the architecture of ancient Rome by its heavily rusticated exterior, its massive Ionic portico and its two-storey main hall – a space inspired by the baths of Rome.

The frescoes in the living rooms include what is said to be a portrait of a woman of the Fóscari family who was exiled here as punishment for an amorous escapade, and whose subsequent misery, according to legend, was the source of the name Malcontenta. The reality is more prosaic – the area was known by that name long before the Fóscari arrived, either because of some local discontent over the development of the land or because of the political *malcontenti* who used to hide out in the nearby salt marshes.

The Villa Pisani

The **Villa Pisani** (or Nazionale) at **STRA** (Tues–Sun: April–Sept 9am–7pm; Oct–March 9am–4pm; €5, or €2.50 for the park only), virtually on the outskirts of Padua, looks more like a product of the *ancien régime* than a house for the Venetian gentry. Commissioned by way of celebration when Alvise Pisani was elected Doge of Venice in 1735, it was the biggest such residence to be built in Venetian territory during that century. It has appealed to megalomaniacs ever since: Napoleon bought it off the Pisani in 1807 and handed it over to Eugène Beauharnais, his stepson and Viceroy of Italy; and in 1934 it was the place chosen for the first meeting of Mussolini and Hitler.

Most of what you see is unexciting and sparsely furnished. But stick with it for the ballroom, its ceiling covered with a fresco of *The Apotheosis of the Pisani Family*, painted by Giambattista **Tiepolo** at the age of 66; a dazzling performance, it's as full of blue space as it could be without falling apart. And if you're trying to puzzle out what's going on – the Pisani family, accompanied by Venice, are being courted by the Arts, Sciences and Spirits of Peace, while Fame plays a fanfare in praise of the Pisani and the Madonna looks on with appropriate pride.

Padua

Extensively reconstructed after the damage caused by bombing in World War II, and hemmed in by the sprawl that has accompanied its development as the most important economic centre of the Veneto, **PADUA** (PADOVA) is not immediately the most alluring city in northern Italy. It is, however, one of the most ancient, and plentiful evidence remains of its impressive lineage. A large student population creates a young, vibrant atmosphere, and yet in spite of having two big attractions – the Giotto frescoes and relics of St Antony – Padua has the feel of a town that is just getting on with its own business. And indeed, for many people Padua's main appeal is as a base from which to make day-trips to its overcrowded neighbour, Venice.

A Roman municipium from 45 BC, the city thrived until the barbarian onslaughts and the subsequent Lombard invasion at the start of the seventh century. Recovery was slow, but by the middle of the twelfth century, when it became a free commune, Padua was prosperous once again. The university was founded in 1221, and a decade later the city became a place of pilgrimage following the death here of St Anthony.

In 1337 the **Da Carrara** family established control. Under their domination, Padua's cultural eminence was secured – Giotto, Dante and Petrarch were among those attracted here – but Carraresi territorial ambitions led to conflict with Venice, and in 1405 the city's independence ended with its conquest by the neighbouring republic. Though politically nullified, Padua remained an artistic and intellectual centre: Donatello and Mantegna both worked here, and in the seventeenth century Galileo researched at the university, where the medical faculty was one of the most ambitious in Europe. With the fall of the Venetian Republic the city passed to Napoleon, who handed it over to the Austrians, after whose regime Padua was annexed to Italy in 1866.

Arrival, information and accommodation

Trains arrive in the north of the town, just a few minutes' walk up Corso del Popolo from the old city walls. The main **bus station** is at Piazzale Boschetti, immediately north of the walls to the east of the Corso – the direct buses from Marco Polo and Treviso airports arrive here; however, you'll find **local buses** for the city and for all the nearby towns described in this chapter also stop at the train station. The main **tourist office** is at Galleria Pedrocchi in the alley behind the café of the same name (Mon–Sat 9.30am–12.30pm & 3–7pm; ☎049.876.7927, ⓦwww.apt.padova.it) and stocks free maps and lists of accommodation. There is another tourist office at the train station (summer Mon–Sat 9.15am–7pm, Sun 9am–noon; winter Mon–Sat 9.20am–5.45pm, Sun 9am–noon; ☎049.875.2077) and there is a booth at Piazza del Santo (March–Oct Mon–Sat 9am–6pm, Sun 9.30am–12.30pm; ☎049.875.3087).

Internet points can be found in the north of town at the large Ludoteca in Collegio on Piazza Petrarca, just behind the Basilica del Carmine (Mon–Fri 9am–2am, Sat & Sun 3pm–2am, except Aug when daily 2/3pm–2am), and in the Il Mago delle Stelle bookshop (Mon–Fri 9am–7.30pm) on Piazzetta Conciapella tucked away on a modern square off Via Matteotti.

A few years ago it was infinitely simpler to find an inexpensive room in Padua than in Venice; it's still the case that the average cost is lower, but availability can be a problem with Venice so near. If you're visiting in high season or during festivals be prepared for a protracted search, but don't despair – Padua has plenty of reasonably priced hotels, and the tourist office has a full list. If you don't mind being a little further from the centre you could try Padua's new "**Bed and Breakfast**" places. This is a good way to see an Italian family home, though bear in mind that this can have its drawbacks in terms of noise, getting home late and so on. Ring or email Kokonor (☎049.864.3394, ⓦwww.bandb-veneto.it/kokonor), the group which coordinates the scheme. The train station has a left-luggage office near the tourist office (€3.87 per item for 12 hours) and cheaper luggage lockers.

Padovacard

Costing €13 and valid for 48 hours, the **Padovacard** allows one visit to the Musei Civici, the Palazzo della Ragione and it also gives reductions to the Duomo baptistry, Scuola del Santo, Museo Antoniano and the Orto Botanico. It only includes the Giotto frescoes if you buy the card when booking for these by phone or on the web – see below. The card also entitles you to free bus rides and free parking in three of the city's car parks. It is available at the tourist office and participating museums and monuments.

Hotels

Eden Via C.Battisti 255 ☎ 049.650.484, ✉ info@hoteledenpadova.it. In a modern block near Piazza del Santo in the university quarter, a mixed bag of rooms, but most are a cut above the average one-star and all doubles have showers and TV. Excellent value given the location. ❸
Al Fagiano Via Locatelli 45 ☎ 049.875.3396, ✆ www.alfagiano.it. Fairly large two-star just off the main road near the basilica. The pleasant rooms are on the small side, but have a/c, TV and hair dryers. Parking in front of hotel for €10. ❹
Majestic Toscanelli Via dell'Arco 2, ☎ 049.663.244, ✆ www.toscanelli.com. The most appealing four-star in town, very near Piazza delle

Erbe. Glitzy and well equipped rooms in this modern hotel. ❼
Mignon Via Belludi 22 ☎ 049.661.722. Comfortable, relatively plush two-star between Prato delle Valle and the basilica. Smallish rooms but with a/c and TV. Rooms at the back quieter. Parking €6. ❹
Sant'Antonio Via San Fermo 118 ☎ 049.875.1393, ✆ www.hotelsantantonio.com. Pleasant two-star with large a/c rooms with slightly faded modern interiors, but decent enough. Double beds as well as twins. Start the day with fresh orange juice and coffee next door at the friendly *Albabar*. ❹

Hostel and campsite

Ostello Città di Padova Via A. Aleardi 30 ☎ 049.875.2219, ✆ 049.654.210. Padua's HI hostel is a short walk west of the Prato della Valle – or take bus #8 or #18 from Bay 3 at the train station. Friendly place with useful information about the town and getting to Venice. 112 beds in rooms of 2–16. Washing machines, Internet access (with phone card) and bike rental, but has an 11pm curfew. Check-in from 4pm. Advisable to book

May–Oct. No IH card needed. €13 (€14 in rooms with two- and five-bed rooms), including breakfast.
Montegrotto Terme Sporting Center Via Roma 123/25 ☎ 049.793.400, ✆ www.sportingcenter.it. This is the nearest campsite to Padua – 15km from the city centre, but frequent trains take around 15min; a very upmarket site, it boasts not merely a swimming pool but thermal baths too. Open March to mid-Nov.

The City

From the train station, the Corso del Popolo and its extension Corso Garibaldi lead south through a gap in the Renaissance city walls towards the centre of the city, passing after a short distance the **Cappella degli Scrovegni** and **Musei Civici degli Eremitani** (Tues–Sun: daily 9am–7pm; free with Padovacard – see above; or €9 for the museum only, €11 including the chapel – see below). For many people the **Giotto frescoes** in the Scrovegni, considered to be one of the key works in the development of European art, are *the* reason for coming to Padua, but even if you're no expert the chapel exerts an extraordinary presence.

It's advisable to **book tickets** at least three or four days in advance, especially in summer. It's not possible to book in person: you'll either have to phone ☎ 049.201.0020 or book via the website ✆ www.cappelladegliscrovegni.it. Tickets cost €10 plus €1 booking fee; entry is free with the Padovacard (see above). Groups of 25 are admitted every quarter of an hour, and you have to be at the museum ticket office an hour before your allotted entry time to pick up your ticket. The new airlock entrance system installed to reverse the damage caused to the frescoes by high levels of humidity borne by the breath and clothing of visitors means at the time printed on your ticket, the glass door to the waiting room slides open to allow the next set of visitors in – and immediately shuts again, anyone left outside being forced to pay up and book another slot. Once inside, a high-tech system adjusts the air humidity of the waiting room down to that of the chapel itself and filters away the worst of the spores and pollution while you are shown a video of the frescoes. The video is useful as it gives you an idea of what to focus on in your short time inside the chapel, and also shows you some of the details of the frescoes. Fourteen minutes later another door leading to the chapel itself opens and you have exactly a quarter of an hour to take in the frescoes before being ejected through a third glass door back into the grounds of the museum.

The chapel was commissioned in 1303 by Enrico Scrovegni in atonement for his father's usury, which was so vicious that he was denied a Christian burial. As soon as the walls were built, Giotto was commissioned to cover them with illustrations of the life of Mary, the life of Jesus and the story of the Passion; the finished cycle, arranged in three tightly-knit tiers and painted against a backdrop of saturated blue, is one of the high points in the development of European art. The Scrovegni series is a marvellous demonstration of Giotto's innovative attention to the inner nature of his subjects. In terms of sheer physical presence and the relationships between the figures and their environment, Giotto's work takes the first important strides towards realism and humanism. The Joachim series on the top row of the north wall (on your right as you walk in) is particularly powerful – note the exchange of looks between the two shepherds in the *Arrival of Joachim*. Beneath the main pictures are shown the vices and virtues in human (usually female) form, while on the wall above the door is a *Last Judgement* – in rather poor condition and now thought to be only partly by Giotto – with rivers of fire leading from God to hell. Directly above the door is a portrait of Scrovegni presenting the chapel; his tomb is at the far end, behind the altar with his statues by **Giovanni Pisano**.

The neighbouring **Musei Civici degli Eremitani** (see above for hours and ticket), formerly the monastery of the Eremitani, is a superbly presented three-part museum complex. The archeological collection, on the ground floor, has a vast array of pre-Roman, Roman and paleo-Christian objects. Upstairs, the vast **Museo d'Arte** houses an extensive assembly of fourteenth- to nineteenth-century art from the Veneto and further afield. The collection is arranged in chronological order, and it's a fairly long walk through tracts of workaday stuff, but names such as Titian, Tintoretto and Tiepolo leaven the mix. Spectacular highpoints are provided by the Giotto *Crucifixion* that was once in the Scrovegni chapel, and a fine *Portrait of a Young Senator* by Bellini. The Capodilista collection, an offshoot of the main gallery, has a pair of mysterious Titian and Giorgione landscapes, and some good Luca Giordano grotesques. The **Museo Bottacin**, for more specialist tastes, was founded in 1865 and contains over 50,000 coins, medals and seals, making it one of the most important museums of its type in the world.

The Chiesa degli Eremitani

The neighbouring church of the **Eremitani**, built at the turn of the fourteenth century, was almost completely wrecked by an Allied bombing raid in 1944 and has been fastidiously rebuilt (summer Mon–Sat 8.15am–12.15pm & 4–6pm, Sun 9.30am–12.15pm & 4–6pm; winter Mon–Sat closes 5.30pm, Sun closes 5pm; free). Photographs to the left of the apse show the extent of the damage, the worst aspect of which was the near-total destruction of Mantegna's frescoes of the lives of St James and St Christopher – the war's severest blow to Italy's artistic heritage.

Produced between 1454 and 1457, when Mantegna was in his mid-twenties, the frescoes were unprecedented in the thoroughness with which they exploited fixed-point perspective – a concept central to Renaissance humanism, with its emphasis on the primacy of individual perception. The extent of his achievement can now be assessed only from the fuzzy photographs and the sad fragments preserved in the chapel to the right of the high altar. On the left wall is the *Martyrdom of St James*, put together from fragments found in the rubble;

and on the right is the *Martyrdom of St Christopher*, which had been removed from the wall before the war.

The central squares

Walking back to the Corso Garibaldi and turning left leads you past the **Caffè Pedrocchi**, which used to be the city's main intellectual salon; it's no longer that, but it does have a multiplicity of functions – chic café, with old ladies in their best hats, concert hall and conference centre. Just beyond, the **Piazza della Frutta** and **Piazza delle Erbe**, the sites of Padua's daily markets, are lined with bars, restaurants and shops. Separating them is the extraordinary **Palazzo della Ragione** or **Salone** (Tues–Sun: Feb–Oct 9am–7pm; Nov–Jan 9am–6pm; €6 or free with Padovacard). At the time of its construction in the 1210s, this vast hall was the largest room to have been built on top of another storey. Its decoration would once have been as astounding as its size, but the original frescoes by Giotto and his assistants were destroyed by fire in 1420, though some by Giustio de'Menabuoi have survived; most of the extant frescoes are by Nicola Miretto (1425–40) depicting an astrological calendar distinctively medieval in its complexity. Mainly used as the city council's assembly hall, it was also a place where Padua's citizens could plead for justice – hence the appellation *della Ragione*, meaning "of reason". The unmissable wooden horse with disproportionately gigantic gonads is modelled on Donatello's *Gattamelata*, and was made for a joust in 1466.

The Duomo and baptistry

Close by is Padua's **Duomo** (Mon–Sat 7.30am–noon & 3.45–7.30pm, Sun 7.45am–1pm & 3.45–8.30pm), an unlovely church whose architect cribbed his design from drawings by Michelangelo. The adjacent Romanesque **baptistry**, though, is one of the unproclaimed delights of Padua (daily 10am–6pm; €2.50, or €1 with Padovacard). Built by the Da Carraras in the thirteenth century, and still in use today, it's lined with fourteenth-century frescoes by Giusto de'Menabuoi, a cycle which makes a fascinating comparison with Giotto's in the Cappella degli Scrovegni. The influence of Giotto is plain, but in striving for greater realism Giusto has lost Giotto's monumentality and made some of his figures awkward and unconvincing. Yet many of the scenes are delightful, and the vibrancy of their colours, coupled with the size and relative quiet of the building, make for a memorable visit.

To the university

If instead of turning right you carry straight on from *Caffè Pedrocchi* you come to the main block of the **university**, the **Palazzo del Bò** (The Ox – named after an inn that used to stand here). Established in September 1221, the University of Padua is older than any other in Italy except that of Bologna, and the coats of arms which encrust the courtyard and Great Hall attest to the social and intellectual rank of its alumni. The first permanent **anatomy theatre** was built here in 1594, a facility that doubtless greatly helped William Harvey, who went on to develop the theory of blood circulation after taking his degree here in 1602. Galileo taught physics here from 1592 to 1610, declaiming from a lectern that is still on show. And in 1678 Elena Lucrezia Corner Piscopia became the first woman to collect a university degree when she was awarded her doctorate in philosophy here – there's a statue of her in the courtyard. The Bò is only open for guided visits (March–Oct Mon, Wed & Fri 3pm, 4pm & 5pm, Tues, Thurs & Sat 9am, 10am & 11am; €2.58); at present, tours set off from the bar, signposted in the courtyard, but it's best to check with the tourist office. A special Paduan tradition takes place in the square in front of the Palazzo in February, May and September. To mark their graduation students are given a poster-sized, caricatured account of their college life and achievements to read out in front of family and friends while drinking a bottle of wine and performing feats or forfeits those around them dare them to do. They are then crowned with a wreath of laurels and cheered with cries of "dottore, dottore".

The Prato della Valle and Santa Giustina

Past the *palazzo*, Via VIII Febbraio turns into Via Roma and then Via Umberto I, before opening up into the sprawling **Prato della Valle**, claimed to be the largest town square in Italy; it's a generally cheerless area, ringed by over-wide roads, but the vast Saturday market and the summer funfair do a lot to make it jollier. As the number of ice cream vendors might suggest, it's also a favourite place for the passeggiata on summer evenings. One side is fronted by the sixteenth-century **Basilica di Santa Giustina** (summer daily 8.30am–noon & 3–7pm; winter Mon–Fri closes 5.30pm, Sat closes 6.45pm, Sun closes 7.30pm). A pair of fifteenth-century griffins, one holding a knight and the other a lion, are the only notable adornments to the unclad brick facade; the freezing interior has little of interest except a huge *Martyrdom of St Justina* by Paolo Veronese (in the apse), some highly proficient carving on the choir stalls, and the sarcophagus which once contained the relics of Luke the Evangelist (apse of left transept).

More appealing are the vestiges of the church's earlier incarnations. In the right transept a stone arch opens onto the **Martyrs' Corridor**, a composite of fifth- to twelfth-century architectural fragments that leads to the **Sacellum di Santa Maria e San Prosdocimo**, burial place of St Prosdocimus. He was the first bishop of Padua back in the fourth century, when the church was founded, and is depicted here on a fifth-century panel. The fifteenth-century **old choir**, reached by a chain of corridors from the left-hand chapel of the right transept, has choir stalls inset with splendid marquetry panels.

Il Santo

At the far end of Via Belludi on Piazza del Santo towers the Basilica di San Antonio, or **Il Santo** (daily 6.30am–7pm). Within eighteen months of his death in 1231, St Anthony had been canonized and his tomb was attracting enough pilgrims to warrant the building of the basilica. It was not until the start of the fourteenth century that the church reached a state that enabled the saint's body to be placed in the **Cappella del Santo** (in the left transept). Plastered with such votive offerings as photographs of healed limbs and car crashes survived with the saint's intervention, the shrine is irresistible to the voyeur. The chapel's more formal decoration includes the most important series of relief sculpture created in sixteenth-century Italy, a sequence of nine marble panels showing scenes from the life of St Anthony. Carved between 1505 and 1577, most have the names of their sculptors incised into the base, Antonio Lombardo, Tullio Lombardo and Jacopo Sansovino being among the most famous.

Adjoining the chapel is the Cappella della Madonna Mora (named after its fourteenth-century French altar statue), which in turn gives onto the Cappella del Beato Luca, whose fourteenth-century frescoes include a lovely image of St James lifting a prison tower to free a prisoner. Back in the aisle, just outside the Cappella del Santo, is Padua's finest work by Pietro Lombardo, the monument to Antonio Roselli (1467). More impressive still are the high altar's bronze sculptures and reliefs by Donatello (1444–45), the works that introduced Renaissance classicism to Padua. Built onto the farthest point of the ambulatory, the **Cappella del Tesoro** (daily 7am–1pm & 2.30–7pm) houses the tongue and vocal chords of St Anthony, as well as a host of lesser relics. For more on St Anthony and the basilica, enter the cloisters (on the south side of the basilica) and follow the signs for the **Musei Antoniani** (Tues–Sun 9am–1pm & 2.30–6.30pm; €2.58, €1.55 with Padovacard), which includes the **Mostra Antoniana** (closes 30min earlier). The former, on the first floor, is a collection of paintings (including the fresco of St Anthony and St Bernardino by **Mantegna**), ornate incense holders, ceremonial robes and other paraphernalia linked to the basilica; the latter, on the ground floor, is a history of votive gifts.

In the shadow of the basilica stands Donatello's **Monument to Gattamelata** (which translates literally as "The Honeyed Cat"), as the *condottiere* Erasmo da Narni was known. He died in 1443 and this monument was raised ten years later, the earliest large bronze sculpture of the Renaissance. A direct precursor to Verrocchio's monument to Colleoni in Venice, it could hardly be more different: Gattemelata was known for his honesty and dignity, and Donatello has given us an image of comparative sensitivity and restraint, quite unlike Verrocchio's image of power through force.

South of Il Santo

To the left as you leave the basilica are the **Oratorio di San Giorgio** and **Scoletta del Santo** (daily: 9am–12.30pm & 2.30–7pm; €2, or €1.50 with Padovacard). The oratory was founded in 1377 as a mortuary chapel, and its frescoes by **Altichiero di Zevio** and **Jacopo Avanzi** were completed soon after. One wall is adorned by the wonderfully titled *St Lucy Remains Immovable at an Attempt to Drag Her with the Help of Oxen to a House of Ill Repute*.

The Scoletta was founded soon after Anthony's canonization, though this building only goes back as far as the early fifteenth century. The ground floor is still used for religious purposes, while upstairs is maintained to look pretty much as it would have in the sixteenth century, with its fine ceiling and paintings dating mainly from 1509–15. Four of the pictures are said to be by Titian.

One way to relax from all this art is to stroll round the corner to the **Orto Botanico**, the oldest botanic gardens in Europe (summer daily 9am–1pm & 3–6pm; winter Mon–Sat 9am–1pm; €2.58, or €2 with Padovacard). Planted in 1545 by the university's medical faculty as a collection of medicinal herbs, the gardens are laid out much as they were originally, and the specimens on show haven't changed too much either. Goethe came here in 1786 to see a palm tree that had been planted in 1585; the selfsame tree still stands.

Eating, drinking and nightlife

Catering for the midday stampede of ravenous students, Padua's **bars** generally produce weightier **snacks** than the routine *tramezzini* – slabs of pizza and sandwiches vast enough to satisfy a glutton are standard; you'll find several amidst the food stalls underneath the Palazzo della Ragione. There are several self-service restaurants offering good-value full menus, open for lunch and dinner, but they turn off their hot-plates by 9pm. For a passeggiata and a place to sit and watch the world go by, the main areas to head for are Piazza dell' Erbe, Piazza Duomo, Piazza Cavour and Prato delle Valle, but for the real action the bars in the narrow streets around these piazzas and the University are the liveliest, with a student-based clientele.

Restaurants

Anfora Via Soncin 13 ☏049.656.629. Boisterous and very reasonable Bohemian restaurant that doubles up as a bar between restaurant hours (12.30–3.15pm & 8–11.30pm), with delicious snacks all day. Get there early or book in advance. Closed Sun.

Belle Parti Via Belle Parti 11 ☏049.875.1822. Delightfully elegant place in all respects, with beautiful decor, a beamed ceiling and gentle lighting. Set in a tiny street running between Via Verdi and Via S. Lucia. This is somewhere to go on a special occasion, with an excellent menu, impeccable service and a relaxed atmosphere. Open till 2am. Closed Mon lunch and Sun.

Al Borgo Via Belludi 56. Wood-fired oven pizzeria with tables outside looking onto the Piazza del Santo; popular with locals and tourists alike. Open till midnight. Closed Sun.

Gastronomica al Portego Via Dante 9. Self-service restaurant, Italian style, with very good local dishes. Closed Sun eve & all day Mon.

L'Isola di Caprera Via Marsilio di Padova 11–15 ☏049.876.0244. Popular, classy restaurant situated just north of Piazza della Fruta and renowned for its fish and seafood dishes. It's moderately priced, and has a tourist menu for €20.70. Service is included in the bill. Closed Sun.

Medina Via S.G. Barbarigo, 18. Small, bustling pizzeria, often packed with students enjoying excellent pizza and salads. Closed Tues.

Nane della Giulia Via Santa Sofia 1. Down in the university quarter, an unusual mix of trendy and unpretentious that attracts a lot of students. Go for the reasonably priced Veneto and vegetarian specialities earlier in the evening and the bar atmosphere later. Live piano Wed and Thurs. Open from 8pm. Closed Mon.

Osteria dei Fabbri Via dei Fabbri 13 ☏049.650.336. Excellent mid-range trattoria with an appealing wooden decor and a friendly atmosphere; you'll be lucky to get a seat without booking. Open till 10.30pm. Closed Sun.

Pepen Piazza Cavour. With a wonderful range of pizzas and seats on the square in the summer, this is one of Padua's best-sited pizzerias. Open till midnight. Closed Sun.

Bars and nightlife

Your best bet, as usual, is to head for the centre and follow the throng. A good place to start is around the unmarked *Bar Nazionale*, at Piazza delle Erbe 40, on the northeast corner (closed Sun). The bar closes at 9pm but the crowds linger for long after, before dispersing – mostly to out-of-town clubs, though the places listed below tend to stay pretty lively until at least 2am during university term time.

Padua's main theatre is the **Teatro Verdi** (closed in summer) on Corso Milano hosting opera and big-name dramatists; details of the season's events can be obtained from the tourist office or in the bilingual information booklet *Padova Today*, distributed in some bars and most hotels. Of the local newspapers, the most comprehensive for listings is *Il Mattino*, but for more offbeat events check out the posters up around the city, particularly in the university area.

Australian Pub Via del Santo 93. One of the best mock pubs in town. It's a lively spot on the edge of the university quarter and is open till 2am daily.

Extra Extra via Ciamician, 145. Padova's flashiest disco. Buzzing after 2am from Thursday to Saturday, dead the rest of the time. If you can't get a taxi, it's an inadvisable thirty-minute walk back to the centre by way of Via Sório.

Limbo Via San Fermo 44. Another popular disco-pub. Open until 3am. Closed Sun.

Miniera Via S. Francesco 144. Dimly lit, trendy bar in the university quarter. Open 8pm–2am. Closed Tues and Wed.

¿Perché no? Via Manzoni 4. Padua's main gay bar, a small, friendly place just beyond the city walls: head along Via Cavazzana out through the walls, turn right and the bar is just before the second major crossroads. Open till 2am daily.

Vicenza

Europe's largest producer of textiles and the focus of Italy's "Silicon Valley", **VICENZA** is a very sleek city, where it can seem that every second car is a BMW. Prosperity hasn't ruined the look of Vicenza, though. The centre of the city, still partly enclosed by medieval walls, is an amalgam of Gothic and Classical buildings that today looks much as it did when the last major phase of construction came to an end at the close of the eighteenth century. This historic core is compact enough to be explored in a day, but the city and its environs really require a short stay to do them justice.

In 1404 Vicenza was absorbed by Venice, and the city's numerous Gothic palaces reflect its status as a Venetian satellite. But in the latter half of the sixteenth century the city was transformed by the work of an architect who owed nothing to Venice and whose rigorous but flexible style was to influence every succeeding generation – Andrea di Pietro (or della Gondola), alias Palladio.

The City

The main street of Vicenza, the **Corso Andrea Palladio**, cuts right through the old centre from the Piazza del Castello down to the Piazza Matteotti, and is lined with palaces, all of them now occupied by shops, offices and banks. Palladio's last palace, the fragmentary **Palazzo Porto-Breganze**, stands on the

VICENZA

0   100 m

RESTAURANTS & BARS
Galleria 15	B
Il Grottino	C
Malvasia	A
Ponte delle Belle	E
Vecchia Guardia	D

Parco Querini

CONTRA PUSTERIA
River Bacchiglione
CONTRA CANOVE
CONTRA V. VENETO
CONTRA S. CORONA
PIAZZA VENTI SETTEMBRE
River Bacchiglione
Padua

Palazzo Leoni-Montanari
Teatro Olimpico
S. Corona
PIAZZA MATTEOTTI

CONTRA PEDAMURO S. BIAGIO
Palazzo Iseppo Porto
CONTRA PORTI
CONTRA S. GAETANO THIENE
C.S. STEFANO
Casa Cogollo
Museo Civico
VIALE A. GIURIOLO
La Rotonda & Monte Bérico

Palazzo Colleoni Porto
S. Stefano
Palazzo Thiene
C.S. FAUSTINO
CONTRA ORACOLO DEL SERVO
CONTRA DELLE SERVO

S. Lorenzo
CORSO A. FOGAZZARO
CONTRA RIALE
Palazzo Barbaran
ANDREA PALLADIO
C. MANIN
C. MORETTE
PIAZZA BIADE
Basilica

S. LORENZO
PIAZZA S. LORENZO
Loggia del Capitaniato
CONTRA MONTE
PIAZZA DEI SIGNORI
PONTE S. MICHELE

CONTRA MOTTON S. LORENZO
Palazzo Valmarana
CORSO
VIA BATTISTI
C. CAVOUR
PIAZZETTA PALLADIO
PIAZZA DELL'ERBE
CONTRA FRANCEI

N
CONTRA GARIBALDI
C. MUSCHERIA
C. PESCHERIE
ORETICO
PONTE S. PAOLO
Oratorio di San Nicola

Duomo
CORSO PALLADIO
PIAZZA CASTELLO
PIAZZA DEL DUOMO
C. ORATORIO PROTI
River Retrone
Monte Bérico

Giardino Salvi
PIAZZALE DE GASPERI
VESCOVADO
CONTRA
Palazzo Porto-Breganze
Train & Bus Stations

ACCOMMODATION
Campo Marzio	6
Due Mori	5
Giardini	2
Palladio	3
Vicenza	4
Youth Hostel	1

Palladio

Born in Padua in 1508, Andrea di Pietro (or della Gondola) began his career as an apprentice stonemason in Vicenza. At thirty he became the protégé of a local noble-man, Count Giangiorgio Trissino, the leading light of the humanist Accademia Olimpico – a learned society which still meets in Vicenza. Trissino gave the architect his classi-cized name, **Palladio**, directed his architectural training, brought him into contact with the dominant class of Vicenza and, perhaps most crucially, took him to Rome – the first of many trips he made through Italy, sketching Imperial Roman remains.

Between 1540 and his death in 1580, Palladio created around a dozen palaces and public buildings in Vicenza, nearly twenty villas in the countryside of the Veneto and two important religious buildings in Venice. But unlike the pioneers of Renaissance Classicism – architects such as Alberti, Brunelleschi and Bramante – Palladio's reputation does not rest on a particular transformation of architectural style. Instead, his fame – and he is arguably the most influential architect in the world – rests on the way he is considered to have perfected existing values of harmony and proportion.

In particular, his lasting influence stems from *I Quattro Libri dell'Architettura* or "The Four Books of Architecture", a treatise he published in 1570, towards the end of his career. Other architects had written important works of theory, but Palladio's is unique in its practical applicability, serving almost as a textbook for Classical architecture. As the style spread into the rest of Europe and beyond, it was to Palladio's book that architects like Inigo Jones (and later, Thomas Jefferson) turned, finding both inspiration and guidance in his examples.

Today, Palladio has perhaps become the victim of his own success. The ubiquity of neo-Classicism in second-rate churches and third-rate bank buildings can make it hard to sense the freshness and brilliance of his designs, though it still shines through in masterpieces like the Basilica in Vicenza, the Villa Barbaro near Ásolo and the churches of the Redentore and San Giorgio Maggiore in Venice. Even if you're inclined to agree with Herbert Read's opinion that "in the back of every dying civi-lization there sticks a bloody Doric column", you might leave the region converted.

southern side of Piazza Castello; no. 163 on the Corso, the **Casa Cogollo**, is known as the Casa del Palladio, though he never lived there and few people think he designed it.

The Museo Civico and Teatro Olimpico

The Corso ends with one of the architect's most imperious buildings, the **Palazzo Chiericati** (begun in 1550), now home of the **Museo Civico**, also known as the Pinacoteca (July & Aug Tues–Sun 9am–7pm; Sept–June 9am–4.45pm; see Vicenza museum box on p.354 for entry). The core of the picture collection is made up of Vicentine artists, none of whose work will knock you flat on your back; it's left to a few more celebrated names – Memling, Tintoretto, Veronese, Tiepolo – and some fine fifteenth-century painting to make the visit memorable.

Across the Piazza Matteotti is the one building in Vicenza you shouldn't fail to go into – the **Teatro Olimpico**, the oldest indoor theatre in Europe (July & Aug Tues–Sun 9am–7pm; Sept–June 9am–4.45pm; see Vicenza museum box on p.354 for entry). Approached in 1579 by the members of the Olympic Academy (a society dedicated to the study of the humanities) to produce a design for a permanent theatre, Palladio devised a covered amphitheatre derived from his reading of Vitruvius and his studies of Roman structures in Italy and France. He died soon after work commenced, and the scheme was then overseen by Scamozzi, who added to Palladio's design the backstage perspective of a classical city, creating the illusion of long urban vistas by tilting the "streets" at an alarming angle. The theatre opened on March 3, 1585, with an extravagant production of *Oedipus Rex*, and is still used for plays and concerts.

The Piazza dei Signori

At the hub of the city, the **Piazza dei Signori**, stands the most awesome of Palladio's creations – the **Basilica**. Designed in the late 1540s (but not finished until the second decade of the next century), this was Palladio's first public project and the one that secured his reputation. The monumental regularity of the basilica disguises the fact that the Palladian building is effectively a stupendous piece of buttressing – the Doric and Ionic colonnades enclose the fifteenth-century hall of the city council, an unstable structure that had defied a number of attempts to prop it up before Palladio's solution was put into effect. The vast Gothic hall is often used for good contemporary architecture exhibitions (Tues–Sun: summer 10am–7pm; winter 9am–5pm; price varies). On Tuesdays and Thursdays a vast market fills the streets between the basilica and the Duomo, though if you're shopping for picnic food, you'll save money by going down the slope and over the river, where the shops are a good bit cheaper.

A late Palladio building, the unfinished **Loggia del Capitaniato**, faces the basilica across the Piazza dei Signori. Built as accommodation for the Venetian military commander of the city, it's decorated with reliefs in celebration of the Venetian victory over the Turks at Lepanto in 1571.

The churches

The **Duomo** was bombed flat in 1944 and carefully reconstructed after the war; it's a rather gloomy place, chiefly distinguished as one of the few Italian cathedrals to be overwhelmed by its secular surroundings. Far more interesting is **Santa Corona** (daily: summer 8.30am–noon & 2.30–6pm; winter 9.30am–noon & 3–6pm), on the other side of the Corso Palladio (at the Piazza Matteotti end), a Dominican church dating from the mid-thirteenth century. Here you'll find two of the three great church paintings in Vicenza – *The Baptism of Christ*, a late work by Giovanni Bellini, and *The Adoration of the Magi*, painted in 1573 by Paolo Veronese. The cloisters now house a run-of-the-mill Museo Naturalistico-Archeologico (Tues–Sun: mid-June to Aug 9am–7pm; Sept to mid-June 9am–5pm; see box below for admission prices).

The nearby **Santo Stefano** (Mon–Sat 8.30–10am & 5.30–7pm) contains the third of the city's fine church paintings: Palma Vecchio's typically stolid and voluptuous *Madonna and Child with SS George and Lucy*.

Vicenza's museums

Two different **biglietti cumulativi** are on offer in Vicenza: the €7 ticket allows you one visit to the Teatro Olimpico, the Museo Civico and the less than enthralling Museo Naturalistico-Archeologico; the €8 ticket gives admission to these three plus the Museo del Risorgimento, a rather specialized museum that's a long way out of the city centre. Two other cards are also available, but these are poor value unless you plan to make a very comprehensive visit. The "Vicenza Card – Musei e Palazzi" costs €11 and gets you into all the places above plus the Gallerie di Palazzo Leoni-Montanari, and gives free entrance to exhibitions at the Palazzo Barbaran. You'd do better paying the individual entrance fees at La Rotonda and the Villa Valmarana than buying the Vicenze e le Ville card at €22. Note that the Basilica is not included in any of the joint tickets. All tickets are valid for three days from purchase.

The palazzi and the parks

Santo Stefano faces a corner of the huge **Palazzo Thiene**, another of Palladio's palaces. It was planned to occupy the entire block down to Corso Palladio, but in the end work progressed no further than the addition of this wing to the existing fifteenth-century house. The facade of the old building is in Contrà Porti, a street that amply demonstrates the way in which the builders of Vicenza grafted new houses onto old without disrupting the symmetry of the street; the palaces here span two centuries, yet the overall impression is one of cohesion. Facing Palazzo Thiene is the **Palazzo Barbaran**, which houses a research institute for Palladian architecture and often has excellent exhibitions, usually, but not always, on classical architects.

Outstanding buildings on Contrà Porti are the fourteenth-century **Palazzo Colleoni Porto** (no. 19) and Palladio's neighbouring **Palazzo Iseppo Porto**, designed a few years after the Thiene palace. The parallel Corso A. Fogazzaro completes the itinerary of major Palladian buildings, with the Palazzo Valmarana (no. 16), perhaps the most eccentric of Palladio's projects – notice the gigantic stucco figures at the sides of the facade, where you'd expect columns to be.

At the end of Contrà Santa Corona, two blocks east of Contrà Porti, the **Palazzo Leoni-Montanari** (Fri–Sun 10am–6pm; €3.30; also see Vicenza museum box on p.354) houses a rather specialized gallery with a collection of art from the Veneto that is respectable enough, if not up to the standards of Venice, or even Padua. Eighteenth-century painting is best represented, including landscape works by Canaletto and Guardi, and there's a rather surprising collection of Russian icons.

Contrà Porti takes you towards the Pusterla bridge and the **Parco Querini**, the biggest expanse of green in the city, enlivened by a decorative hillock populated by ducks, rabbits and peacocks. Vicenza's other refuge for the brick-wearied, the **Giardino Salvi** (at the end of the road running straight up from the train station), is a more modest, artificial affair of winding gravel paths and fountains.

The outskirts – Monte Bérico and the villas

In 1426 Vicenza was struck by bubonic plague, during the course of which outbreak the Virgin appeared twice at the summit of Monte Bérico – the hill on the southern edge of the city – to announce the city's deliverance. The chapel raised on the site of her appearance became a place of pilgrimage, and at the end of the seventeenth century it was replaced by the present **Basilica di Monte Bérico**. Bus #18 (Sundays only) climbs the hill from the bus station every thirty minutes or so; on foot it takes around 25 minutes from the centre of town.

Pilgrims regularly arrive here by the busload, and the glossy interior of the church is immaculately maintained to receive them; a well-stocked shop in the cloister sells devotional trinkets to the faithful. Those in search of artistic fulfilment should venture into the church for Montagna's pietà (in the chapel to the right of the apse) and *The Supper of St Gregory the Great* by Veronese (in the refectory). The latter, the prototype of *The Feast in the House of Levi* in Venice's Accademia, was used for bayonet practice by Austrian troops in 1848 – the small reproduction nearby shows what a thorough job the vandals and subsequent restorers did.

Carry on towards the summit of the hill and you'll come to the **Museo del Risorgimento e della Resistenza**, some ten minutes' walk beyond the basilica. The museum houses an impressively thorough display, paying particular attention to Vicenza's resistance to the Austrians in the mid-nineteenth century and to the efforts of the anti-fascist Alpine fighters a century later, but for many visitors the main attraction will be the extensive wooded parkland laid out on the slopes below the Villa Guiccioli, the main building (mid-June to Aug 9am–7pm; Sept to mid-June 9am–5pm; museum €3.10; park free).

The Villa Valmarana

Ten minutes' walk away from Monte Bérico is the **Villa Valmarana "ai Nani"** – go back down the hill, head along Via M. D'Azeglio for 100m, then turn right into the cobbled Via S. Bastiano, which ends at the villa. This is an undistinguished house made extraordinary by the decorations of Giambattista and Giandomenico Tiepolo (mid-March to Nov Wed, Thurs, Sat & Sun 10am–noon & Tues–Sun 3–5.30pm; €6). *Nani*, by the way, means "Dwarves", the significance of which becomes clear when you see the garden wall.

There are two parts to the house: the Palazzina, containing six rooms frescoed with brilliant virtuosity by Giambattista (scenes based on Virgil, Tasso and Ariosto – you're handed a brief guide to the paintings at the entrance); and the Foresteria, one room of which is frescoed by Giambattista and six by Giandomenico, whose predilections are a little less heroic than his father's.

La Rotonda

From the Villa Valmarana the narrow Strada Valmarana descends the slope to one of Europe's most imitated buildings – Palladio's Villa Capra, known to most people as **La Rotonda** (March 15–Nov 4: villa Wed 10am–noon & 3–6pm; €6 including gardens; grounds only Tues–Thurs same hours; €3) because of its centrally-planned structure: the square outer walls symbolize the physical world while the circle within represents the idea of divine perfection. More obviously, the villa's shape and hill-top position emphasize its domination of the surrounding countryside. La Rotonda is unique among Palladio's villas (see box on p.353) in that it was designed not as the main building of a farm but as a pavilion in which entertainments could be held and the landscape enjoyed. Only a tour of the lavishly decorated interior will fully reveal the subtleties of the Rotonda; the grounds are little more than an attractive belt of grass from which to view the villa and surrounding countryside.

Practicalities

The **train station** is a ten-minute walk southwest of the historic centre; head straight ahead through the park to reach Piazza del Castello. The **tourist office** is at the far end of Corso Palladio, alongside the entrance to the Teatro Olimpico, at Piazza Matteotti 12 (Mon–Sat 9am–1pm & 2.30–6pm, Sun 9am–1pm; ☎0444.320.854, ⓦwww.vicenzae.org). For listings, pick up a copy of the local papers *Il Gazzettino* or *Il Giornale di Vicenza*. **Internet** access can be found in *Matrix* at Piazza della Biade 11a (daily 10am–11pm except Wed & Sun 2–11pm). You can **rent bicycles** at the station and the youth hostel.

Vicenza's a big conference destination, and many of its **hotels** are stuck out in characterless suburbs, so that it pays to be careful where you book. Wherever you decide to stay, phone ahead to book a room if you're going in summer or early autumn – some places close down in August and the main conference season is in September. The only four-star in the historic centre is the *Campo Marzio* by the park near the station at Viale Roma (☎0444.545.700, ⓦwww.hotelcampomarzio.com; out of season prices drop through the floor; ❼), a modern block but with decor in different period styles. The three-star *Giardini*, Via Giuriolo 10 (☎0444.326.458, ⓦwww.promart.it/hotels/giardini.html; ❻), a modern hotel at the southern end of Piazza Matteotti, has comfortable air-conditioned rooms – go for the quieter ones at the back. Of the two-stars within a few yards of the Piazza dei Signori, the following are worth trying – the graceful *Due Mori*, Contrà Do Rode 26 (☎0444.321.886; ❹), which has some beautifully furnished and spacious rooms, especially the ground floor room with disabled access; and the capacious *Vicenza*, Stradella dei Nodari 5/7 (☎0444. 321.512; ❸), which has pleasant, light rooms in what was once an old theatre. The only budget place in town is the **youth hostel** in Viale Giuriolo 7 (☎0444.540.222; €14 for a dorm bed, €16.50 for a single room; non-IH members pay €2.58 membership per night), in a superb position just off Piazza Matteotti. It has Internet access (with phone card) and rents out bikes.

The best budget **restaurant** is the *Antica Casa della Malvasia*, Contrà delle Morette 5 (closed Sun eve & Mon), a bustling, roomy inn just off the Piazza dei Signori: the food is variable but there's live music on Tuesday, and it's open till at least 1am on Friday and Saturday; the bar's superb too. Equally popular, but somewhat less basic, is the *Vecchia Guardia*, close to the basilica at Contrà Pescheria Vecchia 11 (closed Thurs). For a posher, more intimate atmosphere, head just beyond the Piazza del Castello to the *Trattoria Ponte delle Belle*, Contrà Ponte delle Belle 5 (☎0444.320.647; closed Sun & mid-August), which specializes in Tyrolean cuisine, but also does Vicentine specialities. Note that there are few restaurants in central Vicenza and many close in August.

As for **bars** in the centre of the city, the *Malvasia* (see above) is excellent, but the most atmospheric is *Il Grottino*, under the basilica at Piazza delle Erbe 2 (closed Mon). It has a good range of wines and some snacks, stays open till 2am and has a DJ playing jazz and lounge music on Thursday. *Galleria 15* at Piazza delle Biade 15 has live music or a DJ on Friday and Saturday and stays open till 2am (closed Mon). Among the cafés and *pasticcerie* along the Corso and around the basilica, *Sorarù*, in the Piazzetta Andrea Palladio, next to the basilica, is highly recommended (closed Wed), as is the neighbouring *Gran Caffè Garibaldi* (which also does cheap food upstairs and on the terrace in summer). The best ice creams in town are at *Tutto Gelato*, Contrà Frasche 26 (between the basilica and the Duomo), though the *Gran Caffè Garibaldi* runs a close second. If you want to buy your own food, the *alimentari* on the Corso are excellent, especially Il Ceppo at no. 196, near Piazza Matteotti.

Verona

With its wealth of Roman sites and streets of pink-hued medieval buildings, the easy-going city of **VERONA** has more in the way of sights than any other place in the Veneto except Venice itself. Unlike Venice, though, it's not a city overwhelmed by the tourist industry, important though that is to the local economy. Verona is the largest city of the mainland Veneto, its economic success largely due to its position at the crossing of the major routes from Germany and Austria to central Italy and from the west to Venice and Trieste.

Verona's initial development as a **Roman** settlement was similarly due to its straddling the main east–west and north–south lines of communication. A period of decline in the wake of the disintegration of the Roman Empire was followed by revival under the Ostrogoths, who in turn were succeeded by the Franks: Charlemagne's son, Pepin, ruled his kingdom from here. By the twelfth century Verona had become a city-state, and in the following century approached the zenith of its independent existence with the rise of the

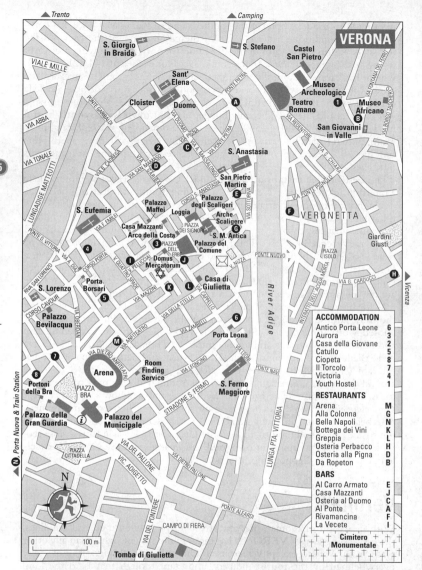

▲ Trento   ▲ Camping

VERONA

VIALE MILLE

S. Giorgio in Braida

S. Stefano

Castel San Pietro

VIA ABBA

Sant' Elena

Cloister   Duomo

VIA DUOMO

Museo Archeologico

Teatro Romano

Ⅰ Museo Africano **Ⓑ**

San Giovanni in Valle

VIA TONALE

Ⓐ

Ⓒ

S. Anastasia

Ⓑ **Ⓒ**

San Pietro Martire

S. Eufemia

Palazzo Maffei

Loggia

Palazzo degli Scaligeri

Arche Scaligere

Ⓕ VERONETTA

Casa Mazzanti

Arco della Costa

Ⓖ

S. M. Antica

Palazzo del Comune

Giardini Giusti

Ⓘ

Domus Mercatorum

Ⓙ

Casa di Giulietta

Ⓗ

Porta Borsari

Ⓚ **Ⓛ**

Palazzo Bevilacqua

Ⓜ

Porta Leona

River Adige

ACCOMMODATION

Antico Porta Leone	6
Aurora	3
Casa della Giovane	2
Catullo	5
Ciopeta	8
Il Torcolo	7
Victoria	4
Youth Hostel	1

RESTAURANTS

Arena	M
Alla Colonna	G
Bella Napoli	N
Bottega dei Vini	K
Greppia	L
Osteria Perbacco	H
Osteria alla Pigna	D
Da Ropeton	B

BARS

Al Carro Armato	E
Casa Mazzanti	J
Osteria al Duomo	C
Al Ponte	A
Rivamancina	F
La Vecete	I

Room Finding Service

Arena

S. Fermo Maggiore

Ⓝ Porta Nuova & Train Station

Portoni della Bra

Palazzo della Gran Guardia

Palazzo del Municipale

Cimitero Monumentale

Tomba di Giulietta

0   100 m

Scaligers. Ruthless in the exercise of power, the Scaligers were at the same time energetic patrons of the arts, and many of Verona's finest buildings date from their rule.

With the fall of their dynasty a time of upheaval ensued, Gian Galeazzo Visconti of Milan emerging in control of the city. Absorption into the Venetian Empire came in 1405, and Verona was governed from Venice until the arrival of Napoleon. Verona's history then shadowed that of Venice: a prolonged interlude of Austrian rule, brought to an end by the Unification of Italy in 1866.

Arrival, information and accommodation

If you're flying to Verona's Valerio Catullo **airport** at Villafranca, 10km away, you can get into the city by a regular APT bus (every 20min 7am–midnight; €3.62) from the airport to the train station and Piazza Cittadella, near the city centre. Flights to **Montichiari** (☎030.965.6511), 23km southeast of Brescia and sometimes optimistically called Verona airport, are served by a daily shuttle bus that takes one and a half hours; a taxi costs around €90.

The **train** and **bus stations** are a fifteen-minute walk from the centre. (Note that Verona Porta Nuova is the town's main station, not Porta Vescovo). To walk to the centre from here, turn right outside the train station (keeping to the right-hand side of the road – there are some busy junctions) then left at the main junction with the broad Corso Porta Nuova, which leads straight to Piazza Bra, site of the Arena and the hub of Verona. If you don't fancy the walk, you can get a bus; tickets must be bought before boarding, either from the machines alongside bay A or from the *tabacchi* inside the train station ticket hall. They cost €0.93 and are valid for any number of journeys within an hour.

The main **tourist office** is on the central Piazza Bra, within the old town walls beside the Palazzo Municipale (Mon–Sat 9am–6pm; ☎045.806.8680, ⓦwww.tourism.verona.it). There are additional offices at the train station (daily 9am–6pm; ☎045.800.0861) and at the airport. You can **rent bikes** in summer from stalls near the tourist office in Piazza Bra. There's **Internet** access at Internetfast, Via Oberdan 16b (Mon–Sat 10am–9.30pm, Sun 3–7pm), at Internet Train, Via Roma 19 (Mon–Fri 10am–10pm, Sat & Sun 4–8pm), and at Via 4 Spade 3b (daily 2.30–8.30pm).

Hotels

Accommodation is hard to find during the opera season (late June to early Sept) so you'll need to book ahead. You could try the room-finding service, Cooperativa Albergatori Veronesi (CAV), at Via Patuzzi 5 (Mon–Sat 9am–7pm; ☎045.800.9844, ⓦwww.cav.vr.it).

Antica Porta Leone Via Corticlla Leoni 3 ☎045.595.499, ⓔhtlanticaportaleone @tiscalinet.it. Large three-star with spacious a/c rooms, some with balconies. Double and twin beds available, and plenty of single rooms. ❻

Aurora Piazzetta XIV Novembre 2 ☎045.594.717, ⓕ045.801.0860. Upmarket two-star hotel with a warm atmosphere and many rooms overlooking the Piazza delle Erbe. The staff are friendly and knowledgeable, and speak good English. ❺

Catullo Via Valerio Catullo 1 ☎045.800.2786. The cheapest hotel in the centre, just off the main shopping artery of Via Mazzini, though the family who run it are not very friendly. Large rooms with shabby gentility and plenty of light, some with shared bathrooms. ❸

Ciopeta Vicolo Teatro Filarmonica 2 ☎045.800.6843, ⓕ045.803.3722. The excellent location behind the Arena and the family atmosphere make this hotel a bargain, especially if you manage to book room 8, which has a balcony. ❹

Il Torcolo Vicolo Listone 3 ☎045.800.7512, ⓕ045.800.4058. Nicely turned-out two-star hotel with comfy rooms within 100m of the Arena. Extremely welcoming owners – and a favourite with the opera crowds, so book ahead. ❺

Victoria Via Adua 8 ☎045.590.566, ⓦwww.hotelvictoria.it. One of the nicer four-star hotels housed in a complex of older buildings with a snazzy modern foyer. Well equipped rooms and gymnasium. If you want to treat yourself, the superior doubles are gorgeous. ❽

Hostels and campsites

Campeggio Castel San Pietro Via Castel S. Pietro 2 ☎045.592.037, ⓦwww.campingcastel-sanpietro.com. Along with the hostel site, this is the most pleasant and convenient place to camp near Verona – take a bus to Via Marsala.

Casa della Giovane Via Pigna 7 ☎045.596.880, ⓕ045.800.5449. Spartan but friendly convent-run hostel for women, with an 11pm curfew, although there is some flexibility for guests with opera tickets. Reservations by fax only. Internet access (with phone card). €11.50, plus some double rooms at €13 per head.

Ostello della Gioventù Salita Fontana del Ferro 15 ☎ 045.590.360. The official HI hostel is in a beautiful old building behind the Teatro Romano; as it's quite a walk from the centre, it's best to take a bus (#73, or 90 on Sundays) to Piazza Isolo,

then walk up the hill. No reservations, but with over 200 beds, there should be room. There's an 11.30pm curfew, but there's some flexibility extended to guests with concert tickets. IH not essential if you're staying for just a night. It does reasonably priced evening meals. €12.50.

The City

Coming from the train station, you pass Verona's south gate, the **Porta Nuova**, and come onto the long Corso Porta Nuova, which ends at the battlemented arches that precede the **Piazza Bra**. Here stands the mightiest of Verona's Roman monuments, the **Arena**. Dating from the first century AD, the Arena has survived in remarkable condition, despite the twelfth-century earthquake that destroyed all but four of the arches of the outer wall. The interior (Tues–Sun 8.30am–7.30pm, Mon from 1.30pm, closes 3.30pm during the opera season late June–early Sept; €3.10) was scarcely damaged by the tremor, and nowadays audiences come to watch gargantuan opera productions where once crowds of around 20,000 packed the benches for gladiatorial contests and the like. Originally measuring 152m by 123m overall, and thus the third largest of all Roman amphitheatres, the Arena is still an awesome sight – and as an added treat offers a tremendous urban panorama from the topmost of the 44 pink marble tiers.

The Casa di Giulietta and San Fermo

North of the Arena, **Via Mazzini** is a narrow traffic-free street lined with generally expensive clothes, shoe and jewellery shops. A left turn at the end leads to the Piazza delle Erbe (see p.348), while a right takes you into **Via Cappello**, a street named after the family that Shakespeare turned into the Capulets – and on the left, at no. 23, is the **Casa di Giulietta** or Juliet's House (Tues–Sun 8.30am–7.30pm, Mon from 1.30pm; €3.10). In fact, although the "Capulets" and the "Montagues" (Montecchi) did exist, Romeo and Juliet were entirely fictional creations. The house itself, constructed at the start of the fourteenth century, is in a fine state of preservation, but is largely empty. It's said that if you stand under the balcony and make a wish about love it will come true.

Via Cappello leads into Via Leoni with its Roman gate, the **Porta Leoni**, and a segment of excavated Roman street, exposed 3m below today's street level. At the end of Via Leoni and across the road rises the red-brick San **Fermo** church (Mon–Sat 10am–6pm, Sun 1–6pm; €2), whose inconsistent exterior betrays the fact that it consists of two churches combined. Flooding forced the Benedictines to superimpose a second church on the one founded in the eighth century. The Gothic upper church has no outstanding works of art but

Verona's churches, museums and monuments

There is a **biglietto unico** for Verona's principal churches, which costs €5 and allows entry to San Zeno, San Lorenzo, the Duomo (including the baptistry and archeological finds), Sant'Anastasia and San Fermo; it can be bought at any of the churches, and at each one you'll be given a useful hand-out in English. Alternatively you can buy individual tickets at €2. If you are planning to be busy, it's worth considering the **Verona Card**, which costs €8 for one day or €12 for three days and gives free access to all the museums, buses and churches in the city. Note that many places are only open from 1.30pm on Mondays.

is graceful enough; the Romanesque lower church, entered from the left of the choir, has impressive low vaulting, sometimes obscured by exhibitions.

Piazza delle Erbe and Piazza dei Signori

Originally a major Roman crossroads and the site of the forum, **Piazza delle Erbe** is still the heart of the city. As the name suggests, the market used to sell mainly vegetables, but nowadays it has been largely taken over by ugly, semi-permanent booths selling clothes, souvenirs, antiques and fast food. The rich variety of buildings framing the square is far more attractive. Most striking are the **Domus Mercatorum** (on the left as you look from the Via Cappello end), which was founded in 1301 as a merchants' warehouse and exchange, the fourteenth-century **Torre del Gardello** and, to the right of the tower, the **Casa Mazzanti**, whose sixteenth-century murals are best seen after dark, under enhancing spotlights.

The neighbouring **Piazza dei Signori** used to be the chief public square of Verona. Much of the right side is taken up by the **Palazzo del Capitano**, which is separated from the Palazzo del Comune by a stretch of excavated Roman street. Facing you as you come into the square is the medieval **Palazzo degli Scaligeri**, residence of the Scaligers; a monument to more democratic times extends from it at a right angle – the fifteenth-century **Loggia del Consiglio**, former assembly hall of the city council and Verona's outstanding early-Renaissance building. The rank of Roman notables along the roof includes Verona's most illustrious native poet, Catullus. For a dizzying view of the city, take a sharp right as soon as you come into the square, and go up the twelfth-century **Torre dei Lamberti** (Tues–Sun 9.30am–7.30pm, Mon from 1.30pm; €2.10 by lift, €1.50 on foot).

The Scaliger tombs

Passing under the arch linking the Palazzo degli Scaligeri to the Palazzo del Capitano, you come to the little Romanesque church of Santa Maria Antica, in front of which are ranged the **Arche Scaligeri**, some of the most elaborate Gothic funerary monuments in Italy. Over the side entrance to the church, an equestrian statue of **Cangrande I** ("Big Dog"; d1329) gawps down from his tomb's pyramidal roof; the statue is a copy, the original being displayed in the Castelvecchio (see p.362). The canopied tombs of the rest of the clan are enclosed within a wrought-iron palisade decorated with ladder motifs, the emblem of the Scaligers – the family name was della Scala, "scala" meaning ladder. **Mastino I** ("Mastiff"; d1277), founder of the dynasty, is buried in the simple tomb against the wall of the church; **Mastino II** (d1351) is to the left of the entrance, opposite the most florid of the tombs, that of **Cansignorio** ("Top Dog"; d1375).

Sant'Anastasia, San Pietro Martire and the Duomo

Going on past the Arche Scaligeri, and turning left along Via San Pietro, you come to **Sant'Anastasia** (Mon–Sat 9am–6pm, Sun 1–6pm; €2), Verona's largest church. Started in 1290 and completed in 1481, it's mainly Gothic in style, with undertones of the Romanesque. The fourteenth-century carvings of New Testament scenes around the doors are the most arresting feature of its bare exterior; the interior's highlight is Pisanello's delicately coloured fresco of *St George and the Princess* (high above the chapel to the right of the altar), a work in which the normally martial saint appears as something of a dandy.

To the left of Sant'Anastasia's facade is an eye-catching tomb, the free-standing monument to Guglielmo di Castelbarco (1320) by Enrico di Rigino. To its left, on one side of the little piazza fronting Sant'Anastasia, stands **San Pietro Martire** (open occasionally in the afternoon and for concerts), deconsecrated since its ransacking by Napoleon. Numerous patches of fresco dot the walls, making for an atmospheric interior, though the highlight is the vast lunette fresco on the east wall. Easily the strangest picture in Verona, it is thought to be an allegorical account of the Virgin's Assumption, though the bizarre collection of animals appears to have little connection with a bemused-looking Madonna.

Verona's red-and-white-striped **Duomo** (Mon–Sat 10am–5.30pm, Sun 1.30–5.30pm; €2) lies just round the river's bend, past the Roman Ponte Pietra. Consecrated in 1187, it's Romanesque in its lower parts, developing into Gothic as it goes up; the two doorways are twelfth century – look for the story of Jonah and the whale on the south porch, and the statues of Roland and Oliver, two of Charlemagne's paladins, on the west. The interior has fascinating architectural details around each chapel and on the columns – particularly fine is the Cappella Mazzanti (last on the right). In the first chapel on the left, an *Assumption* by Titian occupies an architectural frame by Sansovino, who also designed the choir.

To the Castelvecchio

After the Arena and the Teatro Romano, Verona's most impressive Roman remnant is the **Porta dei Borsari** (on the junction of Via Diaz and Corso Porta Borsari), a structure which was as great an influence on the city's Renaissance architects as the amphitheatre. Now reduced to a monumental screen straddling the road, it used to be Verona's largest Roman gate; the inscription dates it at 265, but it's almost certainly older than that.

Heading down Corso Cavour which starts at the Porta dei Borsari, past the small twelfth-century **San Lorenzo** (Mon–Sat 10am–6pm, Sun 1–6pm; €2), you come to the **Arco dei Gavi**, a first-century Roman triumphal arch which was rebuilt in 1930 after Napoleon's troops tore down the original. This is your best vantage point from which to admire the **Ponte Scaligero**, built by Cangrande II between 1355 and 1375. It was the turn of the German army to indulge in wanton destruction this time: they blew up the bridge in 1945, but the salvaged material was used for reconstruction. The stretch of shingle on the opposite bank is a popular spot for picnics, sunbathing and just watching the water flow by, rich in colour from the glacial deposits upstream.

The fortress from which the bridge springs, the **Castelvecchio** (Tues–Sun 8.30am–7.30pm, Mon from 1.30pm; €3.10), was commissioned by Cangrande II at around the same time and became the stronghold for Verona's subsequent rulers. Opened as the city museum in 1925, it was damaged by bombing during World War II, but opened again after scrupulous restoration in 1964. The Castelvecchio's collection of paintings, jewellery, weapons and other artefacts flows through a labyrinth of chambers, courtyards and passages that is fascinating to explore in itself. The equestrian figure Cangrande I, removed from his tomb, is strikingly displayed on an outdoor pedestal; his expression is disconcerting at close range, the simpleton's grin being difficult to reconcile with the image of the ruthless warlord. Outstanding among the paintings are two works by Jacopo Bellini, two Madonnas by Giovanni Bellini, another Madonna by Pisanello, Veronese's *Descent from the Cross*, a Tintoretto *Nativity*, a Lotto portrait and works by Giambattista and Giandomenico Tiepolo. The real joy of the museum, however, is in wandering round the medieval pieces: beautiful sculpture and frescoes by the often nameless artists of the late Middle Ages.

San Zeno Maggiore

A little over 1km northwest of the Castelvecchio is the **Basilica di San Zeno Maggiore** (Mon–Sat 8.30am–6pm, Sun 1–6pm; €2), one of the most significant Romanesque churches in northern Italy. A church was founded here, above the tomb of the city's patron saint, as early as the fifth century, but the present building and its campanile were put up in the first half of the twelfth century, with additions continuing up to the end of the fourteenth. Its large rose window, representing the Wheel of Fortune, dates from the early twelfth century, as does the magnificent portal, whose lintels bear relief sculptures representing the months – look also for St Zeno trampling the devil. The reliefs to the side of the portal are also from the twelfth century and show scenes from the Old Testament on the right, and scenes from the New Testament on the left (except for the bottom two on both sides, which depict scenes from the life of Theodoric). Extraordinary bronze panels on the doors depict scenes from the Bible and the *Miracles of San Zeno*, their style influenced by Byzantine and Ottoman art; most of those on the left are from around 1100, and most of the right-hand panels date from a century or so later. Areas of the lofty and simple interior are covered with frescoes, some superimposed upon others, some defaced by ancient graffiti. Diverting though these are, the one compulsive image in the church is the high altar's luminous *Madonna and Saints* by Mantegna.

North of the Adige

On the other side of Ponte Garibaldi, and right along the embankments or through the public gardens, is **San Giorgio in Braida**, in terms of its works of art the richest of Verona's churches. A *Baptism* by Tintoretto hangs over the door, while the main altar, designed by Sanmicheli, incorporates a marvellous piece by Paolo **Veronese** – the *Martyrdom of St George*.

It's a short walk along the embankments, past the twelfth-century church of Santo Stefano and the Ponte Pietra, to the first-century-BC **Teatro Romano** (Tues–Sun 8.30am–7.30pm, Mon open from 1.30pm; €2.60, free first Sun of month); much restored, the theatre is now used for concerts and plays. High above it, and reached by a rickety-looking lift, the **Museo Archeologico** (same hours & ticket) occupies the buildings of an old convent; its well-arranged collection features a number of Greek, Roman and Etruscan finds.

If you continue up via Santa Chiara from the Teatro Romano you'll come to the finest formal gardens in Verona, the **Giardini Giusti** at Via Giardini Giusti 2 (daily: summer 9am–8pm; winter 9am–sunset; €4.50). Full of fountains and shady corners, the Giusti provides the city's pleasantest respite from the streets. If you've got any energy left to walk up the hill, the **Museo Africano** (Tues–Sat 9am–noon & 3–6pm, Sun 3–7pm; €4) is just off Via San Giovanni in Valle at Vicolo Pozzo 1 – containing musical instruments, fetishes and masks collected over the years by the Combonian missionaries.

Eating, drinking and entertainment

The best **restaurants** tend to be packed after 9pm, so it's best to book or go out early. Your money goes a lot further in Verona than it does in Venice: numerous trattorias offer full meals for around €13 (especially in the Veronetta district, on the east side of the river), while on almost every street corner there's a bar where a glass of house wine costs only €0.60. As the Veneto produces more DOC wine than any other region in Italy, it's not surprising that Italy's main **wine fair**, Vinitaly, is held in Verona; it takes place in April and offers abundant sampling opportunities. For non-alcoholic pleasure, sit outside one of the *gelaterie* in Piazza delle Erbe and indulge in an incredible concoction of fruit, cream and ice cream; However, by far the best ice cream is at *Balu*, at Corso Porta Borsari 57 just inside the roman gate (take-away only, open till 8pm, closed Mon). In the week before and after the Arena season you may find places close early or shut completely as the city takes a rest.

Restaurants

Arena (Pizzeria da Sergio) Vicolo Tre Marchetti 1. Good pizzeria for a late-night bite, as it's open till 1am. Situated in a tiny alley between Via Mazzini and Via Anfiteatro off the northeast side of the Arena. Closed Mon.

Alla Colonna Largo Pescheria Vecchia 4 ☎045.596.718. Simple but superb food and a lively atmosphere in this packed restaurant. The prices are attractive too (menu €13). Turn up early or book. Open till 2am. Closed Sun.

Bella Napoli Via Marconi 14. The best pizzas – and the largest – in Verona, in a distinctly Neapolitan atmosphere. Open till 1am daily.

Bottega dei Vini Vicolo Scudo di Francia 3a, ☎045.800.4535, ⓦwww.bottegavini.it. Just off Via Mazzini, this is one of the best (and most expensive) restaurants in Verona and has one of the largest selections of wines you'll find any-where in Italy, but it's not at all stuffy. Popular with tourists – but with locals, too. Open until midnight. Closed Tues.

Greppia Vicolo Samaritana 3. Small family-run trattoria near the Piazza delle Erbe that has an excellent reputation and moderate prices. Closed Mon.

Osteria Perbacco Via Carducci 48. Moderately priced Veronetta restaurant with a very attractive garden. Especially good fish and vegetarian dishes. Closed Wed.

Osteria alla Pigna Via Pigna 4 ☎045.800.8040. Elegant, traditional restaurant in between the Duomo and Piazza delle Erbe, where you are given a glass of prosecco to start off your meal. Easily among the top five of the thirty or so *osterie tipiche* dotted around the historic centre. Moderately priced. Closed Sun & Mon lunch.

Da Ropeton Via Fontana del Ferro 1, Veronetta. Located just below the youth hostel, this place does superb food and has a great atmosphere – the owner, Silvano, sings and shouts and clowns around with the regulars. In summer a terrace is opened across the road, and waiters defy the traf-fic to bring the food. Open till midnight; closed Tues.

Bars and cafés

Al Carro Armato Vicolo Gatto 2a ⓦwww .carroarmato.it. One of the most atmospheric bars in the city, with live music on Sunday evenings in winter. Friendly staff, good bar snacks. Open until 2am, till midnight on Sunday. Closed Wed.

Casa Mazzanti Caffè Piazza delle Erbe 32. The *Mazzanti* is the loudest, youngest and coolest of the late-opening bars on the square. Closed Mon.

Caffè Coloniale Piazza Viviani 14c. Best hot chocolate in the city, and good snacks in this mock-colonial setting. Open till midnight. Closed Mon (except in July & Aug).

Osteria al Duomo Via Duomo 7a. Best of the city's bars, impervious to the changing fashions around it, and enlivened on Wednesday afternoons (5–8pm) and Friday nights in winter by a tradition-al singalong. Open 4pm–midnight. Closed Thurs.

Al Ponte Via Ponte Pietra 26. Sip a glass in the gar-den here and enjoy a marvellous view from the terrace across the river. Open till 3am. Closed Wed.

Rivamancina Vicolo Quadrelli 1, Veronetta. Popular late bar across the Porta Nuovo that does pasta dishes too. Mon–Sat 8pm–2am.

La Vecete Via Pelliccial 32. Atmospheric osteria that does good food and excellent wines. Let the expert – and English-speaking – barman recom-mend some gems from the superb range of wines from the region; and don't be afraid to check the price on the blackboard behind him – the wines range from cheap to very very expensive. Open till 11pm, or up to 3am during the opera season. Closed Sun.

Nightlife and entertainment

Music and **theatre** are the dominant art forms in the cultural life of Verona. In July and August an **opera festival** takes place in the Arena, always featur-ing a no-expense-spared production of *Aida*. To get the best (or last-minute) seats, call in at the office on Via Dietro Anfiteatro 6b, which opens late on performance nights; if you can't make it in person you can book by phone or online (☎045.800.5151, ⓦwww.arena.it). Big **rock** events crop up on the Arena's calendar too. A season of ballet and of Shakespeare and other dramatists in Italian is the principal summer fare at the **Teatro Romano**. Some of the Teatro events are free; for the rest, cheapskates who don't mind inferior acoustics can park themselves on the steps going up the hill alongside the theatre. The box office at the Teatro Romano also sells tickets for the Arena and vice versa.

From October to May **English-language films** are shown at the Cinema Stimate in Piazza Cittadella. The **disco** scene is much more lively than in Venice, but venues come and go fast, and many of them are outside the centre; look in the local paper, *L'Arena* (there's a copy in every bar), to find out where they are and what days they're open. The *Spettacoli* section of *L'Arena* is the best source of up-to-date information on entertainment in Verona – in Italian. One the most popular clubs is *Alter Ego*, a couple of kilometres north of the centre across the Ponte Pietra at Via Torricelle 9 – best reached by taxi.

One of the most enjoyable days in the calendar is Verona's **Carnevale**: on the Friday before Shrove Tuesday a huge procession of more than eighty floats winds through the centre from Piazza Bra. Totally unlike its Venice counterpart, this is a local event with none of the masks and posing; just lots of people dressing up, loud music and confetti everywhere. However, it's worth avoiding the streets around Piazza Bra later, when youths with snow spray think the funniest thing on earth is to spray unsuspecting people in the face with this foul stuff – the only blight on a good-humoured day.

Treviso

One of the undiscovered gems in the Veneto is **TREVISO**, a charming quiet town with an easy-going air that is also an ideal jumping-off point both for Venice and for the northern Veneto. Treviso was an important town long before its assimilation by Venice in 1389, and plenty of evidence of its early status survives in the form of Gothic churches, public buildings and, most dramatically of all, the paintings of **Tomaso da Modena** (1325–79), the major artist in north Italy in the years immediately after Giotto's death. The general townscape within Treviso's sixteenth-century walls is often appealing too – long porticoes and frescoed house facades give many of the streets an appearance quite distinct from those of other towns in the region.

The City

These features are well preserved in the main street of the centre, **Calmaggiore**, where modern commerce has reached the sort of compromise with the past that the Italians seem to arrange better than anyone else. Modern building techniques have played a larger part than you might think in shaping that compromise – Treviso was pounded during both world wars and on Good Friday 1944 was half destroyed in a single bombing raid.

The early thirteenth-century **Palazzo dei Trecento**, at the side of the **Piazza dei Signori**, was one casualty of 1944 – a line round the exterior shows where the restoration began. The adjoining **Palazzo del Podestà** is a nineteenth-century structure, concocted in an appropriate style.

Of more interest are the two churches at the back of the block: **San Vito** and **Santa Lucia** (usually open daily 9am–noon). The tiny, dark chapel of Santa

Lucia has extensive frescoes by Tomaso da Modena and his followers; San Vito has even older paintings in the alcove through which you enter from Santa Lucia, though they're not in a good state. The cathedral of Treviso, **San Pietro**, stands at the end of Calmaggiore (Mon–Sat 7.30am–noon & 3.30–7pm, Sun 7.30am–1pm & 3.30–8pm). Founded in the twelfth century, San Pietro was much altered in succeeding centuries, and then rebuilt to rectify the damage of 1944. The interior is chiefly notable for the crypt – a thicket of twelfth-century columns with scraps of medieval mosaics – and the Cappella Malchiostro, with fragmentary frescoes by Pordenone and an *Annunciation* by Titian.

Just over the River Sile from the railway station is the severe Dominican church of **San Nicolò** (Mon–Fri 8am–12.30pm & 3.30–7pm), which has frescoes dating from the thirteenth to the sixteenth centuries. Some of the columns are decorated with paintings by Tomaso da Modena and his school, of which the best are the *SS Jerome* and *Agnes* (by Tomaso) on the first column on your right as you enter; there's also a towering *St Christopher*, on the wall of the right aisle, painted around 1410 and attributed to Antonio da Treviso. Equally striking, but far more graceful, is the composite *Tomb of Agostino d'Onigo* on the north wall of the chancel, created in 1500 by Antonio Rizzo (who did the sculpture) and Lorenzo Lotto (who painted the attendant pages). The figures of Agnes and Jerome are an excellent introduction to Tomaso da Modena, but for a comprehensive demonstration of his talents you have to visit the neighbouring **Seminario**, where the chapter house is decorated with a series of forty *Portraits of Members of the Dominican Order*, executed in 1352 (Mon–Fri: summer 8am–6pm; winter 8am–12.30pm & 3–5.30pm; free).

The Santa Caterina district

Treviso has a second great fresco cycle by Tomaso da Modena – *The Story of the Life of St Ursula*, housed in the newly opened **Museo di Santa Caterina**, a deconsecrated church on the other side of the centre from San Nicolò (Tues–Sat 9am–12.30pm & 2.30–6pm; €3, or €5 joint ticket with the Museo Civico). The area around the church is a pleasant one, with its antiques sellers and furniture restorers and the hubbub of the stalls around the market in Piazza Matteotti. There are a couple of other churches worth a look, too. To the north of Santa Caterina is the rebuilt thirteenth-century church of **San Francesco**, an airy building with a ship's-keel roof and patches of fresco, including a *Madonna and Saints* by Tomaso da Modena (chapel to north of chancel). To the south, at the end of Via Carlo Alberto – one of the most attractive streets in the town – stands the **Basilica di Santa Maria Maggiore**, which houses the most venerated image in Treviso, a fresco of the Madonna originally painted by Tomaso but subsequently retouched. Beyond the church on the banks of the Sile is Treviso's brand-new **university**, one of the forces behind a rash of building and restoration work in town.

The Museo Civico

From the centre the recommended route to the **Museo Civico** (Museum Luigi Bailo; Tues–Sat 9am–12.30pm & 2.30–5pm, Sun 9am–noon; €3 or joint ticket with Museo di Santa Caterina) at Borgo Cavour 24 is along Via Riccati, which has a number of fine old houses. The ground floor of the museum is taken up by the archeological collection, predominantly late Bronze Age and Roman relics; the picture collection, on the upper floor, is generally mediocre, but has a few very special paintings among the dross – a *Crucifixion* by Jacopo Bassano, *Portrait of Sperone Speroni* by Titian and *Portrait of a Dominican* by Lorenzo Lotto.

Practicalities

The **tourist office** is right in the centre, at Piazza Monte di Pietà 8 (Mon 9am–12.30pm, Tues–Fri 9am–12.30pm & 2–6pm, Sat & Sun 9am–12.30pm & 3–6pm; ☏0422.547.632, ⓦwww.trevisotour.org); it dispenses useful leaflets not just on Treviso but on attractions throughout Treviso province. From the **train station**, head straight across the bridge, bending slightly left at the first roundabout to reach the centre. Ryanair lays on buses to meet its **flights** to Treviso but these only go to Venice – to get into town take bus 6 from the bus stop on the main road (tickets from the bar across the road or on the bus; it runs every twenty minutes and takes twenty minutes to the station). If you arrive on the late flight take a taxi, which should cost around €15. There is **Internet** access at Servicepoint, Via Toniolo 17, a computer shop in the centre of town.

There are only three **hotels** in the centre, and you'd only choose to stay at one of them, the reasonably priced and pleasant *Campeol*, just behind the tourist office at Piazza Ancilotto 8 (☏ & ⓕ0422.56.601; ⑤). Second choice would be the four-star *Continental*, a short walk from the train station at Via Roma 16 (☏0422.411.216, ⓦwww.hcontinental.it; ⑦); aimed at Eurobusiness types, it's not the most charismatic hotel in the Veneto, but it is conveniently located, well maintained and, with 142 beds, is almost certain to have space. The tourist office can also help with B&B accommodation.

Treviso's **restaurants** have a far higher reputation than its hotels, the leader of the pack being the expensive *El Toulà da Alfredo*, at Via Collalto 26 (☏0422.540.275; closed Sun eve & Mon). A cheaper option is the homely *Toni del Spin*, a few steps from the church of San Vito at Via Inferiore 7 (☏0422.543.829; open till 11pm, closed all day Sun & Mon lunchtime), which provides superb Trevisan cuisine at around €25 per head. *Muscoli's* (Mon–Sat till 2am) is a marvellous **bar** with outdoor seating and excellent snacks – the figs and blue cheese on bread is delicious; at lunchtime, the stern owner occasionally breaks into song, accompanied by the old men at the bar, a magical moment. The most popular bars and cafés in Treviso are those clustered underneath the Palazzo dei Trecento – where the crowds gather in the evening – and spread along Calmaggiore and Via XX Settembre. One of these, *Nascimben*, Via XX Settembre 3, serves the best ice cream in town. Treviso's **nightlife** is very low-key, though this may change with the new university population. Currently, if you want to dance you have to head 3km out of town to the places along the Via Fonderia. The best late-night bar is *La Pausa* at Via d'Annunzio 16 (Mon–Sat 9pm–2am; sometimes has live music on Wed, Fri & Sat).

Castelfranco Veneto and Cittadella

CASTELFRANCO VENETO once stood on the western edge of Treviso's territory, and battlemented brick walls that the Trevisans threw round the town in 1199 to protect it against the Paduans still encircle most of the old centre (or *castello*). Of all the walled towns of the Veneto, only two – Cittadella (see overleaf) and Montagnana – bear comparison with Castelfranco, and the place would merit a visit on the strength of this alone. But Castelfranco was also the birthplace of **Giorgione** and possesses a painting that single-handedly vindicates Vasari's judgement that Giorgione's place in Venetian art is equivalent to Leonardo da Vinci's in that of Florence.

At the time of writing, the painting in question, *The Madonna and Child with SS Francis and Liberale,* has been temporarily removed to Venice for restoration, but it usually hangs in the **Duomo** in a chapel to the right of the chancel. Giorgione is the most elusive of all the great figures of the Renaissance: only six surviving paintings can indisputably be attributed to him, and so little is known about his life that legends have proliferated to fill the gaps – for instance, the one that attributes his death in 1510, aged not more than 34, to his catching bubonic plague from a mistress.

To get **from the train station** to the centre, turn left as you leave the station, then follow the curve of the road to the right, heading straight up Borgo Pieve to the southeast corner of the town walls.

When Treviso turned Castelfranco into a garrison, the Paduans promptly retaliated by reinforcing the defences of **CITTADELLA**, 15km to the west, on the train line to Vicenza. The fortified walls of Cittadella were built in the first quarter of the thirteenth century, and are even more impressive than those of its neighbour. You enter the town through one of four rugged brick gateways; if you're coming from the train station it'll be the Porta Padova, the most daunting of the four, flanked by the **Torre di Malta**. The tower was built as a prison and torture chamber by the monstrous Ezzelino da Romano, known to those he terrorized in this region in the mid-thirteenth century as "The Son of Satan". His atrocities earned him a place in the seventh circle of Dante's *Inferno*, where he's condemned to boil eternally in a river of blood. There's not much else to Cittadella, but it's definitely worth hopping off the train for a quick circuit of the walls.

Bassano del Grappa

Situated on the River Brenta, **BASSANO** has expanded rapidly over the last few decades, though its historic centre remains largely unspoiled. It's better known for its manufacturers and produce, and for the events of the two world wars (see below), than for any outstanding architecture or monuments, but the airy situation on the edge of the mountains and the quiet charm of the old streets make it well worth the trip. For centuries a major producer of ceramics and wrought iron, Bassano is also renowned for its **grappa** distilleries and culinary delicacies such as porcini mushrooms, white asparagus and honey.

Bassano's **tourist office** is just within the easternmost ambit of the town walls, upstairs at Largo Corona d'Italia 35 (Mon–Sat 9am–12.30pm & 2–5pm; closed Sat pm; ☎0424.524.351, ⊛www.comune.bassano.vi.it). On the website you can also find information about the town's summer opera festival. From the tourist office you go through the city walls and turn right for the **bus station** on Piazzale Trento – you buy tickets at the newspaper kiosk; for the **train station**, go straight across the main road and down Via Chilesotti.

Almost all of Bassano's sights lie between the Brenta and the train station. Walking away from the station, you cross the orbital Viale delle Fosse to get to **Piazza Garibaldi**, one of the two main squares. Here, the cloister of the fourteenth-century church of San Francesco now houses the **Museo Civico** (Tues–Sat 9am–6.30pm, Sun 3.30–6.30pm; €4.50; ticket includes the Palazzo Sturm – see opposite), devoted to Roman finds and paintings by the da Ponte family (better known as the Bassano family). Jacopo Bassano is the most famous, though his works can be sentimental and derivative; his son Francesco is better represented by some brooding portraits. Don't miss the tucked-away medieval rooms, which conceal a couple of typically luminous Bartolomeo Vivarini works. Other rooms are devoted to a number of plaster works by Canova and to the great baritone Tito Gobbi, who was born in Bassano.

Beyond Piazza Libertà, Piazzetta Montevecchio leads to a little jumble of streets and stairways running down to the river and the **Ponte degli Alpini**, designed by Palladio in 1568. Nardini, a **grappa** distillery founded in 1779 (daily 8am–8pm), stands at this end of the bridge; these days the distilling process takes place elsewhere, but there's still the original shop and bar where you can sample before you select your bottle.

From here, if you follow Via Ferracina downstream for a couple of minutes you'll come to the eighteenth-century **Palazzo Sturm** (April–Oct Tues–Sat 9am–12.30pm, Sun 3.30–6.30pm; Nov–March Fri 9am–12.30pm, Sat & Sun 3.30–6.30pm; same ticket as Museo Civico – see opposite), a showcase for the town's famed majolica ware.

Various streets and squares in Bassano commemorate the dead of the two world wars. In 1944 resistance fighters were rounded up and hanged from trees along the street now called Viale dei Martiri. The major **war memorial**, however, is out of town on **Monte Grappa**. A vast, circular, tiered edifice with a "Via Eroica" leading to a war museum, it holds 12,000 Italian and Austro-Hungarian dead; less a symbol of mourning and repentance than a declaration of future collaboration, it was built by the Fascists in 1935. Ask at the tourist office about buses up to the memorial.

For **accommodation**, there's only one hotel actually in the old centre, the three-star *Al Castello*, Via Bonamigo 19 (T & F 0424.228.665; ❺), right by the castle, though four-star *Belvedere*, at the Piazzale Giardino 14, just east of the walls (T 0424.529.845, W www.bonotto.it; ❹), and the three-star *Victoria*, at Viale Diaz 33, just across the Ponte Nuovo, on the west bank of the Brenta (T 0424.503.620, W www.hotelvictoria-bassano.com; ❺), are just outside the walls and within easy walking distance of the centre. Otherwise, there's a hostel, *Istituto Cremona*, Via Chini 6 (T 0424.522.032; doubles with private or shared bathrooms available; from €18).

As for **food**, the *Antica Osteria*, Via Matteotti 7 (closed Mon), has good bar snacks, while the old-fashioned *Trattoria del Borgo*, Via Margnan 7 (closed Wed & Sat lunch), has a garden, and *Caffè Ponte Vecchio*, Via Angarano 14 (closed Mon), does pizza and surprisingly authentic Cuban food.

Ásolo and the Villa Barbaro

Known as "la Città dai cento orizzonti" (the city with a hundred horizons), the medieval walled town of **ÁSOLO** presides over a tightly grouped range of nearly thirty gentle peaks in the foothills of the Dolomites. In 1234 Ezzelino da Romano wrested the town from the Bishop of Treviso; on his death in 1259 the townspeople ensured that the dynasty died with him by massacring the rest of his family, who were at that time in nearby San Zenone.

The end of the fifteenth century was marked by the arrival of Caterina Cornaro (see below) – her celebrated court was attended by the likes of Cardinal Bembo, one of the most eminent literary figures of his day, who coined the verb *Asolare* to describe the experience of spending one's time in pleasurable aimlessness. Later writers and artists found the atmosphere equally convivial: Gabriele d'Annunzio wrote about the town, and Robert Browning's last published work – *Asolando* – was written here.

There are regular **buses** to Ásolo from Bassano; if you want to get there from Venice, it's quickest to take a train to Treviso, from where there are buses at least hourly (some change at Montebelluna) – all the buses to Bassano go through Ásolo and Masèr (see opposite).

The Town

The bus drops you at the foot of the hill, from where a connecting minibus (€0.80 return) will appear to shuttle up into the town. Memorabilia of Ásolo's celebrated residents are gathered in the **Museo Civico** in Piazza Maggiore, which has long been in the throes of restoration. Especially diverting are the portraits, photos and personal effects of **Elenora Duse**. An actress in the Sarah Bernhardt mould, Duse was almost as well known for her tempestuous love life as for her roles in Shakespeare, Hugo and Ibsen, and she came to Ásolo to seek refuge from public gossip. Although she died in Pittsburgh while on tour in 1924, her wish was to be buried in Ásolo, and so her body was transported back here, to the church of Sant'Anna. The main interest of the art collection is provided by a pair of dubiously attributed Bellinis, a portrait of Ezzelino painted a good couple of centuries after his death and a brace of large sculptures by Canova.

The Teatro Duse occupies a major part of the **Castello**, which has been largely restored, though there's still little to see other than the view from the ramparts. From 1489 to 1509 this was the home of **Caterina Cornaro**, one of the very few women to have played a major part in Venetian history. Born into one of Venice's most powerful families, Caterina was married to Jacques II, King of Cyprus. Within a year of the wedding Jacques was dead, and there followed nearly a decade of political pressure from Venice's rulers, who wanted to get their hands on the strategically vital island. In 1489 she was finally forced to abdicate in order to gain much-needed weapons and ships against a Turkish attack. Brought back to Venice to sign a deed "freely giving" Cyprus to the Republic, she was given the region of Ásolo as a sign of Venice's indebtedness. Eventually Ásolo too was taken away from her by the Emperor Maximilian, and she sought asylum in Venice, where she died soon after, in 1510.

Practicalities

The **tourist office** is at Piazza G. D'Annunzio 2 (Mon–Sat 9am–12.30pm & 3–6pm; ☎0423.529.046, ⓦwww.asolo.it). **Accommodation** is all but impossible to find. The cheapest of the hotels is the *Duse*, a reasonable-quality three-star at Via Browning 190 (☎0423.55.241; ⑥); the place is booked solid on the second weekend of every month, when a large antiques fair takes over the centre of town. Of the two four-star hotels the *Villa Cipriani*, Via Canova 298 (☎0423.523.411, ⓦwww.sheraton.com/villacipriani; ⑨), is a long-standing favourite with Europe's crowned heads and mega-rich showbiz types. Above the main square, at almost half the price, the new *Albergo al Sole*, Via Collegio 33 (☎0423.528.399, ⓦwww.albergoalsole.com; ⑨), is rapidly making a name for itself, with impeccable facilities and a breathtaking view from the breakfast terrace.

For around €25 you can get a fine meal at the best **restaurant** in town, *Ca' Derton*, Piazza G. D'Annunzio (☎0423.529.648; closed Sun & Mon); the more basic *Cornaro* just off Piazza Garibaldi, in Via Regina Cornaro (closed Mon), has a good range of pizzas plus the standard primi and secondi.

The Villa Barbaro at Masèr

Touring the villas of the Veneto, you become used to mismatches between the quality of the architecture and the quality of the decoration, but at the **Villa Barbaro** at **MASÈR** (Tues, Sat & Sun: summer 3–6pm; winter 2.30–5pm; €5; ⓦ www.villadimaser.it), a few kilometres northeast of Ásolo, you'll see the best of two of the central figures of Italian civilization in the sixteenth century – **Palladio** (see p.353) and **Paolo Veronese**, whose careers crossed here and nowhere else. If you're reliant on public transport, a visit is best made by bus from Bassano via Ásolo (at least 9 daily), or from Treviso – the services from Treviso to Ásolo all pass through Masèr.

The **villa** was built in the 1550s for Daniele and Marcantonio Barbaro, men whose humanist training and diverse cultural interests made the process of designing the house far more of a collaborative venture than were most of Palladio's other projects. The entire ground floor was given over to farm functions – dovecotes in the end pavilions, stables and storage space under the arcades, administrative offices on the lower floor of the central block. The avenue of trees, the sculptures and the very structure of the villa draw you in from the fields, down the projecting central axis of the building and through to the extravagant nymphaeum watered by a spring – the source of the fertility of the land.

This theme of fertility is echoed again and again in the living quarters of the *piano nobile*, in a series of **frescoes** by Veronese that has no equal in northern Italy. The more abstruse scenes are decoded in an excellent guidebook on sale in the villa, but most of the paintings require no footnotes. The walls of the Villa Barbaro are the most resourceful display of trompe l'oeil you'll ever see: servants peer round painted doors, a dog sniffs along the base of a flat balustrade in front of a landscape of ruins, a huntsman (probably Veronese himself) steps into the house through an entrance that's a solid wall. (Inevitably, it's speculated that the woman facing the hunter at the other end of the house was Veronese's mistress.)

In the grounds in front of the villa stands Palladio's **Tempietto** (currently closed for restoration), the only church by him outside Venice and one of his last projects; commissioned by Marcantonio a decade after his brother's death, it was built in 1580, the year Palladio himself died.

Just by the bus stop and crossroads, 300m from the villa, the *Locanda di Masèr* (closed Wed) is a gem, serving superb local cuisine at bargain prices – perfect for a late **lunch** before the villa opens.

Conegliano

North of Treviso, around the amiable town of **CONEGLIANO**, the landscape ceases to be boring. The surrounding hills are patched with vineyards, and the production of wine (prosecco in particular) is central to the economy of the district. Italy's first wine-growers' college was set up in Conegliano in 1876, and there's a large grape festival in the last weekend of September, with parades and a banquet. It's a rewarding place for tourists too, as two well-established **wine routes** meet here: the Strada dei Vini del Piave, which runs for 68km southeast to Oderzo, and the more rewarding Strada del Prosecco, the first to be established in Italy, a 42-kilometre journey west to Valdobbiádene (ⓦ www.altamarca.it). Access to Conegliano itself is straightforward, as nearly all the regular Venice-to-Udine trains stop here.

The old centre of Conegliano is right in front of you as you come out of the station; just follow the road ahead and climb the steps to Via XX Settembre. This is the original main street, whose most decorative feature is the unusual facade of the **Duomo**: a fourteenth-century portico, frescoed in the sixteenth century, which joins seamlessly the buildings on each side. The interior of the church has been much rebuilt, but retains fragments of fifteenth-century frescoes; the major adornment of the church, though, is the magnificent altarpiece of *The Madonna and Child with Saints and Angels*, painted in 1493 by Giambattista Cima, the most famous native of Conegliano. Cima's birthplace, no. 24 Via G.B. Cima (at rear of duomo), has now been converted into the **Casa Museo di G. B. Cima** (May–Aug last Sunday of month 10am–noon & 5–7pm, or book on ☎0438.21.660; donations accepted), which consists mainly of reproductions of his paintings and archeological finds made during the restoration of the house.

The **Museo Civico** (Tues–Sun: 10am–12.30pm & 3.30–6.30pm; €2) is housed in the tallest surviving tower of the reconstructed *castello* on top of the hill. It's reached most quickly by the steep and cobbled Calle Madonna della Neve, which begins at the end of Via Accademia, the street beside the palatial Accademia cinema, and follows the town's most impressive stretch of ancient wall. The museum has some damaged frescoes by Pordenone and a small bronze horse by Giambologna, but most of the paintings are "Workshop of . . ." or "School of . . . ", and the displays of coins, maps, war memorabilia, armour and so forth are no more fascinating than you'd expect. But it's a lovingly maintained place, and the climb through the floors culminates on the tower's roof, from where you get a fine view across the gentle vine-clad landscape.

Practicalities

Conegliano's **tourist office** is on Via XX Settembre (Tues–Sun 9am–12.30pm & 3–6pm; ☎0438.21.230, Ⓦwww.conegliano2000.it). Via XX Settembre has all you'll need in the way of cafés, bars and food shops; the three-star *Canon d'Oro* **hotel** at no. 129 (☎0438.34.246, Ⓦwww.hotelcanondoro.it; ❺) is the best base for a tour of the Conegliano vineyards. If money's tight, you could stay at one of the very basic one-stars a couple of kilometres from the centre of town, such as the *Parè*, Via Vecchia Trevigiana 3/5 (☎0438.64.140; ❸), which has shared bathrooms. Bus #1 from the train station and buses to Treviso go past the former; ask to be let off at *Parè*. Top recommendation for low-cost **eating** is the superb *Alla Corona* trattoria, Via Beato Ongaro 29 (closed Mon), where a meal of genuine local dishes should cost around €22; you get to it by continuing along Via XX Settembre past the *Canon d'Oro*. The town hosts a **wine festival** in September and the main square is given over to a medieval pageant in October, the **Dama Castellana** (Ⓦwww.dama.tv.it).

Vittorio Veneto to Belluno

The name **VITTORIO VENETO** first appeared on the map in 1866 when, to mark the Unification of Italy and honour the first king of the new country (Vittorio Emanuele II), the neighbouring towns of Cèneda and Serravalle (not previously the best of friends) were knotted together and rechristened. A new town hall was built midway along the avenue connecting the two towns, and the train station was constructed opposite, thus ensuring that the visitor steps straight from the train into a sort of no-man's-land. It's here, too, that you'll find the tourist office and bus station. Bus #1 runs between the two halves every fifteen minutes.

Cèneda

CÈNEDA, the commercial centre of Vittorio Veneto, is primarily worth a visit for the **Museo della Battaglia** (Tues–Sun: May–Sept 10am–noon & 4.30–6.30pm; Oct–April 10am–noon & 3–5pm; €3 – the same ticket covers Vittorio Veneto's three main attractions) at Piazza G. Paolo 1, whose loggia was built by Sansovino. The dull cathedral is right next door; turn right out of the station and keep going until you see the sign for the centre. The museum is dedicated to the climactic Battle of Vittorio: fought in October 1918, this was the final engagement of World War I for the Italian Army and marked the end of the Austro-Hungarian empire, which is why most towns in Italy have a Via Vittorio Veneto.

Overlooking town is the imposing Castello di San Martino, once a Lombard stronghold and now the bishop's palace, which is why you won't be allowed in. The only other building that merits a look in Cèneda is the church of **Santa Maria del Meschio**, where you'll find a splendid *Annunciation* by Andrea Previtali, a pupil of Giovanni Bellini. If you turn left off the Cèneda–Serravalle road instead of going right for the cathedral square, you'll soon come across it.

Serravalle

SERRAVALLE, wedged up against the mouth of the gorge between the Col Visentin and the Cansiglio, is an entirely different proposition from its reluctant twin. Once through its southern gate you are into a town that has scarcely seen a demolition since the sixteenth century, though the effect is spoiled by the main road which tears right through the centre. Most of the buildings along Via Martiri della Libertà, Via Roma and Via Mazzini, and around the stage-like Piazza Marcantonio Flaminio, date from the fifteenth and sixteenth centuries – the handsomest being the shield-encrusted Loggia Serravallese. This is now the home of the **Museo del Cenedese** (Tues–Sun: May–Sept 10am–noon & 4–6.30pm; Oct–April 10am–noon & 3–5pm; same ticket as Museo della Battaglia – see above), a jumble of sculptural and archeological bits and pieces, detached frescoes and minor paintings. The **Palazzo Minucci de Carlo** (daily 9am–noon; ☎0438.571.93; €5.50) has a ragbag collection of minor paintings, tapestries and old furniture, but you'll need to make an appointment to get inside.

Your time will be more profitably spent in **San Lorenzo dei Battuti** (same times and ticket as Museo del Cenedese – see above), immediately inside the south gate, which is decorated with frescoes painted around 1450. Uncovered in 1953 and restored to rectify the damage done when Napoleon's lads used the chapel as a kitchen, this is one of the best-preserved fresco cycles in the Veneto. If it's closed, ask at the museum.

Practicalities

The **tourist office**, at Piazza del Popolo 18 (daily 9.30am–12.30pm & 3–6pm, closed Mon afternoon; ☎0438.57.243, ⓦ www.comune.vittoro-veneto.tr.it), is good for information on the ski resorts and walking terrain around the town, as well as accommodation. The nearest **hotel** is the *Flora* just across the main road at Viale Trento e Trieste 28 (☎0438.536.25, Ⓔ hotelflora@libero.it, ❹), which has a good fish restaurant (closed Mon). If you're determined to save money, join the locals for good but simple fare at the packed *Hostaria Vecchia Pieve* at Via del Carso 53 (closed Sun), about fifteen minutes' walk from the tourist office: head along Viale della Vittoria towards Serravalle, turn right at the first big junction down Via Antonello de Serravalle, and at the far end by the church turn right again.

Belluno

The northernmost of the major towns of the Veneto, **BELLUNO** was once a strategically important ally of Venice, and today is the capital of a province that extends mainly over the eastern Dolomites. Although the urban centres to the south are not far away, Belluno's focus of attention lies clearly to the north – the network of the Dolomiti-Bus company radiates out from here, trains run regularly up the Piave Valley to Calalzo, and the tourist handouts are geared mostly to hikers and skiers. Just one train a day runs from Venice to Belluno directly, but it's just as quick anyway to go from Venice to Conegliano and change there; from Padua there are twelve trains daily.

Its position is Belluno's main attraction, but the old centre calls for an hour or two's exploration if you're passing through. The hub of the modern town, and where you'll find its most popular bars and cafés, is the wide **Piazza dei Martiri**, off the south side of which a road leads to the Piazza del Duomo, the kernel of the old town. The sixteenth-century **Duomo**, an amalgam of the Gothic and classical, and built in the pale yellow stone that is a feature of the buildings in Belluno, was designed by Tullio Lombardo; it has had to be reconstructed twice after earthquake damage, in 1873 and 1936. There are a couple of good paintings inside: one by Andrea Schiavone (first altar on right) and one by Jacopo Bassano (third altar on right). The stately **campanile**, designed in 1743 by Filippo Juvarra, offers one of the great views of the Veneto.

Occupying one complete side of the Piazza del Duomo is the residence of the Venetian administrators of the town, the **Palazzo dei Rettori**, a frilly late-fifteenth-century building dolled up with Baroque trimmings. A relic of more independent times stands on the right – the twelfth-century **Torre Civica**, all that's left of the medieval castle. Continuing round the piazza, in Via Duomo, along the side of the town hall, you'll find the **Museo Civico** (Mon & Sat 10am–noon, Tues–Fri 10am–noon & 3–6pm; €2.13): the collection is strong on the work of Belluno's three best-known artists – the painters Sebastiano and Marco Ricci and the sculptor-woodcarver **Andrea Brustolon** – all of whom were born between 1659 and 1673.

Via Duomo ends at the **Piazza del Mercato**, a tiny square hemmed in by porticoed Renaissance buildings. The principal street of the old town, **Via Mezzaterra**, goes down to the medieval **Porta Rugo** (veer left along the cobbled road about 50m from the end), from where the view up into the mountains will provide some compensation if you haven't managed to find the campanile open.

Practicalities

The **tourist office**, at Piazza dei Martiri 7 (Mon–Sat 9am–12.30pm & 3–6pm, Sun 10am–12.30pm; ☎0437.940.083, ⊛www.comune.belluno.it), is a good source of leaflets on Belluno and its province. The cheapest **hotel** in town is the one-star *Centrale*, Via Loreto 2 (☎0437.943.349; ❷), very close to Piazza dei Martiri, with basic rooms with or without private bathrooms. The pick of the central three-stars is the *Astor*, Piazza dei Martiri 26e (T0437.942.094; E astorhotel@libero.it; ❺), but it's functional rather than atmospheric. The best **restaurant** in town is *Terracotta*, near the train station, at Borgo Garibaldi 61 (T0437.942.644; closed Sat); a three-course meal should cost around €23.

Travel details

Trains

Belluno to: Calalzo (10 daily; 1hr); Conegliano (15 daily; 1hr–1hr 30min); Vittorio Veneto (15 daily; 30min).

Conegliano to: Belluno (15 daily; 1hr–1hr 30min); Udine (30 daily; 1hr 15min); Venice (34 daily; 1hr); Vittorio Veneto (15 daily; 25min).

Monsélice to: Padua (9 daily; 20min); Venice (6 daily; 50min).

Padua to: Bassano (10 daily; 1hr 5min); Belluno (12 daily; 2hr); Milan (25 daily; 2hr 30min); Venice (every 30min; 35min); Verona (25 daily; 55min); Vicenza (25 daily; 20min).

Treviso to: Udine (hourly; 1hr 10min–1hr 30min); Venice (30 daily; 30min); Vicenza (hourly; 1hr).

Venice to: Bassano (14 daily; 1hr); Belluno (1 daily; 2hr); Conegliano (34 daily; 1hr); Milan (25 daily; 2hr 50min–3hr 50min); Padua (every 30min; 35min); Treviso (30 daily; 30min); Trieste (14 daily; 2hr 10min); Udine (hourly; 2hr); Verona (at least 25 daily; 1hr 30min); Vicenza (25 daily; 55min); Vittorio Veneto (4 daily; 1–2hr).

Verona to: Milan (30 daily; 1hr 40min); Padua (25 daily; 50min); Venice (25 daily; 1hr 30min); Vicenza (30 daily; 30min).

Vicenza to: Castelfranco (hourly; 40min); Cittadella (hourly; 30min); Milan (30 daily; 1hr 40min); Padua (25 daily; 20min); Treviso (hourly; 1hr); Venice (25 daily; 55min); Verona (30 daily; 30min).

Buses

Bassano to: Ásolo (15 daily; 30min); Masèr (8 daily; 40min); Possagno (every 1–2hr; 40min).

Padua to: Bassano (every 30 min; 1hr 15min).

Treviso to: Ásolo (hourly; 50min); Bassano (hourly; 1hr 20min); Padua (every 30min; 1hr 10min); Venice (every 20min; 55min).

Venice to: Malcontenta (hourly; 20min); Strà (every 30min; 45min).

Vicenza to: Bassano (hourly; 1hr 10min).

Friuli-Venezia Giulia

CHAPTER 6

Highlights

✳ **Osmizze** Lunch at an osmizza is the best way to experience the Slovene culture of the Carso. **See p.389**

✳ **Aquileia's Basilica** This glorious basilica, with its mosaic pavements by Theodore, ranks among the most important monuments of early Christendom. **See p.393**

✳ **Grotta Gigante** The world's largest accessible cave. **See p.397**

✳ **Udine's Piazza Libertà** The central piazza of Friuli-Venezia Giulia's second town is a perfect ensemble of well preserved historic buildings. **See p.388**

✳ **Tiepolo paintings** Oustanding frescoes by Tiepolo cover every surface of the Gallerie del Tiepolo in Udine. **See p.398**

✳ **Tempietto Longobardo** The exquisite statues in this tiny chapel are among the most splendid surviving works of art from the ninth century. **See p.399**

Friuli-Venezia Giulia

The geographical complexity of **Friuli-Venezia Giulia** – around eight thousand square kilometres of alps, limestone plateaux, alluvial plain and shelving coastlands – is mirrored in its social diversity. The mountainous north is ethnically and linguistically Alpine; the old peasant culture of Friuli, though now waning, still gives a degree of coherence to the area south of the mountains; **Udine** seems Venetian, and **Grado**, slumbering in its Adriatic lagoons, Byzantine-Venetian; while **Aquileia**, a few kilometres north of Grado, is still redolent of its Roman and early Christian past. And **Trieste** itself, the regional capital, is a Habsburg city, developed by Austria to be the empire's great southern port. In spirit and appearance it is central European, more like Ljubljana in Slovenia than anywhere else in the region with the possible exception of **Gorizia**.

If one thing unites the different parts of the region, it's how far removed they are from the conventional image of Italy, a remoteness that intensifies the further east you travel. This area has always been a bridge between the Mediterranean world and central Europe – that hazy multinational entity which begins, according to Eric Newby at least, at Monfalcone, north of Trieste. It has been invaded – sometimes enriched, often laid waste – from east and west and north, by the Romans, Huns, Goths, Lombards, Nazis and even the Cossacks. Venice in its heyday controlled the coast and plain as far as Udine; Napoleonic France succeeded the Venetian Republic, to be supplanted in turn by the Habsburgs. Later, the region saw some of the fiercest fighting of World War I on the **Carso** (the plateau inland from Trieste), where artillery shells splintered the limestone into deadly shrapnel, and the hills are still scarred with trenches. Vast war memorials and ossuaries punctuate the landscape: the bones of 60,000 soldiers lie at Oslavia, near Gorizia; 100,000 at Redipuglia; 25,000 in the Udine ossuary.

There was less loss of life in World War II, but Fascism in Trieste was especially virulent, and the city held one of Italy's two death camps. One of the strangest sideshows of the war was staged north of Udine: Cossack troops, led by White Russian officers, made an alliance with the Nazis and invaded Carnia, on the promise of a Cossack homeland among the Carnian mountains once the Reich was secure. The area also saw the invasion of Tito at the end of the war, which brought just as much terror. Partisan and communist atrocities resulted in mass graves for an estimated 10,000. No more invading armies have taken this road, but the last border dispute between Italy and Yugoslavia was not settled until the 1970s, and when neighbouring Slovenia became independent in June 1991 the border posts with Italy were the scene of brief but fierce confrontations between Slovene and Yugoslav troops. Despite Italian fears, however, the fighting did not spill across the border.

While the Friulani want Italian nationality, they don't care for the baggage of Italian identity. Respect for Rome and the government is in short supply, and enthusiasm for the separatist north Italian Lega Nord movement has spread from Lombardy in recent years. It is unlikely that this marks the birth of Friulian separatism, but there's no doubt that the people here have their own ways and traditions, fostering a strong sense of identity. The local dialect, *friulano*, is undergoing something of an official revival – many road signs are bilingual in Italian and *friulano*, while studies of the dialect's history and many local variants are published by the Società Filologica Friulana in Udine. (Pier Paolo Pasolini, who grew up in Casarsa, near Pordenone, wrote his early poetry in *friulano*.) Economically the region is in fairly good shape: Udine and Pordenone are thriving, while Trieste is a focus for container traffic and is becoming a centre of computer technology and electronics.

Tourism is growing too. Increasing numbers of visitors, mostly Italian and German, are discovering places which almost rival the claims of neighbouring Veneto, with none of the crowds or the cynical attitudes to tourists. Notwithstanding its post-industrial atmosphere, **Trieste** makes a good base for walking trips into the extraordinary, cave-riven landscape of the Carso, with the option of a day at one of the purpose-built beach resorts along the **Triestine Riviera** – which isn't as glamorous as it sounds. **Udine**, with its beautiful Venetian centre and excellent art collections, is within easy reach to the north, as is tiny **Cividale del Friuli**, which preserves a picturesque historic centre perched on the gorge of the Natisone, as well as some fascinating Lombard remains. The archeologically minded will head straight for **Aquileia**, however, which has some of the most important Roman and early Christian remains in Italy, and is fifteen minutes from the lagoon resort of **Grado**, which conceals a tiny early Christian centre amid the beach hotels. Further north, towards the Austrian border, the **Carnia** is struggling to develop itself as a rival to the Dolomites for skiing and hiking, though in truth it has little over its neighbour other than peace and quiet.

Trieste

Backed by the green and white cliffs of a limestone plateau and facing the blue Adriatic, **TRIESTE** has a potentially idyllic setting; close up, however, the place reveals uninviting water and an atmosphere of run-down haughtiness. Grass is pushing up from the concrete in its main squares, and the canal, clustered with open-air cafés, is little more than a sad reminder of the city's lovelier neighbour Venice. The city itself is rather strange: a capitalist creation built to play a role that no longer exists, though like so many ports in Europe, the seediness that long prevailed is now giving way to a nascent optimism. Trieste was Tergeste to the Romans, who captured it in 178 BC, but although signs of their occupancy are scattered throughout the city (the theatre off Corso Italia, for instance, and the arch by Piazza Barbacan), what strikes you straightaway is its modernity. With the exception of the castle and cathedral of San Giusto, and the tiny medieval quarter below, the city's whole pre-nineteenth-century history seems dim and vague beside the massive Neoclassical architecture of the **Borgo Teresiano** – the name given to the modern city centre, after Empress Maria Theresa (1740–80), who initiated the development.

Trieste was constructed largely with Austrian capital to serve as the Habsburg Empire's southern port. It briefly eclipsed Venice as the Adriatic's northern port, but its brief heyday drew to a close after 1918, when it finally became Italian and discovered that, for all its good intentions, Italy had no economic use for it. The city languished for sixty years, and is only now making a new role for itself. Computer-based firms are cropping up while seaborne trade goes through the container port on the south side of Trieste, leaving the old quays as windblown car parks.

Lying on the political and ethnic fault-line between the Latin and Slavic worlds, Trieste has long been a city of political extremes. In the nineteenth century it was a hotbed of *irredentismo* – an Italian nationalist movement to "redeem" the Austrian lands of Trieste, Istria (see D'Annunzio on p.231) and the Trentino. After 1918 the tensions increased, leading to a strong Fascist presence in Friuli-Venezia Giulia. Yugoslavia and the Allies fought over Trieste until 1954, when the city and a connecting strip of coast were secured for Italy, though a definitive border settlement was not reached until 1975. Tito kept the Istrian peninsula, whose fearful Italian population emigrated in huge numbers: Fiume (Rijeka), for example, lost 58,000 of its 60,000 Italians. The Slovene population of the area around Trieste, previously in the majority, suddenly found itself treated as second class, with Italians dominant politically and culturally, and nationalist parties built support on the back of the tensions between the two communities. There is even now little interaction between Slovenes

and Italians. The neo-Fascist MSI party did well here, and Trieste shocked the rest of Italy in 2000 by inviting Jorg Haider, founder of Austria's right-wing Freedom Party, to the city.

Yet nationalism has long provoked the development of its antithesis and there is an intense socialist and intellectual tradition which is intimately connected with the city's café culture. Numerous foreign writers based themselves around Trieste, most famously James Joyce (see below) and Rainer Maria Rilke, and native literati included Umberto Saba and Italo Svevo. Freud also spent some time researching in Trieste as a medical student, and the city became the first Italian centre of psychoanalytical thought under Freud's pupil Edoardo Weiss.

More recently in 1980 Trieste became the first city in Italy to completely close its old psychiatric hospital. The city's alternative care programme in the community pioneered by Dr Franco Basaglia in the 1970s is now considered an exemplar in its field.

Arrival, information and accommodation

Trieste's Piazza Libertà **bus station** is right by the central **train station**, ten minutes' walk from the town centre. The main **tourist office** is on the central Piazza Unità D'Italia (daily 9am–7pm; ☎040.347.8312, ⓦwww.trieste-tourism.it). For information on the Friuli-Venezia Giulia region, go to the tourist office at Via G. Rossini 6 (Mon–Thurs 8.30am–12.30pm & 2–4.30pm, Fri 8.30am–12.30pm; ☎040.365.152, ⓦwww.fvgpromo.it).

Accommodation in Trieste is uninspiring. The cheapest decent **hotels** are all between the train station and the town centre and are fairly uniformly dull but acceptable. The *Alabarda*, Via Valdirivo 22 (☎040.630.269; ❷), is probably the best bet: it also has Internet facilities and TVs in all rooms; otherwise try the large *Marina*, Via Galatti 14 (☎040.369.298; ❷), or the *Centrale*, Via Ponchielli 1 (☎040.639.482; ❷; mid-March to Oct). There's also a **HI hostel**, 7km out of the city at Viale Miramare 331 (☎040.224.102; €12) – take a #36 bus from the station to Grignano and ask the driver to drop you at Bivio al Miramare, from where it's a five-minute walk straight down along Viale Miramare. The facilities are basic but it has stunning sea views, and is just 500m from Castello Miramare. The nearest **campsite** is the *Obelisco* (☎040.211.655), on an airy site 7km away in the hills below Opicina; from Piazza Oberdan take either bus #4 or the *tranvia* (cable tramway), which runs up to 8pm: stop at the obelisk, cross over the tracks where you'll see a sign to the campsite which is a minute's walk away.

The City

Trieste's modern life takes place in the grid-like streets of the Borgo Teresiano, but the focal point of the city's pre-modern history, and its prime tourist site, is the hill of **San Giusto**, named after the patron saint of the city. At the very summit of the hill, overlooking the remnants of the Roman forum, is the **Castello** (daily: April–Sept 9am–7pm; Oct–March 9am–5pm; €1.55 including museum), a fifteenth-century Venetian fortress. There's nothing much to see inside, but a walk round the ramparts is *de rigueur* and there are fine views of the new town and the busy port below, while beyond the city confines the high escarpment of the Carso looms over the Adriatic. Its **museum** (Tues–Sun 9am–1pm) houses a small collection of antique weaponry.

More interesting is the **Cattedrale di San Giusto** (Mon–Sat 8am–noon & 2.30–6.30pm, Sun 8am–1pm & 3.30–8pm), built on the ruins of a first-century AD Roman structure. Some fragments remain – the base of the campanile

From 1905 to 1915, and again in 1919–20, **James Joyce** and his wife Nora lived in Trieste. After staying at Piazza Ponterosso 3 for a month, they moved to the third-floor flat at Via San Nicolò 30. (In 1919 the poet Umberto Saba bought a bookshop on the ground floor at the same address. The two writers seem never to have met, though they had a common friend in the novelist Italo Svevo.) There is no plaque in Via San Nicolò, but there is one on Via Bramante 4, quoting the postcard that Joyce despatched in 1915 to his brother Stanislaus, whose Irredentist sympathies had landed him in an Austrian internment camp. The postcard announced that the first chapter of James's new work, *Ulysses*, was finished. For Joyce fans the tourist office publishes a leaflet listing places associated with him.

has been scalloped away to reveal the original pillars, the columns at the entrance were borrowed from a Roman tomb and part of the Roman floor mosaic is incorporated in the present flooring. In around 1050 an earlier Christian chapel was replaced by two churches, the Basilica di Santa Maria Assunta and the Capella di San Giusto. The site was further expanded in the early thirteenth century in an extraordinary stroke of pragmatic architectural genius: the two adjacent buildings were bridged by a high beamed vault, forming the current cathedral nave and leaving a double aisle on each side. The complex history of the building becomes clearer if you study the arches in the interior, or look down on the apse from the castle wall behind. As it stands today, the cathedral is a typically Triestine synthesis of styles, with a serene, largely Romanesque interior only marred by an ugly modern choir. The **Cappella di Santa Maria Assunta** (north aisle) has fine Venetian-Ravennan mosaics of the *Coronation of the Virgin*, revealing the Byzantine roots of the style, while the **Cappella di San Giusto** (south aisle) has thirteenth-century frescoes of the life of the saint, framed between Byzantine pillars. The facade is predominantly Romanesque, but includes a Gothic rose window.

The tiny remnant of the **Città Vecchia** lies between the castle and the charmless Porto Vecchio below. On the cobbled Via della Cattedrale, the **Museo Civico di Storia ed Arte** (Tues–Sun 9am–1pm, Wed open late until 7pm; €1.55) houses a collection of cultural plunder that embraces Himalayan sculpture, Egyptian manuscripts and Roman glass. Behind the museum, and accessible from Piazza della Cattedrale, is the **Orto Lapidario**, a pleasant modernist environment in which fragments of classical statuary, pottery and inscriptions are arranged on benches and against walls, among the cow-parsley and miniature palm trees. The little Corinthian temple on the upper level contains the remains of J.J. Winckelmann (1717–68), the German archeologist and theorist of Neoclassicism, who was murdered in Trieste by a man to whom he had shown off his collection of antique coins.

Further down Via della Cattedrale are a couple of ill-matched churches. The imposing **Santa Maria Maggiore** is little more than another brutish Baroque creation, but its tiny early Romanesque neighbour, **San Silvestro**, is worth a look for its unusual state of preservation; it's now used by adherents of the rare Helvetic-Waldensian sect. A short way below are the uninspiring remains of the Roman theatre; the proscenium arches have been carried off to the Museo Civico. There's little else of note in the old city, though some of the older buildings are at last being restored and there's an antiques fair on the third Sunday of every month. Mosaic enthusiasts may want to stop off at the remains of the **Basilica Paleocristiana** (Wed 10am–noon; free) under the building at

Via Madonna del Mare 11. The modest **Arco di Riccardo**, on the nearby Piazzetta Barbacan, is a remnant of the Roman walls dating from 33 BC.

To the north, Trieste's new town, the **Borgo Teresiano**, is dominated by heavy Neoclassical architecture imported from nineteenth-century Vienna, with wide boulevards and a waterfront spoilt by a busy main road. The focus of the main grid of streets is **Piazza S. Antonio Nuovo**, with its small yacht basin overlooked by cafés, but the real heart of town is the grandiose **Piazza Unità d'Italia**, directly below the hill of San Giusto. Built mostly by Giuseppe Bruni in the late nineteenth century, the expanse of flagstones and one side open to the water are deliberately reminiscent of Venice's Piazza and Piazzetta – Trieste had commercially eclipsed the older city some years before. Projecting into the harbour nearby, the **Molo Audace**, named after the first boat of Italian soldiers to land here in 1918, is the venue for the evening passeggiata.

Trieste's principal museum is the **Revoltella** (Mon & Wed–Sat 10am–1pm & 3–7.30pm, Sun 10am–6pm; July & Aug open until midnight; €6), Via Armando Diaz 27, housed in a Viennese-style palazzo bequeathed to the city by the financier Baron Pasquale Revoltella in 1869. Its combined display of nineteenth-century stately home furnishings and Triestine paintings is well worth a look and the adjacent palace, redesigned by the architect Carlo Scarpa, houses an extensive collection of modern art. The nearby **Museo Sartorio**, in Largo Papa Giovanni XXIII (closed for restoration at time of writing), has ceramics and icons downstairs and oppressive private rooms upstairs, all dark veneers, Gothic tracery and bad Venetian paintings, but its highlight, the early-fourteenth-century Santa Chiara triptych, is well worth a visit. The backs of its side panels have been attributed to Paolo Veneziano, and the central panel contains thirty-six beautifully restored miniature scenes from the life of Christ. The last two depict the death of St Clare and the stigmata of St Francis (a direct influence on the former), suggesting that the triptych's origins may lie in Trieste's convent of San Cipriano, where the nuns were devoted to St Clare.

A vastly more pleasant domestic interior is the **Museo Morpurgo**, north of San Giusto at Via Imbriani 5 (Tues–Sun 9am–1pm, Wed open late until 7pm; €1.55). The palazzo was left to the city by the merchant and banker Mario Morpurgo di Nilma, and its apartments have not really been touched since their first decoration in the 1880s. With its sepia photographs and other memorabilia, it feels less like a museum than like a home whose owners went on holiday and never came back.

One of the ugliest episodes of recent European history is embodied by the **Risiera di San Sabba**, overlooking the southern flank of Trieste's port at Ratto della Pileria 43 (April to mid-May & Nov 1–5 Tues–Sat 9am–6pm, Sun 9am–1pm; rest of the year Tues–Sun 9am–1pm; free), on the #10 bus route. Once a rice-hulling plant, this was one of only two concentration camps in Italy (the other was near Carpi in Emilia-Romagna; see p.428) and now houses a permanent exhibition that serves as a reminder of Fascist crimes in the region. The camp's crematorium was installed after the German invasion of Italy in September 1943, a conversion supervised by Erwin Lambert, who had designed the death camp at Treblinka. Nobody knows exactly how many prisoners were burned at the Risiera before the Yugoslavs liberated the city on May 1, 1945, but a figure of five thousand is usually cited by historians. Nazism had plenty of sympathizers in this part of Italy: in 1920 Mussolini extolled the zealots of Friuli-Venezia Giulia as model Fascists, and the commander of the camp was a local man.

Eating and drinking

Triestine **cuisine** is as mixed as its population, with goulash, potato noodles and cheese dumplings on many menus, as well as some superb fish dishes. The local *terrano*, a very sharp red wine grown only on the limestone highlands, was reputedly the favourite of the Roman empress Livia and is supposed to be good for the blood. It's delicious in any event and should be tried, ideally as an accompaniment to the heavy Triestine food. For less stolid meals, investigate the **osmizze** (see box on p.389), impromptu eating places, often in the hinterland of the Carso, which offer the simplest of local produce at rock-bottom prices. Trieste is most famous in Italy for its **coffee**, imported and even roasted here – you'll be pushed to find a better or a stronger cup anywhere. Via C. Battisti is a good street for **food shops** – cheeses, cooked meats, olives and pasta in its many guises are piled high in the windows.

Restaurants

Two restaurants in the new town are perfect for snack meals and lunches: *Buffet Pepi*, on Via Cassa di Risparmio 3 (closed Sun), a favourite student place, emphasizes Trieste's Austrian connections with excellent sausages, gammon and bowls of steaming sauerkraut. *Da Giovanni*, Via S. Lazzaro 14 (closed Sun), serves simple meals at bench tables, the hams hanging from the ceiling and the barrels of wine behind the bar lending a distinctly rustic air. For an inexpensive meal, head for the ramshackle streets behind the castle, where the *Arco di Riccardo*, adjoining the Roman arch of the same name, at Via del Trionfo 3, serves excellent meals in a welcoming atmosphere (closed Mon).

More expensive places tend to specialize in fish; *branzino* and *sogliola* – sea bass and sole – are local favourites. *Aquario*, on Via Crispi, serves superb fish and seafood at reasonable prices, while the very popular *Trattoria dell'Antica Ghiacceretta* in Via dei Fornelli (closed Sun) concentrates on the food rather than the decor. Plusher, but still excellent, is *Ai Fiori*, on Piazza Hortis 7 (closed Sun & Mon; ☎040.300.633), a classy trattoria on a leafy square between the Riva and the castle hill. For meat, and steak in particular, the prestigious restaurant of *Antica Trattoria Suban*, way out to the east of the city at Via Comici 2 (closed Mon, Tues, & part of Aug), deserves its reputation, but is pricey.

Viale XX Settembre has a number of lively **pizza** places among the bars and cinemas. *Pizzeria Fattorusso*, just off Viale XX Settembre at Via Rosetti 3, is good, and less canteen-like in atmosphere than its rivals. Otherwise *Il Barattolo*, on Piazza Sant'Antonio (closed Mon in winter), is very popular for pizza and decent Italianate food, and is centrally located.

Cafés and gelaterie

Trieste's association with **coffee** dates back to the mid-eighteenth century, when trading began and when the first coffee shops opened in emulation of Vienna. Even now it's the leading coffee port in the Mediterranean – eighty percent of Italy's coffee arrives here, and the city's mayor is currently one Riccardo Illy, from the famous Illy coffee clan. Triestines treat coffee with great seriousness. One of the pleasures of walking around the city centre is the unexpected scent of roasting beans that wafts through the streets and there's a plethora of places in which to sample the various imports and a vast range of ways in which the coffee can be served.

Trieste's favourite **café** is the *Caffè San Marco* (closed Wed), which has occupied its premises on Via C. Battisti for some eighty years. It's a huge, relaxed place with a clientele of all ages chatting and playing chess in the mahogany and mirrored Art Nouveau-style interior. Much of the historic style of the *Caffè Tommaseo* on Piazza Tommaseo – a rendezvous for Italian nationalists in the nineteenth century – was lost in a recent refurbishment; the same is regrettably true for the famous *Caffè degli Specchi*, in Piazza Unità. For a quick pastry, try the *Caffè Pasticceria Pirona* on Largo Barriera Vecchia, one of whose regulars was James Joyce during his Triestine sojourn. The best place to sample the product however is at a *torrefazione* – a café that roasts and sells beans, as well as grinding them; try the *Caffè Colombiana* in Via Carducci near the Via Coroneo junction, *La Triestina* on Piazza Cavana or the *Crèmcaffè* in Piazza Goldoni.

For **ice cream**, the best spot is the leafy Viale XX Settembre, known as the "Acquedotto", where citizens stroll in the evening. *Zampolli* is superb, but there are many to choose from. The Viale is sometimes less congenial at its Piazza San Giovanni end, a gathering place for young *fascisti*. The original *Zampolli* is at Via Ghega 10 and is still considered the best.

Bars and nightlife

Many of the city's **bars** are as glossy as the top-notch cafés, though there is one survival of old Trieste, the *Osteria de Libero*, on the castle hill at Via Risorta 7 (closed Sun), which can hardly have changed in a hundred years. The bar in the Galleria Protti – which runs north from the Piazza Borsa, inside the Assicurazioni Generali building – has a Thirties' nightclub feel. For late drinking, Via Madonna del Mare, on the castle hill, has a number of bars whose names, managements and popularity come and go each year – it's best to follow your ears to where the crowds are. In the new town, *Public House*, Via San Lazzaro 9 (closed Sun), is a trendy, upmarket wine bar, while the *Caffè della Musica*, at Via Rosetti 6 (closed Sun), off Viale XX Settembre, is younger and more studenty than most, and has occasional live music. After midnight, the most popular **nightspots** are east down the Riva: *Benningans Pub* and *Tender* are fairly tacky, but full to bursting on weekend nights; the most central disco, *Mandracchio*, is on the Passo di Piazza, off Piazza Unità, and comes with similar warnings.

Listings

Airport information ℡0481.773.224.
Bus information freephone ℡800.0166.75 (Mon–Thurs 8am–noon & 2–3.30pm, Fri 8am–noon). For AECT buses down the coast, call freephone ℡800.016.675. Timetables and tickets can be bought from newsagents and *tabacchi*. Town buses cost €0.80 for any journey made within an hour of purchase; provincial buses cost a standard €0.90, except private AECT and SAITA services.
Car rental Avis, Piazza della Libertà ℡040.421.521; Europcar, Via Mazzini 1 ℡040.367.944; Maggiore, at the train station ℡040.421.323.
Club Alpino Italiano Via Donota 2 ℡040.630.464.
Consulates UK, Via Torino 7 (Tues & Fri 2.30–4.30pm; ℡040.347.8303); US Consular Agent, Via Dante 7 (Mon–Fri 10am–noon; ℡040.660.177).

Festivals and events During the summer there are programmes of musical events at the castle of San Giusto, and the Verdi opera house (℡040.672.2500) has a summer season, performing mostly operetta. The Festa dell'Unità runs from the end of July to mid-August – check the timetable in *Il Piccolo*, Trieste's daily paper, which should also have details of the festivals in the Carso villages (see below).
Hospital Ospedale Maggiore, Piazza dell'Ospedale ℡040.399.1111; in an emergency, dial ℡118.
Internet access *Sportnet*, Piazza Squero Vecchio, just west of Piazza Unità (Mon–Sat 9am–1pm & 3.30–7.30pm); Internet Point, via San Francesco 28c (Mon–Sat 10am–1pm & 4–9pm; ℡040.771.190).
Police The *Questura* is on Via Teatro Romano ℡040.379.0111.
Post office The main post office is in Piazza Vittorio Veneto (Mon–Sat 8am–7.30pm).

Taxis Radio Taxi ☏ 040.307.730.
Telephones Telecom Italia, Piazza Tommaseo 4b
(8am–10pm) or at the train station (8am–10pm).
Train information ☏ 147.888.088.

Travel agent Agemar, Piazza Duca degli Abruzzi
1a ☏ 040.363.222 – for ferry tickets to Grado and
Ligano, Pirano (Slovenia), Brioni and Rovigno
(Croatia).

Around Trieste: the Carso

The **Carso** is the Italian name for the limestone uplands that rise from the plain of the Veneto south of Monfalcone and eventually merge into the Istrian plateau. Although within thirty minutes' bus ride of Trieste, it feels like an entirely different country, and is geologically, botanically and socially distinct from anywhere else in Italy. Most of the Carso now lies within Slovenia (its Slovene name is Kras), and even the narrow strip inside Italy, though supporting a population of just 20,000, remains distinctively Slovene in culture, boasting villages with names like Zagradec and Koludrovica. The dour villages of thick-walled houses seem to hunker down against the *bora*, the northeasterly wind which can blast this area at any time of year – when it's especially fierce, ropes are strung along the steeper streets in Trieste.

Like all limestone country, the environment is harsh: arid in summer and sometimes snowbound in winter. The surface of the plateau is studded with sink-holes left by streams which have slowly carved their way underground, sometimes reappearing miles away on the coast. The abundance of caves has even led to the German name for the area, *karst*, becoming the standard geographical term for this type of landscape. In other places – near Aurisina, for instance – the land is scarred with World War I trenches.

The distinctive landscape and natural environment have led to proposals for creating a National Park. There is fine **walking** to be had, and several bus services run to the Carso from Trieste, including the #42 and #44. The tourist office publishes a useful map of the network of numbered footpaths in the Carso; it shouldn't be used for serious navigation, but is a useful guide to what's possible – and it would be difficult to get yourself seriously lost. If the scenery isn't as grand as the Dolomites, the pace is gentler, especially if you can break your expedition at an *osmizza* (see box opposite).

Grotta Gigante and Rupingrande

The most picturesque way up into the Carso is to take the *tranvia* (cable tramway; 7.30am–8pm; every 20min; €0.80) from Trieste's Piazza Oberdan to the village of Opicina, at the edge of the plateau. From here it's a pleasant thirty-minute walk to the **Grotta Gigante** (guided visits daily: April–Sept every 30min 10am–6pm; March & Oct hourly 10am–4pm; Nov–Feb hourly 10am–noon & 2–4pm; €7.50), the world's largest accessible cave, and the second-largest natural chamber anywhere in the world. At 107m deep by 208m broad, the dome of St Peter's would fit comfortably inside. It's a steady 11°C inside, so come prepared.

To get there on foot, walk straight down the road from the tram station, then take the first left along Via di Prosecco. After the railway bridge, take a sharp right down a slip road signposted *Officine Laborante*, then turn left, crossing over the small railway line. A path to the left leads through sparse woods and farmland for twenty minutes, passing through a tunnel under the main road before bringing you out at the approach road to the cave. You can save yourself the walk by taking bus #42 from the far side of the small square opposite the tram stop. You can also skip the *tranvia* altogether if you prefer and take bus #42 direct from the centre of Trieste to the cave.

The cave itself, while impressive in scale, is utterly devoid of life, killed off by the electric lights and the spores and germs brought in by visitors. Like most of the caves in the Carso, it was created by the erosive action of a river, in this case the Timavo, which sank deeper and deeper underground before changing course. The cave is now dry. The stalactites and stalagmites grew later, formed by deposits of calcium carbonate and colourful metal oxides. The two long "pillars" in the centre of the cave are in fact wires sheathed in plastic. At the bottom end two super-accurate pendulums are suspended, used to measure seismic shifts in isolation from surface noise and air currents.

Close to the cave are *Milic*, a pleasant **trattoria** (closed Mon), and the Centro Sportivo Mario Ervatti (℡040.225.047), the only **bike-rental** place in the area – useful should you not have a car but want to explore more of the Carso.

The main sights to head for are in and around the village of **RUPIN-GRANDE**, just 3km northeast of the cave and also on the #42 bus route, which acts as something of a cultural capital. A short walk east of the village is a fortress built in the fourteenth century to defend the area from Turkish incursions, while in Rupingrande itself, the **Casa Carso** (Easter–Sept 3–5pm Sun & public holidays only; free) exhibits old furniture and costumes, as well as works by local artisans. The Casa Carso is signposted from the central crossroads in Rupingrande. Every two years the village hosts an important Slovene folk festival, the **Nozze carsiche** (Carso weddings), on the four days leading up to the last Sunday in August.

Strada Vicentina and Val Rosandra

Two walking areas near the city can be particularly recommended. The **Strada Vicentina** (or Napoleonica) is some 2km long, curving along the hillside above the city, between the *Obelisco* campsite and the hamlet of **BORGO NAZARIO** (near Prosecco). It's a scenic but unstrenuous walk, partly shadowed by trees and partly cut through almost sheer limestone cliffs. Roughly half way along is the truncated pyramid of the **Tempio Mariano** at Monte Grisa, built in 1967 on the site of a local place of pilgrimage. The structure isn't exactly easy on the eye, but the interior is impressive and on a clear day the views are superb. Access to the Strada Vicentina couldn't be simpler: *Obelisco* is a stop on the *tranvia*, and the Borgo Nazario end is near Via San Nazario, where the #42 bus stops on its way back to Trieste station.

Osmizze

Perhaps the best way to experience the Slovene culture of the Carso is to find an **osmizza**, an informal restaurant where farmers sell their own produce, such as home-cured meats, cheese, olives, hard-boiled eggs, bread and wine. They are usually very cheap, and a frequent bonus is a stunning view over the bay of Trieste or the limestone hills behind the city. The problem with *osmizze* is that they are often temporary, don't advertise, and usually lie off the beaten track – which makes them all the more worth tracking down. Your best bet is to ask the tourist office for a list or look at Ⓦ www.interware.it/tsr/Ambiente/carso/osmizze.htm. Otherwise, as long as you don't mind taking a few detours, just take a #44 bus from outside the station in Trieste, get off at the villages Prosecco or Contovello, and start asking if there is an *osmizza* nearby. You'll know you are getting warm when you see arrows on clumps of leaves suspended from archways and lamp-posts: they point the way to the nearest *osmizza*.

The other area, the **Val Rosandra**, is very different. This miniature wilderness of limestone cliffs and sumac trees is the local rock-climbing headquarters and is crisscrossed with paths. Take bus #40 or #41 from Trieste's bus station to **BAGNOLI DELLA ROSANDRA** and follow the road at the back of the square towards the hills. After about 500m or so the tarmac gives way to a path bordered on the right by a miniature Roman aqueduct – now resembling little more than a stone-lined ditch – and on the left by a stream with pools for bathing. After thirty minutes the little sanctuary church of Santa Maria in Siaris appears, perched on a spur of rock high on the right. You can climb up to it easily enough and a steep path continues up to the top of the plateau beyond. Beyond this is a waterfall, accessible by a steep path, then the tiny hamlet of Bottazzo – the last habitation before Slovenia. At the border a sign advertises a friendship path linking communities on either side of the frontier. Don't be tempted to investigate; only locals are allowed to cross unpatrolled borders, and the military are fairly active in the area as it's a busy crossing point for illegal immigrants.

Other paths lead across the valley and up to the villages of **Mocco**, where there's a ruined castle. The most rewarding expedition, although strenuous, is across the slopes of **Monte Carso**. It's simplest to begin at **SAN DORLIGO DELLA VALLE**, where bus #40 terminates. Walk uphill through town past the general store until you leave the village. At a T-junction with a major road cross the road to the fountain and national park signs where there's a signpost to the beginning of the walk. After 100m, the unsurfaced track divides into two paths at a small spring. Take the left fork here and follow the path marked #46 as it rises gently across the contours of Monte Carso. After about an hour the trail steepens to bring you out onto the plateau. Be wary of taking the smaller paths that branch uphill off the main trail; these are local shortcuts, but often peter out among faded signs warning of old mines – the explosive type. At the top of the mountain is a beautiful undulating plateau of mixed woodland and grasses, the path running within metres of the Slovene border. A number of roughly marked steep paths turn down into Val Rosandra, but you'll need good grip and a head for heights; the last, #17, probably has the gentlest gradient.

The Triestine Riviera

The thirty-odd kilometres of coastline either side of Trieste, from Múggia to the south and as far as Duino in the north, are optimistically known as the **Triestine Riviera**. While beaches aren't as good as you'll find further down the Adriatic, or even at nearby Grado or Lignano, some fine walks, historic sites and castles are worth a day-trip. Frequent buses trace the coast road, and in summer ferries (see p.405) call at all the coastal towns.

Múggia

Directly south across the bay from Trieste, 11km away by road, **MÚGGIA**, the last remnant of Venice's Istrian possessions, is now reduced to little more than a popular spot for lunch expeditions from Trieste, though the town comes into its own during carnival time. The ferry-trip across the bay from Trieste (summer only) can be a good enough reason in itself to visit, but there are also appealing signs of the past, particularly in the brightly painted buildings on the main square. On the east side of the piazza, the fifteenth-century **Duomo** reveals its origins in its Venetian-Gothic arches and a bas-relief of Christ

Pantocrator in the lunette above the main door; the handsome **Palazzo dei Rettori**, on the north side of the square, displays the tell-tale *leone marciano*, the lion of St Mark. The piazza is backed by a handful of narrow streets and tumbledown houses, many of which date back to Venetian times, though the only house of any architectural note is the so-called **Casa Veneta**, on Via Dante Aligheri, with more Venetian-Gothic arches. There are plans to turn the house opposite into a museum for local archeological finds.

On the seaward side of the piazza, the tiny *mandracchio* is now used as a basin for pleasure boats, while the working harbour just beyond is spoilt only by the unrivalled view of Trieste's industrial backside. Múggia's handful of **fish restaurants** are all within spitting distance of the water. Top recommendation, and not just for the name, is the *Trattoria Lilibontempo* (closed Tues), at Riva Nazario Sauro 10, known as the *ex-Hitler* after the former proprietor, who bore an unnerving resemblance to the Nazi dictator. The most formal – and expensive – of the trattorias is the *Lido* (closed Mon), 200m along the waterfront, but a decent meal can be had at the inexpensive *Alle Rose*, at Via Roma 5 (closed Mon), the main road running behind town.

Bus #20 runs back to Trieste every 30min, but it's worth visiting **Múggia Vecchia**, on the hilltop hard against the Slovene border and less than 20km from Croatia. It's a steep twenty-minute walk past Múggia's fourteenth-century castle and town walls, but bus #50 from outside the **train station**, 100m inland from the main road, runs every forty minutes for those who don't fancy the climb. The old village has a few oddments of ancient foundations, but the main reason to visit is the lovely **Santuario di Santa Maria Assunta**, a largely tenth-century structure, though much rebuilt in the twelfth and fifteenth centuries. Inside, there is just enough light coming through the narrow Romanesque windows to illuminate some peeling Veneto-Byzantine frescoes, mostly of the thirteenth century, and an unusual pulpit supported on four slender, carved columns. From the hill behind the sanctuary on a clear day you can see as far as Fiume and Grado.

Barcola and Miramare

BARCOLA, 2km west of Trieste and connected to the city by buses #6 and #36 from the bus station, is the nearest beach resort. Developed during Trieste's great days at the end of the nineteenth century, it is now really a suburb that comes to life in summer, when all Trieste seems to come here to chat, play cards, sunbathe and swim. Despite the cargo ships and tankers moored in the harbour, the water is moderately clean. Just short of the resort, perched on the slope of the limestone escarpment, is the **Faro della Vittoria**, the second-tallest lighthouse in the world after New York's Statue of Liberty.

Standing at the tip of a rocky promontory 7km from Trieste, the salt-white castle of **MIRAMARE** is the area's prime tourist attraction. The Archduke Ferdinand Maximilian, Emperor Franz Josef's younger brother, was once forced ashore here by a squall, and resolved to buy the site. He built his dream castle and laid out its grounds between 1856 and 1870, but never lived to see it completed – having accepted Napoleon III's offer to make him the Emperor of Mexico, Maximilian was executed by his Mexican opponents in 1867, in the line of imperial duty. His wife Carlotta later went mad, and the legend was born that anyone who spends a night in Miramare will come to a bad end.

The park makes an excellent spot for a picnic, but the real draw is the castle's kitsch **interior** (daily 9am–7.30pm; €4), a remarkable example of regal decadence, and carved, gilded, and inlaid in every way possible. The "Monarchs' Salon", for instance, is embellished with portraits of a King of Norway, the

Emperor of Brazil, a Czar of Russia – anyone, no matter how fraudulent or despotic, as long as they're nominal monarchs. This softens you up for the bedroom and its images of the most important events in the history of this area, pride of place going to the construction of the castle, of course. Other rooms are panelled and furnished like a ship's quarters, reflecting Maximilian's devotion to the Austrian Navy.

There are a number of ways **to get to Miramare**, of which the simplest is to take the #36 bus from Piazza Oberdan, though the private SAITA service from the bus station is quicker. Trains heading west from Trieste also stop, and in summer there's a boat service from the harbour. In July and August a *son et lumière* called "the Romance of Maximilian of Mexico and Charlotte of Habsburg" is performed beside the sea, with a regular performance in English; check with the tourist office or the castle (℡040.224.143) for information on dates and times.

Duino and Sistiana

The village of **DUINO**, 14km northwest along the coast from Trieste, is dominated by its two castles, the **Castello Vecchio** and the fifteenth-century **Castello Nuovo**, seat of the princes of Thurn and Taxis down to the present day. It was in the latter that Rainer Maria Rilke began the great *Duino Elegies*, a work dedicated to his host, the incumbent princess. Access to the Castello Nuovo is prearranged and granted only to large guided groups (ask at the tourist office in Trieste), while the Castello Vecchio is now just a ruined eyrie above the sea.

A pleasant footpath, the Sentiero Rilke, runs 3km back along the coast to the **campsite** (May–Sept; ℡040.299.264) at **SISTIANA**, where there's a large harbour backed by woods, and a **beach**. Bus #44 and the much faster SAITA bus to Monfalcone run from Trieste's bus station to Sistiana and Duino.

Aquileia, Grado and around

Bordered by the Tagliamento in the west and the Isonzo in the east, and drained by other rivers flowing into the sandy, shallow waters at the head of the Adriatic, the triangle of flatlands west of Trieste and south of Udine seems unpromising territory for a visitor – mile upon mile of maize fields, punctuated by telegraph poles, streams, level roads and newish villages. Yet at **Aquileia,** the dull fields of this secretive region have yielded up a wealth of Roman remains, while the glorious **Basilica** ranks among the most important monuments of early Christendom. Tucked away in the lagoons, just to the south, the popular resort of **Grado** with its beaches and crowds of holiday-makers has a completely different atmosphere, though it too preserves some beautiful early Christian remains. If you don't have your own transport, **buses** are the way to explore the region: they leave Udine for Grado at least every hour, calling at Palmanova and Aquileia on the way; from Trieste, change at **Monfalcone**, from where buses leave hourly for Aquileia and Grado.

Aquileia

Forty-five kilometres west of Trieste, **AQUILEIA** was established as a **Roman colony** in 181 BC, its location at the eastern edge of the Venetian plain – on the bank of a navigable river a few kilometres from the sea – being ideal for defensive and trading purposes. It became the nexus for all Rome's dealings with points east and north, and by 10 BC, when the Emperor Augustus received Herod the Great here, Aquileia was the capital of the Regio Venetia et Histria and the fourth most important city in Italy, after Rome, Milan and Capua. In 314 the famous Patriarchate of Aquileia was founded, and under the first patriarch, Theodore, a great basilica was built. Sacked by Attila in 452 and again by the Lombards in 568, Aquileia lost the patriarchate to Grado, which was protected from invasion by its lagoons. It regained its primacy in the early eleventh century under **Patriarch Poppo**, who rebuilt the basilica and erected the campanile, a landmark for miles around. But regional power inevitably passed to Venice, and in 1751 Aquileia lost its patriarchate for the last time, to Udine. The sea has long since retreated, and the River Natissa is a reed-clogged stream. Aquileia is now a dusty little town of 3500 people.

Aquileia's rich history is made visible in the layers of the vast **Basilica** (daily 8.30am–7.30pm; free), just east of the main road. The earliest part, Theodore's extraordinary **mosaic pavement**, was discovered below the nave floor at the beginning of the twentieth century and is thought to be the earliest surviving remnant of any Christian church. The mosaic undulates the full length of the nave in a riotous sequence of colours, patterns and images, many of which draw on Roman iconography. As far as the red line extending across the nave aisle there is no explicitly Christian imagery, though pagan symbolism was frequently adopted and adapted by the early Church. Look for the blond angel bearing the laurel wreath and palm frond – whether it represents the Pax Romana or Christian Victory, no one can be sure. Beyond the line the Biblical story of Jonah begins, complete with waves, whale and fish everywhere – a motif not unconnected to the nearby Adriatic. Other mosaics from Theodore's original basilica, depicting a whole bestiary, have been discovered around the base of the campanile (access from inside the basilica).

In 1348 an earthquake destroyed much of Poppo's work, but the building is still superb, the Gothic elements of the reconstruction – all points above the capitals – harmonizing perfectly with the Romanesque below. The fine nave ceiling, like the steeple of the campanile, dates from the early sixteenth century. The ninth-century **crypt** under the chancel (€2.60) has very faded twelfth-century frescoes telling the story of St Hermagora, the legendary first bishop of Aquileia, including a gory beheading scene and a moving descent from the cross.

A couple of minutes' walk from the basilica, on the other side of the main road, on Via Roma, is the **Museo Archeologico** (Mon 8.30am–2pm, Tues–Sun 8.30am–7.30pm; €4). Worked stone and everyday items litter the fields around Aquileia, but the finer pieces have been collected here, ranging from precise surgical needles, delicate coloured glass and precious stones to great piles of jumbled masonry. The two courtyards, in particular, resemble a junkyard of Roman stone, with hundreds of funerary monuments, including urns piled in neat pyramids; concerts are occasionally held here in summer. It's worth persevering up to the top floor of the museum where two extraordinary bronze heads are displayed side by side. One is a fantastical relief in the Hellenistic style, the other a naturalistic bust which may portray a dictator of the third century AD; the cruel expression certainly supports the speculation. On the ground floor rows of marble sculptures and busts mostly derive from the Roman tombs which once lined the roads into Aquileia.

The **Museo Paleocristiano** (daily 8.30am–2pm; free), housed in the shell of a Benedictine monastery in the northern part of the town, opposite the campsite on Via Germina, is recommended solely to those insatiable for more mosaic pavements. Most of the patterns are geometric, but the mosaic on the mezzanine level is attractive, with Christ represented as a peacock and the apostles by their various symbols. There's a miscellany of early Christian carving and sculpture, but the fifteen-minute riverside walk to the museum from the basilica is perhaps the best reason to go, taking you past the sad remnants of the quays of Aquileia. From the museum you can loop back along the main road, past the forum, to the basilica.

The **tourist office** is at Piazza Capitolo 4 (Mon–Fri 9am–7pm, Sat & Sun 10am–1pm & 2–5pm; ☎0431.910.87, ⓦwww.aquileia.net), beside the basilica. In the newer part of town, west of the main road past the Museo Archeologico, you'll find the cheaper of Aquileia's two **hotels**, the *Aquila Nera*, Piazza Garibaldi 5 (☎0431.91.045; ❷), with an excellent **restaurant** attached. The more upmarket *Hotel Patriarchi* sits on the main road by the bus stop (☎0431.919.595, ⓦwww.hotelpatriarchi.it; ❺). There's also an unremarkable **HI hostel**, *Domus Augusta*, Via Roma 25 (☎0431.910.24; €13); alternatively head along Via Gemina past the Museo Paleocristiana, where rooms are available in **private houses** (❷). Also on Via Gemina is *Camping Aquileia* (☎0431.919.583; mid-May to mid-Sept). Of the **restaurants**, *Alla Basilicata*, on Via Della Stazione, serves decent pizzas, and *La Pergola* on the main road at Localita Beligna 4 serves good home cooking and home-produced wines.

Grado and around

Some 11km south of Aquileia, isolated among lagoons at the end of a causeway, is the ancient island-town of **GRADO**, through which Aquileia once traded with Syria, Cyprus, Arabia and Asia Minor. But Grado is no miniature Venice, despite its parallel history and situation, the tiny historic centre being all but lost among the concrete buildings of the large, modern resort.

For relaxing on the **beach**, however, this is one of the best places in the northern Adriatic, the resort extending eastwards along the length of the sandy island. The water is warm and safe as a bath, and almost as shallow – indeed, the name of the town comes from the gentle angle of its shore. The free beaches are at the western end; if you want a locker, deckchair and shower facilities, you will have to pay a few euro to one of the businesses on the Lungomare Adriatico.

It's worth finding the **historic centre**, however, for its three early-Christian buildings, grouped close together in the heart of a miniature network of old streets. The exteriors are of fairly rustic brick construction, though enlivened by fragments of carved Roman marble. The sixth-century **Basilica** was heavily restored between the 1930s and 1950s, but preserves a bizarre parade of ill-matched nave pillars topped by an assortment of Corinthian capitals; it's thought that these were borrowed from various Roman buildings in Aquileia. The pulpit is of similarly hybrid origins, perched on six slender Roman columns under a Venetian canopy that resembles an oriental tent. Venice's presence is also felt in the fourteenth-century silver *pala* on the high altar. The mosaic pavement, while not as impressive as Aquileia's, is beautiful, the pattern being formed by an endless knot.

The adjacent octagonal **Baptistery** also dates back to the fifth century and the arrival of the first Christians in the lagoon. The church of **Santa Maria delle Grazie**, on its far side, is from the same period as the basilica, and has another mongrel collection of columns and capitals. From the outside it's possible to see how the ground level has sunk over the centuries.

Ten buses per day make the one-hour run to Udine, and there's also a half-hourly bus connection from Cervignano train station, on the Venice–Trieste line. The best way to visit Grado, though, is by boat from Trieste; on Wednesdays, Fridays and Sundays the little steamer *Dionea* calls morning and evening at the Molo Torpediniere on its way from and to the city (see "Travel Details" on p.405).

Grado's **tourist office**, at Viale Dante Alighieri 72 (daily: June–Aug 8am–7pm; Sept–May 9am–6pm; ☎0431.877.111, Ⓔaptgrado@tin.it), has details of **boats**, which run to Venice and Trieste in summer, and the town's **hotels**, the majority of which are fairly expensive and sometimes insist on your taking full pension. Three cheaper hotels are the *Villa Marin*, Via dei Provveditori 20 (☎0431.80.789, Ⓕ0431.85.534; ❺), overlooking the seafront wall between the two beaches; the *Sirenetta*, Via Milano 1 (☎0431.80.404; ❺), on the western beach; and *Al Sole Meuble*, Viale del Sole 31 (☎ & Ⓕ0431.80.370; ❸), which is near the beach, but at its eastern end, a good ten minutes' walk from the centre. The best local **campsites** are at Grado Pineta, around 3km east of the town and served by regular buses: *Camping al Bosco* (☎0431.80.485; May–Sept), the three-star *Camping Punta Spin* (☎0431.80.732; April–Sept), which has a swimming pool, and *Camping Europa* (☎0431.80.877; mid-April to mid-Sept).

A cluster of good **restaurants** can be found in the old streets around the basilica. The tiny *Santa Lucia* (closed Mon), secreted in an alleyway at Calle Corbato 2, serves good pizza, while the *Tavernetta all'Androna* (closed Mon) is more expensive but has a lovely courtyard under the basilica's east wall. The *Enoteca La Sentina*, opposite, is good for wine and snacks. For Grado's fish specialities, head just west to *Trattoria de Toni*, in Piazza Duca d'Aosta, or the *Trattoria Alla Borsa*, Via Conte di Grado, behind the marina.

Gorizia

As with other towns in this region, the tranquillity of present-day **GORIZIA** – virtually midway along the Trieste–Udine rail line – belies the turbulence of its past. The castle that dominates the old centre was the power-base of the dukes of Gorizia, who ruled the area for four centuries. After their eclipse, Venice briefly ruled the town at the start of the sixteenth century, before the Habsburgs took over. It was controlled from Vienna uninterruptedly until August 8, 1916, when the Italian army occupied it – but only until the rout at Caporetto, some 50km north. The border settlement after World War II literally split houses in Gorizia down the middle. Italy kept the town proper, but lost its eastern perimeter to what was then Yugoslavia, where the new regime resolved to build its own Gorizia: **Nova Gorica** – "New Gorizia"– is the result.

The town's appearance, like that of Trieste, is distinctly central European, stamped with the authority of Empress Maria Theresa. Numerous parks and gardens – thriving in the area's mild climate – further enhance the *fin-de-siècle* atmosphere. Again like Trieste, it's a major shopping town for Slovenes, which explains the large number of electrical goods, clothes and food shops, and the good cafés and restaurants.

The main sight in town is the **Borgo Castello**, the quarter built round the castle by the Venetians, mostly in the sixteenth century. It's a pleasant place to wander, and the collection of local folkloric items and handicrafts passes a half hour or so, but the view from the castle walls is more inspiring. The graceful rooms of the **Castle** itself (Tues–Sun: April–Nov 9.30am–1pm & 3–7.30pm; Oct–March 9.30am–6pm; €4.20) host occasional exhibitions, though these are of mostly local interest. The **Museo Provinciali** (Tues–Sun 10am–7pm; €3.10), in the Borgo just down from the castle entrance, is again fairly dry, with collections on textiles, fashion and World War I – the last interesting enough for Italian speakers.

One of the finest of its Neoclassical buildings is the **Palazzo Attems** in Piazza De Amicis, built by Nicolo Pacassi, Maria Theresa's favourite architect. After restoration work is complete – probably early in 2003 – it is due to house the town archives and picture gallery, the latter including some nice pieces, among them an altarpiece by Antonio Guardi. In what was once the Jewish quarter, the **Synagogue**, at Via Ascoli 19 (Tues & Thurs 6–8pm, also open some Sundays; free), is also of Neoclassical design; the serene interior resembles those in Venice's Ghetto.

Probably the strangest sight in Gorizia is the crypt in the Franciscan monastery at **Castagnavizza** – Kostanjevica, rather, for the monastery lies across the border in Nova Gorica. This is the burial place of the last of the French Bourbons. After Louis Philippe was ousted by the bloodless revolution of July 1830, the Bourbons were exiled from France; the family eventually arrived in Gorizia in 1836, and the Habsburgs allowed them to stay. To judge by the impassioned entries in the visitors' book, the silence of the crypt is regularly disturbed by French royalists, whose withered bouquets line the walls. The French state must reckon that the republic is now strong enough to withstand any monarchist pressure, for there has been a recent agreement to return these royal relics, although the dates have yet to be decided. The monastery was also home to Brother Stanislav Skrabec (1844–1918), an important Slovene linguist, and the library of 10,000 books includes a rare copy of the first Slovene grammar, inscribed by its author, Adam Bohoric (1584). The easiest approach is to take a taxi up the hill once you're across the border; walking is the best way back. Once there, ring the bell; there's no charge, but you should offer a donation.

The **tourist office** is at Via Roma 5, on the first floor (Mon–Fri: May–Sept 9am–1pm & 3–6pm; Oct–April 9am–1pm & 3–5pm; ☎0481.386.225), and also supplies information on the province of Gorizia as a whole. For accommodation, the only one-star **hotel** is the excellent *Sandro* at Via S. Chiara 18 (☎0481.533.223; ❹), not far from the central Piazza della Vittoria. If that's full, try the comfortable but bland *Alla Transalpina* at Via Caprin 30 (☎0481.530.291; ❹); the restaurant is overpriced, and it's a good 2km northeast of the centre, right on the Slovene border, but bus #1 runs every fifteen minutes from the train station through town, terminating opposite the hotel.

Gorizia is better served by **places to eat**. The *Osteria Panesale* (closed Sun), Corso Verdi 11, on the way into the old ghetto, serves beautiful local food in simple, classy surroundings. At the other end of the scale, *Al Sabatino* (closed Sun), at Via Mameli 4, is a traditional workers' trattoria serving local dishes in distinctly ordinary surroundings. More urbane is *Alle Lune*, Via Oberdan (closed Sun eve & Mon), but the prices are still moderate.

Udine and around

It is fitting that the best artworks in **UDINE**, 71km northwest of Trieste, are by Giambattista Tiepolo: his airy brilliance suits this town. Running beside and beneath the streets are little canals called *rogge*, diverted from the Torre and Cormor rivers, and these bright streams reflect light onto the walls and through the roadside greenery. Comfortable and bourgeois, Udine is the second city of Friuli-Venezia Giulia, and some say that although it has less than half the population of Trieste, it will gain the ascendancy sooner or later. Certainly it's already far more attractive to visitors, with its galleries, fine churches and well-preserved historic buildings around Piazza Libertà. Udine seems everything that Trieste is not – delicate, untroubled, successful.

Along with Cividale, Tricesimo and Zuglio, Udine was one of the frontier bastions of Imperial Rome, and by the sixth century AD it was far more than a garrison colony. Legend has it that the castle-topped hill at the heart of Udine was built by Attila's hordes, using their helmets as buckets, so that their leader could relish the spectacle of Aquileia in flames, 36km away. But it was not until the thirteenth century that it started to become a regional centre. Patriarch Bertoldo di Andechs (1218–51) can be seen as the father of Udine – he established two markets (the "old market" in Via Mercatovecchio, and the new one in Piazza Matteotti, still a marketplace), moved the patriarchate from Cividale to the castle of Udine, and set up a city council. In 1362 the dukes of Austria acquired the place by treaty, but not for long: Venice, now hungry for territory, captured Udine in 1420, after several assaults and sieges. The city was ruled by Venetian governors for almost 400 years – until 1797, when the Venetian Republic surrendered to Napoleon. Even now, the old aristocracy of Udine speak a version of Venetian dialect, while the humbler Udinese, many of whom have migrated from the countryside, speak *friulano*.

The City

The place to start any exploration of Udine is at the foot of the hill, in the **Piazza Libertà**, a square whose architectural ensemble is matched by few cities in Italy. The fifteenth-century **Palazzo del Comune** is a clear homage to the Palazzo Ducale in Venice, and the clock tower facing the palazzo, built in 1527, similarly has a Venetian model – the lion on the facade and the bronze "Moors" who strike the hours on top of the tower are explicit references to the Torre dell'Orologio in Piazza San Marco. The statue at the north end of the square is a bad allegory of *Peace*, donated to the town by Emperor Franz I to commemorate the Habsburg acquisition of Udine.

To walk up to the **Castello**, go through the **Arco Bollani**, designed by Palladio, and onwards up the graceful Venetian Gothic gallery, the **Loggia del Lippomano** on the right. The sixteenth-century *castello*, decorated by local artists and once the seat of the Friuli parliament, now houses an excellent **Galleria d'Arte Antica** (Tues–Sat 9.30am–12.30pm & 3–6pm, Sun 9.30am–12.30pm; €2.60, free Sun), containing works by Carpaccio, Bronzino and Tiepolo, as well as an indifferent Caravaggio and an interesting historical painting by Palma Il Giovanni showing St Mark putting the city under the patronage of St Hermagora, first bishop of Aquileia; Piazza Libertà is clearly visible on the right. The best-known painting in its collection is Tiepolo's *Consilium in Arena*, showing a meeting of the Order of the Knights of Malta, said to be a faithful rendering, amazingly painted entirely on the basis of written accounts given to the artist.

North from the Piazza Libertà is **Via Mercatovecchio**, once the mercantile heart of the city and now the town's busiest shopping street. The little chapel of **Santa Maria**, incorporated into the Palazzo del Monte di Pietà in Via Mercatovecchio, is a beauty: viewed through the glass booth from the street, the interior, with its cloudy Baroque frescoes by Giulio Quaglio (1694), has a pristine, subaqueous appearance.

Due west lies the **Piazza Matteotti**, with galleries on three sides and the fine

Baroque facade of San Giacomo on the fourth. The square's importance as the centre of public life in Udine is proved by the outside altar on the first-floor balcony of **San Giacomo**; mass was celebrated here on Saturdays so that selling and buying could go on uninterrupted in the market below. As well as being the town's main market, this was the setting for tournaments, plays and carnivals. The fountain in the middle of the square was designed in 1543 by Giovanni da Udine, a pupil of Raphael, who also had a hand in building the castle.

Off the south side of Piazza Libertà is the **Duomo** (7am–noon & 4–6pm), a Romanesque construction that was given a Baroque refit in the eighteenth century. Altarpieces and frescoes by Giambattista Tiepolo are the main attraction – they decorate the first two chapels on the right and the chapel of the Sacrament, a little way beyond. A series of frescoes painted by Tiepolo in collaboration with his son, Giandomenico, can be seen in the tiny **Oratorio della Purità** opposite – ask the sacristan in the Duomo to show you.

But Udine's outstanding works of art are the Giambattista Tiepolo frescoes in the nearby **Gallerie del Tiepolo** in the beautifully furnished **Palazzo Arcivescovile** (Wed–Sun 10am–noon & 3.30–6.30pm; €4, including Museo Diocesano – see below). Painted in the late 1720s, these luminous and consummately theatrical scenes add up to a sort of Rococo epic of the Old Testament. *Fall of the Rebel Angels* is the first work you see as you climb the staircase, while the finest room, the Gallery, is at the top, immediately on your right. Every surface is painted with either trompe l'oeil architectural details or scenes from the story of Abraham, Isaac and Jacob. To the left is a sequence of rooms decorated in rich colours: watch for Tiepolo's *Judgement of Solomon* in the Red Room, and Bambini's wonderful *Triumph of Wisdom* in the serene Delfino library. Also inside the Palazzo Arcivescovile and arranged around the Tiepolo galleries is the **Museo Diocesano**, with an assortment of sculpture and funerary monuments, as well as an exhibition of naive art – popular sculptures from Friuli's churches spanning the Gothic, Renaissance and Baroque periods.

On the edge of the old town in Piazza Diacono, the **Galleria d'Arte Moderna** (Tues–Sat 9.30am–12.30pm & 3–6pm, Sun 9.30am–12.30pm; €2.58, free Sun) gives a reasonable overview of Italian art in the twentieth century, plus a glimpse of a few foreign greats.

Practicalities

Udine's **train** and **bus stations** are close together in the south of the town, on Viale Europa Unità; Via Roma leads from the train station into the centre. The **tourist office** is at Piazza Maggio 7 (May–Sept Mon–Fri 9am–1pm & 3–6pm; Oct–April 9am–1pm & 3–5pm; ☏0432.295.972, ⓦwww.comune.udine.it). **Internet** access can be found to the north of town, at Tempo Reale, Via Gemona 86. **Hotel** options are surprisingly limited: cheap, central but rather grim is *Al Vecchio Tram*, Via Brennari 32 (☏0432.502.516; ❷). It's worth paying the extra to stay at *Quo Vadis*, Piazzale Cella 28 (☏0432.21.091; ❸), a ten-minute walk east along Viale Europa Unità from the train station, or the new *Al Bue*, at Via Pracchiuso 75 (☏0432.299.070; ❺), just north of Piazza Maggio.

Udine has scores of **restaurants**, including the unpretentious *Trattoria all'Allegria*, Via Grazzano 18 (closed Mon), which does simple local dishes in the dining room beside the bar. Just north of Piazza Marconi, the *Osteria Sbarco dei Pirati*, at Via Bartolini 12 (closed Sun), is lively and has a room built out over the *rogga*, while the excellent *Ai Frati*, on Piazzetta Antonini (closed Sun), serves local dishes on a shaded terrace. Try the Carnian speciality of *cialzons* or little ravioli (available Sundays only) at *Al Vecchio Stallo*, an osteria in a converted stables at Via Viola 7 (closed Wed), just inside the ring road, near Piazzale XXVI Luglio; prices are reasonable, and in summer you can eat in the small inner courtyard, surrounded by greenery and Udine's ancient buildings. South of the old town, the *Spaghetteria Da Ciccio*, on Via Grazzano (closed Sun), serves famously vast portions at budget prices to an appreciative student crowd. For **ice cream**, *Il Buon Gelato*, in the old town at Via Manin 14b, lives up to its name.

Later in the evening, students and young Udinese head for Piazza Matteotti and Via Sarpi. On the latter, *Teresina* is a livelier **enoteca** than most, with a good garden, while the apparently unnamed *Tapas*, at Via Sarpi 1, and *Al Capello*, two doors down (both closed Sun), pull in a young crowd. The inevitable Irish **pub**, *Caffè Caucigh*, at Via Gemona 28, is unsurprisingly popular and has live music on Fridays. Students hang out in the *St James* and *Al Marinaio* bars in Via Grazzano, and the *Locanda Medievale* on Viale Sottomonte is popular for its enterprising mix of cured ham and house music, but **nightlife** is otherwise limited, especially outside term. In summer, however, there's a busy programme of cultural events – theatre, music, dance – in and around the town. Ask the tourist office for the listings magazines *L'Estate in Città* and *La Locandina di Udine*. Throughout the year the Ferroviario arts cinema at Via Cernaia 2 is always worth checking out.

Cividale del Friuli

Lying only 17km east of Udine and connected to it by train and bus, **CIVIDALE DEL FRIULI** is a gem of a town, much prized by the Friulani, but pretty well unknown to outsiders. It was founded in 50 BC by Julius Caesar where the Natisone Valley opens into the plain, and in the sixth century became the capital of the first Lombard duchy. In the eighth century the Patriarch of Aquileia moved here, inaugurating Cividale's most prosperous period.

The Town

The old town lies on the same side as the rail and coach stations, and the visitor need never cross the river; though a walk over the Devil's Bridge is *de rigueur*. Just walking around the town, within the oval ring bisected by Via Carlo Alberto and Corso Mazzini, is a pleasure; the pace of life is provincially serene, and many of the buildings have interesting histories and respectable architecture. Cividale has been the main market town in the Natisone Valley for two hundred years, and today you hear Italian, *friulano* and Slovene dialects spoken in the street. There are some remarkable tourist sights, too.

The tiny **Tempietto Longobardo** (daily 9.30am–12.30pm & 3–6.30pm; €2), poised above the Natisone off Piazza San Biagio, is a uniquely fine example of Lombard art. Constructed in the ninth century, largely from older fragments, much of the elaborate stucco work inside the chapel was reduced to rubble in the terrible earthquake of 1222. The delicate interior preserves faded frescoes and carved stalls from its use as a convent chapel in the late fourteenth century, but the eye is drawn to the east wall where an exquisite stucco arch is flanked by six female figures. Whether they represent saints, queens or nuns is uncertain, but the luminous, smiling statues are among the most splendid surviving works of art from the ninth century.

Two other beautiful Lombard pieces are to be found in the **Museo**

Cristiano (Mon–Sat 9.30am–noon & 3–6.30pm, Sun 10am–1pm & 3–6.30pm; free), housed in the precincts of the fifteenth-century Duomo. The Altar of Ratchis was carved for Ratchis, Duke of Cividale and King of the Lombards at Pavia, who died as a Benedictine monk at Montecassino in 759; the reliefs of *Christ in Triumph* and the *Adoration of the Magi* are delicate and haunting. The other highlight is the Baptistry of Callisto, named after Callisto de Treviso, the first Patriarch of Aquileia to move to Cividale. He lived here from 730 to 756 and initiated the building of the patriarchal palace, the cathedral and this octagonal baptistry, which used to stand beside the cathedral. It's constructed from older Lombard fragments, the columns and capitals dating from the fifth century.

The **Duomo** itself (same hours as Museo Cristiano) houses a twelfth-century masterpiece of silversmithery: the *pala* (altarpiece) named after Pellegrino II, the patriarch who commissioned and donated it to the town; it depicts the Virgin seated between the archangels Michael and Gabriel, who are flanked by 25 saints and framed by saints, prophets and the patron himself.

Also in Piazza del Duomo is the **Museo Archeologico** (daily 9am–7.30pm; €2), which houses an excellent exhibition on the Lombards on the first floor, incorporating local finds including some beautiful gold *fibulae*. On the ground floor is a hotchpotch of late Roman and early Christian pieces, the highlight being a second-century mosaic of a wild-eyed head identified as Neptune, which reveals a subtle sense of perspective.

Just a stone's throw from the fifteenth-century Ponte del Diavolo, in Via Monastero Maggiore, is a cellar-like cavern called the **Ipogeo Celtico** (daily 8am–6pm; key from the bar *All' Ipogeo* on Via P. d'Aquileia if closed, donation requested). The hypogeum was probably used as a tomb for Celtic leaders between the fifth and second centuries BC, but there is still some dispute whether it's artificial or was merely adapted by its users. Either way, the spectral faces carved on the walls make it a most unsettling place.

Practicalities

The **tourist office** is just off Piazza Duomo at Via P. d'Aquileia 4 (Mon–Fri 9am–1pm & 3–6pm; closes 5pm in winter; ☎0432.731.461). Most visitors are day-trippers from Udine, but you could stay at Cividale's least expensive **hotel**, *Pomo d'Oro*, Piazza S. Giovanni 20 (☎0432.731.489; ❸), a little way out of town beyond the train station. More comfortable and with exceptional views is the *Castello*, Via del Castello 20 (☎0432.733.242; ❺), 1km north of town, on a hill above the road to Tarcento and Faedis. The restaurant is good, and on a sunny day its terrace is the best place for a leisurely lunch, well worth the taxi trip from the town centre if you don't feel like walking.

The town's smartest **café** is the *San Marco*, opposite the Duomo in the loggia of the sixteenth-century town hall – well placed for watching passers-by. There are good **restaurants**, but they tend to be expensive and largely aimed at tourists. *Zorutti*, Borgo di Ponte 9 (closed Mon), situated just across the Natisone by the Ponte del Diavolo, and the expensive *Alla Frasca*, Via de Rubeis 10 (closed Mon), one block north from Piazza Duomo, are good, the latter boasting a vast array of truffle and mushroom dishes. For Friulian specialities, *Al Fortino*, Via C. Alberto 46 (closed Mon), heading out of town from Piazza P. Diacono, and *Da Nardini*, Piazzetta de Portis 6 (closed Thurs), off C. Alberto, are good but touristy. A favourite with discerning locals is the excellent *Trattorie Dominissini*, at Stretta Stellini 18 (closed Mon) – take a right just short of the Ponte del Diavolo.

Palmanova

Once ranked as the strongest fortress in all Europe, **PALMANOVA** is a massive Venetian garrison town built in 1593 in the form of a nine-pointed star, its symmetrical streets converging on a large hexagonal piazza. Guided tours are conducted through the tunnels in the fortifications, and the **Civico Museo Storico**, at Borgo Udine 4 (daily except Wed 10am–noon & 4–7pm; €2.58), fills out the story further. Apart from this military curiosity, however, there is no real reason to visit the town.

Pordenone and around

Heading west to **Pordenone**, a workaday provincial capital best known for its favourite son, the architect of the same name, you might think there's little reason to get off the train, particularly with the attractions of the Veneto waiting just a few minutes away. But the frequency of trains – they run hourly from Udine to Venice – means that it is possible to hop on and off, and in the pleasantly low-key towns you'll have most of the sites all to yourself.

Codroipo

CODROIPO is a peaceful little town on the main railway line, midway between Udine and Pordenone, that would have nothing to recommend it were the huge **Villa Manin** not just 3km to the southeast, where it completely dominates the little village of Passariano. As the only public transport to the villa from Codroipo consists of three daily buses, the best way to get there is to walk: straight ahead from the station, and bear left in the main square.

Friuli's best-known country house, the Villa Manin was built in 1738 and later enlarged for Lodovico Manin, the pitiful last doge of Venice. In 1797 Napoleon stayed here when he signed the Treaty of Campoformio, which gave Venice to Austria. The greater part of the interior, much of it coated in run-of-the-mill frescoes, is impressive solely for its size, and is used as an exhibition centre in the summer; the arena created by its great frontal galleries, frequently compared to St Peter's Square in Rome, is used for open-air concerts. The villa contains a mediocre **museum** (Tues–Sun 9am–12.30pm & 3–6pm; free); more alluring is the ramshackle **park** (Tues–Sun 9am–6pm; free), where reedy ponds, birdsong and lichen-green statues create a congenial atmosphere for an afternoon doze.

Pordenone

The westernmost of Friuli-Venezia Giulia's three large towns, **PORDENONE** was once a thriving river port, but is now the region's main manufacturing centre, specializing in light industries, especially white goods, textiles and ceramics. As such, the town is hardly set up for tourism, with few specific sights, but the historic centre is carefully preserved and worth a visit. From the train station go straight ahead along Via Mazzini, then take the third right down **Corso Vittorio Emanuele** to the Gothic-Renaissance **Palazzo Comunale**.

Over the road from the palazzo is the **Museo Civico Ricchieri** (Tues–Fri 9.30am–12.30pm & 3–6pm; €1); it's predominantly a second-string collection of Venetian art, but it does have a clutch of works by the finest local artist, Giovanni Antonio de' Sacchis, better known simply as Il Pordenone. Many of the paintings in the museum were removed from the Duomo after the 1976 earthquake. The **Duomo** itself, mainly a late-Gothic structure, is notable only for its Romanesque campanile and some works by Pordenone – the first altarpiece on the right, and the two (not three, whatever the sign may say) least damaged frescoes belonging to the right-hand pillar at the end of the nave.

If you want to see more of Pordenone's work in his home town, search out the parish churches of Roraigrande, Torre, Villanova and Vallenoncello – for information about access, ask at the helpful **tourist office**, Corso Vittorio Emanuele 38 (Mon–Fri: May–Sept 9am–1pm & 3–6pm; Oct–April 9am–1pm & 3–5pm; ☎0434.21.912). The town's **hotels** tend to be business-oriented with no special charms. You might try the swish *Hotel Moderno*, Viale Martelli 1, a triumphant piece of Fascist-era architecture (☎0434.28.215, ⓦwww.eahotels.it /it/moderno; ❼), or the *Minerva*, Piazzale XX Settembre (☎0434.26.066, ⓦwww.hotelminerva.it; ❺), smart enough, if hardly home from home.

The choices for **eating** are much better. La *Vecia Osteria del Moro* (☎0434.28.658; closed Sun) is a beautiful old restaurant a step away from the Palazzo Comunale where you eat superbly for around €25 a head. For budget meals, *Da Zelina*, just behind the Palazzo, serves good pizza.

San Vito and Sesto Al Reghena

You really need a car to get around, but it is possible to make a short trip across country from Pordenone by bus, to take in a couple of sleepy local attractions. At least six **buses** run from Pordenone's Piazza Risorgimento to **SAN VITO AL TAGLIAMENTO**, which has lapsed into slumber since its medieval heyday, retaining a handsome piazza overlooked by a few minor *palazzi*, the thirteenth-century **Torre Raimonda** and a rather plain cathedral. The Torre Raimonda houses a dull **Museo Civico** (Mon–Fri 10am–noon & 3–6.30pm; free), but the main reason to visit is the **Museo Provinciale della Vita Contadina** (Tues–Sat 9am–12.30pm; free), which gives a sense of the everyday realities of traditional peasant life in Friuli. If you want to stay here there is a plush central HI hostel, *Europa*, Via P. Amalteo 39 (☎0434.876.898; €16.50).

Four **buses** from San Vito (more on weekdays) serve **SESTO AL REGHENA**, 10km south, the chief draw of the area. In the centre of the village, the fortified **Santa Maria in Sylvis** (June–Aug 8am–noon & 2.30–7pm; Sept–May daily 8am–7pm; free) is one of the oldest inhabited abbeys in the world, having been founded by the Lombards in the eighth century. The interior of the tenth-century chapel is heavily frescoed, though much is barely visible now; one exception is the unusual image of Christ crucified on the tree of Jesse – the tree of life – in the south transept. But the abbey's treasures are found in the crypt, which houses three important pieces of stonework: a carved Lombard chest known as St Anastia's Urn, a fourteenth-century altar panel in bas-relief and an extraordinary German pietà from the fifteenth century.

Gemona and the Carnia

The peak district in the north of Friuli is known as the **Carnia**, a name given to it by the Celtic tribes who settled here in the fourth century BC. If you're approaching the area by road or rail from Udine, you could make a stop at **GEMONA**, a little town that was largely destroyed in the 1976 earthquake, when almost 1000 people were killed and around 15,000 houses destroyed.

The historic centre, on the steep-sided hilltop, has been devotedly reconstructed and feels disconcertingly like a film set. The cathedral, once a marvellous Romanesque-Gothic specimen, is notable for the enormous fourteenth-century statue of St Christopher on the facade.

Gemona is a good staging post on the way into the Carnia, with a couple of fine and inexpensive **hotels**. The better one is the *Agli Amici*, a couple of kilometres out of the centre at Via G. Odo 44 (☎0432.981.013; ❷) – turn right outside the station then head along Via Piovega, following the yellow signs; the alternative is the *Si-Si*, Via Piovega 15 (☎0432.981.158, ⓦ www.hotelsisi.it; ❸). There's an excellent **trattoria** at the *Agli Amici*, while *Al Falomo*, Via Bini 11 (closed Wed), on the main street just down from the Duomo, has pizzas and an inexpensive tourist menu.

The Carnia proper begins north of Gemona, around the headwaters of the River Tagliamento, and comprises two distinct areas. To the west, hay meadows and orchards give way to the Alpine uplands and pastures of the **Alpi Carniche**, which share the culture of the eastern Dolomites. To the east, the high, sheer and often barren limestone peaks of the **Alpi Giulie** are divided by deep, forested valleys that radiate towards the borders with Austria in the north and Slovenia in the east. Both of these ranges are hardly known even within Italy, yet the area has a lot to offer the hiker and climber. Linguists should get a kick out of it too, as the villagers speak strange variants of *friulano*, German and Slovene.

If you want to plan a Carnia **walking trip** in advance, call in at the Udine office of the *Società Alpina Friulana*, Via Odorico da Pordenone 3 (daily 5–7.30pm plus Mon, Thurs, Fri 9–11pm; ☎0432.504.290, Ⓔsafcai@tin.it). A useful website on Carnia is ⓦ www.carnia.it.

Western Carnia

The lush valleys and flower-filled meadows of the **western Carnia** attract hundreds of walkers from June to September, when the numerous *rifugi* are open for business. One of the best bases for the northern part of this region is the village of **ARTA TERME**, about 35km north of Gemona – there are buses direct from Udine and services from Gemona, changing at Tolmezzo. There's cheap **accommodation** at the central *Miramonti* at Via Umberto I 22 (☎0433.920.76; ❷) and *Comune Rustico* at Via Fontana 14 (☎0433.922.18; ❷), with slightly dearer rooms at the *Gortani* at Via Umberto I 47 (☎0433.928.754; ❹). At **PIANO D'ARTA**, 1km away, you'll find another option – *Pensione Cozzi* at Via Marconi 13–15 (☎0433.920.39; ❷). The **tourist office**, Via Umberto I 15 (May–Sept Mon–Sat 9am–noon & 4–7pm, Sun 9am–12.30pm; Oct–April Mon–Sat 9am–noon & 3–6pm, Sun 9am–12.30pm; ☎0433.929.290), has masses of information on the beautifully secluded local refuges and on the fourteen waymarked *Club Alpino* **walks** in the surrounding highlands. If these treks sound too energetic, you could always just spend €4.65 on a visit to the **thermal pool** of the pagoda-style spa complex close to the tourist office.

Between **Tolmezzo**, where you're likely to have to change buses, and **FORNI DI SOPRA** is a thickly wooded area. After the rural peasantry moved out to the cities and the trees moved in, the area was designated the **Parco Naturale Dolomite Friulane**. The Forni **tourist office**, at Via Cadore 1 (Mon–Sat 9am–12.30pm & 3–5/6pm; July & Aug also Sun 9.30am–1pm; ☎0433.886.767), has lots of information on activities such as mountain biking, horse-riding and **hikes**. They can also help with *rifugi*, as well as provide lists of **accommodation** in town. The cluster of villages that comprises Forni lies about 70km northwest of Gemona, at the foot of the Passo di Mauria, the mountain pass between the Carnia and the eastern Dolomites. It really feels like the end of the road; seven buses arrive here direct from Udine every day but the services onwards are sporadic. In Forni itself, the *Albergo Centrale* (☎0433.88.062; ❸) is a good choice. The only **campsite** hereabouts is the *Tornerai* (☎0433.88.035), 2km away in **STINSANS**.

The Forni region is celebrated for its **food**, with many of its dishes incorporating some of the wild plants found in the vicinity. The mountain refuges are excellent places to sample these local specialities. Especially good is the nearby and spectacularly sited *Varmost* (June–Sept), on the slopes of Monte Crusicalas – there's a cable car in operation (June–Aug & Dec–March; €8 return ticket). In Forni itself, the places to eat are *Varmost* (closed Wed), with polenta and *frico* (a cheese and potato dish) or hearty sausages and goulash to eat in or take away, or the *Pizzeria Coopera* (no regular closing day); both are on the main road through town, Via Nazionale. Forni also has a branch of the *Club Alpino Italiano* on Via Vittorio Veneto, on the square behind the bus stop (July & Aug daily 5–7pm; Sept–June Fri, Sat & Sun 5–7pm), which organizes walks of varying degrees of difficulty.

Eastern Carnia

The place to head for in the **eastern Carnia** is **TARVISIO**, a small mountain resort 65km northeast of Gemona and just 7km from the Austrian border. Four buses a day come here from Udine, and eight trains – if you're coming by train, make sure you get out at Tarvisio Città station, perversely more central than Tarvisio Centrale.

The town receives a steady flow of Austrian visitors, who pour into town for the cheap Italian booze, the strange mix of *bierkeller* and café nightlife, and the first-rate ski slopes. More robust types set off from here on the Carnia's one high-level **long-distance trail**: the *Traversata Carnica*, which runs all the way to Sesto, just below the border. Information on this and all other healthy Tarvisio pursuits is available from the **tourist office**, right by the bus stop on Via Roma (summer Mon–Fri 9am–12.30pm & 3–7pm; ☎0428.2135, ⓦwww.tarvisiano.org). The nicest place **to stay** in Tarvisio is the *Albergo Valle Verde*, just outside the village on Via Priesnig (☎0428.2342; ❹) – it has a wonderful **restaurant** too, serving such specialities as *gnocchi* with smoked ricotta. There are a couple of cheaper places in Tarvisio itself: the *Al Cacciatore*, on the noisy Via Dante (☎0428.2082; ❷), and *Al Mangart* at Via Vittorio Veneto 39 (☎0428.2246; ❷).

For a taste of the splendours of the **Parco Regionale delle Alpi Giulie**, you could hop onto one of the summer buses to the **Laghi di Fusine** – two peaceful, wooded, blue-green lakes within 9km of Tarvisio. The smaller of the pair, and the nearer to Tarvisio, is **Lago Inferiore**, where there's **accommodation** at the *Capanna Edelweiss* (☎0428.61.050; ❷). However, the best walks are from **Lago Superiore**, a short distance up the road, from where there's a marked five-hour circular trail via the *Rifugio Zacchi* (☎0428.61.195; June–Sept).

Travel details

Trains

Trieste to: Gorizia (25 daily; 30min); Udine (25 daily; 1hr 20min); Venice (15 daily; 1hr 40min).
Udine to: Cividale (hourly; 20min); Conigliano (31 daily; 1hr 15min); Gemona (12 daily; 30min); Gorizia (13 daily; 30min); Palmanova (12 daily; 30min); Pordenone (28 daily; 30min); Tarvisio (11 daily, many including transfer to bus; 2hr); Trieste (13 daily; 1hr 10min); Venice (28 daily; 1hr 45min–2hr 15min).

Buses

Gemona to: Tolmezzo (2 daily; 30min).
Tolmezzo to: Arta Terme (10 daily; 20min); Forni di Sopra (7 daily; 1hr 20min).
Trieste to: Duino (hourly; 30min); Grado (14 daily; 1hr–1hr 30min); Lignano (1 daily in summer; 2hr); Monfalcone (for Aquileia and Grado; hourly; 45 min); Tolmezzo (1 daily; 3hr); Udine (27 daily; 1hr 15min).

Udine to: Aquileia (16 daily; 40min); Arta Terme (10 daily; 1hr); Cividale (20 daily; 20min); Codroipo (hourly; 20min); Pordenone (hourly; 40min); Forni di Sopra (8 daily; 1hr 20min); Gemona (9 daily; 50min); Grado (12 daily; 1hr); Lignano (12 daily; 1hr); Palmanova (16 daily; 20min); Pordenone (hourly; 40 min); Tarvisio (4 daily; 2hr 20min); Tolmezzo (14 daily; 50min); Trieste (9 daily; 1hr).

Ferries

Trieste to: Barcola (July to mid-Sept hourly; 30min); Duino (July–Sept 3 daily via Grignano and Sistiana; 1hr 45min); Grado (June–Sept Wed, Fri & Sun; 1 daily; 1hr); Lignano (Tues, Thurs & Sat 1 daily; 1hr 10min); Múggia (mid-June to Oct every 90min; 30min); CROATIA: Brioni (June–Sept Tues–Sun; 4hr); Rovigno (June–Sept Tues–Sun; 3hr 10min); SLOVENIA: Pirano (Wed, Fri & Sun; 1 daily; 1hr 50min).

Emilia-Romagna

CHAPTER 7 # Highlights

* **Ravenna's mosaics**
Unrivalled both in beauty
and preservation. **See
p.447**

* **Modena's Duomo** One
of the finest
Romanesque buildings
in Italy, with some mag-
nificent decoration inside
and out. **See p.427**

* **Brisighella festivals** This
medieval village is known
for its truffle, polenta and
olive festivals in autumn.
See p.441

* **Bologna food market** In
the gastronomic capital
of Italy everything begins
at the market, a bustling
and magical mix of sights
and smells. **See p.417**

* **Parma and its food**
Parma is inextricably
linked to two great deli-
cacies, Parma ham and
Parmesan cheese, both
of which can be sampled
in the city or in the surrounding region. **See
p.412**

* **Rocca Viscontea**
Northern Emilia
Romagna's most majes-
tic castle. **See p.438**

* **Hot chocolate** On a
cold day, there's no bet-
ter way to warm up than
with a mug of fine hot
chocolate in Bologna's
La Torinese bar. **See
p.423**

7

Emilia-Romagna

S et between Lombardy and Tuscany, and stretching from the Adriatic coast almost to the shores of the Mediterranean, **Emilia-Romagna** is the heartland of northern Italy. It is two provinces really: Emilia to the east and the Romagna to the west – the former Papal States, joined together after Unification. Before the papacy took charge in the area, it was a patchwork of ducal territories, ruled over by a handful of families – the Este in Ferrara and Modena, the Farnese in Piacenza and Parma, and lesser dynasties in Ravenna and Rimini – who created sparkling Renaissance courts, combining autocracy with patronage of the arts alongside a continual jockeying for power with the Church. Their castles and fortresses remain, preserved in small villages and towns with restored medieval centres which, apart from a few notable exceptions, are relatively off the tourist track, since many visitors are put off by the extreme weather (searingly hot in summer, close to freezing in winter), or are sidetracked by the more immediate pleasures of Tuscany and Umbria.

The region's landscape is a varied one, ranging from the foothills of the Apennine mountains in the south to the flat fields of the northern plain, the Pianura Padana, interrupted only by windbreaks of poplars, shimmering in the breeze. The area has grown wheat since Roman times, and nowadays its industry and agribusinesses are among Italy's most advanced – there are currently more pigs than people in the Po Valley. Emilia-Romagna remains one of the richest regions in Italy, holding some of the country's most successful small-scale, specialist industrial enterprises.

Carving a dead-straight route through the heart of Emilia-Romagna, from Piacenza to Rimini on the coast, the **Via Emilia** is a central and obvious reference point, a Roman military road constructed in 187 BC that was part of the medieval pilgrim's route to Rome, and the way east to Ravenna and Venice. The towns that grew up along here are among Emilia's most compelling. **Bologna**, the region's capital, is one of Italy's largest cities. Despite having one of the most beautifully preserved city centres in the country and some of its finest food, it has been relatively neglected by tourists, and most people pass straight through – definitely a mistake.

Bologna also gives easy access to places like **Modena** and **Parma** (each just an hour or so away by train): wealthy provincial towns that form the smug core of Emilia and hold some of its finest and most atmospheric architecture, as well as giving access to routes south into the **Apennines**. With a car you can dip into the foothills at will from any of these points, sampling local cuisine and joining in the festivals; and even by bus it's possible to get a taste of the area, which at its best can be very beautiful, not at all like the functional plain to the north. If you're a keen hiker, you might be tempted by the Grand Escursione Apenninica, a 25-day-long trek following the backbone of the range from refuge to refuge, and which can be accessed from the foothills south of **Reggio Emilia**.

The north of Emilia-Romagna is less interesting than the Via Emilia stretch, the Po disgorging into the Adriatic from its bleak **delta** (which it shares with the Veneto), a desolate region of marshland and lagoons that is mainly of appeal to birdwatchers. However, **Ferrara**, just half an hour north of Bologna, is one of the most important Renaissance centres in Italy, formerly under the tutelage of the Este family; and **Ravenna**, a short way east, preserves probably the finest set of Byzantine mosaics in the world in its churches and mausoleums. The coast south is an overdeveloped ribbon of settlement, although **Rimini**, at its southern end, provides a spark of interest, with its wild seaside strip concealing a surprisingly historic town centre.

Regional food and wine

Emilia-Romagna has a just reputation for harbouring the richest, most lavish food in Italy, with its most famous specialities of **parmesan** cheese (*parmigiano-reggiano*), egg pasta, **Parma ham** (generically known as *prosciutto di Parma*) and balsamic vinegar. Despite its current foodie connotations, **balsamic vinegar** started off as a cottage industry, with many Emilian families distilling and then re-distilling local wine to form a dark liquor that is then matured in wooden barrels for at least twelve years. Bologna is regarded as the gastronomic capital of Italy, and Emilia is the only true home of **pasta** in the North: often lovingly hand-made, the dough is formed into lasagne, tortellini stuffed with ricotta cheese and spinach, pumpkin or pork, and other fresh pastas served with *ragù* (meat sauce), cream sauces or simply with butter and parmesan – *alla parmigiana* usually denotes something cooked with parmesan. Modena and Parma specialize in *bollito misto* – boiled **meats**, such as flank of beef, trotters, tongue and spicy sausage; another Modenese dish is *zampone* – stuffed pig's trotter. Romagna's cuisine is more Southern in orientation. While ingredients such as butter, cheese, mushrooms, chestnuts and meat feature in Emilia, Romagna tends more towards onions, garlic and olive oil; the region is second only to Sicily for the amount of **fish** caught in its waters.

Emilia and Romagna only became one in 1947 – their **wines**, like their respective landscapes and people, are quite different. Emilia is synonymous with **Lambrusco**, but don't despair: buy only DOC Lambrusco and be amazed by the dark, often blackberry-coloured wine that foams into the glass and cuts through the fattiness of the typically meaty Emilian meal. There are four DOC zones for Lambrusco and you get a glimpse of three of them, all around Modena, from the Via Emilia, each supporting neat rows of high-trellised vines. The fourth zone extends across the plains and foothills of the Apennines, in the province of Reggio Emilia. Other wines to try, both whites, are Trebbianino Val Trebbia and Monterosso Val D'Arda, while the lively Malvasia (also white) from the Colli di Parma goes well with the celebrated local ham.

Heading east towards the Adriatic coast, you come to the Romagna, a flatter, drier province where the wines have less exuberance but more body and are dominated by Albana and Sangiovese. The sweeter versions of **Albana** are often more successful at bringing out the peachy, toasted-almond flavours of this white. The robust red of **Sangiovese**, from the hills around Ímola and Rimini, comes in various "weights" – all around the heavy mark. Much lighter is Cagnina di Romagna, which is best drunk young (within six months of harvest) and is particularly good with roast chestnuts.

None of this comes cheap, though: Emilia is a wealthy area that makes few concessions to tourists; the tone is, rather like Lombardy to the north, well mannered, well dressed and comfortable. If you need to economize, it would be a shame to stint when it comes to food, which is where the region excels.

Bologna

Emilia's capital, **BOLOGNA**, is a thriving city, whose light engineering and hi-tech industries have brought conspicuous wealth to the old brick palaces and porticoed streets and squares. It's well known for its food – undeniably the richest in the country – and for its politics. "Red Bologna" became the Italian Left's stronghold and spiritual home, having evolved out of the resistance movement to German occupation during World War II. Consequently, Bologna's train station was singled out by Fascist groups in 1980 for a bomb attack in Italy's worst postwar terrorist atrocity. A glassed-in jagged gash in the

BOLOGNA

▲ Youth Hostel   ▲ Ravenna   ▼ Florence

BERTI PICHAT

Porta S. Donato

Porta S. Vitale

VIALE G. B. ERCOLANI

Porta
Mascarella

Pinacoteca
Nazionale

Museo di
Astronomia

Palazzo
Università

Museo
Davia
Bargellini

Santa Maria
dei Servi

Palazzo
Poggi

Teatro
Comunale

Conservatorio
G.B. Martini

S. Stefano

S. Giacomo
Maggiore

British
Council

Museo
Ebraico

Due
Torri

Palazzo
Podestà

Museo Civico
Archeologico

Parco della
Montagnola

Metropolitana

Museo Civico
Medioevale

Palazzo
Re Enzo

Palazzo
dei Notai

S. Petronio

Porta
Galliera

Train Station ◄
Bus
Station

Palazzo
Comunale

S. Francesco

Porta
Sant'Isaia

Porta
San Felice

VIALE CARLO PEPOLI

VIALE GIOVANNI VICINI

▲ Airport

0   200 m

RESTAURANTS

N	Da Amedeo
C	Belle Arti
B	Da Bertino
J	Broccaindosso
A	C'entro
L	Cesari
K	Clorofilla
I	La Colombina
E	Fantoni
H	Trattoria Gianni
G	Grassilli
D	S. Lorenzo
M	Il Tari
F	Teresina

ACCOMMODATION

Accademia	2
Al Cappello Rosso	9
Centrale	7
Corona d'Oro	4
Marconi	1
Orologio	8
Panorama	6
Roma	10
Rossini	3
San Donato	5

station wall commemorates the tragedy in which 84 people died. In the 1998 mayoral elections, however, even Bologna joined the nationwide swing to the right, as voters became disillusioned with the Left's failure to handle rising crime and drugs. Observers also report a slight shift in attitudes, remarking that many Bolognese seem less open and friendly to outsiders than before and are more willing to blame their troubles on immigration.

After Venice, Bologna is certainly one of the best-looking cities in the country. The centre is startlingly medieval in plan, a jumble of red brick, tiled roofs and balconies radiating out from the great central square of Piazza Maggiore. There are enough monuments and curiosities for several days' leisured exploration, but Bologna is really enjoyable just for itself. Thanks to its university, which makes up one-fifth of the city's population of 500,000, there's always something happening – be it theatre, music, the city's strong summer festival, or just the café and bar scene, which is among northern Italy's most convivial. The only problem is expense; nightlife, particularly, can leave your wallet steamrolled, and finding a low-priced place to stay can be very difficult, especially during one of the major trade shows.

Arrival, information and city transport

Bologna's **train station** lies on the northern edge of the city centre at Piazza delle Medaglie d'Oro, near Porta Galliera; all long-distance buses terminate at the **bus station**, next door on Piazza XX Settembre. Bus #25 connects the train station and Piazza del Nettuno, the city centre. Bologna's **Marconi airport** (℡051.647.9615, ⓦwww.bologna-airport.it) lies northwest of town, linked to the centre and the train station by the Aerobus (€4.50; buy tickets on board), which runs approximately every twenty minutes and takes around twenty-five minutes if the traffic is light. Taxis to the centre cost around €15. The city's "other" airport is at **Forlí** (℡0541.786.233, ⓦwww.forli-airport.it), 60km southeast. This is where Ryanair flights land, and special buses are on hand to take you to Bologna; you can buy tickets on board (€10; 75min).

Bologna's main **tourist office** is in the Palazzo del Podestà at Piazza Maggiore 1 (Mon–Sat 8.30am–7pm, Sun 8.30am–2pm; ℡051.246.541, ⓦwww.comune.bologna.it/bolognaturismo); there are also offices at Marconi airport (daily 8am–8pm; ℡051.647.2036) and the train station (Mon–Sat 9am–7pm; ℡051.251.947).

Once you're in the city centre, the best way to **get around** is on foot: a leisurely stroll downtown beneath some of the 25 miles of porticoes that link together the compact *centro storico* is most appealing. **Buses** (ⓦwww.atc.bo.it) are fast and frequent; tickets cost €0.90 each from *tabacchi*, newsstands or ticket machines and are valid on as many buses as you like within one hour. If you plan to make frequent use of them it might be worth buying a Citypass for €6.20, valid for eight journeys. You can get information from the booth at the junction of Via Delle Lame and Via G. Marconi (daily 7am–8pm; ℡051.290.290). For **taxis**, call ℡051.372.727 or 051.534.141.

Accommodation

In terms of **places to stay**, Bologna is not geared up for tourists, least of all for those travelling on a tight budget: there are only a few cheap **hotels**, and there is no handily placed campsite. Bologna's high season is during trade fairs (March to early May & Sept–Dec) when hotel prices can almost double, whereas in July and August prices are far lower. The price codes here refer to summer prices. The tourist offices have hotel lists, and the CST, the Centre for

Tourist Services, next to the tourist office desk at Piazza Maggiore 6 (Mon–Sat 10am–2pm & 3–7pm, Sun 10am–2pm; ☎051.648.7607 or 800.856.065 tollfree, ⊛www.cst.bo.it), can book rooms for you.

Hotels

Accademia Via Belle Arti 6 ☎051.232.318, ⓕ051.263.590, ⊛www.hotelaccademia.it. In the heart of the university quarter, this large two-star hotel has modest-sized doubles, some with balconies. Prices fall €20 in summer as there is no air-conditioning. ❺

Al Cappello Rosso Via de' Fusari 9 ☎051.261.891, ⓕ051.227.179, ⊛www.alcappellorosso.it. Comfy and unfussy furnishings with efficient four-star luxury right in the heart of the centre. ❽–❾

Centrale Via della Zecca 2 ☎051.225.114, ⓕ051.235.162. Good-value two-star hotel in the heart of the city, with great views from the top floor. The staff are friendly and the spacious rooms come with or without bathrooms. ❹

Corona d'Oro Via Oberdan 12 ☎051.236.456, ⓕ051.262.279, ⊛www.cnc.it/bologna. Four-star opulence in an old palazzo close to the twin towers. Magnificent Art Nouveau hall and medieval ceilings. Closed mid-July to mid-August. ❾

Marconi Via Marconi 18 ☎051.262.832. Although the stairway up to this friendly one-star on the first floor of a modern block is not particularly inviting, inside the rooms are clean and recently refurbished, if basic. It's on a major road, so you might want to ask for a room at the back. No credit cards. ❸

Orologio Via IV Novembre 10 ☎051.231.253, ⓕ051.260.552, ⊛www.cnc.it/bologna. Overlooking a corner of Piazza Maggiore, this is the most appealing of Bologna's hotels, with an air of understated luxury, well-equipped rooms and helpful staff. Free Internet access. Book well in advance. ❽

Panorama Via Livraghi 1 ☎051.221.802, ⓕ051.266.360, ⓔpanorama.hotel@libero.it. Just off Ugo Bassi (no sign), offering a range of accommodation, from three- and four-bedded rooms to ordinary doubles – all sharing clean and pleasant bathrooms down the corridor. Helpful owners. ❸

Roma Via D'Azeglio 9 ☎051.226.322, ⓕ051.239.909, ⊛www.hotelroma.biz. On one of the centre's major pedestrian arteries, friendly, quiet and refined, though the heavily patterned floral wallpaper won't be to everyone's taste. ❻

Rossini Via Bibiena 11 ☎051.237.716, ⓕ051.268.035. In the student quarter, just off Piazza Verdi, a very friendly two-star hotel with spacious, comfortable rooms. ❸

San Donato Via Zamboni 16 ☎051.235.395, ⓕ051.230.547, ⊛www.bestwestern.it/sandonato_bo. Even though the rooms don't quite match the elegance of the first-floor lobby, this is a very comfortable four-star. The rooms overlooking the square have fabulous views of the two towers, and there is a breakfast terrace. ❽–❾

Hostel

The **San Sisto-Due Torri**, Via Viadagola 5 and 14 (☎051.501.810), is the city's official youth hostel, 6km outside the centre of town. To get to the hostel take bus #93 from Via Marconi (last service 10.45pm) or #301 from the bus station on Sundays. It opens at 5pm and there's a curfew at 11.30pm. Beds are €12 per head in a dorm and €14 per head in a double room. It's a busy place and you need to book in advance – though the hassled staff are not always very helpful.

Outside Bologna

Thirty minutes by car northeast of Bologna, just outside the town of Budrio, is the *Villa Montefano*, Via Volpino 13 (☎051.692.9587, ⊛www.montefano.com; ❶), a seventeenth-century country villa that's now best described as a residential cultural centre – the brainchild of a young American, Clark Lawrence. Grand, frescoed rooms can accommodate up to eight guests, family-style; everyone pitches in with cleaning and cooking duties. There's an ongoing cultural programme, known throughout the area, of art exhibitions, classical and jazz concerts and readings, plus impromptu parties and other events that keep the atmosphere lively. A stimulating mix of Italians and foreigners, it makes an excellent base from which to explore Ferrara, Bologna and Ravenna.

The City

Bologna's city centre is quite compact, and most sights are within the main ring road. One of Bologna's main thoroughfares, lined with cinemas and bars and always busy, is **Via dell'Indipendenza**, which runs from the train station to the centre, finishing up at the linked central squares of **Piazza Maggiore** and **Piazza del Nettuno**. West of here is the commercial district, bordered by the office blocks of Via G. Marconi, and in the east lies the university quarter. The one thing you will notice quickly is how well preserved the central area actually is, and although this can be frustrating, too – it's not unusual to find notices on churches suggesting you return in a year's time while restoration is carried out – the reward is a city centre that is a joy to stroll around. Above all you'll notice the famous medieval, ochre-coloured porticoes lining every street into the city centre. Built high enough to accommodate people on horseback, they make a vivid first impression, especially at night, while by day they provide an unofficial catwalk for Bologna's well-turned-out residents.

Piazza Maggiore, Piazza del Nettuno and around

Piazza Maggiore and the adjacent **Piazza del Nettuno** make up the notional pulse of the city and are the obvious area to make for first. The squares are a quintessentially social place, and they host, as you might expect, the city's principal secular and religious buildings: the church of San Petronio, Palazzo Re Enzo and Palazzo Comunale – all impressive for their bulk alone, with heavy studded doors and walls pitted with holes from the original scaffolding.

At the centre of Piazza del Nettuno, the **Neptune Fountain** is a symbol of the city, styled in extravagant fashion by Giambologna in 1566. Across the square, the **Palazzo Re Enzo** takes its name from its time as the prison-home of Enzo, king of Sicily, confined here by papal supporters for two decades after the Battle of Fossalta in 1249. If the building looks rather dour, it's partly thanks to the controversial architect Alfonso Rubbiani, who restored (purists would say rebuilt) many of Bologna's medieval structures in the early part of the last century. Next door to the Palazzo Re Enzo, **Palazzo Podestà** fills the northern side of Piazza Maggiore, built at the behest of the Bentivoglio clan, who ruled the city during the fifteenth century, before papal rule was re-established. On the piazza's western edge, the **Palazzo Comunale** gives some indication of the political shifts in power, its facade adorned by a huge statue of Pope Gregory XIII as an affirmation of papal authority. Through a small courtyard, stairs in the right-hand corner (there is also a lift if you go straight ahead) lead to a magnificent ceremonial hall with every inch covered in frescoes. Occasional free chamber concerts are held in the adjoining rooms, and tickets for the palazzo's two art collections are sold here: the **Collezioni Comunali d'Arte** (Tues–Sat 9am–6.30pm, Sun 10am–6.30pm; €4), galleries of ornate furniture and paintings which include works by Vitale da Bologna, Simone dei Crocefessi and others of the Bolognese School; and the **Museo Morandi** (Tues–Sun 10am–6pm; ⓦ www.museomorandi.it; €4), devoted to the life

---

Bologna museum card

You don't need to do much sightseeing to make the *Carta Bologna dei Musei* worthwhile: available for either one (€6) or three days (€8), the pass grants free access to the city's main museums (though not the Due Torri) and reduced entry into the Pinoteca Nazionale and the Museo Ebraico. You can buy the card at tourist offices or at museums.

and works of one of Italy's most important twentieth-century painters. As well as the two hundred works on display, a faithful reconstruction of Morandi's studio offers a fascinating glimpse into his working methods.

On the southern side of Piazza Maggiore stands the church of **San Petronio**, one of the finest Gothic brick buildings in Italy, an enormous structure that was originally intended to have been larger than St Peter's in Rome, but money and land for the side aisle were diverted by the pope's man in Bologna towards a new university, and the architect Antonio di Vicenzo's plans had to be modified. You can see the beginnings of the planned aisles on both sides of the building: when they stopped work they sliced through the window arches and left only the bottom third of the facade decorated with the marble geometric patterns intended to cover the whole. There are models of what the church was supposed to look like in the museum (daily except Tues 10am–12.30pm; free). Notwithstanding its curtailment, San Petronio is a fine example of late fourteenth-century architecture. Above the central portal is a beautiful carving of *Madonna and Child* by visiting artist Jacopo della Quercia. Within, the side chapels contain a host of treasures; the fourth chapel on the north aisle, the Cappella Bolognini, features remarkable frescoes by Giovanni da Modena and a gilded altarpiece by Jacopo di Paolo. The most unusual feature is the astronomical clock – a long brass meridian line set at an angle across the floor, with a hole left in the roof for the sun to shine through onto the right spot.

The ornately decorated building next door to San Petronio is the Palazzo dei Notai ("Notaries"), a fourteenth-century reminder that it was Bologna's legal scholars who, in the Middle Ages, laid the first foundations of contemporary European law. In the opposite direction, across Via dell'Archiginnasio from San Petronio, the **Palazzo dei Banchi** is more of a set-piece than a palazzo, basically a facade designed by the Renaissance architect Vignola to unify a set of medieval houses that didn't really fit with the rest of the square. Adjacent, the **Museo Civico Archeologico** (Tues–Sat 9am–6.30pm, Sun 10am–6.30pm; €4) is rather stuffy, but has good displays of Egyptian and Roman antiquities, and an Etruscan section that is one of the best outside Lazio, with finds drawn from the settlement of Felsina, which predated Bologna; there are reliefs from tombs, vases and a bronze *situla*, richly decorated, from the fifth century BC. Frustratingly though, there is no information in English about any of the exhibits or their Etruscan background.

Just north of the museum, **Via Clavature** – together with nearby Via Pescerie Vecchie and Via Draperie – is home to a grouping of market stalls and shops that makes for one of the city's most enticing sights and provides proof positive of Bologna's gourmet proclivities. In autumn especially, the market is a visual and aural feast, with fat porcini mushrooms, truffles in baskets of rice, thick rolls of mortadella, hanging pheasants, ducks and hares, and skinned frogs by the kilo. The church of **Santa Maria della Vita**, in Via Clavature, is worth a look for its outstanding pietà by Nicola dell'Arca – seven life-sized terracotta figures that are among the most dramatic examples of Renaissance sculpture you'll see.

Down the street in the other direction, Bologna's old university – the **Archiginnasio** – was founded at more or less the same time as Piazza Maggiore was laid out, predating the rest of Europe's universities, although it didn't get a special building until 1565, when Antonio Morandi was commissioned to construct the present building on the site until then reserved for San Petronio. Centralizing the university on one site was a way of maintaining control over students at a time when the Church felt particularly threatened by the

Reformation. You can wander freely into the main courtyard, covered with the coats of arms of its more famous graduates, and perhaps even attend a lecture – Umberto Eco lectures here on semiotics. In the mornings it's also possible to visit the main upstairs **library**, and, most interestingly, the **Teatro Anatomico** (Mon–Sat 9am–1pm; free), the original medical faculty dissection theatre. Tiers of seats surround an extraordinary professor's chair, covered with a canopy supported by figures known as *gli spellati* – "the skinned ones". Not many dissections went on, owing to prohibitions of the Church, but when they did (usually around carnival time), artists and the general public used to turn up as much for the social occasion as for studying the body.

Outside the old university, **Piazza Galvani** remembers the physicist Luigi Galvani with a statue. One of Bologna's more successful scientists, Galvani discovered electrical currents in animals, thereby lending his name to the English language in the word "galvanize". A few minutes south, down Via Garibaldi, is **Piazza San Domenico**, with its strange canopied tombs holding the bones of medieval law scholars. Bologna was instrumental in sorting out wrangles between the pope and the Holy Roman emperor in the tenth and eleventh centuries, earning itself the title of "La Dotta" (The Learned) and forming the basis for the university's prominent law faculties. The church of **San Domenico** was built in 1251 to house the relics of St Dominic, which were placed in the so-called *Arca di San Domenico*: a fifteenth-century work that was ostensibly the creation of Nicola Pisano – though in reality many artists contributed to it. Pisano and his pupils were responsible for the reliefs illustrating the saint's life; the statues on top were the work of Pisano himself; Nicola dell'Arca was responsible for the canopy (this was the work that earned him his name); and the short-haired angel and figures of saints Proculus, with a cloak over his shoulder, and Petronius, holding the model of the city, were the work of a very young Michelangelo. While you're in the church, try also to see the **Museo di San Domenico** (Mon 3–5pm, Tues–Sat 10am–12.30pm & 3–5pm; free) displaying a very fine polychrome terracotta bust of St Dominic by Nicolò dell'Arca along with paintings, reliquaries and vestments, and, beyond, the intricately inlaid mid-sixteenth-century choir stalls.

Just to the east of San Domenico, on a little hill, stands **San Giovanni in Monte**, worth a visit for its stunning collection of paintings from the Bolognese school. Built on an ancient temple, the present structure dates from the thirteenth to fifteenth centuries. The facade's great portal is by Domenico Berardi, and the harmonious interior features unusual partly frescoed columns, a fifteenth-century stained glass tondo, inlaid choir stalls, and a chapel decorated by Guercino.

The university quarter

Bordered by Via Oberdan to the west and Strada Maggiore to the south, the eastern section of Bologna's *centro storico* preserves many of the older **university** departments, housed for the most part in large seventeenth- and eighteenth-century palaces. This is perhaps the pleasantest part of the city to while away the day – or night – amid a concentration of low-budget bars, restaurants and shops aimed at the student population. It is also the place to scour for information on events around town: posters plaster the walls along Via Zamboni and the lanes off it – Via delle Moline, Via Belle Arti, Via Mentana – and the bars and cafés are often promoting some happening or other. One note of warning, though: there's been a spate of drug-related crime in the area recently and while the main streets are safe enough, it's best to avoid the dark side streets at night.

Via Rizzoli leads into the district from Piazza Maggiore, ending up at Piazza di Porta Ravegnana, where the **Torre degli Asinelli** (daily 9am–6pm; closes 5pm in winter; €3), and the perilously leaning **Torre Garisenda** next to it, are together known as the **Due Torri**, the only two remaining of literally hundreds of towers that were scattered across the city during the Middle Ages. The former makes a good place from which to get an overview of the city centre and beyond, out over the red-tiled roofs across the hazy, flat plains and southern hills beyond.

Southeast of the Due Torri, Via Santo Stefano leads down to its medieval gateway, past a complex of four – but originally seven – churches, collectively known as **Santo Stefano**. It's an attractive complex set in a wide piazza at the conjunction of several narrow porticoed streets. Three of the churches face on to the piazza, of which the striking polygonal church of **San Sepolcro** (daily 9am–noon & 3–6pm; free), reached through the church of **Crocifisso**, is about the most interesting. The basin in its courtyard, called "Pilate's Bowl", dates from the eighth century, while on the inside the bones of St Petronius, held in a tomb modelled on the church of the holy sepulchre in Jerusalem, provide a macabre focus typical of the relic-obsessed Middle Ages. A doorway leads from here through to **Santi Vitale e Agricola**, Bologna's oldest church, built from discarded Roman fragments in the fifth century, while the fourth church, the **Trinità**, lies across the courtyard and is home to a small museum (same times; free) containing a reliquary of St Petronius, a thirteenth-century fresco of the *Massacre of the Innocents*, and a handful of later paintings.

From here, follow Via Gerusalemme up to Strada Maggiore, where, a little way down on the right, stands **Santa Maria dei Servi** dating from 1386 and arguably Bologna's most elegant church, with a beautiful portico and fourteenth-century ceiling frescoes by Vitale da Bologna – a rare chance to see the work of the so-called "father" of Bolognese painting *in situ*. A chapel also holds a *Madonna Enthroned* by Cimabue. Across Strada Maggiore, Piazza Aldrovandi has a daily street market and also the **Museo Davia Bargellini** (Tues–Sun 9am–1pm; free), made up of the eclectic art collection of the Davia family, as well as textiles, glassware and furniture; the entrance is on Strada Maggiore. Further north from here, Via Petroni leads through to **Piazza Verdi**, at the heart of the university district. On summer evenings it draws the crowds with its open-air bars and live music. **Via Zamboni** bisects Piazza Verdi, around and along which are many of the old palaces housing various parts of the university. A large number of these buildings were decorated by members of the Bolognese academies, which were prominent in Italian art after 1600. Tibaldi, better known as an architect, turned his hand to fresco in the main building, the **Palazzo Poggi** at no. 33, where you'll find many of the university's specialist museums (Mon–Fri 9am–5.30pm, Sat & Sun 9am–6.30pm, but times frequently change – check on ☏051.209.9602, ⓦwww.unibo.it/musei-universitari; all free). Tibaldi's fresco of Ulysses here was influenced by Michelangelo's Sistine Chapel and has played a part in the well-publicized row over the latter's restoration, with art historians using Tibaldi's fresco as proof that they have got Michelangelo's colours right. On the fourth floor of the building, the fascinating 300-year-old **Specola**, or observatory, draws most people here, its small **Museo di Astronomia** (times as above; free) home to a number of eighteenth-century instruments and a frescoed map of the constellations – painted just seventy years after Galileo was imprisoned for his heretical statements about the cosmos.

The **Museo di Anatomia Umana**, at Via Zamboni 35 (Mon–Fri 9am–5pm; free), might seem an odd place to visit, but it would be a shame to leave Bologna without seeing its highly idiosyncratic (and beautiful) **waxworks**.

These were used until the nineteenth century for medical demonstration, and they are as startling as any art or sculpture in the city. There were two Italian schools of waxworks: the Florentine method, where they used limbs, organs and bones to make moulds to cast the wax; and the Bolognese, where everything was sculpted, even tiny veins and capillaries, which were rolled like Plasticine. The boundaries between "art" and "science" were not rigidly drawn, and in Bologna in the early eighteenth century the workshops of Anna Morandi Mazzolini and Ercole Lelli turned out figures that were much more than just clinical aids. Mazzolini, for example, created a self-portrait in the midst of a brain dissection, pulling back a scalp with wispy hairs attached; other figures, unnervingly displayed in glass cases, are modelled like classical statues, one carrying a sickle, the other a scythe.

Close by, the collection of paintings in the **Pinacoteca Nazionale** at Via Belle Arti 56 (Tues–Sun 9am–7pm; €4, or €3 with Bologna Card) may provide some light relief, concentrating mainly on the work of Bolognese artists. There are canvases by the fourteenth-century painter Vitale da Bologna, later works by Francia and Tibaldi, and paintings from the city's most productive artistic period, the early seventeenth century, when Annibale and Agostino Carracci, Guido Reni and Guercino ("The Cross-eyed") were active here.

Back towards the centre down Via Zamboni, in Piazza Rossini, is the church of **San Giacomo Maggiore**, a Romanesque structure begun in 1267 and enlarged over the centuries. The target here is the Bentivoglio Chapel, decorated with funds provided by one Annibale Bentivoglio to celebrate the family's victory in a local feud in 1488. Lorenzo Costa painted frescoes of the *Apocalypse*, the *Triumph of Death* and a *Madonna Enthroned* as well as of the Bentivoglio family – a deceptively pious-looking lot, captured in what was a fairly innovative picture in its time for the careful characterizations of its patrons. Further frescoes by Costa, along with Francesco Francia, decorate the **Oratorio di Santa Cecilia**; they show episodes from the lives of saints Cecilia and Valerian. And there's a tomb of Anton Galeazzo Bentivoglio by Quercia opposite the chapel – one of the artist's best works.

Piazza Rossini is named after the nineteenth-century composer, who studied at the **Conservatorio G.B. Martini** on the square. The library here is among the most important music libraries in Europe; some of the original manuscripts are on display to the public along with a few paintings. On the other side of Via Zamboni at Via Valdonica 1/5 is the **Museo Ebraico** (Sun–Thurs 10am–6pm, Fri 10am–4pm; Ⓦ www.museoebraicobo.it; €4.15 or €2.15 with Bologna Card). Situated in the old Jewish ghetto, it's the best Jewish museum in the province and presents the history of the once thriving Jewish community in Emilia-Romagna.

The Metropolitana, Museo Civico and the basilica of San Francesco

There's much less of interest to the north and west of Bologna's central piazzas. The city's cathedral, the **Metropolitana di San Pietro**, is on the right out of Piazza del Nettuno, two blocks down Via dell'Indipendenza from Piazza del Nettuno. Originally a tenth-century building, it's been rebuilt many times and is these days more enjoyable for its stately atmosphere than any particular features. The **Museo Civico Medioevale e dal Rinascimento** (Tues–Sat 9am–6.30pm, Sun 10am–6.30pm; €4), opposite, is of more interest, housed in the Renaissance Palazzo Fava at Via Manzoni 4 and decorated with frescoes by Carracci and members of the Bolognese School depicting the *History of Europa*, *Jason's Feats* and scenes from the *Aeneid*. The museum collection itself includes bits of armour, ceramics, numerous tombs and busts of various popes and other dignitaries, and a *Madonna and SS* by Jacopo della Quercia.

West of Piazza del Nettuno, at the end of Via Ugo Bassi, the basilica of **San Francesco** (daily 6.30am–noon & 3–7pm) is a huge Gothic brick pile supported by flying buttresses that was heavily restored in the 1920s and partly rebuilt after World War II. Inside there are a beautiful and very ornate altarpiece from 1392 and a pleasant cloister.

Eating, drinking and entertainment

Eating and **drinking** are the mainstays of Bolognese social life. Eating especially is important to the Bolognese: the city is known as "La Grassa" ("The Fat"), the result of a rich culinary tradition, and the emphasis on food here can be taken to extremes. People travel a long way to eat at the top restaurants, which are said to be the best in Italy, and even the simplest restaurants the many *osterie* often serve dishes of a very high standard. Certainly the lack of a fancy menu or elaborate decor shouldn't rule out further investigation, and you should endeavour to try some local specialities while you're here. Handmade lasagne, tagliatelle and tortellini (small, shaped pasta with a stuffing of ham, sausage, chopped chicken, pork and veal, eggs, nutmeg and parmesan) are excellent and regarded with great affection by residents of Bologna, to the extent that elaborate stories explain their origin: the first tortellini are said to have been made by a Bolognese innkeeper trying to re-create the beauty of Venus's navel.

Bologna has any number of chic **bars** if all you want to do is drink, most notably on and around Via Zamboni, in the student quarter. It also has a good selection of **osterie**, which have been the mainstay of Bolognese **nightlife** for several hundred years – pub-like places, open late, where you go more to drink than eat, though you can get excellent snacky (if sometimes pricey) food. The Bolognese like to go out late, around 10.30 or 11pm, and most osterie stay open until around 2am. The city also has a good variety of **clubs**, with music to suit most tastes: the more established places are mentioned on p.423, but check for details of what's happening, and look out for posters advertising events around the university quarter and Piazza Verdi in particular. **Open-air raves** are held in summer – the best known being "Made in Bo" (Ⓦ www.madeinbo.it), which costs €13 and takes place north of the centre off Via Stalingrado in the area around the Fiera and the Parco di Nord; take bus #25 from the station.

As for the **arts and cultural attractions**, the city has also tried to curb the general August exodus by mounting a summer arts festival, called Viva Bologna, with concerts and videos at night in the courtyards of the civic buildings. Ferragosto is an especially good time to be here, when everyone takes to the hills for all-night revelry in one of the parks outside town. One of the main venues for opera and classical music is the Teatro Comunale on Piazza Verdi (Ⓦ www.comunalebologna.it).

For **information** the main tourist office in Piazza Maggiore has lists of nightclubs, osterie and forthcoming events. Bologna currently lacks a regular "what's on" guide of its own, but for rock concerts and venues, you could try asking at the Rock Shop, Via Mazzini 146, or looking in the weekly supplement of the national newspaper *La Repubblica*. You can find the magazine *Talk About*, which lists some of the main goings-on around town, in the tourist office – ask for it if it is not on display – or the British Council has copies for reference in its library at Strada Maggiore 19 (Mon, Thurs, Sat 10.30am–12.30pm & Mon–Thurs 5–8pm; ☎051.225.142).

Restaurants

Da Amedeo Via Saragozza 88. A good place to try *tortellini in brodo* (in clear broth) and other Emilian specialities, including game. The vegetable dishes and desserts are reliable. Closed Sat.

Belle Arti Via Belle Arti 14. A noisy, studenty place with friendly service and extra-large pizzas. Closed Wed.

Da Bertino Via Delle Lame 55. The place to come for no-nonsense Bolognese peasant-style cooking. *Bollito* and *arrosto* (boiled and roast meats) are brought to your table on a metal trolley, accompanied by a range of traditional relishes. Open till 10.30pm; closed Mon eve & Sun.

Broccaindosso Via Broccaindosso 7a ☎051.234.153. There's little in the way of signs to alert you to the existence of this friendly and eccentric restaurant east of the centre, and you'll need to ring a bell to get in. The waiters bring no menu, just a succession of fantastic antipasti and desserts; you can have pasta too, if you need it. The uninitiated throw themselves on the first dishes they get without realizing there is more to come: the art is definitely to pace yourself. Very cheap. Worth booking. Open 8.30pm–3am; closed Sun.

C'entro Via dell'Indipendenza 45. Large self-service restaurant midway between the station and the centre with a wide range of cheap quality food, including as much salad as you can pile onto your plate. Tables outside in summer. Open till 9pm. Closed Sun.

Cesari Via dé Carbonesi 8 ☎051.237.710. One of Bologna's perennial top choices for quality Emilian cuisine and friendly service. Open till 10.30pm; closed Sun.

Clorofilla Strada Maggiore 64c. A brightly lit, almost sterile, non-smoking vegetarian restaurant – just the place if the "fat of Bologna" has been weighing you down. Open till 11pm; closed Sun.

La Colombina Vicolo Colombina 5 ☎051.231.706. Very attractive and fairly expensive, but excellent value if you're looking for authentic Bolognese specialities. Open till 11pm; closed Tues.

Fantoni Via del Pratello 11. Family-style Bolognese food on one of the oldest streets in the city, packed with locals at lunchtime. Small terrace in the street. Amazing value for money. Closed Sun eve & Mon.

Trattoria Gianni Via Clavature 18 ☎051.229.434. One of the top options in Bologna: try the ultra-traditional *bolliti*, a variety of meats boiled in the Emilian way. Moderate prices. Closed Sun eve & Mon.

Grassilli Via del Luzzo 3 ☎051.222.961. Semes Emilian dishes that have been adapted with flair to suit modern tastes, accompanied by exceptionally good service. An experience to remember, though you'll definitely need to book ahead. Closed Wed.

S. Lorenzo Via S. Lorenzo 4. Convenient self-service cafeteria/restaurant off Via Marconi, serving traditional Bolognese dishes. Closed Sat eve.

Il Tarì Via Collegio di Spagna 13. A trattoria and pizzeria featuring fish dishes, such as delicious *spaghetti allo scoglio* – with seafood and *galletti* mushrooms. Enormous servings of everything, salads too. Open till midnight. Closed Thurs.

Teresina Via Oberdan 4 ☎051.228.985. A great family-run restaurant serving regional dishes as well as very good southern Italian food, including fish (€30–35 for a full meal), with tables outside in summer. Worth booking. Cash only. Open till 10.30pm; closed Sun.

Osterie

Marione Via San Felice 137. Close to the city gate, an old, smoky and dark osteria, with good wine and snacks, served under the watchful eye of Mario. Open till 2am; closed Wed.

Da Matusel Via Bertoloni 2. Close by the university, a popular, well lit and noisy place with reasonably priced food. Open till 1am. Closed Sun.

Del Montesino Via del Pratello 74b. One of many bars in this lively street, a chatty, convivial place serving snacks, including substantial, southern-inspired salads and good *crostini* (various toppings spread on toasted bread). The house wine is very drinkable, though there are other, more expensive options. Closed Mon.

Del Moretto Via San Mamolo 5. One of Bologna's best osterie, situated just outside Porto San Mamolo. Large and lively, with a mixture of young and old, especially favoured by musicians and artists. Open evenings only 7.30pm–3am; closed Sun.

Dell'Orsa Via Mentana 1f. Has live jazz during the winter. Stick with the bruschetta; the other dishes are fairly pricey. Closed Mon.

Senzanome Via Senzanome 42a. Off Via Saragozza, this was a favourite drinking place for cart drivers in the seventeenth century when the osteria was famed for its sausage – made, it is claimed, from bulls' testicles. The place now serves good home-made pasta and has a wide choice of beers and wines. Open evenings only; closed Mon.

Snacks, bars, cafés and ice cream

Altero Via dell'Indipendenza 33; Via Ugo Bassi 10. The best place for pizza by the slice. Halfway between the centre and the station. Open till 1am daily.

Bolognetti Vicolo Bolognetti 2. More of an open-air bar than a club, set in the middle of an impressive cloister. Open summer only, but a great place to while away balmy evenings.

Caffè Commercianti Strada Maggiore 23c. Atmospheric bar that serves everything from coffee and ice cream to aperitifs. Open till 10pm; closed Sun.

Clauricane Irish Pub Via Zamboni 18. Perhaps the largest bar in town, very popular with students at the university up the road, with punters spilling out onto the street on hot evenings. Also serves food. Open daily till 3am.

Enoteca des Arts Via San Felice 9. Tiny, dark and atmospheric bar serving cheap, local wine. Open Mon–Sat 4.30pm–2am.

Enoteca Italiana Via Marsala 2b. Just off Via dell'Indipendenza, offering a range of excellent Italian wines and good snacks. Open till 8pm, closed Sun.

Faccioli Via Altabella 15b. It's been described as a discreet library of a bar, with bottles, not books, lining the walls. Very pleasant place to taste wines and nibble snacks in the shadow of one of the city's towers. Open from 6pm only; closed Sun, & Sat too in July & August.

Gianni Via Montegrappa 11. Fine spot to eat some of the best ice cream in town with tables outside in the summer. Open noon–1am.

Impero Via dell'Indipendenza 39. Excellent croissants and pastries for breakfast – and later. Open till 8.30pm; closed Mon.

Il Piccolo Bar Piazza Verdi. Famous student hang-out open later than most other bars.

Pino Via Castiglione 65. The main branch of Bologna's best-known ice cream chain (closed Sun). You can also taste them at no. 7, much closer to the centre.

Rosa Rose bistrot Via Clavature 18b. A chic bar with tables outside and an extensive range of free snacks that you can graze from at the bar, but also serves meals. Popular with Bologna's trendy crowd at *aperitivo* hour. Part of the expanding Rosa Rose chain that includes a good café-bar on Piazza Maggiore. Closed Tues.

San Daniele bistrot Via Altabella 3a. Excellent wines, cheese and hams and generally good snacks in a relaxed atmosphere. Open daily till 1am.

La Torinese Piazza Re Enzo 1. Hot chocolate to die for in this bar in the centre of the main square. Closed Thurs.

Zanarini Piazza Galvani 1. Where the chic Bolognese gather for their *aperitivi*; suitably smart and expensive. Closed Mon.

Clubs and live music venues

Café Caracol Piazza Galileo. Centrally placed Mexican bar by the police station that's open until 2am, serves great food, and has a small dance floor. Cheap cocktails too during the club's happy hour (7.30–8.30pm). Closed Sun.

Candilejas Via Bentini 20. Salsa and merengue music, alternating with indie stuff. To get there take bus #27 from Piazza del Nettuno to the suburb of Corticella (a 25min journey); nightbus #62 runs on the hour back into town. Closed Sun.

Cantina Bentivoglio Via Mascarella 4b ☎051.265.416, ⊛www.affari.com/bentivoglio. On the edge of the university quarter, and as much an osteria as a bar. Live bands, often including jazz, play at around 10pm in the cellars of this sixteenth-century palazzo, where the food and wine are excellent. Closed Mon.

Cassero Via Don Minzoni 18 ☎051.649.4416, ⊛www.cassero.it. Housed downstairs in La Salara, one of the old city fortifications, this is the best of the city's gay bars (open from 9pm). Discos start after 11pm. Wed gays & straights, Thurs lesbian, Fri & Sat gay only.

Chet Baker Via Polese 7a ☎051.223.795, ⊛www.chetbaker.com. One of the city's most popular jazz venues, attracting international names. Closed Sun.

Link Via Fioravanti 14 ☎051.370.971. Just behind the train station, this *centro sociale* has a cyber-style bar upstairs and enormous dance floor downstairs. Avant-garde performance art and live bands early on, with ambient or techno sounds later. No entrance fee, except for gigs. Daily 10pm–5am.

Marsalino Via Marsala 13d. This osteria has a reputation for its theatre and cabaret and is also a pleasant place to sit and drink. Closed Mon.

Listings

Books English books from Feltrinelli International, Via Zamboni 7.

Car rental Avis, Viale Pietramellara 27d ☎051.255.024; Europcar, Via Amendola 12f ☎051.247.101; Hertz, Via Amendola 16a ☎051.254.830; Maggiore, Via Cairoli 4 ☎051.252.525. All the major companies also have desks at the airport.

Cinema Nosadella, Via Nosadella 21 (ⓦ www.nosadella.it), shows films in their original language on Monday; Arena Puccini, Via Serlio 25, is a summer-only outdoor cinema; Lumiere, Via Pietralata 55a, is an excellent film club that occasionally offers non-dubbed classics.

Gay life Gay-friendly places abound in Bologna, although there are few gay-specific bars and clubs. These include the music and theatre bars in Via Marsala and Via Mascarella and around the university. Gay saunas include New Vigor at Via San Felice 6b, while the next door *Caffè Casablanca* (closed Sun) and the *Pirata Pizzeria* just behind *Cassero* (see "Clubs and live music venues") at Via del Porto 40 are popular gay hangouts.

Hospital In an emergency, dial ☎118; or go to the Pronto Soccorso (24hr casualty) at the Ospedale San Orsola Generale, Via Massarenti 9 (☎051.636.3111); bus #14 from Via Rizzoli.

Internet access Bar College, Largo Respighi 6d (daily noon–midnight); *Net.arena*, Via dé Guidei 3d (Mon–Sat 10am–8pm); and the *Green Farm* bookshop, at Via Zamboni 16–18, which has computers at the back of the shop.

Laundry Laundromat, Via Petroni 38, is the most central coin-op/drop-service laundry; Onda Blu, Via S. Donato 4b–c, is just beyond the city wall (daily 8am–10pm).

Markets There are a couple of great indoor food markets in the city centre: the large and lively Mercato delle Erbe, Via Ugo Bassi 2 (Mon–Sat 7.15am–1pm & 5–7pm, closed Thurs & Sat afternoon); and another on Via Clavature (same opening hours); there's also a smaller open-air market at Piazza Aldrovandi, along Strada Maggiore, closed Thursday afternoons. Finally, there's the open-air La Montagnola market, held in Piazza VIII Agosto on Fridays and Saturdays, dawn until dusk, which sells just about everything, but is especially good for new and secondhand clothes.

Pharmacy Night services rotate; look outside the Farmacia Comunale in Piazza Maggiore or dial ☎800.218.489.

Police In an emergency dial ☎113. Otherwise their main office is Piazza Galileo 7 ☎051.640.1111.

Post office The main post office is on Piazza Minghetti (Mon–Fri 8.15am–6.30pm, Sat 8.15am–1pm).

Shops Some of Bologna's most colourful sights are inside its many food stores, particularly those between Piazza Maggiore and the Due Torri, epitomized by Tamburini at Via Caprarie 1, which has a sizeable array of the different ways of eating the "fat of Bologna". The most convenient supermarket is the Co-op, at Via Montebello 2, behind the train station.

Travel agents CTS, Largo Respighi 2g ☎051.261.802; University Viaggi, Via Zamboni 16e ☎051.236.255.

On from Bologna: south to Tuscany

In the heat of the summer the need to get out of Bologna becomes pressing, and the hills that start almost as soon as you leave the city gates take you high enough to catch some cooling breezes. The most obvious destination for a short trip is the eighteenth-century shrine of **Santuario di Madonna di San Luca**, close on 4km outside the city but connected by way of the world's longest portico, which meanders across the hillside in a series of 666 arches – a shelter for pilgrims on the trek to the top. Bus #20 from the station drops you at the start of the route, by Porta Saragozza southwest of the centre. Further south, the N325 passes through **PONTECCHIO MARCONI**, where the physicist Guglielmo Marconi lived in the late nineteenth century, and from where, in 1895, he sent the first radio message ever – to his brother on the other side of the hill. Marconi lies in a specially designed mausoleum in the village, close to the remains of the boat, *Elettra*, from which Marconi lit up the warship *Sydney* while anchored in Genoa in 1930.

The route on from here towards Pistoia is a beautiful one, taking you above the Setta Valley, past chestnut groves and small villages. It's a well-trafficked road, though, and the back roads are the greatest attraction. **MARZABOT-TO**, a few kilometres on from Sasso Marconi and accessible by direct bus from Bologna, is known as the site of the massacre by the Nazis of 1800 people during World War II. It also sports the remains of an Etruscan town, **Misa** (daily 8am–7pm; free), just outside. The site marks out the residential areas, the city gates, streets and drains; fragments of foundations from temples and some tombs remain – evidence of a town of highly skilled craft workers that was much more than just a staging-post between Etruria and the Po Valley. The **museum** (daily 9am–noon & 3–6.30pm; €2) contains a variety of finds, from the remains of the piped water system to household objects inscribed *mi Venelus* ("I belong to Venel") or *mi Sualus* ("I belong to Sualu").

Modena and around

Though only thirty minutes northwest by train, **MODENA** has a quite distinct identity from Bologna. It proclaims itself the "spiritual capital" of Emilia, highlighting the two cities' long and sometimes intense rivalry. Indeed, Modena does have a number of claims to fame: its outskirts are fringed with prosperous industry – knitwear and ceramics factories on the surrounding plain make a healthy profit, and great car names such as Ferrari, Lamborghini and Maserati are tied to the town (celebrated in *Modena Terra di Motori* in April, when the squares of the town are filled with classic models); Pavarotti is a native of Modena and gives regular concerts in May in the Parco Novi Sad near the train station; the area's balsamic vinegar has become a cult product in kitchens around the world, duly celebrated in the Balsamica festival in May; while the cathedral is considered perhaps the finest Romanesque building in Italy. Of things to see, top of most people's list are the rich collections of paintings and manuscripts built up by the Este family, who decamped here from Ferrara in 1598, after it was annexed by the Papal States, and ruled the town until the nineteenth century. But really the appeal of Modena is in wandering its labyrinthine old centre, finishing up the day with some good food.

Arrival, information and accommodation

Modena's centre, marked by the main Piazza Grande, is a fifteen-minute walk southwest from the **train station** on Piazza Dante Alighieri, down the wide Corso Vittorio Emanuele II. Bus #7 connects the train station with the main street of Via Emilia. The **bus station** for villages on the plain or in the Apennines is on Via Fabriani, off Viale Monte Kosica, ten minutes' walk east from the train station and northeast from the centre of town. The **tourist office** is just off the main square at Via Scudari 12 (Tues–Sat 9am–1am & 3–6pm, Sun & Mon 3–6pm; ☎059.206.660; ⓦwww.comune.modena.it/info-turismo). The *Modenatur* office next door at no. 8/10 (☎059.220.022, ⓦwww.modenatur.net) has information on visits to balsamic vinegar farms and cookery courses. You can go **online** at Piazza Grande 17 (Mon–Sat 9am–1pm & 3–7pm, closed Wed afternoons and Sundays). There is **free parking** inside the stadium at Parco Novi Sad, though most hotels in the centre either have a garage or can give you free parking permits; driving in the centre's one-way system is a bit of a nightmare though.

Modena makes a nice place to stay for a night or two, and there are a few reasonably priced **hotels** in the centre: these fill up quickly so you'll need to book in advance. The cheapest option, just east of the town centre off the Via Emilia, is *Del Pozzo*, which has basic but good-sized rooms (with or without bathrooms) at Via del Pozzo 72a (signposted off the road down a cul-de-sac; ☎059.360.350; ❷); take bus #7 from the train station. Otherwise, try the friendly but basic *Bonci* near Parco Novi Sad at Via Ramazzini 59 (☎059.223.634; ❸), or the *Sole*, Via Malatesta 45 (☎059.214.245; ❸), both with shared bathrooms. Among the smarter hotels, the *Centrale*, Via Rismondo 55 (☎059.218.808, ⓕ059.238.201, ⓦwww.hotelcentrale.com; garage parking €8; ❹), has pleasant, spacious and air-conditioned rooms with or without private bath, and, on the other side of the main artery of Via Emilia, *La Torre*, Via Cervetta 5 (☎059.222.615, ⓕ059.216.316, see website for *Centrale*; ❺), offers spotless modern rooms in a period building. If you're in the mood for full Modenese elegance in a garden setting, the top of the list is the *Canalgrande*, Corso Canalgrande 6 (☎059.217.160, ⓕ059.221.674, ⓦwww.canalgrandehotel.it; ❼), close to the main piazza.

There is also the more basic accommodation option of the city's **hostel**, the *Ostello San Filippo Neri*, Via Sant'Orsola 52 (T & F 059.234.598; €14.50), very near the station. The nearest **campsite** is *International Camping Modena* at Via Cave di Ramo 111 (T 059.332.252), Località Bruciata, 5km from Modena on the way to Reggio Emilia, though the nearby motorway makes it noisy. To get there take bus #19 from Viale Monte Kosica, close by the train station, to Emilia Ovest 1006, from where it's a ten-minute walk: head up Via Rosmini, turn left at the end and follow the road under the motorway approach road.

The Town

Modena's tight, concentric medieval centre is bisected by **Via Emilia**, which runs past the edge of **Piazza Grande**, the nominal centre of town, its stone buildings and arcades forming the focus of much of its life. Dominating the square, the twelfth-century **Duomo** (daily 6.30am–noon & 3.30–6pm) is one of the finest products of the Romanesque period in Italy and was added to the world heritage list by Unesco in 1997. Its most striking feature is the west façade, just off the piazza, whose portal is supported by two majestic lions and fringed with marvellous reliefs – the work of one Wiligelmus, who also did the larger reliefs that run along the wall. Look also at the sculpture on the south side of the church, some of which is by Wiligelmus, some of which – in the final arch – is much later, from the fourteenth century. Inside, the choir, supported by more lions and crouched figures, is friezed with polychrome reliefs depicting New Testament stories – the *Last Supper* stands out particularly. Under the choir is the plain stone coffin of St Geminianus, the patron saint of Modena – on his feast day, January 31, crowds come to visit his coffin, and a big market is held out in the main square. Have a look too at Begarelli's terracotta tableaux of the *Shepherds* in the south aisle.

Beside the main entrance to the Duomo, the **Museo Lapidario** (Tues–Sun 10am–12.30pm & 4–6pm; €3.10) displays stone bits and pieces from the Duomo, while on the other side of the church lurches the **Torre Ghirlandina**, begun at the same time as the Duomo but not completed until two hundred years later. Until recently it contained the *Secchia Rapita* (now in the Palazzo Comunale), a wooden bucket stolen during a raid by the Modenese on Bologna in 1325, and often cited as evidence of the long-standing rivalry between the two towns. The Modenese, who supported Re Enzo (the son of the emperor), swore enmity when the Bolognese took him prisoner after a thirteenth-century battle, liberating the bucket from Bologna until well into the next century in an attempt to even the score. The seventeenth-century poet Tassoni wrote a mock heroic verse on the subject, which apparently retains its significance in people's minds and is still the object of occasional student stunts.

The other main focus for your wanderings around Modena is at the far, northwestern end of Via Emilia, a five-minute walk from Piazza Grande, where the **Palazzo dei Musei** houses the city museums and art galleries. Through an archway lined with Roman tombstones – Piazza Matteotti was on the site of a necropolis – a staircase leads off to the right up to the Biblioteca Estense, on the first floor (Mon–Sat 8.30am–1pm; €2.60). This is only partly open to non-students, but what is on display is worth a look: letters sent by monarchs, popes and despots, with great wax seals, filed away for hundreds of years, old maps, and the prize treasure, Borso d'Este's bible – the *Bibbia di Borso d'Este* – arguably the most decorated book in the world. The **Museo d'Arte Medievale e Moderna e Etnologia** (Tues–Fri 9am–noon, Sat & Sun 10am–1pm, plus Tues, Sat & Sun 4–7pm; W www.comune.modena.it/museoarte; €3.10), on the second floor, is the newest part of the museum, with a large collection of artefacts of archeological and artistic significance, while on the top floor, the **Galleria Estense** (Tues–Sun 8.30am–7.30pm; ⓦ www.galleriaestense.it; €4) is perhaps the highlight of all the collections. Made up of the picture collection of the Este family, it contains paintings of the local schools, from the early Renaissance through to the works of the Carraccis, Guercino and Guido Reni, a sculpture of St Monica in terracotta attributed to Nicolo Dell'Arca, as well as portable altars, Madonnas and triptychs by lesser-known Emilian artists like Cosmè Tura, who painted the Palazzo Schifanoia in Ferrara (see p.445). There's also a bust of Francesco I d'Este by Bernini, a portrait of the same man by Velázquez, and Venetian works by Tintoretto and Veronese.

Eating, drinking and nightlife

Like Bologna, Modena is a terrific place to **eat**, with a large array of restaurants in all price ranges. Try if you can to sample some of the local pork-based specialities, like *ciccioli* – flaky pork scratchings laid out in bars in the evening – or, in a restaurant, *zampone* (pig's trotters, boned and filled with minced meat) or *cotechino* – the same thing, but stuffed inside an animal bladder.

At the bottom end of the price scale, Giusti, Via Farini 75 (closed 12.30–5.30pm), a delicatessen since the seventeenth century, is a good source of picnic food, and there's a reasonable *mensa* at Via Leodino 9. Up a notch, the tiny *Bar Schiavoni* by the market at Via Albinelli 13 does delectable and inventive panini for around €3 (open during market hours); the *Trattoria Aldina* down the road on the first floor at Via Albinelli 40 (open lunchtime only, closed Sun and Mon) is another popular affordable spot. If you want to try food from the hills head for the buzzy *Trattoria Giardinetto* (open till midnight, closed all day Sat & Sun evening) on Piazzale Boschetti, where people come in droves for the *gnocco e tigelle*: a platter of cold meats and fresh vegetables served with light puff pastry diamonds, little scones and a variety of dips that is a meal in itself. *Da Enzo*, Via Coltellini 17 (☎059.225.177; closed Mon), is a nice, slightly old-fashioned place serving Modenese specialities – though not especially cheap. Nearby *Fini*, off Largo San Francesco (☎059.223.314; open till 10.30, closed Mon & Tues), is a pricey, elegant establishment, where the food is delectable in the extreme.

The big **evening spot** in Modena is the large *Café Concerto* on Piazza Grande, where there is occasional live jazz and the crowds spill out onto the square. The new place to be seen is the elegant cocktail bar *Fidelio* at Via del Carmina 3 just off the Via Emilia (open Tues–Sun till 3am), with funky outdoor furniture and generous snacks.

Around Modena

The area immediately around Modena looks rather bland and uninviting with its discount furniture and lighting stores, crumbling farmhouses the size of mansions, and factories. Worth a few hours of your time, however, is **CARPI**, around 15km north of Modena. The town's central **Piazza dei Martiri** is an enormous and impressive open space, almost worth the trip alone, and the sixteenth-century **Castello del Pio**, a mass of ornamental turrets and towers, holds another interesting museum inside – the **Museo al Deportato** (Thurs, Sat, Sun & public hols 10am–12.30pm & 3.30–7pm; €2.07). German occupying forces in World War II held prisoners awaiting deportation to concentration camps at a site in Fóssoli, 6km to the north – the camp sheds still stand, dilapidated, in a field – and the museum has displays on the camps and the conditions in which the prisoners were held, neatly putting them into context with information on political and racial exile. The most sobering aspect of the museum is its layout; you progress through the almost bare rooms accompanied by a long ribbon of quotes painted on the walls, taken from prisoners' letters.

The activity outside in the square provides some welcome relief with slick clothing stores running the length of its sixteenth-century red-brick **Portico Lungo**. At one end of the square are a couple of cafés and the bright ochre **Teatro Comunale**, at the other the Renaissance **Cattedrale** with Baroque facade. The rest of Carpi is unexciting, so it's unlikely that you'll want to hang around town. There are trains and buses every hour to Modena, but if you do want to stay try the **rooms** at *Albergo da Giorgio* at Via G. Rocca 1–5 (℡059.685.365; ❸).

Also worth a detour is the **Galleria Ferrari**, at Via Dino Ferrari 43 in **MARANELLO**, south of Modena (daily 9.30am–6pm; €9.50), an exhibition centre dedicated to the racing dynasty. On display are the cups and trophies won by the Ferrari team over the years, an assortment of Ferrari engines, along with vintage and contemporary examples of the cars themselves and a reconstruction of Enzo Ferrari's study.

Further **south of Modena** lie the foothills of the Apennines, covered by turkey oak, hornbeam and hazel woods. Narrow roads corkscrew into the mountains, from which you can climb by foot onto the *crinale* – the backbone of the Apennine range. Trails lead along the succession of peaks above the treeline, steep slopes on either side, to some glacial lakes, although the routes are most impressive for the views they give across the breadth of Italy on either side.

For many, the main attraction of the **small villages** in the foothills is **food**. The tourist office can advise you on "gourmet itineraries" to find the real Modenese cuisine, but they're not really necessary: restaurant signs by the side of the road invite you in to try cuisine *"alla tua nonna"* – "like grandma used to make" – often involving mortadella, salami or *crescente* (a kind of pitta bread eaten with a mixture of oil, garlic, rosemary and parmesan). Higher in the mountains you can still find *ciacci* – chestnut-flour pancakes, filled with ricotta and sugar – and walnuts (which should be picked on or around the night of St John the Baptist, June 24) that go to make *nocino* liqueur.

You might start your wanderings with **VIGNOLA**, 20km south of Modena. It produces some of the best cherries in Italy and is an impressive sight in April, when it's surrounded by blossom and people come from all around for the spring festival. At other times Vignola is worth a visit for its well-preserved castle, the **Rocca di Vignola** (Tues–Sat 9am–noon & 2.30–6pm, Sun 10am–noon & 2.30–6pm; free), one of many built in the fifteenth and sixteenth centuries to defend the crossings along the River Panaro into the neighbouring state of Bologna. It is a mammoth specimen, with enormous watchtowers on each corner, and fancy brickwork – a castle style you see in other parts of Emilia.

Vignola isn't really somewhere to **stay** – the only hotel is the rather uninviting *Eden*, Via Cesare Battisti 49 (℡059.772.847, ℻059.771.477; ❸) – but there are plenty of decent places to **eat**, especially at the foot of the castle. For a special treat, though, head for **Tavernelle**, 3km southwest on the road to Pavullo nel Frignano where you'll find the moderately priced *Antico Trattoria Moretto*, Via Frignanese (℡059.772.785; closed Mon), a barn of a place, packed with people of all ages enthusiastically tucking into some of the best local fare around.

Reggio Emilia

About 25km northwest up the Via Emilia from Modena, **REGGIO EMILIA** is a very different place from Modena, rather short on sights, with an air of neglect about it, but it's a quiet, ancient town, pleasant for wandering and a good place to rest up for a while. It's also a feasible jumping-off point for travelling into the Reggiano Apennines.

The town is built around two central squares, **Piazza Prampolini** and **Piazza San Prospero**, and the **Palazzo del Municipio** with its fishtail battlements. Like other towns in the area, the centre is closed to traffic, and bicycles clank across the cobbles from all directions. Piazza San Prospero comes alive on market days (Tues & Fri), its stalls and shops selling a staggering array of fruit, vegetables, salami and cheese, including the local *parmigiano-reggiano*. Around the square, the buildings squeeze up so close to the church of **San Prospero** that they seem to have pushed it off balance so that it now lurches to one side. Built in the sixteenth century, its facade is decorated with columns and statues in niches, guarded by six lions in rose-coloured Verona marble – a marked contrast to the unclad octagonal campanile next to it. Via Broletto leads through into **Piazza Prampolini**, skirting the side of the **Duomo**, which displays an awkward amalgamation of styles. Underneath the marble tacked on in the sixteenth century, it's possible to see the church's Romanesque facade, with incongruously Mannerist statues of Adam and Eve lounging over the medieval portal, although all else that remains of the original building are the apse and enormous crypt. The niche of the disproportionate central octagonal tower sports – in gleaming copper – an outsized group of the Madonna and donors looming weirdly over the rest of the facade and the entire piazza. The dusty interior houses a painting of the *Assumption* by Guercino and many tombs, including one for a noted sixteenth-century clockmaker/inventor, Cherubino Sforzani, whose tomb bears a symbolic hourglass carved in marble.

At right angles to the Duomo is the sugar-pink **Palazzo del Capitano del Popolo**. The Italian tricolour of red, white and green was proclaimed here as the official national flag of Italy, when Napoleon's Cispadane Republic was formed in 1797. North of here on the edge of Piazza della Vittoria are the **Musei Civici** (Tues–Sun 9am–noon, Sat & Sun also 3–6pm; free), containing an eighteenth-century private collection of archeological finds, fossils and paintings. In the corner of the square, the **Galleria Parmeggiani** (same hours) houses an important collection of Spanish, Flemish and Italian art, including sculptures and bronzes, as well as costumes and textiles. Nearby stands the church of **Madonna della Ghiara**, built in the seventeenth century and decorated with Bolognese School frescoes of scenes from the Old Testament and a *Crucifixion* by Guercino.

Practicalities

Reggio is on the main rail line between Bologna and Milan. The **train station** is on Piazza Marconi I, just east of the old centre; the **bus station** is on the west side of the public gardens on Via Raimondo Franchetti (but may move near the train station in 2003). The **tourist office** is in the main Piazza Prampolini (Mon–Sat 8.30am–1pm & 2.30–5.30pm, Sun 9am–noon; ☎0522.451.152, ⓦwww.municipio.re.it/turismo), and the helpful **Club Alpino Italiano** office at Viale Mille 32 (☎0522.436.685) has information on walking in the nearby hills, but it's only open Wed–Sat 6–8pm, and is closed for much of August. For **Internet** access head for *Qui Qua Navigator*, Piazza Fontanesi 4 (9am–7.30pm Mon–Sat).

If you're planning **to stay** over, be aware that hotel space is somewhat limited: from Easter to June because of tourists, and then in the autumn owing to endless trade fairs. There's a **youth hostel**, *Ostello Basilica della Ghiara*, 1km from the train station at Via Guasco 6 (℡0522.454.795; €13; open all year), on the first floor of a quiet cloister behind the church of the same name. For a central and reasonably priced hotel try the *Ariosto* on Via San Rocco 12 (℡0522.437.320, ℉0522.452.514; ❸). Or, if you want a taste of fabulous luxury in historic Palazzo del Capitano del Popolo, stay at the *Posta*, Piazza del Monte 2 (℡0522.432.944, ℉0522.452.602, ✉booking@hotelposta.re.it; ❽).

For **food**, *La Zucca*, on the southern edge of the historic centre in Piazza Fontanesi (closed Thurs) is a good place to sample local dishes, as is *Canossa*, at Via Roma 37 (closed Wed), which specializes in various ham antipasti. *La Casseruola*, not far from the central piazza on Via S. Carlo 5a (closed Tues), is a bustling pizzeria, with tables outside.

Around Reggio

Very much in a different vein, the foothills **south of Reggio** are cheese country: you'll see many signs along the roadside advertising the local *parmigiano-reggiano*, and the village of **CASINA**, 27km outside Reggio on the N63 to La Spezia, holds a popular Festa del Parmigiana in August, when the vats of cheese mixture are stirred with enormous wooden paddles. The countryside itself is a mixture of lush pastures and scraggy uplands, with some footpaths around, though there's better walking higher up in the mountains.

With your own transport, you can take the side road leading from Casina to **CANOSSA**. This was the seat of the powerful Da Canossa family, whose most famous member, the Countess Mathilda of Tuscany (La Gran Contessa), was a big name here in the eleventh century – unusually so in a society largely controlled by warlords and the clergy. She was known for donning armour and leading her troops into battle herself, and at the age of 43 scandalized the nobility by marrying a youth of 17. During the battles between Pope Gregory VII and the Holy Roman Emperor Henry IV, she supported the pope and helped draw the excommunicated emperor here as a penitent to apologize to the pontiff. Henry was apparently left waiting outside in the snow for three days before the castle doors were opened. The remains of the **Castle** (summer Tues–Sun 9am–12.30pm & 3–7pm; free) are largely thirteenth-century, but it's really the location – on a rocky outcrop looking towards the mountains in one direction and over the neighbouring castle at Rossena and the towns strung out over the plain in the other – which is impressive. People from the surrounding towns are fond of coming out here at weekends to eat in the local **restaurants**, and it's a popular area for **hiking** or cross-country skiing. You may also see people armed with plastic bags for collecting **mushrooms**, or filling bottles with mineral water from the springs off the mountains.

High in the surrounding hills paths lead onto the mountain *crinale*. **Castelnovo Ne'Monti** in the foothills is a possible base for these walks. Further on, at **Busana**, the road forks to the left, descending through a series of hairpin bends bordered by plenty of falling rock signs, in the Secchia Valley, climbing back up the other side through Cinquecerri to **Ligonchio** – another good starting-point for walks away from cable cars and ski lifts onto nearby **Monte Cusna** (?120m). Close by here are the Prati di Sara, a windswept expanse of grassland with small tarns and the occasional tree. As you ascend, you have more of a view across the layers of ridges, often half-obscured in the mist. It's possible to stay overnight in some of the refuges that group along the

Grand Escursione Apenninica route, a 25-day trek that weaves its way back and forth across the border between Emilia and Tuscany. The Club Alpino Italiano office in Reggio (see p.430) should have information on this route.

Parma

Generally reckoned to have one of the highest standards of living in Italy, **PARMA**, about 30km along the Via Emilia northwest of Reggio, is about as comfortable a town as you could wish for. The measured pace of its streets, the abundance of its restaurants and the general air of affluence are almost cloying, especially if you've arrived from the south. Not surprisingly, if you're travelling on a tight budget, Parma presents a few difficulties – the cheap hotels are usually full, and, although the restaurants are excellent, food too can cost a bomb. That said, it's a friendly enough place, with plenty to see. A visit to the opera can be an experience: the audience are considered one of the toughest outside La Scala and don't pull any punches if they consider a singer to be performing badly. And the city's works of art include the legacy of two great artists – Correggio and Parmigianino.

Arrival, information and accommodation

Parma's **train and bus stations** are fifteen minutes' walk from the central Piazza Garibaldi, or a short ride on buses #1–#6, #8 & #9, or #12–#15. Despite the sign in the Piazza Duomo, the **tourist office** is in fact at Via Melloni 1a (Mon–Sat 9am–7pm, Sun 9am–1pm; ℡0521.218.889, ⓌturisÂmo.comune.parma.it/turismo). The main post office across the road has magÂnificent Art Nouveau decoration inside. You can go **online** for free next door but you need to reserve a time in advance (Mon–Sat 9am–1pm & 3–7pm, Thurs 9am–7pm; ℡0521.218.749). Internet access is easier at the old *Fiaccadori* bookshop in Strada Duomo or at *Polidoro Web* in the Galleria Polidoro, a mall on the corner of Via Mazzini by the river.

Accommodation

Finding a **place to stay** can be tricky and you'd be well advised to book in advance. There's an official **youth hostel**, *Cittadella*, just south of the town cenÂtre in the Parco Cittadella (℡0521.961.434; €10; April–Oct) – take bus #2 or #12 from the station.

Button Borgo Salina 7 ℡0521.208.039. Small but very well-appointed air-conditioned rooms just south of Piazza Garibaldi. ❺

Lazzaro Via XX Marzo 14 ℡0521.208.944. A tiny, homey establishment offering basic rooms with bathrooms above its own very good restaurant, as well as a nearby annexe, on the east side of Piazza Garibaldi. ❸

Moderno Via A. Cecchi 4 ℡0521.772.647. Very cheap two-star near the station: spacious rooms, with pleasant furniture and with or without private baths. ❸

Starhotel du Parc Viale Piacenza 12c ℡0521.292.929, ℻0521.292.828, Ⓦwww.starhotels.it. Luxurious old palace on the north side of the Parco Ducale. ❾

Torino Via A. Mazza 7 ℡0521.281.046, ℻0521.230.725, Ⓦwww.hotel-torino.it. Very comfortable rooms right in the heart of things. ❺

The Town

Parma's main street, **Via Mazzini**, and its continuation, **Strada della Repubblica**, run east from the river, past **Piazza Garibaldi** – which, togethÂer with the narrow streets and alleyways that wind to the south and west, forms the fulcrum of Parma. The mustard-coloured **Palazzo del Governatore** forms the backdrop of the square, behind which the Renaissance church of the **Santa Maria della Steccata** (daily 9am–noon & 3–6pm) was apparently built using Bramante's original plan for St Peter's as a model. Inside there are fresÂcoes by a number of sixteenth-century painters, notably Parmigianino, who spent the last ten years of his life on this work, eventually being sacked for breach of contract by the disgruntled church authorities. A year later he was dead, aged 37, "an almost savage or wild man" who had become obsessed with alchemy, according to Vasari.

Five minutes' walk away – turn right off Strada Cavour – the slightly gloomy **Piazza Duomo** forms part of the old *centro episcopale*, away from the shopping streets of the commercial centre. The Lombard-Romanesque **Duomo** (daily 9am–12.30pm & 3–7pm), dating from the eleventh century, holds earlier work by Parmigianino in its south transept, executed when the artist was a pupil of Correggio – who painted the fresco of the *Assumption* in the central cupola. Finished in 1534, this is among the most famous of Correggio's works, the Virgin Mary floating up through a sea of limbs, faces and swirling drapery, which attracted some bemused comments at the time. One contemporary compared it to a "hash of frogs' legs", while Dickens, visiting much later, thought it a sight that "no operative surgeon gone mad, could imagine in his wildest delirium". Correggio was paid for the painting with a sackful of small change to annoy him, since he was known to be a great miser. The story goes that he carried the sack of coins home in the heat, caught a fever and died at the age of 40. Before you leave, take a look at the relief of the *Deposition* on the west wall of the south transept, an impressive work by the architect Benedetto Antelami that dates from 1178. Look too at the frieze that runs the length of the nave above the arches – also by Correggio.

There's a more significant work by Antelami outside the Duomo, in the form of the beautiful octagonal **Baptistry** (daily 9am–12.30pm & 3–6.45pm; €2.70), its sugary pink Verona marble facing four storeys high, encircled by a band of sculpture and topped off by some slim turrets. The three elaborately carved portals serve as a meeting place in the evening. Bridging the gap between the Romanesque and Gothic styles, this is considered Antelami's finest work; started in 1196, the architect sculpted the frieze that surrounds the building and was also responsible for the reliefs inside, including the polychrome figures above the door and a series of fourteen statues, representing the months and seasons, that have been painstakingly scrubbed down and restored. There's more work by Correggio in the cupola of the church of **San Giovanni Evangelista** behind the Duomo (daily 9am–noon & 3–6pm) – a fresco of the *Vision of St John* at Patmos. Next door, the **Spezieria Storica di San Giovanni Evangelista**, at Borgo Pipa 1 (daily 9am–1.45pm; €2), is a thirteenth-century pharmacy that preserves its medieval interior.

A short walk northwest from here next to the tourist office, the **Camera di San Paolo** in the former Benedictine Convent on Via Melloni (daily 9am–1.45pm; €2) houses more frescoes by Correggio executed in 1519; above the fireplace, the abbess who commissioned the work is portrayed by Correggio as the Goddess Diana. Around the corner on Piazza della Pace, the **Museo Glauco-Lombardi** at Via Garibaldi 15 (Tues–Sat 10am–3pm, Sun 9am–1pm; €4) recalls later times, with a display of memorabilia relating to Marie-Louise of Austria, who reigned here after the defeat of her husband Napoleon at Waterloo. She set herself up with another suitor (much to the chagrin of her exiled spouse) and expanded the Parma violet perfume industry.

Just across from here, it's hard to miss Parma's biggest monument, the **Palazzo della Pilotta**, surrounded by vast expanses of wonderfully green lawn set off by modern fountains. Begun for Alessandro Farnese – the wily Pope Paul III – in the sixteenth century, this building was reduced to a shell by World War II bombing, though it's been rebuilt and now houses a number of Parma's museums, including the main art gallery, the **Galleria Nazionale** (Tues–Sun 9am–1.45pm; €6, including the Teatro Farnese), a modern, hi-tech display that includes more work by Correggio and Parmigianino, and the remarkable *Apostles at the Sepulchre* and *Funeral of the Virgin* by Carracci – massive overwhelming canvases, suspended either side of a gantry at the top of the building.

The **Teatro Farnese** (same times as gallery; €2, or €6 including the Galleria Nazionale), which you pass through to get to the gallery, in the former arms room of the palace, was almost entirely destroyed by bombing in 1944. The restored theatre, still used occasionally, with an extended semicircle of seats three-tiers high, made completely of wood, in a facsimile of Palladio's Teatro Olympico at Vicenza, houses Italy's first revolving stage. On the lower floor, the **Museo Archeologico Nazionale** (daily 9am–7.30pm; €2) is a less essential stop but still worth a glance, with finds from the prehistoric lake villages around Parma, as well as the table top on which the Emperor Trajan notched up a record of his gifts to the poor.

Across the river from the Palazzo della Pilotta, the **Parco Ducale** is a set of formal gardens laid out in the eighteenth century around the sixteenth-century **Palazzo Ducale** (Mon–Sat 9am–noon; €2.58) built for Ottaviano Farnese. Just south, the **Casa di Toscanini** on Via R. Tanzi (Tues–Sat 9am–1pm & 2–6pm, Sun 10am–1pm; €1.50) is the birthplace of the conductor who debuted in the Teatro Regio here (see below), and just one of the sights that recall Parma's strong musical heritage. Further south still, on the same side of the river, the embalmed body of the violinist Niccolo Paganini rests under a canopy in the **Cimitero della Villetta** (daily: summer 8am–12.30pm & 4–7pm; winter 8am–12.30pm & 2.30–5pm).

Eating, drinking and entertainment

Parma is not well known for its nightlife, and the locals tend to prefer long sessions in the various (excellent) restaurants, or else dress up and head for the theatre or opera. **Opera** is big in Parma: the Teatro Regio, at Via Garibaldi 16a (℡0521.218.678, ⓦwww.teatroregioparma.org), is renowned for its discerning audiences. It's not unknown for supporters of one singer to gather in cliques during the opera and discuss his or her virtues with supporters of a rival. Viale Basetti, next to the river, is also the home of one of the top **theatre** companies in Europe, the Colletivo di Parma, who perform between October and April at the Teatro Due, Viale Basetti 12a (℡0521.230.242) and in the Palazzo della Pilotta in June and July, and whose shows draw on a tradition of comedy and political theatre – Dario Fo was a founder member and has often returned.

Reasonably priced **places to eat** include *Enoteca Fontana*, Strada Farini 24, a great authentic old bar, with long wooden tables, a huge choice of different wines and a menu that includes sandwiches, steaming bowls of pasta and hot and cold daily specials – a good bet for lunch (closed Sun and Mon). The *Lazzaro* hotel (see p.433) also has a decent restaurant serving an array of local dishes (closed Sun). Up a bracket in price, opera *apassionati* eat at *Al Canon d'Or*, Via N. Sauro 3a (closed Wed) – not cheap, but entertaining. Top choices for local gourmets are the expensive *La Greppia*, Via Garibaldi 39a (℡0521.233.686; closed Mon & Tues), and much cheaper *Trattoria al Tribunale*, Vicolo Politi 5b, up an alleyway off Strada Farini to the right (℡0521.285.527; open till 10.30, closed Tues), a bustling place serving local specialities. For **picnic food**, the market (Wed & Sat) by the river on Piazza Ghiaia is the best source both of ingredients and of ready-made dishes; there's also a small *tavola calda* (closed Sun & Mon) at Borgo Sant'Ambrogio 2, off the Piazza Garibaldi end of Strada della Repubblica. For **later on** in the evening, *Bottiglia Azzurra*, Borgo Felino 63 (closed Sun), serves a good choice of wines and hot snacks and stays open until 2am.

South of Parma

The countryside **around Parma** is a strange mixture: some of the major roads follow bleak gorges, skirting the edge of blank rock walls for miles; others, looking for all the world as if they lead nowhere, emerge into open meadows and orchards, rich farmland stretching far into the distance.

Prime targets are any of the **medieval castles** strung out across the foothills. There are more than twenty, many built by the powerful Farnese dynasty. The website ⓦwww.castellidelducato.it has a useful map locating all the castles and might help you plan a tour. It's also worth buying a Castelli del Ducato card (€1) which will give you a twenty percent reduction on admission fees. One of the best-sited castles is at **TORRECHIARA**, about 20km south and connected with Parma by hourly buses. The castle provides a superb vantage point over the surrounding area and also has frescoes by Bembo in the **Camera d'Oro** (Tues–Fri 9am–1.45pm, Sat & Sun 9am–6.15pm; €3.10; ⓦwww .comune.langhirano.pr.it).

One of the most famous Parma hams (*Prosciutto di Langhirano*) comes from the foothills around **LANGHIRANO**, which is a few kilometres further on and also linked by regular bus with Parma. The experts say the ham cures so successfully here because of the unique mixture of clear mountain air and sea breezes blowing over the Apennines from Liguria; it is served simply with butter, so as not to mask the fine flavour. The town itself has grown into a mass of stainless steel warehouses – there's no reason to come unless you want to carry a haunch of meat round with you for the rest of your holiday. But the countryside around, particularly near Calestano, is beautiful. Apart from the rail route, the fast way over the mountains is by **autostrada**, the A15, which snakes its way in and out of a succession of tunnels, giving glimpses of lush, hidden valleys, vines and orchards. Women risk life and limb by climbing over the barriers to sell **mushrooms** on the hard shoulder. They tie plastic bags, which fill with air and act like crazy dirigible balloons, to the trees, so you can see them from a distance. Despite this, lots of drivers don't and instead sail across the three lanes at the last minute, screeching to a halt to inspect the latest harvest. You have been warned.

The slower N62 gives access to the *crinale* of the mountains: the trails are a popular attraction for walkers these days, but served a quite different purpose in the last war, when adults and children made the long journey by foot, carrying sacks of salt from the coast to trade for food. The writer Eric Newby was hidden by villagers in these mountains as an escaped prisoner of war in 1943, and the book chronicling his experiences, *Love and War in the Apennines*, captures the beauty of the region and its stupendous views across the full width of Italy.

CORNIGLIO, reached by bus from Parma, is a centre for hiking or skiing, and there are places to stay in most villages nearby – in Bosco di Corniglio, 10km away, try the picturesque and comfortable *Ghirardini* (ⓣ0521.889.123 or 0521.889.001, ⓔinfo100laghi.bosco@libero.it; generally closed Thurs; ❷). More buses squeeze themselves round the tight bends to the small villages of Monchio (16km), Trefiumi (20km) and Prato Spilla (23km from Corniglio), leaving you on the lower slopes of **Monte Malpasso** (1716m) – glistening with small lakes and tarns. Buses also run to **Lagdei** (14km), a starting point for further walks.

West to Piacenza

The Via Emilia continues west from Parma, with small towns mushrooming out from the edges of the road, but mostly it's just a ribbon of shops and roadside cafés. **FIDENZA**, the first place of any size, has a Lombard-Romanesque **cathedral** with a richly decorated facade worked on by followers of the Parma master, Antelami. As Fidenza was a major staging-post on the pilgrimage route to Rome, the carvings depict pilgrims and more domestic subjects – appropriately enough for such an intensive salami-producing region – strings of sausages festoon one figure, others show hunting scenes. The building itself is an important – and relatively rare – example of architecture from the Romanesque-Gothic transition period.

The countryside **to the north** of here is the *bassa*, flat, low country (where Bertolucci filmed *1900*) cut by drainage ditches and open fields growing wheat and corn, sugar beet and vines. In summer it's scorching hot and almost silent, with an odd, still beauty all its own, but generally it's seen as a place to pass through on your way to somewhere else. The small towns and villages of the region are quiet and mainly undistinguished. **SORAGNA** is a good place to be on the first weekend in May for its grand agricultural *festa*, with local wine, cheese and salami tasting. At any time of year, the aroma wafting out of the *salumerie* in the main square may tempt you to sample its array of local produce, also available at *Ristorante Stella d'Oro*, in the side alley Via Mazzini. The small market town is dominated by the tenth-century palace of **Rocca di Soragna** (Tues–Sun 9–11am & 3–5.30pm; €6.75), still owned by the local Meli Lupi family, who ran the town between the fourteenth and eighteenth centuries. The dozen or so rooms are furnished with the original sixteenth-century pieces and decorated with frescoes, some by Parmigianino.

The attractive village of **FONTANELLATO**, a few kilometres northeast of Fidenza, was the site of the camp where Eric Newby was imprisoned, but is perhaps better known as a centre for the production of parmesan cheese. Its central square is dominated by the **Rocca Sanvitale** (April–Oct daily 9.30am–12.30pm & 3–7pm; rest of year Tues–Sun closes 6pm; by tour only – in Italian, last tour an hour before closing; €3.80, plus €2.60 to get into the Sala Di Diana), a fifteenth-century moated castle that the Sanvitale family called home until the onset of World War II. Inside there are some ancient pieces of furniture and a fresco of the legend of *Diana and Actaeon* by Parmigianino.

Five kilometres to the north, the small village of **LE RONCOLE** marks the start of **Verdi** country. By the main road on Piazza Giovannino Guareschi – named after the author of the Don Camillo books who also lived here – you can visit the humble **house** where the great composer was born (Tues–Sun: April–Sept 9.30am–12.30pm & 3–7pm; Oct & Nov 9.30am–noon & 2.30–5pm; €4). Some 5km up the road is **BUSSETO**, the childhood home of Verdi and the centre of the Verdi industry that has grown up around the composer, with regular opera performances during summer. It's an appealing little battlemented town, but the main attractions are strictly for Verdi pilgrims. The **Salone Barezzi** (April–Nov Tues–Sun 9.30am–noon & 2.30–5pm; €3) on the main street, Via Roma 119, now a Verdi museum, was the home of Antonio Barezzi, a wealthy merchant who spotted the young Verdi's talent and brought him in as a teacher for his daughter. Verdi lived here for a while and later married his pupil, Margherita. Now restored to its nineteenth-century state, the museum contains the piano that Verdi played on, the first portrait of the maestro and memorabilia such as the baton that Toscanini used to conduct his Verdi memorial concert in 1926. The rather unfriendly tourist office in Busseto's old *rocca* at Piazza Verdi 10 (☎0524.92.487, ⓦ www.bussetolive.com) may give you information about the sights and about tickets for concerts in the **Verdi Theatre** – which attract international names such as José Carreras. You'll need private transport to get to the last of the Verdi sights, the composer's **villa**, a couple of kilometres west of Busseto at **SANT'AGATA DI VILLANOVA**. The villa, which contains a mock-up of the Milan hotel room where Verdi died, is open for guided tours, lasting forty-five minutes (Tues–Sun: April–Sept 9–11.45am, 3–6.45pm; Feb, March & Oct 9.30–12.30pm & 2.30–5.30pm; €6).

A little way south of here lies **CASTELL'ARQUATO**, a well restored medieval town set on a hillside overlooking the Arda Valley. At the top of the town is Piazza del Municipio, lined with some stunning buildings. The thirteenth-century **Palazzo del Podestà** isn't open to the public, but you can visit the **Basilica**, a magnificently preserved Romanesque monument with an eighth-century baptismal font in the right-hand apse. The **Museo della Collegiata** (opening hours irregular, but generally Tues–Sun 9am–noon & 3–6pm; €2.50) next door has a none too thrilling collection of ecclesiastical art and artefacts, but is worth visiting for its small thirteenth-century brick cloister. The newly restored tower of the fourteenth-century **Rocca Viscontea** (March–Oct Tues–Sun 10am–noon & 3–5pm; €2.60) offers a marvellous view over the surrounding countryside.

The **tourist office** (Mon–Fri 9am–1pm; ☎0523.803.091, ⓦwww.comune .castellarquato.pc.it) is in a hut by the bridge over the river. **Accommodation** is thin on the ground; try the friendly *Leon d'Oro* at Piazza Europa 6 (☎0523.803.651; ❸) at the bottom of the town, which has simply furnished doubles. **Restaurants and cafés** on the other hand are plentiful: *La Rocca da Franco* by the Palazzo at via Asilo 4 (☎0523.805.154; closed Tues & Wed) is well thought of, as is *La Falconiere* (closed Mon), which serves local specialities. For snacks and pastries you can't beat the bakery on the square.

Piacenza

PIACENZA marks the end of the Via Emilia and the border with Lombardy. It's a small, unassuming city, its attractions often passed over in favour of Parma or Modena (or Cremona in Lombardy, see p.188), and, despite a small industrial district across the Po, there's a definite feeling of grass growing between the tracks. Travellers are scarce enough to attract a few stares as they cross the main square, and although there's sufficient interest to merit perhaps half a day of your time, you'd probably be better off staying in one of the Via Emilia's more animated centres, if not pressing on to Milan.

The Town

Marking the centre of town is **Piazza dei Cavalli**, so called because of its two famous bronze equestrian statues, one on each side of the square, often quoted as being among the finest examples of Baroque sculpture. Cast in the early part of the seventeenth century by Francesco Mochi, a pupil of Giambologna, they're impressive works certainly, convincingly poised for action. One of the riders is Alessandro Farnese, a mercenary for Philip II of Spain; the other his son Ranuccio I. Behind, the **Palazzo de Comune**, "Il Gotico", is a fine red-brick palace, built in 1280 – an elegant example of Lombard-Gothic architecture, topped by fishtail battlements.

The church of **San Francesco**, just off the square, dates from the same period and sports an imposing Gothic interior. West of here, back towards the train station, the main shopping street of **Via XX Settembre** leads down to the **Duomo**, a grand Lombard-Romanesque church that has been altered many times since it was built between 1122 and 1233. The interior is lovely, with a high, plain nave supported by stout columns and cupola decorated with frescoes by Guercino – though these may be more difficult to see than the fine frescoes in the transepts and apses. From the Duomo, follow Via Chiapponi up to the church of **San Antonino** – known as "Il Paradiso" for the twelfth-century bas-reliefs on its portal. Beyond, a couple of minutes' walk away from here at Via San Siro 13, the **Galleria Ricci-Oddi** has a large collection of nineteenth- and twentieth-century Italian art (Tues–Sun 10–noon, 3–6pm; €4).

The other place to visit in Piacenza is the **Museo Civico** in the Palazzo Farnese on Piazza Cittadella (Tues–Sun 9.30am–1pm, plus Fri–Sun 3–6.30pm; €5.25), with displays of Romanesque and later sculpture, roomfuls of armour and weapons, lots of paintings, including a depiction of the *Madonna and Child with John the Baptist* by Botticelli, and, in the same room, the so-called "*fegato di Piacenza*": very much the star exhibit of the museum, this is a bronze Etruscan representation of a sliced sheep's liver, marked with the names of Etruscan deities, that was (like real sheep's livers) used to divine the future. As for the building, it's a huge affair, begun by Paciotto in 1558 and only half completed by Vignola some years later for the Farnese family: one room is still decorated with heroic frescoes of Alessandro Farnese, though most were carted off to Naples by the Bourbons, where they remain.

Practicalities

Piacenza's **train station** is fifteen minutes' walk east of Piazza dei Cavalli, on Piazzale Marconi. The **tourist office** at Piazzetta dei Mercanti 7, next to Piazza dei Cavalli (Tues, Wed, Fri & Sat 9.30am–12.30pm & 3–6pm; ☎0523.329.324, ⓦwww.piacenzaturismi.net), has maps of the town and other information. Cheap **hotels** are virtually non-existent; your best bet is the central *Milano* on Viale Risorgimento 47–49 (☎0523.336.843, ⓕ0523.385.101; ❺). Piacenza is considered the gateway to Emilian cooking for people coming from Piemonte and Lombardy, but despite this, **places to eat** in the centre of town are rather thin on the ground. One of the best – and most central – restaurants is the lively *Trattoria Agnello*, right behind the Palazzo del Comune at Via Calzolai 2 (open till 10pm, closed Mon), an unpretentious place with great food and moderate prices that is justifiably popular. *La Pireina*, ten minutes' walk north of Piazza dei Cavalli at Via Borghetto 137 (closed Sun & Mon), is more expensive, but its menu of Piacentine specialities is well worth the splurge.

East along the Via Emilia from Bologna

East of Bologna, the Via Emilia takes in much less of interest than it does on its way west, passing through a clutch of small towns – some of them industrialized and mostly postwar, like Forlì, the unappealing administrative capital of the region, others, like **Faenza**, with medieval piazzas surrounded by towers and battlements. Both started life as Roman way-stations and were under the rule of the Papal States for much of their subsequent history. The **lowlands** to the north are farmed intensively, while on the southern side lie hilly vineyards and pastures, narrow gorges that lead up into the mountains and a couple of ski resorts around Monte Fumaiolo (1407m).

Ímola

About 30km out of Bologna, **ÍMOLA** might be worth a short stop if you're heading east; it's well known as a centre for machinery and ceramic ware, and for the San Marino Grand Prix, which gained a certain notoriety following the death of Ayrton Senna here in 1994. It's a pleasant town, with a thirteenth-century castle, the **Rocca Sforzesca**, and some grey-walled Renaissance palaces, but there is nothing extraordinary about it.

The city's museums tend to open on weekends only, but can be visited on request during the week by phoning ℡0542.602.609. The **Pinacoteca** at Via Sacchi 4 (closed for restoration at the time of writing, but usually open Sat 10am–1pm & 3.30–6pm, Sun 3.30–6pm) holds work by local fifteenth- to eighteenth-century artists; the **Museo Archeologico e Naturalistico** (Museo G. Scarabelli) at Via Verdi 7 (Sun 3.45–6.15pm; free) houses an extensive display of rare plants and beetles; and the **Palazzo Tozzoni** at Via Garibaldi 18 (Sat 9am–noon & 3–6.45pm, Sun 3–6.45pm; €4 joint ticket with the castle) has a vast armoury dating from the thirteenth to the nineteenth centuries.

The place to **eat** in town, if money is no object, is the hallowed *Ristorante San Domenico* at Via G. Sacchi 1 (℡0542.29.000; open till 10.30pm, closed Mon all day & Sun eve; booking essential), which is consistently rated one of the country's top restaurants.

Faenza and Brisighella

East of Ímola, cypress trees and umbrella pines, gentler hills and vineyards signal the fact that you're leaving Emilia and entering the Romagna – although strictly speaking there's no distinct boundary between the two regions. **FAENZA**, 12km from Ímola, gives its name to the faïence-ware it has been producing for the last six hundred years. This style of decorated ceramic ware reached its zenith in the fifteenth and sixteenth centuries, and the town is worth a visit for the vast **Museo delle Ceramiche** alone (April–Oct Tues–Sat 9am–7pm, Sun 9.30am–1pm & 3–7pm; Nov–March Tues–Fri 9am–1.30pm, Sat & Sun 9.30am–1pm & 3–6pm; €6); it's at Viale Baccarini 19 – take Corso D. Baccarini from the station, and it's on the left. The massive collection includes early work painted in the characteristic blue and ochre, and later, more colourful work, often incorporating portraits and landscapes. There's a section devoted to ceramics from other parts of the world, too, including ceramic art by Picasso, Matisse and Chagall.

Faenza is still home to one of Italy's leading ceramics schools, teaching techniques of tin-glazing first introduced in the fourteenth century – the ceramics are decorated after glazing and are given a final lead-based, lustrous wash. The town is also a major production centre, with small workshops down most of its side streets; details of where to buy are available from the **tourist office** in Piazza del Popolo 1 (June–Oct Mon–Sat 9.30am–12.30pm & 3.30–6.30pm, Sun 9.30am–12.30pm; Nov–May Tues–Sat 9.30am–12.30pm & 4–6pm; ℡0546.25.231, ⓦwww.racine.ra.it/faenza).

The rest of Faenza is fairly ordinary, although the town's medieval centre is appealing enough. The long, crenellated **Palazzo del Podestà**, the **Piazza del Popolo** and the **Piazza della Libertà** together make up Faenza's medieval heart. These two squares host the market here on Tuesday, Thursday and Saturday mornings together with the **Piazza Martiri della Libertà**, through an archway from Piazza del Popolo, where you'll find stalls selling cheese and other local foodstuffs. Another good time to be in Faenza is for the Palio del Niballo (jousting and flag twirling), which takes place on the last Sunday in June. If you want to **stay** in Faenza, you might consider a bed-and-breakfast, around half the price of a hotel – ask the tourist office for the list of *affitta-camere*. The best hotel in town is the *Vittoria*, Corso Garibaldi 23 (℡0546.21.508, ℗0546.29.136, ⓦwww.hotel-vittoria.com; ❹), a few blocks away from the Duomo, featuring nineteenth-century decor and a dining room with a frescoed ceiling. **Eating** prospects are favourable – try the *Osteria del Mercato* in Piazza Martiri della Libertà (closed Sun), a good, lively place frequented by locals.

South of Faenza, and accessible by train, the village of **BRISIGHELLA**, halfway up a hillside, is famed for its restaurants (visited by people from as far afield as Milan) and its **Via degli Asini** – a raised, covered lane once part of the town fortifications, used to protect mule trains carrying olive oil and clay for making ceramics. The medieval fortress topping the cliffs over the town was held first by the local Manfredi family, then successively by Cesare Borgia, the Venetians and the pope. It now houses a **Museo del Lavoro Contadino** (summer daily 10am–noon & 3.30–7pm; winter Sat 2.30–4.30pm only; €2) with a collection of tools and other objects evoking the region's traditional rural life. The thirteenth-century **Torre dell'Orologio** sits on a spur of rock opposite, while below the town, down by the River Lamone, is the **Pieve del Tho** – an eleventh-century church, built on top of the remains of an earlier temple to Jupiter. It's worth coming here at carnival time and in late June/early July for the Feste Medievali (ⓦwww.festemedioevali.org). Other high points in the year are the Sagra della Polenta (October), del Tartufo (truffle) and dell' Ulivo (both in November).

One of Brisighella's best **restaurants** is *La Grotta Osteria con Uso di Cucina* serving excellent Romagnolo dishes; it's not cheap, but does have an affordable fixed-price menu (ⓣ0546.81.829; closed Tues); or there's the *Cantina del Bonsignore* at Via Recuperati 4 (ⓣ0546.81.889; open till midnight, closed Wed) offering an interesting menu and good wine in a romantic setting. You'll need to book well in advance if you wish to **stay** in the old town, especially during the food festivals in November. Top choice is the imposing *Albergo Gigiole* on the main square at Piazza Carducci 5 (ⓣ0546.81.209, ⓕ0546.81.275, ⓦwww.gigiole.it; ❼), offering four-star luxury; the chef here started the whole food thing off when his restaurant (closed Mon) proved a magnet for aspiring chefs. *La Rocca*, just up the hill at Via delle Volte 10 (ⓣ0546.81.180, ⓕ0546.80.289, ⓦwww.albergo-larocca.com; ❸), has cheaper and simpler rooms, or you can stay in one of the numerous agriturismo places, details of which are available at the very helpful **tourist office** at Porta Gabolo 5 (Easter–Nov daily 9am–noon & 4–6pm; Dec–Easter Wed–Sat 10.30am–12.30pm; ⓣ0546.81.166, ⓦwww.racine.ra.it/sda).

Ferrara

Thirty minutes' train ride north of Bologna, **FERRARA** was the residence of the Este dukes, an eccentric dynasty that ranked as a major political force throughout Renaissance times. The Este kept the main artists of the day in commissions and built a town which, despite a relatively small population, was – and still is – one of the most elegant urban creations of the period.

When there was no heir, the Este were forced to hand over Ferrara to the papacy and leave for good. Life in Ferrara effectively collapsed: eighteenth-century travellers found a ghost town of empty streets and clogged-up canals infested with mosquitoes. Since then Ferrara has picked itself up, dusted itself down, and is now the centre of a key fruit-producing area, to which the expanse of neat, pollarded trees outside town testifies. It's a popular stop for tourists travelling up from Bologna to Venice, but they rarely stay, leaving the city centre enjoyably tourist-free by the evening.

FERRARA

RESTAURANTS & CAFÉS

Osteria degli Angeli	F
Antica Osteria delle Volte	G
Armando Orsucci	H
Al Brindisi	C
Duca d'Este	B
Enoteca I Contrari	E
L'Osteria	D
Al Postiglione	A

ACCOMMODATION

Casa degli Artisti	4
Corte Estense	3
Ostello Estense	1
Hotel de Prati	2
San Girolami dei Gesuati	5

▼ *Bologna* ▼ *Ravenna*

▶ *Pomposa*

Arrival, information and accommodation

Ferrara's **train station** is west of the city walls, a fifteen-minute walk along Viale Cavour to the centre of town; you can also get a bus: either #1, #2 or #9, though #2 is the most direct. The **bus station** lies just southwest of the main square, on Corso Isonzo. The main **tourist office** can be found in the *castello* courtyard (daily 9am–1pm & 2–6pm; ☎0532.209.370, ⓦwww .ferraraterraeacqua.it) and has plenty of maps and bumph on the town. You can check your **email** at the *Centro Servizio Link*, Via Ariosto 57a (daily 9am–1pm & 3–6.30pm; Aug 9am–1pm only), or at *Speedy Web*, Corso Porta Po 37 (Mon–Fri 10am–10pm, Sat 10am–1pm). Ferrara is known as a *città della bici- cletta* with bikes and cycle paths everywhere, though the cobbled streets don't make for a particularly smooth ride; bikes can be rented at the station (to the left as you come out) or inside the city walls on Piazza Travaglio (€6.20–7 per day). There is free **parking** for cars with foreign number plates in Largo Castello by the castle.

Ferrara has a number of affordable **hotels**, most of them handily placed in the centre, though you need to book ahead, especially in summer. By far the best-value three-star is the *San Girolamo dei Gesuati*, a quiet, friendly hotel over-looking a green courtyard near the Palazzo Schifanoia at Via Madama 40a (☎0532.207.448, ℱ0532.207.264, ⓦwww.sangirolamodeigesuati.it; ❸). More central is the refurbished *Hotel de Prati*, close by the *castello* at Via Padiglioni 5 (☎0532.241.905, ⓦwww.hoteldeprati.com; ❺), where the pleasantly furnished rooms have balconies. Finer still, with an elegant courtyard, is the *Corte Estense*, Via Correggiari 4a, close to the Duomo (☎0532.242.176, ℱ0532.246.405, ⓦwww.corteestense.it; ❻). The cheapest rooms in town (with or without bathrooms) are at the very basic *Casa degli Artisti*, a modern block in the medieval quarter at Via Vittoria 66 (☎0532.761.038; ❷). Ferrara's **youth hostel**, *Ostello Estense*, lies just to the northwest of the centre at Corso Biagio Rossetti 24 (☎0532.204.227; €13), while the **campsite**, *Estense* (May–Sept), is on the northeast edge of town at Via Gramicia 76 (☎ & ℱ0532.752.396, ⓔcampeggio.estense@libero.it); take bus #1 from the train station to Piazzale San Giovanni by the walls, from where it's a ten-minute walk north.

The big **market** day is Friday, taking over the centre of town, and on the first weekend of the month (except Aug) there is a large **antiques** market in the centre between the Castello and the Duomo. One of the big annual events, held the last weekend in May, is the **Palio**, smaller than the famous Siena race, but still an exciting – and more local – event (ⓦwww.comune.fe.it /associa/ente_palio/index.htm). In August, the streets of the town ring to the sounds of the annual **buskers' festival**, drawing participants from far and wide.

The Town

The bulky, moated **Castello Estense** (Tues–Sun 9.30am–6.30pm; €4.10, an extra €1 for the tower) dominates the centre of Ferrara, built in response to a late-fourteenth-century uprising and generally held at the time to be a major feat of military engineering. Behind its grim brick walls, the Este court thrived, supporting artists like Pisanello, Jacopo Bellini, Mantegna, and the poets Ariosto and Tasso. The Este dukes were a pragmatic lot, with various ways of raising cash: keeping tax levels just ahead of their court expenses, boosting cashflow by selling official titles, putting up the tolls for traffic along the Po, and supplying troops for the rulers of Naples, Milan or Florence.

The first of the **Este** to live here was Nicolò II, who commissioned the castle, though descendants were really responsible for its decoration. One of the most famous members of the family was Nicolò III d'Este, who took over in 1393. Nicolò was a well-known patron of the arts and notorious for his amorous liaisons. He was also a ruthless man, who is said to have murdered his wife Parisina and his son by another woman, Ugo, when he discovered that they were having an affair. Three other sons, Leonello, Borso and Ercole (Nicolò's heir), also made their mark and oversaw some of Ferrara's most civilized years. Leonello was a friend of the Renaissance man Alberti and became a caricature of the time by virtue of his habit of consulting his horoscope before he chose what to wear in the morning. Borso loved hunting and thundered through the woods at Mesola on horseback, dressed in velvet and jewels. Ercole's children, Beatrice and Isabella, married into the Sforza and Gonzaga families, thus sealing the Este's status as one of the most glittering of Renaissance dynasties. Ercole's grandson, Alfonso I, married Lucrezia Borgia, who continued to support the retinue of artists and poets, patronizing Titian and Ariosto – as did the last Este duke, Alfonso II, who invited Tasso and Guarini to his court.

It's hard to credit all this as you walk through the castle now, most of which is used as offices and inaccessible to the public. The few rooms that you can see go some way to bringing back the days of Este magnificence, especially the *saletta* and Salone dei Giochi, or games rooms, decorated by Sebastiano Filippi with vigorous scenes of wrestling, discus-throwing, ball-tossing and chariot-racing – beautifully restored and full of interest.

Just south of here, the crenellated **Palazzo Municipio**, built in 1243 but much altered and restored since, holds statues of Nicolò III and another son, Borso, on its facade – though they're actually twentieth-century reproductions. Walk through the arch into the pretty, enclosed square of **Piazza Municipio** for a view of the rest of the building. Opposite the Palazzo Municipio, the **Duomo** is a mixture of Romanesque and Gothic styles and has an undeniably impressive facade, centring on a carved central portal that was begun in the mid-twelfth century by Wiligelmus (of Modena cathedral fame) and finished a century or so later. Much of the carving depicts the *Last Judgement*, with the damned souls grimacing on the central frieze and hell itself depicted on the central lunette, while below the frieze bodies climb out of their coffins. Inside, the main part of the church has the grandeur of a ball-room, with sparkling chandeliers, but is much less intriguing than the exterior carving, and it's in the **Museo della Cattedrale**, housed in the former church of San Romano across the square (Tues–Sun 9am–noon & 3–5pm, Sun 10am–noon & 3–6pm; €4.20), that the real treasures are kept. The highlight of the collection is a set of bas-reliefs illustrating the labours of the months, which formerly adorned the outside of the cathedral. There are also illuminated manuscripts, two organ shutters decorated by Cosimo Tura, one of the *Annunciation*, another showing St George killing the dragon, and a beautiful *Madonna* by della Quercia.

The long arcaded south side of the Duomo flanks **Piazza Trento e Trieste**, whose rickety-looking rows of shops herald the arcades of the appealing **Via San Romano** that runs off the far side of the square past the museum, and – beyond – the labyrinth of alleyways that make up Ferrara's medieval quarter; the arched **Via delle Volte**, a long street running east, parallel to Via Carlo Mayr, is one of the most characteristic. At Via Mazzini 95 a couple of **synagogues** and a small **Jewish museum** (guided tours only Sun–Thurs 10am, 11am & noon; €4), with a display of ritual objects, preserve the memory of the town's small Jewish community. On the wider streets above the tangled medieval district are a number of the Renaissance palaces once inhabited by Ferrara's better-heeled families. Most give nothing away with their anonymous facades – all you get is the occasional glimpse of a roof garden or courtyard inside a closing doorway – but a handful are open to the public and give an idea of what life must have been like for the privileged few during Ferrara's heyday. The **Casa Romei**, at Via Savonarola 30 (Tues–Sun 8.30am–7.30pm; €2), is a typical building of the time, with frescoes and graceful courtyards alongside artefacts rescued from various local churches. Just beyond is the house, at no. 19, where the monk Savaranola was born and lived for twenty years, while behind the palace, the monastery church of **Corpus Domini** at Via Pergolata 4 (Mon–Fri 9.30–11.30am & 3.30–5.30pm; free) holds the tombs of Alfonso I and II d'Este and Lucrezia Borgia.

Palaces and museums

Two minutes southeast of Corpus Domini, the **Palazzo Schifanoia** – the

"Palace of Joy" – at Via Scandiana 23 (Tues–Sun 9am–6pm; €4.20) is one of the grandest of Ferrara's palaces. It belonged to the Este family, and Cosimo Tura's frescoes inside transplanted their court to Arcadia. In the Salone dei Mesi (the "rooms of the months"), the blinds are kept closed to protect the colours, and the room seems silent and empty compared with what's happening on the walls, which are split into three bands. Borso features in many of the court scenes on the lowest band, surrounded by friends and hunting dogs, along with groups of musicians, weavers and embroiderers with white rabbits nibbling the grass at their feet. Above, each section is topped with a sign of the zodiac and, above that, various mythological scenes.

On nearby Corso della Giovecca, at no. 170, the **Palazzina di Marfisa d'Este** (Tues–Sun 9.30am–1pm & 3–6pm; €2) has more frescoes, this time by Filippi, and although its gloomy interior is less impressive than the Schifanoia complex, in summer the loggia and orange grove are a welcome refuge from the heat. In the other direction, to the south, the **Palazzo di Lodovico Il Moro**, Via XX Settembre 124 (Tues–Sun 9am–2pm; €4), holds the city's well-organized archeological museum, with finds from Spina, the Graeco-Etruscan seaport and trading colony near Commachio, displayed together with a dugout canoe from one of the prehistoric lake villages in the Po Delta.

Down in the southeast corner of the town is a gem of a place: the **Monastero di Sant'Antonio in Polesine**, with exquisite frescoes (Mon–Sat 9.30–11.30am & 3–5pm, Sat closes at 4pm; donations accepted). Knock at the door of the convent and the nuns shepherd you into a chapel covered with works by the school of Giotto, including a rare *Flight from Egypt* in which Joseph carries Jesus on his shoulders.

There are some more impressive palaces north of the *castello*, on and around **Corso Ercole I d'Este** – named after Ercole I, who succeeded to the throne in 1441 after his father Nicolò III died, probably poisoned, and who prompt-ly disposed of anyone likely to pose a threat. His reputation for coldness earned him the names "North Wind" and "Diamond", but he certainly got things done, consolidating his power by marrying Eleanor of Aragon, daughter of the Spanish King of Naples, and laying out the northern quarter of the city, the so-called "Herculean Addition", on such a grand scale that Ferrara was tagged the first modern city in Europe. He wasn't a puritanical ruler either; writers of the time describe grand events consisting of many hours of feasting, with sugar cas-tles full of meat set up for the crowd to storm. The **Palazzo dei Diamanti**, a little way down the Corso on the left, named after the diamond-shaped bricks that stud its facade, was at the heart of Ercole's town-plan and is nowadays used for temporary modern art exhibitions as well as being home to several muse-ums, of which the most interesting is the **Pinacoteca Nazionale** (Tues & Wed 9am–2pm, Thurs 9am–7pm, Sat & Sun 9am–1pm; €4), holding works from the Ferrara and Bologna schools, notably paintings by Dossi, Garofalo and Guercino, and a spirited St Christopher by "Il Bastianino" (Sebastiano Filippi).

Eating and drinking

Ferrara has a good range of **restaurants** and trattorias with prices to suit most pockets. Probably the best all-round choice for charm, fun, good food and drink is *Al Brindisi*, Via degli Adelardi 11 (closed Mon), just to the left of the Duomo. It's Ferrara's oldest osteria, once frequented by the likes of Cellini, Titian and Copernicus, with a magnificent wine selection. Food prices are very reasonable, but some of the wines are Italy's finest and are priced accordingly. Moderately priced fare is available at *Osteria degli Angeli*, Via delle Volte 4 (open till 10pm, closed Mon), a convivial place, with lots of different wines and good food, and at the popular *Antica Osteria delle Volte* (open till 11pm, closed Tues) further along the same street at no.37. Slightly more expensive is *L'Osteria*, Via Romei 51 (closed Mon), where the *tortelli di zucca* (pumpkin ravioli) is definitely something special. At the bottom end of the scale, but one of the most charming options, is *Pizzeria da Armando Orsucci*, Via Saraceno 116 (open till 1am, closed Thurs), whose speciality besides pizza is *torta di ceci*, a kind of chickpea-flour pie eaten by the slice right out of the oven, with a dash of black pepper – locals line up for it. Lighter fare is also available at *Al Postiglione*, off Corso Martiri di Libertà at Vicolo del Teatro 4, a *paninoteca* with any number of sandwich combinations, hot and cold, as well as home-made pasta and lots of different beers and wines (open until midnight). Other good, friendly spots for drinking are the *Enoteca I Contrari* at Via Contrari 50 (daily 6pm–1am, plus Mon–Fri noon–3pm) and the bustling *Duca d'Este* at Piazza Castello 22 (closed Tues).

Some 20km west of the town is a place that food buffs will adore: the *Ristorante Tassi* in **Bondeno** (accessible by bus from Ferrara) at Viale Repubblica 23 (T & F 0532.893.030). There is no menu, you just let Signor Tassi lead you through an amazing succession of fine dishes, including meats served with fruit crystallized in a mustard syrup. It's not cheap (€30 per head without drinks) but it is unforgettable, and if you are wise, you will book one of the comfortable large rooms upstairs (❸) so you don't have too far to stagger to bed.

The Po Delta

"So ugly it's beautiful" is a somewhat contrary summing up of the **Po Delta**, east of Ferrara: an expanse of marshland and lagoons culminating in small fingers of land poking out into the Adriatic. Most of the traffic is just passing through, and it's not surprising that the tourist authorities have decided on some heavy promotion.

The River Po splits into several channels, trickling to the sea through these wetlands. Etruscan traders set up the port of Spina here between the fourth and third centuries BC, when the sea covered much of the land from Comacchio to Ravenna. Partly owing to drainage schemes, the briny waters have since retreated by 12km, and the area becomes a bit less marshy each year – an advantage for local farmers but a threat to the many varieties of sea and shore **birds** that inhabit the area. The two main lagoons of **Valli di Comacchio** and **Valle Bertuzzi** have been designated as nature reserves to protect at least some of the wetlands and now constitute one of Europe's most highly regarded birdwatching areas, providing a habitat for nesting and migrating birds, including herons, egrets, curlews, avocets and terns.

Another threat to the area's wild (and human) life is **pollution**: 136,000 tonnes of nitrates, 250 tonnes of arsenic and 60 tonnes of mercury are pumped into the River Po every day, and spillages from oil refineries are further cause for anxiety. Not surprisingly, swimming in the river is banned, as is use of the water for irrigation or drinking purposes. Though you might not fancy it having read this, the best way to see the delta is by **boat**. There are a number of locals in the surrounding area who run guided tours. Sig. Schiavi Vincenzino, Via Vicolo del Farol (T 0533.999.815), or Sig. Dante Passarella, c/o *Ristorante USPA* (T 0533.999.817), both in Gorino, take out boats in summer if enough people are interested. Two-hour boat trips also set off from the harbour of Stazione Foce, south of Comacchio (daily April–Oct at 9am, 11am, 3pm & 5pm; ☎348.471.0332, Ⓦwww.vallidicomacchio.it; €8.50), accessible by car only; follow signs for Museo delle Valli. More information is available at the tourist office in Comacchio (see below).

Comacchio

The region's main centre, **COMACCHIO** is a small fishing town intersected by a network of canals, with a famous local attraction in its triple-bridge or **Trepponti**, built in 1634, which crosses three of the canals. Comacchio is an eel-port, and the time to visit is autumn, when wriggling masses of the creatures are fished out of the canals on their way to the Sargasso Sea. Not surprisingly, eel (*anguille*) is a central ingredient in the local cuisine and there are several places around town to try the different ways they're prepared or other regional dishes like fish risotto, or *fritto misto*. Call in at the **tourist office** at Piazza Folegatti 28 (June–Oct daily 9am–noon & 3–6pm; Nov–May Sat & Sun only; ☎0533.310.161, Ⓦwww.comune.comacchio.fe.it) for more information.

The **beach developments** directly east of Comacchio are not particularly inviting, especially bearing in mind the proximity of the nasty waters of the Po, but it's interesting to see the cantilever nets set up either side of the channels running out to the sea. Incidentally, Comacchio's harbour is named Porto Garibaldi, after the Risorgimento hero who was left on the shore with his wife, Anita, and their companion Leggero, as the last Garibaldini were captured off the coast by the Austrian navy.

Pomposa Abbey

About 20km north of Comacchio, and connected by buses from the port, the **Abbey of Pomposa** (daily 8.30am–7pm; €4) is about all the area has to offer in the way of orthodox sights, a lonely collection of buildings, saved from complete oblivion by numerous bus tours in summer. At the centre of a complex that includes a Lombard-Romanesque campanile, a chapter house and refectory is an eighth-century **Basilica** containing frescoes by Vitale di Bologna and the Bolognese School, though the abbey is better known for one of its monks, Guido d'Arezzo, who in the early eleventh century invented the musical scale here. Only a few hundred years after Pomposa was built, it went into decline, the delta becoming marshier and malarial, and those who weren't killed off by the disease were left to scratch a living from hunting and fishing. The monks finally abandoned their abbey in the seventeenth century.

Ravenna and around

When **RAVENNA** became capital of the Western Roman Empire fifteen hundred years ago, it was more by quirk of fate than design. The Emperor Honorius, alarmed by armies invading from the north, moved his court from Milan to this obscure town on the Romagna coast around 402; it was easy to defend, surrounded by marshland, and was situated close to the port of Classis – at the time the biggest Roman naval base on the Adriatic. Honorius's anxiety proved well founded: Rome was sacked by the Goths in 410 and sank into a decline matched only by Ravenna's ensuing prosperity, and the town became the Roman capital almost by default. After enjoying a period of great monu-

▲ A14 to Bologna, Ferrara & Venice

RESTAURANTS

Bizantino	D
Ca' De Ven	F
Caffè Corte Cavour	C
La Gardela	B
Al Rustichello	A
Bar Silvano	E

Mausoleo di
Teodorico

VIA DELLE INDUSTRIE

N

VIA DI ROMA

CIRCONV. S. GAETANINO

Rocca di
Brancaleone

VIA MURA PORTA SERRATA

Porta
Serrata

VIA VENEZIA

VIA ROCCA BRANCALEONE

VIA D'ARSENA

Canale
Candiano

**Museo
Nazionale**

**Mausoleo di
Galla Placidia**

S. Vitale

VIA P. ALIGHIERI

VIA SALARA

VIA GHISELLI

VIA ROCCA AL FOSSI

VIA U. BASSI

PIAZZA
BARRACCA

VIA SAN VITALE

VIA PIER TRAVERSARI

**Covered
Market**

VIA C. CAVOUR

VIA PONTE MARINO

VIA PAOLO COSTA

PIAZZA
A. COSTA

**Arian
Baptistry**

**Basilica dello
S. Spirito**

VIAL RAVA

PIAZZA
MAMELI

VIALE FARINI

PIAZZA
FARINI

VIA MARONCELLI

**Train
Station**

**Bus
Station**

VIA BARBIANI

VIA C. CATTANEO

VIA PASOLINI

VIA XIII GIUGNO

VIA ARMANDO DIAZ

VIA CARDUCCI

VIALE G. PALLAVICINI

VIA MASSIMO D'AZEGLIO

PIAZZA XX
SETTEMBRE

PIAZZA
DEL POPOLO

VIA A. MARIANI

DI ROMA

**S. Apollinare
Nuovo**

VIA G. OBERDAN

PIAZZA
KENNEDY

VIA MENTANA

PIAZZA
GARIBALDI

**Museo
Dantesco**

VIA ALBERONI

VIA GORDINI

Tomba di Dante

San Francesco

Palazzo di Teodorico

Tower

**Neonian
Baptistry**

PIAZZA S.
FRANCESCO

PIAZZA DEL
DUOMO

PIAZZA
CADUTI

VIA G. GUACCIMANNI

**S. Maria
in Porto**

Duomo

PIAZZA
ARCIVESCOVADO

**Museo
Arcivescovile**

V. A. DE GASPERI

VIA A. BACCARINI

VIA MAZZINI

Giardino
Pubblico

PIAZZA
D'ANNUNZIO

VIA CERCHIO

**Accademia di
Belle Arte**

VIA BALDINI

ACCOMMODATION

Centrale Byron	3
Cappello	2
Al Giaciglio	1
Ostello Dante Alighieri	5
Residenzia Galletti Abbiosi	4

**Porta
Nuova**

VIA ZAGARELLI ALLE MURA

VIALE SANTI BALDINI

VIA CESAREA

RAVENNA

0   100 m

▼ S. Apollinare in Classe & Cesena

mental adornment as chief city of the empire, Ravenna, too, was conquered by the Goths in 476. However, the new conquerors – and new emperors – were also Christians and continued to embellish the city lavishly, particularly the Ostrogoth Theodoric, making it one of the most sought-after towns in the Mediterranean. It wasn't long before Byzantine forces annexed the city to the Eastern Empire and made it into an exarchate, under the rule of Constantinople.

The Byzantine rulers were responsible for Ravenna's most glorious era, keen to outdo rival cities with magnificent palaces, churches and art, and the city became one of the most compelling cultural centres in the world. The growing importance of Venice brought some further prosperity, but the sixteenth century saw the sack of the city and its absorption into the Papal States, since when the Adriatic shoreline has receded, and an eleven-kilometre-long canal through a vast industrial complex now links Ravenna's port to the sea. But remnants of the dazzling Byzantine era are still thick on the ground – not least a set of mosaics at San Vitale that is generally acknowledged to be the crowning achievement of Byzantine art extant anywhere in the world.

Unlike Florence or Venice, say, tourism seems almost incidental to the life of the town, although the nearby **Mirabilandia**, a Disneyesque theme-park, helps bring in the crowds during summer. For a city that has such historic monuments Ravenna's centre feels surprisingly modern – a combination of Mussolini's building programme and allied bombs that levelled much of the city in the last world war. It's a pleasant enough place to spend a couple of days and has some excellent bars and restaurants, but the churches and mosaics will easily monopolize your time. Nightlife is sparse, though the lido towns a couple of kilometres away provide some excitement in summer.

Arrival, information and accommodation

It's only a short, ten-minute walk from the **train station** on Piazza Farini in the east along Viale Farini and Via Armando Diaz to Ravenna's central square, Piazza del Popolo, which with the adjoining streets makes up the compact old centre. The **bus station** is across the tracks behind the train station, in Piazzale Aldo Moro.

There's an information office, with maps, just outside the station on the left (Mon–Sat 6.15am–8pm), next to a place that rents bikes, and a helpful main **tourist office** at Via Salara 8 (Mon–Sat 8.30am–6/7pm, Sun 10am–4pm; ☏0544.35.404, ⓦwww.turismo.ra.it).

One of Ravenna's cheapest **hotels**, a short walk from the station, is the basic but friendly *Al Giaciglio*, Via Rocca Brancaleone 42 (☏0544.39.403; ❷), where rooms come with or without bathrooms. If you prefer to stay right in the historic centre, you can choose from two very comfortable places: the *Centrale Byron*, at Via IV Novembre 14 (☏0544.212.225, ⒻF0544.34.114; ❸), and nearby at no. 41, the chic *Albergo Cappello* (☏0544.219.813, Ⓕ0544.218.814; ❻), in an old palazzo with just seven rooms and a good restaurant. East of the station there's a **youth hostel**, the *Ostello Dante Alighieri*, at Via Nicolodi 12 (☏ & Ⓕ0544.421.164; €12.50), with some family rooms and evening meals available. You can get there on bus #1 from outside the train station, or it's a ten-minute walk – south out of the station, east under the tracks, follow Via Candiano and then head southeast down Via T. Gulli; Via Nicolodi goes off to the right. There's a more upmarket hostel, the *Residenzia Galletti Abbiosi* (☏0544.215.127, Ⓔinfo@ostellora.org; ❸), with air-conditioned singles and doubles, at Via di Roma 140 between the station and the centre; the furnishings are plain but some of the large rooms have fine painted ceilings. **Bed-and-breakfast** accommodation is another cheap option – the tourist office can recommend places close to the centre. The closest **campsite** to Ravenna is in the nearby coastal resort of Punta Marina – regular buses go from the train station.

The City Centre

The centre of Ravenna is without question **Piazza del Popolo**, an elegant open space, arcaded in one corner, that was laid out by the Venetians in the fifteenth century and is now filled with café tables. A few blocks south of the square, across Piazza Garibaldi on Via Alighieri, the **Tomba di Dante** is a site of local pride, a small Neoclassical building which was put up in the eighteenth century to enclose the tomb of Dante. The poet had been chased out of Florence by the time he arrived in Ravenna, and he was sheltered here by the Da Polenta family – then in control of the city – while he finished his *Divine*

Comedy. He died in 1321 and was laid to rest in the adjoining church of **San Francesco**, a much-restored building, elements of which date from the fourth century. File down the stairs in front of the choir for a look at the waterlogged crypt, dating from the tenth century, complete with goldfish and remnants of a mosaic floor. You might want to look in, too, on the **Museo Dantesco**, situated in San Francesco's cloister on Via Alighieri (daily 9.30am–noon & 3.30–6pm; €2) – though its collection of paintings, bronzes and various artefacts relating to Dante is pretty deadly unless you're absolutely fanatical about the man.

A couple of minutes' walk west of here, a grouping of buildings around **Piazza del Duomo** shelters the **Duomo** itself, with its cylindrical – and slightly tipsy – tower. Originally a fifth-century building, the Duomo was completely destroyed by an earthquake in 1733 and rebuilt in unexceptional style soon after. It's not particularly worth a second glance, but the **Museo Arcivescovile** in the Bishop's Palace behind is fascinating, with fragments of mosaics from around the city and the palace's sixth-century Oratorio Sant'Andrea, which is adorned with mosaics of birds in a meadow above a Christ dressed in the armour, cloak and gilded leather skirt of a Roman centurion (daily: April–Sept 9.30am–6.30pm; March & Oct 9.30am–5.30pm; rest of year 9.30am–4.30pm; see box above for admission).

The **Neonian Baptistry**, on the same side of the Duomo, by the belltower (same times as Museo Arcivescovile; see box above for admission), is a conversion from a Roman bathhouse. The original floor level has sunk into the marshy ground, and the remains of the previous building are now 3m below. The choice of building was a logical one: baptisms involved total immersion in those days, and the mixture of styles works well – the marble inlaid designs from the bathhouse blend in with the mosaics of prophets on the arches round the sides. Mosaics of the baptism of Christ and portraits of the twelve Apostles decorate the dome, which is made of hollow terracotta tubes.

East of here, **Via di Roma**, lined with bland, official-looking palaces, cuts right through the modern centre of Ravenna and sees much of its traffic. Halfway up on the right stands the basilica of **Sant'Apollinare Nuovo** (same times as the Museo Arcivescovile; see box above for admission) – called Nuovo to distinguish it from the church of the same name at Classe (see p.454). Built by Theodoric in the sixth century, it contains some of Ravenna's most impressive mosaics, running the length of both sides of the nave. Each shows a line of martyrs – one side male, the other female – processing through avenues of date palms and bearing gifts for Christ and the Virgin enthroned. Some of the scenery is more specific to Ravenna: you can make out what used to be the harbour at Classe with the city in the background, from which rises Theodoric's palace. As a Goth, Theodoric belonged to the Arian branch of

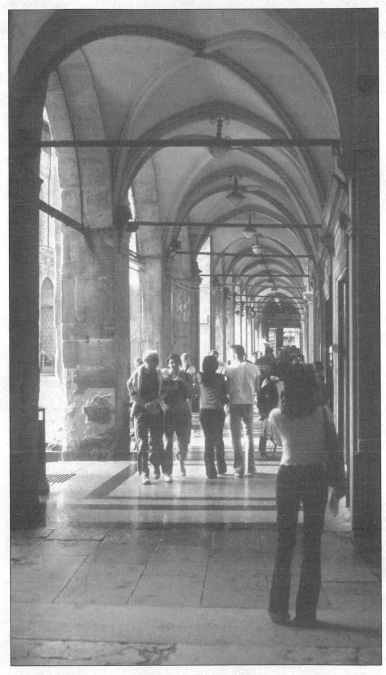

△ Bologna

Christianity which didn't accept the absolute divinity of Christ, a heresy stamped out by Constantinople as much for political as theological reasons. When the Byzantines came along, they removed many of the mosaic figures that had been placed here under Theodoric's reign. In the mosaic drapery above the entrance door you can just make out a figure, not quite obliterated. In fact, if you look at the columns to the left of the building labelled "PALA TIUM", you can still see outstretched hands, possibly Theodoric's, though no one actually knows for sure. When Theodoric built the church in the early 500s, he dedicated it to Jesus, but when the Byzantines took over it was rededicated to St Martin, who was known for his anti-heretic campaigns and is shown at the head of the line of male devotees. Still later, in the ninth century, it was rededicated yet again to the present eponymous saint.

Five minutes' walk away up Via di Roma next door to the Basilica dello Santo Spirito is the **Arian Baptistry** (9am–7pm; free), also built by Theodoric, with a fine mosaic ceiling showing the twelve Apostles and the baptism of Christ.

San Vitale and around

In terms of monuments, Ravenna's biggest draw is the area ten minutes' walk northwest of the city centre, around the basilica of San Vitale, which holds the finest of the mosaics and is now gathered together into one big complex, including the mausoleum of Galla Placidia and the National Museum.

San Vitale (daily: April–Sept 9.30am–6.30pm; March & Oct 9.30am–5.30pm; rest of year 9.30am–4.30pm; see box on p.450 for admission), which was begun in 525 under the Roman emperor Theodoric and finished in 548 under the Byzantine ruler Justinian, is a fairly typical Byzantine church, and its Eastern-inspired arrangement of void and solid, dark and light, was unique for an Italian building of the time. The Byzantines had a mathematical approach to architecture, calling it the "application of geometry to solid matter", and it shows in the building, based on two concentric octagons, its central dome supported by eight columns, and with eight recesses extending from each side – one of which is a semicircular apse that glitters with mosaic. The design was the basis for the great church of Aghia Sofia in Istanbul, built fifteen years later.

There were definite rules about who appeared where in **mosaics** – the higher up and further to the east, the more important or holy the subject. The series in the basilica starts with Old Testament scenes spread across the semi-circular lunettes of the choir; the triumphal arch shows Christ, the Apostles and sons of St Vitalis. Further in, on the semi-dome of the apse, a beardless Christ stands between two angels, presenting a model of the church to St Vitalis and Bishop Ecclesius. But what could have been simply a rigid hierarchy preserved in stone is enlivened by fields and rivers teeming with frogs, herons and dolphins. Of the mosaics on the side walls of the apse, the two processional panels are the best surviving portraits of the Emperor Justinian and his wife Theodora – he's on the left and she's on the right – and a rich example of Byzantine mosaic technique. The small glass *tesserae* are laid in sections, alternate rows set at slightly different angles to vary the reflection of light and give an impression of depth. Colour is used emblematically too, with gold backgrounds denoting either holiness or high status.

Theodora looks a harsh figure under her finery, and she certainly had a reputation for calculated cruelty, arranging "disappearances" of anyone who went against her. According to the sixth-century chronicler Procopius, in his "Secret History" of the court, her rise to power was meteoric. When young she made a living as a child prostitute and circus performer with her two sisters, and later became a courtesan and an actor in bizarre sex shows. She travelled the Middle

East, and when she returned brought herself to the attention of the emperor, Justinian. To the horror of the court, he rejected the well brought-up daughters of his Roman peers and lived with Theodora, giving her the rank of patrician. He was unable to marry her until his mother, the empress, was dead and the law changed; the two then embarked on a reign of staggering corruption and legalized looting.

Across the grass from the basilica is the tiny **Mausoleo di Galla Placidia** (daily: April–Sept 9.30am–6.30pm; March & Oct 9.30am–5.30pm; rest of year 9.30am–4.30pm; see box on p.450 for admission) named after the half-sister of Honorius. The emperor's frequent absences left Galla in charge of the city and she was responsible for much of the grandeur of Ravenna's early days. Despite the name and the three sarcophagi inside, it's unlikely that the building ever held her bones. Galla Placidia was taken hostage when the Goths sacked Rome, and caused a scandal by marrying one of her kidnappers, Ataulf. She went into battle with him as his army forged south, and later they reigned jointly over the Gothic kingdom; when Ataulf was assassinated the Romans took her back for a ransom of corn, after which she was obliged to marry a Roman general, Constantius. Their son formally became the Emperor Valentinian III at the age of 6, and as his regent, Galla Placidia assumed control of the Western Empire.

Inside the basilica, filtered through thin alabaster windows, the light falls on mosaics that glow with a deep blue lustre, most in an earlier style than those of San Vitale, full of Roman and naturalistic motifs. Stars around a golden cross spread across the vaulted ceiling; the Gospels are four volumes on the shelves of a small cupboard, and there are symbolic representations of the Apostles – the lion of St Mark and the ox of St Luke are set in the sky at the points where you would expect to see the constellations of Leo and Taurus. At each end are representations of St Lawrence, with the gridiron on which he was martyred, and at the entrance end is a depiction of the Good Shepherd, with one of his flock.

Adjacent to San Vitale on the southern side, housed in the former cloisters of the church, the **Museo Nazionale** (Tues–Sun 8.30am–6.30pm; €4 or see box on p.450 for joint tickets) contains various items from this and later periods – fifteenth-century icons, early Byzantine glass and embroidery from Florence. Among the most eye-catching exhibits is a sixth-century statue of Hercules capturing a stag, possibly a copy of a Greek original and a very late example of classically inspired subject-matter; and the so-called "Veil of Classis", decorated with portraits of Veronese bishops of the eighth and ninth centuries.

Still within Ravenna, but a bit of a hike north of the train station, lies one more early sixth-century monument that's worth the effort: the **Mausoleo di Teodorico**, Theodoric's Mausoleum (daily 8.30am–7pm; €2 or see box on p.450 for joint tickets). This ten-sided curiosity is unique in Western architecture. Its design owes much to Syrian models of its day, and the whole is constructed of Istrian limestone. The 300-tonne cupola is a single, if cracked, chunk and no one knows exactly how it was manoeuvred into place. Inside the decagonal second storey sits an ancient porphyry bathtub, pressed into use as the royal sarcophagus.

Eating, drinking and entertainment

Central Ravenna is not exactly filled with **places to eat**, and you need to know in advance where to go to avoid fruitless wandering. For lunch, the self-service *Bizantino*, just inside the covered market on Piazza A. Costa, is excellent value, while the market itself stays open until 2pm and is a good source of picnic supplies. *Ca' De Ven*, at Via C. Ricci 24 (open till 10pm, closed Mon, and also Sun June–Aug), is a stunning wood-panelled *enoteca* with painted ceilings and a large selection of Emilia-Romagnan wine, and some food. Another popular restaurant is *Al Rustichello*, at Via Maggiore 21/23 just outside the city walls (booking advised, ☎0544.36043). It's a cheap place where the owner tells you the menu (in English too) with food that your Italian grandmother would be proud of – the *cappelletti with asparagus* is recommended. Two more upmarket places are the restaurant at the *Albergo Cappello* (see above, closed Sun) and *La Gardela*, Via Ponte Marino 3 (closed Thurs), is a pleasant and very central place with a varied menu and moderate prices – ask for the daily specials.

Of the city's **bars and cafés**, the *Bar Silvano*, Piazza Einaudi 7 (closed Sun), just up from Piazza del Popolo, is popular with visitors and offers delicious appetizers with drinks and good sandwiches. On the way to or from San Vitale, at Via S. Vitale 22, you can pop into the *Caffè Corte Cavour*'s inviting inner courtyard for an aperitif. There is an atmospheric bar in the middle of the park inside the walls of the Rocca, the fortification near the station which is a popular venue for concerts.

The **Ravenna Festival** in June and July attracts big names in the rock and classical music world (Ⓦ www.ravennafestival.org), and the Jazz Festival in July and August also draws international stars.

Sant'Apollinare in Classe and Ravenna's seaside resorts

About 6km south of Ravenna by train or buses #4 and #44 from the station, the remains of the old port of **Classe** (daily 9am–dusk; €2) are very thin indeed – the buildings have been looted for stone and the ancient harbour has now completely disappeared under the silt of the River Uniti. One building however, does survive – the church of **Sant'Apollinare in Classe** (Mon–Sat 8.30am–7.30pm, Sun 1–7pm; €2 or see box on p.450 for combined tickets), which was spared because it was the burial place of Ravenna's patron saint. It's a typical basilical church with more fine mosaics. There's a marvellous allegorical depiction of the *Transfiguration* in the apse, with Christ represented by a large cross in a star-spangled universe, flanked by Constantine IV granting privileges to the church of Ravenna, with St Apollinaris pictured in prayer in a naturalistic landscape below. Altogether, it's an odd site, with an otherworldly feel quite at odds with its position close to the *autostrada*.

Nearby is the **Pineta di Classe**, a long belt of umbrella pines that runs the length of the coast, while the **Pineta San Vitale** runs north. The route is closed to visitors during summer owing to the fire risk; at other times it's popular with cyclists – though the thick band of smog that sometimes rests over the tops of the trees can rather destroy any bucolic appeal it might have. There's easy access by bus through Ravenna's heavy industry belt to lido towns. **Marina di Ravenna** or **Punta Marina** are both crowded, lively places; or for something quieter head north to the beaches at **Porto Corsini**, **Casalborsetti** and **Marina Romea**. **PORTO CORSINI**, between Marina Romea and Marina di Ravenna, is also interesting for its working port, large and modern enough to take tankers but still with old-fashioned cantilevered nets used for fishing the side channels. Just before the port, you pass the **Capanno Garibaldi**, a reconstruction of the hut in which Garibaldi hid on his epic 800-kilometre march from Rome after the fall of the short-lived Roman republic in 1849. Garibaldi's life-long partner Anita, who often fought alongside him, died on the way and he was unable to stop for long enough to bury her. After Marina Romea, take a left through the pinewoods towards the

Strada Romea (SS309), where you'll find places to picnic under the umbrella pines well away from the sight of the industrial area – as well as some places for viewing the tolerant bird life that still frequents the lagoon, which is part of the Po Delta nature reserve (see p.446).

Rimini

RIMINI is one of the least pretentious towns in Italy, the archetypal seaside resort, with a reputation for good if slightly sleazy fun that puts it on a par with Blackpool or Torremolinos. It's certainly brash enough to bear the comparison, and there's plenty of money in evidence; but Rimini is rarely downright tacky. Rather, it's a traditional family resort, to which some Italians return year after year, to stay in their customary *pensione* and be looked after by a hardworking *padrona di casa* as if they were relatives. Indeed the warmth of hoteliers in this part of Italy has undoubtedly added to the tourist industry's success. The resort is best avoided in August, unless you feel you can cope with teeming crowds. Out of season, it's a pleasant enough town, but many hotels, restaurants and shops are closed and the atmosphere is almost eerily quiet.

There's another, less savoury side to the town: Rimini is known across Italy for its fast-living and chancy nightlife, and there's a thriving hetero- and transsexual prostitution scene alongside the town's more wholesome attractions. The road between the train station and the beach and on the coast to the south of the centre can be particularly full of kerb-crawlers, and, although it's rarely dangerous, women on their own – after dark at any rate – should be wary in this part of town.

Rimini was 95 percent destroyed in the last war; however, the town does have a much-ignored old centre that is worth at least a morning of your time. But it's the beach, the crowds and the wild cruising that you really come for: Rimini is still the country's best place to party.

Arrival, information and getting around

The **train station** is situated in the centre of Rimini, on Piazzale Cesare Battisti, ten minutes' walk from both the sea and the old centre. The main **bus station** is just south of here on Via Clementini, and bus #9 runs from the airport (information ☎0541.715.711) to the train station (7km) every thirty minutes; tickets cost €1, and can be bought at the airport bar. There's a most helpful **tourist office** right outside the train station to the left (daily: March–Oct 8.30am–7pm; Nov–Feb 10am–4pm; ☎0541.51.331). They have a list of hotels and will help you find a room, or pass you on to the hotel booking office – see below. The main tourist office, at Piazza Federico Fellini 3 on the seafront (April–Sept Mon–Sat 8.30am–7pm, Sun 9.30am–12.30pm; Oct–March Mon–Sat 9.30am–12.30pm & 3.30–6.30pm; ☎0541.56.902, ◍www.rimini-turismo.it), offers the same service and has a board outside showing vacancies when everything else is closed. The Centro di Informazione Comunale, in the Municipio on Piazza Cavour (Mon–Fri 8.30am–1pm & 2–7pm, Sat 9am–1pm; ☎0541.704.112), gives information on cultural events, often in English.

Getting around is best done on foot, at least within the town centre. But if you need to use the buses, buy an orange ticket from a tobacconist or newsstand; it gives 24 hours' unlimited travel in Rimini and the surrounding area (including Santarcángelo, Riccione and Bellaria) for €2.84. There are also a couple of nightbus services – details in "Nightlife" section on p.458.

Accommodation

Despite its 1600 hotels, accommodation can be a problem in Rimini, and in high season especially you may have to take full pension, which can make it very expensive. At the beginning of the season (before Easter) and towards the end (late September), some hoteliers will negotiate a price for a room only, but in the depths of low season you should bear in mind that the town is pretty much dead, and the few hotels that remain open are largely geared to people here on business. You can book accommodation through the tourist office or the town's hotel booking office (summer daily 8am–7.30pm; winter Mon 3–6pm, Tues–Sat 8.30am–12.30pm & 3–6pm; ☎0541.53.399, ⊜riminibooking@iper.net) just opposite the main tourist office itself.

All the hotels listed below are within a five-minute walk of the beach. To get to the beach area from the station, go out to the right – northwest – all the way to the end of the plane trees, and then turn right again – northeast – through the underpass. The name of the beach area's main artery changes every ten blocks or so, but the section nearest the station underpass is called Viale Amerigo Vespucci.

One of the first nice **hotels** you'll come to along the tree-lined streets is the bright and friendly *Villa Lalla*, Viale Vittorio Veneto 22 (☎0541.55.155, Ⓕ0541.23.570, ⓌVwww.villalalla.com; ⓪). A little closer to the beach is the delightful *Villa Adriatica*, Viale Vespucci 3 (☎0541.54.599, Ⓕ0541.26.962, Ⓦwww.villaadriatica.it; ⓪), with a pool and all amenities. Further down the main thoroughfare towards the south, there's the luxurious four-star *Gradisca*, Viale Fiume 1 (☎0541.25.200, Ⓕ0541.56.299, Ⓦwww.hotellagradisca.it; ⓪), where the decor inside and out is like the over-the-top set of a Fellini film. Next, a few blocks further south, comes one of the best of Rimini's more affordable hotels, the *Verudella*, Viale Tripoli 238 (☎0541.391.124; ⓪), quite smart, and run by a friendly brother-and-sister management. Down another leafy side street between Piazzale Tripoli and Piazzale B. Croce, the welcoming, if rather basic, *Donau*, Viale Alfieri 12 (☎0541.381.302; ⓪), does a wonderful buffet breakfast, as does the *Nancy*, Viale Leopardi 11 (☎0541.381.731; ⓪), an attractive villa in a lush garden, in a parallel street one block further south. Rooms are even simpler at the *Bel Ami* at Via Metastasio 4 (☎0541.381.643; ⓪), located in a peaceful, shady side street, three blocks south of Piazzale B. Croce.

Among the **campsites** reachable by bus #4 from Rimini station *Torre Pedrera* at Via S. Salvador 200 is open the longest (☎0541.720.563; mid–March to Oct). Alternatives are *Camping Italia International,* 2km along the coast at Via Toscanelli 112, Viserba (☎0541.732.882; bus #2, #4 or #8; late May to Sept 20); and *Camping Belvedere*, 5km up the coast at Via Grazia Verenin 9, Viserbella (☎0541.720.960; bus #4; June–Sept). Further from the city, there are also smaller, more attractive sites, worth considering if you have your own transport – *Comunità Agro-Turistica La Ruspante* (☎0541.758.890; open from June), at Via Balduccia 862, San Ermete, 9km from Rimini, with a swimming pool, bungalows and facilities for the disabled.

The Town

There are two parts to Rimini. The belt of land east of the rail line is taken up mostly by holiday accommodation, leading down to the main drag of souvenir shops, restaurants and video arcades that stretches 9km north to the suburbs of Viserba and Torre Pedrera and 7km south to Miramare. Out of season, hotel windows are boarded up and neon signs are wrapped in black plastic to protect against the gales, and Rimini's activity contracts around the Parco dell'Indipendenza and the old town, inland. This is the second, often unseen part of Rimini, a ten-minute walk west from the train station – stone buildings clustered around the twin squares of Piazza Tre Martiri and Piazza Cavour, bordered by the port-canal and town ramparts.

On the southern and northern edges of the old centre respectively sit the **Arco d'Augusto** and **Ponte Tiberio**, testifying to Rimini's importance as a Roman colony. The patched-up Arco was built at the beginning of the first century AD at the point where Via Emilia joined Via Flaminia. Rimini's other Roman remains consist of the **Anfiteatro**, of which there are sparse foundations off Via Roma, just south of the train station.

Just south of the Ponte Tiberio, **Piazza Tre Martiri** and **Piazza Cavour** are the two main squares. Piazza Cavour has a statue of Pope Paul V and the Gothic **Palazzo del Podestà**; the square was rebuilt in the 1920s, and purists argue that it was ruined, although the palazzo's fishtail battlements are still impressive enough. Buskers play here, and bikes and Vespas converge from all directions. Opposite, beyond the sixteenth-century fountain incorporating Roman reliefs, the beautiful **old fish market** often shades antiques stalls worth a browse. The **Museo della Città** at Via L. Tonini 1 (Tues–Sat 10am–12.30pm & Tues–Sun 4.30–7pm; €3.62; ⓦwww.comune.rimini.it/musei/citta/index.htm) has a collection of works of art dating from the fourteenth to the nineteenth centuries, the highlight of which is Giovanni Bellini's pietà.

Just east of here on Via 4 Novembre is Rimini's best-known monument, the **Tempio Malatestiano** (daily 9am–12.30pm & 3.30–6.30pm; free), which serves as the town's cathedral. Built by the Guelph family of Malatesta, it's a strange-looking building, having been left unfinished, but is nevertheless one of the masterworks of the Italian Renaissance. Originally a Franciscan Gothic church, it was transformed in 1450 by Leon Battista Alberti into a building for Sigismondo Malatesta, a *condottiere* with an unparalleled reputation for evil, and it's an odd mixture of private chapel and personal monument. Malatesta's long list of alleged crimes include rape, incest, plunder and looting, not to mention the extreme oppression of his subjects. The church kept, rather disingenuously, its dedication to St Francis, but this didn't faze the pope at the time, Pius II, who condemned its graceful blend of pagan ornaments and classical hedonism, branding it "a temple of devil-worshippers". Indeed, Pius was angered enough to publicly consign Sigismondo to hell, burning an effigy of him in the streets of Rome. This had no effect on Sigismondo, who treated the *tempio* as a private memorial chapel to his great love, Isotta degli Atti. Their initials are linked in emblems all over the building, and the Malatesta armorial bearing – the elephant – appears almost as often. Trumpeting elephants, with their ears flying upwards, or elephants with their trunks entwined, decorate the screens between the side aisles and naves; chubby putti, nymphs and shepherds play, surrounded by bunches of black grapes, in a decidedly un-Christian celebration of humanism. There are a number of fine artworks, now restored: a *Crucifix* attributed to Giotto, friezes and reliefs by Agostino di Duccio and a fresco by Piero della Francesca of Sigismondo himself. All in all, it's an appropriate attraction for Rimini, its qualities of pleasurable extravagance almost an emblem for a town that thrives on excess.

Eating and drinking

The seafront is the best place to **eat** cheaply, with hundreds of pizza bars for on-your-feet refuelling. There are also some extremely ritzy places, where formal dress is obligatory, but most of the interesting restaurants are in the old town. For **snacks**, Via Garibaldi, which leads inland from Piazza Tre Martiri, has several pizza-by-the-slice places, or seek out a shop on Via Bonsi selling *piadina* – a flatbread cooked on a hot griddle and filled with mozzarella, tomato or prosciutto. There are good **bars** around the old fish market – such as *Caravaggio*, where the smart set go.

For **sit-down food**, *Osteria de Börg*, at Via Forzieri 12 (closed Mon), is definitely the place to head for first, a relaxed and moderately priced place serving Romagnolo cooking with innovations, such as *cappelletti* (filled pasta) in carrot sauce, fish kebabs, meat roasted over an open fire and a dozen different vegetable dishes. *Pic-Nic*, Via Tempio Malatestiano 30 (closed Mon), does reasonably priced pizzas, as well as pasta, crêpes – and game. *Rimini Key* (closed Tues) has a number of good-value set menus, as well as pizzas, and is in a prime location for catching Rimini's evening cruising along the seafront on Piazzale Croce, while *Acero Rosso*, at Viale Tiberio 11 (closed Mon), is a more expensive, but excellent, fish restaurant. One of the best restaurants on the seafront is *Lo Squero* (closed Tues), Lungomare Tintori 7, offering great shellfish on a leafy terrace with beach views.

In the suburb of **Covignano**, en route to *Paradiso* (see "Nightlife" below), the *Dalla Maria* at Via Grazie 81 is a good-value restaurant serving dependable Romagnolo cooking for €25 (closed Mon). Another restaurant that merits the journey is *Bastian Contrario* (the name means "Awkward Customer"; closed Mon), 5km out of town at Via Marecchiese 312 in Spadarolo (bus #20), serving well-priced regional cooking. A bargain version of this is available at *La Baracca* (closed Wed) on the same road at no. 373.

Nightlife

Rimini's **nightlife** is concentrated on the seafront, mainly to the south of the centre. Above all, Rimini is a place to go **clubbing**: the town has become the Italian Ibiza and is a favourite destination for those who want to club the summer away. The evening's cruising starts at 10pm or 11pm, at one of the seafront bars, shortly after which people then move on to the first club, either in their cool convertibles and jeeps or by a nightbus called the Blue Line, which operates through the night (10.30pm to sunrise) and serves two routes: the first along the length of the coast, from Bellariva to Cattólica; the second from Rimini to Covignano for club *Paradiso*. Pick up either route at Piazzale Kennedy; nightly bus passes cost €3, tickets available on board. For up-to-date information on the Rimini club scene, check the **listings** in the Italian weekly *Chiamami Città* (free in the tourist office or click on Ⓦ www.chiamamicitta.com). Another useful website is Ⓦ www.rimininightandday.com, with information on places and transport.

Paradiso, at Via Covignano 260 (☎ 0541.751.132, Ⓦ www.paradisoclub.it), is perhaps the most consistently popular club, with great dance music as well as various happenings, such as fashion shows, performances and other, often art-based events, featuring guest spots by DJs, designers and artists from other European countries.

Other places with style and good dance music are scattered among the small resorts that fringe Rimini, again all served by the Blue Line bus. **Riccione** has a lively club scene centred around garage and techno with *Pascià* at Via Sardegna 30 (℡0541.604.207, ⊛www.pasciariccione.it), *Prince* at Via Tre Baci 49 (℡0541.691.209, ⊛www.princericcione.it) and, probably the most famous club in Italy, *Cocoricò*, at Via Chieti 44 (℡0541.605.183), where thousands congregate every weekend under an enormous glass pyramid to rave to the latest in Italian techno. To the south of Riccione in **Misano Monte** are *Byblos* – revival/house – at Piazza Castello 24 (℡0541.690.252, ⊛www.byblosclub .com) and *Villa delle Rose* at Via Camiluccia 16 (℡0541.694.311, ⊛www .villadellerose.net).

For **quieter evenings**, *Arena Astra*, Viale Vespucci 131, Misano Adriatico, to the south, shows alternative and rerun movies in the open air in July and August. More sedately still, there's a classical music festival, the Sagra Musicale Malatestiana, throughout the summer in the Convention Centre in Via della Fiera.

Listings

Airport enquiries ℡0541.715.711, ⊛www.rlm-iniairport.com.
Car rental Avis, Viale Trieste 16d ℡0541.51.256; Europcar, Via Giovanni XXIII 126 ℡0541.54.746; Mondaini, Viale Tripoli 16 ℡0541.782.646.
Emergency ℡112.
Doctor Rimini Soccorso on 24hr call on ℡118, or Infermi hospital ℡0541.705.111.
Internet access The tourist office has a list of Internet cafés – two good ones are the *Email Beach* at Viale Vespucci 29c (Mon–Sat 2–8pm) near the shore and *Cyber Pub* at Viale Mantova 70 (daily 8pm–midnight, closed Sun in winter) in Rivazzurre south of the centre.

Laundry Lavanderia Italia '90, 11e Viale Giusti, just off the seafront between Piazzale Tripolo and Piazzale B. Croce.
Pharmacy Via IV Novembre 39/41 (daily except Thurs 8.30am–12.30pm & 4–8pm; ℡0541.24.414); when closed, details of all-night services are posted outside.
Post office Main office on Largo Giulio Cesare (Mon–Fri 8.15am–5.30pm, Sat 8.15am–1pm); smaller branch at Piazzale Tripoli 4 (Mon–Fri 8.10am–1.30pm, Sat 8.10–11.50am).
Taxis Radiotaxi Cooperative ℡0541.50.020 or 0541.51.488; 24hr rank outside the train station.

Around Rimini: Santarcángelo and San Marino

The countryside around Rimini is attractive: small hilltop towns and lush gentle valleys covered with firs and chestnuts, much of it connected to the coast by bus. **SANTARCÁNGELO**, 11km inland and easily accessible by bus (#9) or train from Rimini, is worth the short trip for its steep medieval streets and thirteenth-century **fortress** (ask at the tourist office about opening times; €3). Carved into the hillside on the edge of the village are some artificial caves, a dank hide-out for early Christians in the seventh century. Local **accommodation** includes the campsite at *La Ruspante* (see p.456), or follow signs to the **tourist office** at Via C. Battisti 5 (May–Sept; ℡0541.624.270, ⊜sauiat@ libero.it) for advice on other options. It's also worth visiting Santarcángelo for the village's **restaurants**, of which *Da Lazaroun* at Via del Platano 21 (closed Thurs) is recommended. *Osteria della Violina*, Vicolo d'Enzi 4 (booking advisable, ℡0541.620.416; closed Wed), occupies a seventeenth-century palazzo with an internal courtyard, and has a cheaper section downstairs serving *piatti poveri* ("poor dishes"), which are chalked up on a board and washed down with Sangiovese wine.

Santarcángelo is very different from the region's second tourist attraction (after the beach), the **REPUBLIC OF SAN MARINO** – an unashamed, though not entirely unpleasant, tourist destination that trades on its nearly two millennia of precariously maintained autonomy. Said to have been founded around 300 AD by a monk fleeing the persecutions of Diocletian, it has its own mint, produces its own postage stamps, and has an army of around a thousand men. The ramparts and medieval-style buildings of the citadel above Borgomaggiore, also called "San Marino", restored in the last century, are mildly interesting; there is a trumped-up **waxworks museum** in Via Lapicidi Marini 17 (daily:April–Sept 8.30am–6.30pm; Oct–March 8.30am–12.30pm & 2–5.30pm; €5), a **stamp museum** in Piazza Belzotti in Borgomaggiore (Mon & Thurs 8.15am–6pm,Tues,Wed & Fri 8.15am–2.15pm; free), as well as tacky souvenir shops and restaurants. And you can also get your passport officially stamped, for only €1.03, by the border guards or at the **information** office at Contrada del Collegio (Mon–Fri 8.30am–6.30pm, Sat & Sun 9am–1pm & 2–6pm; ☎0549.882.998). All the touristy tawdriness aside, however, it's a good place just to stroll around; the walk up through town to the **rocce**, battlemented castles along the highest three ridges, is worth the effort for the all-round views. Below, in Borgomaggiore, is Giovanni Michelucci's "fearless and controversial" modernist church, built in the 1960s, with a roof that seems to cascade down in waves.

Travel details

Trains

Bologna to: Ancona (hourly; 2hr 15min); Faenza (hourly; 45min); Ferrara (hourly; 30min); Fidenza (hourly; 1hr 10min); Florence (hourly; 1hr); Forlì (hourly; 50min); Ímola (hourly; 30min); Milan (hourly; 2hr 35min); Modena (every 30 min; 20min); Parma (every 30 min; 50min); Piacenza (hourly; 1hr 30min); Ravenna (13 daily; 1hr 20min); Reggio Emilia (every 30 min; 40min); Rimini (hourly; 1hr 20min).
Faenza to: Brisighella (15 daily; 10min).
Ferrara to: Ravenna (16 daily; 1hr 15min); Rimini (9 daily; 2hr 15min).
Fidenza to: Busseto (14 daily; 15min); Cremona (15 daily; 35min).
Modena to: Carpi (hourly; 12min); Mantua (14 daily; 1hr 20min); Verona (9 daily; 2hr).
Parma to: Brescia (10 daily; 2hr); La Spezia (8 daily; 2hr 15min).
Piacenza to: Cremona (6 daily; 30min).
Rimini to: Santarcángelo (6 daily; 8min).

Buses

Bologna to: Ímola (every 15min; 1hr); Marzabotto (hourly; 15min); Pontecchio Marconi (every 15min; 45min); Vignola (hourly; 1hr).
Ferrara to: Comacchio (10 daily; 1hr 10min).
Fidenza to: Fontanellato (3 daily; 25min); Soragna (9 daily; 20min).
Modena to: Carpi (20 daily; 40min); Maranello (hourly; 30min); Vignola (8 daily; 40min).
Parma to: Busseto/Le Roncole (5 daily; 1hr); Fontanellato (6 daily; 35min); Langhirano (hourly; 45min); Roncole Verdi (5 daily; 50min); Soragna (5 daily; 40min).
Piacenza to: Castell'Arquato (10 daily; 1hr); Rustigazzo (1 daily; 1hr).
Ravenna to: Classe (every 30 min; 10min); Marina di Ravenna (every 30 min; 20min); Marina Romea (10 daily; 20min); Mésola (2 daily; 2hr); Punta Marina (every 30 min; 15min).
Reggio Emilia to: Casina (15 daily; 50min).
Rimini to: Rome (2 daily in summer, 2 weekly in winter; 5hr 30min); San Marino (hourly; 30min); Santarcángelo (hourly; 30min).

Tuscany

CHAPTER 8

Highlights

* **The Duomo, Florence** Climb Brunelleschi's dome, the city's signature building. See p.478

* **The Uffizi** The world's greatest collection of Italian Renaissance paintings. See p.486

* **Medici villas** Explore the country houses of Florence's pre-eminent family. See p.511

* **Chianti** The country's most famous vineyards. See p.512

* **Lucca** An amazing array of Romanesque churches in this most urbane of Tuscan towns. See p.527

* **The Leaning Tower, Pisa** Now saved from imminent collapse, the tower is once again open to visitors. See p.522

* **The Campo** Soak up the atmosphere in Siena's scallop-shell main square. See p.550

* **The Palio** Siena's historic, chaotic horse-race, run over three frenetic laps of the Campo. See p.556

* **Monte Oliveto Maggiore** A mighty monastery set amidst wonderful upland countryside. See p.577

Tuscany

Tuscany harbours the classic landscapes of Italy, familiar from Renaissance paintings and TV travel shows alike, with their backdrop of medieval hill-towns, rows of slender cypress trees, vineyards and olive groves, and artfully sited villas and farmhouses. It's a picture that has long held an irresistible attraction for northern Europeans.

The expat's perspective may be distorted, but Tuscany is indeed the essence of Italy in many ways. The national language evolved from Tuscan dialect, a supremacy ensured by Dante, who wrote the *Divine Comedy* in the vernacular of his birthplace, Florence; and Tuscan writers such as Petrarch and Boccaccio. But what makes this area pivotal to the culture of Italy and all of Europe is the **Renaissance**, which fostered painting, sculpture and architecture that comprise an intrinsic part of a Tuscan tour. The very name by which we refer to this extraordinarily creative era was coined by a Tuscan, Giorgio Vasari, who wrote in the sixteenth century of the "rebirth" of the arts. **Florence** was the most active centre of the Renaissance, flourishing principally through the all-powerful patronage of the Medici dynasty. Every eminent artistic figure from Giotto onwards – Masaccio, Brunelleschi, Alberti, Donatello, Botticelli, Leonardo da Vinci, Michelangelo – is represented here, in an unrivalled gathering of churches, galleries and museums.

Few people react entirely positively to Florence's crowds and its rather draining commercialism. **Siena** provokes less ambiguous responses. This is one of the great medieval cities of Europe, almost perfectly preserved, and with superb works of art in its religious and secular buildings. Its beautiful Campo – the central, scallop-shaped market square – is the scene, too, of Tuscany's one unmissable festival, the **Palio**, which sees bareback horse-riders careering around the cobbles amid the brightest display of pageantry this side of Rome. Other major cities, **Pisa** and **Lucca**, provide convenient entry points to the region, either by air (via Pisa's airport) or along the coastal rail route from Genoa. **Arezzo** serves as the classic introduction to Tuscany if you're approaching from the south (Rome) or east (Perugia). All three have their splendours – Pisa its Leaning Tower, Lucca a string of Romanesque churches, Arezzo an outstanding fresco cycle by Piero della Francesca.

Tucked away to the west and south of Siena are dozens of small **hill-towns** that, for many, epitomize the region. **San Gimignano** is the best-known, and is worth visiting as much for its spectacular array of frescoes as for its much-photographed bristle of medieval tower-houses, though it's now a little too popular for its own good. **Montepulciano**, **Pienza** and **Cortona** are each superbly located and dripping with atmosphere, but the best candidates for a

Tuscan hill-town escape are little-mentioned places such as **Volterra**, **Massa Maríttima** or **Pitigliano**, in each of which tourism has yet to undermine local character.

If the Tuscan **countryside** has a fault, it's the popularity that its seductiveness has brought, and you may find lesser-known sights proving most memorable – remote monasteries like **Monte Oliveto Maggiore**, the sulphur spa of **Bagno Vignoni**, or the striking open-air art gallery of the **Tarot Garden**. The one area where Tuscany fails to impress is its over-developed **coast**, with uninspired beach-umbrella compounds filling every last scrap of sand. The Tuscan **islands** have rather more going for them – **Elba** may be a victim of its own allure, but the smaller islands such as **Capraia** retain a tranquil isolation.

Tuscany's **tourist office** is based at Via di Novoli 26, I-50127 Firenze (☎055.438.2111, ⓦwww.turismo.toscana.it) – their website gives access to a comprehensive accommodation database and links to all fifteen of Tuscany's area tourist offices. Finding **accommodation** can be a major problem in the

Regional food and wine

Tuscan cooking has been a seminal influence in Italian cuisine generally. Its guiding principle is simplicity: classic Tuscan *antipasti* are peasant fare: *bruschetta* is stale bread, toasted and dressed with oil and garlic, *crostini* is toast and pâté. **Olive oil** is the essential flavouring, used as a dressing for salads, a medium for frying and to drizzle over bread or vegetables and into soups and stews just before serving.

Soups are very popular – Tuscan menus always include either *ribollita*, a hearty stew of vegetables, beans and chunks of bread and/or *zuppa di farro*, thick with spelt (a barley-like grain). Fish restaurants around the region try to copy *cacciucco*, a spiced fish and seafood soup, but the best place in Italy to try it is the town of its birth, Livorno. White cannellini **beans** (*fagioli*) are another favourite, turning up in salads, with pasta (*tuoni e lampo*) or just dressed with olive oil. Tuscany is not known for its **pasta**, but many towns in the south serve *pici*, a local variety of thick spaghetti. **Meat** is kept plain, often grilled, and Florentines will often profess to liking nothing better than a good *bistecca alla fiorentina* (rare char-grilled steak), or the simple rustic dishes of *arista* (roast pork loin stuffed with rosemary and garlic) or *pollo alla diavola* (chicken flattened, marinated and then grilled with herbs). Hunters' fare such as *cinghiale* (wild boar) and *coniglio* (rabbit) often turns up in hill-town *trattorie*. Spinach is often married with ricotta to make gnocchi, used as a pasta filling, and in *crespoline* (pancakes) or between two chunks of *focaccia* and eaten as a street or bar snack. Sheep's milk *pecorino* is the most widespread Tuscan **cheese** (best in Pienza), but the most famous is the oval *marzolino* from the Chianti region, which is eaten either fresh or ripened. **Dessert** menus will often include *cantuccini*, hard, almond-flavoured biscuits to be dipped in a glass of Vinsanto (sweet dessert wine) – best known as *biscottini* in Prato – but Siena is the main source of sweet treats, such as almond macaroons and *panforte*, a rich and sticky cake full of nuts and fruit.

Tuscany has some of Italy's finest **wines**. Three top names, which all bear the exclusive DOCG mark (and price-tags to match), are Chianti Classico, Brunello di Montalcino and Vino Nobile di Montepulciano – not the sort of thing you'd knock back at a trattoria. There are dozens of other Chianti varieties, most of them excellent, but it can be difficult to find a bargain: it's worth finding out which labels to aim for before buying. Both Montalcino and Montepulciano produce *rosso* varieties that are more pocket-friendly, and other names to look for include Carmignano and Rosso delle Colline Lucchesi. Two notable whites are dry Vernaccia di San Gimignano and the fresh Galestro. Tuscany is also renowned for Vinsanto, a sweet, strong dessert wine made from grapes left to dry in the sun.

summer: you should definitely reserve in advance, even at budget level. Be warned that the region is also expensive, with few hotel doubles costing less than €50 in high season (€70 in Florence). **Agritourism** is big business, with a plethora of family-run places dotted around the countryside offering anything from budget rooms in a farmhouse up to luxury apartments within restored castles or Renaissance villas set amidst wine estates; the regional government's website (Ⓦ www.agriturismo.regione.toscana.it) has plenty of information.

Florence (Firenze)

Since early in the nineteenth century **FLORENCE** has been celebrated as the most beautiful city in Italy. Stendhal staggered around its streets in a perpetual stupor of delight; the Brownings sighed over its idyllic charms; and E.M. Forster's *Room with a View* portrayed it as the great southern antidote to the sterility of Anglo-Saxon life. For most people Florence comes close to living up to the myth only in its first, resounding impressions. The pinnacle of Brunelleschi's stupendous cathedral dome dominates the cityscape, and the close-up view is even more breathtaking, with the multicoloured **Duomo** rising behind the marble-clad **Baptistry**. Wander from there down towards the River Arno and the attraction still holds: beyond the broad Piazza della Signoria, site of the towering **Palazzo Vecchio**, the river is spanned by the medieval shop-lined **Ponte Vecchio**, with the gorgeous church of **San Miniato al Monte** glistening on the hill behind it.

Yet after registering these marvellous sights, it's hard to stave off a sense of disappointment, for much of Florence is a city of narrow streets and heavy-set, oppressively dour *palazzi* that show only iron-barred windows and massive, studded doors to the outside world. The alienating effects of this physical entrenchment are redoubled by an unending tide of **mass tourism.** You'll find light relief to be in short supply.

The fact is, the best of Florence is to be seen indoors. Under the patronage of the **Medici** family, the city's artists and thinkers were instigators of the shift from the medieval to the modern world-view, and churches, galleries and museums are the places to get to grips with their achievement. The development of the Renaissance can be plotted in the vast picture collection of the **Uffizi** and in the sculpture of the **Bargello** and the **Museo dell'Opera del Duomo**. Equally revelatory are the fabulously decorated chapels of **Santa Croce** and **Santa Maria Novella**, forerunners of such astonishing creations as Masaccio's superb frescoes in the **Cappella Brancacci**, and Fra' Angelico's serene paintings in the monks' cells at **San Marco**. The Renaissance emphasis on harmony and rational design is expressed with unrivalled eloquence in Brunelleschi's architecture, specifically in the churches of **San Lorenzo**, **Santo Spirito** and the **Cappella dei Pazzi**. The full genius of Michelangelo, the dominant creative figure of sixteenth-century Italy, is on display in the fluid design of San Lorenzo's **Biblioteca Laurenziana** and the marble statuary of the **Cappelle Medicee** and the **Accademia** – home of the *David*. Every quarter of Florence can boast a church or collection worth an extended call, and the enormous **Palazzo Pitti** south of the river constitutes a museum district on its own.

Some history

The Roman colony of Florentia was established in 59 BC; expansion was rapid, based on trade along the Arno. In the sixth century AD the city fell to the barbarian hordes of Totila, then the **Lombards** and then Charlemagne's **Franks**. In 1078 Countess Mathilda of Tuscia supervised the construction of new fortifications, and in the year of her death – 1115 – granted Florence the status of an **independent city**. Around 1200, the first *Arti* (Guilds) were formed to promote the interests of traders and bankers in the face of conflict between the pro-imperial **Ghibelline** faction and the pro-papal **Guelphs**. In 1260, the Guelph-backed regime of Florence's *Primo Popolo*, a government of the mercantile class, was ousted after Siena's Ghibelline army defeated Florence. By the 1280s the Guelphs were back in power through the *Secondo Popolo*; the exclusion of the nobility from government in 1293 was the most dramatic measure in a programme of political reform that invested power in the *Signoria*, a council drawn from the major guilds. The mighty Palazzo della Signoria – now known as the **Palazzo Vecchio** – was raised as a visible demonstration of authority over a huge city: at this time, Florence had a population around 100,000, a thriving mercantile sector and a highly developed banking system (the **florin** was common currency across Europe). Strife within the Guelph camp marked the start of the fourteenth century, and then in the 1340s the two largest banks collapsed and the **Black Death** struck, destroying up to half the city's population.

The political rise of **Cosimo de' Medici**, later dubbed Cosimo il Vecchio ("the Old"), was to some extent due to his family's sympathies with the smaller guilds. The **Medici** fortune had been made by the banking prowess of Cosimo's father, Giovanni Bicci de' Medici, and Cosimo used the power conferred by wealth to great effect. Through his patronage of such figures as Brunelleschi and Donatello, Florence became the centre of artistic activity in Italy.

The ascendancy continued under Cosimo's grandson **Lorenzo il Magnifico**, who ruled the city at the height of its artistic prowess. Papal resentment of Florentine independence found an echo in the jealousy of the Pazzi family, one of the city's main rivals to the Medici. The two camps colluded in the **Pazzi conspiracy** of 1478, in which Lorenzo was wounded and his brother Giuliano murdered. Before Lorenzo's death in 1492, the Medici bank failed, and in 1494 Lorenzo's son Piero was obliged to flee. Florentine hearts and minds were seized by the charismatic Dominican monk **Girolamo Savonarola**, who preached on the decadence and corruption of the city. Artists departed in droves. In a symbolic demonstration of the new order, Savonarola and his child spies set about collecting all the trappings of Florence's Medicean culture – books, paintings, tapestries, fancy furniture and clothes – and piled them high in Piazza della Signoria in a **Bonfire of the Vanities**. But such a graphic assault on the past signalled a turning-point: within a year, Savonarola had been found guilty of heresy and treason, and burned alive at the same spot.

After Savonarola, the city functioned peaceably under a republican constitution headed by Piero Soderini, whose chief adviser was his friend **Niccolò Machiavelli**. In 1512 the Medici returned, and in 1516, Giovanni de' Medici

FLORENCE

TUSCANY | Florence

8

ACCOMMODATION	
Anna, Armonia, Azri etc	7
Benvenuti	3
Brunetta	11
Liana	8
Monna Lisa	9
Ostella Villa Camerata	1
Pio X-Artigianelli	12
Residenza Johanna Uno	4
Residenza Johanna Due	2
Suore Oblate dell'Assunzione	10
Villa Betania	13
Villa Il Castagno	5
Vilino La Magnolia	6
RESTAURANTS	
Alla Vecchia Bettola	C
Cibreo	A
I Tarocchi	D
Il Pizzaiuolo	B

Stadio Comunale

Fiesole

Museo Stibbert

Prato & Pistoia

Stazione Campo di Marte

Cimitero degli Inglesi

Museo Archeologico

Spedale degli Innocenti

SS. Annunziata

Accademia

Museo di San Marco

Scalzo

Museo Botanico

Giardino dei Semplici

Giardino della Gherardesca

Sant'Apollonia

Cenacolo di Foligno

Palazzo delle Mostre
Fortezza da Basso

Stazione Santa Maria Novella

Bus Station

See "Central Florence" map for detail

River Mugnone

▲ *S. Salvi*

200 m

0

S. Ambrogio
Mercato Sant'Ambrogio
Synagogue
Santa Maria Maddalena dei Pazzi **10**
Ospedale S. Maria Nuova **11**
Casa Buonarroti
Santa Croce
Museo Horne
Museo dell'Opera del Duomo
Pal. Medici Riccardi
Duomo
Badia Fiorentina
Bargello
Palazzo Vecchio
Uffizi
Orsanmichele
Baptistry
Campanile
Cappelle Medicee
San Lorenzo
Pal. Strozzi
Palazzo Davanzati
Santa Maria Novella
Pal. Rucellai
Santa Trinita
Ognissanti
Santo Spirito
Cappella Brancacci
Santa Maria del Carmine
Santa Felicita
Palazzo Pitti
La Specola
Giardino di Boboli
Forte di Belvedere
Museo Bardini
San Niccolò
Camping Michelangiolo
San Salvatore al Monte
San Miniato al Monte
Porta Romana

River Arno

OLTRARNO

PONTE VECCHIA
PONTE SAN NICCOLÒ
VIALE MICHELANGELO
VIALE GALILEO GALILEI
VIALE GIOVANNI AMENDOLA
VIALE ANTONIO GRAMSCI

became **Pope Leo X**, granting Michelangelo and Leonardo da Vinci major commissions. After the assassination of the tyrannical transvestite Alessandro de' Medici in 1537, Florentine power was handed to a new Cosimo, who seized the Republic of Siena and, in 1569, took the title **Cosimo I**, Grand Duke of Tuscany. The great traditions of Florentine art descended into farce as sycophants such as **Giorgio Vasari** plastered the city with fawning images of Medici power and glory.

Florence's decline was slow and painful. The later Medicis were each more ridiculous than the last: **Francesco** spent most of his thirteen-year reign indoors, obsessed by alchemy; **Ferdinando II** sat back as harvests failed, plagues ran riot and banking and textiles slumped to nothing; the virulently anti-Semitic **Cosimo III** spent 53 years in power cracking down on dissidents; and **Gian Gastone** spent virtually all his time drunk in bed. When Gastone died, in 1737, the Medici line died with him.

Under the terms of a treaty signed by Gian Gastone's sister, **Anna Maria Ludovica**, Florence – and the whole Grand Duchy of Tuscany – passed to Francesco of Lorraine, the future Francis I of Austria. Austrian rule lasted until the coming of the French in 1799; after a fifteen-year interval of French control, the Lorraine dynasty was brought back, remaining in residence until the Risorgimento upheavals of 1859. Absorbed into the united Italian state in the following year, Florence became the **capital** of the Kingdom of Italy in 1861, a position it held until 1875.

After 1890, large swathes of the medieval city were **demolished** by government officials and developers; buildings that had stood in the area of what is now Piazza della Repubblica since the early Middle Ages were pulled down to make way for undistinguished office blocks, and old quarters around Santa Croce and Santa Maria Novella were razed. In 1944, the retreating German army blew up all the city's bridges except the Ponte Vecchio and destroyed swathes of medieval architecture. A disastrous **flood** in November 1966 drowned several people and wrecked buildings and works of art. Restoration of damage caused by the flood, and by a 1993 **Mafia car-bomb** that killed five people outside the Uffizi, is still going on. Indeed, monuments and paintings are the basis of Florence's survival in the new century, a state of affairs that gives rise to considerable popular discontent. The development of new industrial parks on the northern outskirts is the latest and most ambitious attempt to break Florence's ever-increasing dependence on its seven million annual tourists.

Arrival

Florence's main **train station** is Santa Maria Novella, or "Firenze SMN". Many city and all inter-urban **buses** stop outside Between 1.30am and 4am, trains stop instead at the eastern Campo di Marte station, served by nightbus #70. **Pisa's Galileo Galilei** airport (☎050.500.707; ⓦwww.pisa-airport.com), lies 95km west of Florence. Direct trains leave roughly every hour and take an hour. Tickets (€4.40) can be bought from the tourist office halfway down the arrivals concourse on the right. Note that on the return journey you don't have to haul your bags all the way out to the airport, as there's a check-in desk for most airlines by platform 5 at Santa Maria Novella station in Florence, open daily from 7am to 5pm; bags have to be checked in at least thirty minutes before the departure of the train, which must arrive at Pisa airport at least thirty minutes before the departure of the flight, and there's a charge of around €3 for the service.

An increasing number of international air services use Florence's **Aeroporto Amerigo Vespucci** (ⓦwww.aeroporto.firenze.it), 5km northwest in Perétola, linked to SMN station by the"Vola in Bus" shuttle bus (every 30min; €4). Tickets can be bought on board or from machines at the airport and bus station. In Florence buses arrive and depart from the main SITA bus terminal on Via di Santa Caterina da Siena, just a few steps west of Santa Maria Novella railway station; after 9pm, however, the buses depart from outside the Bar Cristallo in Largo Alinari, off the eastern side of Piazza della Stazione.

Information, orientation and transport

The main **tourist office** is just north of the Duomo at Via Cavour 1r (Mon–Sat 8.30am–6.30pm, Sun 8.30am–1.30pm; ☎055.290.832/3, ⓔinfoturismo@ provincia.fi.it). Handy if you're arriving by train or bus is the smaller office at **Piazza della Stazione 4** (Mon–Sat 8.30am–7pm, Sun 8.30am–1.30pm; ☎055.212.245); there's another one at **Borgo Santa Croce 29r** (Mon–Sat 9am–7pm, Sun 9am–2pm; ☎055.234.0444); an information counter within the APT's headquarters at **Via Manzoni 16** (Mon–Fri 9am–1pm; ☎055.23.320); and a desk at **Vespucci airport** (daily 7.30am–11.30pm; ☎055.315.874). Aside from maps and brochures, the most useful item these offices can give you is a photocopied list of the up-to-date opening hours and entrance charges for all the city's museums, which change often. They can also give you the fat little freebie magazine *Firenze City Guide*, crammed with ads, walking itineraries and practical information. Florence's excellent what's-on guide is *Firenze Spettacolo*, available monthly from newsagents (€1.60). On the **Internet**, the APT (ⓦwww.firenze.turismo.toscana.it), the province (ⓦwww.provincia.fi.it) and the municipality (ⓦwww.comune.fi.it) are outclassed by some very useful commercial sites, notably ⓦwww.mega.it, ⓦwww.arca.net/florence.htm and ⓦwww .english.firenze.net.

Finding your way around the centre of town is very easy – it's just ten minutes' walk from Santa Maria Novella to the central Piazza del Duomo, along Via de' Panzani and Via de' Cerretani; stand with your back to the train station and they form the main thoroughfare sweeping away in front of you and to the left. The great majority of the major sights are within a few minutes of the Duomo.

Within the historic centre walking is generally the most efficient way of getting around, but to cross town quickly or get to outlying sights the best form of transport is the ATAF **buses**; they have a range of tickets (€1 for 1hr; €1.80 for 3hr; €4 for 24hr; or the *biglietto multiplo* giving four one-hour rides for €3.90). They can be bought from the main **ticket and information office** (daily 7am–8pm; ☎055.565.0222) in the bays to the east of Santa Maria Novella train station, from shops and stalls displaying the ATAF sign, and from automatic machines all over Florence. Make sure you stamp the ticket in the machine on board. Most routes originate at or pass by the train station, where you can get more information from the ATAF kiosk (freephone ☎800.424.500, ⓦwww.ataf.net).

8

Pedestrianized street

Stazione Santa Maria Novella

★ ATAF Bus Bays ★ ★ ★ ★ ★

❶ Desirée

VIA CHIARA

Mercato Centrale

PIAZZA MERCATO CENTRALE

VIA FIUME

VIA VALFONDA

VIA NAZIONALE

VIA PANICALE

VIA FAENZA

VIA DELL'ARIENTO

BORGO LA NOCE

SITA Bus Station

PIAZZA DELLA STAZIONE

LARGO FRATELLI ALINARI

ⓘ

❸

PIAZZA DELLA STAZIONE

VIA S. C. DA SIENA

VIA DEGLI ORTI ORICELLARI

VIA L. ALAMANNI

VIA S. ANTONINO

VIA SANT'ANTONINO

VIA GUELFA

VIA FAENZA

VIA DEL MELARANCIO

Cappelle Medicee

VIA D. CANTO DE'

VIA D'CANTO DE

PIAZZA MADONNA ALDOBRANDINI

Santa Maria Novella

Museo di Santa Maria Novella

PIAZZA DELL'UNITÀ ITALIANA

VIA DEI CONTI

VIA ZANNETTI

Biblioteca Laurenziana

VIA DELL'ALLORO

VIA DELL'ALBERO

VIA DELLA SCALA

VIA DE CANACCI

VIA DELLA SCALA

VIA DI BELFREDELLI

Ⓐ ❺

PIAZZA SANTA MARIA NOVELLA

VIA DEGLI AVELLI

VIA DEI BANCHI

VIA DEI CERRETANI

S. Maria Maggiore

Pal. Orlandini

PIAZZA PAOLINO

VIA DEL PORCELLANA

VIA DEL MORO

VIA CORNINO

VIA DEI PANZANI

VIA RONDINELLI

Pal. Antinori

❼

S. Gaetano

VIA DEGLI AGLI

VIA DEI PECORI

Ognissanti

PIAZZA OGNISSANTI

BORGO OGNISSANTI

S. Paolino

PIAZZA DEGLI OTTAVIANI

VIA DELLA SPADA

VIA DEL SOLE

VIA DELLE BELLE DONNE

❽

VIA DE' CORSI

VIA DE CERRETANI

VIA CAMPIDOGLIO

VIA DEI

Ospedale S. Giovanni di Dio

Museo Marini

Pal. Rucellai

VIA DE' FOSSI

VIA DE' FEDERIGHI

VIA DE' PESCIONI

Pal. Corsi

VIA DEGLI STROZZI

V. BRUNELLESCHI

PIAZZA DELLA REPUBBLICA

LUNGARNO AMERIGO VESPUCCI

VIA DELLA VIGNA NUOVA

❾

Loggia

VIA DEI PALCHETTI

VIA DE' TORNABUONI

Pal. Strozzi

VIA DEGLI ANSELMI

V. PELLICCERIA

PIAZZA CARLO GOLDONI

Pal. Corsini

VIA DEL PARIONE

VIA DELLA SPADA

Pal. Giaconi

Pal. Strozzino

VIA DE' SASSETTI

VIA PORTA ROSSA

PONTE ALLA CARRAIA

LUNGARNO CORSINI

VIA DEL PURGATORIO

PIAZZA S. TRINITA

Pal. Altovita

Ⓖ

Pal. Bartolini

Pal. Davanzati

Mercato Nuovo

VIA DELLE TERME

LUNGARNO SODERINI

Santa Trinita

PIAZZA N. SAURO

Pal. Spini Ferroni

BORGO SANTI APOSTOLI

Pal. d. Parte Guelfa

VIA PUR S. MARIA

BORGO SAN FREDIANO

PIAZZA BORGO STELLA DEL CARMINE

Chiesa Scozzese

Pal. Guicciardini

LUNGARNO GUICCIARDINI

PONTE S. TRINITA

LUNGARNO ACCIAIUOLI

SS. Apostoli

❶❷

VIA DEL

R i v e r   A r n o

S. Stefano

❶❸

Cappella Brancacci

Ⓛ

Santa Maria del Carmine

Ⓛ

VIA DE' SERRAGLI

VIA DELL'ARDIGLIONE

VIA DI S. MONACA

VIA S. AGOSTINO

Ⓙ

Pal. Frescobaldi

VIA DELLO SPRONE

S. Jacopo Oltrarno

BORGO SAN JACOPO

❶❺

Corridoio Vasariano

PONTE VECCHIO

OLTRARNO

VIA MAFFIA

VIA S. MAFFIA

Ⓚ

Santo Spirito

VIA MAGGIO

VIA DELLO SPRONE

V. DI BARBRANDANO

VIA DE' BARDI

VIA GUICCIARDINI

Santa Felicita

PIAZZA DE' ROSSI

❶❻

Ⓛ

Ⓜ ❶❼

PIAZZA DI SANTO SPIRITO

Ⓝ

VIA DEL PRESTO DI SAN MARTINO

VIA DELLO SPRONE

ACCOMMODATION								
Alessandra	**12**	Dali	**8**	Firenze	**6**	Lungarno	**15**	Sorelle Bandini	**17**
Bavaria	**10**	Desirée	**1**	Hermitage	**13**	Orchidea	**11**	Suore Oblate dello
Casci	**4**	Elite	**5**	Istituto Gould	**16**	Santa Monaca	**14**	Spirito Santo	**3**
		Ferretti	**7**	Loggiato dei Serviti	**2**	Scoti	**9**	

CENTRAL FLORENCE

▲ San Marco

SS Annunziata ✚
PIAZZA SANTISSIMA ANNUNZIATA

Accademia

Opificio delle Pietre Dure

Spedale degli Innocenti

Museo Archeologico

Pal. Gerini

VIA DELLA COLONNA

VIA LAURA

Pal. Medici Riccardi

S. Maria d. Angeli

PIAZZA F. BRUNELLESCHI

Pal. Niccolini

Pal. Pucci

San Lorenzo

Ospedale S. Maria Nuova

N

Palazzo Niccolini

Duomo

Museo dell'Opera del Duomo

PIAZZA S.M. NUOVA ✚

Museo di Firenze com'era

Teatro della Pergola

Baptistery

Campanile

Pal. d. Canonici

S. Maria in Campo

Loggia d. Bigallo

Museo d. Antropologia

Pal. Altoviti

Pal. Albizi

Pal. Salviati

BORGO DEGLI ALBIZI

Pal. Alessandri

PIAZZA G. SALVEMINI

Casa di Dante

Pal. Pazzi

S. Martino

Casino Borghese

Orsanmichele

Bargello

VIA GHIBELLINA

Badia

Teatro Verdi

Casa Buonarroti

▲ Sant'Ambrogio

Pal. Gondi

San Firenze

S. Simone

Loggia d. Signoria

Palazzo Vecchio

Uffizi

PIAZZA SANTA CROCE

Santa Croce

Pal. Vita

Casa dell'Antella

Museo di Storia della Scienza

Pal. Corsini

Pal. Rasponi

Museo dell'Opera di Santa Croce

Borsa

Museo Horne

Biblioteca Nazionale

LUNGARNO GENERALE DIAZ

LUNGARNO DELLA ZECCA VECCHIA

0   100 m

8

TUSCANY | Florence

473

RESTAURANTS

Acqua al Due	E	Belle Donne	B
Angiolino	J	Benvenuto	I
Baldovino	H	Borgo Antico	M
		Caff Italiano	D
Cantinetta dei Verrazzano	C	Oliviero	G
La Casalinga	N	Osteria Santo Spirito	L
Il Contadino	A	Quattro Leoni	K
Enoteca Pinchiorri	F		

Accommodation

On the whole, Florence's **accommodation** is over-priced: it is true to say that the welcome and the service you receive are often not on a par with that of other places in Italy. You should **book in advance**, especially between March and October. If you leave it to the last minute, the easiest solution is to queue up at the **Consorzio Informazioni Turistiche Alberghiere** (ITA) inside the train station (Mon–Sat 8.30am–7pm, Sun 9am–5.30pm; ℡055.282.893, ℻055.288.429) – they charge from €2 to ten times that, according to the class of hotel, and only take bookings over the counter. Five upmarket hotels offer substantial **discounts to students** – see the APT's excellent brochure *Studying in Florence: A Guide* for details. The other option is to save money staying outside Florence, at Fiesole, Prato, Pistoia, Empoli or Greve in Chianti, all of which are within a thirty-minute radius by bus or train.

Hotels

Prices at the down-market end of Florence's **hotels** have a high-season average in one-star places of around €80 – and that's without breakfast, which is virtually compulsory in summer, slapping as much as an extra €8 per person onto the bill. From October to April prices come down a little, and if you arrive in the low season – roughly January to Easter, plus November – you'll find many discounts.

The central area

Alessandra Borgo Santi Apostoli 17 ℡055.283.438, ⍵www.hotelalessandra.com. Occupying a sixteenth-century palazzo, steps from the Uffizi, this stylish two-star, with 25 rooms (16 with bathroom) furnished in a mixture of antique and modern styles, is justifiably popular. ❼

Bavaria Borgo degli Albizi 26 ℡ & ℻ 055.234.0313, ⍵weidinet.com/hotelbavaria. Installed in a sixteenth-century palazzo, a simple and acceptable one-star with just nine rooms, most with shared bathroom. Be sure to book, as it's popular with long-stay language students. No credit cards. ❺

Dali Via dell'Oriuolo 17 ℡055.234.0706, ⍵www.hoteldali.com. Discreet little one-star on a street just behind the Duomo, with nine plain and rather basic rooms (three en suite), a peaceful courtyard and limited parking. The friendly young owners speak good English. ❹

Firenze Piazza dei Donati 4 ℡055.214.203, ℻055.212.370. Modernized one-star bang in the heart of things, with 57 clean, generic doubles, the best on the upper floors. ❺

Hermitage Vicolo Marcio 1 ℡055.287.216, ⍵www.hermitagehotel.com. This welcoming 28-room three-star is steps from the Ponte Vecchio; reception is alongside the roof garden, and above-average guest rooms fill the front rooms on the lower floors, some with river views; rooms from the former *Archibusieri* hotel, now incorporated into the *Hermitage*, are slightly less appealing. ❾

Orchidea Borgo degli Albizi 11 ℡055.248.0346, ℮hotelorchidea@yahoo.it. Lovely little *locanda* in a twelfth-century palazzo run by a friendly Anglo-Italian couple. Four singles and three doubles, with shared bathrooms. ❹

Scoti Via Tornabuoni 7 ℡055.292.128, ℮hotelscoti@hotmail.com. A hotel with bags of character and a superb central location. The lounge features amazing floor-to-ceiling frescoes and the rooms are light and spacious (none with private bathrooms). ❹

The western city centre

Anna (℡055.239.8322), **Armonia** (℡055.211.146), **Azzi** (℡055.213.806, ℮hotelazzi@hotmail.com), **Marini** (℡055.284.824), **Merlini** (℡055.212.848, ⍵www.hotelmerlini.it) and **Paola** (℡055.213.682), all Via Faenza 56. With most of its rooms overlooking the garden, the *Azzi* is the pleasantest of the six one-stars occupying the upper floors of this building, but it tends to get block-booked by a tour operator. The others are all at least tolerable. ❸–❹

Desirée Via Fiume 20 ℡055.238.2382, ⍵www.desireehotel.com. A comfortable two-star

Street-numbering runs in relation to the river. If the street or square is parallel to the river, numbers start from the east and proceed towards the west. If the street is perpendicular to the river, the numbering starts from the end nearest the river bank. Odd numbers are on the left side of the street, even on the right.

However, beware that Florence has a complicated double system of street-numbering: commercial establishments (such as bars and restaurants) have **red** numbers (*rosso*), while private buildings have black or blue numbers – and the two systems don't run in tandem. This means, for example, that Via Mosca 35r might be next-door to Via Mosca 89, but several hundred metres from Via Mosca 33. There's no logic or purpose to it at all.

with stained-glass windows, simulated antique furniture, and a bath in every room. ❻
Elite Via della Scala 12 ☎055.215.395, ⓕ055.213.832. Usefully located, tiny two-star with pleasant, friendly management and occasional bargain prices. ❺

The northern city centre

Casci Via Cavour 13 ☎055.211.686, ⓦwww.hotelcasci.com. A welcoming, excellent, family-run two-star. Only two of its 25 rooms face onto busy Via Cavour, both of which are triple-glazed; some of the others look onto the peaceful rear garden. Big buffet breakfast and free Internet access. ❼
Loggiato dei Serv26 Piazza Santissima Annunziata 3 ☎055.289.592, ⓦwww.loggiatodeiservitihotel.it.

South of the river

Lungarno Borgo San Jacopo 14 ☎055.27.261, ⓦwww.lungarnohotels.com. Picture windows in all public rooms take full advantage of the romantic Arno view, as do the balconies attached to the best of the blue-and-cream liveried guest rooms. ❾
Sorelle Bandini Piazza Santo Spirito 9 ☎055.215.308, ⓕ055.282.761. Some of the rooms are vast, with gorgeous decor, but others are grim, so make sure you inspect before paying.

Further north and east

Benvenuti Via Cavour 112 ☎055.572.141, ⓔbensecc@iol.it. A first-choice two-star in the university quarter, on the corner of Piazza Libertà and Via Matteotti. Bus #1 or #7 to Libertà ❺
Brunetta Borgo Pinti 5 ☎055.240.360, ⓕ055.247.8134. Inexpensive and well placed, a five-minute walk to the east of the Duomo, with functional shared bathrooms. Bus #14 to Salvemini. ❺
Liana Via V. Alfieri 18 ☎055.245.5303,

Ferretti Via delle Belle Donne 17 ☎055.238.1328, ⓔpensioneferretti@pronet.it. Pleasant little place in a side street, with clean bathrooms, better-than-average breakfasts, helpful and informative staff and Internet access. ❺

A monastery overlooking one of Florence's loveliest squares, with vaulted ceilings, original antiques and all mod cons. ❾
Residenza Johanna Via Bonifacio Lupi 14 ☎055.481.896, ⓕ055.482.721, ⓦwww.johanna.it. Comfortable old place on a residential street just north of San Marco offering peace and quiet in TV-free, phone-free rooms, some of them en suite. No credit cards. ❹

One of its main assets is the grandstand views from the top-deck loggia of the piazza below. ❻
Villa Betania Viale Poggio Imperiale 23 ☎055.222.243, ⓦwww.villabetania.it. Fifteenth-century villa 1km south of Porta Romana that has its own, lush gardens and private parking. Ten percent student discount (July, Aug & Nov–Feb). Bus #11. ❼

ⓔhotelliana@dada.it. A small hotel that was once the British Embassy and maintains a similar tone, with refined interior decor and a cool, discreet atmosphere. Bus #6 to D'Azeglio. ❽
Monna Lisa Borgo Pinti 27 ☎055.247.9751, ⓦwww.monnalisa.it. A grim facade conceals a charming and elegant hotel, furnished with original antiques and decor. Go for one of the larger rooms overlooking the lovely internal garden. Bus #6 to Colonna. ❾

❽

TUSCANY | Florence

Ruth's Via delle Cinque Giornate 12
☎ 055.473.377, ✉ cinquegiornate@johanna.it.
Quiet villa on a residential street way north; you're
given a set of keys and left alone. It has a nice little garden, six good-value en-suite doubles, and
private parking. Bus #4 or #28 to Statuto. ❹

Villa Il Castagno Via A. del Castagno 31
☎ 055.571.701, ℻ 055.572.027. Pleasant two-star
in a residential area, with plenty of on-street parking. Rooms are generically comfortable. Bus #10,
#11 or #17 to Ponte al Pino. ❺

Villino La Magnolia Via Mannelli 135
☎ 055.246.6015, 🌐 www.villinolamagnolia. it.
Tasteful conversion of a family home near Campo
di Marte, with marble floors, spacious high-
ceilinged guest rooms and modern bathrooms.
Internet access and easy parking. Bus #12 to
Campo Marte. ❺

Hostels and campsites

As well as **hostels**, Florence has student houses, most of them run by religious
bodies, which are open to young tourists in summer (June–Oct).

Hostels

Istituto Gould Via dei Serragli 49 ☎ 055.212.576,
✉ gould.reception@dada.it. Excellent place occupying part of a seventeenth-century palazzo near
Santo Spirito: ask for a quieter back room. Singles
(with/without private bathroom) are €38/32, doubles €27/25; also triples €22/19 and quads
€21/19. Check in Mon–Fri 9am–1pm & 3–7pm,
Sat 9am–1pm. Bus #36 or #37 from the station to
Serragli.

Ostello Villa Camerata Viale Righi 2–4
☎ 055.601.451, ℻ 055.610.300. HI hostel occupying a sixteenth-century frescoed villa in a beautiful
park below Fiesole. Films in English; inexpensive
meals; midnight curfew. Dorms €13 per person
per night. Bus #17b from the train station, plus a
walk up the hill.

Pio X – Artigianelli Via dei Serragli 106
☎ 055.225.044. Quality hostel with friendly, relaxed
staff. Aim to arrive by 9am, as its 64 beds soon get
snapped up. Minimum stay two nights, maximum
five. €14 per person per night. Midnight curfew.

Santa Monaca Via Santa Monaca 6

☎ 055.268.338, 🌐 www.ostello.it. Very popular
115-bed non-HI hostel near Santo Spirito.
Separate male and female dorms, kitchen and
laundry facilities, free hot showers and inexpensive meals. €16 for a dorm bed. Credit cards
accepted. It's open to check-in 9.30am–1pm and
2pm–12.30am. Curfew 1am. Bus #11, #36 or #37
to Serragli.

Suore Oblate dell'Assunzione Via Borgo Pinti 15
☎ 055.248.0583, ℻ 055.234.6291. Just east of
the Duomo. Run by nuns and open to men and
women. Singles €25.80; doubles €51.70, both
with private bathrooms. Triple and quad rooms are
also available. No breakfast; midnight curfew.

Suore Oblate dello Spirito Santo Via Nazionale
8 ☎ 055.239.8202, ℻ 055.239.8129. Also run by
nuns, this clean and pleasant hostel, a few steps
from the station, is open to women, families and
married couples only; minimum stay two nights.
Beds are arranged in double, triple and quad
rooms, all with private bathroom; breakfast included. Doubles €41.30, triples €46.50.

Campsites

Michelangelo Viale Michelangelo 80
☎ 055.681.1977, 🌐 www.ecvacanze.it. Always
crowded, owing to a superb hillside location and
regular late-night disco. Kitchen facilities. Around
€9 per person, €6 per tent. Bus #13 from the station. April–Oct.

Panoramico Via Peramonda 1, Fiesole. See p.511.

Villa Camerata Viale Righi 2–4 ☎ 055.600.315.
Small, basic, year-round site in the grounds of the
HI hostel. Midnight curfew. €7 per person, €6 per
tent.

The City

Greater Florence now spreads several kilometres down the Arno Valley and
onto the hills north and south of the city, but the major sights are contained in
an area that can be crossed on foot in under thirty minutes.

Florence has a **telephone booking service**, Firenze Musei (☎055.294.883), which allows you to pre-book visits to the Uffizi, the Accademia and the Bargello. You call the number and an English-speaking operator will reserve you a ticket for a specific day and time; the ticket is collected at the museum, again at a specific time, shortly before the time allocated for entry. Though the service is so badly under-resourced that the number is engaged for long periods at a stretch, in the case of the Uffizi and the Accademia it's worth persevering, because at both of these the queue to buy tickets on the door can be enormous – it's not unusual to have to wait three or four hours in summer. Alternatively, you may find that your hotel will be able to make a reservation for you – with four- and five-star hotels this will certainly be an option. If you're going to pre-book a visit, you should do it as soon as possible, because the allocation of reservable tickets is often completely sold out many days in advance.

Note that nearly all of the big museums are routinely **closed on Monday**, though some are open for a couple of Mondays each month. In the majority of cases, museum ticket offices close thirty minutes before the museum itself. At the Palazzo Vecchio and Museo Stibbert however, it's one hour before, while at the Uffizi, Bargello, Museo dell'Opera del Duomo, the dome of the Duomo, the Campanile and Pitti museums it's 45 minutes.

A short walk southeast from the train station brings you to **Piazza del Duomo**, site of the **Duomo** itself and the neighbouring **Baptistry**. The compact district from here south to the river is the inner core, the area into which most of the tourists are packed, and which boasts the best-preserved medieval parts of Florence and the majority of its fashionable streets. Just south of the Duomo is Florence's outstanding sculpture gallery, the **Bargello**. The large **Piazza della Signoria**, some 300m south of the Duomo, is overlooked by the **Palazzo Vecchio** and the famous picture gallery of the **Uffizi**.

West of the Duomo, and backing onto the train station, is the unmissable church of **Santa Maria Novella**. Immediately north of the Duomo is the grand church of **San Lorenzo**, at the heart of a throng of market stalls around the covered **Mercato Centrale**. Clustered together just northeast of San Lorenzo are the monastery of **San Marco**, with its paintings by Fra' Angelico; the **Accademia**, home of Michelangelo's *David*; and **Piazza Santissima Annunziata**, Florence's most attractive square. The main attraction in the eastern quarters of the city centre is the vast Franciscan church of **Santa Croce**.

South of the river – preferably via the medieval **Ponte Vecchio**, which is still picturesquely lined with shops perched over the water – lies the **Oltrarno** district, where the array of museums within the **Palazzo Pitti** exerts the strongest pull, and the church of **Santo Spirito** stands at the focus of a lively student quarter. Overlooking the city from the south is the lavish hilltop church of **San Miniato al Monte**.

Piazza del Duomo

Traffic and people gravitate towards the square at the heart of Florence, **Piazza del Duomo**, beckoned by the pinnacle of Brunelleschi's extraordinary dome, which dominates the cityscape in a way unmatched by any architectural creation in any other Italian city. Yet even though the magnitude of the **Duomo** is apparent from a distance, the first full sight of the church and the adjacent **Baptistry** still comes as a jolt, the colours of their patterned exteriors making a startling contrast with the dun-coloured buildings around them. The square is at its romantic best in the very early morning, lit by low, pale sunlight and free from the heaving crowds that gather soon after 8am.

The Duomo (Santa Maria del Fiore) and around

It was some time in the seventh century when the seat of the Bishop of Florence was transferred from San Lorenzo to the ancient church that stood on the site of the **Duomo**. In the thirteenth century, it was decided that a new cathedral was required, to reflect more accurately the wealth of the city and to put the Pisans and Sienese in their place. **Arnolfo di Cambio**, entrusted with the project in 1294, designed a massive vaulted basilica focused on a domed tribune embraced by three polygonal tribunes. He died eight years later, but by 1418 everything was in place to bear the weight of the dome which he had envisaged as the church's crown. The conception was magnificent: the dome was to span a distance of nearly 42m and rise from a base some 54m above the floor of the nave. It was to be the largest dome ever constructed – but nobody had yet worked out how to build the thing.

A committee of the masons' guild was set up to ponder the problem, and it was to them that **Filippo Brunelleschi** presented himself. Some seventeen years before, in 1401, Brunelleschi had been defeated by Ghiberti in the competition to design the Baptistry doors (see p.479), and had spent the intervening time studying classical architecture and developing new theories of engineering. He won the commission on condition that he work jointly with Ghiberti – a partnership that did not last long (though Ghiberti's contribution to the project was probably more significant than his colleague ever admitted). The key to the dome's success was the construction of two shells: a light outer shell about one metre thick, and an inner shell four times thicker. Brunelleschi's genius was to lay the brickwork in a herringbone pattern in cantilevered rings, thus allowing the massively heavy dome to support itself as it grew, without the use of scaffolding. On March 25, 1436 – Annunciation Day, and the Florentine New Year – the completion of the dome was marked by the papal consecration of the cathedral.

The Duomo's overblown and pernickety main **facade** is a nineteenth-century imitation of a Gothic front, its marble cladding quarried from the same sources as the first builders used – white stone from Carrara (see p.534), red from the Maremma, green from Prato. The south side is the oldest part, but the most attractive adornment is the **Porta della Mandorla**, on the north side. This takes its name from the almond-shaped frame that contains the relief of *The Assumption of the Virgin*, sculpted by Nanni di Banco around 1420. Note that limited numbers of people are permitted inside the Duomo at any one time, and long **queues** often form outside. If you can, come early.

Inside the Duomo

The Duomo's **interior** (Mon–Wed & Fri 10am–5pm, Thurs 10am–3.30pm, Sat 10am–4.45pm, Sun 1.30–4.45pm, closes 3.30pm on first Sat of month) is a vast enclosure of bare masonry in stark contrast to the fussy exterior. Today the fourth-largest church in Europe, it once held a congregation of ten thousand to hear Savonarola preach – the ambience is more that of a public assembly hall than of a devotional building. Initially, the most conspicuous pieces of decoration are two memorials to *condottieri* (mercenary commanders) in the north aisle – Uccello's monument to **Sir John Hawkwood**, painted in 1436, and Castagno's monument to **Niccolò da Tolentino**, created twenty years later. Just beyond, Domenico do Michelino's *Dante Explaining the Divine*

Comedy makes the dome only marginally less prominent than the mountain of Purgatory. The enamelled terracotta reliefs over the doorways to the two **sacristies**, on each side of the altar, are by Luca della Robbia, who also cast the bronze doors of the north sacristy. Judged by mere size, the major work of art in the duomo is the fresco of *The Last Judgement* inside the dome, though a substantial number of Florentines are of the opinion that Vasari's and Zuccari's effort does nothing but deface Brunelleschi's masterpiece and want it stripped away. Below the fresco are seven stained-glass roundels designed by Uccello, Ghiberti, Castagno and Donatello; they are best inspected from the gallery immediately below them, which forms part of the route up **inside the dome** (Mon–Fri 8.30am–7pm, Sat 8.30am–5.40pm; first Sat of the month 8.30am–4pm; €6). The gallery is the queasiest part of the climb, most of which winds between the brick walls of the outer and inner shells of the dome, up to the very summit with its stunning views over the city.

In the 1960s remnants of the Duomo's predecessor, the **Cripta di Santa Reparata**, were uncovered beneath the west end of the **nave** (Mon–Sat 10am–5pm; €3). A detailed model helps make sense of the jigsaw of Roman, early Christian and Romanesque remains, areas of mosaic and patches of fourteenth-century frescoes. Also down here is the **tomb of Brunelleschi**, one of the few Florentines ever honoured with burial inside the Duomo.

The Campanile

Alongside Italy's most impressive cathedral dome is perhaps its most elegant bell-tower. The **Campanile** (daily: 8.30am–7.30pm; €6) was begun in 1334 by **Giotto**, who was no engineer: after his death in 1337 Andrea Pisano and Francesco Talenti took over the teetering, half-built edifice, and immediately doubled the thickness of the walls to stop it collapsing. The first storey is studded with two rows of remarkable bas-reliefs; the lower, illustrating the *Creation of Man* and the *Arts and Industries*, was carved by Pisano himself, the upper by his pupils. The figures of *Prophets* and *Sibyls* in the second-storey niches were created by Donatello and others. The parapet at the top of the tower has the advantage of letting you view the dome as a foreground counterpoint to Florence's cityscape.

The Baptistry

The **Baptistry** (Mon–Sat noon–7pm, Sun 8.30am–2pm; €3) is the oldest building in Florence, generally thought to date from the sixth or seventh century. Although its mysterious origins lie in the depths of the Dark Ages, no building better illustrates the special relationship between Florence and the Roman world. Throughout the Middle Ages the Florentines chose to believe that the baptistry was originally a Roman temple to Mars, a belief bolstered by the interior's inclusion of Roman granite columns. The pattern of its marble cladding, applied in the eleventh and twelfth centuries, is clearly classical in inspiration, and the baptistry's most famous embellishments – its gilded bronze doors – mark the emergence of a self-conscious interest in the art of the ancient world, the birth of the Renaissance.

After Andrea Pisano's success with the **south doors** in 1336, the merchants' guild held a competition in 1401 for the job of making a new set of doors. The two finalists were Brunelleschi and **Lorenzo Ghiberti** – and the latter won the day. Ghiberti's **north doors** show a new naturalism and classical sense of harmony, but their innovation is timid in comparison with his sublime **east doors**. These remarkable works of art are these days reverentially dubbed "The Gates of Paradise", supposedly after a remark made by Michelangelo – but, in fact, the area between a baptistry and a cathedral is formally known in Italy as the *paradiso*. Unprecedented in the subtlety of their modelling, these Old Testament scenes are a primer of early Renaissance art, using perspective, gesture and sophisticated grouping of their subjects to convey the human drama of each scene. Ghiberti has included a self-portrait in the frame of the left-hand door – his is the fourth head from the top of the right-hand band. All the panels now set in the door are replicas, with the originals on display in the Museo dell'Opera (see below); the original competition entries are in the Bargello (see p.483).

You **enter** through the south doors. Inside, both the semi-abstract mosaic floor and the magnificent mosaic ceiling – including a fearsome platoon of demons at the feet of Christ in judgement – were created in the thirteenth century. To the right of the altar is the **tomb of John XXIII**, the schismatic pope who died in Florence in 1419. The monument, draped by an illusionistic marble canopy, is the work of Donatello and his pupil Michelozzo.

The Museo dell'Opera del Duomo

At Piazza del Duomo 9, behind the east end of the duomo, is the **Museo dell'Opera del Duomo** (Mon–Sat 9am–7.30pm, Sun 9am–1.40pm; €6), second only to the Bargello and far easier to take in on a single visit. In the large ground-floor hall are a glassy-eyed *Madonna* by **Arnolfo di Cambio**, a ramrod-straight statue of *Boniface VII*, one of the most unpleasant of all medieval popes (in comedy hat), and four seated figures of the Evangelists (including **Donatello**'s fine *St John*) wrenched from the Duomo's demolished sixteenth-century facade. Giovanni di Bondo's *St Sebastian* is in the end room, eye-catching if only for the ludicrous number of arrows piercing the hapless saint. On the mezzanine is the highlight of the museum – **Michelangelo**'s angular and anguished pietà. This was one of his last works, carved when he was almost eighty and intended for his own tomb; Vasari records that the face of the hooded Nicodemus is a self-portrait. **Upstairs** in room II are **Donatello**'s figures for the campanile, the most powerful of which is the prophet *Habbakuk*, the intensity of whose gaze allegedly prompted the sculptor to seize it and yell "Speak, speak!" Donatello also created one of the ornate *cantorie* (choir-lofts) here, competing with **Luca della Robbia**'s opposite, created at the same time and featuring crowds of laughing, dancing children. Room III is dominated by expression of a very different side of Donatello: his haggard wooden figure of *Mary Magdalene* stares into the middle distance, a wild presence amidst cases full of rich vestments, jewelled reliquaries, and a huge silver-gilt **altar** from the Baptistry, a dazzling meditation on the life of John the Baptist. Returning through room II leads you through a corridor lined with ropes and pulleys used in the construction of the dome (as well as Brunelleschi's **death-mask**) to a room full of wooden models submitted as part of a 1588 facade-designing competition and plans from the nineteenth-century reconstruction. The second upper floor was under restoration at the time of writing.

You return to ground level into the newly covered **courtyard** – where Michelangelo worked from 1501 to 1504 on his *David*. Today, it displays in sealed cases of nitrogen Ghiberti's original **bronze panels** for the baptistry's east doors.

Orsanmichele and the Badia

The main route south from Piazza del Duomo is the arrow-straight **Via dei Calzaiuoli**, Florence's main street, today – as in Roman times – a catwalk for

△ Montepulciano

the Florentine passeggiata between the campanile and Piazza della Signoria. Halfway down the street is the opening into **Piazza della Repubblica**, created in the nineteenth century by razing the old Jewish quarter and markets which once stood here in an attempt to give Florence a grand public square. It's a characterless place, impressive solely for its size.

Partway along Via dei Calzaiuoli is the church of **Orsanmichele** (daily 9am–noon & 4–6pm; closed first & last Mon of month; free). Often unintentionally bypassed by visitors dazzled by the ice-cream parlours and shoe-shops, it stands three storeys high like a military tower. From the ninth century, the church of *San Michele ad Hortum* ("at the garden") stood here, replaced in 1240 by a grain market and after a fire in 1304 by a merchants' loggia. In 1380 the loggia was walled in and dedicated exclusively to religious functions, while two upper storeys were added for use as emergency grain stores. Its **exterior** has some impressive sculpture: outstanding on the east side (Via dei Calzaiuoli) are *John the Baptist* by Ghiberti, the first life-size bronze statue of the Renaissance; on the north side Donatello's *St George*; and on the west side *St Matthew* and *St Stephen* by Ghiberti. The rectangular **interior** is dominated by the vast tabernacle by Orcagna, carved with delicate reliefs and studded with coloured marble and glass. It frames a *Madonna* painted in 1347 by Bernardo Daddi as a replacement for a miraculous image of the Virgin destroyed by the 1304 fire, whose powers this picture is said to have inherited. You can get to the vaulted halls of the **upstairs granary** – one of the city's most imposing medieval interiors – via the building opposite the church door. The halls now house the **Museo di Orsanmichele**, open for tours daily (9am, 10am & 11am) except for the first and last Mondays of the month. If you get the chance be sure to visit, not only for the fine interior, but also for the chance to see several of the most important original exterior statues. As restoration work is completed, it is planned that all the statues will eventually be exhibited here.

Opposite Orsanmichele, the narrow Via Tavolini heads east a block or two to **Via del Proconsolo**, the other main route between Piazza del Duomo and Piazza della Signoria. On the corner, more or less across the road from the Museo del Bargello, is the huge **Badìa Fiorentina**, finally approaching the end of a lengthy restoration. Tourist visits are allowed on Monday afternoons (3–6pm); at other times the church is open for prayer only. This ancient Benedictine abbey was founded late in the tenth century. In the 1280s it was overhauled, probably under the direction of Arnolfo di Cambio; later work has smothered much of the old church, but the narrow campanile – Romanesque at its base, Gothic higher up – has come through intact. The **interior** is deliciously musty and gloomy. Immediately on the left as you enter is Filippino Lippi's *Madonna and St Bernard*. An unmarked door from the choir, immediately right of the high altar, leads to a staircase giving access to the upper storey of the tranquil, fifteenth-century **Chiostro degli Aranci** (Cloister of Oranges – named after the fruit trees that the monks cultivated here), the walls of which are brightened by a vivid fresco cycle of the life of St Benedict, thought to be the work of Giovanni di Consalvo, a Portuguese contemporary of Fra Angelico.

The Bargello

To get a comprehensive idea of the Renaissance achievement in Florence, two museum calls are essential: one to the Uffizi and one to the **Museo Nazionale del Bargello** (Tues–Sat 8.15am–1.50pm; also open on second & fourth Sun, and first, third & fifth Mon of month same times; €4). This outstanding museum is installed in the dauntingly fortress-like Palazzo del Bargello on Via del Proconsolo, halfway between the Duomo and the Palazzo Vecchio. Nowhere else in Italy is there so full a collection of sculpture from the period, and yet the Bargello is normally uncrowded. The palazzo was built in 1255, and soon became the seat of the *Podestà*, the chief magistrate. Numerous malefactors were tried, sentenced and executed here and the building acquired its present name in the sixteenth century, after the resident *Bargello*, or police chief.

The courtyard and ground floor

From the ticket desk, you enter the beautiful Gothic **courtyard**, which is plastered with the coats of arms of the *Podestà* and contains, among many other pieces, six allegorical figures by **Ammannati** from the fountain of the Palazzo Pitti courtyard. The left room holds **Tino di Camaino**'s accomplished *Madonna and Child*, and the others hold paraphernalia as well as some pieces removed from Orsanmichele. At the foot of the courtyard steps is the **Michelangelo Room** (room B). The tipsy, soft-bellied figure of *Bacchus* was his first major sculpture, carved at the age of 22 – a year before the great pietà in Rome. A decade later, Michelangelo's style had evolved into something less immediately seductive, as is shown by the *Pitti Tondo*, the stern grandeur of which prefigures the prophets of the Sistine Chapel ceiling, on which he was then about to start work. The square-jawed bust of *Brutus*, Michelangelo's sole work in the genre, is a coded celebration of anti-Medicean republicanism, having been made in 1540 soon after the murder of the tyrannical Duke Alessandro de' Medici. Works by Michelangelo's followers and contemporaries are ranged in the immediate vicinity; some would command prolonged attention in different company, including **Cellini**'s *Bust of Cosimo I*, and **Giambologna**'s voluptuous *Florence Defeating Pisa*, eclipsed by his more famous *Mercury*. Comic relief is provided by the reliably awful **Bandinelli**, whose coiffured *Adam and Eve* look like a grandee and his wife taking an *au naturel* stroll through their estate.

The upper floors

At the top of the courtyard staircase, the **loggia** has been turned into an aviary for Giambologna's bronze birds, brought here from the Medici villa at Castello (see p.511). The doorway to the right at the top of the stairs opens into the fourteenth-century Salone del Consiglio Generale (room H), where the presiding genius is **Donatello**. Vestiges of the sinuous Gothic manner are evident in the drapery of his marble *David*, placed against the left wall, but there's nothing antiquated in the *St George*, carved just eight years later for the tabernacle of the armourers' guild at Orsanmichele and installed in a replica of its original niche at the far end of the room. If any one sculpture could be said to embody the shift of sensibility that occurred in Renaissance Florence, this is it: whereas St George had previously been little more than a symbol of valour, this alert, tense figure represents not the act of heroism but the volition behind it. In front stands Donatello's sexually ambiguous bronze *David*, cast in the early 1430s as the first freestanding nude figure since classical times and memorably described by Mary McCarthy as "a transvestite's and fetishist's dream." Back opposite the entrance door is Donatello's strange, jubilant figure known as *Amor Atys*, dating from the end of the 1430s, while his breathtakingly vivid bust of *Niccolò da Uzzano* nearby shows that he was just as comfortable with portraiture. The less complex humanism of **Luca della Robbia** is embodied in the glazed terracotta Madonnas set round the walls, while Donatello's master, **Ghiberti**, is represented by his relief of *The Sacrifice of Isaac*, his successful entry in the competition for the baptistry doors. The treatment of the same theme submitted by **Brunelleschi** – and rejected – is displayed close by. Most of the rest of this floor is occupied by a collection of **European and Islamic applied art**, of so high a standard that it would constitute an engrossing museum in its own right. Elsewhere is dazzling carved **ivory** from Byzantium and medieval France.

The sculptural display resumes upstairs, with **Giovanni della Robbia**'s pietà and **Andrea della Robbia**'s exquisite busts of a young woman and a boy. The Sala dei Bronzetti (room P) is Italy's best assembly of small Renaissance bronzes, with plentiful evidence of Giambologna's virtuosity at table-top scale. Lastly, rooms Q and R are devoted mainly to Renaissance portrait busts, including a small bronze group of *Hercules and Antaeus* by **Antonio Pollaiuolo**, possessing a power out of all proportion to its size.

Piazza della Signoria

Even though it sets the stage for the **Palazzo Vecchio** and the **Uffizi**, Florence's main civic square – the frenetic **Piazza della Signoria** – doesn't quite live up to its role. Too many of its buildings are bland nineteenth-century efforts, and the surface of the square resembles the deck of an aircraft carrier. In the 1970s, it was decided to restore the piazza's ancient paving stones, but when the "restorers" returned the first batch, it was found that they had sandblasted chunks off them rather than rinsing them carefully. Some of the original stones then turned up in the yard of a builders' merchant and on the front drives of a number of Tuscan villas.

What little charm the Piazza della Signoria does possess comes from its peculiar array of **statuary**, a miscellany collected at the foot of the Palazzo Vecchio. The line-up starts with Giambologna's equestrian statue of *Cosimo I* and continues with Ammannati's fatuous *Neptune Fountain* and copies of Donatello's *Marzocco* (the city's heraldic lion), his *Judith and Holofernes* and Michelangelo's *David*. Near Ammannati's fountain is a small plaque set into the pavement to mark the location of Savonarola's **Bonfire of the Vanities** (see p.467) and his execution pyre. The square's grace-note, the **Loggia della Signoria**, was built in the late fourteenth century as a dais for city officials during ceremonies; only in the late eighteenth century did it become a showcase for some of the city's more melodramatic sculpture. In the corner nearest the Palazzo Vecchio usually stands a figure that has become one of the iconic images of the Renaissance, Benvenuto Cellini's *Perseus*. However, it's currently being restored inside the Uffizi (in a special area open to the public) and may well be permanently replaced by a copy. Equally attention-seeking is Giambologna's last work, *The Rape of the Sabines*, epitome of the Mannerist obsession with spiralling forms.

The Palazzo Vecchio

Florence's fortress-like town hall, looming above the square as an icon of the city's power and authority, is the **Palazzo Vecchio** (Mon–Wed & Fri–Sun 9am–7pm, Thurs 9am–2pm; €5.70; Ⓦwww.nuovopalazzovecchio.org). The building was begun in 1299 to serve as the home of the Signoria, the highest tier of the city's republican government. Local folklore has it that its misshapen plan was due to the fact that the Guelph government refused to encroach on land previously owned by the hated Ghibellines, and so squeezed the building instead. The most radical overhaul came in 1540, when **Cosimo I** – recently installed as Duke of Florence – moved his retinue here from the Palazzo Medici. The Medici were only in residence for nine years before moving to the

Palazzo Pitti, but the enlargement and refurbishment instigated by Cosimo continued throughout the period of his rule. Much of the decoration of the state rooms comprises a relentless eulogy of Cosimo and his clan, but in among the propaganda are some excellent works of art, including some seminal examples of Mannerism, Cosimo I's court style. The **entrance**, which is alongside the copy of Michelangelo's *David* mobbed night and day by snap-happy crowds, leads into a lovely internal **courtyard** designed by Michelozzo.

Giorgio Vasari, court architect from 1555 until his death in 1574, was responsible for much of the sycophantic decor in the state apartments. His limited talents were given full rein in the huge **Salone dei Cinquecento** at the top of the stairs, built at the end of the fifteenth century as a council assembly hall. This room might have become one of Italy's most extraordinary showcases of Renaissance art, when in 1503 Leonardo da Vinci and Michelangelo were commissioned to fresco opposite walls of the chamber. Unfortunately, Leonardo abandoned the project after his experimental fresco technique went wrong, and Michelangelo's ideas existed only on paper when he was summoned to Rome by Pope Julius II. A few decades later, the hack Vasari stepped in, and painted over Leonardo's failed attempts with drearily bombastic murals celebrating Cosimo's military prowess. Michelangelo's *Victory*, facing the entrance door, was sculpted for Julius's tomb but was donated to the Medici by the artist's nephew; Vasari installed it here to mark Cosimo's defeat of the Sienese.

Stairs rise from the corridor past an intriguing fireworks fresco of 1558 showing the Piazza della Signoria during celebrations for the feast of John the Baptist. Turn left at the top and you enter the **Quartiere degli Elementi** – the decor plays second fiddle to the romantic rooftop views from the terrace. Back at the top of the stairs, head straight on and you cross a gallery at the rear

Secret passageways

The various so-called **"Secret Passageways"** (guided tours Mon–Sat; €6.70, includes ticket to Palazzo Vecchio) allow access to parts of the Palazzo Vecchio that are normally off limits. Most visually impressive is the trip up through the palace and into the Attic of the Salone del Cinquecento. From the vantage point of a balcony high above the hall, the guide describes the complex way in which Vasari created such a huge space within the medieval structure, and explains the allegorical meaning of the paintings. You are then led up into the vast attic itself, where a forest of pungent timber supports the roof above and the ceiling below.

Less magnificent, but still worth it for the guides' commentary, is the route leading from the street up through the secret Stairway of the Duke of Athens. The doorway was knocked through the exterior wall of the Palazzo in 1342 as an emergency escape route for the Duke, who briefly took up the reins of power here. He never in fact used the staircase, but only because his fall from grace came rather sooner than he had imagined. Another route leads into the Studiolo and Tesoretto, and further *percorsi* are planned, depending on the success of the existing tours.

All three tours last roughly an hour, and you can do further tours for €2.60. How many tours are given in English rather depends on how many people are asking, and when: during quieter periods it's likely that you'll have a guide to yourself, but in high season and at weekends it's worth booking in advance at the main ticket office (℡055.276.8224). On weekdays, guides take one party on each Percorso Segreto at 9.30am, 10.30am, 11.30am, 3.30pm, 4.30pm and 5.30pm. On Saturday all three tours run concurrently, leaving hourly from 10am, and at least one every hour should be in English.

of the Salone dei Cinquecento into the private apartments of **Eleanor**, Cosimo I's wife. Star turn here is the tiny and exquisite **chapel**, superbly and vividly decorated by Bronzino in the 1540s.

Through a handful of rooms is the frescoed **Sala d'Udienza**, once an audience chamber, which boasts lovely views over the piazza below and a stunning gilt-coffered ceiling by Giuliano da Maiano, who was also responsible, with his brother Benedetto, for the intarsia work on the doors and the lovely doorway that leads into the **Sala dei Gigli**, a room that takes its name from the lilies (*gigli*) that adorn most of its surfaces. The room has another splendid ceiling by the Maiano brothers, and frescoes by Domenico Ghirlandaio. The highlight of the room is **Donatello**'s original *Judith and Holofernes*, a copy of which sits down below in the piazza. Commissioned by Cosimo il Vecchio, the piece originally served as a fountain in the Palazzo Medici, but was removed to the Piazza della Signoria after the expulsion of the Medici in 1494, to be displayed as a mark of vanquished tyranny. Donatello froze the action at the moment Judith's arm begins its scything stroke, a dramatic conception that no other sculptor of the period would have attempted.

The two small side-rooms are the Cancellaria, **Machiavelli**'s office for fifteen years and now containing a bust and portrait of the much-maligned political thinker; and the lovely **Sala delle Carte**, decorated with 57 maps painted in 1563 by the Medici court astronomer Fra' Ignazio Danti, depicting in some detail what was then the entire known world.

The Museo di Storia della Scienza

At the rear of the Palazzo Vecchio runs Via dei Leoni, named after lions that were moved here from the piazza after Cosimo I objected to the smell. Heading down to the river the street becomes Via dei Castellani, which then opens into **Piazza dei Giudici**, so called because of the tribunal that met in what's now the excellent **Museo di Storia della Scienza** (Mon & Wed–Fri 9.30am–5pm, Tues & Sat 9.30am–1pm, plus second Sun of month 10am–1pm from Oct to May; €6.50). Stop in if you fancy a glimpse of the Renaissance that includes neither heroic male nudes nor tortured saintly visages.

Long after Florence had declined from its artistic apogee, the intellectual reputation of the city was maintained by its scientists. Grand Duke Ferdinando II and his brother Leopoldo, both of whom studied with **Galileo**, founded the Academy of Experiment at the Pitti in 1657, and the instruments made and acquired by this academy are the core of the museum, which has extensive English notes. The **first upper floor** features timepieces and measuring instruments (such as beautiful Arab astrolabes), as well as a massive armillary sphere made for Ferdinando I to prove the fallacy of Copernicus's heliocentric universe. Galileo's original instruments are on show here, such as the lens with which he discovered the four moons of Jupiter. On the **top floor** is the huge lens made for Cosimo III, with which Faraday and Davy managed to ignite a diamond by focusing the rays of the sun. The medical section is full of alarming surgical instruments and wax anatomical models for teaching obstetrics.

The Uffizi

Ranged around a grand U-shaped courtyard between Piazza della Signoria and the river, the **Galleria degli Uffizi** (Tues–Sun 8.15am–6.50pm, also Sat 8.15am–10pm in summer; €8.50, free to under-18s and over-65s; see box on p.477 for details of advance reservations; ⓦ www.uffizi.firenze.it) holds Italy's greatest art collection, and is the city's key attraction. Perhaps that's why the gallery's directors feel no shame in making you queue for two hours or more for admission – there are often queues even to pick up reserved tickets – then climb dozens of internal stairs to reach the gallery level (or queue again for two ancient six-person lifts). Should you fancy a spot of refreshment, there's a rooftop café with excellent views – which charges an insulting amount for a thimbleful of bitter espresso. The single set of public toilets is located at the far end of the uppermost storey. You'd be justified in wondering where all those admission fees end up.

The main picture rooms open off a corridor that runs all the way round the uppermost level of the U-shaped building, is crammed higgledy-piggledy with **classical statuary**, and boasts a **ceiling** decorated in ornate Grotesque style that is an artwork in itself. The paintings are hung chronologically, with each block of rooms forming a neat, self-contained unit. So many masterpieces are collected here that you should put aside **three or four hours** as the minimum to be able to take in the gallery's key works. If time or energy is short, it makes sense to limit yourself to an hour or two exploring the first fifteen rooms, where the Florentine Renaissance works are concentrated.

The elongated building originated in 1560, when Duke Cosimo I ordered **Giorgio Vasari** to design a block of government offices (*uffizi*) to fill a site between the Palazzo Vecchio and the river that was, at that time, occupied by houses and a church. After Vasari's death, work was continued by **Buontalenti**, who – under orders from Francesco I – glazed the upper storey so that it could house his art collection. Each of the succeeding Medici added to the family's trove of art treasures, and the accumulated collection was preserved for public inspection by the last member of the family, Anna Maria Lodovica, whose will specified that it should be left to the people of Florence and never be allowed to leave the city. During the nineteenth century, a large proportion of the sculpture was transferred to the Bargello, while many of the antiquities went to the Museo Archeologico, leaving the Uffizi itself as essentially a gallery of paintings.

Rooms 1–9: from Cimabue to Fra' Filippo Lippi

Room 1 (often closed) houses an assembly of antique sculpture, used as a source-book by Renaissance artists. The gestation period of the Renaissance can be studied in **room 2**, where three altarpieces of the Maestà (*Madonna Enthroned*) by Cimabue, Duccio and Giotto dwarf everything around them, and demonstrate the softening of the Byzantine style into a more tactile form of representation. A high point in the comparatively conservative art of four-teenth-century Siena (room 3) is Martini's *Annunciation*, with its eloquently expansive background of plain gold. Florence's only first-rank Gothic painter, Lorenzo Monaco, features amid the collection of other *trecento* artists (**rooms 5 & 6**), with a majestic *Coronation of the Virgin* and an *Adoration of the Magi*; the spangled version of the latter subject by Gentile da Fabriano is the epitome of International Gothic, cramming every inch of the flattened picture plane with often highly naturalistic detail.

In **room 7**, Piero della Francesca is represented by paired portraits of *Federico da Montefeltro* and *Battista Sforza*; the panels are backed by images of the Duke surrounded by the cardinal virtues and his wife by the theological virtues. Paolo Uccello's curiously measured *Battle of San Romano* once hung in Lorenzo il Magnifico's bedchamber, in company with depictions of the same skirmish that now reside in the Louvre and London's National Gallery. Among the plentiful works by Fra' Filippo Lippi in **room 8** is his celebrated *Madonna and Child with Two Angels*. Close by there's a fine *Madonna* by Botticelli.

Rooms 10–16: from Botticelli to Leonardo da Vinci

The works upon which Botticelli's reputation rests are gathered in the merged **rooms 10–14**: *Primavera*, *The Birth of Venus*, *Adoration of the Magi* and *The Madonna of the Magnificat*. The *Birth of Venus* shows a radiantly beautiful Venus being blown to shore by Zephyrus, god of the west wind, and the nymph Cloris; she is about to step – with oddly filth-lined toenails – onto land, to be clothed by Hora, daughter of Aurora, goddess of the dawn. The *Primavera* on the nearby wall is generally held to show the triumph of Venus, who stands as the central focus of the painting. Zephyrus, on the right, chases Cloris and transmutes her into Flora, symbol of natural fertility (who is endowed with one of the most reproduced smiles in the history of art). The Three Graces, expressions of physical beauty, dance together while Mercury, tantalizingly clad only in a loose robe, chases away the clouds of winter.

Though the Uffizi doesn't own a finished painting entirely by Leonardo da Vinci, works in **room 15** comprise a full sketch of his career. From his formative years there's the celebrated and precisely handled *Annunciation* (mainly by Leonardo) along with the landscape and single angel in profile that he painted aged 18 in Verrocchio's *Baptism*. The incomplete sketch for *The Adoration of the Magi* in the same room encapsulates Leonardo's later radicalism, with its vortex of figures round Mary and the infant Christ. **Room 16**, the enigmatically titled Map Room, is usually kept closed.

Rooms 17–24: from Bronzino to Holbein

Room 18, the octagonal **Tribuna**, was the original Medici gallery and now houses the most important of the Medici sculptures, principal among which is the Medici Venus, a first-century BC copy of the Praxitelean Aphrodite of Cnidos. Also in this room are del Sarto's flirtatious *Portrait of a Girl* and some chillingly precise portraits by Bronzino – especially compelling are *Bartolomeo Panciatichi*, *Lucrezia Panciatichi* and *Eleanor of Toledo with Giovanni de' Medici*. Vasari's portrait of Lorenzo il Magnifico and Bronzino's of Cosimo il Vecchio are deceptively immediate – each was painted long after the death of its subject.

Room 20 is largely devoted to Cranach and Dürer, including the latter's *Portrait of the Artist's Father*, his earliest authenticated painting. Highlights in the following sequence of rooms (**21–23**) are a perplexing *Sacred Allegory* by Giovanni Bellini and Holbein's *Portrait of Sir Richard Southwell*.

Rooms 25–45: from Michelangelo to Goya

The main attraction in **room 25** is Michelangelo's only completed easel painting, the virtuoso *Holy Family*, widely known as the "Doni Tondo" (a *tondo* – a circular artwork – commissioned by the Doni family). An unusually robust and powerful, bare-armed Mary reaches back to take the Christ child from Joseph, watched by a young John the Baptist in an animal skin. The contorted gestures and cold, almost metallic, colours were revolutionary for the time, as was the innovation of including nude figures in an ostensibly religious painting. The *maniera*, or style and execution, of this work was studied and imitated by Florentine painters of the sixteenth century in what became known as the Mannerist movement – as can be gauged from *Moses Defending the Daughters of Jethro* in **room 27** by Rosso Fiorentino, one of the pivotal figures of Mannerism, and works by Bronzino and the mercurial Pontormo. Separating the two Mannerist groups is **room 26** containing Andrea del Sarto's sultry *Madonna of the Harpies* and a number of compositions by Raphael, including the lovely *Madonna of the Goldfinch* and *Pope Leo X with Cardinals Giulio dei*

Medici and Luigi de' Rossi – as shifty a group of ecclesiastics as ever was gathered in one frame. **Room 28** is almost entirely given over to another of the titanic figures of sixteenth-century art, Titian. His *Flora* and *A Knight of Malta* are stunning, but most eyes tend to swivel towards the famous *Venus of Urbino*, just about the most fleshy and provocative of all Renaissance nudes.

A brief diversion through the painters of the sixteenth-century Emilian school follows, centred on Parmigianino, whose *Madonna of the Long Neck* is one of the definitive Mannerist creations. **Rooms 31 to 35** feature artists from Venice and the Veneto, with outstanding paintings by Paolo Veronese (*Holy Family with St Barbara*), Tintoretto (*Leda*) and G.B. Moroni (*Count Pietro Secco Suardi*). Sebastiano del Piombo's *Death of Adonis* which formerly hung here was torn to shreds in 1993 by a Mafia bomb and is still being pieced together.

In **room 41**, dominated by Rubens and Van Dyck, it is one of the less demonstrative items that makes the biggest impact – Rubens' *Portrait of Isabella Brandt*. His equally theatrical contemporary, Caravaggio, has a cluster of pieces in **room 43**, including a sultry, come-hither *Bacchus*. Next is a showcase for the portraiture of Rembrandt – the *Self-Portrait as an Old Man*, painted five years or so before his death, is one of his most melancholic works, its poignancy enhanced by the proximity of another self-portrait from decades earlier. Portraits also seize the attention in the following room of eighteenth-century works (**room 45**), especially the two of Maria Theresa painted by Goya. **Room 42** between these is an impressively ceilinged hall packed with classical statuary, while in an alcove at the top of the exit stairs – misleadingly entitled **rooms 36 & 37** – squats one of Florence's talismans, the Wild Boar, a Roman copy of third-century-BC Hellenistic sculpture. This tusked beast was the model for the Porcellino which stands today in the Mercato Nuovo.

The Corridoio Vasariano

A door on the west corridor between rooms 25 and 34 opens onto the **Corridoio Vasariano**, a passageway built by Vasari to link the Palazzo Vecchio to the Palazzo Pitti through the Uffizi. Winding its way down to the river, over the Ponte Vecchio on an upper level, through the church of Santa Felicità and into the Giardino di Bóboli, it gives a fascinating series of clandestine views of the city, and is completely lined with paintings, the larger portion of which comprises a **gallery of self-portraits**. Once you're past the portrait of Vasari, the series proceeds chronologically, its roll-call littered with illustrious names: Andrea del Sarto, Bronzino, Bernini, Rubens, Rembrandt, van Dyck, Velázquez, Hogarth, Reynolds, Delacroix, Ingres, and others.

Guided tours (€26.08) have to be arranged by phone (☎055.265.4321) or at the gallery's ticket office. Tours are conducted in the morning, usually on Wednesday and Friday only, the precise time varying with the availability of staff. The numbers are limited to thirty people on each tour, so the tours tend to get booked up months in advance.

The western city centre

Several streets in central Florence retain their medieval character, especially in the district west of Piazza della Signoria. Forming a gateway to this quarter is the **Mercato Nuovo** (summer daily 9am–7pm; winter Tues–Sat 9am–5pm), whose souvenir stalls are probably the busiest in the city; there's been a market here since the eleventh century, though the present loggia dates from the sixteenth. Usually a small group is gathered round the bronze boar known as **Il Porcellino**, trying to gain some good luck by getting a coin to fall from the animal's mouth through the grill below his head. An aimless amble through the streets beyond will give you some idea of the feel of Florence in the Middle Ages, when every important house was an urban fortress. The fourteenth-century **Palazzo Davanzati**, Via Porta Rossa 13, looks much as it did when first inhabited, and nowadays houses the **Museo della Casa Fiorentina Antica** (closed indefinitely for long-term restoration; ask at the tourist office for latest details). Virtually every room of the reconstructed interior is furnished and decorated in medieval style, using genuine artefacts assembled from a variety of sources.

Santa Trinitá and around
Via Porta Rossa culminates at Piazza Santa Trinità, not so much a square as a widening of the city's classiest street, **Via de' Tornabuoni**, which heads south across the Arno on the city's most stylish bridge, the **Ponte Santa Trinità**. This was ostensibly designed by Ammannati, but the curve of its arches so closely resembles the arc of Michelangelo's Medici tombs that the credit probably should be his; it was rebuilt stone by stone after the retreating Nazis had blown up the original in 1944. **Santa Trinità** (Mon–Sat 8am–noon & 4–6pm, Sun 4–6pm) was founded in the eleventh century, but piecemeal additions have lent it a pleasantly hybrid air: the largely Gothic interior contrasts with Buontalenti's Mannerist facade of 1594. The interior is notable for **Ghirlandaio's** decoration of the **Cappella Sassetti** (second to the right of the altar). His frescoes of the *Life of St Francis* are concerned as much with a portrayal of fifteenth-century Florence as with their religious themes. Elsewhere in the church is **Luca della Robbia's** powerful composition for the tomb of Benozzo Federighi, Bishop of Fiesole, occupying a wall of the chapel second to the left of the altar and framed by a ceramic border of flowers and greenery.

Heading north from Santa Trìnita is **Via de' Tornabuoni**, home to Cartier, Versace, Armani and the famous local firms Ferragamo and Gucci. Conspicuous wealth is nothing new here, for looming above everything is the vast **Palazzo Strozzi**, the last, the largest and the least subtle of Florentine Renaissance palaces. Filippo Strozzi bought and demolished a dozen town houses to make space for Giuliano da Sangallo's strongbox in stone (1536). When Giovanni Rucellai – one of the richest businessmen in the city and an esteemed scholar into the bargain – decided in the 1450s to commission a new house, he turned to Leon Battista Alberti. The **Palazzo Rucellai**, just west of the Strozzi house in Via della Vigna Nuova, was the first building in Florence to follow the rules of Classical architecture. You can see an even more refined example of Alberti's work, the Cappella di San Sepolcro, in the **Cappella Rucellai** behind the house at Via della Spada 18 (Mon–Sat 10am–noon; free). The church of San Pancrazio on Via della Spada has been converted into the slick **Museo Marino Marini** (Mon & Wed–Fri 10am–5pm; closed Aug; €4). Marini (1901–80) was one of Italy's foremost sculptors of the twentieth century, and this spacious conversion displays variations on his familiar horse-and-rider theme.

Ognissanti
In medieval times a major area of cloth production – the foundation of the Florentine economy – lay in the west of the city. **Ognissanti** (daily 7.30am–12.30pm & 3.30–7.30pm), or All Saints, the main church of this quarter located on Borgo Ognissanti, five minutes' walk west of Via de' Tornabuoni, was founded in 1256 by a Benedictine order who wove woollen cloth. Three hundred years later the Franciscans took it over and renovated it in Baroque

style; inside is the habit worn by St Francis of Assisi when he received the stigmata atop Monte Verna in September 1224. The young face squeezed between the Madonna and the dark-cloaked man in **Ghirlandaio**'s *Madonna della Misericordia* fresco, over the second altar on the right, is said to be that of Amerigo Vespucci – later to set sail on voyages that would give his name to America. Just beyond this, on opposite sides of the nave, are mounted **Botticelli**'s *St Augustine* and Ghirlandaio's more earthbound *St Jerome*, both painted in 1480. In the same year Ghirlandaio painted the bucolic *Last Supper* that covers one wall of the **refectory**, reached through the cloister entered to the left of the church (Mon, Tues & Sat 9am–noon; free).

Santa Maria Novella

The focus of the western city centre is the large, pleasant **Piazza Santa Maria Novella** in front of the church it was named after, which has a lethargic backwater atmosphere, favoured as a spot for picnic lunches and after-dark loitering.

From the beguiling green, white and pink patterns of its marble facade, you'd never guess that the church of **Santa Maria Novella** was the Florentine base of the Dominican order, fearsome vigilantes of thirteenth-century Catholicism. The architects of the Gothic **interior** (Mon–Thurs 9.30am–5pm, Fri & Sun 1–5pm; €2.50) were capable of great ingenuity – the distance between the columns diminishes with proximity to the altar, a device to make the nave appear from the entrance to be longer than it is. **Masaccio**'s extraordinary 1427 fresco of *The Trinity*, one of the earliest works in which perspective and classical proportion were rigorously employed, is painted onto the wall halfway down the left aisle. **Filippino Lippi**'s frescoes for the **Cappella di Filippo Strozzi** (immediately to the right of the chancel) are a fantasy vision of classical ruins in which the narrative often seems to take second place, and one of the first examples of an archeological interest in Roman culture. As a chronicle of fifteenth-century life in Florence, no series of frescoes is more fascinating than **Domenico Ghirlandaio**'s behind the high altar; the work was commissioned by Giovanni Tornabuoni – which explains why certain ladies of the Tornabuoni family are present at the birth of John the Baptist and of the Virgin. **Brunelleschi**'s *Crucifix*, popularly supposed to have been carved as a response to Donatello's uncouth version at Santa Croce, hangs in the Cappella Gondi, left of the chancel. At the end of the left transept is the raised **Cappella Strozzi**, whose faded frescoes by Nardo di Cione (1350s) include an entire wall of visual commentary on Dante's *Inferno*. The magnificent altarpiece by Nardo's brother Andrea (better known as **Orcagna**), is a piece of propaganda for the Dominicans – Christ is shown bestowing favour simultaneously on both St Peter and St Thomas Aquinas, a figure second only to St Dominic in the order's hierarchy.

The Museo di Santa Maria Novella

More remarkable paintings are on display in the spacious Romanesque conventual buildings to the left of the church, entered through a separate door into the **Museo di Santa Maria Novella** (Mon–Thurs & Sat 9am–5pm, Sun 9am–2pm; €2.60). The cloisters, just beyond the ticket desk, are more richly decorated than any others in Florence. The first set, the Romanesque **Chiostro Verde**, features frescoes of *Stories from Genesis* by **Paolo Uccello** and his workshop. Look out for Uccello's windswept image of *The Flood*, on the right as you enter, rendered almost unintelligible by the telescoping perspective and the double appearance of the ark (before and after the flood), the flanks of which form a receding corridor in the centre of the image. On the left, the ark is rising on the deluge; on the right it has come to rest as the waters subside. In the foreground, two men fight each other in their desperation to stay alive (the chequered lifebelt that one of them is wearing is a favourite Uccello device for demonstrating a mastery of perspective). In the right foreground there's a preview of the universal devastation, with a crow gobbling an eyeball from one of the drowned.

Off the cloister opens what was once the chapter-house of the immensely rich convent, the **Cappellone degli Spagnuoli** (Spanish Chapel), which received its new name after Eleanor of Toledo reserved it for the use of her Spanish entourage. Its fresco cycle by Andrea di Firenze, an extended depiction of the triumph of the Catholic Church, was described by Ruskin as "the most noble piece of pictorial philosophy in Italy". The left wall depicts the *Triumph of Divine Wisdom*: Thomas Aquinas is enthroned below the Virgin and Apostles amidst winged Virtues and biblical notables. The more spectacular right wall depicts the *Triumph of the Church*, and includes at the bottom a building supposed to be Florence's cathedral, a pinky-purple creation imagined eighty years before its actual completion. Before it stand the pope and the Holy Roman Emperor, society's ultimate spiritual and temporal rulers. To the right is a group of pilgrims; the saved are shown being marshalled towards a friar who hears their confession (which removes the taint of mortal sin) before dispatch towards St Peter and the Gate of Paradise.

The northern city centre

The busy quarter north of the Duomo and east of the train station is packed with shops and commerce. Focus of the area is Florence's main food market, the vast covered **Mercato Centrale** (Mon–Sat 7am–2pm; winter also Sat 4–8pm). Butchers, *alimentari*, tripe sellers, greengrocers, pasta stalls and bars are all gathered under one roof, charging prices lower than you'll readily find elsewhere. All around is a hectic **street market** (Mon–Sat 8.30am–7pm; Ⓦ www.sanlorenzo-market.com), thronged with stalls selling leather bags, belts, clothes and shoes – plus racks of football shirts from all the most famous teams in Europe.

San Lorenzo

Founded in the fourth century, **San Lorenzo**, on the piazza of the same name (Mon–Sat 10am–5pm; €2.50), has a claim to be the oldest church in Florence, and was the city's cathedral for almost three centuries. Although Michelangelo sweated to produce a scheme for San Lorenzo's facade, the bare brick of the exterior has never been clad; it's a stark, inappropriate prelude to the powerful simplicity of Brunelleschi's interior, one of the earliest Renaissance church designs. Inside are two striking **bronze pulpits** by **Donatello**. Covered in densely populated and disquieting reliefs, chiefly of scenes preceding and following the *Crucifixion*, these are the artist's last works and were completed by his pupils. Close by, at the foot of the altar steps, a large disc of multicoloured marble marks the grave of Cosimo il Vecchio, the artist's main patron. Further pieces by Donatello (who is buried here) adorn the **Sagrestia Vecchia** off the left transept – the two pairs of bronze doors, the large reliefs of *SS Cosmas and Damian* and *SS Lawrence and Stephen*, the cherub-filled frieze, and the eight terracotta tondi. The table of milky marble in the centre of the room is the tomb of Cosimo il Vecchio's parents, Giovanni Bicci de' Medici and Piccarda Bueri.

At the top of the left aisle of San Lorenzo a door leads out to the cloister, and the staircase immediately on the right goes up to the **Biblioteca Laurenziana**

(Mon–Fri 8.30am–1.30pm; free, except during special exhibitions). Wishing to create a suitably grandiose home for the precious manuscripts assembled by Cosimo il Vecchio and Lorenzo il Magnifico, Pope Clement VII (Lorenzo's nephew) asked **Michelangelo** to design a new Medici library in 1524. The vestibule of the building he came up with is a revolutionary showpiece of Mannerist architecture, delighting in paradoxical display – brackets that support nothing, columns that sink into the walls rather than stand out from them, and a flight of steps so large that it almost fills the room, spilling down like a solidified lava flow. You pass from this deliberately eccentric space into the tranquil, architecturally correct reading room. Almost everything here is the work of Michelangelo, even the inlaid desks.

The Cappelle Medicee

Some of Michelangelo's most celebrated Florentine works are in San Lorenzo's Sagrestia Nuova, part of the **Cappelle Medicee** (Tues–Sun 8.15am–5pm, plus same hours first, third & fifth Sun and second & fourth Mon of month; €6). Entrance to the chapels is round the back of San Lorenzo, on Piazza Madonna degli Aldobrandini, and leads directly into the low-vaulted **crypt**, last resting-place of a clutch of minor Medici tossed down here in 1791 by Ferdinand III. After filing through the crypt, you climb steps into the **Cappella dei Principi** (Chapel of the Princes), a gloomy, marble-plated octagonal hall built as a mausoleum for Cosimo I and his ancestors. Morbid and dowdy, it was the most expensive building project ever financed by the family.

Follow the corridor leading on to the **Sagrestia Nuova**, one of the earliest Mannerist buildings, begun by Michelangelo in 1520 and intended as a tribute to, and subversion of, Brunelleschi's Sagrestia Vecchia. Architectural connoisseurs go into raptures over the complex cornices of the alcoves and other such sophistications, but you might be more drawn to the fabulous **Medici tombs**, carved by Michelangelo. To the left is the **tomb of Lorenzo**, Duke of Urbino, grandson of Lorenzo il Magnifico. Michelangelo depicted him as a man of thought, and his sarcophagus bears figures of *Dawn* and *Dusk*, the times of day whose ambiguities appeal to the contemplative mind. Opposite is the **tomb of Giuliano**, Duke of Nemours, youngest son of Lorenzo il Magnifico. As a man of action, his character is symbolized by *Day* and *Night*. Contrary to these idealized images, Giuliano was in fact an easygoing but feckless individual, while Lorenzo combined ineffectualness with arrogance; both died young and unlamented of tuberculosis, combined in Lorenzo's case with syphilis. Michelangelo was not unaware of the ironies – critics have suggested that Lorenzo's absurd hat may well be a gentle hint as to the subject's feeble-mindedness. Their effigies were intended to face the equally grand tombs of Lorenzo il Magnifico and his brother Giuliano, two Medici who had genuine claims to fame and honour, but the only part of the project realized by Michelangelo is the serene **Madonna and Child**, the last image of the Madonna he ever sculpted and one of the most affecting, now flanked by *Cosmas* and *Damian*, patron saints of doctors (*medici*) and thus of the dynasty.

The Palazzo Medici-Riccardi

On the northeastern edge of Piazza San Lorenzo stands the **Palazzo Medici-Riccardi** (9am–7pm, closed Wed; €4), built by Michelozzo in the 1440s for Cosimo il Vecchio and for a century or more the principal seat of the Medici in the city. With its heavily rusticated exterior, this monolithic palace was the prototype for such houses as the Palazzo Pitti and Palazzo Strozzi, but was greatly altered in the seventeenth century by its new owners, the Riccardi family, who took over after Cosimo I moved out. Thanks to its restored Gozzoli **frescoes** – some of the most charming in all Florence – it now rates as a major sight. However, as only fifteen people are allowed to view these paintings at any one time, the queues can be overwhelming. You should visit the ticket office (through the palace courtyard to the rear) or call ✆055.276.0340 and **book in advance** for a timed visit the following day.

Of Michelozzo's original scheme, only the upstairs **chapel** remains intact, its interior covered by a brilliantly colourful narrative fresco of the *Procession of the Magi*, painted around 1460 by Benozzo Gozzoli. It shows the pageant of the Compagnia dei Magi, the most patrician of the city's religious confraternities, through a glowing, dream-like landscape dotted with castles; dogs and fabulous animals trot along beside. It's known that several of the Medici household are featured, but putting names to these prettified faces is a problem. The man leading the cavalcade on a white horse is certainly Piero il Gottoso, sponsor of the fresco. Lorenzo il Magnifico is probably the young king in the foreground, riding the grey horse seen in full profile, while his brother, Giuliano, is probably the one preceded by the black bowman. The artist himself is in the crowd on the far left, his red beret signed with his name in gold. A second staircase ascends from the courtyard to the **Sala di Luca Giordano**, a gilded and mirrored gallery notable for its *Madonna and Child* by Fra' Filippo Lippi, kept in a grotesque black metal box to the left of the door. Luca Giordano's overblown ceiling fresco of *The Apotheosis of the Medici*, painted after the Riccardi family had bought the building in 1659, is either deftly tongue-in-cheek or utterly shameless.

The Accademia

Florence's first Academy of Drawing – indeed, Europe's first – was founded northeast of San Lorenzo on Via Ricasoli in the mid-sixteenth century by Bronzino, Ammannati and Vasari. In 1784, Grand Duke Pietro Leopoldo opened the onsite **Galleria dell'Accademia** (Tues–Sun 8.15am–6.50pm; €8.50). The gallery has an impressive collection of paintings, especially of Florentine altarpieces from the fourteenth to the early sixteenth centuries – but the pictures are not what pull the crowds. Everyone comes here to see the most famous sculpture in the world, **Michelangelo**'s *David*.

Seeing the *David* for the first time can be something of a shock. The conception of the piece was revolutionary. Instead of, as was common, portraying a static warrior David in full armour, with the head of Goliath lying trophy-like at his feet, Michelangelo chose to emphasize human thought and motivation. This David, as well as breaking with tradition by being completely nude (thus recalling classical statuary), is frozen in mid-movement. He is gazing intently over his left shoulder with a stone in his other hand, sizing up Goliath while shifting his weight onto his right foot prior to loading his sling and firing off the stone. The poise of the figure comes in its balance between head and hands, between thought and action.

Michelangelo spent almost three years working beneath a temporary shelter set up in the courtyard of the Opera del Duomo, sculpting the *David* from a tall but very narrow block of flawed Carrara marble which had already been partly worked by others and abandoned. The completed statue is one of the few that Michelangelo created with a main frontal view, as opposed to being viewable in the round – largely because of the block's limitations. He finished it, the largest nude to have been sculpted since classical times, in early 1504 at the age of 29. It was then carted on a four-day procession through the city to its display site in front of the Palazzo Vecchio, suffering attacks as it went from pro-Medici supporters who saw it as symbolizing the recent overthrow of Medicean and Savonarolan rule. Since then, the *David* has become an emblem of the city's pride and of the illimitable ambition of the Renaissance artist. In 1873, it was moved to this specially designed tribune in the Accademia for conservation reasons, and was replaced outside the Palazzo Vecchio by a marble copy.

But herein lies the shock of a first viewing, which so upsets many in the scrum that gathers at *David*'s feet. Michelangelo seems blithely to have abandoned all normal human **proportion**. *David*'s head and hands are obviously far too big, his arms are too long, his legs are too short. Laser-wielding scientists even determined in 2000 that he is wall-eyed. For many people this undermines the whole work: the *David* is an incomparable show of technical bravura but how can it represent the ideal of male beauty? And yet this piece of monumental public sculpture was not designed to be examined up close. On the plinth in Piazza della Signoria *David*'s feet would have been way above head height. In the Accademia, you could reach out and touch his toes (but for a perspex shield installed after a tourist took a hammer to the sculpture's left foot in 1991). Without the benefit of being able to view the work from a position well back as Michelangelo envisaged – which would give the illusion of lengthening the legs and shortening the trunk and arms – the *David* appears hopelessly gangling. Equally, scrutinizing a close-up, full-face image of *David*'s frowning features is a modern preoccupation: from below, in profile and at a distance, the eyes that do in fact point in slightly different directions appear perfectly focused. In the words of Marc Levoy, the scientist from Stanford University who discovered the squint, "He optimized each eye for its appearance as seen from the side – It's a typical Michelangelo trick." Proportion, it seems, is in the eye of the beholder.

Michelangelo once described the process of sculpting as being the liberation of the form from within the stone, a notion that seems to be embodied by the stunning unfinished **Slaves** that line the approach to the *David*. His procedure, clearly demonstrated here, was to cut the block as if it were a deep relief, and then to free the three-dimensional figure. Carved in the 1520s and 1530s, these immensely powerful creations, writhing as if to pull themselves free of the stone, were intended for the tomb of Pope Julius II; in 1564 the artist's nephew gave them to the Medici, who installed them in the grotto of the Bòboli gardens. In their midst here is another unfinished work, *St Matthew*.

The Museo di San Marco

Just north of the Accademia is the lively **Piazza San Marco**, a meeting-place for Florence's many art students. One side of the square is taken up by the Dominican convent and church of San Marco, now deconsecrated to house the **Museo di San Marco** (Tues–Fri 8.15am–1.50pm, Sat 8.15am–6.50pm, plus first, third & fifth Mon of each month 8.15am–1.50pm, and second & fourth Sun 8.15am–6.50pm; €4). In the 1430s, the convent was the recipient of Cosimo il Vecchio's most lavish patronage: he financed Michelozzo's enlargement of the buildings, and went on to establish a vast public library here. Ironically, the convent became the centre of resistance to the Medici later in the century – Savonarola was prior of San Marco from 1491. Meanwhile, as Michelozzo was altering and expanding the convent, its walls were being decorated by one of its friars, **Fra' Angelico**, a painter in whom a medieval simplicity of faith was uniquely allied to a Renaissance sophistication of manner.

The **Ospizio dei Pellegrini** (Pilgrims' Hospice) contains around twenty paintings by Fra'Angelico, most brought here from other churches in Florence.

A *Deposition* and a small *Last Judgement* are outstanding – the former remarkable for its aura of tranquillity, as though the minds of its protagonists were already fixed on the Resurrection. Across the cloister, in the **Sala Capitolare**, is a powerful fresco of the *Crucifixion*, painted by Angelico and assistants in 1441. At the rear of this room, the **refectory** – with a lustrous *Last Supper* by Ghirlandaio – forms an ante-room to the *foresteria* (guest rooms). The key work, for the drama of its setting and the lucidity of its composition, is the famous **Annunciation** at the summit of the main staircase. All round this upper floor are ranged 44 tiny **dormitory cells**, each frescoed either by Angelico himself or by his assistants – don't miss the *Noli me tangere* (cell 1), the *Annunciation* (cell 3), the *Transfiguration* (cell 6) and the *Coronation of the Virgin* (cell 9). In all likelihood, the marvellous *Madonna Enthroned*, on the facing wall, is by Angelico too. The anachronistic monastic onlookers in several of the scenes are St Dominic (with the star above his head) and St Peter Martyr (with the split skull); the latter, responsible for a massacre of Florentine heretics in the thirteenth century, is the city's home-produced Dominican saint. Michelozzo's **library**, a room that seems to exude an atmosphere of calm study, is off the corridor to the right, at the end of which is the pair of rooms used by Cosimo il Vecchio when he came here on retreat.

The **church** of San Marco, greatly altered since Michelozzo's intervention, is worth a visit for two works on the second and third altars on the right: a *Madonna and Saints*, painted in 1509 by Fra' Bartolommeo (like Fra' Angelico, a friar at the convent), and an eighth-century mosaic of *The Madonna in Prayer*, brought here from Constantinople.

Piazza Santissima Annunziata

The Accademia stands between Piazza San Marco to the west and, to the east, **Piazza Santissima Annunziata**, the locals' favourite square on account of its lovely porticoes and church. Until the seventeenth century the Florentine year used to begin on March 25, the Feast of the Annunciation – hence the city's predilection for paintings of the Annunciation, and the popularity of the Annunziata church, which is still the place for society weddings. The festival is marked by a huge fair in the square and the streets leading off it. Giambologna's final work, the equestrian statue of Grand Duke Ferdinando I, holds the centre of the square; it was cast by his pupil Pietro Tacca, creator of the two bizarre **fountains**, on each of which a pair of aquatic monkeys dribble water at two bewhiskered sea-slugs.

The tone of the square is set by Brunelleschi's **Spedale degli Innocenti** (8.30am–2pm, closed Wed; €3), opened in 1445 as the first foundlings' hospital in Europe, and which still incorporates an orphanage – Luca della Robbia's ceramic tondi of swaddled babies advertise the building's function. The convent, centred on two beautiful cloisters, now contains a miscellany of Florentine Renaissance art including one of Luca della Robbia's most charming Madonnas and an incident-packed *Adoration of the Magi* by Ghirlandaio.

The church of **Santissima Annunziata** (daily 7am–12.30pm & 4–6.30pm) is the mother church of the Servite order, which was founded by seven Florentine aristocrats in 1234. Its dedication took place in the fourteenth century, in recognition of its miraculous image of the Virgin which, left unfinished by the monastic artist, was purportedly completed by an angel. It attracted so many pilgrims that the Medici commissioned **Michelozzo** to rebuild the church in the second half of the fifteenth century in order to accommodate them. In the Chiostro dei Voti, the atrium that Michelozzo built onto the church, are some beautiful frescoes mainly painted in the 1510s, including a

TUSCANY | Florence

Visitation by **Pontormo** and a series by **Andrea del Sarto**, whose *Birth of the Virgin* achieves a perfect balance of spontaneity and geometrical order. Much of the church interior's gilt and stucco fancy dress was perpetrated in the seventeenth and eighteenth centuries, but the ornate tabernacle of the miraculous image, cordoned by candles and lanterns to the left of the entrance, was produced by Michelozzo. His patron, Piero il Gottoso, made sure that nobody remained unaware of his largesse: an inscription in the floor reads "The marble alone cost 4000 florins". The painting encased in marble has been repainted into obscurity, and is rarely shown anyway; far more interesting are the frescoes of *The Vision of St Jerome* and *The Trinity* by **Andrea del Castagno** in the first two chapels on the left. Separated from the nave by a triumphal arch is the unusual tribune, begun by Michelozzo but completed to designs by Alberti. The adjoining Chiostro dei Morti, entered from the left transept, is worth visiting for Andrea del Sarto's calculatedly informal *Madonna del Sacco*, painted over the door.

The Museo Archeologico

Just off the square is the **Museo Archeologico**, Via della Colonna 38 (Mon 2–7pm, Tues & Thurs 8.30am–7pm, Wed & Fri–Sun 8.30am–2pm; €4; see box on p.477 for details of advance reservations). This is the pre-eminent collection of its kind in northern Italy, though modernization is perpetually in progress, and they are still rectifying damage caused by the flood of 1966. Its special strength is its **Etruscan** finds. On the ground floor, pride of place goes to the *François Vase*, an Attic bowl from the sixth century BC. It's been restored twice – once after its discovery in Chiusi in 1845, and again after a butter-fingered member of staff converted it into a 638-piece jigsaw in 1900. The two upper floors are arranged with variable clarity. Outstanding among the **Roman** pieces is the nude known as the *Idolino*, probably a copy of a fifth-century BC original. The **Greek** head of a horse, in the same room, once adorned the garden of the Palazzo Medici, where it was studied by Donatello and Verrocchio. In the long gallery stand the *Arringatore* (Orator), the only known Etruscan large bronze from the Hellenistic period; and a *Chimera*, a bizarre triple-headed bronze monster of the fifth century BC discovered at Arezzo and much admired by Cosimo I's retinue of Mannerist artists.

The eastern city centre

The 1966 flood permanently changed the character of the eastern city centre. Before the deluge it had been one of the more densely populated districts of the city, packed with tenements and small workshops. But **Piazza Santa Croce**, a short stroll east of Piazza della Signoria, and the streets around it lie lower than the surrounding area, and were devastated when the Arno burst its banks. Many of the residents moved out permanently in the following years. Leather shops and jewellers are still in evidence, but the souvenir stalls are now a more conspicuous presence.

The piazza has traditionally been one of the city's main arenas: the Medici used it for self-aggrandizing pageants, and under Savonarola it was the principal site for the ceremonial execution of heretics. It's still sometimes used for the **Gioco di Calcio Storico**, a football tournament between the city's four *quartieri*; the game is held three times in St John's week (the last week of June), and is characterized by incomprehensible rules and a degree of violence from which the heavy sixteenth-century costumes offer inadequate protection.

Santa Croce

Florence's two most lavish churches after the Duomo were the headquarters of the two preaching orders: the Dominicans occupied Santa Maria Novella, while the Franciscans were based at the giant church of **Santa Croce** (Mon–Sat 9.30am–5.30pm, Sun 1–5.30pm; €3), famed as the mausoleum of Florence's eminent citizens. Over 270 tombstones pave the floor of the church, while grander monuments commemorate the likes of Ghiberti, Michelangelo, Machiavelli and Galileo. **Dante** has a monument in the church as well as a supremely dramatic statue overlooking the piazza outside – although he is actually buried in Ravenna, where he died.

Inside the door is Vasari's monument to **Michelangelo**, whose body was brought back from Rome to Florence in July 1574; he requested this position so that when the graves of the dead fly open on Judgement Day, the first thing to catch his eye would be Brunelleschi's cathedral dome. On the opposite side of the church is the tomb of **Galileo**, made in 1737, when it was finally agreed to give the great scientist a Christian burial. Back in the right aisle, the Neoclassical cenotaph to **Dante** is immediately after the second altar, while against the third pillar there's a beautiful pulpit by Benedetto da Maiano, carved with scenes from the life of St Francis. The side door at the end of the aisle is flanked by Donatello's gilded stone relief of *The Annunciation* and Bernardo Rossellino's tomb of the humanist **Leonardo Bruni**, a design which has spawned innumerable imitations.

The dazzling chapels at the east end of Santa Croce are a compendium of Florentine fourteenth-century art, showing the extent of Giotto's influence and the full diversity of his followers. The two immediately to the right of the chancel are entirely covered with frescoes by **Giotto**: beside the chancel is the **Cappella Bardi**, featuring scenes from the life of St Francis, while next to it is the **Cappella Peruzzi** with a cycle on the lives of St John the Baptist and John the Evangelist. On the south side of the right transept is the **Cappella Baroncelli**, featuring the first night scene in Western painting, Taddeo Gaddi's *Annunciation to the Shepherds*. On the north side of the left transept, the second **Cappella Bardi** houses a wooden Crucifix by **Donatello** – supposedly criticized by Brunelleschi as resembling a "peasant on the Cross".

The Museo dell'Opera di Santa Croce

Santa Croce's most celebrated attractions have been hived off to form the separate, and little-explored, **Museo dell'Opera di Santa Croce** (entry included with ticket to church), entered to the right of the main steps of the church. Standing at the far end of the **Primo Chiostro**, a peaceful expanse of grass hard up against the church wall, is one of Florence's architectural gems, Brunelleschi's **Cappella dei Pazzi**. If one building could be said to typify the spirit of the early Renaissance, this is it. Brunelleschi designed the chapel in the 1430s and worked on it between 1442 and 1446, though it was only completed after his death. The building is geometrically perfect without seeming pedantic, and is exemplary in the way its decorative detail harmonizes with the design. The polychrome lining of the portico's shallow cupola is by **Luca della Robbia**, as is the tondo of *St Andrew* over the door; inside, Luca also produced the blue-and-white tondi of the *Apostles*.

As you exit the chapel, to your left hides Santa Croce's spacious **Secondo Chiostro**, also by Brunelleschi, and perhaps the most peaceful spot in the centre of Florence (although restoration means access is often restricted). A building between the two houses a damaged *Crucifixion* by **Cimabue** on the right wall, which has become the emblem of the havoc caused by the 1966 flood –

six metres of filthy water surged into the church, tearing the artwork from its mounting. Also in this room are Taddeo Gaddi's fresco of the *Last Supper* and *Crucifixion* and **Donatello**'s enormous gilded *St Louis of Toulouse*, made for Orsanmichele.

South of the river

Visitors to Florence might perceive the Arno as merely a brief interruption in the urban fabric, but Florentines talk as though a ravine divided their city. North of the river is *Arno di quà* ("over here"), while the south side is *Arno di là* ("over there"), also known as the **Oltrarno**, literally "Beyond the Arno". Though traditionally an artisans' quarter, the Oltrarno has always contained prosperous enclaves, and many of the ruling families chose to settle in this area. Nowadays some of the city's swankiest shops line Borgo San Jacopo, while the windows of Via Maggio are an amazing display of palatial furnishings.

The direct route from the city centre to the heart of Oltrarno crosses the river on the **Ponte Vecchio**, the only bridge not mined by the retreating Nazis in 1944. Built in 1345 to replace an ancient wooden bridge, the bustling thoroughfare has always been loaded with shops propped over the water. Up until the sixteenth century, butchers, fishmongers and tanners occupied the bridge, but in 1565 the Medici had the Corridoio Vasariano (see p.489) constructed over the arcades as a private passageway between the Palazzo Vecchio and the Palazzo Pitti. For a generation, the noble nostrils suffered the stench rising from the bridge, until in 1593 Ferdinando I ejected the butchers and installed goldsmiths instead. Today, still replete with jewellery firms, the bridge is crammed with sightseers and big-spending shoppers during the day, and also remains busy after the shutters come down, when street traders set out their stalls and the local lads hang around the bust of Cellini.

Santa Felicità, at the southern end of the bridge, is worth a visit (Mon–Sat 9am–noon & 3–6pm) for the paintings by **Pontormo** in the Cappella Capponi, just inside the door on the right. His weirdly erotic *Deposition* is one of the masterworks of Florentine Mannerism, its jarring colours slicing through the chapel's gloom. There's no sign of any standard imagery, or even the Cross: instead, androgynous figures clad in billows of drapery – metallic blue, puce green and bubblegum pink – bear the lifeless body of Christ like a mournful trophy, backed only by a solitary, ghostly cloud.

The Palazzo Pitti

Although the Medici later took possession of the largest palace in Florence – the **Palazzo Pitti** – it still bears the name of the man for whom it was built. Luca Pitti was a prominent rival of Cosimo il Vecchio, and much of the impetus behind the building of his new house came from a desire to trump the Medici. No sooner was the palace completed, however, than the Pitti's fortunes began to decline. By 1549 they were forced, ironically, to sell out to the Medici. The palace then became the Medici's family pile, growing in bulk until the seventeenth century, when it achieved its present gargantuan proportions. Today, the palazzo and the pavilions of the grand **Giardino di Bóboli** hold eight museums.

Many of the paintings gathered by the Medici in the seventeenth century are now arranged in the **Galleria Palatina**, a labyrinthine suite of 26 rooms in the right-side upper-floor wing of the palace (Tues–Sun 8.15am–6.50pm; €8.50, including admission to the Appartamenti Reali). The ticket office is on the ground floor, just off the main courtyard. You'll need at least a couple of hours to do the gallery justice. The pictures are hung three deep in places, as they would have been in the days of their acquisition, and conform to no ordering principle except that of making each room as varied as possible. There are half-a-dozen excellent works by **Raphael** here, including, in room 5, portraits of Angelo Doni and his wife Maddalena – her pose copied directly from the *Mona Lisa* – and the celebrated *Madonna della Seggiola*, or Madonna of the Chair, in which the figures are curved into the rounded shape of the picture with no sense of artificiality. An even larger contingent of supreme works by **Titian** includes a number of his most trenchant portraits – among them *Pietro Aretino*, the preening *Cardinal Ippolito de' Medici*, and the disconcerting *Portrait of an Englishman* in room 2, a picture that makes the viewer feel as closely scrutinized as was the subject. **Rubens**' *Consequences of War* packs more of a punch than most other Baroque allegories. The gallery's outstanding sculpture is **Canova**'s *Venus Italica* in room 1, commissioned by Napoleon.

Much of the rest of this floor comprises the **Appartamenti Reali** – the Pitti's state rooms, renovated by the dukes of Lorraine in the eighteenth century, and then again by Vittorio Emanuele when Florence became Italy's capital. On the floor above is the **Galleria d'Arte Moderna** (Tues–Sat 8.15am–1.50pm; also open on first, third & fifth Sun and second & fourth Mon of month same times; joint ticket with Galleria del Costume €5). This displays a chronological survey of primarily Tuscan art from the mid-eighteenth century to 1945. Most rewarding are the products of the Macchiaioli, the Italian division of the Impressionist movement; most startling, however, are the sublime specimens of sculptural kitsch, such as Antonio Ciseri's *Pregnant Nun*. The left-side wing of the palace is given over to the **Museo degli Argenti**, entered from the garden courtyard (8.15am–2pm; closed first & last Mon of month; €4, includes porcelain museum and Giardino di Bóboli) – a collection of luxury artefacts, including Lorenzo il Magnifico's trove of antique vases, displayed in one of the four splendidly frescoed reception rooms on the ground floor. The **Galleria del Costume** (same hours and ticket as Galleria d'Arte Moderna) is housed in the Palazzina della Meridiana, the eighteenth-century southern wing of the Pitti, and across the palace gardens is the **Museo delle Porcellane** (Museum of Porcelain; Mon–Sat 9am–1.30pm; also open on first, third & fifth Sun and second & fourth Mon of month same times; included in ticket for Giardino di Bóboli – see below, but closes at 2.30pm).

The Bóboli Gardens and the Belvedere

The **Giardino di Bóboli** is the Pitti's enormous formal garden (daily: opens 8.15am, closes 4.30pm Jan, Feb, Nov & Dec, 5.30pm March, 6.30pm April, May, Sept & Oct, 7.30pm June–Aug; closed first & last Mon of month; €4, includes porcelain and silver museums). Created when the Medici took possession of the Palazzo Pitti, it continued to expand into the early seventeenth century. Today, it is the only extensive area of greenery in the centre of the city, and thus tends to get crowded in the areas close to the gates; it gets quieter in the heart of the garden, however, as the sharp gradients of its avenues take their toll. Of all the garden's Mannerist embellishments, the most celebrated is the **Grotta del Buontalenti**, close to the entrance to the left of the palace facade, beyond the turtle-back figure of Cosimo I's court dwarf (as seen on a thousand postcards). In amongst the fake stalactites are shepherds and sheep that look like calcified sponges, while embedded in the corners are replicas of Michelangelo's *Slaves*, replacing the originals that were here until 1908. In the deepest recesses of the cave stands Giambologna's *Venus Emerging from her Bath*, leered at by attendant imps. The vast **amphitheatre** facing the palace courtyard was designed in the early seventeenth century as an arena for Medici festivities. A set-piece of comparable scale is the fountain island **Isolotto**, best approached along the central cypress avenue known as the *Viottolone*, many of whose statues are Roman originals. Carry straight on from here and you'll come to the **Porta Romana** entrance, which takes its name from the fourteenth-century city gate in the street outside.

It's sometimes possible to leave the gardens by the gate that leads to the precincts of the **Forte di Belvedere**. This star-shaped fortress was built on the orders of Ferdinando I in 1590, ostensibly for the city's protection but really to intimidate the Grand-Duke's fellow Florentines. The **urban panorama** from here is superb and art exhibitions are sometimes held in the box-like palace in the centre of the fortress. The city's new Museo delle Arme (Arms and Armour Museum) is also due to open here soon. East from the Belvedere, and also accessible on Costa San Giorgio which coils up from Piazza Santa Felìcita, stretches the best-preserved section of Florence's fortified walls, an attractive if tiring route to San Miniato (see p.502).

Santo Spirito

The charmingly lived-in **Piazza Santo Spirito**, on the south side of the Ponte Santa Trinità, with its lolling students, market stalls and cafés, and the neighbouring streets with their furniture workshops and antiques showrooms, together encapsulate the self-sufficient character of the quarter, a character not yet hopelessly compromised by the encroachments of tourism. Don't be deterred by the vacant facade of the church of **Santo Spirito** (Mon, Tues, Thurs & Fri 8.30am–noon & 4–6pm, Wed 8am–noon, Sat & Sun 4–6pm) – the interior, one of Brunelleschi's last projects, prompted Bernini to describe it as "the most beautiful church in the world". It's so perfectly proportioned it seems artless, yet the plan is extremely sophisticated – a Latin cross with a continuous chain of 38 chapels round the outside and a line of 35 columns running in parallel right round the building. Unfortunately a Baroque baldachin covers the high altar, but this is the sole disruption of Brunelleschi's arrangement.

The Cappella Brancacci

In 1771 fire wrecked the Carmelite convent and church of **Santa Maria del Carmine** some 300m west of Santo Spirito, but somehow the flames did not damage the frescoes of the church's **Cappella Brancacci**, a cycle of paintings that is one of the essential sights of Florence (Mon & Wed–Sat 10am–5pm, Sun 1–5pm; €3.10). The frescoes adorn one side-chapel of the Carmine, which is barricaded off from the chancel and nave and instead has to be entered on a back route through the cloister. The ticket office is to the right of the church entrance, and your money allows you to view the stunning frescoes, in a maximum group of thirty, for an utterly inadequate fifteen minutes.

The decoration of the chapel was begun in 1424 by **Masolino** and **Masaccio**, the former aged 41 and the latter 22. Within a short time the elder was taking lessons from the younger, whose grasp of the texture of the real world, of the principles of perspective, and of the dramatic potential of the biblical texts they were illustrating far exceeded that of his precursors. Three years later Masaccio was dead, but (in the words of Vasari) "All the most celebrated sculptors and painters since Masaccio's day have become excellent and illustrious by studying their art in this chapel." Michelangelo used to come here to make drawings of Masaccio's scenes – and had his nose broken on the chapel steps by a young sculptor whom he enraged with his condescending attitude.

The Brancacci frescoes are as startling a spectacle as the restored Sistine Chapel in Rome, the brightness and delicacy of their colours and the solidity of the figures exemplifying what Bernard Berenson singled out as the tactile quality of Florentine art. The small scene on the left of the entrance arch is the quintessence of Masaccio's art. Depictions of **The Expulsion of Adam and Eve** had never before captured the desolation of the sinners so graphically – Adam presses his hands to his face in bottomless despair, Eve raises her head and screams. In contrast to the emotional charge of Masaccio's couple, Masolino's almost dainty *Adam and Eve* on the opposite arch pose as if to have their portraits painted – highly reminiscent of Bandinelli's unintentionally comic sculpture in the Bargello.

St Peter is chief protagonist of most of the remaining scenes, two of which are especially compelling. The *Tribute Money* on the upper left wall is the most widely praised, a complex narrative by Masaccio showing Peter, under Christ's instruction, fetching money from the mouth of a fish to pay a sum demanded by the city authorities of Capernaum. Masaccio's *St Peter Healing the Sick*, to the left of the altar, depicts the shadow of the stern saint curing the infirm as it passes over them, a miracle invested with the aura of a solemn ceremonial.

The cycle was suspended in 1428 when Masaccio left for Rome, where he died, and work did not resume until 1480, when the frescoes were completed by **Filippino Lippi**. He finished the *Raising of Theophilus's Son and St Peter Enthroned* (lower left wall), which depicts St Peter bringing the son of the Prefect of Antioch to life and then preaching to the people of the city from a throne. The three figures to the right of the throne are thought to be portraits of Masaccio, Alberti and Brunelleschi. Masaccio originally painted himself touching Peter's robe, but Lippi considered such physical contact to be improper and painted out the arm; you can clearly see where the arm used to be. There's another portrait in the combined scene of *St Peter before Agrippa* and *St Peter's Crucifixion* (lower right wall): the central figure looking out from the painting in the trio right of the crucifixion is Botticelli, Lippi's teacher. Lippi's most distinctive contribution, though, is *The Release of St Peter* on the right-hand side of the entrance arch, where there's a touching intimacy in the relationship between saint and counselling angel.

San Miniato al Monte

The brilliant, multicoloured facade of **San Miniato al Monte** on a steep hillside in the Oltrarno lures troops of visitors up from the south bank of the Arno. Most routes pass through or alongside the broad **Piazzale Michelangelo** just below the church: buses #12 and #13 stop here, there's free parking or it's twenty minute's walk from the city centre. The spectacular views from here of Brunelleschi's dome floating above the city are worth a special journey in themselves.

The church itself more than fulfils the promise of its appearance from a distance: **San Miniato** is the finest Romanesque church in Tuscany. The church's dedicatee, St Minias, belonged to a Christian community that settled in Florence in the third century; according to legend, after his martyrdom his corpse was seen to carry his severed head over the river and up the hill to this spot, where a shrine was subsequently erected to him. Construction of the present building began in 1013 with the foundation of a Cluniac monastery. The gorgeous marble facade – alluding to the baptistry in its geometrical patterning – was added towards the end of that century, though the external mosaic of *Christ between the Virgin and St Minias* dates from the thirteenth. The **interior** (daily: summer 8am–7.30pm; winter 8am–noon & 2.30–7.30pm) is like no other in the city, with the choir raised on a platform above the large crypt; its general form has changed little since the mid-eleventh century. The main structural addition is the Cappella del Cardinale del Portogallo, a paragon of artistic collaboration: the basic design was by Antonio Manetti (a pupil of Brunelleschi), the tomb was carved by Antonio Rossellino, and the terracotta decoration of the ceiling is by Luca della Robbia. The majority of the frescoes along the aisle walls were painted in the fifteenth century; the most extensive are the sacristy's *Scenes from the Life of St Benedict*, painted in the 1380s by Spinello Aretino.

Eating, drinking and entertainment

Florence's gastronomic reputation has suffered under the pressure of mass tourism, and many locals swear there's scarcely a single genuine Tuscan **restaurant** left in the city. But don't despair – this is an exaggeration – a decent meal isn't hard to come by if you explore away from the touristy central streets.

Florentines have always seemed to prefer wine to coffee, and the city can't really claim to have a **café** tradition like that of Rome or Turin – **bars** are both more plentiful and generally more attractive places to rest your weary limbs. The university and the annual influx of language students and other young visitors keep the **nightlife** lively, while **classical music** events such as the prestigious Maggio Musicale maintain Florence's standing as the cultural focus of Tuscany.

Restaurants, pizzerias and snack-bars

In gastronomic circles, Florentine cuisine is often accorded as much reverence as Florentine art but quality cooking doesn't come cheap in Florence – most of the **restaurants** that meet with local approval cost €30 plus per person, including wine. Yet there are some more affordable and congenial places in districts that have a bit of local colour to them, such as Santa Croce and around Santo Spirito. One thing to be aware of is that many restaurants in Florence will only serve full meals – check the menu outside if you're thinking of just popping in for a quick lunchtime plate of pasta.

At the lower end of the market, one option for a rapid stomach-filler is the **friggitoria**, a frequently nameless place serving fried food such as polenta and croquettes, while a **rosticceria** is usually a bit less basic, serving first courses and roast meat dishes often for takeaway only, although some have seating. We've divided the listings below by price: **expensive** means an average full meal (excluding wine) costs €40–60 per person; **inexpensive** means you can eat for €15 or less; **mid-priced** is between the two. These are loose definitions, though, because you can keep costs down even in more expensive places by having just two courses (pasta and main), and retiring to a bar for ice cream or coffee and *digestif*. Remember, too, that you often needn't buy a whole bottle of wine: ask for a half-bottle or quarter-bottle/jug of house wine (*mezza bottiglia* or *un quartino*).

Inexpensive

Benvenuto Via della Mosca 15r, corner Via de'Neri. Don't be misled by the entrance, which looks more like the doorway to a delicatessen than a trattoria; the *gnocchi* and *arista* are delicious and straightforward. Closed Wed & Sun.
Cantinetta dei Verrazzano Via dei Tavolini

18–20r. Great central place for pizza, sandwiches or pastries, owned by a prestigious Chianti vineyard. Take away, sit down briefly by the counter, or grab a table in the pleasant rooms at the back to sample the wine. Mon–Sat 8am–9pm. Closed Aug.
La Casalinga Via del Michelozzo 9r

T 055.218.624. Long-established, traditional family-run trattoria east of Santo Spirito that serves up some of the best low-cost authentic Tuscan dishes in town. Paper tablecloths and brisk service add to the allure. Closed Sun & Aug.

Il Contadino Via Palazzuolo 69r. Very basic but good meals at around €15, with often a lot of backpackers in the queue. Closes at 9.30pm. Closed Sun & Aug.

Il Pizzaiuolo Via de' Macci 113r T 055.241.171.

Many Florentines reckon the pizzas here are the best in the city, something not unconnected with the fact that the owners are Neapolitan. The ambience is friendly and high-spirited, but space is at a premium: booking advised, at least in the evening. No credit cards. Closed Sun & Aug.

I Tarocchi Via dei Renai 12 T 055.234.3912. Quality basic pizzeria – one of the best in the city. Closed Mon.

Mid-priced

Acqua al Due Via della Vigna Vecchia 40r T 055.284.170. Always packed, chiefly on account of its *assaggio di primi* – a succession of pasta dishes shared by everyone at the table. Closed Mon.

Angiolino Via Santo Spirito 36r T 055.239.8976. One of the city's prettiest trattorias. Dried flowers and chillis hang from the brick-vaulted ceiling, set off by wicker-clad Chianti bottles and red-checked tablecloths. The menu is short, Tuscan and to the point, though quality can be erratic. Closed Mon.

Baldovino Via San Giuseppe 22r T 055.241.773. First-rate and very stylish contemporary-looking restaurant run by a charming Scottish couple. It's especially known for pizzas, but the menu is chock-full of other excellent Tuscan and Italian dishes. The wine bar across the way is just as good. Closed Mon.

Belle Donne Via delle Belle Donne 16r. Bustling trattoria with banks of fresh flowers. Share a table and choose from the blackboard menu; especially busy at lunchtime. Open daily, except for Aug holiday.

Borgo Antico Piazza Santo Spirito 6r T 055.210.437. A popular and boisterous trattoria, with quieter tables outside in summer. Choose from ten different pizzas, a daily set-price menu or

a range of Tuscan standards. Servings are generous. Open daily.

Osteria del Caffè Italiano Via Isola delle Stinche 11–13r T 055.289.368. This rambling wood-panelled place, with casual lunch parlour, wine bar and smarter restaurant sections serves first-rate Tuscan food throughout (steer clear of the lacklustre vegetarian offering). Closed Mon.

Osteria Santo Spirito Piazza Santo Spirito 16r T 055.238.2383. Trendy, modern-looking osteria, serving simple, hearty Tuscan dishes with contemporary flair. There's no problem ordering a snack or single course. Outside tables in summer. Open daily.

Quattro Leoni Via Vellutini 1r T 055.218.562. A young, relaxed place arranged around an impressive three-room medieval interior. They only serve full meals, and direct you across the road to the *Caffè degli Artigiani* if you just want a snack. The menu is very Florentine: as a starter try the *finocchiona*, a type of Tuscan salami. Closed Wed in winter.

Alla Vecchia Bettola Viale Lodovico Ariosto 32–34r T 055.224.158. Long trestle tables give this place something of the atmosphere of a drinking den, which is what it once was; the menu has a good repertoire of Tuscan meat dishes. Closed Sun & Mon.

Expensive

Cibrèo Via de'Macci 118r T 055.234.1100. Superb food with creative takes on Tuscan classics in a relaxed, tasteful dining room with friendly and professional service. You'll need to book days in advance for the main part of the restaurant, but next door there's a small backroom section where the food is virtually the same and prices are far lower – around €10 for a main course as opposed to €30 in the main restaurant. Closed Sun, Mon & Aug.

Enoteca Pinchiorri Via Ghibellina 87 T 055.242.777. Florence's best restaurant, with two Michelin stars. The food is sublime and sophisticated, and as for wine, you've a choice of 80,000 different bottles. None of this comes cheap

– you easily could spend in excess of €150 per person, excluding wine – but there's nowhere better for the never-to-be repeated Florentine treat. Closed Mon & Wed lunch, all day Sun & Aug.

Oliviero Via delle Terme 52r T 055.240.618. *Oliviero* currently enjoys a reputation for some of Florence's best food, but at a price. It has a welcoming and old-fashioned feel – something like an Italian restaurant of the Sixties. The innovative food is predominantly Tuscan, but includes other Italian dishes, and puddings, for once, are excellent. The menu includes fresh fish when available, something of a rarity in Florence. Closed lunch, Mon & Aug.

One way to cut eating costs is to retire with a **picnic** to the Bóboli gardens or squares such as Santissima Annunziata, Santa Croce or Santa Maria Novella. The easiest option is to call in at San Lorenzo's **Mercato Centrale** (Mon–Sat 7am–2pm, plus Sat 4–8pm), where everything can be bought under one roof. Almost as comprehensive, and even cheaper, is the **Mercato Sant'Ambrogio** over by Santa Croce (Mon–Fri 7am–2pm). The American bakery Mr Jimmy's, Via San Niccolòl 47, has bagels, brownies, muffins, banana bread and cheesecake. If you're in the centre with closing time approaching Via dei Tavolini, off Via dei Calzaiuoli, is a good street in which to assemble a picnic: Grana Market at no. 11r has cheeses and Semelino at no. 18r bakes wonderful bread. Every district has its *alimentari*, selling the choicest Tuscan produce. The unnamed one close to Santa Trinità at Via Parione 19 prepares delicious sandwiches (eg smoked salmon and *stracchino* cheese), and has a few seats, so you can linger over a glass of wine. Vera, at the southern end of Ponte Santa Trinità at Piazza Frescobaldi 3r, takes the prize for the ultimate Florentine deli; other excellent central *alimentari* include Tassini at Borgo Santi Apostoli 24r and Alessi Paride at Via delle Oche 27–29r.

Cafés, gelaterie, bars and pubs

Pavement **cafés** are not really part of the Florentine scene. Smaller, less ostentatious venues are more the city's style – one-room cafés, bars or *pasticcerie*, or places that combine the functions of all three. Many line the big tourist streets around Piazza della Signoria, but it takes only a little effort to find places where prices are lower and non-Florentine faces fewer: a short walk north from the Duomo gets you into the university area around San Marco, and it's just as easy to cross the river into Oltrarno, the city centre's most down-to-earth quarter. Many of the café/pasticceria-style places are at their busiest first thing in the morning, as the locals stop off for a quick coffee and a pastry such as a *budino di riso* (small rice cake) or a simple brioche or *cornetto*. Devotees of Italian **ice cream** will find plenty of *gelaterie* in Florence to sample some wacky concoctions without straying far off the main drags. The city has a fair spread of **bars** and **pubs** to fuel an evening's entertainment, and classier, specialist **wine-bars** are coming back into fashion after a hiatus: one of the focal points of a Florentine parish is the *vinaio*, an institution that's part wine cellar, part snack bar and part social centre.

Cafés

Caffè Amerini Via della Vigna Nuova 63r. Stylish and intimate, with a clientele like the medieval/Art Deco/modern decor: eclectic. Ideal for a snack lunch, aperitif, or lingering on a rainy afternoon. Closed Sun.

Caffè Cibrèo Via A. del Verrocchio 5r. It's a long way to come just for a drink, but the glorious wood-panelled interior is the prettiest in the city, and the cakes and desserts are outstanding. Tues–Sat 8am–1am.

Caffè Italiano Via della Condotta 56r. A veritable oasis just steps away from the madness of Via dei Calzaiuoli. Elegant downstairs bar with silver teapots and wonderful cakes, and a secret little room upstairs with red velvet banquettes. Lunch is

excellent. Closed Sun.

Caffèlatte Via degli Alfani 39r. This vaguely alternative place is good for breakfast and brunch, featuring a wide range of teas and healthy snacks as well as terrific organic bread baked onsite. The caffè latte, served piping hot in big bowls, is phenomenal. Mon–Sat 8am–midnight.

Caffè Rivoire Piazza Signoria 5r. If you want to people-watch on Florence's main square, this is the place to do so. The café was founded in 1872 and its main claim to fame is the thick hot chocolate, but in summer, go for the refreshing *apcritivo della casa* (Campari, Martini, tonic and Punt & Mes). Closed Mon.

Capocaccia Lungarno Corsini 12–14r. Voted as

the locals' favourite night-time rendezvous, this stylish, trendy haunt doubles as a daytime café and evening snackery; there's also a DJ from Tuesday to Thursday. Tues–Sat noon–4pm & 6pm–1am.

Hemingway Piazza Piattellina 9r. Chocolate is the owners' passion (they're big cheeses in the Chocolate Appreciation Society, and offer desserts to die for), and the swathes of speciality teas,

gourmet coffees, cocktails, food and wines are all excellent, too. Open until 1am. No smoking. Tues–Fri 4pm–1/2am, Sun 11am–8pm.

Procacci Via de'Tornabuoni 64r. Famous café-shop that doesn't serve coffee, just cold drinks. Its fame comes from the extraordinary truffle rolls (*tartufati*), which are delicious if not very filling. Closed Mon.

Gelaterie

Festival del Gelato Via del Corso 75r. Over 100 varieties, with some exotic combinations (including carrot and spinach) and good *semifreddi*. Closed Mon.

Frilli Via San Niccolò 57. Excellent ice creams made from seasonal fruit. Closed Wed.

Perchè No! Via de' Tavolini 19r. Very central and highly regarded *gelateria* with a vast range of

flavours; go for the rum-laced *tiramisù* ice cream. Closed Tues.

Vivoli Via Isola delle Stinche 7r. Operating from unprepossessing premises in a side street close to Santa Croce, this is the best ice cream maker in Florence – some say in Italy. An institution, creating subtle and sublime flavours. Closed Mon & Aug.

Pubs, bars and wine bars

All'Antico Vinaio Via de' Neri 65r. Though recently revamped, the Antico Vinaio preserves much of the rough-and-ready atmosphere that's made it one of Florence's most popular wine bars for the last hundred years. Tues–Sat 8am–8pm, Sun 8am–1pm.

Cabiria Piazza Santo Spirito 4r. Cultish alternative bar, though still cosy and laid-back. Plenty of punters (locals and foreigners) sit out on the piazza. There's a DJ-run soundtrack most nights from around 9pm. Closed Tues.

Caracao Via Ginori 10r. Pseudo-Latin American dive, with a big wooden bar and ranks of tequila bottles. Half-price happy hour 7–10pm. Closed Mon.

Casa del Vino Via dell'Ariento 16r. Wine bar located just west of the Mercato Centrale, and passed by thousands of tourists daily but visited by only a handful. Florentines pitch up for a drink, a natter and an assault on a fine range of panini and *crostini*. Mon–Fri 8am–2.30pm & 5–8pm; Sat 9am–2.30pm. Closed Aug.

Dolce Vita Piazza del Carmine 6r. Trendy, modern-looking bar that's often a venue for small-scale art exhibitions. Dress to preen. Summer Mon–Sat 10.30am–1.30am, Sun 6pm–1.30am; winter daily 6pm–1.30am.

Enoteca Baldovino Via San Giuseppe 18r. Bright, modern and painted in warm ochre tones, this is a stylish, friendly little place to buy a range of gastronomic goodies and sample wines by the bottle or glass. Very convenient for Santa Croce. Summer daily noon–midnight; winter Tues–Sun noon–4pm

& 6pm–midnight

Enoteca de' Giraldi Via de' Giraldi 4r. Old-fashioned central wine-bar and bistro, with vaulted ceilings, stone columns and marble-topped tables. Concentrates on local wines. Mon–Sat noon–4pm & 7pm–1am.

Fiddler's Elbow Piazza Santa Maria Novella. Florence's most popular Irish pub is an invariably heaving affair, though fortunately outside tables relieve the crush. Mon–Thurs 3pm–1am, Fri 3pm–2am, Sat 2pm–2am, Sun 2pm–1am.

Fuori Porta Via del Monte alle Croci. If you're climbing up to San Miniato you could take a breather at Florence's most famous wine-bar. There are over 400 wines by the bottle – the choice by the glass changes every few days – and a wide selection of grappas and malt whiskies. Mon–Sat 12.30–3.30pm & 7pm–12.30am.

Rex Via Fiesolana 25r. Long-established night-time fixture near Santa Croce, friendly and with eye-catching decor. Cocktails are good, tapas are excellent. DJs provide the sounds at weekends. Mon–Thurs & Sun 5pm–1.30am, Fri & Sat closes 2.30am. Closed June–Aug.

Le Volpi e L'Uva Piazza dei Rossi 1r. This discreet little daytime place just over the Ponte Vecchio typifies the atmosphere of the Oltrarno – relaxed, mellow and welcoming. The owners concentrate on the interesting wines of small producers, and provide high-quality snacks to help them down (the cheeses in particular are tremendous). Mon–Sat 11am–8pm.

Nightlife and entertainment

Florentine **nightlife** has a reputation for catering primarily to the middle-aged and affluent, but like every university town it has its pockets of activity, and by hanging around the San Marco or Santo Spirito quarters you should pick up news of any impromptu events. For gay and lesbian nightlife, see Listings, p.508. The city's sizeable population of British and American students ensures a supply of English-language **films**, and the highbrow cultural calendar is filled out with seasons of **classical music, opera and dance** to rival the best in Europe.

You can find **information** in English about concerts and shows at the kiosks in Piazza Repubblica and inside the Palazzo Vecchio; otherwise, consult the tourist offices, check out advertising hoardings around town or get hold of the *Firenze Spettacolo* monthly listings magazine (see p.471 for details). The **ticket agency** Box Office, at Via Alamanni 39 (℡055.210.804, Ⓦwww.boxoffice.it) and Chiasso de' Solderini 8r off Via Porta Rossa (℡055.219.402), has information and tickets for all events, concerts and festivals – but permanently busy phones.

Clubs and live music venues

Be Bop Via dei Servi 28r. Classy rock, jazz and blues cellar, often crammed solid with students. No dance floor as such – more a place to sit and chill out to the music. Daily 6pm–1am.

Central Park Via Fosso Macinante 2, Parco delle Cascine. Currently one of the city's best clubs, with adventurous, wide-ranging music and a superb sound system. A card system operates for drinks, and the first drink is included in the admission, around €18. Wandering in the park outside is unsafe, especially for women. Summer Tues–Sat 11pm–4am; winter Fri & Sat same hours.

Chiodo Fisso Via Dante Alighieri 16r. Good central venue for folk and sometimes jazz. Open nightly.

Jazz Club Via Nuova de' Caccini 3. Florence's foremost jazz venue has been a fixture for years in this side street off Borgo Pinti. The €6 annual membership fee gets you down into the medieval brick-vaulted cellar, where the atmosphere is informal and there's live music most nights. Closed Sun.

Tenax Via Pratese 46 ℡055.308.160, Ⓦwww.dada.it/tenax. *Tenax* is the city's leading venue for new and established bands as well as big-name international acts. Keep an eye open for posters around town or call at the tourist office for upcoming gigs. The place is enormous but easy-going, and doubles as a club after hours. There are ranks of bars, pool tables, computer games and plenty of seating.

Film

There are a couple of **cinemas** showing films undubbed. Cinema Astro, in Piazza San Simone near Santa Croce (no phone), screens English-language films six nights weekly, while Cinema Goldoni, Via dei Serragli 109 (℡055.222.437), and Odeon Original Sound, Via Sassetti 1 (℡055.214.068, Ⓦwww.cinehall.it), run VO (original-language) films once or twice a week. Most cinemas close in the summer months, when **open-air screens** take over – usually at the Forte Belvedere, above the Bóboli gardens, and at the Palacongressi, near the train station on Viale Strozzi.

Classical music, opera and dance

The **Maggio Musicale Fiorentino** is one of Europe's leading festivals of **opera** and **classical music**, lasting from late April to early July. Events are staged at the Teatro Comunale, the tiny Teatro Goldoni, the Teatro della Pergola, the Palazzo dei Congressi, and occasionally in the Bóboli gardens. Information and tickets are available from the Teatro Comunale box office, Corso Italia 16 (℡055.211.158 or 055.213.535, Ⓦwww.maggiofiorentino.com).

The Teatro Comunale is the city's major concert venue, hosting the **symphony orchestra**, which performs a new programme every week during the winter concert season (Jan–March), as well as a prestigious **opera and ballet** season in the autumn (Sept–Dec). The Teatro della Pergola, at Via della Pergola 18 (T055.247.9651), built in 1656 and believed to be Italy's oldest theatre, hosts seasons of **chamber concerts** by the Amici della Musica that draw in world-class performers (Oct–April), while the Florence Chamber Orchestra (T055.783.374, Wwww.videosoft.it/orchest) performs every two weeks (April–June, Sept & Oct) in Orsanmichele church. The **Estate Fiesolana** summer festival concentrates on chamber and symphonic music, with most events held in Fiesole's open-air Teatro Romano (see p.510). July's three-week **Florence Dance Festival** showcases first-rate classical, traditional and contemporary dance; get tickets and information from the festival offices at Borgo Stella 23r (T055.289.276, Wwww.florencedance.org) or the Box Office agency (see p.507).

Listings

Airlines Alitalia, Lungarno Acciaiuoli 10–12r (T055.27.881); British Airways (toll-free T147.812.266); Lufthansa, Piazza Antinori 2 (T055.373.140); Meridiana, Lungarno Vespucci 28r (T055.230.2416); TWA, Via dei Vecchietti 4 (T055.284.691).

Airport information Aeroporto Galileo Galilei, Pisa (T050.500.707, Wwww.pisa-airport.com); information also from the check-in desk at Santa Maria Novella train station, platform 5 (daily 7am–8pm). Peretola-Amerigo Vespucci airport, Via del Termine 11 (T055.373.498, Wwww.safnet.it).

Banks and exchange Florence's main bank branches are on or around Piazza della Repubblica, but exchange booths (*cambio*) and ATM cash card machines (*bancomat*) for Visa, Mastercard and Eurocheque advances can be found across the city. Banks generally open Mon–Fri 8.20am–1.20pm and 2.35–3.35pm, though some are open longer hours. The main Thomas Cook branch is at Lungarno Acciaiuoli 6–12 (Mon–Sat 9am–6pm, Sunday 9am–2pm; T055.289.781); American Express are at Via Dante Alighieri 22r (Mon–Fri 9am–5.30pm, Sat 9am–12.30pm; T055.50.981).

Bike, scooter and moped rental Alinari, Via Guelfa 85r (T055.280.500); Florence by Bike, Via San Zanobi 120–122r (T055.488.992).

Books Aside from the chain bookshops Feltrinelli, Via Cavour 12r, and Seeber, Via de' Cerretani 54r, good general outlets are Paperback Exchange, Via Fiesolana 31r ; and BM Bookshop, Borgo Ognissanti 4r. Il Viaggio, Borgo degli Albizi 41r, specializes in travel books, guides and maps.

Car rental Avis, Borgo Ognissanti 128r T055.239.8826; Europcar, Borgo Ognissanti 53r T055.290.437/8; Hertz, Via Maso Finiguerra 23r

T055.282.260; Italy by Car/Thrifty, Borgo Ognissanti 134r T055.287.161; Maggiore, Via Maso Finiguerra 31r T055.210.238; Program, Borgo Ognissanti 135r T055.282.916.

Consulates UK, Lungarno Corsini 2 T055.284.133; USA, Lungarno Vespucci 38 T055.239.8276. For the Rome embassies of Australia, Canada, Ireland and New Zealand, see p.782.

Emergencies Police T112 or 113; Fire T115; Car breakdown T116; First aid T118. Lost or stolen passports: report loss to police and contact your consulate (see above).

Gay and lesbian life Florence's history is scattered with some of history's greatest gay and bisexual artists (Michelangelo, Leonardo and Botticelli, among others). The leading gay venue is *Crisco Bar*, Via S. Egidio 43r ((T055.248.0580, Wwww.crisco.it; Mon & Wed–Sun 10/11pm till late), though the ambience can be a bit heavy for some tastes. *Il Piccolo Caffè*, Borgo Santa Croce 23r (T055.241.704; daily 5pm till late), has a more chilled-out atmosphere, while *Y.A.G. B@r*, also near Santa Croce at Via de' Macci 8r (T055.246.9022, Wwww.yagbar.com), is stylish and draws a trendy, mixed crowd. The key bar-club is the pioneering *Tabasco*, which has been going for more than thirty years at Piazza Santa Cecilia 3r (T055.213.000, Wwww.tabascogay.it; daily 10pm till late, with music Thurs–Sun). The women's bookshop Libreria delle Donne, Via Fiesolana 2b, has contacts and information for lesbian visitors.

Internet access Florence has dozens of cyber-cafés. Prices hover around €5 per hour, but offers for students, "happy hours" and the like make it possible to spend as little as €2.60 an hour, and

Inter-urban buses

Florence has an alphabet soup of **bus companies** operating on different routes to destinations within Tuscany and in the neighbouring regions. All of them are headquartered at one or other of the bays around Santa Maria Novella train station. **ATAF**, Piazza Stazione ☎055.565.0222, ⓦwww.ataf.net; **CAP**, Largo Alinari 9 ☎055.214.637; **CLAP**, c/o Lazzi, Piazza Stazione 1 ☎0583.587.897; **COPIT**, Largo Alinari 9 ☎0571.74.194; **Eurolines**, c/o Lazzi Express ☎055.215.155; **Lazzi**, Piazza Stazione 1 ☎055.215.155; **LFI**, c/o Lazzi, Piazza Stazione 1 ☎0575.39.881; **RAMA**, c/o Lazzi, Piazza Stazione 1 ☎0564.454.169; **SITA**, Via Santa Caterina da Siena 15 (local and regional ☎800.373.760; long-haul ☎055.214.721); **SULGA**, Piazza Adua ☎075.500.9641.

Arezzo SITA	**Poggibonsi†** SITA
Assisi SULGA	**Prato CAP**, Lazzi
Bettolle* LFI	**Sansepolcro** SITA
Empoli Lazzi	**Siena** SITA
Fiesole ATAF	**Viareggio** Lazzi
Greve in Chianti SITA	**Vinci** COPIT
Grosseto RAMA	**Volterra** SITA
Livorno Lazzi	* change for Montepulciano
Lucca CLAP, Lazzi	† change for San Gimignano
Perugia Lazzi, SITA, SULGA	
Pisa Lazzi	**Florence city buses** ATAF
Pistoia COPIT, Lazzi	**International buses** Eurolines
Poggio a Caiano CLAP	

the price drops the longer you stay on. The two biggest companies, with branches all over the city, are Net Gate and Internet Train, both of which operate a rechargeable card-based system. Central internet points can be found in the following places: near the Duomo at Via Sant' Egidio 10r, Via degli Alfani 11r and Via dell' Oriuolo 40r; near Piazza Signoria at Via dei Cimatori 17r and Via dei Neri 37r; in the train station itself and its underground arcade, and nearby at Via Nazionale 156r and Via Guelfa 24; near San Lorenzo at Via dei Conti 22r; near San Marco at Via delle Ruote 14r.

Laundry Ask your hotel for the nearest, or try Wash & Dry (Via Ghibellina 143r, Via Nazionale 129r, Via della Scala 52r, Via dei Serragli 87r, Via dei Servi 105r, and Via del Sole 29r), all open daily 8am–10pm.

Left luggage There's a staffed counter at the train station, near platform 16 (daily 6am–midnight; €3 per piece for 12hr, then €2 for every every succeeding 12hr).

Lost property The city office, Via Circondaria 19 (Mon–Wed, Fri & Sat 9am–noon; ☎055.367.943), receives property handed in to police or the railway police; take bus #23 to Viale Corsica. There's also a lost property office at Santa Maria Novella station, on platform 16 next to left luggage; open daily 4.15am–1.30am (☎055.235.2190).

Medical facilities The Tourist Medical Service (IAMAT) is a private service used to dealing with foreigners; they have doctors on call 24 hours a day (☎055.475.411), or you can visit their clinic at Via Lorenzo il Magnifico 59 (Mon–Fri 11am–noon & 5–6pm, Sat 11am–noon). Note that you'll need insurance cover to recoup the cost of a consultation, which will be at least €50. Alternatively, you'll find Florence's central hospital on Piazza Santa Maria Nuova.

Parking The only legal street parking is in a blue space (max 2hr, 8am–8pm). Firenze Parcheggi (☎055.272.011, ⓦwww.firenzeparcheggi.it) controls all city car parks, including the 24-hour guarded car park "Parterre" at Piazza della Libertà; with a chit from your hotel you pay €9.30 for 24 hours here. The most central parking is on Piazza Brunelleschi, northeast of the Duomo (€1 per hour). There's free parking south of the river at Piazzale Michelangelo – watch out for a long-running scam whereby bogus parking attendants direct you into a free space, thus implying there's a charge (there isn't). If you've been towed, phone ☎055.308.249 and be prepared for a cash fine of around €80.

Pharmacies Comunale della Stazione inside the train station (☎055.289.435) and All'Insegna del Moro, Piazza San Giovanni 20r (☎055.284.013), are both open 24hr every day. All pharmacies display a late-night roster in their window; otherwise ring ☎182 for information.

Police Emergency: Carabinieri ☎112; Police ☎113. The Questura, where you should report a lost passport or a theft, is at Via Zara 2 (daily 8.30am–12.30pm; ☎055.49.771; dedicated foreigners' office ☎055.497.7235). The special Tourist Aid Police may be useful if you're having communication problems: Via Pietrapiana 50 (Mon–Fri 8.30am–7.30pm, Sat 8.30am–1.30pm; ☎055.203.911). If you do report a theft or other crime, you will have to fill out a form (*una denuncia*): this may be time-consuming, but it's essential

if you want to make a claim on your travel insurance on returning home.

Post office Central post office is at Via Pellicceria 8 (Mon–Fri 8.15am–6pm; Sat 8.15am–noon; telegram office open 24hr; poste restante is through the door immediately on the left as you enter from the street). Other post offices are at Via Pietrapiana 53, Via Cavour 71r (same hours).

Taxis Radio taxis are on ☎055.4798, 055.4242 and 055.4390. Main stands are the train station and Piazza della Repubblica.

Train information ☎147.888.088, ⊛ www .treniitalia.com.

Around Florence

Within the area of Greater Florence, city buses run northeast to the hill-village of **Fiesole** and to the nearest of the various **Medici villas** – originally country retreats, now all but consumed by the suburbs. To the south towards Siena lie the hills and vineyards of **Chianti**, Italy's premier wine region. Around thirty minutes northwest of Florence on the train or bus route towards Lucca lie the neighbours **Prato** and **Pistoia**, both of them full of art and historic architecture, and both serving as fine day-trips or alternative bases in the area. Finally, on the train or bus journey west to Pisa, there are worthwhile diversions to **Vinci** – Leonardo's birthplace – and hilltop **San Miniato**.

Fiesole

A long-established Florentine retreat from the summer heat and crowds, **FIESOLE** spreads over a cluster of hilltops 8km northeast of the city. It predates Florence by several millennia: the Etruscans held out so long up here that the Romans were forced to set up permanent camp in the valley below – thus creating the beginnings of the settlement that was to become Florence. The **views** of Florence, which highlight just how extraordinary Brunelleschi's cathedral dome is, are unmissable, and the airiness of the place makes it great for kicking back.

The central square of Fiesole, **Piazza Mino**, is a long, gently sloping arena lined with shaded cafés and named after the fifteenth-century sculptor Mino da Fiesole, who has two fine pieces in the **Duomo** that dominates the north side of the square. Nineteenth-century restoration ruined the Duomo's exterior, and the interior is something like a stripped-down version of Florence's San Miniato, although there's relief from the austerity in the Cappella Salutati, to the right of the choir: it contains Mino's panel of the *Madonna and Saints*. Behind the Duomo lie the **Museo Archeologico** (9.30am–7pm; closed Tues in winter), containing pieces excavated from the Teatro Romano; and the **Museo Bandini** (summer daily 10am–7pm; winter Mon & Wed–Sat 10am–5pm, Sun 10am–7pm; €6.20, includes entrance to Fiesole's other museums), housing a local canon's collection of medieval Florentine and Tuscan art. Gates give onto the Area Archeologica behind (9.30am–7pm; closed Tues in winter), featuring a 2000-seat **Teatro Romano** built in the first century BC, a baths complex and an **Etruscan temple** dedicated to Minerva.

Fiesole's two other major churches are reached by Via San Francesco, which rises steeply from Piazza Mino, partway up broadening into a terrace giving a spectacular panorama of Florence. **Sant'Alessandro** (daily 10am–noon & 3–5pm) was founded in the sixth century on the site of Etruscan and Roman temples and has beautiful *marmorino cipollino* (onion marble) columns adorning its basilical interior. The Gothic church of **San Francesco** occupies the site of the acropolis; across one of the convent's tiny cloisters there's a chaotic museum of pieces brought back from Egypt and China by missionaries. An alternative descent back to Piazza Mino is through the public park, entered by a gate facing San Francesco's facade. Another lovely walk heads southwest from Piazza Mino for 1.5km down the narrow, winding Via Vecchia Fiesolana (which branches off the main road) to the hamlet of **SAN DOMENICO**. Fra' Angelico was once prior of the Dominican **monastery** here, and the church retains a 1420 *Madonna and Angels* by him (first chapel on the left), and the chapter house also has a Fra' Angelico fresco of *The Crucifixion* (ring the bell at no. 4 for entry).

Practicalities

ATAF city **bus** #7 runs every fifteen minutes from Florence train station through Piazza San Marco to the Piazza Mino. The **tourist office** is just off the square, behind the cathedral on Via Portigiani 3 (Mon–Sat 8.30am–1.30pm; ☎055.598.720, ⓦwww.comune.fiesole.fi.it).

Best of Fiesole's few **hotels** is the stunning *Villa San Michele*, a fourteenth-century former monastery at Via Doccia 4 (☎055.567.8200, ⓦwww.villasan-michele.orient-express.com; ⓐ), surrounded by gorgeous parkland and with a great restaurant. The cheapest option closest to the centre is the pleasant, unfussy *Villa Sorriso*, Via Gramsci 21 (☎055.59.027, ⓕ055.597.8075, ⓔs.benigni@inwind.it; ⓐ); a couple of kilometres farther out, *Villa Baccano*, Via Bosconi 4 (☎ & ⓕ055.59.341, ⓦwww.villabaccano.it; ⓐ), is fractionally more expensive. The **campsite** *Panoramico*, 3km east at Via Peramonda 1 (☎055.599.069, ⓦwww.florencecamping.com), is Florence's best.

The Medici villas

The finest country houses of the Florentine hinterland are, predictably enough, those built for the **Medici**. The earliest of these grand villas were intended as fortified refuges to which the family could withdraw when the political temperature in the city became a little too hot, but as the Medici became established and the risk of challenge lessened, the villas became more ostentatious, signifying the might of the dynasty through their sheer luxuriousness. The **northern outskirts** of Florence hold a clutch of them, these days often to be reached through unattractive industrial sprawl. All, however, boast delightful gardens.

The **Villa Medicea La Petraia** (opens 8.15am; closes 5pm Jan, Feb, Nov & Dec, 6pm March & Oct, 7pm April, May & Sept, 8pm June–Aug; closed first and third Mon of month; €2, including gardens of Villa di Castello; bus #28 from train station to castello) was adapted from a medieval castle in the 1570s and 1580s by Buontalenti. Vittorio Emanuele II glassed over the interior courtyard to convert it into a ballroom; its walls are covered by a seventeenth-century fresco cycle glorifying the Medici. Giambologna's bronze statue of *Venus*, now transplanted to a small room indoors, used to adorn the marble fountain on the upper terrace of the magnificent **garden**. A little under 1km northwest down the hill from La Petraia stands the Baroque **Villa di Castello** (villa closed to public; gardens same hours and ticket as Villa della Petraia). This house was bought in 1477 by Lorenzo and Giovanni de' Medici, principal patrons of Botticelli – the *Birth of Venus* and *Primavera* both used to hang here. The fame of the villa rests on its spectacular **garden**: Montaigne was delighted by its labyrinths, fountains and myriad tricks, and judged it the best garden in Europe. The outstanding eccentricities are Ammannati's shivering figure of *January*, the triple-bowled fountain topped by the same artist's *Hercules and Antaeus*, and the Grotto degli Animali, an artificial cave against whose walls stands a menagerie of sculpted creatures. Also within walking distance of Petraia is **Villa di Careggi**, the meeting place for Lorenzo il Magnifico's academy of Platonic scholars and now a nursing home set amidst expansive woodland visitable by appointment (℡055.427.9755; visits Mon–Fri 9am–6pm & Sat 9am–noon).

Nothing remains of Francesco I's favourite villa, the **Villa Demidoff** at **PRATOLINO**, 12km north of Florence, except its expansive **park** (April–Sept Thurs–Sun 10am–8pm; €3; bus #25), and even this is but a shadow of its earlier self. The mechanical toys, trick fountains and other practical jokes that Buontalenti installed here were the most ingenious of their day. Only Giambologna's immense *Appennino* sculpture – a grizzled man-mountain who gushes water – survives from the original garden, but the park is still one of the most pleasant green spaces near Florence.

In the small town of **POGGIO A CAIANO**, 18km northwest of Florence and 7km south of Prato, is the romantic **Villa Medici di Poggio a Caiano** (daily: Nov–Feb 8.15am–3.30pm; March & Oct 8.15am–4.30pm; April, May & Sept 9am–5.30pm; June–Aug 9am–6.30pm; closed second and third Mon of month; €2). A COPIT bus leaves from Piazza Santa Maria Novella every half-hour, and takes around half an hour to get there; an alternative approach is the #M local CAP service from Prato.

Lorenzo il Magnifico bought a farmhouse on this site in 1480 and had it rebuilt as a grand rural palace by Giuliano da Sangallo. An impressive double-staircase sweeps up to the imposing entrance loggia, commissioned by Lorenzo's son Giovanni, the future Pope Leo X. Inside, the focal point is the double-height *salone*, which the architect made out of the original courtyard; its sixteenth-century frescoes include works by Pontormo and del Sarto. The **gardens**, modified by the Lorraine princes into an English-style landscape, contain some magnificent old trees. To cap the afternoon in style, take a local bus 5km west to the village of **CARMIGNANO** where, in the church of San Michele, hangs Pontormo's *Visitazione* (c.1530), one of the outstanding works of the Mannerist period: its combination of superbly realized colour in the women's drapes, profound emotion and the mesmeric quality of all four faces is electrifying.

The Chianti region

Ask a sample of northern Europeans to describe their idea of paradise, and the odds are it will sound much like **Chianti**, the territory of vineyards and hill-towns that stretches between Florence and Siena. The climate is drenched in luminescent sunlight during the long summer and rarely grim even in the pit of winter. And to cap it all, there's the **wine** – the one Italian vintage everyone's heard of (ⓦwww.chianticlassico. com). Visitors from Britain and other similarly ill-favoured climes were long ago alerted to Chianti's charms, and the rate of immigration has been so rapid since the 1960s that the region is now wryly dubbed "**Chiantishire**". Yet it would be an exaggeration to say that

Chianti is losing its character in the way that many of Italy's coastal towns have lost theirs. The tone of certain parts has been altered, but concessions to tourism have been more or less successfully absorbed into the rhythm of local life.

If you're relying on **buses**, the best targets are the two main towns, **Greve in Chianti** and **Radda in Chianti**. Three SITA **buses** a day run from Florence through Greve and Castellina to Radda. Five TRA-IN buses a day run from Radda through Castellina (but not Greve) to Siena. But the only realistic way to get to know the region is with **your own transport**, following the "Chiantigiana", the SS222 that snakes its way between Florence and Siena through the most beautiful parts of Chianti. The Florence APT's excellent *Il Chianti cartoguida turistica* 1:70,000 contour map pinpoints every lane and farmhouse.

Greve in Chianti

The "Chiantigiana" road meanders south through picture-pretty wine-villages for 28km to the amiable market town of **GREVE IN CHIANTI**. The venue for Chianti's biggest **wine fair** (usually held during the second weekend in September), this is a town with wine for sale on every street: the best outlets are the Enoteca di Gallo Nero, Piazzetta Santa Croce 8, and the Cantinetta di Checucci Sandro, Via Vittorio Veneto. Its hub is the attractive central **Piazza Matteotti**. This long, sloping triangle hosts the regular Saturday market and is overlooked by a statue of local boy **Giovanni da Verrazzano**, who became, in 1524, the first European to see Manhattan island.

Greve's vineyard-oriented **tourist office** in Via Luca Cini (Mon–Sat 10am–1pm & 2–5pm; ☎055.854.5243, ⍟www.comune.greve-in-chianti.fi.it) can also give information on accommodation in local farmhouses and trekking in Chianti. There are also a number of interesting **villas** a stone's throw from Greve, including **Verrazzano**, five minutes drive north of Greti, and **Vignamaggio**, just south of Greve, where Kenneth Branagh filmed *Much Ado about Nothing*. Comfortable accommodation on Piazza Matteotti is offered by *Del Chianti* at no. 86 (☎055.853.763, ⍟albergodelchianti.it; ⑤) and *Da Verrazzano* at no. 28 (☎055.853.189, ⍟www.verrazzano.it; ⑤). The latter also has a very good **restaurant**, at around €35 for a full meal (closed Mon & Jan 15–Feb 15). There are several decent pizzeria-restaurants too: *Gallo Nero*, Via Cesare Battista 9; *La Cantina*, Piazza Trento; and *Torre delle Civette*, Via Veneto. For travellers on a tight rein, there's a **youth hostel** in Lucolena, 10km east of Greve and unconnected by public transport – the *Villa San Michele*, Via Casole 42, with a restaurant and bar (mid-April to Nov; ☎ & ⍟055.851.034, ⍟www.villasanmichele.it; €12).

Radda in Chianti

A ridge 22km south of Greve is occupied by the well-heeled town of **Castellina in Chianti**: its walls, fortress and the covered perimeter walkway all bear testimony to an embattled past on the frontline between Florence and Siena, which lies a further 21km south. From Castellina, the SS429 branches east 22km to **RADDA IN CHIANTI**. The street plan of this minuscule but historic town is focused on **Piazza Ferrucci**, where the frescoed and shield-studded Palazzo Comunale faces a church raised on a high platform.

Close to the piazza, at Via Roma 41, there is the simple one-star *Girarrosto* **hotel and restaurant** (☎0577.738.010; restaurant closed Wed; ②). The two-star *Villa Miranda*, a short distance east of the village in Villa a Radda (☎0577.738.021, ⍟0577.738.668; ③), has scruffy rooms and a rather grubby if occasionally inspired restaurant. Meals at around €35 are served at the *Vignale*, Via XX Settembre 23 (☎0577.738.094; closed Thurs & Jan 10–March 10), but for consistently better food, and spectacular scenery, visit either *Le Vigne* (☎0577.738.640), just off the road between Villa a Radda and Radda in Chianti, where you'll pay around €30, or the restaurant of the three-star *Vescine* hotel (☎0577.741.144; ❹), on the road to Castellina, where meals cost about €10 more.

Prato

Taking its name from the meadow (*prato*) where a great market was held in antiquity, **PRATO** – capital of its own little province 15km northwest of Florence – has been Italy's chief textile city since the early Middle Ages. Even though recent recession has cut into export sales, it still produces three-quarters of all Italy's woollen cloth. Its proximity to Florence (just half-an-hour away) makes it feasible as a cut-price alternative base.

Prato's *centro storico* is enclosed within a rough hexagon of walls, making orientation straightforward. From the square in front of Stazione Centrale, cross the bridge to Piazza Europa and continue on Viale Vittorio Veneto to Piazza San Marco, which is framed by the city walls. Directly ahead, past the prominent **Henry Moore** sculpture *Square Form with Cut* (1974) in the centre of the piazza, rises the white-walled **Castello Imperatore** (Mon & Wed–Sun 9am–1pm; €2, or €5 *biglietto unico*, with Museo dell'Opera del Duomo & Museo di Pittura Murale), built in the thirteenth century for Emperor Frederick II. Concerts are held in the courtyard in summer, and the ramparts offer fine views. Just below the castle to the north is Prato's major Renaissance monument, Giuliano Sangallo's church of **Santa Maria delle Carceri** (daily 7am–noon & 4–7pm), which makes a decorative gesture towards the Romanesque with its bands of green and white marble. The interior is lightened by an Andrea della Robbia frieze. The route to the Duomo passes through Piazza del Comune, home to the **Museo Civico e Galleria Comunale** (under restoration at the time of writing; most of the paintings have been removed to the Museo di Pittura Murale; see below), which contains a ramshackle collection of Florentine art, including work by Fra' Filippo Lippi and a predella by Bernardo Daddi narrating the story of Prato's holy relic, the Girdle of the Madonna (see below).

Piazza Duomo, one block north of Piazza del Comune, forms an effective space for the Pisan-Romanesque facade of the **Duomo** (July–Sept daily 7.30am–12.30pm & 4–7pm, Sun 4–7pm), distinguished by an Andrea della Robbia terracotta over the portal and Donatello and Michelozzo's beautiful **Pulpit of the Sacred Girdle**. This unique addition was constructed for the ceremonial display of the girdle of the Madonna, a garment handed to the ever-incredulous apostle Thomas at her Assumption. The girdle (or *Sacro Cingolo*) was supposedly bequeathed by Thomas to a priest, one of whose descendants married a crusader from Prato, who in turn brought it back to his home town in the twelfth century. Replicas have replaced the Donatello reliefs of gambolling children, the originals now being housed in the cathedral museum. The girdle itself is displayed five times a year: on Easter Sunday, May 1, August 15, September 8 and Christmas Day.

The sensuous frescoes behind the high altar were created between 1452 and 1466 by **Fra' Filippo Lippi**, and depict the martyrdoms of St John the Baptist and St Stephen. During the period of his work, Lippi – though nominally a monk – became infatuated with a young nun called Lucrezia; they later had a child together, Filippino. Lucrezia is said to be the model for the dancing figure of Salome, while Filippo has painted himself as one of those mourning St Stephen; he's third from the right. For several years the Lippi cycle has been undergoing restoration, but it's possible to view the pictures at close range, from the restorers' scaffolding, if you book a ticket in advance at the tourist office (see below), either in person or by phone; the fee is €8 per person.

Housed alongside the Duomo, around the cloister of the bishop's palace, the **Museo dell'Opera del Duomo** (Mon & Wed–Sat 9.30am–12.30pm & 3–6.30pm, Sun 9.30am–12.30pm; €5, with Castello & Museo Pittura Murale) contains the Donatello panels from the great pulpit. The museum's other main treasure is Maso di Bartolomeo's tiny reliquary for the Sacred Girdle, while further important works by Filippo Lippi, including his *Madonna del Ceppo*, are housed in the **Museo di Pittura Murale** (Mon & Wed–Sat 10am–6pm, Sun 10am–1pm; €5, includes entrance to the Museo dell'Opera del Duomo & Castello), a five-minute walk west of the Duomo.

Practicalities

All **trains** (including services direct from Bologna) stop at Stazione Centrale; slow Florence–Pistoia trains also stop at the more convenient Stazione Porta al Serraglio, 150m north of Piazza Duomo. CAP and Lazzi **buses** from Florence stop at Piazza Duomo, while Lazzi buses from Pistoia, Lucca and local villages pass through both train station forecourts. The **tourist office** (Mon–Sat: summer 9am–7pm; winter 9am–1pm & 3–6pm; ☎0574.24.112, Ⓦww.comune.prato.it) is on Piazza delle Carceri, 500m west of Stazione Centrale in the centre of the old town.

At the budget end of the scale, it has a single one-star **hotel**, the *Roma*, outside the southern gate at Via Carradori 1 (☎0574.31.777; ❸), and two two-stars: *Il Giglio* at Piazza San Marco 14 (☎0574.37.049, Ⓕ0574.604.351; ❹) and *La Toscana* at Piazza Ciardi 3 (☎0574.28.096, Ⓕ0574.25.163; ❸). Prato's more expensive hotels tend to be featureless concrete blocks, catering for business visitors. One exception is the three-star *Flora*, Via Cairoli 31 (☎0574.3352; Ⓦwww.prathotels.it; ❼), which occupies a handsome nineteenth-century building very close to the Piazza del Comune. Of the rest, the pick is the *Giardino*, Via Magnolfi 2–6 (☎0574.606.588, Ⓕ0574.606.591; ❻), which has the advantage of being just twenty metres from the Duomo.

Prato has a strong team of decent **restaurants**. For a basic trattoria you can't beat *Lapo*, at Piazza Mercatale 141 (☎0574.23.745; closed Sun). *Lo Scoglio*, Via Verdi 42 (☎0574.22.760; closed Mon), does good pizzas and inexpensive fish dishes, while the slightly pricier *Il Baghino*, Via dell'Accademia 9 (☎0574.27.920; closed Sun evening & Mon lunch), is a long-standing local favourite, serving Prato specialities in a traditional atmosphere. *Enoteca Barni*, near Piazza San Marco at Via Ferrucci 22 (☎0574.607.845; closed all Sat & Sun lunch), is an excellent family-run restaurant/wine bar, where you'll spend in the region of €30–40 a head; a similar bill can be expected at the homely *Osteria 900*, Via Banchelli 14 (☎0574.24.353; closed Mon lunch).

Pistoia

PISTOIA, 18km northwest of Prato and also capital of its own province, is one of the least visited cities in Tuscany – an unjustified ranking for this quiet, well-preserved medieval city just 35 minutes by train from Florence (and about the same by bus). Pistoia was known throughout medieval times for its feuding and was condemned by Dante, Machiavelli and others; Michelangelo referred to the Pistoiese as "the enemies of heaven". An important metalworking centre, it left a legacy to the world in the *pistole*, originally the name of a dagger but later the title given to the first local firearms.

Piazza Duomo and around

The superb medieval complex of **Piazza Duomo** is the heart of the town, and scene of many events and celebrations throughout Pistoia's July festival (see below). If you've arrived from Pisa or Lucca, the style of the **Duomo** itself will be immediately familiar, with its tiered arcades and striped decoration of black and white marble. Set into this soberly refined front is a tunnel-vault portico of bright terracotta tiles by Andrea della Robbia, creator also of the *Madonna and Child* above the door. The **interior** (daily 8.30am–12.30pm & 4–7pm) has an outstanding array of sculptural pieces, one of which is part of the entrance wall – a font designed by Benedetto da Maiano, showing incidents from the life of John the Baptist. Off the right aisle is the Cappella di San Jacopo (€2), endowed with one of the richest pieces of silverwork to be seen in Italy, the **Altarpiece of St James**. Weighing almost a ton and populated with 628 figures, it was begun in 1287 and completed by Brunelleschi in 1456.

Adjoining the Duomo is the Palazzo dei Vescovi housing the **Museo di San Zeno** (guided tours summer Tues, Thurs & Fri 10am, 11.30am & 3.30pm; winter on second Sun of month, 4.30pm; €3; book ahead at the tourist office). The chief exhibit is the huge golden **reliquary of St James** by Lorenzo Ghiberti (1407), and there's a modest archeological collection, with relics from the Roman settlement.

Opposite is the dapper Gothic **Baptistry**, possibly designed by Nicola Pisano; there's nothing under the vast conical brick ceiling but a font, made by Lanfranco da Como in 1226, and the interior's emptiness is sometimes filled by shows of contemporary art. On the opposite side of the piazza, the Palazzo Comunale contains the **Museo Civico** (Tues–Sat 10am–7pm, Sun 9am–12.30pm; €3.20, or €6.20 *biglietto cumulativo*, including Marini and Rospigliosi museums), where the customary Tuscan welter of medieval and Renaissance pieces is bolstered by an impressive showing of Baroque hyperactivity. To the side of the Palazzo Comunale, the Palazzo Rospigliosi on Via Ripa del Sale houses the combined **Museo Diocesano** and **Museo Rospigliosi** (Tues–Sat 10am–1pm, plus Wed–Fri 4–7pm; €3.20, or €6.20 *biglietto cumulativo*, including Museo Civico and Marini museum), a typical small-town collection of historical and ecclesiastical oddments.

The rest of the town

Behind the Palazzo Comunale, across Via Pacini, is **San Bartolomeo in Pantano**, or "St Bartholomew in the Swamp", named for the marshy ground on which the church was raised in the eighth century, and with a rectangular pulpit sculpted in 1250 by Guido da Como. The **Ospedale del Ceppo**, 100m north along Via Pacini, was embellished in the fifteenth century with a portico emblazoned with Giovanni della Robbia's startlingly colourful terracotta frieze of the *Theological Virtues* and the *Seven Works of Mercy*, a panoply of Renaissance types and costume. A couple of minutes over to the west, the twelfth-century **Sant'Andrea** (daily 8.30am–12.30pm & 3–6.30pm) has a corridor-slim aisle with a spectacular pulpit carved by Giovanni Pisano in 1297, showing scenes from the life of Christ and the Last Judgement.

Barely 100m south of the baptistry, Via Cavour is now the main street of the city's inner core, but was once the settlement's outer limit – as the name of the majestic **San Giovanni Fuorcivitas** ("outside the walls") proclaims. The church was founded in the eighth century, but rebuilt between the twelfth and fourteenth centuries, when it received the dazzlingly striped green-and-white flank that serves as its facade. The interior (daily 7.30am–noon & 5–6.30pm), though lit only feebly by the slit windows, is just as remarkable for its pulpit, another of Pistoia's exquisite thirteenth-century trio, carved in 1270 by a pupil of Nicola Pisano.

Via Crispi leads due south to Piazza Garibaldi, where the **Cappella del Tau** (Mon–Sat 9am–1pm) preserves a chaos of fourteenth- and fifteenth-century frescoes. A couple of doors away, in the Palazzo del Tau, is the **Museo Marino Marini** (Tues–Sat 9am–1pm & 3–7pm, Sun 9am–12.30pm; €3.50, free Sat pm; or €6.20 *biglietto cumulativo*, including Museo Civico and Rospigliosi museum), showing a selection of etchings, engravings, sculptures, drawings and watercolours by this important modern artist and Pistoia local.

Four kilometres east of town at **SANTOMATO**, reachable by COPIT bus #19 (direction Tobbiana or Bagnolo), is the remarkable **Fattoria di Celle** art centre, featuring an array of contemporary sculpture and installations set amidst a large area of parkland around a seventeenth-century villa, including constructions in steel and wire by Dennis Oppenheim, in polished green and white marble by Robert Morris, and in stone by Richard Serra. The centre is open from April to September and visitors must first write for an appointment: Fattoria di Celle, 51030 Santomato di Pistoia (℗0573.479.486). The entrance gate is not signposted, but rather signalled by a huge spherical metal construction by Alberto Burri.

Practicalities

Arriving by train or bus from Florence you are just a couple of minutes' walk south of the historic centre – Viale XX Settembre points the way north to Piazza Treviso and the gate into the old town. The **tourist office** is at Piazza del Duomo 4 (Tues–Sun 9am–1pm & 3–6pm; ☎0573.21.622; ⓦwww.comune.pistoia.it).

The city's low tourist profile means a dearth of **accommodation** – so if you plan to stay, phone ahead. There's just one one-star hotel, the clean and friendly *Albergo Autisti*, Viale Pacinotti 89 (☎0573.21.771; ❸), and there's only one two-star within the city walls, the *Albergo Firenze*, a short walk west of Piazza del Duomo at Via Curtatone e Montanara 42 (☎ & ℗573.231.141; ❹). Central alternatives are the three-star *Leon Bianco*, Via Panciatichi 2 (☎0573.26.675, ⓔinfo@hotelleonbianco.it; ❺), or the *Patria*, Via Crispi 6 (☎0573.25.187, ⓦwww.patriahotel.it; ❻) – both are within a minute of San Giovanni Fuorcivitas.

There are two excellent **osterie** in Via del Lastrone, off Piazza della Sala: *La Bottegaia*, at no. 4 (closed Sun lunch & all Mon), which has a terrific range of *crostini* and *bruschette* in addition to its more substantial offerings (the €25 *menu degustazione* is very good value); and *Lo Storno*, at no. 8, where the food is somewhat more robust (eg tripe and *baccalà*), and the emphasis is on lunch (open for lunch daily, but only Wed & Sat evening). There's also a straightforward, inexpensive and good-quality Tuscan menu at *S. Jacopo*, Via Crispi 15 (closed all Mon & Tues lunch), while Pistoia's top pizzas are to be found at *Da Piero*, a pizzeria-trattoria just outside the walls in the southwest corner of town, at Viale Pacinotti 91.

Key festival is the **Luglio Pistoiese**, a programme of concerts and events throughout July which includes openair performances in Piazza Duomo by world-class jazz and blues acts under the "Pistoia Blues" banner. The *Giostra dell'Orso* medieval pageant and joust is on July 25.

Leaving Pistoia, Lazzi **buses** for Florence and Prato run from by the train station; COPIT buses for Empoli, where you can change for Vinci, from Piazza San Francesco.

West to Pisa

Two main roads and rail lines head west from Florence. The A11 *autostrada* shadows the train track northwest through Prato and Pistoia to Lucca. An alternative is the SS67 road, which heads due west from Florence down the valley of the Arno to Pisa, a pleasant enough journey of an hour or so. Along the way you'll pass through the industrial town of **Empoli**, marking the turnoff into the hills north to **Vinci**. A little west of Empoli, past the turning south to Siena and across the border in the Provincia di Pisa, is the medieval village of **San Miniato**, perched high on its rock above the pretty Valdarno.

Vinci

Occupying the picturesque vine- and olive-planted southern slopes of Montalbano 11km north of the industrial town of Empoli, **VINCI** is inextricably associated with **Leonardo da Vinci**, who was born on April 15, 1452, in nearby Anchiano and baptized in Vinci's church of Santa Croce. Vinci itself is a torpid little village that suffers from a surfeit of tour-groups (especially at weekends). The main sight is the thirteenth-century castle, now home to the **Museo Leonardiano** (daily: 9.30am–7pm; winter closes 6pm; €5), packed with models reconstructed from Leonardo's notebook drawings – his celebrated bicycle, helicopter and multi-barrelled machine-gun are all on display.

San Miniato

The strategic hill-top village of **SAN MINIATO**, midway between Pisa and Florence (around 40km from both), was given its landmark fortress by the Holy Roman Emperor Frederick II in 1236. Today it's an attractive mid-journey stopoff, split between a modern valley-floor settlement with train and bus stations (see below) and the original medieval village on its hilltop with a warren of attractive cobbled alleys. Dominating the old quarter's central **Piazza del Popolo** is the fourteenth-century church of **San Domenico**; its windows, glazed with odd greenish-yellow glass, do nothing to aid appreciation of its frescoes and trompe l'oeil decoration. There's a market in its cloisters every Sunday. A narrow street climbs to **Piazza della Repubblica**, which is jazzed up by seventeenth-century *sgraffiti* on the long facade of the religious seminary; part of the ground floor is a row of rare, restored fourteenth-century shops. Opposite the seminary a flight of steps rises to the **Prato del Duomo**, where a tower of the imperial fortress now houses the three-star *Miravalle* hotel (℡0571.418.075; ➎) and its more affordable restaurant next door on the site of the **Palazzo dei Vicari dell'Imperatore**. The red-brick **Duomo** itself, dedicated to St Genesius, the patron saint of actors, is hacked-about Romanesque, with an interior of Baroque gilding and marbling. Next door, the tiny **Museo Diocesano** (April–Nov Tues–Sun 10am–1pm & 3–7pm; Dec–March Sat & Sun only, same hours; €2) has a *Crucifixion* by Fra' Filippo Lippi and a terracotta bust of Christ by Verrocchio. From the Prato del Duomo it's a short walk up to the tower of the **Rocca** (daily 10am–7pm), which was restored after damage in the last war; the spectacular view from the top is worth the climb. Dante's *Inferno* perpetuates the memory of Pier della Vigna, treasurer to Frederick II, who was imprisoned and blinded here, a fate that drove him to suicide by jumping from the tower – as the inscription on a graffitied stone at the base of the tower records.

The **train station**, down in the Arno valley, is a ten-minute walk from the modern part of town, **San Miniato Basso**, from where it's a steep 4km climb to **San Miniato Alto**, the old quarter. A mini orange **bus** runs from the train station every thirty minutes or so (6.30–10.30am & 3.45–7.30pm) to San Miniato Alto. It will deposit you just below the walls in **Piazzale Dante Alighieri**, which is also the place to park. Beyond the town gate, down the road on the right, is Piazza del Popolo and the **tourist office** (summer daily 9am–1pm & 4–7.30pm; winter Mon–Sat 10am–1pm & 3–6.30pm; ☎0571.42.745, ⓦwww.comune.san-miniato.pi.it).

Pisa, Lucca and the coast

Thanks to its Leaning Tower, **Pisa** is known by name to just about every visitor to Italy, though it remains an underrated place, seen by most people on a whistle-stop day-trip that takes in little of its majestic architecture, less of its atmospheric medieval quarters, and none of its street life. Genteel **Lucca** nearby, its walled old town crammed with Romanesque churches, is even less explored.

Tuscany's **coast** is a mixed bag, too over-developed to be consistently attractive. North of Pisa, the succession of beach resorts feature the backdrop of the mighty Alpi Apuane, which harbour the marble quarries of Carrara. South from Pisa, past the untouristed port of **Livorno**, are a hundred scrubby strips of hotels and campsites. The Tuscan shoreline is at its best in the **Maremma** region, where you'll find the protected **Monti dell'Uccellina** reserve and the wild, wooded peninsula of **Monte Argentario**. Tuscany's **islands** offer a breath of fresh air, from the scenic walks on **Elba** to the remoteness of little **Capraia**.

Pisa

Since the beginning of tourism, **PISA** has been known for just one thing – the **Leaning Tower**, which serves around the world as a shorthand image for Italy. It is indeed a freakishly beautiful building, a sight whose impact no amount of prior knowledge can blunt. Yet it is just a single component of Pisa's breathtaking **Campo dei Miracoli**, or Field of Miracles, where the **Duomo**, **Baptistry** and **Camposanto** complete a dazzling architectural ensemble. These, and a dozen or so churches and palazzi scattered about the historic centre, belong to Pisa's "Golden Age", from the eleventh to the thirteenth centuries, when the city was one of the maritime powers of the Mediterranean. The so-called "Pisan Romanesque" **architecture** of this period, with its black and white marble facades inspired by the Moorish designs of Andalucia, is complemented by some of the finest medieval **sculpture** in Italy, much of it from the workshops of Nicola and Giovanni Pisano. The city's political zenith came late in the eleventh century with a series of victories over the **Saracens**: the Pisans brought back from Arab cultures long-forgotten ideas of science, architecture and philosophy. Decline set in with defeat by the Genoese in

ACCOMMODATION
Europa Park	2
Grand Hotel Duomo	5
Gronchi	4
Helvetia	3
Milano	9
Ostello	1
Rinascente	6
Royal Victoria	7
Verdi	8

RESTAURANTS
Bruno	A
La Grotta	D
Mensa Universitaria	B
La Mescita	E
Osteria dei Cavalieri	C
Al Ristoro dei Vecchi Macelli	G
Lo Schiaccianoci	I
Taverna Kostas	H
Il Vecchio Dado	F

PISA

1284, followed by the silting-up of Pisa's harbour. From 1406 the city was governed by Florence, whose Medici rulers re-established the University of Pisa, one of the intellectual forcing houses of the Renaissance; **Galileo** was one of the teachers there. Subsequent centuries saw Pisa fade into provinciality.

Arrival, information and orientation

Pisa Centrale **train** station (information ☎1478.88.088) is about 1km south of the Arno. Lazzi **buses** from Florence, Prato, Pistoia and Carrara arrive at the nearby Piazza Vittorio Emanuele II, while other buses from Volterra, Lucca and Livorno arrive at Piazza San Antonio alongside it. From here, the Leaning Tower is about 25 minutes' walk north, or a ride on CPT city bus #1 from outside the station. Alternatively, you could hop on a local train for the five-minute journey to the more convenient **Pisa San Rossore** station, 200m west of Piazza Manin (also served by local trains from Lucca and some from Viareggio).

Pisa's **Aeroporto Galileo Galilei** (information ℡050.500.707, ⓦwww.pisa-airport.com) is 2km south of Centrale station. Hourly trains run from Pisa Aeroporto station to Pisa Centrale and on to Florence, an hour and fifteen minutes away. CPT city bus #3 departs from the airport every fifteen minutes, and passes the train station, runs along the south bank of the Arno, over Ponte Solferino, to Piazza Manin and then out to the hostel. A taxi to the centre costs around €6.

Pisa's APT **tourist office** is behind the Leaning Tower on the northern side of the Campo dei Miracoli (summer Mon–Sat 9am–7pm, Sun 10.30am–4.30pm; winter Mon–Sat 9am–5.30pm; ℡050.560.464, ⓦwww.pisa.turismo.toscana.it). There's also a small APT office at the **train station** (℡050.42.291), and another at the **airport** (℡050.503.700).

Accommodation

Most visitors hurry through Pisa on a day-trip – this is their loss, but it means that **accommodation** is usually not too hard to find. Staying in the centre of town brings you away from the touristy haunts and into local life a bit more, though note that many low-end hotels are filled by students during the academic year.

Hotels

Europa Park Via Andrea Pisano 23 ℡050.500.732, Ⓕ050.554.930. Smallish, comfortable and well-run modern three-star hotel, with parking. It's on a characterless street, but is barely two minutes' stroll from the Campo dei Miracoli. ❺

Grand Hotel Duomo Via Santa Maria 94 ℡050.825.088, Ⓕ050.560.418. A good, modern four-star with comforts (including parking), a couple of minutes' stroll from the Leaning Tower. ❽

Gronchi Piazza Arcivescovado 1 ℡050.561.823. Most characterful of Pisa's low-end hotels, in a perfect position within spitting distance of the Tower. Twenty-three rooms share four bathrooms. Midnight curfew. ❶

Helvetia Via G. Boschi 31 ℡050.553.084. One-star in an excellent location just off the Campo dei Miracoli with en-suite and shared-bath rooms, kept spotless by the friendly staff. ❸

Milano Via Mascagni 14 ℡050.23.162, Ⓕ050.44.237. One of the better low-end choices around Piazza Stazione, in a side street right opposite the station, with shared-bath and en-suite rooms. ❸

Rinascente Via del Castelletto 28 ℡ & Ⓕ050.580.460. Very popular budget rooms – en suite and not – occupying an old *palazzo* just off Piazza dei Cavalieri. ❸

Royal Victoria Lungarno Pacinotti 12 ℡050.940.111, Ⓕ050.940.180. Tastefully furnished palazzo overlooking the Arno, with character, old-fashioned elegance and private parking. Also some bargain non-en-suite rooms. ❺

Verdi Piazza della Repubblica 5 ℡050.598.947, Ⓕ050.598.944. A competent, welcoming three-star hotel in a restored *palazzo* in a quiet square near San Matteo. ❺

Campsite and hostel

Campeggio Torre Pendente Viale delle Cascine 86 ℡050.561.704, Ⓕ050.561.734. A large, well-maintained site signposted 1km west of the Campo dei Miracoli, with a laundry, bar, restaurant and shop. April to mid-Oct.

Ostello della Gioventù Via Pietrasantina 15 ℡ & Ⓕ050.890.622. Despite the misleading signs, this non-HI hostel is a 45-minute hike from Campo dei Miracoli; take bus #3 from the station or Piazza Manin, which stops outside. There's a supermarket and pizzeria nearby. Make sure you have mosquito repellent in summer, as it's right by a marsh. €15 per person with sheets or €21 for a double room.

The City

Laid out in the mid-eleventh century, Pisa's ecclesiastical centre is known as the **Campo dei Miracoli** (Field of Miracles; also Piazza dei Miracoli or Piazza Duomo; Ⓦ www.opapisa.it). The four major buildings – the **Duomo**, its Bell-tower (which almost immediately slipped to become the **Leaning Tower**), the **Baptistry** and the monumental cemetery of the **Camposanto** – were built on a broad swathe of grassy lawn just within the northern walls of the city. Nowhere else in Italy are the key buildings of a city arrayed with such precision, and nowhere is there so beautiful a contrast of stonework and open meadow. However, the turf rests on highly unstable sandy soil, which accounts for the tower's lean; take a look at the baptistry and you'll see that it leans the other way from the tower.

The rest of the city centre makes for some fine wandering, through alleys that have largely retained their medieval appearance. Southeast, on the river, is the **Museo Nazionale di San Matteo**, a fine collection of ecclesiastical art and sculpture, while west along the Arno is the lavish **Palazzo Reale** and the huge **Arsenale**, the latter currently housing a display of items taken from ongoing excavations at the newly discovered site of Pisa's ancient harbour. One of Pisa's biggest surprises lurks in an unregarded piazza south of the river near the train station: covering one wall of an open bus station is the last-ever mural by US artist **Keith Haring**.

The Leaning Tower of Pisa

The view from the Porta Nuova gate over the serene architectural ensemble laid out on the Campo dei Miracoli would be memorable enough, even were it not for the desperately comic sight of the **Leaning Tower** (April–Sept 8am–7.50pm; March & Oct 9am–7.10pm; Nov–Feb 9am–4.40pm; guided tours; €15) – open again after a lengthy period of restoration – sticking out jauntily from behind the Duomo, wearing its rakishly angled bell-chamber like a pork-pie hat. It is a lunatic vision, slouched over far enough to topple any second – or so it seems.

Two of the most telling facts about the tower (*Torre Pendente* in Italian) are that it has always tilted, and that no one ever put their name to the project, as though the masons involved somehow knew it was doomed. Twelve years after work began on the tower in 1173, it started to subside, but in the opposite direction from the current lean. Masons inserted wedge-shaped stones to correct the problem, whereupon the whole tower tilted crazily the other way. Work was halted when it was only three storeys high. A century or so later, after much calculation, architects added three more uneven storeys, tilted to counterbalance the lean, and then in 1350 Tommaso Pisano completed the stack with a lopsided bell-chamber. A couple of centuries later, **Galileo** exploited the overhang in one of his celebrated experiments, dropping items of different mass off the top to demonstrate the constancy of gravity.

The five museums and monuments in and around Campo dei Miracoli – the Duomo, Baptistry, Museo dell'Opera, Camposanto and Museo delle Sinopie – share a complicated system of **ticketing**. Admission to the Duomo costs €2. Admission to any one sight costs €5. Admission to any two plus the Duomo costs €8. Admission to the four excluding the Duomo costs €8.50. Admission to all five costs €10.50. You can get tickets from the **ticket office** next to the tourist office in the Campo dei Miracoli.

An ill-advised attempt to correct the southerly lean in the mid-nineteenth century involved digging a trench all the way round the base of the tower; this made things considerably worse and, along with the lowering of the water table, has brought the structure to the edge of crisis. By 1990, the top leant more than five metres from vertical and the tower was finally declared off-limits to visitors. Scientists and engineers joined forces to save the thing. The main operation involved using **rotating drills** to remove silt and sand from beneath the foundations on the north side. The tower slowly began to correct its lean and settle. Eleven years and $30 million dollars later the tower was officially reopened to the public in November 2001, its overhang now reduced by 50cm – back to how it was in 1838.

Tours to the top of the tower take place every half hour or so with a maximum of forty people per group; no under-8s are allowed. You can save yourself a long wait by booking tickets in advance on Ⓦ www.opapisa.it (€2 booking fee). The narrow climb up 294 worn steps at a 5 degree angle can be fairly disorienting, and sadly you can no longer step out onto the surrounding balconies, but you do get good views of Pisa's spires and rooftops, with the Monte Pisano hills in the background.

The rest of the Campo dei Miracoli

Pisa's breathtaking **Duomo** (April–Sept Mon–Sat 10am–7.40pm, Sun 1–7.40pm; Oct–March Mon–Sat 10am–4.40pm, Sun 1–4.40pm; €2; see box opposite for details of combined tickets) was begun in 1064 and completed around a century later. With its four levels of variegated colonnades and its subtle interplay of dark-grey marble and white stone, the Duomo is the archetype of Pisan Romanesque, a model often imitated in buildings across Tuscany, but never surpassed. Squares and discs of coloured marble are set into the magnificent facade, but the soberly graceful effect of the primary grey and white is such that you notice these strong tones only when you look closely. Entry is through the huge bronze doors of the **Portale di San Ranieri**, close to the Leaning Tower. These were cast in 1180 by Bonnano Pisano, first architect of the tower, with powerfully diagrammatic biblical scenes. The vast interior is defined by the crisp black and white marble of the long arcades, which recalls the Moorish architecture of Cordoba. A notable survivor from the medieval building is the apse mosaic of *Christ in Majesty*, completed by Cimabue in 1302. The acknowledged highlight, however, is the **pulpit** sculpted by **Giovanni Pisano**. This was packed away after a 1595 fire and was only rediscovered in 1926. The last of the great series of three pulpits created in Tuscany by Giovanni and his father Nicola (the others are in Siena and Pistoia), it is a work of amazing virtuosity with, for instance, the story of the Passion condensed into a single panel.

You exit the Duomo at the main western facade. Directly ahead is the circular **Baptistry** (daily: April–Sept 8am–7.40pm; Oct–March 9am–4.40pm; €5), a bizarre but pleasing building with its three storeys of Romanesque arcades peaking in a crest of Gothic pinnacles and a dome shaped like the stalk end of a lemon. This is the largest baptistry in Italy, begun in 1152 by a certain Deotisalvi ("Godsaveyou"), who left his name on a column to the left of the door; it was worked on in the thirteenth century by Nicola and Giovanni Pisano, and completed late in the fourteenth century. Inside you're immediately struck by the plainness of the vast interior, with its unadorned arcades and bare dome, and by its astonishing acoustics. Overlooking the massive raised font is Nicola Pisano's **pulpit**, sculpted in 1260, half a century before his son's work in the cathedral. There are **stairs** to the upper gallery, and more stairs from there up inside the dome.

The screen of sepulchral white marble running along the north edge of the Campo dei Miracoli is the perimeter wall of what has been called the most beautiful cemetery in the world – the **Camposanto** (same hours as baptistry). According to legend, the Archbishop Ubaldo Lanfranchi had Pisan knights on the Fourth Crusade of 1203 bring a cargo of soil back to Pisa from the hill of Golgotha, in order that eminent Pisans might be buried in holy earth. The building enclosing this sanctified site was completed almost a century later and takes the form of an enormous Gothic cloister. However, when Ruskin described the Camposanto as one of the most precious buildings in Italy, it was the **frescoes** that he was praising. Paintings once covered over two thousand metres of cloister wall, but now the brickwork is mostly bare: **incendiary bombs** dropped by Allied planes on July 27, 1944 set the roofing on fire and drenched the frescoes in molten lead. The most important survivor is the remarkable *Triumph of Death* cycle, a ruthless catalogue of morbid horrors painted within a few months of the Black Death of 1348.

Near the Leaning Tower is the absorbing **Museo dell'Opera del Duomo** (daily: April–Sept 8am–7.40pm; Oct–March 9am–4.40pm; €5). Room 7 contains Giovanni Pisano's affecting *Madonna del Colloquio*, so called because of the intensity of the gazes exchanged by the Madonna and Child. In room 11 is the *Pisan Cross*, which incited the Pisan contingent on the First Crusade to invade Jerusalem. Upstairs, room 15 has beautiful examples of intarsia, the art of inlaid wood, much practised in Pisa in the fifteenth and sixteenth centuries.

On the south side of the Campo, the only gap in the souvenir stalls is for the **Museo delle Sinopie** (same hours as baptistry). After the damage wreaked on the Camposanto, restorers removed its *sinopie* (a *sinopia* is a monochrome sketch over which a fresco is painted). These great plates of plaster now hang from the walls of this hi-tech museum, but getting sense from them is a rather scholastic enterprise. You may get more reward from **walking on the ramparts**; access is at the northwest corner of the lawns (daily: March–Dec; €2), and you can also climb up inside the medieval **Torre di Santa Maria** here to look down into the Camposanto.

Piazza dei Cavalieri and the eastern quarters

Away from the Campo dei Miracoli, Pisa takes on a very different character. Few tourists penetrate far into its squares and arcaded streets, with their Romanesque churches and – especially along the Arno's banks – ranks of fine palazzi. With the large student population it can be a lively place, particularly during the summer festivals and the monthly market, when the main streets on either side of the river become one continuous bazaar.

Piazza dei Cavalieri opens unexpectedly from the narrow backstreets, the central civic square of medieval Pisa. The curving **Palazzo dei Cavalieri**, covered in sgraffiti and topped with busts of the Medici, adjoins the church of **Santo Stefano**, which still houses banners captured from Turkish ships by the Knights of St Stephen – a grand title for a gang of state-sponsored pirates. On the other side of the square is the Renaissance-adapted **Palazzo dell'Orologio**, in whose tower the military leader Ugolino della Gherardesca was starved to death with his sons and grandsons in 1208, as punishment for his alleged duplicity with the Genoese enemy – as described in Dante's *Inferno* and Shelley's *Tower of Famine*. Via Dini heads east to the arcaded **Borgo Stretto**, Pisa's smart street, its windows glittering with consumer desirables that seem out of kilter with the city's unshowy style. More typically Pisan is the atmospheric **market** in and around Piazza Vettovaglie (Mon–Fri morning &

all day Sat). The Borgo meets the river at the traffic-knotted **Piazza Garibaldi**, at the foot of the Ponte di Mezzo.

At the eastern end of the riverfront road Lungarno Mediceo is the **Museo Nazionale di San Matteo** (Tues–Sat 8.30am–7.30pm, Sun 8.30am–1.30pm; €4; joint ticket with Palazzo Reale €6.50). Most of the major works of art from Pisa's churches are now gathered here, including a *St Paul* by a young Masaccio, an oddly festive *Crucifixion* by Gozzoli, and another *Crucifixion* by Turino Vanni that clearly shows the Leaning Tower. The sculpture collection is led by two outstanding works – Donatello's gilded bronze bust of an introspective *San Lussorio*, and Andrea and Nino Pisano's *Madonna del Latte*, a touchingly crafted work showing Mary breastfeeding the baby Jesus.

The western quarters

A main route south from the Campo dei Miracoli is **Via Santa Maria**, which starts out clogged with touristy shops. Where Via dei Mille heads east for Piazza dei Cavalieri, the smaller Via Ghini cuts west to the gate of the **Orto Botanico**, the oldest university botanical gardens in the world, founded in 1543 (March–Oct Mon–Fri 8am–5.30pm, Sat 8am–1pm; Nov–Feb Mon–Fri 8am–5pm, Sat 8am–1pm; free). Via Santa Maria continues south in a much more subdued vein, crooking its way down to meet the river alongside the second of Pisa's leaning towers, the campanile of **San Nicola**, which starts off cylindrical, then becomes octagonal, then finally hexagonal on top.

Alongside San Nicola, fronting onto the Arno, is the **Museo Nazionale di Palazzo Reale**, Lungarno Pacinotti 46 (Mon–Fri 9am–2.30pm, Sat 9am–1.30pm; €3; joint ticket with San Matteo €6.50), displaying painting, sculpture and furniture belonging to the Medici, Lorraine and Savoy dynasties which occupied the house. Lavish sixteenth-century Flemish tapestries share space with antique weaponry, ivory miniatures and porcelain. A largely undistinguished collection of paintings is led by **Bronzino**'s famous portrait of Cosimo I's wife, Eleanor of Toledo. Just as memorable, however, is the lovely river **view** from the balcony.

West along the Arno is the vast **Arsenale**, built in the late sixteenth century to house the ships of the Order of St Stephen. In a twist of fate, it is again housing a naval fleet, though one from much earlier. In December 1998, during excavations to expand Pisa San Rossore train station, archeologists stumbled on the extensive, well-preserved remains of port facilities and ships dating from Etruscan and Roman times. Sixteen ships were uncovered, dating from between the first century BC and the sixth century AD – one of which may turn out to be the only complete Roman warship yet discovered – along with a vast hoard of artefacts. Currently, the museum, known as **Le Navi Antiche di Pisa**, occupies one wing of the arsenal (May–Sept Tues–Fri 10am–1pm & 2–7pm, Sat & Sun 11am–1pm; Oct–April Tues–Sun 10am–1pm & 3–6pm; €3), but the authorities are planning to expand the displays to fill the whole building in the near future.

Just west of the arsenal rises the **Torre Guelfa** of the Fortezza Vecchia or Cittadella Vecchia (May–Sept Tues–Fri 10am–1.30pm & 2.30–5pm, Sat & Sun 10am–1.30pm & 2.30–7pm; €1.60; joint ticket with Santa Maria della Spina €2.50). This ancient fortress, originally built in the thirteenth century, once stood guard over Pisa's harbour but now punctuates an otherwise little-explored district. Pisa is a low-rise city, and the **view** from the tower is spectacular.

South of the river

The middle of the **Ponte di Mezzo**, the city's central bridge, is a perfect spot from which to admire the sweep of Pisa's palazzo-lined waterfront and the **Logge di Banchi** on the south side of the bridge. Formerly the city's silk and wool market, this is now the scene for student gatherings and assignations after dark; it stands at the head of the main **Corso Italia**, a street that gets progressively shabbier as it nears the train station. On the church of San Antonio, just off Piazza Vittorio Emanuele II, is the last work of US artist **Keith Haring**. Haring completed the vibrant, imaginative mural in a week in June 1989 while seriously ill; he died eight months later. His bendy, cartoonish figures radiate colour above what is now the bus station, tragically unregarded, and indeed, quite often obscured by parked buses.

A five-minute walk west of the Ponte di Mezzo is the turreted oratory of **Santa Maria della Spina**. The little church dates from 1230, but was rebuilt in 1323 in the finest flourish of Pisan Gothic by a merchant who had acquired a thorn (*spina*) of Christ's crown. The tiny single-naved **interior** (same hours as Torre Guelfa, above; €1.10; joint ticket with Torre Guelfa €2.50) has mullioned windows on the riverside, but has lost most of its furnishings.

Eating and drinking

Restaurants in the environs of the Leaning Tower are not good value (although the many **bars** and **cafés** benefit from the views). A few blocks south, around Piazza Cavalieri and Piazza Dante, you'll find predominantly local places, many with prices reflecting student finances. Although most kitchens serve up standard Tuscan fare, you'll also find Pisan dishes, including *baccalà alla Pisana* (dried cod) and plenty of seafood.

Bruno Via Bianchi 12 ☏050.560.818. Outside the historic centre, northeast of the Leaning Tower, this traditional *antica trattoria* is known for its top-notch, and pricey, Pisan cuisine. Closed Mon eve & Tues.

La Grotta Via San Francesco 103 ☏050.578.105. Comfortable, quiet old osteria in a cave-like setting, with the motto "wine, bread and company". Locals crowd in at the benches to sample unfussy Tuscan nosh. Closed for lunch and all day Sun.

Mensa Universitaria Via Martiri. Student refectory off Piazza Cavalieri; the cheapest meals in town. Closed Sat & Sun eve, and mid-July to mid-Sept.

La Mescita Via Cavalca 2. This small restaurant in the warren of the Piazza Vettovaglie market is an academic institution, patronized by students and professors alike. Set menus (including vegetarian) from €20. Closed Mon, and Tues & Wed lunch.

Osteria dei Cavalieri Via San Frediano 16 ☏050.580.858, ⊛www.toscana.net/pisa/odc. Outstanding quality, with English-speaking staff and a calm, fresh atmosphere. The fish is exquisite, Tuscan meat and game dishes are expertly prepared, and their vegetarian options are excellent. Eat à la carte or choose from a welter of set menus from €25. Closed Sat lunch & Sun.

Al Ristoro dei Vecchi Macelli Via Volturno 49 ☏050.20.424. Acclaimed as Pisa's best restaurant, with a wide range of sophisticated, innovative takes on Tuscany's gourmet traditions – choose from meat or fish set menus for upwards of €40. Closed Sun lunch & Wed.

Lo Schiaccianoci Via Vespucci 104 ☏050.21.024. Wonderful, if tiny mid-priced fish and seafood restaurant in a hard-to-reach location east of the station. Closed Sun.

Taverna Kostas Via del Borghetto 39. Longstanding local favourite, offering a mix of Greek and Mediterranean cooking, as well as Pisan seafood. Closed Sun lunch & Mon.

Il Vecchio Dado Lungarno Pacinotti 21 ☏050.580.900. Quality pizzeria on the waterfront with a friendly welcome, classy food (the fish dishes are excellent) and lively atmosphere. Closed Wed & Thurs lunch.

Entertainment

Pisa's big traditional event is the **Gioco del Ponte**, held on the last Sunday in June every year, when twelve teams from the north and south banks of the city stage a series of battles, pushing a seven-tonne carriage over the Ponte di Mezzo. The event, first mentioned in 1568, is still held in medieval costume with much ceremony. June 17 sees the **Regata di San Ranieri**, where four rowing teams race in costume in honour of the patron saint of Pisa; it is preceded the night before by the **Luminaria di San Ranieri**, when all the waterfront buildings and the Leaning Tower are illuminated. Italy's four great maritime republics (Amalfi, Pisa, Genoa and Venice) take turns to host the **Regata delle Antiche Repubbliche Marinare**, which will next come round to Pisa in late May/early June 2006. Four eight-man crews from each of the cities race against each other on the Arno, in between festivities and parades.

Look out for **concerts** at the Teatro Comunale Verdi, Via Palestro 40, and for more offbeat and contemporary shows (even the odd rock concert) held in a former church at the end of Via San Zeno. The city also has an adventurous **arts cinema**, Cinema Nuove, in Piazza Stazione.

Listings

Airlines Air Dolomiti ☏ 800.013.366; Air France ☏ 848.884.466; Alitalia ☏ 848.865.643; Britiish Airways ☏ 199.712.266; Lufthansa ☏ 02.8066.3025; Meridiana ☏ 050.43.048; Ryanair ☏ 050.503.770; Transavia Airlines ☏ 02.218.981.
Books Libreria Internazionale, Via Rigattieri 33, stocks English books.
Car rental Autoeuropa ☏ 050.506.883, Avis ☏ 050.42.028, Europcar ☏ 050.41.017, Hertz ☏ 050.43.220, Liberty Rent ☏ 050.48.088, National/Maggiore ☏ 050.42.574, Program ☏ 050.500.296, Sixt ☏ 050.46.209, Thrifty ☏ 050.45.490, Travelcar ☏ 050.44.424. All are based at the airport.
Hospital Santa Chiara, Via Roma 67 ☏ 050.992.111.
Internet access Internet Planet, Piazza Cavallotti 3 ☏ 050.830.702, ⊛ www.internetplanet.it; Internet Point, Via dei Mille 3 ☏ 050.830.701, ⊛ www.koinepisa.it. Both have long opening hours and charge €4 for 30min (less for students).

Internet Surf, open daily until 1am at Via Carducci 5 (☏ 050.830.800, ⊛ www.internetsurf.it) lets you pay by credit card.
Laundry OndaBlu, Via San Francesco 8a.
Left luggage At the airport (daily 10am–8pm; ☏ 050.500.707; €6 per piece per day).
Lost property At the airport ☏ 050.849.400.
Parking There are car parks outside the Porta Nuova, just west of the Campo dei Miracoli, and west of the train station on Via Battisti. Parking in the historic centre is severely restricted: yellow spaces are off-limits, blue spaces are charged by the hour, day and night, and white spaces are free only if you display a chit from your hotel, signed, stamped and dated. The airport long-term car park P2 is free.
Police The *Questura* is at Via Mario Lalli 1 ☏ 050.583.511.
Post office Piazza Vittorio Emanuele II (Mon–Fri 8.15am–7pm, Sat 8.15am–noon).
Taxi Radio Taxi ☏ 050.541.600, Piazza Stazione ☏ 050.41.252, Piazza Duomo ☏ 050.561.878.

Lucca

LUCCA, 17km northeast of Pisa, is the most graceful of Tuscany's provincial capitals, set inside a ring of Renaissance walls fronted by gardens and huge bastions. It's quiet without being dull and absorbs its few tourists with ease.

The city lies at the heart of one of Italy's richest agricultural regions, and it has prospered since Roman times. Its heyday was the eleventh to fourteenth centuries, when the silk trade brought wealth and, for a time, political power. Lucca first lost its independence to Pisa in 1314, then, under Castruccio Castracani, forged an empire in the west of Tuscany. Pisa and Pistoia both fell, and, but for Castracani's untimely death in 1325, Lucca might well have taken

LUCCA

▲ *Pistoia*   ▲   ▲ **5** & **6**

RESTAURANTS	
Da Giulio	A
Da Guido	B
Da Leo	C
Puccini	D

VIALE GUGLIELMO MARCONI

VIALE CARLO DEL PRETE DELLA LIBERTÀ

PIAZZALE MARTIRI

Porta
S. Jacopo

S. Francesco

Villa
Guinigi

Porta
Elisa

VIA DELLA QUARQUONIA

Giardino
Botánico

Porta
S. Maria

Youth Hostel

S. Frediano

San Pietro
Somaldi

S. Pietro

Casa-Torre
Guinigi

S. Maria
Forisportam

Palazzo
Pfanner

Torre
delle Ore

Museo della
Cattedrale

Palazzo
Mansi

S. Agostino

Casa di
Puccini

S. Cristoforo

Duomo

S. Michele
in Foro

S. Paolino

S. Giovanni

Porta S. Pietro

Porta
S. Donato

Porta V.
Emanuele

Palazzo Ducale

S. Romano

Bus
Station

Train
Station

PIAZZALE
B. RICASOLI

CORSO GARIBALDI

VIA VITTORIO VENETO

VIALE GIOSUE CARDUCCI

VIALE LAZZARO PAPI

▲ *Viareggio*

▲ *7* & *Pisa*

N

ACCOMMODATION	
Bernardino	5
Diana	4
La Luna	1
Melecchi	6
Piccolo Hotel Puccini	2
Universo	3
Villa La Principessa	7

0   200 m

Florence. In subsequent centuries it remained largely independent until falling into the hands of Napoleon and the Bourbons. The composer **Giacomo Puccini** was born here in 1858. Today Lucca is reckoned among the wealthiest and most conservative cities in Tuscany, its prosperity gained largely through **silk** and high-quality **olive oil**.

Arrival and information

Lucca's **train station** (information ☎1478.88.088) is just outside the walls to the south. Frequent Lazzi and CLAP **buses** from Florence, and Lazzi ones from Pisa and Livorno, arrive at the western Piazzale Verdi. The focus of Lucca's compact historic centre is the vast Piazza Napoleone, but its social heart is **Piazza San Michele** just to the north. The "long thread", Via Fillungo, heads northeast to the extraordinary circular **Piazza Anfiteatro**. Further east, beyond the Fosso ("ditch"), lies San Francesco.

The main **tourist office** is in the north of town, at Piazza Santa Maria (daily: April–Sept 9am–7pm; Oct–March 9am–5pm; ☎0583.919.931, ⓦ www.lucca-turismo.it). Other offices are in the Cortile degli Svizzeri, behind Piazza Napoleone (same times; ☎0583.4171), and on Piazzale Verdi (daily: April–Sept 9am–7pm; Oct–March 9am–2pm; ☎0583.419.689). They all have (English) **audioguides** for a self-guided town walk (€8) which lasts one hour twenty minutes, or you can dot around between the sights. The **Lucchese Settembre** festival features plenty of activity throughout September, centred on a candlelit procession on the 13th. Consult the tourist office for details of affiliated events, such as jazz and classical **concerts** (including Puccini opera) and **art** shows.

Accommodation

Accommodation can be difficult at almost any time of year; if you turn up without a booking, be prepared to move on to Pisa or Pistoia. There are very few **hotels** within the walls, although some good-value **private rooms** ease the burden (consult the tourist office). Lucca has one HI hostel, the **Ostello San Frediano**, Via della Cavallerizza 12 (☎0583.469.957, ⓔostellosanfrediano @virgilio.it; midnight curfew; €16), which is conveniently located just inside the walls.

Bernardino Via di Tiglio 108 ☎0583.953.356, ⓔhotelber@tin.it. A two-star 600m east of Porta Elisa that is a shade higher-quality than the nearby *Stipino*, with all-en-suite rooms. ❹

Diana Via del Molinetto 11 ☎0583.492.202, ⓦwww.albergodiana.com. Located within the walls a block west of the Duomo, this nine-room two-star has seven double rooms with private bathroom and two singles without. ❸–❹

La Luna Corte Compagni 12 ☎0583.493.634, ⓦwww.hotellaluna.com. A thirty-room three-star within the walls, with characterful rooms ranged around an internal courtyard and free parking – but well-beaten for price by the *Puccini*. ❺

Melecchi Via Romana 37 ☎0583.950.234. This recently restored hotel has fourteen en-suite

rooms and is about 750m east of Porta Elisa. ❹

Piccolo Hotel Puccini Via di Poggio 9 ☎0583.55.421, ⓦwww.hotelpuccini.com. Friendly three-star with just fourteen rooms, steps from the Casa di Puccini and San Michele. First choice within the walls for character and welcome. ❹

Universo Piazza del Giglio 1 ☎0583.493.678, ⓦwww.hoteluniverso.com. Lucca's not-so-grand grand hotel, a venerable old three-star pile right in the centre with a varying set of rooms that match the staff for unpredictable charm. ❼

Villa La Principessa SS del Brennero 1616, Massa Pisana ☎0583.370.037, ⓦwww.hotel-principessa.com. A beautifully appointed nine-teenth-century country villa set in lovely grounds (with pool) 3km south of town. ❽

The City

Lucca is a delightful place simply to wander at random, with much of the centre free from traffic. The historical heart of town is the site of the Roman forum, now the square surrounding **San Michele in Foro** (daily 7.40am–noon & 3–6pm), a church with one of Tuscany's most exquisite **facades**. Most of the present structure dates from the century after 1070, but the church is unfinished, as the money ran out before the body of the building could be raised to the level of the facade. The effect is wonderful, the upper loggias and the windows fronting air. Its Pisan-inspired intricacy is a triumph of poetic eccentricity: each of its myriad columns is different – some twisted, others sculpted or candy-striped. The impressive **campanile** is Lucca's tallest. It would be hard to follow this act and the **interior** barely tries; the best work of art is a beautifully framed painting of SS *Jerome, Sebastian, Roch and Helena* by Filippino Lippi in the right-hand nave.

The composer **Giacomo Puccini** was born a few metres away, on December 22, 1858, at Corte San Lorenzo 9; his father and grandfather had both been organists at San Michele. The family home is now a study centre and small museum, the **Casa di Puccini** (Tues–Sun: June–Sept 10am–6pm; Oct–May 10am–1pm & 3–6pm; €3; ⓦwww.puccini.it). Inside you'll find the Steinway on which Puccini wrote *Turandot* and some scores and ephemera. Just west of here is the **Museo Nazionale di Palazzo Mansi**, Via Galli Tassi 43 (Tues–Sat 9am–7pm, Sun 9am–2pm; €4; joint ticket with Museo Guinigi €6.50). This seventeenth-century palazzo is worth seeing for its magnificent Rococo decor: from a vast, frescoed **Music Salon**, you pass through three drawing-rooms hung with seventeenth-century Flemish tapestries to a gilded **bridal suite**, complete with lavish canopied bed. Rooms 11–14 in the far wing hold an indifferent **Pinacoteca**, the highlight of which is Pontormo's portrait of Alessandro de' Medici.

The Duomo and around

It needs a double-take before you realize why the **Duomo** looks odd. The building is fronted by a severely asymmetric facade – its right-hand arch and loggias are squeezed by the belltower, which was already in place from an earlier building. Nonetheless, little detracts from its overall grandeur, created by the repetition of tiny columns and loggias and by the stunning **atrium**, whose bas-reliefs are some of the finest sculptures in the city. The carvings over the left-hand door – a *Deposition, Annunciation, Nativity* and *Adoration of the Magi* – are by **Nicola Pisano**. Other panels display a symbolic labyrinth, a Tree of Life (with Adam and Eve at the bottom and Christ at the top), a bestiary of grotesques and the months of the year.

The **interior** (daily: summer 7am–7pm; winter 7am–5pm) is best known for the contribution of **Matteo Civitali** (1435–1501), who is represented here most famously by the *Tempietto*, a gilt-and-marble octagon halfway down the church. Some fanatically intense acts of devotion are performed in front of it, directed at the **Volto Santo** (Holy Face), a cedarwood crucifix with bulging eyes popularly said to be a true effigy of Christ carved by Nicodemus, an eye-witness to the Crucifixion. Legend has it that the *Volto Santo* came to Lucca of its own volition, first journeying by boat from the Holy Land, and then brought by oxen guided by divine will. The effigy attracted pilgrims from all over Europe: King William Rufus of England used to swear by it (*"Per sanctum vultum de Lucca!"*). The **Tomb of Ilaria del Carretto** (1410), originally situated in the north transept, is now in the sacristy to the south following lengthy restoration (April–Oct daily 9.30am–5.45pm; Nov–March Mon–Fri 9.30am–4.45pm, Sat 9.30am–6.45pm, Sun 11.30am–4.45pm; €2, or €5.50 combined ticket with the Museo della Cattedrale and San Giovanni). Considered the masterpiece of Sienese sculptor **Jacopo della Quercia**, it consists of a raised dais and the sculpted body of Ilaria, second wife of Paolo Guinigi, one of Lucca's medieval big shots. In a touching, almost sentimental gesture, the artist has carved the family dog at her feet. Also within the sacristy is a superb *Madonna Enthroned* by **Ghirlandaio**.

Occupying a converted twelfth-century building opposite the Duomo is the **Museo della Cattedrale** (April–Oct daily 10am–6pm; Nov–March Mon–Fri 10am–2pm, Sat & Sun 10am–5pm; €3.50, or €5.50 with the cathedral sacristy and San Giovanni). This contains some unnerving Romanesque stone heads, human and equine, and, in room II on the upper floor, a reliquary from Limoges decorated with stories from the life of St Thomas à Becket alongside the *Croce dei Pisani*, an ornate fifteenth-century gold crucifix. West of the Duomo is the church of **San Giovanni** (same hours; €2.50; combined ticket with Tomb of Ilaria and Museo della Cattedrale €5.50). This was Lucca's cathedral until 715, and excavations here have unearthed a tangle of remains, from Roman mosaics to traces of a Carolingian church.

North to San Frediano

Via Cenami leads from the duomo north to the **Torre delle Ore**, the city's clock tower since 1471. From here, **Via Fillungo** cuts through Lucca's luxury shopping district.

San Frediano is again Pisan-Romanesque, featuring a magnificent thirteenth-century exterior mosaic of *Christ in Majesty*, with the Apostles gathered below. The **interior** (Mon–Sat 8.30am–noon & 3–5pm; Sun 10.30am–5pm except during services; free) lives up to the facade's promise – a delicately lit, hall-like basilica. Facing the door is the **Fonta Lustrale**, a huge twelfth-century font executed by three unknown craftsmen. Set behind the font is an *Annunciation* by Andrea della Robbia, festooned with trailing garlands of ceramic fruit. The left-hand of the two rear chapels houses the incorrupt body of **St Zita** (died 1278), a Lucchese maidservant who achieved sainthood from a white lie: she used to give bread from her household to the poor, and when challenged one day by her boss as to the contents of her apron, she replied "only roses and flowers" – into which the bread was transformed. She is commemorated on April 27 by a flower market outside the church. Lucca's best frescoes – **Amico Aspertini**'s sixteenth-century scenes of the *Arrival of the Volto Santo*, the *Life of St Augustine* and *The Miracle of St Frediano* – occupy the second chapel of the left aisle. Frediano, an Irish monk, is said to have brought Christianity to Lucca in the sixth century and is depicted here saving the city from flood.

A short distance south, at Via degli Asili 33, is the **Palazzo Pfanner** (March–Nov 10am–6pm; garden and palace €4, garden only €2.50). The *palazzo*, housing a textiles collection, is less interesting than its rear loggia and exquisite statued gardens with fountain. They can be seen to good effect from the city walls just nearby, which also yield a good overview of another fine church, **Sant'Agostino**.

East of San Frediano is the remarkable **Piazza Anfiteatro**. This ramshackle circuit of medieval buildings, built on the foundations of the Roman amphitheatre that once stood here (arches and columns of which can still be discerned), is now ringed by cafés. South past a covered market looms the **Torre Guinigi**, the fifteenth-century home of Lucca's leading family and one of the strangest sights in town: its battlemented tower is surmounted, 44m up, by a **holm oak** whose roots have grown into the room below. You can climb the tower from Via Sant'Andrea (daily: March–Sept 9am–7.30pm; Oct–Feb 10am–5.30pm; €3.10).

East to San Francesco

Running from north to south across town is a canal and Via del Fosso, across which is the church of **San Francesco**, fronted by a relatively simple facade and adjoining a crumbling brick convent. Behind the church is Lucca's key collection of painting, sculpture, furniture and applied arts, the **Museo Nazionale di Villa Guinigi**, housed in the family's much-restored mansion (Tues–Sat 9am–7pm, Sun 9am–2pm; €4, or €6.50 combined ticket with Palazzo Mansi). Its lower floor has mainly sculpture and archeological finds, with numerous Romanesque pieces and works by della Quercia and Matteo Civitali. Upstairs are lots of big sixteenth-century paintings and more impressive works by early Lucchese and Sienese masters, as well as fine Renaissance offerings from such as Fra' Bartolommeo.

Eating, drinking and entertainment

Lucca has some high-quality **restaurants**. Local specialities include *zuppa di farro*, a thick soup made with spelt (a type of grain) and *capretto*, mountain goat, often roasted. *Puccini*, opposite the composer's house at Corte San Lorenzo 1 (☏0583.316.116; closed Tues & Wed lunch in summer; all day Tues in winter), has a light touch and classy approach to its exquisite pasta and especially good fish dishes: not cheap, this is top choice for a lunch to remember, or a romantic dinner date. *Da Giulio in Pelleria*, Via della Conce 45 (☏0583.55.948; closed Sun & Mon), is a lively trattoria always packed in the evenings – the food is not exceptional, but the atmosphere is. *Da Leo*, Via Tegrini 1 (closed Sun), is an inexpensive locals' haunt with solid Tuscan cooking; and *Da Guido*, Via Cesare Battisti 28 (closed Sun), is a heartwarming place with much joviality and truly unbeatable prices. Lucca's most famous **café–bar** is *Caffè di Simo* at Via Fillungo 58, once Puccini's favourite haunt and still with an appealing late nineteenth-century ambience. Of the bars around Piazza San Michele, *Casali* at no. 40 is the most alluring.

The town's **food shops** are equally good. Caniparoli in Via San Paolina is a wonderful chocolate shop; La Cacioteca, Via Fillungo 242, sells a wide variety of cheeses; Forno Amedeo Giusti, Via Santa Lucia 18, is the town's top bakery, with delicious fresh *focaccia*; Pellegrini on Piazza San Michele has pizza by the slice; and Pasticceria Taddeucci on the same square has a stunning interior of wood-panelling and mosaic tiles to match its selection of cakey delights.

The **Lucchese Settembre** festival features plenty of activity throughout September, centred on a **candlelit procession** on the 13th, when the bejewelled *Volto Santo* is carried through the streets from San Frediano to the Duomo. Consult the tourist office for details of affiliated September events, such as **classical concerts** (including performances of a Puccini opera) at the intimate, four-tiered Teatro Comunale in Piazza del Giglio, as well as **jazz** happenings and **art** exhibitions. Another key musical event is the "Summer Festival" (⊛www.summer-festival.com) often featuring big-name international stars performing in Piazza Anfiteatro.

Listings

Bike rental The tourist office in Piazzale Verdi; Barbetti Cicli, Via dell'Anfiteatro 23; Cicli Bizzarri or Biciclette Poli, either side of the tourist office in Piazza Santa Maria – reckon on about €2.10 per hour.

Hospital Campo di Marte, in Via dell'Ospedale ☏0583.9701.

Internet access Tourist office at Piazza Santa Maria or any of the many outlets on Via San Paolino.

Lost property c/o Comune di Lucca, Via Battisti 10 ☏0583.442.388.

Parking Outside the walls, parking is free for all; inside, only hotel customers can park for free.

Police The *Questura* is at Via Cavour 38 ☏0583.4551.

Post office Via Vallisneri 2 (Mon–Fri 8.15am–7pm, Sat 8.15am–12.30pm).

North of Pisa

The coast from near Pisa north to the Ligurian border is a solid strip of unattractive beach resorts. This **Riviera della Versilia** ought to be otherwise, given the backdrop of the **Alpi Apuane** mountains, but the beaches share the coastal plain with a railway, *autostrada* and clogged urban roads – and, on top of this, the sea is not the cleanest in Italy. The resort of **Viareggio** provides a lively diversion on a coastal journey north to the stunning Cinque Terre (see p.144). Otherwise, the only real appeal lies inland, hiking in the Alpi Apuane and exploring the famed marble quarrying centre of **Carrara**.

Viareggio

VIAREGGIO, 22km northwest of Pisa, is a large and once-elegant nineteenth-century resort, which continues to aim – with limited success – for a well-heeled clientele. It has its attractions, with a fair amount of nightlife (including big-name concerts and hot dance clubs) complemented by some neat Art Deco buildings along Passeggiata Margherita. But the beaches are private and charge upwards of €18 for admission, and in season the hotels are either full or demand *pensione completa*. Aim instead for Viareggio's famously boisterous **Carnevale** (in February); for four consecutive Sundays there's an amazing parade of floats, or *carri* – colossal, lavishly designed papier-mâché models of politicians and celebrities (ⓦwww.viareggio.ilcarnevale.com).

Walks in the Alpi Apuane

There are **walks** throughout the **Alpi Apuane**, which loom behind the Riviera della Versilia and are now protected as a Parco Regioale. Altitudes are relatively low (the summits crest 1900m), conditions are easy and distances are short – you're never very far from civilization. **Ufficio Promozione del Parco delle Apuane**, Via Corrado del Greco 11 in Seravezza, partway between Viareggio and Massa, has leaflets, maps and guidance for walkers (Mon–Sat 10am–noon; ☏0584.75821, ⓦwww.parks.it/parco.alpi.apuane).

One access point is the lovely village of **STAZZEMA**, served by bus from Pietrasanta and with the simple **hotel** *Procinto*, Via IV Novembre 21 (☏0584 .777.004; ❷). Trail #5 is a gentle climb from Stazzema through chestnut woods to the Procinto, a huge table-top crag, below which is the **Rifugio Forte dei Marmi** (open daily June 5–Sept 5; rest of the year, weekends only; ☏0584.777.051; bed only €12). This is an easy day-trip, with time to explore above the *rifugio* and drop in for a snack on the way back down to Stazzema on trails #121 or #126.

The **train station** is 600m back from the seafront. **Buses** (Lazzi, CAT and CLAP) stop nearer the centre; turn right along the seafront, past Piazza Mazzini, to find the **tourist office**, at Viale Carducci 10 (Mon–Fri 9am–1pm & 3-6.30pm, Sat 9.30am–12.30pm & 3.30–6.30pm, Sun 10am–noon; ☎0584.962.233, ℮viareggio@versilia.turismo.toscana.it). The town has literally hundreds of **hotels** in all price brackets; one inexpensive option is *Villa Amadei*, just west of the tourist office at Via F. Gioia 23 (☎0584.45.517, ℮amadei@caen.it; ❸). For the best **restaurant** the town has to offer make for the Michelin-starred *Romano*, Via Mazzini 120 (☎0584.31.382; closed Mon), for its sublime fish and seafood cooking.

Carrara

The capital of Massa-Carrara, Tuscany's northernmost province, is **Massa**, a modern, unappealing town that is more or less merged with its adjacent beach resort of **Marina di Massa** in a sprawl of undistinguished holiday development. Nearby **CARRARA** sits just inside the Ligurian border, 28km north of Viareggio, and enjoys a fame that far outstrips its modest size. For the mountains here have been a principal source of **marble** since the ancient Romans; everyone from Michelangelo to Henry Moore has tramped up here in search of the perfect block. Carrara is still the world's largest producer and exporter of marble, shipping out 1.5 million tonnes a year from the container port plumb in the middle of **Marina di Carrara**. But quiet Carrara itself has a pleasant, rural feel and comes as a relief after the holiday coast.

From the central **Piazza Matteotti**, the pedestrianized Via Roma heads north to the attractive Piazza Accademia, with steps down (west) to the old town and Carrara's Romanesque-Gothic **Duomo**, graced with a lovely Pisan-style marble facade. Heart of the old town is gracious **Piazza Alberica**. This is the focus for the town's display of contemporary marble sculpture, the biennial **Scolpire all'Aperto** (late July to early Oct), when the town invites internationally renowned artists to create new works in public. For the low-down on marble, there's an impressive **Museo Civico di Marmo** on Viale XX Settembre, 2km south of town (July & Aug Mon–Sat 10am–8pm, Sun 9.30am–noon & 5–8pm; May, June, Sept Mon–Sat 10am–6pm; Oct–April 8.30am–1.30pm; ☎0585.845.746; €3.10), served by CAT buses from Piazza Matteotti. Any short trip into the interior brings you to the startling sight of the marble **quarries**. To get a closer view, take a bus (hourly from Via Minzoni) towards **Colonnata**, 8km northeast of Carrara, and get off before the village at the *"Visita Cave"* signs by the mine – if you're driving, follow the *"Cava di Marmo"* signs from the village. You'll see a huge, blindingly white marble basin, its floor and sides perfectly squared by the enormous wire saws used to cut the blocks that litter the surroundings.

Carrara-Avenza **train station** is close to the Marina di Carrara seafront, and is served by regular **buses** which run 4km inland to drop off at Carrara's central Piazza Matteotti. The town has a summer-only **tourist office** at Via XX Settembre 46 (9am–7pm; ☎0585.844.003), though you'll find more information on the coast at Marina di Carrara, from where Navigazione Golfo dei Poeti (see p.150) runs **boats** to Portovenere and the Cinque Terre (June–Sept daily; around €18). Carrara's two **hotels** are the spartan *Da Roberto* on Via Apuana (☎0585.70.634; ❷), and the more salubrious *Michelangelo*, Corso Fratelli Rosselli 3 (☎0585.777.161, ℮hm.carrara@tin.it; ❸), with parking and a jolly manager. The HI **hostel**, *Ostello Albergo Apuano per la Gioventù* (☎0585.780.034, ℮aig@uni.net; April–Sept; curfew 11.30pm; €8.25), is on the seafront between Marina di Carrara and Marina di Massa at Via delle Pinete 237, alongside plenty of **campsites**. The excellent *Il Via* **restaurant**, Via Roma 17 (ⓣ0585.779.423; closed Sun in winter), has a quality meat or fish menu at moderate prices. Elsewhere are the moderately priced *Roma*, Piazza Cesare Battisti 1 (closed Sat), and *Osteria della Contrada*, Via Ulivi 2 (ⓣ0585.776.961; closed Mon). A good little spot for a drink is the *Bar Fuori Porta* Piazza Battisti 1 (closed Sun) which also serves inexpensive antipasti and primi.

Livorno

LIVORNO, 18km southwest of Pisa, is Tuscany's third-largest city and one of Italy's largest ports – a status which invited blanket bombing during World War II. Its rebuilt commercial centre is not pretty, but a poke around the back streets will reveal a network of picturesque canals and hump-backed bridges, a lively streetlife that benefits from a very un-Tuscan ethnic diversity, and plenty of places to sample top-quality **seafood**. What you won't find are the very things Tuscany is famous for: art, architecture and tourists.

Livorno's port was developed under the **Medici**. In 1618, they declared it a **free port** and instituted a liberal constitution which prompted an influx of Jews, Greeks, Spanish Muslims, English Catholics and a cosmopolitan throng of other refugees. Livorno flourished, and attracted a community of English expatriates (including Shelley) whose cack-handed anglicization of the city's name into **Leghorn** is still in use.

The old **Porto Mediceo** has fishing boats spilling back into the canal quarter and unfortunately often a cruise liner blocking the view out to sea. Sangallo's **Fortezza Vecchia** flanks the harbour, about 100m north of Livorno's sole surviving nod to Renaissance art – the statue of the **Quattro Mori**, overlooking the busy waterfront road at Piazza Micheli. This bizarre work decorates an inept 1595 statue of Ferdinando I with the addition of four chained Moors by Pietro Tacca (1623), tacked on either as a celebration of the success of Tuscan raids against North African shipping, or merely as slaves cowering beneath Medici glory. Either way they stand as a poignant and shocking harbourside symbol for this multiracial city. The **Museo Civico Giovanni Fattori**, devoted to Fattori and the late-nineteenth-century Macchiaioli movement, Italy's milk-and-water version of Impressionism, is housed in the extravagant Villa Mimbelli, in via San Jacopo in Acquaviva 65 (Tues–Sun 10am–1pm & 4–7pm; €6.50; bus #1).

The broad Via Grande heads inland to **Piazza Grande**, which features the **Duomo**, a postwar reconstruction. Via Cairoli curls around the Duomo, and partway along, Via Buontalenti leads off to the ochre **Mercato Centrale** that stands at the heart of a boisterous street-market. The canal near here was the limit of the Medici port city; follow it northeast to the ugly treeless expanse of Piazza della Repubblica on one side, and Piazza XX Settembre on the other. The latter is the home of the **Mercatino Americano** – a cultural endowment of stationed American troops – that sells army surplus clothing, fishing and camping gear and flick-knives. From the Mercato Centrale, Via della Madonna strikes north into the **Venezia** district, Livorno's most attractive quarter, with crumbling old tenement buildings and the Fortezza Nuova ringed around by a network of quiet canals. August sees the area come alive for the *Effetto Venezia*, a free **street carnival** of jazz and world music.

Ferries from Livorno

There are dozens of **ferry** sailings from Livorno, to **Corsica** (Bastia or Porto Vecchio), **Sardinia** (Olbia, Golfo Aranci or Cagliari), **Sicily** (Palermo) and the Tuscan islands. Nearly all ferries to Corsica and Sardinia leave from alongside the **Stazione Marittima**, west of the centre behind the Fortezza Vecchia, although some (and boats to Sicily) depart from **Varco Galvani**, a long way west of town. Ferries to Capraia and Elba leave from the central **Porto Mediceo**. Check with the tourist office and the companies themselves for times and prices, and **reserve** well ahead in summer. If you're taking a car to Sardinia, most companies offer discount deals if you cross to Corsica and drive the 180km to the southern tip of the island – often this means the subsequent ferry to Sardinia is free. For a full list of ferries to Sardinia, see p.1070 and to Elba, see opposite.

Ferry Companies

Corsica Ferries Stazione Marittima, Calata Carrara ☎019.215.511, ⓦwww.corsica-ferries.com. To Bastia (Corsica).

Corsica Marittima Stazione Marittima, Calata Carrara ☎0586.210.507, ⓦwww.corsicamarittima.com. To Bastia and Porto Vecchio (Corsica).

Etruria Shipping Porto Mediceo ☎0586.263.319. To Portoferraio (Elba).

Grandi Navi Veloci (Grimaldi) Varco Galvani, Calata Tripoli, Porto Nuovo ☎010.589.331, ⓦwww.grimaldi.it. To Palermo (Sicily).

Lloyd Sardegna/Linea dei Golfi Varco Galvani, Calata Assab, Porto Industriale ☎0565.222.300, ⓦwww.lloydsardegna.it. To Olbia and Cagliari (Sardinia).

Moby Lines Stazione Marittima, Calata Carrara ☎0586.826.823, ⓦwww.mobylines.it. To Bastia (Corsica) and Olbia (Sardinia).

Sardinia Ferries Stazione Marittima, Calata Carrara ☎019.215.511, ⓦwww.sardiniaferries.com). To Golfo Aranci (Sardinia).

Toremar Porto Mediceo ☎0586.896.113, ⓦwww.toremar.it. To Capraia.

Practicalities

The **train station** is 2km east of the centre; take city bus #1 or #2 to Piazza Grande. ATL **buses** from Piombino drop off on Piazza Grande; Lazzi buses from Florence, Pisa and Lucca arrive on Piazza Manin. The **tourist office** is just off Via Cairoli at Piazza Cavour 6 (Mon–Fri 9am–1pm & 3–5pm, Sat 9am–1pm: ☎0586.204.611).

The best **hotel** is the eighteenth-century villa *La Vedetta*, on the Montenero hill at Via della Lecceta 20 (☎0586.579957, ⓦwww.hotellavedetta.it; ❼), with modern decor, parking and spectacular panoramic views. Livorno has a rash of cheap hotels, some of which – around the harbour and station – are grim dives. *Milano*, Via degli Asili 48 (☎0586.219.155, Ⓕ0586.210.118; ❸), is a pleasant exception. *Villa Morazzana* is a **hostel** in the hills, Via di Collinet 86 (☎0586.500.076, Ⓕ0586.502.426; €13). The **campsite** *Miramare*, Via del Littorale 220 (☎0586.580.402, ⓦwww.campingmiramare.com; May–Sept), is a short way south of town.

Italians travel to Livorno just to eat seafood and, specifically, to feast on the local dish *cacciucco*, a spicy seafood stew served with garlic toast. A choice **restaurant** if you can spare €35 a head is *Le Chiave*, Scali delle Cantine (☎0586.888.609; closed Wed). There are dozens of more affordable options: *Antico Moro*, Via Bertelloni 59 (☎0586.884.659; closed Wed and lunchtime), is a pleasant locals' haunt with excellent *cacciucco*. *Café d'Etoile*, Via Indipendenza

13 (closed Sun), off Piazza Cavour, serves fresh salads and snacks. On Venezia's canalsides you'll find the moderately priced couscous-house *Mediterraneo*, Scali Ponte di Marmo 14 (closed Tues), and *The Barge*, a waterside pub with English beers and food, Scali Ancore 6 (closed Sun).

Elba

Mountainous **ELBA** is the third-largest Italian island after Sicily and Sardinia – 29km long by some 19km wide. It has exceptionally clear water, fine white-sand beaches, and a lush, wooded interior, superb for walking. It's now well and truly embracing package tourism – planes bring in a million tourists during August alone – and yet almost everyone comes for the beach resorts: even in the height of summer, inland villages remain mostly quiet. **Portoferraio** is very much the capital, a characterful port town overlooked by a warren of old alleys. Elsewhere, the most attractive towns are **Capoliveri** and **Porto Azzurro** in the southeast and little **Marciana** in the west, the last of these providing access to woodland hikes and the impressive chair lift up to **Monte Capanne** (1018m). **Biodola** occupies an idyllic sweeping bay near Portoferraio that is largely free from the island's otherwise remorseless beach culture. You can also take a ferry from Portoferraio or Porto Azzurro to the largely unspoilt island of **Capraia**, some 30km off Elba.

Ferries to Elba

The main port of departure to Elba is **PIOMBINO**, 75km south of Livorno – not a great place to stay, since it was flattened in World War II and these days makes its living from a giant steelworks. If you're arriving by train, you'll probably have to change at **Campiglia Maríttima** station, from where connecting trains run through the town to Piombino Maríttima. At the port, you'll find plenty of ticket outlets for all ferry companies. Most people head for Portoferraio, to where ferries run every day of the year, the first around 6am and the last around 9pm (earlier and later in high summer; from €6.50, plus about €26 for a car). If you're looking to cut costs get the slightly cheaper ferry to Rio Marina with Toremar. Port taxes add a few thousand lire.

From Piombino Toremar and Moby **ferries** shuttle regularly to Portoferraio (summer every 30min; winter every 2hr; takes 1hr); Toremar also serves Rio Marina (2–3 daily) and Porto Azzurro (summer 1 daily). Toremar's **rapid ferry**, or *linea veloce*, serves Portoferraio (summer 2 daily; takes 40min) and Rio Marina (summer 3 daily; takes 30min). Toremar's **hydrofoil**, or *aliscafo*, glides to Cavo (summer 5 daily; winter 3 daily; takes 20min) and Portoferraio (summer 4 daily; takes 30min). Etruria Shipping ferries run **from Livorno** to Portoferraio (1 daily; 3hr).

Ferry company offices

To book a place on any ferry, phone or visit the office at your port of departure.

Etruria Shipping Porto Medíceo, Livorno ☎0586.263.319.

Moby Nuova Stazione Marittima, Piombino ☎0565.225.211, ⊛www.mobylines.it; Via Ninci 1, Portoferraio ☎0565.9361 or Viale Elba 4, Portoferraio ☎0565.914.133.

Toremar Nuova Stazione Marittima, Piombino ☎0565.31.100, ⊛www.toremar.it; Calata Italia 23, Portoferraio ☎0565.918.080, ⊛www.toremar-elba.it; Calata Voltoni 20, Rio Marina ☎0565.962.073; Banchina IV Novembre 26, Porto Azzurro ☎0565.95.004; Via Michelangelo 54, Cavo ☎0565.949.871.

ELBA

Piombino

Piombino

Piombino

Livorno

Capraia

Bastia (Corsica)

Pianosa & Montecristo

Punta dei Ripalti

Pianosa

N

0   2 km

I. Palmaiola

Cavo

Rio Marina

Nisportino

Rio nell' Elba

Bagnáia

Ottone

Madonna del Monserrato †

Porto Azzurro

Naregno

Capoliveri

M. Calamita 413m

Morcone

Pareti

Innamorata

Portoferráio

Enfola

Viticcio

Carpani

San Martino

Scaglieri

Biódola

Prócchio

La Pila

Lacona

Capo di Stella

Capo di Fonza

Marina di Campo

S. Ilário in Campo

S. Piero in Campo

Cávoli

Sant'Andrea

Marciana Marina

Póggio

Zanca

Marciana

Patresi

P. Polveráia

Cable car

M. Capanne 1018m

Seccheto

Fetováia

Pomonte

Chiessi

Punta Nera

Historically, Elba has been well out of the mainstream. The principal industry from ancient times until World War II was **mining**, both of iron ore and of
the extensive mineral deposits. The **Romans** wrote of "the island of good
wines" (Elban wines are still among Tuscany's finest). In later centuries control
passed from Pisa to Genoa and on to the Medici, Spain, Turkey and finally
France – a cosmopolitan mix that has left its legacy on both architecture and
cultivation. Most people know the island as the place of exile for **Napoleon**,
who, after he was banished here in May 1814, revamped education and the
legal system, built roads and modernized the economy before escaping back to
France in February 1815. The epic "Hundred Days" that followed culminated
in his final defeat at Waterloo.

All seven Tuscan islands, and the seas around them, form the **Parco
Nazionale dell'Arcipelago Toscano**, the largest protected marine park in
Europe, administered from Via Guerrazzi 1 in Portoferraio (☎0565.919.411,
Ⓦwww.islepark.it).

Getting around the island

ATL **buses** serve just about every settlement on the island (no service after
8pm). One-way **fares** are between €0.80 and €3.10 depending on distance,
or you could get a **pass** for €6.50 (one day) or €18 (six days). In addition,
council minibuses run several times a day between town centres and their outlying beaches in the summer season. **Boats** are also much used to reach out-
of-the-way beaches, and are well advertised at all ports. Renting a **bike** or a
scooter is a good way of exploring the island, see p.541, but **car rental** is less
advisable: roads to the beaches and around the major resorts can get nastily
congested in high season, and winter bookings can be hard to come by, since
companies don't pay insurance off-season.

Portoferraio and around

PORTOFERRAIO is the hub of the island's transport system, has an atmospheric old quarter of stepped alleys and old churches, and lives a life quite separate from the hectic comings-and-goings of the huge ferries which dock
nearby. All **boats** slide past the old quarter with its Medici-built harbour to
dock at the main Calata Italia. The **tourist office** (summer Mon–Sat
8am–8pm; winter 8am–2pm & 3–6pm; ☎0565.914.671, Ⓦwww.aptelba.it) is
at Calata Italia 23, and the websites Ⓦwww.elbalink.it and Ⓦwww.elbatut-
tanatura.com are a good source of information. Hiking maps can be bought at
the newsagent opposite the bus stop (Kompass "Isola d'Elba", €7.20; Carta
Turistica e dei Sentieri, €5.50).

From the quayside, head up a short flight of steps to the old quarter's "back
entrance", the **Porta a Terra**. From here, steep alleys fan out on different levels; follow Via del Carmine up to the picturesque little tree-shaded **Piazza
Gramsci**, perched above the old port with a café and romantic views. Via
Victor Hugo (the novelist spent his boyhood in Portoferraio) continues
through another tunnelled gateway up to the highest point of the old quarter
and Napoleon's residence-in-exile, the **Villa dei Mulini** (Mon–Sat 9am–7pm,
Sun 9am–1pm; closed Tues; €3 or €5 joint three-day ticket with Villa di San
Martino). The villa was purpose-built on a well-chosen site with grand views
of the bay, and is a fair-sized old building – though undoubtedly not what the
emperor was used to. Inside you'll find a gallery with Empire-style furniture, a
Baroque bedroom with an absurdly over-gilded bed, a library of two thousand
books sent over from Fontainebleau, and various items of memorabilia. The
peaceful back garden looks down over the rocky headland.

Stepped alleys head down from the villa through the old quarter, passing the arts centre **Pinacoteca Foresiana** (Mon–Sat 9.30am–12.30pm; July & Aug also 6pm–midnight; €2), with a small collection of paintings and Napoleonic ephemera. The heart of the old town is **Piazza della Repubblica**, lined with cafés. Adjacent is the rather drab Piazza Cavour, from where the old Medici gate, the **Porta a Mare**, heads through to the U-shaped port. In the shadow of the Martello tower on the farthest point of the U is the fascinating **Museo Archeologico** (daily 9am–1.30pm & 3–7pm; €2), whose best displays are the various jars and amphorae salvaged from Roman shipwrecks, still full of preserved olives and fish.

From the bus station on Viale Elba take bus #1 southwest into the hills for 5km to the **Villa di San Martino** (same hours at Villa dei Mulini but closed on Mon; €3, or €5 joint three-day ticket with Villa dei Mulini). The arrow-straight avenue leading up to the house is designed to impress, even if the villa itself – bought by Napoleon's sister Elise just before the emperor left the island for good – is a rather chilly affair, with a drab Neoclassical facade enlivened with "N" motifs. The monograms were the idea of Prince Demidoff, husband of Napoleon's niece, and it was he who created the Napoleonic museum. The interior halls of the Neoclassical palazzo are devoted to temporary art exhibitions. Instead, head left of the facade to the ticket office, and then up flights of stairs to the back of the site; here you'll find Napoleon's modest summer retreat. Of the handful of Empire-style rooms, the best is the **Sala Egizio**, decorated with Nilotic scenes to commemorate the Egyptian campaign.

West of Portoferraio, buses head 7km to **ÉNFOLA**, a headland flanked by sandy beaches, and then wind above the coast to the village at the end of the road, **VITICCIO**. From here a footpath covers ground inaccessible to vehicles for 2km south across a prominent headland to picturesque **SCAGLIERI**, fronted by a shop, a bar (which rents bikes and mopeds) and a pizzeria-restaurant. The beaches here are some of the best on the island. Just round the bay sits **BIODOLA** – little more than a road, a couple of hotels and a superb stretch of white sand. The main town of the area, **PROCCHIO**, lies around the next headland to the south: with its traffic, buzzing bars and shops, it's not a place to get away from it all, but the sea is good and the white sand similarly excellent.

Practicalities

You should book a **ferry ticket** for your return journey well in advance in summer (see box above). The Associazione Albergatori, Calata Italia 20 (Mon–Fri 9am–1pm & 3.30–7pm, Sat 9.30am–12.30pm; ☎0565.914.754, ⓦwww.albergatorielbani.it), will phone around to help find **accommodation**. Otherwise, you could ask in bars about **private rooms** or book a self-catering **apartment** through the tourist office. The best **hotel** in terms of its sense of exclusive isolation and impeccable service is the *Park-Hotel Napoleone*, a nineteenth-century mansion beside the emperor's villa at San Martino (☎0565.911.111, Ⓔphnapoleone@elbalink.it; ❾). The white-sand beach at Biodola is overlooked by the luxury *Hermitage* (☎0565.974.811, Ⓔhermitage @elbalink.it; ❾); north along this coast is the decent *Danila* in Scaglieri (☎0565.969.915, ⓦwww.hoteldanila.it; ❻). Portoferraio's best choices are the comfortably done-up old *Ape Elbana*, Salita Cosimo dei Medici 2 (☎0565.914.245, Ⓔapelbana@elba2000.it; ❹), pleasant *Villa Ombrosa*, Viale De Gasperi 3 (☎0565.914.363, ⓦwww.villaombrosa.it; ❾), and clean but spartan *Nobel*, Via Manganaro 72 (☎0565.915.217, Ⓔnobel@elbalink.it; ❸).

The Associazione Campeggi (FAITA), Viale Elba 7 (☎0565.930.208,

@www.campingelba.net), can help out with bookings for the island's **camp-sites**. The shaded *Enfola* (℡0565.939.001, ℻0565.918.613; April to mid-Oct) is west from Portoferraio on the scenic coast road. On the hillside above Biodola beach is *Scaglieri* (℡0565.969.940, @www.campingscaglieri.it; April to mid-Oct). Lacona, Elba's camping hotspot on the coast 7km south of Portoferraio, has a flat foreshore crowded with bars and discos and nearby *Lacona* (℡0565.964.161, @www.camping-lacona.it) set in pine woods.

Portoferraio's **restaurants** can be poor value. Notable exceptions include the characterful, mid-priced *Osteria Libertaria*, on the Medici harbourfront at Calata Matteotti 12 (closed Mon), and *Trattoria La Barca*, one street back at Via Guerrazzi 60 (℡0565.918.036; closed Wed), considered the best restaurant in town. For a real treat, book well ahead at the expensive terrace restaurant of the *Park-Hotel Napoleone* at San Martino (℡0565.918.502; closed in winter); the classic Tuscan cuisine is exquisite, but the multilingual maître d's service really stands out as something special. Back in town, upmarket *Caffè Roma* fronts the harbour, a bright, lively place open all day for coffee and snacks, and then during the evening as a **bar**.

Listings

Bike, scooter, car and boat rental Main agencies are all near the quay: TWN, Viale Elba 32 ℡0565.914.666; BW's, Via Manganaro 15 ℡0565.930.491, @www.bwsplanet.com; Rent Chiappi, Piazza Citi 5 ℡0565.930.681, @www.rentchiappi.it; and Tesi (Maggiore/Budget), Calata Italia 8 ℡0565.930.222, @tesi@elbalink.it. Cicli Brandi, Via Carducci 33 ℡0565.914.128, are mountain-bike specialists. From any of these outlets, the per-day rate for a small car is around €40–60; a 50cc scooter €35; a mountain-bike €15, and an ordinary bike €9. A 5m boat (35–40hp) costs €70–100 a day (no licence needed).
Internet access Joinelba, Via Concia di Terra 40 ℡0565.919.178, @www.joinelba.com.
Left luggage In the bus station (daily 8am–8pm;

€1.30 per piece per day).
Markets Behind Piazza Cavour is the covered food market (Mon–Sat 7am–1pm & 4–8pm, Sun 7am–1pm) which, aside from fruit and veg, has bottles of Elba's acclaimed DOC wines, *rosso* and *bianco*. The weekly Friday market in Piazza della Repubblica focuses on clothes and bric-a-brac.
Parking The car park opposite the bus station on Viale Elba is free. Cars are banned from the old quarter during the summer.
Pharmacy Centrale, Via Cavour 20 ℡0565.914.026.
Post office Piazza della Repubblica in the old town (Mon–Fri 8.15am–7pm, Sat 8.15am–12.30pm).

Eastern Elba

Eastern Elba comprises two tongues of land, each of them dominated by mountain ridges. The northeast corner was formerly mining country, as the reddish rocks bear testament, but is these days given over entirely to beach tourism. The main road east from Portoferraio heads through **Rio nell'Elba**, once the major mining town of the east, to **RIO MARINA**. Tourism and ferry links have replaced iron ore as the town's principal source of revenue; if you're stuck here, the one **hotel** is the *Rio*, Via Palestro 31 (℡0565.924.225, @hotel-rio@elba2000.it; ❼), next to the public gardens overlooking the port. Some boats stop at picturesque **CAVO**, 9km north of Rio Marina; its clutch of **hotels** includes the three-star *Maristella* on the water (℡0565.949.859, @www.hotelmaristella.com; ❺; April–Sept), and one of its pleasantest **restaurants** is mid-priced *La Scogliera*, with tables overlooking the beach.

Porto Azzurro and Capoliveri

The resort of **PORTO AZZURRO** was heavily fortified by Philip III of Spain in 1603. Today his fortress is the island's prison; a walk round the outer ramparts brings you to a shop selling crafts made by the inmates. The town's small, pretty old quarter, closed to traffic, centres on bustling **Via d'Alarcon**. Choice of the lacklustre **hotels** is *Belmare*, Banchina IV Novembre 21 (℡0564.95.012, ✉belmare@elbalink.it; ➎). The *Arrighi* **campsite** north of town at Barbarossa (℡0565.95.568, ℻0565.957.822; April–Nov) gives straight onto the beach. Busy town **restaurants** serve Identikit pasta-based nosh, including the friendly *Lo Scoglio*, Via Cavour 15 (closed Wed in winter). *All'Arco Antico* on Via d'Alarcon has snacks and pizzas from €4. Plenty of places rent **bikes**, boats and scooters, including BW's, Via Provinciale 10 (℡0565.920.196, ⊛www.bwsracing.it). Motorboats shuttle across the bay to the sandy beach at **Naregno**.

CAPOLIVERI, 3.5km southwest of Porto Azzurro and overlooked by Monte Calamita, is the best of the towns on Elba's eastern fringe, a prosperous inland centre whose close-knit lanes have made few concessions to tourism. Capoliveri makes an ideal base for visits south to the fine **beaches** at Morcone, Pareti and Innamorata, but **accommodation** is limited: try at the comfortable two-star *Villa Miramare* in Pareti (℡0565.968.673, ℻0565.939.097; ➍). The *Sugar Reef* **bar** and music venue 1km south of Capoliveri at La Trappola (℡338.917.9026, ⊛www.sugar-reef.com) feeds the town's nightlife image, with dance parties all summer long (daily 11pm–5am). In summer, municipal minibuses run hourly between Capoliveri and nearby beach towns until 1am.

Western Elba

The main road west from Portoferraio heads to prim **MARCIANA MARINA**, whose traffic-filled promenade of bars, restaurants and trinket shops does nothing to lure you into staying. You can **rent a bike** or scooter for a trip inland from TWN, Via Dussol 45 (℡0565.997.027), and access the **Internet** at Foto Berti, Via Cavour 5 (daily 9am–1pm, 5–8pm & 9–11.30pm). Aquavision (℡328.709.5470) operates trips on the **M/N Nautilus**, which has glass panels below the waterline (daily: April–Oct 3.30pm; also July to mid-Sept 2.30pm & 5pm; €15 low season, €20 high season; takes 2hr).

A winding road heads south for 5km into the hills to **POGGIO**, a village renowned for its mineral water and its tight medieval centre, with decorated doorways and a patchwork of cheerful gardens. One of Elba's leading **restaurants**, *Da Publius*, Piazza XX Settembre 13 (℡0565.99.208; closed Mon), has great views and steep prices for its classic Elban cooking (including *cacciucco* and wild boar with mushrooms). The nearby *Monte Capanne*, Via Pini 1 (℡ & ℻ 0565.99.083), serves more affordable food in a lovely, peaceful setting and doubles up as Poggio's **hotel** (➌).

Marciana and Monte Capanne

The high, isolated village of **MARCIANA**, up 4km of switchbacks from Poggio, is the oldest settlement on Elba. It's the most alluring place on the island, perfectly located between great beaches and the mountainous interior. Its steep **old quarter** is a delight, narrow alleys, arches, belvederes and stone stairs festooned with flowers and climbing plants that culminate at the twelfth-century **Fortezza Pisano** (closed to the public, but with great views). The only **accommodation** options are a handful of rooms and apartments available at *Bar La Porta*, Piazza Fuor di Porta (℡0565.901.275; closed Wed). The best **restaurant** is the award-winning *Osteria del Noce*, high up at Via Della Madonna 19 (℡0565.901.284; closed Tues except in summer), with excellent mid-priced food and a terrace with spectacular views. Way up beside the Fortezza at Via del Pretorio 64 is little *Monilli*, a bar and paninoteca open daily until 2am, perched over a wooded hillside.

Various **walking** trails head out from Marciana, both up to Monte Capanne and on scenic, quiet routes down to the coast. Before setting off, you should pick up the local *Comunità Montana* **map** from the Portoferraio tourist office, and make sure you have water and a sunhat.

Trail #1 is a circular route starting from the southern end of the village, which passes the fifteenth-century **Oratorio di San Cerbone** (1hr) and continues beyond the junction with trail #6 and up to the summit of the mountain (where you could take the *cabinovia* down again); you then retrace your steps and take trail #6 west across open country to La Stretta, then skirt Monte Giove back to Marciana (total 8.5km; 4hr 30min).

A different route heads uphill west of Marciana – the path begins at the *Osteria del Noce* – for about 30min to the **Santuario della Madonna del Monte**, the island's most celebrated shrine, a Renaissance church built to house a stone mysteriously painted with an image of the Virgin. From the church, trail #3 again skirts round Monte Giove to La Stretta, then continues jigging on switchbacks west and down through fragrant woodland and scrub to hit the coast at **Chiessi** (total 12km; 6hr).

The main draw of Marciana is 0.5km south of the village – the base-station of a **cabinovia** (cable car) that climbs 650m to the summit of **Monte Capanne** (1018m), Elba's highest point. "Cable car" is a misnomer: it's a series of small exposed cages, each of which is big enough for two people to stand up in, hooked onto a continually running cable: the open-air ride might give you the flutters. It runs in summer only (June–Sept daily 10am–12.15pm & 2.30–6pm; Oct–May 10am–12.15pm & 2.30–5.30pm; €12 return; takes 20min), lifting you slowly above the wooded hills and eventually above the tree line to a levelled platform with a café. From here, it's a short scramble to the summit, from where the views are suitably stupendous. Another local attraction is one of Tuscany's very few **vegetarian restaurants**, *Vegetariano alla Cabinovia* (☎0565.901.029; closed in winter), by a brook in the woods alongside the *cabinovia* base-station, which boasts an affordable menu of falafel and tabbouleh, lentils, seitan and tofu, wholewheat pasta and organic wine.

The western coast and Marina di Campo

The spread-out village of **SANT'ANDREA**, 6km west of Marciana, just off the coast road, is one of Elba's trendiest retreats; divers are drawn here by the crystal-clear seas. **Hotels** are not expensive, most of them discreetly set amid near-tropical vegetation; just above the beach is the eco-friendly *Ilio* (☎0565.908.018, ⓦwww.ilio.it; ❺), which uses all biodegradable materials and has a pleasant, helpful manager. A little west, the road hugs the coast for a lonely, scenic drive round to **CHIESSI** and **POMONTE**, each with a small stony beach, beautifully clear water and little commercialism. By **FETOVAIA** on the southwestern tip of the island you're back to beach development, but the sandy beach is superb – and a big car park prevents some of the chaos of other Elban resorts. About 2km east of Fetovaia is a stretch of **nudist** beach.

MARINA DI CAMPO was the first resort on Elba and is now the largest. The huge white **beach** and clean water are what make the place suffocatingly popular. There's also all the tourist frippery and nightlife you'd expect in any major seaside centre, as well as a **tourist office**, Piazza dei Granatieri (Mon–Wed, Fri & Sat 8am–8pm; ☎0565.977.969). Internet Planet on Via Carducci has **Internet** access (daily 10am–midnight). The moderately priced **restaurant** *L'Aragosta*, Via Bologna 3 (closed winter), has fresh fish served daily, while *Il Gazebo*, Piazzetta Torino, is a **bar** specializing in wholewheat panini, pizzas, *calzoni* and hot-dogs.

Capraia

CAPRAIA, 30km northwest of Elba, is lovely and largely unspoilt. Its former use as a penal colony (up until 1996) ensured that the terrain remained largely untouched, and the local council has since backed environmental protection. The scrubby, almost tree-less island has a knobbly spine of 400m hills, with the eastern slope shallow and riven with valleys, and the western coast featuring cliffs rising almost sheer from the sea. Most people come for the excellent deep-sea **diving**. Toremar **ferries** run from Livorno (at least 1 daily; takes 2hr 30min; €10) – their pre-sunrise service (Thurs 4.50am summer only) is a memorable way to make the crossing. You can also make the crossing with Linee di Navigazione Arcipelago Toscano from Porto Azzurro (☎0565 .921.009, ⓦwww.elbacrociere.com) or from Portoferraio (☎0565.914.797).

From the harbour to the village of **CAPRAIA ISOLA**, overlooked by the **Fortezza di San Giorgio**, is a gentle walk. The Pro Loco **tourist office** is on Via Assunzione (☎0586.905.138). The Cooperativa Parco Naturale, Via Assunzione 42 (☎0586.905.071, ⓔagparco@tin.it), **rents boats** – motorized dinghies (€100) and kayaks (€30). The Capraia Diving Service (☎0586.905.137, ⓦwww.capraiadiving.it) on Via Assunzione has equipment for rent. The main **hotel** is the comfortable four-star *Il Saracino*, Via L. Cibo 40 (☎0586.905.018, ⓕ0586.905.062; ❽), although there's also the small, attractive *Pensione Da Beppone* near the water (☎0586.905.001, ⓕ0586.905.842; ❹), numerous private rooms, and the **campsite** *Le Sughere* (☎ & ⓕ0586.905.066; May–Sept) behind the church. One of the best **restaurants** is the moderately-priced *Vecchio Scorfano*, Via Assunzione 44 (closed winter). A good, well-signposted **walk** leads up from the village into the uninhabited interior, passing springs and – on a branch trail – an isolated tarn known as **Lo Stagnone**. The path leads up to **Il Semaforo**, just below the summit of Monte Arpagna (410m), where a ravine between peaks gives a stunning view westwards across open water to Corsica. The rough trail heads steeply down to a lighthouse on the rugged western coast. Alongside a watchtower on the southernmost tip of land is the narrow inlet of **Cala Rossa** – a spectacular place to swim, in sparkling clear water beneath cliffs of fiery red.

The Maremma coast

The **Maremma** is a loose term derived from *maríttima* that refers to the coastal strip and inland hills of the Provincia di Grosseto, Tuscany's southernmost province. This was the northern heartland of the Etruscans but was depopulated in the Middle Ages as wars disrupted the drainage schemes and allowed malarial swamps to build up behind the dunes. The area became almost synonymous with disease, and nineteenth-century guides advised strongly against a visit – even though *butteri* cowboys roamed freely then, as now, taking care of the region's half-feral horses and its celebrated white cattle. Today, the provincial capital of **Grosseto** remains pretty uninspiring, though there are some patches of scenery – notably the **Monti dell'Uccellina**, protected in the **Parco Naturale della Maremma**, and the wooded peninsula of **Monte Argentario**.

Grosseto and around

Until the mid-nineteenth century, **GROSSETO** was a malaria-ridden back-water. The draining of the marshes, however, which was finally effected under Mussolini, has transformed it into a provincial capital for the Maremma. Grosseto was rebuilt after the war with a rash of dreary condominiums and is deservedly undervisited, though you may well find yourself passing through.

Piazza Dante, at the heart of the old town, has a quirky statue showing Leopoldo II protecting Mother Maremma and crushing the serpent malaria under his foot. The adjacent **Duomo** was started in 1294 but virtually nothing is left to suggest antiquity: the white-and-pink marble facade is a product of the nineteenth century, while the interior has suffered repeated modifications. Its finest artworks are on display in the **Museo Archeologico**, Piazza Baccarini 3 (Tues–Sun: May–Oct 10am–1pm & 5–8pm; Nov–April 9am–1pm & 4–6pm; Nov–Feb closed Tues–Fri afternoons; €5); most interest is in rooms 24–34, the **Museo d'Arte Sacra**, with a handful of good Sienese paintings, notably Sassetta's *Madonna of the Cherries* and a Byzantine *Last Judgement* by Guido da Siena. **San Francesco**, just north of the museum, has a few patches of fresco and an early crucifix by Duccio; from here you can walk round the **walls**, a trip of about forty minutes and one of the more rewarding things Grosseto has to offer.

Most mainline **trains** on the Pisa–Rome coastal line stop in Grosseto, where you can change for Siena or Orbetello. The **tourist office** is inconveniently situated out of town at Via Monterosa 206 (Mon–Fri 8.30am–2.30pm & 3–6pm, Sat 8.30am–12.30pm; ☎0564.462.611, ⓦwww.grosseto.turismo .toscana.it); they have information on the whole province, which includes Massa Maríttima (see p.575) and Pitigliano (see p.587). To reach the **old town**, head up Via Roma from the station past a Fascist-era post office and piazza. Central **hotels** include the *Appennino*, Viale Mameli 1 (☎0564.23.009, Ⓕ0564.416.134; ❷).

The Monti dell'Uccellina

The hills and coastline of the Monti dell'Uccellina are protected as the **Parco Naturale Regionale della Maremma**, set to be upgraded to a Parco Nazionale – recognition for an area that, it is claimed, is the last virgin coastal landscape on the Italian peninsula, 12km south of Grosseto. This breathtaking piece of countryside combines cliffs, coastal marsh, *macchia*, forest-covered hills, pristine beaches and some of the most beautiful stands of umbrella pines in the country. It is a microcosm of all that's best in the Maremma, devoid of the bars, marinas, hotels, roads and half-finished houses that have destroyed much of the Italian littoral. There is no public road access – all drivers should park in **ALBERESE** (scene, in August, of a *butteri* rodeo), near the Visitors' Centre on Via del Fante (☎0564.407.098, ⓔparcomar@gol.grosseto.it). RAMA city **buses** #15, #16 and #17 run irregularly from Grosseto station to Alberese (Mon–Sat); otherwise, take a taxi (€15).

Admission to the park (daily: July to Sept 7.30am–dusk, rest of year 9am–dusk; €6) secures a basic **map** and a place on an hourly bus that runs 10km into the hills, dropping you at the trailhead **Pratini**. From Pratini, you're left to your own devices, or you can book ahead for a place on a three- or five-hour **guided walk** (summer only; tour in English Friday 4.30pm; €8). Most people head straight onto the *Strada degli Olivi*, which leads to the superb **beach**, an idyllic curving bay backed by cliffs and wooded hills. The circular **Trail A1** (*San Rabano*; 6km; 5hr) climbs a ridge and passes the ivy-covered eleventh-century ruined abbey of San Rabano. The last return buses from Pratini or Alberese are around 6.30pm in summer, earlier in winter. For **horse riding**, **canoeing** or **bike rental** in the park contact Il Rialto Centro Turismo Equestre (☎0565.407.102, ⓔilrialto@katamail.com).

Monte Argentario

The high, rocky terrain of **Monte Argentario** (ⓦwww.monteargentario.it), 37km south of Grosseto, is as close to wilderness as southern Tuscany comes. The interior is mountainous, reaching 635m at its highest point, and the coast is sectioned dramatically into headlands, bays and shingle beaches. Much of the area is still uninhabited scrub and woodland, badly prone to forest fires but still excellent walking country.

Long ago, Monte Argentario was an island. Over several thousand years, inshore currents built up two narrow sand spits (*tomboli*) between the mountain and the mainland, creating a lagoon between them. The ancient town of **Orbetello** occupied a peninsula sticking out into the lagoon; then the Romans built a causeway to link Orbetello to the Argentario, forming a third spit of land and dividing the lagoon in two. Orbetello's strange location is the most exciting thing about it, and on summer weekends the roads over the northern Tombolo della Giannella sandbar and through Orbetello become bottlenecks as tourists pile in to resorts such as **Porto Ercole**.

Orbetello and around

ORBETELLO is an unassuming place, graced with palm trees, the pastel-coloured remnants of its Spanish walls, and a lively passeggiata each evening along its main street, Corso Italia. It was probably Etruria's leading port, though little evidence of an ancient past remains: the sixteenth-century Spanish fortifications are the town's conspicuous feature. The **train station** is 4km east at Orbetello Scalo. **Buses** originating in Rome or Grosseto run from Orbetello station to the bus stops near the **tourist office** at Piazza della Repubblica 1 (Mon–Sat 10am–12.30pm & 4.30–8.30pm; ☎0564.860.447, ⓔinfo@proloco-orbetello.it). Choice **hotel** is the simple, friendly and very central *Piccolo Parigi*, Corso Italia 169 (☎0564.867.233, ⒻFAX0564.867.211; ❸). Most of the area's thirteen **campsites** are on and around the lagoon; plump for the *Feniglia* (☎0564.831.090, ⓦwww.emmeti.it/campingfeniglia; open all year), the only site on the southern Tombolo di Feniglia. One of Orbetello's best fish **restaurants** is the moderately priced *Osteria il Nocchino* just behind Piazza della Repubblica on Via Furio Lenzi (☎0564.860.329; open only at weekends in winter), otherwise there is plenty of choice on and around the main Corso Italia.

Roads from Orbetello head north and south around the base of Monte Argentario. On the south side is intimate **PORTO ERCOLE**, with an attractive old quarter and a fishing-village atmosphere. Though founded by the Romans, its chief historical monuments are two **Spanish fortresses**, facing each other across the harbour. At the entrance to the old town, a plaque on the stone gate commemorates the painter **Caravaggio**, who in 1610 keeled over with sunstroke on a beach nearby and died of a fever; he was buried in the parish church of Sant'Erasmo. From the village, you can easily **walk** across the Tombolo di Feniglia, which is barred to traffic and is a prime spot for bird-watching over the lagoon. Finest **restaurant** for fish and seafood is the classy *Gambero Rosso*, Lungomare Andrea Doria (☎0564.832.650; closed Wed).

The Tarot Garden

Unbroken sand stretches down the coast east of Orbetello, with a lagoon and nature reserve at **Lago di Burano** and plenty of opportunities for camping in the dunes. The gently shelving seabed makes for good swimming.

Bang on the Lazio border 20km east of Orbetello, in a landscape of dust, scrub and clammy heat, is one of the oddest and most engaging works of modern art in the region. The **Giardino dei Tarocchi**, or Tarot Garden, is the lifelong dream of Niki de St-Phalle, wife of the late Swiss artist Jean Tinguely. Since 1978, St-Phalle has been devoting herself to constructing this physical interpretation of the tarot deck – chunky, brightly coloured cartoon figures of the **Devil**, the **Guardian Angel**, the **Hanged Man** and others loom well above the treetops, arranged around a curvaceous, arcaded **courtyard** tiled in shards of mirror and shimmering, multi-coloured plastic. The symbolism of the garden may be obscure, but kids of all ages will love it. Don't let its isolation or its priciness put you off: you might well find this fiery-loined Devil speaking to you more clearly from his remote hillside than Michelangelo's "must-see" *David* in the heart of Florence ever could. The garden has limited **opening hours** (mid-May to Oct Mon–Sat 2.30–7.30pm; €10.50; Nov–May first Sat of month 9am–1pm; free ℡0564.895.122). There's no public **transport**, but the sculptures are visible about 1km north of the main Livorno–Rome "Via Aurelia" highway, near the village of Pescia Fiorentina. The nearest **train station** is Chiarone, 4km south – a **taxi** from here will save on the €25 fare you're likely to run up from Orbetello.

Siena and around

SIENA is the perfect antidote to Florence, a unified, modern city at ease with its medieval aspect, ambience and traditions – indeed, exultant about them. It's a place not easily read by outsiders, and to get anything meaningful from a visit you'll need to stay at least one night; too many visitors breeze through on a day-trip.

Self-contained and still part-rural behind its medieval walls, Siena's great attraction is its cityscape, a majestic Gothic ensemble that could be enjoyed without venturing into a single museum. The physical and spiritual heart of the city is the great scallop-shaped piazza **il Campo**, loveliest of all Italian squares and scene of the thrilling **Palio** bareback horse-race. Siena's **Duomo** and **Palazzo Pubblico** are two of the purest examples of Italian Gothic architecture, and the best of the city's paintings – collected in the **Museo Civico** and **Pinacoteca Nazionale** – are in the same tradition; the finest example of Sienese Gothic is Duccio's *Maestà*, on show in the outstanding **Museo dell'Opera del Duomo**. More frescoes fill the halls of **Santa Maria della Scala**, the city's hospital for over 900 years and now its premier exhibition space.

For a hundred years or so, in the twelfth and thirteenth centuries, Siena was one of the major cities of Europe. Virtually the size of Paris, it controlled most of southern Tuscany and its wool industry, dominated the trade routes between France and Rome, and maintained Italy's richest pre-Medici banks. This era reached an apotheosis with the defeat of a much superior Florentine army at the battle of **Montaperti** in 1260. Although the result was reversed permanently nine years later, Siena embarked on an unrivalled urban development under the guidance of its mercantile governors, the **Council of Nine**. From 1287 to 1355 the city underwrote the completion of its cathedral and then the **Campo** and its exuberant **Palazzo Pubblico**. The prosperity came to an abrupt halt with the **Black Death**, which reached Siena in May 1348; by October, two-thirds of the 100,000 population had died. The city never fully recovered (the population today is 60,000) and its politics, always factional, descended into chaos. In 1557 Philip II gave up Siena to **Cosimo de' Medici** in lieu of war services, and the city subsequently became part of Cosimo's Grand Duchy of Tuscany, and fell into decline. The lack of subsequent development explains Siena's astonishing state of preservation: little was built and still less demolished. Since World War II, Siena has again become prosperous, owing partly to **tourism** and partly to the resurgence of the **Monte dei Paschi di Siena**. This bank, founded in Siena in 1472 and currently the city's largest employer, is one of the major players in Italian finance. It today sponsors much of Siena's cultural life, co-existing, apparently easily, with one of Italy's strongest left-wing councils.

The most popular trip from Siena is northwest to the picturesque multi-towered village of **San Gimignano**. Far fewer people take the trouble to sample the ancient Etruscan town of **Volterra**, a highly rewarding stop en route west from Siena to Pisa.

Arrival and information

Siena's **train station** is 2km northeast of town, down in the valley. It has a counter selling city bus tickets (Mon–Sat 5.50am–7.30pm; €0.75). To get into town, cross the road and take just about any city **bus** heading left (#3, #9 to Tozzi; #4, #7, #8, #14, #17, #77 to Garibaldi/Sale; #10 to Gramsci), all of which drop off about 100m north of Piazza Matteotti on the northern edge of the centre. Most **intercity buses** arrive on Viale Tozzi, the road running alongside Piazza Gramsci, or at La Lizza nearby, but note that many now avoid the centre and terminate at the train station instead. Coming from Florence **by train**, you may need to change at Empoli (takes 1hr 45min); **by bus**, there are hourly TRA-IN or SITA expresses (takes 1hr 15min). The **tourist office** is at no. 56 on the Campo (Mon–Sat 8.30am–7.30pm, Sun 9am–3pm; T0577.280.551, W www.terresiena.it).

Accommodation

Finding **accommodation** is barely less of a struggle than in Florence. An alternative to contacting hotels directly is to let **Siena Hotels Promotion** do the work for you – phone, fax or email bookings through them for any of the city's thirty-odd hotels are free (T0577.288.084, W www.hotelsiena.com). If you arrive without a reservation, go to their booth on Piazza Madre Teresa di Calcutta in front of San Domenico (Mon–Sat 9am–8pm; winter closes 7pm), where over-the-counter bookings for the same night cost €1.55. **Vacanze**

Senesi offers a similar service, based within the Parcheggio Il Campo parking garage at Via Fontanella 9 (Mon–Fri 9am–1pm & 3–7pm, Sat 9am–1pm; ☏0577.45.900, ⓦwww.vacanzesenesi.it). Note that hotels are booked solid at **Palio** time (early July and mid-Aug).

Hotels

Bernini Via della Sapienza 15 ☏0577.289.047, ⓦwww.albergobernini.com. Friendly, well-situated one-star hotel near San Domenico, with good-value shared-bath rooms. Midnight curfew. ❺

Cannon d'Oro Via Montanini 28 ☏0577.44.321, ⓔcannondoro@libero.it. A stylish, friendly and well-maintained thirty-room two-star hotel tucked down an alleyway east of Piazza Matteotti. ❺

Centrale Via C Angioleri 26 ☏0577.280.379, ⓕ0577.42.152. A block north of the Campo, up on the third floor. Friendly staff, good location, but no lift. ❹

Certosa di Maggiano Via Certosa 82 ☏0577.288.180, ⓦwww.certosadimaggiano.com. A former monastery in the countryside 1km south-east of Siena that offers luxurious comfort in its few, tasteful rooms and an alluring retreat from worldly affairs in its library, cloister and tranquil terrace. ❾

Chiusarelli Viale Curtatone 15 ☏0577.280.562, ⓦwww.chiusarelli.com. Pleasant old three-star hotel with fifty airy rooms, a garden and private parking steps from Piazza Matteotti. ❻

Duomo Via Stalloreggi 38 ☏0577.289.088, ⓦwww.hotelduomo.it. Pleasant three-star, located in a residential area. Rooms are unremarkable, other than those with rooftop views of the Duomo. Free parking at Parcheggio Il Campo. ❼

Garibaldi Via Duprè 18 ☏0577.284.204. Seven no-nonsense rooms above a quality low-price trat-toria just south of the Campo. Midnight curfew. ❹

Palazzo Ravizza Pian dei Mantellini 34 ☏0577.280.462, ⓦwww.palazzoravizza.it. Genteel old-style hotel in a pleasant backwater of town, also with a quality restaurant and charming little garden for afternoon tea. Free parking. ❾

La Perla Via delle Terme 25 ☏0577.47.144. Regular one-star pensione with all en-suite rooms, in a very central location overlooking Piazza Indipendenza, just north of the Campo. Curfew 1am. ❸

Piccolo Hotel Etruria Via delle Donzelle 3 ☏0577.288.088, ⓔetruria@tin.it. Small, central two-star, with some pokey rooms and a 12.30am curfew, but with parking nearby. Beats the *Tre Donzelle* next door. ❹

Piccolo Hotel Il Palio Piazza del Sale 19 ☏0577 .281.131, ⓕ0577.281.142. Perfectly located for bus arrivals (right near all the bus stops), but 200m north of the centre, with clean, good-sized rooms and extremely friendly, helpful staff. ❺

Santa Caterina Via E.S. Piccolomini 7 ☏0577.221.105, ⓦwww.hscsiena.it. A three-star hotel ten minutes' walk southeast of the Campo, with the benefit of air-conditioning and private parking. ❼

Villa Scacciapensieri Via di Scacciapensieri 10 ☏0577.41.441, ⓦwww.villascacciapensieri.it. Glorious country villa 3km north of Siena, with every luxury including a pool. ❾

Hostel and campsite

Campeggio Siena Colleverde Strada di Scacciapensieri 47 ☏0577.280.044, ⓕ0577.333.298. Secure, well-maintained campsite 2km north of town (bus #3 or #8), with a pool. Mid-March to mid-Nov.

Ostello Guidoriccio Via Fiorentina 89, Stellino ☏0577.52.212. Non-HI 111-bed hostel 2km northwest of the centre; take bus #3, #10 or #15 from Piazza Matteotti or, if you're coming from Florence, ask the bus driver to let you off at "Lo Stellino" (just after the Siena city sign). Curfew 11pm. €14.60 with breakfast.

The City

Everything is easily walkable from the great central square of the **Campo**, which is built at the intersection of a configuration of hills that looks, on the map, like an upside-down Y. Each arm of the Y counts as one of the city's *terzi*, or thirds, and each has its principal thoroughfare, leading out from the Campo on elevated ridges: humdrum **Banchi di Sotto** in the Terzo di San Martino on the southeast; bustling, shop-lined **Via di Città** in the Terzo di Città on the southwest; and elegant **Banchi di Sopra** in the Terzo di Camollia on the north. The central core of alleys – almost entirely medieval in plan and appearance, and closed to traffic – can get a little disorienting, and it's surprisingly easy to lose your fix on the Campo, masked as it is by high buildings. The huge **Duomo** (and attendant museums, including the unmissable **Museo dell'Opera del Duomo** and **Santa Maria della Scala**) sits on a hill above Via di Città, looking across the deep Fontebranda valley north to the equally huge church of **San Domenico** occupying its own hill; getting from one to the other involves a lot of stairs, or a big semi-circular detour in order to stay on a level.

The Campo

The Campo is the centre of Siena in every sense: the main streets lead into it, the Palio is held around its perimeter, and in the evenings it is the natural place to gravitate towards, for visitors and residents alike. Don't spurn the chance to soak up the atmosphere last thing at night, when the amphitheatre curve of the piazza throws the low hum of café conversation around in an invisible spiral of sound, drowned out in the daytime. Four hundred years ago, Montaigne described it as the most beautiful square in the world; you'd find it hard to dispute his words.

When the Council of Nine were planning the piazza in 1293, this old marketplace, which lay at the convergence of the city quarters but was a part of none, was the only possible site. The piazza, completed in 1349, was created in nine segments in honour of the council. It was, from the start, a focus of city life, the scene of executions, bullfights, communal boxing matches, and, of course, the Palio. St Bernardino preached here, holding before him the monogram of Christ's name in Greek ("IHS"), which the council placed on the facade of the Palazzo Pubblico, alongside the city's she-wolf symbol – a reference to Siena's legendary foundation by Senius, son of Remus.

At the highest point of the Campo the Renaissance makes a fleeting appearance with the **Fonte Gaia** (Gay Fountain), designed and carved by Jacopo della Quercia in the early fifteenth century but now replaced by a poor nineteenth-century reproduction. The badly eroded original has been newly restored for display in Santa Maria della Scala.

The Museo Civico

The Palazzo Pubblico (also known as Palazzo Comunale), with its 97m bell-tower, the Torre del Mangia, is the focus of the Campo, occupying virtually its entire south side. Its three-part windows pleased the council so much that they ordered their emulation on all other buildings on the square. The palazzo is still in use as Siena's town hall, but its principal rooms have been converted into the **Museo Civico** (daily: July & Aug 10am–11pm; March–Oct 10am–7pm; Nov–Feb 10am–5.30pm; ⓦwww.comune.siena.it/museocivico) – a series of grand halls frescoed with themes integral to the secular life of the medieval city. If you have time or inclination for only one of Siena's museums, make it this one. **Admission** to the Museo Civico is €6.50, to the Torre del Mangia €5.50. A joint ticket for them both is €9.50 or for multi-entry tickets see box opposite.

At the top of the stairs, you're directed through a disappointing five-room picture gallery to the **Sala del Risorgimento**, painted with nineteenth-century scenes of Vittorio Emanuele, first king of Italy. Across the corridor is a series of frescoed rooms, the **Sala di Balìa** (or dei Priori; room 10), the **Anticamera del Concistoro**, and the grand **Sala del Concistoro**. Room 13, the **Vestibolo**, holds a gilded bronze of the *She-Wolf suckling Romulus and Remus* (1429), an allusion to Siena's mythical founding. Alongside is the **Anticappella**, decorated between 1407 and 1414 by Taddeo di Bartolo. Behind a majestic wrought-iron screen by Jacopo della Quercia is the **Cappella del Consiglio**, also frescoed by di Bartolo and holding an exceptional altarpiece by Sodoma and exquisite inlaid choir-stalls.

All these are little more than a warm-up for room 16, the great **Sala del Mappamondo**. Taking its name from the now scarcely visible frescoed cosmology – a circular map by Lorenzetti – the room was used for several centuries as the city's law court, and contains one of the greatest of all Italian frescoes. Simone Martini's fabulous *Maestà* (Virgin in Majesty) is a painting of almost translucent colour, painted in 1315 when Martini was thirty. The richly decorative style is archetypal Sienese Gothic and Martini's great innovation was the use of a canopy and a frieze of medallions to frame and organize the figures – lending a sense of space and hint of perspective that suggest a knowledge of Giotto's work. The fresco on the opposite wall, the *Equestrian Portrait of Guidoriccio da Fogliano*, is a motif for medieval chivalric Siena and was, until recently, also credited to Martini. Art historians, however, have long puzzled over the anachronistic castles, which are of a much later style than the painting's signed date of 1328. A number of historians – led by the American Gordon Moran (whom the city council accused of being a CIA agent and for a while banned from the building) – interpret the *Guidoriccio* as a sixteenth-century fake, while others maintain that it is a genuine Martini overpainted by subsequent restorers. The newly revealed fresco below the portrait, of two figures in front of a castle, is meanwhile variously attributed to Martini, Duccio and Pietro Lorenzetti.

The adjacent **Sala della Pace** holds Ambrogio Lorenzetti's *Allegories of Good and Bad Government*, frescoes commissioned in 1338 to remind the councillors of their duties. This is one of Europe's most important cycles of medieval secular

SIENA

N

◄ Chianti

◄ Osservanza

◄ Train Station & campsite

◄ Florence

VIA CHIANTIGIANA

VIALE PIETRO TOSELLI

VIA SIMONE MARTINI

RAVACCIANO

VIA DUCCIO DI BONINSEGNA

VIA R. PERUZZI

See Central Siena map for detail

VIALE SARDEGNA

VIA GIUSEPPE MAZZINI

VIALE LIPPO MEMMI

VIA SIMONE MARTINI

Fonte d'Ovile

VIA DOMENICO BECCAFUMI

San Francesco

Oratorio di San Bernardino

VIALE GIUSEPPE MAZZINI

VIA GARIBALDI

VIA GIUSEPPE MAZZINI

Barriera San Lorenzo

TERZO DI CAMOLLIA

Porta Ovile

VIA DEL COMUNE

Santa Maria di Provenzano

VIA R. PIANDIOVILE

VIA DI VALLEROZZI

San Donato

Palazzo Salimbeni

VIA DEL PARADISO

VIA N. PISO

VIALE DON GIOVANNI MINZONI

VIA CAMPANSI

VIA DEI PISPINI

VIA DI CAMOLLIA

PIAZZA DEL SALE

Sant'Andrea

Fonte Nuova

VIA DELLA STUFA SECCA

VIA DEI MONTANINI

VIA DEL PARADISO

PIAZZA GRAMSCI

PIAZZA MATTEOTTI

La Lizza

VIALE TOZZI

VIALE CESARE MACCARI

Stadio Comunale

VIALE RINALDO FRANCI

VIALE DEI MILLE

VIALE CURTATONE

Porta Camollia

Fontegiusta

VIA DI CAMOLLIA

VIALE A. DIAZ

VIA B. PERUZZI

VIA A. SAVO

VIA BLASIO DI MONTLUC

VIA RICASOLI

VIALE VITTORIO EMANUELE I

VIALE V. VENETO

VIALE V.

Fortezza

3

1 2

▲ Arezzo

ACCOMMODATION
Certosa di Maggiano	6
Ostello Guidoriccio	2
Palazzo Ravizza	4
Piccolo Hotel Il Palio	3
Santa Caterina	5
Villa Scacciapensieri	1

0 _____ 200 m

▼ Buonconvento

▼ Autostrada

▼ Autostrada

CENTRAL SIENA

★★ Bus Stops ★★

▲ Piazza Gramsci & La Lizza ▲
▲ Piazza Sale & Via Garibaldi ▲

DRAGO

Stadio Comunale

PIAZZA G. MATTEOTTI

San Donato

1 Palazzo Tantucci

S. Maria delle Nevi

PIAZZA ABBADIA

Palazzo Salimbeni

PIAZZA SALIMBENI

Palazzo Spannocchi

Oratorio delle Suore

Siena Hotels Promotion **2**

PIAZZA MADRE TERESA DI CALCUTTA

3

San Pellegrino

San Cristoforo

Santa Caterina

Palazzo Tolomei

B
4
5

San Domenico

OCA

Fonte Branda

6 PIAZZA INDIPENDENZA

C

Loggia della Mercanzia

i

Fonte Gaia

IL CAMPO

Baptistry

PIAZZA S. GIOVANNI

F

H

Palazzo Pubblico

7

SELVA

Palazzo Arcivescovile

Duomo

PIAZZA JACOPO D. QUERCIA

Museo dell'Opera del Duomo

Palazzo Chigi-Saracini

AQUILA

San Sebastiano

Santa Maria della Scala

PIAZZA DEL DUOMO

I

Palazzo delle Papesse

J

Museo Archeologico

PIAZZA DI POSTIERLA

@

Pinacoteca Nazionale

San Giuseppe

ACCOMMODATION

Bernini	3
Cannon d'Oro	1
Centrale	4
Chiusarelli	2
Duomo	8
Garibaldi	7
La Perla	6
Piccolo Hotel Etruria	5

PIAZZA DELLE DUE PORTE

M

8

L

San Pietro

PANTERA

San Quirico

N

Sant'Ansano

ONDA

TARTUCA

Sant'Agostino

Santa Maria del Carmine

Orto Botanico

▼ Porta San Marco ▼
▼ Porta Tufi ▼

▲ Porta Ovile

San Francesco
PIAZZA S. FRANCESCO

San Pietro a Ovile Ⓐ
V. PROVENZANO
VIA DEL BARONCELLI
VIA PROV. SALVANI
VIA DELLE VERGINI

Oratorio di S. Bernardino

Santa Maria di Provenzano
PIAZZA PROVENZANO SALVANI
VIA DEL FOSSO
GIRAFFA
VIA LUCHERINI

CIVETTA
VIA SALLUSTIO BANDINI
VIA S. VIGILIO
ANGIOLIERI
RINALDINI

San Vigilio

San Giovannino della Staffa
PIAZZA GRASSI
VIA DI VALLEROMICA
LEOCORNO

BANCHI DI SOTTO

Logge del Papa
Palazzo Piccolomini Ⓓ Ⓔ
VIA DEL PORRIONE
San Martino Ⓖ
@
VIA DI PANTANETO

VIA DI VIC D. SCOTTE
VIA DI LUPARELLO
VIA D. SALICOTTO
V. D. FORTUNA
VIA DEL RIALTO

PIAZZA DEL MERCATO
VIA D. MALCONTENTI
VIA DI SALICOTTO
V. D'ARELLO
V. D. CONTRADINO
V. D. SCALELLE
V. D. MANNA
VIA DI PANTANETO

San Giorgio
VIA S. MARTINO
VIA DELL'ORO
VIA PAGLIARESI Ⓚ

San Giacomo
VIA DEL SOLE
VIA PORTA GIUSTIZIA
VIA SAN GIROLAMO
VIA SAN

San Girolamo
VIA DELLE CANTINE
VIA DEI SERVI

Santo Spirito
VIA DEI PISPINI
VIA DELL'OLIVIERA
VICO DEL SASSO
V. FIERA NOVA
VIA FIERA VECCHIA
VIA ROMA

San Raimondo
VIC. DEL RIFUGIO

VIC. D. SAN CLEMENTE

VALDIMONTONE
VIA DI MONTONE

Santa Maria dei Servi

VIA FONTANELLA

VIA BALDASSARE PERUZZI

Ⓑ

N

0   100 m

RESTAURANTS
Al Marsili	I
Le Campane	H
Cane e Gatto	K
La Cina	J
Da Divo	F
Due Porte	M
Gallo Nero	G
Mensa Universitaria	N
Nello	E
Osteria Castelvecchio	L
Osteria Le Logge	D
Renzo	C
La Taverna di Cecco	B
Tullio ai Tre Cristi	A

painting, and includes the first-known panorama in Western art. The walled
city shown is clearly Siena, and the paintings are full of details of medieval life;
their moral theme is expressed in a complex iconography of allegorical virtues

The Siena Palio

The **Siena Palio** (Ⓦwww.comune.siena.it/palioprova) is the most spectacular festival event in Italy: a twice-yearly bareback horse race around the Campo, preceded by days of preparation, medieval pageantry and chicanery. Only ten of the *contrade* can take part in any one race; these are chosen by lot, and their horses and jockeys are also assigned at random. The only rule is that riders cannot interfere with each others' reins. Otherwise, anything goes: each *contrada* has a traditional rival, and ensuring that it loses is as important as winning oneself. Jockeys may be bribed to throw the race or whip a rival or a rival's horse; *contrade* have been known to drug horses and even to ambush a jockey on his way to the race. This is primarily a show for the Sienese; for visitors, in fact, the undercurrent of brutality and the bragging, days-long celebration of victory can be quite a shock.

The race has been held since at least the thirteenth century. Originally it followed a circuit through the town, but since the sixteenth century it has consisted of three laps of the **Campo**, around a track covered with sand and padded with mattresses to minimize injury to riders and horses (though this does occur, and the Palio is a passionate subject for animal-rights supporters). There are normally two Palios a year, with the following build-up:

June 29/August 13: The year's horses are presented in the morning at the town hall and drawn by lot. At 7.15pm the first trial race is held in the Campo.

June 30/August 14: Further trial races at 9am and 7.45pm.

July 1/August 15: Two more trial races at 9am and 7.45pm, followed by a street banquet in each of the *contrade*.

July 2/August 16: The day of the Palio opens with a final trial at 9am. In the early afternoon each *contrada* takes its horse to be blessed in its church (it's a good omen if the horse shits). At around 5pm the town hall bell begins to ring and riders and *comparse* – equerries, ensigns, pages and drummers in medieval costume – proceed to the Campo for a display of flag-twirling and other pageantry. The **race** itself begins at 7.45pm on July 2, or 7pm on August 16, and lasts little more than ninety seconds. There's no PA system to tell you what's going on. At the start (in the northwest corner of the Campo) all the horses except one are penned between two ropes; the free one charges the group from behind, when its rivals least expect it, and the race is on. It's a hectic and violent spectacle; a horse that throws its rider is still eligible to win. The jockeys don't stop at the finishing line but keep going at top speed out of the Campo, pursued by a frenzied mass of supporters. The **palio** – a silk banner – is subsequently presented to the winner.

There are viciously expensive stands for dignitaries and the rich (booked months ahead), but most spectators crowd for free into the centre of the Campo. For the **best view**, you need to have found a position on the inner rail by 2pm (ideally at the start/finish line), but be prepared to stand your ground; people keep pouring in right up until a few minutes before the race, and the swell of the crowd can be quite overwhelming. Toilets, shade and refreshments are minimal, and you won't be able to leave the Campo until at least 8.30pm. **Hotel rooms** are extremely difficult to find, and if you haven't booked, reckon on either staying up all night or travelling in from a neighbouring town. The races are shown live on national TV and repeated endlessly all evening.

The Cinema Moderno on Piazza Tolomei regularly screens a twenty-minute **film** explaining the history and drama of the race, dubbed into various languages (closed for restoration at time of writing).

and figures. *Good Government* (the better-preserved half) is dominated by a throned figure representing the *comune*, flanked by the Virtues and with Faith, Hope and Charity buzzing about his head. To the left, Justice (with Wisdom in the air above) dispenses rewards and punishments, while below her throne Concordia advises the Republic's councillors on their duties. *Bad Government* is ruled by a horned demon, while over the city flies the figure of Fear, whose scroll reads: "Because he looks for his own good in the world, he places justice beneath tyranny. So nobody walks this road without Fear: robbery thrives inside and outside the city gates."

Some fine panel paintings by Lorenzetti's contemporaries are displayed in the **Sala dei Pilastri** to one side. Take time to climb the stairs up to the rear **loggia**, where you can crane your neck to see the current council chambers, also frescoed. From the loggia you can see how abruptly the town ends: buildings rise to the right and left for a few hundred metres along the ridges of the Terzo di San Martino and Terzo di Città, holding a rural valley in their embrace.

Off to the left of the Palazzo Pubblico's internal courtyard, opposite the entrance to the Museo Civico, a door gives access to the 503 steps of the **Torre del Mangia** (daily: July–Sept 10am–11pm; March–June & Oct 10am–7pm; Nov–Jan 10am–4pm; see p.551 for admission), which gives fabulous views across town and countryside. The tower takes its name from its first watchman – a slothful glutton (*mangiaguadagni*) who is commemorated by a statue in the courtyard.

The Loggia della Mercanzia and around

Gaps between buildings behind the Fonte Gaia lead up to the junction-point of the three main streets of Siena, marked by the fifteenth-century **Loggia della Mercanzia** – reluctantly Renaissance, with its Gothic niches for the saints – that was designed as a tribune house for merchants to do their deals. From here, Banchi di Sopra heads north (see p.562), and Via di Città curves west (see p.561). If you follow **Banchi di Sotto** east, you soon reach the **Logge del Papa** with, alongside it, the **Palazzo Piccolomini**, a committed Renaissance building by Bernardo Rossellino, the architect employed at Pienza by the Sienese Pope Pius II (Aeneas Sylvius Piccolomini).

The Duomo and around

Few buildings reveal so much of a city's history and aspirations as Siena's **Duomo**. Complete to virtually its present size around 1215, it was subjected to constant plans for expansion. An initial project, early in the fourteenth century, attempted to double its extent by building a baptistry on the slope below and using this as a foundation for a rebuilt nave, but the work ground to a halt as walls and joints gaped under the pressure. Eventually the chapter hit on a new scheme to reorient the cathedral, using the existing nave as a transept and building a **new nave** out towards the Campo. Again cracks appeared, and then, in 1348, came the Black Death. With the population halved and funds suddenly cut off, the plan was abandoned once and for all. The part-extension still stands at the north end of the square – a vast structure that would have created the largest church in Italy outside Rome. Despite all the abandoned plans, the Duomo is a delight. Its style is an amazing conglomeration of Romanesque and Gothic, delineated by bands of black and white marble. The **facade** was designed in 1284 by Giovanni Pisano, who with his workshop created much of the statuary – philosophers, patriarchs and prophets, now replaced by copies. In the next century the **Campanile** and a Gothic **rose window** were added.

The mosaics in the gables, however, had to wait until the nineteenth century, when money was found to employ Venetian artists.

The use of black and white decoration is continued in the *sgraffito* marble **pavement**, which begins outside the church and takes off into a startling sequence of 56 panels adorning the **interior** (daily: mid-March to Oct 7.30am–7.30pm; rest of year 7.30am–5pm; free). They were completed between 1349 and 1547, with virtually every artist who worked in the city trying his hand at a design. The finest are reckoned to be Beccafumi's *Moses Striking Water from a Rock* and *Sacrifice of Isaac*, just beyond the dome area. However, you're unlikely to see much of the pavement, which is now protected by underfoot boarding for all but a few weeks a year in August, when the full effect is on show (exact dates vary). The zebra-striped interior is equally arresting above floor level, with its line of popes' heads set above the pillars, the same hollow-cheeked scowls cropping up repeatedly. The greatest individual artistic treasure is Nicola Pisano's **pulpit**, with its elaborate high-relief detail of the *Life of Jesus* and *Last Judgement*. In the north transept is a bronze statue by **Donatello** of an emaciated *St John the Baptist*, companion piece to his equally ragged *Mary Magdalene* in Florence, and the Renaissance High Altar is flanked by superb candelabra-carrying angels by Beccafumi.

Midway along the nave, on the left, is the entrance to the stunning **Libreria Piccolomini** (same hours; €1.50, for multi-entry tickets see box on p.550; Ⓦ www.operaduomo.it). The library was commissioned by Francesco Piccolomini (who for ten days was Pius III) to house the books of his uncle Aeneas (Pius II), and to celebrate Aeneas's life in a series of crystal-sharp, brilliantly colourful frescoes by Pinturicchio. The cycle begins to the right of the window, with Aeneas attending the Council of Basel as a secretary, then, in subsequent panels around the walls, presenting himself as envoy to James II of Scotland; being crowned poet laureate by Holy Roman Emperor, Frederick II; representing Frederick on a visit to Pope Eugenius IV; and then – as Bishop of Siena – presiding over the meeting of Frederick III and his bride-to-be Eleanora outside Siena's Porta Camollia. The next panels show Aeneas' being made a cardinal in 1456; being elected pope two years later; and then launching a call for a crusade against the Turks, who had just seized Constantinople. His best-remembered action was the canonization of St Catherine, shown in the penultimate panel. The last fresco shows his death at Ancona.

Santa Maria della Scala

Opposite the Duomo is the **Ospedale di Santa Maria della Scala** (daily: April–Oct 10am–6pm; Nov–March 10.30am–4.30pm; €5.20; for multi-entry tickets see box on p.550; Ⓦ www.santamaria.comune.siena.it). For nine hundred years up until the 1980s, this vast complex served as the city's main hospital. Today its wonderful interiors are being gradually converted into a major centre for art and culture, revealing works that have been inaccessible to all but the most determined of visitors for centuries.

To the left of the ticket desk is the church of **Santissima Annunziata** (also with its own door onto the piazza), blandly remodelled in the fifteenth century but with a bronze statue on the high altar of the *Risen Christ* by Vecchietta, with features so gaunt the veins show through the skin. The other way from the ticket desk leads into a vestibule, the **Cappella del Manto**, with a strikingly beautiful fresco of *St Anne and St Joachim* (1512) – parents of the Virgin – by Beccafumi. Having failed to conceive during twenty years of marriage, the pair are each told by an angel to meet at Jerusalem's Golden Gate and kiss (the scene depicted in the fresco), a moment which symbolizes the Immaculate Conception of their daughter. Adjacent is a long hall, partly used as a bookshop; left off this hall is the vast **Sala del Pellegrinaio**, formerly used as the main hospital ward and entirely frescoed with scenes intended to record the hospital's history and promote the notion of charity toward the sick and orphaned. Their almost entirely secular content was extraordinary at the time they were painted (after 1440 and well before Renaissance ideas took hold). Off to the left, in room 12, is the frescoed **Cappella del Sacro Chiodo** (also known as the Sagrestia Vecchia), which once housed a nail (*chiodo*) from the Passion.

Stairs lead down to the **Oratorio di Santa Caterina della Notte**, an oratory that belonged to one of a number of medieval confraternities that maintained places of worship in the basement vaults of the hospital. It's a dark and strangely spooky place, despite the plethora of decoration – you can easily imagine St Catherine passing nocturnal vigils down here. Also on this level is a series of rooms devoted to documenting the continuing restoration of the original **Fonte Gaia** from the Campo. Stairs lead down again to the oratory and meeting-room of the **Società di Esecutori di Pie Disposizioni** (Executors of Benevolent Legacies), oldest of the lay confraternities, which house a wooden crucifix said to be the one which inspired St Bernadino to become a monk.

In the south wing of the hospital, with its own entrance from the piazza, is the small **Museo Archeologico** (Mon–Sat 9am–2pm; also second & fourth Sun of month 9am–1pm; free), displaying mostly Etruscan artefacts.

The Museo dell'Opera del Duomo

Tucked into a corner of the proposed new nave of the Duomo is the impressive **Museo dell'Opera del Duomo** (daily: mid-March to Sept 9am–7.30pm; Oct 9am–6pm; Nov to mid-March 9am–1.30pm; €5.50; Ⓦwww.operaduomo.it). A tour starts on the top floor: room 1 houses the stark, haunting Byzantine icon known as the **Madonna dagli Occhi Grossi** (of the Big Eyes), the Duomo's original altarpiece, as well as panels depicting St Bernardino preaching in the Campo and Piazza San Francesco. Pass through to the tiny entrance to the **Panorama dal Facciatone** – this leads to steep spiral stairs climbing the walls of the abandoned nave. The sensational view is definitely worth the two-stage climb, but beware that the topmost walkway is narrow and scarily exposed.

Siena's contrade

Siena takes great pride in its division into neighbourhoods, or **contrade**, ancient self-governing wards that formed a patchwork of tribal identity within the fabric of the city and that still flourish today, helping to foster tight bonds of community and contributing to Siena's surprisingly low crime rate. Each of the seventeen *contrade* has its own church, social club and museum. Each, too, has a heraldic animal motif, displayed in a fountain-sculpture in its neighbourhood piazza. Allegiance to one's *contrada* – conferred by birth – remains a strong element of civic life, and identification with the *contrade* is integral to the competition of the Palio. You'll often see groups of *comparse* practising flag-waving and drum-rolling around town.

The *contrade* **museums**, with their displays of Palio trophies, are open to visitors during the build-up to the Palio and at other times by appointment (ask the tourist office to book for you at least a week in advance).

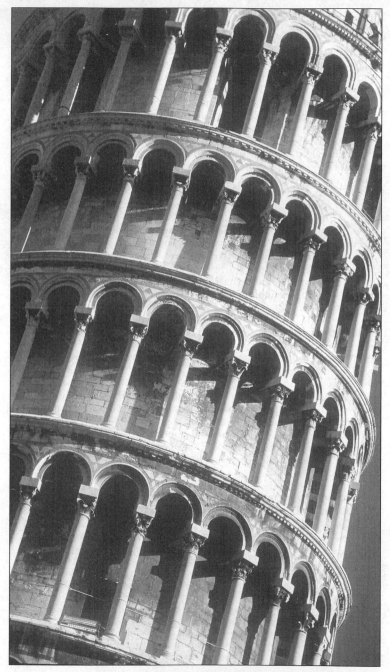

△ The Leaning Tower of Pisa

Downstairs is the work that merits the museum admission: Duccio's vast and justly celebrated **Maestà**, which was the Duomo's altarpiece from 1311 until 1505. This is one of the superlative works of Sienese art, its iconic, Byzantine spirituality accentuated by Duccio's flowing composition, his realization of the space in which action takes place, and a new attention to narrative detail in the panels of the predella and the reverse of the altarpiece which are now displayed to its side. Downstairs again, back on ground-floor level, is the **Galleria delle Statue**, with Donatello's delicate ochre *Madonna and Child* flanked by huge, elongated, twisting figures by Giovanni Pisano. You exit the museum through the atmospheric, late-Baroque church of **San Niccolò in Sasso**, emerging onto Via del Poggio in front of a handy little café.

The Baptistry

The **Baptistry** (daily: mid–March to Sept 9am–7.30pm; Oct 9am–6pm; Nov to mid–March 10am–1pm & 2.30–5pm; €2.50) is unusual in being placed beneath the main body of the Duomo; it is on Piazza San Giovanni, reached by steps which curl around the back of the Duomo. The chapter responsible for the font (1417–30) must have had a good sense of what was happening in Florence at the time, for they commissioned panels by **Ghiberti** (*Baptism of Christ* and *John in Prison*), local sculptor **Jacopo della Quercia** (*The Angel Announcing the Baptist's Birth*), and a superbly dramatic *Herod's Feast* by **Donatello**. The lavishly frescoed walls, largely by Vecchietta, almost overshadow the font.

Along Via di Città

Via di Città is the main thoroughfare linking the Duomo with the Campo, and is lined with shops and plenty of explorable side-alleys, as well as being fronted by some of Siena's finest private palazzi. The **Palazzo Chigi–Saracini** at no. 82 is a Gothic beauty, with its curved facade and rear courtyard. Almost opposite, at Via di Città 126, is the fifteenth-century **Palazzo delle Papesse**, Siena's museum of contemporary art (Tues–Sun noon–7pm; €5). Its four airy floors house excellent temporary exhibits covering anything from architecture to video art, displayed in rooms, some with nineteenth-century frescoes, that still conserve many of their original Renaissance structural and decorative features.

Via di Città continues to a small piazza from where Via San Pietro leads left (south) to the fourteenth-century Palazzo Buonsignori, now the home of the **Pinacoteca Nazionale** (Mon 8.30am–1.30pm, Tues–Sat 8.15am–7.15pm, Sun 8.15am–1.15pm; €4). The collection is a roll of honour of Sienese Gothic painting. The first rooms – two storeys up – hold a host of gilded, thirteenth-century Madonnas; in rooms 7–8, two tiny panels recently attributed to Sassetta – *City by the Sea* and *Castle by a Lake* – are described as the first-ever landscape paintings entirely devoid of religious purpose. Down one flight are Renaissance works by such as Sodoma, whose panel of the *Deposition* (room 32) and frescoes from Sant'Agostino (room 37) show his characteristic drama and delight in costume and landscape. The gallery's topmost storey is devoted to the **Collezione Spannocchi**, a miscellany of Italian, German and Flemish works, including the only painting in the museum by a female artist – *Bernardo Campi Painting Sofonisba's Portrait* by Sofonisba Anguissola, a neat little joke in which the artist excels in her portrait of Campi, but depicts his portrait of her as a flat stereotype.

South of the Pinacoteca Nazionale is the church of **Sant'Agostino** (mid–March to Oct daily 10.30am–1.30pm & 3–5.30pm; €2), with outstanding paintings by Perugino (a *Crucifixion* in the second altar of the south aisle) and Sodoma (*Adoration of the Magi* in the Cappella Piccolomini). A nice walk loops southwest along Via della Cerchia into a studentish area around the church of **Santa Maria del Carmine** (which contains a hermaphrodite *St Michael and the Devil* by Beccafumi). Via del Fosso di San Ansano, north of the Carmine square, is a country lane above terraced vineyards which leads to the Selva (Rhinoceros) *contrada*'s square, from where the stepped Vicolo di San Girolamo leads up to the Duomo.

North of the Campo

Exploring only slightly beyond the touristed central alleys between the Campo and the Duomo reveals much more of the bustling everyday life of the city. North of the Campo, the main street **Banchi di Sopra** leads through the commercial heart of town to **Piazza Matteotti**, home of the main post office, north of which lies the workaday neighbourhood of the Terzi di Camollia. The church of **Santo Stefano** fronts one of the nicest *contrada* squares in the city, home of the Istrici (Porcupine), while the road emerges from the walls at the northern Porta Camollia, inscribed "Siena opens her heart to you wider than this gate." The northwest corner of the city is occupied by a stadium and the gardens of **La Lizza**, which lead up to the bastions of the **Fortezza di Santa Barbara**, rebuilt by the Medici and now housing the comprehensive wine collection of the *Enoteca Italiana* (see p.565).

San Domenico

Monasteries were essentially rural until the beginning of the thirteenth century, when the idea of an exclusively meditative retreat was displaced by the preaching orders of friars. Suddenly, in the space of a few decades, orders began to found monasteries on the periphery of the major Italian cities. In Siena the two greatest orders, the Dominicans and Franciscans, located themselves respectively to the west and east. **San Domenico**, a vast brick church west of Piazza Matteotti (daily: April–Oct 7am–1pm & 3–6.30pm; Nov–March 9am–1pm & 3–6pm), was founded in 1125 and is closely identified with St Catherine of Siena (see box below). Inside on the right is a raised chapel with a contemporary portrait of the saint by her friend Andrea Vanni. Her own chapel, on the south side of the enormous, airy nave, has frescoes by Sodoma of her swooning (to the left of the altar) and in ecstasy (to the right), as well as a reliquary containing her head.

The **Casa Santuario di Santa Caterina** – St Catherine's family house, where she lived as a Dominican nun – is just south of the church, down the hill on Via Santa Caterina (daily: 9am–12.30pm & 3–6pm; free). The building has been much adapted, with a Renaissance loggia and a series of oratories – one on the site of her cell. At the bottom of the hill, through the Oca (Goose) *contrada*, is the **Fonte Branda**, the best-preserved of Siena's medieval fountains and, according to Sienese folklore, the haunt of werewolves, who would throw themselves into the water at dawn to return in human form.

The Oratorio di San Bernardino

St Bernardino, born in the year of St Catherine's death, began his preaching life at the chill monastic church of **San Francesco**, across the city to the east. Alongside the church is the **Oratorio di San Bernardino** (mid-March to Oct daily 10.30am–1.30pm & 3–5.30pm; €2.50; for multi-entry tickets see box on p.550), with a beautifully wood-panelled upper chapel frescoed by Sodoma and Beccafumi. In the lower chapel are seventeenth-century scenes from the saint's life, which was taken up by incessant travel throughout Italy, preaching against usury and denouncing political strife; his sermons in the Campo, it is said, frequently went on for the best part of a day. He was canonized in 1444, and – because of his dictum on rhetoric, "make it clear, short and to the point" – was made patron saint of advertising in the 1980s. The attached **Museo Diocesano di Arte Sacra** (same hours and ticket) contains an array of devotional art from the thirteenth to the seventeenth centuries.

Eating, drinking and nightlife

Although Siena has a swathe of places at which to **eat** well, the city feels distinctly provincial after Florence. The main action of an evening is the passeggiata from Piazza Matteotti along Banchi di Sopra to the Campo – and there's not much in the way of **nightlife** to follow. For most visitors, though, the Campo, the city's universal gathering place, provides diversion enough, while the presence of the university ensures a bit of life in the **bars**.

Restaurants

Siena used to have a poor reputation for **restaurants** but over the last few years a range of new, imaginative *osterie* has signalled a general rise in standards. Local **specialities** include *pici* (thick, hand-rolled spaghetti with toasted breadcrumbs), *finocchiona* (minced pork flavoured with fennel), *pappa col pomodoro* (bread and tomato soup), and *fagioli all'uccelletto* (white bean and sausage stew).

Putting together a **picnic** in the Campo or elsewhere is easy: you can buy pizza by weight from many central hole-in-the-wall places, or phone an order ahead for quality, fresh-baked pizza (whole or by the slice) from *Mister Pizza*, Via delle Terme 94 (☎0577.221.746; closed Sun). Gourmet supplies are at the extravagantly stocked food store Manganelli, Via di Città 71. *Natural Planet*, Via delle Terme 70, has organic foods. The **covered market** south of the Campo in Piazza del Mercato is also good for picnic provisions, and every quarter has its bakery.

We've divided the listings below by price: **expensive** means an average full meal (excluding wine) costs above €40 per person; **inexpensive** means you can eat for €20 or less; **moderate** is between the two.

Inexpensive and moderate

La Cina Casato di Sotto 56. Quiet, affordable Chinese restaurant 150m from the Campo. The food is adequate, and makes a change from pizza and spaghetti. No closing day.

Due Porte Via di Stalloreggi 62 ℡0577.221.887. One place to head for in the quiet southwestern districts, with pizza and a large Tuscan menu, lower prices than you'd expect and an open terrace at the back. Closed Mon. Inexpensive.

Mensa Universitaria Via Sant'Agata 1. The university canteen has full meals for around €7, pasta dishes for less. Closed Aug. Inexpensive.

Renzo Piazza Indipendenza ℡0577.289.296. Light, uncomplicated meals at terrace tables on a quiet enclosed piazza off Via di Città. Closed Thurs. Inexpensive.

Gallo Nero Via del Porrione 65 ℡0577.284.356. Quirky, vaulted place, offering a Tuscan menu for around €18, or a six-course medieval menu for half as much again, boasting dishes such as bittersweet duck with cheese ravioli and chicken in sweet wine with fruit. Closed Mon lunch. Inexpensive–moderate.

Osteria Castelvecchio Via di Castelvecchio 65 ℡0577.49.586. Adventurous, first-rate and nicely informal mid-priced osteria, the best bet for vegetarians (plus plenty of meat too). Menus change daily. Closed Tues. Moderate.

La Taverna di Cecco Via Cecco Angiolieri 19 ℡0577.288.518. Attentive service, moderate prices and heavenly rabbit and rocket salad. Closed Wed.

Tullio ai Tre Cristi Vicolo Provenzano 1 ℡0577.280.608. A Sienese institution since 1830, this is the neighbourhood restaurant of the Giraffa contrada and is draped with heraldic banners to accompany its traditional fare – roast boar, steaks, tripe and some pastas. Terrace tables in summer. Closed Wed. Moderate.

Al Marsili Via del Castoro 3 ℡0577.47.154. Elegant and upmarket large restaurant with good local dishes (including some choice for vegetarians) and attentive service. The *risotto al limone* is worth dallying over, plus they have more exotic dishes such as guineafowl with prunes, pine-nuts and almonds. Closed Mon. Moderate.

Nello Via del Porrione 28 ℡0577.289.043. Sienese specialities at their best: try pumpkin-flower ravioli, roast rabbit, or beef fillet with rocket and *pecorino*, all bolstered by pasta freshly made daily. Closed Mon. Moderate.

Expensive

Le Campane Via delle Campane 6 ℡0577.284.035. High-quality Sienese cuisine at a small, formal restaurant just below the Duomo. Set menus – *di terra* or *di mare* – cost around €40. Closed Mon.

Cane e Gatto Via Pagliaresi 6 ℡0577.287.545. Don't be put off by the absence of a menu: this restaurant serves superb Tuscan *cucina nuova* on its seven-course *menu degustazione*. Closed Thurs.

Da Divo Via Franciosa 29 ℡0577.286.054. Book a table in the atmospheric subterranean vaulted dining-room to savour hearty Tuscan food that, on its day, is well above average. Closed Sun in winter.

Osteria Le Logge Via del Porrione 33 ℡0577.48.013. The best-looking restaurant in Siena, in an old bookcase- and cabinet-lined pharmacy off the Campo. Good pasta and some unusual *secondi*, though the quality of the food – once exceptional – is these days merely above average; Closed Sun.

Sweet treats

Most Sienese buy **ice cream** at one or the other end of the passeggiata – either at the *Nannini Gelateria* at the northern end of Banchi di Sopra, or *La Costarella*, where Via di Città meets Via dei Pellegrini. Siena is also famous for a whole range of **cakes**, including the trademark **panforte** – a dense and delicious wedge of nuts, fruit and honey – and biscuits like *cavallucci* (aniseed, nut and spice) and *ricciarelli* (almond). All are best bought fresh by the *etto* (hectogram – 100g) in any of the bakeries or *pasticcerie* along Banchi di Sopra; the gift-packaged boxes aren't as good.

Bars and cafés

There are pleasant **bars** all over town. *L'Officina*, Piazza del Sale 3a, has around a hundred bottled beers and others on tap. Of the terrace **cafés** ringing the Campo, *Bar Fonte Gaia* stays open later than most, but otherwise they're much of a muchness. The garden of the *Palazzo Ravizza* hotel, Pian dei Mantellini 34, is a lovely tranquil spot for a cup of tea on a hot afternoon. The *Enoteca Italiana* inside the Fortezza (Mon noon–8pm, Tues–Sat noon–1am) is the country's only national **wine** collection. Its cellar stocks and exhibits every single Italian wine (almost a thousand of them) and there's a **bar** – at its best in the early evening – where you can order by the glass or bottle. At various times of year it stages promotions highlighting particular wine regions, and even hosts the odd concert.

Nightlife and entertainment

You'll spot posters for city **events** at Piazza Matteotti, and the Siena supplement of *La Nazione* newspaper has details of the day's concerts and films. You can catch **live bands** at *L'Officina* bar, Piazza del Sale 3a, and at the disco-bar *Al Cambio*, Via di Pantaneto 48, but otherwise your only chances are at the low-key **Siena Jazz** in the last week of July and the gigs organized for the PDS-Communist Party **Festa dell'Unità** throughout the summer.

Siena has prestigious **classical** concerts throughout the year. The Accademia Chigiana is the driving force, staging the *Estate Musicale Chigiana* cycle all summer, and the *Settimana Musicale Senese* in late July, often featuring a major opera production. Venues vary from the Duomo and Sant'Agostino to out-of-town locations such as the atmospheric ruined abbey of San Galgano. Tickets start at €10, bookable through the tourist office or from mid-July onwards in person at the Accademia Chigiana, Via di Città 89 (daily 3–7pm; ☎0577.22.091, ⓦwww.chigiana.it).

Listings

Bike rental DF Bike, Via Massetana Romana 54 ☎0577.271.905; Automotocicli Perozzi, Via del Romitorio 5 ☎0577.223.157.

Bus information Ticket offices beneath Piazza Gramsci have information on all routes. The Sienese bus company is called TRA-IN – and despite appearances has nothing to do with trains. They run roughly half-hourly to Poggibonsi, where you must change for San Gimignano (buy a through ticket), and half-a-dozen times daily to Montalcino and Montepulciano. Note that some buses to the hill-towns south of Siena depart from the train station, not from Piazza Gramsci. TRA-IN and SITA also run regularly to Florence (take an express).

Car rental Avis, Via Simone Martini 36 ☎0577.270.305; Hertz, Viale Sardegna 37 ☎0577.45.085.

Guided walks "Ecco Siena" walking tours (in English) start from outside San Domenico (April–Oct Mon–Fri 4.30pm; €18; last 2hr 30min); bookings can be made at Siena Hotels Promotion, Piazza Madre Teresa di Calcutta ☎0577.288.084 before 1pm on the same day.

Hospital Loc. Le Scotte ☎0577.585.111.

Internet access Internet Train, Via di Città 121 and Via Pantaneto 54; MegaWeb, Via Pantaneto 132; MediaNet, Via Paradiso 10 (closed Sun). All have long daily opening hours and charge around €1.50 for 15min (less for students).

Laundry Wash & Dry, Via Pantaneto 38 (daily 8am–9pm); OndaBlu, Casato di Sotto 17 (daily 8am–10pm).

Left luggage At the TRA-IN bus information centre below Piazza Gramsci (daily 7am–7.45pm; €3.50 per piece for one day only). At the train station, there are self-service lockers on platform 1.

Lost property Comune di Siena, Casato di Sotto 23 (Mon–Fri 9am–12.30pm, Tues & Thurs also 3–5pm).

Market A huge weekly market sprawls over La Lizza (Wed 8am–1pm).

Parking The two biggest parking garages – run by the same company and clearly signposted – charge around €1.30 per hour (daily 7am–11pm) but are misleadingly named: "Parcheggio Il Campo" and "Parcheggio Il Duomo" are a long way south of either the Campo or the Duomo, just inside the Porta Tufi and Porta San Marco respectively (Ⓦ www.sienaparcheggi.it). Parking outside the city gates is free. Tourists are permitted to drive through the old town alleys only in order to check in at their hotel.

Police The *Questura* is on Via del Castoro ☎0577.201.111.

Post office Piazza Matteotti (Mon–Sat 8.15am–7pm).

Taxi Radio Taxi ☎0577.49.222; taxis wait on Piazza Matteotti.

Train information ☎848.888.088, Ⓦ www.trenitalia.it.

San Gimignano

SAN GIMIGNANO, 27km northwest of Siena, is perhaps the most-visited small village in Italy. Its stunning hilltop skyline of towers, built in aristocratic rivalry by the feuding nobles of the twelfth and thirteenth centuries, evokes the appearance of medieval Tuscany more than any other sight. And the town is all that it's cracked up to be: quietly monumental, very well preserved, enticingly rural, and with a fine array of religious and secular frescoes. However, from Easter until October, San Gimignano has very little life of its own, and a lot of day-trippers. If you want to reach beyond its facade of quaintness, you should come well out of season; if you can't, then aim to spend the night here – the town takes on a very different pace and atmosphere in the evenings.

San Gimignano was quite a force to be reckoned with in the early Middle Ages. It was controlled by two great families – the Ardinghelli and the Salvucci – and its 15,000 population (twice the present number) prospered on agricultural holdings and its position on the Lombardy-to-Rome pilgrim route. At its heyday, the town's walls enclosed five monasteries, four hospitals, public baths and a brothel. **Feuds**, however, had long wreaked havoc: the first Ardinghelli–Salvucci conflict erupted in 1246. Whenever the town itself was united, it picked fights with Volterra, Poggibonsi and other neighbours. These were halted only by the **Black Death**, which devastated the population and – as the pilgrim trade collapsed – the economy. Subjection to Florence broke the power of the nobles and so their tower-houses, symbolic in other towns of real control, were not torn down; today, 15 of an original 72 survive. At the beginning of the nineteenth century, travellers spoke of San Gimignano as "miserably poor"; its postwar history has been one of ever-increasing affluence, through **tourism** and the production of an old-established but recently rejuvenated white **wine**, Vernaccia. The famous *Festival Internazionale* (Ⓦ www.fts.toscana.it) fills a couple of weeks in late July with **opera**, **ballet** and concerts of symphonic and chamber **music** on an open-air stage in Piazza Duomo; consult the tourist office for full details.

Arrival, information and accommodation

San Gimignano has very few direct buses from anywhere other than **Colle Val d'Elsa** and the ugly industrial town of **Poggibonsi**: you're likely to have to call in here to transfer. There is an hourly connecting bus from Poggibonsi train station (on the Florence–Empoli–Siena line) which drops off at both of San Gimignano's main gates, **Porta San Giovanni** in the south and **Porta San Matteo** in the north. From each, the main streets Via San Giovanni and Via San

SAN GIMIGNANO

N

Certaldo & Pontedera

VIA GHIACCIAIA

VIALE GARIBALDI

VIA CEPPARELLI

VIA N. CANNICCI

Sant'Agostino

VIA BAGNAIA

San Iacopo

Porta
San Iacopo

P

PIAZZA
S. AGOSTINO

Museo Archeologico
& Spezieria di S. Fina

San Pietro

Porta
San Matteo

V. CELLOLESE

VIA FOLGORE DA S. GIMIGNANO

A

VIA SAN MARTINO

VIA XX SETTEMBRE

VIA CELLE FONTI

Palazzo
Tinacci

VIA DELLA VERGINA

VIA CAPASSI

B 1

VIA MAINARDI

VIA DIACCETO

VIA SAN MATTEO

Casa
Pesciolini

VIA DELLE ROMITE

Porta delle
Fonti

Fonti

San Bartolo
Palazzo della
Cancelleria

Torri Salvucci

Mistero Etrusco

Palazzo del
Podestà

VIA D. CASTELLO

Collegiata

PIAZZA DEL
DUOMO

Museo della
Tortura

C

VIA S. STEFANO

Rocca

Museo
d'Arte
Sacra

2

San Lorenzo in Ponte
& Farmacia

Palazzo
del Popolo

PIAZZA DELLA
CISTERNA

Palazzo
Tortoli

VIA PRUNELLO

3

Arco dei
Becci

VIA D. QUERCECCHIO

VIA D. INNOCENTI

VIA PANDOLFINELLA

VIA PALESTRO

D 4

Porta
Quercecchio

Palazzo
Pratellesi

VIA BERIGNANO

VIA S. GIOVANNI

VIA DI RONDA

VIALE DEI FOSSI

San Francesco

5

Porta San Giovanni

VIALE DEI FOSSI

STRADA DI RACCIANO

PIAZZALE
DEI MARTIRI DI
MONTE MAGGIO

P

VIA ROMA

P

VIA VECCHIA

Poggibonsi, Volterra, Siena & Campsite

P

VIALE DEL FOSSI

| 0 | 200 m |

ACCOMMODATION

L'Antico Pozzo	**1**
Bel Soggiorno	**5**
La Cisterna	**3**
Leon Bianco	**2**
Le Vecchie Mura	**4**

RESTAURANTS

Osteria del Carcere	**C**
Osteria del Catene	**B**
Il Pino	**A**
Le Vecchie Mura	**D**

8

TUSCANY | San Gimignano

Matteo climb to meet in the middle of town at the interlocking squares of **Piazza Duomo** and **Piazza della Cisterna**, where you'll find the Pro Loco **tourist office**, Piazza Duomo 1 (daily: 9am–1pm & 3–7pm; ☎0577.940.008, ⓦ www.sangimignano.com).

Accommodation is bookable for free through a branch of Siena Hotels Promotion, located just inside the southern gate at Via San Giovanni 125 (summer Mon–Sat 9am–7pm; winter Mon–Sat 9.30am–12.30pm & 3–6pm; ☎0577.940.809, ⓦ www.sangimignano.com). They can also give details of **private rooms**.

Hotels

L'Antico Pozzo Via San Matteo 87 ☎0577.942.014, ⓦ www.anticopozzo.com. An upmarket eighteen-room three-star, occupying a fifteenth-century town house. **❼**

Bel Soggiorno Via San Giovanni 91 ☎0577.940.375, ⓦ www.hotelbelsoggiorno.it. Similar quality, price and facilities to the *Leon Bianco*. The 22 rooms are smallish but beautifully appointed. **❼**

La Cisterna Piazza Cisterna 24 ☎0577.940.328, ⓦ www.hotelcisterna.it. Elegant town hotel (estab-

lished 1919), built into a medieval ensemble; some rooms have views onto the piazza or over the valley. **❻**

Leon Bianco Piazza Cisterna 13 ☎0577.941.294, ⓦ www.leonbianco.com. Tasteful three-star hotel with air-con, in a fourteenth-century town mansion opposite the *Cisterna*. Also with a roof terrace for breakfast, drinks and lounging. **❼**

Le Vecchie Mura Via Piandornella 15 ☎0577.940.270, ⓔ vecchiemura@iol.it). A couple of doubles above a restaurant with superb views. **❷**

Campsite

Campeggio Il Boschetto di Piemma ☎0577.940.352, ⓔ bpiemma@tiscalinet.it; April–Oct). The nearest campsite (with bar, restau-

rant and pool), 3km downhill from Porta San Giovanni at Santa Lucia, off the Volterra road.

The Town

You could walk from one end of San Gimignano to the other in about fifteen minutes. It deserves at least a day, however, both for its frescoes and for its lovely surrounding countryside. From the southern gate, **Porta San Giovanni**, the palazzo-lined **Via San Giovanni** leads to the interlocking main squares, the Piazza della Cisterna and Piazza del Duomo. On the right of the street, about 100m up, is the former church of San Francesco – a Romanesque building converted, like many of the *palazzi*, to a wine shop. You enter the **Piazza della Cisterna** through another gateway, the **Arco dei Becci**, part of the original fortifications built before the town expanded in the twelfth century. The square itself is flanked by an anarchic cluster of towers and *palazzi*, and is named after the thirteenth-century public cistern, still functioning in the centre. To the left (northwest) of the square is one of the old Ardinghelli towers; a Salvucci rival rears up behind. An arch leads through to the more austere **Piazza Duomo**, with further towers and civic *palazzi*.

Museum Tickets

There are two different combined tickets or *biglietto cumulativo*: the first, at €7.50, covers admission to the Museo Civico, Torre Grossa, Museo Archeologico/Spezieria /Galleria di Arte Moderna and the Museo Ornitologico; the second, at €5.50, covers admission to the Cappella di Santa Maria and the Museo d'Arte Sacra. You can buy them from any of the participating places, but are only worthwhile if you're planning to visit most of them. Not included are the wackier private concerns such as the Museo della Tortura.

The Collegiata

The plain facade of the Duomo, or more properly the **Collegiata**, since San Gimignano no longer has a bishop, could hardly provide a greater contrast with its interior (March–Oct Mon–Fri 9.30am–7.30pm, Sat 9.30am–5pm, Sun 1–5pm; Nov to mid-Jan closes 5pm daily, €3.50; for details of combined entry ticket see box opposite). This is one of the most comprehensively frescoed churches in Tuscany, with cycles of paintings filling every available space, their brilliant colours set off by Pisan-Romanesque arcades of black and white striped marble. Entrance is from the side courtyard, where you'll also find the small **Museo d'Arte Sacra** (April–Oct daily 9.30am–7.30pm; Nov–March 9.30am–5pm; €3; for details of combined entry ticket see box opposite).

The Collegiata's three principal **fresco cycles** fill the north and south walls, plus two short side walls which protrude from the east (exit) wall of the facade. The **Old Testament** scenes on the north wall, completed by Bartolo di Fredi around 1367, are full of medieval detail in the costumes, activities and interiors. They are also quirkily naturalistic: there are few odder frescoes than the depiction of Noah exposing himself in a drunken stupor. The cycle (which reads from left to right, top to bottom) follows the story of the **Flood** with those of **Abraham and Lot** (their trip to Canaan), **Joseph** (his dream; being let down the well; having his brothers arrested, and being recognized by them), **Moses** (changing a stick into a serpent before the Pharaoh; the Red Sea; Mount Sinai) and **Job** (temptation; the devil killing his herds; thanking God; being consoled). Above, note the beautiful fresco depicting the *Creation of Eve*, in which Eve emerges from the rib of the sleeping Adam. The **New Testament** scenes opposite (begun 1333) have a disputed attribution – either Barna da Siena or Lippo Memmi. They impress most by the intensity of their emotional expression: in *The Kiss of Judas*, the focus of eyes is startlingly immediate. One of the most dramatic scenes is the *Resurrection of Lazarus*, in which a dumbstruck crowd witnesses the removal of a door to reveal the living Lazarus in the winding bandages of burial. An altogether different vision pervades Taddeo di Bartolo's **Last Judgement** (1410), with paradise to the left and hell to the right. This is one of the most gruesome depictions of a customarily lurid subject, with no-holds-barred illustrations of the Seven Deadly Sins.

San Gimignano's most important Renaissance artwork is the superb fresco cycle made by Domenico Ghirlandaio for the small **Cappella di Santa Fina**. The subject is a local saint, born in 1238, who was struck by a dreadful and incurable disease at the age of ten. She gave herself immediately to God, repented her sins (the worst seems to have been accepting an orange from a boy), and insisted on spending the five agonizing years until her death lying on a plank on the floor. The fresco of the right-hand lunette shows Fina experiencing a vision of St Gregory. Opposite it is a much more accomplished work, the *Funeral of St Fina* – Raphael is said to have been especially impressed with it – showing the saint on her deathbed with the towers of San Gimignano in the background. Ghirlandaio left a self-portrait: he's the figure behind the bishop who is saying Mass.

The Museo Civico

The Palazzo Popolo, the other key component of Piazza Duomo, is partly given over to council offices, but most of the building is devoted to the **Museo Civico** and the **Torre Grossa**, the only one of San Gimignano's towers which you can climb (daily: March–Oct 9.30am–7.20pm; Nov–Feb 10am–5.50pm; €5, or for details of combined entry ticket see box opposite).

The lovely courtyard was built in 1323. A loggia opens on the right, from which justice and public decrees were occasionally proclaimed (hence the subject matter of its frescoes). Stairs lead up to a picturesque little balcony and the ticket office. The first room, frescoed with hunting scenes, is the **Sala di Dante** – the poet visited as Florence's ambassador to the town in 1299, making a plea here for Guelph unity. Most of the paintings are Sienese in origin or inspiration, and the highlight is Lippo Memmi's *Maestà* (1317). Off the Sala di Dante are busts of a winsome *Santa Fina* (1496) and *San Gregorio* by Pietro Torrigiano. Highlights upstairs include two outstanding tondi by **Filippino Lippi**. Rooms off to the right hold a triptych by **Taddeo di Bartolo** depicting *Scenes from the Life of St Gimignano* (1393) – with the saint holding the eponymous town on his lap – and **Lorenzo di Niccolò**'s *Scenes from the Life of St Bartholomew* (1401), which includes a graphic depiction of the saint being flayed alive. The most enjoyable paintings are hidden away in a small room off the stairs, frescoes of wedding scenes completed in the 1320s by the Sienese painter Memmo di Filipuccio that are unique in their subject matter: they show a tournament where the wife rides on her husband's back, followed by the lovers taking a shared bath and then climbing into bed – the man managing to keep on the same red hat throughout.

The rest of the town

A few steps east of Piazza della Cisterna at Via del Castello 1 is the new Museo Criminale Medioevale, or **Museo della Tortura** (daily: mid-July to mid-Sept 9am–midnight; rest of year 10am–7pm; €8). This offers an array of instruments (most, chillingly enough, sourced from private collections) designed to inflict pain or death – everything from thumbscrews and chastity belts to an electric chair. The historical notes are scholarly but the place reeks of a distasteful, seedy prurience. Via di Castello continues east past the Romanesque **San Lorenzo in Ponte** (with fragments of a dramatic *Last Judgement* fresco) to a rural lane which winds down between vineyards to the city walls; just beyond the public wellhouse or **Fonti** stretches open countryside.

A signposted lane leads from Piazza Duomo up to the **Rocca**, the old fortress, with its one surviving tower and superb views. It was built, at local expense, by the Florentines "in order to remove every cause of evil thinking from the inhabitants" after their union with the *comune*. Later, its purpose presumably fulfilled, it was dismantled by Cosimo de' Medici. Nowadays it encloses an orchard-like public garden, with figs, olives and a central well.

Via San Matteo is one of the grandest and best preserved of the city streets, running north from Piazza Duomo to the main **Porta San Matteo** gate. Before the gate, Via XX Settembre heads east to the former convent of Santa Chiara, which now houses both the **Galleria d'Arte Contemporaneo**, with work by nineteenth- and twentieth-century Tuscan artists, and the interesting **Museo Archeologico** (both open daily 11am–6pm; closed Friday; €3.50 or see box on p.568 for details of combined entry ticket). In the same complex is the **Spezieria di Santa Fina**, fragrant halls filled with exhibits from the sixteenth-century spice and herb pharmacy of the town's Santa Fina hospital – ceramic jars full of strange potions and hanging bunches of dried herbs. The northernmost corner of town is occupied by the large church of **Sant'Agostino** (daily 7am–noon & 3–7pm; winter closes 6pm), with an outstanding fresco cycle behind the high altar by Benozzo Gozzoli on the *Life of St Augustine* (1465), which provides a superb record of life in Renaissance Florence. Read from low down on the left, the panels depict the saint – who was born in what is now Tunisia in 354 – being taken to school and being flogged by his teacher, studying grammar at Carthage university, crossing the sea to Italy, his teaching in Rome and Milan and being received by Emperor Theodosius. Then comes the turning-point, when he hears St Ambrose preach and, while reading St Paul, hears a child's voice extolling him *"Tolle, lege"* (take and read). After this, he was baptized and returned to Africa to found a monastic community. The depiction of his death almost exactly prefigures Ghirlandaio's Collegiata fresco of the death of St Fina.

Eating and drinking

San Gimignano isn't famous for its **food** – there are too many tourists and too few locals to ensure high standards. However, the tables set out on the car-free squares and lanes, and the good local wines, make for pleasant dining. The recommended places below are all moderately priced.

Little *Gelateria di Piazza*, Piazza della Cisterna 4, has unquestionably the best **ice cream** in Tuscany. Owner Sergio stopped entering competitions after he retained the *Gelatissimo d'Italia* in 1998 – because he kept winning. Framed plaudits cover the walls. His incomparable pistachio flavour is made from finest-quality Sicilian nuts, and his trademark *crema di Santa Fina* is perfumed with saffron, but you'd be hard-pushed on a hot afternoon to beat the trio of peach, champagne with grapefruit, and *vernaccia*, the last a fragrant sorbet made from the crisp local white wine. Avoid poor-quality imitators on the same piazza.

Il Pino Via San Matteo 102 ☎0577.942.225. First choice: a lovely interior, with a specialist focus on *antipasti* and dishes sprinkled with truffle.
Osteria del Carcere Via del Castello 13 ☎0577.941.905. A relatively new and informal place with young owners, serving Tuscan cuisine with an innovative edge. Closed Wed.
Osteria del Catene Via Mainardi 18 ☎0577.941.966. Thoroughly reliable spot for straightforward Tuscan cooking, plus an extensive wine list. Closed Wed.
Le Vecchie Mura Via Piandornella 15 ☎0577.940.270. Housed in an old vaulted stable off Via San Giovanni, with a good atmosphere, fair-value pizzas and quality set meals. Closed Tues & lunch.

Listings

Bike and scooter rental Bruno Bellini, Via Roma 41 ☎0577.940.201, ⊚www.bellinibruno.com.
Bus information You can buy tickets and get timetables from the tourist office in Piazza Duomo. Last buses to Poggibonsi and Colle leave from Porta San Giovanni about 8.30pm.
Internet access Cartoleria La Tuscia, just outside Porta San Matteo, or the craft shop at Via XX Settembre 24b.

Market Piazza Duomo and Piazza Cisterna (Thurs morning).
Parking There are four pay car-parks dotted around the walls. Driving within the walls is forbidden unless you have a chit from your hotel, and the police will ticket you if you try (or if you park outside the Porta San Giovanni).
Taxis ☎0577.940.499 and ☎0577.940.049.

Volterra

The dramatic location of **VOLTERRA** – built on a high plateau enclosed by volcanic hills midway between Siena and the sea – prompted D.H. Lawrence to write that "it gets all the wind and sees all the world – a sort of inland island." Its walled medieval core is atmospheric and not excessively touristed. Everything is made from the yellow-grey stone *panchino*, and you can often find seashells embedded in the paving of streets and squares. **Etruscan** Volterra (Velathri) flourished through a combination of its alabaster mines and an impregnable position, attributes that ensured its survival through the Roman era and beyond. Its isolation was, however, its downfall. Under **Florentine** control from 1360, it proved unable to keep pace with changing and expanding patterns of trade, and the town itself began to subside, its walls and houses slipping away to the west over the **Balze** cliffs, which form a dramatic prospect from the Pisa road. Today, Volterra – part of the Provincia di Pisa – occupies less than a third of its ancient extent.

The Town

Dominating the almost totally medieval square of **Piazza dei Priori**, the **Palazzo dei Priori** is the oldest town hall in Tuscany, begun in 1208, which may have served as the model for Florence's Palazzo Vecchio. If you find the tower open, it's worth climbing to the top for the spectacular views (which reputedly stretch to Corsica). Upstairs inside the palazzo (Sat & Sun 10am–1pm & 2–6pm; €1) is the **Sala del Consiglio**, used as the town's council chamber without interruption since 1257. Its end wall is frescoed with a huge *Annunciation* by Orcagna; just outside, workers are currently restoring Francesco Fiorentino's fresco of the *Crucifixion*.

Leaving the square west past the tourist office, you come to a crossroads overlooked by the **Torre Buomparenti**. South (left) on Via Roma is the **Museo d'Arte Sacra**, a rich four-room collection (daily: March–Oct 9am–1pm & 3–6pm; Nov–Feb 9am–1pm; joint ticket with Museo Guarnacci and Pinacoteca €7), which includes a silver reliquary bust of *St Ottaviano* by Antonio dell Pollaiuolo and a beautiful sixteenth-century alabaster ciborium. Via Roma continues into the slightly down-at-heel cathedral square, with the Pisan-Romanesque **Duomo** (consecrated in 1120) and **Baptistry** (late-thirteenth century). The best of the Duomo's works is a sculpture of the *Deposition* (1228) in the south transept, disarmingly repainted in its original bright colours. Behind the baptistry is an old foundling's hospital decorated by della Robbia. Via Marchesi heads south to a lush area of grass, trees and shade known as the **Parco Archeologico** (daily 10am–noon & 4–7pm; free). There's not much archeology about the place – a few odd lumps of rock, said to be part of a Roman bathhouse – but it's a beautiful part of the town to lie around for a few hours, and there is a good-value café in one corner. Overlooking the park to the east is the Medicean **Rocca**, with rounded bastions and a central tower;

it's one of the great examples of Italian military architecture and for the last 150 years has been a prison for lifers and hard cases. The first turning off Via Marchesi is Via Porta dell'Arco, which runs downhill to the **Arco Etrusco**, an Etruscan gateway, third-century BC in origin, built in cyclopean blocks of stone. The gate was narrowly saved from destruction in the last war during a ten-day battle between the partisans and Nazis.

North (right) from the Torre Buomparenti is the beautiful Renaissance Palazzo Minucci-Solaini, now housing the **Pinacoteca Comunale** (daily: March–Oct 9am–7pm; Nov–Feb 9am–2pm; joint ticket with Museo Guarnacci and Museo d'Arte Sacra €7). The key works are Florentine: Ghirlandaio's marvellous *Christ in Glory*, Luca Signorelli's *Annunciation* and, best of all, Rosso Fiorentino's extraordinary *Deposition*. This is one of the masterpieces of Mannerism, its figures, without any central focus, creating an agitated tension from sharp lines and blocks of discordant colour. It's been described as symbolizing the dilemma of a lost generation (it was painted in the decade which culminated in the sack of Rome) and has also been dubbed blasphemous for its vision of a smiling Christ. On the same street as the Pinacoteca is **Palazzo Viti**, Via dei Sarti 41 (April–Oct daily 10am–1pm & 2.30–6.30pm; Nov–March by appointment only; €4), an extensively frescoed Renaissance mansion filled with alabaster, everything from two-metre-high alabaster candelabras to alabaster tiles laid in the floor of the ballroom.

The Museo Guarnacci

The **Museo Guarnacci**, 500m east of Piazza dei Priori at Via Don Minzoni 15 (same hours and ticket as Pinacoteca, see above) is one of Italy's major archeological museums. On display are entirely local finds, including some 600 Etruscan **funerary urns**. Carved in alabaster, terracotta or local sandstone or limestone, they date from the fourth to first centuries BC, and follow a standard pattern: below a reclining figure of the subject (always leaning on their left side), bas reliefs depict domestic events, Greek myths or simply a symbolic flower – one for a young person, two for middle-aged, three for elderly. The vast collection is organized by theme, with informative notes in each room. Key highlights are **upstairs**: past a large Roman mosaic transferred here from Volterra's baths is the **Urna degli Sposi**, a rare and artistically unique clay urn lid which features a disturbing double portrait of a husband and wife, all piercing eyes and dreadful looks. The star piece is the exceptional **Ombra della Sera** ("Evening Shadow"), an elongated nude that is unique in that it has been personalized and individualized – most of the figurines in nearby cases are generic. This piece was much admired by the twentieth-century Swiss sculptor Alberto Giacometti, who drew inspiration for his famous elongated figures from this Etruscan artist's visualization of the long evening shadows cast in hilltop Volterra.

A short walk away in Piazza XX Settembre is the new **Museo Storico dell'Alabastro** (daily: mid-March to Oct 9am–7pm; Nov to mid-March 9am–1pm; Ⓦ www.museodellalabastro.it; €3) which traces the history of Volterra's alabaster industry and has a collection of over 300 sculptures, vases and other artefacts dating from the end of the eighteenth century.

The Balze cliffs

To reach the much-photographed eroded **Balze** cliffs, follow the Via Ricciarelli northwest from the Piazza dei Priori. As Via San Lino, this passes the church of **San Francesco**, with fifteenth-century frescoes of the *Legend of the True Cross* by Cenni di Cenni, before leaving town through the Porta San

Francesco. From here, follow Borgo Santo Stefano and its continuation, Borgo San Giusto, past the Baroque church and former abbey of **San Giusto**, its dilapidated but striking facade framed by an avenue of cypress trees. At the *Balze* (almost 2km west of Piazza dei Priori) you gain a real sense of the extent of Etruscan Volterra, whose old walls drop away into the chasms. Gashes in the slopes and the natural erosion of sand and clay are made more dramatic by alabaster mines, ancient and modern. Below are buried great tracts of the Etruscan and Roman city, and landslips continue – as evidenced by the ruined eleventh-century **Badia** monastery ebbing away over the precipice.

Practicalities

Irregular **buses** run to Volterra from Larderello, Pisa and Colle Val d'Elsa; all arrive on the south side of the walls at Piazza Martiri, from where it's a two-minute walk to the central Piazza dei Priori. The helpful **tourist office** is at no. 20 (daily: April–Oct 9am–1pm & 2–8pm; Nov–March 10am–1pm & 2–6pm; ☎0588.87.257, Ⓦwww.volterratur.it). They can book accommodation for free and rent you an **audioguide** (€7), available in English, for a self-guided town tour. Avoid the Pro Volterra information office round the corner at Via Turazza 2 – they're not half as helpful or clued-in. There are free **car parks** on the northern side of the walls. Walking and mountain-bike tours are run by the COOP Viaggio Antico (☎0588.81.527, Ⓦwww.viaggioantico.com) – or contact the tourist office. There's an **Internet point** at SESHA computers, Piazza XX Settembre 10. Volterra's most attractive **hotel** is the sixteenth-century *Villa Nencini*, in a peaceful, panoramic setting west of the centre at Borgo Santo Stefano 55 (☎0588.86.386, Ⓕ0588.80.601; ❹). At the eastern end of town is the *San Pietro* independent **hostel**, Via del Poggetto 2 (☎ & Ⓕ 0588.85.577; €15 per person), and anyone can stay in a cell-with-a-view at the *Sant'Andrea* **convent** in the northeast outskirts (☎0588.86.028; €34 per person). The **campsite** *Le Balze* is 1km west of town, Via di Mandringa 115 (☎ & Ⓕ0588.87.880; April–Sept).

As a renowned centre for hunting, Volterra's **restaurant** menus are dominated by wild boar (*cinghiale*), hare (*lepre*) and rabbit (*coniglio*). Most places are moderately priced. *Ombra della Sera*, Via Gramsci 68 (closed Mon), is a pleasant local haunt, while the vaulted gloom of *Vecchia Osteria dei Poeti*, Via Matteotti 55 (closed Thurs), is the most characterful spot for Volterra's gamey cuisine. *Don Beta*, Via Matteotti 39 (closed Mon), offers relief in the form of inexpensive pizzas and light meals.

Southern Tuscany

The inland hills of **southern Tuscany** are the region at its best, an infinite gradation of trees and vineyards that encompasses the *crete* – a sparsely populated region of pale clay hillsides – before climbing into the hills around Monte Amiata. Southwest of Siena towards the sea is gentle **Massa Maríttima**, a memorable but little-visited hill-town that presides over a marshy coastal plain. Magnificent monastic architecture survives in the tranquil settings of **San**

Galgano and, a short distance east, **Monte Oliveto Maggiore**, which boasts the additional attraction of some marvellous frescoes. The finest of the hill-towns to the south of Siena is **Montepulciano**, with its superb wines and an ensemble of Renaissance architecture that rivals neighbouring **Pienza**.

Further south, the tourist crush is noticeably eased in smaller towns and villages that are often overlooked by visitors gorged on Florentine art and Sienese countryside. Wild **Monte Amiata** offers scenic mountain walks, **Saturnia** has some remarkable sulphur springs, and isolated **Pitigliano** is one of the most dramatically sited medieval towns in the region, nurturing the amazing story – and scant remains – of what was once Tuscany's strongest Jewish community.

Massa Maríttima

The road south from Volterra over the mountains to **MASSA MARÍTTIMA** is little explored and scenically magnificent: classic Tuscan countryside which is given an added surreal quality around **Larderello** by the presence of *soffioni* (hot steam geysers), huge silver pipes snaking across the fields, and sulphurous smoke rising from chimneys amid the foliage. There are three **buses** daily to Massa from Volterra (change at Lardarello), one from Grosseto and two from Siena. It sees none of the crowds of San Gimignano, and even Volterra looks crowded in comparison.

Massa, like Volterra, has been a wealthy **mining** town since Etruscan times. In 1225, on the heels of a declaration of independence, it passed Europe's first-ever charter for the protection of miners; in the century afterwards, before Siena took over in 1335, its exquisite **Duomo** went up and the population doubled. The trend was reversed in the sixteenth century, and by 1737, after bouts of plague and malaria, it was a virtual ghost town. Massa gained its "Maríttima" suffix in the Middle Ages when it became the leading hill-town of this coastal region, even though the sea is 20km distant across a silty plain. Its recovery began with the draining of coastal marshes in the 1830s.

Blocks of new buildings mar an approach, but the medieval splendour of **Piazza Garibaldi**, just up from the bus stops, overshadows all that. This exquisite example of Tuscan town planning showcases the thirteenth-century **Duomo**, set on broad steps at a dramatically oblique angle to the square. The cathedral is dedicated to the sixth-century St Cerbone, whose claim to fame was to persuade a flock of geese to follow him when summoned to Rome on heresy charges. Its airy **interior** (daily: 8am–noon & 3–6pm) features eleventh-century carvings of grinning, cross-eyed faces – powerful and primitive, in dramatic contrast to the severe, polished Roman sarcophagus nearby. A modest **Museo Archeologico** occupies the Palazzo del Podestà opposite (April–Oct Tues–Sun 10am–1pm & 4–10pm; Nov–March closes 5pm; €3) – worth visiting for the town's undisputed masterpiece, a superb *Maestà* altarpiece by Ambrogio Lorenzetti, coloured in vivid pink, green and tangerine, with Cerbone and his geese lurking in the corner. Off the other side of the piazza is the **Centro Espositivo di Arte Contemporanea**, Via Goldoni 5 (closed at time of writing), which includes an engaging collection of late-nineteenth-century painting.

Otherwise, barring a couple of limited-interest museums devoted to mining, aim for the picturesque lane Via Moncini, which climbs steeply to the quiet Gothic **upper town**: as you emerge beneath an impressive but militarily useless arch onto **Piazza Matteotti**, facing you is the **Torre del Candeliere**, part of the thirteenth-century *Fortilizio Senese*. The tower is climbable for a stupendous panorama (summer daily 11am–1pm & 3.30–7.30pm; €2.50).

Practicalities

The **tourist office** is just below Piazza Garibaldi at Via Norma Parenti 22 (Mon–Sat 9am–12.30pm & 3.30–7pm, Sun 10am–1pm; ℡0566.902.756, Ⓔamatur@cometanet.it). Massa's only central **hotel** is *Il Sole*, Via Libertà 43 (℡0566.901.971, Ⓔhotelilsole@tin.it; ❹); otherwise go for the pleasant, refurbished *Duca del Mare*, just below town at Via Dante Alighieri 1 (℡0566.902.284, Ⓔducadelmare@libero.it; ❺). Better **restaurants** than those lining Piazza Garibaldi include the characterful *Trattoria dei Cavalieri*, Via Norma Parenti 35 (℡0566.902.093; closed Mon), with moderately priced Tuscan staples, and *Osteria da Tronco* at Vicolo Porte 5 (℡0566.901.991; closed Wed), offering inexpensive osteria-style fare in rustic stone wall setting. *Pizzeria Barbablu*, up at Piazza Matteotti 5, has excellent *pizza gialla* (a pizza base sprinkled with saffron, scamorza and parmesan cheeses, and rocket) and outside tables where you can watch your afternoon vanish as the hands on the Torre del Candeliere's eccentric clock scoot round twelve hours in a single hour. The **pub** *Del Priore*, Via Libertà 34, has good beer and a blues jukebox.

Make time in summer for the **Toscana Foto Festival** (℡0566.901.526, Ⓦwww.toscanafotofestival.it), with photo exhibits and workshops at venues around town in late July, and a prestigious show of the cream of the crop running until late August.

The Crete

South of Siena stretches classic Tuscan countryside known as the *crete* – a sparsely populated region of pale clay hillsides dotted with sheep, cypresses and the odd monumental-looking farmhouse. These tranquil lands were one of the heartlands of medieval monasticism in Tuscany. The Vallombrosan order maintained their main house at Torri just south of Siena, the Benedictine order had theirs at Sant'Ántimo near Montalcino (see p.585), while the Cistercians founded the convent and abbey of **San Galgano**; now ruined, this is one of the most alluring sights in Tuscany, complete with its hilltop chapel housing the **sword-in-the-stone**. The region's grandest monastery is southeast of Siena at **Monte Oliveto Maggiore**.

San Galgano

The **Abbazia di San Galgano**, 26km northeast of Massa Maríttima, midway on the road to Siena, is perhaps the most evocative Gothic building in all Italy – roofless, with a grass field for a nave, nebulous patches of fresco amidst the vegetation, and panoramas of the sky, clouds and hills through a rose window. In the twelfth and thirteenth centuries, local **Cistercian** monks were the leading power in Tuscany. The abbots exercised powers of arbitration in city disputes, and at Siena the monks were the city's accountants. Through them, the ideas of Gothic building were imported to Italy. The order began a hilltop **church** and monastical buildings here in 1218, but their project to build a grand abbey on the fertile land below was doomed to failure. Building work took seventy years up to 1288, but then famine struck in 1329, the Black Death in 1348, and mercenaries ran amok in subsequent decades. By 1500, all the monks had moved to the security of Siena. The buildings mouldered until 1786, when the belltower was struck by lightning and collapsed. Three years later, the church was deconsecrated, and the complex was abandoned for good. These days, the main appeal of the **abbey** (open all day and illuminated at night until 11.30pm) is its state of ruin, although work to halt the advance of Mother Nature is under way and there are concerts of classical music held during the summer (see p.565 for more). Andrei Tarkovsky filmed the finale of *Nostalgia* here.

On the hill above, the unusual round Romanesque church of **Monte Siepi** commemorates the spot where Galgano – a local twelfth-century knight – renounced his violent past by thrusting his sword into a stone. Amazingly enough, Galgano's **sword in the stone** has survived, protected under glass as an object of veneration. A side-chapel preserves the decaying remains of a man's hands: local legend has it that two wolves – companions of Galgano – tore them from a robber who had broken into the saint's tomb.

There are two or three **buses** daily between Massa Maríttima and Siena which pass within sight of the abbey. To one side of the abbey building, in the old vaulted scriptorium, is a small **tourist office** (daily: summer 10.30am–6pm; winter 10.30am–1.30pm & 3–5pm; ☏0577.756.738, ✉prolocochiusdino@tin.it). The small café on the approach to the abbey, run by the *Cooperativa Agricola San Galgano*, has **rooms** (☏0577.756.292; ❷), and can stump up sandwiches and simple meals. In its grounds is the **Centro Italiano Rapaci**, or Raptor Centre; it's open all summer with unreliable opening times (☏347.704.9732), but restricts displays of falconry to August only.

Monte Oliveto Maggiore

It takes some effort to visit the **Abbazia di Monte Oliveto Maggiore**, but the rewards are clear: Tuscany's grandest monastery is sited 26km southeast of Siena in one of the most beautiful tracts of Sienese countryside, and houses one of the most absorbing Renaissance **frescoes** you'll find anywhere. By car, you can approach from the crossroads town of Buonconvento, climbing quickly into forests of pine, oak and cypress, and then into the olive groves that enclose the monastery. One afternoon **bus** daily from Siena's train station goes to the village of Chiusure, 2km east of the abbey.

When Pius II visited in 1463, it was the overall scene that impressed him: the architecture, in honey-coloured Sienese brick, merging into the woods and gardens that the monks had created from the eroded hills of the *crete*. A wealthy Sienese noble, who had been struck blind and had experienced visions of the Virgin, came to this remote wilderness in 1313 and lived the life of a hermit, soon drawing a following. Within six years, the pope recognized his order – the **Olivetans**, or White Benedictines – and over the following two centuries this, their principal house, was transformed into one of the most powerful monasteries in the land. It was only in 1810, when the monastery was suppressed by Napoleon, that it fell from influence. It is today maintained by a small group of Olivetan monks, who supplement their state income with a hi-tech centre for the restoration of ancient books. At the **gatehouse**, there's a good café-restaurant, *La Torre* (☏0577.707.022; closed Tues), from where an avenue of cypresses leads down the hill to the abbey. Signs at the bottom of the slope direct you along a walk to **Blessed Bernardo's grotto** – a chapel built on the site where the founder lived as a hermit – and there's also a **shop**, selling herbal cures and liquors (Mon–Sat 10am–noon & 3.45–6pm, Sun 9.30–10.45am & 3.45–6pm), and a small **tourist office** (Tues–Sun 10am–1pm & 2.30–5.30pm).

The **abbey** (daily 9.15am–noon & 3.15–6pm; winter closes 5pm) is a huge complex, though much of it remains off-limits to visitors. The entrance leads to the **Chiostro Grande**, covered by a series of frescoes depicting the *Life of St Benedict*, the man traditionally regarded as the founder of Christian monasticism. The cycle begins on the east wall, just on the right of the door into the church, and was begun in 1497 by Luca Signorelli who painted nine panels in the middle of the series that start with the depiction of a collapsing house. The colourful Antonio Bazzi, known as Il Sodoma, painted the remaining 27 scenes between 1505 and 1508; he was by all accounts a lively presence, bringing with him part of his menagerie of pets, which included badgers, depicted at his feet in a self-portrait in the third panel. There's a sensuality in many of the secular figures – the young men especially, as befits his nickname, and also the "evil women" (originally nudes, until protests from the abbot). The **church** (entered off the Chiostro Grande) was given a Baroque remodelling in the eighteenth century and some superb stained glass in the twentieth. Its main treasure is the choir stalls, inlaid by Giovanni di Verona and others with architectural, landscape and domestic scenes (including a nod to Sodoma's pets with a cat in a window). Stairs lead from the cloister up to the **library**, again with carving by Giovanni; sadly, it has had to be viewed from the door since the theft of sixteen of its twenty codices in 1975.

BUONCONVENTO, 9km southwest, has unappealing outskirts but a perfectly preserved medieval village at its heart, sheltering the **hotel–restaurant** *Roma* (T0577.806.021, F0577.807.284; ❸; restaurant closed Mon). Regular **buses** from Siena's train station to Buonconvento head on to Montalcino, or to Pienza and Montepulciano.

Montepulciano and around

The highest of the Tuscan hill-towns, at more than 600m, **MONTEPUL-CIANO** is built on a long, narrow ridge 65km southeast of Siena, along which coils the main street, the **Corso**, flanked by a series of dark alleys which drop away to the walls, providing slivers of views between Renaissance *palazzi* out over the rolling countryside. Henry James, who compared the town to a ship, spent most of his time here drinking – a sound policy, in view of the excellent local table wine and the more refined and much-celebrated **Vino Nobile**. The town is set in superb walking country and is not yet overrun by day-trippers. A short distance east is the little Etruscan town of **Chiusi**.

Arrival, information and accommodation

TRA-IN **buses** run roughly every hour between Buonconvento, Torrenieri (change for Montalcino), San Quírico d'Órcia, Pienza and Montepulciano – some of them begin from Siena – while LFI buses run regularly between Montepulciano, Chiusi, and its **train** station.

Montepulciano's spiralling, tortuous streets are incredibly steep, and **orientation** can get confusing. The main entrance to the town – at the lowest point – is the northern gate, the **Porta al Prato**, terminus of all buses; from here, the Corso climbs south through the town (changing its name from Via di Gracciano to Via di Voltaia, then to Via dell'Opio) until it reaches the southern gate, the **Porta delle Farine**, where intercity buses also drop off. From here, the main street (Via del Poliziano, then Via di San Donato) continues its coiling path up and around to enter the main **Piazza Grande** from the south. The

MONTEPULCIANO

▲ *Cortona*

Sant'Agnese

PIAZZA
S. AGNESE

Bus
Stop ★

Giardino di
Poggiofanti

Porta al Prato

A San Bernardo

B C

VIALE D. SANGALLO

VIALE I MAGGIO

P

❶

VIA ROMA

Sant'Agostino

ⓘ

RUGA DI MEZZO

RUGA DI FUORI

Santa
Lucia

PIAZZA
MICHELOZZO

CORSO

VIA PIANA

VIA DEGLI ARCHI

Loggia di
Mercato

PIAZZA
DELL'ERBE

VIA DI GRACCIANO NEL CORSO

San
Francesco

VIA DEL PAOLINO

VIA DEL POGGIOLO

VIA DI ORIOLO

VIA DEL GIARDINO

Palazzo
Cervini

VIA DI VOLTAIA NEL CORSO

D

Porta di Grassi

VIA RICCI

VIA DI PIE' AL SASSO

VIA DI S. BIAGIO

Museo
Civico

E

Palazzo
Tarugi

❷

Gesù

Palazzo
Comunale

PIAZZA
GRANDE

❸ ❹

Palazzo
Cantucci

Duomo

VIA DEL TEATRO

VIA DI ORIOLO

❺

VIA DI COLLAZZI

VIA DI S. DONATO

VIA FIORENZUOLA VECCHIA

▲ F & S. Biagio

Porta
delle Farine

★ Bus
Stop

Fortezza

Casa di
Poliziano

VIA DI POLIZIANO

VIA DEL VECCHIO CIMITERO

VIA DI S. DONATO

Santa Maria
dei Servi

VIA DEI FILOSOFI

VIA DI CIRCONVALLAZIONE

VIA DEI FILOSOFI

▼ *Pienza, Chianciano & Chiusi*

TUSCANY | Montepulciano and around

0 _____ 100 m

ACCOMMODATION

Il Cittino	2
Duomo	5
Marzocco	1
Il Riccio	3
La Terrazza	4

RESTAURANTS

La Briciola	B
Caffè Poliziano	D
Il Cantuccio	C
La Grotta	F
Osteria della	
Porta di Bacco	A
Rosticceria di Voltaia	E

579

stiff climb on foot takes an unrelenting quarter-hour; or you could resort to the LFI town minibuses which run on a loop every 20min, starting and ending at the Porta al Prato (€0.75). The official **tourist office** is on Via Gracciano nel Corso (April–Sept Mon–Sat 9am–12.30pm & 3–8pm, Sun 9am–12.30pm; Oct–March Mon–Sat 9.30am–12.30pm & 3–6pm, Sun 9.30–12.30; ☎0578.757.341, ⓦwww.comune.montepulciano.si.it). For information about Montepulciano's **vino nobile** visit the Strada del Vino office in Piazza Grande 7 (☎0578.717.484, ⓦwww.stradavinonobile.it). **Parking** is free below the eastern walls.

Cheapest **accommodation** is the three rooms above *Ristorante Il Cittino*, Vicolo della Via Nuova 2 (☎0578.757.335; ❷); another reasonable option is *La Terrazza*, a pleasant two-star **hotel** at Via Piè al Sasso 16 (☎0578.757.440, ⓦwww.laterrazzadimontepulciano.com; ❺). The elegant *Marzocco* is at Piazza Savonarola 18 (☎0578.757.262, Ⓕ0578.757.530; ❺), but it's beaten for location and facilities by *Albergo Duomo*, Via San Donato 14 (☎0578.757.473; ❺). You might also consult the tourist office about **private rooms** – most notably those at *Il Riccio*, Via Talosa 21 (☎0578.757.713; ❹). As a last resort, you could get the bus 8km east to **Chianciano Terme**, a huge, characterless spa resort with over 200 hotels.

The Town

Montepulciano's unusually consistent array of Renaissance *palazzi* and churches is a reflection of its remarkable development after 1511, when, following intermittent alliance with Siena, the town finally threw in its lot with Florence. In that year the Florentines sent **Antonio Sangallo the Elder** to rebuild the town's gates and walls, which he did so impressively that the council took him on to work on the town hall and a series of churches. The local nobles meanwhile hired him, his nephew, Antonio Sangallo the Younger, and later the Modena-born **Vignola** – a founding figure of Baroque – to work on their own *palazzi*. The work of this trio is totally assured in conception and execution, and makes a fascinating comparison with Rossellino's Pienza.

Sangallo's first commission was Montepulciano's main gate, the **Porta al Prato**, at the north end of town. Inside the gate the **Corso** begins. In the first square, beside the *Albergo Marzocco*, is a stone column bearing the heraldic lion (*marzocco*) of Florence. Just beyond is the church of **Sant'Agostino**, designed by the earlier Medici protégé, Michelozzo, who also carved the relief above the door. Within are good Sienese paintings by Lorenzo di Credi and Giovanni di Paolo. Across the street a medieval **tower house**, a rare survival in Montepulciano, is surmounted by the commedia dell'arte figure of Pulcinella, who strikes out the hours on the town clock; most un-Tuscan, it is said to have been put up by an exiled bishop from Naples.

About 100m further along is **Piazza delle Erbe** overlooked by the Renaissance **Loggia di Mercato**, which marks a fork in the street. A right turn off the Corso brings you up steeply to a beautiful little piazza fronting the church of **Santa Lucia**, which has a fabulous *Madonna* by Signorelli in a chapel on the right. Just below Santa Lucia, Via del Poggiolo runs down to the church of San Francesco and continues – as the imposing Via Ricci – up to the Piazza Grande past the Sienese-Gothic Palazzo Neri-Orselli, home to the **Museo Civico** (Tues–Sat 10am–1pm & 3–6pm, Sun 10am–6pm; €4.13), an extensive collection of small-town Gothic and Renaissance works.

From Piazza delle Erbe, the Corso continues to the left past further *palazzi*. A long, pleasant stroll through an untouristed part of town brings you onto the quiet, countrified lane of Via di Poliziano, which loops briefly outside the walls and alongside south-facing vistas up to the Baroque **Santa Maria dei Servi**, before climbing steeply back into town alongside the old **Fortezza**, now part-occupied by houses.

Piazza Grande, Montepulciano's theatrical flourish of a main square, is built on the highest point of the ridge, and is worth the climb. Its most distinctive building is the **Palazzo Comunale**, a thirteenth-century Gothic mansion to which Michelozzo added a tower and rustication in imitation of the Palazzo Vecchio in Florence. You can climb the **tower** (daily 10am–6pm; €1.55), and on fabled clear days the view supposedly stretches to Siena. Two of the *palazzi* on the square were designed by Sangallo. The **Palazzo Tarugi**, by the lion and griffin fountain, is a highly innovative building, with a public loggia cut through one corner; it originally had an extension on the top floor, though this has been bricked in. Headier pleasures await at the **Palazzo Cantucci**, one of many buildings scattered about the town that serve as *cantine* for the wine trade, offering free *degustazione* (tastings) and sale of the Vino Nobile. Sangallo and his contemporaries never got around to building a facade for the plain brick **Duomo** across the square (daily 9am–1pm & 3.30–7pm). Its interior is an elegant Renaissance design, and it's scattered with superb sculptures by Michelozzo. The finest of the church's paintings is the Sienese **Taddeo di Bartolo**'s iridescent altarpiece of the *Assumption*, a favourite subject among Sienese artists. The piece was commissioned in 1401 at a time when Montepulciano was briefly under Siena's sway; the choice of an artist and a subject with resonance for Florence's old enemy must have been as much political as aesthetic.

Sangallo's greatest commission came in 1518, when he was invited to design the pilgrimage church of **San Biagio** on the hillside below the town. It's a fifteen-minute walk from the centre: aim for the Porta di Grassi, a couple of levels below the north side of Piazza Grande, from where Via San Biagio slopes down to the church. This was the second-largest church project of its time after St Peter's in Rome, and exercised Antonio until his death in 1534. The result is one of the most serene Renaissance creations in Italy, constructed from a porous travertine whose soft honey-coloured stone blends perfectly into its niche in the landscape. A deeply intellectualized building, its major architectural novelty was the use of freestanding towers to flank the facade (only one was completed). Within, it is spoilt a little by Baroque trompe l'oeil decoration, but remains supremely harmonious. Scarcely less perfect is the nearby **Canonica** (rectory), endowed by Sangallo with a graceful portico and double tiered loggia.

Eating, drinking and entertainment

One **café** is worth a special mention. *Caffè Poliziano*, at Via di Voltaia nel Corso 27 (daily 7am–midnight), is a tearoom from 1868 restored to a classic Art Nouveau design; it serves pastries and pots of tea as well as moderately priced full meals. *Rosticceria di Voltaia*, Via di Voltaia nel Corso 86 (no closing day), is a plain, sociable little **restaurant**; cosy *La Briciola* on Via delle Cantine (closed Wed) serves quality wood-fired pizza. Just inside the Porta al Prato are a clutch of moderately priced options. *Osteria della Porta di Bacco*, Via di Gracciano nel Corso 106 (☎0578.757.948), is a quiet, characterful old stone-arched place; nearby is *Il Cantuccio*, Via delle Cantine 1 (☎0578.757.870; closed Mon), with a standard Tuscan menu enlived by items such as *coniglio alla medievale* (roast rabbit). Opposite San Biagio church is the very pleasant *La Grotta*

(☎0578.757.479; closed Wed), serving mid-priced classic Tuscan cuisine in a sixteenth-century building with its own garden.

Vino Nobile di Montepulciano has been acclaimed since medieval times and today boasts a top-rated DOCG mark. Local vineyards offer tastings in the town (generally free, but often requiring advance notice) – the tourist office has a complete list, and can organize a **wine-tasting** ramble for you. Some of the many places to check out include the venerable *Contucci*, Via San Donato 15 (☎0578.757.006), which can trace the family line in Montepulciano back a thousand years, and the *Cantina Del Redi*, Via di Collazi 5 (☎0578.716.092, ⓦ www.cantinadelredi.com). Even if you can't afford Vino Nobile, ordering a cheap carafe of house *rosso* anywhere in Montepulciano will turn up a fragrant, silky smooth and highly memorable wine.

Every July, the three-week **Cantiere Internazionale d'Arte** (☎0578 .757.089, ⓦ www.cantiere.toscana.nu) presents exhibitions and concerts around town, and the last Sunday in August sees the **Bravìo delle Botti**, a barrel-race in medieval costume.

Chiusi

CHIUSI, 14km east of Montepulciano, is a useful transport hub, but this sleepy place is worth more than an hour or two's stopover – its quietly extraordinary cathedral, Christian catacombs and an Etruscan labyrinth could well entice you into delaying an onward journey. **Chiusi Scalo**, an unattractive suburb, is the default stop for all intercity buses, and is where the train station is located. The town centre, **Chiusi Città**, is 2km west; it's a short walk from the bus stop up Via Marconi to the main street, **Via Porsenna**, named after a semi-mythical Etruscan king of the sixth century BC. Here you'll find the modest **Museo Etrusco** (daily 9am–8pm; €4), with numerous sarcophagi, a few terracottas with traces of ancient paint, and the odd treasure – notably the enigmatic Gualandi Urn. If you're interested in seeing some of the Etruscan **tombs** outside town, ask one of the museum guards to take you (they hold the keys); the famous frescoed Tomba della Scimmia (of the Monkey), off-limits for many years, was opened to the public with much fanfare in May 2000 and is now visitable on pre-booked guided tours (Tues, Thurs & Sat 11am & 4pm; ☎0578.20.177).

Outside the museum is Piazza Duomo, an elegant little square paved in glittering marble with the Romanesque **Duomo**, one of Tuscany's oldest, which was built in the sixth century almost entirely from Etruscan and Roman blocks. Inside is a wealth of decoration; although much of the mosaic work on the walls is nineteenth-century, the marble columns – each with a different capital – the mosaic floor and the alabaster font are all Roman. The **Museo della Cattedrale** alongside (daily: June to mid-Oct 9.45am–12.45pm & 4–7pm; mid-Oct to May Mon–Fri 9.30am–12.45pm, Sat & Sun 9.30am–12.45pm & 3–6pm; €2) has a small collection of silverware and codices, and gives access to the **Labyrinth of Porsenna** (€3 extra or €4 combined ticket), which leads you through the atmospheric tunnels of the Etruscan water-catchment system below the piazza to a huge Roman cistern and then up inside the twelfth-century campanile. You can also arrange here to meet a guide at the entrance to the **Catacombs of Santa Mustiola**, 2km east of town, which were used by early Christians in the fourth and fifth centuries (tours daily 11am; June to mid-Oct also 5pm; €5).

The **tourist office** (Mon–Sat 9.30am–12.30pm & 3–7pm, Sun 9.30am–12.30pm; ☎0578.227.667, ⓔ prolocochiusi@bcc.tin.it) is opposite the

Duomo. There's one central **hotel**, the basic *La Sfinge*, Via Marconi 2 (℡0578.20.157, Ⓦwww.albergolasfinge.it; ❹), with more options at Chiusi Scalo. The best **restaurant** is friendly *La Solita Zuppa*, Via Porsenna 21 (℡0578.21.006; closed Tues), with an inventive menu offering lots of soups and items such as *tagliolini al ginger*. The gourmet-oriented *Zaira*, nearby at Via Arunte 12 (℡0578.20.260; closed Mon in winter), is listed in various gastronomic guides for its moderately priced "Etruscan" fare – boar, pigeon and the like.

Pienza and around

PIENZA, 11km west of Montepulciano, is as complete a Renaissance creation as any in Italy, established in an act of considerable vanity by **Pope Pius II** as a Utopian "New Town". The transformation of the village of Cortignano, where Pius was born, began in 1459 under the architect **Bernardo Rossellino**. The cost was astronomical, but the cathedral, papal and bishop's palaces, and the core of a town (renamed in Pius's honour) were completed in just three years. Pius lived just two more years, and of his successors only his nephew paid Pienza any regard: the city, intended to spread across the hill, stayed village-sized. Today, with a population of 2500, it still has an air of emptiness and folly – a natural stage set, where Zeffirelli filmed *Romeo and Juliet*.

Traffic converges on **Piazza Dante**, just outside the main gate, Porta al Murello, and from here the **Corso** leads straight to Rossellino's centrepiece, **Piazza Pio II**, which deliberately juxtaposes civic and religious buildings – the Duomo, Palazzo Piccolomini (papal palace), Bishop's Palace and Palazzo Pubblico – to underline the balance between Church and Town. The square

---

Hikes in the Parco della Val d'Orcia

There are plenty of interesting **hikes** in the area around San Quírico and Montalcino comprising the **Parco della Val d'Orcia**, full details of which are in *Walking the Val d'Orcia*, an English pamphlet by the Touring Club Italiano, available at the park office, Via Dante Allghieri 33 in San Quírico (℡0577.898.303, Ⓦwww.parcodellavaldorcia.it).

A moderately challenging trail runs from **Bagno Vignoni** out to the castle restaurant at Ripa d'Orcia and back (12km; 4hr). From 100m before the car-park, a cart-track rises through vineyards and olive groves to Rocca di Vignoni, the hamlet of Vignoni and on to Podere Bellaria, after which is a junction. One route heads right (north) to San Quírico, the other left (south) through a scenic landscape up to the castle. Backtracking 500m down the castle hill you'll find a signposted path leading right, down through foliage to a broken bridge over the Orcia river; don't cross, but follow the left-hand riverbank back to Bagno Vignoni.

There's an easy trail from **Montalcino** to San Quírico, crossing shadeless clay hills and dipping through vineyards (13km; 4hr), or you could cycle it, with rental bikes from *Lorenzo Minocci*, Viale Strozzi in Montalcino (℡0577.848.282). From the northern Porta Burelli, a track drops down to Gli Angeli and crosses the paved road in front of Podere La Casaccia, heading into an area of hummocks until you reach the provincial highway. Follow the road right for a few hundred metres, coming off at Podere Fiesole and heading east across clay ground to Podere Casello and Poderi Pian dell'Asso. Cross the train track and a couple of streams before climbing to Podere Belladonna and the chapel of Madonna di Riguardo. A rising and falling path covers the last 1.5km into San Quírico.

8

TUSCANY | Pienza and around

makes the usual medieval nod to Florence in its town hall, but it is otherwise entirely Renaissance in conception.

The **Duomo** has one of the earliest Renaissance facades in Tuscany; the interior, on Pius's orders, took inspiration from the German hall-churches he had seen on his travels, and remains essentially Gothic. The chapels house an outstanding series of Sienese altarpieces, commissioned from the major painters of the age – Giovanni di Paolo, Matteo di Giovanni, Vecchietta and Sano di Pietro. How long the building itself will remain standing is uncertain. Even before completion a crack appeared, and after an earthquake in the nineteenth century it has required much buttressing – the nave currently dips crazily towards the back of the church. The airy **crypt**, with a separate entrance (Mon, Tues & Thurs–Sat 10am–noon & 3.30–5.30pm; €1), displays some sixteenth-century tapestries. Pius's residence, the **Palazzo Piccolomini**, is alongside the Duomo. You're free to walk into the courtyard and through to the original "hanging garden" behind to the left, with a triple-tiered loggia offering a superb view over the valley. The **apartments** above (Tues–Sun 10am–12.30pm & 3–6pm; €3) include Pius II's bedroom, library and other rooms filled with collections of weapons and medals. Further mementoes of the pope – notably his English-made embroidered cope – are across the piazza in the excellent **Museo Diocesano** (mid-March to Oct 10am–1pm & 3–6.30pm; Nov to mid-March Sat & Sun 10am–1pm & 3–6pm; €4.13).

Practicalities

Regular **buses** between Montepulciano and Buonconvento pass through Pienza and San Quírico d'Orcia. Pienza is also a gentle day's **walk** from Montepulciano on an old cross-country route through the walled village of Monticchiello. The **tourist office** (Mon–Sat 9.30am–1pm & 3–6.30pm; ☎0578.749.071, ⓦwww.comunedipienza.it) is in Piazza Pio II opposite the Duomo and offers a self-guided fifty-minute Walkman tour of the town (€5.16). Pienza has pleasant self-catering **apartments** at *Giardino Segreto*, Via Condotti 13 (☎0578.60.452, ⓔmucci@ftbcc.it; ❸), and the fabulously romantic **hotel** *Chiostro di Pienza*, a converted Franciscan monastery at Corso Rossellino 26 (☎0578.748.400, ⓔilchiostro@jampy.it; ❻). Its **restaurant** (closed Mon), with expansive terrace views, is the best in Pienza, but pricier than most. The *Falco*, a simple trattoria in Piazza Dante (closed Fri), and friendly *Latte di Luna*, just inside the walls at Via San Carlo 2 (closed Tues), are more affordable. You can get sandwiches and wine at the *Enoteca Le Crete* on Piazza Martiri, and there's plenty of **picnic food**: Pienza is centre of a region producing *pecorino* sheep's cheese, and has gone overboard on natural food shops.

San Quírico d'Orcia and Bagno Vignoni

SAN QUÍRICO D'ORCIA, a rambling old village, stands at a crossroads 8km west of Pienza. Despite being a major stop for TRA-IN (Siena–Montepulciano), RAMA (Siena–Arcidosso) and SIRA (Montalcino–Rome) buses, its old town is quiet and rather decayed, with an exceptionally pretty Romanesque **Collegiata** church. With your own transport, head for the stunning *Castello Ripa d'Orcia*, an isolated castle **hotel-restaurant** 5km southwest of town down a gravel road (☎0577.897.376, ⓦwww.castelloripadorcia.com; ❹).

You can **rent bikes** from Cicloposse, Via Primo Maggio 27 in Pienza (☎0578.749.983), to follow a country track south to the medieval baths at **BAGNO VIGNONI**, 6km southeast of San Quírico (also served by bus). Its central square is occupied by an arcaded Roman *piscina*, or open pool; the springs still bubble up at a steamy 51°C, and the old, flooded piazza with its backdrop of the Tuscan hills and Renaissance **loggia** – built by the Medici, who, like St Catherine of Siena, took the sulphur cure here – made a memorable scene in Tarkovsky's film *Nostalgia*. The *piscina* has been out of bounds for bathing for some years, but you can bathe in the sulphur springs at the characterful *Posta Marcucci* **hotel** just below the village (☎0577.887.112, ⓦwww.hotelpostamarcucci.it; ❻; pool free to guests, €10.30 per day to others). Pius II's fifteenth-century summer retreat overlooking the *piscina* is now the romantic *Albergo Le Terme* (☎0577.887.150, ⓦwww.albergoleterme.it; ❺). Best **restaurant** is the excellent *Antica Osteria del Leone*, Via dei Mulini 3 (☎0577.877.300; closed Mon).

Montalcino

MONTALCINO is another classic Tuscan hill-town, 20km west of Pienza. Set within a full circuit of walls and watched over by a *rocca*, it looks tremendous from below – and from above, the surrounding countryside strewn with vineyards, orchards and olive groves is equally impressive. Montalcino produces a top-notch DOCG **wine**, Brunello di Montalcino, reckoned by many to be the finest in Italy, and is a quiet place, affluent in an unshowy way from its tourist trade. For a time in the fifteenth century, though, the town was of great symbolic importance: it was the last of the Sienese *comune* to hold out against the Medici, the French and the Spanish after Siena itself had capitulated. This role is acknowledged at the Siena Palio, where the Montalcino contingent – under its medieval banner proclaiming "The Republic of Siena in Montalcino" – takes pride of place.

The main street, Via Mazzini, leads from **Piazza Cavour** at the north end of town to the **Piazza del Popolo**, an odd little square set beneath the elongated tower of the town hall, based in all but its dimensions on that of Siena. An elegant double loggia occupies another side with, opposite, a wonderful and rather Germanic nineteenth-century café, the *Fiaschetteria Italiana*, that is very much the heart of town life. Steps beside the café lead up to the excellent **Museo Civico e Diocesano** (Tues–Sun: April–Dec 10am–6pm; Jan–March 10am–1pm & 2–5.30pm; €4.50). The quality of the art on show is out of all proportion to the size of the town, and takes in a wealth of Sienese painting and early sculpture. Following Via Ricasoli south brings you to the **Rocca** fortress (daily 9am–8pm; winter closes 6pm). Impressively complete, this encloses a public park and plush *enoteca*. You can also get access to the ramparts from here (€3).

Regular buses arrive from Buonconvento and Siena, most of which pass first through **Torrenieri**, from where connections head to Pienza and Montepulciano, and to Arcidosso and Abbadia San Salvatore. Montalcino's bus stop is at the north end of town in Piazza Cavour. The tiny Pro Loco **tourist office** is near the Piazza del Popolo at Costa del Municipio 8 (Tues–Sun 10am–1pm & 2–5.40pm; ☎0577.849.331, ⓦwww.prolocomontalcino.it). **Hotels** are uninspiring, with the *Giardino*, Via Cavour 2 (☎ & ⓕ0577.848.257; ❸), prone to street noise; and the *Giglio*, Via Saloni 49 (☎0577.848.167, ⓔhotel-giglio@tin.it; ❹), generically renovated. **Private rooms** are a better bet: try *Casali*, Via Spagni 3 (☎0577.847.150; ❷). The best **restaurant** is *Il Re di Macchia*, Via Saloni 21 (☎0577.846.116; closed Thurs), swanky and a tad pretentious; *Grappolo Blu*, on Via Scale di Moglio off Via Mazzini (℡0577.847.150; closed Fri), is more down-to-earth. Best pizza in town is at *San Giorgio* on Via Saloni (closed Mon), while *La Griglieria del Corso*, Via Matteotti 19 (closed Mon), has a chill cabinet full of salads and meats to eat in or take out, plus wood-fired pizzas and fresh pasta. *Circolo Arci* is a pleasant **bar-café** in an arcaded courtyard opposite the Museo Civico.

Monte Amiata

At 1738m, the extinct volcano of **Monte Amiata** is the highest point in southern Tuscany. Rising from the comparative desolation of the *crete* in a succession of hills forested in chestnut and fir, it is visible for miles around. A circle of towns rings its lower slopes, but the only one worth visiting for its own sake is **Abbadia San Salvatore**; nonetheless, old castles and bucolic countryside makes the area a good detour. Towns such as Abbadia and, on the western slope, **Arcidosso** are refreshingly cool for summer walking, and in winter are the nearest ski resorts to Rome. **Buses** serve Abbadia San Salvatore from Siena, Buonconvento, Chiusi and Montepulciano; those from Rome and Grosseto to Abbadia pass first through Arcidosso. Avoid the Monte Amiata **train** station – it's 45km away.

The centre of activity is **ABBADIA SAN SALVATORE**, which shelters at its heart a perfect, self-contained medieval quarter. The Benedictine **abbey**, around which the village developed, was founded under the Lombards and rebuilt in 1036. Today a mere fraction remains of the original, and most remnants date from the Middle Ages; the highlight is a large and beautiful eighth-century **crypt**, its 35 columns decorated with Lombard motifs. The town sees plenty of summer visitors, up here for the landscape, cool breezes and some good easy walks: best is the **Anello della Montagna**, a 29km path which circles the mountain between 900m and 1300m – a long day's walk, or easily manageable in sections round to Arcidosso. In July and August, buses shuttle up to the **summit**, offering a panorama that stretches to the sea. The **tourist office**, Via Adua 25 (Mon–Sat 9am–1pm & 4–6pm; ℡0577.775.811, ⓌWww.amiataturismo.it), is headquarters for the Amiata region. Best of the numerous **hotels** are the *Cesaretti*,Via Trento 37 (℡0577.778.198; ❷), and the central *San Marco*,Via Matteotti 13 (℡ & ℗0577.778.089; ❹).

ARCIDOSSO is another summer walking centre, with prosperous new development surrounding a well-preserved medieval quarter. Six buses daily connect to Abbadia. The *Gatto d'Oro* is a modern **hotel** on Via dei Venti (℡ & ℗0564.967.074; ❸), and there's a small **tourist office** at Via Ricasoli 1 (℡0564.966.083, ⓌWww.arcidosso.galamiata.it). Good **walks** include a ramble to the village of Montelaterone, 3km northwest, passing the Romanesque **Abbadia Santa Maria ad Lamulas**. More demanding is the hike up **Monte Labbro** (1193m) 10km south (also accessible by dirt road), which has, on its summit, the ruins of a church established by Davide Lazzaretti, founder of the Jurisdavidical Church, a Christian movement which campaigned for social reform in the turbulent 1870s. Lazzaretti was murdered by the Carabinieri in 1878, and is still remembered by locals.

Pitigliano and around

Tuscany's deep south, on the Lazio border, is its least-touristed corner. **PIT-IGLIANO**, the largest town of the area, is best approached along the road from Manciano, 15km west. As you draw close, the town soars above you on a spectacular outcrop of tufa, its quarters linked by the arches of an immense aqueduct. **Etruscan** tombs honeycomb the cliffs, but the town was known for centuries for its flourishing **Jewish** community (see box below). It has today a slightly grim grandeur, owing to its mighty **fortress** and the tall and largely unaltered alleys of the old Jewish ghetto.

Immediately through the main city gate is **Piazza Garibaldi**, flanked by the fortress and aqueduct (1543) and with views across of houses wedged against the cliffside. Within the fortress is the Renaissance **Palazzo Orsini** (Tues–Sun 10am–1pm & 4–7pm; winter 3–6pm; €3), its lovely interiors filled with jewellery and ecclesiastical ephemera; also in the fortress is the **Museo Civico** (same hours; €2.50), with an interesting collection of Etruscan vases and trinkets. The fortress backs onto **Piazza della Repubblica**, Pitigliano's elongated main square. Beyond lies the old town proper, a tight huddle of arches and medieval alleys. The left fork, Via Zuccarelli, brings you to Vicolo Manin and the **synagogue** and attached **Mostra Ebraico** (closed for restoration at time of writing). Pitigliano's eighteenth-century synagogue part-collapsed in the 1960s, and lay derelict until renovation in 1995. The grand stone arch and the stairs leading up to the women's gallery are the only survivors of the old building, along with plaques commemorating visits made by grand dukes Ferdinand III in 1823 and Leopold II in 1829. Although the Jewish community is virtually gone (see box below), Florentine, Livornese and even American couples still choose to tie the knot here. Staff are happy to show you around the old ghetto, which includes a **bakery** on Via Marghera with a Star of David in its barred window. A few minutes' walk beyond, at the western end of town, you can see traces of the **Etruscan wall** below the Porta Capisotto.

The Jews of Pitigliano

Jews began moving to Pitigliano from Rome in the thirteenth century. The community flourished until the annexation of the area by the Medici in 1608, when new laws forced the Jews to live in a **ghetto** and wear red clothing as a mark of identification. The granting of **religious freedom** throughout Tuscany by the last Medici ruler, Gian Gastone, in 1735, gave the town a new lease of life. Over the next 125 years, Jewish workshops and artisans on present-day **Via Zuccarelli** thrived, and there was even a Jewish university that attracted students from around Europe. By 1860, a third of the town, or some 2200 people, were Jewish.

It was Italian **Unification**, not the Holocaust, which brought about the end. In the new Italy, individuals felt freer than before to marry across religious lines, and the removal of a Catholic Papal State in central Italy gave Jews a new freedom to travel; many headed to the southern ports to take ship for Palestine. By 1900, there were barely a hundred Jews left in Pitigliano. With the surrender of Italian forces in 1943, the town's Jews were forced into **hiding**, and virtually all were protected from the Nazis by local Christian families. But by 1945 most felt unable to stay on, and departed for Rome, Livorno and Florence (all of which have large Jewish communities). Pitigliano's **synagogue** closed in the late 1950s, and today, in what was formerly one of the centres of Jewish learning in southern Europe, there are just three Jewish residents left.

TUSCANY | Pitigliano and around

Three RAMA **buses** daily from Manciano and Grosseto, two from Orbetello and one from Siena drop off on **Piazza Pettruccioli** just outside the city gate. The helpful **tourist office** at Piazza Garibaldi 51 (Tues–Sat 10.20am–1pm & 3–7pm; ☎0564.617.111, ⓦwww.collidimaremma.it) has maps of the *Vie Cave*, ancient Etruscan paths that weave between tombs and cliffside caves all around the town. With its untouristed lanes and the drama of its cliff-edge site, Pitigliano makes a memorable overnight stop. The only **hotel** is *Guastini*, Piazza Petruccioli (☎0564.616.065, ⓦwww.laltramaremma.it/alberghi/guastini; ❸), with a good **restaurant**; also check out the award-winning mid-priced *Osteria Il Tufo Allegro*, Vicolo della Costituzione 1 (closed Tues).

Terme di Saturnia

SATURNIA, 23km northwest of Pitigliano, is renowned for its sulphurous **hot springs**. Several daily buses run from Pitigliano to Orbetello on the coast (see p.546), and there are three daily **buses** north along the minor road from Manciano to Saturnia Be sure to get off at the springs (*Le Terme*) and not at Saturnia village. The last return bus is at 1pm, but it shouldn't be too hard to hitch back. The large **spa complex**, with fierce admission charges, a vast pool and a four-star hotel (☎0564.600.111, ⓦwww.termedisaturnia.it), is 6km north of the village of Montemerano; some 200m before it (as the road takes a sharp curve) follow a dirt track off to the right, unsignposted but usually signalled by a cluster of cars and vans. Two minutes' walk from here brings you to the **cascatelle**, sulphur springs that burst from the ground, forming natural rock-pool jacuzzis of warm, turquoise water, in which you can lie around for hours submerged up to your neck. Entrance is unrestricted and free, but you'll need a shower to wash off the sulphur smell, which can linger for days. The nearest **hotel** is the excellent *Albergo-Ristorante Stellata* (☎0564.602.978; ❻), in an isolated spot 1km down from the falls on the road to Manciano, while the **campsite** *Poggio alle Querce* (☎0564.602.568; open all year) is at Montemerano.

Eastern Tuscany

The Valdarno, or Arno Valley, upstream from Florence is a solidly industrialized district; there's no compelling stop before you reach the provincial capital, **Arezzo**, visited by foreigners in their thousands for its Piero della Francesca frescoes, and by Italians in even greater numbers for its antiques trade. South of Arezzo is the ancient hill-town of **Cortona**, whose picturesquely steep streets and sense of hilltop isolation make it an irresistible place for a stopover.

Arezzo

AREZZO, 65km southeast of Florence, has a charming old quarter, unspoilt enough to catch the eye a few years back of local folk-hero and deliberate

AREZZO

Fortezza
Medicea

S. Domenico

PIAZZA
S. DOMENICO

Casa
Vasari

Passeggio
del
Prato

VIA SAN DOMENICO

VIA MADONNA LAURA

Duomo

VIA SASSOVERDE

VIA XX SETTEMBRE

Santa Maria
in Gradi

VIA RICASOLI

Casa
Petrarca

Loggia
di Vasari

VIA PELLICCERIA

VIALE BRUNO BUOZZI

BORGO S. CROCE

PIAGGIA DI MURELLO

Palazzo
Comunale

VIA ALBERGOTTI

VIA VASARI

PIAZZA
GRANDE

VIA SANSOVINO

VIA GUACCIMANNI MATTEOTTI

Museo
d'Arte

Palazzo
Pretorio

S. Pier
Piccolo

Fraternità dei Laici

VIA CAVOUR

VIA CESARPINO

S. Maria
della Pieve

VIA BORGUNTO

VIA PESCIONI

VIA MINERVA

VIA DELLE MURA

Palazzo
Bacci

SS. Flora e
Lucilla in Badia

VIA GARIBALDI

PIAZZA
S. FRANCESCO

VIA MAZZINI

B A

PIAZZA
S. GIMIGNANO

VIA FONTANELLE

VIA GARIBALDI

SS.
Annunziata

C

S. Francesco

D

VIA OBERDAN

VIA ASMARI

VIA ALDI

PIAZZA
DEL
POPOLO

VIA S. FRANCESCO

San
Michele

CORSO ITALIA

VIA PORTA BUIA

VIA GUIDO MONACO

PIAZZA
SANT'AGOSTINO

Sant
Agostino

VIA LEONE LEONI

VIA PETRARCA

PIAZZA
GUIDO
MONACO

VIA MADONNA DEL PRATO

VIA ROMA

VIA ARETINO

VIA FRANCESCO CRISPI

VIA GIOTTO

VIALE P. FRANCESCA

VIA TRAY GUITTONE

VIA TESTA

VIA MARCONI

PIAZZA
RISORGIMENTO

CORSO ITALIA

VIA MAGGHERITONE

Anfiteatro
Romano

VIALE LUCA SIGNORELLI

VIA GUADAGNOLI

0   100 m

Bus
Station

VIA GUIDO MONACO

VIA SPINELLO

VIA N. ARETINO

Museo
Archeologico

VIALE MICHELANGELO

ACCOMMODATION
Astoria	3
Cavaliere Palace	4
La Toscana	2
Villa Severi	1

VIALE P. FRANCESCA

PIAZZA DELLA
REPUBBLICA

Train Station

RESTAURANTS
Antica Osteria L'Agania	B
La Buca di San Francesco	C
Fiaschetteria de'Redi	D
Il Saraceno	A

8

TUSCANY | Arezzo

clown of Italian cinema **Roberto Benigni**. Many key scenes in his Oscar-winning *La Vita è Bella* (Life is Beautiful) were filmed in Arezzo, and strolling on its quiet streets is like a breath of fresh air after days spent doing battle with Florence's big-city grind.

Arezzo was a major Etruscan and Roman city, and was a prosperous independent republic in the Middle Ages, until, in 1289, its Ghibelline loyalties precipitated military defeat at the hands of Guelph Florentines. In the arts, Petrarch, Pietro Aretino and Vasari, all native Aretines, brought lasting prestige to the city, yet it was an outsider who gave Arezzo its permanent Renaissance monument – **Piero della Francesca**, whose extraordinary **frescoes** belong in the same company with Masaccio's in Florence and Michelangelo's in Rome. Today, the local economy relies on innumerable jewellers and goldsmiths (the city has the world's largest gold manufacturing plant) and on the **antiques** trade: Piazza Grande has showrooms filled with the sort of furniture you put in a bank vault rather than in your living room and once a month – on the first Sunday and the Saturday preceding it – a vast **Fiera Antiquaria** occupies the square. The array of some 600 stalls is fun to browse though, but don't expect any bargains, even among the more junk-laden stalls on the fringes.

Arrival, information and accommodation

Arezzo is a major stop for **trains** between Florence and Rome, and is also served by a branch line from Perugia. **Buses** from Siena and elsewhere arrive diagonally opposite the train station. There are two distinct parts to Arezzo: the **old town**, on the higher parts of the hill, and the newer quarters which occupy the gentler slopes directly in front of the train station.

The main **tourist office** is on the right as you come out of the train station, at Piazza della Repubblica 28 (Mon–Sat 9am–1pm & 3–6.30pm, Sun 9am–1pm; ☎0575.377.678, ⓦwww.arezzocitta.com); the helpful staff speak English and have masses of information on Arezzo and its province. The **post office** is at Via Guido Monaco 34.

Accommodation is hard to come by – doubly so on the first weekend of every month when the antiques fair is on. In addition, the town is booked solid at the end of August and beginning of September, when the *Concorso Polifonico Guido d'Arezzo* and the *Giostra del Saracino* follow in quick succession. Geared to commercial visitors, Arezzo's hotels are generally rather bland and cheerless – certainly the city doesn't have any hotel as appealing as those on offer in nearby Cortona (see p.594).

The best **hotel** is the centrally situated *Cavaliere Palace*, Via Madonna del Prato 83 (☎0575.26.836, ⓦwww.cavalierehotels.com; ❼). Two cheaper options are *La Toscana*, Via Marco Perennio 56 (☎0575.21.692; ❸), a quality one-star (rooms without private bathroom are €10 cheaper); and central *Astoria*, Via Guido Monaco 54 (☎0575.24.361, ⓕ0575.24.362; ❹). Arezzo's excellent **hostel** *Villa Severi* is 1km east of the old town at Via Francesco Redi 13 (☎0575.299.047, ⓦwww.peterpan.it/OSTELLO.HTM; half-board €25, full-board €33).

The Basilica di San Francesco

In the heart of the old town, off to the left of the main Corso Italia and not far from its summit, stands the church of **San Francesco**, home to Piero della Francesca's celebrated **fresco** cycle in the choir (which has now been walled off and renamed the Cappella Bacci; see below). After centuries of damp and neglect, and some poor restoration early in the twentieth century that did more harm than good, work began in 1985 to consolidate and restore the badly damaged frescoes. On April 7, 2000 the brilliantly coloured frescoes were revealed in full, with details visible that had been obscured by dust and grime for centuries. They are worth as much time as you can give them.

You can visit the church during normal hours (summer Mon–Fri 9am–7pm, Sat 9am–6pm; winter Mon–Fri 9am–6pm, Sat 9am–5.30pm; Sun all year tourists allowed to visit 9.45–10.45am). You can see the frescoes from the nave of the church, but you need to get closer to really appreciate them, and you're not allowed any closer than the altar steps unless you've bought a ticket: visits are limited to 25 people at a time (same hours as the church), and to thirty minutes per group, and **tickets** (€5.10) have to be booked in advance. You're encouraged to reserve your tickets by phone (Mon–Fri 9am–1pm & 2–6pm, Sun 9am–1pm; ☎0575.900.404), but outside the peak summer months you can usually make a reservation in person, an hour or so ahead, at the ticket office beside the church.

Built after 1322, the plain basilica earned its renown in the early 1450s, when the local Bacci family commissioned **Piero della Francesca** to continue the decoration of the choir. The theme chosen was **The Legend of the True**

Cross, a story in which the wood of the Cross forms the link in the cycle of redemption that begins with humanity's original sin. Piero painted the series in narrative sequence, working continuously until about 1457. However, he preferred to arrange them according to the precepts of symmetry: the two battle scenes, for example, face each other across the chapel, rather than coming where the story dictates. As is always the case with this mystical painter, smaller-scale symmetries are present in every part of the work: the retinue of the Queen of Sheba (middle right wall) appears twice, in mirror-image arrangement, and the face of the queen is the same as that of the Empress Helena (middle left wall). This orderliness, combined with the pale light and the statuesque quality of the figures, create an atmosphere of spirituality that is unique to Piero, a sense of each incident as a part of a greater plan.

The fresco cycle

The complex story begins with the **Death of Adam** (top right wall), when a sprig from the Tree of Knowledge is planted in Adam's mouth. Below (to the left), **Solomon** orders a bridge to be built from wood taken from the tree that grew from Adam's grave. The visiting **Queen of Sheba** kneels, sensing the holiness of the wood, and then later (to the right) tells Solomon of her prophecy that the same wood will be used to crucify a man. Solomon then orders the beam to be buried (back wall, middle right).

The two most striking scenes have benefited hugely from cleaning. With the encrustation of dirt over the centuries, the **Dream of Constantine** (back wall, lower right) was always thought to be a night scene, but restoration has shown it in fact to depict early morning. As the angel descends to the tent of the sleeping emperor, bringing a vision of victory under the sign of the Cross, dawn is breaking behind the mountains to banish the constellation of Ursa Minor. Constantine's stolid guards keep watch, waiting, stiff with cold, for sunrise. Alongside, the **Victory of Constantine** (lower right wall) shows the emperor's defeat of his rival Maxentius, and his later baptism; part of the wall is damaged, but the sky is suffused with what the critic Sir Kenneth Clark has called "the most perfect morning light in all Renaissance painting".

Under torture, **Judas the Levite** (back wall, middle left) reveals to St Helena, mother of Constantine, the burial places of the three crosses from Golgotha, and then the three are excavated (middle left wall); the **True Cross** is recognized when it brings about a man's resurrection. Arezzo appears as Jerusalem in the top left. Then the Persian king Chosroes, who had stolen the Cross, is defeated by Emperor **Heraclius** (lower left wall); on the right he kneels awaiting execution. Heraclius returns the Cross to Jerusalem (upper left wall).

The rest of the town

Piero della Francesca's frescoes are the main reason to visit Arezzo, but the town's other highlights fit nicely into a pleasant afternoon stroll through the hilly lanes. Further up the Corso northeast of San Francesco you'll come to the steeply sloping **Piazza Grande**, which may look familiar from the film *La Vita è Bella*. The grand, imposing piazza is bordered on the east side by wooden balconied apartments and on the west by the apse of Santa Maria (see below) and the tiered facade of the **Palazzetto della Fraternità dei Laici**, with a Gothic ground floor and fifteenth-century upper storeys. The northern side is formed by the beautiful **Loggia di Vasari**, designed by Giorgio Vasari, court architect to the Medici, in the sixteenth century. Backing onto the square is the twelfth-century **Pieve di Santa Maria** (daily: summer 8am–noon & 3–7pm; winter

closes 6pm) with its unmistakable fourteenth-century campanile, known locally as "the tower of the hundred holes" for its many double-arched windows.
The arcaded facade, elaborate yet severe, belongs to a Romanesque type associated more with Pisa and western Tuscany, and the church is doubly unusual
in presenting its front to a narrow street rather than to the town's main square.
The carvings of the months over the portal are a perfect Romanesque group,
dating from the 1210s; in the tranquil interior, the raised sanctuary – the oldest section of the church – supports Pietro Lorenzetti's *Madonna and Saints*
polyptych, painted in 1320 and restored rather nastily.

At the highest point of town looms the large and unfussy **Duomo** (daily
7am–12.30pm & 3–7pm), its harmonious appearance belying its history. Begun
in the late thirteenth century, it was virtually finished by the sixteenth, but the
campanile comes from the nineteenth and the facade from the twentieth. The
stained-glass windows, made by Guillaume de Marcillat around 1520, let in so
little light that his other contributions to the interior – the paintings on the
first three bays of the nave – are virtually invisible. The tiny fresco nestled
against the right side of the tomb is **Piero della Francesca**'s *Maddalena*, his
only work in the town outside San Francesco.

A short distance west of the Duomo is the thirteenth-century church of **San
Domenico** (summer Mon–Sat 10am–1pm & 2–7pm, Sun 10–11am &
12.30–7pm; winter closes 6pm). The high altar has a *Crucifix* painted by a
twenty-year-old **Cimabue** in 1260, and there are tatters of frescoes all round
the walls. Signs point the way to the nearby **Casa Vasari**, Via XX Settembre
55 (Mon & Wed–Sat 9am–7pm, Sun 9am–1pm; free), designed in lurid style by
the celebrated biographer-architect-painter for himself. Down the slope, at Via
San Lorentino 8, the fifteenth-century Palazzo Bruni-Ciocchi houses the
Museo Statale d'Arte Medioevale e Moderna (Tues–Sun 8.30am–
7.30pm; €4), with a collection of paintings by local artists and majolica work
dating from the thirteenth to the eighteenth centuries.

All the principal sights are in the upper part of town, with the exception of
the **Museo Archeologico** (daily 8.30am–7.30pm; €4), which occupies part
of a monastery built into the wall of the town's Roman amphitheatre, to the
right of the station at Via Margaritone 10. Most impressive are the marvellously coloured coralline vases produced here in the first century BC – their skill
and artistry demonstrate how the Aretines achieved a reputation throughout
the Roman world as consummate craftspeople.

Eating and drinking

Arezzo's **restaurants** more than atone for its dull hotels. *Fiaschetteria de' Redi*,
Via de' Redi 10 (☎0575.355.012; closed Mon), is a busy old stone-floored
wine-bar-cum-osteria. Cosy *Antica Osteria L'Agania*, Via Mazzini 10
(☎0575.295.381; closed Mon), has rustic-style food, as does *Il Saraceno*, Via
Mazzini 6a (☎0575.27.644; closed Wed). *La Buca di San Francesco*, alongside San
Francesco church (☎0575.23.271; closed Mon eve & Tues), is a pricier spot for
Tuscan cooking and is a little tourist-oriented, but it's not at all bad – count on
around €45 per head.

The busiest **bars** and **cafés** are around piazzas Guido Monaco, Grande and
San Francesco, and along Corso Italia. For **ice cream** the first choice is *Il
Gelato*, off Corso Italia at Via de' Cenci 24, while for picnic provisions you can't
do better than *Sbarbacipolle*, Via Garibaldi 120.

Cortona

Travelling south from Arezzo you enter the **Valdichiana**, reclaimed swampland that is now prosperous cattle country, producing the much-prized Florentine *bistecca*. From the valley floor a long road winds up through terraces of vines and olives to the hill-town of **CORTONA**, 20km south of Arezzo, from whose heights you can see Lago Trasimeno. A scattering of Etruscan tombs aside, the steep streets are dominated by medieval architecture that claws its way around a knife-edge ridge, with barely a patch of level ground anywhere. Traffic is restricted, which accentuates the sense of hilltop isolation – although the quantity of summer visitors can diminish the atmosphere. Even without its art treasures, Cortona would be a good place to rest up, with pleasant hotels, excellent restaurants, and an amazing view at night of the villages of southern Tuscany glittering in the distance.

The main arrival point for buses and cars is **Piazza Garibaldi**, from where the only level street in town, Via Nazionale, connects to **Piazza della Repubblica**, which is overlooked by the grandstand staircase of the squat Palazzo del Comune. Just behind is **Piazza Signorelli**, named after Luca Signorelli (1441–1523), Cortona's most famous son, and site of the **Museo dell'Accademia Etrusca** (Tues–Sun: April–Oct 10am–7pm; Nov–March 10am–5pm; €4.50), where an enormous hall contains cabinets of prized Etruscan stuff, surrounded by second-rate paintings. The major exhibit – honoured with its own bijou temple – is an Etruscan bronze lamp from the fifth century BC, its circumference decorated with alternating male and female squatting figures. Elsewhere there are ranks of Etruscan figurines, jewellery and masses of unlabelled domestic odds and ends. The painter Gino Severini (1883–1966), another native of Cortona and an acolyte of the Futurist firebrand Filippo Marinetti, gets a room to himself. With pre-booking (℡0575.630.415), museum experts can guide you around a handful of Etruscan tombs outside town.

Piazza Signorelli links with Piazza Duomo, where the **Duomo** sits hard up against the city walls, overlooking the precipice. It was raised on the ruins of a pagan temple, but progressive rebuilding work has muffled the original Renaissance construction. It remains a cool and tranquil refuge from the sometimes wearing commercialism of the town centre. To the right of the altar is an illuminated vitrine holding a reliquary said to contain a fragment of the True Cross. Across the little piazza, a couple of churches have been knocked together to form the **Museo Diocesano** (April–Sept 9.30am–1pm & 3.30–7pm; Oct 10am–1pm & 3.30–6pm; Nov–March 10am–1pm & 3–5pm; €5), with a small collection of Renaissance art plus a fine Roman sarcophagus, carved with fighting centaurs.

Climbing from Piazza della Repubblica on Via Santucci and then Via Berrettini brings you into the upper town. A further work by Signorelli can be found in the unassuming church of **San Nicolò**, reached by veering right across Piazza della Pescaia at the far end of Via Berettini, then heading up the stepped Via San Nicolò. Ring the bell on the left-hand side wall, and the caretaker will take you to Signorelli's double-sided altarpiece, revealed by a neat hydraulic system that swivels the picture away from the wall. Signorelli's fresco of the *Madonna, Child and Saints* on the left is reminiscent of his more famous work in Orvieto.

From Piazza della Pescaia, a steep path leads up to **Santa Margherita**, resting place of St Margaret of Cortona, the town's patron saint. The daughter of a local farmer, she spent her long years of widowhood helping the poor and sick of Cortona, founding a hospital that stood close to the site of this church. Her tomb, with marble angels lifting the lid of her sarcophagus, was created in the mid-fourteenth century, and is now mounted on the wall to the left of the chancel, while her remains are on display in a glass coffin directly behind the chancel.

Practicalities

There are hourly LFI **buses** between the Arezzo and Cortona, and stopping **trains** from Arezzo call at Camucia-Cortona station (6km), from where a shuttle (roughly every half an hour) takes ten minutes to run up to the old town. Buy tickets at the station bar. The fast Florence–Rome trains stop at Teróntola, 10km south, which is also served by a shuttle roughly every hour (25 minutes to Cortona's Piazza Garibaldi); Teróntola is the station to get off at if you are approaching from Umbria. The centre is closed to traffic, so if you're driving you should park the car in Piazza del Mercato, in Piazza Mazzini by Porta Colonia, in Piazza Garibaldi (the most convenient and therefore busiest), or in front of Santa Margherita below the Fortezza, though this leaves quite a walk back uphill from the centre of town.

The **tourist office** is at Via Nazionale 42 (May–Sept Mon–Sat 9am–1pm & 3–7pm, Sun 9am–1pm; Oct–April Mon–Fri 9am–1pm & 3–6pm, Sat 9am–1pm; ☎0575.630.352, ⓦ www.cortona.net). There are half a dozen **hotels** in the historic centre, the budget option being the one-star, 22-room *Athens*, Via S. Antonio 12 (☎0575.630.508, ⓕ0575.604.457; ❸). Moving up a couple of rungs, there's a pair of decent three-stars: the 26-room *Italia*, very near Piazza della Repubblica at Via Ghibellina 5 (☎0575.630.254, ⓔhotel.italia@technet.it; ❺); and the eight-room *Sabrina*, close by at Via Roma 37 (☎0575.630.397, ⓕ0575.605.763; ❹). The large four-star San Luca, at Piazza Garibaldi 2 (☎0575.630.460, ⓦwww.sanlucacortona.com; ❺), is a charmless modern building, but many of its rooms have lovely views over the Valdichiana. Considerably more expensive, the most luxurious in-town choice is the *San Michele*, Via Guelfa 15 (☎0575.604.348, ⓦwww.hotelsanmichele.net; ❼), a handsome four-star converted from a patrician medieval town house – recently expanded to 55 rooms, it has twenty rooms with whirlpool baths. An atmospheric alternative to these central hotels is the *Oasi Neumann*, Via delle Contesse 1 (☎0575.630.354, ⓦwwwhoteloasi.org; ❺; open April–Oct), located about twenty minutes' walk south from Via Garibaldi. Occupying a converted monastic complex, this charismatic three-star hotel commands splendid views of the Valdichiana, but sometimes accepts guests only on a full-board or half-board basis - no great hardship, as its restaurant is good.

Cortona's HI **youth hostel**, the *Ostello San Marco*, is situated in the heart of the town at Via G. Maffei 57 (☎0575.601.765, ⓦwwwcortonahostel.com; €10.50; doubles and family rooms available; open daily mid-March to mid-Oct 7–10am & 3.30pm–midnight). It's a clean and spacious hostel in an old monastery, with fantastic views from the dormitories and friendly management.

Cortona has numerous **restaurants**, several of which are highly recommendable. Good for a quick lunch or a light evening meal is the *Taverna Pane e Vino*, at Piazza Signorelli 27 (closed Wed), offering *bruschetta*, a wide selection of salamis and cheeses, plus a few more substantial dishes – and the wine list runs to some 550 different vintages. For a more substantial meal, you can't beat the *Osteria del Teatro*, just round the corner at Via Maffei 5 (☎0575.630.556;

closed Wed). Set in a handsome and rambling old house, it's a good-naturedly busy place, featuring delicious home-made pastas on a meat-heavy menu; count on around €35 per person. A good alternative is *Tonino* on Piazza Garibaldi (☎0575.630.500; closed Tues), where there's the bonus of a panoramic view from the terrace.

On summer evenings a favourite night-time hang-out is the *Caffè del Teatro*, on the terrace of the Teatro Signorelli, with live music from Friday to Sunday. You'll occasionally get music at the glossy *Caffè La Saletta*, on Via Nazionale, which also does excellent crêpes and home-made ice cream, and has a terrific wine list.

East of Arezzo

Arezzo is the springboard for the Piero della Francesca art itinerary. Once you've taken in della Francesca's paired portraits of the Duke and Duchess of Urbino in the Uffizi in Florence, and the *Legend of the True Cross* and *Maddalena* in Arezzo, head east into the attractive Valtiberina (Tiber Valley) for more.

MONTERCHI is famous as the home of the *Madonna del Parto*, the only representation of the pregnant Madonna in Renaissance art. The village is off the main SS73 road to Sansepolcro, and is served by four buses daily from Arezzo. Signposts direct you to an ex-primary school on Via della Reglia, the painting's new home (Tues–Sun: summer 9am–1pm & 2–7pm; winter closes 6pm; €3.20). Della Francesca shows two attendant angels drawing back the flap of a small pavilion to reveal the pregnant Virgin, who places her hand on the upper curve of her belly, her eyes downcast. No other Renaissance artist produced anything comparable to its poise and gravity. Note that the picture is an object of pilgrimage: attendants clear the museum of visitors when local pregnant women come to pray to the Madonna.

SANSEPOLCRO, 25km northeast of Arezzo by regular SITA **buses** (also served by **trains** from Perugia and Città di Castello), makes its living as a manufacturer of lace and Buitoni pasta. Piero della Francesca was born here in the 1410s, and, despite short periods away, he spent much of his life in the town. Sansepolcro's modest, wheelchair-friendly **Museo Civico**, in the centre at Via Aggiunti 65 (daily; May–Sept 9am–1.30pm & 2.30–7.30pm; Oct–April 9.30am–1pm & 2.30–6pm; €6.20), houses perhaps della Francesca's greatest painting. The spectral *Resurrection* – originally painted for the adjoining town hall in the 1450s and moved here in the sixteenth century – is an image that has occasioned plenty of exotic prose. Kenneth Clark's description at least has the virtue of being provocative: "This country god, who rises in the grey light while humanity is asleep, has been worshipped ever since man first knew that the seed is not dead in the winter earth, but will force its way upwards through an iron crust." In a more prosaic vein, Aldous Huxley's pronouncement that this is the greatest painting in the world may have saved Sansepolcro from bombing in 1944: before the attack, a British officer recalled Huxley's description and delayed the air-raid. Occupying German forces peacefully withdrew from the town shortly afterwards. Elsewhere in the museum, an earlier della Francesca masterpiece, the *Madonna della Misericordia* polyptych, epitomizes the graceful solemnity of his work. Other pieces that attract attention are a sadistic *Martyrdom of St Quentin* by Pontormo and a painted standard by Luca Signorelli, a student of della Francesca.

Around the town, lesser art treasures are to be found in the **Duomo**, with its tenth-century carved image of the crucified Christ, and in the church of **San Lorenzo**, which has a *Deposition* by Rosso Fiorentino, painted within half-a-century of della Francesca's last works but seeming to belong to another world.

Sansepolcro's little **tourist office** is on Piazza Garibaldi behind the museum (daily: April–Oct 9.30am–noon & 2–7pm; Nov–March 10am–noon & 2–6pm; ⓣ0575.730.231, ⓦwww.sansepolcro.net). Best **hotel** is the welcoming *Fiorentino*, Via Pacioli 60 (ⓣ & ⓕ0575.740.350, ⓦwww.albergofiorentino.com; ❹), in business since 1807 and with rooms both en suite and not. It also has a characterful **restaurant** (closed Fri), in which you can expect to pay €35. Another excellent restaurant in the same price range is the family-run *Da Ventura*, Via Niccolò Aggiunti 30 (ⓣ0575.742.560; closed Sun eve & all Mon, plus Aug & 2 weeks in Jan).

❽ Travel details

Trains

Arezzo to: Assisi (12 daily; 1hr 35min); Bibbiena (hourly; 50min); Bolzano (5 daily; 7hr 30min); Camucia-Cortona (hourly; 20min); Chiusi (hourly; 1hr); Florence (hourly; 1hr); Foligno (every 2hr; 1hr 50min); Orvieto (7 daily; 1hr 20min); Perugia (every 2hr; 1hr 15min); Poppi (hourly; 57min); Rome (hourly; 1hr 40min); Teróntola-Cortona (hourly; 25min); Trento (5 daily; 7hr); Udine (5 daily; 7hr); Venice (5 daily; 5hr 10min); Verona (5 daily; 5hr 15min).

Empoli to: Florence (every 30min; 25min); Pisa (every 30min; 25min); Siena (every 30min; 50min–1hr 20min).

Florence to: Ancona (hourly; 2hr 30min–4hr); Arezzo (hourly; 1hr); Assisi (11 daily; 2hr 35min); Bari (12 daily; 8hr 15min–9hr); Bologna (every 30min; 1hr–1hr 40min); Bolzano (14 daily; 4hr 10min–5hr 50min); Empoli (every 20min; 25min); Foligno (11 daily; 2hr 55min); Genoa (hourly; 3hr 10min–4hr 30min); Lecce (7 daily; 10hr 25min–12hr); Livorno (12 daily; 1hr 30min); Lucca (hourly; 1hr 5min–1hr 50min); Milan (18 daily; 2hr 50min–4hr 50min); Naples (2 daily; 4hr); Perugia (12 daily; 2hr 10min); Pisa central (every 30min; 55min); Pisa airport (hourly; 1hr); Pistoia (hourly; 30–45min); Prato (every 30min; 20min); Reggio Calabria (from Campo Marte, 4 direct trains daily; 11hr, from Santa Maria Novella, changing at Rome, 7 daily; 11hr); Rimini (hourly; 3hr 30min–6hr); Rome (hourly; 2hr 15min–3hr 30min); Siena (via hourly connection at Empoli; 50min–1hr 20min); Trieste (9 daily; 5hr–6hr 15min); Udine (10 daily; 5hr 20min–6hr); Venice central (hourly; 3hr 25min–4hr 10min); Venice-Mestre (10 daily; 2hr 45min–3hr 20min); Verona (14 daily; 2hr 40min–3hr 40min); Viareggio (hourly; 1hr 30min–2hr 25min).

Grosseto to: Cécina (10 daily; 1hr); Florence (1 daily; 2hr 20min); Livorno (15 daily; 1hr 15min); Orbetello (10 daily; 30min); Pisa (15 daily; 1hr 30min); Rome (10 daily; 1hr 30min); Siena (6 daily; 1hr 20min).

Livorno to: Florence (12 daily; 1hr 30min); La Spezia (5 daily; 1hr 20min); Pisa (every 20min; 15–30min); Rome (every 30min; 3–4hr).

Lucca to: Florence (every 30min; 1hr 5min–1hr 50min); Pisa (every 30min; 30min); Pistoia (every 30min; 45min); Prato (every 30min; 1hr); Viareggio (every 30min; 30min).

Pisa to: Empoli (every 30min; 35min); Florence (hourly; 1hr); Livorno (every 20min; 15min); Lucca (every 30min; 30min); Viareggio (every 30min; 20min).

Pistoia to: Bologna (hourly; 1hr); Florence (hourly; 30–45min); Lucca (hourly; 45min); Viareggio (hourly; 1hr 15min).

Prato to: Bologna (10 daily; 1hr); Florence (every 30min; 20min); Lucca (every 30min; 1hr); Pistoia (hourly; 15min); Viareggio (hourly; 1hr 30min).

Siena to: Asciano (12 daily; 35min); Buonconvento (11 daily; 25min); Chiusi (12 daily; 1hr 35min); Empoli (hourly; 50min–1hr 20min); Grosseto (8 daily; 1hr 20min).

Buses

Arezzo to: Città di Castello (12–15 daily; 1hr 30min); Cortona (hourly; 1hr); Sansepolcro (17 daily; 1hr); Siena (5 daily Mon–Fri).

Chiusi to: Montepulciano (14 daily; 45min).

Cortona to: Arezzo (hourly; 50min); Chianciano (4 daily; 1hr), changing for Montepulciano.

Florence to: Bibbiena (8 daily; 2hr 15min); Castellina in Chianti (3 daily; 1hr 35min); Greve in Chianti (3 daily; 1hr 5min); Poggibonsi (10 daily; 1hr 20min); Poppi (9 daily; 2hr 5min); Radda in Chianti (1 daily Mon–Sat; 1hr 40min); Siena (12 express daily, plus 9 stopping services; 1hr 15min express); Volterra (6 daily; 2hr 25min). In addition to these state-owned SITA services, numerous independent bus companies operate from Florence to most Tuscan towns, including Arezzo, Grosseto, Lucca, Pisa, Pistoia, Prato, Sansepolcro and Viareggio.

Livorno to: Piombino (8 daily; 2hr); Pisa (every 30min; 20min).

Lucca to: Florence (30 daily; 1hr 15min); La Spezia (7 daily; 2hr 20min); Livorno (3 daily; 1hr 20min); Pisa (35 daily; 40min); Pisa airport (3 daily; 1hr 30min); Prato (9 daily; 2hr 15min); Viareggio (30 daily; 40min).

Massa Maríttima to: Piombino (2 daily; 25min); San Galgano (2 daily; 1hr); Siena (2 daily; 1hr 40min).

Montalcino to: Buonconvento (hourly; 35min); Monte Amiata (2 daily; 1hr); Siena (6 daily; 1hr).

Montepulciano to: Buonconvento (7 daily; 1hr); Chianciano (every 30min; 25min); Chiusi (every 30min; 50min); Pienza (7 daily; 20min); San Quírico (7 daily; 40min); Torrenieri (7 daily; 50min).

Pisa to: Florence (hourly; 1hr 10min); La Spezia (7 daily; 1hr 20min); Livorno (every 30min; 20min); Viareggio (hourly; 20min).

San Gimignano to: Poggibonsi (hourly; 35min).

Siena to: Abbadia San Salvatore (3 daily; 1hr 20min); Arezzo (4 daily; 2hr); Buonconvento (10 daily; 35min); Florence (30 daily; 1hr 30min–3hr); Grosseto (4 daily; 2hr); Massa Maríttima (4 daily; 1hr 40min); Montalcino (6 daily; 1hr); Montepulciano (4 daily; 1hr 20min); San Galgano (3 daily; 40min); San Gimignano (16 daily; 1hr–1hr 30min); Volterra (6 daily; 2hr).

Viareggio to: Pisa (every 30min; 35min).

Volterra to: Colle Val d'Elsa (for connections to Florence & Siena; 4 daily; Pisa (1 daily).

Ferries

Livorno to: Capraia (1–2 daily; 3hr); Portoferraio (1 daily; 4hr).

Piombino to: Portoferraio (10–18 daily; 1hr).

Umbria

* **Galleria Nazionale dell'Umbria** The region's finest and largest collection of medieval and Renaissance Umbrian paintings. See p.607

* **Gubbio** The best-looking of Umbria's medieval hill towns, and without Assisi's crowds and commercialism. See p.615

* **Basilica di San Francesco** The burial place of St Francis and one of Italy's great buildings, with frescoes by Giotto and Simone Martini. See p.623

* **San Francesco, Montefalco** One of Umbria's best small galleries, with a major fresco cycle by Benozzo Gozzoli. See p.630

* **Valle di Spoleto** A swathe of country with four of the region's most compelling villages: Spello, Bevagna, Trevi and Montefalco. See p.627

* **Piano Grande** A glorious upland plain, the centrepiece of the Monti Sibillini national park. See p.642

* **Valnerina** A verdant, mountain-edged valley dotted with hill villages and spectacular views. See p.639

* **Duomo, Orvieto** On a par with the cathedrals in Milan and Siena, Orvieto's Duomo has a glorious facade and a majestic fresco cycle by Luca Signorelli. See p.651

Umbria

Often referred to as "the green heart of Italy", Umbria is a predominantly beautiful region of rolling hills, woods, streams and valleys, and despite the growing number of visitors has largely retained an unspoilt air. Within its borders it also contains a dozen or so classic hill-towns, each resolutely individual and crammed with artistic and architectural treasures to rival bigger and more famous cities. To the east, pastoral countryside gives way to more rugged scenery, none better than the dramatic twists and turns of the Valnerina and the high mountain landscapes of the Parco Nazionale dei Monti Sibellini.

Umbria was named by the Romans after the mysterious **Umbrii**, a tribe cited by Pliny as the oldest in Italy, and one that controlled territory reaching into present-day Tuscany and the Marche. Although there is scant archeological evidence pertaining to them, it seems that their influence was mainly confined to the east of the Tiber; the darker and bleaker towns to the west – such as Perugia and Orvieto – were founded by the **Etruscans**, whose rise forced the Umbrii to retreat into the eastern hills. Roman domination was eventually undermined by the so-called barbarian invasions, in the face of which the Umbrians withdrew into fortified hill-towns, paving the way for a pattern of bloody rivalry between independent city-states that continued through the Middle Ages. Weakened by constant warfare, most towns eventually fell to the papacy, entering a period of economic and cultural stagnation that continued to the very recent past.

Historically, however, Umbria is best known as the birthplace of several saints, **St Benedict** and **St Francis of Assisi** being the most famous, and for a religious tradition that earned the region such names as *Umbra santa*, *Umbra mistica* and *la terra dei santi* ("the land of saints"). The landscape itself has contributed much to this mystical reputation, and even on a fleeting trip it's impossible to miss the strange quality of the Umbrian light, an oddly luminous silver haze that hangs over the gentle curves of the land.

After years as an impoverished backwater, Umbria has begun to capitalize on its charms. Foreign acquisition of rural property is now as rapid as it was in Tuscany thirty years ago, though outsiders have done nothing to curb the region's renewed sense of identity and youthful enthusiasm, nor to blunt the artistic initiatives that have turned Umbria into one of the most flourishing cultural centres in Italy. Headline-grabbing earthquakes in 1997 briefly dented tourist numbers, but they have had a negligible long-term effect – at least as far as visitors are concerned – as the majority of sights suffered little damage.

Most visitors head for **Perugia**, **Assisi** – the latter with its extraordinary frescoes by Giotto in the Basilica di San Francesco – or **Orvieto**, whose Duomo is one of the greatest Gothic buildings in the country. For a taste of the region's more understated qualities, it's best to concentrate on lesser-known places such as **Todi**, **Gubbio**, ranked as the most perfect medieval centre in Italy, and **Spoleto**, for many people the outstanding Umbrian town. Although there are few unattractive parts of the Umbrian landscape (the factories of Terni and the Tiber Valley being the largest blots), some districts are especially enticing: principally the mountainous **Valnerina**, **Piano Grande** and **Lago Trasimeno**, the last of which is the largest lake in the Italian peninsula, with plenty of opportunities for swimming and watersports.

Getting around the region by public transport presents no problems. Distances between the main sights are short, and there are excellent rail links both within the region and to Florence and Rome. There is an excellent website (ⓦwww.umbriatrasporti.it) with links to full and updated timetables for all bus and train services, including the private FCU and state FS rail services and the ATC, Apm and Ssit bus services. The official tourist board **websites** on the area are ⓦwww.umbria-turismo.it and ⓦwww.umbria2000.it.

The cuisine of landlocked, hilly Umbria relies heavily on rustic staples – pastas and roast meats – and in the past tended to be simple and homely. The region is also the only area outside Piemonte where **truffles** are found in any abundance, and their flavourful shavings, particularly in the east of the region, find their way onto eggs, pasta, fish and meat – but at a price that prohibits overindulgence.

Meat plays a leading role – especially **lamb** and **pork**, which is made into hams, sausage, salami and, most famously, *la porchetta*, whole suckling pig stuffed with rosemary or sage, roasted on a spit. **Game** may also crop up on some menus, most often as pigeon, pheasant or guinea fowl, though it's not unknown to be offered songbirds such as thrush (*tordo*), usually as a paté. The range of **fish** is restricted by the lack of a coast, but trout and crayfish are pulled out of the Nera, Clitunno and Scordo rivers, while the lakes of Piediluco and Trasimeno yield eels, pike, tench and grey mullet. **Vegetable** delicacies include tiny lentils from Castelluccio, beans from Trasimeno, and celery and cardoons from around Trevi. Umbrian **olive oil**, though less hyped than Tuscan oils, has a high reputation, particularly that from around Trevi and Spoleto.

As for desserts, Perugia is renowned for its **chocolate** and pastries. **Cheeses** tend to be standard issue, although some smaller producers survive in the mountains around Norcia and Gubbio.

Umbria used to be best known outside Italy for fresh, dry white **wines**. Orvieto, once predominantly a medium-sweet wine, has been revived in a dry style, though the original *abboccato* is still available. However, the pre-eminence of Orvieto in the domestic market has been successfully challenged by Grechetto, a cheap and almost unfailingly reliable wine made by countless producers across the region. Umbria's quest for quality is also increasingly reflected in a growing number of small producers, many of whom have followed the lead of Giorgio Lungarotti, one of the pioneers of Umbrian viticulture (almost any wine with his name on is reliable), and in some outstanding reds, notably the tiny Montefalco DOCG region close to Spoleto.

Perugia

The provincial capital, **PERUGIA** is the most obvious, if not the most picturesque, base to kick off a tour of Umbria. Although the centre of town is still medieval, it's surrounded by miles of fairly ugly suburbs and not a little industry. Buitoni, the pasta people, have a big works, and Italy's best chocolate, Perugino, is made here. In summer, the streets become claustrophobic and exhausting, so you probably won't want to spend a lot of time here. On the other hand, there's at least a day's worth of good sightseeing, and it's not a bad place to base yourself if you want to explore the surrounding area: it has big-city amenities and trains run out to all the major highlights, complemented by fast new roads and an extensive if complicated bus network.

The town's main draw in summer is **Umbria Jazz**, Italy's foremost jazz event, whose line-ups may well tempt you into staying – past stars have included Sting, Stan Getz, Gil Evans and Wynton Marsalis. Information and tickets are best sussed out well in advance from the tourist office (see below).

The presence of the **Università Italiana per Stranieri** (the Italian University for Foreigners) is another plus. Set up by Mussolini to improve the image of Italy abroad, it's now run as a private concern and gives the town a welcome dash of style and an unexpectedly cosmopolitan flavour. The big state university also means there's an above-average number of films, concerts and miscellaneous cultural events, which can be somewhat lacking in the rest of the region.

PERUGIA

San Pietro & Ipogeo dei Volumni ▶

ACCOMMODATION

Anna	3
Aurora	10
Brufani Palace	9
Eden	8
Etruria	6
Locanda della Posta	7
Ostello Spagnoli	11
Paola	5
Priori	2
Umbria	4
Youth hostel	1

RESTAURANTS

Aladino	B
Cesarino	G
Dal mi Cocco	A
Falchetto	C
Il Gufo	E
Pizza a Taglio	F
Pizzeria Mediterranea	D
Segreto di Pulcinella	H
Scalino	I

Sant'Angelo
Porta Sant'Angelo
S. Colomba
Sant'Agnese
San Benedetto
Sant'Agostino
Porta Bulagaio
Porta Elce
Università per Stranieri
Arco di Augusto
Santa Maria Nuova
Porta Pesa
San Severo
Oratorio di San Bernardino
San Francesco
San Filippo Neri
Duomo
Pozzo Etrusco
Madonna della Luce
Santa Teresa
Casa di Perugino
Palazzo dei Priori
Collegio di Cambio
Porta Santa Susanna
Scala Mobile
Giardini Carducci
Sant'Ercolano
Porta Marzia
Museo Archeologico
San Domenico
Santo Sprito
Porta Eburnea
Scala Mobile
FCU Station Sant'Anna
Car Park/ Bus Station
Stadium
Santa Giuliana

VIA DEL BULAGAIO
CORSO GARIBALDI
VIA ZEFFERINO FAINA
VIA ZEFFERINO FAINA
VIA F. INNAMORATI
VIA A. FABRETTI
VIA ELCE DI SOTTO
VIA A. PASCOLI
VIA S. GALIGANO
VIALE O. ANTINORI
VIA A. PASCOLI
VIA DELL'EREMITA
VIA PINTURICCHIO
VIA E. DAL POZZO
VIA DEL ROSCETTO
VIALE BRUNAMONTI
PIAZZA FORTEBRACCIO
VIA BARTOLO
MALL ROCCHI
VIA DEL SOLE
VIA BONTEMPI
VIA C. BATTISTI
PIAZZA MORLACCHI
VIA S. PAOLO
VIA A. FRATTI
VIA FRANCOLINA
VIA AQUILONE
PIAZZA DANTI
VIA CARTOLARIA
VIA G. ALESSI
VIA DELLA VIOLA
VIALE O. ANTINORI
VIA DEI PRIORI
VIALE INDIPENDENZA
PIAZZA IV NOVEMBRE
CORSO VANNUCCI
VIA MAZZINI
PIAZZA MATTEOTTI
VIA DELLA CUPA
VIA XIV SETTEMBRE
VIA P. COLOMBATA
VIA DELL'ANTINORA
VIA ARTURO CECCHI
VIALE POMPEO PELLINI
VIA DEL CORSO
VIA BONAZZI
VIA BAGLIONI
VIA OBERDAN
VIA UMBRIA
PIAZZA ITALIA
VIA SAN PROSPERO
PIAZZALE BELLUCCI
CORSO CAVOUR
BORGO VENTIGIORNI
VIA DEL PARIONE
VIA MARCONI
VIA MASI
VIA DEL BUCACCIO
VIA L. CAPITINI
VIA S. LORENZO
VIA FRATELLI PELLAS
PIAZZA DEI PARTIGIANI
VIA CACCIATORI DELLE ALPI
VIALE ROMA
VIALE XX SETTEMBRE
VIALE XX SETTEMBRE

N

0   200 m

▼ **11**, Campsites, train station & Fontignano hostel

Arrival and information

Arriving on the state train network you'll find yourself to the southwest of the centre at **Piazza Vittorio Veneto**: from here it's a fifteen-minute ride by bus (bus #6, #7, #9 or #11 – anything to Piazza Italia or Piazza Matteotti will do). City bus tickets (€0.80 for any number of journeys in 70min) are available from the station newsagents (turn right as you enter the ticket hall from the platforms) or a small booth over to the left as you exit the station. You can also purchase tickets on board the bus for €1.50, but you must have the right change. A tourist ticket, the Carta Turistico, valid for 24 hours, costs €3, though you're unlikely to be using enough buses to make it worthwhile. You'll probably want to avoid walking to the centre – it's a steep haul on busy roads. If you're coming on the private FCU (Ferrovie Centrale Umbra) lines from Todi or Terni to the south, or from Città di Castello or Sansepolcro to the north, you'll arrive at the much more central **Stazione Sant'Anna**, near the bus terminal at **Piazza dei Partigiani**. From this large square you can jump on a *scala mobile* (escalator) as it wends its way through weird subterranean streets to **Piazza Italia**.

If you're arriving by **car** be prepared for considerable hassle: all the town's approaches are up steep hills and the signposting leaves plenty to be desired. The centre is closed to traffic at peak times, and you'll do best to leave your car at the main train station and take a bus. Alternatively you could head towards one of the big peripheral car parks – Piazza dei Partigiani is the largest and most convenient.

There's a **tourist office** just behind the Palazzo dei Priori in the Sala San Severo at Piazza IV Novembre 3 (Mon–Sat 8.30am–1.30pm & 3.30–6.30pm, Sun 9am–1pm; ☏075.573.6458, ✉info@iat.perugia.it). It provides a good map, advice on city events and help in finding accommodation. There is also a private information office, the **Infotourist Point**, on the northeast corner of Piazza dei Partigiani (Mon–Fri 9am–2pm & 2.30–6.30pm, Sat 10am–6pm; ☏075.573.2933, ⓦwww.infoumbria.com), which is a useful source of information on organized half-day and day tours and operates as a **box office** for many events and concerts; it also has a left-luggage facility and **Internet access** during office hours. Another good source of information is the monthly **listings magazine** *Vivaperugia*, available from newsstands for €0.52.

Accommodation

Perugia has plenty of **accommodation** in all price ranges, although during term time long-stay students tend to monopolize the cheapest options. As in most of Umbria's main towns, it's a good idea to book in advance, especially during the Jazz festival in July, when room rates may well be raised.

Hotels

Aurora Viale Indipendenza 21 ☏ & ☏075.572.4819, ⓦwww.paginegialle.it. Basic, clean and pleasant two-star hotel with 14 rooms, though on a busy street. ❸
Brufani Palace Piazza Italia 12 ☏075.573.2541, ☏075.572.0210, ⓦwww.sinahotels.com. Perugia's smartest and most luxurious option. Very centrally located. ❾
Eden Via C. Caporali 9 ☏075.572.8102, ☏075.572.0342. A two-star with 18 rooms, all with private bathroom, in a quiet location close to the Corso. ❸
Etruria Via della Luna 21 ☏075.572.3730. A one-star with just eight rooms (seven with private bathrooms) in an unbeatable position immediately off the Corso. ❷

Locanda della Posta Corso Vannucci 97 ☏075.572.8925, ☏075.573.2562, ✉novelber@tin.it. Perugia's first choice if you want an upmarket treat, not as slick as the *Brufani* but just as central and a historic building where the likes of Goethe and Hans Christian Andersen once stayed. ❼
Paola Via della Canapina 5 ☏075.572.3816. Popular place with eight nice rooms, all with shared bathrooms. Hard to find – follow signs for the *Umbria* (see below) off the Corso and then bear left. ❷
Priori Via Vermiglioni 3 ☏075.572.3378, ☏075.572.9155, ✉hotelpriori@perugia.com. Perugia's first-choice mid-range two-star hotel. The 49 rooms (all with private bathroom) are

tastefully fitted out and there's a terrace overlooking the rooftops. The rooms vary greatly so ask to see a selection. ❹
Umbria Via Boncambi 37 ☎075.572.1203,

℗075.573.7952, ⓦwww.hotelumbria.com. Basic, centrally located two-star; all of the 18 rooms have private bathrooms. ❸

Hostels and camping

The town's original **youth hostel**, the Centro Internazionale di Accoglienza per la Gioventù, is two minutes from the Duomo, at Via Bontempi 13 (☎075.572.2880, ℗075.573.9449, ⓦwww.ostello.perugia.it; closed 9.30am–4pm & mid-Dec to mid-Jan; dorm beds €12). It has 134 beds in four-, six- and eight-bed dorms, and is perfectly situated. The newer **Ostello per la Gioventù Maria Luisa Spagnoli**, Località Pian di Massiano (☎075.501.1366, ℗075.502.6805, ⓔperugiahostel@tiscalinet.it; €13), is down near the main station and has its own restaurant and 186 beds in 33 four- and six-bed dorms.

The **campsites** *Il Rocolo*, Strada Fontana 1n (☎ & ℗075.517.8550, ⓦwww.ilrocolo.it; 1 April–15 Oct), and *Paradise d'Été*, Via del Mercato 29a, Strada Fontana (☎075.517.3121, ℗075.517.6056, ⓦwww.wel.it/cparadis; open year round), are 5km out of town at Località Colle della Trinità (Sulga bus marked "Colle della Trinità" from Piazza Italia or #9 bus from the station and a short uphill walk from the crossroads), but you're perhaps better off heading to the more rural sites on Lago Trasimeno (see p.612).

The Town

Once you're safely in Piazza Italia **orientation** is straightforward. The town hinges around a single street, the Corso Vannucci, one of the country's greatest people-watching streets, packed from dawn through to the early hours with a parade of tourists and Umbria's trendsetters and wannabes. Named after the city's most celebrated artist, Pietro Vannucci, better known simply as Perugino, the Corso contains several of the key sights and a couple of Perugia's most atmospheric little cafés.

Piazza Quattro Novembre and the Palazzo dei Priori

At the far end of the Corso Vannucci is the big and austere **Piazza IV Novembre** (once a Roman reservoir), backed by the plain-faced **Duomo**, fully restored after damage caused by the 1983 earthquake. While the Baroque interior is big on size, it's pretty small on works of art and comes as a disappointment after the fifteenth-century facade. As a change from pieces of the True Cross, the chapel almost immediately on your right as you enter, behind a heavy metal grille, contains the Virgin's "wedding ring", an unwieldy 2cm-diameter piece of agate that apparently changes colour according to the character of the person wearing it. The Perugians keep it locked up in fifteen boxes fitted into one another like Russian dolls, each opened with a key held by a different person. It's brought out for general public edification once a year on July 30. In one of the transepts there's an urn holding the ashes of Pope Martin IV, who died in the city after eating too many eels. Urban IV's remains are here too – he was reputedly poisoned with *aquetta*, an imaginative brew made by rubbing white arsenic into pork fat and distilling the unpleasantness that oozes out.

Outside in the piazza (which is the town's main hangout), the centrepiece is the **Fontana Maggiore**, designed by Fra' Bevignate, the monk who had a hand in the shaping of Orvieto's cathedral, and sculpted by the father-and-son team, Nicola and Giovanni Pisano. Sculptures and bas-reliefs – depicting episodes from the Old Testament, classical myth, Aesop's fables and the twelve months of the year – on the two polygonal basins were part of a carefully conceived decorative scheme designed to illustrate the city's glory and achievements. By some canny design work they never line up directly, encouraging you to walk round the fountain chasing a point of repose that never comes.

Just opposite rises the gaunt mass of the **Palazzo dei Priori**, often – and rightly – described as one of the greatest public palaces in Italy. Sheer bulk aside, it's certainly impressive – with rows of trefoil windows (from which convicted criminals were once thrown to their deaths), majestic Gothic doorway, and business-like Guelph crenellations – though the overall effect is rather forbidding; its real beauty derives from the harmony set up by the medieval buildings around it. The lawyers' meeting hall, the **Sala dei Notari** (daily 9am–1pm & 3–7pm, closed Mon Oct–May; free), at the top of the fan-shaped steps, is noted for its frescoes portraying scenes from the Bible, Aesop's fables and the coats of arms of medieval civic worthies: lots of colour, fancy flags, swirls and no substance – but certainly worth a glance.

The small **Collegio della Mercanzia** (March–Oct & 20 Dec–6 Jan Mon–Sat 9am–1pm & 2.30–5.30pm, Sun 9am–1pm; rest of year Tues, Thurs & Fri 8am–2pm, Wed & Sat 8am–4.30pm, Sun 9am–1pm; €1.03; €3.10 with Collegio di Cambio) lies further down the Corso side of the palace at Corso Vannucci 15 hidden behind an innocuous door. The seat of the Merchants' Guild, it is covered entirely in intricate and beautiful fifteenth-century panelling. A few doors down at Corso Vannucci 25, the impressive **Collegio di Cambio** (March–Oct & 20 Dec–6 Jan Mon–Sat 9am–12.30pm & 2.30–5.30pm, Sun 9am–12.30pm; rest of year Tues–Sat 8am–2pm, Sun 9am–12.30pm; €2.60, or €3.10 with the Collegio della Mercanzia) was the town's money exchange in medieval times. The superb frescoes on the walls were executed by Perugino at the height of his powers and are considered the artist's masterpiece; in true Renaissance fashion, they attempt to fuse ancient and Christian culture. Up on the door-side wall there's a famous but unremarkable self-portrait in which the artist looks like he had a bad lunch. The small chapel to the right of the Collegio is frescoed by Giannicola di Paolo (1519), the last important Umbrian painter influenced by Perugino.

The **Galleria Nazionale dell'Umbria** (daily 8.30am–7.30pm, closed first Mon of every month; €6.50) is on the upper floor of the palace complex (lift or stairs), with the entrance through its opulently carved **doorway**. One of central Italy's best and most charming galleries, this takes you on a romp through the history of Umbrian painting, with masterpieces by Perugino, Pinturicchio and many others, plus one or two stunning Tuscan masterpieces (Duccio, Fra' Angelico, Piero della Francesca) thrown in for good measure. The entrance is worth every penny if you're the slightest bit interested in early and mid-Renaissance art, and the paintings are further enhanced by a recent restoration of the rooms. Plans are also in hand to extend the gallery across a large part of the palace's lower floors.

Just east of Piazza Danti behind the cathedral at Piazza Piccinino 1 lies the entrance to the **Pozzo Etrusco** (April–Sept daily 10am–1.30pm & 2.30–6.30pm; Oct–March Mon–Fri 10.30am–1.30pm & 2.30–4.30pm; €1.80), a massive and extraordinary well that does more than hint at the dazzling engineering and technical skills of its Etruscan builders.

A few minutes' walk farther east along Via del Sole brings you to the church of **San Severo** (same hours and ticket as Pozzo Etrusco) in Piazza Raffaello, known for its painting *Holy Trinity and Saints* by Raphael, who spent some five formative years in Umbria. Today it's the only **painting** by him still left in the region – Napoleon carted many of the artist's works off to France – except for a painted banner in the art gallery in Città di Castello (see p.614). The lower third of the painting, depicting *Six Saints*, was completed in 1521 after Raphael's death by Perugino, his erstwhile teacher.

North and west of Corso Vannucci

The best streets to wander around for a feel of the old city are to the east and west of the Duomo, **Via dei Priori** being the most characteristic. Just behind the Palazzo dei Priori in Via della Gabbia there once hung a large iron cage used to imprison thieves and sometimes even clergy. In January 1442, according to a medieval chronicler, priest Angelo di Ferolo "was put back into the cage at midday, and it was very cold and there was much snow, and he remained there until the first day of February both night and day and that same day he was brought out dead". You can still make out long spikes on some of the lower walls, used as hooks for the heads of executed criminals. Medieval Perugia was evidently a hell of a place to be. "The most warlike of the people of Italy", wrote the historian Sismondi, "who always preferred Mars to the Muse". Male citizens played a game (and this was for pleasure) in which two teams, thickly padded in clothes stuffed with deer hair and wearing beaked helmets, stoned each other mercilessly until the majority of the other side were dead or wounded. Children were encouraged to join in for the first two hours to promote "application and aggression".

In 1265 Perugia was also the birthplace of the **Flagellants**, who had half of Europe whipping itself into a frenzy before the movement was declared heretical. In addition to some hearty scourging they took to the streets on moonlit nights, groaning and wailing, dancing in white sheets, singing dirges and clattering human bones together, all as expiation for sin and the wrongs of the world. Then there were the infamous **Baglioni**, the medieval family who misruled the city for several generations, their spell-binding history – full of vendetta, incest and mass-slaughter – the stuff of great medieval soap opera.

Via dei Priori passes the rarely open **Madonna della Luce** on the north side after the medieval Torre degli Scirri, little more than a chapel dominated by an impressive altarpiece by G. B. Caporali, a follower of Perugino. The church takes its name from the story that in 1513 a young barber swore so profusely on losing at cards that a Madonna in a wayside shrine closed her eyes in horror and kept them closed for four days. The miracle prompted celebrations, processions and the building of a new church. Some way beyond, as the street bears right, is a nice patch of grass perfectly placed for relaxing with the crowd from the art school next door or for admiring Agostino di Duccio's colourful **Oratorio di San Bernardino**, whose richly embellished facade (1461) is far and away the best piece of sculpture in the city. Again to the north is what's left of San Francesco, once a colossal church, now ruined by centuries of earthquakes and neglect, but with a curiously jumbled and striking facade still just about standing.

From here you can wander along the rather uninspiring Via A. Pascoli, past the hideous university buildings, to the **Università Italiana per Stranieri** in Piazza Fortebraccio. The big patched-up gateway here is the **Arco di Augusto**, its lowest section one of the few remaining monuments of Etruscan Perugia. The upper remnant was added by the Romans when they captured the city in 40 BC. Terms run from April to December, and posters around the place give details of concerts and English films (especially in the summer).

About a minute's walk north on Corso Garibaldi is the sadly half-defunct **Sant'Agostino**, once Romanesque, now botched Baroque and filled with wistful signs explaining what paintings used to hang in the church before they were spirited to France by light-fingered Napoleonic troops. The church, however, is not entirely ruined: there's a beautiful choir (probably based on a drawing by Perugino) and a couple of patches of fresco on the left-hand (north) wall, giving a tantalizing idea of what the place must once have been. Next door to the north side is the fifteenth-century **Oratorio di Sant'Agostino**, its ludicrously ornate ceiling looking as if it's about to erupt in an explosion of gilt, stucco and chubby plaster cherubs. Fifteen minutes' walk up the street is the fifth-century church of **Sant'Angelo**, situated in a tranquil spot (with a pretty little patch of grass and trees – perfect for picnics and siestas) and based on a circular pagan temple; the 24 columns, each made from a different stone, are from the earlier building.

Corso Cavour

The rest of Perugia's highlights are on the other side of town, grouped together on **Corso Cavour**, a busy and dustily unpleasant road in the summer, and just plain unpleasant the rest of the time. On the way over you could join the smooching couples in the small but well-kept **Giardini Carducci** (by Piazza Italia) to see why Henry James called Perugia the "little city of the infinite views". When the usual cloak of haze lifts on crisp winter mornings, half of Umbria is laid out before you, with the mountains of Tuscany in the distance.

Below the piazza stands the strange octagonal, rarely open, church of **Sant'Ercolano** – built on the site where the head of Perugia's first bishop miraculously re-attached itself to his body after the Goths chopped it off. It's worth taking a short walk past here to look into the Porta Marzia, where a subterranean road of medieval houses, **Via Baglioni Sotteranea**, leads under the ruins of the Rocca Paolina, a once-enormous papal fortress destroyed by the Perugians at Unification. This amazing underground labyrinth can also be accessed from the escalators to Piazza dei Partigiani from the west side of Piazza Italia.

Continuing on to Corso Cavour and heading south, you come to **San Domenico**, Umbria's biggest church. It has a desolate and unfinished air from the outside, with pigeons nesting where they shouldn't and grass growing from the pinky-orange marble, but it's also appealing in a big and rather melancholy sort of way. The original Romanesque interior collapsed in the sixteenth century and the Baroque replacement is vast, cold and bare. Like Sant'Agostino, however, it's full of hints as to how beautiful it must have been – nowhere more so than in the fourth chapel on the right, where a superb **carved arch** by Agostino di Duccio is spoilt only by Victorian Christmas card-style decorations and a doll-like Madonna. In the east transept, to the right of the altar, is the **tomb of Benedict XI** (1324), another pope who died in Perugia, this time from eating poisoned figs. It's an elegant and well-preserved piece by one of the period's three leading sculptors: Pisano, Lorenzo Maitani or Arnolfo di Cambio, no one knows which. There's also another good choir, together with some impressive **stained-glass** windows – the second biggest in Italy after those in Milan Cathedral and a welcome splash of colour in the midst of all the mud-coloured paint.

Housed in the church's cloisters is the **Museo Archeologico Nazionale dell'Umbria** (Mon 2.30–7.30pm, Tues–Sun 8.30am–7.30pm; €2). Before being hammered by Augustus, Perugia was a big shot in the twelve-strong Etruscan federation of cities, which is why the city has one of the most extensive Etruscan collections around. The museum has recently undergone a major overhaul, turning what had been a dusty and uninspiring set of displays into a far brighter and more appealing ensemble. The place is definitely worth a visit, even if the Etruscans normally leave you cold, for there's far more here than the usual run of urns and funerary monuments. Particulary compelling are the Carri Etruschi di Castel San Marino, some exquisite sixth-century bronze chariots; a witty collection of eye-opening artefacts devoted to fashion and beauty in the Etruscan era; and the bewildering **Bellucci Collection**. The last is a private hoard of charms and amulets through the ages: everything from the obvious – lucky horseshoes – to strange and often sinister charms such as snakeskins and dried animals. The exhibits span several thousand years, and form a unique and oddly poignant picture of people's fears and superstitious hopes across the millennia.

If the Etruscans get you going you might try the outstanding local tombs, the **Ipogeo dei Volumni** (daily: July & Aug 9am–noon & 4.30–7pm; Sept–June 9.30am–1pm & 3.30–6.30pm; €2), 7km east of the town at Via Assisana 53, Ponte San Giovanni (bus or train to Ponte San Giovanni and then a short walk). Though the best in Umbria, they're quite small and without any of the racy paintings found in some Tuscan tombs; and certainly not a patch on the graves at Tarquinia or Cerveteri (see p.788 and p.787). Visits are also restricted to a maximum of seven people at a time and you're only officially allowed five minutes in the tombs themselves.

Farther down Corso Cavour, advertised by a rocket-shaped belltower, is the tenth-century basilica of **San Pietro**, the most idiosyncratic of all the town's churches. Tangled up in a group of buildings belonging to the university's agriculture department, the none-too-obvious entrance is through a frescoed doorway in the far left-hand corner of the first courtyard off the road. Few churches can be so sumptuously decorated: every inch of available space is covered in gilt, paint or marble, though a guiding sense of taste seems to have prevailed, and in the candle-lit gloom it actually feels like the sacred place it's meant to be. All the woodwork is extraordinary; the **choir** has been called the best in Italy, and there is a host of works by Perugino, Fiorenzo di Lorenzo and others.

Eating and drinking

Perugia's student population ensures that there is a plethora of reasonably priced places to eat out, from the many snack bars around the centre of town to simple osterie serving traditional Umbrian cuisine. Local dishes feature wild mushrooms, truffles and game often succulently combined with home-made egg pasta.

Pizzerias and restaurants

Aladino Via della Prome 11 ☎075.572.0938. Just up Via del Sole from Piazza Danti and the cathedral, this well-regarded restaurant serves an inspired mixture of Umbrian and Sardinian cooking and has an interesting wine list. You'll need to book. Closed lunchtimes & all day Mon.
Cesarino Piazza IV Novembre 45 ☎075.572.8974. A great central restaurant and a Perugia tradition which hasn't suffered too much from a recent interior redecoration. Booking advised. Closed Wed.
Dal mi Cocco Corso Garibaldi 12 ☎075.573.2511. Good-value traditional dishes

with a variety of set menus. Closed Mon.
Falchetto Via Bartolo 20, just off Piazza Danti. A reliably good and easygoing place with a medieval interior. Closed Mon.
Il Gufo Via della Viola 18 at Via Alessi. Excellent osteria with moderately priced regional cooking. Closed Sun & Mon.
Pizza a Taglio Via dei Priori 3, corner Via della Gabbia. A little place just a few steps from Corso Vannucci for inexpensive pizza by the slice to take away.
Pizzeria Mediterranea Piazza Piccinino 11. Simple and tasteful pizzeria with small wood-fired

oven and a couple of brick-vaulted rooms a few steps beyond the entrance to the Pozzo Etrusco. **Segreto di Pulcinella** Via Larga 8 ☎075.573.6284. A bustling pizzeria that's very popular with students. Closed Tues.

Scalino Via Sant'Ercolano. Authentic old-fashioned pizzeria and trattoria, staffed by little old ladies and patronized almost entirely by locals. Fabulous brick-vaulted dining room and very reasonable prices. Closed Fri.

Cafés and nightlife

The city's liveliest **cafés** are clustered on Corso Vannucci, with the atmospheric old-world *Pasticceria Sandri* at no. 32 (closed Mon) a high spot for the sweet-toothed. For **ice cream** in more-than-generous helpings, join the queues at the *gelateria* at Via Bonazzi 3 on the corner of Piazza della Repubblica. The best place to indulge in local wines is at the *Enoteca Provinciale* at Via Ulisse Rocchi 16–18 (closed Sun pm), which also does good light snacks in a room to the rear, or for a selection of beers and whiskies, there are the inevitable Irish **pubs** – one of the best is *Sullivan's* close to Sant'Ercolano at Via del Bovaro 2 (closed Tues). Several places lay on **live music**: two of the longest-established places are the *Bar Morlacchi*, Piazza Morlacchi 6–8 (closed Sun), and the *Contrappunto Jazz Club*, Via Scortici 4a (closed Mon), open until 1am and 2am respectively. The majority of big **clubs** and discos are out of town; the most popular exception is the central *Domus Deliri*, near Piazza Morlacchi at Via del Naspo 3 (closed Mon).

Lago Trasimeno

The most tempting option around Perugia – whose surroundings are generally pretty bleak – is **LAGO TRASIMENO**, an ideal spot to hole up in for a few days, and particularly recommended if you want to get in some swimming, windsurfing or sailing. The lake is about 30km from Perugia and is well served by both train and bus. It's the biggest inland stretch of water on the Italian peninsula, the fourth largest in Italy overall, and, though you wouldn't think so to look at it, never deeper than 7m – hence bath-like warm water in summer. And, because the tourist and fishing industries are the economic bread and butter of the surrounding towns, it's also clean. Large banks of weed drift in during the summer, but the council takes care of these, dumping them with little subtlety on the shore.

A winning combination of tree-covered hills to the north, Umbria's subtle light, and placid lapping water produces some magical moments, but on overcast and squally days the mood can turn melancholy. Not all the reed-lined shore is uniformly pretty either; steer clear of the northern coast and head for the stretches south of Magione and Castiglione if you're after relative peace and quiet. Be warned, too, that **unofficial camping** is not as easy as it looks, partly because a lot of the immediate shoreline is marshy, but mainly because most of the good spots have already been grabbed by locals.

There's some good **walking** in the vicinity, with treks possible up Monte Castiglione on the mule track from the Passo di Gosparani (7km north of Tuoro); up Monte Acuto from Montacuto (15km northeast on the Umbértide road); or up Monte Murlo from **Preggio**, a hill-village 7km north of Castel Rigone and worth a visit in its own right. If you feel less adventurous, you could try some of the twelve waymarked trails around the lake, starting from centres such as Panicale, Passignano and Castiglione del Lago; pick up the map-brochure *Itinerari Turistici del Trasimeno* from tourist offices.

For visitors with a car, this area is also a good point to cross the border into Tuscany to visit Cortona (see p.593).

Passignano

Strung out along the northern shore, **PASSIGNANO**, a newish town with a medieval heart, is the lake's most accessible point, served by seven daily buses and hourly trains from Perugia and Terontola. In summer it can get a bit clogged with traffic, but in the evenings, the joint is jumping, with bars, discos and fish restaurants aplenty. There's a **tourist office** at Piazza Trento e Trieste 6 (June–Sept Mon–Sat 10am–12.30pm & 4–7pm, Sun 10am–12.30pm; Oct–May Fri & Sat 3–6.30pm, Sun 10am–12.30pm; ☎075.827.635), and about a dozen **hotels** – the best value of which are the fifteen-room *Florida*, Via II Giugno 2 (☎075.827.228; ❷), and eleven-room *Del Pescatore*, Via San Bernardino 5 (☎075.829.6063, ✉delpescatore@libero.it; ❷), both comfortable one-stars with en-suite rooms; and the larger, smarter three-star *Trasimeno*, Via Roma 16a (☎075.829.355, ℻075.829.267, ☹www.hoteltrasimeno.com; ❸).

Somewhere along the lakeshore towards Tuoro, probably at Sanguineto ("the Place of Blood") or Ossaia ("the Place of Bones"), is the spot where the Romans suffered their famous clobbering at the hands of **Hannibal** in 217 BC. Hannibal was headed for Rome, having just crossed the Alps, when he was met by a Roman force under the Consul Flaminius. Things might have gone better for Flaminius if he'd heeded the omens that piled up on the morning of battle. First he fell off his horse, next the legionary standards had to be dug out of the mud, then – and this really should have raised suspicions – the sacred chickens refused their breakfast. Poultry accompanied all Roman armies and, by some means presumably known to the legionnaire in charge of chickens, communicated the will of the gods to waiting commanders in the field. With the chickens against him Flaminius didn't stand a chance. Hannibal lured him into a masterful ambush, with the only escape a muddy retreat into the lake. Sixteen thousand Romans, including the hapless commander, were killed.

Tuoro and Castel Rigone

The rambling village of **TUORO**, 4km west of Passignano and a three-kilometre walk from the Trasimeno battlefield, is a quiet, dull little place giving road access into the desolate, beautiful mountains north of the lake – the best of the scenery within easy reach of Perugia. A hard-to-find drive and walkway have been laid out, starting and finishing just west of the village on the road to Cortona, that take in salient features of the old battlefield. Accommodation here is restricted to a single **hotel**, the eight-roomed *Volante Inn*, at Via Sette Martiri 52 (☎075.826.107, ℻075.825.088, ✉volanteinn@libero.it; ❷), plus a **campsite**, the *Punta Navaccia*, Via Navaccia 4 (☎075.826.357, ℻075.825.8147, ✉navaccia@camping.it; April–Sept), in the nearby hamlet of **Punta Navaccia**.

The village of **CASTEL RIGONE**, 8km northeast of Passignano, sits in the mountains, with superb views and a small, geranium-strewn medieval centre. There are two smart, rather staid, hotels, the better of which is the immediately obvious four-star *Relais La Fattoria*, Via Rigone 1 (☎075.845.322, ℻075.845.197, ☹www.relaislafattoria.com; ❺). The restaurants at the hotels are the only places for a bite to eat, though neither is terribly good.

Castiglione del Lago

CASTIGLIONE DEL LAGO is the most appealing town on the lake and cuts a fine silhouette from other points around the shore, jutting out into the water on a fortified promontory. In the event it doesn't really live up to its distant promise, but is still a friendly, unpretentious place with enough charm and action to hold anyone's interest for a couple of days – longer if all you want to do is crash out on a (albeit modest) beach. It's easy to reach by slow train either from Chiusi (heading north) or Teróntola if you're coming from Arezzo or Perugia. There are also nine buses daily from Perugia.

There's a good **tourist office** at no. 10 in the main Piazza Mazzini (Mon 8am–1.30pm, Tues–Sat 8am–1.30pm & 3–7.30pm, Sun 9am–1pm; ⓣ075.965.2484 or 075.965.2738, ⓔinfo@iat.castiglione-del-lago.pg.it), whose flashiness in such a small place gives a good idea of the town's considerable appeal to tourists. They have a lot of reasonable but generally characterless **rooms** on their books and apartments to rent on a weekly basis, usually a cheaper option if you can get a party together. Among the **hotels**, the top dog is the three star *Duca della Corgna*, Via B. Buozzi 143 (ⓣ075.953.238, ⓕ075.962.2446, ⓔhotelcorgna@trasinet.com; ❺), with the *Trasimeno*, Via Roma 174 (ⓣ075.965.2494, ⓕ075.952.5258; ❸), hot on its heels; more atmospheric is the *Miralago*, Piazza Mazzini 6 (ⓣ075.951.157 or 075.953.063, ⓕ075.951.924, ⓦwww.hotelmiralago.com; ❺), with views of the lake behind. Most of the **campsites** are off the main road some way north or south of the town. The most highly rated is the *Badiaccia*, Via Trasimeno I, 91, Località Badiaccia (ⓣ075.965.9097, ⓕ075.965.9019, ⓦwww.badiaccia.com). Aside from the summer-only **restaurants** on the promenade, the place to eat game, fish fresh from the lake and other dishes is the *L'Acquario*, Via Vittorio Emanuele II 69 (ⓣ075.965.2432; closed Wed, also Tues in winter) on the old town's single main street. The best **swimming** is at the public lido on the southern side of the promontory.

Regular boats make the trip out to the **Isola Maggiore**, one of the lake's three islands, a fun ride if you don't mind the summer crowds. There's a pretty walk round the edge of the island, and you should have no problem discreetly pitching a tent once everyone else has packed up and gone home. If not, there's one good, popular **hotel**, the three-star *Da Sauro*, Via Guglielmi 1 (ⓣ075.826.168, ⓕ075.825.130; ❹), which also doubles as a fine restaurant that's especially known for its fish. Boats also run to the **Isola Polvese** hostel, the 98-bed *Ostello Il Poggio* (ⓣ075.965.9550, ⓕ075.965.9551, ⓦwww.isoapovese.it; €12.91). The hostel has no formal address, but a map near the jetty shows its location, and in any case, the owners will generally meet guests and help with luggage.

The Upper Tiber

Rome's great and famously polluted river, the Tiber, actually spends most of its short life in Umbria, rising in the Alpe della Luna above Sansepolcro. In its moderately pretty but rather unexciting upper reaches north of Perugia – largely given over to sheep and fields of tobacco – you're faced with the familiar problem that everything you don't want to see is easily accessible and everything you do is out of reach without your own transport. The **Ferrovia Centrale Umbra** and the fast N3 to Sansepolcro are perfect for **Città di Castello**, the area's only town of note, after which you'll probably want to strike east on the N257 across the mountains to Urbino (70km). The best reason to follow the Tiber is to stay on the trail of **Piero della Francesca's** mysterious and unsettling masterpieces at Sansepolcro, Arezzo and Monterchi.

The region's best aspect, in fact, is not the valley but the desolate countryside on either side, areas which, like the Valnerina in the east, give the lie to the notion of Umbria as some sort of pastoral idyll. With few roads and fewer villages, but thousands of hectares of natural woodland and abandoned pasture, it teems with wildlife, including many rare species of birds, deer, wild boar and even wolves, now apparently pushing further up the Italian peninsula every year. **Pietralunga** and **Apecchio** to the north are the best exploring bases, with a **campsite** – *La Pineta* (☎075.946.0080, ℉075.946.0646; May–Sept) – at Candeleto close to the former, but there's obviously plenty of scope for freelance camping if you're geared up.

Città di Castello and around

CITTÀ DI CASTELLO is a charming and little-visited town, with a sedate and ordered medieval centre that's well worth a few of hours of your time. It's also increasingly the focus for visitors staying in the many rented villas and farmhouses in hills to the east and west. During August the town becomes busier than usual during its renowned **Festival of Chamber Music**.

Once an important Roman centre – the grid-iron of streets is the only legacy – today the plain-bound site is drab and preserves only a handful of fairly mediocre medieval monuments. The town's main attractions are a trio of museums, along with some quiet, pleasant medieval streets and a bargain restaurant (see below). Foremost among the museums is the **Pinacoteca** at the southern edge of town at Via della Cannoniera 22 (Tues–Sun 10am–1pm & 2.30–6pm; €5), one of the region's best art galleries after Perugia's. The collection makes up in quality what it lacks in quantity, taking in works by **Raphael**, **Signorelli**, **Ghirlandaio** and **Lorenzetti**, plus a wondrous *Maestà* by the anonymous fourteenth-century Maestro di Città di Castello. There are also several sculptures, the most notable by Ghiberti, and a glittering reliquary of Florentine origin, dating from 1420.

The banal reworked **Duomo** in Piazza Gabriotti warrants a call for its smart and newly-revamped museum, the **Museo del Duomo**, entered to the right of the church (Tues–Sun: April–Sept 9.30am–1pm & 2.30–7pm; Oct–March 10am–1pm & 2.30–6.30pm; €5). It contains a completely unexpected collection of big-name paintings, including major works by Rosso Fiorentino, Giulio Romano and Pinturicchio. Even better is the **treasure of Canoscio**, a precious hoard of sixth-century silver chalices dug up in 1932.

The third of the town's triumvirate of museums is the fascinating **Collezione Tessile di Tele Umbra**, just off the main square at Via Sant'Antonio 3 (Tues–Sat 10am–noon & 3.30–6pm, Sun 10.30am–1pm & 3–5.30pm; €2.60). The museum is annexed to a small textile factory set up in 1908 by the Franchetti, a local aristocratic family determined to keep alive the centuries-old traditions of linen-making in the region. The museum traces the history of textiles in the Upper Tiber valley, though in many ways the more interesting part of the concern is the original workshop, which still employs local women and still – almost uniquely in Italy – uses traditional hand-worked looms (workshop open museum hours Mon–Fri only; €1 in addition to museum entrance).

Città di Castello's **tourist office** in the Logge Bufalini just off Piazza Matteotti (Mon–Sat 9am–1pm & 3.30–6.30pm, Sun 10am–1pm; ☎075.855.4922, ℮info@iat.citta-di-castello.pg.it) deals with the whole Upper Tiber region and so is a useful stop if you're spending any time locally. There is a **hostel** on the southern edge of town near the art gallery at Via San Florido

23, the Ostello San Florido (☎075.855.6840; €21), but in practice it operates more or less as a hotel, with accommodation in double rooms and prices that barely undercut those of the town's less expensive hotels. A step up is the excellent, modern, one-star **hotel** *Umbria*, Via dei Galanti 4, off Via Sant'Antonio (☎075.855.4925, ℱ075.852.0911; ❸), just inside the medieval walls, in the east of the old centre. Top of the range is the central four-star *Tiferno*, Piazza Raffaello Sanzio 13 (☎075.855.0331, ℱ075.852.1196, ✉info@hoteltiferno.it; ❺). There's also a pleasant, rural **campsite** at La Montesca, 1km west of town on the minor road to Monte San Marina – the *Montesca* (☎075.855.8566, ℱ075.852.0786; May–Sept). Best of several good **restaurants** is *Amici Miei*, downstairs in a medieval cellar at Via del Monte 2 (closed Wed), off Corso Garibaldi just south of the main Piazza Matteotti: there's no choice, but the menu changes daily and you get four wonderful courses, excluding wine, for a bargain €16. Alternatively, try *Lea*, a locals' favourite at Via San Florido 28 (closed Mon), a short way south of the cathedral.

A couple of kilometres south of Città di Castello, in the hamlet of **GAR-AVELLE**, is one of Umbria's best **folk museums**, the Centro delle Tradizioni Popolari (Tues–Sun: summer 8.30am–12.30pm & 3–7pm; winter 8.30am–12.30pm & 2–6pm; €3.50). It's located in an eighteenth-century farmhouse, preserved with all the accoutrements of daily life – pots, pans, furniture and so forth, plus a range of exhibits covering rural activities such as wine making and weaving.

Gubbio

GUBBIO is the most thoroughly medieval of the Umbrian towns, an immediately likeable place that's hung onto its charm despite an ever-increasing influx of tourists. The streets are picture-book pretty, with houses of rosy-pink stone and seas of orange-tiled roofs; the setting is equally gorgeous with the forest-clad mountains of the Apennines rearing up behind. A broad and largely unspoilt plain stretches out in front of the town, and the whole ensemble – especially on grey, windswept days – maintains Gubbio's tough, mountain outpost atmosphere.

A powerful medieval commune, and always important as the gateway to Ravenna and the Adriatic (it was a key point on the Roman Via Flaminia), these days it's a town apart, not really part of Umbria, Tuscany or Marche – the reason it's been spared the onslaught of modernity.

Gubbio is easiest approached by **bus** from Città di Castello or Perugia on the intermittently pretty cross-country SS298 **road**. The nearest **train station** is at Fossato di Vico, 19km south on the Rome–Foligno–Ancona line; there are ten connecting shuttle buses to Gubbio from Monday to Saturday, six on Sundays.

The Town

Centre-stage is the immense and austere fourteenth-century **Palazzo dei Consoli**, whose crenellated outline and 98-metre campanile immediately grab your attention. Probably designed by Matteo Gattapone, who was also responsible for Spoleto's Ponte delle Torri, the palace took a couple of hundred years to build and required the levelling of vast tracts of the medieval town, mainly to accommodate the huge and windswept Piazza Grande. The lesser **Palazzo**

GUBBIO

RESTAURANTS

Bosone Garden	**C**
Il Campanone	**A**
Grotta dell'Angelo	**D**
Taverna del Lupo	**B**

ACCOMMODATION

Aquilone	**6**	Gattapone	**4**	Park Hotel ai Cappuccini	**1**
Bosone	**7**	Grotta dell'Angelo	**8**	Relais Ducale	**5**
dei Consoli	**2**	Locanda del Duca	**3**		

Pretorio opposite was built to the same plan. Deliberately dominating and humbling, it was what medieval civic pride was all about, an attempt to express power and supremacy in bricks and mortar. Behind a plain square facade (there's a small hole top right where criminals were hung in a cage called *la gogna* – from *vergogna* or "shame") is a cavernous baronial hall, the Salone dell'Arengo, where council officials and leading citizens met to discuss business. The word "harangue" derives from *arengo*, suggesting proceedings frequently boiled over.

The **Museo Civico** (daily: April–Sept 10am–1pm & 3–6pm; Oct–March 10am–1pm & 2–5pm; €4) is also based here and includes a small archeological collection, entered from the rear of the building; this houses a typical miscellany, unremarkable except for the famous **Eugubine Tablets** (upstairs to the left), Umbria's most important archeological find. Discovered in 1444 by an illiterate shepherd, later conned into swapping his priceless treasure trove for a worthless piece of land, the seven bronze tablets are more or less the only extant record of the ancient Umbrian language, a vernacular tongue without written characters. The bastardized Etruscan and Latin of their religious texts was aimed at producing a phonetic translation of the dialect using the main languages of the day. Gubbio was close to the shrine of the so-called Apennine Jove, a major pagan deity visited by pilgrims from all over Italy, so the tablets were probably the work of Roman and Etruscan priests taking advantage of the established order to impose their religious cults in a region where their languages weren't understood. Most importantly, they suggest Romans, Etruscans and Umbrians achieved some sort of coexistence, refuting a long-held belief that succeeding civilizations wiped one another out.

Admission to the museum also gets you into the five-roomed **Pinacoteca** at the top of the palace, worth a look for works by the Gubbian School – one of central Italy's earliest, and a collection of ponderous fourteenth-century furniture. Try the door at the back for views from the palace's **loggia**. The palace also boasted 26 toilets; apparently it was the first in medieval Italy to have interior piped water.

To the north of the Piazza Grande lurks a not very inspiring thirteenth-century **Duomo**, partly redeemed by the odd fresco, twelfth-century stained glass, and some arches gracefully curved apparently to emulate the meeting of hands in prayer. There are also a pair of carved **organ lofts** that for once don't look as if they'd be more at home in a fairground. The adjoining **Museo Diocesano** (Tues–Fri 10am–1pm & 3–6/7pm, Sat & Sun 10am–6/7pm; €4.13), to the right as you face the facade at the corner of Via Federico da Monefeltro, is well worth a few minutes, mainly for a florid Flemish cope, presented to the cathedral by Pope Marcellus II, who was born in Gubbio.

The plain-faced Gothic cathedral is overshadowed by the **Palazzo Ducale** in Via Federico da Montefeltro opposite (Mon, Tues & Thurs–Sun 8.30m–7.30pm; closed Wed; €2), built over an earlier Lombard palace by the Dukes of Montefeltro as a scaled-down copy of their more famous palace in Urbino. The **courtyard** is particularly attractive, but the interior, stripped of most of its original furniture and other trappings, is a trifle dull, despite some fine views from the windows and the harmonious scale of the rooms.

On the hillside above the town stands the **Basilica of Sant'Ubaldo**, which has some great views (even better ones if you climb up to the **Rocca**). There's not much to see in the basilica itself, except the body of the town's patron saint, St Ubaldo, missing three fingers – they were hacked off by his manservant as a religious keepsake. You can't miss the big wooden pillars (*ceri*) featured in Gubbio's annual **Corsa dei Ceri** (May 15), little known outside Italy but second only to Siena's Palio in terms of exuberance and bizarre pageantry. The rules and rigmarole of the 900-year-old ceremony are mind-boggling, but they boil down to three teams racing from Piazza della Signoria to the basilica, carrying the *ceri* (each representing a different saint) on wooden stretchers. By iron-clad tradition, the *cero* of St Ubaldo always wins, the other teams having to ensure they're in the basilica before the doors are shut by the leaders. There's hours of involved ritual at either end, vast crowds and plenty of drinking. A scholarly debate rages as to whether the whole thing's intrinsically religious (commemorating the day in 1155 Ubaldo talked Barbarossa out of flattening Gubbio), or a hangover from some pagan fertility rite. Nowadays the Church, not surprisingly, claims it as its own, but judging by the very phallic *ceri*, and the roar that goes up when they're raised to the vertical, there's something more than religion at play here.

There are several ways up to the basilica, one being via the steep track that strikes off from behind the Duomo. However, it's quicker and far more fun – unless you have no head for heights – to take the **funicular** (summer 8.30am–7.30pm; winter reduced hours; return €4.65, one way €3.62) from Porta Romana, over on the eastern side of town; you jump on small two-person cradles, which then dangle precariously over the woods and crags below as you shudder slowly upwards. While you're waiting you could take in more of Ottaviano Nelli's paintings, tucked away in the thirteenth-century **Sant'Agostino** and **Santa Maria Nuova** nearby. The unusually lovely *Madonna del Belvedere* (1408) in the latter is a masterpiece of the detailed and highly decorative style for which he was famous. His most majestic efforts – seventeen frescoes on the life of the Virgin – are in **San Francesco**, the big church that dominates the Piazza dei Quaranta Martiri – the bus terminal – at the foot of the town. The piazza's named in memory of forty citizens shot by the Germans in 1944, a reprisal for partisan attacks in the surrounding hills.

Gubbio's **Porte della Morte**, the "doors of death", are as controversial as the phallic *ceri*. Almost unique to the town (there are a few others in Assisi and southern France), these are narrow, bricked-up doorways wedged into the facades of its medieval townhouses (with the best examples in Via dei Consoli). The party line is that they were used to carry a coffin out of a house, and then having been tainted with death, were sealed up out of superstitious fear. Nice theory, and very Italian, but judging by the constricted stairways behind the doors, their purpose was probably defensive – the main door could be barricaded, leaving the more easily defended passageway as the only entrance.

There are dozens of picturesque odds and ends around the streets, which are as wonderfully explorable as any in the region. The **Bargello** in Via dei Consoli – the main medieval street (and home to most of the ceramic shops) – the medieval police station, is worth tracking down and gives you the chance to survey the adjacent **Fontana dei Matti** (the "fountain of the mad"), undistinguished but for the tradition that anyone walking round it three times will wind up mad. There's usually someone wondering whether to give it a go.

Practicalities

You shouldn't have any problem **staying** in Gubbio, though the place does get busy, and many of the hotels and restaurants are rather smart affairs aimed at well-heeled Italians. Check for cheap **rooms** in private houses with the **tourist office**, Piazza Odersi 6 (Mon–Fri 8.30am–1.45pm & 3.30–6pm, Sat 9am–1pm & 3.30–6pm, Sun 9.30am–12.30pm; ☎075.922.0790 or 075.922.0693, ℮info@iat.gubbio.pg.it). You can look up your **email** at the *Global Shop*, Via Mazzini 14b.

There's a **hostel**, the *Aquilone* (℡075.927.1105, Ⓕ075.929.1144, Ⓔaquilone@quilone.it; €7.75), with 49 beds in eight dorms, in the hamlet of Ghigiano, about 10km from the centre off the N219 road southeast towards Branca. For **hotel** accommodation, try the straightforward one-star *Locanda del Duca*, just off Via Quaranta Martiri in a quiet side street at Via Piccardi 1 (℡075.927.7753; ❹), with seven en-suite rooms; the reliable two-star *Grotta dell'Angelo*, Via Gioia 47 (℡075.927.1747, Ⓕ075.927.3438; ❸); or the popular and perfectly placed *Albergo dei Consoli* at Via dei Consoli 59 (℡075.927.3335; ❹) – though the nine rooms here are extremely plain. The best mid-range choice is the spacious three-star *Gattapone*, Via G. Ansidei 6 (℡075.927.2489, Ⓕ075.927.2417, Ⓔhotel.gattapone@libero.it; ❺), with its peaceful garden, while if you want a taste of a medieval palace with frescoed ceilings and lots of antiques, treat yourself to the three-star *Bosone*, Via XX Settembre 22 (℡075.922.0688, Ⓕ075.922.0552; ❹). For luxury, opt for the classy new four-star *Relais Ducale* (℡075.922.0157, Ⓕ075.922.0159, Ⓔinfo@relaisducale.com; ❼), just below the cathedral and entered from one of two tiny alleys – Via Ducale or Via Galleotti (signed off Piazza east side of Piazza Grande). Equally smart, but much larger and outside the walls, is the *Park Hotel ai Cappuccini*, Via Tifernate (℡075.92.34, Ⓕ075.922.0323, Ⓔinfo@parkhotelaicappuccini.it; ❼) – an elegantly converted fourteenth-century monastery in parkland, featuring a pool, gym, sauna and garden. Less than 2km south of town, the Città di Gubbio **campsite** (℡ & Ⓕ075.927.2037, Ⓔinfo@gubbiocamping.com; April–Sept) is in a pleasant setting and has a swimming pool.

Gubbio boasts a good selection of **restaurants**, including the smart *Taverna del Lupo* (closed Mon) at Via Ansidei 21, well worth a splurge for its classic Umbrian dishes and excellent truffle risotto; the much cheaper *Grotta dell'Angelo* (closed Tues), annexed to the *Grotta dell'Angelo* hotel, does very good basic meals in its wonderful dining room; and, if you want to dine outdoors, head for the *Bosone Garden* restaurant (closed Wed) on Via Mastro Giorgio, attached to the *Bosone* hotel. Several inexpensive places can be found at the northern end of Via dei Consoli, though in this part of town the best bet is *Il Campanone* at Via Piccardi 22 on the corner with Via Baldassini, with several attractive medieval vaulted dining rooms.

Gualdo Tadino and around

GUALDO TADINO, like Gubbio, is distinct from the rest of Umbria and has a similarly rugged mountain-outpost character. Much the same goes for **Nocera Umbra**, 15km to the south, but it was devasted by the 1997 earthquake and will be under scaffolding for years to come. Sprawling over the lower slopes of the Apennines, Gualdo Tadino has a bleakly medieval centre, hedged about with light industry and unplanned housing. Its single historical claim to fame is as witness to the death of Totila the Hun, who was slain by the Romans under the town walls.

The only remarkable thing about the thirteenth-century Gothic **Duomo** is that the facade has two tiers instead of Umbria's usual three; the interior, done to death in the nineteenth century, has absolutely nothing to recommend it. The **Pinacoteca** was recently transferred – permanently it seems – from its old home in San Francesco to the **Museo Civico** (July–Sept Tues–Sun 10.30am–1pm & 3.30–6.30pm; rest of year Thurs–Sun 10.30am–1pm & 3–5pm; €2.58) in the Rocca Flea, a thirteenth-century castle in Via della

Rocca. Space is given to archeological finds, a collection of ceramics on the upper floor, and to local painters such as fifteenth-century Matteo da Gualdo: the centrepiece is a polyptych by **Nicolò Alunno**, considered unsurpassed among the central Italian artists before Perugino. Without the sugary quality of some Umbrian offerings – all soft-focus saints and dewy-eyed Madonnas – Alunno has a harder edge and a wider and more genuine range of emotion.

With little to detain you, you could easily soak up the atmosphere of the place between the frequent trains from Foligno and Fabriano. The cheapest **accommodation**, however, if you need it, is at the two-star *Centro Sociale Verde Soggiorno*, Via Bosco 50 (☎075.916.263, ℱ075.914.2951, 🄴sdbgulado@ pcn.net; ❷), or the two-star *Dal Bottaio*, Via Casimiri 17 (☎075.913.230; ❷), which also has a restaurant. The best food is at the restaurant of the *Gigiotto* hotel (restaurant closed Wed & Nov), Via Morone 5, though the service can be wanting. For **pizzas** in the old centre, visit Baccus in Via R. Calai (closed Mon). The **tourist office** *Pro Tadino* at Via Calai 39 (May–Sept Mon–Sat 9am–1pm & 3.30–7.30pm; ☎075.912.172) will fill in the gaps.

Parco Regionale del Monte Cucco

Some of Umbria's best upland scenery is to be found in the mountains east and north of Gualdo on the border with the Marche, much of it protected by the **Parco Regionale del Monte Cucco**. Where this area really scores is in its organized trails and backup for outdoor activities of every kind; if you want to don walking boots without too much fuss, this is one of the areas to do it – and **access** is easy, with buses from Gualdo to Valsorda and from Perugia, Gualdo, Gubbio and Assisi to Costacciaro.

The southernmost base for exploration of the park is the resort of **VAL-SORDA** (1000m), 8km northeast of Gualdo on the southern extremity of the park. You can tackle the straightforward trek (1hr) up **Serra Santa** (1421m) on a track of motorway proportions carved out by pilgrims over the years. From the summit you could drop into the spectacular **Valle del Fonno** gorge and follow it down to Gualdo. Paths follow the main ridge from Valsorda north and south, and it's feasible to walk all the way to Nocera Umbra (6hr). Accommodation is thin on the ground, but there's a **campsite**, the *Valsorda* (☎075.913.261; June–Sept).

To get closer to the heart of the mountains head to the unpretentious and appealing **COSTACCIARO**, centre for all the park's outdoor pursuits and access point for the **Grotta di Monte Cucco**, at 922m the fifth-deepest cave system in the world. Above, the huge, bare-sloped Monte Cucco (1566m) is the main playground for **walkers**. The best place to go if you want to get seriously wet or muddy, or just tag along with a tour party, is the **Centro Nazionale di Speleologia**, Via Galeazzi 5 (off Corso Mazzini; ☎ & ℱ075.917.0400 for details of tours; 🅦www.cens.it), one of the country's most energetic and organized outdoor centres; in the past the *centro* has also offered hostel accommodation, but call ahead for current status. There is a 44-bed **hostel** about 1km to the southeast on the N3 road at the hamlet of Scira, the Università Volo Libero (☎ & ℱ075.917.0761, 🄴universitadelvolo@libero.it; €10.33), aimed at the hang-gliding fraternity.

There are other places to stay in and around Costacciaro, the best of them being the two-star *Monte Cucco da Tobia* in the Val di Ranco (☎075.917.7194; ❷; Easter–Oct), a fabled mountaineers' and cavers' hangout. Also convenient for walkers is the *Cappelloni*, Val di Ranco (☎075.917.7131; ❷; May–Sept). Both hotels have restaurants. The nearest **campsite** is the *Rio Verde* (℡075.917.0138; April–Sept) at **Fornace**, 3km north of Costacciaro. Freelance camping is prohibited within the *parco regionale*, but elsewhere you'll have few problems finding a discreet pitch for a tent.

Assisi

ASSISI is already too well known, thanks to **St Francis**, Italy's premier saint and founder of the Franciscan order, which, with its various splinter groups, forms the world's biggest. Had the man not been born here in 1182 the town wouldn't be thronged with tourists and pilgrims for ten months of the year, but then neither would it have the **Basilica of St Francis**, one of the greatest monuments to thirteenth- and fourteenth-century Italian art. You'll probably feel it's worth putting up with the crowds and increasingly overwhelming commercialism, but you may not want to hang around once you've seen all there is to see – something which can easily be done in a day. That said, Assisi quietens down in the evening, and it does retain some medieval hill-town charm.

Arrival and information

Getting here is easy. **Buses** connect regularly with surrounding towns – especially Perugia – putting down and picking up in Piazza Matteotti, in the east of the town above the Duomo. In addition, one bus a day leaves for Rome and two for Florence, from Piazza Unità d'Italia. There are hourly **trains** to Foligno (via Spello) and Teróntola (via Perugia), with connecting half-hourly bus services between the town and the station, which is 5km away to the southwest of the centre. If you are driving, however, note that the centre of town is closed to traffic. Your best bet is to park either in Piazza Matteotti at the top (eastern) end of the town, or below the Basilica in Piazza Unità d'Italia: either way, you will have a stiff uphill walk if you explore the whole town. The staff at the **tourist office**, at the western end of Piazza del Comune (Mon–Fri 8am–2pm & 3–6pm, Sat 9am–1pm & 3–6pm, Sun 9am–1pm; ℡075.812.534, ⓔinfo@iat.assis.pg.it), do their best to help with accommodation and provide some useful maps and pamphlets. You can go **online** at the *Bar del Corso* in Corso Mazzini (daily 8am–11pm).

> ### Assisi and the 1997 earthquakes
>
> In the spring of 1997, earthquakes brought part of Assisi's famed **Basilica** crashing down, killing four people and destroying some of the building's less significant frescoes. But on no account be put off. While the event made world headlines, the damage to the rest of the town was overstated, the epicentre actually being near Coltiorito. Occasional precautionary scaffolding aside, there are very few tangible signs that anything ever happened and none of the most famous frescoes was greatly affected. After several years of intense international support and dedicated work, both the Basilica's **Lower and Upper Church** are now open, along with every other important monument in the town.

Map labels:

▲ Cemetery & Car Park

ASSISI

Porta San Giacomo

Basilica di San Francesco

PIAZZA SUPERIORE DI S.FRANCESCO

S. Marguerita

VIA MERRY DEL VAL

VIA SERMETTAI

VIA SANTA CROCE

VIA DEL COLLE

PIAZZA INFERIORE DI S.FRANCESCO

Santa Croce

VIA METASTASIO

Pinacoteca

VIA S.PAOLO

3

VIA FRATE ELIA

STRADA PIAGGIA S. FRANCESCO

Casa dei Maestri Comacini

VIA SAN FRANCESCO

Oratorio dei Pellegrini

VIA SEMINARIO

VIA ALUGI

SS. Stefano e Fortunato

B PIAZZA GARIBALDI

VIA BRIZI

VIA FONTEBELLA

9

Porta San Francesco

P. UNITA D'ITALIA

P

VIA DEL FOSSO CUPO

Porta S. Pietro

PIAZZA S. PIETRO

VIA ANCAIANI

VIA BORGO S. PIETRO

VIA PENNACCHI

VIA A

San Pietro

VIALE MARCONI

VIALE VITTORIO EMANUELE

VIA S. APOLLINARE

Porta Sermentone

SS 147

Perugia ◄

Umbria | Assisi (side tab) **9**

ACCOMMODATION

Anfiteatro Romano	4
Il Duomo	2
Fontebella	9
Italia	6
La Fortezza	7
Ostello di Fontemaggio	5
Ostello della Pace	12
Pallotta	8
Dei Priori	10
La Rocca	1
Sole	11
Subasio	3

Train Station & Santa Maria degli Angeli (5km) ▼   ▼ **12**

Accommodation

Assisi offers a wide range of **accommodation**, but the supply is often only just adequate for the number of visitors, so advance booking is highly advisable, and essential if you plan to visit over Easter or during the Festa di San Francesco (Oct 3–4) or Calendimaggio (May 21–22). The tourist office has a full list of lodgings, including over fifty **rooms** for rent, and will make reservations for you, too. Spello is close enough to make seeing Assisi easy, and see below for options just outside town. Wherever you choose to stay, try to avoid the concentration of rooms and hotels in Santa Maria degli Angeli or the grim village of Bastia, 4km out of Assisi.

Hotels

Anfiteatro Romano Via Anfiteatro 4 ☎075.813.025, ℱ075.815.110. A good-value one-star in a very pleasant part of town. Choice of rooms with or without bathrooms. **2**

Fontebella Via Fontebella 25 ☎075.812.883, ℱ075.812.941. The town's most elegant and intimate choice. Ask for a room on one of the top floors for great panoramas. **9**

La Fortezza Vicolo della Fortezza 19b ☎075.812.418, ℱ075.819.8035. Friendly two-star with just seven rooms in a perfect position just off Piazza del Comune: the co-owned restaurant is also excellent. **3**

Italia Vicolo della Fortezza 2 ☎075.812.625, ℱ075.804.3749; March–Oct. Basic rooms, but the most central one-star, next to *La Fortezza* (see above). **1**

Pallotta Via San Rufino 6 ☎ & ℱ075.812.307. A two-star in a good location between the Duomo and Piazza del Comune; also has a first-rate co-owned trattoria just off Piazza del Comune (see p.627). **2**

Dei Priori Corso Mazzini 15 ☎075.812.237, ℱ075.816.804. A three-star slightly east of Piazza del Comune. Rooms vary greatly. **7**

La Rocca Via di Porta Perlici 27 ☎ & ℱ075.812.284. A one-star situated at the end of the street beyond the Duomo. Quiet rooms, some with views, most have private bathrooms. **2**

Sole Corso Mazzini 35 ☎075.812.373, ℱ075.813.706. Functional two-star one minute's walk from the Basilica di Santa Chiara. Good option if everywhere else is full. **3**

Subasio Via Frate Elia 2 ☎075.821.206,

622

Rocca Maggiore

Porta Perlici

0   100 m

VIA DELLA ROCCA

San Lorenzo ❶

S. M. delle Rose

Rocca Minore

Foro Romano e Collezione Archeologica

VIA S. MARIA DELLE ROSE

Anfiteatro Romano

Tempio di Minerva

PIAZZA SAN RUFINO

VIA DEL TORRIONI

PIAZZA MATTEOTTI

ⓘ   PIAZZA DEL COMUNE

VIA PORTICA

VIA S RUFINO

VIA SANTUARIO DELLE CARCERI

VIA VECCHI

San Gregorio

Chiesa Nuova

CORSO MAZZINI

Duomo

Bus Terminal

Porta Cappuccini

DA QUINTAVALLE

VIA SANT'AGNESE

PIAZZA DEL VESCOVADO

PIAZZA S. CHIARA

VIA G. ALESSI

CRISTOFANI

VIA BORGO ARETINO

Giardino Pubblico

RESTAURANTS
La Fortezza	A
Medioevo	D
I Monaci	B
Pallotta	C

S. Maria Maggiore

Santa Chiara

Porta Moiano

VIA PORTA MOIANO

VIA DELLE FONTI DI MOIANO

Porta Nuova

VIALE UMBERTO I

VIALE UMBERTO I

LARGO PROPERZIO

VIA MADONNA DELL'OLIVO

▼ San Damiano

9

UMBRIA | Assisi

Ⓣ075.816.691. Assisi's four-star grande dame, old-world comfort with valley views and an envi-

able position – right next to the porticoes of the Basilica. ❽

Outside Assisi

Relais La Corte di Bettona Via Santa Caterina 2, Bettona Ⓣ075.987.114, Ⓕ075.986.9130, Ⓦwww.hotelsantandrea.it. Very comfortable converted medieval building, with an excellent restaurant, and a complimentary bus shuttle service to both Assisi and Perugia. ❽

Castello di Petrata Pieve San Nicolò 22 Ⓣ & Ⓕ075.815.451, Ⓦwww.castellopetrata.com. An elegantly converted medieval castle, 5km north of Assisi, with wonderful views over the valley and its own fine restaurant. ❼

Rooms, hostels and camping

The pick of the **private lodgings** is *Il Duomo*, Vicolo San Lorenzo 2 (Ⓣ075.812.742; ❷), located in a tiny, flower-decked medieval alley (second left off Via di Porta Perlici, heading away from the Duomo); full lists are available from the tourist office, which can also supply details of **pilgrim hostels**. There are two **regular hostels**: the *Ostello di Fontemaggio*, 3km east of town on Via San Rufino Campagna, the road to the Eremo delle Carceri (Ⓣ075.813.636 or 075.812.317, Ⓕ075.813.749; €18.50), with a **campsite**; and the larger 66-bed *Ostello della Pace* at Via di Valecchie 177 (Ⓣ075.816.767; €13), off Viale Marconi, a ten-minute downhill walk from Piazza Unità d'Italia – follow Viale Marconi until it bends sharp right, at which point a minor road leads off left (ignore the minor road straight on at the same point) and downhill, passing the *Country House* hotel on the left after five minutes and reaching the hostel on the right shortly afterwards.

The Basilica di San Francesco

Pilgrims and art lovers alike usually make straight for the **Basilica di San Francesco** (daily 6.30am–7.30pm; free), justifiably famed as Umbria's single greatest glory, and one of the most overwhelming collections of art outside a

623

gallery anywhere in the world. Started in 1228, two years after the saint's death, and financed by donations that flooded in from all over Europe, it's not as grandiose as some religious shrines, though it still strikes you as being a long way from the embodiment of Franciscan principles. If you don't mind compromised ideals, the two churches making up the basilica – one built on top of the other – are a treat.

Most people start with Giotto in the **Upper Church**, mainly because it's the first one they come to, but the sombre **Lower Church** – down the steps to the left – comes earlier, both structurally and artistically. The complicated floor plan and claustrophobic low-lit vaults were intended to create a mood of calm and meditative introspection – an effect added to by brown-robed monks and a ban on photography, though the rule of silence is pretty much ignored by the scrums around the Cavallini frescoes. Francis lies under the floor in a **crypt** only brought to light in 1818 after 52 days of digging (entrance midway down the nave). He was hidden after his funeral for safekeeping, and nowadays endures almost continuous Masses in dozens of languages.

Frescoes cover almost every available space and span a century of continuous artistic development. Stilted early works by anonymous painters influenced by the Byzantines sit alongside Roman painters such as Cavallini, who with Cimabue pioneered the move from mosaic to naturalism and the "new" medium of fresco. They were followed by the best of the Sienese School, **Simone Martini** and **Pietro Lorenzetti**, whose paintings are the ones to make a real point of seeing.

Martini's frescoes are in the **Cappella di San Martino** (1322–26), the first chapel on the left as you enter the nave. He was given free rein in the chapel, and every detail, right down to the floor and stained glass, follows his drawings, adding up to a unified scheme that's unique in Italy. Lorenzetti's works, dominated by a powerful *Crucifixion*, are in the transept to the left of the main altar. Vaults above the altar itself contain four magnificent frescoes, complicated but colourful allegories of the virtues on which Francis founded his order: Poverty, Chastity and Obedience. Once thought to have been the work of Giotto, they're now attributed to one of the church's army of unknown artists. The big feature in the right transept is Cimabue's over-restored *Madonna, Child and Angels with St Francis*, a painting Ruskin described as "the noblest depiction of the Virgin in Christendom." Look out for the famous portrait of Francis and for the much-reproduced fresco of St Clare on the wall to its left.

The more straightforward **Upper Church**, built to a light and airy Gothic plan – that was to be followed for countless Franciscan churches – is a completely different experience. It's less a church than an excuse to show off **Giotto**'s dazzling frescoes on the life of St Francis. *Francis Preaching to the Birds* and *Driving the Devils from Arezzo* are just two of the famous scenes reproduced worldwide on cards and posters. The cycle starts on the right-hand wall up by the main altar and continues clockwise. Giotto was still in his twenties when he accepted the commission, having been recommended for the job by Cimabue, whose own frescoes – almost ruined now by the oxidation of badly chosen pigments and further damaged in the 1997 'quake – fill large parts of the apse and transepts. In the vaults, several harsh areas of bare plaster stand as graphic monuments to the collapse of that year.

If time allows check out the **cloisters**, accessible from the rear right-hand side of the Lower Church, and the Treasury, or **Museo del Tesoro e Collezioni F. M. Perkins** (April–Oct Mon–Sat 9.30am–noon & 2.30–6pm; €1.55), reached via the apse of the Lower Church. The latter, often passed by, contains a rich collection of paintings – including works by Pietro Lorenzetti and Masolino da Panicale.

St Francis is the most extraordinary figure that the Italian church has produced, a revolutionary spirit who took Christianity back to basics. The impact that he had upon the evolution of the Catholic Church stands without parallel, and everything he accomplished in his short life was achieved by nothing more persuasive than the power of preaching and personal example. Dante placed him alongside another Messianic figure, John the Baptist, and his appeal has remained undiminished – Mussolini called him "il piu santo dei santi" (the most saintly of the saints).

The events of his life, though doubtless embellished by myth, are well chronicled. He was born in Assisi in 1182, the son of a wealthy merchant and a Provençal woman – which is why he replaced his baptismal name, Giovanni, with Francesco (Little Frenchman). The Occitan literature of Provence, with its troubadour songs and courtly love poems, was later to be the making of Francis as a poet and speaker. One of the earliest writers in the vernacular, Francis laid the foundation of a great Franciscan literary tradition – his *Fioretti* and famous *Canticle to the Sun* ("brother sun . . . sister moon") stand comparison with the best of medieval verse.

In line with the early life of most male saints, his formative years were full of drinking and womanizing; he was, says one chronicler, "the first instigator of evil, and behind none in foolishness". Illness and imprisonment in a Perugian jail incubated the first seeds of contemplation. Abstinence and solitary wanderings soon followed. The call from God, the culmination of several visions, came in Assisi in 1209, when the crucifix in San Damiano bowed to him and told him to repair God's Church. Francis took the injunction literally, sold his father's stock of cloth and gave the money to Damiano's priest, who refused it.

Francis subsequently renounced his inheritance in the Piazza del Comune: before a large crowd and his outraged father, he stripped naked in a symbolic rejection of wealth and worldly shackles. Adopting the peasant's grey sackcloth (the brown Franciscan habit came later), he began to beg, preach and mix with lepers, a deliberate embodiment of Christ's invocation to the Apostles "to heal the sick, and carry neither purse, nor scrip [money], nor shoes". His message was disarmingly simple: throw out the materialistic trappings of daily life and return to a love of God rooted in poverty, chastity and obedience. Furthermore, learn to see in the beauty and profusion of the natural world the all-pervasive hand of the Divine – a keystone of humanist thought and a departure from the doom-laden strictures of the Dark Ages.

In time he gathered his own twelve apostles and, after some difficulty, obtained permission from Pope Innocent III to found an order that espoused no dogma and maintained no rule. Francis himself never became a priest. In 1212 he was instrumental in the creation of a second order for women, the Poor Clares, and continued the vast peregrinations that took him as far as the Holy Land with the armies of the Crusades. In Egypt he confronted the sultan, Melek el-Kamel, offering to undergo a trial by fire to prove his faith. In 1224 Francis received the stigmata on the mountaintop at La Verna. Two years later, nursing his exhausted body, he died on the mud floor of his hovel in Assisi, having scorned the offer of grander accommodation at the bishop's palace. His canonization followed swiftly, in 1228, in a service conducted by Pope Gregory.

However, a split in the Franciscan order was inevitable. Francis's message and movement had few sympathizers in the wealthy and morally bankrupt papacy of the time, and while his popularity had obliged the Vatican to applaud while he was alive, the papacy quickly moved in to quash the purist elements and encourage more "moderate" tendencies. Gradually it shaped the movement to its own designs, institutionalizing Francis's message in the process.

Despite this, Francis's achievement as the first man to fracture the rigid orthodoxy of the hierarchical Church remains beyond question. Moreover, the Franciscans have not lost their ideological edge, and their views on the primacy of poverty are thought by many to be out of favour with the current pope.

The rest of the town

Via San Francesco leads back to the town centre from the basilica. Partway along the street on the left is the Palazzo Vallemani, the new site of Assisi's excellent **Pinacoteca** (daily: mid-March to mid-Oct 10am–1pm & 2–6/7pm; rest of year till 5pm; €2.20, or €5.20 with the Foro Romano museum and Rocca Maggiore). It would be easy to ignore this after the rich artistic pickings of the Basilica, but the gallery is well worth the admission, not least for the wonderful paintings moved here on a semi-permanent basis from the earthquake-ravaged gallery in Nocera Umbra, near Gualdo Tadino. These include the impressive *Immaculate Conception of the Virgin* (1495–1505) by Matteo da Gualdo, a work complemented by many detached frescoes rescued from churches and other buildings around Assisi, among them important works by the Gubbian artist Ottaviano Nelli. The displays are enhanced by good English commentaries.

A little farther down the street on the right are the remains of the fifteenth-century **Oratorio dei Pellegrini** (daily 9am–noon & 3–8pm; free), the hospice for pilgrims, frescoed inside and out by local painters Mezzastris and Matteo da Gualdo – appealing but modest offerings after the basilica (and often out of bounds because of praying nuns).

Of more limited appeal is the **Foro Romano e Collezione Archeologica** entered just off Piazza del Comune at Via Portica 2 (daily 10am–1pm & 2–5/6pm; €2.50, or €5.20 with Pinacoteca and Rocca Maggiore), housed in the crypt of the now defunct church of San Nicolò. The classical remains include an excavated street – probably part of the old Roman forum – buried under the Piazza del Comune. The piazza itself is dominated by the so-called **Tempio di Minerva**, an enticing and perfectly preserved classical facade from the first century, concealing a dull, if beautifully restored, seventeenth-century Baroque conversion; it was the only thing Goethe was bothered about seeing when he came to Assisi – the basilica he avoided, calling it a "Babylonian pile". Francis's birthplace lies just south of the piazza, marked by the Chiesa Nuova, a dreary church.

A short hike in the other direction up the steep Via di San Rufino brings you to the thirteenth-century **Duomo**, with a typical and very lovely three-tiered Umbrian facade and sumptuously carved central doorway. The only point of interest in a boring interior is the font used to baptize St Francis, St Clare and – by a historical freak – the future Emperor Frederick II, born prematurely in a field outside the town. Off the right (south) nave, there's the small **Museo Capitolare** (daily: April–Sept 10am–noon & 3–7pm; Oct–March 10am–noon & 3–6pm; €3), with a handful of good paintings, including a 1470 work by Nicolò Alunno, and an atmospheric **crypt** (same hours and ticket), entered outside down steps to the right of the facade. The cathedral makes a good point from which to strike off for the **Rocca Maggiore** (daily 10am–dusk; €2.20, €5.20 with Pinacoteca and Museo Civico e Foro Romano), one of the bigger and better preserved in the region, with some all-embracing views the reward after a stiff climb.

Below the Duomo, on the pedestrianized Piazza Santa Chiara, stands the **Basilica di Santa Chiara** (daily 7am–noon & 2pm–dusk; free), burial place of St Francis's devoted early companion, who at the age of 17 founded the Order of the Poor Clares, the female wing of the Franciscans. By some peculiar and not terribly dignified quirk she's also the patron saint of television. The church was consecrated in 1265 and is a virtual facsimile of the basilica up the road, down to the simple facade and opulent rose window. Its engineering wasn't up to the same standards, however, and arches had to be added in 1351 to prevent the whole thing being undermined by crumbling foundations. Instead of art, the scantily decorated interior has the once-withered (it was restored by a specialist in Rome) and macabrely blackened body of St Clare herself and a Byzantine crucifix famous for having bowed to Francis and commanded him to embark on his sacred mission to repair God's Church.

You're not long off the Francis trail in Assisi. **San Damiano** (daily 10am–12.30pm & 2–6pm; free), a peaceful spot of genuine monastic charm, is one of its highlights, and is easily reached by taking the Via Borgo Aretino beyond the basilica and following signs from the Porta Nuova, a steep downhill walk of about fifteen minutes. Original home to the Poor Clares, and one of St Francis's favourite spots (he is thought to have written his well-known *Canticle to the Sun* here), the church, cloisters and rustic setting preserve – almost uniquely in Assisi – a sense of the original Franciscan ideals of humility and simplicity often absent in the rest of the town.

From the train station you can see the town's other major attraction, the vast and majestically uninspiring **Santa Maria degli Angeli**, built in the seventeenth century and rebuilt after an earthquake in 1832. Somewhere in its Baroque bowels are the remains of the **Porziuncola**, a tiny chapel that was effectively the first Franciscan monastery. Francis lived here after founding the order in 1208, attracted by its then remote and wooded surroundings, and in time was joined by other monks and hermits who built a series of cells and mud huts in the vicinity. Today the church is crammed full of largely fourth-rate works of art and bears no relation to the Franciscan ideal.

After you've exhausted the myriad Francis connections, Assisi has the usual wonderful back streets, churches, Roman remains and miscellaneous odds and ends that characterize most Italian towns of similar age. If you have time you could check out the **Roman amphitheatre** near Porta Perlici (east of the Duomo) or the Romanesque church of **San Pietro**, brilliantly restored for once, in Piazza San Pietro.

Eating and drinking

Multilingual tourist menus proliferate in the town's **restaurants**, and prices can be steep. For straight pizzas there's the superb *I Monaci*, Scaletti del Metastasio, whose entrance is in a stepped alley off the north side of Via Fontebella, a few steps down from Piazzetta Garibaldi (closed Wed). The excellent *Pallotta*, just south of Piazza del Comune at Via Volta Piana 2 (closed Tues), is an unpretentious and welcoming trattoria – arrive early for a table at lunch. More upmarket, *La Fortezza*, Vicolo della Fortezza 2 (reservations essential in summer, ☎075.812.418; closed Thurs & Feb), has great food but slightly slow service. *Medioevo*, Via dell'Arco dei Priori 4b (booking advised, ☎075.813.068; closed Wed, Jan & July 1–21), just south off the Piazza del Comune, is highly recommended for a splurge on some eclectic cuisine that draws its inspiration from France, Germany and Austria as well as Italy. For wonderful **ice cream** and mouthwatering **pastries**, head for the *Gran Caffè*, Corso Mazzini 16a.

Spello to Trevi

Ranged on broad terraces above the Vale of Spoleto, medieval and pink-stoned **SPELLO** is the best place for a taste of small-town Umbria if you haven't time or means to explore further, being easy to reach by road and rail (20min from Assisi or Spoleto). Emperor Augustus gave land in the adjacent valley to faithful legionaries who had reached the end of their careers, turning the town (Hispellum) into a sort of Roman retirement home in the process, an ambience it still rather retains.

The walls and three gateways are the most obvious Roman remnants. Don't bother walking out to the paltry and overgrown remains of the old amphitheatre hidden away beyond the main highway to Assisi: you can see all you need to from the top of the town. By far the most distinguished sight is **Pinturicchio's fresco cycle** in the thirteenth-century church of Santa Maria Maggiore, about a third of the way up the town's winding and steep main street on Piazza G. Matteotti. The number-two Umbrian painter after Perugino, he left other important works in Siena (the Duomo), Rome (the Sistine Chapel, Borgia apartments) and a host of churches scattered over central Italy. The frescoes themselves are fresh and glowing from restoration, with Pinturicchio's famous details and colouring brought out to stunning effect. Unfortunately they're behind glass, which also means you can't get a closer look at the chapel's praised but faded fifteenth-century **ceramic pavement**. Almost immediately to the north of the church stands an excellent little art gallery, the **Pinacoteca Civica** (April–June 10.30am–1pm & 3–6.30pm; July–Sept Tues–Sun 10am–1pm & 4–7pm; Oct–March Fri–Sun 10.30am–12.30pm & 3–5pm; €2.58). It contains a handful of masterpieces by local Umbrian painters, notably Nicolò Alunno, as well as several rare pieces of sculpture. Look out in particular for the figure of Christ with movable arms, once common, now extremely rare: during Holy Week the arms could be raised for ceremonies involving depictions of the Crucifixion and lowered for those depicting the Deposition and Resurrection. Farther up the busy, steep main street on the right stands **Sant'Andrea**, a striking Gothic church with another Pinturicchio painting in the right transept brightening up the gloomy interior. Also look out for the looming crucifix attributed to the school of Giotto, and the mummified body of the beatific Andrea Caccioli, an early follower of St Francis, in the left transept. A pleasing antidote to the busy main drag are the little streets at the top of the street and the many small alleys off it.

Spello makes a reasonable base for visiting Assisi, with a good range of **accommodation** (albeit quite pricey), fair restaurants and a small **tourist office** at the northern end of Piazza Matteotti at no. 3 (daily 9.30am–12.30pm & 3.30–5.30pm; ☎0742.651.408). *Il Cacciatore*, Via Giulia 42 (☎0742.651.141, ☏0742.301.603, ✉ilcacciatore@mclink.it; ➎), is a reasonable-value two-star hotel, with fine views from some rooms and potentially noisier rooms looking out over the street. At the smarter four-star *La Bastiglia*, Via dei Molini 17 (☎0742.651.277, ☏0742.301.159, ✉fancelli@lasbastiglia.com; ➐), most of the rooms command a fine view.

Spello's best **restaurant**, set in a vaulted medieval town house, is *Il Molino*, a few steps up from Santa Maria Maggiore at Piazza Matteotti 6–7 (closed Tues), a fairly smart place serving plenty of regional specialities – and wonderful fresh pasta – but with the unfortunate odd pretension. *Il Cacciatore* (closed Mon), attached to the hotel (see above), has middling food and service but a great terrace for al fresco dining. Further up the main street, the *Hosteria de Dadà* at no. 47 on the left is a tiny place with a handful of shared tables and is good for cheap, light meals at lunch or dinner (daily April–Oct noon–4pm & 7pm–midnight). Towards the top of the main street, look out for *Bar Giardino* on the right at no. 12, with a vast garden and panoramic terrace at the back. A little farther along, opposite the church of San Lorenzo, sits the *Pinturicchio*, a cheap and reliable trattoria; the *Bar Tullia*, to its left, is also good and has outside tables from which to take in the street life.

Foligno

To move on anywhere from Spello by public transport means a trip to **FOLIGNO** and a lull in proceedings, because it's a large modern town and flat in every sense of the word. Most of its star-turns were bombed out of existence in the war, and the place is now a mediocre provincial backwater sprawled over an unattractive plain. Its appearance wasn't helped by the 1997 earthquake, which hit the town relatively hard. However, much of what's left is conveniently grouped together in the central **Piazza della Repubblica**, and as you're likely to be passing through, a quick look isn't going to hurt. The town's also brimful of hotels and acts as a nodal point for trains and local village buses.

For the **tourist office** – at Corso Cavour 126 (☏0742.354.459, ✉info@iat.foligno.pg.it) – and bus station (Porta Romana), follow Viale Mezzetti west from the train station to Piazzale Alunno, and the office is on the southernmost corner. Continue up Corso Cavour and you hit the historic centre two minutes later. The graceful twelfth-century **Duomo** has two good Romanesque facades, but the interior was finished off in the eighteenth century to predictable effect. The nearby **Palazzo Trinci** is the only thing worth making a real effort to see. The Trincis were Foligno's medieval big shots, with territory and influence extending over great swaths of Umbria, and their palace is an art-filled monument to wealth and power – all frescoed stairways, carved ceilings and general opulence, most of it restored in the 1990s. Inside are a small **archeological museum** (Tues–Sun 10am–7pm; €5) and a **pinacoteca** (currently closed for restoration), with good frescoes by the fifteenth-century Gubbian painter Ottaviano Nelli.

The only other monument that hints at Foligno's former glory is **Santa Maria Infraportas** (off Piazza San Domenico), a church of pagan origins in which St Peter himself is said to have conducted a Mass. The oldest bit of the current building (eighth century) is the Cappella dell'Assunta off the left nave, dominated by the town's most precious piece of art, a twelfth-century Byzantine mural.

If you need **to stay**, try pleasant *Belvedere Hotel*, Via Flavio Ottaviani 19 (☏0742.353.990, ✆0742.356.243; ❸), just to the right of the station as you come out, on the same piazza. There's also a **hostel**, the *Pierantoni*, Via Pierantoni 23 (☏0742.342.566, ✆0742.343.559, ✉folhostel@tiscalinet.it; €13). For snacks and full **meals**, *La Bottega Barbanera*, right next to the side facade of the Duomo, at Piazza della Repubblica 34, serves gourmet dishes in charming surroundings.

Bevagna

Connected to Foligno (8km) by a regular bus service, the serene, attractive backwater of **BEVAGNA** is quieter and less visited than Spello, with a windswept **central square** of stark perfection. Flanked by two of Umbria's finest Romanesque churches – both untouched and creaking with age – the Piazza S. Silvestri dates from around the thirteenth century. The only exception is the fountain which, while blending perfectly, was installed in 1889. Look out particularly for the surreal gargoyles over the doorway of the larger church, San Michele. And if it's open, check out the Palazzo Comunale, which was converted in the nineteenth century into one of Umbria's prettiest provincial theatres. Also worth seeking out is the impressive **Roman mosaic** (north side of Via Porta Guelfa; free), once part of a bath complex. This fine work shows octopus, lobsters, sea-centaurs and other creatures. To get to see it you'll need to find a guide at the small **Museo di Bevagna** to take you there (Aug daily

10.30am–1pm & 3–7.30pm; April–Sept Tues–Sun 10.30am–1pm & 3.30–6/7pm; Oct–March Fri–Sun 10.30am–1pm & 2.30–5pm; €3). Located at Corso G. Matteotti 70, the museum is devoted to the history of the village and divided into three modest sections: archeological displays, art and history, and maps, letters and other documents.

There's not a lot else to the town, other than the quaint attractiveness of the streets, but Bevagna does boast three charming **hotels**. The most central is the one-star *Il Chiostro di Bevagna*, Corso G. Matteotti 103 (☎0742.361.987, ⓕ0742.369.231, ⓔchiostro.bevagna@katamail.com; ➍), just off Piazza S. Silvestro, in an atmospheric renovated Dominican convent, with an original cloister. Down the same street, the three-star *Palazzo Brunamonti*, Corso G. Matteotti 79 (☎0742.361.932, ⓕ0742.361.948, ⓦwww.brunamonti.com; ➏), is a sumptuous place with a period setting and trompe l'oeil decorations. *L'Orto degli Angeli* (☎0742.360.130, ⓕ0742.361.756, ⓦwww.ortoangeli.it; ➐), just off the Corso G. Matteotti at the eastern end of town, is the most luxurious and historic of them all; the mansion, with porticoes, gardens and a gourmet restaurant, has been in the same family since 1788. If you book in advance, it is possible to stay in the Santa Maria del Monte **convent** (☎0742.360.133, ⓕ0742.369.315, ⓔmonastero@mclink.it; ➋) courtesy of the Benedictine nuns at Corso G. Matteotti 15: all fourteen rooms have private bathrooms, though standards are very basic. There are also a few good **restaurants** in town: try the *Ottavio*, Via del Gonfalone 4 (closed Mon), immediately south of Piazza S. Silvestri in the square in which the buses from Foligno and Montefalco stop; or the *Enoteca di Piazza Onofri*, just behind the Palazzo Comunale at Piazza Onofri 1 (closed Wed, lunchtimes except at weekends & late July to early Aug), perfect for light meals or a snack and a glass of wine. Alternativley, go for the long-established and traditional *Da Nina*, Piazza Garibaldi 6 (closed Tues), a few steps beyond San Francesco.

Montefalco

Bus is the only means of public transport from Foligno to **MONTEFALCO**, a pleasing and intimate medieval village that's home to a superb collection of paintings. Its name, meaning Falcon's Mount, was glorified with the appendage *la ringhiera dell'Umbria* – "the balcony of Umbria" – a tribute to its wonderful views. It was also the birthplace of eight saints, good going even by Italian standards. Nowadays the town's sleepy rather than holy, with only a stupendously ugly water tower and very slight urban sprawl to take the edge off its medieval appeal. The strong, blackberry-flavoured **local wine**, *Sagrantino Passito*, made from a grape variety found nowhere else in Europe, is well worth a try; it's available in several shops in the main square – notably the *Enoteca Benozzo Gozzoli*. Recommended producers are Adanti and Caprai, also makers of the excellent Rosso di Montefalco.

The town's lofty location was a godsend to Spoleto's papal governors, left high, dry and terrified by the fourteenth-century defection of the popes to Avignon. They took refuge here, and their cowering presence accounts for some of the rich decoration of Montefalco's churches, a richness out of all proportion to the town's size. The cavernous ex-church of San Francesco, off the central Piazza del Comune at Via Ringhiera Umbra 6, is now the **Museo Civico di San Francesco** (June–Aug daily 10.30am–1pm & 3–7pm; March–May, Sept & Oct daily 10.30am–1pm & 2–6pm; Nov–Feb Tues–Sun 10.30am–1pm & 2.30–5pm; €6), housing the town's big feature, Benozzo Gozzoli's sumptuous **fresco cycle** on the life of St Francis. With Fra' Angelico,

Gozzoli was one of the most prolific and influential Florentine painters to come south and show the backward Umbrians what the Renaissance was all about. Resplendent with colour and detail, the cycle copies many of the ideas and episodes from Giotto's Assisi cycle but, with two hundred years of artistic know-how to draw on, is more sophisticated and more immediately appealing, if lacking Giotto's austere dignity. Among numerous other paintings in the church and excellent adjoining gallery are works by most of the leading Umbrians (Perugino, Nicolò Alunno, Tiberio d'Assisi), as well as a host of more minor efforts by local fifteenth-century artists. There are more early frescoes in **Sant'Agostino** across the main piazza in Via Umberto I.

The rest of the town is relatively low key but nice for a wander. Probably the most bizarre sight is the mummified body of St Clare (St Chiara), which languishes in the otherwise dismal church of the same name, five minutes' walk from San Francesco in Via Verdi (this is a second St Clare, not to be confused with the one in Assisi). Ring the bell and, if the nuns aren't deep in prayer, they may show you round the adjoining convent: in what turns out to be a fascinating behind-the-scenes look at monastic life, you're shown the remains of the saint's heart and the scissors used to hack it out. The story goes that Christ appeared to Clare, saying the burden of carrying the cross was becoming too heavy; Clare replied she would help by carrying it in her heart. When she was opened up after her death, a cross-shaped piece of tissue was duly found on her heart. Other strange exhibits include three of her kidney stones and a tree that miraculously grew from a staff planted in the garden here by Christ, during one of his appearances to Clare; the berries are used to make rosaries and are said to have powerful medicinal qualities.

Fifty metres beyond the church, preceded by a triple-arched Renaissance porch, is the chapel of **Sant'Illuminata**, strikingly if not terribly well frescoed by local painter Melanzio and others in 1510. Keep on heading out of town, turn left at the T-junction, and fifteen minutes of tedious walking brings you to **San Fortunato**, nicely situated amongst ilex woods and noted for the frescoes by Tiberio d'Assisi (1512), in the Cappella delle Rose (left of the main courtyard).

Practicalities

There's no need to spend more than a morning in Montefalco, but if you do decide **to stay** – and it's a peaceful spot to rest up – try the *Hotel "Degli Affreschi"*, Via G. Mameli 45 (℡0742.379.243, ℻0742.379.643, ❹), not far from the main square. Residents have use of the swimming pool at the ugly modern sister hotel *Hotel Nuovo Mondo*, 2km outside of town on the main road. One of the best restaurants is *Coccorone*, on the corner of Largo Tempestivi and Via Fabbri (closed Wed) – the *crespelle* (stuffed pancakes) and the *tiramisù* are especially good.

If you want more **information** on the town, contact the tourist desk inside San Francesco (summer 10.30am–7.30pm, winter closes at 5pm; ℡0742.379.598).

Trevi

The best way to move southwards without your own transport from Foligno is by train, which skirts the plain of Spoleto and whisks past the light industrial sites that blight the whole stretch of the valley towards Terni and beyond. Not many people stop before Spoleto itself, giving **TREVI** and its towering position no more than an admiring glance. Its daunting inaccessibility is one of the reasons for its easy-going, old-fashioned charm; the feeling is of a pleasant, ordinary provincial town, unspoilt but just beginning to feel the first effects of tourism. All around it lie vast expanses of olive groves, renowned for producing central Italy's finest oil.

The medieval centre, looming high on its hill, is 4km from the station, connected by bus. The main square inside the walls, Piazza Mazzini, has a small and obliging Pro Loco **tourist office** at no. 6 (daily 9am–1pm & 3–6/7pm; ☎0742.781.150), supplemented in a corner of the same piazza by a very helpful Tourist Co-Op (Mon–Sat 8.30am–2pm; ☎0742.780.066, ⓦwww.bedandbreakfastumbria.it). The latter can organize all manner of accommodation locally, from rooms to villas, as well as a variety of tours and activities: despite the official afternoon closing times (see above), there is generally someone in the office most of the day.

The key sight in town is the new **Pinacoteca Comunale** (April–July & Sept Tues–Sun 10.30am–1pm & 3.30–6/7pm; Aug daily 10.30am–1pm & 3–7.30pm; Oct–March Thurs–Sun 10.30am–1pm & 2.30–5pm; €3) in Largo Don Bosco, in the former Convento di San Francesco, reached by taking Via di San Francesco from the northern end of Piazza Mazzini. It houses a well-presented display of coins, ceramics and Roman fragments, several paintings by Umbrian masters and one outstanding work, a *Coronation of the Virgin* (1522) by Lo Spagna. Trevi's medieval governors commissioned this last painting as a copy of a more famous work by the Florentine Ghirlandaio, mainly because they couldn't afford the real thing. In the same complex is the **Museo della Civiltà dell'Ulivo** (same hours and ticket), a smart museum devoted to history of the olive and olive oil production. It's packed with interesting information, in English as well as Italian, though the number of exhibits is small.

Accommodation is limited to the rather bland but adequate three-star *Trevi*, at the southern edge of town at Via Fantosati 2 (☎0742.780.922, ⒻFAX0742.780.772; ❺), and to the more recent two-star *Il Terziere* (☎ & ⒻFAX0742.78.359, ⓦwww.ilterziere.it; ❹), which has the bonus of a pleasant garden: it lies east of the vast square and car park by which you enter Trevi on its eastern side at Via Salerno 1. The tourist offices (see above) will be able to come up with **private rooms** to rent in and around town. For food try the *Osteria La Vecchia Posta*, Piazza Mazzini 14 (closed Thurs except in July & Aug), or the half-hidden *La Prepositura*, Vicolo Oscura 2a, just below Piazza della Rocca, which has lovely medieval dining areas and set *degustazione* menus at €25 and €40.

Fonti di Clitunno

A short hop from Trevi on the road south are the sacred **FONTI DI CLITUNNO** (daily: March–Oct 9am–1pm & 2–6/7pm; Nov–Feb 10am–1pm & 2–4.30pm; €1), an unexpected beauty spot given the pockmarked surroundings. There's a certain amount of commercialized fuss and bother at the entrance, but the springs, streams and willow-shaded lake beyond – painted by Corot and an inspiration to poets from Virgil to Byron – are pure, languid romanticism. Unfortunately, the proximity of the noisy road, with its roaring trucks and buses, comes very close to ruining the effect. The spa waters have attracted people since Roman times – the likes of Caligula and Claudius came here to party – but their major curative effect is allegedly the dubious one of completely extinguishing any appetite for alcohol. Earthquakes over the years have upset many of the underground springs, so the waters aren't as plentiful as they were, but they still flow as limpid as they did in Byron's day, the "sweetest wave of the most living crystal . . . the purest god of gentle waters . . . most serene of aspect and most clear . . . a mirror and a bath for Beauty's youngest daughters." A mini tourist office doles out background information in the summer.

A few hundred metres north is the so-called **Tempietto di Clitunno** (Tues–Sun: April–Oct 8am–8pm; Nov–March 8am–6pm; free), looking for all the world like a miniature Greek temple but actually an eighth-century Christian church, cobbled together with a mixture of idiosyncrasy, wishful thinking and old Roman columns. It's only a small, one-off novelty, but still evocative, and with the bonus inside of some faded frescoes said to be the oldest in Umbria.

Spoleto

SPOLETO is perhaps Umbria's most charming town. Known mainly for its big **summer festival** (see box on p.635), it's remarkable also for its thoroughgoing medievalism, an extremely scenic setting, and several of Italy's most ancient Romanesque **churches**. Far more graceful and provincial a city than Perugia, nowadays it plays second fiddle politically to its long-time historical enemy, though for several centuries it was among the most influential of Italian towns. Two kilometres of well-preserved walls stand as testament to the one-time grandeur of its Roman colony, though its real importance dates from the sixth century when the Lombards made it the capital of one of their three Italian dukedoms. The autonomous **Duchy of Spoleto** eventually stretched to Rome, and by 890 its rulers had become powerful enough to lay claim to the imperial throne itself, making Spoleto, for a short time at least, the capital of the entire Holy Roman Empire. Barbarossa flattened the city in a fit of pique in 1155, and in 1499 the 19-year-old Lucrezia Borgia was appointed governor by her father, Pope Alexander VI. After that it was one long decline until about forty years ago and the arrival of the festival.

Arrival, information and accommodation

Spoleto is easily reached by **train**, with regular services on the main Rome–Ancona line and local links with Foligno, Terni, Orte and elsewhere. The train station is just northwest of the lower town; shuttle buses to the centre depart from outside the station – buy tickets (€0.80) from the station newspaper stand – as do services for Norcia (see p.639); other **buses** leave from central Piazza Libertà and Piazza Garibaldi in the north of the town. The Spoleto **tourist office** is at Piazza Libertà 7 (daily 9am–1pm & 4–6.30/7.30pm; ☎0743.220.311, ✆info@iat.spoleto.pg.it).

There is a **hostel** in the lower town, the *Villa Redenta*, Via di Villa Redenta 1 (☎0743.224.936, ✆villaredenta@hotmail.com; €12.91), with some double rooms available at double the dorm-bed price. From the station walk the length of Viale Trento e Trieste and turn left at the end on Via Flaminia Vecchia: the hostel is another seven or eight minutes' walk on the left almost opposite Via delle Lettere.

Other inexpensive **rooms** are hard to come by when the festival's in full swing, but at other times you shouldn't have too many problems. Cheapest rooms in town are at the central, though small and slightly dingy, *Dell'Angelo*, above a busy trattoria at Via Arco di Druso 25 (☎0743.222.385, ✆0743.207.965, ✆hoteldellangelo@libero.it; ❸). Otherwise try the good, if slightly overpriced, *Aurora*, a perfectly situated two-star in an alley off Piazza Libertà at Via dell'Apollinare 3 (☎0743.220.315, ✆0743.221.885,

SPOLETO

N

ACCOMMODATION

Dell'Angelo	5
Aurora	4
Charleston	2
Nuovo Clitunno	3
Villa Redenta	1

RESTAURANTS

Apollinare	D
Osteria del Matto	C
Il Panciolle	A
Pentagramma	E
Sabatini	B

0　　　　100 m

▼ Terni, San Pietro & Monteluco Campsite   ▼ Monteluco

ⓔinfo@hotelauroraspoleto.it; ❹), or the seven quiet and excellent rooms above *Il Panciolle* restaurant at Via del Duomo 4 (☎0743.45.677; ❸). The best of the central three-stars is the *Nuovo Clitunno*, Piazza Sordini 6 (☎0743.223.340, ℱ0743.222.663, ⓔhotelclitunno@spoleto1.com; ❺), followed by the *Charleston*, Piazza Collicola 10 (☎0743.220.052, ℱ0743.221.244, ⓔinfo@hotelcharleston.it; ❺), by the church of San Domenico.

For **campers** the closest site is *Camping Monteluco* (☎0743.220.358, ⓔprimaver@caribusiness.it; April–Sept), behind San Pietro, with (officially) only 35 places. *Il Girasole* (☎ & ℱ0743.51.335, ⓔcampingilgirasole@libero.it) in the village of **Petrognano** (10km northwest of Spoleto; hourly buses from the train station) is a bigger and flashier affair, with a public swimming pool nearby and tennis courts.

The Festival dei Due Mondi

Hosting Italy's leading international arts festival, the **Festival dei Due Mondi** (Festival of Two Worlds), has been a double-edged blessing for Spoleto – crowds and commercialism being the price it has had to pay for culture. Having already rejected thirty other Italian locations, the influential arts guru Giancarlo Menotti plumped for the town in 1958, attracted by its scenery, small venues and general good vibes. The ensuing jamboree is a great attraction if you're into music, dance or theatre, though the place forgoes a good part of its charm as a result. On top of the crowds, ticket prices for top companies and world-class performers can be off-putting, as can the jet-set, well-heeled cut of the audiences. Be warned too that while the festival's in progress you can expect packed hotels, madness in the restaurants and the chance of higher prices all round. At the same time there's an Edinburgh-type fringe and plenty of fellow travellers (plus lots of film, jazz, buskers and so on). Organizers, moreover, are increasingly looking to more avant-garde acts and wacky shows to recover the artistic edge of the festival's early days. Check out **information** from the **tourist office** on Piazza Libertà or the festival's own **office** at Piazza del Duomo 8 (☎0743.28.120, ⓦwww.spoletofestival.it). Advance tickets can also be bought online at ⓦwww.amitonline.it or by phone on ☎06.808.8352 or in Spoleto itself in the box office at Piazza Libertà 12 (☎0743.44.700, ⓕ0743.40.546).

The Lower Town

The lower town was badly damaged by World War II bombing and its only real interest lies in a couple of first-rate churches, most impressive of which is the fourth-century paleo-Christian **San Salvatore** (daily 7am–5pm; free), built by Christian monks from the eastern Mediterranean in the fourth century, since when it's hardly been touched. Conceived when the only models for religious buildings were Roman temples, that's pretty much what the monks came up with, the net result leaning more to paganism than Christianity. The walls inside are bare, the floors covered in fallen stone, and the dusty gloom is heavy with an almost eerie antiquity. Crumbling Corinthian columns from different ages are wedged awkwardly alongside one another, and at some point the arches in the nave were filled in to prevent total collapse.

In the vicinity is **San Ponziano**, unremarkable but for its distinctive Romanesque facade and an ancient-looking tenth-century crypt, which you should be able to visit by calling on the caretaker at the house on the left of the facade as you face it. The lower town's other attraction is the church of San Gregorio (daily 9am–noon & 3.30–6pm), started in 1069. The tower and intriguing portico are made from a patchwork of fragments clearly pinched from earlier Roman remains, but it's the interior that commands most attention. Stripped back to their Romanesque state, the walls are dotted with substantial patches of fresco and interrupted by a series of unusual stone confessionals. The presbytery is raised several metres above the level of the naves to allow for a masterful little crypt, supported by dozens of tiny pillars.

Tradition has it that somewhere under the church are the bones of ten thousand Christian martyrs killed by the Romans in the amphitheatre close by in the military barracks up the road. No one seems to mind if you just walk straight in; bear right from the gateway for the best of the amphitheatre's remains The ever-ingenious Romans apparently constructed special gutters to drain blood from the arena into the nearby Torrente Tessino, which ran crimson as a result. Now the river's often full of rubbish and a long way from being a puddle, let alone a torrent.

The Upper Town

There's really no single central piazza in Spoleto, but the place to head for is **Piazza Libertà**. Here you'll find the much-restored first-century **Roman theatre**, complete enough, if overshadowed by the gaudily painted buildings on all sides. The worst of these offenders, the church and convent of **Sant'Agata**, absorbed much of the stage area in the Middle Ages, and houses, among other things, the **Museo Archeologico** (daily 8.30am–7.30pm; €2), entered from Via Sant'Agata, the street that drops west from the piazza. The museum ticket gives access to the theatre stage, such as it is, used for festival and other performances throughout the summer. Its past includes a grisly episode in 1319 when four hundred Guelph supporters were rounded up by the Spoletans and dumped on the stage with their throats cut; the corpses were then pushed into a pile and burnt. The highlights of the little museum are the *Lex Spoletina*, two Roman inscriptions that forbade the chopping down of trees in the sacred woods of **Monteluco**. The injunction must have worked because the forests, home to hermits in the second century and later to St Francis, are still there, 8km east of the town. Take one of the hourly #9 buses from Piazza Libertà if you're not up to the very long, stiff walk, and head away from the hotel-restaurant complex and accompanying crowds into the footpaths that cross the woods. You don't have to walk far before you're alone. The views are great on a good day, and it's a welcome relief from the summer maelstrom down in Spoleto itself.

Cutting into the adjoining **Piazza della Fontana** are more Roman remains, all far humbler than the tourist blurb leads you to expect. Of the town's many arches from the period, the **Arco di Druso** (23 AD) straddling the entrance to the Piazza del Mercato is the only one not embedded in a wall. It was intended as a triumphal gateway to the old forum, and built to honour what must have been very minor campaign victories on the part of Drusus, son of Tiberius. The patched-up walls behind it are the city's oldest, built in the sixth century BC by the Umbrians, who otherwise are as mysterious and elusive as ever. To the right of the arch is what is described as a **Roman temple**, but unless you've a vivid imagination it's difficult to see it as anything other than a ditch. Pop into the adjacent church of **San Ansano** for a look at more of the temple and the wonderful fresco-covered crypt (down the stairs to the left of the high altar), originally the home of sixth-century monks.

Nowhere do you get a better sense of Spoleto's market-town roots than in the homely **Piazza del Mercato** beyond, whose two bars on the west side offer a fine opportunity to take in some streetlife. Old women wash fruit and vegetables in a fountain, its crown embellished with an impressive clock, the men drink in the bars and swap unintelligible stall-holders' gossip, and tourists make barely a dent in the proceedings. The *alimentari* on all sides are a cornucopia of goodies, with a definite bias towards truffles and sticky liqueurs.

Turning the corners of the attractive streets hereabouts, you'll soon come to the **Duomo** (daily: March–Oct 7.30am–12.30pm & 3–6pm; Nov–Feb closes 5pm; free), whose facade of restrained elegance is one of the most memorable in the region. The careful balance of Romanesque and Renaissance elements is framed by a gently sloping piazza and lovely hanging gardens, but the broad background of sky and open countryside is what sets the seal on the whole thing. The church suffered like many in Italy from the desire of rich communities to make their wealth and power conspicuous, a desire usually realized by tearing the guts out of old churches and remodelling them in the latest style. This worked well on the thirteenth-century **facade**, which has an arched portico tacked on in 1491, but less well in the interior where Pope Urban VIII's architect, Luigi Arrigucci, applied great dollops of Baroque midway through the seventeenth century. His "improvements", luckily, are eclipsed by the apse's superlative **frescoes** by the great Florentine artist Fra' Filippo Lippi, dominated by his final masterpiece, a *Coronation of the Virgin* (1469).

The artist died shortly after their completion, the rumour being that he was poisoned for seducing the daughter of a local noble family, his position as a monk having had no bearing on his sexual appetite. The Spoletans, not too perturbed by moral laxity, were delighted at having someone famous to put in their cathedral, being, as Vasari put it, "poorly provided with ornaments, above all with distinguished men", and so refused to send the dead artist back to Lorenzo de' Medici, his Florentine patron. Interred in a **tomb** designed by his son, Filippino Lippi (now in the right transept), the corpse disappeared during restoration two centuries later, the popular theory being that it was spirited away by descendants of the compromised girl – a sort of vendetta beyond the grave.

You should also make a point of seeing the **Erioli Chapels** at the beginning of the right nave, primarily for a faded *Madonna and Child* (with Lago di Trasimeno in the background) by Pinturicchio (1497), and for the cruder frescoes in the adjoining chapel by the Sicilian artist Jacopo Santori. There's also a good **Cosmati marble floor**; Umbria's earliest documented painting (a *Crucifix* of 1187, by Alberto Sotio, behind glass at the beginning of the left nave); a colourful chapel further down the left nave containing a framed letter written by St Francis (one of only two to survive); and the inevitable **icon**, which Barbarossa gave to the town in 1185 to try to make amends for having flattened it thirty years earlier.

The **Pinacoteca**, in the Palazzo Comunale, is destined to remain closed until a new home is found for its paintings (the Palazzo Rosari-Spada in Corso Mazzini is the likely candidate), which include a couple of big canvases by a local follower of Perugino, Lo Spagna. In a tiny side street below the Palazzo is the **Casa Romana**, Via di Visiale (daily: 27 March–15 Oct 10am–8pm; rest of year 10.30am–1pm & 3–6.30pm; €2.07), a dark and atmospheric little corner that contains the remains of a Roman house.

Very close by is the medieval town's most celebrated **church**, the twelfth-century **Sant'Eufemia** (seen with Museo Diocesano – see below), architecturally unique in Umbria for its *matronei*, high-arched galleries above the side-naves that segregated women from the men in the main body of the church. It was built over the site of the eighth-century Lombard ducal palace and appears to have been partly constructed from the remains of this and earlier Roman monuments; one or two of the completely mismatched columns are carved with distinctive Lombard motifs. The general dank solemnity of the place clearly points to an early foundation.

Sant'Eufemia is visited in conjunction with the outstanding **Museo Diocesano**, located in the same courtyard as the church (April–Sept Mon & Wed–Sat 10am–1.30pm & 4–7pm, Sun 10.30am–1pm & 3–6pm; Oct–March 10am–12.30pm & 3–6pm, Sun 11–5pm; closed Tues; €3). The half-dozen rooms contain several surprisingly good paintings, including a *Madonna* by Fra' Filippo Lippi and an early Beccafumi, a room of old wooden statues and some wonderfully graphic votive panels offering thanks for salvation from a host of vividly illustrated mishaps.

The Rocca, Ponte delle Torri and San Pietro

If you do nothing else in Spoleto you should take the short walk out to the **Ponte delle Torri**, the town's picture-postcard favourite and an astonishing piece of medieval engineering. It's best taken in as part of a circular walk around the base of the Rocca or on the longer trek out to San Pietro (see below). Within a minute of leaving shady gardens in Piazza Campello you suddenly find yourself looking out over superb countryside (blighted only by the busy roadway below, but this doesn't dominate), with a dramatic panorama across the Tessino gorge and south to the mountains of Castelmonte. There's an informal little bar, on the left before the bend, to help you enjoy the views.

The **Rocca**, everyone's idea of a cartoon castle, with towers, crenellations and sheer walls, was another in the chain of fortresses with which the tireless Cardinal Albornoz hoped to re-establish Church domination in central Italy, a primacy lost during the fourteenth-century papal exile to Avignon. It served until the early 1980s as a high-security prison – testimony to the skill of its medieval builders – and was home to, amongst others, Pope John Paul II's would-be assassin and leading members of the Red Brigade. It's approaching the end of some fifteen years of restoration, and will house, among other things, a museum devoted to the Duchy of Spoleto, but despite prodding from the EU – who put up much of the money for restoration – no date has been set for the grand opening. In the meantime it's possible to visit on a **guided tour** (Mon–Fri at 10am, 11am, 11.45am, 3pm, 4pm, 5pm & 6pm; Sat & Sun hourly from 10am to 6pm inclusive; €4.65). The tours last 45 minutes and depart from the gate at the edge of Piazza Campello: the ticket includes a minibus ride and a guide with limited English, though in the event there is little to be explained: the best bits of the tour are the superb views, the imposing twin courtyards and the sheer scale of the building.

The **bridge**, too, is a genuinely impressive affair, with a 240-metre span supported by ten eighty-metre arches that have been used as a launching pad by jilted lovers for six centuries. Designed by the Gubbian architect Gattapone, who was also responsible for Gubbio's Palazzo dei Consoli, it was initially planned as an aqueduct to bring water from Monteluco, replacing an earlier Roman causeway whose design Gattapone probably borrowed and enlarged upon. In time it also became used as an escape from the Rocca when Spoleto was under siege. The remains of what used to be a covered passageway connecting the two are still visible straggling down the hillside.

It's well worth crossing the bridge and picking up the **footpath**, which zigzags up from the left-hand side of the road and then contours left into peaceful countryside within a few hundred metres, giving great views back over the gorge. Alternatively, turn right on the road and make for the church of **San Pietro**, whose facade beckons from a not-too-distant hillside. If the idea of another church doesn't appeal you can easily double back to town on the circular Via della Rocca.

Though the walk to San Pietro is a longish one (2km), it's pleasantly shady with some good glimpses of Spoleto; the only thing to beware of on the country road (no pavements) are crazed Italians taking the bends too fast. The church would be undistinguished were it not for the splendid **sculptures** adorning its facade. Taken with Maitani's bas-reliefs in Orvieto, they are the best Romanesque carvings in Umbria, partly Lombard in their inspiration, and drawing variously on the Gospels and medieval legend for their complicated narrative and symbolic purpose. A particularly juicy scene to look out for includes the *Death of a Sinner* (left series, second from the top) where the Archangel Michael abandons the sinner to a couple of demons who bind and torture him before bringing in the burning oil to finish the job. Fourth panel from the top (right series) shows a wolf disguised as a friar before a fleeing ram – a dig at dodgy monastic morals.

Eating and drinking

The best place for light **meals** and a glass of wine is the *Osteria del Matto*, a few steps west of Piazza del Mercato at Vicolo del Mercato 3: the single room is dark and snug and the owner very welcoming. A good basic trattoria – though this being chic Spoleto, prices are not terribly basic – is *Il Panciolle,* at Via del Duomo 3 (closed Wed), which has a wonderful terrace for al fresco meals, though service can be slow. For something more special, go to *Sabatini,* at Corso Mazzini 54 (closed Mon), the town's smartest spot (again with outside tables), or the nicely intimate *Apollinare,* Via Sant'Agata 14 (closed Tues) with superb food. More informal is the slightly cheaper and bistro-like *Pentagramma*, signposted off Piazza Libertà at Via T. Martani 4 (closed Mon). The place to drink in the evening is the main bar on the west side of Piazza del Mercato.

The Valnerina and Norcia

The **VALNERINA** is the most beautiful part of Umbria. Strictly translated as the "little valley of the Nera", it effectively refers to the whole eastern part of the region, a self-contained area of high mountains, poor communications, steep wooded valleys, upland villages and vast stretches of barren nothingness. Wolves still roam the summit ridges and are to be protected by a proposed (but long awaited) regional nature reserve. The area is a genuine "forgotten corner", deserted farms everywhere bearing witness to a century of emigration.

The region is best explored with a car, as public transport is limited. The easiest way to get to the region without a car is by bus from Spoleto: six **buses** daily run from Spoleto station to Norcia (1hr 15min), calling at Piedipaterno (2 daily connections to Monteleone), Borgo Cerreto, Serravalle and villages in between (timetables from the tourist office in Spoleto; see p.633). A new road tunnel links Spoleto to the valley, but for scenery stick to the old and tortuous N395 from Spoleto until you hit the "main" SS209 and the more pastoral run up the Nera Valley towards Norcia. Mountains roundabout are around 1500m high, with excellent walking, creeping up as you move east to about 2500m in the **Monti Sibillini**. It's difficult to explore with any sort of plan (unless you stick to the Nera), and the best approach is to follow your nose, poking into small valleys, tracing high country lanes to remote hamlets.

More deliberately, you could make for **VALLO DI NERA**, the most archetypal of the **fortified villages** that pop up along the Lower Nera. Medieval **TRIPONZO** is a natural focus of communications, little more than a quaint staging post and fortified tower (and a better target than modernish Cerreto nearby). **MONTELEONE** is the only place of any size for miles, with a fine church, and popular with trippers.

CASCIA figures large on the map, but is disappointing in actuality – largely modern, thanks to countless earthquakes over the years – and only recommendable to pilgrims in search of **St Rita**, whose presence, enshrined in the stupendously ugly twentieth-century **Basilica**, dominates both the new and earthquake-damaged hill-town.

Norcia

The very pleasant mountain retreat of **NORCIA** is the only place of any size or substance in the Valnerina. Noted on the one hand as the birthplace of **St Benedict** – founder of Western monasticism – and on the other as the producer of Italy's top **salami**, it has an air of charming dereliction, and its low, sturdy houses (built to be earthquake-resistant) are a world away from the pastoral, fairy-tale cities to the west. If transport allows, it could be the base for some good trips into neighbouring territory, particularly the famed Piano Grande (see p.642) and the mountains to the east and north. A big new road through the mountains into Marche has opened and should bring in more visitors – good news for local employment, which is scarce, but a possible challenge to the environment. Hang-gliders and winter-sports enthusiasts have also recently discovered the area, another mixed blessing.

It doesn't take long to see the town, but you may want to stay on for the wonderful air and atmosphere. Most of the action is in the central **Piazza San Benedetto**, site of the Roman forum and presided over by a statue of Benedict. Apart from its facade, you can largely forget about the **Duomo** – destroyed by several earthquakes (the last big one was in 1979), and patched up to look like nothing on earth. The **Castellina** is more captivating: a papal fortress full of gaunt medieval echoes, it contains a fine little **museum** with fascinating old wooden sculptures and several surprisingly accomplished paintings. Unfortunately there doesn't seem to be enough money around to keep it open on a regular basis; if you're lucky enough to find it open, be sure to pop in. The fortress makes a strange bedfellow for the labyrinthine church of **San Benedetto**, which supposedly was built over the saint's birthplace but more likely was raised from the ruins of an earlier Roman temple. Inside there are a few paltry frescoes, nothing more, though the crypt contains the remains of a Roman-era house.

Meat-eaters would be daft not to try the deservedly famous **local pork products**. Anything that can be done to a pig, the Norcians apparently do – and supposedly better than anyone else. Even today, you still see butchers in other parts of Italy called *un nurcino*, after the town. If finances stretch, you could also indulge in the area's prized black **truffle**. The season runs from January to April (though you may come across the lesser prized summer truffles too), and several thousand lire will buy a light dusting over your tagliatelle. Plenty of shops, an attraction in themselves, are on hand to sell you all manner of local specialities, not just truffles, but also hams, the famed lentils of Castelluccio (see p.642) and lots of rare mountain cheeses.

Moderate **hotels** comprise the central eight-roomed *Da Benito*, Via Marconi 4 (T0743.816.670, F0743.824.242, E ristorante.benito@libero.it; ❸), and the bigger *Casa Religiosa San Benedetto*, Via delle Vergini 13 (T & F0743.828.208; ❷), located at the far northwest corner of the upper town, open to all even though it's still a working convent. For a very comfortable modern option, try the *Salicone*, Via Montedoro (T0743.828.076, F0743.828.081, E info-booking@bianconi.com; ❸) just outside the walls. Under the same management is the *Grotta Azzurra*, a comfortable three-star on Via Alfieri 12 (T0743.816.513, F0743.817.342, E info-booking@bianconi.com; ❻), whose restaurant – *the Granaro del Monte* – is *the* best place to **eat** in Norcia; it's relatively inexpensive and set in large medieval banqueting halls (a former papal granary) complete with suits of armour and huge, roaring fires. A more economical place to eat, but still central and excellent, is the *Taverna de' Massari* (Via Roma 13; T0743.816.218; summer daily, winter closed Tues), located northeast of the central piazza, just behind the Basilica of San Benedetto.

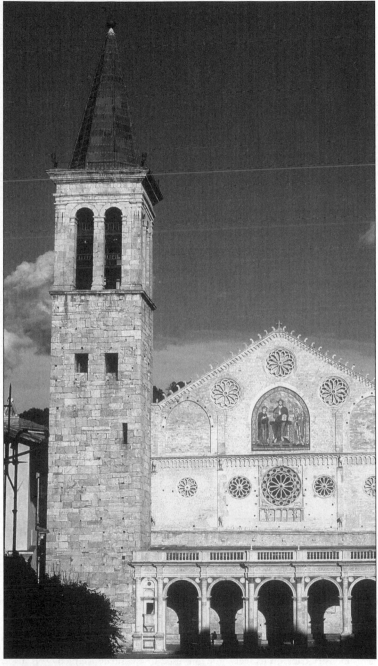

△ The Duomo, Spoleto

The eerie, expansive **Piano Grande**, 20km east of Norcia, is an extraordinary prairie ringed by bare, whaleback mountains and stretching, uninterrupted by tree, hedge or habitation, for miles and miles. It's much photographed – especially in spring when it's ablaze with poppies – and was used by Zeffirelli as a setting in his Franciscan film *Brother Sun, Sister Moon*. The desperately isolated village of **CASTELLUCCIO** hangs above it at around 1400m, and although no longer the sole preserve of shepherds, it remains an unspoilt base and the ideal starting point for any number of straightforward mountain walks. To plan routes, get hold of the 1:50,000 Kompass map no. 666 or the more detailed 1:25,000 CAI maps (the latter are often available in Norcia or Castelluccio's bars). There's no public transport into the area, though you might try your luck at catching lifts in high season, when the skies are filled with hang-gliders. Rough **camping** is generally no problem, and there are a couple of two-star **hotel-restaurants** convenient for the plain and many walks: *La Sibilla*, in Castelluccio itself (booking advised, ☎0743.821.113; ❸), which has an excellent restaurant, and the *Forca Canapine* (☎0743.823.005, 🖷0743.823.006; ❹), a big and comfortable ski-hotel (but with some tiny rooms and even tinier bathrooms) on the Norcia-Arquata road, above the southern edge of the Piano Grande. You might also find rooms above the *Taverna di Castelluccio* bar (☎0743.870.158; ❷), 100m from *La Sibilla*.

If you can't get out here the smaller **Piano di Santa Scolastica**, due south of Norcia, will give you a very watered-down idea of what you're missing. Another worthwhile trip, if you're short of time to spend in aimless exploration, is the road north to **PRECI** and thus to Visso in Marche. Walled and castled Preci was known throughout Europe in the sixteenth century as a school for surgeons, their main trade being removal of kidney stones. However, they had a more notorious sideline – castrating young boys who were foolish enough to show operatic potential. The town has a good place to **eat**: *Il Castoro*, Via Roma (☎0743.939.248; closed Thurs in winter), which offers pizza or good local food such as boar, trout or chewy *stringozzi* pasta. A kilometre above nearby **PIEDIVALLE** is the beautifully sited Abbey of San Eutizio, one of the cradles of the Benedictine movement. Now only a pretty – if over-restored – twelfth-century Romanesque church stands on the site, but in its day the community of monks held sway over more than a hundred castles and local churches. Above the church you can still see the caves used by the earliest hermits and by Benedict himself, who discovered his vocation while visiting the hermits from Norcia.

Terni and around

TERNI was the unlikely birthplace of one of the world's most famous saints, **St Valentine**, bishop of the town until his martyrdom in 273 and now entombed in his personal basilica at San Valentino, a village 2km to the southwest. A less romantic city, however, would be hard to imagine. Terni's important arms and steel industries made it a natural target for Allied bombing in 1944, and eighty percent of the town was reduced to rubble, including, sadly, the best part of its Roman and medieval heritage. Rebuilding replaced what was lost with a grey grid-iron city straight out of postwar eastern Europe; it also put the arms industry back on its feet – the gun used to assassinate Kennedy was made here – and though the town no longer lives up to its nineteenth-century nickname of "the Manchester of Italy", hi-tech weaponry and the stench of chemicals aren't the most enticing of prospects. The **tourist office** (Mon–Sat 9am–1pm & 4–7pm; ☎0744.423.047, ℻0744.427.259, ℮info@iat.terni.it), should you need it, is at Viale Battisti 7a – take Viale della Stazione from the station, and Viale Battisti is 300m up, on the right, at the first major piazza.

The Marmore waterfall

The best place to make for locally is the **Cascate delle Marmore** (train or bus from Terni), created by the Romans in 271 BC when they diverted the River Velino into the Nera during drainage of marshlands to the south. The highest waterfall in Europe (at 165m), it is boosted by the damming of Lago di Piediluco in the 1930s to satisfy the demands of industry for cheap hydroelectric power. Pictures of the falls in full spate adorn most Umbrian tourist offices, but what they neglect to tell you is that the water can be turned off at the flick of a switch (in favour of electric turbines), leaving a none-too-spectacular trickle. No two sources agree on when exactly the water is likely to be switched on, but the best chances of finding it running seem to be weekend lunchtimes and evenings when there's often a *son et lumière*. From July 15 to August 11 it also does the business on weekdays, between 5pm and 6.30pm. The Terni tourist office has current times. The observation platforms are below on the SS209 and above in the village of Marmore, with a steep path between the two. The green and luxuriant setting, tumbling water and expanses of gleaming polished marble add up to a spectacular show – shame about the factories round the corner, though.

Lago di Piediluco

For visitors wishing to carry on up the Velino Valley, **Lago di Piediluco** makes an attractive target. Surrounded by steep and thickly wooded hills, it's Umbria's prettiest lake, something like a miniature version of one of the northern Alpine lakes. Very dark and deep, the water's a bit on the cold side for swimming (and in places unsafe), though it's a big sailing and canoeing centre. The train station is at the western end, some distance from the town of **PIEDILUCO** itself, but perfect if you want to put up a tent on the southern, less-visited shore, or walk the scenic minor road on this shore to Monte Caperno. There's a quay here with boats to and from Piediluco, as well as a famous four-second **echo**, constantly and enthusiastically being tested. Piediluco is picturesque – with the lake on its doorstep it doesn't have to try too hard – but is filled by people escaping from Terni at the weekends. This said, if you're a fishing or watersports fan, or just need a quiet spot for your tent, you may want to go to ground for a couple of days. **Accommodation** can be tight: try the two-star *Lido* on the lake shore at Piazza Bonanni 2 (☎0744.368.292, ℻0744.368.354; ❸), also a popular **restaurant** (no closing day). A top-notch place to eat is the *Tavoletta*, Via Forca 4 (closed Wed and some of June and Oct). There's a big, and in high season usually packed, **campsite**, *Il Lago* (☎0744.369.199, ℮c.marmore@cuoreverde.com).

The Abbazia di San Pietro in Valle

A worthwhile excursion from Terni, particularly if you're making for Norcia and the Valnerina from the south rather than Spoleto, is the **Abbazia di San Pietro in Valle** (daily: 10am–noon & 2–5pm; free), 18km from Terni and signposted from Colleponte. Buses make the run up to **Triponzo**, passing the

UMBRIA | Terni and around

9

abbey en route. Founded by the Lombard duke Faroaldo II, who retired to monastic life after being deposed by his son in 720, the abbey was amongst the most powerful religious houses in Umbro-Romano, controlling vast tracts of land and dominating the lives of thousands of people. It's set high on the hillside near a thickly wooded cleft, the first impression being of a dull blockhouse affair, with nothing to hint at the splendour of the Lombard and Byzantine art inside. The faded frescoes (1190) that cover the body of the main church are the first tentative attempts to create a distinctively Italian art and move away from the stylized influence of Byzantine painting, an influence that nonetheless was to prevail until the advent of Pietro Cavallini, Cimabue and Giotto a century later. The **altar**, beautifully set off by the rose-coloured stone and rich Romanesque display all around, is a rare and important example of Lombard sculpture, carved with what look like pagan, almost Celtic figures and motifs. To each side are well-preserved Roman sarcophagi, backed by a profusion of gorgeously coloured frescoes. A doorway (not always open) leads to the twelfth-century campanile, a Lombard import of a type common in Rome and Lazio and distinguished by fragments and reliefs salvaged from the eighth-century church. There's also a faultless double-tiered cloister from the twelfth century, though access to this may be restricted as the complex's private owners – only the church belongs to the state – have opened an appealing agriturismo (℡0744.780.129, Ⓔchiasco@tin.it; ❼) in part of the abbey.

By following the SS209 past the walled, medieval village of **SCHEGGINO** you can pick up the Spoleto road into the Valnerina, a route covered on p.639. If you need to **stay** locally, Scheggino's *Albergo-Trattoria del Ponte*, Via del Borgo 17 (℡0743.61.253, Ⓕ0743.61.131; ❸), is the best bet. Even if you're just passing through, give their excellent **restaurant** (closed Mon & Sept 1–15) a try – the trout dishes with truffles, in particular, are superb.

Carsulae

The building of the Via Flaminia in 220 BC between Rome and Ancona cemented Umbria's strategic importance as the crossroads of central Italy. Staging-posts and fully fledged colonies sprang up along its route, turning into modern-day Narni, Terni, Spoleto, and Spello. Some settlements, however, such as **CARSULAE**, 15km north of Terni, were subsequently abandoned in the wake of earthquakes and civil war. In its day this particular pile of stones was known as the Pompeii of central Italy, and both Tacitus and Pliny the Younger praised its beauty.

The surrounding plain, though rustic and peaceful, has little real interest, but the excavated remains are surprisingly impressive. The freely-accessible site – the largest Roman site in Umbria – is dominated by a church, **San Damiano**, made from materials filched from the ruins (other stones and precious marbles went to build local houses), behind which runs a stretch of the original Via Flaminia, complete with grooves made by carts and chariots, part of the arched northern gate, tombs, baths, wells, an amphitheatre and all the other trappings of an ex-Roman town.

Narni and around

It's an easy thirty-minute hop on the train from Terni to **NARNI**, which claims to be the geographical centre of Italy, with a hilltop site jutting into the Nera Valley on a majestic spur and crowned by another of Albornoz's formidable papal fortresses. Commanding one end of a steep gorge (about ten minutes of fairly spectacular train travel), it was once the gateway into Umbria, the last post before the Tiber Valley and the undefended road to Rome. However, while the town retains a fine medieval character, the views from its heights are marred by steel and chemical works around **Narni Scalo**, the new town that's grown up in the valley below. The trick is to keep your gaze firmly fixed on the gorge side of the walls and pretend the factories don't exist.

The heart of the **old town** (bus from the train station) has all the standard fittings: the medieval piazzas, the warren of streets, a modest art gallery, the usual crop of Romanesque churches, and a huge *rocca*, currently being restored. There's a **Roman bridge** on the outskirts, the subject of considerable local hype. Goethe arrived in Narni in the middle of the night and was peeved not to have seen it; he was only missing a solitary arch in the middle of the river – just as easily viewed from the train.

In what's an appealing but relatively low-key centre, things revolve around the narrow **Piazza dei Priori**, where pride of place goes to the fourteenth-century **Palazzo dei Priori**, unremarkable except for a fountain and graceful **loggia** designed by the Gubbian architect Gattapone. The gaunt and somewhat eccentric building opposite is the Palazzo del Podestà, cobbled together by amalgamating three town houses and adding some token decoration. The thirteenth-century Romanesque sculptures above the main door are worth a glance, and there's a small **Pinacoteca** on the first floor whose main feature is a superlative and much-copied canvas by Ghirlandaio. The bulk of the town's paintings are due to go on show at a new site in the Palazzo Vescovile, though at the time of writing the opening date was still unknown. When it does open, you'll be able to see key works by Benozzo Gozzoli and Fiorenzo di Lorenzo, plus fourteenth- to sixteenth-century frescoes removed from churches in surrounding villages. On the town's main street is the tiny and easily overlooked church of Santa Maria in Pensole, unaltered since 1175 – you can still see the date above the door – and adorned across the width of its facade with a marvellous carved frieze.

The twelfth-century **Duomo** merits a brief mention, chiefly because its front steps are where the town hangs out. Inside, the Cosmati marble floor and a ninth-century mosaic of Christ don't give much cause to linger.

There's no real reason for staying overnight in Narni, but should you want to your best bet would be the cosy, central *Dei Priori*, Vicolo del Comune 4 (T0744.726.843, Wwww.loggiadeipriori.it; ❸), which offers first-class meals at the lovely *La Loggia* restaurant (closed Mon & second half of July). There's also a collection of cheap but deeply uninspiring **rooms** around the station, and a **campsite** out of town at Monte del Sole (T & F0744.796.336, Emontesole@libero.it; April–Sept). The **tourist office** is at Piazza dei Priori 3 (summer daily 9.30am–12.30pm & 4.30–7pm; T0744.715.362, Einfo@iat.narni.tr.it).

Amelia

AMELIA, 11km northwest of Narni and plonked on top of a sugar-loaf hilltop, is by far the most tempting local excursion if the ruins don't appeal. Though not big on monuments, it's fairly interesting and unvisited, noted mainly for its extraordinary cyclopean walls, claimed as some of the oldest and mightiest in Italy. Supported by their own weight and comprising vast polygonal blocks up to 7m across, they reach a height of over 20m in places and date back, according to early Roman historians, to the Umbrian settlement of the eleventh century BC. Most of the town's churches were ruined in the nineteenth century, and art's thin on the ground – San Giacomo's **double cloister**

and a **tomb** by **Agostino di Duccio** are the only highlights – but Amelia's charm is the typically Umbrian mixture of good views, medieval streets and lovely countryside close at hand.

The **tourist office** is at Via Orvieto 1 (summer: daily 9.30am–12.30pm & Tues–Sat 2.30–6.30pm; winter closes 5.30pm; ℡0744.981.453, ⓔinfo@iat.amelia.tr.it). The local culinary speciality is a tooth-rotting combination of white figs, chocolate and crushed nuts (only available in winter), but for more substantial fare there are two good **restaurants**, both with rooms to rent: the three-star *Anita*, Via Roma 31 (℡0744.982.146, ⓕ0744.983.079; ❸; restaurant closed Mon); and, just 1km north of town, *Le Colonne*, Via Roma 191 (℡0744.983.529; ❷; restaurant closed Wed). The nicest place to **stay**, however, is the small 14-room *Il Carleni*, Via Pellegrino Carleni 21 (℡0744.983.925, ⓦwww.ilcarleni.com; ❺), an "historic residence" with pretty garden, good views and a restaurant. For food, also try the *Gabelletta*, Via Tuderete 20 (℡0744.982.159; closed Mon), in an elegant villa 3.5km northeast, on the road to Montecastrilli.

The drive on to Orvieto along the back roads is a treat: plenty of oak forests and fine walks, and the chance to catch one of Umbria's Romanesque highlights, the twelfth-century church of **Santa Maria Assunata** at Lugnano in Teverina.

Otricoli

OTRICOLI, 15km south of Narni, is almost the last town in Umbria before you enter Lazio and a reasonable miniature of all the region's hill-towns. Its medieval delights, though, are eclipsed by the remains of Roman **Otriculum**, a ramshackle collection of ruins within easy walking distance of the village. To reach them get on the main road that bypasses the village, head downhill for 200m and take the signposted track that strikes off right towards the Tiber. So far no more than a trickle of tourists visits the colony – still largely unexcavated and evocatively draped in clinging undergrowth – but plans by the state to make them the centre of a vast archeological park mean they're headed for the big time.

Unusually, the settlement has no walls, mainly because it was more a pleasure garden than a defensive site, built as a sort of holiday village for Rome's hoi polloi, who travelled up from the capital by boat on the then still navigable Tiber. Turner stopped off to paint a picture (now in the Clore wing of the Tate Gallery in London), and in the sixteenth century Montaigne described the spot as "infinitely pleasant". You can find **rooms** up in Otricoli at the small *Umbria*, Via Roma 72 (℡0744.709.013; ❷).

Todi

TODI is one of the best-established Umbrian hill-towns, at heart still a thriving and insular agricultural centre, but also a favoured trendy retreat for foreign expats and Rome's arts and media types. In the way of these things the tourists haven't been far behind, but neither fact should deter you from making a daytrip: few places beat it for sheer location and fairy-tale medievalism. With a stunning and extremely daunting position, it makes a highly inviting prospect from below.

Getting there and sussing out how to fit it into an itinerary are likely to be your biggest problems. Basically you come either from Terni on the hourly

FCU train or from Perugia, again by FCU or on one of the regular buses that stop below the town by the church of Santa Maria della Consolazione or higher up, just off the main square near San Fortunato. Moving on, in addition to the train, you have the option of a daily bus to Orvieto. Todi's **train stations** (there are two) are both in the middle of nowhere, and **buses** to the centre don't always connect with the trains. Ponte Rio is the station to go for; Ponte Naia, 5km distant, is marginally closer, but fewer trains stop there, bus shuttles are few and far between, and the uphill walk to town is one long slog.

The Town

The central **Piazza del Popolo** is widely held to be the most perfect medieval piazza in Italy and is the reason why most people come here. The **Duomo** at the far end, atop a broad flight of steps, is the main feature – a meeting point of the last of the Romanesque and the first of the Gothic forms filtering up from France in the early fourteenth century. The square, three-tiered **facade** is inspired simplicity; just a sumptuous rose window (1520) and ornately carved doorway to embellish the pinky weathered marble – the classic example of a form found all over Umbria. Inevitably the interior is less impressive. There's some delicate nineteenth-century stained glass in the arched nave on the right, and a good altarpiece by Giannicolo di Paolo (a follower of Perugino), but an appalling sixteenth-century *Last Judgement*, loosely derived from Michelangelo's, defaces the back wall. The strikingly carved **choir** (1530) – of incredible delicacy and precision – is the region's best, with panels at floor level near the front depicting the tools used to carve the piece. The crypt contains a rambling collection of ancient Roman – and possibly Etruscan – fragments.

Back in the piazza, the other key buildings are the three **public palaces**, squared off near the Duomo in deliberately provocative fashion as an expression of medieval civic pride – definitely trying to put one over on the Church. The adjoining Palazzo del Capitano (1290) and adjacent Palazzo del Popolo (begun 1213) are most prominent, thanks mainly to the stone staircase that looks like the setting for a thousand B-movie sword fights. Several films *have* actually been shot in Todi, filmakers lured by its relative proximity to Cinecittà and scenographic "authenticity".

The Palazzo del Capitano houses a superb new museum, the **Museo-Pinacoteca di Todi** (Tues–Sun: April–Aug 10.30am–1pm & 2.30–6pm; March & Sept 10.30am–1pm & 2–5pm; Oct–Feb 10.30am–1pm & 2–4.30pm; €3.10), which brilliantly weaves an open-plan sequence of rooms into the existing medieval structure. The first section of the museum delves into Todi's history, followed by rooms devoted to archeology, coins and medallions, fabrics, ceramics and a picture gallery. In many cases the rooms are more alluring than their displays – particularly the lovely frescoed salon devoted to ceramics – but numerous individual exhibits merit a closer look, none more so than the museum's star painting: the sumptuous *Coronation of the Virgin* (1507) by Lo Spagna.

The **Palazzo dei Priori** (1293–1337) is the southernmost building in the square, with all the various crenellations, battlements and mullioned windows of the other palaces but with the difference that they've been recently restored. It's been the seat of all the town's various rulers and today is still the town hall; if you can look like you're on council business you should be able to peep inside. The best place to enjoy the streetlife is from the **bar** down on its right-hand side, more of a locals' local than the flashy place halfway down the piazza (but which does do a good line in sandwiches).

Streets to the right of the Duomo are quiet and dozy and worth a wander, though the single most celebrated sight in the town after the piazza is the church of **San Fortunato**, set above some half-hearted gardens a very short stroll from the centre. It's an enormous thing given the size of the town – testimony to Todi's medieval wealth and importance. The squat, messy and clearly unfinished facade, an amalgam of Romanesque and Gothic styles, reflects the time it took to build (1292–1462) and at first glance doesn't exactly raise expectations. A florid **Gothic doorway** of arched swirls and carved craziness, however, is the first of several surprises, second of which is the enormous light, airy interior, recently highlighted by cleaning and several dazzling coats of whitewash. It marks the pinnacle of the Umbrian tradition for large vaulted churches, a style based on the smaller and basic "barn churches" common in Tuscany, which were distinguished by a single, low-pitched roof and naves and aisles of equal height. (San Domenico in Perugia, p.609, is another example.) It also marks a trend for side-chapels, a habit picked up from Catalonia and southern France in the thirteenth century and made necessary by the rising demand for daily Masses as the Franciscans became a more ministering order. There's another good **choir**, heavier and with more hints of the Baroque than the one in the Duomo, as well as a few scant patches of Sienese fresco. The fresco by **Masolino di Panicale** in the fourth chapel on the right is a good example of this rare painter's work, though a bit battered. Some lovely **cloisters** to the rear (outside and to the right) round off a distinctive and worthwhile church.

Santa Maria della Consolazione (closed daily 1–3pm), completed in 1607, is thought to have been based on an earlier Bramante draft for St Peter's in Rome; the alternating window types in the cupola are a Bramante trademark. Victorian writers called it the best Renaissance church in Italy (pretty close to saying the best in the world). It's worth a look to judge for yourself, but doesn't merit a special journey.

An ideal place for a siesta is the rambling **Giardino Pubblico**, full of shady nooks and narrow pathways, and a cut above the normal town plot. There's also a kids' playground and a very small **Rocca**, both less noteworthy than the views, which are extensive though usually hazy. The gardens are best tackled via the stony track to the right of San Fortunato, less of a sweat than the path which comes up from Piazza Oberdan.

Todi's tourist offerings are soon exhausted, but if you want to go the whole hog, check the so-called **niches** in Piazza del Vecchio Mercato, all that's left of the Roman colony. The town's proud of them, but they don't amount to much: four big and slightly overgrown arches of completely unknown purpose. Two minutes' walk down the lane in the lowest corner of the piazza brings you to the tiny **San Carlo** or **Ilario** (1020), an ancient Lombard chapel well off the beaten track that's all too often locked to protect a set of frescoes by Lo Spagna. A few metres beyond the church, and next to a crumbling flower-strewn arbour, is the **Fonte Scarnabecco** (1241), an unusual arched fountain that was the town's lifeblood and social meeting place until the advent of piped water. In your wanderings look out for the **three sets of walls**, concentric rings that mark Todi's Umbrian, Roman and medieval limits; they're seen to best effect on Via Matteotti.

Practicalities

The **tourist office** is on the left as you walk up the stepped approach to San Fortunato (daily 9am–1pm & 4–7pm, closed Sun pm in winter; ☎075.894.3395, ⓔinfo@iat.todi.pg.it). **Hotels** are in demand, especially during the increasingly popular Todi Festival (first ten days of Sept), and – except for one very nice but expensive four-star, the *Fonte Cesia*, Via Lorenzo Leoni 3 (☎075.894.3737, ⓕ075.894.4677; ❻) – are characterless, modern affairs some way out of town. Ten minutes' dispiriting walk straight down the main road from Porta Romana brings you to the *Tuder*, Via Maestà dei Lombardi 13 (☎075.894.2184, ⓕ075.894.3952, ⓔhoteltuder@libero.it; ❺), an overpriced and functional place in an uninspiring spot. A short distance beyond it is the marginally better located but rather fancy *Villa Luisa*, Via Angelo Cortesi 147 (☎075.894.8571, ⓕ075.894.8472, ⓔvillaluise@villaluisa.it; ❻).

The town's best-known **restaurant** is the *Umbria* (☎075.882.390; closed Wed), beneath the museum; prices are high and service can be slapdash, but the panorama from the terrace makes it all worthwhile; in season, book to be sure of an outside table. Cheaper alternatives include the unpretentious *Cavour* at Corso Cavour 21 (closed Wed) – just a shame about the piped music – and the basic *Pizzeria Giubilei Italo*, off Corso Cavour in Piazza B. d'Alviano (closed Mon after 8pm). Opposite this is a good **bar** with outside tables, the *Pianiggiana*, though the bars in the main square give you more to look at with your drink or ice cream.

Deruta and the Tiber Valley

North of Todi, the Tiber Valley broadens out into a flat plain edged with moderately pretty low hills and dotted with light industry. It's not somewhere you'll want to spend a lot of time, but there are one or two things worth catching if you're in no hurry to get to Perugia, though Marsciano, the area's main town, certainly isn't one of them.

Instead try to take in some of the **hill-villages** along the route – almost any you choose will boast a Romanesque church. Most are built over the graves of early monks and martyrs, the Tiber and Naia valleys having been amongst the earliest to be colonized by Christians fleeing Roman persecution, and thus the springboard of Umbria's powerful monastic tradition. The most rewarding churches are those you come upon by accident, in crumbling hamlets or in the midst of the ilex woods that blanket surrounding hills, but if you prefer to plan a visit you should make the following a priority: Viepri, Villa di San Faustino, Santa Maria in Partano, San Teranzano and the Abbazia di San Fidenzo.

If you don't get to the peripheral villages, head for **Madonna dei Bagni**, the one church on the main N3 that's definitely worth a look. Its walls are covered with hundreds of votive tiles left by pilgrims over three hundred years, constituting a unique social document and giving occasionally wacky insight into the peculiarities of religious belief. Day-to-day life in the fields, the insides of houses, transport (from horse to carriage to car), clothes and so on are represented almost as cartoons, though the most entertaining tiles are those offered as thanks for "miraculous" escapes from dangerous and not so dangerous corners – a fall from a cow, a bite from a donkey, fire, flood and famine. A hundred tiles were stolen in 1980, and opening times have been curtailed to reduce the risk of a recurrence. The best time to try is Saturday morning, when it's not unknown for bus tours to show up; otherwise ask at the tourist office in Deruta, 2km up the road.

If you're travelling by car, you could make for one of the most charming options for **accommodation** in the area, and handy for Todi, Perugia, Deruta and Assisi: the bucolic *San Orsola* (☎0338.855.5361, ⓔadimc@tiscalinet.it; ❸), a restored twelfth-century *casale*, just a few kilometres off the main highway, near Schiavo di Marsciano. It offers spacious, comfortable rooms with a hearty buffet breakfast featuring their own fresh hens' eggs. An excellent **restaurant** 5km to the north is the *Piccolo Mondo*, at San Vito in Monte (☎075.870.8186; closed Mon), with an extensive menu of substantial regional dishes; phone for directions.

Deruta

The town of **DERUTA** is best known for its **ceramics** and seems to be devoted to nothing else. Some of the stuff is mass-produced trash, and some pieces so big you'd need a trailer to get them home, but most are beautiful – hand-made, hand painted and, by general consent, Italy's best. The Romans worked local clay, but it was the discovery of distinctive blue and yellow glazes in the fifteenth century, allied with the Moorish-influenced designs of southern Spain, that put the town on the map. Some fifty workshops traded as far afield as Britain, and pieces from the period have found their way into most of the world's major museums. Designs these days are mainly copies, with little original work, though it's still very much the place for browsing and buying; avoid the roadside stalls and head for the workshops of the new town for the best choice and prices.

   The **old town** on the hill isn't particularly compelling, but there's a recently revamped **Museo Regionale della Ceramica** next to the church of San Francesco (April–Sept daily 10.30am–1pm & 3.30–6pm; Oct–March Wed–Mon 10.30am–1pm & 2.30–5pm), which traces the history of ceramic production in the town: one of the highlights is a tiled floor (1524) lifted wholesale from the town's parish church.

Orvieto

Out on a limb from the rest of Umbria, **ORVIETO** is perfectly placed between Rome and Florence to serve as a historical picnic for tour operators. Tourists flood into the town in their millions, drawn by the **Duomo**, one of the greatest Gothic buildings in Italy. However, once its facade and Signorelli's frescoes have been admired, the town's not quite as exciting as guides and word of mouth make out. This is partly to do with the gloominess of the dark volcanic rock (tufa) from which it's built, and, more poetically, because it harbours something of the characteristic brooding atmosphere of Etruscan towns (it was one of the twelve-strong federation of Etruscan cities). Two thousand years on, it's not difficult to detect a more laid-back atmosphere in the cities east of the Tiber – founded by the Umbrians, a sunnier and easier-going people. All the same Orvieto is likeable, the setting superb, the Duomo unmissable, and the rest of the town good for a couple of hours' visit. And you could always indulge in its renowned white **wine** if you're stuck with time on your hands.

Arrival, information and accommodation

First impressions of Orvieto from afar tend to be the ones that linger; its position is almost as remarkable and famous as its cathedral. The town, rising 300m sheer from the valley floor, sits on a tabletop plug of volcanic lava, one of four such remnants in the vicinity. Without a doubt, the best approach is by car through the hills to the southwest (from Bolsena, see p.796). It starts to look fairly average again from the dismal town around the train station, but hit the twisting three-kilometre road up to the old centre and you begin to get a sense of its drama and one-off weirdness. If you arrive by train, take the restored nineteenth-century **funicular** (tickets at €0.80 from the funicular ticket office or station newsagent or bar) from the station forecourt to Piazza Cahen: it's a pleasant walk along Corso Cavour to the centre of town (allow five to ten minutes), or you can take one of the regular minibus shuttles (tickets €0.80) that stop outside the funicular every few minutes for the run to Piazza del Duomo. Buses replace the funicular when it closes at 8.30pm. Inter-town buses take you directly to Piazza Cahen, Piazza XXIX Marzo, or Piazza della Repubblica, depending on the service.

The **tourist office** is at Piazza del Duomo 24 (Mon–Fri 8am–2pm & 4–7pm, Sat & Sun 10am–1pm & 3.30–6.30pm; ☎0763.341.772, ✉info@ iat.orvieto.tr.it). Check your **email** at *Caffè Montanucci*, Corso Cavour 19–23 (8am–midnight, closed Wed).

Most of the town's nightlife and budget **rooms** are in Orvieto Scalo, the unlovely district around the station. The only low-cost central **hotel** is the pleasantly dated *Posta*, Via Signorelli 18 (☎ & ℱ0763.341.909, ⓦwww.orvietohotels.it; ❸), two minutes from the Duomo and offering a wide range of single and double rooms with and without private bathrooms. Even better placed are the newly restored three-star *Duomo*, Via Vicolo di Maurizio 7 (☎0763.341.887, ℱ0763.394.973, ✉hotelduomo@tiscalinet.it; ❺), in a comfortable restructured medieval building; and the pleasant, three-star *Italia*, Piazza del Popolo 13 (☎0763.342.065, ℱ0763.342.902, ✉hotelitalia@libero.it; ❹), the biggest central place (45 rooms) and thus likely to have space in an emergency. A little farther from the centre, and therefore quieter, but still within easy walking distance of everything, are the good-value and well-appointed *Corso*, Corso Cavour 343 (☎ & ℱ0763.342.020, ✉hotelcorso@libero.it; ❹), and the slightly larger *Valentino*, Via Angelo da Orvieto 30–32 (☎ & ℱ0743.342.464, ✉hotelvalentino@libero.it; ❹). The nearest **campsite**, the *Scacco Matto*, is 10km away on the SS448 road near Lago di Corbora (bus to Baschi/Civitella); it's a lowly one-star job but is open all year (☎0744.950.163).

The Duomo

Burckhardt described Orvieto's Duomo as "the greatest and richest polychrome monument in the world", while Pope Leo XIII called it "the Golden Lily of Italian cathedrals", adding that on the Day of Judgement it would float up to heaven carried by its own beauty. According to a tradition fostered by the Church, it was built to celebrate the so-called **Miracle of Bolsena** (1263), involving a Bohemian priest who was travelling to Rome to shake off a heretical disbelief in transubstantiation – the idea that the body and blood of Christ

UMBRIA | Orvieto

◀ Viterbo

are physically present in the Eucharist. While he celebrated Mass in a church near Lago di Bolsena, blood started to drip from the host onto the corporale, the cloth underneath the chalice on the altar. The stained linen was whisked off to Pope Urban IV, who like many a pope was in Orvieto to escape the heat and political hassle of Rome. He immediately proclaimed a miracle, and a year later Thomas Aquinas, no less, drew up a papal bull instigating the feast of **Corpus Domini**. The Church at the time, however, was in retreat, and the Umbrian towns were at the height of their civic expansion. It's likely that the building of an awe-inspiring cathedral in one of the region's most powerful *comuni* was less an act to commemorate a miracle than a shrewd piece of political opportunism designed to remind errant citizens of the papacy's power.

It was miraculous that the Duomo was built at all. Medieval Orvieto was so violent that at times the population thought about giving up on it altogether. Dante wrote that its family feuds were worse than those between Verona's Montagues and Capulets – the original inspiration for *Romeo and Juliet*. The

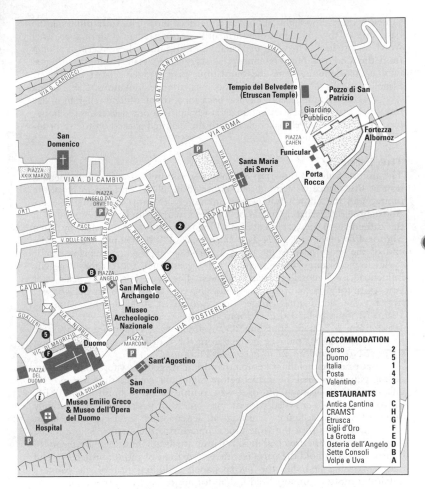

Within image: map labels

ACCOMMODATION

Corso	2
Duomo	5
Italia	1
Posta	4
Valentino	3

RESTAURANTS

Antica Cantina	C
CRAMST	H
Etrusca	G
Gigli d'Oro	F
La Grotta	E
Osteria dell'Angelo	D
Sette Consoli	B
Volpe e Uva	A

UMBRIA | Orvieto

building was also dogged by a committee approach to design – even the plans took thirty years to draw up. Yet though construction dragged on for three centuries and exhausted 33 architects, 152 sculptors, 68 painters and 90 mosaicists, the final product is a surprisingly unified example of the transitional Romanesque-Gothic style. Credit for guiding the work at its most important stage goes to the Sienese architect **Lorenzo Maitani** (c1270–1330), with the initial plans probably drawn up by Arnolfo di Cambio, architect of Florence's Palazzo Vecchio.

The facade

The facade is the star-turn, owing its undeniable impact to a decorative richness just the right side of overkill. It's a riot of columns, spires, bas-reliefs, sculptures, dazzling and almost overpowering use of colour, colossally emphasized doorways and hundreds of capricious details just about held together by four enormous fluted columns. Stunning from the dwarfed piazza, particularly at

653

sunset or under floodlights, it's not all superficial gloss. The **four pillars** at the base, one of the highlights of fourteenth-century Italian sculpture, are well worth a close look. The work of Maitani and his pupils, they describe episodes from the Old and New Testaments in staggering detail: lashings of plague, famine, martyrdoms, grotesque mutilation, mad and emaciated figures, the Flagellation, the Massacre of the Innocents, strange visitations, Cain slaying Abel (particularly juicy), and only the occasional touch of light relief. In its day it was there to point an accusing finger at Orvieto's moral slackers, as the none-too-cheerful final panel makes clear, with the damned packed off to fire, brimstone and eternal misery.

The interior

The inside (daily 7.30am–1pm & 2.30pm–dusk; free) is a disappointment at least at first glance, as if the facade either took all the enthusiasm or all the money and the church was tacked on merely to prop everything else up. Adorned with alternating stripes of coloured marble similar to those found in the cathedrals of Siena, Florence and Pisa, it's mainly distinguished by **Luca Signorelli's** fresco cycle, *The Last Judgement* (1499–1504), in a chapel at the end of the south nave. Some claim it surpasses even Michelangelo's similar cycle in the Sistine Chapel, painted forty years later and obviously heavily influenced by Signorelli's earlier treatment. The cycle is on view again after years of restoration, and though you now have to pay for the privilege of seeing it, the admission's more than worth it (March–Oct Mon–Sat 10am–12.45pm & 2.30–6.15/7.15pm, Sun 2.30–5.45pm; Nov–Feb Mon–Sat 10am–noon & 2.30–5.15pm, Sun 2.30–5.45pm; €3.) Tickets are not available in the cathedral, but must be bought from the tourist office or the souvenir shops at No. 25 and no. 27 in Piazza del Duomo.

Several painters, including Perugino and Fra' Angelico (who completed two ceiling panels), tackled the chapel before Signorelli – a free-thinking and singular artist from nearby Cortona – was commissioned to finish it off. All but the lower walls are crowded with the movement of passionate and beautifully observed muscular figures, creating an effect that's realistic and almost grotesquely fantastic at the same time. Draughtsmanship and a delight in the human form are the frescoes' most obvious attributes, but there are plenty of bizarre details to hold the narrative interest. A mass of monstrous lechery and naked writhing flesh fills the *Inferno* panel, including that of the painter's unfaithful mistress, immortalized in hell for all to see. In another an unfortunate is having his ear bitten off by a green-buttocked demon. Signorelli, suitably clad in black, has painted himself with Fra' Angelico in the lower left corner of *The Sermon of the Antichrist*, both calmly looking on as someone is garrotted at their feet.

All this overshadows the twin **Cappella del Corporale**, which contains the sacred corporale itself, locked away in a massive, jewel-encrusted casket (designed as a deliberate copy of the facade), plus some appealing frescoes by local fourteenth-century painter Ugolino di Prete, describing events connected with the Miracle of Bolsena. The entire apse is covered in more frescoes by Ugolino, many of which were partly restored by Pinturicchio, who was eventually kicked off the job for "consuming too much gold, too much azure and too much wine". Also worth a mention are an easily missed *Madonna and Child* by Gentile da Fabriano and a beautifully delicate fifteenth-century font, both near the main doors.

The rest of the town

Next to the Duomo on the right as you look at it is the **Museo dell'Opera del Duomo** (closed for restoration, excepting the Emilio Greco section). Higlights are paintings by Martini and Pastura (an artist from Viterbo influenced by Perugino), several important thirteenth-century sculptures by Arnolfo di Cambio and Andrea Pisano, and a lovely font filled with Escher-like carved fishes. The **Emilio Greco** section of the museum (daily: April–Sept 10.30am–1pm & 2–6.30pm; Oct–March 10.30am–1pm & 2–5.30pm; €2.50, €4.50 for Biglietto Cumulativo, which includes Il Pozzo di San Patrizio – see below) comprises nearly a hundred works donated to the city by the artist who created the Duomo's bronze doors in the 1960s, none of them profoundly interesting – peek through the door beyond the ground-floor ticket office and you'll see enough of the exhibits to know if you want a closer look.

The wonderfully restored **Museo Claudio Faina** (incorporating the Museo Civico and Museo dei Ragazzi) opposite the Duomo (Tues–Sun: April–Sept 9.30am–6pm; Oct–March 10am–5pm; €4.20) has a predictable but superbly displayed collection of vases and fragments excavated from local tombs (it also offers some great **views** of the cathedral facade). These sixth-century-BC **tombs** (daily: summer 9am–7pm; winter closes 1hr before dusk; €2.20) are still visible just off the road which drops towards the station from Piazza Cahen and are worth tracking down for their rows of massive and sombre stone graves – though none has the grandeur or paintings of the more famous necropoli in Cerveteri and Tarquinia (see p.787 & p.788). Before leaving Piazza del Duomo enquire at the tourist office (see p.651) for details of the fascinating **Orvieto Underground** (ⓦ www.orvietounderground.it) tours into the vast labyrinth of **tunnels**, caves and store rooms that riddle the soft volcanic rock on which Orvieto is built: most date back to medieval times, some to the Etruscan era. Tours leave from the tourist office daily at 11am, 12.15pm, 4pm and 5.15pm (€5.50), but there is some flexibility: ask at the separate desk in the tourist office or call ⓣ 0763.344.891 or 0339.733.2764 for details and bookings.

As far as the town's **churches** go, they all naturally pale beside the Duomo, though most have something worthwhile to see. The tiny Romanesque **San Lorenzo di Arari** was built in 1291 on the site of a church destroyed by monks from nearby San Francesco because the sound of its bells got on their nerves. Four recently restored **frescoes** on the left of the nave depict typically traumatic scenes from the life of St Lawrence. There's also an Etruscan sacrificial slab, which rather oddly serves as the Christian altar (*arari* meaning "altar").

From Piazzale Cacciatore there's a decent **walk** around the city's southern walls (Via Ripa Medici) with views over to a prominent outcrop of rock in the middle distance, part of the old volcanic crater. Ten minutes or so brings you to **San Giovenale**, whose rustic surroundings, on the very western tip of the *rupa*, Orvieto's volcanic plateau, are a far cry from the bustle of the Duomo. It's not much to look at from the outside, but the musty **medieval interior** is the best (and oldest) in the town, though virtually no one makes the trek out to see it. The thirteenth-century Gothic transept, with its two pointed arches, rather oddly stands a metre above the rounded Romanesque nave, making for a hybrid and distinctive church, all of it exhaustively decorated with thirteenth- and fifteenth-century **frescoes**. Check out the *Tree of Life* fresco right of the main door and the macabre *Calendar of Funeral Anniversaries* partly covered by the side entrance.

From the church back to the centre of town Via Malabranca and Via Filippeschi are the best of the **medieval streets**, all tantalizing doorways and tiled roofs, but second-rate by the standards of neighbouring hill-towns. For an overview, climb the **Torre del Moro**, a medieval tower in Corso Cavour just south of Piazza del Popolo (daily: March–Oct 10am–7/8pm; Nov–Feb 10.30am–1pm; €2.60).

The central **Sant' Andrea** on Piazza della Repubblica is worth a mention, more for its strange twelve-sided **campanile** than the bits and pieces of the Roman and Etruscan city in the crypt. In the Piazza del Popolo, further up Corso Cavour (the town's pedestrianized main drag), there's a daily fruit and veg market plus the odd craft stall – in front of the restored and impressive **Palazzo del Popolo** (closed to the public).

Il Pozzo di San Patrizio (daily: April–Sept 10am–6.45pm; Oct–March 10am–5.45pm; €3.50, or €4.50 with the Emilio Greco museum – see above), just off Piazzale Cahen, is the town's novelty act, a huge cylindrical well commissioned in 1527 by Pope Clement VII to guarantee the town's water supply during an expected siege by the Imperial Army (which never came). Water was brought to the surface by donkeys on two broad staircases, cannily designed never to intersect. It's a striking piece of engineering, 13m wide and 62m deep, named after its supposed similarity to the Irish cave where St Patrick died in 493, aged 133.

Eating and drinking

Cheap **restaurants** are grouped together at the bottom (eastern end) of Corso Cavour, though one of the best places on this street, *Antica Cantina*, recently opened and already popular with locals, is midway down in Piazza Monaldeschi 18–19 (closed Wed evening). It's reasonably priced and succeeds in reproducing the old-fashioned trattoria atmosphere. Even better value – though less atmospheric – eating can be found close to the Duomo at the co-operatively run *CRAMST*, Via Maitani 15 (closed Sun). Again deservedly popular with locals, it's a 450-seat canteen affair, offering a choice between restaurant and self-service pizzeria. *La Grotta*, Via Signorelli 5 (closed Mon), is good value, friendly and has been around longer than most. A touch cheaper and probably with better food to boot is the *Volpe e L'uva*, Via Ripa Corsica 1 (closed all day Mon & Tues lunch), tucked away off Via della Pace north of Piazza del Popolo. Up a notch in price, both the *Sette Consoli*, Piazza Sant'Angelo 1a (closed Wed), and *Osteria dell'Angelo*, Corso Cavour 166 (closed Mon), are highly rated by Italian foodie guides, the *Osteria* being the better and slightly cheaper of the two. More traditional, and guaranteed to give you a reliable meal in old-world surroundings, is the *Etrusca*, Via Maitani 10 (closed Mon). If it's romance you're after (and money's no object), head for the *Gigli d'Oro* in Piazza del Duomo (closed Wed), in the shadow of the cathedral facade.

The **wine bars** around the Duomo are an expensive way of sampling the well-known Orvietan white. For great **ice cream** head for *Gelateria Pasqualetti*, an ivy-covered *gelateria* in the main piazza, to the north side of the Duomo: it also has an outlet at Corso Cavour 56.

Around Orvieto

Moving on from Orvieto, you have are plenty of choices of destination. The obvious targets are Rome and Florence, both about ninety minutes away by train, but if you're in no hurry you might just as well head west. There are buses from Piazza Cahen to Viterbo (see p.792) and Bolsena (see p.796), both in Lazio. The road to Bolsena has some of the best views of Orvieto: it's where the postcard shots are taken from and was also where Turner set up his easel (the resulting picture's now in the Clore wing of London's Tate Gallery). The wooded pocket of countryside west of Orvieto around Castel Giorgio is pretty enough, but probably only worth bothering with if you're in a car. Depending on the route you've taken so far you could stay in Umbria and take a slow train north through Città della Pieve or follow one of two good routes east to Todi. The first of these runs through Monte Peglia, some of the region's classic hill country.

Monte Peglia

Monte Peglia is the generic name for the triangular expanse of land that rises between the Chiani Valley in the west and the Tevere in the east. It's wild, sparse and timeless countryside, with hilltop hamlets, olives, vines, herds of white oxen and miles of deserted roads and tracks – the archetype of the pastoral lowlands you find all over the region. Although the map marks several villages, most turn out to be no more than scattered farms, many of them abandoned. The only realistic way of tackling the remoteness is with your own transport.

You'll get the best quick taste of the area on the circuitous and beautifully deserted N79 from Orvieto Scalo to Todi; most of the traffic these days takes the newer and infinitely quicker route south of Lago di Corbara. Superb initial views of Orvieto peter out as the road climbs through many a hairpin into densely wooded hill country, with occasional glimpses (haze allowing) as far as Perugia.

The best of the scenery is north of the road, where the area's woods, rivers and fields are a haven for **wildlife**. It's about the only place in Umbria you'll see otters, for example, and is well known for the variety of its birds, who owe their immunity from the Sunday morning blast-anything-that-flies fraternity to an ancient tract of land – *una bandita demeniale di caccia* – where hunting has traditionally been forbidden.

It's quicker and almost equally scenic to take the N448 to Todi, which after meandering along the flattish southern shore of Lago di Corbara takes off into an unexpectedly dramatic **gorge** for the rest of the run onto Todi. Nobody seems keen to swim in the lake, and it's not used for any sort of watersports – and to be honest it doesn't actually look that inviting. Further on things get better, when the strange purple-red rocks of the gorge, along with sheer cliffs and forested slopes, add up to a more enticing package. The road's pretty quiet, with plenty of free-style **camping** and **picnic** opportunities as the valley flattens out towards Todi.

Città della Pieve

Città della Pieve is most famous as the birthplace of Perugino (1445–1523), but it has a modicum of charm that merits a short visit in its own right. Again, you're better off in a car, for the station is a long haul from the town and it's the sort of place that can easily be seen in an hour. From below, the town looks vaguely and mysteriously enticing as it straggles along a distant ridge to the east, but once up close it lacks the impact of other Umbrian towns, the chief appeal being the tiny red-bricked houses (there was no local building stone), old women knitting, and geraniums in profusion at every window. One of the streets, Via della Baciadonna, claims to be the narrowest in Italy, the width of a "woman's kiss", the translation suggests. If you prefer your poetry liquid, try and get to the April *festa* when the town's fountains run with wine.

Otherwise its only real interest lies in the handful of **Perugino's paintings**, which lie scattered around the town's fairly dismal churches, palaces and oratories, some of which – the **Palazzo della Corgna**, the church of **Sant'Agostino** and the **Oratorio di Santa Maria dei Bianchi** – have been united in a self-contained "circuit" known as the **Museo Aperto** with a single-ticket admission, available from any of the relevant attractions (daily: June–Sept 9.30am–1pm & 4–7.30pm; Oct–April 10am–12.30pm & 3–6pm; €2.70). If the small **tourist office** at Piazza Matteotti 4 (Mon–Sat 10.30am–12.30pm & 4–6/7pm; ☎0578.299.375) is shut, there's a map of the town's few highlights outside the unremarkable Duomo in Piazza Gramsci (or Piazza Plebiscito, depending on your politics).

The cathedral itself has a couple of late works that show **Perugino** in his worst light. The painter's reputation today, though still very high, is lower than it was in his own time, when contemporaries spoke of him in the same breath as Leonardo and Michelangelo. He trained with Leonardo da Vinci in Florence but largely remained faithful to the tenets of the Umbrian School – sublime misty landscapes behind ethereal religious subjects. His great facility enabled him to produce vast numbers of dewy-eyed saints and Madonnas, whose occasional absence of genuine religious sentiment horrified those who demanded sincerity above all else in devotional art. What in his youth had been profound and innovative gradually came to seem stilted and repetitive. Accused of merely replicating a successful formula, he also did nothing to discourage pupils finishing his works, adding his signature to some real shockers – especially in old age. He remains, however, one of the most influential of the Renaissance painters. The painting not to miss is *The Adoration of the Magi* in Santa Maria dei Bianchi, considered his greatest work still resident in Italy (Napoleon removed many to the Louvre in Paris), with lesser paintings in nearby **San Antonio Abate**, **San Pietro** and **Santa Maria dei Servi**.

Travel details

Trains

Assisi to: Foligno (hourly; 15min); Perugia (hourly; 20min); Spello (hourly; 10min); Teróntola (hourly; 1hr).

Città di Castello to: Perugia (hourly; 1hr); Sansepolcro (hourly; 15min).

Foligno to: Ancona (13 daily; 1hr 30min–2hr); Assisi (21 daily; 15min); Fabriano (14 daily; 40min–1hr); Fossato di Vico (14 daily; 40min); Gualdo Tadino (10 daily; 35min); Narni (18 daily; 1hr); Orte (hourly; 1hr–1hr 10 min); Perugia (hourly; 20–35 min); Rome (14 daily; 1hr 45min); Spello (hourly; 5min); Spoleto (hourly; 25min); Terni (hourly; 50min); Teróntola (17 daily; 1hr 15min).

Orvieto to: Arezzo (12 daily; 1hr 20min); Chiusi (12 daily; 40min; connections to Siena, 1hr 30min); Florence (10 daily; 1hr 30min); Orte (17 daily; 30min); Rome (19 daily; 1hr 20min).

Perugia to: Assisi (hourly; 20min); Città di Castello (hourly; 1hr); Deruta (hourly; 20min); Foligno (hourly; 40min); Sansepolcro (hourly; 1hr 30min); Spello (hourly; 30min); Terni (hourly; 1hr 40min); Teróntola (hourly; 35min); Todi (hourly; 50min).

Spoleto to: Foligno (hourly; 25min); Fossato di Vico (10 daily; 50 min); Narni (17 daily; 40min); Nocera Umbra (6 daily; 35min); Terni (hourly; 30min).

Terni to: Città di Castello (FCU line hourly; 2hr 30 min); Foligno (12 daily; 40min); Narni (17 daily; 15min); Orte (hourly; 25min); Perugia (FCU line; 4hourly; 1hr 20min); Sansepolcro (FCU line; hourly; 3hr); Spoleto (hourly; 20min); Todi (FCU line; hourly; 50min).

Buses

Assisi to: Bettona (1 daily; 50 min); Foligno (10 daily; 50min); Gualdo Tadino (1 daily; 1hr 15min);

Gubbio (2 weekly); Norcia and the Valnerina (1 daily; Mon–Sat from Santa Maria degli Angeli); Perugia (10 daily; 30min); Spello (10 daily; 40min).

Bevagna to Montefalco (3 daily; 20 min)

Foligno to Bevagna (3 daily Mon–Fri; 30 min); Montefalco (5 daily; 35min); Perugia (4 daily; 1hr 10min); Spello (7 daily; 15min); Trevi (4 daily; 30min)

Gubbio to: Fossato di Vico (10 daily; 30min); Perugia (10 daily Mon–Sat, 4 daily Sun; 1hr 10min).

Montefalco to: Bevagna (4 daily Mon–Sat; 20 min)

Narni to: Amelia (4–12 daily; 15min); Orvieto (5 daily; 1hr); Otricoli (7–10 daily; 40min); Terni (4–6 daily; 30min).

Norcia to: Castelluccio (2 daily Thurs only; 50min); Perugia (1 daily; 1hr 30min); Rome (1 daily; 3hr); Spoleto (5 daily Mon–Sat, 1 Sun; 1hr 10min); Terni (1 daily; 1hr).

Orvieto to: Amelia (6–7 daily; 1hr 15min); Baschi (5–7 daily; 30min); Bolsena (2 daily; 1hr); Lugnano in Tevere (5–7 daily; 1hr); Narni (6 daily; 1hr 5min); Perugia (1 daily; 2hr 45min); Todi (1 daily; 50min); Terni (6–7 daily; 1hr 40min).

Perugia to: Ascoli Piceno (1–4 daily; 3hr); Assisi (3–12 daily; 30min); Bettona (2 daily; 40min); Castiglione del Lago (7–9 daily Mon–Sat; 1hr 15min); Florence (1 daily; 2hr); Foligno (4 daily; 1hr 10min); Gubbio (10 daily Mon–Sat, 4 daily Sun; 1hr 10min); Norcia (1 daily; 2hr 50min); Orvieto (1 daily; 2hr 25min); Passignano (7 daily Mon–Sat; 1hr 30min); Rome (2–6 daily; 2hr 30min); Rome Fiumicino airport (1–3 daily; 3hr); Siena (3–7 daily; 1hr 30min); Spello (4 daily Mon–Sat; 55min); Spoleto (1 direct daily Mon–Sat; 1hr 20min); Todi (5–7 daily; 1hr).

Spoleto to: Foligno (7 daily; 40min); Fonti di Clitunno (7 daily; 20min); Montefalco (2–3 daily Mon–Sat; 1hr); Monteleone via Valle di Nero and Gavelli (1 daily in winter; 1hr 30min); Norcia (5 daily Mon–Sat; 1 Sun; 1hr 10min); Perugia (5 daily; 1hr 20min); Rome (1 daily; 2hr 20min); Scheggino (5 daily; 1hr 10min); Terni (6 daily; 45min); Trevi (7 daily; 25min).

Terni to: Amelia (10 or more daily Mon–Sat, 1 daily Sun; 50min); Cascata delle Marmore (11–15 daily; 40min); Ferentillo (12–17 daily; 40min); Orvieto (via Baschi, Guardea, Montecchio and Amelia; 5 daily Mon–Sat; 2hr); Piediluco (6–9 daily; 35min); Scheggino (5–8 daily; 50min); Todi (via Sangemini, Acquasparta or Avigliano; 3 daily Mon–Sat; 1hr); Also long-distance services to Bolsena (connection at Orvieto) and Rome.

Todi to: Marsciano (2 daily; 1hr 30min); Orvieto (1 daily; 50min); Perugia (3 daily; 1hr); Terni (8 daily; 45min).

Marche

✳ **Urbino** "Ideal city" and art capital created by Federico da Montefeltro, the ultimate Renaissance man. See p.666

✳ **San Leo** A spectacular ancient town on a rocky outcrop that makes a landmark for miles around. See p.672

✳ **Cónero promontory** This hilly promontory is ideal for walks or cycle rides, or a swim in the clear waters of one of several small bays. See p.683

✳ **Áscoli Piceno** You'll find interesting food and many architectural gems in this relatively undis-

covered medieval town. See p.701

✳ **Macerata and the road to Sarnano** Catch a summer opera in the university town of Macerata and then drive south through some of central Italy's most beautiful countryside. See p.696

✳ **Monti Sibillini** These mountains are a hiker's paradise. See p.699

✳ **Lorenzo Lotto** Don't miss paintings by the Renaissance's best portraitist at Jesi, Loreto, Ancona and Recanati. See p.682, p.688, p.680 & p.689

Marche

L ying between the Apennines and the Adriatic, **Marche** (sometimes anglicized as The Marches) is a varied region, and one you could spend weeks exploring. Large areas of it are unspoilt, particularly in the south-west, where crumbling hill-villages make atmospheric bases for hikes into the stunning **Monti Sibillini** range. Not that all of Marche is free from tourism; much of its coastline is studded with modern grid-plan resorts, and ranks of sun-umbrellas fill many of its beaches. The area also has a fair amount of industry – in particular light engineering, shoe manufacturing and ceramics – heaviest around the port of **Ancona** and along the main road and rail route from Umbria.

Regional food and wine

Marche is very much a rural region, its food a mixture of **seafood** from the long coastline and **country cooking** from the interior, based on locally grown produce – tomatoes, fennel and mushrooms. The most distinctive dish, often served at summer *festas*, is a sweet-and-sour mix of olives stuffed with meat and fried, then served with *crema fritta*, little squares of fried cream. Rabbit and lamb are popular, as is *papardelle alla papara*, wide, flat pasta with duck sauce and, as in many other regions, truffles are considered a delicacy. The grand dish of **porchetta**, whole roast suckling pig, is ubiquitous in the Marche, both in its original large-scale form and in a fast-food version used to fill crisp bread rolls. Baked, stuffed dishes such as *vincisgrassi*, a rich layered dish of pasta, minced meat, mushrooms, giblets and brain, bechamel and truffles, are found everywhere. A typical seafood dish from Ancona is *zuppa di pesce*, a fish soup flavoured with saffron, though you'll find excellent fish broths – known simply as *brodetto* – all along the coast. Puddings include *cicerchiata*, balls of pasta fried and covered in honey, and *frappé*, fried leaves of filo-like pastry dusted with icing sugar.

Although it produces many very drinkable **wines**, the Marche region is best known for just one, **Verdicchio**, a greeny-gold white, excellent with fish, which is instantly recognizable due to its amphora-shaped bottle. This is in fact a hangover from a 1950s marketing ploy inspired by the ancient Greek custom of shipping wine from Ancona in clay amphorae, and, reputedly, by the shape of the actress Gina Lollobrigida. Today, however, many producers are selling their best Verdicchio in standard-shaped bottles – the one to look out for is Verdicchio dei Castelli di Jesi (see p.682). The less well known local **reds** include one of Italy's finest, Rosso Conero, a light wine based on the Montepulciano grape and full of fruit; more common is Rosso Piceno, based on the Sangiovese grape. A Marche aperitif now back in fashion is **mistrà**, an aniseed liqueur generally drunk with coffee.

Of Marche's old-fashioned and slightly forgotten seaside resorts, **Pésaro** is the largest, with a Renaissance centre maintaining its dignity behind the package-tour seafront; for more interesting sunning and swimming it's better to head south of Ancona to the **Cónero Riviera**, a spectacular stretch of coast, with small beaches nestling beneath the dramatic cliffs of Monte Cónero. **San Benedetto del Tronto** has six kilometres of beach, five thousand palm trees, and numerous discos, but is not exactly a happening place compared with say

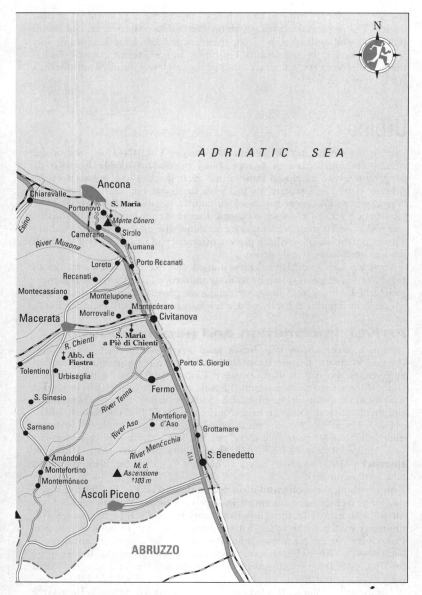

Rimini (see p.455). Really, though, the most appealing – and best known – of Marche's sights are the small hilltop town of **Urbino**, with its spectacular Renaissance palace, and the fortress of **San Leo**, just across the border from San Marino. Further south, **Macerata** is a sleepy university town surrounded by lovely countryside, and, right on the regional border, the fascinating city of **Áscoli Piceno** is a worthy stop-off on the way into Abruzzo (see p.815).

Getting around on public transport is not too much of a problem, though you'll obviously save time in the remotest parts of the region with your own vehicle. The provincial capitals – Urbino, Pésaro, Macerata, Ancona and Áscoli Piceno – are all well served by public transport; and Ancona is also a major port for ferries to Greece and Croatia. For hiking in the Sibillini, **Amandola** has the best bus service; if you don't mind relying on fewer buses, **Montefortino** is a prettier base.

Urbino

During the second half of the fifteenth century, **URBINO** was one of the most prestigious courts in Europe, ruled by the remarkable Federico da Montefeltro, who employed some of the greatest artists and architects of the time to build and decorate his palace in the town. Baldassarre Castiglione, whose sixteenth-century handbook of courtly behaviour, *Il Cortegiane* (The Courtier), is set in the palace, reckoned it to be the most beautiful in all Italy, and it does seem from contemporary accounts that fifteenth-century Urbino was an extraordinarily civilized place, a measured and urbane society in which life was lived without indulgence.

Nowadays Urbino is Marche's most immediately likeable town, saved from an existence as a museum-piece by its lively university. There's a refreshing, energetic feel to the place, plenty of conducive places to eat and drink, and, although its nightlife is hardly wild, a few bars host local bands and the like.

Arrival, information and accommodation

Urbino is served by regular **buses** from Pésaro, where they depart from Piazzale Matteotti and the **train station**, with the last one going at around 8pm. Buses also run regularly between Fano and Urbino. All buses stop in Borgo Mercatale, a terminus-cum-car park at the foot of the Palazzo Ducale which can be reached by spiral staircase, a lift or a series of steep narrow streets and flights of steps. Once up in the old centre, you'll find the **tourist office** at Piazza Duca Federico 35, directly opposite the Palazzo Ducale (mid-May to mid-Sept Mon–Sat 9am–1pm & 3–7pm, Sun 9am–1pm; rest of year Mon–Sat 9am–1pm & 3–6pm; ☎0722.2613, ⓦwww.comune.urbino.ps.it). There's an **Internet point**, *Europ@net*, at Via G. Mazzini 72 (Mon–Sat 10am–midnight, Sun 4pm–midnight).

An economical **accommodation** option that becomes cost-effective if you stay for a week or more is a **room in a private house**. You can get hold of a list at the tourist office, though during term time you will be competing with the many students who lodge with families, so be sure to book in advance. Prices vary but expect to pay about the same as for a two-star **hotel** (price band ❷–❸). Otherwise, the cheapest hotel is the *Fosca*, Via Raffaello 67 (☎0722.2542; ❶), a small studenty *pensione* on the top floor of a residential palazzo in the old town – if the owner isn't there, call ☎0722.329.622 and someone will be along. Another good option is *San Giovanni*, Via Barocci 13 (☎0722.2827; closed July; ❷), in the old town. This sixteenth-century Patrician house known as Palazzo della Spillara is a lovely old-style hotel with very courteous service and its own restaurant serving typical Marche dishes. *Hotel Raffaello*, Via Santa Margherita 38/40 (☎0722.4896, ⓦwww.poliedrosnc.com /hotelraffaellourbino; ❺), behind the Casa di Raffaello in the old town, has wide views over the pan-tiled roofs of Urbino. This former seminary provides three-wheelers to pick up guests and luggage from the lower town.

URBINO

N

RESTAURANTS
Angolo Divino   F
Balestra   H
Franco   C
Girarrosto   B
Mensa   G
Piccolo Bar   D
Raffaello   A
Punto Macrobiotico   E
Tre Piante   J
Vecchia Urbino   I

ACCOMMODATION
Boncorte   6
Fosca   2
Italia   4
Hotel Raffaello   1
San Domenico   5
San Giovanni   3

Porta S. Lucia

VIALE A. GRAMSCI

VIALE DON G.

VIALE COMANDINO

VIA N. PELLIPARIO

VIA GIRO DEI DEBITORI

PIAZZALE ROMA

VIA DEL POPOLO

VIALE B. BUOZZI

Giardini Pubblici

Forteza Albornoz

VIALE FRATELLI ROSSELLI

VIA DELLE VIGNE

Porta Valbona

Bus Station

Lift

P

VIA NAZIONALE 73 BIS

VIA NAZIONALE 73 BIS

University

VIA PIAVE F. SALVAI AI

VIA SAFFI

VIA MATTEOTTI

PIAZZA RINASCIMENTO

VIA S. GEROLAMO

VIA S. MARIA

VIA S. CHIARA

Palazzo Ducale

PIAZZA DUCA FEDERICO

S. Domenico

PIAZZA GHERARDI

V. D. POGGIO

VIA S. DOMENICO

CORSO GARIBALDI

Duomo

VIA G. MAZZINI

VIA BAROCCI

P. S. MARGHERITA

VIA S. MARGHERITA

VIA DEI MACELLI

Oratorio di S. Giovanni

Casa di Raffaello

VIA RAFFAELLO

V. T. VITI

PIAZZA S. FRANCESCO

S. Francesco

PIAZZA DELLA REPUBBLICA

VIA POSTA VECCHIA

V. S. MARGHERITA

VIA BRAMANTE

PIAN DI S. LUCA

VIA S. ANDREA

VIA C. BATTISTI

VIA VETERANI

VIA F. PUCCINOTTI

VIA VALERIO

VIA BUDASSI

VIA PESARESE

VIA S. BARTOLI

VIA FORO POSTERLA

VIA FORO DEL FRANCALE

VIA NUOVA

VIA VEXNN

POZZO NUOVO

PIAZZA SAN FILIPPO

VIA S. FILIPPO

VIA S. VENTO

VIA LAVAGINE

VIA LAVASARI

VIA DELLE MURA

VIA DEI MORTI

VIALE DI VITTORIO

VIALE DI VITTORIO

VIA DELLE MURA

VIA NAZIONALE 73 BIS

VIA DELLA STAZIONE

ROND O MERCATALE

i

0   50 m

▼ La Pineta Campsite & S. Bernardino

10

MARCHE | Urbino

667

Alternatively try *Italia*, Corso Garibaldi 32 (℡0722.2701; ❻), all pale marble and crisp decoration since renovation; or old-fashioned *Boncorte*, Via delle Mura 28 (℡0722.2463, ⓦwww.viphotels.it; ❻), just inside the city walls with views over the countryside. Breakfast is served in the tiny courtyard garden in summer. Its sister hotel *San Domenico*, in a former religious complex just opposite the Palazzo Ducale at Piazza Rinascimento 3 (℡0722.2626; ⓦwww.viphotels.it; ❽), recently reopened and has large rooms, big beds and polished wood floors.

For a much cheaper and more low-key option with good food and an open-air swimming pool, *Balcone sul Metauro* at Peglio near Urbania (℡0722.310.104, ⓔbalconesulmetauro@tin.it; ❷), a thirty-minute drive southwest from Urbino, is a sound choice. There's a **campsite**, the *Pineta* (℡0722.4710, ⓕ0722.4734; April to mid-Sept), 2km south of Urbino beyond San Bernardino (see p.671); bus #4 or #7 drops you close by.

The Palazzo Ducale

The **Palazzo Ducale** (Mon 8.30am–2pm, Tues–Sun 8.30am–7.15pm; €4, 18–25 year olds €2; free to under-18s and over-65s; entrance fee includes Galleria Nazionale – see below), whose *Facciata dei Torricini* overlooks the surrounding countryside, is a fitting monument to Federico. An elegant combination of the aesthetic and the practical, the facade comprises a triple-decked loggia in the form of a triumphal arch flanked by twin defensive towers. In contrast, the Palazzo's bare south side, forming one side of the long central Piazza Rinascimento, looks rather bleak, and it's only once you get inside that you begin to understand its reputation as one of the finest buildings of the Renaissance. Whereas a tour of most palaces of this size tends to reduce the visitor to a state of crabby exhaustion, the spacious rooms of the Palazzo Ducale instil a sense of calm. Although the Palazzo now houses the **Galleria Nazionale delle Marche**, only the few remaining original Urbino works justify much attention, and until you hit these it's the building itself that makes the biggest impression.

Just inside the entrance, the **Cortile d'Onore** is your first real taste of what Urbino is about. The courtyard is not immediately striking – in fact if you've spent any amount of time in Italy, you'll have seen a host of similar ones already – but this is a prototype of the genre. Designed by Dalmatian-born Luciano Laurana, who was selected by Federico after he'd failed to find a suitably bold artist in Florence, it's at once elegant and restrained. Although each element, from the furling Corinthian capitals to the inscription proclaiming Federico's virtues, is exquisitely crafted, it's the way they work together that is Laurana's real achievement. Pilasters on the first floor echo columns on the ground floor, pale stone alternates with dark, and the whole is enhanced by the subtle interplay of light and shadow.

Off the cortile is the room that housed Federico's **library**, which in its day was more comprehensive than Oxford University's Bodleian Library. He spent fourteen years and over thirty thousand ducats gathering books from all over Europe, and employed forty scribes to make illuminated copies on kidskin, which were then covered in crimson and decorated with silver. They disappeared into the vaults of the Vatican after Urbino fell to the papacy in 1631, and all that's left of the room's former grandeur is one of the more outrageous representations of Federico's power – the Eagle of the Montefeltros surrounded by tongues of fire, symbolizing the artistic and spiritual gifts bestowed by Federico.

A monumental staircase, one of the first ever built in Italy, takes you up to the first floor. Wandering through the white, airy rooms, you'll see wooden doors inlaid with everything from gyroscopes and mandolins to armour, representing the various facets of Federico's personality. On carved marble fireplaces, sphinxes are juxtaposed with angels and palm trees with dolphins, while ceilings are stuccoed with such symbols of Montefeltro power as ermines, eagles and exploding grenades.

A famous portrait of Federico da Montefeltro by the Spanish artist **Pedro Berruguete** is worth seeking out (it's been moved about in recent years). Painted, as he always was, in profile (having lost his right eye in battle), Federico is shown as warrior, ruler, scholar and dynast; wearing an ermine-fringed gown over his armour, he sits reading a book, with his pale and delicate son, Guidobaldo, standing at his feet.

The most elaborately decorated part of the palazzo is the suite of rooms known as the **Appartamento del Duca**, behind the Facciata dei Torricini. Displayed here are **Piero della Francesca**'s two great works: the *Madonna of Senigallia*, a subtly coloured, haunting depiction of foreboding in which Mary flanked by two angels offers up her child; and the more perplexing *Flagellation*, where at the back of a cubic room Christ is being almost casually beaten, while in the foreground, in the courtyard, stand three figures: a beautiful youth and two older men. Perhaps the most persuasive intepretation of this much debated painting is that which holds that the foreground figure on the left is Ottaviano Ubaldini (Federico Montefeltro's senior counsellor), while the one on the right is Ludovico Gonzaga (grandfather of Federico's son-in-law), both of whom had been bereaved at the time the picture was commissioned; by this account the beautiful boy between them is the idealized projection of the boys they were mourning, and the picture as a whole is a meditation on the consolations of Christian faith. Also here is Raphael's compelling portrait of a gentlewoman, *La Muta*.

Still in the Appartamento del Duca, no painting better embodies the notion of perfection held by Urbino's elite than *The Ideal City*, long attributed to Piero but now thought to be by one of his followers. Probably intended as a design for a stage set, this famous display of perspective skill depicts a perfectly symmetrical and utterly deserted cityscape, expressing the desire for a civic order which mirrors that of the heavens.

Paolo Uccello 's last work, the six-panelled *Profanation of the Host*, tells the story of a woman who sold a consecrated host to a Jewish merchant. She was hanged, and the merchant and his family were burned at the stake – the angels and devils are arguing over the custody of the woman's soul. The morbid theme and fairy-tale atmosphere that pervade the work may reflect the artist's depression at getting old: shortly after completing it, he filled in his tax return with the statement, "I am old, infirm and unemployed, and my wife is ill."

It's in the three most intimate rooms of the Duke's apartment you come to next that you get most insight into Federico's personality. A spiral staircase descends to two adjoining chapels, one dedicated to Apollo and the Muses, the other to the Christian God. This dualism typifies a strand of Renaissance thought in which mythology and Christianity were reconciled by positing a universe in which pagan deities were seen as aspects of the omnipotent Christian deity.

Back on the main floor you come to the most interesting and best preserved of the palace's rooms, Federico's **Studiolo**, a triumph of illusory perspective created not with paint but with intarsia (inlaid wood). Shelves laden with geometrical instruments appear to protrude from the walls, cupboard doors seem

Federico da Montefeltro

Federico was a formidable soldier, a shrewd and humane ruler, and a genuine intellectual, qualities which were due in part to his education at the Mantua school of the most prestigious Renaissance teacher, Vittorino da Feltre. Poor scholars and young nobles were educated together in Vittorino's classes and were taught self-discipline and frugal living as well as the more usual Latin, maths, literature and the courtly skills of riding, dancing and swordsmanship.

As the elder but illegitimate son of the Montefeltro family, Federico only became ruler of Urbino after his tyrannical half-brother Oddantonio fell victim to an assassin during a popular rebellion. Federico promptly arrived on the scene – fuelling rumours that he'd engineered the uprising himself – and was elected to office after promising not to punish those responsible for Oddantonio's death, to cut taxes, to provide an educational and medical service, and to allow the people some say in the election of magistrates.

Urbino was a small state with few natural resources and a long way from any major trading routes, so selling the military services of his army and himself was Federico's only way of keeping Urbino solvent. In high demand because of his exceptional loyalty to his employers, Federico's mercenary activities yielded an annual income equivalent to £7,000,000/US$11,200,000, a substantial portion of which was used to keep taxes low, thus reducing the likelihood of social discontent during his long absences. When he was at home, he seems to have been a remarkably accessible ruler: he would leave his door open at mealtimes so that any member of his 500-strong court might speak to him between courses, and used to move around his state unarmed (unusual in a time when assassination was common), checking up on the welfare of his people.

Between his military and political commitments, Federico found time to devote to the arts – he delighted in music, but his first love was architecture, which he considered to be the highest form of intellectual and aesthetic activity. He was a friend of the leading architectural theorist, Alberti, and according to his biographer, Vespasiano di Bisticci, Federico's knowledge of the art was unequalled: "Though he had his architects about him, he always first realized the design and then explained the proportions and all else; indeed, to hear him discourse . . . it would seem that his chief talent lay in this art, so well he knew how to expound and carry out its principles." The Dalmatian architect Luciano Laurana was scarcely known until taken up by Federico, while his later commissions included works from the more established Francesco di Giorgio Martini and one of the greatest of all painters and theorists of architecture, Piero della Francesca.

to swing open to reveal lines of books, a letter lies in an apparently half-open drawer. Even more remarkable are the delicately-hued landscapes of Urbino as if viewed from one of the surrounding hills, and the lifelike squirrel perching next to an equally realistic bowl of fruit. The upper half of the room is covered with 28 portraits of great men ranging from Homer and Petrarch to Solomon and St Ambrose – another example of Federico's eclecticism.

The rest of the town – and San Bernardino

Urbino is a lively place, and its bustling streets – a pleasant jumble of Renaissance and medieval houses – can be a refreshing antidote to the rarefied atmosphere of the Palazzo Ducale. Next door to the palace, the town's **Duomo** is a pompous Neoclassical replacement for Francesco di Giorgio Martini's Renaissance church, destroyed in an earthquake in 1789. There's a **museum** inside (daily 9am–noon & 2.30–6pm; €2), but the only reason for going in would be to see Barocci's *Last Supper*, with Christ surrounded by the chaos of washers-up, dogs and angels. Afterwards, trek up to the gardens within the **Fortezza Albornoz** (9am–6pm; free), from where you'll get great views of the town and the countryside. Close by is the **Oratorio di San Giovanni** (Mon–Sat 10am–12.30pm & 3–5.30pm, Sun 10am–12.30pm & 3.30–6pm; €2), behind whose unfortunate modern facade is a stunning cycle of early fourteenth-century frescoes, depicting the *Life of St John the Baptist* and the *Crucifixion*. Vividly coloured and full of expressive detail, so different from the cool economy of later Renaissance artists, the frescoes are at their liveliest in such incidental details as the boozy picnic in the background of the *Baptism of the Multitude*, or the child trying to escape from its mother in the *Crucifixion*. On Via Raffaello, the **Casa Natale di Raffaello**, birthplace (in 1483) of Urbino's most famous son, the painter Raphael (Mon–Sat 9am–1pm & 3–7pm, Sun 10am–1pm; €3), proudly displays the "stone" where Raphael and his father Giovanni Santi mixed their pigments and sizes. There's one work by Raphael, an early *Madonna and Child*; the other walls are covered with reproductions and minor works by his contemporaries and Santi.

There's another fine Renaissance church just outside Urbino, that of **San Bernardino**, built atop a hill 2km south of town. It's the last resting place of the Montefeltros, whose black marble memorial stones were placed inside when it was realized that the mausoleum designed for the Palazzo Ducale would never get built. It was long thought to have been the work of Bramante, but is now attributed to Francesco di Giorgio Martini.

Eating, drinking and nightlife

There are plenty of reasonable places to **eat** in Urbino. The cheapest deal is the university *mensa* on Piazza San Filippo, which is open to student ID card-holders only. For those on a budget, there are any number of fast-food and self-service outlets: try the *Piccolo-Bar* at Via V. Veneto 32; *Raffaello*, Via Raffaello 41 (closed Sun), for sit-down or takeaway *piadine* and *crescia sfogliata* (a bit like a pizza folded in half); or *Franco* at Via del Poggio 1 (closed Sun), which is both a self-service place and a restaurant. *Le Tre Piante*, Via Foro Posterula 1 (closed Mon), just off Via Budassi, is a restaurant worth seeking out for its small terrace overlooking the hills, and such pasta dishes as *strozzapreti* – "strangled priests", with sausage, cream, mushrooms and peppers – or tagliatelle with lemon and prawns. The tempting smells of grilled meats and truffles coming from Piazza San Francesco make *Girarrosto* (closed Mon) much easier to find; there are plenty of pasta dishes, *funghi* and a few veggie options too. *La Balestra*, Via Valerio 16 (closed Tues), has tables inside and out and serves typical food from Montefeltro (as this part of the Marche is sometimes called) and pizzas in the evening until 3am, while the more upscale *Vecchia Urbino*, Via Vasari 3/5 (closed Tues; booking advisable on ☎0722.4447), and *Osteria l'Angolo Divino*, Via San Andrea 14 (closed Mon), are highly regarded for delicacies from Le Marche. For bargain **vegetarian** dishes head for *Un Punto Macrobiotico*, Via Nuova 6 (closed Sun).

As for drinking and **nightlife**, the curiously named *Bosom Pub*, Via Budassi 24, has a good range of bottled beers, including Belgian classics, as well as decent sandwiches; there's also the *El Pequèro* a kind of pub-restaurant at Via San Domenico 1, and *Gula* at Corso Garibaldi 23, where you can get cheap pizzas and good beer. If you're in search of live music, local bands tend to play at *Underground*, Via Barocci 12.

North of Urbino: Sassocorvaro and San Leo

The villages of northern Marche, though pleasant enough, cannot compete with the crumbling hill settlements further south, and the rarity of buses makes exploration by public transport something of an ordeal. There are a couple of places, however, that justify the effort.

Perched above a twee artificial lake some 30km northwest of Urbino by road, **SASSOCORVARO** is dominated by one of Francesco di Giorgio Martini's most ambitious fortresses (April–Sept daily 9.30am–12.30pm & 3–7pm; Oct–March Sat & Sun 9.30am–12.30pm & 2.30–6pm; €4). Like San Leo (see below) it was built to withstand the onslaught of the cannon, but as the site lacked San Leo's natural advantages, Francesco was forced to seek a strictly architectural solution. As far as possible, he did away with straight walls and built a grim and cunning fortress bulging with hourglass towers. Inside, it's something of a surprise to find an elegant Renaissance courtyard and an intimate and frescoed theatre – the fortress was built on the orders of Federico da Montefeltro for one of his condottieri, Ottaviano degli Ubaldini. It's a tribute to the strength of Francesco's architecture that the fortress was selected as a safe house for some of Italy's greatest works of art during World War II, including Piero della Francesca's *Flagellation* and Giorgione's *La Tempesta*, reproductions of which are on show.

There's also a museum of **folk life** (same hours and included in the castle admission ticket), with displays of traditional weaving, winemaking equipment and a mock-up of an old kitchen.

San Leo

The menacing fortress of **SAN LEO** (Mon–Fri 9am–6.30pm, Sat & Sun 9am–7pm; closes at least 1hr earlier in winter; €7), clamped to the summit of a dizzying precipice in the northern tip of the Marche, has staggered generations of visitors with its intimidating beauty. Machiavelli praised it, Dante modelled the terrain of his Purgatory on it, and Pietro Bembo considered it Italy's "most beautiful implement of war". In fact it's not as impregnable as it seems: it fell to a succession of powers, most recently to the Fascists in World War II, who used it as an aircraft-sighting post. One of the few invaders to have been repelled was Cesare Borgia, despite his having first persuaded a weak-willed retainer to give him the key.

There's been a fortress at San Leo since the Romans founded a city on the rock. Later colonizers added to it as necessary until the fifteenth century, when Federico da Montefeltro realized that it was no match for the new gunpowder-charged weapons, and set his military architect, Francesco di Giorgio Martini, the task of creating a new one. The walls were built on a slight inward slope and backed with earth, thus reducing the impact of cannonballs and providing a rampart. Three large squares were incorporated for the manoeuvring of heavy cannons, and every point was defended with firing posts. San Leo's greatest advantage, however, remained its position, which allows unwelcome visitors to be spotted from a great distance.

From the eighteenth century San Leo was used as a prison for enemies of the Vatican, of whom the most notorious was the womanizing Count of Cagliostro, a self-proclaimed alchemist, miracle doctor and necromancer. At first the charismatic heretic was incarcerated in a regular prison, but on the insistence of his guards, who were terrified of his diabolic powers, he was moved to the so-called Pozzetto di Cagliostro (Cagliostro's Well), now the fortress's most memorable sight. The only entrance was through a trap door in the ceiling, so that food could be lowered to him without the warden running the risk of engaging Cagliostro's evil eye. There was one window, triple-barred and placed so that the prisoner couldn't avoid seeing San Leo's twin churches. Not that this had any effect – Cagliostro died of an apoplectic attack, unrepentant after four years of being virtually buried alive.

As well as the fortress, there's the pleasant old village to explore. St Leo arrived in the third century and converted the local population to Christianity, and the two village churches, though they failed to impress Cagliostro, are worth a visit. The **Pieve** was built in the ninth century, with material salvaged from a Roman temple to Jupiter, by Byzantine-influenced architects from Ravenna. The capitals, dimly lit by the tiny windows, are carved with stylized foliage; also notable is the raised sanctuary, designed to impress upon the common worshippers the elevated position of their social superiors. Sunk into the ground behind the church is a sixth-century chapel founded by and later dedicated to St Leo, whose body lay here until 1014 when Henry II, emperor of Germany, calling in at the town on his way home from defeating the Greeks and Saracens in Rome, decided to remove it to Germany. His plans were thwarted by the horses bearing the saint's body – after a short distance they refused to go any further, so St Leo's body was left in the small village of Voghenza near Ferrara.

The heavy lid of the sarcophagus remains in the twelfth-century **Duomo**, dedicated to the saint. Like the Pieve it's built of local sandstone and incorporates fragments from the Jupiter temple, on whose site it was raised. The best of these are the Corinthian capitals sitting on the stubby Roman columns in the raised sanctuary. Above them, vaults are supported on the heads of crouching caryatids – which are more aesthetically pleasing than structurally efficient, for the church walls and arches have been distorted by bearing the brunt of the weight – so much so that the raised sanctuary was closed for restoration at the time of writing. The lid of St Leo's sarcophagus is in the crypt (not always open), which is far older than the church and was perhaps once used for pagan worship, as evidenced by the primitive carvings on the wall behind the altar.

Getting to San Leo on public transport is a pain: you need to travel up the coast to Rimini (see p.455), then catch the one daily bus to the village from the train station. Once here, you'll find a **tourist office** at Piazza Dante 14 (daily: mid-July to 31 Aug 9am–9pm; autumn & winter 9am–6.30pm; rest of year 9am–7.30pm; ☎0541.916.306). There are only two **hotels** in San Leo: the rambling *La Rocca*, Via G. Leopardi 16 (☎0541.916.241; ✆rist.larocca@libero.it; ❸), which has a rustic **restaurant** beneath its seven rooms; and the spick-and-span *Castello*, Piazza Dante Alighieri 11/12 (☎0541.916.214; ❹), a family-run hotel, bar and restaurant on the main square. Camper vans are allowed to make overnight stops in the car park below the main square.

Pésaro and around

Most of the tourists who come to **PÉSARO** visit for a beach holiday, attracted by the string of affordable three-star hotels and the easy, low-key family fun on offer. Germans and Brits are attracted by the cheap package holidays to

Port (100 m)

ADRIATIC
SEA

ACCOMMODATION
Atlantic   1
Hotel des Bains 5
Caravelle   4
Clipper   3
Napoleon   2

N

VIALE GORIZIA
VIALE TRENTO
VIA M. PATERINI
VIALE C. BATTISTI
VIALE DELLA VITTORIA
VIALE POLA
VIALE ROVERETO
VIALE TRIESTE
VIALE CECCHI
VIALE MONTEFALCONE
VIALE FIUME
VIALE DA VINCI
VIALE MARCONI
VIALE DANTE
VIALE ZARA
VIALE TRIESTE
PIAZZALE DELLA LIBERTA
VIA DELLA ROBBIA
VIALE DEI PARTIGIANI
VIALE DELLA VITTORIA
VIALE C. BATTISTI
VIALE LANFRANCO
VIALE D. REPUBBLICA
VIALE VACCAJ
VIA MAMELI
VIALE RISORGIMENTO
VIALE DELLA LIBERAZIONE
VIA MAZZINI
CORSO XI SETTEMBRE
VIA G. BOVIO
VIA CASTELFIDARDO
VIA MAZZOLARI
VIA MAZZA
VIA BRANCA
VIA ROSSINI
VIA DON MINZONI
VIALE R. SANZIO
VIALE TRENTO
VIA BUONARROTI
VIALE MASCAGNI
VIALE VERDI

LARGO ALDO MORO

Sant'
Agostino

A

Museo
Civico

Casa
Rossini

B

Rocca
Constanza

Museo
Oliveriano

Palazzo
Ducale

PIAZZA DEL POPOLO

Madonna
delle Grazie

S. FRANCESCO

PIAZZA D. MONTE

VIA G. BRUNO

C

VIA DIA

VIA BAVIERA

Bus
Station

PIAZZALE MATTEOTTI

VIA BUOZZI

VIA MANZONI

Teatro
Rossini

PIAZZA LAZZARINI

D

VIA G. ABBATI

E

VIA CATTANEO

F

PIAZZALE GARIBALDI

VIA XI FEBBRAIO

Train Station

VIALE XXIV MAGGIO

0   200 m

RESTAURANTS
Antica Osterie La Guercia   B
C'era una Volta   E
Esedra   F
Harnold's   D
Pasqualon   C
Sante   A

Fano

i

Pésaro but it's a popular place with Italians too, going through the daily ritual of beach, lunch, beach, passeggiata and ice-cream before dinner back at the hotel. The town is a bit of a backwater but pleasant enough nonetheless: with its long stretch of sandy beach and old centre with small craft and design shops to wander around. A lot of Pésaro dates from the 1920s and 1930s so it has rather had its day. Nevertheless, if you do find yourself strolling along the prom with an ice cream in hand among all the grannies, you couldn't exactly call that unpleasant, and with regular transport connections to lesser-known towns like Gradara and Fano it makes a feasible base from which to explore the northern Marche.

The Town

The centre of town is the coolly dignified **Piazza del Popolo**, in which the rituals of the pavement café scene are played out against the sharp lines of sundry Fascist-period buildings and the Renaissance restraint of the **Palazzo Ducale**.

The most significant relic of Renaissance Pésaro, however, is Giovanni Bellini's magnificent *Coronation of the Virgin* polyptych, housed in the art gallery of the **Museo Civico** (July & Aug Wed, Fri–Sun 9.30am–12.30pm & 5–8pm, Tues & Thurs 9.30am–12.30pm & 5–11pm; Sept–June Tues & Wed 9.30am–12.30pm, Thurs–Sun 9.30am–12.30pm & 4–7pm; €2.58, or €4.13 including Casa di Rossini). Painted in the 1470s for a church now known as Madonna delle Grazie (in Via San Francesco), the altarpiece situates the coronation not in some starry heaven but in the countryside around Pésaro, dominated by the castle of Gradara. Portraits of saints flank the central scene, ranging from the hesitant St Lawrence to the dreamy St Anthony, and below are a *Nativity* and scenes from the saints' lives. Although none of the gallery's other paintings can compare with the Bellini, don't miss Marco Zoppo's *pietà*, in which the dead Christ's muscled sensuousness prompts speculation on the artist's necrophiliac tendencies. Renaissance Pésaro was famous for its ceramics, and the museum houses a fine collection – ranging from a *Madonna and Child* surrounded by pine cones, lemons and bilberries from the workshop of Andrea della Robbia, to plates decorated with an Arabian bandit. The most striking piece, however, stands above the entrance to the museum – a ferocious snake-haired *Medusa* by the local artist Ferruccio Mengaroni.

A block beyond the museum, the old and narrow Via Castelfidardo leads down to Pésaro's most attractive street, the porticoed Corso XI Settembre. If you want to do more than just browse in its shops, take a look inside the church of **Sant'Agostino** – the choir stalls are inlaid with landscapes, Renaissance cityscapes, and, displaying a wit to rival the *studiolo* in the Palazzo Ducale in Urbino, half-open cupboards and protruding stacks of books.

On Via Mazza, the continuation of Via Castelfidardo, is Pésaro's archeological museum in the Palazzo Almerici, the **Museo Oliveriano** (July & Aug Mon–Sat 4–7pm; rest of year Mon–Sat 9am–noon; free; you may need to apply at the adjacent library if there is no one there), with a small but unusual collection of local finds. Among the relics from the Iron Age necropolis at nearby Novilara are a child's tomb filled with miniature domestic utensils and a tomb slab carved with pear-shaped figures rowing a square-sailed boat into battle. Even more intriguing is the collection of ex-votives – breasts, feet, heads and even a dog – collected not from an early Catholic church but from a Roman sacred grove at San Veneranda (3km from Pésaro), consecrated in the second century BC. Pride of place, however, goes to a bronze statue of a Grecian youth, exquisite even though it's a facsimile of a Roman copy of a fifth-century-BC Greek original.

In the other direction, the tree-lined grid of stucco hotels and gleaming apartments marks Pésaro's long sandy beachfront, punctuated by a handful of Art Deco villas, including one on Piazzale della Libertà whose eaves are supported by white plaster lobsters. On the way, at Via Rossini 34, the **Casa di Rossini** (same hours as Museo Civico above; €2.58) houses a modest shrine of memorabilia to the composer, who was born here in 1792. The Teatro Rossini on Piazza Lazzarini hosts an opera festival in his honour every August.

Practicalities

Finding your way around Pésaro is no problem – Viale Risorgimento leads from the **train station** to the town's main axis, Via Branca–Via Rossini–Viale della Repubblica, which cuts straight through the historical town to the beach. Bisecting it at Piazza del Popolo are Corso XI Settembre, scene of the evening *passeggiata*, and Via San Francesco, which leads to the **bus station** on Piazzale Matteotti. The main **tourist office** (daily 9am–1pm & 3.30–6.30pm; closed Sun in winter; ☎0721.69.341, ⓦ www.comune.pesaro.ps.it) is on the seafront on Piazzale della Libertà, at the end of Viale della Repubblica.

Pick of the reasonably priced and convenient **hotels** along the seafront are *Caravelle*, Viale Trieste 269 (☎0721.370.450, ⓦ www.hotel-caravelle.net; ❺), a light, airy place with a swimming pool, bikes, a games room, and room prices that drop by almost a half in May and September; *Des Bains*, Viale Trieste 221 (☎0721.34.957; ❻), dating back to 1905 and, though modernized many times since then, still with something of the "belle époque" about it; *Napoleon*, Viale Fiume 118 (☎0721.31.160; ❻), is geared up for families with its mini-suites, play room and water slides. Other hotels line the avenues which run parallel to the sea: at the less expensive end of the scale, *Clipper*, Viale Marconi 53 (☎0721.30.915, ⓦ www.hotelclipper.it; ❹), is relaxed and friendly despite the old-fashioned furniture and offers an alfresco buffet breakfast on the terrace. On the edge of town on the road south to Fano, *Villa Serena* at Via S Nicola 6/3 (☎0721.55.211, ⓦ www.villa-serena.it; ❻) is an atmospheric family-owned hotel stuffed with antiques and heirlooms, with a handful of guest rooms and a swimming pool in the rambling garden. The nearest **campsites** to Pésaro are at Fano and at Fiorenzuola (see opposite and below).

There's no shortage of affordable places to **eat**. For food on your feet, try *Harnold's* on Piazza Lazzarini; among pizzerias, *C'era una volta*, at Via Cattaneo 26 (closed Mon), is good, cheap and popular – so long as you don't mind rustic decor and loud rock music. There's a fine ristorante/pizzeria called *Pasqualon* at Via G. Bruno 37 (closed Sun and first two weeks of June). Among the notable fish restaurants are *Trattoria Da Sante*, on Via G. Bovio (closed Mon), in the east of town and with rock-bottom prices; *Antica Osteria La Guercia* at Via Baviera 33, just off the Piazza del Popolo (closed Sun), which does amazing pasta and fish dishes like *mal tagliati* and *cece e vongole* and is very reasonably priced; and *Esedra*, on the small piazza of the same name just off Via C Cattaneo (closed Mon), which serves wonderful ravioli with fresh sole and tomatoes, mixed fish kebabs and spaghetti with squid ink.

North of Pésaro

The most pleasant route north from Pésaro is the Strada Panoramica, a minor road winding through the coastal hills to **Gabicce Mare**, a large resort with a fine beach and an expensive clifftop disco.

If you want beaches without crowds, catch a bus to **FIORENZUOLA** and **CASTEL DI MEZZO**, just a few kilometres along the Strada Panoramica from Pésaro – tiny fishing villages, with minuscule beaches reached only by steep, narrow tracks. Most people visit them to eat at the **fish restaurants**, so you should have the beaches to yourself. You can enjoy a fine *brodetto di pesce* at *Il Vento di Focara*, Via Fossa 1 (☎0721.208.522), in Fiorenzuola – though it's wise to reserve in advance. En route, in a beautiful setting some 7km north of Pésaro, you'll also pass the *Panorama* **campsite** (☎0721.208.145; May–Sept).

Gradara

Inland, to the north, is the castle of **GRADARA** (Mon 8.30am–2pm, Tues–Sun 8.30am–7.15pm; €4) – not a place to go in season if you want to avoid crowds, as it's one of the main package-tour excursions. A fairy-tale confection of mellow red-brick and swallow-tail turrets, it's said to be the scene of a thirteenth-century scandal involving Francesca da Rimini, who committed adultery with Paolo da Malatesta, her husband's brother. The lovers were killed for their transgression and later consigned to hell by Dante – he meets their spirits in Canto V of the *Inferno*, where they are caught in a ceaseless whirlwind.

Inside the castle is a room decked out as the scene of the crime, with a sumptuously refurbished four-poster bed, fake wall hangings and an open book – Francesca tells Dante in hell that it was while reading the story of Lancelot and Guinevere that she and Paolo first succumbed to their passion. Further reminders of the story are found in two nineteenth-century paintings: one showing the lovers (either dead or in a state of post-coital collapse) watched by the crippled husband; the other, less ambiguous, of the naked couple. Other rooms are furnished as a torture chamber, complete with spiked iron ball, handcuffs and lances, and as the guards' room, a strange mixture of tavern and armoury. After touring the castle, it's well worth taking a walk round the walls for the fine views over the surrounding hills. Incidentally, Francesca's unhappy spirit is said to wander the castle when the moon is full.

Fano

Fifteen minutes south of Pésaro by half-hourly bus lies **FANO**, no longer quite the haven it was when Robert Browning came here in 1848, seeking relief from the heat and crowds of Florence. Although its beaches remain splendid, they now attract thousands of package tourists every year. Between the sandy and sheltered Lido and the long, pebbly Sassonia are good stretches where you don't have to pay, and there are further beaches at Torrette and Marotta to the south, both easily reached by bus. Fano is a pleasant enough place if a little humdrum, and comfortably combines its role as resort with that of small fishing port and minor historical town.

If you're coming to Fano by bus, you could ask to be dropped off at the crenellated **Porta Maggiore** and the remnants of the medieval defensive walls, on the southwestern side of the town centre. Behind them is a Roman gate, the **Arco di Augusto**, impressive despite having been truncated in the fifteenth century when Federico da Montefeltro blasted away its upper storey. You can see what it used to look like in a relief on the facade of the adjacent church of San Michele.

The Roman precursor of Fano, named Fanum Fortunae after its Temple of Fortune, stood at the eastern end of the Via Flaminia, which cut across the Apennines to Rome. The town is still built around a Roman crossroads plan: Via Arco di Augusto and Corso Matteotti follow the routes of the cardus and decumanus, and their junction is marked with a copy of a Roman milestone stating its distance from the capital (195.4 Roman miles). There are few other relics of Roman Fano, although the fifteenth-century **fountain** in the main square, along Via Mazzini, is dedicated to Fortune.

Overlooking the fountain are the reconstructed thirteenth-century Palazzo della Ragione and the fifteenth-century **Corte Malatestiana**, dating from the time Fano was ruled by the Malatesta family. Its most notorious member was

Sigismondo, whose disagreements with the pope led to the siege of Fano (when the Arco di Augusto lost its top) and his excommunication. After the death of his first wife – whom he was suspected of having poisoned – Sigismondo remarried in Fano in 1449, holding a three-day banquet in the Corte Malatestiana. Rumours about Sigismondo's sinister interest in his wives' diet revived when, seven years later, his second wife also died unexpectedly, leaving him free to marry his long-time mistress, Isotta degli Atti (for more on the Malatestas, see p.677). The Corte is at its best nowadays on summer evenings, when its loggias, turrets and trefoil windows provide a backdrop for concerts. Inside there's a small **museum and art gallery** (Tues–Sun 9am–12.30pm & 4–7pm, and also 9–11pm mid-June to mid-Sept; €3), whose most striking exhibit is a mosaic of a winged figure riding a panther. Upstairs, the art gallery is worth visiting for an insight into the Victorian psyche, as it's here that you'll find Guercino's *The Guardian Angel*, a painting that entranced Browning during his stay here and inspired a poem of the same title. Expressing a wistful desire to take the place of the child depicted here learning how to pray, the gushingly sentimental poem became incredibly popular, and Italy was flooded with reproductions of the painting for holidaying Browning fans. The keenest disciples set up a club, membership of which was gained by travelling to Fano and sending the founder a postcard.

Less saccharine paintings are to be found in the Renaissance church of **Santa Maria Nuova** on Via de Pili, off the main square. The two works by Perugino, a *Madonna, Child and Saints* and an *Annunciation*, are both suffused with a calm luminosity.

Practicalities

The **train station**, where buses also stop, is ten minutes' walk from the seafront, at the end of Via Cavallotti. Fano's **tourist office**, at Via C. Battisti 10 (July & Aug daily 9am–1pm & 3.30–6.30pm; Sept–June Mon–Fri 9am–1pm & 3.30–6.30pm, Sat 9am–1pm; ☎0721.803.534), is well organized, with additional offices at Torrette (Via Boscomarina 10) and Marotta (Via Viale C. Colombo 31) during July and August.

The site Ⓦwww.turismofano.com is worth checking out for B&B, agri-tourism and "*agricampeggio*" (informal camping on farms). Two of the most reasonable **hotel** options are *Mare*, Viale Colombo 20 (☎0721.805.667; ❷), an easy-going family-run pension with a shady garden and verandah a few blocks back from the sea, offering good home cooking and an excellent full-board deal; and the more formal *Corallo*, at Via Leonardo da Vinci 3 (☎0721.804.200, Ⓦwww.hotelcorallo-fano.it; ❹), on the seafront. There are plenty of **campsites** on the coast between Pésaro and Fano, such as *Norina* (☎0721.55.792; winter ☎0721.391.352; April to mid-Oct) and *Marinella* (☎0721.55.795, Ⓦwww.campingmarinella.it; April–Sept), both easily reached by bus.

For **eating**, apart from numerous pizzerias and snack bars, there's *Da Pep*, Via Garibaldi 19 (closed Mon), in the old town serving home-made pasta and fish dishes at reasonable prices, with tables outside in the shady cobbled street. Alternatively try the cheap and earthy fish taverna, *Da Quinta*, in the fishing harbour at Viale Adriatico (closed Sun), which caters mostly for fishermen, and with prices that reflect this. Just around the corner from the port don't miss *Self Service "Al Pesce Azzurro"*, at Viale Adriatico 48 (May–Sept), run by a co-operative of fishermen's wives, and offering a great value three-course set meal of the freshest fish.

Senigállia

Further down the coast, **SENIGÁLLIA** is an unprepossessing family resort with a good beach and most of its tourist activity packed into a short season. The town centre focuses on the rickety **Foro Annonario**, a semi-circular Neoclassical marketplace, behind which stands the imposing thirteenth-century **Rocca Roveresca** (May–Sept Tues–Sat 9am–1pm & 5–10pm, Sun 9am–1pm; €2). The rocca, or castle, was built for Federico da Montefeltro's son-in-law by Luciano Laurana, architect of the Palazzo Ducale in Urbino. Below the elegant Renaissance halls lies an underground warren of vaulted storage rooms and dungeons. Upstairs, the fireplaces and beautiful spiral staircase show little sign of use. The cells, however, are a different matter: converted from cannon positions when the region fell to the pope, they have tiny airholes designed to inflict a slow and agonizing death on their occupants. Fine views are to be had from the towers, built in the fifteenth century when the Adriatic coast was plagued by Turkish bandits.

Ancona and around

Severely damaged by war and earthquakes, workaday **ANCONA** has a few historical monuments embedded in a tangle of commercial buildings. The modern centre is a grid of broad avenues and palm-shaded piazzas, while the station area, with its heavy trucks travelling noisily to and from the port, will probably make you want to take the next train out. However, as the Adriatic's largest port it's a convenient departure point, and you may well pass through in order to catch one of the regular ferries to Greece and Croatia. The city is even more of a gateway to the Marche region of late with Ryanair's direct flights from the UK to Falconara airport 10km away – so it's quite possible you may make an overnight stop.

Regular buses run along the seafront from the train station to the port, passing the pentagonal **Lazzaretto**, built within the harbour in the eighteenth century as a quarantine station for immigrants. The port itself is headed by a well-preserved Roman arch, the **Arco di Traiano**, raised in honour of Emperor Trajan, under whose rule Ancona first became a major port. Behind it is the **Arco Clementino**, a piece of architectural self-congratulation by Pope Clement XII, who made Ancona a free port in the eighteenth century and thus considered himself Trajan's equal.

On a steep hill overlooking the port rises the town's Romanesque Duomo. What survives of old Ancona is spread out below it, and a wander up the hill is the most pleasant way of filling in time here. At the foot of the hill is Piazza della Repubblica, from which Via della Loggia leads past the **Loggia dei Mercanti**, whose Gothic splendours can be seen in all their glory now that the layers of grime have been cleaned off – you can make out the figures of medieval dignitaries and horsemen below its elaborately carved windows. Walk along the narrow road into Piazza del Plebiscito and you come to the new **Museo della Città** (June–Sept Sat & Sun 7–11pm; rest of year Thurs–Sat 10am–1pm, plus 5–8pm Sat & Sun; €2.60), with models, paintings, sculptures and original documents showing key events in Ancona from 2000BC to 2000AD. Backtracking to Piazza della Repubblica, take a left into Corso Mazzini, where there's a long sixteenth-century **fountain** with thirteen spouting heads, all with great expressions, attributed to Pellegrino Tibaldi.

Equally appealing is the Romanesque church of **Santa Maria della Piazza**, its facade a fantasia of blind loggias and its portal carved with chunky figures and elegant birds. Behind the church, on Via Pizzecolli, is the town's **Pinacoteca Comunale** (Mon 9am–1pm, Tues–Fri 9am–7pm, Sat 8.30am–6.30pm, Sun 3–7pm; €4). The highlight here is Titian's *Apparition of the Virgin*, a sombre yet impassioned work, with the Virgin appearing to a rotund and fluffy-bearded bishop in a stormy sunset sky. There's also a glorious *Sacra Conversazione* by Lotto, a view of sixteenth-century Ancona by Andrea Lilli, and an exquisite yet chilling *Madonna and Child* by Carlo Crivelli, with a mean-looking Mary pinching the toe of a rather pained Christ, incongruously flanked by bunches of apples and a marrow.

Beyond the gallery is the church of **San Francesco delle Scale**, named for the steps leading up to it. Titian's *Apparition* was painted for this church, but today its most remarkable work is an almost orgasmic *Assumption* by Lotto. Further up the hill, the **Museo Archeologico** is not a bad place to spend an hour (Tues–Sun 8.30am–7.30pm; €4), its wacky moulded ceilings vaulting over a collection of finds ranging from red- and black-figure Greek craters to a stunning Celtic gold crown.

Passing the remains of the Roman amphitheatre, now capped with graffitied earthquake-shattered buildings, you climb up to the pink-and-white **Duomo** (or San Ciriaco). Though mostly built in a restrained Romanesque style, there's an outburst of Gothic exuberance in the doorway's cluster of slender columns, some plain, others twisted and carved. The simple and calm interior is built on a Greek-cross plan, enlivened by a cupola that from below resembles an elongated umbrella. The most memorable feature, however, is a screen along the edge of the raised right transept, one section of which is carved with eagles, fantastic birds and storks entwined in a tree, the other with saints.

Practicalities

Via Marconi and its continuation, Via XXIX Settembre, run straight along the coast up from the train station to the port and the centre of town. Via XXIX Settembre ends in the adjacent piazzas of Kennedy and Repubblica, from which the modern centre's three parallel avenues – Corso Stamira, Corso Garibaldi and Corso Mazzini – slice up to Piazza Cavour, while Via della Loggia runs up above the port to the alleyways of the old town. The main **tourist office** for Ancona and the Marche region is at Via Thaon de Revel 4 at the end of Viale della Vittoria (Mon–Sat 9am–1pm & 3–6pm; July open till 7.30pm; ☎071.358.991, ⓦ www.le-marche.com); there's also a seasonal office (mid-June to Aug Sun–Tues 3–7pm, Wed–Sat 10am–2pm & 3–7pm; ⓔ iat.ancona@regione.marche.it) at the Stazione Maríttima. The main **bus terminus** is Piazza Cavour, connected by regular bus with the **train station** on Piazza Rosselli. The **Stazione Maríttima**, where ferries dock, is connected with the train station by bus. A bus (more or less hourly; less frequent on Sun) connects the **airport** with the train station; buy tickets (€1.25) before boarding from the nearest bar/newspaper kiosk (timetable at ⓦ www.ancona-airport.com under "*Dove Siamo*").

If you want to **stay** the night in Ancona you'll find no shortage of cheap and cheerful places: the *Dorico*, Via Flaminia 8 (☎071.42.761; ❷), and *Gino*, Via Flaminia 4 (☎071.42.562; ❸), are both fine, with the *Gino* serving good-value food. The centrally located *Milano*, Via Montebello 1 (☎071.201.147; ❶), is distinctly no-frills; the most pleasant budget place to stay in Ancona is *Viale*, Viale della Vittoria 23 (☎071.201.861; ❹), whose tiny courtyard garden is decked out with geraniums (breakfast is included in the price) – it's on the long avenue that leads to the blindingly white war memorial (take buses #1, or #1/4 from the train station). Of the more upmarket options there's the new and slick *Fortuna*, Piazza Rosselli 15 (℡071.42.633; ❺); *Roma e Pace*, Via G. Leopardi 1 (℡071.202.007; ❺), which is conveniently near the port; or if you can't get by without a pool, cocktail bar and health club aim for *Grand Hotel Passetto*, Via Thaon de Revel 1 (℡071.31.307; ❽), at the far end of Viale della Vittoria.

Piazza Roma is the place to hang out – there are plenty of **cafés** with tables outside in the pedestrianized cobbled square, the busiest being *Caffè Lombardo* at the top of Corso Mazzini. If you're waiting for a bus on Piazza Cavour, *Caffè Cavour* is conveniently placed for good sandwiches and great pastries. Of Ancona's **restaurants**, the first choice is *Clarice*, on Via del Traffico (closed Sat eve and Sun), off Corso Garibaldi (on the right as you walk up from the sea), an old-style, family restaurant in a cobbled side street with tables outside. It serves traditional, very reasonably priced food, with many local dishes on the menu. Second choice is *Osteria del Pozzo*, on Via Bonda (closed Sun), a narrow lane off Piazza del Plebiscito, where diners tuck into seafood and pasta dishes, or *La Cantinetta* on Via Gramsci (closed Sun), just off Piazza del Plebiscito, a simple restaurant whose speciality is *Stoccafisso all'Anconetana*, a traditional recipe involving salt cod. For a good, inexpensive spread of roasted vegetables, pasta and seafood salads, cold meats and mozzarella head for the help-yourself lunchtime buffet at *Caffè Giuliani* on via Traffico with tables outside in a shady covered arcade (closed and Sun). For pizza, try *La Bussola* on Via Leopardi (closed Sun).

Onwards to Greece, Turkey and Croatia

Ferries leave from the Stazione Maríttima, a couple of kilometres (bus #1 or #1/4) north of the train station, close to the centre of town. The **tourist office** here (mid-June to mid-Sept daily 8am–8pm; ℡071.201.183) has timetables, and each of the main ferry lines has a ticket office (closed at lunchtime) – you can also buy tickets from the agencies all around the port. Among the main lines are Blue Star (℡071.202.034 or 071.207.1068, ⓦwww.strintzis.gr), which goes to Cephalonia, Ithaca, Igoumenitsa and Patras in Greece and Çeşme in southwest Turkey; and Minoan (℡071.201.708, ⓦwww.minoan.it) and Superfast (℡071.202.033, ⓦwww.superfast.com) which sail to Igoumenitsa and Patras. There's also Jadrolinija (℡071.204.305, ⓦwww.amatori.com) and Adriatica di Navigazione (℡071.204.915, ⓦwww.adriatica.it) which sail to Croatia and the Dalmatian islands.

Charges on ferry lines depend on the speed of the crossing, with one-way fares starting at around €44 per person to Croatia; if you are taking a car add another €57.50. For the nineteen-hour overnight journey to Patras in July and August, reckon on paying €96 for an aircraft-style seat for the crossing (cabins are available) with Superfast; add €105 for a car. For the mammoth crossing to Turkey (41hr 30min) with Blue Star, you can expect to pay €185 plus €20 tax one-way in high season: students with proof of status get a fifteen percent discount. Blue Star also allows access to your camper van during all crossings, providing free water and electricity, and offers some good five-adult/one-car deals. There are no discounts for holders of InterRail and Eurail passes, but outside high season prices drop by 25–30 percent, and there are 30 percent discounts on return journeys. Boarding tax of €3 is payable to the port agency at the time of embarkation. You should book in advance, and you should always aim to arrive at the Stazione Maríttima two to three hours before your ferry is due to depart.

Inland: the Esino Valley

Cutting right across the Marche, the **Esino Valley** is broad and bland in the east, but narrows to a dramatic limestone gorge – the Gola di Rossa – just before the town of **FABRIANO** and the border with Umbria. Famous for two things – paper-making and Gentile da Fabriano, the best of the International Gothic artists – Fabriano is now heavily industrialized and a dismal town at first sight. You're most likely to pass through on your way to Umbria and Rome. Although Fabriano and Jesi are built up, most of the valley is given over to agriculture and is best known for Verdicchio, a dry white wine produced in the hilltop villages around Jesi. What most visitors come for, however, are the vast Frasassi caves.

Jesi

Though its industrial development has led to **JESI** being known as "the little Milan of the Marche", the historic centre of the town is well preserved. Clinging to a long ridge, it's fringed by medieval walls and retains a scattering of Renaissance and Baroque palaces. One of the most majestic of these, the Palazzo Pianetti, is home of the **Pinacoteca Civica** (mid-June to mid-Sept Tues–Sun 10am–1pm & 5–11pm; rest of year Tues–Sat 10am–1pm & 4–7pm, Sun 10am–1pm & 5–8pm; €3.20). The highlight of its opulent interior is the magnificent 72-metre-long stuccoed, gilded and frescoed gallery – a Rococo fantasy of shells, flowers and festoons framing cloud-backed allegorical figures. The collection of paintings is best known for some late works by **Lorenzo Lotto**, who unlike his contemporaries Titian and Giorgione, chose to be an outsider from the Venetian artworld, opting instead for obscurity, working in such provincial Italian towns as Ancona and Recanati, Treviso and Bergamo. As a result he was long-neglected, though his use of colour and the expressive intensity of his portraits is exceptional, and he was unique in combining this meticulous realism with the southern European traditions of the High Renaissance.

In two graceful *Annunciation* panels (once part of a triptych), a hurried angel Gabriel delivers the news to a more than slightly taken aback Virgin; and in the *Visitation*, the setting is a simple domestic interior. Scenes from the refreshingly assertive life of St Lucy (a polyptych) show Lotto's freshness of colour; the *Madonna delle Rose* is interesting for its naturalistic setting – with a baby Jesus trying to jump into the arms of a grandfatherly St Joseph – as well as its allusions to Christian mysticism.

A stroll around town takes you past the Teatro Pergolesi, a vast eighteenth-century opera house in Piazza della Repubblica, named after local-born composer Giovanni Battista Pergolesi. Encircling the town are the massive ramparts, restructured in the fourteenth century and built on top of the foundations of Roman walls – an escalator takes you through the ramparts, several metres thick, from the lower town to the upper town (with steps back down again).

Verdicchio country

No wine is produced in Jesi itself – if you want to indulge in some wine sampling, head for **CUPRAMONTANA**, accessible by bus from Ancona and Jesi, where one of the best producers is Vallerosa Bonci, at Via Torre 17 (℡0731.789.129, Ⓦwww.assivip.it/aziende/bonci.htm). Otherwise try Colonarra, whose cellars, although disappointingly modern, have good wines, including a champagne-like sparkler called, naturally enough, Colonarra. The best time to visit is on the first Sunday in October, when there's a parade and dancing, and the village streets are lined with stalls of wine and food for the **grape festival**. Theoretically, this marks the eve of the harvest but, owing to hangovers, it's usually a couple of days before anyone feels fit enough to start work.

The Frasassi caves and San Vittore Terme

Further up the Esino Valley, just after the Gola di Rossa, a road leads up from Genga train station to the Frasassi gorge, carved by the River Sentino, which was also responsible for creating the eighteen kilometres of caves beneath it. The largest cave of the **Grotte di Frasassi** (daily March–July & Sept–Oct: tours at 9am, 11am, 12.30pm, 3pm, 4.30pm & 6pm; Aug entry every 10min from 8am–6.30pm; 10 July–25 Aug also open 9–10.30pm; Nov–Feb 11am & 3pm; closed 10–30 Jan; tours last 70min; €10.50; Ⓦ www.frasassi.com) was discovered only in 1971, and just over a kilometre of its caverns and tunnels is now open to the public.

Inevitably, the most remarkable stalactite and stalagmite formations have been named: there's a petrified Niagara Falls, a giant's head with a wonderfully Roman profile, a cave whose floor is covered with candles, complete with holders, and a set of organ pipes. The vast Cave of the Great Wind, at 240m high, is one of the biggest in Europe – large enough to contain Milan Cathedral – and has been used for a series of experiments, ranging from sensory deprivation (as a possible treatment for drug addicts) to a subterranean version of *Big Brother* when a group of people were shut away for a month.

The Cónero Riviera

Just south of Ancona the white cliffs of **Monte Cónero** plunge straight into the sea, forming the northern Adriatic's most spectacular and enjoyable stretch of coastline. It's easily accessible, with the major resorts of **Portonovo**, Sirolo and Numana all linked by bus from Ancona, either from the train station or Piazza Cavour. **Sirolo** and **Numana** are now almost as crowded in July and August as the rest of the Adriatic resorts, the main difference being that their cliff-backed beaches are more picturesque. The most stunning stretch of coast, a series of tiny coves at the base of Monte Cónero between Portonovo and Sirolo, is best explored by boat – they leave from both bays. You can go just for the scenery or ask to be dropped off somewhere along the way for a few hours of swimming.

This stretch of coast is the home of Rosso Cónero wine, made from the same Montepulciano grape as Chianti, though less well-known than its Tuscan counterpart. Rarely found outside Italy, there's a chance to sample it at the Rosso Cónero **festival** at Camerano, 8km inland from Monte Cónero in the first week in September, with tastings, music and theatre.

Portonovo

Only 11km from Ancona, **PORTONOVO** nestles beneath Monte Cónero, a pleasant resort of a couple of campsites and a clutch of expensive hotels, one of which is sited in the Napoleonic fort that dominates the bay. Although its pebbly beach gets very busy in summer, the scenery is unbeatable, and you can escape the worst of the crush if you're prepared to paddle and clamber to the few tiny beaches to the south. There's also a lovely Romanesque church, **Santa**

Maria, perched above the beach at the end of an oleander-lined path. At present you can see it only from the outside (ask at the nearby Hotel Fortino Napoleonico for details of how to get into the grounds), but this is enough – the clear light reflected from the sea bathes it in a golden glow, the shadows adding to the delicate interplay of arcades and wavily tiled roof. **The trail across Monte Cónero to Sirolo** begins in Portonovo, at a stairway to the right of the Hotel Internazionale. Though rewarding, it's a steep and tricky hike, so don't attempt it without a map.

Portonovo is linked with Ancona by regular urban buses. Unfortunately all of the town's **hotels** are expensive – but at least there are some stylish choices. *Emilia*, Via Collina di Portonovo (℡071.801.117, Ⓦwww.hotelemilia.com; ❽), is a five-minute car journey inland – and uphill – from the beach. A light, modern hotel, the walls are covered with a huge contemporary art collection, a legacy of the Fifties and Sixties when artists were invited to pay for their stay with a piece of their work. The pool and many places to lounge tempt you to stay put but there are electric bikes on loan for short rides up into the Monte Cónero Park, and a shuttle service down to the beach. Down by the seashore in a converted fortress is *Fortino Napoleonico* (℡071.801.450, Ⓦwww.hotelfortino.it; ❾) built on the orders of Napoleon to stop the English landing to take on fresh water from Monte Cónero's springs, and now an upmarket hotel. There are some military touches in the suites but generally the hotel is chi-chi and grand. Otherwise there are two **campsites**: *Camping Comunale La Torre* (℡071.801.257; June to mid-Sept) is slightly cheaper; if it's full, try the *Camping Club Adriatico* (℡071.801.170; May to mid-Sept). For food, there's no better place to watch the sun go down than from the chilled beach bar and restaurant *Il Clandestino* (to find it, follow the "Torre" signs). *Susci Italiano* is on the menu – like sushi in concept but using speciality olive oils and balsamic vinegar rather than wasabi and soy sauce. *Da Anna*, on the beach (summer only), is a great family-run fish **restaurant**.

Sirolo

Further south, **SIROLO** has an old centre of terraced cottages divided by neat cobbled streets. The main square, Piazza Veneto, is on the clifftop, with good views of the coast and Monte Cónero. What used to be a quiet bolt-hole has taken off in the last few years and the place now gets packed-out on weekends from June to September. In season, buses run roughly every half-hour to the two beaches below, Sassi Neri and San Michele, of which San Michele, just to the north, is the better, with a section at the far end where nudism is tolerated. The town has won a blue flag for its clean waters every year since 1994. Particularly inviting is the small beach close to the jagged mid-sea islets of the Due Sorelle, although you won't have it to yourself in peak season.

There is a good choice of **accommodation**: beach lovers should head for *Arturo*, Via Spiaggia 1 (℡071.933.0975, Ⓔinfo@conerohotels.it; ❹; June–Sept), right on the white shingle strand, a yellow house with green shutters and just seven rooms. It's a bus ride from Sirolo proper (or a long walk down and then back uphill), but it's one of the least expensive options in town. It has its own restaurant and there are other places to eat and drink in the evenings down at the beach. At the other end of the scale is *Rocco*, Via Torrioni 1 (℡071.933.0558, Ⓦwww.locandarocco.it; ❼), built into the town gate and a short walk down the main street of Via Italia from the piazza. Once a thirteenth-century inn where St Francis is said to have slept, it's now a stylish seven-room hotel with an upmarket restaurant (closed Tues in winter) serving refined, imaginative and very expensive food. Many Sirolese are offering B&B

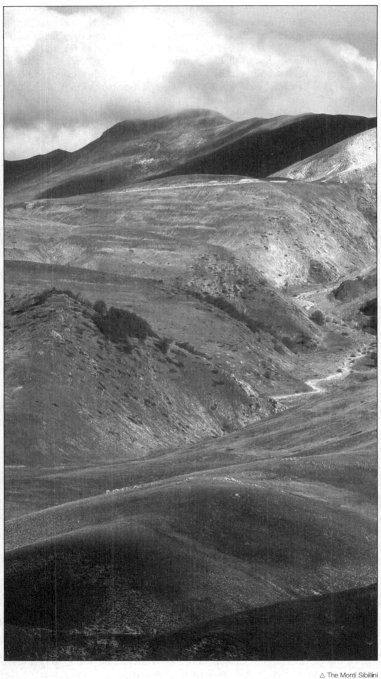

△ The Monti Sibillini

these days – look out for the "*camere*" signs around town. On Via Giulietti, for example, there are **rooms** at number 46 (☎071.736.0593; ❸) with good triple and quadruple rooms as well as inexpensive doubles. Across the road at number 9 is *Stella* (☎071.933.0704, ✉hotelstellasirolo@libero.it; ❺), and a short walk away *Emiliana*, Via Raffaello Sanzio 2 (☎071.933.0932, ✉hotelemiliana@virgilio.it; ❸), both pleasant, modern hotels. Another good choice is *Panoramic*, Via San Michele 8 (☎071.933.0659, ✉hotelpanoramic.sirolo@katamail.com; ❻), just off Via Giulietti, a friendly place with a sun terrace and a stunning view of the coastline. Sirolo's closest campsite is the *Internazionale* (☎071.933.0884; April–Sept; ⓦwww.internazionale.com), set on a terraced, wooded hillside below Piazza Veneto, within sight and sound of the sea.

If you can afford to splurge in Sirolo, do it on a **meal** at the hotel *Rocco* (see above), or the equally expensive *Il Grottino* (closed Tues in winter) on Via Ospedale, just off Via Italia, which specializes in fish in its stone-vaulted restaurant or outside on a terrace scented with jasmine plants. Otherwise there's *La Taverna* (closed Thurs in winter), Via Italia 10, offering *enogastronomia*: local wine and several fish and pasta combinations plus the local cheese, *formaggio di Fossa*. At *Trattoria Sara* next door at number 9 (closed Wed in winter) diners can sample robust dishes in a no-nonsense atmosphere; the seafood antipasti, risotto and tagliatelle with fish sauce are especially recommended. Otherwise, a great eatery down at the beach is *Da Peppe*, where workers from town go for lunch in summer. Back in town, for cocktails and **ice creams** with a sea view head to *Il Grillo*, on Via Giulietti just below Piazza Veneto.

Numana

NUMANA, a small port with a large pebble beach, is where you can take a boat to the offshore islets of Due Sorelle (June–Sept, roughly hourly 9am–3pm) for a spot of swimming and sunbathing. There is also the added attraction of a **museum** (daily 8.30am–7.30pm; €2), filled mostly with relics of the Piceni tribe, who occupied the area between Senigállia and Pescara from the seventh century BC; the extent to which they were influenced by the Greeks, who set up a trading post nearby, is clearly visible in the red-and-black pots decorated with scenes from Greek mythology. If you want **to stay**, *Teresa a Mare*, Via del Golfo 26 (☎071.933.0623; ❼), and the *Scogliera*, Via del Golfo 21 (☎071.933.0622; ❾), on a small headland at the northern edge of the bay, are both modern, appealing places among Numana's handful of two- and three-star hotels. But unless you are set on staying here, you might be better off in Sirolo, where there is also more choice of places to eat.

Loreto

One of Italy's most popular sites of pilgrimage, attracting four million visitors every year, **LORETO** owes its existence to one of the Catholic Church's more surreal legends. The story goes that in 1292, when the Muslims kicked the Crusaders out of Palestine, a band of angels flew the **house of Mary** from Nazareth to Dalmatia, and then, a few years later, whisked it across the Adriatic to Loreto. In the face of growing scepticism, the Vatican came up with the more plausible story that the Holy House was transported to Loreto on board a Crusader ship. Not surprisingly, though, this theory doesn't seem to have the same hold on the Catholic imagination, and the Madonna of Loreto continues to be viewed as the patron of aviators: Lindbergh took an image of the

Madonna of Loreto on his landmark Atlantic flight in 1927, and a medallion inscribed with her image also accompanied the crew of Apollo 9. Among the Madonna of Loreto's more unlikely fans were Galileo, denounced and imprisoned as a heretic, and Descartes, who reckoned she'd helped him refine his philosophical method. For centuries she was also credited with military victories (presumably she was thought to have power over projectiles), though the builders of Loreto's basilica, aware that the site was vulnerable to Turkish pirates, decided not to rely on the Madonna's defensive capabilities, and accordingly constructed a formidable fortified church here.

Loreto's treasures were indeed covetable, the most costly and idiosyncratic being a golden baby donated by Louis XIII of France, weighing exactly the same as his long-awaited heir, the future Louis XIV. The basilica was ransacked in 1798 by Napoleonic troops, most of the plunder ending up on the shelves of the Louvre in Paris. Following Napoleon's demise, subsequent popes managed to retrieve many of the valuables, but the majority were stolen again in 1974, in what became known as the "holy theft of the century".

Numbering among its contributors such figures as Bramante, Antonio da Sangallo, Sansovino, Lotto and Luca Signorelli, the basilica is a must for anyone even mildly interested in the Renaissance. However, for the non-believer the atmosphere of devotional hard-sell can soon become stifling. Loreto can also be a distressing or a moving place, depending on your attitude to faith – between April and October so-called "white trains" bring the sick and terminally ill on three-day missions of hope, the main event being a Mass in Piazza della Madonna, outside the basilica.

The pilgrimage site

Had it been completed according to Bramante's design, the **Piazza della Madonna** would have been an ideal Renaissance square. It still looks pretty good, although Bramante's **Palazzo Apostolico** has only two of its projected three wings, and his low facade for the basilica, designed to make its elegant dome the piazza's focal point, was never built. Instead, the dome, masked by a fluid late-Renaissance facade, is best seen from the back. Here you can see how Baccio Pontelli, who had a hand in most of the Marche's fifteenth-century military architecture, fortified the church – the loggia that runs along the sides and around the nine apses has a dual role as a walkway for meditating monks and a battlement, looking down over the sturdy defensive walls.

Inside the basilica

The church's **interior** (daily: April–Sept 6.15am–8pm; Oct–March 6.45am–7pm) is the jumbled result of Bramante's, Sansovino's and Sangallo's attempts to graft Renaissance elements onto the late-Gothic structure. Clashing with the pointed arches of the nave, Loreto's raison d'être, the Santa Casa (Holy House), is encased in a marble cuboid designed by Bramante and encrusted with statues and reliefs. With typical Renaissance panache, pagan sibyls are juxtaposed with Old Testament prophets, all sharing in the honour of foreseeing Mary's life, scenes from which decorate the rest of the walls. The best are by Sansovino: a *Nativity* on the south side and an *Annunciation* on the front.

You may not be able to look around the Holy House itself as a service is usually being conducted for visiting pilgrims and it is closed from 12.30pm to 2.30pm. A primitive stone building, it has no foundations and only three walls – cited by believers as proof of its authenticity (the basement and fourth wall were formed by a grotto which can still be seen in Nazareth), but seen by sceptics simply as evidence of the research undertaken by its fakers. Pride of place is given to a copy of the famous *Black Madonna of Loreto*; the medieval original, once crazily attributed to St Luke, was destroyed in a fire in 1921. Madonna and Child are usually to be seen swathed in an ornate but ill-fitting wrap known as a dalmatic, a practice started by Pope Pius VII in 1801 in celebration of the statue's return from the Louvre. Pope Julius II contributed the cannon shell hanging on the right-hand wall, attributing his miraculous escape from it to the Madonna of Loreto's missile-deflecting powers.

One of the most recent of the church's 25 chapels is the **Cappella Americana**, featuring a plane in recognition of the Madonna's role as patron of aviators. Of more artistic interest is the **Cappella del Crocifisso**, whose wooden *Crucifixion* is a triumph of Baroque ingenuity: viewed from the left, Christ appears to be still alive; from the centre, to be drawing his last agonized breath; and from the right, to be dead. Less theatrical is the **Sagrestia di San Giovanni**, frescoed by Luca Signorelli – most striking is the Conversion of St Paul, with its panic-stricken courtiers. The sacristy's inlaid cupboards, featuring a jumble of trompe l'oeil bric-a-brac, are influenced by those in the *studiolo* of Urbino's palace (see p.669).

Next door, in the **Cappella dei Duchi di Urbino**, commissioned by the last duke, Francesco Maria II della Rovere, is an *Annunciation* by Barocci, taking place before an open window through which the Palazzo Ducale can be seen. By far the most entertaining chapel, however, is the **Sagrestia di San Marco**, where vaulted frescoes feature prophets who seem to be resolving the knotty problem of the sex of angels by peering up their skirts. Ezekiel looks appalled, Zacharias flushed and embarrassed, Jeremiah delighted, and David utterly overwhelmed.

To the left of the Chapel of the Crucifix, a corridor leads to the sumptuously stuccoed atrium and the **Treasury**, its vault unremarkably frescoed by Pomerancio. The artist won the competition for the commission in 1604 thanks to Vatican manoeuvring, much to the chagrin of the loser, Caravaggio, who hired a cutthroat to slash Pomerancio's face.

The Museo-Pinacoteca

The items left behind in the treasury after the 1974 burglary are now kept in the **Museo-Pinacoteca** (Tues–Sun: April–Oct 9am–1pm & 4–7pm; Nov–March 10am–1pm & 3–6pm; donations requested) housed in the west wing of the Palazzo Apostolico. It shouldn't be missed, principally for the eight paintings by Lorenzo Lotto that are held here, nearly all dated between 1549 and 1556, including his final work, *The Presentation in the Temple*. Plagued by neurosis and lack of money, Lotto finally joined the religious community at Loreto, painted some of the canvases shown here, and died here in 1556. Looking at *The Presentation*, with its rotund, crumbling priest and frail, almost skeletal nun, it would appear that he never found much inner peace. *Christ and the Adulteress* is an even more powerful work, with Christ surrounded by maniacally intense men and a swooning adulteress. For some light relief, take a look at the best of all the depictions of the Holy House's angel-powered flight – a copy of a fluffy-clouded fantasy by Giambattista Tiepolo.

Practicalities

Loreto is easily accessible by **train** from Ancona; the station is some way out of town but connected with the centre by regular buses. The busiest periods are December 8–12 (the anniversary of the legendary flight), August 1–20, September 5–10, Easter, and from Christmas through to January 7; it's also pretty crowded throughout the summer, and finding accommodation can be difficult so it's worth visiting Ⓦwww.le-marche.com or the **tourist office** at Via Solari 3 (Mon–Sat 9am–1pm & 4–6.30pm; Sun 9am–12.30pm; ☎071.970.276, Ⓔiat.loreto@regione.marche.it) for a complete list. The one-star **hotels** are run by religious orders, among them the *Sorelle Francescane*, Via Marconi 26 (☎071.970.306; ❸). For something less spartan, try the central 1970s-style *Il Giardinetto*, just inside the Porta Romana on Corso Boccalini (☎071.977.135, Ⓦwww.hotelgiardinetto.it; ❹), or *Centrale*, Via Solari 7 (☎071 .970.173, Ⓔrist.girarrosto@fastnet.it; ❺), a comfortable two-star with good reductions in low season and a vast and popular restaurant, *Girarrosto* (see below). Within the city walls there are good deals in low-season at the *Pellegrino e Pace* on the edge of the main square at Piazza della Madonna 5 (☎071 .977.106, Ⓦwww.pellegrinoepace.it; ❹), especially if you are looking for a triple or quadruple room. Leading away from the piazza, at Corso Boccalini 69, is *Delfino Azzurro* (☎071.977.283; ❺), a friendly two-star with a private garage. A couple of kilometres beyond the city walls, and connected by bus from the train station, is the **youth hostel** at Via Aldo Moro 46 (☎071.750.1026; €13.50–19).

Your best bet for places to **eat** is the *Ristorante Girarrosto* in Via Solari (closed Wed) for good, fresh pasta dishes, while the *Garibaldi*, further down the same street (closed Wed), serves great pizza as does the *Antica Pizzeria del Corso* at Corso Boccalini 74 (closed Mon).

Recanati and Porto Recanati

A few kilometres along the Macerata road from Loreto is **RECANATI**, a small town that makes a comfortable living from having been the birthplace of the opera singer Beniamino Gigli and the nineteenth-century poet Giacomo Leopardi. The visitor can wallow in Gigli memorabilia in the civic art gallery, or visit places that feature in Leopardi's poems; if such acts of homage don't appeal, there's little point in coming to Recanati. It's attractive in a forgettable sort of way, but the provinciality soon becomes stultifying – Leopardi himself, though loving Recanati for its views of sea, hills and mountains, found most of its inhabitants stodgy and narrow-minded.

Recanati

On the central Piazza Leopardi, the **Museo Beniamino Gigli** (Tues–Sun 10am–1pm & 3–6pm; €2.10) is housed in the nineteenth-century **Palazzo Comunale**, a fussy mock-Renaissance symbol of Recanatese obtuseness – in order to build it they ripped down a fine medieval palace. All that remains of the original palace is the vast **Torre del Borgo**, glowering down on the municipal architecture that surrounds it. Once inside the gallery you can forget all this and lose yourself in Gigli's world, evoked by costumes worn by the great tenor, presents received by him (including a dagger from D'Annunzio), and, best of all, a replica of his dressing room. A crackly recording of his voice is often playing on a wind-up gramophone as a fitting accompaniment to the exhibits. It's worth dropping in, too, at the patrician house on Via Gregorio XII where the **Museo Civico Villa Colloredo Mels** (Tues–Fri 9am–noon & 3–7pm; Sat & Sun 9am–1pm & 3–8pm; €4.65) is housed, with four paintings by **Lotto** the highlight of the small collection. Among them there's a polyptych, complete save for its predella (which somehow ended up in Russia), a *Transfiguration* and an *Annunciation*, better known as *The Madonna of the Cat* for the cat scuttling between the Madonna and angel – thought by some critics to represent the devil.

Left out of Piazza Leopardi, the main street leads down to the **Palazzo Leopardi** where the poet was born in 1798 and which still contains his vast library of over 25,000 volumes. The odd name of the square in front of it, **Piazzuola Sabato del Villagio**, comes from one of Leopardi's poems, in which he observes a typical Recanati Saturday, with "a swarm of children shouting on the piazzuola". You're almost bound to meet crowds of schoolkids here, but their elation tends to come from relief at finishing the tedious tour of Leopardi's gloomy house. The best-known thing about the poet is his lack of success in love, which is typically blamed on his smothering mother, who still cut up his meat for him when he was 25. Leopardi sought solace in the view from the edge of town – on a good day it extends as far as the Apennines. The lower hills, which seem to roll endlessly towards the mountains, inspired his most famous poem, *Colle Infinito* ("Infinite Hills"), and a plaque with a line from it has been stuck on a wall, above a heap of rocks from Naples, where he died and is buried. Adding insult to injury, the place where he came to forget his failures with women has become a lovers' lane.

Porto Recanati

If you're not a fan of either Gigli or Leopardi, you may well head straight to **PORTO RECANATI**, the nearest resort to Loreto. Its main street, Corso Matteotti, is headed by the turreted tower of a medieval castle; off it is a tiny old quarter of terraced cottages surrounded by hotels and apartment buildings. Apart from the beach, limited attractions include a **sailing and windsurfing school** (June–Aug) – details from the **tourist office** (summer daily 9am–12.30pm & 4.30–7pm; winter Mon, Wed, Fri 9am–12.30pm & 4–6.30pm; ✆071.979.9084, ✉iat.portorecanati@regione.marche.it) on the Corso – and four discos. If you tire of the beach you can visit an art gallery inside the **castle** (Mon–Fri 5–7pm; free) which is undergoing a long pro-gramme of restoration but is usually open in summer: among the pictures is a portrait of a peasant at work attributed to Millet. Even better, the castle court-yard has an **arena** – a wonderfully atmospheric place to see films and theatre.

The website ⓦwww.portorecanatiturismo.it lists a couple of B&B options or there are two mid-range **hotels** in town: the seventeen-room *Bianchi Nicola*, Via Rosselli 2 (✆071.979.9016; ❹), or the *Bianchi Vincenzo* at Via Garibaldi 15 (✆071.979.9040; ❺), whose rooms have balconies overlooking the sea. *Enzo* at Corso Matteotti 21/23 (✆071.759.0734, ✉hotelenzo@libero.it; ❻) is a glossy four-star. The *Pineta* **campsite**, to the south on Viale della Repubblica (✆071.979.9237), is reasonably convenient and has four-person bungalows as well.

Porto Recanati is best known for its *brodetto*, a classy fish soup cooked with nine varieties of fish, spiced with saffron and served with squares of toast. One of the best places to try it is the **restaurant** inside the *Bianchi Vincenzo* hotel (see above; closed to non-residents Mon) on the seafront – the chef is justifi-ably known as the *l'uomo del brodetto* (the "brodetto man") and conjures up other equally delicious dishes, including delicate seafood starters and a superb fish risotto. The *mago del brodetto*, however (the "brodetto magician"), is the chef at the other Bianchi family hotel, *Bianchi Nicola* (also closed to non-residents Mon).

Macerata

A little-known provincial capital surrounded by Marche's loveliest countryside, **MACERATA** is one of the region's liveliest historical towns, thanks to its ancient university. Easy-paced and unpretentious, it's an ideal place to wind down in the evenings after exploring the province. For opera and ballet fans, its annual *Stagione Lirica*, held in Italy's best open-air venue outside Verona, is a must: in recent years it has drawn such heavyweights as Placido Domingo, Birgit Nilsson and José Carreras. And if you're the slightest bit interested in contemporary art, Macerata has a gallery that alone is reason enough for visiting the town.

The Town

Piazza della Libertà is the heart of the old town, an odd square in which the disparate buildings vie for supremacy. The Renaissance **Loggia dei Mercanti** was supplied by Alessandro Farnese, better known as Pope Paul III, the instigator of many architectural improvements to sixteenth-century Rome; sadly he did nothing else for the square, and the loggia is elbowed out by the bland **Palazzo del Comune** and overlooked by the dull **Torre del Comune**. The dreariest feature, however, is the mournful brick facade of **San Paolo**, a deconsecrated seventeenth-century church now used as an exhibition space.

Things buzz a bit more along the main *passeggiata* route, the boutique- and bar-lined **Corso della Repubblica**, which ends at **Piazza Vittorio Veneto** and the **Pinacoteca Civica** (June–Sept daily 9am–7pm; Oct–May daily 9am–1pm & 4–7pm except Mon am and Sun pm; free). The collection here, ranging from the Renaissance perfectionist Crivelli to Ancona-born futurist Cagli, isn't bad, but you might find the artworks on show in the **Palazzo Ricci** (Tues & Thurs 4–6pm, Sat 10am–noon; free), off the square on Via Ricci, more challenging; they make up what is by any standards a fine collection of Italian contemporary art. There are two thrilling sculptures by Francesco Messina – a nerve-tingling nude of a dancer putting on her shoes, and a leaping horse. Enrico Baj's *Military Head* depicts a general decorated with assorted fabric on a background of upholstery material, and you might see a similarly satiric intent in Manzu's bronze bas-relief of a clutch of cardinals. There's also a good cross-section of work by the Italian futurists, followed by de Chirico's weird *Worried Muse*; de Chirico's brother, Alberto Savinio, provides the gallery's jokiest piece of social satire in the form of a painting of a richly dressed society woman whose long neck ends in a goose's head.

Seeing the rest of Macerata's sights doesn't take long. Via Ricci leads along towards the bleak **Piazza Mazzini**, below which is the Neoclassical **Sferisterio**, built in the early nineteenth century as an arena for *sphaera*, a traditional game that involved bashing a ball with a spiked iron glove. It was also used for bullfights, horse racing and mock jousts until, in 1921, the opera festival was inaugurated and the musicians took it over. It's rather dismal and not worth visiting, except for a performance.

Up Via Ciccarelli from Piazza Mazzini, the town's **Duomo** on Piazza Strambi is no architectural showpiece either – a workaday chunk of Baroque, which might have looked slightly more appetizing had its facade been finished. Inside there's a statue of Macerata's patron saint, Giuliano, whose path to sainthood sounds like something out of a Sunday tabloid. He arrived home to find two people in his bed and, thinking they were his wife and her lover, promptly killed them. Discovering he'd murdered his parents, he hacked one of his arms off in remorse – the severed limb is now kept in a church strongroom, encased in a sleeve of gold and silver. The relic is displayed on request, but a day's notice is required.

Practicalities

Old Macerata is wrapped around a hill, surrounded by modern suburbs that are home to the **train station**, a ten-minute walk south at the end of Viale Don Bosco. This is connected with Piazza della Libertà by frequent buses. **Buses** stop at the Giardini Diaz, directly below the old town on the western side, across Viale Puccinotti; some, however, do continue to a second, more convenient stop, from which it's a five-minute climb up stepped Piaggia delle Torre to Piazza della Libertà.

The **tourist office** is on Piazza della Libertà (Mon–Fri 9am–1pm & 3–6pm, Sat 9am–1pm; ℡0733.234.807, ⓦwww.comune.macerata.it). and the website for the province is ⓦwww.sinp.net. There are just a handful of **hotels** in Macerata, and if you're looking for somewhere fairly cheap you should try to book in advance; during the opera season (mid-July to mid-Aug), this is absolutely crucial. The top budget choice is the **youth hostel**, Via dell'Asilo 36 (℡0733.232.515; €12.91 including breakfast), opened in 2000 in a converted nineteenth-century palazzo that once housed Macerata's first infant school. Spotlessly clean, air-conditioned in summer and heated in winter, the hostel offers ninety beds in a choice of dorms or smaller rooms – some of them vaulted and frescoed. Ask at the tourist office (ⓔiat.macerata@regione.marche.it) for the **B&B** options too – these fall in the ❸ price band. Among the central hotel choices are the *Arcadia*, *Da Rosa* and the *Arena*; the *Arcadia*, Via P. Matteo Ricci (℡0733.235.961; ❹), in a quiet cobbled street in the historic centre between Piazza della Libertà and Piazza Mazzini, has newly decorated bedrooms with huge beds and TVs; *Da Rosa*, Via Armaroli 94 (℡0733.232.670; ❸), is more old-fashioned, and is near Piazza della Libertà; while the modern, friendly *Arena* at nearby Vicolo Sferisterio, off Piazza Mazzini (℡0733.230.931; ❹), is tucked away in a small courtyard in a group of ancient stone buildings. Otherwise there's the *Residenza Lauri* at Via T. Lauri 6 (℡0733.232.376; ❹), also central and reached via Corso Matteotti; its rooms are pleasant and there are triples and quadruples with kitchenettes also available. Macerata's four-star option is *Hotel Claudiani*, Via Ulissi 8 (℡0733.261.400; ❻), in a modernized palazzo just off Corso Matteotti in the historic centre. A pleasant option **out of town** is *Il Vecchio Granaio*, località Chiaravalle, Passo di Treia (℡0733.843.488, ⓔturigest@tin.it; ❹), a former hunting lodge and now an *agriturismo* complex a twenty-minute drive from Macerata on the SS361 at the km 40,500 marker (there are five buses a day to Passo Treia from Macerata). The large guest rooms in the converted stable block are decorated with antiques and hunting prints, and superlative views of the hills are available from the communal sun terrace. There's a large swimming pool in the garden and the restaurant serves excellent food.

On presentation of an ISIC card you can have an hour's free access to the **Internet** at the Facoltà di Scienze della Comunicazione, Via XX Settembre (Mon–Thurs 9am–1pm & 4–8pm, Fri 9am–1pm & 3–6pm; book) near Palazzo Ricci. Or there's the *Internet Center* at Piazza Mazzini 52 (erratic hours).

As for **food**, at lunchtime the Maceratese head for *Il Ghiottone*, a self-service restaurant at Via Gramsci 30 which runs between the tourist office and Palazzo Ricci. The student *mensa* is at Viale Don Bosco 12 outside the centre on the Piazza Mazzini side of town. *Da Silvano* on Piaggia delle Torre, just off Piazza della Libertà (closed Mon and most of May), is a good sit-down pizzeria. *Trattoria da Ezio*, Via Crescimbeni 65 (closed Sun), serves very reasonably priced food with fish specials on Wednesday and Friday, and "Thursday gnocchi". For a more indulgent meal, head for Macerata's most famous restaurant, *Da Secondo*, on Via Pescheria Vecchia (℡0733.260.912; closed Mon); they do a superlative *vincisgrassi*, the rich Marche version of lasagne, along with excellent roast lamb and pigeon.

For more dedicated **drinking** (or indeed daytime sandwiches), there's the *Firenze* music bar on Via Pescheria Vecchia, and the popular *Il Pozzo*, Via Costa 5 (off Piazza Oberdan), a student pub-birreria since the 1970s that, sadly, closes at around 8pm. Most of Macerata's pubs are busiest around midnight or 1am, and Wednesday and Thursday are the big nights out: for more on local **nightlife**, check out Ⓦwww.maceratagallery.it. The *Pub Palace-Restaurant and Rhythmic Bar* at Vicolo Coltelli 13 goes on all night, and you can sometimes catch live jazz and ska at *Terminal-Music* at Via Fontemaggiore just outside the city walls by Porta San Giuliano. In a different vein, *Osteria Il Giardinetto*, at Piazza San Giovanni 8 is Macerata's oldest and most authentic osteria and the place to head for a few carafes of wine. Seats for the **opera** are bookable at the Biglietteria dell'Arena Sferisterio, Piazza Mazzini 10 (℡0733.230.735, Ⓕ0733.261.570, Ⓔmacerataopera@mercurio.it). Ticket prices range from €15 in the balcony (not bookable) to €100 (plus ten percent booking fee) in the front stalls.

East of Macerata

With its hills rising from the coast and rippling towards the Apennines, its medieval villages and scattering of Romanesque abbeys and churches, the area around Macerata is interesting to explore. You can get to most places by bus within a day, although if you're wanting to visit some of the more out-of-the-way hill-villages, you may find it more convenient to sleep over.

The Chienti Valley

From Macerata the road and rail lines run east to the coast through the **Chienti Valley**, taking in some of the region's most characteristic hill-towns and two of its finest churches. About 10km from Macerata, close to the turn-off for Morrovalle, is the Romanesque church of **San Claudio al Chienti**, approached along a cypress-lined avenue. Carefully restored after years of use as a farm outbuilding, the church appears to be none the worse for its undignified past – you'd certainly never guess that the two cylindrical towers flanking its facade used to serve as grain silos. The upper storey, intended for church dignitaries, was entered through the elegant marble portal, while lesser mortals were directed to the tunnel-like door on the ground floor. The marble for the portal, like much of the church's fabric, was scavenged from a Roman village, Pausula, which once stood in the adjacent field.

Morrovalle and Montelupone

Above San Claudio is the hill-village of **MORROVALLE**, skirted by a stepped street which disappears through arched gates. Hemmed inside the main piazza at the top of the village is the squat Palazzo del Podestà, where Italy's first pawnshop was set up by St Bernard in 1428. The building next to it is the Palazzo Lazzarini, seat of the ruling family who survived their internecine battle for the privilege of ruling Morrovalle. The palazzo, though built in the fourteenth century, incorporates an earlier Romanesque-Gothic portal, possibly taken from a local church.

The even more remote **MONTELUPONE** is served by (rare) bus from Macerata, and offers views from Monte Cónero across to the most beautiful of the Apennines, the Monti Sibillini. A good time to go is during the *passeggiata*, when the stone buildings look handsome in the early evening sun, and the village is at its liveliest.

Santa Maria a Piè di Chienti

Back in the valley, road and railway pass the ex-monastery of **Santa Maria a Piè di Chienti** (daily 8am–8pm) just after the fork for Montecósaro. It was built by Cluniac monks, who came to the area in the tenth century, draining the flood-prone river into channels and creating fertile land out of what had been a fever-ridden marsh. Situated close to the coast, the monastery was vulnerable to Saracen invasions, so the monks encircled it with ditches, which could be flooded in the event of a raid. The monastery survived until the early nineteenth century, when it was destroyed by Napoleonic troops, and now all that remains is the church itself. The facade was rebuilt in the eighteenth century, and the church's best external features are now its apses, decorated with fake pilasters and scalloped arcades. However, it's the interior (key from the adjacent bar) that's really special, its columns and arches bathed in the half-light that falls from the windowpanes of alabaster. After wandering around the vaulted chamber beneath the raised presbytery, and up the stairs to the galleries (narrow to ensure that they were climbed slowly, with a prayer on every step), you'll need to switch the lights on (by the right transept) to see the fifteenth-century frescoes properly. The best-preserved are in the apse, showing New Testament scenes in Renaissance settings, framed by fake mosaics and dominated by a stony-faced Christ.

West of Macerata

Heading southwest of Macerata towards the Monti Sibillini, you might stop off briefly at **TOLENTINO** to see the **Basilica di San Nicola** (daily 7.30am–12.30pm & 3.30–7pm; free). Its west front is a real feast for the eyes – a curly Baroque facade with a grinning sun instead of a rose window and a fancily twisting Gothic portal topped by an oriental-style arch enclosing a dragon-slaying saint. Inside, the most intriguing feature is the **Cappellone di San Nicola**, whose Gothic frescoes create a kaleidoscope of colourful scenes of medieval life. In fact, they are episodes from the life of Christ, painted in the fourteenth century by one of Giotto's followers, known only as the "Maestro di Tolentino". The most striking are *The Wedding at Cana*, with hefty servants carrying massive jugs of wine on their shoulders, *The Slaughter of the Innocents*, and *The Entry into Jerusalem*, in which an attempt at perspective is made by peopling the trees with miniature figures.

Just east of Tolentino is the imposing, fourteenth-century **Castello della Rancia**. This vast fort was the main grain store for the Cistercian abbey of Fiastra (see p.696) back in the twelfth century. It was transformed into a castle in the fourteenth century and became the focal point of a number of armed clashes, at one time harbouring the notorious Renaissance mercenary Sir John Hawkwood.

San Severino Marche

Twelve kilometres north of Tolentino lies the old, silvery-grey town of **SAN SEVERINO MARCHE**, a pretty little place whose modern centre converges on an unusual elliptical square, **Piazza del Popolo**, surrounded by porticoes. Just above the piazza on Via Salimbeni the town's art gallery, known as the **Pinacoteca Tacchi e Venturi** after a local historian (July–Sept Tues–Sun 9am–1pm & 4.30–6.30pm, Fri open until 8pm; Oct–June Tues–Sat 9am–1pm plus alternate Sundays 9am–1pm; €2.07), is as good a reason as any for a visit, with a quite memorable assembly of pieces. A gilded polyptych of saints by Paolo Veneziano is followed by an even more sumptuous altarpiece by Vittore Crivelli, which centres on a china-doll Madonna weighed down in heavy gold embroidery. It's the frame that really catches your eye, though – an opulent confection of scalloped arches topped with urns from which spring gesticulating ecclesiastics. Other highlights are the works by the Salimbeni brothers, who were born and worked in San Severino in the fifteenth century; they are represented by delicate and expressive frescoes detached from local churches and a wooden polyptych of *The Marriage of St Catherine*. The finds that used to make up the **Museo Archeologico** in the same building are in the process of being transferred to new premises next to the Duomo Vecchio. They were excavated from the Roman valley town of Septempeda, whose inhabitants, driven out by barbarian invasions in the sixth century, escaped up the nearest hill to found the forerunner of San Severino.

Other works by the Salimbeni brothers adorn two of San Severino's churches. One of these, the ancient **San Lorenzo in Doliolo**, at the top of Via Salimbeni, looks slightly odd thanks to a medieval brick tower standing on top of its stone portal. The Salimbeni frescoes, illustrating the story of St Andrew, are on the vault of the tenth-century crypt, looking far older and more primitive than they really are because of their antique surroundings; the back part of the crypt is thought to be a pagan temple dating back to the time of the refugees from Septempeda.

The other church – actually the old cathedral – is up in **CASTELLO**, the upper part of San Severino, a long and steep walk – although there are occasional buses from the main square. A lonely, evocative place, it was here that the Romans from Septempeda came, though as Castello continued to be the hub of religious and political life until the eighteenth century, any traces of them have long been covered over. Close to its thirteenth-century walls, sheltered by a Gothic portico, is the **Fontana dei Sette Canelle**, a seven-spouted fountain where you'll occasionally see women doing their washing. Right at the top, dwarfed by the medieval Torre del Comune, is the **Duomo Vecchio**, founded in the tenth century but with a Romanesque-Gothic facade, simple Gothic cloisters, and a much rebuilt interior. Not surprisingly, it's lost a bit of atmosphere with all these reconstructions, but the baptistry vault still has its Salimbeni frescoes. Also worth a look are the inlaid choir stalls and tomb of the town's patron, St Severinus.

For a congenial **place to stay** in San Severino, head for the *Due Torri*, Via San Francesco 21(℡0733.645.419, ⓔduetorri@wnt.it; ❺), high above town in the Castello; it has spotless bedrooms in an old stone wing with green shutters, tiled floors and simple furnishings. There's a popular restaurant attached, which doubles as a shop, selling local delicacies, wines and spirits.

Visso, Ússita and hiking territory

Some way south of San Severino, close to the border with Umbria and the Monti Sibillini, **VISSO** (reachable by bus from Macerata) is the gateway to the Sibillini Mountain National Park. A pleasant village with narrow streets bordered by medieval stone houses, Visso was more prominent back in the fifteenth and sixteenth centuries when it was at a strategic point on the route between Marche and Umbria. Now you may well stop off here if you're visiting the park: there's good food to be had at *Trattoria da Richetta*, Piazza Garibaldi 7, and a **Casa del Parco** at Via Battisti 15 (July & Aug daily 9.30am–12.30pm & 4–7pm; Sept Thurs–Sun same times; rest of year Sat & Sun only; ☎0737.95262, ⓦwww.sibillini.net) for information on walks and wildlife. For access to the **mountain hiking** trails, you'll need to head up the narrow valley to **ÚSSITA**, a rather anonymous winter sports resort at the foot of Monte Bove. Several walks of 7 or 8km start from the basic *Rifugio Forcella del Fargno* (June & Oct Sat only; July & Sept Sat & Sun; Aug daily; from within Italy ☎0330.280.690; from abroad phone the warden's private number ☎0733.230.812). Among them is the ascent of the three-peaked mountain known as the **Pizzo Tre Vescovi** because it resembles three mitred bishops. The going can be tricky, as the upper peaks are covered in snow for most of the year, so you'll need a good map (Kompass 666 is the best).

If you have your own transport or you don't mind road walking, you can also head up to the **Santuario di Macereto** (daily 7.30am–12.30pm & 3.30–7pm; free), set on a wild high plain above Ússita. It's no rustic chapel but a classy Bramantesque church built in the sixteenth century as a spiritual stopover for shepherds bringing their flocks up from their winter grazing grounds in the south, and it's surrounded by arcaded stalls for the animals.

South of Macerata: the road to Sarnano

With the Sibillini mountains on the horizon, snow-capped for most of the year, the route south from Macerata towards Sarnano ranks as one of the Marche's most beautiful. Ten kilometres along the road, on the edge of a dense wood, is the Romanesque-Gothic complex of the **Abbazia di Fiastra** (mid-June to mid-Sept daily 10am–1pm & 3–7pm; rest of year same times Sun and national holidays only; €3 for abbey and museum), a Cistercian abbey with a simple, pan-tiled brick cloister and monastic quarters adjoining a grandiose aisled church. The latter is lit by an impressive rose window and contains fifteenth-century frescoes of the *Crucifixion with St Benedict and St Bernard*. From the typically Cistercian central cloister, doors lead into side rooms, among them the refectory, with a vaulted roof resting on seven columns borrowed from the ancient Roman colony of Urbs Salvia a few kilometres down the road. Other buildings in the complex include the eighteenth-century **Palazzo Giustiniani–Bandini**, where Wagner once stayed and whose wedding-cake facade was modelled on Buckingham Palace.

Just as interesting as the bricks and mortar is the vivid picture you get of the monks' influence on the surrounding area: it was they who first drained the marshy land back in the twelfth century and started farming here. Their huge granary, the Castello della Rancia (see p.694), can still be seen by the roadside on the way to Tolentino, giving some clue as to the size of their domain. At the height of their power there were more than two hundred monks here and the abbey was an important religious centre for three centuries. In the fifteenth century the abbey was ransacked by mercenaries, but is once again occupied by monks, who occasionally can be seen flitting across the cloister in their white hooded robes.

The abbey complex is a popular day out with locals and you'll see a steady stream of visitors looking round the building and its grounds, now a nature reserve. The trails through the woods are a popular Sunday stroll, and you should take time to see the **Museo della Civiltà Contadina** (due to reopen after restoration in 2003; same times as abbey, see above), a folk museum laid out in the abbey's low-vaulted outhouses. Among the agricultural and weaving equipment is a decorated wagon such as most farming families would have owned right up until the middle of the twentieth century, using it as a manure cart, a wedding carriage, or whatever form of transport was needed. For some insight into the economics of marriage, take a look at the dowry lists, itemizing the value of household goods. There's also a small **archeological museum**, visitable on the same ticket, containing finds from the nearby Roman town of Urbisaglia.

A five-minute bus ride away, the site of **Urbisaglia** (April–Sept Sun–Wed 9.30am–1.30pm, Thurs–Sat 9.30am–1.30pm & 2.30–7.30pm; Oct–March Mon–Sat 9.30am–1.30pm; free), or Urbs Salvia, was one of the Marche's most important Roman towns until it was sacked by Alaric in 409 AD. Its fame continued into the Middle Ages, when Dante invoked it as an example of a city fallen from glory in his *Paradiso*. So far an amphitheatre, theatre, baths and parts of the walls have been excavated, and frescoes of hunting scenes have been discovered in an underpassage.

South of Urbisaglia, the hill-town health resort of **SAN GINESIO** is justifiably known as the balcony of the Sibillini: the panoramic view from the gardens of the Colle Ascarano, just outside the town walls, stretches from the Adriatic and Monte Cónero to the Sibillini mountains and the highest of the Apennines, the Gran Sasso in Abruzzo. There's a fair amount to see in the town itself: its central piazza is dominated by one of the Marche's most unusual churches, the **Collegiata della Annunziata**, whose late-Gothic facade is decorated with filigree-like terracotta moulding. Rising above it are two campaniles, one capped by an onion dome and the other by what looks like a manicured cactus. Gothic frescoes adorn some of the chapels, and the crypt has frescoes by the Salimbeni brothers – including a pietà in which Mary looks completely demented and Christ is so covered with nail-holes that he appears to have chicken pox.

Sarnano

Until a few years ago, **SARNANO**, south of San Ginesio, was a poor and virtually abandoned village. Recently, however, the town has woken up to the potential of its radioactive springs, known since Roman times to have wide-ranging curative properties, and has begun to develop itself into a spa resort and weekend day-trip destination. The medieval core, coiling in concentric circles around a gentle hill, has been subtly restored, and though it's now more of a showpiece than a living village, its narrow interconnecting cobbled streets and picturesque old houses make it an ideal place for an undemanding day's wandering. On the last weekend in May until mid-June every year, an arts and crafts fair draws in the crowds, with work by Italian craftsmen on sale at scores of temporary shop/exhibition spaces in and around the historic centre.

It's worth getting a map from the **tourist office**, Lago Enrico Ricciardi 1 just off Piazza della Libertà in the new town (daily: summer 9am–1pm & 3.30–6.30pm; winter 9am–1pm & 3–6pm; ☎0733.657.144), before heading up through **Porta Brunforte** into old Sarnano. Just inside is the fourteenth-century church of **San Francesco**, decorated with Palestinian plates, thought to have been brought to Sarnano by souvenir-collecting Crusaders. Its convent is now the seat of the *comune* and houses a fine **Pinacoteca** (July & Aug Tues–Sun 10.30am–12.30pm & 4.30–7.30pm; April–June & Sept–Dec same times Sat, Sun & national hols only; €2.50), the major item being a *Madonna and Child* by Vittore Crivelli.

Continue climbing to the summit of the town and you hit **Piazza Alta**, once the political and religious centre. When Sarnano fell under papal rule in the sixteenth century, the limitation of local power made participation in public life lose its allure; eventually, in the nineteenth century, the underused four-teenth-century **Palazzo del Popolo** was converted into a theatre. It also proved increasingly difficult to ordain priors, as Rome refused to accept those chosen by the people, and the **Palazzo dei Priori** became the prison. These and the square's other medieval buildings have all been restored in recent years and are worth a look; keys are held by the comune at Via Leopardi 1. At present the most interesting of the piazza's buildings is the thirteenth-century church of **Santa Maria di Piazza**, whose fifteenth-century frescoes include a figure known as the *Madonna with Angels*, for the host of celestial musicians and choristers surrounding her. The wooden statue of Christ on the altar has been saddled with one of popular tradition's looniest myths – if it's about to rain, his beard is supposed to grow. On the second Sunday in August, Santa Maria is the starting-point for Sarnano's annual medieval knees-up, or palio – though apart from the costumes and processions, it has more in common with a kids' sports day, featuring a tug-of-war, pole climbing, and a race in which the competitors have to balance jugs of water on their heads.

The two most affordable **hotels** in Sarnano are *Villa*, Via Rimembranza 46 (☎0733.657.218; ❷), a shuttered villa in its own substantial garden 300m uphill from the tourist office, and *Ai Pini*, Via F. Corridoni 101 (☎0733.657.183; ❷), a similar hotel just past the sports ground. But for a few euros more, you could stay at *Terme*, Piazza Libertà 82 (☎0733.657.166; ❸), a substantial nineteenth-century brick palazzo with Art Nouveau flourishes and simple rooms with tiled floors. If you want to **ski** in winter, or to spend a few summer days in the mountains, there's a small resort, **Sasso Tetto**, 10km away – the cheapest hotel there is *La Sibilla* (June to mid-Sept & Dec–March; ☎0733.651.102; ❶).

Southeast of Macerata: Fermo and Porto San Giorgio

Southeast of Macerata, a short distance from the coast, is the attractive old town of **FERMO**. Its web of streets is lined with medieval and Renaissance build-ings, erupting out of which is a wooded peak crowned with a Romanesque-Gothic cathedral. The town's most spectacular monument, however, is hidden from view – a first-century underground complex of thirty filter beds known as the **Piscina Epuratoria Romana** (mid-June to Sept Tues–Sun 10am–1pm & 3.30–7.30pm; Oct to mid-June Tues–Sun 9.30am–1pm & 3.30–7pm; €2.58), originally designed to supply the Roman Imperial fleet with fresh water when it docked at the nearby port. It's worth joining one of the guided tours (no additional charge) which leave Fermo's small museum every half-hour during opening times in summer, every hour in winter; the night tours are especially atmospheric (9pm, 10pm & 11pm every Thurs in July and daily in mid-August). Entered from Via Aceti, off the main Piazza del Popolo, the cistern is something akin to a flooded cathedral, with its well-preserved vault and arches subtly lit and reflected in the dark, still water. From Fermo a road descends to the resort of **PORTO SAN GIORGIO**, with a small fishing and sailing port and a long sandy beach.

The Monti Sibillini

With a mountain lake reddened by the blood of the devil, a narrow pass known as the gorge of hell and a cave reputed to have been the lair of an enchantress, the **Monti Sibillini** are not only the most beautiful of the Apennines, but they teem with ancient legends too.

The best way of exploring the Sibillini is on foot; even if you're not a seasoned hiker there are easy but stunning trails, while for diehard backpackers there are challenging long treks, too. The most agreeable bases are the medieval hill-villages that crown the Sibillini foothills, but there are also a number of *rifugi* if you want to be closer to the starting-points for walks. Most villages are served by buses, but they're few and far between and you'll do better with your own transport.

Amándola and around

AMÁNDOLA is easy to get to on public transport and makes one of the best bases for seeing the region. Its main sight is a **Museo della Civiltà Contadina** (open on request ☎0736.840704; free), housed in the ex-convent of the church of San Francesco. The collection is fascinating, ranging from wine-making and grappa-distilling apparatus to a hand-pulled ambulance and carts decorated with Fascist symbols. It's in the kitchen, though, that things really come alive – the clutter includes a jar of roasted barley (a coffee substitute), a sausage-making machine, mosquito spray, a primitive potty and a wooden baby-walker. Amándola is also a rather forward-looking place, holding an excellent week-long international **theatre festival** in the first week of September. Low on pretension and high on participation, the festival overcomes language barriers with mime and movement performances and workshops – the atmosphere is irresistible, and it's well worth sticking around for the whole week.

Otherwise, Amándola is a great place to unwind after a day's hiking. It has an excellent **hostel** in a converted eighteenth-century palazzo, the *Casa per Feria*, Via Indipendenza 73 (☎0736.848.598, ⓦ www.montesibillini.it; €36.15 for a double room; Oct to Easter only open to groups of 15 or more), run by a co-operative and aimed particularly at school parties – but open to individuals too.

Montefortino

A few kilometres south of Amándola, the hill-village of **MONTEFORTINO** is perhaps a prettier base than Amándola, touristy in season and dead quiet out, but less well-served by buses. Primarily a place to wander and admire the Sibillini views, Montefortino also has a small **Pinacoteca** (open on request, ☎0736.859101), whose chief attractions are a polyptych by Alemanno – a follower of the Crivelli who took as much delight in painting embroidery as they did – and an arresting twelfth-century portrait of a man with a pipe and candle emerging from the darkness. Appropriately, given the necromantic traditions of the area, there's also an eighteenth-century painting of Circe with her occult apparatus. There's nowhere **to stay** actually in town, though for a minimum two-night stay there are some small apartments with kitchen on the outskirts: call Signora Sergio (☎0736.859019, ℮agropelloni@libero.it; ❸). If you have a car, however, you can take the road signposted Sanctuaria dell'Ambro, and head 5km west to Località Ambro, where you'll find a cluster of bars and market stalls at the weekend selling delicacies of the region, and two places to stay. The friendly bar-restaurant with rooms, *Peppiné* (☎0736.859.171; ❸), offers simple accommodation and a menu including *tagliatelle casarecce* and lamb *cacciatore* (hunter style), while the *Ambro* (☎0736.859.170; ❺) is a bigger, slightly dour albergo also above a busy bar-restaurant, with a menu which includes pasta with *funghi porcini* and *gorbani* (mountain greens), wild boar, kid and truffles.

Montemonaco and around

A short way south of Montefortino, **MONTEMONACO**, a walled medieval village of cobbled streets and yellow stone houses, is close to some of the Sibillini's most legendary sights. One, the **cave of the sibyl**, whose occupant gave her name to the mountain group (see p.873 for more on sibyls), is a two-hour walk west from the village, though periodic rockfalls can make this a less-than-rewarding excursion. The other, through the **Gola dell'Infernaccio** (Gorge of Hell), southwest of the village, is an easy and spectacular hike in summer. You can take a bus to the Infernaccio fork, from where it's a three-hour walk to the gorge. The approach through a narrow valley is evocative: silent, except for the distant roar of the River Tenna, with memorial plaques on the cliffs at the entrance to commemorate those who've taken the harder way up. The path squeezes its way under jagged rocks, accompanied by the deafening sound of raging water. After a second bridge it forks, the lower path leading to the tranquil source of the Tenna and the upper, more interestingly, in about half an hour, to the **Hermitage of San Leonardo**, occupied by a solitary monk.

Back down in the valley, *Agriturismo La Cittadella* (☎0736.856.361, ⓦwww.cittadelladeisibillini.it; ❸), 2.5km down an unmetalled road from the northern end of Montemonaco, is a congenial place for an overnight stay. For local information call the *comune* at Montemonaco (☎0736.856.141) or the seasonal Pro Loco office on ☎0736.856.411. If you are going to attempt a climb up Monte Sibilla, the *Rifugio Monte Sibilla* (June–Sept Sat & Sun; mid-July to mid-Sept daily; ☎0736.856.422), is the best base. It lies about 6km east of Montemonaco along the path which eventually leads to the cave (see above). As the path is only barely visible you'd be advised to take the Kompass *Monti Sibillini* map.

To do the best of the Sibillini treks, however, you need to drive or take a taxi 8km east from Montemonaco to the quiet village of **FOCE**, where you can stay and eat well in the *Taverna della Montagna* (☎0736.856.327; ❷). There's now also a spot where you can put up a tent or park your camper for a nominal fee at the end of the village: no comforts, but magnificent views. The hike, through the **Valle del Lago di Pilato** and up to the **Lago di Pilato** and **Pizzo di Diavolo** (Devil's Peak), is fairly tough; you'll need the Kompass map, and you shouldn't attempt it at all outside the high summer months and only in good conditions, as the snows don't melt until June. Here, guarding the entrance to Umbria, stands **Monte Vettore** (2477m), the highest of the Sibillini peaks.

According to the legend of the lake, Pilate's body was dispatched from Rome on a cart pulled by two wild oxen, who climbed up into the Sibillini and ditched the corpse in the water here. In the Middle Ages it became a favourite haunt for necromancers seeking dialogues with the devil – stones inscribed with occult symbols have been found on its shores. Deciding they wanted to be rid of the magicians, the local lords one night put soldiers on guard around its shores. Nothing happened until the morning, when the soldiers discovered that the lake had turned red; assuming it was with the devil's blood, they fled. What in fact turned the water red was a mass of minuscule red *Chircephalus marchesonii*, a species of fish indigenous to Asia; a shoal was stranded here millions of years ago when the sea receded, and its descendants still thrive.

Áscoli Piceno and the coast

ÁSCOLI PICENO owes its existence to a woodpecker that led a band of nomadic shepherds to the wedge of land between two rivers on which the city now stands. At least, that's one of the many legends to have grown up around the origins of Áscoli and the Piceni tribe for whom it is named; other versions replace the woodpecker-guide with Diomedes or the son of Saturn, and the nomadic shepherds with veterans of the Trojan War or Greek traders. Whatever the truth, the Piceni were real enough, and the relics of their civilization suggest that they were a pretty emotional and impetuous lot: writing curses on missiles before firing them, gauging the intensity of grief by measuring the volume of tears, and losing a critical battle against the Romans when they interpreted an earthquake as a sign of divine wrath, and abandoned the fight.

Today the Ascolani seem initially to be reserved, as if in obedience to the aphorisms urging moderation, hard work and reticence that are inscribed on many of their houses. However, one taste of the exuberance that fills the central piazza of this good-looking medieval town in the early evening is enough to dispel such an impression. If you come for Mardi Gras, you'll be able to participate in the Marche's most flamboyant carnival, while on the second Saturday in July and first Sunday in August there's the Quintana, a medieval festival that incorporates a spectacular joust.

The Town

The central **Piazza del Popolo**, the stage for the evening *passeggiata*, is the place to get the feel of Áscoli. Paved with gleaming travertine and flanked by Renaissance porticoes, it's the setting for two of the city's finest buildings, the pleasantly jumbled **Palazzo dei Capitani del Popolo** and the refined Romano-Gothic San Francesco. The former dates from the late twelfth century, when the free commune of Áscoli was at its height. That anything of the building has survived is something of a miracle, for in 1535 a certain Giambattista Quieti set it on fire so as to incinerate a rebel barricaded inside. The interior was gutted but enough remained of the facade for a swift facelift to suffice. Rectangular windows were slotted into medieval arches, and a grand portal affixed, on top of which sits a statue to Pope Paul III, who reintroduced peace by replacing Quieti with a neutral outsider. Not that peace lasted long; a few years after the portal had been completed, the Ascolani, finding themselves under the rule of an overbearing papal representative, solved the problem by murdering him in the sacristy of the Duomo.

When they weren't slaughtering each other, at least some of Áscoli's rulers found time to collect public money in order to finance city improvements. The

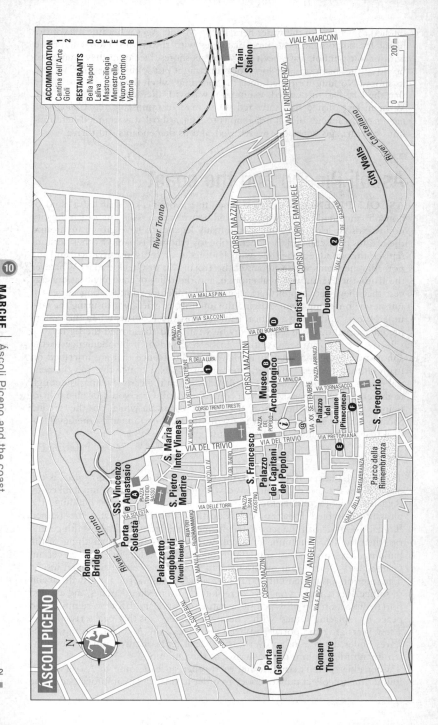

ÁSCOLI PICENO

N

ACCOMMODATION
Cantina dell' Arte 1
Gioli 2

RESTAURANTS
Bella Napoli D
Laliva C
Mastrociliegia F
Menestrello E
Nuovo Grottino A
Vittoria B

Train Station

VIALE MARCONI

0   200 m

City Walls

River Castellano

CORSO MAZZINI

CORSO VITTORIO EMANUELE

VIALE INDIPENDENZA

VIALE ALCIDE DE GASPERI

Duomo

Baptistry

2

VIA DEI BONAPARTE

D

VIA MALASPINA

VIA SACCONI

PIAZZA GIACOMINI

R. DELLA LUPA

VIA DELLE CANTERINE

1

Museo
Archeologico
B

PIAZZA
ARRINGO

V. MINUCIA

VIA TORNASACCO

Palazzo
del
Comune
(Pinacoteca)

F

S. Gregorio

VIA DI VESTA

CORSO TRENTO TRIESTE

V. VIDACILIO

PIAZZA
DEL
POPOLO

i

VIA XX SETTEMBRE

VIA PRETORIANA

E

S. Francesco
Palazzo
dei Capitani
del Popolo

VIA DEL TRIVIO

Parco della
Rimembranza

VIALE DELLA RIMEMBRANZA

VIA DEL TRIVIO

VIA NICOLÒ IV

VOL. TEMPIO

PIAZZA
S.SAN
AGOSTINO

VIA DELLE TORRI

RUA DEI PROGRAMMATICO

S. Pietro
Martire

S. Maria
inter Vineas

SS. Vincenzo
e Anastasio

PIAZZA
VENTIDIO
BASSO

A

Porta
Solesta

VIA SOLESTA

Palazzetto
Longobardi
(Youth Hostel)

RUA MANILA

VIA MANILA

FLOGRAMMATICO

VIA SOFFITTI

River
Tronto

Roman
Bridge

River Tronto

River
Tronto

CORSO MAZZINI

OZZO

VIA DINO ANGELINI

VIA F. RICCI

Porta
Gemina

Roman
Theatre

sixteenth-century **loggias** that enclose the piazza are one of the results – each of a slightly different width, to correspond to the size of the contribution made by the various merchants and shopkeepers who worked there.

The church of **San Francesco**, on the other hand, was financed by the sale of a Franciscan convent outside the city, after Pope Alexander IV had given the Franciscans permission to move within its walls. Construction started in 1258 but wasn't completed until 1549, when the low cupola was added. It's a somewhat restrained church, with little to seize the attention except for the intricate west portal on Via del Trivio, but a good place to cool and calm down after the heat and bustle of Áscoli's narrow streets. Adjoining the south side of the church is the sixteenth-century **Loggia dei Mercanti**, once attributed to Bramante. Formerly the scene of commercial wheeling and dealing, there are still niches cut into the back wall in which bricks could be checked for size before being purchased. The cloister to the north of the church is now also used for commerce as it is the site of a daily market, where the female smallholders who bring in their produce from the countryside could give anyone a lesson in hard-sell. The church's smaller and older cloister is far prettier and remains tranquil, despite having been pressed into service as the garden of a Fascist-era office block.

San Vincenzo and around

Via Trivio continues up towards Piazza Ventidio Basso, the medieval commercial centre of town, of interest for its two churches. **San Vincenzo e San Anastasio** is Áscoli's most distinctive church, with a fifteenth-century chessboard facade that was once filled out with frescoes. Beneath the mainly eleventh-century body of the building is a primitive crypt erected over a spring which was supposed to have leprosy-curing properties. Although the plunge bath is still there, the spring was diverted elsewhere in the last century.

Across the square, **San Pietro Martire** is a far less appealing building, erected by Dominican monks in the thirteenth century in order not to be outdone by their Franciscan rivals down the road. It's as austere and intimidating as Saint Peter the Martyr himself, who, between founding Dominican communities like that at Áscoli, gained such a reputation as a persecutor of religious sects that he became the patron of inquisitors after his murder by a couple of so-called heretics.

The dark **Via Soderini**, leading out of the square, forms the spine of Áscoli's riverside medieval quarter. Lined with buildings out of which the occasional defensive tower sprouts, it's an evocative street, giving you a clear idea of how rigorously the town was defended. Tiny streets fan out from it, many of them spanned by covered passages which in times of siege served as escape routes and as stations from which to pour oil down onto the heads of attackers. Of the defensive tower houses, one of the best preserved is the **Palazzetto Longobardi**, a virtually windowless twelfth-century building, now converted into a youth hostel (see p.705).

After exploring the quarter you can cut through to the river and the thirteenth-century gate, the **Porta Solestà**, from which one of Italy's largest and most impressively preserved **Roman bridges** spans the river. An underpassage tunnels through it, which unfortunately has flooded with water and is currently being restored. When it has been repaired, it's worth making the effort to arrange to have it opened for you at the tourist office, as much for the uncanny experience of walking across an unseen river with traffic crossing just above your head as for the opportunity to examine colossal Roman masonry at close quarters.

To San Gregorio

There's little else of Roman Áscoli to see, except some sparse remains of a **Roman theatre**, on the southwest edge of town, close to the Roman **Porta Gemina**, or twin gate, at the beginning of the road to Rome. From the theatre a road leads up to the **Parco della Rimembranza**, for a great rooftop view of the town, and on to the steep and picturesque **Via Pretoriana**, whose small craft shops make it a good hunting ground for gifts. Close by, the fourteenth-century church of San Gregorio was ingeniously built around the remains of a Roman temple. Incorporated into the facade are two lofty Corinthian columns, originally imported by the Romans from Greece, and patches of *opus reticulatum* (diamond brickwork). In the adjoining convent is a tiny revolving door with the inscription *Qui si depositano gli innocenti* ("Here you deposit the innocent"), designed so that parents could remain anonymous when leaving unwanted children to the care of priests and nuns.

The Duomo, Pinacoteca and Museo Archeologico

With the pregnant caryatids on the facade of the **Palazzo del Comune** overlooked by the pompous **Duomo**, **Piazza Arringo** is a testimony to the flamboyance of Áscoli's Baroque architects. However, as the Duomo shelters what is reckoned to be Carlo Crivelli's best work, and the Palazzo del Comune one of the Marche's best art galleries, the square's eccentric architecture does have its positive side.

In the Duomo's flashy interior, chandeliers are suspended on strings of illuminated beads, the apse is painted with a fake Persian carpet, the pillar capitals and vault ribs are gaudily gilded, and the cupola is painted with late nineteenth-century frescoes of obscure Áscolani saints against a backdrop of impossibly blue skies and feather-mop palm trees. In the midst of this, the **Crivelli polyptych**, in the Cappella del Sacramento, is worth seeking out. Even if his penchant for rarefied opulence isn't to your taste, this work's style and psychological insight are impressive. The most arresting of the ten panels is the central pietà, in which the haggard expression of Mary, the torment that distorts Christ's face, and the Magdalene's horror as she examines the wound in his hand are given heightened impact by the strict semi-circular composition.

The **Pinacoteca Civica** in the Palazzo Comunale (daily 9am–1pm & 3.30–7.30pm; closes half an hour earlier in winter; €5) contains other pieces by Crivelli, and though they are in lousy condition and not as sophisticated as the Duomo's polyptych they are engaging nonetheless. One shows the sprawling baby Christ, chin in hand, apparently mesmerized by an apple. Pietro Alemanno, Crivelli's follower, contributes an *Annunciation* featuring a view of medieval Áscoli bristling with towers, and there are also a few foreign works, most notably a *Portrait of a Woman* by Van Dyck.

If you want to know more about ancient Áscoli, you should also visit the **Museo Archeologico** (Tues–Sun 8.30am–7.30pm; €2), across the square. The collection includes Piceni projectiles inscribed with curses against their Roman enemies, jewellery, heavy bronze rings that were placed on the stomachs of dead women, and small test-tube-like containers used to assess the quality of grief by measuring the volume of tears.

Practicalities

Áscoli's **train station** is just east of the town centre, ten minutes' walk away, left off Viale Indipendenza. The **tourist office** is on the ground floor of the Palazzo dei Capitani del Popolo on Piazza del Popolo (Mon–Fri

8.30am–1.30pm & 3–6.30pm, Sat 9am–1pm & 3–6.30pm, Sun 9am–1pm; ℡0736.253.045, ✉iat.ascolipiceno@regione.marche.it). You're likely to want to stay over, although there are only a couple of **hotels** in the centre and you will certainly need to book in advance. The most affordable option is a **youth hostel**, the *Ostello de' Longobardi*, open all year round and housed in a medieval tower bang in the historic centre at Via Soderini 16 (℡0736.261.862; €11). The two central hotels are the *Cantina dell'Arte*, Rua della Lupa 8 (℡0736.255.620; ❷), with only eleven rooms and its own reasonably priced restaurant, and the smart *Gioli*, Viale de Gasperi 14 (℡0736.255.550; ❻), which caters mostly for the business market. If you have a car, the options widen, as there are some good *agriturismo* places to stay outside town, among them *Villa Cicchi* (℡0736.252272; ❼) on the road to Rosara (2km southwest of Ascoli) and *Le Sorgenti* (℡0736263.725; ❹), a farm keeping goats and making olive oil 7km from town in the hamlet of Lago Castel Trosino. Of the four **Internet points** in Ascoli, *Rinascita Comunicazione*, Piazza Roma 7, has the longest opening hours (Mon 4–8pm, Tues–Thurs 9am–8pm, Fri & Sat 9am–10pm, Sun 10am–1pm & 4–8pm).

You can **eat** quite inexpensively, particularly at the lively *Bella Napoli*, Via Bonaparte 18–20 (closed Sun), off Piazza Arringo, Ascoli's best pizzeria. Ascoli's most imaginative cooking is at *Trattoria Laliva*, Piazza della Viola 13 (closed Tues eve and all day Wed), offering a modern take on Marchegiana cuisine. *Trattoria Nuovo Grottino*, Piazza Ventidio Basso 2 (near the youth hostel), is a popular neighbourhood place with tables outside and offering meaty dishes. Alternatively *Vittoria*, Via dei Bonnacorsi 7 (closed Sun), offers a good-value fixed-price menu at lunchtime and dishes like *fritto misto Ascolana* and fish kebabs. For more refined cuisine, try the *Mastrociliegia*, Via di Vesta 28 (booking advised ℡0736.250.034; closed Sun), a convivial osteria-restaurant with a beamed ceiling and bare brick walls; the wine list is excellent and so is the food, in particular the polenta with boar or hare, gnocchi with butter and sage, tagliatelle with kid, and funghi porcini and truffles. For a **drink**, there are many places to linger over a coffee or a cocktail in Piazza del Popolo. Among them is the famous Art Nouveau-style *Caffè Meletti* which makes its own superb amaro and anisette and is lined with mahogany cases filled with obscure bottles; the old men of Ascoli sit outside and converse on the topics of the day.

The Ascoli coast

Easily accessible by bus or train from Ascoli Piceno, **SAN BENEDETTO DEL TRONTO** is the most extravagant of the Marche's resorts. Known as the "Riviera delle Palme" for the five thousand palms that shade its promenade, and with 6km of sandy white beach, it makes a nice break on a hot afternoon if you're in Ascoli and fancy a swim. There are more exciting resorts in Italy, but if you're determined to stay there are something like 120 **hotels**, details of which are available on the searchable database at ⓦwww.turismo.marche.it or from the **tourist office** on Viale delle Tamerici (Mon–Sat 9am–1pm & 4–7pm, Sun 9am–1pm; ℡0735.592.237, ✉iat.sanbenedetto@regione.marche.it). Note that most places will insist on a full-pension arrangement in August.

GROTTAMARE, a few minutes further up the coastal rail line, is a lower-key resort on the same model, but without San Benedetto's panache. If you have a car head instead the 8km inland to *La Campana*, at Contrada Menocchia 39, near the hill-town of Montefiore d'Aso (℡0734.939.012, ⓦwww.lacampana.it; ❻), an *agriturismo* complex made up of a farm that breeds sheep and alpaca, old stone buildings containing guest rooms with a great swimming pool on a terrace overlooking the Adriatic. The garden catches cooling breezes when the resorts are sweltering on the coast below. Bed and breakfast is available from July to December except from late-July to late-August when full board is obligatory; meals are made from vegetables from their organic garden and meat, cheese and buttermilk from their flock of sheep.

Travel details

Trains

Ancona to: Bologna (33 daily; 1hr 55min–2hr 52min); Jesi (25 daily; 25min); Loreto (24 daily; 20min); Rome (10 daily; 3hr 8min/3hr 53min); Porto S Giorgio (29 daily; 52min); San Benedetto (31 daily; 1hr 14min); Senigállia (10 daily; 24min).
Áscoli Piceno to: San Benedetto del Tronto (11 daily; 40min).
Macerata to: San Severino Marche (18 daily; 30min); Tolentino (18 daily; 20min).
Pésaro to: Ancona (19 daily; 40–50min); Fabriano (20 daily; 2hr 15min); Marotta (every 25 min; 20min); Torrette (every 25 min; 25min).

Buses

(NB much reduced service Sundays and public holidays)
Amándola to: Áscoli Piceno (3 daily; 1hr 10min); Fermo (4 daily; 1hr); Montefortino (5 daily; 25min); Montemonaco (5 daily; 25min); Porto San Giorgio (4 daily; 1hr 15min); Sarnano (7 daily; 30min).
Ancona to: Jesi (8 daily; 30min); Loreto (8 daily Mon–Sat; 1hr 5min); Macerata (6 daily; 1hr 30min); Numana (18 daily, 9 on Sun; 40min); Porto Recanati (5 daily Mon–Sat; 1hr); Senigállia (23 daily; 1hr); Sirolo (18 daily, 9 on Sun; 35min).

Áscoli Piceno to: Amándola (3 daily Mon–Sat; 1hr 10min); Montefortino (3 daily Mon–Sat; 1hr 20min); Montemonaco (3 daily Mon–Sat; 1hr 30min); Rome (5 daily; 3hr); San Benedetto del Tronto (every 30min; hourly on Sun; 1hr).
Macerata to: Amándola (7 daily; 1hr 15min); Ancona (1 daily; 1hr); Abbazia di Fiastra (11 daily; 15min); Loreto (10 daily; 50min); Morrovalle Scalo (hourly; 15min); Porto Recanati (10 daily; 1hr); Recanati (14 daily; 35min); San Severino (5 daily; 35min); Sarnano (11 daily; 55min); Tolentino (12 daily; 30min); Visso (5 daily; 2hr).
Pésaro to: Fabriano (3 daily; 2hr); Fano (roughly every 30min; 15min); Gradara (hourly; 55min); Sassocorvaro (5 daily; 1hr); Torrette (7 daily; 15min); Urbino (22 daily; 50min).
Porto San Giorgio to: Fermo (every 30min; 15min).
San Leo to: Rimini (1 daily; 45min)
Urbino to: Fano (10 daily; 1hr 15min); Pesaro (22 daily; 55min).

International ferries

Ancona to: Cephalonia (April–Oct 1 daily; 16hr 45min); Croatia (summer 4 weekly; winter 3 weekly; 8–9hr); Igoumenitsa (summer at least 1 daily; winter 2–4 weekly; 15hr 30min); Ithaca (April–Oct 4 weekly; 26hr); Patras (at least 1 daily; 19hr); Turkey (May–Oct 1 weekly; 41hr 30min).

Rome and Lazio

CHAPTER 11

Highlights

* **Vatican Museums** Quite simply the largest and richest collection of art and culture in the world. See p.767

* **Capitoline Museums** The august and impressive home of some of Rome's finest ancient sculpture and paintings. See p.726

* **Roman Forum** The heart of ancient Rome. See p.742

* **Pantheon** The most complete ancient Roman structure in the city. See p.729

* **Colosseum** One of ancient Rome's best-known and most impressive monuments. See p.746

* **Piazza Navona** The city's most beautiful square. See p.730

* **Tivoli** The site of Hadrian's villa, as well as many Renaissance residences and their splendid landscaped gardens. See p.784

* **Viterbo** An old medieval town well worth exploring for its Etruscan remains and museums. See p.792

Rome and Lazio

O f all Italy's historic cities, it's perhaps Rome which is the most compelling. There's more to see here than in any other city in the world, with the relics of over two thousand years of habitation packed into its sprawling urban area. You could spend a month here and still only scratch the surface. As a historic place, it is special enough; as a contemporary European capital, it is utterly unique.

Perfectly placed between Italy's North and South, and heartily despised by both, Rome is perhaps the perfect **capital** for a country like Italy. Once the seat of a great empire, and later the home of the papacy, which ruled its dominions from here with a distant and autocratic hand, it's still seen as a place somewhat apart from the rest of Italy, spending money made elsewhere on the corrupt and bloated government machine that runs the country. Romans, the thinking seems to go, are a lazy lot, not to be trusted and living very nicely off the fat of the rest of the land. Even Romans find it hard to disagree with this analysis: in a city of around four million, there are around 600,000 office-workers, compared to an industrial workforce of one sixth of that.

For the traveller, all of this is much less evident than the sheer weight of **history** that the city supports. There are of course the city's classical features, most visibly the Colosseum, and the Forum and Palatine Hill; but from here there's an almost uninterrupted sequence of monuments – from early Christian basilicas, Romanesque churches, Renaissance palaces, right up to the fountains and churches of the Baroque period, which perhaps more than any other era has determined the look of the city today. There is the modern epoch too, from the ponderous Neoclassical architecture of the post-Unification period to the self-publicizing edifices of the Mussolini years. All these various eras crowd in on one another to an almost overwhelming degree: there are medieval churches atop ancient basilicas above Roman palaces; houses and apartment blocks incorporate fragments of eroded Roman columns, carvings and inscriptions; roads and piazzas follow the lines of ancient amphitheatres and stadiums.

Inevitably, Rome is not an easy place to absorb on one visit, and you need to take things slowly, even if you only have a few days here. You can't see everything on your first visit to Rome, and there's no point in even trying. Most of the city's sights can be approached from a variety of directions, and it's part of the city's allure to stumble across things by accident, gradually piecing together the whole, rather than marching around to a timetable on a predetermined route. In any case, it's hard to get anywhere very fast. It's easy to lose a sense of direction in the twisting old streets, and despite regular pledges to ban motor vehicles from the city centre, the congestion can be awful.

Beyond Rome, the region of **Lazio** inevitably pales in comparison, with relatively few centres of note and a landscape that varies from the gently undulating green hills of its northern reaches to the more inhospitable mountains south and east of the capital. It's a fairly poor region, its lack of identity the butt of a number of Italian jokes, and it's the closest you'll get to the feel of the Italian south without catching the train to Naples. Much, however, can be easily seen on a day-trip from the capital, not least the ancient sites of **Ostia Antica** and the Roman Emperor Hadrian's villa at **Tivoli** – two of the area's most important ancient sites. Further afield, in the north of Lazio the Etruscan sites of **Tarquinia** and **Cerveteri** provide the most obvious tourist focus, the slightly gloomy town of **Viterbo** the best base; Romans, meanwhile, head out at weekends to soak up the gentle beauty of lakes **Vico** and **Bolsena**. The region east of Rome is sparsely populated and poor, though scenically appealing, its high hills unfolding beyond the main, rather dull, regional centre of **Rieti**. The south, on the other hand, is the one part of Lazio where you might want to spend a little longer, especially if you're beating a leisurely path to Naples. You can see coastal resorts like **Anzio** and **Nettuno** as a day-trip too, and they make the best places to swim while based in the capital. But the coast beyond demands more attention: resorts like **Terracina** and **Sperlonga** are relatively unknown outside Italy; and islands like **Ponza** one of the loveliest spots, out of season at least, on the entire west coast. Inland, much is mountainous and fairly inaccessible, but that's part of its appeal: the monasteries at **Subiaco** and **Montecassino** are just two worthwhile stops on what might be a rewarding and original route south.

Rome

Rome's early **history** is caked with legend. Rea Silvia, a vestal virgin and daughter of a local king, Numitor, had twin sons – the product, she alleged, of a rape by Mars. They were supposed to be sacrificed to the god but the ritual wasn't carried out, and the two boys were abandoned and found by a wolf, who nursed them until their adoption by a shepherd, who named them **Romulus and Remus**. As they grew into manhood, under the protection of the gods, they became leaders in the small community, and later laid out the boundaries of the city on the Palatine Hill. However, it soon became apparent that there was only room for one ruler, and, unable to agree on the signs given to them by the gods, they quarrelled, Romulus killing Remus and becoming in 753 BC the city's first **monarch**, to be followed by six further kings.

Whatever the truth of this story, there's no doubt that Rome was an obvious spot to build a city: the Palatine and Capitoline hills provided security, and there was, of course, the river Tiber, which could easily be crossed here by way of the Isola Tiberina, making this a key location on the trade routes between Etruria and Campania. Rome as a kingdom lasted until about 507 BC, when the people rose up against the tyrannical King Tarquinius and established a **Republic**, appointing the first two consuls and instituting a more democratic form of government. The city prospered under the Republic, growing greatly in size and subduing the various tribes of the surrounding areas – the **Etruscans** to the north, the **Sabines** to the east, the **Samnites** to the south. By the time it had fought and won the third Punic War against its principal rival, **Carthage**, in 146 BC, it had become the dominant power in the Mediterranean.

The history of the Republic was, however, also one of **internal strife**, marked by factional fighting among the patrician ruling classes, as everyone tried to grab a slice of the riches that were pouring into the city from its plundering expeditions abroad – and the ordinary people, or plebeians, enjoying little more justice than they had under the Roman monarchs. This all came to a head in 44 BC, when **Julius Caesar**, having proclaimed himself dictator, was murdered on 15 March, by conspirators concerned at the growing concentration of power into one man's hands. A brief period of turmoil ensued, giving way, in 27 BC, to the founding of the **Empire** under **Augustus** – a triumph for the new democrats over the old guard. Augustus heaved Rome into the Imperial era: he was determined to turn the city – as he claimed – from one of stone to one of marble, building arches, theatres and monuments of a magnificence suited to the capital of an expanding empire. Under Augustus, and his successors, the city swelled to a population of a million or more, its people housed in cramped apartment blocks or *insulae*; crime in the city was rife, and the traffic problem apparently on a par with today's, leading one contemporary writer to complain that the din on the streets made it impossible to get a good night's sleep. But it was a time of peace and prosperity, the Roman upper classes living a life of indolent luxury, in sumptuous residences with proper plumbing and central heating, and the empire's borders being ever more extended, into other parts of Europe and the Middle East, reaching their maximum limits under the Emperor Trajan, who died in 117 AD. This period constitutes the heyday of the Roman Empire, a time which Gibbon called "the happiest times in the history of humanity".

The **decline of Rome** is hard to date precisely, but it could be said to have started with the Emperor **Diocletian**, who assumed power in 284 and divided the empire into two parts, east and west, while becoming known for his relentless persecution of Christians. The first Christian emperor, **Constantine**, shifted the seat of power to Byzantium in 330, and Rome's heady period as capital of the world was over, the wealthier members of the population moving east and a series of invasions by Goths in 410 and Vandals about forty years later only serving to quicken the city's ruin. By the sixth century the city was a devastated and infection-ridden shadow of its former self.

After the fall of the empire, the pope – who was based in Rome owing to the fact that St Peter (the Apostle and first pope) was martyred here in 64 AD – became the temporal ruler over much of Italy, and it was the papacy, under Pope **Gregory I** ("the Great") in 590, that rescued Rome from its demise. In an eerie echo of the empire, Gregory sent missions all over Europe to spread the word of the Church and publicize its holy relics, so drawing pilgrims, and their money, back to the city, and in time making the papacy the natural authority in Rome. The pope took the name "Pontifex Maximus" after the title of the high priest of classical times (literally "the keeper of the bridges", which were vital to the city's well-being). The crowning a couple of centuries later of Charlemagne as Holy Roman Emperor, with dominions spread Europe-wide but answerable to the pope, intensified the city's revival, and the pope and city became recognized as head of the Christian world.

There were times over the next few hundred years when the power of Rome and the papacy was weakened: Robert Guiscard, the Norman king, sacked the city in 1084; a century later, a dispute between the city and the papacy led to a series of popes relocating to Viterbo; and in 1308 the French-born Pope **Clement V** transferred his court to Avignon. In the mid-fourteenth century, Cola di Rienzo seized power, setting himself up as the people's saviour from the decadent ways of the city's rulers and forming a new Roman republic. But the increasingly autocratic ways of the new ruler soon lost popularity; Cola di Rienzo was deposed, and in 1376 Pope **Gregory XI** returned to Rome. As time went on, power gradually became concentrated in a handful of **families**, who swapped the top jobs, including the papacy itself, between them. Under the burgeoning power of the pope, the city began to take on a new aspect: churches were built, the city's pagan monuments rediscovered and preserved, and artists began to arrive in Rome to work on commissions for the latest pope, who would invariably try to outdo his predecessor's efforts with ever more glorious self-aggrandizing buildings and works of art. This process reached a head during the **Renaissance**; Bramante, Raphael and Michelangelo all worked in the city, on and off, throughout their careers. The reigns of Pope

Julius II, and his successor, **Leo X**, were something of a golden age: the city was once again the centre of cultural and artistic life, and site of the creation of great works of art like Michelangelo's frescoes in the Sistine Chapel, Raphael's *Stanze* in the Vatican Palace and fine buildings like the Villa Farnesina, Palazzo Farnese and Palazzo Spada, not to mention the commissioning of a new St Peter's. However, in 1527 all this was brought abruptly to an end, when the armies of the Habsburg monarch, Charles V, swept into the city, occupying it – and wreaking havoc – for a year, while Pope **Clement VII** cowered in the Castel Sant'Angelo.

The ensuing years were ones of yet more restoration, and perhaps because of this it's the **seventeenth century** that has left the most tangible impression on Rome today, the vigour of the **Counter-Reformation** throwing up huge sensational monuments like the Gesù church that were designed to confound the scepticism of the new Protestant thinking. This period also saw the completion of St Peter's under **Paul V**, and the ascendancy of Gian Lorenzo Bernini as the city's principal architect and sculptor under the Barberini pope, **Urban VIII** – a patronage that was extended under the Pamphili pope, **Innocent X**.

The **eighteenth century** saw the decline of the papacy as a political force, a phenomenon marked by the occupation of the city in 1798 by Napoleon; **Pius VI** was unceremoniously sent off to France as a prisoner, and Napoleon declared another Roman republic, with himself at its head, which lasted until 1815, when papal rule was restored. Thirty-four years later a pro-Unification caucus under **Mazzini** declared the city a republic but was soon chased out, and Rome had to wait until **Garibaldi** stormed the walls in 1870 to join the unified country – symbolically the most important part of the Italian peninsula to do so. "Roma o morte", Garibaldi had cried, and he wasted no time in declaring the city the capital of the new kingdom – under **Vittorio Emanuele II** – and confining the by now quite powerless pontiff, **Pius IX**, to the Vatican until agreement was reached on a way to coexist.

The Piemontese rulers of the new kingdom set about building a city fit to govern from, cutting new streets through Rome's central core (Via Nazionale, Via del Tritone) and constructing grandiose buildings like the Altar of the Nation. **Mussolini** took over Rome in 1922, and in 1929 signed the **Lateran Pact** with Pope **Pius XI**, a compromise which forced the Vatican to accept the new Italian state and in return recognized the Vatican City as sovereign territory, independent of Italy, together with the key basilicas and papal palaces in Rome, which remain technically independent of Italy to this day. Mussolini's motivations weren't dissimilar to the popes, however, when he bulldozed his way through the Roman Forum and began work on the futuristic, self-publicizing planned extension to the city known as EUR.

Since **World War II**, Italy has become renowned as a country which changes its government, if not its politicians, every few months, and for the rest of Italy Rome has come to symbolize the inertia of their nation's government – at odds with both the wealthy north and the poor south. Despite this, the city's growth has been phenomenal in the post-war years, its population soaring to close on four million. Though famous in the **Sixties** as the home of Fellini's *Dolce Vita* and Italy's bright young things, Rome is still, even by Italian standards, a relatively provincial place, and one which is in some ways still trying to lug itself into the twenty-first century. Great efforts were, however, made to prepare the city for the arrival of the Millennium, and the city is looking better than ever. In many ways there has never been a better time to visit Rome.

Arrival, city transport and information

Rome has two **airports**: Leonardo da Vinci, better known simply as Fiumicino, which handles most scheduled flights, and Ciampino, where you'll arrive if you're travelling on a charter, or with one of the low-cost European airlines. **Taxis** to the city centre from either airport cost around €45, more at night, and take 30–45 minutes; they're worth considering if you are in a group but otherwise the public transport connections are reasonable. Beware of unlicensed taxis operating in the area – a number of visitors have been badly ripped

TRAINS AND METRO

Metro A
Metro B
F.S. line

TO VITERBO
TO ORTE

LA GIUSTINIANA
PRIMA PORTA
LA CELSA
LABARO
CENTRO RAI
SAXA RUBRA
GROTTA ROSSA
DUE PONTI
TOR DI QUINTO

FARA SABINA
PIANA BELLA DI MONTELIBRETTI
MONTEROTONDO
SETTEBAGNI
FIDENE
NUOVO SALARIO

TO VITERBO
OTTAVIA
S. FILIPPO NERI
MONTE MARIO
PINETA SACCHETTI
TO GROSETTO
BALDUINO

River Tiber
MONTE ANTENNE
CAMPI SPORTIVI
ACQUA ACETOSA
EUCLIDE

FREGENE
AURELIA
CIPRO-MUSEI VATICANI
OTTAVIANO S. PIETRO
VALLE AURELIA
FLAMINIO
SPAGNA
BARBERINI
BOLOGNA

REBIBBIA
River Aniene
NOMENTANA
F.S. TIBURTINA
QUINTILIANI
PONTE MAMMOLO
S. MARIA DEL SOCCORSO
PIETRALATA
MONTI TIBURTINI

F.S. SAN PIETRO
LEPANTO
REPUBBLICA
POLICLINICO
CASTRO PRETORIO
TERMINI
LAZIALI
PORTA MAGGIORE
TOR SAPIENZA
PRENESTINA
TO TIVOLI & SULMONA

CAVOUR
COLOSSEO
VITTORIO
MANZONI
LODI
ALESSI

F.S. TRASTEVERE
VILLA BONELLI
MAGLIANA
MURATELLA
MURATELRIA
PONTE GALERIA

CIRCO MASSIMO
PIRAMIDE/ LIDO DI OSTIA
F.S. OSTIENSE
GARBATELLA
SAN PAOLO
MARCONI
MAGLIANA

S. GIOVANNI
RE DI ROMA
PONTELUNGO
F.S. TUSCOLANA
FURIO CAMILLO
COLLI ALBANI
A. TRAVERTINO
PORTA FURBA
N. QUADRATO
LUCIO SESTIO
G. AGRICOLA
SUBAUGUSTA
CINECITTA

TOR PIGNATTARA
CENTOCELLE
TOGLIATTI
TORRE SPACATA
PANTANO
TORRE MAURA
GIARDINETTI
TORRE NOVA
TORRE ANGELA
TORRE GAIA
GROTTE CELONI
BORGHESIANA
FINOCCHIO

EUR PALASPORT
EUR FERMI
LAURENTINA
ANAGNINA

AEROPORTO FIUMICINO
FIUMICINO CITTA
TOR DI VALLE
VITINIA
CAS. BERNOCCHI
ACILIA
OSTIA ANTICA
LIDO CENTRO
STELLA POLARE
CAST. FUSANO
C. COLOMBO

TORRICOLA
CAPANNELLE
CIAMPINO

TO NETTUNO
TO VELLETRI
TO ALBANO LAZIALE

off and have even had luggage stolen. You can recognize licensed taxis by their taxi light and City of Rome logo with a serial number on the side of the car.

Fiumicino is connected to the centre of Rome by direct trains, which take thirty minutes to get to Termini and cost €8.50; services begin at 7.37am, and then leave hourly from 8.07am until 10.07pm. Alternatively, there are more frequent trains to Trastevere, Ostiense and Tiburtina stations, each on the edge of the city centre, roughly every twenty minutes from 6.27am to 11.27pm; tickets to these stations cost €4.50 and Tiburtina and Ostiense are just a short metro ride from Termini, making it a much cheaper (and not necessarily slower) journey; or you can catch city bus #175 from Ostiense, or city bus #492 or #649 from Tiburtina, to the centre of town. These cheaper alternatives do inevitably, however, involve more bag-hauling.

There are no direct connections between the city centre and **Ciampino**. Hourly buses run from the airport to the Anagnina metro station, at the end of line A – a thirty-minute journey (€1.20), from where it's a twenty-minute ride into the centre. Failing that, you can take a bus from the airport to Ciampino overground train station, a ten-minute journey, and then take a train into Termini, which is a further twenty minutes (€2.50). The airline Go, incidentally, lays on a bus to Piazza Santa Maria Maggiore, half an hour after the arrival of each of its flights, but it's no quicker and it costs €10.40 one-way.

Travelling by **train** from most places in Italy, or indeed Europe, you arrive at **Stazione Termini**, centrally placed for all parts of the city and meeting-point of the two metro lines and many city-bus routes. There's a **left-luggage** facility here (daily 5.15am–midnight; €2.40 per piece every 12hr). Among **other train stations** in Rome, Tiburtina is a stop for some north–south intercity trains; selected routes around Lazio are handled by the Regionali platforms of Stazione Termini (a further five-minute walk beyond the end of the regular platforms); and there's also the COTRAL urban train station on Piazzale Flaminio, which runs to La Giustiniana – the so-called Roma-Nord line.

Arriving by **bus** can leave you in any one of a number of places around the city. The main stations include Ponte Mammolo (trains from Tivoli and Subiaco); Lepanto (Cerveteri, Civitavecchia area); EUR Fermi (Nettuno, Anzio, southern Lazio coast); Anagnina (Castelli Romani); Saxa Rubra (Viterbo and around). All of these stations are on a metro line, except Saxa Rubra, which is on the Roma-Nord line and connected by trains every fifteen minutes with the station at Piazzale Flaminio, on metro line A. Eurolines buses from outside Italy terminate on Piazza della Repubblica.

Coming into the city by **road** can be quite confusing. If you are on the A1 highway coming from the north take the exit "Roma Nord"; from the south, follow exit "Roma Est". Both lead you to the Grande Raccordo Anulare, which circles the city and is connected with all of the major arteries into the city centre – the Via Cassia from the north, Via Salaria from the northeast, Via

Line #110

Good for general orientation and a quick glance at the sights is the ATAC-run #110 tour bus with guided commentary. It leaves from Piazza Cinquecento outside Stazione Termini and stops at all the major sights, including Piazza di Spagna, Castel Sant'Angelo, the Vatican and Appia Antica. The whole round trip takes about three hours. In summer, departures are every half hour from 9am until 8pm daily, including holidays and Sundays. Tickets for a single journey cost €7.75, or you can buy a day pass for €12.91 which allows you to hop and off throughout the day.

Tiburtina or Via Nomentana from the east, Via Appia Nuova and the Pontina from the south, Via Prenestina and Via Casilina from the southeast, or Via Cristoforo Colombo from the southwest, and Via Aurelia from the northwest.

City transport

Like most Italian cities, even the larger ones, the best way to get around Rome is to **walk**. That said, its **bus service**, run by ATAC, is, on the whole, a good one – cheap, reliable and as quick as the clogged streets allow. There are also four **tram** lines, including the brand-new and relatively fast #8 which runs from Viale Trastevere to Largo Argentina.

Rome's **metro** operates from 5.30am to 11.30pm, though it's not as useful as you might think, since its two lines cater more for commuters from the suburbs than tourists in the city centre. Nonetheless, there are a few useful city-centre stations: Termini is the hub of both lines, and there are stops at the Colosseum, Piazza Barberini and Spanish Steps.

When the buses and the metro stop – at around midnight – a network of **night buses** click into service, accessing most parts of the city and operating through to about 5am; they are easily identified by the owl symbol above the "*bus notturno*" schedule. They normally have conductors, so you can buy a ticket on board (though it may be worth keeping spare tickets handy just in case).

Flat-fare **tickets** on all forms of transport currently cost €1 each and are good for any number of bus rides and one metro ride within 75 minutes of validating them – bus tickets should be validated in machines on board the bus. You can buy tickets from *tabacchi*, newsstands and ticket machines located in all metro stations and at major bus stops. If you're using transport extensively it's worth getting a **day pass**, valid on all city transport until midnight of the day purchased, for €3.10, or a **seven-day pass** for €12.40.

⑪

Useful transport routes

Buses

#23 Piazza Clodio–Piazza Risorgimento–Ponte Vittorio Emanuele II–Ponte Garibaldi–Via Marmorata–Piazzale Ostiense–Basilica di S. Paolo.

#40 Termini, Via Nazionale, Piazza Venezia, Corso Vittorio Emanuele II, Piazza Pia.

#64 Termini–Piazza della Repubblica–Via Nazionale–Piazza Venezia–Corso Vittorio Emanuele II–Stazione S. Pietro.

#492 Stazione Tiburtina–Termini–Piazza Barberini–Via del Corso–Piazza Venezia–Largo Argentina–Corso del Rinascimento–Piazza Cavour–Piazza Risorgimento.

#660 Largo Colli Albani–Via Appia Nuova–Via Appia Antica.

#714 Termini–Santa Maria Maggiore–San Giovanni in Laterano–Baths of Caracalla–EUR.

#910 Termini–Piazza della Repubblica–Via Piedmonte–Via Pinciana (Villa Borghese)–Piazza Euclide–Palazzetto dello Sport–Piazza Mancini.

Trams

#3 Stazione Trastevere, Piramide, Colosseum, S. Giovanni, Sta Croce, Porta Maggiore, Largo Thorwaldsen.

#8 Viale Trastevere–Largo Argentina.

#19 Porto Maggiore–Viale Regina Margherita–Viale Belle Arti–Ottaviano–Piazza Risorgimento.

#30 Piramide–Viale Aventino–Colosseum–San Giovanni–Viale Regina Margherita–Villa Giulia.

The easiest way to get a **taxi** is to find the nearest taxi stand (*fermata dei taxi*) – central ones include Termini, Piazza Venezia, Piazza San Silvestro, Piazza di Spagna and Piazza Barberini. Alternatively, taxis can be radio-paged (☎06.3570, 06.4994, 06.4157 or 06.5551), though these usually cost more, as the meter starts ticking the moment the taxi is dispatched to collect you. Only take licensed yellow or white cabs and make sure the meter is switched on. To give you a rough idea of what you can expect to pay, a journey from one side of the city centre to the other will cost around €7 – the supplement after 10pm is €2.75 and €1 extra is added to every trip on a Sunday. Note that all taxis carry a rate card in English giving the current tariff.

Information

There are **tourist information booths** at Fiumicino (daily 8.15am–7.15pm; ☎06.6595.6074) and at Termini (daily 8.15am–7.15pm; ☎06.487.1270), although the long queues that often develop at both of these mean you're usually better off heading straight for the main **tourist office** at Via Parigi 5 (Mon–Fri 8.15am–7.15pm, Sat 8.15am–1.45pm; ☎06.4889.9253 or 06.4889.9255), five minutes' walk from Termini. They have free maps that should – together with our own – be ample for finding your way around.

There are also **information kiosks** (see box below) in key locations around the city centre (daily 9am–6pm) that are useful for free maps, directions (the staff usually speak English) and details about nearby sights. Another good source of information is the privately run **Enjoy Rome**, Via Varese 39 (Mon–Fri 8.30am–2pm & 3.30–6pm, Sat 8.30am–2pm; ☎06.445.1843), whose friendly, English-speaking staff operate a free room-finding service; they also organize tours and have a left-luggage service for customers. Their information is often more up-to-date and reliable than that handed out by the various tourist offices.

For what's-on information, the city's best source of **listings** is perhaps *Roma c'è* (€1.20, Thursdays), which has a helpful section in English giving information on tours, clubs, restaurants, services and weekly events. The English expat bi-weekly, *Wanted in Rome* (€1, every other Wednesday), is also a useful source of information, especially if you're looking for an apartment or work. For those with a bit of Italian, there's *Time Out Roma* (€1.20; Thursdays), a weekly review full of listings as well as articles on the trendiest everything in Rome; and the daily arts pages of the Rome **newspaper**, *Il Messaggero*, listing movies, plays and major musical events. The newspaper *La Repubblica* also includes the "Trova Roma" section in its Thursday edition, another handy guide to current offerings. All of these publications are available from newsstands all over the city.

Information kiosks

Spanish Steps Largo Goldoni ☎06.6813.6061.
San Giovanni Piazza San Giovanni in Laterano ☎06.7720.3535.
Via Nazionale Palazzo delle Esposizioni ☎06.4782.4525.
Piazza Navona Piazza delle Cinque Lune ☎06.6880.9240.
Castel Sant'Angelo Piazza Pia ☎06.6880.9707.
Forum Piazza del Tempio della Pace ☎06.6992.4307.
Trastevere Piazza Sonnino ☎06.5833.3457.
Santa Maria Maggiore Via del'Olmata ☎06.4788.0294.

Accommodation

As you might expect, there is plenty of **accommodation** in Rome, and for much of the year you can usually expect to find something, although it's always worth booking in advance, especially when the city is at its busiest – from Easter to the end of October, and over the Christmas period. If you haven't booked, the Enjoy Rome office (see p.717) is your best bet; or try the Free Hotel Reservation Service (daily 7am–10pm; ☎06.699.1000), where multilingual staff will check out vacancies for you. The rooms offered by touts at Termini are rarely a good deal, and can often be rather dodgy; be sure you establish the (full) price beforehand, in writing if necessary, and only use them as a last resort.

Hotels and pensions

Many of the city's cheaper places are located conveniently close to **Termini**, and you could do worse than hole up in one of these, so long as you can tolerate the seediness of the district. The streets both sides of the station – Via Amendola, Via Principe Amedeo, Via Marghera, Via Magenta, Via Palestro – are stacked full of bargain hotels, and some buildings have several pensions to choose from, though you should be somewhat circumspect in the streets to the southwest of the station, parts of which can be a little *too* unsavoury, especially for women travelling alone. If you want to stay somewhere more central and picturesque, go for one of the many hotels in the **centro storico**, some of them not that expensive, but they fill quickly – it's best to phone in advance before heading down there. For more luxury surroundings, the area **east of Via del Corso**, towards Via Veneto and around the Spanish Steps is the city's prime hunting ground for beautiful, upscale accommodation – although there are a few affordable options close by Piazza Spagna. Consider also staying across the river in **Prati**, a pleasant neighbourhood, nicely distanced from the hubbub of the city centre proper, and handy for the Vatican and St Peter's, or in the lively streets of **Trastevere**, again on the west side of the river but an easy walk into the centre of town.

Centro Storico and east of Via del Corso

Abruzzi Piazza della Rotonda 69 ☎06.679.2021. Bang in front of the Pantheon, and as such you pay for the location. Rooms are clean but very simple, all with wash basins but none with private baths. No credit cards. Bus #64 or #492. ❹

Arenula Via S. Maria de'Calderari 47 ☎06.687.9454, ℱ06.689.6188, ⓦwww.hotel.arenula@ flashnet.it. Simple, clean rooms, each with their own bath, TV and telephone. A great location, just a few minutes' walk from Trastevere, the Jewish Ghetto and Campo de' Fiori. Bus #H or #63. ❻

Campo de' Fiori Via del Biscione 6 ☎06.6880.6865, ℱ06.687.6003, ⓦwww.hotel-campodefiori.com. A friendly place in a great location close to Campo de' Fiori. Rooms come in all shapes and colours but are clean and pleasant. After six floors of stairs there are some great views to be had from their large roof terrace. Bus #64 or #492. ❺

Della Lunetta Piazza del Paradiso 68 ☎06.686.1080, ℱ06.689.2028. An unspectacular hotel, but in a nice location close to Campo de' Fiori. Simple, smallish rooms. No breakfast. Bus #64 or #492. ❹

Eradelli Via due Macelli 28 ☎06.679.1265. A rather plain hotel with no-frills rooms, but well priced for its location just up the street from the Spanish Steps. Metro A Spagna. ❹

Firenze Via due Macelli 106 ☎06.679.7240, ℱ06.785.636. Just up the street from *Eradelli*, this recently renovated hotel is a bit more expensive but is worth it for its smart new rooms. Metro A Spagna. ❻

Grand Hotel Plaza Via del Corso 126 ☎06.6992.1111, ℱ06.6994.1575, ⓦwww.hotelplazarome.com. There's a wonderful early 1900s atmosphere to this hotel: its lobby and

main bar are worth cropping into just to admire its glorious gilded and frescoed ceilings; the rooms are a little more faded, but still very comfortable, and for the location the rates are about as low as you could reasonably expect. Metro A Spagna. **❾**
Julia Via Rasella 29 ☎06.488.1637, ⓕ06.481.7044, ⓦwww.hoteljulia.it. Absolutely charming three-star hotel with 33 rooms all with direct (ISDN) hook-ups for Internet just a few steps from Palazzo Barberini. Metro A Barberini. **❼**
Margutta Via Laurina 34 ☎06.322.3674, ⓕ06.320.0395. Popular hotel handily located in the Corso/Piazza del Popolo shopping area. Three rooms have tiny private balconies. Reserve well ahead. Metro A Spagna. **❺**
Navona Via dei Sediari 8 ☎06.686.4203, ⓕ06.6880.3802. Completely renovated *pensione*-turned-hotel in a building that dates back to the first century AD. Very close to Piazza Navona and run by a friendly Italian-Australian couple. No credit cards; a/c available for €15.49 extra a night. Bus #64 or #492. **❺**
Primavera Piazza San Pantaleo 3 ☎ & ⓕ06.6880.3109. Worth it for the location alone – a grand building with a peaceful courtyard, a world away from the noisy square outside. Its simple rooms, overlooking Corso Vittorio Emanuele, are a couple of minutes' walk away from both Piazza Navona and Campo de' Fiori. Bus #64. **❺**
Santa Chiara Via di Santa Chiara 21 ☎06.687.2979, ⓕ06.687.3144. A friendly, family-run hotel in a great location, on a quiet piazza behind the Pantheon. Nice rooms too, hard to beat for the price, which includes breakfast. Bus #64 or #492. **❽**
Smeraldo Vicolo dei Chiodaroli 9 ☎06.687.5929, ⓕ06.6880.5495. Clean and comfortable hotel with a modern interior. All rooms have been recently renovated, with shiny new baths, televisions and a/c. Breakfast not included in the price. Bus #64. **❺**
Sole Via del Biscione 76 ☎06.687.9446, ⓕ06.689.3787. Almost overlooking Piazza del Campo de' Fiori, this place has pleasant rooms with televisions and phones, and a lovely, view-laden roof terrace. No breakfast, no credit cards. Bus #64. **❻**
Zanardelli Via G. Zanardelli 7 ☎06.6821.1392, ⓕ06.6880.3802. A new hotel run by the same family as the *Navona* – to which it is a more lavish alternative. Located just north of Piazza Navona, the building used to be a papal residence and has many original fixtures and furnishings. The rooms are elegant, with antique iron beds, silk-lined walls, and all modern amenities. Bus #70. **❼**

Termini and around

Hotel des Artistes Via Villafranca 20 ☎06.445.4365, ⓕ06.446.2368, ⓦwww.hoteldesartistes.com. One of the better hotels in the Termini area. Exceptionally good value, spotlessly clean, with a breezy roof terrace and Internet access. Also has dorm beds for €20. Metro B Castro Pretorio. **❺**
Astoria Garden Via Bachelet 8 ☎06.446.9908, ⓕ06.445.3329. In a peaceful area east of Termini, a newly renovated hotel that was once the home of an Italian count. Rooms are pleasant, quiet and some have balconies. Metro Termini. **❺**
Casa Kolbe Via di San Teodoro 44 ☎06.679.4974, ⓕ06.6994.1550. In a quiet location not far from the Colosseum, this is a favourite with students and tour groups. Its rooms are simple, clean, and good value for the location. Metro B Colosseo. **❹**
Residenza Cellini Via Modena 5 ☎06.47.82.52.04, ⓕ06.47.88.18.06, ⓔresidenzacellini@tin.it. A splendid, very small (6 rooms) hotel in the centre of everything, very close to Piazza Repubblica. Metro A Repubblica. **❽**
Cervia Via Palestro 55 ☎06.491.057, ⓕ06.491.056, ⓔhotelcervia@wnt.it. Pleasant rooms in a lively *pensione* in the same building as the *Restivo* (see below). If you don't mind lugging your bags a few more steps, ask for the discounted rooms on the third floor. Metro B Castro Pretorio. **❹**
Elide Via Firenze 50 ☎06.474.1367, ⓕ06.4890.4318. A *pensione* for the last fifty years, with clean, simple rooms and a friendly staff, a few minutes from Piazza della Repubblica. Metro A Repubblica. **❸**
Fawlty Towers Via Magenta 39 ☎06.445.4802. Playfully named accommodation, owned by the people who run Enjoy Rome, this place has both dorm beds (€18) and clean, comfortable rooms, some with private bath. There's a communal kitchen, Internet access and a pleasant roof terrace. Metro Termini. **❹**
Katty Via Palestro 35 ☎06.490 079, ⓕ06.444.1216. A good-value *pensione* located in one of the nicer buildings on the east side of Termini. Rooms are quite pleasant and some have shiny new bathrooms. If you want to spend a bit extra, go up a floor to *Katty 2*, where all rooms have private baths, minibar, TV, phone and a/c. Metro B Castro Pretorio. **❸–❹**
Marsala Via Marsala 36 ☎06.444.1262, ⓕ06.441.397. Handily situated two-star hotel 50m east of the station. Very clean, good-value rooms, and a friendly English-speaking staff. Metro Termini. **❹**

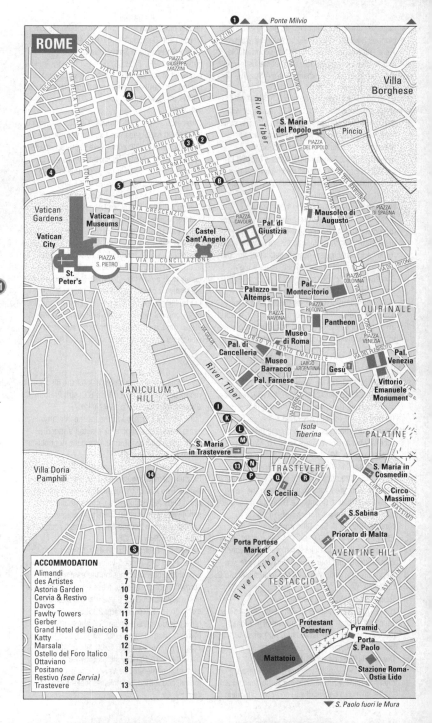

ROME

Ponte Milvio

Villa Borghese

Villa Doria Pamphili

JANICULUM HILL

Vatican Gardens

Vatican City

Vatican Museums

St. Peter's

PIAZZA S. PIETRO

Castel Sant'Angelo

Pal. di Giustizia

Pal. di Conciliazione

Mausoleo di Augusto

S. Maria del Popolo

Pincio

PIAZZA DEL POPOLO

Palazzo Altemps

Pal. Montecitorio

Pantheon

Museo di Roma

Pal. di Cancelleria

Museo Barracco

Pal. Farnese

Gesù

Pal. Venezia

Vittorio Emanuele Monument

S. Maria in Trastevere

TRASTEVERE

S. Cecilia

Isola Tiberina

PALATINE

S. Maria in Cosmedin

Circo Massimo

S.Sabina

Priorato di Malta

AVENTINE HILL

Porta Portese Market

TESTACCIO

Protestant Cemetery

Pyramid

Porta S. Paolo

Mattatoio

Stazione Roma-Ostia Lido

S. Paolo fuori le Mura

ACCOMMODATION

Alimandi	4
des Artistes	7
Astoria Garden	10
Cervia & Restivo	9
Davos	2
Fawlty Towers	11
Gerber	3
Grand Hotel del Gianicolo	14
Katty	6
Marsala	12
Ostello del Foro Italico	1
Ottaviano	5
Positano	8
Restivo (see Cervia)	
Trastevere	13

RESTAURANTS

Africa	C
Asinocotto	R
Baia Chia	J
Casetta de' Trastevere	M
Il Dito e la Luna	H
Formula 1	G
La Grotta Azzura	B
L'Insalatiera 2	A
Ivo	P
Magna Roma	O
Ai Marmi	O
Monzù Vladi	K
Da Paris	N
Il Podista	D
Dar Poeta	L
Pommicoro	F
Romolo	I
Tram Tram	E
Il Vascello	S

0   200 m

Positano Via Palestro 49 ☎ 06.490.360, ⓕ 06.446.9101, ⓔ hotposit@tin.it. Not glamorous, but certainly reasonably priced, with comfortable rooms two minutes' walk from Termini. Helpful management too. Metro Termini. ❷

Restivo Via Palestro 55 ☎ 06.446.2172. Spotless rooms in a small *pensione* run by a sweet old lady. She stays up until all guests are safely back home, so it's best avoided if you're planning to party into the small hours. No private bathrooms. Metro B Castro Pretorio. ❸

Rosetta Via Cavour 295 ☎ & ⓕ 06.4782.3069. Family-run *pensione* in a nice location very close to the Colosseum. The small rooms are a bit shabby, but they're comfortable enough, and have private baths, TV, and telephone. No breakfast. Metro B Colosseo. ❹

Across the river: Trastevere and the Vatican

Alimandi Via Tunisi 8 ☎ 06.3972.3948, ⓕ 06.3972.3943. Close to the Vatican, this place boasts friendly staff, a roof-top garden, and nicely furnished, good-value doubles, all with telephone and TV. Metro A Ottaviano. ❻

Arcangelo Via Boezio 15 ☎ 06.687.4143, ⓕ 06.689.3050. Clean, reliable hotel, with comfortable rooms in a quiet street not far from the Vatican. Metro A Ottaviano. ❺

Colors Via Boezio 31 ☎ & ⓕ 06.687.4030. Run by the people from Enjoy Rome, this is a smaller version of their popular *Fawlty Towers*, a hostel/hotel in a quiet neighbourhood near the Vatican. Both dorm beds (€18) and private rooms are available. Everyone is very friendly, and there are kitchen facilities, a lounge with satellite TV, and a small terrace. Metro A Ottaviano. ❹

Davos Via degli Scipioni 239 ☎ 06.321.7012, ⓕ 06.323.0367. Simple, affordable *pensione* on a quiet street not far from the Vatican. Rooms are clean and quite basic, but all except one has a private bath. No credit cards. Metro A Lepanto. ❹

Gerber Via degli Scipioni 241 ☎ 06.321.6485, ⓕ 06.322.1001. A friendly staff and elegant comfortable rooms make this hotel great value for its convenient location on a quiet street not far from the Vatican. Even better, they give a 10 percent discount to *Rough Guide* readers. Metro A Lepanto. ❻

Ottaviano Via Ottaviano 6 ☎ 06.3973.8138, ⓦ www.pensioneottaviano.com. A simple *pensione*-cum-hostel near to the Vatican that is very popular with the backpacking crowd; book well in advance. No private bathrooms. Metro A Ottaviano. Dorm beds €18; rooms ❷

Trastevere Via Luciano Manara 24a/25 ☎ 06.581.4713, ⓕ 06.588.1016. The place to come if you want to be in the heart of Trastevere, with all new furnishings, terracotta floors, and newly installed bathrooms in every room. They also have apartments with kitchens. Bus #H or #63. ❹

Hostels, convents and student accommodation

Nostra Signora di Lourdes Via Sistina 113 ☎ 06.474.5324. A swankily located convent – just a few minutes' walk from the Spanish Steps – with singles and doubles for women or married couples who can put up with a 10.30pm curfew. Bus #175. No en-suites; €30 per person.

Ostello del Foro Italico Viale delle Olimpiadi 61 ☎ 06.324.2571. Rome's official HI hostel, though not particularly central or easy to get to from Termini. You can call ahead to check out availability, but they won't take bookings – of any kind, and staff are not especially helpful. Midnight curfew. Metro A to Ottaviano, then bus #32 to the hostel – ask the driver for the "*ostello*". €15 including breakfast.

Sandy Via Cavour 136 ☎ 06.488.4585. Run by the same folk as the *Ottaviano*, but with dormitories only. No breakfast. Metro B Cavour. €18 per person.

Suore Pie Operaie Via di Torre Argentina 76 ☎ 06.686.1254. For women only, this place offers the cheapest beds in the city centre, although you need to book well in advance and there's a 10.30pm curfew. Closed Aug. Bus #64. €16 per person.

YWCA Via C. Balbo 4 ☎ 06.488.0460, ⓕ 06.487.1028. Though only open to women and married couples, this is more conveniently situated than the HI hostel, just ten minutes' walk from Termini. Singles, doubles, and three-bedded rooms; all rooms include breakfast except Sun mornings and August. Midnight curfew. Metro Termini. €26–74.

Camping

All Rome's **campsites** are some way out of the city, and, although easy enough to get to, they are not especially cheap. The closest site is *Camping Flaminio*, 8km north of the centre on Via Flaminia Nuova (€8.50 plus €6.75 per person; ☎06.333.2604; take bus #910 to Piazza Mancini, then transfer to bus #200 (ask the driver to drop you at the "fermata più vicina al campeggio"; March–Oct). *Camping Tiber*, on Via Tiberina at Km1400 (€8.50 plus €6.75 per person; ☎06.3361.2314; March–Oct), is another good bet – right beside the Tiber, quiet, spacious and friendly, with a bar/pizzeria, a swimming pool and really hot showers. It has a free shuttle service (every 30min) to and from the nearby Prima Porta station, where you can catch the Roma-Nord service to Piazzale Flaminio (about 20min).

The City

Rome's **city centre** is divided neatly into distinct blocks. The warren of streets that makes up the **centro storico** occupies the hook of land on the left bank of the River Tiber, bordered to the east by Via del Corso and to the north and south by water. From here Rome's central core spreads east across Via del Corso to the major shopping streets and alleys around the **Spanish Steps** down to the main artery of **Via Nazionale**; to the major sites of the **ancient city** to the south; and to the huge expanse of the **Villa Borghese** park to the north. The left bank of the river is oddly distanced from the main hum of this part of the city, home to the **Vatican** and **Saint Peter's**, and, to the south of these, **Trastevere** – even in ancient times a distinct entity from the city proper, as well as the focus of much of the city's nightlife.

Piazza Venezia and the Capitoline Hill

Piazza Venezia is not so much a square as a road junction, and a busy one at that. But it's a good central place to start your wanderings, close to both the medieval and Renaissance centre of Rome and the bulk of the ruins of the ancient city. Flanked on all sides by imposing buildings, it's a dignified focal point for the city in spite of the traffic, and a spot you'll find yourself returning to time and again.

Visiting Rome's museums and ancient sites

There are a number of ways you can make visiting Rome's most important museums and ancient sites easier and cheaper. Museums and sites that are under the jurisdiction of the City of Rome – the Capitoline Museums, Palazzo Barberini, Palazzo Altemps and Palazzo Massimo, among others – can be visited on an all-in-one five-day ticket, which costs €15.50 and is sold at any of those places it's valid. You can also visit the Palazzo Altemps and Palazzo Massimo, together with the Palatine and Colosseum, on a €12.95 **combined ticket** – again available at any of the participating museums. Some sites and museums give discounts or even free admission to students or EU citizens under 18 or over 65 – make sure you can produce the relevant card or ID.

CENTRAL ROME

0   100 m

N

▲ Piazza del Popolo

ACCOMMODATION

Abruzzi	12
Arcangelo	16
Arenula	24
Campo di' Fiori	20
Casa Kolbe	25
Residenza Cellini	19
Colors	10
Elide	3
Eradelli	8
Firenze	7
Grand Hotel Plaza	6
Julia	5
Della Lunetta	18
Margutta	1
Navona	23
Nostra Signora	
di Lourdes	4
Primavera	22
Rosetta	13
Sandy	21
Santa Chiara	17
Smeraldo	15
Sole	11
Suore Pie Operaie	
YWCA	9
Zanardelli	2

RESTAURANTS

Armando al Pantheon	J
Da Baffeto	N
Beltramme	D
Café Capranica	I
La Carbonara	Q
Ciccia Bomba	M
Colline Emiliane	G
L'Enoteca Antica	C
Da Gigetto	T
Grappolo d'Oro	P
La Grotta	S
L'Insalata Ricca	O
Il Leoncino	E
La Montecarlo	L
Myosotis	H
Naturist Club-L'Isola	F
Otello alla Concordia	B
Der Pallaro	R
Pizza Re	A
Da Vito	K

Via Piave · Via XX Settembre · Via Sicilia · Via Lucania · Via Sardegna · Via Piemonte · Via Sistina · Via Veneto · Via Ludovisi

S. Maria degli Angeli
Stazione Termini
Piazza dei Cinquecento
Piazza della Repubblica
S. Maria della Vittoria
Palazzo Massimo
S. Maria Maggiore
S. Prassede
Palazzo Barberini
Capuchin Church
S. Carlo alle Quattro Fontane
S. Pietro in Vincoli
Palazzo del Quirinale
Palazzo del Quirinale
Domus Aurea
Colosseum
Trinità dei Monti
Spanish Steps
Fontana di Trevi
Forum of Trajan & Imperial Fora
Galleria Colonna
Roman Forum
Palazzo Chigi
Time Elevator
Palazzo Doria Pamphilj
Palazzo Venezia
S. Maria in Aracoeli
Capitoline Museums
S. Maria sopra Minerva
Vittorio Emanuele Monument
Palazzo Montecitorio
S. Luigi dei Francesi
S. Ignazio
Pantheon
S. Ivo
Gesù
Teatro di Marcello
Palazzo Altemps
S. Agostino
S. Agnese
Palazzo della Cancelleria
S. Andrea della Valle
Synagogue
Palazzo Farnese
Palazzo Spada
Chiesa Nuova
Villa Farnesina
Palazzo Corsini
S. Maria in Trastevere
S. Clemente
Ara Pacis
Mausoleo di Augusto
Castel S. Angelo
Palazzo di Giustizia

Ponte Cavour · Ponte Umberto · Ponte Sant'Angelo · Ponte Principe Amedeo · Ponte Mazzini

Lungotevere · Via del Corso · Corso Vittorio Emanuele II · Corso Rinascimento · Via Giulia

Palazzo Venezia and the church of San Marco

Forming the western side of the piazza, the **Palazzo Venezia** (Tues–Sat 9am–1.30pm, Sun 9am–1pm; €4.65) was the first large Renaissance palace in the city, built for the Venetian Pope Paul II in the mid-fifteenth century and for a long time the embassy of the Venetian Republic. More famously, Mussolini moved in here while in power, occupying the vast *Sala del Mappamondo* and making his declamatory speeches to the huge crowds below from the small balcony facing onto the piazza proper. These days it's a much more peripheral building, home to a museum of Renaissance arts and crafts made up of the magpie-ish collection of Paul II, and a venue for temporary exhibitions. Adjacent to the palace on its southern side, the church of **San Marco**, accessible from Piazza San Marco (daily except Mon morning and Wed afternoon 8.30am–12.30pm & 4–7pm), is a tidy basilica rebuilt in 833 and added to by various Renaissance and eighteenth-century popes. Under restoration at the time of writing, it's a warm, cosy church, with an apse mosaic dating from the ninth century showing Pope Gregory offering his church to Christ.

The Vittorio Emanuele Monument

Everything pales into insignificance beside the marble monstrosity rearing up across the street – the **Vittorio Emanuele Monument** (Tues–Sun 9am–4.30pm; free), erected at the beginning of the twentieth century as the "Altar of the Nation" to commemorate Italian Unification. Variously likened in the past to a typewriter (because of its shape), and, by American GIs, to a wedding cake (the marble used will never mellow with age), King Vittorio Emanuele II, who it's in part supposed to honour, probably wouldn't have thought much of it – he was by all accounts a modest man; indeed, the only person who seems to have benefited from the building is the prime minister at the time, who was a deputy for Brescia, from where the marble was supplied. The monument was opened for the first time a few years ago, and you can now climb the 246 steps to the immense semi-circular colonnade at the top. The views are perhaps the best in Rome – not least because this is the one place from which you can't see the Vittorio Emanuele Monument. At the top of the first set of stairs is the Tomb of the Unknown Soldier, flanked by eternal flames and a permanent guard of honour. Incidentally, the equestrian statue of the king is claimed to be the world's largest (its moustache is 3m long).

The Capitoline Hill

The real pity about the Vittorio Emanuele Monument is that it obscures views of the **Capitoline Hill** behind – once, in the days of Imperial Rome, the spiritual and political centre of the Roman Empire. Apart from anything else, this hill has contributed key words to the English language, including, of course, "capitol", and "money", which comes from the temple to Juno Moneta that once stood up here and housed the Roman mint. The Capitoline also played a significant role in medieval and Renaissance times: the flamboyant fourteenth-century dictator Cola di Rienzo stood here in triumph in 1347, and was murdered here by an angry mob seven years later – a humble statue marks the spot.

Santa Maria in Aracoeli

The church of **Santa Maria in Aracoeli** (daily: summer 7am–noon & 4–6.30pm; winter closes 5.30pm) crowns the highest point on the Capitoline Hill, built on the site of a temple to Jupiter where, according to legend, the

Tiburtine Sybil foretold the birth of Christ. It's a steep climb to the top, reached by a flight of steps erected by Cola di Rienzo in 1348, but the church is worth it, one of Rome's most ancient basilicas. Inside, in the first chapel on the right, there are some fine frescoes by Pinturicchio recording the life of San Bernardino – realistic tableaux of landscapes and bustling town scenes. The church is also known for its role as keeper of the so-called "Bambino", a small statue of the Christ child, carved from the wood of a Gethsemane olive tree, that is said to have healing powers and was traditionally called out to the sickbeds of the ill and dying all over the city, its coach commanding instant right of way through the heavy Rome traffic. The Bambino was stolen in 1994, however, and a copy now stands in its place, in a small chapel to the left of the high altar.

The Campidoglio and Capitoline Museums

Next door to the steps up to Santa Maria is the **cordonata**, an elegant, gently rising ramp, topped with two Roman statues of Castor and Pollux, leading to the **Campidoglio**, one of Rome's most elegant squares. Designed by Michelangelo in the last years of his life for Pope Paul III, the square wasn't in fact completed until the late seventeenth century. Michelangelo balanced the piazza, redesigning the facade of what is now **Palazzo dei Conservatori** and projecting an identical building across the way, known as **Palazzo Nuovo**. Both are angled slightly to focus on **Palazzo Senatorio**, Rome's town hall. In the centre of the square Michelangelo placed an equestrian statue of Emperor Marcus Aurelius, which had previously stood for years outside San Giovanni in Laterano; early Christians had refrained from melting it down because they believed it to be of the Emperor Constantine. After careful restoration, the original is behind a glass wall in the Palazzo Nuovo, and a copy has taken its place at the centre of the piazza.

The Palazzo dei Conservatori and Palazzo Nuovo together make up the **Capitoline Museums** (Tues–Sun 9am–7pm; €6.20), containing some of the city's most important ancient sculpture. Of the two museum buildings it's the **Palazzo Nuovo** (on the left) that really steals the show. Just inside the entrance is the original Marcus Aurelius statue, and the first floor concentrates some of the best of the city's Roman copies of Greek sculpture into half a dozen or so rooms and a long gallery crammed with elegant statuary. There's a remarkable, controlled statue of the *Dying Gaul*, a Roman copy of a Hellenistic original; a naturalistic *Boy with Goose* – another copy; an original depiction of *Eros and Psyche*; a *Satyr Resting*, after a piece by Praxiteles, which was the inspiration for Hawthorne's book the *Marble Faun*; and the red marble *Laughing Silenus*, another Roman copy of a Greek original. Walk through, too, to the so-called *Sala degli Imperatori*, with its busts of Roman emperors and other famous names, including a young Augustus, a cruel Caracalla, and a portrait of Helena, the mother of Constantine, reclining gracefully. And don't miss the *Capitoline Venus*, housed in a room on its own – a coy, delicate piece, again based on a work by Praxiteles.

The same ticket gets you into the **Palazzo dei Conservatori** across the square (though it must be on the same day) – a larger, more varied collection, with more ancient sculpture but also later pieces. You can either walk across the square itself, or follow a set of stairs down to the *Tabularium*, built in 78 BC as the state archives and recently converted into a gallery to connect the two museums. This way gives a marvellous view over the Forum and the chance to see the remains of the Temple of Vejovis, built here in 196 BC, directly under the Palazzo Senatorio, in the saddle between the two summits of the

Capitoline Hill. Once on the other side, littered around the courtyard of the Palazzo dei Conservatori are the feet and other fragments of a gigantic statue of Constantine. Inside, in various **first-floor wings**, there are friezes and murals showing events from Roman history, a couple of enormous statues of popes Innocent X (by Algardi) and Urban VIII (by Bernini), the exquisite *Spinario* – a Hellenistic work from the first century BC showing a boy plucking a thorn from his foot – and the sacred symbol of Rome, the Etruscan bronze she-wolf nursing the mythic founders of the city; the twins themselves are not Etruscan but were added by Pollaiuolo in the late fifteenth century.

Upstairs, the **second floor Pinacoteca** houses Renaissance painting from the fourteenth century to the late seventeenth century – well-labelled, with descriptions of each painting in Italian and English. The paintings fill half a dozen rooms or so, and highlights include a couple of portraits by Van Dyck and an intense *Portrait of a Crossbowman* by Lorenzo Lotto, a pair of paintings from 1590 by Tintoretto – a *Flagellation* and *Christ Crowned with Thorns* – and a very fine early work by Carracci, *Head of a Boy*. In one of two large main galleries, there's a vast picture by Guercino, depicting the *Burial of Santa Petronilla* (the legendary daughter of St Peter, who died young), which used to hang in St Peter's and arrived here via the Quirinale palace and the Louvre, to hang alongside several other works by the same artist, notably a lovely, contemplative Persian Sybil and a wonderful picture of Cleopatra cowed before a young and victorious Octavius. In the same room, there are also two paintings by Caravaggio, one a replica of the young *John the Baptist* which hangs in the Palazzo Doria-Pamphili, the other a famous canvas known as the *Fortune-Teller*. By this time you may be ready for a break, in which case you should go the building's **restaurant-bar**, whose roof terrace gives unparalleled views over the city.

The Tarpeian Rock and San Pietro in Carcere

After seeing the museums, walk around behind the Palazzo Senatorio for a great view down onto the Forum, with the Colosseum in the background. On the right, Via del Monte Tarpeio follows, as its name suggests, the brink of the old **Tarpeian Rock**, from which traitors would be thrown in ancient times – so-called after Tarpeia, who betrayed the city to the Sabines. On the left side of the Palazzo Senatorio (as you face it from the Campidoglio) steps lead down to the little church of **San Pietro in Carcere** (daily: summer 9am–noon & 2.30–6pm; winter 9am–noon & 2–5pm; donation expected), built above the ancient Mamertine Prison, where spies, vanquished soldiers and other enemies of the Roman state were incarcerated, and where St Peter himself was held. Steps lead down into the murky depths of the jail, where you can see the bars to which he was chained, along with the spring the saint is said to have created to baptize the other prisoners down here. At the top of the staircase, hollowed out of the honeycomb of stone, is an imprint claimed to be of St Peter's head as he tumbled down the stairs (though when the prison was in use, the only access was through a hole in the ceiling). It's an unappealing place even now, and you won't be sorry to leave – through an exit cunningly placed to lead you through the gift shop.

North of Piazza Venezia

Immediately **north of Piazza Venezia** is the *centro storico* proper. It's here that most people find the Rome they have been looking for – the Rome of small crumbling piazzas, churches and fountains, blind alleys and streets humming with scooters and foot-traffic. This area was known in Roman times as the *Campus Martius*, a low-lying area outside the ancient city centre that was given over to barracks and sporting arenas, together with the odd temple. Later it became the heart of the Renaissance city, and nowadays it's the part of the town that is densest in interest, an unruly knot of narrow streets and alleys that holds some of the best of Rome's classical and Baroque heritage and its most vivacious street- and nightlife. Whichever direction you wander in there's something to see; indeed it's part of the appeal of Rome that even the most aimless ambling leads you past some breathlessly beautiful and historic spots.

Via del Corso

The boundary of the historic centre to the east, **Via del Corso** is Rome's main thoroughfare, leading all the way from Piazza Venezia at its southern end up to the Piazza del Popolo to the north. On its eastern side, it gives onto the swish shopping streets that lead up to Piazza di Spagna, on the western side the web of streets that tangles its way right down to the Tiber. Nowadays it is Rome's principal shopping street, home to a mixture of upmarket boutiques and chain stores that make it a busy stretch during the day, full of hurrying pedestrians and crammed buses, but a relatively dead one come the evening.

Galleria Doria Pamphili

North of Piazza Venezia, the first building on the left of Via del Corso is the Palazzo Doria Pamphili, among the city's finest Rococo palaces. Inside, through an entrance on Piazza di Collegio Romano, the **Galleria Doria Pamphili** (10am–5pm closed Thurs; €7.30, or €5.30 if you present a used ticket from the Galleria Borghese within five days; tours of private apartments every 30min 10.30am–12.30pm; €3.05; ⓦwww.doriapamphilj.it) is one of Rome's best private late-Renaissance art collections. The Doria Pamphili family still lives in part of the building, and the first part of the gallery is made up of a series of **private apartments**, furnished in the style of the original palace, through which you're guided by way of a free audio-tour narrated by the urbane Jonathan Pamphili. Beyond here, the **picture gallery** extends around a courtyard, the paintings displayed in the style of the time, crammed in frame-to-frame, floor-to-ceiling. Just inside, at the corner of the courtyard, there's a badly cracked bust of Innocent X by Bernini, which the sculptor apparently replaced in a week with the more famous version down the hall, in a room off to the left, where Bernini appears to have captured the pope about to erupt into laughter. In the same room, Velázquez's famous painting of the same man is quite different, depicting a rather irritable character regarding the viewer with impatience. The rest of the collection is just as rich in interest. There is perhaps Rome's best concentration of Dutch and Flemish paintings, including a rare Italian work by Brueghel the Elder, showing a naval battle being fought outside Naples, a highly realistic portrait of two old men, by Quentin Metsys, and a Hans Memling *Deposition*, in the furthest rooms, as well as another Metsys painting – the fabulously ugly *Moneylenders and their Clients* – in the main gallery. There is also Carracci's bucolic *Flight into Egypt*, painted shortly before the artist's death; two paintings by Caravaggio – *Mary Magdalene* and *John the Baptist*; and *Salome with the head of St John*, by Titian.

Sant'Ignazio

The next left off Via del Corso after the palace leads into **Piazza Sant'Ignazio**, a lovely little square, laid out like a theatre set and dominated by the facade of the Jesuit church of **Sant'Ignazio** (daily 7.30am–12.30pm &

4–7.15pm). The saint isn't actually buried here; appropriately, for the founder of the Jesuit order, he's in the Gesù church a little way south. But it's a spacious structure, worth visiting for its marvellous Baroque ceiling by Andrea del Pozzo showing the entry of St Ignatius into paradise, a spectacular work that employs sledgehammer trompe l'oeil effects, notably in the mock cupola painted into the dome of the crossing. Stand on the disc in the centre of the nave, the focal point for the ingenious rendering of perspective: figures in various states of action and repose, conversation and silence, fix you with stares from their classical pediment.

The Pantheon

Via del Seminario leads down to Piazza della Rotonda, where the main focus of interest is of course the **Pantheon** (Mon–Sat 9am–6.30pm, Sun 9am–1pm; free), which forms the square's southern edge, easily the most complete ancient Roman structure in the city and, along with the Colosseum, visually the most impressive. Though originally a temple that formed part of Marcus Agrippa's redesign of the Campus Martius in around 27 BC – hence the inscription – it's since been proved that the building was entirely rebuilt by the Emperor Hadrian and finished around the year 125 AD. It's a formidable architectural achievement even now, although, like the city's other Roman monuments, it would have been much more sumptuous in its day. It was consecrated as a Christian site in 609 AD and dedicated to Santa Maria ai Martiri in allusion to the Christian bones that were found here; a thousand years later, the bronze roof was stripped from the ceiling of the portico by Pope Urban VIII, to be melted down for the baldachino in St Peter's and the cannons of the Castel Sant'Angelo. (Interestingly, some of the "stolen" bronze later found its way back here when, after Unification, the cannons were in turn melted down to provide materials for the tombs of two Italian kings, which are housed in the right and left chapels.) Inside, you get the best impression of the engineering expertise of Hadrian: the diameter is precisely equal to its height (43m), the hole in the centre of the dome – from which shafts of sunlight descend to illuminate the musty interior – a full 9m across. Most impressively, there are no visible arches or vaults to hold the whole thing up; instead they're sunk into the concrete of the walls of the building. Again, it would have been richly decorated, the coffered ceiling heavily stuccoed and the niches filled with the statues of gods. Now, apart from the sheer size of the place, the main thing of interest is the tomb of Raphael, between the second and third chapel on the left, with an inscription by the humanist bishop Pietro Bembo: "Living, great Nature feared he might outvie Her works, and dying, fears herself may die."

Santa Maria Sopra Minerva

There's more artistic splendour on view behind the Pantheon, though Bernini's **Elephant Statue** doesn't really prepare you for the church of Santa Maria Sopra Minerva beyond. The statue is Bernini's most endearing piece of work, if not his most characteristic: a cheery elephant trumpeting under the weight of the obelisk he carries on his back – a reference to Pope Alexander VII's reign and supposed to illustrate the fact that strength should support wisdom. **Santa Maria Sopra Minerva** (Mon–Sat 7am–7pm, Sun 8am–7pm) is Rome's only Gothic church, and worth a look just for that, though its soaring lines have since been overburdened by marble and frescoes. Built in the late thirteenth century on the ruins of a temple to Minerva, it is also one of Rome's art-treasure churches, crammed with the tombs and self-indulgences of wealthy Roman families. Of these, the Carafa chapel, in the south transept, is the best known, holding Filippino Lippi's fresco of *The Assumption*, a bright, effervescent piece of work, below which one painting shows a hopeful Carafa (the religious zealot, Pope Paul IV) being presented to the Virgin Mary by Thomas Aquinas; another depicts Aquinas confounding the heretics in the sight of two beautiful young boys – the future Medici popes Leo X and Clement VII (the equestrian statue of Marcus Aurelius, destined for the Capitoline Hill, is just visible in the background). You should look too at the figure of *Christ Bearing the Cross*, on the left-hand side of the main altar, a serene work that Michelangelo completed for the church in 1521.

Sant'Ivo

A few steps west of the Pantheon, on Corso del Rinascimento, the rather blank facade of the **Palazzo della Sapienza** cradles the church of **Sant'Ivo** (Sun 10am–1pm) – from the outside at least, one of Rome's most impressive churches, with a playful facade designed by Borromini. Though originally built for the Barberini pope, Urban VIII, the building actually spans the reign of three pontiffs. Each of the two small towers is topped with the weird, blanc-mange-like groupings that are the symbol of the Chigi family (representing the hills of Monti di Pasci di Siena), and the central cupola spirals helter-skelter-fashion to its zenith, crowned with flames that are supposed to represent the sting of the Barberini bee, their family symbol. The inside, too, is very cleverly designed, very light and spacious given the small space the church is squeezed into, rising to the tall parabolic cupola.

San Luigi dei Francesi

A short walk from here, at the bottom of Via della Scrofa, the French national church of **San Luigi dei Francesi** (daily except Thurs afternoon 7.30am–12.30pm & 3.30–7pm) is another church in the vicinity of the Pantheon that is worth a look, mainly for the works by Caravaggio. In the last chapel on the left are three paintings (€0.25 to switch on the lights): the *Calling of St Matthew*, in which Christ points to Matthew, who is illuminated by a shaft of sunlight; Matthew visited by an angel as he writes the Gospel; and the saint's martyrdom. Caravaggio's first public commission, these paintings were actually rejected at first, partly on grounds of indecorum, and it took considerable reworking by the artist before they were finally accepted.

Piazza Navona and around

Just west of San Luigi dei Francesi lies **Piazza Navona**, Rome's most famous square. Lined with cafés and restaurants, pedestrianized and often thronged with tourists, street artists and pigeons, it is as picturesque – and as vibrant, day and night – as any piazza in Italy. It takes its shape from the first-century AD Stadium of Domitian, the principal venue of the athletic events and later chariot races that took place in the Campus Martius. Until the mid-fifteenth century the ruins of the arena were still here, overgrown and disused, but the square was given a facelift in the mid-seventeenth century by Pope Innocent X, who built most of the grandiose palaces that surround it and commissioned Borromini to design the facade of the church of **Sant'Agnese in Agone** on the piazza's western side. The story goes that the thirteen-year-old St Agnes was stripped naked before the crowds in the stadium as punishment for refusing to marry, whereupon she miraculously grew hair to cover herself. This church, typically squeezed into the tightest of spaces by Borromini, is supposedly built on the spot where it all happened.

Opposite, the **Fontana dei Quattro Fiumi**, one of three that punctuate the square, is a masterpiece by Bernini, Borromini's arch-rival. Each figure represents one of the four great rivers of the world – the Nile, Danube, Ganges and Plate – though only the horse, symbolizing the Danube, was actually carved by Bernini himself. It's said that all the figures are shielding their eyes in horror from Borromini's church facade (Bernini was an arrogant man who never had time for the work of the less successful Borromini, and their rivalry is well documented), but the fountain had actually been completed before the facade was begun. The grand complexity of rock is topped with an Egyptian obelisk, brought here by Pope Innocent X from the Circus of Maxentius.

Bernini also had a hand in the fountain at the southern end of the square, the so-called **Fontana del Moro**, designing the central figure of the Moor in what is another fantastically playful piece of work, surrounded by toothsome dolphins and other marine figures. In the opposite direction, just off the north side of Piazza Navona, there are some visible remains of the **Stadium of Domitian** (Sat & Sun 10am–12.30pm; €5.20). You can visit these on one of the short, thirty-minute guided tours that leave regularly at weekends, in English or Italian, and in doing so you can learn a little more about the stadium and its relationship with present-day Piazza Navona. But to be honest there's not a lot more to see than you can view from the street.

You might be better off spending any money you save on the Stadium in the antique dealers of narrow **Via dei Coronari**, almost opposite. This street, and some of the streets around, are the fulcrum of Rome's antiques trade, and, although the prices are as high as you might expect in such a location, there is a huge number of shops (Via dei Coronari consists of virtually nothing else), selling a tremendous variety of stuff, and a browse along here makes for one of the city's absorbing bits of sightseeing.

Palazzo Altemps

Just across the street from the north end of Piazza Navona, Piazza Sant'Apollinare is home of the beautifully restored **Palazzo Altemps** (Tues–Sat 9am–7.45pm; €5 or for details of combined ticket, see box on p.723; Sat & Sun guided tours every hour, in English by request; €3.10), nowadays home to part of the Museo Nazionale Romano (the other half is in the Palazzo Massimo – see p.751), and the cream of its collections of Roman statuary. On the ground floor, at the far end of the courtyard's loggia, there's a statue of the Emperor Antoninus Pius, and, around the corner, a couple of marvellous heads of Zeus and Pluto, a bust of Julia, the daughter of the Emperor Augustus, and a likeness of the philosopher Demosthenes, from the second century AD. There are two almost identical statues of *Apollo the Lyrist*, a magnificent statue of Athena taming a serpent, pieced together from fragments found near the church of Santa Maria Sopra Minerva, an *Aphrodite* from an original by Praxiteles, and, in the far corner of the courtyard, a shameless *Dionysus* with a satyr and panther, found on the Quirinal Hill. Upstairs you get a slightly better sense of the original sumptuousness of the building – some of the frescoes remain and the north loggia retains its original, late-sixteenth-century decoration, simulating a vine-laden pergola. Among the objects on display there is a fine statue of Hermes, a wonderful statue of a warrior at rest, and, most engagingly, a charmingly sensitive portrayal of *Orestes and Electra*, from the first century AD by a sculptor called Menelaus – his name is carved at the base of one of the figures. In a later room there is a colossal head of Hera, and – what some consider the highlight of the entire collection – the famous *Ludovisi throne*: an original fifth-century-BC Greek work embellished with a delicate relief portraying the birth of Aphrodite. Further on, the Fireplace Salon, whose huge fireplace is embellished with caryatids and lurking ibex – the symbol of the Altemps family – has the so-called *Suicide of Galatian*, apparently commissioned by Julius Caesar to adorn his Quirinal estate; at the other end of the room, an incredible sarcophagus depicts a battle between the Romans and barbarians in graphic, almost viscerally sculptural, detail.

Sant'Agostino

Just east of Palazzo Altemps, through an arch, the Renaissance facade of the church of **Sant'Agostino** (daily 7.45am–noon & 4–7.30pm) takes up one side of a drab piazza of the same name. It's not much to look at from the outside, but a handful of art treasures might draw you in. Just inside the door, the serene statue of the *Madonna del Parto*, by Sansovino, is traditionally invoked during pregnancy, and is accordingly surrounded by photos of new-born babes and their blissful parents. But the biggest crowds gather around the first chapel on the left, where the *Madonna and Pilgrims* by Caravaggio (€0.25 to switch on the lights) is a characteristic work of what was at the time almost revolutionary realism, showing two peasants with dirty clothes praying at the feet of a sensuous Mary and Child.

Piazza Montecitorio and around

Further on, **Piazza Montecitorio** takes its name from the bulky **Palazzo di Montecitorio** on its northern side, home since 1871 to the Italian parliament – though the building itself is a Bernini creation from 1650. The obelisk in the centre of the square was brought to Rome by Augustus and set up in the Campus Martius, where it formed the hand of a giant sundial. Just beyond, off Via del Corso, the **Palazzo Chigi** flanks the north side of **Piazza Colonna**, official residence of the prime minister. The **Column of Marcus Aurelius**, which gives the square its name, was erected between 180 and 190 AD to commemorate military victories in northern Europe, and, like the column of Trajan which inspired it, is decorated with reliefs depicting scenes from the campaigns.

The Mausoleum of Augustus

A little further up Via del Corso, off to the left, cut through to **Piazza del Augusta Imperatore**, an odd square of largely Mussolini-era buildings surrounding the massive **Mausoleum of Augustus** (guided tours Sat & Sun 11am; €5.20), the burial place of the emperor and his family but these days not much more than a peaceful ring of cypresses, circled by paths, flowering shrubs and the debris of tramps. The mausoleum has been transformed into many buildings over the years, not least a fortress, like Hadrian's mausoleum across the river, but only recently has been opened to the public – although inside, the passageways and central crypt, where the ashes of the members of the Augustan dynasty were kept, don't add much to the picture you get from the outside.

Piazza del Popolo

The other side of Piazza del Augusto Imperatore, **Via di Ripetta** leads north to the oval-shaped expanse of **Piazza del Popolo** – a dignified meeting of roads laid out in 1538 by Pope Paul III (Alessandro Farnese) to make an impressive entrance to the city. The monumental **Porta del Popolo** went up in 1655, the work of Bernini, whose patron Alexander VII's Chigi family symbol – the heap of hills surmounted by a star – can clearly be seen above the main gateway. During summer, the steps around the obelisk and fountain, and

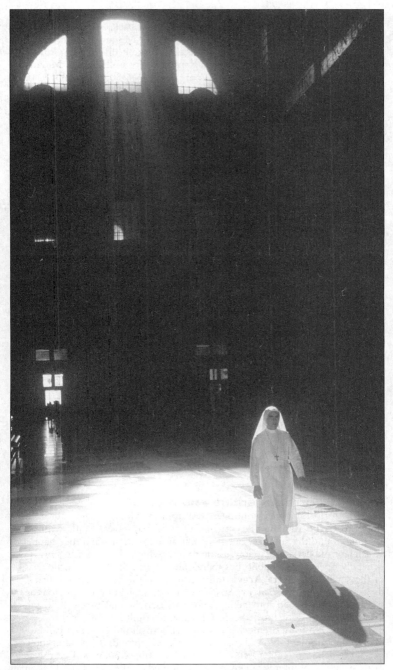

△ St Peter's, Rome

the cafés on either side of the square, are popular hangouts. But the square's real attraction is the unbroken view it gives all the way back down Via del Corso, to the central columns of the Vittorio Emanuele Monument. If you get to choose your first view of the centre of Rome, make it this one.

On the far side of the piazza, hard against the city walls, **Santa Maria del Popolo** (Mon–Sat 7am–noon & 4–7pm, Sun 8am–1.30pm & 4.30–7.30pm) holds some of the best Renaissance art of any Roman church. It was originally erected here in 1099 over the supposed burial place of Nero, in order to sanctify what was believed to be an evil place, but took its present form in the fifteenth century. Inside there are lovely frescoes by Pinturicchio in the first chapel of the south aisle, and the same artist also did some work in the Bramante-designed apse, which in turn boasts two fine tombs by Andrea Sansovino. The Chigi chapel, the second from the entrance in the northern aisle, was designed by Raphael for Agostino Chigi in 1516, though most of the work was actually undertaken by other artists and not finished until the seventeenth century. Michelangelo's protégé, Sebastiano del Piombo, was responsible for the altarpiece, and two of the sculptures in the corner niches, of Daniel and Habakkuk, are by Bernini. But it's two pictures by Caravaggio that attract the most attention, in the left-hand chapel of the north transept. These are typically dramatic works – one, the *Conversion of St Paul*, showing Paul and horse bathed in a beatific radiance, the other, the *Crucifixion of St Peter*, showing Peter as an aged but strong figure, dominated by the muscular figures hoisting him up.

West of Piazza Venezia

Via del Plebiscito, a dark, rather gloomy thoroughfare, forges west from Piazza Venezia to the **Piazza del Gesù**, where the church of **Gesù**, a symbol of the Counter-Reformation and the Jesuit order (daily 6am–12.30pm & 4–7.15pm), was ideal for the large and fervent congregations the Jesuits wanted to draw – indeed, high and wide, with a single-aisled nave and short transepts edging out under a huge dome, it has since served as the model for Jesuit churches everywhere. The facade is by Giacomo della Porta, the interior the work of Vignola. Today it's still a well-patronized church, notable for its size (the glittery tomb of the order's founder, St Ignatius, is topped by a huge globe of lapis lazuli – the largest piece in existence) and the staggering richness of its interior, especially the paintings of Baciccia in the dome and the ceiling's ingenious trompe l'oeil.

Largo di Torre Argentina and around

Corso Vittorio Emanuele continues west from the Gesù, opening out eventually onto **Largo di Torre Argentina**, a good-sized square frantic with traffic circling around the ruins of four (Republican-era) temples and the channel of an ancient public lavatory, now home to a thriving colony of cats. This is not generally open to the public, but there's not a lot to see here. On the far side of the square, the **Tetra Argentina** was in 1816 the venue for the first performance of Rossini's *Barber of Seville*, not a success at all on the night: Rossini was apparently booed into taking refuge in Bernasconi's pastry shop which used to be next door (now the *Brek* restaurant). Built in 1731, it is today one of the city's most important theatres, and has a small museum that can be visited by appointment. Nowadays, however, the **Crypta Balbi**, around the corner at Via delle Botteghe Oscure 31 (Tues–Sun 9am–7.30pm; €4), is the area's principal point of interest, a new museum housed on the site of an old Roman imperial theatre and with displays covering the period from the fall of the Roman Empire to the late Middle Ages.

Sant'Andrea delle Valle

From Largo Argentina you can either push on down Corso Vittorio Emanuele or cut left towards the Tiber and right at Piazza Cairoli into the network of streets that centres on Campo de' Fiori. Taking the Corso route, you pass the church of **Sant'Andrea della Valle** (daily 7.30am–noon & 4.30–7.30pm), which has the distinction of sporting the city's second-tallest dome (after St Peter's). Inside, it's one of the most Baroque of Rome's churches, a high, barn-like building, in which most of your attention is drawn not only to the dome, decorated with frescoes of the *Glory of Paradise* by Giovanni Lanfranco, but also to a marvellous set of frescoes in the apse by his contemporary Domenichino, illustrating the life of St Andrew, and centring on the monumental scene of his crucifixion on the characteristic transverse cross. In a side chapel on the right, you may recognize some good-looking copies of not only Michelangelo's *Pietà* (the original is in St Peter's), but also of his figures of Leah and Rachel, from the same artist's tomb of his patron, Julius II, in the church of San Pietro in Vincoli (see p.749).

Piazza Pasquino and around

Immediately behind the Palazzo Braschi, just south of Piazza Navona, the small space of **Piazza Pasquino** isn't quite what you'd expect from the scene of centuries of satire, but the battered torso of Pasquino itself, anonymous poker of fun at the rich and famous during the Middle Ages, still stands in the corner. It's most famous among a number of so-called "talking statues" in Rome, upon which anonymous comments on the affairs of the day would be attached – comments that had a serious as well as a humorous intent. Pasquino gave us our word "pasquinade", but nowadays the graffitied comments and photo-copied poems that occasionally grace the statue are usually somewhat lacking in wit. **Via del Governo Vecchio** leads west from here into one of Rome's liveliest quarters, the narrow streets noisy at night, and holding some of the city's most vigorous restaurants and bars.

Piazza Campo de' Fiori

At the southern end of Piazza della Cancelleria, in front of the palace, is one of several entrances to **Piazza Campo de' Fiori**, in many ways Rome's most appealing square, home to a lively **fruit and vegetable market** (Mon–Sat 8am–1pm), and flanked by restaurants and cafés. No one really knows how the square came by its name, which means "field of flowers", but one theory holds that it was derived from the Roman Campus Martius, which used to cover most of this part of town; another claims it is after Flora, the mistress of Pompey, whose theatre used to stand on what is now the northeast corner of the square – a huge complex by all accounts, which stretched right over to Largo Argentina. You can still see the foundations in the basement of the *Da Pancrazio* restaurant, on the tiny Piazza del Biscione, and the semicircular Via di Grotta Pinta retains the rounded shape of the theatre. Later, Campo de' Fiori was an important point on papal processions between the Vatican and the major basilicas of Rome (notably San Giovanni in Laterano) and a site of public executions. The most notorious killing is commemorated by the statue of **Giordano Bruno** in the middle of the square. Bruno was a late-sixteenth-century freethinker who followed the teachings of Copernicus and was denounced to the Inquisition; his trial lasted for years under a succession of different popes, and finally, when he refused to renounce his philosophical beliefs, he was burned at the stake.

Palazzo Farnese and Galleria Spada

Just south of Campo de' Fiori, **Piazza Farnese** is a quite different square, with great fountains spurting out of lilies – the Farnese emblem – into marble tubs brought from the Baths of Caracalla, and the sober bulk of the **Palazzo Farnese** itself, begun in 1514 by Antonio di Sangallo the Younger and finished off after the architect's death by Michelangelo, who added the top tier of windows and cornice. The building now houses the French Embassy and is closed to the public.

Make do instead with the Palazzo Spada, back towards Via Arenula at Piazza Capo di Ferro 3, and the **Galleria Spada** inside (Tues–Sat 8.30am–7.30pm; €5; guided tours every hour, on the hour, included in the price); walk right through the courtyard to the back of the building. Its four rooms, decorated in the manner of a Roman noble family, aren't spectacularly interesting unless you're a connoisseur of seventeenth- and eighteenth-century Italian painting. But there are two portraits of the cardinal Bernadino Spada by Reni and Guercino, and the building itself is a treat: its facade is frilled with stucco adornments, and, left off the small courtyard, there's a crafty trompe l'oeil by Borromini – a tunnel whose actual length is multiplied about four times through the architect's tricks with perspective – though to see this you have to wait for one of the guided tours.

The Jewish Ghetto and around

Cross over to the far side of Via Arenula and you're in what was once the city's **Jewish Ghetto**, a crumbling area of narrow, switchback streets and alleys, easy to lose your way in, and with a lingering sense of age. There was a Jewish population in Rome as far back as the second century BC, and with the accruing of Middle Eastern colonies, their numbers eventually swelled to around 40,000. Revolts in the colonies led to a small tax on Jews and a special census and they were effectively ghettoized here in the mid-sixteenth century when Pope Paul IV issued a series of punitive laws that forced them into what was then one of Rome's most squalid districts: a wall was built around the area and all Jews, in a chilling omen of things to come, were made to wear yellow caps and shawls when they left the district. Later, after Unification, the ghetto was opened up, and although the Nazi occupation brought the inevitable deportations, the majority of Rome's Jewish population survived, and currently numbers 16,000 (around half Italy's total). This is nowadays, however, spread all over the city, and a couple of kosher restaurants and butchers are pretty much all that remains to mark this out from any other quarter of the city.

Via Portico d'Ottavia

The main artery of the Jewish area is **Via Portico d'Ottavia**, which leads down to the **Portico d'Ottavia**, a not terribly well-preserved second-century BC gate, rebuilt by Augustus and dedicated to his sister in 23 BC, that was the entranceway to the adjacent **Teatro di Marcello**. This has served many purposes over the years: begun by Julius Caesar, finished by Augustus, it was pillaged in the fourth century and not properly restored until the Middle Ages, after which it became a formidable fortified palace for a succession of different rulers, including the Orsini family. The theatre has been recently restored and provides a grand backdrop for classical concerts in the summer. Crossing to the other side of Via Portico d'Ottavia, follow your nose to **Piazza Mattei**, whose **Fontana delle Tartarughe**, or "turtle fountain", is a delightful late-sixteenth-century creation, perhaps restored by Bernini.

The Synagogue

The Ghetto's principal Jewish sight is the huge **Synagogue** by the river (Mon–Thurs 9am–5pm, Fri 9am–2pm, Sun 9am–12.30pm; closed Sat & Jewish holidays; €5 15), built in 1904 and very much dominating all around with its bulk – not to mention the carabinieri who stand guard 24 hours a day outside, ever since a PLO attack on the building in 1982. The only way to see the building is on one of the short guided tours it runs in English, afterwards taking in the small two-room museum. The interior of the building is impressive, rising to a high, rainbow-hued dome, and the tours, which are included in the price and leave very regularly, are excellent, giving good background on the building and Rome's Jewish community in general.

Piazza Bocca della Verità and around

Further along the river from the Synagogue lies **Piazza Bocca della Verità**, home to two of the city's better-preserved Roman temples – the **Temple of Portunus** and the **Temple of Hercules Victor**, long known as the temple of Vesta because, like all vestal temples, it is circular. Both date from the end of the second century BC. and although you can't get inside, they're actually fine examples of republican-era places of worship; and the Temple of Hercules Victor is, for what it's worth, the oldest surviving marble structure in Rome. More interesting is the church of **Santa Maria in Cosmedin** on the far side of the square (daily 9am–noon & 3–5pm), a typically Roman medieval basilica with a huge marble altar and a colourful and ingenious Cosmati-work marble mosaic floor – one of the city's finest. Outside in the portico, and giving the square its name, is the **Bocca della Verità** (Mouth of Truth), an ancient Roman drain cover in the shape of an enormous face that in medieval times would apparently swallow the hand of anyone who hadn't told the truth. It was particularly popular with husbands anxious to test the faithfulness of their wives; now it is one of the city's biggest tour-bus attractions. On the northern side, the square peters out peacefully at the **Arch of Janus**, perhaps Rome's most weathered triumphal arch, beyond which the campanile of the church of **San Giorgio in Velabro** (daily 10am–12.30pm & 4–6.30pm) is a stunted echo of that of Santa Maria across the way. Inside, recently opened after a major restoration, this is one of the city's barest and most beautiful ancient basilicas; only the late-twelfth-century fresco in the apse, the work of Pietro Cavallini, lightens the melancholy mood. Cavallini's fresco shows Christ and His mother, and various saints, including St George on the left, to whom the church is dedicated – and whose cranial bones lie in the reliquary under the high altar canopy, placed here in 749 AD, shortly after the original basilica was built.

Isola Tiberina

Back by the river, you can see the remains of **Ponte Rotto** (Broken Bridge) – all that remains of the first stone bridge to span the river. Built between 179 and 142 BC, it collapsed at the end of the sixteenth century. Further upstream is **Ponte Fabricio**, which crosses to **Isola Tiberina**. Built in 62 BC, it's the only classical bridge to remain intact without help from the restorers (the Ponte Cestio, on the other side of the island, was partially rebuilt in the nineteenth century). As for the island, it's a calm respite from the city centre proper, its originally tenth-century church of **San Bartolomeo** worth a peep on the way across the river to Trastevere, especially if you're into modern sculpture – Padre Martini, a well-known local sculptor, used to live on the island, and the church holds some wonderful examples of his elegant, semi-abstract religious pieces.

East of Via del Corso

The triangular area on the **eastern side of Via del Corso**, bounded by Piazza del Popolo, the Corso, the edge of the Villa Borghese and Piazza di Spagna, is travellers' Rome, historically the artistic quarter of the city, for which eighteenth- and nineteenth-century Grand Tourists would make in search of the colourful, exotic city. Keats and Giorgio de Chirico are just two of those who used to live on Piazza di Spagna; Goethe had lodgings on Via del Corso; and institutions like *Caffè Greco* and *Babington's Tea Rooms* were the meeting-places of a local artistic and expat community for close on a couple of centuries. Today these institutions have given ground to more latter-day traps for the tourist dollar: American Express and *McDonald's* have settled into the area, while Via dei Condotti and around is these days strictly international designer territory, with some of Rome's fanciest stores; the local residents are more likely to be investment bankers than artists or poets. But the air of a Rome being discovered, even colonized, by foreigners persists, even if most of them hanging out on the Spanish Steps are flying-visit InterRailers.

Piazza di Spagna and the Keats-Shelley Memorial House

Via del Babuino leads down from Piazza del Popolo to **Piazza di Spagna**, a long straggle of a square almost entirely enclosed by buildings and centring on the distinctive boat-shaped **Barcaccia** fountain, the last work of Bernini's father. It apparently remembers the great flood of Christmas Day 1598, when a barge from the Tiber was washed up on the slopes of Pincio Hill here.

Fronting the square, opposite the fountain, is the house where the poet John Keats died in 1821. It now serves as the **Keats–Shelley Memorial House** (Mon–Fri 9am–1pm & 3–6pm, Sat 11am–6pm; €2.50), an archive of English-language literary and historical works and a museum of manuscripts and literary mementoes relating to the Keats circle of the early nineteenth century – namely the poet himself, Shelley and Mary Shelley, and Byron (who at one time lived across the square). Among many bits of manuscript, letters and the like, there's a silver scallop shell reliquary containing locks of Milton's and Elizabeth Barrett Browning's hair, while Keats's death mask, stored in the room where he died, captures a resigned grimace. Keats didn't really enjoy his time in Rome, referring to it as his "posthumous life": he was tormented by his love for Fanny Browne, and spent months in pain before he died, confined to the rooming house with his artist friend Joseph Severn, to whom he remarked that he could already feel "the flowers growing over him".

The Spanish Steps

As for the **Spanish Steps**, which sweep down in a cascade of balustrades and balconies beside the house, the only Spanish thing about them is the fact that they lead down to the Spanish Embassy, which also gave the piazza its name. In the nineteenth century they were the hangout of young hopefuls waiting to be chosen as artists' models; nowadays the scene is not much changed, as the venue for international posing and fast pick-ups late into the summer nights. At the top is the **Trinità dei Monti**, a largely sixteenth-century church designed by Carlo Maderno and paid for by the French king. Its rose-coloured Baroque facade overlooks the rest of Rome from its hilltop site, and it's worth clambering up just for the views. But while here you may as well pop your head around the door for a couple of faded works by Daniele da Volterra, notably a soft flowing fresco of *The Assumption* in the third chapel on the right, which includes a portrait of his teacher Michelangelo, and a poorly lit *Deposition* across the nave.

Piazza Barberini

From the church you can either continue left past the Villa Medici, now housing the French Academy, to the Pincio terrace and the gardens of the Villa Borghese (see p.754), or head south down Via Sistina to **Piazza Barberini**, a frenetic traffic junction at the top end of the busy shopping street of Via del Tritone – named after Bernini's **Fontana del Tritone**, which gushes a high jet of water in the centre of the square. Traditionally, this was the Barberini quarter of the city, a family who were the greatest patrons of Gian Lorenzo Bernini, and the sculptor's works in their honour are thick on the ground around here. He finished the Tritone fountain in 1644, going on shortly after to design the **Fontana delle Api** ("Fountain of the Bees") at the bottom end of Via Veneto. Unlike the Tritone fountain you could walk right past this, a smaller, quirkier work, its broad scallop shell studded with the bees that were the symbol of the Barberinis.

Santa Maria della Concezione: the Capuchin Cemetery

A little way up Via Veneto, the Capuchin church of **Santa Maria della Concezione** was another sponsored creation of the Barberini, though it's not a particularly significant building in itself, only numbering Guido Reni's androgynous *St Michael Trampling on the Devil* among its treasures. The devil in the picture is said to be a portrait of Innocent X, whom the artist despised and who was apparently a sworn enemy of the Barberini family. But the **Capuchin cemetery** (Mon–Wed & Fri–Sun 9am–noon & 3–6pm; compulsory "donation"), on the right of the church, is one of the more macabre and bizarre sights of Rome. Here, the bones of 4000 monks are set into the walls of a series of chapels, a monument to "Our Sister of Bodily Death", in the words of St Francis, that was erected in 1793. The bones appear in abstract or Christian patterns or as fully clothed skeletons, their faces peering out of their cowls in various twisted expressions of agony – somewhere between the chilling and the ludicrous.

Via Veneto and Via Rasella

Via Veneto, which bends north from Piazza Barberini up to the southern edge of the Borghese gardens, is a cool, materialistic antidote to the murky atmosphere of the Capuchin grotto. The pricey bars and restaurants lining the street were once the haunt of Rome's Beautiful People, made famous by Fellini's *La Dolce Vita*, but they left a long time ago, and Via Veneto isn't really any different from other busy streets in central Rome – a pretty tree-lined road, but with a fair share of high-class tack trying to cash in on departed glory.

Just off to the right of Via Veneto, **Via Rasella** was the scene of an ambush of a Nazi military patrol in 1944 that led to one of the worst Italian wartime atrocities – the reprisal massacre of 35 innocent Romans at the Ardeatine Caves outside the city walls. A memorial (see p.1169) now stands on the sight of the executions, and the event is commemorated every March 24.

Palazzo Barberini

On the other side of Piazza Barberini, the **Palazzo Barberini**, at Via Barberini 18, is home to the **Galleria di Arte Antica** (Tues–Sun 9am–7pm; €6, or for details of combined ticket, see box on p.723), consisting of a rich patchwork of mainly Italian art from the early Renaissance to late Baroque period. The building alone is worth the entrance fee, the epitome of Baroque grandeur, with a first-floor *salone* frescoed by Pietro da Cortona in one of the best examples of exuberant trompe l'oeil work there is – a manic rendering of *The Triumph of Divine Providence* that almost crawls down the walls to meet you. Broadly speaking, the collection proceeds chronologically across three floors of the building, starting with the first floor and ending on the third. Across the hall from the *salone*, the first floor displays early Renaissance works, notably Fra' Filippo Lippi's warmly maternal *Madonna and Child*, a richly coloured and beautifully composed *Annunciation* by the same artist, and Raphael's beguiling *Fornarina*, a painting of the daughter of a Travesteran baker thought to have been Raphael's mistress (Raphael's name appears clearly on the woman's bracelet) – although some experts claim the painting to be the work of a pupil. Look out also, in nearby rooms, for Bronzino's portrait of Stefano Colonna and an anguished *St Jerome* by Tintoretto – full of interesting detail, and clever use of light and shade. Among the upstairs works, there is a famous painting of *Beatrice Cenci*, fomerly attributed to Guide Reni, which moved Shelley to write a play about her tragedy, and a portrait of *Henry VIII* by Hans Holbein which feels almost as well-known – probably because the painter produced so many of the monarch. It's a stark contrast to the rather ascetic figure of *Erasmus of Rotterdam* by Quentin Matsys, which hangs next to it.

San Carlo alle Quattro Fontane and the Palazzo del Quirinale

Continue on up Via delle Quattro Fontane and you're at a seventeenth-century landmark, the church of **San Carlo alle Quattro Fontane** (Mon–Fri 9am–12.30pm & 4–6pm, Sat 9am–12.30pm). This was Borromini's first real design commission, and in it he displays all the ingenuity he later became famous for, cramming the church elegantly into a tiny and awkwardly shaped site that apparently covers roughly the same surface area as one of the dome-supporting piers inside St Peter's. Tucked in beside the church, the newly restored cloister is also squeezed into a tight but elegant oblong, topped with a charming balustrade. Outside the church are the four **fountains** that give the street and church their name, each cut into a niche in a corner of the cross-roads that marks this, the highest point on the Quirinal Hill, while to the left is the featureless wall of the **Palazzo del Quirinale** (second & fourth Sun morning each month September–May 8am–1pm; €5.20), a sixteenth-century structure that was the official summer residence of the popes until Unification, when it became the royal palace. It's now the home of Italy's president, but you can appreciate its exceptional siting from the **Piazza del Quirinale** at the far end on the right, from which views stretch right across the centre of Rome. The main feature of the piazza is the huge statue of the **Dioscuri**, or Castor and Pollux – massive five-metre-high Roman copies of classical Greek statues, showing the two godlike twins, the sons of Jupiter, who according to legend won victory for the Romans in an important battle.

Fontana di Trevi

Via della Dataria winds down from Piazza del Quirinale into the tight web of narrow, apparently aimless streets below, bringing you shortly to one of Rome's more surprising sights, easy to stumble upon by accident – the **Fontana di Trevi**, a huge, very Baroque gush of water over statues and rocks built onto the backside of a Renaissance palace; it's fed by the same source that surfaces at the Barcaccia fountain in Piazza di Spagna. There was a Trevi fountain, designed by Alberti, around the corner in Via dei Crociferi, a smaller, more modest affair by all accounts, but Urban VIII decided to upgrade it in line with his other grandiose schemes of the time and employed Bernini, among others, to design an alternative. Work didn't begin, however, until 1732, when Niccolò Salvi won a competition held by Clement XII to design the fountain, and even then it took thirty years to finish the project. Salvi died in the process, his lungs shot by the time spent in the dank waterworks of the fountain. The Trevi fountain is now, of course, the place you come to chuck in a coin if you want to guarantee your return to Rome, though you might remember Anita Ekberg throwing herself into it in *La Dolce Vita* (there are police here to discourage you from doing the same thing). Newly restored, it's one of the city's most vigorous outdoor spots to hang out.

Galleria Colonna and the Time Elevator Roma

A short stroll south from the Fontana di Trevi brings you to the **Galleria Colonna**, at Via della Pilotta 17 (Sat 9am–1pm; €7; English guided tours at 11am, included in the price), part of the Palazzo Colonna complex and, although outranked by many of the other Roman palatial collections, worth forty minutes or so if you happen by when it's open, if only for the chandelier-decked Great Hall where most of the paintings are displayed. Best on the whole is the gallery's collection of landscapes by Dughet (Poussin's brother-in-law), but other works that stand out are Carracci's early – and unusually spontaneous – *Bean Eater* (though this attribution has been questioned), a *Narcissus* by Tintoretto and a *Portrait of a Venetian Gentleman* caught in supremely confident pose by Veronese.

Near Galleria Colonna at Via SS. Apostoli 20 is the newly opened **Time Elevator Roma** (daily 9am–midnight; 45 min; every 15 min; €11), a multimedia film show of the history of Rome from its founding to the present day. You're strapped into a chair which moves around a bit like a flight simulator and takes you on a "ride" through time. It's quite a fun introduction if you don't know much about the history of the city.

The Roman Forums and the Palatine Hill

From Piazza Venezia **Via dei Fori Imperiali** cuts south through the heart of Rome's ancient sites, a soulless boulevard imposed on the area by Mussolini in 1932. Before then, this was a warren of medieval streets that wound around the ruins of the ancient city centre, but as with the Via della Conciliazione up to St Peter's the Duce preferred to build something to his own glory rather than preserve that of another era. There is a long-standing plan to make this entire ancient part of the city into a huge archeological park which would stretch right down to the catacombs on the Via Appia Antica. However, although excavations have been undertaken in recent years, they are continuing slowly. For the moment, if you want tranquil sightseeing you'll have to settle for coming on Sunday, when a long stretch from Piazza Venezia to Via Appia Antica is closed to traffic and pedestrians take to the streets to stroll past the ruins of the ancient city.

The Imperial Forums and around

One of the major victims of Mussolini's redesign was the **Forum of Trajan** on the north side of the road, a complex of basilicas, monuments, apartments

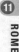

and shops that was in its day the most sumptuous of the imperial forums, built here after the Forum proper had become too small at what was probably the very pinnacle of Roman power and prestige. It's currently fairly unrecognizable, the main section no more than a sunken area of scattered columns to the left of the road, fronting the semicircle of **Markets of Trajan** (summer Tues–Sat 9am–6pm, Sun 9am–1.30pm; winter Tues–Sat 9am–4pm, Sun 9am–1.30pm; €4), a tiered ancient Roman shopping centre that's also accessible from Via IV Novembre. Down below the markets, the Basilica Ulpia was a central part of the Forum of Trajan, an immense structure, now mostly hidden below ground level. It had five aisles and a huge apse at either end, and measured 176m long by 59m wide. At the head of the basilica, the enormous **Column of Trajan** was erected to celebrate the emperor's victories in Dacia (modern Romania) in 112 AD, and is covered from top to bottom with reliefs commemorating the highlights of the campaign. The carving on the base shows the trophies brought back and there's an inscription saying that the column was dedicated by the Senate and People of Rome in 113 AD in honour of Trajan. Behind the Forum of Trajan, the **Torre delle Milizie** (summer open Sat & Sun 9am–7pm; €4) is fondly imagined to be the tower from which Nero watched Rome burning, although it's actually a twelfth-century fortification left over from days when Rome was divided into warring factions within the city walls. The views from the top are unparalleled and well worth the exhausting climb.

The Roman Forum

The **Roman Forum** (summer Tues–Sat 9am–6pm, Sun 9am–1pm; winter Tues–Sat 9am–3pm, Sun 9am–1pm; free) is very near the top of most visitors' things to see in Rome. However, for many it's also one of the city's most disappointing sights, and you need an imagination and some small grasp of history to really appreciate the place at all. Certainly it holds some of the most ruined Roman ruins you'll see: the area was abandoned (and looted) for so long that very little is anything like intact. But these five or so acres were once the heart of the Mediterranean world, and are a very real and potent testament to a power that held a large chunk of the earth in its thrall for close on five centuries and whose influence reverberates right up to the present day – in language, architecture, political terms and systems, even in the romance that the last couple of hundred years have lent to its ruins.

Even in ancient times Rome was a very large city, stretching out as far as the Aurelian Wall in a sprawl of apartment blocks or *insulae*. But the Forum was its centre, home to its political and religious institutions, its shops and market stalls, and a meeting-place for all and sundry – which it remained until the Imperial era, when Rome's increased importance as a world power led to the extensions nearby. The Forum never really recovered from this: neglect set in, a fire in the third century AD destroyed many of the buildings, and although the damage was repaired, Rome was by this time in a general state of decay, the coming of Christianity only serving to accelerate the process, particularly with regard to its pagan temples and institutions. After the later downfall of the city to various barbarian invaders, the area was left in ruin, its relics quarried for the construction in other parts of Rome during medieval and Renaissance times and the odd church or tower being constructed *in situ* out of the more viable piles. Excavation of the site didn't start until the beginning of the nineteenth century, since when it has continued pretty much without stopping: you'll notice a fair part of the site, especially up on the Palatine, closed off for further digs.

The **Via Sacra** runs directly through the core of the Forum, from below the Capitoline Hill in the west to the far eastern extent of the site and the Arch of Titus (where there's a handy exit for the Colosseum, see p.746). It was the best-known street of ancient Rome, along which victorious emperors and generals would ride in procession to give thanks at the Capitoline's Temple of Jupiter. The steps that line it just inside the main entrance are part of the **Regia**, or house of the kings, an extremely ancient group of foundations that date probably from the reign of the second King of Rome, Numa, who ruled from 715 to 673 BC. There was a shrine of Mars here, housing the shields and spears of Mars, which generals embarking on a war rattled before setting off. If the shields and spears rattled of their own accord it was a bad omen, requiring purification and repentance rites. The Regia later became the residence of Julius Caesar, who moved here in 45 BC – an imperious act which at least in part led to his downfall. Opposite the Regia, the Temple of Antoninus and Faustina is the best-preserved temple in the forum, mainly because of its preservation since the seventh century as the church of **San Lorenzo in Miranda**. Next to the Regia, the pile of rubble with the little green roof is all that remains of the grandeur and magnificence that comprised the **temple to Julius Caesar** – the round brick stump under the roof marks the spot where Caesar was cremated, and around which the temple was built. The football pitch of broken columns to the right of the Via Sacra marks the site of the **Basilica Emilia**, built in the second century BC to house law courts, and, in the little booths and boutiques flanking it on the Via Sacra side, money-changers. Close by, a little marble plaque dedicated to **Venus Cloacina** marks the site of a small shrine dedicated to Venus where the Cloaca Maxima canal drained the Forum, which was originally marshland. The Cloaca Maxima reaches all the way to the Tiber from here, and still keeps the area drained.

A little way beyond, the large cube-shaped building is the **Curia**, built on the orders of Julius Caesar, although what you see now is a Diocletian reconstruction. One of the few whole structures left in the Forum, the Senate met here during the Republican period, and augurs would come to announce the wishes of the gods. Inside, three wide stairs rise left and right, on which about 300 senators could be accommodated with their folding chairs. In the centre is the speaker's platform, with a porphyry statue of a togaed figure. Otherwise, apart from the floor, elegantly patterned in red, yellow, green and white marble, there's not much left of its ancient decor, only the grey and white marble facing each side of the speaker's platform, which would once have covered the entire hall.

Immediately outside the Curia, the black, fenced-off paving of the **Lapis Niger** marks the traditional site of the tomb of Romulus, the steps beneath (usually closed) leading down to a monument that was considered sacred ground during classical times. To the right, the **Arch of Septimius Severus** was constructed in the early third century AD by his sons Caracalla and Galba to mark their father's victories in what is now Iran. The friezes on it recall Severus and his son Caracalla, who ruled Rome with a reign of undisciplined terror for seven years. There's a space where Galba was commemorated – Caracalla had him executed in 213AD, and his name expediently removed from the arch altogether.

To the left of the arch, the low brown wall is the **Rostra**, facing the wide-open scatter of paving, dumped stones and beached columns that makes up the central portion of the Forum, the place where most of the life of the city was carried on, and which, in ancient times, was usually crowded with politicians, tribunes and traders. Left of the Rostra are the long stairs of the **Basilica Julia**, built by Julius Caesar in the 50s BC after he returned from the Gallic wars. A bit further along, on the right, the guard rails lead into a kind of alcove in the pavement, which marks the site of the **Lacus Curtius** – the spot where, according to legend, a chasm opened during the earliest days and the sooth-sayers determined that it would only be closed once Rome had sacrificed its most valuable possession into it. Marcus Curtius, a Roman soldier who declared that Rome's most valuable possession was a loyal citizen, hurled him-self and his horse into the void and it duly closed. Around the corner to the right, the enormous pile of rubble topped by three graceful Corinthinan columns is the **Temple of Castor and Pollux**, the Forum's oldest temple, dedicated in 484 BC to the divine twins or Dioscuri, the offspring of Jupiter by Leda, who appeared miraculously to ensure victory for the Romans in a key battle. The story goes that a group of Roman citizens were gathered around a water fountain on this spot fretting about the war, when Castor and Pollux appeared and reassured them that the battle was won – hence the temple, and their adoption as the protectors of Rome.

Beyond here, the **House of the Vestal Virgins** is a second-century AD reconstruction of a building originally built by Nero. Vesta was the Roman goddess of the hearth and home, and her cult was an important one in ancient Rome. Her temple was in the charge of the famed vestal virgins, who had the responsibility of keeping the sacred flame of Vesta alight, and were obliged to remain chaste for the thirty years that they served (they usually started at around age ten). If the flame should go out, the woman responsible was scourged; if she should lose her chastity, she was buried alive (her male part-ner-in-crime was flogged to death in front of the Curia). A vestal virgin could resign her post if she wished, and she had the benefit of residing in a very com-fortable palace: four floors of rooms around a central courtyard, with the round **Temple of Vesta** at the near end. The rooms are mainly ruins now, though they're fairly recognizable on the Palatine side, and you can get a good sense of the shape of the place from the remains of the courtyard (temporarily closed, but you can look through the fence), still with its pool in the centre and fringed by the statues or inscribed pedestals of some of the Vestals themselves.

Opposite the Vestals' house, the curved facade of the **Temple of Romulus** (the son of the emperor Maxentius), dating from 309 AD, has been sanctified and serves as vestibule for the church of **Santi Cosma e Damiano** behind. Just past the temple, a shady walkway to the left leads up to the **Basilica of Maxentius**, which rises up towards the main road – in terms of size and inge-nuity probably the Forum's most impressive remains. By the early fourth cen-tury, when this structure was built, Roman architects and engineers were expert at building with poured concrete. Begun by Maxentius, it was contin-ued by his co-emperor and rival, Constantine, after he had defeated him at the Battle of the Milvian Bridge in 312 AD. It's said that Michelangelo studied the hexagonal coffered arches here when grappling with the dome of St Peter's, and apparently Renaissance architects frequently used its apse and arches as a model.

Back on the Via Sacra, past the church of Santa Maria Nova, the **Antiquarium of the Forum** (daily except Mon 9am–5pm; free) houses a collection of statue fragments, capitals, tiles, mosaics and other bits and pieces. From the basilica the Via Sacra climbs more steeply to the **Arch of Titus**, which stands commandingly on a low arm of the Palatine Hill, looking one way down the remainder of the Via Sacra to the Colosseum, and back over the Forum proper. The arch was built by Titus's brother, Domitian, after the emperor's death in 81 AD, to commemorate his victories in Judea in 70 AD, and his triumphal return from that campaign. It's a much restored structure, and you can see, in reliefs on the inside, scenes of Titus riding in a chariot with Nike, goddess of Victory, being escorted by representatives of the Senate and Plebs, and, on the opposite side, spoils being removed from the Temple in Jerusalem. It's a long-standing tradition that Jews don't pass under this arch, though at the moment it's chained off anyway.

The Palatine Hill

Turning right at the Arch of Titus takes you up to the ticket booth and entrance to the **Palatine Hill** (summer Tues–Sat 9am–6pm, Sun 9am–1pm; winter Tues–Sat 9am–3pm, Sun 9am–1pm; €6.20, including admission to Colosseum, or for details of combined ticket, see box on p.723, last tickets 1hr before closing), supposedly where the city of Rome was founded and holding some of its most ancient remnants. In a way it's a more pleasant site to tour than the Forum, larger, greener and more of a park – a good place to have a picnic and relax after the rigours of the ruins below. In the days of the Republic, the Palatine was the most desirable address in Rome (from it is derived our word "palace"), and the big names continued to colonize it during the imperial era, trying to outdo each other with ever larger and more magnificent dwellings.

Following the main path up from the Forum, you come to the **Domus Flavia**, one of the most splendid residences, and, although it's now almost completely ruined, the peristyle is easy enough to identify, with its fountain and hexagonal brick arrangement in the centre. To the left, the top level of the gargantuan **Domus Augustana** spreads to the far brink of the hill – not the home of Augustus as its name suggests, but the private house of any emperor (or "Augustus"). You can look down from here on its vast central courtyard with maze-like fountain and wander to the brink of the deep trench of the **Stadium**. On the far side of the stadium, the ruins of the **Baths of Septimius Severus** cling to the side of the hill, the terrace giving good views over the Colosseum and the churches of the Celian Hill opposite.

Walking in the opposite direction from the Domus Flavia, steps lead down to the **Cryptoporticus** (currently closed for restoration), a long passage built by Nero to link the vestibule of his Domus Aurea with the Domus Augustana and other Palatine palaces, and decorated along part of its length with well-preserved Roman stucco-work. You can go either way along the passage: a left turn leads to the **House of Livia**, originally believed to have been the residence of Livia, the wife of Augustus, though now identified as simply part of Augustus's house (the set of ruins beyond). Its courtyard and some of the inner rooms are decorated with scanty frescoes.

Turn right down the passage and up some steps on the left and you're in the **Farnese Gardens**, among the first botanical gardens in Europe, laid out by Cardinal Alessandro Farnese in the mid-sixteenth century and now a tidily planted, shady retreat from the exposed heat of the ruins. The terrace here looks back over the Forum, while the terrace at the opposite end looks down on the church of San Teodoro, across to St Peter's, and on the new excavations immediately below – the traces of an **Iron Age village** that perhaps marks the real centre of Rome's ancient beginnings. The large grey building here houses the Palatine **Antiquarium** (free), which contains a vast assortment of statuary, pottery, terracotta antefixes and architectural fragments that have been excavated on the Palatine during the last 150 years. Much like the Forum Antiquarium, its most interesting exhibits are the very oldest, including models of how the Palatine looked in the Iron Age.

The Colosseum, Celian Hill and beyond

Leaving the Forum by way of the Via Sacra, under the Arch of Titus, you see the huge **Arch of Constantine** to your right, placed here in the early decades of the fourth century AD after Constantine had consolidated his power as sole emperor. The arch demonstrates the deterioration of the arts during the late stages of the Roman Empire, in that there were hardly any sculptors around good enough to produce original work and most of the sculptural decoration here had to be removed from other monuments.

Across from here, the **Colosseum** (summer Tues–Sat 9am–6pm, Sun 9am–1pm; winter Tues–Sat 9am–3pm, Sun 9am–1pm; €6.20, including admission to the Palatine or for details of combined ticket, see box on p.723) is perhaps Rome's most awe-inspiring ancient monument, and one which – unlike the Forum – needs little historical knowledge or imagination to deduce its function. Originally known as the Flavian Amphitheatre (the name Colosseum is a much later invention), it was begun around 72 AD by the Emperor Vespasian, who was anxious to extinguish the memory of Nero, and so chose the site of Nero's outrageous Domus Aurea (see p.749) for the stadium; the Colosseum is sited on a lake that lay in front of the vestibule of the palace, where Nero had erected a statue of himself as sun god. The lake was drained, and the Colosseum was – incredibly, given the size of the project – inaugurated by Vespasian's son Titus about eight years later, an event celebrated by a hundred days of continuous games; it was finally completed by Domitian, Titus's brother, the third of the Flavian emperors. It is said that seventy thousand Hebrew slaves did the heavy work at the Colosseum. Fifty thousand cartloads of pre-cut travertine stone were hauled from the quarries at Tivoli, a distance of seventeen miles. In the depths of what must have been the muddy bottom of the lake, a labyrinth was laid out, walling in passages for the contestants and creating areas for assembling and storing scenery and other requirements for gladiatorial contests.

The overall structure was tastefully designed, with close attention paid to decoration. On the outside, the arena's three arcades rose in strict classical fashion – Ionic, topped by Doric, topped by Corinthian, columns – to a flat surface at the top punctuated only by windows, where there was a series of supports for masts that protruded at the upper limit. These masts, 240 in total, were used to array a canvas awning over the spectators inside the arena. Inside, beyond the corridors that led up to the seats, lavishly decorated with painted stuccoes, there was room for a total of around 60,000 people seated and 10,000 or so standing; and the design is such that all 70,000 could enter and be seated in a matter of minutes – surely a lesson for designers of modern stadiums. The seating was allocated on a strict basis, with the emperor and his attendants naturally occupying the best seats in the house, and the social class of the spectators diminishing as you got nearer the top. There were no ticket sales as we conceive of them; rather, tickets were distributed through – and according to the social status of – Roman heads of households. These "tickets" were in fact wooden tags, with the entrance, row, aisle and seat number carved on them. Inside the amphitheatre, the labyrinth below was covered over with a wooden floor, punctuated at various intervals with trap doors, which could be opened as required, and lifts for raising and lowering the animals that were to take part in the games. The floor was covered with canvas to make it waterproof and the canvas was covered with several centimetres of sand to absorb blood; in fact, our word "arena" is derived from the Latin word for sand.

The Celian Hill

Some of the animals that were to die in the Colosseum were kept in a zoo up on the **Celian Hill**, just behind the arena, the furthest south of Rome's seven hills and probably its most peaceful, still clothed almost entirely in woodland and with the park of **Villa Celimontana** at its heart. You can get in here by way of the entrance on **Piazza della Navicella**, a little way down Via Claudia, and you could do worse than take a stroll through, before moving on to a couple of worthwhile churches. Continuing up to the summit of the hill, you'll come to the church of **Santi Giovanni e Paolo** (daily 8.30am–noon & 3.30–6.30pm), marked by its colourful campanile and set in a once-peaceful square that's been invaded by adolescent autograph hunters since Silvio Berlusconi's TV studios moved in opposite. Originally founded by a Roman senator called Pammachius, the church is in a way a memorial to conscientious objection, dedicated to two dignitaries in the court of Constantine who were beheaded here in 361 AD after refusing military service. The relics of their house are downstairs, although this is currently closed for restoration – around twenty rooms in all, frescoed with pagan and Christian subjects. Inside the church, the railed-off square in mid-nave marks the shrine where the saints were martyred and buried.

From the church the road descends under a succession of brick arches to the church of **San Gregorio Magno** on the left (daily 9am–noon & 3–6.30pm), in a commanding position above the traffic drone of the road below, and looking over to the lollipop pines of the Palatine Hill opposite. Again, it's the story behind the church that's most interesting. It was from here that St Gregory dispatched St Augustine in the early seventh century to convert England to Christianity, and although the rather ordinary Baroque interior shows little evidence of it, the chapel of the saint does have a beautifully carved altar showing scenes from his life, and there's a room containing his marble throne. More impressive is the structure to the left of the church, made up of three chapels and surrounded by cypress trees. **Santa Silvia** and **Sant'Andrea** contain **frescoes** by Guido Reni, Domenichino and Pomarancio, while **Santa Barbara** treasures the table at which St Gregory fed twelve paupers daily with his own hands for years.

San Clemente

From the Colosseum, it's a short walk east down Via San Giovanni in Laterano to the church of **San Clemente** (Mon–Sat 9am–12.30pm & 3–6pm, Sun opens 10am), a cream-coloured twelfth-century basilica that encapsulates perhaps better than any other the continuity of history in the city – being in fact a conglomeration of three places of worship. The ground-floor church is a superb example of a medieval basilica: its facade and courtyard face east in the archaic fashion, and there are some fine, warm mosaics in the apse and a chapel with frescoes by Masolino. Downstairs (same hours as church; €2.30) there's the nave of an earlier church, dated back to 392 AD, with a frescoed narthex depicting, among other things, the *Miracle of San Clemente*. And at the eastern end of this church, steps lead down to a third level: a labyrinthine set of rooms including a dank Mithraic temple of the late second century, set among several rooms of a Roman house built after the fire of 64 AD. In the temple is preserved a statue of Mithras slaying the bull and the seats upon which the worshippers sat during their ceremonies. The underground river that formerly fed the lake in front of the Domus Aurea can be heard rushing to its destination in the Tiber, behind the Circo Massimo, a reminder that Rome is built on very shaky foundations indeed.

San Giovanni in Laterano

Continuing down the same street brings you out eventually at the basilica of **San Giovanni in Laterano** (daily: summer 7am–7pm; winter 7am–6pm). Officially Rome's cathedral and the seat of the pope as bishop of Rome, this was for centuries the main papal residence. However, when the papacy returned from Avignon at the end of the fourteenth century, the Lateran palaces were in ruin and uninhabitable, and the pope moved across town to the Vatican, where he has remained ever since. There has been a church on this site since the fourth century, the first established by Constantine, and the present building, reworked by Borromini in the mid-seventeenth century, evokes – like San Clemente or San Stefano – Rome's staggering wealth of history, with a host of features from different periods. The doors to the church, oddly enough, were taken from the Curia of the Roman Forum.

The **interior** has been extensively reworked over the centuries. Much of what you see today dates from 1600, when Clement VIII had the church remodelled for that Holy Year. The first pillar on the left of the right-hand aisle shows a fragment of Giotto's fresco of Boniface VIII, proclaiming the first Holy Year in 1300. Further on, a more recent monument commemorates Sylvester I – "the magician pope", Bishop of Rome during much of Constantine's reign – and incorporates part of his original tomb, said to sweat and rattle its bones when a pope is about to die. Kept secure behind the papal altar are the heads of St Peter and St Paul, the church's prize relics. Outside, the **cloisters** (daily 9am–5pm; €2) are one of the most pleasing parts of the complex, decorated with early thirteenth-century Cosmati work and with fragments of the original basilica arranged around in no particular order, including a remarkable papal throne assembly and various papal artefacts (not least the vestments of Boniface VIII) in a room off to the side.

Adjoining the basilica is the **Lateran Palace**, home of the popes in the Middle Ages and also formally part of Vatican territory. Next door, the **Baptistry** (daily: summer 9am–1pm & 5–7pm; winter 9am–1pm & 4–6pm; free) has been carefully restored, along with the side of the church itself, after a car bombing in 1993. It is the oldest surviving baptistry in the Christian world, a mosaic-lined, octagonal structure built during the fifth century that has been the model for many such buildings since. There are more ancient remains on the other side of the church, on Piazza di Porta San Giovanni, foremost of which is the **Scala Santa** (daily 6.15am–12.15pm & 3.30–6.30pm), claimed to be the staircase from Pontius Pilate's house down which Christ walked after his trial. The 28 steps are protected by boards, and the only way you're allowed to climb them is on your knees, which pilgrims do regularly – although there is also a staircase to the side for the less penitent. At the top, the chapel of **San Lorenzo** holds an ancient (sixth- or seventh-century) painting of Christ said to be the work of an angel, hence its name – *acheiropoeton*, or "not done by human hands".

Santa Croce in Gerusalemme

Across the far side of the square, the **Porta Asinaria**, one of the city's grander gateways, marks the Aurelian Wall, which leads around on its city side by way of Viale Carlo Felice to another key Roman church, **Santa Croce in Gerusalemme**, one of the seven pilgrimage churches of Rome (daily 6am–noon & 3.30–7pm). Built on the site of the palace of Constantine's mother St Helena, it houses the relics of the true cross she had brought back from Jerusalem. The building is mainly Baroque in style following an eighteenth-century renovation, but the relics of the cross are stored in a surreal Mussolini-era chapel at the end of the left aisle, and there are some very fine Renaissance apse frescoes, recording the discovery of the fragments. North of here, towards the rail tracks, the **Porta Maggiore** is probably the most impressive of all the city gates, built in the first century AD to carry water into Rome from the aqueducts outside.

The Esquiline Hill, Termini and beyond

On the far side of the main road, Via Labacana, from the Colosseum, the **Esquiline Hill** is the highest and largest of the city's seven hills. Nowadays it's a mixed area, but one which almost every traveller to Rome encounters at some point – not just because of key sights like Nero's Domus Aurea and the basilica of Santa Maria Maggiore, and the grand developments of post-Unification Rome around Via Nazionale and Via XX Settembre, but also because of Stazione Termini, whose tawdry environs are home to the lion's share of Rome's budget hotels.

The Domus Aurea

One of the Esquiline Hill's most intriguing sights is without doubt Nero's **Domus Aurea** or "Golden House" (daily 9am–8pm, guided tours obligatory; €8.25, plus €1.05 reservation fee – booking recommended, ☎06.3974.9907). The entrance is off Via Labacana, in the Parco Oppio, almost opposite the Colosseum. Built on the summit of the Oppian and into its sides after a fire of 64 AD devastated this part of Rome, the "house" was a vast undertaking, but it was not intended to be a residence at all; rather it was a series of banqueting rooms, nymphaeums, small baths, terraces and gardens, facing what at the time was a small lake fed by the underground springs that drained from the surrounding hills. Rome was used to Nero's excesses, but it had never seen anything like the Golden House before. The facade was supposed to have been coated in solid gold, there was hot and cold running water in the baths, one of the dining rooms was rigged up to shower flowers and natural scent on guests, and the grounds – which covered a full square mile – held vineyards and game. Nero didn't get to enjoy his palace for long – he died a couple of years after it was finished, and Vespasian tore a lot of the exposed facade down in disgust, draining its lake and building the Colosseum on top. Later Trajan built his baths on top of the rest of the complex, and it was pretty much forgotten until its wall paintings were discovered by Renaissance artists, including Raphael. When these artists first visited these rooms, they had to climb down ladders into what they believed at first was some kind of mystical cave, or grotto – giving us the word *grotesque*, which they used to describe their attempts to imitate this style of painting in their own work. The guided tours take in various covered fountains, service corridors, terraces and, most spectacularly, the Octagonal Room – domed, with a hole in the middle, which is supposed to have rotated as the day progressed to emulate the passage of the sun. Most of the rooms are decorated with fanciful depictions of people looking out of windows at you, garlands of flowers, fruit, vines and foliage, interspersed with mythical animals. Perhaps the best-preserved frescoes are in the room of Achilles at Skyros, illustrating Homer's story of Achilles being sent to the island of Skyros disguised as a woman to prevent him being drawn into the Trojan wars.

San Pietro in Vincoli

Steps lead up from Colosseum metro station to Via Terme di Tito and left into Via Eudossia, which leads to the tranquil piazza of the restored church of **San Pietro in Vincoli** (daily 8am–12.30pm & 3.30–6pm) – one of Rome's most delightfully plain churches, built to house an important relic, the chains that held St Peter when he was in Jerusalem and those that held him in Rome, which miraculously joined together. The chains can still be seen in the *confessio* beneath the high altar, in a beautiful gold and rock crystal reliquary, but most people come for the tomb of Pope Julius II at the far end of the southern aisle, which occupied Michelangelo on and off for much of his career and was the cause of many a dispute with Julius and his successors. Michelangelo reluctantly gave it up to paint the Sistine Chapel, and never again found the time to return to it for very long, being always at the beck and call of successive popes – who understandably had little interest in promoting the glory of one of their predecessors. No one knows how the tomb would have looked had it been finished, and the only statues that Michelangelo completed are the Moses, Leah and Rachel, which remain here in the church, and two Slaves which are now in the Louvre. The figure of Moses, however, pictured as descended from Sinai to find the Israelites worshipping the golden calf, and flanked by the gentle figures of Leah and Rachel, is one of the artist's most captivating works, the rest of the composition – completed by later artists – seeming dull and static by comparison.

Via Cavour and Santa Maria Maggiore

Steps lead down from San Pietro in Vincoli to **Via Cavour**, a busy central thoroughfare which carves a route between the Colosseum and Termini station. After about half a kilometre the street widens to reveal the basilica of **Santa Maria Maggiore** (daily: summer 7am–7pm; winter 7am–6pm), one of the city's five great basilicas, and with one of Rome's best-preserved Byzantine interiors – a fact belied by its dull eighteenth-century exterior. Unlike the other great places of pilgrimage in Rome, Santa Maria Maggiore was not built on any special Constantinian site, but instead went up during the fifth century after the Council of Ephesus recognized the cult of the Virgin and churches venerating Our Lady began to spring up all over the Christian world. According to legend, the Virgin Mary appeared to Pope Liberius in a dream on the night of August 4, 352 AD, telling him to build a church on the Esquiline hill, on a spot where he would find a patch of newly fallen snow the next morning. The snow would outline exactly the plan of the church that should be built there in her honour – which of course is exactly what happened, and the first church here was called Santa Maria della Neve ("of the snow"). The present structure dates from about 420 AD, and was completed under the reign of St Sixtus III, and survives remarkably intact, the broad nave fringed on both sides with strikingly well-kept mosaics, most of which date from the church's construction and recount incidents from the Old Testament. The chapel in the right transept holds the elaborate tomb of Sixtus V – another, less famous, Sistine Chapel, decorated with frescoes and stucco reliefs portraying events from his reign. It also contains the tomb of another zealous and reforming pope, St Pius V, whose statue faces that of Sixtus. Outside the Sistine Chapel is the tomb slab of the Bernini family, including Gian Lorenzo himself, while opposite, the Pauline Chapel is even more sumptuous, home to the tombs of the Borghese pope, Paul V, and his immediate predecessor Clement VIII. The altar, of lapis lazuli and agate, contains a Madonna and Child dating from the twelfth or thirteenth century. Between the two chapels, the *confessio* contains a kneeling statue of Pope Pius IX, and, beneath it, a reliquary that is said to contain fragments of the crib of Christ, in rock crystal and silver. Finally, the thirteenth-century mosaics of *Christ Pantocrator and the Legend of the Snow*, in the loggia above the main entrance, are definitely worth a look (daily 9.30am–6pm; €2.60).

Santa Prassede and Santa Pudenziana

Behind Santa Maria Maggiore, off Via Merulana, the ninth-century church of **Santa Prassede** occupies an ancient site, where it's claimed St Prassede harboured Christians on the run from the Roman persecutions. She apparently collected the blood and remains of the martyrs and placed them in a well where she herself was later buried; a red marble disc in the floor of the nave marks the spot. In the southern aisle, the Chapel of Saint Zeno was built by Pope Paschal I as a mausoleum for his mother, Theodora, and is decorated with marvellous ninth-century mosaics that make it glitter like a jewel-encrusted bowl. The chapel also contains a fragment of a column supposed to be the one to which Christ was tied when he was scourged. On the other side of Via Cavour, the church of **Santa Pudenziana** on Via Urbana has equally ancient origins, dedicated to St Prassede's supposed sister and for many years believed to have been built on the site where St Peter lived and worshipped – though this has since been entirely discredited. There were for years two relics in the church, the chair that St Peter used as his throne and the table at which he said Mass, though both have long gone – to the Vatican and the Lateran, respectively. But the church still has one feature of ancient origin, the superb fifth-century apse mosaics – some of the oldest Christian figurative mosaics in Rome, though they've been tampered with and restored over the years.

Via Nazionale and Piazza della Repubblica

A couple of minutes' walk north-west from Santa Maria Maggiore, **Via Nazionale** connects Piazza Venezia and the centre of town with the area around Termini and the eastern districts beyond. A focus for much development after Unification, its heavy, overbearing buildings were constructed to give Rome some semblance of modern sophistication when it became capital of the new country, but most are now occupied by hotels and bland shops and boutiques. At the top of Via Nazionale, **Piazza della Repubblica** – formerly Piazza Esedra – is typical of Rome's nineteenth-century regeneration, a stern, once dignified but now rather shabby semicircle of buildings given over to cheap hotels, street vendors, travel agents and fast-food joints, and centring on a fountain surrounded by languishing nymphs and sea monsters.

The piazza actually follows the outlines of the exedra of the Baths of Diocletian, the remains of which lie across the piazza and are partially contained in the church of **Santa Maria degli Angeli** – not Rome's most welcoming church but giving the best impression of the size and grandeur of Diocletian's bath complex. It's a huge, open building, with an interior standardized by Vanvitelli into a rich eighteenth-century confection after a couple of centuries of piecemeal adaptation (started by an aged Michelangelo). The pink granite pillars, at nine feet in diameter the largest in Rome, are original, and the main transept formed the main hall of the baths; only the crescent shape of the facade remains from the original caldarium (it had previously been hidden by a newer facing), the vestibule (the tepidarium) and main transept. The meridian that strikes diagonally across the floor here was, until 1846, the regulator of time for Romans (now a cannon shot fired daily at noon from the Janiculum Hill).

Palazzo Massimo

Across from Santa Maria degli Angeli, through a seedy little park, the snazzily restored **Palazzo Massimo** at Largo di Villa Perretti is home, together with the Palazzo Altemps (see p.731), to the Museo Nazionale Romano (Tues–Sat 9am–7pm, Sun 9am–2pm; €6, or, for details of combined ticket, see box on p.723), a superb collection of Greek and Roman antiquities, second only to the Vatican's, which has been entirely reorganized and features many pieces that have remained undisplayed for decades. The ground floor of the museum is devoted to statuary of the early Empire, including an unparalleled selection of busts of the emperors and their families. There are silver and gold coins from the seventh century BC to the first century AD, and, further on, a painted frieze from the first century BC showing scenes from the Trojan War and the legend of the founding of Rome. The top-floor gallery has a room devoted to the Flavian emperors – look out for the bust of Vespasian – and beyond there's more statuary from the imperial era, a room of bronze fittings from ships found at Lake Nemi, south of Rome, and some stunning frescoes from the country villa, north of Rome, of the emperor Augustus's wife Livia, depicting an orchard dense with fruit and flowers and patrolled by partridges, doves and other feathered friends. On the same floor, there are also some of the best mosaics ever found in Roman villas around the world – highlight of which are the floors from the Villa di Baccano on Via Cassia, including four mosaic panels taken from a bedroom, featuring four chariot drivers and their horses, so finely crafted that from a distance they look as if they've been painted.

Stazione Termini

Across the street is the low white facade of **Stazione Termini** (so named for its proximity to the Baths of Diocletian, nothing to do with being the termini of Rome's rail lines) and the vast, bus-crammed hubbub that is Piazza dei Cinquecento in front. The station is an ambitious piece of modern architectural design that was completed in 1950 and still entirely dominates the streets around with its low-slung, self-consciously futuristic lines. It recently received a huge and sleek renovation that converted part of its cavernous ticket hall to retail and restaurant space and upgraded the building in general – making it a nice spot for a browse and a wander, and a marvellous place to catch a train. As for **Piazza dei Cinquecento**, it's a good place to find buses and taxis, but otherwise it and the areas around are pretty much low-life territory, and although not especially dangerous, not a place to hang around for long either.

Via XX Settembre and Santa Maria della Vittoria

Just to the north of Termini, **Via XX Settembre** spears out towards the Aurelian Wall from Via del Quirinale – not Rome's most appealing thoroughfare by any means, flanked by the deliberately faceless bureaucracies of the national government, erected after Unification in anticipation of Rome's ascension as a new world capital. It was, however, the route by which Garibaldi's troops entered the city on September 20, 1870, and the place where they breached the wall is marked with a column. The church of **Santa Maria della Vittoria** here (Jan–July & Sept–Dec daily 6.30am–noon & 4.30–7.00pm) was built by Carlo Maderno and its interior is one of the most elaborate examples of Baroque decoration in Rome: almost shockingly excessive to modern eyes, its ceiling and walls are pitted with carving, and statues are crammed into remote corners as in an over-stuffed attic. The church's best-known feature, Bernini's carving of the *Ecstasy of St Theresa*, the centrepiece of the sepulchral chapel of Cardinal Cornaro, continues the histrionics – a deliberately melodramatic work featuring a theatrically posed St Theresa.

Via Nomentana

At the north end of Via XX Settembre, the **Porta Pia** was one of the last works of Michelangelo, erected under Pope Pius IV in 1561, beyond which the wide boulevard of **Via Nomentana** leads up eventually to the church of **Sant'Agnese fuori le Mura** (Mon 9am–noon, Tues–Sat 9am–noon & 4–6pm, Sun 4–6pm), served by bus #36/60 from Termini. Dedicated to the same saint who was martyred in Domitian's Stadium in 303 AD, the church was built by Honorius I in the seventh century, when he reworked Constantine's original structure. The apse mosaic is Byzantine in style and contemporary with Honorius's building, showing Agnes next to the pope, who holds a model of his church. Out of the narthex the custodian will lead you down into the **catacombs** (same hours as church; €4.15) that sprawl below the church, which are among the best-preserved and most crowd-free of all the city's catacombs. Indeed, if you only have time for one set of catacombs during your stay in Rome (and they really are all very much alike), these are among the best.

After the catacombs the guide will show you a further part of what is really a small complex of early Christian structures, the church of **Santa Constanza** (usually open the same hours as Sant'Agnese; free), which more than any other building in Rome, perhaps, illustrates the transition from the pagan to Christian city in its decorative and architectural features. Built in 350 AD as a mausoleum for Constantia and Helena, the daughters of the Emperor Constantine, it's a round structure which follows the traditional shape of the great pagan tombs (consider those of Hadrian and Augustus elsewhere in the city), and the mosaics on the vaulting of its circular ambulatory – fourth-century depictions of vines, leaves and birds – would have been as at home on the floor of a Roman *domus* as they were in a Christian church.

San Lorenzo

South and east of Via Nomentana, a short walk from Termini, the neighbourhood of **San Lorenzo** spreads from the main campus of Rome's university, on the far side of Via Tiburtina, to the railway tracks – a solidly working-class district that retains something of its local air and is home to some good and often inexpensive local restaurants (see p.775). The area takes its name from the church of **San Lorenzo fuori le Mura** on Via Tiburtina, one of the seven great pilgrimage churches of Rome, and a typical Roman basilica, fronted by a columned portico and with a lovely twelfth-century cloister to its side (daily: summer 7am–noon & 4–7.30pm; winter closes 5.30pm). The original church here was built over the site of St Lawrence's martyrdom by Constantine – the saint was reputedly burned to death on a gridiron, halfway through his ordeal apparently uttering the immortal words, "Turn me, I am done on this side." Where the church of San Lorenzo differs is that it is actually a combination of three churches built at different periods – one a sixth-century reconstruction of Constantine's church by Pelagius II, which now forms the chancel, another a fifth-century church from the time of Sixtus III, both joined by a basilica from the thirteenth century by Honorius II. Because of its proximity to Rome's rail yards, the church was bombed heavily during World War II, but it has been rebuilt with sensitivity, and remains much as it was originally. Inside there are features from all periods: a Cosmetic floor, thirteenth-century pulpits and a Paschal candlestick. The mosaic on the inside of the triumphal arch is a sixth-century depiction of Pelagius offering his church to Christ; while below stairs, catacombs (currently closed for restoration) – where St Lawrence was apparently buried – lead a dank path from the pillars of Constantine's original structure. There's also a Romanesque cloister with well-tended garden that you can get into through the sacristy.

Villa Borghese and North Central Rome

Immediately above Piazza del Popolo, the hill known as the Pincio marks the edge of the city's core and the beginning of a collection of parks and gardens that forms Rome's largest central open space – the **Villa Borghese**, made up of the grounds of the seventeenth-century pleasure palace of Scipione Borghese, which were bought by the city at the beginning of the last century. It's a huge area, and its woods, lake and grass criss-crossed by roads are about as near as you can get to peace in the city centre without making too much effort. There are any number of attractions for those who want to do more than just stroll or sunbathe: a tiny boating lake, a zoo – a cruel affair well worth avoiding – and some of the city's finest museums.

The **Pincio Hill** isn't formally part of the Villa Borghese, but its terrace and gardens, laid out by Valadier in the early nineteenth century and fringed with dilapidated busts of classical and Italian heroes, give fine views over the roofs, domes and TV antennae of central Rome. South of here are more gardens in the grounds of the **Villa Medici**, though as the villa is home to the French Academy, they can usually only be visited on selected days, when they host concerts and art shows.

Galleria Borghese

Situated on the far eastern edge of the Villa Borghese park is the **Galleria Borghese** (Tues–Sat 9am–7.30pm; pre-booked visits only, every 2hr; reservations Mon–Fri 9am–7pm, Sat 9am–1pm on ☎06.32.81.02; €6.20 plus €1.05 reservation fee), built in the early seventeenth century by Cardinal Scipione Borghese and turned over to the state when the gardens became city property in 1902. Reopened some years ago after a lengthy restoration, it has taken its place as one of Rome's great treasure houses and should not be missed.

The **ground floor** contains mainly sculpture: a mixture of ancient Roman items and seventeenth-century works, roughly linked together with late-eighteenth-century ceiling paintings showing scenes from the Trojan War. Highlights include, in the first room off the entrance hall, Canova's famously erotic statue of *Pauline Borghese* posed as Venus – Pauline Borghese, the sister of Napoleon and married (reluctantly) to the reigning Prince Borghese, was a shocking woman in her day, with grand habits. There are tales of her jewels and clothes, of the Negro who used to carry her from her bath, of the servants she used as footstools, and, of course, her long line of lovers. Next door, there's a marvellous statue of David by Bernini – the face of which is a self-portrait of the sculptor – and, further on, a dramatic, poised statue of Apollo and Daphne that captures the split second when Daphne is transformed into a laurel tree, with her fingers becoming leaves and her legs tree trunks. Next door, the walls of the Room of the Emperors are flanked by seventeenth- and eighteenth-century busts of Roman emperors, facing another Bernini sculpture, *The Rape of Persepone* dating from 1622, a coolly virtuosic work that shows in melodramatic form the story of the abduction to the underworld of the beautiful nymph Persepone. Finally, the so-called Room of Silenus contains a variety of paintings by Cardinal Scipione's faithful servant Caravaggio – notably the *Madonna of the Grooms* from 1605, a painting that at the time was considered to have depicted Christ far too realistically to hang in a central Rome church, so Cardinal Scipione happily bought it for his collection. Look also at *St Jerome*, captured writing at a table lit only by a source of light that streams in from the upper left of the picture, and his *David holding the Head of Goliath*, sent by Caravaggio to Cardinal Scipione from exile in Malta, where he had fled to escape capital punishment for various crimes, in the hope of winning a reprieve.

Upstairs is the Galleria Borghese's **Pinacoteca**, literally one of the richest collections of paintings in the world, although unfortunately you're only allowed half an hour up here before having to leave. In the first room are several important paintings by Raphael, his teacher Perugino and other masters of the Umbrian school from the late fifteenth and early sixteenth centuries, not least some Raphaels, including his *Deposition*, painted in 1507 for a noble of Perugia in memory of her son, and pillaged from Perugia cathedral by associates of Cardinal Scipione. In further rooms there are more early-sixteenth-century paintings, prominent among which is Cranach's *Venus and Cupid with a Honeycomb*, of 1531, Lorenzo Lotto's touching *Portrait of a Man*, and, at the back of the building, a series of self-portraits done by Bernini at various stages of his long life. Next to these are a lifelike bust of Cardinal Scipione executed by Bernini in 1632, portraying him as the worldly connoisseur of fine art and fine living that he was, and a smaller bust of Pope Paul V, also by Bernini. Beyond here, in a further room, there is a painting of *Diana* by Domechino, showing the goddess and her attendants doing a bit of target practice, and Titian's *Sacred and Profane Love*, painted in 1514 when he was about 25 years old, to celebrate the marriage of the Venetian noble Nicolò Aurelio (whose coat of arms is on the sarcophagus).

Galleria Nazionale d'Arte Moderna

The Villa Borghese's two other major museums are situated on the other side of the park, about 1km away along the Viale delle Belle Arti, and of these, the **Galleria Nazionale d'Arte Moderna**, at no. 131 (Tues–Sat 9am–7.30pm; shorter hours in winter; €6.50), is probably the least compulsory, a lumbering, Neoclassical building housing a collection that isn't really as grand as you might expect, made up of a wide selection of nineteenth- and twentieth-century Italian (and a few foreign) names. The nineteenth-century collection, on the upper floor, contains a lot of marginal Italian masters (as well as a Van Gogh). The twentieth-century collection is more appealing, and includes work by Modigliani, De Chirico, Giacomo Balla, Boccione and other Futurists, along with the odd Cézanne, Mondrian and Klimt, and some post-war canvases by the likes of Mark Rothko and Jackson Pollock.

Museo Nazionale di Villa Giulia

The **Museo Nazionale di Villa Giulia** (Tues–Sat 8.30am–7.30pm; €4), five minutes' walk away in the direction of Via Flaminia, is more of an essential stop, housing as it does the world's primary collection of Etruscan treasures (along with the Etruscan collection in the Vatican), and a good introduction – or conclusion – to the Etruscan sites in Lazio, which between them contributed most of the artefacts on display here. It's not an especially large collection, but it's worth taking the trouble to see the whole. The **east wing** houses bronze objects dating from the seventh and sixth centuries BC, as well as terracottas of Apollo and Hercules from the temple complex at Veii near Rome and a number of terracotta votive offerings of anatomical parts of the human body, their detail alluding to the Etruscans' accomplishments in medicine. The most famous piece though is the remarkable Sarcophagus of the Married Couple from Cerveteri (see p.787), a touchingly lifelike portrayal of a husband and wife lying on a couch. Upstairs is an exhibition devoted to the **Ficaroni Cista**, a superb example of the Etruscan *cistae*, drum-like metal objects, engraved and adorned with figures, which were supposed to hold all the things needed for the care of the body after death. The upper floor of the museum's **west wing** is devoted to the Faliscians, a people from northeast Lazio, who were closely affiliated with the Etruscans. There are gaudily coloured terracotta figures that leer, run, jump and climb, a drinking horn in the shape of a dog's head that is so lifelike you almost expect it to bark, and a bronze disc breastplate from the seventh century BC decorated with a weird, almost modern pattern of galloping creatures. The ground floor of the west wing of the museum displays artefacts found outside Etruria proper but of obvious Etruscan provenance or heavily influenced by the Etruscans.

North Central Rome

In the northeast of the city lies the enormous public park of the **Villa Ada**, connected with Villa Borghese by Via Salaria – the old trading route between the Romans and Sabines, so called because the main product transported along here was salt. The Villa Ada was once the estate of King Vittorio Emanuele III and is a nice enough place in which to while away an afternoon, but otherwise not really worth the special journey from the centre of town. The **Catacombe di Priscilla** (Feb–Dec Tues–Sun 8.30am–noon & 2.30–5pm; €4.15 including tour), which you can reach from Via Salaria, are the only real thing to see – a frescoed labyrinth of tunnels that is visitable on regular (obligatory) guided tours and are home to a number of obviously Christian frescoes – Daniel in the lions' den, the resurrection of Lazarus, the sacrifice of Isaac – painted between the second and fourth centuries AD. One of the frescoes is claimed to be the earliest known depiction of the *Virgin and Child*, though it could in fact simply be a picture of a mother and child, both of whom were probably buried here.

To the northwest the Tiber sweeps around in a wide hook-shaped bend. These northern outskirts of Rome aren't particularly enticing, though the **Ponte Milvio**, the old, originally Roman, footbridge where the emperor Constantine defeated Maxentius in 312 AD, still stands and provides wonderful views of the meandering Tiber, with the city springing up green on the hills to both sides and the river running fast and silty below. On the northern side of the river, **Piazzale di Ponte Milvio** sports a cheap and cheerful market (Mon–Sat 8am–1.30pm) and a handful of bars and restaurants, and is ten minutes' walk southwest from the **Foro Italico** sports centre, one of the few parts of Rome to survive intact pretty much the way Mussolini planned it.

South Central Rome

On its southern side, the Palatine Hill drops down to the **Circo Massimo**, a long, thin, green expanse bordered by heavily trafficked roads that was the ancient city's main venue for chariot races. At one time this arena had a capacity of up to 400,000 spectators, and if it were still intact it would no doubt match the Colosseum for grandeur. As it is, a litter of stones at the Viale Aventino end is all that remains, together with – at the southern end – a little medieval tower built by the Frangipani family.

The Baths of Caracalla

Across the far side of Piazza di Porta Capena, the **Baths of Caracalla**, Viale Terme di Caracalla 52 (summer Mon & Sun 9am–1pm, Tues–Sat 9am–6pm; winter Mon & Sun 9am–1pm, Tues–Sat 9am–3pm; €4.20), are much better preserved, and they give a far better sense of the scale and monumentality of Roman architecture than most of the extant ruins in the city – so much so that

Shelley was moved to write *Prometheus Unbound* here in 1819. The baths are no more than a shell now, but the walls still rise to very nearly their original height. There are many fragments of mosaics – none spectacular, but quite a few bright and well preserved – and it's easy to discern a floor plan. As for Caracalla, he was one of Rome's worst and shortest-lived rulers, and it's no wonder there's nothing else in the city built by him. The baths have until recently been used for occasional opera performances during the summer (one of Mussolini's better ideas), but these have largely stopped owing to damage to the site. Watch out for their re-emergence, though – it's a thrilling and inexpensive way to see the baths at their most atmospheric.

The Aventine Hill

Cross back over Viale Aventino after seeing the baths and scale the **Aventine Hill** – the southernmost of the city's seven hills and the heart of plebeian Rome in ancient times. These days the working-class quarters of the city are further south, and the Aventine is in fact one of the city's more upscale residential areas, covered with villas and gardens and one of the few places in the city where you can escape the traffic. A short way up Via Santa Sabina, the church of **Santa Sabina** (daily 7am–12.45pm & 3.30–6pm) is a strong contender for Rome's most beautiful basilica: high and wide, its nave and portico restored back to their fifth-century appearance in the 1930s. Look especially at the main doors, which are contemporary with the church and boast eighteen panels carved with Christian scenes, forming a complete illustrated Bible, which includes one of the oldest representations of the Crucifixion in existence. Santa Sabina is also the principal church of the Dominicans, and it's claimed that the orange trees in the garden outside, which you can glimpse on your way to the restrained cloister, are descendants of those planted by St Dominic himself. Whatever the truth of this, the views from the gardens are splendid – right across the Tiber to the centre of Rome and St Peter's.

There are other churches on the Aventine, and in any case it's a nice place to wander. Follow the road south past the **Priorato di Malta**, one of several buildings in the city belonging to the Knights of Malta, which has a celebrated view of the dome of St Peter's through the keyhole of its main gate. The little piazza in front of the main gate has marble triumphal insignia designed and placed here by Piranesi to celebrate the knights' dramatic history.

Testaccio

On the far side of Via Marmorata, below, the solid working-class neighbourhood of **TESTACCIO** groups around a couple of main squares, a tight-knit community with a market and a number of bars and small trattorias that was for many years synonymous with the slaughterhouse that sprawls down to the Tiber just beyond. In recent years the area has become a trendy place to live, property prices have soared, and some uneasy contradictions have emerged, with vegetarian restaurants opening their doors in an area still known for the offal dishes served in its traditional trattorias, and gay and alternative clubs standing cheek-by-jowl with the car-repair shops gouged into Monte Testaccio.

The slaughterhouse, or **Mattatoio**, once the area's main employer, is now home to the *centro sociale* "Villaggio Globale", a space used for concerts, raves and exhibitions, along with stabling for the city's horse-and-carriage drivers, a gymnasium, and a small gypsy camp. For years there has been talk of sprucing it up into a *chi-chi* affair of shops and restaurants, but so far nothing has happened, and it's likely to remain as it is for some time to come. Opposite the slaughterhouse, **Monte Testaccio**, which gives the area its name, is a 35-metre-high mound created out of the shards of Roman amphorae that were dumped here over some 600 years. The ancients were not aware of the fact that the terracotta amphorae could be recycled, and consequently broke them up into small shards and laid them down in an orderly manner, sprinkling quicklime on them to dissolve the residual wine or oil and so creating the mountain you see today. It's an odd sight, the ceramic curls visible through the tufts of grass that crown its higher reaches.

The Protestant Cemetery

On the opposite side of Via Zabaglia, Via Caio Cestio leads up to the entrance of the **Protestant Cemetery** (Tues–Sun 9am–5pm; donation expected), one of the shrines to the English in Rome and a fitting conclusion to a visit to the Keats-Shelley Memorial House (see p.738), since it is here that both poets are buried, along with a handful of other well-known names. In fact, the cemetery's title is a misnomer – the cemetery is reserved for non-Roman Catholics so you'll also find famous Italian atheists, Christians of the Orthodox persuasion, and the odd Jew or Muslim, buried here. It's a small and surprisingly tranquil enclave, crouched behind the mossy pyramidal **tomb** of one Caius Cestius, who died in 12 BC, and home to a friendly colony of well-fed cats. Part of Cestius's will decreed that all his slaves should be freed, and the white pyramid you see today was thrown up by them in only 330 days of what must have been joyful building.

Most visitors come here to see the grave of Keats, who lies next to his friend, the painter Joseph Severn, in a corner of the old part of the cemetery near the pyramid, his stone inscribed as he wished with the words "Here lies one whose name was writ in water". Severn died much later than Keats but asked to be laid here nonetheless, together with his brushes and palette. Shelley's ashes were brought here at Mary Shelley's request and interred, after much obstruction by the papal authorities, in the newer part of the cemetery, at the opposite end. The Shelleys had visited several years earlier, the poet praising it as "the most beautiful and solemn cemetery I ever beheld". It had been intended that Shelley should rest with his young son, William, who was also buried here, but his remains couldn't be found (although his small grave lies nearby). Among other famous internees, Edward Trelawny lies next door, the political writer and activist, Gramsci, on the far right-hand side in the middle, to name just two – though if you're at all interested in star-spotting you should ask to have a look at the English booklet at the entrance.

From the Protestant Cemetery, you could make a long (hour or so) detour back into the city centre following the **Aurelian Wall**, built by the emperor Aurelian (and his successor Probus) in 275 AD to enclose Rome's seven hills. One of the best-preserved stretches runs between Porta San Paolo and Porta San Sebastiano: walk through Porta San Paolo and turn left, and follow the walls keeping them always on your left.

San Paolo fuori le Mura

Two kilometres or so south of the Porta San Paolo, the basilica of **San Paolo fuori le Mura** (daily 7.30am–6.30pm) is one of the five patriarchal basilicas of Rome, occupying the supposed site of St Paul's tomb, where he was laid to rest after being beheaded at Tre Fontane (see p.760). Of the five, this basilica has probably fared the least well over the years. It was apparently once the grandest of them all, connected to the Aurelian Wall by a mile-long colonnade of 800 marble columns, but a ninth-century sacking by the Saracens and a devastating fire in 1823 means that the church you see now is largely a nineteenth-century reconstruction, sited in what is these days a rather unenticing neighbourhood.

For all that, it's a very successful if somewhat clinical rehash of the former church, succeeding where St Peter's tries (but ultimately fails) by impressing with sheer size and grandeur: whether you enter by way of the cloisters or the west door, it's impossible not to be awed by the space of the building inside, its crowds of columns topped by round-arched arcading. Some parts of the building did survive the fire. In the south transept, the paschal candlestick is a remarkable piece of Romanesque carving, supported by half-human beasts and rising through entwined tendrils and strangely human limbs and bodies to scenes from Christ's life, the figures crowding in together as if for a photocall. The bronze aisle doors date from 1070 and were also rescued from the old basilica, as was the thirteenth-century tabernacle by Arnolfo di Cambio. The arch across the apse is original too, embellished with mosaics donated by the Byzantine queen Galla Placidia in the sixth century that show Christ giving a blessing, angels, the symbols of the Gospels, and saints Peter and Paul. There's also the cloister, just behind here – probably Rome's finest piece of Cosmatesque work, its spiralling, mosaic-encrusted columns enclosing a peaceful rose garden.

EUR

From San Paolo, Via Ostiense leads south to join up with Via Cristoforo Colombo which in turn runs down to **EUR** (pronounced "eh-oor") – the acronym for the district built for the "Esposizione Universale Roma". It's quite a walk, so you'd be better off taking bus #714 from Termini or Metro line B. This is not so much a neighbourhood as a statement in stone: planned by Mussolini for the aborted 1942 World Fair and not finished until well after the war, it's a cold, soulless grid of square buildings, long vistas and wide processional boulevards linked tenuously to the rest of Rome by metro but light years away from the city in feel. Come here for its numerous museums, some of which *are* worth the trip, or if you have a yen for modern architecture and urban planning; otherwise, stay well clear.

The great flaw of EUR is that it's not built for people: the streets are wide thoroughfares designed for easy traffic flow and fast driving, shops and cafés are easily outnumbered by offices. Of the buildings, the post-war development of the area threw up bland office blocks for the most part, and it's the pre-war Fascist-style constructions that are of most interest. The **Palazzo della Civiltà del Lavoro** in the northwest corner stands out, Fascist-inspired architecture at its most assured – the "square Colosseum" some have called it, which sums up its mixing of modern and classical styles perfectly. To the south, **Piazza Marconi** is the nominal centre of EUR, where the wide, classically inspired boulevards intersect to swerve around an obelisk in the centre.

All the museums are within easy reach of here. On the square itself, the **Museo Nazionale delle Arti e delle Tradizioni Popolari** (Mon–Sat 9am–8pm; €4) is a run-through of applied arts, costumes and religious artefacts from the Italian regions. The **Museo Nazionale Preistorico ed Etnografico Luigi Pigorini**, Viale Lincoln 1 (daily 9am–8pm; €4), is arranged in manageable and easily comprehensible order; the ethnographic collection displays artefacts from South America, the Pacific and Africa. In the same building, further down the colonnade, at Viale Lincoln 3, is the **Museo dell'Alto Medioevo** (Tues–Sat 9am–2pm; €2), which concentrates on artefacts from the fifth century to the tenth century – local finds mainly, including some beautiful jewellery from the seventh century and a delicate fifth-century gold fibula found on the Palatine Hill. But of all the museums, the most interesting is the **Museo della Civiltà Romana**, Piazza Agnelli 10 (Tues–Sat 9am–7pm, Sun 9am–2pm; €4.15), which has, among numerous reproductions of ancient Roman finds, a large-scale model of the fourth-century city – perfect for setting the rest of the city in context.

The Abbazia delle Tre Fontane

The antidote to EUR is just a short walk away, at the **Abbazia delle Tre Fontane**, a complex of churches founded on the spot where St Paul was martyred; it's said that when the saint was beheaded his head bounced and three springs erupted where his head touched the ground. In those days this was a malarial area, and it was all but abandoned during the Middle Ages, but in the second half of the nineteenth century Trappist monks drained the swamp and planted eucalyptus trees in the vicinity; they still distil a eucalyptus-based chest remedy here, as well as an exquisite liqueur, both sold – alongside wonderful chocolate bars – at the small shop by the entrance.

Via Appia Antica: the Catacombs

During classical times the **Via Appia**, reachable by bus #218 from Piazza San Giovanni in Laterano, was the most important of all the Roman trade routes, the so-called "Queen of Roads", carrying supplies right down through Campania to the port of Bríndisi. It's no longer the main route south out of the city, but it remains an important part of early Christian Rome, its verges lined with the underground burial cemeteries or **catacombs** of the first Christians. Laws in ancient Rome forbade burial within the city walls – most Romans were cremated. Although there are catacombs in other parts of the city, this is by far the largest concentration, around five complexes in all, dating from the first to the fourth century, almost entirely emptied of bodies now but still decorated with the primitive signs and frescoes that were the hallmark of the then-burgeoning Christian movement. Despite much speculation, no one really knows why the Christians decided to bury their dead in these tunnels: the rock here, tuff, is soft and easy to hollow out, but the digging involved must still have been phenomenal, and there is no real reason to suppose that the burial places had to be secret – they continued to bury their dead like this long after Christianity became the established religion. Whatever the reasons, they make intriguing viewing now. The three principal complexes are within walking distance of each other, though it's not really worth trying to see them all – the layers of shelves and drawers aren't particularly gripping after a while.

Via Appia Antica begins at the **Porta San Sebastiano**, built in the fifth century, a little way on from which the church of **Domine Quo Vadis** signals the start of the catacomb stretch of road. Legend has this as the place where St Peter saw Christ while fleeing from certain death in Rome and asked "Where goest thou, Lord?", to which Christ replied that he was going to be crucified once more, leading Peter to turn around and accept his fate. Continuing on for 1km or so you reach the catacombs of **San Callisto** (Jan–Oct & Dec Thurs–Tues 8.30am–noon & 2.30–5pm; €4.15) – the nearest bus stop on the #218 route is Largo Martiri Fosse Ardeatine. All third-century popes (of whom San Callisto was one) are buried here in the papal crypt, and the site features some well-preserved seventh- and eighth-century frescoes. A little way west from here, the catacombs of **San Domitilla** (Feb–Dec Mon & Wed–Sun 8.30am–noon & 2.30–5pm; €4.15) are quieter than those of San Callisto and adjoin the remains of a fourth-century basilica erected here to the martyrs

Achilleus and Nereus. The labyrinth itself is Rome's largest, stretching for around 17km in all, and contains more frescoes and early wall etchings.

The catacombs of **San Sebastiano** (Jan–Oct & Dec Fri–Wed 9am–noon & 2.30–5pm; €4.15), 500m further on, are probably best for a visit, situated under a much renovated basilica that was originally built by Constantine on the spot where the bodies of the apostles Peter and Paul are said to have been laid for a time. Downstairs, half-hour tours wind around dark corridors showing signs of early Christian worship – paintings of doves and fish, a contemporary carved oil lamp and inscriptions dating the tombs themselves. The most striking features, however, are not Christian at all, but three pagan tombs (one painted, two stuccoed) discovered when archeologists were burrowing beneath the floor of the basilica upstairs. Just above here, Constantine is said to have raised his chapel to Peter and Paul, and although St Peter was later removed to the Vatican, and St Paul to San Paolo fuori le Mura, the graffiti above records the fact that this was indeed, albeit temporarily, where the two Apostles rested.

Trastevere

Across the river from the centre of town, on the right bank of the Tiber, the district of **TRASTEVERE** was the artisan area of the city in classical times, neatly placed for the trade that came upriver from Ostia and was unloaded nearby. Outside the city walls, Trastevere (the name means literally "across the Tiber") was for centuries heavily populated by immigrants, and this separation lent the neighbourhood a strong identity that lasted well into the last century. Nowadays the area is a long way from the working-class quarter it used to be, and although you're still likely to hear Travestere's strong Roman dialect, you're also likely to bump into some of its many foreign residents, lured by the charm of its narrow streets and closeted squares. However, even if the local *Festa de' Noantri* ("celebration of we others"), held every July, seems to symbolize the slow decline of local spirit rather than celebrate its existence, there is good reason to come to Trastevere. It is among the more pleasant places to stroll in Rome, particularly peaceful in the morning, and lively come evening, as dozens of trattorias set tables out along the cobblestone streets – Trastevere has long been known for its restaurants (see p.776). The neighbourhood has also become the focus of the city's alternative scene and is home to much of its most vibrant and youthful nightlife (see p.778).

The obvious way to approach Trastevere is to cross over from Isola Tiberina or from the pedestrian Ponte Sisto at the end of Via Giulia, both of which leave you five minutes from the heart of the neighbourhood. On a Sunday it's worth walking over the Ponte Sublicio to Porta Portese, from which the **Porta Portese** flea market stretches down Via Portuense to Trastevere train station in a congested medley of antiques, old motor spares, cheap and trendy clothing and assorted junk – more touristy than it used to be, but still above all a Romans' market. Haggling is the rule, and keep a good hold of your wallet or purse. Come early if you want to buy, or even move – most of the bargains have gone by 10am, by which time the crush of people can be intense.

Santa Cecilia in Trastevere

Further north, on Via Anicia, is the church of **Santa Cecilia in Trastevere** (daily 10am–noon & 4–5.30pm), a cream, rather sterile church – apart from a pretty front courtyard – whose antiseptic eighteenth-century appearance belies its historical associations. A church was originally built here over the site of the second-century home of St Cecilia, whose husband Valerian was executed for refusing to worship Roman gods and who herself was subsequently persecuted for Christian beliefs. The story has it that Cecilia was locked in the caldarium of her own baths for several days but refused to die, singing her way through the ordeal (Cecilia is patron saint of music). Her head was finally half hacked off with an axe, though it took several blows before she finally succumbed. Below the high altar, Stefano Maderno's limp, almost modern statue of the saint shows her incorruptible body as it was found when exhumed in 1599, with three deep cuts in her neck – a fragile, intensely human piece of work that has helped make Cecilia one of the most revered Roman saints.

Santa Maria in Trastevere

There's more life on the far side of Viale Trastevere, the wide boulevard that cuts through the centre of the district, where **Piazza Santa Maria in Trastevere** constitutes the heart of old Trastevere. It was named after the church of **Santa Maria in Trastevere** in its northwest corner (daily 7.30am–12.40pm & 4–7pm), held to be the first Christian place of worship in Rome, built on a site where a fountain of oil is said to have sprung on the day of Christ's birth. These days people come here for two things. The church's mosaics are among the city's most impressive: those on the cornice by Cavallini were completed a century or so after the rebuilding and show the Madonna surrounded by ten female figures with lamps – once thought to represent the Wise and Foolish Virgins. Inside, there's a nineteenth-century copy of a Cosmatesque pavement of spirals and circles, and apse mosaics contemporary with the building of the church – Byzantine-inspired works depicting a solemn yet sensitive parade of saints thronged around Christ and Mary. Beneath the high altar on the right, an inscription – "FONS OLIO" – marks the spot where the oil is supposed to have sprung up.

Galleria Nazionale di Palazzo Corsini and the Orte Botanico

Cutting north through the backstreets towards the Tiber, you'll come to the **Galleria Nazionale di Palazzo Corsini** at Via della Lungara 10 (Tues–Sun 8.30am–7pm; €4), an unexpected cultural attraction on this side of the river, counting among its highlights works by Rubens, van Dyck, Guido Reni and Caravaggio. You can also visit the chambers of Queen Christina, who renounced Protestantism, and, with it, the Swedish throne in 1655, and brought her library and fortune to Rome, to the delight of the Chigi pope, Alexander VII. She died here, in the palace, in 1689, and she is one of only four women to be buried in St Peter's.

The park of the Palazzo Corsini is now the site of the **Orto Botanico** (Mon–Sat 9.30am–5.30pm; €2.10), a good example of eighteenth-century garden design, with a wood of century-old oaks, cedars and conifers, a grove of acclimatized palm-trees, a herbal garden with medicinal plants and a collection of orchids that bloom in springtime and early summer.

Villa Farnesina

Across the road from the Palazzo Corsini is the **Villa Farnesina** (Mon–Sat 9am–1pm; €3.10), built during the early sixteenth century by Baldassare Peruzzi for the banker Agostino Chigi and famous for its Renaissance frescoes. Inside you can view the Raphael-designed painting of *Cupid and Psyche* in the now glassed-in loggia, completed in 1517 by the artist's assistants, Giulio Romano, Francesco Penni and Giovanni da Udine. Vasari claims Raphael didn't complete the work because his infatuation with his mistress – "La Fornarina", whose father's bakery was situated nearby – was making it difficult to concentrate, and says that Chigi arranged for her to live with the painter in the palace while he worked on the loggia. More likely he was simply so overloaded with commissions that he couldn't possibly finish them all. He did, however, manage to finish the *Galatea* in the room next door, which he fitted in between his Vatican commissions for Julius II; "the greatest evocation of paganism of the Renaissance", Kenneth Clark called it, although Vasari claims that Michelangelo, passing by one day while Raphael was canoodling with La Fornarina, finished the painting for him.

The Janiculum Hill

From the Villa Farnesina, it's about a fifteen-minute walk up Via Garibaldi (bus #870 goes up from Piazza della Rovere) to the summit of the **Janiculum Hill** – not one of the seven hills of Rome, but the one with the best and most accessible views of the centre. Via Garibaldi leads up past the church of **San Pietro in Montorio** (daily 7.30am–noon & 4–6pm), built on a site once – now, it's thought, wrongly – believed to have been the place of the saint's crucifixion. The compact interior is particularly intimate – it's a favourite for weddings – and features some first-rate paintings, among them Sebastiano del Piombo's graceful *Flagellation*. Don't miss Bramante's little **Tempietto** (daily 9am–noon & 4–6pm) in the courtyard on the right, one of the seminal works of the Renaissance, built on what was supposed to have been the precise spot of St Peter's martyrdom. The small circular building is like a classical temple in miniature, perfectly proportioned and neatly executed.

The Janiculum was the scene of a fierce 1849 set-to between Garibaldi's troops and the French, and the white marble **memorial** opposite the church is dedicated to all those who died in the battle. A little further up the hill, the **Acqua Paola** – constructed for Paul V with marble from the Roman Forum – gushes water at a bend in the road. At the top, the **Porta San Pancrazio** was built during the reign of Urban VIII, destroyed by the French in 1849, and rebuilt by Pope Pius IX five years later. It's currently being restored and will eventually house the new Museum of the Roman Republic 1848–49. Turn right to the crest of the hill, where, on Piazzale Garibaldi, there's an equestrian monument to Garibaldi – an ostentatious work from 1895. Just below is the spot from which a cannon is fired at noon each day for Romans to check their watches. Further on, a statue marks the grave of Anita Garibaldi and recalls the important part she played in the 1849 battle – it's a fiery, melodramatic work (she cradles a baby in one arm, brandishes a pistol with the other, and is galloping full speed on a horse). Spread out before her are some of the best views over the city.

The Vatican

On the west bank of the Tiber, directly across from Rome's historic centre, the **VATICAN CITY** was established as an independent sovereign state in 1929, a tiny territory surrounded by high walls on its far, western side and on the near side opening its doors to the rest of the city and its pilgrims in the form of St Peter's and its colonnaded piazza. It's believed that St Peter himself was buried in a pagan cemetery here, giving rise to the building of a basilica to venerate his name and the siting of the headquarters of the Catholic Church here. After reaching an uneasy agreement with Mussolini, the Vatican became a sovereign state, and nowadays has its own radio station, newspaper, currency and postal service, and indeed security service in the colourfully dressed Swiss Guards. Despite these trappings, you wouldn't know at any point that you had left Rome and entered the Vatican; indeed the area around the Vatican, known as the Borgo, is one of the most cosmopolitan districts of Rome, full of hotels and restaurants, and scurrying tourists and pilgrims. You may find yourself staying in one of many mid-range hotels located here, although unless you're a pilgrim it's a better idea to base yourself in the more atmospheric city centre and travel back and forth on the useful bus #64. However much you try, one visit is never anywhere near enough.

The Vatican Museums and St Peter's are open to visitors year-round – see individual accounts below for opening times. It's also possible to visit the **Vatican Gardens**, though only on a guided tour departing at 10am (Mon, Tues & Thurs–Sat except religious holidays; €10); visits last about two hours and tickets must be bought a few days ahead from the **Vatican Information Office** in Piazza San Pietro (Mon–Sat 8.30am–6pm; ☎06.6988.4466). You can also, if you wish, attend a **papal audience**: these happen once a week, usually on Wednesdays at 11am in the Audiences Room, and are by no means one-to-one affairs. It's often possible to get a place on one if you apply not more than a month and no fewer than two days in advance: send a fax with your name, your home address, your Rome address, and your preferred date of audience, to the Prefettura della Casa Pontificia (☎06.6988.3273, ℱ06.6988.5863). If you want to send a postcard with a Vatican postmark, there are Vatican **post offices** on the north side of Piazza San Pietro and inside the Vatican Museums.

Castel Sant'Angelo

The best route to the Vatican and St Peter's is across **Ponte Sant'Angelo**, flanked by angels carved to designs by Bernini – his so-called "breezy maniacs". On the far side is the great circular hulk of the **Castel Sant'Angelo** (Tues–Sun 9am–8pm; €6.50, free guided tours in English Sat & Sun at 4.30pm), designed and built by the Emperor Hadrian as his own mausoleum (his ashes were interred here until a twelfth-century pope appropriated the sarcophagus, which was later destroyed in a fire). It was a grand monument, faced with white marble, surrounded by statues and topped with cypresses, similar in style to Augustus's mausoleum across the river. Renamed in the sixth century, when Pope Gregory the Great witnessed a vision of St Michael here that ended a terrible plague, the mausoleum's position near the Vatican was not lost on the papal authorities, who converted the building for use as a fortress and built a passageway to link it with the Vatican as a refuge in times of siege or invasion – a route utilized on a number of occasions, most notably when the Medici pope, Clement VII, sheltered here for several months during the Sack of Rome in 1527.

Inside, from the monumental entrance hall a spiral ramp leads up into the centre of the mausoleum itself, passing through the chamber where the emperor was entombed, to the main level at the top, where a small palace was built to house the papal residents in appropriate splendour. After the Sack of Rome, Pope Paul III had some especially fine renovations made, including the beautiful frescoed *Sala Paolina* – you'll notice Paul III's personal motto, *Festina Lenta* ("make haste slowly"), scattered throughout the ceilings and in various corners of all his rooms. Elsewhere, rooms hold swords, armour, guns and the like, others are lavishly decorated with grotesques and paintings; don't miss the bathroom of Clement VII on the second floor, with its prototype hot and cold water taps and mildly erotic frescoes. Below are dungeons and storerooms (not visitable), testament to the castle's grisly past as the city's most notorious Renaissance prison – Benvenuto Cellini and Cesare Borgia are just two of its more famous detainees. From the quiet bar upstairs you'll also get one of the best views of Rome and excellent coffee.

Piazza San Pietro

The approach to St Peter's – **Via della Conciliazione** – is disappointing: typically, Mussolini swept away the houses of the previously narrow street and replaced them with this wide sweeping avenue, and nowadays St Peter's somehow looks too near, the vast space of Bernini's **Piazza San Pietro** not really becoming apparent until you're right on top of it. In fact, in tune with the spirit of the Baroque, the church was supposed to be even better hidden than it is now: Bernini planned to complete the colonnade with a triumphal arch linking the two arms, so obscuring the view until you were well inside the square, but this was never carried out and the arms of the piazza remain open, symbolically welcoming the world into the lap of the Catholic Church. The obelisk in the centre was brought to Rome by Caligula in 36 AD, and it stood for many years in the centre of Nero's Circus on the Vatican Hill (to the left of the church); according to legend, it marked the site of St Peter's martyrdom. It was moved here in 1586, when Sixtus V ordered that it be erected in front of the basilica, a task that took four months and was apparently done in silence, on pain of death.

Basilica di San Pietro

The piazza is so grand that you can't help but feel a little let down by the **Basilica di San Pietro** (daily: summer 7am–7pm; winter 7am–6pm), its facade – by no means the church's best feature – obscuring the dome that signals the building from just about everywhere else in the city. Built to a plan initially conceived at the turn of the fifteenth century by Bramante and finished off, heavily modified, over a century later by Carlo Maderno, St Peter's is a strange hotchpotch of styles, bridging the gap between the Renaissance and Baroque eras with varying levels of success. It is, however, the principal shrine of the Catholic Church, built as a replacement for the run-down structure erected here by Constantine in the early fourth century on the site of St Peter's tomb. As such, it can't help but impress, having been worked on by the greatest Italian architects of the sixteenth and seventeenth centuries, and occupying a site rich with historical significance.

In size, certainly, Saint Peter's beats most other churches hands down. Bramante had originally conceived a Greek cross plan rising to a high central dome, but this plan was altered after his death and only revived with the (by then) very elderly Michelangelo's accession as chief architect. Michelangelo was largely responsible for the dome, but he too died shortly afterwards, in 1564, before it was completed. He was succeeded by Vignola, and the dome was completed in 1590 by Giacomo della Porta. Carlo Maderno, under orders from Pope Paul V, took over in 1605, and stretched the church into a Latin cross plan, which had the practical advantage of accommodating more people and followed more directly the plan of Constantine's original basilica. But in so doing he completely unbalanced all the previous designs, not least by obscuring the dome (which he also modified) from view in the piazza. The inside, too, is very much of the Baroque era, largely the work of Bernini, who created many of the most important fixtures.

Inside St Peter's

You need to be properly dressed to enter St Peter's, which means no bare knees or shoulders – a rule that is very strictly enforced. Inside on the right is Michelangelo's other legacy to the church, his **Pietà**, completed at the opposite end of his career when he was just 24. Following an attack by a vandal a few years back, it sits behind glass, strangely remote from the life of the rest of

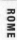

the building. Looking at the piece, you can see why the statue is so famous: it's a sensitive and individual work, and an adept one too, draping the limp body of a grown man across the legs of a woman with grace and ease. As you walk down the **nave**, the size of the building becomes more apparent – and not just because of the bronze plaques set in the floor that make comparisons with the sizes of other churches. The **dome** is breathtakingly imposing, rising high above the supposed site of St Peter's tomb. With a diameter of 44m it is only 1.5m smaller than the Pantheon (the letters of the inscription inside its lower level are over six feet high); it is supported by four enormous piers, decorated with reliefs depicting the basilica's so-called **major relics**: St Veronica's hand-kerchief, which was used to wipe the face of Christ, and is adorned with His miraculous image; the lance of St Longinus, which pierced Christ's side; and a piece of the True Cross, in the pier of St Helen (the head of St Andrew, which was returned to the Eastern Church by Pope Paul VI in 1966, was also formerly kept here). On the right side of the nave, near the pier of St Longinus, the bronze statue of **St Peter** is another of the most venerated monuments in the basilica, carved in the thirteenth century by Arnolfo di Cambio and with its right foot polished smooth by the attentions of pilgrims. On holy days this stat-ue is dressed in papal tiara and vestments. Bronze was also the material used in Bernini's **baldacchino**, the centrepiece of the sculptor's Baroque embellish-ment of the interior, a massive 26m high (the height, apparently, of Palazzo Farnese), cast out of 927 tonnes of metal removed from the Pantheon roof in 1633. To modern eyes, it's an almost grotesque piece of work, with its wild spi-ralling columns copied from columns in the Constantine basilica. But it has the odd personal touch, not least in the female faces expressing the agony of child-birth and a beaming baby carved on the plinths – said to have been carried out for a niece of Bernini's patron (Urban VIII), who gave birth at the same time as the sculptor was finishing the piece.

Bernini's feverish sculpting decorates the apse too, his **cattedra** enclosing the supposed (though doubtful) chair of St Peter in a curvy marble and stucco throne. On the right, the **tomb of Urban VIII**, also by Bernini, is less grand but more dignified. On the left, the **tomb of Paul III**, by Giacomo della Porta, was moved up and down the nave of the church before it was finally placed here as a counter to that of Urban VIII. More interesting is Bernini's **monument to Alexander VII** in the south transept, with its winged skele-ton struggling underneath the heavy marble drapes, upon which the Chigi pope is kneeling in prayer. The grim reaper significantly clutches an hourglass – the Baroque at its most melodramatic, and symbolic. On the left sits Charity, on the right, Truth Revealed in Time; to the rear are Hope and Faith.

An entrance off the aisle leads to the steeply priced **Treasury** (daily: summer 9am–6pm; winter 9am–5pm; €4). Along with some more recent additions, this holds artefacts from the earlier church: a spiral column (the other survivors form part of the colonnade around the interior of the dome); a wall-mounted tabernacle by Donatello; a rich blue-and-gold dalmatic that is said once to have belonged to Charlemagne (though this has been called into question); the vest-ments and tiara for the bronze statue of St Peter in the nave of the basilica; and the massive, though fairly ghastly, late-fifteenth-century bronze tomb of Sixtus IV by Pollaiuolo – said to be a very accurate portrait. Back at the central cross-ing, steps lead down under Bernini's statue of St Longinus to the **Grottoes** (daily: summer 8am–6pm; winter 7am–5pm), where a good number of popes are buried, though to be honest none is particularly interesting. Far better is the ascent to the **roof and dome** (daily: May–Sept 8am–6pm; Oct–April 8am–5pm; €5 with elevator, €4 by stairs); the entrance is in the northern courtyard between the church and the Vatican Palace, on your way out as you exit through the crypt. You'll probably need to queue and, even with the lift, it's a long climb up a narrow stairway that spirals up the dome. The views from the gallery around the interior of the dome give you a sense of the enormity of the church. From there, the roof grants views from behind the huge statues onto the piazza below, before the ascent to the lantern at the top of the dome, from which the views over the city are as glorious as you'd expect.

The Vatican Museums

A fifteen-minute walk from St Peter's (follow the signs out from the north side of the piazza), the only part of the Vatican Palace you can visit independently is the **Vatican Museums** at Viale Vaticano 13 (April–Nov Mon–Sat 8.45am–2.20pm, last exit 3.45pm; rest of year Mon–Sat 8.45am–12.20pm, last exit 1.45pm; €10; closed Sun, holidays and religious holidays, except the last Sunday of each month when admission is free) – quite simply, the largest, richest, most compelling and perhaps most exhausting museum complex in the world. If you have found any of Rome's other museums disappointing, the Vatican is probably the reason why: so much booty from the city's history has ended up here, from both classical and later times, and so many of the Renaissance's finest artists were in the employ of the pope, that not surprisingly the result is a set of museums so stuffed with antiquities as to put most other European collections to shame.

As its name suggests, the Vatican Palace actually holds a collection of museums on very diverse subjects – displays of classical statuary, Renaissance painting, Etruscan relics, Egyptian artefacts, not to mention the furnishings and decoration of the palace itself. There's no point in trying to see everything, at least not on one visit. Once inside, you have a choice of **routes**, but the only features you really shouldn't miss are the Raphael Stanze and the Sistine Chapel. Above all, decide how long you want to spend here, and what you want to see before you start; you could spend anything from 45 minutes to the better part of a day here, and it's easy to collapse from museum fatigue before you've even got to your most important target of interest. Be conservative – the distances between different sections alone can be vast and very tiring.

The Museo Pio-Clementino, Museo Egizio and Museo Gregoriano Etrusco

To the left of the entrance, the small **Museo Pio-Clementino** and its octagonal courtyard is home to some of the best of the Vatican's classical statuary, including two statues that influenced Renaissance artists more than any others: the serene *Apollo Belvedere*, a Roman copy of a fourth-century BC original – and the first-century BC *Laocoön*, discovered near Nero's Golden House in 1506 and depicting a Trojan priest being crushed with his sons by serpents sent to punish him for warning his fellow citizens of the danger of the Trojan horse. It is perhaps the most famous classical statue ever, referred to by Pliny who thought it carved from a single piece of marble, and written about by Byron – who described its contorted realism as "dignifying pain".

The nearby **Museo Egizio** isn't one of the Vatican's highlights. It has some vividly painted mummy cases (and two mummies), along with *canopi*, the alabaster vessels into which the entrails of the deceased were placed. There is also a partial reconstruction of the Temple of Serapis from Hadrian's Villa near Tivoli, along with a statue of his lover, Antinous, who drowned close to the original temple in Egypt and so inspired Hadrian to build his replica. Past the entrance to the Egyptian Museum a grand staircase leads up to the **Museo**

Gregoriano Etrusco, which holds sculpture, funerary art and applied art from the sites of southern Etruria – a good complement to Rome's specialist Etruscan collection in the Villa Giulia. Especially worth seeing are the finds from a seventh-century BC tomb discovered near Cerveteri, which contained the remains of three Etruscan nobles, two men and a woman; the breastplate of the woman and her huge fibia (clasp) are of gold. Take a look at the small ducks and lions with which they are decorated, fashioned in the almost microscopic beadwork for which Etruscan goldsmiths were famous.

The Galleries of Candelabra, Tapestries and Maps

Outside the Etruscan Museum, the large monumental staircase leads back down to the main route, taking you first through the **Gallery of Candelabra**, the niches of which are adorned with huge candelabra taken from imperial Roman villas. Beyond here the **Gallery of Tapestries** has on the left Belgian tapestries to designs by the school of Raphael which show scenes from the life of Christ, and on the right tapestries made in Rome at the Barberini workshops during the 1600s, showing scenes from the life of Maffeo Barberini, who became Pope Urban VIII. Next, the **Gallery of Maps**, which is as long (175m) as the previous two galleries put together, was decorated in the late sixteenth century at the behest of Pope Gregory XIII, the reformer of the calendar, to show all of Italy, the major islands in the Mediterranean, the papal possessions in France, as well as the siege of Malta, the battle of Lepanto and large-scale maps of the maritime republics of Venice and Genoa.

The Raphael Stanze

Beyond the Gallery of the Maps, all visitors are directed to a covered walkway suspended over the palace courtyard of the Belvedere which leads through to the **Raphael Stanze**. The first of these, the **Stanza di Constantino**, was not in fact done by Raphael at all, but painted in part to his designs about five years after he died by his pupils, Giulio Romano, Francesco Penni and Raffello del Colle, between 1525 and 1531. It shows scenes from the life of the Emperor Constantine, who made Christianity the official religion of the Roman Empire. The enormous painting on the wall opposite the entrance is the *Battle of the Milvian Bridge* by Giulio Romano and Francesco Penni – a depiction of a decisive battle in 312 AD between the warring co-emperors of the West, Constantine and Maxentius. Further on, **Stanza di Eliodoro** is the first of the Raphael rooms proper, in which the fresco on the right of the entrance, *The Expulsion of Heliodorus from the Temple*, is an exciting piece of work, painted in 1512–1514 for Pope Julius II. The images of Heliodorus, the horseman and the flying men are adeptly done, the figures almost jumping out of the painting into the room, but the group of people on the left is more interesting – Pope Julius II, in his papal robes, Giulio Romano, the pupil of Raphael, and, to his left, Raphael himself in a rare self-portrait. On the left wall as you enter, the *Mass of Bolsena* relates a miracle that occurred in the town in northern Lazio in the 1260s, when a German priest who doubted the transubstantiation of Christ found the wafer bleeding when he broke it during a service. The pope facing the priest is another portrait of Julius II. On the window wall opposite is the *Deliverance of St Peter*, showing the saint being assisted in a jail-break by the Angel of the Lord – a night scene, whose clever chiaroscuro predates Caravaggio by nearly one hundred years. Finally, on the large wall opposite Heliodorus, *Leo I Repulsing Attila the Hun* is an allegory of the difficulties that the papacy was going through in the early 1500s, and shows the chubby cardinal, Giovanni dei Medici, who succeeded Julius II as Leo X in 1513.

The next room, the **Stanza della Segnatura** or pope's study, is probably the best known – and with good reason. Painted in the years 1508–11, when Raphael first came to Rome, the subjects were again the choice of Julius II, and, composed with careful balance and harmony, it comes close to the peak of the painter's art. The *School of Athens*, on the near wall as you come in, steals the show, a representation of the triumph of scientific truth, in which all the great minds from antiquity are represented. Plato and Aristotle discuss philosophy at the centre of the painting: Aristotle, the father of scientific method, motions downwards; Plato, pointing upwards, indicating his philosophy of otherworldly spirituality, is believed to be a portrait of Leonardo da Vinci. Spread across the steps is Diogenes, lazily ignorant of all that is happening around him, while to the left Raphael added a solitary, sullen portrait of Michelangelo – a homage to the artist, apparently painted after Raphael saw the first stage of the Sistine Chapel almost next door.

The last room, the **Stanza Incendio**, was the last to be decorated, to the general glorification of Pope Leo X, and in a sense it brings together three generations of work. The ceiling was painted by Perugino, Raphael's teacher, and the frescoes were completed to Raphael's designs by his pupils (notably Giulio Romano), most striking of which is the *Fire in the Borgo*, facing the main window – an oblique reference to Leo X restoring peace to Italy after Julius II's reign but in fact describing an event that took place during the reign of Leo IV, when the pope stood in the loggia of the old St Peter's and made the sign of the cross to extinguish a fire.

The Borgia apartments

Outside the Raphael Stanze, on the other side of the Sistine Chapel steps, the **Borgia Apartments** were inhabited by Julius II's hated predecessor, Alexander VI – a fact which persuaded Julius to move into the new set of rooms he called upon Raphael to decorate. Nowadays it's host to a largely missable collection of modern religious art, including liturgical vestments designed by Matisse, a *Landscape with Angels* by Salvador Dalí, and one of Francis Bacon's studies of Innocent X after Velázquez. But it's Pinturicchio's ceiling frescoes in the *Sala dei Santi* that are most worth seeing, typically rich in colour and detail, depicting the legend of Osiris and the Apis bull – a reference to the Borgia family symbol, a bull. Among other images is a scene showing St Catherine of Alexandria disputing with the Emperor Maximillian, in which Pinturicchio has placed his self-portrait behind the emperor – and also, clearly visible in the background, the Arch of Constantine. The figure of St Catherine is said to be a portrait of Lucrezia Borgia, and the room was reputedly the scene of a decidedly un-papal party to celebrate the first of Lucrezia's three marriages, which ended up with men tossing sweets down the fronts of the women's dresses.

The Sistine Chapel

Steps lead up from here to the **Sistine Chapel**, a huge barn-like structure built for Pope Sixtus IV between 1473 and 1481. It serves as the pope's official private chapel and the scene of the conclaves of cardinals for the election of each new pontiff. The ceiling paintings here, and the *Last Judgement* on the wall behind the altar, together make up arguably the greatest masterpiece in Western art, and the largest body of painting ever planned and executed by one man – Michelangelo. They are also probably the most viewed paintings in the world: it's estimated that on an average day about 15,000 people trudge through here to take a look; and during the summer and on special occasions the number of visitors can exceed 20,000. Bear in mind that the taking of pictures of any kind, including video, is prohibited in the chapel, and it is also officially forbidden to speak – although this is something that is rampantly ignored.

Upon completion of the structure, Sixtus brought in several prominent painters of the Renaissance to decorate the **walls**. The overall project was under the management of Pinturicchio and comprised a series of paintings showing (on the left as you face the altar) scenes from the life of Moses and, on the right, scenes from the life of Christ. Sixtus didn't have just anybody work on these: there are paintings by, among others, Perugino, who painted the marvellously composed cityscape of *Jesus giving St Peter the Keys to Heaven*, Botticelli – *The Trials of Moses* and *Cleansing of the Leper* – and Ghirlandaio, whose *Calling of St Peter and St Andrew* shows Christ calling the two saints to be disciples, surrounded by onlookers, against a fictitious medieval landscape of boats, birds, turrets and mountains. Some of the paintings were in fact collaborative efforts, and it's known that Ghirlandaio and Botticelli in particular contributed to each other's work. Anywhere else they would be pored over very closely indeed. As it is, they are entirely overshadowed by Michelangelo's more famous work.

It was Pope Julius II who turned his attention to the **ceiling**; he was an avid collector and patron of the arts, and summoned to Rome the best artists and architects of the day, among them Michelangelo, who, through a series of political intrigues orchestrated by Bramante and Raphael, was assigned the task of decorating the Sistine Chapel. Oddly enough, Michelangelo hadn't wanted to do the work at all: he considered himself a sculptor, not a painter, and was more eager to get on with carving Julius II's tomb (now in San Pietro in Vincoli, see p.750) than painting the ceiling, which he regarded as a chore. Pope Julius II, however, had other plans, drawing up a design of the twelve Apostles for the vault and hiring Bramante to design a scaffold for the artist from which to work. Michelangelo was apparently an awkward, solitary character: he had barely begun painting when he rejected Bramante's scaffold as unusable, fired all his staff, and dumped the pope's scheme for the ceiling in favour of his own. But the pope was easily his match, and there are tales of the two men clashing while the work was going on – Michelangelo would lock the doors at crucial points, ignoring the pope's demands to see how it was progressing.

The **frescoes** depict scenes from the Old Testament, from the *Creation of Light* at the altar end to the *Drunkenness of Noah* over the door. The sides are decorated with prophets and sibyls and the ancestors of Jesus. Julius II lived only a few months after the Sistine Chapel ceiling was finished, but the fame of the work he had commissioned soon spread far and wide. Certainly, it's staggeringly impressive, all the more so after its restoration some years ago, which has lifted centuries of accumulated soot and candle grime off the paintings to reveal a much brighter, more vivid painting than anyone thought existed. The restorers have also been able to chart the progress of Michelangelo as he moved across the vault. Images on fresco must be completed before the plaster dries, and each day a fresh layer of plaster would have been laid, on which Michelangelo would have had around eight hours or so before having to finish for the day. Comparing the different areas of plaster, it seems the figure of Adam, in the key *Creation of Adam* scene, took just four days; God, in the same fresco, took three days. You can also see the development of Michelangelo as a painter when you look at the paintings in reverse order. The first painting, over the door, the *Drunkenness of Noah*, is done in a stiff and formal style, and is vastly different from the last painting he did, over the altar, which shows the artist at his best, the perfect master of the technique of fresco painting.

The **Last Judgement**, on the altar wall of the chapel, was painted by

Michelangelo more than twenty years later (1535–41). Michelangelo wasn't especially keen to work on this either – he was still engaged on Julius II's tomb, under threat of legal action from the late pope's family – but Pope Paul III, an old acquaintance of the artist, was keen to complete the decoration of the chapel. The painting took five years, again single-handed, but it is probably the most inspired and most homogeneous large-scale painting you're ever likely to see, the technical virtuosity of Michelangelo taking a back seat to the sheer exuberance of the work. The human body is fashioned into a finely captured set of exquisite poses: even the damned can be seen as a celebration of the human form. Perhaps unsurprisingly, the painting offended some, and even before it was complete Rome was divided as to its merits, especially regarding the etiquette of introducing such a display of nudity into the pope's private chapel. But Michelangelo's response to this was unequivocal, lampooning one of his fiercer critics, the pope's master of ceremonies at the time, Biago di Cesena, as Minos, the doorkeeper of hell, with ass's ears and an entwined serpent in the bottom right-hand corner of the picture. Later the pope's zealous successor, Pius IV, objected to the painting and would have had it removed entirely had not Michelangelo's pupil, Daniele da Volterra, appeased him by carefully – and selectively – adding coverings to some of the more obviously naked figures, earning himself forever the nickname of the "breeches-maker". During the recent work, most of the remaining breeches have been discreetly removed, restoring the painting to its former glory.

The Braccio Nuovo and Museo Chiaramonti

Walking back from the Sistine Chapel takes you through the **Braccio Nuovo** and **Museo Chiaramonti**, which both hold classical sculpture, although be warned that they are the Vatican at its most overwhelming – close on a thousand statues crammed into two long galleries – and you need a keen eye and much perseverance to make any sense of it all. The **Braccio Nuovo** was built in the early 1800s to display classical statuary that was particularly prized, and it contains, among other things, probably the most famous extant image of Augustus, and a bizarre-looking statue depicting the Nile, whose yearly flooding was essential to the fertility of the Egyptian soil. The 300-metre-long **Chiaramonti gallery** is especially unnerving, lined as it is with the chill marble busts of hundreds of nameless, blank-eyed ancient Romans, along with the odd deity. It pays to have a leisurely wander, for there are some real characters here: sour, thin-lipped matrons with their hair tortured into pleats, curls and spirals; kids, caught in a sulk or mid-chortle; and ancient old men with flesh sagging and wrinkling to reveal the skull beneath.

The Pinacoteca

The **Pinacoteca** is housed in a separate building on the far side of the Vatican's main spine and ranks possibly as Rome's best picture gallery, with works from the early to High Renaissance right up to the nineteenth century. Among early works, there are pieces by Crivelli, Lippi and the stunning Simoneschi triptych by Giotto of the *Martyrdom of SS Peter and Paul*, painted in the early 1300s for the old St Peter's. There are the rich backdrops and elegantly clad figures of the Umbrian School painters, Perugino and Pinturicchio, and Raphael has a room to himself, including, in climate-controlled glass cases, the tapestries that were made to his designs to be hung in the Sistine Chapel during conclave, and three paintings including the *Transfiguration*, which he had nearly completed when he died in 1520, and which was finished by his pupils; the *Coronation of the Virgin*, done when he was only 19 years old; and, on the left, the *Madonna* *of Foglino*, showing saints John the Baptist, Francis of Assisi, and Jerome. Leonardo's *St Jerome*, in the next room, is unfinished too, but it's a remarkable piece of work, with Jerome a rake-like ascetic torn between suffering and a good meal. Caravaggio's *Descent from the Cross* in the next room but one, however, gets more attention, a warts and all canvas that unusually shows the Virgin Mary as a middle-aged mother grieving over her dead son, while the men placing Christ's body on the bier are obviously models that the artist recruited from the city streets – a realism that is imitated successfully by Reni's *Crucifixion of St Peter* in the same room. Take a look also at the most gruesome painting in the collection, Poussin's *Martyrdom of St Erasmus*, which shows the saint stretched out on a table with his hands bound above his head in the process of having his small intestine wound onto a drum – basically being "drawn" prior to "quartering".

The museums Gregoriano Profano and Pio Cristiano

Leaving the Pinacoteca, you're well placed for the further grouping of museums in the modern building next door. The **Museo Gregoriano Profano** holds more classical sculpture, mounted on scaffolds for all-round viewing, including mosaics of athletes from the Baths of Caracalla and Roman funerary work, notably the Haterii tomb friezes, which show backdrops of ancient Rome and realistic portrayals of contemporary life. The adjacent **Museo Pio Cristiano** has intricate early Christian sarcophagi and, most famously, an expressive third-century AD statue of the *Good Shepherd*. And the **Museo Pio Cristiano** displays art and artefacts from all over the world, collected by Catholic missionaries, and seems to be inspired by the Vatican's desire to poke fun at non-Christian cults as well as pat itself on the back for its own evangelical successes.

Eating

Rome is a great place to **eat**: its denizens know a good deal about freshness and authenticity, and can be very demanding when it comes to the quality of the dishes they are served. Consequently, eating out is a major, often hours-long, activity, and the meals you'll enjoy generally range from good to truly remarkable. You'll find that most city-centre **restaurants** offer standard Italian dishes, although a few more adventurous restaurants have been popping up of late. At the geographical centre of the country, Italy's capital also has numerous establishments dedicated to a variety of regional cuisines, and a reasonable number of excellent ethnic restaurants. Rome is blessed with an abundance of good, honest **pizzerias** as well, churning out thin, crispy-baked pizza from wood-fired ovens. We've also listed a range of places serving **snacks** and, at the end of the section, the best of the city's **gelaterie** and **pasticcerie**. One final caveat: although generally speaking it's hard to find truly bad food and rip-off prices in Rome, it may be wise to avoid places that are adjacent to some major monuments, such as the Pantheon, Piazza Navona or the Vatican.

Lunch, snacks and self-service

Rome has plenty of places in which to refuel during a long day's sightseeing, and they don't all cater for tourists. Most bars sell panini and *tramezzini*, and there are plenty of stand-up *rosticerrie*, but the following are some of our favourite places for a good-quality, unpretentious **lunch or snack,** or just a sustaining cup of coffee.

Roman food and wine

Roman cooking is traditionally dominated by the offal-based earthy cuisine of the working classes, with a little influence from the city's centuries-old Jewish population thrown in. Although you'll find all sorts of pasta served in Roman restaurants, spaghetti is probably the most popular, as it stands up well to the coarse, gutsy sauces the Romans prefer: *aglio e olio* (garlic and oil), *cacio e pepe* (pecorino and ground black pepper), *alla carbonara* (with beaten eggs, cubes of pan-fried *guanciale* – cured pork jowl – or bacon, and pecorino or parmesan), and *alle vongole* (with baby clams). Fish is an integral, though usually pricey, part of Roman cuisine, and is most frequently eaten in Rome as salt cod – *baccalà*; best eaten Jewish-style, deep-fried. Offal is also important and although it has been ousted from many of the more refined city-centre restaurants, you'll still find it on the menus of more traditional places, especially those in Testaccio. Most favoured is *pajata*, the intestines of an unweaned calf, but you'll also find *lingua* (tongue), *rognone* (kidney), *milza* (spleen – delicious as a pat on toasted bread) and *trippa* (tripe). Look out too for *coda alla vaccinara*, oxtail stewed in a rich sauce of tomato and celery; *testerelle d'abbacchio*, lamb's head baked in the oven with herbs and oil; and *coratella*, lamb's heart, liver, lungs and spleen cooked in olive oil with lots of black pepper and onions. More conventional meat dishes include *abbacchio*, milk-fed lamb roasted to melting tenderness with rosemary, sage and garlic; *scottadito*, grilled lamb chops eaten with the fingers; and *saltimbocca alla romana*, thin slices of veal cooked with a slice of prosciutto and sage on top. Artichokes (*carciofi*) are the quintessential Roman vegetable, served "alla romana" (stuffed with garlic and roman mint and stewed) and in all their unadulterated glory as *alla giudea* – flattened and deep fried in olive oil. Another not-to-be-missed side dish is batter-fried squash or courgette blossom, stuffed with mozzarella and a sliver of marinated anchovy. Roman pizza has a thin crust and is best when baked in a wood-burning oven (*cotta a legna*), but you can also find pizza by the slice (*pizza al taglio*), always sold by weight.

Wine comes mainly from the Castelli Romani (most famously Frascati) to the south, and from around Montefiascone (Est! Est! Est!) in the north. Both are basic, straightforward whites, fine for sunny lunchtimes but otherwise not all that noteworthy. However, in most places you'll find a complete selection of Italy's best and most famous wines.

Centro Storico and east of Via del Corso

Antico Forno Via delle Muratte. The last thing you'd expect just by the Trevi Fountain: fresh pizza, a sandwich bar, a bakery and grocery store, all rolled into one – and open on Sundays.

Brek Largo di Torre Argentina 1. A self-service restaurant, part of a chain, with a colourful cinema-theme decor. Everything is prepared fresh. Good for both a snack or a full meal.

Caffè Leonardo Piazza Mignanelli 21a. Just around from the Spanish Steps, this bistro offers sandwiches and dozens of big, satisfying salads at amazing prices for the chic zone it's in.

Caffè Sant'Eustachio Piazza Sant'Eustachio 82. Just behind the Pantheon you'll find what many feel is absolutely Rome's best coffee, usually served Neapolitan-style – that is, very, very sweet.

Filetti di Baccalà Largo dei Librari 88. A fish-and-chip shop without the chips. Paper-covered Formica tables (outdoors in summer), cheap wine,

beer and fried cod, a timeless Roman speciality. Located near Campo de' Fiori. Closed in August.

Il Forno di Campo de' Fiori Campo de' Fiori 22. The *pizza bianca* here is a Roman legend, and their *pizza rossa* (with a smear of tomato sauce) follows close behind. Get it hot from the oven.

Herbier Natura Via San Claudio 87. Just off Piazza San Silvestro, inside a lovely inner courtyard, this is a real oasis of calm away from the hectic and fumy traffic. Snacks or even a full lunch.

La Scaletta Via della Maddalena 46–49. Very centrally placed *birreria* that's good for its great, reviving snacks, hot meals, or just a drink between sights.

Self-Service Luncheonette Salita di San Nicola da Tolentino 19/21. Just up from Bernini's spouting Triton fountain at Piazza Barberini, this place has great food served cafeteria-style.

Zi Fenizia Via Santa Maria del Pianto 64–65. Kosher takeaway pizza in the heart of the Jewish Ghetto, and also roasted chicken, *suppli*, burgers and *shawarma*.

Termini and around

Caffè Fantini Via A. Depretis 77b. Cafeteria-style service, sandwiches, and a hot and cold buffet. A convenient place to break after seeing Santa Maria Maggiore.

Enoteca Cavour 313 Via Cavour 313. At the Forum end of Via Cavour, a lovely old wine bar that makes a handy retreat after seeing the ancient sites. Lots of wines and delicious (though not cheap) snacks and salads.

Bar Pompili Via Napoli 77. The low prices at this little place make it a worthwhile detour for breakfast or a snack. Decent cappuccinos, *cornetti* and *tramezzini* are all at least half the price you'd pay elsewhere. Closed Sun.

Trimani Via Cernaia 37b. Classy wine bar (Rome's biggest selection of Italian regional vintages) good for a lunchtime tipple and gastronomic indulgence.

Across the river: Trastevere and the Vatican

Fidelio Via degli Stefaneschi 3/7. Tucked away behind Piazza Sonino in Trastevere, a *vineria* with lunch and dinner possibilities, too.

Il Mondo in Tasca Via della Lungaretta 169. This great little place, whose name translates as "The World in Your Pocket", offers *shawarma*, felafel, hummus, curry, pizza, chili con carne, couscous, salads, tandoori, moussaka, goulash, etc. Plus you can check your email and get a tarot reading.

Non Solo Pizza Via degli Scipioni 95–97. Try a slice of pizza with sausage and broccoli. There's

also the whole range of Roman fritters – *suppli*, *olive ascolane, fiori di zucca, crocchette* – and a complete selection of hot dishes.

Ombre Rosse Piazza Sant'Egidio 12. A people-watching spot that has become a Trastevere institution, especially for a morning cappuccino, but also for interesting light meals.

Da Venanzo Via San Francesco a Ripa 137. Hole-in-the-wall pizzeria that does great slices, as well as roast chickens and potatoes, *suppli* and all the usual *rosticceria* fare.

Restaurants and pizzerias

There are lots of good restaurants in the **centro storico**, and it's still surprisingly easy to find places that are not tourist traps – prices in all but the really swanky places remain pretty uniform throughout the city. The area around **Via Cavour** and **Termini** is packed with cheap restaurants, although some of them are of dubious cleanliness; if you are not in a hurry, you might do better heading up to the nearby student area of **San Lorenzo**, where you can often eat far better for the same money. South of the centre, the **Testaccio** neighbourhood is also well endowed with good, inexpensive trattorias, and, across the river, **Trastevere** is Rome's traditional restaurant enclave. Even though the number of authentic "Trast" trattorias has declined over recent years, you'll easily find good-to-great meals there, at all price levels.

Centro Storico and east of Via del Corso

Armando al Pantheon Salita de' Crescenzi 30 ✆06.6880.3034. Surprisingly unpretentious surroundings and hearty food in a spot close to the Pantheon. Good prices, too. Closed Sat pm & all day Sun.

Da Baffetto Via del Governo Vecchio 114 ✆06.686.1617. A tiny, highly authentic pizzeria that has long been a Rome institution. Amazingly it's still good value, and has tables outside in summer, though you'll always have to queue.

Beltramme Via della Croce 39. This very old-fashioned *fiaschetteria* (originally it sold only wine, by

the *fiasco* or flask), two blocks from the Spanish Steps, is just about always packed and is fairly pricey, but if you want authentic Roman food, atmosphere and service the way it used to be, this is the place. No credit cards.

Caffè Capranica Piazza Capranica 104 ✆06.679.0860. This restaurant, taverna and pizzeria all in one is admirably located on a quiet piazza near the Pantheon. Standard fare, well prepared, and average prices.

La Carbonara Campo de' Fiori 23 ✆06.686.4783. The most expensive of the square's restaurants, but always busy, with plenty of outdoor seating and an excellent selection of antipasti. Try their home-made ravioli, *pappardelle* in wild boar sauce, or their namesake, *spaghetti alla carbonara*. Closed Tues.

Ciccia Bomba Via del Governo Vecchio 76 ⌾06.6880.2108. Very central, versatile pizzeria/trattoria that serves quality food for reasonable prices. Closed Wed.

Colline Emiliane Via degli Avignonesi 22 ⌾06.481.7538. Many Italians consider the cuisine of the Emilia Romagna region to be the country's best. Try it for yourself, lovingly prepared by a family, oddly enough, from Le Marche. Closed Fri.

L'Enoteca Antica Via della Croce 76b ⌾06.679.0896. An old Spanish Steps-area wine bar with a selection of hot and cold dishes, including soups and attractive desserts.

Da Giggetto Via del Portico d'Ottavia 21–22 ⌾06.686.1105. Roman-Jewish fare in the Jewish Ghetto, featuring deep-fried artichokes, *baccalà*, and *rigatoni con pajata*, along with good non-offal pasta dishes, eaten outside in summer by the ruins of the Portico d'Ottavia. Not cheap, but worth it. Closed Mon.

Grappolo d'Oro Piazza della Cancelleria 80 ⌾06.686.4118. Curiously untouched by the hordes in nearby Campo de' Fiori. Genuine Roman cuisine in traditional trattoria atmosphere. Closed Sun.

La Grotta Via delle Grotte 27 ⌾06.686.4293. An out-of-the-way, cosy trattoria with a traditional, limited menu and the deeply authentic feel of old Rome. Outdoor seating in summer, towards the river from Campo de' Fiori. Closed Sun.

L'Insalata Ricca Largo dei Chiavari 85/86 ⌾06.6880.3656. An Anglo-American presence in a relaxed and slightly out-of-the-ordinary place, although it is just one of a Roman chain of six. Interesting, big salads, as the name suggests, wholefood options and reasonably priced Italian fare.

Il Leoncino Via del Leoncino 28 ⌾06.687.6306. Genuine, cheap and hectic pizzeria, just off Via del Corso – really one of the best for lovers of crispy Roman-style pizza, baked in wood ovens. No credit

Wed.

Termini and around

Africa Via Gaeta 26 ⌾06.494.1077. Arguably the city's most interesting (Eritrean) food, testimony to its significant Ethiopian and Somalian population. No credit cards. Closed Sat.

Baia Chia Via Machiavelli 5 ⌾06.7045.3452. Near Santa Maria Maggiore, this Sardinian restaurant has lots of good fish starters and tasty first

cards. Closed weekday lunchtimes.

Magna Roma Via Capo d'Africa 26 ⌾06.700.9800, ⌾www.magnaroma.com. Fancy a taste of what the ancient Romans ate at dinner? Then try this: Pompeiian decor, oil lamps and an authentic, reconstructed menu featuring such delicacies as beef stew with quince and chestnut soup. Reckon on €35 a head without wine. Closed Sun.

La Montecarlo Vicolo Savelli 12 ⌾06.686.1877. Hectic pizzeria owned by the daughter of *Da Baffetto* (see opposite) and serving similar crisp, blistered pizza, along with good pasta dishes. Tables outside in summer, but be prepared to queue.

Myosotis Via della Vaccarella 3–5 ⌾06.686.5554. Excellent food, service and value at this slightly upscale restaurant a short walk from the Pantheon. Try the *maltagliati* or *stracci* if you like fresh pasta. Closed Sun.

Naturist Club – L'Isola Via della Vite 14 ⌾06.679.2509. A friendly vegetarian, semi-self-service restaurant at lunchtime, *Naturist Club* features wholegrain risottos, vegetable pies and fresh juices. In the evenings it becomes *L'Isola*, an affordable restaurant specializing in fish dishes. Closed Sun.

Otello alla Concordia Via della Croce 81 ⌾06.678.1454. This place used to be one of Fellini's favourites – he lived just a few blocks away on Via Margutta – and remains an elegant, yet affordable choice in the heart of Rome. Closed Sun.

Der Pallaro Largo del Pallaro 15 ⌾06.6880.1488. An old-fashioned trattoria serving a set daily menu for €17, including wine. Located in a quiet piazza between Campo de' Fiori and Largo Argentina. No credit cards. Closed Mon.

Pizza Re Via di Ripetta 14 ⌾06.321.1468. Authentic Neapolitan pizzeria made in a wood-stoked oven. Busy, so book. Closed Sun lunch.

Da Vito Via delle Colonnelle 5 ⌾06.679.3842. Close by the Panetheon but hidden away, and very authentic, this trattoria has several set menus and an extensive à la carte selection. All the standards plus their own typically Roman specialities. Closed

courses. Closed Sun.

Il Dito e la Luna Via dei Sabelli 49/51 ⌾06.494.0726. Creative Sicilian cuisine in a bistro-like San Lorenzo restaurant popular with thirty-something-ish Romans. Closed Sun.

Formula 1 Via degli Equi 13 ⌾06.445.3866. Justifiably popular San Lorenzo pizzeria, with tables outside in summer. Closed Sun.

Il Podista Via Tiburtina 224 ☎06.4470.0967. Owned and run by marathon-runners – hence, perhaps, the quickly served pizzas and fried food, along with typically Roman fare. Closed Sun.

Pommidoro Piazza dei Sanniti 44 ☎06.445.2692. A typical, family-run Roman trattoria, with a breezy open veranda in summer and a fireplace in winter.

Closed Sun.

Tram Tram Via dei Reti 44–46 ☎06.490.416. Trendy, animated and smoky San Lorenzo restaurant, serving some fine Pugliese pasta dishes, notably seafood lasagne, and unusual salads. Reservations are recommended. Closed Mon.

Across the river: Trastevere and the Vatican

Asinocotto Via Vascellari 48 ☎06.589.8985, ⓦwww.asinocotto.it. A fabulous restaurant, one of the few really fine gourmet establishments in Rome serving up inventive cuisine such as zucchini flowers stuffed with green ricotta, fettucini in a sauce of red lettuce, or chocolate mousse with celery syrup. The wine list stretches to 65 pages. It's rather pricey (€45 not including wine) but worth it. Booking advised.

Casetta de' Trastevere Piazza de' Renzi 31–32 ☎06.580.0158. A traditional Trastevere eatery in every way. Beautiful setting, good food, low prices. Delicious *spaghetti alle vongole*. Closed Mon.

Dino Via San Girolamo Emiliani 8. For a sample of how real Romans eat try this little trattoria. Strictly Roman cuisine, no credit cards, no reservations, just good food and excellent house wines at a very reasonable price. Take tram 8 to Ospedale San Callisto, walk up the hill to the traffic lights, take a left and *Dino* is on your left. Closed Mon.

La Grotta Azzurra Via Cicerone 62a ☎06.323.4490. Quiet, relaxing refuge after a day at the Vatican. Fish specialities and impeccable service at moderate prices. Closed Thurs.

L'Insalatiera 2 Via Trionfale 94 ☎06.3974.2975. A vegetarian restaurant specializing in regional Italian cuisine. Everything is home-made, including the wonderful desserts, such as chocolate and ricotta pie. No smoking. Closed Sun.

Ivo Via di San Francesco a Ripa 158 ☎06.581.7082. *The* Trastevere pizzeria, almost in danger of becoming a caricature, but still good. Arrive early to avoid a chaotic queue. Closed Tues.

Ai Marmi Viale Trastevere 53/59 ☎06.580.0919. Nicknamed "the mortuary" because of its stark

interior and marble tables, this place serves unique "*suppli al telefono*" (deep-fried rice balls, so named because of the string of mozzarella it forms when you take a bite), fresh *baccalà* and the best pizza in Trastevere. A lively feel of the real Rome. Closed Wed.

Monzù Vladi Piazza San Giovanni della Malva 2 ☎06.589.5640. A welcome newcomer to Trastevere, this great restaurant specializes in fine Neapolitan cuisine. Go on Mon, Wed, or Fri, when the cheeses arrive fresh from Campania. Closed Sun.

Da Paris Piazza San Callisto 7a ☎06.581.5378. Fine Roman Jewish cookery in one of Trastevere's most atmospheric piazzas. Also other traditional dishes. Closed Sun.

Dar Poeta Vicolo del Bologna 45 ☎06.588.0516. Without any doubts, one of the top-ten pizzerias in Rome. Don't expect the typical crusty Roman pizza here; the margherita (ask for it *con basilico* – with basil) comes out of the oven soft and with plenty of good mozzarella on top. Be prepared to wait for a table; you might prefer to ask for outside seating because inside the roar is deafening. Closed Mon.

Romolo Via Porta Settimiana 8 ☎06.581.3873. A Trastevere institution, apparently located in the very building where Raphael's lover, "La Fornarina", lived. Great garden setting in fine weather. Traditional Roman menu. Closed Mon.

Il Vascello Via G. Masari 8 ☎06.580.6517. A charming and popular Sardinian restaurant/pizzeria in the heart of Monteverde Vecchio frequented by academics, scholars, artists and locals. Great food and great wines at low prices. Reservation recommended. Closed Tues.

Gelaterie and pasticcerie

Dolci & Doni Via delle Carrozze 85. A truly sumptuous array of pastries right in the heart of the city, just a few steps away from Piazza di Spagna. Tea and other snacks, too.

Doppia Coppia Via della Scala 51. This Sicilian-owned Trastevere joint has some of the very best ice cream in town. Sublime consistency and unusual flavours.

Il Forno del Ghetto Via del Portico d'Ottavia 1.

Marvellous kosher Jewish bakery whose pies and pastries draw quite a crowd.

Il Gelato di San Crispino Via della Panetteria 42. Considered by many to be the best ice cream in Rome. Wonderful flavours – all natural – will make the other *gelato* you've tasted pale by comparison.

Giolitti Via Uffici del Vicario 40. An Italian institution that once had a reputation – now lost – for the country's top ice cream. Still pretty good, however, with a choice of seventy flavours.

Palazzo del Freddo di Giovanni Fassi Via Principe Eugenio 65/7. A wonderful, airy 1920s ice-cream parlour not far from Termini. Brilliant fruit ice creams and good milk shakes.

Pascucci Via di Torre Argentina 20. *Frullati* central for the *centro storico*. Your choice of fresh fruit whipped up with ice and milk – the ultimate

Roman refreshment on a hot day.

Tre Scalini Piazza Navona 30. Bus #64 or #492. Piazza Navona institution that is renowned for its famous *tartufo* – death by dark chocolate. Open Thurs–Tues, 8am–1.30am.

Valzani Via del Moro 37. One of the oldest of the city's pastry shops, still keeping up traditions. Closed June–15 Sept.

Drinking

There are plenty of **bars** in Rome, and although, as with the rest of Italy, most are functional daytime haunts and not at all the kinds of places you'd want to spend an evening, owing in part to the considerable presence of Anglo-Americans and the changing tastes of Italian youth, there are plenty of more conducive bars and pubs nowadays – and there's now an Irish pub practically on every corner in central Rome. There's also been a recent upsurge of interest in **wine bars** (*enoteche* or *vinerie*): the old ones have gained new cachet, and newer ones, with wine lists the size of dictionaries, are weighing in too, often with accompanying gourmet menus.

Bear in mind that there is sometimes considerable **crossover** between Rome's bars, restaurants and clubs: for the most part, the places listed below are drinking spots, but you can eat, sometimes quite substantially, at many of them, and several could be classed just as easily as nightclubs, with loud music and occasionally even an entrance charge. Although we've divided these listings into the usual **neighbourhoods**, the truth is the areas around Campo de' Fiori and the Pantheon, plus Trastevere and Testaccio, are the densest and most happening parts of town.

Centro Storico and east of Via del Corso

Bar del Fico Piazza del Fico 26–28. Currently one of several hotspots in the area – just around the corner from *Bar della Pace*, and slightly cheaper. Outdoor heating in winter.

Bar della Pace Via della Pace 5. Just off Piazza Navona, this is *the* summer bar, with outside tables full of Rome's self-consciously beautiful people.

Bevitoria Navona Piazza Navona 72. Right by the Fountain of Neptune, a wine-tasters' tradition. Regulars swear it's the *only* place in Rome to drink Italian wine.

La Curia di Bacco Via dei Biscione 79. This lively place looks like it was hollowed out of the ruins of the ancient Teatro di Pompeii, near Campo de' Fiori – and, in fact, it was. A young crowd, some good wines and interesting snacks.

The Drunken Ship Campo de' Fiori 20–21. A lively meeting-point, with great music, tremendously popular with young Romans and foreign students. Happy hour 7–9pm.

Jonathan's Angels Via della Fossa 18. This quirky bar, just behind Piazza Navona, certainly

wins the "most decorated" award. Every inch (even the toilet, which is worth a visit on its own) is plastered, painted or tricked out in outlandish style by the artist-proprietor.

Lowenhaus Via della Fontanella 16d. Just off Piazza del Popolo, a Bavarian-style drinking establishment with beer and snacks to match. Live jazz from 10pm onwards on Fridays.

Miscellanea Via delle Paste 110a. Located halfway between Via del Corso and the Pantheon, this place was the first American-style bar in Rome, a boozy hangout of US students, and inevitably packed at night. Reasonable prices and the best-value sandwiches in town.

Rock Castle Caf Via B. Cenci 8. In the Jewish Ghetto, just across from Trastevere, a student hangout consisting of six medieval-style rooms, all for dancing and mingling.

Trinity College Via del Collegio Romano 6. A warm and inviting establishment offering international beers and food. Food includes complete pub meals until 1am.

Victoria House Via Gesù e Maria 18. Authentically

dingy English-style pub, just a stone's throw from Piazza di Spagna. There's a non-smoking room, and a happy hour from 6pm to 9pm. **Vineria** Campo de' Fiori 15. Long-established

bar/wine shop right on the Campo, patronized by devoted regulars, although it's now been refurbished, and also offers light meals. Closed Sun lunchtime.

Termini and around

Druid's Den Via San Martino ai Monti 28. Appealing Irish pub near Santa Maria Maggiore with a genuine Celtic feel (and owners). It's not just for the homesick: it has a mixed expat/Italian clientele. Closed Mon.
Fiddler's Elbow Via dell'Olmata 43. One of the two original Irish bars in Rome, one block closer to Santa Maria Maggiore than its rival, the *Druid's*, and roomier, with a decidedly more Latin feel.

Monti D.O.C. Via G. Lanza 93. Comfortable Santa Maria Maggiore neighbourhood wine bar, with a good wine list and some nice food: quiches, salads and pastas. Closed Sun.
Rive Gauche 2 Via dei Sabelli 43. The San Lorenzo district's mythic dive, a smoky, noisy, cavernous evocation of intellectual Left Bank Paris – more or less. Happy hour till 9pm.

Across the river: Trastevere and the Vatican

Il Cantiniere di Santadorotea Via di Santa Dorotea 9. In the heart of Trastevere, this place has some great wines and a range of delicious snacks. Closed Tues.
Clamur Piazza del'Emporio 1. Large yet cosy Irish pub, on the trendy Testaccio side of the Porta Portese (Trastevere) bridge, offering the usual beers plus snacks.
Fiestaloca Via degli Orti di Cesare 7. Mexico-by-the-Tiber-in-Trastevere with very mixed music and very Tex-Mex menu. You have to pay to get in at weekends – Friday €5, drink included, Saturday €8, drink included. Closed Mon.
Enoteca Malafemmina Via San Crisogono 31. This Trastevere wine bar is one of the friendliest places in town. Some amazing wines and delicious

light snacks ordered fresh from the first-class restaurant next door. Closed Wed.
Mr Brown Vicolo del Cinque 29. This popular night-time hangout is on one of Trastevere's most charming detours. A young, fun-loving crowd, happy hour from 9pm to 10pm daily, cheap beers, and an assortment of salads, sandwiches and crepes. Closed Sun.
La Scala Piazza della Scala 60. Perhaps the most popular Trastevere *birreria* – big, bustling and crowded, with a Texan-ranch-meets-McDonald's decor. Food too and occasional (dire) music.
Stardust Vicolo de' Renzi 4. One of Trastevere's most authentic haunts, and just the place for all-night partying, with occasional live jazz.

Nightlife

Roman **nightlife** retains some of the smart ethos satirized in Fellini's film *La Dolce Vita*, and designer dressing-up is still very much a part of the mainstream scene. Rome's **clubs** run the gamut. There are vast glitter palaces with stunning lights and sound systems, predictable dance music and an over-dressed, over-made-up clientele – good if you can afford it and just want to dance (and observe Romans in their natural Saturday-night element). But there are also places that are not much more than ritzy **bars** with music, and other, more down-to-earth places to dance, playing a more interesting selection of music to a younger, more cautious-spending crowd. Whichever you prefer, all tend to open and close late, and some charge a heavy entrance fee – as much as €15, which usually includes a drink. During the hot summer months, many clubs close down or move to outdoor locations.

On the **live music scene**, there are plenty of small-scale summer offerings, but the chances of catching major rock and pop acts are virtually non-existent, and getting worse. Big promoters book the cities up north, especially Milan and Bologna, and leave Rome entirely out of the loop. The city is also a bit of a backwater for the **performing arts**, and very few international performers of renown in any of the arts regularly put in an appearance here. Nevertheless, there is cultural entertainment available, and the quality is sometimes better than you might expect. In any case, what the arts here may lack in professionalism, they often make up for in the charm of the setting. Rome's **summer festival**, for example, organized by "Estate Romana", means that there's a good range of classical music, opera, theatre and cinema running throughout the warm months, often in picturesque locations. Other summer live-music offerings include **Testaccio Village** and the **Festa dell'Unità**, both held in and around the old slaughterhouse in Testaccio. The Festa dell'Unità charges no admission and includes live music, dancing and an array of other entertainments, as well as ethnic eateries. **Testaccio Village** offers a different group every night during the warm months, followed by three outdoor **discos**, all for free on production of a very low-priced weekly pass – available at the ticket booth near the entrance.

Tickets and information

Rome has no comprehensive **ticket service**; you usually have to go to the venue in person some time before the event. However, you can first try Orbis, near Santa Maria Maggiore, at Piazza Esquilino 37 (Mon–Sat 9.30am–1pm & 4–7.30pm; ☎06.474.4776), or, not far from the Vatican, Box Office, Viale Giulio Cesare 88 (Mon 3.30–7pm, Tues–Sat 10am–1.30pm & 2.30–7pm; ☎06.372.0216), but these two provide only information by phone. If you have a credit card you may be able to save time by calling the Italian-language Prenoticket (Mon 3.30–5pm, Tues–Fri 10am–1pm & 2.30–5pm, Sat 10am–1pm; ☎06.520.721); let the recorded voice speak for about a minute, then dial 1 to select the reservation service. For **what's on information**, see p.717.

Clubs

Alien Via Velletri 13/19 ☎06.841.2212. Currently one of the hippest clubs in Rome, with art and fashion shows, performance art and exhibitions as well as lots and lots of house music. Admission price €20, though women are sometimes let in free. It also has a summer venue, *Alien 2 Mare*, at the nearby seaside resort of Fregene, at Piazzale Fregene 5 ☎06.6656.4761.

Black Out Via Saturnia 18 ☎06.7049.6791. Punk, trash and indie music, with occasional gigs by US and UK bands. Located out by San Giovanni in Laterano. Admission price €5.20–7.75. Closed in summer.

Gilda Via Mario de' Fiori 97 ☎06.678.4838. A few blocks from the Spanish Steps this slick, stylish and expensive club is the focus for the city's minor (and would-be) celebs. Jacket required. Admission price €25. Their summer venue, *Gilda-on-the-Beach*, is in Fregene, at Lungomare di Ponente 11 ☎06.6656.0649.

Goa Via Libetta 13 ☎06.574.8277. Opened by famous local DJ Giancarlino and playing techno, house, and trance. There are sofas to help you recover after high-energy dancing; the decor changes every few weeks. Located near San Paolo. Admission price €25.

Jam Session Via del Cardello 13a ☎06.6994.2419. Just off Via Cavour, this place hosts a young crowd bopping to 1970s & 1980s disco tunes they couldn't possibly have heard first-time around. Wed is gay night. Admission price €5.25 includes a drink.

Gay bars, clubs and restaurants

L'Alibi Via Monte Testaccio 44 ☎06.574.3448. Predominantly – but by no means exclusively – male venue that's one of Rome's oldest and best gay clubs. Downstairs there's a multi-room cellar disco and upstairs an open-air bar. There's a big terrace to enjoy in the warm months. Free admission Wed & Thurs; other nights €10.50.

Baronato Quattro Bellezze Via di Panico 23 ☎06.687.2865. Definitely one-of-a-kind, this place is owned and run by the inimitable Dominot, life-long drag chanteuse, who performs Piaf here on Thursday evenings. There's nothing else like it, at least not in Rome. Dominot is Tunisian by birth and the fare here is accordingly his home-made couscous. No admission charge.

Garbo Vicolo di Santa Margherita 1A ☎06.5832.0782. A friendly Trastevere bar, with a relaxed atmosphere and a nice setting, just behind the main piazza. No admission charge.

L'Hangar Via in Selci 29 ☎06.488.1397. One of Rome's oldest and least expensive gay spots, always crammed with young people. No charge to get in, you just take a ticket and pay when you leave for whatever you've had to drink.

Le Sorellastre Via San Francesco di Sales 1b ☎06.718.5288. This Trastevere bar and restaurant, serving Italian and international cuisine, is the only *exclusively* lesbian place in town. Closed Sun.

Rock and pop venues

Accademia Vicolo della Renella 90 ☎06.589.6321. A popular Trastevere eatery and party spot for a youngish crowd, with live rock Mon & Wed evenings, otherwise a DJ.

Alpheus Via del Commercio 36 ☎06.574.7826. Housed in an ex-factory off Via Ostiense, a little way beyond Testaccio, this has space for three simultaneous events – usually a disco, concert and exhibition or piece of theatre. Currently Fri night is gay night. Admission price €7–8, Wed free for students.

Blue Knight Via delle Fornaci 8–10 ☎06.630.011. Right near St Peter's, the main floor here is a bar and *gelateria*, while downstairs there is almost always live acoustic music Thurs–Sat, usually starting at 10.30pm. No admission charge.

Caffè Latino Via Monte Testaccio 96 ☎06.5728.8384. Multi-event Testaccio club with varied live music almost every night, as well as cartoons, films, and cabaret. There's also a disco playing a selection of funky, acid jazz and black music. Best at weekends when it gets more crowded. Admission price €7.75–10.50.

Circolo degli Artisti Via Casilina Vecchia 42 ☎06.7030.5684. A very large venue located beyond Porta Maggiore. A good range of bands, with frequent discos and theme nights, etc. Officially members only: €5 for a three-month membership.

Il Locale Vicolo del Fico 3 ☎06.687.9075. Trendy joint that enjoys a lively, not to say chaotic, atmosphere, and some up-to-the-minute (mainly indie) music. Admission price €3.

RipArte Café Via Orti di Trastevere 7 ☎06.586.1852. Live music at 11pm every evening in an elegantly modern environment, where you can also eat – but best reserve ahead. Entrance €16.

Villaggio Globale Lungotevere Testaccio ☎06.5730.0329. Situated in the old slaughterhouse on the river, this hosts concerts, club nights, performances and exhibitions almost every night; check newspaper listings. Opening hours depend on events.

Jazz and Latin venues

Alexanderplatz Via Ostia 9 ☎06.3974.2171. Rome's top live jazz club/restaurant with reasonable membership and free entry, except when there's star-billing. Reservations recommended.

Berimbau Via dei Fienaroli 30b ☎06.581.3249. Plenty of live samba and strong Brazilian drinks and food in the heart of Trastevere. Admission price €7.75–10.50, drink included.

Big Mama Vicolo San Francesco a Ripa 18 ☎06.581.2551. Trastevere-based jazz/blues club of long standing. Technically members only, but only costs €5.20 a month, €10.50 for a year. Closed July–Oct.

Escopazzo Via d'Aracoeli 41 ☎06.6920.0422. Friendly bar that attracts a thirty-something crowd and offers food and wine along with live concerts or jam sessions most nights. Free entrance.

Fonclea Via Crescenzio 82a ☎06.689.6302. Located near the Vatican, this jazz/soul, funk and rock venue is fitted out like a British pub and has live music most nights. Happy hour 7–8pm. Free admission Mon–Fri & Sun, Sat €5.25.

Gregory's Via Gregoriana 54d ☎06.679.6386. Just up the Spanish Steps and to the right, an elegant night-spot featuring live jazz improvised by Roman and international musicians. Always crowded. Snacks on offer, too.

New Mississippi Jazz Club Borgo Angelico 18a ☎06.6880.6348. Historical Vatican area jazz venue which also runs a music school. They serve cold buffet dinners, and concerts start at 10pm. Officially members only, but the annual fee is a mere €2.50.

Classical music and opera

Rome's own **orchestras** are not of an international standard, and the city attracts far fewer prestigious orchestras and artists than you might expect of a capital. The city's main classical venue is the *Accademia Santa Cecilia* (see below), and we've listed a number of other places where the city's other orchestras and musical associations perform. In the summer, concerts are staged in cloisters, in the Villa Giulia and Teatro di Marcello, just off Piazza Venezia, and in the ancient Roman theatre at Ostia Antica.

Rome's **opera** scene has long been overshadowed by that of Milan but is improving. The **Teatro dell'Opera** is located near Stazione Termini and Piazza della Repubblica, at Via Firenze 72 (box office daily 9am–4.30pm; English spoken; ☎06.4816.0255; metro A Repubblica). Rome's opera season runs from November to May. Nobody compares it to *La Scala*, but cheap tickets are a lot easier to come by, and important singers do sometimes perform here. Expect to pay at least €16. In summer, the opera moves **outdoors** and ticket prices come down. Summer performances used to be held in a stunning setting at the ancient Baths of Caracalla, but that practice was terminated a few years ago owing to excessive damage to the monument. The last few years the venue has been the Stadio Olimpico, but now the Teatro dell'Opera is air-conditioned that too may change.

Accademia Filarmonica Romana Teatro Olimpico, Piazza Gentile da Fabriano 17 ☎06.326.5991. Classical standards and occasional contemporary works. Performances are on Thurs and run from October to early May. Tickets cost €15.50–31.
Accademia di Santa Cecilia Via della Conciliazione 4 (information ☎06.361.1064; box office ☎06.6880.1044). Year-round, the focus of the Rome classical music scene, with concerts by its own orchestra (Rome's best) and by visiting orchestras and artists. Most of the tickets are pre-sold by season pass, but for certain special events tickets can go for as little as €7.75.
Gonfalone Oratorio del Gonfalone, Via del Gonfalone 32a ☎06.687.5952. The season here runs from November to early June, offering performances of chamber music with an emphasis on the Baroque, every Thursday at 9pm. Tickets cost €13 and you can reserve by phone.
Istituzione Universitaria dei Concerti Aula Magna of the Sapienza University, Piazzale Aldo Moro 5 ☎06.361.0051. Musical offerings ranging from Mozart to Miles Davis. Tickets cost €7.75–26, and the season runs from October to April.

Film

There tends to be more and more **English-language cinema** on offer in Rome, partly owing to foreign demand, but also because Italians are finally beginning to realize that they've been at a disadvantage culturally, linguistically and economically by being spoon-fed a steady diet of dubbed travesties. If you can understand Italian, you'll naturally also find current Italian productions available all over town.

Alcazar Via Merry del Val 14 ☎06.588.0099. Trastevere cinema featuring mainstream American and English films.
Nuovo Olimpia Via in Lucina 16 ☎06 686.1068. Very central, with two screens, and always featuring at least one foreign film in the original language.
Nuovo Sacher Largo Ascianghi 1 ☎06.581.8116. Trastevere film theatre showing mainly foreign independent films in their original versions. €4.15, during the day, €5.15 at night.
Pasquino Piazza Sant'Egidio 10 ☎06.580.3622. Long-established as Rome's premier English-language cinema, with three screens showing recent general releases and the odd indie from Sundance, etc.
Quirinetta Via. M. Minghetti 4 ☎06.679.0012. Centrally located, near the Trevi Fountain, and always showing films in the original language – most of them first-run mainstream American fare. A huge screen and great Dolby surround-sound.

Listings

Airlines Alitalia, Via Bissolati 11 (information ℡06.65.643; 24hr domestic flight information ℡06.65.641; international flights ℡06.65.642); British Airways, Viale Città d'Europa, 681 ℡848.81.22.66; Fiumicino airport ℡06.6501.1513; U.S. Airways Via Bissolati, 20 ℡064.203.261; Continental Airlines, Via Parigi, 11 ℡0666.053.030. Note that many airlines are either in or very close by Via Bissolati and Via Barberini.

Airport enquiries Fiumicino ℡06.659.51; Ciampino ℡06.794.941.

American Express Travel office and exchange facilities at Piazza di Spagna 38 (Mon–Fri 9am–5.30pm, Sat 9am–12.30pm; longer hours in the summer; ℡06.67.641).

Auto Club Italia (ACI) ℡06.49.981; 24hr recorded information ℡06.44.77. Italy's automobile club has an English-speaking staff that can help you with driving or repair information at little or no cost.

Bike and scooter rental Collalti, Via del Pellegrino 82 ℡06.6880.1084 (closed Mon) does bike rental and repairs; Rent-a-Scooter Motoservices, Via F. Turati 50 ℡06.446.9222, is the best deal for scooters and offers a 10 percent discount to *Rough Guide* readers.

Books The Lion Bookshop, Via dei Greci 33 ℡06.3265.0437, is one of the city's biggest and best-stocked English-language bookshops, and has an English-speaking staff for enquiries. Try also the Anglo-American Book Co, Via della Vite 102 ℡06.679.5222; the Corner Bookshop, Via del Moro 48 ℡06.583.6942 (no closing day), a tiny gem run by an English lady and her cat; the Economy Book Center, Via Torino 136 ℡06.474.6877; and Feltrinelli International, Via Orlando 84 ℡06.482.7878 (no closing day), which has an excellent selection of English books and travel guides.

Car rental All the big names have desks at Fiumicino and Termini. In the city centre itself, there are, among others, Avis, Via Sardegna 38a ℡06.4282.4728, Hertz, Via Veneto 156 ℡06.321.6831, and Maggiore, Via Po 8 ℡06.854.8698.

Car repair Call ℡116 for emergency breakdown service. Otherwise, consult the ACI (see above) or the Yellow Pages under "Autoriparazioni" for repair shops.

Club Alpino Italiano Corso Vittorio Emanuele 305 ℡06.683.2684.

Dentist The Ospedale di Odontoiatria G. Eastman, Viale Regina Elena 287b ℡06.8448.3232, has a 24-hour emergency service.

Embassies Australia, Corso Trieste 25c ℡06.852.721, emergencies toll free at ℡800.877.790; Britain, Via XX Settembre 80a ℡06.482.5441; Canada, Via Zara 30 ℡06.445.981; Ireland, Piazza Campitelli 3 ℡06.697.9121; New Zealand, Via Zara 28 ℡06.441.7171; USA, Via Veneto 119 ℡06.46.741.

Emergencies Call ℡113. Both the Police and the Carabinieri have offices in Termini. Otherwise the most central police office is off Via del Corso in Piazza del Collegio Romano 3 ℡06.46.861, and there's a Carabinieri office in Piazza Venezia to the right of Via del Corso.

Exchange American Express (see above); Thomas Cook, Piazza Barberini 21a (Mon–Sat 9am–8pm, Sun 9.30am–5pm); Via della Conciliazione 23 (Mon–Sat 9am–8pm, Sun 9.30am–5pm).

Football Rome's two teams, Roma and Lazio, play at the Stadio Olimpico, on Via del Foro Italico, on alternate Sundays from September till May. The stadium is reachable by metro line A to Ottaviano, then bus #32, or by bus #910 from Termini. Lazio fans traditionally occupy the Curva Nord end of the ground, where a seat costs around €15; seats elsewhere, in the *distinti* (or corners) or the *tribuna* (or main stand) are quite a lot more expensive – reckon on paying around €50 for a decent *tribuna* ticket. Roma fans occupy the Curva Sud, and this is completely sold out to season ticket holders so you can expect to pay more to see Roma play. For information about ticket outlets and availability, try Lazio Point, Via Farini 34 ℡06.482.6688, Mon–Sat 9am–1pm & 2.30–5pm), the Lazio ticket office (℡06.323.7333), or the Roma team office (℡06.506.0200).

Gay contacts ARCI-Gay Caravaggio, Via Lariana 8 ℡06.855.5522, and ARCI-Lesbica Roma, Via dei Monti di Pietralata 16 ℡06.418.0369, are the Rome branches of the nation-wide Italian gay organization. Otherwise there's gay information in English on ℡06.541.398, Mon evenings, 8.30–10.30pm, or gay information in Italian on ℡167.162.966, Mon–Fri 2–4pm.

Hospital In case of emergency phone ℡113 or ℡118. Otherwise the most central hospitals with casualty departments are the Policlinico Umberto I, Viale del Policlinico 155 ℡06.49.971, and the Santo Spirito, Lungotevere in Sassia 1 ℡06.68.351, near the Vatican. The Rome American Hospital, Via E. Longoni 81 ℡06.22.551 or 06.678.6209, is a private multi-speciality hospital with bilingual staff.

Internet Bibli, Via dei Fienaroli 28 ☎06.588.4097, offers Internet access in a large, multipurpose bookstore in Trastevere; an hour costs €6. Try also Internet Caf, Via Cavour 213 ☎06.4782.3051, an efficiently run, pleasant environment with Internet access, scanning and printing.

Laundry Onda Blu, at Via Principe Amedeo 70b and Via Lamarmora 12 (both daily 8am–10pm); Wash and Dry, Via Della Pelliccia 35 and Via Della Chiesa Nuova 15–16 (both daily 8am–10pm). All offer a wash including soap and tumble-drying for €7.75 for a 6kg (15lb) load. Slightly cheaper and offering Internet access while you wait is Splashnet, Via Varese 33 (6kg for €6 including 15 minutes free internet).

Libraries The British Council, Via delle Quattro Fontane 20 (Mon, Tues, Thurs & Fri 10am–1pm, Wed 2–5pm; closed Aug & Christmas; ☎06.478.141), has a lending library, for which yearly membership costs €51.65. Non-members are, however, allowed to use it for reference purposes for free. There's also a library at the American church of Santa Susanna, Via XX Settembre 14 ☎06.482.7510, which also has a good noticeboard for finding work, accommodation and so on.

Lost Property For property lost on a train call ☎06.4730.6682 (daily 7am–11pm); on a bus ☎06.581.6040 (Mon & Fri 8.30am–1pm, Tues–Thurs 2.30–6pm); on the metro ☎06.487.4309.

Pharmacies Piram, Via Nazionale 228 ☎06.488.0754, and Farmicia della Stazione, Piazza dei Cinquecento ☎06.488.0019, are both open 24hr, year-round.

Post Rome's main post office is at Piazza San Silvestro 18–20 (Mon–Fri 9am–6pm, Sat 9am–2pm; closes midday last Sat of each month). This is the place to pick up poste-restante mail.

Swimming pools The city's most central open-air pool is at the *Grand Hotel del Gianicolo*, Viale delle Mura Gianicolensi 107 ☎06.58.33.34.05 (Mon–Fri 9am–7.30pm, €16; Sat & Sun €25 plus €5 obligatory bathing cap, unless you bring your own). There's also an open-air pool, Piscina delle Rose, at Viale America 20 in EUR, metro line B (June–Sept 15 daily 9am–7pm; €7.50 half-day; ☎06.592.6717).

Train enquiries For general enquires about schedules and prices call ☎848.888.088 (daily 7am–9pm) or look up ⓦwwww.trenitalia.it.

Travel agents For discount tickets try CTS at Via Genova 16 ☎06.462.0431, and Corso Vittorio Emanuele II 297 ☎06.687.2672; both are open on Saturday mornings, when all the other travel agents are closed. Other good places to try are Viaggiare, Via San Nicola da Tolentino 15 ☎06.421.171, who have some English-speaking staff, and Elsy Viaggi, Via di Torre Argentina 80 ☎06.689.6460.

Tour Guides For personalized tours of all the sights, museums and even out of the city contact Laila Thea Volpe, Licensed Tour Guide, ☎06 582.8519, Ⓔsailawaywind@yahoo.com. Rome Revealed Tours, a cultural association, offers daily (except Wed, Sun & holidays) tours of the Vatican museums. The tour lasts about two hours and the guides are all English mother-tongue speakers. Book on ☎06 9016 0167, Ⓔromerevealed@libero.it.

Out from the city: Tivoli and Ostia Antica

You may find there's quite enough in Rome to keep you occupied during your stay. But Rome can be a hot, oppressive city, its surfeit of churches and museums intensely wearying, and if you're around long enough you really shouldn't feel any guilt about getting out to see something of the countryside around. Two of the main attractions visitable on a day-trip are, it's true, Roman sites, but just the process of getting to them can be energizing. **Tivoli**, about an hour by bus east of Rome, is a small town famous for the travertine quarries nearby, the landscaped gardens and parks of its Renaissance villas, and a fine ancient Roman villa just outside. **Ostia**, in the opposite direction from the city near the sea, and similarly easy to reach on public transport, is nowadays the city's main seaside resort (though one worth avoiding, see p.800 for more attractive options just a little further south), but it was home to the port of Rome in classical times, and the site is well preserved and worth seeing. Bear in mind, too, that a number of **other places in Lazio** – the Etruscan sites north of Rome, the Castelli Romani (p.800), Palestrina and Subiaco (pp.802–803), and parts of the southern coast (p.805) – are close enough to the city to make a feasible day-trip, especially if you have access to a car.

Tivoli

Just 40km from Rome, perched high on a hill and looking back over the plain, **TIVOLI** has always been something of a retreat from the city. In classical days it was a retirement town for wealthy Romans; later, during Renaissance times, it again became the playground of the moneyed classes, attracting some of the city's most well-to-do families, who built their country villas out here. Nowadays the leisured classes have mostly gone, but Tivoli does very nicely on the fruits of its still-thriving travertine business, exporting the precious stone world-wide (the quarries line the main road into town from Rome), and supports a small airy centre that preserves a number of relics from its ritzier days. To do justice to the gardens and villas – especially if Villa Adriana is on your list, as indeed it should be – you'll need time, so it's worth setting out early.

Most people head first for **Villa d'Este** (summer daily 9am–1hr before sunset; winter Tues–Sun 9am–1hr before sunset; €4.20 for house and grounds), across the main square of Largo Garibaldi – the country retreat of Cardinal Ippolito d'Este that was transformed from a convent by Pirro Ligorio in 1550, and now often thronged with visitors even outside peak season. They mainly come to see the fountains of the landscaped gardens, but the restored ground-floor apartments alone make the trip well worthwhile, frescoed with scenes of mythology and the history of Tivoli by Girolamo Muziano and Federico Zuccari in 1555–1560. Unfortunately, restoration is still going on in the gardens below, and you may find many of the famous fountains are temporarily closed. However, you can see the theatrical, magnificent Organ Fountain, which has been returned to its original glory and makes a most imposing sight as it gushes millions of gallons of water down the hillside. Among the other fountains you can see are the Fontana dell'Ovato, near the Organ Fountain, fringed with statues, behind which is a rather dank arcade, and the Rometta or "Little Rome", on the opposite side of the garden, which has reproductions of the city's major buildings and a boat holding an obelisk. Finally a word of warning: be sure to drink only from those fountains marked *acqua potabile*, and don't wade or splash in the other fountains – the water is basically sewage from the town above.

Tivoli's other main attraction is **Villa Gregoriana**, currently closed for restoration, but usually open daily from 10am to one hour before sunset (€4). It's a park with waterfalls created when Pope Gregory XVI diverted the flow of the river here to ease the periodic flooding of the town in 1831. Less well-known and less touristed than the d'Este estate, it has none of the latter's conceits – its vegetation is lush and overgrown, descending into a gashed-out gorge over 60m deep. There are two main waterfalls – the larger Grande Cascata on the far side, and a small Bernini-designed one at the neck of the gorge. The path winds down to the bottom of the canyon, scaling the drop on the other side past two grottoes, where you can get right up close to the pounding water, the dark, torn shapes of the rock glowering overhead. It's harder work than the Villa d'Este – if you blithely saunter down to the bottom of the gorge, you'll find that it's a long way back up the other side – but in many ways more rewarding; the path leads up on the far side to an exit and the substantial remains of a **Temple of Vesta**, which you'll have seen clinging to the side of the hill. This is now incorporated into the gardens of a restaurant, but it's all right to walk through and take a look, and the view is probably Tivoli's best – down into the chasm and across to the high green hills that ring the town.

Villa Adriana

Once you've seen these two sights you've really seen Tivoli – the rest of the town is nice enough but there's not that much to it. But just outside town, at the bottom of the hill, fifteen minutes' walk off the main Rome road (ask the Rome–Tivoli bus to drop you or take the local CAT #4 from Largo Garibaldi), **Villa Adriana** (daily 9am–1hr before sunset; €6.20) casts the invention of the Tivoli popes and cardinals very much into the shade. This was probably the largest and most sumptuous villa in the Roman Empire, the retirement home of the Emperor Hadrian for a short while between 135 AD and his death three years later, and it occupies an enormous site. You need time to see it all; there's no point in doing it at a gallop and, taken with the rest of Tivoli, it makes for a long day's sightseeing. Spending €3.81 on the large-scale map they sell at the bookstore near the ticket booth helps make it all understandable.

The site is one of the most soothing spots around Rome, its stones almost the epitome of romantic, civilized ruins. The imperial palace buildings proper are in fact one of the least well-preserved parts of the complex, but much else is clearly recognizable. Hadrian was a great traveller and a keen architect, and parts of the villa were inspired by buildings he had seen around the world. The massive Pecile, for instance, through which you enter, is a reproduction of a building in Athens; and the Canopus, on the opposite side of the site, is a liberal copy of the sanctuary of Serapis near Alexandria, its long, elegant channel of water fringed by sporadic columns and statues leading up to a Temple of Serapis at the far end. Nearby, a museum displays the latest finds from the ongoing excavations, though most of the extensive original discoveries have found their way back to Rome. Walking back towards the entrance, make your way across the upper storey of the so-called Pretorio, a former warehouse, and down to the remains of two bath complexes. Beyond is a fishpond with a *cryptoporticus* (underground passageway) winding around underneath, and behind that the relics of the emperor's imperial apartments. The Teatro Maríttimo, adjacent, with its island in the middle of a circular pond, is the place to which it's believed Hadrian would retire at siesta time to be sure of being alone.

Practicalities

Buses leave Rome for Tivoli and Villa Adriana every twenty minutes from Ponte Mammolo metro station (line B) – the journey time is fifty minutes. Be sure to get on the buses that follow the Via Tiburtina route – they're much quicker. In Tivoli, the **bus station** is in Piazza Massimo near the Villa Gregoriana, though you can get off earlier, on the main square of Largo Garibaldi, where you'll find the **tourist office** (Mon 9am–2pm, Tues–Fri 9am–6.30pm, Sat 9am–3pm; ☎0774.334.522), which has free maps and information on **accommodation**.

Ostia Antica

There are two Ostias: one a rather over-visited seaside resort, **Lido di Ostia**, which is best avoided; the other, one of the finest ancient Roman sites – the excavations of the port of **OSTIA ANTICA** – which are on a par with anything you'll see in Rome itself and easily merit a half-day journey out. The stop before Lido di Ostia on the train from Rome, the site of Ostia Antica marked the coastline in classical times, and the town which grew up here was the port of ancient Rome, a thriving place whose commercial activities were vital to the city further upstream. The **excavations** are relatively free of tourists (daily

9am–1hr before sunset; €4), and it's much easier to reconstruct a Roman town from these than from any amount of pottering around the Forum. It's also very spread out, so be prepared for a fair amount of walking.

The **Decumanus Maximus** is the main street, leading west from the entrance, past the **Baths of Neptune** on the right (where there's an interesting mosaic) to the town's commercial centre, otherwise known as the **Piazzale delle Corporazioni**, for the remains of shops and trading offices that still fringe the central square. These represented commercial enterprises from all over the ancient world, and the mosaics just in front denote their trade – grain merchants, ship-fitters, ropemakers and the like. Flanking one side of the square, the **theatre** has been much restored but is nonetheless impressive, enlarged by Septimius Severus in the second century AD to hold up to 4000 people. On the left of the square, the **House of Apulius** preserves mosaic floors and, beyond, a dark-aisled *mithraeum* with more mosaics illustrating the cult's practices. Behind here – past the substantial remains of the *horrea* or warehouses that once stood all over the city – the **Casa di Diana** is probably the best-preserved private house in Ostia, with a dark, mysterious set of rooms around a central courtyard, and again with a *mithraeum* at the back. You can climb up to its roof for a fine view of the rest of the site, afterwards crossing the road to the **Thermopolium** – an ancient Roman café, complete with seats outside, a high counter, display shelves and even wall paintings of parts of the menu.

North of the Casa di Diana, the **museum** (Tues–Sat 9am–4.30pm, Sun 9am–1pm; entry with ticket for the excavations – see above) holds a variety of articles from the site, including a statue of Mithras killing a bull, wall paintings depicting domestic life in Ostia and some fine sarcophagi and statuary from the imperial period. Left from here, the **Forum** centres on the **Capitol** building, reached by a wide flight of steps, and is fringed by the remains of baths and a basilica. Further on down the main street, more **horrea** superbly preserved and complete with pediment and names inscribed on the marble merit a detour off to the right; although you can't enter, you can peer into the courtyard. Beyond, the **House of Cupid and Psyche** has a courtyard you can walk into, its rooms clearly discernible on one side, a colourful marbled floor on the other.

Northern Lazio

Northern Lazio is a quite different entity from the region south of the capital. Green and wooded in its central areas, its steadily more undulating hills hint at the landscapes of Tuscany and Umbria further north. There are few large centres, though, and interest is sparse: with determination (and, in some cases, a car), you can see much of it on day-trips from Rome. Foremost among the area's attractions is the legacy of the **Etruscans**, some of whose most important sites, scattered along the southern stretch of coast, are readily accessible by road or rail – necropolises mainly, but the only remains of a civilization that ruled the area for close on a thousand years. The **coast** itself is of very little appeal until you get close to the Tuscan border, and if you want to swim you'd be better off doing so inland, around lakes **Vico** or **Bolsena** – playgrounds for hot and bothered Romans on summer weekends. Between these, **Viterbo** is the main centre, a dour provincial town that can make a good base for visiting both the lakes and the region's **Mannerist villas and gardens**, though all over this central area bear in mind that touring without your own transport can be an uphill struggle. Over to the east, **Rieti** is the big centre, a rather bland and somewhat deservedly unvisited town on the way to Abruzzo. Beyond it lie the **lakes and mountains** of Terminillo and Amatrice, scenically spectacular, but again virtually out of reach without your own vehicle.

Etruria and the coast

D.H. Lawrence had pretty much the last word on the plain and low hills stretching north from Rome towards the Tuscan border: "A peculiarly forlorn coast," he lamented, "the sea peculiarly flat and sunken, lifeless looking, the land as if it had given up its last gasp and was now forever inert." His *Etruscan Places*, published in 1932, is one of the best introductions to both the Etruscans and their cities, which, one or two beaches excepted, are the main reasons for venturing out here.

Cerveteri

CERVETERI provides the most accessible Etruscan taster if you're commuting from Rome. The nearest train station is 7km away at **LADISPOLI**, also incidentally the best of the rather uninspiring seaside resorts just outside Rome – there are plenty of places to swim about ten minutes' walk from the station, although the best spot is further north, around half-an-hour away from the station at the **Torre Flavia** – a medieval construction restored in 1565 by an Orsini cardinal and now collapsing elegantly into the water in four equal parts.

If you want to head straight for Cerveteri itself, however, you're best off getting a **bus** from the Lepanto metro station (line A) in Rome; they leave every thirty minutes and will drop you off at Piazza Aldo Moro in the town centre (a 1hr 20min journey).

There's been a settlement at Cerveteri since the tenth century BC, when it was already known to the Greeks as an important trading centre. Cerveteri, the Roman *Caere*, was among the top three cities in the twelve-strong Etruscan federation, its wealth derived largely from the mineral riches of the **Tolfa hills** to the northeast – a gentle range which gives the plain a much-needed touch of scenic colour. In its heyday the town spread over 8km (something like thirty times its present size), controlling territory that stretched for 50km up the coast. The rot set in from 351 BC, when it became a dependency of Rome, having failed, like most of Etruria, to maintain a neutrality with the new power.

The present town is a thirteenth-century creation, dismissed by D. H. Lawrence – and you really can't blame him – as "forlorn beyond words". On arrival, make straight for the Etruscan **necropolis** (Tues–Sun: May–Sept 9am–7pm; Oct–April 9am–4pm; €4.15), just 1km away and signposted from the central piazza. The Etruscans constructed a literal **city of the dead** here, weird and fantastically well preserved, with complete streets and houses, some formed as strange round pillboxes carved from the living rock, others still covered in earth to create the tumuli effect that ripples over the surrounding plateau. The general span of the graves is seventh to first century BC: as far as anyone can make out, women were buried in separate small chambers within the "house" – easy to distinguish – while the men were laid on death beds (occasionally in sarcophagi) hewn directly from the stone. Slaves were cremated and their ashes placed in urns alongside their masters – civilized by comparison with the Romans, who simply threw their slaves into mass burial pits. The twelve or so show-tombs, lying between the two roads that bisect the city, are grouped together beyond the entrance; they close in random rotation, so it's difficult to know in advance which ones are going to be open. If possible don't miss the **Tomba Bella** (Tomb of the Bas-Reliefs), **Tomba dei Letti Funebri** (Tomb of the Funeral Beds) and the **Tomba dei Capitelli**.

You could spend several hours wandering about here, but you might be better off heading back into town to the **Museo Nazionale di Cerveteri**, at the top of the old quarter in the sixteenth-century **Castello Ruspoli** (Tue–Sun 9am–7pm; free). This has two large rooms containing a fraction of the huge wealth that was buried with the Etruscan dead – vases, sarcophagi, terracottas and a run of miscellaneous day-to-day objects; most of the best stuff has been whisked away to Villa Giulia in Rome (see p.755). On the way to the museum, if the tombs have whetted your appetite you might want to make a stop at the little **trattoria**, *Tulchulcha*, on the necropolis road, where they serve a hearty country-style food backed up by crisp Cerveteri white wines (no credit cards; closed Mon).

Civitavecchia

The only reasons to break a journey in **CIVITAVECCHIA**, 30km north, are to change trains or to pick up a **ferry to Sardinia** (see p.812 for details of crossings); try to take a night crossing to save yourself the dubious pleasure of spending a night in town. The tourist office sells tickets, but you can book ahead (essential in the summer months) from many travel agents both in the town and in other parts of Italy. The **ferry docks** (closed Mon) are in the centre of the town at the end of Viale Garibaldi, ten minutes' walk from the train station. There's a **tourist office** between the two at Viale Garibaldi 40 (Mon–Fri 8am–1pm & 4.30–7pm; ☎0766.25.348). Should you get stuck, however, head for the modern **hotel** *Medusa* (☎0766.24.327; ❹), which is near the 68,300km marker on Via Aurelia and has nice, clean rooms. As for **eating**, try the *Santa Lucia*, Viale Garibaldi 38 (closed Wed in winter), close by the tourist office, which does decent pizzas, or *Trattoria Sora Maria*, off Largo Plebiscito on Via Zara (closed Fri in winter), a nice place and good for fish.

Tarquinia

TARQUINIA, about 15km further north, is the most touted of the Etruscan necropolises, and with good reason. As long as it is not overrun with fellow visitors, the site can be quite evocative and the actual town, partly walled and with a crop of medieval towers, is a pleasant place to pass an afternoon. The museum is the finest in the region outside of Rome and should not be missed.

The Town

Apart from its old fortified district, which commanded the town approaches for several centuries and holds within its walls a twelfth-century Romanesque church, **Santa Maria di Castello** – notable for its rib vaulting, the first known example in Italy – it's the **Museo Nazionale Tarquiniense**, right on the main town square of Piazza Cavour (Tues–Sun 9am–7pm; €6.20, including admission to the necropolis) that draws the crowds. It's not a large museum, and is all the better for that and for the fact that it is sensitively housed in an attractive Gothic-Renaissance palazzo. The ground-floor rooms contain some superb sculpted sarcophagi, many decorated with warm and human portraits of the deceased, while upstairs are displays of exquisite Etruscan gold jewellery, painted ceramics, bronzes, candlesticks, figures and heads, including the renowned winged terracotta horses (fourth century BC), probably from a temple frieze – a striking example of the Etruscans' skill in decorative terracotta. As well as having fine views over the surrounding countryside and down to the sea, the top floor is probably the most impressive part of the museum, with some of the best of the wall paintings from the nearby necropolis – relocated here owing to their on-site deterioration, and displayed in re-creations of the tomb chambers.

The site

It's the **necropolis** itself (Tues–Sun 9am–1hr before sunset; €6.20 including admission to museum), though, which really makes the journey worthwhile, a warren of graves spread across a plateau on the southeast edge of the town that is all that's left of a city – the site of which is across the valley to the northeast of the necropolis – that was once the artistic, cultural and probably political capital of Etruria. The city was founded in the tenth century BC and its population is estimated to have been around 100,000, going into a gradual decline from the fourth century BC under the growing influence of Rome. Etruscan cities were built almost entirely of wood, so most vanished quickly – and those that didn't were redeveloped by the Romans, making this necropolis one of the few extant remnants of the Etruscan culture.

There are about four buses a day from Piazza Cavour to the necropolis, or it's a fifteen-minute walk: take Via Umberto I from Piazza Cavour, pass through the Porta Romana, skip the roundabout (Piazza Europa), follow Via IV Novembre/Via delle Croci up the hill, and the site is on the left. Excavations started in 1489, the first recorded in modern times, since when 6000 tombs have been uncovered (900 in 1958 alone), with many more apparently still to be unearthed. Grave-robbing is common (thieves are known as *i tombaroli*), and there are patrols; together with the growing influx of visitors, this means that only a limited number of tombs (usually about 12 each day) are open at any time. Etruscan burial places were often straight copies of houses (though less literally so here than at Cerveteri), filled with the clutter of daily life to provide the dead with all they might need in the afterlife. But the Tarquinia tombs have something else besides – **wall paintings**, the oldest of which date from about the seventh or eighth century BC. There's been much speculation about the purpose and style of these. The earliest paintings emphasize mythical and ritualistic scenes, but later works from the fourth to the sixth century – in the

Orco, Auguri, Della Caccia and Della Pescia tombs – show greater social realism, giving an insight into the habits, customs and scenes from the life of the deceased. The style of these later works is a mixture of Greek, indigenous Etruscan and even Eastern influences, their ease and fluidity pointing to a civilization that was at the pinnacle of its development. The Greek aspects are particularly important, representing the only allusions to Hellenistic monumental painting, a form that otherwise has largely vanished without trace. From the fourth century BC decadence sets in, with the appearance of increasingly morbid and purely necromantic drawings.

Practicalities

Tarquinia's **train station** is 2km below the town centre, connected with the central Barriera San Giusto, hard up against the city walls, by regular local bus; **buses** from Viterbo and Rome also drop you in Barriera San Giusto. The **tourist office** is just through the city gate at Piazza Cavour 1 (Mon–Sat 8am–2pm; ☎0766.856.38, ⓦ www.comune.tarquinia.vt.it) and doles out maps of the town and other information. There are few places to **eat** and even fewer places to **stay** in town; indeed if you want to stay you're really better off on the coast at Tarquinia Lido (see below), where there's more choice. As for **eating**, there's a cosy trattoria-pizzeria, *Campanari*, at Piazza Cavour 11 (closed Mon), or the more upscale *San Marco* at Piazza Cavour 20 (closed Mon). Perhaps the most atmospheric place to **drink** is *Osterina il Grottino*, a rather dingy cave-like bar at Alberata Dante Aligheri 8 that serves wine siphoned out of barrels piled in the corner.

Tarquinia Lido

TARQUINIA LIDO, reachable by hourly bus from Barriera San Giusto via the FS station, is home to most of Tarquinia's real action. The *Albergo Miramare*, Viale dei Tirreni 36 (☎0766.864.020, no phone bookings accepted; ❸), has reasonably priced en-suites, and there are three huge **campsites** here – and at Riva di Tarquinia to the north – hosting great herds of holiday-makers. The beaches are heavily developed, with restaurants, discos, sports facilities, "pubs", even cinemas, but might be just what you're looking for after dismal Tarquinia proper. The best bet, though, is to round off a day-trip with a quick dip and head back to the station.

Lago di Vico and Caprarola

The smallest but most appealing of northern Lazio's lakes, and the only one deemed worthy of being declared a nature reserve, **Lago di Vico** is a former volcanic crater, ringed by appreciable mountains, the highest of which – Monte Fogliano – rises to 963m on the western shore. The **Via Cimina** traverses the summit ridges and is a popular scenic drive, dotted with restaurants, but there's a quieter road lower down (closed to cars) that skirts closer to the shoreline. The flatter northern edge, marshy in places, is the spot for discreet unofficial **camping**.

Getting around this part of Lazio is a sweat, and in an ideal world you'd have your own transport. Buses between Viterbo and Rome skirt the area, and two rickety branch rail lines spear around the lake from Orte. With careful scrutiny of the timetables both can just about be made to work for you. One of the rail lines ties in to the Rome–Viterbo line (from the Roma Nord

Station) at Capranica, with halts at Ronciglione and Caprarola; the other winds up to Viterbo via Bomarzo.

Caprarola: the Palazzo Farnese

Over and above the lake's sheer prettiness, there's not much besides the odd attractive village and a scattering of Roman and Etruscan remains – none terribly interesting in their own right, but worthwhile if you can string several together. More properly deserving of individual attention is the **Palazzo Farnese** at **CAPRAROLA**, which, like the villas at Bagnaia and Bomarzo (see p794), ranks among the high points of seventeenth-century Italian Mannerism.

The **palace** stands huge and imposing at the top of the town's steep main street (Tues–Sun: March–Oct 9am–6.30pm; Nov–Feb 9am–4pm; €2.10, includes garden tour; ⓦ www.isa.it/tuscia/caprarola). The building is clearly a masterpiece; Stendhal described it as a building where "architecture married Nature". Begun by Antonio di Sangallo the Younger for Pierluigi Farnese in the early 1520s, it was originally more a castle than a palace, situated at the centre of the lands belonging to the Farnese family. Later, Cardinal Alessandro Farnese took up residence here, in 1559 hiring Vignola to modify the building while retaining the peculiar pentagonal floor-plan. Vignola was an inspired choice: apprenticed at Fontainebleau, he was among the most accomplished architects of the late Renaissance, and exemplifies the Mannerist style at its best in his creation at Caprarola, which celebrates the period's values of superiority of art over nature and style over substance, together with a self-satisfied, almost gloating eulogizing of the patron's virtues.

Of the palace's five floors only the *piano nobile* is open to the public. Although all the furniture has gone, the interior is still impressive. There are frescoes from 1560, most of them by the brothers Zuccari chronicling the Farnese family's greatness, much lauded as the building's highlight (though some are embarrassingly crude and others terribly knocked about), and a monumental spiral staircase up to a circular courtyard. The courtyard gives onto the main rooms of the *piano nobile*, huge and heavy with its thirty pairs of columns but considered to be one of Vignola's finest moments. The first and last rooms are perhaps the best, however, the first with a super-embellished grotto-like fireplace and pictures of local communities like Caprarola itself (the central scene is an imaginary one), the last, the *Sala del Mappomondo* decorated with huge painted maps of the known world and a wonderful ceiling fresco of the constellations.

Outside there are twin **gardens** (guided tours Mon–Sat 10am, 1.30pm, 3pm & 5pm; same ticket as palace), divided into a south-facing summer terrace and an east-facing winter terrace, with plants and design appropriate to each. Look out for the artificial grotto and the stalactites, brought from a real cave and stuck on.

Practicalities

Without your own car, it's best to use Viterbo (see overleaf) as a base and take one of the seven **buses** a day from there to Caprarola. This entails a very pleasant 45-minute ride through the wooded hills of the Monti Cimini that leaves you at the foot of the main street, from where it's a ten-minute walk to the palace at the top. In any case Caprarola only has one **hotel**, the *Farnese* (☎0761.646.029; ❷), a modern place way out on Via Circonvallazione on the Viterbo side of town (the Viterbo bus goes right past) that should be used in emergencies only. For **food**, there's the *Trattoria del Cimino* midway down the main street at Via F. Nicolai 44 (closed Fri), and a pizzeria off to the left of Piazza Romei in front of the palace (closed Sun).

Viterbo and around

The capital of its province, and indeed of northern Lazio as a whole, **VITERBO** is easily the region's most historic centre, a medieval town that during the thirteenth century was once something of a rival to Rome. It was, for a time, the residence of popes, a succession of whom relocated here after friction in the capital. Today there are some vestiges of its vanquished prestige – a handful of grand palaces and numerous medieval churches, enclosed by an intact set of medieval walls. The town is a well-kept place and refreshingly untouched by much tourist traffic but only really worth staying in if you're keen to visit the surrounding area. If you aren't, it's worth knowing that buses and trains run frequently from Rome (buses are fastest) and you can comfortably see the town in a day.

The Town

If there is a centre to Viterbo it's **Piazza del Plebiscito**, an appropriately named square girdled almost entirely by the fifteenth- and sixteenth-century buildings that make up the town's council offices. The lions and palm trees that reflect each other across the square are Viterbo's symbol, and you'll see them repeated, in grandiose echoes of Venice, all over town. You can look in on the fine Renaissance courtyard of the main, arcaded building of the **Palazzo dei Priori** and also see the council chamber itself, decorated with a series of murals depicting Viterbo's history right back to Etruscan times in a weird mixture of pagan and Christian motifs – a mixture continued across the square in the church of **Sant'Angelo**.

There are a number of directions you can walk in from the piazza. Most interesting is to take a right off the square down Via San Lorenzo, which leads past the pretty Piazza di Gesù to the macabrely named Piazza del Morte. Left from here takes you through Viterbo's oldest quarter, the **Quartiere San Pellegrino** – a tight mess of hilly streets, home to a number of art and antique shops. In the opposite direction, Piazza San Lorenzo is flanked by the town's most historic group of buildings, notably the **Palazzo Papale** itself, a thirteenth-century structure whose impressive site, looking over the green gorge that cuts into central Viterbo, is best appreciated from its open Gothic loggia. You can peep into the Great Hall, venue of the election of half a dozen or so popes, but otherwise the palace is closed to the public, and you have to content yourself with a wander into the **Duomo** opposite, a plain Romanesque church that has an elegant striped floor and an understated beauty unusual among Italian churches.

East of Piazza del Plebiscito, Via Roma soon becomes **Corso Italia**, Viterbo's main shopping street and the scene of a busy *passeggiata* of an evening. At its far end, steps lead up from Piazza Verdi to the nineteenth-century church of **Santa Rosa**, which holds the saint's corpse in a chapel in the south aisle – a faintly grotesque, doll-like figure with a forced grin, dressed up in a nun's habit. A good time to be in Viterbo is September 3 during the **festa**, when the *macchina* of Santa Rosa – the platform and altarpiece that hold the icon – is carried through the streets of the town to the accompaniment of much revelry and, later, fireworks.

After seeing Santa Rosa, the rest of Viterbo can't help but seem a bit sinister, and in any case you've seen it all except for one quarter, which is at the top of the hill above Piazza Verdi. Follow Via Matteotti up to **Piazza della Rocca**, a large square dominated by the fierce-looking **Rocca Albornoz**, home of the small **Museo Nazionale** (Tues–Sun 9am–7pm; €2), whose archeological collection includes displays of locally unearthed Roman and Etruscan artefacts. Just off the opposite side of the square, the church of **San Francesco** is also worth a quick look, a high and unusually plain Gothic church that is the burial place of two of Viterbo's popes – Clement IV and Adrian V – both laid in now heavily restored but impressive Cosmatesque tombs on either side of the main altar.

Outside the walls is the twelfth-century church of **Santa Maria della Verità**, whose fine early-Renaissance frescoes by little-known master Lorenzo da Viterbo in the Capella Mazzatosta were recently damaged by vandals and are under restoration. In the convent next door is the recently restored **Museo Civico** (Tues–Sun: summer 9am–7pm; winter 9am–6pm; €3.10), containing locally found antiquities from the Iron Age to the Roman imperial period, while the upper floors house an art gallery with paintings from the thirteenth to nineteenth centuries, including works by Sebastiano del Piombo.

Practicalities

Unusually for a small town, Viterbo has two **main train stations**: one, Porta Romana, is situated just outside the Porta Romana to the south of the town centre, around fifteen minutes' walk from Piazza del Plebiscito; and the other, Porta Fiorentina, is on Viale Trento just north of the city walls, close by Piazza della Rocca and handier for hotels and the centre of town. There's also a station serving the **COTRAL** Roma-Nord line in Località Riello, next door to Porta Fiorentina and about ten minutes' walk from Piazza del Plebiscito, where trains from Rome's Piazzale Flaminia station arrive. By far the best way, though, to get to Viterbo is the FM3 train from Stazione Trastevere. Departures are at least hourly throughout the day, less frequent at night, and journey time is an hour and twenty minutes to Porta Fiorentina. There's a **tourist office** on Piazza San Carluccio 5 (Mon–Sat 9am–1pm; ☎0761.304.795) in the medieval part of town, which has free maps of Viterbo and the surrounding area and information on **accommodation**. Close by, Via della Cava, which winds up to Piazza della Rocca, has a couple of Viterbo's inexpensive hotels: the *Leon D'Oro*, Via della Cava 36 (☎0761.344.444; ❹), is a friendly and decent three-star, with off-street parking; or you could try the more basic *Roma*, down the street at Via della Cava 26 (☎0761.226.474; ❸).

Finding **somewhere to eat** is no problem. Although it's now partly given over to a *McDonald's*, *Schenardi*, Corso Italia 11 (closed Wed), preserves its Art Nouveau interior and is still one of the nicest places for a lunchtime snack or a drink and a wide selection of tea. There are a number of cheap pizzerias on Via Matteotti and Via della Cava. The *Porta Romana*, in Via della Bonta, has excellent food, and is supremely friendly. Otherwise, try *La Scaletta*, Via Marconi 43 (closed Mon), for reasonably priced pizzas, or *Tre Re*, Via Marcel Gattesco 3 (closed Thurs), off Piazza delle Erbe – a cosy place, popular with locals and a good venue for trying regional specialities. If you're feeling indulgent, treat yourself to the wonderful food at the *Enoteca la Torre*, Via della Torre 5 (☎0761.226.467; evenings only; closed Sun), Viterbo's culinary highlight: a slightly precious place, but not overly costly if you select sparingly from the five or six courses on offer – and go easy on the huge and pricey wine list.

Around Viterbo: Bagnaia, Bomarzo and Tuscania

Viterbo makes by far the best base besides Rome for seeing much of northern Lazio, especially the places that aren't really feasible on a day-trip from the capital. The Mannerist villas of **Caprarola** (see p.791) and **Bagnaia** are a short distance away and easily reached on public transport, as are – from the same era – the bizarre gardens of **Bomarzo** and the shores of **Lago di Bolsena** (see p.796). Less excitingly, Viterbo is also connected by regular bus with **Tuscania**.

Bagnaia

BAGNAIA, about 5km east of Viterbo, isn't much of a town, but like Caprarola further south it's completely dominated by a sixteenth-century palace, the **Villa Lante**, whose small but superb **gardens** are considered Vignola's masterpiece and one of the supreme creations of Renaissance garden art – "the most lovely place of the physical beauty of nature in all Italy or in all the world", according to Sacheverell Sitwell. The villa is easily visited from Viterbo using the hourly **bus** #6 from Piazza Martiri dei Ungheria or from the stop at the beginning of Viale Trento, or the less frequent trains of the Roma-Nord line.

A short walk up the hill from the main square, the **villa** is actually two villas, built twenty years apart for different cardinals but symmetrically aligned as part of the same architectural plan. They are closed to the public, but there's nothing much to write home about anyway; in contrast to Caprarola it's the **gardens** (Tues–Sun 9am–1hr before sunset; €2.10) that take pride of place – some of the best-preserved from the period and a summing up of Mannerist aspirations. The main group lie behind the villas, ranged over five gently sloping terraces, and are only visitable in the company of a guide. An attempt at a stylized interpretation of the natural world, they were an ambitious project, even by the standards of the time, depicting the progress of a river from its source in the hills to its outlet in the sea – represented here by a large parterre. The route takes in various watery adventures – waterfalls, lakes and the like – and among numerous fountains and low hedges there are plenty of humorous (or plain silly) touches, such as a maiden whose breasts spout water, a cascade designed as an elongated crayfish, and the so-called "wetting sports" – hidden sprays of water that drenched unsuspecting onlookers and were a big favourite of Mannerist pranksters. Only the guide gets to play with these.

The adjoining **park** (Tues–Sun 9am–1hr before sunset; free), through which you can wander at will, has an even more ambitious narrative, attempting to describe through horticulture the progress of civilization from primitive times to the glories of the sixteenth century. In true Mannerist style almost as much weight is given to allegory as to architecture, both here and on the villas. The various square motifs that appear around the buildings, for example, were supposed to represent the perfection of heaven brought to earth.

Bomarzo

Twelve kilometres north-east of Bagnaia, the village of **BOMARZO** is home to another Mannerist creation, the **Parco dei Mostri** (daily 9am– 1hr before sunset; €7.75) and a greater contrast to the former's restrained elegance would be hard to find. It's still ostensibly a garden, but one look at the tangled wood and its huge, completely crazed sculptures is enough to see that this is Mannerism gone mad. Salvador Dalí loved the surreal flavour of the place, even making a film here, and its strange otherworldly qualities – like a sixteenth-century theme park of fantasy and horror – have made it one of northern Lazio's primary tourist attractions.

Built in 1552 by the hunchbacked Duke of Orsini, the *Sacro Bosco,* or "Sacred Wood", as he called it, set out to parody Mannerist self-glorification by deliberate vulgarity. Knocking the intellectual pretentions of the day through its mockery of idealized Arcadian retreats from society and Art's supposed "triumph" over Nature, it still retains the typically Mannerist calculated attempts at sensationalism. Apparently built by Turkish prisoners captured at the Battle of Lepanto (though this smacks of a Christian rationalization of the park's "heretical" features), the park has an Etruscan influence too, manifest in the plentiful urns and pine cones, and its madder moments are said to have been induced by a popular epic of the time, Ariosto's *Orlando Furioso,* a tale of lost sanity. The giant warrior at the entrance tearing apart a woodcutter comes from the story, a symbol of Orlando's madness, and deeper into the park an English prince pours Orlando's brains down an elephant's trunk – another symbol apparently, this time of the restoration of sanity. There are many other dank, mossy sculptures of tortoises, elephants, a whale, a mad laughing mask, dragons, nymphs, butterflies, and plenty of things you couldn't put a name to. There's a perfect octagonal temple, dedicated to Orsini's wife, and a crooked, slanting house that makes your head spin. Numerous cryptic inscriptions all over the park only add to the mystery.

Eight **buses** a day run from Viterbo to Bomarzo, from where the Parco dei Mostri is a signposted ten-minute walk. You can also get here by **train** – the nearest station is Attigliano-Bomarzo, on the Orte–Montefiascone–Viterbo link, but this is a five-kilometre walk from the park.

Tuscania

Sheep and then more sheep are the only thing that breaks the monotony of the wide, desolate country between Viterbo and Tarquinia until the towers of **TUSCANIA** come into view – an impressive sight, especially early in the morning when the sun is striking them full on. The town was used as the location of the Franco Zefferelli films *Romeo and Juliet* and *The Taming of the Shrew* but in 1971 it was flattened by an earthquake which killed several hundred people. A concentrated effort of civic planning and a healthy budget has restored it, and it's now a very tidy and clean reconstruction of what was once a run-down and seedy medieval town – well worth a wander.

The real point of a visit to Tuscania, however, lies in two justly celebrated **Romanesque churches** on the eastern edge of the town, close to the rocky outcrop of the old Etruscan settlement. From the central Piazza Basile take the Via Clodia until the unmistakable bulk of **San Pietro** (daily: summer 9am–1pm & 3–7pm; winter 9am–1pm & 2–5pm) looms into view. Considered one of the gems of the Italian Romanesque, it's an essentially thirteenth-century construction with eighth-century fragments of Lombard origin. Fronted by a threadbare grass piazza, which produces an odd courtyard effect, it's also flanked by the remains of a Bishop's Palace and two sturdy towers, the whole church having once been fortified as part of the town's defensive scheme. The intrinsic marble carving on the facade is a bizarre mix of mythological figures and Christian symbolism – look out for the dancer and a three-headed man spewing out a twisting vine – and may well come from an Etruscan temple. The interior is solemn and cavernous, with huge blunt pillars supporting curious notched arches, a feature known in Italian as *dentati* (literally "toothed"), a spiralling Cosmatesque pavement and some early twelfth-century frescoes in the transept, somewhat the worse for wear after the earthquake in 1971. Steps lead down underneath the chancel to a mosque-like crypt made up of 28 columns and ribbed vaulting.

The town's other focal point, **Santa Maria Maggiore** (same hours as San Pietro), is a stone's throw away down the hill, a less gracious affair than San Pietro, despite the fact that it was built slightly earlier in the same style. The arched marble doorway was probably added by Pisan sculptors in the twelfth century, and is surmounted by an almost naive white-marble Madonna and Child, and flanked by saints and biblical scenes. The rest of the ruddy stone facade is largely Gothic, only the left portal preserving the zigzags of Norman motif. Inside is the usual bare simplicity of the Romanesque – stone walls, the odd fresco (including entertaining scenes of the Last Judgement in the apse, now, alas, fading fast) and, most remarkably, a font designed for total immersion.

Montefiascone, Lago di Bolsena and around

Heading north from Viterbo by road, you've little choice but to take the Via Cassia to **MONTEFIASCONE**, an unattractive journey, not improved by opting for the train, which runs alongside. Montefiascone rears up high, perched on the rim of an old volcanic crater, an Etruscan city and possibly the site of a huge temple to Voltumna – a sort of parliament for the heads of the twelve-city Etruscan Federation. The seventeenth-century **Duomo** is immediately striking, a huge octagonal pile that totally dominates the skyline, though it's less interesting than the twelfth-century church of **San Flaviano** a little way out of town on the road to Orvieto. An extraordinary Romanesque work, consisting of two interconnected but opposite-facing basilicas, the lower church contains several fourteenth- and fifteenth-century frescoes as well as the tomb of Bishop Giovanni Fugger, who reputedly died from knocking back too much of the local wine. Bumph from the **tourist office**, Via Cassia Vecchia (8.30am–1pm; ☎0761.83.201), regales you with other unlikely legends surrounding this potable brew and has details of **accommodation**, which includes the inexpensive hotel *Italia* at Piazzale Roma 9 (☎0761.826.058, Ⓕ0761.831.091, Ⓔhotelitalia@inwind.it; ❸) and a **campsite**, the *Amalasunta*, Via del Lago 77 (☎0761.825.294), out on the Marta road at Prato Roncone.

Buses run from Montefiascone to Orvieto (see p.650) and to most points on **Lago di Bolsena** – a popular destination, though rarely overcrowded. If you want to get away from it all and plan on spending some time here, head for the less-visited western shore, which is better for camping rough and more picturesque into the bargain. The lake occupies the remains of a broad volcanic crater and is the largest of its kind in Europe. The surrounding soil is immensely fertile, and there's a super-mild microclimate, with most of the shores intensely cultivated as a result. Dante praised the quality of its eels, though fishermen today are hampered by the so-called *sesse* – odd tide-like variations in the lake's level.

CAPODIMONTE, on the southern shore, is one of the more developed spots, an attractive town that pushes into the lake on a partly forested peninsula. The only sight worth a mention is the sixteenth-century **Castello Farnese** (closed to the public), an octagonal tower commanding the tip of the promontory, but there's good **swimming** from a tree-lined shore, and boat trips run out to the **Isola Bisentina**, which sports Etruscan tombs, five frescoed chapels, and another Farnese villa – the summer retreat of several popes. The nearest **campsite** is 1500m away at Località San Lorenzo, *Camping Bisenzio* (☎0761.871.202; May–Sept).

On the opposite shore, **BOLSENA** is the lake's main focus, a relaxed and likeable place that's worth a stop even if you don't intend to hang around. Medieval nooks and alleyways run off the single main drag, with a well-preserved fourteenth-century **castle** perched over the western end. Inside is the local **museum** (Tues–Sun: summer 9.30am–1.30pm & 4–8pm; winter 9.30am–1.30pm; free) with a modest collection of local Roman and Etruscan finds. The de-consecrated thirteenth-century church of **San Francesco** adds character to the town's main Piazza Matteotti and occasionally hosts concerts and small exhibitions, and the eleventh-century **Santa Cristina** conceals a good Romanesque interior behind a wide Renaissance facade added in 1494. St Cristina was the daughter of the town's third-century Roman prefect, who tortured her for her Christian beliefs, eventually throwing her into the lake with a stone round her ankles. Miraculously the stone floated and saved her life, becoming marked with the imprint of her feet – though she died at the tender age of 12 as a result of further mistreatment. The stone makes up the altar of the Cappella del Miracolo, off the left-hand aisle – an altar that also starred in the Mass of Bolsena (see p.768), when a sceptical priest was assured of the mystery of transubstantiation by real blood. Adjoining the chapel is the Grotta di Santa Cristina, once part of early Christian catacombs.

Set back 1km from the lake, the town itself tends to shut down come nightfall, when the **bars and restaurants** on the shore get into full swing. The closest of the **campsites**, most of which are a short walk out of town, is the *Campeggio Il Lago*, less than 1km away at Viale Cadorna 6 (℡0761.799.191; March–Sept). *La Pineta* is a similar distance from town at Viale Diaz 48 (℡0761.799.801; May–Sept). The cheapest **hotel** is the *Italia*, Corso Cavour 53 (℡0761.799.193; ❷). For full details, call in at the **tourist office** at Piazza Matteotti 9 (summer Mon–Sat 9am–1pm & 4–8pm; winter Sat & Sun 9am–1pm & 4–8pm; ℡0761.799.923).

Rieti and around

Pleasantly situated but rather dull, **RIETI** is the capital of Lazio's largest province, occupying the plumb geographical centre of Italy – and with a plaque in Piazza di San Rufo to prove it. In the days of the Romans this was a key region, the so-called *Umbilicus Italiae*, and the Via Salaria or "Salt Road" traversing these parts formed an essential route for trading salt (extracted from the Tiber estuary) with the Sabines who lived up in these hills. But nowadays it's on its last legs, with the second-lowest population density in the country (after Aosta) and a drift from the land that's more often associated with the south. Three-quarters of the rural population has moved from the countryside since 1950, most of them to Rome, and it doesn't look like changing: poor communications have deterred any sort of industrial initiative – something that is to the visitors' if not the locals' advantage, leaving Rieti's mountain-ringed plain almost entirely unscarred by factories or housing.

The Town

Rieti is really just somewhere to while away an hour waiting for a bus, unless you want to use it as a base for walks in the area (see below). Despite the tourist office's artful pictures of medieval walls and arches, the only traces of the medieval town you'll find are the **Duomo** and the **Palazzo Vescovile** off the main street and a short stretch of twelfth-century wall to the north of the centre. For those planning serious walking or camping trips, it's worth visiting the main **tourist office** at Piazza Vittorio Emanuele II (Mon–Sat 9.30am–1pm & 4–6pm; ☎0746.201.146, ⓦwww.apt.rieti.it), which has maps of the town and, more importantly, detailed routes for **high-level walks** around Terminillo (see below). With their help you also shouldn't have problems planning a tour of the four **Franciscan monasteries** around Rieti, all connected one way or another with important episodes in the saint's life. They're all scenic enough, though without an abiding interest in St Francis you may not find them terribly exciting. The most famous is at **GRECCIO**, where Francis created the first ever Christmas crib, a real-life nativity scene complete with cows, for the benefit of locals; this is re-enacted every year on December 24, December 26 and at Epiphany on January 6.

Practicalities

Rieti's **train station** is just north of the town centre on the far side of Viale L. Morroni. By **train** from Rome it's around three hours to Rieti: there's no direct link and you have to change at Terni (and sometimes Orte) for a line that eventually continues to L'Aquila and Sulmona. The **bus station** is in Via Fratelli Sebastiani off Via Salaria, and several **buses** a day ply back and forth to Rome (a 2hr journey). For somewhere **to stay**, the *Serena*, Viale della Gioventù 17 (☎0746.270.930; ❸), is probably the cheapest option close to the centre of town, and has a few cheaper rooms without baths. If you want to be in the centre itself, try the *Europa*, Via San Rufo 49 (☎0746.495.149; ❸), which also has some cheaper rooms. You can **eat** inexpensively at *Pizzeria Il Pappamondo*, Piazza Cavour 63 (closed Tues), or, for a little more money, try *Bistrot*, on Piazza San Rufo 25 (closed Sun), a family-run place whose adventurous and varied menu changes daily.

Around Terminillo

Less than 20km from Rieti, reachable by way of a heart-stopping bus ride, **TERMINILLO** lies amidst 2000-metre-high mountains and scenery of almost Alpine splendour, a winter ski-resort that likes to think of itself as something of an elite tourist centre. As such it's dominated by clusters of big modern hotels, ski lifts and associated winter-sports paraphernalia. Terminillo is not an especially attractive place, more a string of ski-centres than a town, with facilities that seem rather out of place and redundant in summer, but there's plenty of off-season scope for walking and climbing in the hills around, including a series of refuges if you want to do more than stroll.

Advice on ski conditions and accommodation is available from the **tourist office** at Via dei Villini 33 in Terminillo/Pian de Valli (daily: summer 9am–1pm & 4–8pm; winter 9am–1pm & 4–6pm; ☎0746.261.121). There's a **youth hostel**, the *Ostello della Neve*, at Terminillo/Campoforogna (☎0746.261.169; €9.30). Contact the **Club Alpino Italiano**, Via Garibaldi 264b, in Rome (☎06.686.1011), for advance information on some of the most challenging hikes in the countryside around. One tremendous low-level hike is by way of **La Valle Scura**, 12km across country to Sigillo; ask at the tourist office for details. If you plan on trekking off into the wilderness, bear in mind that many slopes away from the ski-runs are thickly wooded, especially in the Vallonina towards Leonessa, and you often have to climb quite high before finding open country.

Another good base for hikes is **AMATRICE**, 65km north-east of Rieti, a

rather drab grid-iron town laid out in 1529, famous only for having given birth
to a pasta dish, *spaghetti all'Amatriciana*, with a spicy bacon and tomato sauce.
Behind, the Monti della Laga rise to seriously high peaks – 2400m up – which
continue on into Abruzzo's Gran Sasso (see p.821). The **tourist office** at
Corso Umberto I 93 (☎0746.826.344) issues a detailed map with several
marked paths, most of which start from rough roads above the hamlets of San
Martino and Cappricchia. If you plan on staying, try the two-star **hotel** *La
Conca* on Via della Madonnella 24 (☎0746.826.791; ❷).

The Sabine Hills

The **Sabine Hills**, south of Rieti, are an altogether softer option than the
mountains to the east. For an area so close to Rome this sees only a trickle of
tourism – partly because there are no big sights and partly because it's difficult
to get around in what is essentially a landscape of small villages and secondary
roads. If you decide to bother with the region it'll be for the scenery, the best
of which is east of the Via Salaria around **Lago del Turano** and **Lago del
Salto**, where the village of **ROCCA SINIBALDA** provides a focus – though
it's really no more than a fortified castle, surrounded by high wooded hills.
Northeast of here, a great swath of desolate country centres around Monte
Nuria (1888m) and Monte Moro (1524m) – walking and backpacking territory mostly, with the small **Lago Rascino** providing a wild and unspoilt destination, especially good for camping.

On the other side of the Via Salaria, many of the villages have been doubly
destroyed, first in the Fifties by people emigrating to Rome, and then more
recently – and ironically – by richer Romans returning to buy up holiday
homes. The villages still look much as they always did – small self-contained
nuclei on the tops of low hills – and varying degrees of medieval character are
about all they've got going for them, though the rolling countryside between
is moderately pretty. One undoubted highlight in a lacklustre area is the old
Benedictine abbey at **FARFA**, situated in fine olive-covered countryside 6km
from the village of Faro. Getting there by bus is difficult as connections are
required, but the Rieti tourist office will be able to advise on the latest schedules. Founded in the fifth century and endowed by Charlemagne, it was one of
the single most powerful abbeys in Europe for a while, with a huge economic
base, a merchant fleet, even its own army, and rights to Aquila, Molise, Viterbo,
Spoleto, Tarquinia and Civitavecchia – central Italy in effect. By the end of the
Middle Ages, however, it was in decline, and most of its early medieval splendour has since been submerged under fifteenth- and sixteenth-century additions. The **Abbey Church** (summer Tues–Sat 9.30am–1pm & 4.30–7pm, Sun
10am–1pm & 4–7pm; winter daily 3.30–6pm; €2.60) is stacked with various
treasures, including parts of the Carolingian pavement, the sculptural relief
forming the pulpit base and a few eleventh-century frescoes in the belltower,
but the **museum** (closed for restoration) is the main focus, collecting together parts of the abbey's heritage as well as local archeological fragments. Most
fascinating is the **Cures Pillar**, a sixth-century BC Sabine inscription found
in a local riverbed in 1982. It's the only example known, and, still undeci-
phered, it remains an emblem for studies of the previously ignored Sabine culture.

Southern Lazio

The saying goes that the Italian South begins with the first petrol station south of Rome, and certainly there's a radically different feel to the **southern part of Lazio**, the green wooded hills north of the city giving way to a mix of flat marshy land and harsh unyielding mountains that has a poor, almost desperate look in places. Many skate straight through the area on their way south to Naples, and you may want to do the same. But if you've time, the **coast** is worth taking in on a more unhurried route south: its resorts, especially **Terracina** and **Sperlonga**, are fine places to take it easy after the rigours of the capital, and the **Pontine Islands**, a couple of hours offshore, are – out of high season at least – among Italy's undiscovered treasures. **Inland**, too, the landscape can be rewarding: the towns of the **Castelli Romani** are the most accessible taste of the region, easily assimilated on a day-trip from Rome; **Subiaco** to the east and the **Ciocaria** region to the south are more remote, but hold some of Lazio's most inspiring scenery – broad tree-clad hills and valleys sheltering small, unassuming towns.

The Castelli Romani and Alban Hills

Just free of the sprawling southern suburbs of Rome, the thirteen towns that make up the **Castelli Romani** date back to medieval times, since when these hills – the **Colli Albani** – have served as an escape for the rich and powerful from the summer heat of the city. It's a wine-growing area (the vines grow easily on the volcanic soil) and is now pretty heavily built-up, with most of the historic centres ringed by unprepossessing suburbs; and summer weekends can see Romans trooping out in huge numbers for lunch at local trattorias. But if you avoid the rush-hour times and peak-season holidays, the region is still worth the journey, either as a day-trip from Rome or on the way south through Lazio. By car, there are two obvious routes, both starting with Frascati and Grottaferrata and then spearing off at Marino along either the eastern or western side of Lago Albano. On public transport from Rome, COTRAL buses serve the area (every 30min; a 35min journey) from the terminus upstairs from the metro station Anagnina (line A).

Frascati and around

At just 20km from Rome, **FRASCATI** is the nearest of the Castelli towns and also the most striking, dominated by the majestic **Villa Aldobrandini**, built by Giacomo della Porta in 1598 for one Cardinal Aldobrandi. Since it still belongs to the family you can't actually get inside, but the **gardens** are open to the public (Mon–Fri: summer 9am–1pm & 3–6pm; winter 9am–1pm & 3–5pm; free). These are somewhat neglected these days, and sadly the potentially spectacular water garden at the rear of the villa is often switched off. But the view from the terrace in front of the house is superb, with Rome visible on a clear day. Frascati is also about the most famous of the Colli Albani wine towns: ask at the **tourist office** on Piazza Marconi 1 (Tues–Fri 8am–2pm & 4–7pm, Sat 8am–2pm; ☎06.942.0331) for details of local wine producers that run tours and tastings, or simply indulge at one of the many trattorias in town.

Better yet, pick up a *porchetta* (whole roasted pork) sandwich from one of the stands on Piazza del Mercato and head for one of the town's many *cantine* – you can take food in with you – where wine is sold by the litre from giant wooden barrels.

The tourist office can also give you more details of **Tusculum**, beautifully sited on a hilltop just outside Frascati. This was a favourite retreat of Roman patricians: Cicero had a villa here, but the resort was destroyed in 1191 by Pope Celestine III, the inhabitants moving down the hill to modern-day Frascati. Most of the Roman remains seem to have disappeared forever beneath the undergrowth; there's a small theatre, and the views, again, are fine.

Three kilometres or so down the road, **GROTTAFERRATA** is also known for its wine and its eleventh-century **Abbey** – a fortified Basilian (Greek Orthodox) monastery surrounded by high defensive walls and a now empty moat (daily 6am–12.30pm & 3.30–7pm; winter till sunset; free). It's a timeless spot; the little church of Santa Maria inside has a Byzantine-style interior decorated with thirteenth-century mosaics and, in the chapel of St Nilo off the right aisle, frescoes by Domenichino. Through the inner courtyard there's a small museum (closed for restoration) displaying classical and medieval sculptures. **MARINO**, another 4km further on, isn't a particularly attractive place, though its wine is perhaps the region's best after Frascati and is distributed free on the first Sunday of October during its Sagra dell'Uva festival.

East of Lago Albano

The scenic Via dei Laghi skirts the eastern rim of **Lago Albano** until a winding road leads up to **Monte Cavo**, at 949m the second highest of the Colli Albani and topped with the masts and satellite dishes of the Italian military – who operate from nearby Ciampino airport. A temple to Jupiter once stood here, but now the only extant antiquity is the Via Sacra, which, about 1000m from the top, emerges from dense undergrowth, snaking down through the woods before disappearing again into thick bush.

On the far side of Monte Cavo, the road bears right for **ROCCA DI PAPA**, at 680m the highest of the Castelli Romani towns and one of its most picturesque, with a medieval quarter tumbling down the hill in haphazard terraces, and motor traffic kept to a strictly enforced minimum. Make for the small Piazza Garibaldi, a lively place in summer with a bar and restaurant, and soak up the views.

Castel Gandolfo and west of Lago Albano

Leaving Marino, the road joins up with the old Roman Via Appia, which travels straight as an arrow down the west side of Lago Albano. **CASTEL GANDOLFO** is the first significant stop, best known as the summer retreat of the pope. At over 400m above the rim of Lago Albano, it's a pleasantly airy place, but inevitably papal business predominates, especially on those Sundays between July and September when the pope traditionally gives a midday address from the courtyard of the Papal Palace. Unless you actually want to see the pope, it's best to avoid this. Better, if it's hot, to take advantage of the lake: there's a pleasant **Lido** just below the town, from where, if you've the energy, you can walk right around the lake in about two hours.

From Castel Gandolfo a panoramic road leads to **ALBANO LAZIALE**, probably the most appealing of the towns along the Via Appia, its large Piazza Mazzini looking south to the lovely Villa Comunale park, with sketchy remains of a villa that once belonged to Pompey. The town also has other Roman remains. Along the high street, Corso Matteotti, the church of **San Pietro** was built over the foundations of the baths of a Roman garrison, which you can see built into the walls. Near the church of Santa Maria della Stella is the **museo civico** (Mon–Sat 9am–12.30pm, Sun 9am–noon, plus Wed & Thurs 4–7pm; €2.10), with a small but high-quality archeological collection. Walk along Via della Stella to the **Tomb of Horatii and the Curiatii**, just outside town on the Ariccia road, whose strange "chimneys" date from the Republican era. There's an **amphitheatre** too, on the hill above – in heavy ruin now, and currently closed, but once with room for 15,000 spectators.

The Via Appia continues on to **ARICCIA** across the nineteenth-century **Ponte di Ariccia** – from where you can see the arches of the old Roman viaduct just below – into the central piazza of the town, a well-proportioned square embellished with Bernini's round church of **Santa Maria dell'Assunzione**. Ariccia, incidentally, is famous for its *porchetta* – roast pork.

Palestrina, Subiaco and the Ciociaria

Considering its proximity to the capital, it's a surprise that the **southeastern rim of Lazio** isn't more discovered; in fact it's one of the areas of Italy least known to tourists, for the most part a poor region of low hills edging into the mountains of Abruzzo that is bypassed by those heading south on the fast Autostrada del Sole.

Palestrina

PALESTRINA was built on the site of the ancient Praeneste, originally an Etruscan settlement and later a favoured resort for patrician Romans. "Cool Praeneste", as Horace called it, was the site of an enormous Roman Temple of Fortune, whose foundations more or less determine the extent of the modern town centre, which steps up the hillside in a series of terraces constructed on the different levels of the once vast edifice – the ruins of which you can see at every turn.

Buses run to Palestrina about every 45 minutes from Rome and take about 45 minutes, dropping you on Via degli Arcioni, from where you have to walk up the steep incline to the town centre. You can see this in no time. There's a much-changed **Duomo** with fragments of a Roman road at the top end of the right aisle and a copy of Michelangelo's *Pietà di Palestrina* – the original is now in Florence. And the stepped streets of the place are appealing enough for some casual strolling. But you have to climb to the top of the town for the real attraction – the **Palazzo Colonna-Barberini**, which houses the **Museo Nazionale Archeologico Prenestino** (daily 9am–1hr before sunset; €2). Originally built in the eleventh century and greatly modified by Taddeo Barberini in 1640, this occupies the uppermost level of the Temple of Fortune, now largely modernized inside and containing an excellent display of artefacts. Among a number of Roman pieces, there's a torso of a statue of Fortune in slate-grey marble, a recently found sculpture, *Il Triade Capitolina*, other bits from the temple, and funerary *cistae* much like those displayed at the Villa Giulia in Rome. The museum's prize exhibit is the marvellous first-century BC *Mosaic of the Nile*, which depicts the flooding of the river with a number of Egyptian scenes of life along the waterway from the source to the delta. Look closely and you'll notice a wealth of detail: there's a banquet going on under the vines on the left, soldiers and priests are grouped in front of the Serepaeum on the right, while the source of the river among the mountains is pictured at the top of the mosaic, where hunters and wild animals, labelled with Greek lettering, congregate. Outside the museum, your ticket admits you to the top **terrace** of the temple, the ruins of which command fine views over the surrounding countryside.

Subiaco

Around 15km northeast of Palestrina, **SUBIACO** (accessible by bus from Tivoli or direct from Rome) is beautifully set, pyramided around a hill topped by the Rocca Abbazia castle, close to Monte Liviato – one of Lazio's premier ski resorts. Founded as a purpose-built settlement to accommodate workmen building Nero's grand villa nearby (very meagre traces of which survive), during the fifth century Subiaco became the chosen contemplative base of St Benedict, who lived a life of seclusion and prayer in a cave on the slopes of a nearby mountain. St Benedict left after three years to found the monastery at Montecassino (see p.805), but his legacy lives on in the town, in the shape of two monastic complexes just outside.

The **Abbazia di Santa Scolastica** (daily 9am–12.30pm & 4–7pm; free) is the closer (and larger) of the two, a pleasant five-kilometre walk out of town along the Ienne road from the main bus stop and following the signs off to the left before the bridge. Dedicated to Benedict's sister, it's been heavily restored over the years: the facade, with the Benedictine motto *Ora et Labora* over the entrance, isn't original and the only features of any real age in the church inside are two cipolino marble pillars from Nero's villa. The three cloisters, though, are delightful: the first is from the Renaissance period; the second one is among the oldest Gothic works in Italy, lushly planted and fragrant; and the third a Cosmati work with lovely arcades of pillars.

Further up the same road, the landscape grows more dramatic, after about fifteen minutes reaching the **Abbazia di San Benedetto** (daily 9am–12.30pm & 3–6pm; free) – a complex of two churches, chapels and other buildings clasping the rocky hillside on the precise site of St Benedict's cave. This is much the more interesting of the two monasteries: its church divides into several levels, the upper part decorated with frescoes of the fourteenth-century Sienese school and fifteenth-century Perugian school, the lower leading into the Sacro Speco – the actual cave where St Benedict lived, now left in its natural condition but for a serene statue by Raggi, a disciple of Bernini. From here a spiral staircase leads up to the chapel of San Gregorio, containing a thirteenth-century picture of St Francis that's reckoned to be the first ever portrait of the saint painted from life. In the other direction, stairs lead down to another chapel, from which Benedict would preach to shepherds, and a terrace which looks out onto the so-called "Holy Rose Tree" – in fact, a three-forked bush said to have been created by St Francis from a bramble.

Practicalities

You can comfortably see Subiaco and its monasteries on a **day-trip** from Rome, even using public transport: the bus journey takes around two-and-a-half hours and you can arrive in the town by lunchtime, eat, visit the monasteries in the afternoon and take an evening bus back to Rome (the last one leaves at 8.30pm).

The town's location may, however, make you want to linger: there's a reasonable **hotel** in the centre of town, the *Aniene*, at Via Cadorna 18 (℡0774.85.565; ❷), which has an adequate **restaurant**, and the more upmarket two-star *Miramonti*, Via Papa Giovanni XXIII, 4 (℡0774.83.243; ❺), which has an excellent, if pricey, restaurant (€40 per person for dinner; closed Tues). The **tourist office** at Via Cadorna 59 (Mon 8am–2pm, Tues–Sat 8am–2pm & 3.30–6.30pm; ☎0774.822.013) has full details of accommodation and transport links. If you're **heading south** by public transport take the early bus out to Frosinone – from where you can get train or bus connections on to other points in Lazio and Campania.

The Ciociaria

From Subiaco the road heads south into a region known as the **Ciociaria**, a relatively remote corner of Lazio that takes its name from the bark sandals, or *ciocie*, worn here in days gone by. This hilly country was settled several centuries before the Romans by the Italic tribes – the Hernici, the Equii, the Volscians and the Sanniti – who built inaccessible and heavily fortified towns, the remains of which, owing to their shrewd foreign policy of allying themselves with Rome, can still be seen today in the form of the extraordinary cyclopean walls of their citadels, quite unlike anything else in Italy.

The first town you come to, **FIUGGI**, is a spa resort whose bottled mineral water you will probably have already noticed in supermarkets. It's not an especially appealing spot and fills up with health-conscious Italian tourists in summer. From Fiuggi there's a choice of two routes, either west to Anagni or south to Alatri. **ANAGNI**, a former Hernici stronghold, is a well-preserved old place that produced a number of medieval popes from its powerful local Segni family, including Boniface VIII, whose **palace** (daily 9am–12.30pm & 3–6pm; €1.55) here was invaded in 1303 by representatives of Philip IV of France when he attempted to assert the absolute authority of the papacy. You can visit a few rooms in the palace, including the one where Colonna is said to have slapped Boniface – a statue of whom stands on the outside of Anagni's **Duomo**, an imposing Romanesque basilica dating from the eleventh century. Inside there's a fine Cosmatesque pavement, a thirteenth-century baldacchino, some important proto-Renaissance thirteenth-century frescoes in the crypt and a treasury containing some of the pontifical effects of Pope Boniface VIII.

In the opposite direction, **ALATRI** – the Hernici Aletrium – preserves its cyclopean walls from the sixth-century-BC acropolis. Built long before the more sophisticated stone-cutting techniques of the Romans, they are still very much intact – most impressively, perhaps, in the Porta di Falli, with its strident fertility symbols carved on the lintel. The town's streets wind around the citadel beneath the walls, cut by two square gateways (the arch hadn't yet been invented in Europe when this was built), inside of which the cathedral and Episcopal Palace stand on the site of the Hernici's ancient temples, since lost. The views, incidentally, are terrific.

FERENTINO, 10km west, also sports a good set of walls, though a hybrid one, modified by the Romans. You can get up to the old citadel here too, though it's 5km from the modern town's station (bus connection), and the cathedral there is regularly open. **FROSINONE**, 10km or so further south, is the main town of the Ciociaria but is of little interest, being a bland sprawling place with barely any remains of the Hernici settlement. But it's a good place to pick up bus and train connections on to other points in Lazio and Campania: buses run west to Priverno from here, and from near there, you can pick up trains south or north and visit Fossanova abbey (see p.807). Trains also connect Frosinone's FS station (some way out of town but connected by bus) with Naples, Cassino and Caserta.

Further south: Cassino and the Abbey of Montecassino

The town of **CASSINO**, fifty minutes down the railway line from Frosinone, is the site of another important monastery, the **Abbey of Montecassino** (daily 9.30am–12.30pm & 3.30–6pm; free; ⓦ www.osb.org), founded in 529 by St Benedict after he left Subiaco (see p.803), on a spot to which he was guided by three ravens. This was for many years one of the most important and influential monastic complexes in the Christian world, its monks spreading the word as far away as Britain and Scandinavia in between developing the tradition of culture and learning that was at the core of the Benedictine order. Ironically, its strategically vital position, perched high on a mountaintop between Rome and Naples, has been its downfall: this vantage point has been coveted and fought over by a succession of invaders, and over the years the abbey has been repeatedly destroyed. During World War II, the abbey came to be the lynchpin of the German presence in this part of Italy and, after a battle that lasted almost six months, the Allies – a mixture of Poles, New Zealanders and Indian troops – eventually bombed it to ruins in May 1944, sacrificing several thousand lives in the process. It was subsequently rebuilt, and the austere medieval style of its buildings has been faithfully re-created, but it's really more impressive for its position than for itself: much of the complex is not open to the public, and its sterile white central courtyard is engaging only for the views it gives over the surrounding hills and the Polish war cemetery below. The church, off here, in a hideously ornate Baroque style, has a small **museum** (same hours as abbey; €1) containing incunabula, old manuscripts and suchlike. But otherwise you can't help but feel that Montecassino's glory days ended firmly with the war.

The **town** below was fairly comprehensively destroyed, too, and has very little appeal. There's a **tourist office** at Piazza de Gasperi 10 (Mon–Sat 8.30am–1pm & 3.30–6.30pm, Sun 9am–noon; ☎0776.25.629, ⓦ www.apt.frosinone.it), on the opposite side of the centre to the train and bus station, and another at Corso della Repubblica 23 (Mon–Sat 9am–noon & 4–7pm; ☎0776.26.842). Buses scale the mountain to the abbey from Piazza San Benedetto twice daily. If you need to stay, **hotels** are at least inexpensive – pick up a list from the tourist office.

The southern Lazio coast

The **Lazio coast to the south** of Rome is a much more attractive proposition than that to the north. Its towns have a bit more charm, the water is less polluted, and in the further reaches, beyond the dreary flats of the Pontine Marshes and Monte Circeo, the shoreline begins to pucker into cliffs and coves that hint gently at the glories that await in Campania further south – all good either for day-trips and overnight outings from the city, or for a pleasingly wayward route to Naples.

Anzio and Nettuno

About 40km south of Rome, and easily seen on a day-trip, **ANZIO** is the first town of any note, centre of a lengthy spread of settlement that focuses on a lively central square and a busy fishing industry. Much of the town was damaged during a difficult Allied landing here on January 22, 1944, to which two military cemeteries (one British, another, at nearby Nettuno, American) bear testimony. But despite a pretty thorough rebuilding it's a likeable resort, still depending as much on fish as tourists for its livelihood. The town's seafood **restaurants**, crowding together along the harbour and not unreasonably priced, are reason enough to come – try *Pierino* at Piazza C. Battisti 3 (closed Mon) – while the **beaches**, which edge the coast on either side, don't get unbearably thronged outside of August. Anzio is also a possible route on to the island of Ponza; for timings of **hydrofoils**, which leave daily in summer, ask at the **tourist office** on Piazza Pia 19 (daily 9am–1pm & 3.30–6pm; ☎06.984.5147) or consult the website ⓦwww.vetor.it.

NETTUNO, a couple of kilometres down the coast (and walkable by the coast road), is more of the same, but with slightly less beach space and water that's not quite so clear and calm. Again it's a mostly modern town, but there's a well-preserved old quarter, still walled, with a couple of decent trattorias on the main square – information from the **tourist office** at the port (daily 9.30am–12.30pm & 5–7.30pm, but closed Sun afternoon in winter; ☎06.980.3335).

The Pontine Marshes, Monte Circeo and San Felice Circeo

Beyond Anzio and Nettuno lie the **Pontine Marshes**, until seventy-odd years ago a boggy plain prone to malaria and populated by only a few inhabitants and some water buffalo. Julius Caesar had planned to drain the area but was assassinated before he could carry out his plan, and it was left to Mussolini to reclaim the region in 1928 – in a scheme that built a series of spanking new towns and provided an expanse of fertile, fresh farmland.

At the centre of the development lies **LATINA**, the provincial capital, founded in 1932, and centre of the thriving local agricultural economy, though of little interest now save for its transport connections. Buses run from here to the medieval town of **SERMONETA**, remarkable for its series of defensive walls erected over the centuries to protect it from the depredations of the Saracens and later from the wars between the papacy and Naples which raged throughout the Middle Ages. The outer walls have a massive gleaming white aspect that's reminiscent of Fascist architecture, but in fact they were put up by Cesare Borgia in the late 1400s when his father Alexander VI awarded this town to him. The earlier walls surround the historical centre and the defences around the well-preserved castle (Mon–Wed & Fri–Sun 9am–12.30pm & 2–5pm, closed Thurs; €2.60), erected in the 1200s by the feudal Caetani family and a near-perfect example of the medieval system of moats, portcullis, drawbridges and final defence tunnels designed to render the place practically impregnable. As well as all the defence technology, there is a huge display of arms, armour, catapults and ancient cannon, and you can also see the vast cisterns and silos used to lay in supplies in times of conflict. To get a feel for Sermoneta, it's worth staying over, and the *Principe di Serrone* **hotel**, in the heart of the historic centre (☎0773.30.342; ❹), is as good a place as any. There are also a number of good **restaurants and bars** nearby: *La Catena*, a moderately priced trattoria in the centre of town, serves decent local specialities (closed Mon; ☎0773.319.119), and on the way up the mountain there's *La Taparita*, a restaurant well favoured by the locals (closed Mon; ☎0773.318.417).

Similarly easy to reach by bus from Latina (or by train and then taxi from Latina Scalo), **NINFA**, with its enchanting gardens, was another Caetani family stronghold. From the twelfth century, it was a thriving little fortified village with a castle keep in its centre, but it was abandoned during the Renaissance because of the spread of malaria. The inhabitants moved up the nearby mountain to Sermoneta, leaving a number of ruined medieval buildings, around which gardens here were created in the early twentieth century. There are all kinds of wild and domestic flowers, shrubs and trees, situated among little streams, waterfalls and ponds – very pretty, and worth the detour (April–Nov open first weekend of each month; guided tours only, last tour at 6pm; €6.20).

Buses from Latina take about fifty minutes to reach **PRIVERNO**, another hilltop town, whose pretty main square is flanked by a Gothic town hall and a cathedral from 1283 that apparently holds the relics of St Thomas Aquinas. About 5km south of the town, an hour or so walk or reachable by regular bus from Piazza XX Settembre, the **Abbey of Fossanova** (daily: summer 7am–noon & 4–7.30pm; winter 3–5.30pm; free) was where Aquinas died in 1274, en route between Naples and Lyon. This monastery of the Cistercian order may tempt you if you have time to spare before catching a train at the nearby Priverno-Fossanova train station, 2km beyond. Although it has been rather heavily restored, the simplicity of its thirteenth-century Burgundian Gothic church is refreshing after the gaudiness of Baroque churches. A door leads from here out to a plain Romanesque cloister, with a garden in the centre and a chapter house off to one side, with wide windows through which lay brothers could watch the services (the corridor on the far side of the cloisters was for their use). A door to the left leads through a small separate courtyard to the guest wing where, at the northern end, St Thomas is supposed to have breathed his last.

The area around **SABAUDIA**, a Mussolini-era new town, 20km from Latina on the coast, gives some impression of what the marshes were like before they were drained, poised between two lagoons that make up the coastal Lago di Sabaudia. A large area to the north of the town, the Selva del Circeo, four coastal lakes, the huge bulk of Monte Circeo to the south and the offshore island of Zannone together form the **Parco Nazionale del Circeo**, set up in 1934 to preserve something of the marshes' wildlife and almost sinister natural beauty. It's a fine spot for birds: all kinds of water species can be seen here – herons, buzzards, storks, fish hawks, and rare species like the peregrine falcon and Cavaliere d'Italia; and the flora includes eucalyptus groves, oaks, elms, ash and wild flowers in spring. **Monte Circeo** itself lies to the south of Sabaudia across several kilometres of gleaming water, the sandy beach coming to an end at the sixteenth-century **Torre Paola**, perched at the entrance of a canal linking Lago di Sabaudia to the sea. There's a little pier usually occupied by a group of fishermen, from where the road turns inland and skirts the northern slopes of the mountain, passing through splendid woods.

After about 4km a road branches off to the right and rounds the mountain to emerge at **SAN FELICE CIRCEO**, a picturesque village of pretty stone houses bleached yellow by the sun. In summer it becomes a fairly trendy spot, the marina chock-a-block with fancy motor launches and yachts, its sandy beaches crowded with glistening oiled bodies and its roads bumper to bumper with flashy cars. The small **Piazza Municipio** has a **tourist office** (summer daily 10am–noon & 5–8pm; winter Sat & Sun 10am–noon; ☎0773.547.77, Ⓦwww.circeoprimo.it) and an interesting local **museum** (July–Sept daily 6–10pm; free), from behind which a road winds its way up to the summit of the **mountain** and the site of an ancient **temple**. The views from here are marvellous: there's a large car park at the top, with a summer bar, near to which is the entrance to the sparse relics of a Roman town – *Circeii* – and its rather better preserved cyclopean walls, not unlike the constructions in the Ciociaria (see p.804).

Back in the village you can rest up on the beaches or, in season, rent a boat (℡0773.543.263) out to the famous **Grotta della Maga Circe**. For quieter swimming spots, take the road towards the lighthouse, the "Faro di Torre Cervia", which after a couple of kilometres reaches a secluded rocky spot – great for snorkelling. The area is also well supplied with campsites and inexpensive hotels.

Terracina

A further 15km down the coast from San Felice (hourly buses), or, if you're coming from Rome take the bus from EUR Fermi, **TERRACINA** is an immediately likeable little town, divided between a tumbledown old quarter high on the hill above and a lively newer area down by the sea. During classical times it was an important staging-post on the Appian Way, which reaches the sea here; nowadays it's primarily a seaside resort and one of the nicest along this stretch of coast, with good, ample beaches and frequent connections with the other points of interest around.

The centre of the old quarter is **Piazza Municipio**, which occupies the site of the old Roman forum, complete with the original slabs, and now focuses on the colonnade of the town's **Duomo**, with its elegant mossy campanile. An endearing little church with a fine mosaic floor and a beautiful mosaic-studded pulpit, it was built within the shell of a Roman temple dedicated to Augustus.

Terracina's main attraction, and rightly so, is the **Temple of Jupiter Anxurus**, which crowns the hill above the town. Take the steps up from Piazza Municipio onto Via Anxur and follow this for 200m, from where a road winds to the top (forty minutes). There's a convenient bar (closed lunchtimes) at the top to aid your recovery. The temple is believed to date back to the first century BC and was connected to Terracina by some lengthy walls, although all that's now visible is the base of the structure, in the form of an arched terrace from which the views are stupendous – Terracina boxed neatly below and the bay curving round on either side.

As for **beaches**, apart from a scrubby oval of sand fringing the town centre, they stretch north pretty much indefinitely from beyond the main town harbour and are large enough not to get overcrowded.

Practicalities

The **tourist office**, just off Via Leopardi, in the park behind Piazza Mazzini (summer Mon–Sat 9am–1pm & 5–8pm, Sun 9am–1pm; winter shorter hours; ℡0773.727.759), has more information, hotel lists and a map of the town. **Bikes** are for rent at Caccia e Pesca, Via Roma 9, for around €5 a day. **Taxis** are available from Umberto Azzoli's taxi garage on Piazza della Repubblica (℡0773.703.888).

One of the best places to stay is the *Hegelberger*, up in the old town at Via San Domenico 2 (℡0773.701.697; ❹), a very informal *pensione* where the guest rooms are off the owner's lounge; rooms are basic, but there's a self-catering kitchen and the rooms share a spacious balcony with a spectacular view. The nearest **campsite** is the *Costazzurra* (℡0773.702.589), a fifteen-minute walk south along the coast road, and there are numerous other campsites outside town, especially on the stretch called Salto di Fondi.

The top **restaurant** is the reasonably priced *Ai Trioni* in the old town at Via S.Valentino 6, which does local specialities, especially fresh fish and seafood and is set in ancient stone vaults. Another good choice is the lively *Vesuvio* on Via

San Domenico above the old town, (closed Wed), which serves seafood and pizzas.

Sperlonga

The coast south of Terracina is probably Lazio's prettiest stretch, the cliff punctured by tiny beaches signposted enticingly from the road. **SPERLONGA**, built high on a rocky promontory, is a fashionable spot locally, its whitewashed houses and narrow streets more Greek in feel than Italian, and sadly given over entirely to tourists during summer (though cars are not allowed into the centre). There are some excellent **restaurants** specializing in seafood on Via Cristoforo; a basic, modern **hotel**, the *Grazie* at Via M. A. Colonna 110 (☎0771.54.223; ❸); and a few pricey *pensioni*, though these are often full and you might find it easier to hole up in Terracina and come to Sperlonga for the day, taking advantage of the half-hourly buses. Another possibility is the many **rooms** and apartments for rent at the height of the season; ask at the local **information office** (Thurs–Tues 9am–1pm; ☎0771.54.796). The **beach** is certainly worth stopping for: a lengthy strand to the south with the town as backdrop and abundant space.

Beyond Sperlonga the coast steepens markedly, with yet more appealing beaches and, if you're camping, any number of handy campsites. A couple of kilometres from Sperlonga, there's a small museum and the remains of the **Villa of Tiberius** (daily: summer 9am–9pm; winter 9am–4pm; €2.20) – worth a stop if you've got your own transport. The house was built around a large ornamental pool which extends into a grotto in the cliff face. The **museum** (same hours and ticket as villa) holds finds from the villa, centrepiece of which is a large, complex group of statues depicting scenes from Homer's *Odyssey* in the style of the Vatican's *Laocoön* (see p.767), possibly by the same sculptors.

Formia

Some 20km around the bay, hard under the glowering backdrop of the Monti Aurunci, lies **FORMIA**, a largely modern town but an important resort during Roman times. Cicero was murdered at his villa here by Mark Antony's soldiers in 44 AD for his opposition to the triumvirate that succeeded Caesar. There are good **beaches** to the north of the town centre and a **tourist office** at Viale Unità d'Italia 30–34 (summer Mon–Sat 8.30am–2pm & 5–8pm, Sun 9am–1pm; winter Mon, Wed, Fri–Sun 8.30am–2pm, Tues & Thurs 8.30am–2pm & 5–8pm; ☎0771.771.386). But otherwise Formia is more a stopover than a stop in its own right, with plentiful connections on to Naples, Rome and inland to Cassino, and regular ferries and hydrofoils to Ponza (see below). If you're taking an early boat, the *Ariston* at Via Cristoforo Colombo 19 (☎0771.770.405; ❸) is the most convenient **hotel** to the harbour but is expensive for what it is, and rather characterless; the *Del Golfo*, Piazzale Stazione Ferroviaria 1 (☎0771.790.037; ❷), is much cheaper and not a great deal less convenient. For **food**, check out *Zi Anna Mare* on Largo Paone (closed Tues) for fresh fish and pizzas served on a terrace.

Minturno

A few kilometres south of Formia – and the next stop on the train – **MINTURNO** is the last town before the Campania border, a maze of tiny lanes and vaulted streets oddly reminiscent of an Arab *medina*. The main square is dominated by a massive crumbling **castle**, which was owned until the middle of the last century by the Carraciolo-Carafa dynasty. Behind, the town's **Duomo** is a Norman structure not unlike that of nearby Sessa Arunca or Ravello, with a similar colourful mosaic pulpit. About 4km south of town are the ruins of the ancient Roman port of **Minturnae** (daily 9am–7pm; €2.10), a once flourishing town afflicted by depopulation as this low-lying area became malarial. Most striking are the remains of a restored amphitheatre (still used for concerts in summer), below which there's a small antiquarium containing finds from around the site and a broken-down aqueduct that runs for 2km southwest.

The Pontine Islands

Scattered across the sea between Rome and Naples, the **Pontine Islands** are one of Italy's least-known island groupings. Volcanic in origin, only two of the islands are inhabited, **Ponza** and **Ventotene**, of which only Ponza supports any kind of tourist industry. Visit between mid-June and the end of August and you'll find this thriving, as people seek an alternative to crowded Capri; at any other time the island is yours for the asking.

As for **getting to the islands**, you can reach **Ponza** from a number of points on the mainland during the summer. From **Formia**, there are year-round services every day except Wednesday, consisting of a twice-daily ferry and a twice-daily hydrofoil offered by, among others, the company CARE-MAR (ⓦwww.caremar.it). There are also year-round ferries scheduled once daily from **Terracina** (much more frequently in July and August), and at least twice-daily hydrofoils from **Anzio** between June and September (ⓦwww.snavali.com). Fares are similar from all ports, with ferries at around €10 one-way and hydrofoils about double that – although they take less than half as long.

To reach **Ventotene** from the mainland you can go from **Formia** or **Anzio**: ferries run once daily; hydrofoils run twice daily except Tuesday. You can also travel **between the islands** of Ponza and Ventotene using the services of Cooperativa Barcaioli Ponzesi (ⓦwww.ponza.com/barcaioli).

Ponza

Even **PONZA**, the main island of the Pontine group, is manageably small, a sharp, rocky hunk of land only 8km end to end and at its widest point just under 2km across. Ferries sail to **PONZA TOWN**, one of the most beautiful small towns in these parts: heaped around the bay in a series of neat pastel-coloured pyramids, its flat-roofed houses radiate out from the pink semicircle that curls around the fishing harbour. It makes a marvellous place to rest up for a while, having so far escaped the clutches of designer boutiques and souvenir shops; and, although there are not a lot of specific sights on the island, the town is a fun place for aimless wanderings, particularly at passeggiata time, when the crowds turn out to parade along the yellow-painted **Municipio** arcade of shops and cafés. For lazing and swimming, there's a small, clean **beach** in the town; and a ten-minute walk away, across the island, the **Chiaia di Luna** beach, a sheer sickle of cliff edged by a slender rim of sand – though be warned that the waves here are much choppier than those on the sheltered mainland-facing side of the island.

The only other real settlement on the island is **LA FORNA**, a wide green bay dotted with huddles of houses. There's a beach here, but a small grubby one, and you'd be better off following the path down from the road around the bay to the rocks and swimming from there: the water is lovely and clear, and, with the so-called **Piscina Naturale**, perfect for sheltered swimming when the fishing boats have finished for the day. For really secluded swimming, you can also take a boat from here (€4 per person return) around the headland to **Spiaggia Santa Lucia**, where you may well have the beach to yourself. Settlement straggles on from La Forna towards the sharp northern end of the island, where the road ends abruptly and a steep stony path (to the right) leads down to more rocks from which you can swim.

Practicalities

The **tourist office** in Ponza Town (Mon–Sat 9am–1pm & 4.30–7.30pm, Sun 9am–1pm; ℡0771.80.031) is on Via Molo Musco, up the hill from the Banca di Napoli on the right side of the harbour, and has maps and accommodation lists. You may well be accosted with offers of **rooms** as you get off the ferry: if so, a fair price is around the €30–50 mark; otherwise, the woman at Via Chiaia di Luna 8 (℡0771.80.043) takes in visitors for a negotiable fee. **Hotels** are pricier; the cheapest in Ponza Town is the *Silvia*, 200m through the Roman tunnel and on the Santa Maria waterfront (℡077180075, ℱ077180742; ❸). *Gennarino al Mare* (0771.80.071, ⓦwww.emmeti.it/Gennarino; ❽), next to the town beach, is worth the splurge for its great seascape views, and boasts its own restaurant. You might also try the helpful people at *Immobiliare Turistica*, Via Roma 2 (℡0771.809.886), who rent out rooms and apartments year-round. In La Forna, the *Ortensia* (℡0771.808.922; ❺) is the best and most convenient option location-wise. There's an island **bus service** connecting the port with other points on the island, including La Forna, roughly hourly. You can **rent scooters** from a place by the main harbour in Ponza Town, by the first tunnel, for €31 a day. **Boats**, too, are a good (sometimes the only) way of seeing the most dramatic parts of the island. For around €4 per person Barcaioli (see above) will drop you off and return to pick you up at a designated time at any of the points around the island. Motorboats can be rented from a number of outlets around the harbour and cost around €36–41 a day, or you could negotiate with Signora Lucia (℡0771.80.516).

For **food** you're spoilt for choice: there are plenty of restaurants in Ponza Town and most are good, albeit expensive. Try *Al Aragosta* in the harbour, which serves the local speciality of *zuppa di lenticchie* (lentil soup); the *Ippocampo*, in the Municipio above, does good pasta and fish; or check out the restaurant attached to the *Gennarino al Mare* hotel (see above).

Ventotene

The only other inhabited Pontine island, **VENTOTENE** is quite distinct from Ponza, situated a fair way south, flatter and much less lush and green. It's also much smaller and, although it makes a nice stop on a leisurely route to Naples, it's unlikely to detain you for long. However, if you do decide to linger, there are a couple of places renting out rooms. The single town – village really – has a population of around 500, and its dusty piazza is home to a museum displaying finds from an imperial-era villa, remains of which you can see spread over the headland to the left of the village. On the other side, there's a small beach of grey volcanic sand.

Travel details

Trains

Frosinone to: Caserta (8 daily; 1hr 10min); Cassino (12 daily; 1hr 10min); Naples (6 daily; 1hr 55min).

Priverno-Fossanova to: Terracina (10 daily; 40min).

Rome (Termini) to: Ancona (8 daily; 3hr 15min–6hr); Anzio/Nettuno (hourly; 1hr); L'Aquila (5 daily; 4hr 40min); Bologna (12 daily; 3hr 20min); Cerveteri* (11 daily; 45min); Civitavecchia* (8 daily; 45min); Florence (hourly; 2hr–3hr 30min); Formia (hourly; 1hr 25min); Latina (hourly; 35min); Milan (12 daily; 3hr–5hr 40min); Naples (hourly; 2hr 30min); Pescara (4 daily; 3hr 40min); Priverno-Fossanova (hourly; 1hr); Tarquinia* (5 daily; 3hr 30min).

Rome (Laziale) to: Anagni (14 daily; 55min); Palestrina (5 daily; 35min); Viterbo (6 daily 2hr).

Rome (Magliania/metro B) to: Ostia Lido (every 20min; 30min).

Rome (Piazzale Flaminio/Roma-Nord line) to: Viterbo (5 daily; 2hr 45min).

Rome (San Pietro) to: Viterbo* (12 daily; 1hr 30min).

* Trains also run from Rome Trastevere.

Buses

Frosinone to: Priverno (hourly; 50min).

Latina to: Sermoneta (Mon–Sat 12 daily, Sun 6 daily; 1hr).

Rome (Anagnina) to: Palestrina (16 daily; 45min).

Rome (EUR Fermi) to: Sabaudia (12 daily; 2hr 15min); San Felice (12 daily; 2hr 15min); Terracina (12 daily; 2hr 30min).

Rome (Ponte Mammolo) to: Subiaco (18 daily; 1hr 15min); Tivoli (every 20min; 1hr).

Rome (Via Lepanto) to: Cerveteri (every 30min; 1hr 20min); Civita Castellana (via Nepi and Castel S. Elia) (12 daily; 1hr 30min); Civitavecchia (20 daily; 1hr 50min); Tarquinia (10 daily; 2hr 15min); Blera, via Barbarano Romano (Mon–Sat 6 daily, Sun 2 daily; 2hr).

Rome (Saxa Rubra) to: Viterbo, via Sutri and Vetralla (every 30min; 1hr 30min).

Rome (Tiburtina) to: Rieti (every 20min; 1hr 50min).

Subiaco to: Frosinone (3 daily; 2hr).

Terracina to: Cassino (3 daily; 2hr 30min); Formia (every 30min; 1hr 10min); Sabaudia (8 daily; 1hr 20min); San Felice Circeo (17 daily; 30min); Sperlonga (every 30min; 1hr).

Viterbo to: Bagnaia (11 daily; 20min); Bomarzo (6 daily; 30min); Caprarola (7 daily; 45min); Civitavecchia (8 daily; 1hr 30min); Tarquinia (11 daily; 1hr); Tuscania (14 daily; 30min).

Ferries

Civitavecchia to: Cagliari (1 daily; 13hr); Golfo Aranci (2 daily; 9hr); Olbia (1 daily; 7hr).

Formia to: Ponza (2 daily; 2hr 30min); Ventotene (2 daily; 2hr 10min).

Terracina to: Ponza (2 daily; 1hr).

Hydrofoils (*aliscafi*)

Anzio to: Ponza (3 daily; 1hr 10min); Ventotene (2 daily; 1hr 10min).

Formia to: Ponza (2 daily; 1hr 15min); Ventotene (2 daily; 1hr 15min).

Ponza to: Ventotene (2 daily; 40min).

Abruzzo and Molise

CHAPTER 12

Highlights

* **Corno Grande** Hike in the wild and craggy Gran Sasso massif, out of which rises Italy's highest peak, the Corno Grande. See p.821

* **Costumes in Scanno** It's not often you come across such traditional costumes as those worn every day in the intriguing medieval village of Scanno. See p.825

* **Virtù** Téramo is the place to sample this thick and spicy minestrone, the town's speciality. See p.831

* **Atri** The hilltop town of Atri, set in a luscious landscape, has spectacular frescoes in the cathedral, and appealing museums to explore. See p.832

* **Archeological museum at Chieti** Head here for the best and most comprehensive display of Abruzzese antiquities, including the unique Capestrano warrior. See p.835

* **Villa Vignola, near Vasto** Worth saving up for is this perfect, secluded hideaway, with lush garden, pebbled beach and terraced restaurant. See p.837

* **Bull race at Ururi** The ordinary town of Ururi turns into a scene of frenetic activity once a year as horses, bulls and carts career through the streets. See p.842

Abruzzo and Molise

bruzzo and Molise, one region until 1963 known simply as the Abruzzi, together make Italy's transition from north to south. Both are sparsely populated, mountainous regions prone to earthquakes, and both have always been outside the mainstream of Italian affairs. You could spend a whole holiday exploring the **Abruzzo**. Bordered by the Apennines, it holds some of Italy's wildest terrain: silent valleys, abandoned hill-villages and vast untamed mountain plains, once roamed by wolves, bears and chamois. Legends of werewolves and witches abound and there's a strong sense of the provincial. There are villages where life is hard and strangers something of a novelty. And although the region's costumes, crafts and festivals naturally appeal to visitors, there is little hype or sham. The Abruzzesi have done much to pull their region out of the poverty trap, though, developing resorts on the long, sandy Adriatic coastline and exploiting the tourist potential of a large, mountainous national park. It also has some great historic towns. Most visited are **L'Aquila**, at the foot of Gran Sasso, and **Sulmona** just to its south. Both are good bases: Sulmona is more convenient if you're coming by train from Rome, L'Aquila if you're approaching from Umbria. The hill-villages around L'Aquila are worth visiting if you're based here for any length of time: those below the **Gran Sasso**, the Apennines' highest peak, are deeply rural places, where time can seem to have stopped in the fifteenth century; **Bominaco**, to the east, has two impressive churches, one a perfect and pristine example of the Romanesque, the other covered with Byzantine-style frescoes. The rail route from the Marche runs down the coast through Abruzzo's numerous grid-plan resorts – few of them anything special, but adequate sun-and-sand stopovers. The best of them is **Vasto**, with a gently shelving sandy beach and bus connections inland to the lively upper old town. Among other hill-towns worth visiting is **Atri**, whose cathedral contains a stunning cycle of frescoes.

South of Sulmona, Abruzzo feels more traditional. In **Scanno** the women wear costumes that – like the Scannese – originated in Asia Minor, and they make intricate lace on cylindrical cushions known as *tomboli*. Just down the road, the scruffy hill-village of **Cocullo** hosts one of Europe's most bizarre religious festivals, in which a statue of the local saint is draped with live snakes before being paraded through the streets.

Gentler, less rugged and somewhat poorer than Abruzzo, **Molise** has more in common with southern than central Italy. Much of the region still seems to be struggling out of its past, its towns and villages victims of either economic neglect or hurried modern development. The cities, **Isernia** and **Campobasso**, are large and bland, rebuilt after earthquakes and fringed with factories erected by northern money that has been lured here by the low price of land and labour.

But Molise has its compensations. Just as the modern-day industrial tycoons have invaded the area, scattering it with formula-built Anytowns, so, over 2000 years ago, the Romans charged into the region, forcing the native Italic Samnite tribes to leave their small villages and live in equally formula-built set-tlements. Molise still has a scattering of low-key Roman ruins – most interest-ingly at **Saepinum**, Italy's most complete example of a Roman provincial town and a site that's still well off the tourist track. Wandering among the ruins, and looking out over the green fields to the mountains beyond, you get some inkling of what it must have been like to be Italy's first Grand Tourists.

Molise has some interesting contradictions: traditions that would have been ancient two hundred years ago still persist. In many a new apartment block, Benetton-clad girls will be making lace alongside their grandmothers, and in the village of **Ururi**, settled by Albanian refugees in the fourteenth century, there's an annual chariot race, as barbaric as anything the Romans dreamed up.

Finally there's the sheer physical aspect of the place. Forty percent of Molise is covered by **mountains**, and although they are less dramatic than Abruzzo's, there are masses of possibilities for hiking. A must is the trail up **Monte La Gallinola** in the **Matese** mountains, from where on a clear day the whole of the peninsula, from the Bay of Naples to the Adriatic, stretches out before you. Visitors are also starting to explore the area's ancient sheep-droving routes,

Abruzzo is a mountainous region where agriculture is difficult and sheep-farming dominates. Consequently, **lamb** tends to feature strongly in the local cuisine. You'll come across *abbacchio*, unweaned baby lamb that is usually cut into chunks and roasted; and *castrato*, castrated lamb, when the meat is often cooked as a casserole with tomatoes, wine, herbs, onion and celery (*intingolo di castrato*), while the innards are typically roasted in the oven (*alenoto di castrato*). Look out as well for *agnello a cutturo*, an aromatic herby casserole served with bread.

The other crucial ingredient in the region's cuisine is **chilli** (*peperoncino* in the rest of Italy, but known locally as *pepedinie* or *diavolini*), used liberally in all kinds of dishes and believed by many locals to be a cure for ailments ranging from neuralgia to arthritis.

Probably Abruzzo's most famous dish is *maccheroni alla chitarra*, made by pressing a sheet of **pasta** over a wooden frame wired like a guitar, and usually served with a tomato or lamb sauce. Other local pastas include the roughly cut *strangozze* and *maltagliati*, both inevitably served with a lamb sauce. Cheese tends to be *pecorino* – most often mature and grainy like parmesan, but you may come across young cheeses that are still mild, soft and milky.

The **wines** of Molise are rarely found outside the region. The most interesting vintages come from the Biferno Valley between Larino and Guglionesi, where a hearty Biferno red is made from a combination of the Montepulciano, Trebbiano Toscano and Aglianico grapes. The best-known wine of Abruzzo is Montepulciano d'Abruzzo, a heavy **red** made from the Montepulciano grape with up to 15 percent Sangiovese, commonly found as house red in the restaurants of Abruzzo, Molise and Rome. Montepulciano d'Abruzzo Cerasuola is a light **rosato** made from the same grapes; and Trebbiano d'Abruzzo is an often insipid dry **white** made from the Trebbiano d'Abruzzo and Trebbiano Toscano grapes. There are, however, a few quality producers: look out for wines from the Azienda Agricola Illuminati Dino and from the Azienda Agricola Pepe Emidio, both in the province of Téramo.

known as *tratturi*, 111m wide, which are gaining new life as mountain–bike or horseback–riding trails, served by occasional farmhouse guesthouses and riding stables along the way.

Don't expect to rush through Abruzzo and Molise if you're relying on public transport; in both regions, **getting around** on bus and train demands patience and the careful studying of timetables.

L'Aquila

The pleasant town of **L'AQUILA** is overlooked by the bulk of the Gran Sasso mountain and is the main access point to the national park of the same name. The city was founded by a German emperor, and the story of its foundation is itself worthy of a Brothers Grimm fairy-tale: in 1242 Frederick II drew together the populations from 99 Abruzzesi villages to form a new city. Each village built its own church, piazza and quarter: there's a medieval fountain with 99 spouts, and the town-hall clock still chimes 99 times every night. These days only two churches remain, though, albeit magnificent ones. The city is an appealing blend of ancient and modern, with a university, smart shops, bustling streets and a daily market where you can buy anything from black-market cassettes to traditional Abruzzese craftwork.

L'AQUILA

Castello
(Museo
Nazionale
d' Abruzzo)

VIALE DUCA DEGLI ABRUZZI

VIALE GRAN SASSO

VIA
GARIBALDI

VIA ROMA

VIA
XX SETTEMBRE

VIA ROMA

VIA GIOVANNI XXIII

V. FONTE PRETURO

VIA CASCINA

VIA SAN MARTINO

Bus
Station

PIAZZA
BATTAGLIONE
ALPINI

VIA CASTELLO

PIAZZA
DELL'
ANNUNZIATA

VIA PAGANICA

PZA S. MARIA
PAGANICA

Santa Maria
Paganica

VIA SAN VANELLI

CORSO PRINCIPE UMBERTO

San
Bernardino

PZA'S.
MARGHERITA

CORSO VITTORIO EMANUELE

PIAZZA
DEL
TEATRO

PIAZZA
PALAZZO

VIA ANNUNZIATA

VIA SALLUSTIO

Casa Museo
Signorini Corsi

VIA SAN BERNARDINO

VIA FONTESECCO

VIA TESORA

VIA SASSA

Fontana delle
99 Cannelle

Duomo

PIAZZA DEL
DUOMO

LARGO SILVESTRO
DELL'AQUILA

VITTORIO TERRACCIO

VIA STRINELLA

PZA S.
VITO, V. SAN JACOPO

San
Vito

V.S. MADONNA DEL PONTE

VIA DEL CARDINALE

Santuario
del Suffragio

VIA CIMINO

Porta
Bazzano

Train Station (200 m)

River Aterno

VIA XX SETTEMBRE

VIA DELLA CROCE ROSSA

CORSO FEDERICO II

VIA DRAGONETTI

Santa
Giusta

VIALE CADORNA

VIA FRANCESCO CRISPI

VIALE PANTONIATRO MAGGI

VIA PIAVE

VIALE DI
COLLEMAGGIO

Santa Maria
di Collemaggio

VIA S. MARIA DEGLI ANGELI

N

0   100 m

ACCOMMODATION
Castello   2
Duomo   3
Orazi   1

RESTAURANTS
Antico Borgo   F
Antiche Mura   A
Cantina dell Boss   C
Ernesto   E
Trattoria del Giaguaro B
Casa Jacopo   D
Renato   G

A & Via XXV Aprile

Arrival, information and accommodation

L'Aquila's **train station** is a good way downhill from the centre, connected with the main part of town by regular buses. Long-distance **buses** stop on Piazza Battaglione Alpini at the beginning of the old centre's main street, Corso Vittorio Emanuele. The **information booth** there has bus timetables covering L'Aquila province and connections to Rome. The main **tourist office** is at Piazza Santa Maria Paganica 5, just south of the bus station (daily: mid-May to mid-Sept 8am–1pm & 3–6pm; mid-Sept to mid-May closed Sun; ☎0862.410.808). The **Centro Turistico Gran Sasso** (☎0862.22.147) at Corso Vittorio Emanuele 49 provides more information on outdoor activities in the Gran Sasso. There's an **Internet** café, *Internauti*, at Via Cimino 51 (Tues–Sat 6pm–1am).

The main drawback of L'Aquila is its lack of cheap **hotels**, and you should definitely book in advance if you're planning to stay. The cheapest option is functional *Orazi*, at Via Roma 175 (☎0862.412.889; ❶), a ten-minute walk from Piazza dell' Annunziata. Up from there is the modern, but more classy, *Castello* on Piazza Battaglione Alpini (☎0862.419.147, ℉0862.419.140; ❺) and the *Duomo* at Via Dragonetti 6 (☎0862.410.893, ℉0862.413.058; ❹), housed in a quiet, eighteenth-century palace with views over Piazza del Duomo.

The City

L'Aquila's centre is relatively compact and easily seen on foot. Marking the northeastern entrance to the city centre is **Piazza Battaglione Alpini**, with the unusual Fontana Luminosa at its centre. Viale delle Medaglie d'Oro leads to the formidable **Castello**, built by the Spanish in the sixteenth century to keep the citizens of L'Aquila in order after an uprising. The Spanish forced the *Aquilani* to pay for the castle by imposing an annual tax and heavy fines. In the Fascist period the castle's surroundings were landscaped as a park, and, following the devastation wreaked by the Nazis in 1943, the building was renovated and the **Museo Nazionale d'Abruzzo** (Tues–Sun 9am–8pm; €4) established in the former barracks. The most popular exhibit here is the skeleton of a prehistoric mammoth found about 14km from L'Aquila in the 1950s, but the collection of works of art rescued from abandoned and earthquake-ravaged churches is also worth a visit. Among the polychrome wooden Madonnas, those by Silvestro dell'Aquila stand out, spare, ascetic and nerved with inner strength, while the best of the paintings are the dreamy and mystical works attributed to Andrea Delitio, a fifteenth-century Abruzzese artist responsible for the region's best fresco cycle – in the cathedral at Atri (see p.832). The exhibit with the most sensational history is an elaborate silver crucifix by Nicola da Guardiagrele: after being stolen from L'Aquila's Duomo and auctioned at Sotheby's, it's now kept for safety in the museum. The museum also hosts concerts throughout the year – check with the tourist office for details.

From Piazza Battaglione Alpini, arcaded **Corso Vittorio Emanuele** is L'Aquila's main street, lined with upmarket clothes shops, jewellers and cafés, and liveliest in the evenings when L'Aquila's youth turn out for the *passeggiata*. To the left down Via San Bernadino, the church of **San Bernardino** (daily 7–11am & 4–7.30pm) has a sumptuous facade, with three magnificent white tiers bedecked with classical columns, pediments, friezes and inscriptions. Inside, the ceiling is luxuriously gilded and skilfully carved – in some places bold and chunky, in others as complex and sinuous as oriental embroidery. The glazed blue and white terracotta altarpiece by Andrea della Robbia on the right as you enter is very fine, as is San Bernardino's mausoleum, sculpted by Silvestro dell'Aquila. San Bernardino was originally from Siena but died in L'Aquila, where his relics remain, ritually visited every year on his feast day by Sienese bearing gifts of Tuscan oil.

On the opposite side of the Corso, Via Sallustio leads to Via Patini and the **Casa Museo Signorini Corsi** (July & Aug Tues–Sun 10am–7pm; Sept–June Tues–Sun 10am–1pm plus Tues–Fri 4–7pm; €3.10), a sixteenth-century *palazzo* whose intimate rooms aim for a lived-in look. Among the religious paintings, mainly from the fifteenth to seventeenth centuries, there is an appealing *Madonna with Cat* and a luminous *Holy Family* attributed to Botticelli. The art is set off by displays of decorative items and period furniture. The main Corso carries on up to the central **Piazza del Duomo**, more noted for its **market**

(Mon–Sat 8am–2pm) and as the focus for the *passeggiata* than for its architecture; the numerous surrounding cafés make a pleasant spot for a coffee and a snack. The Duomo, having been destroyed on several occasions by earthquakes, now features a tedious Neoclassical front. The façade of the eighteenth-century **Santuario del Suffragio**, however, is a voluptuous combination of curves, topped by a flamboyant honeycombed alcove. Tumbling down the hill below the piazza, steep-stepped streets of ancient houses lead down to **Porta Bazzano**, one of the old city gates. Rather than heading straight there, take time to wander the abutting streets, lined with Renaissance and Baroque palaces. Some of these are still opulent, others decaying, providing an evocative backdrop for the church of **Santa Giusta**, whose rose window is decorated with twelve figures representing the various artisans who contributed to the building.

From Porta Bazzano, Via Porta Bazzano leads to the church of **Santa Maria di Collemaggio** (Mon–Fri 8.30am–1pm & 3–8pm, Sat & Sun 8.30am–8pm). One of Abruzzo's most distinctive churches, its massive rectangular bulk is faced with a geometric jigsaw of pink and white stone, more redolent of a mosque than a church, pierced by delicate, lacy rose windows and entered through a fancy Romanesque arch. It was founded in the thirteenth century by Peter of Morrone, a hermit unwillingly dragged from his mountain retreat to be made pope by power-hungry cardinals who reckoned he would be easy to manipulate. When he turned out to be too naive even for the uses of the cardinals, he was forced to resign and was posthumously compensated for the ordeal by being canonized. Thieves stole his relics in April 1988, intending to hold them to ransom, but they were soon safely retrieved and returned to their grandiose Palladian-style sarcophagus. One of the few things Peter managed to do during his short reign was to install a Holy Door in the church – opened every year on August 28, when sinners pass through it to procure absolution.

Finally there's L'Aquila's best-known sight, the **Fontana delle 99 Cannelle**, outside the town centre close to the train station, tucked behind the medieval **Porta Riviera**. Set around three sides of a sunken piazza and overlooked by abandoned houses and the tiny church of **San Vito**, each water spout is a symbol for one of the villages that formed the city. This constant supply of fresh water sustained the *Aquilani* through the plagues, earthquakes and sieges to which the city was subjected, and was used for washing clothes until after the war.

Eating and drinking

L'Aquila has a decent selection of good, reasonably priced **places to eat**, ranging from restaurants serving traditional Abruzzese fare to cheap and cheerful pizzerias catering for the town's student population. For a real treat head for *Ernesto*, in Piazza Palazzo (closed Mon & Sun), where you can indulge in risotto with saffron and mushrooms, a soup of *farro* (emmer, a barley-like grain) with wild chicory, or lamb in a sauce of egg, local goat's cheese and artichoke hearts. *Le Antiche Mura*, at Via XXV Aprile 2 (closed Sun), is another good traditional restaurant, with a wide variety of local specialities – try *ceci e castagne* (chickpeas and chestnuts) or *coniglio allo zafferano* (rabbit scented with locally collected saffron) – as is *Trattoria del Giaguaro*, on Piazza Santa Maria Paganica (closed Mon evening & all day Tues); neither is especially expensive. Not far from here at Via Bominaco 24, *Casa Jacopo di Notar Nanni* (closed Mon), formerly a fifteenth-century *palazzo*, puts on a good tourist menu for €16. Another reliable choice is *Renato* at Via della Indipendenza 9, close to Piazza del Duomo (closed Sun), where the waiter will reel off the specials of the day based on produce from the market nearby. Away from the centre down the hill next to the Fontana delle 99 Cannelle is *L'Antico Borgo*, Piazza San Vito 1 (closed Tues), which serves good fish dishes and makes a peaceful spot for lunch outside in summer. If all you want is a **snack** washed down with good wine, first choice is *La Cantina del Boss* (closed Sat lunch & all Sun), Via Castello 3. Alternatively, several shops on Via Patini (between Piazza Palazzo and Piazza del Duomo) have all you need for a good picnic or lunch on the go.

The Gran Sasso and Campo Imperatore plain

Whether you approach Abruzzo from the Marche in the north or Rome in the west, your arrival will be signalled by the spectacular bulk of the **Gran Sasso** massif, containing by far the highest of the Apennine peaks. If you come by *autostrada* from the Marche, you'll actually travel underneath, through a ten-kilometre tunnel, passing the entrance to a trailblazing particle-physics research laboratory bored into the very heart of the mountain range.

The massif itself consists of two parallel chains, flanking the vast **Campo Imperatore** plain which stretches for 27km at over 2000m above sea-level. This is a bleak but atmospheric place, overlooked by abandoned and semi-abandoned hill-villages, its rolling grassland in places laid bare to reveal rocks, carved into moonscape ripples by the wind.

The itinerary below is an easy day's drive from L'Aquila. If you're dependent on public transport, it will take two days and you may have to content yourself with viewing the plain by cable car and taking buses up to the hill-villages from L'Aquila via the less interesting southern route.

Fonte Cerreto and the Corno Grande

The first leg, however, is easy. Bus #6 from L'Aquila's Corso Vittorio Emanuele runs regularly up to **FONTE CERRETO**, the gateway to Campo Imperatore – basically two hotels, a restaurant and a campsite clustered around a cable-car station. Most of these were built in the Thirties as part of Mussolini's scheme to keep Italians fit by encouraging them to take exercise in the mountains. Ironically, he was imprisoned here in 1943, first at the *Villetta* inn in Fonte Cerreto, and then at the *Albergo Campo Imperatore*, a grim hotel at the top of the cable-car route. Apparently it was with some trepidation that Mussolini stepped into the cable car, enquiring whether it was safe and then hastily covering his cowardice by adding, "Not for my sake, you understand, because my life is over. But for those who accompany me." *Il Duce* apparently spent his days at the hotel on a diet of eggs, rice, boiled onions and grapes, contemplating suicide. Hitler came to his rescue, dispatching an ace pilot to airlift him out in a tiny aeroplane, which is supposed to have terrified him almost as much as the cable car.

The **cable car** that so spooked Mussolini has been replaced by a new one which runs in winter for skiing and for the summer hiking season (July to mid-Sept daily 8.30am–6pm; winter reduced service depending on snowfall; return journey €9). A small **information office** (July & Aug daily 9am–1pm) near the *Villetta* hotel has details of walks and wildlife to be seen in the Gran Sasso park. You can still stay at the *Villetta* (☎0862.606.171, ℱ0862.606.674; ❹), though it's now a pleasantly modernized hotel over a snack-bar; alternatively,

try *Villetta's* larger sister hotel *Fiordigigli* (☎0862.606.172, ⓕ0862.606.674; ❹),
also at the base of the cable car. There's cheaper accommodation in two mountain refuges run by CAI: one of these is the *Ostello Campo Imperatore*
(☎0862.400.011; €15, or €30 for dinner, bed and breakfast; 1 June–Sept 15),
which occupies the old cable-car station; the other is the *Duca degli Abruzzi
rifugio* (☎0862.606.657, ⓕ3476.232.101; €25 for dinner, bed and breakfast; 1
June–Sept 15), several metres beyond. It's now the most popular starting-point
for assaults on the Gran Sasso's highest peak, the **Corno Grande** (2912m).

Outside the summer months, the ascent of Corno Grande should only be
attempted by experienced climbers, and at all times includes some fairly killing
scree-climbing and alarming descents. Perhaps the most challenging route is
the tough trek from the *Ostello Campo Imperatore* right across the mountain
range, taking in the Corno Grande, sleeping over at the *Rifugio Franchetti*
(☎0861.959.634; €13.50, or €35 for dinner, bed and breakfast; June–Sept),
and then walking across to the Arapietra ridge. From here a ski lift will take
you down to the ugly ski resort of Prati di Tivo – which nevertheless offers
some of the best views of Gran Sasso – from where you can get a bus to the
town of Téramo. If you're going to do any of the Gran Sasso trails, you'll need
the CAI *Gran Sasso d'Italia* map, and should check out weather conditions from
either the tourist or the CAI office in L'Aquila.

The Campo Imperatore plain

For non-hikers the road continues from Fonte Cerreto across **Campo
Imperatore**, backed by awesome rocky massifs that have been prime fodder
for film-makers over the years, masquerading as everything from the surface of
Mars to a remote region of Tibet. Film crews and the occasional hiker apart,
the only people you're likely to meet here are nomadic shepherds, who bring
their flocks up to the plain for summer grazing after wintering in the south –
a practice that has been going on since Roman times. Although the sheep are
now transported by lorry rather than on foot, the shepherds' shacks sprinkled
across the plain suggest that their living standards have changed very little.

South to Sulmona: Bominaco

From L'Aquila, the SS17 follows the ancient route of the local shepherds across
the saffron fields south to Sulmona. If you have your own transport, it's worth
making a short detour on the way to see two of Abruzzo's most beautiful
churches at **BOMINACO** (also accessible by bus from L'Aquila). The village
itself is an inauspicious knot of grubby houses, but the endearingly askew and
lichen-mottled facade of **San Pellegrino** conceals floor-to-ceiling frescoes in
vivid hues reminiscent of a peacock's plume (daily 8am–2pm & 4–7pm).
There's also an intriguing thirteenth-century calendar, with the signs of the
zodiac looking down over lists of religious festivals and miniatures of men
engaged in supposedly typical activities for the time of year – boozing in
January, chopping wood in February, sleeping in March . . .

The church of **Santa Maria dell'Assunta** (daily 8am–2pm & 4–7pm), just
beyond, has a more coolly refined exterior, but its aloofness is tempered by
monsters carved at the bases of the windows – notably a chimera with the face
of a diabolic lion, flexing its talons and flicking its serpentine tail. Inside, the
creamy-white carvings are so exquisitely precise that it seems the mason has
only just put down his chisel; in fact they're 800 years old. There's been some

restoration, but this is scarcely discernible, and the lack of the usual cracks and crumblings is uncanny. This is particularly striking in the extraordinary free-standing column, consisting of two entwined rolls of stone so supple and sensuous that you expect them to dimple to the touch. If the churches are closed, you can get the keys from Signora Alessandrina Tiberi at Via Ripa 4 (☎0862.93.756).

Sulmona and around

Flanked by bleak mountains and bristling with legends about its most famous son, Ovid, **SULMONA** is a rich and comfortable provincial town owing its wealth to gold jewellery and sugared almonds. An atmospheric little place, with a dark tangle of a historical centre lined with imposing palaces, its sights can be seen in a day, but the town makes a good base for exploring the surroundings, and you may want to stay longer.

Arrival, information and accommodation

Arrive in Sulmona **by bus** and you'll be dropped at the Parco Fluviale, just down the hill from the western end of the main street, Corso Ovidio. The **train station** is about 1km outside the centre of town; bus #A runs from the station along Corso Ovidio. The **tourist office** (June–Sept Mon–Sat 9am–1pm & 4–7pm, Sun 9am–1pm; Oct–May Mon–Fri 9am–1pm & 4–6pm, Sat 9am–1pm; ☎0864.53.276) is at Corso Ovidio 208. There's a second **information office** in the old pharmacy of the Palazzo SS Annunziata with very helpful staff, maps and details of Sulmona's churches and palaces (daily 9am–1.30pm & 4–8pm; ☎0864.210.216).

The best of the cheaper **places to stay** is the *Centro Celestiniano*, a **hostel** in a former school between the bus station and the town centre at Via Matteotti 14 (☎0864.56.549; €15–18 per person); call them from the station and they will pick you up in their bus. Other cheap hotels are the *Stella*, at Via Mazara 18, off Corso Ovidio (☎ & ℱ0864.52.653, ⓦwww.albergostellaristorante.com; ❷), a relaxed, family-run establishment, though often full. The most atmospheric of the town's affordable **hotels** is the creeper-covered *Italia* (☎ & ℱ0864.52.308; no credit cards; ❷), just behind Piazza XX Settembre at Piazza Salvatore Tommasi – a little ramshackle, though with plenty of personality and a nice owner (it's often fully booked by American students on summer courses). More upmarket is *Armando's*, on the edge of town at Via Montenero 15 (☎0864.210.783, ℱ0864.210.787; ❹).

The Town

Corso Ovidio, Sulmona's main street, cuts through the centre from the parkside bus terminus, leading up to the intimate square **Piazza XX Settembre**. A couple of minutes back up Corso Ovidio stands Sulmona's architectural showpiece, the **Annunziata**, a Gothic-Renaissance *palazzo* adjoining a flamboyant Baroque church. These days, its steps are a hangout for the town's lads during the evening *passeggiata*, but once they would have been crowded with Sulmona's ill and destitute: the Annunziata housed a hospital, a pharmacy and a store of grain, donated by the rich and shared out to the needy. It was established by a confraternity to take care of the citizens from birth until death, and most of the external decoration is designed to remind onlookers of the life process: around the first door is a tree of life; an allegorical frieze with scenes from the cultivation of the vine representing birth, marriage and death stretches right across the facade; a sunburst-style wheel of life stands above a window; and statues of saints gaze piously down from pedestals, firmly placing the symbolism in a Christian context. The most intriguing statue, however, is just inside the entrance: Ovid, metamorphosed from pagan poet of love into an ascetic friar. Inside the Annunziata are three **museums**: one (currently being restored) with exhibits on local costume and transhumance – the practice of moving sheep to summer pastures – and examples of work by Sulmona's Renaissance goldsmiths, a trade that continues here today, as evidenced by the number of jewellers' shops along the Corso. Another, the **Museo Civico** (Tues–Sun 10am–1pm & 10am–1pm & 4–7pm; €1), has local sculpture and paintings from the sixteenth to seventeenth centuries; and a third, the **Museo 'in situ'** (currently being restored), shows the excavations of a Roman villa inhabited from the first century BC to the second century AD, abandoned suddenly along with many other houses in the valley when a landslide or an earthquake struck. Among the fragments of fabulously coloured wall painting are depictions of Pan, Eros, Dionysus and Ariadne, and there are several floor mosaics, all well-labelled.

The Corso's **shops** are also full of Sulmona's other great product – *confetti*, originally a confection of sugared almonds, but nowadays consisting of sugar-coated chocolate and hazelnuts wired into elaborate flowers with the aid of coloured cellophane, crepe paper and ribbons. Any number of designs – giant daisies, elegantly contrived orchids, even Pokemon characters – can be seen in the many specialist shops on the Corso. Through ingenious marketing the Sulmonese *confetti* barons have made gifts of their intricate sculpture *de rigueur* at christenings and confirmations throughout Catholic Europe. At Abruzzese weddings, bride and groom are painfully pelted with loose white *confetti*.

At Piazza del Carmine, the weighty Romanesque portal of **San Francesco della Scarpa** was the only part of the church solid enough to withstand the 1703 earthquake. The church gets its name – della Scarpa – "of the shoe" – from the fact that Franciscans wore shoes instead of the sandals worn by other monastic orders. Opposite, the impressive Gothic aqueduct, built to supply water to the town and power to its wool mills, ends at a fifteenth-century fountain, the **Fontana del Vecchio**, named for the chubby-cheeked old man on top. On the other side of the aqueduct is **Piazza Garibaldi**, a vast square dominated by the austere slopes of Monte Morrone, on which the hermit Pietro Morrone lived until he was dragged away to be made pope (see p.820). There's a former nunnery in the corner – take a look at the courtyard, where there's a tiny door at which unmarried mothers were permitted to abandon their babies.

Eating and drinking

Sulmona has some excellent reasonably priced **restaurants**. The chef at the *Italia* on Piazza XX Settembre (closed Mon) bases his dishes on traditional Abruzzese fare, but is ever inventing new variations – try his fresh cannelloni stuffed with ricotta and various secret ingredients. *Al Quadrivio*, Via Mazara 38 (closed all Mon & Sun eve), also serves up some memorable food, like *carrati* – home-made *bucatini* with fresh tomato – while *Mafalda* at Via Solimo 20 (closed Sun in winter) is enjoyable in summer, when you can eat dishes like *maccheroni alla chitarra* in its walled garden. *Clemente*, Vico Quercia 20 (closed Thurs), serves home-produced salami and dishes such as *linguine d'Ovidio* (with pancetta and truffles), spicy *farfalle* with prosciutto and spinach, sausages, lamb roasted or grilled, and pastries made in-house. *Cesidio*, Via Solimo 25 (closed Mon), does some great pasta dishes and good crepes. The best **ice cream** is to be had at *Schiazza* and *di Marzio*, both at the western end of Corso Ovidio. For an excellent choice of **wines** head for *La Cantina di Biffi*, an elegantly countrified place in Via Barbato off Corso Ovidio (closed Mon), where you can eat as well; or try the quintessentially Italian *Black Bull* (closed Sun), across the river by the Ponte Capograssi.

South of Sulmona: Cocullo and Scanno

A tatty hill-village, connected with Sulmona by infrequent trains and even less frequent buses, **COCULLO** is understandably neglected by outsiders for 364 days of the year. However, on the first Thursday in May it's invaded by TV crews, journalists, beggars, buskers, street-vendors and what seems like half the population of central Italy. The reason for all this activity is Cocullo's weird **festival of snakes**, an annual event celebrated in memory of St Dominic, the patron saint of the village, who allegedly rid the area of venomous snakes back in the eleventh century.

The festival is an odd mixture of the modern and archaic. Everyone pours into the main square, while a wailing Mass is relayed from the church over aged speakers, competing with pulsing pop music and the cries of the beggars. After the service a number of snake-charmers in the crowd drape a wooden statue of St Dominic with a writhing mass of live but harmless snakes, which is then paraded through the streets in a bizarre celebration of the saint's unique powers (he was apparently good at curing snake-bites too). Actually, it is thought that Cocullo's preoccupation with snakes dates back to before the advent of the saint. In the pre-Christian era, local tribes worshipped their goddess Angitia with offerings of snakes, and it seems too much of a coincidence that Dominic's powers also related to the creatures. Scholars have attempted to rationalize the festival by drawing a parallel between snakes shedding their skins and the ancient Cocullans shedding their paganism for Christianity – but whatever the origins, Cocullo's festival is today more than anything a celebration of St Dominic's power to attract enough tourist lucre in a day to keep the village going for a year. Incidentally, if you're suffering from toothache, he's also reckoned to have the power to cure it, the only snag being that you have to ring the church bell with the rope in your teeth.

Lago di Scanno . . . and Scanno

Twenty kilometres down the road, but most easily accessible by bus from Sulmona, Scanno is another popular tourist destination, reached by passing through the narrow and rocky Saggitario Gorge, a spectacular drive along galleries of rock and around blind hairpin bends which widen out at the glassy green **Lago di Scanno**. Perched over the lake is a church, **Madonna del Lago**, with the cliff as its back wall, and nearby there are boats and pedalos for rent, and a good restaurant, the *Trattoria sul Lago*. If you're planning on staying there's a **campsite** *I Lupi* (℡0864.740.100; open all year), 4km away at Villalago, but be warned that it is normally packed out in summer, especially during August.

A couple of kilometres beyond, **SCANNO** itself is a well-preserved medieval village encircled by mountains. Many of the women of the village still wear the traditional costume of long, dark, pleated skirts and bodices, with either a patterned apron for day-to-day wear or a brocade skirt and embroidered fez with coils of cord looped behind to conceal the hair on special occasions (with a white skirt for weddings). The skirts are made of wool – the village's staple industry in former times – and weigh around 12 kilos, but their heaviness doesn't prevent them from being worn for household tasks. As you wander round the village it soon becomes clear that far from being dismissed as an anachronism, older women dressed in this way are accorded great respect. The hat, and the fact that at Scannese weddings the tradition was for women to squat on the floor of the church, has led scholars to believe that the Scannese originated in Asia Minor; Scannese jewellery also has something of the Orient about it – large, delicately filigreed earrings, and a star, known as a *presuntuosa*, given to fiancées to ward off other men. If you want to see the costume and jewellery at close quarters head for the shop at Strada Silla 32.

It's a pleasure strolling around the old town built into the steep hillside, the squares and alleyways lined with solid stone houses built by wool barons when business was good. However, Scanno is not some sort of museum piece. Though the population has dwindled, it's a living village, with enough work available in Sulmona to keep people from moving away. Now that shepherding as a way of life is virtually finished, sheep have been replaced by tourists. A chair lift takes **skiers** up to a handful of runs on Monte Rotondo, operating also in the short summer season (July & Aug) when it's worth going up just for the view of lake and mountains, especially at sunset.

Scanno practicalities

The **tourist office** (mid-May to mid-Sept daily 9am–1pm & 4–7pm; rest of year Mon–Fri 3–6pm; ☎0864.74.317) is at Piazza Santa Maria della Valle 12. Every August Scanno holds a **classical music festival**, and on January 17 a **lasagne festival** – more properly called the *Festa di San Antonio Abate*, involving the cooking of a great cauldron of lasagne and beans outside the door of the church, which is then blessed and doled out with a somewhat unholy amount of pushing and shoving. The best restaurants for traditional Abruzzese fare are *Gli Archetti* (closed Tues) on Via Silla inside the Porta della Croce entrance to the old town; *La Volpe e l'Uva*, a small, laid-back bar with music, a good wine list, and snacks in the form of crepes, cheese and salumi on Piazza San Rocco (closed Wed in winter); and *Birreria La Baita*, above the village near the chair lift, serving excellent pasta dishes and snacks, with live music some Saturday nights.

The most atmospheric **place to stay** is *Mille Pini* next to the chair lift at Via Pescara 2 (☎0864.74.387, ℱ0864.749.818; ❹), a large chalet overlooking the village. There are also slightly cheaper pine-clad mountain cabin rooms (with baths – a rarity in these parts – as well as showers) above *Birreria La Baita* – same phone number as *Mille Pini*. The cheapest options are the *Eden*, Viale della Pineta 10–12 (☎0864.74.328; no credit cards; ❷), and the family-run *Pensione Nilde* between the lake and the village at Viale del Lago 101 (☎ & ℱ0864.74.359; no credit cards; ❷); or for somewhere central and modern try *Seggiovia*, Via D. Tanturri 42 (☎0864.74.371, ℱ0864.747.966; ❷).

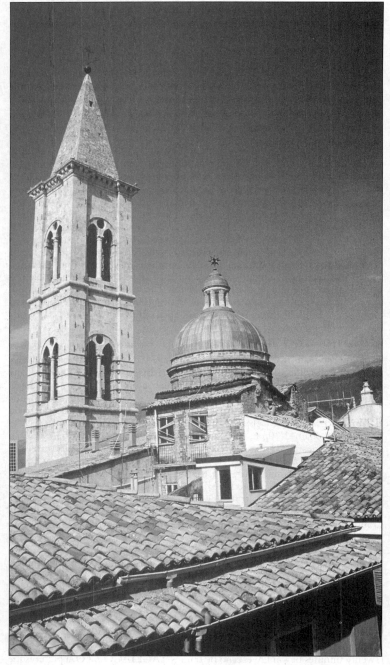

△ Sulmona, Abruzzo

Southwest Abruzzo and the national park

Heading west towards Rome from Sulmona, road and railway skirt the **Fucino Plain**, an endless, unreal and utterly flat expanse of agricultural land whose only landmarks are the satellite dishes of Telespazio, Italy's biggest telecommunications complex. The Fucino was once Italy's third-largest lake, and is the largest lake in the world to have been artificially drained. Attempts to empty it began nearly two thousand years ago. The Marsi people who lived on its shores, fed up with the fact that it flooded every time the mountain snows melted, managed to persuade Emperor Claudius to build a six-kilometre-long outlet tunnel, designed to transfer the water from the lake into a nearby valley. On the day of the draining, the shores and surrounding mountains were packed with spectators: the proceedings were inaugurated by a mechanical Triton who rose up from the lake blowing a trumpet, whence a mock battle ensued, with warships manned by condemned criminals, after which Claudius gave the signal for the outlet gates to be opened. Unfortunately, the tunnel couldn't cope with the vast volume of water, and thousands of spectators, including members of the imperial party, only narrowly escaped being washed away. Frederick II attempted to open up the tunnel in 1240, but the lake was only finally drained in 1875, as much to gain agricultural land as to solve the flooding problem – though it has brought associated problems. The climate has grown humid, misty and mosquito-ridden, and it's clear that lakeside tourist developments would have been far more profitable than agriculture.

Celano and Avezzano

Fringing the plain is **CELANO**, a pretty village crowned by the turreted toy-town Castello Piccolomini, home of the **Museo d'Arte Sacra** (daily 8am–8pm; closed Mon Sept–June; €2), which displays a range of medieval paintings, sculpture and vestments. More interesting, but difficult to reach without your own transport, is the striking, turf-roofed **Museo della Preistoria d'Abruzzo**, south of Celano, 3km from the Aielli–Celano exit off the A25 (Mon–Sat 8.30am–1.30pm; free; sometimes open Sun – call ☎0863.790.357). Finds from a nearby Bronze Age lake village and tomb reconstructions are well displayed, as are the arresting *Capestrano Warrior* statue (see p.835) with his trademark wide-brimmed hat, and the intricate bone artefacts, the best and largest of which is a complete funeral bed from the first century BC. *Hotel Le Gole* on Borgo Sardellino (☎0863.711.009, ☎0863.711.101, ☻www.hotellegole.it; ❺) makes an excellent night stop. Built in 1998 in faux-Francescan style around a central cloister it's a comfortable, professionally run, well-organized place to stay, with great food at reasonable prices in its *Da Guerrinuccio* restaurant. It's situated on the Aielli-Celano road off the A25 *autostrada*.

A little further west is **AVEZZANO**, destroyed – along with 10,000 inhabitants – by an earthquake in 1915. It was rebuilt, but flattened again by World War II bombings. It's since been reconstructed, but the only reason to stop here is to get a bus (from outside the train station) south to the Parco Nazionale d'Abruzzo (see below).

Tagliacozzo

Twenty minutes beyond Avezzano by train is **TAGLIACOZZO**, a picturesque town nestling beneath a pine-wooded cliff with an unspoilt Renaissance core that's well worth a wander. There are few focuses as such; the pleasure is more in discovering hidden corners, craft and gourmet food shops. The warren of small squares is enclosed by fourteenth- and fifteenth-century houses, a tangle of narrow streets and alleys, and the church of **San Francesco**, with its paper-doily rose window and column capitals carved with twisting flowers and leaves. Above the church is the impenetrable **Palazzo Ducale** and the small **Teatro Thalia** – named, like Tagliacozzo itself, after the Greek muse of theatre. The story goes that the town was founded by Greeks from Mount Parnassus: next to San Francesco is a church dedicated to two Greek saints, Cosmo and Damiano, and there are supposedly still traces of Greek in Tagliacozzo's dialect.

There's a **tourist office** at Via Vittorio Veneto 6 (June–Sept daily 9am–1pm & 4–7pm; Oct–May Mon–Fri 9am–1pm & 3.30–6pm; ☎0863.910.622). Unfortunately, many of Tagliacozzo's **hotels** have seen better days, so it's not such a great stop-off. The cheapest places are *La Lucciola* on Via Tiburtina Valeria, a busy main road behind the station (☎0863.6501; ❷), and the pleasant *Gatto d'Oro* on Viale Aldo Moro (☎0863.610.369; ❷). For somewhere with marginally more facilities try the *Miramonti* also near the station on Via Vittorio Veneto (☎0863.6581; ❸). There are several scenic **places to eat** around Piazza dell'Obelisco near the entrance to the old town; *Al Corradino di Svevia* (closed Tues Oct–May) at no. 48 is friendly and popular with the locals.

The Parco Nazionale d'Abruzzo

At four hundred square kilometres, the **Parco Nazionale d'Abruzzo** is Italy's third-largest national park and holds some of its wildest mountain land, providing a hunter-free haven for wolves, brown bears, chamois and a pair of royal eagles, along with some great walking. There are said to be around eighty bears in the park and half that number of wolves. The central village, **PESCASSÉROLI**, is the most commercialized spot, liberally decorated with the park's cute logo – a cuddly brown bear – and surrounded by campsites, holiday flats and hotels.

The best way to get away from the valley is to hike, and if you're not up for this there's not much point in coming here. The trick is to take advantage of the comprehensive information service, and get walking as quickly as possible: as soon as you get away from the vicinity of the tourist villages, the wild Apennine beauty really makes itself felt.

Information and walking routes

There is a **tourist office** in Pescasséroli, opposite the police station on Via Piave (mid-May to late Sept daily 9am–1pm & 4–7pm; rest of year Mon–Fri 9am–1pm & 3–6pm; ☎0863.910.097). The village also has a natural history **museum** on Viale Sant Lucia (daily 10am–1pm & 3–7pm; €5.20), which fills you in on the park's flora and fauna. The helpful **Ufficio di Zona** (daily 9am–noon & 3–7pm; ☎0863.91.955), behind the *municipio* (town hall), offers information on hiking in the park and has a good map you can refer to. For organized trekking, mountain biking, horse riding and cross-country skiing, plus CTS bus tickets, head for **Ecotur**, a co-operative at Piazza Vittorio Veneto 24 (daily 9am–1pm & 3.30–7pm; winter closed Sun; ☎0863.912.760, ⓦwww.pescasseroli.online.it).

There are other tourist offices in **Opi** (July–Sept daily 9am–12.30pm & 4–7pm; Oct–June Thurs–Tues 9am–12.30pm & 3.30–6pm; ☎0863.910.622), which also has a **chamois museum** (Easter & June–Sept daily 10am–1pm & 3–7pm; free); in **Villetta** (mid-July to mid-Sept daily 10am–1pm & 4–7pm; rest of year Sat & Sun 9.30am–1pm; ☎0864.89.333); and in **Barrea** (Aug &

Sept daily 9am–1pm & 4–8pm; ☏0864.88.227). All have leaflets outlining specific walks that take less than an hour, and are gentle and very popular. They can also sell you a map (€5.20) on which all **walking routes** are marked, along with an indication of the difficulty involved (F=easy, M=moderate, D=difficult), the time needed, and the flora and fauna you're likely to see on the way; there are nearly 150 different routes, starting from 25 letter-coded points, so making a choice can be difficult. The following are just suggestions, taking into account the ease of reaching the starting-point by bus.

From point #F2, 1km out of Opi on the SS83 (car park available) there's a two-and-a-half-hour walk through the **Valle Fondillo** – one of the loveliest parts of the park. This route is best followed very early in the morning, to avoid other hikers and have a small chance of seeing bears and chamois: if you do catch a glimpse of one, take care, keep quiet and don't panic – though they're extremely strong and will attack if under threat, it is almost unknown for them to harm walkers. Off this path runs #F1 via which you can climb **Mont'Amaro** (1862m) for great views over to Lake Barrea. Another good climb is up **Monte Tranquillo** (route #C3, about 2hr) about 1km out of Pescasséroli, taking the road to the left on entering the village, past the *Hotel Ivy*. The mountain (1841m) is crowned by a small sanctuary, dedicated to the black Madonna of Monte Tranquillo. From the summit you can either retrace your steps or take path #Q3 into the next valley, where you'll probably meet fewer fellow walkers. Your best chance of seeing some of the park's chamois is to take path #I1, turning left just before the youth hostel at Civitella Alfedena, and through the forested **Val di Rosa**, until the forest gives way to the grassy slopes where the chamois graze. A path zigzags from here up the slope to **Passo Cavuto**, and beyond to the *Rifugio Forca Resuni*. From here a path (#K6) descends into the **Valle Ianna'nghera** – where you may see bears – and back to Civitella Alfedena. This circuit should take six hours.

Note that from July to September, the two most popular routes – #F1 to Mont'Amaro and #I1 through Val di Rosa – are open by reservation **only**. For #F1, book onto a guided tour (in English by request; €8) at the information point in Valle Fondillo. Access to #I1 is free in June but restricted from July 8 to September 10 to fifty walkers per day and a hundred on Sundays and holidays. From September 16 to Nov 5 it is free to walk #I1 during the week, but access is restricted at weekends; book in person at the information point at Civitella Alfedena (€8). During the rest of the year these two routes are open without restriction or fee, though guided tours can still be arranged.

Accommodation and restaurants

Pescasséroli is fairly well served by buses (from Avezzano, from Castel di Sangro on the border with Molise, and one bus daily to Rome in summer), so you may find it a convenient place to stay. In high season, there's little chance of finding a **room** on arrival; you need to book at least a month in advance and be prepared for compulsory half-board in August. The cheaper places include *Al Castello*, a small, stone-built guesthouse with squeakily clean and pretty rooms on Via Gabriele d'Annunzio off the main piazza (☏ & ℻0863.910.757; ❷), and the friendly *Peppe di Sora*, across the river on Viale B. Croce (☏0863.91.908, ℻0863.910.023; ❷). Outside town, the chalet-style *Paradiso*, Loc. Fronte Fracassi (☏0863.910.422, ℻0863.910.498; ❹), is an appealing place to stay. If you're coming here for a week or more, you might consider B&B accommodation in a private house or an apartment rental – the tourist office will supply you with a list – though again, it's wise to book a month in advance. Campers should manage to find space on one of the five **campsites**.

The simplest to reach are *dell'Orso* (℡0863.91.955), which also has a *rifugio* (E5), on the main approach road (SS83); and *Club Alto Sangro* (℡0863.910.083) and *Sant'Andrea* (℡0863.912.173), both at Località Sant'Andrea off the SS83. *Panoramica* (℡0863.912.257) is out of the village at the foot of the *funivia* up to Monte Vitelle.

Among other nearby villages, **CIVITELLA ALFADENA**, situated high above Lago Barrea, has a small and jolly **hotel**, *La Torre* (℡0864.890.121; ❷), where the owner speaks good Scottish, and a **camping** area, *Wolf*, close by (℡0864.890.360; June–Oct). Across the lake at Villetta Barrea is the highly polished and quiet *Degli Olmi* hotel, Via Fossata 8b (℡0864.89.159, ℱ0864.89.185; ❸); and on the outskirts of the village the campsite, *Le Quite* (℡0864.89.141; June–Oct). At Barrea *La Genziana* campsite (℡0864.88.101) is convenient for walk-point #K up to the tiny mountain Lago Vivo or the larger Lago Montana Spaccata.

As for **eating out**, in most villages you'll find fairly cheap pizza and pasta, and general stores that will make up sandwiches for picnics. For local specialities and good location it's worth heading for *La Baita*, on Piazzale Cabinovia (closed Tues in winter), 2.5km from the centre of Pescasséroli; slightly more expensive is *Il Pescatore* on Via Roma in Villetta Barrea, a large restaurant where you can feast on superlative fresh trout from the lake and pasta dishes.

Northeast Abruzzo: Téramo and around

Rising from the Adriatic and rolling towards the eastern slopes of the Gran Sasso, the landscape of northeast Abruzzo is gentle, and its inland towns are usually ignored in favour of its long, sandy and highly popular coastline. **TÉRAMO**, capital of the province of the same name, is a modern town with an elegant centre harbouring the remains of a Roman amphitheatre, theatre and baths and a treasure-filled cathedral. Maybe not much to draw you, but Téramo does have good bus and train connections with the northern Abruzzo coast, and if you're heading for the sea you may well pass through. **Buses** stop at **Piazza Garibaldi**, to which the **train station** is linked by regular city buses. To reach the **tourist office** (May–Sept daily 9am–1pm & 4–7pm; Oct–April closed Sun; ℡0861.244.222) at Via Carducci 17, take Corso S. Giorgio from Piazza Garibaldi and then turn right. In the other direction off the piazza, at Via del Castello 62, is a reasonable **hotel**, the *Castello* (℡ & ℱ0861.247.582; no credit cards; ❶), which has some rooms with baths, as well as showers. **Restaurants** with the classic Teramano *virtù* on the menu – a hefty version of minestrone accompanied by a chilli sauce – include *Antico Cantinone*, at Via Ciotti 5 (closed Sun). A newer place with an excellent wine list is *Sotto Le Stelle* at Via Nazario Sauro 50 (closed Sun), a good bet for local specialities including *chitarre*: pasta with meaty accompaniments. If you don't want to stay in Téramo itself, you could head for *Zunica* (℡ & ℱ0861.91.319, ⓦwww.hotelzunica.it; ❺), Piazza Filippi Pepe 14, in the hill-village of **Civitella del Tronto**, between Téramo and Ascoli Piceno in the Marche; it has small, modern rooms, superb food in the restaurant, and a lively locals' bar on the ground floor.

Even if you're just passing through, look in on Téramo's main attraction, the **Duomo** (7.30am–noon & 4–7pm), at the top of Corso San Giorgio and behind whose patchy facade lies a remarkable silver altarfront. It's worth squatting down for a good look at this (ask the sacristan to switch the lights on). Crafted by the fifteenth-century Abruzzese silversmith Nicola da Guardiagrele

– also responsible for the statues of Mary and Gabriel that flank the church doorway – it has 35 panels with lively reliefs of religious scenes, starting with the *Annunciation* and moving through the New Testament, punctuating the narrative with portraits of various saints. Nicola was famous enough to feature in a sumptuous polyptych by a Venetian artist, Jacobello del Fiore, in a Baroque chapel to the left. Set into an ornate gilded frame are static portraits of saints, in rich blue, red and gold gowns, flanking the *Coronation of the Virgin*, and beneath it a model of Téramo, set against a gilded sky, with Nicola wearing a monk's habit on the left, Jacobello in the red gown on the right.

To the right of the Duomo, Via Irelli leads to the heart of Roman Téramo, with fragments of the **amphitheatre**, and the more substantial walls of the **theatre**, where two of the original twenty entrance arches remain. Just behind Piazza Garibaldi at Viale Bovio 1 is the town's modest **pinacoteca** (mid-May to mid-Sept daily 10am–7pm; rest of year Mon–Sat 9am–1pm & 3–7pm, Sun 10am–1pm & 4–7pm; €5.16 joint ticket with the *museo archeologico* below), whose collection of local art over the centuries is best represented by the *Madonna Enthroned with Saints* – a polyptych in which the colours are lucid and the forms almost sculpted, the work of the local fifteenth-century artist Giacomo da Campli. The **museo archeologico** off Via Carducci on Via Delfico (same hours as the art gallery) is strong on Roman finds from excavations in Téramo and includes a first-century mosaic of an appealing lion among the forum columns and marble busts.

The northern Abruzzo coast

The **northern Abruzzo coastline** isn't at first sight the region's most appealing stretch, its ribbon of sand hugged for most of its considerable length by road and railway, studded with grids of beach umbrellas and flimsy cabins and lined with concrete-box apartment blocks and hotels. However, the beaches are good and frequently palm-fringed, there are plenty of campsites, and though the resorts may look bland they can be fun – especially if you just want a few days resting up.

The coastal rail line ensures that access to the resorts couldn't be easier, though finding a hotel may be a problem, as they get booked up in advance for most of the summer and the cheaper ones tend to be closed out of season – your best bet at most of the coastal towns is to head straight for the tourist office on arrival.

Atri

The approach to **ATRI**, about 10km inland from Pineto, is like travelling through the background of a Renaissance painting, with gently undulating hills planted with orderly olive groves giving way to a surrealist landscape of sleek clay gullies known as *calanchi*, water-eroded into smooth ripples, wrinkles and folds. Atri's Duomo contains Abruzzo's greatest cycle of frescoes, and the town itself, with its narrow stepped and bridged streets, is one you're likely to be reluctant to leave.

A decision to stay may be helped along by the fact that the town has a great hotel – three-star quality at one-star prices – the *San Francesco* (☎ & ℱ085.87.0305; ❷), which is housed in an ex-convent next to the church of San Francesco on Corso Adriano, and also has a decent **restaurant** *Alla Corte* (closed Wed).

Regular **buses** make the trip from Pescara and Téramo and drop you near **Porta San Domenico**, the town's only surviving defensive gate. To get to the centre, walk through the gate and cut down one of the narrow side streets to the main thoroughfare, which leads up to the central piazza, dominated by the thirteenth-century **Duomo** (daily 8.30am–noon & 3–7.30pm). Its facade is understated, pierced by a rose window and perforated by the holes in which scaffolding beams were slotted during construction. The inside is similarly simple, with patches of frescoes on the brick columns and – visible through glass set into the floor of the apse – an octagonal mosaic pavement decorated with sea horses, dolphins and fish, from the Roman baths over which the church was built. The Duomo's highlight, however, is the cycle of **fifteenth-century frescoes** by Andrea Delitio on the apse walls. Delitio has been called the "Piero della Francesca" of Abruzzo for his sophisticated use of architecture and landscape; but in contrast to Piero's cool intellectualism and obscure symbolism, Delitio places the religious scenes in realistic contexts. *The Birth of Mary*, for example, has servants giving the newly born baby a bath; in the apse vault the four Evangelists are placed in natural settings, the animals that are the emblems of the saints behaving as domestic pets; and back on the walls, the lives of the rich – especially in the *Wedding at Cana* and *Presentation in the Temple* – contrast with the lives of the poor, notably Mary, Joseph and the shepherds in the *Nativity*. The most emotionally charged scene is the *Slaughter of the Innocents*, in which the horror is intensified by the refined Renaissance architectural setting and the fact that the massacre is coolly observed from a balcony by Herod's party of civic bigwigs.

For a touch of light relief, head back up the right-hand aisle to see a piece of Renaissance kitsch – a font with four oversized frogs clinging to the basin. The attached **museum** (June–Sept daily 10am–noon & 4–8pm; Oct–May Thurs–Tues 10am–noon & 3–5pm; €3) reveals large, seventeenth-century majolica dishes and jugs, silverware and baptismal shells. It also lets you into the cloisters, the site of a cavernous Roman cistern. Concentrating on more recent history, the **museo civico etnografico** (June–Sept Tues–Sun 4–8pm; Oct–May Tues–Sat 10am–1pm; €1.55), near the post office in Via S. Pietro, is good on old radiograms, prams, nineteenth-century costume and shoes, and has an intriguing 1950s machine for making liquorice. If you've had your fill of museums, stroll out to the belvedere for views, or simply sit in a café and watch the small-town life around you.

Loreto Aprutino

One of the most important market towns in the region is **LORETO APRUTINO**, a quiet hilltop settlement with medieval origins 24km inland from Pescara. The labyrinthine old town is home to a score of **artisans' workshops**, open to the public (daily 4–7pm) and making knives, copper and iron pots and items in terracotta and decorated glass. Some tiny cantinas in the old town sell olive oil, for which the area has been awarded a DOP (*denominazione di origine protetta*), the equivalent of the DOC designation for wine. Loreto heaves with people on market day (Thurs) and in the evenings during the late-running *passeggiata*, when it's a pleasure simply to do nothing and for a moment be part of small-town life. If you want a focus for your wanderings, head just outside town for the fourteenth-century church of **Santa Maria in Piano** (daily 8am–noon & 3–7pm). It's noted for its series of frescoes in the right aisle, painted in diverse styles dating from the fourteenth to sixteenth centuries and celebrating the devotions of saints and apostles, including St Thomas of

Aquinas, protector of the city. At the top of the old town, on the end of a row of nineteenth-century *palazzi*, stands the church of **San Pietro Apostolo**. The church dates from the fifteenth and sixteenth centuries, with a Renaissance doorway decorated with the coat of arms of the Borboni, who chose this as their castle abbey.

Practicalities

Regular **buses** make the trip from Pescara, dropping you near the **tourist office** at Via dei Normanni 8 (Tues–Sat 8.30am–12.30pm & 4–7.30pm, Sun 8.30am–12.30pm; ☎085.829.0213). There are plenty of interesting **places to stay**. The ninth-century castle which tops the town is now a grand hotel, the *Castello Chiola* (☎085.829.0690, ⓕ085.829.0677; ❻). The huge, high-ceilinged rooms have been decorated in stately style and it has a glass-roofed, inner courtyard lounge, and a small swimming pool on a terrace overlooking the surrounding countryside. Also central is the airy B&B *Loreblick* at Via Fiorano 42 (☎ & ⓕ085.829.0323, ⓔloreblick@inwind.it; ❷) with good food at its *Florano* restaurant, while out of town you can **eat** very well at hotel-restaurant *La Bilancia*, Contrada da Palazzo 11 (☎085.828.9321; closed Mon). There's a welcoming agriturismo guesthouse *Le Magnolie*, at Contrada da Fiorano 83 (☎ & ⓕ085.828.9534, ⓦwww.lemagnolie.com; ❹), on a mixed farm cultivating olives, fruit trees, vegetables and cereal crops; the six bedrooms and three mini-apartments are furnished with flair; lunch and dinner are served on request. It's on a minor road between the SS151 between Penne and Loreto Aprutino, and the SS81 between Penne and Pianella; look out for the signposts.

Pescara

The main town and resort of the Abruzzo coast is **PESCARA**, a bustling, modern place that's probably the region's most commercial and expensive city. If you're looking for somewhere to sunbathe there are much quieter places than Pescara's sixteen-kilometre beach; but if you're aiming to take a ferry over to Croatia or the islands of the Dalmatian coast, you might find yourself using the city as a departure point, or there's a chance you might pass through for the train or bus connections.

Architecturally, Pescara isn't a distinguished town. Opposite the new train station, the main street, **Corso Umberto**, is lined with designer boutiques and packed with the label-conscious Pescarese, who also hang out in the elegant cafés on **Piazza Rinascita**, known as Pescara's *salone*. If you've time to kill, you could visit the **Museo delle Genti d'Abruzzo** at Via delle Caserme 22 (July to mid-Sept, Mon–Fri 9am–1pm; mid-Sept to June Mon–Sat 9am–1pm plus Tues & Thurs 3.30–6pm, Sun 10am–1pm; €4), devoted to the life and popular traditions of the region; or visit the birthplace of the poet and mentor of Mussolini, **Gabriele d'Annunzio** (see p.231), at Corso Manthonè 101 (Tues–Sat 9am–1.30pm, Sun 9am–12.30pm; €2). A third museum, the **Museo e Pinacoteca Cascella**, at Viale G. Marconi 45 (Mon–Sat 9am–1pm, plus Tues & Thurs 4.30–6.30pm; €1.50), is for devotees of Art Nouveau and later twentieth-century art, with five hundred lithographic prints, paintings, ceramics and sculptures, including a stunning set of portraits (mounted on dinner plates) by the prolific Cascella family who lived and worked here.

Practicalities

Pescara has two **train stations**, though unless you're leaving the country you only need to use one, Stazione Centrale (the other, Porta Nuova, is only for ferry connections). Conveniently, **buses** to Rome (quicker than the train) and

Naples leave from outside Stazione Centrale. Ryanair flights from London Stansted touch down at the **airport**, around 5km southwest of the city and connected by #38 bus (every 10min). The **tourist office** is on the first floor at Via Paolucci (June–Sept Mon–Sat 8am–1pm & 3–6pm, Sun 8.30am–1pm; Oct–May Mon–Fri 8am–1pm & 3–6pm, Sat 8.30am–1pm; ☎085.421.9981), close to the seafront.

The nearest **campsites** are *Francivilia* (☎085.810.715; June–Sept) and *Paola* (☎085.817.525; June–Sept) at Francivalla al Mare – buses #1 and #2 stop outside. Most of the **hotels** are on the beach-front north of the river and the old town, although you can sleep more cheaply at somewhere like the *Corso* (☎085.422.4210; no credit cards; ❶), to the right of the train station at Corso Vittorio Emanuele 292, or *Planet*, Via Piave 142 (☎ & ☎085.421.1657; ❶), up Corso Umberto from the train station, left onto Via M. Forti and then right. A more upmarket choice (book a couple of weeks in advance) is the comfortable, shiny and businesslike *Alba*, Via M. Forti 14 (☎085.389.145, ☎085.292.163; ❹). For **meals**, try the *Cantina di Jozz* at Via delle Caserme 61 (closed all day Mon & Sun evening) which does great Abruzzese food. Otherwise, try the gastronomically inclined and slow-food advocate *La Lumaca*, just down the road from the *Cantina* at no. 51 (☎085.451.0880; closed Tues). Corso Mathonè is the main street running through what remains of the old town of Pescara next to the river; here, among other good places to eat, you'll find *Locanda Manthonè*, recommended by the Pescarese for its quality food at reasonable prices.

Chieti

Just twenty minutes by train from Pescara, **CHIETI** is a more pleasant place to stop over between trains. It holds Abruzzo's best museum by far, with an extensive collection of finds from the region, and the town itself has a relaxed and appealing provincial air.

Coming by train you arrive at Chieti Scalo, from where it's a short journey on bus #1 up the hill to Chieti proper, 5km away, which spreads over a curving ridge and has great views of the Maiella and Gran Sasso – and, when it's clear, out to sea. Buses arrive at **Piazza Vittorio Emanuele** alongside the chunky and much-reconstructed cathedral, from where the main **Corso Marrucini** cuts through the town centre to **Piazza Trento e Trieste**. Behind the post office, off Via Spaventa, are the remains of three little Roman temples. However, it's the **Museo Archeologico Nazionale di Abruzzo** (daily 9am–8pm; €4) which is of most interest, laid out in the dignified Villa Comunale, and encircled by a park, beyond Piazza Trento e Trieste. It holds finds from Abruzzo's major sites: on the ground floor there's a Roman portrait-bust of an old man, in which the stone appears as soft, wrinkled and flaccid as real skin, a massive and muscly white-marble Hercules from the temple at Alba Fucens and an elegant, bone funeral bed from a tomb at Amiternum. Upstairs, most striking are the bronze Hercules from the sanctuary outside Sulmona (see p.823) and the *Capestrano Warrior*, a statue of a Bronze Age warrior prince. It dates back to the time (sixth century BC) when a deified, hero-worshipped warrior leader was key to Bronze Age society. Statues like these in characteristic pose with the arms across the torso were set on the top of burial mounds to mark territory throughout the Adriatic and Central Europe and must have made an awesome feature of the landscape.

Remains of the occupants of Bronze Age tombs are laid out in the adjacent rooms – the men buried with armour and weapons, the women with jewellery, kitchen utensils, spindles, and in one case even a nail-brush.

Further digs in Chieti have uncovered the core of Teate, the main town of the Marrucini (an Italic tribe) which became a Roman colony in the first century BC. The site lies on the edge of central Chieti at the **Civitella archeological park** (daily 9am–8pm; €4) and includes the remains of temples, theatre, amphitheatre, thermal baths and a new museum.

Practicalities

The **tourist office** is at Via Spaventa 29, just off Corso Marrucino (May–Sept daily 9am–1pm & 4–7pm; Oct–April Mon–Fri 9am–1pm & 3–6pm; ☏0871.63.640). An affordable, central **hotel** is the *Garibaldi* at Piazza Garibaldi 25 (☏ & ℻0871.345.318; no credit cards; ❸). Around 3km away in the hills southwest of Chieti there's a place worth going out of your way to stay at: the welcoming, well-organized farmhouse guesthouse *Il Quadrifoglio* at Strada Licini 22, Colle Marconi (☏ & ℻0871.63.400, ✉anndora@tin.it; ❷). There are six newly furnished bedrooms, an apartment with full kitchen and log-burning fire, and a lounge, balcony, garden and barbecue with olive groves and oakwoods in one direction and far-reaching views in the other. Proprietor Anna Maria D'Orazio will cook an evening meal (€13) for guests if they want and also runs gourmet cooking courses (she speaks excellent English). If you're arriving by plane, you can arrange to be picked up from Pescara airport. Good-value **meals** can also be had in central Chieti at *Trattoria Nino*, Via Principessa di Piemonte 7 (closed Fri), near Piazza Trento e Trieste, and at *Primavera*, Viale B. Croce 69, in Chieti Scalo, the lower town (closed Sun).

The southern Abruzzo coast

The coast south of Pescara is less developed than the northern stretch; the long ribbon of sand continues, followed by the train line and punctuated with mostly small resorts. **ORTONA**, further along, is of most interest for its daily summer ferries to the Trémiti Islands (see p.924), its mainly reconstructed centre dominated by the shell of a castle and the massive dome of its cathedral.

Twenty kilometres south of Ortona lies the small resort of **FOSSACÉSIA MARINA**, where it's advisable to book **hotels** well ahead in summer; be prepared for compulsory half-board in July and August. The *Levante* hotel is right on the beach (☏0872.60.169, ℻0872.607.706; ❸), while 3km inland at Via S. Giovanni in Venere 40 is the *Golfo di Venere* (☏ & ℻0872.60.541; ❸) and a **campsite**, *Valle di Venere* (☏0872.608.291; June–Oct). Another campsite, *La Foce* (☏0872.609.110), lies 4km up the coast next to the beach, just off the SS16 at the km 484,3 mark, and is well equipped with shady pitches, bar, sailing and surfing facilities. On the way inland to Fossacésia itself is the creamy-gold Romanesque church of **San Giovanni in Venere**, which owes its name to the fact that it was built over a Roman temple dedicated to Venus the Conciliator and is visited by anyone seeking the return of peace within their family. The church, with its finely carved sandstone door and triple apse, is superbly sited among the undulating fields above the coast and is still a favourite outing for Abruzzese families – harmony now being sought by the treat of a hearty meal in the restaurant outside the church. If you're visiting at the weekend or during holidays and want the church to yourself, aim to get there at lunchtime, while everyone else is safely ensconced behind plates of pasta.

Vasto

VASTO, further south, close to the border with Molise, is a fine old city, overlooking the resort of **VASTO MARINA**. There are boats in the summer to the Trémiti Islands, plenty of campsites, and a handful of reasonable hotels along the broad sandy beach – palm-lined and beach-hutted in the centre, wilder and rockier to the north.

Vasto is all about beach, though if you're here for a day or so you should definitely get a bus from the new train station on the seafront to the upper town (they run roughly every 30min, a 10min journey), whose rooftops and campaniles rise above palms and olive groves. The centre of town is **Piazza Rossetti**, its gardens dominated by the chunky **Castello Calderesco**. The piazza is named after Gabriele Rossetti, a local eighteenth-century poet who is better known as the father of the Pre-Raphaelite poet Dante Gabriele Rossetti.

Just off the piazza, next to the small Duomo, stands the splendid Renaissance **Palazzo d'Avalos** (July & Aug Tues–Sun 8am–midnight; Sept–June Tues–Sun 9.30am–12.30pm & 4.30–8.30pm). This was once the home of the poet and friend of Michelangelo, Vittoria Colonna, who was famous in her time for the bleak sonnets she wrote after her husband's death; nowadays it houses the town's **museum** (same hours as palazzo; €1.05 for the archeological museum; €3.65 for the art gallery; €1.05 for the costume museum; or €5.15 for the whole lot). The best of its exhibits are some bellicose second-century bronzes, a third-century warrior with an arm missing, a collection of Greek coins – evidence of Vasto's early importance as an international trading city, and the beautiful clothes and battered old hobby-horse in the costume museum.

Alongside the palazzo, **Piazza del Popolo** is the site of the **tourist office** (mid-May to Sept Mon–Sat 9am–1pm & 4–7pm; rest of year Mon–Sat 9am–1pm & 3–6pm; ☎0873.367.312) and opens onto a panoramic promenade that takes you to Vasto's most memorable sight, the door of the church of **San Pietro**, surrounded by Romanesque twists and zigzags, standing isolated against a backdrop of sky, sea and trees, the rest of the church having been destroyed in a landslide in 1956.

Pleasant as the upper town is, most of the action is down by the beach in **Vasto Marina**, and best placed for this are the numerous **campsites** along the coast. Most of them are off the SS16 towards Foggia; *Il Piopetto* is right on the beach and has pine-trees for shade (☎0873.801.466, mid-May to mid-Sept). Among the **hotels**, good value is spacious and airy *La Bitta*, close to the free beach on Lungomare Cardella, but open only from June to September (☎ & ℱ0873.801.979; no credit cards; ❶). If you do want to stay in the upper town, try either *Dei Sette*, on Via San Michele, a ten-minute walk out of the centre past the stadium and the public gardens (☎ & ℱ0873.362.819; ❷), or the *Palizzi,* a ten-minute walk in the opposite direction on the busy Corso Mazzini (☎0873.367.361, ℱ0873.363.814, ✆cdivirgilio@mail.clio.it; ❷). The most peaceful bolthole has got to be *Villa Vignola* (☎0873.310.050, ℱ0873.310.060; ❺), a small white villa with five rooms, a tiny pebble beach, a garden for lounging in and a romantic terrace restaurant serving such delicacies as home-made ravioli with saffron sauce and prawns, stuffed baby squid and simple grilled fish (at least €45 a head). Book well ahead; to find it, take the SS16 north out of Marina di Vasto, pass the turn-off for Vasto itself and keep going until you get to a sign pointing to the "Porto". Turn right here, right again immediately after the railway line and right again after the bridge. Note that half-board is compulsory at all Vasto's hotels in July and August. As for **eat-**

ing and drinking, there are loads of pizzerias and "pubs" in Vasto Marina, although you might prefer to consider splashing out at *Villa Vignola* in Contrada Vignola (see above).

Isernia and around

ISERNIA was severely damaged for the eighth time by an earthquake in 1984, but after a slow recovery it has rebuilt its commercial centre so that it's now comparatively busy and bustling. Historically the city hasn't had much luck: much of the centre was destroyed in a bombing raid on September 10, 1943, and a monument to the 4000 who were killed – an anguished nude ankle-deep in fractured tiles, bricks and gutters – is the centrepiece of the square called, understandably, Piazza X Settembre.

Not surprisingly, little of old Isernia survives. The city's main attraction is the **Museo Nazionale Santa Maria delle Monache** (daily 8.30am–7.30pm; €2), in the heart of the old town at Piazza Santa Maria 8. In 1979 local road-builders unearthed traces of a million-year-old village here, the most ancient signs of human life yet found in Europe. The exhibits are backed up by a video in English, which reconstructs the village and puts the ancient civilization in context. Contrary to the misleading publicity, there were no human remains found, just weapons, traps, traces of pigment thought to have been used as body paint, and animal bones, laid out to create a solid platform on the marshy land for the village.

Though unbeguiling in itself, Isernia can be a useful starting-point for exploring the rest of Molise: **buses** to local villages leave from Via XXIV Maggio, parallel with Corso Garibaldi, and longer-distance buses, including those to Rome and Naples, from outside the train station. The **tourist office** is at Via Farinacci 1 (Mon–Sat 8am–2pm; ☎0865.3992). You probably won't need to stay over, but if you do, head for *Sayonara*, a modern three-star at Via G. Berti 131 (☎0865.50.992, ⓕ0865.415.919, ⓔinfo@sayonara.it; ➌) and the only central hotel. **Eating** prospects are better: there's a good traditional restaurant, *Taverna Maresca*, in the old town on Corso Marcelli (closed Sun). Their filling pasta-, bean- or polenta-based first courses are meals in themselves, though try and leave room for their mains of roast kid or lamb cooked in various mysterious but delicious ways.

Around Isernia

The countryside **around Isernia** is lush and gentle, at its best in spring, when the meadows are sprinkled with wild flowers. The valleys are headed by hill-villages, most of them run-down places ringed with new housing estates, and the rewards of exploring are principally those of being the first foreigner to have visited in ages. Getting around, though, isn't easy: buses are often organized around the school day, which means you'll have to leave either very early in the morning or at around 2pm – after that there may be no other bus until the next day.

Just outside **PIETRABBONDANTE**, northeast of Isernia, are the remains of a pre-Roman Samnite village, notably a well-preserved theatre (Tues–Sun 9am–dusk; €2) set in a green field at the foot of Monte Caraceno. Further along the road, **AGNONE** is best known for having produced church bells for over a thousand years. The **Marinelli Pontifical Foundry** still makes bells in the traditional way, using a priest to bless the molten bronze as it's poured into the mould, which supposedly ensures that the bell's tones will be pure. A small **museum** can be visited (guided tours Mon–Sat noon–4pm; €4.50). Agnone is also famous for its coppersmiths, most of whom work on the main street.

To the west of Isernia, the bus calls at **Cerro al Volturno**, crowned by one of Molise's more spectacular castles, almost growing out of the grey rock on which it is perched. A few kilometres further on is **CASTEL SAN VIN-CENZO**, another pretty-from-a-distance hill-village: get off the bus below the village at the Cartiera (paper mill) and walk along the road to the left for about 1km, until you come to the abbey of **San Vincenzo al Volturno** (℡0865.955.246, Ⓦwww.sanvincenzoabbey.org) – a much-reconstructed complex now run by American nuns, with a crypt covered by a complete cycle of ninth-century frescoes in rich Byzantine colours, the only surviving example of ninth-century Benedictine art. Unfortunately the frescoes are not open to the public; to see them you will need to contact the abbey well in advance to make an appointment. At the **zona archeologico** nearby are the remains of a seventh-century monastery (in theory open daily 9am–noon & 3–6pm but call ℡0865.951.006 to book; guided tours €2.50).

About 20km to the south, but most easily accessible by train from Isernia, is the village of **VENAFRO**, topped by a derelict castle and with a Roman amphitheatre (just by the railway station) that was converted into an oval piazza in the Middle Ages. Most of the local finds are on display in the **Museo Archeologico Santa Chiara** (daily 8.30am–7.30pm; €2) on Via Garibaldi.

Campobasso, Saepinum and the Matese

Home of a top-security prison and the National Carabinieri School, **CAM-POBASSO**, the regional capital, is about as appealing as you'd expect – a modern, rather faceless town that was once known for its cutlery industry. It's a good base, though, for the remarkable ruins at **Saepinum**, and if you're around in early June, don't miss the town's spectacular Corpus Christi *Sagra dei Misteri* procession, in which citizens are dressed as saints, angels and devils, inserted into fantastic contraptions and transported, seemingly suspended in midair, through the streets.

At any other time of the year the most notable attraction is the **Samnite Museum** (daily 8.30am–7.30pm; free) at Via Chiarizia 12, with statues and archeological finds from the area. Steep alleys of the small, old upper town lead up to a couple of Romanesque churches – **San Bartolomeo**, which has eerily contorted figures carved around its main door, and **San Giorgio**, whose entrance displays a dragon surrounded by stylized flowers. The views at least are extensive, though they consist mostly of Campobasso's suburban sprawl. And there's little point carrying on up the hill to the monastery and sixteenth-century castle: the monastery is modern, and the castle now a weather station.

The nicest, most central **hotel** is the *Skanderbeg*, near the station and museum at Via Novelli 31 (℡0874.413.341, Ⓕ0874.416.340; ❹), or there's the *Tricolore*, outside the centre on the road to Térmoli (℡ & Ⓕ0874.63.190; ❷). The **tourist office** (Mon–Sat 8am–2pm; ℡0874.415.662) at Piazza Vittoria 14 in the new town has details of local events and bus routes to elsewhere in the province.

Saepinum

It's **SAEPINUM**, a ruined Roman town to the south, close to the border with Puglia, that makes the stopover in Campobasso worthwhile. Three kilometres from the nearest village, surrounded by a lush plain fringed with the foothills of the Matese mountains, it's the best example in Italy of a provincial Roman town – and is tourist-free.

The main reason Saepinum is so intact is that it was never very important: nothing much ever happened here, and after the fall of the Roman Empire it carried on as the sleepy backwater it had always been – until the ninth century when it was sacked by Saracens. Over the centuries its inhabitants added only a handful of farms and cottages, incorporating the odd Roman column or architrave, and eventually moved south to the more secure hilltop site of present-day Sepino. Some have now moved back and rebuilt the farms and cottages on Saepinum's peripheries, contributing if anything to the site's appeal. Their sheep graze below an ancient mausoleum, chickens scratch around the walls, and the only sounds are the tinkling of the sheep's bells.

Saepinum is accessible by **bus**, and there's **information** and a good **restaurant** at the *centro turistico Il Grifo*, though be prepared for the noise of school parties. There are also two bar-restaurants at the Porta Boiano and the Porta Tammaro. From Campobasso, either catch one of the two services that stop at Altilia (right outside the site) which leave the Campo Sportivo daily except Sunday at 7.50am and 1pm; or get a bus to **Sepino** (7 daily except Sun; to check schedules call ☏0874.64.744) and walk the remaining 3km to Saepinum. Buses return to Campobasso from the archeological site at 8.15am and 1.35pm.

The site

Depending on whether you arrive by bus or by car, entrance to Saepinum (always open; free) is through the **Porta Terravecchia** or the **Porta Tammaro**, two of the town's four gates. The site is bisected by the *cardus maximus*, still paved with the original stones, and crossed by the *decumanus maximus* – centre of town and home to the public buildings and trading quarters. On the left, grass spills through the cracks in the pavement of the **forum**, now used by the few local kids as a football pitch, bordered by the foundations of various municipal buildings: the comitium, the curia, a temple, baths, and in the centre a fountain with a relief of a griffin. Beyond the forum, on the left of the decumanus, the **Casa Impluvio Sannitico** contains a vat to collect rainwater, from the Samnite town that stood on the site before the Romans sacked it in 293 BC. Until quite recently the village was passed through, as it had been for over 2000 years, by nomadic shepherds, moving their flocks between their winter grazing lands in the south and summer pastures in Abruzzo. The *trattura*, as it's called, still takes place, but in much reduced form by lorry and motorway. Further along the road is what must have been a welcome, if bizarre, landmark for generations of shepherds – an enormous stone cylinder resembling a modern water tower that is in fact the mausoleum of one of Saepinum's Roman citizens.

Back down the decumanus on the other side of the crossroads is the well-preserved **Basilica** that served as the main courthouse. Beyond is the most interesting part of the town – the octagonal macellum (marketplace), with its small stone stalls and central rain-collecting dish, and a series of houses fronted by workshops, with the small living quarters behind. This leads down to the best-preserved gate, the **Porta Boiano**, flanked by cylindrical towers and statues of prisoners celebrating some victory over barbarian invaders.

The Matese

One of Italy's least visited mountain ranges, scattered with high plains, forests and lakes, the **Matese** stretches between Molise and Campania. Wolves still wander its woods, and the peaks are home to eagles, falcons and hawks. The streams are well stocked with fish and the valleys full of the much-coveted porcini mushrooms.

Trains running between Isernia and Campobasso stop at **BOIANO**, a pleasant town overlooked by a densely wooded hill crowned with the remains of a castle. If you want to stay, try the *Hotel Mary* at Via Barcellona 21 (T & F0874.778.375; ❷). There's also a good traditional **osteria**, the *Filomena* at Via Garibaldi 16 (closed Mon), featuring dishes such as *orrecchiette con broccoletti* and *spaghetti alla chitarra*. The town is a handy starting-point for the hike (around 2hr) up **Monte Gallinola** – best done on a clear day when the views take in Italy's eastern and western coastlines. The road leads from beyond the central Piazza Pasquino up to a *rifugio*; from here a steep road, later a footpath, climbs through a forest to the Costa Alta, a mile-high pass whose views are good – though nothing compared to what you'll see when you get to the summit. The path then leads across ski-slopes to the base of Monte la Gallinola, where a track heads up to the top, from which you look down over the Lago del Matese, and, if weather permits, get the much-touted panoramic view.

You can, of course, see something of the Matese in more comfort, by taking a bus to the winter-sports centre of **CAMPITELLO MATESE** from either Boiano or Campobasso; or by staying over at the *Matese* (T0874.780.378, F0874.780.379; ❹), 9km from Campitello Matese at **SAN MASSIMO**, northwest of Boiano. From Boiano, take the road marked Castellone and San Massimo and, coming down from the mountains, take the left branch when the road forks.

Towards the coast: Larino and the Albanian villages

Halfway between Campobasso and Térmoli, **LARINO** is considerably more attractive than most Molise towns, its medieval centre clasped in the valley, relatively untouched by the concrete and pace of the modern industrial town that supports it. The highlight is its cathedral, but there are also some minor Roman relics in its small museum and a neglected amphitheatre in the modern town.

To the left of the **train station**, Via Gramsci leads down to old Larino. The main street widens out at Piazza Vittorio Emanuele, backing onto which is the **Palazzo Ducale**, whose **museum** (Mon–Fri 8.30am–1.30pm & 3–6pm, closed Wed afternoon; free) contains large Roman mosaics and a hoard of coins. On Via Gramsci, about halfway between the station and the *centro storico*, there's a garden that also has Roman ruins, including capitals and columns, and a sacrificial altar called the Ara Frentana. Close by is the **Duomo**, built in the early fourteenth century just after the town had been flattened by an earthquake and sacked by the Saracens, with an intricately carved Gothic portal.

The oldest part of the town starts beyond the Duomo but, appealing as the houses and steep alleys are, it is the glimpses of centuries-old streetlife that are more memorable – women making lace and preparing vegetables outside their houses, while the kids play at their feet and the men do absolutely nothing when they're not boozing in the bar.

If you take a bus from Piazza Vittorio Emanuele to the upper city, you'll jump a couple of centuries in five minutes. Modern Larino is a bustling place, built on the site of the original Samnite/Roman town. The large and overgrown **amphitheatre** off Via Viadotto Frentano is visible from the street (Tues–Sat 9am–7pm, Sun 9am–1pm; free) and gives some idea of the importance of early second-century BC Larinum, though apart from this the mosaic pavement off Viale Molise and a few fragments of walls, behind the Scuola Materna off Viale Giulio Cesare, are hardly sufficient clues to how Larino once looked. If you want to **stay**, your only choice is the *Park Hotel Campitelli 2* (☎0874.823.541, ⊕0874.822.339; ❸) at Via San Benedetto 1, an air-conditioned four-star, about 1km from the station.

The Albanian villages

URURI, 12km from Larino, and **PORTOCANNONE**, closer to the coast, are isolated villages, most easily reached by bus from Térmoli. Their isolation is such that six hundred years after their ancestors emigrated from Albania, the locals still speak an Albanian-Italian dialect incomprehensible to outsiders. Portocannone's Romanesque church contains an icon of the Madonna of Constantinople, brought over by the original émigrés, and in Ururi, at the beginning of May, a **festival** is staged: a fierce and furious race through the village streets on gladiator-style carts, pulled by bulls and pushed by men on horseback with spiked poles. It's a ruthless business: the horses are fed beer before the race to excite them, and although the riders are supposed to push only the back of the carts, they are not averse to prodding the flanks of the bulls, who have already been given electric shocks to liven them up. The race itself is terrifying, but unforgettable, with bulls, carts and spikes hurtling past the frenzied crowds, nowadays protected by wire fences. There are almost inevitably injuries, and at least one person has been killed. If you want to go, the tourist offices at Campobasso and Térmoli will have the precise date.

The Molise coast

The brief stretch of the **Molise coast** is less developed than Abruzzo's. Its only real town, **TÉRMOLI**, a fishing port and quiet, undistinguished resort, makes for a relaxing place to spend a day. The beach is long and sandy and the old town, walled and guarded by a castle, has an interesting cathedral. It's also a departure point for ferries (mid-June to Sept) to the Trémiti Islands (see p.924).

Térmoli is the place where Italian and Central European time is set – from the observatory inside the stark castle built above the beach in 1247 by Frederick II. Beyond the castle the road follows the old walls around the headland, holding what's left of the old town, focus of which is the **Duomo**. This is most notable for its Romanesque exterior, decorated all the way round with a series of blind arcades and windows – a feature introduced by Frederick II's Norman-influenced architects. Inside are the relics of St Timothy, best known for the letters he received from St Paul, who advised him on how to go about converting the Greeks. That he ended up in Térmoli is thanks to Térmolese Crusaders, who brought his bones back from Constantinople as a souvenir. The Térmolese hid them, fearing that if the Turks ever succeeded in penetrating the city they would seize and destroy them. In fact the relics were hidden so well they weren't discovered until 1945, during restoration work to repair bomb damage (the sacristan will show you them).

Térmoli's **tourist office** (June–Sept Mon–Fri 8am–2pm plus Mon & Wed 3–6.30pm & Tues, Thurs & Fri 5–6.30pm, Sat 8am–1pm; Oct–May Mon–Fri 8am–2pm, Sat 8am–1pm; ☎0875.706.754) on Piazza M. Bega is difficult to find, tucked into a grotty car park behind a Benetton shop and opposite the local bus station. There's a second office open in summer (daily 6pm–midnight) in Piazza Duomo in the old town, which promotes local crafts and Molise in general. Long-distance **buses** pull up in Via Martiri della Resistenza, 1km from the centre and the **train station**. The cheapest **hotel** is *Al Caminetto*, off the SS16 in Villaggio Airone, Via Europa 2 (☎ & ⑤0875.52.139; no credit cards; ❷; half-board compulsory in July & Aug), 4 km from the town centre and served in high season by rare buses from Piazza Bega; on the same route are two **campsites**, *Cala Saracena* (☎0875.52.193; June to mid-Sept) and *Azzurra* (☎0875.52.404; June–Sept). In a more convenient location, just opposite the train station, but rather more expensive, is the spacious *Corona* (☎0875.84.041, ⑤0875.84.043; ❺). A two-hundred-metre walk from the station, *Rosary,* Lungomare Corso Colombo 24 (☎0875.84.944, ⑤0875.84.947; ❷), has plenty of rooms with balconies facing the beach. While here you should certainly have a meal in one of Térmoli's seafood **restaurants**. *Squalo Blu*, Via A. De Gasperi 49 (closed Mon), is worth a splurge – there's a splendid *menu degustazione* for €30, though you can, of course, eat more modestly for less; and there are plenty of pizzerias and simple trattorias along Via Fratelli Brigada, the seafront and the parallel Via V. Emanuele III, if you want somewhere cheaper.

Travel details

Trains

Avezzano to: Tagliacozzo (7 daily; 10min).
Campobasso to: Térmoli (9 daily; 1hr 45min).
L'Aquila to: Sulmona (11 daily; 1hr); Terni (10 daily; 2hr).
Isernia to: Campobasso (13 daily; 1hr.10min).
Pescara to: Alanno (15 daily; 25min); Ancona (24 daily; 1hr 30min–2hr); Rome (5 daily; 3hr 30min); Sulmona (21 daily; 1hr–1hr 20min); Térmoli (18 daily; 1hr); Vasto (16 daily; 55min).
Sulmona to: Alanno (11 daily; 45min); Avezzano (10 daily; 1hr 15min); Celano (9 daily; 1hr); L'Aquila (12 daily; 1hr).
Térmoli to: Foggia (16 daily; 1hr).

Buses

Atri to: Pescara (12 daily; 1hr).
L'Aquila to: Bominaco (4 daily; 1hr); Rome (18 daily; 1hr 40min); Sulmona (7 daily; 1hr 30min); Téramo (6 daily; 1hr 20min).
Avezzano to: Pescasséroli (8 daily; 1hr 30min).
Chieti to: Rome (8 daily; 2hr 30min).

Isernia to Campobasso: (4–5 daily; 45min).
Pescara to: Áscoli Piceno (6 daily; 2hr 30min); Atri (12 daily; 1hr); Chieti (every 20min; 40min); L'Aquila (9 daily; 1hr 50min); Loreto Aprutino (6 daily; 45min); Rome (7 daily; 3hr); Sulmona (4 daily; 1hr 30min).
Sulmona to: Cocullo (1 daily; 45min); Scanno (7 daily; 1hr).
Téramo to: Atri (3 daily; 1hr 10min).
Térmoli to: Campobasso (hourly; 1hr 10min); Pescara (3 daily; 2hr 20min).

Ferries

Pescara to: Vela Luka and Stari Grad (2 weekly, Mon & Fri; 4hr 30min & 6hr 15min); Bol and Stari Grad (1 weekly, Tues; 4hr 40min & 5hr 30min); Spalato and Stari Grad (1 weekly, Tues; 4hr 30min & 5hr 45min); Hvar, Bol and Stari Grad (1 weekly, Sat; 4hr 15min, 5hr 15min & 6hr).
Ortona via Vasto to: Trémiti Islands (1 daily; 2 hr).
Térmoli to: Trémiti Islands (2 ferries & 3 hydrofoils daily; 40min–1hr 40min).
Vasto to: Stari Grad (1 weekly, Thurs; 4hr).

Campania

CHAPTER 13

Highlights

* **Museo Archeologico Nazionale** A superb museum with a wealth of Greek and Roman artefacts. See p.864

* **Pizza in Naples** Choose between any number of traditional, family-run restaurants for a sample pizza, crisp and sizzling hot straight from a wood-fired oven. See p.849

* **Miracle of San Gennaro** The liquefaction of the saint's blood in Naples cathedral is an occasion charged with emotion and often accompanied by much festivity. See p.859

* **Pompeii and Herculaneum** These sites afford an unparalleled glimpse into ancient Roman daily life and architecture. See p.874 & 877

* **Cápri** A jewel of an island with stunning scenery and cliff walks. See p.883

* **Ravello** The beautiful medieval town of Ravello is a balcony onto the stunning Amalfi coast. See p.901

* **Paestum** Majestic Greek temples and the colourful tomb paintings. See p.904

13

Campania

The region immediately south of Lazio, **Campania**, marks the real beginning of the Italian south or *mezzogiorno*. It's the part of the south too, perhaps inevitably, that most people see, as it's easily accessible from Rome and home to some of the area's (indeed Italy's) most notable features – Roman sites, spectacular stretches of coast, tiny islands. It's always been a sought-after region, first named by the Romans, who tagged it the *campania felix*, or "happy land" (to distinguish it from the rather dull *campagna* further north), and settled down here in villas and palatial estates that stretched right around the bay. Later, when Naples became the final stop on northerners' Grand Tours, the bay became no less fabled, the relics of its heady Roman period only adding to the charm for most travellers.

You might, of course, find this hard to believe now, and anyone coming in search of the glories of the Bay of Naples is likely to be disappointed. Industry has eaten into the land around the city and the once-grand vistas are often cluttered by cranes and smoke-belching chimneys. But give the area time. **Naples** is the obvious focus, an utterly compelling city and one that dominates the region in every way. At just two-and-a-half hours by train from the capital, there's no excuse for not seeing at least this part of Campania, though of course you need three or four days to absorb the city properly, before embarking on the remarkable attractions surrounding it. The **Golfo di Napoli**, certainly, is dense enough in interest to occupy you for a good week: there are the ancient sites of **Pompeii**, **Herculaneum** and the **Villa Oplontis**, just half an hour away – Italy's best-preserved and most revealing Roman remains; there is the odd, volcanic **Campi Flegrei** area to the north of the city; and of course there are the islands, **Cápri**, **Ischia** and **Prócida** – Cápri swarms with visitors but is so beautiful that a day here is by no means time squandered, while Ischia, which is the largest island and absorbs tourists more readily, is a lively and attractive base from which you can explore the bay by ferry.

Inland Campania is, by contrast, a poor, unknown region for the most part, but the nearby towns of **Cápua** and **Caserta** repay visits and are easily seen on day-trips. Similarly **Benevento**, an old stop on the Roman route to Bríndisi, has its moments, though you might want to make this part of a wider trip through Campania's interior (or on to Puglia), bearing in mind that it's a difficult and not especially rewarding area to travel through. The area **south of Naples** however, has more immediate appeal. **Sorrento**, at the far east end of the bay, is a major package-holiday destination but a cheery and likeable place for that; and the **Amalfi coast**, across the peninsula, is probably Europe's most dramatic stretch of coastline, harbouring some fantastically enticing – if crowded – beach resorts. Further south, the lively port of **Salerno** gives access to the Hellenistic site of **Paestum** and the uncrowded coastline of the **Cilento** just beyond.

Naples

Whatever your real interest in Campania, the chances are that you'll wind up in **NAPLES** – capital of the region and, indeed, of the whole Italian south. It's the kind of city that is laden with visitors' preconceptions, and it rarely disappoints: it is filthy, it is very large and overbearing, it is crime-infested, and it is most definitely like nowhere else in Italy – something the inhabitants will be keener than anyone to tell you. In all these things lies the city's charm. Perhaps the feeling that you're somewhere unique makes it possible to endure the noise and harassment, perhaps it's the feeling that in less than three hours you've travelled from an ordinary part of Europe to somewhere akin to an Arab bazaar. One thing, though, is certain: a couple of days here and you're likely to be as staunch a defender of the place as its most devoted inhabitants. Few cities on earth inspire such fierce loyalties.

In Naples, all the pride and resentment of the Italian south, all the historical differences between the two wildly disparate halves of Italy, are sharply brought into focus. This is the true heart of the *mezzogiorno*, a lawless, petulant city that has its own way of doing things. It's a city of extremes, fiercely Catholic, its

The flavour of **Naples** dominates the whole of Campania. Nowhere else in Italy is street food so much part of the culture. Most importantly, perhaps, Naples is the true home of the **pizza**, rapidly baked in searingly hot wood-fired ovens and running with olive oil. There's no such thing as "Pizza Napoletana" here; in Naples, the crucial one is the *marinara* – not, as you might think, anything to do with seafood, but the basic Neapolitan pizza, topped with just tomato, garlic and a leaf or two of basil, *no* cheese. Street food also comprises fried pizzas topped with a smear of tomato and a square of mozzarella, and *calzone*, a stuffed fried pizza with ham and cheese or vegetables. *Friggiotore* sell other fried food: heavenly *krocche* (potato croquettes), *arancini* (rice balls) and *fiorilli* (courgette flowers in batter).

Naples is also the home of pasta and tomato sauce, made with fresh tomatoes and basil, and laced with garlic; it's a curious aspect of Neapolitan sauces that garlic, onion and parmesan are rarely combined. Aubergines and courgettes turn up endlessly in **pasta sauces**, as does the tomato-**mozzarella** pairing (the regions to the north and east of Naples are both big mozzarella-producing regions), the latter particularly good with *gnocchi*. **Seafood** is excellent all along the coast: clams combine with garlic and oil for superb *spaghetti alle vongole*; mussels are prepared as *zuppa di cozze* (with hot pepper sauce); fresh squid and octopus are ubiquitous. **Pastries** are good, too. Absolutely not to be missed is the *sfogliatella*, a flaky triangular pastry case stuffed with ricotta and candied peel, and the Easter cake, *pastiera*, made with ricotta and softened wheat grain. Further to the south, the marshy plains of the **Cilento** produce fabulous strawberries, artichokes and mozzarella cheese – much of the mozzarella that comes from here is made from pure buffalo milk, unmixed with cow's milk.

The volcanic slopes of Vesuvius are among the most ancient **wine-producing** areas in Italy: Ischia nowadays produces good **white** wine, notably Biancolella, while Cápri's is more everyday. Lacryma Christi, from the slopes of Mount Vesuvius and available in red and white varieties, can be reasonable. The best choices for a Campanian white, however, are Greco di Tufo and Fiano di Avellino; the **red** to go for is Taurasi, a rich wine made from the *aglianico* grape that can command high prices.

streets punctuated by bright neon Madonnas cut into niches, its miraculous cults regulating the lives of the people much as they have always done. Football, too, is something of a religion here, though support is not as fanatical as it used to be since the demise of the club from Italy's *serie* A to B status.

Music, also, has played a key part in the city's identity: there's long been a Naples style, bound up with the city's strange, harsh dialect – and, to some extent, the long-established presence of the US military: American jazz lent a flavour to Neapolitan traditional songs in the Fifties; and the Seventies saw one of Italy's most concentrated musical movements in the urban blues scene of Pino Daniele and the music around the radical Alfa Romeo factory out at Pomigliano. More recently, a distinctive style of Neapolitan rap emerged from the *centri sociali* or "social centres" – groups of left-wing urban activists who challenge the establishment, of which the most famous exponents are 99 Posse.

Some history

There was a settlement here, **Parthenope**, as early as the ninth century BC, but it was superseded by a colony formed by the Greek settlers at nearby Cumae, who established an outpost here in 750 BC, giving it the name Neapolis. It prospered during Greek and later Roman times, escaping the disasters that befell the cities around and eventually declaring itself independent

Ospedale Cardarelli
(Cardarelli Hospital)

Policlinico

TANGENZIALE OVEST DI NAPOLI

Rione
Alto

Montedonzelli

Materdei

VIA PIETRO CASTELLINO

VIA GIUSEPPE ROSSI

PIAZZA
MEDAGLIE
D'ORO

PIAZZA
MAZZINI

Salvatore
Rosa

P. Medaglie d'Oro

VIA E. SUAREZ

VIA

PIAZZA DEGLI
ARTISTI

VIALE MICHELANGELO

Montesanto

Cilea

VIA BERNINI

VIA TITO ANGELINI

VIA GRAMSCI

LUCA GIORDANO

VÓMERO

Funicolare di Montesanto

P. Vanvitelli

PIAZZA
VANVITELLI

Castel
Sant'Elmo

FRANCESCO CILEA

D

VIA BELVEDERE

VIA

Certosa
San Martino

VIA A. FALCONE

Funicolare Centrale

VIA S. STEFANO

Funicolare di Chiaia

CORSO EUROPA

CORSO VITTORIO EMANUELE

TANGENZIALE OVEST DI NAPOLI

Ferrovia Cumana
Stazione Corso
Vitt. Emanuele

Villa
Floridiana

Piazza Amedeo

PIEDIGROTTA

6

CORSO VITTORIO EMANUELE

CHIAIA

7

PIAZZA
AMEDEO

VIA DEI MILLE

VIA G. NICOTERA

VIA M. SCHIPA

VIA FRANCESCO CRISPI

F

VIA FLANGIERI

G

VIA A. D'ISERNIA

Villa
Pignatelli

E

V. S. TERESA A
CHIAIA

V. CAVALLERIZZA

H

VIA CHIAIA

VIA CARLO POERIO

S. Francesco
di Paola

Virgil's
Tomb

PIAZZA
DELLA
REPUBBLICA

Villa
Comunale

RIVIERA DI CHIAIA

i

PIAZZA
DEI MARTIRI

8

Mergellina

PIAZZA
PIEDIGROTTA

Aquarium

PIAZZA
VITTORIA

9

SANTA
LUCIA

VIALE ANTONIO GRAMSCI

J

VIA CARACCIOLO

PIAZZA
SANNAZZARO

10

MERGELLINA

11

VIA PARTENOPE

K

Marina

Castel
dell'Ovo

VIA MERGELLINA

Funicolare di
Mergellina

M

Hydrofoils to Cápri, Ischia & Prócida

S. Paolo Stadium & Posillipo

13

CAMPANIA | Naples

ACCOMMODATION

Ausonia	10
Casanova	2
Crispi	7
Eden	4
Excelsior	11
Ginevra	3
Grand Hotel Parker's	6
Mancini	5
Parteno	9
Villa Capodimonte	1
Youth hostel	8

RESTAURANTS & CAFÉS

Alla Brace	B
Antonio & Antonio	F
Attanasio	A
Avellinese	C
Bersagliera	L
Brandi	G
Da Ciciotto	M
Da Ettore	I
Gorizia	D
Da Pasqualino	K
Remy Gelo	J
Da Tonino	E
Umberto	H

in 763 – which it remained for close on 400 years, until the **Normans** took the city in 1139. The Normans weren't here for long: like the rest of this region, the city soon came under the rule of the Hohenstaufen dynasty, who stayed rather half-heartedly until 1269, when their last king, Conradin, was beheaded in what's now Piazza del Mercato, and the **Angevins** took over the city. With one exception – Robert the Wise, who was a gentle and enlightened ruler and made the city a great centre for the arts – the Angevin kings ruled badly, in the end losing Naples to Alfonso I of Aragon in 1422, thus establishing a **Spanish** connection for the city for the next 300 years. Following the War of the Spanish Succession, Naples was briefly ceded to the Austrians, before being taken, to general rejoicing, by **Charles of Bourbon** in 1734. Charles was a cultivated and judicious monarch, but his dissolute son Ferdinand presided over a shambolic period in the city's history, abandoning it to the republican French. Their "Parthenopean Republic" here was short-lived, and the British reinstalled the Bourbon monarch, carrying out vicious reprisals against the rebels. The instigator of these reprisals was Admiral Nelson – fresh from his victory at the Battle of the Nile – who was famously having an affair with Lady Hamilton, the wife of the British ambassador to Naples. Under continuing Bourbon rule, or more accurately misrule, the city became one of the most populated in Europe, and one of the most iniquitous, setting a trend which still holds good today. For the rest of Europe, Naples was the requisite final stop on the **Grand Tour**, a position it enjoyed not so much for its proximity to the major classical sites as for the ready availability of sex. The city was for a long time the prostitution capital of the Continent, and its reputation drew people from far and wide, giving new meaning (in the days when syphilis was rife) to the phrase "see Naples and die".

More recently, Naples and its surrounding area have been the recipient of much of the money that has poured into the south under the **Cassa per il Mezzogiorno** scheme, and its industry is spreading, if not exactly booming. But the real power in the area is still in the hands of organized crime or the **Camorra**: much of the coastline west of the city – to Bagnoli – was built by Camorra money, and, although it's not at all publicized, little happens that matters here without the nod of the larger families. Not surprisingly, much government money has found its way into their hands too, with the result that there's been little real improvement in the living standards of the average Neapolitan: a very high percentage remain unemployed, and a disgraceful number still inhabit the typically Neapolitan one-room *bassi* – slums really, letting in no light and housing many in appallingly overcrowded conditions. In the late 1970s there was a cholera outbreak in part of the city, and until recently it was thought that the same thing could happen again. However, **Antonio Bassolino**, mayor of the city from 1993 until 2000 and currently president of Campania, did much to promote Naples and its attractions. Bassolino was confident that supporting Naples' cultural strengths would boost local pride. Scores of neglected churches, museums and palaces were restored and now have extended opening times, particularly in the month of May, in a festival called Maggio dei Monumenti. There's been a burst of creative activity from local filmmakers, songwriters, artists and playwrights, and saying that you are from Naples gives you instant credibility in Rome, Milan and other northern cities.

From time to time, however, Mafia violence raises its ugly head, as in 2000 when an alliance between the Camorra families concocted by godmother Maria Licciardi, known as "La Madrina", resulted in the death of sixty people in a series of tit-for-tat killings. Licciardi was arrested in June 2001, since when violent activity has quietened down.

Arrival, information and city transport

Naples' Capodichino **airport** (℡081.789.6259, flight enquiries ℡848.888.777, ⓦwww.gesac.it) is around 7km north of the city centre. It is connected with Piazza Garibaldi (the stop is in front of the station at the McDonald's corner) by bus #3S approximately every fifteen minutes, and the journey takes twenty to thirty minutes; buy tickets (€0.77) from the *tabacchi* in the departures hall. There is also an official airport bus, *Alibus*, operated by ANM (℡081.763.2177), which runs to Piazza Garibaldi every thirty minutes between 6.30am and 11.30pm (6am–midnight in the opposite direction), although it isn't very much quicker and is double the price (€2); however, it does have the advantage of continuing to the Piazza Municipio and Stazione Marittima, from where hydrofoils depart for the islands. Taxis, too, tend to take almost as long as buses to reach the centre, and cost up to €20; if you do use one, make sure the meter is switched on when you get in (see overleaf for more on taxis).

By train, you're most likely to arrive at Napoli Centrale, situated on the edge of the city centre at one end of Piazza Garibaldi, at the main hub of city (and suburban) transport services; there's a **left luggage** office here (open 24hr). Some trains also pull into Stazione Mergellina, on the opposite side of the city centre, which is connected with Piazza Garibaldi by the underground *metropolitana*. For train enquiries phone ℡848.888.088 or go to the information booths at Napoli Centrale and be prepared to queue (daily 7am–9pm).

City and suburban **buses** also stop on Piazza Garibaldi, though you'll need to check the stops carefully as they are not well signed. CTP (℡081.700.1111) run buses to Caserta, FABN (℡800.127.157) to Benevento and Trasporti Irpinia buses (℡081.553.4677) to Avellino from here, but the main company, SITA (℡081.552.2176, ⓦwww.sita-on-line.it), which connects with Pompeii, Sorrento, the Amalfi coast and Salerno, leaves from Via G. Ferraris, just south of the Stazione Centrale and from their main office at Via Pisanelli, just off Piazza Municipio.

Information

The most convenient of Naples' **tourist offices** is in the Stazione Centrale (Mon–Sat 8am–8pm, Sun 9am–2pm; ℡081.268.779); its opening times are a little unreliable and the queues can be long and slow-moving, but it's a good place to pick up a free city **map** and an English-language copy of the monthly *Qui Napoli*, a useful reference on the city and an indicator of **what's on**; the more youth-oriented *Pagine dell'Ozio* also appears monthly (€0.95). In the centre, you'll find a tourist office on Piazza del Gesù Nuovo (Mon–Sat 9am–8pm, Sun 9am–3pm; ℡081.551.2701) and another at Piazza dei Martiri 58 (Mon–Fri 8.30am–3.30pm; ℡081.410.7211).

City transport

The only way to really **get around** Naples and stay sane is to **walk**. Driving can be a nightmare, and to negotiate the narrow streets, hectic squares and racetrack boulevards on a moped or scooter takes years of training. In any case, *not* to walk would mean you'd miss a lot – Naples is the kind of place best appreciated from street level.

For longer journeys – and Naples is a big, spread-out city – there are a number of alternatives, both for the city itself and the bay as a whole. **Public transport** comes under the care of Azienda Napoletana Mobilità (ANM). Its city **buses** are efficient, if crowded and slow, and are much the best way of making short hops across the city centre. The bus system is supplemented by

#R2 Piazza Garibaldi–Corso Umberto–Via Sanfelice–Via Medina–Via Emanuele III–Via San Carlo–Piazza Trieste e Trento–Piazza Municipio–Via Medina–Via Sanfelice–Corso Umberto–Piazza Garibaldi
#R3 Piazza Trieste e Trento–Piazza Municipio–Riviera di Chiaia–Mergellina
#140 Via Santa Lucia–Via Mergellina–Via Posillipo Piazza Garibaldi–Pozzuoli
#152 Piazza Garibaldi–Piazza Municipio–Piazza Vittoria–Mergellina–Pozzuoli
#401 (night bus) Piazza Garibaldi–Riviera di Chiaia–Mergellina–Fuorigrotta–Pozzuoli
#435D/435S (night bus) Circular route from Stazione Centrale via Via Toledo and Piazza Trieste e Trento
For details on the frequency of the rail lines, see "Travel details", p.907.

the **metropolitana**, a small-scale underground network that crosses the city centre, stopping at about four places between Piazza Garibaldi and Mergellina, and runs eventually out to Pozzuoli and Solfatara in about half an hour; the new metro station at Piazza Dante has a useful stop at the Museo Nazionale Archeologico. In addition, three **funiculars** scale the hill of the Vómero: one, the Funicolare di Chiaia, from Piazza Amedeo; another, the Funicolare Centrale, from the station at the bottom of Via Mattia, just off Via Toledo; and a third, the Funicolare di Montesanto, from the station on Piazza Montesanto. Another, the Funicolare di Mergellina, runs up the hill above Mergellina from Via Mergellina. *Giranapoli* **tickets** for all ANM modes of transport cost a flat €0.77 (valid ninety minutes) and are available in advance from *tabacchi*, stations, or the transport booth on Piazza Garibaldi; an all-day ticket costs €2.32. Any combination of journeys by bus, tram, metro, funicular, Ferrovia Cumana and Circumflegrea lines is allowed.

If you need to take a **taxi** – and you should realize that they can be interminably slow – make sure the driver switches on the meter when you start (they often don't); fares start at €2.58 for the initial journey – minimum fare €4.13. Note that journeys to and from the airport incur an extra charge of €2.58; trips after 10pm or before 7am cost an extra €2.07; and those on public holidays an extra €1.55; all of which gives plenty of scope for confusion, and even resident Neapolitans are wary of the stunts taxi drivers pull to get a higher fare. There are taxi ranks at the train station, on Piazza Dante and Piazza Trieste e Trento, or phone ☏081.556.4444 or 081.556.0202.

For solely **out-of-town trips** – around the bay in either direction – there are three more rail systems. The **Circumvesuviana** runs from its station on Corso Garibaldi right round the Bay of Naples about every thirty minutes, stopping everywhere, as far south as Sorrento, which it reaches in about an hour. The **Ferrovia Cumana** operates every ten minutes from its terminus station in Piazza Montesanto west to Pozzuoli and Báia. And the **Circumflegrea** line runs every twenty minutes, again from Piazza Montesanto, west to Cuma. Tickets are available at the stations, and are very reasonable.

Accommodation

Accommodation **prices** in Naples may come as a refreshing change after the north of Italy, but they're still not cheap, and the city being the kind of place it is you need to choose carefully from among the cheaper dives. A good many of these are conveniently situated around Piazza Garibaldi, spitting distance from the train station and not badly placed for the rest of town, but rather insalubrious and noisy; others can be found in the lively and more atmospheric group on the far side of the *centro storico*, near the university. The station tourist office may point you to something good (it's certainly worth enquiring); if not, just follow the listings below – and don't, whatever you do, go with one of the touts hanging around the station. It's unlikely you'll be getting into anything dangerous but it *is* a possibility and in any case the room probably won't be up to much and you'll be charged commission, too. If you can, try to **book in advance**, as the city does get crowded.

Hotels

Ausonia Via Caracciolo 11 ☎081.682.278, ℱ081.664.536. A two-star with a nautical theme, neatly placed in Mergellina, next to the stop for hydrofoils to the islands. Bus #R3 or #152. **④**

Bella Capri Via Melisurgo 4 ☎081.552.9494, ℱ081.552.9265, ⓦwww.bellacapri.it. Right opposite the ferry port and airport bus stop, this small and welcoming sixth-floor *pensione* has a great view of the bay and includes breakfast in the rate. Ten percent discount with this book. **④**

Casanova Via Venezia 2 ☎081.268.287, ℱ081.269.792. Best of the station-area budget options, this creeper-clad hotel is quiet, run by an affable team, has pleasant rooms and a communal roof terrace. **②**

Crispi Via Francesco Crispi 104 ☎ & ℱ081.668.048, ⓔlovenap@tin.it. Well-established one-star quite close to the Piazza Amedeo metropolitana stop. **⑤**

Duomo Via Duomo 228 ☎ & ℱ081.265.988. Quiet and friendly place near the cathedral, prettily decorated and with vivid blue bathrooms. No credit cards. **③**

Eden Corso Novara 9 ☎081.285.344, ℱ081.285.690. One of the more comfortable station-area choices, if rather noisy. Good rates for carriers of this book. **②**

Excelsior Via Partenope 48 ☎081.764.0111, ℱ081.764.9743, ⓦwww.excelsior.it. An extremely plush upmarket hotel, wonderfully sited on the waterfront opposite the Castel dell'Ovo. **⑨**

Ginevra Via Genova 116 ☎081.554.1757, ℱ081.283.210, ⓦwww.mds.it/ginevra. Welcoming place very close to the station that has modern rooms looking onto a large plant-filled courtyard. Discount with this book if you're paying cash. **③**

Grand Hotel Parker's Corso Vittorio Emanuele 135 ☎081.761.2474, ℱ081.663.527,

ⓦwww.thecharminghotels.com. This upmarket and extremely comfortable hotel claims to be the oldest in Naples, and has hosted Oscar Wilde and Virgina Woolf, as well as King Vittorio Emanuele himself. With a high vantage-point over the city, the views from the dining room over the bay and east to Vesuvius are unparalleled. **⑨**

Napolit'amo Via Toledo 148 ☎ & ℱ081.552.3626, ⓦwww.napolitamo.it. A restored palace which offers spacious and elegant rooms in the pedestrianized part of Via Toledo. Staff are very courteous and breakfast is included. Discount with this book. **④**

Le Orchidee Corso Umberto 7 ☎081.551.0721, ℱ081.251.4088. A good central location, not far from the ferry port and just a short bus ride from Stazione Centrale. Large and elegantly furnished rooms, all with private bath. **⑤**

Parteno Via Partenope 1 ☎081.245.2095, ℱ081.247.1303, ⓦwww.parteno.it. Seven individually designed and beautifully furnished rooms in an eighteenth-century building on the waterfront. Great breakfasts. **⑦**

Soggiorno Imperia Piazza Luigi Miraglia 386 ☎ & ℱ081.459.347, ⓔmalgorzatagajo@hotmail.com. Friendly hotel with English-speaking management and a marvellous location in the heart of old Naples, a short walk from Piazza Dante. Nice rooms, with kitchen facilities and Internet access as well; the only drawback is its location at the top of five arduous flights of stairs. No credit cards. **②**

Villa Capodimonte Via Moiariello 66 ☎081.459.000, ℱ081.299.344. Ideally sited for seeing the Palazzo Reale di Capodimonte, this modern option is very comfortable, and attractively located. It sits above the Sanità district (see p.866), which can be dangerous. **⑧**

Hostels and campsites

The large official **youth hostel**, *Ostello Mergellina*, Salita della Grotta 23 (€16, including breakfast; ☎081.761.2346, ℱ081.761.2391), is in a nice location, if somewhat removed from the life of the city centre, and offers two-, four- and six-bedded rooms. The drawbacks are a curfew at 12.30am and a three-day maximum stay during July and August. It's conveniently located right next to the Mergellina *metropolitana* station. If you prefer something more central, opt for the *Hostel/Pensione Mancini* (℡081.553.6731, ℻081.554.6675, ⓦwww .hostelpensionemancini.com) at Via Mancini 33, just west of Piazza Garibaldi. There's not a lot of space, but the English-speaking management is attentive, and there are laundry and Internet facilities. Dorm beds (no bunks) cost €16, and doubles are available (no credit cards; ❷) at a discount to carriers of this book.

There are a number of **campsites** within a feasible distance of Naples. The closest is the *Vulcano Solfatara* site in Pozzuoli (see p.872) at Via Solfatara 47 (℡081.526.7413; April–Oct); take the *metropolitana* to Pozzuoli and walk ten minutes up the hill. When this is closed, you're probably best off going to one of the other sites around the bay – perhaps at Pompeii (see p.880), or, rather nicer, Sorrento (p.882), neither of which is more than an hour out from the city.

The City

Naples is a surprisingly large city, and a sprawling one, with a centre that has many different focuses. The area between Piazza Garibaldi and Via Toledo, roughly corresponding to the old Roman Neapolis (much of which is still unexcavated below the ground), makes up the old part of the city – the **centro storico** – the main streets still following the path of the old Roman roads. This is much the liveliest and most teeming part of town, an open-air kasbah of hawking, yelling humanity that makes up in energy what it lacks in grace. Buildings rise high on either side of the narrow, crowded streets, cobwebbed with washing; there's little light, not even much sense of the rest of the city outside – certainly not of the proximity of the sea.

But the insularity of the *centro storico* is deceptive, and in reality there's another, quite different side to Naples, one that's much more like the sunwashed Bay of Naples murals you've seen in cheap restaurants back home. **Via Toledo**, the main street of the city, edges the old centre from the **Palazzo Reale** up to the **Museo Nazionale Archeologico** and the heights of **Capodimonte**; to the left rises the **Vómero**, with its fancy housing and museums, and the smug neighbourhood of **Chiaia**, beyond which lies the long green boulevard of **Riviera de Chiara**, stretching around to the districts of **Mergellina** and **Posillipo**: all neighbourhoods that exert quite a different kind of pull – that of an airy waterfront city, with views, seafood eaten *al fresco* and peace and quiet.

Piazza Garibaldi to Via Toledo: the centro storico

However you actually get to Naples, there's a good chance that the first place you'll see is **Piazza Garibaldi**, a long, wide square crisscrossed by traffic lanes

---

Napoli artecard

If you're considering doing the rounds of the musems, it's worth investing in a **Napoli artecard** (℡800.600.601, ⓦwww.napoliartecard.com; €13, €8 for 18–25 year-olds), which gives you free admission to two museums and a fifty per cent reduction to four others over a period of sixty hours, as well as free travel on public transport. You can buy it at any of the participating museums or from the airport, stations and newsagents. The museums covered by the ticket are the Museo Nazionale Archeologico, Museo Nazionale di Capodimonte, Museo Nazionale di San Martino, Castel Sant'Elmo, Museo Civico di Castel Nuovo and the Palazzo Reale.

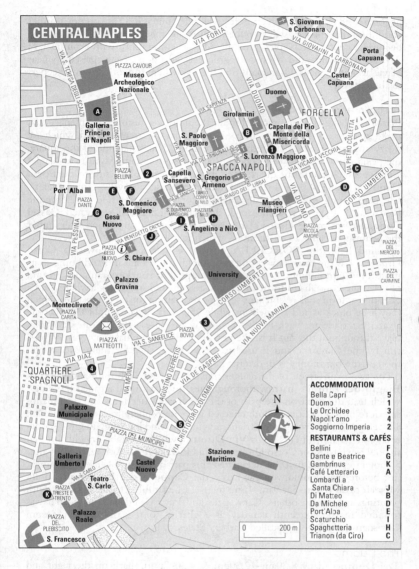

that cuts into the city centre from the modern train station. It's the city's transport hub – most of the city buses leave from here, as do the *metropolitana* and Circumvesuviana lines – and one of its most hectic junctions; indeed it's Piazza Garibaldi, perhaps more so than any other part of the city, that puts people off Naples. The buildings aren't particularly distinguished and you're likely to be accosted on all sides by street hawkers selling a dubious array of pirate cassettes, cigarettes, baseball caps and sunglasses; do not on any account be tempted by the digital cameras or mobile phones on offer as you're more than likely to be sold an empty box. You need to have all your wits about you to successfully negotiate the traffic, which comes from all sides, but as long as you don't dither you'll find that the cars will stop for you. Of late, the area around here has also become a centre for Naples' growing African community, with a number of African restaurants and Moroccan groceries, and don't be surprised to hear Slavic accents – many Ukrainians find their way here to work as housekeepers in the city.

Forcella and around

Piazza Garibaldi is good preparation for the noise, confusion, even menace that make up the rest of the city centre – especially in the streets around, which are sleazy and best avoided at night if you're alone. The other side of the square, the *centro storico* spreads west as far as Via Toledo – the tangled heart of Naples and its most characteristic quarter. Off the right corner of the square, the **Porta Capuana** is one of several relics from the Aragonese city walls, a sturdy defensive gate dating from 1490, delicately decorated on one side in Florentine Renaissance style. Across the road, the white and much renovated **Castel Capuano** was the residence of the Norman king William I, and later, under the Spanish, became a courthouse – which it still is.

Behind here, the **FORCELLA** quarter, which spreads down to Corso Umberto I, is the main city-centre stronghold of the Camorra and home to its most important families. It's also the city's open-air **market**, stamping-ground of yet more contraband tobacco dealers, cassette and sunglasses hawkers, and a quantity of food stalls – chickens sit in boxes waiting for the chop, after which they'll be plucked and cleaned up while you wait. As you might fast become aware, the trade in black-market ciggies is an old-established one and takes place throughout the city. It is, like just about every criminal activity in Naples, run by the Camorra, and it used to be a high earner for them. Nowadays, though, the big money is in drugs.

The two main streets of the *centro storico* are **Via dei Tribunali** and **Via San Biagio dei Librai** – narrow thoroughfares, lined with old arcaded buildings, which lead due west on the path of the decumanus maximus and decumanus inferiore of Roman times, both charged with atmosphere throughout the day, a maelstrom of hurrying pedestrians, revving cars and buzzing, dodging scooters. Via dei Tribunali cuts up to **Via Duomo**, which ploughs straight through the old town to meet Corso Umberto I and Piazza Nicola Amore, laid out after a cholera epidemic in 1884 decimated this part of the city. On Via Tribunali, just before Via Duomo, you can't miss the **Cappella del Pio Monte della Misericorda** (Mon–Sat 9am–1pm; free) – a beautiful octagonal chapel, with paintings by, among others, Caravaggio and Luca Giordano. The chapel was founded in the sixteenth century as a charity to raise money to ransom Christians held in the so-called Barbary States.

The Duomo

The **Duomo** (daily 8.30am–12.30pm & 4.30–7pm), sharp on the right and tucked away unassumingly from the main street, is a Gothic building from the early thirteenth century (though with a late nineteenth-century neo-Gothic facade) dedicated to the patron saint of the city, San Gennaro. The church – and saint – are key reference points for Neapolitans: San Gennaro was martyred at Pozzuoli, just outside Naples, in 305 AD under the purges of Diocletian. Tradition has it that, when his body was transferred here, two phials of his blood liquefied in the bishop's hands, since which time the "miracle" has continued to repeat itself no less than three times a year – on the first Saturday in May (when a procession leads from the church of Santa Chiara to the cathedral) and on

The miracle of San Gennaro

If you're in Naples at the right time it's possible to attend the service to witness the **liquefaction of San Gennaro's blood**, but you must be sure to arrive at the cathedral early. The Mass starts at 9am, and queues begin to form two hours before that; arrive much after 7am and there's a chance you won't get in. Once the line of Carabinieri have opened up the church everyone will make a dash for the front; for a good view of the proceedings you'll have to join them – and pushing and shoving is, incidentally, very much part of the procedure. The atmosphere in the church throughout the service is a boisterous one. The preliminary Mass goes on for some time, the chancel of the church ringed by armed policemen and flanked by a determined press and photographic corps, until a procession leads out of the saint's chapel holding the (still solid) phial of the blood aloft, to much applause and neck-craning, and cries of "Viva San Gennaro". After ten minutes or so of emotional imprecations the reliquary is taken down from its holder and inspected – at which point, hopefully, it is declared to tumultuous applause and cheering that the saint's blood is indeed now liquid, and the phial is shaken to prove the point. Afterwards the atmosphere is a festive one, stallholders setting up outside the church and the devout queuing up to kiss the phial containing the liquefied blood – a process that goes on for a week.

September 19 and December 16. There is still much superstition surrounding this event: San Gennaro is seen as the saviour and protector of Naples, and if the blood refuses to liquefy – which luckily is rare – disaster is supposed to befall the city, and many still wait with bated breath to see if the miracle has occurred. Interestingly, one of the few occasions in recent times that Gennaro's blood hasn't turned was in 1944, an event followed by Vesuvius's last eruption. The last times were in 1980, the year of the earthquake, and in 1988, the day after which Naples lost an important football match to their rivals, Milan.

The miraculous liquefaction takes place during a special Mass in full view of the congregation – a service it's perfectly possible to attend (see box above), though the church authorities have yet to allow any close scientific examination of the blood or the "miraculous" process. Whatever the truth of the miracle, there's no question it's still a significant event in the Neapolitan calendar, and one of the more bizarre of the city's institutions.

The first chapel on the right as you walk into the cathedral is dedicated to San Gennaro and holds the precious phials of the saint's blood and his skull in a silver bust-reliquary from 1305. On the other side of the church, the basilica of **Santa Restituta** is almost a church in its own right, officially the oldest structure in Naples, erected by Constantine in 324 and supported by columns that were taken from a temple to Apollo on this site. The **Baptistry**, too (Mon–Sat 9am–noon & 4.30–7pm, Sun 9am–noon; €3), contains relics from very early Christian times, including a late fifth-century structure preserving fragments of contemporary mosaics and a font believed to have been taken from a temple to Dionysus. Downstairs, the **crypt** (same ticket as for the baptistry) of San Gennaro is one of the finest examples of Renaissance art in Naples, founded by Cardinal Carafa and holding the tombs of both San Gennaro and Pope Innocent IV.

Spaccanapoli

Across Via Duomo, Via Tribunali continues on past **Piazza Girolamini**, on which a plaque marks the house where, in 1668, Giambattista Vico was born – now the home of a well-known Camorra family. Vico was a late-Renaissance

Neapolitan philosopher who advanced theories of cyclical history that were far ahead of their time and still echo through twentieth-century thinking: James Joyce's *Finnegans Wake* was based on his writings. Vico lived all his life in this district and was buried in the church of **Girolamini** (entrance on Via Duomo). Next door, you can look in on the impressive **Chiostro dei Girolamini**, built around a courtyard containing orange and medlar trees, and the **Quadreria dei Girolamini** (Mon–Sat 9.30am–1pm; free), a gallery containing paintings by Ribera, Solimena and Dürer, among many others.

Further down Via Tribunali, on the left, the church of **San Lorenzo Maggiore** is a light, spacious Gothic church, unspoiled by later additions and with a soaring Gothic ambulatory at its apse – unusual in Italy, even more so in Naples, where garishly embellished church interiors are the order of the day. It's a mainly thirteenth- and fourteenth-century building, though with a much later facade, built during the reign of the Angevin king Robert the Wise on the site of a Roman basilica – remains of which are in the cloisters. In a way it was at the centre of the golden age that Naples enjoyed under Robert, the focus of its cultural activity. Petrarch stayed for a while in the adjacent convent, and Boccaccio is said to have met the model for his Fiammetta, believed to be Robert's daughter, during Mass here in 1334.

Excavations beneath the church (April–Oct Mon–Sat 9am–5pm, Sun 9am–1pm; Nov–March Mon–Sat 9am–1pm & 3–5pm, Sun 9am–1pm; €4) have revealed what was once the Roman forum, and before that, the Greek agora. You can walk along the old Roman pavement, passing a barrel-vaulted bakery, a laundry and an area of sloping stone banquettes that were warmed underneath by a fire, where it is thought that people reclined and debated the great issues of the day. What was likely to have been the town's treasury shows a remarkable resemblance to a contemporary bank, with visitors having to negotiate a security-conscious double doorway before reaching the main area for business. The great tufa foundations of the Roman forum were built over the earlier Greek agora; a scale model shows how the latter was laid out, with the circular tholos, where some goods were sold, at its centre. It's a rare chance to see exactly how the layers of the city were built up over the centuries, and to get some idea of how Naples must have looked back in the fifth century BC.

You're now in the city's busiest and most architecturally rich quarter, the so-called **Spaccanapoli** or "split-Naples" that's the real heart of the old city. Cut down to its other main axis, **Via San Biagio dei Librai**, by way of **Via San Gregorio Armeno**, one of the old city's most picturesque streets, lined with places specializing in the making of *presepi* or Christmas cribs (see box below) – the last courtyard on the left is a good place to see one of them in action if you're here at the right time of year.

Almost opposite is the arched portal of the church of **San Gregorio Armeno** (daily 8.30am–noon & 5–7pm), a sumptuous Baroque edifice with frescoes by the late seventeenth-century Neapolitan artist Luca Giordano, not to mention two stupendously ornate gilded organs, one on each side of the nave. Up above the south aisle, you'll notice a series of grilles through which the Benedictine nuns of the **Chiostro di San Gregorio Armeno** next door would view the services. You can visit the courtyard of the convent (entrance up the street and on the left; daily 9.30–11.30am; free), which is a wonderfully peaceful haven from the noise outside, planted with limes and busy with nuns quietly going about their duties.

There's more work by Giordano back on Via Duomo, at no. 288 in the **Museo Filangieri**, which unfortunately is closed indefinitely for restoration; contact the tourist office for updates.

Heading west down Via San Biagio leads to the **Largo di Corpo di Nilo**, where you'll find a Roman statue of a reclining old man, sculpted in Nero's time; it's a representation of the Nile and has a habit, it's claimed, of whispering to women as they walk by. The church nearby, **Sant'Angelo a Nilo**, has sculptures by Michelozzo and Donatello, the first Renaissance work to be seen in Naples. Further on, **Piazza San Domenico Maggiore** is marked by the **Guglia di San Domenico** – one of the whimsical Baroque obelisks that were originally put up after times of plague or disease, built in 1737. The **church** (daily 8am–noon & 4.30–7pm) of the same name flanks the north side of the square, an originally – though much messed about – Gothic building from 1289, one of whose chapels holds a miraculous painting of the *Crucifixion* which is said to have spoken to St Thomas Aquinas during his time at the adjacent monastery.

North of here, Via de Sanctis leads off right to one of the city's odder monuments, the **Capella Sansevero** (Mon & Wed–Sat 10am–7pm, closes 5pm in winter, Sun 10am–1.30pm; €5), the tomb-chapel of the di Sangro family, decorated by the sculptor Giuseppe Sammartino in the mid-eighteenth century. The decoration, at least, is extraordinary, the centrepiece a carving of a dead Christ, laid out flat and covered with a veil of stark and remarkable realism, not least because it was carved out of a single piece of marble. Even more accomplished is the veiled figure of *Modesty* on the left, and, on the right, its twin *Disillusionment*, in the form of a woeful figure struggling with the marble netting of his own disenchantment. Look, too, at the effusive *Deposition* on the high altar and the memorial above the doorway, which shows one Cecco di Sangro climbing out of his tomb, sword in hand. You might also want to descend downstairs. The man responsible for the chapel, Prince Raimondo, was a well-known eighteenth-century alchemist, and down here are the results of some of his experiments: bodies of an upright man and woman, behind glass, their capillaries and most of their organs preserved by a mysterious liquid developed by the prince – who, incidentally, was excommunicated by the pope for such practices. Even now the black entanglements make for a gruesome sight.

Continuing west, Via San Biagio becomes Via San Benedetto Croce, named after the twentieth-century philosopher who spent much of his life in this neighbourhood, living in the palace at no. 12. A little way down, the street broadens out at Piazza del Gesù Nuovo, centring on another ornate **Guglia**, much larger than the San Domenico one and dating from 1750. On the right, the **Gesù Nuovo** (daily 8am–1pm & 4–7pm) church is most notable for its lava-stone facade, originally part of a fifteenth-century palace which stood here, prickled with pyramids that give it an impregnable, prison-like air. The inside is as gaudy as you might expect, in part decorated by the Neapolitan-Spanish painter Ribera.

Facing the Gesù church, the church of **Santa Chiara** is quite different, a Provençal-Gothic structure built in 1328 that was completely gutted during the last war and rebuilt with a bare Gothic austerity that's pleasing after the excesses opposite. There's not very much to see inside, only the tombs of the Angevin monarchs in the last chapel on the right, including Robert the Wise at the altar, showing the king in a monk's habit. But the attached convent, established by Robert's wife, Sancia, has a **cloister** (entrance to the left of the church: Mon–Fri 9.30am–1pm & 3.30–5.30pm, Sat & Sun 9.30am–1pm) that is truly one of the gems of the city, a shady haven lushly planted, and furnished with benches and low walls covered with colourful majolica tiles depicting bucolic scenes of life outside.

Corso Umberto I, Piazza Municipio and the Palazzo Reale

Off the far left corner of Piazza Garibaldi, **Via Garibaldi** runs down to the sea, past the main Circumvesuviana terminal and, on the right, the **Porta Nolana**, a solid-looking Aragonese gateway that signals the entrance to Naples' main fish market – a grouping of streets lined with a wonderful array of stalls piled high with wriggling displays of fish and seafood. Behind, towards the water, the church of **Santa Maria del Carmine** dates back to the thirteenth century and is traditionally the church of the poor in Naples, particularly fishermen and mariners – the main port area is close by. Axel Munthe, the Swedish writer and resident of Cápri, used to sleep here after tending to victims of the 1884 cholera outbreak.

Just west, the still war-damaged **Piazza del Mercato** was for centuries home to the city's scaffold, and is a bleak, dusty square even now. There's little to detain you in this part of town, and you may as well cut back up to **Corso Umberto I**, which spears through the old part of the city, a long straight journey from the seedy gatherings of prostitutes and kerb-crawlers at its Piazza Garibaldi end, past many of the city's more mainstream shops, to the symmetrical **Piazza Bovio** and its elegant seventeenth-century Fontana del Nettuno.

From Piazza Bovio it's a short walk down to **Piazza del Municipio**, a busy traffic junction that stretches from the ferry terminal on the water up to the Palazzo Municipale at the top, dominated by the brooding hulk of the **Castel Nuovo** opposite – the "Maschio Angioino" – erected in 1282 by the Angevins and later converted as the royal residence of the Aragon monarchs. The entrance incorporates a triumphal arch from 1454 that commemorates the taking of the city by Alfonso I, the first Aragon ruler, and shows details of his triumph topped by a rousing statue of St Michael. These days the castle is mainly taken up by the offices of the Naples and Campania councils, but part is given over to the **Museo Civico** (Mon–Sat 9am–7pm; €5.16), comprising a rather dull collection of fourteenth- and fifteenth-century frescoes and sculpture in the chapel and an array of silver and bronze objects.

Just beyond the castle, on the left, the **Teatro San Carlo** is an oddly unimpressive building from the outside; inside, however, you can see why this theatre was the envy of Europe when it opened in 1737 in time for Charles of Bourbon's birthday, for whom it was built. Destroyed by fire in 1816 and rebuilt, it's still the largest opera house in Italy and one of the most distinguished in the world. Opposite, the **Galleria Umberto I** has fared less well over the years, its high arcades, erected in 1887, comparatively empty of the teeming life that characterizes the rest of Naples, and in the evening even something of a danger spot.

Come out of the Galleria and you're on **Piazza Trieste e Trento**, more a roundabout than a piazza, whose life you can watch while sipping a pricey drink on the terrace of the sleek **Caffè Gambrinus**. To the left, **Piazza del Plebiscito** is another attempt at civic grandeur, with a curve of columns modelled on Bernini's piazza for Saint Peter's in Rome and a favourite place to stroll of an evening. Art features here have included a monumental pyramid of salt by Mimmo Paladino, a mountain of ancient furniture, armoires and kitchen tables by Jannis Kounellis and low-key *son et lumière* events. The church of **San Francesco di Paola** is floodlit at night, when it is at its most impressive. At other times its attempts at classical majesty (it's a copy of the Pantheon in Rome) only really work once you're standing under its enormous dome.

Opposite, the **Palazzo Reale** (Thurs–Tues 9am–8pm; last entry 7pm; €4) manages better than most of the buildings around here to retain some semblance of its former glories, though it's a bland, derivative building for the most part and even a bit of a fake, thrown up hurriedly in 1602 to accommodate Philip III on a visit here and never actually occupied by a monarch long-term. Indeed it's more of a monument to monarchies than monarchs, with the various dynasties that ruled Naples by proxy for so long represented in the niches of the facade, from Roger the Norman to Vittorio Emanuele II, taking in among others Alfonso I and a slightly comic Murat on the way. Upstairs, the palace's first-floor rooms are decorated with fine Baroque excesses of gilded furniture, trompe l'oeil ceilings, great overbearing tapestries and lots and lots of undistinguished seventeenth- and eighteenth-century paintings. Best bits are the chapel, on the far side of the central square (you may have to ask someone to open this for you), with its finely worked altarpiece; the little theatre – the first room on the right – which is refreshingly restrained after the rest of the palace; and the terrace, which gives good views over the port and the forbidding Castel Nuovo. Look also at the original bronze doors of the palace at the bottom of the dwarfing main staircase, cast in 1468 and showing scenes from Ferdinand of Aragon's struggle against the local barons. The cannonball wedged in the bottom left-hand panel dates from a naval battle between the French and the Genoese that took place while the former were pillaging the doors from the palace.

Just south of Piazza del Plebiscito, Via Santa Lucia curves around towards the sea, the main artery of the **SANTA LUCIA** district – for years the city's most famed and characteristic neighbourhood, site of a lively fish market and source of most of the *O Sole Mio*-type clichés about Naples you've ever heard. It's a much less neighbourly place now, home to most of the city's poshest hotels on the streets around and along the seafront Via Partenope, though one or two decent restaurants make it a better-than-average place to come and eat. Down on the waterfront, the grey mass of the **Castel dell'Ovo** or "egg-castle" (Mon–Sat 9am–6pm, Sun 9am–2pm; free) takes its name from the whimsical legend that it was built over an egg placed here by Virgil in Roman times: it is believed that if the egg breaks, Naples will fall. Actually it was built by the Hohenstaufen king Frederick II and extended by the Angevins. You can walk over the short causeway that connects its small island to the mainland and eat at one of the surrounding restaurants – which make an atmospheric if not always culinarily memorable place to spend the evening; *Bersagliera* on the landward side has great seafood and is the best option (see p.869).

From Piazza Trieste e Trento to Capodimonte

Piazza Trieste e Trento marks the beginning of the city's main shopping street, **Via Toledo** – or, to give it its official name, Via Roma – which leads north in a dead straight line, climbing the hill up to the national archeological museum and separating two very different parts of Naples. To its right, across as far as Piazza del Gesù Nuovo, the streets and buildings are modern and spacious, centring on the unmistakable mass of the Fascist-era central **Post Office**. The streets to the left, on the other hand, scaling the footslopes of the Vómero, are some of the city's most narrow and crowded, a grid of alleys that was laid out to house Spanish troops during the seventeenth century and hence now known as the **Quartiere Spagnoli**. It's an enticing area, at least for visitors, in that it's what you expect to find when you come to Naples, with the buildings so close together as to barely admit any sunlight. But it's as poor a part of Italy as you'll find, home to the notorious Neapolitan *bassi* – one-room windowless dwellings that open directly onto the street – and as such a national disgrace.

Further up Via Toledo, just north of Piazza Carità on the edge of the old part of the city, the church of **Monteoliveto** (Tues–Sat 8.30am–12.30pm) was rebuilt after a sound wartime bombing, but it holds some of the city's finest Renaissance art, including a sacristy frescoed by Vasari, a rather startling almost life-size pietà of eight figures by Guido Mazzoni (the faces are said to be portraits) and two sculptural works by Antonio Rossellino – a nativity scene and the tomb of Mary of Aragon, daughter of Ferdinand I.

Continuing on up the hill, you come to **Piazza Dante**, another Neapolitan square that looks as if it has seen better days, designed by Luigi Vanvitelli during the eighteenth century and cutting an elegant semi-circle off to the right of the main road that focuses on a statue of the poet. There are a couple of restaurants here, and it's a turnaround point for buses, but otherwise – unless you want to take a right through the seventeenth-century **Port'Alba** into Piazza Bellini and the old part of the city – you may as well push on up the street to the archeological museum, housed in a grandiose, late-sixteenth-century army barracks on the corner of Piazza Cavour.

The Museo Archeologico Nazionale

Naples isn't really a city of museums – there's more on the streets that's worth observing on the whole, and most displays of interest are kept *in situ* in churches, palaces and the like. However, the **Museo Archeologico Nazionale** (Mon & Wed–Sun 9am–7.30pm; €6.50; from Piazza Garibaldi take bus #C40 or the *metropolitana*) is an exception, home to the Farnese collection of antiquities from Lazio and Campania and the best of the finds from the nearby Roman sites of Pompeii and Herculaneum. You'd be mad to miss seeing them; it's worth investing in a guidebook (€7.75) or an audio guide (€4), both in English, to get the most out of your visit, and allow yourself at least half a day to see everything.

The ground floor of the museum concentrates on sculpture from the **Farnese collection**, displayed at its best in the mighty Great Hall, which holds imperial-era figures like the *Farnese Bull* and *Farnese Hercules* from the Baths of Caracalla in Rome – the former the largest piece of classical sculpture ever found. Don't miss *Ephesian Artemis*, an alabaster and bronze statue with rows of bulls' scrota peeling off her chest, and bees, mini-beasts and sphinxes adorning her lower half. The mezzanine floor holds the museum's collection of **mosaics** – remarkably preserved works all, giving a superb insight into ordinary Roman customs, beliefs and humour. All are worth looking at – images of fish, crustacea, wildlife on the banks of the Nile, a cheeky cat and quail with still-life beneath, masks and simple abstract decoration. But some highlights include a realistic *Battle Scene* (no. 10020), the *Three Musicians with Dwarf* (no. 9985), an urbane meeting of the *Platonic Academy* (no. 124545), and a marvellously captured scene from a comedy *The Consultation of the Fattucchiera* (no. 9987), with a soothsayer giving a dour and doomy prediction.

At the far end of the mezzanine is the fascinating **Gabinetto Segreto** (Secret Room), containing erotic material taken from the brothels, baths, houses and taverns of Pompeii and Herculaneum; to see the display, which lurks tantalizingly behind a grilled gate, you need to obtain a timed ticket (no extra charge) from the entrance hall. The objects in the collection weren't always segregated in this way; it was the shocked Duke of Calabria who, having taken his wife and daughter to view the museum, decided that the offending objects should be removed from the gaze of ladies. From then until the time of Garibaldi they were kept under lock and key, disappearing again from public view in the twentieth century for long periods. The artefacts, from languidly sensual wall-paintings to preposterously phallic lamps, bear testimony to Roman licentiousness, although the phallus was often used as a kind of lucky charm rather than as a sexual symbol – cheerfully hung outside taverns and bakeries to ward off the evil eye. Free English-language tours of the Gabinetto are admirably serious and smut-free, though it is hard to repress a giggle at the sculpture of a man whose toga is failing to mask an erection, or at the graphic but elegantly executed marble of Pan "seducing" a goat.

Upstairs through the Salone della Meridiana, which holds a sparse but fine assortment of Roman figures (notably a wonderfully strained *Atlas* and a demure *Venus* adjusting her sandal – Roman replicas of Greek originals), a series of rooms holds the **Campanian wall paintings**, lifted from the villas of Pompeii and Herculaneum, and rich in colour and invention. There are plenty here, and it's worth devoting some time to this section, which includes works from the Sacrarium – part of Pompeii's Egyptian temple of Isis, the most celebrated mystery cult of antiquity – the discovery of which gave a major boost to Egyptomania at the end of the eighteenth century. In the next series of rooms, some of the smallest and most easily missed works are among the most exquisite. Among those to look out for are a paternal *Achilles and Chirone* (no. 9109); the *Sacrifice of Iphiginia* (no. 9112) in the next room, one of the best preserved of all the murals; the dignified *Dido abandoned by Aeneas and the Personification of Africa* (no. 8998); and the series of frescoes telling the story of the Trojan horse. Look out too for the group of four small pictures, the best of which is a depiction of a woman gathering flowers entitled *Allegoria della Primavera* – a fluid, impressionistic piece of work capturing both the gentleness of spring and the graceful beauty of the woman.

Beyond the murals are the actual **finds from the Campanian cities** – everyday items like glass, silver, ceramics, charred pieces of rope, even foodstuffs (petrified cakes, figs, fruit and nuts), together with a model layout of Pompeii in cork. On the other side of the first floor, there are finds from one particular house, the **Villa dei Papiri** in Herculaneum – sculptures in bronze mainly. The *Hermes at Rest* in the centre of the second room is perhaps the most arresting item, rapt with exhaustion, but around are other adept statues – of athletes, suffused with movement, a languid *Resting Satyr*, the convincingly woozy *Drunken Silenus*, and, in the final room, portrait busts of soldiers and various local big cheeses.

Piazza Cavour and Sanità

To the left of the archeological museum as you come out, **Piazza Cavour** is a busy traffic junction and bus stop. A short walk east, at 223 Via Foria, lies the **Orto Botanico** (Mon–Fri 9am–2pm, by appointment only; ☏081.449.759), founded in 1807 by Joseph Bonaparte and a detour worth making if you're interested in such things. Perhaps more intriguing is the enormously long facade, actually only one fifth of the originally conceived size, of the **Albergo dei Poveri** alongside, a workhouse built in 1751 that has been empty for years and forms a vast, oddly derelict landmark along the top side of **Piazza Carlo III**.

North of Piazza Cavour, you can stroll up through the old quarter of **SANITÀ**, following the tangle of streets for ten minutes or so up to the church of **Santa Maria della Sanità** on the piazza of the same name, a Dominican church from the early seventeenth century whose design was based loosely on Bramante's for Saint Peter's in Rome. There are paintings by Giordano and other Neapolitan artists inside, if you can get in, although perhaps of more interest are the **Catacombe di San Gaudioso** (guided tours 9.30am–12.30pm, afternoons by appointment only ☏081.544.1305; €3) underneath, an intriguing early-Christian burial ground full of skeletons and the fifth-century tomb of St Gaudioso, who was known, apparently, as the "African", owing to the fact that he was a fifth-century bishop from North Africa.

Lifts link Sanità with Corso Amedeo up above, the main road up to Capodimonte. Walk under the bridge through to the rest of the teeming district, home to a couple of the city centre's larger hospitals and, close by one of them, another burial place, the **Catacombe di San Gennaro** (currently closed for restoration; ring ☏081.741.1071 for times of guided visits) behind the huge Madre del Buon Consiglio church. These were discovered only recently, next to the originally eighth-century church of San Gennaro in Moenia, and hold early Christian frescoes and mosaics, newly restored and amazingly bright.

The Palazzo Reale di Capodimonte

At the top of the hill, accessible by bus #C40 from Piazza Garibaldi and Piazza Dante, the **Palazzo Reale di Capodimonte** – and its beautiful **park** (9am–1hr before dusk; free) – was the royal residence of the Bourbon King Charles III, built in 1738 and now housing the picture gallery of the Naples museum, the **Museo Nazionale di Capodimonte** (Tues–Sun 8.30am–7.30pm; €7.50). The royal apartments, on the first floor, are smaller and more downbeat than those at Caserta (see p.893) but in many ways more enjoyable, not least because you can actually walk through the rooms freely. That said, you'll need a keen interest in the Bourbon dynasty to want to linger: high spots are the ballroom, lined with portraits of various Bourbon monarchs and other European despots, and a number of rooms of porcelain, some painted with local scenes and one in particular a sticky confection of Chinese scenes, monkeys and fruit and flowers from the Capodimonte factory here.

The museum is organized, not chronologically, but by collections: between them the Farnese and Bourbon rulers amassed some superb Renaissance and Flemish works, including a couple of Brueghels – *The Misanthrope* and *The Blind* – and two triptychs by Joos van Cleve. There are also canvases by Perugino and Pinturicchio, an elegant *Madonna and Child with Angels* by Botticelli and Lippi's soft, sensitive *Annunciation*. Later works include many Titians, with a number of paintings of the shrewd Farnese Pope Paul III in various states of ageing and the lascivious *Danae*; Raphael's austere portrait of *Leo X* and a worldly *Clement VII* by Sebastiano del Piombo; and Bellini's impressively coloured and composed *Transfiguration*.

Chiaia, Villa Comunale, Mergellina and Posillipo

Via Chiaia leads west from Piazza Trieste e Trento into a quite different Naples from the congested *vicoli* of the *centro storico* or Quartiere Spagnoli, lined with the city's fanciest shops and bending down to the **Piazza dei Martiri** – named after the nineteenth-century revolutionary martyrs commemorated by the column in its centre. This part of town, the **Chiaia** neighbourhood, displays a sense of order and classical elegance that is quite absent from the rest of the city centre, its buildings well preserved, the people noticeably better heeled – although the upper part of the district, which spreads up the hill towards Vómero, is as maze-like and evocative as anywhere in the city.

From Piazza dei Martiri, you can stroll down to the waterfront and **Villa Comunale**, Naples' most central city park and the place from where it's possible to appreciate the city best as a port and seafront city, the views stretching right around the bay from the long lizard of its northern side to the distinctive silhouette of Vesuvius in the east, behind the cranes and far-off apartment blocks of the sprawling industrial suburbs. The park itself sometimes hosts a large antiques and bric-a-brac market on Sunday mornings.

The road that skirts the park, **Via Caracciolo**, makes a nice way to walk around the bay to Mergellina, particularly in the early evening when the lights of the city enhance the views. On the way you might want to take in the century-old **Aquarium** (currently closed for restoration). Across from here, on the other side of Riviera di Chiaia, the gardens of the **Villa Pignatelli** (Tues–Sun 9am–2pm; €2) are a peaceful alternative to the Villa Comunale, and the house itself, now a museum, is kept in much the same way as when it was the home of a prominent Naples family and a meeting place for the city's elite in the 1900s. It's tastefully furnished and by Naples standards low-key, its handful of rooms holding books, porcelain, the odd painting and a set of photos signed by various aristocrats and royal personages.

Villa Comunale stretches around the bay for a good mile, at the far end of which lie the harbour and main square – Piazza Sannazzaro – of the **Mergellina** district, a good place to come and eat at night and a terminus for hydrofoils to the bay's islands. There's not a lot else here, only the dense and lovely **Parco Virgiliano** (Tues–Sun 9am–1pm), north of Piazza Sannazzaro, where the supposed burial place of the Roman poet Virgil is marked by a Roman monument. Of the other neighbourhoods nearby, the **Fuorigrotta** district, the other side of the Mergellina hill, is not of interest unless you're going to a football match, since it's home to Napoli's **San Paolo** stadium (see p.871 for details). Ditto **Posillipo**, further along the shore, which is an upmarket suburb of the city stacked with fat villas and pockets – though, again, people do come out here to eat.

Vómero

Like Chiaia below and Mergellina to the west, **VÓMERO** – the district topping the hill immediately above the old city – is one of Naples' relatively modern additions, a light, airy and relatively peaceful quarter connected most directly with the teeming morass below by funicular railway. It's a large area but mostly residential, and you're unlikely to want to stray beyond the streets that fan out from each of the three funicular stations, centring on the grand symmetry of **Piazza Vanvitelli**.

Come up on the Montesanto funicular (see map on pp.850–851) and you're well placed for a visit to two of the buildings that dominate Naples, way above the old city. Five minutes' walk away, the **Castel Sant'Elmo** (Tues–Sun 9am–7pm; €1) occupies Naples' highest point and is an impressive fortification, a fourteenth-century structure once used for incarcerating political prisoners and now lording it grandly over the streets below. Though still in use primarily as a military fortification, it nowadays hosts exhibitions, concerts and an annual antiques fair, as well as boasting the very best views of Naples.

Beyond the castle, the fourteenth-century **Certosa San Martino** has the next-best views over the bay and is also accessible, now being home to the **Museo Nazionale di San Martino** (Tues–Fri 8.30am–7.30pm, Sat & Sun 9am–7.30pm; €6). Much of this, too, often appears to be under restoration, but the monastery itself, thoroughly Baroqued in the seventeenth century, and the views from its cunningly constructed terrace, are well worth the entrance fee – short of climbing Vesuvius as good a vista of the entire Bay of Naples as you'll get. The church, on the left of the entrance, is typically garish Baroque, with a colourful pavement and an *Adoration of the Shepherds* by Reni above the altar. In the museum proper, there are paintings by Neapolitan masters – Ribera, Stanzione, Vaccaro – and other rather dusty bits and pieces rescued from churches and the odd minor aristocrat, as well as historical and maritime sections displaying models of ships, and documents, coins and costumes recording the era of the Kingdom of Naples. The Baroque cloisters are lovely, though again rather gone to seed. The display of *presepi* or Christmas cribs (see box on p.861) is probably the most remarkable – and unique – aspect of the museum.

There's another museum up here, ten minutes' walk away in the Neoclassical **Villa Floridiana**, close to the Chiaia funicular, whose lush grounds (daily 9am–1hr before sunset) make a good place for a picnic. The **Museo Duca di Martina** (Tues–Sun 9am–2pm; €2.50) is, however, of fairly specialist interest, a porcelain collection varying from the beautifully simple to the outrageously kitsch – hideous teapots, ceramic asparagus sticks and the like. There are examples (of course) of Capodimonte and Meissen, and eighteenth-century English, French, German and Viennese work – as well as a handful of pieces of Qing dynasty Chinese porcelain and Murano glass and exquisite non-ceramic items like inlaid ivory boxes and panels. On the whole, it's a small museum that's worth taking in before salivating over yet another view, this time from just below the villa.

Eating, drinking and nightlife

Neapolitan cuisine consists of simple dishes cooked with fresh, healthy ingredients (see box on p.849 for more on regional specialities). Also, as Naples is not primarily a tourist-geared city, most restaurants are family-run places used by locals and as such generally serve good food at very reasonable prices. There's no better place in Italy to eat pizza, at a solid core of almost obsessively unchanging places that still serve only the (very few) traditional varieties. You're never far from a food stall for delectable snacks on the move, or you can always pick something up from the city's street markets in La Forcella or the fish market at Porta Nolana.

We've categorized recommended restaurants below as "Inexpensive" (under €15), "Moderate" (€15–25), or "Expensive" (€25–40) according to the amount you can expect to pay per head for a full meal including wine and cover charge.

Restaurants and pizzerias

Alla Brace Via S. Spaventa 14–16. Good choice just off Piazza Garibaldi that has we l-priced pasta dishes and main courses. Closed Sun. Inexpensive.

Antonio & Antonio Via Francesco Crispi 89. A cheery no-nonsense place which dishes up enormous pizzas from €2.58. Inexpensive.

Trattoria Avellinese Via S. Spaventa 31. The most welcoming and best-value of the many options on and around Piazza Garibaldi, with terrific antipasti. Used by tourists and locals alike. Closed Sun in winter. Inexpensive.

Bellini Via Santa Maria di Constantinopoli 80. One of the city's most famous and longest established restaurants, which dishes up delicious pizzas and a very good selection of other, especially seafood, dishes. It also has a great convivial outside terrace on the street, screened by foliage. Closed Sun evenings. Moderate.

Bersagliera Borgo Marinaro. Fine food, especially seafood, though inevitably you pay for the location, slap next to the Castel dell'Ovo, and for the "O Sole Mio" minstrels who wander between the tables outside. Closed Tues. Expensive.

Brandi Salita Sant'Anna di Palazzo 1–2, off Via Chiaia. One of Naples' most famous pizzerias, said to be where they invented the *pizza margherita* in 1889 in honour of the visiting Queen Margherita of Savoy. Very friendly, serving pasta and (excellent) pizzas from €4.13. In the evening, the tables outside in the candlelit alley are a lovely place to sit. Closed Mon. Inexpensive–moderate.

Da Ciciotto off Via Marechiaro, Posillipo. Hole-in-the-wall place where in fine weather you can sit outside and enjoy the bay. Good seafood and fish. To get there, follow Via Marechiaro to the end, where it opens out onto a small piazza. Take the steps off the far end that lead down to the sea. Turn sharp right at the bottom of the first flight. Closed Wed. Inexpensive–moderate.

Dante e Beatrice Piazza Dante 44. A long-established restaurant that trades slightly on its reputation, but pleasant location for eating outside. Neapolitan specialities come with guitar accompaniment. Closed Wed & late Aug to mid-Sept. Moderate–expensive.

Da Ettore Via Santa Lucia 56. A popular neighbourhood restaurant, famous for its *pagnotielli* – calzoni stuffed with mozzarella, ham and mushrooms. Closed Sun. Moderate.

Gorizia Via Bernini 29. Unpretentious Vómero restaurant close to the Centrale and Chiaia funicular stops that does good antipasti, great mini-pizzas as well as a good selection of main courses. Try the speciality of the house – veal wrapped around prosciutto and mozzarella. Closed Wed. Moderate.

Lombardi a Santa Chiara Via B. Croce 59. Another well-known and wel -respected pizza restaurant, and with a varied menu besides pizza. Closed Sun & most of Aug. Moderate.

Di Matteo Via Tribunali 94. A terrific and well-located pizzeria – one of the best and most famous in the city. Photos advertise a famous erstwhile customer – Bill Clinton. Closed Sun. Inexpensive.

Da Michele Via Cesare Sersale 1–3. Tucked away off Corso Umberto I in the Forcella district, this is the most determinedly traditional of all the Naples pizzerias, offering just two varieties (allegedly the only two worth eating) – *marinara* and *margherita*. Don't arrive late, as they sometimes run out of dough. Closed Sun. Inexpensive.

Da Pasqualino Piazza Sannazzaro 79. Mergellina restaurant with outdoor seating and great seafood and pizzas. A good bet also for takeaway pizzas if you're staying at the nearby youth hostel. Closed Tues. Inexpensive.

Port'Alba Via Port'Alba 18. Old-established pizzeria (said to be the oldest in Italy) just off Piazza Dante that has a wide-ranging menu including very good fish dishes, besides its excellent pizza. Closed Wed. Inexpensive–moderate.

Spaghetteria Via G. Paladino 7. Inexpensive plates of pasta in a youthful restaurant patronized by students from the nearby university. Also features a great-value *menu turistico* (€8). Closed Sat lunchtime & Mon evening. Inexpensive.

Da Tonino Via Santa Teresa a Chiaia 47. Friendly and frenetic restaurant with large tables, around which everyone sits. Try their *pasta e fagioli* and *pasta e ceci* soups and, on Fridays especially, the *spaghetti alle seppie* – spaghetti with cuttlefish. Closed Sun. Moderate.

Trianon (da Ciro) Via P. Colletta 46. Lively Forcella pizzeria that is a nearby rival to *Da Michele* (above), but serving a wider range of pizzas. Open daily. Inexpensive.

Umberto Via Alabardieri 30–31. A long-time popular choice among the professional classes of the Chiaia district, serving marvellous food in somewhat smooth and old-fashioned surroundings. Closed Mon. Expensive.

13

Cakes, snacks, ice cream

Attanasio Vico Ferrovia, off Via Milano. Bakery that specializes in *sfogliatelle* (ricotta-stuffed pastries).

Gambrinus Via Chiaia 1–2. The oldest and best-known of Neapolitan cafés, founded in 1861. Not cheap, but its aura of chandeliered gentility – and outside seating on Piazza Trieste e Trento – makes it worth at least one visit.

Café Letterario Galleria Principe di Napoli 6–7. An elegant café inside the galleria, within striking distance of the Museo Nazionale. Also sells books and posters, and has Internet access.

Remy Gelo Via F. Galiani 29a. Off Via Caracciolo, near the hydrofoil terminal, this place does superb ice creams and *granite*.

Scaturchio Piazza San Domenico. Another elegant old Naples standard, it's been serving coffee and pastries in the heart of Spaccanapoli for decades.

Bars, clubs and theatres

The old part of the city is crammed with **bars**; the best thing to do is head for one of the lively and glamorous central squares where the local *ragazzi* hang out – try Piazza Bellini, a focal point for the gay community, or Piazza del Gesù Nuovo. Bear in mind though, that things don't really get going till at least 9pm. For **nightclubs** you may – owing to the licensing laws – have to obtain a *tesserino* or membership card to gain entry, which will cost upwards of €10. For the best of the clubs head around the bay, ideally with your own transport, to the places situated in the beach areas north or south of the city; the *pagine dell'Ozio* magazine has club listings.

For more highbrow **culture** there's the Teatro San Carlo, whose opera season runs from December to May. You'll find tickets hard to come by, however, as they are mostly sold on a subscription basis, but if you do manage to get hold of one, dress up. The rest of the year is given over to classical concerts and ballet (box office Tues–Sun 10am–1pm & 4.30–6.30pm; ☏081.797.2111). The Teatro Mercadante on Piazza Municipio (☏081.551.3396; tickets from €14) is a stunning little eighteenth-century building, featuring the best of touring Italian theatre.

Bars and clubs

Chez Moi Parco Margherita 13, near Piazza Amedeo. A great club which has been going strong since the Seventies, with a small dance floor and intimate lounges with waiter service. Frequented by an elegant crowd. Thurs–Sun 8pm–2am.

Internet Bar Piazza Bellini 44 🌐www.internetbar-napoli.it. A central and stylish little bar where you can surf the Web. Mon–Sat 9am–2am.

Intra Moenia Piazza Bellini 70. One of several trendy haunts on Piazza Bellini, where tables spread across the square. A lovely place to sit and read under the wisteria on a sunny day – it styles itself a "literary café". Substantial snacks and fancy ice creams are served, and there's a computer for Internet access. Daily 10am–2am.

La Mela Via dei Mille 40. A legendary and long-established club with an exclusive clientele and a resident DJ. Dress up to get past the doorman. Thurs–Sun midnight–4am.

Madison Street Via Sgambati 30c. A huge upmarket disco with themed events and a gay night on Saturdays. Open till late.

Michelemma Club, Via Campana 12, Pozzuoli ☏081.526.9743. An out-of-town option that's definitely worth the trip; centred round a lemon and orange plantation, it features a vibrant dancefloor and a concert hall, as well as a handy pizzeria.

My Way Via Cappella Vecchia 30c, off Piazza dei Martiri. A funky nightclub with a cave-like dancefloor which plays a range of music, from salsa to house. Oct–April Thurs–Sat 10pm–4am.

Notting Hill Piazza Dante 88a. A non-mainstream club geared to Brit pop plus garage and drum 'n' bass, with live music on Tuesday, Thursday and Saturday. Oct–May Tues–Sun 10.30pm–5am.

Otto Jazz Club Piazzetta Cariati 23. A popular jazz club off Corso Vittorio Emanuele which also dips its toes into Neapolitan folk song. Has 200 cocktails on the menu. Daily 10pm–3am.

Virgilio Club Via Lucrezio Caro 6, just below the Parco della Rimembranza, Posillipo. A fun and leafy outdoor disco that gets jam-packed on summer nights. June–Sept Sat 11pm–4am.

Listings

Airlines Alitalia (☎848.865.643; Capodichino airport desk ☎081.709.3333); British Airways (☎848.812.266; Capodichino airport desk ☎081.780.3087); Go (☎848.887.766); TWA, Via Cervantes 55 (☎081.551.3063).

Car rental Avis, Via Piedigrotta 44 ☎081.761.1365; Europcar, Via Scarfoglio 10 ☎081.762.8808; Hertz, Piazza Garibaldi 91 ☎081.206.228; Maggiore, Via Cervantes 92 ☎081.552.1900. These agents also have desks at Stazione Centrale and at the airport.

Consulates Canada, Via Carducci 29 ☎081.401.338; UK, Via dei Mille 40 ☎081.423.8911; USA, Piazza della Repubblica ☎081.583.8111.

Exchange Outside normal banking hours you can change money and travellers' cheques at the booth inside Stazione Centrale (daily 8am–7.30pm).

Football The Stadio di San Paolo in Fuorigrotta is the home of the Napoli side, currently in Serie B. To get to the ground, take the Ferrovia Cumana from Montesanto to Mostra and the stadium is right in front of you. Tickets, available from the offices facing you as you approach, or from the club's outlets in town, cost from €12.

Hospital To call an ambulance, dial ☎081.752.8282, 081.752.0696 or 081.752.0850, or go to the Guardia Medica Permanente in the Palazzo Municipio, open 24hr.

Internet As well as the cafés and bars listed opposite, handy places are *Promhotel*, inside the station on the lower ground floor (☎081.266.908), and above the *Bar Mexico* on Piazza Garibaldi 73 (☎081.563.4836).

Laundry Bolle Blu, Corso Novara 62–4, just up from the Stazione Centrale, open daily 8.30am–8pm.

Lottery Along with San Gennaro, the lottery is a fanatically observed institution in Naples. Winning the lottery is seen, in a way, as the ultimate triumph over the system, and superstitions around it are rife – to the extent that there's even a book, *La Smorfia*, which interprets the meaning behind each lottery number. There are also people, called

assisti (literally "guided ones"), who claim to have supernatural access to knowledge of what the winning numbers will be. The draw is made every Saturday noon at the Ufficio Lotto on Via San Biagio dei Librai, to the accompaniment of much hysteria.

Markets The Mercato dei Fiori (Flower Market) at Castel Nuovo kicks off every morning at sunrise, while Pignasecca on via Pignasecca is an atmospheric daily market, the stalls piled with fresh fruit, vegetables and seafood.

Pharmacies The pharmacy at Napoli Centrale is open 24 hrs and there's a list of those open at night in the newspaper *Il Mattino*.

Police ☎112; you can speak to an operator in English. The main police station (*questura*) is at Via Medina 75 (☎081.794.1111); you can also report crimes at the small police station in Stazione Centrale. To report theft of a car call ☎081.794.1435.

Post office The main post office is in the enormous building on Piazza Matteotti, just off Via Toledo (Mon–Sat 8.15am–7.20pm).

Tours A Neapolitan Legends walk takes place every Sunday morning at 11am starting from Piazza San Domenico Maggiore (☎081.542.2088). You can also experience underground Naples on tours run by LAES (Sat & Sun 10am; ☎081.400.256), which leave from *Bar Gambrinus* on Piazza Trieste e Trento and take you through sewers and passageways that date back as far as 4000 years. Napoli Sotterranea runs a similar tour daily (☎081.296.944, ⓦwww.lanapolisotterranea.it); the meeting point is Piazza San Gaetano. In summer you can also cruise Naples harbour by boat at night with Pelagus, Piazza Municipio 84 (☎081.552.0105); there are regular departures from Largo Nazario Sauro near Mergellina harbour between July and September.

Travel agents CTS, Via Mezzocannone 25 (☎081.552.7960), for discount tickets, budget flights and so on. You could also try Wasteels, Stazione Centrale (☎081.201.071; Mon–Sat 9am–7.30pm).

West from Naples: Pozzuoli and the Campi Flegrei

The area around Naples is one of the most unstable in the world. Vesuvius is only the best known of the many and varied examples of volcanic activity in the province, the most concentrated instances – volcanic craters, hot springs, *fumaroles* – being northwest of the city in the region known as the **Campi Flegrei** (Fiery Fields). This is the Phlegrean Fields of classical times, a mysterious place in turn mythologized by Homer and Virgil as the entrance to Hades and eulogized as the Elysian Fields for its beauty. These days most of the mystery is gone – like most of the bay, the presence of Naples dominates in the form of new building and suburbs – and much of the volcanic activity is extinct. But parts of the area still retain some of the doomy associations that first drew the ancients here, and there are some substantial remains of their presence.

Pozzuoli and the Solfatara

The first town that can really be considered free of Naples' sprawl is **POZZUOLI**, which sits on a stout promontory jutting out from the slender crescent of volcanic hills behind. Despite achieving some glamour as the hometown of Sophia Loren, it's an ordinary little place, nothing special but likeable enough, with ferry connections to the islands of Prócida and Ischia (see p.892 and p.888). And although you wouldn't want to stay here (unless you're a camper; see "Accommodation", p.856), it's a good first stop before travelling on to the rest of the Campi Flegrei. You can get there from Naples on the *metropolitana* from Piazza Garibaldi, or on the Ferrovia Cumana line from Montesanto station; both take about twenty minutes. Bus #152 also runs direct from Piazza Garibaldi.

Pozzuoli has suffered more than most of the towns around here from the area's volcanic activity and subsidence is still a major – and carefully monitored – problem. The best time to come is on Sunday, when the whole town turns out for the morning fish market, afterwards eating lunch in one of several waterfront restaurants: *Il Capitano* (closed Tues) near the dock on Lungomare C. Colombo is decent; or there's *Don Antonio*, up narrow Via Magazzini off the old port, which specializes in excellent fresh fish and seafood. In town there are a number of relics of the Romans' liking for the place. The rather overgrown **Anfiteatro Flavio** (daily 8.30am–1hr before sunset; €4 combined ticket with excavations at Báia and Cumae), on Via Domiziana just north of the centre, was at one time the third largest in Italy and is still reasonably well preserved, although some parts are shut off to the public – a little illicit clambering over fences might enable you to get a better sense of the place. Not far from here, beyond the Cumana station between Via Roma and Via Sacchini, a **Temple of Serapide** sits enclosed within a small park, often flooded in winter, but, otherwise, accessible – and in fact since proved to be not a temple at all but a market hall from the first century AD. It's pretty ruined, but it is still possible to make out the shape of the building, its three freestanding marble columns eaten away halfway up by shellfish.

Just north of town, ten minutes' walk up the hill from the *metropolitana*/FS station (bus #152 from Piazza Garibaldi in Naples stops outside), the **Solfatara** (daily 9am–1hr before sunset; €4.60) is further, and tangible, evidence of the volcanic nature of the area, the exposed crater of a semi-extinct volcano – into which you can walk – that hasn't erupted for a couple of thousand years; in fact, it was a major tourist attraction in Roman times too. Not surprisingly, it's a weird place: steam rises from the rocks around and the grey-yellow ground is hot to the touch (and sounds hollow underfoot), emitting eerily silent jets or *fumaroles* that leave the air pungent with sulphurous fumes. Some of the *fumaroles* have been covered artificially with brick, creating an almost unbearably warm, sauna-like environment into which you can bend if you can stand it, while others are just left open.

A short, three-minute walk further up the hill on the right, the sixteenth-century **Santuario di San Gennaro** (daily 9am–noon & 4.30–8pm) was built on the supposed site of the martyrdom of Naples' patron saint and holds a stone stained with splashes of his blood (he was beheaded) that apparently glows when his blood liquefies in Naples, which it does three times a year – see "The Miracle of San Gennaro" box on p.859.

Báia and Cumae

The next town along from Pozzuoli, reached in fifteen minutes by train from the Cumana station, by the Temple of Serapide, is **BÁIA**, a small port with a tiny, rather unattractive bit of beach and a set of imperial-era Roman ruins piling up on the hill above. This was one of the bay's most favoured spots in Roman times, a trendy resort at which all the most fashionable of the city's patricians had villas: the Emperor Hadrian died here in 138 AD and Nero was rumoured to have murdered his mother in Báia. You can take a **tour** organized by the Associazione Aliseo (☎081.526.5780) in a glass-bottomed boat which explores the submerged villas along the coastline at Báia. Trips run from March to November on Saturday at midday and 4pm, and on Sunday at 10.30am, midday and 4pm.

Immediately behind the station, remains of some enormous Roman baths leave you in no doubt of the town's function in ancient times. Steps lead up from the station square to the entrance to the **excavations** (daily 9am–1hr before sunset; €4 combined ticket with Anfiteatro Flavio and Cumae) of a Roman palace of the first to the fourth century AD, structured across several levels and an evocative location. Follow the steps down from the entrance level to the first terrace of the palace: the rooms on the right contain patches of Roman stucco-work depicting birds and mythical creatures and a statue of Mercury, beheaded by vandals in recent years. Below are the remains of a small theatre and an open space – a former *piscina* – bordered on one side by a pretty loggia.

There are more ruins inland from Báia at **Lago d'Averno**, where Agrippa constructed a military harbour in 37 BC. The lake itself is the Lake Avernus of antiquity, a volcanic crater that the Greeks believed – and Virgil later wrote – was the entrance to Hades: birds flying over were said to suffocate with the toxic fumes that rose from the lake's murky waters, and sacrifices were regularly made here to the dark deities that lurked beneath the gloomy surface. Today it's more cheerful, no longer surrounded by thick forest (this was cut down by Agrippa), although there's not really any other reason to come – the water of the nearby sea is much more enticing for swimming.

Further up the coast, the town of **Cumae** was the first Greek colony on the Italian mainland, a source of settlers for other colonies (Naples was originally settled by Greeks from Cumae) and a centre of Hellenistic civilization. Later it was home to the so-called Cumaean Sibyl, from whom Tarquinius purchased the Sibylline Books that laid down the laws for the Republic. The **site** (daily 9am–1hr before sunset; €4 combined ticket with Anfiteatro Flavio and Báia), a short walk from the bus stop, is spread over a large area and not at all comprehensively excavated. But the only part you're likely to want to see forms a tight nucleus close to the entrance. The best-known feature is the Cave of the Sibyl, a long, dark corridor that was home to the most famous of the ancient oracles. The cave is rectangular in shape, with light admitted from a series of niches in the western wall; the Sibyl used to dispense her wisdom from the three large chambers at the far end of the forty-foot passageway, the most famous occasion being when Aeneas came here to consult her – an event recorded by the lines of Virgil posted up either side of the entrance.

But the best of Cumae is still to come. Climb up the steps to the right of the cave entrance and follow the winding Via Sacra past a constructed belvedere on the left and the fairly scanty remains of a temple on the right to the Acropolis. Here you'll find the remains of a temple to Jupiter, but it's the **views** that you really come for: from the far side of the temple way south across the shellfish-filled **Lago Fusaro** and the bottom corner of the coast; and, if you clamber down from the other side of the temple, north up the curving coast to the Gulf of Gaeta.

East from Naples: Ercolano to Sorrento

The coast **east from Naples** is no better, perhaps even a little worse than the coast west of the city – the Circumvesuviana train edging out through derelict industrial buildings and dense housing that squeezes ever closer to the track. Most people come here for the ancient sights of **Herculaneum** and **Pompeii**, or to scale **Vesuvius** – or they skip the lot for the resort town of **Sorrento**. All are easy day-trips, though Sorrento is easily worth a little more time and is a good base for seeing some of the Amalfi coast.

Ercolano: Vesuvius and the site of Herculaneum

East of Naples the first real point of any interest is the town of **ERCOLANO**, the modern offshoot of the ancient site of Herculaneum, which was destroyed by the eruption of Vesuvius on August 2, 79 AD. It's worth stopping here for two reasons: to see the excavations of the site and to climb to the summit of Vesuvius – to which buses run from outside the train station. A word of warning, though: if you're planning to both visit Herculaneum and scale Vesuvius in one day (and it is possible), be sure to see Vesuvius first, and set off reasonably early – buses stop running up the mountain at around lunchtime, leaving you the afternoon free to wander around the site.

Herculaneum
Situated at the seaward end of Ercolano's main street, the site of **Herculaneum** (March–Sept 8.30am–7.30pm; Oct–Feb 8.30am–6pm; €8.50, or combined ticket with Pompeii and the Villa Oplontis valid 3 days €13.50; audio guide €5.16) was discovered in 1709, when a well-digger accidentally struck the stage of the buried theatre. Excavations were undertaken throughout the eighteenth and nineteenth centuries, during which period much of the marble and bronze from the site was carted off to Naples to decorate the city's palaces, and it wasn't until 1927 that digging and preservation began in earnest. Herculaneum was a residential town, much smaller than Pompeii, and as such it makes a more manageable site, less architecturally impressive and less outside the modern mainstream (Ercolano virtually abuts the site), but better preserved and more easily taken in on a single visit. Archeologists held for a long time that unlike in Pompeii, on the other side of the volcano, most of the inhabitants of Herculaneum managed to escape. However, recent discoveries of entangled skeletons found at what was the shoreline of the town suggest oth-

erwise, and it's now believed that most of the population was buried by huge avalanches of volcanic mud, which later hardened into the tufa-type rock that preserved much of the town. In early 2000 the remains of another 48 people were found; they were carrying coins, which suggests they were attempting to flee the disaster.

There are always plenty of **guides** hanging around, some English-speaking: it's a good way to get the most out of the site, but be sure to negotiate the fee before you start.

Because Herculaneum wasn't a commercial town, there was no central open space or forum, just streets of villas and shops, cut as usual by two very straight main thoroughfares that cross in the centre. Start your tour just inside the entrance at the bottom end of Cardo III, where you'll see the **House of the Argus** (Casa d'Argo) on the left, a very grand building judging by its once-impressive courtyard – although even this is upstaged by the size of the place across the street, the so-called **Hotel** (Casa del Albergo), which covers a huge area, though you can only really get a true impression of its size from the rectangle of stumpy columns that made up its atrium. Further up, Cardo III joins the Decumanus Inferiore, just beyond which it's the large **Thermae** or bath complex which dominates – the domed frigidarium of its men's section decorated with a floor mosaic of dolphins, its caldarium containing a plunge bath and a scallop-shell apse. Still intact are the benches where they sat and the wooden, partitioned shelves for clothing. The women's section has a well-preserved black and white mosaic of Triton and sea creatures, and original glass shards in its window. On the far side of the baths, across Cardo IV, the **Samnite House** (Casa Sannitica) has an attractive atrium, with a graceful loggia all the way round and a hole in the roof still decorated with animal spouts. Three doors down, the **House of Neptune and Amphitrite** (Casa di Nettuno ed Anfitrite) holds sparklingly preserved and richly ornamental wall mosaics featuring the gods themselves on one wall, hunting dogs and deer on a vibrant blue background on another. Adjacent is the **House of the Beautiful Courtyard** (Casa del Bel Cortile) where skeletons of bodies still lie in the positions they fell, and there's a **wine shop** (Casa con Botteghe), stocked with shelves of amphorae.

Turning right at the top of Cardo IV takes you around to Cardo V and most of the rest of the town's **shops** – a variety of places including a baker's, complete with ovens and grinding mills, a weaver's, with loom and bones, and a dyer's, with a huge pot for dyes. Behind the ones on the left you can see the **Palestra**, where public games were held, although it's not actually possible to reach this. Further down on the right, the shop on the corner of Cardo V and Decumanus Inferiore has a well-preserved counter and urns for cereals or some such merchandise; another, further down Cardo V on the right, has a Priapic painting behind its counter. Cutting through to Cardo IV from here takes you to the **House of the Wooden Partition** (Casa del Tramezzo di Legno) with its original partition doors (now under glass) – evidence that it was the home of a poorer class of person than many of the buildings here. The next-door **House of Opus Craticium** (Casa a Graticcio) is a plebeian artisans' residence, originally divided into separate apartments, and with an upper storey balcony overhanging the streetfront. The term "opus craticium" refers to the building method of using poor-quality material held together by wooden frames, of which this is a very well-preserved example. At the bottom end of Cardo IV, the **House of the Mosaic Atrium** (Casa del Atrio Mosaico), was a grand villa in its day and retains its mosaic-laid courtyard, corrugated by the force of the tufa. It's currently closed, but you can still see inside. Behind here, the **House of the Deer** (Casa dei Cervi) on Cardo V was another luxury villa, its two storeys built around a central courtyard and containing corridors decorated with richly coloured still-lifes.

Close by, from the end of Cardo IV, a covered passageway leads down to another **baths** building on the left (currently closed), which is in fact one of the most impressive – and intact – structures in Herculaneum, complete with extremely well-preserved stucco work and a pretty much intact set of baths; it also has a complete original Roman door, the only one in Herculaneum that wasn't charred by fire. If you find it open, the damp mustiness makes it certainly the most evocative stop on a tour of the site.

Mount Vesuvius

Since its first eruption in 79 AD, when it buried the towns and inhabitants of Pompeii and Herculaneum, **Mount Vesuvius** has dominated the lives of those who live on the Bay of Naples, its brooding bulk forming a stately backdrop to the ever-growing settlements that group around its lower slopes. It's still an active volcano, the only one on mainland Europe. There have been more than a hundred eruptions over the years, but only two others of real significance – one in December 1631 that engulfed many nearby towns and killed 3000 people; and the last, in March 1944, which caused widespread devastation in the towns around, though no one was actually killed. The people who live here still fear the reawakening of the volcano, and with good cause – scientists calculate it should erupt every thirty years or so, and it hasn't since 1944. It's carefully monitored, of course, and there is apparently no reason to expect any movement for some time. But the subsidence in towns like Ercolano below is a continuing reminder of the instability of the area, one of southern Italy's most densely populated: around half a million people would be immediately threatened by another eruption.

There are several ways of making the **ascent**. Buses, run by Trasporti Vesuviani (⊕081.559.2582; April–Oct at 9.10am, 10.10am, 11.30am, 1.30pm & 2.10pm, last bus back 4.15pm; Nov–March at 10.30am, 11.30am, 12.40pm, last bus back 3pm; €3.10 return), leave from the bar by the train station and drop you at the car park and huddle of souvenir shops and cafés close to the crater. There is a **charge** of €6 to approach the crater, which includes a brief explanatory talk (in English). The bus is much the cheapest way of doing things, but you can look out for minibus taxis which charge around €6 per person and wait while you see the crater. Or you can take the infrequent local bus (#5) from the roundabout near the train station to the end of the line and walk from there – a good couple of hours to the crater. The walk is certainly a pleasant one, winding through the fertile lower slopes of the volcano, covered with vines and olives, past the main lava flows of the 1944 eruption as far as the car park, which sits just above the greenery among the bare cinders of Vesuvius's main summit.

Walking up to the crater from the car park takes about half an hour, a stony stroll across reddened, barren gravel and rock on marked-out paths, though with nothing on your right to prevent you falling down the smooth side of the mountain – take care. At the top is a deep, wide, jagged ashtray of red rock swirled over by midges and emitting the odd plume of smoke, though since the last eruption effectively sealed up the main crevice this is much less evident than it once was.

The bay to Sorrento

Beyond Ercolano the bay doesn't really pick up: it's still hard to distinguish much countryside between the towns – most of which sadly seem more in tune with their proximity to the city than to the sea. **TORRE DEL GRECO**, the first place you reach, is famous for its coral industry, and you can still buy coral jewellery here, but the business is threatened by the polluted nature of the waters of the bay.

Further along, **TORRE ANNUNZIATA** is no more appealing at first sight, though about half a kilometre down from the train station is the **Villa Oplontis** (April–Oct 8.30am–7.30pm, last entry 6pm; Nov–March 8.30am–5pm, last entry 3.30pm; €5 combined ticket with Pompeii and Herculaneum valid 3 days €13.50), one of the best preserved of all Roman villas. Also a victim of the 79 AD eruption, this sumptuous residence is now thought to have belonged to Poppaea, the second wife of Emperor Nero, and is remarkable for the scale and beauty of its architecture, wall paintings and gardens. From the vast atrium, adorned with intricate architectural paintings of columns and shields, the vista extends right through the house, to the colonnaded portico surrounding it and the restored, formal gardens bordered with box hedges. Like villas of today, this one also had its own sun terrace and swimming pool, and bones discovered under the lawn suggest that a goat kept the grass in check. Inside, most striking is the bright-red and tawny-yellow caldarium in the bath complex where a pastoral painting portrays Hercules, draped in lion skin, in the garden of the Hesperides, while above him, astride a seahorse, sits a sultry Nereid. Other rooms yield peacocks galore, bowls of figs and pomegranates, theatrical masks and impressionistic scenes of daily life.

As the site is off the main tour-group track, you're likely as not to have it to yourself; look out for the car opposite the entrance selling guidebooks from its boot – you'll probably want to buy one, as there is no information at the ticket office and nothing is labelled.

The only reason for stopping at **CASTELLAMMARE DI STABIA**, a few kilometres further round the bay, is to take the funicular from Circumvesuviana station (daily every 30min: mid-June to Aug 7.25am–7.15pm; rest of year 9.25am–4.25pm; €6.71 return) up to the top of **Monte Faito** (1100m), a ten-minute journey that gives predictably dazzling views, although you need to walk for fifteen minutes or so at the top to get clear of the trees. Alternatively, hurry on south to Salerno or west to Sorrento – both feasible jumping-off points for the Amalfi coast.

Pompeii

The other Roman town to be destroyed by Vesuvius – **Pompeii** – was a much larger affair than Herculaneum and one of Campania's most important commercial centres in its day. After a spell as a Greek colony, Pompeii came under the sway of the Romans in 200 BC, later functioning as both a moneyed resort for wealthy patricians and a trading town that exported wine and fish products, notably its own brand of fish sauce. A severe earthquake destroyed much of the city in 63 AD, and the eruption of Vesuvius sixteen years later only served to exacerbate what was already a desperate situation.

Vesuvius had been spouting smoke and ash for several days before the eruption and in fact most of the town had already been evacuated when disaster struck: out of a total population of 20,000 it's thought that only 2000 actually perished, asphyxiated by the toxic fumes of the volcanic debris, their homes buried in several metres of volcanic ash and pumice. **Pliny**, the Roman naturalist, was one of the casualties – he died at nearby Stabiae (now Castellammare) of a heart attack. But his nephew, Pliny the Younger, described the full horror of the scene in two vivid letters to the historian Tacitus, who was compiling a history of the disaster, writing that the sky turned dark like "a room when it is shut up, and the lamp put out".

In effect the eruption froze the way of life in Pompeii as it stood at the time – a way of life that subsequent excavations have revealed in precise and remarkable detail; indeed Pompeii has probably yielded more information about the ordinary life of Roman citizens during the imperial era than any other site: its social conventions, class structure, domestic arrangements and its (very high) standard of living. Some of the buildings are even covered with ancient graffiti, either referring to contemporary political events or simply to the romantic entanglements of the inhabitants; and the full horror of their way of **death** is apparent in plaster casts made from the shapes their bodies left in the volcanic ash – with faces tortured with agony, or shielding themselves from the dust and ashes.

The first parts of the town were discovered in 1600, but it wasn't until 1748 that **excavations** began, continuing more or less without interruption – after 1860 under the auspices of the Italian government – until the present day. Indeed, exciting discoveries are still being made, and a flood of new funds is being used to excavate a further twenty hectares of the site; it is hoped to resolve whether or not the survivors attempted, vainly, to resettle Pompeii after the eruption. A privately funded excavation has recently revealed a covered heated swimming pool, whose erotic wall-paintings have been deemed by the Vatican to be unsuitable for children. And, in a further development, a luxury "hotel" complex was uncovered in May 2000 during the widening of a motorway, slabs of stacked cut marble suggesting it was still under construction when Vesuvius erupted.

Bear in mind that most of the best mosaics and murals (from Herculaneum too) are in the archeological museum in Naples, and that as you can only see a small proportion of those found *in situ*, visits to both sites really need to be supplemented by an additional one to the museum (see p.864).

The site

The **site** of Pompeii (daily: April–Oct 8.30am–7.30pm, last entry 6pm; Nov–March 8.30am–5pm, last entry 3.30pm; €8.50; combined ticket with Herculaneum and Villa Oplontis valid 3 days €13.50; ⓦ www.pompei.it) covers a wide area, and seeing it properly takes half a day at the very least; really you should devote most of a day to it and take plenty of breaks – unlike Herculaneum there's little shade, and the distances involved are quite large: flat comfortable shoes are a must.

All of this makes Pompeii sound a bit of a chore – which it certainly isn't. But there is a lot to see, and you should be reasonably selective: many of the streets aren't lined by much more than foundations, and after a while one ruin begins to look much like another. Again, many of the most interesting structures are kept locked and only opened when a large group forms or a tip is handed over to one of the many custodians. It's worth studying the **site map**, which you'll find at every entrance – pins on the map indicate which areas are currently closed. To be sure of seeing as much as possible you could take a tour, although one of the pleasures of Pompeii is to escape the hordes and absorb the strangely still quality of the town, which, despite the large number of visitors, it is quite possible to do.

Entering the site from the Pompeii-Villa dei Misteri side, through the Porta Marina, the **Forum** is the first real feature of significance, a long, slim open space surrounded by the ruins of what would have been some of the town's most important official buildings – a basilica, temples to Apollo and Jupiter, and a market hall. Walking north from here, up the so-called Via di Mercurio, takes you towards some of the town's more luxurious houses. On the left, the **House of the Tragic Poet** (Casa del Poetica Tragico) is named for its mosaics of a theatrical production and a poet inside, though the "Cave Canem" (Beware of the Dog) mosaic by the main entrance is more eye-catching. Close by, the residents of the **House of the Faun** (Casa del Fauno) must have been a friendlier lot, its "Ave" (Welcome) mosaic outside beckoning you in to view the atrium and the copy of a tiny bronze dancing faun (the original is in Naples) that gives the villa its name.

On the street behind, the **House of the Vettii** (Casa dei Vettii) is one of the most delightful houses in Pompeii and one of the best maintained, a merchant villa ranged around a lovely central peristyle that gives the best possible impression of the domestic environment of the city's upper middle classes. The first room on the right off the peristyle holds the best of Pompeii's murals actually viewable on site: the one on the left shows the young Hercules struggling with serpents; another, in the corner, depicts Ixion tied to a wheel after offending Zeus, while a third shows Dirce being dragged to her death by the bull set on her by the sons of Antiope. There are more paintings beyond here, through the villa's kitchen in a small room that's normally kept locked – erotic works showing various techniques of lovemaking (Greek-style, woman on top; Roman-style, man on top) together with an absurdly potent-looking statue of Priapus from which women were supposed to drink to be fertile; phallic symbols were also, it's reckoned, believed to ward off the evil eye.

Cross over to the other side of the site for the so-called **new excavations**, which began in 1911 and actually uncovered some of the town's most important quarters, stretching along the main Via dell'Abbondanza. The **Grand Theatre**, for one, is very well preserved and is still used for performances, overlooking the small, grassy, column-fringed square of the **Gladiators' Barracks** (Caserma dei Gladiatori) – not in fact a barracks at all but a refectory and meeting-place for spectators from the nearby amphitheatre. Walk around to the far left side of the Grand Theatre, down the steps and up again, and you're in front of the **Little Theatre** – a smaller, more intimate venue also still used for summer performances and with a better-kept corridor behind the stage space. As for the **Amphitheatre**, it's one of Italy's most intact and accessible, and also its oldest, dating from 80 BC; it once had room for a crowd of some 12,000 – well over half the town's population. Next door, the **Palestra** is a vast parade ground that was used by Pompeii's youth for sport and exercise – still with its square of swimming pool in the centre. It must have been in use when the eruption struck Pompeii, since its southeast corner was found littered with the skeletons of young men trying to flee the disaster. Just north of the Palestra, off Via Abbondanza, is the **House of Loreius Tiburtinus** (Casa di Loreio Tiburtino), a gracious villa fronted by great bronze doors. Paintings of Narcissus gazing rapt at his reflection and Pyramus and Thisbe frame a water cascade; the water flowed down a channel and into the villa's lovely garden, which has been replanted with vines and shrubs.

One last place you shouldn't miss at Pompeii is the **Villa dei Misteri**, outside the main site, a short walk from the Porta Ercolano (same hours and ticket as main site). This is probably the best-preserved of all Pompeii's palatial houses, an originally third-century BC structure with a warren of rooms and courtyards that derives its name from a series of paintings in one of its larger chambers: depictions of the initiation rites of a young woman into the Dionysiac Mysteries, an outlawed cult of the early imperial era. Not much is known about the cult itself, but the paintings are marvellously clear, remarkable for the surety of their execution and the brightness of their tones and colours. They follow an obvious narrative, starting with the left-hand wall and continuing around the room with a series of freeze-frames showing sacrifice, flagellation, dancing and other rituals, all under the serene gaze of the mistress of the house.

Practicalities

To **reach Pompeii from Naples**, take the Circumvesuviana east from Torre Annuziata to Pompeii-Villa dei Misteri – about thirty minutes; this leaves you right outside the western entrance to the site. The Circumvesuviana also runs to Pompeii-Santuario, outside the site's eastern entrance, or you can take the roughly hourly mainline train (direction Salerno) to the main Pompeii FS station, on the south side of the fairly characterless modern town. From the main station ignore the taxi drivers offering to take you to the entrance for an extortionate fee – it only takes around ten minutes to walk. Head away from the station towards the tall belltower, turning left at the main square to follow the signs to "Pompeii Scavi". After around 200m you come to the eastern entrance, Porta di Nuceria, on the right-hand side, the site itself screened by an avenue of trees.

If you want to make Pompeii an overnight stop, there are plenty of **hotels** and an excellent new **youth hostel**, *Casa del Pellegrino*, Via Duca d'Aosta 4 (℡081.850.8644; dorms €13), with family rooms (❶) as well, situated 300m from the Pompeii-Santuario station. There are also a couple of handy **campsites** including *Pompei* (℡081.862.2882) at Via Plinio 113, south of the main entrance. Modern Pompeii's **tourist office** at Via Sacra 1 (Mon–Sat 9am–3pm; ℡081.850.7255), just off the main square, has plans of the site.

Sorrento

Topping the rocky cliffs close to the end of its peninsula, 25km south of Pompeii, the last town of significance on this side of the bay, **SORRENTO** is solely and unashamedly a resort, its inspired location and mild climate drawing foreigners from all over Europe for close on 200 years. Ibsen wrote part of *Peer Gynt* in Sorrento, Wagner and Nietzsche had a well-publicized row here, and Maxim Gorky lived for over a decade in the town. Nowadays it's strictly package-tour territory, but really none the worse for it, with little of the brashness of its Spanish and Greek equivalents but all of their vigour, a bright, lively place that retains its southern Italian roots. Cheap restaurants aren't hard to find, nor – if you know where to look – is reasonably priced accommodation; and there's really no better place outside Naples itself from which to explore the rugged peninsula (even parts of the Amalfi coast) and the islands of the bay.

Sorrento's centre is **Piazza Tasso**, built astride the gorge that runs through the centre of town; it was named after the wayward sixteenth-century Italian poet to whom the town was home and has a statue of him in the far corner. There's nothing much to see in Sorrento itself, but it's nice to wander through the streets that feed into the square, some of which are pedestrianized for the lively evening passeggiata. The local **Museo Correale di Terranova**, housed in the airy former palace of a family of local counts at the far end of Via Correale (Mon & Wed–Sun 9am–2pm; €6), might kill an hour or so, with its examples of the local inlaid wood *intarsio* work – most of it much nicer and more ingenious than the mass-produced stuff you see around town – along with various paintings of the Neapolitan school, the odd foreign canvas, including an obscure Rubens, lots of views of Sorrento and the Bay of Naples, and various locally unearthed archeological knick-knacks. Otherwise the town

ACCOMMODATION		RESTAURANTS	
Bellevue Syrene	2	Angelina Lauro	A
City	5	Il Buco	B
Désirée	8	La Fenice	G
Elios	9	Il Giardiniello	C
Excelsior Victoria	3	Da Gigino	D
Hotel del Corso	6	Minervetta	F
Lorelay et Londres	1	Parruchiano	E
Nice	4		
Youth Hoste	7		

SORRENTO

is entirely given over to pleasure and there's not much else to see, although it's nice to linger in the shady gardens of the **Villa Comunale**, whose terrace has lovely views out to sea, and peek into the small thirteenth-century cloister of the church of **San Francesco** just outside, planted with vines and bright bougainvillea – a peaceful escape from the bustle of the rest of Sorrento.

Strange as it may seem, Sorrento isn't particularly well provided with **beaches**, and in the town itself you either have to make do with the small strips of sand of the **Marina Piccola** lido, right below the Villa Comunale gardens and accessible by a lift or steps, or the rocks and tiny, crowded strip of sand at **Marina Grande** – fifteen minutes' walk or a short bus ride (roughly every 30min) west of Piazza Tasso. Both places cost around €3 a head for the day, plus charges for parasol and chair rental, although there is a small patch of sand, immediately right of the lift exit at Marina Piccola, that is free. If you do come down to either of these spots, it's a good idea to rent a pedal-boat (from €10 an hour) and get free of the shore, since both beaches can get busy.

If you don't fancy the crowds in Sorrento, you can try the beaches further west. Twenty minutes' walk from the centre of Sorrento along Via del Capo (which is the continuation of Corso Italia), or a short bus ride from Piazza Tasso, there are a couple of options. You can either walk ten minutes or so from the bus stop down the Ruderi Villa Romana Pollio to some nice rocks, swathed with walkways, around the ruins of a Roman villa; or you could stroll 100m further west and take a path off to the right past the *Hotel Dania*, which shortcuts in ten minutes or so to **Marina Puolo** – a short stretch of beach lined by fishing boats and a handful of trattorias.

Practicalities

Sorrento's **train station** is located in the centre of town, five minutes from the main Piazza Tasso along busy Corso Italia. There's a **tourist office** in the large

CAMPANIA | Ercolano to Sorrento

13

yellow Circolo dei Forestieri building at Via Luigi de Maio 35, just off Piazza San Antonino (Mon–Sat 8.45am–7/8pm; ☎081.807.4033, ⓦwww.sorrento-tourism.it or ⓦwww.sorrento-online.com), which has maps, details on accommodation, transport and information about excursions The travel offices on Piazza San Antonino can deal with bus and ferry enquiries and reserve tickets. If you don't want to rely on public transport, Sorrento, Corso Italia 210 (☎081.878.1386), close by the train station, rents cars and scooters, and Guarracino, Via Sant'Antonino 19 (☎081.878.1728), just off the piazza of the same name, rents bikes.

Accommodation

Accommodation isn't really a problem, although during peak season you should definitely book in advance. There's a private **youth hostel**, *Le Sirene* at Via degli Aranci 156 (☎ & ⓕ081.807.2925; €14, including breakfast), which also has double rooms (❷). To get there from the train station, turn left on the main road and Via degli Aranci is 200m down on the left. The closest of the **campsites** is the *Nube d'Argento* site, near the *Elios* hotel at Via del Capo 21 (☎081.878.1344; April–Dec); if that's full, try the *Santa Fortunata*, which comes with private beach, about 1.5km from the centre at Via del Capo 41 (☎081.807.3579; April–Oct).

Bellevue Syrene Piazza della Vittoria 5 ☎081.878.1024, ⓕ081.878.3963. A lovely nineteenth-century hotel, built on the remains of a Roman villa. Boasts glorious views and a private beach. ❾

City Corso Italia 221 ☎ & ⓕ081.877.2210, ⓔhotelcity@libero.it. Fairly basic, but well placed for the action in town. ❸

Hotel del Corso Corso Italia 134 ☎ & ⓕ081.807.3157, ⓦwww.hoteldelcorso.com. Right by Piazza Tazzo, the *del Corso* is furnished in pleasant, modern style and has a breakfast terrace overlooking the street. ❺

Désirée Via Capo 31 ☎ & ⓕ081.878.1563. Great option beautifully situated on top of the cliff to the west of town, with stunning views and a private beach (accessible by lift). Rooms are stylish and the owners go out of their way to be helpful. Breakfast is included in the price. Closed mid-Nov to Feb. No credit cards. ❹

Elios Via del Capo 33 ☎081.878.1812. A good ten minutes' walk from the centre to the west of town,

the *Elios* has terrific sea views and private parking. Seaward rooms are quieter. Closed Dec–March. No credit cards. ❷

Excelsior Vittoria Piazza Tasso 34 ☎081.807.1044, ⓕ081.877.1206, ⓦwww.exvitt.it. This fabulously grand hotel has been owned by the same family since 1834; it sits right in the centre of town in a formal garden with a lemon and orange grove and a large pool; the lift from the swish terrace bar plunges straight down to the seafront. Immaculate, friendly service. ❾

Loreley et Londres Via Califano 2 ☎081.807.3187, ⓕ081.532.9001. Situated in a beautiful ancient building high on the cliffs on the eastern edge of the town centre, this is wonderful value. Breakfast is included in the price. Closed mid-Nov to mid-March. ❺

Nice Corso Italia 257 ☎081.807.2530, ⓕ081.807.1154. A very convenient and centrally placed option; the attractive en-suite rooms are air-conditioned, but a trifle noisy. ❹

Eating

Sorrento has no shortage of **restaurants**, but in the more touristy places service can be slow and the food not up to scratch. If you just want a snack, *Bar Rita*, Corso Italia 219, can't be bettered, with a wide array of sandwiches, cakes and other delicious lunch items. We've categorized recommended restaurants below as "Inexpensive" (under €15), "Moderate" (€15–25), or "Expensive" (€25–40) according to the amount you can expect to pay per head for a full meal including wine and cover charge.

Angelina Lauro Piazza Angelina Lauro 39. A self-service place that does snacks and full meals and has good options for vegetarians. No credit cards.

Closed Tues. Inexpensive.

Il Buco Rampa Marina Piccola 11, Piazza San Antonino. Just off the square and down a cobbled alley, this former monastic wine cellar, now decorated with photos of old Sorrento, comes up trumps for lunch or dinner. Closed Wed. Moderate–expensive.

La Fenice Via degli Aranci 11. A great place with decorative stained glass, covered patio and lively atmosphere. Closed Mon. Moderate.

Giardiniello Via Accademia 7. Just off Corso Italia, between Piazza Sant'Antonio and Via Tasso, this pizzeria-ristorante with a small garden specializes in fish, shellfish and barbecued meats. Moderate.

Da Gigino Via degli Archi 15. A great, no-nonsense choice, with excellent pizzas and good pasta and main courses. Closed Tues except July & Sept. Inexpensive–moderate.

Minervetta Via del Capo 30. Scenically sited in a pension whose terrace restaurant perches a little way along Via del Capo on the right. Inexpensive.

Parruchiano Corso Italia 67. More of a conservatory than a restaurant, this vast place is very popular with locals and tour groups alike. The fine food is great value. Closed Wed. Moderate.

Nightlife

For **drinking**, stylish *Bar Ercolano*, right on Piazza Tasso, isn't as pricey as you'd think and is vibrantly sited. The terrace bar in the *Circolo dei Forestieri* is a genteel place to drink and has wonderfully romantic night-time views, as well as a dance floor, and for some vicarious glamour head for the beautiful outside bar at the *Grand Hotel Excelsior Vittoria* (see above), which looks across the bay to Vesuvius. *Bollicine*, a small wood-panelled wine bar on Via Accademia, is a smart place to sample a wide range of good Campanian wines. For late-night drinking, the pubs along Corso Italia are as good a place as any: try the capacious *English Inn*, Corso Italia 55, which has a free outside dance floor upstairs that gets packed in the summer; and *Chaplin's*, almost opposite, which provides Internet access, is open till late.

The islands

Guarding each prong of the Bay of Naples, the islands of Cápri, Ischia and Prócida between them make up the best-known group of Italian islands. Each is a very different creature, though. **Cápri** is a place of legend, home to the mythical Sirens and a much-eulogized playground of the super-rich in the years since – though now settled down to a lucrative existence as a target for day-trippers from the mainland. Visit by all means, but bear in mind that you have to hunt hard these days to detect the origins of much of the purple prose. **Ischia** is a target for package tours (predominantly from Germany) and weekenders from Naples, but its size means that it doesn't feel as crowded as Cápri, and plentiful hot springs, sandy beaches and a green volcanic interior make the island well worth a few days' visit, especially as you can easily visit other sites in the bay (including Pompeii and Herculaneum) by ferry from here. Pretty **Prócida**, the smallest of the islands and the least interesting – though the best venue for fairly peaceful lazing – remains reasonably untouched by the high season.

Cápri

Sheering out of the sea just off the far end of the Sorrentine peninsula, the island of **Cápri** has long been the most sought-after part of the Bay of Naples. During Roman times Augustus retreated to the island's gorgeous cliffbound scenery to escape the cares of office; later Tiberius moved the imperial capital here, indulging himself in legendarily debauched antics until his death in 37 AD. After the Romans left, Cápri was rather neglected until the early nineteenth century, when the discovery of the Blue Grotto and the island's remarkable natural

Ferries and hydrofoils to the islands operate from Naples, Pozzuoli and Sorrento, with some connections from Salerno, Amalfi and Positano. There are two departure points in Naples: the main harbour (the Molo Beverello) at the bottom of Piazza Municipio and the quayside at Mergellina. Whichever route you take, day-trips are quite feasible; usually the last connection delivers you back on the mainland in time for dinner. On foot, you can simply buy tickets when you turn up at the offices at the port; in general it's better to buy a single rather than a return ticket since it doesn't work out more expensive and you retain more flexibility on the time you come back. Having said that, on summer Sundays (especially on Cápri, and especially by hydrofoil), it's a good idea to buy your return ticket as soon as you arrive, to avoid the risk of finding the last boat or hydrofoil fully booked.

The following gives a rough idea of frequencies during the summer (they're greatly reduced off-season). For specific timings you can look in *Qui Napoli* or *Il Mattino*, check with the local tourist office or look up the companies online: Caremar (℡081.551.3882, ＠www.caremar.it); Alilauro (℡081.761.1004, ＠www.alilauro.it); SNAV (℡081.761.2348, ＠www.snavali.com), NLG (℡081.552.0763, ＠www.navlib.it), Prócida Lines (℡081.896.0328) and Traghetti Pozzuoli (℡081.526.7736).

Hydrofoils and fast ferries
Naples (Molo Beverello)–Cápri (25 daily; 40min).
Naples (Molo Beverello)–Casamicciola, Ischia (4 daily; 1hr).
Naples (Molo Beverello)–Forio, Ischia (4 daily; 50min).
Naples (Molo Beverello)–Ischia (20 daily; 40–60min).
Naples (Molo Beverello)–Prócida (6 daily; 35–40min).
Naples (Mergellina)–Cápri (6 daily; 35min).
Naples (Mergellina)–Casamicciola, Ischia (6 daily; 45min).
Naples (Mergellina)–Prócida (3 daily; 20min).
Casamicciola, Ischia–Prócida (10 daily; 20min).
Ischia–Prócida (3 daily; 15min).
Prócida–Ischia (3 daily; 15min).
Salerno–Cápri (2 daily; 2hr).
Sorrento–Ischia (via Naples: 4 daily; 1hr); also 1 daily direct, and 1 daily via Cápri.
Sorrento–Cápri (20 daily; 20–25min).

Ferries
Naples (Molo Beverello)–Cápri (3 daily; 1hr 20min).
Naples (Molo Beverello)–Ischia (7 daily; 1hr 30min).
Naples (Molo Beverello)–Prócida (6 daily; 1hr).
Pozzuoli–Ischia (3 daily; 1hr).
Pozzuoli–Casamicciola, Ischia (12 daily; 1hr 30min).
Pozzuoli–Prócida (13 daily; 35min–50min).
Ischia–Prócida (6 daily; 25min).
Sorrento–Cápri (5 daily; 40min).
Salerno–Cápri (via Amalfi; 1 daily; 2hr).
Salerno–Ischia (via Amalfi and Positano; 1 daily; 2hr 30min).

landscape coincided nicely with the rise of tourism, and the island has never looked back, attracting a steady flow of artists and writers and, more recently, inquisitive tourists, ever since. The English especially have always flocked here: D.H. Lawrence and George Bernard Shaw were among more illustrious visitors, Graham Greene and Gracie Fields had houses here; and even Lenin visited for a time after the failure of the 1905 uprising.

Cápri tends to get a mixed press these days, the consensus being that while it might have been an attractive place once, it's been pretty much ruined by the crowds and the prices. And Cápri *is* crowded, to the degree that in July and August, and on *all* summer weekends, it would be sensible to give it a miss. But reports that the island has been irreparably spoilt are way overstated. Ischia is busy too. Prócida isn't nearly as interesting – or beautiful – and it would be hard to find a place with more inspiring views. It's expensive, though prices aren't really any higher than at other major Italian resorts, and you can find very reasonably priced and attractive accommodation in Anacápri or just visit on a day-trip, which should give you time enough to see the whole island.

Marina Grande, Cápri town and around

Ferries and hydrofoils dock at **MARINA GRANDE**, the waterside extension of the island's main town, which perches on the hill above. You can take boats to the Blue Grotto (see opposite) from here, and there's a tourist office that doles out plenty of information, and hires out an audio guide (€5.16), as well as any number of pricey waterside cafés and restaurants. It is, however, quickly exhausted, and you may as well take the **funicular** (daily 6.30am–9pm; till 12.30am June–Sept; €1.30 one-way) up the steep hill to Cápri town itself; if the funicular is too crowded (as it surely will be in high season) you can also walk, which takes about twenty minutes; follow the road up from the far end of the harbour, from where steps lead all the way up across the crisscrossing road.

CÁPRI is the main town of the island, nestled between its two mountains, its houses connected by winding, hilly alleyways that give onto the dinky main square of **Piazza Umberto**, crowded with café tables and lit by twinkling fairy lights in the evenings. On the far side of town is the **Certosa San Giacomo** (Tues–Sat 9am–2pm, Sun 9am–1pm; free), a run-down old monastery, though due for lengthy restoration at the time of writing, with a handful of paintings, a couple of shapeless Roman statues dredged up from the deep and an overgrown cloister. To the right of the monastery, the **Giardini Augustos** give tremendous views of the coast below and the towering jagged cliffs above, and from there you can wind down to either the beach (rocks really), or, beyond, to **MARINA PICCOLA** – a small huddle of houses and restaurants around a few patches of pebble beach: reasonably uncrowded out of season, though in July or August you might as well forget it. Marina Piccola is also accessible by bus.

Up above the Certosa, and a further pleasant walk fifteen minutes through Cápri town, the **Belvedere del Cannone** has marvellous views, especially over the **Faraglioni** rocks to the left and Marina Piccola to the right. Further out of Cápri town, there are two walks worth doing to the eastern edge of the island. One, up to the ruins of Tiberius's villa, the **Villa Jovis** (daily 9am–1hr before sunset; €2), is a steep thirty-minute hike from Piazza Umberto following Via Botteghe out of the square and Via Tiberio up the hill. It was here that Tiberius retired in 27 AD to lead a life of vice and debauchery and to take revenge on his enemies, many of whom he apparently had thrown off the cliff-face. You can see why he chose the site: it's among Cápri's most exhilarating, with incredible vistas of Ischia, Prócida and the bay; on a clear day you can even see Salerno and beyond. There's not much left of the villa, but you can get a good sense of the shape and design of its various parts from the arched halls and narrow passageways that remain. Below, there's another villa, the more recent **Villa Fersen** of one Count Fersen-Adelsward, a gay Swedish millionaire who built the house in the early 1900s apparently to entertain pick-ups from the town. Unfortunately its new owner has not seen fit to open it up to the public.

The other walk is to the **Arco Naturale**, an impressive natural rock formation at the end of a high, lush valley, a 25-minute hike from Cápri town, again following Via Botteghe out of the square but branching off up Via Matermania after ten minutes or so; you can get quite close to the arch owing to the specially constructed viewing platforms. Just before the arch, steps lead down to the **Grotta di Matermania**, ten minutes away down quite a few steps – a dusty cutaway out of the rock that was converted to house a shrine to the Sybil by the Romans. Steps lead on down from the cave, sheer through the trees, before flattening into a path that you can follow back to the **Tragara Belvedere**, and, eventually, Cápri town – reachable in about an hour.

Anacápri and around

The island's other main settlement, **ANACÁPRI**, is more sprawling than Cápri itself and less obviously picturesque, its main square, **Piazza Vittoria**, flanked by souvenir shops, bland fashion boutiques and restaurants decked with tourist menus – Cápri without the chic. A chair lift operates from Piazza Vittoria up to **Monte Solaro** (March–Oct daily 9.30am to sunset; Nov–Feb 10.30am–3pm; return €5.50, one-way €4), the island's highest point (596m). At the top there's only a ruined castle and a café, but the location is very tranquil and the views are marvellous.

A short walk away from Piazza Vittoria down Via G. Orlandi, the church of **San Michele** is the village's principal sight, its tiled floor painted with an eighteenth-century depiction of the *Fall* that you view from an upstairs balcony – a lush work after a drawing by the Neapolitan painter **Solimena**, in rich blues and yellows, showing cats, unicorns and other creatures.

Continuing in the same direction, a good 45-minute hike away starting off down Via Lo Pozzo (or reachable by bus every twenty minutes from Piazza Vittoria), you come to the **Blue Grotto** or Grotta Azzurra, probably the island's best-known feature – though also its most exploitative, the boatmen here whisking visitors onto boats and in and out of the grotto in about five minutes flat (daily 9am–1hr before sunset; €4, plus €4.10 for the rowing boat). The grotto is quietly impressive, the blue of its innards caused by the sun entering the cave through the water, but it's rather overrated. Technically, you can swim into the cave – it's not the exclusive preserve of the boatmen, though they'll try to persuade you otherwise – but the route through is so busy that unless you're a strong swimmer it's only advisable to try at the end of the day after the tours have finished. You can also get here by boat direct from Marina Grande (€6–9).

Time is much better spent walking in the opposite direction from Piazza Vittoria, past a long gauntlet of souvenir stalls to Axel Munthe's **Villa San Michele** (daily: March, April & Oct 9.30am–4.30pm; May–Sept 9am–6pm; Nov–Feb 10.30am–3.30pm; €5), a light, airy house with lush and fragrant gardens that is one of the real highlights of the island. The Swedish writer and healer Munthe lived here for a number of years, and it's filled with his furniture and knick-knacks, as well as Roman artefacts ingeniously incorporated into the villa's rooms and gardens. Busts and bronzes abound: one statue of Hermes was given to Munthe by the city of Naples in thanks for his work in the city during the cholera epidemic of 1884 (see p.862); Corinthian capitals are converted as coffee tables, other surfaces topped with intricate Cosmati mosaic-work. His book *The Story of San Michele* – more the story of his life – is well worth a read. There's also an attractive, small natural history exhibition in the gardens, which fills you in on local flora and fauna, to the (recorded) accompaniment of the golden oriole and nightingale.

Practicalities

There are **tourist offices** in Marina Grande (May–Oct daily 8.30am–11pm; Nov–April Mon–Sat 9am–5pm; ☎081.837.0634, ⓦwww.capritourism.com), and on Piazza Umberto in Cápri town (same hours; ☎081.837.0686). In Anacápri the tourist office is on Via G. Orlandi (May–Oct daily 8.30am–8.30pm; Nov–April Mon–Sat 9am–3pm; ☎081.837.1524). You'll find an **Internet point** at the *Caffè Augusto*, Via Cristoforo Colombo 20 in Marina Grande (☎081.837.8518). For **getting around** the island, there's a decent bus service connecting all the main centres – Marina Grande, Cápri, Marina Piccola, Anacápri – every fifteen minutes; buses also run regularly down to the Blue Grotto from Anacápri. Tickets cost €1.30 for a single trip, €2.10 for an hour and €6.70 for a day and are available from *tabacchi*. For travel in real style, however, go for one of the many white, soft-top taxis that swish about the island (☎081.837.0543).

If you're contemplating **staying overnight** on Cápri in peak season – and the island is a lot quieter after the day-tripping crowds have gone home – book well ahead as space is extremely limited. Prices in Cápri itself can go through the roof, but there are very acceptable and much cheaper alternatives in Anacápri. Best bet in Cápri itself is the very obliging *Quattro Stagioni*, Via Marina Piccola 1 (☎ & ℻081.837.0041, ⓦwww.hotel4stagionicapri.com; closed Nov–March; ❺), with well-furnished rooms and basketwork furniture. Those without views are compensated with a bath-tub, and there's a ten per-cent discount to carriers of this book. It's a little out of town at the fork of the roads to Marina Piccola and Anacápri. The modern *Stella Maris*, Via Roma 27 (☎081.837.0452, ℻081.837.8682; ❹), is more centrally placed just opposite the bus station, and has good facilities. *La Prora*, very appealingly situated up above the *Stella Maris* on Via Castello (☎ & ℻081.837.0281; closed Nov–March; ❻), has great views, as has the intimate *Villa Esperia* on Via Sopramonte (☎081.837.0262, ℻081.837.0933; ❼), a former Englishwoman's villa with charming rooms, some of which have their own terrace. In Anacápri, there are two excellent options, both of which offer breakfast in the price and a pick-up service from the port if you phone ahead. *Villa Eva*, Via La Fabbrica 8 (☎081.837.1549, ℻081.837.2040, ⓦwww.villaeva.com; closed Nov–Feb; no credit cards; ❺), has rooms in its main house and cottages dotted through the extensive gardens, an outdoor pool in summer and free-range chickens. The very friendly *Bussola di Hermes* (☎ & ℻081.838.2010, ✉bus.hermes@libero.it; no credit cards; ❸), Via Traversa La Vigna 14, must be the best value on the island, is open all year and has laundry and Internet facilities. If the weather is not good enough for breakfast on the terrace (it does sometimes rain here), it will be brought to your light and stylish room.

As for **eating**, one of the best places is *Da Gemma*, under the arches of old Cápri at Via Madre Serafina 6 (closed Mon & Jan), a friendly, long-established place whose plant-filled window overlooks the bay; it's good for seafood and antipasti and not that pricey. Down below, *Da Giorgio* is a surprisingly inexpensive restaurant in a good location (closed Jan & Feb plus Tues in Nov & Dec), while on the other side of Piazza Umberto, the oldest restaurant on the island, *Pizzeria Aurora* (closed Tues & Jan–March), on Via Fuorlovado – the continuation of Via Botteghe – is pretty good value too, has tables outside and a good wine list. At the other end of the scale *La Capannina* (☎081.837.0732), Via Le Botteghe 14, pretty and pink, beneath high plant-filled windows, is reckoned the island's best restaurant. In Anacápri, *Materita* on Via G Orlandi, off Piazza Diaz, is a fairly reasonable place, and those staying at *Villa Eva* can get a bargain "tourist menu" at *Il Cucciolo*, five minutes away at Nuova Traversa

CAMPANIA | The islands

Veterino 50. Somewhat nicer, though, *Da Giovanni* (closed mid-Oct to April), near the Blue Grotto is a great-value place to eat, especially by Cápri's standards. To find it take the cliffside path to the left of the Blue Grotto bus stop, away from the Grotto; ignore the pricey seafood places along the way, and follow the path right to the end. You can always knock yourself up a picnic lunch if you prefer: in Cápri town there are a supermarket and bakery a little way down Via Botteghe off Piazza Umberto, and well-stocked *salumerie* at Via Roma 13 and 30.

Ischia

Largest of the islands in the Bay of Naples, **Ischia** rises out of the sea in a series of pointy green hummocks, German, Scandinavian and British tourists flocking in large numbers during peak season to its charming beach resorts, thermal springs and therapeutic sands. Its reputation has always been poorer than Cápri's: it is perhaps not so dramatically beautiful, but you can at least be sure of being alone in exploring parts of the mountainous interior, and **La Mortella**, the exotic garden cultivated by the British composer William Walton and his widow Susana, is an unmissable attraction. Indeed, if you're after some beach lounging, good walking and lively nightlife within striking distance of Naples and the rest of the bay, it might be just the place.

   Public transport is regular and easy to negotiate: buses #CS and #CD circle the island – one in each direction – every thirty minutes, stopping just about everywhere. Tickets cost €0.93 and are valid for an hour, day tickets are €2.74.

Ischia Porto and Ischia Ponte

The main town of Ischia is **ISCHIA PORTO**, where the ferries dock, an appealing stretch of hotels, ritzy boutiques and beach shops planted with lemon trees and Indian figs fronted by golden sands: **Spiaggia San Pietro** is to the right of the port, accessible by following Via Buonocore off Via Roma; and the inexplicably named **Spiaggia degli Inglesi**, on the other side of the port, is reachable by way of the narrow path that leads over the headland from the end of Via Jasolino.

   Otherwise the main thing to do is to window-shop and stroll along the main Corso Vittoria Colonna, either branching off to a further beach, the **Spiaggia dei Pescatori**, or following it all the way down to the other part of Ischia's main town, **ISCHIA PONTE**, also reachable by bus #7, a quieter and less commercialized centre. Here the focus is the **Castello Aragonese** (March–Nov 9.30am to sunset; €8, includes the lift to the top), which crowns an offshore rock but is accessible from a short causeway; its stunningly distinctive pyramid was one of the backdrops in the film *The Talented Mr Ripley*. Vittoria Colonna, the Renaissance poet and close friend of Michelangelo, spent much of her life here, following the seizure of her family's land by Alexander VI. The citadel itself where she lived is rather tumbledown now and closed to the public, but below is a complex of buildings, almost a separate village really, around which you can stroll. There's the weird open shell of a cathedral destroyed by the British in 1806, a prison that once held political prisoners during the upheavals of the Unification, and the macabre remnants of a convent, in which a couple of dark rooms ringed with a set of commode-like seats served as a cemetery for the dead sisters – placed here to putrefy in front of the living members of the community.

Practicalities

Ischia Porto's helpful **tourist office** is right by the quayside ferry ticket offices (Mon–Sat 9am–2pm & 3–8pm; ☎081.507.4211, ⓦwww.ischiaonline.it); the **bus terminus**, with buses going to all other parts of the island, is just behind here.

There is plenty of **accommodation**, though bear in mind that many places close in low season. The *Monastero*, high in the *castello* in Ischia Ponte (☎081.992.435, ⓦwww.castelloaragonese.it; closed Nov–Feb; ❺), is perfect if you fancy a bit of seclusion and has tremendous views. The simple and elegantly furnished rooms were once the nuns' cells. Ischia Porto is better for access to the island's nightlife: the prettily furnished *Antonio Macri*, off the portside at Via Jasolino 96 (☎ & Ⓕ081.992.603; ❹), is a good-value place. Close by, the idiosyncratically decorated and very pleasant *Locanda sul Mare*, Via Jasolino 90 (☎ & Ⓕ081.981.470, ⓦwww.locandasulmare.it; closed Dec–Feb; ❸), is a great bargain. Towards the pricier end of the scale is the *Hotel Continental Mare*, west of town at Via B. Cossa 25 (☎081.982.577, Ⓕ081.992.505, ⓦwww.continentalmare.it; ❼), which enjoys a splendid location above the sea and its own stretch of beach. Best of all though, is luxurious *Il Moresco* (☎081.981.355, Ⓕ081.992.338, ⓦwww.ilmoresco.it; ❾), Via E. Gianturco 16. Housed in an elegant 1950s villa in the heart of Ischia Porto, but still managing to feel secluded, it has lovely swimming and thermal pools, and friendly, attentive service. For a **campsite**, *Eurocamping dei Pini*, Via delle Ginestre 28 (☎081.982.069), is not far from the port and also has bungalows.

There's no shortage of **eating** options: *Mastù Peppe*, right by the tourist office and ferry quay (closed Mon), is cheap and quite good, though the service can be slow; with a little more money, try *Gennaro*, across the harbour at Via Porto 59. For a real splash-out option, go for the superb *Alberto*, right on the seafront on Viale C. Colombo – the pretty restaurant, on stilts, over the sea, has immaculate service and beautifully presented seafood. In Ischia Ponte, *Coco* (closed Wed in winter), just to the right of the causeway which leads to the *castello*, has lovely sea views and dishes up great seafood.

As for **nightlife**, head for the lively run of late-night bars and cafés along Via Porto; best is the *Millennium Bar* which has a free dancefloor as well as serving during the day as a café with **Internet** access (2pm till late).

Casamicciola Terme and Lacco Ameno

The island is at its most developed along its northern and western shores – heading west from Ischia Porto. The first village you reach, **CASAMICCIO-LA TERME**, is a spa centre with many hotels and a crowded central beach – though you can find a quieter one on the far side of the village. Ibsen spent a summer here, and the waters are said to be full of iodine (apparently beneficial for the skin and the nervous system), but otherwise you may as well push on to **LACCO AMENO**, a brighter little town, again with a beach and with spa waters that are said to be the most radioactive in Italy.

Above the main square away from the sea in Villa Arbusto is the **Museo Archeologico di Pithecusa** (daily: April–Oct 9.30am–1pm & 5–7pm; Nov–March 9.30am–1pm & 3–5pm; €5.16; ⓦwww.pithecusae.it) with well-displayed finds from the acropolis of Monte di Vico, in continuous use from the eighth to the first centuries BC. Pithecusa (modern Ischia) was the first and northernmost Greek settlement in the West, a thriving and vital staging post at the western end of routes from the Aegean and the Levant – in addition to local artefacts, the museum displays grave goods imported from Syria, Egypt and Etruria. The epigram on the modest-looking Coppa di Nestore makes a light-hearted challenge to the cup mentioned in Homer's *Iliad*, while a shipwreck scene on a locally made bowl is thought to be the oldest example of figurative painting in Italy.

La Mortella

Between Lacco Ameno and Forio is one of Ischia's highlights: the stunning garden of **La Mortella** (April–Nov Tues, Thurs, Sat & Sun 9am–7pm; €8; ask the bus driver to drop you off), created by the English composer William Walton and his Argentinian widow Susana, who still lives here. The Waltons moved to Ischia, then sparsely populated and little-known to tourists, in 1949, forerunners of a coterie of writers and artists including Auden and Terence Rattigan. With the garden designer Russell Page they created La Mortella from an unpromising volcanic stone quarry, just the first phase of landscaping taking seven years to complete.

Paths wind up through the abundant site, which has some 300 rare and exotic plants. Near the entrance is a glasshouse sheltering the world's largest waterlily, **Victoria amazonica**, a gender-bending giant which flowers as a female with white petals, imprisons beetles for pollination purposes, and reopens later in the day with male organs developed and deep crimson petals. Above the glasshouse sits a charming terraced **tearoom/bar**, where the strains of Walton's music can be heard, and an enclosure with bright hummingbirds flitting about. Paths loop through luxuriant foliage to the pyramid-shaped rock that holds Walton's ashes, a cascade guarded by a sculpted crocodile and a pretty **Thai pavilion** surrounded by heavy-headed purple agapanthus. At the garden's summit, a belvedere provides superb views across the island.

Devotees of Walton's music shouldn't miss the prettily theatrical **museum** above the tearoom, which shows a video about the composer and features portraits by Cecil Beaton, a bust by Elizabeth Frink, and paintings and set-designs by John Piper. And it's well worth combining your visit to the garden with free **concerts** (April–July, Sept & Oct Sat & Sun 5pm), held in the adjoining recital hall, which provide a forum for students from Fiesole and Naples.

Forio

FORIO sprawls around its bay, another growing resort that is quite pretty behind its seafront of bars and pizzerias, focusing around the busy main street of Corso Umberto. Out on the point on the far side of the old centre (turn right at the far end of Corso Umberto), the simple **Chiesa Soccorso** is a bold, whitewashed landmark from which to survey the town.

There are good **beaches** either side of Forio: the **Spiaggia di Chiaia**, a short walk to the north; to the south **Cava del Isola** which is popular with a young crowd; and the **Spiaggia di Citara**, a somewhat longer walk to the south along Via G. Mazzella. Here you'll find the **Giardini Poseidon** (April–Oct daily 8.30am–7pm; €25 per day, €20 for a half-day), an extensive complex of blissfully relaxing thermal baths on the seafront.

If you decide to **stay**, try the charming and central *Punta del Sole* on Piazza Maltese (℡081.989.156, ℻081.998.209, ⓦwww.hotelpuntadelsole.it; ❻), with balconied rooms set in a beautiful garden – or there's the more basic, but friendly, *Nettuno*, Via C. Piro 1 (℡081.997.140, ℻081.507.1055; ❹). For the island's inviting **youth hostel**, *Il Gabbiano* (℡081.909.422; €16), with its own swimming pool, you'd be advised to book well ahead; it's on the bus route just over 1km south of Forio. There are some good **eating** options here: head for the delightful *Umberto a Mare* (closed Nov–March) tucked under the Chiesa Soccorso, whose pretty whitewashed interior looks out onto the sea. If you have a car, take the road to Monte Epomeo and head for *Peppina di Renato* (closed Wed Nov–Feb) where you sit on barrel seats to consume great pizzas; or just off the coast road heading south is *Il Melograno* (closed Mon & Tues in winter), which does a modern take on traditional Ischia cuisine.

Sant'Angelo and around

Ischia is most pleasant on its southern side, the landscape steeper and greener, with fewer people to enjoy it. **SANT'ANGELO** is probably its loveliest spot, a tiny fishing village crowded around a narrow isthmus linking with a humpy islet that's out of bounds to buses, which drop you right outside. It's inevitably quite developed, centring on a harbour and square crowded with café tables and surrounded by pricey boutiques, but if all you want to do is laze in the sun it's perhaps the island's most appealing spot to do so. There's a reasonable **beach** lining one side of the isthmus that connects Sant'Angelo to its islet, as well as the nearby stretch of the **Spiaggia dei Maronti**, 1km east, which is accessible by plentiful taxi boats from Sant'Angelo's harbour (€3), or on foot in about 25 minutes – take the path from the top of the village.

Taxi boats will drop you at one of a number of specific features: one, the **Fumarole**, is where steam emerges from under the rocks in a kind of outdoor sauna; further along close by a couple of hotels is a path that cuts inland through a mini-gorge to the **Terme Cavascura**, where hot springs have been harnessed for you to pamper yourself thoroughly (daily 8.30am–1.30pm & 2.30–6pm; €9 for swim & sauna; €19 upwards for mud treatments).

Up above Sant'Angelo looms the craggy summit of Ischia's now dormant volcano, **Monte Epomeo**. Ischia Porto-bound buses make the twenty-minute trip up to **FONTANA**, a superb ride, with wonderful views back over the coast, from where you can climb up to the summit of the volcano. Follow the signposted road off to the left from the centre of Fontana: after about five minutes it joins a larger road; after another ten to fifteen minutes take the left fork, a stony track off the road, and follow this up to the summit – when in doubt, always fork left and you can't go wrong. It's a steep hour or so's climb, especially at the end when the path becomes no more than a channel cut out of the soft rock. However, there are a couple of scenically placed cafés in which to gather your energies at the top, where the views are stunning. Bear in mind, too, that you can drive to within about twenty minutes of the summit, leaving your vehicle by the signs for the military exclusion zone.

There are plenty of places to **stay** in and around Sant'Angelo; the cheaper places tend to be outside the village proper. Centrally situated, with balconies fronting the sea, *Casa Celestino* (℡081.999.213, ℻081.999.149; closed Nov–March; ❾) is an attractive option. Up in Succhivo, ten minutes' walk back in the direction of Forio (the bus passes right by), *Casa Guiseppina*, on the main Via D'Iorio (℡ & ℻081.907.771; half board obligatory €35), is excellent. On a rocky headland above Sant'Angelo itself, the *San Michele* (℡081.999.276, ℻081.999.149; ❾) is pricier but has a beautifully lush garden and terrace and a seawater pool. When it comes to **eating**, you might be wise to walk up to the next village along from Succhivo, Panza, where the *Da Leopoldo* restaurant (℡081.907.086; closed Mon–Sat lunchtimes March–Oct, and Jan, Feb & Dec) is famous in these parts for its Ischian specialities (rabbit, great sausages and good antipasto table), cosy atmosphere and moderate prices. It is, however, a bit difficult to find: follow Via S. Gennaro from the main square of Panza for about ten minutes, and it's a little way past the *Hotel Al Bosco*. In Sant'Angelo itself you could do worse than stoke up on the fine pizzas at the unpretentious *Da Pasquale*, up in the old centre of the village; everywhere else is much of a muchness.

Prócida

A serrated hunk of volcanic rock that's the smallest (population 10,000) and nearest island to Naples, **Prócida** has managed to fend off the kind of tourist numbers that have flooded into Cápri and Ischia. It lacks the spectacle, or variety, of both islands, though it compensates with extra room and extra peace. Its main town, **MARINA GRANDE**, where you arrive by ferry, is a slightly run-down but picturesque conglomeration of tall pastel-painted houses rising from the waterfront to a network of steep streets winding up to the fortified tip of the island – the so-called **Terra Murata**. Part of this was once given over to a rather forbidding prison, now abandoned, but it's worth walking up anyway to see the abbey church of **San Michele** (daily 9.30am–12.45pm & 3–6pm, closed Sun afternoon), whose domes are decorated with a stirring painting by Giordano of St Michael beating back the Turks from Prócida's shore. The views, too, from the nearby belvedere are among the region's best, taking in the whole of the Bay of Naples, from Capo Miseno bang in front of you right around to the end of the Sorrentine peninsula and Cápri on the far left.

For the rest, Prócida's appeal lies in its opportunities to swim and eat in relative peace. There are **beaches** in Marina Grande itself, on the far side of the jetty, and, in the opposite direction, beyond the fishing harbour, though both are fairly grubby. Similarly, **Spiaggia Chiaia**, just beyond the fishing harbour of nearby Coricella, is a reasonable bathing beach but isn't very large and can get crowded. You can walk there, or the Chiaioella bus stops nearby.

On the whole if you want to swim you're better off making the fifteen-minute bus journey from Marina Grande to **CHIAIOELLA**, where there's a handful of bars and **restaurants** around a pleasant, almost circular bay and a long stretch of sandy beach that is the island's best. By taking the road up from behind the beach you can cross the bridge onto the islet of **Vivara**, a nature reserve, very peaceful and overgrown. It's a refreshingly bucolic affair after the rest of the island, where the settlement is pretty much continuous.

Practicalities

The island has no tourist office as such, but you can get **information** from the Graziella Travel Agency (Mon–Sat 9am–1pm & 4–7pm; closed Sat pm in winter; ☎081.896.9594, ⓦwww.procida.net) on Via Roma. For **getting around**, a bus service connects Marina Grande with Chiaioella roughly every twenty minutes and coincides with all ferry and hydrofoil arrivals. There's not much choice if you want to **stay** on the island: there are only a handful of hotels, together with a couple of *pensioni*. Nicest, if your budget stretches to it, is *La Casa Sul Mare* (☎ & ⓕ081.896.8799; ⓦwww.lacasasulmare.it; ❼), at Via Salita Castello 13, on the way to San Michele. Rooms are simple, fresh and elegant and all have a sea-view terrace. Alternatively, in Chiaioella there is the *Riviera* hotel, ten minutes' walk from the beach at Via G. de Procida 36 (☎081.896.7197, ⓦwww.hotelrivieraprocida.it; closed Oct–March; ❹) – the bus goes right by. *Crescenzo*, at Via Marina Chiaiolella 33, is a three-star with a fine ristorante-pizzeria whose speciality is spaghetti with crab meat and courgette (☎081.896.7255, ⓕ081.810.1260, ⓦwww.campnet.it/procida/crescenzo; ❻). If these are full, there's the *Albergo*, between the *Riviera* and the harbour on the left, at Via Rivoli 6 (☎081.896.7488, ⓕ081.896.7670, ⓦwww.campnet.it/celeste; ❻), with nice gardens. Be aware that at all of these places you *must* book in advance. For **camping**, there are five sites on the island, most within easy walking distance of the sea: try one of the two on Via IV Novembre: the *Caravella* (☎081.896.9230;

May–Sept) and the *Vivara* (☎081.896.9242; mid-June to mid-Sept) – both around 200m from the sea. To get to them, take the Chiaioella bus and get off at Piazza Olmo.

Eating is rather easier. In Marina Grande, restaurants line the waterfront Via Roma: *La Medusa*, opposite the ferry terminal (closed Tues), is not cheap but is very good; or economize at the friendly *Ristorante Il Cantinone*, Via Roma 55 (closed Tues), a popular locals' joint where wood-panelled walls add to the marine flavour and the antipasto is unmissable. In Chiaioella, you could try *Il Galeone*, right by the bus stop between the bay and the beach. A number of **café–bars** in Marina Grande serve drinks and *gelati* – try *Capriccio* at Via Roma 99 which also acts as an **Internet** point – while the *Number Two* on Via Libertà, which leads off Via Roma, is the main **nightclub**.

North of Naples: Caserta, Cápua and around

There's not much to draw you to the territory immediately north of Naples. The towns just outside the city – Casoria, Afragola, Acerra – are collectively known as the "**Triangle of Death**" for their Camorra connections and make up a bleak conurbation of poor housing and industrial messiness.

Caserta

Further inland, a short train or bus ride direct from Naples, **CASERTA**, incongruously surrounded by a sprawl of industrial complexes and warehouses that stretches all the way back to Naples, is known as the "Versailles of Naples" for its vast eighteenth-century royal palace, which utterly dominates the town. There's not much point in coming here if you don't want to see this; if you do, be sure to also see the old village of **Caserta Vecchia**, 10km north of the modern town, where the population lived before the building of the palace. To get there by car, more or less the only way, make a left onto Piazza Vanvitelli from the palace and carry straight on to the edge of town, following the road from there up into the hills. It's now almost entirely deserted but is a bucolic antidote to Caserta's soulless streets and has a nice main square and fine twelfth-century cathedral. Should you want to stay, the *Bed and Breakfast Caserta* at Via San Michele 3 (☎0823.329.455, ℱ0823.323.550, ⓦwww.bedandbreakfastcaserta.it; no credit cards; ❻) makes a charming spot. The elegant rooms are furnished with antiques and have a private garden. There are a couple of **restaurants** up here geared to wedding parties and Sunday excursionists from Naples and Caserta: try *A Marchesina*, on the right of the street leading off the square from under the church tower; they do hearty sandwiches and strong local wine – which you can also buy in the adjacent shop. The local speciality, incidentally, is wild boar (and wild boar ham – *prosciutto di cinghiale*) – the animals are still plentiful in the surrounding hills.

The Palazzo Reale

The palace (visible from the bus/train stations) and its grounds are royal creations on the grandest of scales and made a fitting setting for the signing of the German–Italian armistice in 1945. Begun in 1752 for the Bourbon King

Charles III to plans drawn up by Vanvitelli, and completed a little over twenty years later, it's an awesomely large complex, built around four courtyards, with a facade 245m long, nestling between two curving brick arms and overlooking a massive, classically ordered square. However, it's ultimately a dull structure that substitutes size for inspiration. Only the majestic central staircases up to the **royal apartments** (Tues–Sun 8.30am–6.30pm; €4.20) hit the right note. And the apartments themselves are a grand parade of heavily painted and stuccoed rooms, sparsely furnished in empire style, some with great, overbearing classical statues and all, in their brazen, overstated display of wealth, pretty disgusting – not least in the smug portraits of the Bourbon dynasty, especially the one of the podgy Francis I with his brat-like children. There's little point in singling out anything of special significance: there isn't anything really, and it's the feel of the building and its pitiless overstatement that are the real attractions.

Behind the palace, the **gardens** too (Tues–Sun 8.30am–5pm; €2) are classically ordered and on no less huge a scale, stretching out behind along one central three-kilometre-long axis and punctured by myth-inspired fountains. The main promenade is longer than it looks from the palace (it's a good half an hour's walk or a short bicycle ride), and regular buses make the round trip, dropping you off at selected intervals along the way and turning round by the main cascade at the top, completed in 1779, which depicts Diana turning Actaeon into a stag. Walk to the top, look back at the palace, hop on a bus . . . and depart.

Santa Maria Cápua Vetere and Cápua

Regular buses run from Caserta, either from the bus/train station or the stop just to the left as you exit the palace, for the 6km to **SANTA MARIA CÁPUA VETERE** – a not especially pleasant journey past jutting signs, petrol stations and run-down housing. There's not much to Santa Maria itself either, but in its day this originally Etruscan, later Samnite, city, then known as Cápua, was the second city of Italy, centre of the rich and important region of Campania and famous for its skill in working bronze. Its first-century-AD **amphitheatre** was once the largest in Italy after the Colosseum, and parts of it remain on the far side of town, a right turn shortly after Piazza San Francesco d'Assisi. It held a reputed Roman gladiator school and barracks, and it was here that the gladiators' revolt, led by Spartacus, broke out in 73 BC – a revolt that was only put down after two years and four lost battles. The amphitheatre (Tues–Sun 9am–sunset; combined ticket with Mithraeum €2.50) now is less well preserved than the Colosseum (though better than Pozzuoli's), having lost most of the surrounding tiers – and many of the remaining ones have been concreted over. But the network of tunnels underneath survives reasonably intact, and is accessible. The **Mithraeum** across the road, down Via Antifeatro and then left down Via Morelli, is one of the best preserved in the country and redolent with the bizarre, bloodletting rites that accompanied the cult of Mithraism and has a well-preserved fresco of Mithras himself in action.

There are heaps of rubble and a handful of artefacts dotted around the amphitheatre, not least a large piece of mosaic, but most of the finds have found their way to the **Museo Provinciale** in **CÁPUA**, 4km down the road (Tues–Sat 9am–12.30pm, Sun 9am–1pm; €4.13). Sited on the broad curve of the Volturno River, it's a marginally more attractive place than Santa Maria, but it's not really worth the trek (or even bus ride) if you're without a car.

Benevento

BENEVENTO, further inland than Cápua or Caserta and reachable in about an hour and a half from Naples by bus or train, was another important Roman settlement, a key point on the Via Appia between Rome and Brindisi and as such a thriving trading town. Founded in 278 BC, it was at the time the farthest point from Rome to be colonized, and even now it has a remote air about it, circled by hills and with a centre that was (pointlessly) bombed to smithereens in the last war and even now seems only half rebuilt. Its climate also ranks among southern Italy's most extreme.

The Town

Buses from Naples drop you on the main square, where the **Duomo** is an almost total reconstruction of its thirteenth-century Romanesque original; what's left of its famous bronze doors, believed to be Byzantine, is now stashed inside. Left from here, the main street, **Corso Garibaldi**, leads up the hill, a once elegant thoroughfare lined with ancient palaces. Off to the left about halfway up, the **Arch of Trajan** is the major remnant of the Roman era, a marvellously preserved triumphal arch that is refreshing after the scaffolding and netting of Rome's arches, since you can get close enough to study its friezes. Built to guard the entrance to Benevento from the Appian Way, it's actually as heavy-handed a piece of self-acclaim as there ever was, showing the Emperor Trajan in various scenes of triumph, power and generosity. Further up Corso Garibaldi, the **Museo Sannio** (Tues–Sun 9am–1pm; €2.58), in the cloister behind the eighth-century church of Santa Sofia, holds a selection of Roman finds from the local area, including a number of artefacts from a temple of Isis – various sphinxes, bulls and a headless statue of Isis herself. There are also terracotta votive figurines from the fifth century BC, and the cloister itself has capitals carved with energetic scenes of animals, humans and strange beasts – hunting, riding and attacking.

There are more bits and pieces from Roman times scattered around the rather battered old quarter of town, the **Triggio** – reached by following Via Carlo Torre off to the left of the main road beyond the cathedral. The **Bue Apis**, at the far end of Corso Dante, is another relic from the temple of Isis, a first-century BC sculpture of a bull. And in the heart of the old quarter there are the substantial remains of a **Teatro Romano** built during the reign of Hadrian – though it's been a little over-restored for modern use. In Hadrian's time it seated 20,000 people, rather less today as the upper level remains mossily decrepit, but it's still an atmospheric sight – looking out over the green rolling countryside of the province beyond and, like most of Benevento, relatively unvisited by tourists.

Practicalities

Benevento is roughly 60km from Naples, and **buses** run roughly every two hours from Piazza Garibaldi – an hour-and-a-half trip. **Trains** stop down the hill from the centre and if you're coming from Naples, the private FBN line is the quicker option. Benevento is easily seen on a day excursion and there's no need **to stay**, but if you're pushing on east to Fóggia and Puglia (to which there are regular train connections), or if you get stuck, the small and affable *Della Corte* (T & F 0824.54.819; no credit cards; ❷), Piazza Piano di Corte, is the best bet. For **food**, if you're just here for the day you're likely to be content with the snacks, pizza and *tavola calda*-style dishes at *Pizzeria Romana*, next door to the cathedral on the corner of Via Carlo Torre. For evening eating there are passable restaurants dotted on and around the main Corso Garibaldi.

The Amalfi coast

Occupying the southern side of Sorrento's peninsula, the **Costiera Amalfitana** lays claim to being Europe's most beautiful stretch of coast, its corniche road winding around the towering cliffs that slip almost sheer into the sea. By car or bus it's an incredible ride (though it can get mighty congested in summer), with some of the most spectacular stretches between Salerno and Amalfi. If you're staying in Sorrento especially it shouldn't be missed on any account; in any case the towns along here hold the beaches that Sorrento lacks. The coast as a whole has become rather developed, and these days it's in fact one of Italy's ritzier bits of shoreline, villas atop its precarious slopes fetching a bomb in both cash and kudos. But the cliffs are so steep, and the towns' growth so inevitably constrained, that it seems unlikely that the Amalfi coast can ever become completely spoilt.

Coming **from Sorrento**, buses normally join the coast road a little way **west of Positano**. If the coast road is closed, however, which it is from time to time due to landslides and forest fires, the bus from Sorrento will take the alternative route, via Castellammare and Agerola, right over the backbone of the Sorrentine peninsula, which is itself a journey worth making – the bus zigzagging down the other side in a crazy helter-skelter of hairpin bends to join the road a few kilometres **west of Amalfi**.

Positano, Praiano and the Grotta dello Smeraldo

There's not much to **POSITANO**, only a couple of decent beaches and a great many boutiques; the town has long specialized in clothes made from linen, georgette and cotton, as well as handmade shoes and sandals. But its location, heaped up in a pyramid high above the water, has inspired a thousand picture postcards and helped to make it a moneyed resort that runs a close second to Cápri in the celebrity stakes. Since John Steinbeck wrote up the place in glowing terms back in 1953, the village has enjoyed a fame quite out of proportion to its tiny size. Franco Zefferelli is just one of many famous names who have villas nearby, and the people who come here to lie on the beach consider themselves a cut above your average sun-worshipper.

Positano is, of course, expensive, although its beaches are nice enough and don't get too crowded. The main one, the Spiaggia Grande right in front of the village, is reasonable, although you'll be sunbathing among the fishing boats unless you want to pay over the odds for the pleasanter bit on the far left; there's also another, larger stretch of beach, Spiaggia del Fornillo, around the headland to the west, accessible in five minutes by a pretty path that winds around from above the hydrofoil jetty – although its central section is also a pay area. Nonetheless the bar-terrace of the *Puppetto* hotel (see opposite), which runs along much of its length, is a cheaper place to eat and drink than anywhere in Positano proper.

Buses to Positano drop off at the top of the village, from where it's a steep walk down or a short bus ride (every 30min) to the little square at the bottom end of Via Cristoforo Colombo, five minutes' walk from the seafront; **ferries** and **hydrofoils** from Cápri, Naples, Amalfi and Salerno pull in at the jetty just to the right of the main beach. There's a busy **tourist office** just back from the beach by the church steps (June–Sept Mon–Sat 8am–2pm & 3–8pm; Oct–May Mon–Fri 8am–2pm; ℡089.875.067, ⓦwww.positanonline.it). By far the cheapest **accommodation** in Positano is the private *Ostello Brikette* (℡089.875.857, ⓕ089.812.814, ⓦwww.brikette.com; €20; doubles ➋; curfew

Mon–Fri midnight, Sat & Sun 1am, 2am in summer; lockout 10am–4pm; closed Nov–March), on Via G. Marconi 358, a 200-metre walk uphill from the main bus stop at the *Bar Internazionale* on the coastal road from Sorrento to Amalfi. It's a friendly, efficient and clean **hostel** with stunning Mediterranean views, bar and Internet access, but mattresses are wrapped in polythene and dorms can be airless. Alternatively, the *Bougainville*, right by the bus stop (℡089.875.047, ℱ089.811.150, ⓦwww.bougainville.it; closed Nov to mid-March; ❹), is very pleasant and very central. Less central, but handy for the Fornillo beach on Via Fornillo, are the *Maria Luisa* (℡ & ℱ089.875.023; closed Jan & Dec; ❹), with a plant-filled terrace and four cats, the nicely furnished and amenable *Casa Guadagno* (℡089.875.042, ℱ089.811.407; closed Nov–March; ❺), and the more expensive *Vittoria* (℡089.875.049, ℱ089.811.037, ⓦwww.hotelvittoriapositano.com; ❼). Consider also the *Pupetto* hotel (℡089.875.087, ℱ089.811.517, ⓦwww.hotelpupetto.it; closed Nov–Feb; ❼), which is very enticingly placed right by the beach and has a good restaurant.

For **food**, *Chez Black*, right behind Positano's beach (closed Jan), is a very popular long-established seafood restaurant – their pizzas are the closest you'll get to a budget sit-down lunch in this location. *O Caporale*, just around the corner (closed Nov–March), has a nicely painted fish-themed ceiling and isn't too expensive whatever you have. If you're really strapped for cash, check out the *alimentari* by the tourist office at the foot of the church steps. At the other end of the price spectrum is *La Cambusa*, on the right as you approach the beach (closed Tues in winter), where a full fish blowout will set you back around €50–60 a head. The *Brigantino* bar, Via del Saracino 35, is open for **Internet** access every day.

PRAIANO is a little further along to the east, squeezed into a cleft in the rocks. Much smaller and very much quieter than Positano, it consists of two tiny centres – Véttica Maggiore on the Positano side and Marina di Praiano on the Amalfi side. There is a small patch of beach, together with a couple of sandy coves close by, but food and **rooms** are still fairly pricey. In Véttica Maggiore, the *Casa Colomba pensione* (℡089.874.079, ℱ089.874.392; half-board in July & Aug; no credit cards; ❸), high above the main road just after the first tunnel, has great views from its location at the top of 180 steps. Conveniently sited by the bus stop, the *Continental* hotel (℡089.874.084, ℱ089.874.779, ⓦwww.continental.praiano.it; half-board in Aug; closed mid-Nov to March; ❺) has a choice between frescoed rooms furnished with antiques in the main house or smart bungalows right on the cliff edge. It comes with a private beach, and on the terraces above it a **campsite** *La Tranquillità*, which must be one of the best sited in the country. *Onda Verde* (℡089.874.143, ℱ089.874.125, ⓦwww.ondaverde.it; ❺) is similarly well placed, perched on the cliff edge at Marina di Praiano, or there are rooms to rent right on the harbour front – ask at *La Conchiglia* restaurant in Marina di Praiano (℡089.874.313; ❷). There's a concentration of **restaurants** in Véttica Maggiore; try the *Trattoria San Gennaro*, next to the church (closed Wed), which has a good choice of local dishes, or *La Brace*, above the pharmacy (closed Wed Oct–March), with pizzas straight from the wood-fired oven, which you can eat on the covered terrace.

Shortly after Praiano you pass the **Furore** gorge, which gashes into the mountainside just above the coast road, and a little further along, about 4km out of Praiano (reachable direct by taxi boat from either Praiano or Amalfi), the **Grotta dello Smeraldo** (daily: March–Oct 9am–5pm; Nov–Feb 10am–4pm; €5), one of the most highly touted local natural features. A lift descends to the level of the grotto, where you can tour the interior by boat – a mildly impressive but certainly not unmissable sight which includes a rather startling sub-aquatic nativity scene.

Amalfi

Set in a wide cleft in the cliffs, **AMALFI**, a mere 4km or so further east, is the largest town and perhaps the highlight of the coast, and a good place to base yourself. It has been an established seaside resort since Edwardian times, when the British upper classes found the town a pleasant spot to spend their winters. Actually Amalfi's credentials go back much further: it was an independent republic during Byzantine times and one of the great naval powers, with a population of some 70,000; Webster's *Duchess of Malfi* was set here, and the city's traders established outposts all over the Mediterranean, setting up the Order of the Knights of St John of Jerusalem. Amalfi was finally vanquished by the Normans in 1131, and the town was devastated by an earthquake in 1343, but there is still the odd remnant of Amalfi's past glories around today, and the town has a crumbly attractiveness to its whitewashed courtyards and alleys that makes it fun to wander through.

The Town

The **Duomo** (daily 7.30–10am & 5–7.30pm), at the top of a steep flight of steps, utterly dominates the town's main piazza, its tiered, almost gaudy facade topped by a glazed tiled cupola that's typical of the area. The bronze doors of the church came from Constantinople and date from 1066. Inside it's a mixture of Saracen and Romanesque styles, though now heavily restored, with a major relic in the body of St Andrew buried in its crypt. The cloister – the so-called **Chiostro del Paradiso** (daily: July–Sept 9am–9pm; Oct–June 10am–5pm; €2.50) – is the most appealing part of the building, oddly Arabic in feel with its whitewashed arches and palms. There's an adjacent **museum** (same hours and ticket as the cloisters), with various medieval and episcopal treasures, most intriguingly an eighteenth-century sedan chair from Macau, which was used by the bishop of Amalfi; a thirteenth-century mitre sewn with myriad seed pearls, gold panels and gems; and three silver reliquary heads – two gravely bearded and medieval, the third an altogether more relaxed and chubby Renaissance character, with elaborately braided hair.

Almost next door to the Duomo, in the small **museo civico** (Mon–Fri 8am–2pm; free), part of the Municipio, you can view the *Tavoliere Amalfitana*, the book of maritime laws that governed the republic, and the rest of the Mediterranean, until 1570. On the waterfront, the old **Arsenal** is a reminder of the military might of the Amalfi republic, and its ancient vaulted interior now hosts art exhibitions and suchlike. In the opposite direction you can follow the main street of **Via Genova** up through the heart of Amalfi and out the other side, to where the town peters out and the gorge narrows into the **Valle dei Mulini** (Valley of Mills), once the centre of Amalfi's high-quality paper industry. Apart from a rather desultory paper museum, there's not much to see here nowadays, despite the grandiose claims inferred by name, and it's hard to find a mill that is still functioning – although there is a shop on the left that makes and bottles its own *limoncello* (lemon liqueur), a speciality of the region.

Practicalities

Amalfi's most immediate focus is the seafront, a humming, cheerfully vigorous strand given over to street stalls, a car park for the town's considerable tourist traffic, and an acceptably crowded **beach**, although once again the best bits are

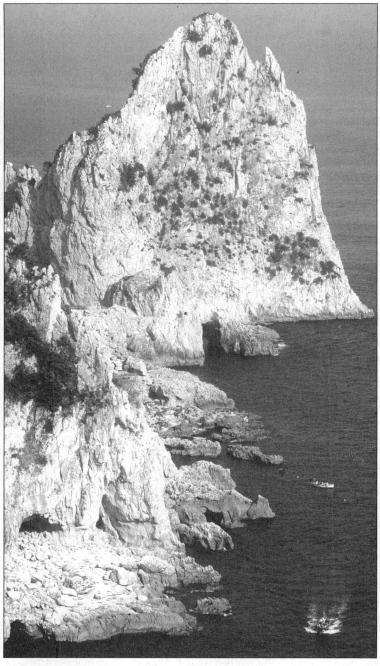

△ The Faraglioni rocks, Cápri

pay areas only. The **tourist office** (Mon–Fri 8.30am–2.30pm & 3–5pm, Sat 8.30am–1pm; ☎089.871.107, ⓦwww.azienturismoamalfi.com), not overburdened with information, is situated in the courtyard next to the **post office** in Corso Repubblica Marinara, the road that runs along the waterfront, and close to the *Bar Sirena* at no. 21, which provides **Internet** access. **Ferries** and **hydrofoils** to Salerno, Positano, Cápri and Ischia (see p.884) leave from the landing stage in the tiny harbour.

If you're staying, you'll find a number of fair-priced **hotels**, among the cheapest of which are the centrally placed *Sant'Andrea* on the main square (☎089.871.145; closed Oct & Nov; ❹), which is pretty and stuffed full of pictures and ornaments, and beyond it the family-run *Lidomare*, tucked away up to the left of the main square at Via Piccolomini 9 (☎089.871.332, ⓕ089.871.394, ⓦwww.lidomare.it; ❺). Once a ducal palace, it's full of antiques and though it's nicely old-fashioned, some bathrooms come equipped with hydromassage. On the western edge of the town is the swish *Hotel Santa Caterina* (☎089.871.012, ⓕ089.871.351, ⓦwww.hotelsantacaterina.it; ❾), an elegant villa with period furnishings; it has a great lift which plummets down from the bougainvillea-wreathed terrace to an arc of rocky beach. You might also consider staying in the adjacent village of Atrani (see below). If you're on a tight budget you could opt for the cosy **youth hostel** *Beata Solitudo* located in Agerola, 16km north of Amalfi (☎081.802.5048; €9), which also has a small **campsite**. A regular bus connects with Amalfi.

As for **eating**, *Trattoria da Gemma*, a short walk up Via Genova on the left (closed Wed), has a small, carefully considered menu, strong on fish and seafood, and a lovely terrace overlooking the street, although it's not one of the town's cheaper places. *Il Tari*, a little further up on the left after Via Genova has become Via P. Capuano, *is* cheap and not at all bad; further up again, *Taverna del Duca* on Piazza Spirito Santo 26 (closed Thurs) has a cosy atmosphere, and their *fusilli del Duca* is well worth a try; while *Il Mulino*, right at the top of the main street ten minutes' walk from the Duomo, is a cheery and inexpensive family-run place used by locals that does good pizza and pasta dishes. If you fancy a bit of **nightlife**, carry on up the main street to the *Roccoco Discopub* in the otherwise quiet Valle dei Mulini. Back in the centre of town, if all you want is a snack, the *Green Bar*, Via P. Capuano 46, has sandwiches, pizza slices, *calzone* and the like.

Atrani

A short walk around the headland (take the path off to the right just before the tunnel through the *Zaccaria* restaurant), **ATRANI** is an extension of Amalfi really, and was indeed another part of the maritime republic, with a similarly styled church sporting another set of bronze doors from Constantinople, manufactured in 1086. It's a quiet place, which benefits from all the attention bestowed upon its neighbour, with a pretty, almost entirely enclosed little square, Piazza Umberto, giving onto a usually gloriously peaceful (and free) patch of sandy **beach** – hard to believe the bustle of Amalfi is just around the corner. Another good reason for coming here is that it has a great **place to stay** in the *A'Scalinatella*, Piazza Umberto 1 (☎ 089.871.492, ⓕ089.871.930, ⓦwww.hostelscalinatella.com), hostel and hotel – a friendly, family-run establishment that offers excellent-value hostel beds (Easter–Sept €21; Oct–Easter €13; price includes dinner) and regular private rooms (❹) in various different buildings around town. For the reception, look for the telephone box and take the steps up to the right just beyond it. Otherwise for **eating**, try *A'Paranza*, Traversa Dragone 2 (closed Tues), a friendly seafood trattoria with fabulous home-made pasta and a speciality of *zuppa di pesce*. You'll find the restaurant on the road that leads inland from the main square.

Ravello

The best views of the coast can be had inland from Amalfi in **RAVELLO**: another renowned spot, "closer to the sky than the seashore", wrote André Gide – with some justification. Ravello was also an independent republic for a while, and for a time an outpost of the Amalfi city-state; now it's not much more than a large village, but its unrivalled location, spread across the top of one of the coast's mountains, 335m up, makes it more than worth the thirty-minute bus ride through the steeply cultivated terraces up from Amalfi – although, like most of this coast, the charms of Ravello haven't been recently discovered. Wagner set part of *Parsifal*, one of his last operas, in the place; D.H. Lawrence wrote some of *Lady Chatterley's Lover* here; John Huston filmed his languid movie *Beat the Devil* in town (a film in which the locations easily out-shine the plot); and Gore Vidal is just one of the best known of many celebrities who spend at least part of the year here.

The Town

Buses drop off on the main **Piazza Vescovado**, outside the **Duomo**: a bright eleventh-century church, renovated in 1786, that's dedicated to St Pantaleone, a fourth-century saint whose blood – kept in a chapel on the left-hand side – is supposed to liquefy like Naples' San Gennaro once a year on July 27. It's a richly decorated church, with a pair of twelfth-century bronze doors, cast with 54 scenes of the Passion; inside, there are two monumental thirteenth-century ambones (pulpits), both wonderfully adorned with intricate and glittering mosaics. The more elaborate one to the right of the altar, the Gospel ambo, dated 1272, sports dragons and birds on spiral columns supported by six roaring lions, and with the coat of arms and the vivacious profiles of the Rufolo family, the donors, on each side. On the left, the Epistle ambo illustrates the story of Jonah and the whale. Downstairs in the crypt the **museo** (daily 9.30am–1pm & 3–7pm; €1.50) holds the superb bust of Sigilgaita Rufolo and the silver reliquary of Saint Barbara, alongside a collection of highly decorative, fluid mosaic and marble reliefs from the same era.

The Rufolos figure again on the other side of the square, where various left-overs of their **Villa Rufolo** (daily: June–Sept 9am–8pm; Oct–May 9am–6pm; €4) lie scattered among rich gardens overlooking the precipitous coastline; this is the spectacular main venue for the prestigious chamber concerts held from March to October. The programme is widely advertised and tickets cost €20 (details from the Ravello Concert Society ☎089.858.149, ⓦ www.ravelloarts .org). If the crowds (best avoided by coming early in the morning) put you off, turn left by the entrance and walk up the steps over the tunnel for the best (free) view over the shore, from where it's a pleasant stroll through the back end of Ravello to the main square. Failing that, walk in the opposite direction to the **Villa Cimbrone** (daily 9am–sunset; €4.10), ten minutes away, whose formal gardens spread across the furthest tip of Ravello's ridge. Most of the villa itself, once frequented by the Bloomsbury Group, is not open to visitors, though it's worth peeping into the crumbly, flower-hung cloister as you go in and the open crypt down the steps from here – probably the only crypt with views over cliffs and open sea. But the gardens are entirely accessible, dotted with statues and leading down to what must be the most gorgeous spot in Ravello – a belvedere that looks down to Atrani below and the sea beyond.

Practicalities

Small orange SITA buses run up to Ravello from Amalfi roughly hourly from Piazza Flavio Gioià. If you can't tear yourself away, the **tourist office** in Piazza Duomo (Mon–Sat: May–Sept 8am–8pm; Oct–April 8am–7pm; ☎089.857 .096, ⓦ www.ravello.it/aziendaturismo) has information on **rooms**. If you have money to burn, the *Palumbo*, Via San Giovanni del Toro 16 (☎089 .857.244, ⓕ089.818.133,ⓦ www.hotelpalumbo.it; ➒), is definitely the place to do it – one of Italy's best opportunities to experience real, old-world luxury in a magnificent location. If this seems too much, the *Parsifal*, back down the road (☎089.857.144, ⓕ089.857.972, ⓦ www.hotelparsifal.com; ➏), easily competes on great views for quite a lot less. The *Garden* (☎089.857.226, ⓕ089.858.110; ➏), all of whose cool, blue rooms have a terrace with a vista, is just off the main piazza, and next to the cathedral on Viale Wagner the charming *Toro* (☎089.857.211, ⓕ089.858.592, ⓦ www.hoteltoro.it; ➎) makes up for its lack of view with a lovely garden.

There are some marvellous places **to eat**, all doing their best to exploit the location. The restaurant at the *Garden* (closed Tues Nov–March) boasts a marvellous panoramic terrace, while the *Palazzo della Marra* in Via della Marra 7 (closed Tues Nov–March), full of abstract paintings and huge ceramic plates, has an enticingly good tourist menu at €32. The *Cumpà Cosimo* restaurant at Via Roma 48 is good too, with great local food and wine at moderate prices.

⑬ Salerno

Capital of Campania's southernmost province, the lively port of **SALERNO** is much less pell-mell than Naples and, being well off most travellers' itineraries, has a good supply of cheap accommodation – making it a good base for both the Amalfi coast and the ancient site of Paestum further south. During medieval times the town's medical school was the most eminent in Europe. More recently, it was the site of the Allied landing of September 9, 1943 – a landing that reduced much of the centre to rubble. The subsequent rebuilding has restored neither charm nor efficiency to the town centre, which is an odd mixture of wide, rather characterless boulevards and a small medieval core full of intriguingly dark corners and alleys. But the town's siting, strung along the top of its gulf and looking across to the sheer wall of the Amalfi coast, is fine.

Arrival, information and accommodation

Salerno's **train station** lies at the southern end of the town centre on Piazza Vittorio Veneto. City and local **buses** pull up here; those from Paestum and further south arrive and leave from Piazza della Concordia, down by the waterside nearby; buses from Naples use the SITA bus station at Corso Garibaldi 119. **Ferries** and **hydrofoils** from Amalfi, Càpri and Positano (see p.884) arrive in the harbour.

For information, there's an enthusiastic and helpful **tourist office** outside the train station on Piazza Vittorio Veneto (Mon–Sat 9am–2pm & 3–8pm; ☎089.231.432, ⓦ www.salernocity.com), which has bags of information on the Salerno area; the fortnightly *Memo* (€0.50) has listings of what's on. The town's cheaper **hotels** are handily placed along (or just off) Corso V. Emanuele, which leads north into the town centre from the station: try friendly *Santa Rosa*, at Corso V. Emanuele 16 (☎ & ⓕ089.225.346; ➋); you can use the **Internet** at the language school one floor down in the same building

(Mon–Sat 9am–2pm & 3.30–8pm). Right by the station is the more upmarket *Plaza*, Piazza Vittorio Veneto 42 (℡089.224.477, ℱ089.237.311; ❹). Alternatively there's a new **youth hostel**, *Ave Gratia Plena*, a few minutes' walk west of the cathedral at Via dei Canali (℡089.790.251; €12).

The Town

There isn't a great deal to see in Salerno, but it's pleasant to wander through the vibrant streets of the centre, especially the ramshackle old medieval quarter, which starts at the far end of **Corso V. Emanuele**, lined with designer shops and heaving with people (especially on Saturdays), and has **Via dei Mercanti** as its main axis. To the right of Via dei Mercanti, up Via Duomo, the **Duomo** (daily 7am–noon & 4–7.30pm) squeezes into the congested streets, an enormous church built in 1076 by Robert Guiscard and dedicated to St Matthew. The main features are yet another set of bronze doors from Constantinople and, in the heavily restored interior, two elegant mosaic pulpits dating from 1173, as well as the quietly expressive fifteenth-century tomb of Margaret of Anjou, wife of Charles III of Durazzo. The polychrome marble crypt holds the body of St Matthew himself, brought here in the tenth century. Outside, the courtyard is cool and shady, its columns plundered from Paestum, centring on a gently gurgling fountain.

From the cathedral, turn right at the bottom of the steps for the **Museo Diocesano** (daily 9am–6pm; free), which, although its opening times are erratic, is worth a hammer on the door to see its large altar-front, embellished with ivory panels in the late eleventh century and the largest work of its kind in the world. Failing that, turn left out of the church, left at the bottom of the steps, left again and then first right, and 100m or so further on is the **Museo Provinciale** (Mon–Sat 9am–1pm & 4–8pm, Sun 9am–1.30pm; free) – a largely dull museum that occupies two floors of an over-restored Romanesque palace. It's worth heading upstairs though, past the deadening array of fossils and fragments of ancient sculpture, to see the sensual *Head of Apollo*, a Roman bronze fished from the Gulf of Salerno in the 1930s.

Eating and drinking

Salerno isn't a tourist town, but it's a very sociable place with plenty of street life and an intriguing choice of **eating places**. If all you want is a bite at lunchtime, there is a good *tavola calda* at *Pranz Express*, Corso V. Emanuele 15, and the fruit and vegetable market off to the left just before the end of Corso V. Emanuele is a good source for picnics, as are the *alimentari* and *panificio* outside the station by the *Plaza* hotel. Among sit-down options, the nearby *Trattoria da Sasa*, tucked away at Via degli Orti 22 (closed Mon lunchtime & Sun–Thurs eves), a right turn off Corso V. Emanuele immediately after Via Diaz, is a reliable restaurant, used by locals, serving decent fish and seafood. Other than that, there are a number of places in and around the old town, and on the main roads – Via Roma and Lungomare Trieste – that sweep around by the sea. *Antica Pizzeria Vicolo delle Neve*, left off Via dei Mercanti about 50m past the Duomo (closed Wed & lunchtimes) – in the old city – is a deliciously downbeat place with both pizzas and local specialities; *Il Caminetto*, five minutes' away at Via Roma 232 (closed Wed), is a little pricey but friendly; while *Ristorante Santa Lucia*, in between the two at Via Roma 182 (closed Mon), is the elegant haunt of Salerno's young and trendy. *Trianon*, Piazza F. Gioia (closed Sun lunchtime), sells many variations on the traditional, huge Neapolitan pizza – the best in the town.

As for **bars**, *Mennir* at Vicolo Giudaica 50 is a friendly, stylish place open in the evening for as long as its customers want to drink. A few doors away, *La Cantinella* offers a more traditional Italian atmosphere and cheap drinks. **Via Roma** is lined with good bars, from the unnamed, bustling place tucked into a corner at the northern end of the street, past *Easy Rider* which, despite the name, is an Irish pub, to the more ostentatiously trendy *Zen*.

Salerno hosts what claims to be the oldest **fair** in Europe – the Fieravecchia – on the first weekend in May, when townsfolk parade in medieval gear, food stalls are set up along the waterfront and a 2000-egg omelette is cooked down at the beach on a giant metal contraption.

Paestum

About an hour's bus ride south of Salerno, the ancient site of **Paestum** (daily 9am–1hr before sunset; €4, €6.50 for site plus museum) spreads across a large area at the bottom end of the **Piana del Sele** – a wide, flat plain grazed by the buffalo that produce a good quantity of southern Italy's mozzarella cheese. Paestum, or Poseidonia as it was known, was founded by Greeks from Sybaris in the sixth century BC, and later, in 273 BC, colonized by the Romans, who Latinized the name. But by the ninth century a combination of malaria and Saracen raids had decimated the population and left the buildings deserted and gradually overtaken by thick forest, and the site wasn't rediscovered until the eighteenth century during the building of a road through here. It's a desolate, open place even now ("inexpressibly grand", Shelley called it), mostly unrecognizable ruin but with three golden-stoned **temples** that are among the best-preserved Doric temples in Europe. Of these, the Temple of Neptune, dating from about 450 BC, is the most complete, with only its roof and parts of the inner walls missing. The Basilica of Hera, built a century or so earlier, retains its double rows of columns, while the Temple of Ceres at the northern end of the site was used as a Christian church for a time. All are now sectioned off from the public and are undergoing various stages of restoration, though it's still possible to appreciate their scale and proportion. In between, the forum is little more than an open space, and the buildings around are mere foundations.

The splendid **museum** (daily 9am–7pm; closed first and third Mon every month; €4, €6.50 including site), across the road, holds Greek and Roman finds from the site and around. Straight ahead of you as you enter are some stunning sixth-century bronze vases (*hydriae*), decorated with rams, lions and sphinxes; behind them more bronze – gleaming helmets, breastplates and greaves. Make a point of seeing the rare Greek tomb paintings, the best of which are from the Tomb of the Diver, graceful and expressively naturalistic pieces of work, including a diver in mid-plunge, said to represent the passage from life to death, and lovers banqueting. Attractive fourth-century terracotta plates depict all sorts of comestibles – fruit, sweets, fruit and cheese, and a set of weathered archaic period Greek metopes from another temple at the mouth of the Sele River, a few kilometres north, shows scenes of fighting and hunting. On the first floor, which is devoted to Roman finds, highlights are a statue of an abstracted looking Pan with his pipes, a third-century relief showing a baby in pointed hat and amulets, and a sarcophagus cover of a tenderly embracing couple.

Practicalities

It's perfectly feasible to see Paestum on a day-trip from either Salerno or Agrópoli (see below) – it's much nearer to the latter. However, you can also stay in one of the many hotels or campsites that are strewn along the sandy shore beyond the site. The **tourist office** on the main road opposite the site entrance (Mon–Sat 9am–1pm & 2–7pm, closes 5pm in winter, Sun 9am–1pm; ☎0828.811.016, ⓦwww.paestumtourism.it) has details. For **hotels** just walk down to the beach (about fifteen minutes) and take your pick: close by the site to the left of where the main road hits the beach is the attractively tiled *Calypso*, Via Mantegna 63 (☎0828.811.031, ⓕ0828.721.191, ⓦwww.calypso.paestum.com; ❸), one of the few hotels around that can cope with vegan, macrobiotic and organic diets (with traditional food as well). The cheerful and very good value *Baia del Sole*, Via Torre 48 (☎ & ⓕ0828.811.119; ❸), is one of the few places that does not require half-board in high season. If you prefer to be a little more secluded, *Villa Rita* (☎0828.811.081, ⓕ0828.722.555, ⓦwww.hotelvillarita.it; ❺) is pleasantly situated in relaxing gardens just south of the archeological site. Or for a stopover in real style, head 4km northwards to the *Tenuta Seiiano* (☎0828.724.544, ⓦwww.agriturismoseliano.it; ❺), a farm run by the Bellelli family, where the buffalo herd produces milk for mozzarella. You can either stay in the main house where the rooms are loaded with antiques, or in more modern rooms near the rose garden and swimming pool; the food here is excellent. Most of the **campsites** are much of a muchness: the *Apollo* (☎0828.811.178; April–Sept) on Via Principe di Piemonte and the *Villagio dei Pini* (☎0828.811.030; open all year) are two of the most central and are well signposted. As for the **beach** itself, the development behind it is fairly tacky, and it's a bit grimy in places. But space, even in peak season, is rarely too much of a problem. For **food**, the *Apollo* restaurant, right by the temples, is not bad and is pleasantly located in an old building, or for something more intimate and upmarket try the *Ristorante Enoteca Tavernelle* at Via Tavernelle 14, around 1km out on the Salerno road.

The Cilento coast

Immediately south of Paestum, the coastline bulges out into a broad mountainous hump of territory known as the **Cilento** – one of the remotest parts of Campania, thickly wooded with olives and chestnuts. **AGRÓPOLI**, the first town you reach, fifteen minutes out from Paestum, is a good base for the ruins (buses every hour), and its blend of the peaceful old quarter, heaped on a headland, and the new modern centre down below makes for a nice place to spend a few days, with a vivacious main-street *passeggiata*. The beaches aren't great, but you can swim from the flat rocks in the harbour and the water's perfectly clean. For **accommodation**, the *Hotel Carola* in the harbour (☎0974.826.422, ⓕ0974.826.425; ❸), on Via Carlo Pisacane, has attractive double rooms with balconies, or there's the *Serenella*, at Lungomare San Marco 150 (☎0974.823.333, ⓕ0974.825.562; full-board in Aug; ❸), which has its own private beach. Agrópoli is also on the main Salerno–Reggio railway line and there's an excellent **youth hostel**, *La Lanterna*, about 1km from the station and conveniently close to the bus stop for Paestum, at Via Lanterna 8 (☎0974.838.364; closed Nov–mid-March; €10), which also has family rooms (❶) and does full dinners for €8.

Acciaroli, Marina d'Ascea and Velia

Buses run down to **ACCIAROLI**, about 25km south of Salerno – one of the Cilento's larger resorts and a port for the hydrofoils plying the coast during summer. The railway joins the shoreline again at **MARINA D'ASCEA**, a fairly indifferent resort but surrounded by hotels and campsites, especially along the lengthy sand beach that stretches north to Marina del Casalvelino.

Close by, **MARINA DI VELIA** gives access to the site of **Velia** (daily 9am–1hr before sunset; €2.50) – comprising the ruins of the Hellenistic town of Elea, founded around 540 BC and an important port and cultural centre, home to its own school of philosophy. Later it became a favourite holiday resort for wealthy Romans, Horace just one of many who came here on the advice of his doctor. The decline of Velia parallels that of Paestum – malarial swamp rendering much of the area uninhabitable – though the upper reaches were lived in until the fifteenth century. There, however, the comparison ends: the remains of Velia are considerably more decimated than those of Paestum and the town was never as crucial a centre, with nothing like as many temples. At the centre of the ruins the **"Porta Rosa"**, named after the wife of the archeologist who conducted the first investigations, is one of the earliest arches ever found – and the first indication to experts that the Greeks knew how to construct such things. Up from here, the **Acropolis** has relics of an amphitheatre and a temple, together with a massive Norman tower – visible for some distance around.

Outside the site there's a restaurant, the *Amoroso*, and beyond here a small beach – though this can get crowded in summer. There's another decent restaurant, too, *La Torre*, 200m up the road going towards Agrópoli.

Palinuro

Cheerful **PALINURO**, too, further south, is worth a stop, named after the legendary pilot of the *Aeneid*, who is supposed to have drowned here. It's a much livelier place than anywhere else on the Cilento coast, and so can be packed out. But it's a good alternative to Agrópoli, both as a base for the site of Velia and a beach-bumming spot – the sea here is one of the cleanest spots on the coast – and the harbour area to the east of town retains a certain fishing port authenticity. From the harbour, you can explore the stunning craggy coast of the Capo Palinuro, studded with a series of caves, either by taking a guided **boat tour** (€8) or – more fun – by renting a **motorboat** (€25 for 2hr, plus around €10 for petrol).

The best **hotel** option is *Hotel Residence La Torre* (T0974.931.107, F0974.931.264; ❹), just 10m from the glorious sandy beach by the harbour, where you'll find a sociable bar – a great place for a sundowner. In town, the attractive central **campsite** provides shade and has a rudimentary restaurant, with access to a sandy beach where steps from a series of rock pools take you straight into the sea. A number of good unpretentious **eating** options line Via Indipendenza, the best of which is friendly *L'Ancora* at no. 115; their speciality is *zuppa di pesce*, and the wood-fired oven turns out large and delicious pizzas. Alternatively, blow your last few euros at the *Da Carmelo* restaurant (sometimes closed Wed out of season), 2km south of town at Località Isca, whose fish and seafood are said to be the best for miles around.

Travel details

Metropolitana/FS Naples

Gianturco–Piazza Garibaldi–Piazza Cavour–
Montesanto–Piazza Amedeo–Mergellina–Piazza
Leopardi (Fuorigrotta)–Campi Flegrei–Cavalleggeri
d'Aosta–Bagnoli–Pozzuoli. Trains every 8min.
Circumflegrea (information ☎ 800.001.616).
Connects Naples Montesanto to Cuma, Lido Fusaro
and Torregaveta with 6 departures daily.
Departures every 20min for all stations to Licola.
Circumvesuviana (information ☎ 081.772.2444).
This line runs between Naples and Sorrento, with
many stops around the southern part of the bay,
including Ercolano and Pompeii, every 30min.
Ferrovia Cumana (information ☎ 800.001.616).
Connects Naples Montesanto with Fuorigrotta,
Agnano, Bagnoli, Pozzuoli, Báia, Fusaro and
Torregaveta. Departures every 10min.

Trains

Benevento to: Fóggia (12 daily; 1hr 15min);
Naples (17 daily; 1hr 5min–1hr 50min).
Naples to: Agrópoli (15 daily; 1hr 40min);
Benevento (18 daily; 1hr 5min–1hr 55min);
Caserta (every 20min; 35–45min); Fóggia (4 daily;
2hr 20min–3hr); Formia (hourly; 50min); Paola
(Calabria) (7 daily; 3hr); Rome (hourly; 2hr 20min);
Salerno (hourly; 50min); Santa Maria Cápua Vetere
(9 daily; 50min); Sapri (7 daily; 2hr).
Salerno to: Paestum/Agrópoli (9 daily; 35min);
Sapri (10 daily; 1hr 20–50min).

Buses

Agrópoli to: Acciaroli (6 daily; 1hr); Paestum
(hourly; 10min); Salerno (hourly; 1hr 20min); Sapri
(1 daily; 3hr 30min).

Naples to: Amalfi (5 daily; 1hr 55min); Benevento
(6 daily; 1hr 30min); Cápua (hourly; 1hr 15min);
Caserta (every 20min; 1hr); Salerno (every
15–30min; 1hr 5min); Sorrento (1 daily Mon–Sat at
8.45am; 1hr 20min); Pompeii Scavi (every 30min;
30min); Positano (1 daily Mon–Sat at 8.45am; 1hr
55min).
Naples Capodichino airport to: Sorrento (6 daily;
1hr).
Ravello to: Amalfi (10 daily; 30min).
Salerno to: Agrópoli (hourly; 1hr 20min); Amalfi
(hourly; 1hr 10min); Naples (every 15–30min; 1hr
5min); Padula (2 daily; 1hr 50min–2hr); Paestum
(hourly; 1hr); Positano (every 1–2hr; 2hr); Sorrento
(every 1–2hr; 2hr 45min); Vietri (every 30–min;
1hr).
Sorrento to: Amalfi (10 daily; 1hr 25min); Naples
(1 daily at 6.35pm; 1hr 20min); Naples
Capodichino Airport (6 daily; 1hr min); Positano (10
daily; 35min); Salerno (12 daily; 2hr 45min).

Ferries and hydrofoils

Naples to: Aeolian Islands/Milazzo (ferry:
twice/thrice weekly in high season at 9pm; 9hr
30min/18hr 50min) Aeolian Islands (hydrofoil:
June–Sept twice daily 4–6hr); Cagliari (ferry:
weekly/thrice weekly in high season at 7.15pm;
16hr 15min); Palermo (ferry: daily at 8.45pm; 9hr
45min; hydrofoil: daily at 5.30pm; 4hr); Sorrento (7
daily hydrofoils; 35min).
Salerno to: Amalfi (April–Sept 6 daily hydrofoils;
35min) Positano (5 daily hydrofoils; 1hr 10min).
For details of ferry and hydrofoil connections
between Naples, the Amalfi coast and Salerno and
the islands, see p.884.

Puglia

CHAPTER 14

Highlights

* **Lecce** In the southern tip of Italy, Lecce is an exuberant city of Baroque architecture and opulent churches. **See p.945**

* **Péschici and Vieste** For sun and sea, head for these resorts, with the option of travelling onwards to the Trémiti islands. **See p.922**

* **Ostuni** One of the most stunning hill-top towns in southern Italy, with a sun-bleached old quarter and a sandy coastline 7km away. **See p.944**

* **Castles** Puglia's Swabian castles are monuments to thir-teenth-century engineering. See impressive examples at Lucera and Castel del Monte. **See p.915 & p.931**

* **Martina Franca** This lively town with its Moorish feel makes a good base for exploring the surrounding area's *trulli* – Puglia's traditional conical white-washed buildings. **See p.935**

* **Bari** Not a traditional tourist destination, but the maze-like old city makes for fascinating wandering and there are excellent restaurants in all price brackets. **See p.926**

14

Puglia

Puglia is the long strip of land, 400km from north to south, that makes up the "heel" of Italy. For centuries it was a strategic province, colonized, invaded and conquered (like its neighbours, Calabria and Sicily) by just about every major power of the day – from the Greeks through to the Spanish. As elsewhere in the south, each ruling dynasty left its own distinctive mark on the landscape and architecture – as seen, for example, in the surviving traces of Roman agricultural schemes and the fortified medieval towns. There's no escaping some of the historical influences in Puglia. Perhaps most distinctive are the Saracenic kasbah-like quarters of many towns and cities, the one at **Bari** being the biggest and most atmospheric. The Normans endowed Puglia with splendidly ornate cathedrals; there's one at **Trani** which skilfully blends many strands of regional craft traditions from north and south. And the Baroque exuberance of towns like **Lecce** and **Martina Franca** are testament to the Spanish legacy. But if there's one symbol of Puglia that stands out, it's the imposing castles built by the Swabian Frederick II all over the province – foremost of which are the **Castel del Monte** and the remnants of the palace at **Lucera**.

Clean seas and reliable sunshine have made Puglia a popular spot for holidays, with acres of campsite-and-bungalow-type tourist villages – as well as a large number of flashy four-star hotels – principally serving tourists from Italy and Germany. The cities, however, including Bari, have little that's characteristic enough to warrant long stays: **Táranto** and its surroundings have fought a losing battle with the local steel industry, while **Bríndisi** is known and visited only for its ferry connections with Greece; even **Lecce** has little to hold you once you've trekked your way along modern boulevards to see the crazed confectionery of its Baroque churches.

Nevertheless, there's a geographical diversity to Puglia that can be very attractive. The very southern tip, the **Salentine peninsula**, is rocky and dry, more Greek than Italian, while there's plenty of barren mountain scenery in the undulating plateau of **Le Murge**, in the centre of the province. The best escape, though, is north to the hills, forests and beaches of the **Gargano promontory**. Though the beaches have been monopolized by mega-campsites and hotels, this is where you'll find some of the finest unpolluted sand and sea anywhere on the Adriatic.

Getting around Puglia by public transport is fairly easy, at least as far as the main towns and cities go. FS **trains** connect nearly all the major places, while small, private lines head into previously remote areas – in the Gargano and on the edges of Le Murge. Most other places can be reached by **bus**, though as ever services are often infrequent or inconveniently early – a problem that can only really be solved by taking, or renting, your own **car**.

Fóggia and the Tavoliere

The broad sweep of the **Tavoliere plain** stretches from the Basilicata border to the edge of the Gargano massif – flat, fertile lands that are southern Italy's wheat bowl, and the source of the country's best pasta. It was the Romans who attempted the first intense cultivation of the area, parcelling the land up into neat squares for distribution to its pensionable centurions. This lent the land its chessboard appearance, from which the Tavoliere takes its name, but for the centurions the gift was a mixed blessing. **Fóggia** province proved to be an unhealthy place, an earthquake-prone swampland rife with malarial mosquitoes, and settlements here suffered from disease and disaster in fairly equal proportions. It wasn't until the advent of irrigation schemes in the 1920s that the mosquitoes lost their malarial bite and the area began to take on its present rich appearance. As the transport hub of the province, Fóggia is somewhere you'll probably pass through, though for more of an idea of what the Tavoliere is like, head for the walled town of **Lucera** or the little village of **Tróia**.

Fóggia

The Tavoliere's main town, **FÓGGIA**, looms out of the plain without warning, a fine starting-point for exploring northern Puglia and the Gargano promontory though not an encouraging stop in itself. Although Fóggia flourished under Frederick II, who declared it an imperial residence and built a palace here, the town was devastated in turn by the French in 1528, an earthquake in 1731 and Allied bombs during World War II. Today the city's streets

Igoumenitsa, Corfu, Patras, ▲ ▲ *Kefallonia, Ithaca & Paxi*

are all reassuringly earthquake-proof, wide and low-built, a modern layout that is handsome enough, but you're going to have to search hard in between the tree-lined boulevards for what is left of the old town.

What little there is lies scattered around the **Duomo**, which is to the left off Corso Vittorio Emanuele, the main drag that runs down from the central, fountained Piazza Cavour. The cathedral is an odd Romanesque–Baroque sandwich, the top part tacked on in the eighteenth century after the earthquake.

While you're here, take a look at the nearby **Museo Cívico** on Piazza Nigri (Sun–Fri 9am–1pm; €1.50), reached by walking down the Corso to Via Arpi. Incorporated into the side of the building are three portals, one of which – the Porta Grande, with the thoughtful-looking eagles – is all that remains of Frederick II's imperial palace. The museum underwent major renovations recently and should have reopened by early 2003. Duck inside and there are the usual regional archeological finds and a more interesting section on local life and folklore. If you're interested in such things, the modest **Museo di Storia Naturale** at Via Bellavia 1 (Tues–Sun: summer 9am–1pm & 5–9pm; winter 5–7pm; €1.50; take bus #8 or #12 from the train station) is dedicated to local flora and fauna, with a couple of dinosaur casts including a Pterosaur among the birds and insects on show.

That really is it, as far as Fóggia's sights go, though there are enough green spaces and shopping streets up in the new town to occupy any remaining time – something you might well have, as Fóggia is an important rail junction on the main Bologna–Lecce and Naples–Bari lines.

14

PUGLIA | Fóggia and the Tavoliere

913

The influence of Puglia's former rulers is evident in the region's food. Like the **Greeks**, Pugliesi eat lamb and kid spit-roast over herb-scented fires and deep-fried doughnut-like cakes steeped in honey; and like the **Spanish** they drink almond milk, *latte di mandorla*. Puglia is the source of eighty percent of Europe's pasta and most of Italy's fish; it produces more wine than Germany and more olive oil (even if it is not always of the finest quality) than all the other regions of Italy combined. It's famous for olives (from Cerignola), almonds (from Ruvo di Puglia), dark juicy tomatoes (often sun-dried), fava beans, voluptuous figs (fresh and dried), *cotognata* (a moulded jam made from quinces) and for its melons, grapes and green cauliflower. The most distinctive local **pasta** is *orecchiette*, ear-shaped pasta which you will still see women making in their doorways in the old part of Bari. Look out too for *panzarotti alla barese*, pockets of pasta stuffed with *ragù* (meat sauce), egg and cheese or *ricotta* and *prosciutto* that are deep-fried in olive oil. Otherwise, there is a marked preference for short stubby varieties of pasta, which you'll find served with peppers, cauliflower, or even turnip tops (*cime di rapa*). Not surprisingly, fish and shellfish dominate many a menu. There are some good fish soups (*zuppe di pesce*) whose ingredients and style vary from place to place – the Bríndisi version, for example, is dominated by eels.

As elsewhere in the south, lamb is the most common **meat**, often roast over rosemary and thyme branches, which impart a wonderful flavour. A local speciality is *gnummerieddi*, a haggis-like dish, made by stuffing a lamb gut with minced offal, herbs and garlic – best grilled over an open fire. There is little beef or pork, poultry is uncommon, and game is virtually nonexistent; as a result, horsemeat is popular, especially in the Salento area. To confound your prejudices, go for *braciole di cavallo*, horsemeat steaks cooked in a good rich tomato sauce.

Cheeses are a strong point, including *ricotta*, *cacioricotta*, *mozzarella*, *burrata*, *caprini* (small fresh goat's cheeses preserved in olive oil), and *fagottini* (small smoked cheeses, a speciality of the Fóggia area). If you're in Andria, try *burrata*, a creamy soft cow's cheese.

Puglia is the land of the grape. In recent years the region has exploited its hot, fertile plain to become one of the wealthiest parts of the south, and while much of its **wine** is pretty basic (the vast majority is used in Torinese vermouths) there have recently been immense improvements. Yields have been severely reduced, grapes have been picked at precisely the right moment, and modern technology has been introduced to great advantage. Wine-maker Kym Milne, for example, has created an excellent Chardonnay del Salento and a huge red Salice Salentino. Other wines to look out for include Primitivo di Manduria (another huge red) and Locorotondo, a straightforward, clean-tasting white, as well as dessert wines.

Practicalities

The **train station** is on Piazzale Vittorio Veneto, on the northern edge of town, a short walk from Piazza Cavour and the centre. FS services (information ☎0881.727.234) from here run to Manfredonia, while Ferrovie del Gargano (FG; ☎0881.772.491; office to the left of the station entrance) trains go to Péschici Calenella. SITA **buses**, which serve the whole region, arrive at and depart from just outside the train station; their ticket office (☎0881.773.117) is under the porticoes opposite the station; when this is closed, buy tickets at the *Kiwi Bar*, on the corner of Viale XXIV Maggio. There are also Ferrovie del Gargano buses (ⓦwww.ferroviedelgargano.com) to Manfredonia and Vieste. The **tourist office** (Mon–Fri 8am–1pm; ☎0881.723.650 or ☎0881.723.141, Ⓔaptfoggia@pugliaturismo.com); a twenty-minute walk into town, on the first floor at Via E. Perrone 17, off

Piazzale Puglia, has a lot of good information on the province as a whole. If you are headed for the Gargano, it's worth picking up *Tutto Gargano* (€3 from newsstands or free from the tourist office), a great resource for accommodation and information on festivals and events; check out its site at ⓦwww.tuttogargano.com, too.

Staying in Fóggia may be necessary if you arrive late or need to leave early: *Hotel Venezia*, Via Piave 40 (ⓣ0881.770.903; ❸), is a good, cheap hotel that's been recently renovated; to get to it go down Viale XXIV Maggio from the station, then third right. *Hotel Europa*, Via Monfalcone 52 (ⓣ0881.721.743, ⓦwww.italiaabc.com; ❼), is more upmarket with smart rooms and helpful staff – again it's down Viale XXIV Maggio from the station, then second right. The grandest place in town is *Cicolella*, at Viale XXIV Maggio 60 (ⓣ0881.688.890, ⓦwww.cicolella.isnet.it; ❽), a businesslike hotel clad in black marble and cherry wood dating back to the early 1900s and offering attentive service. The only time that bed space will be short is at the beginning of May, during the **Fiera di Fóggia**, a huge international agricultural affair held on the outskirts of the town.

There are several good **food** options: try *Il Rugantino*, Via Luigi Sturzo 23 (closed Mon) – head down Corso Roma and turn left at the sanatorium – which offers great pizzas and other dishes; *Osteria Chacaito*, Via Arpi 62 (closed Sun), a typically Foggiese osteria with excellent wines near the Museo Civico; or spend a little more at *Da Pompeo*, Vico al Piano 14 (closed Sun), down Corso Vittorio Emanuele II and right at the Palazzo Vescovile – a good place to indulge in Pugliese specialities. For **drinking**, *Coniglio Mannaro* (closed Mon) is an interesting pub-type bar at Via Bruno 26 in the historic centre, sometimes with live music and art exhibitions; *Nessun Dorma* (closed Tues), Via Duomo 20, does good snacks.

Lucera

Just 18km west, within easy reach of Fóggia (hourly buses), **LUCERA** is a far better introduction to Puglia. A small town with a bright and bustling centre, it was once the capital of the Tavoliere and has a distinct charm, its vast castle dominating the landscape for miles around. It was once a thriving Saracen city: Frederick II, having forced the Arabs out of Sicily, resettled 20,000 of them here, on the site of an abandoned Roman town, allowing them complete freedom of religious worship – an almost unheard of act of liberalism for the early thirteenth century.

Buses arrive in Piazza del Popolo, from where it's only a short walk up Via Gramsci to the **Duomo**, which marks the centre of the medieval walled town. The cathedral – a dark, rather miserable building – was built in the early fourteenth century after Frederick II's death when the Angevins arrived and a conflict with the Saracens began. The Angevins won and built the cathedral on the site of a mosque; by the end of their rule, few of the town's original Arab-influenced buildings were left. However, the Arabic layout of Lucera survived and there's a powerful atmosphere here – best appreciated by wandering the narrow streets of the old town, peering into the courtyards and alleyways. Close to the cathedral, a little way down Via de' Nicastri, is the **Museo Cívico** (Tues–Sat 9am–1pm & 4–7pm, Sun 9am–1pm; €1), well stocked with Greek pottery and their Puglian copies. There are some fine mosaics and terracotta heads too, and the bust of a Greek youth said – rather optimistically – to be that of Alexander the Great.

The other sights are all outside the old centre, most notably the **Castello** (Tues–Sun: summer 9am–1pm & 3–8pm; winter 9am–2pm; free), built by

Frederick and designed to house a lavish court which included an exotic collection of wild beasts. To get there from Piazza Duomo follow Via Bovio and Via Federico II to Piazza Matteotti and look for the signs. The largest in southern Italy after Lagopésole in Basilicata (see p.977), the castle commands spectacular views over the Tavoliere, stretching across to the foothills of the Apennines to the west and the mountains of Gargano to the east. Contained within the kilometre-long walls are the evocative remains of Frederick's great palace, fragments of mosaic work and fallen columns peering out of a dense undergrowth of wild flowers. The Roman **amphitheatre** (same hours as castle) is on the western edge of town and often holds concerts in summer.

Stopping over in Lucera wouldn't be a bad thing: you can **stay** in town at the functional *La Balconata 2* at Viale Ferrovia 15 (℡0881.546.725; ❸) or *Al Passetto* at Piazza del Popolo 24 (℡0881.520.998, ⓦ www.hotellabalconata.it; ❸) – the latter has a fine restaurant (closed Mon). Or there's a good farm B&B 5km outside Lucera, *Masseria Mezzana Grande*, on the road to Bíccari (℡0881.529.915; ❼), with large rooms, modern bathrooms and a private kitchen and sitting room for guests. Bear in mind that the B&B comes second to the farm's main business of growing grain, olives and almonds, and that sometimes they have problems with their water supply and can't take guests so you should ring ahead. As for **places to eat**: *La Tavernetta*, Via Schiavone 7–9, behind the cathedral (closed Wed), is an excellent place for crispy pizzas cooked in a wood-fired oven, pasta dishes and local wine, while the lively, informal *Lupus in Fabula*, Via Gramsci 10 (closed Tues in winter & July), in the old town, offers typically Luceran dishes and a good wine list at moderate prices.

Tróia

Frequent buses also make the short ride (from either Lucera or Fóggia) to **TRÓIA**, 18km due south of Lucera. The locals seem curiously blasé as to the origin of their village's name; it means "slut" in Italian, which probably has its origins in Helen of Troy, but no one is able to offer a logical connection with the village. Whatever the reason, the Tróiani atone for the name by having five patron saints, whose statues are paraded around town in a procession every July 9.

At all other times of the year Tróia is a quiet, dusty village, its only sight the fine **Duomo**, an intriguing eleventh-century blend of Byzantine and Apulian–Romanesque styles, with a generous hint of Saracen influence, too. The great bronze doors are covered with reliefs of animals and biblical figures, while above, surrounded by a frenzy of carved lions frozen in stone, is an extraordinary rose window. Distinctly Saracen in flavour, the window resembles a finely worked piece of oriental ivory, being composed of eleven stone panels, each one delicately carved. There's more exact detail inside too, including a curiously decorated pulpit and some ornate capitals.

Manfredonia and Siponto

By Puglian standards, **MANFREDONIA** is a new town, a mere 600 years old, founded – as the name suggests – by Manfred, illegitimate son of Frederick II. The Austrians struck the first blow of World War I on Italian soil here by bombing the town's station in 1915, but this is really Manfredonia's only claim to fame. Heavy industry on the northern outskirts and the flat, featureless landscape mean that for most vistitors it's little more than a gateway to the Gargano promontory, and most people pass quickly through. Still, what the town lacks in ambience and historical sights is more than made up for by its sandy beaches, which stretch for miles down the coast.

The **Castello**, on Corso Manfredi, was started by Manfred and extended by the Angevins. Its huge bastions were added in 1607 by the Spanish to stave off a Turkish attack: they failed to do so, the Turks landing in 1620, ravaging the hapless inhabitants and destroying much of the town – though most of the protective walls still survive. The castle now houses the **Museo Nazionale** (daily except first and last Mon of the month: 8.30am–7.30pm; €2.50), largely devoted to Daunic finds from the seventh and sixth centuries BC. The prize exhibits are several stone stelae, thought to be tombstones, richly carved with images of armoured warriors, female figures and scenes from daily life. There are also relics from a water-worshipping cult from the Grotta Scaloria – a reaction perhaps to the drought that struck the Tavoliere in Neolithic times.

Practicalities

The easiest way to reach Manfredonia is by train from Fóggia: from the **station** turn right and it's a short walk along Viale Aldo Moro to Piazza Marconi. Just across the square, Corso Manfredi leads up to the **tourist office** in the *comune* building in Piazza del Popolo (Mon–Fri 9am–1pm, plus Tues 4.30–7.30pm; ☎0884.581.998; ✉manfredonia@pugliaturismo.com), a pro loco rather than a full-blown tourist office, but which has some information on the Gargano area. A **hydrofoil** service runs to the Trémiti Islands from the harbour via Vieste (June–Sept 1 daily; a 2hr journey; €20.71 single); **tickets** can be purchased from the Adriatica office (🌐www.adriatica.it) in the harbour itself at least thirty minutes before departure. Taking the hydrofoil means you will probably have to **stay** overnight: the large hotel *Azzurro* (☎0884.581.498; ❸), around 200m west of the station at Via G. di Vittorio 56, is friendly and conveniently central.

There are plenty of **restaurants** in Manfredonia, one of the best of which is *Coppola Rossa*, Via dei Celestini 13 (booking advisable ☎0884.582.522; closed all day Mon & Sun eve), where you can feast on grilled antipasti, *troccoli alla scoglio* (tiny pasta in a sauce of clams, eels, tomatoes and oil), *orecchiette* with scampi, or *ciambotta* (fish soup).

The Gargano promontory

The **Gargano promontory** rises like an island from the flat plains of the Tavoliere, geographically and culturally different from the rest of Puglia. Its landscape is remarkably diverse: beaches and lagoons to the north, a rocky, indented eastern coast and a mountainous, green heartland of oaks and beech trees – reminiscent of a Germanic forest rather than a corner of southern Italy. For centuries the promontory was extremely isolated, visited only by pilgrims making their way along the valley to Monte Sant'Angelo and its shrine. Nowadays tourism has taken off in a big way, especially on the coast around Vieste, but in 1991 the whole peninsula became a national park, helping to protect the Gargano from overbearing development and ensuring that much of the interior remains supremely unspoiled and quiet.

Approaches to the promontory are pretty straightforward. **FS trains** run from Fóggia to Manfredonia on the southeast side of Gargano, from where it's only 16km by **bus** to Monte Sant'Angelo. Alternatively, in the north of the region, **Ferrovie del Gargano** (🌐www.ferroviedelgargano.com) operates

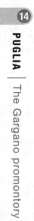

THE GARGANO PROMONTORY

10 km

0

N

◀ *Trémiti Islands (Late April–Early October)*

◀ *Trémiti Islands*

▶ *Barletta*

▶ *Fóggia*

▶ *Fóggia*

Vieste

Péschici

San Menaio

Ischitella

Vico del Gargano

Rodi Garganico

Lago di Varano

Lago di Lésina

Cagnano Varano

Sannicandro Garganico

Apricena

San Severo

San Marco in Lamis

San Giovanni Rotondo

S. Maria di Pulsano

Monte Sant'Angelo

Manfredonia

Siponto

Mattinata

Mattinatella

Pugnochiuso

Testa del Gargano

FORESTA UMBRIA

Summer only

- – Ferry
- – Hydrofoil

trains between Fóggia and San Severo. You then change here for onward travel to Péschici-Calenella, from where a bus connects with Péschici. Note that most FG stations are quite a distance from the towns and villages they serve, so always go for the connecting bus if there is one.

Getting around in the interior can be a little more tortuous. **Buses** are run by two companies: SITA (☎0881.773.117) serves the inland towns and operates the inland route to Vieste; and FG (☎0881.725.188 or 0881.772.4918), which runs the trains and connecting buses in northern Gargano, including a coastal bus route to Vieste, via Manfredonia, Mattinata and Pugnochiuso. There is also a **ferry service** connecting Manfredonia, Vieste, Péschici, Rodi Garganico and most coastal towns, which goes on to the Trémiti Islands (p.924).

Monte Sant'Angelo and the pilgrim route

Just north of Manfredonia, perched almost 800m up in the hills, **MONTE SANT'ANGELO** is the highest – and coldest – settlement in the Gargano. Pilgrims have trudged up the switchback paths and roads for centuries to visit the spot where the archangel Michael is said to have made four separate appearances, mostly at the end of the fifth century – making the sanctuary here one of the earliest Christian shrines in Europe and one of the most important in Italy. Today, the pilgrims come by bus, and the major festivals on May 8 and September 28, 29 & 30 every year attract locals from miles around, some of whom turn up in traditional dress.

SITA **buses** – which run every two hours from Manfredonia – drop you in Piazza Duca d'Aosta, from where you should follow the road uphill to the edge of the old town and the Via Reale Basilica, where you'll find the **Santuario di San Michele Arcangelo** itself (July–Sept daily 6.30am–7.30pm; April, June & Oct Mon–Sat 7.30am–12.30pm & 2.30–6pm, Sun 6.30am–7pm; Nov–March closes at 5pm). Apart from a lean octagonal thirteenth-century campanile, the sanctuary seems rather plain on the outside, but from the small courtyard on the right a flight of stone steps leads down to the crypts – heralded by a magnificent pair of eleventh-century bronze doors, made in Constantinople, that form the entrance to the church built on the site of the cave in which the archangel first appeared (in 490). Opposite the campanile, another set of steps leads down to the nearby ruins of the **Chiesa di San Pietro**, behind which is the so-called **Tomba di Rotari** (9am–noon, otherwise see the custodian in San Michele) – an imposing domed tower once thought to be the tomb of Rothari, a seventh-century Lombard chieftain who was converted to Christianity. More prosaically, it's more likely to have been a twelfth-century baptistry; the large baptismal font is just on the right as you enter the tower. Little remains of the church itself, wrecked by an earthquake, but look out for the rose window – a Catherine wheel of entwined mermaids.

Back on Via Reale Basilica, it's an easy clamber up to the ruined Norman **Castello** for good views over the town and valley. From here, you can cut down through the narrow whitewashed streets of the old town to Piazza San Francesco d'Assisi and the **Museo Tancredi** (May–Sept Mon 8am–2pm, Tues–Sun 8.30am–2pm & 3–7pm; Oct–April Mon, Wed & Fri 8am–2pm, Tues & Thurs 8.20am–2pm & 3–7pm; €1.55), an arts and crafts museum with some interesting displays on the production of olive oil, wheat, wine and coal.

Practicalities

For overnight stays (though don't count on available beds at the main pilgrimage times), the only **hotels** are the peaceful *Rotary*, in a panoramic position 1km along the road to Pulsano (☎0884.562.146; ❹); the *Sant'Angelo* nearby (☎0884.565.536; ❺); and *Michael* (as in the Saint), Via R. Basilica 86 (no phone; ❹). For snacks try *Drengot's Pub* in the historic centre at Via Castello 25, which does good sandwiches and cold collations as well as lots of foreign beers. One of the nicest **restaurants** in town is the *Medio Evo*, Via Castelli 21 (closed Mon in winter), serving home-made bread and produce from its own garden.

The pilgrim route: San Giovanni Rotondo

The ancient **pilgrim route** weaved its way along the Stignano Valley between San Severo in the west and Monte Sant'Angelo and until comparatively recently was the only road that linked the villages of the Gargano interior. With your own transport, it's still a good route for exploring a couple of the region's most important religious centres. If you want to follow any part of the pilgrim route by bus, you'll have to plan your itinerary carefully and be prepared to travel in leisurely fashion.

Direct bus services between Monte Sant'Angelo and the first village on the route, **SAN GIOVANNI ROTONDO**, run every couple of hours, although the village is better connected by bus with Manfredonia, a SITA service from there making around fourteen trips a day. Nestling under the highest peak hereabouts, Monte Calvo, San Giovanni Rotondo is a modern centre for pilgrimage on a massive scale: it's the burial place of Padre Pio, a local priest who died in 1968 and was canonized in 2002. Pio received the stigmata and "appeared" before cardinals in Rome while asleep in San Giovanni Rotondo, and won an immense following – especially among Italian Catholics – for his model piety and legendary ability to heal the sick. There's no escaping his frail portrait throughout the Gargano peninsula, but it's especially prominent in San Giovanni Rotondo. A whole industry has grown up in San Giovanni, fuelled by the seven million and more pilgrims who pass through every year, making it the most visited pilgrimage site in the world after Lourdes. It's steadily transforming the town: a new stadium-sized church by Renzo Piano will hold Padre Pio's remains when it is complete (which should be sometime in 2003). The town takes its name from the **Rotonda di San Giovanni**, a building of indeterminate origin on the edge of the old town – like the Tomba di Rotari, it's thought to have been a baptistry, built on the site of an earlier pagan temple.

Nine kilometres further west, and looking splendidly out over the Tavoliere plain, **SAN MARCO IN LAMIS**, though considerably smaller than San Giovanni, is dominated by a huge sixteenth-century Convento di San Matteo, with a modern interior. Every Good Friday the town holds a noisy, lively – and originally pagan – affair called the **fracchie**, when huge bundles of burning wood are hauled through the streets to illuminate the town for the Madonna as she seeks Jesus.

Vieste and the Costa Garganica

About 15km north of Manfredonia, the road tunnels under a mountain to emerge in a softer, greener landscape. **MATTINATA**, a small but popular resort with good campsites, sits back from the coast, overlooking olive groves and pine trees that drop down gently to a magnificent stretch of beach. There's a nice **agriturism** place to stay 1.5km from the roundabout where the buses stop: *Agriturismo Madonna Incoronata* (☎0884.582.317 or ☎0336.285.486, Ⓔagriturismo@gargano.it; ❹) offers well-furnished apartments with kitchen, bathroom and private terrace from €75 per night (minimum two-night stay) on an organic farm growing mostly olives, making a great base for exploring the Gargano. Beyond Mattinata the road splits: one branch (which the SITA bus takes) winds its way through the eastern part of the Foresta Umbra (see p.924) to Vieste; the coastal route (and the FG bus) runs up to **PUG-NOCHIUSO**, a panoramic bay dominated by a grim-looking holiday village surrounded by barbed-wire fences. If you're interested, one of the easiest of the local **hiking trails** starts close by. The path is clearly marked off the Mattinata–Pugnochiuso road, about 3km north of Baia di Zagare, and the trail (around 3km each way) runs sharply down to a beach, the Spiaggia di Vignanótica. To reach the start of the trail, take the FG bus from Mattinata for Pugnochiuso/Vieste and ask to be let off at Località Mégoli.

Vieste

VIESTE juts out into the Adriatic on two promontories, the easternmost point of the Gargano peninsula. Fifty years ago there wasn't even a proper road here, but today Vieste, with its excellent beaches, is the holiday capital of Gargano (and Puglia), and the streets and sands are packed in August. Despite this it has managed to survive as a lively and inviting town, with an interesting historic core and active nightlife that warrant a stop of a day or two – certainly if you're planning to take the ferry from here to the Trémiti Islands.

The **old town** sits on the easternmost of the two promontories, at the tip of which stands the **Chiesa di San Francesco**, once a thriving monastery, and a **trabucco** – a cantilevered arrangement of beams, winches and ropes still used by fishermen to catch mullet. Made of wood, these structures are a feature peculiar to the rocky Gargano coast, probably Phoenician in origin, and the principle at least is straightforward. As mullet swim head to tail, a live mullet is attached to a line and used to entice others to swim over a net suspended below, which is then hoisted up to the platform. Visits can be arranged through the agency Sinergie (℡0884.706635, ✉sinergie@viesteonline.it).

From the church, climb up Via Mafrolla, walking into the old town to Piazza Seggio. Straight ahead, Via Duomo is site of the so-called **Chianca Amara**, the "bitter stone", where as many as 5000 local people were beheaded when the Turks sacked the town in 1554. Further down, beyond the stone, the **Cattedrale**, eleventh century in origin but tampered with in the eighteenth century, is a cool retreat from the fierce glare of the sun in the whitewashed streets; and beyond here the **Castello** is another of Frederick II's installations – owned by the military now and not open to the public, but giving good views over the beaches and town.

You **arrive** by bus at Piazza Mazzini, to the west of the town centre; bear right from here along Viale XXIV Maggio, which becomes Corso Lorenzo Fazzini – the main street. At no. 8 is the main **tourist office** (Mon–Fri 8am–2pm, plus Tues & Thurs 4–7pm; ℡0884.707.495), and there's another at Piazza Kennedy, in the centre of the old town (Mon–Sat: June–Sept 8am–2pm & 4–10pm; Oct–May 8am–2pm & 4–8pm; ℡0884.708.806).

Though there's no shortage of **accommodation** in Vieste, you will need to book ahead in high season and budget options are hard to come by. First choice is the atmospheric *Pensione ai Centro Storico*, Via Mafrolla 32 (℡0884.707.030; ❹), in the old town, with large, simple rooms, and a sun terrace overlooking the promontory where you can bring your own beer and take-out pizza and enjoy the sunset. With just thirteen rooms and many people coming back year after year you need to book well in advance (at Easter for August) and those wanting a stay of three days to a week will be given preference. Perhaps a more straightforward option in the old town is *Seggio*, Via Vesta 7 (℡0884.708.123,

@www.iqsnet.it/hotelseggio; **❼**), with vertiginous views down to its swimming pool and private rocky beach, while around 1.5km north of the castle along the shore, the good-value *Albergo Vela Velo*, Lungomare Europa 19 (☎0884.701.462; **❺**), is a small, modern two-star. A little more upmarket is the *Hotel Punta San Francesco* at Via D. Francesco 2 (☎0884.701.422; **❻**), with lovely views over the promontory and comfortable whitewashed rooms with terracotta tile floors.

There's a huge variety of **places to eat** within the narrow streets and tiny piazzas of the old town. Among the many choices are *Osteria degli Archi*, Via Ripe 2 (booking advisable; ☎0884.705199; closed Mon in winter), which specializes in seafood. *Dragone*, via Duomo 8 (closed Nov–March), located in a natural cave, is also good for fish. The strangely named *Box 19*, Via Santa Maria di Merino 13 (closed Mon & Nov), serves excellent seafood such as *linguine all'astice* (lobster). There are some cheap and cheerful pizzerias on the Piazza Vittorio Emanuele II; and the terrace bar at *Hotel Seggio* (see above) is a good place to chill before dinner.

From June to September there are catamaran and hydrofoil connections to the **Trémiti Islands** (June, July & Sept 1 daily, Aug 3 daily; a 1hr journey; €13.43 single) from Vieste; tickets are available from a number of agencies around town, including Gargáno Viaggi at Piazza Roma 7 (daily 9am–12.30pm & 5–9pm; ☎0884.708.501, @www.garganoviaggi@tiscalinet.it), or from the Adriatica office (@www.adriatica.it) in the harbour. Otherwise, foot-passenger **ferries** (*motonave*) run the rest of the year once a week; buy tickets from the agencies above or from the ticket office at the harbour (look for the "Vieste 1" sign).

Around Vieste

There are a number of day-trips worth making **around Vieste**. The most obvious move is to the **beaches**: there's a small one between the promontories, a second, San Lorenzo, to the north, and a third, Pizzomunno, just south of town; the last is much the nicest and is home from May to September to the *Ghironda Beach* **bar**, a good place for a sandwich or a beer during the day, and heaving at night when the live music and dancing start. Best of all, though, and certainly less crowded, is the marvellous Scialmarino beach, 4km up the coast towards Péschici – walkable if you don't have transport.

Vieste is also an excellent base for seeing the grotto-ridden **coastline** around the Testa del Gargano, south of town, though the only way to do it properly is on an organized trip. Excursion boats for the grottoes leave from next to San Francesco church at around 9am and 2.30pm, a three-hour trip; tickets, costing €13, are again available from Gargáno Viaggi (see above) and SOL (daily March–Oct 9am–1pm & 4–9pm, July & Aug until 11pm; ☎0884.701.558, @www.solvieste.it) at Via Tre Piccioni 5.

Péschici and northern Gargano

Atop its rocky vantage point overlooking a beautiful sandy bay, **PÉSCHICI** is a little smaller than Vieste and one of the most attractive village resorts in the Gargano. Though originally built in 970 as a buffer against Saracen incursions, its labyrinth of tiny streets and houses sporting domed roofs has a distinctly Arabic tinge. Beach-lazing is the focus, although the town also makes a good base for exploring some of the caves and defensive medieval towers of the nearby coastline. The easiest trips are to the grotto at **San Nicola**, 3km east of town (some buses), or 5km west to the **Torre di Monte Pucci** for some fine coastal views.

The FG **train** line ends at Calenella, a few kilometres west of Péschici but connected to the town by a bus. This, and other **buses**, drop you in the newer, beach resort part of Péschici, from where it's a short walk down to the main street – Corso Garibaldi – and the sea. For **accommodation**, the *Locanda Al Castello*, Via Castello 29 (☎0884.964.038; ❹), is a stiff walk away up in the old town, down a narrow lane of whitewashed houses and with an excellent restaurant/pizzeria. For hotels in the newer part of town there's plenty of choice: *Hotel d'Amato* off the SS89 next to the beach (☎0884.963.415, ⓦwww.hoteldamato.it; ❼) offers modern rooms, a restaurant, bar, two swimming pools and sometimes ayurvedic and shiatsu massage. The *Elisa*, right next to the beach at Via Marina 20 (☎0884.964.012; ❺), is a simple place with a so-so restaurant below. You can get cheaper rooms if you are prepared to be a few minutes walk from the beach: *Piccolo Paradiso*, a family-run hotel on Viale Kennedy 29 (☎0884.963.466; ❸), has magnificent sea views and a deservedly popular terraced restaurant. There's also a choice of **campsites** – the *Baia San Nicola* (☎0884.964.231), 2km east along the coast at Punta San Nicola, and *Calenella* (☎0884.968.105) and the much smaller *Baia Calenella* (☎0884.968.212), both west along the SS89 coast road just past the train station at Peschici-Calenella, towards San Menaio. For **eating**, there are scores of resturants, pizzerias, *gelaterie* and bars in the old town, scene of a lively *passeggiata* that goes on all evening. The *Fra Stefano* at Via Forno 8 (closed Nov–March) serves good grilled fish and *orechiette* among other dishes. For a more unusual setting, head for the *Grotta delle Rondini* (closed Nov–March) situated in a natural cave near the port outside the old town, with some good antipasti specialities on the menu, while *La Collinetta* (☎0884.964.151) on the coast road to Vieste (closed Nov to mid-March) serves interesting fish, including seafood gratin and red mullet baked in foil, at reasonable prices. The latter is a hotel too, and their half-pension deals are worth considering: prices range from €39 per person in April–June and September to €67 per person in July and August.

    Ferries to the Trémiti islands from Péschici (calling at Rodi Garganico on the way) leave at around 9am from the port, taking 1hr 15min and costing €25 for the return trip (the ferry brings everyone back at around 5pm). You can buy tickets onshore next to the boat right up until departure.

West along the coast and onwards

Further along the coast, there's a string of white sandy beaches stretching from San Menaio to **RODI GARGANICO** – originally a Greek settlement ("Rodi" is derived from Rhodes) and nowadays, with its beaches and fast hydrofoil links with the Trémiti Islands, a highly popular resort in summer. Again, it's full and expensive in August, but come a couple of months either side and it can be delightful. **SAN MENAIO** is much quieter than Rodi – more compact and with fewer villas – and even in high season it's easy to get away from it all by walking a few hundred yards south along the strand. *Sole, Lungomare* 2 (☎0884.968.621, ⓦwww.hoteldamato.it; ❽), is an attractive 1920s **hotel** built right next to the sea, and room prices include sunlounger and umbrella on their private sandy beach. There's also a pleasant, shaded **campsite** called *Internazionale* (☎0884.968.528; May–Sept), just off the SS89 a few minutes' walk from the beach. From Rodi Garganico, both road and rail skirt the large **Lago di Varano**, a once-malarial swamp which swallowed the ancient Athenian town of Uria in the fourth century BC. The region around the lake, its villages traditionally poor and backward, is probably the least-visited part of the Gargano promontory – though the lake itself is full of eels and attracts a great variety of birdlife, particularly curlews and warblers. Further west, the thin **Lago di Lésina** is a highly saline shallow lagoon, cut off from the sea by a twenty-seven-kilometre stretch of sand dunes. It's still mercifully free from development – unlike the northern spit of Varano, which is slowly beginning to fill with campsites.

Alternatively, from Cagnano Varano the FG train line cuts southwest, skirting the promontory, inland to **SAN SEVERO**, a small market town known for its wines but otherwise not a place where you'll want to do much more than change transport. The FG line from here terminates at Fóggia, but the FS trains that stop here carry on down the coast to Bari.

Inland Gargano: Vico del Gargano and the Foresta Umbra

The **interior** of the Gargano promontory can make a cool break from its busy coast, and though there's not much public transport, apart from the odd bus from Vieste, San Menaio and Rodi Garganico, you can rent mountain bikes or fix up jeep safaris or pony trekking via the park website (see below) or the SOL agency (see p.922) to get to the best of it. **VICO DEL GARGANO** is the nicest of the villages and firmly off the beaten track, sited on a hill surrounded by citrus groves and with a creakingly ancient centre full of steep, tangled streets. It's on the edge of the **Foresta Umbra** (or "Forest of Shadows") which stretches right across the centre of the Gargano massif – 11,000 hectares of pines, oaks and beeches, hiding a rich variety of wildlife, roe deer especially – and is the last remnant of an ancient forest which once covered most of Puglia. Even if you're not a botanist or a birdwatcher you may find yourself appreciating the amazing biodiversity of the forest, which is a kind of "biological island", resulting in its designation as a national park in 1991. There are more than 70 species of orchid to be found in the park, for example, and if you're lucky you may see wild-boar piglets rooting around by the side of the road. If you fancy following any of the marked **walks** through the forest head for the **Centro di Vísita** (☎0884.565.579, ⓦ www.parcogargano.it) in the middle which doles out advice and information.

The Trémiti Islands

A small group of islands 40km off the Gargano coast, the **Trémiti Islands** – Isole Trémiti – are almost entirely given over to tourism in the summer, when the tiny population is swamped by visitors. Despite this, they remain relatively unspoilt and the sea crystal clear.

The islands were traditionally a place of exile and punishment in the past. Augustus banished his granddaughter Julia to the islands, while Charlemagne packed his father-in-law off here (minus eyes and limbs) in the eighth century. Monks from Montecassino, on the mainland, first set about building a formidable fortress-abbey on one of the islands in the eleventh century, which managed to withstand frequent assault by the Turks. Later, during the eighteenth century, the islands returned to their old role as a place of confinement for political prisoners, though the Bourbons, concerned at the decline in the local population, shipped in two hundred women from the Neapolitan taverns to encourage a recovery.

Hydrofoils and catamarans run to San Nicola from Manfredonia (see p.916) and there's a service from Vieste (see p.922) during the summer.

Ferries, or *motonave* (foot passengers only), from Vieste, Péschici and Rodi Gargánico operate once a week at quieter times of the year.

The main Trémiti group consists of three islands: San Nicola, San Domino – the biggest – and Capraia, of which only the first two are inhabited. Most **ferries** arrive at **SAN NICOLA**, where you can wander around the monastic fortress and the tiny church of **Santa Maria a Mare**, built by the monks in the eleventh century on the site of an earlier ninth-century hermitage. San Nicola is rugged and rocky with no beaches, although there is nude bathing on its east side and good swimming to be had off the whole island.

Ignore the offers of pricey boat trips to the other islands and instead jump on the regular ferry which takes about a minute to cross to **SAN DOMINO**. It's a greener island than its neighbour, its pines offering a welcome shade from the heat. Although there is a sandy **beach** – Cala delle Arene – right where the ferry lands on the northeast side of the island, it gets packed in the summer. Your best bet is to follow the signs for the *Villaggio TCI* (see below) and make for the west of the island and its quieter coves such as Cala dello Spido. For walking, head for the Punta di Diamante; **maps** are pinned up in some of the bars or can be bought from souvenir shops. Accommodation on the islands is limited to San Domino and is largely full-board only in high season: count on paying about €50–60 a night per person. The *municipio* on San Domino holds a list of private rooms, or you could try the most appealing of the small hotels, *Pensione Pineta* (☎0882.463.202; ❸), a whitewashed villa in pine trees near some quiet rocky coves just outside the tiny village centre. Alternatively, there's the *Albergo La Nassa* (☎0882.463.345; ❸), on the footpath into the village, or *Albergo Gabbiano* (☎0882.463.410; ❼) in the village itself at Piazza Belvedere; it's essential to book ahead for all three. A cheaper alternative is to camp at the *Villaggio TCI* (☎0882.463.402). Bear in mind, too, that provisions have to be ferried across from the mainland, so eating out can be a costly exercise – buy some picnic food before you get on the boat. Mosquitoes tend to be a serious problem in the summer months.

Along the coast to Bari

The first part of the coastal route south from Manfredonia is unremarkable, flat lands given up to saline extraction. You won't, anyway, be able to come this way by train or bus – though there is a direct coastal road. First stop, by rail at least, isn't until **MARGHERITA DI SAVOIA**, at the edge of the Tavoliere, a small town that boasts the country's oldest working salt pans, dating to the third century BC. Beyond here, though, the rest of the coastline is easily accessible by public transport; most places have stations on the main Bologna–Lecce rail line.

Among them is **TRANI**, a place with a cosmopolitan air not found in any of the other towns nearby. One of the most important medieval Italian ports, it was a prosperous trading centre with a large mercantile and Jewish community, during the Middle Ages rivalling Bari as a commercial port and in the fourteenth century powerful enough to take on the domineering Venetians.

Modern-day Trani is still a prosperous place, its elegant buildings spruce and smart. Centrepiece of the town is the cream-coloured eleventh-century **Duomo** (daily 8.30am–noon & 3–6pm), overlooking the sea on a large open piazza at the edge of the old town. Dedicated to San Nicola Pellegrino, it consists of no fewer than three churches, stacked on top of each other like an inverted wedding cake – the facade austere but lightened by a pretty rose window. The **Chiesa di Ognissanti**, close by, was a twelfth-century chapel of the

Knights Templar, once part of a hospital for injured Crusaders. Sadly, it's unlikely to be open, but if you hang around someone may appear with a key.

The rail line continues south to **MOLFETTA**, a working port, unashamedly non-touristy and all the better for it, its waterfront active with visiting ships and thronged by an evening *passeggiata* that sweeps down to the docks to watch the sunset.

Bari

Commercial and administrative capital of Puglia, a university town and southern Italy's second city, **BARI** has its fair share of interest. But although an economically vibrant place, it harbours no pretensions to being a major tourist attraction. People come here primarily for work or to leave for Greece on its many ferries.

Bari was already a thriving centre when the Romans arrived. Later the city was the seat of the Byzantine governor of southern Italy, while under the Normans Bari rivalled Venice, both as a maritime centre and, following the seizure of the remains of St Nicholas, as a place of pilgrimage. Since those heady days Bari has declined considerably. Its fortunes revived briefly in 1813 when the king of Naples foisted a planned expansion upon the city – giving the centre its contemporary gridded street pattern, wide avenues and piazzas. And Mussolini instituted a university and left a legacy of strident Fascist architecture. But the city was heavily bombed during the last war, and today its vigorous centre is a symbol of the south's zeal for commercial growth.

Arrival and information

Bari is a fairly compact city, running from the train station in the gridded new city down to the bulging old centre, the *cittavecchia*, in just ten blocks. There are three train stations in Bari. The **Stazione Centrale** is in Piazza Aldo Moro, on the southern edge of the modern centre; it serves regular FS trains and those of the private Ferrovia del Sud-Est line (FSE information ☎080.546.2111), which run down via Alberobello, Locorotondo and Martina Franca to Gagliano del Capo (see p.934 for more on this route). Nearby, at Piazza Aldo Moro, the separate **Stazione Bari-Nord** is for trains run by the private FerroTramViaria company (FTV information ☎080.523.2202), connecting Bari with Andria, Barletta, Bitonto and Ruvo di Puglia. Adjacent to this, on Corso Italia, is the **Stazione FAL Apulo-Lucane**; trains and buses from here are run by Ferrovia Apulo-Lucane (FAL train information ☎080.572.5227; bus information ☎080.572.5215) and go to Altamura, Gravina, and Matera and Potenza in Basilicata.

Buses complicate the issue even further: from the coastal towns north of Bari you'll arrive at Piazza Eroi del Mare; SITA buses from inland and southern

The Baresi bag snatchers

A **word of warning**: the Baresi take positive delight in portraying the old city as a den of thieves, and certainly strolling through the narrow alleys with your camera in full view isn't particularly wise. Bag snatching by young kids on mopeds (the *topini*, or "little mice") isn't as rife as it once was, but neither is it extinct, so it's best to keep your wits about you.

Ferries to Greece, Albania & Croatia

Porto Nuovo

PIAZZALE
C. COLOMBO

PIAZZA
S. PIETRO

MOLO S. VITO

**Stazione
Marrittima**

Porto
Sen. Antonio
de Tullic

◄ Palese, Youth Hostel (8km)

**Chiesa di
San Gregorio**

PIAZZA
S. NICOLA

**Basilica di
San Nicola**

OLD CITY

CORSO SEN. ANTONIO DE TULLIO

LUNGOMARE IMPERATORE AUGUSTO

**Cattedrale
di San Sabino**

PIAZZA
ODEGITRIA

**Colonna della
Giustizia**

A

MOLO SANT' ANTONIO

**Castello
Normanno-
Svevo**

PIAZZA ISABELLA
D'ARAGONA

PIAZZA FEDERICO II

PIAZZA MASSARI

B

PIAZZA
MERCANTILE

C

**Palazzo
Sedile**

D

LARGO CHIURLIA

PIAZZA
FERRARESE

E

Porto Vecchio

VIA G. MURAT

VIA S. FRANCESCO D'ASSISI

CORSO VITTORIC EMANUELE II

VIA PICCINNI

LUNGOMARE IMPERATORE AUGUSTO

F

VIA ABATE GIMMA

VIA MARCHESE DI MONTRONE

VIA CALEFATI

VIA CAIROLI

VIA ROBERTO DA BARI

VIA PUTIGNANI

VIA SPARANO

VIA AGIRO

LUNGOMARE DI CROLLALANZA

MOLO S. NICOLA

**Bus
Station**

**Teatro
Petruzzelli**

H

CORSO CAVOUR

VIA COGNETTI

VIA MELO

G ◄

VIA QUINTINO SELLA

VIA DE ROSSI

VIA PRINCIPE AMEDEO

VIA DANTE ALIGHIERI

VIA NICCLAI

VIA DE GIOSA

VIA IMBRIANI

VIA CARDASSI

**Università
& Museo
Archeologico**

PIAZZA UMBERTO I

VIA BEATILLO

VIA CRISANZIO

VIA SPARANO

VIA P. PETRONI

1

@

**Stazione
Bari-
Nord**

PIAZZA ALDO MORO

ⓘ

**Stazione FAL
Apulo-
Lucane**

VIA

CORSO ITALIA

VIA ZUPPETTA

2

0   100 m

Stazione Centrale (FS)

N

Pinacoteca Provinciale (300 m) ►

Stazione FSR (Largo Ciaia) ►

ACCOMMODATION	
Adria	2
Costa	1
Giulia	1
Romeo	1

RESTAURANTS	
Ai 2 Ghiottoni	H
Antica Osteria Vini e Cucina	E
Credenza	C
Locanda di Federico	A
Pedro	F
Pescatore	B
Terranima	G
Travi	D

towns pull up in Largo Sorrentino (behind the train station); Marozzi buses from Rome arrive either here or on Piazza Aldo Moro. Buses of the private rail line FAL, from Basilicata, arrive at their station on Corso Italia, while FSE buses from Bríndisi pull in at their station on Largo Ciaia. **Ferries** from Albania, Croatia, Turkey, Israel, Montenegro and Greece (Igoumenitsa, Corfu and Patras) all use the Stazione Maríttima, next to the old city, connected with the main FS train station by bus #20. The **airport** is about 9km northwest up the coast; there is an Alitalia bus that connects with arrivals and drops at the central train station.

 Getting around, your best bet is to walk – not a bad option in such a small city. The **tourist office** is at Piazza Aldo Moro 33a, in a small cul-de-sac to the right as you come out of the main train station (Mon–Fri 8am–1pm plus Tues & Thurs 3–6pm; ℡080.524.2361, ⓌWww.pugliaturismo.com/aptbari).

Accommodation

There are several handy and affordable **hotels** one block from the station in the apartment building at Via Crisanzio 12: *Costa* (℡080.521.9015; ❺) is the nicest, with simple but attractive rooms and air conditioning on the way. Next door, on the ground floor, the rooms at the *Romeo* (℡080.523.7253; ❸) are all doubles with TVs and bathrooms, while upstairs is *Giulia* (℡080.521.6630; ❸), run by a pleasant couple, with some rooms en suite. A similar choice in the same area is the *Adria*, right out of the station on Via Zuppetta (℡080.524.6699; ❸); prices are cheaper if you opt for an inward-facing room without private bathroom or TV. The **youth hostel** near the beach at Palese, 8km up the coast, has been closed for years and shows no signs of reopening; if it ever does, it can be reached on bus #1 from Piazza Aldo Moro; get off at the Villaggio dell'Aeronautica and walk 300m. The nearest campsite is *Camping Sea World*, 6km south of the city at SS Adriatica 78 (℡080.549.1175); take bus #12 (or #12/) from Teatro Petruzzelli.

The City

There's not a lot to the **new city** of Bari, bar a good museum or two. Its straight streets are lined with shops and offices, relieved occasionally by the odd bit of greenery and piazza, best of which is the starting-point of the evening *passeggiata*, **Piazza Umberto I** – usually full of stalls selling jewellery, books and prints. Off the piazza, the university building houses an excellent **Museo Archeologico**, currently closed for restoration. If it's reopened by the time of your visit, it's well worth a look: it holds a good selection of Greek and Puglian ceramics and a solid collection of artefacts from the Daunic, Messapian and Peucetic peoples – Puglia's earliest inhabitants. Afterwards, cut to the right for tree-lined **Corso Cavour**, Bari's main commercial street, which leads down to the waterfront. Right along here, in the Palazzo della Provincia, the **Pinacoteca Provinciale** (Tues–Sat 9am–1pm & 4–7pm, Sun 9am–1pm; €2.50) contains mostly southern Italian art ranging from the twelfth- to nineteenth-century, but there are also works by Tintoretto and Paolo Veronese that were moved from the cathedral, and a recent acquisition of paintings by the twentieth-century painter from Bologna, Giorgio Morandi.

The old city

Even if you're only in Bari to catch a ferry, try to make time for a wander around the **old city**, an entrancing jumble of streets at the far end of Corso Cavour that's possibly the most confusing place to walk around in southern

Ferries from Bari

International ferry services run from Bari to Greece, Albania and Croatia. Travel agents around town often have a wide variety of offers on **tickets**; as a general rule, you will save twelve to twenty percent if you buy a return ticket. Once you've got your ticket, you must report to the relevant desk at the Stazione Maríttima at least two hours before departure. The embarkation tax of €6 per passenger should be included in your ticket, but it's worth checking when you buy it (and note that if you are coming back from Durazzo/Durres in Albania to Bari, departure tax payable in Albania is USD6 per adult, USD7 per car and USD16 per camper). Prices given below are for travel in high season.

Albania
Hydrofoil services to **Albania** are operated by La Vikinga Lines, bookable through Portrans at the Stazione Maríttima (℡080.523.2429), or at Corso A. de Tullio 6 (℡080.521.1416), departing Bari twice daily in the morning and the afternoon; the journey takes 3hr 30min and costs €89 one way.

Adriatica runs a car ferry to Durazzo/Durres four times a week in July and August; the journey takes eight hours overnight (from €60 one way). Adriatica has offices at Via Liside 4 (℡080.553.1555) and Stazione Maríttima (℡080.523.5825, ⓦwww .adriatica.it).

Croatia
Jadrolinija operates fast catamaran services to the coastal towns of Dubrovnik, Rijeka, Zadar and Split and the islands of Hvar, Korcula, Dugi Otok and Mljet in **Croatia**. Services to Dubrovnik and Split operate four times a week in August and two to three times a week mid-June to mid-Sept. Journey time is 7–8 hr. For the full timetable check out ⓦwww.jadrolinija.hr. Contact Jadrolinija through P. Lorusso & Co, Via Piccinni 133 (℡080.521.7643), and at the Stazione Maríttima (℡080.527.5439), or book online.

Greece
Ferry services to **Greece** are operated by Ventouris and Superfast. Ventouris tickets are bookable at ⓦwww.ferries.gr/ventouris or through P. Lorusso & Co (contact details see above). Superfast ferries can be booked on ⓦwww.superfast.com or through Portrans (details above). Ventouris runs daily services to Corfu (end of July to mid-August) and Igcumenitsa (mid-June to mid-Sept) with between two and four weekly sailings the rest of the year; one-way prices start at €42 per person, €52 extra for a car. The service to Igoumenitsa takes 11hr 30min and the service to Corfu takes 10hr. Superfast runs a daily overnight sailing to both Igoumenitsa and Patras year-round and the seats cost from €78 (cars €52); the journeys take 9hr and 15hr respectively.

Italy. Its labyrinth of seemingly endless passages weaving through courtyards and under arches was originally designed to spare the inhabitants from the wind and throw invaders into a state of confusion. This it still does admirably, and even with the best of maps you're going to get lost. Life is lived very much outdoors, and on summer evenings, it's full of people sitting outside their kitchen doors.

Specific sights are few. The **Basilica di San Nicola** (daily 9am–1pm & 4–7pm; museum Tues–Fri 10am–noon), in the heart of the old city, was consecrated in 1197, as an inscription at the side of the main door testifies, to house the relics of the saint plundered a century earlier from southern Turkey. From the outside it all looks thoroughly Norman, especially the twin fortress-like towers, but it's a misleading impression: the right-hand tower predates the church, the other was added later for balance, and even the simple nave is shattered by three great arches and an ornate seventeenth-century ceiling. The real beauty of the church lies in its stonework: the twelfth-century altar canopy is one of the finest in Italy, the motifs around the capitals the work of stonemasons from Como; and the twelfth-century carved doorway and the simple, striking mosaic floor behind the altar are lovely, prey to a very heavy Saracen influence. Best of all is the twelfth-century episcopal throne behind the altar, a superb piece of work supported by small figures wheezing beneath its weight. Down in the crypt are the remains of the saint, patron of pawnbrokers and sailors (and of Russians, who made the pilgrimage here until 1917). Behind the tomb-altar, the richly decorated fourteenth-century icon of the saint was a present from the King of Serbia.

It's not far from the basilica to Bari's other important church, the **Cattedrale di San Sabino** (daily 8.30am–1pm & 4–7pm), off Piazza Odegitria, dedicated to the original patron saint of Bari, before he was usurped by Nicholas, and built at the end of the twelfth century. It's well worth coming just for the contrast: uncluttered by arches, it retains its original medieval atmosphere, and – unlike the basilica – a timbered roof. The cathedral houses an icon, too, an eighth-century work known as the *Madonna Odegitria*, brought here for safety from Constantinople by Byzantine monks. It's said to be the most authentic likeness of the Madonna in existence, having been taken from an original sketch by Luke the Apostle, and it's paraded around the city at religious festivals.

Across the piazza the **Castello Normanno-Svevo** (Tues–Sat 9am–1pm & 3.30–7pm, Sun 9am–1pm; €2) sits on the site of an earlier Roman fort. Built by Frederick II, much of it is closed to the public, but it has a vaulted hall that provides a cool escape from the afternoon sun. You can also see a gathering of some of the best of past Puglian artistry in a display of plaster-cast reproductions from churches and buildings throughout the region – specifically from the Castel del Monte, the cathedral at Altamura, and an animated frieze of griffins devouring serpents from the church of San Leonardo at Siponto.

Eating and drinking

If you want something more than the fast food you'll find in Via Sparano across from the station, two inexpensive **restaurants** worth seeking out in the old city are *Le Travi* on Largo Chiurlia (closed Mon) and *Antica Osteria Vini e Cucina* (closed Sun), just off Piazza del Ferrarese on an alleyway called Via Vallisa, both offering typical Barese cuisine. Nearby on traffic-free Piazza Mercantile, *La Locanda di Federico* (closed Mon) is a popular place that's slightly more upscale, and has tables outside. Also worth trying is the good self-service *El Pedro,* at Via Piccinni 152 (closed Sun), which specializes in traditional Italian cuisine. Not much more expensive is the *Cafe Batafobrele/Restaurant Terranima*, at Via Putignani 213–215 (closed Sun), with a daily menu of regional specialities, and a relaxed atmosphere. The no-nonsense *Ristorante al Pescatore*, Via Federico II di Svevia 8 (closed Sun), just east of the castle, does fine fish; reckon on paying around €25–30 a head; at *La Credenze*, Via Verrone 15/Arco Sant'Onofrio (closed Wed), in the old city you can eat such typically Barese dishes as *orecchiette* with cauliflower. For a euro-busting blow-out, *Ai 2 Ghiottoni* [sic], Via Putignani 11/b (booking advisable ☏080.523.2240; closed Sun), is one of the top restaurants in town, with good shellfish and a refined version of Pugliese cuisine.

Listings

Beach The nearest beach is north of the city; take bus #1 from Teatro Petruzzelli to Palese/Santo Spirito. To the south, there are beaches at Torre a Mare and San Giorgio – both reached on bus #12 from Stazione Centrale or #12/ from Teatro Petruzzelli.

Exchange Outside banking hours in Piazza Aldo Moro, inside Stazione Centrale.
Police Via G. Murat ☎080.529.1111.
Post office The main office is behind the university in Piazza Battisti (Mon–Fri 8am–7.30pm, Sat 8.30am–noon).

Le Murge

Rising gently from the Adriatic coast, **Le Murge** – a low limestone plateau – dominates the landscape to the south and west of Bari. The towns in the region are not natural holiday destinations: the area is sparsely populated and the small settlements that exist are rural backwaters with a slow pace of life. But they do make an interesting day out or a good stopover if you're heading for the region of Basilicata. There are some buses and trains from Bari, but, as always, without your own car travelling very extensively can be difficult.

The Low Murge

The main town of the Low Murge is **ANDRIA**, a large agricultural centre easily reached from Barletta or Bari that's at its best during its Monday-morning market – otherwise it has little to hold you. It was, though, a favourite haunt of Frederick II, who was responsible for the main local attraction these days, the **Castel del Monte**, 17km south – the most extraordinary of all Puglia's castles and one of the finest surviving examples of Swabian architecture (daily: April–Sept 10am–1.30pm & 2.30–7pm; Oct–March 9am–1pm & 2.30–5.30pm; €3; ☎0883.569.848). Official guides here offer free tours in English, although donations are appreciated; from April to September they are based at the castle's Pro Loco cabin, but from October to March you need to contact the Pro Loco office in Andria (☎0883.592.283, ⓦwww.proloco.andria.ba.it). Sadly, there is only an infrequent bus service from Andria – contact the Pro Loco office there or the castle itself for timetables.

Begun by Frederick in the 1240s, the Castel is a high, isolated fortress precisely built around an octagonal courtyard in two storeys of eight rooms. A mystery surrounds its intended purpose. Although there was once an iron gate which could be lowered over the main entrance there are no other visible signs of fortification, and the castle may have served as a mere hunting lodge. Nonetheless the mathematical precision involved in its construction, and the preoccupation with the number eight, have excited writers for centuries. It's argued the castle is in fact an enormous astrological calendar, also that Frederick may have had the octagonal Omar mosque in Jerusalem in mind when he designed it; but despite his recorded fascination with the sciences, no one really knows. There is only one record of its use. The defeat of Manfred, Frederick's illegitimate son, at the battle of Benevento in 1266 signalled the end of Swabian power in Puglia; and Manfred's sons and heirs were imprisoned in the castle for over thirty years – a lonely place to be incarcerated.

East of Andria (but best reached by hourly bus from Molfetta), the old centre of **RUVO DI PUGLIA** is an attractive stop, with a quiet, timeless atmosphere. In the autumn, the pavements of the old town are strewn with almonds, spread out to dry in the sun as they have been for centuries. Just across from the **tourist office** on Via Vittorio Veneto 48 (Mon–Fri 10am–noon & 7.30–9pm, Sat 10am–noon; ☎080.361.5419), the **Museo Jatta** in Piazza Bovio (daily 8.30am–1.30pm, plus Sat 2.30–7.30pm; free) houses a dusty collection of local copies of ancient Greek pottery as well as some beautiful originals, including a fifth-century BC crater depicting the death of Talos. Ruvo's thirteenth-century **Duomo**, tucked into the tightly packed streets of the town's old quarter, is also well worth a look. Its beautiful portal is guarded by animated griffins balancing on fragile columns, with a staggering amount of decoration on the outer walls, like the rose window and the arches tapering off into human and animal heads.

The High Murge

Around 45km south of Bari (and reachable by train), **ALTAMURA** is the largest town in the High Murge, an originally fifth-century-BC settlement fortified by the Peucetians – parts of whose town still remain. Given its many historical layers, it's perhaps appropriate that Altamura is home to one of southern Italy's best **archeological museums** (July & Aug daily 8.30am–7.30pm; Sept–June Tues–Sat 8am–2pm & 4.30–7.30pm, Sun 8.30am–1.30pm; free) on Via Santeramo 88. The collection here traces the history of the people of the Murge from prehistory to late medieval times, with plenty of first-rate finds from all over the peninsula.

Altamura's most striking feature, however, is its **Duomo**, a mixture of styles varying from Apulian-Romanesque to Gothic and Baroque. Take a look, too, at the tiny church of **San Niccolò dei Greci** on Corso Federico di Svevia; built by the Greek colonists in the thirteenth century and in which they celebrated their Orthodox religion for more than 400 years.

Some 12km west, not far from the border with Basilicata, lies **GRAVINA DI PUGLIA** – a castle-protected town clinging to the edge of a deep ravine. During the early barbarian invasions the locals took refuge in the caves along the sides of the ravine, a move that seems to have paid off until the arrival of the Saracens, who promptly massacred every cave-dwelling inhabitant. Under the Normans, though, the shattered town settled down to a quieter life as a fiefdom of the wealthy pope-producing Orsini family, whose mark – an enormous spread eagle – is all over town. In the dilapidated old quarter, the cave-church of **San Michele delle Grotte**, a dark, dank affair hewn out of the rock, holds bones that are said to be the remains of victims of the last Saracen attack, almost a thousand years old. The **Santomasi museum** (Tues–Sat 9am–noon & 4–6pm, Sun 9am–1pm; €3) in Piazza Santomasi contains archeological finds, Bourbon arms and uniforms as well as sixteenth- and seventeenth-century paintings, but more engaging, certainly if you couldn't get into San Michele, is the reconstruction of San Vito Vecchio, another cave-church, set up on the ground floor with some remarkable tenth-century Byzantine frescoes. There's also a new **archeological museum** on Piazza Benedetto Tredicésimo (Tues–Sat 9am–1pm & 5–8pm; €2) with artefacts found around the ancient town. Ask here for guided **tours** in English of this and other cave-churches.

Down the coast from Bari

The coast south of Bari is a craggy stretch, with rock-hewn villages towering above tiny sandy coves. Just ten minutes by FS train from Bari (or bus #12 from

Piazza Aldo Moro), **TORRE A MARE** provides one of the easiest escapes from the city, situated on a rocky ledge high above two large caves, though its ease of access from Bari means it can get quite crowded. There'll be fewer people around another twenty minutes on, at **POLIGNANO A MARE**, which, despite a newfound popularity, remains fairly low-key. It's a small port, with a scuffed, whitewashed medieval centre, perching on the edge of the limestone cliffs, and the kind of place people head for on a Sunday to watch the waves crashing against the rocks or to sunbathe on the clifftops. If you don't have a car it is best reached by train, although there is a bus service, run by FSE, from Largo Ciaia in Bari. If you'd like to **stay**, head for the appealing *Covo dei Saraceni*, Via Conversano 1A (☎080.424.1177; ⑥), which sits right on the rocks and has modern rooms – some with large balconies and private terraces – a restaurant with panoramic views, and a laid-back atmosphere. Don't miss a meal in a **cave restaurant** high above the crashing waves at the nearby *Hotel Grotta Palazzese*. Sufferers of vertigo may prefer to make their way to the **restaurant** attached to the hotel *Castellinaria*, Contrada S. Giovanni, (☎080.424.0233; ⑦) for dishes based on the freshest fish.

Egnázia and Fasano

Some 8km further on lies the commercial port of **MONÓPOLI**, with a nice old town, but not much else to see. There's more of interest south, at the site of the ancient city of **Egnázia** (daily 8.30am–7.30pm or dusk in winter; €3; ☎080.482.9056), or Gnathia; if you don't have your own transport, it's best reached from **Fasano** (call Fasano's tourist office for timetable; ☎080.441.3086). Egnázia was an important Messapian centre during the fifth century BC, fortified with over 2km of walls, large parts of which still stand in the northern corner of the ruined town – up to 7m high. It was later colonized by the Greeks and then the Romans (in 244 BC), who built a forum, amphitheatre, a colonnaded public hall and temples: one was dedicated to Syria, a goddess popular with the early Romans who – according to Lucian – was worshipped by men dressed as women. Horace is known to have dropped by here to see the city's famous altar, which ignited wood without a flame.

At the turn of the first century AD, the Emperor Trajan constructed the **Via Egnázia**, a road that ran down to Bríndisi and continued from what is now Durres in Albania, via Thessaloniki, all the way to Constantinople, marking Egnázia's importance as a military and commercial centre. Parts of the road survive, running alongside the Roman public buildings. With the collapse of the Roman Empire, however, the city fell to subsequent barbarian invasions, and was almost completely destroyed by the Gothic king Totila in 545 AD. A community struggled on here, seeking refuge in the Messapian tombs, until the tenth century when the settlement was finally abandoned. There's a new on-site **museum** (same hours and ticket) housing a fascinating array of artefacts, including examples of the distinctive earthenware for which the ancient town was prized.

There are some good **places to stay** in **Selva di Fasano**, a hill station of villas in lush gardens above the town of Fasano. Try *La Silvana*, Viale dei Pini 87 (☎080.433.1161, ✉hotellasilvana@tiscalinet.it; ④), an unpretentious hotel with large, simply decorated rooms, Moorish arches over balconies and plenty of terrace space. Alternatively, there's the modern, glitzy *Sierra Silvana*, Via Don Bartolo Boggia (☎080.433.1322, ✉sierrasilvana@tin.it; ⑦), with regular rooms and *trulli* in the grounds that you can stay in; it's the perfect place to lounge by the pool for the day or take their free shuttle bus to the beach 15km away.

The FSE line: Castellana Grotte to Martina Franca

Meandering lazily down towards the **Valle d'Itria**, the Ferrovia Sud-Est passes through some of the prettiest of Puglia's landscapes. The olive gradually loses ground to vineyards and cherry and peach orchards, neatly partitioned off by dry-stone walls. The barren limestone terrain of Le Murge swallows rivers whole (south of the Ofanto, near Barletta, few rivers make it to the sea), producing a landscape cut by deep ravines and pitted with caverns and grottoes. About 40km out of Bari are the **Grotte di Castellana**, a spectacular set of underground caves (April–Sept 8.30am–1pm & 2.30–7pm; Oct–March 9.30am–12.30pm & 3–4pm; plus night tours at 9pm from end of July to end of Aug; €13 for a full 3km/2hr tour, €10.50 for 1km/50min tour excluding Grotta Bianca; ☎080.499.8211 or freephone in Italy ☎800-213976). Check out the site ⓦwww.grottedicastellana.it for full information on when tours depart: at the time of writing there were short tours in English at 1pm and 6.30pm and full tours at 11am and 4pm in high season only. A lift takes you down to the largest of the caverns, La Grave, 60m below ground, which was used as the local rubbish dump until its accidental discovery in 1938. From here, there's over 1km of strangely formed caves to explore, ending in the most impressive of them all, the Grotta Bianca – a shimmering sea of white stalagmites and stalactites. To **get to the caves**, simply follow the signs from the station, from where it's about 500m to the grotto.

After **PUTIGNANO** (next stop down the line), **trulli** come to dominate the landscape: cylindrical, whitewashed buildings with grey conical roofs tapering out to a point or sphere, often adorned with painted symbols. Confined to this part of Puglia, their ancient origins are obscure, though few today date back more than a couple of hundred years. Apart from their intrinsic beauty, there seems no special reason for building houses like this, and certainly no reason for them popping up here – though many theories abound, one claiming that the dome-shaped houses are much cooler in the baking Puglian summers. Certainly they make full use of local building materials and are remarkably easy to adapt: when you need more room, you simply knock a hole in the wall and build another next door (see p.1164 for more on *trulli*).

If you want to take a closer look, **ALBEROBELLO** is the best place, where there's a large local concentration of *trulli* – around 1500 packing Alberobello's narrow streets; most are south of the town centre, on and around Largo Martellotta. For orientation, you can pick up a town map from the **tourist office** in the centre at Piazza Ferdinando IV (Mon–Fri 8am–2pm plus Tues & Thurs 3–6.30pm; ☎080.432.5171, ⓔcasadamorealberobello@hotmail.com), about a ten-minute walk from the station; for information ⓦwww.tuttoalberobello.it is a useful site. Inevitably, there is a certain amount of tourist tat to go with the cute conical stone huts, and proprietors of *trulli* given over to displays of woolly shawls, liqueurs and other souvenirs practically drag in passers-by. If you want to complete the *trulli* experience by **staying** in one, look at ⓦwww.trullinet.com/alberghi which lists private *trulli* for rent; or check in at *Hotel Dei Trulli*, Via Cadore 31 (☎080.432.3555; ❼), which comprises a dozen or so of the conical cottages, shaded by pine trees and with a pool next door. A five-minute stroll from the *trulli* area of town is *Casa Albergo S Antonio*, Via Isonzo 8a (☎080.432.2913; ❷), a former seminary run by a religious institution, with bright, simply furnished rooms. For a spick and span, more central, choice, try *Lanzillotta* at Piazza Ferdinando IV, 31 (☎080.432.1511, ⓔhotellanzillotta@tiscalinet.it; ❸)

As for **food**, *Il Poeta Contadino*, at Via Indipendenza 21 (Sept–June; closed Mon), has specialities including *purè di fave con cicoria* (broad beans with wild chicory) and *cavatelli con cime di rapa* (pasta with turnip tops). Wine buffs shouldn't pass up a browse around the *Enoteca Anima del Vino*, on Largo Martellota 93, with its good assortment of local **wines** and excellent *cotognata* from Maglie; *Bar Ailanto* (across the way) serves an excellent **coffee** *granita*. For a quick **Internet** fix, head for Centre TIM Emmegi at Via T Cucci 23, between Largo Martellotta and Piazza Ferdinando IV (Mon–Sat 9am–1pm & 5–9pm; daily July & August).

Just a few kilometres south, **LOCOROTONDO**, which owes its name to its circular layout, gives good views over the whole area, speckled with red- and grey-roofed *trulli* in a sea of olives, vines and almond trees. It's a great place to wander for an hour or so, and to sample edible **local specialities**: check out *Centro Storico* at Via Eroi di Dogali 6 (closed Wed in winter), an excellent trattoria where you can savour hearty *crecchiette,* served with meat sauce and creamy white cheese (*ragù e caciotta*).

Martina Franca

The *trulli* are still plentiful by the time you reach **MARTINA FRANCA**, a surprising town with a tangible Moorish flavour and a lively *passeggiata* at weekends. It is reputed to have been founded by Tarentine settlers fed up with constant Saracen attacks during the tenth century, but it was the Angevin prince of Táranto who bolstered the community in the early fourteenth century by granting it certain tax privileges. The town derives its name from this – *franca* meaning duty or stamp. Today its medieval core is adorned with some of the most subtle and least overbearing examples of architecture from the Baroque period you'll find.

Through the **Porta di Santo Stefano**, which marks the entrance to the old town, Piazza Roma is dominated by the vast **Palazzo Ducale**, dating from 1688 and now housing the town hall, but with a handful of rooms open to the public most mornings – most of them smothered in classical eighteenth-century Arcadian murals by a local artist. Just across the square, narrow Via Vittorio Emanuele leads right into the old town and Piazza Plebiscito, fronted by the vast Baroque facade of the **Chiesa di San Martino**, an eighteenth-century church built on the site of an earlier Romanesque structure, of which only the campanile survives. From adjacent Piazza Immacolata you can either bear left down Via Cavour, with its Baroque *palazzi* and balconied streets, or wander further into the old town, the roads running around the edge of the surviving fourteenth-century town walls offering an excellent panorama of the Valle d'Itria, with its neatly ordered fields dotted with *trulli*.

Southern Italy's top performing arts festival, the **Festival della Valle d'Itria** (T080.480.5100), takes place in Martina Franca in late July/early August every year. On a par with the *Maggio Musicale* in Florence, the festival is mainly operatic, with performances in the appropriately grand Palazzo Ducale. It's a congenial and unpretentious event, though tickets aren't cheap: they're available from the festival office in the Palazzo Ducale. For more information look up W www.euro-festival.net.

Practicalities

There's a spasmodic bus service from the **FSE train station** up to the centre of town; otherwise you'll have to walk for fifteen minutes – left out of the station and up Viale della Libertà to Corso Italia, which leads to the old town centre. The **tourist office** on Piazza Roma 35 (Mon–Fri 8.30am–1pm & 5–7pm;

Sat 9am–12.30pm; ☎080.480.5702) has good maps of the town. The cheapest **hotel** is the *Hotel da Luigi* on Via Táranto, Zona G (☎080.430.1324; ❷), though this is 2km out of town and at festival time you won't get a room here. One of the best of the pricier options in town is the comfortable *Dell'Erba*, Via dei Cedri 1 (☎080.430.1055, ✉hoteldellerba@italiainrete.net; ❺), with a swimming pool, restaurant and plenty of sun terraces. There's also the opportunity to stay in a traditional apartment in the old town – an atmospheric choice. Studio apartments for two work out at €68 per night, plus linen charge (no minimum stay); contact *Villaggio In* (☎080.480.5911, ⊛www.villaggioin.it).

As for **eating** in Martina Franca, you'll get an excellent meal at *La Cantina*, Vico 1 Lanucara 12 (closed Mon), signposted off Piazza Settembre, the main gate to the old town – try the pasta with beans (*bucatini con fagioli*) or lamb (*orecchiette con sugo di castrato*) and broad beans with wild chicory. Or head straight for the town's best pizzas at *La Panca* (closed Mon), Via Spirito Santo 14, off Via Bellini; and *Il Chiostro*, Via Principe Umberto 55 (closed Tues), which leads off the main square in the old town, off Piazza M. Immacolata. If you're after **snacks** or picnic food, try *Fratelli Ricci*, the butcher at Via Cavour 19 (closed Mon), selling roast meats in the evenings and a wonderful example of *capocollo*, a local cured pork salami.

Táranto

There are numerous legends connected with the origins of **TÁRANTO**. It was variously founded by the Spartan deity Phalanthus; Taras, the son of Neptune; or – perhaps more likely – illegitimate Spartans born while their fathers were away fighting. Whatever the truth is, Taras, as it was known to the Greeks, was a well-chosen site and soon became the first city of Magna Graecia, renowned for its wool, its oysters and mussels, and its dyes – the imperial purple was the product of decayed Tarentine molluscs. Resplendent with temples, its acropolis harboured a vast bronze of Poseidon that was one of the wonders of the ancient world. Sadly, little remains of ancient Taras or even of later Roman Tarentum, their monuments and relics confined to the great museum in the modern city. After being destroyed by the Romans, Táranto was for years little more than a small fishing port, its strategic position on the sea only being recognized in Napoleonic times. It was home to the Italian fleet after Unification, and consequently heavily bombed during the last war, since when attempts to rejuvenate the town have left its medieval heart girdled by heavy industry, including the vast Italsider steel plant that throws its flames and lights into the skies above.

Finding your way around is easy. The city divides neatly into three distinct parts: the northern spur is the industrial part of town, home of the steel works and train station. Cross the Ponte di Porta Napoli and you're on the central island containing the old town. And the southern spur holds the modern city centre (the Borgo Nuovo), the administrative and commercial hub of Táranto, linked to the old town by a swing-bridge.

The City

In Greek times the island holding the **old town** wasn't an island at all but part of the southern peninsula, connected by an isthmus to the southern spur. Here the Greeks raised temples and the acropolis, while further south lay the resi-

N

PIAZZA
DUCA D'AOSTA

**Train
Station**

VIA DUCA D'AOSTA

VIA NAPOLI

PIAZZA
FONTANA

Mare Piccolo

**Fish
Market**

VIA CARIATI

**San Domenico
Maggiore**

VIA GIUSEPPE GARIBALDI

VIA D. MEZZO

**Palazzo
Pantaleo**

Cattedrale

VIA DEL DUOMO

CORSO VITTORIO EMANUELE

**Colonna
Romana**

PIAZZA
CASTELLO

PIAZZA
MUNICIPIO

Castello

**Museo
Nazionale**

Ramparts

VIA ROMA

CORSO DUE MARI

VIA REGINA MARGHERITA

VIA PITAGORA

**Villa
Peripato**

B

VIA CAVOUR

PIAZZA
ARCHITA

1

CORSO UMBERTO I

PIAZZA
VITTORIA

i

VIA MIGNOGNA

**Palazzo
di Uffici**

VIA D'AQUINO

VIA MASSARI

VIA GIOVINAZZI

VIA ANFITEATRO

PIAZZA
MARIA
IMMACOLATA PALMA

V. DI
PALMA

Mare Grande

LUNGO VITTORIO EMANUELE

VIA PRINCIPE AMEDEO

VIA BERABDI

VIA G. MAZZINI

VIA G. OBERDAN

ACCOMMODATION
Plaza   **1**
RESTAURANTS
Ristorante Basile   **A**
Da Mimmo   **B**

0   200 m

PUGLIA | Táranto

dential districts. There's one extant fragment of ancient Táranto – the Doric
columns, re-erected in a corner of **Piazza Castello**, which once adorned a
temple of Poseidon. The rest of the tiny island is a mass of poky streets and
alleyways, buttressed by scaffolding seemingly to prevent the whole place from
falling down. The Aragonese **Castello** (now owned by the navy) at the southern end surveys the comings and goings of warships and fishing boats. The nar-

row canal they slide through, between the city's two inland "seas", was built in the late nineteenth century, on the site of the castle's old moat. "Seas" is a bit of a misnomer: the Mare Piccolo is really a large lagoon, home to Táranto's famous oysters and the Italian navy; and the Mare Grande is really a vast bay, protected by sea walls and the offshore fortified island of San Pietro.

At the heart of the old town lies the eleventh-century **Cattedrale**, which once did duty as a mosque – dedicated to Táranto's patron saint, Cataldo (Cathal), a seventh-century Irish monk who on returning from a pilgrimage to the Holy Land was so shocked by the licentiousness of the town's inhabitants that he decided to stay and clean the place up. His remains lie under the altar of a small chapel that bears his name – "a jovial nightmare in stone", Norman Douglas thought. As for the rest of the church, recent restoration has stripped away most of the Baroque alterations, and fragments of a Byzantine mosaic floor have been revealed. The columns of the nave, too, are ancient, pillaged from the temples that once stood on the island, their delicately carved capitals depicting tiny birds nestling among the stone foliage. A few blocks away, check out the city's **fish market**, on Via Cariati, a lively affair where the best of the local catch is displayed at the crack of dawn: octopuses lie dazed, clams spit defiantly at you, while other less definable creatures seem preoccupied with making a last dash for freedom before the restaurateurs arrive – some of the city's finest restaurants are just across the road.

It's a short walk across the swing-bridge to Táranto's **modern centre** – though this, like Bari's, has limited charms, its wide streets laid out on a grid pattern that forms the centre of the city's passeggiata, around piazzas Vittoria and Archita. Nearby, the **Villa Peripato** was *the* place for the Tarentini to take their early-evening stroll at the beginning of the last century, but today's gardeners seem to be fighting a losing battle with the undergrowth.

The only real attraction in this part of town – and it's a gem when it's fully functioning – is the **Museo Nazionale** on Corso Umberto I at no. 41, which offers a fascinating insight into the ancient splendour of Taras. With something in excess of 50,000 pieces of Greek terracotta alone, it's one of the largest collections in the world. Part of the museum was due to reopen in September 2002 after a lengthy restoration and expansion; in the meantime while the works continue, just some of the collection is on view, split between here and the **Palazzo Pantaleo** at Via Pantaleo (daily 8.30am–7.30pm; €2) near the church of San Domenico in the old town. Among the highlights are some of the best examples of the work of the goldsmiths of Taras, which give just a hint of Magna Graecia's wealth. They crafted earrings, necklaces, tiaras and bracelets with minute precision, all delicately patterned and finely worked in gold filigree. Informative commentary in English gives some insight into Greek artistocratic culture, and explains that athleticism and athletic beauty were considered a gift from the gods, in conjunction with red-and-black Lekythos pots decorated with athletes and found in a Greek tomb dating from the fifth century. Most prominent in the collection is the Greek sculpture – including two beautiful busts of Apollo and Aphrodite dating from the fifth century BC, but there's Roman sculpture too, including an elegant head of Diana from the first century AD.

Practicalities

All **buses** arrive at and depart from Piazza Castello, except FS connections with Metaponto and Potenza, which arrive at Piazza Duca d'Aosta, just outside the **train station**. You can save yourself the half-hour walk in from the station by hopping on bus #1, #3 or #8 which run to Corso Umberto in the modern city. Get off just after Palazzo di Uffici and you're close to the **tourist office** on Corso Umberto I at no. 113 (Mon–Fri 9am–1pm & 4.30–6.30pm, Sat 9am–noon; T 099.453.2392, E apttaranto@pugliaturismo.com). Timetables for **city buses** are posted in the AMAT office just around the corner on Via Margherita 34.

    Accommodation can be a real headache, as Taranto isn't really geared up for tourism: one of the few central, inexpensive hotels is *Plaza*, Via d'Aquino 46 (T 099.459.0775, E plaza@euronline.net; ❹).

    For **meals**, check out the tourist menu at the *Ristorante Basile*, Via Pitagora 76 (closed Sat), and the good – and very fairly priced – local specialities at *Da Mimmo*, one block up at Via Giovinazzi 18 (closed Wed).

Northwest of Táranto

Inland and **northwest** of Táranto, the scenery changes dramatically, gorges and ravines marking a landscape that's closer to that of Basilicata than Puglia. **MAS-SAFRA**, about 15km from Táranto (regular trains and FSE buses from Piazza Castello), is split in two by a ravine, the Gravina di San Marco, lined with grottoes dating mainly from the ninth to the fourteenth centuries. Many contain cave-churches, hewn out of the rock by Greek monks and decorated with lavish frescoes. All such sites in Massafra are visitable only by guided tours arranged with the **tourist office** at Piazza Garibaldi 33 (Mon–Fri 9am–noon & 4–7pm; T 099.880.6128, W www.prolocomassafra.it). A Baroque staircase runs down to the eighteenth-century **Santuario della Madonna della Scala**, built onto an earlier cave-church, which features a beautiful fresco of a *Madonna and Child*, dating from the twelfth to the thirteenth centuries – beyond which more steps lead down to an eighth-century crypt. The nearby **Cripta della Buona Nuova** houses a thirteenth-century fresco of the Madonna and a striking painting of Christ Pantocrator. About 200m away, at the bottom of the ravine, is a mass of interconnected caves known as the **Farmacia del Mago Greguro**, now in a pretty pitiful state but once used by the medieval monks as a herbalist's workshop.

    Easily the most spectacular of the ravine towns is **LATERZA**, close to the border of Basilicata, also reachable by bus from Piazza Castello, and situated on the Puglian equivalent of the Grand Canyon, complete with buzzards and kites.

Brindisi

Across the peninsula, 60km east of Táranto on the opposite coast, lies **BRÍNDISI**, once a bridging point for Crusading knights and still strictly a place for passing through. The natural harbour here, the safest on the Adriatic coast, made Brindisi an ideal choice for early settlers. In Roman times, the port became the main crossing point between eastern and western empires, and later, under the Normans, there came a steady stream of pilgrims heading east towards the Holy Land. The route is still open, and now Bríndisi – primarily – is where you come if you're **heading for Greece** from Italy. On arrival, you may well think that the entire town is full of shipping agents: this, when all is said and done, is the town's main business. But even if you're leaving the same night you'll almost certainly end up with time on your hands. You could just while away time in a bar or restaurant down the main Corso Garibaldi, but the old town is pretty compact and, although it isn't brimming with ancient monuments, has a pleasant, almost oriental, flavour about it – and a few hidden gems tucked down its narrow streets. What's more, the town's evening *passeggiata* is one of the south's most boisterous.

The Town and around

The top of a broad flight of steps known as the **Scalinata Virgiliana** (Virgil's Steps) marks the end of the ancient Via Appia, which ran all the way from the Porta Capena in Rome. Two columns stood here for years – useful navigation points for ships coming into harbour. The single column left is being restored and this area is currently under reconstruction. A marble tablet in the corner of the piazza marks the supposed site of the house in which Virgil died, in 19 BC. Via Colonne, with its seventeenth- and eighteenth-century *palazzi*, runs up to the **Duomo** – a remarkable building, if only for the fact that it's survived seven earthquakes since its construction in the eleventh century. Just outside is

Onwards to Greece and Turkey: ferries, tickets and some tips

Agents

There is a staggering array of **agents** selling ferry tickets to Greece, and you should take care to avoid getting ripped off. Ignore the touts clustered around the train station in high season, who specialize in selling imaginary places on non-existent boats, and *always* buy your ticket direct from the company's office or an approved agent. Among the **reliable agencies** are Utac Viaggi, near the Standa at Via Santa Lucia 11 (℡0831.524.921, ⓦwww.utacviaggi.it); Grecian Travel, near the harbour at Corso Garibaldi 79 (℡0831.568.333); Discovery, Corso Garibaldi 49 (℡0831.527.667, ℮discovership@libero.it) which also sells onward ferry tickets to the Cyclades and Crete; and Appia Travel, Via Regina Margherita 8/9 (℡0831.521.684), which sells Transalpino tickets and bus tickets to Rome and other destinations, as well as ferry tickets. **Peak period** (roughly mid-July to mid-Aug) is calamitous, and less reputable agents make crass overbookings: book well in advance or travel a month either side of these dates.

Ferry companies

Ferry companies can't always be trusted either. Many appear overnight in July and August operating craft of questionable seaworthiness. As a rule (though there are honourable exceptions), nearly all the reliable companies' ferries sail in the evening. It's worth visiting Viaggi Fazzina's website ⓦwww.traghettiamo.it for links to the major companies. Among them are: Adriatica (ⓦwww.adriatica.it), c/o Adria (℡0831.523.825) on the first floor of the Stazione Maríttima; to Corfu, Igoumenitsa and Patras; Hellenic Mediterranean Lines, Corso Garibaldi 8 (℡0831.528.531, ℮resa@hml.it), to the same destinations, and also to Paxi and Zante; Fragline, Corso Garibaldi 88 (℡0831.590.310, ⓦwww.fragline.gr), to Corfu and Igoumenitsa; and Blue Star (ⓦwww.bluestarferries.com), Costa Morena (℡0831.548.115) and Med Link (contact through Discovery, see above) to the same destinations plus Çesme.

Adriatica run three times a week throughout the year and daily late June to mid-Sept; the others operate frequent services between May and September. **Schedules** are posted on their sites.

Prices and boarding

Prices vary considerably according to season. On the whole, Adriatica is the most expensive, Fragline the cheapest: you'll be looking at a one-way, high-season fare to Corfu/Igoumenitsa or Patras of €48–65 per person, depending on whether you want a cabin or not; €50 extra for a car. There are reductions of around 20–40 percent on the return fare if you book with the same company you are travelling out with. InterRail and Eurail **passes** are valid, while holders of Italian rail passes get discounts on some services. Check on purchase whether your ticket includes **embarkation tax** – currently €6 per person or per car, €15 per camper van.

Leaving Italy, you must present your boarding card to the authorities at the Stazione Maríttima (first floor); it's best to do it as soon as you have your ticket to avoid the crowds. Then, you should go to the terminal **at least two hours** before the ship's departure, and make sure that any stopover you are making on the way to Patras is clearly marked on your ticket. It's advisable to **stock up on food and drink** in Brindisi's supermarkets, as there are the inevitable mark-ups once on board.

---

the **Museo Archeologico Provinciale** (Mon & Fri–Sun 9am–1.30pm, Tues 9am–1.30pm & 3.30–7pm, Thurs 9am–8pm; free). In addition to ornaments and statues from the necropolises that lined the Via Appia in Roman times, several rooms accommodate bronzes recovered in underwater exploration nearby, as well as finds from the excavations at Egnázia (see p.933). Follow Via Tarentini from here and bear left for the tiny round church of **San Giovanni al Sepolcro**, an eleventh-century baptistry. It's a little dark and decrepit inside, but you can just make out some of the original thirteenth-century frescoes. And there are more frescoes, this time a century older, in the **Chiesa di Santa Lucia**, just off Piazza del Popolo.

Brindisi's most important medieval monument is further afield: the **Chiesa di Santa Maria del Casale** (check with the tourist office for hours and ring for entrance at the gate) – a three-kilometre bus ride towards the airport from town; take bus #4 (from the train station) and ask the driver when to get off. Built by Philip of Anjou at the end of the thirteenth century, it's an odd mixture of styles, the facade an Arabic mass of geometric patterns, worked in two shades of sandstone, and the portal with an almost Art Deco touch to it. The stark interior is rescued from gloom by some fourteenth-century frescoes depicting allegorical scenes relating to the Day of Judgement, a vision of hell designed to scare the living daylights out of the less devout.

Practicalities

Arriving by **ferry** from Greece leaves you at one of three landing stages: two of these are on Via del Mare, at the **Stazione Maríttima** from where it's a few minutes' walk to Piazza Vittorio Emanuele and the bottom of Corso Garibaldi, and another twenty minutes up to the central **train station** the other side of the town centre in Piazza Crispi. The other disembarkation point is at **Costa Moreno**, a couple of kilometres south-east of town; a shuttle bus run by the port authority links this with the town centre, dropping off and picking up at the intersection of Corso Garibaldi and Lungomare R. Margherita, in front of the maritime station. Marozzi **coaches** linking the town with Rome (3 daily; ☎06.4424.9519) and Miccolis coaches connecting it with Naples (3 daily; ☎0831.560.678) arrive at and depart from near the tourist office on Lungomare R. Margherita. Central Brindisi is small enough to walk around, but for **transport around town**, lots of buses run down Corso Umberto and Corso Garibaldi; taxis sit in ranks outside the train station. The **tourist office** has moved to Lungomare R. Margherita 43/44 (summer daily 9am–1pm & 3–10pm; winter Mon–Sat 8.30am–2pm & 4–8pm; ☎0831.523.072, ✉apt-brindisi@pugliaturismo.com). A website primarily for the inhabitants of Brindisi, ⓦwww.brindisiweb.com, has some useful tourism links; for an **Internet point** Italian-style, head for Giovanni Tateo's *Abacus*, Via Conserva 4 (daily 9am–midnight; closed 1 week in Sept), a locals' café serving snacks, appetizers and pizzas.

Nearly all the ferries leave in the evening, so **accommodation** isn't usually a problem. If you do need to stay, try the renovated *Regina*, Via Cavour 5 (☎0831.562.001, ⓦwww.hotelreginaweb.com; ❹), down a quiet side street 150m from the station; the nearby helpful and professional *Barsotti*, Via Cavour 1 (☎0831.560.877, ⓦwww.hotelbarsotti.com; ❺); or the smaller, nicely done-up *Torino*, Largo Palumbo 6 (☎0831.597587, ⓦwww.brindisiweb.com/torino; ❼), a few steps away. *L'Approdo*, Via del Mare 50 (☎0831.529.667; ❹), several minutes' walk from the maritime station, next to a popular pizza restaurant, offers special triple and quadruple deals; or there's the slick *Mediterraneo*, Via Aldo Moro 70 (☎0831.582.811; ❼), a Best Western hotel out of the centre towards the Lecce-to-Bari road. All the hotels mentioned here have air con. There's also a **youth hostel**, 2km out of town in Casale at Via Brandi 2 (☎0831.413.123 or contact the warden Maurizio on his mobile ☎+39.338.323.5545; ✉hostelbrindisi@hotmail.com; €13), with no lock-out

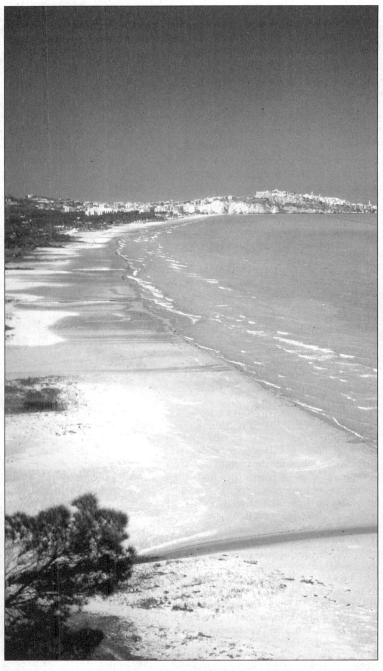

△ Vieste, The Gargano promontory

and a homely atmosphere, where you can rent a bed for the day (€5) if you've got a night departure, with full use of their facilities, including hot showers, email, laundry, bar and café. The hostel is reachable on bus #3 or #4 from the train station, walkable in fifteen minutes by following the strategically placed yellow signs through town, or you can call them for a pick-up service from town (they'll drive you back to the port or to the beach later too if you ask nicely).

It's not difficult to **eat** cheaply in Bríndisi; the whole of Corso Garibaldi (particularly the port end) is smothered in mostly uninspiring fast-food joints. For a nicer sit-down meal in a **restaurant**, stroll around Piazza Dionisi and you will soon be accosted by waiters doing the hard-sell. Among the appealing choices is *Skipper* pizzeria (closed Fri) at number 2 with its own shady garden planted with large stands of bamboo. *Ristorante Penny* (closed Mon; ☎0831.563.013) in a thirteenth-century *palazzo* by the port at Via S. Francesco 1 serves such delights as *tagliolini* with crab meat and calamari, along with a vast wine list. You can have an equally memorable meal at the acclaimed *Trattoria Pantagruele*, Via Salita di Ripalta 13 (closed all day Mon & Sun eve, plus weekends in July & Aug), which serves very good local dishes, especially seafood.

Listings

Car rental at the airport: Avis ☎0831.418.826; Europcar ☎0831.412.061; Maggiore ☎0831.418.155; Sixt ☎0831.418.083.
Overnight doctor ☎0831.537.111.
Police station ☎0831.543.111.
Post office Main office on Piazza Vittoria (Mon–Fri 8.30am–1pm & 3–6pm, Sat 8.30am–noon), anoth-

er at the Stazione Maríttima (Mon–Sat 8.30am–1pm).
Train station ☎0831.521.975; train information (number functions in Italy only) ☎848.88088; timetables and prices on Ⓦwww.fs-on-line.it
Taxis ☎0831.597.901 & ☎0831.597.503.

West of Bríndisi: Ostuni

OSTUNI, 40km northwest of the town and just 35 minutes away by train, is one of the most stunning small towns of southern Italy. Situated on three hills at the southernmost edge of Le Murge, and an important Greco-Roman city in the first century AD, its old centre spreads across the highest of the hills, a gleaming white splash of sun-bleached streets and cobbled alleyways, dominating the plains below. The maze of well-preserved winding streets makes for a fascinating amble, the town buzzes on summer nights and there are some exceptional views – particularly from Largo Castello over the woods to the north. Bits of cavorting Baroque twist out of unexpected places, including an ornamented eighteenth-century obelisk, 21m high, dedicated to St Oronzo, which stands in Piazza della Libertà (aka Piazza St Oronzo) on the southern edge of the old town. This is the focal point on summer Saturday nights for hordes of people who drive in from the countryside around, meet up with their friends, pack out the **bars and cafés** and listen to the music coming from the sound system.

The **Chiesa delle Monacelle**, on the main drag from the upper town to the main piazza, has displays on prehistory (daily 9am–1pm & 4.30–10pm; winter closes 7.30pm; €1.50), the highlight of which is "Delia", the skeleton of a pregnant young woman found in a crouched position, her bones decorated before burial. You'll find the **tourist office** at Corso Mazzini 8 in the old town (summer Mon–Fri 8am–1.30pm & 4.30–9.30pm, Sat 4.30–9.30pm; winter Mon–Fri 9am–12.30pm & 3.30–6.30pm; ☎0831.301.268).

Ostuni's proximity to a popular sandy coastline with Blue Flag beaches, 7km away, makes budget **accommodation** tricky to find. The tourist office can help with private **rooms** in town, or there are a couple of unremarkable but cheap, central hotels: the *Hotel Orchidea Nera* on Via Mazzini 118 (T0831.301.366; ❸), or the *Tre Torri*, at Via Vittorio Emanuele 298 (T0831.331.114; ❸). If your budget can stand it, you could always opt for the beautiful, antique-filled four-star hotel *Al Castello Marchesale*, Via Scipione Petrarolo 7 (T0831.305.925; ❽). An alternative is to stay in one of the many excellent **agriturismo** places out of town: *Il Frantoio* (T0831.440.276, Wwww.trecolline.it; ❼) on the SS16 at the km874 milestone is a traditional white farmhouse in 72 hectares of olive grove, with eight rooms furnished with family furniture and antique beds. Rates include breakfast and access to a private beach; you can also dine at *Il Frantoio* if you book ahead. This makes a good winter option, as the rooms have fireplaces and old wood burning stoves. *Masseria La Salìnola* (T0831.330.683, Wwww.agriturismo.com/Salinola; €452 per person per week in high season) has doubles and small apartments on a traditional estate surrounded by olive groves, with a swimming pool (in high season) and bikes. The only snag is, there's a one week minimum stay. It's quite tricky to find: in town, look out for the neon sign of *Bar Manhattan* on the ring road, turn right at the roundabout, then head for San Michele; after 1.7km you'll see the *Masseria* on your left.

There are a number of excellent **restaurants** in Ostuni: try *Osteria del Tempo Perso*, at Via Tanzarella 47 (closed all day Mon & lunchtimes except Sun; reservations advised T0831.303.320), for good-value *fave e cicoria* (broad beans with chicory), *orecchiette con cime di rapa* (pasta with turnip tops) and grilled meat. *Vecchia Ostuni*, Largo Lanza 9, just off Piazza della Libertà, is another good choice with a vast array of antipasti including deep-fried courgette flowers, snails in a piquant tomato sauce, twists of mozzarella, and pickled peppers. At the top of the town, *Antiche Pietanze*, on Via P.Vincenti, is a small place up a set of narrow whitewashed steps offering regional food at moderate prices and a good-value set menu.

Lecce and the Salentine peninsula

A fast 40km south from Bríndisi, Baroque **Lecce** is a place to linger, with some diverting Roman remains and a wealth of fine architecture scattered about an appealing old town area. It's also a good starting-point for excursions further into the **Salentine peninsula**, which begins south of the city. In keeping with the city's long association with traders and settlers, the landscape here begins to take on a distinctive Greek flavour, a mildly undulating region planted with carob, prickly pear and tobacco. The Adriatic coast is pitted with cliffs, topped with ruined watchtowers, with rugged coves and caves right the way down to the **southern cape**. The hinterland, by comparison, is more barren, although there's again a Greek element to it, with its tiny, sun-blasted villages growing out of the dry, stony, red earth and the flat-roofed houses painted in bright pastel colours.

Lecce

Whether or not you like the Baroque style, you can't fail to be impressed by the exuberant building styles on display in **LECCE**, though the fact that they are firmly in the grip of a largely unremarkable modern city does detract from the enjoyment. The arrival of religious orders (Jesuits, the Teatini and Franciscans) at the end of the sixteenth century brought an influx of wealth

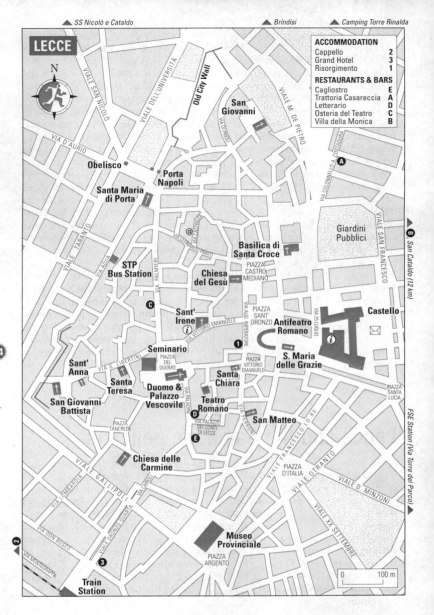

which paid for the opulent churches and *palazzi* that still pervade today's city. The flowery style of "Leccese Baroque" owed as much to the materials to hand as to the skills of the architects: the soft local sandstone could be intricately carved and then hardened with age. Unfortunately, modern pollution is in danger of ruining many of the buildings, keeping the mass of stonemasons and carpenters who still work in Lecce well occupied.

The City

Start in **Piazza Sant'Oronzo**, the hub of the old town, named after the first-century bishop of Lecce who went to the lions under Nero. His bronze statue lurches unsteadily from the top of the **Colonna di Sant'Oronzo** that once stood at the end of the Via Appia in Brindisi. It resurfaced here in 1666 to honour Oronzo, who was credited with having spared the town from plague ten years earlier. The south side of the piazza is taken up by the weighty remains of the **Anfiteatro Romano**, which probably dates from the time of Hadrian. In its heyday it seated 20,000 spectators, and it's still used in summer for concerts and plays. Sadly, though, most of its decorative bas-reliefs, of fighting gladiators and wild beasts, have been removed to the town's museum for safekeeping, and nowadays it looks rather depleted.

The best of Lecce's Baroque churches are all a short distance from Piazza Sant'Oronzo. The finest, certainly the most ornate, is the **Basilica di Santa Croce**, just to the north, whose florid facade, the work of the local architect Antonio Zimbalo, took around 150 years to complete, its upper half a riot of decorative garlands and flowers around a central rose window. The **Church of Santa Chiara**, in the opposite direction on Piazza Vittorio Emanuele, is an essential stop; loaded down with ornament, its interior is full of little chapels groaning with garlands and gilt. There's more Baroque extravagance on offer on Via Vittorio Emanuele, where the **Church of Sant'Irene** houses the most sumptuous of Lecce's Baroque altars – lavishly frosted and gilded, and smothered with decoration. Nearby, facing onto Piazza del Duomo, the **Seminario** holds an impressively ornate well, carved stone masquerading as delicately wrought iron. Next door, the balconied **Palazzo Vescovile** adjoins the **Duomo** itself, twelfth century in origin but rebuilt entirely in the mid-seventeenth century by Zimbalo. He tacked on two ornate facades and an enormous five-storeyed campanile that towers 70m above the square. The plain **Castello di Carlo V**, to the east of Piazza Sant'Oronzo, is currently under restoration.

There's further work by Zimbalo in the **Church of San Giovanni Battista** (or del Rosario), by the Porta Rudiae in the southwest corner of town – the ornate facade and twisting columns fronting some extremely odd altars, dumpy cherubim diving for cover amid scenes resembling an exploding fruit bowl. But if the Baroque trappings of the town are beginning to pall, there's the odd relic from other eras too, not least a well-preserved **Teatro Romano** (sometimes used as a concert venue) near the **church of Santa Chiara**, the only one of its kind to be found in Puglia, with its rows of seats and orchestra floor still remarkably intact. There's also the fine Romanesque church of **Santi Nicolò e Cataldo** (entrance through the cemetery gate; generally open mornings) built by the Normans in 1190, with a cool interior that reveals a generous hint of Saracen influence in the arches and the octagonal rounded dome. Little remains of the frescoes that once covered its walls, though an image of St Nicolò can be found on the south side, together with a delicately carved portal. One more stop to make, when it reopens after restoration, is the **Museo Provinciale Castromediano** near the railway station on the other side of town, which has finds from the old Roman town, including decorative panels from the amphitheatre and some religious gold- and silverwork.

Practicalities

Regional **buses** arrive at the Porta Napoli, the FSE bus station (℡0832.347.634) on Via Torre del Parco, or the STP bus station on Via Adua. FSE and FS **trains** (℡0832.668.233) use the same station, 1km south of the centre at the end of Via Oronzo Quarta. The **tourist office** is at Via Vittorio

Emanuele II, 24 (Mon–Fri 9am–1pm & 4–7pm, Sat 9am–1pm; ℡0832 .248.092).

The cheapest **place to stay** is *Cappello*,Via Montegrappa 4 (℡0832.308.881, Ⓦwww.hotelcapello.it; ❷), a friendly and efficiently run large hotel just outside the station – for once, a fairly salubrious area. If your budget will run to it, give yourself a treat and book in at the Art Nouveau *Grand Hotel*, Viale Oronzo Quarta 28 (℡0832.309.405; ❺); the bedrooms are pretty plain, but the building is gorgeous. More imposing is *Risorgimento*,Via Augusto Imperatore (℡0832.242.125; ❺), a sandstone *palazzo* dating back to the early 1900s with elegant interiors, just off Piazza S. Oronzo. Otherwise, the tourist office can help you find a reasonably priced private **room** (just call in and check out their noticeboard) or simply search on Ⓦwww.bedandbreakfast.lecce.it. Another site, Ⓦwww.caffeletto.it, lists B&B options in historic buildings in the old town and on the outskirts of Lecce – many are beautiful, albeit at a price.The closest **campsites** are *Namastè* (℡0832.329.547, Ⓦwww.camping-lecce.it) on the road to **NOVOLI** (at the 4.5km marker) and *Camping Torre Rinalda* (℡0832.382.161, Ⓦwww.torrerinaldi.it) at **TORRE RINALDA** on the Salentine coast 10km north of Lecce; hourly buses run from the Piazza Sant'Oronzo.

Lecce's burgeoning **bar scene** is a bonus, with *Caffe Letterario* (closed Sat & Sun lunch & Aug),Via G. Paladini 46, an arty little book-café with tasty snacks at lunchtime and in the evening (you will need to fill out a free membership card). A few doors away in Via Cairoli, there's a laid-back cocktail bar and eatery *Cagliostro* in the courtyard and garden of the *palazzo* at number 25 from May to October. For **Internet access**, international newspapers, books and travel guides, *Chatwin* café is atVia Isabella Castriota (Mon–Sat 10am–1.30pm & 4.30–10pm; Ⓦwww.chatwin.netcafe.it).

For **meals**, *Villa della Monica*,Via SS. Giacomo e Filippo 40 (closed Tues), is worth tracking down where, in summer, you can sit in the gleaming marble, fountain-studded courtyard and sip a cocktail, lunch or dine.Their specialities include pasta with crayfish, beef with rocket and parmesan, Salentine chickpea soup, and grilled smoked scamorza cheese. At the other end of the scale, the best choice in town for homely cuisine is *Trattoria Casareccia* onVia Colonnello A. Costadura 19 (closed all day Mon & Sun evening). More centrally, *Osteria del Teatro* onVia Palmieri 26 (closed Sun) serves up a good *purè di fave e cicoria*.

The eastern peninsula: Otranto and the southern cape

The quickest escape from Lecce to the coast is to **SAN CATALDO**, popular with the locals, and with sandy beaches served by buses from Lecce's Villa Comunale.Without your own transport, though, you won't be able to see anything else of the coast south of San Cataldo until Otranto. With a car it's a pleasant route south along a rocky shoreline littered with ruined towers, a legacy of the defences erected against Turkish incursions.

Otranto

OTRANTO, a minuscule town nestling around its harbour, is only an hour by train from Lecce (change at Maglie) and still very much a quiet Puglian backwater set in an arid, rocky and windblown landscape, with translucent seas to swim in and a comparatively undeveloped coastline – though summer ferry services to Albania and a Club Med affair nearby attract visitors in the height of summer. Its history, however, is decidedly grim. One of the last Byzantine towns to fall to the Normans, in 1070, Otranto remained a thriving port for Crusaders, pilgrims and traders. But in 1480 a Turkish fleet laid siege to the town, which held out for fifteen days before capitulating. It's said that as a punishment the archbishop, upon capture, suffered the indignity of being sawn in half, a popular Turkish spectacle. Nearly 12,000 people lost their lives and the 800 survivors, refusing to convert, were taken up a nearby hill and beheaded. Otranto never really recovered, though the town does feature one glorious survivor of the Turkish attack inside its cathedral.

This, the **Cattedrale di Santa Maria Annunziata** (daily 8.30am–noon & 4–7pm), down a small alleyway just to the left of the castle, is a Romanesque structure with a rose window added in the fifteenth century and a marble-columned nave adorned by an extraordinary **mosaic floor**, a multicoloured tapestry in stone. The central theme is the "Tree of Life". Historical and animal figures are shown as a mix of myth and reality – Alexander the Great, King Arthur, the Queen of Sheba, crabs, fish, serpents and mermaids. The work of a twelfth-century monk, for all its rough simplicity the mosaic provides a captivating picture, empowered by a delightful child-like innocence.

Not far from the cathedral, the town's Aragonese **Castello** (daily 10am–noon & 6–10pm; free) juts out into the bay, defending the harbour. Its walls incorporate fragments of Roman and medieval inscriptions, while Charles V's coat-of-arms looms from its portal. Outside on a dusty square, old men still play a highly animated form of *boules*, impervious to passers-by. Out on the southern edge of town is the hill, covered with cypress trees, where the survivors of the Turkish siege were beheaded. At the top of the hill, the sixteenth-century **Chiesa di San Francesco di Paola** holds inscriptions of the names of the victims, together with a vivid description of the terrible events of July 1480.

There's a variety of musical and theatrical events in Otranto throughout the summer, usually centred around the castle, and an annual **festival** commemorating the "800 Martyrs" on August 13–15. Details and other information are available from the **tourist office**, Via Pantaleone 12 in the new town (July & Aug daily 8.30am–1.30pm & 4.30–9pm; Sept–June Mon–Sat 8am–2pm; ☎0836.801.436). If you want **to stay** in Otranto, your best bet is the light, modern *Bellavista*, Via Vittorio Emanuele 4 (☎0836.801.058; ❺), right in the centre of things near the beach, just outside the old town; the nearest **campsite**, *Camping Hydrusa*, is on Via del Porto (☎0836.801.255; May–Sept), signposted from the port. There are some excellent **restaurants** in town, such as *Da Sergio* on Corso Garibaldi (closed Sun in winter), and *La Duchesca* at Piazza Castello 17 (closed Mon in winter), while the air-conditioned self-service restaurant *Boomerang*, at 13/14 Via Vittorio Emanuele II, by the park next to the beach, serves delicious well-priced fresh antipasti, pasta and simple meals. Alternatively, in nearby Frassanito, *Da Umberto*, along the road to San Cataldo (closed Sun in winter), does great fish dishes.

Ferry services occasionally run to **Albania** from Otranto. During 2002 they were suspended, but should be up and running again in 2003. To book, call Ella de Viaggi (☎0836.801.005).

To the southern cape

From Otranto, all the way down to the cape at Santa Maria di Leuca, the coastline is steep and rugged. **CAPO D'OTRANTO**, 5km south of Otranto, is the easternmost point on the Italian peninsula, topped by a lighthouse and the rather desolate ruins of a seventh-century abbey. On clear mornings there's a commanding view across the straits, the mountains of Albania visible about 80km away. (On seriously clear days they say you can even see Corfu, 100km away.) The relative remoteness of the coast means that refugees from Albania as well as Pakistanis, Kurds and North Africans who have passed through Greece head for the coast around Otranto on a regular basis. They have often made the sea voyage in inflatable dinghies run by traffickers and their beach landings can make a bizarre and poignant contrast to the happy crowds on Sunday outings.

There isn't really much to draw you down as far as **SANTA MARIA DI LEUCA**, a somewhat barren spot that's a fitting "land's end", with a scattering of Neolithic remains and an uninspiring marina. The once-supposed "end of the world" is marked by the tiny church of **Santa Maria Finibus Terrae**, built on the site of an ancient temple dedicated to Minerva, which stands perched on the white limestone cliffs. But it's all a bit of an anticlimax: even the cape isn't really the southernmost point, that distinction going to the Punta Ristola, a little to the west. You can get down this far, or at least as far as **Gagliano del Capo**, by train: it's at the end of the FSE rail line, just 5km from the cape.

The western peninsula: Galatina, Nardo and Gallipoli

About half an hour down the rail line from Lecce, **GALATINA** is an intriguing Salentine town on the edge of an area known as Grecia Salentina, a key Greek colony well into medieval times, which retained Greek customs and language up until the present. Today, it's an important centre of the Italian tobacco industry, with much of the weed grown in the fields around, as well as being famed for its excellent local **wine**; stop by at *Bellone* on Via Soleto 2 (closed Thurs afternoon & all day Sun) for good pasta and wine, including hard-to-find local pasta shapes that are produced in-house. In the old part of town, the church of **Santa Caterina in Galatina** (daily 9am–noon & 5–7pm) is also well worth a look for the stunning fourteenth-century frescoes that cover its interior.

Most interestingly, Galatina is the prime place in the Salentine where the phenomenon of **tarantism** still survives. Once a year, on the feast day of Saints Peter and Paul (June 28/29), the devout – together with musicians, dancers, academics, photographers and curious bystanders – gather at the chapel of St Paul near the cathedral to pay their respects. In earlier centuries and as recently as the 1950s, victims of an unexplained illness with various conflicting symptoms that could range from lassitude to paranoia and a compulsion to dance were brought to the chapel to be cured. The sickness was commonly attributed to the dreaded tarantula bite and those who got over the sickness by going into a sort of music-inspired trance-dance would then come here every year to give thanks to St Paul for their cure. Modern scholars say that the sufferers – mostly women – usually hadn't been bitten but that the ruse of the "spider bite" was a metaphor for poisoning and entrapment at an existential level. Various medical explanations have been put forward, with other theories linking it to exorcism and ecstatic religion. These days the festa is enjoying something of a revival, due in part to the resurgence of *pizzica* music which is typical of the Salento peninsula. You'll need to get to Galatina by 4.30am or 5am on the 29th for the most intriguing part of the action – which may range from music and dancing outside the doors of the candle-lit chapel (open only on the weekend of the festa) to some present-day *tarantati* shyly turning up to pay their respects to St Paul before the crowds arrive for the official early morning mass at the church next door at around 6am. A huge fair of rides and market stalls then takes over the town with the festivities going on until late.

The beat of the tambourine is a vital feature of *pizzica* music. Until now there have been three kinds: the *pizzica di cuore*, danced for fun and as part of courtship by couples or groups at festas; the *pizzica scherma*, a knife or sword dance which originally was a way of settling disputes; and the *pizzica tarantata*, the trance-dance enacted by the sick to get over their illness. A resurgence in regional pride has given rise to a new *pizzica* style which encompasses "techno-pizzica", as well as rave and rap music by bands such as *Sud Sound System* who perform a mix of reggae and southern Italian music in the Leccese dialect, passing round the microphone and inviting anyone who wants to to improvise a few lines. It's possible to catch bands like these at the summer festivals and fairs around the Salento. One of the most important in recent years has been "the night of the tarantula" (*La notte della taranta*) in mid-August at Melpignano (between Galatina and Otranto), an all-night music festival which drew a 25,000-strong crowd in 2001. Another *festa* in honour of St Rocco in the small village of Torre Paduli (25km southeast of Galatina, near Ruffano) is the scene for a mass *pizzica scherma* dance, accompanied by musicians of all ages who beat their tambourines, it is said, until their fingers bleed.

The **tourist office** at Via V Emanuele II (daily 9.30am–8pm; ☏0836.569.984, ⓔiat.galatina@libero.it) will give the lowdown on events surrounding the *festa* which is gaining a higher profile these days after years of "discouragement" by both the church and the municipality. There's only one central **place to stay**: the plush *Palazzo Baldi* in a courtyard a few steps from the cathedral at Corte Baldi (☏0836.568.345; ⓺).

By way of contrast, first impressions of **GALLIPOLI** (not the World War I battlefield in Turkey) are fairly uninspiring. The new town sprouted on the mainland once the population outgrew its original island site in the eighteenth century, and all that remains of the once-beautiful city (the Kalli-pollis) of the Greeks is a rather weather-beaten fountain, which sits in the new town near the bridge. Over the bridge things get more interesting: the old town itself is a maze of meandering and twisting whitewashed streets, with tiny tomatoes, hanging on the walls to dry, providing a sudden blaze of colour alongside the fishing nets. Only the familiar Aragonese castle, which squats in one corner of the island, serves as a reminder that this is still Italy.

For **accommodation**, try *Pescatore* on Riviera C. Colombo 39 (☏0833.264.331; ⓸), an attractive hotel in the old quarter with some rooms which overlook the sea and a good restaurant (closed Mon) serving seafood-oriented home cooking. Alternatively, there's the simpler hotel, *Le Conchiglie*, Via delle Perle 12 (☏0833.209.039; ⓶), outside the centre at Località Conchiglie. There's a good **campsite** 5km to the north: *La Vecchia Torre* (☏0833.209.083, ⓔsundar@libero.it; June–Sept) at Rivabella on the coast road to Santa Maria al Bagno.

Travel details

Trains

Altamura to: Gravina in Puglia (7 daily; 20min).
Bari to: Alberobello (FSE, 15 daily; 1hr 30min); Altamura (13 daily; 1hr 10min); Andria (hourly;

1hr); Barletta (hourly; 55min); Bitonto (hourly; 20min); Brindisi (hourly; 1hr–1hr 30min); Fasano (20 daily; 40min–1hr); Gravina in Puglia (3 daily; 1hr 15min); Grotte di Castellana (FSE, hourly; 50min); Lecce (hourly; 1hr 30min–2hr); Lecce (hourly; 1hr 30min); Locorotondo (FSE, 15 daily; 1hr 40min); Martina Franca (FSE, 15 daily; 1hr 45min); Molfetta (hourly; 30min); Naples (2 daily; 3hr 45min); Ostuni (hourly; 1hr); Péschici (1 daily, change at Rodi Gargánico; 5hr 20min); Polignano a Mare (hourly; 45min); Putignano (FSE, hourly; 1hr); Rome (9 daily; 4hr 30min–5hr 30min); Ruvo di Puglia (hourly; 40min); Spinazzola (3 daily; 1hr 15min–1hr 45min); Táranto (11 fast trains daily; 1hr 5min–1hr 26min); Torre a Mare (hourly; 10min); Trani (hourly; 40min).

Bríndisi to: Fasano (hourly; 37min); Lecce (hourly; 24–34min); Ostuni (hourly; 22–34min).

Fóggia to: Bari (hourly; 1hr–1hr 30min); Barletta (17 daily; 30min); Brindisi (17 daily; 2hr 50min); Fasano (17 daily; 2hr 15min); Manfredonia (9 daily; 30min); Molfetta (hourly; 1hr 5min); Ostuni (17 daily; 2hr 30min); Péschici (4 daily; 2hr 8min); San Severo (5 daily; 22min); Trani (hourly; 50min).

Lecce to: Bari (hourly; 1hr 30min–2hr); Otranto (7 daily; 1hr); Gallipoli (9 daily; 1hr); Gagliano del Capo (10 daily; 1hr 30min); Rome (6 daily; 6hr 30min–7hr).

Martina Franca to: Táranto (9 daily; 40min).

San Severo to: Péschici (9 daily; 1hr 40min).

Táranto to: Bari (15 daily; 1hr 15min); Bríndisi (10 daily; 1hr); Grottaglie (11 daily; 15min); Martina Franca (9 daily; 40min); Massafra (12 daily; 15min); Metaponto (8 daily; 45min); Naples (3 fast trains daily; 4hr 18min); Reggio di Calabria (3 daily; 6hr).

Buses

NB: the bus service on Sundays is drastically reduced.

Bari to: Andria (6–7 daily; 1hr 30min); Barletta (3–4 hourly; 1hr 25min); Canosa di Puglia (10 daily; 2hr 10min); Margherita di Savoia (8 daily; 1hr 45min); Molfetta (3–4 hourly; 40min); Trani (3–4 hourly; 1hr 5min).

Fasano to: Martina Franca (12 daily; 20min); Savelletri and Egnazia (6 daily; 20 min); Selva Fasano (4 daily; 10min).

Fóggia to: Manfredonia (18 daily; 45min); Mattinata (9 daily; 1hr 15min); Vieste (5 daily; 2hr 45min); Troia (24 daily; 40min).

Manfredonia to: Bari (1 daily; 2hr 20min); San

Giovanni Rotondo (14 daily; 40min); San Marco in Lamis (10 daily; 1hr); Mattinata (10 daily; 30min); Monte Sant'Angelo (every 2hr; 55min); Vico del Gargano (2 daily; 2hr 15min); Vieste (2 daily; 1hr 55min).

Molfetta to: Ruvo di Puglia (hourly; 30min).

Péschici to: Rodi Gargánico (3 daily; 35min); Rome (2 daily; 6hr 40min); San Severo (3 daily; 2hr 25min); Vico del Gârgano (1 daily; 45min); Vieste (13 daily; 45min).

Rodi Gârgánico to: Foresta Umbra (2 daily; 1hr 5min); Vico del Gârgano (2 daily; 40min).

Vico del Gârgano to: Ischitella (9 daily; 15min).

Vieste to: Fóggia (1 daily; 2hr 45min); Manfredonia (3 daily; 1hr 40min); Péschici (9 daily; 45min); Rome (2 daily; 7hr 15min).

Ferries

Manfredonia to: Vieste/Péschici/Rodi Gargánico (mid-June to mid-Sept 1 daily; early June & late Sept 4 weekly; April–May 2 weekly; 2hr 40min–5hr 20min).

Vieste to: Trémiti (1 weekly Jan–May & Oct–Dec; 1hr 10min–2hr 15min).

Péschici to: Trémiti via Rodi Gargánico (1 daily June–Sept; 1hr 15min).

Hydrofoils

Trémiti Islands to: Manfredonia (1 daily June, July & Sept; 2 daily Aug; 2hr); Vieste (June, July & Sept 1 daily; Aug 3 daily; 1hr).

International ferries

Bari to: Corfu (daily end July to mid Aug; 5 weekly mid-Jun to end July & mid-Aug to mid-Sept; 2 weekly in winter; 9hr); Dubrovnik, Croatia (4 weekly August, between 2 and 3 weekly June, July & Sept; 7–8hr); Durres/Durazzo, Albania (2–3 daily; 3hr 30min–8hr); Igoumenitsa (daily; from 9hr); Patras (daily from 15hr).

Bríndisi to: Çesme (2 weekly; from 28hr); Corfu (at least 1 daily; 9hr 30min); Igoumenitsa (at least 1 daily; from 9hr); Kefallonia (daily; 14hr); Patras (daily; 15hr); Paxi (4–6 weekly July & Aug; from 10hr 30min); Zante (2 weekly July & Aug; 19hr 30min).

Calabria and Basilicata

CHAPTER 15 Highlights

✳ **Matera** Sliced by a ravine containing thousands of *sassi* – cave dwellings gouged out of rock that were inhabited till the 1950s – Matera's urban landscape is truly unique, and the town is also one of the most cultured in the south of Italy. **See p.979**

✳ **Tropea promontory** This region has it all – beautiful white sandy beaches, turquoise water, hills tumbling down to the coast and – in Tropea town and Pizzo – two of the most characterful old centres in Calabria. **See p.967**

✳ **Aspromonte** Right at Italy's southern tip, the Aspromonte massif has some of Calabria's most spectacular mountain scenery. **See p.973**

✳ **Bronzi di Riace** Two extraordinary seven-foot high bronze statues of Greek athletes housed in Reggio's Museo Nazionale. **See p.972**

✳ **Cosenza** In a region of few big cities, Cosenza's absorbing old quarter and cultural attractions stand out, and it also makes a great base for skiing and hill-walking in the nearby Sila. **See p.960**

Calabria and Basilicata

More than any other of the regions of the Italian South, **Calabria** and **Basilicata** represent the quintessence of the *mezzogiorno*. Underdeveloped and – owing to emigration – sparsely populated, these rural regions were long considered only good for taxation, and even then they were mismanaged. Although agriculture was systematized to an extent when these lands formed a part of Magna Graecia, by the time the Normans arrived there was little infrastructure or defence against the depredations of maritime raiders. Moreover, the feudal era didn't really die here until the Bourbons were ejected at Unification, and remnants of the older society persist in the widespread system of patronage and an exaggerated use of titles. Respect for authority co-exists with a deep scepticism and an apathy and inertia vividly described by Carlo Levi in his *Christ Stopped at Eboli* – a book that for many Italians was the introduction to the very deep problems besetting the *mezzogiorno*.

Indeed, this area is if anything even more marginalized than it was before Unification, when it was at least the geographical centre of the Bourbon state, and today talk of the Two Nations of Italy is most strikingly manifest in what can seem a very distant region from the emphatically European north – to which its people provide a reluctant supply of cheap labour. But despite lingering attitudes on both sides that perpetuate this gulf, much has changed in the south, to the extent that the picture drawn in Levi's book would hardly be recognized today, thanks largely to a massive channelling of funds since the war to finance huge irrigation and land-reclamation schemes, industrial development and a modern system of communications. Malaria has been eradicated, previously unproductive land made fertile, and construction is under way everywhere – though often hand-in-hand with the forces of organized crime and with frequently dire consequences for the physical aspect of the land.

The **landscape** provides the main reason to come to Basilicata and Calabria: although they're the least fertile regions in Italy, the combination of mountain grandeur and a relatively unspoilt coastline, often in close proximity, gives them a powerful appeal, and one only beginning to be exploited by the tourist industry. Two of the main cities, **Cosenza**, lying just inland of the Tyrrhenian coast, and **Reggio**, at its southern tip, lie within the shadow of the forested slopes of the **Sila massif** and the craggy wilderness of **Aspromonte**,

Regional food and wine

The food of Calabria is similar to that of Campania, but tends to have a rougher approach. **Greek influence** still pervades in the form of aubergines, swordfish and sweets incorporating figs, almonds and honey; otherwise it has the common trademarks of the south – plenty of pasta, pork and cheeses such as mozzarella, *caciocavallo*, mature provolone and pecorino. Basilicata is another poor region, mountainous and sparsely populated, relying on pasta, tomatoes, bread, olives and pork. A fondness for **spicy food** shows in the popularity of all types of peppers and, unusually in Italy, ginger (*zenzero*), which is thrown into many dishes. **Strong cheeses**, like matured ricotta – to match the strength of other ingredients – are favoured.

Cirò is the success story of Calabrian wine making, an old **wine** that has been given some modern touches and now shifts bottles outside its home territory. Not surprisingly, given its far-south position, Calabria also turns out sweet whites such as Greco di Bianco. The **aglianico** grape makes a star appearance in Basilicata: Aglianico del Vulture is the region's only DOC, but other wines worth trying are the sweet, sparkling Malvasia and Moscato.

respectively, and Cosenza also holds Calabria's most compelling old centre, in striking contrast to the progressive and prosperous sheen of its modern counterpart. In Basilicata, **Potenza** is useful as a transport hub for the string of medieval towns lying to the north, although the town holds none of the fascination of the region's second city, **Matera**, whose distinctive *sassi* – cavelike dwellings in the heart of the town – give it a uniquely dramatic setting. Of the coasts, it's the **Tyrrhenian** that is most engaging, with spots like **Maratea**, **Tropea** and **Scilla** favourite hideaway resorts for discerning Italian and foreign visitors. The **Ionian** coast, on the other hand, can be bleak and is visited mainly for its **ancient sites** – relics of the once mighty states that comprised the Greek colonies known as Magna Graecia.

Good **transport** services exist, but in hilly and coastal areas a car is useful, especially to penetrate some of the more far-flung inland areas. Once you've arrived somewhere, park up as soon as you can, as a vehicle can only be an encumbrance in the smaller places. The old suspicion of strangers may still persist in rural areas, but more often than not you'll find the inhabitants welcoming, and fiercely proud of their region. As for sexual harassment, this is still a reality in some parts of the south – macho values prevail and women travelling alone will often be stared at (see p.53 for some hints on dealing with the more persistent specimens of southern manhood).

The northern Tyrrhenian coast

The northern stretch of the Tyrrhenian coast takes in both Calabria and Basilicata, of which the latter – a brief mountainous slice – is the most inspiring stretch and probably the most visited part of the entire region, its sheer cliffs and rocky coves refreshingly unspoilt by the holiday industry.

The obvious stop here is **Maratea**, hemmed in by the mountains and offering some first-rate beaches, which get overcrowded in summer. Once you're in Calabria, the holiday complexes intrude on the mainly mountainous littoral, though there are some absorbing places to break the journey, notably the towns of **Diamante**, **Belvedere** and **Amantea**, and plenty of good swim-stops in between. Following the coast down, the main SS18 runs alongside the railway line, though the frequent trains don't always stop at smaller places.

Maratea

The main – indeed the only – town on Basilicata's Tyrrhenian seaboard, **MARATEA** is a picturesque cluster of localities scattered along the cliffy coastline, mostly dedicated to the holiday industry during summer but perfectly peaceful outside the peak period. The old inland centre, known simply as **Maratea Paese**, is a knot of steep, narrow alleys and squares worth nosing around, though lacking any vital attractions. More compelling are the straggling, long-abandoned ruins of **Maratea Antica** behind and above town up the five-kilometre road to **Monte San Biagio** (624m), from which memorable views extend over the Golfo di Policastro. The peak is dominated by the **Redentore**, an enormous marble Christ, arms akimbo, symbolically positioned with its back to the sea, looking towards the mountains of the interior. Opposite the statue, and looking as if it were about to be crushed under the giant's feet, is the **Santuario di San Biagio**, built on the site of a pagan temple dedicated to Minerva and now the destination of a procession during the town's main festivities on the second Sunday of May, when a statue of the patron saint is carried up the hill.

Maratea's chief allure, however, is the beautiful rocky coastline hereabouts and the string of coastal offshoots where the hotels and restaurants are located. Most of the action – and accommodation – is in or around the *frazione* of **Fiumicello**, 5km north of Maratea Paese, though the chic elite who have colonized much of the area prefer to be seen in the snazzier bars and restaurants of **Maratea Porto**, directly below Maratea Paese – if nothing else, a pleasant place to stroll around and gawp at the yachts. The whole area is well endowed with sandy **beaches**, including a good one below Fiumicello; most are well signposted, but don't hesitate to explore the less obvious ones.

Practicalities

Most **trains** stop at the main Maratea station, at the bottom of Maratea Paese, from where it's a five-minute minibus or taxi ride (or a fifteen-minute walk) to Fiumicello. There is a second, less-used station, Maratea Scalo (at Marina di Maratea), 5km south of the main station. For **getting around**, a summer-only minibus service (every 1hr–1hr 30min; €0.52, tickets bought on board) connects Maratea Porto, Fiumicello, Marina di Maratea and Maratea Paese in that order. The **tourist office** is on Fiumicello's main square (Mon–Sat: May–Sept 8am–2pm & 3–8pm; Oct–May 8am–2pm, also Tues & Thurs 3–6pm; ☎0973.876.908, ✉aptmaratea@tiscalinet.it).

Accommodation can be hard to come by at any time, and in high season is often expensive, with many hotels requiring half-board during the peak period. Many close outside the summer months, though one good choice that's open all year, and has plenty of space, is the *Fiorella* (☎0973.876.921; ❸), just outside Fiumicello at Via Santa Vénere 21 (near the petrol station). If you want to stay by the sea, try the *Settebello* (☎0973.876.277; May–Oct; ⓦwww.costadimaratea.com/settebello; ❺), which overlooks the beach at Fiumicello. A cheaper alternative to hotels around Maratea, and one that avoids the half-board requirement, is to rent **rooms** (lists available from the tourist offices); in central Fiumicello, for example, Giovanni Talarico offers spotless accommodation with sparkling views across to the mountains at Via Santa Vénere 29 (☎0973.877.040; ❷; July & Aug). The nearest **campsite** is *Camping Maratea* at Castrocucco (☎0973.877.580; mid-June to mid-Sept), 5km south of Maratea Scalo station and 10km south of Maratea Paese; it's reachable on infrequent minibuses in July and August only, or by taxi.

There are dozens of **restaurants** in the area. Some of the best are in Fiumicello, where, on the main Via Santa Vénere, *La Bússola*'s good and cheap pizzas generally pull in a strong local crowd (no closing day). Further down the main road towards the beach, at no. 97, *Da Felicia* has outdoor seating and serves fresh fish at reasonable prices (closed Sun in winter).

Into Calabria

South of Maratea, the road soon drops to reveal the flat coast of Calabria, on the other side of the River Noce. The first town you reach, **PRAIA A MARE**, is typical of the resorts along this coast – lively in the summer, deserted the rest of the time, and with a handful of **campsites**, **hotels** and **pizzerias** to choose from. On the beach, a sixteenth-century bastion faces the rocky **Isola di Dino** a little way out, where there are caves and grottoes visitable by renting a boat from the pebbly beach. Behind the town another **grotto** is the home of a widely venerated Madonna. The story goes that the people of nearby Aieta repeatedly attempted to remove this image to their own church, but each time it disappeared and was found back here, where they were eventually forced to let it be. More recently, however, the image disappeared for good, though a replacement was quickly and pragmatically installed.

Beyond Praia, **SAN NICOLA ARCELLA** has a lovely wide **beach**, from which – through a series of passages and a tunnel – you can get to other, emptier beaches. There is a good **pizzeria** here – *L'Incontro*, in Via Aldo Moro (June–Oct, closed Sun) – and a couple of **hotels**, the *Brillantino*, in the old centre (℡0985.3280; ❷), and *Villa Príncipe* (℡0985.3125; ❸), with fine views, near the south entrance to the village at Corso Umberto 8. Further on, the seaside town of **CIRELLA** was a Sybarite colony, devastated by Hannibal, then Romanized; the theatrical ruins of **Cirella Vecchia**, overlooking the SS18, are of a later date, the result of a French bombardment in 1806 (though local lore attributes other, more sinister explanations, most notably a plague of ants). From behind the ruins a road forks inland to the hilltop villages of **Grisolia** and **Maiera**, close together on the map but actually divided by a gully, across which villagers conduct conversations with each other.

Five kilometres down the coast, the chic seaside town of **DIAMANTE** glistens on its small promontory. The walls of the narrow whitewashed lanes have been adorned with striking modern murals, making for an intriguing wander around, and there are a couple of good, moderately priced fish **restaurants** with outside seating down by the seafront at Spiaggia Piccola (beyond the *mole*): most relaxed is the *Taverna del Pescatore* (Oct–May, closed Tues), with views over the small port.

BELVEDERE MARITTIMO, some 10km down the coast, overlooks its unexceptional marina from a spur a little way inland; it's an imposing and elegant town, full of greenery and having little of the air of neglect typical of Calabria's older centres. At the top, an impressive **castle** stands guard, originally a Norman construction but rebuilt under the Aragonese, whose coat-of-arms can be seen above the main gate. The inside has been gutted, however, and it's closed to the public. Down in **Belvedere Marina**, the best place to eat is the *Milleluci* on Via Grossi (mid-Sept to mid-May, closed Tues), which serves pizzas baked in a wood-fired oven alongside such specialities as *gnocchi di patata alla pescatora*.

Paola and San Lúcido

A little way down the coast, the sizeable town of **PAOLA** is an important rail and road junction for Cosenza, and the site of the **Santuario di San**

Francesco di Paola, in a ravine above the town. Not to be confused with Francis of Assisi, this St Francis spent most of his life in the town and, as Calabria's principal saint, is venerated throughout the south. People visit the shrine at all times of year, but particularly during the week leading up to the May 4 **festa** – when a fair occupies the town, with daily festivities culminating in the carrying of his statue into the sea and a grand display of fireworks on the beach at midnight.

There are several **hotels** and **trattorias** around the station by the sea and, a stiff ten-minute climb up, a couple of good **pizzerias** near the central piazza above – the *Eureka*, in Via del Cannone (closed Tues), with outdoor eating in summer, and *Le Arcate*, through the arch at Via Valitutti 5 (mid-Sept to June, closed Mon). If you're looking for a place **to stay**, however, **SAN LÚCIDO**, 6km south, is a more attractive town with a satisfying warren of alleys and squares in its clifftop old quarter; the spruce *Hotel Irma* (T 0982.81.330; ❸) is a handy *pensione* near the station and the seafront, and there are **trattorias** nearby.

Cosenza and around

COSENZA is the region's most interesting town, and makes a useful base for exploring the surrounding area, particularly the **Sila** mountains. Historically it has always played an important role in the commercial and intellectual life of Calabria (Norman Douglas wrote, with characteristic hyperbole, "for acute and original thought this town can hardly be surpassed by any other of its size on earth"), and recently the town has generated a degree of wealth which – while still some way below most of Italy – has in the last twenty years or so literally transformed the landscape. New construction, much of it featureless and ugly, has sprouted everywhere, while its boldly designed university is expanding fast, helping to create a strong regional awareness and self-confidence.

Completely enclosed by mountains – the Sila on the east, the Catena Costiera separating it from the sea to the west – Cosenza is the meeting point of two rivers, the Crati and the Busento. Somewhere beneath the latter, tradition has the burial place of **Alaric the Goth**, the barbarian who gave the western world a jolt when he prised open the gates of Rome in 410 AD. Struck down for his sins by malaria while journeying south, he was interred here along with his booty, and the course of the river deviated to cover the traces, lending Cosenza a place in history and giving rise to countless, fruitless projects to discover the tomb's whereabouts.

The Town

The two rivers form a neat division between old and new Cosenza, with the main artery of the newer town, **Corso Mazzini**, running off north from near their junction. This is where most of the shops and banks are, and – by day – it's the liveliest place to be. Most of the things worth seeing, however, are located in the old part, the **centro storico**, a compact knot of steps and alleys rising up to a sturdy Swabian castle in the southern part of town. Much of the old town has been abandoned in favour of the newer suburbs to the north, but the area has recently pulled itself out of a long period as the haunt of *mafiosi*, delinquents and prostitutes, and attracted many small businesses in the form of boutiques and bars, making it a pleasant focus for walking and drinking until

COSENZA

ACCOMMODATION
Bruno   2
Excelsior   3
Grisaro   1

RESTAURANTS & BARS
All'Acquedotto   B
American Bar   A
L'Arco Vecchio   J
The Beat   F
Calabria Bella   E
Calò   I
Gran Caffè Renzelli   G
James Joyce   H
El Mojito   C
Per Bacco   D

0   200 m

late. By day there's a tranquillity here that the rest of the town lacks, while by
night the main street, **Corso Telesio**, is the place to be, especially in summer
when it is closed to traffic.

From Piazza Valdesi on the far side of the bridge, Corso Telesio curves up into
the old quarter's confusion of narrow streets. The road is named after Cosenza's
most famous son, **Bernardino Telesio**, the sixteenth-century humanist
philosopher and major influence on the other great Calabrian philosopher,
Tommaso Campanella. Halfway up, Cosenza's stately **Duomo** stands in a
square of tall *palazzi*. Consecrated on the occasion of Frederick II's visit to the
city in 1222, its Provençal Gothic style was later modified by Baroque accre-
tions – though sporadic restorations have undone much of the damage to the
facade. The interior – a mixture of Romanesque, Gothic and Baroque styles –
has a Roman sarcophagus carved with a hunting scene, in a good state of
preservation, and, in the north transept, the lovely tomb of Isabella of Aragon,

who died in Cosenza in 1271 while returning with her husband Philip III –
seen kneeling beside her – from an abortive Crusade in Tunisia. But the
Duomo's most venerated item lies in the first chapel on the left: a copy of a
thirteenth-century Byzantine icon, the *Madonna del Pilerio*, which was once
carried around the country during times of plague. The original is in the
Laboratorio di Restauro (usually Mon–Fri 8am–2pm; free), a restoration
workshop behind the cloisters of the church and convent of **San Francesco
d'Assisi** on the street of the same name, reached from Via del Seggio, an alley
leading up from Corso Telesio. Also displayed here is a Byzantine reliquary crucifix made by Greek craftsmen in Palermo and presented by Frederick II at the
consecration of the cathedral. The church itself, a much-restored thirteenth-
century complex badly damaged in World War II, has paintings by Wilhelm
Borremans in the sumptuous St Catherine chapel on the right of the nave.

From San Francesco, climb up to Corso Vittorio Emanuele, following it until
you reach the little track on the right leading to the formidable **Castello**
(summer Mon–Fri 9am–12.30pm & 4–6pm; winter closed; free), another
Frederick II construction reduced to its present condition by a series of earthquakes. The inside is bare but sensitively restored, and hosts occasional exhibitions and concerts in summer, but it makes a good spot at any time for a breath
of clean air and to enjoy the superb view over Cosenza and the surrounding
mountains. You can also reach the castle from Cosenza's most elegant square,
Piazza XV Marzo, at the top of Corso Telesio, where there is a shady public
garden (currently closed for renovation), and the **Accademia Cosentina**
houses the **Museo Civico** (Mon & Thurs 9am–1pm & 3.30–6pm, Tues, Wed
& Fri 9am–1pm; free), which sports a rather scanty collection of prehistoric
and classical bric-a-brac from the surrounding area and a few paintings.

Practicalities

The **bus station** is below Piazza Fera, from where it's a twenty-minute walk
down the length of Corso Mazzini to the hotels and the *centro storico*. Arriving
by train, you will have to take a bus (every 20min) from the **train station** a
little way outside town – tickets from the bar inside the station. There's a **left-
luggage** office here (7am–8pm) and two **car rental** agencies charge identical
prices – useful for excursions into the Sila – Hertz (☎0984.31.081) and
Maggiore (☎0984.482.144); note, however, that parking spaces in Cosenza
itself are a valuable commodity.

The main **tourist office** is at Corso Mazzini 92 (Mon–Fri 7.30am–1.30pm,
plus Mon & Wed 2–5pm; ☎0984.27.271), and there is an office specifically for
the *centro storico* behind the Duomo in Via Toscano (Mon–Thurs 9am–1pm &
4–6pm, Fri 9am–1pm; ☎0984.813.336). The town's only **Internet** point is the
huge *Internet Café Cosenza*, some way out of the centre, at Via XXIV Maggio
23 (Mon–Sat 7am–1am, Sun 3pm–1am). Primarily used by business travellers,
Cosenza's **hotels** are mainly brash and expensive, but there are some more
modest choices close to each other in the centre, namely the spacious and
comfortable *Excelsior* in Piazza Matteotti (☎0984.74.383; ❸), the rather
gloomy pension *Bruno* at Corso Mazzini 27 (☎0984.73.889; ❷), and the more
business-like *Grisaro*, around the corner on Viale Trieste (☎0984.27.838; ❸),
which has parking for guests.

There is more choice when it comes to **restaurants**. In summer the most
congenial place to be is *All'Acquedotto*, a pizzeria/*birreria* below the old aqueduct, at the end of the winding Via Arnone and Viale della Repubblica, with

great views over the valley (no closing day). In the old town, *Per Bacco* is a stylish wood-beamed *enoteca*-restaurant where a meal of Calabrian specialities will set you back around €25 a head without wine. *L'Arco Vecchio*, above Piazza XV Marzo on Via Archi di Ciaccio (closed Sun), and *Calabria Bella*, in Piazza Duomo, which has outside seating in summer, are more formal choices, both serving traditional local dishes. But it's the **cafés** and **bars** of Cosenza's old quarter that are most fun. There's a lively Cuban bar at the foot of Corso Telesio, *El Mojito* (closed Mon), serving seventy different varieties of rum, as well as light meals. Further up the Corso, meanwhile, are two raucous *birrerie* that stay open late: *The Beat*, opposite the Duomo, and one of the town's two local Irish pubs, the *James Joyce*, on Via Cornelio (open evenings only, closed Mon), which charges up to €5 for entry when there's live music in the basement (usually at weekends). Just up from here, at Via Liceo 6, *Calò* is another congenial – and quieter – place for a late-night drink or meal, serving a range of cocktails, beers, and *frullati*, and highly reminiscent of an outdoor café in Rome's Trastevere. For coffees and *cornetti* during your daytime strolling, stop off at the old-fashioned *Gran Caffè Renzelli*, up past the Duomo. The best **ice creams** in town are from *Zorro*, at the bottom of Corso Telesio.

Around Cosenza

People spending any time in Cosenza will be mostly interested in excursions into the **Sila** (see below), but some of the villages dotted around the surrounding hills, where most of the Cosentine population have their roots and family homes, shouldn't be ignored. In summer, the streets are thronged until late, and at night the view over the bowl of the valley is magnificent, with glittering threads and clusters of light. It is also in the summer that the village **festas** normally take place, with each *comune* vying to outdo the others in terms of spectacle and expense.

The villages of the **Presila**, on the eastern slope of the valley, have a reputation for late-night revelry and some good **trattorias** – try *U'Fuccularu*, in **Pedace** (closed Mon), or *Dal Barone* in **Pianette di Rovito** (closed Wed) – and **birrerias**, such as *La Grotta* in **Spezzano della Sila**, which also serves snacks. On the other side of the valley the hilltop village of **RENDE** holds the prize for the tidiest village in the region: it has good views and an absorbing little **museum** (daily 9am–6pm; free) in the Palazzo Zagarese, on Via de Bártolo, devoted to local folk art, costumes, cuisine, music, the Albanian community and emigration. Rende also boasts a decent choice of places to eat and drink, including the good-value **pizzeria** *L'Arco*, at Via Costa 4 (closed lunchtime & Tues), with a panoramic terrace. Northeast of Cosenza, above the village of **LUZZI**, stands the **Abbazia di Sambucina**. A Cistercian abbey founded in the twelfth century and long the centre of this order of monks throughout the south, it has a beautiful, lightly pointed portal (rebuilt in the fifteenth century) and the original presbytery.

Buses for the villages depart from the **bus station** in Cosenza, below Piazza Fera, but to get the most out of these places you should ideally have your own transport, as services normally stop at nightfall. An interesting (but slow) way to get to the Presila during the day (and beyond, into the Sila) is by **train**, on the Cálabro-Lucane (FCL) line: this leaves twice a day from the small station east of Piazza Matteotti for Camigliatello (see p.964), offering marvellous glimpses over the Cosenza valley as it twists and grinds up the mountain through woods and over rivers.

The Sila

Covering the widest part of the Calabrian peninsula, the **Sila** massif is more of an extensive plateau than a mountain range, though the peaks on its western flank reach heights of nearly 2000m. It's divided into three main groups, the Sila Greca, Sila Grande and Sila Piccola, the last two of which are little more than an administrative division, while the former – although the least entrancing scenically – is distinguished by the Albanian villages from which it takes its name.

At one time the Sila was one huge forest and was exploited from earliest times to provide fuel and material for the construction of fleets, fortresses and even for church-building in Rome, resulting in a deforestation that helped bring about the malarial conditions that for centuries laid much of Calabria low. The cutting of trees is now strictly controlled, and since the regional government recognized the potential of the area and imposed restrictions on building and hunting, there is plenty here for the outdoors enthusiast, in summer as a relief from the heat of the towns or coasts and in winter for downhill or cross-country skiing. The other seasons have their own charms: spring, when the woods are a riot of wild flowers, and autumn, for the full gamut of decaying colour and – a local speciality – wild mushrooms.

The Sila Greca

Deforestation has had the most devastating effect on the **Sila Greca**, the northernmost part of the massif, leaving mainly cultivated rolling highlands in place of the dense woods. But the area is easily accessible from the Ionian coast or the autostrada inland, and if you have a car it's worth the detour to investigate some of the **Albanian villages** scattered around these hills, originally settled in the fifteenth century by colonies of Albanians in flight from Muslim invasions. **SAN DEMETRIO CORONE** is the most interesting, containing an Italo-Albanian *Collegio* charged with the task of guarding what remains of the Albanian heritage. Annexed to this is the church of **Sant'Adriano**, a structure that still shows elements of its Byzantine and Norman origins. Really, though, it's the annual festivals that show these villages at their best. Along with the opportunity to see their elaborate costumes and hear some gutsy singing, going to one may be the only chance of hearing the authentic language – a fifteenth-century version of modern Albanian – which has only recently been replaced by *calabrese* dialect as the everyday language in these parts. Festivals take place in the villages of **Santa Sofia** (July 15 & 16), **San Cosmo** (September 26 & 27), **Vaccarizzo** (March 31–April 2), and **San Giorgio** (April 2).

The Sila Grande

Densely forested, and the highest, most extensive part of the Sila range, the **Sila Grande** has Calabria's main **ski slopes** as well as the region's three principal **lakes** – all artificial (for hydroelectric purposes) and much loved by fishing enthusiasts, who come out in force at weekends. The best base for day-trips is Cosenza, but if you want to spend any time up here it would be much better either to camp or lodge in a hotel; campsites enjoy good lakeside locations, but the hotels are mainly in the towns and villages, and many close out of season (March–July, Oct & Nov).

The towns vary greatly. **SAN GIOVANNI IN FIORE**, in the heart of the Sila, is the area's biggest, but also the dreariest. For winter-sports enthusiasts and summer trekkers alike, **CAMIGLIATELLO** is the best-known of the resorts, a functional place that's well connected by bus with Cosenza, though it lacks any intrinsic charm. Centred on Via Roma, the town has three ski slopes of its own and another at Moccone (3km to the west) and a confusion of hotels, restaurants and souvenir shops; if you fancy **skiing**, the slopes have facilities for renting equipment (about €15 per day) and offer tuition (group lessons are about €10 per person per hour). The Sila terrain also makes ideal **riding** country, though most stables are open in summer only; one exception that's open all year is Maneggio Sila (☏0360.283.252), 3km from Camigliatello on the Cecita road. The numerous **hotels** in town can be expensive; for moderate rates in plain rooms try the *Miramonti* in Via Forgitelle (☏0984.579.067; ❷) or the *Leonetti* at Via Roma 42 (☏0984.578.075; ❷), or opt for more comfort at only slightly higher prices at the *Meranda* (☏0984.578.022; ❸) just off Via Roma. For a **snack** in Camigliatello, *Lo Spuntino* on Via Repaci, off the other side of Via Roma, has excellent panini and other fast food, while Moccone has a good-value **trattoria**, the aptly named *Si Mangia Bene Si Paga Poco* (closed Mon) which has a well-deserved reputation and a €13 set menu. At the time of writing, the Pro Loco **tourist office** at the top of Via Roma had closed, though you may still be able to find brochures and maps on **walking routes** in the area in some of the bars scattered around the Sila. You need to understand Italian to read the route descriptions, and the map is not perfect, but it can be helpful as a broad guide to the relative lengths of the paths, and for switching from one to another.

From Camigliatello, you could hike for 15km – or take the bus – to **Lago Cecita**, the best starting-place for expeditions to **La Fossiata**, a conservation area that resembles a national park on the American model, with tidy wooden fences along the roads and numerous picnic spots. It is always possible to find your own space, but it's a good idea, too, to follow the planned routes set out by the *Corpo Forestale* – paths can run out on you when you least expect it. There's a **hotel** here, the *Cecita* (☏0983.579.074; ❸), on the lakeside at Località San Giovanni Paliático. Owing to concerns about littering and the risk of fires, camping in the area is forbidden except in the **campsite** near the hotel – also called *Cecita* (☏0983.24.039). Elsewhere, there are a couple of sites 15km south on the banks of Lago Arvo (see below). If you choose to descend the steep slopes from La Fossiata to remote **LONGOBUCCO**, atmospherically enclosed at the bottom of a narrow valley, there's the useful *Hotel Stella* (☏0983.72.082; ❷), offering simple accommodation and a restaurant – phone ahead.

Camigliatello is also a useful starting-point for a ramble that takes in the area's highest peaks, following the *strada delle vette* ("road of the peaks") for 13km through pine and beech woods before forking off and up to the three **peaks** of Monte Scuro, Monte Curcio and, highest of all, Monte Botte Donato (1928m). The trail, which is often snowbound between December and May, continues on down to **Lago Arvo** and the resort of Lorica, from which it is a shorter distance than following the *strada delle vette* to reach Botte Donato. Or you can save the sweat and take the chair lift from the località Cavaliere, just outside town. **LORICA**, like Camigliatello, is dedicated to tourism in the height of the winter and summer seasons, but its lakeside location makes it a more relaxed spot, with lots of places for picnicking under the pines and observing the antics of the black squirrels that inhabit them. The town is connected with Cosenza by **bus**, arriving in the morning and returning in the afternoon, and there is a **campsite** which also rents out bungalows, *Lago Arvo*, occupying a picturesque lakeside location just outside the town (☏0984.537.060). There's a handful of hotels, most of which require half-board in high season – although the comfortable but pricey *Park 108* (☎0983.537.077; ❹) at Via Nazionale 86 doesn't.

The Sila Piccola

Bounded by Lago Ampollino in the north, Catanzaro and the Ionian coast in the south, the **Sila Piccola** is the region's most densely forested section, centring on the **Foresta di Gariglione**, thick with fir, beech and the gigantic turkey oak from which it derives its name. It's not so well adapted for walking as La Fossiata though, and apart from the odd resort, it's a sparsely populated area and most of its villages are in any case unattractive.

More interesting than most is **BELCASTRO**, on the southern fringes of the range. Watched over by a Norman castle, it is claimed to be the birthplace of St Thomas Aquinas, whose family once held the town in fief. Further west, on the SS109, the mountain village of **TAVERNA** has long historical associations but is best-known today as the home of Calabria's foremost seventeenth-century painter, **Mattia Preti**, whose Spanish-looking works can be seen in four of the local churches, notably **San Domenico**. From the village it's 25km down a winding road to the regional capital of Catanzaro.

The southern Tyrrhenian coast

The province of Catanzaro begins at the Savuto River, and from here down to Reggio the SS18, autostrada and main rail line all run parallel along the coast, apart from the stretch of the Tropea promontory. Immediately after the river, a few kilometres inland from the resort of Lido di Falerna, the hill-village of **NOCERA TIRINESE** (buses run from the station on the coast) is famed for the flagellants who – literally – paint the streets red every Easter during a religious festival that grips the whole village with fervour. Wailing processions sway through the streets, and teams of two sprint between churches, one holding a cross, the other beating himself with a spiked brush; his freely flowing blood is then splashed over the doors of the houses to protect those within – not to be washed off until it happens naturally with the rain. One of the few examples of this kind of ritual bloodletting still to be found in the south, and not at all a mere tourist event, it's worth catching if you're around here at the right time.

Thirteen kilometres further down the coast, between Capo Súvero (marked by its lighthouse) and Lido di Gizzeria, is a fine **swimming spot**, a sandy spit with a freshwater lake close by, surrounded by palms and bamboo. The plain that stretches east from here, the **Piana di Sant'Eufemia**, is the narrowest part of the Calabrian peninsula, much of it reclaimed only in the last hundred years from malarial swamp: the mosquitoes remain but they no longer carry the disease. **LAMEZIA** has Calabria's main **airport** (most international flights are summer only), while **SANT'EUFEMIA-LAMEZIA** is the **rail and road junction** for Catanzaro and the Ionian coast. Heading south on the highway you begin a slow ascent on the long viaduct that is one of the engineering feats of the Autostrada del Sole, the views growing more inspiring as it rises above the coast to the high tableland of the Tropea promontory.

Pizzo

Following the railway or the SS18, you might want to spend some time in the picturesque little town of **PIZZO**, neatly placed for the **beaches** around

Tropea and site of a small **castle** (daily: summer 9am–1pm & 5–10pm; winter 9am–1pm & 3–7pm; free) overlooking the sea just off the main Piazza della Repubblica. Built in 1486 by Ferdinand I of Aragon, it holds the room in which the French general **Murat** was imprisoned, with some of his personal effects and copies of the last letters he wrote, and the terrace where he was shot in October 1815. Murat, Napoleon's brother-in-law and one of his ablest generals, met his ignominious end here after attempting to rouse the people against the Bourbons to reclaim the throne of Naples given to him by Napoleon; the people of Pizzo ignored his haughty entreaties, and he was arrested and court-martialled.

A couple of kilometres north of the centre, you might drop in on the **Chiesetta di Piedigrotta** (daily 9am–1pm & 3–7.30pm), a curious rock-hewn church by a sandy beach, signposted off the coastal SS22. Created in the seventeenth century by Neapolitan sailors rescued from a shipwreck, the church was later enlarged and its interior festooned with eccentric statuary depicting episodes from the Bible. Most of this was the work of a local father-and-son team, and it was augmented by another scion of the family in 1969, who restored the works and contributed some of his own, including a quirky scene showing Fidel Castro kneeling before Pope John XXIII and President Kennedy. You can see some of the inside through the windows if the church is closed.

Pizzo has a Pro Loco **tourist information** office which doubles as an insurance agency (or visa versa), located under the arches at the bottom of Piazza della Repubblica (Mon–Sat: summer 9am–1pm & 5–9pm; winter 9am–1pm; T0963.531.310). There's a comfortable **place to stay** in Pizzo, right on the main square, the *Hotel Murat*, with good views over the coast from some rooms (T0963.534.201; ❺); alternatively, there's the rather characterless *Sonia*, right by the Chiesetta di Piedigrotta on Via Prangi (T0963.531.315; ❷), which requires at least half-board in August. If you have transport, you might consider a first-rate agriturismo further north on the main road out of town (200m before the Agip station), *A Casa Janca* (T0963.264364; ❻), where full-board weighs in at an extra €80 per person per night. Furnished in traditional rustic style, the place is locally renowned for its **restaurant**, where non-guests can also dine. Other places to eat in the centre of town include a good trattoria under the arcade in Piazza della Repubblica, *Il Porticato* (closed Wed), or walk down to the port area for a range of seafood restaurants, one of them, *La Nave* (closed Wed), in the form of a ship. Between April and July sample the **tuna** or **swordfish**, for which Pizzo is a fishing centre. Make sure you also sample the famous local **ice cream**, *tartufo di Pizzo*, though you can also find it in bars and restaurants up and down the coast.

Vibo and the Tropea promontory

Pizzo is a starting-point for the coastal rail line that rings the **Tropea promontory**; trains run from a separate **station**, Pizzo Calabro, near the port (if you're coming from the north, you need to change at Lamezia). The first stop, **VIBO MARINA**, is the major port and industrial centre of this stretch of coast, with regular departures to the Aeolian Islands (see p.1018) between June and September. Some 10km above the port and served by the mainline station of Pizzo-Vibo Valentia, the larger town of **VIBO VALENTIA** has a history that goes back to Greek times, when it was known as **Hipponion** (fragments of whose walls are still standing 2km north of town). Because of its strategic importance, Vibo has always held a prominent position in Calabria's history: under Murat it was a provincial capital with a flourishing cultural life, inhabited by grandees whose memory lives on in the street names and in the many surviving palaces – mostly now in a state of decay. Vibo's restoration as a provincial capital may change the town's backwater feel, but in the meantime it's a place to stop at chiefly to view the impressive **Museo Archeologico**, housed in the Norman castle superbly sited at the top of the town (daily 9am–7.30pm; €2; take bus #A from Via Vittorio Emanuele). The display includes Greek and Roman vases, figurines, *pinakes* (terracotta plaques) and military hardware from the sixth century BC on. The museum is brilliantly designed, incorporating the towers and stairs from the Norman construction, and you should leave time for a walk afterwards round the lofty walls for the distant views out to sea and inland over the rolling countryside. Back in the town centre, there's an **information office** (Mon–Fri 7.30am–1.30pm, plus Mon & Wed 2–5pm; ☎0963.42.008) on Via Forgiari, off the main Corso Vittorio Emanuele. Central **hotels** in town include the stylish *Risorgimento* on Via Colletta (☎0963.41.125; ❸) and the plainer *Miramonti* on Via Protetti (☎0963.41.053; ❷), and there's a good **trattoria** just up the hill from the *Risorgimento* at Via Francica 2, *Le Arcate* (closed Sun lunch).

West of Vibo the golden sands of the Tropea promontory stretch invitingly into the Tyrrhenian Sea – one of the least spoilt and most scenic parts of Calabria. Take your choice from among the numerous **beaches** – mostly clean and sandy, though relatively crowded at the height of the season – and **campsites**, for example *Squalo 33* (☎0963.391.945) at picturesque **BRIÁTICO**; all sites around here are open summer only.

Tropea and around

Twelve kilometres southwest along the coast from Briático, **TROPEA** can claim to be the prettiest town on the whole of the southern Tyrrhenian coast, and (after Maratea) the most fashionable, with a seaside charm missing from many of the other Calabrian resorts, and not yet entirely eroded by the annual influx of tourists. The buildings have character without being twee – see particularly the lovely Norman **Cathedral** at the bottom of Via Roma, whose interior harbours a couple of unexploded American bombs from the last war (one accompanied by a grateful prayer to the Madonna), a Renaissance ciborium and a statue of the Madonna and Child from the same period. The central apse also has a much-venerated fourteenth-century icon of the Virgin Maria of Romania. The views from the upper town over the sea and the church of **Santa Maria dell'Isola** on its rock (daily 9.30am–12.30pm, 3–8.30pm) are superb, and on a clear day you will see the cone of Strómboli and sometimes other Aeolian Islands looming on the horizon. If the sun's not out, the **museum** (summer only daily 9am–1pm & 4pm–midnight; €1.30) is worth a look, devoted to traditional Calabrian crafts and trades (wood turning, olive oil making and so forth) and featuring dozens of meticulously hand-made mechanical models of Calabrian peasants going about their daily business.

There are good beaches all around Tropea and plenty of **accommodation** – though in August booking ahead is vital. The bland but comfortable *Virgilio* in Viale Tondo (☎0963.61.978; ❸), requires half- or full-board in high season, as do most of the other hotels – one that doesn't is the *Miramare* (☎0963.61.570; ❹) on Via Libertà, the road heading south out of town, a fairly standard hotel with small rooms. If you're here for a week or more, renting an **apartment** may be worthwhile; the rooms at *Gurnella* (☎0963.61427, ⓦwww.tropea.biz/appartamenti_gurnella.htm), just outside the centre, are clean and modern and have lovely views over the town and out to sea (€210–730 for a week in a five-bed apartment, depending on the season).

As for **eating**, Tropea has more trattorias per square metre than any other town in Calabria, often with budget-priced tourist menus. There's a clutch around central Piazza Ércole, some with outside seating. *El Sol* at Largo Mercato 15 has a large terrace overlooking the valley, as well as a varied menu, and fish fans will appreciate the *Osteria del Pescatore*, a vaulted cellar around the corner from the cathedral in Via del Monte (closed in winter). For other evening entertainment, *Donegan's*, the **pub** attached to the *Miramare* hotel, serves Guinness on tap as well as panini and other snacks, and hosts occasional live music. The Pro Loco **tourist office** is in Piazza Ércole (summer daily 9am–1pm & 4.30–9/10pm; winter daily 9am–1pm & 4–8pm; ℡0963.61.475). There's now an official tourist office website for Tropea, Ⓦwww.casadei.it, though the privately-run Ⓦwww.tropea.biz is much more comprehensive, with details of accommodation and lots of background information about the local area.

Further around the promontory, **CAPO VATICANO** holds some of the area's most popular beaches, including **Grotticelle** and **Tonicello**, both spacious enough to allow you to get away from the bustle. Grotticelle has a **campsite** immediately above it, *Quattro Scoglie*, where you can rent self-contained **apartments** for about €22 a head in low season, rising to €35 (℡0963.663.126; May–Oct). The nearest **hotel** to this beach, the *Grotticelle* (℡0963.663.157; ❸), lies a few minutes' walk further up the road, but if you have transport you'd do better trying the excellent agriturismo 2km away at the edge of the hamlet of Brivadi, *Donna Orsola*, where, if you wish, you can even help with the cooking (℡0963/665111, Ⓦwww.donnaorsola.com; ❹).To the south of Capo Vaticano, the road teeters high above the sea before reaching **NICÓTERA**, 11km down, built in its present position by Robert Guiscard. The Castello Ruffo here contains a small **archeological museum** of finds from the area and a collection of folkloric items (both free), but keeps very irregular hours: you're most likely to find someone to let you in during the mornings. There's also a **Cathedral**, with work by Antonello Gagini, and far-reaching views south over the **Piana**, Calabria's second plain of any size, mostly dedicated to olive cultivation. Directly below the town, Nicótera's marina has wide beaches with a couple of summer-only **campsites** at their southern end.

South to Reggio

The Mesima river marks the border of the province of Reggio di Calabria. The towns around here are mostly new and unattractive, partly owing to the fact that the area is one of the most seismically active in Italy – the epicentre of the notorious 1783 earthquake was at nearby Oppido. The small Tropea rail line connects with the main line at Rosarno, 18km beyond which is **PALMI**. Situated a little way above the town (take Via San Giorgio, close to the exit onto the SS18) is the excellent museum complex in **La Casa della Cultura Leonida Repaci** (Mon & Thurs 8am–2pm & 3–6pm, Tues, Wed & Fri 8am–2pm; €1.55), named after a local writer and artist. It incorporates an archeological section, holding pieces of pottery and various excavations from the sea bed; paintings including work by Tintoretto and Guercino; a gallery of modern art and sculpture, mainly by southern Italian artists such as Guttuso but also including works by Modigliani, De Chirico and Carlo Levi; a section devoted to local composer Francesco Cilea; and Calabria's best collection of folklore items.

From Palmi the tall TV mast on Sicily's northern tip is already visible, but the best view of Sicily and the Calabrian coast is some 5km down the road, at

15

Monte Sant'Elia, the first elevation of the Aspromonte massif (see p.973). From this balcony, perched on cliffs that plunge vertically down to the sea, you can see the two volcanoes of Etna and Stromboli on a clear day; there is a **campsite** behind and a tourist village. The spot is believed to have been named after St Elia Speleotes, who lived in these parts (in a cave, which can be visited on the road leading into Aspromonte from Melicucca) and whose body, when he died aged 94, proved unburnable by the Saracens. Earlier, when his body was washed, the water was used for curing another holy man's toothache.

From here south, the proximity of Sicily becomes the dominant feature looking out to sea, and the stretch of the autostrada that dives down to Villa San Giovanni can claim to be one of the most panoramic in Italy, burrowing high up through mountains with the Straits of Messina glittering below. Travelling by train or following the old coastal road, you skirt the so-called Costa Viola, passing through **Bagnara**, famous for its swordfish, and **SCILLA**, ancient Scylla, with a fine sandy **beach** and lots of action in the summer. This was the legendary location of a six-headed cave monster, one of two hazards to mariners mentioned in the **Odyssey**, the other being the whirlpool Charybdis, corresponding to the modern Cariddi located 6km away on the other side of the Strait. Crowning a hefty rock, a **castle** separates the main beach from the fishing village to the north. The only **place to stay** in town is the *Pensione Le Sirene* (booking advisable in summer, ℡0965.754.121; ❷): try to get one of the four front rooms facing the sea – the others are just mediocre. There are several good fish **restaurants** along the seafront, including *U Bais* (closed Mon lunch); on the piazza in the upper town, *Vertigine* has a terrace with tables for snacks or full meals overlooking the sea (June–Sept, closed Mon).

From Scilla it's just 9km to **VILLA SAN GIOVANNI** (hourly buses), worth stopping at only as a point of embarkation for Sicily. The state-run FS **ferries** leave from directly behind the station about every thirty minutes and arrive at the train station in Messina (see p.1024) in about forty minutes; if you're travelling by **car** it's more convenient to catch one of the private Caronte ferries (under the train tracks to the right of the station), which leave approximately every fifteen minutes and pull in closer to the entrance to the autostrada. Both companies charge around €1 for foot passengers and €18 for cars. If you're heading for Reggio, take a train or one of the hourly Salzone **buses** from outside the station.

Reggio di Calabria and around

As you approach **REGGIO DI CALABRIA**, the provincial capital, you travel through some of the most extreme landscapes in the South. Dilapidated villages lie stranded among mountains, which are themselves torn apart by wide *fiumare*, or riverbeds – empty or reduced to a trickle for nine-tenths of the year, but swelling with the melting of the winter snows to destructive torrents. Reggio itself was one of the first ancient Greek settlements on the Italian mainland; today, it's Calabria's biggest town by some distance, with a population of over 180,000 – but also one that's been synonymous for years with urban decline. Happily, there are now signs that Reggio may be turning the corner. Efforts to regenerate the city are evident wherever you look, not least in the superb seafront and its gleaming, newly-restored promenade that faces Messina across the Straits – finally living up to its billing by Gabriele

REGGIO DI CALABRIA

The Port

A & Autostrada

VIALE AMENDOLA

1 Museo Nazionale

PIAZZA NAVA

PIAZZA INDIPENDENZA

VIA TORRIONE

Train Station (Reggio Lido)

VIA D'ANNUNZIO

B

CORSO GARIBALDI

CORSO VITTORIO EMANUELE

LUNGAMARE MATTEOTTI

VIA II SETTEMBRE

VIA TRIPPI

VIA TORRONE

VIA POSSIDONEA

VIA GIULIA

@

VIA GIUDECCA

Straits

of

Messina

C

VIA OSANNA

i

VIA CATTÓLICA DEL GRECI

VIA ASCHENEZ

PIAZZA ITALIA

VIA FOTI

VIA CAMPANELLA

VIA FURNARI

VIA POSSIDUNEA

CORSO VITTORIO EMANUELE

2 Castello

CORSO GARIBALDI

VIA VITRIOLI

Duomo

PIAZZA DUOMO

VIA CROCEFISSO

VIA XXI AGOSTO

VIA SPANO

ACCOMMODATION
Diana	2
Lido	1
Mundial	3

RESTAURANTS & BARS
Bonaccorso	D
London Bistro	C
Pub	B
Ritrovo Morabito	A

VILLA COMUNALE

VIA SAN FRANCESCO DI PAOLA

VIA BIXIO

D

VIA BATTISTI

Train Station (Reggio Centrale)

0   100 m

PIAZZA GARIBALDI

i

3

Airport & SS 106

d'Annunzio as "the most beautiful kilometre in Italy". Meanwhile, the *passeggiata* down Reggio's main street, Corso Garibaldi, stretching for 2km across the centre of town, is one of the most animated in Calabria.

Nevertheless, Reggio's grim suburbs, with their half-finished housing and potholed streets, are testament to its enduring and deep-seated social problems, specifically the stranglehold that the Calabrian Mafia, or **'ndrangheta**, continues to have on the town. Locally this phenomenon is referred to as the *piovra*, or octopus, whose tentacles penetrate all aspects of the city's life (*tangente*, or protection money, is tacitly understood to be paid by all shopkeepers and business people in most parts of Reggio), although the bloody *faide* (feuds) between rival families over control of the drugs trade which have periodically convulsed the city seem to be on the decline.

Most visitors to Reggio, however, will see little of this darker side of the town. There are few, in any case, who choose to spend much time here, since Reggio isn't exactly bulging with unmissable attractions, largely owing to the violence of the earthquakes that have repeatedly devastated the area, the most recent – and most destructive – of which flattened the city in 1908. It does possess, however, the **Museo Nazionale** at the Lido end of Corso Garibaldi (daily except first and third Mon of the month 9am–8pm, May–Sept also open until 11pm on Sat; €5), which holds the most important collection of archeological finds in Calabria. Most of the items inside date from the Hellenic period, with examples from all the major Greek sites in Calabria, including the famous *pinakes* or carved tablets from the sanctuary of Persephone at Locri. The most renowned exhibits in the museum are the **Bronzi di Riace**: two bronze statues dragged out of the Ionian Sea in 1972 near the village of Riace. They are shapely examples of the highest period of Greek art (fifth century BC), attributed to Phidias or followers of his school, and especially prized because there are so few finds from this period in such a good state of repair. Around them are detailed explanations of the recovery and cleaning-up of the statues that preceded their tour around the country, when they caused a minor sensation. Now they seem almost forgotten in the well-lit basement they share with another prize exhibit – a philosopher's head from the fourth century BC. Upstairs, you can see examples of Byzantine and Renaissance art, including work by Antonello da Messina.

A stroll along the **lungomare** seaside esplanade is the other chief pleasure of a visit to Reggio, affording wonderful views of the Sicilian coastline and Mount Etna. However, as you gaze over the Straits of Messina, you probably won't catch sight of the semi-mythical phenomenon known as the **Fata Morgana**, which appears as a shimmering, magical city of turrets and towers – quite unlike the city of Messina. The legend is said to be connected with Arthurian myths brought south by the Normans, but some locals swear they have witnessed it, suggesting it may be a meteorological phenomenon – best conditions are apparently an absolute stillness of the air and water.

The city's sights are rounded off by the **Duomo**, rebuilt after the earthquake of 1908 and resembling an ice cream confection, while remains of the **Castello Aragonese** on Piazza Castello make a pleasant backdrop for summer festivities.

Practicalities

If you're **arriving** by train, get off at **Reggio Lido** for the port or museum. Buses end up at the **Reggio Centrale** station, 1km or so down the long Corso Garibaldi. You may want to make use of **city buses** for getting from one end of town to the other; tickets cost €0.52 from kiosks and *tabacchi*. There's a small **tourist office** inside the Centrale station (Mon–Sat 3–8pm; ☎0965.27.120), and a larger one at Corso Garibaldi 329 (Mon–Sat 7.45am–1.45pm & 2–8pm; ℡0965.892.012). *Sweet@Web* at Via Giudecca 35 has fast **Internet** access (open evenings only).

The Centrale station area is also where you'll find Reggio's best-value **hotel**, the basic, but clean and modern, *Mundial* at Via Gaeta 9 (℡0965.332.255; ❸). At the other end of the Corso, near the Lido station, the *Lido* at Via Tre Settembre has cheerful rooms (℡0965.25.001; ❹), while the large and shabby *Diana* (℡0965.891.522; ❸) at Via Vitrioli 12, mid-way along the Corso, should be a last resort. There are a handful of **eating** places around Corso Garibaldi, ranging from the pricey but rated *Bonaccorso* near the main train station at Via Bixio 5 (closed Sun), which offers a €20 set-price menu, to the *London Bistro* with its excellent fish, some way further up the Corso at Via Osanna 9. There's a pub near the museum on the corner of Via d'Annunzio and Corso Vittorio Emanuele serving crepes, panini and other snacks, or you could venture out to the far more fashionable *Ritrovo Morabito*, a bar with tables selling ice cream and pastries on Via Vallone Petrara (from Piazza Nava, follow Viale Améndola for nine blocks, turning right onto Via Cardinale Portanova and right again onto Via Vallone Petrara). More centrally, the **bars** around Piazza Duomo have good – though pricey – snacks, while the best **gelateria** in town is *Césare*, a kiosk on Piazza Indipendenza. Off Viale Améndola, Piazza del Pópolo has a daily morning fruit and veg **market** and occasional evening concerts in summer.

From Reggio's port you can reach Messina in fifteen minutes by *nave veloce*, or **fast ferry** (Mon–Sat 12 daily, Sun 6 daily; €2.58); by car you have to go from Villa San Giovanni (see p.970). There's also a regular **hydrofoil** service (summer 5 daily; winter 1 daily; €21.69) to the Aeolian Islands (see p.1018).

Aspromonte

Most visitors to Reggio province leave without having ventured into the great massif of **Aspromonte**, the last spur of the Apennines on the tip of Italy's boot, and displaying an even more pronounced dialogue between mountain scenery and seascape than elsewhere in Calabria. You can be on a beach and a ski slope within the same hour, passing from the brilliant, almost tropical vegetation of the coast to dense forests of beech and pine that rise to nearly 2000m. The physical aspect of the range varies enormously, depending on which side you enter from: coming up from the Tyrrhenian coast you pass through endless olive groves that are the thickest and tallest in the region, whereas on the Ionian side the mountains have the empty, arid look of desert peaks.

Santo Stefano

Access to the Aspromonte range is easiest from the Tyrrhenian side, with several buses a day leaving Reggio's Piazza Garibaldi for Gambarie and winding their way up the highly scenic SS184 from Gállico, through profusely terraced groves of vine and citrus to the village of **SANTO STEFANO**, famous as the birthplace and final resting-place of the last of the great brigands who roamed these parts, **Giuseppe Musolino** (1875–1956). Occupying a sort of Robin Hood role in the popular imagination, Musolino was a legend in his own lifetime, the last thirty years of which he spent in jail and, finally, a lunatic asylum – the penalty for having led the *Carabinieri* on a long and humiliating dance up and down the slopes of Aspromonte during his profitable career.

While he was alive, he was warmly regarded by all who might otherwise have paled at the mention of brigandage, and even now he is seen as a local hero – described even by a village policeman as "*una persona onestissima*", the most honest of people. Musolino's victims were rich, or corrupt, or informers, and he was never known to refuse a plea for help from those in need. It is hard to know how much is myth, but the romantic aura that surrounds him is partly due to the fact that brigandage, with which the region was rife during the Bourbon period and for which the tormented mountainscape of Aspromonte provided a natural refuge, was also a political gesture of rebellion and little to do with the organized crime that has succeeded it. Just above the village, in the cemetery, you can see Musolino's grave, now renovated but until recently daubed with the signatures of people come to pay their respects.

Gambarie

GAMBARIE, a little further up amid thick woods, is a fully fledged holiday town, used as a cooling-off place for overheated *reggini* (from Reggio) in the summer and as a skiing resort in the winter – a sporadically working chair lift goes up to the **ski slope** at the top of **Monte Scirocco** (1660m). There's a handful of **restaurants** on the main square and a small choice of **hotels**, pick of which is the bright and clean *Miramonti* with its wood-panelled rooms (☎0965.743.190; ❷), alongside the ski lift. Ask here or at any of Gambarie's larger hotels about rental facilities for skiing equipment. When the mountain is not snowbound, Gambarie is also a good base for walks in the area: for Aspromonte's highest peak, **Montalto** (1955m), start down along the SS183 towards Melito, turning off left after 3 or 4km onto a broken road, after which it's another 16km to the top, marked by a bronze statue of Christ gazing steadily out over the Straits of Messina – a memorable view. If you still have any energy there is another track that descends steeply for another 10km to the **Santuario della Madonna di Polsi**, inhabited only by the monks of the monastery there. A large **fair** takes place here every year on the first two days of September – an unashamedly pagan event that involves the slaughter and sale of large numbers of goats. The monastery can put you up, or else camp in the area.

Delianuova and the coastal route

Continuing on down along the SS183 will bring you eventually to the Ionian coast at Melito di Porto Salvo, a tortuous but highly scenic route with views over towards Sicily. Going up the same road from Gambarie (in the opposite direction) leads 26km along a plain and through more forest to **DELIAN-UOVA**, another resort, though not as busy as Gambarie, with a trattoria, a *birreria* and one **hotel**, the *Aspromonte 2001* (☎0966.963.012; ❷). A path from here leads up to Montalto (about a five-hour hike). Halfway between Gambarie and Delianuova, a turn-off on the right will take you to the **Cippo Garibaldi**, a modern monument in the woods commemorating the spot where the hero, having emerged from his retirement in the summer of 1862 with the intention of marching on Rome, was ignominiously captured by the troops of King Vittorio Emanuele II, in whose name he had raised the banner.

The **coastal route** along Italy's toe-tip also offers some interesting excursions into the mountainous inland Aspromonte, road and rail line running south out of Reggio through the series of small nondescript towns adorned by a profusion of cactus, agave, banana trees and date palms, and surrounded by the extensive plantations of citrus that are a feature of the Reggio area. Look out in particular for the bergamot, a fruit resembling a yellow orange whose essence is used as a base for expensive perfumes – one of the principal exports of this area and until recently, because of the precise conditions required for its cultivation, not found anywhere else in the world.

Campsites abound along this coast, attached to sandy beaches in varying states of cleanliness, and mostly open only in summer. Visible to the right, as you travel eastwards, is the inland village of **PENTEDÁTTILO**, which owes its name to the Greek word for "five-fingered", on account of the curiously shaped rock on which it stands. Norman Douglas likened it more to an upturned molar, and Edward Lear, travelling through the area in 1848, thought it "perfectly magical" – though its old Byzantine centre has largely been abandoned in favour of a new and ugly town just below.

You are now in the **Zona Grecánica**, named after the villages on these southern slopes of Aspromonte that were settled by Greeks some two thousand years ago and still retain some traces of the Greek language in the local dialect. One such village is **BOVA**, perched on a crag 15km inland from its seaside satellite, Bova Marina. Bova is a remote place, with a view justifiably described by Lear as "truly magnificent", although the thick oak forests he saw then no longer exist. From the remains of the **castello** at the top, you can map out some alluring excursions into the wild country around: there are no hotels here but the countryside is one of the loveliest and most isolated parts of Aspromonte.

Around the corner of the coast, another route into Aspromonte takes you by way of the village of **SAN LUCA**, known to *Calabresi* as the home of the writer **Corrado Alvaro,** whose novels (*Gente di Aspromonte* is one) describe the lives of the people living in these mountains. The region is also known for its reputation as a *'ndrangheta* stronghold: the triangle of land between the villages of San Luca, Plati and Cimina is a favourite area for holding kidnap victims, often for months at a time, and is periodically – usually following accusations of apathy on the part of the government – a target for army operations to root out the hiding places. From San Luca a road continues up, leading after 20km to the Santuario della Madonna di Polsi (see opposite and from there to the peak of Montalto. The road is asphalted for only half the way and careers up some pretty hairy mountainsides, but is worth the sweat for the near-Himalayan landscape and the numerous possibilities for picnicking and walking. Local people will warn you against travelling alone in these parts, to which you should pay heed without necessarily following their advice.

Potenza and around

Basilicata's regional capital, **POTENZA**, has suffered more than most southern towns from the effects of earthquake and war, which have robbed it of much of its historical heritage. There is still considerable restoration work in progress, and despite the dust in summer, continuing improvements have helped to make Potenza a lively, go-ahead place and an excellent base for visiting some of the smaller towns and villages of inland Basilicata, most of which are conveniently situated on the main routes to – or from – the outside world.

The Italian mainland's highest provincial capital, Potenza is built on a spur between two valleys, and presents an unpromising vista from afar, seemingly consisting of nothing but characterless modern blocks surrounded by unsightly and polluting industrial works. The town is also a trial for drivers, its confusing one-way streets clogged with traffic and almost devoid of parking spaces (make sure you're not parked illegally – tickets and fines are freely distributed). But perseverance pays off, for the animated centre, focused on the narrow, partly pedestrianized **Via Pretoria**, is a maze of alleys and small, sequestered squares, well stocked with bars and restaurants and at its best during the nightly *passeggiata*. The most important sight here, off the main **Piazza Prefettura** (also known as Piazza Pagano), is the church of **San Francesco**, which contains a Byzantine-style icon of the Madonna del Terremoto and an elaborate sixteenth-century tomb. In the modern districts spread out below, the only compelling attraction is the **Museo Archeologico Provinciale** (Mon, Wed & Sun 9am–1pm, Tues, Thurs & Sat 9am–1pm & 4–7pm; free) in Rione Santa Maria (north of the centre), home to the region's most important collection of finds from the prehistory of Lucania, and some good ceramics, terracottas and statuettes from Greek Metapontum.

Potenza has three **train stations**. The central Potenza Città station has a line to Acerenza and Gravina in Puglia, and links with Potenza Inferiore, on the other side of town, which in turn has trains to Rionero, Melfi, Ferrandina (for Matera), Metaponto, Taranto, Fóggia and Salerno; Stazione Superiore in Rione Santa Maria is a stop on the line to Rionero, Melfi and Fóggia. The independent Ferrovie Appulo-Lucane (FAL) line links all three and also serves Bari and the Potenza area. **Drivers** would be well advised to park below the centre around Viale Marconi, from where escalators and lifts connect with Via del Pópolo, a few steps away from Piazza Prefettura. Most **buses** leaving for destinations within Basilicata leave from Piazza Crispi; buses for Salerno, Naples and Rome leave from Piazza Bologna. Frequent **city buses** connect the modern districts with Via Vaccaro and Corso Umberto in the city centre (tickets from *tabacchi* and bars; €0.52), as do several lifts (free) and rickety stairways. There is a **tourist office** at Via Alianelli 4, off Piazza Prefettura (Mon–Fri 9am–1pm & 4.30–7pm, Sat 9am–12.30pm; ☏0971.21.812).

Central **accommodation** includes the small and basic *Europa*, at the bottom of Via Pretoria (☏0971.34.014; ❶), and the rather gloomy *Miramonti* at Via Caserma Lucania 30 (☏0971.22.987; ❷), whose rooms are adequate though charmless. For a little more comfort, pay extra at the *Tourist*, Via Vescovado 4 (☏0971.25.955; ❹), a big place with good facilities at the eastern end of Via Pretoria, below Piazza Bonaventura. If these are full, there's the very ordinary *Galgano* at Via Vaccaro 428 (☏0971.52.125; ❷), a brief bus ride or a thirty-minute walk from the centre and difficult to find: it's signposted from a roundabout at the bottom of Via Vaccaro (from Potenza Inferiore station, turn left and keep walking for twenty minutes).

You can **eat** well and cheaply at the *Trattoria al Duomo* in Via Serrao (closed Sun), in a brick-vaulted cellar just around the corner from Potenza's cathedral (to the right of it), which serves excellent pasta dishes, including a delicious *orecchiette alla boscaiola* (pasta with a rich sauce of mushrooms and ham). Alternatively, the *Taverna Oraziana* on Via Flacco is a pleasant, casual place, occupying yet another cellar at the bottom of steps at the western end of Via Pretoria (closed Sun evening). On the northern edge of the old town, the *Due Torri*, on the street of the same name, is a more upmarket place, though the prices are reasonable (closed Sun).

Potenza has a few good **pubs**: the *Barracuda*, in Via Caserma Lucania (closed daytime and Mon), near Piazza Matteotti, serving panini and other **snacks**, and *Goblin's*, right on the central Piazza Pagano, which serves Irish draught beer and also makes a good breakfast stop for its *cornetti* and chocolate *faggotti*. Another good drinking-spot, popular with a younger crowd, is *Carpe Diem* (evenings only; no sign on the door), round the corner from *Barracuda* at Via XX Settembre 23, enjoying a view over the valley. The management here also operates Potenza's main venue for **live music**, located in the suburbs; just check the posters, consult the website ⓦ www.carpediemlive.net, or ask for details of what's on.

North of Potenza

North of Potenza lie several towns from the Norman era with some good examples of their brand of hybrid architecture. All are connected by bus with Potenza, and most are on the main Potenza–Fóggia rail line.

Acerenza and Castel Lagopésole

The venerable stronghold of **ACERENZA**, northeast of Potenza, is not so easy to reach by public transport, although it does have a station on the FAL line to Gravina, in Puglia, a few kilometres below the town itself, connected by a regular bus service to the top. It's worth the effort for the grand panorama and its famous **Cattedrale** (daily 9.30am–12.30pm & 4–7pm), from which it is thought the name of Basilicata derives (it was the bishop of this basilica who exercised jurisdiction over the territory around). Constructed in the eleventh century but rebuilt in its present Romanesque form in 1281, probably by French Angevin architects, the cathedral has a time-worn exterior, though the cupola at the top is a recent addition, following the earthquake of 1930. Inside, its crypt is a rare example of the impact of the Renaissance in Basilicata. West of here, on the main road north out of Potenza towards Fóggia, the massive castle of **Castel Lagopésole** (daily: summer 9.30am–1pm & 4–7pm; winter 9.30am–1pm & 3–5pm; free) is visible long before you reach it, dominating the surrounding country and dwarfing the village at its base. This was the last and greatest of Frederick II's castles, and was said to be his favourite for the rich hunting grounds in the woods around (now farmland), though the building itself was still unfinished by the time of the emperor's death in 1250. You can visit the chapel and some of the royal apartments. Note the two sculpted heads on the outside of the keep, one representing Beatrice, Frederick Barbarossa's second wife, the other Barbarossa himself (Frederick II's grandfather), on whom you may just distinguish the ass's ears for which he was famous. If you need a **meal** around here, *Falcon's Castle* at the bottom of the hill should fit the bill.

Melfi

About 25km north from Lagopésole on the SS93, on the far side of the imposing Monte Vulture, is the historic town of **MELFI**, long a centre of strategic importance, taken by the Normans in 1041 and their first capital in the south of Italy. It was in the formidable **Castle** at the top of the town that Pope Nicholas II formally recognized the conquests of Robert Guiscard over the Byzantines and Saracens, thereby legitimizing the piratical Normans and confirming their place in the embattled history of the south. It was here also that Guiscard imprisoned his first wife Aberada, and from where, in 1231, Frederick II issued his *Constitutiones Augustales*, reckoned to be the most comprehensive body of legislation promulgated since the time of Charlemagne. Repeatedly damaged by earthquakes, the castle now contains a **museum** (Mon 2–8pm, Tues–Sun 9am–8pm; €2.50) housing prehistoric finds and objects from the Greek, Roman and Byzantine eras, including ceramics, jewellery and a candelabra carved with the goddess Ea abducting the manly looking infant Kephalos. A separate door from the courtyard gives access to the museum's most celebrated item, an exquisitely carved Roman sarcophagus from the second century, the so-called *sarcofago di Rapolla*, showing the image of the dead girl for whom it was made, reclining on cushions, with five statuettes of gods and heroes on the sides.

In the centre of town off Via Vittorio Emanuele, is the **Duomo**, originally twelfth-century but rebuilt following earthquakes. After the 1930 quake, a

Byzantine-style Madonna and Child fresco was brought to light, which you can see to the left of the altar; a chapel on the right also has a Madonna, in her role as protectress of the city – a copy of the original statue stolen from here in 1982. The cathedral's campanile has miraculously survived the various cataclysms: the two black stone griffins symbolized the Norman hegemony in the South and are visible everywhere in Melfi, having been adopted as the town's emblem.

Melfi has a decent, very cheap **hotel**, the *Savoia* at Viale Savoia 21 (℡0972.23.710; ❶), though it's rather difficult to find: behind the cathedral turn right at Piazza IV Novembre, then left at Via Camassa, then left again onto Viale Savoia. You'll find a pleasant **restaurant/pizzeria** a little way down from the cathedral at Via Vittorio Emanuele 29, the *Delle Rose* (closed Mon), with outdoor seating in summer.

Venosa

If Melfi preserves the appearance of a dark medieval town, **VENOSA** has an attractive airiness, a harmonious place, rich with historical associations. Known in antiquity as Venusia, it was in its time the largest colony in the Roman world, and much is made of the fact that it was the birthplace of Quintus Horatius Flaccus, known to Italians as Orazio and to the English as **Horace** (68–65 BC); his supposed house lies past the cathedral on the right. Venosa's web of narrow streets is full of reminders of the town's long past. The tomb of the Roman general Marcellus, ambushed and killed by Hannibal here in 208 BC, is off Via Melfi, while a medieval washing-place lies near the Duomo on the old town's long main street, Corso Vittorio Emanuele. At the top of this street, a formidable Aragonese **Castello** dominates the spacious and arcaded Piazza Umberto, and houses a well-presented **archeological museum** (Wed–Mon 9am–8pm, Tues 2–8pm, sometimes open until 11pm on Sat; €2.50; joint ticket with archeological park), displaying finds from local excavations, mainly coins, frescoes, fragments of mosaics and older prehistoric remains from the Vulture area. Many of the Roman exhibits here were unearthed in Venosa's **archeological park**, a twenty-minute walk away at the far end of the *corso* (daily except Tues am: March–Oct 9am–7pm; Nov–Feb 9am–5pm; €2.50; joint ticket with archeological museum). Here you can see the sketchy remains of Roman baths and houses as well as a paleo-Christian baptistry, while across the road lies an amphitheatre (for which you must ask at the ticket-office for entry), and there are Jewish catacombs further along the road.

The excavations are overlooked by Venosa's most striking attraction, the **Abbazia della Trinità** (daily 8.30am–1.30pm & 3–5.30pm), a complex of churches begun in the mid-eleventh century that was the resting place of a number of Norman bigwigs, including Robert Guiscard. The first and greatest of the Norman adventurers in southern Italy, he's thought to be buried along with three of his brothers in a single uninscribed tomb on the right of the nave, while his divorced first wife Aberada occupies a slightly nobler tomb on the opposite side. The church also displays murals and mosaics, including a good fresco of the Byzantine St Apollonia hidden in the recess of an arch in front of Guiscard's supposed tomb; more frescoes showing Christian imagery can be seen in the crypt. Backing on to the older church, the Chiesa Nuova was begun in around 1100, a gigantic construction that was too ambitious to be properly finished – only the lower part of the walls and the apse were completed, incorporating fragments from the Roman ruins.

Venosa has an excellent **place to stay**, the *Orazio*, a beautifully restored old house with friendly management at Corso Vittorio Emanuele 142

(☎0972.31.135; ❸): it's well worth phoning ahead to guarantee a room. If it's full, you'll have to make do with the *Villa del Sorriso*, a modern place a couple of kilometres west of the centre at Via Appia 135 (☎0972.35.975; ❷). As for **restaurants**, your best bet is the *Taverna Ducale*, halfway down the Corso on Piazza Municipio, where for under €20 you can enjoy a feast of rustic but delicious Lucanian cuisine – the antipasto of local salami, porcini mushrooms and grilled vegetables would feed an army in itself.

Matera and around

The interior of the **province of Matera** has a great deal in common with Potenza province – a wide, empty terrain, much of it given over to agriculture and pasture, much of it good for nothing in particular. Run-down, depopulated, its bare clay hills appear, in Carlo Levi's words, "a sea of white, monotonous and treeless", dotted with solitary villages that are cut off from each other and the rest of the world. Little to recommend for an action-packed tour, then, but plenty of the timeless atmosphere portrayed by film-makers like Rosi and Bertolucci.

Matera

The town of **MATERA** itself is unique, with a degree of culture and elegance unusual by southern standards and, in its **sassi** – dwellings dug out of the ravine in tiers – one of the country's oddest urban features. The *sassi* are mainly abandoned now, an eerie troglodyte enclave occupying the lower regions of the city. But until thirty-odd years ago this part of the city was still populated by the poorest of the *materani*.

During the 1950s and 1960s, fifteen thousand people were forcibly removed from the *sassi* and rehoused in modern districts on the outskirts of town. Since then the area has been officially cleaned up and is being gradually repopulated, and in 1993 was made a World Heritage Site. Nowadays it's hard to picture the squalor that previously existed here, as described by Levi's sister, in *Christ Stopped at Eboli*, who compared the *sassi* to Dante's *Inferno*, so horrified was she by their disease-ridden inhabitants. "Never before have I seen such a spectacle of misery," she said. The children had "the wrinkled faces of old men, emaciated by hunger, with hair crawling with lice and encrusted with scabs. Most of them had swollen bellies and faces yellowed and stricken with malaria." Pursuing her, they begged not for coins but for quinine.

The Town

Divided into two sections – the Sasso Caveoso and Sasso Barisano – the *sassi* district can be entered from a number of different points around the centre of town, some signposted, some not. The **Strada Panoramica dei Sassi**, newly built with an eye to tourism, weaves through both zones and is a useful reference point, but you need to leave this to penetrate the warren and its *chiese rupestri* or **rock-hewn churches**. One, **Madonna de Idris** (all *chiesi rupestri* open daily 10am–1.30pm & 2.30–6.30pm; €2.10), perched on the conical Monte Errone that rises in the midst of the *sassi*, has frescoes dating from the fourteenth century. Another, the tenth-century **Santa Lucia alle Malve** in the so-called Albanian quarter (settled by refugees in the fifteenth century), has Byzantine-style frescoes dating from 1250. Other churches have a more orthodox appearance but are worth a visit; **San Pietro Caveoso**, for example, at the centre of the Caveoso district (Santa Lucia alle Malve lies behind it), is rather over-zealously restored and has a wooden ceiling and frescoes. For a fascinating glimpse of what life was like for the *sassi*-dwellers, head for the **Casa Grotta**, just below Madonna de Idris (daily: April–Oct 9am–8pm; Nov–March 9am–5pm; €1.50). Reconstructed inside a *sasso* with the help of the family who lived here until the 1950s and using original furniture, utensils and clothes, it gives an insight into how families with several children and livestock managed to live together in small holes in the rock without running water or electricity. If you want to explore the **caves** and more *chiese rupestri* on the far side of the ravine, you can cross the river further up towards the Sasso Barisano, though you'd do well to take a supply of drinking water – the excursion is further than it looks – up to an hour if you don't stray off the track. To get the most out of the whole area equip yourself with an *itinerario turistico* and a map, both available from the tourist office (see opposite). Better still, for a commentary and access to parts of the *sassi* you might otherwise miss on your own, you can join a guided **tour**; the Nuovi Amici dei Sassi, at Piazza Sedile 20 (☎0835.331.011), or Tour Service Matera, at Piazza Vittorio Veneto 42 (☎0835.334.633), charge around €8 per person for groups of four or more; or negotiate with one of the freelancers on the spot, who ask around €8–15 according to the length of the tour and the size of your party.

The more animated face of the old town has its centre at **Piazza Vittorio Veneto**, a large and stately square which in the evening is cleared of traffic and given over to a long procession of shuffling promenaders. The *materani* take their evening *passeggiata* seriously, and the din of the crowds rising up out of this square can be like the noise from a stadium. Matera's modern quarters stretch out to the north and west of here, but most of the things worth seeing are along the Via San Biagio and Via del Corso.

Winding off from the bottom end of the piazza, the narrow Via del Corso leads down to the seventeenth-century church of **San Francesco d'Assisi**, whose ornate Baroque style was superimposed on two older churches, traces of which, including some eleventh-century frescoes, can be visited through a passage in the third chapel on the left. In the main church are eight panels of a polyptych by Bartolomeo Vivarini, set above the altar. From San Francesco, you can cut across neighbouring Piazza Sedile onto Via Duomo – a good place to view the sprawling *sassi* below. Further on, the **Duomo**, which effectively divides this area into two, was built in the late thirteenth century and retains a strong Apulian-Romanesque flavour. Between the figures of Peter and Paul on the facade is a sculpture of the patron of Matera, Madonna della Bruna. Her feast day, the Sagra di Santa Bruna, is celebrated on July 2, when her statue is carried in procession three times round the piazza before being stormed by the onlookers, who are allowed to break up the papier-mâché float and carry off bits as mementos. At the back of the building you can see a recently recovered fresco from 1270 showing scenes from the Last Judgement.

From Piazza San Francesco, continue down into Via Rídola to admire the elliptical facade of the **Chiesa del Purgatorio**, gruesomely decorated with skulls. A little further on is the essential **Museo Rídola** (Mon 2–8pm; Tues–Sun 9am–8pm; €2.50), housed in the ex-monastery of Santa Chiara and containing an extensive selection of prehistoric and classical finds from the Matera area, including Bronze Age weaponry and beautifully decorated Greek plates and amphorae. A few metres on, at the end of Piazza Pascoli, the Palazzo Lanfranchi holds a **Pinacoteca** with an assortment of seventeenth- and eighteenth-century paintings.

Practicalities

Matera's **train station** is on Piazza Matteotti and is served by the FAL line, linked to Altamura (in Puglia, for connections to Bari and Gravina) and to Ferrandina (for connections to Metaponto or Potenza); **buses** also stop here. Trailing down from Piazza Matteotti, Via Roma has the town's **tourist office** – actually just off it at Via de Viti de Marco 9 (Mon & Thurs 9am–1pm & 4–6.30pm, Tues, Wed, Fri & Sat 9am–1pm; ℡0835.331.983, ℮info@aptbasilicata.it). Via del Corso, leading off the main Piazza Veneto (at the bottom of Via Roma), is the location of the **telephone** office and the **main post office**. *Greenfax*, at the Biblioteca Provinciale T. Stigliani on Via Roma, offers **Internet** access (Mon–Fri 9am–1.30pm & 4–6.30pm, Sat 9am–1.30pm).

Apart from Maratea, Matera is the only place in Basilicata where you might have difficulty finding a room for the night – booking a week or so in advance is highly recommended. The best **hotel** is the *Sassi*, right in the heart of the Sasso Barisano district and not far from the Duomo at Via San Giovanni Vecchio 89 (℡0835.331.009; ➎), its rooms gouged out of the tufa and affording marvellous views. Other choices in town include the *Piccolo*, a smart, modern place at Via de Sariis 11 (℡0835.330.201; ➍), the elegant but pricey *Albergo Italia* in Via Rídola (℡0835.333.561; ➏), or the *Casa d'Imperio* **bed and breakfast** in a beautifully refurbished sixteenth-century house at Via d'Addozio 39 (℡0835.330503, ⓦwww.casadimperio.it ➍). There is also an unofficial **youth hostel** in two converted guest rooms in the *Sassi Hotel* (see above), well-sited and with dormitory beds going for €15.60 per night: apply at the hotel.

There is more choice and better value among Matera's **restaurants**. The *Trattoria Lucana* is a good family-run place at Via Lucana 48 (closed Sun & 2 weeks in Sept), or enjoy the view over the *sassi* at the atmospheric *Il Terrazzino*, Vico San Giuseppe 7 (closed Tues). There is a pizzeria in Piazza Sedile, and a much rowdier affair, *La Panca*, a bit further out from the centre in Via Giolitti (closed Mon), ten minutes' walk from Piazza Vittorio Veneto up Via XX Settembre and Via Annunziatella. There's also a pizzeria, *Il Castello*, at the Angevin castle above Via Lucana, with outdoor seating in summer (closed Wed). *Hemingway*, in Via Rídola (closed Mon), is an elegant bar/pasticceria with tables in the square, while in Sasso Barisano, the *Caffè del Cavaliere* in Piazza San Pietro Barisano (closed daytimes and Mon) – the more populous end of the ravine dwellings – is an evocative place for a coffee or late-night drink.

Around Matera

Twenty kilometres south of Matera and connected by rail, the hilltop town of **MONTESCAGLIOSO** was once a Greek settlement and is now the site of a magnificent ruined eleventh-century Benedictine abbey, the **Abbazia di Sant'Angelo**. There are good views from here over the Bradano Valley. On the same line, but more conveniently reached by bus (the train station is 10km below the town), is the lively medieval town of **MIGLIÓNICO**, with a finely preserved fifteenth-century bastion at one end, with views all around. It was here in 1481 that the *congiura dei baroni* was held, a meeting of rebellious barons who formed a league in opposition to Ferdinand II of Aragon, from which the castle assumed the name *Castello del Malconsiglio*.

The SS7, which heads west from here, is the Roman Via Appia, and is a far preferable route to the SS407 (Basentana) that runs parallel. Buses only touch on it intermittently, so it's best covered with your own transport. Tracing the ridge between the Bradano and Basento valleys, it takes in some magnificent country and a number of good stopoffs. **TRICÁRICO** is another old hilltop village, quite important in its time, with a **Duomo** originally constructed by Robert Guiscard. Further south, **ALIANO** is the village described by Carlo Levi in *Christ Stopped at Eboli*. Called Gagliano by Levi, it's reachable by bus from **Pisticci**, on the Matera train line. Apart from the yellow "welcome" sign on the outskirts of the village and a general air of well-being, the place has not significantly changed since he was there. Nothing is missing: the church, the piazza where the Fascist mayor gave his regular addresses to the impassive peasants, the steep drop of the *fossa del bersagliere* and a striking view over the Agri and the "endless sweep of clay, with the white dots of villages, stretching out as far as the invisible sea" that Levi knew so well. A recent and useful addition is the series of plaques identifying key buildings mentioned in the book, along with appropriate quotes. You can see the rather grand house where he stayed at the bottom of the village ("away from the gaze of the mayor and his acolytes"), being converted at the time of writing into a full-scale **museum** to house some of his paintings, personal items and articles of folkloric interest. It's due to open soon; for the latest, phone ☎0835.568.529 or 0339.1332234, or call at the *Parco Letterario Carlo Levi* next to the church (Mon–Fri 9am–1pm & 3–6pm).

The northern Ionian coast

From Táranto (see p.936) to Reggio at Italy's toe-tip (see p.970), the **Ionian coast** is a mainly flat sandy strip, sometimes monotonous but less developed than the Tyrrhenian side of the peninsula, and with cleaner water. The **northern** section, from **Metaponto** to **Capo Colonna**, consists of a mountainous interior backing onto an empty seaboard, punctuated only by holiday resorts, a plethora of campsites – overflowing in the summer months with legions of Italians – and some notable historical sites. Of these, the most significant are connected with the periods of Greek occupation, the most recent of which was that of the Byzantines, who administered the area on and off for 500 years, leaving their traces most strikingly in the hilltop town of **Rossano**. A thousand years earlier, the clutch of Greek colonies collectively known as Magna Graecia rose and fell, of which Metapontion, Sybaris and Kroton, all on this stretch of the Ionian coast, were some of the greatest. Although only the first of these has been properly excavated, there are museums in all, describing an era that was – culturally and intellectually – the brightest moment in the history of Basilicata and Calabria. All the coastal towns are well connected by rail and bus, while places inland are linked by local buses from the coast. The SS106 road, which skirts this coastline, is mostly straight and fast.

The Basilicata coast

The most extensively excavated of the Greek sites, and the only place of any real significance on the Ionian coast of Basilicata, is at **METAPONTO**, an important road and rail junction connecting the coastal routes between Táranto and Reggio with the interior of Basilicata – to Potenza by train and Matera by bus. Metapontion was settled in the eighth century BC and owed its subsequent prosperity to the fertility of the surrounding land – perfect for cereal production (symbolized by the ear of corn stamped on its coinage) and its position as a commercial centre. Pythagoras, banished from Kroton, established a school here in about 510 BC that contributed to an enduring philosophical tradition. The city's downfall came as a result of a series of catastrophes: absorbed by Rome, embroiled in the Punic Wars, sacked by the slave-rebel Spartacus, and later desolated by a combination of malaria and Saracen raids.

Lido di Metaponto and the Zona Archeologica

Metaponto today is a straggling, amorphous place, comprising train station, museum and ruins. Arriving at the station, you're 3km from the **LIDO DI METAPONTO**, where there are sandy, well-equipped **beaches**, numerous **campsites** and a handful of hotels. Two of the campsites – the *Lido* (T0835.741.884) and *Magna Grecia* (T0835.741.855) – also have bungalows available (both ❸); all have their own beaches and the bigger ones have tennis, discos and other facilities. The best-value **hotel** is the well-equipped *Kennedy,* at Via Jonio 1 (T0835.741.960; ❷), about 1km from the station, off the Lido road.

For the first batch of ruins, take the next turning on the right after the Lido junction (coming from the station) and follow the narrow lane down to the wide site – signposted **Zona Archeologica** – which has the remains of a theatre and a Temple of Apollo Licius. The latter is a sixth-century BC construction that once possessed 32 columns, but you need some imagination to picture its original appearance. In a better state of preservation is the **Temple of Hera**, or Tavole Palatine, 2–3km north, where the main SS106 crosses the Bradano (take one of the buses to Táranto from Metaponto station). With fifteen of its columns remaining, it is the most suggestive remnant of this once mighty state. A selection of other survivals can be seen at the **Museo Archeologico Nazionale** (Mon 2–8pm, Tues–Sun 9am–8pm; €2.58), opposite the sanctuary of Apollo Licio, about 1km outside Metaponto town (and well signposted). The exhibits are mainly fourth- and fifth-century statuary, ceramics and jewellery, though administrative and financial problems have meant that only a small fraction of the finds are displayed, and work on a new wing has stopped indefinitely. Nonetheless, there is a fascinating section on the new insights revealed by the study of fingerprints on shards found in the artisans' quarter, and look out too for examples of the famous coins.

Policoro

There's a similar collection of antiquities at the **Museo Nazionale della Siritide**, 25km down the coast, just behind the village of **POLICORO**. The museum (Mon & Wed–Sun 9am–8pm, Tues 2–8pm; €2.50) contains clay figurines and jewel-bedecked skeletons among other material taken from the zone between the Sinni and Agri rivers, in its time one of the richest areas on this coast and site of the two Greek colonies of **Siris** and **Heraclea**. The first of these, after which the museum is named, reached such a position of wealth and eminence that the other colonies were persuaded to gang together in the middle of the sixth century BC to put an end to Sirian ambitions. Heraclea was founded on the same spot by Tarentines in 432 BC with the aim of driving a wedge between the Achaean cities of Metapontion and Sybaris to the north and south. It was here that Pyrrhus, king of Epirus, first introduced elephants to the Romans, and, although winning the first of two battles in 280 BC, suffered such high losses that he declared another such victory would cost him the war – so bequeathing to posterity the term "Pyrrhic victory".

Into Calabria

Shortly after crossing the Sinni River you enter Calabria, skirting the base of the lofty Monte Pollino. Inland, look out for the **Castle** at **ROCCA IMPE-RIALE**, built by Frederick II in the style of Lagopésole and Lucera. Imposing from a distance, its state of abandon becomes more obvious as you approach, but the views from its crumbling walls are impressive. Further inland, at the medieval village of **ORIOLO**, there's another **Castle**, this one from the fifteenth century and in a better state of preservation, from which you can continue inland into Basilicata and the woods around **Senise**, or loop back to the coast at **ROSETO**, the site of another of Frederick II's castles, prominent at the side of the road. In Norman times this spot marked the boundary between the territories controlled by Robert Guiscard and his brother Roger.

Síbari

The mountainous slopes soon give way to the wide **Piana di Síbari**, the most extensive of the Calabrian coastal plains, bounded by Pollino to the north, the Sila Greca to the west and the Sila Grande in the south. The rivers flowing off these mountains, which for centuries kept the land well watered and rich, also helped to transform it into a stagnant and malarial mire, and although land reclamation has restored the area's fertility, without visiting the museum and excavations at **Síbari** you could pass through the area with no inkling of the civilization that once flourished on these shores.

Long one of the great archeological mysteries tantalizing generations of scholars, the site of ancient Sybaris was only definitely identified in the late 1960s, when aerial and X-ray photography confirmed that the site previously known to be that of Roman Thurium was also that of Sybaris. There are in fact three separate levels of construction that have been unearthed here, one Greek and two Roman, one on top of the other. Together these make up one of the world's largest archeological sites, covering 1000 hectares (compared to Pompeii's 50), though only 10 hectares have so far been dug up, and the great riches that the excavations were expected to yield have not yet come to light; there have been too many other settlements on this same spot, not to mention the marauders who regularly passed through the area.

The wealth of the city – said to number 100,000 in population and have dominion over half a million – was only one factor in its fame, around which myth and documentary evidence have combined to produce a colourful muddle of anecdotes. The city's laws and institutions were apparently made to ensure the greatest comfort and well-being of its citizens, including the banning from the city of all noisy traders, such as metalworkers, and the planting of trees along every street for shade. Cooks were so highly prized that they were apparently bought and sold in the marketplace for great sums and were allowed to patent their recipes, while inventions ascribed to the Sybarites include pasta and the chamberpot. This was all too much for the Crotonians, who, under their general Milo (more famous as a much-garlanded Olympic athlete) destroyed the city in 510 BC, diverting the waters of the river over the site to complete the job.

The **excavations** lie across the rail lines some 4km south down the SS106, on the right-hand side (daily 9am–1hr before sunset; free). Most of the excavations belong to the Roman period, but something of the earlier site might still be turned up – the silt and sand of the river bed has yet to be explored properly, work having been effectively halted for much of the last twenty years owing to shortage of funds. Of the Roman city, the remains are at least impressively displayed and maintained, including baths, a patrician's house with mosaics, and a decumanus (claimed to be the widest in existence). Just off the site, a small room contains individual finds including some Greek exhibits, mainly ceramic shards, though nothing that would have raised much excitement in the numerous enthusiasts who long sought this spot. There's more to be seen, from here and other local sites, at the **Museo della Sibarite** (daily 9am–7.30pm; €2), down a left-turn about 1km before the excavations, on the banks of the River Crati.

Monastery of Pathirion and Rossano

There are remnants from more recent times further south, near the village of **SANTA MARIA DEL PATIRE**, where the **Monastery of Pathirion** sits among groves of olive and holm-oak at the end of a road built by Austrian prisoners during World War I. Its well-preserved church – a simple basilica – has sweeping views over the Sibari plain and the mountains around, but is the only intact relic of the monastery, which lies in ruins below – an extensive complex that had its centre at nearby Rossano and rivalled the holy mountain of Athos in Greece as a centre of monastic learning.

Twelve kilometres away, the resort of **ROSSANO SCALO** has far outstripped its parent-town of **ROSSANO** in terms of size and bustle, and most of the holiday-makers who frequent its beaches never even get round to visiting the hilltop town, 7km up an awkward winding road – something that has helped preserve the old centre from excessive development. The foremost Byzantine centre in the south, Rossano was the focus of a veritable renaissance of literature, theology and art between the eighth and eleventh centuries, a period to which the town's greatest treasures belong. Its majolica-tiled **Cattedrale** is an Angevin construction largely rebuilt after the 1836 earthquake but has a much-venerated ninth-century Byzantine fresco, *Madonna Achiropita*, whose Greek epithet, meaning "not painted by hand", refers to its divine authorship. The over-decorated interior boasts a wooden ceiling and a mosaic floor near the altar, though most of the artworks here suffer from neglect. Next to the cathedral, the **Museo Diocesano** (Mon–Wed, Fri & Sat 10am–noon; €2.07) contains the famed *codex purpureus Rossanensis*, or Purple Codex, a unique sixth-century manuscript on reddish-purple parchment illustrating the life of Christ. The book, which was brought from Palestine by monks fleeing the Muslim invasions, is open at one page, but you can leaf through a good copy and see, among other things, how the Last Supper was originally depicted, with Christ and his disciples not seated but reclining on cushions round the table, and all eating from the same plate. Other items in this tiny museum include a fifteenth-century icon painted on both sides and formerly at Pathirion, and several pieces of silverware of superb artistry. In contrast to the Duomo's grandiosity, the diminutive church of **San Marco**, at the end of Corso Garibaldi on the edge of town, retains a primitive spirituality. The five cupolas of the tenth- or eleventh-century construction, surrounded by palms on a terrace that looks out over the gorge below, impart an almost Middle Eastern flavour. The stark white interior, recently restored, is enlivened only by six frail columns and two Byzantine frescoes. To visit, ask at the Cooperativa Neilos at their office at Piazza Duomo 25 (℡0983.525.263). They are also equipped to supply **information** on the area.

Hotels are few and far between, all in the lower town, and not especially cheap. Try the *Murano*, right by the sea on Lido Sant'Angelo (℡0983.511.788; ❸), or, 50m up from the level crossing, the *Scigliano* (℡0983.511.846; ❺), though if you have transport you'll find a better deal at the *President* (℡0983.511.375; ❹), a couple of kilometres north up the SS106. All are rather characterless, modern places, but prices should include breakfast. Alternatively, 1km north from Rossano Scalo on the seafront road, you'll find chalets for rent at the local **campsite**, *Torino* (℡0983.512.394). Back in the old town, the best **trattoria** lies just off Piazza Anargiri, *La Villa*, in Via San Bartolomeo, with alfresco eating in summer (closed lunchtimes & Tues); there's another, more casual evenings-only place, *La Bizantina*, right outside San Marco, or try *Le Arcate* near the cathedral. All of these places also serve pizzas.

Crotone and around

South of Rossano there is an empty stretch of beaches; inland are the vineyards of Cirò, the source of Calabria's best-known **wine**. Crossing the River Neto into the fertile **Marchesato** region, you'll have your approach to **Crotone** (the ancient Greek city of Kroton) blighted by a smoky industrial zone – not the most alluring entry into a city, but a rare thing in Calabria, and a reminder of the false hopes once vested in the industrialization of the region.

Crotone

The site of ancient Kroton has been entirely lost, but in its day this was among the most important colonial settlements of Magna Graecia, overshadowed by its more powerful neighbour Sybaris but with a school of medicine that was famous throughout the classical world and closely linked with the prowess of the city's athletes, who regularly scooped all the honours at the Olympic Games back in Greece. In 530 BC the mathematician and metaphysician Pythagoras took up residence in Kroton and established an aristocratic party based on his ideas which eventually gained control, though the political turmoil that resulted from the sack of Sybaris led to their banishment from the city. Kroton went on to be the first of the Greek cities in Calabria but was increasingly destabilized by internal conflicts and the external threat of the encroaching barbarians, eventually being destroyed by the Romans. A resurgence of sorts occurred in the thirteenth century when it was made the main town of the Marchesato region, a vast feudal domain extending from the Neto to the Simeri rivers, held by the powerful Ruffo family of Catanzaro. But its prosperity was always hindered by the scourge of malaria, which poisoned every initiative and debilitated its people, provoking the author George Gissing – himself a victim of malaria during his visit in 1897 – to condemn Crotone as "a squalid little town".

In recent times Crotone has been mired in drugs and crime, though the city's elevation in 1995 as one of Calabria's new provincial capitals may finally revitalize the area. In fact, past the ugly industry defacing the northern approaches, the old centre retains an agreeable, unspoiled character, and the town makes a good base for the **beaches** that spread to the south and for the Greek ruins at Capo Colonna (see p.989). On the old town's main Corso Vittorio Emanuele, the **Duomo**'s chief draw is an icon of the Black Madonna, usually locked away, but displayed during May when, at midnight on the third Saturday, it is paraded through the town en route to Capo Colonna; the following evening it's transported back to the Duomo by sea – the highlight of a week of festivities during which the seafront is jammed with stalls. At the end of the Corso, the church of the **Immacolata** has an ossuary in its crypt, containing hundreds of neatly piled skulls grinning under electric candle-light. Further up Via Risorgimento, the brand new **Museo Archeologico Nazionale** (daily except first and third Mon of month 9am–7.30pm; €2)

△ Cosenza, Calabria

holds the best collection of finds from Magna Graecia on the Ionian coast. Alongside good examples of Greek and Roman coins, information about and fragments from the excavations at Crotone and its various colonies, lists of the Olympic winners who hailed from the city and maps of the digs (the main one right next to the main industrial complex), the cool and airy rooms display an array of items from Capo Colonna. Most noteworthy of these is the so-called **Treasure of Hera**, a beautifully restored group of bronze statuettes – including a sphinx, a gorgon, a horse, a winged siren and a very rare nuraghic boat from Sardinia – found in a tomb at Capo Colonna in 1987, and dating from the seventh to the fifth centuries BC. The most dazzling item is a gold diadem, expertly worked with garlands of leaves and sprigs of myrtle.

At the top of the road, the eighteenth-century **Palazzo Morelli**, which stands on the corner of Piazza Castello, is one of several palaces built by Spanish nobility that surround the **Castello**, itself locally referred to as Charles V's but actually constructed by the Spanish viceroy Don Pedro di Toledo in 1541. Within, you can gaze over the sturdy ramparts to the town and sea below, and visit the **Museo Cívico** (Tues–Sat 9am–1pm & 3–8pm, Sun 9.30am–12.30pm; €1.55), a diverting exhibition of old maps and photos of Crotone and around, plus coins and sundry heraldic devices. The ticket also allows you into the **Torre Comandante**, one of the sentinel towers (same hours).

Arriving by **train** you will need to take either a taxi or bus to cover the 1.5km to the centre of town, Piazza Pitagora, and most of the hotels. There's a **tourist office** at Via Torino 148, obscurely sited halfway between the station and the old town (Mon & Wed 9am–1pm & 3–5pm, Tues, Thurs & Fri 7.30am–1pm; ☎0962.23.185). The **bus** station is on Via Ruffo, a couple of streets east of Piazza Pitagora, where most provincial and regional buses arrive. Nearby, the small and clean *Pace* at Via Cutro 56 (☎0962.22.584; ❶) is central Crotone's cheapest **accommodation** choice, after which comes the rather dingy *Italia*, over the arcades of Piazza Vittoria, just off Corso Vittorio Emanuele (☎0962.23.910; ❷), and the much fancier *Capitol* (☎0962.24.996; ❹), at the bottom of the Corso at Piazza Umberto 61.

Below the *Italia*, the *Caffè Italia* (closed Mon) is good for snacks, *cornetti* and refreshing *latte di mándorla* (almond milk). For something more substantial, you'll also find a few **restaurants** in this part of town, ranging from the basic *Mary* pizzeria with its wood-fired oven, opposite the *Pace* hotel, to the *Ristorante Da Peppino* in Piazza Umberto (closed Mon), a high-quality trattoria that draws a strong local crowd. The pick of the restaurants on the seafront, meanwhile, is *Casa Rosa* (closed Sun) at Via Gramsci – pricey but well worth it for good seafood and Calabrian specialities like the fiery *sardelle con ricotta*.

Inland to Santa Severina

From Crotone's bus office on Via Ruffo there are a couple of departures daily to **SANTA SEVERINA**, on the eastern fringes of the Sila Piccola (see p.966). A Byzantine fortified town built on a hilltop, it's well worth a detour, principally for the Norman castle that dominates it. Rebuilt by Robert Guiscard on the ruins of a Byzantine stronghold and remodelled by the Swabians and Angevins, the newly renovated castle holds a first-rate **museum** (Aug daily 9am–1pm & 3–8pm; Sept–July Tues–Sun 9am–1pm & 3–6pm; €3.10), ranging through all parts of the construction from the foundations to the first-floor rooms. Exhibits include Byzantine artefacts, sundry arms and artillery and a scale model of the castle, as well as an informative overview of military architecture in Calabria and temporary exhibitions upstairs. From the stout battlemented walls long views extend over the hilly surroundings towards the mountains of Sila, and nearer at hand over the elongated square of the old town. On the other side of the piazza, whose flagstones are studded with symbols of the zodiac, the **Duomo** lies adjacent to an eighth-century Byzantine **baptistry** (9am–noon & 3–7pm) which preserves traces of frescoes of the saints, Greek inscriptions on the capitals and its original font. On the other side of the Duomo, the **Museo Diocesano** also repays a visit (Mon–Sat 9am–1pm & 3–8pm, Sun 3–10pm; €2.07), containing a painfully graphic fifteenth-century Christ on the cross, an early printed edition of the Bible, and – its greatest treasure – the *Spilla Angioina*, a brooch from about 1300, studded with gold, pearls and rubies. The bars in the square serve snacks, and if you're looking for a full **meal** in Santa Severina, try the *Locanda del Re* on the steps below the castle (closed Mon & 2 weeks in Sept) – which, incidentally, also has comfortable **rooms to rent** by the night (℡0962.51.734; **➊**).

Capo Colonna to Le Castella

Another worthwhile excursion from Crotone is to the famed column at **Capo Colonna** on Calabria's extreme eastern point, for which you have to drive or walk 11km along the coast. The column is a solitary remnant of a vast structure which served as the temple for all the Greeks in Calabria. Dedicated to Hera Lacinia, the temple originally possessed 48 of these Doric columns and was the repository of immense wealth before being repeatedly sacked as Magna Graecia and Hellenism itself declined. The object of Gissing's pilgrimage to Crotone, and a feature of his fevered visions as he lay on his sick bed (he eventually left without seeing it), it remained forever a mirage for him as he strained his eyes on the Crotone seafront, as unattainable as his attempts to recapture the glories of ancient Greece.

There are some excellent **bathing spots** not far south of here. **CAPO RIZZUTO** is a spit of land with a choice of sandy or rocky inlets to swim from. In winter the resort is dead, but it can get quite congested in the height of summer and difficult to find a place to stay. Nearby **LE CASTELLA** is another busy holiday spot, but not yet strangled by tourism. It would be hard to spoil the beautifully sited Aragonese **castle** on an islet just off the main town. As the Golfo di Squillace's only anchorage for large ships, the site was fortified from the fourth century BC and was later held by the Aragonese and Angevins, sold in perpetuum to the Duke of Carafa for 9000 ducats in 1496, and, the target of repeated Turkish raids, was finally abandoned at the end of the eighteenth century. You can wander round the outside of the castle; the interior, however, is currently closed – the word is that it's being converted into an archeological museum. You could swim off the rocks here, though you'll probably be more tempted by the arc of beach to the south. If you're seduced into **staying**, you can't do better than *L'Aragonese* (℡0962.795.013; **➋**; full-board only in Aug), right opposite the castle, with a **restaurant** below – ask for a sea-facing room. There are a couple of other hotel options in town if this is full; alternatively look for houses advertising *camere*. The nearest **campsites** are the *Costa Splendente* (℡0962.795.131) and *Marinella* (℡0962.799.810), both a couple of kilometres to the west and open June to September.

The southern Ionian coast

The southern part of Calabria's Ionian seaboard is less developed than the rest of the region, perhaps because it's less interesting scenically and most of the seaside towns and villages strung along it are unappealing. If you like sandy

beaches, though, this is where to find them – either wild and unpopulated or, if you prefer, glitzy and brochure-style, as at **Soverato**. At **Locri** there is the region's best collection of Greek ruins and, overlooking the coast a short way inland, the craggy medieval strongholds of **Squillace** and **Gerace**, and **Stilo**, with its jewel of Byzantine church-building, the **Cattólica**.

Catanzaro, La Roccelletta and Squillace

Despite its fine position, set high up in the foothills of the Sila and with good views out to sea, Calabria's regional capital, **CATANZARO**, has little innate charm: it's a crowded, overdeveloped, traffic-ridden city, within a short ride of some five-star beaches, but otherwise best avoided. There's more interest further on down the coast at the ruined basilica of Santa Maria della Roccella, or **La Roccelletta,** 100m down the road that branches off the SS106, signposted towards San Floro and Borgia. Half-hidden in an olive grove, this partly restored red brick shell is all that remains of what was once the second-largest church in Calabria (after Gerace). Of uncertain date, though probably Norman in origin and founded by Basilian monks, it still has a mighty impact on the unsuspecting viewer. Much of the building material used in its construction came from the remains of the Roman town of Scolacium, the excavations of which can be seen in the **zona archeologica** (daily 9am–1hr before sunset; free) nestled among the olives behind the church. The best-preserved item here is a **theatre**, once able to hold some 3500 spectators, and thought to have been abandoned following a fire some time after 350 AD. Elsewhere on the site are the scanty remains of baths, and an **antiquarium** displaying finds from the site – mainly statuary, pottery and coins.

Five kilometres further south along the coast, at Lido di Squillace, is the turn-off for the old town of **SQUILLACE**, 8km up in the hills, once an important centre but now just a mountain village, isolated on its high crag. There are lofty views to be enjoyed over the Gulf and beyond Catanzaro as far as the Sila Piccola, and the **Castle** (currently under restoration) is one of the most romantic collections of ruins in Calabria. But the place is probably most renowned for its associations with **Cassiodorus**, whose monastery was located in the vicinity – though all trace of it has long since disappeared. Cassiodorus (480–570), scholar and secretary to the Ostrogoth, Theodoric, used his position to preserve much of Italy's classical heritage against the onset of the Dark Ages and the book-burning propensities of the Christians. Retiring to spend the last thirty years of his life in seclusion here, Cassiodorus composed histories and collections of documents – of invaluable use to historians. There's a **restaurant** below the castle, *La Cripta*, which also serves pizzas (closed Mon).

The coast to Locri

South of Squillace, the golden sands of **COPANELLO** and **SOVERATO** beckon, two resorts that are increasingly attracting the international market. The private lidos hold sway here, charging €3–6 for a day under a parasol on a clean **beach** with access to a bar, but it's easy to find free beaches if you fancy more seclusion. Soverato has a handful of two-star **hotels** among the grander establishments, for example the *San Vincenzo* (℡0967.21.106; ❷), at Corso Umberto 296, and the *Riviera*, on Via Regina Elena (℡0967.25.738; ❷), both of which have **restaurants**. If you want to go up a peg or two, opt instead for the well-equipped *Gli Ulivi*, Via Moro 1 (℡0967.21.487; ❺), which has its own strip of beach, or the more modest *Del Golfo* on Via Marina (℡0967.21.307; ❹), well-sited by the sea but without a restaurant. The local **campsite**, *Glauco,* lies in Località San Nicola, 1km north (☎0967.25.533; closed winter).

The coast south assumes a bare, empty look that it keeps until the outskirts of Reggio, though with views of the distant mountains of the Serre and Aspromonte to stave off monotony. Regular **buses and trains** connect the towns along the coast, and buses link inland villages. On the far side of Monasterace a turn-off where the bus stops leads to **STILO**, 11km up the side of the rugged Monte Consolino. An influential centre at different periods, Stilo is best known for the tiny tenth-century Byzantine temple, the **Cattólica** (daily: summer 8am–8pm; winter 7am–7pm; donations requested), which can be reached by car by taking the first hairpin on the right at the end of the village, or on foot by climbing a series of alleys from the village's main street, Via Tommaso Campanella. Once a base for hermits and Basilian monks in the south of Calabria, this perfectly proportioned temple is reckoned to be the best-preserved monument of its kind, though little of its former glory remains inside, apart from some damaged frescoes and four slim, upturned columns taken from an older temple.

The name of **Tommaso Campanella** occurs everywhere in Stilo, a reminder of the village's links with this Dominican friar and utopian philosopher (1568–1639). Campanella was hounded by the Inquisition principally for his support of the Copernican model of the solar system, and spent some thirty years in prison for the heretical theories expounded in his book, *City of the Sun*. Eventually fleeing to Paris, he became the protégé of Cardinal Richelieu. The shell of **San Domenico** church, part of the convent where he lived, can be seen by following Via Campanella to the Porta Stefanina at the end of the village. Halfway along the road, look into the thirteenth-century **Duomo**, its ogival Gothic portal the only part remaining from the original construction. Note, too, along with other Byzantine and Norman reliefs, the surreal pair of feet stuck onto the wall on the left of the door, taken from a pagan temple and symbolizing the triumph of the Church.

Stilo has a pair of **hotels**, both open from May to September only. The more appealing of the two is the *San Giorgio* at Via Citarelli 8 (☎0964.775.047; ❸), just off the main Via Campanella, housed in the seventeenth-century palace of the Lamberti counts and furnished in nineteenth-century style, with a garden and pool. The *Città del Sole*, on Viale Roma heading towards the Cattólica (☎0964.775.588; ❹), has a contrastingly impersonal, corporate atmosphere, with modern rooms and facilities. In both, make sure you get a room enjoying the wide views over the Ionian. Both have **restaurants** (open to non-guests), though the *San Giorgio*'s is only open June to September. The only other place in town to eat is a basic pizzeria, *Oenotria*, on Viale Roma (closed Sun).

The resort of **RIACE**, where the Bronzi di Riace were found (see p.972), lies 7km south of Monasterace, though there's little to stop for beyond its sandy beaches – a far better place to pause would be **ROCCELLA IÓNICA**, another resort 13km down the coast, surmounted by the remains of a medieval castle. Once the stronghold of local feudal overlords, the princes of Caraffa, the ruins are now too precarious to allow entry, but they make a striking backdrop for a **jazz festival** at the end of August which takes place in an amphitheatre below, attracting international names: contact the tourist office at Reggio for details (p.972). At sea-level, the town is lively enough to make a decent overnight stop, with one **hotel**, the functional and reasonably priced *Mediterraneo*, in the central Piazza XXV Aprile (☎0964.863.388; ❷), near the train station. There's a fish **restaurant** and pizzeria, *Il Veliero* (closed Wed), just beyond the level-crossing at the bottom of the square, though if you have transport it's well worth heading 3km south out of town on the SS106, where

La Cascina, a well-restored farmhouse from 1899, serves up excellent meals at very moderate prices (closed Tues).

Locri and Gerace

Continuing south, you soon come to the most famous classical site on this coast, **Locri Epizefiri** (daily 9am–1hr before sunset; free), some 3km beyond the resort town of **LOCRI**. Founded some time in the seventh century BC, the city of Locris was responsible for the first written code of law throughout the Hellenic world. Its moment of glory came in the second half of the sixth century when, supposedly assisted by Castor and Pollux, 10,000 Locrians defeated 130,000 Crotonians on the banks of the River Sagra, 25km north. Founding colonies and gathering fame in the spheres of horse rearing and music, the city was an ally of Syracuse but eventually declined during Roman times. The walls of the city, traces of which can still be seen, measured some 8km in circumference, and the excavations within are now interspersed over a wide area among farms and orchards. Your own transport would be useful for some of the more far-flung features, though the most interesting can be visited on foot without too much effort, including a fifth-century-BC Ionic temple, a Roman necropolis and a well-preserved Graeco-Roman theatre. In any case make a stop at the **museum** (daily except first & third Mon of month; 9am–8pm; €2.07) to consult the plan of the site, and examine the most recent finds, including a good collection of **pinakes**, or votive ceramics – though some of the best items have been appropriated by the Museo Nazionale in Reggio.

After the Saracens devastated Locris in the seventh century AD, the survivors fled inland to found **GERACE**, on an impregnable site that was later occupied and strengthened by the Normans. At the end of a steep and tortuous road 10km up from modern Locri, its ruined **castle** stands at one end of the town on a sheer cliff; it's usually accessible, though officially the site is out of bounds due to the very precarious state of the paths and walls. Easier to visit is the **Duomo** (daily: April–July 9.30am–1pm & 3–8pm; Aug 9.30am–1pm & 3–9pm; Sept–March 9.30am–1pm & 3–6pm), founded in 1045 by Robert Guiscard, enlarged by Frederick II in 1222 and today still the biggest church in Calabria. Its simple and well-preserved interior has twenty columns of granite and marble, each different and with various capitals; the one on the right nearest the altar in *verde antico* changes tone according to the weather. The Treasury below (€1), which you pass on the way up to the nave, contains religious knick-knacks. Two other churches from the same period that are worth a look are **San Francesco** and **San Giovanello**, at the end of Via Caduti sul Lavoro (to the left of the Duomo's main entrance), both showing a nice mix of Norman, Byzantine and Saracenic influences. They are usually closed: ask at the nearby *tabacchi* about access.

Travel details

Trains

Cosenza to: Camigliatello (Ferrovia Cálabro-Lucane; 2 daily; 1hr 20min); Naples (every 2hr; 3hr 40min–4hr 15min); Paola (hourly; 20min); Rome (2 daily; 5hr 30min–6hr 15min).

Matera to: Bari (Ferrovia Appulo-Lucane; 8 daily; 1hr 30min).

Metaponto to: Bari (5 daily; 2hr); Cosenza (3 daily; 1hr30–2hr30); Ferrandina (for Matera) (10 daily; 30min); Reggio (4 daily; 4hr 40min–6hr 30min); Síbari (hourly; 1hr–1hr 35min); Táranto (hourly; 45min).

Paola to: Cosenza (hourly; 30min); Naples (hourly; 2hr 30min–4hr30min); Reggio (hourly; 2hr); Rome (every 1–2hr; 4hr 30min–5hr 30min).
Potenza (Inferiore) to: Fóggia (every 2hr; 2hr); Metaponto (9 daily; 1hr 30min); Salerno (hourly; 2hr); Táranto (6 daily; 2hr 15min).
Reggio to: Catanzaro (10 daily; 2hr 20min–4hr 30min); Naples (every 1–2hr; 4hr 35min–9hr 10 min); Paola (hourly; 1hr 45min–6hr); Rome (hourly; 6hr 15min–11hr); Táranto (4 daily; 5–8hr).

Buses

Cosenza to: Camigliatello (hourly; 1hr); Catanzaro (Mon–Sat 8 daily; 1hr 45min); Naples (1 daily; 5hr); Rome (3 daily; 6hr).

Matera to: Metaponto (Mon–Sat 4 daily; 50min); Potenza (Mon–Sat 2 daily; 1hr 30min).
Potenza to: Matera (Mon–Sat 2 daily; 1hr 30min); Naples (4 daily; 2hr); Rome (2 daily; 4hr 30min).
Reggio to: Rome (3 daily; 8 hr); Florence (2 daily, 12hr).
Tropea to: Capo Vaticano (June–Sept 4 daily; 20min).

Ferries and hydrofoils

Reggio to: Messina (12 daily; 20min).
Villa San Giovanni to: Messina (every 15min; 45min).

Sicily

CHAPTER 16 Highlights

✳ **Cappella Palatina, Palermo** Admire the colour and beauty of the chapel's Byzantine mosaics, carved Arab ceiling and decorative marble floor. See p.1006

✳ **The ascent of Etna** It's an eerie climb up the blackened lunar landscape of this smoking volcano, which dominates the landscape of eastern Sicily. See p.1029

✳ **Performance in Siracusa's Teatro Greco** Choose between classical dramas or more modern productions, staged every summer in the city's spectacular Greek theatre. See p.1039

✳ **Villa Romana del Casale, Piazza Armerina** The vitality, colour and diversity of the grand-scale mosaics at this Roman villa are not to be missed. See p.1049

✳ **Noto** The apotheosis of Baroque town planning, Noto offers glorious golden vistas, from extravagant balconied *palazzi* to soaring church facades. See p.1043

✳ **Agrigento** The Valley of the Temples at Agrigento is a spectacular sight. See p.1044

16

Sicily

I like Sicily extremely – a good on-the-brink feeling – one hop and you're out of Europe . . .

D. H. Lawrence in a letter to Lady Cynthia Asquith, 1920

The Sicilians aren't the only people to consider themselves, and their island, a separate entity. Coming from the Italian mainland, it's easy to spot that **Sicily** (Sicilia) has a different feel, that socially and culturally you *are* all but out of Europe. Occupying a strategically vital position, and as the largest island in the Mediterranean, Sicily's history and outlook are not those of its modern parent but of its erstwhile foreign rulers – from the Greeks who first settled the east coast in the eighth century BC, through a dazzling array of Romans, Arabs, Normans, French and Spanish, to the Bourbons seen off by Garibaldi in 1860. Substantial relics of these ages remain: temples, theatres and churches are scattered about the whole island. But there are other, more immediate hints of Sicily's unique past. A hybrid Sicilian language, for a start, is still widely spoken in the countryside; the food is noticeably different, spicier and with more emphasis on fish and vegetables; even the flora echoes the change of temperament – oranges, lemons, olives and palms are ubiquitous.

Sicily also still promotes a real sense of **arrival**. The standard approach for those heading south from the mainland is to cross the Straits of Messina, from Villa San Giovanni or Reggio di Calabria: this way, the train-ferry pilots a course between *Scylla* and *Charybdis*, the twin hazards of rock and whirlpool that were a legendary threat to sailors. Coming in by plane, too, there are spectacular approaches to either of the coastal airports at Palermo and Catania.

Once you're on land, deciding **where to go** is largely a matter of time. Inevitably, most points of interest are on the coast: the interior of the island is often mountainous, sparsely populated and relatively inaccessible. The capital **Palermo** is a memorable first stop, a bustling, noisy city with an unrivalled display of Norman art and architecture and Baroque churches, combined with a warren of medieval streets and markets. From modern and earthquake-ravaged **Messina**, the most obvious trips are to the chic resort of **Taormina** and the lava-built second city of **Catania**. A skirt around the foothills, and even up to the craters of **Mount Etna**, shouldn't be missed, while to the south sit **Siracusa**, once the most important city of the Greek world, and a Baroque group of towns centring on **Ragusa**. The south coast's greatest draw are the Greek temples at **Agrigento**, while inland, **Enna** is typical of the mountain towns that provided defence for a succession of the island's rulers. Close by is

Piazza Armerina and its Roman mosaics, and to the west, most of Sicily's fishing industry – and much of the continuing Mafia activity – focuses on the area around **Trápani**. To see all these places, you'll need at least a couple of weeks – more like a month if you want to travel extensively inland, a slower and more traditional experience altogether.

The Mafia

Whatever else the **Mafia** is, it isn't an organization that impinges upon the lives of tourists, and it's unlikely you'll come into contact with Mafia activity of any kind. That said, the Mafia does exist – and for very real historical and social reasons. But what began as an early medieval conspiracy, to protect the family from oppressive intrusions of the state, has developed along predictable lines. Alongside the endemic poverty, Sicily continues to endure a system of allegiance, preferment and patronage of massive self-perpetuating proportions, from which few local people profit. Most of the towns and villages of western Sicily are tainted, and Palermo and Trápani have been noted Mafia centres for decades. But travellers won't be much aware of the problem, due to the power of *omertà*, the law of silence. All this is not to say that **petty crime** won't make itself felt. Take all the usual precautions concerning your money and valuables, and have extra care in the cities – Palermo and Catania in particular.

Getting around

Getting around Sicily can be a protracted business. **Trains** along the northern and eastern coasts (Messina–Palermo and Messina–Siracusa) are extensions of – or connected with – the "express" trains from Rome/Naples, which means that they are frequently delayed. At least an hour late is normal. Also, Sicily's geographical oddities often conspire to place train stations miles away from the relevant town – check the text for details, and don't expect a rail pass to be as much use as on the mainland. **Buses** are generally quicker though more expensive. There's no single bus company – Interbus, SAIS and AST are the main three – but the local tourist office can point out where to catch what. Pick up timetables wherever you go and, despite the assertions to the contrary, expect there to be little (if any) service anywhere on a Sunday.

SICILY

16

SICILY

999

Égadi Islands

Ferry
Hydrofoil

0   50 km

Palermo and around

Unmistakably the capital of Sicily, **Palermo** is fast, brash, loud and exciting. Here the Sicilian fusion of all things foreign – art, architecture, culture and lifestyle – exists at its most extreme: elegant Baroque cheek by jowl with Arabic cupolas, high fashion shops competing with Byzantine street markets, Vespas parked against Spanish *palazzi*. And all to a background of sputtering, swirling traffic.

You could easily spend two or three days in Palermo without ever leaving the city's limits. But make time for at least one day-trip: the capital has several traditional bolt-holes if you want a break from the bustle, most obviously the heights of **Monte Pellegrino** and the fine beach at **Mondello**. If your interest has been fired by the city's great Norman heritage, you won't want to miss the famous medieval cathedral of **Monreale**, just a few kilometres west; or you might like to take one of the year-round ferries or hydrofoils to **Ústica**, 60km northwest of Palermo – a tiny volcanic island with enough impressive grottoes and coastal walks to occupy any remaining time.

Palermo

In its own wide bay underneath the limestone bulk of Monte Pellegrino, and fronting the broad, fertile Conca d'Oro (Golden Shell) Valley, **PALERMO** is stupendously sited. Originally a Phoenician, then a Carthaginian colony, this remarkable city was long considered a prize worth capturing. Named Panormus (All Harbour), its mercantile attractions were obvious, and under Saracen and Norman rule in the ninth to twelfth centuries Palermo became the greatest city in Europe – famed for the wealth of its court, and peerless as a centre of learning. There are plenty of relics from this era, but it's the rebuilding of the sixteenth and seventeenth centuries that shaped the city as you see it today.

It's worth making Palermo your first stop in Sicily; it's the island's main transport centre, and has Sicily's greatest concentration of sights. Money from Rome and the EU has facilitated the regeneration of the historic centre – the signs are obvious – but the obstacles remain huge. This is partly owing to the age-old system of kickbacks for contracts and tenders to bent politicians and the Mafia, which have creamed off much of the money. One of the few to stand up against this state of affairs was **Leoluca Orlando**, who, following his deposition by his own Christian Democrat party in 1990, went on to found and lead the anti-Mafia and anti-Masonic party, **La Rete**. As Palermo's mayor (1993–2001), his prominence on the national stage forced attention on reform of the city's institutions and reversed the tendency of neglect and decay that had characterized the city for centuries.

The essential sights are all pretty central and easy to cover on foot. Paramount are the hybrid **Cattedrale** and nearby **Palazzo dei Normanni** (Royal Palace), with its superb, mosaic-decorated chapel, the **Cappella Palatina**; the glorious Norman churches of **La Martorana** and **San Giovanni degli Eremeti**; the Baroque opulence of **San Giuseppe dei Teatini** and **Santa Caterina**; and first-class **museums** of art, archeology and ethnography.

1000

This historical jumble of treasures has its downside. Many people have continued to live in their medieval ghettos, unemployment is endemic, the old port largely idle and petty crime commonplace. Don't be paranoid, though: things are not significantly worse than any other European city. By taking the usual precautions, not flashing bulging wallets or cameras around and avoiding any quiet neighbourhood, especially at night, you should feel perfectly safe.

Arrival, information and transport

Palermo's Falcone Borsellino **airport** (☎848.865.643, ⓦ www.gesap.it) is at Punta Raisi, 31km west of the city, from where buses run every thirty minutes into the centre, stopping outside the Politeama Garibaldi theatre on Piazza Ruggero Séttimo, and finally outside the *Hotel Elena*, at the Stazione Centrale; buy your ticket on board. Buses run from 6.45am until the last incoming flight, and journey time is 45 minutes (Prestia & Commandè buses; ☎091.580.457; €4.65). For the return journey, departures are every thirty minutes from 5am to about 9.30pm from outside the *Hotel Elena*, and follow the same route. Taxi fares for the same trip cost around €40 per car.

Trains all pull in at the Stazione Centrale (enquiries ☎848.888.088), at the southern end of Via Roma, close to the cheap accommodation; buses #101 and #102, and two circular minibus services – *linea gialla* and *linea rossa* – connect with the modern city from outside the station.

The majority of the country- and island-wide **buses** (including those in the following list) operate out of Via Paolo Balsamo beside the train station: AST (☎091.680.0031) serves Corleone, Módica and Ragusa; Cuffaro (☎091.616 .1510) Agrigento; Interbus (☎091.304.0900) Catania, Naples, Rome and Siracusa; SAIS (☎091.616.6028, ⓦ www.saisautolinee.it) Naples, Catania, Enna, Piazza Armerina, Messina, Noto and Cefalù; Salemi (☎091.617.5411) Marsala and Mazara del Vallo; Segesta (☎091.616.7919) Rome and Trápani.

All **ferry** and **hydrofoil** services dock at the Stazione Maríttima, just off Via Francesco Crispi, from where it's a ten-minute walk up Via E. Amari to Piazza Castelnuovo; see p.1012 for details of ferry companies and destinations.

Driving in the city is best avoided if possible. Parking attendants will guide you to a space and charge you around €0.60 per hour, and meters are installed over a large part of the centre. Renting a **bike** (see listings) can be an exhilarating alternative; provided you don't hesitate and you always go for the gap, it's perfectly safe.

Information

Palermo's main **tourist office** is at Piazza Castelnuovo 34 (May to mid-July Mon–Fri 8.30am–2pm & 2.30–7pm; mid-July to Sept daily 9am–1pm; October–May Mon–Fri 8.30–11am & 2.30–6pm; ☎091.605.8351, ⓦ www .palermotourism.com); it has free maps of the city and province, a free booklet published every two months (*Agenda*) containing reams of tourist information, including current events and transport information, and also provides a list of accommodation in and around the city. There are two smaller offices at the Stazione Centrale (same hours as above; ☎091.616.5914) and the airport (open for incoming flights; ☎091.591.698). You'll also find numerous information kiosks dotted about the centre. For more complete **city listings** and a rundown of what's on. pick up a copy of the local paper, *Il Giornale di Sicilia*, or look out for the more youth-oriented *Lapis* (free) updated every few weeks.

CENTRAL PALERMO

ACCOMMODATION

Alessandra	6
Cortese	7
Florio	2
Grand Hotel Villa Igiea	1
Letizia	5
Orientale	8
Posta	4
Sausele	9
Sicilia	6
Tonic	3

RESTAURANTS

Bellini	H
Caffé d'Oriente	F
Charleston	A
Trattoria-Pizzeria Enzo	I
Pizzeria Italia	D
Peppino	B
Trattoria dal Pompiere	C
Primavera	G
Santandrea	E

N

Stazione Marittima

Ucciardone Prison

Giardino Inglese

Villino Basile

Teatro Politeama Garibaldi

Bus to Airport

Sant'Ignazio All' Olivella

A La Favorita & Mondello ▲

Museo Mormino ▲

VIA DUCA DELLA VERDURA
VIALE DELLA LIBERTÀ
VIA DI GIARDINO
VIA CONSOLAZIONE
VIA ARCHIMEDE
VIALE ALBANESE
VIA CARINI
VIA LA LUMIA
VIA P. CALVI
VIA G. DAITA
VIA MAZZINI
VIA SPASIMO
VIA CATANIA
VIA MESSINA
VIA CARDUCCI
VIA VILLAFRANCA
VIA PRINCIPE DI VILLAFRANCA
VIA DANTE
VIA LATINI
VIA RUGGERO SETTIMO
VIA VILLAREALE
VIA CAVOUR
VIALE GIARDINARA
VIA CERDA
VIA MARIANO STABILE
VIA PRINCIPE DI GRANATELLI
VIA ROBERTO
VIA AMMIRAGLIO GRAVINA
VIA AMARI
VIA EMERICO AMARI
VIA FRANCESCO CRISPI
CORSO DOMENICO SCINÀ
PIAZZA UCCIARDONE
PIAZZA STURZO
PIAZZA POLITEAMA
PIAZZA RUGGERO SETTIMO
PIAZZA CASTELNUOVO
PIAZZA XIII VITTIME
PIAZZA F. CRISPI
PIAZZA MORDINI
LUPO

La Zisa ▲   ◀ Convento dei Cappuccini   La Cuba & Morreale ▲ (8 km)

La Cala

Porta Felice

Museo delle Marionette

FORO ITALICO

Palazzo Butera

PIAZZA DELLA KALSA

Santa Maria della Catena

Palazzo Chiaramonte

Santa Maria dei Miracoli

Galleria Regionale

Lo Spasimo

Giardino Garibaldi

Palazzo Mirto

San Francesco d'Assisi

La Gancia

LA KALSA

Villa Giulia

CORSO VITTORIO EMANUELE

PIAZZA MARINA

La Magione

Botanical Gardens

VUCCIRIA

San Giorgio

Oratorio di Santa Zita

Oratorio del Rosario

San Domenico

Oratorio di San Lorenzo

Cassa di Risparmio

Palazzo della Cassa di Risparmio

Palazzo Gancì

Palazzo Aiutamicristo

VIA LINCOLN

VIA ARCHIRAFI

Museo Archeologico Regionale

Palazzo delle Poste

Santa Caterina

Municipio

La Martorana

San Cataldo

Palazzo S. Croce

Bus Station

Bus to Airport ★

Stazione Centrale

Teatro Massimo

Quattro Canti

San Giuseppe dei Teatini

Università

Il Gesù

San Nicolò

Carmine

PIAZZA VERDI

Sant'Agostino

PIAZZA PRETORIA

ALBERGHERIA

Cattedrale

Palazzo Sclafani

Palazzo Arcivescovile

Villa Bonanno

Palazzo dei Normanni

Porta Carini

Palazzo di Giustizia

CAPO

Porta Nuova

San Giovanni degli Eremiti

Parco d'Orleans

VIA VOLTURNO

VIA MAQUEDA

VIA ROMA

VIA LINCOLN

CORSO TUKORY

0   100 m

City transport

City buses (AMAT ℡091.350.111, ⓦwww.amat.pa.it) are easy to use, covering every corner of Palermo and stretching out to Monreale and Mondello. There's a flat fare of €0.77 for any number of journeys made within ninety minutes, or you can buy an all-day ticket for €2.58, while tickets for the *linea gialla* and *rossa*, and the *circolare* (which covers the *centro storico*) minibus services cost €0.52 for a day's use – all are available from the AMAT glass booths outside Stazione Centrale, or at the southern end of Viale della Libertà, in *tabacchi*, and wherever else you see the AMAT sign; validate tickets in the machine at the back of the bus the first time you use them. The main city **bus rank** is outside Stazione Centrale and buses run until midnight (11.30pm on Sundays). Otherwise, don't be afraid of jumping into a **taxi** (ranks outside the train station and in other main piazzas, or call ℡091.513.311); just make sure the meter is switched on.

Accommodation

Most of Palermo's budget **hotel accommodation** choices lie on and around the southern ends of Via Maqueda and Via Roma, roughly in the area between Stazione Centrale and Corso Vittorio Emanuele. The drawback of the new **youth hostel** *Baia del Corallo* on Via Plauto (℡091.336.595; €16) is that it's 12km northwest of the city; it's reachable by taking the metro to the Tommaso Natale stop and then bus #628 to the terminus. If you're **camping**, take bus #616 from Piazza Vittorio Veneto (itself reached by #101 or #106 along Viale della Libertà from Piazza Castelnuovo) out to **Sferracavallo**, 13km northwest, where there are two all-year sites: the *Trinacria* on the seafront on Via Barcarello (℡091.530.590) and the cheaper *Ulivi* on Via Pegaso (℡091.533.021).

Alessandra Via Divisi 99 ℡091.617.3958, Ⓕ091.616.5180, ⓦwww.albergoalessandra.com. Small, modern rooms with air-conditioning in a well-maintained building. It's at the corner with Via Maqueda, which means rooms overlook that noisy street. Internet access. ❸

Cortese Via Scarparelli 16 ℡091.331.722. Buried in back streets just a step away from the Ballarò market, it's a ten-minute walk from Via Maqueda and Piazza Pretoria, but it's comfortable, air-conditioned and safe. Follow the signpost down Via dell'Università. ❷

Florio Via Principe di Belmonte 33 ℡ & Ⓕ091.609.0852. On the corner of Piazza Florio and handy for the port, this is a colourful and cosy choice with lots of rugs and plants. ❸

Grand Hotel Villa Igiea Via Belmonte 43 ℡091.543.744, Ⓕ091.547.654, ⓦwww.villaigiea.thi.it. At Acquasanta, 3km north of the city, this classic Art Nouveau building, originally a villa of the Forio family (the first people to put tuna fish into cans), was designed by Ernesto Basile in 1900. It's still sumptuous, and often full, so book ahead. ❾

Letizia Via dei Bottai 30 ℡ & Ⓕ091.589.110, ⓦwww.hotelletizia.com. Each room in this charming hotel, just off Piazza Marina, has its own colour scheme and furnishings. There's an enclosed courtyard for breakfast. ❸

Orientale Via Maqueda 26 ℡091.616.5727. This marble-studded *palazzo* near the station has plenty of atmosphere, but rooms are mostly pokey. No credit cards. ❷

Posta Via Gagini 77 ℡091.587.338, Ⓕ091.587.347. On a street parallel to Via Roma, the hotel is central but quiet with stylish modern rooms and polite service. Garage parking available at €11 per day. ❺

Sausele Via V. Errante 12 ℡091.616.1308, Ⓕ091.616.7525, ⓦwww.hotelsausele.it. Well-kept and secure, this Swiss-managed hotel represents good value though can be noisy at night. Take the first right off Via Oreto, behind the station. Parking costs €8 a night. ❹

Sicilia Via Divisi 99 ℡091.616.8460, Ⓕ091.616.3606, ⓦwww.albergosicilia.com. Pleasantly run and good-value rooms with air-conditioning; those around the small downstairs courtyard are quieter. There's parking nearby (€13). ❸

Tonic Via Mariano Stábile ℡091.581.754, Ⓕ091.585.560. Smart, spacious hotel in the modern town. Caters mainly to the business fraternity and has two rooms for the disabled. ❺

The City

Historical Palermo sits around one central crossroads, the **Quattro Canti**, which is at the core of four distinct quarters. The **Albergheria** and the **Capo** quarter, the latter beyond the cathedral, lie roughly west of Via Maqueda; the **Vucciria** and old harbour of La Cala and the **La Kalsa** lie to the east, closest to the water. You'll find virtually all the surviving ancient monuments and buildings of the city in these areas.

Around the Quattro Canti

Heart of the old city is the **Quattro Canti**, or "Four Corners", erected in 1611: a newly restored and gleaming Baroque crossroads that divides old Palermo into its quadrants. You'll pass this junction many times, and it's worth one turn around to check the tiered statues – respectively a season, a king of Sicily and a patron of the city – in each concave "corner".

On the southwest corner (entrance on Corso Vittorio Emanuele), **San Giuseppe dei Teatini** (Mon–Sat 7.30am–noon & 6–8pm, Sun 8.30am–1pm & 6–8pm), begun in 1612, is the most harmonious of the city's Baroque churches. Inside there's a wealth of detail – especially in the lavish side chapels – given plenty of contrasting space by 22 enormous supporting columns in nave and dome. Outside, across Via Maqueda, is **Piazza Pretoria**, floodlit at night to highlight the nude figures of its great central fountain (currently boarded for restoration), a racy sixteenth-century Florentine design. The piazza also holds the restored *municipio*, plaque-studded and pristine, while towering above both square and fountain is the massive flank of **Santa Caterina** (currently closed for restoration), Sicilian Baroque at its most exuberant, every inch of the enormous interior covered in a wildly decorative, pustular relief-work, deep reds and yellows filling in between sculpted cherubs, Madonnas, lions and eagles.

Piazza Bellini, just around the corner, is the site of two more wildly contrasting churches. The little Saracenic red golfball domes belong to **San Cataldo**, a squat twelfth-century chapel on a palm-planted bank above the piazza (Mon–Fri 9am–3.30pm, Sat 9am–12.30pm, Sun 9am–1pm). Never decorated, it retains a good mosaic floor in an otherwise bare and peaceful interior. The understatement of this little chapel is more than offset by the splendid intricacy of the adjacent **La Martorana** (Mon–Sat 8am–1pm & 3.30–7pm, closes 5.30pm in winter, Sun 8.30am–1pm) – one of the finest survivors of the medieval city. With a Norman foundation, the church received a Baroque going-over – and its curving northern facade – in 1588. Happily, the alterations don't detract from the power of the interior, entered through the slim twelfth-century campanile, which retains its ribbed arches and slender columns. A series of spectacular **mosaics**, animated twelfth-century Greek works, are laid on and around the columns supporting the main cupola. A gentle Christ dominates the dome, surrounded by angels, the Apostles and the Madonna to the sides. Two more original mosaic panels have been set in frames on the walls just inside the entrance to the church: a kneeling George of Antioch (the church's founder) dedicating La Martorana to the Virgin, and King Roger being crowned by Christ – the diamond-studded monarch contrasting with a larger, more dignified Christ.

The Albergheria and the Palazzo dei Normanni

The district just to the northwest of the train station – the **Albergheria** – hasn't changed substantially for several hundred years. A maze of tiny streets and

16

tall leaning buildings, it's an engaging place to wander, much of the central area taken up by a street market that all but conceals several fine churches. Via Ponticello leads down past the Baroque church of **Il Gesù** or **Casa Professa** (Mon–Sat 7.30–11.30am & 5–6.30pm, Sun 7am–12.30pm), the first Jesuit foundation in Sicily and gloriously decorated inside, to **Piazza Ballarò** – along with adjacent **Piazza del Carmine**, the focus of a raucous daily market, with bulging vegetable stalls, unmarked drinking dens and some good snack stalls.

At the westernmost edge of the quarter, over Via Benedettini, is the Albergheria's quietest haven, the deconsecrated church of **San Giovanni degli Eremiti** (Mon–Sat 9am–7pm, Sun 9am–1pm; €4.13) – St John of the Hermits. Built in 1132, it's the most obviously Arabic of the city's Norman relics, with five ochre domes topping a small church that was built upon the remains of a mosque.

From San Giovanni it's a few paces to the main road, where, if you turn right and then veer left up the steps, you'll climb out of the fast traffic to gaze on the vast length of the **Palazzo dei Normanni** or Palazzo Reale (entrance on Piazza Indipendenza). A royal palace has always occupied the high ground here, above medieval Palermo. Originally built by the Saracens, the palace was enlarged considerably by the Normans, under whom it housed the most magnificent of medieval European courts – a noted centre of poetic and artistic achievement. Sadly, there's little left from those times in the current structure. The long front was added by the Spanish in the seventeenth century and most of the interior is now taken up by the Sicilian regional Parliament (which explains the security guards and the limited opening hours). Be prepared to queue.

Of the **Royal Apartments**, the only part now open to the public is happily the most sumptuous, the so-called **Sala di Ruggero** (Mon, Fri & Sat 9am–noon; free guided visit), decorated with lively twelfth-century mosaics of hunting scenes. Descend a floor to the beautiful **Cappella Palatina** (Mon–Fri 9–11.45am & 3–4.45pm, Sat 9–11.45am, Sun 9–9.45am & noon–12.45pm; free), central Palermo's undisputed artistic gem. The private royal chapel of Roger II, built between 1132 and 1143, its interior is immediately overwhelming – cupola, three apses and nave entirely covered in twelfth-century **mosaics** of outstanding quality. As usual, it's the powerful representation of Christ as Pantocrator which dominates the senses, bolstered here by other secondary images – Christ blessing, open book in hand, and Christ enthroned, between Peter (to whom the chapel is dedicated) and Paul. Unlike the bright pictures of La Martorana the mosaics here give a single, effective impression, fully expressing the faith that inspired their creation.

The Cattedrale, the Capo and the modern city

Spanning Corso Vittorio Emanuele, on the far side of the Palazzo dei Normanni, the early sixteenth-century **Porta Nuova** commemorates Charles V's Tunisian exploits, with suitably grim, turbaned figures adorning the western entrance. This gate marked the extent of the late medieval city, and the long road beyond heads to Monreale.

The Corso runs back towards the centre, past the huge bulk of the **Cattedrale** (Mon–Sat 7am–7pm, Sun 8am–1.30pm & 4–7pm; free) – a more substantial Norman relic than the palace. It's an odd building, with the fine lines of the tawny stone spoilt by the late eighteenth century addition of a completely out-of-character dome. Still, the triple-apsed eastern end and the lovely matching towers are all original, dating from 1185. And despite the

Catalan-Gothic facade and arches, there's enough Norman carving and detail to rescue the exterior from mere curiosity value. The same is not true, however, of the inside: it is grand enough but cold and Neoclassical, the only items of interest are the fine portal and wooden doors (both fifteenth century) and the royal **tombs**, containing the mortal remains of some of Sicily's most famous monarchs – including Frederick II and his wife Constance. There's also a **treasury** (daily 9.30am–5.30pm; €2) to the right of the choir, the highlights of which are a jewel- and pearl-encrusted skull cap and three simple, precious rings, all enterprisingly removed from the tomb of Constance of Aragon in the eighteenth century.

From the cathedral you can bear left, around the apses, and up into the **CAPO** quarter, one of the oldest areas of Palermo and another tight web of impoverished streets, unrelieved by space or greenery. Just around the corner from Piazza del Monte is the fine church of **Sant'Agostino** (Mon–Sat 7am–noon & 4–5.30pm, Sun 7am–noon), built in the thirteenth century. Above the main door (on Via Raimondo) there's a gorgeous latticework rose window; inside, some calm sixteenth-century cloisters; and – along Via Sant'Agostino, behind the market stalls – a sculpted fifteenth-century doorway attributed to Domenico Gagini.

The stalls of the clothes **market** (daily 8am to around 8pm) along **Via Sant'Agostino** run all the way down to Via Maqueda and beyond, the streets off to the left gradually becoming wider and more nondescript as they broach the area around the late-nineteenth-century **Teatro Mássimo**. Strictly Neoclassical in style, this is a monumental structure, supposedly the largest theatre in Italy, and beautifully cleaned up after years of closure. To appreciate the interior fully take a tour (every 30min Tues–Sun 10am–3.30pm; €2.60), or attend one of the classical concerts or operas held here between October and June.

The theatre marks the dividing line between old and new Palermo and beyond here there's little that's vital, though plenty that is grand and modern. Via Maqueda becomes **Via Ruggero Séttimo**, which cuts up through the gridded shopping streets to the huge double square made up of **Piazza Castelnuovo** and **Piazza Ruggero Séttimo** (commonly referred to as **Piazza Politeama**). Dominating the whole lot is Palermo's other massive theatre, the **Politeama Garibaldi**, which also houses the city's **Galleria d'Arte Moderna** (Tues–Sat 9am–8pm, Sun 9am–1pm; €3.10) – a vibrant collection of twentieth-century Sicilian art and sculpture. A kilometre or so along Viale della Libertà, the road that strikes north from here, is **Museo Mormino** (Mon–Fri 9am–1pm & 3–7pm; free) where there's a horde of attractive nineteenth-century paintings, a wide representation of Italian majolica, Greek vases, and a splendid Etruscan mirror.

The Vucciria, archeological museum and old harbour

Via Roma, running from Stazione Centrale, is a fairly modern addition to the city, all clothes and shoe shops. It's nothing like as interesting as the parallel Via Maqueda, consisting mostly of tall apartment blocks that conceal hotels, but stick with it as far as the church of Sant'Antonio. Behind here – down the steps – is the sprawling **Vucciria market** (daily 8am to around 8pm): winding streets radiating out from a small enclosed piazza, wet from the ice and waste of the fish stalls and where you'll find a couple of restaurants, some very basic bars and all manner of food and junk on sale.

The northern limit of the market is marked by the distinctive church of **San Domenico** (daily 9am–11.30pm, plus Sat & Sun 5–7pm), with a fine eighteenth-century facade and an interior of tombs containing a host of famous Sicilians. Parliamentarians, poets and painters, they're of little interest to foreigners except to explain the finer points behind Palermitan street naming. The **oratory** behind the church (Oratorio del Rosario; Mon–Fri 9am–1pm & 2–5.30pm, Sat 9am–1pm; free but tipping is usual) contains fine stucco work by Serpotta and a masterful van Dyck altarpiece, painted in 1628 before the artist fled Palermo for Genoa to escape the plague.

From Piazza San Domenico, Via Roma continues north, passing (on the left) Palermo's main post office, the gargantuan **Palazzo delle Poste**. Built by the Fascists in 1933, it's a severe concrete block, with a wide swath of steps running up to ten unfluted columns that run the length and height of the building itself. The grandiosity of the post office is brought down to size by the sixteenth-century convent behind, which now houses the **Museo Archeologico Regionale** (Mon–Fri 8.30am–6.45pm, Sat & Sun 8.30am–1.45pm; €4.50), a magnificent collection of artefacts, mainly from the western half of the island, displayed on three floors. Two cloisters hold anchors and other retrieved hardware from the sea off the Sicilian coast, Egyptian and Punic remains in rooms to either side, and Roman sculpture – notably a giant enthroned Zeus. In rooms at the far end of the cloisters are numerous stelae and other inscribed tablets, and reconstructions of the assembled stone **lion's head water spouts** from the so-called "Victory Temple" at Himera (fifth century BC), the fierce animal faces tempered by braided fur and a grooved tongue which channelled the water. There are also finds from the temple site of Selinunte, on the southwest coast of the island, highpoint of which – indeed of the museum – is the **Salone di Selinunte**, a room that gathers together the richly carved metopes from the various temples. Sculpted panels from the friezes which once adorned the temples, the metopes are appealing works of art depicting lively mythological scenes: the earliest, dating from the sixth century BC, are those representing the gods of Delphi, the Sphynx, the rape of Europa, and Hercules and the Bull. But it's the friezes from Temples C and F that really catch the eye, vivid fifth-century-BC works – such as Perseus beheading the Medusa with a short sword. Upstairs has also plenty to reward a lengthy dawdle: some 12,000 votive terracotta figures, and two bronze sculptures – the life-like figure of an alert ram (third century BC), originally one of a pair, and the glistening, muscular study of Hercules subduing a stag, found at Pompeii. The beautifully preserved Roman mosaics from Piazza della Vittória in Palermo on the second floor are well worth seeing, too.

The juxtaposition of different styles begins again in earnest if you cross back over Via Roma and head towards the water. The church of **Santa Zita** (also known as Santa Cita or San Mamiliano), on quiet Via Squarcialupo, is justly known for its marvellous **oratory** (Mon–Fri 8am–noon, Sat 9am–1pm; ring the bell if closed, or ask in the church in front): repository of one of Serpotta's finest works – the *Battle of Lépanto* – and some rich mother-of-pearl benches. From here streets spread back to the thumb-shaped inlet of the old harbour, **La Cala**. This was once the main port of Palermo, stretching as far inland as Via Roma, but the rot set in during the sixteenth century when silting caused the water to recede to its current position. All the heavy work eventually moved northwards to docks off the remodelled postwar streets, and La Cala now does duty as a yachting marina.

La Kalsa and the Galleria Regionale

This southeastern quarter of old Palermo was worst hit by the war, but after years of decay, it's sloughing off its desolate image, as the numerous cranes and tiers of scaffolding testify. It's here that you'll find some of Palermo's most remarkable buildings and churches, as well as its only central park, **Villa Giulia**, just a few minutes' walk along Via Lincoln from the train station and home to an extensive botanical garden (Mon–Fri 9am–5pm, Sat & Sun 8.30am–1.30pm; €3.50).

Cutting back to Piazza Garibaldi and walking north, turn off down Via Magione for the church of **La Magione** (daily 9.30am–7pm), one of the city's more graceful spots, approached through a palm-lined drive. Built in 1151, the simple, sparse Norman church was subsequently given to the Teutonic knights as their headquarters by Henry VI. The church marks the edge of **La Kalsa** (its name is from the Arabic *khalisa*, meaning "pure"), an area subjected to saturation bombing during World War II, because of its proximity to the port. The worst of the bombsite is now greened over and a popular spot for football practice. Across the square, set back off Via Spasimo, is the complex of Santa Maria dello Spasimo (daily 8am–midnight; free), a former church, now roofless except for its Gothic apse, and an atmospheric night-time venue for jazz concerts.

Beyond Piazza della Kalsa is Via Alloro with, at its seaward end, the **Palazzo Abatellis**, a fifteenth-century palace revamped since the war to house Sicily's **Galleria Regionale** (Mon, Wed, Fri & Sat 9am–1.30pm, Tues & Thurs 9am–1.30pm & 3–7.30pm, Sun 9am–1pm; €4.50), a stunning medieval art collection. Inside, there's a simple split: sculpture downstairs, paintings upstairs, the one exception to which, a magnificent fifteenth-century fresco of the *Triumph of Death*, is displayed in the former chapel, coating an entire wall. It's a chilling study by an unknown (possibly Flemish) painter in which Death is cast as a skeletal archer astride a galloping, spindly horse, trampling bodies planted by his arrows. The other masterpiece on the ground floor is among the works of fifteenth-century sculptor Francesco Laurana (room 4), whose white marble bust of Eleonora of Aragon is a calm, perfectly studied portrait.

Upstairs there's no shortage of excellent Sicilian work, including a four-teenth-century Byzantine mosaic of the Madonna and Child, and paintings and frescoes from the fifteenth century vivid in their portrayal of the coronation of the Virgin, a favourite theme. This floor, too, contains a collection of works by Antonello da Messina (1430–79), including three small portraits of Saints Gregory, Jerome and Augustine and the celebrated *Annunciation*, a placid depiction of Mary, head and shoulders covered, right hand slightly raised.

Via Paternostro, which runs west off Via Alloro, curves north passing the striking thirteenth-century church of **San Francesco d'Assisi** (Mon–Fri 9.30am–5pm, Sat & Sun 9.30am–12.30pm), whose portal, picked out with a zigzagged decoration, is topped by a wonderful rose window. To the side of the church, at Via Immacolatella 5, is the renowned **Oratorio di San Lorenzo** (Mon–Fri 9am–noon), harbouring stucco scenes from the lives of St Lawrence and St Francis by Serpotta.

East of here on Via Merlo is the late eighteenth-century **Palazzo Mirto** (Mon–Sat 9am–7pm, Sun 9am–1pm; €2.50), one of the few *palazzi* in the city to have retained its imposing original fixtures and fittings. Passing through the Giardino Garibaldi and Piazza Marina brings you to Corso Vittorio Emanuele, which runs down to the water and ends in the Baroque gate, **Porta Felice**, begun in 1582 as a balance to the Porta Nuova. The whole area beyond the gate was flattened in 1943, and has since been rebuilt as the ugly **Foro Italico** promenade, from where you can look back over the harbour to Monte Pellegrino. Back beyond the Porta Felice, around the corner from the **Palazzo Chiaramonte**, second largest of Palermo's palaces and ex-headquarters of the Inquisition, is the engaging **Museo delle Marionette** at Via Butera

1 (Mon–Fri 9am–1pm & 4–7pm, Sat 9am–1pm; ⓦ www.museomarionet-
tepalermo.it; €3), the definitive collection of puppets, screens and painted
scenery in Palermo. A traditional Sicilian entertainment, puppet theatres are
now mainly staged for the benefit of tourists. The stories are usually based on
the exploits of the hero Roland (Orlando), a dashing knight in combat against
Saracen invaders, usually culminating in a great battle. It's all great fun, and in
summer the museum puts on free shows (the *Spettácolo dei pupi*), currently on
Fridays at 5.30pm.

The outskirts

The **Museo Etnografico Pitrè** (daily except Fri 8.30am–7.30pm; €3.10) lies
3km north of Piazza Castelnuovo (bus #106 or #806 from Politeama or Viale
della Libertà). Although its main attraction – the brightly painted Sicilian carts
– are currently in the hands of the restorers, you'll still get a good insight into
Sicilian folklore and culture. In addition to a reconstructed puppet theatre,
expressive puppets and scenery backdrops there's a whole series of intricately
worked terracotta figures, dolls and games, bicycles, painted masks and even a
great, flowery iron bedstead.

Tracking down the rest of central Palermo's **Norman relics** entails a bit of
a trek or using public transport. Bus #124 runs west from the Politeama to **La
Zisa** (from the Arabic, *el aziz*, "magnificent"), a huge palace begun by William
I in 1160, with a fine exterior and a rich, well-crafted Islamic interior
(Mon–Sat 9am–7pm, Sun 9am–1.30pm; €2.50). Closer to the centre, about
1km beyond Porta Nuova at Corso Calatafimi 100, is **La Cuba**, the remains
of a slightly later Norman pavilion that formed part of the same royal park as
La Zisa, now tucked inside an army barracks, but well-restored and open to the
public (Mon–Sat 9am–7pm, Sun 9am–1.30pm; €2).

But for real attention-grabbing stuff, take bus #327 from Piazza
Indipendenza southwest along Via dei Cappuccini as far as Via Pindemonte.
Close by, in Piazza Cappuccini, the **Convento dei Cappuccini** (daily
9am–noon & 3–5pm; €1.50, donation to poor also requested) retained its own
burial ground for several hundred years, placing its dead in catacombs under
the church. Later, right up until 1881, others were also interred here. The bodies (some 8000 of them) were preserved by various chemical and drying
processes – including the use of vinegar and arsenic baths – and then placed in
niches along corridors, dressed in suits of clothes provided for the purpose.
Descending into the catacombs is quite unnerving, especially if you arrive in a
lull between coach parties. The rough-cut stone corridors are divided according to sex and status, different caverns reserved for men, women, the clergy,
doctors, lawyers and surgeons. Suspended in individual niches, hand-written
notes about their necks, the bodies have become vile, contorted, grinning figures – some decomposed beyond recognition, others complete with skin, hair
and eyes fixing you with a steely stare; most harrowing are the tiny babies and
children.

Eating

For **snacks**, the *Ferrara*, just to the left of the train station in Piazza Giulio
Cesare, and the *Mediterraneo*, Corso Vittorio Emanuele 244, are reliable options
and you can eat good **ice cream** and snack lunches including *arancini* at
Mazzara, a bar-pasticceria at Via Magliocco 15 (on the corner of Piazza
Ungheria). The *Antico Caffè*, Via Principe di Belmonte 111, is the perfect place

for delectable cakes and ice cream with a piano accompaniment. For authentic Sicilian fast food, *Antica Focacceria San Francesco*, off Corso Vittorio Emanuele at Via A. Paternostro 58, is an old-time place with marble-topped tables within, and outside seating in the square. You can also stock up from the **markets**; best are the Ballarò, in the Albergheria (see p.1005), and the Vucciria, off Via Roma (p.1007). And there's a GS **supermarket** on Piazza Marina (Mon–Sat 8.30am–8.30pm). The most popular restaurants get packed at weekends, full of people intent on a night out rather than just a meal. The recommended restaurant options below range from "Inexpensive" (under €15) to "Moderate" (€15–25), "Expensive" (€25–40) and "Very Expensive" (over €40) according to the amount one person might expect to pay for a full meal including wine and cover charge.

Bellini Piazza Bellini. The best bet for alfresco pizzas; outdoor tables are in the shadow of La Martorana church. Closed Tues. Moderate.

Caffè d'Oriente Piazza Cancellieri. Hidden away at the top of Via Celso (an alley off Via Maqueda near Corso Vittorio Emanuele), this place swims with North African atmosphere. Couscous and other specialities are served in the square. Closed Mon. Moderate.

Charleston Viale Regina Elena, Mondello ☎091.450.171. Palermo's most celebrated high-class restaurant just offshore at Mondello. Formal and stylish, it serves exquisite cuisine, with regular forays into other Italian regions to supplement its Sicilian specialities. Reservations advised. Closed Sun. Very Expensive.

Trattoria-Pizzeria Enzo Via Maurolico 17/19. The city's best bargain for three-course meals – hefty portions and daft prices. Large range of salads. Closed Mon. Inexpensive.

Pizzeria Italia Via Orologio 54 (opposite Teatro

Mássimo). The best place in town for pizzas, attracting large queues. Closed lunchtime except Sun. Inexpensive.

Peppino Piazza Castelnuovo 49. A full restaurant menu is offered alongside some good pizzas. It's touristy, but in a good location. Closed Wed & Aug. Moderate.

Trattoria dal Pompiere Via Bara Olivella 107 (opposite Teatro Mássimo). It's a bit seedy, but the pizzas are spot on. Inexpensive.

Primavera Piazza Bologni 4. Not far from the cathedral, off Via Vittorio Emanuele, with outdoor seating, this is a popular trattoria with home-style cooking. Closed Mon. Moderate.

Santandrea Piazza Sant'Andrea ☎091.334.999. Chic restaurant a stone's throw from Piazza San Domenico and the Vucciria market. There are no menus, dishes are seasonal and generally delicious. Book early to eat alfresco. Closed Tues & Jan. Expensive.

16

Bars and nightlife

The strangest thing about Palermo's fast lifestyle is that it virtually stops at around 8pm. Apart from a perfunctory *passeggiata* between the Teatro Massimo and Piazza Castelnuovo, in most areas everything is quiet outside after dark. In summer, most young people head for Mondello (see overleaf), and buses run there and back till late. Still, for an outdoor, early-evening **drink**, Via Principe di Belmonte is a good spot – closed to traffic, and with several popular places – for coffees and beers. Evening crowds also congregate at the nearby *Bottiglieria del Mássimo*, a wine bar with pavement seating at Via Spinuzza 59, and in the bars on Piazza Olivella, opposite the archeological museum. New bars are opening up just northeast of the Vucciria market; try *I Grilli Giu* on Piazza Cavalieri di Malta for a candlelit cocktail (there's a restaurant above as well).

If it's **discos** and **video bars** you're after, what exists is all in the new, northern section of the city, on Viale Strasburgo and Via Generale Arimondi (beyond the Giardino Inglese).

Listings

American Express Via E. Amari 40 (Mon–Fri 9am–1pm & 4–7pm, Sat 9am–1pm; ☏091.587.144).

Bike rental Kursaal Kahlesa, Foro Umberto I 21 ☏091.616.2828, rents out bikes for €8 a day.

Car rental Avis, Via Francesco Crispi 115 ☏091.586.940; Hertz, Via Messina 7c ☏091.331.668; Maggiore, Viale Alcide de Gásperi 79 ☏091.681.2811; Sicily By Car, Via Mariano Stábile 6a ☏091.581.045. All of these also have desks at Punta Raisi airport.

Consulates Netherlands, Via Roma 489 ☏091.581.521; UK, Via Cavour 117 ☏091.326.412; US, Via Vaccarini 1 ☏091.305.857. For nationals of most other countries, the nearest consulates are in Naples or Rome.

Exchange There are exchange offices open outside normal banking hours at Punta Raisi airport (daily 8am–9pm) and Stazione Centrale (daily 8am–8pm).

Ferry and hydrofoil companies Grandi Navi Veloci (Grimaldi), services to Genoa and Livorno (at the port at Calata Marinai d'Italia; ☏091.587.404, ⓦwww.gnv.it); Siremar, to Ústica (Via F. Crispi 120; ☏091.582.403, ⓦwww.siremar.it); SNAV, to Naples and the Aeolian Islands (Via Principe di Belmonte 55; ☏091.333.333,

ⓦwww.snavali.com); Tirrenia, to Naples, Genoa and Cágliari (at the port on Via Molo; ☏091.602.1111, ⓦwww.tirrenia.it).

Gay and lesbian information ARCI Gay, Via Genova 7 ☏091.335.688.

Hospital Civico Regionale Generale, Via Carmelo Lazzaro ☏091.666.1111. For emergency first aid ☏091.288.141.

Internet access *Aboriginal Internet Café*, Via Spinuzza 51, opposite the Teatro Massimo (Tues–Sun 11am–2pm); *Internet Café*, Via dei Candelai 65 (Tues–Sun from 7pm).

Left luggage Stazione Centrale (daily 6am–10pm; €2.50 per 12hr); Stazione Maríttima (daily 7am–8pm; €1.50 per 24hr).

Pharmacist All-night service at Via Roma 1, Via Roma 207 and Via Mariano Stábile 177. There's also a list in *Il Giornale di Sicilia*.

Police Central city station at Piazza Vittoria ☏091.210.111.

Post office Main post office is the Palazzo delle Poste on Via Roma (Mon–Fri 8am–6.30pm, Sat 8.30am–1.30pm). Poste Restante closes at 1.30pm daily.

Travel agents CTS, Via Garzilli 28 (Mon–Fri 9am–1pm & 4–7.30pm; ☏091.611.0713); Le Vie dei Canti (Mon–Fri 9am–1pm & 4–7.30pm; ☏091.612.1285).

Monte Pellegrino and Mondello

Splitting the city from the bay at Mondello (see below) is **Monte Pellegrino**, to which the ride itself is as good a reason as any to go (bus #812 from the Politeama theatre) – an impressive route through a green belt of trees, cacti and scrub, and with views over Palermo and its plain. The bus drops you at the **Santuario di Santa Rosalia** (daily 7am–8pm), a cave in the hillside where the bones of the city's patron were discovered. A chapel was promptly built over the entrance in 1625: supposedly miraculous water trickles down the walls, channelled and collected by steel plates, and fancy lighting illuminates a bier containing a statue of the saint, around which there's invariably a scrum. A small road to the right of the chapel leads to the summit, a half-hour's walk, affording more splendid views, while paths and trails cover the rest of the mountain top.

If this isn't your bag, the other obvious trip from central Palermo is the short (11km) run to **MONDELLO**, a small seaside resort tucked under the northern bluff of Monte Pellegrino. It features one of Sicily's best stretches of sand (rather than the more usual stones), the two-kilometre beach curving round to a tiny working harbour and the remnants of a medieval tower. There's a line of restaurants overlooking the water and the fish, naturally, is temptingly fresh. Alternatively, you could grab some of the excellent snack food from the water-

△ The Oreccio di Dionigi, Siracusa

front stalls and hit the beach. Although often crowded, summer nights at Mondello are fun – the scene of Palermo's real *passeggiata*. In winter it's more laid-back, and rarely very busy, but the restaurants and snack stalls are still open. To get to Mondello, take bus #806, or #833 in summer, from the Politeama theatre or Viale della Libertà – a half-hour ride.

Monreale

Whether or not you get to mountain or beach, you really shouldn't miss Sicily's most extraordinary medieval mosaics in the cathedral at **MONREALE** (Royal Mountain). This small hill-town, 8km southwest of Palermo, commands unsurpassed views down the Conca d'Oro Valley, with the capital shimmering in the distant bay. Buses #309 and #389 run frequently from Piazza dell'Indipendenza, and the journey up the valley takes twenty minutes. Monreale's Norman **Duomo** (daily 8am–6pm) flanks one side of Piazza Vittorio Emanuele. The rather severe, square-towered exterior – though handsome enough – is no preparation for what's inside: the most impressive and extensive area of Christian medieval mosaic work in the world, the apex of Sicilian-Norman art.

The cathedral, and the town that grew up around it in the twelfth century, both owe their existence to young King William II's rivalry with his powerful Palermitan archbishop, the Englishman Walter of the Mill. William endowed a new monastery in his royal grounds in 1174; the abbey church – this cathedral – was thrown up in a matter of years. This haste accounts for the splendid uniformity of the cathedral's galaxy of coloured mosaics, all bathed in a golden background.

The **mosaics** were almost certainly executed by Greek and Byzantine craftsmen, and they reveal a unitary plan and inspiration. What immediately draws your attention is the all-embracing half-figure of Christ in benediction in the central apse: an awesome and pivotal mosaic, the head and shoulders alone almost twenty metres high. Underneath sit an enthroned Madonna and Child, attendant angels and, below, ranks of saints, each individually and subtly coloured and identified by name. Worth singling out here is the figure of Thomas à Becket (marked *SCS Thomas Cantb*), canonized in 1173, just before the mosaics were begun, and presumably included as a show of support by William for the papacy. The nave mosaics are no less remarkable, an animated series that starts with the Creation (to the right of the altar) and runs around the whole church. Most scenes are instantly recognizable: Adam and Eve, Abraham on the point of sacrificing his son, a positively jaunty Noah's Ark; even the Creation, shown in a set of glorious, simplistic panels portraying God filling his world with animals, water, light . . . and people.

Ask at the desk by the entrance to climb the **tower** (daily 9.30am–noon & 3.30–5.30pm; €1) in the southwest corner of the cathedral. The steps give access to the roof and leave you standing right above the central apse – an unusual and precarious vantage point. It's also worth visiting the **cloisters** (Mon–Sat 9am–7pm, Sun 9am–1pm; €4.50), part of William's original Benedictine monastery. The formal garden is surrounded by an elegant arcaded quadrangle, 216 twin columns supporting slightly pointed arches – a legacy of the Arab influence. No two capitals are the same, each a riot of detail and imagination: armed hunters doing battle with winged beasts; flowers, birds, snakes and foliage. Entrance to the cloisters is from Piazza Guglielmo, in the corner by the right-hand tower of the cathedral.

Ústica

A volcanic, turtle-shaped island 60km northwest of Palermo, **ÚSTICA** is one of the more appealing destinations for a quick jaunt away from the city. Colonized originally by the Phoenicians, the island took its name from the Latin *ustum*, or "burnt", a reference to its blackened, lava-strewn appearance. Exposed and isolated, it had a rough time throughout the Middle Ages, its scant population repeatedly harried by pirates who used the island as a base. Even as late as the 1890s the few inhabitants were nearly all exiled prisoners. Today, Ústica's fertile uplands are just right for a day's ambling, while the rough coastline is touted as a skin-diver's paradise, the clear water bursting with fish, sponges, weed and coral. Less adventurous types can easily take a boat trip through Ústica's rugged grottoes and lava outcrops.

The little port of **ÚSTICA TOWN**, where the boats dock, features nothing much besides a few bars, a bank, a dozen restaurants and a handful of places to stay. All these facilities sit around a sloping double piazza, just five minutes' walk uphill from the harbour. **Ferries** and **hydrofoils** operate roughly once or twice daily from Palermo (from the Stazione Maríttima): the cheapest summer passage is around €10.80 one-way by ferry, rising to €16 on the hydrofoils. (Tickets are from Siremar – see "Listings" for Palermo, p.1012). Ústica town has a couple of good **hotel** choices: the attractive *Clelia*, at Via Magazzino 7 (T091.844.9039, W www.hotelclelia.it; ❹), with a roof terrace overlooking the sea, and the more basic but friendly *Ariston*, Via della Vittoria 5 (T091.844.9042, F091.844.9335, ❸), which can arrange diving and boat trips. Alternatively, ask about **private rooms** at the *Bar Centrale* on the piazza, or look for *camere* signs. An excellent and central place to **eat** is *Da Mario*, opposite the *Bar Centrale*, a small, simple trattoria where superb fish dinners with wine cost around €20, or if you want a view, dine at *La Luna sul Porto* below the piazza and above the port on Via Vittorio Emanuele (closed Tues).

The Tyrrhenian coast

From Palermo, the whole of the rugged **Tyrrhenian coast** is accessible by rail and road, offering at times a spectacular ride past deserted coves and rocky beaches. The first real attraction is **Cefalù**, a beach resort and cathedral town. There are few essential stops beyond, though the quiet seaside towns further east are all nice enough for a short break. Also, buses run inland from the larger resorts, providing access to the northern **mountain chains**, the Madonie and the Nebrodi, with their quiet hill-towns. Unfortunately, the easternmost part of the coast, around **Milazzo** – Sicily's second-largest port – is fairly grim and industrial. However, there's an easy escape route to the desolate **Aeolian Islands**, visible from much of the Tyrrhenian coast and reached by ferries and hydrofoils from Milazzo, hydrofoils from Messina, and, during the summer, hydrofoils from Palermo and Cefalù.

Cefalù

Despite the recent attentions of Club Med and a barrage of modern building outside town, **CEFALÙ** remains a fairly small-scale fishing port, partly by virtue of its geographical position – tucked onto every available inch of a shelf of land beneath a fearsome crag, La Rocca. Roger II founded a mighty cathedral here in 1131 and, as befitting one of the most influential early European rulers, his church dominates the skyline, the great twin towers of the facade rearing up above the flat roofs of the medieval quarter. Naturally, it's the major attraction in town, but most visitors are equally tempted by Cefalù's fine curving sands – the main reason why the holiday companies have moved in in such great numbers in recent years. Still, it's a pleasant town, and nothing like as developed as Sicily's other package resort of Taormina.

Halfway along Corso Ruggero, the main pedestrianized road through the old town, stands the **Duomo** (daily: summer 8am–noon & 3.30–7pm; winter closes 5pm) built – partly at least – as Roger's thanks for fetching up at Cefalù's safe beach in a violent storm. Inside, covering the apse and presbytery, are the earliest and best-preserved of the Sicilian church mosaics, dating from 1148. The **mosaics** follow a familiar pattern. Christ Pantocrator dominates the central apse, underneath is the Madonna flanked by archangels, and then the Apostles. Although minuscule in comparison with those at Monreale (see p.1014), these mosaics are just as appealing and, most interestingly, display a quite marked artistic tradition. Forty years earlier than those in William's cathedral, they are thoroughly Byzantine in concept: Christ's face is elongated, the powerful eyes set close together, the outstretched hand flexed and calming.

In high season, when Cefalù's tangibly Arabic central grid of streets is crowded with tourists, you'd do best to visit the cathedral early in the morning, before succumbing to the lure of the long sandy **beach** beyond the harbour. There are a couple of other places that are also worth venturing to: the **Museo Mandralisca** (daily: 9am–7pm €4), at Via Mandralisca 13 (across from Piazza Duomo), has a wry *Portrait of an Unknown Man* by the fifteenth-century Sicilian Master Antonello da Messina and a huge shell collection; and **La Rocca**, the mountain above the town, holds the megalithic so-called Tempio di Diana, from where paths continue right around the crag, inside medieval walls, to the sketchy fortifications at the very top. If you want to stay over, best priced **accommodation** is the small *Locanda Cangelosi*, centrally placed at Via Umberto I 26 (☏0921.421.591; no credit cards; ❷). Pricier are the very pleasant *Pensione delle Rose* (☏ & Ⓕ0921.421.885; half-board in July & Aug; ❸), at Via Gibilmanna, twenty minutes out of town along Umberto I, where some of the rooms have private terraces, and *La Giara*, in the heart of the old town at Via Veterani 40 (☏0921.421.562, Ⓕ0921.422.518; ❺), well-equipped, with an affable management and a big terrace. The best place to **eat** on a budget is the *Arkade Grill*, off Corso Ruggero at Via Vanni 9 (closed Thurs in winter), which offers a good-value tourist menu in summer; a hike up in price is the elegant *L'Antica Corte*, Corso Ruggero 193 (☏0921.423.228; closed Thurs). The **tourist office** is at Corso Ruggero 77 (Mon–Sat 8am–2.30pm & 3.30–8pm, Sun 9am–1pm; ☏0921.421.050, Ⓦwww.cefalu-tour.pa.it) and has free maps and accommodation lists. There are three **hydrofoils** a week to the Aeolian Islands from mid-June to mid-September.

Tíndari and the coast to Milazzo

East of Cefalù the train stops at several small seaside resorts, including **SANTA STEFANO DI CAMASTRA**, a ceramics town, and another 30km on, the fishing village of **SANT'AGATA DI MILITELLO**, popular with Italian holidaymakers. Further down the coast, rounding the cape, you'll find good **beaches** at Capo d'Orlando itself and also at **Oliveri**. From **Patti**'s main square you can catch a bus (3 daily) to Tíndari and the best site of this stretch of coast, the ruins of ancient **Tyndaris** (daily 9am–1hr before sunset; €2). Founded in 396 BC, it was one of the last Greek settlements in Sicily and retains its Greek walls. Most of the remains, though, are Roman, including some house ruins and a beautifully situated theatre.Visible on the hilltop as you approach the site is the **Santuario della Madonna Nera** (Mon–Sat 6.45am–12.30pm & 2.30–7pm, Sun 12.30–8pm), a lavishly kitsch temple built in the 1960s, where pilgrims come for the Byzantine Black Madonna. From here there's a marvellous seaward view to the tongue of white sand and the Marinella lagoons.

Milazzo

At the base of a thin spit of land poking into the Tyrrhenian Sea, **MILAZZO** is not the sort of place you're likely to make a beeline for. Disfigured by a giant oil refinery, the coast around is noisy and smelly. However, it's the main port of departure for the **Aeolian Islands** (see box below for details of sailings), which means, at best, a couple of hours in town awaiting the ferry/hydrofoil – at worst a night in one of the **hotels**. Near the dock, try the *Central*,Via del Sole 8 (T090.928.1043; no credit cards; ❸), a cheery little place with shared bathrooms, or the *California*, opposite, at Via del Sole 9 (T090.922.1389; no credit cards; ❷), which has rooms with private facilities. More upmarket is *La Bussola*, Via XX Luglio 29 (T & F090.928.2955; ❹), which is opposite the Mylarum 2 **garage**, a secure place to leave your car if you're heading for the islands (€7.75 per day). The local favourite for fish **meals** is *Il Covo del Pirata*, Lungomare Garibaldi 47–48 (closed Wed except Aug), while good for pizzas is *Da Tonino*, at Via Cavour 27 (closed Thurs in winter), right in the centre. **Buses** (including the Giuntabus service from Messina) stop on the quayside. The **train station** is 3km south of the centre, but local buses run into town every

16

Getting to the Aeolian Islands

Sailings **from Milazzo** operate daily and are frequent enough to make it unnecessary to book (unless you're taking a car), although bear in mind that there is a reduced service between October and May – and that even moderately rough weather can disrupt the schedules. The **shipping agencies** are down by the harbour and open usual working hours as well as just before all departures – Siremar (Via dei Mille 19; T090.928.3242, W www.siremar.it) for ferries and hydrofoils, SNAV (Via dei Mille 33; T090.928.7821, W www.snavali.com) for hydrofoils only, and NGI (Via dei Mille 26; T090.928.3415) for ferries only. Hydrofoils are more frequent and twice as quick, but almost twice the price of the ferries: Milazzo to Lípari costs around €6 one way on the ferry, €10 on the hydrofoil.

There are summer services, too, from **Naples** and **Reggio di Calabria** on the Italian mainland; elswhere in Sicily, services run from **Messina** and, in summer, **Palermo** and **Cefalù** (see "Travel details", p.1060, for an outline of schedules and crossing times).

thirty minutes during the day, dropping you on the quayside or further up in Piazza della Repubblica. Milazzo's helpful **tourist office** is at Piazza Duilio 20 (Mon–Fri 8am–2pm & 3–6.30pm, Sat 8am–2pm; ☎090.922.2865, ⓦwww.aastmilazzo.it), just back from the harbour.

If there's time to kill, you might like to poke around the restored **Castle** (guided tours hourly Tues–Sun: June–Aug 10am–noon & 5–7pm; Sept–May 10am–noon & 3–5pm; €2.50), which sits inside a much larger and older walled city, complete with its own cathedral.

The Aeolian Islands

Volcanic in origin, the **Aeolian Islands** lead a precarious existence in the buffeted waters off the northern Sicilian coast. They are named after Aeolus, the Greek god who kept the winds he controlled shut tight in one of the islands' many caves. According to Homer, Odysseus put into the Aeolians and was given a bag of wind to help him home, but his sailors opened it too soon and the ship was blown straight back to port. More verifiably, the islands were coveted for their mineral wealth, the mining of obsidian (hard, glass-like lava) providing the basis for early prosperity. Later their strategic importance attracted the Greeks, who settled on Lípari in 580 BC. The Greeks' powerful fleet kept rivals at bay until the islands fell to the Carthaginians, who in turn were pushed out by the Romans in 252 BC. Thereafter began a period of decline: the islands became a haven for pirates and a place of exile, a state of affairs that continued right into the twentieth century with the Fascists exiling their political opponents to Lípari.

It's only comparatively recently that the islanders stopped scratching a subsistence living and started welcoming tourists. Emigration had virtually depopulated some of the islands, and even now the more remote ones are sorely stretched to maintain a decent living. That said, you won't be alone if you come to the islands during the summer months: the central group of Vulcano, Lípari, Panarea and Salina are pretty well known to an increasing crowd of devotees. Lípari, particularly, is expensive in high season. But get out to the minor isles or come in blustery winter for a taste of what it was like twenty – or a hundred – years ago: unsophisticated, rough and beautiful.

Getting there is easiest from Milazzo (see box overleaf), with year-round ferries and hydrofoils connecting the port with all the islands. **Getting around** in summer is easy, as ferries (*traghetti*) and hydrofoils (*aliscafi*) link all the islands. In winter, services are reduced and in rough weather cancelled altogether, particularly on the routes out to Alicudi and Filicudi. You can take cars to Lípari and Salina, but bikes are better and you can rent them on the spot.

In high season (Easter and July/August), **accommodation** is scarce and you'd be wise to phone in advance, especially if you want to visit Strómboli. You may also find that many places insist that you pay for **half-board**. Most hotels and *pensioni* drop their prices by up to fifty percent from October to March, while **renting apartments** or **private rooms** is an economical option too. There are **campsites** on Vulcano, Lípari and Salina – but note that camping rough is illegal. **Restaurants** can be expensive, since much of the food (as well as much of the water on some islands) has to be imported. In many places there's not always the option of a cheap pizzeria, so if money is tight, expect to do some self-catering.

There are **banks** on Lípari, Salina and Vulcano (summer only), and you can change money in post offices, travel agencies and major hotels throughout the islands, but the rates aren't good. **Electricity** has only slowly come to some islands, and if you're spending any time on Alicudi, Filicudi or Strómboli, a torch isn't a bad investment. Don't be surprised if hotels ask you to go sparingly with the **water**.

Vulcano

Closest to the Sicilian mainland, **VULCANO** is the first port of call for ferries and hydrofoils – around an hour and a half on the slowest crossing. From the harbour of **PORTO DI LEVANTE** you can walk up to the main crater of the volcano in around an hour: the last volcanic explosion here was in 1890. A second hike is to **Vulcanello**, the volcanic pimple just to the north of the port, spewed out of the sea in 183 BC, and there's good walking to be had around the rest of the island, too. Less energetically, just fifteen minutes' walk from Porto di Levante, across the neck of land separating it from Porto di Ponente, there's an excellent black-sand **beach**. On the way you'll pass Vulcano's sulphurous mud baths and hot springs bubbling into (and warming) the sea. If you opt for a wallow in the mud, be warned you'll reek of it for days afterwards, and don't wear any jewellery, because it will be stained and corroded.

A summer-only **tourist office** operates at Porto di Levante (June–Sept daily 8am–2pm; ☎090.985.2028) and has information on **rooms**. There isn't a huge choice, but *La Giara* at Via Provinciale 18 is welcoming and quiet (☎090.985.2229, ℱ090.985.2451, ℗www.netnet.it/pensionelagiara; ❻; closed Nov–March), or there's the functional *Torre*, in the piazzetta near the mud baths (☎090.985.2342; no credit cards; ❹). On the Porto Ponente side, *Residence Lanterna Bleu* (☎ & ℱ090.985.2178; ❹; closed mid-Dec to mid-Jan) is a series of one- and two-bedroom apartments with kitchen. The cost of **food** on the island is exorbitant, and you have to choose carefully from the battery of restaurants along the road that bends around from the port. *Da Maurizio* (closed Nov–Easter), just beyond the Siremar agency, has a nice shady garden and a reasonable tourist menu on offer, while *Il Palmento* (closed Nov–Easter), just up from the mud baths, isn't bad for pizzas. A more upmarket choice is the *Belvedere* (☎090.985.3047; closed Nov–Easter) in the Piano district.

Lípari

There are regular, daily hydrofoil services from Vulcano on to **Lípari**, by far the most popular of the islands – and the most diverse. The group's main port and capital, **LÍPARI TOWN** is a thriving little place prettily bunched between two harbours, **arrival** at which is one of *the* island experiences: hydrofoils dock at the Marina Corta, a tiny harbour formed by a church-topped mole and dwarfed by the castle that crowns the hill above; ferries steam straight past, around the mighty sixteenth-century walls of the fort, to dock at the Marina Lunga, a deep-water harbour curving around to the north as a long beach.

The upper town within the fortress walls, the **Castello**, forms the main focus of interest. Finds from the site, which has been continuously occupied since Neolithic times, have enabled archeologists to date other Mediterranean cultures. Alongside the well-marked **excavations**, there's a tangle of dilapidated churches flanking the main cobbled street, and several buildings (including the seventeenth-century bishop's palace) that make up the separate arms of the **Museo Eoliano** (daily: summer 9am–1.30pm, classical section also 3–7pm; winter 9am–1.30pm, classical section also 3–6pm; €4.50) – a lavish collection of Neolithic pottery, late Bronze Age artefacts, and decorated Greek and

Roman vases and statues, most of it dug up outside. Highlights are the towering banks of amphorae, a stunning array of Greek theatrical masks, and statuettes of dancers and actors – early Greek pin-ups. Down below, the streets wind around the base of the fortified hill and down to the harbours. The town is reliant upon tourism these days – as the restaurants and craft shops testify – but it's all fairly small-scale.

The **tourist office** at Corso Vittorio Emanuele 202 (July & Aug Mon–Sat 8am–2pm & 4–10pm; Sept–June Mon–Fri 8am–2pm & 4.30–7.30pm, Sat 8am–2pm; ☎090.988.0095, ⓦwww.netnet.it/aasteolie) can provide the useful *Ospitalità in blu* booklet, which contains a list of hotels and information for all the Aeolian islands. In July and August it makes sense to listen to the offers of **rooms** as you step off the boat. Expect to pay around €25–40 per person in August, €20 at other times of the year, for something with a shower, kitchen and balcony or terrace. Otherwise, good places to try include *Enza Marturano*, Via Maurolico 35 (☎368.322.4997 or 090.981.2544; no credit cards; ❸), whose four bright rooms are ranged around a communal lounge/kitchen; *Enzo Il Negro*, Via Garibaldi 29 (☎090.981.3163; closed Dec; ❹), a roomy place with a roof terrace near the hydrofoil port; *Diana Brown* at Vico Himera 3 (☎090.981.2584, ⓕ090.981.3213, ⓔdbrown@net.net.it; no credit cards; ❹), a spotlessly clean place with fridges and kettles and a book exchange, run by a South African expat; and the *Neri*, Via G. Marconi 43 (☎090.981.1413, ⓕ090.981.3642, ⓦwww.pensioneneri.it; closed mid-Nov to Feb; ❻), a fine old mansion that serves breakfast on a lovely terrace. The nearest **campsite**, *Baia Unci* (☎090.981.1909; mid-March to mid-Oct), is 3km away at the southern end of the fishing village of Canneto (see below); the bus from Lípari stops outside. There's an UPIM **supermarket** and various *alimentari* and bakeries on the main Corso.

The town's numerous **restaurants and pizzerias** have (often poor) tourist menus at around €10–15; even the cheaper places impose exorbitant 15 or 20 percent service charges that'll boost your bill. *Bartolo*, Via Garibaldi 53 (closed Fri in autumn & spring, & Dec–March), has great wood-fired pizzas, while *Trattoria d'Oro*, Via Umberto I, 32 (closed Oct–Dec), and *A Sfiziusa*, Via Roma 29 (closed Fri Oct–June), are both decent backstreet trattorias. For a gastronomic treat, the expensive *E'Pulera*, Via Diana (☎090.981.1158; closed mid-Oct to mid-May), specializes in traditional Aeolian food and is set in a romantic courtyard-garden.

The **rest of the island** is easy to reach on a network of regular **buses**, which leave from a stop by the Marina Lunga, opposite the service station. Around here too are a couple of **scooter and bike rental** outfits, such as Da Marcello, Via Sottomonastero (☎090.981.1234), which charges €18 (€42 in Aug) a day for scooters and €10 a day for bikes; Lípari is a good place to book a **boat excursion**: the main agencies are Viking, Vico Himera 3 (☎090.981.2584 or 338.640.7572), also with a kiosk at the Marina Corta; and La Cava, Corso Vittorio Emanuele 124 (☎090.981.1242). Typically, you'll pay around €34 for an all-day trip which lets you visit and swim off Panarea and then see the evening explosions off Strómboli; day-trips to Panarea or Vulcano, allowing plenty of swimming, are around half that price.

CANNETO, a fishing village with a pebbled beach and a couple of hotels, also makes a pleasant excursion. From here the road climbs north, passing an excellent sandy beach (the Spiaggia Bianca) a couple of kilometres out of Canneto, before reaching the stony beach at **Porticello**. West of Lípari, the road clambers up the hill to **Quattrocchi** ("Four Eyes"), a three-kilometre hike that ends in glorious and much-photographed views over Vulcano and the spikey *faraglioni* rocks that puncture the sea between the two islands. Keep on the road to **Pianoconte**, which has a couple of pizza restaurants that are popular in the evenings, and just after the village, a side road slinks off down to the old Roman thermal baths at **San Calógero**. This is a particularly fine walk, across a valley and skirting some impressive cliffs. It takes about half-an-hour from Pianoconte.

Salina

North of Lípari, **Salina**'s two extinct volcanic cones rise out of a fertile land which produces capers and white *malvasia* wine by the bucketload. Again, it's excellent walking country (though there are bus services between the main villages) and you get some marvellous vantage points over the other islands.

The main island port is **SANTA MARINA DI SALINA**, on the east coast, visually unexciting but a relaxed enough spot to linger awhile. You can find **private rooms** here if you ask around, or try *Catena de Pasquale* at Via Francesco Crispi 17 (☎090.984.3094; no credit cards; ❸). Of the **hotels** and *pensioni*, you're most likely to find room at the very nicely furnished *Mamma Santina*, Via Sanità 40 (☎090.984.3054, ℻090.984.3051, ⓦwww.mammasantina.it; ❽), signposted to the left off the main street of Via Risorgimento, but half- or full-board is the requirement here. The *Portobello* **restaurant** above the port (closed Wed in winter & all Nov) serves excellent local antipasto, slabs of swordfish and wine by the carafe. **LINGUA**, 3km south, makes a pleasant alternative base, with accommodation at '*A Cannata* (☎ & ℻090.984.3161, ⓦwww.netnet.it/salina/cannata; ❸), near the church, where some of the rooms come with a terrace and wonderful views of Lípari; and *Il Delfino*, right on the *lungomare* at Via Garibaldi 19, with attractive rooms attached to its locally renowned restaurant (☎090.984.3024, ℻090.984.3298; ❷). Half-board is compulsory at both in July and August.

Trails cut right across Salina, in particular linking Santa Marina with the peak of **Monte Fossa delle Felci** (962m), the sanctuary of Madonna del Terzito and the south coast at Rinella. Take the bus to the sanctuary – any between Santa Marina/Malfa and Leni/Rinella pass right by it – and start there, saving yourself the first three hundred metres of climbing. Don't go overloaded, wear strong shoes, and take plenty of water.

Most ferries and hydrofoils also call at the little port of **RINELLA**, on the island's south coast; if you want to move straight on, **buses** meet the boat arrivals on the quayside (and call here several times a day in addition). Notices at the port advertise **rooms** for rent and there's a nice little **hotel**, too, *L'Ariana* (☎090.980.9075, ℻090.980.9250, ⓦwww.hotelariana.it; half-board in Aug; closed mid-Nov & Dec; ❺), above the port to the left. The village is also the site of the island's one **campsite**, *Tre Pini* (☎090.980.9155; May–Sept), with a bar-restaurant.

Panarea

Panarea, to the east, is the smallest of the Aeolians but easily the most scenic. Only 3km by 1.5km, no cars can squeeze onto the island's narrow lanes to disturb the tranquillity, though heavily laden three-wheelers are common. Indeed, Panarea's cosy intimacy has made it into something of a ghetto for the idle rich. Nevertheless, either side of high season you can find reasonably priced accommodation if you persevere. Panarea's population divides itself among three hamlets on the eastern side of the island, Ditella, San Pietro and Drauto, with the boats docking at **SAN PIETRO**. It's always worth asking around for rented rooms – *Trattoria da Francesco* (☎090.983.3023; no credit cards; half-board in Aug; ❸) on the harbourside and several houses on Via San Pietro, up from the port, oblige – but bear in mind that the supply of accommodation on the island simply can't meet the demand in July and August. The two cheapest **hotels** are the *Casa Rodà* (☎090.983.006, ℱ090.983.212; closed Oct–March; ❺) and the *Tesoriero* (☎090.983.098, ℱ090.983.007, ⓦwww.hoteltesoriero.it; closed mid-Oct to mid-March; ❼), both on Via San Pietro. For a splurge, you could try one of the two more luxurious hotels at San Pietro, the *Raya* (☎090.983.013, ℱ090.983.103, ⓦwww.hotelraya.it; ❾; closed Nov–March), on a hill to the left, or the nearby *Cincotta* (☎090.983.014, ℱ090.983.211; ❽; closed Nov–Easter): both have wonderful terraces and facilities, and rates plummet outside high season. The hotels also house Panarea's best **restaurants**, though you can eat more modestly by the harbour at *Trattoria da Francesco*, while *Casa Rodà* has a garden-restaurant serving pizzas in the evenings (both closed in winter).

Half an hour's walk south of San Pietro is the island's one sandy **beach** and, high above here on the other side, **Punta Milazzese**, where a Bronze Age village of 23 huts was discovered in 1948. The site is thought to have been inhabited since the fourteenth century BC, and pottery found here (displayed in Lípari's museum) shows a distinct Minoan influence. Elsewhere, there are hot springs at San Pietro and, at **CALCARA** to the north, a beach and sea that sometimes steam – one effect of the island's fumaroles.

Strómboli

Despite the regularity of the volcanic explosions, people have always lived on **Strómboli**. Usually, little more than flashes and noise are thrown up, though sometimes the explosions are more serious, as in January 2003, when a burst of gas sent rocks into the sea and caused a tidal wave. A constant flow of lava is always to be seen, slowly sliding down the northwest side of the volcano into the sea. Most of the many hotels and rooms to let on the island are on the eastern side, in the adjacent parishes of San Vincenzo, San Bartolo and Piscità, often grouped together as **STRÓMBOLI** town and something of a chic resort since Rossellini and Ingrid Bergman immortalized the place in the 1949 film *Strómboli*. From the quayside, the lower coastal road runs around to the main beaches of **Ficograndi** and, further on, **Piscità**, the island's best ashy beach. It's around 25 minutes on foot from the port to here. The other road from the dock cuts up into the "village", where as Via Roma it runs to the church of **San Vincenzo**, whose square offers glorious views of the offshore islet of **Strombolicchio**. Beyond the square, along Via Vittorio Emanuele III, it's another fifteen minutes' walk to the second church of **San Bártolo**, above Piscità.

In summer, the quayside is thick with three-wheelers and touts from the various rooms places waving cards; prices start at around €25 per person. If you want to try and book a **room** in advance, the following places are all worth contacting: *Villa Petrusa*, Via Soldato Panettieri 4 (☎090.986.045, ℱ090.986.126; closed Nov–March; ❺), with an attractive garden, or further out, the friendly *Pensione Brasile*, Via Soldato Cincotta, in the Piscità district (☎090.986.008, ⓦwww.pensionebrasile.it; closed Nov–March; ❸), where half-board is required in July and August, and the *Casa del Sole*, at Via Soldato Cincotta (☎ & ℱ090.986.017; closed Nov–Easter; no credit cards; ❷), which has kitchen facilities and a sun terrace. The best **restaurant** in the village is *Il Canneto* (closed Oct–Easter), up from the port, though you'll find cheaper fare and good **pizzas** further up the road at *La Trottola*, a popular place where you can eat for well under €25 (closed Oct–Easter, though pizzas available in winter at weekends). At night, there's no better spot for lingering than *Bar Ingrid*, in the square by San Vincenzo church, open until late.

On the other side of the island, the hamlet of **GINOSTRA** is a peaceful place of typical white Aeolian houses on terraces. There's excellent accommodation here, too, at the *Locanda Petrusa* (☎ & ℻090.981.2305; closed Oct–April; half-board in July & Aug; no credit cards; ❸), which has three spacious rooms with terraces and a shared bathroom, and also serves meals. **Hydrofoils** run back to Strómboli three times a day in summer (three a week in winter), but these are susceptible to cancellation because of rough waters.

Guides for the **ascent of the volcano** (depending on the level of activity) are readily available in Strómboli village and cost around €20 per person. The climb up takes three hours; you get an hour or so at the top watching the pyrotechnics, and it then takes another two hours to descend. Although there are signs suggesting otherwise, many people make the hike alone: it's not dangerous provided you stick to the marked paths. The **route** starts a few minutes' walk beyond San Bártolo church (see opposite), where a fork bears left and then climbs upwards for an easy forty minutes to *L'Osservatorio*, a bar-pizzeria (closed in winter) with a wide terrace and a view of the volcano. Beyond this point, you'll need to be properly equipped: good shoes, a sunhat and plenty of water (a minimum of two litres per person) are essential. If you intend to spend the night at the top take a sweater, waterproofs, groundsheet, sleeping bag, torch and food, and bed down in one of the lava shelters until dawn. Do not, under any circumstances, come down in the dark without a guide, and if it clouds over or starts to rain heavily, stay put until it clears.

The main **boat trips** offered are tours around the island, calling at Ginostra and Strombolicchio (3hr; €13); and trips out at night to see the Sciara del Fuoco by boat (1hr; €13). A friendly outfit is run by Pippo – of Società Navigazione Pippo (☎090.986.135 or 338.985.7883) – who has a stand in front of the *Beach Bar*.

The Ionian coast: Messina to Siracusa

It's Sicily's eastern **Ionian coast** which draws most visitors, attracted by some of the island's most exciting sights – natural and constructed. The most likely arrival point is **Messina**, which receives a constant stream of ferries bearing trains across the Straits from Calabria. **Taormina**, most chic of the island's resorts and famed for its remarkable Graeco-Roman theatre, is an hour's train ride south, and lava-built **Catania**, Sicily's second city, is another hour beyond: both places (indeed the whole of this part of the coast) are dominated by the massive presence of **Mount Etna**, Europe's highest volcano. A road and a narrow-gauge, single-track railway circumnavigate the lower slopes of Etna, passing through a series of hardy towns surrounded by swirls of black rock spat from the volcano. Further south, out of the lee of Etna, lie traces of the ancient Greek cities that once lined the southeastern coast. **Megara Hyblaea** has the most extensive remains, and the route concludes in **Siracusa** – formerly the most important and beautiful city in the Hellenistic world.

Messina and south

MESSINA may well be your first sight of Sicily; and – from the ferry – it's a fine one, the glittering town spread up the hillside beyond the sickle-shaped harbour. Sadly, the image is shattered almost as soon as you step into the city, bombed and shaken to a shadow of its former self by a record number of disasters. Plague, cholera and earthquakes all struck throughout the eighteenth and nineteenth centuries, culminating in the great earthquake of 1908 that killed 84,000 people, levelled the city and made the shore sink by half a metre overnight. Allied bombing raids in 1943 didn't help, undoing much of the post-earthquake restoration.

Today, the remodelled city guards against future natural disasters, with wide streets and low, reinforced concrete buildings marching off in all directions. Not surprisingly, it is a pretty dull spectacle, and most of what interest there is resides in Messina's active port area. Take time at least to walk up Via I Settembre from the train station to Piazza del Duomo. The traffic-cluttered paved square was laid out in the eighteenth century, while the **Duomo** itself (daily 7.30am–noon & 4.30–6.30pm, 3.30–6pm in winter) is a faithful reconstruction of the medieval cathedral built by Roger II. The facade retains its grand doorways and some original sculpture: inside, most of what you see – from the marble floor to the painted wooden ceiling – has been retouched and rebuilt. The detached **campanile** reputedly contains the largest astronomical clock in the world. Be there at noon and you get the full show, a visually impressive panoply of moving gilt figures including a crowing cock, roaring lion and a succession of doves and angels accompanying the Madonna.

Much of what was salvaged from the various disasters now resides in the **Museo Regionale** (Tues–Sat 9am–2pm, Sun 9am–1pm, plus Tues, Thurs & Sat 4–7pm, 3–6pm in winter; €4), 3km north of the centre – a 45-minute walk along Via della Libertà, or bus #28 from Piazza Cairoli or Via Garibaldi, or buses #76, #77, #78 and #79 from Via Garibaldi or the train station. A great deal has been painstakingly stuck and plastered back together in this beautifully laid-out museum, including a couple of Caravaggios, commissioned by the city in 1604. There are also damaged works by Antonello da Messina, a few good Flemish pieces and the city's rescued archeological remains. Look out for the striking painting of *St Peter* by Girolamo Alibrandi and a writhing Scilla, adorned with lions' heads, a sixteenth-century sculpture by da Montorsoli.

If you're in Messina in mid-summer, you may coincide with the feast of the Assumption, or **ferragosto**, August 15, when a towering carriage, the *Vara* – an elaborate column supporting dozens of papier-mâché putti and angels, topped by the figure of Christ stretching out his right arm to launch Mary heavenwards – is hauled through the city centre. Late at night, one of Sicily's best **firework displays** is held on the seafront near Via della Libertà.

Practicalities

Trains all use the **Stazione Centrale** by the harbour, adjacent to the **Stazione Maríttima** – where the train-ferries from Calabria dock. Other **ferries** and **hydrofoils** (to and from Villa San Giovanni, Reggio di Calabria and the Aeolian Islands) dock at quays further to the north, on Via Vittorio Emanuele and Via della Libertà. Interbus and SAIS **buses** for Taormina and Catania leave from Piazza della Repubblica by the train station, while those for Milazzo (for onward connections to the Aeolian Islands) depart from the Giuntabus office at Via Terranova 8 (at the corner of Viale San Martino). There are two **tourist offices** just outside the train station: one on Piazza della Repubblica (Mon–Thurs 9am–1pm & 3–5pm, Fri 9am–1pm; ☎090.672.944), where good English is spoken, the other just beyond on Via Calabria (Mon–Sat 8am–6.30pm; ☎090.674.236); both can supply you with free maps, Aeolian Island ferry timetables and accommodation lists.

Unless you arrive late in the day, it's hardly necessary to **stay over** in Messina. Still, there are a couple of basic options on Via N. Scotto, an alley on the south side of Piazza della Repubblica, beyond the SAIS office: the *Mirage*, at no. 3 (☎090.293.8844; ❷); and the sprucer *Touring*, at no. 17 (☎ & ℱ090.293.8851; ❷). A slicker option is the modern *Excelsior* (☎090.293.1431, ℱ090.293.8721; ❹), near Piazza Cairoli at Via Maddalena 32. There's a **campsite**, *Il Peloritano* (☎090.348.496), out beyond Punta del Faro on the northern coast; take bus #81 to Rodia from the train station. Messina has a good choice of **restaurants**, in which you should try the swordfish, freshly caught and a local speciality; May and June are the best months for this, before the water gets too warm. *Lungomare da Mario* is a good choice, opposite the hydrofoil dock at Via Vittorio Emanuele 108 (closed Wed except Aug); otherwise try *Osteria del Campanile*, Via Loggia dei Mercanti 9, off Piazza del Duomo (closed Sun except July & Aug), for surprisingly good pasta, or the basic but good *Pizzeria del Capitano* at Via dei Mille 88, close to Piazza Cairoli (closed Mon). For panini and other cold **snacks**, head for *Salumeria Nucita*, an *alimentari* at Via Garibaldi 125 (closed Wed evening & Sun). There's an **Internet point** at Via dei Mille 200, off Piazza Cairoli (Mon–Sat 9am–1pm & 4–8pm).

The coastal route south

Try to take the train, rather than the slower bus or road option, **south from Messina**, since the line follows the rough, stony shore pretty much all the way: on a clear day there are spanking views over to Calabria.

Santa Teresa Di Riva is the first recognizable resort, with an oversized beach, though it's nothing to shout about. The straggling village is more attractive as a jumping-off point for the foothills of the **Monti Peloritani**, the long mountain range that cuts south from Messina. Buses from Santa Teresa twist the 4km up to **SAVOCA**, a peaceful hill-village, evocatively sited up in the clouds. Houses and three churches perch precariously on the cliff sides in clumps, a tattered castle topping the pile. Signs in the village point you to the **Cappuccini monastery** whose catacombs (Tues–Sun: summer 9am–1pm & 4–7pm; winter 9am–1pm & 3–5pm; donation requested) maintain a selection of mummified bodies, two to three hundred years old, in niches, dressed in their eighteenth-century finery, the skulls of less complete compatriots lining the walls above. More offbeat delight is at hand in the village's *Bar Vitelli*, used as the scene of Michael Corleone's betrothal in Coppola's film *The Godfather*.

Taormina

TAORMINA, high on Monte Tauro and dominating two grand sweeping bays below, is Sicily's best-known resort. The outstanding remains of its classical theatre, with Mount Etna as an unparalleled backdrop, arrested passing travellers when Taormina was no more than a medieval hill-village. Goethe and D.H. Lawrence are the two big names touted by the tourist office; Lawrence was so enraptured that he lived here (1920–23) in a house at the top of the valley cleft behind the theatre. Although international tourism has taken its toll over recent years, Taormina still retains much of its small-town charm. The one main traffic-free street is an unbroken line of fifteenth- to nineteenth-century *palazzi* and small, intimate piazzas, and there is an agreeably crumbly castle and rows of flower-filled balconies. The downside is that between June and August it's virtually impossible to find anywhere to stay, and the narrow alleys are shoulder-to-shoulder with tourists. April, May or September are slightly better, but to avoid the crowds completely come between October and March, when it's often still warm enough to swim.

Arrival, information and accommodation

Trains pull up at the handsome Taormina-Giardini station (left-luggage office 6am–9pm) on the water's edge, way below town. It's a very steep thirty-minute walk up to Taormina (turn right out of the station and then, after 200m, left through a gap in the buildings, marked "Centro"). Much better (certainly if you have luggage) is to arrive by bus or take one of the fairly frequent local buses that pick up outside the train station. The **bus terminal** is on Via Pirandello in Taormina itself: bear left up the road from the terminal, turn through the Porta Messina, and the main street, **Corso Umberto I**, lies before you. If you're arriving by car for the day, make for the Lumbi car park (24hr). The **tourist office** (Mon–Sat 8.30am–2pm & 4–7pm; ☎0942.23.243, ⓦwww.gate2taormina.com) is in the fourteenth-century Palazzo Corvaja, off Piazza Vittorio Emanuele, the first square you come to. You'll find an **Internet** café at Corso Umberto 214, opposite the *municipio* (Mon–Fri 9am–1pm & 4–8pm, Sat & Sun from 10am).

Finding a bed in summer is a time-consuming business; only a handful will be both available and affordable, so start looking early. The best prices are for **rented rooms**, for example close to the public gardens at the *Leone*, Via Bagnoli Croce 126 (☎0942.23.878, ⑤0942.21.182; no credit cards; ❷); or nearer the Greek theatre, at Via Iallia Bassa 20, the *Pensione Grazia* (☎ & ⑤0942.24.776; no credit cards; ❷), with incredible roof-terrace views; or else the tiny but cheap and central *Diana* at Via di Giovanni 6 (☎0942.23.898; no credit cards; ❷). A big step up in price gets you a **hotel** room at the pleasant *Elios* at Via Bagnoli Croce 98 (☎ & ⑤0942.23.431; ❹), with a great roof terrace, or the *Pensione Svizzera*, at Via Pirandello 26 (☎0942.23.790, ⑤0924.625.906, ⓦwww.pensionesvizzera.com; ❺), just up from the bus terminal and enjoying excellent views from its spacious rooms. A family-run place, the *Pensione Villa Greta* (☎0942.28.286, ⑤0942.24.360; ❹) is warmly recommended: fifteen minutes' walk out of town on the road up to Castelmola, it has superb balcony views, as well as a dining room with good home cooking. There's a small **youth** hostel, *Ulisse* (☎0942.23.193; closed Nov–Jan; €14.50), at Vico San Francesco di Paola, 200m west of the cathedral; book well ahead to secure a bed.

The Town

The **Teatro Greco** (daily 9am–1hr before sunset; €4.50) – signposted from just about everywhere – is where you should make for first, if only to acquaint yourself with Taormina's remarkable siting, with panoramic views encompassing southern Calabria, the Sicilian coastline and snow-capped Etna. That it was founded by Greeks in the third century BC is the extent of the theatre's Hellenistic connections, for the visible remains are almost entirely Roman. It was rebuilt at the end of the first century AD, when Taormina thrived under imperial Roman rule, and the reconstruction changed the theatre's character entirely. The impressive Roman scene building, for example, is Sicily's only surviving example but can only have obscured the views of Etna – presumably a major reason for the theatre's original siting. Likewise, the stage and lower seats were cut back to provide more room and a deep trench dug in the orchestra to accommodate the animals and fighters used in Roman gladiatorial contests. Between July and August the theatre hosts an international **arts festival** including film, theatre and music (tickets and information from the tourist office).

There are a few other Roman vestiges around town, including a much smaller **Odeon** (originally used for musical recitations) next to the tourist office. Really, though, Taormina's attractions are all to do with strolling the flower-decked streets and alleys, and window shopping in the converted ground floors of the mansions along the Corso. Centre of town is Piazza IX Aprile, with its restored twelfth-century **Torre dell'Orologio** and terrace overlooking Etna and the bay – though don't sit down at the inviting outdoor cafés unless you have a substantial bankroll. Give yourself time to hike up to the **Castello** by way of a stepped path leading up from the main road behind the tourist office, from where you can continue on to **Castelmola**, 5km above and seemingly growing out of its severe crag. It's about an hour's climb to the village (though there are buses), while another couple of hours beyond are the heights of **Monte Venere** (885m) – take the path behind Castelmola's cemetery – for the last word in local vistas.

Eating

Eating in Taormina can be an expensive business, though most places have tourist menus of varying standards and prices. Among the **trattorias**, *Il Baccanale* in Piazza Filea, off Via Bagnoli Croce (closed Thurs Nov–March), serves good grilled sardines at outdoor tables, while below Porta Messina the *Trattoria da Nino* cooks up basic but good pasta and seafood dishes at Via Pirandello 37 (closed Fri Nov–Feb), and *Terrazza Angelo*, Corso Umberto 38 (closed Thurs Nov–Easter), does good seafood and pizzas, and has a panoramic terrace. For **pizzas** and pasta in lively surroundings, there's *Mamma Rosa*, Via Naumachia 10 (closed Nov), and the more secluded *La Botte*, Piazza Santa Domenica 4 (closed Mon in winter), both touristy but serving good hearty meals at their outdoor tables. For snacks, there's an indoor **market** off Via Cappuccini (mornings only, Mon–Sat) and a good **rosticceria** just up from Porta Messina, on the corner of Via Timeo and Via Patricio.

Taormina's beaches – and Naxos

The **coastline** below the town is unquestionably appealing – a mixture of grottoes and rocky coves – but too many of its beaches are either private lidos (paying) or simply too packed in summer to be much fun.

The closest beach to town is at **Mazzarò** with its much-photographed islet. There's a **cable car** service (€1.60 single) that runs every fifteen minutes from Via Pirandello and a steep path that starts just below the cable car station. If you're still searching for a bed there are a dozen small **hotels** here, though get the tourist office to phone first. The beach-bars and restaurants at **Spisone**, north again, are also reachable by path from Taormina, this time from below the cemetery in town. From Spisone, the coast opens out and the beach gets wider. With more time you might explore **Letojanni**, a little resort in its own right with rather more ordinary bars and shops, a few fishing boats on a sand beach, and regular buses and trains back to Taormina. For **campers** there's a site called *Paradise International* (☎0942.36.306; March–Oct), 1km north along the coast.

Roomier and better for swimming are the sands south of Taormina at **GIARDINI-NAXOS**, and to a lesser extent at the holiday village of Recanati, beyond. Be prepared to pay to use the beach. The wide curving bay of Giardini – easily seen from Taormina's terraces – was the launching-point of Garibaldi's attack on the Bourbon troops in Calabria (1860) and, as significantly, the site of the first Greek colony in Sicily. An obvious stop for ships running between Greece and southern Italy, it was the site of a settlement in 734 BC, named Naxos after the Naxian colonists. It was never very important, and the extensive **excavations** (daily 9am to 1hr before sunset; €2) are very low-key – a long section of ancient, lava-built city wall, two covered kilns and a sketchy temple. But it's a pleasant walk there through the lemon groves (bus from Taormina to Naxos/Recanati and follow the "Scavi" signs), and you can see some of the finds in a **Museo Archeologico** by the entrance to the site (same ticket).

Giardini itself, the long town backing the good beach, is an excellent alternative source of accommodation and food. Prices tend to be a good bit cheaper than in Taormina, and in high season, if you arrive by train, it's probably worth trying here first. Recommended **places to stay** are *La Sirena*, Via Schisò 36 (☎0942.51.853; ❷), by the pier with views over the bay, and *Villa Mora*, Via Naxos 47 (☎ & ℱ0942.51.839; ❸), near the tourist office, both of which require half-board in August. For **eating**, the best and the cheapest is the restaurant-pizzeria attached to the seafront, *Lido d'Angelo* on Via Tysandros, while good pizzas and fresh pasta are also to be had at *Fratelli Marano*, Via Naxos 181. **Buses** run half-hourly to Giardini from Taormina, the last one returning from the station at 10.15pm.

Around Mount Etna

Mount Etna's massive bulk looms over much of the coastal route south from Taormina. One of the world's largest volcanoes, it really demands a separate visit, but if you're pushed for time you'll have to content yourself with the ever more imminent views of its eastern flank as you head along the coast to Catania. With time, you can make the circular route to Catania on the slow train around the volcano, the **Circumetnea** – one of Sicily's most interesting rides – and stop off on the **volcano** itself. Reaching the lower craters below the summit is eminently possible, on foot or by mountain-bus – either way a thrilling experience.

The Circumetnea railway: Giarre-Riposto to Catania

If you don't have the time to reach the summit of Etna, then the **Circumetnea** railway provides alternative volcanic thrills. A private line, 114km long, it runs around the base of the volcano through fertile vegetation and strewn lava – a marvellous ride. The line begins in the twin town of **Giarre–Riposto**, thirty minutes by train or bus from Taormina; mainline FS trains will drop you at Giarre, the second stop of the Circumetnea line. Rail passes are not valid on this route, and if you make the entire trip to Catania, allow five hours; tickets cost €5.16 one-way, €10.32 return.

The closest town to the summit is dark, medieval **RANDAZZO**, built entirely of lava. Although dangerously near Etna, Randazzo has never been engulfed; when the 1981 eruption took it to the point of evacuation, the lava-flow finally stopped just outside town. Poke around the gloomy streets – dingily authentic despite the fact that much of the town has been heavily restored after being bombed to bits in 1943, when it figured as the last Sicilian strong-hold of the Axis forces. The **Museo Vagliasindi** in Via Castello (daily 9am–1pm & 3–8pm; €1.60), housed in the former castle, has good displays of small-scale objects mainly from nearby Greek metropolis, and ranks of dangling puppets.

If you want to break the journey around Etna, then Randazzo is probably the place to **stay**, though the only choice is the tidy *Scrivano* (℡095.921.126, ℻095.921.433; ❸), behind the Agip petrol station on Via Regina Margherita.

Mount Etna: the ascent

The bleak lava wilderness around the summit of **Etna** is one of the most mem-orable landscapes Italy has to offer. While circling its lower slopes by road or rail is fine for the views, it can only be second best to the spectacular ascent. At 3323m, Etna is a fairly substantial mountain, and one of the world's biggest active volcanoes. Some of its eruptions have been disastrous: in 1169, 1329 and 1381 the lava reached the sea and in 1669 Catania was wrecked and its castle surrounded by molten rock. The Circumetnea railway line has been repeated-ly ruptured by lava flows: nine people were killed on the edge of the main crater in 1979 and in 2001 military helicopters were called in to water-bomb blazing fires.

This unpredictability means that it is no longer possible to get close to the main crater. An **eruption** in 1971 destroyed the observatory supposed to give warning of just such an event, and the volcano has been in an almost contin-ual state of eruption since 1998, the most recent being in 2002 when the resort of Piano Provenzana on the northern side was engulfed with lava. If you do attempt the summit, be sure to heed the warnings as you get closer to the top.

There are several **approaches** to the volcano. If you have a car you can enjoy some of the best scenery on the north side of the volcano, by taking the road that leads up from Linguaglossa. On **public transport**, though, you'll need to come via **Nicolosi**, on the southern side of Etna and an hour from Catania by bus. A winter ski resort and last main stop before the steeper slopes begin, it's a good place to pick up information – from the small **tourist office** at Via Garibaldi 63 (daily 8.30am–1pm, summer also 4–7.30pm; ℡095.911.505), the main road that runs through Nicolosi. There are several **hotels** too, a couple in town, the rest on the road out, as well as a **campsite** – all signposted and detailed on full lists available from the information office.

Although there are frequent buses to Nicolosi from Catania, only one (around 8am from outside Catania train station) continues to the **Hotel/Rifugio Sapienza** which marks the end of the negotiable road up the south side of Etna. In the summer of 2001 and winter of 2002 this was a scene of frenetic activity, when dams and channels were cut to contain the molten lava which threatened to engulf the whole area. However the row of souvenir shops, the couple of restaurants, and the totally refurbished *Hotel/Rifugio Sapienza* (℡095.914.141; ❹) are still standing, but surrounded by rills of lava. Arriving on the early-morning bus, you should have enough time to make the top and get back for the return bus to Catania – it leaves around 4.30pm from the hotel.

There are two ways **up the volcano** from the refuge. Until the cable car service is restored, you can either take one of the **four-wheel drive minibuses** (known as jeeps) with a guide, that leave on demand from the cable-car station (daily 9am to sunset, weather permitting; €38 return) to just below the main crater, or you can **walk**, following the rough minibus track. Really it all depends on finances and time: walking up will take around four hours, the return obviously a little less. However you go, at whatever time of year, take warm clothes, good shoes or boots and glasses to keep the flying grit out of your eyes. You can rent boots and jackets (€1 each) from the cable-car station.

The lower slopes have been newly planted with trees; higher up, the cindery texture of previous eruptions is in sharp contrast with the darker new crust of buckled folds and jagged piles. The highest you're allowed to get (on foot or in the bus) is currently 2760m, where signs forbid further access. To go further would be a foolish act – gaseous explosions and molten rock are common this far up. From here you can feel the heat through your feet and view the new fumaroles exuding smoke. Higher still is the main crater and, depending on weather conditions, you may see smoke from here too. Disappointingly, there's often haze or cloud which mars the unsurpassed panorama to the sea.

Catania

Bang in the middle of the Ionian coast, **CATANIA** is Sicily's second-largest city and despite the ever-looming presence of Etna – even the city's main street is named after the volcano – and the ubiquitous black-grey volcanic stone in pavements and buildings, there's more openness and space than in the island's capital. A major transport hub, and predominantly a businesslike, commercial centre, it's nevertheless one of the island's most historic and intriguing cities.

Some of the island's first Greek colonists settled the site as early as 729 BC, becoming so influential that their laws were eventually adopted by all the Ionian colonies of Magna Graecia. Later, a series of natural disasters helped shape the city as it appears today: Etna erupted in 1669, engulfing the city, the lava swamping the harbour, which was then topped by an earthquake in 1693 that devastated the whole of southeastern Sicily. The swift rebuilding was on a grand scale, and making full use of the local building material, Giovanni Vaccarini, the eighteenth-century architect, gave the city a lofty, noble air. Despite the neglect of many of the churches and the disintegrating, grey mansions, there's still interest in what, at first, might seem intimidating. Delving about throws up lava-encrusted Roman relics, surviving alongside some of the finest Baroque work on the island.

CATANIA

Palazzo
di Giustizia

Stazione
Metropolitana

Orto
Botánico

Villa
Bellini

Teatro
Metropolitan (i)

Anfiteatro
Romano

Sant'Agata al
Cárcere

San
Nicolò   San
Giuliano   Collegiata
San
Benedetto   University   Teatro
Bellini   Collegio
Cutelli
Municipio   Sant'
Agata
Odeon
Museo   Duomo
Teatro   Belliniano
Romano   Porta
Ujeda

Castello
Ursino

Molo
Vecchio

ACCOMMODATION				RESTAURANTS	
Centrale Europa	6	Rubens	2	Don Turiddu	B
La Collegiata	3	Savona	5	Finocchiaro	C
Gresi	1	Youth Hostel	7	La Siciliana	A
Holland International	4			Trattoria Tripoli	D

▼ Airport, Beaches & Campsites

Arrival, information and accommodation

The **airport**, Fontanarossa (☎095.340.505, ⓦ www.aeroporto.catania.it), is
5km south and is the entry point for most charter flights to Sicily. The Alibus
(every 20min 5am–midnight; €0.80) runs from right outside to the central

Piazza Stesicoro (on Via Etnea) and to Stazione Centrale in around twenty minutes. A taxi from the rank outside the airport will cost around €18 for the same journey. The **Stazione Centrale**, for all mainline trains, is in Piazza Giovanni XXIII, northeast of the centre (enquiries ℡848.888.088). If you're changing on to the round-Etna train, the **Stazione Circumetnea** (℡095.541.250) is at Via Caronda at the northern end of Via Etnea, by the Borgo metro station.

All **buses**, both regional from Catania province and island-wide, stop at various points in Piazza Giovanni XXIII, across from the train station. Of the bus companies, AST (℡095.746.1096), whose timetables are pinned to posts and whose ticket office is at Via L. Sturzo 230, on the east side of the square, stop opposite the station and serve Etna (*Hotel/Rifugio Sapienza*), Nicolosi and Siracusa; Interbus/Etna Trasporti (℡095.532.716) leave from Via d'Amico 185, at the back of the piazza, for Enna, Giardini-Naxos, Noto, Piazza Armerina, Ragusa, Rome, Siracusa and Taormina; SAIS (℡095.536.201) to Agrigento, Enna, Messina, Rome and Palermo also leaves from Via d'Amico.

Immediately outside the Stazione Centrale you'll find ranks of AMT **city buses**: #1/4, #4/7, #432 and #448 run into the centre, along Via VI Aprile and Via Vittorio Emanuele to Piazza del Duomo. Other central pick-up points are Piazza del Duomo itself, Piazza Stesícoro, and Piazza Borsellino (below Piazza del Duomo), where there's a stop for the airport Alibus and for buses #4/27 and #5/38, which serve the campsites. **Tickets** (€0.80) are valid for any number of journeys within ninety minutes and are available from *tabacchi*, the newsagents inside Stazione Centrale or the booth outside the station. The same outlets also sell a *biglietto giornaliero* (€2), valid for one-day's unlimited travel on all local AMT bus routes. **Driving** and parking in Catania is a stressful experience. Take advice from your hotel or seek a parking attendant who will guide you to a spot for around €60 an hour.

There's a **tourist office** (daily 9am–7pm; ℡095.730.6255) inside Stazione Centrale, but the main office (daily 9am–7pm; ℡095.730.6222, ⓦwww.apt.catania.it) is signposted off Via Etnea, at Via Cimarosa 10. There's also an **information office** at the airport (daily 8am–9pm; ℡095.730.6266). For **what's on** check out Catania's daily newspaper *La Sicilia* and the free fortnightly arts and entertainment guide *Lapis*.

Accommodation

There's a fairly good choice of **places to stay** in Catania, though it's always wise to book ahead in summer. Around Via Etnea, the newly refurbished *Pensione Gresi*, Via Pacini 28 (℡095.322.709, Ⓕ095.715.3045; ❸), retains its painted ceilings, and the *Rubens*, Via Etnea 196 (℡095.317.073, Ⓕ095.715.1713; ❷), sports antiques and a suave, English-speaking owner. Further down at Via Vasta 10, on the corner with Via Etnea, *La Collegiata* (℡095.315.256, Ⓕ095.322.848; ❹) occupies a restored Baroque *palazzo*. If you want to stay nearer the station, the *Holland International* is a good choice at Via Vittorio Emanuele 8 (℡095.533.605, Ⓕ095.746.5892; no credit cards; ❷), with a multilingual Dutch owner and vaulted frescoed ceilings. Around Piazza del Duomo you can choose between the spick-and-span *Centrale Europa*, Via Vittorio Emanuele 167 (℡095.311.309, Ⓕ095.317.531; ❷), or the more upmarket and elegant *Savona* at Via Vittorio Emanuele 210 (℡095.326.982, Ⓕ095.715.8169; ❻). The private **youth hostel** *Agorá* near the fish market in Piazza Currò (℡095.723.3010, ⓦwww.agorahostel.hypermart.net; €15.50) has dorm bunks and a couple of doubles (❷), Internet and laundry facilities. There are three **campsites** (with lidos and cabins available) a short way south of the city on

Lungomare Kennedy; take bus #4/27 or #5/38 (the latter service operates in summer only) from the train station or Via Etna.

The City

Catania's main square, **Piazza del Duomo**, is a handy orientation point and a stop for most city buses: Via Etnea steams off north, lined with the city's most fashionable shops and cafés; fish market and port lie behind to the south; train station to the east; the best of the Baroque quarter to the west. It's also one of Sicily's most attractive city squares, rebuilt completely in the first half of the eighteenth century by Vaccarini and surrounded with fine Baroque structures. Most striking of these is the **Municipio** on the northern side of the piazza, finished in 1741, though to admire it properly you'll have to gain the central reserve of the piazza. Here, the **elephant fountain** is the city's symbol, the eighteenth-century lava elephant supporting an Egyptian obelisk on its back.

Cross back for the **Duomo** (daily 8am–noon & 4.30–7pm) on the piazza's eastern flank. Apart from the marvellous volcanic-rock medieval apses (seen through the gate at Via Vittorio Emanuele 159), this was pretty much entirely remodelled by Vaccarini, whose heavy Baroque touch is readily apparent from the imposing facade on which he tagged granite columns from Catania's Roman amphitheatre (see below). The interior is no less grand: adorned by a rich series of chapels, notably the Cappella di Sant'Agata to the right of the choir, which conceals the relics paraded through the city on the saint's festival at the beginning of February.

Nearby is Catania's open-air **market**, a noisome affair with slabs and buckets full of twitching fish, eels and shellfish and endless lanes full of vegetable and fruit stalls, as well as one or two excellent lunchtime trattorias. The roads wind through a pretty dilapidated neighbourhood to an open space punctured by the **Castello Ursino**, once the proud fortress of Frederick II. Originally the castle stood on a rocky cliff, over the beach, but following the 1669 eruption, which reclaimed this entire area from the sea, all that remains is the blackened keep. The **Museo Cívico** (Tues–Sat 9am–1pm & 3–6pm, Sun 9am–1pm; free) is housed inside, its central chambers hung with retrieved mosaic fragments, stone inscriptions and tombstones, while other rooms hold an extraordinarily delightful range of items, including a Greek terracotta statuette of two goddesses being pulled in a sea carriage by mythical beasts and a seventeenth-century French pistol, inlaid in silver and depicting rabbits, fish and cherubs.

Back towards the centre, dingy **Piazza Mazzini** heralds perhaps the most interesting section of the city. Everything close by is big and Baroque, and **Via Crociferi** – which strikes north from the main road, under an arch – is lined with some of the most arresting religious and secular examples, best seen on a slow amble, peering in the eighteenth-century courtyards and churches. At the bottom of the narrow street, the house where the composer Vincenzo Bellini was born in 1801 now houses the **Museo Belliniano** (Mon–Fri 9am–1pm plus Tues & Thurs 3–6pm, Sun 9am–12.30pm; free), an agreeable collection of photographs, original scores, his death mask and other memorabilia. A local boy, Bellini notches up several tributes around the city, including a piazza, theatre and park named after him, a berth in the Duomo and the ultimate accolade, *spaghetti alla Norma*. Cooked with tomato, ricotta and aubergine sauce, and named after one of Bellini's operas, it's a Catanian speciality.

West from here, the **Teatro Romano** (daily: 9am–1.30pm & 2.30–7pm; €2) was built of lava in the second century AD on the site of an earlier Greek theatre, and much of the seating and the underground passageways are preserved, though all the marble which originally covered it has disappeared. Further west, down Via

16

Teatro Greco, the pretty crescent of Piazza Dante stares out over the unfinished facade of **San Nicolò** (daily 9am–1pm), the biggest church in Sicily, stark and empty of detail both outside and in – save for a meridian line drawn across the floor of the transept – following its partial eighteenth-century restoration.

Nearby, a few minutes' walk north, the little twelfth-century church of **Sant'Agata al Cárcere** was built on the site of the prison where St Agatha was confined before her martyrdom. From here, you drop down into **Piazza Stesicoro**, the enormous square that marks the modern centre of Catania, one half of which is almost entirely occupied by the closed-off, sunken, black remains of Catania's **Anfiteatro Romano**, dating back to the second or third century AD. In its heyday, the amphitheatre could hold around 16,000 spectators, and from the church steps above you can see the seating quite clearly, supported by long vaults.

Eating and drinking

You'll rarely do better for eating than in Catania, where fresh **fish** is a speciality. Try the fried fish and *spaghetti alla Norma* specialities at the *Trattoria Tripoli*, Via Pardo 30 (closed Sun), close by the fish market. For a more expensive meal, *Ristorante Finocchiaro*, off Piazza dell'Università at Via E. Reina 13 (closed Wed & lunchtime), has excellent antipasti and unusual local dishes, and at *Don Turiddu*, Via Musumeci 50, there's no menu, just a splendid parade of antipasti and fish at the entrance for you to take your pick (closed Sun & Aug). *La Siciliana* (closed Sun eve & Mon; ☎095.376.400), in the north of the city at Viale Marco Polo 52a, is worth the journey for its pasta and puddings; a full meal here will cost around €40. For **snacks**, *Savia*, Via Etnea 302 (closed Mon), opposite the main entrance to the Villa Bellini, is one of the town's finest stand-up café-bars, open since 1899.

Catania's student population ensures a fair choice of youthful **bars and pubs** – some with live music – which stay open late. *La Collegiata*, Via Collegiata 3, has a pleasant terrace for a night-time drink, and the *Nievski*, Via Alessi 15 (closed Sun lunch & Mon), offers organic food at lunchtime and has **Internet** access. In addition, the *comune* operates *café concerto* periods during the summer, when the streets and squares of the old town, between Piazza Università and Piazza Bellini, are closed to traffic between 9pm and 2am. The bars here all spill tables out onto the squares and alleys, and live bands keep things swinging until the small hours.

Listings

American Express c/o La Duca Viaggi, Via Etnea 63 ☎095.316.155; Mon–Fri 9.30am–1pm & 4.30–7.30pm, Sat 9am–noon.

Car rental Avis, at airport (☎095.340.500) and Via V. Giuffrida 19 (☎095.445.536); Maggiore/Budget, at airport (☎095.340.594); Sixt, at airport (☎095.340.252); Hertz, at airport (☎095.341.595) and Via P. Toselli 16 (☎095.322.560); Holiday Car Rental, at airport (☎095.346.769).

Emergencies ☎113 for all emergency services.

Hospital Ospedale Vittorio Emanuele, Via Plebiscito; Ospedale Generale Garibaldi, Piazza S. Maria di Gesù 7; S. Tomaselli, Via Passo Gravina 185; for any of these, call ☎095.759.1111.

Pharmacies Cutelli, Via Vittorio Emanuele II 54 ☎095.531.400; Croce Rossa, Via Etnea 274 ☎095.317.053; Europa, Corso Italia 105 ☎095.383.536. All are open at night.

Police Emergencies ☎112; Carabinieri, Piazza Giovanni Verga 8 ☎095.537.822.

Post office Main post office and poste restante at Via Etnea 215, close to the Villa Bellini (Mon–Sat 8.15am–6.30pm).

Travel agents La Duca Viaggi, Via Etnea 63–65 ☎095.316.155; Elisea, Corso Sicilia 31 ☎095.312.321; Etnea Viaggi, Corso Sicilia 109 ☎095.327.080; Viaggi Wasteel, Piazza Giovanni XXIII ☎095.531.511.

The plain of Catania

Buses from Catania run around the southern spur of the Golfo di Catania to **AUGUSTA**, oil port and naval base. It's pleasanter than it sounds, built (like Siracusa) on a small islet connected to the mainland, and there are beach resorts to the north, one at **BRUCOLI**, together with a fifteenth-century castle. But the real reason to stay would be as a base for visiting the nearby site of **Megara Hyblaea**, around 10km south, across the bay. Founded by Greeks a few years before Siracusa, the city enjoyed a fair living from sea-trade and pottery until destroyed by first Gelon in 483 BC and later the Romans. The large **site** shows a Doric temple, some tombs and houses, an eighth-century BC agora, as well as a small **museum** (Mon–Sat 9am–7pm; free) with plans, photos and some finds. Unfortunately, it's not easy to get to without your own transport: the only possibility is to take a local train from Augusta to Megara-Giannalena, from where it's still a fair hike, though you could reduce it to a kilometre by walking along the rails and climbing up at the road bridge.

The last stretch of the journey to Siracusa, by train especially, is a nightmare of **rampant industrialization**. As far as Priolo, the track skirts the largest concentration of chemical plants in Europe, a stinking, Meccano-built mesh of pipes and tanks that has irreversibly polluted the local sea and air. People living in the coastal villages have had to be evacuated and their houses destroyed, the environment deemed unfit for human habitation.

Siracusa

It's hardly surprising that **SIRACUSA** (ancient Syracuse) – an easily defendable offshore island with fertile plains across on the mainland and two natural harbours – should attract the early Greek colonists, in this case Corinthians who settled the site in 733 BC. Within a hundred years, the city was so powerful that it was sending out its own colonists to the south and west; and later Siracusa was the island's main power base – indeed, the city's history reads as a list of Sicily's most famous and effective rulers.

Syracuse first assumed its almost mythic eminence under **Gelon**, the tyrant of Gela, who moved his rule to the city in 485 BC to increase his power: it was he who began work on the city's Temple of Athena, later to become the Christian cathedral of Syracuse. It was an unparalleled period of Greek prosperity in Sicily, while the extent of a wider Siracusean influence was indicated by the defeat of the Etruscans (474 BC), who had been causing trouble for Greek towns on mainland Italy. It was a growing influence which troubled Athens, and in 415 BC a fleet of 134 triremes was dispatched to take Syracuse – only to be blockaded and the fleet destroyed. Those who weren't slaughtered as they ran were imprisoned in the city's stone quarries.

Under **Dionysius the Elder**, the city became a great military base, the tyrant building the first of the Euryalus forts and erecting strong city walls. As the leading European power, Syracuse more or less retained its prime position for two hundred years until it was attacked by the Romans in 215 BC. The subsequent two-year siege was made long and hazardous for the attackers by the mechanical devices contrived by **Archimedes** – who, as the Romans finally forced victory, was killed by a foot soldier.

From this time, Syracuse withered in importance. It became, briefly, a major religious centre in the early Christian period, but for the most part its days as

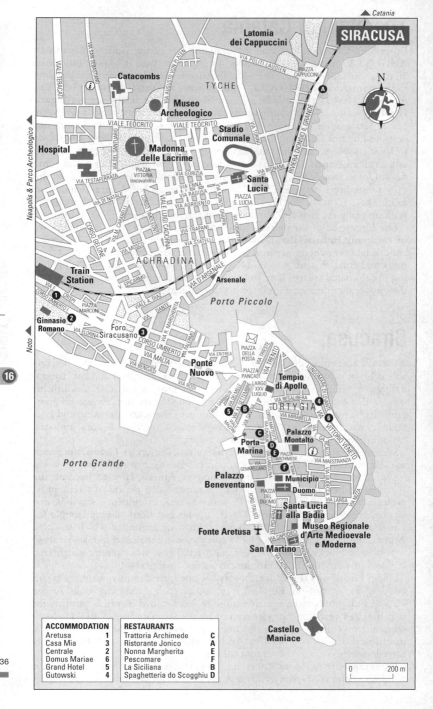

▲ Catania

SIRACUSA

Latomia dei Cappuccini

VIA POLITI LAUDIEN

PIAZZA CAPPUCCINI

VIALE TERACATI

VIA SAN SEBASTIANO

VIA AUGUSTO VON PLATEN

Catacombs

T Y C H E

VIA TORINO

Museo Archeologico

VIALE TEÓCRITO VIALE TEÓCRITO

Stadio Comunale

RIVIERA DIONISIO IL GRANDE

A

Hospital

VIA DEL SANTUARIO

Madonna delle Lacrime

PIAZZA VITTORIA (excavations)

VIA BIGNAMI

Santa Lucia

VIA GORIZIA

VIA TESTAFERRATA

VIA ENNA

VIA RAGUSA

VIA MONTE GRAPPA

PIAZZA S. LUCIA

VIA DI NATALE

VIALE LUIGI CADORNA

VIA TRAPANI

VIA AGRIGENTO

VIA TIMONOLEONTE

VIA STATELLO

VIA MOSCO

VIA ADRIANO

A C H R A D I N A

VIA D'ARSENALE

Train Station

Arsenale

V. EPICARMO

Porto Piccolo

VIA A. DIAZ

CORSO GELONE

CORSO UMBERTO

VIA A. DIAZ

PIAZZA MARCONI

VIA DANTE

1

CRISPI

2

Ginnasio Romano

VIA ELORINA

Foro Siracusano

3

CORSO UMBERTO

VIA R. MARGHERITA

VIA PALERMO

VIA ERITREA

PIAZZA DELLA POSTA

VIA TRIESTE

VIA TRENTO

LUNGOMARE DI LEVANTE

Ponte Nuovo

VIA MALTA

VIA BENGASI

VIA ROOI

PIAZZA PANCALI

Tempio di Apollo

LARGO XXV LUGLIO

VIA RESALIBERA

O R T Y G I A

4

Porto Grande

RIVA GARIBALDI

5

B

VIA XX SETTEMBRE

VIA SAVOIA

VIA MIRABELLA

VIA VITTORIO VENETO

6

VIA GARIBALDI

VIA CAVOUR

C

Porta Marina

VIA DIOMEDE

CORSO MATTEOTTI

Palazzo Montalto

D

E

PIAZZA ARCHIMEDE

VIA MAESTRANZA

i

VIA GEMMELLARO

F

Palazzo Beneventano

Municipio

Duomo

PIAZZA DEL DUOMO

VIA LARGA

VIA GIUDECCA

VIA NIZZA

FORO ITALICO

Santa Lucia alla Badia

Fonte Aretusa ⊤

VIA CAPODIECI

Museo Regionale d'Arte Medioevale e Moderna

LUNGOMARE ORTIGIA

San Martino

VIA CASTELLO MANIACE

Castello Maniace

N

◄ Neapolis & Parco Archeologico

◄ Noto

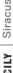

ACCOMMODATION		RESTAURANTS	
Aretusa	1	Trattoria Archimede	C
Casa Mia	3	Ristorante Jonico	A
Centrale	2	Nonna Margherita	E
Domus Mariae	6	Pescomare	F
Grand Hotel	5	La Siciliana	B
Gutowski	4	Spaghetteria do Scogghiu	D

0 — 200 m

a power were done: it was sacked by the Saracens and most of its later Norman buildings fell in the 1693 earthquake. Passed by until the twentieth century, the city suffered a double blow in World War II when it was bombed by the Allies and then, after its capture, by the Luftwaffe in 1943. Luckily, the extensive ancient remains were little damaged, and although decay and new development have reduced the attractions of the modern city, it's an essential stop on any tour of the island.

Some **orientation** pointers are useful. The original Greek settlement was on the fortified island of **Ortygia**, compact enough to see in a good half-day's stroll and almost completely late medieval in character. The Greek city spread onto the mainland in four distinct areas: **Achradina**, over the water from Ortygia, was the city's commercial and administrative centre and today encompasses the new streets that radiate out from the train station; **Tyche**, to the northeast, was residential and now holds the archeological museum and the city's extensive catacombs; **Neapolis**, to the west, is the site of the fascinating archeological park based on ancient Syracuse's public and social amenities; while **Epipolae** stretches way to the northwest, to the city's outer defensive walls and the Euryalus fort.

Arrival, information and accommodation

The **train station** is on the mainland, about a twenty-minute walk from either Ortygia or Neapolis. If you're not staying, dump your bags in the **left-luggage office** in the station (7am–9pm; €3.87 for 12hr) and strike off for one or the other. AST city and regional **buses** (☎0931.462.711) arrive in Piazza (or Riva) della Poste, just over the bridge on Ortygia, or else in Piazzale Marconi, in the modern town; the Interbus office (☎0931.66.710) and their regional buses stop in Via Trieste, close by Piazza della Poste.

The main **city bus** stops are in Piazza Archimede and Largo XXV Luglio on Ortygia, and along Corso Umberto on the mainland; tickets cost €0.77, valid for ninety minutes. **Drivers** will find the city a breeze after Palermo and Catania, and parking places relatively easy to come by. For maps, accommodation listings, details of performances in the Greek theatre, and other **information**, visit the **tourist office** at Via Maestranza 33 (Mon–Fri 8am–2pm & 2.30–5.30pm, Sat 8.30am–2pm; ☎0931.464.255, ⓦwww.apt-siracusa) or at Via San Sebastiano 43 (Mon–Fri 8.30am–1.30pm & 3–6pm, Sat 8.30am–1pm; ☎0931.481.200). The main **post office** is in Piazza della Poste and there's an **Internet** point in the Aleph bookshop at Corso Umberto I 106 (Mon–Sat 9am–9pm).

There's a fair spread of **accommodation** choices, but in high season it's wise to book in advance. For staying on Ortygia the elegant *Domus Mariae*, Via Vittorio Veneto 76 (☎0931.24.854, ⓕ0931.24.858, ⓦwww.sistemia.it/domus-mariae; ❻), is efficiently run by nuns and has views to the sea; close by at Lungomare Vittorini 26 the *Gutowski* (☎0931.465.861, ⓕ0931.480.505, ⓦwww.guthotel.it; ❺) has tastefully plain rooms. Most stylish of all, though, is the *Grand Hotel* (☎0931.464.600, ⓕ0931.464611, ⓦwww.grandhotelsr.it; ❾), a veteran haunt of the rich and famous in a prime position overlooking the

It's worth buying a **combined ticket** (valid two days) if you're planning to see Siracusa's major sights: a ticket for the Museo Regionale, Parco Archeologico and the Museo Archeologico costs €8, and for the Museo Archeologico and the Parco Archeologico €6.

Porto Grande, at Viale Mazzini 12. The cheaper hotels are all on the mainland. The best option, and closest to Ortygia, is *Casa Mia*, Corso Umberto 112 (℡0931.463.349, Ⓦwww.bbcasamia.it; no credit cards; ❸), a friendly B & B place furnished with antique beds, and with an inner terrace for breakfast. Around the train station you'll find the *Aretusa*, at Via Francesco Crispi 75 (℡ & Ⓕ0931.24.211, Ⓦwww.hotelaretusa.it; ❷), with plain, modern furniture and ten percent discount to carriers of this book, and the newly spruced-up *Centrale*, at Corso Umberto 141 (℡0931.60.528, Ⓕ0931.61.175; ❷). The nearest **campsite**, *Agriturist Rinaura* (℡0931.721.224), is 5km away – take bus #21, #22 or #23 from Corso Umberto or Piazza delle Poste.

Central Siracusa: Ortygia and Achradina

A fist of land with the thumb downturned, **ORTYGIA** stuffs more than 2700 years of history into a space barely 1km long and 0.5km across. The island was connected to the mainland at different times by causeway or by bridge: today you approach over the wide Ponte Nuovo to Piazza Pancali, where the sandstone remnants of the **Tempio di Apollo** sit in a little green park surrounded by railings. Erected around 570 BC in the colony's early years, it was the first grand Doric temple to be built in Sicily, though there's not much left to provoke the senses: a few column stumps, part of the inner sanctuary wall and the stereobate can be made out.

Follow Via Savoia towards the water and you fetch up on the harbour front, an active place overlooking the main harbour, the Porto Grande. Set back from the water, a curlicued fifteenth-century limestone gateway, the **Porta Marina**, provides one entrance into the webbed streets of the old town. The walk uphill ends on a terrace looking over the harbour, from where you slip down to a piazza encircling the **Fonte Aretusa**, probably the most enduring of Siracusa's romantic locations. The freshwater spring – now neither fresh nor a spring – fuelled an attractive Greek myth: the nymph Arethusa, chased by the river god Alpheus, was changed into a spring by the goddess Artemis and, jumping into the sea off the Peloponnese, reappeared as a fountain in Siracusa. Actually, there are natural freshwater springs all over Ortygia, but the landscaped, papyrus-covered fountain – complete with fish and ducks – is undeniably pretty. Admiral Nelson took on water supplies here before the Battle of the Nile, though you'd be better advised to sip a coffee in one of the cafés nearby.

The old town's roads lead on, down the "thumb" of Ortygia, as far as the **Castello Maniace** on the island's southern tip. Thrown up by Frederick II in 1239, the solid square keep is now a barracks and is off-limits to visitors. Back on the main chunk of Ortygia, the severe thirteenth-century Palazzo Bellomo houses the **Museo Regionale d'Arte Medioevale e Moderna** (Tues–Sat 9am–1.30pm, plus Fri & Sat 3–6.30pm; €2.50), an outstanding collection of medieval art. There are some wonderful pieces in here, including notable works by the omnipresent Gagini family and a damaged fifteenth-century *Annunciation* by Antonello da Messina, the museum's most famous exhibit.

Ortygia's most obvious attractions, though, surround the **Piazza del Duomo**, the island's most appealing spot. The piazza is an elongated space from which impressive buildings radiate out up either flank, including the seventeenth-century **Municipio** with the remains of an early Ionic temple in its basement. This was abandoned when work began on the most ambitious of all Siracusa's temples, the **Tempio di Atena**, which was raised in the fifth century BC and now forms the basis of the Duomo. In the normal run of things it might be expected to have suffered the eventual ruination that befell most of

16

the Greek temples in Sicily. Yet much of it survives, thanks to the foundation in the seventh century AD of a Christian church which incorporated the temple in its structure – thus keeping the masonry scavengers at bay. The **Duomo** (daily 8am–noon & 4–7pm) itself makes the grandest statement about Ortygia's continuous settlement, with twelve of the temple's fluted columns, and their architrave, embedded in its battlemented Norman wall. Inside, the nave of the Christian church was formed by hacking eight arches in the cella walls.

Buses run from Largo XXV Luglio over Ponte Nuovo and into **ACHRADINA**, the important commercial centre of ancient Syracuse. Although nowadays there's little of interest here, you may find yourself staying in one of the hotels scattered around its modern streets. The **Foro Siracusano** was the site of the agora, the marketplace and public square, and there are a few remains still to be seen – though the dominant feature is the war memorial in its garden, a Fascist monument of 1936. The only other ancient attraction left in the area is the **Ginnasio Romano**, off Via Elorina behind the train station: not a gymnasium at all, but a small first-century AD Roman theatre – partly sunken under moss-covered water – and a few pieces of a temple and altar.

Tyche and Neapolis: the archeological museum and park

TYCHE, north of the train station, is mainly new and commercial, and if you want to see the best of Siracusa's archeological delights you might as well take the bus straight from Ortygia and save your legs. Buses #3, #5, #12 and #15 leave from Largo XXV Luglio – all running up Corso Gelone. Get off at Viale Teocrito and signposts point you east for the archeological museum and west for Neapolis. It's best to take the museum first: it's good for putting the site into perspective and is unlikely to be packed first thing in the morning.

The **Museo Archeologico** (Tues–Sat 9am–7pm, plus Aug & Sept Sun 9am–1pm; €4.50) holds a wealth of material, starting with geological and prehistoric finds, moving through entire rooms devoted to the Chalcidesian colonies (Naxos, Lentini, Zancle) and to Megara Hyblaea, and finally to the main body of the collection: an immensely detailed catalogue of life in ancient Syracuse and its sub-colonies. Most famous exhibit is the *Venus*, at the entrance to the Syracuse section: a headless figure arising from the sea, the clear white marble almost palpably dripping. Attempt also to track down the section dealing with the temples of Syracuse; fragments from each (like the seven lion-gargoyles from the Tempio di Atena) are displayed alongside model and video reconstructions. There's an explanatory diagram at the entrance to the circular building and everything is colour coded: pick the sector you're interested in and follow the arrows, prehistory starting just to the left of the entrance.

NEAPOLIS, to the west, is now contained within a large **Parco Archeologico** (daily 9am–2hr before sunset). Although you don't pay for the initial excavations, seeing the Greek theatre and quarries – easily the most interesting parts – costs €4.50, paid at a separate entrance. The **Ara di Ierone II**, an enormous altar of the third century BC on a solid white plinth, is the first thing you see, across the way from which is the entrance to the theatre and quarries. The **Teatro Greco** is very prettily sited, cut out of the rock and looking down into trees below. It's much bigger than the one at Taormina, capable of holding around 15,000 people, though less impressive scenically. But the theatre's pedigree is impeccable: Aeschylus put on works here, and around the top of the middle gangway are a set of carved names which marked the various seat blocks occupied by the royal family. Greek dramas are still played here in May and June, as wooden planking over the surviving seats testifies.

Walk back through the theatre and another path leads down into a leafy quarry, the **Latomia del Paradiso**, best known for its unusually shaped cavern that Dionysius is supposed to have used as a prison. This, the **Orecchio di Dionigi** (or "Ear of Dionysius"), is a high, S-shaped cave 65m long: Caravaggio, a visitor in 1586, coined the name after the shape of the entrance, but the acoustic properties are such that it's not impossible to imagine Dionysius eavesdropping on his prisoners from a vantage point above. A second cave, the **Grotta dei Cordari**, used by the ancient city's ropemakers, is shored up at present.

Keep your ticket from the theatre and Latomia del Paradiso, as it will also get you into the elliptical **Anfiteatro Romano**, back up the main path past the altar and through a gate on your right; you have to see this last. A late building, dating from the third century AD, it's a substantial relic with the tunnels for animals and gladiators clearly visible. Again, some of the seats are inscribed with the owners' names.

Castello Eurialo

For terrific views over the city and relief on hot and crowded days, it's worth the brief excursion a few kilometres west of Siracusa to the military and defensive works begun under Dionysius the Elder to defend the port from land attack. Added to and adapted over a couple of centuries, they basically consisted of a great wall which defended the ridge of **Epipolae** (the city's western limit), and the massive **Castello Eurialo** (daily until 1hr before sunset; free) – *the* major extant Greek fortification in the Mediterranean. There are three defensive trenches, the innermost leading off into a system of tunnels and passages. Climb up to the castle proper, its long keep and the lower walls and towers providing hearty views over the oil refineries and tankers of the coast north of the city, and over Siracusa itself.

Bars and pizzerias share the view, and make this a viable place for an evening out. **Buses** #9, #11 and #25 run from the Corso Gelone, outside the archeological park, to the village of Belvedere; the site is just before the village, on the right, a fifteen-minute ride.

Eating and drinking

Many of Siracusa's **restaurants** are overpriced, but there are some good-value places. *Spaghetteria do Scogghiu*, Via Scina 11 (no credit cards; closed Mon), has a huge pasta selection, and *La Siciliana*, Via Savoia 17 (no credit cards; closed Mon), and *Nonna Margherita* at Via Cavour 12 on Ortygia (closed Wed) have a wide range of good pizzas and often draw queues. For fish, the *Trattoria Archimede*, Via Gemmellaro 8 (closed Sun eve), is frequented by locals, while *Pescomare* (closed Mon), just off Piazza del Duomo at Via Landolina 6, serves pizzas too, in an atmospheric, plant-filled old courtyard. For top-quality nosh, take a taxi or hike out to the rustic *Ristorante Jonico*, Riviera Dionisio il Grande 194 (☎0931.655.40; closed Tues), where a meal of superb antipasti and staggeringly delicious fresh fish will cost up to €40. Good **bars** and cafés are easy to come by, some of the best being the *Gran Caffè del Duomo*, right in front of the cathedral, the outdoor *Bar Ortygia*, at the Fonte Aretusa, and the *Bar Del Ponte* at the end of the Ponte Nuovo on Ortygia – a good breakfast place, this one.

The southern coast and the interior

It's tempting to give Sicily's long **southern coast** a miss, especially if you're short on time as there are few major sites. But to do so would be to ignore some of the most appealing places on the island. The whole region, coast and hinterland, marks a welcome break from the volcanic fixation of the blacker lands to the north: here the towns are largely spacious and bright, strung across a gentler, unscarred landscape that rolls down to the sea.

Sicily's southeastern bulge was devastated by a calamitous seventeenth-century earthquake and the inland rebuilding, over the next century, was almost entirely Baroque in concept and execution. **Ragusa** dominates, a splendid town on two levels, the older lower town much abandoned but still with its share of grandiose buildings. Elsewhere, similar vigorous Baroque towns mushroomed, like little **Módica** to the south and – the undisputed gem – **Noto** to the east.

Down on the **coast** itself there's a line of small-town resorts which stretches from the southeastern cape, **Capo Passero**. There are decent beaches but often the coastline is marred by industrial development and pollution. More vital, further west, is **Agrigento**, sitting on a rise overlooking the sea above its famed series of Greek temples.

Slow cross-country trains and limited exit motorways do little to encourage stopping in the island's **interior**, but it's only here that you really begin to get off the tourist trail. Much of the land is burned dry during the long summer months, sometimes a dreary picture, but in compensation the region boasts some of Sicily's most curious towns. **Enna** is the obvious target, as central as you can get, the blustery mountain town a pace apart from the dry hills below. There are easy trips to be made from here, north into the hills and south to **Piazza Armerina** and the fabulous Roman mosaics.

Ragusa and the southeast

The **earthquake of 1693**, which destroyed utterly the towns and villages of southeastern Sicily, had one positive and lasting effect. Where there were ruins, a new generation of confident architects raised new planned towns in an opulent Baroque style. All were harmonious creations, Catania the grandest, Noto the most eagerly promoted by the tourist board. But there is a bagful of other towns too, less visited but all providing surprising pockets of grandeur amid the bare hills and deep valleys of the region.

Ragusa

RAGUSA is a busy and likeable provincial capital with an encouraging, friendly atmosphere. The destructive earthquake split the city in two: the old town of Ragusa Ibla, on a jut of land above its valley, was comprehensively flattened, and within a few years a new town emerged, on the higher ridge to the west. Ibla was stubbornly rebuilt around its medieval ruins, while its new rival developed along grander, planned lines. All the business and industry relocated in the prosperous upper town, where oil is the latest venture – derricks are scattered around modern Ragusa's higher reaches.

You'll arrive here, in the **upper town**: all **buses** stop outside the **train station**, and a left turn takes you along the main road and over the exposed Ponte Nuovo, spanning a huge cleft in the ridge. All the interest in modern Ragusa is on the other side, the gridded Baroque town slipping off to right and left on either side of the steeply sloping Corso Italia. To the right, down the Corso on a wide terrace above Piazza San Giovanni, stands the **Duomo**, conceived on a grand, symmetrical scale. Finished in 1774, its tapered columns and fine doorways are a fairly sombre background to the vigorous small-town atmosphere around. Back towards the train station, underneath the Ponte Nuovo, there's an important **Museo Archeologico** (daily 9am–1.30pm & 4–7.30pm; €2) dealing mainly with finds from the archeological site of Kamarina (sixth century BC) on the coast to the southwest.

But it's **RAGUSA IBLA**, the original **lower town**, where you'll probably while away much of the day, its weather-beaten roofs straddling the outcrop of rock about twenty minutes' walk away. The main attraction, situated in the newly restored and gleaming central core of the town, is the church of **San Giorgio** (daily 9am–noon & 4–7pm). Stridently placed at the top of Piazza Duomo, it's one of the masterpieces of Sicilian Baroque, built by Rosario Gagliardi and finished in 1784. The glorious three-tiered facade, sets of triple columns climbing up the wedding cake exterior to a balconied belfry, is an imaginative work, though typically not much enhanced by venturing inside. As with Gagliardi's other important church in Módica (see below), all the beauty is in the immediacy of the powerful exterior.

The whole town – deathly quiet at lunchtime – is ripe for aimless wandering. Gagliardi gets another credit for the elegant rounded facade of **San Giuseppe** in Piazza Pola, a few steps below the Duomo, while Corso XXV Aprile continues down past abandoned *palazzi* to the **Giardino Ibleo** (daily 8am–8pm) – gardens that mark the very edge of the spur on which the town is built. If you can't face the walk back to the upper town, bus #1 or #3 makes the trip, hourly, from Piazza Pola.

Sadly, **accommodation** is limited to a choice of hotels in the upper town. The cheapest, *San Giovanni*, Via Traspontino 3 (T0932.621.013, F0932.621 .294; ❷), is at the train station end of the lower Ponte dei Cappuccini, while the *Montreal* on Via San Giuseppe is far better equipped but considerably more expensive (T & F0932.621.133; ❺). In the upper town there's a good, basic **restaurant** in Via S. Anna 117, the *Ristorante Orfeo*, with large, full meals for around €15 (closed Sun), while *La Grotta* at Via Cartia, off Via Roma, is good for pizzas (closed Wed). The best deal in Ibla is to be had at *U Saracinu*, on Via del Convento (closed Wed), near the Duomo, which does good Sicilian cooking with North African touches. Also in Ragusa Ibla, you can sit outside for nourishing meals at *La Béttola* in Largo Camarina (closed Mon). The *Caffè Trieste*, Corso Italia 76–78, is a decent **café-bar** with an enticing savoury snack and pastry selection.

Comiso and Módica

The best of the rest of the Baroque southeast can be seen in easy trips from Ragusa. If you came from the west you might already have passed through

16

Comiso, its green centre dominated by the twin domes of two impressive churches. If you didn't, the journey in itself is worth making, up over a barren 600-metre-high plateau looking away to the distant sea. The wild countryside hereabouts continues to impress as you head beyond Ragusa, the route to **Módica**, half an hour to the south, a case in point. As the bus swirls down past Ragusa Ibla and climbs through some rugged hills, all the vegetation seems to have been pulled into the valleys below, the tiered slopes bare and rocky. Módica itself is an enjoyable place to spend half a day. A powerful medieval base of the Chiaramonte, the upper town is watched over by the magnificent eighteenth-century facade of **San Giorgio**, a worthy rival to the church of the same name in Ragusa Ibla. It's thought that Gagliardi was responsible for this too: the elliptical facade is topped by a belfry, the church approached by a symmetrical double staircase which switchbacks up across the upper roads of the town.

Noto

The real highlight of any tour of the Baroque southeast, despite the collapse of its Duomo, is further afield at **NOTO**. Easily the most harmonious post-earthquake creation, for a time, in the mid-nineteenth century, it replaced Siracusa as that region's provincial capital. Indeed, despite its architectural identification with the Baroque towns around Ragusa, Noto is best reached from Siracusa – around half an hour's journey by bus or train. Planned and laid out by Giovanni Battista Landolina and adorned by Gagliardi, there's not a town to touch Noto for uniform excellence in design and execution. Each year sees an increase in the number of monuments to have shaken off the grime of traffic pollution and regained their original honey-coloured facades.

The pedestrianized main Corso is lined with some of Sicily's most captivating buildings, from the flat-fronted church of **San Francesco**, on the right, along as far as Piazza XVI Maggio and the graceful, curving church of **San Domenico**. And Piazza Municipio is arguably Sicily's finest piazza with its perfectly proportioned, tree-planted expanses. The **Duomo**, finished in 1770, but now closed due to the unfortunate collapse of the dome in 1996, is hemmed in by two palaces of remarkable decorative quality. Opposite, the **Municipio** (or Palazzo Ducezio) is flanked by its own green spaces, the arcaded building presenting a lovely, simple facade of columns and long stone balconies. Head up the steep **Via Corrado Nicolaci**, an eighteenth-century street that contains the extraordinary **Palazzo Villadorata** at no. 18 (Tues–Sun 9am–1pm and 3–6pm; €3), its six balconies supported by a panoply of griffins, galloping horses and fat-cheeked cherubs.

Staying in Noto wouldn't be a bad alternative to Siracusa, though options in the town itself are more limited. There's an excellent new **youth hostel**, *Il Castello*, housed in a converted *palazzo* on Via Fratelli Bandiera in the upper part of town (℡0931.571.534; €14.50). You can find out about the numerous **rented rooms** and **bed-and-breakfast** places from the **tourist office** in Piazza XVI Maggio (Mon–Sat 8am–2pm & 3.30–6.30pm, plus Sun in summer 8am–2pm; ℡0931.836.744, ⓦwww.comune.noto.sr.it). Try the *Centro Storico* (℡0931.573.967; no credit cards; ❸) at Corso Vittorio Emanuele 64, an eighteenth-century *palazzo*, or *L'Arca*, Via Rococco Pirri 14 (℡0931.838.656, ⓟ0931.573.360, ⓦwww.notobarocca.com/arcarooms; no credit cards; ❸), which are both central. The other alternative is to stay at Noto Marina, 8km southeast, where there is a cluster of holiday hotels. In Noto, you can **eat** at the straightforward *Trattoria Giglio*, just to the side of the town hall at Piazza Municipio 8–10, where the cooking has a Spanish flavour, the small *Trattoria del*

*Carmine,*Via Ducezio 9, for *cucina casalinga* at low prices, or more expensively at *Ristorante Neas*, Via Rocco Pirri 30 (☎0931.573.538; closed Mon), a knock-out for fish dishes and a good place to sample the local wine *moscato di Noto*.

Agrigento

Though handsome, well sited and awash with medieval atmosphere, **AGRI-GENTO** is not visited for the town itself. The interest instead focuses on the substantial remains of Pindar's "most beautiful city of mortals", a couple of kilometres below. Here, strung out along a ridge facing the sea, is a series of Doric temples – the most captivating of Sicilian Greek remains and a grouping unique outside Greece.

The site

In 581 BC colonists from nearby Gela and from Rhodes founded the city of Akragas between the rivers of Hypsas and Akragas. They surrounded it with a mighty wall, formed in part by a higher ridge on which stood the acropolis (and, today, the modern town). The southern limit of the ancient city was a second, lower ridge and it was here, in the so-called "Valley of the Temples", that the city architects erected their sacred buildings during the fifth century BC.

A road winds down from the modern city to the **VALLE DEI TEMPLI**, buses dropping you at a car park between the two separate sections of archeological remains (the eastern and western zones), and then the museum (see opposite). The **eastern zone** is unenclosed and is at its crowd-free best in early morning or late evening. A path climbs up to the oldest of Akragas's temples, the **Tempio di Ercole** (Hercules). Probably begun in the last decades of the sixth century BC, nine of the original 38 columns have been re-erected, everything else scattered around like a waiting jigsaw puzzle. Retrace your steps back to the path which leads to the glorious **Tempio della Concordia**, dated to around 430 BC: perfectly preserved and beautifully sited, with fine views to the city and the sea, the tawny stone lending the structure warmth and strength. That it's still so complete is explained by its conversion (in the sixth century AD) to a Christian church. Restored to its (more or less) original layout in the eighteenth century, it's kept its lines and slightly tapering columns, although it's fenced off to keep the crowds at bay. The path continues, following the line of the ancient city walls, to the **Tempio di Giunone** (or Hera), an engaging half-ruin standing at the very edge of the ridge. The patches of red visible here and there on the masonry denote fire damage, probably from the sack of Akragas by the Carthaginians in 406 BC.

The **western zone** (daily 8.30am–1hr before sunset; €4.50, joint ticket with archeological museum €6), back along the path and beyond the car park, is less impressive, a vast tangle of stone and fallen masonry from a variety of temples. Most notable is the mammoth construction that was the **Tempio di Giove**, or Temple of Olympian Zeus. The largest Doric temple ever known, it was never completed, left in ruins by the Carthaginians and further damaged by earthquakes. Still, the stereobate remains, while on the ground, face to the sky, lies an eight-metre-high *telamone*: a supporting column sculpted as a male figure, arms raised and bent to bear the temple's weight. Other scattered remains litter the area, including the so-called **Tempio dei Dioscuri** (Castor and Pollux), rebuilt in 1832 and actually made up of unrelated pieces from the confused rubble on the ground.

Via dei Templi leads back to the town from the car park via the excellent **Museo Nazionale Archeologico** (daily 9am–1.30pm, plus Tues–Sat 2–5.30pm; €4.50) – the bus passes by outside. The extraordinarily rich collection is devoted to finds from the city and the surrounding area; best displays are the cases of vases (sixth to third century BC) and a reassembled *telamone* stacked against one wall. Nip over the road on the way out for the **Hellenistic-Roman quarter** (daily 9am–1hr before sunset; free), which contains lines of houses, inhabited intermittently until the fifth century AD, many with mosaic designs still discernible.

The modern city

It would be a mistake not to scout round modern Agrigento, modern only in comparison with the temples. Thoroughly medieval at its heart, its tiny stepped streets and fine churches look down over the Valle dei Templi (dramatically floodlit at night) and beyond to the sea. The main street, **Via Atenea**, starts at the eastern edge of the old town, above the train station, the streets off to the right harbouring ramshackle *palazzi* and the church of **Santa Maria dei Greci**. Built over a Greek temple of the fifth century BC, the flattened columns are visible in the nave, while an underground tunnel reveals the stylobate and column stumps, all part of the church's foundations.

Practicalities

Trains arrive at Agrigento Centrale station at the edge of the old town; don't get out at Agrigento Bassa, as it's 3km north of town. **Buses** use the terminal in Piazza Roselli, near the post office, while **city buses** to the temples and the beach at San Leone leave from Piazza Marconi, outside the train station. Buy city bus **tickets** (€0.78) from kiosks or *tabacchi*. The old town stetches west of the three main interlocking squares, piazzas Marconi, Aldo Moro and Vittorio Emanuele. Via Atenea is Agrigento's principal artery, running west from Piazza Aldo Moro, off which runs Via Empedocle with the **tourist office** at no. 73 (Mon–Fri 8.30am–1.30pm plus Wed 4–7pm; ☎0922.20.391).

Finding **somewhere to stay** in Agrigento shouldn't be a problem, except perhaps in peak season. The *Bella Napoli*, Piazza Lena 6 (☎ & ℱ0922.20.435; ❷), at the western end of the old town, is one of the better budget choices, but can be a little noisy; otherwise try the unexciting *Belvedere*, Via San Vito 20 (☎ & ℱ0922.20.051; ❷). With a little more money, the obliging and smart *Amici* (☎ & ℱ0922.402.831, ⓌWwww.hotelamici.com; ❹) just by the train station is an excellent choice, and for real luxury, you can stay at the *Villa Athena*, Via dei Templi (☎0922.596.288, ℱ0922.402.180, Ⓦwww.athenahotels.com; ❾), right in the archeological zone, with a pool and big windows soaking up the views. You can **camp** 6km away at the coastal resort of **SAN LEONE**, at *Internazionale San Leone* (☎0922.416.121); bus #2 from outside the train station (every 30min until 9pm).

As for **food**, there's a budget choice at the *Atenea*, a friendly family-run trattoria in Via Ficari, in a quiet courtyard just off the Via Atenea (no credit cards; closed Sun except July & Aug). In the same neighbourhood, at Via Giambertoni 2, the folksy *Ambasciata di Sicilia* (☎0922.20.526; closed Mon) is small but has a view-laden terrace and serves good *antipasto rustico* and fresh fish. For the best pizzas head for the basic *Chez Jean 2* in Via Cicerone (no credit cards; closed Sun), but if you want something near the temples, *Trattoria Caio* on Via Nettuno in San Leone is the locals' choice for pasta and pizza. With a car and a little more money in your pocket, you could head out to *Del Vigneto* at Via Cavaleri

16

Magazzeni 11, south of the temples off the SS115 (☎0922.414.319; closed Tues & Nov); the regional dishes served here are superb.

Eraclea Minoa

From Agrigento you're well poised for moving on into western Sicily, and frequent buses get you to Sciacca in around two and a half hours. If you can, though, first drop in on the other important local Greek site, **ERACLEA MINOA** – originally named Minoa after the Cretan king Minos, who chased Daedalus from Crete to Sicily and founded a city where he landed. The Greeks settled here in the sixth century, later adding the tag Heraklea. A buffer between the two great cities at Akragas, 40km to the east, and Selinus, 60km west, Eraclea Minoa was dragged into endless border disputes, but in spite of this it flourished. Most of the remains date from the fourth century BC, Eraclea Minoa's most important period, three hundred years or so before the town declined.

The **site** (daily 9am–1hr before sunset; €2) is finely situated right on the coast, at the mouth of the River Platani. Apart from the good **walls**, once 6km long, which survive in interrupted sections, the main attraction is the sandstone **theatre**; some of the finds are held in a small on-site **museum**. While you're here, you'll be hard put to resist a trip down to the **beach**, one of the best on Sicily's southern coast, backed by pine trees and chalky cliffs. At the foot of the road from the site, a couple of bar-restaurants sit right on the beach which have **rooms** advertised; or there's a **campsite** nearby with cabins, *Eraclea Minoa Village* (☎0922.847.310; May–Oct). Without your own transport, you can get here between June and September by buses from Cattolica Eraclea or from the SS115, both accessible from Agrigento, but outside the summer months you're going to have to do some tough walking: take any bus running between Agrigento and Sciacca and ask the driver to let you off at the turning; it's 5km west of Montallegro, on the SS115, and the site is another 3.5km from there. Heading on, walk west from the site turning and you should be able to flag down a bus going to Sciacca.

Inland to Enna

The most scenically rewarding parts of Sicily's **interior** are in the east, primarily the hill-towns and villages that lie in a wide half-circle to the north of Enna – which is where you should head if you want to see the region by public transport.

From Agrigento, however, there are several worthwhile routes – most only practicable for travellers with transport. One route goes by way of **Sant'Angelo Muxaro** (daily buses from Agrigento), beyond which begins the most convoluted **approach to Palermo**, the twisting road climbing up to 1000m at Prizzi, from where there are occasional bus services down to **Corleone**. A fairly large town for these parts, it lent Mario Puzo's fictional Godfather, Don Corleone, his adopted family name – and it's the name of one of Sicily's most notorious real-life Mafia clans. There is a bus from Corleone to Palermo, another 60km.

The other option from Agrigento, better if you want to head on to the most appealing parts of the interior, is the **route to Enna**. There's a local bus service that connects up the nearer places, while trains make the journey too, up through gentle, tree-planted slopes and then across the hilltops. At Canicatti the line splits, trains running south to Licata, on the coast.

Enna

From a bulging V-shaped ridge almost 1000m up, **ENNA** lords it over the surrounding hills of central Sicily. The approach to this doughty mountain stronghold is still as formidable as ever, the bus climbing slowly out of the valley and looping across the solid crag to the summit and the town. For obvious strategic reasons, Enna was a magnet for successive hostile armies, who in turn besieged and fortified the town, each doing their damnedest to disprove Livy's description of Enna as *inexpugnabilis*.

Despite the destructive attention, most of Enna's remains are medieval and in good shape, with the prize exhibit the thirteenth-century **Castello di Lombardia** (daily: Easter–Oct 8am–8pm; Nov–Easter 9am–1pm & 3–5pm; free), dominating the easternmost spur of town. A mighty construction with its strong walls complete, it guards the steep slopes on either side of Enna, its six surviving towers (out of an original twenty) providing lookouts. From the tallest, the Torre Pisana, the magnificent views take in Enna itself, some rugged countryside in all directions and, if you're lucky, Mount Etna.

In the centre of town virtually all the accredited sights lie stretched out along and around **Via Roma**, which descends from the castle. It's a narrow street, broken by small piazzas – one of which fronts the hemmed-in **Duomo**, dating in part from 1307. The spacious sixteenth-century interior (9am–noon & 4–7pm) features huge supporting alabaster columns, the bases of which are covered with an amorphous writhing mass of carved figures. Outside, behind the apses, the **Museo Alessi** (daily 8am–8pm; €2.60) fields a rich collection of local church art, old coins and the impressive contents of the cathedral's own treasury. There's a second museum, too, equally good: the **Museo Archeologico** (daily 8am–6pm; €2), just over the way in Piazza Mazzini, covering Neolithic to Roman times and including a fine series of painted Greek vases.

Via Roma slopes down to the rectangular **Piazza Vittorio Emanuele**, focal point of the evening *passeggiata*. Off here, there's a long cliff-edge belvedere, while the bottom of the piazza is marked by the plain, high wall of the **Chiesa di San Francesco**, whose massive sixteenth-century tower previously formed part of the town's system of watchtowers. This linked the castle with the **Torre di Federico**, which stands in isolation in its little park in the largely modern south of the town. An octagonal tower, 24m high, it's a survivor of the alterations to the city made by Frederick of Aragon who added a (now hidden) underground passage linking it to the *castello*.

Practicalities

All long-distance and most local buses use the **bus terminal** on Viale Diaz in the new town – turn right out of the terminal, right again down Corso Sicilia and it's around a ten-minute walk to Piazza Vittorio Emanuele. Enna's **train station** is 5km below town, though a local bus runs roughly hourly to the centre (but only at selected times on Sunday, when you may have to take a taxi). You can reach everywhere in Enna itself very easily on foot, though **buses for Pergusa** (#5; roughly every 30min, 7am–9.30pm) leave from outside San Francesco church; tickets (€0.80) are bought from *tabacchi* and valid for one hour. Information, as well as a good, free **map** of Enna, is available from the **tourist office** at Via Roma 413 (Mon–Sat 9am–1pm & 3–7pm; closed Sat in winter; ☎0935.528.228).

There's only one **hotel** in Enna, the dead-central *Grande Albergo Sicilia* in Piazza Colaianni (☎0935.500.850, ⓕ0935.500.488; ❺), which has bright, well-furnished rooms, some with views. There's also a pleasant bed-and-breakfast place, *Da Pietro* (☎ & ⓕ0935.33.647; no credit cards; ❷), with a garden, on Contrada Longobardi in neighbouring Calscibetta (accessible by frequent buses). Alternatively, you can take a bus to nearby **PERGUSA**, supposedly the site of Hades' abduction of Persephone to the underworld. These days the famed Lago di Pergusa is encircled by a motor-racing track, alongside which are several hotels, including the *Miralago* (☎ & ⓕ0935.541.272; no credit cards; ❷), its functional exterior revealing attractive rooms, and by the racetrack on Via Autostrada, the *Riviera* (☎0935.541.267, ⓕ0935.541.260; ❺), with its own swimming pool.

For **meals** in Enna, *Tiffany*, near the cathedral at Via Roma 487 (closed Thurs), provides pizzas and pastas. *La Fontana*, Via Vulturo 6 (closed Fri in winter), has good home-cooking and friendly service, while considerably more costly is the *Ristorante Ariston*, Via Roma 353 (closed Sun); expect to pay €26–30 for a full meal with wine. The **market** in Enna is held on Tuesdays (8am–2pm) in Piazza Europa, below the Torre di Federico II.

Piazza Armerina and around

To the **south of Enna**, less than an hour away by bus, **PIAZZA ARMERINA** lies amid thick tree-planted hills, a quiet, unassuming place mainly seventeenth and eighteenth century in appearance, its skyline pierced by towers, the houses huddled together under the joint protection of castle and cathedral. All in all, it is a thoroughly pleasant place to idle around, though the real local draw is an imperial Roman **villa** that stands in rugged countryside at Casale, 5km southwest of Piazza Armerina. Hidden under mud for 700 years, the excavated remains reveal a rich villa, probably a hunting lodge and summer home, decorated with polychromatic mosaic floors that are unique in the Roman world for their quality and extent.

Buses drop you in Piazza Sen. Marescalchi, in the lower town. The old town is up the hill, centred around Piazza Garibaldi, off which is the **tourist office**, at Via Cavour 15 (Mon–Fri 8am–2pm, plus Wed 3–6.30pm; ☎0935.680.201, ⓦwww.piazza-armerina.it). The only central **hotel** choices are the rather noisily sited *Villa Romana*, Via A. de Gasperi 18 (☎ & ⓕ0935.682.911; ❹), or a refurbished fifteenth-century monastery, the *Ostello del Borgo*, Largo San Giovanni 6 (☎0935.687.019, ⓕ0935.686943, ⓦwww.ostellodelborgo.it; ❸). There are several options out of town: signposted everywhere by a red fox is the agriturismo *Agricasale* (☎ & ⓕ0935.686.034, ⓦwww.piazza-armerina.it/agricasale; half-board only; ❺), a good spot for peaceful rooms, large swimming pool, and great food; you can also camp here. The *Mosaici da Battiato*, in Contrada Paratore (☎ & ⓕ0935.685.453; closed late Nov to late Dec; ❷), is just at the turn-off to the villa which is a further 1km from the hotel, and has a grill-restaurant popular with tour groups during the day. The bus to the mosaics passes right by. Immediately across from here, *La Ruota* (☎0935.680.542; March–Oct) has space for **camping**. For **eating**, *La Tavernetta*, in town at Via Cavour 14 (closed Sun), isn't bad value for money, or

alternatively try *Da Pepito*, Via Roma 140 (closed Tues evening & Dec), opposite the park, which serves tasty Sicilian dishes.

The Villa Romana del Casale

A regular **bus service** runs to the villa between May and September from
Piazza Sen. Marescalchi in Piazza Armerina; the first bus leaves at 10.30am, and
the last returns at 6.30pm. Otherwise you'll have to take a taxi (around €10)
or **walk** the 6km: head down Via Matteotti or Via Principato and follow the
signs; it takes around an hour on foot and is an attractive walk. It's also feasible
to visit on a day-trip **from Enna** (see p.1047), but check the bus schedules
before setting out.

The **Villa Romana** (daily 8am–6.30pm; €4.50) dates from the early fourth
century BC and was used right up until the twelfth century when a mudslide
kept it largely covered until comprehensive excavations in the 1950s. It's been
covered again since to protect the mosaics, with a hard plastic and metal roof
and walls designed to indicate the original size and shape, while walkways lead
visitors through the rooms in as logical an order as possible. The mosaics themselves are identifiable as fourth-century Roman-African school, which explains
many of the more exotic scenes and animals portrayed; they also point to the
villa having had an important owner, possibly Maximianus Herculeus, co-
emperor with Diocletian.

The **main entrance** leads into a wide courtyard with fountains, where the
thermae (baths) group around an octagonal *frigidarium* and a central mosaic
showing a lively marine scene. A walkway leads out of the baths and into the
villa proper, to the massive central court or **peristyle**, whose surrounding corridors are decorated with animal head mosaics. From here, a balcony looks
down upon one of the villa's most interesting pictures, a boisterous **circus
scene** showing a chariot race. Small rooms beyond, on either side of the peristyle, reveal only fragmentary geometric patterns, although one contains probably the villa's most famous image, a two-tiered scene of ten girls, realistically
muscular **figures** in Roman "bikinis", taking part in various gymnastic and
athletic activities.

Beyond the peristyle, a long, covered corridor contains the most extraordinary of the mosaics: the **great hunting scene**, which sets armed and shield-
bearing hunters against a panoply of wild animals. Along the entire sixty-metre
length of the mosaic are tigers, ostriches, elephants, even a rhino, being trapped,
bundled up and down gangplanks and into cages, destined for the Games back
in Rome. The square-hatted figure overseeing the operation is probably
Maximianus himself: his personal area of responsibility in the imperial
Tetrarchy was North Africa, where much of the scene is set.

Other rooms beyond are nearly all on a grand scale. The **triclinium**, a dining room with three apses, features the labours of Hercules, and a path leads
around the back to the **private apartments**, based around a large basilica. Best
mosaics here are a **children's circus**, where tiny chariots are drawn by colourful birds, and a **children's hunt**, the kids chased and pecked by the hares and
peacocks they're supposed to snare.

Trápani and the west

The **west** of Sicily is a land apart. Skirting around the coast from **Trápani** –
easily the largest town in the region – it looks immediately different: the cubic

16

whitewashed houses, palm trees, active fishing harbours and sunburned low-lands seem more akin to Africa than Europe; and historically, the west of the island has always looked south. The earliest of all Sicilian sites, the mountain haunt of **Érice**, was dominated by Punic influence, the Carthaginians them-selves entrenched in **Marsala**, at Sicily's westernmost point, for several hundred years; while the Saracen invaders took their first steps on the island at **Mazara del Vallo**, a town still strongly Arabic at heart. The Greeks never secured the same foothold in Sicily's west as elsewhere, although the remains at **Segesta** and **Selinunte** count among the island's best.

Trápani

Out on something of a limb, **TRÁPANI** is an attractive enough town, though with little to keep you long – more a stopover, perhaps, en route to the off-shore Égadi Islands (see p.1053) or inland to Érice (see opposite). A rich trad-ing centre throughout the early Middle Ages, halfway point for Tunis and Africa, Trápani has suffered years of decline since then, and today suffers from its remote position on Sicily's western tip, despite the revitalization of the huge salt pans to the south of town.

The Town

Trápani's **old town**, broadly speaking the area west of the train station, sports a mix of often incongruous architectural styles, something that harks back to Trápani's past as a complex medieval Mediterranean trading centre. It's partic-ularly true of the medieval Jewish quarter, a wedge of hairline streets and alleys that holds one of the city's most characteristic buildings, the **Palazzo della Giudecca** on Via Giudecca – sixteenth-century, with a stone-studded tower and finely wrought Spanish-style Plateresque windows. Just up from here, Trápani is at its most engaging, Corso Italia preceding a confused set of three piazzas, enlivened by their surrounding churches: one doorway of the six-teenth-century **Chiesa di Santa Maria di Gesù** (Via San Pietro) is defiant-ly Renaissance in execution, and further up, on Piazzetta Saturno, the church of **Sant'Agostino** is even earlier, fourteenth-century and retaining a Gothic portal and delicate rose window.

Off the Piazzetta, Via Torrearsa neatly splits the old town. West of here Trápani's layout becomes more regularly planned, while the main drag and shopping street, the elegant **Corso Vittorio Emanuele**, changes name to Via Carolina and then Via Torre di Ligny as it runs towards the **Torre di Ligny** – utmost point of the scimitar of land that holds the old town. Finish off your circuit at the daily **market**, at the northern end of Via Torrearsa – fish, fruit and veg sold from the arcaded Piazza Mercato di Pesce, and with several lively bars in the area.

Celebrations and processions at Easter in Trápani are given added piquancy by the carriage around town on Good Friday of the **Misteri**, a group of life-sized eighteenth-century wooden figures representing scenes from the Passion. At other times they are on display in the exuberantly sculpted **Chiesa del Purgatorio** (in theory daily 4–6.30pm, plus Lent daily 10am–noon & 4–7pm; free), on Via Domenico Giglio, near the junction with Via Francesco d'Assisi.

Except on arrival, you hardly need to set foot in the newer parts of the city. The only incentive is the interesting **Museo Regionale Pépoli** (Mon–Sat 9am–1.30pm, Sun 9am–12.30pm, plus Aug & Sept daily 3.30–7pm; €2.50), a good three-kilometre bus ride away in the drab heart of modern Trápani: take bus #24, #25 or #30 from Corso Vittorio Emanuele, Via Libertà or Via

Garibaldi, and get off at the garden outside the Santuario dell'Annunziata, the fourteenth-century convent which houses the museum. The **Cappella della Madonna** contains the city's sacred statue, the *Madonna di Trápani*, attributed to Nino Pisano, which stands under a grandiose marble canopy by Antonello Gagini. Approached through bird-filled cloisters, the museum includes a bit of everything, from local archeological finds to delicate seventeenth-century coral craftwork and a good medieval art section. Look out for the grim wooden guillotine of 1789 downstairs and the eighteenth-century majolica-tiled scene of La Mattanza (the annual tuna-fish kill).

Practicalities

Come to Trápani by land from the east of the island and you'll arrive in the modern part of town: most **buses** (including those to and from Érice) pull up at the terminal in Piazza Malta (Piazza Montalto); **trains** stop just around the corner in Piazza Umberto I. Exceptions to the rule are the fast **buses** for Palermo and Agrigento, which leave from the ferry terminal as well as the bus station. **Ferries** and **hydrofoils** for the Égadi Islands, Pantelleria, Cagliari and Tunis dock at the adjacent Molo di Sanità. Trápani's **airport**, 15km south of the centre at Birgi, connects with Italian cities and Pantelleria. For well-written information in English, accommodation listings and free maps, visit the **tourist office** in Piazzetta Saturno (Mon–Sat 8am–8pm, Sun 9am–noon; ☏0923.29.000, ⓦwww.apt.trapani.it). There's an **Internet point** at the *Grimon Café* at Via G.B. Fardella (Mon 6am–9pm & Tues–Sun 6am–midnight).

Finding somewhere to stay at Easter will be tricky, unless you book well in advance, but at other times rooms are easy to come by. Cheapest of the **hotels** is the *Messina*, Corso Vittorio Emanuele 71 (☏ & ⒻF0923.21.198; no credit cards; ❶), a bit dingy and often booked out; alternatively, try the bright *Nuovo Russo* at Via Tintori 4 (☏0923.22.166, ⒻF0923.26.623; ❸). The **youth hostel** *G. Amodeo* is 3km out of town on Contrada Raganzili (☏0923.26.350; April–Oct; €11); take bus #23 from Via Fardella and get off at the Ospedale Villa dei Gerani, from where take the second on the right and walk 600m uphill. The nearest **campsite** *Lido Valdérice* is a twenty-minute bus ride away in Bonagia (☏0923.573.477; June–Sept) – there are around eight buses daily (not Sun in winter) to the turn-off, from which it's a fifteen-minute walk.

Eating is particularly enjoyable in Trápani. The *Trattoria Safina*, opposite the train station at Piazza Umberto I (closed Fri except July & Aug), is a real bargain; for fine pizzas seek out *Calvino*, Via N. Nasi 77 (no credit cards; closed Tues), parallel to the *corso*; try the speciality *oreganata*. Better-class meals are on offer at *P&G*, Via Spalti 1, near the station (☏0923.547.701; closed Sun & Aug), a semi-formal place with local *busiate* pasta.

Érice and Segesta

The nearest and most exhilarating ride from Trápani is to **ÉRICE**, forty minutes away by bus. It's a mountain town with creeping hillside alleys, stone buildings, silent charm and powerful associations. Founded by Elymnians, who claimed descent from the Trojans, the original city was known to the ancient world as Eryx, and a magnificent temple, dedicated to Venus Erycina, Mediterranean goddess of fertility, once topped the mountain. Though the city was considered impregnable, Carthaginian, Roman, Arab and Norman forces all forced entry over the centuries. But all respected the sanctity of Érice: the

Romans rebuilt the temple and set two hundred soldiers to serve as guardians of the shrine; while the Arabs renamed the town Gebel-Hamed, or Mohammed's mountain.

When it's fine, the views from the terraces of Érice are stupendous – over Trápani, the slumbering whales of the Égadi Islands and on very clear days as far as Cape Bon in Tunisia. Scout around the town at random: the most convoluted of routes is only going to take you a couple of hours and every street and piazza is a delight. You enter through the Norman **Porta Trápani**, just inside which the battlemented fourteenth-century campanile of the **Duomo** did service as a lookout tower for Frederick III of Aragon. From here there's no set route, though passing through pretty **Piazza Umberto** with its couple of outdoor bars is a good idea; and a natural start or finish could be made at the ivy-clad Norman **Castello** at the far end of town. This was built on the site of the famed ancient temple, chunks of which are incorporated in the walls.

Hardly surprisingly, **staying** in Érice means paying through the nose and booking in advance. The only relatively cheap choices are the smart *Edelweiss*, in Cortile Padre Vincenzo, a cobbled alley off Piazzetta San Domenico (℡0923.869.420, ℻0923.869.158; ❺), and, just outside town, the *Ermione*, Via Pineta Comunale 43 (℡0923.869.138, ℻0923.869.587; ❺), with a brighter interior than exterior. The helpful **tourist office** (Mon–Sat 8am–2pm; winter closed Sat; ℡0923.869.388) is on Viale Conte Pepoli and dishes out maps. If you're coming for the day you may want to bring a picnic since **restaurant** prices in Érice are vastly inflated. However, many places offer a tourist menu, such as the *Re Aceste*, Viale Conte Pepoli 45 (closed Wed & Nov), whose terrace overlooks the plain below town. There's higher-quality fare at *La Pentolaccia*, Via Guarnotti 17, housed in an old monastery and moderately priced (closed Tues), and at the more formal and correspondingly pricier *Monte San Giuliano*, entered through a medieval gateway at Vicolo San Rocco 7 (℡0923.869.595; closed Mon & 2 weeks in Nov & Jan). Don't leave without a visit either to the *Caffè Maria* at Corso Vittorio Emanuele 4 or the associated *pasticceria* a few doors down for the marzipan goodies or exquisite *cannoli*.

The Temple of Segesta

If time is limited, it's hard to know which to recommend most: the heights of Érice or Trápani's other local attraction, the temple at **Segesta** (daily 9am–1hr before sunset; €4.50). Although unfinished, this Greek construction of 424 BC is one of the most inspiring of Doric temples anywhere and, along with the theatre, virtually the only relic of an ancient city whose roots – like those of Érice – go back to the twelfth century BC. Unlike Érice, though, ancient Segesta was eventually Hellenized and spent most of the later period disputing its borders with Selinus to the south. The temple dates from a time of prosperous alliance with Athens, the building abandoned when a new dispute broke out with Selinus in 416 BC.

The **temple** itself crowns a low hill, beyond a café and car park. From a distance you could be forgiven for thinking that it's complete: the 36 regular white stone columns, entablature and pediment are all intact, and all it lacks is a roof. However, get closer and you see just how unfinished the building is: stone studs, always removed on completion, still line the stylobate, the tall columns are unfluted and the cella walls are missing. Below the car park, a road winds up through slopes of wild fennel to the small **theatre** on a higher hill beyond; there's a half-hourly minibus service if you don't fancy the climb. The view from the top is justly lauded, across green slopes and the plain to the sea, the deep blue of the bay a lovely contrast to the theatre's white stone – not much damaged by the stilted motorway snaking away below.

Without your own transport, **getting to Segesta** involves a twenty-minute uphill walk from Segesta-Tempio, to which there are at least three buses a day from Piazza Malta in Trápani, the last one returning at around 6.15pm, and four trains (Mon–Sat), two on Sunday, from Trápani stopping here on their way to Palermo. There are more frequent trains connecting Trápani and Palermo with the station of **CALATAFIMI**, signposted 4km away (the town itself is a further 4km away). There's also a cheap and modern **hotel** in Calatafimi, the *Mille Pini*, Piazza F. Vivona 4 (☎0924.951.260, ℱ0924.950.223, ℮millepini@tin.it; ❷), if you want to stay the night in the quiet surroundings.

The Égadi Islands

Of the various islands, islets and rock stacks that fan out from the west coast of Sicily, the three **Égadi Islands** (Isole Égadi) are best for a quick jaunt – connected by ferry and hydrofoil with Trápani. Saved from depopulation by tourism, in season at least you're not going to be alone, certainly on the main island, Favignana. But a tour of the islands is worthwhile, not least for the caves that perforate the splintered coastlines. Out of season things are noticeably quieter: come between April and July and you may witness the bloody Mattanza, an age-old slaughter in this noted centre of tuna fishing.

All **transport** (ferries and hydrofoils several times daily in summer) to the islands departs from Trápani's Molo di Sanità; tickets are available from the booth on the dockside on Via Ammiraglio Staiti. Though less frequent, ferries are, as always, much cheaper.

FAVIGNANA, island and port town, is first stop for the boats from Trápani, a good base since it has virtually all the accommodation and the Égadi's only campsites. Only 25 minutes by hydrofoil from the mainland, the island attracts a lot of day-trippers, keen to get onto its few rocky beaches. But get out of the main port and it's easy enough to escape the crowds, even easier with a bike. (There's a bike rental shop, Isidoro, at Via Mazzini 40; around €5.20 a day.) Caves all over the island bear prehistoric traces and many are accessible if you're determined enough. Otherwise, the two wings of the island invite separate walks; best is the stroll around the eastern part, past the bizarre ancient quarries at Cala Rossa and taking in Lido Burrone, the island's best beach, only 3km from the port. Best **hotel** choice for value and comfort is the modern *Égadi*, Via C. Colombo 17 (☎ & ℱ0923.921.232; no credit cards; ❹), right in the centre of Favignana town, and there are two **campsites** outside town – an easy walk and both well signposted.

LÉVANZO, to the north, looks immediately inviting, its white houses against the turquoise sea reminiscent of the Greek islands. The steep coast is full of inlets and, again, is riddled with caves. One, the **Grotta del Genovese**, was discovered in 1949 and contains some remarkable Paleolithic incised drawings, 6000 years old, as well as later Neolithic pictures. To arrange to see the cave you'll have to contact the guardian, Natale Castiglione, who lives at Via Calvario 11 (call ☎0923.924.032 during summer; weekends only in winter), near the hydrofoil quay. There are two **hotels** on Lévanzo, both just above the only road and with good views over the sea; the cheaper one is the *Paradiso* (☎ & ℱ0923.924.080; ❸), and a little further up the side road, the *Pensione Dei*

Fenici (☎ & ℱ 0923.924.083; no credit cards; ❸) is much fancier. In summer, both places demand half- or full-board. However, you should be able to get **rooms** in private houses if you ask around the port.

MARÉTTIMO, furthest out of the Égadi Islands, is the place to come for solitude. Very much off the beaten track, it's reached by only a few tourists. More white houses are scattered across the rocky island, while there's a bar in the main piazza and two restaurants. The spectacular fragmented coastline is pitted with rocky coves sheltering hideaway **beaches**, and there are numerous gentle **walks** which will take you all over the island. Again, although there are no hotels on Maréttimo you should be able to rent a room by asking at the café in the main square.

Trápani to Palermo: the coastal route

Frequent buses run north from Trápani, cutting away from the coast until reaching **SAN VITO LO CAPO** at the very nib of the northwestern headland. There are some good sands nearby, while the cape itself is only a stride away; and there are several **campsites** too – good options are the central *La Fata* (☎ 0923.972.133) and *La Pineta* (☎ 0923.972.818, ⓦ www.campinglapineta.it), a twenty-minute walk in the Scopello direction. San Vito is a popular local holiday spot and you don't have to camp – there are several fairly good **pensioni** in the village, as well as trattorias and bars catering to the summer crowds. Best value is the nicely furnished *Eden*, Via Mulino 62, a ten-minute walk from the beach (☎ 0923.972.460; closed Nov–Feb; no credit cards; ❷). A step up in price is the *Ocean View*, behind the church at Via Santuario 49 (☎ 0923.972.508, ℱ 0923.621.163, ⓦ www.hotelsabbiadoro.com; closed Nov–Feb; ❹), which has pleasant rooms and an inner courtyard garden. The main Via Savoia has at least three places offering rooms up to ❹; cheapest is the *Costa Gaia* (☎ 0923 .972.268, ℱ 0923.621.531, ⓦ www.albergocostagaia.com; no credit cards; ❸). *Hotel Capo San Vito*, right on the beach at Via San Vito 3 (☎ 0923.972.284, ℱ 0923.972.559, ⓦ www.caposanvito.it; ❼; closed Dec–March), is unprepossessing from the outside, but pukka within, and has a Moorish-style terrace restaurant. At least half-board is compulsory in July and August at the last three. There's no shortage of good places to **eat**; couscous is the thing to try here. Go for the elaborately decorated *Tha'am* at Via Duca degli Abruzzi 32 (☎ 0923.972.836; closed Tues in winter), off Via Savoia.

You'll have to return to Trápani for onward transport. Buses or, more frequently, **trains** cut across the headland to **CASTELLAMMARE DEL GOLFO**, another popular resort built on and around a hefty rocky promontory which is guarded by the squat remains of an Aragonese castle. The local **train station** is 4km east of town; a bus meets arrivals and shuttles you into Castellammare. However, if you're looking for a place to stay you could do much better by moving the 10km west up the coast to Scopello; there are four buses a day (Mon–Sat) from the **bus station** on Via della Repubblica off the main Via Segesta.

The road to **SCOPELLO** from Castellammare forks just before the village, with one strand running the few hundred metres down to the **Tonnara do Scopello**, set in its own tiny cove. This old tuna fishery is where the writer Gavin Maxwell lived and worked in the 1950s, basing his *Ten Pains of Death* on his experiences there. It's almost too picturesque to be true – not least the row of abandoned buildings on the quayside and the ruined old watchtowers tottering on jagged pinnacles of rock above the sea. The actual village of Scopello perches on a ridge a couple of hundred metres above the coastline, comprising little more than a paved square and a fountain, off which run a couple of alleys. In summer, particularly, you'd do well to book in advance if you want **to stay** here. *La Tranchina* at Via A. Diaz 7 (ⓣ & ⓕ0924.541.099; ❸, including breakfast) has comfortable rooms with an English-speaking owner. *La Tavernetta*, next door at no. 3 (ⓣ & ⓕ0924.541.129; ❸), has similarly pleasant rooms, some with distant sea views. The food at the *Torre Benistra*, just around the corner at Via Natale di Roma 19 (ⓣ & ⓕ0924.541.128; ❷), is probably best in the village. Half-board is compulsory in July and August at all three. The nearest **campsite** is *Baia di Guidaloca* (ⓣ0924.541.262; April–Sept), 3km south of Scopello and a stone's throw from the lovely bay of **Cala Bianca**, where there's good swimming; the bus from Castellammare passes right by.

The southern entrance to the **Riserva Naturale dello Zíngaro** is just 2km from Scopello, the first nature reserve to have been established in Sicily, comprising a completely unspoiled seven-kilometre stretch of coastline backed by steep mountains. At the entrance, there's an **information hut**, where you can pick up a plan showing the trails through the reserve. It's less than twenty minutes to the first beach, **Punta della Capreria**, and 3km to the successive coves of **Disa**, **Berretta** and **Marinella**, which should be a little more secluded.

East of here (and the train from Trápani stops at every town before Palermo) it's a strange – often unpleasant – coastal mixture of industrialization and tourist development. The wide and fertile gulf provides some good views though, and there's the occasional beach that beckons. The last few towns that line the gulf, **Balestrate**, **Trappeto** and, inland, **Partinico**, are more interesting for what they were, and to some extent still are – infamous centres of Mafia influence and social and political neglect. **Daniel Dolci**, a social reformer of remarkable persistence, first came to Trappeto in 1952 from wealthy northern Italy. He was appalled. "Looking all around me, I saw no streets, just mud and dust. Not a single drugstore – or sewer. The dialect didn't even have a word for sewer." Dolci inaugurated a programme of self-help among the local people, building community and cultural centres, promoting local education – things that cut right across the traditional areas of influence in the Mafia-ridden west of Sicily. It's a story told in the words of the local people in Dolci's extraordinary book *Sicilian Lives*: vital reading if you intend to pass this way.

Mózia, Marsala and Mazara del Vallo

Around 15km **south of Trápani**, the unique Phoenician settlement of **MÓZIA** (also known as Mothia or Motya) lies just offshore from the crystalline patchwork of saltpans which line this part of the coast. Situated on one of the islands in the shallow Stagnone lagoon, it was excavated in the late nineteenth century by an Englishman, Joseph Whitaker. You can explore the ruins (daily: April–Oct 9am–1pm & 3–6pm; Nov–March 9am–3pm; €6 including ferry) and visit the museum he established, which alone is worth a visit for its magnificent and sensual sculpture, *Il Giovannetto di Mozia*. If you're reliant on public transport, the island is more easily reached from Marsala: regular buses run from Piazza del Pópolo to the ferry-landing. And should you want to **stay** in the area, the peaceful *Baglio Vajarassa* (ⓣ0923.968.628, ⓦwww.bagliovajarassa.com; no credit cards; ❺) on Contrada Spagnola 176, a couple of kilometres south of the ferry landing, offers rooms furnished with antiques, and dinner (included in the price) around a communal table.

By-passing Mózia, and pretty much keeping within sight of the sea all the way, the western rail loop runs down the coast from Trápani to **MARSALA**, a distance of around 25km. The city, which takes its name from the Arabic Marsah-el-Allah, the port of Allah, was once the main Saracenic base in Sicily, but since the late eighteenth century it has been better known for the dessert wine that carries its name, something every bar and restaurant will sell you.

The centre of Marsala is extremely attractive, a clean sixteenth-century layout that's free of traffic and littered with high, ageing buildings and arcaded courtyards. But – pleasant as the town is – save your energy for two excellent museums. The most central, behind the cathedral at Via Garraffa 57, is the **Museo degli Arazzi** (Tues–Sun 9am–1pm & 4–6pm; €1.50), whose sole display is a series of eight enormous hand-stitched wool and silk tapestries depicting the capture of Jerusalem – sixteenth-century and beautifully rich, in burnished red, gold and green. Afterwards, walk out to the cape (follow the main Via XI Maggio to Piazza della Vittoria and bear left towards the water); one of the stone-vaulted warehouses that line the promenade holds the equally impressive **Museo Marsala** (daily 9am–1.30pm, plus Wed & Fri–Sun 4–7pm; €2). An archeological museum of quality, its major exhibit is a reconstructed Punic warship once rowed by 68 oarsmen, probably sunk during the First Punic War, and rediscovered in 1971. Other bits and pieces on display are from the excavated site (mostly Roman) of Lilybaeum. If you want a **meal** in Marsala, head for the wood-panelled *Trattoria Garibaldi* at Piazza Addolorata 5 (closed Mon) for good local dishes.

Half an hour's driving further on, **MAZARA DEL VALLO** is Sicily's most important fishing port and a place of equal distinction for the Arabs and Normans who dominated the island a thousand years ago. The first Saracen gain in Sicily, Mazara, was Arabic for 250 years until captured by Count Roger in 1075: the island's first Norman parliament met in the town 22 years later, and a relic of that period is the tiny pink-domed Norman chapel of **San Nicolò**, on the edge of the harbour. North Africans crew the colourful fishing boats that block the harbour and river, the old city kasbah once more houses a Tunisian community. Wandering around the harbour area is the most rewarding thing to do in Mazara, although you can spend an enjoyable hour or so as well in the remodelled Norman **Duomo**, which shelters some Roman and Byzantine remains, and poking around the **Museo Civico** (Mon–Fri 9am–1pm, plus Tues & Thurs 3.30–5.30pm; free) in Piazza del Plebiscito, just off Mazara's main square. The only hotel **accommodation** is the dauntingly large but very comfortable *Hopps Hotel*, at Via G. Hopps 29 (℡0923.946.133, ℻0923.946.075; ❺), at the eastern end of the Lungomare Mazzini. A good **restaurant** for regional dishes in the town is *La Béttola* at Corso Diaz 20, opposite the train station (closed Wed).

Marinella, Selinunte and Sciacca

There's very little else to stop for around the western coast; even less inland, which is crossed by one major road, the SS188, which runs from Marsala to Salemi, centre of a prosperous wine-making region. But the southernmost chunk of Sicily's western bulge is easily reached by train and has several places worth more than a cursory glance if you have the time.

MARINELLA, together with the nearby Greek ruins of Selinunte, is one of them. To get there you'll need to take a bus from Piazza Reina Margherita (5 daily; 25min) in Castelvetrano, a little way inland from Marzara dell Vallo. The village, right next to the Greek ruins of **Selinunte**, is no longer the isolated place it once was, with new buildings in the centre and the seafront slightly top-heavy with trattorias and *pensioni* these days. But it remains an attractive place, certainly if you're planning to make use of the fine sand **beach** that stretches west from the village to the ruins. **Buses** pull up on the road that leads down to the seafront, where the main **hotels** and restaurants are situated. First choice here is the *Lido Azzurro*, Via Marco Polo 98 (ⓣ & ⓕ0924.46.256; half-board in July & Aug; ❸), a charming villa with sea-facing balconies. Opposite the temple car park, the sign pointing to "Chiesa" leads to the old abandoned train station, just before which you'll find *Il Pescatore*, at Via Castore e Polluce 31 (ⓣ0924.46.303; no credit cards; ❶), with a very genial host, fruit breakfasts (€3) on the terrace and rooftop camping. There are also two **campsites** virtually next to each other on the main road, though they are 1500m north of the village: the *Athena* (ⓣ0924.46.132) and *Il Maggiolino* (ⓣ0924.46.044, ⓦwww.campingmaggiolino.it); the bus from Castelvetrano passes right by them. Of the many **restaurants**, *Baffo's*, at Via Marco Polo 51, is good value, with a wide selection of fish dishes. In the residential district, the ristorante-pizzeria *da Bruno* (closed Thurs except July & Aug), in Via Alceste, serves crispy pizzas from a wood-burning stove, good antipasti and a reasonable tourist menu. For a meal by the sea, *La Pineta* on the east beach, Mare Pineta, can't be bettered for its location, fish dishes and speciality bread.

Selinunte: the site

The westernmost of the Hellenic colonies, the Greek city of Selinus – **Selinunte** in modern Italian – reached its peak in the fifth century BC when a series of mighty temples was erected. A bitter rival of Segesta (see p.1052), whose lands lay adjacent to the north, the powerful city and its fertile plain attracted enemies hand over fist, and it was only a matter of time before Selinus caught the eye of Segesta's ally, Carthage. Geographically vulnerable, the city was sacked by Carthaginians, any recovery forestalled by earthquakes that later razed the city. Despite the destruction, which left the site completely abandoned until it was rediscovered in the sixteenth century, the ruins of Selinus have exerted a romantic hold ever since.

The **site** of Selinus is set back behind the main part of Marinella village, split into two parts with temples in each, known only as Temples A–G. The two parts are enclosed within the same site, with the car park and **entrance** (daily 9am–1hr before sunset; €4.50, tickets sold until 2hr before sunset) lying through the landscaped earthbanks that preclude views of the east group of temples from the road. The first stop is at the **East Group**. Shrouded in the wild celery which gave the ancient city its name, the temples are in various stages of reconstructed ruin: the most complete the one nearest the sea (Temple E), the northernmost (Temple G) a tangle of columned wreckage six metres high in places. The road leads down from here, across the (now buried) site of the old harbour to the second part of excavated Selinus, the **acropolis**, a site containing what remains of the other temples (five in all), as well as the well-preserved city streets and massive, stepped walls which rise above the duned beach below. Temple C stands on the highest point of the acropolis, and there are glorious views from its stones out over the sparkling sea: from this temple were removed some of the best metopes, now on show in Palermo's archeological museum (see p.1008).

Sciacca

FS **buses** leave from outside Castelvetrano train station three times daily (1 on Sun) for Sciacca, picking up at the abandoned Selinunte station in Marinella village. **SCIACCA**'s upper town is skirted by good medieval walls which form high sides to the steep streets, rising to a ruined Spanish castle. Below, the lower town sits on a clifftop terrace overlooking the harbour, a place where it's easy to while away time drinking in the coastal views. Hot springs at **Monte San Calogero**, 8km from town, kept the Romans healthy and are still in use. Get there on bus #5 every ninety minutes from Sciacca; ask for details at the **tourist office**, Corso Vittorio Emanuele 84 (Mon–Sat 9am–2pm; ☎0925.22.744, ⓦwww.aziendaturismosciacca.it).

With an active harbour here and some good beaches close by, Sciacca makes a nice place to **stay** over, though there's precious little choice – the only central option being the obliging *Paloma Bianca* at Via Figuli 5 (☎0925.25.667, ⓕ0925.25.130; ❸), a rather uninspiring business-travellers' hotel, but comfortable enough. You could spend a little more money on the plusher *Grand Hotel delle Terme*, Viale Nuove Terme 1 (☎0925.23.133, ⓕ0925.87.002; ❼), on the cliffs to the east of town, set in its own park with outstanding views out to sea. The nearest **campsite**, *Baia Makauda* (☎0925.997.001), 9km east of town at Località San Giorgio Tranchina, also has bungalows and is best reached by taxi if you don't have your own transport.

Pantelleria

Forty kilometres nearer to Tunisia than to Sicily, **PANTELLERIA** is the most singular of Sicily's outlying islands. Volcanic, it has been settled since Neolithic times and later supported a Phoenician colony in the seventh century BC. Its strategic position kept it in the mainstream of Sicilian history for years: developed as one of the main Mediterranean bases by the Fascists during World War II, Pantelleria was bombed without mercy by the Allies in May 1943 as they advanced from North Africa. In part, this explains the morose appearance of the island's main town (also called Pantelleria) – thrown up in unedifying concrete.

There are no beaches of any kind in Pantelleria, its rough black coastline mainly jagged rocks, but the **swimming** is still pretty good in some exceptionally scenic spots. Inland, the largely mountainous country offers plenty of **rambling** opportunities, all an easy moped- or bus-ride from the port. If you're spending any length of time on Pantelleria, a novel accommodation option is to stay in one of the local **dammuso** houses: a throwback to the buildings of Neolithic times, their strong walls and domed roofs keep the temperature down indoors; many are available for rent (through Call Tour, Via Cágliari 52 ☎0923.911.065). The main drawback is the **cost of living**: there are only a few hotels, where there may be a minimum three-day stay in July and August, while food (and water) is mostly imported and therefore relatively expensive. The best times to visit are May/June or September/October, to avoid the summer's ferocious heat.

Practicalities

PANTELLERIA TOWN is the site of most of the island's accommodation and facilities. For online information, consult ⓦwww.pantelleria.it. The **airport** is 5km southeast of town; a bus connects with flight arrivals and drops

Siremar **ferries** from Trápani (June–Sept 1 daily; Oct–May 1 daily Mon–Sat) take just under six hours to reach Pantelleria, for a deck-class fare of around €22.44 one way, less outside the high season. The **hydrofoil service**, also from Trápani, is twice as fast and twice the price; it currently operates from mid-June to mid-September, on Wednesday, Friday and Sunday.

Pantelleria is thirty minutes' **flight** from Trápani (1–2 daily), or 50 minutes from Palermo (at least 2 daily): the normal one-way fare from either is around €70, but there are special offers at weekends, and discounts are available from mainland travel agencies and the Cossira office on the island.

you in the central Piazza Cavour. **Arriving by sea**, you'll disembark right in the centre of town. The local **buses** leave from Piazza Cavour, with regular departures to all the main villages on the island – there are no services on Sundays. The few **hotels** in town include the *Miryam*, Corso Umberto I (℡0923.911.374, ℱ0932.911.777; ❹), which is at the far end of the port, near the castle, and is bright and pleasant inside despite rather glum external appearances; the *Port Hotel* (℡0923.911.299, ℱ0923.912.203; ❻), nearer the dock at Via Borgo Italia 6, with harbour-facing rooms; and the nearby *Khamma*, at Via Borgo Italia 24 (℡0923.912.680, ℱ0923.912.570; ❻). Rates fall considerably out of high season. There's no **campsite** on the island. Probably the best place to **eat** in town is *Il Cappero*, Via Roma 31, just off the main piazza (no credit cards; closed Mon in winter), which serves the local ravioli stuffed with *tumma*, fresh fish (including large tuna steaks) and popular pizzas. There's a good antipasto table too. The best-placed trattoria in town is *Il Dammuso*, Via Borgo Italia (near the *Miryam*), a trendy place with large windows opening right onto the harbour; the long menu includes great fish and pizzas.

Around the island

There are seven daily **buses** along the southwest coast to Scauri, passing on the way the first of the island's strange **sesi**, massive black Neolithic funeral mounds of piled rock, with low passages leading inside. On foot, it's just over an hour from the *sesi* to **Sataria**, where concrete steps lead down to a tiny square-cut sea pool. In the cave behind are more pools where warm water bubbles through, reputed to be good for curing rheumatism and skin diseases.

Along the northeast coast to Kamma and Tracino (6 daily buses), get the bus to drop you at the top of the route down into **Gadir**, a small anchorage with just a few houses hemmed in by volcanic pricks of rock. From here it's an easy, fairly flat hour's stroll to the charming **Cala Levante**, a huddle of houses around another tiny fishing harbour. Where the road peters out, bear right along the path at the second anchorage and keep along the coast for another five minutes until the **Arco dell'Elefante**, or "Elephant Arch", hoves into view, named after the hooped formation of rock that resembles an elephant stooping to drink.

The main inland destination is Pantelleria's main volcano, the Montagna Grande, whose summit is the island's most distinctive feature seen from out at sea. Buses (4 daily) run from the port for the crumbly old village of **Siba**, perched on a ridge below the volcano. To climb the peak of **Montagna Grande** (836m), keep left at the telephone sign by the *tabacchi* here, and strike off the main road. From Siba, another (signposted) path – on the left as you follow the road through the village – brings you in around twenty minutes to the **Sauna Naturale** (or Bagno Asciutto). It's little more than a slit in the rock-face, where you can crouch in absolute darkness, breaking out into a heavy sweat as soon as you enter.

Travel details

Trains

Agrigento to: Palermo (10 daily; 2hr); Términi Imerese (10 daily; 1hr 35min).

Catania to: Enna (7 daily; 1hr 25min); Messina (1–2 hourly; 1hr 30min–2hr); Palermo (3 daily; 3hr 30min); Siracusa (1–2 hourly; 1hr 30min); Taormina (1–2 hourly; 50min).

Enna to: Caltanissetta (10 daily; 25min); Catania (8 daily; 1hr 25min); Palermo (3 daily; 2hr).

Messina to: Catania (1–2 hourly; 1hr 30min–2hr); Cefalù (hourly; 2hr 35min); Palermo (hourly daily; 2hr 55min–4hr 25min); Taormina (1–2 hourly; 20min–1hr).

Palermo to: Agrigento (10 daily; 2hr); Castelvetrano (3 daily; 2hr); Catania (3 daily; 3hr 30min); Cefalù (1–2 hourly; 1hr); Enna (3 daily; 2hr); Marsala (3 daily; 3hr); Mazara del Vallo (3 daily; 2hr 30min); Messina (hourly daily; 2hr 45min–4hr 10min); Milazzo (hourly daily; 2hr 20min–4hr); Términi Imerese (1–2 hourly; 30–40min); Trápani (9 daily; 2hr 30min).

Ragusa to: Módica (7 daily; 20min); Noto (6 daily; 1hr 30min).

Randazzo to: Riposto (6 daily; 45min).

Siracusa to: Catania (1–2 hourly; 1hr 30min); Messina (hourly daily; 2hr 40min–3hr 20min); Noto (9 daily; 30min); Ragusa (4 daily; 2hr 20min).

Taormina to: Catania (1–2 hourly; 50min); Messina (1–2 hourly; 45min–1hr 15min); Siracusa (1–2 hourly; 2hr 15min).

Trápani to: Calatafimi (9 daily; 40min); Castelvetrano (hourly; 1hr 10min); Marsala (hourly; 30min); Mazara del Vallo (hourly; 50min); Palermo (5 daily; 3hr 25min); Segesta-Tempio (4 daily; 25min).

Buses

Schedules below are for Monday–Saturday services; on Sundays, services are either drastically reduced or non-existent.

Agrigento to: Catania (9 daily; 2hr 50min); Palermo (hourly; 2hr); Trápani (4 daily; 3hr 30min).

Castelvetrano to: Agrigento (4 daily; 2hr); Marinella (5 daily; 20min); Marsala (3 daily;

40min); Mazara del Vallo (3 daily; 20min); Trápani (6 daily; 1hr 30min).

Catania to: Agrigento (11 daily; 2hr 50min); Enna (6 daily; 1hr 25min); Messina (1–2 hourly; 1hr 35min); Nicolosi (hourly; 40min); Noto (7 daily; 1hr 25 min–2hr 15min); Palermo (hourly; 2hr 40min); Piazza Armerina (4 daily; 2hr 50min); Ragusa (12 daily; 1hr 55min); Siracusa (hourly; 1hr 20min); Taormina (hourly; 1hr 5min–1hr 55min).

Enna to: Catania (7 daily; 1hr 20min); 1hr 20min); Piazza Armerina (6 daily; 40min).

Messina to: Catania (hourly; 1hr 35min); Catania airport (8 daily 1 hr 45min); Giardini-Naxos (7 daily; 50min–1hr 50min); Milazzo (hourly; 50min); Palermo (6 daily; 3hr 10min); Randazzo (4 daily; 2hr); Taormina (hourly; 1hr).

Milazzo to: Messina (hourly; 50min).

Palermo to: Agrigento (hourly; 2hr); Catania (hourly; 2hr 40min); Cefalù (3 daily; 1hr); Enna (6 daily; 1hr 35min–2hr); Marsala (hourly; 2 hr 30min); Messina (7 daily; 3hr); Siracusa (hourly; 3hr 15min); Trápani (hourly; 2hr).

Piazza Armerina to: Enna (5 daily; 30min); Palermo (7 daily; 2hr–2hr 30min).

Siracusa to: Catania (hourly; 1hr 25min); Noto (hourly; 40min); Piazza Armerina (1 daily; 2hr 30min); Ragusa (7 daily; 1hr 30min).

Taormina to: Castelmola (6 daily; 15min); Catania (hourly; 1hr 5min–2hr 5min).

Trápani to: Agrigento (3 daily; 3hr 30min); Érice (10 daily; 40min); San Vito Lo Capo (7 daily; 1hr 15min).

Ferries

The services detailed here refer to the period from June to September; you should expect frequencies to be greatly reduced or suspended outside these months, especially to the Aeolian Islands.

Lípari to: Alicudi (5 weekly; 3hr 10min–3hr 50min); Filicudi (6 weekly; 2hr–2hr 45min); Milazzo (6–9 daily; 1hr 15min–2hr 30min); Naples (3–6 weekly; 14hr); Panarea (1–2 daily; 1hr 55min); Salina (2 daily; 50min); Strómboli (1–2 daily; 3hr–4hr 15min); Vulcano (3–5 daily; 25min).

Messina to: Lípari (4 daily; 1hr 30min); Villa San

Giovanni (every 20min; 40min).

Milazzo to: Alicudi (5 weekly; 5hr 5min); Filicudi (5–6 weekly, 5hr); Ginostra (3–6 weekly; 5hr 10min); Lípari (6–9 daily; 1hr 5min–2hr); Naples (6 weekly; 16hr 30min); Panarea (6 weekly; 4hr 10min–5hr); Salina (3–4 daily; 2hr 35min–3hr 50min); Strómboli (9 weekly; 6hr–6hr 25min); Vulcano (4 daily; 1hr 25min–2hr).

Palermo to: Cágliari (1 weekly; 13hr 30min); Genoa (1 daily; 20hr); Livorno (3 weekly; 17hr); Naples (1 daily; 10hr 15min); Ústica (1 daily; 2hr 20min).

Trápani to: Cágliari (1 weekly; 11hr); Favignana (1 daily; 55min–1hr 25min); Lévanzo (3 daily; 50min–1hr 30min); Maréttimo (1 daily; 2hr 35min); Pantelleria (1 daily; 5hr 45min).

Hydrofoils and fast ferries

Again, most of the services listed are greatly reduced or suspended outside the summer season.
Cefalù to: Lípari (3 weekly; 3hr 15min); Palermo (3 weekly; 1hr); Vulcano (3 weekly; 3hr).

Lípari to: Alicudi (4 daily; 1hr 20min–2 hr); Cefalù (3 weekly; 3hr 15min); Filicudi (4 daily; 1hr 5min–1hr 30min); Ginostra (3 daily; 1hr–1hr 25min); Messina (5 daily; 1hr 25min–3hr 40min); Milazzo (hourly; 55min); Naples (2 daily; 5hr 35min); Palermo (2 daily; 3hr 55min); Panarea (6 daily; 25min–1hr 20min); Salina (hourly; 20–45min); Strómboli (6 daily; 1hr–1hr 55min);

Vulcano (hourly; 10min).

Messina to: Lípari (5 daily; 1hr 20min–2hr 35min); Réggio di Calabria (hourly; 15–25min); Vulcano (5 daily; 1hr 20min–2hr 50min).

Milazzo to: Alicudi (3 daily; 2hr 35min–3hr); Filicudi (3 daily; 2hr 20min–2hr 45min); Ginostra (3 daily; 1hr 5min–2hr 35min); Lípari (hourly; 35min–1hr); Panarea (6 daily; 1hr 50min–2hr 20min); Salina (hourly; 1hr 20min–1hr 50min); Strómboli (6 daily; 1hr 25min–2hr 20min); Vulcano (hourly; 40min–1hr).

Palermo to: Cefalù (3 weekly; 1hr); Lípari (2 daily; 3hr 25min–3hr 55min); Naples (1 daily; 4hr); Ústica (2–3 daily; 1hr 15min).

Pantelleria to: Trápani (3 weekly; 2hr 15min).

Trápani to: Favignana (14 daily; 25min); Lévanzo (10 daily; 35min); Maréttimo (3 daily; 1hr); Naples (3 weekly; 6hr 45min); Pantelleria (3 weekly; 2hr 10min–3hr); Ústica (3 weekly; 2hr 30min).

Ústica to: Favignana (3 weekly; 2hr); Naples (3 weekly; 4hr); Trápani (3 weekly; 2hr 30min).

Flights

Palermo to: Pantelleria (2–4 daily; 50min).
Trápani to: Pantelleria (1 daily; 45min).

International ferries and catamarans

Catania to: Malta (3 weekly–2 daily; 3–11hr).
Trápani to: Tunis (1 weekly; 8hr 15min).

SICILY | Travel details

16

Sardinia

CHAPTER 17 # Highlights

* **Cágliari's old town**
Cágliari's Castello quarter is the most atmospheric part of town, a dense warren of alleys girded by thick walls. See p.1073

* **Nora** Although much of this Carthaginian and Roman archeological site is submerged under the sea, what remains – including mosaics, a theatre and baths – gives a good indication of the town's former importance. See p.1076

* **Sa Sartiglia, Oristano** One of the island's most spectacular festivals, involving brilliant feats of equestrian prowess, fab-

ulous costumes and lashings of medieval pageantry. See p.1081

* **Tiscali** A vast cave housing the remains of a prehistoric village. See p.1087

* **Nuraghe Su Nuraxi** Sardinia's mysterious prehistoric *nuraghi* are strewn throughout the island, and this is one of the most impressive. See p.1077

* **La Pelosa** You don't need to venture far to find idyllic beaches in Sardinia, but this one, on the island's northwestern tip, is a classic. See p.1103

Sardinia

A little under 200km from the Italian mainland, slightly more than that from the North African coast at Tunisia, Sardinia is way off most tourist itineraries of Italy: D.H. Lawrence found it exotically different when he passed through here in 1921 – "lost", as he put it, "between Europe and Africa and belonging to nowhere." Your reasons for coming will probably be a combination of plain curiosity and a yearning for clean beaches. The island is relatively free of large cities or heavy industry, and its beaches are indeed some of the cleanest in Italy and on the whole uncrowded, except perhaps for peak season, when ferries bring in a steady stream of sun-worshippers from what the islanders call il continente, or mainland Italy. But Sardinia offers plenty besides sun and sea – the more so if you are prepared to penetrate into its lesser-known interior.

Although not known for its cultural riches, the island does hold some surprises, not least the remains of the various civilizations that passed through here. Its central Mediterranean position ensured that it was never left alone for long, and from the Carthaginians onwards the island was ravaged by a succession of invaders, each of them leaving some imprint behind: Roman and Carthaginian ruins, Genoan fortresses, a string of elegant Pisan churches, not to mention some impressive Gothic and Spanish Baroque architecture. Perhaps most striking of all, however, are the remnants of Sardinia's only significant native culture, known as the **nuraghic** civilization after the 7000-odd *nuraghi* that litter the landscape. These mysterious, stone-built constructions, unique to Sardinia, are often in splendid isolation, which means they're fairly difficult to get to without your own transport, but make the effort to see at least one during your stay – or failing that, drop in on the museums of Cágliari or Sássari to view the lovely statuettes and domestic objects left by this culture.

On the whole, Sardinia's smaller centres are the most attractive, but the capital, **Cágliari** – for many the arrival point – shouldn't be written off. With good accommodation and restaurants, it makes a useful base for exploring the southern third of the island. The other main ferry port is **Olbia** in the north, little more than a transit town but well geared for accommodation and conveniently close to the jagged northern coast. The **Costa Smeralda**, a few kilometres distant, is Sardinia's best-known resort area and lives up to its reputation for opulence. The prices may preclude anything more than a brief visit, although there are campsites for those outside the ranks of the super-rich.

Both Olbia and Cágliari have airports, as does Sardinia's main package destination of **Alghero** – a fishing port in the northwest of the island that has been known to British holiday-makers for years, yet retains a friendly, unspoiled air.

Sardinian cooking revolves around scintillatingly fresh ingredients simply prepared: seafood – especially **lobster** – is grilled over open fires scented with myrtle and juniper, as is meltingly tender **suckling pig**. This means that there is little pork left to be made into salami and other cured meats, although a few wild boar escape the fire long enough to be made into *prosciutto di cinghiale*, a ham with a strong flavour of game. Being surrounded by sparkling seas, Sardinians also make rich, Spanish-inspired **fish stews** and produce **bottarga**, a version of caviar made with mullet eggs. **Pasta** is substantial here, taking the form of *culurgiones* (massive ravioli filled with cheese and egg) or *malloreddus* (saffron-flavoured, *gnocchi*-like shapes), while cheeses tend to be made from ewe's milk and are either fresh and herby or pungent and salty – like the famous **pecorino sardo**. The island is also famous for the quality and variety of its bread, ranging from parchment-like *carta da musica* wafers to chunky rustic loaves intended to sustain shepherds on the hills. As in Sicily, there is an abundance of light and airy **pastries**, frequently flavoured with lemon, almonds or orange flower water.

Vernaccia is the most famous Sardinian wine: a hefty drink reminiscent of sherry and treated in a similar way – the bone-dry version as an **aperitif** and the sweet variant as a **dessert wine**. Other wines worth seeking out are Mandrolasi, an easy-drinking **red**, and Cannonau di Sardegna, a heady number much favoured by locals. Among the **whites**, look out for dry Torbato or the full-flavoured Trebbiano Sardo, both perfect accompaniments to local fish and seafood.

But Alghero's main attraction is its Spanish ambience, a legacy of long years in which the town was a Catalan colony, giving it a wholly different feel from the rest of the island. Inland, **Nuoro** has impressive literary credentials and a good ethnographical museum. As the biggest town in Sardinia's interior, it also makes a useful stopover for visiting some of the remoter mountain areas, in particular the **Gennargentu** range, covering the heart of the island. This is where you can find what remains of the island's traditional culture, best embodied in the numerous village **festivals**.

Some history

Anyone seeking the true Sard identity must refer all the way back to the island's prehistory, the one period when it enjoyed undisturbed prosperity. Although little is known about the society, plenty of traces of this era survive, most conspicuous of which are the rough constructions known as *nuraghi*, mainly built between 1500 and 500 BC both for defensive purposes and as habitations. They can be seen everywhere in Sardinia, the biggest ones all in the heart of the island: at **Su Nuraxi**, north of Cágliari, and, between Oristano and Sássari, at **Sant'Antine**.

This nuraghic culture peaked between the tenth and eighth centuries BC, trading with the **Phoenicians**, amongst others, from the eastern Mediterranean. But from the sixth century the more warlike **Carthaginians** entered the scene, with their capital less than 200km away near present-day Tunis. Their campaign to control the island was halted only by their need to concentrate on the new military threat to their power, the Romans. Caught in the middle, the Sards fought on both sides until their decisive defeat in a campaign in 177 and 176 BC, during which some 27,000 islanders were slaughtered. A core of survivors fled into the impenetrable central and eastern mountains, where they retained their independence in an area called Barbaria by the Romans, known today as the **Barbágia**.

I. La Maddalena
I. Caprera
Santa Teresa
di Gallura
Palau
Porto Cervo
Arzachena
Costa
Smeralda
Olbia
Golfo Aranci
Tempio
Pausania
GALLURA

Genoa

I. Asinara

Punta
Falcone
Stintino
Castelsardo

Porto Torres
Sássari

Anghelu
Ruju
Alghero
Capo
Caccia
Torralba

Chilivani
Posada
Siniscola

Nuraghe di
Sant'Antine
SS131

Orosei
Bosa
Nuoro
Maconner
Oliena
Cala Gonone
Dorgáli
Mamoiada
Orgósolo
Abbasanta
Fonni
BARBAGIA
Monte La
Mármora

Sinis
Sórgono
Désulo
Tonara
MONTI DEL
GENNARGENTU
Tortolì
Arbatax

Tharros
Oristano
Aritzo

Ísili
Giara di
Gesturi
Gestúri
Su
Nuraxi
Barúmini
Las Plassas
Mandas

Sanluri
SS131

Muravera
Iglésias

I. di
San Pietro
Portoscuso
Carbonia
Villasimius
Carloforte
Cágliari
Calasetta
Sant'
Antíoco
Pula
Nora
I. di Sant'Antíoco

N

0   20 km

1067

The most impressive remains left by the Romans can be seen in **Cágliari**, on the coast south of the capital at **Nora**, and at **Tharros**, west of Oristano – all Carthaginian sites later enlarged by Roman settlers – and there still survive strong Latin traces in the Sard dialect today. The fall of Rome was followed by barbarian raids, then, briefly, in the sixth century AD, by the **Byzantines**, whose only significant monument is **Cágliari**'s church of **San Saturno**.

The relative emptiness of Sardinia's coasts today is largely due to the twin effects of malaria and the Muslim raids which continued sporadically for over 500 years, prompting the construction of the numerous watchtowers which can still be seen. In the eleventh century ecclesiastical rights over Sardinia were granted to the rising city-state of Pisa. **Pisan** influence was mainly concentrated in the south, based in **Cágliari**, where the defences they built still stand, and Pisan churches can be found throughout Sardinia, often marooned in the middle of the Sardinian countryside.

By the end of the thirteenth century, Pisa found itself out-manoeuvred by its rival **Genoa**, which established power-bases in Sássari and the north. But when, in 1297, Pope Boniface VIII gave James II of Aragon exclusive rights over both Sardinia and Corsica in exchange for surrendering his claims to Sicily, **Spain** entered the scene. The islanders' cause was led by **Arborea**, the area around present-day Oristano, and championed in particular by **Eleanor of Arborea**, a warrior along the lines of Boadicea and Jeanne d'Arc. Eleanor succeeded in stemming the Spanish advance, but after her death in 1404 Sardinian resistance crumbled and the Aragonese triumphed.

Traces of Spain's long dominion survive in the island's dialects and in the sprinkling of Gothic and Baroque architecture in churches and palaces. The best example of both is at **Alghero**, where the people still speak a strong Catalan dialect and the whole town has the air of a Spanish enclave. Nearby **Sássari** also shows strong Spanish influence.

During the War of the Spanish Succession (1701–20), **Cágliari** was bombarded by an English fleet and briefly occupied. Treaties followed, ceding the island first to Austria, then to Victor Amadeus, Duke of Savoy. His united possessions became the new **Kingdom of Sardinia**.

The years that followed saw a new emphasis on reconstruction, with the opening of schools, investment in industry and agriculture, and the building of roads, most famously the **Carlo Felice highway** which runs the length of the island – today the SS131. But Savoy's quarrels became Sardinia's, and in 1793 the island found itself threatened by **Napoleon**, who led an unsuccessful attempt at invasion in 1793. Later, **Nelson** spent fifteen months hovering around the island's coasts in the hunt for the French fleet that led up to the rout at Trafalgar in 1805. Throughout this long wait, during which Nelson never once set foot on shore, he sent a stream of letters to London urging that steps be taken to secure Sardinia – at the time the only neutral shore in this part of the Mediterranean: "God knows", he wrote, "if we could possess one island, Sardinia, we should want neither Malta, nor any other."

Garibaldi embarked on both his major expeditions from his farm on one of Sardinia's outlying islands, **Caprera**, and the Kingdom of Sardinia ended with the **Unification of Italy** in 1861. Since then, Sardinia's role as part of a modern nation-state has not always been easy. The phenomenon of **banditry**, for example, associated with the hinterland and the Gennargentu mountains in particular, was largely the continuation of old habits into the new age. Outbreaks of lawlessness were ruthlessly suppressed, but there was little money available to improve the root causes of the problem, nor much interest in doing so.

However, the island benefited from Mussolini's land reforms, including the harnessing and damming of rivers, the draining of land, and the introduction of agricultural colonies from the mainland, which founded the towns of **Arborea** and **Fertília**.

After World War II, Sardinia was granted the same autonomous status as Sicily, Valle d'Aosta and Alto-Adige, giving the island control over such areas as transport, tourism, police, industry and agriculture. The *Cassa per il Mezzogiorno* fund was extended to Sardinia, and the island was saturated with enough DDT to rid it of malaria forever. Such improvements, together with the increasing revenues from tourism, have helped to marginalize local opposition towards the central government, eroding the support of the local separatist groups **Partito Sardo d'Azione** and the more extreme **Sardigna Natzione**, which, among other things, have campaigned vociferously against the siting of one of the Mediterranean's largest concentrations of NATO forces in the **Maddalena Islands**.

Getting to Sardinia

If you're coming direct from the UK, you'll find Ryanair's **flights** to Alghero's Fertília airport hard to beat for price; see p.13 of the "Basics" for contact details. From the Italian mainland there are frequent daily flights to **Alghero** and to the island's two other main airports, at **Cágliari** and **Olbia**. These are mainly operated by Alitalia, Air One and Sardinia's own Meridiana, and cost €100–130 for a one-way ticket from Rome or Milan, with a myriad of special deals and weekend discounts worth asking about. A cheaper option are the **ferries** from mainland Italy, as well as from Sicily, Corsica and France (see box overleaf). You should make bookings several months in advance for summer crossings, even if you're on foot; August sailings can be fully booked up by May.

Basic **prices** range from about €25 to €55 per person, depending on the season and the route taken: the ticket includes use of a reclining armchair; a **berth** provides a better night's sleep, but adds another €10–15. The charge for a vehicle starts at around €65 for a small **car** in low season. Fares on the **high-speed ferries** (*mezzi veloci*) are €30–50 travelling second-class (up to 50 percent more in the peak season), plus €65–100 for a small car. Look out for discounts applying to return tickets bought in advance within certain periods, and for special deals for car plus two or three passengers.

Getting around the island

Once on the island, you can rely on a good network of public transport covering most localities. There is the island-wide bus service run by ARST and the private PANI for longer hauls between towns, while trains connect the major towns of **Cágliari**, Oristano, Sássari and Olbia, with smaller narrow-gauge lines linking with Nuoro and Alghero.

If you're planning to use the buses a lot between June and September, it's worth considering investing in a **biglietto turístico**, available from main ARST offices and valid on all ARST buses. The seven-day pass costs €31.76; fourteen days costs €54.60, and they are also available for 21 or 28 days.

Ferries to Sardinia

From	To	Line	No. per week	Duration
Civitavécchia	Arbatax	Tirrenia	2	11hr
Civitavécchia	Cágliari	Tirrenia & Sardinia	7–10	13–16hr 45min
Civitavécchia	Golfo Aranci	Sardinia	7 (mid-June to Sept only)	6hr 45min–9hr
Civitavécchia	Olbia	Tirrenia & Moby Lines	7–21	5–8hr
Genoa	Arbatax	Tirrenia	2	19hr
Genoa	Cágliari	Tirrenia	2 (mid-July to early Sept only)	20hr
Genoa	Olbia	Tirrenia, Grimaldi & Moby Lines	3–28	8hr–13hr 15min
Genoa	Palau	Tris	3–7 (April–Sept only)	13hr
Genoa	Porto Torres	Tirrenia & Grimaldi	13–23	8–11hr
La Spezia	Palau	Tris	2 (mid-June to early Sept only)	12hr
Livorno	Cágliari	Linea dei Golfi	1 (April–Sept only)	19hr
Livorno	Golfo Aranci	Sardinia	1–12 (March –Oct)	7hr 30min–10hr
Livorno	Olbia	Linea dei Golfi & Moby Lines	6–24	8–11hr
Livorno	Golfo Aranci	Sardinia	4–7 (March to early Nov only)	7hr 30min–10hr
Marseille	Porto Torres	SNCM	1 (April–Sept only)	16hr
Naples	Cágliari	Tirrenia	1–2	16hr 15min
Naples	Palau	Linee Lauro	1–2 (mid-June to mid-Sept only)	14hr
Piombino	Olbia	Linea dei Golfi	5–16 (April–Sept only)	8–9hr
Palermo	Cágliari	Tirrenia	1	13hr 30min
Porto Vecchio (Corsica)	Palau	Tris	1–2 (April–Sept only)	2hr 30min
Savona	Palau	Tris	2 (mid-June to early Sept only)	13–14hr
Toulon	Porto Torres	SNCM	2 (July–Aug only)	9hr 15min–16hr 15min
Trápani	Cágliari	Tirrenia	1	11hr 30min

High-speed ferries

From	To	Line	No. per week	Duration
Civitavécchia	Golfo Aranci	Sardinia	9–14 (late March to early Oct only)	3hr 35min
Civitavécchia	Olbia	Tirrenia	7–28 (June to early Sept only)	4–6hr
Fiumicino	Arbatax	Tirrenia	2 (mid-July to early Sept only)	4hr 45min
Fiumicino	Golfo Aranci	Tirrenia	7–11 (late June to early Sept only)	4hr
Genoa	Olbia	Tirrenia	7 (late June to early Sept only)	6hr
Genoa	Palau	Tris	7 (July–Sept only)	5hr 30min
Livorno	Golfo Aranci	Sardinia	4–5 (late March to mid-Oct only)	6hr

Cágliari and the south

Cágliari has been Sardinia's capital at least since Roman times and is still its biggest town, with the busiest port and the greatest concentration of industry. Intimidating as this may sound, you won't want to stray far out of the old centre surrounding the port, which is compact enough to negotiate on foot, and offers both sophistication and charm in the raggle-taggle of narrow lanes crammed into its high citadel.

The main attractions here are the **archeological museum** with its unique collection of nuraghic statuettes, the city walls with their two **Pisan towers** looking down over the port, and the **cathedral** – all within easy distance of each other. There is also a sprinkling of Roman remains, including an impressive **amphitheatre**. Forty kilometres down the coast, more ruins from this period can be seen at **Nora**, the most complete ancient site on the island. Other places worth visiting from Cágliari include the famous *nuraghe* of **Su Nuraxi**, a compelling sight surrounded by the brown hills of the interior, and the islands of **Sant'Antíoco** and **San Pietro**, moored off the coast west of Cágliari.

Cágliari

Viewing Cágliari from the sea at the start of his Sardinian sojourn in 1921, D.H. Lawrence compared it to Jerusalem: ". . . strange and rather wonderful, not a bit like Italy". Today, still crowned by its historic nucleus squeezed within a protective ring of Pisan fortifications, **CÁGLIARI** is less frenetic than any town of equivalent size on the Italian mainland, most of its quarter-million population housed in mushrooming apartment blocks away from the centre. Its setting is enhanced by the calm lagoons (*stagni*) west of the city and along the airport road, the habitat for cranes, cormorants and flamingoes. In the centre, the evening promenades along Via Manno are the smartest you'll see in Sardinia, dropping down to the noisier Piazza Yenne and Largo Carlo Felice, around which most of the shops, restaurants, banks and hotels are located. At the bottom of the town, the arcades of Via Roma shelter more shops and bars, across from the port.

Arrival, information, transport and accommodation

Just steps away from the heart of town, Cágliari's port is dominated by the **Stazione Maríttima**, which houses a **tourist office** (Mon–Fri 8.30am– 1.30pm & 3–6pm, Sat & Sun 8.30am–1.30pm; ☎070.668.352) and a **left-luggage office** which holds bags for free until 6pm daily. Arrivals at the Sabaudo dock to the west are met by a free **shuttle bus** which runs to and from the Stazione Maríttima.

Cágliari's **airport** sits beside the city's largest *stagno* (lagoon): facilities include a **bureau de change** and a tourist office (☎070.240.200). An ARST bus service into town runs at least every ninety minutes from 6.15am until midnight to Piazza Matteotti and takes fifteen minutes (tickets from the shop behind the information office); otherwise a taxi ride costs around €15.

Piazza Matteotti holds the **train** and **bus stations** and is the terminus for most **local buses**, tickets for which are sold at the booth (€0.77 for 90min); FMS buses for Sant'Antioco leave from Via Roma (unmarked stop outside the farmacia, tickets from the nearby news kiosk) and Via C. Colombo (behind Piazza Deffenu, tickets from *Bar Muro*); and the FdS station, for slow trains to Arbatax (see p.1090), is a twenty-five minute walk from Piazza Matteotti, at Piazza Repubblica (on Via Dante).

17

CÁGLIARI

0   200 m

RESTAURANTS
La Damigiana	B
Da Fabio	F
Il Gatto	D
L'Isola del Gelato	E
Da Lillicu	G
Il Merlo Parlante	A
Da Serafino	H
Sotto la Torre	C

ACCOMMODATION
Aurora	1
Calamosca	7
Italia	4
Miramare	6
Palmas	2
La Perla	3
Pensione Vittoria	5

S. Caterina

VIA ANTONIO SCANO

Palazzo di Giustizia

FdS Train Station

S. Saturno

Cemetery

PIAZZA CIMITERO

VIALE DEL CIMITERO

▼ & Poetto (4 km)

VIA PRAGA

VIA PALESTRINA

VIA PERGOLESI

VIA G. PUCCINI

VIA DANTE

VIA S. BENEDETTO

VIA B. TUVERI

VIA PESSINA

VIA EUROPA

VIA DANTE

VIA A. MANZONI

V.F. COCCO ORTU

VIA PAOLI

VIA G. DELEDDA

VIA S. FARINA

VIA ALGHERO

San Domenico

VIA S. GIOVANNI

VIA ROCCA

VIA S. OZIERI

VIA S. DOMENICO

VIA G. GARIBALDI

VIA SONNINO

VIA S. LUCIFERO

VIA LOGUDORO

VIA NUORO

VIA BONARIA

VIALE ARMANDO DIAZ

VIA SONNINO

VIA S. SETTEMBRE

VIA XX SETTEMBRE

VIALE REGINA MARGHERITA

FMS Bus Station

Cittadella dei Musei

Anfiteatro Romano

Orto Botánico

Viale Buon Cammino

Torre S. Pancrazio

V. REG. ELENA

Palazzo Viceregio

PIAZZA DELL' ARSENALE

PIAZZA PALAZZO

V. DEI GENOVESI

VIALE REGINA ELENA

Cattedrale

University

Bastione San Remy

PIAZZA COSTITUZIONE

San Michele

VIA OSPEDALE

V.S. DOMENICO

V.A. AZUNI

Torre dell'Elefante

PIAZZA YENNE

VIA UNIVERSITÁ

VIA MANNO

VIA GARIBALDI

VIA SASSARI

VIA S. MARGHERITA

VIA ANGIOY

CORSO VITTORIO EMANUELE

VIA MAMELI

VIA G. MAMELI

Palazzo Comunale

LARGO CARLO FELICE

PIAZZA MATTEOTTI

FMS

Bus Stop ★ 5

PANI

Bus Stop

VIA SARDEGNA

VIA NAPOLI

VIA CONCEZIONE

VIA LEPANTO

VIA DESPANI

VIA BAYLLE

VIA ROMA

Stazione Marittima

Port

Bus Station

Train Station

PIAZZA CARMINE

VIA S. AGOSTINO

VIA MADDALENA

VIALE TRENTO

VIALE TRIESTE

VIA ROMA

VIALE LA PLAIA

VIALE RIVA DI PONENTE

V. OSTAIA

V. TIGELLIO

VIALE FRA IGNAZIO DA LACONI

VIA CARPEA

MIRELLO

N

1072

▼ Airport & SS131

▼ Ferry to Genoa, Civitavecchia, Naples, Palermo & Trápani

Piazza Matteotti also has a tourist information kiosk (March–Oct Mon–Sat 8am–8pm, July to mid-Sept also Sun 8am–7pm; Nov–Feb Mon–Sat 8am–2pm; ☎070.669.255), but the **main tourist office** covering the whole island is at Via Mameli 97 (mid-Feb to mid-May Mon–Sat 9am–7pm, Sun 9am–2pm; mid-May to mid-Sept daily 8am–8pm; mid-Sept to mid-Oct Mon–Sat 9am–7pm, Sun 9am–2pm; mid-Oct to mid-Feb Mon–Sat 9am–6pm; ☎070.60.231, ⓦ www.esit.net). There's also a toll-free information line for the whole island (☎800.013.153).

Accommodation

Cágliari has a good selection of **hotels**, though availability may be restricted in high season, and single rooms are at a premium at all times. The biggest concentration of places is on or around the narrow Via Sardegna, running parallel to Via Roma. The nearest **campsite** is beyond **Quartu Sant'Elena**, a 45-minute bus ride east along the coast, where the *Pini e Mare* (☎070.803.103, ⓦ web.tiscalinet.it/piniemare; mid-June to mid-Sept) has bungalows as well.

Aurora Salita Santa Chiara 19 ☎070.658.625. A modest *pensione* in a dilapidated *palazzo* behind Piazza Yenne. The plain and reasonably clean rooms are always popular so it's best to book ahead. No credit cards. ❷

Calamosca Viale Calamosca ☎070.371.628, ⓦ www.hotelcalamosca.it. Comfortable upmarket option; this is the nearest hotel to Poetto (see p.1075), Cágliari's summer suburb, and also has its own beach, but space is limited in peak season and there's no direct bus link to the centre of Cágliari. ❹

Italia Via Sardegna 31 ☎070.660.410, ⓕ070.650.240. Smart but rather characterless choice, mainly used by business travellers and groups. All rooms are modern and well-equipped, without views. ❺

Miramare Via Roma 59 ☎ & ⓕ070.664.021. Located on the second floor of a block facing the port (but no views), the bathless rooms just scrape into this price category and are somewhat pokey, but modernization is underway, and each has air-conditioning and TV. ❷

Palmas Via Sardegna 14 ☎070.651.679. Good value at this cheapie on the main tourist strip, with box showers in some rooms but no private facilities. No credit cards. ❷

La Perla Via Sardegna 18 ☎070.669.446. Very similar to its neighbour *Palmas*, though smaller and more old-fashioned, with slightly higher rates. No credit cards. ❷

Pensione Vittoria Via Roma 75 ☎070.657.970. Undisturbed by street-noise, this central choice has clean and pleasant rooms, though you may prefer the air-conditioned, slightly pricier ones in the *AeR Bundes Jack*, on the floor below and run by the same friendly family. ❸

The City

Almost all the wandering you will want to do in Cágliari is encompassed within the old Castello quarter, on the hill overlooking the port. The most evocative entry to this is from the monumental **Bastione San Remy** on Piazza Costituzione, whose nineteenth-century imperialist tone is watered down by the graffiti and weeds sprouting out of its walls. It's worth the haul up the grandiose flight of steps inside for Cágliari's best views over the port and the lagoons beyond. Sunset is a good time to be here, or whenever you feel like a pause from sightseeing-fatigue, its shady benches conducive to a snatched siesta.

From the bastion, you can wander off in any direction to enter the intricate maze of Cágliari's citadel, traditionally the seat of the administration, aristocracy and highest ecclesiastical offices. It has been little altered since the Middle Ages, though the tidy Romanesque facade on the **Cattedrale** (Mon–Sat 8am–12.30pm & 4.30–8pm, Sun 8am–1pm & 4–8pm) in Piazza Palazzo is in fact a fake, added in the twentieth century in the old Pisan style. The structure dates originally from the thirteenth century but has gone through what Lawrence called "the mincing machine of the ages, and oozed out Baroque and sausagey".

Inside, a pair of massive stone **pulpits** flank the main doors: they were crafted as a single piece in around 1160 to grace Pisa's cathedral, but were later presented to Cágliari along with the same sculptor's set of lions, which now adorn the outside of the building. Other features of the cathedral that are worth a glance include the ornate seventeenth-century **tomb** of Martin II of Aragon (in the left transept), the **aula capitolare** (off the right transept), containing some good religious art, and, under the altar, a densely adorned **crypt**. Hewn out of the rock, little of this subterranean chamber has been left undecorated, and there are carvings by Sicilian artists of the Sardinian saints whose ashes were said to have been found under the church of San Saturno (see opposite) in 1617. Also here are the tombs of the wife of Louis XVIII of France, Marie-Josephine of Savoy, and the infant son of Vittorio Emanuele I of Savoy and Maria-Teresa of Austria, Carlo Emanuele, who died in 1799.

The cathedral stands in one corner of the square, to the left of which are the archbishop's palace and – also eighteenth-century – the **Palazzo Viceregio** or Governor's Palace, formerly the palace of the Piedmontese kings of Sardinia (though rarely inhabited by them), its stately rooms today holding occasional exhibitions.

At the far end of Piazza Palazzo a road leads into the smaller Piazza Indipendenza, location of the **Torre San Pancrazio**, one of the main bulwarks of the city's defences erected by Pisa after it had wrested the city from the Genoans in 1305 (though these did not prevent the Aragonese from walking in just fifteen years later). It's worth ascending the tower (Tues–Sun: May–Sept 9am–1pm & 3.30–7.30pm; Oct–April 9am–4.30pm; free) for the magnificent views seawards over the old town and port. From here it's only a short walk to Via dell'Università and the city's second major bulwark, the **Torre dell'Elefante** (same hours as above), named after a small carving of an elephant on one side. Like the other tower, it has a half-finished look, with the side facing the old town completely open.

Through the arch at the top of Piazza Indipendenza, Piazza dell'Arsenale holds a plaque recording the visit made by Cervantes to Cágliari in 1573, shortly before his capture and imprisonment by Moorish pirates. Across the square, the **Cittadella dei Musei** stands on the site of the former royal arsenal, housing the city's principal museums. The main attraction is the **Museo Archeologico** (Tues–Sun 9am–8pm; €4, or €5 with Pinacoteca), a must for anyone interested in Sardinia's past. The island's most important Phoenician, Carthaginian and Roman finds are gathered here, including busts and statues of muses and gods, jewellery and coins, and funerary items from the sites of Nora and Tharros. But everything pales beside the museum's greatest pieces, from Sardinia's **nuraghic** culture. Of these, the most eye-catching is a series of bronze statuettes, ranging from about thirty to ninety centimetres in height, spindly and highly stylized but packed with invention and quirky humour. The main source of information about this phase of the island's history, these figures represent warriors and hunters, athletes, shepherds, nursing mothers, bulls, horses and wild animals. Most were votive offerings, made to decorate the inside of temples, later buried to protect them from the hands of foreign predators.

The other museums, all very different, are also worth exploring. The smallest and most surprising is the **Mostra di Cere Anatomiche** (Tues–Sat 9am–1pm & 4–7pm, Sun 9am–1pm; free), which displays 23 wax models of anatomical sections, gruesome reproductions of works made by the Florentine Clemente Susini at the start of the nineteenth century. Further up, the **Museo d'Arte Siamese** (Tues–Sun 9am–1pm & 4–7.30pm; €2) holds a fascinating assemblage of items from Southeast Asia – the collection of a local engineer who spent twenty years in the region – including Siamese paintings of Hindu and Buddhist legends, Chinese bowls and boxes, Japanese statuettes and a fearsome array of weaponry. Lastly, the excellent **Pinacoteca** (Tues–Sun 9am–8pm; €2, or €5 with Museo Archeologico) contains mostly Catalan and Italian religious art from the fifteenth and sixteenth centuries. Look out in particular for the trio of panel paintings next to each other on the top level: the panel frame of *San Bernardino* by Joan Figuera and Rafael Thomas, *Annunciation* by Joan Mates, and *Visitation* by Joan Barcelo.

From Piazza dell'Arsenale Viale Buon Cammino leads to Viale Fra Ignazio and the entrance to the **Anfiteatro Romano** (Tues–Sun: April–Oct 10am–1pm & 3–6pm; Nov–March 9am–1pm & 2–5pm; free). Cut out of solid rock in the second century AD, the amphitheatre could hold the entire city's population of about 20,000. Despite the decay, with much of the site cannibalized to build churches in the Middle Ages, you can still see the trenches for the animals, the underground passages and several rows of seats. Music, dance and theatre performances take place here in the summer months (tickets from Box Office, Viale Regina Margherita 43, ℡070.657.428). Turn left out of the amphitheatre and walk a few minutes down Viale Fra Ignazio da Laconi to the **Orto Botánico** (daily: April–Sept 8am–1.30pm & 3–7pm; Oct–March 8am–1.30pm; €0.50), one of Italy's most famous botanical gardens, with over five hundred species of Mediterranean and tropical plants – a shady spot on a sizzling afternoon.

East of the centre there's little to see in Cágliari's traffic-thronged modern quarters beyond the banks and businesses, the one exception being the fifth-century church of **San Saturno** (Mon–Sat 9am–1pm), Sardinia's oldest and one of the most important surviving examples of early Christian architecture in the Mediterranean. Set in its own piazza off the busy Via Dante, looking Middle Eastern with its palm trees and cupola, the basilica was erected on the spot where the Christian martyr Saturninus met his fate during the reign of Diocletian. Around the sturdy walls, which withstood severe bombardment during World War II, lie various pieces of flotsam from the past: four cannonballs, fragments of Roman sarcophagi and slabs of stone carved with Latin inscriptions. The interior is bare of decoration, though it's nonetheless impressive, with tall glass walls added to the sides, through which you can see an excavated necropolis.

Poetto

If you need a break and a bathe, head for the suburb of **Poetto**, a fifteen-minute bus ride from Piazza Matteotti past Cágliari's Sant'Elia football stadium. Poetto has 6km of fine sandy **beach**, with small bars and showers conveniently nearby; some stretches are lidos where you pay a standard daily rate for entry (about €5), and deckchairs and parasols are available for rent, along with pedalos and wind-surfing equipment.

Rearing above a small marina, the western end of the strip is dominated by the **Sella del Diávolo** ("Devil's Saddle"), a massive outcrop jutting into the sea; most of it is now a military zone and therefore off limits. The name is connected with a legend relating how the Archangel Gabriel won a battle here against the devil himself. The name of Cágliari's gulf, Golfo degli Angeli, is also a reference to this celestial tussle.

Eating, drinking and nightlife

Cágliari has a great range of **restaurants**, many clustered around Via Sardegna. Almost all have competitively-priced tourist menus, which aren't at all bad though don't offer very much choice. We've categorized recommended restaurants below as "Inexpensive" (under €15), "Moderate" (€15–25), or "Expensive" (€25–40) according to the amount you can expect to pay per head for a full meal including wine and cover charge. For a morning **coffee** or afternoon tea, Piazza Yenne makes a pleasant, relatively traffic-free alternative to the bustling cafés on Via Roma, while, outside the centre, Poetto is a blitz of bars, fairgrounds and ice-cream kiosks – a good place for a summer evening outing. Cágliari also has a couple of lively places for **ice creams** and late-night **drinking**, listed below.

La Damigiana Corso Vittorio Emanuele 115. Good fixed-price meals are served in this simple trattoria off the tourist track. Closed Mon evening. Inexpensive.

Da Fabio Via Sardegna 90, on the corner with Via Concezione. Easy-going trattoria which offers tourist menus and pizzas and has an English-speaking boss. Closed Mon & two weeks in Nov. Moderate.

Il Gatto Viale Trieste 15, just off Piazza del Cármine. Away from the port, and with a smarter feel than the places there, this little restaurant offers immaculately prepared seafood and meat dishes. Closed lunch Sat & Sun. Moderate.

L'Isola del Gelato Piazza Yenne 35. Cágliari's top ice-cream parlour offers a range of scrumptious concoctions, as well as yoghurt with fresh fruit, making this a good breakfast stop. Closed Mon Oct–Feb.

Da Lillicu Via Sardegna 78 ☎070.652.970. Serves a small but reliable range of authentic Sard specialities on marble tables. It's very popular with locals, so you'll need to book ahead. Closed Sun. Moderate.

Il Merlo Parlante Via Portascalas. Hidden down an alley off the middle of Corso Vittorio Emanuele, this small but popular students' hangout offers beer, panini and music until late. Closed daytime. Inexpensive.

Da Serafino at Via Sardegna 109 and Via Lepanto 6. Popular place offering honest, local dishes served without formality, extremely good value. Closed Thurs. Inexpensive.

Sotto La Torre Piazza San Giuseppe. Located opposite the Torre dell'Elefante, a great place for a snack and a drink from early morning to late at night. Tables in small, stylish rooms help create a relaxed atmosphere. Closed Sun June–Sept, Wed Oct–May. Inexpensive.

Listings

Airlines Tickets from travel agents or airport desks. For airport call ☎070.212.8263. Flight information for Air Dolomiti ☎800.013.366, ⓦwww.airdolomiti.it; Air One ☎848.848.880, ⓦwww.flyairone.it; Alitalia ☎848.865.643, ⓦwww.alitalia.it; Alpi Eagles ☎041.599.7788, ⓦwww.alpieagles.com; Meridiana ☎199.111.333, ⓦwww.meridiana.it; Volare ☎848.858.870, ⓦwww.volare-airlines.com.
Bus operators ARST, Piazza Matteotti ☎070.409.8324 or 800.865. 042, ⓦwww.arst.sardegna.it; FMS, Viale Colombo ☎800.044.553, ⓦwww.ferroviemeridionalisarde.it; PANI, Stazione Maríttima ☎070.652.326.
Car rental Cara, Piazza Deffenu 13 (☎070.658.992); Ruvioli, Via dei Mille 11 (☎070.658.955) and airport (☎070.240.323); Hertz, Piazza Matteotti 8 (☎070.651.078) and airport (☎070.240.037).

Ferries Tirrenia, Stazione Maríttima ☎199.123.199, ⓦwww.tirrenia.it.
Festivals Sant'Efisio: May 1–4, including a procession to the saint's church at Nora.
Hospital Via Peretti 21 ☎070.543.266.
Internet access Le Librerie della Costa, Via Roma 63; Saxophone, Via Baylle 6.
Laundry Coin-operated laundry at Corso Vittorio Emanuele 232 (daily 9am–9pm).
Post office Piazza del Cármine (Mon–Fri 8.10am–6.40pm, Sat 8.10am–1.20pm). Closes at 4pm on last day of month (or noon, if this falls on a Sat).
Telephones Via Angioy (daily 8am–10pm).
Train information FS ☎848.888.088, ⓦwww.trenitalia.it; FdS ☎070.491.304, ⓦwww.ferroviesardegna.it.
Travel agents CTS, Via Balbo 12 ☎070.488.260; Sardamondial, Via Roma 9 ☎070.668.094; Viaggi Orrù, Via Roma 95 ☎070.659.858.

Nora

The easiest excursion you can make from Cágliari is to the waterside archeological site at **NORA**, 40km south of the city. In summer there's a bus service direct to the site; the rest of the year the nearest stop is the village of **PULA**, 3km away and served by ten daily ARST buses. It's worth going to Pula anyway, as the village **museum** (daily: 9am–8pm; €5.50 including site at Nora) gives a good explanation of the Nora finds.

Founded by the Phoenicians and settled later by Carthaginians and Romans, **Nora** (daily 9am–1hr before sunset; €5.50 including museum) was abandoned around the third century AD, possibly as a result of a natural disaster. Now partly submerged under the sea, the remains on land include houses, Carthaginian warehouses, a temple, baths with some well-preserved mosaics, and a theatre in an equally good state of repair. The rest is rubble, though its position on the tip of a peninsula gives it plenty of atmosphere.

Outside the site stands the rather ordinary-looking eleventh-century church of Sant'Efisio, site of the saint's martyrdom and the ultimate destination of Cágliari's four-day May Day procession. Behind the church is an exquisite sandy bay, lapped by crystal-clear water, but rapidly transformed into day-tripper hell in season. There's a fine **hotel** 1km away on the road back to Pula, *Su Gunventeddu* (℡070.920.9092, ✉hotelsugunventeddu@hotmail.com; ❹), just 100m from a good beach and offering bright, quiet rooms and a recommended **restaurant** also open to non-guests; in Pula itself there's the good-value, flower-bedecked *Quattro Mori* at Via Cágliari 10 (℡070.920.9124; ❶; no credit cards), and, further along the same road at no. 30, the better-equipped *Sandalyon* (℡070.920.9151; ❹), where most rooms have a balcony.

The coast south holds some of Sardinia's most exclusive hotels, biggest and flashiest of which is the *Forte Village*, spread over a wide area, and catering largely to package groups (late March to mid-Nov; ℡070.92.171, ⓦwww.fortevillageresort.com; ❾), though luxury-lovers might prefer the more select *Flamingo* (mid-April to late Oct; ℡070.920.8361, ⓦwww.hotelflamingo.it; ❽), where you can stay in hotel rooms or in detached villas; the half-board requirement bumps up the price. There are fine beaches all down this coast, especially around **Chia**, while beyond **Capo Spartivento**, the coastal road offers terrific views over a deserted cliff-hung coastline, sheltering a few small sand beaches which are accessible on an infrequent bus service in summer.

Su Nuraxi and around

If you only have time to see one of Sardinia's *nuraghi*, you should make it **SU NURAXI** (daily 9am–1hr before sunset; €4.20), the biggest and most famous of them, and a good taste of the primitive grandeur of the island's only indigenous civilization. The snag is access: the site lies 1km outside the village of **BARÚMINI**, 50km north of Cágliari, to which there are only three daily ARST buses, calling here en route to Láconi, Désulo and Samugheo. The site lies fifteen minutes' walk west of the main crossroads at Barúmini's centre.

Su Nuraxi's dialect name means simply "the *nuragh*", and not only is it the largest nuraghic complex on the island, but it's also thought to be the oldest, dating probably from around 1500 BC. Comprising a bulky fortress surrounded by the remains of a village, Su Nuraxi was a palace complex at the very least – possibly even a capital city. The central tower once reached 21m (now shrunk to less than 15m), and its outer defences and inner chambers are connected by passageways and stairs. The whole complex is thought to have been covered with earth by Sards and Carthaginians at the time of the Roman conquest, which may account for its excellent state of preservation: if it weren't for a torrential rainstorm that washed away the slopes in 1949, the site may never have been revealed at all.

If you want to stay in the area, there are several **accommodation** possibilities in the village. Of these, the swankiest is *Sa Lolla* (☎070.936.8419; ❸), a ranch-style hotel on Via Cavour with a fantastic **restaurant** attached – open to non-guests, and worth a journey in itself. Barúmini also offers a choice of B&Bs, of which there is a cluster near the post office on Viale Umberto, all of a similar standard and identically priced (❷): try *Casa Sanna* at Viale Umberto 61 (☎070.936.8157 or 347.825.5160); *Casa del Rio*, Trav. I Principessa Maria (☎070.936.8141 or 328.675.6025), or *Casa Piras*, Trav. II Principessa Maria (☎070.936.8372 or 349.883.7015). They are not marked so you may have to ask around to find them.

The skyline south of Barúmini is punctuated by the extraordinary conical hill of **Las Plassas**, its round peak strewn with the fragments of a twelfth-century **castle** sticking up like broken teeth – a landmark for miles around. North and west of the town extends the high plain of **Giara di Gésturi**, the last refuge of Sardinia's wild ponies. You'll need a little luck and a lot of cunning to spot these small, shy creatures, but in any case it's excellent high ground for walking, at an altitude of around 600m. Spring is the best season to visit, when the area is a stopover for migrating birds. Again, though, the problem is access. Dedicated hikers can explore a good part of the plain on foot from the village of Gésturi, a stop on the bus routes from Cágliari to Láconi, Désulo and Samugheo.

West of Cágliari: Sant'Antíoco and San Pietro

West of Cágliari, the landscape is mountainous and empty, but cut through by the fast SS130 and the rail line as far as the mining towns of Iglesias and Carbonia. FMS buses also run this way, crossing a causeway south of Carbonia to reach the island of **Sant'Antíoco**. This and the neighbouring isle of **San Pietro** – reachable on ferries – can just about be visited from Cágliari on a day-trip, but you'd do better staying over and sampling the local beaches. Although well-frequented holiday destinations in summer, the islands have not yet become over-developed; in fact accommodation is on the scarce side, and if you're thinking of staying, be sure to book ahead.

Sant'Antíoco

SANT'ANTÍOCO, the larger of the southwest islands, is served by four daily FMS buses from Cágliari, about a two-hour ride. The port area of the island's main town (also called Sant'Antíoco) is just on the other side of the causeway. The sheltered harbour made this an important base for the Carthaginians and the Romans, allowing them to command the whole of Sardinia's southwest coast. More recently, Nelson's storm-damaged flagship, the *Vanguard*, put in here shortly before the Battle of the Nile in 1798.

It is the upper part of the town which holds all the interest, however, having been continuously inhabited since Phoenician times. Here, on Piazza Parrochia, at the top of Via Regina Margherita, the twelfth-century church of **Sant'Antíoco** was built over Christian **catacombs**, which were in turn enlarged from an existing Carthaginian burial place; you can visit these dingy corridors, with authentic skeletons and reproductions of ceramic objects unearthed during excavation, on a guided tour (summer Mon–Sat 9am–noon, 3–6pm & 7–8pm, Sun 10–11am & 4–8pm; winter Mon–Sat 10am–noon & 3–6pm, Sun 10–11am & 4–6pm; €2.50). Near the entrance to the catacombs, the musty, rather cavernous church holds a statue of St Antiochus, plainly showing his Mauretanian origins; his feast day, on the second Sunday after Easter, is a four-day affair with traditional songs, poetry recitations, dancing, fireworks and a procession to the sea.

Further down Via Regina Margherita, a small **Museo Archeologico** (daily: summer 9am–1pm & 3.30–7pm; winter 3.30–7pm; €5.16, including archeological zone and Museo Etnográfico, see below) displays finds from the excavations of the Phoenician, Carthaginian and Roman cities that once occupied the surrounding territories. The exhibits represent a tiny fraction of the second-largest collection of Carthaginian discoveries after Carthage itself, the bulk of which is presently stored away. Nonetheless, this small collection is worth a cursory glance for its few ceramic objects and items of jewellery, and for the maps and diagrams of the site.

Sant'Antíoco's archeological zone (same times as Museo Archeologico) is signposted up a side road outside the church, about a kilometre's walk towards the sea. The most impressive remains are of an extensive **Punic tophet**, or burial site, dedicated to the Carthaginian goddess Tanit; this burial site once covered the entire hill where the old city now stands. The numerous urns scattered about here (interspersed with modern reproductions) were long believed to contain the ashes of sacrificed first-born children, but this is now thought to have been Roman propaganda: the urns, it seems, contained the cremated remains of children still-born or dead from natural causes. Apart from the *tophet*, the archeological zone also contains the well-preserved ruins of a temple and an exhibition of more bits and pieces dug up from the area.

Returning into the town on Via Necrópoli, you can use your ticket for the museum and archeological zone for a small but engrossing **Museo Etnográfico** (same times): one capacious room crammed to the rafters with examples of rural culture – tools, agricultural implements, craftwork, bread- and pasta-making equipment, most of them only recently superseded by modern machinery – all enthusiastically explained (in Italian) by a guide.

There are three **hotels** in town: the somewhat dowdy *Eden* (☎0781.840.768; ❹), right next to the church of Sant'Antíoco, where half- or full-board is required in August, and two smaller places on the main road between the port and the church: the *Hotel del Corso*, at Corso Vittorio Emanuele 32 (☎0781.800.265, ⓦwww.hoteldelcorso.it; ❺), which has a panoramic roof-terrace, and the more modest *Moderno* at Via Nazionale 82 (☎0781.83.105; ❸), which also rents out bikes and scooters. More inspiring places lie 6km south of town, where the *Scaia Longa* (☎0781.817.202; ❷) overlooks the beach at **Maladroxia**, and 10km north of town, in or around the small resort of **Calasetta**, the terminus for the FMS bus from Cágliari, where choices include *Cala di Seta*, Via Regina Margherita 61 (☎0781.88.304, ⓦwww.caladiseta .qo.to; ❹), and the *Bellavista*, standing above a lovely arc of beach a short walk north of town (☎ & ☏0781.88.211; ❹) – both require half-board in August. There's also a **campsite**, *Le Saline* (☎0781.88.615, ⓦwww.campinglesaline .com), just beyond the *Bellavista*.

San Pietro

Every day, nine to thirteen **ferries from Calasetta** do the five-kilometre hop to **SAN PIETRO** (40min; €2.17): in summer, drivers should join the queue in good time – and make sure they get a return ticket. San Pietro's dialect is pure *piemontese*, two and a half centuries after the Savoyan king Carlo Emanuele III invited a colony of Ligurians to settle here after their eviction from the island of Tabarca, near Tunisia. The settlers were later abducted and taken back to Tunisia in one of the last great pirate raids, but were returned once the ransom demands had been met. The island's only town, attractive **CARLOFORTE** (named after the king), is lively in summer and close to panoramic beauty spots and mainly rocky beaches.

The few **hotels** are concentrated in Carloforte, where the most stylish choice is undoubtedly the *Hieracon* at Corso Cavour 63 (☎0781.854.028; ❺) – right from the port, as you leave the ferry – though the plainer *California* is more affordable, a ten-minute walk left along the port at Via Cavallera 15 (☎0781.854.470, ⓔcalifornia.hotel@tiscalinet.it; ❹). Availability is extremely limited in summer, but if you are stuck without a booking, ask about **rooms for rent** at the Pro Loco **tourist office**, opposite the port on Piazza Carlo Alberto III (Mon–Sat 9.30am–1pm & 4.30–7pm, closed winter afternoons; ☎0781.854.009, ⓦwww.carloforte.it/proloco).

Oristano and Nuoro

Sardinia's smallest province, Oristano, was only created in 1975, out of bits hacked off the provinces of Cágliari and Nuoro, though it roughly corresponds to the much older entity of Arborea, the medieval *giudicato* which championed the Sardinian cause in the struggle against the Spaniards. Then as now, **Oristano** was the region's main town, and today it retains more than a hint of medieval atmosphere.

The Punic-Roman town of **Tharros** is similar to Nora in appearance and worth a visit if you gave Nora a miss. Further north up the coast, the predominant flavour at the riverside town of **Bosa** is also medieval, with its sturdy fort, and is within striking distance of a lovely unspoilt stretch of coastline.

Bosa is the only west-coast point of the province of Nuoro, which covers most of Sardinia's interior and its barren eastern coast. This area is little travelled by tourists, though for many it's the most interesting part of the island, dotted with small and isolated villages, of which the provincial capital, **Nuoro**, is only a larger version, though it makes a useful transport junction and base for excursions. The region's inhabitants have retained a fierce sense of independence and loyalty to their traditions, and this is especially true in the ring of the once almost impenetrable **Gennargentu mountains**, centred on the island's highest peak, La Mármora (1834m). These mountains form the core of the **Barbágia** region, called Barbaria by the Romans who, like their successors, were never able to subdue it, foiled by the guerrilla warfare for which these hidden recesses proved ideal.

Nuoro province's long **eastern seaboard** is highly developed around the resorts of Siniscola and Posada, but further south it preserves its desolate beauty, virtually untouched apart from a couple of isolated spots around **Cala Golone**, and, further down, **Tortolì** and the small port of **Arbatax**.

Oristano

ORISTANO is a flat, unprepossessing place, whose old walls have been mostly replaced by busy boulevards. However, the centre has a relaxed and sophisticated ambience, and although it is 4km from the sea, the town is attractively surrounded by water, its lagoons and irrigation canals helping to make this a richly productive agricultural zone. The southern lagoon, the **Stagno di Santa Giusta**, is one of the two homes of Sardinia's flamingo population: if they're not at Cágliari they're bound to be here, sharing the water with the coracle-like flat-bottomed boats still used by the lagoon's fishermen.

The Town

In the heart of the town is Oristano's central symbol, the marble statue of **Eleonora d'Arborea**, presiding over the piazza named after her. Eleanor was the *giudice* of the Arborea region from 1384 to 1404 and is the best known and best loved of Sardinia's medieval rulers, having been the only one who enjoyed any success against the island's aggressors. Ensconced in the last of Sardinia's *giudicati* to remain independent of the Aragonese, Eleanor united local resistance and, despite the desertion of her husband, Brancaleone Doria, to the enemy, succeeded in negotiating a treaty in 1388 that guaranteed her a measure of independence. She later backed this up by a tactical alliance with the Genoans, and it was with Genoan help that Brancaleone, having returned to the fold, managed to occupy Sássari on her behalf.

Eleanor's military achievements collapsed soon after her death from plague in 1404, though the most enduring benefit of her reign survived her by several centuries: the formulation of a **Code of Laws** (*Carta di Logu*), first mooted by her father Mariano IV but embodied by Eleanor in a legal document in 1395. Covering every aspect of civil legislation, this document was adopted in 1421 by the Aragonese and extended throughout the island. As the eighteenth-century English lawyer and traveller John Tyndale put it: "The framing of a body of laws so far in advance of those of other countries, where greater civilizations existed, must ever be the brightest ornament in the diadem of the Giudicessa." Eleanor's statue, carved in 1881, shows her bearing the scroll on which the laws were written, while inset panels depict her various victories.

Although it's called the **Casa di Eleonora**, the fine house – now derelict – at Via Parpaglia 6–12 (left off Via La Marmora, which leads off the piazza) could not in fact have been her home, as it was built over a century after her death. She is unequivocally buried in the fourteenth-century church of **Santa Chiara**, in the parallel Via Garibaldi.

Off Via Parpaglia, Piazzetta Corrias holds Oristano's **Antiquarium Arborense** (Tues–Sun 9am–2pm & 3–8pm; €3), one of Sardinia's most absorbing museums, housed in a sixteenth-century merchant's house. As well as rotating exhibitions of its extensive collection of nuraghic, Phoenician, Roman and Greek artefacts, there's a gallery of medieval and Renaissance art and an imaginative scaled-down reconstruction of Roman Tharros.

Sa Sartiglia

The rituals of Oristano's flamboyant **Sa Sartiglia** festival perhaps originated with knights on the Second Crusade, who in the eleventh century may well have imported the trappings of Saracen tournaments to Sardinia. In the period of the Spanish domination, similarly lavish feasts were held for the ruling knights at regular intervals throughout the year. In time, these celebrations took on a more theatrical aspect and became merged with the annual Carnival – the Sa Sartiglia is now a three-day festival that closes the Carnival period, ending on Shrove Tuesday. Highlights of this costumed pageant include horseback parades and trials of equestrian prowess, all judged by a white-masked arbiter known as **Su Componidori**. Selected from among the "knight" contestants, the *Componidori* represents the continuation of the *giudice*'s role and is decked out in a bizarre pastiche of medieval garb – the process of dressing him is itself a highly formal ceremony, conducted in public at the beginning of each day.

In fact all the participants are masked and costumed, and the whole affair exudes a drama unrivalled by Sardinia's other festivals. The climax of the proceedings is the joust after which the festival is named, when the mounted contestants attempt to lance a ring, or *sartiglia*, suspended in the air, charging towards it at full gallop.

At one end of Via Parpaglia, linked to Piazza Eleonora by the narrow pedestrianized Corso Umberto, is Piazza Roma, where pavement bars are clustered around the base of the **San Cristóforo** bastion, erected by the *giudice* Mariano II in 1291. This was the fulcrum of Oristano's fortifications, the only other survivor of which is the smaller **Portixedda** ("little gate") tower, at the bottom of Via Mazzini (off Via Roma). Both are open for visits during the summer, each holding a small display of odds and ends relating to local history.

Oristano's **Duomo** stands in a spacious square up Via Duomo, which is behind Piazza Eleonora. Though started in the thirteenth century, most of the present Duomo is a Baroque renovation, retaining only parts of the apses from its original construction. With the fourteenth-century onion-roofed belltower and the next-door seminary, it forms an atmospheric ensemble.

At the other end of Via Duomo stands the nineteenth-century church of **San Francesco**, incorporating the remains of a much older Gothic building. The space in front, merging with Piazza Eleonora, forms the main arena for Oristano's annual **Sa Sartiglia** (see box on p.1081).

Practicalities

Oristano's **train station** is at the eastern end of town, a half-hour walk from the centre, also linked by the local *linea verde* and *linea rossa* local buses, which run every twenty minutes or so – buy tickets from the bar outside the station. The ARST **bus station** is on Via Cágliari, while PANI buses pull in at Via Lombardia, ten minutes from Piazza Roma down Via Tirso (tickets from *Blu Bar*). The **Pro Loco** is off Via Duomo at Via Vittorio Emanuele 8 (Mon–Fri 9am–12.30pm & 4.30–7.30pm; mid-July to mid-Sept also Sat 9am–noon; ☎0783.70.621), and the **main tourist office** is round the corner at Piazza Eleonora 19 (Mon–Fri 8am–2pm & 4–7pm, Sat 9am–1pm; ☎0783.36.831).

Accommodation

Oristano is badly off for accommodation, with just six **hotels** listed, and these often full. You'll need to book way ahead if you want to stay during the Sa Sartiglia festivities in particular. The cheapest and friendliest is also the most difficult to find – the *Píccolo*, at Via Martignano 19 (☎0783.71.500; ❸; no credit cards), in an area of unmarked streets behind Piazza Martini, near Via del Cármine. Also centrally located, the *Isa* on Piazza Mariano (☎0783.360.101; ❺) is posh and rather bland, while, north of the centre, *Villa delle Rose* (☎0783.310.101, ☏0783.310.117; ❹) is a comfortable choice on the quiet Piazza Italia (at the end of Via Lombardia), with spacious bathrooms, and there's the business-traveller's *Mistral* on Via Mártiri di Belfiore, off Via Cágliari (☎0783.212.505, ☏0783.210.058; ❹). You'll get more personal attention, however, at one of Oristano's **B&Bs**: try the very central *Eleonora*, right on Piazza Eleonora at no. 12 (☎0783.704.35; ❷), or, further out, the friendly *Antonella*, Via Sardegna 140 (☎0783.73.863; ❷), a five-minute walk from Piazza Mariano.

The nearest **campsites** lie 6km away at **MARINA DI TORRE GRANDE**, Oristano's lido: the *Torre Grande* (☎0783.22.228), 150m from the sea, and the better-equipped but pricier *Spinnaker* (☎0783.22.074), nearer the beach; both are open from May to September, and they're reachable on frequent buses from the ARST bus station.

Eating and drinking

Oristano is better off for **restaurants**, including the central and reliable *Trattoria Gino*, off Piazza Roma at Via Tirso 13 (no smoking; closed Sun), which features traditional Sardinian items like *ravioli sardi* (made with butter and sage) and *sebadas* (cheese-filled pastry-cases topped with honey). A few doors along, the stylish *Ciccio & Dessi* offers a complete contrast, serving snacks and full, moderately priced meals; some tables are in the garden (closed Sun evening & Mon). Via Parpaglia's *Antica Trattoria del Teatro* is fancy but good-value (closed Tues), with a long wine list. For a cheap and basic pizza, head for *La Torre* on Piazza Roma (closed Mon), where the speciality is *pizza ai funghi porcini*. You might like to finish your meal with a glass of Oristano's celebrated Vernaccia dessert wine. For late-night drinking or daytime snacks, the hip *Lolamundo Café* in Piazzetta Corrias has tables in the piazza and occasional DJs in the evenings (closed Sat & Sun).

Around Oristano: Tharros

Many people come to Oristano just to visit the Punic and Roman ruins at **Tharros**, about 20km west of Oristano and served by five ARST buses daily in July and August only. Like Nora, Tharros is pitched on a limb of land surrounded by water, though in this case it's a clenched fist, dominated by a sturdy Spanish watchtower. The peninsula, which forms the northern tip of the mouth of the Golfo di Oristano, was settled by Phoenicians as early as 800 BC. Tharros grew under Carthaginian occupation and then, after 238 BC, was revitalized by the Romans, who furnished it with the baths and streets that you see today. The town was finally abandoned in 1070 in favour of the more secure Oristano, then a small village.

The **site** (daily: April–Sept 9am–8pm; Oct–March 9am–5pm; €4) consists mostly of Punic and Roman houses arranged on a grid of streets, of which the broad-slabbed Decumanus Maximus is the most impressive. Another, the Cardo Maximus, has a deep open sewer visible alongside it. But the things you'll notice immediately on entering the site are the solitary remnants of a first-century BC Roman temple, with only two of its four Corinthian columns still upright. There are also baths and fragments of mosaics from the Roman city, and a wall and remains of a tophet from the earlier Punic settlement. Like Nora, there is much more submerged underwater, as a result of subsidence.

Near the site stands the fifth-century church of **San Giovanni di Sinis**, which vies with Cágliari's San Saturno for the title of oldest Christian church in Sardinia. Further back up the road towards Oristano (signposted off the Tharros road) is the sanctuary of **San Salvatore**, whose main interest is in a subterranean fourth-century chamber dedicated to Mars and Venus, complete with faded frescoes of Venus, Cupid and Hercules – ask the custodian to let you see it. The sanctuary forms the focus of a wild **festival** on the first weekend of September, the main feature of which is a race run at dawn to the village of **Cabras**, 8km away, by the town's boys. Barefoot and clad in white shirts and shorts, they bear aloft the statue of San Salvatore in a re-enactment of a frantic rescue mission undertaken four centuries ago to save the saint from Moorish attackers.

Bosa

North of Oristano, a brief bus ride from the rail and road junction of **Macomer** takes you to **BOSA** and the coast. Stranded in the middle of one of Sardinia's last remaining stretches of deserted coastline, and so far overlooked by the tourist industry, the town huddles on the banks of the Temo river around a hilltop castle. From the riverside the corridor-like lanes of the old district, **Sa Costa**, ascend the contours of the hillside, full of medieval gloom. To explore these backstreets, take any road leading up from the **Cathedral**, on the northern side of Bosa's main bridge. Keep climbing for about twenty minutes to reach Bosa's **Castello Malaspina** (currently closed for renovation), erected by the Malaspina family in 1122 – there's also a road that skirts the back of town, leading round to the castle gate. From the castle ramparts you can pick out Bosa's former cathedral of **San Pietro**, an eleventh-century construction with a Gothic facade added by Cistercian monks a couple of hundred years later. From the bridge, it's a 1.5-kilometre walk along the river to the church.

In the other direction, **BOSA MARINA** lies 5km downstream on what was the town's original site before its inhabitants shifted to a more defensible position. Today it is a conventional minor resort with a small choice of hotels and bars, its tiny port and sandy beach in the lee of the islet of Isola Rossa, now linked to the mainland and guarded by an old Spanish watchtower. Across the river, you can also swim from the rocks at the mouth of the Temo, or further north off the beautiful rocky coast accessible from the Alghero road.

Practicalities

Bosa's **Pro Loco** tourist office is at Via Azuni 5 (June–Sept daily 9.30am–1pm & 6–9.30pm; ☎0785.376.107), and there's another seasonal office in Bosa Marina, on the main Via C. Colombo (mid-June to mid-Sept daily 10am–1pm & 6–9pm; ☎0785.377.108). Most of the **hotels** are in Bosa Marina, though Bosa does have one fine old *palazzo* just across the river, *Sa Pischedda* (☎0785.373.065; ❸), and there's also an attractive **agriturismo** on the road to San Pietro, where much of the food is homegrown and all is organic (☎0785.373.793 or 380.705.2674; ❸). While convenient for the beach, Bosa Marina has a fairly uninspiring bunch of hotels, though these include the friendly *Costa Corallo* on Via C. Colombo (☎0784.375.162; ❹), and you will also find here one of Sardinia's rare **youth hostels**, close to the beach on Via Sardegna (☎0785.375.009; €10.33; June–Sept). The nearest **campsite**, *Turas* (☎0785.359.270; June–Sept), is a couple of kilometres south down the coast from Bosa Marina (connected by bus in summer). **Bikes to rent** are available from *Sa Pischedda*, and there's an **Internet point** at Via Gioberti 12 (Mon–Sat until 8.30pm).

There are surprisingly few decent **restaurants** in Bosa Marina, though there's a good choice in the centre of town. One of the best is the semi-formal *Borgo Sant'Ignazio* (☎0785.374.662; closed Tues Oct–April), in an alley above the Corso, Via Sant'Ignazio 33, which cooks up delicious local specialities. The restaurant attached to *Sa Pischedda* is also worth a visit, and has some outdoor seating, while west of the centre on Viale Alghero, you can eat sumptuously at the *Mannu* hotel (☎0785.375.306), which serves superlative Italian and Sard dishes at rather steep prices – and the rooms above offer a further accommodation option (❹), if you don't mind the uninspiring location. For lunchtime **snacks** and refreshments, avoid the pricey bars on the main Corso in favour of the *Taverna*, on Piazza Cármine (closed Tues in winter).

Nuoro

"There is nothing to see in Nuoro: which to tell the truth, is always a relief. Sights are an irritating bore," wrote D.H. Lawrence, though he omitted to mention the town's superb position beneath the soaring peak of Monte Ortobene and opposite the sheer and stark heights of Supramonte. In many respects **NUORO** is little different from the other villages of the region, but no place on the island can match its extraordinary literary fame. This was the town Lawrence made for in his Sardinian excursion of 1921, when it appeared to him "as if at the end of the world, mountains rising sombre behind". The best-known Sard poet, **Sebastiano Satta** (1867–1914), was Nuorese, as was the author **Grazia Deledda** (1871–1936), who won the Nobel Prize for Literature in 1927 in recognition of a writing career devoted to recounting the day-to-day trials and passions of local villagers. For **Salvatore Satta** (1902–75) – no relation to Sebastiano – "Nuoro was nothing but a perch for the crows", as he wrote in his semi-autobiographical masterpiece, *The Day of Judgement*; his only novel, it was published posthumously to great acclaim. The last century has witnessed few changes in this insular town despite the unsightly apartment blocks, administrative buildings and banks superimposed upon it.

Nuoro's **old quarter** is the most compelling part of town, spread around the pedestrianized axis of **Corso Garibaldi**, along which a buzzing passeggiata injects a bit of life into the place. Just off here, on Via Satta, drop into the **Museo d'Arte Nuorese** (Tues–Sun 10am–1pm & 4.30–8.30pm; €2.58), a collection of twentieth-century and contemporary art from the whole island, with a preponderance of local artists. Displayed on three floors, the works are refreshingly diverse, and there are also temporary exhibitions of modern Italian art. At the top of the Corso, turn right past the Duomo and along Via Mereu to reach the town's impressive **Museo Etnografico** (daily: mid-June to mid-Sept 9am–8pm; mid-Sept to mid-June 9am–1pm & 3–7pm; €2.58), a modern purpose-built complex which holds Sardinia's most comprehensive range of local costumes, jewellery, masks, carpets and other handicrafts. Examples and explanations of traditional musical instruments from around the island are also displayed, together with a fascinating array of old photographs. Turn left at the eastern end of the Corso and up Via Deledda for the **Casa di Grazia Deledda** (same hours as Museo Etnografico; €2.58), the well-to-do home of Nuoro's literary star, restored and furnished and displaying various photos and mementoes.

Nuoro's biggest annual **festival**, the **Festa del Redentore**, is one of the most vibrant events on the island's calendar, taking place over the penultimate Sunday of August, when dancing and dialect singing are enthusiastically per-formed, and August 29, the day of a long procession to Mount Ortobene (see p.1086). It's a grand spectacle, and a unique opportunity to see as many as 3000 of Sardinia's local costumes, worn by participants from all over the island, in particular the villages of Barbágia (see p.1086).

Practicalities

Heading east from Macomer on the private FdS line, you can reach Nuoro in around two hours; the alternative is to take a PANI bus all the way from Oristano (4 daily; 2hr). Nuoro's **train station** is a twenty-minute walk from the centre of town along Via La Mármora, on which stop frequent **city buses** (tickets from the shop inside the station). ARST **buses** stop at Via Sardegna, a few minutes' walk south of the station, while PANI buses stop at Via Brigata Sássari (parallel to Via La Mármora). The main **tourist office** is on Piazza Italia (March–Sept daily 9am–1pm & 4–7pm; ☎0784.30.083); in winter go directly to the administration office on the third floor (Mon, Thurs & Fri 9am–1pm, Tues & Wed 9am–1pm & 3.30–6.30pm; ☎0784.30.083, ⓦwww.provincia .nuoro.it). There's another private information office at Corso Garibaldi 155, which can arrange excursions beyond Nuoro (Mon–Sat 9.30am–1pm, also Sun in Aug; ☎0784.38.777, ⓦwww.viazzos.it).

Nuoro is hopelessly ill-equipped for accommodating the few tourists who pass through, and your best option is to find lodgings outside town on Monte Ortobene or even further afield in Oliena (see below for both). In town, the best options are the **hotels** *Grillo*, near the ethnographic museum at Via Monsignor Melas 14 (📞0784.38.678; ❹), and *Euro*, near the train station on Via Trieste (📞0784.34.071; ❹) – both rather charmless business-class places.

The town is better off for **restaurants**, often featuring regional specialities, best of which is the *Rifugio* at Via Mereu 28 (📞0784.232.355; closed Wed), where pizzas are also available. Other places include the arty *Tascusi*, Via Aspromonte 13 (closed Sun), and the slightly more formal *Il Portico*, Via Monsignor Bua 13 (closed Tues), both places off the top end of the Corso. You'll find a more boisterous atmosphere at *Ciusa*, a pizzeria-restaurant at Viale Ciusa 55, a few minutes' walk from Via Deledda at the eastern end of town (closed Tues Oct–May). For a lunchtime **snack**, there's *Il Mio Bar*, a handy sit-down **bar** on Via Mereu (closed Sun), while *Bar Nuovo* at the top of Corso Garibaldi (closed Wed) and *Bar Cambosu* round the corner on Piazza Vittorio Emanuele (closed Mon) are amenable places for breakfasts and evening drinks.

Monte Ortobene

From Nuoro's Piazza Vittorio Emanuele a local bus runs from June to August only (3–10 daily) up to the summit of **Monte Ortobene**, 8km away, from where there are striking views over the gorge separating Nuoro from the Supramonte massif. This is the venue for Nuoro's **Festa del Redentore** on August 29, when a procession from town weaves up the mountain to the bronze **statue** of the Redeemer at the top (955m). Poised in an attitude of swirling motion, the statue is probably the best vantage point, with dizzying views down to the valley floor. The woods round about are perfect for walks and picnics, and there are possibilities for horse riding at Farcana, signposted left near the top, where there's also a grand open-air public swimming pool. There's an excellent **B&B** on the mountain, the friendly *Casa Solotti* (📞0784.33.954 or 328.602.8975, 🌐www.casasolotti.it; ❷), right after the Farcana turn-off, offering wonderful mountain views and great breakfasts; ring ahead for a pick-up from Nuoro or to be guided to the right place.

The Barbágia

South of Nuoro extends the mountainous region known as the **Barbágia**, characterized by forested slopes, lush meadows and a scattering of villages still much as Salvatore Satta described them a century ago, "minuscule settlements as remote from one another as are the stars". The elderly folk in these tight communities are just about the only people on the island who still routinely wear the traditional local costumes, which otherwise are likely to be seen only during one of the numerous small festivals that punctuate the year. Each village has at least one, for which preparations are made months in advance.

Barbágia's villages evolved primarily as shepherds' settlements, whose isolated circumstances and economic difficulties in the postwar years led to widescale emigration and, among those who stayed behind, a crime wave. Sheep-rustling and internecine feuding came to be replaced by the infinitely more lucrative practice of the **kidnapping** and ransoming of wealthy industrialists or their families. This phenomenon reached epidemic proportions during 1966–68 when scores of Carabinieri were drafted into the area to comb the mountains for the hide-outs, rarely with any success. Recent years, however, have seen a lull in the kidnaps, apart from occasional high-profile cases such as that of Farouk Kassam, an eight-year-old who was abducted on the Costa Smeralda and held for seven months in 1992, having part of his ear cut off by his kidnappers to accelerate the ransom payment.

Nowadays, shepherds send their children to university, or they go to seek work in mainland Italy and don't come back. They leave behind slowly atrophying communities whose salvation is deemed to lie in a greater awareness of their tourism potential. Without the pulling power of the coastal regions, however, the area has to rely on its appeal to **skiing** and **hiking** enthusiasts. Mountain trekking at all levels is a particular draw; ask at Nuoro's tourist office for a booklet outlining routes (see p.1085).

Oliena and around

Visible across the valley, the nearest village to Nuoro is **OLIENA** (4–11 buses daily), 12km southeast, famed as the haunt of bandits until relatively recent times. However, the village prefers its reputation as the producer of one of the island's best wines, a dry, almost black concoction that turns lighter and stronger over the years. Oliena lies on the slopes of **Monte Corrasi**, a dramatically rugged limestone elevation which forms part of the Supramonte massif and rises to 1363m. There are numerous organized **excursions** you can make around its various caves and crags, the most famous of which is to the remote Valle Lanaitta and the nuraghic village of **Tiscali** (daily: May–Sept 9am–7pm; Oct–April 9am–5pm; €5), spectacularly sited within a vast mountain-top cavern, a half-day jaunt from Oliena. All hikes should be accompanied by a guide, which can be arranged through Oliena's helpful **tourist office** on the main Via Deledda (Mon–Sat 9am–1pm & 4–7pm; ☎0784.286.078). Bilingual staff here can also book **accommodation** in the area: the best options are *Ci Kappa*, Via M. Luther King (☎0784.288.733; ❷), a smart hotel in the centre of the village; *Su Marimundu* (☎0784.287.360 or 388.338.4892; ❷), a well-equipped country B&B about 1km north of the village (call to be met); and *Cooperativa Turística Enis*, 3km south in Località Maccione (☎0784.288.363; ❸), which also has pitches for **camping** and a superb **restaurant** with lofty views over the valley.

Orgósolo and around

Deeper into the mountains, at the end of a straggly eighteen-kilometre road running south from Oliena, **ORGÓSOLO** is stuck with its label of bandit capital of the island. The clans of Orgósolo, whose menfolk used to spend the greater part of the year away from home with their flocks, have always nursed an animosity towards the settled crop-farmers on Barbágia's fringes, a tension that occasionally broke out into open warfare. On top of this there was tension between rival clans, which found expression in large-scale sheep-rustling and bloody vendettas, such as the one that broke out at the beginning of the last century and lasted for fourteen years, virtually exterminating the two families involved. Between 1901 and 1954, Orgósolo – population 4000 – clocked up an average of one murder every two months.

Perhaps the village's most infamous son is **Graziano Mesina**, the so-called "Scarlet Rose", who won local hearts in the 1960s by robbing only from the rich to give to the poor and only killing for revenge against those who had betrayed him. Roaming at will through the mountains, even granting interviews to reporters and television journalists, he was eventually captured and incarcerated in Sássari prison. Escaping in 1968, he was recaptured near Nuoro and flown by helicopter the same day to appear on television in Cágliari. Mesina last surfaced in July 1992, when he was dispatched to Sardinia from a mainland prison to help negotiate the release of Farouk Kassam (see above).

Visitors to the village won't find much evidence of its violent past amid the shabby grey, breeze-blocked houses, but they will come across a vivid collection of **murals**, some of them covering whole houses and shops, portraying village culture, most illustrating the oppression of the landless by the landowners, or demanding Sardinian independence.

Orgósolo has two **hotels**: the basic *Petit* on Via Mannu (℡0784.402.009; ❷) and the panoramic and slightly smarter *Sa 'e Jana*, on Via Lussu, at the southern edge of the village (℡0784.402.437; ❷), with stupendous views and a good **restaurant**.

The Gennargentu massif

The central region of the Barbágia holds the **Gennargentu** chain of mountains – the name means "silver gate", referring to the snow that covers them every winter. Here, you'll find the island's only skiing facilities on **Monte Bruncu Spina**, Sardinia's second-highest peak (1829m). In spring and summer, you can explore this and other areas on **mountain treks**, best undertaken in the company of guides for which the tourist office at Nuoro can supply a list. Along the way you may see wild pigs, vultures and deer, though you would be lucky to spot one of the rare mouflon, an elegant wild goat with long curved horns – its numbers have been decimated by hunting.

The nearby settlements make useful bases for both skiers and trekkers, for example **FONNI**, 13km due south of Mamoiada and at 1000m the island's highest village. Try to coincide your visit with one of Fonni's costumed festivals, principally the Madonna dei Mártiri, on the Monday following the first Sunday in June, and on San Giovanni's day on June 24. There are a couple of comfortable **hotels** here, both with their own restaurants, the flashy modern *Cualbu* (℡0784.57.054; ❹) on Viale del Lavoro and the *Cinghialetto* on Via Grazia Deledda (℡0784.57.660; ❸), with only seven rooms.

From **DÉSULO**, a further 26km south, it is possible to reach the area's highest peak, La Mármora, by a twelve-kilometre path. **Hotels** here include the good-value *Maria Carolina*, on Via Cágliari (℡0784.619.310; ❷), and the basic *La Nuova* on Via Lamármora (℡0784.619.251; ❶), which has shared bathrooms.

Other good bases for the area include **TONARA**, 14km west of Désulo, where the *Belvedere* (℡0784.63.756; ❷) and *Su Toni* (℡0784.63.420; ❶) make good **accommodation** options – both with restaurants – and there's also a **youth hostel** (℡0784.610.005; €10.30), signposted on the northern edge of the village, with ample dormitory space as well as en-suite doubles (❶). Finally, **ARITZO**, 15km south, has a choice of four **hotels**: try the old-fashioned but comfortable *Moderno*, at the top of the village on Via Kennedy (℡0784.629.229; ❸), with a small garden and restaurant, or the more modern but blander *Castello*, on the main Corso Umberto (℡0784.629.266; ❷). For **bus** services linking these villages see "Travel Details" on p.1103.

Dorgali and Cala Gonone

Centre of the renowned **Cannonau** wine-growing region, **DORGALI** attracts a lot of tourists in summer, both for its craftwork and on account of the recent growth of Cala Gonone, a small port 10km east. Dorgali's **restaurants** and **hotels** are generally cheaper than its neighbour's: for bargain lodgings try the *Sant'Elene*, a couple of kilometres south of town (℡0784.94.572; ❸; April–Oct).

CALA GONONE is reached by heading south out of town and turning left into the long tunnel through the rock wall, from which the road plunges down to the bay. Beautifully sited at the base of the 900-metre-high mountains, this once tiny settlement was until recently accessible only by boat. Now hotels and villas dominate the scene, though these have not entirely spoilt the sense of isolation, and it is worth a visit if only to take advantage of the numerous boat tours to the secluded beaches up and down the coast. Among the best are **Cala Luna** and **Cala Sisine**, though if you are here for a short time you would do well to choose a tour that combines pauses at these swimming stops with exploration of the deep grottoes that pit the shore.

Most famous of these is the **Grotta del Bue Marino** – one of the last refuges of the Mediterranean monk seal, or "sea ox", in Italian waters, before the last colony moved on, probably at about the same time that the tourists moved in. It's a worthwhile expedition, anyway, since this is among Sardinia's most spectacular caves, a luminescent gallery filled with remarkable natural sculptures, resembling organ pipes, wedding cakes and even human heads – one of them is known as *Dante*, after a fondly imagined resemblance to the poet. Boat trips from Cala Gonone cost around €6, and entry to the cave is €7.

Ticket offices for the various excursions are in the port area, and there's a summer–only **tourist office** on Via Bue Marino (daily: April–June & Sept 9.30am–1pm & 3–6.30pm; July & Aug 9am–11pm; ☎0784.93 696). There's no lack of **hotels** hereabouts. Near the port and beaches are the lively, bougainvillea-covered *Cala Luna* (April–Oct; ☎0784.93.133; ❹), with direct access to the beach; *La Conchiglia* (March to mid-Oct; ☎0784.93.448; ❸), smaller and smarter, and also with seafront views; and the *Piccolo*, just up the hill from the harbour (☎0784.93.235; ❸), a fairly plain place that – unlike most choices here – is open year-round and does not require half-board in August. There's also an excellent, well-equipped **campsite**, a brief walk up from the beach and near the tourist office (☎0784.93.165, ⓦwww.campingcalagonone.it; April–Oct). The numerous **places to eat** in town range from fast food to gourmet seafood parlours (most places are closed in winter). The restaurant attached to the *Miramare* hotel on Piazza Giardini is both highly rated and moderately priced (closed mid-Oct to March), while the restaurant at the *Pop* hotel on Via Marco Polo is cheap and boisterous.

Hikes from Cala Gonone and Dorgali

South of Cala Gonone lies one of Sardinia's last truly untouched tracts: swerving inland along the ridge of the Flumineddu River, walled on the other side by the Supramonte massif, the new road brings you into a majestic mountain landscape, largely devoid of human life. There are several long-distance hikes which can be made in these wild parts, one of which – a two- to three-day hike – follows the coast **from Cala Gonone** to Cala Sisine, at which point the route wanders inland, up the Sisine canyon, as far as the solitary church of San Pietro, from which a track leads down to Baunei. A second, shorter hike follows the course of the Flumineddu River **from Dorgali** and takes you after a couple of hours into the **Gorroppu gorge**, though further exploration requires climbing skills and even dinghies to negotiate the small lakes in the heart of the gorge, which also terminates at Baunei.

A good first port of call for those interested in **walks** and excursions is Sa Domu De S'Orku, a bunker-like building near the turn-off for Urzulei, housing a bar, a shop and the Società Gorroppu (☎0782.649.282 or 347.423.3650), an informal hiking centre where you can look at routes and maps and talk to the staff about destinations, such as the Supramonte massif. Guided walks are also on offer, costing €15.50–52 per person per day, according to the size of your party.

Tortolì and Arbatax

From Baunei the road descends steeply to **TORTOLÌ**, 5km inland from the port of **ARBATAX**, itself little more than a paper factory, a few bars and restaurants, and a port from which ferries ply twice weekly to Genoa, Civitavecchia and (summer only) Fiumicino. The small beach here is famous for its red rocks, but there are better bathing spots outside town – especially to the south, where there is a series of sand and rock beaches at **Lido Orrì**. There's a summer-only **tourist office** at Arbatax station (daily: mid-June to mid-Sept 7.30am–12.30pm & 5–8pm, July & Aug closes 10.30pm; ☎0782.667.690) that has information on sea **excursions**, including to the Grotta del Bue Marino for around €23 (see p.1089); in winter, Tortolì's Pro Loco on Via Mazzini is open 9am–12.30pm (☎0782.622.824). **Ferry tickets** are available from the Tirrenia office near the port, on your right as you walk towards the station (Mon–Fri 8.30am–1pm & 4–7.30pm, Sat 8.30am–1pm, plus Wed & Sun 10pm–midnight).

Frequent daily **buses** connect Cágliari and Nuoro with Tortolì, which, along with Arbatax, is also on the narrow-gauge FdS railway. The train follows an inland route to Cágliari, with a change at Mandas; the full journey from the coast to Cágliari takes seven dawdling hours (mid-June to Sept only).

There are several small **hotels** in the Arbatax area, most of them difficult to reach on foot. The only reasonably priced one lies a couple of kilometres south of the port in the Porto Frailis district, near a good beach, the *Gabbiano* (☎0782.623.512; ❸). Otherwise, head towards Tortolì, where there is a small selection, including the pleasant *Splendor* on Viale Arbatax (☎0782.623.037; ❸) – opposite the Esso station on the other side of the rail tracks – and, further up on the left (on the corner with Via Sarcidano), *Dolce Casa* (☎0782.623.484; ❸; mid-June to mid-Sept), a clean and comfortable place run by an expatriate Englishwoman and her husband. There are several **campsites** in the area, including *Telis* at Porto Frailis (☎0782.667.323, ⓦ www.campingtelis.com) and *Orrì* at Lido Orrì (☎0782.624.695); all are open in summer only and have bungalows to rent. As for **restaurants**, there are few seafront places in Arbatax itself; rather, head for the Porto Frailis district, where *Il Faro*, overlooking the beach, has a good choice of fish. A frequent summer **bus** service connects Tortolì, Arbatax, Lido Orrì and Porto Frailis.

Olbia, Gallura and the Costa Smeralda

The largest town in Sardinia's northeastern wedge, **Olbia** owes its recent phenomenal growth to the huge influx of tourists bound for one of the Mediterranean's loveliest stretches of coast, the **Costa Smeralda**, whose five-star development has helped to transform the economy of the entire island. Elsewhere on the coast it's still possible to have fun without stacks of money: there are miles of shoreline still undeveloped and a profusion of minor islands, over sixty in all, which you can explore on various boat tours. A daily ferry service from **Palau** links the biggest islands of **Maddalena** and **Caprera**, while further west **Santa Teresa di Gallura** boasts some superb coves and beaches.

This indented northern shore fringes the region of **Gallura**, whose raw red and wind-sculpted granite mountains imbue the area with its unique edge-of-the-wilderness appeal. There is a hidden world within here that most tourists never discover, thickly forested with the cork-oaks which, after tourism, provide most of Gallura's revenue.

Olbia

Awash with traffic and ugly apartment blocks, **OLBIA** is the least Sardinian of all the island's towns. Its port and airport, however, make it an inevitable stop for some and its numerous bars and restaurants are generally crowded with tourists, sailors from the port and US service personnel from the nearby NATO bases.

If you're stuck for an afternoon here, you might as well visit the town's only item of historical interest, the little basilica of **San Símplicio**, on the street of the same name. The simple granite structure is set in a piazza apart from Olbia's bustle, making it a good spot for a sit down. Claimed to be the most important medieval monument in the whole of Gallura – a region hardly famed for its artistic heritage – the church formed part of the great Pisan reconstruction programme of the eleventh and twelfth centuries, though, it must be said, it is

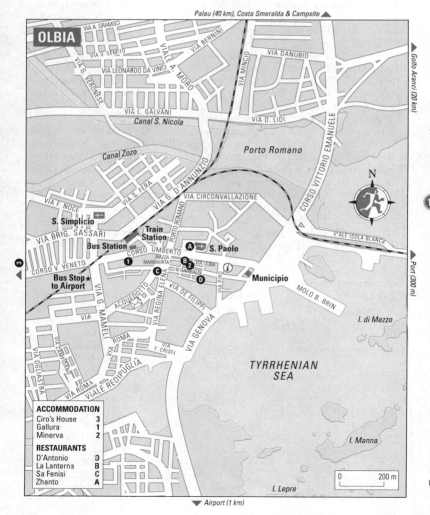

Palau (40 km), Costa Smeralda & Campsite

OLBIA

VIA A. GRAMSCI
VIA V. GEMITO
VIA G. VERONESE
VIA G. LEONARDO DA VINCI
VIALE A. MORO
VIA BERNINI
VIA MINCIO
VIA DANUBIO

VIA L. GALVANI
Canal S. Nicola
VIA D. LIDI

Canal Zozo
Porto Romano

VIA F. NOCE
VIA S. FERA
VIA G. D'ANNUNZIO
VIA CIRCONVALLAZIONE
CORSO VITTORIO EMANUELE

S. Simplicio
VIA BRIG. SASSARI
Train Station
Bus Station
CORSO UMBERTO
S. Paolo
V'ALE ISOLA BLANCA

CORSO V. VENETO
PIAZZA MARGHERITA
VIA ULBIA
V. GARIBALDI
VIA PIRI
Municipio

Bus Stop to Airport
VIA G. MAMELI
ACQUEDOTTO
VIA REGINA ELENA
VIA DE FILIPPI
VIA GENOVA
MOLO B. BRIN

I. di Mezzo

VIA
ROMA
VIA F. CRISPI

VIA OGLIASTRA
VIA CAMPANIA
VIA ROMA
VIALE REDIPUGLIA

TYRRHENIAN SEA

N

Golfo Aranci (20 km)
Port (300 m)

17

3

ACCOMMODATION
Ciro's House 3
Gallura 1
Minerva 2

RESTAURANTS
D'Antonio D
La Lanterna B
Sa Fenisi C
Zhanto A

I. Manna

0   200 m

I. Lepre

Airport (1 km)

the least interesting example of it. Its murky interior has three aisles separated by pillars and columns recycled from Roman constructions, and even the stoup for the holy water was formerly an urn that held cremated ashes.

The church is the venue for Olbia's biggest **festa**, six days of processions, costumed dancing, poetry recitations, traditional games and fireworks around May 15, commemorating San Símplicio's martyrdom in the fourth century.

Arrival, transport and information
Ferries from Civitavecchia, Piombino, Genoa and Livorno (see box on p.1070) dock at the island of Isola Bianca, connected to the mainland by a two-kilometre causeway; hourly buses (#3) run into town, or you can take the less frequent trains to Olbia's main station. There are Tirrenia offices at the port (daily 8.30am–1pm & 4.45pm–12.15am; ☎199.123.199), and agencies at the bottom of Corso Umberto, where you can pick up tickets for Tirrenia, Moby Lines and Sardinia Ferries services (all agencies Mon–Sat 8.30am–1pm & 4.30–7.30pm). Sardinia and some Tirrenia ferry services leave from Golfo Aranci, 15km up the coast (8 buses daily summer only, or regular trains). Book early for all departures.

Olbia's **airport** is connected by half-hourly buses (#2) to the central Piazza Regina Margherita until 8pm; tickets cost €0.57 and can be bought from the airport bar. Taxis cost about €15. Note that there is a summer-only bus service (6 daily) that departs from the airport to the **resorts** of Arzachena, Palau and Santa Teresa di Gallura (see p.1103), obviating the need to go to Olbia at all if you're bound for the beach-chequered coast or for Corsica.

Trains for Sássari and Cágliari run several times daily from the station just off Corso Umberto, which has a **left-luggage office** (Mon–Sat 7.30am–noon & 2–5pm). There is also a station at the ferry quay, though not all trains stop here. The ARST **bus station** is round the corner on the Corso (also reachable by walking along the train station platform).

The **tourist office** is on Via Piro, a side street running off the Corso (mid-June to mid-Sept Mon–Sat 8am–1pm & 3.30–7pm, Sun 8.30am–1pm; mid-Sept to mid-June Mon–Sat 8.30am–1pm; ☎0789.21.453). There are further offices at the port and airport, but these are open in summer only, and then only for arrivals and departures. You can **rent bikes and scooters** from On the Road, Via Sássari 8.

Accommodation and eating
Olbia has several good, central **hotels**, though most are on the expensive side. The cheapest choice lies round the corner from the tourist office on Via Garibaldi, the *Minerva* (☎0789.21.190; ❸), while the *Gallura* at Corso Umberto 145 (☎0789.24.648; ❺) offers more comforts in the form of TVs, minibars, air-conditioning and breakfast thrown in, as well as a first-class restaurant on the ground floor. Otherwise, there's a good-value **B&B** at Via Aspromonte 7, *Ciro's House* (☎0789.24.075; ❸; closed Jan–March), a twenty-minute walk from the station west of the level-crossing on Corso Umberto, offering rooms with or without bath, while the nearest **campsite** is at Località Cugnana (☎0789.33.184, ⓦwww.cugnana.it; May–Sept), 10km north of town; it's also the closest to the Costa Smeralda, and consequently can get crowded. There's a pool and bungalows are also available (❹); from Olbia, four to five buses daily stop right outside.

As for **eating**, you'll find good food, smart surroundings and plenty of locals at the *Gallura* (see above) and at *Zhanto*, just off the Corso on Via delle Terme (closed Sun), which also serves pizzas and has a small garden. Alternatively, if it's just a pizza you're after, head for the subterranean *Lanterna*, off the other side of the Corso on Via Olbia (closed Wed), which includes a **vegetarian** choice. *D'Antonio*, Via Garibaldi 48, has good set-price menus, and *Sa Fenisi* has tables outside on Piazza Matteotti (behind Piazza Margherita). *Caffè Cosimino*, on Piazza Margherita (closed Sun), is a nice spot for coffees, fresh *cornetti* and **drinks**, with seating both inside – where the walls have faded photos of old Olbia – and out.

The Costa Smeralda

The **Costa Smeralda** is a strictly defined ten-kilometre strip between the gulfs of Cugnana and Arzachena, beginning about 12km north of Olbia. Legend has it that the Aga Khan stumbled upon the charms of this jagged coast when his yacht took shelter from a storm in one of the narrow creeks here in 1958. Four years later the fabulously wealthy tycoon headed a consortium of businessmen with the aim of exploiting this wild coastal strip, and was easily able to persuade the local farmers to part with their largely uncultivable land – though stories have circulated ever since of the stratagems used to dupe the locals into selling their property for a fraction of its value.

The consortium's plans were on a massive scale, limited only by the conditions imposed by the regional government. These included proper sewage treatment and disposal, restrictions on building, and the insistence that the appearance of the landscape should not be unduly changed. On this last point the developers were only partly successful. Although you won't see any multi-storey hotels, advertising hoardings, fast-food restaurants or garish filling stations, neither will you find a genuine fishing village surviving in these parts, nor anything like the kind of busy local markets you'll see in other parts of the island, and the luxurious holiday villages have a bland, almost suburban feel about them.

You can judge for yourself by taking a look at the "capital" of Costa Smeralda, **PORTO CERVO**, connected to Olbia by ARST buses (3–6 daily Mon–Sat). The "local"-style rustic-red architecture here is overwhelming in its artifice, embodying the dream of an idyllic Mediterranean village without any of the irritations of real life. Fascinating to wander round, graffiti- and litter-free, Porto Cervo exults in its exclusivity. The huge yachting marina is a curiosity in itself, a succession of ultra-sleek floating palaces. Their gleaming ranks are overlooked by the **Stella Maris** church, a modern whitewashed design by the Roman architect Michel Busiri Vici, who was also responsible for the grotto-like shopping arcade in Porto Cervo's centre; inside there's a good *Mater Dolorosa* by El Greco.

You'll need your own transport to get to the sequestered **beaches**, none of them clearly marked; just follow any dirt track down to the sea – the rougher it is, the more promising. Try ones at **Capriccioli, Rena Bianca** and **Liscia Ruia**, all dotted down the coast south of Porto Cervo.

The Golfo di Arzachena

At least five buses daily leave Olbia on the northward-bound SS125 that takes in Arzachena, Palau and Santa Teresa di Gallura. **ARZACHENA** is a not particularly inspiring inland town, though it has a useful **tourist office** in its central Piazza Risorgimento (Mon–Fri 8am–1.30pm & 3–7pm, Sat 8am–1.30pm; July & Aug also open Sat afternoon & Sun; ☎0789.82.624) and a handful of mostly expensive **hotels**. Most affordable of these, the *Citti*, lies just outside town on the main road to Palau at Viale Costa Smeralda 197 (☎0789.82.662;

❹), and boasts a small pool, while *Casa Mia*, on the other side of Arzachena off the Olbia road at Via Torricelli 3 (☎0789.82.790, ⓦwww.hotelcasamia.it; ❻) ,has a garden and restaurant; both have significantly lower rates outside the peak season.

Outside the luxury zone but sharing many of the Costa Smeralda's natural advantages, the **Golfo di Arzachena** is a deep narrow bay with facilities concentrated in and around **CANNIGIONE** – a small fishing port and yachting resort linked by buses (Mon–Sat 3–5 daily) with Arzachena. Virtually all Cannigione's hotels are over the ❺ mark, and most are open only from Easter to October. One of the few open all year, and also the cheapest, is the *Hotel del Porto*, right in front of the port on Lungomare Andrea Doria (☎0789.88.011; ❺), offering fairly standard holiday accommodation with good views. There's a **campsite** a kilometre or two inland and south of Cannigione, the *Golfo di Arzachena* (☎0789.88.583, ⓦwww.campingarzachena.com; March–Oct), which also has bungalows and a large pool, but the more attractive site lies a couple of kilometres beyond Cannigione round the bay in the **LACONIA** district, the *Villaggio Isuledda* (☎0789.86.003, ⓦwww.isuledda.it; April to mid-Oct), right on the shore, with excellent bathing spots. Five **buses** a day link the area to Cannigione and Arzachena (summer only).

The Maddalena Islands

From **PALAU**, 10km up the coast from Cannigione, ferries leave once or twice an hour (up to €2.17 per person, €5.20 for a medium-sized car) for the main island of the Maddalena archipelago, **La Maddalena**, from which you can reach **Caprera**, the island on which Garibaldi spent the last years of his life. Drivers should be warned that, in high season, it's a hectic bustle for tickets, and long queues are common.

La Maddalena

It takes twenty minutes to cross what Nelson called "Agincourt Sound" from Palau to the port and sole town on **LA MADDALENA**. The town, bearing the same name as the island, is a cheerful place with a population of about 15,000, swollen by a large number of Italian and US sailors who lend the town a garrison feel. Their headquarters are on the eastern side of town, a drab area of barracks and sentries, though the main military installations and submarine base are situated on the neighbouring island of Santo Stéfano – briefly captured by Napoleon in 1793 in an abortive attempt to take Sardinia.

Most of the action takes place in the narrow lanes between Piazza Umberto I and Cala Gavetta (the marina for small boats), a five-minute walk from the ferry port (heading left) and site of the **tourist office** (summer Mon–Sat 8.30am–1pm & 4–6.30pm, Sat 8am–7pm, also Sun 4–6.30pm mid-June to Sept; winter closes 1.30pm Sat; ☎0789.736.321). The town is not particularly well off for **hotels**. Cheapest are the *Arcipélago* at Via Indipendenza Traversa 2 (☎0789.727.328; ❹), which is hard to find (but signposted), offering modern, quiet rooms a fifteen-minute walk east from the ferry port, and the old-fashioned *Gabbiano*, Via Giúlio Césare 20 (☎0789.722.507; ❹), panoramically sited on the shore beyond Cala Gavetta. Addresses of **rooms and apartments** to rent are available from the tourist office. There are also three **campsites**, all outside town: *Il Sole*, on Via Indipendenza (☎0789.727.727; mid-June to Oct), and *Maddalena*, in the Moneta district (☎0789.728.051; mid-April to mid-Oct) are both on the way to Caprera; or there's *Abbatoggia* (☎0789.739.173; June–Sept), close by some good beaches in the north of the island. *Maddalena* also has bungalows available (❷).

17

Buses run to various parts of the island from near the Banco di Sardinia at the end of Via XX Settembre (every 30min in summer; every 2hr in winter). A good way of getting round the island is on a **bike or moped**, which can be rented from any of the outlets on the seafront towards Cala Gavetta for about €20 a day for a bike, or €50 a day for a moped (though prices are halved outside the peak season). The island invites aimless wandering and offers a variety of sandy and rocky beaches in mostly undeveloped coves. The **beaches** on the northern and western coasts are most attractive, particularly those around the tiny port of Madonetta, 5km west of La Maddalena, and at Cala Lunga, 5km north of town.

Caprera

Between October and May half of **CAPRERA** is closed off for military purposes, but there is always plenty of space left to roam this protected woody parkland, which is undeveloped apart from Garibaldi's house in the centre and a Club Med complex that offers the island's only tourist facilities.

Giuseppe Garibaldi (1807–82) came to live in Caprera in 1855, after a twenty-year exile from Italy. It was from here that he embarked on his spectacular conquest of Sicily and Naples in 1861, accompanied by his thousand Red-Shirts, and it was here that he returned after his campaigns to resume a simple farming life. Having bought the northern part of the island for £360, he spent much of his time writing his memoirs and some bad novels. His neighbour was an Englishman named Collins, with whom he had some celebrated disagreements concerning their wandering goat-herds, as a result of which Garibaldi built a wall dividing their properties, which can still be seen. After Collins's death in 1864 a group of English admirers provided the money for Garibaldi to buy the rest of Caprera from his ex-neighbour's family.

The **museum** (mid-June to mid-Sept Tues–Sat 9am–1.30pm & 2–6.30pm, Sun & Mon 9am–1.30pm; mid-Sept to mid-June daily 9am–1.30pm; €2) is in Garibaldi's old house, the elegant South American-style **Casa Bianca**, which has been preserved pretty much as he left it. Visitors are escorted past the bed where he slept, a smaller one where he died, various scrolls, manifestos and pronouncements, a pair of ivory-and-gold binoculars given to him by Edward VII and a letter from London, dated 1867, conferring on him honorary presidency of the National Reform League. A stopped clock and a wall-calendar indicate the precise time and date of his death.

The tour ends with Garibaldi's tomb in the garden, its rough granite contrasting with the more pompous tombs of his last wife and five of his children. Garibaldi had requested to be cremated, but following the wishes of his son Menotti his corpse was embalmed. In 1932, fifty years after his death, his tomb was opened to reveal the body perfectly intact.

Santa Teresa di Gallura

The bus from Olbia and Palau to **SANTA TERESA DI GALLURA**, Sardinia's northernmost port, passes a succession of lovely bays, some dramatic rocky coastline, and a handful of campsites. Santa Teresa's **tourist office** is on the main Piazza Vittorio Emanuele (mid-June to late Oct daily 8.30am–1pm & 3–8pm; rest of year Mon–Fri 8.30am–1pm & 3.30–6.30pm, Sat 8.30am–1pm; ☎0789.754.127); there is also a summer-only booth down by the port. Moby Lines and Saremar operate sailings from here to Bonifacio in Corsica (2–14 daily; 1hr; €9.70–11.50, vehicles extra).

Santa Teresa's plentiful central **hotels** range from the plain, family-run *Scano* on Via Lázio (☎0789.754.447; ❷) to the more elegant *Da Cecco*, at Via Po 3

(☎0789.754.220; Easter–Oct; ⑤), both of which, like most places here, demand at least half-board in July and August. There are several more hotels outside town, where they are best placed to take advantage of some of Sardinia's most alluring **beaches**, all with superb views over to Corsica, just 11km away. To the east, **Punta Falcone** and **La Marmorata** are popular spots, while 3km west of Santa Teresa, **Capo Testa** is one of Sardinia's finest bathing localities, a rocky promontory surrounded by turquoise sea. In the latter area, you can stay comfortably and cheaply at *Bocche di Bonifacio* (☎0789.754.202; April to mid-Oct; ③), which also has good-value **apartments** to let, though these are usually booked up in peak period. The nearest **campsite** is *Gallura* (☎0789.755.580; mid-May to Sept), 1km west of town, but you can be nearer the beach at *La Liccia* (☎0789.755.190, ⓦwww.campinglaliccia.com; May–Sept), 6km along the Castelsardo road.

Sássari and Alghero

The western half of the province is a green, fertile region, hilly but not so craggily scenic as Gallura. The provincial capital, **Sássari**, is for many the island's most interesting town, with its crowded medieval centre and secluded squares.

ACCOMMODATION
Frank	3
Il Gatto e la Volpe	2
Giusy	1

RESTAURANTS
Da Bruno	B
Che Farò	C
Fainè Sassu	D
Da Peppina	A
Il Posto	E

As a holiday destination, however, it has limited appeal, being inland and lacking enough entertainment to fill more than a couple of afternoons or evenings here. More popular is **Alghero**, the island's oldest resort as well as its major fishing port.

Sássari

Sardinia's second city, **SÁSSARI**, combines an insular, traditional feel, as embodied in its well-preserved tangle of lanes in the old quarter, with a forward-looking, confident air that is most evident in its modern centre. Historically, while Cágliari was Pisa's base of operations during the Middle Ages, Sássari was the Genoan capital, ruled by the Doria family, whose power reached throughout the Mediterranean. Under the Aragonese it became an important centre of Spanish hegemony, and the Spanish stamp is still strong, not least in its churches. In the sixteenth century the Jesuits founded Sardinia's first **university** here, and the intellectual tradition has survived, particularly in the political sphere. In recent years, Sássari has produced two national presidents – Antonio Segni and Francesco Cossiga – as well as the long-time head of the Italian Communist Party, Enrico Berlinguer (1922–84) – a cousin, incidentally, of the Christian Democrat Cossiga. Note that if you're coming to Sássari by **train**, you'll probably have to change at Ozieri-Chilivani station, outside the nondescript town of Chilivani.

The City

The **old quarter**, a network of alleys and piazzas bisected by the main Corso Vittorio Emanuele, is a good area for strolling around. At the heart of it is the **Duomo**, whose florid facade is Sardinia's most imposing example of Baroque architecture, added to a simpler Aragonese-Gothic base from the fifteenth and sixteenth centuries. Behind it, the eighteenth-century **Palazzo Ducale** now houses the town hall. On the other side of the Corso, **Piazza Tola** retains its medieval feel and is the venue of a daily market, overlooked by the Renaissance facade of the **Palazzo d'Usini**.

Sássari's festivals

One of Sardinia's showiest festivals – the **Cavalcata** – takes place in Sássari on **Ascension Day** (the fortieth day after Easter, usually the penultimate Sunday of May), the highlight of a month of cultural activities. Northern Sardinia's equivalent to Cágliari's Sant'Efisio festival, it attracts hundreds of richly costumed participants from villages throughout the province and beyond. Originally staged for the benefit of visiting Spanish kings or other dignitaries, it lapsed until its revival fifty years ago. The festival is divided into three stages, the morning featuring a horseback parade and a display of the embroidered and decorated costumes unique to each village, after which there is a show of stirring feats of horsemanship at the local race course, ending with traditional songs and dances back in Piazza Italia.

On the afternoon of **August 14** there is a much more local affair – **I Candelieri**, linked to the Pisan devotion to the Madonna of the Assumption. It became a regular event when an outbreak of plague in Sássari in 1652 mysteriously abated on the eve of the feast of the Assumption, since when the ritual has been repeated annually as a token of thanks. The rumbustious event involves bands of *gremi*, or medieval guilds of merchants, artisans and labourers, decked out in Spanish-style costumes and bearing gigantic wooden "candlesticks", 8m tall, through the old town.

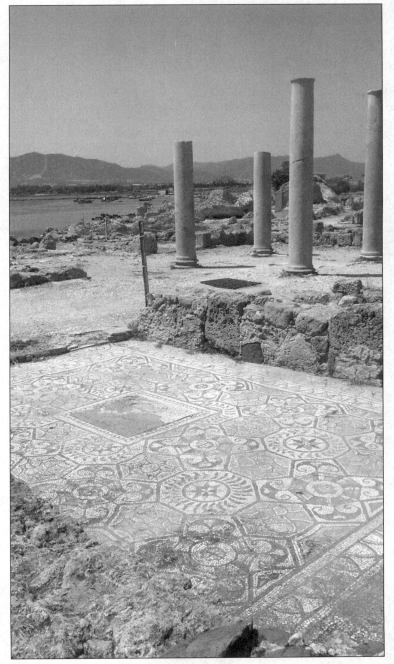

△ Ancient Roman mosaics, Nora, Sardinia

The only other item worth searching out in the old quarter is the late-Renaissance **Fonte Rosello**, at the bottom of a flight of grassy steps accessible from Corso Trinità, at the northern end of the old town. Fed by a spring in which throngs of the city's women used to scrub their clothes, the fountain is elaborately carved with dolphins and four statues representing the seasons, the work of Genoese stonemasons. Next to it stands a reconstructed wash-house.

Connected by a series of squares to the old quarter, the **newer town** is centred on the grandiose Piazza Italia. Leading off the piazza is Via Roma, site of the **Museo Sanna** (Tues–Sun 9am–7.30pm; €2), Sardinia's second archeological museum. It's a good substitute if you've missed the much bigger collection at Cágliari; like the Cágliari museum, its most interesting exhibits are nuraghic sculptures.

Practicalities

The **train station** is at the bottom of the old town's Corso Vittorio Emanuele, with a left-luggage office (daily 7.30am–8.50pm). All local and ARST services arrive at and depart from the **bus station** on Corso Vico, a right turn out of the train station; PANI buses run from Via Bellieni 5, just off Via Roma. ARST buses connect **Fertília airport** with the bus station.

Sássari's **main tourist office** is at Viale Umberto 72 (Mon–Thurs 9am–1.30pm & 4–6pm, Fri 9am–1.30pm; ℡079.231.331), and there's a smaller office next to the museum at Via Roma 62 (same hours; ℡079.231.777). Staying in Sássari can be a real problem, and you'd do well to phone ahead to ensure availability. The only reasonably-priced **hotel** is the lacklustre *Giusy* (℡079.233.327; ❷), conveniently near the station on Piazza Sant'Antonio, and the next step up is quite a leap, the relatively luxurious *Frank*, Via Armando Diaz 20 (℡079.276.456; ❹), in the modern town. If you don't mind staying outside the centre, *Il Gatto e La Volpe* (℡079.318.0012 or 333.695.7118; ❷), a rustic **B&B**, makes a great alternative; it's a large country house with friendly owners and lots of rooms, located in Caniga, 6km west of town – call to be met.

At least Sássari has a good range of **restaurants**, such as *Il Posto*, a smart and friendly trattoria in the new town at Via Enrico Costa 16 (closed Sun). In the old town, the basic *Da Peppina*, in Vícolo Pigozzi (closed Sun), an alley off Corso Vittorio Emanuele, is a good place to sample the local specialities of horsemeat, donkey and snails. At *Fainè Sassu*, off Piazza Castello at Via Usai 17 (closed Sun & June–Sept), the menu is confined to another *sassarese* speciality: *fainè*, a sort of pancake made of chickpea flour, either plain or cooked with onions, sausage or anchovies. Further along this street, *Che Farò* serves **pizzas** by the metre to eat in or take away (closed Mon), or sit outside *Da Bruno*, a cheap pizzeria on Piazza Matteotti (closed Wed in winter). For a daytime **snack** or a late drink, try *Coffee Break*, a cosy bar at Piazza Azuni 19 (closed daytime Sun).

Alghero

ALGHERO is a very rare Italian phenomenon: a tourist town that is also a flourishing fishing port, giving it an economic base entirely independent of the summer masses. The predominant flavour here is Catalan, owing to a whole-sale Hispanicization that followed the overthrow of the Doria family by Pedro IV of Aragon in 1354, a process so thorough that it became known as "Barcelonetta". The traces are still strong in the old town today, with its flamboyant churches, wrought-iron balconies and narrow cobbled streets named in

17

ALGHERO

ACCOMMODATION
Normandie 3
San Francesco 2
San Giuan 1

RESTAURANTS & BARS
Café Latino A
La Lépanto D
Maristella E
Ristorante Mazzini B
Da Pietro C
Poco Loco F

both Italian and Catalan. Beyond the stout girdle of walls enclosing this historic core, the new town's grid of parallel streets has little of interest beyond its restaurants and hotels.

Arrival and accommodation

Visitors arriving on Alitalia flights at **Fertília airport** will be met by buses for the centre of town (tickets from the bar); there are also direct services to Sàssari, Olbia and Nuoro. Buses for the Ryanair flights run every two hours only. If you've just missed one and can't face a long wait for the next, your only option is a taxi (around €20). Timetables and other information can be obtained from the airport's **tourist office** (daily 8.30am–7.30pm; ☏079.935.124). **Trains** arrive some way out of the centre, but regular city buses connect the station to the port. Out-of-town **buses** arrive on Via Catalogna, in the Giardino Púbblico. Alghero's main **tourist office** (Mon–Sat 8am–8pm, May–Sept also Sun 9am–1pm; ☎079.979.054, ⓦwww.infoalghero.it) is at the top end of the Giardino Púbblico, its multilingual staff equipped with reams of maps, accommodation lists and tour details.

Alghero's best-value **hotel**, and the only one located in the old town, is the *San Francesco*, at Via Machin 2 (☎079.980.330; ❹), just behind San Francesco church, with clean and quiet en-suite rooms. If it's full, try the basic but adequate *Normandie*, on Via Enrico Mattei, south of the old town, between Via Kennedy and Via Giovanni XXIII (☎079.975.302; ❷), or the *San Giuan*, a modern holiday villa with bland, airy rooms, located north of the centre and near the beaches at Via Angioy 2 (☎079.951.222; ❹). Two kilometres out of town, *La Mariposa* **campsite** (☎079.950.360, ⓦwww.lamariposa.it; April–Oct) has direct access to the beach. There's a useful **youth hostel** 6km along the coast at **FERTILIA**, reachable by local bus, but call first to check availability (☎079.930.353; €13).

A good way to get around the town and its environs is by **bike**: Cicloexpress, off Via Garibaldi at the northern end of the port, charge from €35 per day for a scooter, €10 for a mountain bike.

The Town

A walk around the old town should take in the series of seven defensive **towers** which dominate Alghero's centre and its surrounding walls. From the **Giardino Púbblico**, the **Porta Terra** is the first of these massive bulwarks – known as the Jewish Tower, it was erected at the expense of the prosperous Jewish community before their expulsion in 1492. Beyond is a puzzle of lanes, at the heart of which the pedestrianized Via Carlo Alberto, Via Principe Umberto and Via Roma have most of the bars and shops. At the bottom of Via Umberto stands Alghero's sixteenth-century **Cattedrale**, where Spanish viceroys stopped to swear a preliminary oath before taking office in Cágliari. Its incongruously Neoclassical entrance is round the other side on Via Manno; inside, the lofty nave's alternating pillars and columns rise to an impressive octagonal dome.

Most of Alghero's finest architecture dates from the same period and is built in a similar Catalan-Gothic style. Two of the best examples are a short walk away: the **Palazzo d'Albis** on Piazza Cívica and the elegantly austere Jewish palace **Palau Reial** in Via Sant'Erasmo (now a restaurant).

Outside the old quarter, most of the tourist activity revolves around the **port**, its wide quay nudged by rows of colourful fishing boats and bordered by bars. The town's beaches begin further north, backed by hotels, many of the older ones converted from villas formerly owned by the expatriate community of central Europeans who fled here after World War I.

Neptune's Grotto and ancient sites

The best of the excursions you can take from the port is to **Neptune's Grotto**, with boats departing several times daily in summer: tickets cost €10, not counting the entry charge to the grotto. The forty-five-minute boat ride west along the coast takes you past the long bay of Porto Conte as far as the point of **Capo Caccia**, where the spectacular sheer cliffs are riddled by deep marine caves. They include the **Grotta Verde** and **Grotta dei Ricami** – visited on some tours – but the most impressive is the **Grotta di Nettuno** itself (daily: April–Sept 9am–7pm; Oct 10am–5pm; Nov–March 9am–2pm; €8), a long snaking passage, into which forty-five-minute tours are led, single-file, on the hour every hour, past dramatically lit and fantastical stalagmites and stalactites.

A cheaper alternative to the boat is to drive to Capo Caccia or take a **bus** from the main bus terminal (3 daily in summer; 1 in winter; €3.25 return; 50min). Once you are deposited at the end of the line, there's a 654-step descent down the Escala del Cabirol, a highly scenic route whose Catalan name means "goat's steps", presumably a reference to the only animal that could negotiate the perilous path before the construction of the stairway in 1954. Make sure you time your arrival at the cave in time for the next tour: the descent takes 10–15 minutes. On the way back, leave some time before the bus goes for a well-earned ice cream at the bar opposite the steps.

With your own vehicle, you can also visit two sites 10km outside Alghero. The necropolis of **Anghelu Ruju**, a pre-nuraghic cave complex of thirty-six hypogea (daily: April–Oct 9am–7pm; Nov–March 9.30am–4pm; €2.10, or €3.60 with guide; with Nuraghe Palmavera – see below – €3.60, or €6.20 with guides), is on the road to Porto Torres, near the airport. On the road to Porto Conte, you'll pass the **nuraghe di Palmavera** (same hours and price as Anghelu Ruju) on your right, comprising a ruined palace dating from around 1100 BC and surrounded by fifty or so circular huts, one of which, with a central stool surrounded by a stone bench, is believed to have been used for meetings and religious gatherings.

Eating and drinking

Alghero's **restaurants** are renowned for their seafood, always fresh, inventively prepared and tastefully presented; spring and winter are the best seasons. Remember when ordering that most places price fish by weight: two-to-three *etti* (an *etto* is 100g) usually gets you a healthy portion. For a first-rate – and fairly pricey – fishy feast, head for *La Lépanto*, off Piazza Sulis at Via Carlo Alberto 135 (☎079.979.116; closed Mon in winter), also offering delicious meat dishes. Less expensive, but less atmospheric, *Da Pietro* deals out straight-forward seafood dishes at Via Machin 20 (closed Wed in winter). Off the tourist circuit, *Maristella* on Via Kennedy offers reasonable prices and tasty fare – it's popular with locals so worth booking (☎079.978.172) – while the no-non-sense *Ristorante Mazzini* at Via Mazzini 59 serves standard Italian dishes at low prices, and has a wood-fired oven for pizzas. For snacks, the fast-food joints by the port aren't bad.

There is an abundant supply of decent **bars**. The *Café Latino* (closed Tues), with an entrance in Via Manno, has parasols on the city wall overlooking the port, and serves ices and snacks as well as drinks, while *Poco Loco* on Via Gramsci has beers, pizzas, live music and **Internet access**.

Stintino and Pelosa

The tiny village of **STINTINO**, on Sardinia's northwestern tip, was until recently nothing more than a remote jumble of fishermen's cottages jammed between two narrow harbours. Fortunately its discovery by the tourist indus-try has not drastically altered it, and it remains a small, laid-back village and the only centre in the tongue of land forming the western arm of the **Golfo di Asinara**. Most of the sunning and swimming takes place further up the coast at La Pelosa, but the only cheapish **accommodation** in the area is in Stintino itself: the simple *Lina* at Via Lepanto 38 (☎079.523.071; ❹), overlooking the Porto Vecchio; the smarter and more central *Silvestrino* at Via Sássari 14 (☎079.523.007; ❻), which has an excellent trattoria that specializes in lobster soup; and the small and neat *Geranio Rosso*, Via XXI Aprile (☎079.523.292; ❺), which has a pizzeria on site – the last two require at least half-board in summer. It's worth finding out about renting **apartments** in and around Stintino, usually only available weekly (€580–680 inland, or €850–960 by the sea), but you may pick something up for just two or three days, especially out of season when prices are lower: contact Stintours (☎079.523.777) on Lungomare C. Colombo for information and bookings, where you can also rent **cars**, **mopeds** and **bikes**. Between two and six **buses** a day go to Stintino from Sássari, and there are organized bus trips from Alghero in the summer months.

Four kilometres up the road from Stintino a collection of tourist villages clutter up the otherwise idyllic promontory of **La Pelosa** – reached by bus in summer, otherwise taxi or rented transport from Stintino. Hotels and self-catering apartments back some of Sardinia's most deluxe **beaches**, with views out to the isles of Piana and the larger, elongated **Asinara**, the only known habitat of a miniature white ass from which the island takes its name, and previously a prison-island. In summer, you can explore it on daily boat excursions from Stintino, leaving at 9.30am, returning at about 5.45pm; the full visit including swimming-stops and guide costs €27; bring your own lunch. Book at Stintours (see above).

Travel details

Trains

Alghero to: Sássari (6–11 daily; 35min).
Arbatax to: Cágliari (mid-June to Sept 2 daily via Mandas; 7hr).
Cágliari to: Arbatax (mid-June to Sept 2 daily via Mandas; 7hr); Macomer** (8 daily; 2–3hr); Olbia** (4–5 daily; 3hr 50min–4hr 15min); Oristano (hourly; 1hr–1hr 40 min); Sássari** (4 daily; 3hr 20min–4hr 15min).
Macomer to: Nuoro (Mon–Sat 6 daily; 1hr 30min).
Nuoro to: Macomer (Mon–Sat 6 daily; 1hr 30min).
Olbia to: Cágliari** (4 daily; 3hr 50min–4hr 15min); Golfo Aranci (4–7 daily; 25min); Macomer* (4 daily; 2hr–2hr 15min); Oristano* (4 daily; 3hr); Sássari* (4–6 daily; 2hr).
Oristano to: Cágliari (hourly; 1hr 15min–1hr 45 min); Macomer (10 daily; 1hr); Olbia* (5–6 daily; 2hr 50min–3hr 20min); Sássari* (4–5 daily; 2hr 20min–3hr).
Sássari to: Alghero (6–11 daily; 35min); Cágliari** (4 daily; 3hr 25min–4hr); Macomer* (4 daily; 1hr 45min); Olbia* (4 daily; 2hr); Oristano* (4 daily; 2hr 40min).

*may involve changing trains at Ozieri-Chilivani
**may involve changing trains at Oristano and/or Ozieri-Chilivani

Buses

Alghero to: Bosa (2–4 daily; 55min–1hr 40min); Nuoro (2 daily; 3hr 15min–3hr 45min); Olbia (1 daily; 2hr); Sássari (hourly; 45min–1hr).
Cágliari to: Macomer (4 daily; 2hr 30min); Nuoro (4 daily; 3hr 30min); Oristano (4 daily; 1hr 35min); Sant'Antíoco (4 daily; 2hr); Sássari (7 daily; 3hr 15min–3hr 50min).
Macomer to: Bosa (3 daily; 30min); Cágliari (4 daily; 2hr 15min); Nuoro (4 daily; 1hr); Oristano (4 daily; 50min); Sássari (4 daily; 1hr 15min).
Nuoro to: Alghero (2 daily; 2hr 45min–3hr); Aritzo (1–2 daily; 2hr 10min); Cágliari (4 daily; 3hr 30min); Désulo (1 daily Mon–Sat; 1hr 30min); Fonni (3–7 daily; 50min); Olbia (6 daily; 1hr 45min); Orgósolo (8 daily; 35min). Sássari (6 daily; 2hr 25min); Tonara (1–2 daily; 1hr 40min).
Olbia to: Alghero (1 daily; 2hr); Arzachena (8–13 daily; 1hr 40min); Nuoro (6–7 daily; 1hr 45min); Palau (8–13 daily; 1hr); Porto Cervo (4–6 daily, not Sun in winter; 45min); Santa Teresa di Gallura (5–8 daily; 2hr); Sássari (5–7 daily; 1hr 30min).
Oristano to: Cágliari (4 daily; 1hr 25min); Macomer (4 daily; 1hr); Nuoro (4 daily; 2hr); Sássari (4 daily; 2hr 15min).
Sássari to: Alghero (hourly; 45min–1hr); Bosa (3–7 daily; 2hr 10min–2hr 30min); Cágliari (7

daily; 3hr 15min–3hr 45min); Nuoro (6 daily; 2hr 30min); Olbia (5–6 daily; 1hr 30min); Oristano (4 daily; 2hr 20min); Stintino (2–6 daily; 1hr 15min).

Ferries

Arbatax to: Civitavécchia (2 weekly; 10hr 30min); Fiumicino (mid-July to early Sept 2 weekly; 5hr 30min); Genoa (2 weekly; 20hr).
Cágliari to: Civitavécchia (1–2 daily; 14–17hr); Genoa (mid-July to early Sept 2 weekly; 20hr); Naples (1–2 weekly; 16hr 15min); Palermo (1 weekly; 13hr 30min); Trápani (1 weekly; 11hr).
Calasetta to: San Pietro (9–13 daily; 40min).
Golfo Aranci to: Civitavécchia (late March to early Oct 1–21 weekly; 3hr 30min–8hr); Fiumicino (late June to early Sept 1–2 daily; 4hr–5hr 30min); Livorno (4–14 weekly; 9–10hr).
Olbia to: Civitavécchia (1–6 daily; 5–8hr); Genoa (3–28 weekly; 6–13hr 30min); Livorno (6–24 weekly; 9–11hr); Piombino (April–Sept 3–16 weekly; 8–9hr).
Palau to: Genoa (April–Sept 3–14 weekly; 5hr 30min–13hr); La Maddalena (3–5 hourly; 20min); La Spezia (mid-June to early Sept 2 weekly; 12hr); Naples (mid-June to mid-Sept 1–2 weekly; 14hr); Savona (mid-June to early Sept 2 weekly; 14hr).
Porto Torres to: Genoa (1–4 daily; 8–11hr).

International ferries

Palau to: Porto Vecchio, Corsica (April–Sept 1–2 weekly; 2hr 30min).
Porto Torres to: Marseille, France (April–Sept 1 weekly; 16hr); Toulon, France (July–Aug 2 weekly; 9hr 15min–16hr 15min).
Santa Teresa di Gallura to: Bonifacio, Corsica (2–14 daily; 1hr).

Contexts

Contexts

A history of Italy

A specific Italian history is hard to identify. Italy wasn't formally a united country until 1861, and the history of the peninsula after the Romans is more one of warring city states and colonization and annexation by foreign powers. It's almost inconceivable now that Italy should fragment once again, but the regional differences remain strong and have even, in recent years, become a major factor in Italian politics.

Early times

A smattering of remains exist from the Neanderthals who occupied the Italian peninsula half a million years ago, but the main period of colonization began after the last Ice Age, with evidence of **Paleolithic** and **Neolithic** settlements dating from around 20,000 BC and 4000 BC respectively. More sophisticated tribes developed towards the end of the prehistoric period, between 2400 and 1800 BC; those who left the most visible traces were the **Ligurians** (who inhabited a much greater area than modern Liguria), the **Siculi** of southern Italy and Latium, and the **Sards**, who farmed and raised livestock on Sardinia. More advanced still were migrant groups from the eastern Mediterranean, who introduced the techniques of working copper. Later, various **Bronze Age** societies (1600–1000 BC) built a network of farms and villages in the Apennines, and on the Sicilian and southern coasts, the latter population trading with Mycenaeans in Greece.

Other tribes brought Indo-European languages into Italy. The Veneti, Latins and Umbrii moved down the peninsula from the north, whilst the Piceni and the Messapians in Puglia crossed the Adriatic from what is now Croatia. The artificial line between prehistory and history is drawn around the eighth century BC with the arrival of the **Phoenicians** and their trade links between Carthage and southern Italy. This soon encouraged the arrival of the **Carthaginians** in Sicily, Sardinia and the Latium coast – just when **Greeks** and **Etruscans** were gaining influence.

Etruscans and Greeks

Greek settlers colonized parts of the Tuscan coast and the Bay of Naples in the eighth century BC, moving on to **Naxos** on Sicily's Ionian coast, and founding the city of Syracuse in the year 736 BC. The colonies they established in Sicily and southern Italy came to be known as **Magna Graecia**. Along with Etruscan cities to the north they were the earliest Italian civilizations to leave substantial buildings and written records.

The Greek settlements were hugely successful, introducing the vine and the olive to Italy, and establishing a high-yielding agricultural system. Cities like **Syracuse** and **Tarentum** were wealthier and more sophisticated than those on mainland Greece, dominating trade in the central Mediterranean, despite competition from Carthage. Ruins such as the temples of **Agrigento** and

Selinunte, the fortified walls around Gela, and the theatres at Syracuse and Taormina on Sicily attest to a great prosperity, and Magna Graecia became an enriching influence on the culture of the Greek homeland – Archimedes, Aeschylus and Empedocles were all from Sicily. Yet these colonies suffered from the same factionalism as the Greek states, and the cities of Tarentum, Metapontum, Sybaris and Croton were united only when faced with the threat of outside invasion. From 400 BC, after Sybaris was razed to the ground, the other colonies went into irreversible economic decline, to become satellite states of Rome.

The **Etruscans** were the other major civilization of the period, mostly living in the area between the **Tiber** and **Arno** rivers. Their language, known mostly from funerary texts, is one of the last relics of an ancient language common to the Mediterranean. Some say they arrived in Italy around the ninth century BC from western Anatolia, others that they came from the north, and a third hypothesis places their origins in Etruria. Whatever the case, they set up a cluster of **twelve city states** in northern Italy, traded with Greek colonies to the south and were the most powerful people in northern Italy by the sixth century BC, edging out the indigenous population of Ligurians, Latins and Sabines. Tomb frescoes in Umbria and Lazio depict a refined and luxurious culture with highly developed systems of divination, based on the reading of animal entrails and the flight of birds. Herodotus wrote that the Etruscans recorded their ancestry along the female line, and tomb excavations in the nineteenth century revealed that women were buried in special sarcophagi carved with their names. Well-preserved chamber tombs with wall paintings exist at **Cerveteri** and **Tarquinia**, the two major sites in Italy. The Etruscans were technically advanced, creating new agricultural land through irrigation and building their cities on ramparted hilltops – a pattern of settlement that has left a permanent mark on central Italy. Their kingdom contracted, however, after invasions by the **Cumans**, **Syracusans** and **Gauls**, and was eventually forced into alliance with the embryonic Roman state.

Roman Italy

The growth of **Rome**, a border town between the Etruscans and the Latins, gained impetus around 600 BC from a coalition of Latin and Sabine communities. The **Tarquins**, an Etruscan dynasty, oversaw the early expansion, but in 509 BC the Romans ejected the Etruscan royal family and became a **republic**, with power shared jointly between two consuls, both elected for one year. Further changes came half a century later, after a protracted class struggle that resulted in the **Law of the Twelve Tables**, which made patricians and plebeians equal. Thus stabilized, the Romans set out to systematically conquer the northern peninsula and, after the fall of Veii in 396 BC, succeeded in capturing **Sutri** and **Nepi**, towns which Livy considered the "barriers and gateways of Etruria". Various wars and truces with other cities brought about agreements to pay harsh tributes.

The **Gauls** captured Rome in 390, refusing to leave until they had received a vast payment, but this proved a temporary reversal. The Romans took **Campania** and the fertile land of Puglia after defeating the **Samnites** in battles over a period of 35 years. They then set their sights on the wealthy Greek colonies to the south, including Tarentum, whose inhabitants turned to the

Greek king, **Pyrrhus of Epirus**, for military support. He initially repelled the Roman invaders, but lost his advantage and was defeated at **Beneventum** in 275 BC. The Romans had by then established their rule in most of southern Italy, and now became a threat to Carthage. In 264 they had the chance of obtaining **Sicily**, when the Mamertines, a mercenary army in control of Messina, appealed to them for help against the Carthaginians. The Romans obliged – sparking off the **First Punic War** – and took most of the island, together with Sardinia and Corsica. With their victory in 222 BC over the Gauls in the Po Valley, all Italy was now under Roman control.

They also turned a subsequent military threat to their advantage, in what came to be known as the **Second Punic War**. The Carthaginians had watched the spread of Roman power across the Mediterranean with some alarm, and at the end of the third century BC they allowed **Hannibal** to make an Alpine crossing into Italy with his army of infantry, horsemen and elephants. Hannibal crushed the Roman legions at Lago Trasimeno and Cannae (216 BC), and then halted at Capua. With remarkable cool, considering Hannibal's proximity, **Scipio** set sail on a retaliatory mission to the Carthaginian territory of **Spain**, taking Cartagena, and continuing his journey into **Africa**. It was another fifty years before Carthage was taken, closely followed by all of Spain, but the Romans were busy in the meantime adding **Macedonian Greece** to their territory.

These conquests gave Roman citizens a tax-free existence subsidized by captured treasure, but society was sharply divided into those enjoying the benefits, and those who were not. The former belonged mostly to the **senatorial party**, who ignored demands for reform by their opposition, the popular party. The radical reforms sponsored by the tribune **Gaius Gracchus** came too close to democracy for the senatorial party, whose declaration of martial law was followed by the assassination of Gracchus. The majority of people realized that the only hope of gaining influence was through the army, but **General Gaius Marius**, when put into power, was ineffective against the senatorial clique, who systematically picked off the new regime.

The first century BC saw civil strife on an unprecedented scale. Although Marius was still in power, another general, Sulla, was in the ascendancy, leading military campaigns against northern invaders and rebellious subjects in the south. Sulla subsequently took power and established his dictatorship in Rome, throwing out a populist government which had formed while he was away on a campaign in the east. Murder and exile were common, and cities which had sided with Marius during their struggle for power were punished with massacres and destruction. Thousands of Sulla's war veterans were given confiscated land, but much of it was laid to waste. In 73 BC a gladiator named **Spartacus** led 70,000 dispossessed farmers and escaped slaves in a revolt, which lasted for two years before they were defeated by the legions.

Julius Caesar and Augustus

Rome became calmer only after Sulla's death, when **Pompey**, another general, and **Licinus Crassus**, a rich builder, became masters of Rome. Pompey's interest lay in lucrative wars elsewhere, so his absence from the capital gave Julius Caesar the chance to make a name for himself as an orator and raiser of finance. When Pompey returned in 60 BC, he made himself, Crassus and Caesar rulers of the **first Triumvirate**.

Caesar bought himself the post of consul in 59 BC, then spent the next eight years on campaigns against the **Gauls**. His military success needled Pompey, and he eventually turned against his colleague, giving Caesar the chance to hit back. In 49 BC he crossed the river **Rubicon**, committing the offence of entering Roman territory with an army without first informing the Senate, but when he reached the city there was no resistance – everyone had fled, and Caesar became absolute ruler of Rome. He spent the next four years on civil reforms, writing his history of the Gallic wars, and chasing Pompey and his followers through Spain, Greece and Egypt. A group of enemies within the Senate, including his adopted son **Brutus**, conspired to murder him in 44 BC, a few months after he had been appointed ruler for life. **Octavian**, Caesar's nephew and heir, Lepidus and Marcus Antonius (**Mark Antony**) formed the **second Triumvirate** the following year. Again, the arrangement was fraught with tensions, the battle for power this time being between Antony and Octavian. While Antony was with **Cleopatra**, Octavian spent his time developing his military strength and the final, decisive battle took place at **Actium** in 31 BC, where Antony committed suicide.

As sole ruler of the new regime, Octavian, renaming himself **Augustus Caesar**, embarked on a series of reforms and public works, giving himself complete powers despite his unassuming official title of "First Citizen".

The emperors

Tiberius (AD 14–37), the successor to Augustus, ruled wisely, but thereafter began a period of decadence. During the psychopathic reign of **Caligula** (37–41) the civil service kept the empire running; **Claudius** (41–54) conquered southern Britain, and was succeeded by his stepson **Nero** (54–68), who violently persecuted the **Christians**. Nero committed suicide when threatened by a coup, leading to a rapid succession of four emperors in the year 68. The period of prosperity during the rule of the **Flavian** emperors (Vespasian and his sons Titus and Domitian) was a forerunner for the **Century of the Antonines**, a period named after the successful reigns of Nerva, Trajan, Hadrian, Antonius and **Marcus Aurelius**. These generals consolidated the empire's infrastructure, and created an encouraging environment for artistic achievement. A prime example is the formidable bronze equestrian statue of Marcus Aurelius in Rome – a work not equalled in sophistication until the Renaissance.

A troubled period followed under the rule of Marcus Aurelius' son **Commodus** (180–93) and his successors, none of whom were wholly in control of the legions. Artistic, intellectual and religious life stagnated, and the balance of economic development tilted in favour of the north, while the agricultural south grew ever more impoverished.

Barbarians and Byzantines

In the middle of the third century, incursions by **Goths** in Greece, the Balkans and Asia, and the **Franks** and **Alamanni** in Gaul foreshadowed the collapse of the empire. **Aurelian** (270–275) re-established some order after terrible civil wars, to be followed by **Diocletian** (284–305), whose persecution of Christians produced many of the Church's present-day saints. **Plagues** had decimated the population, but problems of a huge but static economy were compounded by the doubling in size of the army at this time to about half a million men. To ease administration, Diocletian **divided the empire** into two halves, east and west, basing himself as ruler of the western empire in Mediolanum (Milan). This measure brought about a relative recovery, coinciding with the rise of **Christianity**, which was declared the state religion during the reign of **Constantine** (306–337). **Constantinople**, capital of the eastern empire, became a thriving trading and manufacturing city, while Rome itself went into decline, as the enlargement of the senatorial estates and the impoverishment of the lower classes gave rise to something comparable to a primitive feudal system.

Barbarians (meaning outsiders, or foreigners) had been crossing the border into the empire since 376 AD, when the **Ostrogoths** were driven from their kingdom in southern Russia by the **Huns**, a tribe of ferocious horsemen. The Huns went on to attack the **Visigoths**, 70,000 of whom crossed the border and settled inside the empire. When the Roman aristocracy saw that the empire was no longer a shield against barbarian raids, they were less inclined to pay for its support, seeing that a more comfortable future lay in being on good terms with the barbarian successor states.

By the fifth century, many legions were made up of troops from conquered territories, and several posts of high command were held by outsiders. With little will or loyalty behind it, the **empire floundered**, and on New Year's Eve of 406, Vandals, Alans and Sueves crossed the frozen Rhine into Gaul, chased by the Huns from their kingdoms in what are now Hungary and Austria. By 408, the imperial government in Ravenna could no longer hold off **Alaric** (commander of Illyricum – now Croatia) who went on to **sack Rome** in 410, causing a crisis of morale in the west. "When the whole world perished in one city," wrote Saint Jerome, "then I was dumb with silence".

The bitter **end of the Roman Empire** in the west came after **Valentinian III**'s assassination in 455. His eight successors over the next twenty years were finally ignored by the Germanic troops in the army, who elected their general **Odoacer** as king. The remaining Roman aristocracy hated him, and the eastern emperor, **Zeno**, who in theory now ruled the whole empire, refused to recognize him. In 488, Zeno rid himself of the Ostrogoth leader **Theodoric** by persuading him to march on Odoacer in Italy. By 493, Theodoric had succeeded, becoming ruler of the western territories.

A lull followed. The Senate in Rome and the civil service continued to function, and the remains of the empire were still administered under Roman law. Ostrogothic rule of the west continued after Theodoric's death, but in the 530s the eastern emperor, **Justinian**, began to plan the reunification of the Roman Empire "up to the two oceans". In 536 his general **Belisarius** landed in Sicily and moved north through Rome to Ravenna; complete reconquest of the Italian peninsula was achieved in 552, after which the Byzantines retained a presence in the south and in Sardinia for 500 years.

During this time the **Christian Church** developed as a more or less independent authority, since the emperor was at a safe distance in Constantinople. Continual invasions had led to an uncertain political scene in which the **bishops of Rome** emerged with the strongest voice – justification of their primacy having already been given by Pope Leo I (440–461), who spoke of his right to "rule all who are ruled in the first instance by Christ". A confused period of rule followed, as armies from northern Europe tried to take more territory from the old empire.

Lombards and Franks

During the chaotic sixth century, the **Lombards**, a Germanic tribe, were driven southwest into Italy, and by the eighth century, when the **Franks** arrived from Gaul, they were extending their power throughout the peninsula. The Franks were orthodox Christians, and therefore acceptable to Gallo-Roman nobility, integrating quickly and taking over much of the provincial administration. They were ruled by the Merovingian royal family, but the mayors of the palace – the Carolingians – began to take power in real terms. Led by **Pepin the Short**, they saw an advantage in supporting the papacy, giving Rome large endowments and forcibly converting pagans in areas they conquered. When Pepin wanted to oust the Merovingians, and become King of the Franks, he appealed to the pope in Rome for his blessing, who was happy to agree, anointing the new Frankish king with holy oil.

This alliance was useful to both parties. In 755 the pope called on the Frankish army to confront the Lombards. The Franks forced them to hand over treasure and 22 cities and castles, which then became the northern part of the **Papal States**. Pepin died in 768, with the Church indebted to him. According to custom, he divided the kingdom between his two sons, one of whom died within three years. The other was Charles the Great, or **Charlemagne**.

An intelligent and innovative leader, Charlemagne was proclaimed King of the Franks and of the Lombards, and patrician of the Romans, after a decisive war against the Lombards in 774. On Christmas Day of the year 800, Pope Leo III expressed his gratitude for Charlemagne's political support by crowning him **Emperor of the Holy Roman Empire**, an investiture that forged an enduring link between the fortunes of Italy and those of northern Europe. By the time Charlemagne died, all of Italy from south of Rome to Lombardy, including Sardinia, was part of the huge **Carolingian Empire**. The parts which didn't come under his domain were Sicily and the southern coast, which were gradually being reconquered by Arabs from Tunisia; and Puglia and Calabria, colonized by Byzantines and Greeks.

The task of holding these gains was beyond Charlemagne's successors, and by the beginning of the tenth century the family was extinct and the rival Italian states had become prizes for which the western (French) and eastern (German) Frankish kingdoms competed. Power switched in 936 to **Otto**, king of the eastern Franks. Political disunity in Italy invited him to intervene, and in 962 he was crowned emperor; Otto's son and grandson (Ottos II and III) set the seal on the renewal of the Holy Roman Empire.

Popes and emperors

On the death of **Otto III** in 1002, Italy was again without a recognized ruler. In the north, noblemen jockeyed for power, and the papacy was manipulated by rival Roman families. The most decisive events were in the south, where Sicily, Calabria and Puglia were captured by the **Normans**, who proved effective administrators and synthesized their own culture with the existing half-Arabic, half-Italian south. In **Palermo** in the eleventh century they created the most dynamic culture of the Mediterranean world.

Meanwhile in Rome, a series of reforming popes began to strengthen the church. **Gregory VII**, elected in 1073, was the most radical, demanding the right to depose emperors if he so wished. **Emperor Henry IV** was equally determined for this not to happen. The inevitable quarrel broke out, over a key appointment to the archbishopric of Milan. Henry denounced Gregory as "now not pope, but false monk"; the pope responded by excommunicating him, thereby freeing his subjects from their allegiance. By 1077 Henry was aware of his tactical error and tried to make amends by visiting the pope at **Canossa**, where the emperor, barefoot and penitent, was kept waiting outside for three days. The formal reconciliation that did nothing to heal the rift, and Henry's son, **Henry V**, continued the feud, eventually coming to a compromise in which the emperor kept control of bishops' land ownership, while giving up rights over their investiture.

After this symbolic victory, the papacy developed into the most comprehensive and advanced centralized government in Europe in the realms of law and finance, but it wasn't long before unity again came under attack. This time, the threat came from **Emperor Frederick I** (Barbarossa), who besieged many northern Italian cities from his base in Germany from 1154. **Pope Alexander III** responded with ambiguous pronouncements about the imperial crown being a "benefice" which the pope conferred, implying that the emperor was the pope's vassal. The issue of papal or imperial supremacy was to polarize the country for the next two hundred years, almost every part of Italy being torn by struggles between **Guelphs** (supporting the pope) and **Ghibellines** (supporting the emperor).

Henry's son, **Frederick II**, assumed the imperial throne at the age of three and a half, inheriting the Norman **Kingdom of Sicily**. Later linked by marriage to the great **Hohenstaufen** dynasty in Germany, he inevitably turned his attentions to northern Italy. However, his power base was small, and opposition from the Italian commune and the papacy snowballed into civil war. His sudden death in 1250 marked a major downturn in imperial fortunes.

The emergence of city states

Charles of Anjou, brother of King Louis IX of France, defeated Frederick II's heirs in southern Italy, and received **Naples** and **Sicily** as a reward from the pope. His oppressive government finally provoked an uprising on Easter Monday 1282, a revolt that came to be known as the **Sicilian Vespers**, as some two thousand occupying soldiers were murdered in Palermo at the sound of the bell for vespers. For the next twenty years the French were at war with **Peter of Aragon**, who took Sicily and then tried for the southern mainland.

If imperial power was on the defensive, the papacy was in even worse shape. Knowing that the pontiff had little military backing or financial strength left, **Philip of France** sent his men to the pope's summer residence in 1303, subjecting the old man to a degrading attack. Boniface died within a few weeks; his French successor, Clement V, promptly moved the papacy to **Avignon**.

The declining political power of the major rulers was countered by the growing autonomy of the cities. By 1300, a broad belt of some three hundred virtually **independent city states** stretched from central Italy to the northernmost edge of the peninsula. In the middle of the century the population of Europe was savagely depleted by the **Black Death** – brought into Europe by a Genoese ship returning from the Black Sea – but the city states survived, developing a concept of citizenship quite different from the feudal lord-and-vassal relationship. By the end of the fourteenth century the richer and more influential states had swallowed up the smaller **comune**, leaving four as clear political front runners. These were **Genoa** (controlling the Ligurian coast), **Florence** (ruling Tuscany), **Milan**, whose sphere of influence included Lombardy and much of central Italy, and **Venice**. Smaller principalities, such as Mantua and Ferrara, supported armies of mercenaries, ensuring their security by building impregnable fortress–palaces.

Perpetual vendettas between the propertied classes often induced the citizens to accept the overall rule of one **signore** in preference to the bloodshed of warring clans. A despotic form of government evolved, sanctioned by official titles from the emperor or pope, and by the fifteenth century most city states were under princely rather than republican rule. In the south of the fragmented peninsula was the **Kingdom of Naples**; the **States of the Church** stretched up from Rome through modern-day Marche, Umbria and the Romagna; **Siena, Florence, Modena, Mantua** and **Ferrara** were independent states, as were the **Duchy of Milan**, and the maritime republics of **Venice** and **Genoa**, with a few odd pockets of independence like Lucca, for example, and Rimini.

The commercial and secular city states of late medieval times were the seed bed for the **Renaissance**, when urban entrepreneurs (such as the Medici) and autocratic rulers (such as Federico da Montefeltro) enhanced their status through the financing of architectural projects, paintings and sculpture. It was also at this time that the Tuscan dialect – the language of Dante, Petrarch and Boccaccio – became established as Italy's literary language; it later became the nation's official spoken language.

By the mid-fifteenth century the five most powerful states – Naples, the papacy, Milan, and the republics of Venice and Florence – reached a tacit agreement to maintain the new balance of power. Yet though there was a balance of power at home, the history of each of the independent Italian states became inextricably bound up with the power politics of other European countries.

French and Spanish intervention

The inevitable finally happened when an Italian state invited a larger power in to defeat one of its rivals. In 1494, at the request of the Duke of Milan, **Charles** VIII of France marched south to renew the Angevin claim to the Kingdom of Naples. After the accomplishment of his mission, Charles stayed for three months in Naples, before heading back to France; the kingdom was then acquired by **Ferdinand II of Aragon**, subsequently ruler of all Spain.

The person who really established the Spanish in Italy was the Habsburg Charles V (1500–1558), who within three years of inheriting both the Austrian and Spanish thrones bribed his way to being elected Holy Roman Emperor. In 1527 the imperial troops sacked **Rome**, a calamity widely interpreted at the time as God's punishment of the disorganized and dissolute Italians. The French remained troublesome opposition, but they were defeated at Pavia in 1526 and Naples in 1529. With the treaty of Cateau-Cambresis in 1559, Spain held Sicily, Naples, Sardinia, the Duchy of Milan and some Tuscan fortresses, and they were to exert a stranglehold on Italian political life for the next 150 years. The remaining smaller states became satellites of either Spanish or French rule; only the papacy and Venice remained independent.

Social and economic troubles were as severe as the political upheavals. While the papacy combated the spread of the **Reformation** in northern Europe, the major manufacturing and trading centres were coming to terms with the opening up of the Atlantic and Indian Ocean trade routes – discoveries which meant that northern Italy would increasingly be bypassed. Mid-sixteenth-century **economic recession** prompted wealthy Venetian and Florentine merchants to invest in land rather than business, while in the south high taxes and repressive feudal regimes produced an upsurge of banditry and even the raising of peasant militias – resistance that was ultimately suppressed brutally by the Spanish.

The seventeenth century was a low point in Italian political life, with little room for manoeuvre between the papacy and colonial powers. The Spanish eventually lost control of Italy at the start of the eighteenth century when, as a result of the War of the Spanish Succession, Lombardy, Mantua, Naples and Sardinia all came under Austrian control. The machinations of the major powers led to **frequent realignments** in the first half of the century. Piemonte, ruled by the Duke of Savoy, Victor Amadeus II, was forced in 1720 to surrender Sicily to the Austrians in return for Sardinia. In 1734 Naples and Sicily passed to the Spanish Bourbons, and three years later the House of Lorraine acquired Tuscany on the extinction of the Medici.

Relatively enlightened Bourbon rule in the south did little to arrest the economic polarization of society, but the northern states advanced under the intelligent if autocratic rule of Austria's **Maria Theresa** (1740–80) and her son **Joseph II** (1780–92) who prepared the way for early industrialization. Lightning changes came in April 1796, when the French armies of Napoleon invaded northern Italy. Within a few years the French had been driven out again, but by 1810 Napoleon was in command of the whole peninsula, and his puppet regimes remained in charge until Waterloo. Napoleonic rule had profound effects, reducing the power of the papacy, reforming feudal land rights and introducing representative government to Italy. Elected assemblies were provided on the French model, giving the emerging middle class a chance for political discussion and action.

Unification

The fall of Napoleon led to the Vienna Settlement of 1815, by which the Austrians effectively restored the old ruling class. **Metternich**, the Austrian Chancellor, did all he could to foster any local loyalties that might weaken the appeal of unity, yet the years between 1820 and 1849 became years of revolution. Uprisings began in Sicily, Naples and Piemonte, when **King Ferdinand** introduced measures that restricted personal freedom and destroyed many farmers' livelihoods. A makeshift army quickly gained popular support in Sicily, and forced some concessions, before Ferdinand invited the Austrians in to help him crush the revolution. In the north, the oppressive laws enacted by **Vittorio Emanuele I** in the Kingdom of Piemonte sparked off student protests and army mutinies in Turin. Vittorio Emanuele abdicated in favour of his brother, Carlo Felice, and his son **Carlo Alberto**; the latter initially gave some support to the radicals, but Carlo Felice then called in the Austrians, and thousands of revolutionaries were forced into exile. Carlo Alberto became King of Piemonte in 1831. A secretive, excessively devout and devious character, he did a major volte-face when he assumed the throne by forming an alliance with the Austrians.

In 1831 further uprisings occurred in Parma, Modena, the Papal States, Sicily and Naples. Their lack of co-ordination, and the readiness with which Austrian and papal troops intervened, ensured that revolution was short-lived. But even if these actions were unsustained, their influence grew.

One person profoundly influenced by these insurgencies was **Giuseppe Mazzini**. Arrested as Secretary of the Genoese branch of the Carbonari (a secret radical society) in 1827 and jailed for three months in 1830, he formulated his political ideology and set up "**Young Italy**" on his release. Among the many to whom the ideals of "Young Italy" appealed was **Giuseppe Garibaldi**, soon to play a central role in the **Risorgimento**, as the movement to reform and unite the country was known.

Crop failures in 1846 and 1847 produced widespread **famine** and **cholera outbreaks**. In Sicily an army of peasants marched on the capital, burning debt collection records, destroying property and freeing prisoners. Middle- and upper-class moderates were worried, and formed a government to control the uprising, but Sicilian **separatist** aims were realized in 1848. Fighting spread to Naples, where **Ferdinand II** made some temporary concessions, but nonetheless he retook Sicily the following year. At the same time as the southern revolution, serious disturbances took place in Tuscany, Piemonte and the Papal States. Rulers fled their duchies, and Carlo Alberto altered course again, prompted by Metternich's fall from power in Vienna: he granted his subjects a constitution and declared war on Austria. In Rome, the pope fled from rioting and Mazzini became a member of the city's republican triumvirate in 1849, with Garibaldi organizing the defences.

None of the uprisings lasted long. Twenty thousand revolutionaries were expelled from Rome, Carlo Alberto abdicated in favour of his son Vittorio Emanuele II after military defeats at the hands of the Austrians, and the dukes returned to Tuscany, Modena and Parma. One thing which did survive was Piemonte's constitution, which throughout the 1850s attracted political refugees to this cosmopolitan state.

Cavour and Garibaldi

Nine years of radical change began when **Count Camillo Cavour** became Prime Minister of Piemonte in 1852. The involvement of Piemontese troops in the Crimean War brought Cavour into contact with Napoleon III at the Congress of Paris, at which the hostilities were ended, and in July 1858 the two men had secret talks on the "Italian question". Napoleon III had decided to support Italy in its fight against the Austrians – the only realistic way of achieving unification – as long as resistance was non-revolutionary. Having bargained over the division of territory, they waited for a chance to provoke Austria into war. This came in 1859, when Cavour wrote an emotive anti-Austrian speech for Vittorio Emanuele at the opening of parliament. His battle cry for an end to the **grido di dolore** (cry of pain) was taken up over Italy. The Austrians ordered demobilization by the Piemontese, who did the reverse.

The war was disastrous from the start, and thousands died at Magenta and Solferino. In July 1859, Napoleon III made a truce with the Austrians without consulting Cavour, who resigned in fury. Provisional governments remained in power in Tuscany, Modena and the Romagna. Cavour returned to government in 1860, and soon France, Piemonte and the papacy agreed to a series of plebiscites, a move which ensured that by mid-March of 1860, **Tuscany** and the new state of **Emilia** (duchies of Modena and Parma plus the Romagna) had voted for **union with Piemonte**. A secret treaty between Vittorio

Emanuele and Napoleon III ceded Savoy and Nice to France, subject to plebiscites. The result was as planned, no doubt due in part to the presence of the French Army during voting.

Garibaldi promptly set off for Nice with the aim of blowing up the ballot boxes, only to be diverted when he reached Genoa, where he heard of an **uprising in Sicily**. Commandeering two old paddle steamers and obtaining just enough rifles for his thousand Red Shirts, he headed south. More support came when they landed in Sicily, and Garibaldi's army outflanked the 12,000 Neapolitan troops to take the island. After that, they crossed to the mainland, easily occupied Naples, then struck out for Rome. Cavour, anxious that he might lose the initiative, hastily dispatched a Piemontese army to **annexe the Papal States**, except for the Patrimony around Rome. Worried by the possibility that the anti-Church revolutionaries who made up the Red Shirt army might stir up trouble, Cavour and Vittorio Emanuele travelled south to Rome, accompanied by their army, and arranged plebiscites in Sicily, Naples, Umbria and the Papal Marches that offered little alternative but to vote for annexation by Piemonte. After their triumphal parade through Naples, they thanked Garibaldi for his trouble, took command of all territories and held elections to a new parliament. In February 1861, the members formally announced the **Kingdom of Italy**.

Cavour died the same year, before the country was completely unified, since Rome and Venice were still outside the kingdom. Garibaldi marched unsuccessfully on Rome in 1862, and again five years later, by which time Venice had been subsumed. It wasn't until Napoleon III was defeated by Prussia in 1870 that the French troops were ousted from Rome. Thus by 1871 **Unification** was complete.

The world wars

After the Risorgimento, some things still hadn't changed. The ruling class were slow to move towards a broader based political system, while living standards actually worsened in some areas, particularly in Sicily. When Sicilian peasant farmers organized into **fasci** – forerunners of trade unions – the prime minister sent in 30,000 soldiers, closed down newspapers and interned suspected troublemakers without trial. In the 1890s capitalist methods and modern machinery in the Po Valley created a new social structure, with rich **agrari** at the top of the pile, a mass of farm labourers at the bottom, and an intervening layer of estate managers.

In the 1880s Italy's **colonial expansion** began, initially concentrated in bloody – and ultimately disastrous – campaigns in Abyssinia and Eritrea in 1886. In 1912 Italy wrested the Dodecanese islands and Libya from Turkey, a development deplored by many, including **Benito Mussolini**, who during this war was the radical secretary of the PSI (Partito Socialista Italiano) in Forlì.

World War I and the rise of Mussolini

Italy entered **World War I** in 1915 with the chief aims of settling old scores with Austria and furthering its colonial ambitions through French and British support. A badly equipped, poorly commanded army took three years to force Austria into defeat, finally achieved in the last month of the war at Vittorio Veneto. Some territory was gained – Trieste, Gorizia, and what became Trentino-Alto Adige – but at the cost of over half a million dead, many more wounded, and a mountainous war debt.

The middle classes, disillusioned with the war's outcome and alarmed by inflation and social unrest, turned to Mussolini, now a figurehead of the Right. In 1921, recently elected to parliament, Mussolini formed the Partito Nazionale Fascista, whose **squadre** terrorized their opponents by direct personal attacks and the destruction of newspaper offices, printing shops, and socialist and trade union premises. By 1922 the party was in a position to carry out an insurrectionary "**March on Rome**". Plans for the march were leaked to Prime Minister Facta, who needed the king's signature on a martial law decree if the army were to meet the march. Fears of civil war led to the king's refusal. Facta resigned, Mussolini made it clear that he would not join any government he did not lead, and on October 29 **was awarded the premiership**. Only then did the march take place.

Zealous **squadristi** now urged Mussolini towards **dictatorship**, which he announced early in 1925. Political opposition and trade unions were outlawed, the free press disintegrated under censorship and Fascist takeovers, elected local governments were replaced by appointed officials, powers of arrest and detention were increased, and special courts were established for political crimes. In 1929, Mussolini ended a sixty-year feud between Church and State by reorganizing the **Vatican** as an autonomous Church state within the Kingdom of Italy. (As late as 1904, anyone involved in the new regime, even as a voter, had been automatically excommunicated.) By 1939, the motto "Everything within the State; nothing outside the State; nothing against the State" had become fact, with the government controlling the larger part of Italy's steel, iron and ship-building industries, as well as every aspect of political life.

World War II

Mussolini's involvement in the **Spanish Civil War** in 1936 brought about the formation of the "**Axis**" with Nazi Germany. Italy entered **World War II** totally unprepared and with outdated equipment, but in 1941 invaded Yugoslavia to gain control of the Adriatic coast. Before long, though, Mussolini was on the defensive. Tens of thousands of Italian troops were killed on the Russian front in the winter of 1942, and in July 1943 the Allied forces gained a first foothold in Europe, when Patton's American Seventh Army and the British Eighth Army under Montgomery landed in Sicily. A month later they controlled the island.

In the face of these and other reversals Mussolini was overthrown by his own Grand Council, who bundled him away to the isolated mountain resort of Gran Sasso, and replaced him with the perplexed **Marshal Badoglio**. The Allies wanted Italy's surrender, for which they secretly offered amnesty to the king, Vittorio Emanuele III, who had coexisted with the Fascist regime for 21 years. On September 8 a radio broadcast announced that an **armistice** had been signed, and on the following day the Allies crossed onto the mainland. As the Anglo-American army moved up through the peninsula, German divisions moved south to meet them, springing Mussolini from jail to set up the **republic of Salò** on Lago di Garda. It was a total failure, and increasing numbers of men and women from Communist, Socialist or Catholic parties swelled the opposing partisan forces to 450,000. In April 1945 Mussolini fled for his life, but was caught by partisans before reaching Switzerland. He and his lover, Claretta Petacci, were shot and strung upside down from a filling station roof in Milan's Piazzale Loreto.

The postwar years

A popular mandate declared Italy a republic in 1946, and Alcide de Gasperi's **Democrazia Cristiana** (DC) party formed a government. During the 1950s Italy became a front-rank industrial nation, massive firms such as Fiat and Olivetti helping to double the GDP and triple industrial production. American financial aid – the Marshall Plan – was an important factor in this expansion, as was the availability of a large and compliant workforce, a substantial proportion of which was drawn from the villages of the south.

The DC at first operated in alliance with other right-wing parties, but in 1963, in a move precipitated by the increased politicization of the blue-collar workers, they were obliged to share power for the first time with the **Partito Socialista Italiano** (PSI). The DC politician who was largely responsible for sounding out the socialists was **Aldo Moro**, the dominant figure of Italian politics in the 1960s. Moro was prime minister from 1963 to 1968, a period in which the economy was disturbed by inflation and the removal of vast sums of money by wealthy citizens alarmed by the arrival in power of the PSI. The decade ended with the "**autunno caldo**" ("hot autumn") of 1969, when strikes, occupations and demonstrations paralysed the country.

The 1970s and 1980s

In the 1970s the situation continued to worsen. More extreme forms of unrest broke out, instigated in the first instance by the far right, who were almost certainly behind a bomb which killed sixteen people in Piazza Fontana, Milan, in 1969, and the Piazza della Loggia bombing in Brescia five years later. **Neo-fascist terrorism** continued throughout the next decade, reaching its hideous climax in 1980, when 84 people were killed and 200 wounded in a bomb blast at Bologna train station. At the same time, a plethora of left-wing terrorist groups sprang up, many of them led by disaffected intellectuals at the northern universities. The most active of these were the **Brigate Rosse** (Red Brigades). They reached the peak of their notoriety in 1978, when a Red Brigade group kidnapped and killed Aldo Moro himself. A major police offensive in the early 1980s nullified most of the Brigate Rosse, but a number of hardline splinter groups from the various terrorist organizations are still in existence.

Inconsistencies and secrecy beset those trying to discover who was really responsible for the terrorist activity of the Seventies. One Red Brigade member who served 18 years in jail for his part in the assassination of Aldo Moro recently asserted that it was spies working for the **Italian secret services** who masterminded the operation. A report prepared by the PDS (Italy's party of the democratic left) in 2000 stirred up further controversy: it alleged that in the 1970s and 1980s the Establishment pursued a "**strategy of tension**" and that indiscriminate bombing of the public and the threat of a right-wing coup were devices to stabilize centre-right political control of the country. The perpetrators of bombing campaigns were rarely caught, said the report, because "those massacres, those bombs, those military actions had been organized or promoted or supported by men inside Italian state institutions and, as has been discovered more recently, by men linked to the structures of United States intelligence". "Other bombing campaigns were attributed to the left to prevent the

Communist Party from achieving power by democratic means," said Valter Bielli, PDS MP, and one of the report's authors. The report drew furious rebuttals from centre-right groups and the US embassy in Rome.

By whatever means, the DC government certainly clung to power. It was partly sustained by the so-called "historic compromise" negotiated in 1976 with **Enrico Berlinguer**, leader of the **Partito Comunista Italiano** (PCI). By this arrangement the PCI – polling 34 percent of the national vote, just three points less than the DC – agreed to abstain from voting in parliament in order to maintain a government of national unity. The pact was rescinded in 1979, and after Berlinguer's death in 1984 the PCI's share of the vote dropped to around 27 percent. The combination of this withdrawal of popular support and the collapse of the Communist bloc led to a realignment of the PCI under the leadership of **Achille Occhetto**, who turned the party into a democratic socialist grouping along the lines of left-leaning parties in Germany or Sweden – a transformation encapsulated by the party's new name – the **Partito Democratico della Sinistra** ("Democratic Party of the Left").

In its efforts to exclude the left wing from power, the DC had been obliged to accede to demands from minor parties such as the **Radical Party**, which gained eighteen seats in the 1987 election, one of them going to the porn star Ilona Staller, better known as **La Cicciolina**. Furthermore, the DC's reputation was severely damaged in the early 1980s by a series of scandals, notably the furore surrounding the activities of the P2 Masonic lodge, when links were discovered between corrupt bankers, senior DC members, and fanatical right-wing groups. As its popularity fell, the DC was forced to offer the premiership to politicians from other parties. In 1981 Giovanni Spadolini of the Republicans became the first non-DC prime minister since the war, and in 1983 **Bettino Craxi** was installed as the first premier from the PSI, a position he held for four years.

Even through the upheavals of the 1970s the national income of Italy continued to grow, and there developed a national obsession with **Il Sorpasso**, a term signifying the country's overtaking of France and Britain in the economic league table. Experts disagreed as to whether Il Sorpasso actually happened (most thought it hadn't), and calculations were complicated by the huge scale of tax evasion and other illicit financial dealings in Italy. All strata of society were involved in the withholding of money from central government, but the ruling power in this **economia sommersa** (submerged economy) was, and to a certain extent still is, the **Mafia**, whose contacts penetrate to the highest levels in Rome. The most traumatic proof of the Mafia's infiltration of the political hierarchy came in May 1992, with the murders of anti-Mafia judges **Giovanni Falcone** and **Paolo Borsellino**, whose killers could only have penetrated the judges' security with the help of inside information.

To the present day

The murders of the immensely respected Falcone and Borsellino might well come to be seen as marking a fault-line in the political history of modern Italy, and the late 1980s and early 1990s saw the rise of a number of new political parties, as people became disillusioned with the old DC-led consensus. One was the right-wing **Lega Nord** (Northern League), whose autocratic leader, **Umberto Bossi**, capitalized on northern frustration with the state, which they saw as supporting a corrupt south on the back of the hard-working, law-abiding north. The **Alleanza Democratica**, or Democratic Alliance, led by the more circumspect **Mario Segni**, offered a less divisive alternative to middle-of-the road voters, while the fascist MSI, renamed the **Alleanza Nazionale** (AN), or National Alliance, and now a wide coalition of right-wingers led by the persuasive Gianfranco Fini, has gained ground in recent years.

In 1992 the new government of **Giuliano Amato** – a politician untainted by any hint of corruption – instigated the biggest round-up of Mafia members in nearly a decade, leading to the arrest, at the beginning of 1993, of Salvatore "Toto" Riina, the Mafia **capo di tutti capi** (boss of bosses) and the man widely believed to have been behind the Falcone and Borsellino killings. The arrest of Riina followed the testimony of numerous supergrasses, who also implicated key members of the establishment in Mafia activities. For example, it was exposed that a murdered associate of the former prime minister **Giulio Andreotti** was the Mafia's man in Rome, a top-level fixer who would arrange acquittals from the Supreme Court in exchange for support. (Bettino Craxi once called Andreotti a fox, adding "sooner or later all foxes end up as fur coats.")

However, it was **Craxi** himself who was one of the first to fall from grace. Craxi was at the centre of the powerful Socialist establishment that ran the key city of Milan, when in February 1992 a minor party official was arrested on corruption charges. This represented just the tip of a long-established culture of kickbacks and bribes that went right to the top of the Italian political establishment, not just in Milan, nicknamed **tangentopoli** ("bribesville"), but across the entire country. By the end of that year thousands were under arrest and the net was spreading. What came to be known as the **Mani Pulite** or Clean Hands investigation, led by the crusading Milan judge, Antonio di Pietro, was under way.

The established Italian parties, most notably the Christian Democrats and the Socialists, were almost entirely wiped out in the municipal elections of 1993. The establishment wasn't finished yet, however, and the national **elections of 1994** saw yet another political force emerge to fill the power vacuum: the centre-right **Forza Italia** or "Come On Italy", led by the media mogul **Silvio Berlusconi**, who used the power of his TV stations to build support, and swept to power as prime minister in a populist alliance – his "Freedom Pole" coalition – with Bossi's Lega Nord and the fascist National Alliance. The fact that Berlusconi was not a politician was perhaps his greatest asset, and most Italians, albeit briefly, saw this as a new beginning – the end of the old, corrupt regime, and the birth of a truly modern Italian state. However, as one of the country's top northern industrialists, and a former crony of Craxi, Berlusconi was as bound up with the old ways as anyone. Not only did he resist all attempts to reduce the scope of his media business, with which, as prime minister, there was a clear conflict of interest, but in time he himself came under investigation concerning the tax dealings of his Fininvest group. At the end of 1994 Berlusconi was himself forced to resign after the withdrawal of Bossi's Lega Nord from the coalition, and the government collapsed. The next administration, led by the relatively colourless finance man **Lamberto Dini**, managed to stagger on into 1995, but a year later things had once again descended into chaos, with none of a number of compromise candidates able to put together a government. In an attempt to break the deadlock, Scalfaro called elections for April 1996. For the first time in Italy's history a broad centre-left alliance was formed, known as the **ulivo** ("olive tree"), led by **Romano Prodi**, head of the small **Partito Popolare Italiano** (the PPI, or Italian People's Party). In terms of numbers, *l'ulivo* was made up mostly of the PDS, though in order to gain a majority in the Chamber of Deputies the government formed alliances with most of the other parties, including the Lega Nord and the newly created Italian Communist Party, the Rifondazione Comunista.

Meanwhile, the trial of **Giulio Andreotti**, perhaps the most potent symbol of the sleazy postwar years, at last went ahead in Palermo and he had to answer charges of a long-term conspiracy with the Mafia. Andreotti, seven times Prime Minister of Italy and a senator for life, denied any association, and was acquitted in October 1999 aged 80. In 2002, however, he was back in court, this time charged with complicity in the murder of a journalist. Andreotti denied the charge, but was found guilty and sentenced to 24 years in prison. He is currently appealing, but even if he loses, the worst he can expect is house arrest – Italian law does not allow the jailing of anyone over 75 years old.

In January 1999, Craxi was convicted with twenty others of corruption in connection with kickbacks involving ENEL, the state electrical company. He was sentenced to five years in prison, but died a year later in exile in Tunisia. The most influential public figure to be tried in the late Nineties, however, was **Berlusconi**, who was **convicted** and sentenced in August 1998 to two years and nine months in jail. Perhaps not surprisingly, Berlusconi has since been acquitted of a number of the charges against him, and, although further offences have come to light (bribing the judiciary among them), the ongoing proceedings have served more as a background to his resurgent political career than anything else.

Compared with the turmoil of the early 1990s, the political situation had reached a fairly even plateau. The Christian Democratic party had dissolved; the shift from proportional representation to a first-past-the-post system had begun; and a trend towards two large coalitions – one on the centre-left and the other on the centre-right – indicated a major break from the fragmented, multiparty political landscape of the postwar era. In the mid- to late-1990s attention shifted to the economy and a series of austerity measures to bring down inflation and reduce public spending began as a prelude to the entry of the lira into the **ERM**. In October 1998, the relatively prolonged period of stability ended when the Prodi government was defeated in a parliamentary vote of no confidence. President Scalfaro quickly appointed the former leader of the PDS, **Massimo D'Alema**, as Prime Minister designate. The government lasted for eighteen months before he quit after overwhelming defeat in regional elections in April 2000 and Giuliano Amato was re-appointed as Italy's 58th prime minister since World War II. The left coalition replaced him with **Francesco Rutelli**, the slick and successful ex-mayor of Rome, in the lead-up to the April 2001 elections, only to be crushingly defeated by Berlusconi's Forza Italia. A year and a half on, Berlusconi has so far failed to fulfil any of his electoral promises, but a number of bills have been passed that conveniently protect his own business interests and thwart any attempts by the judiciary to pursue charges of corruption. He has been condemned by many Italians for his mismanagement of events at the G8 Summit in Genoa in 2001, during which demonstrator Carlo Giuliani was shot dead by a *carabiniere*, and for his labour reforms at the beginning of 2002. At the time of writing, unemployment is at a current high, economic growth at a standstill and inflation on the rise – the future of yet another Italian government cannot be guaranteed.

Painting and Sculpture

taly's contribution to European painting and sculpture far surpasses that of any other nation. This is in part due to the triumph of the Renaissance period, but Italy can also boast many other remarkable artistic achievements, from the seventh century BC to modern times. The country's fragmented political history has led to strong regional characteristics in Italian art: Rome, Pisa, Siena, Florence, Milan, Venice, Bologna and Naples all have distinctive and recognizable traditions.

The Etruscans

Italian artistic history begins with the **Etruscans**, whose culture spanned the seventh to the first centuries BC. Etruscan art was distinct from that of Greece, then the dominant nation both politically and artistically, though in many other respects it consistently shows the impact of contemporary trends in Greece. Many of the finest Etruscan **sculptures** date from the sixth century BC. Among the best examples, both now in the Villa Giulia in Rome, are the *Apollo and Herakles* from Veio, and the *Sarcophagus of a Married Couple* from Cerveteri, the reclining figures of the latter a typical motif of Etruscan art – the faces realistic and expressive, with prominent eyes and enigmatic smiles, but otherwise scant attention paid to human anatomy. Depictions of animals, real and imaginary, were also common, most famous among which are the *Chimera* from Arezzo, now in the Museo Archeologico in Florence, and Rome's own emblem, the *She-Wolf*, in the Palazzo dei Conservatori – both from the fifth century BC.

Surviving Etruscan **wall paintings** are surprisingly numerous, especially considering that (apart from a few at Paestum) all of their Greek counterparts in Italy have vanished. The most outstanding array is in Tarquinia, which preserves examples ranging from the sixth to the first century BC; another fine group is at Chiusi. These paintings were at first of a religious or magic nature, initially intending to provide an amenable environment for the dead. Later, visionary views of the afterlife were attempted. With their bold drawing, bright colours and lively details, they have an immediate visual appeal.

The Romans

Like the Etruscans, the **Romans** were heavily indebted to the Greeks for their art forms, happily adapting Greek models to suit their own purpose, though they had little taste for the aesthetic values that had played such a key role in Greek art. Admittedly, the great heroic statues of the Greeks were highly prized. Many were brought to Rome, while others were extensively imitated and copied, and some of the most famous pieces of Roman **sculpture** – the *Apollo Belvedere* and the *Venus of Cnidos* in the Vatican, the *Medici Venus* in the Uffizi – are actually Roman copies of lost Greek originals, though they are successful pieces of work in their own right.

The Empire's own contribution to artistic development is exemplified by Roman **portraiture**, which usually eschewed idealization in favour of an objective representation of the physical features, typically showing a bony facial structure, bare forehead, pursed lips and large eyes. Only occasionally, as in the reigns of Augustus and Hadrian, was this image softened. Marble portrait busts have survived in vast quantities, but the bronze equestrian statues – a particularly effective means of stressing the power and charisma of the emperor – were later melted down. Only that of Marcus Aurelius in Rome survives.

The Romans also made full and varied use of relief sculpture, not least in the carvings which adorned the front of **sarcophagi**, their main form of funerary art, and on the **triumphal arches** and **columns** erected to celebrate military victories. Some of these, like Trajan's Column in Rome, which dates from the second century AD, display a virtuoso skill and attention to detail in their depiction of great deeds and battles.

In the domestic environment, **wall paintings** were an essential feature, though relatively few survive. In Rome itself, there are the *Esquiline Landscapes* and *Aldobrandini Wedding*, and the frescoes from the Villa Livia, while the best examples are those preserved in the towns of Pompeii and Herculaneum after their submersion by the eruption of Mount Vesuvius in 79 AD. Some of these remain in situ, notably the spectacular paintings in the Villa dei Misteri; others have been moved to the Museo Nazionale in Naples. In general, a huge range of subject matter was tackled – landscapes, portraits, still lifes, mythologies and genre scenes – while both realistic and stylized approaches to the depiction of nature were attempted.

Early Christian art

The **early Christian** period saw an almost total rejection of sculpture, other than for sarcophagi, though the remarkable wooden doors of Santa Sabina in Rome – featuring the earliest known representation of the Crucifixion – are a notable exception. The earliest murals were created in the Roman catacombs, and show no great stylistic innovation, but increasingly Christian painters began to render a sense of expression to the facial features, in order that the emotions of pain, sorrow and ecstasy could be depicted, along with a richly symbolic pictorial vocabulary. But the early Christians favoured **mosaics** rather than painting as a medium. This painstaking art form had hitherto been associated with floor decoration, but it proved ideal for the decoration of the early churches, its inappropriateness for the depiction of movement in many ways responsible for the rigid artistic forms which took an increasing grip. The earliest surviving cycle, in Santa Maria Maggiore in **Rome**, dates from the second quarter of the fifth century, and is fairly small-scale. The slightly later group in the Mausoleo di Galla Placidia in **Ravenna**, the city which had by then assumed the status of capital of the western empire, are more monumental, their daring geometric patterns, elaborate imagery and sublime colouring representing perhaps the first great milestone of Christian art.

Ravenna continued as a centre of artistic innovation when a century later it became in effect the Italian capital of **Byzantine** culture and politics. Many magnificent mosaic series were created, and three sets in particular far surpass in quality anything produced in Constantinople itself, or indeed anywhere else in its empire: at the church of San Vitale, where the mosaics are the central focus of the architecture itself; Sant'Apollinare Nuovo, whose two frieze processions were quite unlike anything previously seen in Italian art; and the church of Sant'Apollinare in Classe, whose apse mosaics exude a unique sense of peace and mystery.

The middle ages

Italy at first played a rather subsidiary role in the Europe-wide re-emergence from the Dark Ages. The **Byzantine tradition** proved surprisingly durable, particularly in Venice and Sicily, which both retained strong trading links with Constantinople. Throughout the twelfth century, Byzantine craftsmen proved that the art of mosaic was far from exhausted, providing works that are worthy successors to those at Ravenna in the Cappella Palatina of Palermo and the duomos of Cefalù and Monreale, and of course the Basilica of San Marco in Venice.

Many Italian **fresco cycles** of the period still show traces of Byzantine influence, and the style was also a feature of the great eleventh-century Benedictine art movement fostered by the abbey of Montecassino. Sadly, nearly all the products of this school have vanished, though the murals in Sant'Angelo in Formis near Capua give an approximate idea of what they must have looked like.

Because of the cost of frescoes, from the second quarter of the twelfth century **panel paintings** became increasingly important, particularly in Tuscany. Subjects fell into three main categories: the Madonna and Child with saints; the portrait of a saint surrounded by scenes from his life; or the *Christus Triumphans*, a large painted crucifix showing an open-eyed Christ with outstretched hands.

The art of **sculpture** was initially slow to revive after its long period in the doldrums, but it came to occupy a crucial role throughout Europe during the Romanesque period, with Lombard and Emilian masons playing a key role in its dissemination. Just after the turn of the twelfth century, a master by the name of **Wiligelmo** carved at Modena what may well be the earliest of the great cathedral porches – a form that was to become one of the outstanding features of European medieval art. His bas-reliefs feature expressive figures grouped with considerable narrative skill, and they suggest at least some familiarity with classical works. The same sculptor may also have carved the magnificent episcopal throne in San Nicolò in Bari. **Nicolò**, a pupil of Wiligelmo, seems to have been responsible for most of the other great portals of northern Italy – those of the Sacra di San Michele, San Zeno in Verona, and of the cathedrals of Verona, Ferrara, Piacenza and Cremona. Towards the end of the century, this style was developed in and around Parma by **Benedetto Antelami**, who created the graceful *Deposition* relief in the cathedral, the profuse and lively decoration of the baptistry.

The precursors of Renaissance

The distinction between **Gothic** and **Renaissance**, so marked in the painting and sculpture of other countries, is very blurred in Italy. In the mid-thirteenth century, what is normally considered one of the key planks of the Renaissance

– the rediscovery of the full sense of form, beauty and modelling characteristic of classical art – had already occurred with the statues of the Porta Romana in **Capua**, fragments of which are preserved in the town's museum. These were commissioned by Emperor Frederick II, who wished to revive memories of the grandeur that was Rome. Increasingly, Italians came to believe that it was northern barbarians who had destroyed the arts, which it was now their own duty to revive.

A sculptor of south Italian origin who was doubtless familiar with the work at Capua, **Nicola Pisano** (c1220–84), developed this style, in four major surviving works – the pulpits of the Pisa Baptistry and the Duomo in Siena, the Arca San Domenico in Bologna and the Fonte Gaia in Perugia. His figures have a sure sense of volume, with varying levels of relief used to create an illusion of space. **Arnolfo di Cambio** (c1245–1310), his assistant on some of these projects, developed the mix of classical and Gothic features in his own works, which include the famous bronze *St Peter* in Rome, and the *Tomb of Cardinal de Braye* in San Domenico in Orvieto. The latter defined the format of wall tombs for the next century, showing the deceased lying on a coffin below the Madonna and Child, all set within an elaborate architectural framework.

Of even greater long-term significance was the achievement of **Giovanni Pisano** (c1248–1314), who abandoned his father's penchant for paganism, adopting instead new and dramatic postures for his figures which were quite unlike anything in the previous history of sculpture. This is nowhere more evident than in the statues he created for the facade of the Duomo in Siena, which are placed high up rather than round the portals, and are a world away from their static counterparts on French cathedrals.

It was only in the last three decades of the thirteenth century that Italian painters finally began to break away from the time-honoured Byzantine formulas, a new sense of freedom initiated by **Pietro Cavallini** (active 1273–1308) in Rome and developed by the Florentine **Cimabue** (c1240–1302), who introduced rounded forms to his fresco of *The Madonna of St Francis* in the lower church at Assisi. His masterpiece, the Passion cycle in the upper church, is sadly ruined, but enough remains to give evidence of the overwhelming tragic grandeur it must once have possessed.

Whereas Cimabue's works were still rooted in the Byzantine tradition, and made no attempt to break away from a flat surface effect, a huge leap was made by his pupil and fellow Florentine, **Giotto di Bondone** (1266–1337), whose innovations were to define the entire subsequent course of Western art. Giotto decisively threw off the two-dimensional restrictions of painting, managing to give his pictures an illusion of depth. Thanks to having better materials at his disposal than Cimabue, his *Life of St Francis* in the upper church at Assisi survived remarkably well until the 1997 earthquake, now since restored; his frescoes in the Scrovegni Chapel in Padua survived less well and had to be restored recently to save them from being ruined by humidity and pollution. These two great cycles are the best examples of Giotto's genius in all its many facets. Among these are such basic principles as a sense for the significant, unencumbered by surplus detail; the convincing treatment of action, movement, gesture and emotion; and total command over technical matters like figure modelling, foreshortening, and effects of light and shade.

The fourteenth and early fifteenth centuries

In spite of these momentous developments, the path towards the Renaissance was not to follow a continuous or consistent course. Indeed, the leading local school of painters in the fourteenth century was not that of Florence, but of neighbouring **Siena**, which had very different preoccupations. This had a great deal to do with the father figure, **Duccio di Buoninsegna** (c1255–1318), who did not go along the revolutionary path of Giotto, but instead breathed a whole new life into the Byzantine tradition. Duccio's sense of grandeur is well conveyed by the central panel of his masterpiece, the *Maestà*, in the Museo dell Opera del Duomo of his native city. However, it is the small scenes of this vast altarpiece which bring out his best quality: that of a masterful storyteller, adept at arrangement, grouping and the depiction of expression, feeling and movement. Colour, which in Giotto is merely used to bring out the forms, becomes a leading component in its own right.

In spite of the presence in the city of the vibrant statues of Giovanni Pisano, subsequent Sienese painters found Duccio's narrative art the more potent model. **Simone Martini** (c1284–1344) began his career by painting a fresco counterpart of Duccio's *Maestà* in the Palazzo Pubblico, though his most celebrated work in this building, the commemorative *Equestrian Portrait of Guidoriccio da Fogliano*, is now widely regarded as a fake. His refined, graceful style depended above all on line, colour and decorative effects – seen to best effect in the cycle of *The Life of St Martin* in the lower church in Assisi and in the sumptuous, cunningly designed *Annunciation* in the Uffizi. The latter was painted in collaboration with his brother-in-law **Lippo Memmi** (d1357), who independently painted the *Maestà* in the Palazzo Pubblico in San Gimignano, and may also have been responsible for the dramatic New Testament frescoes in the Collegiata of the same town, traditionally ascribed to the otherwise unknown **Barna**.

Another Sienese painter who worked at Assisi was **Pietro Lorenzetti** (active 1306–45); his frescoes there show the impact of Giotto, and have a sense of pathos which is uncharacteristic of Sienese painting. His brother **Ambrogio Lorenzetti** (active 1319–47) was a more original artist, whose main achievement was the idiosyncratic *Allegory of Good and Bad Government* in the Palazzo Pubblico, which shows painting being used for a secular, didactic purpose for the first time and raises the landscape background to a new, higher status, with an awareness of perspective uncommon for this date. The other notable Sienese sculptor of the period was the mysterious **Lorenzo Maitani** (c1270–1330), who is associated with one work only – the wonderfully lyrical reliefs on the most sumptuous facade in Italy, that of the Duomo in Orvieto.

In **Florence**, meanwhile, a whole group of painters consciously followed Giotto's style, without materially adding to it. The most talented was **Maso di Banco** (active 1320–1350), who was particularly skilled at conveying the master's sense of plastic form, while the most faithful was **Taddeo Gaddi** (d1366), whose son **Agnolo Gaddi** (d1396) carried the Giottesque tradition on to nearly the end of the century. **Bernardo Daddi** (c1290–1349), on the other hand, combined this tradition with aspects of the Sienese style. The sculptor **Andrea Pisano** (c1290–1348) succeeded Giotto as master mason of the campanile. The reliefs he executed for it, plus the bronze door he made for the baptistry, translate Giotto's pictorial language back into a three-dimensional format.

A reaction against the hegemony of the Giottesque style came with **Andrea Orcagna** (c1308–68) who was equally prominent as a painter and sculptor, developing a flowery, decorative idiom seen to best effect in the tabernacle in Orsanmichele. The paintings of Orcagna and his school re-established the hierarchical tradition of the Byzantines, and rejected the importance of spatial depth.

At the very end of the fourteenth century, the **International Gothic** style, originating in the Burgundian courts, swept across Europe. This introduced a new richness to the depiction of landscape, animals and costume, though it was unconcerned with intellectual matters. Its dissemination in Italy was largely due to **Gentile da Fabriano** (c1370–1427), whose *Adoration of the Magi* in the Uffizi (one of his relatively few surviving compositions) shows the gorgeously opulent surface effects of this style at its best. Another leading practitioner was **Masolino da Panicale** (c1383–1447), who is best known for having begun the famous fresco cycle in Santa Maria del Carmine in Florence. In the same city, the new movement influenced **Lorenzo Monaco** (c1372–1425), whose work bridges the Florentine and Sienese traditions.

International Gothic took a particularly firm grip in Verona, chiefly through **Antonio Pisanello** (1395–1455). The latter's fame rests partly on his prowess as a medallist, and only a tantalizing handful of his paintings remain, notably the frescoes in the Veronese churches of Sant'Anastasia and San Fermo, and the Palazzo Ducale in Mantua, which magically evoke the idealized courtly world of fairy tales. Numerous drawings prove these were based on patient observations of nature – something that was to be a key element in the unfolding of the Renaissance.

The Florentine Renaissance

A date often given for the start of the **Renaissance** is 1401, when the Florentine authorities announced a public competition for the right to make a second door for the baptistry. Candidates had to submit a trial piece of *The Sacrifice of Isaac*, a stiff test presenting problems of narrative, expression, movement and spatial arrangement, in which scenery, animals and both nude and draped figures had to be adequately depicted. The most audacious solution, which can be seen in the Bargello, was provided by **Filippo Brunelleschi** (1377–1446), who in the process fully mastered the science of perspective. He failed to win, and in disgust gave up sculpture in favour of architecture, but the new possibilities opened up by his command over visuals, and the impetus they provided for other artists to experiment and discover, mark the transition from medieval art to modern.

Brunelleschi's mantle was taken over by **Donatello** (c1386–1466), who began his long career by creating a new kind of freestanding statue to adorn Florence's churches, which became the artistic symbol of the city. These heroic, larger-than-life figures are shown with their feet planted firmly on the ground, displaying facial expressions of great energy and concentration. A typical example is the *St George* made for Orsanmichele, below which was placed an extraordinary carving of the saint slaying the dragon which uses the art of perspective for the first time in stone sculpture, as well as pioneering the technique of very low relief. With the bronze *David*, now in the Bargello, Donatello helped bring the nude – the ultimate figurative challenge – back into the mainstream of art; and he also revived another lost art, the bronze equestrian statue, with the *Monument to Gattamelata* in Padua.

The victor of the baptistry door competition was **Lorenzo Ghiberti** (1378–1455), who thereafter devoted almost the rest of his life to the project. Ghiberti initially showed no interest in perspective, and remained loyal to most of the old Gothic formulas, his first set of doors merely refining Andrea Pisano's techniques. However, his second set of doors, known as the *Gates of Paradise*, show how his style evolved under the influence of classical antecedents, creating a sense of space and illusion, and imbuing the grouping and characterization of the figures with a gently lyrical touch.

Donatello's collaborator **Nanni di Banco** (c1384–1421) was another to achieve an individual mix of the Gothic and Renaissance idioms, notably in *The Four Saints* on Orsanmichele. Another architect-sculptor, **Bernardo Rossellino** (1409–64), created in the *Monument to Leonardo Bruni* in Santa Croce the prototype of the sort of niche tomb that was to prevail for the rest of the century.

Luca della Robbia (1400–82) began his career as a sculptor of marble and bronze, working in a classically derived style, but a very different one from the essentially serious approach of his contemporaries. However, after Luca invented the art of glazed terracotta, he abandoned other forms of sculpture, laying the foundation for a highly lucrative family business which was continued by his nephew **Andrea della Robbia** (1435–1525).

The painter **Masaccio** (1401–28) belongs with Brunelleschi and Donatello as a key figure of the early Renaissance. His *Trinity* fresco in Santa Maria Novella must have startled his contemporaries, its perfect sense of depth and perspective giving the illusion of peering into the solid wall on which it was painted. Masaccio collaborated with Masolino, most notably in the fresco cycle in Santa Maria del Carmine. In this, the scenes are pared down to the essentials; the figures have a heroic quality and dignity, with their gestures depicted at the moment of maximum intensity. A single source of light is used, with shadows cast accurately.

Fra' Angelico (c1400–55), like Ghiberti in sculpture, combined new techniques with the Gothic tradition. A devout Dominican monk, his pictures show a rapt, heavenly vision. Colour is a telling ingredient: Angelico's ethereal blue was inimitable, the rest of his palette hardly less fetching. Frescoes in the cells of his own monastery of San Marco, intended as aids to contemplation, rank as his most important body of work. Late in his career, Angelico was called to the Vatican, where he frescoed the Cappella Niccolina, employing a style which had by then lost all Gothic traces.

Fra' Filippo Lippi (c1406–69) gradually moved away from the style of his master Masaccio to develop a greater sense of drama, seen to best effect in the frescoes in the cathedral at Prato. His later panels show a highly personal, mystical vision, characterized by wistful Madonnas, playful children and poetic landscapes. Fra' Angelico's only follower of note was **Benozzo Gozzoli** (c1421–97), whose work lacks any sense of profundity, but possesses undeniable decorative charm, best seen in the frescoes in the Palazzo Medici-Ricardi in Florence.

The city's most eccentric painter was **Paolo Uccello** (1396–1475), who was obsessed by the problems of perspective and foreshortening. His *Sir John Hawkwood* in the Duomo was a deliberate piece of trompe l'oeil, though its effect is marred by the use of different vantage points, a characteristic common to his paintings, in which he tried to find as many lines as possible to lead the eye inwards. **Domenico Veneziano** (1406–61) was one of the most admired artists of the day, but only a few works by him survive, notably the serene **St Lucy Altar** in the Uffizi, which shows his talent for spatial arrangement and gentle, pastel-like colouring. **Andrea del Castagno** (c1421–57), in contrast, favoured harsh, strong colours, and an exaggerated dramatic pose for his figures, as can be seen in *The Last Supper* in Sant'Apollonia. In the series of *Famous Men* in the Uffizi he initiated a Florentine trend by vividly translating onto canvas the late sculptural types of Donatello.

Halfway through the century, a new versatility was brought to Florentine art by **Antonio Pollaiuolo** (c1432–98), who was active as a painter, sculptor, engraver, goldsmith and embroidery designer. Pollaiuolo was renowned for the advances he made in the depiction of anatomy and movement; he was also one of the first to grapple with the next great challenge facing Renaissance painters, namely how to move beyond making all parts of a picture accurate and realistic, while at the same time creating a satisfying compositional whole. Another painter-sculptor was **Andrea del Verrocchio** (c1435–88), whose fame as a teacher has unfairly drawn attention away from his own wide-ranging achievements. His *Christ and St Thomas* on Orsanmichele shows crafty compositional skills in fitting two statues into a space intended for one, and marks a move away from classicism, as does his equestrian *Monument to Bartolommeo Colleoni* outside San Zanipolo in Venice. Other Florentine sculptors of this period preferred a much softer approach. **Desiderio da Settignano** (1428–64) made sensitive busts of women and children, and used Donatello's technique of low relief to create scenes of the utmost delicacy. **Mino da Fiesole** (1429–84), **Antonio Rossellino** (1427–79) and **Benedetto da Maiano** (1442–97) showed broadly similar preoccupations, all concentrating on grace and beauty of line.

Subjects drawn from classical mythology became an increasingly important part of the repertoire of Florentine painters in the second half of the fifteenth century, in large part owing to the humanist culture fostered at the court. One of Italy's most distinctive artists, **Sandro Botticelli** (c1445–1510), created the most famous and haunting images in this field, notably *The Birth of Venus* and *Primavera*, both now in the Uffizi. His late work shows a deliberate archaism, perhaps as a result of the religious fanaticism of the time.

Filippino Lippi (1457/8–1504), the result of Fra' Filippo's affair with a nun, came to fame with his completion of Masaccio's frescoes in Santa Maria del Carmine. He developed a style based on that of Botticelli, though with a more consciously antique feeling. Another painter with pagan tastes was the reclusive **Piero di Cosimo** (c1462–1521), who was at his best in enigmatic mythological scenes. Meanwhile, vivid new frescoes were created for Florence's churches by **Domenico Ghirlandaio** (1449–94), whose works are now chiefly remembered for their documentary interest, being filled with portraits of contemporary notables and vivid anecdotal details.

The fifteenth century elsewhere in Italy

Although the fifteenth century brought a rich crop of artists working throughout Italy, including many places which previously had little tradition of their own to draw on, no other city came near to matching the depth and consistency of the fifteenth-century Florentine School.

However, although the technical innovations pioneered in Florence were to have an enormous influence, they were by no means slavishly followed. Sienese painters proved the continuing vitality of the colourful narrative approach of the previous century, modified by the impact of International Gothic. The works of **Sassetta** (c1392–1450), which are often impregnated by a sense of mysticism, do make some concessions to the new theories of spatial composition, but this is an essentially subordinate feature. The finest Sienese artist of the century was the sculptor **Jacopo della Quercia** (1374–1438), whose style is essentially linear, though with classical tendencies modified by knowledge of the most advanced northern European art of the day. He was given important public commissions in his native city, such as the overall supervision of the baptistry font and the Fonte Gaia. However, his masterpiece is his last work, the reliefs on the facade of San Petronio in Bologna, which show a vigorous approach fully comparable with those of the great Florentines. His main follower was the Florentine-born **Agostino di Duccio** (1418–81), another sculptor heavily dependent on line, whose work abounds with nervous energy. His masterpiece, executed in collaboration with **Matteo de' Pasti** (c1420–67), is the joyous series of low reliefs in the Tempio Malatestiano in Rimini.

Another artist associated with the Rimini project was the Tuscan **Piero della Francesca** (1410/20–92), who cast an overwhelming influence over the development of painting in central Italy. A painstaking worker, Piero was also active as a mathematician, hence the importance of perspective and symmetry in his compositions. His figures are painted with a cool sense of detachment yet have a grave, monumental beauty. Piero was also one of the great painters of light, in the blue skies which illuminate his gentle landscapes, and in more dramatic effects, such as in *The Dream of Constantine*, part of his most substantial commission – the fresco cycle in San Francesco, Arezzo.

Melozzo da Forlì (1438–94) was the closest follower of Piero della Francesca, showing a similar interest in perspective, and apparently inventing a favourite Renaissance trick device called *sotto in su*, an extreme form of illusion in which figures painted on a ceiling appear to float in space. Another inventive pupil of the same master was **Luca Signorelli** (1450–1523), who developed the ideas of dramatic movement pioneered by Pollaiuolo. In spite of obvious defects, such as harsh colours, stiff drawing and a tendency to overcrowd his compositions, Signorelli was responsible for some of the most heroic paintings of the day. His profound knowledge of anatomy was to be an enormous influence on the succeeding generation, and he used the nude to achieve the most spectacular effects, notably in the frescoes in Orvieto's Duomo.

Pietro Perugino (1445–1523), probably yet another pupil of Piero, developed in a quite different way from Signorelli, producing calm altarpieces featuring soft and beautifully rounded figures set against serene Umbrian landscapes. His collaborator **Bernardino Pinturicchio** (c1454–1513) was a purely decorative artist whose work has no pretensions to depth, but is nearly always fresh and pleasing, particularly in his larger schemes such as the Libreria Piccolomini in the Duomo in Siena.

The first important Renaissance painter in northern Italy was **Andrea Mantegna** (c1431–1506), who represents the apogee of classical influence. Steeped from an early age in the art of the Romans, Mantegna's ideal vision of the antique world permeates nearly all his work, even becoming the predominant element in many of his sacred compositions, together with a phenomenal technical skill, and daring use of unorthodox vantage points – best seen in the grief-laden *Dead Christ* in the Brera, Milan. In total contrast is the exuberant decoration for the Camera degli Sposi in Mantua, one of the artist's few works based on direct observation rather than classical inspiration.

Padua in the mid-fifteenth century became an important training ground for artists, thanks to the early successes of Mantegna, and the ten-year stay of Donatello. One of its offshoots was the group of painters active in Ferrara: **Cosmè Tura** (c1431–95), **Francesco del Cossa** (1435/6–77) and **Ercole de' Roberti** (1448/55–96). Tura's figures are highly charged, with mannered poses and claw-like hands, typically set against fanciful architecture very different from the idealized townscapes painted by other Renaissance artists. Cossa's outline is sharper, his figures energetic rather than theatrical, his colours more resplendent; he too favoured architectural backgrounds, particularly of ruins. Roberti's essentially small-scale style combines something of the pathos of Tura with Cossa's emphasis on colour and line.

Also trained in Padua was the Brescian **Vincenzo Foppa** (1427/30–1515/6), who subsequently became the leader of the Milanese school. His best works have a certain grandeur of conception, and a subdued sense of colouring. His main follower was **Ambrogio Bergognone** (1450/60–1523), who is particularly associated with the Certosa di Pavia. This great building project was also the main outlet for the talents of the leading Lombard sculptors of the day, notably **Giovanni Antonio Amadeo** (1447–1522), whose other main work is the decoration of the Cappella Colleoni in Bergamo.

Venice, as always, remained something of a law unto itself. Even in mid-century, the sculptures of **Bartolomeo Bon** (c1374–1464/7) and the crowded panels of **Michele Giambono** (active 1420–62) showed the city's continuing preference for late-Gothic forms. Something of a transition can be seen with the **Vivarini** family – **Antonio** (c1419–80), his brother **Bartolomeo** (c1430–91) and his son **Alvise** (c1445–1505) – who gradually introduced a sense of spatial perspective and an increased attempt at characterization. **Carlo Crivelli** (c1430–95) was also associated with them. One of the most inventive and idiosyncratic artists of the day, Crivelli abandoned Venice, preferring commissions from churches in small towns in Marche, which he executed in a deliberately archaic style. His altarpieces are claustrophobically opulent, characterized by strong drawing, rich colours, elaborate detail and a superfluity of decoration, with incidental still lifes a common ingredient.

Another, and far more influential, artistic dynasty was that of the **Bellini** family – **Jacopo** (c1400–70) and his sons **Gentile** (c1429–1507) and **Giovanni** (c1430–1516). The latter was the most significant, standing as a major influence on Venetian painters to come. Though influenced by his brother-in-law Mantegna, Bellini's overall effect is very different, with a soft beauty of both colour and outline. He painted a seemingly endless series of variations on subjects such as the *Madonna and Child* and pietà, yet always managed to make each very different. His larger altarpieces concentrate attention on the foreground, and arrange the figures in such a way that there is a parallel plane behind, rather than the more usual receding landscape. Gentile Bellini was essentially a history painter who epitomized the penchant for highly detailed depictions of Venetian life.

Vittore Carpaccio (c1460–1523) continued this narrative tradition, and two complete cycles by him can still be seen in Venice: that of *St Ursula* in the Accademia, and of *St George and St Jerome* in the Scuola di San Giorgio degli Schiavoni. A love of the picturesque also pervades his altarpieces, which generally give due prominence to fantastic landscapes and resplendent Renaissance buildings.

Venetian Renaissance sculpture was dominated by yet another dynasty, the **Lombardo** family: **Pietro** (c1438–1515) and his sons **Antonio** (c1458–1516) and **Tullio** (c1460–1532). Their strongly classical style was particularly suited to funerary monuments, the best of which are in San Zanipolo. They were also talented decorative carvers, as can be seen in the interior scheme for their own church of Santa Maria dei Miracoli.

Closely associated with the Venetian school was the only important southern Italian painter of the Renaissance, **Antonello da Messina** (c1430–79), who spent the last years of his life in the city. Antonello combined Italian painters' achievements in perspective and foreshortening with the ability to reproduce a variety of textures (skin, velvet, hair, wood) in the naturalistic way that was typical of contemporary Flemish artists; and it was through contact with their work that he introduced oil painting to Italy. His pictures have a strong sense of pathos, and some of his most arresting images are simple devotional pictures, which follow the same format he favoured for his secular portraits.

The High Renaissance

Just as the beginning of the Renaissance is linked to the specific circumstances of the competition for the Florence Baptistry doors, so the climactic part of the era, known as the High Renaissance, is sometimes considered to have started with the mural of *The Last Supper* in Santa Maria delle Grazie in Milan, painted in the last years of the fifteenth century by **Leonardo da Vinci** (1452–1519). Apart from its magnificent spatial and illusory qualities, this painting endowed each of the characters with identifiable psychological traits, and successfully froze the action to capture the mood of a precise moment. His use of *sfumato*, a blurred outline whereby tones gradually but imperceptibly changed from light to dark, was of crucial importance to his ability to make his figures appear as living beings with a soul – a technique best seen in his portraits.

In Florence, the most original painter of the generation after Leonardo was **Fra' Bartolommeo della Porta** (c1474–1517), who was caught up in the religious fanaticism that also influenced Botticelli. As a device to stress the otherness of the divine, he clad the figures in his religious compositions in plain drapery, rather than the colourful contemporary costumes which had hitherto been fashionable. He also did away with elaborate backgrounds and anecdotal detail, concentrating instead on expression and gesture. **Mariotto Albertinelli** (1474–1515), who worked with him in the same workshop in San Marco that had once been run by Fra' Angelico, painted in a broadly similar but less austere manner. **Andrea del Sarto** (1486–1530), on the other hand, was the one Florentine artist who shared the Venetian precept of colour and shade as being the most important ingredients of a picture. His figures are classical in outline, aiming at a balance of nuance, proportion and monumentality.

These Florentines, however, stood very much in the shadow of **Michelangelo Buonarroti** (1475–1564), with whom the Renaissance period reaches its climax. Michelangelo's first love was the creation of marble statues. He had little interest in relief, and none at all in bronze or clay, believing that the slow building up of forms was too simple a task for a great artist. His technique is illustrated most graphically in the unfinished *Slaves* in Florence's Accademia, who seem to be pushing their way out of the stone. The colossal early *David*, also in the Accademia, shows his mastery of the nude, which thereafter became the key focus of his art. In spite of claiming to be a reluctant painter, Michelangelo's single greatest accomplishment was the ceiling fresco of the Sistine Chapel, one of the world's most awe-inspiring acts of individual human achievement. Its confident and elated mood is offset by the overpowering despondency of *The Last Judgement* on the end wall, painted three decades later. His later works are more abstract, as seen in the *pietàs* in the Museo dell'Opera in Florence and the Milan Castello, which contrast sharply with the formal beauty of his youthful interpretation of the scene in St Peter's.

Raphael (1483–1520) stands in almost complete antithesis to his rival Michelangelo, though the personal friendships he forged with his powerful patrons were as significant in raising the status of the artist as was the latter's less compromising approach. A pupil of Perugino, he quickly surpassed his teacher's style, going to Florence where he became chiefly renowned for numerous variants of the *Madonna and Child* and *Holy Family*. Raphael also developed into a supreme portraitist, skilled at both the psychological and physical attributes of his sitters. His greatest works, however, are the frescoes of his Roman period, notably those in the Stanze della Segnatura in the Vatican and the Villa Farnesina. Influenced by Michelangelo's achievement in the Sistine Chapel, Raphael's late works show him moving towards a large-scale, more dramatic and mannered style, but his early death meant that the continuation of this trend was left to his pupils.

Closely related to the classicizing tendency of Raphael is that of the Florentine-born sculptor **Andrea Sansovino** (c1467–1529), whose grandiose tombs in Santa Maria del Popolo in Rome, with standing effigies of the *Virtues*, set the tone for sixteenth-century funerary monuments. His pupil **Jacopo Sansovino** (1486–1570) took his name and carried on his tradition, spending the latter part of his career in Venice, where although principally active as an architect, he also made monumental sculptures which are inseparable from the buildings they adorn. **Sebastiano del Piombo** (c1485–1547), on the other hand, stood as a direct rival to Raphael in Rome, striving to transfer Michelangelo's heroic manner to panel painting. In this, he was only variably successful, though he was a highly sensitive portraitist.

Meanwhile **Antonio Correggio** (1489/94–1534) managed to carve out a brilliant career for himself in Parma. His three ceiling frescoes there develop the illusionistic devices of Mantegna, marking Correggio out as a precursor of the Baroque. One of the great painters of mythological scenes, he was also a relentless explorer of the dramatic possibilities of light and shade. Another fine exponent of the contrasts of light was the Ferrarese **Dosso Dossi** (1479/90–1542), a romantic spirit who created fantastic landscapes peopled with sumptuously dressed figures.

The golden period of Venetian painting, ushered in by Bellini, continued with his elusive pupil, **Giorgione** (1475–1510), whose short life is shrouded in mystery. One of the few paintings certainly by him is *The Tempest* in the Venice Accademia, whose true subject matter baffled even his contemporaries. In it, the figures are, for the first time in Italian art, completely subsidiary to the lush landscape illuminated by menacing shafts of light. The haunting altarpiece in the Duomo of his native town of Castelfranco Veneto is also almost certainly his, but many other paintings attributed to him may actually be by one of many painters who maintained something of his poetic, colourful style. Some of these, notably **Vincenzo Catena** (c1480–1531) and **Palma il Vecchio** (c1480–1528), developed recognizable artistic personalities of their own. **Lorenzo Lotto** (c1480–1556) was the most distinctive of this circle, travelling widely throughout his career, assimilating an astonishing variety of influences.

Giorgione's influence is also marked in the early works of **Titian** (c1485–1576), the dominant personality of the Venetian school and one of the most versatile painters of all time. His art embraced with equal skill all the subjects that were required by the Renaissance – altarpieces, mythologies, allegories and portraits. Even more than Michelangelo, he was able to pick and choose his patrons, and was the first artist to build up a truly international clientele. As a portraitist of men of power, Titian was unrivalled, setting the vocabulary for official images which was to prevail until well into the seventeenth century. His complete technical and compositional mastery was already apparent in relatively early works such as the *Assumption* in I Frari, the first example of what was to become a Venetian speciality: a panel painting specially designed to fit an architectural space. Towards the end of his life, Titian abandoned his bravura and brilliant palette in favour of a very free style, stretching the possibilities of oil paint to their very limits.

Giovanni Antonio Pordenone (1483/4–1539) was a provincial north Italian painter strongly influenced by Giorgione and Titian. More obviously in direct descent from the Venetian masters was the school of Brescia. **Giovanni Girolamo Savoldo** (active 1508–48) showed particular adeptness at light effects, and was a pioneer of night scenes, while **Alessandro Moretto** (c1498–1554) was one of the most incisive portraitists of the Renaissance, and seems to have been responsible for introducing the full-length form to Italy. His altarpieces are more variable, but often have a suitably grand manner.

The Late Renaissance

The perfection of form achieved in the late Renaissance was the culmination of centuries of striving. As artists could not hope to improve on the achievements of Michelangelo and Raphael at their peak, they had to find new approaches. As a result, **Mannerism** was born. This was a deliberately intellectual approach, aimed at flouting the accepted rules, notably by distorting the senses of scale and perspective, exaggerating anatomical details, adopting unlikely poses for the figures, and using unnaturally harsh colours.

One artist commonly labelled a Mannerist is **Giulio Romano** (c1499–1546), one of the most gifted of Raphael's assistants, whose frescoes in the Palazzo Te in Mantua, which he himself built, show the style at its most grandiose, notably in *The Fall of the Giants*, occupying a room to itself. A leading light in the adoption of Mannerism in Florence was **Rosso Fiorentino** (1494–1540), together with **Jacopo Pontormo** (1494–1556) and **Agnolo Bronzino** (1503–72). Pontormo, a brilliant draughtsman, was the most talented of this group, an able decorator and an inquiring if understated portraitist. Bronzino was highly prolific, but only his portraits of royal and noble personages have much appeal today, their detachment, concentrating more on the beauty of their clothing, casting an enormous influence on official portraitists down the centuries. **Giorgio Vasari** (1511–74), originally from Arezzo, was responsible for many of the frescoes in the Palazzo Vecchio, although he is now chiefly famous for his series of biographies of artists, which marked the birth of art history as a discipline.

Another Florentine Mannerist whose writings have helped secure his fame is the sculptor **Benvenuto Cellini** (1500–71), the author of a racy *Autobiography* which offers a fascinating insight into the artistic world of the time. Though he was successful in finding favour at courts all over Europe, only a few of his sculptures, all of a very high quality, survive. The *Bust of Cosimo I*, in the Bargello, marks the departure of the portrait from realism, creating instead a new heroic image. His *Perseus*, in the Loggia dei Lanzi, forms a fitting counterpart to Donatello's late *Judith*, and completely outclasses the *Hercules and Cacus* in the square outside by his rival **Baccio Bandinelli** (1493–1560).

By far the most influential Florentine Mannerist, however, was **Giambologna** (1529–1608), a sculptor of French origin. His favourite medium was bronze, and he established a large workshop which churned out miniature replicas of his most important compositions. These typically show figures in combat, and are designed for the spectator to walk around, rather than examine from only one viewpoint. His most famous image is the typically androgynous *Mercury*; in a conscious rebuttal of the approaches of both Donatello and Michelangelo, this figure appears to float in the air, in the boldest attempt ever made by a sculptor to defy the laws of gravity.

One of the most individualistic Mannerists was **Domenico Beccafumi** (1486–1551), who provided a somewhat unusual end to the long line of Sienese painters, though his emphasis on colour was utterly typical of that city. He was a master of decorative effect, as witnessed by his illusionist frescoes in the Palazzo Pubblico, and his large altarpieces for Sienese churches, which show a particular concern for light and shade, perspective effects, and deep emotions. In Parma, the paintings of Francesco Mazzola, known simply as **Parmigianino** (1503–40), retained something of the consciously refined approach of Correggio, with their exaggeratedly sinuous figures, though his portraits reveal considerable spiritual insight. His decorative scheme for Santa Maria della Steccata typifies the Mannerist penchant for surplus ornament and demonstrates the fertility of his imagination.

Venice, as ever, followed its own distinctive late-Renaissance path, having no taste for the sort of Mannerism practised elsewhere in Italy. **Jacopo Tintoretto** (1518–94) aimed at an ideal based on the drawing of Michelangelo and the colour of Titian, though in fact the heroic style he forged had only superficial resemblances to his mentors. To heighten the sense of drama, he used a battery of other methods: unorthodox vantage points, elongated figures, and unexpected positioning of the main subject on the canvas.

In strong contrast to Tintoretto, the other leading Venetian painter of the day, **Paolo Veronese** (1528–88), was a supreme decorator on a grand scale. Indeed, some of his best work was conceived for architectural settings, such as San Sebastiano in Venice and the Villa Barbara in Masèr. Veronese's love of pomp and splendour, however, is carried over into his easel paintings, which revel in warm, glowing colours and monumental figures, with little sense of gravitas. He fell foul of the Inquisition as a result of the inclusion of German soldiers (which put him under suspicion of Protestant sympathies) and other anachronistic and surplus detail in a huge banquet scene (now in the Venice Accademia) purporting to represent *The Last Supper*. He responded by changing the title to *A Feast in the House of Levi*.

Alessandro Vittoria (1525–1608), a pupil of Jacopo Sansovino, embellished Venice's churches with sculptures that have much in common with Mannerist productions elsewhere in Italy, but are more classically modelled. **Jacopo Bassano** (1510–92) was trained in the city, but preferred to work in the provincial town after which he takes his name, where he was by far the most remarkable of a dynasty of painters. As a setting for his religious panels, he painted the small town and country life of his day as it really was. He also popularized the inclusion of animals and heaped piles of fruit and vegetables – features eagerly taken up by later northern European artists – and was a superb painter of light and shade, using heavy daubs of colour and strong chiaroscuro.

Another remarkable artist working well away from the main centres was **Federico Barocci** (1535–1612) of Urbino. His paintings were painstakingly executed, their soft rounded forms mirroring the comforting religious image propagated by the Counter-Reformation, and with an emphasis on light and movement that was to some extent anticipatory of the Baroque to come.

The Baroque age

The leadership of Italian art away from the sterility of late Mannerism came initially from cities that had hitherto played a minor role in its development. Bologna was the first to come to prominence, through the academy founded there in 1585 by members of the **Carracci** family – **Lodovico** (1555–1619), **Agostino** (1557–1602) and **Annibale** (1560–1609). This was by no means the first attempt to set up a training school for artists, a concept rendered necessary by the blow the Renaissance had dealt to the old workshop tradition, but it was far more successful than any previous venture. Annibale was easily the greatest and most versatile artist of the three, breathing a whole new life into the classical tradition. His frescoes in the Palazzo Farnese in Rome offer a fresh and highly imaginative approach to mythological scenes, as well as being brilliant examples of illusionism. A more serious intent is noticeable in the artist's canvases, which introduce an emotional yet untheatrical content to well-ordered religious subjects. He was also a major landscape painter, pioneering the sort of luscious scene with a subsidiary subject from the Bible or classical literature which was later to be developed in Rome by the great French painters, Claude and Poussin.

An entirely different but equally novel approach was taken by **Michelangelo da Caravaggio** (1573–1610), whose violent and wayward life led him from Milan to Rome, Naples, Malta, Sicily and most of the way back again. Caravaggio was the great master of chiaroscuro, which he used to even more dramatic effect than Tintoretto. He also used what seemed like shock tactics to his patrons in the Church, stripping away centuries of idealized tradition to present biblical stories as they might have seemed at the time. Real-life peasants, beggars, ruffians and prostitutes were all used as models for the figures, to enhance the realistic impact. His original canvases for commissions such as those for the Roman churches of San Luigi dei Francesi and Santa Maria del Popolo were sometimes rejected, though he always managed to find a private buyer. His impact on the great European Golden Age of seventeenth-century painting was immense, spawning whole schools of Dutch and French derivatives, along with Rembrandt, Rubens, and most of the great Spanish masters.

In Italy, Caravaggio's art had an immediate impact on the older **Orazio Gentileschi** (1563–1639), who was particularly keen on its tenebrist effects. The Mantuan **Bartolomeo Manfredi** (c1580–1620) extended the master's style to such genre subjects as card games and soldiers in guardrooms. And Caravaggio's style was brought to Naples by **Giovanni Battista Caracciolo** (c1578–1635), inspiring the city's painters to raise Naples from its traditionally marginal position in Italian art to a place, throughout the seventeenth century, at the very forefront.

The first important follower of the Carracci in Bologna was **Guido Reni** (1575–1642). In the nineteenth century, Reni was ranked as one of the supreme artists of all time, but suffered a slump in reputation when a reaction against artistic sentimentality set in; it is only very recently that his genuine gifts for the expression of feeling have been given their proper due. Among other Carracci pupils, **Domenichino** (1581–1641) was a faithful follower of the style, extending its hold on Rome, though he was better at its more decorative and idealized aspects. **Guercino** (1591–1666) merged the classical and realistic styles, imbuing chiaroscuro effects with a subtlety very different to that favoured by Caravaggio and his followers.

Giovanni Lanfranco (1582–1647), originally from Parma, combined the Carracci style with elements borrowed from Correggio. His frescoes in Rome and Naples have a greater sense of movement and technical trickery than those Domenichino was painting at the same time, and mark the beginnings of High Baroque painting. In turn, his own work was made to seem out-of-date by **Pietro da Cortona** (1596–1669), who introduced a sense of fantasy and freedom that was far more ambitious than anything previously attempted. His ceiling in the Palazzo Barberini presented the illusion of opening on to the heavily populated heavens above, with figures seen *di sotto in su* – apparently teeming down into the hall below. For a century, this was to be the sort of monumental painting favoured in Rome; it was also spread to Florence by Cortona himself, by means of a series of frescoes in the Palazzo Pitti.

The High Baroque style was essentially a Roman phenomenon, born out of the super-confident mood in the world capital of Catholicism as a result of the success of the Counter Reformation. Its overwhelmingly dominant personality was **Gianlorenzo Bernini** (1598–1680), a youthful prodigy who had created an entirely new sculptural language while still in his early twenties. Such works as *David* and *Apollo and Daphne*, both in the Villa Borghese, were the first great marble statues since Michelangelo, yet in their independence of form showed a decisive rejection of the concept of belonging to the block from which they were carved, drawing the spectator into the scene and asserting the primacy of the emotions – a key concept of the Baroque. Though only an occasional painter (he in fact spent more time as an architect), Bernini adopted painterly techniques for his work, using different materials for contrast, exploiting sources of light, and using illusionist techniques, producing a drama best seen in *The Ecstasy of St Theresa* in Rome's Santa Maria della Vittoria, which goes so far as to re-create the atmosphere of a theatre by the inclusion of a gallery of onlookers.

So overwhelming was the impact of Bernini's art that most other sculpture of the period is but a pale imitation of it. One of the few sculptors not to be overawed was the Tuscan **Francesco Mochi** (1580–1654), who made two magnificent equestrian monuments in Piacenza. **Alessandro Algardi** (1598–1654) of Bologna managed a brilliant career in Rome as a bitter rival of Bernini, promoting a sculptural version of the Carracci style.

In Venice, the versatile Genoese **Bernardo Strozzi** (1581–1644) tried to revive memories of the great sixteenth-century masters. His exuberant early works are generally more successful, showing the influence of Rubens: they typically have very free brushwork, luminous colours and pronounced modelling. In Naples, **Massimo Stanzione** (1585–1656) combined something of the approaches of Carracci and Caravaggio, though his most original works are his detailed, colourful portraits. A much more aggressively Caravaggesque idiom is apparent in the work of **Artemisia Gentileschi** (c1597–1651), daughter of Orazio, who was particularly adept at lurid subjects. She enjoyed a remarkable degree of independence and status for a woman of her day, and has attracted a great deal of attention from modern feminists, having a fair claim to the title of "the greatest ever female painter". **Salvator Rosa** (1615–73) painted landscapes that have a wild, mystical quality very different from those of the classical painters of Bologna and Rome. Characteristically, they are populated by bandits or witches, or have an allegorical theme. **Mattia Preti** (1613–99), who originally hailed from the artistic backwater of Calabria, painted some of the most effective canvases in Caravaggio's idiom, excelling at its tenebrist aspects. His later work is more influenced by Roman Baroque, using brighter colours and pronounced spatial effects. In these, he resembles **Luca Giordano** (1632–1705), the main Neapolitan painter of the second half of the century. Giordano was renowned for his ability to paint quickly, and he ranks among the most prolific artists of all time. His output employs a whole variety of styles and is uneven in quality, but shows remarkable technical facility. The last major Baroque painter active in Naples was **Francesco Solimena** (1657–1747), whose large crowded compositions show the full theatricality of the style.

Meanwhile, the Roman vogue for spectacular illusionistic ceilings was continued by **Giovanni Battista Baciccia** (1639–1709), who was warmer in colour and even more audacious in approach than Pietro da Cortona. His most famous decoration is that in the Gesù, which boldly mixes painted and stucco figures. An even greater command of pyrotechnics, however, was displayed by the Jesuit **Andrea Pozzo** (1642–1709) on the ceiling of Sant'Ignazio, whose illusion is designed to be seen from only one specific point.

The eighteenth century

The decline of Italian art in many of its most celebrated strongholds gathered pace in the eighteenth century, a slump from which only Venice and Rome stood apart. In the case of the former, its pre-eminence was due to a revival of its grand decorative tradition after a century's gap. This gave it a leading position in European **Rococo**, the ornate derivative of late Baroque.

An updated version of the style of Veronese was first fostered by **Sebastiano Ricci** (1659–1734), whose work is superficially similar to Veronese's, but has an airier, lighter feel. A more individual approach is apparent in the work of **Giovanni Battista Piazzetta** (1683–1754), an outstanding draughtsman whose joyful and harmonious paintings give the impression of a free and easy approach, yet which were actually the result of meticulous planning. Venice also boasted a notable female portraitist in **Rosalba Carriera** (1675–1757), who was the first artist to use pastel as an independent medium.

By far the most accomplished exponent of Venetian Rococo, and one of the greatest decorative artists of all time, was **Giovanni Battista Tiepolo** (1696–1770). His work is best seen in an architectural setting, where his illusionistic approach compares favourably with those of the earlier Roman artists in its colour, handling, spatial awareness, sense of fantasy and depth of feeling. The finest schemes were made for foreign patrons (in Würzburg and Madrid), but there are some excellent examples in Udine, Vicenza and Stra, and several in Venice itself, notably the Palazzo Labia and Ca'Rezzonico.

His son**, Giovanni Domenico Tiepolo** (1727–1804), aided him on many projects and painted in a broadly similar style, though he had a more obvious eye for satire. Also active in Venice were a number of painters who specialized in painting views of the city as mementos for its aristocratic visitors. The best known of these was **Antonio Canaletto** (1697–1768), whose images, often painted on the spot and with the use of a camera obscura, have defined the popular conception of the buildings and lifestyle of Venice ever since. However, they are an idealized representation, with spatial arrangements and even individual buildings altered. Canaletto's nephew, **Bernardo Bellotto** (1721–80), closely followed his style and applied it to cities all over Europe, but took a more literal approach, stressing topographical exactness. A more sombre, musing mood is present in the Venetian views of **Francesco Guardi** (1712–93), who used a darker palette. His emphasis on transitory light effects foreshadowed the French Impressionists, while his figures have a greater vivacity than those of Canaletto. Genre scenes were also much in demand with visiting tourists, and **Pietro Longhi** (1702–85), who had a limited technique but ready sense of humour, vividly characterized the Venetian life of his day for the benefit of this market.

Among non-Venetian painters, the Genoese **Alessandro Magnasco** (1667–1749) is particularly distinctive, often combining into one picture his two favourite themes of mannered landscapes ravaged by the elements and ecstatic monks at prayer. In Rome, the tourist demand for views was met by **Giovanni Paolo Panini** (c1692–1765), who painted both the ruins of the classical period and the modern buildings of the day. These are surpassed, however, by the grandiose large-scale etchings of **Giovanni Battista Piranesi** (1720–78), which fully exploit the dramatic contrasts of light and shade possible in the black-and-white medium.

The latter can be seen as an early manifestation of **Neoclassicism**, a movement which began in the middle of the century, inspired partly by a reaction against Baroque excesses, and partly by the excitement caused by the discovery of Pompeii and Herculaneum, though many of its leading exponents were foreigners resident in Rome. Neoclassicism aimed at the complete revival of the arts of the ancients, a trend that was particularly marked in sculpture, which had a far larger legacy to borrow on than painting. It is best seen in the works of **Antonio Canova** (1757–1822), which show great beauty in modelling, though a certain frigidity in the depiction of emotions. His statues are often highly erotic in effect: the several monuments he made in honour of Napoleon include life-sized nude depictions, one of which is now in the Brera, Milan.

The nineteenth century

If the eighteenth century was a lean time for Italian art, the nineteenth century was even worse, Paris becoming the overwhelmingly dominant European trendsetter. **Francesco Hayez** (1791–1882) was perhaps the most successful painter at work in the first half of the century, continuing the Neoclassical manner in his history scenes and highly finished portraits.

Towards the 1850s the Romantic taste for realism was reflected in an interest in the country's scenery, immortalized by various local schools: the **Scuola di Posillipo** and the Palizzi brothers (Giuseppe, 1812–88, and Filippo, 1818–99) in Naples; the **Scuola di Rivara** in Piedmont; **il Piccio** (1804–73) in Lombardy; and the **Macchiaioli** in Tuscany. The Macchiaioli were a group of painters based in Florence, who held comparatively modern and definable aims. Their name derives from the Italian word for a blot, as they made extensive use of individual patches of light and dark colour, which was used to define form, in opposition to the super-smooth Neoclassical approach then in vogue. The guiding spirit of the movement was **Giovanni Fattori** (1825–1905), who painted scenes of military life (based on his experiences fighting in the Wars of Independence of 1848–9) and broad landscapes using very free brushwork and compositional techniques. The group's chief theorist, **Telemaco Signorini** (1835–1901), came to be influenced by the painting of Corot and the Barbizon

School, and later followers moved to Paris, to become accepted as peripheral members of the Impressionist circle.

The turn of the century drew, once again, on international trends. Symbolism was chiefly represented by the haunting *femmes fatales* of **Gaetano Previati** (1852–1920) and the subtler compositions of **Giovanni Segantini** (1858–99), who coupled naturalism with imagination. **Giuseppe Pellizza da Volpedo** (1868–1907) experimented with **Divisionismo**, the Italian version of Seurat's Pointillisme. His most famous work, *The Fourth State*, is a striking depiction of the inevitable progress of the working class as outlined by Marx.

Compared with painting, the development of nineteenth-century **sculpture** was somehow delayed. The Canova influence seems to have been hard to escape, and works from this period often demonstrate great skill but little originality. Favourite subjects were portraits and, in typically Romantic fashion, historical characters with heavy revolutionary overtones, such as *Spartacus* by **Vincenzo Vela** (1820–91). Vela's work, together with the later efforts of **Lorenzo Bartolini** (1777–1850), introduced a more naturalistic touch while still retaining a high degree of finish. A more dramatic change of direction occurred through the Neapolitan **Vincenzo Gemito** (1852–1929), who dared to leave smoothness aside and concentrated on movement. **Mario Rutelli** (1859–1941) developed a naturalistic and lively style, taking inspiration from Hellenistic sculpture and specializing in bronze figures for fountains and equestrian monuments, which have since become famous Roman landmarks (the Fontana delle Naiadi in Piazza della Repubblica and **Anita Garibaldi**, on the Janiculum Hill, for example).

Yet the most innovative experiments would only be made by **Medardo Rosso** (1858–1928), who managed to capture the fluidity and elusiveness of the fleeting moment in the third dimension, influencing, among others, Rodin. After the latter's death in 1917, Guillaume Apollinaire acclaimed Rosso as "the greatest living sculptor"; his wax and bronze sculptures, when properly lit, seem to emerge softly from the shadows. Rosso, however, lived and worked in Paris for most of his life.

The twentieth century

The only Italian artist born within the last two hundred years to have gained truly universal recognition is **Amedeo Modigliani** (1884–1920). Although most of his adult life was spent in Paris, Modigliani's work is recognizably Italian, being rooted in the tradition of the Renaissance and Mannerist masters. Primitive African art, then being appreciated in Europe for the first time, was the other main influence on his highly distinctive and essentially linear style. His output consists almost entirely of sensuous reclining female nudes, and strongly drawn, psychologically penetrating portraits.

In 1909 an attempt to break France's artistic monopoly was launched – ironically enough, in Paris – by the **Futurists**, who aimed to glorify the dynamism of the modern world, including the key role of warfare. Their approach was similar to the recently founded Cubist movement in aiming to reproduce several sides of an object at the same time, but differed in striving to convey movement as well. **Umberto Boccioni** (1882–1916) was the most resourceful member of the group, which never recovered from his death in World War I – for which, true to his principles, he had volunteered. His erstwhile colleagues later developed in different directions. **Giacomo Balla** (1871–1958) painted in a variety of styles, ranging from the academic to the abstract. **Gino Severini** (1883–1966) joined the Cubists after the latter had become more interested in colour, then turned to mural and mosaic decorations, before reverting, towards the end of his life, to a sense of fantasy that was characteristic of his Futurist phase. **Carlo Carrà** (1881–1966) did a complete about-face from his Futurist origins, aiming to revive the representationalism of the old Italian masters.

Carrà teamed up in 1917 with **Giorgio de Chirico** (1888–1978) to form **Pittura Metafisica**, which reacted against both the mechanical approach of Cubism and Futurism's infatuation with the modern world, cultivating instead a nostalgia for antiquity. The movement, which established a school in Ferrara, was influenced by Surrealism, and had in particular a penchant for the presence of unexpected, out-of-place objects; de Chirico's **Metaphysical Interiors** show rooms littered with all the fetishes of modern civilization. Architectural forms of a strange and rigid nature are another recurring theme in his work of this period, though like Carrà he later abandoned this in favour of a consciously archaic approach.

Other Italian painters of the twentieth century to have gained an international reputation include **Giorgio Morandi** (1890–1964), who was strongly influenced by de Chirico and specialized in haunting still lifes – very precisely drawn and often in monochrome. Also touched by the Metaphysical tradition was **Filippo de Pisis** (1896–1956), whose huge output is experimental in nature, often exploring sensation and the unexpected; consequently, it is highly uneven in quality.

If Futurism had been the official art of the Fascist regime, after World War II any self-respecting artist had to be a Communist, or at least display left-wing sympathies. However, unanimity in political ideas didn't generate agreement on how these ideas should be expressed. Realists such as **Renato Guttuso** (1912–1987), who believed in figurative painting and focused on dramatic subjects, were opposed by Formalists like Renato Birolli (1905–1959), who were moving towards experimental, non-figurative art. Italy's leading practitioner of abstraction was **Alberto Burri** (1915–95), best known for his collages of waste materials with a thick blob of red or black paint. One of the most successful experiments in Formalism was **Spazialismo**, a group founded by **Lucio Fontana** (1899–1968) with the aim of integrating the third dimension with the two-dimensional format of traditional painting.

Between 1960 and 1970 the antithesis between Realism and Formalism was resolved with the so-called **Informal Art** that originated from a rejection of the establishment, an attitude shared by both European and American artists (New York having by now become the modern alternative to Paris). Since contemporary society was viewed as hostile, the artist wanted to affirm his or her own individuality without even attempting to communicate or to represent reality in any immediately recognizable way. The work of art became equated with the artist's individual gestures, such as Lucio Fontana's sharp cuts in the canvas. Particular importance was attached to the materials on which the informal artist impressed his mark: wood, cloth, metal scraps, plastic were cut, torn, and burned to emphasize the purely "gestural" value of the work.

However, not all artists took themselves that seriously. **Piero Manzoni** (1933–1963) parodied both "the artist's gesture" and the deliberate lack of any communicative content by a series of provocative experiments à la Warhol, from *Consecration of the Art of the Hard-boiled Egg*, where cooked eggs available for public consumption were given added value by the artist's thumb print, to *Lines*, traced on a piece of paper rolled up and sealed into a container. But the most sensational of these statements was perhaps his *Merda d'Artista* (literally,

"Artist's Shit"), mercifully tinned and sealed but outrageously sold by weight at the current price of gold.

After this eloquent comment on art as self-expression, the focus shifted once more to materials and techniques, particularly as a response to an exhibition of American pop art at the prestigious Venice Biennale in 1964. Italian artists such as **Michelangelo Pistoletto** (b1933) rediscovered the creative possibilities of the mixed media collage (pioneered by Burri), with cheap materials still enjoying popularity and sometimes even attaining subject-matter status. Meanwhile, politics made a quiet exit from the art scene.

A parallel development in terms of a "return to reality" was Minimalism (yet another US creature), which concentrated on the mechanical process of constructing the artwork, again using unsophisticated materials (steel, iron, concrete) and elementary geometrical shapes. The traditional divide between painting and sculpture, already blurred by Fontana, seemed to be gone for good, as Minimalist artists such as **Rodolfo Aricò** (b1930) and **Mario Surbone** (b1932) played ambiguous games with depth and surface.

Along these lines came the so-called **Arte Povera** ("Poor Art"), a post-Minimalist movement whose leading figure was **Jannis Kounellis** (b1936), an artist of Greek origin who produced 3D installations and performances using odd media mixes (such as cotton and steel). Another representative of this "school", which flourished mainly between the late Sixties and the mid-Seventies, is **Mario Merz** (b1925), who uses found objects and materials (glass sheets, twigs, metal scraps) to create installations that convey a sense of fragility and danger.

Figurative art made a comeback at the end of the Seventies with the work of **Francesco Clemente** (b1952), **Enzo Cucchi** (b1949), **Sandro Chia** (b1946) and **Mimmo Paladino** (b1948), usually referred to, in the veritable jungle of twentieth-century art movements, as **Transavanguardia** or **Neo-Expressionist** painters. Not only was the human figure rehabilitated but so too were the traditional media, from oil on canvas, to watercolour, pastel, and even fresco. After a long spell of sulky anti-commercialism, Italian painting seemed to have finally made up with the public.

Generally speaking, modern Italian sculptors have been more successful than painters in reinterpreting Italy's heritage in a novel way. **Giacomo Manzù** (1908–91) aimed to revive the Italian religious tradition, in a highly personal manner reminiscent of Donatello, whose technique of very low relief he used extensively. His best-known work is the bronze door of St Peter's on the theme of death, a commission awarded following a highly contentious competition in 1949. **Marino Marini** (1901–80) specialized in another great theme of Italian art, that of the equestrian monument – examples of his work are now displayed in a museum specially devoted to Marini in Florence – while the elegant portraits and female nudes of **Emilio Greco** (1913–95) stand as an updated form of Mannerism.

Although there is nothing truly ground-breaking about the Italian sculpture or painting of the last few years, there are a couple of interesting artists who have been well-received in the international forum. Video-artist **Grazia Toderi** (b1963) uses images of water to discuss transformation and existence, while Padua-born **Maurizio Cattelan** (b1960) creates witty, thought-provoking installations that explore themes of Italian popular culture. Unnerving work like *bidibidobidiboo* (1996) and *La Nona Ora* (1998) hide a lonely despondency behind their laconic humour.

Gordon McLachlan,
with contributions by **Catherine McBeth**

Architecture

With an almost unbroken tradition stretching back over 2500 years, Italy has had an unrivalled influence on Western architecture. From Roman times through the Renaissance and Baroque to Palladio, no other country could claim so great a contribution to building styles and construction techniques for such an extended length of time. The country still boasts a remarkable legacy of historic buildings, and wherever you visit in Italy you won't be far from some of the most inspirational architecture in the world.

The Greeks and Etruscans

The earliest important structures still standing in Italy were built by the peninsula's **Greek** colonizers of the sixth century BC. These exhibit the same qualities characteristic of the classical architecture of Greece itself: a strong but simple outline, a rigorous adherence to balanced proportions, a total unity of design featuring a logical system of horizontals and verticals, and extensive use of decoration to emphasize the structure. This architecture, which principally made use of marble, was based on three great **classical orders**, each of which consisted of an upright column, sometimes resting on a base, topped by a capital and an entablature of architrave, cornice and frieze.

Doric, the grandest and plainest of these orders, was used for the **temples** which are the chief glory of the Greek style, dedicated to gods yet always human in scale, never rising very high, nor appearing in any way overblown. A fine group can be seen on the Italian mainland at **Paestum**; the others – at Agrigento, Selinunte, Segesta and Siracusa – are in **Sicily**. They are older and less refined than the Parthenon in Athens, but their state of preservation compares favourably with any of their counterparts in Greece. Significantly, the Temple of Concord in Agrigento, the most complete of all, was saved by being transformed into a Christian church, while the Temple of Athena in Syracuse was incorporated into the Duomo, where it still remains.

The Greeks were also inveterate builders of open-air **theatres** – generally set against hillsides, with seats for the spectators hollowed out of the rock. Siracusa's Greek theatre is one of the best preserved of its period; that of Taormina, with the peerless backdrop of Mount Etna, also dates back to the Greeks, but was extensively remodelled by the Romans.

A very different form of architecture was practised during the same period in central Italy by the **Etruscans**, but unfortunately little Etruscan architecture remains above ground, as their Roman conquerors engaged in a deliberate programme of obliteration. The few surviving examples include the city walls of Volterra and Cortona, from the sixth century BC, and the gateways at Volterra and Perugia, from about three centuries later. However, Etruscan tombs survive in abundance, mainly at Cerveteri and Tarquinia in northern Lazio.

The Roman period

In architecture, as in many other fields, the **Romans** borrowed from and adapted Greek models. Just as was the case with other art forms, however, their approach to building shows marked differences, particularly in their preference for order and usefulness above beauty. Functional building materials were favoured, and only from the time of Augustus, which marked the softening of the Roman image, are marble and stucco much in evidence, and then usually for facing purposes only. Furthermore, towns were laid out wherever possible in a regular planned grid format, to the model of a military camp.

Although they used the three Greek orders (preferring the Corinthian, with its elaborate acanthus leaf capital), and invented two more of their own (Composite and Tuscan), the Romans relegated the column from the essential structural role it had performed under the Greeks to one that was merely decorative. Instead, they concentrated on solid constructions, employing the rounded forms of the arch and dome, and focusing attention on the end walls. **Vaulting** was the Romans' major contribution to architectural development. Their use of an early type of concrete enabled them to span much larger spaces and build much higher than the Greeks had ever done; indeed, their achievements were unequalled until the nineteenth century. Accordingly, they were able to create an architecture that perfectly expressed their own preoccupations of power and glory.

Roman architecture once dominated Europe, showing no appreciable regional variations, and many of the most impressive individual monuments still standing lie outside Italy. However, the most important ensembles are to be found in **Rome** itself, its original seaport of **Ostia**, and the residential towns of **Pompeii** and **Herculaneum** (which were both submerged by the massive eruption of Mount Vesuvius). The heart of a Roman city was its **forum**, a square usually set at the intersection of the two main streets. Its buildings were the focus of all the main aspects of public life: worship, politics, law, finance, trading, shopping and meeting. In time, it often became too small for all these functions: the Roman Forum itself, which largely dates from the days of the Republic, is an extreme case in point, and successive emperors found it necessary to lay out separate new forums in the city.

Each forum usually contained several **temples**, of which notable examples survive in Palestrina, Tivoli, Assisi and Brescia. At first, these tended to follow the Greek model, with the front entrance given due prominence, and often preceded by a flight of steps. Later, circular designs were increasingly favoured, as with the Temples of Vesta in Rome. A circular design was also chosen for the **Pantheon** in Rome, which is not only the greatest temple of all, and the only complete building to have survived from the days of imperial Rome, but is also one of the all-time masterpieces of both engineering and architecture, its dome still one of the largest in the world.

The main public building in Roman towns was the **basilica**, which was used for meetings, markets and administration. In many respects, it was rather like a Greek temple turned inside out, consisting of a large hall terminating in an apse, with aisles to the side, often bearing galleries and with a sloping vault which was lower than that of the main section. No complete examples survive in Italy, but some idea of the development of this type of building can be had by comparing the fragments of the basilicas of Trajan and Maxentius in Rome, which are nearly two centuries apart in date. The former was colonnaded, and had a flat wooden roof, while the latter (as can clearly be seen in the surviving aisle) had a sturdy concrete vault borne by five massive piers.

In the field of leisure, the **thermae** played a key role. These vast edifices had hot, warm and cold baths, as well as halls for all kinds of other activities – those of the Emperors Caracalla and Diocletian, both in Rome, from the third and fourth centuries AD, provide the most potent reminder of their splendour. There were a number of differences between Roman **theatres** and those of the Greeks: usually, they were free-standing structures built on level ground rather than built against a hillside, and the *orchestra* was smaller and semi-circular in shape. However, the Romans as a rule much preferred the atmosphere of their **amphitheatres**, which were used to stage gladiatorial contests and other public spectaculars. These were elliptical in shape, and of very solid construction, using a variety of materials. The outer wall, pierced by rows of arches, had a massive effect; inside, the seats were grouped in tiers. Rome's so-called Colosseum is the best preserved; others are to be found in Verona, Cápua, Pozzuoli and Pompeii.

Roman **residences** fall into three main categories. The *domus* or town dwelling was grouped symmetrically around an atrium and one or more peristyle courts. A more rambling plan characterizes the *villa*, a patrician country residence which tended to be decorated with porticoes and colonnades, and have rooms specially aligned to catch both the sun and the shade. Poorer Romans lived in *insulae*, tenement-type constructions with several floors, which were often vaulted throughout and grouped symmetrically in streets and squares. Few Roman **palaces** remain. The most important is the Villa Adriana in Tivoli, replete with fantastical re-creations of buildings the Emperor Hadrian had seen on his travels, along with grottoes, terraces and fountains. From a century earlier, Nero's fabled Domus Aurea in Rome survives only in part.

Roman law forbade burial inside the city walls, and the Via Appia became the favoured site, lined by cylindrical, tower-like **mausoleums**, the finest being that of Cecilia Metella. A similar but larger structure, of the Emperor Augustus, was the first to be built in the city centre. Another in honour of Hadrian was by far the most spectacular funerary monument built by the Romans, but was later converted into the Castel Sant'Angelo.

The **triumphal arch** was a specifically Roman creation, usually erected to celebrate military victories and richly adorned with bas-reliefs, the whole surmounted by a large sculptural group, usually of a horse-drawn triumphal chariot. Several of these arches can be seen in Rome; others are in Ancona, Aosta, Benevento, Rimini and Susa.

Another Roman invention was the **aqueduct**, which was built to transport water to the towns. These were undecorated and purely functional, with the water running down a very gentle gradient along a channel at the top. Nonetheless, they often have a majestic sweep, particularly when the lie of the land dictated the building of several tiers. Traces of aqueducts can be seen south of Rome, though the most impressive surviving examples are in other countries. The Romans also excelled at building **bridges**. There were eleven spanning the Tiber in the capital in imperial times; these have mostly been replaced or altered, but the Pons Fabricius remains substantially intact. Other bridges which have changed little are the graceful Ponte di Solesta in Ascoli Piceno, which is of a single arch only, and the five-arched Ponte di Tiberio in Rimini.

Early Christian and Byzanthine

The **early Christians** in Italy initially had to practise their religion in private houses and underground in **catacombs** hollowed out of the rock. Those in Rome are the most famous, but other impressive groups can be seen in Naples and Siracusa. When Christianity was legalized and officially adopted by the Roman Empire, it was hardly surprising that its architecture should base itself very directly on secular imperial models. In general, **churches** adopted a basilican format, but when they were raised over the graves of martyrs, whose tombs were often kept in the crypt directly below the high altar, they adopted a central plan-type known as a Martyrium. In time, they would invariably be oriented towards the east, though in the early churches it was quite normal to face exactly the opposite way. For the interior, columns were often taken from demolished secular buildings.

In **Rome** itself, much the best-preserved church of this time is Santa Sabina, which dates from the fifth century. Its exterior is of a stark simplicity, the plain brick walls pierced only by large windows; the interior shows the move towards regular columns. The larger contemporary basilicas of Santa Maria Maggiore and San Paolo fuori le Mura, though both much altered down the centuries, still clearly show the variations in the basilican plan. **Transepts** were introduced, as a result of a conscious desire to simulate the shape of the Cross; double aisles were also employed, except at Santa Maria Maggiore. Also of this period is San Giovanni in Laterano, which pioneers the Italian preference for a separate, octagonal **baptistry**.

The basic basilican style flourished in the city for centuries, and little in the way of development is discernible between the seventh-century Sant'Agnese and the ninth-century Santa Maria in Cosmedin, or even the twelfth-century San Clemente, though the last is unusually archaic.

The next significant buildings are those of the subsequent imperial capital, **Ravenna**. These are understandably more famous for the resplendent mosaics which adorn their interiors, but they are also of major architectural significance, marking the appearance in Italy of the **Byzantine** style, whose most distinctive characteristic was the development of the dome. Under the Romans, this by necessity had to rest on a circular base; by the use of pendentives, the Byzantines were able to erect a dome on square foundations. The earliest of the surviving Ravenna monuments, the Mausoleum of Galla Placida, dating from about 430, provides a good illustration of this. The church of San Vitale, an ingenious design of an octagon within an octagon, is also remarkable. The other churches here are basilican in form; a curiosity is that the apse is semicircular inside, but has a polygonal exterior. Their cylindrical **campaniles** were added later, probably in the ninth century. These are the earliest freestanding belltowers – from then on, a popular characteristic of Italian churches – to have survived, though the form was actually pioneered in Rome.

Italy's most purely Byzantine buildings are to be found in the Venetian lagoon, whose prosperity was dependent on its eastern trade. The Duomo of **Torcello**, originally seventh-century but extensively remodelled in the early eleventh century, is the oldest of these; Santa Fosca on the same island is in the same style. However, the Byzantine heritage is seen to best effect in the basilica of San Marco in **Venice** itself. This was also much altered in the eleventh century, but the basic layout of the original ninth-century building, modelled on the Church of the Holy Apostles in Constantinople, was preserved. With its five bulbous domes, its Greek-cross plan and sumptuous mosaic decoration, it stands as the supreme Byzantine monument of its time.

Romanesque

The European emergence from the Dark Ages in the tenth and eleventh centuries is associated in architecture with the **Romanesque** style, which in Italy draws heavily on the country's own heritage. Features not commonly found in other countries include a continued attachment to the basilical plan, and to cupolas raised on domes, the use of marble for facing, the presence of separate baptistries and campaniles, and the employment of the arch for decorative rather than purely structural reasons.

Strong regional variations are apparent. The churches of the **Lombard plain** most resemble those of northern Europe, and were among the most internationally influential. Their most dominant features are their tall, stately towers, which are unbuttressed and adorned with pilaster strips. They usually have a projecting vaulted porch on the facade, resting on a base of lions, above which a wheel window serves as the principal source of light for the nave. Decoration is otherwise concentrated in the apse, which often has an open dwarf gallery and corbels delicately carved with grotesque heads. Rib vaulting – revolutionary in its day – was sometimes used inside. The Duomo in **Modena** is particularly outstanding, as are the characteristic trios of duomo, campanile and baptistry at **Parma** and **Cremona**.

All these are surpassed by the highly distinctive style of **Pisa**, which can be seen all over the city, but is particularly associated with the Campo dei Miracoli, which adds a burial ground (the Camposanto) to the normal group of three – a Duomo, bell-tower and baptistry – and has the rare advantage of a spacious, verdant setting away from the commercial centre. Although the ensemble was begun in the mid-eleventh century and only finished three hundred years later, it shows a remarkable sense of unity. The buildings all have marble facing, and their exteriors, in a design conducive to catching wonderful light effects, have open arcaded galleries, which rise all the way to the facade gable – and all the way round the building. A broadly similar approach was adopted in the neighbouring cities of **Lucca** and **Pistoia**.

An even more idiosyncratic Romanesque style was fostered in the earliest surviving buildings of **Florence** – the baptistry, San Miniato and Santi Apostoli, plus the Badia in Fiesole. The overall layout of these buildings is typical enough of the time, but the continued use of mosaics and marble panelling in the interiors is suggestive of the Byzantine era, while the overall elegance of form shows a debt to Roman models.

In **southern Italy** there was a marriage of Byzantine and Romanesque styles, as can be seen at San Nicola in Bari and the Duomos of Salerno, Amalfi, Troia, Trani, Molfetta and Bitonto. An even more intoxicating mix is found in **Sicily**, where the island's traditions were freely welded into an exotic confection which is wholly unique. Sturdy Norman towers were often found in concert with Byzantine domes and mosaics and Saracenic horseshoe arches and stalactite vaulting. The Duomo of **Monreale** – and in particular its fabulous cloister with dazzling mosaics and richly carved capitals – is particularly outstanding. Those of Cefalù and Palermo are also notable, as are three surprising parish churches, all in the capital – La Martorana, San Cataldo and San Giovanni degli Eremiti. Palermo also has two outstanding palaces which show the same mix of styles: the Palazzo dei Normanni and La Zisa.

The Gothic period

The **Gothic** style, which placed great emphasis on light and verticality, and was associated with the pointed arch, rib vault, flying buttress and large traceried windows, progressed from its mid-twelfth-century French origins to become the dominant architectural force of medieval Europe. But although it was used in Italy from the early thirteenth to the early fifteenth centuries, its lifespan here was far shorter than elsewhere, and the forms it took quite different from those of other countries. In many ways, Italy was wholly unsuited to the Gothic – the pointed arch was foreign to a country steeped in classicism – which remained essentially a northern European creation. For the same reason, the giant portals of northern Gothic were unwanted; moreover, the large numbers of statues in the round they required were anathema to a nation reared on relief carvings.

In Italian Gothic architecture the emphasis is still on the **horizontal**: buildings seldom rise very high, and often have wooden roofs rather than stone vaults. **Colour** plays a far more important role than in any other country, as do walls covered with marble facing, mosaics and frescoes. A great deal of attention was lavished on **facades**, but these were again often purely decorative, with no architectural relationship to the structure behind. Many of the most characteristic features of Gothic, such as soaring steeples and graceful pinnacles, flying buttresses and elaborate vaults, are hardly to be found in Italy at all.

As elsewhere in Europe, the spread of the plain early-Gothic style in Italy is associated with the reforming Cistercian order of monks. The abbey of **Fossanova**, which was completed in the first decade of the thirteenth century, is an outstanding example of their architecture, as well as an unusually complete example of a medieval monastic complex. In a similar manner are the monasteries of San Galgano near Siena (now in ruins) and the collegiate church of Sant'Andrea in Vercelli. However, the most outstanding early-Gothic church in Italy is the basilica of San Francesco in **Assisi**, which was built in the wake of the saint's death in 1226. It is a wholly original, symbolical design, with the lower church dark and mysterious, the upper light and airy, each provided with ample wall space, which in time was duly filled with appropriate fresco cycles.

Nothing quite like San Francesco was ever built again, but the churches of the Franciscan and Dominican orders became a dominant feature of many cities. In accordance with the emphasis placed on preaching, these were typically barn-like structures, intended to hold a large congregation. They were invariably of brick, but differed considerably in plan. The most imposing are the late-thirteenth-century Santa Croce and Santa Maria Novella in **Florence**, and their fourteenth-century counterparts in **Venice** – I Frari and San Zanipolo.

Though there were relatively few important building projects of the Gothic period, they generally took on a spectacular nature. The Duomo in **Siena** is arguably the most sumptuous Gothic cathedral ever built, and boasts a resplendent facade in which sculptures were used in a wholly unorthodox and challenging way. **Florence**'s Duomo has gained world fame through its Renaissance dome, but in essentials it is a highly inventive Gothic design, whose final shape had already been determined by the mid-fourteenth century. Its detached campanile, unbuttressed and faced with coloured marbles and reliefs, illustrates the continuing Italian preference for this form. **Orvieto** shows the tendencies of Italian Gothic at its most extreme: the interior archi-

C

tecture is plain, and remarkably close in spirit to an early Christian basilica, whereas the facade surpasses even Siena's for ornateness, with its narrative bas-reliefs, brightly coloured marbles and mosaics. Only the Duomo of **Milan**, begun in the late fourteenth century but not finally completed until the nineteenth century, uses much of the stock vocabulary of northern European cathedral architecture, no doubt owing to the fact that German masons were partly responsible for its construction. Yet even here the gleaming white marble and pronounced geometric nature of the design are wholly Italianate.

The scale of this project seems to have inspired that of the nearby Certosa di Pavia, near **Pavia**, the most extensive monastic complex in the country. Here, however, notice was paid to changing artistic tastes, with the result that it progressively moved away from its Gothic origins. San Petronio in **Bologna**, which was started around the same time, was a parish church intended to rival any cathedral, and to surpass them all in length. Work, however, was abandoned on the belated completion of the nave. From a century earlier, another idiosyncratic design worthy of mention is the Basilica di Sant'Antonio in **Padua**. This has an essentially Gothic plan, even including a French-style chevet with radiating chapels. However, the facade is derived from the Lombard Romanesque, while the seven large domes are evidence of the continued attraction of Byzantinism.

In the field of military architecture, the most imposing thirteenth-century **castles** were built in southern Italy by Emperor Frederick II, most impressive of which is the celebrated **Castel del Monte**, which combined classical and Gothic elements in a plan of monotonous regularity, with an octagonal shape used for towers, perimeter walls and courtyard. Frederick's castle at **Lucera** was transformed later in the century, by the Angevins, who also built the Castel Nuovo in **Naples** – later altered to serve as a palace in succeeding centuries.

Among fourteenth-century constructions, the Fortezza at **Volterra** is an archetypal medieval castle set high on a hill, with cylindrical keep, round towers, massive outer walls and machicolations. Of the palatial fortresses begun around this time, those of **Mantua**, **Ferrara** and **Verona** are particularly outstanding, the last guarded by a strongly fortified **bridge** over the Adige. Italy's other famous Gothic bridge, the Ponte Vecchio in Florence, presents a total contrast, with jewellers' shops along its length.

In the late thirteenth century, the rise of civic pride led to a passion for building majestic **town halls**, often crowned by a slender tower. The most imposing are the Palazzo Pubblico in Siena and the Palazzo Vecchio in Florence. These same cities, along with many more in central Italy, are rich in Gothic **mansions** of the patrician class. However, the most distinctive residences in the country were built in **Venice**. The Ca' d'Oro is the most refined, whereas the Ca' Fóscari and Palazzo Giustinian have a compensating monumental grandeur. All were modelled on the **Palazzo Ducale** in Mantua, arguably the greatest secular European building of its time, which ingeniously combines Gothic and Islamic styles on its exterior walls, with evidence of the classical influence in its courtyards and interiors.

The Early Renaissance

The Gothic style maintained a firm hold over northern European architecture until well into the sixteenth century. In **Florence**, however, it had been supplanted by the second decade of the fifteenth century by the new, classically derived **Renaissance** style, which soon spread throughout Italy. Its conquest of the rest of Europe, if belated, was absolute, establishing an architectural vocabulary which remained fundamentally unchallenged until the nineteenth century. From here on, the history of architecture becomes a history of architects, with full-time practitioners emerging for the first time.

Both the format of modern architecture and the profession of architect were in many respects the single-handed creation of **Filippo Brunelleschi** (1377–1446). Having been unsuccessful in the competition for the Florence Baptistry doors, he turned away from his original training as a sculptor, devoting himself to a careful study of the building practices and techniques of the ancients. He subsequently won another major local competition, that for the Duomo's dome. It was only by reviving Roman methods of herringbone brickwork, and by inventing suitable hoisting machinery, that Brunelleschi was able to give the final shape to this otherwise Gothic construction, which ever since has served as the focal point of the city, and provided a model for all subsequent domes. In his key original buildings – the Ospedale degli Innocenti, the churches of San Lorenzo and Santo Spirito and the Cappella Pazzi – Brunelleschi seems to have been inspired as much by the distinctive Romanesque legacy of his native city as by ancient Rome. His designs are majestic but uncomplicated; they are entirely original, and in no sense an archeological revival of any previous style.

Three more Renaissance innovations – a new type of urban palace, a central plan for church design and a new type of library – are best illustrated in buildings by **Michelozzo di Bartolommeo** (1396–1472). The Palazzo Medici-Riccardi established the form of Florentine mansions for the rest of the century – a severe facade of three bands: rusticated stonework in the basement, smoother stones in the middle and smooth ashlar upstairs, an overhanging cornice, and a compensatingly light inner courtyard. In the church of Santissima Annunziata, Michelozzo modelled the tribune on a circular Roman temple in the first centrally planned church design to be completed in the Renaissance period; with Santa Maria delle Grazie in **Pistoia** he extended this concept to the entire building. His light and airy library in San Marco is a mould-breaker in its own right; its format of a central nave flanked by aisles was used throughout the Renaissance.

Even more influential was **Leon Battista Alberti** (1404–72). One of the most complete personifications of Renaissance Man, Alberti was above all a writer and theorist, the author of the first architectural treatise since Roman times; he designed buildings, but always relied on other architects to build them. Far more archeological in taste than Brunelleschi, he set out to give new life to such Roman forms as triumphal arches and pedimented temple fronts. He also articulated the theory of harmonic proportions, which, in emulation of musical intervals, adopted certain ratios of measurement – first put into practice in the facade of Santa Maria Novella. With the Palazzo Rucellai, he solved the problem of how to make the facades of Florentine palaces seem less austere and Gothic in feel by the simple expedient of introducing thin pilaster strips. Alberti's most original creations, however, are outside Florence. Although unfinished, his design for the Tempio Malatestiano in **Rimini** is a magnificent fragment, cloaking the old Franciscan church with a covering inspired by the same town's great Roman monuments. An even more resplendent facade was designed for Sant'Andrea in **Mantua**. Its elements are carefully repeated in the interior, a vast space which daringly omits aisles in favour of a single nave with side chapels.

Bernardo Rossellino (1409–64), who was the builder of the Palazzo Rucellai, used its basic form again in the Palazzo Piccolomini in **Pienza**, where he was also responsible for the Duomo and the surrounding buildings. This was part of the most ambitious planning scheme of the day, the laying out of a complete new papal town. Like many subsequent Renaissance projects, it remains incomplete, available funds failing to match the grandeur of inspiration. The creation of ideal towns was the main preoccupation of Antonio Averlino known as **Filarete** (c1400–69), the second main architectural theorist of the day. He himself built very little, other than part of the Castello Sforzesco and the huge, symmetrical Ospedale Maggiore, both in **Milan**.

Of the next generation of Florentine architects, **Giuliano da Maiano** (1432–90) introduced the Renaissance style to **Siena** with the Palazzo Spannocchi, and also built the Duomo in **Faenza**. The last phase of his career was spent in **Naples**, where he was responsible for the Porta Capuana and chapels in the church of Monteoliveto. **Giuliano da Sangallo** (1445–1516) was the first to apply Renaissance principles to the layout of villas in the Villa Medicea di Poggio a Caiano, and his work in **Florence** includes the project for the Palazzo Strozzi, the most ambitious palace of the century, and the heavily antique cloister of Santa Maria Maddalena dei Pazzi, in which Ionic columns boldly take the place of arches.

The most complete and refined early-Renaissance palace was built in the comparative obscurity of **Urbino**, where a cultivated humanist court flourished. **Luciano Laurana** (c1420–79), an obscure architect of Dalmatian origin, is credited with the overall plan, as well as the building of the elegant courtyard, and the ornate chimneypieces and doorways which are key features of the interior. Also attached to Urbino was the Sienese **Francesco di Giorgio Martini** (1439–1501/2), who is thought to have built the exquisite loggia of the Palazzo Ducale overlooking the hills, as well as two domed churches: San Bernardino in Urbino itself and Santa Maria delle Grazie al Calcinaio in Cortona. Like many other Renaissance architects, he worked extensively on military projects, specializing in hilltop castles with pioneering defences against artillery. **Ferrara** was another small court where the Renaissance prospered, thanks in large part to an ambitious extension to the town designed by **Biagio Rossetti** (1447–1516), which included numerous churches and palaces, the most original of which is the Palazzo dei Diamanti, named after the diamond shapes used on its facade. **Venice** remained attached to the Gothic style until the 1460s. When the Renaissance finally took root, it was given a pronounced local accent, with hangovers from Byzantinism in the preference for rich surfaces and mystical spatial effects. Architects still enjoyed nothing like the prestige they had gained in Florence, and it was only as a result of nineteenth-century research that **Mauro Coducci** (c1440–1504) emerged from obscurity to be identified as the builder of many of the city's best buildings of this time – the churches of San Michele in Isola, San Giovanni Crisostomo and the reconstruction of Santa Maria Formosa. His rival **Pietro Lombardo** (c1435–1515) was less concerned with the central tenets of the Florentine Renaissance than with using them to update the Venetian-Byzantine tradition. The tiny church of Santa Maria dei Miracoli, for which he and his sons also made the decoration, shows his highly ornate style at its best.

The High Renaissance and Mannerism

The first architect of the High Renaissance was **Donato Bramante** (1444–1514) who began his working life in **Milan**. His early masterpieces include the church of Santa Maria presso San Satiro, which ingeniously incorporates a ninth-century chapel and makes up for the lack of space to build an apse by including a convincing trompe l'oeil of one; the centrally planned east end of Santa Maria delle Grazie, which completely outclasses the Gothic nave; and a series of cloisters for Sant'Ambrogio. With the French invasion of the city in 1499, Bramante fled to **Rome**, where his enthusiasm coincided nicely with the papal authorities' desire to rebuild the city in a manner worthy of its imperial heyday. This centred on the demolition of the fourth-century basilica of **St Peter's**, and its replacement by a vast new church. Bramante provided a design that was the ultimate in central planning, a Greek cross with four smaller Greek crosses in its arms. This project took well over a century to complete, by which time Bramante's plan had been altered out of all recognition, with only the piers of the dome surviving. Bramante's surviving masterpieces in Rome are the Chiostro in Santa Maria della Pace – his first work in the city – and the tiny Tempietto of San Pietro in Montorio, where the Renaissance perfectly captures the spirit of Classical architecture without imitating it.

Bramante's position as leading architect in Rome was taken over by **Raphael** (1483–1520). His painting activities left him little time for this, but his few buildings were enormously influential. The Chigi chapel in the church of Santa Maria del Popolo brought to fruition the interest in centralized temples first evident in his early panel of *The Marriage of the Virgin* (now in the Pinacoteca Brera, Milan). It is deliberately set apart from the rest of the church, and opulently adorned with statues, bronze reliefs, paintings, marbles and mosaics, its richness reflecting that of the patron, the papal banker. His pupil **Giulio Romano** (1492/9–1546) was active mainly in **Mantua**, where he consciously rejected the ideal of perfect harmony and balance in Classical architecture, thus beginning the Mannerist style. The Palazzo Te establishes a new relationship between house and garden, as well as between architecture and interior decoration. The artist's own house in the same city is very different but equally inventive, while his design for the Duomo is an early example of a building concerned above all with effect, the intention being to "suck" the viewer towards the high altar.

Baldassarre Peruzzi (1481–1536), originally from Siena, built the most graceful of **Rome**'s High Renaissance palaces, the Villa Farnesina, which is arguably the outstanding secular monument of the time, featuring an unusual U-shaped plan with two superbly frescoed ground floor loggias and an upstairs hall with illusionistic architectural perspectives. The Palazzo Massimo alle Colonne from late in his career successfully overcomes the difficulties of its curved site by means of a highly original convex facade.

Michelangelo Buonarroti (1475–1564) only took up architecture in middle age. His approach was in direct contrast to Alberti's, using plans as a rough guide only, and making constant changes throughout the period of execution. None of his major buildings were finished in his lifetime: his earliest commissions in **Florence** – San Lorenzo's Sagrestia Nuova (which forms a piece with his own sculptures) and the Biblioteca Laurenziana (where every element of the sculpture is closely tied to the architecture) – already show an original approach to building. Like Giulio Romano, he adopted an entirely new attitude to space, and turned the vocabulary of classicism to suit his own ends. In **Rome,** he invented the giant order – columns and pilasters rising through two or more storeys – in his design of the Piazza del Campidoglio. Other major projects were his work on St Peter's and the completion of the Palazzo Farnese begun by Antonio da Sangallo the Younger, transforming it into the most spectacular palace of its time.

The High Renaissance was introduced to **Venice** by **Jacopo Sansovino** (1486–1570), who fled from Rome after its sacking by French troops in 1527. Sansovino quickly became the leading architect in the city, and erected a series of public edifices – the Zecca, the Loggetta and the Libreria Sansoviniana – which transformed the area around San Marco. The last-named is one of the most joyous, festive designs of the Renaissance, a highly successful compromise between classical precision and Venetian love of surface ornament.

Michele Sanmicheli (c1484–1559) spent much of his career on military projects, building the fortifications of his native **Verona**, including three dignified gateways, and the Fortezza at the entrance to Venice's Lido. He also built very grandiose palaces in both cities, which are especially notable for their facades of richly detailed stonework: the Palazzo Grimani on the Canal Grande and the Palazzo Bevilacqua in Verona are among the finest. The Cappella Pellegrini in San Bernardino, Verona, develops the idea of Raphael's Chigi chapel, while the later pilgrimage church of Madonna di Campagna in the same city is one of the most ambitious centrally planned churches of the sixteenth century.

Italy's most erudite and internationally influential architect was the Paduan **Andrea Palladio** (1508–80), who distilled features from all his great predecessors, welding them into a distinctive personal style. Palladio is associated above all with the city of **Vicenza**, which he adorned with a magnificent series of palaces, beginning with the so-called Basilica. In a spectacular piece of conjectural archeology in the same city, he built the Teatro Olimpico, the first permanent theatre since the days of antiquity. The villas he created for aristocratic clients in the surrounding countryside were much imitated elsewhere; indeed, they served as the model for British country houses until well into the nineteenth century. In the most famous, La Rotonda, Palladio put the architect's ideal of a central plan to secular use for the first time, and introduced identical temple-like fronts on all four sides of the building.

Genoa developed a distinctive architectural character of its own during the High Renaissance thanks to **Galeazzo Alessi** (1512–72), who made the most of the sloping sites common to this hilly city. His huge palaces typically feature monumental staircases and courtyards set on different levels. He also designed the commanding hilltop church of Santa Maria in Carignano, which borrows Bramante's plan for St Peter's.

In **Florence**, the Mannerist style took firm root in the wake of Michelangelo. **Bartolomeo Ammannati** (1511–92) is best known for his additions and amendments to the Palazzo Pitti, which more or less determined its final form, and for the graceful Ponte Santa Trinità. **Bernardo Buontalenti** (c1536–1608) was the city's quirkiest architect, celebrated mainly for the grottoes in the Bóboli Gardens and his designs for court spectaculars. Yet he also worked in a conventional idiom, as witnessed by the Fortezza Belvedere, the Galleria e Tribuna of the Uffizi and the facade of Santa Trinità.

The most important architect in Rome after the death of Michelangelo was Jacopo Barozzi, known as **il Vignola** (1507–73). In collaboration with

Ammannati and Vasari (1511–74), he worked on the project for the Villa Giulia, the city's finest expression of the Mannerist delight in architecture mingled with landscape gardening. Vignola also succeeded Michelangelo as architect of St Peter's, but his chief importance lies in the way he prepared the ground for the new Baroque style. The Gesù, mother church of the Jesuits, the order on which the Counter-Reformation was to depend so much, was Vignola's most important commission, and one which was imitated all round the world. His design was based on Alberti's Sant'Andrea in Mantua, eliminating the aisles and using the nave pilasters and lighting effects to draw the eye towards the high altar.

Vignola died before the Gesù was complete, leaving the facade to be built by **Giacomo della Porta** (c1533–1602). This imperious front places emphasis on the portal, and presents a highly unified design in which every component plays an essential role. Della Porta was also responsible for the construction and final shape of the dome of St Peter's, making it more ornate than Michelangelo had intended.

While Rome moved confidently into a new era, the High Renaissance was kept alive in northern Italy by Palladio's most faithful follower, **Vincenzo Scamozzi** (1552–1616). He completed many of Palladio's unfinished designs, and added the brilliant perspective stage set to the Teatro Olympico. Many of his original works imitate Palladio's most famous buildings: he built a broadly similar theatre at Sabbioneta, and modelled San Nicolò da Tolentino in Venice on Il Redentore.

The Baroque

Although it may be difficult to pinpoint the exact period when **Baroque** began, it is recognizably a distinctive style in its own right. Politically, its birth is inexorably linked to **Rome**, a city which needed to reflect in a wealth of new buildings the brash, self-confident mood it had acquired as a result of the Counter Reformation, its architecture expressing both the pomp and mystery of the religious approach then being propagated. Architects became concerned with daring spatial effects, with rendering movement by the use of curvaceous lines and dazzling tricks of light, and with rich decoration of which painting and sculpture were integral components.

The first architect to build wholly within the new idiom was **Carlo Maderno** (1556–1629). Maderno's reputation has been sullied by his association with a major architectural failure, the completion of St Peter's by the addition of a nave and facade, which destroyed the balance of the Greek-cross plan and masked the view of the dome. Yet Maderno was really only marginally at fault: the clergy had always disliked the democratic nature of centrally planned churches, and it was the new hieratic spirit of the age which prompted the need for the extensions. The highly original facade of Santa Susanna and the dome of Sant'Andrea della Valle prove that Maderno was actually a highly capable designer. He also started Rome's most important seventeenth-century palace, the Palazzo Barberini, though this was much altered by later hands.

The overall appearance of Baroque Rome is owed above all to **Gianlorenzo Bernini** (1598–1680). Like Michelangelo, Bernini only took up architecture in mid-career, by which time he had established his reputation as the leading sculptor of the day. His fusion of the arts was to be one of the keynotes of the

Baroque. His principal architectural achievements were in the field of town planning: he revamped the Piazza Navona, in the centre of which he placed a monumental fountain to his own design. Most brilliant of all was his surprisingly simple rearrangement of the square in front of St Peter's into an oval shape, with two sets of colonnades grouped to symbolize the embracing arms of the Church. The nearby Scala Regia is an equally clever design, with the steps, columns and vault all diminishing in size towards the summit to give a far greater feeling of grandeur than the restricted space would seem to allow.

Francesco Borromini (1599–1667), at first Bernini's assistant, but later his bitter rival, was the most daring and inventive Baroque architect. His attitude to decoration was very different to Bernini's, whose sculptural training he did not share. To him, architecture was sculpture in its own right, and he treated the entire wall surface plastically, favouring monochromal effects instead of colours. Even in his first commission, the church of San Carlino alle Quattro Fontane, Borromini showed his total disregard for convention, creating a stunning spatial design based on a complex series of shapes, with two equilateral triangles resolved into an oval at the level of the dome, and a circle in the lantern above. The facade, added later, was highly influential in its mixed use of concave and convex effects. Other noteworthy buildings were the facade of Sant'Agnese in Piazza Navona with its seemingly independent towers flanking the dome – a motif that was subsequently much imitated – and Sant'Ivo alla Sapienza, where again he uses a complex scheme based on the inter-connection of triangles.

The third main architect of Baroque Rome was **Pietro da Cortona** (1596–1669). Surprisingly, Cortona desisted from the union of the arts beloved of Bernini, preferring instead whitewashed interior walls. Nonetheless, his mature work combines elements from both Borromini and Bernini: the facade of Santa Maria della Pace, for example, makes considerable play with concave and convex shapes, yet takes this further by rearranging the square in which it is set to form a kind of foyer.

Elsewhere in Italy, only a handful of seventeenth-century architects stand comparison with their Roman contemporaries. One of these was **Francesco Maria Ricchino** (1583–1658), whose buildings in **Milan** bear direct comparison with the most progressive designs in Rome. **Bartolomeo Bianco** (1590/1657) adorned **Genoa** with some of the century's finest palaces, proving a worthy successor to Alessi in the way he turned the sloping ground to his advantage.

The leading Baroque architect in **Naples** was the Lombard **Cosimo Fanzago** (1591–1678), whose early buildings, notably the cloisters of the Certosa di San Martino, are restrained and classically inspired. Another south Italian centre for a distinctively exuberant, wilful form of Baroque was the little town of **Lecce**, which was adorned with a series of churches and public buildings by a group of architects whose leading light was **Giuseppe Zimbalo** (1617/20–1710).

The only major Baroque architect in **Venice** was **Baldassarre Longhena** (1598–1682). His fame rests chiefly on the votive church of Santa Maria della Salute, whose distinctive domed silhouette makes the most of its prominent site. Longhena also built two of the Canal Grande's finest palaces, the Ca' Pésaro and the Ca' Rezzonico, though here he did little more than update Sansovino's forms.

Turin, which had previously played no significant part in Italian art and architecture, progressively took over from Rome as the leading centre of the Baroque. **Carlo Castellamonte** (1560–1641) drew up an ambitious plan of the city, and built the Piazza San Carlo as its centrepiece. Even more significant was the arrival of the monk **Guarino Guarini** (1624–83), who was a brilliant mathematician as well as architect. Guarini was unusual among Italians in his interest in both Gothic and Islamic styles of building, but the prime influence on his development was Borromini. He used his mathematical skills to inflate the Roman architect's essentially small-scale approach into the grand manner in such commissions as the Collegio dei Nobili and the Palazzo Carignano. Both the Cappella della Sacra Sidone, built at the east end of the Duomo to house the Turin Shroud, and the church of San Lorenzo feature fantastic conical domes and pyrotechnic spatial effects using a wide variety of shapes.

After a gap of a generation, Turin attracted another remarkable architect, the Roman-trained Sicilian **Filippo Juvarra** (1678–1736). In a twenty-year sojourn in the city, he was responsible for a wealth of buildings, including the planning of new districts, churches, palaces and countryside villas. His imposingly sited Superga basilica combines the pilgrimage church and monastery in a single unit, and is by far the finest of its type in Italy, fully worthy of comparison with its central European counterparts. However, Juvarra's masterpiece is the Palazzina di Stupinigi, an extravagantly decorous villa which uses a triaxial hexagonal design instead of the conventional rectangle.

In **Sicily**, the disastrous earthquake of 1693 led to a wholesale demand for new buildings. Accordingly, the island is richly endowed with flowery late-Baroque creations which are the nearest Italian equivalents to French and German Rococo. Essentially, they are derivative in nature, paying a heavy debt to Borromini as well as to the Churrigueresque style of Spain. The most individualistic architect was **Giovan Battista Vaccarini** (1702–68), who was particularly associated with the laying out of **Catania**. However, the much smaller planned town of **Noto** provides an even more visually satisfying ensemble.

Neoclassicism

In the mid-eighteenth century the **Neoclassical** style reacted against the sumptuousness of late Baroque by returning to the most basic principles of classicism. Yet long before that, while the century was still young, a number of architects in **Venice** had decisively moved against Baroque excesses, notably **Giovanni Scalfarotto** (1690–1764), whose San Simone Piccolo is demonstrably derived from the Pantheon.

Giovanni Battista Piranesi (1720–78) did more than anyone to popularize the Neoclassical approach in Rome. His inspired large-scale engravings of the city's ruins rank among the all-time masterpieces of graphic art, and were to have a wide circulation. His theoretical writings asserted the superiority of the architecture of classical Rome over Greece, and advocated a reinterpretation of its forms as the basis for a new style. As a practising architect, Piranesi is known only for Santa Maria del Priorato, a heavily symbolical church for the Knights of Malta, set in a pentagonal square in Rome.

A remarkable synthesis of late Baroque and Neoclassicism was achieved by **Luigi Vanvitelli** (1700–73) in the colossal royal palace of **Caserta**, whose ornate apartments with their long vistas show all the swagger of the old style, whereas the exterior has all the calm restraint of the new. His pupil **Giuseppe Piermarini** (1734–1808) became the leading Neoclassical architect in Milan, where he designed several severe palaces with long, unadorned facades, along with what became Italy's most prestigious opera house, Teatro alla Scala.

Another celebrated theatre, La Fenice in **Venice**, was the best-known build-ing by the city's most committed exponent of Neoclassicism, **Giannantonio Selva** (1751–1819); gutted by fire early in 1996, the opera house is being rebuilt as it was after an earlier fire in 1836. A certain French influence per-vades the work of **Giuseppe Valadier** (1762–1839), who was given responsi-bility for remodelling the interiors of the cathedrals of Spoleto and Urbino while still in his twenties. Later he was based in Rome, where his commissions included the triumphal arch on the Ponte Milvio and the laying out of the Piazza del Popolo.

As with the other visual arts, architecture in Italy was in the doldrums for most of the nineteenth century. Because of the all-pervasiveness of the classi-cal tradition, there was little of the confident modern reinterpretation of other styles which characterizes northern European building of this period. Only **Giuseppe Japelli** (1783–1852) stands as an exception to this. His masterpiece, the Caffè Pedrocchi in **Padua**, is firmly Neoclassical, but its extension is neo-Gothic, while his Teatro Verdi in the same city is based on Rococo, and his vil-las are modelled on Palladio.

The nineteenth century also saw some impressive examples of town plan-ning. One of these was in **Trieste**, where the waterfront area was redesigned. In **Turin**, the work of the previous century was continued by the laying out of the Piazza Vittorio Veneto and Piazza Carlo Felice at opposite ends of the city. Later, **Alessandro Antonelli** (1798–1888) adorned the city with a huge iron supported tower, the Mole Antonelliana, originally intended as a syna-gogue, but converted into a museum.

The most original piece of planning was in **Milan**, whose status as the com-mercial hub of the emergent nation-state is symbolized by the construction of the Galleria Vittorio Emanuele II by **Giuseppe Mengoni** (1829–77) – Italy's first important example of design in iron and glass, and the initiator of a trend for covered shopping areas throughout Europe.

With the accomplishment of complete Italian Unification in 1871, **Rome** had to be supplied with new streets and buildings worthy of a great modern capital; inevitably, the most monumental classical style possible was chosen, and it was only a partial success. The most strikingly visible – if not the most aes-thetically pleasing – late-Neoclassical addition to the city's patrimony is the Vittoriano, a huge white marble monument to Vittorio Emanuele II by **Giuseppe Sacconi** (1853–1905).

The twentieth century

A reaction against the nineteenth-century infatuation with the imitation of historical styles came with the **Art Nouveau** movement, whose sinewy forms dominated European architecture and design in the early years of the new cen-tury. In Italy, where it was known as **Liberty**, its impact was less extensive than in most other countries and also more restrained. **Giuseppe Sommaruga** (1867–1917) was the most talented exponent; the most important of his build-ings is the Palazzo Castiglioni in Milan.

Of far more long-lasting significance to the overall direction of Italian archi-tecture was the **Futurist** movement, manifested in the visionary drawings of **Antonio Sant'Elia** (1888–1916), who envisaged a vibrant high-rise metrop-olis of the future dominated by frenetic activity and rapid transport systems operating on several levels. Sant'Elia's death in World War I meant that none of these visionary projects was ever realized. The only construction that gives a vague idea of what Futurist architecture might have been is the Monument to the Fallen in **Como**, which is based on a design by Sant'Elia for a lighthouse. The executant architect was **Giuseppe Terragni** (1904–43), the major exponent of **Rationalism** in Italy. This movement was strongly influenced by the ideas of the Bauhaus movement in Germany, and sought to use new materials in a modern way, to capitalize on space and light for a modern revolution where rational lines were cleared of the decorations and elaborations of past styles. Terragni founded the Gruppo 7, composed of Italy's seven most progressive inter-war architects, who fought to have Rationalism accepted above classicist architecture as the official architecture of Fascism. Terragni built several other works in Como, the most accomplished of which is the Casa del Fascio, originally the local Fascist Party headquarters.

During the twenty years of **Fascism**, Mussolini directed a massive building programme which left cities, towns and villages across the country shadowed by institutional buildings built in a monumental style reminiscent of those of ancient Rome. The colossal dimensions and imperial paraphernalia adopted by architects like **Marcello Piacentini** (1880–1960), Mussolini's favourite architect, who was responsible for the Piazza della Vittoria in **Brescia**, tended to be favoured over Rationalism. New towns like Sabaudia and Littoria near Rome were designed as prototype communities for the new "empire". But World War II put a stop to the building programmes and later caused the destruction of much of the built fabric of Italy's urban centres.

After the war the themes of memory, relationship with history and the search for a new identity became the central concerns of Italian architecture. The story of postwar architecture begins with two **memorials**: the monument to the 35 civilians killed in the massacre of the Ardeatine Caves in Rome and the monument to the victims of the German concentration camps in Milan's Cimitero Monumentale. The latter was designed by the studio BPR, a successful practice before the war called BBPR: the first "B", Gian Luigi Banfi, was killed in Mauthausen concentration camp towards the end of the war. The postwar years were also the years when **New Realism** dominated Italian culture from cinema to literature. It was a new language, free from the ties of the recent Fascist past. The critic **Bruno Zevi** (1918–1999) wrote about organic architecture as the architecture of democracy, where forms were freed from the strictures of straight lines in favour of curves.

Huge rebuilding programmes were undertaken as much to provide employment as to repair the devastation suffered during the war. Endless motorways were laid across the country and working class neighbourhoods were built on the outskirts of cities, public money often being used to subsidize private financial and speculative interests. The architecture was often subordinate to the political interests involved, and in the worst cases New Realism became synonymous with nostalgia and populism. However, as this approach flourished in Rome, there was a different atmosphere in Milan. **Ernesto Nathan Rogers** (1909–1969) of BPR (a close relative of the British architect Richard Rogers) was the personality behind the theory of continuity, the necessity for continuity with the ideals of prewar Rationalism without negating its critical revision. The most significant example of this architecture is the Torre Velasca by BPR in Milan. The giant *torre civica* is an intellectual interpretation of the disappearing medieval city.

During the Fifties and Sixties architectural tendencies or movements were overshadowed by the work carried out by several individual characters who defy categorization, the most important being Ignazio Gardella, Carlo Scarpa and Pier Luigi Nervi. **Ignazio Gardella** (1905–1999) rejected exhibitionism in favour of the value of materials and forms. His most representative works are the Casa Borsalino in **Alessandria** and the Padiglione d'Arte Contemporanea (PAC) in the Villa Reale in **Milan**, reconstructed after being destroyed by a Mafia bomb in 1993. The work of **Carlo Scarpa** (1906–1978) on the other hand was infused with a very personal poeticism, always on the verge of refined excess. His exquisite detailing is superbly exemplified in the restoration of the Castelvecchio in **Verona** as a museum, and the reorganization of the Fondazione Querini Stampalia in Venice. **Pier Luigi Nervi** (1891–1979), an engineer, practised throughout the political turmoil of the twentieth century, unaffected by fashions or prevailing styles, and popularized the use of reinforced concrete. Among his prestigious postwar commissions are various exhibition halls in **Turin**, whose amazing wide-span vaults recall his aircraft hangars destroyed during the war; the sports centres for the 1960 Olympic Games in **Rome** and the Papal audience chamber in the Vatican. Nervi also provided the engineering core of Italy's most famous skyscraper, the Grattacielo Pirelli in Milan by **Gio Ponti** (1891–1979).

In the mid-Sixties the myths of New Realism were substituted by technological myths and egalitarian utopias. But the projects remained on the drawing board and paradoxically the radical social architects, like Andrea Branzi (b1938) and Ettore Sottsass (b1917), found their only creative outlet was through **industrial design**, in particular, pieces commissioned by a wealthy, cultured elite.

For the next thirty years, Italian architecture was essentially architecture on the page – written or drawn – characterized by a lack of common thinking. The most important contributions to this theoretical school came from Giorgio Grassi (b1935) and Aldo Rossi (1931–1997). A number of other architects even became painters or writers (Massimo Scolari and Arduino Cantafora).

The few Italians who made their name for architecture during this period were only able to do so by building abroad: for example **Renzo Piano** (b1937), with the Pompidou Centre in Paris, in collaboration with Richard Rogers, and **Massimiliano Fuksas** (b1944), with numerous works in France, including the Médiathèque Rezé.

In the last few years, however, there have been signs of a reviving interest in architecture. International competitions have multiplied and the generation of Italian architects who had to work abroad have been given important commissions at home, for example Piano with the Padre Pio Pilgrimage Church in San Giovanni Rotondo in Foggia and the Rome auditorium, and Fuksas with the Italian Space Agency Headquarters and the new Congress Centre at the EUR in Rome. Renowned architects from abroad have also been called in to work on historically and culturally important projects: **Zaha Hadid** (b1950) for the contemporary arts centre in Rome; **David Chipperfield** (b1953) for the extension to the cemetery of San Michele in Venice; and **Enric Miralles** (1955–2000) and **Benedetta Tagliabue** (b1963) for the new school of architecture in Venice. It remains to be seen whether this will lead to more work for home-grown talent.

Gordon McLachlan and **Lucy Ratcliffe**

C

Vernacular architecture

Architecture isn't just about palaces and churches, and it's interesting to see how domestic architecture has developed, especially with regard to the siting and layout of small towns and farming settlements, both of which have had at least as much impact on the landscape of Italy as the country's better-known monumental architecture.

The hill-towns

Throughout the Middle Ages in Italy, the countryside was unsafe and unhealthy and the land in many places remained uncultivated, either swamp or barren. As late as the fifteenth century, wolves still prowled within a few miles of Florence, in a landscape populated largely by brigands and deer. The topography of the countryside, with its abundance of hills and mountains rising steeply from fertile plains, provided natural sites for fortified settlements which could both remove the population from the malarial swamps and bandits and preserve the limited fertile land for cultivation.

In the period of their greatest expansion – between the twelfth and fourteenth centuries – **hill-towns** sprang up all over. Many were superimposed on early Etruscan cities – **Chiusi** and **Cortona** – or cave dwellings, as in **Sorano**. **Matera**, in Basilicata, grew from a very early settlement of grottoes formed by the natural erosion of volcanic rock (tufa) along the side of a high ravine. The houses that evolved from these caves (called sassi – literally "rocks") remained in use until 1952 when they were condemned. Though most hill-towns were built within high and sometimes battlemented perimeter walls, the fortress aspects of many sites obviated the need for additional protection. Houses in **Pitigliano** (in Tuscany), for example, rise like a natural extension of the rock outcropping on which they sit. The sheer drop afforded by these sites (often extended by the use of towers) enabled inhabitants to make good use of gravity by dropping a crushing blow onto the heads of enemies attempting to scale the walls. It was also a good way of dispatching the dead as well as a simple form of rubbish disposal. After the revolution in fortifications between the thirteenth and fifteenth centuries, and the introduction of gunpowder and cannon reduced the need for enormous vertical drops, towers grew shorter and were adapted to newer methods of warfare.

Although many hill-towns were genuinely self-contained communities, the countryside remained under the political and economic control of the cities and of the communes, and the Grand Dukes and Church officials who ran them, particularly in north and central Italy. Each city-state set up satellite towns of its own, to protect trade routes (whether at sea or on land), or to operate as garrisons for soldiers, weaponry and food in case of war (or civil insurrection). Siena established the fortified hill-town of **Monteriggioni** in the early thirteenth century along an important route from Rome into France which also passed through **San Gimignano. San Miniato** was also set up as a fortified town by Emperor Frederick II (still quarrelling with the papacy) to take advantage of and protect this same route. At roughly the same time, Florence founded similar frontier outposts, setting up **San Giovanni Valdarno**, **Scarperia** and **Firenzuola**, all within ten years. Fewer towns emerged in the south during this period, partly because there were fewer cities: of the 26 Italian towns with populations of more than 20,000 in the thirteenth century, only three were in the south.

Hill-towns share many features, whatever the impetus for their original development. They are almost always densely built settlements, constructed with materials found on or near their site, which adds to the impression that they arise naturally from their geological foundations. They usually rely on just one or two simple dwelling types endlessly repeated. **Strómboli**, one of the Aeolian islands off the north coast of Sicily, is an example of the rich effects created by repetition of a single, very basic dwelling type, in this case a simple cube. In most hill-towns, houses are built right up to the edge of – and often open out directly onto – the narrow passageways and streets. This reflects the more integral links between the productive activities of the medieval household (carried out on the ground floor) and the street immediately outside which not only became an extension of the works inside but also served as a kind of shop, linked to a wider network of merchants, traders and exchange. Altogether, many more functions were carried out publicly in the streets, traces of which are still visible in the surviving evidence of public fountains and wash-houses, wells and communal ovens. Streets in medieval hill-towns were even more crowded than they are today; houses had overhanging wooden balconies, used to dry and store a variety of foods. Supports for these balconies (or the holes which held them) can still be seen on the fronts of many houses.

Hill-towns still preserve a great deal of their medieval character. The very characteristics which made them useful for purposes of defence and isolation made them unsuitable for later growth and redevelopment in response to changing circumstances. There are exceptions – in the late-fifteenth century the village of Corsignano near Montepulciano was transformed into the little Renaissance town of **Pienza** to commemorate the birthplace of Pope Pius II. But in general, there is little evidence of urban planning, or the country's more recent economic history, in hill-towns.

Settlements of the plain

Though variations abound, the basic types of settlements on the plains and in coastal areas reveal a great deal about the impact of urban political and economic activity on the development of the countryside. Distinct waves of development correspond to changes in the fortunes of city merchants and in the accumulation of capital required for agricultural investment. Accumulation, in turn, depended on economic prosperity and on relatively long and uninterrupted periods of peace.

The North

Just as the economic incentive for rural development derived from the towns, so did the building style. The **house-tower** (*la casa-torre*), which spread first through the Mugello, Chianti and Casentino districts between the thirteenth and fifteenth centuries, was really a transplanted version of the tall, square, fortified city house, using construction techniques borrowed from urban models, particularly from the fortified towns of Bologna, Perugia and Siena. The defensive character of the house-tower can be read from the thickness of its walls, from its restricted openings high off the ground and from its height.

Over successive centuries, the house-tower gradually lost its defensive character, re-emerging as a **dove tower** (*la torre colombaia*), protruding from the centre of a new form of extended dwelling which had been wrapped around it. Doves and pigeons were not only adept at killing snakes and consuming weeds but also provided valuable meat for the table and manure for agricultural use. Though this functional role gradually fell away, the dove tower became a ubiquitous feature of domestic architecture across almost all of central and southern Italy, and still remains an important decorative element in contemporary villas.

The house to which the dove tower belongs is the **casa della mezzadria**, the classic Renaissance country villa, widespread across Tuscany, Umbria and Marche as well as other areas in central and northern Italy. Usually square in plan, it was built using a combination of brick, stone and terracotta under a tent-like roof with the dove tower at its apex. Depending on its location and the urban models to which it harks back, it might boast a portico at ground level (typically Florentine), and a loggia at first-floor level (typically Arentine), or neither a portico nor loggia but a flat wall on the front facade (more common in the area around Siena).

The house derives its name from the system of sharecropping by which most of the land was farmed. Under this system, *la mezzadria* (based on the word *mezza* – "half"), the peasant farmer yielded up half the annual produce to his landowner. This gave the landlord no incentive either to invest in stock or to introduce new agricultural methods. At the same time, it impoverished the labour force, compelled by increasing debt to supply free labour – which was used, among other things, to build the main house. Used only occasionally by the landlord, the house was the primary residence of the estate manager *(il fattore)*, who was the agent and overseer of urban capital invested in the countryside. Because this system paid workers in kind rather than in cash, it inevitably tied agriculture to the limited production of subsistence goods and so failed to encourage specialization (based on natural advantages) and the commercial innovations that modern agriculture required.

By contrast, the alluvial plain across north and central Italy encouraged specialization very early on. Large-scale investment in reclamation and irrigation is necessary to create and sustain arable land, something that was first undertaken by the Benedictines and Cistercians in the eleventh to thirteenth centuries. The enormous commercial enterprises that resulted from this catered for commercial markets in rice, silk and dairy products. Square in plan and built around a massive enclosed courtyard which could extend for 150 metres or more, the architecture of the farming complex *(la cascina)* was often stark with high rectangular porticoes supported by square columns sometimes running along three sides of the enclosed interior space.

Normally, the estate accommodated four basic elements which were architecturally distinct: the owner-manager's house which was more elaborate in design and often taller than the other buildings; housing for workers, tenement-like in character, with external balconies running along the upper floors used to dry and store crops like rice; stables for cows and other animals; and stables for horses with hay lofts above. This last feature is easily recognizable from a distance by virtue of the striking patterns of brickwork used to create large grates for the ventilation of hay. An overall operation of this kind of enterprise was convincingly portrayed in Bertolucci's *Novecento*, set in nineteenth-century Lombardy. Today many of these courtyards are inhabited by independent small farmers, each cultivating their own smallholding; others are abandoned. On the eastern side of the plain, around the Ferrara district, where agriculture has become most mechanized, the stables and storage areas of enclosed-court complexes have become truly vast.

At the more modest end of the spectrum, the house of the **independent farmer** (*la casa colonica*) is to be found all over Italy, adapted to local materials and customs. Of simpler construction, it often consists of a kitchen and bedrooms sitting on top of animal sheds and agricultural stores (common in central and north Italy), but equally, the barn and house might form separate wings or entirely separate buildings, as is typically found along the slopes of the Apennines running the entire length of the country.

The South

In southern Italy (particularly Campania and Puglia), the **masseria** is a more common type of farming settlement. Dominating vast tracts of land which were derived from feudal estates and ultimately from the landed properties of the Roman emperors (*latifondia*), these complex structures are massive and set in isolated countryside where they are entirely closed to the outside world. Consisting of a dense cluster of separate buildings, *masserie* were sometimes enclosed by a high perimeter stone wall into which round defence towers were built. They could, however, also consist of a lower grouping of buildings more loosely bound within a larger area. At its largest a *masseria* virtually operated as a self-contained village incorporating church, school, medical clinic and shop within its precinct, in addition to accommodating the full range of agricultural requirements for stabling, housing (of day labourers called *braccianti*) and a wide variety of storage. In their purest, least-altered form, village *masserie* are still visible in parts of Sicily.

Trulli, found along the coast of Puglia and inland, form one of the most remote, curious and ancient types of farm settlement in Italy. Of uncertain origin (possibly Cretan or North African), and appearing in Italy some time between 2000 and 1000 BC, *trulli* consist of clusters of single circular rooms, each covered by a conical roof made of overlapping rough stone tiles and topped by decorative symbolic pinnacles. Built as primitive agricultural communities, the profusion of conical roofs (each dwelling contributing two or three) produces a startling effect on the landscape.

Cinema

From the earliest days of the cinema, the Italians have always been passionate movie-lovers and movie-makers. But it was with their films of the postwar period, and the shift from studio-based films to the use of the country's actual town and landscapes, that Italy came to the forefront of world cinema. Their style and technique were ground-breaking, and the use of real locations added a dimension, a mood, which made Italian cinema linger longer in the memory. The endless expanse of the Po Valley plain in *Obsession*, the steaming sulphur springs outside *Naples in Voyage to Italy*, the deserted, off-season seaside resort of Rimini in *I Vitelloni*, created an atmosphere that could never have been achieved in a studio.

The background

The Italians were once famous for their silent costume epics, pre-World War I dramas that had monumental backdrops and crowd scenes – a leftover from the Italian grand opera tradition. They were often set in the period of the Roman Empire, anticipating the Fascist nostalgia for ancient Rome by at least a decade. **Giovanni Pastrone's Cabiria** (1913), set in Babylon, was the most sophisticated and innovative of these, with spectacular sets and lighting effects that the American director D. W. Griffiths imitated in his masterpiece **Intolerance** (1916). This borrowing of Italian expertise by Hollywood gave the Taviani brothers the story for their **Good Morning Babylon** (1986).

Even in its early stages the Italian cinema was handicapped by the economic problems that were destined to keep it lagging behind the American industry. The reason for this was not simply lack of funds, but also an inability on the part of the government to realize what a moneyspinner the indigenous film-making talent could be, and what the unregulated influx of foreign films into Italy would mean for the home market. In addition to this, the Americans themselves began making films in Italy, attracted by the cheap labour, the locations, and the quality of the light, thereby devastating the already fragile indigenous industry. An American film crew arrived in 1923 to make an epic version of **Ben Hur**. Three years prior to this, 220 films were made in Italy; by 1927 the number had dropped to around a dozen a year.

The Fascist regime (1922–43) was surprisingly slow to recognize the potential, in both economic and propaganda terms, of the cinema. But in 1934 Mussolini did begin to mete out financial support. He also limited the number of foreign imports, had film added to the arts festival in Venice, and in 1937 inaugurated "Cinecittà", the film studio complex just outside Rome. From 1938 to 1944 the proportion of Italian productions to imports rose rapidly, though home-produced films would never account for more than a third of the total number of films distributed in the country.

Films made during the Fascist period featured glorious victories from the past (the Romans again), and from the present – the war in Ethiopia, for example. During this time, although not all movies were vehicles for propaganda, no films could be made that were overtly critical of the regime. Most popular at the time were the escapist, sentimental, "white telephone" films, so-called because the heroine would have a gleaming white telephone in her boudoir,

Hollywood-style – a touch of the exotic for the average Italian at the time, who rarely even saw such a thing, let alone owned one.

Italians were not, however, cut off from what was going on in world cinema between the wars, and the ideas and techniques of Eisenstein and, even more so, of French directors, particularly Renoir, Pagnol and Carne, began to filter through. Likewise with literature: probably the biggest single influence on the emerging generation of Italian film-makers was the American novel. Hemingway, Faulkner and Steinbeck spoke directly to the young generation: their subjects were realistic, their stylistic approach was fresh, even raw, and the emotion seemed genuine.

It was not surprising, then, that the late 1930s and early 1940s should see an element of documentary-style realism creep into film-making. Contemporary social themes were addressed; non-professional actors were sometimes used. Directors – even those with the official stamp of approval – made the occasional realistic documentary, with none of the bombast or gloss of the typical Fascist film. It was on films such as these that future neo-realist directors such as Visconti, Rossellini and De Sica, and the writer Zavattini, worked their apprenticeships, learning techniques that they would draw on a few years later when they were allowed to unleash their creative imaginations.

A film made in 1943 caused a considerable stir. When it was first shown, Mussolini's son, Vittorio, walked out, exclaiming "This is not Italy!" But Mussolini allowed it to be distributed anyway, probably because there was nothing politically controversial in it. The film was **Luchino Visconti**'s **Obsession**, an unauthorized adaptation of the American novel **The Postman Always Rings Twice** by James M. Cain. Visconti transposed this low-life story of adultery and murder to northern Italy, the characters playing out their seedy tragedy in the relentlessly flat landscape of the Po Valley and among the surreal carnival floats in Ferrara. It showed two ordinary people in the grip of a violent passion, so obsessed with each other that they bring about their own destruction. The original negative was deliberately destroyed when the official film industry was moved north to Mussolini's Saló Republic on Lago di Garda. **Obsession** was something new in the Italian cinema: it had an honesty and intensity, a lack of glamour, that pointed the way to the "neo-realist" films of the immediate postwar period.

The neo-realists

The end of the war meant the end of Fascist domination of everything, including the film industry; but Italy was left emotionally as well as physically shattered. It now seemed important to film-makers to make sense of the intense experience the Italian people had undergone, to rebuild in some way what had been destroyed.

As the tanks were rolling out of Rome in 1945, **Roberto Rossellini** cobbled together the bare minimum of finances, crew and equipment and started shooting **Rome, Open City**. He used real locations, documentary footage, and low-grade film, and came up with a grainy, idiosyncratic style that influenced not only his Italian contemporaries, but also the American films noirs of the late 1940s, and the grittily realistic films of the early 1950s – as well as the French New Wave of the 1960s.

Neo-realism had no manifesto, but its main exponents – Rossellini, De Sica and Visconti – expounded the following aims, even if they didn't always stick to them: to show real people rather than conventional heroes (using non-actors), real time, real light, real places (shooting on location, not in studios). Their intention was to present the everyday stuff of life and not romantic dreams.

Unusually for an "art" film, **Rome, Open City** was a box office hit. It had a good emotional, even melodramatic, story, with touches of humour, and packed a terrific moral punch. Set in a downbeat quarter of occupied Rome, it is about a partisan priest and a communist who join forces to help the resistance. The Nazis are depicted as effeminate and depraved, while the partisans – including a band of children – are the true heroes, though Rossellini seems to pursue immediacy at the expense of making political statements.

This was the first in Rossellini's so-called "war trilogy". It was followed by **Paisà** (1946), which traced the Allied occupation north from Sicily to the Po Valley, in six self-contained episodes; and the desolate **Germany, Year Zero** (1947), set in the ruins of postwar Berlin, about a child whom circumstances push to suicide.

In these, as in other neo-realist films, children are seen as the innocent victims of adult corruption. **Vittorio De Sica's Shoeshine** (1946) is an anatomy of a friendship between two Roman boys, destroyed first by black-marketeers, then by the police. A young boy is the witness to his father's humiliation in De Sica's **Bicycle Thieves** (1948) – also set in the poorer quarters of Rome – when he sees him steal a bicycle out of desperation (a bicycle means getting his job back) and immediately get caught. The child's illusions are dashed, and the blame is laid on society for not providing the basic human requirements. At the time *Bicycle Thieves* was called the only truly communist film of the postwar decade, but in retrospect the message, as in *Rome, Open City*, seems politically ambiguous. Crowds are seen as hostile and claustrophobic, and the only hope seems to lie in the family unit, which the hero falls thankfully back on at the end.

This conflict between Catholic and Marxist ideology is a recurrent theme in Italian cinema, from Rossellini through to Pasolini, and the Taviani brothers in the 1980s, and it's often this that gives their films the necessary tension. More than anyone, Visconti exemplifies this dichotomy. Born an aristocrat in the famous Milanese family, and sentenced to death (though not executed) for being anti-Fascist in 1944, he was influenced by the writings of Antonio Gramsci, and right up until his death in 1976 veered between two milieux for his films – the honest, suffering sub-proletariat, and the decadent, suffering upper classes.

In 1948 Visconti made a version of the nineteenth-century Sicilian author Giovanni Verga's novel **The House by the Medlar Tree**, about a family of fishermen destroyed by circumstance, which he filmed as **The Earth Trembles**. It was shot on location on the stark Sicilian coast, using an entire village as cast, speaking in their native Sicilian (with an Italian voice-over and subtitles). He adapted the story to incorporate a Marxist perspective, but this fades from view in the pervading atmosphere of stoic fatalism, closer to Greek tragedy than to the party line. Something else that detracted from the intended message was the sophisticated visual style: stunning tableaux such as the one where the wives, dressed in black, stand waiting for their husbands on the skyline, looking out to sea, prompted Orson Welles to remark that Visconti shot fishermen as if they were Vogue models. Indeed, style constantly threatened to overtake content in Visconti's work, culminating in the emotionally slick **Death In Venice** (1971).

The end of neo-realism

By the early 1950s, neo-realism was on the way out. Social problems no longer occupied centre stage, and film-makers now concentrated on the psychological, the historical, even the magical side of life. There were several reasons for this, not least that the trauma of World War II had receded, and cities (and lives) were being rebuilt. As Rossellini said in 1954, "you can't go on making films about heroism among the rubble for ever". Directors wanted to move on to new themes. Another reason for the break was government intervention. The cinema industry was in the doldrums, and the Christian Democrat minister Giulio Andreotti had banned any more neo-realist films from being made on the grounds that social criticism equalled communism. The Cold War was just beginning.

Neo-realist films had in any case, with one or two exceptions, rarely been good box office. Of Italian-made films, the general public tended to prefer farces, historical dramas or comedies. The Neapolitan comic actor Totò – who had a colossal career spanning scores of films and several decades – was a particular favourite. In **Toto looks for a Home** (1949), he and his family search for somewhere to live in the postwar ruins of Rome, in a comic variation on a neo-realist theme. It was a sign of the times that people preferred to laugh at their problems rather than confront them.

De Sica meanwhile had moved on from the unremitting pessimism of *Bicycle Thieves* to a fantastic fable set in Milan, **Miracle in Milan** (1950), about a young man who is given a white dove which possesses the power to grant the wishes of everyone living in his slummy suburb. Surreal special effects are used to create a startling impact, for example in a shot of the hero and heroine flying high above the pinnacles of Milan cathedral on a broomstick. The moral is still a neo-realist one, but with a change of emphasis: art and imagination can help your problems disappear for a while, but won't solve them.

In 1954 **Visconti** made **Senso**, another adaptation of a nineteenth-century novel but worlds away from **The Earth Trembles**. It opens to the strains of Verdi in the Venice opera house, La Fenice, one night in 1866, and is Visconti's view of the politically controversial Unification, portrayed through the lives of a few aristocratic individuals. It was a theme he would return to in **The Leopard** (1963). **Senso** was the first of Visconti's historical spectaculars, and the first major Italian film to be made in colour.

The Fifties and the next generation of directors

Neo-realism was dead, but the next generation of film-makers – Fellini, Pasolini, Bertolucci, Antonioni, Rosi – could not help but be influenced at first by its ideals and techniques, though the style each of them went on to evolve was highly personal.

Federico Fellini, for one, saw neo-realism as more a world-view than a "school". His early films, such as **La Strada** (1954), follow a recognizably realistic storyline (unlike his later movies), but the whole feeling is different to the films of the 1940s. His characters are motivated by human values rather than social ones – searching for love rather than solidarity. All through his long career Fellini used films as a kind of personal notebook in which to hark back to his youth. **I Vitelloni** (1953) is set in an unrecognizable Rimini, his birth-place, before the days of mass tourism; **Amarcord** (1974) is again set in Rimini, this time under Fascism. He also explores his own personal sexual fantasies and insecurities, as in **Casanova** (1976) and **The City of Women** (1980).

But Fellini isn't all nostalgia and sex. There are philosophical themes that run through his work, not least the gap between reality and illusion. The heroine of **The White Sheikh** (1952) falls in love with the Valentino–type actor play-ing the romantic lead for "photo romance" comics (being shot on the coast outside Rome), and has her illusions dashed when reality intervenes and he makes a bungling attempt to seduce her. **Casanova** too is an oddly (and delib-erately) artificial-looking film. It wasn't actually shot in Venice, and the water in the lagoon is in fact a shaken plastic sheet – an odd backlash against the real landscapes of the neo-realists.

Religion is also a theme in Fellini's work, and he's at his best when satirizing the Roman Catholic Church, as in the grotesque clerical fashion parade in **Roma** (1971), or the malicious episode in **La Dolce Vita** (1960) where a couple of children claim to have had a vision of the Virgin Mary, and create the press event of the month.

Pier Paolo Pasolini, murdered in mysterious circumstances in 1975, was a practising Catholic, a homosexual and a Marxist, as well as a poet and novelist. His films reflected this cocktail of ideological and sexual tendencies, though in a less autobiographical way than Fellini's. They're also far more disturbing and challenging: **Theorem** (1968) intercuts shots of a spiritually empty middle-class Milanese family, into which a mysterious young stranger insinuates him-self, with desolate scenes of a volcanic wasteland. **The Gospel According to Matthew** (1963) is a radical interpretation of a familiar story (and an excellent antidote to Zeffirelli's syrupy late-Seventies **Jesus of Nazareth**) in which Jesus is not a man of peace but the champion of the sub-proletariat and the enemy of hypocrisy. It was filmed in the surprisingly biblical-looking landscape of the poorer regions of southern Italy – Puglia and Calabria – and used the peasants of the area in the cast. Pasolini's **Decameron** (1971) was a record hit at the box office because of its explicit sex scenes, though the director's intention had been political rather than salacious, with Boccaccio's fourteenth-century tales transposed from their original middle-class Florentine setting to the dispos-sessed of Naples.

Otherwise, the real box-office earners in the 1960s and 1970s were the so-called "spaghetti westerns", shot in the Arizona-look-alike interior of Sardinia, the best of which were directed by **Sergio Leone**.

Bernardo Bertolucci started out as Pasolini's assistant, and shared his poli-tics, though his own films are more straightforward and accessible. **The Spider's Strategem** (1969), filmed in the strange, star-shaped Renaissance town of Sabbioneta near Mantua, was the first of many feature films sponsored by RAI, the Italian state TV network, and is about the anatomy of a destruc-tive father-son relationship with constant flashbacks to the Fascist era. Another early film, **The Conformist** (1970), adapted from the novel by Alberto Moravia, had the spiritually empty hero (or rather, anti-hero) search for father-substitutes in Fascist Rome – again a dream-like jumble of flashbacks. **The Conformist** was Bertolucci's first step on the path to world recognition; sub-sequent projects, from **Last Tango in Paris** (1971), through **1900** (1976), **La Luna** (1979), the Oscar-winning **The Last Emperor** (1988) and the ill-judged **The Sheltering Sky** (1990), have made him one of the country's most commercially successful directors.

Michelangelo Antonioni again had a neo-realist background, but in the films he made in the 1960s and 1970s he shifted the emphasis from outward action and social realism to internal and psychological anguish. The locations he chose – the volcanic landscape of Sicily for **L'Avventura** (1964), the bleak townscape of industrial Milan in **La Notta** (1961), the impersonal Stock Exchange building in Rome for **The Eclipse** (1962), the alienating oil refineries and power plants at Ravenna for **The Red Desert** (1964) – made perfect settings for what were almost cinematic equivalents of existential novels.

The Neapolitan director **Francesco Rosi** made a series of semi-documentary "inquiry" films attacking various aspects of the Italian establishment: the Sicilian mafia in **Salvatore Giuliano** (1962), the construction industry mafia in Naples in **Hands Over the City** (1963), the army in **Just Another War** (1970), and vested interests of all kinds in **The Mattei Affair** (1972). Not that these are dry analyses of Italian society: the viewer has to sort through the pieces of evidence – the newsreel footage, the half-heard comments, the absence of comment – to come to his or her own conclusions about the truth, in kind of do-it-yourself mystery stories.

Later on, in the late 1970s and 1980s, Rosi went in a more personal direction. **Christ Stopped at Eboli** (1979) is a surprisingly unincisive critique of "the problem of the south", set in a poverty-stricken mountain village in Basilicata. **Three Brothers** (1980) looks at three different political attitudes, as the brothers of the title, reunited for their mother's funeral back home in Puglia, argue, reminisce and dream. Oddly enough, in 1983 Rosi made a completely apolitical film of the opera **Carmen**.

Nostalgia... to the present

Italian cinema of the Seventies and Eighties was dominated by foreign co-productions and TV-sponsored films, which, like elsewhere, led to a loss of national identity. Audiences were steadily eroded by the successive onslaughts of television, video and TV deregulation. Some directors tried to address this problem by focusing on purely Italian themes, others by looking to the past.

Ermanno Olmi's The Tree of Wooden Clogs (1978) has a Bergamasque cast speaking dialect with Italian subtitles, and did well at the box office worldwide. Also prominent among Italian directors of the time were the **Taviani brothers**, whose **Padre Padrone** (1977), a mini-epic set in Sardinia that details the showdown between an overbearing father and his rebellious son, and **Kaos** (1984), an adapation of Pirandello stories shot in scenic Sicily, are both loving of the Italian landscape and redolent of a time past. Together with **Good Morning Babylon** (1986), these films put the brothers' work centre-stage internationally.

Nostalgia was a keynote of the time. **Giuseppe Tornatore's** Oscar-winning **Cinema Paradiso** (1988) was shot in the director's native village near Palermo, and tells its story through a series of flashbacks. The central figure, a successful film director named Salvatore, returns to the village for a funeral, only to find that the magical Cinema Paradiso of his childhood is about to be razed to make way for a car park. Similarly, in **Ettore Scola's Splendor** (1989), the owner of the cinema in a small provincial town is forced to sell up to a property developer because of declining audiences and debt. In equally poignant vein, **Michael Radford**'s **Il Postino** (1994) is a humorous tale set in 1930s Italy, which follows the artistic and political awakening of the central character, played by Italian comic Massimo Troisi (who sadly died soon after the film's completion).

In this rather soul-searching period of Italian film-making, the films of **Gabriele Salvatores** dealt with groups of Italians abroad, often cut adrift, or seeking escape. His **Mediterraneo** (1991) shows eight reluctant Italian sailors stranded on a Greek island in 1941, and recounts their gradual integration into local life, while **Marrakech Express** (1989) has a group of seven setting off for Morocco in search of their friend, and **Puerto Escondido** (1992) explores life for an Italian in a commune in Mexico.

If the films best known outside Italy were rather escapist in their subject matter, it was a different story at home. During the late 1980s and early 1990s, film-makers began to address the major preoccupation of the time, namely the corruption at the heart of Italian society. The nicely titled **The Brownnose** (**Il Portaborse**; 1991) by **Daniele Luchetti** satirizes the favoured Italian way of outwitting the system and getting things done – the oiling of the wheels of bureaucracy by means of gifts and bribery involves the anti-hero in all manner of scrapes.

Gianni Amelio's political drama **Open Doors** (**Porte Aperte**, 1989), from Leonardo Sciascia's novel of the same name, is set in Fascist Palermo just before World War II, but its subject matter – a liberal judge being obstructed in his investigations of all-pervasive corruption – was particularly apposite at the time. The same director's **Stolen Children** (**Il Ladro di Bambini**; 1992) is a better-known film outside Italy, and deals with corrupt society as seen through the eyes of a child. Amelio made no new work for five years until **The Way We Laughed** (**Così Ridevamo**; 1998), the story of two brothers leaving rural Sicily for Turin in the late 1950s, a film which suggests that the present-day malaises that Italy is experiencing have their roots in the betrayals and violence in the late Fifties and early Sixties.

Films with a much more hard-hitting, realistic edge also began to emerge, among them **Mario Martone**'s **Rehearsal for War** (**Teatro di Guerra**, 1998), which examines the Yugoslav conflict and the power of the imagination in our perception of evil. Meanwhile, such directors as **Marco Risi** dealt with specific social problems – his **Ragazzi Fuori** follows the lives of half a dozen youngsters fresh out of prison, and the sequel, **Mery per Sempre** (1988), shows them back inside.

More provocative still, **Daniele Cipri** and **Franco Maresco**'s **Toto Che Visse Due Volte** (Totò And His Two Lives; 1998), set in Sicily, ruffled a few feathers with its violation of religious and sexual taboos (including a depiction of a statue of the Virgin Mary being assaulted). Critics disliked the film's clumsiness, but this iconoclastic work didn't trouble the establishment. When the film censors banned its release, the deputy prime minister – a film buff – stepped in and disbanded their board.

A sea change

In the 1990s a sea change took place in Italian film as screenplay writers, cinematographers and directors began to shake free of nostalgia and corruption themes and explore contemporary life in an idiosyncratic, amusing and penetrating way. Director, actor and screenwriter **Nanni Moretti** achieved great acclaim with his **Dear Diary** (**Caro Diario**; 1994). In three parts, the film covers such diverse subjects as twentieth-century architecture, children and telephones, Pasolini's unsolved murder, the myth of rural idyll, as well as Moretti's own fight against cancer. Much of the film is spent following Moretti on his scooter through Rome, or travelling by ferry from one island to another. His latest film **The Son's Room** (**La Stanza del Figlio**, 2001), however, is a much darker work exploring a family's grief; the film won a Palme d'Or at Cannes and much critical attention.

In his films, Moretti appears to be continually questioning the worth of everything, including his own work; indeed, he went too far for some critics in **Aprile** (1998), which focuses on his inability to decide how to finish his films – or even whether to finish them. Although it wasn't as well received as his other works, it's still a very funny film; in it, Moretti feels obliged to make a film about Italian politics, but is continually sidetracked by his real passions, including the birth of his first child.

An Oscar-winning work by **Roberto Benigni**, known for such slapstick-style movies as **Johnny Stecchino** (1992) and **The Monster** (1996), marks another brave foray into new territory. Benigni's **Life is Beautiful** (**La Vita è Bella**, 1997) addresses the Holocaust and dares to combine comedy with genocide. A parent's desire to protect the innocence of their child, rather than the Holocaust itself, is the theme of the film, and Benigni (who also plays the lead role with his wife, Nicoletta Braschi, as his co-star) distinguishes between laughing *at* the Holocaust and laughing *in* the Holocaust; visual gags, dramatic tension and a poignancy that's almost unbearable at times permeate the film. In answer to critics who accuse him of treating a painful subject with too much levity, Benigni claims that Italian Holocaust survivors are only just beginning to talk about the events of more than fifty years ago and that a film like *La Vita è Bella* is justified if it opens up debate.

At the same time as film-makers have found a new assurance, cinema audiences are flocking to the box office, not least because of the mediocrity (at best) of what's on TV. Benigni's **Pinocchio** (2002) grossed US$7m in its first weekend, a new record at the Italian box office. The story is adapted from the Italian writer Carlo Collodi's 1880 fable, and as he did in **Life is Beautiful**, Benigni doubles as star and director, playing opposite his wife, Braschi, who is the blue-haired fairy. True to the original story, the film is a moral tale in which the puppet who dreams of becoming a real boy has to learn honesty first through a series of adventures. Benigni's film represents a reclaiming of cultural property: Disney reportedly tried to trademark the character Pinocchio, claiming that it was their animation that everyone thought of first when they heard the name, but they lost their claim.

Other directors to have enjoyed both success at home and abroad include **Gabriele Muccino**, whose coming-of-age story **Come te nessuno mai** ("But Forever in the Mind", 1999) is an interesting take on the US high-school comedy genre: his very Italian students are highly politicized, planning strikes and taking part in a 24-hour sit-in, both of which provide a backdrop for the inevitable angsting and first love. Muccino's romantic comedy **The Last Kiss** (**L'Ultimo Baccio**, 2002), a film dealing with panic at parenthood and the chasing of vanishing youth, won a flurry of awards and universal approval. **Ferzan Ozpetek**, a Turk who has lived in Rome for more than twenty years, made a name for himself with **Turkish Bath** and **Harem Suare**. His latest, more mainstream film, **Ignorant Fairies** (**Le fate Ignoranti**, 2001), deals with the themes of love, loss and deception wrapped up in a soundtrack of Middle Eastern and Latin music. Commenting on the current changes in Italian film, Ozpetek says, "The public is more demanding now. At the same time, people have become more willing to experiment, to go to see quality Italian films with fully developed stories and interesting characters. Before they would have looked to foreign films for that type of cinema."

An example of one such quality film is **Giuseppe Piccioni**'s **Light of My Eyes** (**Luce Dei Miei Occhi**, 2001). Set in Rome, it's a haunting exploration of the alienation that many feel in their lives and their romantic relationships. The story is particularly strong thanks to the character of Maria, the female lead, free of the usual stereotypes and beautifully acted.

Many have been looking to Naples and Sicily as the most vibrant sector of the film industry, part of a general resurgence in artistic activity in southern Italy that's connected with a new pride in regional identity. First-time director **Vincenzo Marra**'s **Sailing Home** (**Tornando a Casa**, 2001) is just one of the experimental films to have been made in the region. Made on a shoestring budget, it uses fishermen rather than professional actors, is spoken in Neapolitan dialect (at home it was released with Italian subtitles) and was shot in semi-documentary style.

More accessible to an international audience perhaps is Neapolitan director **Antonio Capuano**'s **Luna Rossa** (2001), a mesmerizing portrayal of a Camorra family from the inside, borrowing from Greek tragedy for its structure and with a soundtrack by indie-rockers Almamegretta. Visually rich, brooding, confusing and violent, the film is artistically assured in a way that few others have been in recent years.

Front of House

Film director **Martin Scorsese** has been active in restoring copies of the classic Italian movies and trying to work out a systematic distribution in the US and other English-speaking countries. His aim is to bring a whole new audience to Italian cinema, an aim that his epic documentary **My Voyage in Italy** (**Il Mio Viaggio in Italia**, 2001) supports. Growing up in New York's Little Italy in the 1940s, Scorsese remembers watching the Italian movies of the time with his extended family and neighbours who dropped by. "Italy had just come out of the devastation of World War II," he says "and these films were showing the war's harsh reality with images so intensely moving that my older relatives cried and we kids were overwhelmed." In his "voyage" he takes us through some of these films and in the process the viewer sees three stories unfolding: Scorsese's discovery of his family and his Italian roots, the shaping of his artistic vision, and an overview of some of the classic greats of Italian cinema – a four-hour marathon, and unmissable.

Revitalization has been taking place not just behind the camera, but also in front of the screen, with Rome foremost among Italian cities in wooing the public away from its TV and back into the **cinemas**. The city's old cinema halls of the 1930s, so deeply mourned in films like *Cinema Paradiso* and *Splendor*, are being brought back to life (if they haven't already been pulled down), financed by the film industry itself at the "encouragement" of the city council. New multiscreen complexes have supplemented the historic Pasquino and Nanni Moretti's Nuovo Sacher, and the red-tape restricting filming on location in the city has been much reduced. By all accounts this has been a success: in the *Dolce Vita*-era there were three hundred cinema halls in the city – in 2000, this figure was exceeded and other Italian cities are reported to be set to follow the Roman example.

Sheila Brownlee and **Celia Woolfrey**

Books

A comprehensive background reading list for Italy would run on for dozens of pages, and would include a vast number of out-of-print (OP) titles. Most of our recommendations are in print, but those that aren't shouldn't be too difficult to track down. The book symbol marks titles that are particularly recommended.

Travel and general

Anne Calcagno (ed) *Travelers' Tales: Italy*. Crammed with evocative period detail by the likes of H.V. Morton as well as contemporary writing specifically commissioned for this volume by Tim Parks, Lisa St Aubin de Terán and others, this makes a perfect introduction to the richness and variety of the country. See also *Tuscany: True Stories*, edited by Calcagno and Tara Austen Weaver, with a similar collection.

★ **Vincent Cronin** *The Golden Honeycomb*. Disguised as a quest for the mythical golden honeycomb of Daedalus, this is a searching account of a sojourn in Sicily in the 1950s. Although overwritten in parts, it has colourful descriptions of Sicily's art, architecture and folklore.

Charles Dickens *Pictures from Italy*. The classic mid-nineteenth-century Grand Tour, taking in the sights of Emilia, Tuscany, Rome and Naples, in elegant, measured and incisive prose.

★ **Norman Douglas** *Old Calabria*. A brilliant travel chronicle based on the author's wanderings around Calabria in the early twentieth century. Wide-ranging and digressive, it's a classic of the genre. See also *Siren Land* (OP) and the novel, *South Wind* (OP), which focus on Cápri and the Bay of Naples.

Johann Wolfgang Von Goethe *Italian Journey*. Surprisingly readable account of a journey all through the peninsula at the end of the eighteenth century, a classic of travel writing and a decisive point in Goethe's own transition from Sturm und Drang to classicism.

Henry James *Italian Hours*. Urbane travel pieces from the young James; perceptive about particular monuments and works of art, superb on the different atmospheres of Italy.

Jonathan Keates *Italian Journeys*. Frank yet affectionate journey through the Italian social, cultural and historical landscape. Full of engaging anecdotes, its witty portraits get under the surface of Italy and its people.

★ **D.H. Lawrence** *D.H. Lawrence and Italy*. Lawrence's three Italian travelogues collected into one volume. *Sea and Sardinia* and *Twilight in Italy* combine the author's seemingly natural ill-temper when travelling with a genuine sense of regret for a way of life almost visibly passing away. *Etruscan Places*, published posthumously, consists of his more philosophical musings on Etruscan art and civilization, and remains one of the most illuminating books written on the period.

David Leavitt *Florence, A Delicate Case*. Though a book largely about Florence's expat community over the last 150 years may sound insular and antique, Leavitt injects a good deal of wit and sensitivity into this quirky portrait of Florence. Refreshingly free of cultural overload, the account focuses on the city's more shadowy side – its role as a destination for suicides and taboo-breakers – and there's a flamboyant cast of characters.

Norman Lewis *Naples '44.* Lewis was among the first Allied troops to move into Naples following the Italian surrender in World War II, and this is his diary of his experiences there. Part travelogue, part journalism, this is without question the finest thing you can read on World War II in Italy – and, despite its often bleak subject matter, among the most entertaining. Lewis's more recent *In Sicily* is a broad contemporary portrait of the island he has married into and returns to frequently. Subjects range from reflections on Palermo's ruined *palazzi* to the impact of immigration, and there's plenty on the Mafia.

Charles Lister *Heel to Toe.* Firmly in the tradition of such English travel-writers as Douglas and Gissing, the author sets off on a bicycle, soon transferring to a moped, for a journey along the Ionian coast from Brindisi to Reggio. Mixing history and culture with strong opinions and copious digression, it's chatty and accessible, if somewhat over-written. In a similar style, Lister's *Between Two Seas* (OP) charts his walk along the Appian Way.

Mary McCarthy *The Stones of Florence/Venice Observed.* A mixture of high-class reporting on the contemporary cities and anecdotal detail on their histories; one of the few accounts of these two cities that doesn't read as if it's been written in a library.

Jan Morris *Venice* (titled *The World of Venice* in US). Some people think this is the most acute modern book written about any Italian city, while others find it unbearably fey. At least give it a look. The author has more recently published what she claims is her final book, *Trieste and the Meaning of Nowhere*, an aptly elegiac salute to this curious frontier city.

H.V. Morton *A Traveller in Italy; A Traveller in Rome* and *A Traveller in Southern Italy.* Morton's leisurely and amiable books were written in the 1930s, long before modern tourism got into its stride, and their nostalgic charm has a lot to do with their enduring popularity. But they are also packed with learned details and vivid descriptions.

William Murray *Italy: the Fatal Gift* (OP). Murray spent several years in Italy shortly after the last war, and this is a collection of essays inspired by his time there, and many return visits since. Skilfully combining personal anecdote and contemporary Italian history and politics, it's one of the most insightful introductions to the country and its people you can buy.

Eric Newby *Love and War in the Apennines.* An anecdotal, oddly nostalgic account of the sheltering of the author by local people in the mountains of Emilia-Romagna in the closing months of World War II. Newby's *A Small Place in Italy*, recounting his life in a small farmhouse at the foot of the Alps, is equally evocative, and reads much more "authentically" than other expatriates-in-Italy tales.

History, politics and society

The Longman History of Italy
This eight-volume series covers the history of Italy from the end of the Roman Empire to the present, each instalment comprising a range of essays on all aspects of political, social, economic and cultural history. Invaluable if you've developed a special interest in a particular period.

⭐ **Luigi Barzini** *The Italians*.
Long the most respected work on the Italian nation, and rightly so. Barzini leaves no stone unturned in his quest to pinpoint the real Italy.

R.J.B. Bosworth *Mussolini*. This gripping account of modern Italy's most traumatic period paints a vivid picture of *Il Duce*. Achieving great understanding without succumbing to sympathy for the man, Bosworth explains the context of Fascism and examines Mussolini's legacy, warning of the strong fascination for him that still exists in Italy today.

Jerome Carcopino *Daily Life in Ancient Rome*. Detailed but never dull, this is a seminal work of Roman social history.

John Cornwell *A Thief in the Night*. An investigation into the death of the "three-day pope", John Paul I, told as a fast-paced detective story. A good read for devotees of conspiracy theory, although more cynical types will probably wonder whether it isn't all a lot of fuss about nothing.

Giovanni Falcone *Men of Honour: The Truth about the Mafia* (OP). The most incisive analysis of the *mafioso* mentality by the investigating magistrate assassinated by the mob in May 1992.

Alan Friedman *Agnelli and the Network of Italian Power* (OP). Agnelli didn't like this book when it came out, and no wonder. Friedman's book was among the first pieces of journalism to pull no punches on the dynastic and anti-democratic power network that is at the heart of Italian society. If you're intrigued by the inertia of Italian postwar politics, it's a must.

Edward Gibbon *The Decline and Fall of the Roman Empire*. Awe-inspiring in its erudition, Gibbon's masterpiece is one of the greatest histories ever written, and one of the finest compositions of English prose. Penguin also publish an abridged version for those without the time to tackle the entire work.

⭐ **Paul Ginsborg** *A History of Contemporary Italy*. A very scholarly but readable account of postwar Italian history, illustrating the complexity of contending economic, social and political currents. Bringing the story up to date, Ginsborg's *Italy and its Discontents* unravels the knotty background to Berlusconi's rise to power and his tussles with the judiciary. It's essential reading for anyone intrigued by the present contradictions of Italian society.

Michael Grant *A History of Rome*. A straightforward and reliable summary of an impossibly complicated story.

Christopher Hibbert *Rome: The Biography of a City*. The history of Italy's capital made easy. As ever, Hibbert is readable and entertaining, but never superficial, providing by far the most comprehensive, yet concise, account of the city through the ages. The companion volumes, *Venice: The Biography of a City* (OP) and *Florence: The Biography of a City*, are particularly good on the changing social fabric in those cities, and have more coverage of the twentieth-century than most; excellent illustrations too. Another foray into an episode of Italian history, Hibbert's *Garibaldi and his Enemies* (OP) is a popular treatment of the life and revolutionary works of Giuseppe Garibaldi, thrillingly detailing the exploits of "The Thousand" in their lightning campaign from Marsala to Milazzo.

Tobias Jones *The Dark Heart of Italy*. Written during a three-year period in Parma, *The Dark Heart of Italy* consists of an interconnected sequence of essays dealing with various aspects of modern Italian society, from the legal and political systems to the media and football. Bewildered and fascinated at every turn, Jones reveals a culture in which evasiveness and ethical malleability are as significant as the much-celebrated virtues of vivacity, charm and sophistication – a culture exemplified above all by the character of Silvio Berlusconi, in effect the owner of the Italian state. An affectionate but clear-eyed corrective to the sentimentalizing claptrap perpetrated by so many English and American expats.

Norman Lewis *The Honoured Society*. Famous account of the Mafia, its origins, personalities and customs. Certainly the most enjoyable introduction to the subject available, though much of it is taken up with the story of banditry – really a separate issue – and his lack of accredited sources leaves you wondering how much is conjecture.

Valerio Lintner *A Traveller's History of Italy*. A brief history of the country, from the Etruscans right up to the present day. Well written and sensibly concise, it could be just the thing for the dilettante historian of the country. Lots of tables and chronologies for easy reference.

Patrick McCarthy *The Crisis of the Italian State* (OP). Subtitled *From the Origins of the Cold War to the Fall of*

Berlusconi and Beyond, this is a detailed but quite readable analysis of the root causes and major events of the "Clean Hands" political crisis of the Nineties.

John Julius Norwich *The Normans in Sicily*. Accessible, well-researched story of the Normans' explosive entry into the south of Italy and their creation in Sicily of one of the most brilliant medieval European civilizations. Just as stimulating is his *A History of Venice*, the most engrossing treatment of the subject available.

Giuliano Procacci *History of the Italian People*. A comprehensive history of the peninsula, charting the development of Italy as a nation-state.

Uta Ranke-Heinemann *Eunuchs for the Kingdom of Heaven* (OP). Entertaining, erudite and witty critique of the Catholic Church's attitude to sex.

Donald Sassoon *Contemporary Italy*. Slightly academic background on the country and its institutions.

Renate Siebert *Secrets of Life and Death: Women and the Mafia*, translated by Liz Heron. History and analysis of the patriarchal nature of Mafia organizations, which are held to be the apotheosis of the masculine society of Italy's south. Poignant first-person narratives give background to the account, exploding the myth of the Mafia as protecting the weak and defending women, who continue to be used as drug mules and decoys. The author is a German-born professor of sociology at the University of Calabria.

Denis Mack Smith *The Making of Italy 1796–1866*; *Italy and its Monarchy*. The former is an admirably lucid explanation of the various forces at work in the Unification of Italy, while the latter

C

deals with Italy's short-lived monarchy, whose kings ruled the country for less than a century – it reveals Vittorio Emanuele II and co. as a bunch of irresponsible and rather dim buffoons that the country was glad to be rid of. The same author has also written a couple of excellent biographies, *Mazzini* and *Mussolini*.

Claire Sterling *The Mafia*. Thorough piece of Mafia scholar-ship, showing to a disturbing degree just how little Mafia power has been eroded by the state's onslaught of recent years.

Alexander Stille *Excellent Cadavers*. Stille traces the rise, successes, failures and eventual assassinations of anti-Mafia magistrates Giovanni Falcone and Paolo Borsellino, as well as dishing the dirt on Andreotti and Craxi.

Art, architecture and archeology

Michael Baxandall *Painting and Experience in Fifteenth-Century Italy*. An invaluable analysis, concentrating on the way in which the art of the period would have been perceived at the time.

Anthony Blunt *Artistic Theory in Italy 1450–1600*. A cogent summary of the aesthetic ground rules of Renaissance art, but – contrary to the impression given by the writer's patrician tone – far from the last word. The author's *Baroque Rome* is a broad examination of Rome's Baroque architecture in two volumes.

Jacob Burckhardt *The Civilization of the Renaissance in Italy*. A nineteenth-century classic of Renaissance scholarship.

Robert Etienne *Pompeii, The Day a City Died*. Archeologically and historically rigorous, yet highly accessible, account of the life and death of Pompeii.

J.R. Hale (ed) *Encyclopaedia of the Italian Renaissance*. Exemplary reference book, many of whose summaries are as informative as essays twice their length; covers individual artists, movements, cities, philosophical concepts, the lot.

Frederick Hartt *History of Italian Renaissance Art*. If one book on this vast subject can be said to be indispensable, this is it. In view of its comprehensiveness and acuity, and the range of its illustrations, it's something of a bargain.

Howard Hibbard *Bernini*. A standard overview of the life and work of the central figure of Roman Baroque.

Anthony Hughes *Michelangelo*. Part of the acclaimed Phaidon Art and Ideas series, this is an ideal single-volume introduction to arguably the greatest artist of the Renaissance. Setting Michelangelo within his historical and political context, Hughes examines his work not only as the expression of an individual sensibility but also in the light of the often fraught relations between artist and patron. An accessible and stimulating read.

Peter Humfrey *Lorenzo Lotto*. A lavishly illustrated, scholarly reappraisal of the Renaissance painter who was a contemporary of Titian and Giorgione.

Michael Levey *Early Renaissance*. Precise and fluently written, and well illustrated; probably the best introduction to the subject. Levey's *High Renaissance* continues the story in the same style.

Peter Murray *The Architecture of the Italian Renaissance*. Begins with

Romanesque buildings and finishes with Palladio – valuable both as a gazetteer of the main monuments and as a synopsis of the underlying concepts.

Peter and Linda Murray *Art of the Renaissance*. Serviceable thumbnail sketch, useful for preparing the ground before a trip to Italy.

T.W. Potter *Roman Italy* (OP). A learned illustrated survey of Roman society based on archeological sources. Essential reading if you're interested in the period.

Catherine Puglisi *Caravaggio*. An intelligent and engaging study of one of the most innovative artists of the Renaissance, enhanced with sumptuous colour plates throughout.

★ **Peter Robb** *M*. This highly individual biography of Caravaggio – referred to as "M" throughout – tackles one of the most colourful figures of the late Renaissance. It's a passionately partisan and controversial study, with disconcerting inconsistencies of style, but ultimately hugely enjoyable, pre-

senting an engrossing evocation of the period, rent boys and all.

Ross King *Brunelleschi's Dome*. An intriguing account of the architectural innovations and intense rivalries behind the construction of Florence's Duomo. It also paints an engaging picture of life in the medieval city.

John Shearman *Mannerism*. The self-conscious art of sixteenth-century Mannerism is one of the most complex topics of Renaissance studies; Shearman's brief discussion analyses the main currents, yet never oversimplifies nor becomes pedantic.

Giorgio Vasari *Lives of the Artists*. A new abridgement brought out by OUP of the sixteenth-century artist's classic work on his predecessors and contemporaries. Includes essays on Giotto, Brunelleschi, Mantegna, Leonardo, Michelangelo, Raphael, and more. The first real work of art history and still among the most penetrating books you can read on Italian Renaissance art. The unabridged version was published in 1996 by Everyman's Library.

Specific guides

Helena Attlee and Alex Ramsay *Italian Gardens*. Evocatively photographed (by Alex Ramsay), this is a guide to more than sixty of the peninsula's most beautiful gardens. Both practical and up to date, the guide provides histories and descriptions, as well as detailed information on locations, facilities, opening times and accessibility.

Amanda Claridge *Oxford Archeological Guides: Rome*. A well-written and excellently conceived concise guide to the ancient city, a good investment if that is your particular area of interest.

Tim Jepson *Wild Italy*. Guide to the flora and fauna of the Italian peninsula by a *Rough Guide* contributor.

Gillian Price *Walking in the Dolomites*. A lively and informative specialized guide to the best walks in the Dolomites. Cicerone also publish guides to Alta Via 1 & 2 and to various Vie Ferrate (see p.246 for more on these peculiarly Italian phenomena).

Victoria Pybus *Live and Work in Italy*. Accessible and informative handbook on all aspects of living and working in Italy, including regional differences.

Ancient literature

Catullus *The Poems of Catullus.* Although his name is associated primarily with the tortured love poems addressed to Lesbia, Catullus also produced some acerbic satirical verse; this collection does full justice to his range.

Cicero *Selected Works.* The rhetorical prose of Cicero was for many Renaissance scholars the paragon of literary style, and his political ideas provided similarly fertile material for discussion. Penguin publish half a dozen volumes of his work.

Juvenal *The Sixteen Satires.* Savage attacks on the follies and excesses of Rome at the end of the first century and start of the second.

Livy *The Early History of Rome.* Lively chronicle of the city's evolution from the days of Romulus and Remus; Penguin also publish later instalments of those parts of Livy's history that have survived, including the gripping War with Hannibal.

Marcus Aurelius *Meditations.* The classic text of Stoic thought, written by one of the few Roman emperors it's easy to admire.

★ **Ovid** *Metamorphoses* and *Erotic Poems.* The mythical tales of the Metamorphoses have been so frequently quarried by artists that they can be enjoyed both as literature and as a key to some of the masterworks of Renaissance and later art. His elegiac love poems have a sexual candour that makes them seem almost modern.

Petronius *Satyricon.* Fragmentary, spicy narrative written by one of Nero's inner circle; Fellini's film of the same name gives a pretty accurate idea of the tone.

Plautus *Pot of Gold, and other plays.* The most popular playwright of his time, whose complicated plots provided a model for Renaissance comedies such as The Comedy of Errors.

Seneca *Four Tragedies and Octavia.* Violent, fast-paced drama from Nero's one-time tutor; the only plays to have survived from the Roman Empire.

Suetonius *The Twelve Caesars.* The inside story on such vile specimens as Caligula, Nero and Domitian; elegantly written and appalling.

Tacitus *Annals of Imperial Rome.* Covers much of the terrain dealt with by Suetonius, but from the stance of the diligent historian and serious moralist.

★ **Virgil** *The Aeneid.* The central work of Latin literature, depicting the adventures of Aeneas after the fall of Troy, and thus celebrating Rome's heroic lineage.

Italian classics

Dante Alighieri *The Divine Comedy.* No work in any other language bears comparison with Dante's poetic exegesis of the moral scheme of God's creation; in late medieval Italy it was venerated both as a book of almost scriptural authority and as the ultimate refinement of the vernacular Tuscan language. A new translation, by Mark Musa, is printed in full in *The Portable Dante* (Penguin).

Ludovico Ariosto *Orlando Furioso.* Italy's chivalrous epic, set in Charlemagne's Europe; has its exciting moments, but most readers would be grateful for an abridged version. Penguin's verse translation is pacier and more accessible than Oxford's prose version.

Giovanni Boccaccio *The Decameron*. Set in the plague-racked Florence of 1348, this assembly of one hundred short stories is a fascinating social record as well as a constantly diverting comic sequence.

Baldassare Castiglione *The Book of the Courtier*. Written in the form of a series of dialogues held in the court of Urbino, this subtle, entertaining book defines all the qualities essential in the perfect gentleman; the idealistic converse of Machiavelli.

Benvenuto Cellini *Autobiography*. Shamelessly egocentric record of the travails and triumphs of the sculptor and goldsmith's career; one of the freshest literary productions of its time.

Giacomo Leopardi *Leopardi*, tr. Eamon Grennan. Generally considered the greatest Italian poet since Dante, and a formative influence on the poets who followed, Leopardi has never had a big following in the English-speaking world, a situation that may change with this new, gutsy translation by Grennan, an Irish poet, published by Dedalus Press.

Niccolò Machiavelli *The Prince*. A treatise on statecraft which actually did less to form the political thought of Italy than it did to form foreign-

ers' perceptions of the country; there was far more to Machiavelli than the realpolitik of *The Prince*, as is shown by the selection of writings included in the anthology *The Portable Machiavelli*.

Alessandro Manzoni *The Betrothed*. No pool-side thriller, but a skilful melding of the romance of two young lovers and a sweeping historical drama, all suffused with an almost religious sense of human destiny. First published in 1823, but reissued in 1840 after Manzoni had improved the novel's diction through study of the Tuscan dialect – a landmark in the transition towards linguistic nationalism.

Petrarch (Francesco Petrarca) *Selections from the Canzoniere* (Oxford UP). Often described as the first modern poet, by virtue of his preoccupation with worldly fame and secular love, Petrarch wrote some of the Italian language's greatest lyrics. This slim selection at least hints at what is lost in translation.

Marco Polo *Travels*. Buttonholing account of Polo's journey to the court of Kublai Khan, and his seventeen-year stay there; engaging even when the stories are clearly fanciful.

Leonardo da Vinci *Notebooks*. Miscellany of speculation and observation from the universal genius of Renaissance Italy; essential to any understanding of the man.

Modern Italian literature

Giorgio Bassani *The Garden of the Finzi Continis*. Gentle, elegiac novel, set in the Jewish community of Ferrara during the Fascist period, on the eve of the mass deportations to Germany. Infused with a sense of regret for a Europe that died with the war.

Cinzia Sartini Blum and Lara Trubowitz (eds). *Contemporary*

Italian Women Poets. A bilingual selection of twenty-five very diverse poets working in the last half-century. Among the selections is verse by Dacia Maraini and Mariella Bettarini.

Enrico Brizzi *Jack Frusciante has Left the Band*. Pacy, unrequited-love story set in Bologna. Rebellious Alex D endures life with his parents (whom he calls Matron and The Chancellor) while not getting anywhere with his girlfriend, the enigmatic but totally insecure Aidi. Some great descriptions of the overpowering pressure to conform in an Italian provincial town, the book is also memorably poignant at times.

Gesualdo Bufalino *The Keeper of Ruins*; *The Plague Sower*; *Blind Argus* (OP) and *Night's Lies*. One of Sicily's most esteemed twentieth-century writers, Bufalino arrived late on the literary scene, publishing his first novel, *The Plague Sower*, when he was into his sixties. Most of his output has now been translated.

Aldo Busi *Seminar on Youth* (OP); *Confessions of a Panty-Hose Salesman* and *Sodomies in Eleven Point*. Busi is something of an *enfant terrible* in the Italian literary world, but his tales of gay escapades around northern Italy go beyond the mere showy; indeed his somewhat impenetrable style masks a humanity and wit that is rare in much recent Italian fiction.

Ann and Michael Caesars (eds) *The Quality of Light*. Anthology of contemporary Italian writers, including work by Primo Levi and Gianni Celati, as well as many other less well-known writers like the starkly realistic Pier Vittorio Tondelli.

★ **Italo Calvino** *If on a Winter's Night a Traveller*. Calvino's fiction became increasingly concerned with the nature of fiction itself, and this involuted, witty novel marks the culmination of the process. Other titles include *The Castle of Crossed Destinies* and *Invisible Cities*; *Difficult Loves* and *Mr Palomar*.

Gianni Celati *Voices from the Plains* (OP). Chance encounters on a walk down the Po provide the focus for these atmospheric tales. The four understated novellas in *Appearances* pay similarly close attention to the specific locales of Emilia-Romagna.

Gabriele D'Annunzio *Halcyon* (OP). Self-regarding dandy, war hero and worshipper of Mussolini, D'Annunzio was perhaps the most complex figure of twentieth-century Italian literature; this extended lyric sequence – a troubled idyll set on the Tuscan coast – contains much of his finest poetry.

Umberto Eco *The Name of the Rose*. An allusive, tightly plotted monastic detective story. Check out also his equally hyped, though rather more impenetrable, *Foucault's Pendulum*, and the allegorical *Island of the Day Before*. His most recent work, *Baudolino*, is another medieval fable, this time interspersed with reflections on the postmodern age.

Dario Fo *Plays I*. This collection includes a trio of Fo's most famous plays – *Mistero Buffo*, *Accidental Death of an Anarchist* and *Trumpets and Raspberries* – along with two previously unpublished short works. The Nobel Prize winner fabulously weaves together contemporary politics, surreal farce and the traditions of *commedia dell'arte*.

Carlo Emilio Gadda *That Awful Mess on Via Merulana* (OP). Superficially a detective story, this celebrated modernist novel is so dense a weave of physical reality and literary diversions that the reader is led away from a solution rather than towards it; it enjoys the sort of status in Italian fiction that *Ulysses* has in English.

Natalia Ginzburg *The Things We Used to Say*. The constraints of family life are a dominant theme in Ginzburg's writing, and her own upbringing is the source material for this characteristically rigorous yet lyrical work.

★ **Giuseppe di Lampedusa** *The Leopard*. The most famous Sicilian novel, written after the war but recounting the dramatic nineteenth-century transition from Bourbon to Piemontese rule from an aristocrat's point of view. A good character-study and rich with incidental detail, including some nice description of the Sicilian landscape.

★ **Carlo Levi** *Christ Stopped at Eboli*. First published in 1945, this memoir, describing Levi's exile to a remote region of Basilicata by the Fascists, was the first to awaken modern Italy to the plight of its southern regions.

★ **Primo Levi** *If This is a Man / The Truce; The Periodic Table*. Levi's experiences in Auschwitz are the main subject of *If This is a Man*, while *The Truce* records his eight-month journey back to Turin after his liberation. Levi's training as a chemist forms the background of *Periodic Table,* a mixture of autobiographical reflections and practical observations. The amorality of the Third Reich and its repercussions are the recurrent subjects of Levi's later works, all of which show an unwavering exactitude of recollection and judgement.

Elsa Morante *History*. Capturing daily Roman life during the last war, this is probably the most vivid fictional picture of the conflict as seen from the city.

Alberto Moravia *Roman Tales* (OP). A collection of stories, first published in the Fifties, which show the underbelly of a rapidly changing city; it is evocative of both the city and its people. *The Conformist* is a psychological novel about a man sucked into the abyss of Fascism by his desperation to conform; *The Woman of Rome* is an earlier work, a teeming and sensual novel, centred on the activities of a Roman prostitute.

Pier Paolo Pasolini *A Violent Life*. Pasolini's writing is preoccupied with the demise of local, dialect-based cultures of agrarian Italy in the face of modernization. His supernaturalistic evocation of life in the slum areas of Rome caused a scandal when it was published in 1959, but is now considered one of the classics of Italian postwar fiction. See also the collection of short stories, *Roman Nights and Other Stories*, and *A Dream of Something* – Pasolini's pastoral tale of growing up in Friuli in the late Forties.

Cesare Pavese *Moon and the Bonfire; Devil in the Hills*. Exploring the difficulties of achieving an acceptance of one's past, *Moon and the Bonfire* was written shortly before Pavese's suicide at the age of 42; *Devil in the Hills* is an early collection of tales of adolescence in and around Turin.

Luigi Pirandello *Six Characters in Search of an Author; The Late Mattia Pascal* and *Eleven Short Stories*. His most famous and accomplished work, *Six Characters…*, written in 1921, contains many of the themes that dogged Pirandello throughout his writing career – the idea of a multiple personality and the quality of reality. *The Late Mattia Pascal* is an early novel (1904), entertainingly written despite its stylistic shortcomings; while the collection of short stories is perhaps the best introduction to Pirandello's work.

Umberto Saba *Ernesto* (OP). A lyrical autobiographical novel by the Triestine poet, recollecting youth and homosexuality. Marvellous translation.

★ **Leonardo Sciascia** *Sicilian Uncles; The Wine Dark Sea; Candido* (OP) and *The Day of the Owl*. Writing again and again about his native Sicily, Sciascia has made of that island "a metaphor of the modern world". Economically written, Sciascia's short stories are packed with incisive insights, and infused with the author's humane and sympathetic views of its people. *The Moro Affair* is an illuminating account

C

of the kidnapping of the ex-prime minister Aldo Moro by the Brigate Rosse in 1978.

Ignazio Silone *Fontamara*; *Bread and Wine*. From his exile in Switzerland, Silone wrote about his native Abruzzo, and about the struggle for social justice. *Fontamara* tells the tale of a small village driven to revolt against its landlords and the Fascist thugs sent to enforce their rule; *Bread and Wine*, a more introspective work, examines the parallels between Silone's political commitment and religious belief. The two works, together with *The Seed Beneath the Snow*, are published in one volume by Steerforth Press, titled *The Abruzzo Trilogy*.

Italo Svevo *Confessions of Zeno*. Complete critical indifference to his early efforts so discouraged Svevo that he gave up writing altogether, until encouraged by James Joyce, who taught him English in Trieste. The resultant novel is a unique creation, a comic portrait of a character at once wistful, helpless and irrepressible.

Giovanni Verga *Little Novels of Sicily* (*Sicilian Stories* in US); *Cavalleria Rusticana* and *I Malavoglia, or The House by the Medlar Tree*. Verga, born

in the nineteenth century in Catania, spent several years in various European salons before coming home to write his best work. Much of it is a reaction against the pseudo-sophistication of society circles, stressing the simple lives of ordinary people, though sometimes accompanied by a heavy smattering of "peasant passion", with much emotion, wounded honour and feuds to the death.

Elio Vittorini *Conversations in Sicily*. A Sicilian emigrant returns from the north of Italy after fifteen years to see his mother on her birthday. The conversations of the title are with the people he meets on the way, local villagers and his mother, and reveal a poverty- and disease-ridden Sicily, though the scenes are affectionately drawn. In the US, New Directions publish an excellent anthology of his writings, *A Vittorini Omnibus*.

William Weaver (ed) *Open City: Seven Writers in Postwar Rome*. A nicely produced anthology of pieces by the cream of Italy's twentieth-century novelists – Bassani, Silone, Ginzburg, Moravia, among others – selected and with an introduction by one of the most eminent Italian translators of recent years.

An Italian miscellany

Lindsey Davis *Venus in Copper*, *The Jupiter Myth* and others. These crime novels set in the age of the Emperor Vespasian are shot through with sparkling comedy, and follow super-sleuth Marcus Didius Falco as he unpicks mysteries and dastardly doings. An omnibus containing three tales is also available: *Falco on his Metal*.

Michael Dibdin *Ratking*, *Vendetta*, *Cabal*; *Dead Lagoon*. Dibdin's Aurelio Zen is a classically eccentric, loner detective, and this is a classic series of well-plotted detective yarns.

However, Dibdin is as interested in the country as he is in his characters, and these novels tell us plenty about the way Italian society operates. Among the most recent in the series are *Cosi Fan Tutti* set in Naples, *A Long Finish*, in which Zen is sent to Piemonte on the trail of the murderer of a noted wine maker, and *Blood Rain*, set in Catania, with more of his own personal life revealed along the way. A supremely palatable way to read about Italy and Italians.

E.M. Forster *A Room with a View*. Set in and around Florence, this is the ultimate novel about how the nature of the Italian light, temperament and soul can make the English upper classes lose their heads.

Marius Gabriel *House of Many Rooms*. Psychological thriller and study of human relationships set in San Francisco and Italy.

Annie Hawes *Extra Virgin*. Belonging to the Mayes/Mayle school of expats setting up in sunny rural climes, but superior to most of the genre in every way, this relates how two sisters overcome various adversities and much local incomprehension to find their idyll on a Ligurian mountain. It's funny and smart, interspersed with plenty of culinary culture and peasant lore.

Nathaniel Hawthorne *The Marble Faun*. A nineteenth-century take on the lives of Anglo-American expats in the Eternal City – sculptors, passionate lovers, devotees of Classical Purity – the usual mad mix and excessive goings-on that you'll still find today.

Ernest Hemingway *A Farewell To Arms*. Hemingway's first novel is partly based on his experiences as a teenage ambulance driver on Italy's northeast front during World War 1 – a terse account of the futility of this particular corner of the conflict.

Patricia Highsmith *The Talented Mr Ripley*. The novel follows the fortunes of the eponymous hero through Italy as he exchanges his own identity for that of the man he has murdered. Recently released as a movie, starring Gwyneth Paltrow and directed by Anthony Minghella.

Donna Leon *Death at La Fenice, A Venetian Reckoning, Fatal Remedies*, and others. Venice-based crime thrillers featuring Guido Brunetti, the honest police commissario in a world of high-level intrigue and corruption. Public scandals and Brunetti's private

life are absorbingly interwoven, and these atmospheric tales usually work on several different levels.

Thomas Mann *Death in Venice*. Irascible and ultra-traditional old novelist visits Venice to recover after a breakdown and becomes obsessed with a beautiful young boy, awakening an internal debate about the nature of beauty and art to which the city is a fitting and resonant backdrop.

Allan Massie *Augustus, Tiberius, Caesar*. A trilogy of novels that tells the stories of the three emperors as if they were recently discovered autobiographies. Massie's historical precision and careful dramatization hold up well.

Frances Mayes *Under the Tuscan Sun, Bella Tuscany*. Follow the trials and triumphs of American author and boyfriend as they renovate a farmhouse near Cortona, interspersed with recipes. The echoes of Peter Mayle in Provence will put many off.

Ian McEwan *The Comfort of Strangers*. An ordinary young English couple fall foul of a sexually ambiguous predator in a Venice who is never named, but evoked by means of arch little devices such as quotes from Ruskin.

John Mortimer *Summer's Lease*. The chattering classes revel in Chiantishire. Not exactly profound, but hugely entertaining.

Magdalen Nabb *Death in Springtime* (OP), *Death in Autumn* and many other titles. Thrillers that make the most of their settings in low-life Florence and the wild Sardinian hills where shepherds dabble in a spot of kidnapping.

Michael Ondaatje *The English Patient*. The novel that inspired the Anthony Minghella film starring Juliette Binoche and Ralph Fiennes.

A nurse cares for her patient, burnt beyond recognition, in an abandoned Italian monastery during World War II as his true identity, and the story of the passionate but doomed affair he has survived, are uncovered.

★ **Tim Parks** *Italian Neighbours, An Italian Education, Europa* and *A Season with Verona*. Novelist Tim Parks has lived in Italy since 1981. Through deftly told tales of family life, his books examine what it means to be Italian, and how national identity is absorbed. *Europa* is a bawdy, savage tale of love gone wrong, set among a group of academics travelling to lobby the European Parliament in Strasbourg, while *A Season with Verona* relates his passion for his local football team, but drawing in much more besides.

Daphne Phelps *A House in Sicily*. An Englishwoman inherits a villa in Taormina and turns it into a guesthouse to make ends meet. This allows vignettes of eminent guests – Bertrand Russell, Tennessee Williams, Roald Dahl – as well as of the locals, though her anglocentric and patronizing take on some of these, including the local Mafia don, grate.

★ **Peter Robb** *Midnight in Sicily*. The Australian Robb spent fifteen years in the Italian south tracing the contorted relations between organized crime and politics. Here, he focuses on the structure of the Mafia, the trials of the bosses in the 1980s, the high-profile assassinations that ensued, and the trial of Andreotti. It's a thorough, fast-paced study, providing deep insights into the dynamics of Sicilian society and an authentic portrait of Palermo.

Susan Sontag *The Volcano Lover*. A profound and surprising novel, based on the notorious affair between Nelson and Lady Hamilton, wife of the volcano-fixated English ambassador to Naples. The self-absorbed protagonists indulge their various obsessions – romantic and geological – as Vesuvius smoulders in the background and the Bourbon court wallows in dissolution and incompetence. An absolute must-read for visitors to Naples.

Stendhal *The Charterhouse of Parma*. Panoramic nineteenth-century French novel that dramatizes the struggles and intrigues of the Italian papal states before Unification. A wonderful read, and a good insight into the era to boot.

Irving Stone *The Agony and the Ecstasy*. Stone's dramatized life of Van Gogh is well-known, filmed with a memorably angst-ridden Kirk Douglas in the title role. Here Stone gives the same treatment to Michelangelo, popular "faction" that is entertaining even if it doesn't exactly get to the root of the artist's work and times.

Lowri Turner *Gianni Versace: Fashion's Last Emperor*. Fashion editor Turner's "photo-biography" of the late designer suggests that Versace and the man who allegedly gunned him down were murdered by the Mafia. A strange mix of reportage, interspersed with 90 colour photographs of supermodels and Versace's own glamorous homes.

Barry Unsworth *After Hannibal* and *Stone Virgin*. The author lives in Umbria, where the former novel is set. *After Hannibal* is a black comedy of expat life, where a diverse cast of characters in the process of being betrayed each confide in the same local lawyer. The earlier *Stone Virgin*, set in Venice, is about a conservation expert who falls under the spell of a statue of the Madonna he is working on – and of a member of the family who owns it.

Roger Vailland *The Law*. This evocation of life in a small Pugliese town, of its people, etiquette and harsh tradition, is tight, considered and utterly convincing.

Salley Vickers *Miss Garnet's Angel*. The unique atmosphere of Venice is captured in this tale of a desiccated spinster awakened by the city to the finer things in life. The author's sound knowledge of the place and its art triumphs over a potentially hackneyed tale.

Edith Wharton *Roman Fever and Other Stories*. The title story of this collection recounts two old women's stingingly bitchy reminiscences about their adolescence in Rome.

Jeanette Winterson *The Passion*. Whimsical tale of the intertwined lives of a member of Napoleon's catering corps and a female gondolier.

Food and drink

Burton Anderson *Wines of Italy* and *Best Italian Wines*. The first is an excellent pocket guide to the regional wines and winemaking techniques of Italy, the second an in-depth look at the top two hundred wines.

Antonio Carluccio *Carluccio's Complete Italian Food*. Based on the BBC TV series. Carluccio's passion for food goes right back to basics; his message is that a meal – however humble or grand – is only as good as the land or sea from which its ingredients come.

Elizabeth David *Italian Food*. The writer who introduced Italian cuisine – and ingredients – to Britain. Ahead of its time when it was published in the Fifties, and imbued with all the enthusiasm and diversity of Italian cookery. An inspirational book.

Patience Gray *Honey from a Weed*. The author lived and worked in basic conditions in various Mediterranean countries, and in this intriguing blend of cookbook and autobiography, she describes roughing it and cooking it.

Valentina Harris *Italia! Italia!*; *Recipes from an Italian Farmhouse*. All the classics, pizzas and pastas, with regional recipes and anecdotes from local and regional traditions.

Marcella Hazan *The Classic Italian Cookbook* and *Marcella Cucina*. The best Italian cookbook for the novice in the kitchen, *The Classic Italian Cookbook* is a step-by-step guide that never compromises the spirit or authenticity of Hazan's subject. She draws her recipes from all over the peninsula, emphasizing the intrinsically regional nature of Italian food. Her latest, the fully illustrated *Marcella Cucina*, combines regional dishes and anecdotes.

Fred Plotkin *Italy for the Gourmet Traveller*. Comprehensive, region-by-region guide to the best of Italian cuisine, with a foodie's guide to major towns and cities, a gazetteer of restaurants and specialist food and wine shops, and descriptions of local dishes, with recipes.

Claudia Roden *The Food of Italy*. A culinary classic, this regional guide takes in local recipes from the people for whom they are second nature. Authentic and accessible.

Arthur Schwartz *Naples at Table*. Simple, authentic recipes from Campania, all lavishly photographed. There's impressive attention to detail and care for local traditions, accompanied by entertaining commentary.

Mary Taylor Simeti *Sicilian Food*. Starting with the oldest and most

C

elemental components of the Sicilian diet, this book offers a collection of recipes and evocations of the dishes' origins: from the culinary innovations of Arab and Norman invaders to the ritual luxuries of Sicily's aristocracy.

language

language

Italian

T he ability to speak English confers prestige in Italy, and there's often no shortage of people willing to show off their knowledge, particularly returned *emigrati*. However, even in the main cities and resorts you'll need to use at least some Italian, and in more remote areas you may well find no one speaks English at all.

Pronunciation

Wherever you are, it's a good idea to master at least a little **Italian**, a task made easier by the fact that your halting efforts will often be rewarded by smiles and genuine surprise. In any case, it's one of the easiest European languages to learn, especially if you already have a smattering of French or Spanish, both of which are extremely similar grammatically.

Easiest of all is the **pronunciation**, since every word is spoken exactly as it's written, and usually enunciated with exaggerated, open-mouthed clarity. The only difficulties you're likely to encounter are the few **consonants** that are different from English:

c before e or i is pronounced as in **ch**urch, while ch before the same vowels is hard, as in **c**at.

sci and sce are pronounced as in **sh**eet and **sh**elter respectively.

The same goes with g – soft before e or i, as in geranium; hard before h, as in **g**arlic.

gn has the ni sound of our onion.

gl in Italian is softened to something like li in English, as in stallion.

h is not aspirated, as in honour.

Italian words and phrases

Basics

Good morning - **Buon giorno**
Good afternoon/evening - **Buona sera**
Good night - **Buona notte**
Hello/goodbye - **Ciao** (informal; to strangers use phrases above)
Goodbye - **Arrivederci**
Yes - **Si**
No - **No**
Please - **Per favore**
Thank you (very much) - **Grazie (molte/mille grazie)**
You're welcome - **Prego**
All right/that's OK - **Va bene**
How are you? - **Come stai/sta?** (informal/formal)
I'm fine - **Bene**

Do you speak English? - **Parla inglese?**
I don't understand - **Non ho capito**
I don't know - **Non lo so**
Excuse me - **Mi scusi/Prego**
Excuse me (in a crowd) - **Permesso**
I'm sorry - **Mi dispiace**
I'm here on holiday - **Sono qui in vacanza**
I'm British/Irish/ - **Sono britannico/a irlandese/a**
American/ - **americano/a**
Australian/ - **australiano/a/**
New Zealander - **neozelandese/a**
I live in . . . - **Abito a . . .**
Today - **Oggi**
Tomorrow - **Domani**
Day after tomorrow - **Dopodomani**

Yesterday – **Ieri**
Now – **Adesso**
Later – **Più tardi**
Wait a minute! – **Aspetta!**
Let's go! – **Andiamo!**
In the morning – **Di mattina**
In the afternoon – **Nel pomeriggio**
In the evening – **Di sera**
Here/There – **Qui/Là**
Good/Bad – **Buono/Cattivo**
Big/Small – **Grande/Píccolo**
Cheap/Expensive – **Económico/Caro**
Early/Late – **Presto/Tardi**

Hot/Cold – **Caldo/Freddo**
Near/Far – **Vicino/Lontano**
Vacant/Occupied – **Libero/Occupato**
Quickly/Slowly – **Velocemente/Lentamente**
Slowly/Quietly – **Piano**
With/Without – **Con/Senza**
More/Less – **Più/Meno**
Enough, no more – **Basta**
Mr . . . – **Signor . . .**
Mrs . . . – **Signora . . .**
Miss . . . – **Signorina . . .**
(il Signor, la Signora, la Signorina when
speaking about someone else)

Driving

A sinistra/A destra – Left/right
Sempre diritto – Go straight ahead
Gira a destra/sinistra – Turn to the left/right
Parcheggio – Parking
Divieto di sosta/Sosta vietata – No parking
Senso único – One-way street
Senso vietato – No entry

Rallentare – Slow down
Strada chiusa/ lavoro in corso – Road
closed/under repair
Vietato il transito – No through road
Vietato il sorpasso – No overtaking
Incrocio – Crossroads
Limite di velocità – Speed limit

Some signs

Entrata/Uscita – Entrance/Exit
Ingresso líbero – Free entrance
Signori/Signore – Gentlemen/Ladies
Gabinetto/Bagno – WC/Bathroom
Libero/Occupato – Vacant/Engaged
Aperto/Chiuso – Open/Closed
Arrivi/Partenze – Arrivals/Departures
Chiuso per restauro – Closed for restoration
Chiuso per ferie – Closed for holidays
Tirare/Spingere – Pull/Push
Guasto – Out of order
Acqua potabile – Drinking water

Affítasi – To let
Binario – Platform
Cassa – Cash desk
Avanti – Go/walk
Alt – Stop/halt
Dogana – Customs
Non toccare – Do not touch
Perícolo – Danger
Attenzione – Beware
Pronto soccorso – First aid
Suonare il campanello – Ring the bell
Vietato fumare – No smoking

Italian numbers

1 – uno	11 – undici	21 – ventuno	101 – centuno
2 – due	12 – dodici	22 – ventidue	110 – centodieci
3 – tre	13 – tredici	30 – trenta	200 – duecento
4 – quattro	14 – quattordici	40 – quaranta	500 – cinquecento
5 – cinque	15 – quindici	50 – cinquanta	1000 – mille
6 – sei	16 – sedici	60 – sessanta	5000 – cinquemila
7 – sette	17 – diciassette	70 – settanta	10,000 – diecimila
8 – otto	18 – diciotto	80 – ottanta	50,000 –
9 – nove	19 – diciannove	90 – novanta	cinquantamila
10 – dieci	20 – venti	100 – cento	

Accommodation

Hotel – **Albergo/hotel**
Is there a hotel nearby? – **C'è un albergo qui vicino?**
Do you have a room . . . – **Ha una cámera . . .**
for one/two/three – **per una/due/tre**
person/people – **persona/e**
for one/two/ – **per una/due/**
three night/s – **tre notte/i**
for one/two week/s – **per una/due settimana/e**
with a double bed – **con un letto matrimoniale**
with a shower/bath – **con una doccia/un bagno**
with a balcony – **con una terrazza**
hot/cold water – **acqua calda/freddo**
How much is it? – **Quanto costa?**
It's expensive – **È caro**

Is breakfast included? – **È compresa la prima colazione?**
Do you have anything cheaper? – **Ha niente che costa di meno?**
Full/half board – **Pensione completa/mezza pensione**
Can I see the room? – **Posso vedere la cámera?**
I'll take it – **La prendo**
I'd like to – **Vorrei prenotare una**
book a room – **cámera**
I have a booking – **Ho una prenotazione**
Can we camp here? – **Possiamo campeggiare qui?**
Is there a campsite nearby? – **C'è un camping qui vicino?**
Tent – **Tenda**
Cabin – **Cabina**
Youth hostel – **Ostello per la gioventù**

Questions and directions

Where? (where is/ – **Dove? (Dov'è/**
where are . . . ?) – **Dove sono . . . ?)**
When? – **Quando?**
What? (what is it?) – **Cosa? (Cos'è?)**
How much/many? – **Quanto/Quanti?**
Why? – **Perché?**
It is/there is (is it/is there . . . ?) – **C'e . . . ?**
What time is it? – **Che ora è/Che ore sono?**
How do I get to . . . ? – **Come arrivo a . . . ?**
How far is it to . . . ? – **Cuant'è lontano a . . . ?**

Can you give me a lift to . . . ? – **Mi può dare un passaggio a . . . ?**
Can you tell me when to get off? – **Mi può dire di scendere alla fermata giusta?**
What time does it open? – **A che ora apre?**
What time does it close? – **A che ora chiude?**
How much does it cost – **Quanto costa?**
(. . . do they cost?) – (. . . **Quanto cóstano?**)
What's it called – **Come si chiama**
in Italian? – **in italiano?**

Travelling

Aeroplane – **Aeroplano**
Bus – **Autobus/pullman**
Train – **Treno**
Car – **Macchina**
Taxi – **Taxi**
Bicycle – **Bicicletta**
Ferry – **Traghetto**
Ship – **Nave**
Hydrofoil – **Aliscafo**
Hitch-hiking – **Autostop**
On foot – **A piedi**
Bus station – **Autostazione**
Railway station – **Stazione ferroviaria**
Ferry terminal – **Stazione maríttima**
Port – **Porto**

A ticket to . . . – **Un biglietto per . . .**
One-way/return – **Solo andata/andata e ritorno**
Can I book a seat? – **Posso prenotare un posto?**
What time does it leave? – **A che ora parte?**
When is the next – **Quando parte il prossimo**
bus/train/ferry – **pullman,/treno/traghetto**
to . . . ? – **per . . . ?**
Do I have to change? – **Devo cambiare?**
Where does it leave from? – **Da dove parte?**
What platform does it leave from? – **Da quale binario parte?**
How many kilometres is it? – **Quanti chilómetri sono?**

LANGUAGE | Italian words and phrases

L

1193

How long does it take?– **Quanto ci vuole?**
What number bus is it to . . ? – **Che número di autobus per . . ?**

Where's the road to . . . – **Dové la strada per . .**
Next stop please – **La próssima fermata, per favore**

Eating and drinking

Basics and snacks

Aceto – Vinegar
Aglio – Garlic
Biscotti – Biscuits
Burro – Butter
Caramelle – Sweets
Cioccolato – Chocolate
Focaccia – A kind of pizza
Formaggio – Cheese
Frittata – Omelette
Grissini – Bread sticks
Maionese – Mayonnaise
Marmellata – Jam
Olio – Oil
Olive – Olives
Pane – Bread
Pane integrate – Wholemeal bread
Panino – Bread roll
Patatine – Crisps (potato chips)
Patate fritte – Chips (French fries)
Pepe – Pepper
Pizzetta – Small cheese-and-tomato pizza
Riso – Rice
Sale – Salt
Uova – Eggs
Yogurt – Yoghurt
Zúcchero – Sugar
Zuppa – Soup

Pizzas

Calzone – Folded pizza, often with cheese, ham and tomato
Capricciosa – Literally "capricious"; topped with whatever they've got in the kitchen, usually including baby artichoke, ham and capers
Cardinale – Ham and olives
Funghi – Mushroom (tinned, sliced button mushrooms unless it specifies fresh – funghi freschi)
Frutti di mare – Seafood, usually mussels, prawns, squid and clams
Margherita – Cheese and tomato
Marinara – Tomato and garlic
Napoli/Napoletana – Tomato, cheese, anchovy, olive oil and oregano
Quattro formaggi – "Four cheeses", usually including mozzarella, fontina, gruyere and gorgonzola

Quattro stagioni – "Four seasons", usually including ham, pepper, onion, mushrooms, artichokes, olives, etc

Antipasti and starters

Antipasto misto – Starter of seafood, vegetables and cold meats
Caponata – Mixed aubergine, olives, tomatoes and anchovies
Caprese – Tomato and mozzarella salad with basil
Crespolina – Pancake, usually stuffed
Insalata russa – Salad of diced vegetables in mayonnaise
Melanzane alla parmigiana – Aubergine with tomato and parmesan cheese
Peperonata – Green and red peppers stewed in olive oil
Pomodori ripieni – Stuffed tomatoes
Prosciutto – Ham
Salame – Salami

The first course (*il primo*): soups, pasta...

Brodo – Clear broth
Cannelloni – Large tubes of pasta, stuffed
Farfalle – Butterfly-shaped pasta
Fettuccine – Narrow pasta ribbons
Gnocchi – Small potato and dough dumplings
Minestrina – Clear broth with small pasta shapes
Minestrone – Thick vegetable soup
Pasta al Forno – Pasta baked with minced meat, eggs, tomato and cheese
Pasta e fagioli – Pasta with beans
Pastina in brodo – Pasta pieces in clear broth
Penne – Smaller version of rigatoni
Rigatoni – Large, grooved tubular pasta
Stracciatella – Broth with egg
Tagliatelle – Pasta ribbons
Tortellini – Small rings of pasta, stuffed with meat or cheese
Vermicelli – Thin spaghetti

...and pasta sauce

Amatriciana – Cubed bacon and tomato sauce
Arrabbiata – Spicy tomato sauce, with chillies ("Angry")

Bolognese - Meat sauce
Carbonara - Cream, ham and beaten egg
Funghi - Mushrooms
Panna - Cream
Parmigiano - Parmesan cheese
Pereroncino - Olive oil, garlic and fresh
  chillies
Pesto - Sauce with ground basil, garlic and
  pine nuts
Pomodoro - Tomato sauce
Puttanesca - Tomato, anchovy, olive oil and
  oregano ("Whorish")
Ragù - Meat sauce
Salvia - Sage
Vóngole - Sauce with clams

The second course (*il secondo*): meat (*carne*)...

Agnello - Lamb
Bistecca - Steak
Carpaccio - Thin slices of raw beef
Cervella - Brain, usually calves'
Cinghiale - Wild boar
Coniglio - Rabbit
Costolette or coteletta - Cutlet, chop
Fegatini - Chicken livers
Fegato - Liver
Involtini - Meat slices, rolled and stuffed
Lepre - Hare
Lingua - Tongue
Maiale - Pork
Manzo - Beef
Mortadella - Salami-type cured meat
Ossobuco - Shin of veal
Pancetta/Speck - Bacon
Pollo - Chicken
Polpette - Meatballs
Rognoni - Kidneys
Saclsiccia - Sausage
Saltimbocca - Veal with ham
Spezzatino - Stew
Tacchino - Turkey
Trippa - Tripe
Vitello - Veal

...fish (*pesce*) and shellfish (*crostacei*)

Acciughe - Anchovies
Anguilla - Eel
Aragosta - Lobster
Baccalà - Dried salted cod
Calamari - Squid
Cefalo - Grey mullet

Cozze - Mussels
Dentice - Sea bream
Gamberetti - Shrimps
Gámberi - Prawns
Granchio - Crab
Merluzzo - Cod
Ostriche - Oysters
Pesce spada - Swordfish
Polpo - Octopus
Riccio di mare - Sea urchin
Rospo - Monkfish
Sampiero - John Dory
Sarde - Sardines
Sgombro - Mackerel
Sógliola - Sole
Tonno - Tuna
Triglie - Red mullet
Trota - Trout
Vóngole - Clams

Vegetables (*contorni*), herbs (*erbe aromatiche*) and salad (*insalata*)

Asparagi - Asparagus
Basílico - Basil
Cápperi - Capers
Carciofi - Artichokes
Carciofini - Artichoke hearts
Carotte - Carrots
Cavolfiori - Cauliflower
Cávolo - Cabbage
Cetriolo - Cucumber
Cipolla - Onion
Fagioli - Beans
Fagiolini - String beans
Finocchio - Fennel
Insalata verde/mista - Green salad/mixed
  salad
Lenticchie - Lentils
Melanzane - Aubergine
Origano - Oregano
Patate - Potatoes
Peperoni - Peppers
Piselli - Peas
Pomodori - Tomatoes
Radicchio - Red salad leaves
Spinaci - Spinach
Zucchini - Courgettes

Some terms and useful words

Affumicato - Smoked
Arrosto - Roast
Ben cotto - Well done
Bollito/lesso - Boiled

Alla brace – Barbecued
Brasato – Cooked in wine
Congelato – Frozen
Cotto – Cooked (not raw)
Crudo – Raw
Al dente – Firm, not overcooked
Ai ferri – Grilled without oil
Al forno – Baked
Fritto – Fried
Grattugiato – Grated
Alla griglia – Grilled
Alla Milanese – Fried in egg and
   breadcrumbs
Pizzaiola – Cooked with tomato sauce
Ripieno – Stuffed
Al sangue – Rare
Allo spiedo – On the spit
Stracotto – Braised, stewed
Surgelato – Frozen
In umido – Stewed

Sweets (*dolci*), fruit (*frutta*), cheeses (*formaggi*) and nuts (*noci*)

Amaretti – Macaroons
Ananas – Pineapple
Anguria/Coccómero – Watermelon
Arance – Oranges
Banane – Bananas
Cacchi – Persimmons
Ciliegie – Cherries
Dolcelatte – Creamy blue cheese
Fichi – Figs
Fichi d'India – Prickly pears
Fontina – Northern Italian cheese, used in
   cooking
Frágole – Strawberries
Gelato – Ice cream
Gorgonzola – Soft, strong, blue-veined cheese
Limone – Lemon
Macedonia – Fruit salad
Mándorle – Almonds
Mele – Apples
Melone – Melon
Mozzarella – Soft, white cheese, made from
   buffalo milk

Parmigiano – Parmesan
Pecorino – Strong, hard sheep's cheese
Pere – Pears
Pesche – Peaches
Pignoli – Pine nuts
Pistacchio – Pistachio nut
Provola/Provolone – Mild cheese made
from buffalo or sheep milk, sometimes
smoked
Ricotta – Soft, white sheep cheese
Torta – Cake, tart
Uva – Grapes
Zabaglione – Dessert with eggs, sugar and
   marsala wine
Zuppa inglese – Trifle

Drinks

Acqua minerale – Mineral water
Aranciata – Orangeade
Bicchiere – Glass
Birra – Beer
Bottiglia – Bottle
Caffè – Coffee
Cioccolata calda – Hot chocolate
Ghiaccio – Ice
Granita – Iced drink, with coffee or fruit
Latte – Milk
Limonata – Lemonade
Selz – Soda water
Spremuta – Fresh fruit juice
Spumante – Sparkling wine
Succo – Concentrated fruit juice with sugar
Tè – Tea
Tónica – Tonic water
Vino – Wine
Rosso – Red
Bianco – White
Rosato – Rosé
Secco – Dry
Dolce – Sweet
Litro – Litre
Mezzo – Half
Quarto – Quarter
Caraffa – Carafe
Salute! – Cheers!

Phrasebooks and dictionaries

The most user-friendly phrasebook is the
Rough Guides' own Italian, arranged dictionary-
style for ease of access and with a host of
cultural tips and slang expressions. Among

dictionaries, Collins publish a comprehensive
series: their Gem or Pocket dictionaries are fine
for travelling purposes, while their Concise is
adequate for most language needs.

When speaking to strangers, the third person is the polite form (ie lei instead of tu for "you"); using the second person is a mark of familiarity or disrespect. Italians don't use "please" and "thank you" as much as we do: it's all implied in the tone. If in doubt, err on the polite side.

Most Italian words are **stressed** on the penultimate syllable. In written Italian, **accents** (either ´ or `) have traditionally been used to denote stress on other syllables, but the acute (') accent is more rarely used these days. In the text we've used acute accents only when we feel it's necessary to help you get the pronunciation right – eg Pésaro where the accent indicates that the stress should be on the **e**, not the a. Note that the endings -**ia** or -**ie** count as two syllables, hence trattoria is stressed on the **i**.

You'll find variations in **dialect** all over the country. Neapolitan especially can be difficult to understand, and the Sicilian dialect is different enough from conventional Italian as to be almost a separate language. But everywhere people will slip into more orthodox Italian if they see you're a foreigner.

Glossary of artistic and architectural terms

agora Square or market place in an ancient Greek city.

ambo A kind of simple pulpit, popular in Italian medieval churches.

apse Semicircular recess at the altar (usually eastern) end of a church.

architrave The lowest part of the entablature.

atrium Inner courtyard.

baldachino A canopy on columns, usually placed over the altar in a church.

basilica Originally a Roman administrative building, adapted for early churches; distinguished by lack of transepts.

belvedere A terrace or lookout point.

caldarium The steam room of a Roman bath.

campanile Belltower, sometimes detached, usually of a church.

capital Top of a column.

catalan-gothic Hybrid form of architecture, mixing elements of fifteenth-century Spanish and northern European styles.

cella Sanctuary of a temple.

chiaroscuro The balance of light and shade in a painting, and the skill of the artist in depicting the contrast between the two.

chancel Part of a church containing the altar.

ciborium Another word for Baldachino, see above.

cornice The top section of a classical facade.

cortile Galleried courtyard or cloisters.

cosmati work Decorative mosaic work on marble, usually highly coloured, found in early Christian Italian churches, especially in Rome. Derives from the name Cosma, a common name among families of marble workers at the time.

crypt Burial place in a church, usually under the choir.

cryptoporticus Underground passageway.

cyclopean walls Fortifications built of huge, rough stone blocks, common in the pre-Roman settlements of Lazio.

decumanus maximus The main street of a Roman town. The second cross-street was known as the Decumanus Inferiore.

entablature The section above the capital on a classical building, below the cornice.

ex-voto Artefact designed in thanksgiving to a saint. The adjective is ex-votive.

fresco Wall-painting technique in which the artist applies paint to wet plaster for a more permanent finish.

loggia Roofed gallery or balcony.

metope A panel on the frieze of a Greek temple.

mithraism Pre-Christian cult associated with the Persian god of Light, who slew a bull and fertilized the world with its blood.

nave Central space in a church, usually flanked by aisles.

pantocrator Usually refers to an image of Christ, portrayed with outstretched arms.

piano nobile Main floor of a palace, usually the first.

polyptych Painting on several joined wooden panels.

portico Covered entrance to a building, or porch.

presepio A Christmas crib.

putti Cherubs.

reliquary Receptacle for a saint's relics, usually bones. Often highly decorated.

sgraffito Decorative technique whereby one layer of plaster is scratched to form a pattern. Popular in sixteenth-century Italy.

stereobate Visible base of any building, usually a Greek temple.

stucco Plaster made from water, lime, sand and powdered marble, used for decorative work.

thermae Baths, usually elaborate buildings in Roman villas.

triptych Painting on three joined wooden panels.

trompe l'oeil Work of art that deceives the viewer by means of tricks with perspective.

Glossary of words and acronyms

aliscafo Hydrofoil.
anfiteatro Amphitheatre.
autostazione Bus station.
autostrada Motorway.
biblioteca Library.
cappella Chapel.
castello Castle.
centro Centre.
chiesa Church.
comune An administrative area; also the local council or town hall.
corso Avenue or boulevard.
duomo/cattedrale Cathedral.
entrata Entrance.
festa Festival, holiday.
fiume River.
fumarola Volcanic vapour emission from the ground.
golfo Gulf.
lago Lake.
largo Square.
lungomare Seafront road or promenade.
mare Sea.
mercato Market.

municipio Town hall.
paese Place, area, country village.
palazzo Palace, mansion, or block of flats.
parco Park.
passeggiata The customary early evening walk.
piano Plain.
piazza Square.
pinacoteca Picture Gallery.
ponte Bridge.
santuario Sanctuary.
senso unico One-way street.
sottopassaggio Subway.
spiaggia Beach.
stazione Station.
strada Road.
teatro Theatre.
tempio Temple.
torre Tower.
traghetto Ferry.
uscita Exit.
via Road (always used with name, eg Via Roma).

Acronyms

AAST Azienda Autonoma di Soggiorno e Turismo.
APT Azienda Promozione Turistica.
ACI Automobile Club d'Italia.
CAI Club Alpino Italiano.
DC Democrazia Cristiana (the Christian Democrat party).
EPT Ente Provinciale per il Turismo (provincial tourist office); see also APT .
FS Ferrovie dello Stato (Italian State Railways).
IVA Imposta Valore Aggiunto (VAT).

MSI Movimento Sociale Italiano (the Italian Fascist party).
PCI Partito Comunista Italiano; old name for the Italian Communist party.
PDS Partito Democratico della Sinistra (new name for the Italian Communist party).
PSI Partito Socialista Italiano (the Italian Socialist party).
RAI The Italian state TV and radio network.
SIP Italian state telephone company.
SS Strada Statale; a major road, eg SS18.

Glossary of street names

Italian streets form a kind of outdoor pantheon of historical figures. A jumble of artists, thinkers, politicians, generals and saints, in roughly equal proportions, intersect with each other in blind disregard for sense or chronology. The mad mix of heroes (and a very few heroines) constantly reminds the visitor of just how much Italians relish their past. Almost all of the following appear in every major Italian city.

Bassi, Ugo (1801–1849). A priest from Bologna who, as a fervent and eloquent supporter of Garibaldi and his cause, became one of its most important martyrs when he was condemned to death and shot by the Austrians.

Bellini. The name of both a Venetian family of fifteenth-century painters (Jacopo and sons Gentile and Giovanni) and a nineteenth-century Sicilian composer of operas (Vicenzo), best known for Norma and La Sonnambula.

Bertani, Agostino (1812–1886). A Milanese doctor, who organized the medical and ambulance services for Garibaldi's campaigns and became one of his closest associates and shrewdest strategists.

Bixio, Nino (1821–1873). Loyal companion-at-arms to Garibaldi, who enlisted and disciplined civilian volunteers to fight some of the critical battles of the Unification era.

Buonarroti, Filippo (1761–1837). Tuscan revolutionary and friend of Robespierre, who was involved with Gracchus Babeuf in the short-lived Conspiracy of Equals in Paris, May 1796.

Calatafimi. First decisive battle in Garibaldi's Sicilian campaign, May 1860.

Cappuccini. Monks whose characteristic brown robes and peaked white hoods have lent their names to the Italian coffee drink with hot milk.

Carducci, Giosue (1835–1907). Patriotic poet of the Risorgimento who won the Nobel Prize for literature in 1907.

Cavour, Camillo di (1810–1861). Prime Minister of Piemonte who relied on diplomatic cunning to promote the interests of his northern kingdom in the Unification of Italy.

Crispi, Francesco (1819–1901). Reforming prime minister of the late nineteenth century.

D'Annunzio, Gabriele (1863–1938). Nationalist writer who refurbished Italy's past with sex and violence and who lived out some of his fantasies as a Fascist military adventurer.

Dante Alighieri (1265–1321). Medieval Italian poet known for his three-part poem, The Divine Comedy.

De Gasperi, Alcide (1881–1954). A prominent anti-Fascist imprisoned by Mussolini, and the first Catholic Prime Minister of modern Italy in 1945, aligning his country with the West by joining NATO.

Depretis, Agostino (1813–87). Italian prime minister on three occasions during the late nineteenth century. His administrations are remembered for the stagnation and corruption they engendered.

Foscolo, Ugo (1778–1827). Nineteenth-century poet, dramatist and critic who left Venice under Austrian rule to settle in England where he became a commentator on Petrarch, Dante and Boccaccio.

Garibaldi, Giuseppe (1807–1882). Italy's unquestioned nationalist hero, and the tag on most Italian towns' most prominent boulevards or squares. Streets are full of his exploits and the supporting cast of comrades (see Bassi, Bertani, Bixio, Calatafimi, I Mille, Turr).

Giolitti, Giovanni (1842–1928). Prime minister five times between 1892 and 1921. He sponsored an electoral reform bill which extended male suffrage and won workers the right to organize and strike.

Goldoni, Carlo (1707–1793). Venetian dramatist much influenced by Moliere, who wrote more than 250 comedies.

Gramsci, Antonio (1881–1937). One of the founders of the Italian Communist Party. Arrested by Mussolini in 1928 and held until just before his death, his influential writings from prison on the political role of culture and intellectuals remain controversial fifty years on.

Leopardi, Giacomo (1798–1837). A lyric poet plagued by ill-health and melancholy whose patriotic verses were taken up by the Unification.

Machiavelli, Niccolò (1469–1527). Political scientist and author of The Prince whose name outside Italy has become synonymous with unprincipled political opportunism.

Manin, Daniele (1804–1857). Leader of a revolution in Venice which proclaimed a republic in March 1848 and was overrun by the Austrians shortly thereafter.

Manzoni, Alessandro (1785–1873). Liberal Catholic writer and playwright whose historical novel I promesi sposi (The Betrothed), set in seventeenth-century Milan, is still required reading in Italian schools.

Marconi, Guglielmo (1874–1937). Developer of the wireless system, sending messages across the Straits of Dover in 1899 and across the Atlantic in 1901.

Matteotti, Giacomo. A Socialist in the Italian Parliament who was murdered by Fascist thugs for his public denunciation of the 1924 elections which gave Mussolini majority control. In what has become known as Mussolini's Watergate, the incident had a brief chance of stopping Il Duce in his tracks – but didn't.

Mazzini, Giuseppe (1805–1872). Propagandist of Italian Unification whose influence was spread through the organization (Giovine Italia) Young Italy which he founded to promote the national cause.

I Mille (The Thousand). The name given to the largely untrained band of civilian volunteers (made up of students, workers, artists, journalists and every kind of adventurer) who were mobilized in 1860 for Garibaldi's successful Sicilian campaign.

Moro, Aldo. Post-war prime minister who was kidnapped and murdered by the Brigate Rosse in May 1978.

Puccini, Giacomo (1858–1924). A member of the fifth generation of a family of professional musicians, and composer of many popular operas, including Madame Butterfly, La Bohème and Tosca.

Quattro Novembre (November 4). Anniversary of the 1918 victory in the war.

Ricasoli. An ancient and distinguished Tuscan family name. The nineteenth-century Baron Ricasoli (an ally of Cavour and very briefly prime minister) has been eclipsed by the relatively greater prominence of his family's vineyards, known particularly for their Chianti.

Ricci, Matteo (1552–1610). Early Italian missionary to China.

Risorgimento. The nineteenth-century movement to unify Italy and liberate the country from foreign domination.

Savonarola. A fifteenth-century Dominican friar and prophet of doom, who inspired a famous book-burning (which included Boccaccio's Decameron among the forbidden texts), and was himself burned in 1498.

Togliatti (1893–1964). Co-founder (with Gramsci and others) of the Italian Communist Party, which, in 1956, adopted his programme for an "Italian Road to Socialism".

Turr, Stefan. A Hungarian colonel in Garibaldi's army and close associate who helped acquire arms for the volunteer army (The Thousand) to mount the campaign in Sicily.

Umberto I and II. Kings of Italy, respectively, between 1878 and 1900 and for a brief period in 1946.

Vasari, Giorgio (1511–1574). The father of modern art history, whose Lives of the Artists traced the story of art from ancient Rome through to his own contemporary – and fellow Tuscan – Michelangelo.

Venti Settembre (September 20). The day Italian troops stormed into Rome in 1870, marking the final stage of Unification.

Venticinque Aprile (April 25). Anniversary of the 1945 liberation.

Ventiquattro Maggio (May 24). Date in 1915 when Italy declared war on Austria-Hungary.

Verdi, Giuseppe (1813–1901). Hugely popular and prolific composer of operas who became a national hero.

Vespri Siciliani. Massacre of the Angevin French in Sicily in 1282, carried out (according to legend) while vesper bells were ringing, in retaliation for the savage colonization of the island by the Angevin. Verdi used the story for an opera in 1855.

Vittorio Emanuele II and III. Respectively, the first king of unified Italy, from 1861 to 1878, and from 1900 until 1946. Very often the main street of towns are named after Vittorio Emanuele II – an overly grand accolade for a dull and unenlightened ruler.

Volturno. A river near Capua, and the name given to an important battle led by Garibaldi against the Bourbons in October 1860.

Index

and small print

Index

Map entries are in colour

INDEX

W

Y

Z

INDEX

Ⓘ

Twenty Years of Rough Guides

In the summer of 1981, Mark Ellingham, Rough Guides' founder, knocked out the first guide on a typewriter, with a group of friends. Mark had been travelling in Greece after university, and couldn't find a guidebook that really answered his needs. There were heavyweight cultural guides on the one hand – good on museums and classical sites but not on beaches and tavernas – and on the other hand student manuals that were so caught up with how to save money that they lost sight of the country's significance beyond its role as a place for a cool vacation. None of the guides began to address Greece as a country, with its natural and human environment, its politics and its contemporary life.

Having no urgent reason to return home, Mark decided to write his own guide. It was a guide to Greece that tried to combine some erudition and insight with a thoroughly practical approach to travellers' needs. Scrupulously researched listings of places to stay, eat and drink were matched by careful attention to detail on everything from Homer to Greek music, from classical sites to national parks and from nude beaches to monasteries. Back in London, Mark and his friends got their Rough Guide accepted by a farsighted commissioning editor at the publisher Routledge and it came out in 1982.

The Rough Guide to Greece was a student scheme that became a publishing phenomenon. The immediate success of the book – shortlisted for the Thomas Cook award – spawned a series that rapidly covered dozens of countries. The Rough Guides found a ready market among backpackers and budget travellers, but soon acquired a much broader readership that included older and less impecunious visitors. Readers relished the guides' wit and inquisitiveness as much as the enthusiastic, critical approach that acknowledges everyone wants value for money – but not at any price.

Rough Guides soon began supplementing the "rougher" information – the hostel and low-budget listings – with the kind of detail that independent-minded travellers on any budget might expect. These days, the guides – distributed worldwide by the Penguin group – include recommendations spanning the range from shoestring to luxury, and cover more than 200 destinations around the globe. Our growing team of authors, many of whom come to Rough Guides initially as outstandingly good letter-writers telling us about their travels, are spread all over the world, particularly in Europe, the USA and Australia. As well as the travel guides, Rough Guides publishes a series of dictionary phrasebooks covering two dozen major languages, an acclaimed series of music guides running the gamut from Classical to World Music, a series of music CDs in association with World Music Network, and a range of reference books on topics as diverse as the Internet, Pregnancy and Unexplained Phenomena. Visit **www.roughguides.com** to see what's cooking.

Rough Guide Credits

Text editor: Ruth Blackmore
Series editor: Mark Ellingham
Editorial: Martin Dunford, Jonathan Buckley, Kate Berens, Ann-Marie Shaw, Helena Smith, Olivia Swift, Geoff Howard, Claire Saunders, Gavin Thomas, Alexander Mark Rogers, Polly Thomas, Joe Staines, Richard Lim, Duncan Clark, Peter Buckley, Lucy Ratcliffe, Clifton Wilkinson, Alison Murchie, Matthew Teller, Andrew Dickson, Fran Sandham, Sally Schafer, Matthew Milton, Karoline Densley (UK); Andrew Rosenberg, Yuki Takagaki, Richard Koss, Hunter Slaton (US)
Production: Link Hall, Helen Prior, Julia Bovis, Katie Pringle, Rachel Holmes, Andy Turner, Dan May, Tanya Hall, John McKay, Sophie Hewat

Cartography: Maxine Repath, Melissa Baker, Ed Wright, Katie Lloyd-Jones
Cover art direction: Louise Boulton
Picture research: Sharon Martins, Mark Thomas
Online: Kelly Martinez, Anja Mutic-Blessing, Jennifer Gold, Audra Epstein, Suzanne Welles, Cree Lawson (US)
Finance: Gary Singh
Marketing & Publicity: Richard Trillo, Niki Smith, David Wearn, Chloë Roberts, Demelza Dallow, Claire Southern (UK); Simon Carloss, David Wechsler, Megan Kennedy (US)
Administration: Julie Sanderson

Publishing Information

This sixth edition published May 2003 by **Rough Guides Ltd**,
80 Strand, London WC2R 0RL.
345 Hudson St, 4th Floor,
New York, NY 10014, USA.
Distributed by the Penguin Group
Penguin Books Ltd,
80 Strand, London WC2R 0RL
Penguin Putnam, Inc.
375 Hudson Street, NY 10014, USA
Penguin Books Australia Ltd,
487 Maroondah Highway, PO Box 257,
Ringwood, Victoria 3134, Australia
Penguin Books Canada Ltd,
10 Alcorn Avenue, Toronto, Ontario,
Canada M4V 1E4
Penguin Books (NZ) Ltd,
182–190 Wairau Road, Auckland 10,
New Zealand
Typeset in Bembo and Helvetica to an original design by Henry Iles.

Printed in Italy by LegoPrint S.p.A

© Ros Belford, Martin Dunford and Celia Woolfrey

1232pp includes index
A catalogue record for this book is available from the British Library

ISBN 1-843-530 600

The publishers and authors have done their best to ensure the accuracy and currency of all the information in **The Rough Guide to Italy**, however, they can accept no responsibility for any loss, injury, or inconvenience sustained by any traveller as a result of information or advice contained in the guide.

Help us update

We've gone to a lot of effort to ensure that the sixth edition of **The Rough Guide to Italy** is accurate and up-to-date. However, things change – places get "discovered", opening hours are notoriously fickle, restaurants and rooms raise prices or lower standards. If you feel we've got it wrong or left something out, we'd like to know, and if you can remember the address, the price, the time, the phone number, so much the better.

We'll credit all contributions, and send a copy of the next edition (or any other Rough Guide if you prefer) for the best letters. Everyone who writes to us and isn't already a subscriber will receive a copy of our full-colour thrice-yearly newsletter. Please mark letters: "**Rough Guide Italy Update**" and send to: Rough Guides, 80 Strand, London WC2R 0RL, or Rough Guides, 4th Floor, 345 Hudson St, New York, NY 10014. Or send an email to **mail@roughguides.com**

Have your questions answered and tell others about your trip at
www.roughguides.atinfopop.com

Acknowledgements

Lucia Graves thanks Simone Randino, Claudia Zudini, and all the Trieste crowd.

Charles Hebbert would like to thank Caroline Hoare, Glenda Roth, Charlotte Bradbeer, Caroline Hutchings, Sue Cole, Howard Carter, Jonathan Buckley, Ali Palmer and Amy Erickson for their time, thoughts and suggestions, as well as the staff of the tourist offices.

Kate Hughes would like to thank Alfredo Cefalo, Mario Cascio and Agata Scampornino.

Tim Jepson would like to thank Yasmin Sethna.

Lucy Ratcliffe would like to thank Germana Colombo at Milan APT; Paola Strola from the Distretto turistico dei Laghi; and Babara Mora at Garda APT for their help and support; Ness and Iris for their unbeatable company; and Luca for unlimited grappa and encouragement.

Norman Roberson thanks Dr. Laura Lee Farr for her insights into historical material; Prof. Rainer Tullner for his assistance and guidance on the intricacies of Italian life; Betty and the cats for their invaluable help; and Raffaella and Lorella from the Bar F.R.A.M. in Monteverde Nuovo, for their help in researching the nightlife.

Celia Woolfrey thanks Karen Ludtke in Lecce (for information on tarantism), plus all the APT and IAT tourist offices in Marche and Puglia.

Thanks also to Ken Bell for proofreading; Rachel Holmes for typesetting; The Map Studio, Romsey, Hants, for cartography; Mark Thomas for picture research; Martin Dunford for the introduction and things not to miss; Kate Hughes for indexing; and Stanfords for map recommendations.

Readers' letters

Thanks to all the readers who took the trouble to write in with their comments and suggestions (and apologies to anyone whose name we've misspelt or omitted):

Mrs. Christine O'Brien, Brian K. Tanner, Tony Killilea, Roz Reid, Michael J. Wilson, Claire E. Kirkwood, Liz Phillips, Mike Appleyard, Susanne Christie, Richard Askew and Mhairie McLaughlin, Eva Smith, Chris Bragoli, Roy Bixler, Graeme Muir, Gary Cornwell, Eveline De Jonghe, Pam and John Fletcher, Anne Jackson, Rachel Wakefield, Sonja Wolf, Steve Devereux, Lorenza Bellincampi and Gene Ogle, Linda Stephenson, Geoff Garvey, Darren Colby, Alida Warman, Shevaun McDonnell, James White, Mary Greenwold, Lesley Flischer, Ulla Osterby, Colin Armstrong, Dan Evans, Philip van Lookeren Campagne, Katrin Bocking and Matthew Homer, Sage and Paul Baczuk, Fiona Jarman, Anne Davidson, Daniel Dennis, Brian Mulhern, Hay Sorée, Mariana Varela, Stephen Iseger, Victoria Bull, Neil and Ruth Charlton, Ann Bresnihan, Jeffrey Grenfell-Hill, Mrs M. I. Dodwell, James Bowling, Irene Ball, Philippa Dolphin, Melenie Francis, Linzi Banks, Kajetan Kasinski, William and Amanda Graham, Dr. Barbara Seeney, Ramon Kershner, Liz Ashley, Heather and Peter de Lacey, Christina Breaden, Walter Gundrey, Denise Fitzpatrick, Les Clark, Carosella Dolciaria, Oggy Boytchev, Vivien Uff, Keith Duncan, Petter Tandstad and family, Mark Sellin, Stephie Strunz, Mike Appleton, Fiona Duffy, Nick Gool, Jane McLardie, Les Clark, Patricia Pike, I. J. Lewis, Vicky Jones, Richard and Judith Veal, Katy Owen, Kanvie Wu, Rose-Mary Damiani, Ivana Drazic, Paul Capriotti, Hazel Williams, Teresa Searle and Steve Dew, Tim and Jenny Guerrier, Gary Cole, Ellen Tullo, Malcolm Kennedy, Mark Abbott, Stuart George, J.A. McKinnell, Petra Söderlund, Camilla Wimmer, Bernadette Cook, Z.C.E. Jackson, Herbert Kniep, Elizabeth Schaaf, Scott Amendola, Sheelagh and Bernard Hunter, Jan Portillo, Irene and John Pegley, P. J. L. Hicknes, Clare E. Flynn, Haydn Downey, Michael M nihan, Roy Bixler, Matthias Stephan, Michael Smith, Rupert Allen, Gaye Brown, Mrs E. Robinson, Matt Lucas, Matthias Stephan, Emma Shaw, Mrs W. M. Moisey, Judie Cole, Brian Muchera, Pete Herron, Caroline Harmer, William and Amanda Graham, Jose Acuna, Tom Murray, Rebekah Spanner, Martin Thomas and Carole

SMALL PRINT

Photo Credits

Detail of Ducal Palace in Urbino © Everton
 Macduff/Corbis
Genoa © Neil Setchfield
Capitoline Museum © Neil Setchfield
The Palio, Siena © Jay Dickman/Corbis
Faraglioni rock formations, Cápri © Peter
 Wilson
Carnival Mask, Venice © Neil Setchfield
The Lamentation by Giotto di Bondone
 © Archivo Iconografico S.A./Corbis
Etna Erupting © Michael Jenner
Duomo, Milan © Neil Setchfield
Pizza Slice © Yoav Levy/Robert Harding
Gubbio © Martin Barlow
Staue on Façade of Santa Croce, Lecce
 © John Heseltine/Corbis
Fresco painting of Diana from Stabiae
 © Mimmo Jodice/Corbis
Madonna di Campiglio © Lee Karen Stow
Uffizi, Florence © Martin Barlow
The Last Supper by Leonardo da Vinci
 © EdimEdia/Corbis
Display of Truffles © Martin Barlow
Temple of Apollo, Pompei © Peter Wilson
The Island of Elba, Roman Ruins © Maurice
 Joseph/Robert Harding

Black and whites

Chamois silhouette on skyline, Gran Paradiso
 © Ingo Arndt/Nature Picture Library p.64
Parco Nazionale © Tim Jepson p.75
View over city, Genoa © Neil Setchfield p.106
Portofino © Michael Jenner p.151
The Duomo, Milan © Neil Setchfield p.158
Sant'Andrea and the Rontonda, Mantua
 © Peter Wilson p.179
Alpe di Siusi © Rainer Reisenberger p.240
Madonna d Campiglio © Lee Karen Stow
 p.259
First day of the Carnevale, Venice © Sarah
 Quil, Venice Picture Library p.280
Santa Maria della Salute, Venice © Peter
 Wilson p.293

Canal Grande, Trieste © C. Bowman/Robert
 Harding p.378
Neoni Baptistry in Raverna © Paul Almasy/
 Corbis p.408
Bologna arcades © Tim Jepson p.451
San Galgano © Chris Cce/Axiom p.462
Montepulciano street scene © Michael
 Jenner p.481
The Leaning Tower of Pisa © Neil Setchfield
 p.560
The Duomo, Orvieto © Ruth Tomlinson/
 Robert Harding p.600
The Duomo, Spoleto © Martin Barlow p.641
Detail of Ducal Palace in Urbino © Everton
 Macduff/Corbis p.662
The Monti Sibillini © Martin Barlow p.685
St. Peter's Square, Vatican City, Rome
 © Peter Wilson p.708
Inside St Peter's, Rome © Peter Wilson p.733
Gran Sasso Peaks from Tagliacozzo
 © K.Gillham/Robert Harding p.814
Sulmona, Abruzzo © K.Gillham/Robert
 Harding p.827
Naples, view over the City © Peter Wilson
 p.846
The Faraglioni rocks, Cápri © Peter Wilson
 p.899
Ostuni © Sheila Terry/Robert Harding p.910
Vieste, the Gargano Promontory © Tony
 Gervis/Robert Harding p.943
Sassi dwellings © John Heseltine/Corbis
 p.964
Cosenza, Calabria © Sam Mountford p.987
Mosaic, Villa Romana del Casale, Piazza
 Armerina © Ashworth R./Robert Harding
 p.996
The Ear of Dionysus, Siracusa © J.Lightfoot/
 Robert Harding p.1013
Nuraghe Su Nuraxi © Rob Andrews p.1064
Ancient Roman mosaics, Nora, Sardinia
 © Rob Andrews p.1098

stay in touch

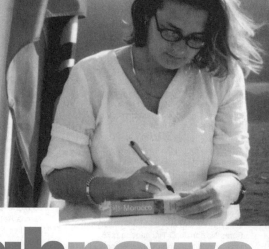

roughnews

Rough Guides' FREE full-colour newsletter

News, travel issues, music reviews, readers' letters and the latest dispatches from authors on the road

If you would like to receive roughnews, please send us your name and address:

Rough Guides, 80 Strand, London WC2R 0RL, UK

Rough Guides, 4th Floor, 345 Hudson St, New York NY10014, USA

newslettersubs@roughguides.co.uk

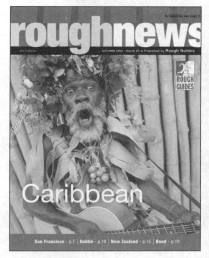

Visit us online
roughguides.com

Information on over 25,000 destinations around the world

- **Read** Rough Guides' trusted travel info
- **Share** journals, photos and travel advice with other readers
- Get exclusive Rough Guide **discounts** and travel **deals**
- Earn membership points every time you contribute to the Rough Guide **community** and get **free** books, flights and trips
- Browse thousands of CD reviews and artists in our **music** area

● TRAVEL ● MUSIC ● REFERENCE ● PHRASEBOOKS ●

Rough Guides travel

Rough Guides publishes new books every month.

Rough Guides music, reference & CDs

THE ROUGH GUIDE TO
cultmovies
THE GOOD, THE BAD AND THE VERY WEIRD INDEED

THE ROUGH GUIDE TO
Man Utd
2001–02 SEASON
Jim White & Andy Mitten
An UNOFFICIAL GUIDE in association with UNITED WE STAND

THE ROUGH GUIDE TO
Videogaming
KATE BERENS AND GEOFF HOWARD

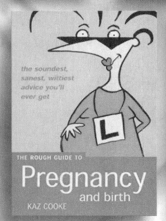

the soundest,
sanest, wittiest
advice you'll
ever get

THE ROUGH GUIDE TO
Pregnancy
and birth
KAZ COOKE

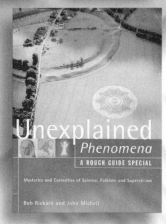

Unexplained
Phenomena
A ROUGH GUIDE SPECIAL

Mysteries and Curiosities of Science, Folklore and Superstition

Bob Rickard and John Michell

THE ROUGH GUIDE TO
Children's Books 0–5 years

THE ROUGH GUIDE TO
Children's Books 5–11 years

THE ROUGH GUIDE TO
Elvis
THE MAN • THE MUSIC • THE MOVIES • THE MYTH Paul Simpson

Pocket History Series

The Rough Guide Chronicle
England

The Rough Guide Chronicle
China

The Rough Guide Chronicle
India

The Rough Guide Chronicle
France

Rough Guide Reference

The ideas expressed in this code were developed by and for independent travellers.

Learn About The Country You're Visiting

Start enjoying your travels before you leave by tapping into as many sources of information as you can.

The Cost Of Your Holiday

Think about where your money goes - be fair and realistic about how cheaply you travel. Try and put money into local peoples' hands; drink local beer or fruit juice rather than imported brands and stay in locally owned accommodation. Haggle with humour and not aggressively. Pay what something is worth to you and remember how wealthy you are compared to local people.

Embrace The Local Culture

Open your mind to new cultures and traditions - it will transform your experience. Think carefully about what's appropriate in terms of your clothes and the way you behave. You'll earn respect and be more readily welcomed by local people. Respect local laws and attitudes towards drugs and alcohol that vary in different countries and communities. Think about the impact you could have on them.

Exploring The World – The Travellers' Code

Being sensitive to these ideas means getting more out of your travels - and giving more back to the people you meet and the places you visit.

Minimise Your Environmental Impact

Think about what happens to your rubbish - take biodegradable products and a water filter bottle. Be sensitive to limited resources like water, fuel and electricity. Help preserve local wildlife and habitats by respecting local rules and regulations, such as sticking to footpaths and not standing on coral.

Don't Rely On Guidebooks

Use your guidebook as a starting point, not the only source of information. Talk to local people, then discover your own adventure!

Be Discreet With Photography

Don't treat people as part of the landscape, they may not want their picture taken. Ask first and respect their wishes.

We work with people the world over to promote tourism that benefits their communities, but we can only carry on our work with the support of people like you. For membership details or to find out how to make your travels work for local people and the environment, visit our website.

www.tourismconcern.org.uk

Tourism Concern
Campaigning for Ethical and Fairly Traded Tourism

Let's get inspired.

Alitalia takes its inspiration from Europe's magnificent scenery, grand architecture and unique culture. Discover the enchantment of Italy and the very best of Europe with Alitalia and Italiatour's Exclusive Vacation Programs. Inspired? Call us today at 800.845.3365 or visit www.italiatourusa.com